Federal

SOCIAL SECURITY LAWS

SELECTED STATUTES AND REGULATIONS

Mat #42139304

This publication was created to provide you with accurate and authoritative information concerning the subject matter covered; however, this publication was not necessarily prepared by persons licensed to practice law in a particular jurisdiction. The publisher is not engaged in rendering legal or other professional advice and this publication is not a substitute for the advice of an attorney. If you require legal or other expert advice, you should seek the services of a competent attorney or other professional.

ISBN 978-0-314-69874-2

PREFACE

WHAT'S NEW

The complete text of the federal statutes relating to Old–Age, Survivors, and Disability Insurance Benefits and to Supplemental Security Income for the Aged, Blind, and Disabled, as amended through Pub.L. 116-9, approved March 12, 2019, is set out in this pamphlet. Social Security Administration regulations, as amended to 84 FR 11655, March 28, 2019, interpreting and applying these statutes, have been extracted from the Code of Federal Regulations and are also set out herein.

CONTACT US

For additional information or research assistance call the Reference Attorneys at 1-800-REF-ATTY (1-800-733-2889). Contact our U.S. legal editorial department directly with your questions and suggestions by e-mail at editors.us-legal@tr.com.

Thank you for subscribing to this product. Should you have any questions regarding this product, please contact Customer Service at 1-800-328-4880 or by fax at 1-800-340-9378. If you would like to inquire about related publications, or to place an order, please contact us at 1-888-728-7677 or visit us at legalsolutions.thomsonreuters.com.

THE PUBLISHER

April, 2019

THOMSON REUTERS PROVIEW™

This title is one of many now available on your tablet as an eBook.

Take your research mobile. Powered by the Thomson Reuters ProView™ app, our eBooks deliver the same trusted content as your print resources, but in a compact, on-the-go format.

ProView eBooks are designed for the way you work. You can add your own notes and highlights to the text, and all of your annotations will transfer electronically to every new edition of your eBook.

You can also instantly verify primary authority with built-in links to WestlawNext® and KeyCite®, so you can be confident that you're accessing the most current and accurate information.

To find out more about ProView eBooks and available discounts, call 1-800-344-5009.

TABLE OF CONTENTS

THE CODE OF THE LAWS OF THE UNITED STATES OF AMERICA

TITLE 42, U.S. CODE, THE PUBLIC HEALTH AND WELFARE

EQUAL ACCESS TO JUSTICE ACT

CODE OF FEDERAL REGULATIONS

TITLE 20, EMPLOYEES' BENEFITS

INDEX

TITLE 42

THE PUBLIC HEALTH AND WELFARE

CHAPTER 7—SOCIAL SECURITY

SUBCHAPTER II—FEDERAL OLD-AGE, SURVIVORS, AND DISABILITY INSURANCE BENEFITS

SUBCHAPTER XVI—SUPPLEMENTAL SECURITY INCOME FOR AGED, BLIND, AND DISABLED

Part A—Determination of Benefits

Part B—Procedural and General Provisions

SUBCHAPTER XVIII—HEALTH INSURANCE FOR AGED AND DISABLED

Part D—Voluntary Prescription Drug Benefit Program

Subpart 1—Part D Eligible Individuals and Prescription Drug Benefits

Sec.

SUBCHAPTER XVIII—HEALTH INSURANCE FOR AGED AND DISABLED—Cont'd

1395w–102. Prescription drug benefits.
1395w–103. Access to a choice of qualified prescription drug coverage.
1395w–104. Beneficiary protections for qualified prescription drug coverage.

Subpart 2—Prescription Drug Plans; PDP Sponsors; Financing

1395w–111. PDP regions; submission of bids; plan approval.
1395w–112. Requirements for and contracts with prescription drug plan (PDP) sponsors.
1395w–113. Premiums; late enrollment penalty.
1395w–114. Premium and cost-sharing subsidies for low-income individuals.
1395w–114a. Medicare coverage gap discount program.
1395w–115. Subsidies for part D eligible individuals for qualified prescription drug coverage.
1395w–116. Medicare Prescription Drug Account in the Federal Supplementary Medical Insurance Trust Fund.

Subpart 3—Application to Medicare Advantage Program and Treatment of Employer-Sponsored Programs and Other Prescription Drug Plans

1395w–131. Application to Medicare Advantage program and related managed care programs.
1395w–132. Special rules for employer-sponsored programs.
1395w–133. State Pharmaceutical Assistance Programs.
1395w–134. Coordination requirements for plans providing prescription drug coverage.

Subpart 4—Medicare Prescription Drug Discount Card and Transitional Assistance Program

1395w–141. Medicare prescription drug discount card and transitional assistance program.

Subpart 5—Definitions and Miscellaneous Provisions

1395w–151. Definitions; treatment of references to provisions in part C.
1395w–152. Miscellaneous provisions.
1395w–153. Condition for coverage of drugs under this part.
1395w–154. Improved Medicare prescription drug plan and MA-PD plan complaint system.

TABLE

The following table shows the classification of each section of the Social Security Act, Act Aug. 14, 1935, c. 531, 49 Stat. 620, to this title. For complete classification, see USCA Popular Name Table for Acts of Congress and Tables.

Social Security Act	This Title
Title I	Subchapter I
1	301
2	302
3	303
4	304
5	305 (Omitted)
6	306
Title II	Subchapter II
201	401
202	402
203	403
204	404
205	405
206	406
207	407
208	408
209	409
210	410
211	411
212	412
213	413
214	414
215	415
216	416
217	417
218	418
219	419 (Repealed)
220	420
221	421
222	422
223	423
224	424a
225	425
226	426
226A	426–1
227	427
228	428
229	429
230	430
231	431
232	432
233	433
234	434
Title III	Subchapter III
301	501
302	502
303	503
304	504
Title IV	Subchapter IV
401	601
402	602
403	603
404	604
405	605
406	606
407	607
408	608
409	609
410	610
411	611
411A	611a
412	612
413	613
414	614 (Repealed)
415	615
416	616
417	617

Social Security Act	This Title
418	618
419	619
420	620 (Repealed)
421	621
422	622
423	623
424	624
425	625
426	626
427	627
428	628
429	628a (Transferred)
429	628b
430	629
431	629a
432	629b
433	629c
434	629d
435	629e
436	629f
437	629g
438	629h
439	629i
440 to 445	640 to 645 (Repealed)
451	651
452	652
453	653
453A	653a
454	654
454A	654a
454B	654b
455	655
456	656
457	657
458	658 (Repealed)
458A	658a
459	659
459A	659a
460	660
461	661 (Repealed)
462	662 (Repealed)
463	663
464	664
465	665
466	666
467	667
468	668
469	669
469A	669a
469B	669b
470	670
471	671
472	672
473	673
473A	673b
473B	673c
474	674
475	675
475A	675a
476	676
477	677
478	678
479	679

Social Security Act	This Title
479A	679b
479B	679c
481 to 487	681 to 687 (Repealed)
Title V	Subchapter V
501	701
502	702
503	703
504	704
505	705
506	706
507	707
508	708
509	709
510	710
511	711
512	712
513	713
514 to 516	714 to 716 (Omitted)
521 to 528	721 to 728 (Repealed)
531 to 533	729 to 729a (Omitted)
541	731 (Omitted)
Title VI	Subchapter VI
601	801 (Repealed)
602 to 605	802 to 805 (Repealed)
Title VII	Subchapter VII
701	901
702	902
703	903
704	904
705	906
706	907 (Repealed)
707	908 (Omitted)
708	909
709	910
710	911
711	912
712	913
713	914
Title VIII	Subchapter VIII
801	1001
802	1002
803	1003
804	1004
805	1005
806	1006
807	1007
808	1008
809	1009
810	1010
810A	1010a
811	1011
812	1012
813	1013
Title IX	Subchapter IX
901	1101
902	1102
903	1103
904	1104

Social Security Act	This Title
905	1105
906	1106
907	1107
908	1108
909	1109
910	1110
911	1111
Title X	Subchapter X
1001	1201
1002	1202
1003	1203
1004	1204
1005	1205 (Omitted)
1006	1206
Title XI	Subchapter XI
1101	1301
1102	1302
1103	1303
1104	1304
1105	1305
1106	1306
1107	1307
1108	1308
1109	1309
1110	1310
1111	1311
1112	1312
1113	1313
1114	1314
1114A	1314b
1115	1315
1115A	1315a
1116	1316
1117	1317
1118	1318
1119	1319
1120	1320
1121	1320a
1122	1320a–1
1123	1320a–2
1123A	1320a–2a
1124	1320a–3
1124A	1320a–3a
1125	1320a–4
1126	1320a–5
1127	1320a–6
1128	1320a–7
1128A	1320a–7a
1128B	1320a–7b
1128C	1320a–7c
1128D	1320a–7d
1128E	1320a–7e
1128F	1320a–7f
1128G	1320a–7h
1128H	1320a–7i
1128I	1320a–7j
1128J	1320a–7k
1129	1320a–8
1129A	1320a–8a
1129B	1320a–8b
1130	1320a–9

Social Security Act	This Title
1130	1320b (Repealed)
1130A	1320a–10
1131	1320b–1
1132	1320b–2
1133	1320b–3
1134	1320b–4
1135	1320b–5
1136	1320b–6
1137	1320b–7
1138	1320b–8
1139	1320b–9
1139A	1320b–9a
1139B	1320b–9b
1140	1320b–10
1141	1320b–11
1142	1320b–12
1143	1320b–13
1144	1320b–14
1145	1320b–15
1146	1320b–16
1147	1320b–17
1147A	1320b–18 (Repealed)
1148	1320b–19
1149	1320b–20
1150	1320b–21
1150A	1320b–23
1150B	1320b–25
1151	1320c
1152	1320c–1
1153	1320c–2
1154	1320c–3
1155	1320c–4
1156	1320c–5
1157	1320c–6
1158	1320c–7
1159	1320c–8
1160	1320c–9
1161	1320c–10
1162	1320c–11
1163	1320c–12
1164	1320c–13 (Repealed)
1165 to 1170	1320c–14 to 1320c–19 (Omitted)
1171	1320d
1172	1320d–1
1173	1320d–2
1174	1320d–3
1175	1320d–4
1176	1320d–5
1177	1320d–6
1178	1320d–7
1179	1320d–8
1180	1320d–9
1181	1320e
1182	1320e–1
1183	1320e–2
Title XII	Subchapter XII
1201	1321
1202	1322
1203	1323
1204	1324

Social Security Act	This Title
Title XIII	Subchapter XIII
1301 to 1306	1331 to 1336 (Repealed)
Title XIV	Subchapter XIV
1401	1351
1402	1352
1403	1353
1404	1354
1405	1355
Title XV	Subchapter XV
1501 to 1511	1361 to 1371 (Repealed)
Title XVI	Subchapter XVI
1601	1381
1602	1381a
1603	1383nt
1604	1384 (Omitted)
1605	1385 (Omitted)
1611	1382
1612	1382a
1613	1382b
1614	1382c
1615	1382d
1616	1382e
1617	1382f
1618	1382g
1619	1382h
1620	1382i
1621	1382j
1622	1382k (Repealed)
1631	1383
1632	1383a
1633	1383b
1634	1383c
1635	1383d
1636	1383e
1637	1383f
Title XVII	Subchapter XVII
1701	1391
1702	1392
1703	1393
1704	1394
Title XVIII	Subchapter XVIII
1801	1395
1802	1395a
1803	1395b
1804	1395b–2
1805	1395b–6
1806	1395b–7
1807	1395b–8
1808	1395b–9
1809	1395b–10
1811	1395c
1812	1395d
1813	1395e
1814	1395f
1815	1395g
1816	1395h

Social Security Act	This Title
1817	1395i
1817A	1395i–1a (Repealed)
1818	1395i–2
1818A	1395i–2a
1819	1395i–3
1820	1395i–4
1821	1395i–5
1831	1395j
1832	1395k
1833	1395*l*
1834	1395m
1835	1395n
1836	1395*o*
1837	1395p
1838	1395q
1839	1395r
1840	1395s
1841	1395t
1841A	1395t–1 (Repealed)
1841B	1395t–2 (Repealed)
1842	1395u
1843	1395v
1844	1395w
1845	1395w–1 (Repealed)
1846	1395w–2
1847	1395w–3
1847A	1395w–3a
1847B	1395w–3b
1848	1395w–4
1851	1395w–21
1852	1395w–22
1853	1395w–23
1854	1395w–24
1855	1395w–25
1856	1395w–26
1857	1395w–27
1858	1395w–27a
1859	1395w–28
1860C–1	1395w–29
1860D–1	1395w–101
1860D–2	1395w–102
1860D–3	1395w–103
1860D–4	1395w–104
1860D–11	1395w–111
1860D–12	1395w–112
1860D–13	1395w–113
1860D–14	1395w–114
1860D–14A	1395w–114a
1860D–15	1395w–115
1860D–16	1395w–116
1860D–21	1395w–131
1860D–22	1395w–132
1860D–23	1395w–133
1860D–24	1395w–134
1860D–31	1395w–141
1860D–41	1395w–151
1860D–42	1395w–152
1860D–43	1395w–153
1861	1395x
1862	1395y
1863	1395z
1864	1395aa
1865	1395bb

Social Security Act	This Title
1866	1395cc
1866A	1395cc–1
1866B	1395cc–2
1866C	1395cc–3
1866D	1395cc–4
1866E	1395cc–5
1867	1395dd
1868	1395ee
1869	1395ff
1870	1395gg
1871	1395hh
1872	1395ii
1873	1395jj
1874	1395kk
1875	1395*ll*
1876	1395mm
1877	1395nn
1878	1395*oo*
1879	1395pp
1880	1395qq
1881	1395rr
1881A	1395rr–1
1882	1395ss
1883	1395tt
1884	1395uu
1885	1395vv
1886	1395ww
1887	1395xx
1888	1395yy
1889	1395zz
1890	1395aaa
1890A	1395aaa–1
1891	1395bbb
1892	1395ccc
1893	1395ddd
1894	1395eee
1895	1395fff
1896	1395ggg
1897	1395hhh
1898	1395iii
1899	1395jjj
1899A	1395kkk (Repealed)
1899B	1395*lll*
Title XIX	Subchapter XIX
1901	1396
1902	1396a
1903	1396b
1904	1396c
1905	1396d
1906	1396e
1906A	1396e–1
1907	1396f
1908	1396g
1908A	1396g–1
1909	1396h
1910	1396i
1911	1396j
1912	1396k
1913	1396*l*
1914	1396m
1915	1396n
1916	1396*o*

Social Security Act	This Title
1916A	1396*o*–1
1917	1396p
1918	1396q
1919	1396r
1920	1396r–1
1920A	1396r–1a
1920B	1396r–1b
1921	1396r–2
1922	1396r–3
1923	1396r–4
1924	1396r–5
1925	1396r–6
1926	1396r–7 (Repealed)
1927	1396r–8
1928	1396s
1929	1396t
1930	1396u
1931	1396u–1
1932	1396u–2
1933	1396u–3
1934	1396u–4
1935	1396u–5
1936	1396u–6
1937	1396u–7
1938	1396u–8
1939	1396v
1940	1396w
1941	1396w–1
1942	1396w–2
1943	1396w–3
1945	1396w–4
1946	1396w–5
Title XX	Subchapter XX
2001	1397
2002	1397a
2003	1397b
2004	1397c
2005	1397d
2006	1397e
2007	1397f
2008	1397g
2009	1397h
2011	1397j
2012	1397j–1
2021	1397k
2022	1397k–1
2023	1397k–2
2024	1397k–3
2031	1397*l*
2041	1397m
2042	1397m–1
2043	1397m–2
2044	1397m–3
2045	1397m–4
2046	1397m–5
Title XXI	Subchapter XXI
2101	1397aa
2102	1397bb
2103	1397cc
2104	1397dd
2105	1397ee

Social Security Act	This Title
2106	1397ff
2107	1397gg
2108	1397hh
2109	1397ii
2110	1397jj
2111	1397kk
2112	1397ll
2113	1397mm

SUBCHAPTER II—FEDERAL OLD-AGE, SURVIVORS, AND DISABILITY INSURANCE BENEFITS

§ 401. Trust Funds

(a) Federal Old-Age and Survivors Insurance Trust Fund

There is hereby created on the books of the Treasury of the United States a trust fund to be known as the "Federal Old-Age and Survivors Insurance Trust Fund". The Federal Old-Age and Survivors Insurance Trust Fund shall consist of the securities held by the Secretary of the Treasury for the Old-Age Reserve Account and the amount standing to the credit of the Old-Age Reserve Account on the books of the Treasury on January 1, 1940, which securities and amount the Secretary of the Treasury is authorized and directed to transfer to the Federal Old-Age and Survivors Insurance Trust Fund, and, in addition, such gifts and bequests as may be made as provided in subsection (i)(1), and such amounts as may be appropriated to, or deposited in, the Federal Old-Age and Survivors Insurance Trust Fund as hereinafter provided. There is hereby appropriated to the Federal Old-Age and Survivors Insurance Trust Fund for the fiscal year ending June 30, 1941, and for each fiscal year thereafter, out of any moneys in the Treasury not otherwise appropriated, amounts equivalent to 100 per centum of—

(1) the taxes (including interest, penalties, and additions to the taxes) received under subchapter A of chapter 9 of the Internal Revenue Code of 1939 (and covered into the Treasury) which are deposited into the Treasury by collectors of internal revenue before January 1, 1951; and

(2) the taxes certified each month by the Commissioner of Internal Revenue as taxes received under subchapter A of chapter 9 of such Code which are deposited into the Treasury by collectors of internal revenue after December 31, 1950, and before January 1, 1953, with respect to assessments of such taxes made before January 1, 1951; and

(3) the taxes imposed by subchapter A of chapter 9 of such Code with respect to wages (as defined in section 1426 of such Code), and by chapter 21 (other than sections 3101(b) and 3111(b)) of the Internal Revenue Code of 1954 with respect to wages (as defined in section 3121 of such Code) reported to the Commissioner of Internal Revenue pursuant to section 1420(c) of the Internal Revenue Code of 1939 after December 31, 1950, or to the Secretary of the Treasury or his delegates pursuant to subtitle F of the Internal Revenue Code of 1954 after December 31, 1954, as determined by the Secretary of the Treasury by applying the applicable rates of tax under such subchapter or chapter 21 (other than sections 3101(b) and 3111(b)) to such wages, which wages shall be certified by the Commissioner of Social Security on the basis of the records of wages established and maintained by such Commissioner in accordance with such reports, less the amounts specified in clause (1) of subsection (b); and

(4) the taxes imposed by subchapter E of chapter 1 of the Internal Revenue Code of 1939, with respect to self-employment income (as defined in section 481 of such Code), and by chapter 2 (other than section 1401(b)) of the Internal Revenue Code of 1954 with respect to self-employment income (as defined in section 1402 of such Code) reported to the Commissioner of Internal Revenue on tax returns under such subchapter or to the Secretary of the Treasury or his delegate on tax returns under subtitle F of such Code, as determined by the Secretary of the Treasury by applying the applicable rate of tax under such subchapter or chapter (other than section 1401(b)) to such self-employment income, which self-employment income shall be certified by the Commissioner of Social Security on the basis of the records of self-employment income established and maintained by the Commissioner of Social Security in accordance with such returns, less the amounts specified in clause (2) of subsection (b).

The amounts appropriated by clauses (3) and (4) of this subsection shall be transferred from time to time from the general fund in the Treasury to the Federal Old-Age and Survivors Insurance Trust Fund, and the amounts appropriated by clauses (1) and (2) of subsection (b) shall be transferred from time to time from the general fund in the Treasury to the Federal Disability Insurance Trust Fund, such amounts to be determined on the basis of estimates by the Secretary of the Treasury of the taxes, specified in clauses (3) and (4) of this subsection, paid to or deposited into the Treasury; and proper adjustments shall be made in amounts subsequently transferred to the extent prior estimates were in excess of or were less than the taxes specified in such clauses (3) and (4) of this subsection. All amounts transferred to either Trust Fund under the preceding sentence shall be invested by the Managing Trustee in the same manner and to the same extent as the other assets of such Trust Fund. Notwithstanding the preceding sentence, in any case in which the Secretary of the Treasury determines that the assets of either such Trust Fund would otherwise be inadequate to meet such Fund's obligations for any month, the Secretary of the Treasury shall transfer to such Trust

Fund on the first day of such month the amount which would have been transferred to such Fund under this section as in effect on October 1, 1990; and such Trust Fund shall pay interest to the general fund on the amount so transferred on the first day of any month at a rate (calculated on a daily basis, and applied against the difference between the amount so transferred on such first day and the amount which would have been transferred to the Trust Fund up to that day under the procedures in effect on January 1, 1983) equal to the rate earned by the investments of such Fund in the same month under subsection (d).

(b) Federal Disability Insurance Trust Fund

There is hereby created on the books of the Treasury of the United States a trust fund to be known as the "Federal Disability Insurance Trust Fund". The Federal Disability Insurance Trust Fund shall consist of such gifts and bequests as may be made as provided in subsection (i)(1), and such amounts as may be appropriated to, or deposited in, such fund as provided in this section. There is hereby appropriated to the Federal Disability Insurance Trust Fund for the fiscal year ending June 30, 1957, and for each fiscal year thereafter, out of any moneys in the Treasury not otherwise appropriated, amounts equivalent to 100 per centum of—

(1) (A) ½ of 1 per centum of the wages (as defined in section 3121 of the Internal Revenue Code of 1954) paid after December 31, 1956, and before January 1, 1966, and reported to the Secretary of the Treasury or his delegate pursuant to subtitle F of the Internal Revenue Code of 1954, (B) 0.70 of 1 per centum of the wages (as so defined) paid after December 31, 1965, and before January 1, 1968, and so reported, (C) 0.95 of 1 per centum of the wages (as so defined) paid after December 31, 1967, and before January 1, 1970, and so reported, (D) 1.10 per centum of the wages (as so defined) paid after December 31, 1969, and before January 1, 1973, and so reported, (E) 1.1 per centum of the wages (as so defined) paid after December 31, 1972, and before January 1, 1974, and so reported, (F) 1.15 per centum of the wages (as so defined) paid after December 31, 1973, and before January 1, 1978, and so reported, (G) 1.55 per centum of the wages (as so defined) paid after December 31, 1977, and before January 1, 1979, and so reported, (H) 1.50 per centum of the wages (as so defined) paid after December 31, 1978, and before January 1, 1980, and so reported, (I) 1.12 per centum of the wages (as so defined) paid after December 31, 1979, and before January 1, 1981, and so reported, (J) 1.30 per centum of the wages (as so defined) paid after December 31, 1980, and before January 1, 1982, and so reported, (K) 1.65 per centum of the wages (as so defined) paid after December 31, 1981, and before January 1, 1983, and so reported, (L) 1.25 per centum of the wages (as so defined) paid after December 31, 1982, and before January 1, 1984, and so reported, (M) 1.00 per centum of the wages (as so defined) paid after December 31, 1983, and before January 1, 1988, and so reported, (N) 1.06 per centum of the wages (as so defined) paid after December 31, 1987, and before January 1, 1990, and so reported, (O) 1.20 per centum of the wages (as so defined) paid after December 31, 1989, and before January 1, 1994, and so reported, (P) 1.88 per centum of the wages (as so defined) paid after December 31, 1993, and before January 1, 1997, and so reported, (Q) 1.70 per centum of the wages (as so defined) paid after December 31, 1996, and before January 1, 2000, and so reported, (R) 1.80 per centum of the wages (as so defined) paid after December 31, 1999, and before January 1, 2016, and so reported, (S) 2.37 per centum of the wages (as so defined) paid after December 31, 2015, and before January 1, 2019, and so reported, and (T) 1.80 per centum of the wages (as so defined) paid after December 31, 2018, and so reported,,[1] which wages shall be certified by the Commissioner of Social Security on the basis of the records of wages established and maintained by such Commissioner in accordance with such reports; and

(2) (A) ⅜ of 1 per centum of the amount of self-employment income (as defined in section 1402 of the Internal Revenue Code of 1954) reported to the Secretary of the Treasury or his delegate on tax returns under subtitle F of the Internal Revenue Code of 1954 for any taxable year beginning after December 31, 1956, and before January 1, 1966, (B) 0.525 of 1 per centum of the amount of self-employment income (as so defined) so reported for any taxable year beginning after December 31, 1965, and before January 1, 1968, (C) 0.7125 of 1 per centum of the amount of self-employment income (as so defined) so reported for any taxable year beginning after December 31, 1967, and before January 1, 1970, (D) 0.825 of 1 per centum of the amount of self-employment income (as so defined) so reported for any taxable year beginning after December 31, 1969, and before January 1, 1973, (E) 0.795 of 1 per centum of the amount of self-employment income (as so defined) so reported for any taxable year beginning after December 31, 1972, and before January 1, 1974, (F) 0.815 of 1 per centum of the amount of self-employment income (as so defined) as reported for any taxable year beginning after December 31, 1973, and before January 1, 1978, (G) 1.090 per centum of the amount of self-employment income (as so defined) so reported for any taxable year beginning after December 31, 1977, and before January 1, 1979, (H) 1.0400 per centum of the amount of self-employment income (as so defined) so reported for any taxable year beginning after December 31, 1978, and before January 1, 1980, (I) 0.7775 per centum of the amount of self-employment income (as so defined) so reported for any taxable year beginning after De-

cember 31, 1979, and before January 1, 1981, (J) 0.9750 per centum of the amount of self-employment income (as so defined) so reported for any taxable year beginning after December 31, 1980, and before January 1, 1982, (K) 1.2375 per centum of the amount of self-employment income (as so defined) so reported for any taxable year beginning after December 31, 1981, and before January 1, 1983, (L) 0.9375 per centum of the amount of self-employment income (as so defined) so reported for any taxable year beginning after December 31, 1982, and before January 1, 1984, (M) 1.00 per centum of the amount of self-employment income (as so defined) so reported for any taxable year beginning after December 31, 1983, and before January 1, 1988, (N) 1.06 per centum of the self-employment income (as so defined) so reported for any taxable year beginning after December 31, 1987, and before January 1, 1990, (O) 1.20 per centum of the amount of self-employment income (as so defined) so reported for any taxable year beginning after December 31, 1989, and before January 1, 1994, (P) 1.88 per centum of the amount of self-employment income (as so defined) so reported for any taxable year beginning after December 31, 1993, and before January 1, 1997, (Q) 1.70 per centum of the amount of self-employment income (as so defined) so reported for any taxable year beginning after December 31, 1996, and before January 1, 2000, (R) 1.80 per centum of the amount of self-employment income (as so defined) so reported for any taxable year beginning after December 31, 1999, and before January 1, 2016, (S) 2.37 per centum of the amount of self-employment income (as so defined) so reported for any taxable year beginning after December 31, 2015, and before January 1, 2019, and (T) 1.80 per centum of the amount of self-employment income (as so defined) so reported for any taxable year beginning after December 31, 2018, which self-employment income shall be certified by the Commissioner of Social Security on the basis of the records of self-employment income established and maintained by the Commissioner of Social Security in accordance with such returns.

(c) Board of Trustees; duties; reports to Congress

With respect to the Federal Old-Age and Survivors Insurance Trust Fund and the Federal Disability Insurance Trust Fund (hereinafter in this subchapter called the "Trust Funds") there is hereby created a body to be known as the Board of Trustees of the Trust Funds (hereinafter in this subchapter called the "Board of Trustees") which Board of Trustees shall be composed of the Commissioner of Social Security, the Secretary of the Treasury, the Secretary of Labor, and the Secretary of Health and Human Services, all ex officio, and of two members of the public (both of whom may not be from the same political party), who shall be nominated by the President for a term of four years and subject to confirmation by the Senate. A member of the Board of Trustees serving as a member of the public and nominated and confirmed to fill a vacancy occurring during a term shall be nominated and confirmed only for the remainder of such term. An individual nominated and confirmed as a member of the public may serve in such position after the expiration of such member's term until the earlier of the time at which the member's successor takes office or the time at which a report of the Board is first issued under paragraph (2) after the expiration of the member's term. The Secretary of the Treasury shall be the Managing Trustee of the Board of Trustees (hereinafter in this subchapter called the "Managing Trustee"). The Deputy Commissioner of Social Security shall serve as Secretary of the Board of Trustees. The Board of Trustees shall meet not less frequently than once each calendar year. It shall be the duty of the Board of Trustees to—

(1) Hold the Trust Funds;

(2) Report to the Congress not later than the first day of April of each year on the operation and status of the Trust Funds during the preceding fiscal year and on their expected operation and status during the next ensuing five fiscal years;

(3) Report immediately to the Congress whenever the Board of Trustees is of the opinion that the amount of either of the Trust Funds is unduly small;

(4) Recommend improvements in administrative procedures and policies designed to effectuate the proper coordination of the old-age and survivors insurance and Federal-State unemployment compensation program; and

(5) Review the general policies followed in managing the Trust Funds, and recommend changes in such policies, including necessary changes in the provisions of the law which govern the way in which the Trust Funds are to be managed.

The report provided for in paragraph (2) of this subsection shall include a statement of the assets of, and the disbursements made from, the Trust Funds during the preceding fiscal year, an estimate of the expected future income to, and disbursements to be made from, the Trust Funds during each of the next ensuing five fiscal years, and a statement of the actuarial status of the Trust Funds. Such statement shall include a finding by the Board of Trustees as to whether the Federal Old-Age and Survivors Insurance Trust Fund and the Federal Disability Insurance Trust Fund, individually and collectively, are in close actuarial balance (as defined by the Board of Trustees). Such report shall include an actuarial opinion by the Chief Actuary of the Social Security Administration certifying that the techniques and methodologies used are generally accepted within the actuarial profession and that the assumptions and cost estimates used are reasonable. Such report shall also include an actuarial analysis of the benefit disbursements made from the Federal Old-

Age and Survivors Insurance Trust Fund with respect to disabled beneficiaries. Such report shall be printed as a House document of the session of the Congress to which the report is made. A person serving on the Board of Trustees shall not be considered to be a fiduciary and shall not be personally liable for actions taken in such capacity with respect to the Trust Funds.

(d) Investments

It shall be the duty of the Managing Trustee to invest such portion of the Trust Funds as is not, in his judgment, required to meet current withdrawals. Such investments may be made only in interest-bearing obligations of the United States or in obligations guaranteed as to both principal and interest by the United States. For such purpose such obligations may be acquired (1) on original issue at the issue price, or (2) by purchase of outstanding obligations at the market price. The purposes for which obligations of the United States may be issued under chapter 31 of Title 31 are hereby extended to authorize the issuance at par of public-debt obligations for purchase by the Trust Funds. Such obligations issued for purchase by the Trust Funds shall have maturities fixed with due regard for the needs of the Trust Funds and shall bear interest at a rate equal to the average market yield (computed by the Managing Trustee on the basis of market quotations as of the end of the calendar month next preceding the date of such issue) on all marketable interest-bearing obligations of the United States then forming a part of the public debt which are not due or callable until after the expiration of four years from the end of such calendar month; except that where such average market yield is not a multiple of one-eighth of 1 per centum, the rate of interest of such obligations shall be the multiple of one-eighth of 1 per centum nearest such market yield. Each obligation issued for purchase by the Trust Funds under this subsection shall be evidenced by a paper instrument in the form of a bond, note, or certificate of indebtedness issued by the Secretary of the Treasury setting forth the principal amount, date of maturity, and interest rate of the obligation, and stating on its face that the obligation shall be incontestable in the hands of the Trust Fund to which it is issued, that the obligation is supported by the full faith and credit of the United States, and that the United States is pledged to the payment of the obligation with respect to both principal and interest. The Managing Trustee may purchase other interest-bearing obligations of the United States or obligations guaranteed as to both principal and interest by the United States, on original issue or at the market price, only where he determines that the purchase of such other obligations is in the public interest.

(e) Sale of acquired obligations

Any obligations acquired by the Trust Funds (except public-debt obligations issued exclusively to the Trust Funds) may be sold by the Managing Trustee at the market price, and such public-debt obligations may be redeemed at par plus accrued interest.

(f) Proceeds from sale or redemption of obligations; interest

The interest on, and the proceeds from the sale or redemption of, any obligations held in the Federal Old-Age and Survivors Insurance Trust Fund and the Federal Disability Insurance Trust Fund shall be credited to and form a part of the Federal Old-Age and Survivors Insurance Trust Fund and the Disability Insurance Trust Fund, respectively. Payment from the general fund of the Treasury to either of the Trust Funds of any such interest or proceeds shall be in the form of paper checks drawn on such general fund to the order of such Trust Fund.

(g) Payments into Treasury

(1)(A) The Managing Trustee of the Trust Funds (which for purposes of this paragraph shall include also the Federal Hospital Insurance Trust Fund and the Federal Supplementary Medical Insurance Trust Fund established by subchapter XVIII) is directed to pay from the Trust Funds into the Treasury—

(i) [2] the amounts estimated by the Managing Trustee, the Commissioner of Social Security, and the Secretary of Health and Human Services which will be expended, out of moneys appropriated from the general fund in the Treasury, during a three-month period by the Department of Health and Human Services for the administration of subchapter XVIII of this chapter, and by the Department of the Treasury for the administration of subchapters II and XVIII of this chapter and chapters 2 and 21 of the Internal Revenue Code of 1986, less

(ii) [2] the amounts estimated (pursuant to the applicable method prescribed under paragraph (4) of this subsection) by the Commissioner of Social Security which will be expended, out of moneys made available for expenditures from the Trust Funds, during such three-month period to cover the cost of carrying out the functions of the Social Security Administration, specified in section 432 of this title, which relate to the administration of provisions of the Internal Revenue Code of 1986 other than those referred to in clause (i) and the functions of the Social Security Administration in connection with the withholding of taxes from benefits, as described in section 407(c) of this title, pursuant to requests by persons entitled to such benefits or such persons' representative payee.

Such payments shall be carried into the Treasury as the net amount of repayments due the general fund account for reimbursement of expenses incurred in connection with the administration of subchapters II and XVIII of this chapter and chapters 2 and 21 of the Internal Revenue Code of 1986. A final accounting of such payments for any fiscal year shall be made at the earliest practicable date after the close thereof. There are hereby authorized to be made available for expenditure, out of any or all of the Trust Funds, such amounts as the Congress may deem appropriate to pay the costs of the part of the administration of this subchapter, subchapter VIII, subchapter XVI, and subchapter XVIII for which the Commissioner of Social Security is responsible, the costs of subchapter XVIII for which the Secretary of Health and Human Services is responsible, and the costs of carrying out the functions of the Social Security Administration, specified in section 432 of this title, which relate to the administration of provisions of the Internal Revenue Code of 1986 other than those referred to in clause (i) of the first sentence of this subparagraph and the functions of the Social Security Administration in connection with the withholding of taxes from benefits, as described in section 407(c) of this title, pursuant to requests by persons entitled to such benefits or such persons' representative payee. Of the amounts authorized to be made available out of the Federal Old-Age and Survivors Insurance Trust Fund and the Federal Disability Insurance Trust Fund under the preceding sentence, there are hereby authorized to be made available from either or both of such Trust Funds for continuing disability reviews—

(i) [2] for fiscal year 1996, $260,000,000;

(ii) [2] for fiscal year 1997, $360,000,000;

(iii) for fiscal year 1998, $570,000,000;

(iv) for fiscal year 1999, $720,000,000;

(v) for fiscal year 2000, $720,000,000;

(vi) for fiscal year 2001, $720,000,000; and

(viii) [3] for fiscal year 2002, $720,000,000.

For purposes of this subparagraph, the term "continuing disability review" means a review conducted pursuant to section 421(i) of this title and a review or disability eligibility redetermination conducted to determine the continuing disability and eligibility of a recipient of benefits under the supplemental security income program under subchapter XVI, including any review or redetermination conducted pursuant to section 207 or 208 of the Social Security Independence and Program Improvements Act of 1994 (Public Law 103–296).

(B) After the close of each fiscal year—

(i) the Commissioner of Social Security shall determine—

(I) the portion of the costs, incurred during such fiscal year, of administration of this subchapter, subchapter VIII, subchapter XVI, and subchapter XVIII for which the Commissioner is responsible and of carrying out the functions of the Social Security Administration, specified in section 432 of this title, which relate to the administration of provisions of the Internal Revenue Code of 1986 (other than those referred to in clause (i) of the first sentence of subparagraph (A)) and the functions of the Social Security Administration in connection with the withholding of taxes from benefits, as described in section 407(c) of this title, pursuant to requests by persons entitled to such benefits or such persons' representative payee, which should have been borne by the general fund of the Treasury,

(II) the portion of such costs which should have been borne by the Federal Old-Age and Survivors Insurance Trust Fund,

(III) the portion of such costs which should have been borne by the Federal Disability Insurance Trust Fund,

(IV) the portion of such costs which should have been borne by the Federal Hospital Insurance Trust Fund, and

(V) the portion of such costs which should have been borne by the Federal Supplementary Medical Insurance Trust Fund (and, of such portion, the portion of such costs which should have been borne by the Medicare Prescription Drug Account in such Trust Fund), and

(ii) the Secretary of Health and Human Services shall determine—

(I) the portion of the costs, incurred during such fiscal year, of the administration of subchapter XVIII for which the Secretary is responsible, which should have been borne by the general fund of the Treasury,

(II) the portion of such costs which should have been borne by the Federal Hospital Insurance Trust Fund, and

(III) the portion of such costs which should have been borne by the Federal Supplementary Medical Insurance Trust Fund (and, of such portion, the portion of such costs which should have been borne by the Medicare Prescription Drug Account in such Trust Fund).

(C) After the determinations under subparagraph (B) have been made for any fiscal year, the Commisioner [4] of Social Security and the Secretary shall each certify to the Managing Trustee the amounts, if any, which should be transferred from one to any of the other such Trust Funds and the amounts, if any, which should be transferred between the Trust Funds (or one of the Trust Funds) and the general fund of the Treasury, in order to ensure that each of the Trust Funds and the general fund of the Treasury have borne their proper share of the costs, incurred during such fiscal year, for—

(i) the parts of the administration of this subchapter, subchapter VIII, subchapter XVI, and subchapter XVIII for which the Commissioner of Social Security is responsible,

(ii) the parts of the administration of subchapter XVIII for which the Secretary is responsible, and

(iii) carrying out the functions of the Social Security Administration, specified in section 432 of this title, which relate to the administration of provisions of the Internal Revenue Code of 1986 (other than those referred to in clause (i) of the first sentence of subparagraph (A)) and the functions of the Social Security Administration in connection with the withholding of taxes from benefits, as described in section 407(c) of this title, pursuant to requests by persons entitled to such benefits or such persons' representative payee.

The Managing Trustee shall transfer any such amounts in accordance with any certification so made.

(D) The determinations required under subclauses (IV) and (V) of subparagraph (B)(i) shall be made in accordance with the cost allocation methodology in existence on August 15, 1994, until such time as the methodology for making the determinations required under such subclauses is revised by agreement of the Commissioner and the Secretary, except that the determination of the amounts to be borne by the general fund of the Treasury with respect to expenditures incurred in carrying out the functions of the Social Security Administration specified in section 432 of this title and the functions of the Social Security Administration in connection with the withholding of taxes from benefits as described in section 407(c) of this title shall be made pursuant to the applicable method prescribed under paragraph (4).

(2) The Managing Trustee is directed to pay from time to time from the Trust Funds into the Treasury the amount estimated by him as taxes imposed under section 3101(a) of the Internal Revenue Code of 1986 which are subject to refund under section 6413(c) of such Code with respect to wages (as defined in section 3121 of such Code). Such taxes shall be determined on the basis of the records of wages maintained by the Commissioner of Social Security in accordance with the wages reported to the Secretary of the Treasury or his delegate pursuant to subtitle F of such Code, and the Commissioner of Social Security shall furnish the Managing Trustee such information as may be required by the Trustee for such purpose. The payments by the Managing Trustee shall be covered into the Treasury as repayments to the account for refunding internal revenue collections. Payments pursuant to the first sentence of this paragraph shall be made from the Federal Old-Age and Survivors Insurance Trust Fund and the Federal Disability Insurance Trust Fund in the ratio in which amounts were appropriated to such Trust Funds under clause (3) of subsection (a) of this section and clause (1) of subsection (b).

(3) Repayments made under paragraph (1) or (2) of this subsection shall not be available for expenditures but shall be carried to the surplus fund of the Treasury. If it subsequently appears that the estimates under either such paragraph in any particular period were too high or too low, appropriate adjustments shall be made by the Managing Trustee in future payments.

(4) The Commissioner of Social Security shall utilize the method prescribed pursuant to this paragraph, as in effect immediately before August 15, 1994, for determining the costs which should be borne by the general fund of the Treasury of carrying out the functions of the Commissioner, specified in section 432 of this title, which relate to the administration of provisions of the Internal Revenue Code of 1986 (other than those referred to in clause (i) of the first sentence of paragraph (1)(A)). The Board of Trustees of such Trust Funds shall prescribe the method of determining the costs which should be borne by the general fund in the Treasury of carrying out the functions of the Social Security Administration in connection with the withholding of taxes from benefits, as described in section 407(c) of this title, pursuant to requests by persons entitled to such benefits or such persons' representative payee. If at any time or times thereafter the Boards of Trustees of such Trust Funds consider such action advisable, they may modify the method of determining such costs.

(h) Benefit payments

Benefit payments required to be made under section 423 of this title, and benefit payments required to be made under subsection (b), (c), or (d) of section 402 of this title to individuals entitled to benefits on the basis of the wages and self-employment income of an individual entitled to disability insurance benefits, shall be made only from the Federal Disability Insurance Trust Fund. All other benefit payments required to be made under this subchapter (other than section 426 of this title) shall be made only from the Federal Old-Age and Survivors Insurance Trust Fund.

(i) Gifts and bequests

(1) The Managing Trustee may accept on behalf of the United States money gifts and bequests made unconditionally to the Federal Old-Age and Survivors Insurance Trust Fund, the Federal Disability Insurance Trust Fund, the Federal Hospital Insurance Trust Fund, or the Federal Supplementary Medical Insurance Trust Fund (and for the Medicare Prescription Drug Account and the Transitional Assistance Account in such Trust Fund) or to the Social Security Administration, the Department of Health and Human Services, or any part or officer thereof, for the benefit of any of such Funds or any activity financed through such Funds.

(2) Any such gift accepted pursuant to the authority granted in paragraph (1) of this subsection shall be deposited in—

(A) the specific trust fund designated by the donor or

(B) if the donor has not so designated, the Federal Old-Age and Survivors Insurance Trust Fund.

(j) Travel expenses

There are authorized to be made available for expenditure, out of the Federal Old-Age and Survivors Insurance Trust Fund, or the Federal Disability Insurance Trust Fund (as determined appropriate by the Commissioner of Social Security), such amounts as are required to pay travel expenses, either on an actual cost or commuted basis, to individuals for travel incident to medical examinations requested by the Commissioner of Social Security in connection with disability determinations under this subchapter, and to parties, their representatives, and all reasonably necessary witnesses for travel within the United States (as defined in section 410(i) of this title) to attend reconsideration interviews and proceedings before administrative law judges with respect to any determination under this subchapter. The amount available under the preceding sentence for payment for air travel by any person shall not exceed the coach fare for air travel between the points involved unless the use of first-class accommodations is required (as determined under regulations of the Commissioner of Social Security) because of such person's health condition or the unavailability of alternative accommodations; and the amount available for payment for other travel by any person shall not exceed the cost of travel (between the points involved) by the most economical and expeditious means of transportation appropriate to such person's health condition, as specified in such regulations. The amount available for payment under this subsection for travel by a representative to attend an administrative proceeding before an administrative law judge or other adjudicator shall not exceed the maximum amount allowable under this subsection for such travel originating within the geographic area of the office having jurisdiction over such proceeding.

(k) Experiment and demonstration project expenditures

Expenditures made for experiments and demonstration projects under section 434 of this title shall be made from the Federal Disability Insurance Trust Fund and the Federal Old-Age and Survivors Insurance Trust Fund, as determined appropriate by the Commissioner of Social Security.

(*l*) Interfund borrowing

(1) If at any time prior to January 1988 the Managing Trustee determines that borrowing authorized under this subsection is appropriate in order to best meet the need for financing the benefit payments from the Federal Old-Age and Survivors Insurance Trust Fund or the Federal Disability Insurance Trust Fund, the Managing Trustee may borrow such amounts as he determines to be appropriate from the other such Trust Fund, or, subject to paragraph (5), from the Federal Hospital Insurance Trust Fund established under section 1395i of this title, for transfer to and deposit in the Trust Fund whose need for financing is involved.

(2) In any case where a loan has been made to a Trust Fund under paragraph (1), there shall be transferred on the last day of each month after such loan is made, from the borrowing Trust Fund to the lending Trust Fund, the total interest accrued to such day with respect to the unrepaid balance of such loan at a rate equal to the rate which the lending Trust Fund would earn on the amount involved if the loan were an investment under subsection (d) (even if such an investment would earn interest at a rate different than the rate earned by investments redeemed by the lending fund in order to make the loan).

(3)(A) If in any month after a loan has been made to a Trust Fund under paragraph (1), the Managing Trustee determines that the assets of such Trust Fund are sufficient to permit repayment of all or part of any loans made to such Fund under paragraph (1), he shall make such repayments as he determines to be appropriate.

(B)(i) If on the last day of any year after a loan has been made under paragraph (1) by the Federal Hospital Insurance Trust Fund to the Federal Old-Age and Survivors Insurance Trust Fund or the Federal Disability Insurance Trust Fund, the Managing Trustee determines that the OASDI trust fund ratio exceeds 15 percent, he shall transfer from the borrowing Trust Fund to the Federal Hospital Insurance Trust Fund an amount that—

(I) together with any amounts transferred from another borrowing Trust Fund under this paragraph for such year, will reduce the OASDI trust fund ratio to 15 percent; and

(II) does not exceed the outstanding balance of such loan.

(ii) Amounts required to be transferred under clause (i) shall be transferred on the last day of the first month of the year succeeding the year in which the determination described in clause (i) is made.

(iii) For purposes of this subparagraph, the term "OASDI trust fund ratio" means, with respect to any calendar year, the ratio of—

(I) the combined balance in the Federal Old-Age and Survivors Insurance Trust Fund and the Federal Disability Insurance Trust Fund, as of the last day of such calendar year, to

(II) the amount estimated by the Commissioner of Social Security to be the total amount to be paid from the Federal Old-Age and Survivors Insurance Trust Fund and the Federal Disability Insurance Trust Fund during the calendar year following such calendar year for all purposes authorized by this section (other than payments of interest on, and repayments of, loans from the Federal Hospital Insurance Trust Fund under paragraph (1), but excluding any transfer payments between such trust funds and reducing the amount of any transfer to the Railroad Retirement Account by the amount of any transfers into either such trust fund from that Account).

(C)(i) The full amount of all loans made under paragraph (1) (whether made before or after January 1, 1983) shall be repaid at the earliest feasible date and in any event no later than December 31, 1989.

(ii) For the period after December 31, 1987, and before January 1, 1990, the Managing Trustee shall transfer each month to the Federal Hospital Insurance Trust Fund from any Trust Fund with any amount outstanding on a loan made from the Federal Hospital Insurance Trust Fund under paragraph (1) an amount not less than an amount equal to (I) the amount owed to the Federal Hospital Insurance Trust Fund by such Trust Fund at the beginning of such month (plus the interest accrued on the outstanding balance of such loan during such month), divided by (II) the number of months elapsing after the preceding month and before January 1990. The Managing Trustee may, during this period, transfer larger amounts than prescribed by the preceding sentence.

(4) The Board of Trustees shall make a timely report to the Congress of any amounts transferred (including interest payments) under this subsection.

(5)(A) No amounts may be borrowed from the Federal Hospital Insurance Trust Fund under paragraph (1) during any month if the Hospital Insurance Trust Fund ratio for such month is less than 10 percent.

(B) For purposes of this paragraph, the term "Hospital Insurance Trust Fund ratio" means, with respect to any month, the ratio of—

(i) the balance in the Federal Hospital Insurance Trust Fund, reduced by the outstanding amount of any loan (including interest thereon) theretofore made to such Trust Fund under this subsection, as of the last day of the second month preceding such month, to

(ii) the amount obtained by multiplying by twelve the total amount which (as estimated by the Secretary) will be paid from the Federal Hospital Insurance Trust Fund during the month for which such ratio is to be determined (other than payments of interest on, or repayments of loans from another Trust Fund under this subsection), and reducing the amount of any transfers to the Railroad Retirement Account by the amount of any transfer into the Hospital Insurance Trust Fund from that Account.

(m) Accounting for unnegotiated benefit checks

(1) The Secretary of the Treasury shall implement procedures to permit the identification of each check issued for benefits under this subchapter that has not been presented for payment by the close of the sixth month following the month of its issuance.

(2) The Secretary of the Treasury shall, on a monthly basis, credit each of the Trust Funds for the amount of all benefit checks (including interest thereon) drawn on such Trust Fund more than 6 months previously but not presented for payment and not previously credited to such Trust Fund, to the extent provided in advance in appropriation Acts.

(3) If a benefit check is presented for payment to the Treasury and the amount thereof has been previously credited pursuant to paragraph (2) to one of the Trust Funds, the Secretary of the Treasury shall nevertheless pay such check, if otherwise proper, recharge such Trust Fund, and notify the Commissioner of Social Security.

(4) A benefit check bearing a current date may be issued to an individual who did not negotiate the original benefit check and who surrenders such check for cancellation if the Secretary of the Treasury determines it is necessary to effect proper payment of benefits.

(n) Payments to Funds in satisfaction of obligations

Not later than July 1, 2004, the Secretary of the Treasury shall transfer, from amounts in the general fund of the Treasury that are not otherwise appropriated—

(1) $624,971,854 to the Federal Old–Age and Survivors Insurance Trust Fund;

(2) $105,379,671 to the Federal Disability Insurance Trust Fund; and

(3) $173,306,134 to the Federal Hospital Insurance Trust Fund.

Amounts transferred in accordance with this subsection shall be in satisfaction of certain outstanding obligations for deemed wage credits for 2000 and 2001.

(Aug. 14, 1935, c. 531, Title II, § 201, 49 Stat. 622; Aug. 10, 1939, c. 666, Title II, § 201, 53 Stat. 1362; Feb. 25, 1944, c. 63, Title IX, § 902, 58 Stat. 93; Aug. 28, 1950, c. 809, Title I, § 109(a), 64 Stat. 521; Aug. 1, 1956, c. 836, Title I, § 103(e), 70 Stat. 819; Pub.L. 85–840, Title II, § 205(a), Aug. 28, 1958, 72 Stat. 1021; Pub.L. 86–346, Title I, § 104(2), Sept. 22, 1959, 73 Stat. 622; Pub.L. 86–778, Title VII, § 701(a) to (e), Sept. 13, 1960, 74 Stat. 992, 993; Pub.L. 89–97, Title I, § 108(a), Title III, §§ 305, 327, July 30, 1965, 79 Stat. 338, 370, 400; Pub.L. 90–248, Title I, §§ 110, 169, Jan. 2, 1968, 81 Stat. 837, 875; Pub.L. 91–172, Title X, § 1005, Dec. 30, 1969, 83 Stat. 741; Pub.L. 92–336, Title II, § 205, July 1, 1972, 86 Stat. 422; Pub.L. 92–603, Title I, §§ 132(a) to (c), 136, Title III, § 305(a), Oct. 30, 1972, 86 Stat. 1360, 1364, 1484; Pub.L. 93–233, § 7, Dec. 31, 1973, 87 Stat. 955; Pub.L. 94–202, § 8(d), Jan. 2, 1976, 89 Stat. 1137; Pub.L. 95–216, Title I, § 102(a), Dec. 20, 1977, 91 Stat. 1513; Pub.L. 96–265, Title III, § 310(a), Title V, § 505(a)(5), June 9, 1980, 94 Stat. 459, 474; Pub.L. 96–403, § 1, Oct. 9, 1980, 94 Stat. 1709; Pub.L. 97–123, § 1(a), Dec. 29, 1981, 95 Stat. 1659; Pub.L. 98–21, Title I, §§ 126, 141(a), 142(a)(1), (2)(A), (3), (4), 152(a), 154(a), Title III, § 341(a), Apr. 20, 1983, 97 Stat. 91, 98 to 100, 105, 107, 135; Pub.L. 98–369, Div. B, Title VI, §§ 2661(a),

2663(a)(1), (j)(2)(A)(i), July 18, 1984, 98 Stat. 1156, 1160, 1170; Pub.L. 99–272, Title IX, § 9213(a), Apr. 7, 1986, 100 Stat. 180; Pub.L. 100–360, Title II, § 212(c)(1), July 1, 1988, 102 Stat. 741; Pub.L. 100–647, Title VIII, § 8005(a), Nov. 10, 1988, 102 Stat. 3781; Pub.L. 101–234, Title II, § 202(a), Dec. 13, 1989, 103 Stat. 1981; Pub.L. 101–508, Title V, §§ 5106(c), 5115(a), Title XIII, § 13304, Nov. 5, 1990, 104 Stat. 1388–268, 1388–274, 1388–627; Pub.L. 103–296, Title I, § 107(b), Title III, §§ 301(a), (b), 321(a)(1), (c)(1)(A)(i), (B)(i), (C), Aug. 15, 1994, 108 Stat. 1478, 1517, 1535, 1537; Pub.L. 103–387, § 3(a), (b), Oct. 22, 1994, 108 Stat. 4074, 4075; Pub.L. 104–121, Title I, § 103(a), Mar. 29, 1996, 110 Stat. 848; Pub.L. 105–277, Div. J, Title IV, § 4005(b), Oct. 21, 1998, 112 Stat. 2681–911; Pub.L. 106–169, Title II, § 251(b)(1), Dec. 14, 1999, 113 Stat. 1854; Pub.L. 106–170, Title III, § 301(b)(1)(B), Dec. 17, 1999, 113 Stat. 1902; Pub.L. 108–173, Title I, § 101(e)(3)(A), (B), Dec. 8, 2003, 117 Stat. 2150; Pub.L. 108–203, Title IV, § 420(a), Mar. 2, 2004, 118 Stat. 535; Pub.L. 114–74, Title VIII, § 833(1), (2), Nov. 2, 2015, 129 Stat. 613.)

1 So in original.

2 So in original. Two cls. (i) and (ii) have been enacted.

3 So in original. Probably should be "(vii)".

4 So in original. Probably should be "Commissioner".

HISTORICAL AND STATUTORY NOTES

References in Text

Subchapter A of chapter 9 of the Internal Revenue Code of 1939, referred to in subsec. (a)(1), (2), (3), was comprised of sections 1400 to 1432, and was repealed (subject to certain exceptions) by section 7851(a)(3) of the Internal Revenue Code of 1954.

Sections 1426 and 1420(c) of the Internal Revenue Code of 1939, referred to in subsec. (a)(3), were a part of subchapter A of chapter 9 of the 1939 Code. See note set out under this section.

Internal Revenue Code of 1954, referred to in subsecs. (a)(3), (4), (b)(1)(A), (2), (2)(A), was redesignated Internal Revenue Code of 1986 by Pub.L. 99–514, § 2, Oct. 22, 1986, 100 Stat. 2095, and is classified as 26 U.S.C.A. § 1 et seq.

Subtitle F of Title 26, referred to in subsecs. (a)(3), (4), (b)(1), is classified to section 6001 et seq. of Title 26, Internal Revenue Code.

Subchapter E of chapter 1 of the Internal Revenue Code of 1939, referred to in subsec. (a)(4), was comprised of sections 480 to 482, and was repealed (subject to certain exceptions) by section 7851(a)(1)(A) of the Internal Revenue Code of 1986.

Section 481 of the Internal Revenue Code of 1939, referred to in subsec. (a)(4), was a part of subchapter E of chapter 1 of the Internal Revenue Code of 1939. See note set out under this section. For provision deeming a reference in other laws to a provision of the Internal Revenue Code of 1939 as a reference to the corresponding provision of the Internal Revenue Code of 1986, see section 7852(b) of Title 26, the Internal Revenue Code. See Tables for distribution of the Internal Revenue Code of 1939 to the Internal Revenue Code of 1986.

Subchapter VIII, referred to in subsec. (g), was in the original "title VIII", meaning Title VIII of the Social Security Act, Act Aug. 14, 1935, c. 531, Title VIII, § 801 et seq., as added Dec. 14, 1999, Pub.L. 106–169, Title II, § 251(a), 113 Stat. 1844, as amended, which is classified to Subchapter VIII of this chapter, 42 U.S.C.A. § 1001 et seq.

Chapters 2 and 21 and subtitle F of the Internal Revenue Code of 1986, referred to in subsec. (g)(1)(A), (2), are classified to 26 U.S.C.A. §§ 1401 et seq., 3101 et seq., and 6001 et seq.

The Social Security Independence and Program Improvements Act of 1994, referred to in subsec. (g)(1)(A), is Pub.L. 103–296, Aug. 15, 1994, 108 Stat. 1464. Sections 207 and 208 of this Act are set out as notes under section 1382 of this title. For complete classification of this Act to the Code, see Short Title note set out under section 1305 of this title and Tables.

Codifications

The authorities provided by each provision of, and each amendment made by, Pub.L. 110–246, as in effect on Sept. 30, 2012, to continue, and the Secretary of Agriculture to carry out the authorities, until the later of Sept. 30, 2013, or the date specified in the provision of, or amendment made by, Pub.L. 110–246, see section 701(a) of Pub.L. 112–240, set out in a note under 7 U.S.C.A. § 8701.

Effective and Applicability Provisions

2015 Acts. Pub.L. 114–74, Title VIII, § 833(3), Nov. 2, 2015, 129 Stat. 614, provided that: "The amendments made by this section [amending this section] shall apply with respect to wages paid after December 31, 2015, and self-employment income for taxable years beginning after such date."

1998 Acts. Section 4005(c) of Pub.L. 105–277 provided that: "The amendments made by subsection (b) [amending subsec. (g) of this section] shall apply to benefits paid on or after the first day of the second month beginning after the month in which this Act is enacted [Oct. 21, 1998]."

1994 Acts. Section 3(c) of Pub.L. 103–387 provided that: "The amendments made by this section [amending this section and enacting provisions set out as a note under this section] shall apply with respect to wages paid after December 31, 1993, and self-employment income for taxable years beginning after such date."

Section 110 of Pub.L. 103–296 provided that:

"(a) In general.—Except as otherwise provided in this title, this title [Title I of Pub.L. 103–296] and the amendments made by such title [enacting section 913 of this title, amending this section and sections 402, 403, 404, 405, 406, 408, 409, 410, 411, 413, 415, 416, 417, 418, 421, 422, 423, 424a, 425, 428, 429, 430, 431, 432, 433, 901, 902, 903, 904, 907, 910, 1301, 1306, 1307, 1310, 1320a–6, 1320a–7, 1320a–8, 1320b–1, 1320b–10, 1320b–11, 1320c–4, 1381a, 1382, 1382a, 1382b, 1382c, 1382d, 1382e, 1382g, 1382h, 1382i, 1382j, 1383b, 1383c, 1383d, 1395i, 1395s, 1395t, 1395cc, 1395ff, 1395ii, 1395mm, 1395rr, 1396a, 1396d, 1396i, and 1396g of this title, sections 5312, 5313, 5315, 8141, and 8347 of Title 5, Government Organization and Employees, sections 9 and 11 of Appendix 3 of Title 5, sections 2015, 2017, 2020, and 2025 of Title 7, Agriculture, section 707 of Title 14, Coast Guard, sections 1402, 3127, 6050F, 6057, 6103, 6402, 6511; 9704, and 9706 of Title 26, Internal Revenue Code, sections 902, 921, 922, 923, 924, 925, 936, 945, and 957 of Title 30, Mineral Lands and Mining, sections 901 and 3720A of Title 31, Money and Finance, and section 5105 of Title 38, Veterans' Benefits, repealing section 907 of this title, enacting provisions set out as notes under sections 901, 904, and 907 of this title, and amending provisions set out as notes under sections 405, 1310, 1382, 1383, 1384, and 1385 of this title], shall take effect March 31, 1995.

"(b) Transition rules.—Section 106 [amending section 5315 of Title 5 and enacting provisions set out as a note under section 901 of this title] shall take effect on the date of the enactment of this Act [Aug. 15, 1994].

"**(c) Exceptions.**—The amendments made by section 103 [amending section 903 of this title], subsections (b)(4) and (c) of section 105 [section 105(b)(4), (c) of Pub.L. 103–296, which is set out in a note under section 901 of this title], and subsections (a)(1), (e)(1), (e)(2), (e)(3), and (*l*)(2) of section 108 [enacting section 913 of this title and amending sections 5312, 5313, and 5315 of Title 5 and section 11 of Appendix 3 of Title 5] shall take effect on the date of the enactment of this Act [Aug. 15, 1994]."

Section 301(c) of Pub.L. 103–296 provided that:

"**(1) In general.**—The amendments made by this section [amending subsecs. (d) and (f) of this section] shall apply with respect to obligations issued, and payments made, after 60 days after the date of the enactment of this Act [Aug. 15, 1994].

"**(2) Treatment of outstanding obligations.**—Not later than 60 days after the date of the enactment of this Act [Aug. 15, 1994], the Secretary of the Treasury shall issue to the Federal Old–Age and Survivors Insurance Trust Fund or the Federal Disability Insurance Trust Fund, as applicable, a paper instrument, in the form of a bond, note, or certificate of indebtedness, for each obligation which has been issued to the Trust Fund under section 201(d) of the Social Security Act [section 401(d) of this title] and which is outstanding as of such date. Each such document shall set forth the principal amount, date of maturity, and interest rate of the obligation, and shall state on its face that the obligation shall be incontestable in the hands of the Trust Fund to which it was issued, that the obligation is supported by the full faith and credit of the United States, and that the United States is pledged to the payment of the obligation with respect to both principal and interest."

Section 321(c)(1)(A)(ii) of Pub.L. 103–296 provided that: "The amendments made by clause (i) [amending subsec. (g)(1) of this section] shall apply only with respect to periods beginning on or after the date of the enactment of this Act [Aug. 15, 1994]."

Section 321(c)(1)(B)(ii) of Pub.L. 103–296 provided that: "The amendments made by clause (i) [amending subsec. (g)(2) of this section] shall apply only with respect to wages paid on or after January 1, 1995."

1990 Acts. Section 5106(d) of Pub.L. 101–508 provided that: "The amendments made by this section [amending this section and sections 406, 1320a–6, 1383 and 1395i of this title] shall apply with respect to determinations made on or after July 1, 1991, and to reimbursement for travel expenses incurred on or after April 1, 1991."

Section 5115(c) of Pub.L. 101–508 provided that: "The amendments made by this section [amending subsec. (a) of this section] shall become effective on the first day of the month following the month in which this Act is enacted [Nov. 1990]."

Amendment by section 13304 of Pub.L. 101–508 effective for annual reports of the Board of Trustees issued in or after calendar year 1991, see section 13306 of Pub.L. 101–508, set out as a note under section 632 of Title 2, The Congress.

1989 Acts. Amendment by Pub.L. 101–234 effective Jan. 1, 1990, see section 202(b) of Pub.L. 101–234, set out as a note under this section.

1988 Acts. Section 8005(b) of Pub.L. 100–647 provided that: "The amendments made by this section [amending subsec. (c) of this section and sections 1395i(b), 1395t(b) of this title] shall apply to members of the Boards of Trustees of the Federal Old–Age and Survivors Insurance Trust Fund and the Federal Disability Insurance Trust Fund, of the Federal Hospital Insurance Trust Fund, and of the Federal Supplementary Medical Insurance Trust Fund serving on such Boards of Trustees as members of the public on or after the date of the enactment of this Act [Nov. 10, 1988]."

1986 Acts. Section 9213(c) of Pub.L. 99–272 provided that: "The amendments made by this section [amending subsec. (c) of this section and sections 1395i(b) and 1395t(b) of this title] shall become effective on the date of the enactment of this Act [Apr. 7, 1986]."

1984 Acts. Section 2664 of Pub.L. 98–369 provided that:

"**(a)** Except as otherwise specifically provided, the amendments made by sections 2661 and 2662 [amending subsec. (*l*) of this section, sections 402, 403, 405, 409, 410, 415, 416, 423, 428, and 429 of this title, sections 86, 134, 422A, 3121, 3306, and 6334 of Title 26, Internal Revenue Code, and enacting provisions set out as notes under sections 402, 403, 415 and 902 of this title, sections 3121 and 3306 of Title 26, Internal Revenue Code and section 3023 of Title 38, Veterans' Benefits] shall be effective as though they had been included in the enactment of the Social Security Amendments of 1983 (Public Law 98–21).

"**(b)** Except to the extent otherwise specifically provided in this subtitle, the amendments made by section 2663 [amending this section and sections 402, 403, 405, 406, 408, 409, 410, 411, 413, 415, 416, 417, 418, 421, 422, 423, 426, 428, 430, 431, 433, 502, 503, 602, 603, 604, 606, 607, 609, 610, 614, 615, 620, 631, 636, 641, 643, 644, 645, 652, 653, 654, 656, 660, 662, 674, 902, 903, 1101, 1104, 1108, 1301, 1302, 1306, 1307, 1314, 1315, 1316, 1320, 1320a–5, 1320b–1, 1331, 1381a, 1382, 1382a, 1382c, 1382d, 1382g, 1382j, 1383, 1395i, 1395s, 1395t, 1395u, 1396, 1397a and 1397e of this title, sections 51, 1402, 3121, 6057, 6103 and 6511 of Title 26, Internal Revenue Code, repealing sections 1331 to 1336 of this title, and enacting provisions set out as notes under sections 1301 and 1307 of this title] shall be effective on the date of the enactment of this Act [July 18, 1984]; but none of such amendments shall be construed as changing or affecting any right, liability, status, or interpretation which existed (under the provisions of law involved) before that date."

1983 Acts. Section 141(c) of Pub.L. 98–21 provided that: "The amendments made by this section [amending subsec. (a) of this section and section 1395i(a) of this title] shall become effective on the first day of the month following the month in which this Act is enacted [April, 1983]."

Section 142(a)(2)(B) of Pub.L. 98–21 provided that: "The amendment made by this paragraph [amending pars. (1) and (2) of subsec. (*l*) of this section] shall apply with respect to months beginning more than thirty days after the date of enactment of this Act [Apr. 20, 1983]."

Section 152(b) of Pub.L. 98–21 provided that: "The amendment made by subsection (a) [enacting subsec. (m) of this section] shall apply with respect to all checks for benefits under title II of the Social Security Act [this subchapter] which are issued on or after the first day of the twenty-fourth month following the month in which this Act is enacted [April, 1983]."

Section 154(e) of Pub.L. 98–21 provided that: "The amendments made by this section [amending subsec. (c) of this section and sections 1395i(b) and 1395t(b) of this title] shall take effect on the date of the enactment of this Act [Apr. 20, 1983]."

Section 341(d) of Pub.L. 98–21 provided that: "The amendments made by this section [amending subsec. (c) of this section and sections 1395i(b) and 1395t(b) of this title] shall become effective on the date of enactment of this Act [Apr. 30, 1983]."

1981 Acts. Section 1(c) of Pub.L. 97–123 provided that: "The amendments made by this section [amending this section and section 1395i of this title] shall be effective on the date of the enactment of this Act [Dec. 29, 1981]."

1980 Acts. Section 2 of Pub.L. 96–403 provided that: "The amendments made by the first section of this Act [amending this section] shall apply with respect to remuneration paid, and taxable years beginning after December 31, 1979."

1977 Acts. Amendment by Pub.L. 95–216 applicable with respect to remuneration paid or received and taxable years beginning after 1977, see section 104 of Pub.L. 95–216, set out as a note under section 1401 of Title 26, Internal Revenue Code.

1972 Acts. Section 132(f) of Pub.L. 92–603 provided that: "The amendments made by this section [amending subsecs. (a) and (b) and enacting subsec. (i) of this section and amending sections 1395i(a) and 1395t(a) of this title] shall apply with respect to gifts and bequests received after the date of enactment of this Act [Oct. 30, 1972]."

Section 305(c) of Pub.L. 92–603 provided that: "The provisions of this section [amending subsec. (g)(1)(A) of this section and enacting provisions set out as a note under this section] shall become effective on the date of enactment of this Act [Oct. 30, 1972]."

1960 Acts. Section 701(f) of Pub.L. 86–778 provided that: "The amendments made by this section [to subsecs. (c), (d) and (e) of this section] shall take effect on the first day of the first month beginning after the date of the enactment of this Act [Sept. 13, 1960]."

1958 Acts. Amendment by Pub.L. 85–840 applicable with respect to monthly benefits under this subchapter for months after Aug. 1958, but only if an application for such benefits is filed on or after Aug. 28, 1958, see section 207(a) of Pub.L. 85–840, set out as a note under section 416 of this title.

1939 Acts. Section 201 of Act Aug. 10, 1939 provided that the amendment made by that section is effective Jan. 1, 1940.

Temporary Employee Payroll Tax Cut

For provisions relating to transfer of funds to the Federal Old–Age and Survivors Trust Fund and the Federal Disability Insurance Trust Fund established under section 201 of the Social Security Act (42 U.S.C. 401) and to the Social Security Equivalent Benefit Account established under section 15A(a) of the Railroad Retirement Act of 1974 (45 U.S.C. 231n–1(a)), see Pub.L. 111–312, Title VI, § 601(d), Dec. 17, 2010, 124 Stat. 3309, set out in a note under 26 U.S.C.A. § 1401.

Protection of Social Security

Pub.L. 110–234, Title XV, § 15361, May 22, 2008, 122 Stat. 1527, and Pub.L. 110–246, Title XV, § 15361, June 18, 2008, 122 Stat. 2289, provided that: "To ensure that the assets of the trust funds established under section 201 of the Social Security Act (42 U.S.C. 401) [this section] are not reduced as a result of the enactment of this Act [the Food, Conservation, and Energy Act of 2008, Pub.L. 110–246, June 18, 2008, 122 Stat. 1651; see Tables for complete classification], the Secretary of the Treasury shall transfer annually from the general revenues of the Federal Government to those trust funds the following amounts:

"(1) For fiscal year 2009, $5,000,000.

"(2) For fiscal year 2010, $9,000,000.

"(3) For fiscal year 2011, $8,000,000.

"(4) For fiscal year 2012, $7,000,000.

"(5) For fiscal year 2013, $8,000,000.

"(6) For fiscal year 2014, $8,000,000.

"(7) For fiscal year 2015, $8,000,000.

"(8) For fiscal year 2016, $6,000,000.

"(9) For fiscal year 2017, $7,000,000.".

[Amendments by Pub.L. 110–246, except as otherwise provided, shall take effect on the earlier of June 18, 2008 or May 22, 2008, see Pub.L. 110–246, § 4(b), set out in a Repeal of Duplicative Enactment note under 7 U.S.C.A. § 8701; Pub.L. 110–234 repealed effective May 22, 2008, see Repeal of Duplicative Enactment by Pub.L. 110–246, § 4(a), set out in a note under 7 U.S.C.A. § 8701.]

No Impact on Social Security Trust Funds

Pub.L. 107–147, Title V, § 501, Mar. 9, 2002, 116 Stat. 58, provided that:

"**(a) In general.**—Nothing in this Act (or an amendment made by this Act [enacting subchapter Y of this chapter (26 U.S.C.A. § 1400L), amending 26 U.S.C.A. §§ 21, 23, 24, 25B, 26, 30, 32, 38, 42, 45, 45A, 45E, 45F, 51, 51A, 56, 62, 63, 108, 131, 137, 151, 168, 170, 172, 179A, 220, 280F, 341, 351, 358, 401, 402, 403, 404, 408, 409, 412, 414, 415, 416, 417, 448, 457, 469, 475, 503, 529, 613A, 741, 809, 857, 904, 943, 953, 954, 995, 1055, 1091, 1221, 1233, 1234A, 1234B, 1256, 1394, 1397E, 1400C, 2016, 2101, 2511, 3304, 3306, 4101, 4980E, 4980F, 6103, 6105, 6224, 6227, 6228, 6229, 6231, 6234, 6331, 6428, 7652, 7702A, and 9812, 29 U.S.C.A. §§ 1003, 1054, 1082, 1104, and 1306, and 42 U.S.C.A. §§ 503, 603, and 1103, and enacting provisions set out as notes under 26 U.S.C.A. §§ 1, 21, 23, 25B, 26, 30, 32, 38, 45, 51, 51A, 56, 62, 108, 131, 151, 168, 172, 179A, 220, 401, 448, 613A, 809, 953, 1256, 1397E, 3304, 4101, 6041, 6103, 6224, 6331, 7652, 7702A, and 9812, and amending provisions set out as notes under 26 U.S.C.A. §§ 1, 38, 415, and 4980F]) shall be construed to alter or amend title II of the Social Security Act [42 U.S.C.A. § 401 et seq.] (or any regulation promulgated under that Act [Act Aug. 14, 1935, c. 531, 49 Stat. 620, as amended]).

"**(b) Transfers.**—

"**(1) Estimate of Secretary.**—The Secretary of the Treasury shall annually estimate the impact that the enactment of this Act has on the income and balances of the trust funds established under section 201 of the Social Security Act (42 U.S.C. 401).

"**(2) Transfer of funds.**—If, under paragraph (1), the Secretary of the Treasury estimates that the enactment of this Act [Mar. 9, 2002] has a negative impact on the income and balances of the trust funds established under section 201 of the Social Security Act (42 U.S.C. 401), the Secretary shall transfer, not less frequently than quarterly, from the general revenues of the Federal Government an amount sufficient so as to ensure that the income and balances of such trust funds are not reduced as a result of the enactment of this Act [Mar. 9, 2002]."

Victims of Terrorism Tax Relief Act of 2001—No Impact on Social Security Trust Funds

Pub.L. 107–134, Title III, § 301, Jan. 23, 2002, 115 Stat. 2444, provided that:

"(a) **In general.**—Nothing in this Act (or an amendment made by this Act) [Victims of Terrorism Tax Relief Act of 2001, Pub.L. 107–134, Jan. 23, 2002, 115 Stat. 2427, which enacted 26 U.S.C.A §§ 139 and 5891, and 29 U.S.C.A. § 1148, amending 26 U.S.C.A. §§ 5, 101, 104, 642, 692, 2011, 2053, 2201, 6013, 6081, 6103, 6105, 6161, 6404, 7213, 7508, 7508A, and 29 U.S.C.A. § 1302, and enacting provisions set out as notes under 26 U.S.C.A. §§ 101, 108, 139, 501, 642, 692, 2011, 5891, 6081 and 6103, and 49 U.S.C.A. § 40101] shall be construed to alter or amend title II of the Social Security Act [Act Aug. 14, 1935, c. 531, 49 Stat. 620, as amended; Title II is classified principally to subchapter II of chapter 7 of Title 42 (42 U.S.C.A. § 401 et seq.); see Tables for complete classification] (or any regulation promulgated under that Act).

"(b) **Transfers.**—

"(1) **Estimate of Secretary.**—The Secretary of the Treasury shall annually estimate the impact that the enactment of this Act [Victims of Terrorism Tax Relief Act of 2001, Pub.L. 107–134, Jan. 23, 2002, 115 Stat. 2427, which enacted 26 U.S.C.A §§ 139 and 5891, and 29 U.S.C.A. § 1148, amending 26 U.S.C.A. §§ 5, 101, 104, 642, 692, 2011, 2053, 2201, 6013, 6081, 6103, 6105, 6161, 6404, 7213, 7508, 7508A, and 29 U.S.C.A. § 1302, and enacting provisions set out as notes under 26 U.S.C.A. §§ 101, 108, 139, 501, 642, 692, 2011, 5891, 6081 and 6103, and 49 U.S.C.A. § 40101] has on the income and balances of the trust funds established under section 201 of the Social Security Act (42 U.S.C. 401).

"(2) **Transfer of funds.**—If, under paragraph (1), the Secretary of the Treasury estimates that the enactment of this Act [Victims of Terrorism Tax Relief Act of 2001, Pub.L. 107–134, Jan. 23, 2002, 115 Stat. 2427, which enacted 26 U.S.C.A §§ 139 and 5891, and 29 U.S.C.A. § 1148, amending 26 U.S.C.A. §§ 5, 101, 104, 642, 692, 2011, 2053, 2201, 6013, 6081, 6103, 6105, 6161, 6404, 7213, 7508, 7508A, and 29 U.S.C.A. § 1302, and enacting provisions set out as notes under 26 U.S.C.A. §§ 101, 108, 139, 501, 642, 692, 2011, 5891, 6081 and 6103, and 49 U.S.C.A. § 40101] has a negative impact on the income and balances of the trust funds established under section 201 of the Social Security Act (42 U.S.C. 401), the Secretary shall transfer, not less frequently than quarterly, from the general revenues of the Federal Government an amount sufficient so as to ensure that the income and balances of such trust funds are not reduced as a result of the enactment of this Act [Victims of Terrorism Tax Relief Act of 2001, Pub.L. 107–134, Jan. 23, 2002, 115 Stat. 2427, which enacted 26 U.S.C.A §§ 139 and 5891, and 29 U.S.C.A. § 1148, amending 26 U.S.C.A. §§ 5, 101, 104, 642, 692, 2011, 2053, 2201, 6013, 6081, 6103, 6105, 6161, 6404, 7213, 7508, 7508A, and 29 U.S.C.A. § 1302, and enacting provisions set out as notes under 26 U.S.C.A. §§ 101, 108, 139, 501, 642, 692, 2011, 5891, 6081 and 6103, and 49 U.S.C.A. § 40101]."

Study by General Accounting Office [now Government Accountability Office] of Existing Coordination of the DI and SSI Programs as They Relate to Individuals Entering or Leaving Concurrent Entitlement

Pub.L. 106–170, Title III, § 303(b), Dec. 17, 1999, 113 Stat. 1904, provided that:

"(1) **Study.**—As soon as practicable after the date of the enactment of this Act [Dec. 17, 1999], the Comptroller General of the United States shall undertake a study to evaluate the coordination under current law of the disability insurance program under title II of the Social Security Act [subchapter II of this chapter] (42 U.S.C. 401 et seq.) and the supplemental security income program under title XVI of such Act [subchapter XVI of this chapter] (42 U.S.C. 1381 et seq.), as such programs relate to individuals entering or leaving concurrent entitlement under such programs. In such study, the Comptroller General shall specifically address the effectiveness of work incentives under such programs with respect to such individuals and the effectiveness of coverage of such individuals under titles XVIII and XIX of such Act [subchapters XVIII and XIX of this chapter] (42 U.S.C. 1395 et seq., 1396 et seq.).

"(2) **Report.**—Not later than 3 years after the date of the enactment of this Act [Dec. 17, 1999], the Comptroller General shall transmit to the Committee on Ways and Means of the House of Representatives and the Committee on Finance of the Senate a written report presenting the results of the Comptroller General's study conducted pursuant to this subsection, together with such recommendations for legislative or administrative changes as the Comptroller General determines are appropriate."

Advances From Trust Funds for Administrative Expenses

Section 305(b) of Pub.L. 92–603, provided that:

"(1) Sums appropriated pursuant to section 1601 of the Social Security Act [section 1381 of this title] shall be utilized from time to time, in amounts certified under the second sentence of section 201(g)(1)(A) of such Act [subsec. (g)(1)(A) of this section], to repay the Trust Funds for expenditures made from such Funds in any fiscal year under section 201(g)(1)(A) of such Act (as amended by subsection (a) of this section) [amending subsec. (g)(1)(A) of this section] on account of the costs of administration of title XVI of such Act (as added by section 301 of this Act) [subchapter XVI of this chapter].

"(2) If the Trust Funds have not theretofore been repaid for expenditures made in any fiscal year (as described in paragraph (1)) to the extent necessary on account of—

"(A) expenditures made from such Funds prior to the end of such fiscal year to the extent that the amount of such expenditures exceeded the amount of the expenditures which would have been made from such Funds if subsection (a) had not been enacted,

"(B) the additional administrative expenses, if any, resulting from the excess expenditures described in subparagraph (A), and

"(C) any loss in interest to such Funds resulting from such excess expenditures and such administrative expenses,

in order to place each such Fund in the same position (at the end of such fiscal year) as it would have been in if such excess expenditures had not been made, the amendments made by subsection (a) shall cease to be effective at the close of the fiscal year following such fiscal year.

"(3) As used in this subsection, the term 'Trust Funds' has the meaning given it in section 201(g)(1)(A) of the Social Security Act [subsec. (g)(1)(A) of this section]."

Advances From Trust Funds for Administrative Purposes; Fiscal Year Transition Period of July 1, 1976, Through September 30, 1976, Deemed Fiscal Year

Fiscal year transition period of July 1, 1976, through Sept. 30, 1976, deemed fiscal year for purposes of section 305(b) of Pub.L. 92–603, set out as a note above relating to advances from trust funds for administrative purposes, see section 201(11) of Pub.L. 94–274, set out as a note under section 343 of Title 7, Agriculture.

Appointment and Compensation of Individuals Necessary to Assist Board of Trustees

Section 8(e) of Pub.L. 94–202 provided that: "Any persons the Board of Trustees finds necessary to employ to assist it in performing its functions under section 201(g)(4) of the Social Security Act [subsec. (g)(4) of this section] may be appointed without regard to the civil service or classification laws, shall be compensated, while so employed at rates fixed by the Board of Trustees, but not exceeding $100 per day, and, while away from their homes or regular places of business, they may be allowed traveling expenses, including per diem in lieu of subsistence, as authorized by law for persons in the Government service employed intermittently."

Construction of 1994 Amendments

Section 321(d) of Pub.L. 103–296 provided that:

"(1) The preceding provisions of this section [amending this section and sections 402, 403, 405, 408–411, 413, 415, 416, 418, 423, 429, 430, and 432 of this title, and enacting provisions set out as notes under this section and sections 402 and 430 of this title] shall be construed only as technical and clerical corrections and as reflecting the original intent of the provisions amended thereby.

"(2) Any reference in title II of the Social Security Act [this subchapter] to the Internal Revenue Code of 1986 [Title 26, Internal Revenue Code] shall be construed to include a reference to the Internal Revenue Code of 1954 to the extent necessary to carry out the provisions of paragraph (1)."

Due Date for 1983 Report on Operation and Status of Trust Fund

Section 154(d) of Pub.L. 98–21 provided that: "Notwithstanding sections 201(c)(2), 1817(b)(2), and 1841(b)(2) of the Social Security Act [subsec. (c)(2) of this section and sections 1395i(b)(2) and 1395t(b)(2) of this title], the annual reports of the Boards of Trustees of the Trust Funds which are required in the calendar year 1983 under those sections may be filed at any time not later than forty-five days after the date of the enactment of this Act [Apr. 20, 1983]."

Effects of Certain Amendments by Pub.L. 96–265; Report

Section 312 of Pub.L. 96–265 provided that: "The Secretary of Health and Human Services shall submit to the Congress not later than January 1, 1985, a full and complete report as to the effects produced by reason of the preceding provisions of this Act [Titles I (section 101 et seq.), II (section 201 et seq.), and III (section 301 et seq.) of Pub.L. 96–265] and the amendments made thereby [see Tables for classification]."

Fiscal Year Transition Period of July 1, 1976, Through September 30, 1976, Deemed Fiscal Year

Fiscal year transition period of July 1, 1976, through Sept. 30, 1976, deemed fiscal year for purposes of subsecs. (a), (b), and (g)(1) of this section, see section 201(12) of Pub.L. 94–274, set out as a note under section 343 of Title 7, Agriculture.

Fiscal Year Transition Period of July 1, 1976, Through September 30, 1976 Deemed Part of Fiscal Year Beginning July 1, 1975

Fiscal year transition period of July 1, 1976, through Sept. 30, 1976, deemed part of fiscal year beginning July 1, 1975, for purposes of subsec. (c) of this section, see section 204(7) of Pub.L. 94–274, set out as a note under section 390e of Title 7, Agriculture.

Gifts and Bequests for Use of United States and for Exclusively Public Purposes

Section 132(g) of Pub.L. 92–603 provided that: "For the purpose of Federal income, estate, and gift taxes, any gift or bequest to the Federal Old–Age and Survivors Insurance Trust Fund, the Federal Disability Insurance Trust Fund, the Federal Hospital Insurance Trust Fund, or the Federal Supplementary Medical Insurance Trust Fund, or to the Department of Health, Education, and Welfare [now Health and Human Services], or any part or officer thereof, for the benefit of any of such Funds or any activity financed through any of such Funds, which is accepted by the Managing Trustee of such Trust Funds under the authority of section 201(i) of the Social Security Act [subsec. (i) of this section], shall be considered as a gift or bequest to or for the use of the United States and as made for exclusively public purposes."

Land Diverted Under 1983 Payment-in-Kind Program

Land diverted from production of agricultural commodities under a 1983 payment-in-kind program to be treated, for purposes of this subchapter, as used during the 1983 crop year by qualified taxpayers in the active conduct of the trade or business of farming, with qualified taxpayers who materially participate in the diversion and devotion to conservation uses under a 1983 payment-in-kind program to be treated as materially participating in the operation of such land during the 1983 crop year, see section 3 of Pub.L. 98–4, set out as a note under section 61 of Title 26, Internal Revenue Code.

Method of Determining Costs Prescribed by Board of Trustees; Certification and Transfer of Funds

Section 8(f) of Pub.L. 94–202, as amended by Pub.L. 99–514, § 2, Oct. 22, 1986, 100 Stat. 2095, provided that: "The Secretary shall not make any estimates pursuant to section 201(g)(1)(A)(ii) of the Social Security Act [subsec. (g)(1)(A)(ii) of this section] before the Board of Trustees prescribes the method of determining costs as provided in section 201(g)(4) of such Act [subsec. (g)(4) of this section]. The determination pursuant to section 201(g)(1)(B) of the Social Security Act [subsec. (g)(1)(B) of this section] with respect to the carrying out of the functions of the Department of Health, Education, and Welfare [now Health and Human Services] specified in section 232 of such Act [section 432 of this title], which relate to the administration of provisions of the Internal Revenue Code of 1986 [formerly I.R.C. 1954] (other than those referred to in clause (i) of the first sentence of section 201(g)(1)(A) of the Social Security Act [subsec. (g)(1)(A) of this section]), during fiscal years ending before the Board of Trustees prescribes the method of making such determinations, shall be made after the Board of Trustees has prescribed such method. The Secretary of Health, Education, and Welfare [now Health and Human Services] shall certify to the Managing Trustee the amounts that should be transferred from the general fund in the Treasury to the Trust Funds (as referred to in section 201(g)(1)(A) of the Social Security Act [subsec. (g)(1)(A) of this section]) to insure that the general fund in the Treasury bears its proper share of the costs of carrying out such functions in such fiscal years. The Managing Trustee is authorized and directed to transfer any such amounts in accordance with any certification so made."

Reimbursement to Trust Funds for Unnegotiated Benefit Checks

Section 152(c) of Pub.L. 98–21 provided that:

"(1) The Secretary of the Treasury shall transfer from the general fund of the Treasury to the Federal Old–Age and Survivors Insurance Trust Fund and to the Federal Disability Insurance Trust Fund, in the month following the month in which this Act is enacted [April, 1983] and in each of the succeeding 30 months, such sums as may be necessary to reimburse such Trust Funds in the total amount of all checks (including interest thereof) which he and the Secretary of Health and Human Services jointly determine to be unnegotiated benefit checks, to the extent provided in advance in appropriation Acts. After any amounts authorized by this subsection have been transferred to a Trust Fund with respect to any benefit check, the provisions of paragraphs (3) and (4) of section 201(m) of the Social Security Act [subsec. (m) of this section] (as added by subsection (a) of this section) shall be applicable to such check.

"(2) As used in paragraph (1), the term 'unnegotiated benefit checks' means checks for benefits under title II of the Social Security Act [this subchapter] which are issued prior to the twenty-fourth month following the month in which this Act is enacted [April, 1983], which remain unnegotiated after the sixth month following the date on which they were issued, and with respect to which no transfers have previously been made in accordance with the first sentence of such paragraph."

Repeal of Changes in Medicare Part B Monthly Premium and Financing

Section 202 of Pub.L. 101–234 provided that:

"**(a) In general.**—Sections 211 through 213 (other than sections 211(b) and 211(c)(3)(B)) of MCCA [which had enacted sections 1395t–1 and 1395t–2 of this title and amended this section and sections 1395i, 1395*l*, 1395r, 1395s, 1395t, 1395w, and 1395mm of this title and enacted provisions set out as a note under section 1395r of this title] are repealed and the provisions of law amended or repealed by such sections are restored or revised as if such sections had not been enacted.

"**(b) Effective date.**—The provisions of subsection (a) shall take effect January 1, 1990, and the repeal of section 211 of MCCA [amending sections 1395r, 1395w, and 1395mm of this title] shall apply to premiums for months beginning after December 31, 1989."

Study of Float Period of Monthly Insurance Benefit Checks

Pub.L. 98–21, Title I, § 153, Apr. 20, 1983, 97 Stat. 106, directed the Secretary of Health and Human Services and the Secretary of the Treasury jointly to undertake a thorough study with respect to the period of time (referred to as the "float period") between the issuance of checks from the general fund of the Treasury in payment of monthly insurance benefits under title II of the Social Security Act [this subchapter] and the transfer to the general fund from the Federal Old–Age and Survivors Insurance Trust Fund or the Federal Disability Insurance Trust Fund, as applicable, of the amounts necessary to compensate the general fund for the issuance of such checks, with the Secretaries to submit a report to the President and the Congress not later than twelve months after April 20, 1983, on their findings as to the necessity of making adjustments in the procedures governing the payment of the monthly insurance benefits. For termination, effective May 15, 2000, of reporting provisions pertaining to transfers from the general fund to the Social Security Trust fund accounts, set out above, see Pub.L. 104–66, § 3003, as amended, set out as a note under 31 U.S.C.A. § 1113, and the 17th item on page 143 of House Document No. 103–7.

Study Relating to Establishment of Time Limitations for Decisions on Claims for Benefits; Report

Section 308 of Pub.L. 96–265 provided that the Secretary of Health and Human Services submit to the Congress, no later than July 1, 1980, a report recommending the establishment of appropriate time limitations governing decisions on claims for benefits under this subchapter, taking into account both the need for expeditious processing of claims for benefits and the need to assure that all such claims will be thoroughly considered and accurately determined.

Taxes on Services Rendered by Employees of International Organizations Prior to January 1, 1946

Section 5(b) of Act Dec. 29, 1945, c. 652, Title I, 59 Stat. 671, prohibited collection of tax under title VIII or IX of the Social Security Act or under the Federal Insurance Contributions Act or the Federal Unemployment Tax Act with respect to services rendered prior to January 1, 1946, which were described in paragraph (16) of sections 1426(b) and 1607(c) of the Internal Revenue Code of 1939, and authorized refund of taxes collected.

Transfer of Equivalent of 1983 Tax Increases to Payor Funds; Reports

Section 121(e) of Pub.L. 98–21, as amended Pub.L. 99–514, § 2, Oct. 22, 1986, 100 Stat. 2095; Pub.L. 103–66, Title XIII, § 13215(c), Aug. 10, 1993, 107 Stat. 476; Pub.L. 104–188, Title I, § 1703(n)(12), Aug. 20, 1996, 110 Stat. 1877, provided that:

"**(1) In general.—(A)** There are hereby appropriated to each payor fund amounts equivalent to (i) the aggregate increase in tax liabilities under chapter 1 of the Internal Revenue Code of 1986 [section 1 et seq. of Title 26, Internal Revenue Code] which is attributable to the application of sections 86 and 871(a)(3) of such Code (as added by this section) [26 U.S.C. 86, 871(a)(3)] to payments from such payor fund, less (ii) the amounts equivalent to the aggregate increase in tax liabilities under chapter 1 of the Internal Revenue Code of 1986 [section 1 et seq. of Title 26] which is attributable to the amendments to section 86 of such Code made by section 13215 of the Revenue Reconciliation Act of 1993 [section 86 of Title 26 as amended by section 13215 of Pub.L. 103–66].

"**(B)** There are hereby appropriated to the hospital insurance trust fund amounts equal to the increase in tax liabilities described in subparagraph (A)(ii). Such appropriated amounts shall be transferred from the general fund of the Treasury on the basis of estimates of such tax liabilities made by the Secretary of the Treasury. Transfers shall be made pursuant to a schedule made by the Secretary of the Treasury that takes into account estimated timing of collection of such liabilities.

"**(2) Transfers.**—The amounts appropriated by paragraph (1)(A) to any payor fund shall be transferred from time to time (but not less frequently than quarterly) from the general fund of the Treasury on the basis of estimates made by the

Secretary of the Treasury of the amounts referred to in such paragraph. Any such quarterly payment shall be made on the first day of such quarter and shall take into account social security benefits estimated to be received during such quarter. Proper adjustments shall be made in the amounts subsequently transferred to the extent prior estimates were in excess of or less than the amounts required to be transferred.

"(3) **Definitions.**—For purposes of this subsection—

"(A) **Payor fund.**—The term 'payor fund' means any trust fund or account from which payments of social security benefits are made.

"(B) **Hospital insurance trust fund.**—The term 'hospital insurance trust fund' means the fund established pursuant to section 1817 of the Social Security Act [section 1395i of this title].

"(C) **Social security benefits.**—The term 'social security benefits' has the meaning given such term by section 86(d)(1) of the Internal Revenue Code of 1986 [26 U.S.C. 86(d)(1)].

"(4) **Reports.**—The Secretary of the Treasury shall submit annual reports to the Congress and to the Secretary of Health and Human Services and the Railroad Retirement Board on—

"(A) the transfers made under this subsection during the year, and the methodology used in determining the amount of such transfers and the funds or account to which made, and

"(B) the anticipated operation of this subsection during the next 5 years."

[For termination, effective May 15, 2000, of provisions relating to submission of annual reports to Congress in section 121(e)(4) of Pub.L. 98–21, set out in note above, see Pub.L. 104–66, § 3003, as amended, set out as a note under 31 U.S.C.A. § 1113 and item 17 on page 143 of House Document No. 103–7.]

[Amendment by section 1703 of Pub.L. 104–188 effective as if included in provision of Revenue Reconciliation Act of 1993 [Pub.L. 103–66, Title XIII, Chapter I, § 13001 et seq., Aug. 10, 1993, 107 Stat. 416, see Tables for classification] to which it relates, see section 1703(*o*) of Pub.L. 104–188, set out as a note under section 39 of Title 26, Internal Revenue Code.]

Use of Continuing Disability Review Funds and Report Requirement

Section 103(d) of Pub.L. 104–121, as amended Pub.L. 104–193, Title II, § 211(d)(5)(D), Aug. 22, 1996, 110 Stat. 2192, provided that:

"(1) **In general.**—The Commissioner of Social Security shall ensure that funds made available for continuing disability reviews (as defined in section 201(g)(1)(A) of the Social Security Act) [subsec. (g)(1)(A) of this section] are used, to the greatest extent practicable, to maximize the combined savings in the old-age, survivors, and disability insurance, supplemental security income, Medicare, and medicaid programs, except that the amounts appropriated pursuant to the authorization and discretionary spending allowance provisions in section 211(d)(2)(5) of the Personal Responsibility and Work Opportunity Reconciliation Act of 1996 [probably means section 211(d)(5) of Pub.L. 104–193, which amended sections 665e and 901 of Title 2, The Congress, enacted provisions set out as a note under section 1382c of this title, and amended this note] shall be used only for continuing disability reviews and redeterminations under title XVI of the Social Security Act [this subchapter].

"(2) **Report.**—The Commissioner of Social Security shall provide annually (at the conclusion of each of the fiscal years 1996 through 2002) to the Congress a report on continuing disability reviews which includes—

"(A) the amount spent on continuing disability reviews in the fiscal year covered by the report, and the number of reviews conducted, by category of review;

"(B) the results of the continuing disability reviews in terms of cessations of benefits or determinations of continuing eligibility, by program; and

"(C) the estimated savings over the short-, medium-, and long-term to the old-age, survivors, and disability insurance, supplemental security income, Medicare, and medicaid programs from continuing disability reviews which result in cessations of benefits and the estimated present value of such savings."

EXECUTIVE ORDERS

EXECUTIVE ORDER NO. 12335

Ex. Ord. No. 12335, Dec. 16, 1981, 46 F.R. 61633, as amended by Ex. Ord. No. 12397, Dec. 23, 1982, 47 F.R. 57651; Ex. Ord. No. 12402, Jan. 15, 1983, 48 F.R. 2311, which related to the National Commission on Social Security Reform, was revoked by Ex. Ord. No. 12534, Sept. 30, 1985, 50 F.R. 40319, set out as a note under section 14 of the Federal Advisory Committee Act in Appendix 2 to Title 5, Government Organization and Employees.

[Ex. Ord. Nos. 12397 and 12402, set out in the credit to this Executive Order, were both revoked by Ex. Ord. No. 12553, Feb. 25, 1986, 51 F.R. 7237.]

§ 401a. Omitted

HISTORICAL AND STATUTORY NOTES

Codifications

Section, Acts Aug. 1, 1956, c. 836, Title I, § 116, 70 Stat. 833; Sept. 13, 1966, Pub.L. 86–778, Title VII, § 704, 74 Stat. 994; July 30, 1965, Pub.L. 89–97, Title I, § 109(b), 79 Stat. 340, which established an initial Advisory Council on Social Security Financing to review the status of the Federal Old-Age and Survivors Insurance Trust Fund and the Federal Disability Insurance Trust Fund in relation to long term commitments to old-age, survivors, and disability insurance programs, appointed personnel and provided for their compensation, required a report of the findings and recommendations of the Council to be submitted to the Secretary of the Board of Trustees of the abovementioned Trust Funds not later than Jan. 1, 1959, at which time the Council terminated, provided for subsequent Advisory Councils to be appointed in 1963, 1966, and every fifth year thereafter and to submit reports to Congress, and required additional information be included in these reports, was omitted from the Code in view of the termination of the initial Advisory Council on submission of their report not later than Jan. 1, 1959, the repeal of subsec. (e) by Pub.L. 89–97, Title I, § 109(b), July 30, 1965, 79 Stat. 340, which provided for the subsequent Advisory Councils, and the obsolescence of subsec. (f), which provided for additional information in reports to Congress, upon the repeal of subsec. (e).

§ 402. Old-age and survivors insurance benefit payments

(a) Old-age insurance benefits

Every individual who—

(1) is a fully insured individual (as defined in section 414(a) of this title),

(2) has attained age 62, and

(3) has filed application for old-age insurance benefits or was entitled to disability insurance benefits for the month preceding the month in which he attained retirement age (as defined in section 416(*l*) of this title),

shall be entitled to an old-age insurance benefit for each month, beginning with—

(A) in the case of an individual who has attained retirement age (as defined in section 416(*l*) of this title), the first month in which such individual meets the criteria specified in paragraphs (1), (2), and (3), or

(B) in the case of an individual who has attained age 62, but has not attained retirement age (as defined in section 416(*l*) of this title), the first month throughout which such individual meets the criteria specified in paragraphs (1) and (2) (if in that month he meets the criterion specified in paragraph (3)),

and ending with the month preceding the month in which he dies. Except as provided in subsection (q) and subsection (w), such individual's old-age insurance benefit for any month shall be equal to his primary insurance amount (as defined in section 415(a) of this title) for such month.

(b) Wife's insurance benefits

(1) The wife (as defined in section 416(b) of this title) and every divorced wife (as defined in section 416(d) of this title) of an individual entitled to old-age or disability insurance benefits, if such wife or such divorced wife—

(A) has filed application for wife's insurance benefits,

(B)(i) has attained age 62, or

(ii) in the case of a wife, has in her care (individually or jointly with such individual) at the time of filing such application a child entitled to a child's insurance benefit on the basis of the wages and self-employment income of such individual,

(C) in the case of a divorced wife, is not married, and

(D) is not entitled to old-age or disability insurance benefits, or is entitled to old-age or disability insurance benefits based on a primary insurance amount which is less than one-half of the primary insurance amount of such individual,

shall (subject to subsection (s)) be entitled to a wife's insurance benefit for each month, beginning with—

(i) in the case of a wife or divorced wife (as so defined) of an individual entitled to old-age benefits, if such wife or divorced wife has attained retirement age (as defined in section 416(*l*) of this title), the first month in which she meets the criteria specified in subparagraphs (A), (B), (C), and (D), or

(ii) in the case of a wife or divorced wife (as so defined) of—

(I) an individual entitled to old-age insurance benefits, if such wife or divorced wife has not attained retirement age (as defined in section 416(*l*) of this title), or

(II) an individual entitled to disability insurance benefits,

the first month throughout which she is such a wife or divorced wife and meets the criteria specified in subparagraphs (B), (C), and (D) (if in such month she meets the criterion specified in subparagraph (A)),

whichever is earlier, and ending with the month preceding the month in which any of the following occurs—

(E) she dies,

(F) such individual dies,

(G) in the case of a wife, they are divorced and either (i) she has not attained age 62, or (ii) she has attained age 62 but has not been married to such individual for a period of 10 years immediately before the date the divorce became effective,

(H) in the case of a divorced wife, she marries a person other than such individual,

(I) in the case of a wife who has not attained age 62, no child of such individual is entitled to a child's insurance benefit,

(J) she becomes entitled to an old-age or disability insurance benefit based on a primary insurance amount which is equal to or exceeds one-half of the primary insurance amount of such individual, or

(K) such individual is not entitled to disability insurance benefits and is not entitled to old-age insurance benefits.

(2) Except as provided in subsections (k)(5) and (q), such wife's insurance benefit for each month shall be equal to one-half of the primary insurance amount of her husband (or, in the case of a divorced wife, her former husband) for such month.

(3) In the case of any divorced wife who marries—

(A) an individual entitled to benefits under subsection (c), (f), (g), or (h), or

(B) an individual who has attained the age of 18 and is entitled to benefits under subsection (d),

such divorced wife's entitlement to benefits under this subsection shall, notwithstanding the provisions of paragraph (1) (but subject to subsection (s)), not be terminated by reason of such marriage.

(4)(A) Notwithstanding the preceding provisions of this subsection, except as provided in subparagraph (B), the divorced wife of an individual who is not entitled to old-age or disability insurance benefits, but who has attained age 62 and is a fully insured individual (as defined in section 414 of this title), if such divorced wife—

(i) meets the requirements of subparagraphs (A) through (D) of paragraph (1), and

(ii) has been divorced from such insured individual for not less than 2 years,

shall be entitled to a wife's insurance benefit under this subsection for each month, in such amount, and beginning and ending with such months, as determined (under regulations of the Commissioner of Social Security) in the manner otherwise provided for wife's insurance benefits under this subsection, as if such insured individual had become entitled to old-age insurance benefits on the date on which the divorced wife first meets the criteria for entitlement set forth in clauses (i) and (ii).

(B) A wife's insurance benefit provided under this paragraph which has not otherwise terminated in accordance with subparagraph (E), (F), (H), or (J) of paragraph (1) shall terminate with the month preceding the first month in which the insured individual is no longer a fully insured individual.

(c) Husband's insurance benefits

(1) The husband (as defined in section 416(f) of this title) and every divorced husband (as defined in section 416(d) of this title) of an individual entitled to old-age or disability insurance benefits, if such husband or such divorced husband—

(A) has filed application for husband's insurance benefits,

(B)(i) has attained age 62, or

(ii) in the case of a husband, has in his care (individually or jointly with such individual) at the time of filing such application a child entitled to a child's insurance benefit on the basis of the wages and self-employment income of such individual,

(C) in the case of a divorced husband, is not married, and

(D) is not entitled to old-age or disability insurance benefits, or is entitled to old-age or disability insurance benefits based on a primary insurance amount which is less than one-half of the primary insurance amount of such individual,

shall (subject to subsection (s)) be entitled to a husband's insurance benefit for each month, beginning with—

(i) in the case of a husband or divorced husband (as so defined) of an individual who is entitled to an old-age insurance benefit, if such husband or divorced husband has attained retirement age (as defined in section 416(*l*) of this title), the first month in which he meets the criteria specified in subparagraphs (A), (B), (C), and (D), or

(ii) in the case of a husband or divorced husband (as so defined) of—

(I) an individual entitled to old-age insurance benefits, if such husband or divorced husband has not attained retirement age (as defined in section 416(*l*) of this title), or

(II) an individual entitled to disability insurance benefits,

the first month throughout which he is such a husband or divorced husband and meets the criteria specified in subparagraphs (B), (C), and (D) (if in such month he meets the criterion specified in subparagraph (A)),

whichever is earlier, and ending with the month preceding the month in which any of the following occurs:

(E) he dies,

(F) such individual dies,

(G) in the case of a husband, they are divorced and either (i) he has not attained age 62, or (ii) he has attained age 62 but has not been married to such individual for a period of 10 years immediately before the divorce became effective,

(H) in the case of a divorced husband, he marries a person other than such individual,

(I) in the case of a husband who has not attained age 62, no child of such individual is entitled to a child's insurance benefit,

(J) he becomes entitled to an old-age or disability insurance benefit based on a primary insurance amount which is equal to or exceeds one-half of the primary insurance amount of such individual, or

(K) such individual is not entitled to disability insurance benefits and is not entitled to old-age insurance benefits.

(2) Except as provided in subsections (k)(5) and (q), such husband's insurance benefit for each month shall be equal to one-half of the primary insurance amount of his wife (or, in the case of a divorced husband, his former wife) for such month.

(3) In the case of any divorced husband who marries—

(A) an individual entitled to benefits under subsection (b), (e), (g), or (h), or

(B) an individual who has attained the age of 18 and is entitled to benefits under subsection (d), by reason of paragraph (1)(B)(ii) thereof,

such divorced husband's entitlement to benefits under this subsection, notwithstanding the provisions of paragraph (1) (but subject to subsection (s)), shall not be terminated by reason of such marriage.

(4)(A) Notwithstanding the preceding provisions of this subsection, except as provided in subparagraph

(B), the divorced husband of an individual who is not entitled to old-age or disability insurance benefits, but who has attained age 62 and is a fully insured individual (as defined in section 414 of this title), if such divorced husband—

(i) meets the requirements of subparagraphs (A) through (D) of paragraph (1), and

(ii) has been divorced from such insured individual for not less than 2 years,

shall be entitled to a husband's insurance benefit under this subsection for each month, in such amount, and beginning and ending with such months, as determined (under regulations of the Commissioner of Social Security) in the manner otherwise provided for husband's insurance benefits under this subsection, as if such insured individual had become entitled to old-age insurance benefits on the date on which the divorced husband first meets the criteria for entitlement set forth in clauses (i) and (ii).

(B) A husband's insurance benefit provided under this paragraph which has not otherwise terminated in accordance with subparagraph (E), (F), (H), or (J) of paragraph (1) shall terminate with the month preceding the first month in which the insured individual is no longer a fully insured individual.

(d) Child's insurance benefits

(1) Every child (as defined in section 416(e) of this title) of an individual entitled to old-age or disability insurance benefits, or of an individual who dies a fully or currently insured individual, if such child—

(A) has filed application for child's insurance benefits,

(B) at the time such application was filed was unmarried and (i) either had not attained the age of 18 or was a full-time elementary or secondary school student and had not attained the age of 19, or (ii) is under a disability (as defined in section 423(d) of this title) which began before he attained the age of 22, and

(C) was dependent upon such individual—

(i) if such individual is living, at the time such application was filed,

(ii) if such individual has died, at the time of such death, or

(iii) if such individual had a period of disability which continued until he became entitled to old-age or disability insurance benefits, or (if he has died) until the month of his death, at the beginning of such period of disability or at the time he became entitled to such benefits,

shall be entitled to a child's insurance benefit for each month, beginning with—

(i) in the case of a child (as so defined) of such an individual who has died, the first month in which such child meets the criteria specified in subparagraphs (A), (B), and (C), or

(ii) in the case of a child (as so defined) of an individual entitled to an old-age insurance benefit or to a disability insurance benefit, the first month throughout which such child is a child (as so defined) and meets the criteria specified in subparagraphs (B) and (C) (if in such month he meets the criterion specified in subparagraph (A)),

whichever is earlier, and ending with the month preceding whichever of the following first occurs—

(D) the month in which such child dies, or marries,

(E) the month in which such child attains the age of 18, but only if he (i) is not under a disability (as so defined) at the time he attains such age, and (ii) is not a full-time elementary or secondary school student during any part of such month,

(F) if such child was not under a disability (as so defined) at the time he attained the age of 18, the earlier of—

(i) the first month during no part of which he is a full-time elementary or secondary school student, or

(ii) the month in which he attains the age of 19,

but only if he was not under a disability (as so defined) in such earlier month;

(G) if such child was under a disability (as so defined) at the time he attained the age of 18 or if he was not under a disability (as so defined) at such time but was under a disability (as so defined) at or prior to the time he attained (or would attain) the age of 22—

(i) the termination month, subject to section 423(e) of this title (and for purposes of this subparagraph, the termination month for any individual shall be the third month following the month in which his disability ceases; except that, in the case of an individual who has a period of trial work which ends as determined by application of section 422(c)(4)(A) of this title, the termination month shall be the earlier of (I) the third month following the earliest month after the end of such period of trial work with respect to which such individual is determined to no longer be suffering from a disabling physical or mental impairment, or (II) the third month following the earliest month in which such individual engages or is determined able to engage in substantial gainful activity, but in no event earlier than the first month occurring after the 36 months following such period of trial work in which he engages or is determined able to engage in substantial gainful activity),

or (if later) the earlier of—

(ii) the first month during no part of which he is a full-time elementary or secondary school student, or

(iii) the month in which he attains the age of 19,

but only if he was not under a disability (as so defined) in such earlier month; or

(H) if the benefits under this subsection are based on the wages and self-employment income of a stepparent who is subsequently divorced from such child's natural parent, the month after the month in which such divorce becomes final.

Entitlement of any child to benefits under this subsection on the basis of the wages and self-employment income of an individual entitled to disability insurance benefits shall also end with the month before the first month for which such individual is not entitled to such benefits unless such individual is, for such later month, entitled to old-age insurance benefits or unless he dies in such month. No payment under this paragraph may be made to a child who would not meet the definition of disability in section 423(d) of this title except for paragraph (1)(B) thereof for any month in which he engages in substantial gainful activity.

(2) Such child's insurance benefit for each month shall, if the individual on the basis of whose wages and self-employment income the child is entitled to such benefit has not died prior to the end of such month, be equal to one-half of the primary insurance amount of such individual for such month. Such child's insurance benefit for each month shall, if such individual has died in or prior to such month, be equal to three-fourths of the primary insurance amount of such individual.

(3) A child shall be deemed dependent upon his father or adopting father or his mother or adopting mother at the time specified in paragraph (1)(C) of this subsection unless, at such time, such individual was not living with or contributing to the support of such child and—

(A) such child is neither the legitimate nor adopted child of such individual, or

(B) such child has been adopted by some other individual.

For purposes of this paragraph, a child deemed to be a child of a fully or currently insured individual pursuant to section 416(h)(2)(B) or section 416(h)(3) of this title shall be deemed to be the legitimate child of such individual.

(4) A child shall be deemed dependent upon his stepfather or stepmother at the time specified in paragraph (1)(C) of this subsection if, at such time, the child was receiving at least one-half of his support from such stepfather or stepmother.

(5) In the case of a child who has attained the age of eighteen and who marries—

(A) an individual entitled to benefits under subsection (a), (b), (c), (e), (f), (g), or (h) or under section 423(a) of this title, or

(B) another individual who has attained the age of eighteen and is entitled to benefits under this subsection,

such child's entitlement to benefits under this subsection shall, notwithstanding the provisions of paragraph (1) but subject to subsection (s), not be terminated by reason of such marriage.

(6) A child whose entitlement to child's insurance benefits on the basis of the wages and self-employment income of an insured individual terminated with the month preceding the month in which such child attained the age of 18, or with a subsequent month, may again become entitled to such benefits (provided no event specified in paragraph (1)(D) has occurred) beginning with the first month thereafter in which he—

(A) (i) is a full-time elementary or secondary school student and has not attained the age of 19, or (ii) is under a disability (as defined in section 423(d) of this title) and has not attained the age of 22, or

(B) is under a disability (as so defined) which began (i) before the close of the 84th month following the month in which his most recent entitlement to child's insurance benefits terminated because he ceased to be under such disability, or (ii) after the close of the 84th month following the month in which his most recent entitlement to child's insurance benefits terminated because he ceased to be under such disability due to performance of substantial gainful activity,

but only if he has filed application for such reentitlement. Such reentitlement shall end with the month preceding whichever of the following first occurs:

(C) the first month in which an event specified in paragraph (1)(D) occurs;

(D) the earlier of (i) the first month during no part of which he is a full-time elementary or secondary school student or (ii) the month in which he attains the age of 19, but only if he is not under a disability (as so defined) in such earlier month; or

(E) if he was under a disability (as so defined), the termination month (as defined in paragraph (1)(G)(i)), subject to section 423(e) of this title, or (if later) the earlier of—

(i) the first month during no part of which he is a full-time elementary or secondary school student, or

(ii) the month in which he attains the age of 19.

(7) For the purposes of this subsection—

(A) A "full-time elementary or secondary school student" is an individual who is in full-time attendance as a student at an elementary or secondary school, as determined by the Commissioner of Social Security (in accordance with regulations prescribed by the Commissioner) in the light of the standards and practices of the schools involved, except that no individual shall be considered a "full-time elementary or secondary school student" if he is paid by his employer while attending an elementary or secondary school at the request, or pursuant to a requirement, of his employer. An individual shall not be considered a "full-time elementary or secondary school student" for the purpose of this section while that individual is confined in a jail, prison, or other penal institution or correctional facility, pursuant to his conviction of an offense (committed after the effective date of this sentence) which constituted a felony under applicable law. An individual who is determined to be a full-time elementary or secondary school student shall be deemed to be such a student throughout the month with respect to which such determination is made.

(B) Except to the extent provided in such regulations, an individual shall be deemed to be a full-time elementary or secondary school student during any period of nonattendance at an elementary or secondary school at which he has been in full-time attendance if (i) such period is 4 calendar months or less, and (ii) he shows to the satisfaction of the Commissioner of Social Security that he intends to continue to be in full-time attendance at an elementary or secondary school immediately following such period. An individual who does not meet the requirement of clause (ii) with respect to such period of nonattendance shall be deemed to have met such requirement (as of the beginning of such period) if he is in full-time attendance at an elementary or secondary school immediately following such period.

(C)(i) An "elementary or secondary school" is a school which provides elementary or secondary education, respectively, as determined under the law of the State or other jurisdiction in which it is located.

(ii) For the purpose of determining whether a child is a "full-time elementary or secondary school student" or "intends to continue to be in full-time attendance at an elementary or secondary school", within the meaning of this subsection, there shall be disregarded any education provided, or to be provided, beyond grade 12.

(D) A child who attains age 19 at a time when he is a full-time elementary or secondary school student (as defined in subparagraph (A) of this paragraph and without application of subparagraph (B) of such paragraph) but has not (at such time) completed the requirements for, or received, a diploma or equivalent certificate from a secondary school (as defined in subparagraph (C)(i)) shall be deemed (for purposes of determining whether his entitlement to benefits under this subsection has terminated under paragraph (1)(F) and for purposes of determining his initial entitlement to such benefits under clause (i) of paragraph (1)(B)) not to have attained such age until the first day of the first month following the end of the quarter or semester in which he is enrolled at such time (or, if the elementary or secondary school (as defined in this paragraph) in which he is enrolled is not operated on a quarter or semester system, until the first day of the first month following the completion of the course in which he is so enrolled or until the first day of the third month beginning after such time, whichever first occurs).

(8) In the case of—

(A) an individual entitled to old-age insurance benefits (other than an individual referred to in subparagraph (B)), or

(B) an individual entitled to disability insurance benefits, or an individual entitled to old-age insurance benefits who was entitled to disability insurance benefits for the month preceding the first month for which he was entitled to old-age insurance benefits,

a child of such individual adopted after such individual became entitled to such old-age or disability insurance benefits shall be deemed not to meet the requirements of clause (i) or (iii) of paragraph (1)(C) unless such child—

(C) is the natural child or stepchild of such individual (including such a child who was legally adopted by such individual), or

(D)(i) was legally adopted by such individual in an adoption decreed by a court of competent jurisdiction within the United States, and

(ii) in the case of a child who attained the age of 18 prior to the commencement of proceedings for adoption, the child was living with or receiving at least one-half of the child's support from such individual for the year immediately preceding the month in which the adoption is decreed.

(9)(A) A child who is a child of an individual under clause (3) of the first sentence of section 416(e) of this title and is not a child of such individual under clause (1) or (2) of such first sentence shall be deemed not to be dependent on such individual at the time specified in subparagraph (1)(C) of this subsection unless (i) such child was living with such individual in the United States and receiving at least one-half of his support from such individual (I) for the year immediately before the month in which such individual became entitled to old-age insurance benefits or disability insurance benefits or died, or (II) if such individual had a period of disability which continued until he had become entitled to old-age insurance benefits, or disability insurance benefits, or died, for the year immediately before the month in which such period of disability began, and (ii) the period during which such child was living with such individual began before the child attained age 18.

(B) In the case of a child who was born in the one-year period during which such child must have been living with and receiving at least one-half of his support from such individual, such child shall be deemed to meet such requirements for such period if, as of the close of such period, such child has lived with such individual in the United States and received at least one-half of his support from such individual for substantially all of the period which begins on the date of such child's birth.

(10) For purposes of paragraph (1)(H)—

(A) each stepparent shall notify the Commissioner of Social Security of any divorce upon such divorce becoming final; and

(B) the Commissioner shall annually notify any stepparent of the rule for termination described in paragraph (1)(H) and of the requirement described in subparagraph (A).

(e) Widow's insurance benefits

(1) The widow (as defined in section 416(c) of this title) and every surviving divorced wife (as defined in section 416(d) of this title) of an individual who died a fully insured individual, if such widow or such surviving divorced wife—

(A) is not married,

(B) (i) has attained age 60, or (ii) has attained age 50 but has not attained age 60 and is under a disability (as defined in section 423(d) of this title) which began before the end of the period specified in paragraph (4),

(C)(i) has filed application for widow's insurance benefits,

(ii) was entitled to wife's insurance benefits, on the basis of the wages and self-employment income of such individual, for the month preceding the month in which such individual died, and—

(I) has attained retirement age (as defined in section 416(l) of this title),

(II) is not entitled to benefits under subsection (a) or section 423 of this title, or

(III) has in effect a certificate (described in paragraph (8)) filed by her with the Commissioner of Social Security, in accordance with regulations prescribed by the Commissioner of Social Security, in which she elects to receive widow's insurance benefits (subject to reduction as provided in subsection (q)), or

(iii) was entitled, on the basis of such wages and self-employment income, to mother's insurance benefits for the month preceding the month in which she attained retirement age (as defined in section 416(l) of this title), and

(D) is not entitled to old-age insurance benefits or is entitled to old-age insurance benefits each of which is less than the primary insurance amount (as determined after application of subparagraphs (B) and (C) of paragraph (2)) of such deceased individual,

shall be entitled to a widow's insurance benefit for each month, beginning with—

(E) if she satisfies subparagraph (B) by reason of clause (i) thereof, the first month in which she becomes so entitled to such insurance benefits, or

(F) if she satisfies subparagraph (B) by reason of clause (ii) thereof—

(i) the first month after her waiting period (as defined in paragraph (5)) in which she becomes so entitled to such insurance benefits, or

(ii) the first month during all of which she is under a disability and in which she becomes so entitled to such insurance benefits, but only if she was previously entitled to insurance benefits under this subsection on the basis of being under a disability and such first month occurs (I) in the period specified in paragraph (4) and (II) after the month in which a previous entitlement to such benefits on such basis terminated,

and ending with the month preceding the first month in which any of the following occurs: she remarries, dies, becomes entitled to an old-age insurance benefit equal to or exceeding the primary insurance amount (as determined after application of subparagraphs (B) and (C) of paragraph (2)) of such deceased individual, or, if she became entitled to such benefits before she attained age 60, subject to section 423(e) of this title, the termination month (unless she attains retirement age (as defined in section 416(l) of this title) on or before the last day of such termination month). For purposes of the preceding sentence, the termination month for any individual shall be the third month following the month in which her disability ceases; except that, in the case of an individual who has a period of trial work which ends as determined by application of section 422(c)(4)(A) of this title, the termination month shall be the earlier of (I) the third month following the earliest month after the end of such period of trial work with respect to which such individual is determined to no longer be suffering from a disabling physical or mental impairment, or (II) the third month following the earliest month in which such individual engages or is determined able to engage in substantial gainful activity, but in no event earlier than the first month occurring after the 36 months following such period of trial work in which she engages or is determined able to engage in substantial gainful activity.

(2)(A) Except as provided in subsection (k)(5), subsection (q), and subparagraph (D) of this paragraph, such widow's insurance benefit for each month shall be equal to the primary insurance amount (as determined for purposes of this subsection after application of subparagraphs (B) and (C)) of such deceased individual.

(B)(i) For purposes of this subsection, in any case in which such deceased individual dies before attaining age 62 and section 415(a)(1) of this title (as in effect after December 1978) is applicable in determining such individual's primary insurance amount—

(I) such primary insurance amount shall be determined under the formula set forth in section

415(a)(1)(B)(i) and (ii) of this title which is applicable to individuals who initially become eligible for old-age insurance benefits in the second year after the year specified in clause (ii),

(II) the year specified in clause (ii) shall be substituted for the second calendar year specified in section 415(b)(3)(A)(ii)(I) of this title, and

(III) such primary insurance amount shall be increased under section 415(i) of this title as if it were the primary insurance amount referred to in section 415(i)(2)(A)(ii)(II) of this title, except that it shall be increased only for years beginning after the first year after the year specified in clause (ii).

(ii) The year specified in this clause is the earlier of—

(I) the year in which the deceased individual attained age 60, or would have attained age 60 had he lived to that age, or

(II) the second year preceding the year in which the widow or surviving divorced wife first meets the requirements of paragraph (1)(B) or the second year preceding the year in which the deceased individual died, whichever is later.

(iii) This subparagraph shall apply with respect to any benefit under this subsection only to the extent its application does not result in a primary insurance amount for purposes of this subsection which is less than the primary insurance amount otherwise determined for such deceased individual under section 415 of this title.

(C) If such deceased individual was (or upon application would have been) entitled to an old-age insurance benefit which was increased (or subject to being increased) on account of delayed retirement under the provisions of subsection (w), then, for purposes of this subsection, such individual's primary insurance amount, if less than the old-age insurance benefit (increased, where applicable, under section 415(f)(5), 415(f)(6), or 415(f)(9)(B) of this title and under section 415(i) of this title as if such individual were still alive in the case of an individual who has died) which he was receiving (or would upon application have received) for the month prior to the month in which he died, shall be deemed to be equal to such old-age insurance benefit, and (notwithstanding the provisions of paragraph (3) of subsection (w)) the number of increment months shall include any month in the months of the calendar year in which he died, prior to the month in which he died, which satisfy the conditions in paragraph (2) of subsection (w).

(D) If the deceased individual (on the basis of whose wages and self-employment income a widow or surviving divorced wife is entitled to widow's insurance benefits under this subsection) was, at any time, entitled to an old-age insurance benefit which was reduced by reason of the application of subsection (q), the widow's insurance benefit of such widow or surviving divorced wife for any month shall, if the amount of the widow's insurance benefit of such widow or surviving divorced wife (as determined under subparagraph (A) and after application of subsection (q)) is greater than—

(i) the amount of the old-age insurance benefit to which such deceased individual would have been entitled (after application of subsection (q)) for such month if such individual were still living and section 415(f)(5), 415(f)(6), or 415(f)(9)(B) of this title were applied, where applicable, and

(ii) 82½ percent of the primary insurance amount (as determined without regard to subparagraph (C)) of such deceased individual,

be reduced to the amount referred to in clause (i), or (if greater) the amount referred to in clause (ii).

(3) For purposes of paragraph (1), if—

(A) a widow or surviving divorced wife marries after attaining age 60 (or after attaining age 50 if she was entitled before such marriage occurred to benefits based on disability under this subsection), or

(B) a disabled widow or disabled surviving divorced wife described in paragraph (1)(B)(ii) marries after attaining age 50,

such marriage shall be deemed not to have occurred.

(4) The period referred to in paragraph (1)(B)(ii), in the case of any widow or surviving divorced wife, is the period beginning with whichever of the following is the latest:

(A) the month in which occurred the death of the fully insured individual referred to in paragraph (1) on whose wages and self-employment income her benefits are or would be based, or

(B) the last month for which she was entitled to mother's insurance benefits on the basis of the wages and self-employment income of such individual, or

(C) the month in which a previous entitlement to widow's insurance benefits on the basis of such wages and self-employment income terminated because her disability had ceased,

and ending with the month before the month in which she attains age 60, or, if earlier, with the close of the eighty-fourth month following the month with which such period began.

(5)(A) The waiting period referred to in paragraph (1)(F), in the case of any widow or surviving divorced wife, is the earliest period of five consecutive calendar months—

(i) throughout which she has been under a disability, and

(ii) which begins not earlier than with whichever of the following is the later: (I) the first day of the seventeenth month before the month in which her application is filed, or (II) the first day of the fifth month before the month in which the period specified in paragraph (4) begins.

(B) For purposes of paragraph (1)(F)(i), each month in the period commencing with the first month for which such widow or surviving divorced wife is first eligible for supplemental security income benefits under subchapter XVI, or State supplementary payments of the type referred to in section 1382e(a) of this title (or payments of the type described in section 212(a) of Public Law 93–66) which are paid by the Commissioner of Social Security under an agreement referred to in section 1382e(a) of this title (or in section 212(b) of Public Law 93–66), shall be included as one of the months of such waiting period for which the requirements of subparagraph (A) have been met.

(6) In the case of an individual entitled to monthly insurance benefits payable under this section for any month prior to January 1973 whose benefits were not redetermined under section 102(g) of the Social Security Amendments of 1972, such benefits shall not be redetermined pursuant to such section, but shall be increased pursuant to any general benefit increase (as defined in section 415(i)(3) of this title) or any increase in benefits made under or pursuant to section 415(i) of this title, including for this purpose the increase provided effective for March 1974, as though such redetermination had been made.

(7) Any certificate filed pursuant to paragraph (1)(C)(ii)(III) shall be effective for purposes of this subsection—

(A) for the month in which it is filed and for any month thereafter, and

(B) for months, in the period designated by the individual filing such certificate, of one or more consecutive months (not exceeding 12) immediately preceding the month in which such certificate is filed;

except that such certificate shall not be effective for any month before the month in which she attains age 62.

(8) An individual shall be deemed to be under a disability for purposes of paragraph (1)(B)(ii) if such individual is eligible for supplemental security income benefits under subchapter XVI, or State supplementary payments of the type referred to in section 1382e(a) of this title (or payments of the type described in section 212(a) of Public Law 93–66) which are paid by the Commissioner of Social Security under an agreement referred to in section 1382e(a) of this title (or in section 212(b) of Public Law 93–66), for the month for which all requirements of paragraph (1) for entitlement to benefits under this subsection (other than being under a disability) are met.

(f) Widower's insurance benefits

(1) The widower (as defined in section 416(g) of this title) and every surviving divorced husband (as defined in section 416(d) of this title) of an individual who died a fully insured individual, if such widower or such surviving divorced husband—

(A) is not married,

(B) (i) has attained age 60, or (ii) has attained age 50 but has not attained age 60 and is under a disability (as defined in section 423(d) of this title) which began before the end of the period specified in paragraph (4),

(C)(i) has filed application for widower's insurance benefits,

(ii) was entitled to husband's insurance benefits, on the basis of the wages and self-employment income of such individual, for the month preceding the month in which such individual died, and—

(I) has attained retirement age (as defined in section 416(*l*) of this title),

(II) is not entitled to benefits under subsection (a) or section 423 of this title, or

(III) has in effect a certificate (described in paragraph (8)) filed by him with the Commissioner of Social Security, in accordance with regulations prescribed by the Commissioner of Social Security, in which he elects to receive widower's insurance benefits (subject to reduction as provided in subsection (q)), or

(iii) was entitled, on the basis of such wages and self-employment income, to father's insurance benefits for the month preceding the month in which he attained retirement age (as defined in section 416(*l*) of this title), and

(D) is not entitled to old-age insurance benefits, or is entitled to old-age insurance benefits each of which is less than the primary insurance amount (as determined after application of subparagraphs (B) and (C) of paragraph (3)) of such deceased individual,

shall be entitled to a widower's insurance benefit for each month, beginning with—

(E) if he satisfies subparagraph (B) by reason of clause (i) thereof, the first month in which he becomes so entitled to such insurance benefits, or

(F) if he satisfies subparagraph (B) by reason of clause (ii) thereof—

(i) the first month after his waiting period (as defined in paragraph (5)) in which he becomes so entitled to such insurance benefits, or

(ii) the first month during all of which he is under a disability and in which he becomes so entitled to such insurance benefits, but only if he was previously entitled to insurance benefits under this subsection on the basis of being under a disability and such first month occurs (I) in the period specified in paragraph (4) and (II) after the month in which a previous entitlement to such benefits on such basis terminated,

and ending with the month preceding the first month in which any of the following occurs: he remarries, dies, or becomes entitled to an old-age insurance benefit equal to or exceeding the primary insurance amount (as determined after application of subparagraphs (B) and (C) of paragraph (3)) of such deceased individual, or, if he became entitled to such benefits before he attained age 60, subject to section 423(e) of this title, the termination month (unless he attains retirement age (as defined in section 416(*l*) of this title) on or before the last day of such termination month). For purposes of the preceding sentence, the termination month for any individual shall be the third month following the month in which his disability ceases; except that, in the case of an individual who has a period of trial work which ends as determined by application of section 422(c)(4)(A) of this title, the termination month shall be the earlier of (I) the third month following the earliest month after the end of such period of trial work with respect to which such individual is determined to no longer be suffering from a disabling physical or mental impairment, or (II) the third month following the earliest month in which such individual engages or is determined able to engage in substantial gainful activity, but in no event earlier than the first month occurring after the 36 months following such period of trial work in which he engages or is determined able to engage in substantial gainful activity.

(2)(A) Except as provided in subsection (k)(5), subsection (q), and subparagraph (D) of this paragraph, such widower's insurance benefit for each month shall be equal to the primary insurance amount (as determined for purposes of this subsection after application of subparagraphs (B) and (C)) of such deceased individual.

(B)(i) For purposes of this subsection, in any case in which such deceased individual dies before attaining age 62 and section 415(a)(1) of this title (as in effect after December 1978) is applicable in determining such individual's primary insurance amount—

(I) such primary insurance amount shall be determined under the formula set forth in section 415(a)(1)(B)(i) and (ii) of this title which is applicable to individuals who initially become eligible for old-age insurance benefits in the second year after the year specified in clause (ii),

(II) the year specified in clause (ii) shall be substituted for the second calendar year specified in section 415(b)(3)(A)(ii)(I) of this title, and

(III) such primary insurance amount shall be increased under section 415(i) of this title as if it were the primary insurance amount referred to in section 415(i)(2)(A)(ii)(II) of this title, except that it shall be increased only for years beginning after the first year after the year specified in clause (ii).

(ii) The year specified in this clause is the earlier of—

(I) the year in which the deceased individual attained age 60, or would have attained age 60 had she lived to that age, or

(II) the second year preceding the year in which the widower or surviving divorced husband first meets the requirements of paragraph (1)(B) or the second year preceding the year in which the deceased individual died, whichever is later.

(iii) This subparagraph shall apply with respect to any benefit under this subsection only to the extent its application does not result in a primary insurance amount for purposes of this subsection which is less than the primary insurance amount otherwise determined for such deceased individual under section 415 of this title.

(C) If such deceased individual was (or upon application would have been) entitled to an old-age insurance benefit which was increased (or subject to being increased) on account of delayed retirement under the provisions of subsection (w), then, for purposes of this subsection, such individual's primary insurance amount, if less than the old-age insurance benefit (increased, where applicable, under section 415(f)(5), 415(f)(6), or 415(f)(9)(B) of this title and under section 415(i) of this title as if such individual were still alive in the case of an individual who has died) which she was receiving (or would upon application have received) for the month prior to the month in which she died, shall be deemed to be equal to such old-age insurance benefit, and (notwithstanding the provisions of paragraph (3) of subsection (w)) the number of increment months shall include any month in the months of the calendar year in which she died, prior to the month in which she died, which satisfy the conditions in paragraph (2) of subsection (w).

(D) If the deceased individual (on the basis of whose wages and self-employment income a widower or surviving divorced husband is entitled to widower's insurance benefits under this subsection) was, at any time, entitled to an old-age insurance benefit which was reduced by reason of the application of subsection (q), the widower's insurance benefit of such widower or surviving divorced husband for any month shall, if the amount of the widower's insurance benefit of such widower or surviving divorced husband (as determined under subparagraph (A) and after application of subsection (q)) is greater than—

(i) the amount of the old-age insurance benefit to which such deceased individual would have been entitled (after application of subsection (q)) for such month if such individual were still living and section 415(f)(5), 415(f)(6), or 415(f)(9)(B) of this title were applied, where applicable, and

(ii) 82½ percent of the primary insurance amount (as determined without regard to subparagraph (C)) of such deceased individual;

be reduced to the amount referred to in clause (i), or (if greater) the amount referred to in clause (ii).

(3) For purposes of paragraph (1), if—

(A) a widower or surviving divorced husband marries after attaining age 60 (or after attaining age 50 if he was entitled before such marriage occurred to benefits based on disability under this subsection), or

(B) a disabled widower or surviving divorced husband described in paragraph (1)(B)(ii) marries after attaining age 50,

such marriage shall be deemed not to have occurred.

(4) The period referred to in paragraph (1)(B)(ii), in the case of any widower or surviving divorced husband, is the period beginning with whichever of the following is the latest:

(A) the month in which occurred the death of the fully insured individual referred to in paragraph (1) on whose wages and self-employment income his benefits are or would be based,

(B) the last month for which he was entitled to father's insurance benefits on the basis of the wages and self-employment income of such individual, or

(C) the month in which a previous entitlement to widower's insurance benefits on the basis of such wages and self-employment income terminated because his disability had ceased,

and ending with the month before the month in which he attains age 60, or, if earlier, with the close of the eighty-fourth month following the month with which such period began.

(5)(A) The waiting period referred to in paragraph (1)(F), in the case of any widower or surviving divorced husband, is the earliest period of five consecutive calendar months—

(i) throughout which he has been under a disability, and

(ii) which begins not earlier than with whichever of the following is the later: (I) the first day of the seventeenth month before the month in which his application is filed, or (II) the first day of the fifth month before the month in which the period specified in paragraph (4) begins.

(B) For purposes of paragraph (1)(F)(i), each month in the period commencing with the first month for which such widower or surviving divorced husband is first eligible for supplemental security income benefits under subchapter XVI, or State supplementary payments of the type referred to in section 1382e(a) of this title (or payments of the type described in section 212(a) of Public Law 93–66) which are paid by the Commissioner of Social Security under an agreement referred to in section 1382e(a) of this title (or in section 212(b) of Public Law 93–66), shall be included as one of the months of such waiting period for which the requirements of subparagraph (A) have been met.

(6) In the case of an individual entitled to monthly insurance benefits payable under this section for any month prior to January 1973 whose benefits were not redetermined under section 102(g) of the Social Security Amendments of 1972, such benefits shall not be redetermined pursuant to such section, but shall be increased pursuant to any general benefit increase (as defined in section 415(i)(3) of this title) or any increase in benefits made under or pursuant to section 415(i) of this title, including for this purpose the increase provided effective for March 1974, as though such redetermination had been made.

(7) Any certificate filed pursuant to paragraph (1)(C)(ii)(III) shall be effective for purposes of this subsection—

(A) for the month in which it is filed and for any month thereafter, and

(B) for months, in the period designated by the individual filing such certificate, of one or more consecutive months (not exceeding 12) immediately preceding the month in which such certificate is filed;

except that such certificate shall not be effective for any month before the month in which he attains age 62.

(8) An individual shall be deemed to be under a disability for purposes of paragraph (1)(B)(ii) if such individual is eligible for supplemental security income benefits under subchapter XVI, or State supplementary payments of the type referred to in section 1382e(a) of this title (or payments of the type described in section 212(a) of Public Law 93–66) which are paid by the Commissioner of Social Security under an agreement referred to in such section 1382e(a) of this title (or in section 212(b) of Public Law 93–66), for the month for which all requirements of paragraph (1) for entitlement to benefits under this subsection (other than being under a disability) are met.

(g) Mother's and father's insurance benefits

(1) The surviving spouse and every surviving divorced parent (as defined in section 416(d) of this title) of an individual who died a fully or currently insured individual, if such surviving spouse or surviving divorced parent—

(A) is not married,

(B) is not entitled to a surviving spouse's insurance benefit,

(C) is not entitled to old-age insurance benefits, or is entitled to old-age insurance benefits each of which is less than three-fourths of the primary insurance amount of such individual,

(D) has filed application for mother's or father's insurance benefits, or was entitled to a spouse's insurance benefit on the basis of the wages and self-employment income of such individual for the month preceding the month in which such individual died,

(E) at the time of filing such application has in his or her care a child of such individual entitled to a child's insurance benefit, and

(F) in the case of a surviving divorced parent—

(i) the child referred to in subparagraph (E) is his or her son, daughter, or legally adopted child, and

(ii) the benefits referred to in such subparagraph are payable on the basis of such individual's wages and self-employment income,

shall (subject to subsection (s)) be entitled to a mother's or father's insurance benefit for each month, beginning with the first month in which he or she becomes so entitled to such insurance benefits and ending with the month preceding the first month in which any of the following occurs: no child of such deceased individual is entitled to a child's insurance benefit, such surviving spouse or surviving divorced parent becomes entitled to an old-age insurance benefit equal to or exceeding three-fourths of the primary insurance amount of such deceased individual, he or she becomes entitled to a surviving spouse's insurance benefit, he or she remarries, or he or she dies. Entitlement to such benefits shall also end, in the case of a surviving divorced parent, with the month immediately preceding the first month in which no son, daughter, or legally adopted child of such surviving divorced parent is entitled to a child's insurance benefit on the basis of the wages and self-employment income of such deceased individual.

(2) Such mother's or father's insurance benefit for each month shall be equal to three-fourths of the primary insurance amount of such deceased individual.

(3) In the case of a surviving spouse or surviving divorced parent who marries—

(A) an individual entitled to benefits under this subsection or subsection (a), (b), (c), (e), (f), or (h), or under section 423(a) of this title, or

(B) an individual who has attained the age of eighteen and is entitled to benefits under subsection (d),

the entitlement of such surviving spouse or surviving divorced parent to benefits under this subsection shall, notwithstanding the provisions of paragraph (1) of this subsection but subject to subsection (s), not be terminated by reason of such marriage.

(h) Parent's insurance benefits

(1) Every parent (as defined in this subsection) of an individual who died a fully insured individual, if such parent—

(A) has attained age 62,

(B) (i) was receiving at least one-half of his support from such individual at the time of such individual's death or, if such individual had a period of disability which did not end prior to the month in which he died, at the time such period began or at the time of such death, and (ii) filed proof of such support within two years after the date of such death, or, if such individual had such a period of disability, within two years after the month in which such individual filed application with respect to such period of disability or two years after the date of such death, as the case may be,

(C) has not married since such individual's death,

(D) is not entitled to old-age insurance benefits, or is entitled to old-age insurance benefits each of which is less than 82½ percent of the primary insurance amount of such deceased individual if the amount of the parent's insurance benefit for such month is determinable under paragraph (2)(A) (or 75 percent of such primary insurance amount in any other case), and

(E) has filed application for parent's insurance benefits,

shall be entitled to a parent's insurance benefit for each month beginning with the first month after August 1950 in which such parent becomes so entitled to such parent's insurance benefits and ending with the month preceding the first month in which any of the following occurs: such parent dies, marries, or becomes entitled to an old-age insurance benefit equal to or exceeding 82½ percent of the primary insurance amount of such deceased individual if the amount of the parent's insurance benefit for such month is determinable under paragraph (2)(A) (or 75 percent of such primary insurance amount in any other case).

(2)(A) Except as provided in subparagraphs (B) and (C), such parent's insurance benefit for each month shall be equal to 82½ percent of the primary insurance amount of such deceased individual.

(B) For any month for which more than one parent is entitled to parent's insurance benefits on the basis of such deceased individual's wages and self-employment income, such benefit for each such parent for such month shall (except as provided in subparagraph (C)) be equal to 75 percent of the primary insurance amount of such deceased individual.

(C) In any case in which—

(i) any parent is entitled to a parent's insurance benefit for a month on the basis of a deceased individual's wages and self-employment income, and

(ii) another parent of such deceased individual is entitled to a parent's insurance benefit for such month on the basis of such wages and self-employment income, and on the basis of an application filed after such month and after the month in which the application for the parent's benefits referred to in clause (i) was filed,

the amount of the parent's insurance benefit of the parent referred to in clause (i) for the month referred to in such clause shall be determined under subparagraph (A) instead of subparagraph (B) and the amount of the parent's insurance benefit of a parent referred to in clause (ii) for such month shall be equal to 150 percent of the primary insurance amount of the deceased individual minus the amount (before the application of section 403(a) of this title) of the benefit for such month of the parent referred to in clause (i).

(3) As used in this subsection, the term "parent" means the mother or father of an individual, a stepparent of an individual by a marriage contracted before such individual attained the age of sixteen, or an adopting parent by whom an individual was adopted before he attained the age of sixteen.

(4) In the case of a parent who marries—

(A) an individual entitled to benefits under this subsection or subsection (b), (c), (e), (f), or (g), or

(B) an individual who has attained the age of eighteen and is entitled to benefits under subsection (d),

such parent's entitlement to benefits under this subsection shall, notwithstanding the provisions of paragraph (1) of this subsection but subject to subsection (s), not be terminated by reason of such marriage.

(i) Lump-sum death payments

Upon the death, after August 1950, of an individual who died a fully or currently insured individual, an amount equal to three times such individual's primary insurance amount (as determined without regard to the amendments made by section 2201 of the Omnibus Budget Reconciliation Act of 1981, relating to the repeal of the minimum benefit provisions), or an amount equal to $255, whichever is the smaller, shall be paid in a lump sum to the person, if any, determined by the Commissioner of Social Security to be the widow or widower of the deceased and to have been living in the same household with the deceased at the time of death. If there is no such person, or if such person dies before receiving payment, then such amount shall be paid—

(1) to a widow (as defined in section 416(c) of this title) or widower (as defined in section 416(g) of this title) who is entitled (or would have been so entitled had a timely application been filed), on the basis of the wages and self-employment income of such insured individual, to benefits under subsection (e), (f), or (g) for the month in which occurred such individual's death; or

(2) if no person qualifies for payment under paragraph (1), or if such person dies before receiving payment, in equal shares to each person who is entitled (or would have been so entitled had a timely application been filed), on the basis of the wages and self-employment income of such insured individual, to benefits under subsection (d) for the month in which occurred such individual's death.

No payment shall be made to any person under this subsection unless application therefor shall have been filed, by or on behalf of such person (whether or not legally competent), prior to the expiration of two years after the date of death of such insured individual, or unless such person was entitled to wife's or husband's insurance benefits, on the basis of the wages and self-employment income of such insured individual, for the month preceding the month in which such individual died. In the case of any individual who died outside the forty-eight States and the District of Columbia after December 1953 and before January 1, 1957, whose death occurred while he was in the active military or naval service of the United States, and who is returned to any of such States, the District of Columbia, Alaska, Hawaii, the Commonwealth of Puerto Rico, the Virgin Islands, Guam, or American Samoa for interment or reinterment, the provisions of the preceding sentence shall not prevent payment to any person under the second sentence of this subsection if application for a lump-sum death payment with respect to such deceased individual is filed by or on behalf of such person (whether or not legally competent) prior to the expiration of two years after the date of such interment or reinterment. In the case of any individual who died outside the fifty States and the District of Columbia after December 1956 while he was performing service, as a member of a uniformed service, to which the provisions of section 410(*l*)(1) of this title are applicable, and who is returned to any State, or to any Territory or possession of the United States, for interment or reinterment, the provisions of the third sentence of this subsection shall not prevent payment to any person under the second sentence of this subsection if application for a lump-sum death payment with respect to such deceased individual is filed by or on behalf of such person (whether or not legally competent) prior to the expiration of two years after the date of such interment or reinterment.

(j) Application for monthly insurance benefits

(1) Subject to the limitations contained in paragraph (4), an individual who would have been entitled to a benefit under subsection (a), (b), (c), (d), (e), (f), (g), or (h) for any month after August 1950 had he filed application therefor prior to the end of such month shall be entitled to such benefit for such month if he files application therefor prior to—

(A) the end of the twelfth month immediately succeeding such month in any case where the individual (i) is filing application for a benefit under subsection (e) or (f), and satisfies paragraph (1)(B) of such subsection by reason of clause (ii) thereof, or

(ii) is filing application for a benefit under subsection (b), (c), or (d) on the basis of the wages and self-employment income of a person entitled to disability insurance benefits, or

(B) the end of the sixth month immediately succeeding such month in any case where subparagraph (A) does not apply.

Any benefit under this subchapter for a month prior to the month in which application is filed shall be reduced, to any extent that may be necessary, so that it will not render erroneous any benefit which, before the filing of such application, the Commissioner of Social Security has certified for payment for such prior month.

(2) An application for any monthly benefits under this section filed before the first month in which the applicant satisfies the requirements for such benefits shall be deemed a valid application (and shall be deemed to have been filed in such first month) only if the applicant satisfies the requirements for such benefits before the Commissioner of Social Security makes a final decision on the application and no request under section 405(b) of this title for notice and opportunity for a hearing thereon is made or, if such a request is made, before a decision based upon the evidence adduced at the hearing is made (regardless of whether such decision becomes the final decision of the Commissioner of Social Security).

(3) Notwithstanding the provisions of paragraph (1), an individual may, at his option, waive entitlement to any benefit referred to in paragraph (1) for any one or more consecutive months (beginning with the earliest month for which such individual would otherwise be entitled to such benefit) which occur before the month in which such individual files application for such benefit; and, in such case, such individual shall not be considered as entitled to such benefits for any such month or months before such individual filed such application. An individual shall be deemed to have waived such entitlement for any such month for which such benefit would, under the second sentence of paragraph (1), be reduced to zero.

(4)(A) Except as provided in subparagraph (B), no individual shall be entitled to a monthly benefit under subsection (a), (b), (c), (e), or (f) for any month prior to the month in which he or she files an application for benefits under that subsection if the amount of the monthly benefit to which such individual would otherwise be entitled for any such month would be subject to reduction pursuant to subsection (q).

(B)(i) If the individual applying for retroactive benefits is a widow, surviving divorced wife, or widower and is under a disability (as defined in section 423(d) of this title), and such individual would, except for subparagraph (A), be entitled to retroactive benefits as a disabled widow or widower or disabled surviving divorced wife for any month before attaining the age of 60, then subparagraph (A) shall not apply with respect to such month or any subsequent month.

(ii) Subparagraph (A) does not apply to a benefit under subsection (e) or (f) for the month immediately preceding the month of application, if the insured individual died in that preceding month.

(iii) As used in this subparagraph, the term "retroactive benefits" means benefits to which an individual becomes entitled for a month prior to the month in which application for such benefits is filed.

(5) In any case in which it is determined to the satisfaction of the Commissioner of Social Security that an individual failed as of any date to apply for monthly insurance benefits under this subchapter by reason of misinformation provided to such individual by any officer or employee of the Social Security Administration relating to such individual's eligibility for benefits under this subchapter, such individual shall be deemed to have applied for such benefits on the later of—

(A) the date on which such misinformation was provided to such individual, or

(B) the date on which such individual met all requirements for entitlement to such benefits (other than application therefor).

(k) Simultaneous entitlement to benefits

(1) A child, entitled to child's insurance benefits on the basis of the wages and self-employment income of an insured individual, who would be entitled, on filing application, to child's insurance benefits on the basis of the wages and self-employment income of some other insured individual, shall be deemed entitled, subject to the provisions of paragraph (2) of this subsection, to child's insurance benefits on the basis of the wages and self-employment income of such other individual if an application for child's insurance benefits on the basis of the wages and self-employment income of such other individual has been filed by any other child who would, on filing application, be entitled to child's insurance benefits on the basis of the wages and self-employment income of both such insured individuals.

(2)(A) Any child who under the preceding provisions of this section is entitled for any month to child's insurance benefits on the wages and self-employment income of more than one insured individual shall, notwithstanding such provisions, be entitled to only one of such child's insurance benefits for such month. Such child's insurance benefits for such month shall be the benefit based on the wages and self-employment income of the insured individual who has the greatest primary insurance amount, except that such child's insurance benefits for such month shall be the largest benefit to which such child could be entitled under subsection (d) (without the application of section 403(a) of this title) or subsection (m) if entitlement to such benefit would not, with respect to any person, result in a benefit lower (after the application of section 403(a) of this title) than the benefit which would be applicable if such child were entitled on the wages and self-employment income of the individual with the greatest primary insurance amount. Where more than one child is entitled to child's insurance benefits pursuant to the preceding provisions of this paragraph, each such child who is entitled on the wages and self-employment income of the same insured individuals shall be entitled on the wages and self-employment income of the same such insured individual.

(B) Any individual (other than an individual to whom subsection (e)(3) or (f)(3) applies) who, under the preceding provisions of this section and under the provisions of section 423 of this title, is entitled for any month to more than one monthly insurance benefit (other than an old-age or disability insurance benefit) under this subchapter shall be entitled to only one such monthly benefit for such month, such benefit to be the largest of the monthly benefits to which he (but for this subparagraph) would otherwise be entitled for such month. Any individual who is entitled for any month to more than one widow's or widower's insurance benefit to which subsection (e)(3) or (f)(3) applies shall be entitled to only one such benefit for such month, such benefit to be the largest of such benefits.

(3)(A) If an individual is entitled to an old-age or disability insurance benefit for any month and to any other monthly insurance benefit for such month, such other insurance benefit for such month, after any reduction under subsection (q), subsection (e)(2) or (f)(2), and any reduction under section 403(a) of this title, shall be reduced, but not below zero, by an amount equal to such old-age or disability insurance benefit (after reduction under such subsection (q)).

(B) If an individual is entitled for any month to a widow's or widower's insurance benefit to which subsection (e)(3) or (f)(3) applies and to any other monthly insurance benefit under this section (other than an old-age insurance benefit), such other insurance benefit for such month, after any reduction under subparagraph (A) of this paragraph, any reduction under subsection (q), and any reduction under section 403(a) of this title, shall be reduced, but not below zero, by an amount equal to such widow's or widower's insurance benefit after any reduction or reductions under such subparagraph (A) and such section 403(a).

(4) Any individual who, under this section and section 423 of this title, is entitled for any month to both an old-age insurance benefit and a disability insurance benefit under this subchapter shall be entitled to only the larger of such benefits for such month, except that, if such individual so elects, he shall instead be entitled to only the smaller of such benefits for such month.

(5)(A) The amount of a monthly insurance benefit of any individual for each month under subsection (b), (c), (e), (f), or (g) (as determined after application of the provisions of subsection (q) and the preceding provisions of this subsection) shall be reduced (but not below zero) by an amount equal to two-thirds of the amount of any monthly periodic benefit payable to such individual for such month which is based upon such individual's earnings while in the service of the Federal Government or any State (or political subdivision thereof, as defined in section 418(b)(2) of this title) if, during any portion of the last 60 months of such service ending with the last day such individual was employed by such entity—

(i) such service did not constitute "employment" as defined in section 410 of this title, or

(ii) such service was being performed while in the service of the Federal Government, and constituted "employment" as so defined solely by reason of—

(I) clause (ii) or (iii) of subparagraph (G) of section 410(a)(5) of this title, where the lump-sum payment described in such clause (ii) or the cessation of coverage described in such clause (iii) (whichever is applicable) was received or occurred on or after January 1, 1988, or

(II) an election to become subject to the Federal Employees' Retirement System provided in chapter 84 of Title 5 or the Foreign Service Pension System provided in subchapter II of chapter 8 of title I of the Foreign Service Act of 1980 made pursuant to law after December 31, 1987, unless subparagraph (B) applies.

The amount of the reduction in any benefit under this subparagraph, if not a multiple of $0.10, shall be rounded to the next higher multiple of $0.10.

(B)(i) Subparagraph (A)(i) shall not apply with respect to monthly periodic benefits based wholly on service as a member of a uniformed service (as defined in section 410(m) of this title).

(ii) Subparagraph (A)(ii) shall not apply with respect to monthly periodic benefits based in whole or in part on service which constituted "employment" as defined in section 410 of this title if such service was performed for at least 60 months in the aggregate during the period beginning January 1, 1988, and ending with the close of the first calendar month as of the end of which such individual is eligible for benefits under this subsection and has made a valid application for such benefits.

(C) For purposes of this paragraph, any periodic benefit which otherwise meets the requirements of subparagraph (A), but which is paid on other than a monthly basis, shall be allocated on a basis equivalent to a monthly benefit (as determined by the Commissioner of Social Security) and such equivalent monthly benefit shall constitute a monthly periodic benefit for purposes of subparagraph (A). For purposes of this subparagraph, the term "periodic benefit" includes a benefit payable in a lump sum if it is a commutation of, or a substitute for, periodic payments.

(*l*) Entitlement to survivor benefits under railroad retirement provisions

If any person would be entitled, upon filing application therefor to an annuity under section 2 of the Railroad Retirement Act of 1974, or to a lump-sum payment under section 6(b) of such Act, with respect to the death of an employee (as defined in such Act) no lump-sum death payment, and no monthly benefit for the month in which such employee died or for any month thereafter, shall be paid under this section to any person on the basis of the wages and self-employment income of such employee.

(m) Repealed. Pub.L. 97–35, Title XXII, § 2201(b)(10), Aug. 13, 1981, 95 Stat. 831

(n) Termination of benefits upon removal of primary beneficiary

(1) If any individual is (after September 1, 1954) removed under section 1227(a) of Title 8 (other than under paragraph (1)(C) of such section) or under section 1182(a)(6)(A) of Title 8, then, notwithstanding any other provisions of this subchapter—

(A) no monthly benefit under this section or section 423 of this title shall be paid to such individual, on the basis of his wages and self-employment income, for any month occurring (i) after the month in which the Commissioner of Social Security is notified by the Attorney General or the Secretary of Homeland Security that such individual has been so removed, and (ii) before the month in which such individual is thereafter lawfully admitted to the United States for permanent residence,

(B) if no benefit could be paid to such individual (or if no benefit could be paid to him if he were alive) for any month by reason of subparagraph (A), no monthly benefit under this section shall be paid, on the basis of his wages and self-employment income, for such month to any other person who is not a citizen of the United States and is outside the United States for any part of such month, and

(C) no lump-sum death payment shall be made on the basis of such individual's wages and self-employment income if he dies (i) in or after the month in which such notice is received, and (ii) before the month in which he is thereafter lawfully admitted to the United States for permanent residence.

Section 403(b), (c), and (d) of this title shall not apply with respect to any such individual for any month for which no monthly benefit may be paid to him by reason of this paragraph.

(2)(A) In the case of the removal of any individual under any of the paragraphs of section 1227(a) of Title 8 (other than under paragraph (1)(C) of such section) or under section 1182(a)(6)(A) of Title 8, the revocation and setting aside of citizenship of any individual under section 1451 of Title 8 in any case in which the revocation and setting aside is based on conduct described in section 1182(a)(3)(E)(i) of Title 8 (relating to participation in Nazi persecution), or the renunciation of nationality by any individual under section 1481(a)(5) of Title 8 pursuant to a settlement agreement with the Attorney General where the individual has admitted to conduct described in section 1182(a)(3)(E)(i) of Title 8 (relating to participation in Nazi persecution) occurring after December 18, 2014, the Attorney General or the Secretary of Homeland Security shall notify the Commissioner of Social Security of such removal, revocation and setting aside, or renunciation of nationality not later than 7 days after such removal, revocation and setting aside, or renunciation of nationality (or, in the case of any such removal, revocation and setting aside, of[1] renunciation of nationality that has occurred prior to December 18, 2014, not later than 7 days after December 18, 2014).

(B)(i) Not later than 30 days after December 18, 2014, the Attorney General shall certify to the Committee on Ways and Means of the House of Representatives and the Committee on Finance of the Senate that the Commissioner of Social Security has been notified of each removal, revocation and setting aside, or renunciation of nationality described in subparagraph (A).

(ii) Not later than 30 days after each notification with respect to an individual under subparagraph (A), the Commissioner of Social Security shall certify to the Committee on Ways and Means of the House of Representatives and the Committee on Finance of the Senate that such individual's benefits were terminated under this subsection.

(3) For purposes of paragraphs (1) and (2) of this subsection—

(A) an individual against whom a final order of removal has been issued under section 1227(a)(4)(D) of Title 8 on grounds of participation in Nazi persecution shall be considered to have been removed under such section as of the date on which such order became final;

(B) an individual with respect to whom an order admitting the individual to citizenship has been revoked and set aside under section 1451 of Title 8 in any case in which the revocation and setting aside is based on conduct described in section 1182(a)(3)(E)(i) of Title 8 (relating to participation in Nazi persecution), concealment of a material fact about such conduct, or willful misrepresentation about such conduct shall be considered to have been removed as described in paragraph (1) as of the date of such revocation and setting aside; and

(C) an individual who pursuant to a settlement agreement with the Attorney General has admitted to conduct described in section 1182(a)(3)(E)(i) of Title 8 (relating to participation in Nazi persecution) and who pursuant to such settlement agreement has lost status as a national of the United States by a renunciation under section 1481(a)(5) of Title 8 shall be considered to have been removed as described in paragraph (1) as of the date of such renunciation.

(4) In the case of any individual described in paragraph (3) whose monthly benefits are terminated under paragraph (1)—

(A) no benefits otherwise available under this section based on the wages and self-employment income of any other individual shall be paid to such individual for any month after such termination; and

(B) no supplemental security income benefits under subchapter XVI shall be paid to such individual for any such month, including supplementary payments pursuant to an agreement for Federal administration under section 1382e(a) of this title and payments pursuant to an agreement entered into under section 212(b) of Public Law 93–66 [2]

(*o*) Application for benefits by survivors of members and former members of uniformed services

In the case of any individual who would be entitled to benefits under subsection (d), (e), (g), or (h) upon filing proper application therefor, the filing with the Administrator of Veterans' Affairs by or on behalf of such individual of an application for such benefits, on the form described in section 5105 of Title 38, shall satisfy the requirement of such subsection (d), (e), (g), or (h) that an application for such benefits be filed.

(p) Extension of period for filing proof of support and applications for lump-sum death payment

In any case in which there is a failure—

(1) to file proof of support under subparagraph (B) of subsection (h)(1), or under clause (B) of subsection (f)(1) as in effect prior to the Social Security Act Amendments of 1950, within the period prescribed by such subparagraph or clause, or

(2) to file, in the case of a death after 1946, application for a lump-sum death payment under subsection (i), or under subsection (g) as in effect prior to the Social Security Act Amendments of 1950, within the period prescribed by such subsection,

any such proof or application, as the case may be, which is filed after the expiration of such period shall be deemed to have been filed within such period if it is shown to the satisfaction of the Commissioner of Social Security that there was good cause for failure to file such proof or application within such period. The determination of what constitutes good cause for purposes of this subsection shall be made in accordance with regulations of the Commissioner of Social Security.

(q) Reduction of benefit amounts for certain beneficiaries

(1) Subject to paragraph (9), if the first month for which an individual is entitled to an old-age, wife's, husband's, widow's, or widower's insurance benefit is a month before the month in which such individual attains retirement age, the amount of such benefit for such month and for any subsequent month shall, subject to the succeeding paragraphs of this subsection, be reduced by—

(A) $\frac{5}{9}$ of 1 percent of such amount if such benefit is an old-age insurance benefit, $\frac{25}{36}$ of 1 percent of such amount if such benefit is a wife's or husband's insurance benefit, or $\frac{19}{40}$ of 1 percent of such amount if such benefit is a widow's or widower's insurance benefit, multiplied by

(B)(i) the number of months in the reduction period for such benefit (determined under paragraph (6)), if such benefit is for a month before the month in which such individual attains retirement age, or

(ii) if less, the number of such months in the adjusted reduction period for such benefit (determined under paragraph (7)), if such benefit is (I) for the month in which such individual attains age 62, or (II) for the month in which such individual attains retirement age.

(2) If an individual is entitled to a disability insurance benefit for a month after a month for which such individual was entitled to an old-age insurance benefit, such disability insurance benefit for each month shall be reduced by the amount such old-age insurance benefit would be reduced under paragraphs (1) and (4) for such month had such individual attained retirement age (as defined in section 416(*l*) of this title) in the first month for which he most recently became entitled to a disability insurance benefit.

(3)(A) If the first month for which an individual both is entitled to a wife's, husband's, widow's, or widower's insurance benefit and has attained age 62 (in the case of a wife's or husband's insurance benefit) or age 50 (in the case of a widow's or widower's insurance benefit) is a month for which such individual is also entitled to—

(i) an old-age insurance benefit (to which such individual was first entitled for a month before he attains retirement age (as defined in section 416(*l*) of this title)), or

(ii) a disability insurance benefit,

then in lieu of any reduction under paragraph (1) (but subject to the succeeding paragraphs of this subsection) such wife's, husband's, widow's, or widower's insurance benefit for each month shall be reduced as provided in subparagraph (B), (C), or (D).

(B) For any month for which such individual is entitled to an old-age insurance benefit and is not entitled to a disability insurance benefit, such individual's wife's or husband's insurance benefit shall be reduced by the sum of—

(i) the amount by which such old-age insurance benefit is reduced under paragraph (1) for such month, and

(ii) the amount by which such wife's or husband's insurance benefit would be reduced under paragraph (1) for such month if it were equal to the excess of such wife's or husband's insurance benefit (before reduction under this subsection) over such old-age insurance benefit (before reduction under this subsection).

(C) For any month for which such individual is entitled to a disability insurance benefit, such individual's wife's, husband's, widow's, or widower's insurance benefit shall be reduced by the sum of—

(i) the amount by which such disability insurance benefit is reduced under paragraph (2) for such month (if such paragraph applied to such benefit), and

(ii) the amount by which such wife's, husband's, widow's, or widower's insurance benefit would be reduced under paragraph (1) for such month if it were equal to the excess of such wife's, husband's, widow's, or widower's insurance benefit (before reduction under this subsection) over such disability insurance benefit (before reduction under this subsection).

(D) For any month for which such individual is entitled neither to an old-age insurance benefit nor to a disability insurance benefit, such individual's wife's, husband's, widow's, or widower's insurance benefit shall be reduced by the amount by which it would be reduced under paragraph (1).

(E) Notwithstanding subparagraph (A) of this paragraph, if the first month for which an individual is entitled to a widow's or widower's insurance benefit is a month for which such individual is also entitled to an old-age insurance benefit to which such individual was first entitled for that month or for a month before she or he became entitled to a widow's or widower's benefit, the reduction in such widow's or widower's insurance benefit shall be determined under paragraph (1).

(4) If—

(A) an individual is or was entitled to a benefit subject to reduction under paragraph (1) or (3) of this subsection, and

(B) such benefit is increased by reason of an increase in the primary insurance amount of the individual on whose wages and self-employment income such benefit is based,

then the amount of the reduction of such benefit (after the application of any adjustment under paragraph (7)) for each month beginning with the month of such increase in the primary insurance amount shall be computed under paragraph (1) or (3), whichever applies, as though the increased primary insurance amount had been in effect for and after the month for which the individual first became entitled to such monthly benefit reduced under such paragraph (1) or (3).

(5)(A) No wife's or husband's insurance benefit shall be reduced under this subsection—

(i) for any month before the first month for which there is in effect a certificate filed by him or her with the Commissioner of Social Security, in accordance with regulations prescribed by the Commissioner of Social Security, in which he or she elects to receive wife's or husband's insurance benefits reduced as provided in this subsection, or

(ii) for any month in which he or she has in his or her care (individually or jointly with the person on whose wages and self-employment income the wife's or husband's insurance benefit is based) a child of such person entitled to child's insurance benefits.

(B) Any certificate described in subparagraph (A)(i) shall be effective for purposes of this subsection (and for purposes of preventing deductions under section 403(c)(2) of this title)—

(i) for the month in which it is filed and for any month thereafter, and

(ii) for months, in the period designated by the individual filing such certificate, of one or more consecutive months (not exceeding 12) immediately preceding the month in which such certificate is filed;

except that such certificate shall not be effective for any month before the month in which he or she attains age 62, nor shall it be effective for any month to which subparagraph (A)(ii) applies.

(C) If an individual does not have in his or her care a child described in subparagraph (A)(ii) in the first month for which he or she is entitled to a wife's or husband's insurance benefit, and if such first month is a month before the month in which he or she attains retirement age (as defined in section 416(*l*) of this title), he or she shall be deemed to have filed in such first month the certificate described in subparagraph (A)(i).

(D) No widow's or widower's insurance benefit for a month in which he or she has in his or her care a child of his or her deceased spouse (or deceased former spouse) entitled to child's insurance benefits shall be reduced under this subsection below the amount to which he or she would have been entitled had he or she been entitled for such month to mother's or father's insurance benefits on the basis of his or her deceased spouse's (or deceased former spouse's) wages and self-employment income.

(6) For purposes of this subsection, the "reduction period" for an individual's old-age, wife's, husband's, widow's, or widower's insurance benefit is the period—

(A) beginning—

(i) in the case of an old-age insurance benefit, with the first day of the first month for which such individual is entitled to such benefit,

(ii) in the case of a wife's or husband's insurance benefit, with the first day of the first month for which a certificate described in paragraph (5)(A)(i) is effective, or

(iii) in the case of a widow's or widower's insurance benefit, with the first day of the first month for which such individual is entitled to such benefit or the first day of the month in which such individual attains age 60, whichever is the later, and

(B) ending with the last day of the month before the month in which such individual attains retirement age.

(7) For purposes of this subsection, the "adjusted reduction period" for an individual's old-age, wife's, husband's, widow's, or widower's insurance benefit is the reduction period prescribed in paragraph (6) for such benefit, excluding—

(A) any month in which such benefit was subject to deductions under section 403(b), 403(c)(1), 403(d)(1), or 422(b) of this title,

(B) in the case of wife's or husband's insurance benefits, any month in which such individual had in his or her care (individually or jointly with the person on whose wages and self-employment income such benefit is based) a child of such person entitled to child's insurance benefits,

(C) in the case of wife's or husband's insurance benefits, any month for which such individual was not entitled to such benefits because of the occurrence of an event that terminated her or his entitlement to such benefits,

(D) in the case of widow's or widower's insurance benefits, any month in which the reduction in the amount of such benefit was determined under paragraph (5)(D),

(E) in the case of widow's or widower's insurance benefits, any month before the month in which she or he attained age 62, and also for any later month before the month in which she or he attained retirement age, for which she or he was not entitled to such benefit because of the occurrence of an event that terminated her or his entitlement to such benefits, and

(F) in the case of old-age insurance benefits, any month for which such individual was entitled to a disability insurance benefit.

(8) This subsection shall be applied after reduction under section 403(a) of this title and before application of section 415(g) of this title. If the amount of any reduction computed under paragraph (1), (2), or (3) is not a multiple of $0.10, it shall be increased to the next higher multiple of $0.10.

(9) The amount of the reduction for early retirement specified in paragraph (1)—

(A) for old-age insurance benefits, wife's insurance benefits, and husband's insurance benefits, shall be the amount specified in such paragraph for the first 36 months of the reduction period (as defined in paragraph (6)) or adjusted reduction period (as defined in paragraph (7)), and five-twelfths of 1 percent for any additional months included in such periods; and

(B) for widow's insurance benefits and widower's insurance benefits, shall be periodically revised by the Commissioner of Social Security such that—

(i) the amount of the reduction at early retirement age as defined in section 416(*l*) of this title shall be 28.5 percent of the full benefit; and

(ii) the amount of the reduction for each month in the reduction period (specified in paragraph (6)) or the adjusted reduction period (specified in paragraph (7)) shall be established by linear interpolation between 28.5 percent at the month of attainment of early retirement age and 0 percent at the month of attainment of retirement age.

(10) For purposes of applying paragraph (4), with respect to monthly benefits payable for any month after December 1977 to an individual who was entitled to a monthly benefit as reduced under paragraph (1) or (3) prior to January 1978, the amount of reduction in such benefit for the first month for which such benefit is increased by reason of an increase in the primary insurance amount of the individual on whose wages and self-employment income such benefit is based and for all subsequent months (and similarly for all subsequent increases) shall be increased by a percentage equal to the percentage increase in such primary insurance amount (such increase being made in accordance with the provisions of paragraph (8)). In the case of an individual whose reduced benefit under this section is increased as a result of the use of an adjusted reduction period (in accordance with paragraphs (1) and (3) of this subsection), then for the first month for which such increase is effective, and for all subsequent months, the amount of such reduction (after the application of the previous sentence, if applicable) shall be determined—

(A) in the case of old-age, wife's, and husband's insurance benefits, by multiplying such amount by the ratio of (i) the number of months in the adjusted reduction period to (ii) the number of months in the reduction period,

(B) in the case of widow's and widower's insurance benefits for the month in which such individual attains age 62, by multiplying such amount by the ratio of (i) the number of months in the reduction period beginning with age 62 multiplied by 19/40 of 1 percent, plus the number of months in the adjusted reduction period prior to age 62 multiplied by 19/40 of

1 percent to (ii) the number of months in the reduction period multiplied by 19/40 of 1 percent, and

(C) in the case of widow's and widower's insurance benefits for the month in which such individual attains retirement age (as defined in section 416(*l*) of this title), by multiplying such amount by the ratio of (i) the number of months in the adjusted reduction period multiplied by 19/40 of 1 percent to (ii) the number of months in the reduction period beginning with age 62 multiplied by 19/40 of 1 percent, plus the number of months in the adjusted reduction period prior to age 62 multiplied by 19/40 of 1 percent,

such determination being made in accordance with the provisions of paragraph (8).

(11) When an individual is entitled to more than one monthly benefit under this subchapter and one or more of such benefits are reduced under this subsection, paragraph (10) shall apply separately to each such benefit reduced under this subsection before the application of subsection (k) (pertaining to the method by which monthly benefits are offset when an individual is entitled to more than one kind of benefit) and the application of this paragraph shall operate in conjunction with paragraph (3).

(r) Presumed filing of application by individuals eligible for old-age insurance benefits and for wife's or husband's insurance benefits

(1) If an individual is eligible for a wife's or husband's insurance benefit (except in the case of eligibility pursuant to clause (ii) of subsection (b)(1)(B) or subsection (c)(1)(B), as appropriate), in any month for which the individual is entitled to an old-age insurance benefit, such individual shall be deemed to have filed an application for wife's or husband's insurance benefits for such month.

(2) If an individual is eligible (but for subsection (k)(4)) for an old-age insurance benefit in any month for which the individual is entitled to a wife's or husband's insurance benefit (except in the case of entitlement pursuant to clause (ii) of subsection (b)(1)(B) or subsection (c)(1)(B), as appropriate), such individual shall be deemed to have filed an application for old-age insurance benefits—

(A) for such month, or

(B) if such individual is also entitled to a disability insurance benefit for such month, in the first subsequent month for which such individual is not entitled to a disability insurance benefit.

(3) For purposes of this subsection, an individual shall be deemed eligible for a benefit for a month if, upon filing application therefor in such month, he would be entitled to such benefit for such month.

(s) Child over specified age to be disregarded for certain benefit purposes unless disabled

(1) For the purposes of subsections (b)(1), (c)(1), (g)(1), (q)(5), and (q)(7) and paragraphs (2), (3), and (4) of section 403(c) of this title, a child who is entitled to child's insurance benefits under subsection (d) for any month, and who has attained the age of 16 but is not in such month under a disability (as defined in section 423(d) of this title), shall be deemed not entitled to such benefits for such month, unless he was under such a disability in the third month before such month.

(2) So much of subsections (b)(3), (c)(4), (d)(5), (g)(3), and (h)(4) as precedes the semicolon, shall not apply in the case of any child unless such child, at the time of the marriage referred to therein, was under a disability (as defined in section 423(d) of this title) or had been under such a disability in the third month before the month in which such marriage occurred.

(3) The last sentence of subsection (c) of section 403 of this title, subsection (f)(1)(C) of section 403 of this title, and subsections (b)(3)(B), (c)(6)(B), (f)(3)(B), and (g)(6)(B) of section 416 of this title shall not apply in the case of any child with respect to any month referred to therein unless in such month or the third month prior thereto such child was under a disability (as defined in section 423(d) of this title).

(t) Suspension of benefits of aliens who are outside United States; residency requirements for dependents and survivors

(1) Notwithstanding any other provision of this subchapter, no monthly benefits shall be paid under this section or under section 423 of this title to any individual who is not a citizen or national of the United States for any month which is—

(A) after the sixth consecutive calendar month during all of which the Commissioner of Social Security finds, on the basis of information furnished to the Commissioner by the Attorney General or information which otherwise comes to the Commissioner's attention, that such individual is outside the United States, and

(B) prior to the first month thereafter for all of which such individual has been in the United States.

For purposes of the preceding sentence, after an individual has been outside the United States for any period of thirty consecutive days he shall be treated as remaining outside the United States until he has been in the United States for a period of thirty consecutive days.

(2) Subject to paragraph (11), paragraph (1) of this subsection shall not apply to any individual who is a citizen of a foreign country which the Commissioner of Social Security finds has in effect a social insurance or pension system which is of general application in such country and under which—

(A) periodic benefits, or the actuarial equivalent thereof, are paid on account of old age, retirement, or death, and

(B) individuals who are citizens of the United States but not citizens of such foreign country and who qualify for such benefits are permitted to receive such benefits or the actuarial equivalent thereof while outside such foreign country without regard to the duration of the absence.

(3) Paragraph (1) of this subsection shall not apply in any case where its application would be contrary to any treaty obligation of the United States in effect on August 1, 1956.

(4) Subject to paragraph (11), paragraph (1) of this subsection shall not apply to any benefit for any month if—

(A) not less than forty of the quarters elapsing before such month are quarters of coverage for the individual on whose wages and self-employment income such benefit is based, or

(B) the individual on whose wages and self-employment income such benefit is based has, before such month, resided in the United States for a period or periods aggregating ten years or more, or

(C) the individual entitled to such benefit is outside the United States while in the active military or naval service of the United States, or

(D) the individual on whose wages and self-employment income such benefit is based died, before such month, either (i) while on active duty or inactive duty training (as those terms are defined in section 410(*l*)(2) and (3) of this title) as a member of a uniformed service (as defined in section 410(m) of this title), or (ii) as the result of a disease or injury which the Secretary of Veterans Affairs determines was incurred or aggravated in line of duty while on active duty (as defined in section 410(*l*)(2) of this title), or an injury which he determines was incurred or aggravated in line of duty while on inactive duty training (as defined in section 410(*l*)(3) of this title), as a member of a uniformed service (as defined in section 410(m) of this title), if the Secretary of Veterans Affairs determines that such individual was discharged or released from the period of such active duty or inactive duty training under conditions other than dishonorable, and if the Secretary of Veterans Affairs certifies to the Commissioner of Social Security his determinations with respect to such individual under this clause, or

(E) the individual on whose employment such benefit is based had been in service covered by the Railroad Retirement Act of 1937 or 1974 which was treated as employment covered by this chapter pursuant to the provisions of section 5(k)(1) of the Railroad Retirement Act of 1937 or section 18(2) of the Railroad Retirement Act of 1974;

except that subparagraphs (A) and (B) of this paragraph shall not apply in the case of any individual who is a citizen of a foreign country that has in effect a social insurance or pension system which is of general application in such country and which satisfies subparagraph (A) but not subparagraph (B) of paragraph (2), or who is a citizen of a foreign country that has no social insurance or pension system of general application if at any time within five years prior to the month in which the Social Security Amendments of 1967 are enacted (or the first month thereafter for which his benefits are subject to suspension under paragraph (1)) payments to individuals residing in such country were withheld by the Treasury Department under sections 3329(a) and 3330(a) of Title 31.

(5) No person who is, or upon application would be, entitled to a monthly benefit under this section for December 1956 shall be deprived, by reason of paragraph (1) of this subsection, of such benefit or any other benefit based on the wages and self-employment income of the individual on whose wages and self-employment income such monthly benefit for December 1956 is based.

(6) If an individual is outside the United States when he dies and no benefit may, by reason of paragraph (1) or (10) of this subsection, be paid to him for the month preceding the month in which he dies, no lump-sum death payment may be made on the basis of such individual's wages and self-employment income.

(7) Subsections (b), (c), and (d) of section 403 of this title shall not apply with respect to any individual for any month for which no monthly benefit may be paid to him by reason of paragraph (1) of this subsection.

(8) The Attorney General shall certify to the Commissioner of Social Security such information regarding aliens who depart from the United States to any foreign country (other than a foreign country which is territorially contiguous to the continental United States) as may be necessary to enable the Commissioner of Social Security to carry out the purposes of this subsection and shall otherwise aid, assist, and cooperate with the Commissioner of Social Security in obtaining such other information as may be necessary to enable the Commissioner of Social Security to carry out the purposes of this subsection.

(9) No payments shall be made under part A of subchapter XVIII with respect to items or services furnished to an individual in any month for which the prohibition in paragraph (1) against payment of benefits to him is applicable (or would be if he were entitled to any such benefits).

(10) Notwithstanding any other provision of this subchapter, no monthly benefits shall be paid under this section or under section 423 of this title, for any month beginning after June 30, 1968, to an individual who is not a citizen or national of the United States and who resides during such month in a foreign country if payments for such month to individuals residing in such country are withheld by the Treasury Department under sections 3329(a) and 3330(a) of Title 31.

(11)(A) Paragraph (2) and subparagraphs (A), (B), (C), and (E) of paragraph (4) shall apply with respect to an individual's monthly benefits under subsection (b), (c), (d), (e), (f), (g), or (h) only if such individual meets the residency requirements of this paragraph with respect to those benefits.

(B) An individual entitled to benefits under subsection (b), (c), (e), (f), or (g) meets the residency requirements of this paragraph with respect to those benefits only if such individual has resided in the United States, and while so residing bore a spousal relationship to the person on whose wages and self-employment income such entitlement is based, for a total period of not less than 5 years. For purposes of this subparagraph, a period of time for which an individual bears a spousal relationship to another person consists of a period throughout which the individual has been, with respect to such other person, a wife, a husband, a widow, a widower, a divorced wife, a divorced husband, a surviving divorced wife, a surviving divorced husband, a surviving divorced mother, a surviving divorced father, or (as applicable in the course of such period) any two or more of the foregoing.

(C) An individual entitled to benefits under subsection (d) meets the residency requirements of this paragraph with respect to those benefits only if—

(i)(I) such individual has resided in the United States (as the child of the person on whose wages and self-employment income such entitlement is based) for a total period of not less than 5 years, or

(II) the person on whose wages and self-employment income such entitlement is based, and the individual's other parent (within the meaning of subsection (h)(3)), if any, have each resided in the United States for a total period of not less than 5 years (or died while residing in the United States), and

(ii) in the case of an individual entitled to such benefits as an adopted child, such individual was adopted within the United States by the person on whose wages and self-employment income such entitlement is based, and has lived in the United States with such person and received at least one-half of his or her support from such person for a period (beginning before such individual attained age 18) consisting of—

(I) the year immediately before the month in which such person became eligible for old-age insurance benefits or disability insurance benefits or died, whichever occurred first, or

(II) if such person had a period of disability which continued until he or she became entitled to old-age insurance benefits or disability insurance benefits or died, the year immediately before the month in which such period of disability began.

(D) An individual entitled to benefits under subsection (h) meets the residency requirements of this paragraph with respect to those benefits only if such individual has resided in the United States, and while so residing was a parent (within the meaning of subsection (h)(3)) of the person on whose wages and self-employment income such entitlement is based, for a total period of not less than 5 years.

(E) This paragraph shall not apply with respect to any individual who is a citizen or resident of a foreign country with which the United States has an agreement in force concluded pursuant to section 433 of this title, except to the extent provided by such agreement.

(u) Conviction of subversive activities, etc.

(1) If any individual is convicted of any offense (committed after August 1, 1956) under—

(A) chapter 37 (relating to espionage and censorship), chapter 105 (relating to sabotage), or chapter 115 (relating to treason, sedition, and subversive activities) of Title 18, or

(B) section 783 of Title 50,

then the court may, in addition to all other penalties provided by law, impose a penalty that in determining whether any monthly insurance benefit under this section or section 423 of this title is payable to such individual for the month in which he is convicted or for any month thereafter, in determining the amount of any such benefit payable to such individual for any such month, and in determining whether such individual is entitled to insurance benefits under part A of subchapter XVIII for any such month, there shall not be taken into account—

(C) any wages paid to such individual or to any other individual in the calendar year in which such conviction occurs or in any prior calendar year, and

(D) any net earnings from self-employment derived by such individual or by any other individual during a taxable year in which such conviction occurs or during any prior taxable year.

(2) As soon as practicable after an additional penalty has, pursuant to paragraph (1) of this subsection, been imposed with respect to any individual, the Attorney General shall notify the Commissioner of Social Security of such imposition.

(3) If any individual with respect to whom an additional penalty has been imposed pursuant to paragraph (1) of this subsection is granted a pardon of the offense by the President of the United States, such additional penalty shall not apply for any month beginning after the date on which such pardon is granted.

(v) Waiver of benefits

(1) Notwithstanding any other provisions of this subchapter, and subject to paragraph (3), in the case of any individual who files a waiver pursuant to section 1402(g) of the Internal Revenue Code of 1986 and is granted a tax exemption thereunder, no benefits or other payments shall be payable under this subchapter to him, no payments shall be made on his behalf under part A of subchapter XVIII, and no benefits or other payments under this subchapter shall be payable on the basis of his wages and self-employment income to any other person, after the filing of such waiver.

(2) Notwithstanding any other provision of this subchapter, and subject to paragraph (3), in the case of any individual who files a waiver pursuant to section 3127 of the Internal Revenue Code of 1986 and is granted a tax exemption thereunder, no benefits or other payments shall be payable under this subchapter to him, no payments shall be made on his behalf under part A of subchapter XVIII, and no benefits or other payments under this subchapter shall be payable on the basis of his wages and self-employment income to any other person, after the filing of such waiver.

(3) If, after an exemption referred to in paragraph (1) or (2) is granted to an individual, such exemption ceases to be effective, the waiver referred to in such paragraph shall cease to be applicable in the case of benefits and other payments under this subchapter and part A of subchapter XVIII to the extent based on—

(A) his wages for and after the calendar year following the calendar year in which occurs the failure to meet the requirements of section 1402(g) or 3127 of the Internal Revenue Code of 1986 on which the cessation of such exemption is based, and

(B) his self-employment income for and after the taxable year in which occurs such failure.

(w) Increase in old-age insurance benefit amounts on account of delayed retirement

(1) The amount of an old-age insurance benefit (other than a benefit based on a primary insurance amount determined under section 415(a)(3) of this title as in effect in December 1978 or section 415(a)(1)(C)(i) of this title as in effect thereafter) which is payable without regard to this subsection to an individual shall be increased by—

(A) the applicable percentage (as determined under paragraph (6)) of such amount, multiplied by

(B) the number (if any) of the increment months for such individual.

(2) For purposes of this subsection, the number of increment months for any individual shall be a number equal to the total number of the months—

(A) which have elapsed after the month before the month in which such individual attained retirement age (as defined in section 416(*l*) of this title) or (if later) December 1970 and prior to the month in which such individual attained age 70, and

(B) with respect to which—

(i) such individual was a fully insured individual (as defined in section 414(a) of this title),

(ii) such individual either was not entitled to an old-age insurance benefit or, if so entitled, did not receive benefits pursuant to a request under subsection (z) by such individual that benefits not be paid, and

(iii) such individual was not subject to a penalty imposed under section 1320a–8a of this title.

(3) For purposes of applying the provisions of paragraph (1), a determination shall be made under paragraph (2) for each year, beginning with 1972, of the total number of an individual's increment months through the year for which the determination is made and the total so determined shall be applicable to such individual's old-age insurance benefits beginning with benefits for January of the year following the year for which such determination is made; except that the total number applicable in the case of an individual who attains age 70 after 1972 shall be determined through the month before the month in which he attains such age and shall be applicable to his old-age insurance benefit beginning with the month in which he attains such age.

(4) This subsection shall be applied after reduction under section 403(a) of this title.

(5) If an individual's primary insurance amount is determined under paragraph (3) of section 415(a) of this title as in effect in December 1978, or section 415(a)(1)(C)(i) of this title as in effect thereafter, and, as a result of this subsection, he would be entitled to a higher old-age insurance benefit if his primary insurance amount were determined under section 415(a) of this title (whether before, in, or after December 1978) without regard to such paragraph, such individual's old-age insurance benefit based upon his primary insurance amount determined under such paragraph shall be increased by an amount equal to the difference between such benefit and the benefit to which he would be entitled if his primary insurance amount were determined under such section without regard to such paragraph.

(6) For purposes of paragraph (1)(A), the "applicable percentage" is—

(A) 1/12 of 1 percent in the case of an individual who first becomes eligible for an old-age insurance benefit in any calendar year before 1979;

(B) 1/4 of 1 percent in the case of an individual who first becomes eligible for an old-age insurance benefit in any calendar year after 1978 and before 1987;

(C) in the case of an individual who first becomes eligible for an old-age insurance benefit in a calendar year after 1986 and before 2005, a percentage equal to the applicable percentage in effect under this paragraph for persons who first became eligible for an old-age insurance benefit in the preceding calendar year (as increased pursuant to this subparagraph), plus 1/24 of 1 percent if the calendar year in which that particular individual first becomes eligible for such benefit is not evenly divisible by 2; and

(D) ⅔ of 1 percent in the case of an individual who first becomes eligible for an old-age insurance benefit in a calendar year after 2004.

(x) Limitation on payments to prisoners, certain other inmates of publicly funded institutions, fugitives, probationers, and parolees

(1)(A) Notwithstanding any other provision of this subchapter, no monthly benefits shall be paid under this section or under section 423 of this title to any individual for any month ending with or during or beginning with or during a period of more than 30 days throughout all of which such individual—

(i) is confined in a jail, prison, or other penal institution or correctional facility pursuant to his conviction of a criminal offense,

(ii) is confined by court order in an institution at public expense in connection with—

(I) a verdict or finding that the individual is guilty but insane, with respect to a criminal offense,

(II) a verdict or finding that the individual is not guilty of such an offense by reason of insanity,

(III) a finding that such individual is incompetent to stand trial under an allegation of such an offense, or

(IV) a similar verdict or finding with respect to such an offense based on similar factors (such as a mental disease, a mental defect, or mental incompetence),

(iii) immediately upon completion of confinement as described in clause (i) pursuant to conviction of a criminal offense an element of which is sexual activity, is confined by court order in an institution at public expense pursuant to a finding that the individual is a sexually dangerous person or a sexual predator or a similar finding,

(iv) is fleeing to avoid prosecution, or custody or confinement after conviction, under the laws of the place from which the person flees, for a crime, or an attempt to commit a crime, which is a felony under the laws of the place from which the person flees, or, in jurisdictions that do not define crimes as felonies, is punishable by death or imprisonment for a term exceeding 1 year regardless of the actual sentence imposed, or

(v) is violating a condition of probation or parole imposed under Federal or State law.

(B)(i) For purposes of clause (i) of subparagraph (A), an individual shall not be considered confined in an institution comprising a jail, prison, or other penal institution or correctional facility during any month throughout which such individual is residing outside such institution at no expense (other than the cost of monitoring) to such institution or the penal system or to any agency to which the penal system has transferred jurisdiction over the individual.

(ii) For purposes of clauses (ii) and (iii) of subparagraph (A), an individual confined in an institution as described in such clause (ii) shall be treated as remaining so confined until—

(I) he or she is released from the care and supervision of such institution, and

(II) such institution ceases to meet the individual's basic living needs.

(iii) Notwithstanding subparagraph (A), the Commissioner shall, for good cause shown, pay the individual benefits that have been withheld or would otherwise be withheld pursuant to clause (iv) or (v) of subparagraph (A) if the Commissioner determines that—

(I) a court of competent jurisdiction has found the individual not guilty of the criminal offense, dismissed the charges relating to the criminal offense, vacated the warrant for arrest of the individual for the criminal offense, or issued any similar exonerating order (or taken similar exonerating action), or

(II) the individual was erroneously implicated in connection with the criminal offense by reason of identity fraud.

(iv) Notwithstanding subparagraph (A), the Commissioner may, for good cause shown based on mitigating circumstances, pay the individual benefits that have been withheld or would otherwise be withheld pursuant to clause (iv) or (v) of subparagraph (A) if the Commissioner determines that—

(I) the offense described in clause (iv) or underlying the imposition of the probation or parole described in clause (v) was nonviolent and not drug-related, and

(II) in the case of an individual from whom benefits have been withheld or otherwise would be withheld pursuant to subparagraph (A)(v), the action that resulted in the violation of a condition of probation or parole was nonviolent and not drug-related.

(2) Benefits which would be payable to any individual (other than a confined individual to whom benefits are not payable by reason of paragraph (1)) under this subchapter on the basis of the wages and self-employment income of such a confined individual but for the provisions of paragraph (1), shall be payable as though such confined individual were receiving such benefits under this section or section 423 of this title.

(3)(A) Notwithstanding the provisions of section 552a of Title 5 or any other provision of Federal or State law, any agency of the United States Government or of any State (or political subdivision thereof) shall make available to the Commissioner of Social Security, upon written request, the name and social security account number of any individual who is confined as described in paragraph (1) if the confinement is under the jurisdiction of such agency and the Commissioner of Social Security requires such information to carry out the provisions of this section.

(B)(i) The Commissioner shall enter into an agreement under this subparagraph with any interested State or local institution comprising a jail, prison, penal institution, or correctional facility, or comprising any other institution a purpose of which is to confine individuals as described in paragraph (1)(A)(ii). Under such agreement—

(I) the institution shall provide to the Commissioner, on a monthly basis and in a manner specified by the Commissioner, the first, middle, and last names, Social Security account numbers or taxpayer identification numbers, prison assigned inmate numbers, last known addresses, dates of birth, confinement commencement dates, dates of release or anticipated dates of release, dates of work release, and, to the extent available to the institution, such other identifying information concerning the individuals confined in the institution as the Commissioner may require for the purpose of carrying out paragraph (1) and clause (iv) of this subparagraph and other provisions of this subchapter; and

(II) the Commissioner shall pay to the institution, with respect to information described in subclause (I) concerning each individual who is confined therein as described in paragraph (1)(A), who receives a benefit under this subchapter for the month preceding the first month of such confinement, and whose benefit under this subchapter is determined by the Commissioner to be not payable by reason of confinement based on the information provided by the institution, $400 (subject to reduction under clause (ii)) if the institution furnishes the information to the Commissioner within 30 days after the date such individual's confinement in such institution begins, or $200 (subject to reduction under clause (ii)) if the institution furnishes the information after 30 days after such date but within 90 days after such date.

(ii) The dollar amounts specified in clause (i)(II) shall be reduced by 50 percent if the Commissioner is also required to make a payment to the institution with respect to the same individual under an agreement entered into under section 1382(e)(1)(I) of this title.

(iii) There are authorized to be transferred from the Federal Old-Age and Survivors Insurance Trust Fund and the Federal Disability Insurance Trust Fund, as appropriate, such sums as may be necessary to enable the Commissioner to make payments to institutions required by clause (i)(II).

(iv) The Commissioner shall maintain, and shall provide on a reimbursable basis, information obtained pursuant to agreements entered into under this paragraph to any agency administering a Federal or federally-assisted cash, food, or medical assistance program for eligibility and other administrative purposes under such program, for statistical and research activities conducted by Federal and State agencies, and to the Secretary of the Treasury for the purposes of tax administration, debt collection, and identifying, preventing, and recovering improper payments under federally funded programs.

(v)(I) The Commissioner may disclose information received pursuant to this paragraph to any officer, employee, agent, or contractor of the Department of the Treasury whose official duties require such information to assist in the identification, prevention, and recovery of improper payments or in the collection of delinquent debts owed to the United States, including payments certified by the head of an executive, judicial, or legislative paying agency, and payments made to individuals whose eligibility, or continuing eligibility, to participate in a Federal program (including those administered by a State or political subdivision thereof) is being reviewed.

(II) Notwithstanding the provisions of section 552a of Title 5 or any other provision of Federal or State law, the Secretary of the Treasury may compare information disclosed under subclause (I) with any other personally identifiable information derived from a Federal system of records or similar records maintained by a Federal contractor, a Federal grantee, or an entity administering a Federal program or activity, and may redisclose such comparison of information to any paying or administering agency and to the head of the Federal Bureau of Prisons and the head of any State agency charged with the administration of prisons with respect to inmates whom the Secretary of the Treasury has determined may have been issued, or facilitated in the issuance of, an improper payment.

(III) The comparison of information disclosed under subclause (I) shall not be considered a matching program for purposes of section 552a of Title 5.

(C) Notwithstanding the provisions of section 552a of Title 5 or any other provision of Federal or State law (other than section 6103 of the Internal Revenue Code of 1986 and section 1306(c) of this title), the Commissioner shall furnish any Federal, State, or local law enforcement officer, upon the written request of the officer, with the current address, Social Security number, and photograph (if applicable) of any beneficiary under this subchapter, if the officer furnishes the Commissioner with the name of the beneficiary, and other identifying information as reasonably required by the Commissioner to establish the unique identity of the beneficiary, and notifies the Commissioner that—

(i) the beneficiary is described in clause (iv) or (v) of paragraph (1)(A); and

(ii) the location or apprehension of the beneficiary is within the officer's official duties.

(y) Limitation on payments to aliens

Notwithstanding any other provision of law, no monthly benefit under this subchapter shall be payable to any alien in the United States for any month during which such alien is not lawfully present in the United States as determined by the Attorney General.

(z) Voluntary suspension

(1)(A) Except as otherwise provided in this subsection, any individual who has attained retirement age (as defined in section 416(*l*) of this title) and is entitled to old-age insurance benefits may request that payment of such benefits be suspended—

(i) beginning with the month following the month in which such request is received by the Commissioner, and

(ii) ending with the earlier of the month following the month in which a request by the individual for a resumption of such benefits is so received or the month following the month in which the individual attains the age of 70.

(2) An individual may not suspend such benefits under this subsection, and any suspension of such benefits under this subsection shall end, effective with respect to any month in which the individual becomes subject to—

(A) mandatory suspension of such benefits under subsection (x);

(B) termination of such benefits under subsection (n);

(C) a penalty under section 1320a–8a of this title imposing nonpayment of such benefits; or

(D) any other withholding, in whole or in part, of such benefits under any other provision of law that authorizes recovery of a debt by withholding such benefits.

(3) In the case of an individual who requests that such benefits be suspended under this subsection, for any month during the period in which the suspension is in effect—

(A) no retroactive benefits (as defined in subsection (j)(4)(B)(iii)) shall be payable to such individual;

(B) no monthly benefit shall be payable to any other individual on the basis of such individual's wages and self-employment income; and

(C) no monthly benefit shall be payable to such individual on the basis of another individual's wages and self-employment income.

(Aug. 14, 1935, c. 531, Title II, § 202, 49 Stat. 623; Aug. 10, 1939, c. 666, Title II, § 201, 53 Stat. 1362; Aug. 10, 1946, c. 951, Title IV, §§ 402, 403(a), 404(a), 405(a), 60 Stat. 986, 987; Aug. 28, 1950, c. 809, Title I, § 101(a), 64 Stat. 482; Aug. 14, 1953, c. 483, § 2, 67 Stat. 580; Sept. 1, 1954, c. 1206, Title I, §§ 102(i), 105(a), 107, 110, 68 Stat. 1073, 1079, 1083, 1085; Aug. 9, 1955, c. 685, § 2, 69 Stat. 621; Aug. 1, 1956, c. 836, Title I, §§ 101(a) to (c), 102(c), (d)(1) to (10), 103(c)(1) to (3), 113, 114(a), 118(a), 121(a), 70 Stat. 807, 810 to 814, 818, 831, 832, 835, 838; Aug. 1, 1956, c. 837, Title IV, §§ 403(a), 407, 70 Stat. 871, 876; Pub.L. 85–238, §§ 1, 3(a) to (g), Aug. 30, 1957, 71 Stat. 518; Pub.L. 85–798, § 1, Aug. 28, 1958, 72 Stat. 964; Pub.L. 85–840, Title I, § 101(e), Title II, § 205(b) to (i), Title III, §§ 301(a)(1), (b)(1), (c)(1), 303, 304(a)(1), 305(a), 306(a), 307(a) to (e), Aug. 28, 1958, 72 Stat. 1017, 1021 to 1024, 1026, 1027, 1029 to 1032; Pub.L. 85–857, § 13(i)(1), Sept. 2, 1958, 72 Stat. 1265; Pub.L. 85–927, § 301, Sept. 6, 1958, 72 Stat. 1783; Pub.L. 86–70, § 32(c)(1), June 25, 1959, 73 Stat. 149; Pub.L. 86–624, § 30(c)(1), July 12, 1960, 74 Stat. 420; Pub.L. 86–778, Title I, § 103(a)(1), (j)(2)(C), (D), Title II, §§ 201(a), (b), 202(a), 203(a), 205(a), (b), 208(d), 211(i) to (*l*), Title III, § 301(a), Title IV, § 403(d), Sept. 13, 1960, 74 Stat. 936, 937, 946, 947, 949, 952, 957 to 959, 969; Pub.L. 87–64, Title I, §§ 102(a), (b)(1), (2)(A), (3), (e), 104(a) to (d), June 30, 1961, 75 Stat. 131, 134 to 136, 138, 139; Pub.L. 89–97, Title I, § 104(a), Title III, §§ 303(d), 304(a) to (j), 306(a), (b), (c)(1) to (9), 307(a), (b), 308(a), (b), (d)(1), (2)(A), (3) to (5), (12), (13), 319(d), 323(a), 324(a), 328(a), 333(a) to (c), 334(e), (f), 339(b), 343(a), July 30, 1965, 79 Stat. 334, 367 to 379, 392, 397, 398, 400, 403 to 405, 410, 412; Pub.L. 90–248, Title I, §§ 103(a) to (d), 104(a) to (c), 112(a), 151(a) to (d)(1), (2), 157(a), (b), 158(c)(1), (2), 162(a)(1), (b)(1), (c)(1), (2), Jan. 2, 1968, 81 Stat. 828 to 832, 838, 860, 867, 868, 871; Pub.L. 91–172, Title X, § 1004(a) to (c), Dec. 30, 1969, 83 Stat. 741; Pub.L. 92–223, § 1, Dec. 28, 1971, 85 Stat. 802; Pub.L. 92–603, Title I, §§ 102(a), (b), (d) to (f), 103(a), (b), 107(a), 108(a) to (e), 109(a), 110(a), 111(a), 112(a), 113(b), 114(a) to (c), 116(b), (c), Oct. 30, 1972, 86 Stat. 1335, 1336, 1338 to 1340, 1343 to 1348, 1350; Pub.L. 93–66, Title II, § 240(a), July 9, 1973, 87 Stat. 161; Pub.L. 93–233, §§ 1(f), (g), 18(b), Dec. 31, 1973, 87 Stat. 947, 948, 967; Pub.L. 93–445, Title III, § 301, Oct. 16, 1974, 88 Stat. 1357; Pub.L. 95–216, Title II, §§ 203, 204(a) to (d), 205(a), (b), Title III, §§ 331(a) to (c), 332(a)(1), (2), 334(a) to (d)(4)(A), (5), (6), (e), 336(a), (b), 337(b), 353(f)(1), Dec. 20, 1977, 91 Stat. 1527 to 1529, 1541 to 1548, 1554; Pub.L. 95–600, Title VII, § 703(j)(14)(A), Nov. 6, 1978, 92 Stat. 2942; Pub.L. 96–265, Title III, §§ 303(b)(1)(B) to (D), 306(a), June 9, 1980, 94 Stat. 451, 452, 457; Pub.L. 96–473, §§ 5(b), 6(a), Oct. 19, 1980, 94 Stat. 2265; Pub.L. 96–499, Title X, § 1011(a), Dec. 5, 1980, 94 Stat. 2655; Pub.L. 97–35, Title XXII, §§ 2201(b)(10), (11), (d), (f), 2202(a)(1), 2203(a), (b)(1), (c)(1), (d)(1), (2), 2205(a)(1), 2206(b)(1), 2210(a), Aug. 13, 1981, 95 Stat. 831 to 838, 841; Pub.L. 97–123, § 2(e), Dec. 29, 1981, 95 Stat. 1660; Pub.L. 97–455, § 7(c), Jan. 12, 1983, 96 Stat. 2501; Pub.L. 98–21, Title I, §§ 111(a)(7), 113(d), 114(a) to (c)(1), 131(a)(1) to (3)(G), (b)(1) to (3)(F), (c), 132(a), 133(a), (b), 134(a), (b), Title II, § 201(b), (c)(1)(A), Title III, §§ 301(a), (b), 302, 306(a), (b), (d) to (h), 307(a), 309(a) to (e), 334(a), 337(a), 339(a), 340(a), (b), Apr. 20, 1983, 97 Stat. 72, 79, 92, 93, 95, 97, 98, 108, 111 to 116, 130, 131, 133 to 135; Pub.L. 98–369, Div. B, Title VI, §§ 2661(b) to (f), 2662(c)(1), 2663(a)(2), July 18, 1984, 98 Stat. 1156, 1159, 1160; Pub.L. 99–272, Title XII, §§ 12104(a), 12107(a), Apr. 7, 1986, 100 Stat. 285, 286; Pub.L. 99–514, Title XVIII, § 1883(a)(1) to (3), Oct. 22, 1986, 100 Stat. 2916; Pub.L. 100–203, Title IX, §§ 9007(a) to (e), 9010(b) to (d), Dec. 22, 1987, 101 Stat. 1330–289 to 1330–293; Pub.L. 100–647, Title VIII, §§ 8004(a), (b), 8007(b), 8010(a), (b), 8014(a), Nov. 10, 1988, 102 Stat. 3780, 3782, 3788, 3790; Pub.L. 101–239, Title X, §§ 10203(a), 10301(a), (b), 10302(a)(1), Dec. 19, 1989, 103 Stat. 2473, 2481; Pub.L. 101–508, Title V, §§ 5103(c)(2)(A), (B), (d), 5116(a), Nov. 5, 1990, 104 Stat. 1388–252, 1388–253, 1388–274; Pub.L. 101–649, Title VI, § 603(b)(5), Nov. 29, 1990, 104 Stat. 5085; Pub.L. 102–40, Title IV, § 402(d)(2), May 7, 1991, 105 Stat. 239; Pub.L. 102–54, § 13(q)(3)(C), June 13, 1991, 105 Stat. 279; Pub.L. 103–296, Title I, § 107(a)(4), Title III, §§ 308(a), 321(a)(2) to (5), (b)(1), (c)(2), Aug. 15, 1994, 108 Stat. 1478, 1522, 1535 to 1538; Pub.L. 103–387, § 4(a), Oct. 22, 1994, 108 Stat. 4076;

Pub.L. 104–121, Title I, § 104(a)(1), (b)(1), (2), Mar. 29, 1996, 110 Stat. 851, 852; Pub.L. 104–208, Div. C, Title III, § 308(g)(1), Title V, § 503(a), Sept. 30, 1996, 110 Stat. 3009–622, 3009–671; Pub.L. 106–169, Title II, § 207(b), Dec. 14, 1999, 113 Stat. 1838; Pub.L. 106–170, Title IV, § 402(a)(1), (b)(1), (d)(1), (2), Dec. 17, 1999, 113 Stat. 1907 to 1909; Pub.L. 106–182, § 4(b), Apr. 7, 2000, 114 Stat. 199; Pub.L. 108–203, Title II, § 203(a), Title IV, §§ 412(a), (b), 418(a) to (b)(4)(B)(vi), (5), 420A(a), Mar. 2, 2004, 118 Stat. 509, 527, 528, 531 to 533, 535; Pub.L. 113–67, Div. A, Title II, § 204(a)(1), (b)(1), Dec. 26, 2013, 127 Stat. 1179, 1180; Pub.L. 113–270, §§ 3, 4, Dec. 18, 2014, 128 Stat. 2948; Pub.L. 114–74, Title VIII, § 831(a)(1), (2), (b)(1), (2), Nov. 2, 2015, 129 Stat. 611, 612, 613.)

[1] So in original. Probably should be "or".

[2] So in original. Probably should be a period at the end.

HISTORICAL AND STATUTORY NOTES

References in Text

The effective date of this sentence, referred to in subsec. (d)(7)(A), is the effective date of section 5 of Pub.L. 96–473, which added such sentence effective with respect to benefits payable for months beginning on or after October 1, 1980. See Effective Date of 1980 Amendments note under this section.

Section 212 of Pub.L. 93–66, referred to in subsecs. (e)(5)(B), (8), (f)(5)(B), (8), (n)(4), is section 212 of Pub.L. 93–66, Title II, July 9, 1973, 87 Stat. 155, as amended, which is set out as a note under section 1382 of this title.

Section 102(g) of the Social Security Amendments of 1972, referred to in subsecs. (e)(6) and (f)(6), is section 102(g) of Pub.L. 92–603, Oct. 30, 1972, 86 Stat. 1329, which is set out as a Redetermination of Widow's and Widower's Benefits note under this section.

Paragraph (3) of subsec. (f) of this section, referred to in subsec. (f)(1), was redesignated par. (2) of subsec. (f) by Pub.L. 108–203, § 418(b)(4)(A)(i). See 2004 Amendment note below.

Section 2201 of the Omnibus Budget Reconciliation Act of 1981, referred to in subsec. (i), is Pub.L. 97–35, Title XXII, § 2201, Aug. 13, 1981, 95 Stat. 830, which enacted section 1382k of this title, amended sections 402, 403, 415, 417, and 433 of this title, and enacted provisions set out as notes under sections 415 and 1382k of this title.

Subsection (k)(4), referred to in subsec. (r)(2), originally read "section 202(k)(4)", which was translated as if it read "subsection (k)(4)" of this section, which is section 202 of the Social Security Act.

Chapter 37, chapter 105 and chapter 115, referred to in subsec. (u)(1)(A), are classified to 18 U.S.C.A. §§ 791 et seq., 2151 et seq., and 2381 et seq., respectively.

Subsection (z), referred to in subsec. (w)(2)(B)(ii), originally read "section 202(z)", which was translated as if it read "subsection (z)" of this section, which is section 202 of the Social Security Act.

Subsection (x), referred to in subsec. (z)(2)(A), originally read "section 202(x)", which was translated as if it read "subsection (x)" of this section, which is section 202 of the Social Security Act.

Subsection (n), referred to in subsec. (z)(2)(B), originally read "section 202(n)", which was translated as if it read "subsection (n)" of this section, which is section 202 of the Social Security Act.

Chapter 84 of Title 5, referred to in subsec. (k)(5)(A)(ii)(II), is 5 U.S.C.A. § 8401 et seq.

The Foreign Service Act of 1980, referred to in subsec. (k)(5)(A)(ii)(II), is Pub.L. 96–465, Oct. 17, 1980, 94 Stat. 2071, as amended. Subchapter II of chapter 8 of title I of the Act is classified generally to part II of subchapter VIII of chapter 52 of Title 22, 22 U.S.C.A. § 4071 et seq. For complete classification, see Short Title note set out under 22 U.S.C.A. § 3901 and Tables.

Section 1227(a) of Title 8, referred to in subsec. (n), was amended generally by Pub.L. 101–649, title VI, § 602(a), Nov. 29, 1990, 104 Stat. 5077, and as amended, does not contain a par. (19).

Subchapter XVI, referred to in subsec. (n)(4), originally read "title XVI", meaning Title XVI of the Social Security Act, Act Aug. 14, 1935, c. 531, 49 Stat. 620, as amended, which is principally classified to subchapter XVI of this chapter, 42 U.S.C.A. § 1381 et seq.

"Clause (B) of subsection (f)(1) of this section as in effect prior to the Social Security Act Amendments of 1950", and "subsection (g) of this section as in effect prior to the Social Security Act Amendments of 1950", referred to in subsec. (p), means such subsections as in effect prior to September 1, 1950, which was the effective date of section 101(a) of Act Aug. 28, 1950. See section 101(b)(1), (3) of Act Aug. 28, 1950, set out as an Effective Date of 1950 Amendment note under this section.

Subsection (c)(4), referred to in subsec. (s)(2), was redesignated subsec. (c)(3) by Pub.L. 108–203, § 418(b)(2)(A). See 2004 Amendments note below.

Subsection (c)(6)(B) of section 416 of this title, referred to in subsec. (s)(3), was redesignated subsec. (c)(1)(F)(ii) of section 416 of this title by Pub.L. 108–203, § 414(a)(1), (2), (4).

Subsection (g)(6)(B) of section 416 of this title, referred to in subsec. (s)(3), was redesignated subsec. (g)(1)(F)(ii) of section 416 of this title by Pub.L. 108–203, § 414(b)(1), (2), (4).

The Railroad Retirement Act of 1937, referred to in subsec. (t)(4)(E), is Act Aug. 29, 1935, c. 812, 49 Stat. 867, as amended generally. See par. for Railroad Retirement Act of 1974 below.

The Railroad Retirement Act of 1974, referred to in subsec. (t)(4)(E), is Act Aug. 29, 1935, c. 812, as amended generally by Pub.L. 93–445, Title I, § 101, Oct. 16, 1974, 88 Stat. 1305, which is classified generally to subchapter IV (45 U.S.C.A. § 231 et seq.) of chapter 9 of Title 45. Pub.L. 93–445 completely amended and revised the Railroad Retirement Act of 1937 (approved June 24, 1937, c. 382, 50 Stat. 307), and as thus amended and revised, the 1937 Act was redesignated the Railroad Retirement Act of 1974. Previously, the 1937 Act had completely amended and revised the Railroad Retirement Act of 1935 (approved Aug. 29, 1935, c. 812, 49 Stat. 967). Section 201 of the 1937 Act provided that the 1935 Act, as in force prior to amendment by the 1937 Act, may be cited as the Railroad Retirement Act of 1935; and that the 1935 Act, as amended by the 1937 Act may be cited as the Railroad Retirement Act of 1937. The Railroad Retirement Acts of 1935 and 1937 were classified to subchapter II (45 U.S.C.A. § 215 et seq.) and subchapter III (45 U.S.C.A. § 228a et seq.), respectively, of chapter 9 of Title 45. For further details and complete classification of these Acts to the Code, see Codifications note set out preceding 45 U.S.C.A. § 231, 45 U.S.C.A. § 231t, and Tables.

The month in which the Social Security Amendments of 1967 were enacted, referred to in the exception provision following (t)(4)(E), was Jan. 1968, date of approval of Pub.L. 90–248 being Jan. 2, 1968.

Part A of subchapter XVIII, referred to in subsecs. (t)(9), (u)(1), and (v), is classified to section 1395c et seq. of this title.

The Internal Revenue Code of 1986, referred to in subsec. (v), is classified generally to Title 26, Internal Revenue Code.

Codifications

Amendment by Pub.L. 99–514, Title XVIII, § 1883(a)(3), which amended subsec. (q)(5)(C) of this section by striking out "she shall be deemed" and inserting in lieu thereof "he or she shall be deemed" was not executed, as no change in text was required, in view of the prior amendment of subsec. (q)(5) by Pub.L. 98–21, Title III, § 309(c)(4).

Phrase "attained retirement age (as defined in section 416(*l*) of this title)" was substituted for "attained age 65" in subsecs. (c)(1) and (f)(1)(C)(ii) of this section as the probable intent of Congress notwithstanding the fact that under the numerical sequence of sections in Pub.L. 98–21 the substitution of language in subsecs. (c)(1) and (f)(1)(C)(ii) of this section [by section 201(c)(1)(A) of Pub.L. 98–21] occurred prior to the insertion of the affected language in subsec. (c)(1) of this section [by section 301(a)(2)(C) of Pub.L. 98–21] and also prior to the enactment of subsec. (f)(1)(C)(ii) of this section [by section 306(g) of Pub.L. 98–21].

In subsecs. (t)(4), (10), "sections 3329(a) and 3330(a) of Title 31" was substituted for "the first section of the Act of October 9, 1940 (31 U.S.C. 123)" on authority of Pub.L. 97–258, § 4(b), Sept. 13, 1982, 96 Stat. 1067, the first section of which enacted Title 31, Money and Finance.

Section 2202(a)(1)(B) of Pub.L. 97–35, set out in the credit of this section, was amended by section 2263(a)(2)(E) of Pub.L. 98–369 to correct an error in the directory language of section 2202(a)(1)(B) of Pub.L. 97–35 which had erroneously quoted language which section 2202(a)(1)(B) of Pub.L. 97–35 had directed should have been deleted from subsec. (i) of this section.

Effective and Applicability Provisions

2015 Acts. Pub.L. 114–74, Title VIII, § 831(a)(3), Nov. 2, 2015, 129 Stat. 612, provided that: "The amendments made by this subsection [amending this section] shall apply with respect to individuals who attain age 62 in any calendar year after 2015."

Pub.L. 114–74, Title VIII, § 831(b)(3), Nov. 2, 2015, 129 Stat. 613, provided that: "The amendments made by this subsection [amending this section] shall apply with respect to requests for benefit suspension submitted beginning at least 180 days after the date of the enactment of this Act [Nov. 2, 2015]."

2014 Acts. Pub.L. 113–270, § 5, Dec. 18, 2014, 128 Stat. 2950, provided that: "The amendments made by this Act [amending subsec. (n) of this section] shall apply with respect to benefits paid for any month beginning after the date of the enactment of this Act [Dec. 18, 2014]."

2004 Acts. Pub.L. 108–203, Title II, § 203(d), Mar. 2, 2004, 118 Stat. 511, provided that: "The amendments made by this section [amending this section and 42 U.S.C.A. §§ 1004 and 1382] shall take effect on the first day of the first month that begins on or after the date that is 9 months after the date of enactment of this Act [Mar. 2, 2004]."

Pub.L. 108–203, Title IV, § 412(c), Mar. 2, 2004, 118 Stat. 528, provided that:

"(1) **In general.**—The amendment made by—

"(A) subsection (a)(1) [amending subsec. (n)(1) of this section] shall apply to individuals with respect to whom the Commissioner of Social Security receives a removal notice after the date of the enactment of this Act;

"(B) subsection (a)(2) [amending subsec. (n)(2) of this section] shall apply with respect to notifications of removals received by the Commissioner of Social Security after the date of enactment of this Act [Mar. 2, 2004]; and

"(C) subsection (a)(3) [amending subsec. (n)(3) of this section] shall be effective as if enacted on March 1, 1991.

"(2) **Subsequent correction of cross-reference and terminology.**—The amendments made by subsections (a)(4) [amending subsec. (n)(3) of this section] and (b)(1) [amending subsec. (n) of this section] shall be effective as if enacted on April 1, 1997.

"(3) **References to the Secretary of Homeland Security.**—The amendment made by subsection (b)(2) [amending subsec. (n) of this section] shall be effective as if enacted on March 1, 2003."

Pub.L. 108–203, Title IV, § 418(c), Mar. 2, 2004, 118 Stat. 533, provided that:

"(1) **In general.**—The amendments made by this section [enacting subsec. (k)(5) of this section and amending subsecs. (b)(2), (4), (5), (c)(2) to (5), (e)(2)(A), (7) to (9), (f)(1)(B), (F), (2) to (9), (g)(2), (4), and (k)(2)(B), (3)(A), (B) of this section and 42 U.S.C.A. § 426] shall apply with respect to applications for benefits under title II of the Social Security Act [this subchapter] filed on or after the first day of the first month that begins after the date of enactment of this Act [Mar. 2, 2004], except that such amendments shall not apply in connection with monthly periodic benefits of any individual based on earnings while in service described in section 202(k)(5)(A) of the Social Security Act [subsec. (k)(5)(A) of this section] (in the matter preceding clause (i) thereof) if the last day of such service occurs before July 1, 2004.

"(2) **Transitional rule.**—In the case of any individual whose last day of service described in subparagraph (A) of section 202(k)(5) of the Social Security Act [subsec. (k)(5)(A) of this section] (as added by subsection (a) of this section) occurs within 5 years after the date of enactment of this Act [Mar. 2, 2004]—

"(A) The 60–month period described in such subparagraph (A) shall be reduced (but not to less than 1 month) by the number of months of such service (in the aggregate and without regard to whether such months of service were continuous) which—

"(i) were performed by the individual under the same retirement system on or before the date of enactment of this Act [Mar. 2, 2004], and

"(ii) constituted 'employment' as defined in section 210 of the Social Security Act [42 U.S.C.A. § 410]; and

"(B) months of service necessary to fulfill the 60–month period as reduced by subparagraph (A) of this paragraph must be performed after the date of enactment of this Act [Mar. 2, 2004]."

Pub.L. 108–203, Title IV, § 420A(b), Mar. 2, 2004, 118 Stat. 535, provided that: "The amendments made by subsection (a) [amending subsec. (d)(6)(B) of this section] shall be effective with respect to benefits payable for months beginning with the 7th month that begins after the date of enactment of this Act [Mar. 2, 2004]."

2000 Acts. Pub.L. 106–182, § 5, April 7, 2000, 114 Stat. 199, provided that: "The amendments made by this Act [amending this section and section 403 of this title] shall apply with respect to taxable years ending after December 31, 1999."

1999 Acts. Pub.L. 106–170, Title IV, § 402(d)(3), Dec. 17, 1999, 113 Stat. 1909, provided that: "The amendments made by this subsection [amending this section] shall apply with respect to benefits for months ending after the date of the enactment of this Act [Dec. 17, 1999]."

Pub.L. 106–170, Title IV, § 402(b)(2), Dec. 17, 1999, 113 Stat. 1908, provided that: "The amendments made by this subsection [amending this section] shall apply to individuals whose period of confinement in an institution commences on or after the first day of the fourth month beginning after the month in which this Act is enacted [December 1999]."

Pub.L. 106–170, Title IV, § 402(a)(4), Dec. 17, 1999, 113 Stat. 1908, provided that: "The amendments made by this subsection [amending this section and section 1382 of this title and section 552a of Title 5] shall apply to individuals whose period of confinement in an institution commences on or after the first day of the fourth month beginning after the month in which this Act is enacted [December 1999]."

Pub.L. 106–169, Title II, § 207(e), Dec. 14, 1999, 113 Stat. 1839, provided that, "The amendments made by this section [enacting section 1320a–8a of this title, amending sections 402 and 1382 of this title and enacting a note set out under section 1320a–8a of this title] shall apply to statements and representations made on or after the date of the enactment of this Act [Dec. 14, 1999]."

1996 Acts. Amendment by section 308 of Div. C of Pub.L. 104–208 effective, with certain exceptions and subject to certain transitional rules, on the first day of the first month beginning more than 180 days after Sept. 30, 1996, see section 309 of Div. C of Pub.L. 104–208, set out as a note under section 1101 of Title 8, Aliens and Nationality.

Section 503(b) of Div. C of Pub.L. 104–208 provided that: "The amendment made by subsection (a) [enacting subsec. (y) of this section] shall apply with respect to benefits for which applications are filed on or after the first day of the first month that begins at least 60 days after the date of the enactment of this Act [Sept. 30, 1996]."

Title V of Div. C of Pub.L. 104–208 effective on Sept. 30, 1996, see section 591 of Pub.L. 104–208, set out as a note under section 1101 of Title 8, Aliens and Nationality.

Section 104(a)(2) of Pub.L. 104–121 provided that: "The amendment made by paragraph (1) [amending subsec. (d)(4) of this section] shall apply with respect to benefits of individuals who become entitled to such benefits for months after the third month following the month in which this Act is enacted [March, 1996]."

Section 104(b)(3) of Pub.L. 104–121 provided that:

"(A) The amendments made by paragraph (1) [enacting subsec. (d)(1)(H) of this section] shall apply with respect to final divorces occurring after the third month following the month in which this Act is enacted [March, 1996].

"(B) The amendment made by paragraph (2) [enacting subsec. (d)(10) of this section] shall take effect on the date of the enactment of this Act [Mar. 29, 1996]."

Amendment by section 107(a)(4) of Pub.L. 103–296 effective Mar. 31, 1995, see section 110 of Pub.L. 103–296, set out as a note under section 401 of this title.

1994 Acts. Section 4(b) of Pub.L. 103–387 provided that: "The amendments made by this section [amending this section] shall apply with respect to benefits for months commencing after 90 days after the date of the enactment of this Act [Oct. 22, 1994]."

Amendment by section 107(a)(4) of Pub.L. 103–296 effective Mar. 31, 1995, see section 110 of Pub.L. 103–296 set out as a note under section 401 of this title.

Section 308(c) of Pub.L. 103–296 provided that: "The amendments made by this section [amending this section and section 415 of this title] shall apply (notwithstanding section 215(f) of the Social Security Act [section 415(f) of this title]) with respect to benefits payable for months after December 1994."

Section 321(b)(1) of Pub.L. 103–296 provided in part that the amendment by section 321(b)(1) of Pub.L. 103–296 of directory language in section 603(b)(5)(A) of Pub.L. 101–649 (which had amended subsec. (n)(1) of this section in 1990) is effective as if the correcting language of Pub.L. 103–296 had been included as part of the original directory language of Pub.L. 101–649.

1990 Acts. Amendment by section 603(b)(5) of Pub.L. 101–649 not applicable to deportation proceedings for which notice has been provided to the alien before Mar. 1, 1991, see section 602(d) of Pub.L. 101–649, set out as a note under section 1161 of Title 8, Aliens and Nationality.

Section 5103(e)(1) of Pub.L. 101–508 provided that: "The amendments made by this section [amending this section and sections 416, 423, 426 and 1383c of this title, and enacting provisions set out as a note under this section] (other than paragraphs (1) and (2)(C) of subsection (c) [amending sections 426 and 1383c of this title]) shall apply with respect to monthly insurance benefits for months after December 1990 for which applications are filed on or after January 1, 1991, or are pending on such date. The amendments made by subsection (c)(1) [amending section 1383c of this title] shall apply with respect to medical assistance provided after December 1990. The amendments made by subsection (c)(2)(C) [amending section 426 of this title] shall apply with respect to items and services furnished after December 1990."

Section 5116(b) of Pub.L. 101–508 provided that: "The amendments made by this section [amending subsec. (a) of this section] shall become effective on the first day of the month following the month in which this Act is enacted [Nov. 1990]."

1989 Acts. Section 10203(b) of Pub.L. 101–239 provided that: "The amendments made by this section [redesignating as subsec. (q)(3)(E) former subsec. (q)(3)(H) and striking subsec. (q)(3)(E) to (G) of this section] shall apply—

"(1) in the case of any individual's old-age insurance benefit referred to in section 202(q)(3)(E) of the Social Security Act [subsec. (q)(3)(E) of this section] (as in effect before the amendments made by this section), only if such individual attains age 62 on or after January 1, 1990, and

"(2) in the case of any individual's disability insurance benefit referred to in section 202(q)(3)(F) or (G) of such Act [subsec. (q)(3)(F) or (G) of this section] (as so in effect), only if such individual both attains age 62 and becomes disabled on or after such date."

Section 10301(c) of Pub.L. 101–239 provided that: "The amendments made by this section [enacting subsec. (d)(8)(D)(ii) and striking subsec. (d)(8)(D)(ii) and (iii) and the last flush sentence] shall apply with respect to benefits payable for months after December 1989, but only on the basis of applications filed on or after January 1, 1990."

Section 10302(a)(2) of Pub.L. 101–239 provided that: "The amendment made by paragraph (1) [enacting subsec. (j)(5) of this section] shall apply with respect to misinformation furnished after December 1982 and to benefits for months after December 1982."

1988 Acts. Section 8004(c) of Pub.L. 100–647 provided that: "The amendments made by this section [amending subsec. (n)(1) and enacting subsec. (n)(3) of this section] shall apply only in the case of deportations occurring, and final orders of deportation issued, on or after the date of enactment of this Act [Nov. 10, 1988], and only to benefits for months beginning (and deaths occurring) on or after such date."

Amendment of this section by section 8007(b) of Pub.L. 100–647 applicable to benefits paid for (and items and services furnished in) months after Dec. 1988, see section 8007(d) of Pub.L. 100–647, set out as a note under section 1402 of Title 26, Internal Revenue Code.

Section 8010(c) of Pub.L. 100–647 provided that: "The amendments made by this section [enacting subsecs. (e)(1)(C)(i), (ii), (8) and (f)(1)(C)(i), (ii), (8) of this section; striking out former subsecs. (e)(1)(C)(i) and (f)(1)(C)(i) of this section; and redesignating as subsecs. (e)(1)(C)(iii) and (f)(1)(C)(iii) former subsecs. (e)(1)(C)(ii) and (f)(1)(C)(ii) of this section] shall apply to benefits payable under section 202(e) or section 202(f) of the Social Security Act [subsec. (e) or (f) of this section] on the basis of the wages and self-employment income of an individual who dies after the month [November] in which this Act is enacted [Nov. 10, 1988]."

Section 8014(c) of Pub.L. 100–647 provided that: "The preceding provisions of this section [Pub.L. 100–647, § 8014(b), set out as a note under this section] (including the amendments made by subsection (a) [amending subsections (b)(4)(A)(ii)(II), (c)(2)(A)(ii)(II), (e)(7)(A)(ii)(II), (f)(2)(A)(ii)(II), and (g)(4)(A)(ii)(II) of this section]) shall apply as if they had been included or reflected in the provisions of section 9007 of the Omnibus Budget Reconciliation Act of 1987 (101 Stat. 1330–289) [Pub.L. 100–203, § 9007(a) to (e), amending this section and § 9007(f), set out as Effective Date of 1987 Amendment note under this section] at the time of its enactment [Dec. 22, 1987]."

1987 Acts. Section 9007(f) of Pub.L. 100–203 provided that: "The amendments made by this section [amending subsecs. (b)(4)(A) to (C), (c)(2)(A) to (C), (e)(7)(A) to (C), (f)(2)(A) to (C), (g)(4)(A) to (C)] shall apply only with respect to benefits for months after December 1987; except that nothing in such amendments shall affect any exemption (from the application of the pension offset provisions contained in subsection (b)(4), (c)(2), (e)(7), (f)(2), or (g)(4) of section 202 of the Social Security Act [subsecs. (b)(4), (c)(2), (e)(7), (f)(2), or (g)(4) of this section]) which any individual may have by reason of subsection (g) or (h) of section 334 of the Social Security Amendments of 1977 [set out as notes under this section].".

Section 9010(f) of Pub.L. 100–203 provided that: "The amendments made by this section [amending subsecs. (d)(1)(G)(i), (e)(1)(F)(II), (f)(1)(F)(II) of this section, sections 416(i)(2)(D)(II), 423(a)(1), (e), and 426(b) of this title] shall take effect January 1, 1988, and shall apply with respect to—

"(1) individuals who are entitled to benefits which are payable under subsection (d)(1)(B)(ii), (d)(6)(A)(ii), (d)(6)(B), (e)(1)(B)(ii), or (f)(1)(B)(ii) of section 202 of the Social Security Act [this section] or subsection (a)(1) of section 223 of such Act for [section 423 of this title] any month after December 1987, and

"(2) individuals who are entitled to benefits which are payable under any provision referred to in paragraph (1) for any month before January 1988 and with respect to whom the 15–month period described in the applicable provision amended by this section has not elapsed as of January 1, 1988."

1986 Acts. Section 1883(f) of Pub.L. 99–514 provided that: "Except as otherwise provided in this section, the amendments made by this section [amending sections 402, 410, 411, 415, 418, 421, 423, 657, 658, 664, 674, 1301, 1320b–6, 1383, 1382a, and 1397b of this title and sections 1402 and 3121 of Title 26, Internal Revenue Code, repealing section 1397f of this title, and enacting a provision set out as a note section 602 of this title] shall take effect on the date of the enactment of this Act [Oct. 22, 1986]."

Section 12104(b) of Pub.L. 99–272 provided that: "The amendment made by subsection (a) [amending subsec. (d)(8)(D)(ii)(III) of this section] shall apply with respect to benefits for which application is filed after the date of the enactment of this Act [Apr. 7, 1986]."

Section 12107(c) of Pub.L. 99–272 provided that: "The amendments made by this section [amending subsec. (d)(6)(E) of this section and section 423(e) of this title] are effective December 1, 1980, and shall apply with respect to any individual who is under a disability (as defined in section 223(d) of the Social Security Act [section 423(d) of this title]) on or after that date."

1984 Acts. Amendment to subsecs. (a) to (f), (q), (r), (w) by section 2661(b) to (d), 2662(c)(1) of Pub.L. 98–369 effective as though included in the enactment of the Social Security Amendments of 1983 [Pub.L. 98–21], see section 2664(a) of Pub.L. 98–369, set out as a note under section 401 of this title.

Amendment to subsecs. (d) to (f), (q), (t), (u) by section 2663(a)(2) of Pub.L. 98–369 effective July 18, 1984, but not to be construed as changing or affecting any right, liability, status or interpretation which existed (under the provisions of law involved) before that date, see section 2664(b) of Pub.L. 98–369, set out as a note under section 401 of this title.

1983 Acts. Section 111(a)(8) of Pub.L. 98–21 provided that: "The amendments made by this subsection [to shift the cost-of-living adjustments to a calendar year basis by amending subsec. (m) of this section and sections 403(f)(8)(A), 415(i)(2)(A)(ii), (iii), (B), and 430(a) of this title] shall apply with respect to cost-of-living increases determined under section 215(i) of the Social Security Act [section 415(i) of this title] for years after 1982."

Section 114(c)(2) of Pub.L. 98–21 provided that: "The amendments made by paragraph (1) [amending subsec. (w)(2)(A), (3), of this section] shall apply with respect to increment months in calendar years after 1983."

Section 131(d) of Pub.L. 98–21 provided that:

"(1) The amendments made by this section [amending this section and section 426 of this title] shall be effective with respect to monthly benefits payable under title II of the Social Security Act [this subchapter] for months after December 1983.

"(2) In the case of an individual who was not entitled to a monthly benefit of the type involved under title II of such Act [this subchapter] for December, 1983, no benefit shall be paid under such title [subchapter] by reason of such amendments unless proper application for such benefit is made."

Section 132(c)(1) of Pub.L. 98–21 provided that: "The amendments made by subsection (a) [amending subsec. (b)(5) of this section] shall apply with respect to monthly insurance benefits for months after December, 1984, but only on the basis of applications filed on or after January 1, 1985."

Section 133(c) of Pub.L. 98–21 provided that: "The amendments made by this section [amending subsecs. (e) and (f) of this section] shall apply with respect to monthly insurance benefits for months after December 1984 for individuals who first meet all criteria for entitlement to benefits under section 202(e) or (f) of the Social Security Act [subsecs. (e) or (f) of this section] (other than making application for such benefits) after December 1984."

Section 134(c) of Pub.L. 98–21 provided that: "The amendments made by this section [amending subsecs. (q) and (m) of this section] shall apply with respect to benefits for months after December 1983."

Section 301(a)(5) of Pub.L. 98–21, as amended Pub.L. 98–369, Title VI, § 2662(d), July 18, 1984, 98 Stat. 1159, provided in part that the enactment of subsec. (c)(5) of this section [by section 301(a)(5) of Pub.L. 98–21] is effective "with respect to monthly insurance benefits for months after December 1984 (but only on the basis of applications filed on or after January 1, 1985)".

Section 307(b) of Pub.L. 98–21 provided that "The amendments made by subsection (a) [amending subsecs. (b)(3), (d)(5), (g)(3), and (h)(4) of this section] shall apply with respect to benefits under title II of the Social Security Act [this subchapter] for months after the month in which this Act is enacted [April, 1983] but only in cases in which the 'last month' referred to in the provision amended is a month after the month in which this Act is enacted."

Section 310 of Pub.L. 98–21 provided that:

"(a) Except as otherwise specifically provided in this title, the amendments made by this part [amending this section and sections 403, 405, 416, 417, 422, 423, 425, 426, 427, and 428 of this title] apply only with respect to monthly benefits payable under title II of the Social Security Act [this subchapter] for months after the month in which this Act is enacted [April, 1983].

"(b) Nothing in any amendment made by this part shall be construed as affecting the validity of any benefit which was paid, prior to the effective date of such amendment, as a result of a judicial determination."

Section 334(b) of Pub.L. 98–21 provided that: "The amendments made by subsection (a) [amending subsec. (j)(4)(B) of this section] shall apply with respect to survivors whose applications for monthly benefits are filed after the second month following the month in which this Act is enacted [April, 1983]."

Section 337(b) of Pub.L. 98–21 as amended by Pub.L. 98–617, § 2(a)(1), Nov. 8, 1984, 98 Stat. 3294, provided that: "The amendments made by subsection (a) of this section [amending this section] shall apply only with respect to monthly insurance benefits payable under title II of the Social Security Act [this subchapter] for months after June 1983."

[Section 2(a)(2) of Pub.L. 98–617 provided that: "The amendments made by this subsection [amending this note] shall apply to benefits payable under title II of the Social Security Act [this subchapter] for months beginning after the month of enactment of this Act [November 1984]."]

Section 339(c) of Pub.L. 98–21 provided that: "The amendments made by subsections (a) [adding subsec. (x) of this section] and (b) [striking out section 423(f) of this title] shall apply with respect to monthly benefits payable for months beginning on or after the date of enactment of this Act [Apr. 20, 1983]."

Section 340(c) of Pub.L. 98–21 provided that: "The amendments made by this section [amending subsec. (t) of this section] shall apply with respect to any individual who initially becomes eligible for benefits under section 202 or 223 [this section and section 423 of this title] after December 31, 1984."

Section 7(d) of Pub.L. 97–455 provided that: "The amendments made by subsections (a) [enacting and amending provisions set out as notes under this section] and (c) [amending subsecs. (b)(4)(A), (c)(2)(A), (e)(8)(A), (f)(2)(A), and (g)(4)(A) of this section] of this section shall be effective with respect to monthly insurance benefits for months after November 1982."

1981 Acts. Amendments by section 2201(b)(10), (11), (d)(1), (2) of Pub.L. 97–35 and section 2(e) of Pub.L. 97–123, applicable with respect to benefits for months after December 1981, and amendment by section 2201(f) of Pub.L. 97–35 applicable with respect to deaths occurring after December 1981, with certain exceptions, see section 2(j)(2) to (4) of Pub.L. 97–123, set out as a note under section 415 of this title.

Section 2202(b) of Pub.L. 97–35 provided that: "The amendments made by subsection (a) [amending subsec. (i) of this section and section 416(c) and (g) of this title] shall apply only with respect to deaths occurring after August 1981."

Section 2203(f)(1), (2) of Pub.L. 97–35 provided that:

"(1) The amendments made by subsections (a) [amending subsec. (a) of this section], (b) [amending subsec. (b)(1) of this section and section 416(b) of this title], and (c) [amending subsec. (c)(1) of this section and section 416(f) of this title] of this section shall apply only to monthly insurance benefits payable to individuals who attain age 62 after August 1981.

"(2) The amendments made by subsection (d) of this section [amending subsec. (d)(1) and (7) of this section and section 416(e) and (h) of this title] shall apply to monthly insurance benefits for months after August 1981, and only in the case of individuals who were not entitled to such insurance benefits for August 1981 or any preceding month."

Section 2205(b) of Pub.L. 97–35 provided that: "The amendments made by subsection (a) [amending subsec. (s)(1) of this section] shall apply with respect to wife's and mother's insurance benefits for months after the month in which this Act is enacted [August, 1981]; except that, in the case of an individual who is entitled to such a benefit (on the basis of having a child in her care) for the month in which this Act is enacted [August, 1981], such amendments shall not take effect until the first day of the first month which begins 2 years or more after the date of the enactment of this Act [Aug. 13, 1981]."

Section 2206(c) of Pub.L. 97–35 provided that: "The amendments made by this section [amending this section and sections 403 and 415 of this title] shall apply only with respect to initial calculations and adjustments of primary insurance amounts and benefit amounts which are attributable to periods after August 1981."

Section 2210(b) of Pub.L. 97–35 provided that: "Except as provided in subsection (c) [set out as a note under this section], the amendments made by subsection (a) [amending this section] shall apply to child's insurance benefits under section 202(d) of the Social Security Act [subsec. (d) of this section] for months after July 1982."

1980 Acts. Section 1011(b) of Pub.L. 96–499 provided that: "The amendment made by subsection (a) [amending this section] shall be effective with respect to applications filed on or after the first day of the first month which begins 60 days or more after the date of the enactment of this Act [Dec. 5, 1980]."

Section 5(d) of Pub.L. 96–473 provided that: "The amendments made by this section [amending subsec. (d)(7)(A) of this section and sections 416 and 423 of this title] shall be effective with respect to benefits payable for months beginning on or after October 1, 1980."

Section 303(d) of Pub.L. 96–265 provided that: "The amendments made by this section [amending this section and sections 416, 422, 423, 1382 and 1382c of this title] shall become effective on the first day of the sixth month which begins after the date of the enactment of this Act [June 9, 1980] and shall apply with respect to any individual whose disability has not been determined to have ceased prior to such first day."

Section 306(d) of Pub.L. 96–265 provided that: "The amendments made by this section [amending subsec. (j)(2) of this section and sections 416 and 423 of this title] shall apply to applications filed after the month in which this Act is enacted [June 1980]."

1978 Acts. Amendment by Pub.L. 95–600 effective Oct. 4, 1976, see section 703(r) of Pub.L. 95–600, set out as an Effective Date of 1978 Amendment note under section 46 of Title 26, Internal Revenue Code.

1977 Acts. Section 206 of Pub.L. 95–216 provided that: "The amendments made by the provisions of this title other than sections 201(d), 204, and 205(a) [amending this section and sections 403, 415, 417, 424a and 1395r of this title] shall be effective with respect to monthly benefits under title II of the Social Security Act [this subchapter] payable for months after December 1978 and with respect to lump-sum death payments with respect to deaths occurring after such month. The amendments made by section 201(d) [amending section 415 of this title] shall be effective with respect to monthly benefits of an individual who becomes eligible for an old-age or disability insurance benefit, or dies, after December 1977. The amendments made by section 204 [amending this section and section 403(a)(8) of this title] shall be effective with respect to monthly benefits for months after May 1978. The amendment made by section 205(a) [amending this section] shall be effective with respect to monthly benefits payable for months after December 1978 based on the wages and self-employment income of individuals who die after December 1978."

Section 331(d) of Pub.L. 95–216 provided that: "The amendments made by this section [amending this section] shall be effective with respect to monthly benefits payable for months after December 1977."

Section 332(b) of Pub.L. 95–216 provided that: "The amendments made by subsection (a) [amending this section and section 426 of this title] shall be effective with respect to monthly insurance benefits under title II of the Social Security Act [this subchapter] to which an individual becomes entitled on the basis of an application filed on or after January 1, 1978."

Section 334(f) of Pub.L. 95–216, as amended by Pub.L. 97–455, § 7(a)(2), Jan. 12, 1983, 96 Stat. 2501, provided that: "Subject to subsections (g) and (h), the amendments made by this section [amending this section and section 426(h)(1)(B) of this title and enacting provisions set out as notes under this section] shall apply with respect to monthly insurance benefits payable under title II of the Social Security Act [this subchapter] for months beginning with the month in which this Act is enacted [Dec., 1977], on the basis of applications filed in or after the month in which this Act is enacted [Dec., 1977]."

Section 336(c)(1) of Pub.L. 95–216 provided that: "The amendments made by this section [amending this section] shall apply only with respect to monthly benefits payable under title II of the Social Security Act [this subchapter] for months after December 1978, and, in the case of individuals who are not entitled to benefits of the type involved for December 1978, only on the basis of applications filed on or after January 1, 1979."

Section 337(c) of Pub.L. 95–216 provided that: "The amendments made by this section [amending subsec. (b)(1)(G) of this section and section 416(d)(1) and (2) of this title] shall apply with respect to monthly benefits payable under title II of the Social Security Act [this subchapter] for months after December 1978, and, in the case of individuals who are not entitled to benefits of the type involved for December 1978, only on the basis of applications filed on or after January 1, 1979."

Section 353(f)(1) of Pub.L. 95–216 provided in part that the amendment of subsec. (u)(1)(C) by Pub.L. 95–216 is effective with respect to convictions after Dec. 31, 1977.

1974 Acts. Section 603 of Pub.L. 93–445 provided that: "The provisions of title II of this Act [set out as a note under section 231 of Title 45, Railroads] and the amendments made by title III and title IV of this Act [amending this section and sections 405, 410, 416, 426, 1395s, 1395u, 1395v, 1395gg, 1395kk of this title and sections 352, 354, 360, 361, and 362 of Title 45, Railroads] shall become effective on January 1, 1975."

1973 Acts. Section 240(b) of Pub.L. 93–66 provided that: "The amendment made by subsection (a) [enacting item III of subsec. (d)(8)(D)(ii) of this section] shall apply with respect to monthly benefits payable under title II of the Social Security Act [this subchapter] for months after the month in which this Act is enacted [July 1973] on the basis of applications for such benefits filed in or after the month in which this Act is enacted [July 1973]."

1972 Acts. Section 102(i) of Pub.L. 92–603 provided that: "The amendments made by this section [amending this section and section 403 of this title and enacting provisions set out as notes under this section] shall apply with respect to monthly benefits under title II of the Social Security Act [this subchapter] for months after December 1972."

Section 103(d) of Pub.L. 92–603 provided that: "The amendments made by this section [amending this section and section 403 of this title] shall be applicable with respect to old-age insurance benefits payable under title II of the Social Security Act [this subchapter] for months beginning after 1972."

Section 107(c) of Pub.L. 92–603 provided that: "The amendments made by this section [amending this section and sections 403, 422, and 425 of this title] shall apply with respect to monthly benefits under title II of the Social Security Act [this subchapter] for months after December 1972, except that in the case of an individual who was not entitled to a monthly benefit under title II of such Act [this subchapter] for December 1972 such amendments shall apply only on the basis of an application filed in or after the month in which this Act is enacted [Oct. 1972]."

Section 108(f) of Pub.L. 92–603 provided that: "The amendments made by this section [amending this section] shall apply only with respect to monthly benefits under section 202 of the Social Security Act [this section] for months after December 1972 except that in the case of an individual who was not entitled to a monthly benefit under such section 202 [this section] for December 1972 such amendments shall apply only on the basis of an application filed after September 30, 1972."

Section 109(b) of Pub.L. 92–603 provided that: "The amendment made by subsection (a) [adding subsec. (d)(7)(D) of this section] shall apply only with respect to benefits payable under title II of the Social Security Act [this subchapter] for months after December 1972."

Section 110(b) of Pub.L. 92–603 provided that: "The amendment made by subsection (a) [amending subsec. (k)(2)(A) of this section] shall apply only with respect to monthly benefits under title II of the Social Security Act [this subchapter] for months after December 1972."

Section 111(b) of Pub.L. 92–603 provided that: "The amendment made by subsection (a) [amending subsec. (d)(8) of this section] shall apply with respect to monthly benefits payable under title II of the Social Security Act [this subchapter] for months after December 1967 on the basis of an application filed in or after the month in which this Act is enacted [Oct. 1972]; except that such amendments shall not apply with respect to benefits for any month before the month in which this Act is enacted [Oct. 1972] unless such application is filed before the close of the sixth month after the month in which this Act is enacted [Oct. 1972]."

Section 112(b) of Pub.L. 92–603 provided that: "The amendment made by subsection (a) [striking out provisions covering this subchapter] shall apply only with respect to monthly benefits under title II of the Social Security Act [this subchapter] for months beginning with the month in which this Act is enacted [Oct. 1972]."

Section 113(c) of Pub.L. 92–603 provided that: "The amendments made by this section [enacting subsec. (d)(9) of this section and amending section 416(e) of this title] shall apply with respect to monthly benefits payable under title II of the Social Security Act [this subchapter] for months after December 1972, but only on the basis of applications filed on or after the date of the enactment of this Act [Oct. 30, 1972]."

Section 114(d) of Pub.L. 92–603 provided that: "The amendments made by this section [amending this sect] shall apply only with respect to benefits payable under title II of the Social Security Act [this subchapter] for months after December 1972 on the basis of applications filed on or after the date of enactment of this Act [Oct. 30, 1972]."

Amendment by section 116(b), (c) of Pub.L. 92–603 effective with respect to applications for widow's and widower's insurance benefits based on disability under this section filed in or after Oct. 1972 or before Oct. 1972 under specified conditions, see section 116(e) of Pub.L. 92–603, set out as a note under section 423 of this title.

1971 Acts. Section 2 of Pub.L. 92–223 provided that: "The amendments made by the first section of this Act [amending this section] shall be effective only in the case of lump-sum death payments under title II of the Social Security Act [this subchapter] made with respect to deaths which occur after December 31, 1970."

1969 Acts. Section 1004(d) of Pub.L. 91–172 provided that: "The amendments made by subsections (a), (b), and (c) [amending this section] shall apply with respect to monthly benefits under title II of the Social Security Act [this subchapter] for months after December 1969."

1968 Acts. Section 103(e) of Pub.L. 90–248 provided that: "The amendments made by subsections (a), (b), (c), and (d) [amending this section] shall apply with respect to monthly benefits under title II of the Social Security Act [this subchapter] for months after January 1968."

Section 104(e) of Pub.L. 90–248 provided that: "The amendments made by this section [amending this section and sections 403, 416, 422, and 425 of this title] shall apply with respect to monthly benefits under title II of the Social Security Act [this subchapter] for and after the month of February 1968, but only on the basis of applications for such benefits filed in or after the month in which this Act is enacted [Jan. 1968]."

Section 112(b) of Pub.L. 90–248 provided that: "The amendments made by subsection (a) [amending this section] shall apply with respect to monthly benefits payable under title II of the Social Security Act [this subchapter] for months after January 1968, but only on the basis of applications filed after the date of enactment of this Act [Jan. 2, 1968]."

Section 151(e) of Pub.L. 90–248 provided that: "The amendments made by this section [amending this section and section 228e of Title 45, Railroads] shall apply with respect to monthly benefits payable under title II of the Social Security Act [this subchapter] (and annuities accruing under the Railroad Retirement Act of 1937 [section 231 et seq. of Title 45]) for months after January 1968, but only on the basis of applications filed in or after the month in which this Act is enacted [Jan. 1968]."

Section 157(d) of Pub.L. 90–248 provided that: "The amendments made by this section [amending this section] shall apply with respect to monthly benefits payable under title II of the Social Security Act [this subchapter] for months after January 1968, but only on the basis of applications filed in or after the month in which this Act is enacted [Jan. 1968]."

Amendment by section 158(c)(1), (2) of Pub.L. 90–248 applicable with respect to applications for disability insurance benefits under section 423 of this title and to disability determinations under section 416(i) of this title, filed in or after Jan. 1968, or before Jan. 1968 if the applicant has not died before such month and if (A) notice of the final decision of the Secretary of Health, Education, and Welfare has not been given to the applicant before such month; or (B) the notice referred to in subparagraph (A) has been so given before such month but a civil action with respect to such final decision is commenced under section 205(g) of the Social Security Act [section 405(g) of this title] (whether before, in, or after such month) and the decision in such civil action has not become final before such month, see section 158(e) of Pub.L. 90–248, set out as a note under section 423 of this title.

Section 162(a)(2) of Pub.L. 90–248 provided that: "The amendment made by paragraph (1) [amending this section] shall apply only with respect to six-month periods (within the meaning of section 202(t)(1)(A) of the Social Security Act [subsec. (t)(1)(A) of this section]) which begin after the date of the enactment of this Act [Jan. 2, 1968]."

Section 162(b)(2) of Pub.L. 90–248 provided that: "The amendment made by paragraph (1) [amending this section] shall apply only with respect to monthly benefits under title

II of the Social Security Act [this subchapter] for months beginning after June 30, 1968."

1965 Acts. Amendment by section 303(d) of Pub.L. 89–97 effective with respect to applications for disability insurance benefits under section 423 of this title, and for disability determinations under section 416(i) of this title, filed in or after July 1965 or before July 1965, if the applicant has not died before such month, and notice of final administrative decision has not been given to the applicant before such month, see section 303(f)(1), of Pub.L. 89–97, set out as a note under section 423 of this title.

Section 304(*o*) of Pub.L. 89–97 provided that: "The amendments made by this section [amending this section and sections 415, 416, and 423 of this title] shall apply with respect to monthly insurance benefits under title II of the Social Security Act [this subchapter] for and after the second month following the month [July 1965] in which this Act [Pub.L. 89–97] is enacted, but only on the basis of applications filed in or after the month [July 1965] in which this Act [Pub.L. 89–97] is enacted."

Section 306(d) of Pub.L. 89–97 provided that:

"The amendments made by this section [amending this section and sections 403, 416, 422, and 425 of this title] shall apply with respect to monthly insurance benefits under section 202 of the Social Security Act [this section] for months after December 1964; except that—

"(1) in the case of an individual who was not entitled to a child's insurance benefit under subsection (d) of such section [subsec. (d) of this section] for the month in which this Act is enacted [July 1965], such amendments shall apply only on the basis of an application filed in or after the month in which this Act is enacted [July 1965], and

"(2) no monthly insurance benefit shall be payable for any month before the second month following the month in which this Act is enacted [July 1965] by reason of section 202(d)(1)(B)(ii) of the Social Security Act [subsec. (d)(1)(B)(ii) of this section] as amended by this section."

Section 307(c) of Pub.L. 89–97 provided that: "The amendments made by this section [amending this section] shall apply with respect to monthly insurance benefits under section 202 of the Social Security Act [this section] for and after the second month following the month [July 1965] in which this Act [Pub.L. 89–97] is enacted, but only on the basis of applications filed in or after the month [July 1965] in which this Act [Pub.L. 89–97] is enacted."

Section 308(e) of Pub.L. 89–97 provided that: "The amendments made by this section [amending this section and sections 403, 405, 416, and 422 of this title] shall be applicable with respect to monthly insurance benefits under title II of the Social Security Act [this subchapter] beginning with the second month following the month in which this Act is enacted [July 1965]; but, in the case of an individual who was not entitled to a monthly insurance benefit under section 202 of such Act [this section] for the first month following the month in which this Act is enacted [July 1965], only on the basis of an application filed in or after the month in which this Act is enacted [July 1965]."

Amendment by section 319(d) of Pub.L. 89–97 applicable with respect to taxable years beginning after Dec. 31, 1950, see section 319(e) of Pub.L. 89–97, set out as a note under section 1402 of Title 26, Internal Revenue Code.

Section 323(b) of Pub.L. 89–97 provided that: "The amendments made by subsection (a) of this section [amending this section] shall be applicable to persons who file applications, or on whose behalf applications are filed, for benefits under section 202(d) of the Social Security Act [subsec. (d) of this section] on or after the date this section is enacted [July 30, 1965]. The time limit provided by section 202(d)(10)(B) of such Act [subsec. (d)(10)(B) of this section] as amended by this section for legally adopting a child shall not apply in the case of any child who is adopted before the end of the 12–month period following the month in which this section is enacted."

Section 324(b) of Pub.L. 89–97 provided that: "The amendments made by this section [to subsec. (p) of this section] shall be effective with respect to (1) applications for lump-sum death payments filed in or after the month [July 1965] in which this Act is enacted, and (2) monthly benefits based on applications filed in or after such month."

Amendment of subsec. (j)(2) by section 328 of Pub.L. 89–97 applicable with respect to applications filed on or after July 30, 1965, applications as to which the Secretary has not made a final decision before July 30, 1965, and, if a civil action with respect to a final decision of the Secretary has been commenced under section 405(g) of this title before July 30, 1965, applications as to which there has been no final judicial decision before July 30, 1965, see section 328(d) of Pub.L. 89–97, set out as an Effective Date of 1965 Amendment note under section 416 of this title.

Section 333(d) of Pub.L. 89–97 provided that: "The amendments made by this section [to subsecs. (e), (f) and (k) of this section] shall apply with respect to monthly insurance benefits under section 202 of the Social Security Act [this section] beginning with the second month following the month in which this Act is enacted [July 1965]; but, in the case of an individual who was not entitled to a monthly insurance benefit under section 202(e) or (f) of such Act [subsec. (e) or (f) of this section] for the first month following the month in which this Act is enacted, only on the basis of an application filed in or after the month in which this Act is enacted."

Section 334(g) of Pub.L. 89–97 provided that: "The amendment made by this section [amending this section and section 416 of this title] shall be applicable only with respect to monthly insurance benefits under title II of the Social Security Act [this subchapter] beginning with the second month following the month in which this Act is enacted [July 1965], but only on the basis of applications filed in or after the month in which this Act is enacted [July 1965]."

Amendment by section 339(b) of Pub.L. 89–97 applicable with respect to monthly insurance benefits under subchapter II of this chapter beginning with Sept. 1965 but only on the basis of an application filed in or after July 1965, see section 339(c) of Pub.L. 89–97, set out as a note under section 416 of this title.

Section 343(b) of Pub.L. 89–97 provided that: "The amendment made by subsection (a) [to subsec. (d)(1)(D) of this section] shall apply only with respect to monthly insurance benefits under title II of the Social Security Act [this subchapter] for months after the month in which this Act is enacted [July 1965]; except that, in the case of an individual who was not entitled to child's insurance benefits under section 202(d) of such Act [subsec. (d) of this section] for the month in which this Act was enacted [July 1965], such amendment shall apply only on the basis of an application filed in or after the month in which this Act is enacted [July 1965]."

1961 Acts. Section 102(f) of Pub.L. 87–64 provided that:

"**(1)** The amendments made by subsection (a) [amending this section] shall apply with respect to monthly benefits for months beginning on or after the effective date of this title [see Effective Date of 1961 Amendments note under this section] based on applications filed in or after March 1961.

"**(2)(A)** Except as provided in subparagraphs (B), (C), and (D), section 202(q) of such Act [subsec. (q) of this section], as amended by subsection (b)(1), shall apply with respect to monthly benefits for months beginning on or after the effective date of this title [see Effective Date of 1961 Amendment note under this section].

"**(B)** Section 202(q)(3) of such Act [subsec. (q)(3) of this section], as amended by subsection (b)(1), shall apply with respect to monthly benefits for months beginning on or after the effective date of this title [see note under this section], but only if the increase described in such section 202(q)(3) [subsec. (q)(3) of this section]—

"**(i)** is not effective for any month beginning before the effective date of this title [see Effective Dates note under this section], or

"**(ii)** is based on an application for a recomputation filed on or after the effective date of this title [see effective date note under this section].

"**(C)** In the case of any individual who attained age 65 before the effective date of this title [see Effective Date of 1961 Amendment note under this section], the adjustment in such individual's reduction period provided for in section 202(q)(6) of such Act [subsec. (q)(6) of this section], as amended by subsection (b)(1), shall not apply to such individual unless the total of the months specified in subparagraphs (A), (B), and (C) of such section 202(q)(6) [subsec. (q)(6) of this section] is not less than 3.

"**(D)** In the case of any individual entitled to a monthly benefit for the last month beginning before the effective date of this title [see Effective Date of 1961 Amendment note under this section], if the amount of such benefit for any month thereafter is, solely by reason of the change in section 202(q) of such Act [subsec. (q) of this section] made by subsection (b)(1), lower than the amount of such benefit for such last month, then it shall be increased to the amount of such benefit for such last month.

"**(3)** Section 202(r) of such Act [subsec. (r) of this section], as amended by subsection (b)(1), shall apply only with respect to monthly benefits for months beginning on or after the effective date of this title [see Effective Date of 1961 Amendment note under this section], except that subparagraph (B) of section 202(r)(2) [subsec. (r)(2) of this section] (as so amended) shall apply only if the first subsequent month described in such subparagraph (B) is a month beginning on or after the effective date of this title [see Effective Date of 1961 Amendment note under this section].

"**(4)** The amendments made by subsection (b)(2) [adding subsec. (a)(3) to section 423 of this title, amending sections 416(i)(2) and 423(a)(1) of this title, and repealing subsec. (s) of this section] shall take effect on the effective date of this title [see Effective Date of 1961 Amendment note under this section].

"**(5)** The amendments made by subsection (b)(3) [to subsec. (j)(3) of this section] shall apply with respect to applications for monthly benefits filed on or after the effective date of this title [see Effective Date of 1961 Amendment note under this section].

"**(6)** The amendments made by subsections (c) and (d)(1) and (2) [amending sections 409, 413, 415, 416, and 423 of this title] shall apply with respect to—

"**(A)** monthly benefits for months beginning on or after the effective date of this title [see Effective Date of 1961 Amendments note under this section] based on applications filed in or after March 1961, and

"**(B)** lump-sum death payments under title II of the Social Security Act [this subchapter] in the case of deaths on or after the effective date of this title [see Effective Date of 1961 Amendments note under this section].

"**(7)** The amendment made by subsection (d)(3) [amending section 415 of this title] shall take effect on the effective date of this title [see Effective Date of 1961 Amendments note under this section].

"**(8)** The amendments made by subsection (e) [amending this section] shall apply with respect to monthly benefits for months beginning on or after the effective date of this title [see Effective Date of 1961 Amendments note under this section].

"**(9)** For purposes of this subsection, the term 'monthly benefits' means monthly insurance benefits under title II of the Social Security Act [this subchapter]."

Section 104(e) of Pub.L. 87–64 provided that: "The amendments made by this section [amending this section] shall apply with respect to monthly benefits under section 202 of the Social Security Act [this section] for months beginning on or after the effective date of this title [see Effective Date of 1961 Amendments note under this section]."

Section 109 of Pub.L. 87–64 provided that: "Except as otherwise provided the effective date of this title is the first day of the first calendar month which begins on or after the 30th day after the date of the enactment of this Act [June 30, 1961]."

1960 Acts. Section 103(v) of Pub.L. 86–778, as amended by Pub.L. 99–514, § 2, Oct. 22, 1986, 100 Stat. 2095, provided that:

"**(1)** The amendments made by subsection (a) [to last two sentences of subsec. (i) of this section and to notes under this section] shall apply only with respect to reinterments after the date of the enactment of this Act [Sept. 13, 1960]. The amendments made by subsections (b), (e), and (f) [to sections 403(k) and 410(h)(i) of this title] shall apply only with respect to service performed after 1960; except that insofar as the carrying on of a trade or business (other than performance of service as an employee) is concerned, such amendments shall apply only in the case of taxable years beginning after 1960. The amendments made by subsections (d), (i), (*o*), and (p) [adding section 410(a)(18) of this title and section 3121(b)(18) of Title 26 and amending section 418(b)(1) of this title and section 3121(e) of Title 26] shall apply only with respect to service performed after 1960. The amendments made by subsections (h) and (*l*) [to section 411(b) of this title and section 1402(b) of Title 26] shall apply only in the case of taxable years beginning after 1960. The amendments made by subsections (c), (n), (q), and (r) [adding sections 3125, 6205(a)(3), 6413(a)(3) and 6413(c)(2)(D), (E) of Title 26 and amending section 410(a)(7) of this title and section 3121(b)(7) of Title 26], shall apply only with respect to (1) service in the employ of the Government of Guam or any political subdivision thereof, or any instrumentality of any one or more of the foregoing wholly owned thereby, which is performed after 1960 and after the calendar quarter in which the Secretary of the Treasury receives a certification by the Governor of Guam that legislation has been enacted by the Government of Guam expressing its desire to have the insurance system established by title II of the Social Security Act [this subchapter] extended to the officers and employees of such Government and such political subdivisions and instrumentalities, and (2) service in the employ of the Government of American Samoa or any political subdivision thereof or any instrumentality of any one or more of the foregoing wholly owned thereby, which is performed after 1960 and after the calendar quarter in which the Secretary of the Treasury receives a certification by the Governor of American Samoa that the Government of American Samoa desires to have the insurance system established by such title II extended to the officers and employees of such Government and such political subdivisions and instrumentalities. The amendments made by subsections (g) and (k) [to section 411(a)(7), (8) of this title and section 1402(a)(8), (9) of Title 26, Internal Revenue Code] shall apply only in the case of taxable years beginning after 1960, except that, insofar as they involve the nonapplication of section 932 of the Internal Revenue Code of 1986 [formerly I.R.C. 1954] [section 932 of Title 26] to the Virgin Islands for purposes of chapter 2 of such Code and section 211 of the Social Security Act [section 411 of this title], such amendments shall be effective in the case of all taxable years with respect to which such chapter 2 (and corresponding provisions of prior law) and such section 211 [section 411 of this title] are applicable. The amendments made by subsections (j), (s), and (t) [adding section 7213(d) of Title 26, amending subsecs. (i) (last sentence), and (t)(14)(D) of this section and sections 405(p)(1), 409(j), 409 (last par.), 410(j) to (n), 411(a)(6), 415(h)(1), 417(e)(1) and 418(c)(6)(C) of this title and section 7701(a)(12) of Title 26, and repealing section 419 of this title] shall take effect on the date of the enactment of this Act [Sept. 13, 1960]; and there are authorized to be appropriated such sums as may be necessary for the performance by any officer or employee of functions delegated to him by the Secretary of the Treasury in accordance with the amendment made by such subsection (t) [to section 7701(a)(12) of Title 26].

"(2) The amendments made by subsections (c) and (n) [to section 410(a)(7) of this title and section 3121(b)(7) of Title 26] shall have application only as expressly provided therein, and determinations as to whether an officer or employee of the Government of Guam or the Government of American Samoa or any political subdivision thereof, or of any instrumentality of any one or more of the foregoing which is wholly owned thereby, is an employee of the United States or any agency or instrumentality thereof within the meaning of any provision of law not affected by such amendments, shall be made without any inferences drawn from such amendments.

"(3) The repeal of section 219 of the Social Security Act [section 419 of this title], and the elimination of other provisions of such Act making reference to such section 219 [elimination of sections 410(h) to (j) and 411(a)(6), (b) of this title making reference to section 419 of this title], shall not be construed as changing or otherwise affecting the effective date specified in such section for the extension to the Commonwealth of Puerto Rico of the insurance system under title II of such Act [this subchapter], the manner or consequences of such extension, or the status of any individual with respect to whom the provisions so eliminated are applicable."

Section 201(c) of Pub.L. 86–778 provided that: "The amendments made by this section [amending this section] shall apply as though this Act had been enacted on August 28, 1958, and with respect to monthly benefits under section 202 of the Social Security Act [this section] for months after August 1958 based on applications for such benefits filed on or after August 28, 1958."

Section 202(b) of Pub.L. 86–778 provided that: "The amendments made by subsection (a) [amending this section] shall apply with respect to monthly benefits under section 202 of the Social Security Act [this section] for months beginning with the month in which this Act is enacted [Sept. 1960], but only if an application for such benefits is filed in or after such month."

Section 203(b) of Pub.L. 86–778 provided that: "The amendment made by subsection (a) [amending this section] shall apply—

"(1) in the case of the death of an individual occurring on or after the date of the enactment of this Act [Sept. 13, 1960], and

"(2) in the case of the death of an individual occurring prior to such date, but only if no application for a lump-sum death payment under section 202(i) of the Social Security Act [subsec. (i) of this section] is filed on the basis of such individual's wages and self-employment income prior to the third calendar month beginning after such date."

Section 205(d) of Pub.L. 86–778 provided that: "The preceding provisions of this section and the amendments made thereby [amending this section] shall apply only in the case of monthly benefits under title II of the Social Security Act [this subchapter] for months after the month in which this Act is enacted [Sept. 1960], on the basis of applications filed in or after such month."

Amendment of subsec. (d)(3) of this section by Pub.L. 86–778, section 208(d), which added sentence following subpar. (B), applicable (1) with respect to monthly benefits under this subchapter for months beginning with Sept. 1960 on the basis of an application filed in or after such month, and (2) in the case of a lump-sum death payment under this subchapter based on an application filed in or after Sept. 1960, but only if no person, other than the person filing such application, has filed an application for a lump-sum death payment under this subchapter prior to Sept. 13, 1960 with respect to the death of the same individual, see section 208(f) of Pub.L. 86–778, set out as a note under section 416 of this title.

Amendment by section 211(i) to (*l*) of Pub.L. 86–778 effective in the manner provided in section 211(p) and (q) of Pub.L. 86–778, see section 211(p) to (s) of Pub.L. 86–778, set out as a note under section 403 of this title.

Section 301(b) of Pub.L. 86–778 provided that: "The amendment made by this section [amending this section] shall apply only with respect to monthly benefits under section 202 of the Social Security Act [this section] for months after the second month following the month in which this Act is enacted [Sept. 1960]."

Amendment by section 403(d) of Pub.L. 86–778 applicable only with respect to benefits under subsec. (d) of this section or section 423(a) of this title for months after Sept. 1960, in the case of individuals who, without regard to such amendment, would have been entitled to such benefits for Sept. 1960, or for any succeeding month, see section 403(e) of Pub.L. 86–778, set out as a note under section 422 of this title.

Section 47(e) of Pub.L. 86–624 provided that: "The amendment made by section 30(c)(1) [amending this section] shall be applicable in the case of deaths occurring on or after August 21, 1959."

1959 Acts. Section 47(e) of Pub.L. 86–70 provided that: "The amendment made by paragraph (1) of subsection (c) of section 32 [to subsec. (i) of this section] shall apply in the case of deaths occurring on or after January 3, 1959."

1958 Acts. Section 302 of Pub.L. 85–927 provided that: "The amendments made by section 301 of this Act [adding subsec. (t)(4)(E) of this section] shall apply with respect to monthly benefits under section 202 of the Social Security Act [this section] for months after December 1956, and with respect to lump-sum death payments under such section 202 [this section] in the case of deaths occurring after December 1956."

Amendment by Pub.L. 85–857 effective Jan. 1, 1959, see section 2 of Pub.L. 85–857, set out as a note preceding section 101 of Title 38, Veterans' Benefits.

Amendment by section 101(e) of Pub.L. 85–840 applicable in the case of monthly benefits under this subchapter for months after Dec. 1958, and in the case of lump-sum death payments under this subchapter, with respect to deaths occurring after such month, see section 101(g) of Pub.L. 85–840, set out as a note under section 415 of this title.

Amendment by section 205(b) to (i) of Pub.L. 85–840 applicable with respect to monthly benefits under this subchapter for months after Aug. 1958, but only if an application for such benefits is filed on or after Aug. 28, 1958, see section 207(a) of Pub.L. 85–840, set out as a note under section 416 of this title.

Section 301(f) of Pub.L. 85–840 provided that: "The amendments made by this section [amending this section and section 416 of this title] shall apply with respect to monthly benefits under section 202 of the Social Security Act [this section] for months beginning after the date of enactment of this Act [August 28, 1958], but only if an application for such benefits is filed on or after such date."

Section 304(a)(2) of Pub.L. 85–840 provided that: "The amendment made by this subsection [amending this section] shall apply with respect to monthly benefits under section 202 of the Social Security Act [this section] for months beginning after the date of enactment of this Act [August 28, 1958], but only if an application for such benefits is filed on or after such date."

Section 305(c) of Pub.L. 85–840 provided that: "The amendments made by this section [amending this section and section 416 of this title] shall apply in the case of lump-sum death payments under such section 202(i) [subsec. (i) of this section] on the basis of the wages and self-employment income of any individual who dies after the month in which this Act is enacted [August 1958]."

Section 306(b) of Pub.L. 85–840 provided that: "The amendments made by this section [amending this section] shall apply with respect to monthly benefits under section 202 of the Social Security Act [this section] for months beginning after the date of enactment of this Act [August 28, 1958], but only if an application for such benefits is filed on or after such date."

Section 307(h)(1) of Pub.L. 85–840 provided that: "The amendments made by this section (other than by subsections (f) and (g)) [amending this section] shall apply with respect to monthly benefits under section 202 of the Social Security Act [this section] for months following the month in which this Act is enacted [August 1958]; except that in any case in which benefits were terminated with the close of the month in which this Act is enacted [August 1958] or any prior month and, if the amendments made by this section had been in effect for such month, such benefits would not have been terminated, the amendments made by this section shall apply with respect to monthly benefits under section 202 of the Social Security Act [this section] for months beginning after the date of enactment of this Act [August 28, 1958], but only if an application for such benefits is filed after such date."

1957 Acts. Section 2 of Pub.L. 85–238 provided that: "The amendments made by the first section of this Act [amending this section] shall apply with respect to monthly benefits under section 202 of the Social Security Act [this section] for months after December 1956, and with respect to lump-sum death payments under such section 202 [this section] in the case of deaths occurring after December 1956."

Section 3(i) of Pub.L. 85–238 provided that:

"(1) Except as provided in paragraph (2), the amendments made by this section [amending this section and section 416 of this title] shall apply in the case of monthly benefits under section 202 of the Social Security Act [this section] for months after the month in which this Act is enacted [August, 1957].

"(2) The amendment made by subsection (f) [amending this section] shall not apply in the case of benefits under section 202(h) of the Social Security Act [subsec.(h) of this section] based on the wages and self-employment income of a deceased individual who died in or prior to the month in which this Act is enacted [August, 1957], for any parent who files the proof of support required by such section 202(h) [subsec. (h) of this section], in or prior to the month in which this Act is enacted [August, 1957]; and the amendment to section 216(h)(1) of such Act [section 416(h)(1) of this title] made by subsection (h) of this section shall not operate to deprive any such parent of benefits to which he would otherwise be entitled under section 202(h) of such Act [subsec. (h) of this section]."

1956 Acts. Section 403(b) of Act Aug. 1, 1956, c. 837, provided that: "The amendment made by subsection (a) [amending this section] shall be effective as though it had been enacted on March 31, 1956."

Section 101(h) of Act Aug. 1, 1956, c. 836, provided that:

"(1) The amendments made by this section, other than subsection (c) [amending this section and section 403 of this title], shall apply with respect to monthly benefits under section 202 of the Social Security Act [this section] for months after December, 1956, but only except as provided in paragraph (2), on the basis of an application filed after September 1956. For purposes of title II of the Social Security Act, as amended by this Act [this subchapter], an application for wife's, child's, or mother's insurance benefits under such title II filed, by reason of this paragraph, by an individual who was entitled to benefits prior to, but not for, December 1956 and whose entitlement terminated as a result of a child's attainment of age eighteen shall be treated as the application referred to in subsection (b), (d), and (g), respectively, of section 202 of such Act [subsecs. (b), (d), and (g) of this section].

"(2) In the case of an individual who was entitled, without the application of subsection (j)(1) of such section 202 [subsec. (j)(1) of this section], to a child's insurance benefit under subsection (d) of such section [subsec. (d) of this section] for December 1956, such amendments shall apply with respect to benefits under such section 202 [this section] for months after December 1956.

"(3) The amendment made by subsection (c) [to subsec. (h)(1) of this section] shall apply in the case of benefits under section 202(h) of the Social Security Act [subsec. (h) of this section] based on the wages and self-employment income of an individual who dies after August 1956."

Section 114(b) of Act Aug. 1, 1956, c. 836, provided that: "The amendment made by subsection (a) [adding subsec. (p) of this section] shall apply in the case of lump-sum death payments under title II of the Social Security Act [this subchapter], and monthly benefits under such title for months after August 1956, based on applications filed after August 1956."

Section 118(b) of Act Aug. 1, 1956, c. 836, provided that: "The amendment made by subsection (a) [adding subsec. (t) of this section] shall apply in the case of monthly benefits under title II of the Social Security Act [this subchapter] for months after December 1956 and in the case of lump-sum death payments under section 202(i) of such Act [subsec. (i) of this section] with respect to deaths occurring after December 1956."

1954 Acts. Section 105(b) of Act Sept. 1, 1954 provided that: "The amendment made by subsection (a) [amending this section] shall be applicable only in the case of applications for monthly benefits under section 202 of the Social Security Act [this section] filed after August 1954; except that no individual shall, by reason of such amendment, be entitled to any benefit for any month prior to February 1954."

1950 Acts. Section 101(b)(1), (3) of Act Aug. 28, 1950 provided that:

"(1) Except as provided in paragraph (3), the amendment made by subsection (a) of this section [amending this section] shall take effect September 1, 1950.

"(3) Section 202(j)(2) of the Social Security Act [subsec. (j)(2) of this section], as amended by this Act, shall take effect on the date of enactment of this Act [Aug. 28, 1950]."

1946 Acts. Section 403(b) of Act Aug. 10, 1946 provided that: "The amendment made by subsection (a) of this section [amending this section] shall be applicable only in cases of applications for benefits under that Act filed after December 31, 1946."

Section 404(b) of Act Aug. 10, 1946 provided that: "The amendment made by subsection (a) of this section [amending this section] shall be applicable only in cases where the death of the insured individual occurs after December 31, 1946."

Subsec. 405(b) of Act Aug. 10, 1946 provided that: "The amendment made by subsection (a) of this section [amending this section] shall be applicable only in cases of applications for benefits under this title [this subchapter] filed after December 31, 1946."

1939 Acts. Amendment by Act Aug. 10, 1939 was made effective Jan. 1, 1940 by section 201 of Act Aug. 10, 1939.

Change of Name

Reference to Administrator of Veterans' Affairs deemed to refer to Secretary of Veterans Affairs pursuant to section 10 of Pub.L. 100–527, set out as a Department of Veterans Affairs Act note under 38 U.S.C.A. § 301.

Transfer of Functions

All functions of the Federal Security Administrator were transferred to the Secretary of Health, Education, and Welfare and all agencies of the Federal Security Agency were transferred to the Department of Health, Education, and Welfare by section 5 of Reorg. Plan No. 1 of 1953, set out as a note under section 3501 of this title. The Federal Security Agency and the Office of Administrator were abolished by section 8 Reorg. Plan No. 1 of 1953. The Secretary and Department of Health, Education, and Welfare were redesignated the Secretary of Health and Human Services by § 509(b) of Pub.L. 96–88 which is classified to section 3508(b) of Title 20, Education.

Savings Provisions

1972 Acts. Section 102(h) of Pub.L. 92–603 provided that: "Where—

"(1) two or more persons are entitled to monthly benefits under section 202 of the Social Security Act [this section] for December 1972 on the basis of the wages and self-employment income of a deceased individual, and one or more of such persons is so entitled under subsection (e) or (f) of such section 202 [subsec. (e) or (f) of this section], and

"(2) one or more of such persons is entitled on the basis of such wages and self-employment income to monthly benefits under subsection (e) or (f) of such section 202 [subsec. (e) or (f) of this section] (as amended by this section) for January 1973, and

"(3) the total of benefits to which all persons are entitled under section 202 of such Act [this section] on the basis of such wages and self-employment income for January 1973 is reduced by reason of section 203(a) of such Act [section 403(a) of this title], as amended by this Act (or would, but for the penultimate sentence of such section 203(a) [section 403(a) of this title], be so reduced),

then the amount of the benefit to which each such person referred to in paragraph (1) is entitled for months after December 1972 shall in no case be less after the application of this section and such section 203(a) [section 403(a) of this title] than the amount it would have been without the application of this section."

Section 114(e) of Pub.L. 92–603 provided that: "Where—

"(1) one or more persons are entitled (without the application of sections 202(j)(1) and 223(b) of the Social Security Act) [subsec. (j)(1) of this section and section 423(b) of this title] to monthly benefits under section 202 or 223 of such Act [this section or section 423 of this title] for December 1972 on the basis of the wages and self-employment income of an insured individual, and

"(2) one or more persons (not included in paragraph (1)) are entitled to monthly benefits under such section 202(g) [subsec. (g) of this section] as a surviving divorced mother (as defined in section 216(d)(3)) [section 416(d)(3) of this title] for a month after December 1972 on the basis of such wages and self-employment income, and

"(3) the total of benefits to which all persons are entitled under such section 202 and 223 [this section and section 423 of this title] on the basis of such wages and self-employment income for any month after December 1972 is reduced by reason of section 203(a) of such Act [section 403(a) of this title] as amended by this Act [Pub.L. 92–603] (or would, but for the penultimate sentence of such section 203(a) [section 403(a) of this title], be so reduced),

then the amount of the benefit to which each person referred to in paragraph (1) of this subsection is entitled beginning with the first month after December 1972 for which any person referred to in paragraph (2) becomes entitled shall be adjusted, after the application of such section 203(a) [section 403(a) of this title], to an amount no less than the amount it would have been if the person or persons referred to in paragraph (2) of this subsection were not entitled to a benefit referred to in such paragraph (2)."

1961 Acts. Section 104(f) of Pub.L. 87–64 provided that: "Where—

"(1) two or more persons were entitled (without the application of subsection (j)(1) of section 202 of the Social Security Act [subsec. (j)(1) of this section]) to monthly benefits under such section 202 [this section] for the last month beginning before the effective date of this title [see Effective Date of 1961 Acts note under this section] on the basis of the wages and self-employment income of a deceased individual, and one or more of such persons is entitled to a monthly insurance benefit under subsection (e), (f), or (h) of such section 202 [subsecs. (e), (f), or (h) of this section] for such last month; and

"(2) no person, other than the persons referred to in paragraph (1) of this subsection, is entitled to benefits under such section 202 [this section] on the basis of such individual's wages and self-employment income for a subsequent month or for any month after such last month and before such subsequent month; and

"(3) the total of the benefits to which all persons are entitled under such section 202 [this section] on the basis of such individual's wages and self-employment income for such subsequent month is reduced by reason of the application of section 203(a) of such Act [section 403(a) of this title],

then the amount of the benefit to which each such person referred to in paragraph (1) of this subsection is entitled for such subsequent month shall be determined without regard to this Act if, after the application of this Act such benefit for such month is less than the amount of such benefit for such last month. The preceding provisions of this subsection shall not apply to any monthly benefit of any person for any month beginning after the effective date of this title [see Effective Date of 1961 Act note under this section] unless paragraph (3) also applies to such benefit for the month beginning on such effective date (or would so apply but for the next to the last sentence of section 203(a) of the Social Security Act [section 403(a) of this title])."

1960 Acts. Section 208(e) of Pub.L. 86–778 provided that: "Where—

"(1) one or more persons were entitled (without the application of section 202(j)(1) of the Social Security Act [subsec. (j)(1) of this section]) to monthly benefits under section 202 of such Act [this section] for the month before the month in which this Act is enacted [Sept. 1960] on the basis of the wages and self-employment income of an individual; and

"(2) any person is entitled to benefits under subsection (b), (c), (d), (e), (f), or (g) of section 202 of the Social Security Act [subsec. (b), (c), (d), (e), (f), or (g) of this section] for any subsequent month on the basis of such individual's wages and self-employment income and such person would not be entitled to such benefits but for the enactment of this section; and

"(3) the total of the benefits to which all persons are entitled under section 202 of the Social Security Act [this section] on the basis of such individual's wages and self-employment income for such subsequent month is reduced by reason of the application of section 203(a) of such Act [section 403(a) of this title],

then the amount of the benefit to which each person referred to in paragraph (1) of this subsection is entitled for such subsequent month shall not, after the application of such section 203(a) [section 403(a) of this title], be less than the amount it would have been (determined without regard to section 301 [section 501 of this title]) if no person referred to in paragraph (2) of this subsection was entitled to a benefit referred to in such paragraph for such subsequent month on the basis of such wages and self-employment income of such individual."

Section 301(c) of Pub.L. 86–778 provided that: "Where—

"(1) one or more persons were entitled (without the application of section 202(j)(1) of the Social Security Act [subsec. (j)(1) of this section]) to monthly benefits under section 202 of such Act [this section] for the second month following the month in which this Act is enacted [Sept. 1960] on the basis of the wages and self-employment income of a deceased individual (but not including any person who became so entitled by reason of section 208 of this Act [section 408 of this title]); and

"(2) no person, other than (i) those persons referred to in paragraph (1) of this subsection (ii) those persons who are entitled to benefits under section 202(d), (e), (f), or (g) of the Social Security Act [subsec. (d), (e), (f) or (g) of this section] but would not be so entitled except for the enactment of section 208 of this Act [section 408 of this title], is entitled to benefits under such section 202 [this section] on the basis of such individual's wages and self-employment income for any subsequent month or for any month after the second month following the month in which this Act is enacted [Sept. 1960] and prior to such subsequent month; and

"(3) the total of the benefits to which all persons referred to in paragraph (1) of this subsection are entitled under section 202 of the Social Security Act [this section] on the basis of such individual's wages and self-employment income for such subsequent month exceeds the maximum of benefits payable, as provided in section 203(a) of such Act [section 403(a) of this title], on the basis of such wages and self-employment income,

then the amount of the benefit to which each such person referred to in paragraph (1) of this subsection is entitled for such subsequent month shall be determined—

"(4) in case such person is entitled to benefits under section 202(e), (f), (g), or (h) [subsecs. (e), (f), (g), or (h) of this section], as though this section and section 208 had not been enacted, or

"(5) in case such person is entitled to benefits under section 202(d) [subsec. (d) of this section], as though (i) no person is entitled to benefits under section 202(e), (f), (g), or (h) for such subsequent month, and (ii) the maximum of benefits payable, as described in paragraph (3) is such maximum less the amount of each person's benefit for such month determined pursuant to paragraph (4)."

1958 Acts. Section 304(b) of Pub.L. 85–840 provided that: "Where—

"(1) one or more persons were entitled (without the application of section 202(j)(1) of the Social Security Act [subsec. (j)(1) of this section]) to monthly benefits under section 202 of such Act [this section] for the month in which this Act is enacted [August 1958] on the basis of the wages and self-employment income of an individual; and

"(2) a person is entitled to a parent's insurance benefit under section 202(h) of the Social Security Act [subsec. (h) of this section] for any subsequent month on the basis of such wages and self-employment income and such person would not be entitled to such benefit but for the enactment of this section; and

"(3) the total of the benefits to which all persons are entitled under section 202 of the Social Security Act [this section] on the basis of such wages and self-employment income for such subsequent month are reduced by reason of the application of section 203(a) of such Act [section 403(a) of this title],

then the amount of the benefit to which each such person referred to in paragraph (1) of this subsection is entitled for such subsequent month shall be increased, after the application of such section 203(a) [section 403(a) of this title], to the amount it would have been if no person referred to in paragraph (2) of this subsection was entitled to a parent's insurance benefit for such subsequent month on the basis of such wages and self-employment income."

1957 Acts. Section 5 of Pub.L. 85–238 provided that: "Where—

"**(a)** one or more persons were entitled (without the application of section 202(j)(1) of the Social Security Act [subsec. (j)(1) of this section]) to parents' insurance benefits under section 202(h) of such Act [subsec. (h) of this section] for the month in which this Act [August 1957] is enacted on the basis of the wages and self-employment income of an individual;

"**(b)** a person becomes entitled to a widow's, widower's or mother's insurance benefit under section 202(e), (f), or (g) of the Social Security Act [subsecs. (e), (f), or (g) or this section] for any subsequent month on the basis of such wages and self-employment income;

"**(c)** the total of the benefits to which all persons are entitled under section 202 of the Social Security Act [this section], on the basis of such wages and self-employment income for such subsequent month are reduced by reason of the application of section 203(a) of such Act [section 403(a) of this title];

then the amount of the benefit to which each such person referred to in paragraph (a) or (b) is entitled for such subsequent month shall be increased, after the application of such § 203(a) [§ 403(a) of this title], to the amount it would have been—

"**(d)** if, in the case of a parent's insurance benefit, the person referred to in paragraph (b) was not entitled to the benefit referred to in such paragraph, or

"**(e)** if, in the case of a benefit referred to in paragraph (b), no person was entitled to a parent's insurance benefit for such subsequent month on the basis of such wages and self-employment income."

Severability of Provisions

If any provision of Division C of Pub.L. 104–208 or the application of such provision to any person or circumstances is held to be unconstitutional, the remainder of Division C of Pub.L. 104–208 and the application of the provisions of Division C of Pub.L. 104–208 to any person or circumstance not to be affected thereby, see section 1(e) of Pub.L. 104–208, set out as a note under section 1101 of Title 8, Aliens and Nationality.

Findings

Pub.L. 113–270, § 2, Dec. 18, 2014, 128 Stat. 2948, provided that:

"Congress finds the following:

"**(1)** Congress enacted social security legislation to provide earned benefits for workers and their families, should they retire, become disabled, or die.

"**(2)** Congress never intended for participants in Nazi persecution to be allowed to enter the United States or to reap the benefits of United States residency or citizenship, including participation in the Nation's Social Security program."

Construction of 1994 Amendments

Section 7 of Pub.L. 103—387 provided that: "Until March 31, 1995, any reference in this Act [see Short Title of 1994 Amendments note, set out under section 1 of Title 26, Internal Revenue Code] (other than section 3(d) [108 Stat. 4075]) or any amendment made by this Act to the Commissioner of Social Security shall be deemed a reference to the Secretary of Health and Human Services.

Adjustment of Benefits Based on Disability Which Began Between Age 18 and 22

Section 108(g) of Pub.L. 92–603 provided that: "Where—

"**(1)** one or more persons are entitled (without the application of sections 202(j)(1) and 223(b) of the Social Security Act) [subsec. (j)(1) of this section and section 423(b) of this title] to monthly benefits under section 202 or 223 of such Act [this section or section 423 of this title] for December 1972 on the basis of the wages and self-employment income of an insured individual, and

"**(2)** one or more persons (not included in paragraph (1)) are entitled to monthly benefits under such section 202 or 223 [this section or section 423 of this title] for January 1973 solely by reason of the amendments made by this section on the basis of such wages and self-employment income, and

"**(3)** the total of benefits to which all persons are entitled under such sections 202 and 223 [this section and section 423 of this title] on the basis of such wages and self-employment income for January 1973 is reduced by reason of section 203(a) of such Act [section 403(a) of this title] as amended by this Act [Pub.L. 92–603] (or would, but for the penultimate sentence of such section 203(a), be so reduced),

then the amount of the benefit to which each person referred to in paragraph (1) of this subsection is entitled for months after December 1972 shall be adjusted, after the application of such section 203(a) [section 403(a) of this title], to an amount no less than the amount it would have been if the person or persons referred to in paragraph (2) of this subsection were not entitled to a benefit referred to in such paragraph (2)."

Application for Benefits by Survivors of Members and Former Members of Uniformed Services

Forms for use by survivors of members and former members of the uniformed services in filing applications for benefits under this subchapter to be prescribed jointly by the Administrator of Veterans' Affairs and the Secretary of Health and Human Services, see section 5105 of Title 38, Veterans' Benefits.

Application Requirements for Certain Individuals on Benefit Rolls

Section 5103(e)(2) of Pub.L. 101–508 provided that: "In the case of any individual who—

"**(A)** is entitled to disability insurance benefits under section 223 of the Social Security Act [section 423 of this title] for December 1990 or is eligible for supplemental security income benefits under title XVI of such Act [subchapter XVI of this chapter], or State supplementary payments of the type referred to in section 1616(a) of such Act [section 1382e(a) of this title] (or payments of the type described in section 212(a) of Public Law 93–66 [set out as a note under section 1382 of this title]) which are paid by the Secretary under an agreement referred to in such section 1616(a) (or in section 212(b) of Public Law 93–66 [set out as a note under section 1382 of this title]), for January 1991,

"(B) applied for widow's or widower's insurance benefits under subsection (e) or (f) of section 202 of the Social Security Act [subsec. (e) or (f) of this section] during 1990, and

"(C) is not entitled to such benefits under such subsection (e) or (f) [subsec. (e) or (f) of this section] for any month on the basis of such application by reason of the definition of disability under section 223(d)(2)(B) of the Social Security Act [section 423(d)(2)(B) of this title] (as in effect immediately before the date of the enactment of this Act [Nov. 5, 1990]), and would have been so entitled for such month on the basis of such application if the amendments made by this section [amending this section and sections 416, 423, 426 and 1383c of this title and enacting provisions set out as a note under this section] had been applied with respect to such application, for purposes of determining such individual's entitlement to such benefits under subsection (e) or (f) of section 202 of the Social Security Act [subsec. (e) or (f) of this section] for months after December 1990, the requirement of paragraph (1)(C)(i) of such subsection shall be deemed to have been met."

[The provisions of section 5103(e)(2) of Pub.L. 101–508, set out as a note above, are to apply with respect to monthly insurance benefits for months after Dec., 1990 for which applications are filed on or after Jan. 1, 1991, or are pending on such date, see section 5103(e)(1) of Pub.L. 101–508, set out as a note under this section.]

Child's Insurance Benefits; Continued Eligibility of Certain Individuals; Limitations

Section 2210(c) of Pub.L. 97–35 provided that:

"(1) Notwithstanding the provisions of section 202(d) of the Social Security Act (as in effect prior to or after the amendments made by subsection (a)) [subsec. (d) of this section], any individual who—

"(A) has attained the age of 18;

"(B) is not under a disability (as defined in section 223(d) of such Act) [section 423(d) of this title];

"(C) is entitled to a child's insurance benefit under such section 202(d) [subsec. (d) of this section] for August 1981; and

"(D) is a full-time student at a post-secondary school, college, or university that is an educational institution (as such terms are defined in section 202(d)(7)(A) and (C) of such Act as in effect prior to the amendments made by subsection (a)) [subsec. (d)(7)(A) and (C) of this section] for any month prior to May 1982;

shall be entitled to a child's benefit under section 202(d) of such Act [subsec. (d) of this section] in accordance with the provisions of such section as in effect prior to the amendments made by subsection (a) [amending subsec. (d) of this section] for any month after July 1981 and prior to August 1985 if such individual would be entitled to such child's benefit for such month under such section 202(d) if subsections (a) and (b) of this section [amending subsec. (d) of this section and enacting a provision set out as a note under this section] had not been enacted, but such benefits shall be subject to the limitations set forth in this subsection.

"(2) No benefit described in paragraph (1) shall be paid to an individual to whom paragraph (1) applies for the months of May, June, July, and August, beginning with benefits otherwise payable for May 1982.

"(3) The amount of the monthly benefit payable under paragraph (1) to an individual to whom paragraph (1) applies for any month after July 1982 (prior to deductions on account of work required by section 203 of such Act) [section 403 of this title] shall not exceed the amount of the benefit to which such individual was entitled for August 1981 (prior to deductions on account of work required by section 203 of such Act), less an amount—

"(A) during the months after July 1982 and before August 1983, equal to 25 percent of such benefit for August 1981;

"(B) during the months after July 1983 and before August 1984, equal to 50 percent of such benefit for August 1981; and

"(C) during the months after July 1984 and before August 1985, equal to 75 percent of such benefit for August 1981.

"(4) Any individual to whom the provisions of paragraph (1) apply and whose entitlement to benefits under paragraph (1) ends after July 1982 shall not subsequently become entitled, or reentitled, to benefits under paragraph (1) or under section 202(d) of the Social Security Act [subsec. (d) of this section] as in effect after the amendments made by subsection (a) unless he meets the requirements of section 202(d)(1)(B)(ii) of that Act [subsec. (d)(1)(B)(ii) of this section] as so in effect."

Cost-of-Living Increase in Social Security Benefits; Effective Date; Consumer Price Index Percentage

Section 201 of Pub.L. 93–66, as amended Pub.L. 93–233, § 1(a) to (e), Dec. 30, 1973, 87 Stat. 947, provided that:

"(a)(1) The Secretary of Health, Education, and Welfare [now Secretary of Health and Human Services] (hereinafter in this section referred to as the 'Secretary') shall, in accordance with the provisions of this section, increase the monthly benefits and lump-sum death payments payable under title II of the Social Security Act [this subchapter] by 7 per centum.

"(2) The provisions of this section (and the increase in benefits made hereunder) shall be effective, in the case of monthly benefits under title II of the Social Security Act [this subchapter], only for months after February 1974 and prior to June 1974, and, in the case of lump-sum death payments under such title [this subchapter], only with respect to deaths which occur after February 1974 and prior to June 1974.

"(b) The increase in social security benefits authorized under this section shall be provided, and any determinations by the Secretary in connection with the provision of such increase in benefits shall be made, in the manner prescribed in section 215(i) of the Social Security Act [section 4151(i) of this title] for the implementation of cost-of-living increases authorized under title II of such Act [this subchapter], except that—

"(1) the amount of such increase shall be 7 per centum,

"(2) in the case of any individual entitled to monthly insurance benefits payable pursuant to section 202(e) of such Act [subsec. (e) of this section] for February 1974 (without the application of section 202(j)(1) or 223(b) of such Act [subsec. (j)(1) of this section or section 423(b) of this title]), including such benefits based on a primary insurance amount determined under section 215(a)(3) of such Act as amended by this section [section 415(a)(3) of this title], such increase shall be determined without regard to paragraph (2)(B) of such section 202(e) [subsec. (e) of this section], and

"(3) in the case of any individual entitled to monthly insurance benefits payable pursuant to section 202(f) of such Act [subsec. (f) of this section] for February 1974 (without the application of section 202(j)(1) or 223(b) of such Act [subsec. (j)(1) of this section or section 423(b) of this title]), including such benefits based on a primary insurance amount determined under section 215(a)(3) of such Act as amended by this section [section 415(a)(3) of this title], such increase shall be determined without regard to paragraph (3)(B) of such section 202(f) [subsec. (f) of this section].

"**(c)** The increase in social security benefits provided by this section shall—

"(1) not be considered to be an increase in benefits made under or pursuant to section 215(i) of the Social Security Act [section 415(i) of this title], and

"(2) not (except for purposes of section 203(a)(2) of such Act [section 403(a)(2) of this title], as in effect after February 1974) be considered to be a 'general benefit increase under this title' [this subchapter] (as such term is defined in section 215(i)(3) of such Act [section 415(i)(3) of this title]);

and nothing in this section shall be construed as authorizing any increase in the 'contribution and benefit base' (as that term is employed in section 230 of such Act [section 430 of this title]) or any increase in the 'exempt amount' (as such term is used in section 203(f)(8) of such Act [section 403(f)(8) of this title]).

"**(d)** Nothing in this section shall be construed to authorize (directly or indirectly) any increase in monthly benefits under title II of the Social Security Act [this subchapter] for any month after May 1974, or any increase in lump-sum death payments payable under such title [this subchapter] in the case of deaths occurring after May 1974. The recognition of the existence of the increase in benefits authorized by the preceding subsections of this section (during the period it was in effect) in the application, after May 1974, of the provisions of sections 202(q) and 203(a) of such Act [subsec. (q) of this section and section 403(a) of this title] shall not, for purposes of the preceding sentence, be considered to be an increase in a monthly benefit for a month after May 1974."

[The Secretary of Health, Education, and Welfare was redesignated the Secretary of Health and Human Services by section 3508(b) of Title 20, Education.]

Death Outside U.S.; Extension of Filing Time for Lump-Sum Payments

Section 5(e)(2) of Act July 18, 1952, c. 945, 66 Stat. 776, as amended Pub.L. 86–778, Title I, § 103(a)(2), Sept. 13, 1960, 74 Stat. 936, provided that: "In the case of any individual who died outside the forty-eight States and the District of Columbia after August 1950 and prior to January 1954, whose death occurred while he was in the active military or naval service of the United States, and who is returned to any of such States, the District of Columbia, Alaska, Hawaii, the Commonwealth of Puerto Rico, the Virgin Islands, Guam, or American Samoa for interment or reinterment, the last sentence of section 202(i) of the Social Security Act [subsec. (i) of this section] shall not prevent payment to any person under the second sentence thereof if application for a lump-sum death payment with respect to such deceased individual is filed under such section by or on behalf of such person (whether or not legally competent) prior to the expiration of two years after the date of such interment or reinterment."

Disregarding OASDI Benefit Increases and Child's Insurance Benefit Payments Beyond Age 18 to the Extent Attributable to Retroactive Effective Date of 1965 Amendments

Authorization to disregard, in determining need for aid or assistance under an approved state plan, amounts paid under this subchapter for months occurring after December 1964 and before October 1965 to the extent to which payment is attributable to the payment of child's insurance benefits under the old-age, survivors, and disability insurance system after attainment of age 18, in the case of individuals attending school, resulting from enactment of section 306 of Pub.L. 89–97, see section 406 of Pub.L. 89–97, set out as a note under section 415 of this title.

Extension of Filing Period for Husband's, Widower's, or Parent's Benefits in Certain Cases

Section 210 of Pub.L. 86–778 provided that:

"**(a)** In the case of any husband who would not be entitled to husband's insurance benefits under section 202(c) of the Social Security Act [subsec. (c) of this section] except for the enactment of this Act, the requirement in section 202(c)(1)(C) of the Social Security Act [subsec. (c)(1)(C) of this section] relating to the time within which proof of support must be filed shall not apply if such proof of support is filed within two years after the month in which this Act is enacted [Sept. 1960].

"**(b)** In the case of any widower who would not be entitled to widower's insurance benefits under section 202(f) of the Social Security Act [subsec. (f) of this section] except for the enactment of this Act, the requirement in section 202(f)(1)(D) of the Social Security Act [subsec. (f)(1)(D) of this section] relating to the time within which proof of support must be filed shall not apply if such proof of support is filed within two years after the month in which this Act is enacted [Sept. 1960].

"**(c)** In the case of any parent who would not be entitled to parent's insurance benefits under section 202(h) of the Social Security Act except for the enactment of this Act, the requirement in section 202(h)(1)(B) of the Social Security Act [subsec. (h)(1)(B) of this section] relating to the time within which proof of support must be filed shall not apply if such proof of support is filed within two years after the month in which this Act is enacted [Sept. 1960]."

Filing of Proof of Support

1968 Acts. Section 157(c) of Pub.L. 90–248 provided that: "In the case of any husband who would not be entitled to husband's insurance benefits under section 202(c) of the Social Security Act [subsec. (c) of this section] or any widower who would not be entitled to widower's insurance benefits under section 202(f) of such Act [subsec. (f) of this section] except for the enactment of this section, the requirement in section 202(c)(1)(C) or 202(f)(1)(D) of such Act [subsec. (c)(1)(C) or (f)(1)(D) of this section] relating to the time within which proof of support must be filed shall not apply if such proof of support is filed within two years after the month following the month in which this Act is enacted [Jan. 1968]."

1961 Acts. Section 103(c) of Pub.L. 87–64 provided that: "In the case of any widower or parent who would not be entitled to widower's insurance benefits under section 202(f) [subsec. (f) of this section], or parent's insurance benefits under section 202(h) [subsec. (h) of this section], of the Social Security Act except for the enactment of this Act (other than this subsection), the requirement in sections 202(f)(1)(D) and 202(h)(1)(B) [subsecs. (f)(1)(D) and (h)(1)(B) of this section], respectively, of the Social Security Act relating to the time within which proof of support must be filed shall not apply if such proof of support is filed before the close of the 2-year period which begins on the effective date of this title [see Effective Date of 1961 Acts note under this section]."

1958 Acts. Section 207(b) of Pub.L. 85–840 provided that: "In the case of any husband, widower, or parent who would not be entitled to benefits under section 202(c), section 202(f), and section 202(h), respectively, of the Social Security Act [subsecs. (c), (f) and (h) of this section] except for the enactment of section 205 of this Act [amending subsecs. (b), (c)(1), (d)(1), (f)(1)(D), (g)(1)(F), (h)(1)(B), (k), and (q)(5), (6) of this section and sections 401(h), 403(c), (h), 414(b), 415(g), 422(b)(3) and 425 of this title], the requirement in such section 202(c), section 202(f) or section 202(h) [subsec. (c), (f) or (h) of this section], as the case may be, that proof of support be filed within a two-year period shall not apply if such proof is filed within two years after the month in which this Act is enacted [August 1958]."

Section 304(c) of Pub.L. 85–840 provided that: "In the case of any parent who would not be entitled to parent's benefits under section 202(h) of the Social Security Act [subsec. (h) of this section] except for the enactment of this section, the requirement in such section 202(h) [subsec. (h) of this section] that proof of support be filed within two years of the date of death of the insured individual referred to therein shall not apply if such proof is filed within the two-year period beginning with the first day of the month after the month in which this Act is enacted [August 1958]."

1954 Acts. Section 113 of Act Sept. 1, 1954 provided that:

"**(a)** For the purpose of determining the entitlement of any individual to husband's insurance benefits under subsection (c) of section 202 of the Social Security Act [subsec. (c) of this section] of the basis of his wife's wages and self-employment income, the requirements of paragraph (1)(D) of such subsection shall be deemed to be met if—

"**(1)** such individual was receiving at least one-half of his support, as determined in accordance with regulations prescribed by the Secretary of Health, Education, and Welfare [now Secretary of Health and Human Services] from his wife on the first day of the first month (A) for which she was entitled to a monthly benefit under subsection (a) of such section 202 [subsec. (a) of this section] and (B) in which an event described in paragraph (1) or (2) of section 203(b) of such Act [section 403(b) of this title] (as in effect before or after the enactment of this Act [Sept. 1, 1954]) did not occur,

"**(2)** such individual has filed proof of such support within two years after such first month, and

"**(3)** such wife was, without the application of subsection (j)(1) of such section 202 [subsec. (j)(1) of this section] entitled to a primary insurance benefit under such Act, for August 1950.

"**(b)** For the purpose of determining the entitlement to any individual to widower's insurance benefits under subsection (f) of section 202 of the Social Security Act [subsec. (f) of this section] on the basis of his deceased wife's wages and self-employment income, the requirements of paragraph (1)(E)(ii) of such subsection shall be deemed to be met if—

"**(1)** such individual was receiving at least one-half of his support, as determined in accordance with regulations prescribed by the Secretary of Health, Education, and Welfare [now Secretary of Health and Human Services] from his wife, and she was a currently insured individual, on the first day of the first month (A) for which she was entitled to a monthly benefit under subsection (a) of such section 202 [subsec. (a) of this section] and (B) in which an event described in paragraph (1) or (2) of section 203(b) of such Act [section 403(b) of this title] (as in effect before or after the enactment of this Act [Sept. 1, 1954]) did not occur,

"**(2)** such individual has filed proof of such support within two years after such first month, and

"**(3)** such wife was, without the application of subsection (j)(1) of such section 202 [subsec. (j)(1) of this section], entitled to a primary insurance benefit under such Act for August 1950.

"**(c)** For purposes of subsection (b)(1) of this section, and for purposes of section 202(c)(1) of the Social Security Act [subsec. (c)(1) of this section] in cases to which subsection (a) of this section is applicable, the wife of an individual shall be deemed a currently insured individual if she had not less than six quarters of coverage (as determined under section 213 of the Social Security Act [section 413 of this title]) during the thirteen-quarter period ending with the calendar quarter in which occurs the first month (1) for which such wife was entitled to a monthly benefit under section 202(a) of such Act [subsec. (a) of this section], and (2) in which an event described in paragraph (1) or (2) of section 203(b) of such Act [subsec. (b)(1) or (2) of this section] (as in effect before or after the enactment of this Act [Sept. 1, 1954]) did not occur.

"**(d)** This section shall apply only with respect to husband's insurance benefits under section 202(c) of the Social Security Act [subsec. (c) of this section] and widower's insurance benefits under section 202(f) of such Act [subsec. (f) of this section], for months after August 1954, and only with respect to benefits based on applications filed after such month."

[The Secretary of Health, Education, and Welfare was redesignated the Secretary of Health and Human Services by section 3508(b) of Title 20, Education.]

1950 Acts. Section 101(c) of Act Aug. 28, 1950 provided that:

"**(1)** Any individual entitled to primary insurance benefits or widow's current insurance benefits under section 202 of the Social Security Act [this section] as in effect prior to its amendment by this Act who would but for the enactment of this Act, be entitled to such benefits for September 1950 shall be deemed to be entitled to old-age insurance benefits or mother's insurance benefits (as the case may be) under section 202 of the Social Security Act [this section], as amended by this Act, as though such individual became entitled to such benefits in such month.

"**(2)** Any individual entitled to any other monthly insurance benefits under section 202 of the Social Security Act [this section] as in effect prior to its amendment by this Act who would, but for the enactment of this Act, be entitled to such benefits for September 1950 shall be deemed to be entitled to such benefits under section 202 of the Social Security Act [this section], as amended by this Act, as though such individual became entitled to such benefits in such month.

"**(3)** Any individual who files application after August 1950 for monthly benefits under any subsection of section 202 of the Social Security Act [section 402 of this title] who would, but for the enactment of this Act, be entitled to benefits under such subsection (as in effect prior to such enactment) for any month prior to September 1950 shall be deemed entitled to such benefits for such month prior to September 1950 to the same extent and in the same amounts as though this Act had not been enacted."

Lump-Sum Payments for Deaths Before 1940; Time Limitation

Lump sum payments of 3½ per cent of total wages paid with respect to employment after Dec. 31, 1936 and before reaching the age of 65 were provided for persons who were not qualified individuals upon reaching that age by section 204 of Act Aug. 14, 1935, before amendment in 1939. Such lump sum payments except to the estate of an individual who died prior to Jan. 1, 1940, were prohibited after Aug. 10, 1939, by section 902(g) of Act Aug. 10, 1939. Section 415 of Act Aug. 10, 1946, provided that no lump sum payments shall be made under said section 204 of the 1935 Act or said section 902(g) of the 1939 Act unless application therefor has been filed prior to the expiration of six months after Aug. 10, 1946.

Lump-Sum Payments Where Death Occurred Prior to September 1, 1950

Section 101(d) of Act Aug. 28, 1950, as amended July 18, 1952, c. 945, § 5(e)(1), 66 Stat. 775; Sept. 13, 1960, Pub.L. 86–778, Title I, § 103(a)(2), 74 Stat. 936, provided that: "Lump-sum death payments shall be made in the case of individuals who died prior to September 1950 as though this Act had not been enacted; except that in the case of any individual who died outside the forty-eight States and the District of Columbia after December 6, 1941, and prior to August 10, 1946 the last sentence of section 202(g) of the Social Security Act [subsec. (g) of this section] as in effect prior to the enactment of this Act shall not be applicable if application for a lump-sum death payment is filed prior to September 1952, and except that in the case of any individual who died outside the forty-eight States and the District of Columbia on or after June 25, 1950, and prior to September 1950, whose death occurred while he was in the active military or naval service of the United States, and who is returned to any of such States, the District of Columbia, Alaska, Hawaii, the Commonwealth of Puerto Rico, the Virgin Islands, Guam, or American Samoa for interment or reinterment, the last sentence of section 202(g) of the Social Security Act [subsec. (g) of this section] as in effect prior to the enactment of this Act [July 18, 1952] shall not prevent payment to any person under the second sentence thereof [subsec. (g) of this section] if application for a lump-sum death payment under such section with respect to such deceased individual is filed by or on behalf of such person (whether or not legally competent) prior to the expiration of two years after the date of such interment or reinterment."

March Through May 1974 Monthly Insurance Benefit for Only Individual Entitled to Benefit on Basis of Wages and Self-Employment Income of Deceased Insured Individual

Section 1(i) of Pub.L. 93–233 provided that: "In the case of an individual to whom monthly benefits are payable under title II of the Social Security Act [this subchapter] for February 1974 (without the application of section 202(j)(1) or 223(b) of such Act [subsec. (j)(1) of this section or section 423(b) of this title]), and to whom section 202(m) of such Act [subsec. (m) of this section] is applicable for such month, such section [this section] shall continue to be applicable to such benefits for the months of March through May 1974 for which such individual remains the only individual entitled to a monthly benefit on the basis of the wages and self-employment income of the deceased insured individual."

Minimum Monthly Insurance Benefits for Months After December 1978, for Widow or Widower and Other Jointly Entitled Individuals

Section 336(d) of Pub.L. 95–216 provided that: "Where—

"(1) two or more persons are entitled to monthly benefits under section 202 of the Social Security Act [this section] for December 1978 on the basis of the wages and self-employment income of a deceased individual, and one or more of such persons is so entitled under subsection (e) or (f) of such section 202 [subsec. (e) or (f) of this section], and

"(2) one or more of such persons is entitled on the basis of such wages and self-employment income to monthly benefits under subsection (e) or (f) of such section 202 (as amended by this section) for January 1979, and

"(3) the total of benefits to which all persons are entitled under section 202 of such Act [section 402 of this title] on the basis of such wages and self-employment income for January 1979 is reduced by reason of section 203(a) of such Act as amended by this Act [section 403(a) of this title] (or would, but for the first sentence of section 203(a)(4) [section 403(a)(4) of this title], be so reduced),

then the amount of the benefit to which each such person referred to in paragraph (1) is entitled for months after December 1978 shall in no case be less after the application of this section [see section 336(c)(1) of Pub.L. 95–216, set out as an Effective Date of 1977 Act note under this section] and such section 203(a) [section 403(a) of this title] than the amount it would have been without the application of this section."

Monthly Payments to Surviving Spouse of Member or Former Member of Armed Forces Where Such Person Has in Care a Child of Such Member; Amount, Criteria, Etc.

Pub.L. 97–377, Title I, § 156, Dec. 21, 1982, 96 Stat. 1920, as amended Pub.L. 98–94, Title IX, § 943, Sept. 24, 1983, 97 Stat. 654; Pub.L. 100–322, Title III, § 314, May 20, 1988, 102 Stat. 535; Pub.L. 102–83, § 5(c)(2), Aug. 6, 1991, 105 Stat. 406, provided that:

"(a)(1) The head of the agency shall pay each month an amount determined under paragraph (2) to a person—

"(A) who is the surviving spouse of a member or former member of the Armed Forces described in subsection (c);

"(B) who has in such person's care a child of such member or former member who has attained sixteen years of age but not eighteen years of age and is entitled to a child's insurance benefit under section 202(d) of the Social Security Act (42 U.S.C. 402(d) for such month or who meets the requirements for entitlement to the equivalent of such benefit provided under section 1312(a) of title 38, United States Code [section 1312(a) of Title 38, Veterans' Benefits]; and

"(C) who is not entitled for such month to a mother's insurance benefit under section 202(g) of the Social Security Act (42 U.S.C. 402(g)), or to the equivalent of such benefit based on meeting the requirements of section 1312(a) of title 38, United States Code [section 1312(a) of Title 38, Veterans' Benefits] by reason of having such child (or any other child of such member or former member) in her care.

"(2) A payment under paragraph (1) for any month shall be in the amount of the mother's insurance benefit, if any, that such person would receive for such month under section 202(g) of the Social Security Act if such child were under sixteen years of age, disregarding any adjustments made under section 215(i) of the Social Security Act [section 415(i) of this title] after August 1981. However, if such person is entitled for such month to a mother's insurance benefit under section 202(g) of such Act by reason of having the child of a person other than such member or former member of the Armed Forces in such person's care, the amount of the payment under the preceding sentence for such month shall be reduced (but not below zero) by the amount of the benefit payable by reason of having such child in such person's care.

"(b)(1) The head of the agency shall pay each month an amount determined under paragraph (2) to a person—

"(A) who is the child of a member or former member of the Armed Forces described in subsection (c);

"(B) who has attained eighteen years of age but not twenty-two years of age and is not under a disability as defined in section 223(d) of the Social Security Act (42 U.S.C. 423(d));

"(C) who is a full-time student at a post-secondary school, college, or university that is an educational institution (as such terms were defined in section 202(d)(7)(A) and (C) of the Social Security Act as in effect before the amendments made by section 2210(a) of the Omnibus Budget Reconciliation Act of 1981 (Public Law 97–35; 95 Stat. 841)) [amending subsec. (d)(7)(A) and (C) of this section]; and

"(D) who is not entitled for such month to a child's insurance benefit under section 202(d) of the Social Security Act (42 U.S.C. 402(d)) or is entitled for such month to such benefit only by reason of section 2210(c) of the Omnibus Budget Reconciliation Act of 1981 (95 Stat. 842) [section 2210(c) of Pub.L. 97–35, set out as a note under this section].

"(2) A payment under paragraph (1) for any month shall be in the amount that the person concerned would have been entitled to receive for such month as a child's insurance benefit under section 202(d) of the Social Security Act [subsec. (d) of this section] (as in effect before the amendments made by section 2210(a) of the Omnibus Budget Reconciliation Act of 1981 (95 Stat. 841)) [section 2210(a) of Pub.L. 97–35], disregarding any adjustments made under section 215(i) of the Social Security Act [section 415(i) of this title] after August 1981, but reduced for any month by any amount payable to such person for such month under section 2210(c) of the Omnibus Budget Reconciliation Act of 1981 (95 Stat. 842) [section 2210(c) of Pub.L. 97–35, set out as a note under this section].

"(c) A member or former member of the Armed Forces referred to in subsection (a) or (b) as described in this subsection is a member or former member of the Armed Forces who died on active duty before August 13, 1981, or died from a service-connected disability incurred or aggravated before such date.

"(d)(1) The Secretary of Health and Human Services shall provide to the head of the agency such information as the head of the agency may require to carry out this section.

"(2) The head of the agency shall carry out this section under regulations which the head of the agency shall prescribe. Such regulations shall be prescribed not later than ninety days after the date of the enactment of this section [Dec. 21, 1982].

"(e)(1) Unless otherwise provided by law—

"(A) each time after December 31, 1981, that an increase is made by law in the dependency and indemnity compensation paid under section 1311 of title 38, United States Code [section 1311 of Title 38, Veterans' Benefits], the head of the agency shall, at the same time and effective as of the same date on which such increase takes effect, increase the benefits paid under subsection (a) by a percentage that is equal to the overall average (rounded to the nearest one-tenth of 1 per centum) of the percentages by which each of the dependency and indemnity compensation rates under section 411 of such title are increased above the rates as in effect immediately before such increase; and

"(B) each time after December 31, 1981, that an increase is made by law in the rates of educational assistance allowances provided for under section 3531(b) of title 38, United States Code, the head of the agency shall, at the same time and effective as of the same date on which such increase takes effect, increase the benefits paid under subsection (b) by a percentage that is equal to the overall average (rounded to the nearest one-tenth of 1 per centum) of the percentages by which each of the educational assistance allowance rates provided for under section 3531(b) of such title are increased above the rates as in effect immediately before such increase.

"(2) The amount of the benefit payable to any person under subsection (a) or (b) and the amount of any increase in any such benefit made pursuant to clause (1) or (2) of this subsection, if not a multiple of $1, shall be rounded to the next lower multiple of $1.

"(f) Payments under subsections (a) and (b) shall be made only for months after the month in which this section is enacted.

"(g)(1) During each fiscal year the Secretary of Defense shall transfer from time to time to the head of the agency such amounts as the head of the agency determines to be necessary to pay the benefits provided for under subsections (a) and (b) during such fiscal year and to pay the administrative expenses incurred in paying such benefits during such fiscal year. During fiscal year 1983, transfers under this subsection shall be made from the 'Retired Pay, Defense' account of the Department of Defense. During subsequent fiscal years, such transfers shall be made from such account or from funds otherwise available to the Secretary for the purpose of the payment of such benefits and expenses. The Secretary of Defense may transfer funds under this subsection in advance of the payment of benefits and expenses by the head of the agency.

"(2) The head of the agency shall establish on the books of the agency over which he exercises jurisdiction a new account to be used for the payment of benefits under subsections (a) and (b) and shall credit to such account all funds transferred to him for such purpose by the Secretary of Defense.

"(h) The head of the agency and the Secretary of Health and Human Services may enter into an agreement to provide for the payment by the Secretary or the head of the agency of benefits provided for under subsection (a) and benefits provided for under section 202(g) of the Social Security Act (42 U.S.C. 402(g)) in a single monthly payment and for the payment by the Secretary or the head of the agency of benefits provided for under subsection (b) and benefits provided for under section 202(d) of the Social Security Act (42 U.S.C. 402(d)) in a single monthly payment, if the head of the agency and the Secretary agree that such action would be practicable and cost effective to the Government.

"(i) For the purposes of this section:

"(1) The term 'head of the agency' means the head of such department or agency of the Government as the

President shall designate to administer the provisions of this section.

"(2) The terms 'active military, naval, or air service' and 'service-connected' have the meanings given those terms in paragraphs (24) and (16), respectively, of section 101 of title 38, United States Code [section 101(24) and (16) of Title 38], except that for the purposes of this section such terms do not apply to any service in the commissioned corps of the Public Health Service or the National Oceanic and Atmospheric Administration."

Nonapplicability of Amendments by Section 334 of Pub.L. 95–216 to Monthly Insurance Benefits Payable to Individuals Eligible for Monthly Periodic Benefits; Savings Provisions

Section 334(g) of Pub.L. 95–216, as amended Pub.L. 98–617, § 2(b)(1), Nov. 8, 1984, 98 Stat. 3294, provided that:

"(1) The amendments made by the preceding provisions of this section [see section 334(f) of Pub.L. 95–216, set out as an Effective Date of 1977 Act note under this section] shall not apply with respect to any monthly insurance benefit payable, under subsection (b), (c), (e), (f), or (g) (as the case may be) of section 202 of the Social Security Act [subsec. (b), (c), (e), (f), or (g) of this section], to an individual—

"(A)(i) to whom there is payable for any month within the 60–month period beginning with the month in which this Act [Dec., 1977] is enacted (or who is eligible in any such month for) a monthly periodic benefit (within the meaning of such provisions) based upon such individual's earnings while in the service of the Federal Government or any State (or political subdivision thereof, as defined in section 218(b)(2) of the Social Security Act) [section 418(b)(2) of this title], or (ii) who would have been eligible for such a monthly periodic benefit (within the meaning of paragraph (2)) before the close of such 60–month period, except for a requirement which postponed eligibility (as so defined) for such monthly periodic benefit until the month following the month in which all other requirements were met"; and

"(B) who at time of application for or initial entitlement to such monthly insurance benefit under such subsection (b), (c), (e), (f), or (g) meets the requirements of that subsection as it was in effect and being administered in January 1977.

"(2) For purposes of paragraph (1)(A), an individual is eligible for a monthly periodic benefit for any month if such benefit would be payable to such individual for that month if such individual were not employed during that month and had made proper application for such benefit.

"(3) If any provision of this subsection, or the application thereof to any person or circumstance, is held invalid, the remainder of this section shall not be affected thereby, but the application of this subsection to any other persons or circumstances shall also be considered invalid."

[Section 2(b)(3) of Pub.L. 98–617 provided that: "The amendments made by this subsection [amending this note and provisions set out as an Offset Against Spouses' Benefits on Account of Public Pensions note set out under this section] shall apply with respect to benefits payable under title II of the Social Security Act [this subchapter] for months beginning after the month of enactment of this Act [November 1984]."]

Offset Against Spouses' Benefits on Account of Public Pensions

Section 334(h) of Pub.L. 95–216, as added Pub.L. 97–455, § 7(a)(1), Jan. 12, 1983, 96 Stat. 2501, and amended Pub.L. 98–617, § 2(b)(2), Nov. 8, 1984, 98 Stat. 3294, provided that: "In addition, the amendments made by the preceding provisions of this section [see section 334(f) of Pub.L. 95–216, set out as a note under this section] shall not apply with respect to any monthly insurance benefit payable, under subsection (b), (c), (e), (f), or (g) (as the case may be) of section 202 of the Social Security Act [subsecs. (b), (c), (e), (f), or (g) of this section], to an individual—

"(1)(A) to whom there is payable for any month prior to July 1983 (or who is eligible in any such month for) a monthly periodic benefit (within the meaning of such provisions) based upon such individual's earnings while in the service of the Federal Government or any State (or political subdivision thereof, as defined in section 218(b)(2) of the Social Security Act [section 418(b)(2) of this title]), or (B) who would have been eligible for such a monthly periodic benefit (within the meaning of subsection (g)(2)) before the close of June 1983, except for a requirement which postponed eligibility (as so defined) for such monthly periodic benefit until the month following the month in which all other requirements were met"; and

"(2) who at the time of application for or initial entitlement to such monthly insurance benefit under such subsection (b), (c), (e), (f), or (g)—

"(A) meets the dependency test of one-half support set forth in paragraph (1)(C) of such subsection (c) as it read prior to the enactment of the amendments made by this section [see section 334(f) of Pub.L. 95–216, set out as an Effective Date of 1977 Act note under this section], or an equivalent dependency test (if the individual is a woman), in the case of an individual applying for or becoming entitled to benefits under such subsection (b) or (c), or

"(B) meets the dependency test of one-half support set forth in paragraph (1)(D) of such subsection (f) as it read prior to the enactment of the amendments made by this section, or an equivalent dependency test (if the individual is a woman), in the case of an individual applying for or becoming entitled to benefits under such subsection (e), (f), or (g)."

[Section 2(b)(3) of Pub.L. 98–617 provided that the amendment to this note shall be applicable with respect to benefits payable under this subchapter for months beginning after November, 1984].

Payment of Annuities to Officers and Employees of United States Convicted of Certain Offenses

Section 121(b) of Act Aug. 1, 1956, c. 836, provided that: "The amendment made by subsection (a) of this section [adding subsec. (u) of this section] shall not be construed to restrict or otherwise affect any of the provisions of the Act entitled 'An Act to prohibit payments of annuities to officers and employees of the United States convicted of certain offenses, and for other purposes', approved September 1, 1954 (Public Law 769, Eighty-third Congress) [formerly sections 2281 to 2288 of Title 5, Executive Departments and Government Officers and Employees, and now covered by sections 8311 et seq. of Title 5, Government Organization and Employees]."

Payments of Aliens' Benefits Withheld Under Foreign Delivery Restriction of Checks Against Federal Funds

Section 162(c)(3) of Pub.L. 90–248 provided that: "Whenever benefits which an individual who is not a citizen or national of the United States was entitled to receive under title II of the Social Security Act [this subchapter] are, on June 30, 1968, being withheld by the Treasury Department under the first section of the Act of October 9, 1940 (31 U.S.C. 123) [section 123 of Title 31, Money and Finance], any such benefits, payable to such individual for months after the month in which the determination by the Treasury Department that the benefits should be so withheld was made, shall not be paid—

"**(A)** to any person other than such individual, or, if such individual dies before such benefits can be paid, to any person other than an individual who was entitled for the month in which the deceased individual died (with the application of section 202(j)(1) of the Social Security Act [subsec. (j)(1) of this section]) to a monthly benefit under title II of such Act [this subchapter] on the basis of the same wages and self-employment income as such deceased individual, or

"**(B)** in excess of the equivalent of the last twelve months' benefits that would have been payable to such individual."

Pilot Study of Efficacy of Providing Individualized Information to Recipients of Old-Age and Survivors Insurance Benefits

Section 106 of Pub.L. 104–121 provided that:

"**(a) In general.**—During a 2-year period beginning as soon as practicable in 1996, the Commissioner of Social Security shall conduct a pilot study of the efficacy of providing certain individualized information to recipients of monthly insurance benefits under section 202 of the Social Security Act [this section], designed to promote better understanding of their contributions and benefits under the social security system. The study shall involve solely beneficiaries whose entitlement to such benefits first occurred in or after 1984 and who have remained entitled to such benefits for a continuous period of not less than 5 years. The number of such recipients involved in the study shall be of sufficient size to generate a statistically valid sample for purposes of the study, but shall not exceed 600,000 beneficiaries.

"**(b) Annualized statements.**—During the course of the study, the Commissioner shall provide to each of the beneficiaries involved in the study one annualized statement, setting forth the following information:

"(1) an estimate of the aggregate wages and self-employment income earned by the individual on whose wages and self-employment income the benefit is based, as shown on the records of the Commissioner as of the end of the last calendar year ending prior to the beneficiary's first month of entitlement;

"(2) an estimate of the aggregate of the employee and self-employment contributions, and the aggregate of the employer contributions (separately identified), made with respect to the wages and self-employment income on which the benefit is based, as shown on the records of the Commissioner as of the end of the calendar year preceding the beneficiary's first month of entitlement; and

"(3) an estimate of the total amount paid as benefits under section 202 of the Social Security Act [this section] based on such wages and self-employment income, as shown on the records of the Commissioner as of the end of the last calendar year preceding the issuance of the statement for which complete information is available.

"**(c) Inclusion with matter otherwise distributed to beneficiaries.**—The Commissioner shall ensure that reports provided pursuant to this section are, to the maximum extent practicable, included with other reports currently provided to beneficiaries on an annual basis.

"**(d) Report to the Congress.**—The Commissioner shall report to each House of the Congress regarding the results of the pilot study conducted pursuant to this section not later than 60 days after the completion of such study."

Redetermination of Widow's and Widower's Benefits for December 1972 and After to Provide for 1972 Increases

Section 102(g) of Pub.L. 92–603 provided that:

"(1) In the case of an individual who is entitled to widow's or widower's insurance benefits for the month of December 1972 the Secretary shall, if it would increase such benefits, redetermine the amount of such benefits for months after December 1972 under title II of the Social Security Act [this subchapter] as if the amendments made by this section [amending this section and section 403 of this title] had been in effect for the first month of such individual's entitlement to such benefits.

"(2) For purposes of paragraph (1)—

"**(A)** any deceased individual on whose wages and self-employment income the benefits of an individual referred to in paragraph (1) are based, shall be deemed not to have been entitled to benefits if the record, of insured individuals who were entitled to benefits, that is readily available to the Secretary contains no entry for such deceased individual; and

"**(B)** any deductions under subsections (b) and (c) of section 203 of such Act [section 403 of this title], applicable to the benefits of an individual referred to in paragraph (1) for any month prior to September 1965, shall be disregarded in applying the provisions of section 202(q)(7) of such Act [subsec. (q)(7) of this section] (as amended by this Act) [Pub.L. 92–603]."

Redetermination of Widow's and Widower's Monthly Insurance Benefits for Months After December 1978

Section 336(c)(2) of Pub.L. 95–216 provided that: "In the case of an individual who was entitled for the month of December 1978 to monthly insurance benefits under subsection (e) or (f) of section 202 of the Social Security Act [subsec. (e) or (f) of this section] to which the provisions of subsection (e)(4) or (f)(5) [subsec. (e)(4) or (f)(5) of this section] applied, the Secretary shall, if such benefits would be increased by the amendments made by this section [see section 336(c)(1) of Pub.L. 95–216, set out as a note under this section], redetermine the amount of such benefits for months after December 1978 as if such amendments had been in effect for the first month for which the provisions of section 202(e)(4) or 202(f)(5) became applicable."

Special $50 Payment Under Tax Reduction Act of 1975

Pub.L. 94–12, Title VII, § 702, Mar. 29, 1975, 89 Stat. 66, provided that the Secretary of the Treasury, at the earliest practicable date after Mar. 29, 1975, make a $50 payment to each individual, who for the month of March, 1975, was entitled, without regard to subsec. (j)(1) of this section, section 423(b) of this title, or section 231d(a)(ii) of Title 45, Railroads, to a monthly insurance benefit payable under this subchapter, a monthly annuity or pension payment under the Railroad

Retirement Act of 1935, the Railroad Retirement Act of 1937, or the Railroad Retirement Act of 1974, or a benefit under the supplemental security income benefits program under subchapter XVI of this title, except that payment be made only to individuals who were paid a benefit for March 1975 in a check issued no later than Aug. 31, 1975, that no payment be made to any individual who is not a resident of the United States as defined in section 410(i) of this title, and if an individual is entitled under two or more programs, this individual receive only one $50 payment, and that this payment received not be considered as income, or for the calendar year 1975, as a resource, for purposes of any Federal or State program which undertakes to furnish aid or assistance to individuals or families, where eligibility for the program is based upon need of the individual or family involved or as income for federal income tax purposes.

Study of Retirement Test and of Drug Standards and Coverage

Section 405 of Pub.L. 90–248 authorized the Secretary of Health, Education, and Welfare [now Secretary of Health and Human Services] to make a study of the existing retirement test and proposals for the modification of the test, the quality and cost standards for drugs for which payments are made under this chapter, and the coverage of drugs under part B of subchapter XVIII of this chapter, and submit a report to the President and to Congress concerning his findings and recommendations on or before Jan. 1, 1969.

Termination of Child's Insurance Benefits by Reason of Adoption

Section 112(c) of Pub.L. 92–603 provided that: "Any child—

"(1) whose entitlement to child's insurance benefits under section 202(d) of the Social Security Act [subsec. (d) of this section] was terminated by reason of his adoption, prior to the date of the enactment of this Act [Oct. 30, 1972], and

"(2) who, except for such adoption, would be entitled to child's insurance benefits under such section for a month after the month in which this Act is enacted [Oct. 1972],

may, upon filing application for child's insurance benefits under the Social Security Act [this chapter] after the date of enactment of this Act [Oct. 30, 1972], become reentitled to such benefits; except that no child shall, by reason of the enactment of this section, become reentitled to such benefits for any month prior to the month after the month in which this Act is enacted [Oct. 1972]."

Termination of Special $50 Payments Under Tax Reduction Act of 1975

Pub.L. 95–30, Title IV, § 406, May 23, 1977, 91 Stat. 156, provided that: "Notwithstanding the provisions of section 702(a) of the Tax Reduction Act of 1975 [see Pub.L. 94–12, § 702, set out as a note under this section], no payment shall, after the date of the enactment of this Act [May 23, 1977], be made under that section".

Treatment of Employees Whose Federal Employment Terminated After Making Election Into Social Security Coverage But Before Effective Date of Election

Section 8014(b) of Pub.L. 100–647 provided that: "Subsections (b)(4)(A)(i), (c)(2)(A)(i), (e)(7)(A)(i), (f)(2)(A)(i), and (g)(4)(A)(i) of section 202 of the Social Security Act (42 U.S.C. 402 (b)(4)(A)(i), (c)(2)(A)(i), (e)(7)(A)(i), (f)(2)(A)(i), (g)(4)(A)(i)) [subsecs. (b)(4)(A)(i), (c)(2)(A)(i), (e)(7)(A)(i), (f)(2)(A)(i), and (g)(4)(A)(i) of this section] shall not apply with respect to monthly periodic benefits of any individual based solely on service which was performed while in the service of the Federal Government if—

"(1) such person made, before January 1, 1988, an election pursuant to law to become subject to the Federal Employees' Retirement System provided in chapter 84 of title 5, United States Code [5 U.S.C.A. § 8401 et seq.], or the Foreign Service Pension System provided in subchapter II of chapter 8 of title I of the Foreign Service Act of 1980 [22 U.S.C.A. § 4071 et seq.] (or such person made such an election on or after January 1, 1988, and before July 1, 1988, pursuant to regulations of the Office of Personnel Management relating to belated elections and correction of administrative errors (5 CFR 846.204) as in effect on the date of the enactment of this Act [Nov. 10, 1988]), and

"(2) such service terminated before the date on which such election became effective."

EXECUTIVE ORDERS

EXECUTIVE ORDER NO. 12436

July 29, 1983, 48 F.R. 34931

PAYMENT OF CERTAIN BENEFITS TO SURVIVORS OF PERSONS WHO DIED IN OR AS A RESULT OF MILITARY SERVICE

By the authority vested in me as President by the Constitution and laws of the United States of America, including § 156 of Public Law 97–377 (96 Stat. 1920; 42 U.S.C. 402 note) [set out as a note under this section], in order to provide certain benefits to the surviving spouses and children of certain persons who died in or as a result of military service, it is hereby ordered as follows:

Section 1. The Administrator of Veterans' Affairs is designated to administer the provisions of § 156 of Public Law 97–377 [set out as a note under this section].

Sec. 2. The Secretary of Health and Human Services [Commissioner of Social Security] shall provide to the Administrator of Veterans' affairs such information and such technical assistance as the Administrator may reasonably require to discharge his responsibilities under § 156. The Administrator of Veterans' Affairs shall reimburse the Department of Health and Human Services for all expenses it incurs in providing such information and technical assistance to the Veterans' Administration. Such expenses shall be paid from the Veterans' Administration account described in § 3 of this Order.

Sec. 3. During fiscal year 1983 and each succeeding fiscal year, the Secretary of Defense shall transfer, from time to time, from the "Retired Pay, Defense" account of the Department of Defense to an account established in the Veterans' Administration, such amounts as the Administrator of Veterans' Affairs determines to be necessary to pay the benefits authorized by § 156 during fiscal year 1983 and each succeeding fiscal year, and the expenses incurred by the Veterans' Administration in paying such benefits during fiscal year 1983 and each succeeding fiscal year. Such transfers shall, to the extent feasible, be made in advance of the payment of benefits and expenses by the Veterans' Administration.

Sec. 4. This Order shall be effective as of January 1, 1983.

Ronald Reagan

[Reference to "Secretary of Health and Human Services" deemed reference to "Commissioner of Social Security", effective Mar. 31, 1995, pursuant to Pub.L. 103–296, Title I, §§ 107(a)(1), 110(a), Aug. 15, 1994, 108 Stat. 1477, 1490.]

§ 403. Reduction of insurance benefits

(a) Maximum benefits

(1) In the case of an individual whose primary insurance amount has been computed or recomputed under section 415(a)(1) or (4) of this title, or section 415(d) of this title, as in effect after December 1978, the total monthly benefits to which beneficiaries may be entitled under section 402 or 423 of this title for a month on the basis of the wages and self-employment income of such individual shall, except as provided by paragraphs (3) and (6) (but prior to any increases resulting from the application of paragraph (2)(A)(ii)(III) of section 415(i) of this title), be reduced as necessary so as not to exceed—

(A) 150 percent of such individual's primary insurance amount to the extent that it does not exceed the amount established with respect to this subparagraph by paragraph (2),

(B) 272 percent of such individual's primary insurance amount to the extent that it exceeds the amount established with respect to subparagraph (A) but does not exceed the amount established with respect to this subparagraph by paragraph (2),

(C) 134 percent of such individual's primary insurance amount to the extent that it exceeds the amount established with respect to subparagraph (B) but does not exceed the amount established with respect to this subparagraph by paragraph (2), and

(D) 175 percent of such individual's primary insurance amount to the extent that it exceeds the amount established with respect to subparagraph (C).

Any such amount that is not a multiple of $0.10 shall be decreased to the next lower multiple of $0.10.

(2)(A) For individuals who initially become eligible for old-age or disability insurance benefits, or who die (before becoming so eligible for such benefits), in the calendar year 1979, the amounts established with respect to subparagraphs (A), (B), and (C) of paragraph (1) shall be $230, $332, and $433, respectively.

(B) For individuals who initially become eligible for old-age or disability insurance benefits, or who die (before becoming so eligible for such benefits), in any calendar year after 1979, each of the amounts so established shall equal the product of the corresponding amount established for the calendar year 1979 by subparagraph (A) of this paragraph and the quotient obtained under subparagraph (B)(ii) of section 415(a)(1) of this title, with such product being rounded in the manner prescribed by section 415(a)(1)(B)(iii) of this title.

(C) In each calendar year after 1978 the Commissioner of Social Security shall publish in the Federal Register, on or before November 1, the formula which (except as provided in section 415(i)(2)(D) of this title) is to be applicable under this paragraph to individuals who become eligible for old-age or disability insurance benefits, or who die (before becoming eligible for such benefits), in the following calendar year.

(D) A year shall not be counted as the year of an individual's death or eligibility for purposes of this paragraph or paragraph (8) in any case where such individual was entitled to a disability insurance benefit for any of the 12 months immediately preceding the month of such death or eligibility (but there shall be counted instead the year of the individual's eligibility for the disability insurance benefits to which he was entitled during such 12 months).

(3)(A) When an individual who is entitled to benefits on the basis of the wages and self-employment income of any insured individual and to whom this subsection applies would (but for the provisions of section 402(k)(2)(A) of this title) be entitled to child's insurance benefits for a month on the basis of the wages and self-employment income of one or more other insured individuals, the total monthly benefits to which all beneficiaries are entitled on the basis of such wages and self-employment income shall not be reduced under this subsection to less than the smaller of—

(i) the sum of the maximum amounts of benefits payable on the basis of the wages and self-employment income of all such insured individuals, or

(ii) an amount **(I)** initially equal to the product of 1.75 and the primary insurance amount that would be computed under section 415(a)(1) of this title, for January of the year determined for purposes of this clause under the following two sentences, with respect to average indexed monthly earnings equal to one-twelfth of the contribution and benefit base determined for that year under section 430 of this title, and **(II)** thereafter increased in accordance with the provisions of section 415(i)(2)(A)(ii) of this title.

The year established for purposes of clause (ii) shall be 1983 or, if it occurs later with respect to any individual, the year in which occurred the month that the application of the reduction provisions contained in this subparagraph began with respect to benefits payable on the basis of the wages and self-employment income of the insured individual. If for any month subsequent to the first month for which clause (ii) applies (with respect to benefits payable on the basis of the wages and self-employment income of the insured individual) the reduction under this subparagraph ceases to apply, then the year determined under the preceding sentence shall be redetermined (for purposes of any subsequent application of this subparagraph with respect to benefits payable on the basis of such wages and self-employment income) as though this subparagraph had not been previously applicable.

(B) When two or more persons were entitled (without the application of section 402(j)(1) of this title and section 423(b) of this title) to monthly benefits under section 402 or 423 of this title for January 1971 or any prior month on the basis of the wages and self-employment income of such insured individual and the provisions of this subsection as in effect for any such month were applicable in determining the benefit amount of any persons on the basis of such wages and self-employment income, the total of benefits for any month after January 1971 shall not be reduced to less than the largest of—

(i) the amount determined under this subsection without regard to this subparagraph,

(ii) the largest amount which has been determined for any month under this subsection for persons entitled to monthly benefits on the basis of such insured individual's wages and self-employment income, or

(iii) if any persons are entitled to benefits on the basis of such wages and self-employment income for the month before the effective month (after September 1972) of a general benefit increase under this title (as defined in section 415(i)(3) of this title) or a benefit increase under the provisions of section 415(i) of this title, an amount equal to the sum of amounts derived by multiplying the benefit amount determined under this subchapter (excluding any part thereof determined under section 402(w) of this title) for the month before such effective month (including this subsection, but without the application of section 422(b) of this title, section 402(q) of this title, and subsections (b), (c), and (d) of this section), for each such person for such month, by a percentage equal to the percentage of the increase provided under such benefit increase (with any such increased amount which is not a multiple of $0.10 being rounded to the next lower multiple of $0.10);

but in any such case **(I)** subparagraph (A) of this paragraph shall not be applied to such total of benefits after the application of clause (ii) or (iii), and **(II)** if section 402(k)(2)(A) of this title was applicable in the case of any such benefits for a month, and ceases to apply for a month after such month, the provisions of clause (ii) or (iii) shall be applied, for and after the month in which section 402(k)(2)(A) of this title ceases to apply, as though subparagraph (A) of this paragraph had not been applicable to such total of benefits for the last month for which clause (ii) or (iii) was applicable.

(C) When any of such individuals is entitled to monthly benefits as a divorced spouse under section 402(b) or (c) of this title or as a surviving divorced spouse under section 402(e) or (f) of this title for any month, the benefit to which he or she is entitled on the basis of the wages and self-employment income of such insured individual for such month shall be determined without regard to this subsection, and the benefits of all other individuals who are entitled for such month to monthly benefits under section 402 of this title on the wages and self-employment income of such insured individual shall be determined as if no such divorced spouse or surviving divorced spouse were entitled to benefits for such month.

(D) In any case in which—

(i) two or more individuals are entitled to monthly benefits for the same month as a spouse under subsection (b) or (c) of section 402 of this title, or as a surviving spouse under subsection (e), (f), or (g) of section 402 of this title,

(ii) at least one of such individuals is entitled by reason of subparagraph (A)(ii) or (B) of section 416(h)(1) of this title, and

(iii) such entitlements are based on the wages and self-employment income of the same insured individual,

the benefit of the entitled individual whose entitlement is based on a valid marriage (as determined without regard to subparagraphs (A)(ii) and (B) of section 416(h)(1) of this title) to such insured individual shall, for such month and all months thereafter, be determined without regard to this subsection, and the benefits of all other individuals who are entitled, for such month or any month thereafter, to monthly benefits under section 402 of this title based on the wages and self-employment income of such insured individual shall be determined as if such entitled individual were not entitled to benefits for such month.

(4) In any case in which benefits are reduced pursuant to the provisions of this subsection, the reduction shall be made after any deductions under this section and after any deductions under section 422(b) of this title. Notwithstanding the preceding sentence, any reduction under this subsection in the case of an individual who is entitled to a benefit under subsection (b), (c), (d), (e), (f), (g), or (h) of section 402 of this title for any month on the basis of the same wages and self-employment income as another person—

(A) who also is entitled to a benefit under subsection (b), (c), (d), (e), (f), (g), or (h) of section 402 of this title for such month,

(B) who does not live in the same household as such individual, and

(C) whose benefit for such month is suspended (in whole or in part) pursuant to subsection (h)(3) of this section,

shall be made before the suspension under subsection (h)(3). Whenever a reduction is made under this subsection in the total of monthly benefits to which individuals are entitled for any month on the basis of the wages and self-employment income of an insured individual, each such benefit other than the old-age or disability insurance benefit shall be proportionately decreased.

(5) Notwithstanding any other provision of law, when—

(A) two or more persons are entitled to monthly benefits for a particular month on the basis of the wages and self-employment income of an insured individual and (for such particular month) the provisions of this subsection are applicable to such monthly benefits, and

(B) such individual's primary insurance amount is increased for the following month under any provision of this subchapter,

then the total of monthly benefits for all persons on the basis of such wages and self-employment income for such particular month, as determined under the provisions of this subsection, shall for purposes of determining the total monthly benefits for all persons on the basis of such wages and self-employment income for months subsequent to such particular month be considered to have been increased by the smallest amount that would have been required in order to assure that the total of monthly benefits payable on the basis of such wages and self-employment income for any such subsequent month will not be less (after the application of the other provisions of this subsection and section 402(q) of this title) than the total of monthly benefits (after the application of the other provisions of this subsection and section 402(q) of this title) payable on the basis of such wages and self-employment income for such particular month.

(6) Notwithstanding any of the preceding provisions of this subsection other than paragraphs (3)(A), (3)(C), (3)(D), (4), and (5) (but subject to section 415(i)(2)(A)(ii) of this title), the total monthly benefits to which beneficiaries may be entitled under sections 402 and 423 of this title for any month on the basis of the wages and self-employment income of an individual entitled to disability insurance benefits shall be reduced (before the application of section 424a of this title) to the smaller of—

(A) 85 percent of such individual's average indexed monthly earnings (or 100 percent of his primary insurance amount, if larger), or

(B) 150 percent of such individual's primary insurance amount.

(7) In the case of any individual who is entitled for any month to benefits based upon the primary insurance amounts of two or more insured individuals, one or more of which primary insurance amounts were determined under section 415(a) or (d) of this title as in effect (without regard to the table contained therein) prior to January 1979 and one or more of which primary insurance amounts were determined under section 415(a)(1) or (4) of this title, or section 415(d) of this title, as in effect after December 1978, the total benefits payable to that individual and all other individuals entitled to benefits for that month based upon those primary insurance amounts shall be reduced to an amount equal to the amount determined in accordance with the provisions of paragraph (3)(A)(ii) of this subsection, except that for this purpose the references to subparagraph (A) in the last two sentences of paragraph (3)(A) shall be deemed to be references to paragraph (7).

(8) Subject to paragraph (7) and except as otherwise provided in paragraph (10)(C), this subsection as in effect in December 1978 shall remain in effect with respect to a primary insurance amount computed under section 415(a) or (d) of this title, as in effect (without regard to the table contained therein) in December 1978 and as amended by section 5117 of the Omnibus Budget Reconciliation Act of 1990, except that a primary insurance amount so computed with respect to an individual who first becomes eligible for an old-age or disability insurance benefit, or dies (before becoming eligible for such a benefit), after December 1978, shall instead be governed by this section as in effect after December 1978. For purposes of the preceding sentence, the phrase "rounded to the next higher multiple of $0.10", as it appeared in subsection (a)(2)(C) of this section as in effect in December 1978, shall be deemed to read "rounded to the next lower multiple of $0.10".

(9) When—

(A) one or more persons were entitled (without the application of section 402(j)(1) of this title) to monthly benefits under section 402 of this title for May 1978 on the basis of the wages and self-employment income of an individual,

(B) the benefit of at least one such person for June 1978 is increased by reason of the amendments made by section 204 of the Social Security Amendments of 1977; and

(C) the total amount of benefits to which all such persons are entitled under such section 402 of this title are reduced under the provisions of this subsection (or would be so reduced except for the first sentence of subsection (a)(4)),

then the amount of the benefit to which each such person is entitled for months after May 1978 shall be increased (after such reductions are made under this subsection) to the amount such benefits would have been if the benefit of the person or persons referred to in subparagraph (B) had not been so increased.

(10)(A) Subject to subparagraphs (B) and (C)—

(i) the total monthly benefits to which beneficiaries may be entitled under sections 402 and 423 of this title for a month on the basis of the wages and self-employment income of an individual whose primary insurance amount is computed under section 415(a)(2)(B)(i) of this title shall equal the total monthly benefits which were authorized by this section with respect to such individual's primary insurance amount for the last month of his prior entitlement to disability insurance benefits, increased for this purpose by the general benefit increases and other increases under section 415(i) of this title that would have applied to such total monthly benefits had the individual remained entitled to disability insurance benefits until the month in which he became entitled to old-age insurance benefits or reentitled to disability insurance benefits or died, and

(ii) the total monthly benefits to which beneficiaries may be entitled under sections 402 and 423 of this title for a month on the basis of the wages and self-employment income of an individual whose primary insurance amount is computed under section 415(a)(2)(C) of this title shall equal the total monthly benefits which were authorized by this section with respect to such individual's primary insurance amount for the last month of his prior entitlement to disability insurance benefits.

(B) In any case in which—

(i) the total monthly benefits with respect to such individual's primary insurance amount for the last month of his prior entitlement to disability insurance benefits was computed under paragraph (6), and

(ii) the individual's primary insurance amount is computed under subparagraph (B)(i) or (C) of section 415(a)(2) of this title by reason of the individual's entitlement to old-age insurance benefits or death,

the total monthly benefits shall equal the total monthly benefits that would have been authorized with respect to the primary insurance amount for the last month of his prior entitlement to disability insurance benefits if such total monthly benefits had been computed without regard to paragraph (6).

(C) This paragraph shall apply before the application of paragraph (3)(A), and before the application of subsection (a)(1) of this section as in effect in December 1978.

(b) Deductions on account of work

(1) Deductions, in such amounts and at such time or times as the Commissioner of Social Security shall determine, shall be made from any payment or payments under this subchapter to which an individual is entitled, and from any payment or payments to which any other persons are entitled on the basis of such individual's wages and self-employment income, until the total of such deductions equals—

(A) such individual's benefit or benefits under section 402 of this title for any month, and

(B) if such individual was entitled to old-age insurance benefits under section 402(a) of this title for such month, the benefit or benefits of all other persons for such month under section 402 of this title based on such individual's wages and self-employment income,

if for such month he is charged with excess earnings, under the provisions of subsection (f) of this section, equal to the total of benefits referred to in clauses (A) and (B). If the excess earnings so charged are less than such total of benefits, such deductions with respect to such month shall be equal only to the amount of such excess earnings. If a child who has attained the age of 18 and is entitled to child's insurance benefits, or a person who is entitled to mother's or father's insurance benefits, is married to an individual entitled to old-age insurance benefits under section 402(a) of this title, such child or such person, as the case may be, shall, for the purposes of this subsection and subsection (f), be deemed to be entitled to such benefits on the basis of the wages and self-employment income of such individual entitled to old-age insurance benefits. If a deduction has already been made under this subsection with respect to a person's benefit or benefits under section 402 of this title for a month, he shall be deemed entitled to payments under such section for such month for purposes of further deductions under this subsection, and for purposes of charging of each person's excess earnings under subsection (f), only to the extent of the total of his benefits remaining after such earlier deductions have been made. For purposes of this subsection and subsection (f)—

(i) an individual shall be deemed to be entitled to payments under section 402 of this title equal to the amount of the benefit or benefits to which he is entitled under such section after the application of subsection (a) of this section, but without the application of the first sentence of paragraph (4) thereof; and

(ii) if a deduction is made with respect to an individual's benefit or benefits under section 402 of this title because of the occurrence in any month of an event specified in subsection (c) or (d) of this section or in section 422(b) of this title, such individual shall not be considered to be entitled to any benefits under such section 402 for such month.

(2)(A) Except as provided in subparagraph (B), in any case in which—

(i) any of the other persons referred to in paragraph (1)(B) is entitled to monthly benefits as a divorced spouse under section 402(b) or (c) of this title for any month, and

(ii) such person has been divorced for not less than 2 years,

the benefit to which he or she is entitled on the basis of the wages and self-employment income of the individual referred to in paragraph (1) for such month shall be determined without regard to deductions under this subsection as a result of excess earnings of such individual, and the benefits of all other individuals who are entitled for such month to monthly benefits under section 402 of this title on the basis of the wages and self-employment income of such individual referred to in paragraph (1) shall be determined as if no such divorced spouse were entitled to benefits for such month.

(B) Clause (ii) of subparagraph (A) shall not apply with respect to any divorced spouse in any case in which the individual referred to in paragraph (1) became entitled to old-age insurance benefits under section 402(a) of this title before the date of the divorce.

(c) Deductions on account of noncovered work outside United States or failure to have child in care

Deductions, in such amounts and at such time or times as the Commissioner of Social Security shall determine, shall be made from any payment or payments under this subchapter to which an individual is entitled, until the total of such deductions equals such individual's benefits or benefit under section 402 of this title for any month—

(1) in which such individual is under retirement age (as defined in section 416(*l*) of this title) and for more than forty-five hours of which such individual engaged in noncovered remunerative activity outside the United States;

(2) in which such individual, if a wife or husband under retirement age (as defined in section 416(*l*) of this title) entitled to a wife's or husband's insurance benefit, did not have in his or her care (individually or jointly with his or her spouse) a child of such spouse entitled to a child's insurance benefit and such wife's or husband's insurance benefit for such month was not reduced under the provisions of section 402(q) of this title;

(3) in which such individual, if a widow or widower entitled to a mother's or father's insurance benefit, did not have in his or her care a child of his or her deceased spouse entitled to a child's insurance benefit; or

(4) in which such an individual, if a surviving divorced mother or father entitled to a mother's or father's insurance benefit, did not have in his or her care a child of his or her deceased former spouse who (A) is his or her son, daughter, or legally adopted child and (B) is entitled to a child's insurance benefit on the basis of the wages and self-employment income of such deceased former spouse.

For purposes of paragraphs (2), (3), and (4) of this subsection, a child shall not be considered to be entitled to a child's insurance benefit for any month in which paragraph (1) of section 402(s) of this title applies or an event specified in section 422(b) of this title occurs with respect to such child. Subject to paragraph (3) of such section 402(s) of this title, no deduction shall be made under this subsection from any child's insurance benefit for the month in which the child entitled to such benefit attained the age of eighteen or any subsequent month; nor shall any deduction be made under this subsection from any widow's or widower's insurance benefit if the widow, surviving divorced wife, widower, or surviving divorced husband involved became entitled to such benefit prior to attaining age 60.

(d) Deductions from dependents' benefits on account of noncovered work outside United States by old-age insurance beneficiary

(1)(A) Deductions shall be made from any wife's, husband's, or child's insurance benefit, based on the wages and self-employment income of an individual entitled to old-age insurance benefits, to which a wife, divorced wife, husband, divorced husband, or child is entitled, until the total of such deductions equals such wife's, husband's, or child's insurance benefit or benefits under section 402 of this title for any month in which such individual is under retirement age (as defined in section 416(*l*) of this title) and for more than forty-five hours of which such individual engaged in noncovered remunerative activity outside the United States.

(B)(i) Except as provided in clause (ii), in any case in which—

(I) a divorced spouse is entitled to monthly benefits under section 402(b) or (c) of this title for any month, and

(II) such divorced spouse has been divorced for not less than 2 years,

the benefit to which he or she is entitled for such month on the basis of the wages and self-employment income of the individual entitled to old-age insurance benefits referred to in subparagraph (A) shall be determined without regard to deductions under this paragraph as a result of excess earnings of such individual, and the benefits of all other individuals who are entitled for such month to monthly benefits under section 402 of this title on the basis of the wages and self-employment income of such individual referred to in subparagraph (A) shall be determined as if no such divorced spouse were entitled to benefits for such month.

(ii) Subclause (II) of clause (i) shall not apply with respect to any divorced spouse in any case in which the individual entitled to old-age insurance benefits referred to in subparagraph (A) became entitled to such benefits before the date of the divorce.

(2) Deductions shall be made from any child's insurance benefit to which a child who has attained the age of eighteen is entitled, or from any mother's or father's insurance benefit to which a person is entitled, until the total of such deductions equals such child's insurance benefit or benefits or mother's or father's insurance benefit or benefits under section 402 of this title for any month in which such child or person entitled to mother's or father's insurance benefits is married to an individual under retirement age (as defined in section 416(*l*) of this title) who is entitled to old-age insurance benefits and for more than forty-five hours of which such individual engaged in noncovered remunerative activity outside the United States.

(e) Occurrence of more than one event

If more than one of the events specified in subsections (c) and (d) and section 422(b) of this title occurs in any one month which would occasion deductions equal to a benefit for such month, only an amount equal to such benefit shall be deducted.

(f) Months to which earnings are charged

For purposes of subsection (b)—

(1) The amount of an individual's excess earnings (as defined in paragraph (3)) shall be charged to months as follows: There shall be charged to the first month of such taxable year an amount of his excess earnings equal to the sum of the payments to which he and all other persons (excluding divorced spouses referred to in subsection (b)(2)) are entitled for such month under section 402 of this title on the basis of his wages and self-employment income (or the total of his excess earnings if such excess earnings are less than such sum), and the balance, if any, of such excess earnings shall be charged to each succeeding month in such year to the extent, in the case of each such month, of the sum of the payments to which such individual and all such other persons are entitled for such month under section 402 of this title on the basis of his wages and self-employment income, until the total of such excess has been so charged. Where an individual is entitled to benefits under section 402(a) of this title and other persons (excluding divorced spouses referred to in subsection (b)(2)) are entitled to benefits under section 402(b), (c), or (d) of this title on the basis of the wages and self-employment income of such individual, the excess earnings of such individual for any taxable year shall be charged in accordance with the provisions of this subsection before the excess earnings of such persons for a taxable year are charged to months in such individual's taxable year. Notwithstanding the preceding provisions of this paragraph but subject to section 402(s) of this title, no part of the excess earnings of an individual shall be charged to any month (A) for which such individual was not entitled to a benefit under this subchapter, (B) in which such individual was at or above retirement age (as defined in section 416(*l*) of this title), (C) in which such individual, if a child entitled to child's insurance benefits, has attained the age of 18, (D) for which such individual is entitled to widow's or widower's insurance benefits if such individual became so entitled prior to attaining age 60, (E) in which such individual did not engage in self-employment and did not render services for wages (determined as provided in paragraph (5) of this subsection) of more than the applicable exempt amount as determined under paragraph (8), if such month is in the taxable year in which occurs the first month after December 1977 that is both (i) a month for which the individual is entitled to benefits under subsection (a), (b), (c), (d), (e), (f), (g), or (h) of section 402 of this title (without having been entitled for the preceding month to a benefit under any other of such subsections), and (ii) a month in which the individual did not engage in self-employment and did not render services for wages (determined as provided in paragraph (5)) of more than the applicable exempt amount as determined under paragraph (8), or (F) in which such individual did not engage in self-employment and did not render services for wages (determined as provided in paragraph (5) of this subsection) of more than the applicable exempt amount as determined under paragraph (8), in the case of an individual entitled to benefits under section 402(b) or (c) of this title (but only by reason of having a child in his or her care within the meaning of paragraph (1)(B) of subsection (b) or (c), as may be applicable) or under section 402(d) or (g) of this title, if such month is in a year in which such entitlement ends for a reason other than the death of such individual, and such individual is not entitled to any benefits under this subchapter for the month following the month during which such entitlement under section 402(b), (d), or (g) of this title ended.

(2) As used in paragraph (1), the term "first month of such taxable year" means the earliest month in such year to which the charging of excess earnings described in such paragraph is not prohibited by the application of clauses (A), (B), (C), (D), (E), and (F) thereof.

(3) For purposes of paragraph (1) and subsection (h), an individual's excess earnings for a taxable year shall be 33⅓ percent of his earnings for such year in excess of the product of the applicable exempt amount as determined under paragraph (8) in the case of an individual who has attained (or, but for the individual's death, would have attained) retirement age (as defined in section 416(*l*) of this title) before the close of such taxable year, or 50 percent of his earnings for such year in excess of such product in the case of any other individual, multiplied by the number of months in such year, except that, in determining an individual's excess earnings for the taxable year in which he attains retirement age (as defined in section 416(*l*) of this title), there shall be excluded any earnings of such individual for the month in which he attains such age and any subsequent month (with any net earnings or net loss from self-employment in such year being prorated in an equitable manner under regulations of the Commissioner of Social Security). For purposes of the preceding sentence, notwithstanding section 411(e) of this title, the number of months in the taxable year in which an individual dies shall be 12. The excess earnings as derived under the first sentence of this paragraph, if not a multiple of $1, shall be reduced to the next lower multiple of $1.

(4) For purposes of clause (E) of paragraph (1)—

(A) An individual will be presumed, with respect to any month, to have been engaged in self-employment in such month until it is shown to the satisfaction of the Commissioner of Social Security that such individual rendered no substantial services in such month with respect to any trade or business the net income or loss of which is includible in computing (as provided in paragraph (5) of this subsection) his net earnings or net loss from self-employment for any taxable year. The Commissioner of Social Security shall by regulations prescribe the methods and criteria for determining whether or not an individual has rendered substantial services with respect to any trade or business.

(B) An individual will be presumed, with respect to any month, to have rendered services for wages (determined as provided in paragraph (5) of this subsection) of more than the applicable exempt amount as determined under paragraph (8) until it is shown to the satisfaction of the Commissioner of Social Security that such individual did not render such services in such month for more than such amount.

(5)(A) An individual's earnings for a taxable year shall be (i) the sum of his wages for services rendered in such year and his net earnings from self-employment for such year, minus (ii) any net loss from self-employment for such year.

(B) For purposes of this section—

(i) an individual's net earnings from self-employment for any taxable year shall be determined as provided in section 411 of this title, except that paragraphs (1), (4), and (5) of section 411(c) of this title shall not apply and the gross income shall be computed by excluding the amounts provided by subparagraph (D) of this paragraph, and

(ii) an individual's net loss from self-employment for any taxable year is the excess of the deductions (plus his distributive share of loss described in section 702(a)(8) of the Internal Revenue Code of 1986) taken into account under clause (i) over the gross income (plus his distributive share of income so described) taken into account under clause (i).

(C) For purposes of this subsection, an individual's wages shall be computed without regard to the limitations as to amounts of remuneration specified in paragraphs (1), (6)(B), (6)(C), (7)(B), and (8) of section 409(a) of this title; and in making such computation services which do not constitute employment as defined in section 410 of this title, performed within the United States by the individual as an employee or performed outside the United States in the active military or naval service of the United States, shall be deemed to be employment as so defined if the remuneration for such services is not includible in computing his net earnings or net loss from self-employment. The term "wages" does not include—

(i) the amount of any payment made to, or on behalf of, an employee or any of his dependents (including any amount paid by an employer for insurance or annuities, or into a fund, to provide for any such payment) on account of retirement, or

(ii) any payment or series of payments by an employer to an employee or any of his dependents upon or after the termination of the employee's employment relationship because of retirement after attaining an age specified in a plan referred to in section 409(a)(11)(B) of this title or in a pension plan of the employer.

(D) In the case of—

(i) an individual who has attained retirement age (as defined in section 416(*l*) of this title) on or before the last day of the taxable year, and who shows to the satisfaction of the Commissioner of Social Security that he or she is receiving royalties attributable to a copyright or patent obtained before the taxable year in which he or she attained such age and that the property to which the copyright or patent relates was created by his or her own personal efforts, or

(ii) an individual who has become entitled to insurance benefits under this subchapter, other than benefits under section 423 of this title or benefits payable under section 402(d) of this title by reason of being under a disability, and who shows to the satisfaction of the Commissioner of Social Security that he or she is receiving, in a year after his or her initial year of entitlement to such benefits, any other income not attributable to services performed after the month in which he or she initially became entitled to such benefits,

there shall be excluded from gross income any such royalties or other income.

(E) For purposes of this section, any individual's net earnings from self-employment which result from or are attributable to the performance of services by such individual as a director of a corporation during any taxable year shall be deemed to have been derived (and received) by such individual in that year, at the time the services were performed, regardless of when the income, on which the computation of such net earnings from self-employment is based, is actually paid to or received by such individual (unless such income was actually paid and received prior to that year).

(6) For purposes of this subsection, wages (determined as provided in paragraph (5)(C)) which, according to reports received by the Commissioner of Social Security, are paid to an individual during a taxable year shall be presumed to have been paid to him for services performed in such year until it is shown to the satisfaction of the Commissioner of Social Security that they were paid for services performed in another taxable year. If such reports with respect to an individual show his wages for a calendar year, such individual's taxable year shall be presumed to be a calendar year for purposes of this subsection until it is shown to the satisfaction of the Commissioner of Social Security that his taxable year is not a calendar year.

(7) Where an individual's excess earnings are charged to a month and the excess earnings so charged are less than the total of the payments (without regard to such charging) to which all persons (excluding divorced spouses referred to in subsection (b)(2)) are entitled under section 402 of this title for such month on the basis of his wages and self-employment income, the difference between such total and the excess so charged to such month shall be paid (if it is otherwise payable under this subchapter) to such individual and other persons in the proportion that the benefit to which each of them is entitled (without regard to such charging, without the application of section 402(k)(3) of this title, and prior to the application of section 403(a) of this title) bears to the total of the benefits to which all of them are entitled.

(8)(A) Whenever the Commissioner of Social Security pursuant to section 415(i) of this title increases benefits effective with the month of December following a cost-of-living computation quarter [1] the Commissioner shall also determine and publish in the Federal Register on or before November 1 of the calendar year in which such quarter occurs the new exempt amounts (separately stated for individuals described in subparagraph (D) and for other individuals) which are to be applicable (unless prevented from becoming effective by subparagraph (C)) with respect to taxable years ending in (or with the close of) the calendar year after the calendar year in which such benefit increase is effective (or, in the case of an individual who dies during the calendar year after the calendar year in which the benefit increase is effective, with respect to such individual's taxable year which ends, upon his death, during such year).

(B) Except as otherwise provided in subparagraph (D), the exempt amount which is applicable to individuals described in such subparagraph and the exempt amount which is applicable to other individuals, for each month of a particular taxable year, shall each be whichever of the following is the larger—

(i) the corresponding exempt amount which is in effect with respect to months in the taxable year in which the determination under subparagraph (A) is made, or

(ii) the product of the corresponding exempt amount which is in effect with respect to months in the taxable year ending after 2001 and before 2003 (with respect to individuals described in subparagraph (D)) or the taxable year ending after 1993 and before 1995 (with respect to other individuals), and the ratio of—

(I) the national average wage index (as defined in section 409(k)(1) of this title) for the calendar year before the calendar year in which the determination under subparagraph (A) is made, to

(II) the national average wage index (as so defined) for 2000 (with respect to individuals described in subparagraph (D)) or 1992 (with respect to other individuals),

with such product, if not a multiple of $10, being rounded to the next higher multiple of $10 where such product is a multiple of $5 but not of $10 and to the nearest multiple of $10 in any other case.

Whenever the Commissioner of Social Security determines that an exempt amount is to be increased in any year under this paragraph, the Commissioner shall notify the House Committee on Ways and Means and the Senate Committee on Finance within 30 days after the close of the base quarter (as defined in section 415(i)(1)(A) of this title) in such year of the estimated amount of such increase, indicating the new exempt amount, the actuarial estimates of the effect of the increase, and the actuarial assumptions and methodology used in preparing such estimates.

(C) Notwithstanding the determination of a new exempt amount by the Commissioner of Social Security under subparagraph (A) (and notwithstanding any publication thereof under such subparagraph or any notification thereof under the last sentence of subparagraph (B)), such new exempt amount shall not take effect pursuant thereto if during the calendar year in which such determination is made a law increasing the exempt amount is enacted.

(D) Notwithstanding any other provision of this subsection, the exempt amount which is applicable to an individual who has attained retirement age (as defined in section 416(*l*) of this title) before the close of the taxable year involved shall be—

(i) for each month of any taxable year ending after 1995 and before 1997, $1,041.66⅔,

(ii) for each month of any taxable year ending after 1996 and before 1998, $1,125.00,

(iii) for each month of any taxable year ending after 1997 and before 1999, $1,208.33⅓,

(iv) for each month of any taxable year ending after 1998 and before 2000, $1,291.66⅔,

(v) for each month of any taxable year ending after 1999 and before 2001, $1,416.66⅔,

(vi) for each month of any taxable year ending after 2000 and before 2002, $2,083.33⅓, and

(vii) for each month of any taxable year ending after 2001 and before 2003, $2,500.00.

(E) Notwithstanding subparagraph (D), no deductions in benefits shall be made under subsection (b) with respect to the earnings of any individual in any month beginning with the month in which the individual attains retirement age (as defined in section 416(*l*) of this title).

(9) For purposes of paragraphs (3), (5)(D)(i), (8)(D), and (8)(E), the term "retirement age (as defined in section 416(*l*) of this title)", with respect to any individual entitled to monthly insurance benefits under section 402 of this title, means the retirement age (as so defined) which is applicable in the case of old-age insurance benefits, regardless of whether or not the particular benefits to which the individual is entitled (or the only such benefits) are old-age insurance benefits.

(g) Penalty for failure to report certain events

Any individual in receipt of benefits subject to deduction under subsection (c), (or who is in receipt of such benefits on behalf of another individual), because of the occurrence of an event specified therein, who fails to report such occurrence to the Commissioner of Social Security prior to the receipt and acceptance of an insurance benefit for the second month following the month in which such event occurred, shall suffer deductions in addition to those imposed under subsection (c) as follows:

(1) if such failure is the first one with respect to which an additional deduction is imposed by this subsection, such additional deduction shall be equal to his benefit or benefits for the first month of the period for which there is a failure to report even though such failure is with respect to more than one month;

(2) if such failure is the second one with respect to which an additional deduction is imposed by this subsection, such additional deduction shall be equal to two times his benefit or benefits for the first month of the period for which there is a failure to report even though such failure is with respect to more than two months; and

(3) if such failure is the third or a subsequent one for which an additional deduction is imposed under this subsection, such additional deduction shall be equal to three times his benefit or benefits for the first month of the period for which there is a failure to report even though the failure to report is with respect to more than three months;

except that the number of additional deductions required by this subsection shall not exceed the number of months in the period for which there is a failure to report. As used in this subsection, the term "period for which there is a failure to report" with respect to any individual means the period for which such individual received and accepted insurance benefits under section 402 of this title without making a timely report and for which deductions are required under subsection (c).

(h) Report of earnings to Commissioner

(1)(A) If an individual is entitled to any monthly insurance benefit under section 402 of this title during any taxable year in which he has earnings or wages, as computed pursuant to paragraph (5) of subsection (f), in excess of the product of the applicable exempt amount as determined under subsection (f)(8) times the number of months in such year, such individual (or the individual who is in receipt of such benefit on his behalf) shall make a report to the Commissioner of Social Security of his earnings (or wages) for such taxable year. Such report shall be made on or before the fifteenth day of the fourth month following the close of such year, and shall contain such information and be made in such manner as the Commissioner of Social Security may by regulations prescribe. Such report need not be made for any taxable year—

(i) beginning with or after the month in which such individual attained retirement age (as defined in section 416(*l*) of this title), or

(ii) if benefit payments for all months (in such taxable year) in which such individual is under retirement age (as defined in section 416(*l*) of this title) have been suspended under the provisions of the first sentence of paragraph (3) of this subsection, unless—

(I) such individual is entitled to benefits under subsection (b), (c), (d), (e), (f), (g), or (h) of section 402 of this title,

(II) such benefits are reduced under subsection (a) of this section for any month in such taxable year, and

(III) in any such month there is another person who also is entitled to benefits under subsection (b), (c), (d), (e), (f), (g), or (h) of section 402 of this title on the basis of the same wages and self-employment income and who does not live in the same household as such individual.

The Commissioner of Social Security may grant a reasonable extension of time for making the report of earnings required in this paragraph if the Commissioner finds that there is valid reason for a delay, but in no case may the period be extended more than four months.

(B) If the benefit payments of an individual have been suspended for all months in any taxable year under the provisions of the first sentence of paragraph (3) of this subsection, no benefit payment shall be made to such individual for any such month in such taxable year after the expiration of the period of three years, three months, and fifteen days following the close of such taxable year unless within such period the individual, or some other person entitled to benefits under this subchapter on the basis of the same wages and self-employment income, files with the Commissioner of Social Security information showing that a benefit for such month is payable to such individual.

(2) If an individual fails to make a report required under paragraph (1) of this subsection, within the time prescribed by or in accordance with such paragraph, for any taxable year and any deduction is imposed under subsection (b) by reason of his earnings for such year, he shall suffer additional deductions as follows:

(A) if such failure is the first one with respect to which an additional deduction is imposed under this paragraph, such additional deduction shall be equal to his benefit or benefits for the last month of such year for which he was entitled to a benefit under section 402 of this title, except that if the deduction imposed under subsection (b) by reason of his earnings for such year is less than the amount of his benefit (or benefits) for the last month of such year for which he was entitled to a benefit under section 402 of this title, the additional deduction shall be equal to the amount of the deduction imposed under subsection (b) but not less than $10;

(B) if such failure is the second one for which an additional deduction is imposed under this paragraph, such additional deduction shall be equal to two times his benefit or benefits for the last month of such year for which he was entitled to a benefit under section 402 of this title;

(C) if such failure is the third or a subsequent one for which an additional deduction is imposed under this paragraph, such additional deduction shall be equal to three times his benefit or benefits for the last month of such year for which he was entitled to a benefit under section 402 of this title;

except that the number of the additional deductions required by this paragraph with respect to a failure to report earnings for a taxable year shall not exceed the number of months in such year for which such individual received and accepted insurance benefits under section 402 of this title and for which deductions are imposed under subsection (b) by reason of his earnings. In determining whether a failure to report earnings is the first or a subsequent failure for any individual, all taxable years ending prior to the imposition of the first additional deduction under this paragraph, other than the latest one of such years, shall be disregarded.

(3) If the Commissioner of Social Security determines, on the basis of information obtained by or submitted to the Commissioner, that it may reasonably be expected that an individual entitled to benefits under section 402 of this title for any taxable year will suffer deductions imposed under subsection (b) by reason of his earnings for such year, the Commissioner of Social Security may, before the close of such taxable year, suspend the total or less than the total payment for each month in such year (or for only such months as the Commissioner of Social Security may specify) of the benefits payable on the basis of such individual's wages and self-employment income; and such suspension shall remain in effect with respect to the benefits for any month until the Commissioner of Social Security has determined whether or not any deduction is imposed for such month under subsection (b). The Commissioner of Social Security is authorized, before the close of the taxable year of an individual entitled to benefits during such year, to request of such individual that he make, at such time or times as the Commissioner of Social Security may specify, a declaration of his estimated earnings for the taxable year and that he furnish to the Commissioner of Social Security such other information with respect to such earnings as the Commissioner of Social Security may specify. A failure by such individual to comply with any such request shall in itself constitute justification for a determination under this paragraph that it may reasonably be expected that the individual will suffer deductions imposed under subsection (b) by reason of his earnings for such year. If, after the close of a taxable year of an individual entitled to benefits under section 402 of this title for such year, the Commissioner of Social Security requests such individual to furnish a report of his earnings (as computed pursuant to paragraph (5) of subsection (f)) for such taxable year or any other information with respect to such earnings which the Commissioner of Social Security may specify, and the individual fails to comply with such request, such failure shall in itself constitute justification for a determination that such individual's benefits are subject to deductions under subsection (b) for each month in such taxable year (or only for such months thereof as the Commissioner of Social Security may specify) by reason of his earnings for such year.

(4) The Commissioner of Social Security shall develop and implement procedures in accordance with this subsection to avoid paying more than the correct amount of benefits to any individual under this subchapter as a result of such individual's failure to file a correct report or estimate of earnings or wages. Such procedures may include identifying categories of individuals who are likely to be paid more than the correct amount of benefits and requesting that they estimate their earnings or wages more frequently than other persons subject to deductions under this section on account of earnings or wages.

(i) Repealed. Pub.L. 103–296, Title III, § 309(a), Aug. 15, 1994, 108 Stat. 1523

(j) Attainment of retirement age

For the purposes of this section, an individual shall be considered as having attained retirement age (as defined in section 416(l) of this title) during the entire month in which he attains such age.

(k) Noncovered remunerative activity outside United States

An individual shall be considered to be engaged in noncovered remunerative activity outside the United States if he performs services outside the United States as an employee and such services do not constitute employment as defined in section 410 of this title and are not performed in the active military or naval service of the United States, or if he carries on a trade or business outside the United States (other than the performance of service as an employee) the net income or loss of which (1) is not includible in computing his net earnings from self-employment for a taxable year and (2) would not be excluded from net earnings from self-employment, if carried on in the United States, by any of the numbered paragraphs of section 411(a) of this title. When used in the preceding sentence with respect to a trade or business (other than the performance of service as an employee), the term "United States" does not include the Commonwealth of Puerto Rico, the Virgin Islands, Guam, or American Samoa in the case of an alien who is not a resident of the United States (including the Commonwealth of Puerto Rico, the Virgin Islands, Guam, and American Samoa); and the term "trade or business" shall have the same meaning as when used in section 162 of the Internal Revenue Code of 1986.

(*l*) Good cause for failure to make reports required

The failure of an individual to make any report required by subsection (g) or (h)(1)(A) within the time prescribed therein shall not be regarded as such a failure if it is shown to the satisfaction of the Commissioner of Social Security that he had good cause for failing to make such report within such time. The determination of what constitutes good cause for purposes of this subsection shall be made in accordance with regulations of the Commissioner of Social Security, except that in making any such determination, the Commissioner of Social Security shall specifically take into account any physical, mental, educational, or linguistic limitation such individual may have (including any lack of facility with the English language).

(Aug. 14, 1935, c. 531, Title II, § 203, 49 Stat. 623; Aug. 10, 1939, c. 666, Title II, § 201, 53 Stat. 1362; Aug. 10, 1946, c. 951, Title IV, § 406, 60 Stat. 988; Aug. 28, 1950, c. 809, Title I, §§ 102(a), 103(a), 64 Stat. 489; July 18, 1952, c. 945, §§ 2(b)(2), 4(a) to (d), 66 Stat. 768, 773; Sept. 1, 1954, c. 1206, Title I, §§ 102(e)(7), 103(a) to (h), (i)(3), 112(a), 68 Stat. 1070, 1073 to 1078, 1085; Aug. 1, 1956, c. 836, Title I, §§ 101(d) to (g), 102(d)(11), 107(a), 112(a), (b), 70 Stat. 808, 814, 829, 831; Pub.L. 85–840, Title I, § 101(f), Title II, § 205(j), (k), Title III, §§ 307(f), 308(a) to (e), Aug. 28, 1958, 72 Stat. 1017, 1024, 1032, 1033; Pub.L. 86–778, Title I, § 103(b), Title II, §§ 209(a), 211(a) to (h), Title III, § 302(a), Sept. 13, 1960, 74 Stat. 936, 953 to 957, 960; Pub.L. 87–64, Title I, § 108(a), June 30, 1961, 75 Stat. 140; Pub.L. 89–97, Title III, §§ 301(c), 306(c)(10) to (12), 308(d)(6) to (8), 310(a), 325(a), July 30, 1965, 79 Stat. 363, 373, 378 to 380, 399; Pub.L. 90–248, Title I, §§ 101(b), 104(d)(1), 107(a), 160, 161(a), (b), 163(a)(1), Jan. 2, 1968, 81 Stat. 826, 832, 834, 870, 872; Pub.L. 91–172, Title X, § 1002(b)(1), Dec. 30, 1969, 83 Stat. 739; Pub.L. 92–5, Title II, § 201(b), Mar. 17, 1971, 85 Stat. 8; Pub.L. 92–336, Title II, §§ 201(b), (h)(1), 202(a)(2)(A), (B), July 1, 1972, 86 Stat. 410, 411, 415; Pub.L. 92–603, Title I, §§ 101(b), 102(c), 103(c), 105(a), (b), 106(a), 107(b)(1), (2), 144(a)(2), (3), Oct. 30, 1972, 86 Stat. 1334, 1336, 1340 to 1343, 1370; Pub.L. 93–66, Title II, § 202(a) to (c), July 9, 1973, 87 Stat. 153; Pub.L. 93–233, §§ 3(k), 18(a), Dec. 31, 1973, 87 Stat. 953, 967; Pub.L. 94–202, § 8(i), Jan. 2, 1976, 89 Stat. 1140; Pub.L. 95–216, Title II, §§ 202, 204(e), Title III, §§ 301(a), (b), (c)(1), (d), 302(a) to (d), 303(a), 353(a), Dec. 20, 1977, 91 Stat. 1524, 1528, 1530, 1531, 1552; Pub.L. 96–265, Title I, § 101(a) to (b)(2), June 9, 1980, 94 Stat. 442; Pub.L. 96–473, §§ 1(a), 3(a), 4(a), 6(b), Oct. 19, 1980, 94 Stat. 2263 to 2265; Pub.L. 97–35, Title XXII, §§ 2201(c)(6), 2206(b)(2) to (4), Aug. 13, 1981, 95 Stat. 831, 838; Pub.L. 97–123, § 2(f), Dec. 29, 1981, 95 Stat. 1661; Pub.L. 98–21, Title I, §§ 111(a)(4), 132(b), Title II, § 201(c)(1)(B), (2), Title III, §§ 306(i), 309(f) to (h), 324(c)(4), 331(a), (b), 347(a), Apr. 20, 1983, 97 Stat. 72, 94, 109, 114, 116, 117, 125, 128, 129, 138; Pub.L. 98–369, Div. B, Title VI, §§ 2602(a), 2661(g)(1)(A), (2)(A), 2262(c)(1), 2663(a)(3), July 18, 1984, 98 Stat. 1127, 1157, 1159, 1161; Pub.L. 99–272, Title XII, § 12108(a), Apr. 7, 1986, 100 Stat. 286; Pub.L. 100–647, Title VIII, § 8002(a), (b), Nov. 10, 1988, 102 Stat. 3779; Pub.L. 101–239, Title X, §§ 10208(b)(1)(A), (B), (d)(2)(A)(i), (ii), (vi), 10305(a), Dec. 19, 1989, 103 Stat. 2477, 2480, 2481, 2483; Pub.L. 101–508, Title V, §§ 5117(a)(3)(B), 5119(c), (d), 5123(a)(1), (2), 5127(a), (b), Nov. 5, 1990, 104 Stat. 1388–277, 1388–279, 1388–280, 1388–284, 1388–286; Pub.L. 103–296, Title I, § 107(a)(4), Title III, §§ 309(a) to (c), 310(a), (b), 314(a), 321(a)(6), (c)(6)(A), (g)(2), Aug. 15, 1994, 108 Stat. 1478, 1523, 1524, 1530, 1536, 1538, 1543; Pub.L. 104–121, Title I, § 102(a), (b)(1), Mar. 29, 1996, 110 Stat. 847, 848; Pub.L. 106–182, §§ 2 to 4(a), Apr. 7, 2000, 114 Stat. 198, 199.)

[1] So in original. Probably should be followed by a comma.

HISTORICAL AND STATUTORY NOTES

References in Text

Section 422(b) of this title, referred to in subsecs. (a)(3)(B)(iii), (4), (b)(1)(ii), (c), and (e), was repealed by Pub.L. 106–170, Title I, § 101(b)(1)(C), Dec. 17, 1999, 113 Stat. 1873.

Section 5117 of the Omnibus Budget Reconciliation Act of 1990, referred to in subsec. (a)(8), means section 5117 of Pub.L. 101–508, Nov. 5, 1990, 104 Stat. 1388–277, which in addition to amending this section, amended sections 413, 415 and 417 of this title. For complete classification of this Act to the Code, see Tables.

The amendments made by section 204 of the Social Security Amendments of 1977, referred to in subsec. (a)(9)(B), means the amendments made by section 204 of Pub.L. 95–216, which enacted subsec. (a)(8) of this section and amended section 402(e)(2)(A), (e)(2)(B)(i), (f)(3)(A), and (f)(3)(B)(i) of this title.

The Internal Revenue Code of 1986, referred to in subsecs. (f)(5)(B)(ii) and (k) is classified principally to Title 26.

Codifications

Section 201(c)(1) of Pub.L. 98–21, set out in the credit of this section, was amended by section 2662(c)(1) of Pub.L. 98–369 to correct an error in the directory language of Pub.L. 98–21 under which the article "the" had been left out in the direction to strike out references to the age of 65 in subsecs. (c) and (f) of this section.

Effective and Applicability Provisions

2000 Acts. Amendment by Pub.L. 106–182 applicable with respect to taxable years ending after December 31, 1999, see section 5 of Pub.L. 106–182, set out as a note under section 402 of this title.

1996 Acts. Section 102(c) of Pub.L. 104–121 provided that: "The amendments made by this section [amending this section and section 423 of this title] shall apply with respect to taxable years ending after 1995."

1994 Acts. Amendment by section 107(a)(4) of Pub.L. 103–296 effective Mar. 31, 1995, see section 110 of Pub.L. 103–296, set out as a note under section 401 of this title.

Section 309(e)(1) of Pub.L. 103–296 provided that: "The amendments made by subsections (a), (b), and (c) [amending this section] shall apply with respect to benefits payable for months after December 1995."

Section 310(c) of Pub.L. 103–296 provided that: "The amendments made by this section [amending subsec. (a)(8) and (10) of this section] shall apply for the purpose of determining the total monthly benefits to which beneficiaries may be entitled under sections 202 and 223 of the Social Security Act [sections 402 and 423 of this title] based on the wages and self-employment income of an individual who—

"(1) becomes entitled to an old-age insurance benefit under section 202(a) of such Act [section 402(a) of this title],

"(2) becomes reentitled to a disability insurance benefit under section 223 of such Act [section 423 of this title], or

"(3) dies,

after December 1995."

Section 314(b) of Pub.L. 103–296 provided that: "The amendment made by subsection (a) [amending this section] shall apply with respect to reports of earnings for taxable years ending on or after December 31, 1994."

Section 321(g)(3)(B) of Pub.L. 103–296 provided that: "The amendment made by paragraph (2) [amending subsec. (f)(8)(b)(ii) of this section] shall be effective with respect to the determination of the exempt amounts applicable to any taxable year ending after 1994."

1990 Acts. Section 5117(a)(4) of Pub.L. 101–508 provided that:

"**(A) In general.**—Except as provided in subparagraph (B), the amendments made by this subsection [amending this section and section 415 of this title] shall apply with respect to the computation of the primary insurance amount of any insured individual in any case in which a person becomes entitled to benefits under section 202 or 223 [section 402 and 423 of this title] on the basis of such insured individual's wages and self-employment income for months after the 18–month period following the month in which this Act is enacted [Nov. 1990], except that such amendments shall not apply if any person is entitled to benefits based on the wages and self-employment income of such insured individual for the month preceding the initial month of such person's entitlement to such benefits under section 202 or 223 [section 402 or 423 of this title].

"**(B) Recomputations.**—The amendments made by this subsection [amending this section and section 415 of this title] shall apply with respect to any primary insurance amount upon the recomputation of such primary insurance amount if such recomputation is first effective for monthly benefits for months after the 18–month period following the month in which this Act is enacted [Nov. 1990]."

Section 5119(e) of Pub.L. 101–508 provided that:

"**(1) In general.**—The amendments made by this section [amending this section and section 416 of this title] shall apply with respect to benefits for months after December 1990.

"**(2) Application requirement.**—

"**(A) General rule.**—Except as provided in subparagraph (B), the amendments made by this section [amending this section and section 416 of this title] shall apply only with respect to benefits for which application is filed with the Secretary of Health and Human Services after December 31, 1990.

"**(B) Exception from application requirement.**—Subparagraph (A) shall not apply with respect to the benefits of any individual if such individual is entitled to a benefit under subsection (b), (c), (e), or (f) of section 202 of the Social Security Act [subsecs. (b), (c), (e) or (f) of section 402 of this title] for December 1990 and the individual on whose wages and self-employment income such benefit for December 1990 is based is the same individual on the basis of whose wages and self-employment income application would otherwise be required under subparagraph (A)."

[Reference to "Secretary of Health and Human Services" deemed reference to "Commissioner of Social Security", effective Mar. 31, 1995, pursuant to Pub.L. 103–296, Title I, §§ 107(a)(1), 110(a), Aug. 15, 1994, 108 Stat. 1477, 1490.]

Section 5123(b) of Pub.L. 101–508 provided that: "The amendments made by this section [amending this section and section 1402 of Title 26, Internal Revenue Code] shall apply with respect to income received for services performed in taxable years beginning after December 31, 1990."

Section 5127(c) of Pub.L. 101–508 provided that: "The amendments made by this section [amending subsecs. (b) and (d) of this section] shall apply with respect to benefits for months after December 1990."

1989 Acts. Amendment by section 10208(b)(1)(A), (B) of Pub.L. 101–239 applicable with respect to computation of average total wage amounts (under amended provisions) for calendar years after 1990, see section 10208(c) of Pub.L. 101–239, set out as a note under section 430 of this title.

Section 10305(f) of Pub.L. 101–239 provided that: "The amendments made by this section [amending this section and sections 404, 423 and 1383 of this title] shall apply with respect to determinations made on or after July 1, 1990."

1988 Acts. Section 8002(c) of Pub.L. 100–647 provided that: "The amendments made by this section [amending subsec. (f)(3) of this section] shall apply to deaths after the date of the enactment of this Act [Nov. 10, 1988]."

1986 Acts. Section 12108(b) of Pub.L. 99–272, as amended Pub.L. 99–514, Title XVIII, § 1895(a), Oct. 22, 1986, 100 Stat. 2931, provided that: "The amendments made by subsection (a) [amending subsec. (a)(4) and (6) of this section] shall apply with respect to benefits payable for months after December 1986."

1984 Acts. Section 2602(b) of Pub.L. 98–369 provided that: "The amendment made by subsection (a) [enacting subsec. (h)(4) of this section] shall be effective upon the date of the enactment of this Act [July 18, 1984]."

Section 2661(g)(1)(B) of Pub.L. 98–369 provided that: "The amendments made by subparagraph (A) [amending subsec. (d) of this section] shall apply only with respect to months beginning with the second month after the month in which this Act is enacted [July, 1984]."

Section 2661(g)(2)(B) of Pub.L. 98–369 provided that: "The amendment made by subparagraph (A) [adding subsec. (f)(9) of this section] shall be effective as though it had been enacted on April 20, 1983, as part of section 201 of the Social Security Amendments of 1983 [Pub.L. 98–21]."

Amendment to subsecs. (c), (f) by section 2662(c)(1) of Pub.L. 98–369 effective as though included in the enactment of the Social Security Amendments of 1983 [Pub.L. 98–21], see section 2664(a) of Pub.L. 98–369, set out as a note under section 401 of this title.

Amendment to subsecs. (a)(8), (d)(2), (f)(5), (8) by section 2663(a)(3) of Pub.L. 98–369 effective July 18, 1984, but not to be construed as changing or affecting any right, liability, status or interpretation which existed (under the provisions of law involved) before that date, see section 2664(b) of Pub.L. 98–369, set out as a note under section 401 of this title.

1983 Acts. Amendment of subsec. (f)(8)(A) by section 111(a) of Pub.L. 98–21 applicable with respect to cost-of-living increases determined under section 415(i) of this title for years after 1982, see section 111(a)(8) of Pub.L. 98–21, set out as a note under section 402 of this title.

Section 132(c)(2) of Pub.L. 98–21 provided that: "The amendments made by subsection (b) [amending subsec. (b), (d), and (f) of this section] shall apply with respect to monthly insurance benefits for months after December 1984."

Amendment by sections 306(i) and 309(f), (g) and (h) of Pub.L. 98–21 applicable only with respect to monthly payments payable under this subchapter for months after April, 1983, except as otherwise specifically provided, see section 310 of Pub.L. 98–21, set out as a note under section 402 of this title.

Amendment by section 324 of Pub.L. 98–21 applicable to remuneration paid after Dec. 31, 1983, except for certain employer contributions made during 1984 under a qualified cash or deferred arrangement, and except in the case of an agreement with certain nonqualified deferred compensation plans in existence on Mar. 24, 1983, see section 324(d) of Pub.L. 98–21, set out as a note under section 3121 of Title 26, Internal Revenue Code.

Section 331(c) of Pub.L. 98–21 provided that: "The amendments made by subsection (a) [amending subsec. (a)(3)(A), (7) of this section] shall be effective with respect to payments for months after December 1983."

Section 347(b) of Pub.L. 98–21 provided that: "The amendment made by subsection (a) [amending subsec. (f)(3) of this section] shall apply only with respect to taxable years beginning after December 1989, and only in the case of individuals who have attained retirement age (as defined in section 216(*l*) of the Social Security Act) [section 416(*l*) of this title]."

1981 Acts. Amendment of subsec. (a)(8) by section 2201(c)(6) of Pub.L. 97–35 and by section 2(f) of Pub.L. 97–123, applicable with respect to benefits for months after December 1981 with certain exceptions, see section 2(j)(2) to (4) of Pub.L. 97–123, set out as a note under section 415 of this title.

Amendment of subsec. (a)(1), (3)(B)(iii), and (8) by section 2206(b)(2) to (4) of Pub.L. 97–35, respectively, applicable only with respect to initial calculations and adjustments of primary insurance amounts and benefit amounts which are attributable to periods after August 1981, see section 2206(c) of Pub.L. 97–35, set out as a note under section 402 of this title.

1980 Acts. Section 1(b) of Pub.L. 96–473 provided that: "The amendment made by subsection (a) [amending subsec. (f)(1)(F) and (2) of this section] shall apply with respect to monthly benefits payable for months after December 1977."

Section 3(b) of Pub.L. 96–473 provided that: "The amendment made by subsection (a) [amending subsec. (f)(5)(D) of this section] shall apply with respect to taxable years ending after December 31, 1977, but only with respect to benefits payable for months after December 1977."

Section 4(b) of Pub.L. 96–473 provided that: "The amendment made by subsection (a) [amending subsec. (f)(1)(E) of this section] shall apply with respect to monthly benefits payable for months after December 1977."

Section 101(c) of Pub.L. 96–265 provided that: "The amendments made by this section [amending this section and section 415 of this title] shall apply only with respect to monthly benefits payable on the basis of the wages and self-employment income of an individual who first becomes eligible for benefits (determined under sections 415(a)(3)(B) and 415(a)(2)(A) of this title, as applied for this purpose) after 1978, and who first becomes entitled to disability insurance benefits after June 30, 1980."

1977 Acts. Amendment of subsec. (a)(1) to (7) by Pub.L. 95–216 effective only with respect to monthly benefits under this subchapter payable for months after December 1978 and with respect to lump-sum death payments with respect to deaths occurring after such month, see section 206 of Pub.L. 95–216, set out as a note under section 402 of this title.

Enactment of subsec. (a)(8) by Pub.L. 95–216 effective only with respect to monthly benefits for months after May 1978, see section 206 of Pub.L. 95–216, set out as a note under section 402 of this title.

Section 301(e) of Pub.L. 95–216 provided that: "The amendments made by this section [amending subsecs. (f)(1)(E), (f)(3), (f)(4)(B), (f)(8)(A), (f)(8)(B), and (h)(1)(A) and enacting subsec. (f)(8)(D) of this section] shall apply with respect to taxable years ending after December 1977."

Section 302(e) of Pub.L. 95–216 provided that: "The amendments made by this section [amending subsecs. (c)(1), (d)(1), (f)(1)(B), (f)(3), (h)(1)(A), and (j) of this section] shall apply only with respect to taxable years ending after December 31, 1981."

Section 303(b) of Pub.L. 95–216 provided that: "The amendment made by subsection (a) [amending subsec. (f)(1)(E) of this section] shall apply only with respect to monthly benefits payable for months after December 1977."

Amendment by section 353(a) of Pub.L. 95–216 [substituting "is" for "was" in subsec. (f)(8)(B)(i) of this section and amending subsec. (f)(8)(B)(ii) of this section] to be effective Jan. 1, 1979, see section 353(g) of Pub.L. 95–216, set out as a note under section 418 of this title.

1973 Acts. Section 202(d) of Pub.L. 93–66 provided that: "The amendments [of subsecs. (f)(1), (3), (4)(B) and (h)(1)(A) of this section] made by this section shall be effective with respect to taxable years beginning after December 31, 1973."

1972 Acts. Amendment of subsec. (a) by section 101(b) of Pub.L. 92–603 applicable with respect to monthly insurance benefits under this subchapter for months after Dec. 1972 and with respect to lump-sum death payments under this subchapter in the case of deaths occurring after such month, see section 101(g) of Pub.L. 92–603, set out as a note under section 415 of this title.

Section 202(a)(2)(A) of Pub.L. 92–336 provided in part that the amendment to subsec. (a) shall take effect Jan. 1, 1974.

Section 202(a)(2)(B) of Pub.L. 92–336 provided in part that the amendment to subsec. (a)(2) shall take effect Jan. 1, 1974.

Amendment of subsec. (a)(2) by § 201(b) of Pub.L. 92–336 applicable with respect to monthly benefits under this subchapter for months after Aug. 1972 and with respect to lump-sum death payments under this subchapter in the case of deaths occurring after such month, see section 201(i) of Pub.L. 92–336, set out as a note under section 415 of this title.

Section 144(b) of Pub.L. 92–603 provided that: "The amendments made by each of the paragraphs in subsection (a) [amending subsec. (a)(2)(B) of this section and subsec. (a)(2)(C), eff. Jan. 1, 1974, and sections 415(a) and 430(b)(2) of this title] shall be effective in like manner as if such amendment had been included in title II of Public Law 92–336 in the particular provision of such title referred to in such paragraph."

Amendment of subsec. (a)(4) by section 201(h)(1) of Pub.L. 92–336 applicable with respect to monthly benefits under this subchapter for months after Dec. 1971, see section 201(i) of Pub.L. 92–336, set out as a note under section 415 of this title.

Amendment of subsec. (c) and (f) by section 102(c) of Pub.L. 92–603 applicable with respect to monthly benefits under this subchapter for months after Dec. 1972, see section 102(i) of Pub.L. 92–603, set out as a note under section 402 of this title.

Amendment of subsecs. (c) and (f)(1)(D) by § 107(b)(1), (2) of Pub.L. 92–603 applicable with respect to monthly benefits under this subchapter for months after Dec. 1972, with specified exceptions, see section 107(c) of Pub.L. 92–603, set out as a note under section 402 of this title.

Section 105(c) of Pub.L. 92–603 provided that: "The amendments made by this section [amending subsecs. (f) and (h) of this section] shall apply with respect to taxable years ending after December 1972."

Section 106(b) of Pub.L. 92–603 provided that: "The amendment made by subsection (a) [amending subsec. (f)(3) of this section to provide for the exclusion of certain earnings in year of attaining age 72] shall apply with respect to taxable years ending after December 1972."

1971 Acts. Amendment by Pub.L. 92–5 applicable with respect to monthly benefits under this subchapter for months after Dec. 1970 and with respect to lump-sum death payments under this subchapter in the case of deaths occurring in and after Mar. 1971, see section 201(e) of Pub.L. 92–5, set out as a note under section 415 of this title.

1969 Acts. Amendment of subsec. (a)(2) by Pub.L. 91–172 applicable with respect to monthly benefits under this subchapter for month after Dec. 1969 and with respect to lump-sum death payments under this subchapter in the case of deaths occurring after Dec. 1969, see section 1002(e) of Pub.L. 91–172, set out as a note under section 415 of this title.

1968 Acts. Amendment of subsec. (a)(2) by section 101(b) of Pub.L. 90–248 applicable with respect to monthly benefits and lump-sum death benefits, in the case of deaths occurring after Jan. 1968, under this subchapter for months after Jan. 1968, see section 101(e) of Pub.L. 90–248, set out as a note under section 415 of this title.

Amendment of subsecs. (c), (f)(1), (2), (4) by section 104 of Pub.L. 90–248 applicable with respect to monthly benefits under this subchapter for and after the month of Feb. 1968, but only on the basis of applications for such benefits filed in or after Jan. 1968, see section 104(e) of Pub.L. 90–248, set out as a note under section 402 of this title.

Section 107(b) of Pub.L. 90–248 provided that: "The amendments made by subsection (a) [to subsecs. (f)(1), (3), (4)(B), and (h)(1)(A) of this section] shall apply with respect to taxable years ending after December 1967."

Section 163(a)(2) of Pub.L. 90–248 provided that: "The amendment made by paragraph (1) [to subsec. (a) of this section] shall apply only with respect to monthly benefits payable under title II of the Social Security Act [this subchapter] with respect to individuals who become entitled to benefits under section 202(d) of such Act [section 402(d) of this title] solely by reason of section 216(h)(3) of such Act [section 416(h)(3) of this title] in or after January 1968 (but without regard to section 202(j)(1) of such Act [section 402(j)(1) of this title]). The provisions of section 170 of this Act [set out as a Savings Provisions note under this section] shall not apply with respect to any such individual."

1965 Acts. Amendment of subsec. (a) by section 301(c) of Pub.L. 89–97 applicable with respect to monthly benefits under this subchapter for months after Dec. 1964 and with respect to lump-sum death benefits payments under this subchapter in the case of deaths occurring in or after July 1965, see section 301(d) of Pub.L. 89–97, set out as a note under section 415 of this title.

Amendment of subsecs. (a)(3), (c)(4), and (d)(1) by section 308 of Pub.L. 89–97 applicable with respect to monthly insurance benefits under this subchapter beginning with the second month following July 1965, but, in the case of an individual who was not entitled to a monthly insurance benefit under section 402 of this title for the first month following July 1965, only on the basis of an application filed in or after July 1965, see section 308(e) of Pub.L. 89–97, set out as a note under section 402 of this title.

Section 310(b) of Pub.L. 89–97 provided that: "The amendments made by subsection (a) [to subsecs. (f)(1), (3), (4)(B) and (h)(1)(A) of this section] shall apply with respect to taxable years ending after December 31, 1965."

Section 325(b) of Pub.L. 89–97 provided that: "The amendments made by subsection (a) [to subsec. (f)(5)(B), (D) of this section] shall apply with respect to the computation of net earnings from self-employment and the net loss from self-employment for taxable years beginning after 1964."

1961 Acts. Section 108(b) of Pub.L. 87–64 provided that: "The amendment made by subsection (a) [to subsec. (f)(3) of this section] shall apply in the case of taxable years ending after the enactment of this Act [June 30, 1961]."

1960 Acts. Amendment of subsec. (k) of this section by section 103(b) of Pub.L. 86–778 applicable only with respect to service performed after 1960, except that insofar as the carrying on of a trade or business (other than performance of service as an employee) is concerned, the amendment shall be applicable only in the case of taxable years beginning after 1960, see section 103(v)(1) of Pub.L. 86–778, set out as a note under section 402 of this title.

Section 211(p) to (s) of Pub.L. 86–778 provided that:

"(p) Section 203(c), (d), (e), (g), and (i) of the Social Security Act as amended by this Act [subsecs. (c), (d), (e), (g), and (i) of this section] shall be effective with respect to monthly benefits for months after December 1960.

"(q) Section 203(b), (f), and (h) of the Social Security Act as amended by this Act [subsecs. (b), (f) and (h) of this section] shall be effective with respect to taxable years beginning after December 1960.

"(r) Section 203(*l*) of the Social Security Act as amended by this Act [subsec. (*l*) of this section], to the extent that it applies to section 203(g) of the Social Security Act as amended by this Act [subsec. (g) of this section], shall be effective with respect to monthly benefits for months after December 1960 and, to the extent that it applies to section 203(h)(1)(A) of the Social Security Act as amended by this Act [subsec. (h)(1)(A) of this section], shall be effective with respect to taxable years beginning after December 1960.

"(s) The amendments made by subsections (i), (j), (k), (*l*), (m), (n), and (*o*) of this section [to sections 402(n)(1), (q)(5), (6), (t)(7), 408(a)(3) and 415(g) of this title and sections 228c and 228e of Title 45], to the extent that they make changes in references to provisions of section 203 of the Social Security Act [this section], shall take effect in the manner provided in subsections (p) and (q) of this section for the provisions of such section 203 to which the respective references so changed relate."

Section 302(b) of Pub.L. 86–778 provided that: "The amendments made by subsection (a) [to subsec. (a)(3) of this section] shall apply only in the case of monthly benefits under section 202 or section 223 of the Social Security Act [section 402 or section 423 of this title] for months after the month following the month in which this Act is enacted [Sept. 1960], and then only (1) if the insured individual on the basis of whose wages and self-employment income such monthly benefits are payable became entitled (without the application of section 202(j)(1) or section 223(b) of such Act [section 402(j)(1) or section 423(b) of this title]) to benefits under section 202(a) or section 223 of such Act [section 402(a) or section 423 of this title] after the month following the month in which this Act is enacted [Sept. 1960], or (2) if such insured individual died before becoming so entitled no person was entitled (without the application of section 202(j)(1) or section 223(b) of such Act [section 402(j)(1) or section 423(b) of this title]) on the basis of such wages and self-employment income to monthly benefits under title II of the Social Security Act [this subchapter] for the month following the month in which this Act is enacted [Sept. 1960] or any prior month."

1958 Acts. Amendment of subsec. (a) by Pub.L. 85–840 applicable in the case of monthly benefits under this subchapter for months after Dec. 1958, and in the case of lump-sum death payments under this subchapter, with respect to deaths occurring after such month, see section 101(g) of Pub.L. 85–840, set out as a note under section 415 of this title.

Amendment of subsec. (c) by section 205 of Pub.L. 85–840 applicable with respect to monthly benefits under this subchapter for months after Aug. 1958, but only if an application for such benefits is filed on or after Aug. 28, 1958, see section 207(a) of Pub.L. 85–840, set out as a note under section 416 of this title.

Amendment of subsec. (h) by section 205(k) of Pub.L. 85–840 applicable with respect to monthly benefits under this subchapter for Aug. 1958 and succeeding months, see section 207(a) of Pub.L. 85–840, set out as a note under section 416 of this title.

Section 307(h)(2) of Pub.L. 85–840, provided that: "The amendments made by subsection (f) [to subsecs. (c)(1), (2) of this section] shall apply with respect to monthly benefits under subsection (d) or (g) of section 202 of the Social Security Act [subsecs. (d) or (g) of section 402 of this title] for months in any taxable year, of the individual to whom the person entitled to such benefits is married, beginning after the month in which this Act is enacted [August 1958]."

Section 308(f) of Pub.L. 85–840 provided that: "The amendments made by this section [to subsecs. (e)(2), (3), (g)(1) and (*l*) of this section] shall be applicable with respect to taxable years beginning after the month in which this Act is enacted [August 1958]."

1956 Acts. Amendment of subsecs. (a), (b), (d), and (h) by section 101(d) to (g) of Act Aug. 1, 1956 applicable with respect to monthly benefits under section 402 of this title for months after Dec. 1956, but only on the basis of an application filed after Sept. 1956, see section 101(h) of Act Aug. 1, 1956, set out as a note under section 402 of this title.

Section 107(a) of Act Aug. 1, 1956 provided in part that the amendment to subsec. (g)(1) of this section should be applicable in the case of monthly benefits under this subchapter for months in any taxable year (of the individual entitled to such benefits) beginning after 1954.

Section 112(c) of Act Aug. 1, 1956 provided that: "The amendments made by subsections (a) and (b) [to subsecs. (e)(4)(C) and (k) of this section] shall be applicable with respect to taxable years ending after 1955."

1954 Acts. Section 103(i)(1) and (2) of Act Sept. 1, 1954 provided that:

"(1) The amendments [to subsecs. (g) and (b)(1)] made by subsection (f) and by paragraph (1) of subsection (a) of this section shall be applicable in the case of monthly benefits under title II of the Social Security Act [this subchapter] for months in any taxable year (of the individual entitled to such benefits) beginning after December 1954. The amendments [to subsec. (c)(1)] made by paragraph (1) of subsection (b) of this section shall be applicable in the case of monthly benefits under such title II for months in any taxable year (of the individual on the basis of whose wages and self-employment income such benefits are payable) beginning after December 1954. The amendments [to subsec. (f), (k), (b)(2), and (c)(2)] made by subsections (e) and (g), and by paragraph (2) of subsection (a) and paragraph (2) of subsection (b), shall be applicable in the case of monthly benefits under such title II for months after December 1954. The remaining amendments made by this section (other than [the adding of subsec. (*l*) by] subsection (h)) shall be applicable, insofar as they are related to the monthly benefits of an individual which are based on his wages and self-employment income, in the case of monthly benefits under such title II for months in any taxable year (of such individual) beginning after December 1954 and, insofar as they are related to the monthly benefits of an individual which are based on the wages and self-employment income of someone else, in the case of monthly benefits under such title II for months in any taxable year (of the individual on whose wages and self-employment income such benefits are based) beginning after December 1954.

"(2) No deduction shall be imposed on or after the date of the enactment of this Act [Sept. 1, 1954] under subsection (f) or (g) of section 203 of the Social Security Act [subsecs. (f) or (g) of this section] as in effect prior to such date, on account of failure to file a report of an event described in subsection (b)(1), (b)(2), or (c)(1) of such section [this section] (as in effect prior to such date); and no such deduction imposed prior to such date shall be collected after such date. In determining whether, under section 203(g)(2) of the Social Security Act [subsec. (g)(2) of this section] as amended by this Act, a failure to file a report is a first or subsequent failure, any failure with respect to a taxable year which began prior to January 1955 shall be disregarded."

Section 103(i)(3) of Act Sept. 1, 1954, provided that: "Subsections (b)(1), (b)(2), (c), (e), and (j) of section 203 of the Social Security Act [this section] as in effect prior to the enactment of this Act, to the extent they are in effect with respect to months after 1954, are each amended by striking out 'seventy-five' and inserting in lieu thereof 'seventy-two', but only with respect to such months after 1954."

Amendment to subsec. (a) by Act Sept. 1, 1954, section 102(e)(7), applicable in the case of lump-sum death payments under section 402 of this title with respect to death occurring, and in the case of monthly benefits under such section for months after Aug. 1954, see note set out under section 415 of this title.

Subsecs. (b)(1), (2), (c), (e) and (j) as in effect prior to Sept. 1, 1954, to the extent that they were in effect with respect to months after 1954, were each amended by Act Sept. 1, 1954, section 103(i)(3), which substituted "seventy-two" for "seventy-five", but only with respect to such months after 1954.

1952 Acts. For effective date of amendment of subsec. (a) by Act July 18, 1952, see section 2(c)(3) of Act July 18, 1952, set out as a note under section 415 of this title.

Section 4(e) of Act July 18, 1952 provided that: "The amendments made by subsection (a) [to subsec. (b)(1) and (c)(1) of this section] shall apply in the case of monthly benefits under title II of the Social Security Act [this subchapter] for months after August 1952. The amendments made by subsection (b) [to subsec. (b)(2) of this section] shall apply in the case of monthly benefits under such title II [this subchapter] for months in any taxable year (of the individual entitled to such benefits) ending after August 1952. The amendments made by subsection (c) [to subsec. (c)(2) of this section] shall apply in the case of monthly benefits under such title II [this subchapter] for months in any taxable year (of the individual on the basis of whose wages and self-employment income such benefits are payable) ending after August 1952. The amendments made by subsection (d) [to subsecs. (e), (g) of this section] shall apply in the case of taxable years ending after August 1952. As used in this subsection, the term 'taxable year' shall have the meaning assigned to it by section 211(e) of the Social Security Act [section 411(e) of this title]."

1950 Acts. Section 102(b) of Act Aug. 28, 1950 provided that: "The amendment made by subsection (a) of this section [amending this section] shall be applicable with respect to benefits for months after August 1950."

Section 103(b) of Act Aug. 28, 1950 provided that: "The amendments made by this section shall take effect September 1, 1950, except that the provisions of subsections (d), (e), and (f) of section 203 of the Social Security Act [subsections (d) to (f) of this section] as in effect prior to the enactment of this Act [Aug. 28, 1950] shall be applicable for months prior to September 1950."

1939 Acts. Amendment by Act Aug. 10, 1939 was made effective Jan. 1, 1940 by section 201 of Act Aug. 10, 1939.

Transfer of Functions

All functions of the Federal Security Administrator were transferred to the Secretary of Health, Education, and Welfare and all agencies of the Federal Security Agency were transferred to the Department of Health, Education, and Welfare by section 5 of Reorg. Plan No. 1 of 1953, set out under section 3501 of this title. The Federal Security Agency and the office of Administrator were abolished by section 8 of Reorg. Plan No. 1 of 1953. The Secretary and Department of Health, Education, and Welfare were redesignated the Secretary and Department of Health and Human Services by section 509(b) of Pub.L. 96–88 which is classified to section 3508(b) of Title 20, Education.

Savings Provisions

1972 Acts. Section 201(h)(2) of Pub.L. 92–336 provided that: "In any case in which the provisions of section 1002(b)(2) of the Social Security Amendments of 1969 [set out as a note below] were applicable with respect to benefits for any month in 1970, the total of monthly benefits as determined under section 203(a) of the Social Security Act [subsec. (a) of this section] shall, for months after 1970, be increased to the amount that would be required in order to assure that the total of such monthly benefits (after the application of section 202(q) of such Act [section 402(q) of this title]) will not be less than the total of monthly benefits that was applicable (after the application of such sections 203(a) and 202(q)) for the first month for which the provisions of such section 1002(b)(2) applied."

1969 Acts. Section 1002(b)(2) of Pub.L. 91–172 provided that: "Notwithstanding any other provision of law, when two or more persons are entitled to monthly insurance benefits under title II of the Social Security Act [this subchapter] for any month after 1969 on the basis of the wages and self-employment income of an insured individual (and at least one of such persons was so entitled for a month before January 1971 on the basis of an application filed before 1971), the total of the benefits to which such persons are entitled under such title for such month (after the application of sections 203(a) and 202(q) of such Act [sections 403(a) and 402(q) of this title]) shall be not less than the total of the monthly insurance benefits to which such persons would be entitled under such title for such month (after the application of such sections 203(a) and 202(q) [sections 403(a) and 402(q) of this title]) without regard to the amendment made by subsection (a) of this section [amending tables set out in section 415(a) of this title]."

1968 Acts. Section 170 of Pub.L. 90–248 provided that: "Where—

"(1) one or more persons were entitled (without the application of section 202(j)(1) of the Social Security Act [section 402(j)(1) of this title]) to monthly benefits under section 202 or 223 of such Act [section 402 or 423 of this title] for January 1968 on the basis of the wages and self-employment income of an individual, and

"(2) one or more persons (not included in paragraph (1)) become entitled to monthly benefits under such section 202 [section 402 of this title] for February 1968 on the basis of such wages and self-employment by reason of the amendments made to such Act [this chapter] by sections 104 [to sections 402(e)(1)(B), foll. (E), (F), (G), 5, 6, (f)(1)(B), (F), (G), 3, 6, 7, (q), (q)(1)(A), (C), (D), 3(A), (C) to (G), 6, 7, 9, 403(c), (f)(1), (2), (4), 416(i)(1), 422(a), (b)(1), (d)(1)(C), (D), and 425 of this title], 112 [to section 402(d)(8)(E) of this title], 150 [to section 416(e) second sent. of this title], 151 [to section 402(d)(3) to (10), (s)(2), (3) of this title and section 228e(*l*)(1) of Title 45], 156 [to section 416(c)(5), (e) first sent., (g)(5), (k) of this title], and 157 of this Act [to section 402(c)(1), (2), (f)(1), (2), and 402 note of this title], and

"(3) the total of benefits to which all persons are entitled under such section 202 or 223 [section 402 or 423 of this title] on the basis of such wages and self-employment for February 1968 are reduced by reason of section 203(a) of such Act [subsec. (a) of this section], as amended by this Act (or would, but for the penultimate sentence of such section 203(a) [subsec. (a) of this section], be so reduced),

then the amount of the benefit to which each such person referred to in paragraph (1) is entitled for months after January 1968 shall be increased, after the application of such section 203(a) [subsec. (a) of this section], to the amount it would have been if the person or persons referred to in paragraph (2) were not entitled to a benefit referred to in such paragraph."

1954 Acts. Section 102(h) of Act Sept. 1, 1954 provided that:

"(1) Where—

"**(A)** an individual was entitled (without the application of section 202(j)(1) of the Social Security Act [section 402(j)(1) of this title]) to an old-age insurance benefit under title II of such Act [this subchapter] for August 1954;

"**(B)** one or more other persons were entitled (without the application of such section 202(j)(1) [section 402(j)(1) of this title]) to monthly benefits under such title for such month on the basis of the wages and self-employment income of such individual; and

"**(C)** the total of the benefits to which all persons are entitled under such title on the basis of such individual's wages and self-employment income for any subsequent month for which he is entitled to an old-age insurance benefit under such title, would (but for the provisions of this paragraph) be reduced by reason of the application of section 203(a) of the Social Security Act, as amended by this Act [subsec. (a) of this section],

then the total of benefits referred to in clause (C) for such subsequent month shall be reduced to whichever of the following is the larger—

"**(D)** the amount determined pursuant to section 203(a) of the Social Security Act, as amended by this Act [subsec. (a) of this section]; or

"**(E)** the amount determined pursuant to such section, as in effect prior to the enactment of this Act [Sept. 1, 1954] for August 1954 plus the excess of (i) the amount of his old-age insurance benefit for such month computed as if the amendments [to section 415 of this title and subsec. (a) of this section] made by the preceding subsections of this section had been applicable in the case of such benefit for such month over (ii) the amount of his old-age insurance benefit for such month, or

"**(F)** the amount determined pursuant to section 2(d)(1) of the Social Security Act Amendments of 1952 [set out as a note under section 415 of this section] for August 1954 plus the excess of (i) the amount of his old-age insurance benefit for such month computed as if the amendments made by the preceding subsections of this section had been applicable in the case of such benefit for such month over (ii) the amount of his old-age insurance benefit for such month.

"(2) Where—

"**(A)** two or more persons were entitled (without the application of section 202(j)(1) of the Social Security Act [section 402(j)(1) of this title]) to monthly benefits under title II of such Act [this subchapter] for August 1954 on the basis of the wages and self-employment income of a deceased individual; and

"**(B)** the total of the benefits to which all such persons are entitled on the basis of such deceased individual's wages and self-employment income for any subsequent month would (but for the provisions of this paragraph) be reduced by reason of the application of the first sentence of section 203(a) of the Social Security Act, as amended by this Act [subsec. (a) of this section],

then, notwithstanding any other provision in title II of the Social Security Act [this subchapter], such deceased individual's average monthly wage shall, for purposes of such § 203(a) [subsec. (a) of this section], be whichever of the following is the larger:

"**(C)** his average monthly wage determined pursuant to section 215 of such Act, as amended by this Act [section 415 of this title]; or

"**(D)** his average monthly wage determined under such section 215, as in effect prior to the enactment of this Act [Sept. 1, 1954], plus $7."

Computation of Benefits for Certain Children

Section 163(b) of Pub.L. 90–248 provided that: "Where—

"**(1)** one or more persons were entitled (without the application of section 202(j)(1) of the Social Security Act [section 402(j)(1) of this title]) to monthly benefits under section 202 or 223 of such Act [section 402 or 423 of this title] for January 1968 on the basis of the wages and self-employment income of an individual, and

"**(2)** one or more persons became entitled to monthly benefits before January 1968 under section 202(d) of such Act [section 402(d) of this title] by reason of section 216(h)(3) of such Act [section 416(h)(3) of this section] (but without regard to section 202(j)(1) [section 402(j)(1) of this title]), on the basis of such wages and self-employment income and are so entitled for January 1968, and

"**(3)** the total of benefits to which all persons are entitled under such section 202 or 223 of such Act [section 402 or 423 of this title] on the basis of such wages and self-employment for January 1968 are reduced by reason of section 203(a) of such Act [subsec. (a) of this section], as amended by this Act (or would, but for the penultimate sentence of such section 203(a) [subsec. (a) of this section], be so reduced),

then the amount of the benefit to which each such person referred to in paragraph (1) above (but not including persons referred to in paragraph (2) above) is entitled for months after January 1968 shall be increased, after the application of such section 203(a) [subsec. (a) of this section], to the amount it would have been if the person or persons referred to in paragraph (2) were not entitled to a benefit referred to in such paragraph (2)."

Computation of Old–Age and Survivor Family Maximum: 1986

By notice of the Secretary of Health and Human Services, Oct. 29, 1985, published in the Federal Register on Oct. 31, 1985, at 50 F.R. 45561, it was determined and announced pursuant to authority contained in subsec. (a)(2)(C) of this section, that for the families of workers who first become eligible for old-age benefits or die (before becoming eligible for such benefits) in 1986 the portions of the primary insurance amounts to be used in 1986 in applying subsec. (a) of this section are determined to be the first $379, the amount between $379 and $548, the amount between $548 and $714, and the amount over $714.

Computation of Old–Age and Survivor Family Maximum: 1985

By notice of the Secretary of Health and Human Services, Oct. 29, 1984, published in the Federal Register on Oct. 31, 1984, at 49 F.R. 43775, it was determined and announced, pursuant to authority contained in subsec. (a)(2)(C) of this section, that for the families of workers who first become eligible for old-age benefits or die (before becoming eligible for such benefits) in 1985 the portions of the primary insurance amounts to be used in 1985 in applying subsec. (a) of this section are determined to be the first $358, the amount between $358 and $517, the amount between $517 and $675, and the amount over $675.

Computation of Old-Age and Survivor Family Maximum: 1984

By notice of the Secretary of Health and Human Services, Oct. 27, 1983, published in the Federal Register on Nov. 1, 1983, at 48 F.R. 50414, it was determined and announced, pursuant to authority contained in subsec. (a)(2)(C) of this section, that for the families of workers who first become eligible for old-age benefits or die (before becoming eligible for such benefits) in 1984 the portions of the primary insurance amounts to be used in 1984 in applying subsec. (a) of this section are determined to be the first $342, the amount between $342 and $493, the amount between $493 and $643, and the amount over $643.

Cost-of-Living Increase in Benefits

For purposes of subsec. (f)(8) of this section, the increase in benefits provided by section 2 of Pub.L. 93–233, revising benefits table of section 415(a) of this title and amending sections 427(a), (b) and 428(b)(1), (2), (c)(3)(A), (B) of this title considered an increase under section 415(i) of this title, see section 3(i) of Pub.L. 93–233, set out as a note under section 415 of this title.

Increased Exempt Amounts for Individuals Described in Subsection (f)(8)(D); Notification in 1977 to 1981; Individuals Other Than Those Described in Subsection (f)(8)(D)

Section 301(c)(2) of Pub.L. 95–216 provided that: "No notification with respect to an increased exempt amount for individuals described in section 203(f)(8)(D) of the Social Security Act [subsec. (f)(8)(D) of this section] (as added by paragraph (1) of this subsection) shall be required under the last sentence of section 203(f)(8)(B) of such Act [subsec. (f)(8)(B) of this section] in 1977, 1978, 1979, 1980, or 1981; and section 203(f)(8)(C) of such Act [subsec. (f)(8)(C) of this section] shall not prevent the new exempt amount determined and published under section 203(f)(8)(A) [subsec. (f)(8)(A) of this section] in 1977 from becoming effective to the extent that such new exempt amount applies to individuals other than those described in section 203(f)(8)(D) of such Act [subsec. (f)(8)(D) of this section] (as so added)."

Penalties for Failure to File Timely Reports of Earnings and Other Events

Section 161(c) of Pub.L. 90–248 provided that: "The amendments made by this section [to subsecs. (h)(2)(A) and (g) of this section] shall apply with respect to any deductions imposed on or after the date of the enactment of this Act [Jan. 2, 1968] under subsections (g) and (h) of section 203 of the Social Security Act [subsecs. (g) and (h) of this section] on account of failure to make a report required thereby."

Prohibition on Imposition of Deduction for Failure to File Certain Reports of Events

Section 209(b) of Pub.L. 86–778 provided that: "No deduction shall be imposed on or after the date of the enactment of this Act [Sept. 13, 1960] under section 203(f) of the Social Security Act [subsec. (f) of this section], as in effect prior to such date, on account of failure to file a report of an event described in section 203(c) of such Act [subsec. (c) of this section], as in effect prior to such date; and no such deduction imposed prior to such date shall be collected after such date."

Prohibition on Payment of Benefits to Certain Spouses or Children

Section 211(t) of Pub.L. 86–778 provided that: "In any case where—

"(1) an individual has earnings (as defined in section 203(e)(4) of the Social Security Act [subsec. (e)(4) of this section] as in effect prior to the enactment of this Act [Sept. 13, 1960]) in a taxable year which begins before 1961 and ends in 1961 (but not on December 31, 1961), and

"(2) such individual's spouse or child entitled to monthly benefits on the basis of such individual's self-employment income has excess earnings (as defined in section 203(f)(3) of the Social Security Act as amended by this Act [subsec. (f)(3) of this section]) in a taxable year which begins after 1960, and

"(3) one or more months in the taxable year specified in paragraph (2) are included in the taxable year specified in paragraph (1),

then, if a deduction is imposed against the benefits payable to such individual with respect to a month described in paragraph (3), such spouse or child, as the case may be, shall not, for purposes of subsections (b) and (f) of section 203 of the Social Security Act as amended by this Act [subsecs. (b) and (f) of this section], be entitled to a payment for such month."

Retirement Test Exempt Amounts for 1986

By notice of the Secretary of Health and Human Services, Oct. 29, 1985, published in the Federal Register on Oct. 31, 1985, at 50 F.R. 45560, it was determined and announced pursuant to authority contained in subsec. (f)(8) of this section, that the retirement test monthly exempt amount for beneficiaries aged 65 through 69 for 1986 is $640, with the corresponding annual retirement test exempt amount for these beneficiaries set at $7,800, and that, for beneficiaries under age 65, the retirement test monthly exempt amount for 1986 is $480, with the corresponding annual retirement test exempt amount for these beneficiaries set at $5,760.

Retirement Test Exempt Amounts for 1985

By notice of the Secretary of Health and Human Services, Oct. 29, 1984, published in the Federal Register on Oct. 31, 1984, at 49 F.R. 43775, it was determined and announced, pursuant to authority contained in subsec. (f)(8) of this section, that the retirement test monthly exempt amount for beneficiaries aged 65 through 69 for 1985 is $610, with the corresponding annual retirement test exempt amount for these beneficiaries set at $7,320, and that, for beneficiaries under age 65, the retirement test monthly exempt amount for 1985 is $450, with the corresponding annual retirement test exempt amount for these beneficiaries set at $5,400.

Retirement Test Exempt Amounts for 1984

By notice of the Secretary of Health and Human Services, Oct. 27, 1983, published in the Federal Register on Nov. 1, 1983, at 48 F.R. 50414, it was determined and announced, pursuant to authority contained in subsec. (f)(8) of this section, that the retirement test monthly exempt amount for beneficiaries aged 65 through 69 for 1984 is $580, with the corresponding annual retirement test exempt amount for these beneficiaries set at $6,960, and that, for beneficiaries under age 65, the retirement test monthly exempt amount for

1984 is $430, with the corresponding annual retirement test exempt amount for these beneficiaries set at $5,160.

Retirement Test Exempt Amount for 1976

By notice of the Secretary of Health, Education, and Welfare [now Secretary of Health and Human Services], Oct. 22, 1975, 40 F.R. 50556, it was determined and announced that, pursuant to authority contained in subsec. (f)(8) of this section, the monthly exempt amount under the retirement test would be $230 with respect to taxable years ending in calendar year 1976.

Temporary Extension of Earnings Limitations to Include All Persons Aged Less Than Seventy-Two

Section 2204 of Pub.L. 97-35 provided that:

"**(a)** Notwithstanding subsection (e) of section 302 of the Social Security Amendments of 1977 (91 Stat. 1531; Public Law 95-216) [set out as an Effective Date of 1977 Act note above], the amendments made to section 203 of the Social Security Act [this section] by subsections (a) through (d) of such section 302 shall, except as provided in subsection (b) of this section, apply only with respect to monthly insurance benefits payable under title II of the Social Security Act [this subchapter] for months after December 1982.

"**(b)** In the case of any individual whose first taxable year (as in effect on the date of the enactment of this Act [Aug. 13, 1981]) ending after December 31, 1981, begins before January 1, 1982, the amendments made by section 302 of the Social Security Amendments of 1977 [amending this section] shall apply with respect to taxable years beginning with such taxable year."

§ 404. Overpayments and underpayments

(a) Procedure for adjustment or recovery

(1) Whenever the Commissioner of Social Security finds that more or less than the correct amount of payment has been made to any person under this subchapter, proper adjustment or recovery shall be made, under regulations prescribed by the Commissioner of Social Security, as follows:

(A) With respect to payment to a person of more than the correct amount, the Commissioner of Social Security shall decrease any payment under this subchapter to which such overpaid person is entitled, or shall require such overpaid person or his estate to refund the amount in excess of the correct amount, or shall decrease any payment under this subchapter payable to his estate or to any other person on the basis of the wages and self-employment income which were the basis of the payments to such overpaid person, or shall obtain recovery by means of reduction in tax refunds based on notice to the Secretary of the Treasury as permitted under section 3720A of Title 31, or shall apply any combination of the foregoing. A payment made under this subchapter on the basis of an erroneous report of death by the Department of Defense of an individual in the line of duty while he is a member of the uniformed services (as defined in section 410(m) of this title) on active duty (as defined in section 410(*l*) of this title) shall not be considered an incorrect payment for any month prior to the month such Department notifies the Commissioner of Social Security that such individual is alive.

(B)(i) Subject to clause (ii), with respect to payment to a person of less than the correct amount, the Commissioner of Social Security shall make payment of the balance of the amount due such underpaid person, or, if such person dies before payments are completed or before negotiating one or more checks representing correct payments, disposition of the amount due shall be made in accordance with subsection (d).

(ii) No payment shall be made under this subparagraph to any person during any period for which monthly insurance benefits of such person—

(I) are subject to nonpayment by reason of section 402(x)(1) of this title, or

(II) in the case of a person whose monthly insurance benefits have terminated for a reason other than death, would be subject to nonpayment by reason of section 402(x)(1) of this title but for the termination of such benefits,

until section 402(x)(1) of this title no longer applies, or would no longer apply in the case of benefits that have terminated.

(iii) Nothing in clause (ii) shall be construed to limit the Commissioner's authority to withhold amounts, make adjustments, or recover amounts due under this subchapter, subchapter VIII or subchapter XVI that would be deducted from a payment that would otherwise be payable to such person but for such clause.

(2) Notwithstanding any other provision of this section, when any payment of more than the correct amount is made to or on behalf of an individual who has died, and such payment—

(A) is made by direct deposit to a financial institution;

(B) is credited by the financial institution to a joint account of the deceased individual and another person; and

(C) such other person was entitled to a monthly benefit on the basis of the same wages and self-employment income as the deceased individual for the month preceding the month in which the deceased individual died,

the amount of such payment in excess of the correct amount shall be treated as a payment of more than the correct amount to such other person. If any payment of more than the correct amount is made to a representative payee on behalf of an individual after the individual's death, the representative payee shall be liable for the repayment of the overpayment, and the Commissioner of Social Security shall establish an overpayment control record under the social security account number of the representative payee.

(3)(A) When any payment of more than the correct amount is made on behalf of an individual who is a represented minor beneficiary for a month in which such individual is in foster care under the responsibility of a State and the State is the representative payee of such individual, the State shall be liable for the repayment of the overpayment, and there shall be no adjustment of payments to, or recovery by the United States from, such individual.

(B) For purposes of this paragraph, the term "represented minor beneficiary" has the meaning given such term in subsection (j)(11)(B)(iii).

(b) Access to financial information for old-age, survivors, and disability insurance waivers

(1) In any case in which more than the correct amount of payment has been made, there shall be no adjustment of payments to, or recovery by the United States from, any person who is without fault if such adjustment or recovery would defeat the purpose of this subchapter or would be against equity and good conscience.

(2) In making for purposes of this subsection any determination of whether any individual is without fault, the Commissioner of Social Security shall specifically take into account any physical, mental, educational, or linguistic limitation such individual may have (including any lack of facility with the English language).

(3)(A) In making for purposes of this subsection any determination of whether such adjustment or recovery would defeat the purpose of this subchapter, the Commissioner of Social Security shall require an individual to provide authorization for the Commissioner to obtain (subject to the cost reimbursement requirements of section 1115(a) of the Right to Financial Privacy Act [1]) from any financial institution (within the meaning of section 1101(1) of such Act [2]) any financial record (within the meaning of section 1101(2) of such Act [2]) held by the institution with respect to such individual whenever the Commissioner determines the record is needed in connection with a determination with respect to such adjustment or recovery.

(B) Notwithstanding section 1104(a)(1) of the Right to Financial Privacy Act [3], an authorization provided by an individual pursuant this paragraph shall remain effective until the earlier of—

(i) the rendering of a final decision on whether adjustment or recovery would defeat the purpose of this subchapter; or

(ii) the express revocation by the individual of the authorization, in a written notification to the Commissioner.

(C)(i) An authorization obtained by the Commissioner of Social Security pursuant this paragraph shall be considered to meet the requirements of the Right to Financial Privacy Act [4] for purposes of section 1103(a) of such Act [5], and need not be furnished to the financial institution, notwithstanding section 1104(a) of such Act [3].

(ii) The certification requirements of section 1103(b) of the Right to Financial Privacy Act [5] shall not apply to requests by the Commissioner of Social Security pursuant to an authorization provided under this paragraph.

(iii) A request by the Commissioner pursuant to an authorization provided under this paragraph is deemed to meet the requirements of section 1104(a)(3) of the Right to Financial Privacy Act [3] and the flush language of section 1102 of such Act [6].

(D) The Commissioner shall inform any person who provides authorization pursuant to this paragraph of the duration and scope of the authorization.

(E) If an individual refuses to provide, or revokes, any authorization for the Commissioner of Social Security to obtain from any financial institution any financial record, the Commissioner may, on that basis, determine that adjustment or recovery would not defeat the purpose of this subchapter.

(c) Nonliability of certifying and disbursing officers

No certifying or disbursing officer shall be held liable for any amount certified or paid by him to any person where the adjustment or recovery of such amount is waived under subsection (b), or where adjustment under subsection (a) is not completed prior to the death of all persons against whose benefits deductions are authorized.

(d) Payment to survivors or heirs when eligible person is deceased

If an individual dies before any payment due him under this subchapter is completed, payment of the amount due (including the amount of any unnegotiated checks) shall be made—

(1) to the person, if any, who is determined by the Commissioner of Social Security to be the surviving spouse of the deceased individual and who either (i) was living in the same household with the deceased at the time of his death or (ii) was, for the month in which the deceased individual died, entitled to a monthly benefit on the basis of the same wages and self-employment income as was the deceased individual;

(2) if there is no person who meets the requirements of paragraph (1), or if the person who meets such requirements dies before the payment due him under this subchapter is completed, to the child or children, if any, of the deceased individual who were, for the month in which the deceased individual died, entitled to monthly benefits on the basis of the same wages and self-employment income as was the deceased individual (and, in case there is more than one such child, in equal parts to each such child);

(3) if there is no person who meets the requirements of paragraph (1) or (2), or if each person who meets such requirements dies before the payment due him under this subchapter is completed, to the parent or parents, if any, of the deceased individual who were, for the month in which the deceased individual died, entitled to monthly benefits on the basis of the same wages and self-employment income as was the deceased individual (and, in case there is more than one such parent, in equal parts to each such parent);

(4) if there is no person who meets the requirements of paragraph (1), (2), or (3), or if each person who meets such requirements dies before the payment due him under this subchapter is completed, to the person, if any, determined by the Commissioner of Social Security to be the surviving spouse of the deceased individual;

(5) if there is no person who meets the requirements of paragraph (1), (2), (3), or (4), or if each person who meets such requirements dies before the payment due him under this subchapter is completed, to the person or persons, if any, determined by the Commissioner of Social Security to be the child or children of the deceased individual (and, in case there is more than one such child, in equal parts to each such child);

(6) if there is no person who meets the requirements of paragraph (1), (2), (3), (4), or (5), or if each person who meets such requirements dies before the payment due him under this subchapter is completed, to the parent or parents, if any, of the deceased individual (and, in case there is more than one such parent, in equal parts to each such parent); or

(7) if there is no person who meets the requirements of paragraph (1), (2), (3), (4), (5), or (6), or if each person who meets such requirements dies before the payment due him under this subchapter is completed, to the legal representative of the estate of the deceased individual, if any.

(e) Adjustments due to supplemental security income payments

For payments which are adjusted by reason of payment of benefits under the supplemental security income program established by subchapter XVI, see section 1320a–6 of this title.

(f) Collection of delinquent amounts

(1) With respect to any deliquent[7] amount, the Commissioner of Social Security may use the collection practices described in sections 3711(f), 3716, 3717, and 3718 of Title 31 and in section 5514 of Title 5, all as in effect immediately after April 26, 1996.

(2) For purposes of paragraph (1), the term "delinquent amount" means an amount—

(A) in excess of the correct amount of payment under this subchapter;

(B) paid to a person after such person has attained 18 years of age; and

(C) determined by the Commissioner of Social Security, under regulations, to be otherwise unrecoverable under this section after such person ceases to be a beneficiary under this subchapter.

(g) Cross-program recovery of overpayments

For provisions relating to the cross-program recovery of overpayments made under programs administered by the Commissioner of Social Security, see section 1320b–17 of this title.

(Aug. 14, 1935, c. 531, Title II, § 204, 49 Stat. 624; Aug. 10, 1939, c. 666, Title II, § 201, 53 Stat. 1362, 1368; Aug. 28, 1950, c. 809, Title I, § 109(b)(1), 64 Stat. 523; Sept. 1, 1954, c. 1206, Title I, § 111(a), 68 Stat. 1085; Pub.L. 89–97, Title III, § 329, July 30, 1965, 79 Stat. 401; Pub.L. 90–248, Title I, §§ 152, 153(a), 154(a), Jan. 2, 1968, 81 Stat. 860, 861; Pub.L. 96–265, Title V, § 501(b), June 9, 1980, 94 Stat. 470; Pub.L. 99–272, Title XII, § 12113(a), Apr. 7, 1986, 100 Stat. 288; Pub.L. 101–239, Title X, § 10305(b), Dec. 19, 1989, 103 Stat. 2483; Pub.L. 101–508, Title V, § 5129(a), Nov. 5, 1990, 104 Stat. 1388–287; Pub.L. 103–296, Title I, § 107(a)(4), Aug. 15, 1994, 108 Stat. 1478; Pub.L. 103–387, § 5(a), Oct. 22, 1994, 108 Stat. 4077; Pub.L. 104–134, Title III, § 31001(z)(2)(A), Apr. 26, 1996, 110 Stat. 1321–379; Pub.L. 104–316, Title I, § 115(g)(2)(E), Oct. 19, 1996, 110 Stat. 3835; Pub.L. 105–306, § 8(b)(1), Oct. 28, 1998, 112 Stat. 2929; Pub.L. 106–169, Title II, §§ 201(a), 203(c), Dec. 14, 1999, 113 Stat. 1831, 1832; Pub.L. 108–203, Title II, § 210(b)(1), Mar. 2, 2004, 118 Stat. 517; Pub.L. 111–115, § 2(a), Dec. 15, 2009, 123 Stat. 3029; Pub.L. 114–74, Title VIII, § 834(a), Nov. 2, 2015, 129 Stat. 614; Pub.L. 115–165, Title I, § 104(a), Apr. 13, 2018, 132 Stat. 1263.)

1 See 12 U.S.C.A. § 3415.

2 See 12 U.S.C.A. § 3401.

3 See 12 U.S.C.A. § 3404.

4 Probably means the Right to Financial Privacy Act of 1978, Title XI of Pub.L. 95–630, which is classified principally to chapter 35 of Title 12, 12 U.S.C.A. § 3401 et seq. See References in Text note set out under this section.

5 See 12 U.S.C.A. § 3403.

6 See 12 U.S.C.A. § 3402.

7 So in original. Probably should be "delinquent".

HISTORICAL AND STATUTORY NOTES

References in Text

This subchapter, referred to in text, originally read "this title", meaning Title II of the Social Security Act, Act Aug. 14, 1935, c. 531, 49 Stat. 620, as amended, which is principally classified to subchapter II of this chapter, 42 U.S.C.A. § 401 et seq.

Subchapter VIII or subchapter XVI, referred to in subsec. (a)(1)(B)(iii), originally read "title VIII or title XVI", meaning title VIII or title XVI of the Social Security Act, Act Aug. 14, 1935, c. 531, 49 Stat. 620, as amended. Title VIII of such Act is principally classified to subchapter VIII of this chapter, 42 U.S.C.A. § 1001 et seq. Title XVI of such Act is principally classified to subchapter XVI of this chapter, 42 U.S.C.A. § 1381 et seq. For complete classification, see Short Title note set out under 42 U.S.C.A. § 1305 and Tables.

The Right to Financial Privacy Act, referred to in subsec. (b)(3)(A), (B), (C), probably means the Right to Financial

Privacy Act of 1978, Title XI of Pub.L. 95–630, Nov. 10, 1978, 92 Stat. 3697, which is classified generally to chapter 35 of Title 12, 12 U.S.C.A. § 3401 et seq. Sections 1101, 1102, 1103, 1104, and 1115 of the Act are classified to 12 U.S.C.A. §§ 3401, 3402, 3403, 3404, and 3415, respectively. For complete classification, see Short Title note set out under 12 U.S.C.A. § 3401 and Tables.

Codifications

Section 31001(z)(2)(A) of Pub.L. 104–134, which directed that subsec. (f) of this section be amended to read "as follows:", followed by provisions beginning with the designation "(f)(1)" and ending with a period, and without either accounting for the existing par. (2) of subsec. (f) or adding a new par. (2), was executed, as the probable intent of Congress, to par. (1) of subsec. (f) only, with existing par. (2) left unchanged. See 1996 Amendments note set out under this section.

Effective and Applicability Provisions

2018 Acts. Pub.L. 115–165, Title I, § 104(c), Apr. 13, 2018, 132 Stat. 1264, provided that: "The amendment made by subsection (a) [amending this section] shall apply with respect to overpayment determinations made on or after the date of the enactment of this Act [Apr. 13, 2018] and to any other overpaid amounts that have not been recovered as of such date."

2015 Acts. Pub.L. 114–74, Title VIII, § 834(c), Nov. 2, 2015, 129 Stat. 615, provided that: "The amendments made by this section [amending this section and 42 U.S.C.A. § 1383] shall apply with respect to determinations made on or after the date that is 3 months after the date of the enactment of this section [Nov. 2, 2015]."

2009 Acts. Pub.L. 111–115, § 2(c), Dec. 15, 2009, 123 Stat. 3030, provided that: "The amendments made by this section [amending this section and 42 U.S.C.A. § 1383] shall be effective for payments that would otherwise be made on or after the date of the enactment of this Act [Dec. 15, 2009]."

2004 Acts. Pub.L. 108–203, Title II, § 210(c), Mar. 2, 2004, 118 Stat. 517, provided that: "The amendments and repeal made by this section [amending subsec. (g) of this section and 42 U.S.C.A. §§ 1008, 1320b–17, and 1383(b)(1)(B), (6), and repealing 42 U.S.C.A. § 1320b–18] shall take effect on the date of enactment of this Act [Mar. 2, 2004], and shall be effective with respect to overpayments under titles II, VIII, and XVI of the Social Security Act [this subchapter and subchapters VIII and XVI of this chapter, 42 U.S.C.A. §§ 401 et seq., 1001 et seq., and 1381 et seq., respectively] that are outstanding on or after such date [Mar. 2, 2004]."

1999 Acts. Amendment by section 203(c) of Pub.L. 106–169 applicable to debt outstanding on or after Dec. 14, 1999, see section 203(d) of Pub.L. 106–169, set out as a note under section 3701 of Title 31.

Pub.L. 106–169, Title II, § 201(c), Dec. 14, 1999, 113 Stat. 1831, provided that: "The amendments made by this section [amending subsec. (a)(2) of this section and section 1383 of this title] shall apply to overpayments made 12 months or more after the date of the enactment of this Act [Dec. 14, 1999]."

1998 Acts. Pub.L. 105–306, § 8(c), Oct. 28, 1998, 112 Stat. 2930, provided that: "The amendments made by this section [enacting section 1320b–17 of this title, amending this section and section 1383 of this title] shall take effect on the date of the enactment of this Act [Oct. 28, 1998] and shall apply to amounts incorrectly paid which remain outstanding on or after such date."

1996 Acts. Amendment by Pub.L. 104–316 effective Oct. 19, 1996, see section 101(e) of Pub.L. 104–316, set out as a note under section 130c of Title 2, The Congress.

Amendment by Pub.L. 104–134 effective Apr. 26, 1996, see section 31001(a)(2)(A) of Pub.L. 104–134, set out as a note under section 3322 of Title 31, Money and Finance.

1994 Acts. Amendment by Pub.L. 103–387 applicable to collection activities begun on or after October 22, 1994, see section 5(c) of Pub.L. 103–387, as amended by section 31001(z)(2)(B) of Pub.L. 104–134, set out as a note under section 3701 of Title 31, Money and Finance.

Amendment by section 107(a)(4) of Pub.L. 103–296 effective Mar. 31, 1995, see section 110 of Pub.L. 103–296, set out as a note under section 401 of this title.

1990 Acts. Amendment by Pub.L. 101–508 effective Jan. 1, 1991, and inapplicable to refunds to which amendments by section 2653 of the Deficit Reduction Act of 1984 do not apply, see section 5129(d) of Pub.L. 101–508, set out as a note under section 6402 of Title 26, Internal Revenue Code.

1989 Acts. Amendment by Pub.L. 101–239 applicable with respect to determinations made on or after July 1, 1990, see section 10305(f) of Pub.L. 101–239, set out as a note under section 403 of this title.

1986 Acts. Section 12113(c) of Pub.L. 99–272 provided that: "The amendments made by this section [amending subsec. (a) of this section and section 1383(b) of this title] shall apply only in the case of deaths of which the Secretary is first notified on or after the date of the enactment of this Act [Apr. 7, 1986]."

1980 Acts. Amendment by Pub.L. 96–265 applicable in the case of payments of monthly insurance benefits under this subchapter entitlement of which is determined on or after July 1, 1981, see section 501(d) of Pub.L. 96–265, set out as a note under section 1320a–6 of this title.

1968 Acts. Section 153(b) of Pub.L. 90–248 provided that: "The amendment made by this section [to subsec. (a)(1) of this section] shall apply with respect to benefits under title II of the Social Security Act [this subchapter] if the individual to whom such benefits were paid would have been entitled to such benefits in or after the month in which this Act was enacted [Jan. 1968] if the report mentioned in the amendment made by subsection (a) of this section had been correct (but without regard to the provisions of section 202(j)(1) of such Act [section 402(j)(1) of this title])."

Report on Overpayment Waivers

Pub.L. 114–74, Title VIII, § 845(c), Nov. 2, 2015, 129 Stat. 619, provided that:

"Not later than January 1 of each calendar year, the Commissioner of Social Security shall submit to the Committee on Ways and Means of the House of Representatives and the Committee on Finance of the Senate a report on—

"(1) the number and total value of overpayments recovered or scheduled to be recovered by the Social Security Administration during the previous fiscal year of benefits under title II and title XVI, respectively, [probably means Title II and Title XVI of Act Aug. 14, 1935, c. 531, which are classified to subchapter II and subchapter XVI of this chapter, 42 U.S.C.A. § 401 et seq. and 42 U.S.C.A. § 1381 et seq., respectively] including the terms and conditions of repayment of such overpayments; and

"(2) the number and total value of overpayments waived by the Social Security Administration during the previous fiscal year of benefits under title II and title XVI, respectively [subchapter II and subchapter XVI of this chapter, 42 U.S.C.A. § 401 et seq. and 42 U.S.C.A. § 1381 et seq., respectively]."

§ 405. Evidence, procedure, and certification for payments

(a) Rules and regulations; procedures

The Commissioner of Social Security shall have full power and authority to make rules and regulations and to establish procedures, not inconsistent with the provisions of this subchapter, which are necessary or appropriate to carry out such provisions, and shall adopt reasonable and proper rules and regulations to regulate and provide for the nature and extent of the proofs and evidence and the method of taking and furnishing the same in order to establish the right to benefits hereunder.

(b) Administrative determination of entitlement to benefits; findings of fact; hearings; investigations; evidentiary hearings in reconsiderations of disability benefit terminations; subsequent applications

(1) The Commissioner of Social Security is directed to make findings of fact, and decisions as to the rights of any individual applying for a payment under this subchapter. Any such decision by the Commissioner of Social Security which involves a determination of disability and which is in whole or in part unfavorable to such individual shall contain a statement of the case, in understandable language, setting forth a discussion of the evidence, and stating the Commissioner's determination and the reason or reasons upon which it is based. Upon request by any such individual or upon request by a wife, divorced wife, widow, surviving divorced wife, surviving divorced mother, surviving divorced father, husband, divorced husband, widower, surviving divorced husband, child, or parent who makes a showing in writing that his or her rights may be prejudiced by any decision the Commissioner of Social Security has rendered, the Commissioner shall give such applicant and such other individual reasonable notice and opportunity for a hearing with respect to such decision, and, if a hearing is held, shall, on the basis of evidence adduced at the hearing, affirm, modify, or reverse the Commissioner's findings of fact and such decision. Any such request with respect to such a decision must be filed within sixty days after notice of such decision is received by the individual making such request. The Commissioner of Social Security is further authorized, on the Commissioner's own motion, to hold such hearings and to conduct such investigations and other proceedings as the Commissioner may deem necessary or proper for the administration of this subchapter. In the course of any hearing, investigation, or other proceeding, the Commissioner may administer oaths and affirmations, examine witnesses, and receive evidence. Evidence may be received at any hearing before the Commissioner of Social Security even though inadmissible under rules of evidence applicable to court procedure.

(2) In any case where—

(A) an individual is a recipient of disability insurance benefits, or of child's, widow's, or widower's insurance benefits based on disability,

(B) the physical or mental impairment on the basis of which such benefits are payable is found to have ceased, not to have existed, or to no longer be disabling, and

(C) as a consequence of the finding described in subparagraph (B), such individual is determined by the Commissioner of Social Security not to be entitled to such benefits,

any reconsideration of the finding described in subparagraph (B), in connection with a reconsideration by the Commissioner of Social Security (before any hearing under paragraph (1) on the issue of such entitlement) of the Commissioner's determination described in subparagraph (C), shall be made only after opportunity for an evidentiary hearing, with regard to the finding described in subparagraph (B), which is reasonably accessible to such individual. Any reconsideration of a finding described in subparagraph (B) may be made either by the State agency or the Commissioner of Social Security where the finding was originally made by the State agency, and shall be made by the Commissioner of Social Security where the finding was originally made by the Commissioner of Social Security. In the case of a reconsideration by a State agency of a finding described in subparagraph (B) which was originally made by such State agency, the evidentiary hearing shall be held by an adjudicatory unit of the State agency other than the unit that made the finding described in subparagraph (B). In the case of a reconsideration by the Commissioner of Social Security of a finding described in subparagraph (B) which was originally made by the Commissioner of Social Security, the evidentiary hearing shall be held by a person other than the person or persons who made the finding described in subparagraph (B).

(3)(A) A failure to timely request review of an initial adverse determination with respect to an application for any benefit under this subchapter or an adverse determination on reconsideration of such an initial determination shall not serve as a basis for denial of a subsequent application for any benefit under this subchapter if the applicant demonstrates that the applicant, or any other individual referred to in paragraph (1), failed to so request such a review acting in good faith reliance upon incorrect, incomplete, or misleading information, relating to the consequences of reapplying for benefits in lieu of seeking review of an adverse determination, provided by any officer or employee of the Social Security Administration or any State agency acting under section 421 of this title.

(B) In any notice of an adverse determination with respect to which a review may be requested under paragraph (1), the Commissioner of Social Security shall describe in clear and specific language the effect on possible entitlement to benefits under this subchapter of choosing to reapply in lieu of requesting review of the determination.

(c) Wage records

(1) For the purposes of this subsection—

(A) The term "year" means a calendar year when used with respect to wages and a taxable year when used with respect to self-employment income.

(B) The term "time limitation" means a period of three years, three months, and fifteen days.

(C) The term "survivor" means an individual's spouse, surviving divorced wife, surviving divorced husband, surviving divorced mother, surviving divorced father, child, or parent, who survives such individual.

(D) The term "period" when used with respect to self-employment income means a taxable year and when used with respect to wages means—

(i) a quarter if wages were reported or should have been reported on a quarterly basis on tax returns filed with the Secretary of the Treasury or his delegate under section 6011 of the Internal Revenue Code of 1986 or regulations thereunder (or on reports filed by a State under section 418(e) of this title (as in effect prior to December 31, 1986) or regulations thereunder),

(ii) a year if wages were reported or should have been reported on a yearly basis on such tax returns or reports, or

(iii) the half year beginning January 1 or July 1 in the case of wages which were reported or should have been reported for calendar year 1937.

(2)(A) On the basis of information obtained by or submitted to the Commissioner of Social Security, and after such verification thereof as the Commissioner deems necessary, the Commissioner of Social Security shall establish and maintain records of the amounts of wages paid to, and the amounts of self-employment income derived by, each individual and of the periods in which such wages were paid and such income was derived and, upon request, shall inform any individual or his survivor, or the legal representative of such individual or his estate, of the amounts of wages and self-employment income of such individual and the periods during which such wages were paid and such income was derived, as shown by such records at the time of such request.

(B)(i) In carrying out the Commissioner's duties under subparagraph (A) and subparagraph (F), the Commissioner of Social Security shall take affirmative measures to assure that social security account numbers will, to the maximum extent practicable, be assigned to all members of appropriate groups or categories of individuals by assigning such numbers (or ascertaining that such numbers have already been assigned):

(I) to aliens at the time of their lawful admission to the United States either for permanent residence or under other authority of law permitting them to engage in employment in the United States and to other aliens at such time as their status is so changed as to make it lawful for them to engage in such employment;

(II) to any individual who is an applicant for or recipient of benefits under any program financed in whole or in part from Federal funds including any child on whose behalf such benefits are claimed by another person; and

(III) to any other individual when it appears that he could have been but was not assigned an account number under the provisions of subclauses (I) or (II) but only after such investigation as is necessary to establish to the satisfaction of the Commissioner of Social Security, the identity of such individual, the fact that an account number has not already been assigned to such individual, and the fact that such individual is a citizen or a noncitizen who is not, because of his alien status, prohibited from engaging in employment;

and, in carrying out such duties, the Commissioner of Social Security is authorized to take affirmative measures to assure the issuance of social security numbers:

(IV) to or on behalf of children who are below school age at the request of their parents or guardians; and

(V) to children of school age at the time of their first enrollment in school.

(ii) The Commissioner of Social Security shall require of applicants for social security account numbers such evidence as may be necessary to establish the age, citizenship, or alien status, and true identity of such applicants, and to determine which (if any) social security account number has previously been assigned to such individual. With respect to an application for a social security account number for an individual who has not attained the age of 18 before such application, such evidence shall include the information described in subparagraph (C)(ii).

(iii) In carrying out the requirements of this subparagraph, the Commissioner of Social Security shall enter into such agreements as may be necessary with the Attorney General and other officials and with State and local welfare agencies and school authorities (including nonpublic school authorities).

(C)(i) It is the policy of the United States that any State (or political subdivision thereof) may, in the administration of any tax, general public assistance, driver's license, or motor vehicle registration law within its jurisdiction, utilize the social security account numbers issued by the Commissioner of Social Security for the purpose of establishing the identification of individuals affected by such law, and may require any individual who is or appears to be so affected to furnish to such State (or political subdivision thereof) or any agency thereof having administrative responsibility for the law involved, the social security account number (or numbers, if he has more than one such number) issued to him by the Commissioner of Social Security.

(ii) In the administration of any law involving the issuance of a birth certificate, each State shall require each parent to furnish to such State (or political subdivision thereof) or any agency thereof having administrative responsibility for the law involved, the social security account number (or numbers, if the parent has more than one such number) issued to the parent unless the State (in accordance with regulations prescribed by the Commissioner of Social Security) finds good cause for not requiring the furnishing of such number. The State shall make numbers furnished under this subclause available to the Commissioner of Social Security and the agency administering the State's plan under part D of subchapter IV in accordance with Federal or State law and regulation. Such numbers shall not be recorded on the birth certificate. A State shall not use any social security account number, obtained with respect to the issuance by the State of a birth certificate, for any purpose other than for the enforcement of child support orders in effect in the State, unless section 7(a) of the Privacy Act of 1974 does not prohibit the State from requiring the disclosure of such number, by reason of the State having adopted, before January 1, 1975, a statute or regulation requiring such disclosure.

(iii)(I) In the administration of section 9 of the Food and Nutrition Act of 2008 (7 U.S.C. 2018) involving the determination of the qualifications of applicants under such Act, the Secretary of Agriculture may require each applicant retail store or wholesale food concern to furnish to the Secretary of Agriculture the social security account number of each individual who is an officer of the store or concern and, in the case of a privately owned applicant, furnish the social security account numbers of the owners of such applicant. No officer or employee of the Department of Agriculture shall have access to any such number for any purpose other than the establishment and maintenance of a list of the names and social security account numbers of such individuals for use in determining those applicants who have been previously sanctioned or convicted under section 12 or 15 of such Act (7 U.S.C. 2021 or 2024).

(II) The Secretary of Agriculture may share any information contained in any list referred to in subclause (I) with any other agency or instrumentality of the United States which otherwise has access to social security account numbers in accordance with this subsection or other applicable Federal law, except that the Secretary of Agriculture may share such information only to the extent that such Secretary determines such sharing would assist in verifying and matching such information against information maintained by such other agency or instrumentality. Any such information shared pursuant to this subclause may be used by such other agency or instrumentality only for the purpose of effective administration and enforcement of the Food and Nutrition Act of 2008 or for the purpose of investigation of violations of other Federal laws or enforcement of such laws.

(III) The Secretary of Agriculture, and the head of any other agency or instrumentality referred to in this subclause, shall restrict, to the satisfaction of the Commissioner of Social Security, access to social security account numbers obtained pursuant to this clause only to officers and employees of the United States whose duties or responsibilities require access for the purposes described in subclause (II).

(IV) The Secretary of Agriculture, and the head of any agency or instrumentality with which information is shared pursuant to clause [1] (II), shall provide such other safeguards as the Commissioner of Social Security determines to be necessary or appropriate to protect the confidentiality of the social security account numbers.

(iv) In the administration of section 506 of the Federal Crop Insurance Act, the Federal Crop Insurance Corporation may require each policyholder and each reinsured company to furnish to the insurer or to the Corporation the social security account number of such policyholder, subject to the requirements of this clause. No officer or employee of the Federal Crop Insurance Corporation shall have access to any such number for any purpose other than the establishment of a system of records necessary for the effective administration of such Act. The Manager of the Corporation may require each policyholder to provide to the Manager, at such times and in such manner as prescribed by the Manager, the social security account number of each individual that holds or acquires a substantial beneficial interest in the policyholder. For purposes of this clause, the term "substantial beneficial interest" means not less than 5 percent of all beneficial interest in the policyholder. The Secretary of Agriculture shall restrict, to the satisfaction of the Commissioner of Social Security, access to social security account numbers obtained pursuant to this clause only to officers and employees of the United States or authorized persons whose duties or responsibilities require access for the administration of the Federal Crop Insurance Act. The Secretary of Agriculture shall provide such other safeguards as the Commissioner of Social Security determines to be necessary or appropriate to protect the confidentiality of such social security account numbers. For purposes of this clause the term "authorized person" means an officer or employee of an insurer whom the Manager of the Corporation designates by rule, subject to appropriate safeguards including a prohibition against the release of such social security account number (other than to the Corporation) by such person.

(v) If and to the extent that any provision of Federal law heretofore enacted is inconsistent with the policy set forth in clause (i), such provision shall, on and after October 4, 1976, be null, void, and of no effect. If and to the extent that any such provision is inconsistent with the requirement set forth in clause (ii), such provision shall, on and after October 13, 1988, be null, void, and of no effect.

(vi)(I) For purposes of clause (i) of this subparagraph, an agency of a State (or political subdivision thereof) charged with the administration of any general public assistance, driver's license, or motor vehicle registration law which did not use the social security account number for identification under a law or regulation adopted before January 1, 1975, may require an individual to disclose his or her social security number to such agency solely for the purpose of administering the laws referred to in clause (i) above and for the purpose of responding to requests for information from an agency administering a program funded under part A of subchapter IV or an agency operating pursuant to the provisions of part D of such subchapter.

(II) Any State or political subdivision thereof (and any person acting as an agent of such an agency or instrumentality), in the administration of any driver's license or motor vehicle registration law within its jurisdiction, may not display a social security account number issued by the Commissioner of Social Security (or any derivative of such number) on any driver's license, motor vehicle registration, or personal identification card (as defined in section 7212(a)(2) of the 9/11 Commission Implementation Act of 2004), or include, on any such license, registration, or personal identification card, a magnetic strip, bar code, or other means of communication which conveys such number (or derivative thereof).

(vii) For purposes of this subparagraph, the term "State" includes the District of Columbia, the Commonwealth of Puerto Rico, the Virgin Islands, Guam, the Commonwealth of the Northern Marianas, and the Trust Territory of the Pacific Islands.

(viii)(I) Social security account numbers and related records that are obtained or maintained by authorized persons pursuant to any provision of law enacted on or after October 1, 1990, shall be confidential, and no authorized person shall disclose any such social security account number or related record.

(II) Paragraphs (1), (2), and (3) of section 7213(a) of the Internal Revenue Code of 1986 shall apply with respect to the unauthorized willful disclosure to any person of social security account numbers and related records obtained or maintained by an authorized person pursuant to a provision of law enacted on or after October 1, 1990, in the same manner and to the same extent as such paragraphs apply with respect to unauthorized disclosures of return and return information described in such paragraphs. Paragraph (4) of section 7213(a) of such Code shall apply with respect to the willful offer of any item of material value in exchange for any such social security account number or related record in the same manner and to the same extent as such paragraph applies with respect to offers (in exchange for any return or return information) described in such paragraph.

(III) For purposes of this clause, the term "authorized person" means an officer or employee of the United States, an officer or employee of any State, political subdivision of a State, or agency of a State or political subdivision of a State, and any other person (or officer or employee thereof), who has or had access to social security account numbers or related records pursuant to any provision of law enacted on or after October 1, 1990. For purposes of this subclause, the term "officer or employee" includes a former officer or employee.

(IV) For purposes of this clause, the term "related record" means any record, list, or compilation that indicates, directly or indirectly, the identity of any individual with respect to whom a social security account number or a request for a social security account number is maintained pursuant to this clause.

(ix) In the administration of the provisions of chapter 81 of Title 5 and the Longshore and Harbor Workers' Compensation Act (33 U.S.C. 901 et seq.), the Secretary of Labor may require by regulation that any person filing a notice of injury or a claim for benefits under such provisions provide as part of such notice or claim such person's social security account number, subject to the requirements of this clause. No officer or employee of the Department of Labor shall have access to any such number for any purpose other than the establishment of a system of records necessary for the effective administration of such provisions. The Secretary of Labor shall restrict, to the satisfaction of the Commissioner of Social Security, access to social security account numbers obtained pursuant to this clause to officers and employees of the United States whose duties or responsibilities require access for the administration or enforcement of such provisions. The Secretary of Labor shall provide such other safeguards as the Commissioner of Social Security determines to be necessary or appropriate to protect the confidentiality of the social security account numbers.

(x) The Secretary of Health and Human Services, and the Exchanges established under section 1311 of the Patient Protection and Affordable Care Act, are authorized to collect and use the names and social security account numbers of individuals as required to administer the provisions of, and the amendments made by, the [2] such Act.

(xi) No Federal, State, or local agency may display the Social Security account number of any individual, or any derivative of such number, on any check issued for any payment by the Federal, State, or local agency.

(xii) No Federal, State, or local agency may employ, or enter into a contract for the use or employment of, prisoners in any capacity that would allow such prisoners access to the Social Security account numbers of other individuals. For purposes of this clause, the term "prisoner" means an individual confined in a jail, prison, or other penal institution or correctional facility pursuant to such individual's conviction of a criminal offense.

(xiii) The Secretary of Health and Human Services, in consultation with the Commissioner of Social Security, shall establish cost-effective procedures to ensure that a Social Security account number (or derivative thereof) is not displayed, coded, or embedded on the Medicare card issued to an individual who is entitled to benefits under part A of subchapter XVIII or enrolled under part B of subchapter XVIII and that any other identifier displayed on such card is not identifiable as a Social Security account number (or derivative thereof).

(D)(i) It is the policy of the United States that—

(I) any State (or any political subdivision of a State) and any authorized blood donation facility may utilize the social security account numbers issued by the Commissioner of Social Security for the purpose of identifying blood donors, and

(II) any State (or political subdivision of a State) may require any individual who donates blood within such State (or political subdivision) to furnish to such State (or political subdivision), to any agency thereof having related administrative responsibility, or to any authorized blood donation facility the social security account number (or numbers, if the donor has more than one such number) issued to the donor by the Commissioner of Social Security.

(ii) If and to the extent that any provision of Federal law enacted before November 10, 1988, is inconsistent with the policy set forth in clause (i), such provision shall, on and after November 10, 1988, be null, void, and of no effect.

(iii) For purposes of this subparagraph—

(I) the term "authorized blood donation facility" means an entity described in section 1320b–11(h)(1)(B) of this title, and

(II) the term "State" includes the District of Columbia, the Commonwealth of Puerto Rico, the Virgin Islands, Guam, the Commonwealth of the Northern Marianas, and the Trust Territory of the Pacific Islands.

(E)(i) It is the policy of the United States that—

(I) any State (or any political subdivision of a State) may utilize the social security account numbers issued by the Commissioner of Social Security for the additional purposes described in clause (ii) if such numbers have been collected and are otherwise utilized by such State (or political subdivision) in accordance with applicable law, and

(II) any district court of the United States may use, for such additional purposes, any such social security account numbers which have been so collected and are so utilized by any State.

(ii) The additional purposes described in this clause are the following:

(I) Identifying duplicate names of individuals on master lists used for jury selection purposes.

(II) Identifying on such master lists those individuals who are ineligible to serve on a jury by reason of their conviction of a felony.

(iii) To the extent that any provision of Federal law enacted before August 15, 1994, is inconsistent with the policy set forth in clause (i), such provision shall, on and after August 15, 1994, be null, void, and of no effect.

(iv) For purposes of this subparagraph, the term "State" has the meaning such term has in subparagraph (D).

(F) The Commissioner of Social Security shall require, as a condition for receipt of benefits under this subchapter, that an individual furnish satisfactory proof of a social security account number assigned to such individual by the Commissioner of Social Security or, in the case of an individual to whom no such number has been assigned, that such individual make proper application for assignment of such a number.

(G) The Commissioner of Social Security shall issue a social security card to each individual at the time of the issuance of a social security account number to such individual. The social security card shall be made of banknote paper, and (to the maximum extent practicable) shall be a card which cannot be counterfeited.

(H) The Commissioner of Social Security shall share with the Secretary of the Treasury the information obtained by the Commissioner pursuant to the second sentence of subparagraph (B)(ii) and to subparagraph (C)(ii) for the purpose of administering those sections of the Internal Revenue Code of 1986 which grant tax benefits based on support or residence of children.

(3) The Commissioner's records shall be evidence for the purpose of proceedings before the Commissioner of Social Security or any court of the amounts of wages paid to, and self-employment income derived by, an individual and of the periods in which such wages were paid and such income was derived. The absence of an entry in such records as to wages alleged to have been paid to, or as to self-employment income alleged to have been derived by, an individual in any period shall be evidence that no such alleged wages were paid to, or that no such alleged income was derived by, such individual during such period.

(4) Prior to the expiration of the time limitation following any year the Commissioner of Social Security may, if it is brought to the Commissioner's attention that any entry of wages or self-employment income in the Commissioner's records for such year is erroneous or that any item of wages or self-employment income for such year has been omitted from such records, correct such entry or include such omitted item in the Commissioner's records, as the case may be. After the expiration of the time limitation following any year—

(A) the Commissioner's records (with changes, if any, made pursuant to paragraph (5) of this subsection) of the amounts of wages paid to, and self-employment income derived by, an individual during any period in such year shall be conclusive for the purposes of this subchapter;

(B) the absence of an entry in the Commissioner's records as to the wages alleged to have been paid by an employer to an individual during any period in such year shall be presumptive evidence for the purposes of this subchapter that no such alleged wages were paid to such individual in such period; and

(C) the absence of an entry in the Commissioner's records as to the self-employment income alleged to have been derived by an individual in such year shall be conclusive for the purposes of this subchapter that no such alleged self-employment income was derived by such individual in such year unless it is shown that he filed a tax return of his self-employment income for such year before the expiration of the time limitation following such year, in which case the Commissioner of Social Security shall include in the Commissioner's records the self-employment income of such individual for such year.

(5) After the expiration of the time limitation following any year in which wages were paid or alleged to have been paid to, or self-employment income was derived or alleged to have been derived by, an individual, the Commissioner of Social Security may change or delete any entry with respect to wages or self-employment income in the Commissioner's records of such year for such individual or include in the Commissioner's records of such year for such individual any omitted item of wages or self-employment income but only—

(A) if an application for monthly benefits or for a lump-sum death payment was filed within the time limitation following such year; except that no such change, deletion, or inclusion may be made pursuant to this subparagraph after a final decision upon the application for monthly benefits or lump-sum death payment;

(B) if within the time limitation following such year an individual or his survivor makes a request for a change or deletion, or for an inclusion of an omitted item, and alleges in writing that the Commissioner's records of the wages paid to, or the self-employment income derived by, such individual in such year are in one or more respects erroneous; except that no such change, deletion, or inclusion may be made pursuant to this subparagraph after a final decision upon such request. Written notice of the Commissioner's decision on any such request shall be given to the individual who made the request;

(C) to correct errors apparent on the face of such records;

(D) to transfer items to records of the Railroad Retirement Board if such items were credited under this subchapter when they should have been credited under the Railroad Retirement Act of 1937 or 1974, or to enter items transferred by the Railroad Retirement Board which have been credited under the Railroad Retirement Act of 1937 or 1974 when they should have been credited under this subchapter;

(E) to delete or reduce the amount of any entry which is erroneous as a result of fraud;

(F) to conform the Commissioner's records to—

(i) tax returns or portions thereof (including information returns and other written statements) filed with the Commissioner of Internal Revenue under Title VIII of the Social Security Act, under subchapter E of chapter 1 or subchapter A of chapter 9 of the Internal Revenue Code of 1939, under chapter 2 or 21 of the Internal Revenue Code of 1954 or the Internal Revenue Code of 1986, or under regulations made under authority of such title, subchapter, or chapter;

(ii) wage reports filed by a State pursuant to an agreement under section 418 of this title or regulations of the Commissioner of Social Security thereunder; or

(iii) assessments of amounts due under an agreement pursuant to section 418 of this title (as in effect prior to December 31, 1986), if such assessments are made within the period specified in subsection (q) of such section (as so in effect), or allowances of credits or refunds of overpayments by a State under an agreement pursuant to such section;

except that no amount of self-employment income of an individual for any taxable year (if such return or statement was filed after the expiration of the time limitation following the taxable year) shall be included in the Commissioner's records pursuant to this subparagraph;

(G) to correct errors made in the allocation, to individuals or periods, of wages or self-employment income entered in the records of the Commissioner of Social Security;

(H) to include wages paid during any period in such year to an individual by an employer;

(I) to enter items which constitute remuneration for employment under subsection (*o*), such entries to be in accordance with certified reports of records made by the Railroad Retirement Board pursuant to section 5(k)(3) of the Railroad Retirement Act of 1937 or section 7(b)(7) of the Railroad Retirement Act of 1974; or

(J) to include self-employment income for any taxable year, up to, but not in excess of, the amount of wages deleted by the Commissioner of Social Security as payments erroneously included in such records as wages paid to such individual, if such income (or net earnings from self-employment), not already included in such records as self-employment income, is included in a return or statement (referred to in subparagraph (F) of this subsection) filed before the expiration of the time limitation following the taxable year in which such deletion of wages is made.

(6) Written notice of any deletion or reduction under paragraph (4) or (5) of this subsection shall be given to the individual whose record is involved or to his survivor, except that (A) in the case of a deletion or reduction with respect to any entry of wages such notice shall be given to such individual only if he has previously been notified by the Commissioner of Social Security of the amount of his wages for the period involved, and (B) such notice shall be given to such survivor only if he or the individual whose record is involved has previously been notified by the Commissioner of Social Security of the amount of such individual's wages and self-employment income for the period involved.

(7) Upon request in writing (within such period, after any change or refusal of a request for a change of the Commissioner's records pursuant to this subsection, as the Commissioner of Social Security may prescribe), opportunity for hearing with respect to such change or refusal shall be afforded to any individual or his survivor. If a hearing is held pursuant to this paragraph the Commissioner of Social Security shall make findings of fact and a decision based upon the evidence adduced at such hearing and shall include any omitted items, or change or delete any entry, in the Commissioner's records as may be required by such findings and decision.

(8) A translation into English by a third party of a statement made in a foreign language by an applicant for or beneficiary of monthly insurance benefits under this subchapter shall not be regarded as reliable for any purpose under this subchapter unless the third party, under penalty of perjury—

(A) certifies that the translation is accurate; and

(B) discloses the nature and scope of the relationship between the third party and the applicant or recipient, as the case may be.

(9) Decisions of the Commissioner of Social Security under this subsection shall be reviewable by commencing a civil action in the United States district court as provided in subsection (g).

(d) Issuance of subpenas in administrative proceedings

For the purpose of any hearing, investigation, or other proceeding authorized or directed under this subchapter, or relative to any other matter within the Commissioner's jurisdiction hereunder, the Commissioner of Social Security shall have power to issue subpenas requiring the attendance and testimony of witnesses and the production of any evidence that relates to any matter under investigation or in question before the Commissioner of Social Security. Such attendance of witnesses and production of evidence at the designated place of such hearing, investigation, or other proceeding may be required from any place in the United States or in any Territory or possession thereof. Subpenas of the Commissioner of Social Security shall be served by anyone authorized by the Commissioner (1) by delivering a copy thereof to the individual named therein, or (2) by registered mail or by certified mail addressed to such individual at his last dwelling place or principal place of business. A verified return by the individual so serving the subpoena setting forth the manner of service, or, in the case of service by registered mail or by certified mail, the return post-office receipt therefor signed by the individual so served, shall be proof of service. Witnesses so subpoenaed shall be paid the same fees and mileage as are paid witnesses in the district courts of the United States.

(e) Judicial enforcement of subpenas; contempt

In case of contumacy by, or refusal to obey a subpoena duly served upon, any person, any district court of the United States for the judicial district in which said person charged with contumacy or refusal to obey is found or resides or transacts business, upon application by the Commissioner of Social Security, shall have jurisdiction to issue an order requiring such person to appear and give testimony, or to appear and produce evidence, or both; any failure to obey such order of the court may be punished by said court as contempt thereof.

(f) Repealed. Pub.L. 91–452, Title II, § 236, Oct. 15, 1970, 84 Stat. 930

(g) Judicial review

Any individual, after any final decision of the Commissioner of Social Security made after a hearing to which he was a party, irrespective of the amount in controversy, may obtain a review of such decision by a civil action commenced within sixty days after the mailing to him of notice of such decision or within such further time as the Commissioner of Social Security may allow. Such action shall be brought in the district court of the United States for the judicial district in which the plaintiff resides, or has his principal place of business, or, if he does not reside or have his principal place of business within any such judicial district, in the United States District Court for the District of Columbia. As part of the Commissioner's answer the Commissioner of Social Security shall file a certified copy of the transcript of the record including the evidence upon which the findings and decision complained of are based. The court shall have power to enter, upon the pleadings and transcript of the record, a judgment affirming, modifying, or reversing the decision of the Commissioner of Social Security, with or without remanding the cause for a rehearing. The findings of the Commissioner of Social Security as to any fact, if supported by substantial evidence, shall be conclusive, and where a claim has been denied by the Commissioner of Social Security or a decision is rendered under subsection (b) of this section which is adverse to an individual who was a party to the hearing before the Commissioner of Social Security, because of failure of the claimant or such individual to submit proof in conformity with any regulation prescribed under subsection (a) of this section, the court shall review only the question of conformity with such regulations and the validity of such regulations. The court may, on motion of the Commissioner of Social Security made for good cause shown before the Commissioner files the Commissioner's answer, remand the case to the Commissioner of Social Security for further action by the Commissioner of Social Security, and it may at any time order additional evidence to be taken before the Commissioner of Social Security, but only upon a showing that there is new evidence which is material and that there is good cause for the failure to incorporate such evidence into the record in a prior proceeding; and the Commissioner of Social Security shall, after the case is remanded, and after hearing such additional evidence if so ordered, modify or affirm the Commissioner's findings of fact or the Commissioner's decision, or both, and shall file with the court any such additional and modified findings of fact and decision, and, in any case in which the Commissioner has not made a decision fully favorable to the individual, a transcript of the additional record and testimony upon which the Commissioner's action in modifying or affirming was based. Such additional or modified findings of fact and decision shall be reviewable only to the extent provided for review of the original findings of fact and decision. The judgment of the court shall be final except that it shall be subject to review in the same manner as a judgment in other civil actions. Any action instituted in accordance with this subsection shall survive notwithstanding any change in the person occupying the office of Commissioner of Social Security or any vacancy in such office.

(h) Finality of Commissioner's decision

The findings and decision of the Commissioner of Social Security after a hearing shall be binding upon all individuals who were parties to such hearing. No findings of fact or decision of the Commissioner of Social Security shall be reviewed by any person, tribunal, or governmental agency except as herein provided. No action against the United States, the Commissioner of Social Security, or any officer or employee thereof shall be brought under section 1331 or 1346 of Title 28 to recover on any claim arising under this subchapter.

(i) Certification for payment

Upon final decision of the Commissioner of Social Security, or upon final judgment of any court of competent jurisdiction, that any person is entitled to any payment or payments under this subchapter, the Commissioner of Social Security shall certify to the Managing Trustee the name and address of the person so entitled to receive such payment or payments, the amount of such payment or payments, and the time at which such payment or payments should be made, and the Managing Trustee, through the Fiscal Service of the Department of the Treasury, and prior to any action thereon by the Government Accountability Office, shall make payment in accordance with the certification of the Commissioner of Social Security (except that in the case of (A) an individual who will have completed ten years of service (or five or more years of service, all of which accrues after December 31, 1995) creditable under the Railroad Retirement Act of 1937 or the Railroad Retirement Act of 1974, (B) the wife or husband or divorced wife or divorced husband of such an individual, (C) any survivor of such an individual if such survivor is entitled, or could upon application become entitled, to an annuity under section 2 of the Railroad Retirement Act of 1974, and (D) any other person entitled to benefits under section 402 of this title on the basis of the wages and self-employment income of such an individual (except a survivor of such an individual where such individual did not have a current connection with the railroad industry, as defined in the Railroad Retirement Act of 1974, at the time of his death), such certification shall be made to the Railroad Retirement Board which shall provide for such payment or payments to such person on behalf of the Managing Trustee in accordance with the provisions of the Railroad Retirement Act of 1974): *Provided*, That where a review of the Commissioner's decision is or may be sought under subsection (g) the Commissioner of Social Security may withhold certification of payment pending such review. The Managing Trustee shall not be held personally liable for any payment or payments made in accordance with a certification by the Commissioner of Social Security.

(j) Representative payees

(1)(A) If the Commissioner of Social Security determines that the interest of any individual under this subchapter would be served thereby, certification of payment of such individual's benefit under this subchapter may be made, regardless of the legal competency or incompetency of the individual, either for direct payment to the individual, or for his or her use and benefit, to another individual, or an organization, with respect to whom the requirements of paragraph (2) have been met (hereinafter in this subsection referred to as the individual's "representative payee"). If the Commissioner of Social Security or a court of competent jurisdiction determines that a representative payee has misused any individual's benefit paid to such representative payee pursuant to this subsection or section 1007 or 1383(a)(2) of this title, the Commissioner of Social Security shall promptly revoke certification for payment of benefits to such representative payee pursuant to this subsection and certify payment to an alternative representative payee or, if the interest of the individual under this subchapter would be served thereby, to the individual.

(B) In the case of an individual entitled to benefits based on disability, the payment of such benefits shall be made to a representative payee if the Commissioner of Social Security determines that such payment would serve the interest of the individual because the individual also has an alcoholism or drug addiction condition (as determined by the Commissioner) and the individual is incapable of managing such benefits.

(2)(A) Any certification made under paragraph (1) for payment of benefits to an individual's representative payee shall be made on the basis of—

(i) an investigation by the Commissioner of Social Security of the person to serve as representative payee, which shall be conducted in advance of such certification and shall, to the extent practicable, include a face-to-face interview with such person, and

(ii) adequate evidence that such certification is in the interest of such individual (as determined by the Commissioner of Social Security in regulations).

(B)(i) As part of the investigation referred to in subparagraph (A)(i), the Commissioner of Social Security shall—

(I) require the person being investigated to submit documented proof of the identity of such person, unless information establishing such identity has been submitted with an application for benefits under this subchapter, subchapter VIII, or subchapter XVI,

(II) verify such person's social security account number (or employer identification number),

(III) determine whether such person has been convicted of a violation of section 408, 1011, or 1383a of this title,

(IV) obtain information concerning whether such person has been convicted of any other offense under Federal or State law which resulted in imprisonment for more than 1 year,

(V) obtain information concerning whether such person is a person described in section 402(x)(1)(A)(iv) of this title,

(VI) determine whether certification of payment of benefits to such person has been revoked pursuant to this subsection, the designation of such person as a representative payee has been revoked pursuant to section 1007(a) of this title, or payment of benefits to such person has been terminated pursuant to section 1383(a)(2)(A)(iii) of this title by reason of misuse of funds paid as benefits under this subchapter, subchapter VIII, or subchapter XVI, and

(VII) determine whether such person has been convicted (and not subsequently exonerated), under Federal or State law, of a felony provided under clause (iv), or of an attempt or a conspiracy to commit such a felony.

(ii) The Commissioner of Social Security shall establish and maintain a centralized file, which shall be updated periodically and which shall be in a form which renders it readily retrievable by each servicing office of the Social Security Administration. Such file shall consist of—

(I) a list of the names and social security account numbers (or employer identification numbers) of all persons with respect to whom certification of payment of benefits has been revoked on or after January 1, 1991, pursuant to this subsection, whose designation as a representative payee has been revoked pursuant to section 1007(a) of this title, or with respect to whom payment of benefits has been terminated on or after such date pursuant to section 1383(a)(2)(A)(iii) of this title, by reason of misuse of funds paid as benefits under this subchapter, subchapter VIII, or subchapter XVI, and

(II) a list of the names and social security account numbers (or employer identification numbers) of all persons who have been convicted of a violation of section 408, 1011, or 1383a of this title.

(iii) Notwithstanding the provisions of section 552a of Title 5 or any other provision of Federal or State law (other than section 6103 of the Internal Revenue Code of 1986 and section 1306(c) of this title), the Commissioner shall furnish any Federal, State, or local law enforcement officer, upon the written request of the officer, with the current address, social security account number, and photograph (if applicable) of any person investigated under this paragraph, if the officer furnishes the Commissioner with the name of such person and such other identifying information as may reasonably be required by the Commissioner to establish the unique identity of such person, and notifies the Commissioner that—

(I) such person is described in section 402(x)(1)(A)(iv) of this title,

(II) such person has information that is necessary for the officer to conduct the officer's official duties, and

(III) the location or apprehension of such person is within the officer's official duties.

(iv) The felony crimes provided under this clause, whether an offense under State or Federal law, are the following:

(I) Human trafficking, including as prohibited under sections 1590 and 1591 of Title 18.

(II) False imprisonment, including as prohibited under section 1201 of Title 18.

(III) Kidnapping, including as prohibited under section 1201 of Title 18.

(IV) Rape and sexual assault, including as prohibited under sections 2241, 2242, 2243, and 2244 of Title 18.

(V) First-degree homicide, including as prohibited under section 1111 of Title 18.

(VI) Robbery, including as prohibited under section 2111 of Title 18.

(VII) Fraud to obtain access to government assistance, including as prohibited under sections 287, 1001, and 1343 of Title 18.

(VIII) Fraud by scheme, including as prohibited under section 1343 of Title 18.

(IX) Theft of government funds or property, including as prohibited under section 641 of Title 18.

(X) Abuse or neglect, including as prohibited under sections 111, 113, 114, 115, 116, or 117 of Title 18.

(XI) Forgery, including as prohibited under section 642 and chapter 25 (except section 512) of Title 18.

(XII) Identity theft or identity fraud, including as prohibited under sections 1028 and 1028A of Title 18.

The Commissioner of Social Security may promulgate regulations to provide for additional felony crimes under this clause.

(v)(I) For the purpose of carrying out the activities required under subparagraph (B)(i) as part of the investigation under subparagraph (A)(i), the Commissioner may conduct a background check of any individual seeking to serve as a representative payee under this subsection and may disqualify from service as a representative payee any such individual who fails to grant permission for the Commissioner to conduct such a background check.

(II) The Commissioner may revoke certification of payment of benefits under this subsection to any individual serving as a representative payee on or after January 1, 2019 who fails to grant permission for the Commissioner to conduct such a background check.

(C)(i) Benefits of an individual may not be certified for payment to any other person pursuant to this subsection if—

(I) such person has previously been convicted as described in subparagraph (B)(i)(III),

(II) except as provided in clause (ii), certification of payment of benefits to such person under this subsection has previously been revoked as described in subparagraph (B)(i)(VI)[3] the designation of such person as a representative payee has been revoked pursuant to section 1007(a) of this title, or payment of benefits to such person pursuant to section 1383(a)(2)(A)(ii) of this title has previously been terminated as described in section 1383(a)(2)(B)(ii)(VI) of this title,

(III) except as provided in clause (iii), such person is a creditor of such individual who provides such individual with goods or services for consideration,

(IV) such person has previously been convicted as described in subparagraph (B)(i)(IV), unless the Commissioner determines that such certification would be appropriate notwithstanding such conviction,

(V) such person is a person described in section 402(x)(1)(A)(iv) of this title,

(VI) except as provided in clause (vi), such person has previously been convicted (and not subsequently exonerated) as described in subparagraph (B)(i)(VII), or

(VII) such person's benefits under this subchapter, subchapter VIII, or subchapter XVI are certified for payment to a representative payee during the period for which the individual's benefits would be certified for payment to another person.

(ii) The Commissioner of Social Security shall prescribe regulations under which the Commissioner of Social Security may grant exemptions to any person from the provisions of clause (i)(II) on a case-by-case basis if such exemption is in the best interest of the individual whose benefits would be paid to such person pursuant to this subsection.

(iii) Clause (i)(III) shall not apply with respect to any person who is a creditor referred to therein if such creditor is—

(I) a relative of such individual if such relative resides in the same household as such individual,

(II) a legal guardian or legal representative of such individual,

(III) a facility that is licensed or certified as a care facility under the law of a State or a political subdivision of a State,

(IV) a person who is an administrator, owner, or employee of a facility referred to in subclause (III) if such individual resides in such facility, and the certification of payment to such facility or such person is made only after good faith efforts have been made by the local servicing office of the Social Security Administration to locate an alternative representative payee to whom such certification of payment would serve the best interests of such individual, or

(V) an individual who is determined by the Commissioner of Social Security, on the basis of written findings and under procedures which the Commissioner of Social Security shall prescribe by regulation, to be acceptable to serve as a representative payee.

(iv) The procedures referred to in clause (iii)(V) shall require the individual who will serve as representative payee to establish, to the satisfaction of the Commissioner of Social Security, that—

(I) such individual poses no risk to the beneficiary,

(II) the financial relationship of such individual to the beneficiary poses no substantial conflict of interest, and

(III) no other more suitable representative payee can be found.

(v) In the case of an individual described in paragraph (1)(B), when selecting such individual's representative payee, preference shall be given to—

(I) a certified community-based nonprofit social service agency (as defined in paragraph (10)),

(II) a Federal, State, or local government agency whose mission is to carry out income maintenance, social service, or health care-related activities,

(III) a State or local government agency with fiduciary responsibilities, or

(IV) a designee of an agency (other than of a Federal agency) referred to in the preceding subclauses of this clause, if the Commissioner of Social Security deems it appropriate,

(vi)(I) With respect to any person described in subclause (II)—

(aa) subparagraph (B)(i)(VII) shall not apply; and

(bb) the Commissioner may grant an exemption from the provisions of clause (i)(VI) if the Commissioner determines that such exemption is in the best interest of the individual entitled to benefits.

(II) A person is described in this subclause if the person—

(aa) is the custodial parent of a minor child for whom the person applies to serve;

(bb) is the custodial spouse of the beneficiary for whom the person applies to serve;

(cc) is the custodial parent of a beneficiary who is under a disability (as defined in section 423(d) of this title) which began before the beneficiary attained the age of 22, for whom the person applies to serve;

(dd) is the custodial court appointed guardian of the beneficiary for whom the person applies to serve;

(ee) is the custodial grandparent of a minor grandchild for whom the person applies to serve;

(ff) is the parent who was previously representative payee for his or her minor child who has since turned 18 and continues to be eligible for such benefit; or

(gg) received a presidential or gubernatorial pardon for the relevant conviction.

unless the Commissioner of Social Security determines that selection of a family member would be appropriate.

(D)(i) Subject to clause (ii), if the Commissioner of Social Security makes a determination described in the first sentence of paragraph (1) with respect to any individual's benefit and determines that direct payment of the benefit to the individual would cause substantial harm to the individual, the Commissioner of Social Security may defer (in the case of initial entitlement) or suspend (in the case of existing entitlement) direct payment of such benefit to the individual, until such time as the selection of a representative payee is made pursuant to this subsection.

(ii)(I) Except as provided in subclause (II), any deferral or suspension of direct payment of a benefit pursuant to clause (i) shall be for a period of not more than 1 month.

(II) Subclause (I) shall not apply in any case in which the individual is, as of the date of the Commissioner's determination, legally incompetent, under the age of 15 years, or described in paragraph (1)(B).

(iii) Payment pursuant to this subsection of any benefits which are deferred or suspended pending the selection of a representative payee shall be made to the individual or the representative payee as a single sum or over such period of time as the Commissioner of Social Security determines is in the best interest of the individual entitled to such benefits.

(E)(i) Any individual who is dissatisfied with a determination by the Commissioner of Social Security to certify payment of such individual's benefit to a representative payee under paragraph (1) or with the designation of a particular person to serve as representative payee shall be entitled to a hearing by the Commissioner of Social Security to the same extent as is provided in subsection (b), and to judicial review of the Commissioner's final decision as is provided in subsection (g).

(ii) In advance of the certification of payment of an individual's benefit to a representative payee under paragraph (1), the Commissioner of Social Security shall provide written notice of the Commissioner's initial determination to certify such payment. Such notice shall be provided to such individual, except that, if such individual—

(I) is under the age of 15,

(II) is an unemancipated minor under the age of 18, or

(III) is legally incompetent,

then such notice shall be provided solely to the legal guardian or legal representative of such individual.

(iii) Any notice described in clause (ii) shall be clearly written in language that is easily understandable to the reader, shall identify the person to be designated as such individual's representative payee, and shall explain to the reader the right under clause (i) of such individual or of such individual's legal guardian or legal representative—

(I) to appeal a determination that a representative payee is necessary for such individual,

(II) to appeal the designation of a particular person to serve as the representative payee of such individual, and

(III) to review the evidence upon which such designation is based and submit additional evidence.

(3)(A) In any case where payment under this subchapter is made to a person other than the individual entitled to such payment, the Commissioner of Social Security shall establish a system of accountability monitoring whereby such person shall report not less often than annually with respect to the use of such payments. The Commissioner of Social Security shall establish and implement statistically valid procedures for reviewing such reports in order to identify instances in which such persons are not properly using such payments.

(B) Subparagraph (A) shall not apply in any case where the other person to whom such payment is made is a State institution. In such cases, the Commissioner of Social Security shall establish a system of accountability monitoring for institutions in each State.

(C) Subparagraph (A) shall not apply in any case where the individual entitled to such payment is a resident of a Federal institution and the other person to whom such payment is made is the institution.

(D)(i) Subparagraph (A) shall not apply in any case where the other person to whom such payment is made is—

(I) a parent, or other individual who is a legal guardian of, a minor child entitled to such payment who primarily resides in the same household;

(II) a parent of an individual entitled to such payment who is under a disability (as defined in section 423(d) of this title) who primarily resides in the same household; or

(III) the spouse of the individual entitled to such payment.

(ii) The Commissioner of Social Security shall establish and implement procedures as necessary for the Commissioner to determine the eligibility of such parties for the exemption provided in clause (i). The Commissioner shall prescribe such regulations as may be necessary to determine eligibility for such exemption.

(E) Notwithstanding subparagraphs (A), (B), (C), and (D), the Commissioner of Social Security may require a report at any time from any person receiving payments on behalf of another, if the Commissioner of Social Security has reason to believe that the person receiving such payments is misusing such payments.

(F) In any case in which the person described in subparagraph (A) or (E) receiving payments on behalf of another fails to submit a report required by the Commissioner of Social Security under subparagraph (A) or (E), the Commissioner may, after furnishing notice to such person and the individual entitled to such payment, require that such person appear in person at a field office of the Social Security Administration serving the area in which the individual resides in order to receive such payments.

(G) The Commissioner of Social Security shall maintain a centralized file, which shall be updated periodically and which shall be in a form which will be readily retrievable by each servicing office of the Social Security Administration, of—

(i) the address and the social security account number (or employer identification number) of each representative payee who is receiving benefit payments pursuant to this subsection, section 1007 of this title, or section 1383(a)(2) of this title, and

(ii) the address and social security account number of each individual for whom each representative payee is reported to be providing services as representative payee pursuant to this subsection, section 1007 of this title, or section 1383(a)(2) of this title.

(H) Each servicing office of the Administration shall maintain a list, which shall be updated periodically, of public agencies and certified community-based nonprofit social service agencies (as defined in paragraph (10)) which are qualified to serve as representative payees pursuant to this subsection or section 1007 or 1383(a)(2) of this title and which are located in the area served by such servicing office.

(4)(A)(i) Except as provided in the next sentence, a qualified organization may collect from an individual a monthly fee for expenses (including overhead) incurred by such organization in providing services performed as such individual's representative payee pursuant to this subsection if such fee does not exceed the lesser of—

(I) 10 percent of the monthly benefit involved, or

(II) $25.00 per month ($50.00 per month in any case in which the individual is described in paragraph (1)(B)).

A qualified organization may not collect a fee from an individual for any month with respect to which the Commissioner of Social Security or a court of competent jurisdiction has determined that the organization misused all or part of the individual's benefit, and any amount so collected by the qualified organization for such month shall be treated as a misused part of the individual's benefit for purposes of paragraphs (5) and (6). The Commissioner shall adjust annually (after 1995) each dollar amount set forth in subclause (II) under procedures providing for adjustments in the same manner and to the same extent as adjustments are provided for under the procedures used to adjust benefit amounts under section 415(i)(2)(A) of this title, except that any amount so adjusted that is not a multiple of $1.00 shall be rounded to the nearest multiple of $1.00. Any agreement providing for a fee in excess of the amount permitted under this subparagraph shall be void and shall be treated as misuse by such organization of such individual's benefits.

(ii) In the case of an individual who is no longer currently entitled to monthly insurance benefits under this subchapter but to whom all past-due benefits have not been paid, for purposes of clause (i), any amount of such past-due benefits payable in any month shall be treated as a monthly benefit referred to in clause (i)(I).

(B) For purposes of this paragraph, the term "qualified organization" means any State or local government agency whose mission is to carry out income maintenance, social service, or health care-related activities, any State or local government agency with fiduciary responsibilities, or any certified community-based nonprofit social service agency (as defined in paragraph (10)), if such agency, in accordance with any applicable regulations of the Commissioner of Social Security—

(i) regularly provides services as the representative payee, pursuant to this subsection or section 1007 or 1383(a)(2) of this title, concurrently to 5 or more individuals,[4]

(ii) demonstrates to the satisfaction of the Commissioner of Social Security that such agency is not otherwise a creditor of any such individual.

The Commissioner of Social Security shall prescribe regulations under which the Commissioner of Social Security may grant an exception from clause (ii) for any individual on a case-by-case basis if such exception is in the best interests of such individual.

(C) Any qualified organization which knowingly charges or collects, directly or indirectly, any fee in excess of the maximum fee prescribed under subparagraph (A) or makes any agreement, directly or indirectly, to charge or collect any fee in excess of such maximum fee, shall be fined in accordance with Title 18, or imprisoned not more than 6 months, or both.

(5) In cases where the negligent failure of the Commissioner of Social Security to investigate or monitor a representative payee results in misuse of benefits by the representative payee, the Commissioner of Social Security shall certify for payment to the beneficiary or the beneficiary's alternative representative payee an amount equal to such misused benefits. In any case in which a representative payee that—

(A) is not an individual (regardless of whether it is a "qualified organization" within the meaning of paragraph (4)(B)); or

(B) is an individual who, for any month during a period when misuse occurs, serves 15 or more individuals who are beneficiaries under this subchapter, subchapter VIII, subchapter XVI, or any combination of such subchapters;

misuses all or part of an individual's benefit paid to such representative payee, the Commissioner of Social Security shall certify for payment to the beneficiary or the beneficiary's alternative representative payee an amount equal to the amount of such benefit so misused. The provisions of this paragraph are subject to the limitations of paragraph (7)(B). The Commissioner of Social Security shall make a good faith effort to obtain restitution from the terminated representative payee.

(6) In addition to such other reviews of representative payees as the Commissioner of Social Security may otherwise conduct, the Commissioner shall provide for the periodic onsite review of any person or agency located in the United States that receives the benefits payable under this subchapter (alone or in combination with benefits payable under subchapter VIII or subchapter XVI) to another individual pursuant to the appointment of such person or agency as a representative payee under this subsection, section 1007 of this title, or section 1383(a)(2) of this title in any case in which—

(i) the representative payee is a person who serves in that capacity with respect to 15 or more such individuals;

(ii) the representative payee is a certified community-based nonprofit social service agency (as defined in paragraph (10) of this subsection or section 1383(a)(2)(I) of this title);

(iii) the representative payee is an agency (other than an agency described in clause (ii)) that serves in that capacity with respect to 50 or more such individuals; or

(iv) the representative payee collects a fee for its services.

The Commissioner shall also conduct periodic onsite reviews of individual and organizational payees, including payees who are related to the beneficiary and primarily reside in the same household, selected on the basis of risk-factors for potential misuse or unsuitability associated with such payees or beneficiaries.

(C)(i) [5] The Commissioner of Social Security shall make annual grants directly to the protection and advocacy system serving each of the States and the American Indian consortium for the purpose of conducting reviews of representative payees in accordance with this subparagraph. The total amount used by the Commissioner for such grants each year—

(I) shall be an amount sufficient, as determined by the Commissioner in consultation with each of the protection and advocacy systems, to carry out all of the activities described in clause (ii); and

(II) shall not be less than $25,000,000.

(ii) A protection and advocacy system awarded a grant under this subparagraph shall use the grant funds to—

(I) conduct all periodic onsite reviews pursuant to this paragraph and such other reviews of representative payees as the Commissioner may request, including reviews conducted in response to allegations or concerns about the performance or suitability of the payee;

(II) conduct additional reviews that the protection and advocacy system has reason to believe are warranted;

(III) develop corrective action plans to assist representative payees in conforming to requirements specified by the Commissioner;

(IV) submit a report to the Commissioner on each completed review containing such information as the Commissioner shall require; and

(V) conduct an initial onsite assessment of any organization that begins collecting a fee for its services as a representative payee to ensure that such organization is established as such a representative payee in accordance with requirements specified by the Commissioner.

A protection and advocacy system may refer beneficiaries to other programs or services as the protection and advocacy system considers appropriate.

(iii) To be eligible to receive grants under this section, a protection and advocacy system shall submit an initial application to the Commissioner at such time, in such form and manner, and accompanied by such information and assurances as the Commissioner may require.

(iv)(I) Subject to subclause (II), the Commissioner shall ensure that any funds used for grants under clause (i) shall be allocated to the protection and advocacy systems serving each of the States and the American Indian consortium in a manner such that the amount provided to each protection and advocacy system bears the same ratio to the total of such funds as the number of represented beneficiaries in the State or American Indian consortium in which such protection and advocacy system is located bears to the total number of represented beneficiaries.

(II) The amount of an annual grant to a protection and advocacy system under clause (i) shall—

(aa) in the case of a protection and advocacy system serving American Samoa, Guam, the United States Virgin Islands, or the Commonwealth of the Northern Mariana Islands, or the American Indian consortium, not be less than $30,000; and

(bb) in the case of a protection and advocacy system serving any other State, not be less than $60,000.

(III) Funds provided to a protection and advocacy system through a grant under clause (i) for a 1-year period shall remain available through the end of the following 1-year period.

(IV) For purposes of this clause, the term "represented beneficiary" means an individual—

(aa) who is entitled to benefits under this subchapter, subchapter VIII, or subchapter XVI; and

(bb) whose benefits have been certified for payment to a representative payee.

(v)(I) The Commissioner shall make annual grants, in an amount equal to 4 percent of the total amount of grants awarded each year under clause (i), to an eligible national association for the provision of training and technical assistance, administrative support, and data collection services to protection and advocacy systems in connection with grants awarded under clause (i).

(II) In this clause, the term "eligible national association" means a national disability association with extensive knowledge and demonstrated experience in providing training, technical assistance, and administrative oversight to protection and advocacy systems that monitor representative payees.

(vi) In conducting reviews under this section, a protection and advocacy system shall have the same authorities, including access to records, facilities, and persons, as such system would have for purposes of providing services under subtitle C of title I of the Developmental Disabilities Assistance and Bill of Rights Act of 2000 (42 U.S.C. 15041 et seq.).

(vii) Whenever benefit amounts under this title are increased by any percentage effective with any month after November 2018 as a result of a determination made under section 415(i) of this title, each of the dollar amounts specified in clauses (i)(II) and (iv)(II) shall be increased by the same percentage.

(viii) No additional funds are authorized to be appropriated to carry out the requirements of this subparagraph. Such requirements shall be carried out using amounts otherwise authorized.

(ix) In this subparagraph:

(I) The term "American Indian consortium" means a consortium established under subtitle C of title I of the Developmental Disabilities Assistance and Bill of Rights Act of 2000 (42 U.S.C. 15041 et seq.).

(II) The term "protection and advocacy system" means a protection and advocacy system established under subtitle C of title I of the Developmental Disabilities Assistance and Bill of Rights Act of 2000 (42 U.S.C. 15041 et seq.).

(III) The term "State" means the several States of the United States, the District of Columbia, the Commonwealth of Puerto Rico, the United States Virgin Islands, Guam, American Samoa, and the Commonwealth of the Northern Mariana Islands.

(7)(A) If the Commissioner of Social Security or a court of competent jurisdiction determines that a representative payee that is not a Federal, State, or local government agency has misused all or part of an individual's benefit that was paid to such representative payee under this subsection, the representative payee shall be liable for the amount misused, and such amount (to the extent not repaid by the representative payee) shall be treated as an overpayment of benefits under this subchapter to the representative payee for all purposes of this chapter and related laws pertaining to the recovery of such overpayments. Subject to subparagraph (B), upon recovering all or any part of such amount, the Commissioner shall certify an amount equal to the recovered amount for payment to such individual or such individual's alternative representative payee.

(B) The total of the amount certified for payment to such individual or such individual's alternative representative payee under subparagraph (A) and the amount certified for payment under paragraph (5) may not exceed the total benefit amount misused by the representative payee with respect to such individual.

(8) For purposes of this subsection, the term "benefit based on disability" of an individual means a disability insurance benefit of such individual under section 423 of this title or a child's, widow's, or widower's insurance benefit of such individual under section 402 of this title based on such individual's disability.

(9) For purposes of this subsection, misuse of benefits by a representative payee occurs in any case in which the representative payee receives payment under this subchapter for the use and benefit of another person and converts such payment, or any part thereof, to a use other than for the use and benefit of such other person. The Commissioner of Social Security may prescribe by regulation the meaning of the term "use and benefit" for purposes of this paragraph.

(10) For purposes of this subsection, the term "certified community-based nonprofit social service agency" means a community-based nonprofit social service agency which is in compliance with requirements, under regulations which shall be prescribed by the Commissioner, for annual certification to the Commissioner that it is bonded in accordance with requirements specified by the Commissioner and that it is licensed in each State in which it serves as a representative payee (if licensing is available in the State) in accordance with requirements specified by the Commissioner. Any such annual certification shall include a copy of any independent audit on the agency which may have been performed since the previous certification.

(11)(A) The Commissioner of Social Security shall—

(i) enter into agreements with each State with a plan approved under part E of subchapter IV for the purpose of sharing and matching data, on an automated monthly basis, in the system of records of the Social Security Administration with each Statewide and Tribal Automated Child Welfare Information System to identify represented minor beneficiaries who are in foster care under the responsibility of the State for such month; and

(ii) in any case in which a represented minor beneficiary has entered or exited foster care or changed foster care placement in such month, redetermine the appropriate representative payee for such individual.

(B) For purposes of this paragraph—

(i) the term "State" has the meaning given such term for purposes of part E of subchapter IV;

(ii) the term "Statewide and Tribal Automated Child Welfare Information System" means a statewide mechanized data collection and information retrieval system described in section 674(a)(3)(C) of this title; and

(iii) the term "represented minor beneficiary", with respect to an individual for a month, means a child (as defined for purposes of section 675(8) of this title) entitled to benefits under this subchapter for such month whose benefits are certified for payment to a representative payee.

(12)(A) Not later than January 31 of each fiscal year, the Commissioner shall submit to the Committee on Ways and Means of the House of Representatives and the Committee on Finance of the Senate a report on the total number of individuals entitled to benefits under subchapters II, VIII, and XVI, respectively, (and the number of individuals concurrently entitled to benefits under more than one such subchapter) who have a representative payee, the total number of such representative payees, and the results of all reviews of representative payees conducted during the previous fiscal year in connection with benefits under this subchapter, subchapter VIII, or subchapter XVI. Such report shall summarize problems identified in such reviews and corrective actions taken or planned to be taken to correct such problems, and shall include—

(i) the number of such reviews;

(ii) the results of such reviews;

(iii) the number of cases in which the representative payee was changed and why;

(iv) the number of reviews conducted in response to allegations or concerns about the performance or suitability of the payee;

(v) the number of cases discovered in which there was a misuse of funds, and the total dollar amount of benefits determined by the Commissioner during such fiscal year to have been misused by a representative payee (regardless of the fiscal year in which such misuse occurred);

(vi) the number of cases discovered in which such misuse of funds resulted from the negligent failure of the Commissioner to investigate or monitor a representative payee;

(vii) the final disposition of such cases of misuse of funds, including—

(I) any criminal, civil, and administrative penalties imposed;

(II) the total dollar amount of misused benefits repaid to beneficiaries and alternative representative payees under each of—

(aa) paragraph (5) (on the basis of a negligent failure of the Commissioner described in such paragraph);

(bb) paragraph (5) (on any other basis); and

(cc) paragraph (7);

(III) the total dollar amount of misused benefits recovered under each of—

(aa) paragraph (5); and

(bb) paragraph (7);

(viii) any updates to prior year reports necessary to reflect subsequent recoveries and repayments pertaining to misuse determinations made in prior years; and

(ix) such other information as the Commissioner deems appropriate.

(B) Each report required under this paragraph for a fiscal year shall include the information described in clauses (i) through (ix) of subparagraph (A) with respect to—

(i) all representative payees reviewed during such fiscal year;

(ii) all such representative payees that are organizations, separated by whether such organization collects a fee for its services as a representative payee;

(iii) all such representative payees that are individuals serving 15 or more individuals; and

(iv) all such representative payees that are individuals serving less than 15 individuals, separated by whether such representative payee is a family member.

(k) Payments to incompetents

Any payment made after December 31, 1939, under conditions set forth in subsection (j), any payment made before January 1, 1940, to, or on behalf of, a legally incompetent individual, and any payment made after December 31, 1939, to a legally incompetent individual without knowledge by the Commissioner of Social Security of incompetency prior to certification of payment, if otherwise valid under this subchapter, shall be a complete settlement and satisfaction of any claim, right, or interest in and to such payment.

(*l*) Delegation of powers and duties by Commissioner

The Commissioner of Social Security is authorized to delegate to any member, officer, or employee of the Social Security Administration designated by the Commissioner any of the powers conferred upon the Commissioner by this section, and is authorized to be represented by the Commissioner's own attorneys in any court in any case or proceeding arising under the provisions of subsection (e).

(m) Repealed. Aug. 28, 1950, c. 809, Title I, § 101(b)(2), 64 Stat. 488

(n) Joint payments

The Commissioner of Social Security may, in the Commissioner's discretion, certify to the Managing Trustee any two or more individuals of the same family for joint payment of the total benefits payable to such individuals for any month, and if one of such individuals dies before a check representing such joint payment is negotiated, payment of the amount of such unnegotiated check to the surviving individual or individuals may be authorized in accordance with regulations of the Secretary of the Treasury; except that appropriate adjustment or recovery shall be made under section 404(a) of this title with respect to so much of the amount of such check as exceeds the amount to which such surviving individual or individuals are entitled under this subchapter for such month.

(*o*) Crediting of compensation under Railroad Retirement Act

If there is no person who would be entitled, upon application therefor, to an annuity under section 2 of the Railroad Retirement Act of 1974, or to a lump-sum payment under section 6(b) of such Act, with respect to the death of an employee (as defined in such Act), then, notwithstanding section 410(a)(9) of this title, compensation (as defined in such Railroad Retirement Act, but excluding compensation attributable as having been paid during any month on account of military service creditable under section 3(i) of such Act if wages are deemed to have been paid to such employee during such month under subsection (a) or (e) of section 417 of this title) of such employee shall constitute remuneration for employment for purposes of determining (A) entitlement to and the amount of any lump-sum death payment under this subchapter on the basis of such employee's wages and self-employment income and (B) entitlement to and the amount of any monthly benefit under this subchapter, for the month in which such employee died or for any month thereafter, on the basis of such wages and self-employment income. For such purposes, compensation (as so defined) paid in a calendar year before 1978 shall, in the absence of evidence to the contrary, be presumed to have been paid in equal proportions with respect to all months in the year in which the employee rendered services for such compensation.

(p) Special rules in case of Federal service

(1) With respect to service included as employment under section 410 of this title which is performed in the employ of the United States or in the employ of any instrumentality which is wholly owned by the United States, including service, performed as a member of a uniformed service, to which the provisions of subsection (*l*)(1) of such section are applicable, and including service, performed as a volunteer or volunteer leader within the meaning of the Peace Corps Act, to which the provisions of section 410(*o*) of this title are applicable, the Commissioner of Social Security shall not make determinations as to the amounts of remuneration for such service, or the periods in which or for which such remuneration was paid, but shall accept the determinations with respect thereto of the head of the appropriate Federal agency or instrumentality, and of such agents as such head may designate, as evidenced by returns filed in accordance with the provisions of section 3122 of the Internal Revenue Code of 1954 and certifications made pursuant to this subsection. Such determinations shall be final and conclusive. Nothing in this paragraph shall be construed to affect the Commissioner's authority to determine under sections 409 and 410 of this title whether any such service constitutes employment, the periods of such employment, and whether remuneration paid for any such service constitutes wages.

(2) The head of any such agency or instrumentality is authorized and directed, upon written request of the Commissioner of Social Security, to make certification to the Commissioner with respect to any matter determinable for the Commissioner of Social Security by such head or his agents under this subsection, which the Commissioner of Social Security finds necessary in administering this subchapter.

(3) The provisions of paragraphs (1) and (2) of this subsection shall be applicable in the case of service performed by a civilian employee, not compensated from funds appropriated by the Congress, in the Army and Air Force Exchange Service, Army and Air Force Motion Picture Service, Navy Exchanges, Marine Corps Exchanges, or other activities, conducted by an instrumentality of the United States subject to the jurisdiction of the Secretary of Defense, at installations of the Department of Defense for the comfort, pleasure, contentment, and mental and physical improvement of personnel of such Department; and for purposes of paragraphs (1) and (2) of this subsection the Secretary of Defense shall be deemed to be the head of such instrumentality. The provisions of paragraphs (1) and (2) shall be applicable also in the case of service performed by a civilian employee, not compensated from funds appropriated by the Congress, in the Coast Guard Exchanges or other activities, conducted by an instrumentality of the United States subject to the jurisdiction of the Secretary of Homeland Security, at installations of the Coast Guard for the comfort, pleasure, contentment, and mental and physical improvement of personnel of the Coast Guard; and for purposes of paragraphs (1) and (2) the Secretary of Homeland Security shall be deemed to be the head of such instrumentality.

(q) Expedited benefit payments

(1) The Commissioner of Social Security shall establish and put into effect procedures under which expedited payment of monthly insurance benefits under this subchapter will, subject to paragraph (4) of this subsection, be made as set forth in paragraphs (2) and (3) of this subsection.

(2) In any case in which—

(A) an individual makes an allegation that a monthly benefit under this subchapter was due him in a particular month but was not paid to him, and

(B) such individual submits a written request for the payment of such benefit—

(i) in the case of an individual who received a regular monthly benefit in the month preceding the month with respect to which such allegation is made, not less than 30 days after the 15th day of the month with respect to which such allegation is made (and in the event that such request is submitted prior to the expiration of such 30-day period, it shall be deemed to have been submitted upon the expiration of such period), and

(ii) in any other case, not less than 90 days after the later of (I) the date on which such benefit is alleged to have been due, or (II) the date on which such individual furnished the last information requested by the Commissioner of Social Security (and such written request will be deemed to be filed on the day on which it was filed, or the ninetieth day after the first day on which the Commissioner of Social Security has evidence that such allegation is true, whichever is later),

the Commissioner of Social Security shall, if the Commissioner finds that benefits are due, certify such benefits for payment, and payment shall be made within 15 days immediately following the date on which the written request is deemed to have been filed.

(3) In any case in which the Commissioner of Social Security determines that there is evidence, although additional evidence might be required for a final decision, that an allegation described in paragraph (2)(A) is true, the Commissioner may make a preliminary certification of such benefit for payment even though the

30-day or 90-day periods described in paragraph (2)(B)(i) and (B)(ii) have not elapsed.

(4) Any payment made pursuant to a certification under paragraph (3) of this subsection shall not be considered an incorrect payment for purposes of determining the liability of the certifying or disbursing officer.

(5) For purposes of this subsection, benefits payable under section 428 of this title shall be treated as monthly insurance benefits payable under this subchapter. However, this subsection shall not apply with respect to any benefit for which a check has been negotiated, or with respect to any benefit alleged to be due under either section 423 of this title, or section 402 of this title to a wife, husband, or child of an individual entitled to or applying for benefits under section 423 of this title, or to a child who has attained age 18 and is under a disability, or to a widow or widower on the basis of being under a disability.

(r) Use of death certificates to correct program information

(1) The Commissioner of Social Security shall undertake to establish a program under which—

(A) States (or political subdivisions thereof) voluntarily contract with the Commissioner of Social Security to furnish the Commissioner of Social Security periodically with information (in a form established by the Commissioner of Social Security in consultation with the States) concerning individuals with respect to whom death certificates (or equivalent documents maintained by the States or subdivisions) have been officially filed with them; and

(B) there will be (i) a comparison of such information on such individuals with information on such individuals in the records being used in the administration of this chapter, (ii) validation of the results of such comparisons, and (iii) corrections in such records to accurately reflect the status of such individuals.

(2) Each State (or political subdivision thereof) which furnishes the Commissioner of Social Security with information on records of deaths in the State or subdivision under this subsection may be paid by the Commissioner of Social Security from amounts available for administration of this chapter the reasonable costs (established by the Commissioner of Social Security in consultations with the States) for transcribing and transmitting such information to the Commissioner of Social Security.

(3) In the case of individuals with respect to whom federally funded benefits are provided by (or through) a Federal or State agency other than under this chapter, the Commissioner of Social Security shall to the extent feasible provide such information through a cooperative arrangement with such agency, for ensuring proper payment of those benefits with respect to such individuals if—

(A) under such arrangement the agency provides reimbursement to the Commissioner of Social Security for the reasonable cost of carrying out such arrangement, and

(B) such arrangement does not conflict with the duties of the Commissioner of Social Security under paragraph (1).

(4) The Commissioner of Social Security may enter into similar agreements with States to provide information for their use in programs wholly funded by the States if the requirements of subparagraphs (A) and (B) of paragraph (3) are met.

(5) The Commissioner of Social Security may use or provide for the use of such records as may be corrected under this section, subject to such safeguards as the Commissioner of Social Security determines are necessary or appropriate to protect the information from unauthorized use or disclosure, for statistical and research activities conducted by Federal and State agencies.

(6) Information furnished to the Commissioner of Social Security under this subsection may not be used for any purpose other than the purpose described in this subsection and is exempt from disclosure under section 552 of Title 5, and from the requirements of section 552a of such title.

(7) The Commissioner of Social Security shall include information on the status of the program established under this section and impediments to the effective implementation of the program in the 1984 report required under section 904 of this title.

(8)(A) The Commissioner of Social Security shall, upon the request of the official responsible for a State driver's license agency pursuant to the Help America Vote Act of 2002—

(i) enter into an agreement with such official for the purpose of verifying applicable information, so long as the requirements of subparagraphs (A) and (B) of paragraph (3) are met; and

(ii) include in such agreement safeguards to assure the maintenance of the confidentiality of any applicable information disclosed and procedures to permit such agency to use the applicable information for the purpose of maintaining its records.

(B) Information provided pursuant to an agreement under this paragraph shall be provided at such time, in such place, and in such manner as the Commissioner determines appropriate.

(C) The Commissioner shall develop methods to verify the accuracy of information provided by the agency with respect to applications for voter registration, for whom the last 4 digits of a social security number are provided instead of a driver's license number.

(D) For purposes of this paragraph—

(i) the term "applicable information" means information regarding whether—

(I) the name (including the first name and any family forename or surname), the date of birth (including the month, day, and year), and social security number of an individual provided to the Commissioner match the information contained in the Commissioner's records, and

(II) such individual is shown on the records of the Commissioner as being deceased; and

(ii) the term "State driver's license agency" means the State agency which issues driver's licenses to individuals within the State and maintains records relating to such licensure.

(E) Nothing in this paragraph may be construed to require the provision of applicable information with regard to a request for a record of an individual if the Commissioner determines there are exceptional circumstances warranting an exception (such as safety of the individual or interference with an investigation).

(F) Applicable information provided by the Commission pursuant to an agreement under this paragraph or by an individual to any agency that has entered into an agreement under this paragraph shall be considered as strictly confidential and shall be used only for the purposes described in this paragraph and for carrying out an agreement under this paragraph. Any officer or employee or former officer or employee of a State, or any officer or employee or former officer or employee of a contractor of a State who, without the written authority of the Commissioner, publishes or communicates any applicable information in such individual's possession by reason of such employment or position as such an officer, shall be guilty of a felony and upon conviction thereof shall be fined or imprisoned, or both, as described in section 408 of this title.

(9)(A) The Commissioner of Social Security shall, upon the request of the Secretary or the Inspector General of the Department of Health and Human Services—

(i) enter into an agreement with the Secretary or such Inspector General for the purpose of matching data in the system of records of the Social Security Administration and the system of records of the Department of Health and Human Services; and

(ii) include in such agreement safeguards to assure the maintenance of the confidentiality of any information disclosed.

(B) For purposes of this paragraph, the term "system of records" has the meaning given such term in section 552a(a)(5) of Title 5.

(s) Notice requirements

The Commissioner of Social Security shall take such actions as are necessary to ensure that any notice to one or more individuals issued pursuant to this subchapter by the Commissioner of Social Security or by a State agency—

(1) is written in simple and clear language, and

(2) includes the address and telephone number of the local office of the Social Security Administration which serves the recipient.

In the case of any such notice which is not generated by a local servicing office, the requirements of paragraph (2) shall be treated as satisfied if such notice includes the address of the local office of the Social Security Administration which services the recipient of the notice and a telephone number through which such office can be reached.

(t) Same-day personal interviews at field offices in cases where time is of essence

In any case in which an individual visits a field office of the Social Security Administration and represents during the visit to an officer or employee of the Social Security Administration in the office that the individual's visit is occasioned by—

(1) the receipt of a notice from the Social Security Administration indicating a time limit for response by the individual, or

(2) the theft, loss, or nonreceipt of a benefit payment under this subchapter,

the Commissioner of Social Security shall ensure that the individual is granted a face-to-face interview at the office with an officer or employee of the Social Security Administration before the close of business on the day of the visit.

(u) Redetermination of entitlement

(1)(A) The Commissioner of Social Security shall immediately redetermine the entitlement of individuals to monthly insurance benefits under this subchapter if there is reason to believe that fraud or similar fault was involved in the application of the individual for such benefits, unless a United States attorney, or equivalent State prosecutor, with jurisdiction over potential or actual related criminal cases, certifies, in writing, that there is a substantial risk that such action by the Commissioner of Social Security with regard to beneficiaries in a particular investigation would jeopardize the criminal prosecution of a person involved in a suspected fraud.

(B) When redetermining the entitlement, or making an initial determination of entitlement, of an individual under this subchapter, the Commissioner of Social Security shall disregard any evidence if there is reason to believe that fraud or similar fault was involved in the providing of such evidence.

(2) For purposes of paragraph (1), similar fault is involved with respect to a determination if—

(A) an incorrect or incomplete statement that is material to the determination is knowingly made; or

(B) information that is material to the determination is knowingly concealed.

(3) If, after redetermining pursuant to this subsection the entitlement of an individual to monthly insurance benefits, the Commissioner of Social Security determines that there is insufficient evidence to support such entitlement, the Commissioner of Social Security may terminate such entitlement and may treat benefits paid on the basis of such insufficient evidence as overpayments.

(Aug. 14, 1935, c. 531, Title II, § 205, 49 Stat. 624; Aug. 10, 1939, c. 666, Title II, § 201, 53 Stat. 1362, 1368; June 25, 1948, c. 646, § 32(b), 62 Stat. 991; May 24, 1949, c. 139, § 127, 63 Stat. 107; Aug. 28, 1950, c. 809, Title I, §§ 101(b)(2), 108(a) to (c), 109(b), 64 Stat. 488, 518, 523; July 18, 1952, c. 945, § 5(b), 66 Stat. 775; Sept. 1, 1954, c. 1206, Title I, § 101(a)(5), (c)(3), 68 Stat. 1052, 1054; Aug. 1, 1956, c. 836, Title I, §§ 107(b), 111(a), 117, 70 Stat. 829, 831, 834; Aug. 1, 1956, c. 837, Title IV, § 402(b), 70 Stat. 871; Pub.L. 86–507, § 1(35), June 11, 1960, 74 Stat. 202; Pub.L. 86–778, Title I, §§ 102(f)(2), 103(j)(2)(E), Title VII, § 702(a), Sept. 13, 1960, 74 Stat. 933, 938, 993; Pub.L. 87–293, Title II, § 202(b)(3), Sept. 22, 1961, 75 Stat. 626; Pub.L. 89–97, Title III, §§ 308(d)(9), (10), 330, July 30, 1965, 79 Stat. 379, 401; Pub.L. 90–248, Title I, § 171(a), Jan. 2, 1968, 81 Stat. 876; Pub.L. 91–452, Title II, § 236, Oct. 15, 1970, 84 Stat. 930; Pub.L. 92–603, Title I, § 137, Oct. 30, 1972, 86 Stat. 1364; Pub.L. 93–445, Title III, §§ 302(a), 303, Oct. 16, 1974, 88 Stat. 1358; Pub.L. 94–202, § 4, Jan. 2, 1976, 89 Stat. 1136; Pub.L. 94–455, Title XII, § 1211(b), Oct. 4, 1976, 90 Stat. 1711; Pub.L. 95–216, Title III, § 353(f)(2), Dec. 20, 1977, 91 Stat. 1554; Pub.L. 95–600, Title VII, § 703(j)(14)(B), Nov. 6, 1978, 92 Stat. 2942; Pub.L. 96–265, Title III, §§ 305(a), 307, June 9, 1980, 94 Stat. 457, 458; Pub.L. 97–455, § 4(a), Jan. 12, 1983, 96 Stat. 2499; Pub.L. 98–21, Title III, §§ 301(d), 309(i), 336, 345(a), Apr. 20, 1983, 97 Stat. 111, 117, 130, 137; Pub.L. 98–369, Div.B, Title VI, §§ 2661(h), 2663(a)(4), (j)(4), July 18, 1984, 98 Stat. 1157, 1162, 1171; Pub.L. 98–460, § 16(a), Oct. 9, 1984, 98 Stat. 1809; Pub.L. 99–509, Title IX, § 9002(c)(2)(A), (B), Oct. 21, 1986, 100 Stat. 1971; Pub.L. 100–485, Title I, § 125(a), Oct. 13, 1988, 102 Stat. 2353; Pub.L. 100–647, Title VIII, §§ 8008(a), 8009(a), 8015(a)(1), 8016(a)(1), Nov. 10, 1988, 102 Stat. 3783, 3787, 3790, 3792; Pub.L. 101–239, Title X, §§ 10303(a), 10304, Dec. 19, 1989, 103 Stat. 2482, 2483; Pub.L. 101–508, Title V, §§ 5105(a)(1)(A), (2)(A)(i), (3)(A)(i), (b)(1)(A), (c)(1), (d)(1)(A), 5107(a)(1), 5109(a)(1), Nov. 5, 1990, 104 Stat. 1388–254, 1388–255, 1388–260, 1388–263, 1388–265, 1388–269, 1388–271; Pub.L. 101–624, Title XVII, § 1735(a), (b), Title XXII, § 2201(b), (c), Nov. 28, 1990, 104 Stat. 3791, 3792, 3951, 3952; Pub.L. 103–296, Title I, § 107(a)(1), (2), (4), Title II, §§ 201(a)(1)(A), (B), (2)(A) to (C), 206(a)(1), (d)(1), Title III, §§ 304(a), 316(a), 318, 321(a)(7) to (11), (c)(3), (6)(B), (f)(2)(A), Aug. 15, 1994, 108 Stat. 1477, 1478, 1490, 1492, 1509, 1514, 1520, 1531, 1533, 1536, 1538, 1541; Pub.L. 104–121, Title I, § 105(a)(2), Mar. 29, 1996, 110 Stat. 852; Pub.L. 104–193, Title I, § 108(a)(1), Aug. 22, 1996, 110 Stat. 2164; Pub.L. 105–34, Title X, § 1090(b)(1), Aug. 5, 1997, 111 Stat. 962; Pub.L. 106–169, Title II, § 251(b)(2), Dec. 14, 1999, 113 Stat. 1854; Pub.L. 107–90, Title I, § 103(i)(3), Dec. 21, 2001, 115 Stat. 882; Pub.L. 107–252, Title III, § 303(a)(5)(C), Oct. 29, 2002, 116 Stat. 1711; Pub.L. 108–203, Title I, §§ 101(a), 102(a)(1), (b)(1), 103(a), 104(a), 105(a), 106(a), Title IV, § 411(a), Mar. 2, 2004, 118 Stat. 495, 497, 498, 500, 503 to 505, 527; Pub.L. 108–271, § 8(b), July 7, 2004, 118 Stat. 814; Pub.L. 108–458, Title VII, §7214(a), Dec. 17, 2004, 118 Stat. 3832; Pub.L. 109–241, Title IX, § 902(n), July 11, 2006, 120 Stat. 568; Pub.L. 110–234, Title IV, § 4002(b)(1)(B), (2)(V), May 22, 2008, 122 Stat. 1096, 1097; Pub.L. 110–246, § 4(a), Title IV, § 4002(b)(1)(B), (2)(V), June 18, 2008, 122 Stat. 1664, 1857, 1858; Pub.L. 111–148, Title I, § 1414(a)(2), Title VI, § 6402(b)(3), Mar. 23, 2010, 124 Stat. 237, 756; Pub.L. 111–318, § 2(a)(1), (b)(1), Dec. 18, 2010, 124 Stat. 3455; Pub.L. 114–10, Title V, § 501(a), Apr. 16, 2015, 129 Stat. 163; Pub.L. 114–74, Title VIII, § 843, Nov. 2, 2015, 129 Stat. 617; Pub. L. 115–165, Title I, §§ 101(a), (b), 102(a), 103(a)(1), 105(a), Title II, §§ 201(a), 202(a), 203(a), Apr. 13, 2018, 132 Stat. 1257, 1259, 1260, 1261, 1262, 1264, 1266, 1267, 1272.)

[1] So in original. Probably should be "subclause".

[2] So in original. The word "the" probably should not appear.

[3] So in original. Probably should be followed by a comma.

[4] So in original. Probably should be followed by "and".

[5] So in original. There are no subpars. (A) or (B).

Enactment of Subsec. (j)(1)(C)

Pub.L. 115–165, Title II, § 201(a), Apr. 13, 2018, 132 Stat. 1266, provided that, effective on the date that is 2 years after April 13, 2018, subsec. (j)(1)(C) is enacted to read as follows:

(C)(i) *An individual who is entitled to or is an applicant for a benefit under this subchapter, subchapter VIII, or subchapter XVI, who has attained 18 years of age or is an emancipated minor, may, at any time, designate one or more other individuals to serve as a representative payee for such individual in the event that the Commissioner of Social Security determines under subparagraph (A) that the interest of such individual would be served by certification for payment of such benefits to which the individual is entitled to a representative payee. If the Commissioner of Social Security makes such a determination with respect to such individual at any time after such designation has been made, the Commissioner shall—*

(I) *certify payment of such benefits to the designated individual, subject to the requirements of paragraph (2); or*

(II) *if the Commissioner determines that certification for payment of such benefits to the designated individual would not satisfy the requirements of paragraph (2), that the designated individual is unwilling or unable to serve as representative payee, or that other good cause exists, certify payment of such benefits to another individual or organization, in accordance with paragraph (1).*

(ii) *An organization may not be designated to serve as a representative payee under this subparagraph.*

HISTORICAL AND STATUTORY NOTES

References in Text

For provisions deeming a reference in other laws to a provision of the 1939 Code as a reference to the corresponding provisions of the 1986 Code, see 26 U.S.C.A. § 7852(b). For a table of comparisons of the 1939 Code to the 1986 Code, see table preceding 26 U.S.C.A. § 1. The Internal Revenue Code of 1986 is classified principally to Title 26.

This subchapter, referred to in text, originally read "this title", meaning the Social Security Act, Act Aug. 14, 1935, c. 531, Title II, 49 Stat. 622, as amended, which is classified as this subchapter, 42 U.S.C.A. § 401 et seq.

Part A of subchapter XVIII, referred to in text, originally read "Part A", meaning part A of Title XVIII of the Social Security Act, Act Aug. 14, 1935, c. 531, Title XVIII, § 1811 et seq., as added July 30, 1965, Pub.L. 89–97, Title I, § 102(a), 79 Stat. 291, and amended, which is classified principally to part A of subchapter XVIII of this chapter, 42 U.S.C.A. § 1395c et seq.

Part B of subchapter XVIII, referred to in text, originally read "Part B of title XVIII," meaning Part B of Title XVIII of the Social Security Act, Act Aug. 14, 1935, c. 531, Title XVIII, § 1831 et seq., as added July 30, 1965, Pub.L. 89–97, Title I, § 102(a), 79 Stat. 301, and amended, which is classified principally to part B of subchapter XVIII of this chapter, 42 U.S.C.A. § 1395j et seq.

Subsecs. (e) and (q) of section 418 of this title, referred to in subsecs. (c)(1)(D)(i), (5)(F)(iii), which related to payments and reports by States, and to time limitation on assessments, respectively, were repealed, and subsec. (f) of section 418 of this title was redesignated as subsec. (e), by Pub.L. 99–509, Title IX, § 9002(c)(1), Oct. 21, 1986, 100 Stat. 1971.

Parts A and D of subchapter IV, referred to in subsec. (c)(2)(C)(ii), (vi), are classified to 42 U.S.C.A. §§ 602 et seq. and 651 et seq., respectively.

Section 7(a) of the Privacy Act of 1974, referred to in subsec. (c)(2)(C)(ii), is set out as a note under section 552a of Title 5, Government Organization and Employees.

The Food and Nutrition Act of 2008, referred to in subsec. (c)(2)(C)(iii)(I), (II), is Pub.L. 88–525, Aug. 31, 1964, 78 Stat. 703, as amended, formerly known as the Food Stamp Act of 1977, which principally enacted chapter 51 (§ 2011 et seq.) of Title 7, Agriculture. Section 9 of the Act is classified to 7 U.S.C.A. § 2018. For complete classification, see Short Title note set out under 7 U.S.C.A. § 2011 and Tables.

The Federal Crop Insurance Act, referred to in subsec. (c)(2)(C)(iv), is subtitle A of Title V of Act Feb. 16, 1938, c. 30, 52 Stat. 72, as amended, which is classified generally to subchapter I of chapter 36 of Title 7, 7 U.S.C.A. § 1501 et seq. For complete classification, see 7 U.S.C.A. § 1501 and Tables.

Section 7212(a)(2) of the 9/11 Commission Implementation Act of 2004, referred to in subsec. (c)(2)(C)(vi)(II), is Pub.L. 108–458, Title VII, § 7212(a)(2), Dec. 17, 2004, 118 Stat. 3828, which is classified in a note set out under 49 U.S.C.A. § 30301.

The Internal Revenue Code of 1986, referred to in subsec. (c)(2)(C)(viii), (II), (H), is classified generally to Title 26, Internal Revenue Code.

The Longshore and Harbor Workers' Compensation Act (33 U.S.C. 901 et seq.), referred to in subsec. (c)(2)(C)(ix), is Act Mar. 4, 1927, c. 509, 44 Stat. 1424, as amended, which is classified generally to chapter 18 (section 901 et seq.) of Title 33, Navigation and Navigable Waters. For complete classification of this Act to the Code, see 33 U.S.C.A. § 901 and Tables.

Section 1331 of the Patient Protection and Affordable Care Act, referred to in subsec. (c)(2)(C)(x), is Pub.L. 111–148, Title I, § 1331, Mar. 23, 2010, 124 Stat. 199, which enacted 42 U.S.C.A. § 18051.

Such Act, referred to in subsec. (c)(2)(C)(x), means the Patient Protection and Affordable Care Act, Pub.L. 111–148, Mar. 23, 2010, 124 Stat. 119; for complete classification, see Tables.

The Railroad Retirement Act of 1937, referred to in subsec. (c)(5)(D), probably means Act Aug. 29, 1935, c. 812, 49 Stat. 867, known as the Railroad Retirement Act of 1935. See par. for Railroad Retirement Act of 1974 under this section.

Subchapter E of chapter 1 and subchapter A of chapter 9 of the Internal Revenue Code of 1939, referred to in subsec. (c)(5)(F)(i), were comprised of sections 480 to 482 and 1400 to 1432, respectively, and were repealed (subject to certain exceptions) by 26 U.S.C.A. § 7851(a)(1)(A), (3).

Title VIII of the Social Security Act, referred to in subsec. (c)(5)(F)(i), probably means former title VIII of the Social Security Act, which was classified to subchapter VIII (42 U.S.C.A. § 1001 et seq.) of this chapter, and was omitted from the Code as superseded by the provisions of the Internal Revenue Code of 1939 and the Internal Revenue Code of 1986 (26 U.S.C.A. § 1 et seq.).

Chapters 2 and 21 of the Internal Revenue Code of 1954 or the Internal Revenue Code of 1986, referred to in subsec. (c)(5)(F)(i), are classified to sections 1401 et seq. and 3101 et seq., respectively, of Title 26, Internal Revenue Code.

Section 5(k)(3) of the Railroad Retirement Act of 1937, referred to in subsec. (c)(5)(I), was classified to section 228e of Title 45, Railroads. See paragraph for Railroad Retirement Act of 1974 under this section.

The Railroad Retirement Act of 1937, referred to in subsec. (i), is Act Aug. 29, 1935, c. 812, 49 Stat. 867, as amended generally. See paragraph for Railroad Retirement Act of 1974 under this section.

The Railroad Retirement Act of 1974, referred to in subsecs. (c), (i), and (*o*) is Title I of Pub.L. 93–445, Oct. 16, 1974, 88 Stat. 1305, and is classified generally to subchapter IV (section 231 et seq.) of chapter 9 of Title 45, Railroads. Such Title I completely amended and revised the Railroad Retirement Act of 1937 (approved June 24, 1937, c. 382, 50 Stat. 307), and as thus amended and revised the 1937 Act was redesignated the Railroad Retirement Act of 1974. Sections 2, 3, 6, and 7 of such Act are classified to 45 U.S.C.A. §§ 231a, 231b, 231e, and 231f, respectively. Previously, the 1937 Act had completely amended and revised the Railroad Retirement Act of 1935 (approved Aug. 29, 1935, c. 812, 49 Stat. 967). Section 201 of the 1937 Act provided that the 1935 Act, as in force prior to amendment by the 1937 Act, may be cited as the Railroad Retirement Act of 1935; and that the 1935 Act, as amended by the 1937 Act may be cited as the Railroad Retirement Act of 1937. The Railroad Retirement Acts of 1935 and 1937 were classified to subchapter II (section 215 et seq.) and subchapter III (section 228a et seq.), respectively, of chapter 9 of Title 45.

Chapter 25 of Title 18 referred to in subsec. (j)(2)(B)(iv)(XI), is classified to 18 U.S.C.A. § 470 et seq.

Subchapter VIII of this chapter, referred to in subsec. (j)(5), (6), originally read "title VIII", meaning the Social Security Act, Act Aug. 14, 1935, c. 531, Title VIII, as added Dec. 14, 1999, Pub.L. 106–169, Title II, § 251(a), 113 Stat. 1844, as amended, which is classified as subchapter VIII of this chapter, 42 U.S.C.A. § 1001 et seq.

Subchapter XVI, referred to in subsec. (j)(5), (6), originally read "title XVI", meaning the Social Security Act, Act Aug. 14, 1935, c. 531, Title XVI, as added Oct. 30, 1972, Pub.L. 92–603, Title III, § 301, 86 Stat. 1465, as amended, which is classified as subchapter XVI of this chapter, 42 U.S.C.A. § 1381 et seq.

The Developmental Disabilities Assistance and Bill of Rights Act of 2000, referred to in subsec. (j)(6)(C)(vi) and (ix), is Pub.L. 106–402, Oct. 30, 2000, 114 Stat. 1677, which is classified principally to chapter 144 of this title, 42 U.S.C.A. § 15001 et seq. Subtitle C of Title I of such Act, is classified principally to part C of subchapter I of chapter 144 of this title, 42 U.S.C.A. § 15041 et seq. For complete classification, see Short Title note set out under 42 U.S.C.A. § 15001 and Tables.

Part E of subchapter IV, referred to in subsec. (j)(11)(A)(i) and (B)(i) originally read, "Part E of title IV," meaning Part E of Title IV of the Social Security Act, Act Aug. 14, 1935, c.531, 49 Stat. 620, as amended. Part E of Title IV of such Act is principally classified to part E of subchapter IV of this chapter, 42 U.S.C.A. § 670 et seq.

Subchapters II, VIII, and XVI, referred to in subsec. (j)(12)(A) originally read "titles II, VIII, and XVI," meaning Titles II, VIII, and XVI of the Social Security Act, Act Aug. 14, 1935, c.531, 49 Stat. 620, as amended, which is principally classified to this chapter, 42 U.S.C.A. § 301 et seq. Titles II, VIII, and XVI of the Act are principally classified to subchapters II, VIII, and XVI of this chapter, 42 U.S.C.A. §§ 401, 1001, and 1381 et seq., respectively. For complete classification, see 42 U.S.C.A. § 1305 and Tables.

The Peace Corps Act, referred to in subsec. (p)(1), is Pub.L. 87–293, Sept. 22, 1961, 75 Stat. 612, which is classified principally to chapter 34 (section 2501 et seq.) of Title 22, Foreign Relations and Intercourse. For complete classification of this Act to the Code, see Short Title note set out under section 2501 of Title 22 and Tables.

Section 3122 of the Internal Revenue Code of 1954, referred to in subsec. (p)(1), redesignated section 3122 of the Internal Revenue Code of 1986 by Pub.L. 99–514, § 2, Oct. 22, 1986, 100 Stat. 2095, and is classified to 26 U.S.C.A. § 3122.

Section 904 of this title, referred to in subsec. (r)(7), was amended generally by Pub.L. 103–296, Title I, § 104(a), Aug. 15, 1994, 108 Stat. 1470, and, as so amended, does not require an annual report.

The Help America Vote Act of 2002, referred to in subsec. (r)(8), is Pub.L. 107–252, Oct. 29, 2002, 116 Stat. 1666, which was classified principally to chapter 146 of this title, 42 U.S.C.A. § 15301 et seq., prior to editorial reclassification and renumbering in Title 52 and is now classified principally to chapter 209 (§ 20901 et seq.) of Title 52. For complete classification of this Act to the Code, see Short Title note set out under 52 U.S.C.A. § 10101 and Tables.

Codifications

The authorities provided by each provision of, and each amendment made by, Pub.L. 110–246, as in effect on Sept. 30, 2012, to continue, and the Secretary of Agriculture to carry out the authorities, until the later of Sept. 30, 2013, or the date specified in the provision of, or amendment made by, Pub.L. 110–246, see section 701(a) of Pub.L. 112–240, set out in a note under 7 U.S.C.A. § 8701.

August 15, 1994, referred to in subsec. (c)(2)(E)(iii), was in the original "the date of the enactment of this subparagraph" and "that date", which were translated as meaning the date of enactment of Pub.L. 103—296, which added subsec. (c)(2)(E) and redesignated former subsec. (c)(2)(E) as (c)(2)(F).

Section 125(a)(2) of Pub.L. 100–485 became effective pursuant to section 125(b) of Pub.L. 100–485 amending subsec. (c)(2)(C)(ii), and without reference to redesignations to subcls. (I) and (II) of cl. (i) by section 2201(b)(2) of Pub.L. 101–624, which made language of subsec. (c)(2)(C)(ii) obsolete.

Amendments by Pub.L. 101–624, § 1735(a), (b), which added subsec. (c)(2)(C)(iii) and (vii) and made accommodating changes in designations have been executed by setting out such cls. and not the accommodating changes which are not capable of execution in view of prior amendments to subsec. (c) by Pub.L. 101–624, § 2201(b), (c).

In subsec. (g), Act June 25, 1948, as amended by Act May 24, 1949, substituted United States District Court for the District of Columbia, for District Court of the United States for the District of Columbia.

In subsec. (h), "section 1331 or 1346 of Title 28" was substituted for "section 24 of the Judicial Code of the United States" on authority of Act June 25, 1948, c. 646, 62 Stat. 869, section 1 of which enacted Title 28, Judiciary and Judicial Procedure. Prior to the enactment of Title 28, section 24 of the Judicial Code was classified to section 41 of Title 28. Jurisdictional provisions previously covered by section 41 of Title 28 are covered by sections 1331 to 1348, 1350 to 1357, 1359, 1397, 1399, 2361, 2401, and 2402 of Title 28.

Amendment by section 5105(b)(1)(A) of Pub.L. 101–508 was executed to subsec. (j)(3) of this section, as the probable intent of Congress, despite language directing that amendment be made to section 605(j) of this title.

Effective and Applicability Provisions

2018 Acts. Pub.L. 115–165, Title I, § 102(d), Apr. 13, 2018, 132 Stat. 1261, provided that: "The amendments made by this section [amending subsec. (j)(3) of this section and 42 U.S.C.A. §§ 1007 and 1383] shall take effect on the date of the enactment of this Act [Apr. 13, 2018]."

Pub.L. 115–165, Title I, § 103(a)(4), Apr. 13, 2018, 132 Stat. 1262, provided that:

"(A) In general.—The amendments made by this subsection [amending subsec. (j)(11) of this section and 42 U.S.C.A. § 671] shall apply with respect to months beginning on or after the date that is 1 year after the date of the enactment of this Act [Apr. 13, 2018].

"(B) Exception if State legislation required.—In the case of a State plan under part E of title IV of the Social Security Act [part E of subchapter IV of this chapter, 42 U.S.C.A. § 670 et seq.] that the Secretary of Health and Human Services determines requires State legislation (other than legislation appropriating funds) in order for the plan to meet the additional requirement imposed by the amendments made under this subsection [amending subsec. (j)(11) of this section and 42 U.S.C.A. § 671], such plan shall not be regarded as failing to comply with the requirements of such title [subchapter IV of this chapter, 42 U.S.C.A. § 601 et seq.] solely on the basis of its failure to meet this additional requirement before the first day of the first calendar quarter beginning after the close of the first regular session of the State legislature that begins after the date of the enactment of this Act [Apr. 13, 2018]. For purposes of the previous sentence, in the case of a State that has a 2-year legislative session, each year of such session shall be deemed to be a separate regular session of the State legislature."

Pub.L. 115–165, Title II, § 201(b), Apr. 13, 2018, 132 Stat. 1266, provided that: "The amendment made by subsection (a) [amending subsec. (j)(1)(C) of this section] shall take effect on the date that is 2 years after the date of the enactment of this section [Apr. 13, 2018]."

Pub.L. 115–165, Title II, § 202(d), Apr. 13, 2018, 132 Stat. 1271, provided that: "Subject to subsection (e) [enacting provisions set out as a note under this section], the amendments made by subsections (a), (b), and (c) [amending this section, 42 U.S.C.A. §§ 1007 and 1383] shall apply with respect to any individual appointed to serve as a representative payee pursuant to section 205(j), 807, or 1631(a)(2) of the Social Security Act [subsec. (j) of this section, and 42 U.S.C.A. §§ 1007, and 1383(a)(2) of this title] on or after January 1, 2019."

Pub.L. 115–165, Title II, § 203(d), Apr. 13, 2018, 132 Stat. 1273, provided that:

"(1) **New appointments.**—Subject to paragraph (2), the amendments made by this section [amending subsec. (j)(2)(C) of this section, and 42 U.S.C.A. §§ 1007 and 1383] shall apply with respect to any individual appointed to serve as a representative payee under title II, title VIII, or title XVI of the Social Security Act [subchapters II, VIII, or XVI of this chapter, 42 U.S.C.A §§ 401 et seq., 1001 et seq., or 1381 et seq.] on or after January 1, 2019.

"(2) **Prior appointments.**—With respect to individuals serving as a representative payee whose benefits under this title, title VIII, or title XVI [this subchapter and subchapter VIII or XVI of this chapter, 42 U.S.C.A §§ 401 et seq., 1001 et seq., or 1381 et seq.] are certified for payment to another representative payee as of January 1, 2019, the Commissioner shall take any steps necessary to terminate such individual's service as a representative payee as soon as possible, but no later than January 1, 2024."

2015 Acts. Pub.L. 114–10, Title V, § 501(d), Apr. 16, 2015, 129 Stat. 164, provided that:

"(1) **In general.**—Clause (xiii) of section 205(c)(2)(C) of the Social Security Act (42 U.S.C. 405(c)(2)(C)), as added by subsection (a)(3) [Pub.L. 114–10, Title V, § 501(a)(3), Apr. 16, 2015, 129 Stat. 163, which added cl. (xiii) to subsec. (c)(2)(C) of this section], shall apply with respect to Medicare cards issued on and after an effective date specified by the Secretary of Health and Human Services, but in no case shall such effective date be later than the date that is four years after the date of the enactment of this Act [Apr. 16, 2015].

"(2) **Reissuance.**—The Secretary shall provide for the reissuance of Medicare cards that comply with the requirements of such clause not later than four years after the effective date specified by the Secretary under paragraph (1)."

2010 Acts. Pub.L. 111–318, § 2(a)(2), Dec. 18, 2010, 124 Stat. 3455, provided that: "The amendment made by this subsection [amending this section] shall apply with respect to checks issued after the date that is 3 years after the date of enactment of this Act [Dec. 18, 2010]."

Pub.L. 111–318, § 2(b)(2), Dec. 18, 2010, 124 Stat. 3455, provided that: The amendment made by this subsection [amending this section] shall apply with respect to employment of prisoners, or entry into contract with prisoners, after the date that is 1 year after the date of enactment of this Act [Dec. 18, 2010]."

2008 Acts. Amendments by Pub.L. 110–246, except as otherwise provided, shall take effect on the earlier of June 18, 2008, or May 22, 2008, see Pub.L. 110–246, § 4(b), set out in a Repeal of Duplicative Enactment note under 7 U.S.C.A. § 8701.

Amendments by Title IV of Pub.L. 110–246, except as otherwise provided, take effect on October 1, 2008, see Pub.L. 110–246, § 4407, set out as a note under 2 U.S.C.A. § 1161.

2004 Acts. Pub.L. 108–458, Title VII, § 7214(b), Dec. 17, 2004, 118 Stat. 3832, provided that: "The amendment made by subsection (a)(2) [amending this section] shall apply with respect to licenses, registrations, and identification cards issued or reissued 1 year after the date of enactment of this Act [Dec. 17, 2004]."

Notwithstanding any other provision of Pub.L. 108–458, Pub.L. 108–458, Title VII, Subtitle B (§§ 7201 to 7220), to take effect on Dec. 17, 2004, see Pub.L. 108–458, § 7219, which is set out as a note under 8 U.S.C.A. § 1202.

Pub.L. 108–203, Title I, § 101(d), Mar. 2, 2004, 118 Stat. 497, provided that: "The amendments made by this section [enacting subsec. (j)(8) of this section and 42 U.S.C.A. §§ 1007(j), 1382b(a)(14), and 1383(a)(2)(A)(iv), and amending subsec. (j)(5) of this section and 42 U.S.C.A. §§ 1007(a), (i), 1382b(a)(12), (13), and 1383(a)(2)(E)] shall apply to any case of benefit misuse by a representative payee with respect to which the Commissioner of Social Security makes the determination of misuse on or after January 1, 1995."

Pub.L. 108–203, Title I, § 102(a)(3), Mar. 2, 2004, 118 Stat. 498, provided that: "The amendments made by this subsection [enacting subsec. (j)(9) of this section and 42 U.S.C.A. § 1383(a)(2)(I) and amending subsec. (j)(2)(C)(v), (3)(F), (4)(B) of this section and 42 U.S.C.A. § 1383(a)(2)(B)(vii), (D)(ii)] shall take effect on the first day of the thirteenth month beginning after the date of the enactment of this Act [Mar. 2, 2004]."

Pub.L. 108–203, Title I, § 103(d), Mar. 2, 2004, 118 Stat. 503, provided that: "The amendments made by this section [enacting subsec. (j)(2)(B)(iii), (C)(i)(IV), and (V) of this section and 42 U.S.C.A. §§ 1007(d)(1)(D), (E), and 1383(a)(2)(B)(iii)(IV), (V), (xiv) and amending subsec. (j)(2)(B)(i), (C)(i)(II) of this section and 42 U.S.C.A. §§ 1007(b)(2)(C) to (E), (3), (d)(1)(B), (C), and 1383(a)(2)(B)] shall take effect on the first day of the thirteenth month beginning after the date of the enactment of this Act [Mar. 2, 2004]."

Pub.L. 108–203, Title I, § 104(c), Mar. 2, 2004, 118 Stat. 504, provided that: "The amendments made by this section [amending subsec. (j)(4)(A)(i) of this section and 42 U.S.C.A. § 1383(a)(2)(D)(i)] shall apply to any month involving benefit misuse by a representative payee in any case with respect to which the Commissioner of Social Security or a court of competent jurisdiction makes the determination of misuse after 180 days after the date of the enactment of this Act [Mar. 2, 2004]."

Pub.L. 108–203, Title I, § 105(d), Mar. 2, 2004, 118 Stat. 505, provided that: "The amendments made by this section [enacting 42 U.S.C.A. § 1007(*l*) and amending subsec. (j)(2)(C)(v), (3)(F), (4)(B), and (7) to (10) of this section and 42 U.S.C.A. § 1383(a)(2)(G)(i)(II), (H)] shall apply to benefit misuse by a representative payee in any case with respect to which the Commissioner of Social Security or a court of competent jurisdiction makes the determination of misuse after 180 days after the date of the enactment of this Act [Mar. 2, 2004]."

Pub.L. 108–203, Title I, § 106(d), Mar. 2, 2004, 118 Stat. 506, provided that: "The amendments made by this section [enacting 42 U.S.C.A. § 1383(a)(2)(C)(v) and amending subsec. (j)(3)(E) to (G) of this section and 42 U.S.C.A. § 1007(h)(3) to (5)] shall take effect 180 days after the date of the enactment of this Act [Mar. 2, 2004]."

Pub.L. 108–203, Title IV, § 411(b), Mar. 2, 2004, 118 Stat. 527, provided that: "The amendment made by this section [amending subsec. (g) of this section] shall apply with respect to final determinations issued (upon remand) on or after the date of the enactment of this Act [Mar. 2, 2004]."

2001 Acts. Pub.L. 107–90, Title I, § 103(j), Dec. 21, 2001, 115 Stat. 882, provided that: "The amendments made by this section [amending this section and sections 231a, 231b, 231c, 231d, 231e, 231f, 231q, 231r of Title 45] shall take effect on January 1, 2002."

1997 Acts. Section 1090(b)(2) of Pub.L. 105–34 provided that:

"**(A)** The amendment made by paragraph (1)(A) [amending subsec. (c)(2)(B)(ii) of this section] shall apply to applications made after the date which is 180 days after the date of the enactment of this Act [Aug. 5, 1997].

"**(B)** The amendments made by subparagraphs (B) and (C) of paragraph (1) [amending this section] shall apply to information obtained on, before, or after the date of the enactment of this Act [Aug. 5, 1997]."

1996 Acts. Amendments by section 108(a)(1) of Pub.L. 104–193 effective July 1, 1997, with transition rules relating to State options to accelerate such date, rules relating to claims, actions, and proceedings commenced before such date, rules relating to closing out of accounts for terminated or substantially modified programs and continuance in office of Assistant Secretary for Family Support, and provisions relating to termination of entitlement under AFDC program, see section 116 of Pub.L. 104–193, set out as a note under section 601 of this title.

Section 105(a)(5) of Pub.L. 104–121, as amended Pub.L. 106–170, Title IV, § 401(a), (b), Dec. 17, 1999, 113 Stat. 1906, provided that:

"**(A)** The amendments made by paragraphs (1) and (4) [amending sections 423 and 425 of this title, respectively] shall apply to any individual who applies for, or whose claim is finally adjudicated with respect to, benefits under title II of the Social Security Act [this subchapter] based on disability on or after the date of the enactment of this Act [Mar. 29, 1996], and, in the case of any individual who has applied for, and whose claim has been finally adjudicated with respect to, such benefits before such date of enactment, such amendments shall apply only with respect to such benefits for months beginning on or after January 1, 1997.

"**(B)** The amendments made by paragraphs (2) and (3) [amending this section and section 422 of this title] shall take effect on July 1, 1996, with respect to any individual—

"**(i)** whose claim for benefits is finally adjudicated on or after the date of the enactment of this Act [Mar. 29, 1996]; or

"**(ii)** whose entitlement to benefits is based upon an entitlement redetermination made pursuant to subparagraph (C).

"**(C)** Within 90 days after the date of the enactment of this Act [Mar. 29, 1996], the Commissioner of Social Security shall notify each individual who is entitled to monthly insurance benefits under title II of the Social Security Act [this subchapter] based on disability for the month in which this Act is enacted [March 1996] and whose entitlement to such benefits would terminate by reason of the amendments made by this subsection [amending this section and sections 422, 423, and 425 of this title]. If such an individual reapplies for benefits under title II of such Act (as amended by this Act) [this subchapter as amended by Pub.L. 104–121] based on disability within 120 days after the date of the enactment of this Act [Mar. 29, 1996], the Commissioner of Social Security shall, not later than January 1, 1997, complete the entitlement redetermination (including a new medical determination) with respect to such individual pursuant to the procedures of such title.

"**(D)** For purposes of this paragraph, an individual's claim, with respect to benefits under title II [this subchapter] based on disability, which has been denied in whole before the date of the enactment of this Act [Mar. 29, 1996], may not be considered to be finally adjudicated before such date if, on or after such date—

"**(i)** there is pending a request for either administrative or judicial review with respect to such claim; or

"**(ii)** there is pending, with respect to such claim, a readjudication by the Commissioner of Social Security pursuant to relief in a class action or implementation by the Commissioner of a court remand order.

"**(E)** Notwithstanding the provisions of this paragraph, with respect to any individual for whom the Commissioner of Social Security does not perform the entitlement redetermination before the date prescribed in subparagraph (C), the Commissioner shall perform such entitlement redetermination in lieu of a continuing disability review whenever the Commissioner determines that the individual's entitlement is subject to redetermination based on the preceding provisions of this paragraph, and the provisions of section 223(f) [42 U.S.C.A. § 423(f)] shall not apply to such redetermination."

[Pub.L. 106–170, Title IV, § 401(c), Dec. 17, 1999, 113 Stat. 1907, provided that: "The amendments made by this section [amending this note] shall take effect as if included in the enactment of section 105 of the Contract with America Advancement Act of 1996 (Public Law 104–121; 110 Stat. 852 et seq.)."]

1994 Acts. Amendment by section 107(a)(1), (2), and (4) of Pub.L. 103–296 effective Mar. 31, 1995, see section 110 of Pub.L. 103–296, set out as a note under section 401 of this title.

Section 201(a)(1)(D) of Pub.L. 103–296 provided that:

"**(i) General rule.**—Except as provided in clause (ii), the amendments made by this paragraph [amending subsec. (j) of this section and enacting provisions set out as notes under this section] shall apply with respect to benefits paid in months beginning after 180 days after the date of the enactment of this Act.

"**(ii) Treatment of current beneficiaries.**—In any case in which—

"**(I)** an individual is entitled to benefits based on disability (as defined in section 205(j)(7) of the Social Security Act, as amended by this section),

"**(II)** the determination of disability was made by the Secretary of Health and Human Services during or before the 180–day period following the date of the enactment of this Act [Aug. 15, 1994], and

"**(III)** alcoholism or drug addiction is a contributing factor material to the Secretary's determination that the individual is under a disability, the amendments made by this paragraph shall apply with respect to benefits paid in months after the month in which such individual is notified by the Secretary in writing that alcoholism or drug addiction is a contributing factor material to the Secretary's determination and that the Secretary is therefore required to make a certification of payment of such individual's benefits to a representative payee."

Section 201(a)(2)(B)(iii) of Pub.L. 103–296 provided in part that the repeal by that section of subsec. (j)(4)(D) of this section is effective July 1, 1994.

Section 201(a)(2)(D) of Pub.L. 103–296 provided that: "Except as provided in subparagraph (B)(iii), the amendments made by this paragraph [amending subsec. (j) of this section and enacting provisions set out as a note under this section] shall apply with respect to months beginning after 90 days after the date of the enactment of this Act [Aug. 15, 1994]."

Section 206(a)(3) of Pub.L. 103–296 provided that: "The amendments made by this subsection [amending subsec. (c)(8) and (9) of this section and section 1383(e)(4) of this title] shall apply to translations made on or after October 1, 1994."

Section 206(d)(3) of Pub.L. 103–296 provided that: "The amendments made by this subsection [enacting subsec. (u) of this section and section 1383(e)(6) of this title] shall take effect on October 1, 1994, and shall apply to determinations made before, on, or after such date."

Section 304(c) of Pub.L. 103–296 provided that: "The amendments made by this section [amending this section and section 1320b–10 of this title] shall take effect on the date of the enactment of this Act [Aug. 15, 1994]."

Section 321(f)(5) of Pub.L. 103–296 provided that: "Each amendment made by this subsection [amending this section and sections 406, 423, 1320a–6, and 1383 of this title] shall take effect as if included in the provisions of the Omnibus Budget Reconciliation Act of 1990 [Pub.L. 101–508, Dec. 19, 1989, 104 Stat. 1388, for classifications to which see Tables] to which such amendment relates, except that the amendments made by paragraph (3)(B) [enacting sections 406(b)(1)(B) of this title and amending section 1320–6(a) of this title] shall apply with respect to favorable judgments made after 180 days after the date of the enactment of this Act [Aug. 15, 1994]."

1990 Acts. Amendment by section 1735(a), (b) of Pub.L. 101–624 effective and implemented the 1st day of the month beginning 120 days after the publication and implementing regulations, which regulations are to be promulgated not later than Oct. 1, 1991, see section 1781(a) of Pub.L. 101–624, set out as a note under section 2012 of this title.

Section 5105(a)(5) of Pub.L. 101–508 provided that:

"(A) Use and selection of representative payees.—The amendments made by paragraphs (1) and (2) [amending subsec. (j)(1) and (2) of this section and section 1383(a)(2)(A) through (C) of this title, and enacting provisions set out as a note under this section] shall take effect July 1, 1991, and shall apply only with respect to—

"**(i)** certifications of payment of benefits under title II of the Social Security Act [this subchapter] to representative payees made on or after such date; and

"**(ii)** provisions for payment of benefits under title XVI of such Act [subchapter XVI of this chapter] to representative payees made on or after such date."

"(B) Compensation of representative payees.—The amendments made by paragraph (3) [amending subsec. (j)(4) and (5) of this section and section 1383(a)(2)(D) and (E) of this title, and enacting provisions set out as notes under this section] shall take effect July 1, 1991, and the Secretary of Health and Human Services shall prescribe initial regulations necessary to carry out such amendments not later than such date."

Section 5105(b)(1)(B) of Pub.L. 101–508 provided that: "The amendments made by subparagraph (A) [amending subsec. (j)(3)(B) to (F) of this section] shall take effect October 1, 1992, and the Secretary of Health and Human Services shall take such actions as are necessary to ensure that the requirements of section 205(j)(3)(E) of the Social Security Act (as amended by subparagraph (A) of this paragraph) [subsec. (j)(3)(E) of this section] are satisfied as of such date."

Section 5105(d)(2) of Pub.L. 101–508 provided that: "The amendments made by paragraph (1) [amending (j)(6) of this section and section 1383(a)(2)(F) of this title] shall apply with respect to annual reports issued for years after 1991."

Section 5107(b) of Pub.L. 101–508 provided that: "The amendments made by this section [amending this section and section 1383 of this title] shall apply with respect to adverse determinations made on or after July 1, 1991."

Section 5109(b) of Pub.L. 101–508 provided that: "The amendments made by this section [amending this section and section 1383 of this title] shall apply with respect to notices issued on or after July 1, 1991."

1989 Acts. Section 10303(c) of Pub.L. 101–239 provided that: "The amendments made by this section [enacting subsec. (t) of this section and section 1383(e)(6) of this title] shall apply to visits to field offices of the Social Security Administration on or after January 1, 1990."

1988 Acts. Section 8009(b) of Pub.L. 100–647 provided that: "The amendments made by this section [amending subsec. (c)(2)(B)(i); enacting subsec. (c)(2)(E); and redesignating as subsec. (c)(2)(F) former subsec. (c)(2)(E) of this section] shall apply to benefits entitlement to which commences after the sixth month following the month [November] in which this Act is enacted [Nov. 10, 1988]."

Amendment by section 8015(a)(1) of Pub.L. 100–647 applicable to determinations relating to service commenced in any position on or after Nov. 10, 1988, see section 8015(a)(3) of Pub.L. 100–647, set out as a note under section 3122 of Title 26, Internal Revenue Code.

Amendment by section 8016(a)(1) of Pub.L. 100–647 effective Nov. 10, 1988, except that any amendment to a provision of a particular Public Law which is referred to by its number, or to a provision of the Social Security Act [42 U.S.C.A. 301 et seq.], or to Title 26, as added or amended by a provision of a particular Public Law which is so referred to, effective as though included or reflected in the relevant provisions of that Public Law at the time of its enactment, see section 8016(b) of Pub.L. 100–647, set out as a note under section 3111 of Title 26.

Section 125(b) of Pub.L. 100–485 provided that: "The amendments made by subsection (a) [amending subsec. (c)(2)(C) of this section] shall become effective on the first day of the 25th month which begins on or after the date of the enactment of this Act [Oct. 13, 1988]."

1986 Acts. Amendment by Pub.L. 99–509 effective with respect to payments due with respect to wages paid after Dec. 31, 1986, including wages paid after such date by a State (or political subdivision thereof) that modified its agreement pursuant to section 418(e)(2) of this title prior to Oct. 21, 1986, with certain exceptions, see section 9002(d) of Pub.L. 99–509 set out as a note under section 418 of this title.

1984 Acts. Section 16(d) of Pub.L. 98–460 provided that: "The amendments made by this section [amending subsec. (j) of this section and sections 408, 1383(a)(2), and 1383a of this title] shall become effective on the date of the enactment of this Act [Oct. 9, 1984], and, in the case of the amendments made by subsection (c) [amending section 1383a of this title], shall apply with respect to violations occurring on or after such date."

Amendment by section 2661(h) of Pub.L. 98–369 effective as though included in the enactment of the Social Security Amendments of 1983 [Pub.L. 98–21], see section 2664(a) of Pub.L. 98–369, set out as of a note under section 401 of this title.

Amendment by section 2663(a)(4), (j)(4) of Pub.L. 98–369 effective July 18, 1984, but not to be construed as changing or affecting any right, liability, status or interpretation which existed (under the provisions of law involved) before that date, see section 2664(b) of Pub.L. 98–369, set out as a note under section 401 of this title.

1983 Acts. Amendment by sections 301(d) and 309(i) of Pub.L. 98–21 applicable only with respect to monthly payments payable under this subchapter for months after April, 1983, except as otherwise specifically provided, see section 310 of Pub.L. 98–21, set out as a note under section 402 of this title.

Section 345(b) of Pub.L. 98–21 provided that: "The amendment made by this section [adding subsec. (c)(2)(D) of this section] shall apply with respect to all new and replacement social security cards issued more than 193 days after the date of the enactment of this Act [Apr. 20, 1983]."

Section 4(b) of Pub.L. 97–455 provided that: "The amendments made by subsection (a) [amending subsec. (b) of this section] shall apply with respect to reconsiderations (of findings described in section 205(b)(2)(B) of the Social Security Act) [subsec. (b)(2)(B) of this section] which are requested on or after such date as the Secretary of Health and Human Services may specify, but in any event not later than January 1, 1984."

1980 Acts. Section 305(c) of Pub.L. 96–265 provided that: "The amendments made by this section [amending sections 405(b) and 1383 of this title] shall apply with respect to decisions made on or after the first day of the 13th month following the month in which this Act is enacted [June, 1980]."

1978 Acts. Amendment by Pub.L. 95–600 effective Oct. 4, 1976, see section 703(r) of Pub.L. 95–600, set out as a note under section 46 of Title 26.

1977 Acts. Amendment by Pub.L. 95–216 effective Jan. 1, 1978, see section 353(g) of Pub.L. 95–216, set out as a note under section 418 of this title.

1976 Acts. Section 5 of Pub.L. 94–202 provided that: "The amendments made by the first two sections of this Act [amending section 1383 of this title], and the provisions of section 3 [set out as a note under section 1383 of this title], shall take effect on the date of the enactment of this Act [Jan. 2, 1976]. The amendment made by section 4 of this Act [amending subsec. (b) of this section] shall apply with respect to any decision or determination of which notice is received, by the individual requesting the hearing involved, after February 29, 1976. The amendment made by the first section of this Act [amending subsec. (c) of section 1383 of this title], to the extent that it changes the period within which hearings must be requested, shall apply with respect to any decision or determination of which notice is received, by the individual requesting the hearing involved, on or after the date of the enactment of this Act [Jan. 2, 1976]."

1974 Acts. Section 302(b) of Pub.L. 93–445 provided that: "The amendment made by this section [amending subsec. (i) of this section] shall apply only with respect to benefits payable to individuals who first become entitled to benefits under title II of the Social Security Act [this subchapter] after 1974."

Amendment by section 303 of Pub.L. 93–445 effective Jan. 1, 1975, see section 603 of Pub.L. 93–445, set out as a note under section 402 of this title.

1970 Acts. Amendment by Pub.L. 91–452 effective the sixtieth day following Oct. 15, 1970, see section 260 of Pub.L. 91–452, set out as a note under section 6001 of Title 18, Crimes and Criminal Procedure.

1968 Acts. Section 171(b) of Pub.L. 90–248 provided that: "The amendment made by subsection (a) of this section [enacting subsec. (q) of this section] shall be effective with respect to written requests filed under section 205(q) of the Social Security Act [subsec. (q) of this section] after June 30, 1968."

1965 Acts. Amendment by section 308(d)(9), (10) Pub.L. 89–97 applicable with respect to monthly insurance benefits under this subchapter beginning with the second month following July, 1965, but, in the case of an individual who was not entitled to a monthly insurance benefit under section 402 of this title for the first month following July, 1965, only on the basis of an application filed in or after July, 1965, see section 308(e) of Pub.L. 89–97, set out as a note under section 402 of this title.

1961 Acts. Amendment by Pub.L. 87–293 applicable with respect to service performed after Sept. 22, 1961, but in the case of persons serving under the Peace Corps agency established by executive order applicable with respect to service performed on or after the effective date of enrollment, see section 202(c) of Pub.L. 87–293, set out as a note under section 3121 of Title 26.

1960 Acts. Amendment by section 102(f)(2) of Pub.L. 86–778 effective the first day of the second calendar year following 1960, see section 102(f)(3) of Pub.L. 86–778, set out as a note under section 418 of this title.

Amendment by section 103(j)(2)(E) of Pub.L. 86–778 effective Sept. 13, 1960, see section 103(v)(1) of Pub.L. 86–778, set out as a note under section 402 of this title.

Section 702(b) of Pub.L. 86–778 provided that: "The amendment made by subsection (a) [to subsec. (g) of this section] shall apply to actions which are pending in court on the date of the enactment of this Act [Sept. 13, 1960] or are commenced after such date."

1956 Acts. Section 111(b) of Act Aug. 1, 1956, c. 836, provided that: "The amendment made by subsection (a) [to subsec. (b) of this section] shall be effective upon enactment [August 1, 1956]; except that the period of time prescribed by the Secretary pursuant to the third sentence of section 205(b) of the Social Security Act, as amended by subsection (a) of this section [subsec. (b) of this section], with respect to decisions notice of which has been mailed by him to any individual prior to the enactment of this Act [August 1, 1956] may not terminate for such individual less than six months after the date of enactment of this Act [August 1, 1956]."

Amendment by Act Aug. 1, 1956, c. 837, effective Jan. 1, 1957.

1954 Acts. Section 101(n) of Act Sept. 1, 1954 provided that: "The amendment made by paragraph (3) of subsection (g) [amending section 411 of this title] shall be applicable only with respect to taxable years beginning after 1950. The amendments made by paragraphs (1), (2), and (4) of such subsection [amending section 411 of this title] shall, except for purposes of section 203 of the Social Security Act [section 403 of this title], be applicable only with respect to taxable years ending after 1954. The amendments made by paragraphs (1), (2), and (3) of subsection (a) [amending section 409 of this title] shall be applicable only with respect to remuneration paid after 1954. The amendments made by paragraphs (4), (5), and (6) of subsection (a) [amending sections 410 and 418 of this title] shall be applicable only with respect to services (whether performed after 1954 or prior to 1955) for which the remuneration is paid after 1954. The amendment made by paragraph (3) of subsection (c) [amending this section] shall become effective January 1, 1955. The other amendments made by this section (other than the amendments made by subsections (h), (i), (j) and (m)[)] [amending section 410 of this title] shall be applicable only with respect to services performed after 1954. For purposes of section 203 of the Social Security Act [section 403 of this title], the amendments made by paragraphs (1), (2), and (4) of subsection (g) [amending section 411 of this title] and by subsection(d) [amending section 411 of this title] shall be effective with respect to net earnings from self-employment derived after 1954. The amount of net earnings from self-employment derived during any taxable year ending in, and not with the close of, 1955 shall be credited equally to the calendar quarter in which such taxable year ends and to each of the three or fewer preceding quarters any part of which is in such taxable year; and, for purposes of the preceding sentence of this subsection, net earnings from self-employment so credited to calendar quarters in 1955 shall be deemed to have been derived after 1954."

1950 Acts. Section 108(d) of Act Aug. 28, 1950 provided that: "The amendments made by subsections (a) and (c) of this section [amending subsecs. (b), *(o)* of this section] shall take effect on September 1, 1950. The amendment made by subsection (b) of this section [amending subsec. (c) of this section] shall take effect January 1, 1951, except that, effective on September 1, 1950, the husband or former wife divorced of an individual shall be treated the same as a parent of such individual, and the legal representative of an individual or his estate shall be treated the same as the individual, for purposes of section 205(c) of the Social Security Act [subsec. (c) of this section] as in effect prior to the enactment of this Act [Aug. 28, 1950]."

Section 101(b)(2) of Act Aug. 28, 1950 provided in part that subsec. (m), relating to filing of application for benefits under this subchapter, was repealed effective with respect to monthly payments under section 402 of this title for the months after August 1950.

1939 Acts. Amendment by Act Aug. 10, 1939 was made effective Jan. 1, 1940, by section 201 of Act Aug. 10, 1939.

Repeals

Pub.L. 110–234 repealed effective May 22, 2008, see Repeal of Duplicative Enactment by Pub.L. 110–246, § 4(a), set out in a note under 7 U.S.C.A. § 8701.

Repeals; Amendments and Application of Amendments Unaffected

Section 202(b)(3) of Pub.L. 87–293, cited as a credit to this section, was repealed by Pub.L. 89–572, § 5(a), Sept. 13, 1966, 80 Stat. 765. Such repeal not deemed to affect amendments to this section contained in such provisions, and continuation in full force and effect until modified by appropriate authority of all determinations, authorization, regulations, orders, contracts, agreements, and other actions issued, undertaken, or entered into under authority of the repealed provisions, see § 5(b) of Pub.L. 89–572, set out as a note under former section 2515 of Title 22, Foreign Relations and Intercourse.

Savings Provisions

Amendment by Pub.L. 91–452 not to affect any immunity to which any individual is entitled under this section by reason of any testimony given before the sixtieth day following Oct. 15, 1970, see section 260 of Pub.L. 91–452, set out as an Effective Date; Savings Provisions note under section 6001 of Title 18, Crimes and Criminal Procedure.

Severability of Provisions

If any provision of Pub. L. 101–624 or the application thereof to any person or circumstance is held invalid, such invalidity not to affect other provisions or applications of Pub.L. 101–624 which can be given effect without regard to the invalid provision or application, see section 2519 of Pub. L. 101–624, set out as a note under section 1421 of Title 7, Agriculture.

Availability of Grant Funds

Pub.L. 115–165, Title I, § 101(c), Apr. 13, 2018, 132 Stat. 1259, provided that:

"(1) Protection and advocacy system grants.—Grants described under clause (i) of subparagraph (C) of section 205(j)(6) of the Social Security Act [subsec. (j)(6)(C)(i) of this section] (as added by subsection (a)) shall be awarded on August 1, 2018, and annually thereafter, and funds provided by such grants to a protection and advocacy system may be used to reimburse the protection and advocacy system for amounts expended by the protection and advocacy system during the period beginning on May 1, 2018, and ending on such date for hiring and start-up costs in preparation to carry out reviews of representative payees in accordance with such subparagraph.

"(2) National association grants.—Grants described under clause (v) of such subparagraph [subsec. (j)(6)(C) of this section] shall be awarded on May 1, 2018, and annually thereafter."

Regulations

Pub.L. 115–165, Title II, § 201(c), Apr. 13, 2018, 132 Stat. 1266, provided that: "Not later than 18 months after the date of the enactment of this section [Apr. 13, 2018], the Commissioner of Social Security shall promulgate regulations specifying the information an individual is required to provide to the Commissioner in order to designate another individual to serve as the individual's representative payee under section 205(j)(1)(C) of the Social Security Act [subsec. (j)(1)(C) of this section] (as added by subsection (a))."

Pub.L. 115–165, Title II, § 202(f), Apr. 13, 2018, 132 Stat. 1272, provided that: "Not later than 1 year after the date of enactment of this section [Apr. 13, 2018], the Commissioner of Social Security shall issue regulations to establish a process for reviewing each individual serving as a representative payee pursuant to section 205(j), 807, or 1631(a)(2) of the Social Security Act [subsec. (j) of this section, and 42 U.S.C.A. §§ 1007, or 1383(a)(2)] (other than individuals with respect to whom an exemption has been granted under section 205(j)(2)(C)(vi), 807(d)(2)(D), or 1631(a)(2)(B)(xvii) [subsec. (j)(2)(C)(vi) of this section, and 42 U.S.C.A. §§ 1007(d)(2)(D), or 1383(a)(2)(B)(xvi)]) not less than once every 5 years to determine whether any such individual has been convicted of a felony as described in subsection (e)(1) of this section [enacting provisions set out as a note under this section]."

Notification to Beneficiaries

Pub.L. 115–165, Title II, § 201(d), Apr. 13, 2018, 132 Stat. 1266, provided that: "Not later than January 1, 2020, and annually thereafter, the Commissioner of Social Security shall notify each individual entitled to a benefit under title II, VIII, or XVI of the Social Security Act [subchapter II, VIII, or XVI of this chapter, 42 U.S.C.A. §§ 401 et seq., 1001 et seq., or 1381 et seq.] of the name of any individual designated to serve as the individual's representative payee under section 205(j)(1)(C) of such Act [subsec. (j)(1)(C) of this section] (as added by subsection (a))."

Application to Prior Appointments

Pub.L. 115–165, Title II, § 202(e), Apr. 13, 2018, 132 Stat. 1271, provided that:

"**(1) In general.**—Not later than January 1, 2024, the Commissioner of Social Security shall conduct a review of each individual serving as a representative payee pursuant to 205(j), 807, or 1631(a)(2) of the Social Security Act [subsec. (j) of this section, and 42 U.S.C.A. §§ 1007 and 1383(a)(2)], to determine whether such individual has been convicted of a felony as described in section 205(j)(2)(B)(i)(VII), 807(b)(2)(G), or 1631(a)(2)(B)(ii)(VII) [subsec. (j)(2)(B)(i)(VII) of this section, and 42 U.S.C.A. §§ 1007(b)(2)(G), or 1383(a)(2)(B)(ii)(VII)], respectively (as such provisions are added by this section). Except as provided in section 205(j)(2)(C)(vi), 807(d)(2)(D), or 1631(a)(2)(B)(xvii) [subsec. (j)(2)(C)(vi) of this title, and 42 U.S.C.A. §§ 1007(d)(2)(D) or 1383(a)(2)(B)(xvii)] (as so added), any individual determined by the Commissioner to have been so convicted may not serve as a representative payee on or after the date of such determination.

"**(2) Priority.**—In conducting reviews under paragraph (1), the Commissioner shall prioritize reviews of the following categories of individuals, in the following order:

"**(A)** An individual serving as representative payee for 15 or more individuals.

"**(B)** An individual serving as representative payee for an individual who is not related to the representative payee.

"**(C)** An individual serving as representative payee for an individual who has attained the age of 18 and is not the spouse of the representative payee."

Social Security Number Fraud Prevention Act of 2017

Pub.L. 115–59, §§ 1, 2, Sept. 15, 2017, 131 Stat. 1152, provided that:

"**Section 1. Short title.**

"This Act [this note] may be cited as the 'Social Security Number Fraud Prevention Act of 2017'.

"**Sec. 2. Restriction of social security numbers on documents sent by mail.**

"**(a) Restriction.**—An agency may not include the social security account number of an individual on any document sent by mail unless the head of the agency determines that the inclusion of the social security account number on the document is necessary.

"**(b) Regulations.**—Not later than 5 years after the date of the enactment of this Act [Sept. 15, 2017], the head of each CFO Act agency shall issue regulations specifying the circumstances under which inclusion of a social security account number on a document sent by mail is necessary. Such regulations shall include—

"(1) instructions for the partial redaction of social security account numbers where feasible; and

"(2) a requirement that social security account numbers not be visible on the outside of any package sent by mail.

"**(c) Report.**—Not later than 30 days after the date of the enactment of this Act [Sept. 15, 2017], and not later than the first, second, third, fourth, and fifth-year anniversary of such date of enactment, the head of each CFO Act agency shall submit to the Committee on Ways and Means and the Committee on Oversight and Government Reform of the House of Representatives, the Committee on Finance and the Committee on Homeland Security and Governmental Affairs of the Senate, and any other appropriate authorizing committees of the House of Representatives and the Senate, a report on the implementation of subsection (a) that includes the following:

"(1) The title and identification number of any document used by the CFO Act agency during the previous year that includes the complete social security account number of an individual.

"(2) For the first report submitted, a plan that describes how the CFO Act agency will comply with the requirements of subsection (a).

"(3) For the final report submitted, the title and identification number of each document used by the CFO Act agency for which the head of the agency has determined, in accordance with regulations issued pursuant to subsection (b), that the inclusion of a social security account number on such document is necessary, and the rationale for such determination.

"(4) For any other report that is not the first or final report submitted, an update on the implementation of the plan described under paragraph (2).

"**(d) Definitions.**—In this section:

"**(1) Agency.**—The term 'agency' has the meaning given that term in section 551 of title 5, United States Code [5 U.S.C.A. § 551], but includes an establishment in the legislative or judicial branch of the Government (except the Senate, the House of Representatives, and the Architect of the Capitol, and any activities under the direction of the Architect of the Capitol).

"**(2) CFO Act agency.**—The term 'CFO Act agency' means the agencies listed in paragraphs (1) and (2) of section 901(b) of title 31, United States Code [31 U.S.C.A. § 901(b)].

"**(e) Effective date.**—Subsection (a) shall apply with respect to any document sent by mail on or after the date that is 5 years after the date of the enactment of this Act [Sept. 15, 2017]."

Implementation of Clause (xiii) of Subsection (c)(2)(C) of this Section

Pub.L. 114–10, Title V, § 501(b), Apr. 16, 2015, 129 Stat. 163, provided that:

"In implementing clause (xiii) of section 205(c)(2)(C) of the Social Security Act (42 U.S.C. 405(c)(2)(C)), as added by subsection (a)(3) [Pub.L. 114–10, Title V, § 501(a)(3), Apr. 16, 2015, 129 Stat. 163, which added cl. (xiii) to subsec. (c)(2)(C) of this section], the Secretary of Health and Human Services shall do the following:

"(1) **In general.**—Establish a cost-effective process that involves the least amount of disruption to, as well as necessary assistance for, Medicare beneficiaries and health care providers, such as a process that provides such beneficiaries with access to assistance through a toll-free telephone number and provides outreach to providers.

"(2) **Consideration of Medicare beneficiary identified.**—Consider implementing a process, similar to the process involving Railroad Retirement Board beneficiaries, under which a Medicare beneficiary identifier which is not a Social Security account number (or derivative thereof) is used external to the Department of Health and Human Services and is convertible over to a Social Security account number (or derivative thereof) for use internal to such Department and the Social Security Administration."

Rules of Construction

Pub.L. 114–10, Title V, § 519, Apr. 16, 2015, 129 Stat. 175, provided that: "Except as explicitly provided in this subtitle, nothing in this subtitle [subtitle A of Title V of Pub.L. 114–10, Title V, §§ 501 to 519, Apr. 16, 2015, 129 Stat. 163], including the amendments made by this subtitle [amending this section and 42 U.S.C.A. §§ 1320a–7a, 1395b–7, 1395*l*, 1395m, 1395w–104, 1395x, 1395y, 1395kk, 1395kk–1, 1395ddd, and 1395iii, and enacting provisions set out as notes under this section and 42 U.S.C.A. §§ 1395a–7a, 1395b–7, 1395*l*, 1395m, 1395y, 1395kk, and 1395kk–1], shall be construed as preventing the use of notice and comment rulemaking in the implementation of the provisions of, and the amendments made by, this subtitle."

Social Security Cards and Numbers

Pub.L. 108–458, Title VII, § 7213, Dec. 17, 2004, 118 Stat. 3830, provided that:

"(a) **Security enhancements.**—The Commissioner of Social Security shall—

"(1) Not later than 1 year after the date of enactment of this Act [Dec. 17, 2004]—

"(A) restrict the issuance of multiple replacement social security cards to any individual to 3 per year and 10 for the life of the individual, except that the Commissioner may allow for reasonable exceptions from the limits under this paragraph on a case-by-case basis in compelling circumstances;

"(B) establish minimum standards for the verification of documents or records submitted by an individual to establish eligibility for an original or replacement social security card, other than for purposes of enumeration at birth; and

"(C) require independent verification of any birth record submitted by an individual to establish eligibility for a social security account number, other than for purposes of enumeration at birth, except that the Commissioner may allow for reasonable exceptions from the requirement for independent verification under this subparagraph on a case by case basis in compelling circumstances; and

"(2) notwithstanding section 205(r) of the Social Security Act (42 U.S.C. 405(r)) and any agreement entered into thereunder, not later than 18 months after the date of enactment of this Act [Dec. 17, 2004] with respect to death indicators and not later than 36 months after the date of enactment of this Act [Dec. 17, 2004] with respect to fraud indicators, add death and fraud indicators to the social security number verification systems for employers, State agencies issuing driver's licenses and identity cards, and other verification routines that the Commissioner determines to be appropriate.

"(b) **Interagency security task force.**—The Commissioner of Social Security, in consultation with the Secretary of Homeland Security, shall form an interagency task force for the purpose of further improving the security of social security cards and numbers. Not later than 18 months after the date of enactment of this Act [Dec. 17, 2004], the task force shall establish, and the Commissioner shall provide for the implementation of, security requirements, including—

"(1) standards for safeguarding social security cards from counterfeiting, tampering, alteration, and theft;

"(2) requirements for verifying documents submitted for the issuance of replacement cards; and

"(3) actions to increase enforcement against the fraudulent use or issuance of social security numbers and cards.

"(c) **Enumeration at birth.**—

"(1) **Improvement of application process.**—As soon as practicable after the date of enactment of this Act [Dec. 17, 2004], the Commissioner of Social Security shall undertake to make improvements to the enumeration at birth program for the issuance of social security account numbers to newborns. Such improvements shall be designed to prevent—

"(A) the assignment of social security account numbers to unnamed children;

"(B) the issuance of more than 1 social security account number to the same child; and

"(C) other opportunities for fraudulently obtaining a social security account number.

"(2) **Report to Congress.**—Not later than 1 year after the date of enactment of this Act [Dec. 17, 2004], the Commissioner shall transmit to each House of Congress a report specifying in detail the extent to which the improvements required under paragraph (1) have been made.

"(d) **Study regarding process for enumeration at birth.**—

"(1) **In general.**—As soon as practicable after the date of enactment of this Act [Dec. 17, 2004], the Commissioner of Social Security shall conduct a study to determine the most efficient options for ensuring the integrity of the process for enumeration at birth. This study shall include an examination of available methods for reconciling hospital birth records with birth registrations submitted to agencies of States and political subdivisions thereof and with information provided to the Commissioner as part of the process for enumeration at birth.

"(2) **Report.**—

"(A) **In general.**—Not later than 18 months after the date of enactment of this Act [Dec. 17, 2004], the Commissioner shall submit a report to the Committee on Ways and Means of the House of Representatives and the Committee on Finance of the Senate regarding the results of the study conducted under paragraph (1).

"(B) **Contents.**—The report submitted under subparagraph (A) shall contain such recommendations for legislative changes as the Commissioner considers necessary to implement needed improvements in the process for enumeration at birth.

"(e) **Authorization of appropriations.**—There are authorized to be appropriated to the Commissioner of Social Security for each of the fiscal years 2005 through 2009, such sums as may be necessary to carry out this section [this note]."

[Notwithstanding any other provision of Pub.L. 108–458, Pub.L. 108–458, Title VII, Subtitle B (§§ 7201 to 7220), to take effect on Dec. 17, 2004, see Pub.L. 108–458, § 7219, which is set out as a note under 8 U.S.C.A. § 1202.]

Annual Reports on Reviews of OASDI and SSI Cases

Section 206(g) of Pub.L. 103–296, as amended Pub.L. 103–296, Title I, § 108(b)(10)(B), Aug. 15, 1994, 108 Stat. 1483, provided that: "The Commissioner of Social Security shall annually submit to the Committee on Ways and Means of the House of Representatives and the Committee on Finance of the Senate a report on the extent to which the Commissioner has exercised his authority to review cases of entitlement to monthly insurance benefits under title II of the Social Security Act [42 U.S.C.A. § 401 et seq.] and supplemental security income cases under title XVI of such Act [42 U.S.C.A. § 1381 et seq.], and the extent to which the cases reviewed were those that involved a high likelihood or probability of fraud."

[Amendment by section 108(b)(10)(B) of Pub.L. 103–296 effective Mar. 31, 1995, see section 110 of Pub.L. 103–296, set out as a note under this section.]

Conduct of Face-to-Face Reconsiderations in Disability Cases

Section 5 of Pub.L. 97–455 provided that: "The Secretary of Health and Human Services shall take such steps as may be necessary or appropriate to assure public understanding of the importance the Congress attaches to the face-to-face reconsiderations provided for in section 205(b)(2) of the Social Security Act (as added by section 4 of this Act) [subsec. (b)(2) of this section]. For this purpose the Secretary shall—

"(1) provide for the establishment and implementation of procedures for the conduct of such reconsiderations in a manner which assures that beneficiaries will receive reasonable notice and information with respect to the time and place of reconsideration and the opportunities afforded to introduce evidence and be represented by counsel; and

"(2) advise beneficiaries who request or are entitled to request such reconsiderations of the procedures so established, of their opportunities to introduce evidence and be represented by counsel at such reconsiderations, and of the importance of submitting all evidence that relates to the question before the Secretary or the State agency at such reconsiderations."

Counterfeiting of Social Security Account Number Cards

Pub.L. 99–603, Title I, § 101(f), Nov. 6, 1986, 100 Stat. 3373, provided that:

"(1) The Comptroller General of the United States, upon consultation with the Attorney General and the Secretary of Health and Human Services as well as private sector representatives (including representatives of the financial, banking, and manufacturing industries), shall inquire into technological alternatives for producing and issuing social security account number cards that are more resistant to counterfeiting than social security account number cards being issued on the date of enactment of this Act [Nov. 6, 1986] by the Social Security Administration, including the use of encoded magnetic, optical, or active electronic media such as magnetic stripes, holograms, and integrated circuit chips. Such inquiry should focus on technologies that will help ensure the authenticity of the card, rather than the identity of the bearer.

"(2) The Comptroller General of the United States shall explore additional actions that could be taken to reduce the potential for fraudulently obtaining and using social security account number cards.

"(3) Not later than one year after the date of enactment of this Act, [Nov. 6, 1986], the Comptroller General of the United States shall prepare and transmit to the Committee on the Judiciary and the Committee on Ways and Means of the House of Representatives and the Committee on the Judiciary and the Committee on Finance of the Senate a report setting forth his findings and recommendations under this subsection."

Demonstration Projects Relating to Provision of Information to Local Agencies Providing Child and Adult Protective Services

Section 5105(b)(3) of Pub.L. 101–508 provided that:

"(A) **In general.**—As soon as practicable after the date of the enactment of this Act [Nov. 5, 1990], the Secretary of Health and Human Services shall implement a demonstration project under this paragraph in all or part of not fewer than 2 States. Under each such project, the Secretary shall enter into an agreement with the State in which the project is located to make readily available, for the duration of the project, to the appropriate State agency, a listing of addresses of multiple benefit recipients.

"(B) **Listing of addresses of multiple benefit recipients.**—The list referred to in subparagraph (A) shall consist of a current list setting forth each address within the State at which benefits under title II [this subchapter] benefits under title XVI [subchapter XVI of this chapter] or any combination of such benefits are being received by 5 or more individuals. For purposes of this subparagraph, in the case of benefits under title II [this subchapter], all individuals receiving benefits on the basis of the wages and self-employment income of the same individual shall be counted as 1 individual.

"(C) **Appropriate State agency.**—The appropriate State agency referred to in subparagraph (A) is the agency of the State which the Secretary determines is primarily responsible for regulating care facilities operated in such State or providing for child and adult protective services in such State.

"(D) **Report.**—The Secretary shall report to the Committee on Ways and Means of the House of Representatives and the Committee on Finance of the Senate concerning such demonstration projects, together with any recommendations, not later than July 1, 1992. Such report shall include an evaluation of the feasibility and desirability of legislation implementing the programs established pursuant to this paragraph on a permanent basis.

"(E) **State.**—For purposes of this paragraph, the term 'State' means a State, including the entities included in such term by section 210(h) of the Social Security Act (42 U.S.C. 410(h) [section 410(h) of this title])."

Development of Prototype of Counterfeit-Resistant Social Security Card Required

Pub.L. 104–208, Div. C, Title VI, § 657, Sept. 30, 1996, 110 Stat. 3009–719, provided that:

"(a) **Development.**—

"(1) **In general.**—The Commissioner of Social Security (in this section referred to as the 'Commissioner') shall, in accordance with the provisions of this section, develop a prototype of a counterfeit-resistant social security card. Such prototype card—

"(A) shall be made of a durable, tamper-resistant material such as plastic or polyester;

"(B) shall employ technologies that provide security features, such as magnetic stripes, holograms, and integrated circuits; and

"(C) shall be developed so as to provide individuals with reliable proof of citizenship or legal resident alien status.

"(2) **Assistance by Attorney General.**—The Attorney General shall provide such information and assistance as the Commissioner deems necessary to achieve the purposes of this section.

"(b) **Studies and reports.**—

"(1) **In general.**—The Comptroller General and the Commissioner of Social Security shall each conduct a study, and issue a report to the Congress, that examines different methods of improving the social security card application process.

"(2) **Elements of studies.**—The studies shall include evaluations of the cost and work load implications of issuing a counterfeit-resistant social security card for all individuals over a 3, 5, and 10 year period. The studies shall also evaluate the feasibility and cost implications of imposing a user fee for replacement cards and cards issued to individuals who apply for such a card prior to the scheduled 3, 5, and 10 year phase-in options.

"(3) **Distribution of reports.**—Copies of the reports described in this subsection, along with facsimiles of the prototype cards as described in subsection (a), shall be submitted to the Committees on Ways and Means and Judiciary of the House of Representatives and the Committees on Finance and Judiciary of the Senate not later than 1 year after the date of the enactment of this Act [Sept. 30, 1996]."

Similar provisions were contained in the following prior Act:

Pub.L. 104–193, Title I, § 111, Aug. 22, 1996, 110 Stat. 2176.

Inclusion of Self-Employment Income in Records of Secretary of Health, Education, and Welfare

Section 331(c) of Pub.L. 89–97 provided that: "Notwithstanding any provision of section 205(c)(5)(F) of the Social Security Act [subsec. (c)(5)(F) of this section], the Secretary of Health, Education, and Welfare [now Secretary of Health and Human Services] may conform, before April 16, 1970, his records to tax returns or statements of earnings which constitute self-employment income solely by reason of the filing of a certificate which is effective under section 1402(e)(5) of such Code [former section 1402(e)(5) of Title 26, Internal Revenue Code]."

Section 101(e) of Pub.L. 86–778 provided that: "The provisions of section 205(c)(5)(F) of the Social Security Act [subsec. (c)(5)(F) of this section], insofar as they prohibit inclusion in the records of the Secretary of Health, Education, and Welfare [now Secretary of Health and Human Services] of self-employment income for a taxable year when the return or statement including such income is filed after the time limitation following such taxable year, shall not be applicable to earnings which are derived in any taxable year ending before 1960 and which constitute self-employment income solely by reason of the filing of a certificate which is effective under Section 1402(e)(3)(B) or (5) of the Internal Revenue Code of 1954 [former section 1402(e)(3)(B) or (5) of Title 26, Internal Revenue Code]."

Ninety-Day Delay in Deferral or Suspension of Benefits for Current Beneficiaries

Section 201(a)(1)(C) of Pub.L. 103–296 provided that: "In the case of an individual who, as of 180 days after the date of the enactment of this Act [Aug. 15, 1994], has been determined to be under a disability, if alcoholism or drug addiction is a contributing factor material to the determination of the Secretary of Health and Human Services that the individual is under a disability, the Secretary may, notwithstanding clauses (i) and (ii) of section 205(j)(2)(D) of the Social Security Act [subsec. (j)(2)(D) of this section], make direct payment of benefits to such individual during the 90–day period commencing with the date on which such individual is provided the notice described in subparagraph (D)(ii) of this paragraph, until such time during such period as the selection of a representative payee is made pursuant to section 205(j) of such Act [subsec. (j) of this section]."

Report by Comptroller General

Section 5105(a)(3)(B)(ii) of Pub.L. 101–508 provided that: "Not later than July 1, 1992, the Comptroller General of the United States shall conduct a study of the advantages and disadvantages of allowing qualified organizations serving as representative payees to charge fees pursuant to the amendments made by subparagraph (A) [amending this section and section 1383 of this title] and shall transmit a report to the Committee on Ways and Means of the House of Representatives and the Committee on Finance of the Senate setting forth the results of such study."

[The provisions of section 5105(a)(3)(B)(ii) of Pub.L. 101–508, set out as a note above, are to take effect on July 1, 1991, except as otherwise provided, see section 5105(a)(5)(B) of Pub.L. 101–508, set out as a note under this section.]

Report by Secretary of Health and Human Services

Section 5105(a)(3)(B)(i) of Pub.L. 101–508 provided that: "Not later than January 1, 1993, the Secretary of Health and Human Services shall transmit a report to the Committee on Ways and Means of the House of Representatives and the Committee on Finance of the Senate setting forth the number and types of qualified organizations which have served as representative payees and have collected fees for such service pursuant to any amendment made by subparagraph (A) [amending this section and section 1383 of this title]."

[The provisions of section 5105(a)(3)(B)(i) of Pub.L. 101–508, set out as a note above, are to take effect on July 1, 1991, except as otherwise provided, see section 5105(a)(5)(B) of Pub.L. 101–508, set out as a note under this section.]

Report on Feasibility of Obtaining Ready Access to Certain Criminal Fraud Records

Section 5105(a)(2)(B) of Pub.L. 101–508 provided that: "As soon as practicable after the date of the enactment of this Act [Nov. 5, 1990], the Secretary of Health and Human Services, in consultation with the Attorney General of the United States and the Secretary of the Treasury, shall study the feasibility of establishing and maintaining a current list, which would be readily available to local offices of the Social Security Administration for use in investigations undertaken pursuant to section 205(j)(2) or 1631(a)(2)(B) of the Social Security Act [subsec. (j)(2) of this section or section 1383(a)(2)(B) of this title], of the names and social security account numbers of individuals who have been convicted of a violation of section 495 of title 18, United States Code [section 495 of Title 18, Crimes and Criminal Procedures]. The Secretary of Health and Human Services shall, not later than July 1, 1992, submit the results of such study, together with any recommendations, to the Committee on Ways and Means of the House of Representatives and the Committee on Finance of the Senate."

[The provisions of section 5105(a)(2)(B) of Pub.L. 101–508, set out as a note above, are to take effect on July 1, 1991, except as otherwise provided, see section 5105(a)(5)(A) of Pub.L. 101–508, set out as a note under this section.]

Study Regarding Feasibility, Cost, and Equity of Requiring Representative Payees for All Disability Beneficiaries Suffering From Alcoholism or Drug Addiction

Section 201(a)(1)(E) of Pub.L. 103–296 provided that:

"(i) **Study.**—As soon as practicable after the date of the enactment of this Act [Aug. 15, 1994], the Secretary of Health and Human Services shall conduct a study of the representative payee program. In such study, the Secretary shall examine—

"(I) the feasibility, cost, and equity of requiring representative payees for all individuals entitled to benefits based on disability under title II or XVI [42 U.S.C.A. § 1381 et seq.] of the Social Security Act who suffer from alcoholism or drug addiction, irrespective of whether the alcoholism or drug addiction was material in any case to the Secretary's determination of disability,

"(II) the feasibility, cost, and equity of providing benefits through non-cash means, including (but not limited to) vouchers, debit cards, and electronic benefits transfer systems,

"(III) the extent to which child beneficiaries are afflicted by drug addiction or alcoholism and ways of addressing such affliction, including the feasibility of requiring treatment, and

"(IV) the extent to which children's representative payees are afflicted by drug addiction or alcoholism, and methods to identify children's representative payees afflicted by drug addiction or alcoholism and to ensure that benefits continue to be provided to beneficiaries appropriately.

"(ii) **Report.**—Not later than December 31, 1995, the Secretary shall transmit to the Committee on Ways and Means of the House of Representatives and the Committee on Finance of the Senate a report setting forth the findings of the Secretary based on such study. Such report shall include such recommendations for administrative or legislative changes as the Secretary considers appropriate."

Study Relating to Feasibility of Screening of Individuals With Criminal Records

Section 5105(a)(4) of Pub.L. 101–508 provided that: "As soon as practicable after the date of the enactment of this Act [Nov. 5, 1990], the Secretary of Health and Human Services shall conduct a study of the feasibility of determining the type of representative payee applicant most likely to have a felony or misdemeanor conviction, the suitability of individuals with prior convictions to serve as representative payees, and the circumstances under which such applicants could be allowed to serve as representative payees. The Secretary shall transmit the results of such study to the Committee on Ways and Means of the House of Representatives and the Committee on Finance of the Senate not later than July 1, 1992."

Study Relating to More Stringent Oversight of High-Risk Representative Payees

Section 5105(b)(2) of Pub.L. 101–508 provided that:

"(A) **In general.**—As soon as practicable after the date of the enactment of this Act [Nov. 5, 1990], the Secretary of Health and Human Services shall conduct a study of the need for a more stringent accounting system for high-risk representative payees than is otherwise generally provided under section 205(j)(3) or 1631(a)(2)(C) of the Social Security Act [subsec. (j)(3) of this section or section 1383(a)(2)(C) of this title], which would include such additional reporting requirements, record maintenance requirements, and other measures as the Secretary considers necessary to determine whether services are being appropriately provided by such payees in accordance with such sections 205(j) and 1631(a)(2) [subsec. (j) of this section and section 1383(a)(2) of this title].

"(B) **Special procedures.**—In such study, the Secretary shall determine the appropriate means of implementing more stringent, statistically valid procedures for—

"(i) reviewing reports which would be submitted to the Secretary under any system described in subparagraph (A), and

"(ii) periodic, random audits of records which would be kept under such a system,

in order to identify any instances in which high-risk representative payees are misusing payments made pursuant to section 205(j) or 1631(a)(2) of the Social Security Act [subsec. (j) of this section and section 1383(a)(2) of this title].

"(C) **High-risk representative payee.**—For purposes of this paragraph, the term 'high-risk representative payee' means a representative payee under section 205(j) or 1631(a)(2) of the Social Security Act (42 U.S.C. 405(j) and 1383(a)(2), respectively) [subsec. (j) of this section and section 1383(a)(2) of this title] (other than a Federal or State institution) who—

"(i) regularly provides concurrent services as a representative payee under such section 205(j) [subsec. (j) of this section], such section 1631(a)(2) [section 1383(a)(2) of this title], or both such sections, for 5 or more individuals who are unrelated to such representative payee,

"(ii) is neither related to an individual on whose behalf the payee is being paid benefits nor living in the same household with such individual,

"(iii) is a creditor of such individual, or

"(iv) is in such other category of payees as the Secretary may determine appropriate.

"(D) **Report.**—The Secretary shall report to the Committee on Ways and Means of the House of Representatives and the Committee on Finance of the Senate the results of the study, together with any recommendations, not later than July 1, 1992. Such report shall include an evaluation of the feasibility and desirability of legislation implementing stricter accounting and review procedures for high-risk representative payees in all servicing offices of the Social Security Administration (together with proposed legislative language)."

Termination of Trust Territory of the Pacific Islands

For termination of Trust Territory of the Pacific Islands, see note set out preceding 48 U.S.C.A. § 1681.

§ 405a. Regulations pertaining to frequency or due dates of payments and reports under voluntary agreements covering State and local employees; effective date

Notwithstanding any other provision of law, no regulation and no modification of any regulation, promulgated by the Secretary of Health and Human Services, after January 2, 1976, shall become effective prior to the end of the eighteen-month period which begins with the first day of the first calendar month which begins after the date on which such regulation or modification of a regulation is published in the Federal Register, if and insofar as such regulation or modification of a regulation pertains, directly or indirectly, to the frequency or due dates for payments and reports required under section 418(e) of this title.

(Pub.L. 94–202, § 7, Jan. 2, 1976, 89 Stat. 1137; Pub.L. 96–88, Title V, § 509(b), Oct. 17, 1979, 93 Stat. 695.)

HISTORICAL AND STATUTORY NOTES

References in Text

Subsec. (e) of section 418 of this title, referred to in text, which related to payments and reports by States, was repealed, and subsec. (f) of section 418 of this title was redesignated as subsec. (e), by Pub.L. 99–509, Title IX, § 9002(c)(1), Oct. 21, 1986, 100 Stat.1971.

Codifications

Section was not enacted as part of the Social Security Act which comprises this chapter.

Change of Name

"Secretary of Health and Human Services" was substituted for "Secretary of Health, Education, and Welfare" in text pursuant to section 509(b) of Pub.L. 96–88 which is classified to section 3508(b) of Title 20, Education.

Time for Making Social Security Contributions With Respect to Covered State and Local Employees

Pub.L. 96–265, Title V, § 503(c), June 9, 1980, 94 Stat. 471, provided that: "The provisions of section 7 of Public Law 94–202 [this section] shall not be applicable to any regulation which becomes effective on or after July 1, 1980, and which is designed to carry out the purposes of subsection (a) of this section [amending section 418 of this title]."

§ 405b. Reducing identity fraud

(a) Purpose

The purpose of this section is to reduce the prevalence of synthetic identity fraud, which disproportionally affects vulnerable populations, such as minors and recent immigrants, by facilitating the validation by permitted entities of fraud protection data, pursuant to electronically received consumer consent, through use of a database maintained by the Commissioner.

(b) Definitions

In this section:

(1) Commissioner

The term "Commissioner" means the Commissioner of the Social Security Administration.

(2) Financial institution

The term "financial institution" has the meaning given the term in section 509 of the Gramm-Leach-Bliley Act (15 U.S.C. 6809).

(3) Fraud protection data

The term "fraud protection data" means a combination of the following information with respect to an individual:

(A) The name of the individual (including the first name and any family forename or surname of the individual).

(B) The social security number of the individual.

(C) The date of birth (including the month, day, and year) of the individual.

(4) Permitted entity

The term "permitted entity" means a financial institution or a service provider, subsidiary, affiliate, agent, subcontractor, or assignee of a financial institution.

(c) Efficiency

(1) Reliance on existing methods

The Commissioner shall evaluate the feasibility of making modifications to any database that is in existence as of May 24, 2018, or a similar resource such that the database or resource—

(A) is reasonably designed to effectuate the purpose of this section; and

(B) meets the requirements of subsection (d).

(2) Execution

The Commissioner shall make the modifications necessary to any database that is in existence as of May 24, 2018, or similar resource, or develop a database or similar resource, to effectuate the requirements described in paragraph (1).

(d) Protection of vulnerable consumers

The database or similar resource described in subsection (c) shall—

(1) compare fraud protection data provided in an inquiry by a permitted entity against such information maintained by the Commissioner in order to confirm (or not confirm) the validity of the information provided;

(2) be scalable and accommodate reasonably anticipated volumes of verification requests from permitted entities with commercially reasonable uptime and availability; and

(3) allow permitted entities to submit—

(A) 1 or more individual requests electronically for real-time machine-to-machine (or similar functionality) accurate responses; and

(B) multiple requests electronically, such as those provided in a batch format, for accurate electronic responses within a reasonable period of time from submission, not to exceed 24 hours.

(e) Certification required

Before providing confirmation of fraud protection data to a permitted entity, the Commissioner shall ensure that the Commissioner has a certification from the permitted entity that is dated not more than 2 years before the date on which that confirmation is provided that includes the following declarations:

(1) The entity is a permitted entity.

(2) The entity is in compliance with this section.

(3) The entity is, and will remain, in compliance with its privacy and data security requirements, as described in title V of the Gramm-Leach-Bliley Act (15 U.S.C. 6801 et seq.), with respect to information the entity receives from the Commissioner pursuant to this section.

(4) The entity will retain sufficient records to demonstrate its compliance with its certification and this section for a period of not less than 2 years.

(f) Consumer consent

(1) In general

Notwithstanding any other provision of law or regulation, a permitted entity may submit a request to the database or similar resource described in subsection (c) only—

(A) pursuant to the written, including electronic, consent received by a permitted entity from the individual who is the subject of the request; and

(B) in connection with a credit transaction or any circumstance described in section 1681b of Title 15.

(2) Electronic consent requirements

For a permitted entity to use the consent of an individual received electronically pursuant to paragraph (1)(A), the permitted entity must obtain the individual's electronic signature, as defined in section 7006 of Title 15.

(3) Effectuating electronic consent

No provision of law or requirement, including section 552a of Title 5, shall prevent the use of electronic consent for purposes of this subsection or for use in any other consent based verification under the discretion of the Commissioner.

(g) Compliance and enforcement

(1) Audits and monitoring

The Commissioner may—

(A) conduct audits and monitoring to—

(i) ensure proper use by permitted entities of the database or similar resource described in subsection (c); and

(ii) deter fraud and misuse by permitted entities with respect to the database or similar resource described in subsection (c); and

(B) terminate services for any permitted entity that prevents or refuses to allow the Commissioner to carry out the activities described in subparagraph (A).

(2) Enforcement

(A) In general

Notwithstanding any other provision of law, including the matter preceding paragraph (1) of section 505(a) of the Gramm-Leach-Bliley Act (15 U.S.C. 6805(a)), any violation of this section and any certification made under this section shall be enforced in accordance with paragraphs (1) through (7) of such section 505(a) by the agencies described in those paragraphs.

(B) Relevant information

Upon discovery by the Commissioner, pursuant to an audit described in paragraph (1), of any violation of this section or any certification made under this section, the Commissioner shall forward any relevant information pertaining to that violation to the appropriate agency described in subparagraph (A) for evaluation by the agency for purposes of enforcing this section.

(h) Recovery of costs

(1) In general

(A) In general

Amounts obligated to carry out this section shall be fully recovered from the users of the database or verification system by way of advances, reimbursements, user fees, or other recoveries as determined by the Commissioner. The funds recovered under this paragraph shall be deposited as an offsetting collection to the account providing appropriations for the Social Security Administration, to be used for the administration of this section without fiscal year limitation.

(B) Prices fixed by Commissioner

The Commissioner shall establish the amount to be paid by the users under this paragraph, including the costs of any services or work performed, such as any appropriate upgrades, maintenance, and associated direct and indirect administrative costs, in support of carrying out the purposes described in this section, by reimbursement or in advance as determined by the Commissioner. The amount of such prices shall be periodically adjusted by the Commissioner to ensure that amounts collected are sufficient to fully offset the cost of the administration of this section.

(2) Initial development

The Commissioner shall not begin development of a verification system to carry out this section until the Commissioner determines that amounts equal to at least 50 percent of program start-up costs have been collected under paragraph (1).

(3) Existing resources

The Commissioner may use funds designated for information technology modernization to carry out this section.

(4) Annual report

The Commissioner shall annually submit to the Committee on Ways and Means of the House of Representatives and the Committee on Finance of the Senate a report on the amount of indirect costs to the Social Security Administration arising as a result of the implementation of this section.

(Pub.L. 115–174, Title II, § 215, May 24, 2018, 132 Stat. 1323.)

HISTORICAL AND STATUTORY NOTES

References in Text

The Gramm-Leach-Bliley Act, referred to in text, is Pub.L. 106–102, Nov. 12, 1999, 113 Stat. 1338, also known as the Financial Services Modernization Act of 1999, which principally enacted chapters 93, 94 and 95 of Title 15, 15 U.S.C.A. § 6701 et seq., 15 U.S.C.A. § 6801 et seq., and 15 U.S.C.A. § 6901 et seq., respectively, and amended chapters 16 and 17 of Title 12, 12 U.S.C.A. § 1811 et seq., and 12 U.S.C.A. § 1841 et seq. For complete classification, see Tables.

Title V of the Act is classified to chapter 94 of Title 15, 15 U.S.C.A. § 6801 et seq.

Codifications

This section was enacted as part of the Economic Growth, Regulatory Relief, and Consumer Protection Act, and not as part of the Social Security Act, which otherwise comprises this chapter.

§ 406. Representation of claimants before Commissioner

(a) Recognition of representatives; fees for representation before Commissioner

(1) The Commissioner of Social Security may prescribe rules and regulations governing the recognition of agents or other persons, other than attorneys as hereinafter provided, representing claimants before the Commissioner of Social Security, and may require of such agents or other persons, before being recognized as representatives of claimants that they shall show that they are of good character and in good repute, possessed of the necessary qualifications to enable them to render such claimants valuable service, and otherwise competent to advise and assist such claimants in the presentation of their cases. An attorney in good standing who is admitted to practice before the highest court of the State, Territory, District, or insular possession of his residence or before the Supreme Court of the United States or the inferior Federal courts, shall be entitled to represent claimants before the Commissioner of Social Security. Notwithstanding the preceding sentences, the Commissioner, after due notice and opportunity for hearing, (A) may refuse to recognize as a representative, and may disqualify a representative already recognized, any attorney who has been disbarred or suspended from any court or bar to which he or she was previously admitted to practice or who has been disqualified from participating in or appearing before any Federal program or agency, and (B) may refuse to recognize, and may disqualify, as a non-attorney representative any attorney who has been disbarred or suspended from any court or bar to which he or she was previously admitted to practice. A representative who has been disqualified or suspended pursuant to this section from appearing before the Social Security Administration as a result of collecting or receiving a fee in excess of the amount authorized shall be barred from appearing before the Social Security Administration as a representative until full restitution is made to the claimant and, thereafter, may be considered for reinstatement only under such rules as the Commissioner may prescribe. The Commissioner of Social Security may, after due notice and opportunity for hearing, suspend or prohibit from further practice before the Commissioner any such person, agent, or attorney who refuses to comply with the Commissioner's rules and regulations or who violates any provision of this section for which a penalty is prescribed. The Commissioner of Social Security may, by rule and regulation, prescribe the maximum fees which may be charged for services performed in connection with any claim before the Commissioner of Social Security under this subchapter, and any agreement in violation of such rules and regulations shall be void. Except as provided in paragraph (2)(A), whenever the Commissioner of Social Security, in any claim before the Commissioner for benefits under this subchapter, makes a determination favorable to the claimant, the Commissioner shall, if the claimant was represented by an attorney in connection with such claim, fix (in accordance with the regulations prescribed pursuant to the preceding sentence) a reasonable fee to compensate such attorney for the services performed by him in connection with such claim.

(2)(A) In the case of a claim of entitlement to past-due benefits under this subchapter, if—

(i) an agreement between the claimant and another person regarding any fee to be recovered by such person to compensate such person for services with respect to the claim is presented in writing to the Commissioner of Social Security prior to the time of the Commissioner's determination regarding the claim,

(ii) the fee specified in the agreement does not exceed the lesser of—

(I) 25 percent of the total amount of such past-due benefits (as determined before any applicable reduction under section 1320a–6(a) of this title), or

(II) $4,000, and

(iii) the determination is favorable to the claimant,

then the Commissioner of Social Security shall approve that agreement at the time of the favorable determination, and (subject to paragraph (3)) the fee specified in the agreement shall be the maximum fee. The Commissioner of Social Security may from time to time increase the dollar amount under clause (ii)(II) to the extent that the rate of increase in such amount, as determined over the period since January 1, 1991, does not at any time exceed the rate of increase in primary insurance amounts under section 415(i) of this title since such date. The Commissioner of Social Security shall publish any such increased amount in the Federal Register.

(B) For purposes of this subsection, the term "past-due benefits" excludes any benefits with respect to which payment has been continued pursuant to subsection (g) or (h) of section 423 of this title.

(C) In any case involving—

(i) an agreement described in subparagraph (A) with any person relating to both a claim of entitlement to past-due benefits under this subchapter and a claim of entitlement to past-due benefits under subchapter XVI, and

(ii) a favorable determination made by the Commissioner of Social Security with respect to both such claims,

the Commissioner of Social Security may approve such agreement only if the total fee or fees specified in such agreement does not exceed, in the aggregate, the dollar amount in effect under subparagraph (A)(ii)(II).

(D) In the case of a claim with respect to which the Commissioner of Social Security has approved an agreement pursuant to subparagraph (A), the Commissioner of Social Security shall provide the claimant and the person representing the claimant a written notice of—

(i) the dollar amount of the past-due benefits (as determined before any applicable reduction under section 1320a–6(a) of this title) and the dollar amount of the past-due benefits payable to the claimant,

(ii) the dollar amount of the maximum fee which may be charged or recovered as determined under this paragraph, and

(iii) a description of the procedures for review under paragraph (3).

(3)(A) The Commissioner of Social Security shall provide by regulation for review of the amount which would otherwise be the maximum fee as determined under paragraph (2) if, within 15 days after receipt of the notice provided pursuant to paragraph (2)(D)—

(i) the claimant, or the administrative law judge or other adjudicator who made the favorable determination, submits a written request to the Commissioner of Social Security to reduce the maximum fee, or

(ii) the person representing the claimant submits a written request to the Commissioner of Social Security to increase the maximum fee.

Any such review shall be conducted after providing the claimant, the person representing the claimant, and the adjudicator with reasonable notice of such request and an opportunity to submit written information in favor of or in opposition to such request. The adjudicator may request the Commissioner of Social Security to reduce the maximum fee only on the basis of evidence of the failure of the person representing the claimant to represent adequately the claimant's interest or on the basis of evidence that the fee is clearly excessive for services rendered.

(B)(i) In the case of a request for review under subparagraph (A) by the claimant or by the person representing the claimant, such review shall be conducted by the administrative law judge who made the favorable determination or, if the Commissioner of Social Security determines that such administrative law judge is unavailable or if the determination was not made by an administrative law judge, such review shall be conducted by another person designated by the Commissioner of Social Security for such purpose.

(ii) In the case of a request by the adjudicator for review under subparagraph (A), the review shall be conducted by the Commissioner of Social Security or by an administrative law judge or other person (other than such adjudicator) who is designated by the Commissioner of Social Security.

(C) Upon completion of the review, the administrative law judge or other person conducting the review shall affirm or modify the amount which would otherwise be the maximum fee. Any such amount so affirmed or modified shall be considered the amount of the maximum fee which may be recovered under paragraph (2). The decision of the administrative law judge or other person conducting the review shall not be subject to further review.

(4) Subject to subsection (d), if the claimant is determined to be entitled to past-due benefits under this subchapter and the person representing the claimant is an attorney, the Commissioner of Social Security shall, notwithstanding section 405(i) of this title, certify for payment out of such past-due benefits (as determined before any applicable reduction under section 1320a–6(a) of this title) to such attorney an amount equal to so much of the maximum fee as does not exceed 25 percent of such past-due benefits (as deter-

mined before any applicable reduction under section 1320a–6(a) of this title).

(5) Any person who shall, with intent to defraud, in any manner willfully and knowingly deceive, mislead, or threaten any claimant or prospective claimant or beneficiary under this subchapter by word, circular, letter or advertisement, or who shall knowingly charge or collect directly or indirectly any fee in excess of the maximum fee, or make any agreement directly or indirectly to charge or collect any fee in excess of the maximum fee, prescribed by the Commissioner of Social Security shall be deemed guilty of a misdemeanor and, upon conviction thereof, shall for each offense be punished by a fine not exceeding $500 or by imprisonment not exceeding one year, or both. The Commissioner of Social Security shall maintain in the electronic information retrieval system used by the Social Security Administration a current record, with respect to any claimant before the Commissioner of Social Security, of the identity of any person representing such claimant in accordance with this subsection.

(b) Fees for representation before court

(1)(A) Whenever a court renders a judgment favorable to a claimant under this subchapter who was represented before the court by an attorney, the court may determine and allow as part of its judgment a reasonable fee for such representation, not in excess of 25 percent of the total of the past-due benefits to which the claimant is entitled by reason of such judgment, and the Commissioner of Social Security may, notwithstanding the provisions of section 405(i) of this title, but subject to subsection (d) of this section, certify the amount of such fee for payment to such attorney out of, and not in addition to, the amount of such past-due benefits. In case of any such judgment, no other fee may be payable or certified for payment for such representation except as provided in this paragraph.

(B) For purposes of this paragraph—

(i) the term "past-due benefits" excludes any benefits with respect to which payment has been continued pursuant to subsection (g) or (h) of section 423 of this title, and

(ii) amounts of past-due benefits shall be determined before any applicable reduction under section 1320a–6(a) of this title.

(2) Any attorney who charges, demands, receives, or collects for services rendered in connection with proceedings before a court to which paragraph (1) of this subsection is applicable any amount in excess of that allowed by the court thereunder shall be guilty of a misdemeanor and upon conviction thereof shall be subject to a fine of not more than $500, or imprisonment for not more than one year, or both.

(c) Notification of options for obtaining attorneys

The Commissioner of Social Security shall notify each claimant in writing, together with the notice to such claimant of an adverse determination, of the options for obtaining attorneys to represent individuals in presenting their cases before the Commissioner of Social Security. Such notification shall also advise the claimant of the availability to qualifying claimants of legal services organizations which provide legal services free of charge.

(d) Assessment on attorneys

(1) In general

Whenever a fee for services is required to be certified for payment to an attorney from a claimant's past-due benefits pursuant to subsection (a)(4) or (b)(1), the Commissioner shall impose on the attorney an assessment calculated in accordance with paragraph (2).

(2) Amount

(A) The amount of an assessment under paragraph (1) shall be equal to the product obtained by multiplying the amount of the representative's fee that would be required to be so certified by subsection (a)(4) or (b)(1) before the application of this subsection, by the percentage specified in subparagraph (B), except that the maximum amount of the assessment may not exceed the greater of $75 or the adjusted amount as provided pursuant to the following two sentences. In the case of any calendar year beginning after the amendments made by section 301 of the Social Security Protection Act of 2003 take effect, the dollar amount specified in the preceding sentence (including a previously adjusted amount) shall be adjusted annually under the procedures used to adjust benefit amounts under section 415(i)(2)(A)(ii) of this title, except such adjustment shall be based on the higher of $75 or the previously adjusted amount that would have been in effect for December of the preceding year, but for the rounding of such amount pursuant to the following sentence. Any amount so adjusted that is not a multiple of $1 shall be rounded to the next lowest multiple of $1, but in no case less than $75.

(B) The percentage specified in this subparagraph is—

(i) for calendar years before 2001, 6.3 percent, and

(ii) for calendar years after 2000, such percentage rate as the Commissioner determines is necessary in order to achieve full recovery of the costs of determining and certifying fees to attorneys from the past-due benefits of claimants, but not in excess of 6.3 percent.

(3) Collection

The Commissioner may collect the assessment imposed on an attorney under paragraph (1) by offset from the amount of the fee otherwise required by subsection (a)(4) or (b)(1) to be certified for payment to the attorney from a claimant's past-due benefits.

(4) Prohibition on claimant reimbursement

An attorney subject to an assessment under paragraph (1) may not, directly or indirectly, request or otherwise obtain reimbursement for such assessment from the claimant whose claim gave rise to the assessment.

(5) Disposition of assessments

Assessments on attorneys collected under this subsection shall be credited to the Federal Old-Age and Survivors Insurance Trust Fund and the Federal Disability Insurance Trust Fund, as appropriate.

(6) Authorization of appropriations

The assessments authorized under this section shall be collected and available for obligation only to the extent and in the amount provided in advance in appropriations Acts. Amounts so appropriated are authorized to remain available until expended, for administrative expenses in carrying out this subchapter and related laws.

(e) Extension of fee withholding and assessment procedures to qualified non-attorney representatives

(1) The Commissioner shall provide for the extension of the fee withholding procedures and assessment procedures that apply under the preceding provisions of this section to agents and other persons, other than attorneys, who represent claimants under this subchapter before the Commissioner.

(2) Fee-withholding procedures may be extended under paragraph (1) to any nonattorney[1] representative only if such representative meets at least the following prerequisites:

(A) The representative has been awarded a bachelor's degree from an accredited institution of higher education, or has been determined by the Commissioner to have equivalent qualifications derived from training and work experience.

(B) The representative has passed an examination, written and administered by the Commissioner, which tests knowledge of the relevant provisions of this chapter and the most recent developments in agency and court decisions affecting this subchapter and subchapter XVI.

(C) The representative has secured professional liability insurance, or equivalent insurance, which the Commissioner has determined to be adequate to protect claimants in the event of malpractice by the representative.

(D) The representative has undergone a criminal background check to ensure the representative's fitness to practice before the Commissioner.

(E) The representative demonstrates ongoing completion of qualified courses of continuing education, including education regarding ethics and professional conduct, which are designed to enhance professional knowledge in matters related to entitlement to, or eligibility for, benefits based on disability under this subchapter and subchapter XVI. Such continuing education, and the instructors providing such education, shall meet such standards as the Commissioner may prescribe.

(3)(A) The Commissioner may assess representatives reasonable fees to cover the cost to the Social Security Administration of administering the prerequisites described in paragraph (2).

(B) Fees collected under subparagraph (A) shall be credited to the Federal Old-Age and Survivors Insurance Trust Fund and the Federal Disability Insurance Trust Fund, or deposited as miscellaneous receipts in the general fund of the Treasury, based on such allocations as the Commissioner determines appropriate.

(C) The fees authorized under this paragraph shall be collected and available for obligation only to the extent and in the amount provided in advance in appropriations Acts. Amounts so appropriated are authorized to remain available until expended for administering the prerequisites described in paragraph (2).

(Aug. 14, 1935, c. 531, Title II, § 206, 49 Stat. 624; Aug. 10, 1939, c. 666, Title II, § 201, 53 Stat. 1372; Aug. 28, 1950, c. 809, Title I, § 109(b)(1), 64 Stat. 523; Pub.L. 85–840, Title III, § 309, Aug. 28, 1958, 72 Stat. 1034; Pub.L. 89–97, Title III, § 332, July 30, 1965, 79 Stat. 403; Pub.L. 90–248, Title I, § 173, Jan. 2, 1968, 81 Stat. 877; Pub.L. 98–369, Div. B, Title VI, § 2663(*l*)(1), July 18, 1984, 98 Stat. 1171; Pub.L. 101–239, Title X, § 10307(a)(1), (b)(1), Dec. 19, 1989, 103 Stat. 2484, 2485; Pub.L. 101–508, Title V, § 5106(a)(1), Nov. 5, 1990, 104 Stat. 1388–266; Pub.L. 103–296, Title I, § 107(a)(4), Title III, § 321(f)(3)(B)(i), (4), Aug. 15, 1994, 108 Stat. 1478, 1541, 1542; Pub.L. 106–170, Title IV, § 406(a), (b), Dec. 17, 1999, 113 Stat. 1911, 1912; Pub.L. 108–203, Title II, § 205, Title III, § 301(a), Mar. 2, 2004, 118 Stat. 512, 519; Pub.L. 111–142, § 3(a), Feb. 27, 2010, 124 Stat. 38.)

[1] So in original. Probably should be "non-attorney".

HISTORICAL AND STATUTORY NOTES

References in Text

This subchapter, referred to in text, originally read "this title", meaning Title II of the Social Security Act, Act Aug. 14, 1935, c. 531, 49 Stat. 622, as amended, which is classified to this subchapter, 42 U.S.C.A. § 401 et seq.

This chapter, referred to in text, originally read "this Act" meaning the Social Security Act, Act Aug. 14, 1935, c. 531, 49 Stat. 620, as amended, which is classified to this chapter, 42 U.S.C.A. § 301 et seq. For complete classification, see 42 U.S.C.A. § 1305 and Tables.

Section 301 of the Social Security Protection Act of 2003, referred to in subsec. (d)(2)(A), probably means Section 301 of the Social Security Protection Act of 2004, which is Pub.L. 108–203, Title III, § 301, Mar. 2, 2004, 118 Stat. 519, which amended this section and enacted provisions set out as an Effective and Applicability Provisions note under this section.

Subchapter XVI, referred to in subsec. (e)(2)(B), (E), originally read "title XVI", meaning Title XVI of the Social Security Act, Act, Aug. 14, 1935, c. 531, 49 Stat. 622, as amended, which is principally classified to subchapter XVI of this chapter, 42 U.S.C.A. § 1381 et seq.

Codifications

Pub.L. 101–239, Title X, § 10307(a)(1), (3), Dec. 19, 1989, 103 Stat. 2485, effective June 1, 1991, added at the end of subsec. (a) the following sentence: "The Secretary shall maintain in the electronic information retrieval system used by the Social Security Administration a current record, with respect to any claimant before the Secretary, of the identity of any person representing such claimant in accordance with this subsection.". Such amendment could not be executed to the present text in view of complete revision of the subsection.

Effective and Applicability Provisions

2010 Acts. Pub.L. 111–142, § 3(c), Feb. 27, 2010, 124 Stat. 39, provided that: "The Commissioner of Social Security shall provide for full implementation of the provisions of section 206(e) of the Social Security Act [42 U.S.C.A. § 406(e)] (as added by subsection (a)) and the amendments made by subsection (b) [amending 42 U.S.C.A. § 1383, and provisions set out in a note under this section] not later than March 1, 2010."

2004 Acts. Pub.L. 108–203, Title III, § 301(b), Mar. 2, 2004, 118 Stat. 519, provided that: "The amendments made by this section [amending subsec. (d)(2)(A) of this section] shall apply with respect to fees for representation of claimants which are first required to be certified or paid under section 206 of the Social Security Act on or after the first day of the first month that begins after 180 days after the date of the enactment of this Act [Mar. 2, 2004]."

1999 Acts. Pub.L. 106–170, Title IV, § 406(d), Dec. 17, 1999, 113 Stat. 1913, provided that: "The amendments made by this section [amending this section and enacting provisions set out as notes under this section] shall apply in the case of any attorney with respect to whom a fee for services is required to be certified for payment from a claimant's past-due benefits pursuant to subsection (a)(4) or (b)(1) of section 206 of the Social Security Act [subsec. (a)(4) or (b)(1) of this section] after the later of—

"(1) December 31, 1999, or

"(2) the last day of the first month beginning after the month in which this Act is enacted [Dec. 1999]."

1994 Acts. Amendment by section 107(a)(4) of Pub.L. 103–296 effective Mar. 31, 1995, see section 110 of Pub.L. 103–296, set out as a note under section 401 of this title.

Amendments by section 321(f)(3)(B)(i), (4) of Pub.L. 103–296 to subsecs. (b)(1) and (a), respectively, of this section effective as if included in the provisions of Pub.L. 101–508 to which they relate, except that enactment of subsec. (b)(1)(B) of this section applicable with respect to favorable judgments made after 180 days after Aug. 15, 1994, see section 321(f)(5) of Pub.L. 103–296, set out as a note under section 405 of this title.

1990 Acts. Amendment by section 5106 of Pub.L. 101–508 applicable with respect to determinations made on or after July 1, 1991, and to reimbursements for travel expenses incurred on or after April 1, 1991, see section 5106(d) of Pub.L. 101–508, set out as a note under section 401 of this title.

1989 Acts. Section 10307(a)(3) of Pub.L. 101–239 provided that: "The amendments made by this subsection [amending this section and section 1383 of this title] shall take effect June 1, 1991."

Section 10307(b)(3) of Pub.L. 101–239 provided that: "The amendments made by this subsection [amending this section and section 1383 of this title] shall apply with respect to adverse determinations made on or after January 1, 1991."

1984 Acts. Amendment by section 2663(*l*)(1) of Pub.L. 98–369 effective July 18, 1984, but not to be construed as changing or affecting any right, liability, status, or interpretation which existed (under the provisions of law involved) before that date, see section 2664(b) of Pub.L. 98–369, set out as a note under section 401 of this title.

1939 Acts. Amendment by Act Aug. 10, 1939 was made effective Jan. 1, 1940 by section 201 of Act Aug. 10, 1939.

Transfer of Functions

All functions of the Federal Security Administrator were transferred to the Secretary of Health, Education and Welfare and all agencies of the Federal Security Agency were transferred to the Department of Health, Education, and Welfare by section 5 of 1953 Reorg. Plan No. 1, set out under section 202 of this title. The Federal Security Agency and the office of Administrator were abolished by section 8 of said 1953 Reorg. Plan No. 1. The Secretary and Department of Health, Education, and Welfare were redesignated the Secretary and Department of Health and Human Services by section 509(b) of Pub.L. 96–88 which is classified to section 3508(b) of Title 20, Education.

Nationwide Demonstration Project Providing for Extension of Fee Withholding Procedures to Non-Attorney Representatives

Pub.L. 108–203, Title III, § 303, Mar. 2, 2004, 118 Stat. 521, as amended Pub.L. 111–142, § 3(b)(2), Feb. 27, 2010, 124 Stat. 39, provided that:

"(a) In general.—The Commissioner of Social Security (hereafter in this section referred to as the 'Commissioner") shall develop and carry out a nationwide demonstration project under this section with respect to agents and other persons, other than attorneys, who represent claimants under titles II and XVI of the Social Security Act [this subchapter and subchapter XVI of this chapter, 42 U.S.C.A. § 1381 et seq.] before the Commissioner. The demonstration project shall be designed to determine the potential results of extending to such representatives the fee withholding procedures and assessment procedures that apply under sections 206 and section 1631(d)(2) of such Act [this section and 42 U.S.C.A. § 1383(d)(2)] to attorneys seeking direct payment out of past due benefits under such titles and shall include an analysis of the effect of such extension on claimants and program administration.

"(b) Standards for inclusion in demonstration project.—Fee- withholding procedures may be extended under the demonstration project carried out pursuant to subsection (a) [of this note] to any non-attorney representative only if such representative meets at least the following prerequisites:

"(1) The representative has been awarded a bachelor's degree from an accredited institution of higher education, or has been determined by the Commissioner to have equivalent qualifications derived from training and work experience.

"(2) The representative has passed an examination, written and administered by the Commissioner, which tests knowledge of the relevant provisions of the Social Security Act and the most recent developments in agency and court decisions affecting titles II and XVI of such Act [this subchapter and subchapter XVI of this chapter, 42 U.S.C.A. § 1381 et seq.].

"(3) The representative has secured professional liability insurance, or equivalent insurance, which the Commissioner has determined to be adequate to protect claimants in the event of malpractice by the representative.

"(4) The representative has undergone a criminal background check to ensure the representative's fitness to practice before the Commissioner.

"(5) The representative demonstrates ongoing completion of qualified courses of continuing education, including education regarding ethics and professional conduct, which are designed to enhance professional knowledge in matters related to entitlement to, or eligibility for, benefits based on disability under titles II and XVI of such Act [this subchapter and subchapter XVI of this chapter, 42 U.S.C.A. § 1381 et seq.]. Such continuing education, and the instructors providing such education, shall meet such standards as the Commissioner may prescribe.

"(c) Assessment of fees.—

"(1) In general.—The Commissioner may assess representatives reasonable fees to cover the cost to the Social Security Administration of administering the prerequisites described in subsection (b) [of this note].

"(2) Disposition of fees.—Fees collected under paragraph (1) shall be credited to the Federal Old-Age and Survivors Insurance Trust Fund and the Federal Disability Insurance Trust Fund, or deposited as miscellaneous receipts in the general fund of the Treasury, based on such allocations as the Commissioner of Social Security determines appropriate.

"(3) Authorization of appropriations.—The fees authorized under this subparagraph shall be collected and available for obligation only to the extent and in the amount provided in advance in appropriations Acts. Amounts so appropriated are authorized to remain available until expended for administering the prerequisites described in subsection (b) [of this note].

"(d) Notice to Congress and applicability of fee withholding procedures.—Not later than 1 year after the date of enactment of this Act [Mar. 2, 2004], the Commissioner shall complete such actions as are necessary to fully implement the requirements for full operation of the demonstration project and shall submit to each House of Congress a written notice of the completion of such actions [Such notices submitted Feb. 28, 2005]. The applicability under this section [this note] to non-attorney representatives of the fee withholding procedures and assessment procedures under sections 206 and 1631(d)(2) of the Social Security Act [this section and 42 U.S.C.A. § 1381(d)(2)] shall be effective with respect to fees for representation of claimants in the case of claims for benefits with respect to which the agreement for representation is entered into by such non-attorney representatives during the period beginning with the date of the submission of such notice by the Commissioner to Congress and ending with the termination date of the demonstration project.

"(e) Reports by the Commissioner; termination.—

"(1) Interim reports.—On or before the date which is 1 year after the date of enactment of this Act [Mar. 2, 2004], and annually thereafter, the Commissioner shall transmit to the Committee on Ways and Means of the House of Representatives and to the Committee on Finance of the Senate an annual interim report on the progress of the demonstration project carried out under this section [this note], together with any related data and materials that the Commissioner may consider appropriate.

"(2) Termination date.—The termination date of the demonstration project under this section [this note] is the date which is 5 years after the date of the submission of the notice by the Commissioner to each House of Congress pursuant to subsection (d) [of this note]. The authority under the preceding provisions of this section shall not apply in the case of claims for benefits with respect to which the agreement for representation is entered into after the termination date."

GAO Study Regarding the Fee Payment Process for Claimant Representatives

Pub.L. 108–203, Title III, § 304, Mar. 2, 2004, 118 Stat. 523, provided that:

"(a) Study.—

"(1) In general.—The Comptroller General of the United States shall study and evaluate the appointment and payment of claimant representatives appearing before the Commissioner of Social Security in connection with benefit claims under titles II and XVI of the Social Security Act [this subchapter and subchapter XVI of this chapter] (42 U.S.C. 401 et seq., 1381 et seq.) in each of the following groups:

"(A) Attorney claimant representatives who elect fee withholding under section 206 or 1631(d)(2) of such Act [this section and 42 U.S.C.A. § 1381(d)(2)].

"(B) Attorney claimant representatives who do not elect such fee withholding.

"(C) Non-attorney claimant representatives who are eligible for, and elect, such fee withholding.

"(D) Non-attorney claimant representatives who are eligible for, but do not elect, such fee withholding.

"(E) Non-attorney claimant representatives who are not eligible for such fee withholding.

"(2) Matters to be studied.—In conducting the study under this subsection, the Comptroller General shall, for each of group of claimant representatives described in paragraph (1)—

"(A) Conduct a survey of the relevant characteristics of such claimant representatives including—

"(i) qualifications and experience;

"(ii) the type of employment of such claimant representatives, such as with an advocacy group, State or local government, or insurance or other company;

"(iii) geographical distribution between urban and rural areas;

"(iv) the nature of claimants' cases, such as whether the cases are for disability insurance benefits only, supplemental security income benefits only, or concurrent benefits;

"(v) the relationship of such claimant representatives to claimants, such as whether the claimant is a friend, family member, or client of the claimant representative; and "(vi) the amount of compensation (if any) paid to the claimant representatives and the method of payment of such compensation;

"(B) assess the quality and effectiveness of the services provided by such claimant representatives, including a comparison of claimant satisfaction or complaints and benefit outcomes, adjusted for differences in claimant representatives' caseload, claimants' diagnostic group, level of decision, and other relevant factors;

"(C) assess the interactions between fee withholding under sections 206 and 1631(d)(2) of such Act [this section and 42 U.S.C.A. § 1381(d)(2)] (including under the amendments made by section 302 of this Act [amending 42 U.S.C.A. § 1383(a)(2)(F)(i)(II), (10)(A) and (d)(2)(A) to (D), and enacting provisions set out as an Effective and Applicability Provisions note under that section] and under the demonstration project conducted under section 303 of this Act [Pub.L. 108–203, Title III, § 303, Mar. 2, 2004, 118 Stat. 521, which is set out in a note under this section]), the windfall offset under section 1127 of such Act [42 U.S.C.A. § 1320a–6], and interim assistance reimbursements under section 1631(g) of such Act [42 U.S.C.A. § 1383(g)];

"(D) assess the potential results of making permanent the fee withholding procedures under sections 206 and 1631(d)(2) of such Act [this section and 42 U.S.C.A. § 1381(d)(2)] under the amendments made by section 302 of this Act [amending 42 U.S.C.A. § 1383(a)(2)(F)(i)(II), (10)(A), and (d)(2)(A) to (D), and enacting provisions set out as an Effective and Applicability Provisions note under that section] and under the demonstration project conducted under section 303 of this Act [Pub.L. 108–203, Title III, § 303, Mar. 2, 2004, 118 Stat. 521, which is set out in a note under this section] with respect to program administration and claimant outcomes, and assess whether the rules and procedures employed by the Commissioner of Social Security to evaluate the qualifications and performance of claimant representatives should be revised prior to making such procedures permanent; and

"(E) make such recommendations for administrative and legislative changes as the Comptroller General of the United States considers necessary or appropriate.

"**(3) Consultation required.**—The Comptroller General of the United States shall consult with beneficiaries under title II of such Act [this subchapter], beneficiaries under title XVI of such Act [subchapter XVI of this chapter, 42 U.S.C.A. § 1381 et seq.], claimant representatives of beneficiaries under such titles, and other interested parties, in conducting the study and evaluation required under paragraph (1).

"**(b) Report.**—Not later than 3 years after the date of the submission by the Commissioner of Social Security to each House of Congress pursuant to section 303(d) of this Act [Pub.L. 108–203, Title III, § 303(d), Mar. 2, 2004, 118 Stat. 522, which requires such submission not later than 1 year after Mar. 2, 2004, and which is set out in a note under 42 U.S.C.A. § 406] of written notice of completion of full implementation of the requirements for operation of the demonstration project under section 303 of this Act [Pub.L. 108–203, Title III, § 303, Mar. 2, 2004, 118 Stat. 521, which is set out as a note under 42 U.S.C.A. § 406], the Comptroller General of the United States shall submit to the Committee on Ways and Means of the House of Representatives and the Committee on Finance of the Senate a report on the results of the study and evaluation conducted pursuant to subsection (a) [of this note]."

GAO Study and Report

Pub.L. 106–170, Title IV, § 406(c), Dec. 17, 1999, 113 Stat. 1912, provided that:

"**(1) Study.**—The Comptroller General of the United States shall conduct a study that—

"(A) examines the costs incurred by the Social Security Administration in administering the provisions of subsection (a)(4) and (b)(1) of section 206 of the Social Security Act (42 U.S.C. 406) and itemizes the components of such costs, including the costs of determining fees to attorneys from the past-due benefits of claimants before the Commissioner of Social Security and of certifying such fees;

"(B) identifies efficiencies that the Social Security Administration could implement to reduce such costs;

"(C) examines the feasibility and advisability of linking the payment of, or the amount of, the assessment under section 206(d) of the Social Security Act (42 U.S.C. 406(d)) to the timeliness of the payment of the fee to the attorney as certified by the Commissioner of Social Security pursuant to subsection (a)(4) or (b)(1) of section 206 of such Act (42 U.S.C. 406);

"(D) determines whether the provisions of subsection (a)(4) and (b)(1) of section 206 of such Act (42 U.S.C. 406) should be applied to claimants under title XVI of such Act [subchapter XVI of this chapter] (42 U.S.C 1381 et seq.);

"(E) determines the feasibility and advisability of stating fees under section 206(d) of such Act (42 U.S.C. 406(d)) in terms of a fixed dollar amount as opposed to a percentage;

"(F) determines whether the dollar limit specified in section 206(a)(2)(A)(ii)(II) of such Act (42 U.S.C. 406(a)(2)(A)(ii)(II)) should be raised; and

"(G) determines whether the assessment on attorneys required under section 206(d) of such Act (42 U.S.C. 406(d)) (as added by subsection (a)(1) of this section) impairs access to legal representation for claimants.

"**(2) Report.**—Not later than 1 year after the date of the enactment of this Act [Dec. 17, 1999], the Comptroller General of the United States shall submit a report to the Committee on Ways and Means of the House of Representatives and the Committee on Finance of the Senate on the study conducted under paragraph (1), together with any recommendations for legislation that the Comptroller General determines to be appropriate as a result of such study."

§ 407. Assignment of benefits

(a) In general

The right of any person to any future payment under this subchapter shall not be transferable or assignable, at law or in equity, and none of the moneys paid or payable or rights existing under this subchapter shall be subject to execution, levy, attachment, garnishment, or other legal process, or to the operation of any bankruptcy or insolvency law.

(b) Amendment of section

No other provision of law, enacted before, on, or after April 20, 1983, may be construed to limit, supersede, or otherwise modify the provisions of this section except to the extent that it does so by express reference to this section.

(c) Withholding of taxes

Nothing in this section shall be construed to prohibit withholding taxes from any benefit under this subchapter, if such withholding is done pursuant to a request made in accordance with section 3402(p)(1) of the Internal Revenue Code of 1986 by the person entitled to such benefit or such person's representative payee.

(Aug. 14, 1935, c. 531, Title II, § 207, 49 Stat. 624; Aug. 10, 1939, c. 666, Title II, § 201, 53 Stat. 1372; Pub.L. 98–21, Title III, § 335(a), Apr. 20, 1983, 97 Stat. 130; Pub.L. 105–277, Div. J, Title IV, § 4005(a), Oct. 21, 1998, 112 Stat. 2681–911.)

HISTORICAL AND STATUTORY NOTES

References in text

The Internal Revenue Code of 1986, referred to in subsec. (c), is classified to 26 U.S.C.A. § 1 et seq.

Codifications

In subsec. (b), "April 20, 1983" was substituted for "the date of the enactment of this section", which was translated as meaning the date of enactment of this subsection, as the probable intent of Congress.

Effective and Applicability Provisions

1983 Acts. Section 335(c) of Pub.L. 98–21 provided that: "The amendments made by subsection (a) [amending this section] shall apply only with respect to benefits payable or rights existing under the Social Security Act [classified principally to this chapter] on or after the date of the enactment of this Act [Apr. 20, 1983]."

1939 Acts. Amendment by Act Aug. 10, 1939 effective Jan. 1, 1940, see section 201 of Act Aug. 10, 1939.

§ 408. Penalties

(a) In general

Whoever—

(1) for the purpose of causing an increase in any payment authorized to be made under this subchapter, or for the purpose of causing any payment to be made where no payment is authorized under this subchapter, shall make or cause to be made any false statement or representation (including any false statement or representation in connection with any matter arising under subchapter E of chapter 1, or subchapter A or E of chapter 9 of the Internal Revenue Code of 1939, or chapter 2 or 21 or subtitle F of the Internal Revenue Code of 1954) as to—

(A) whether wages were paid or received for employment (as said terms are defined in this subchapter and the Internal Revenue Code), or the amount of wages or the period during which paid or the person to whom paid; or

(B) whether net earnings from self-employment (as such term is defined in this subchapter and in the Internal Revenue Code) were derived, or as to the amount of such net earnings or the period during which or the person by whom derived; or

(C) whether a person entitled to benefits under this subchapter had earnings in or for a particular period (as determined under section 403(f) of this title for purposes of deductions from benefits), or as to the amount thereof; or

(2) makes or causes to be made any false statement or representation of a material fact in any application for any payment or for a disability determination under this subchapter; or

(3) at any time makes or causes to be made any false statement or representation of a material fact for use in determining rights to payment under this subchapter; or

(4) having knowledge of the occurrence of any event affecting (1) his initial or continued right to any payment under this subchapter, or (2) the initial or continued right to any payment of any other individual in whose behalf he has applied for or is receiving such payment, conceals or fails to disclose such event with an intent fraudulently to secure payment either in a greater amount than is due or when no payment is authorized; or

(5) having made application to receive payment under this subchapter for the use and benefit of another and having received such a payment, knowingly and willfully converts such a payment, or any part thereof, to a use other than for the use and benefit of such other person; or

(6) willfully, knowingly, and with intent to deceive the Commissioner of Social Security as to his true identity (or the true identity of any other person) furnishes or causes to be furnished false information to the Commissioner of Social Security with respect to any information required by the Commissioner of Social Security in connection with the establishment and maintenance of the records provided for in section 405(c)(2) of this title; or

(7) for the purpose of causing an increase in any payment authorized under this subchapter (or any other program financed in whole or in part from Federal funds), or for the purpose of causing a payment under this subchapter (or any such other program) to be made when no payment is authorized thereunder, or for the purpose of obtaining (for himself or any other person) any payment or any other benefit to which he (or such other person) is not entitled, or for the purpose of obtaining anything of value from any person, or for any other purpose—

(A) willfully, knowingly, and with intent to deceive, uses a social security account number, assigned by the Commissioner of Social Security (in the exercise of the Commissioner's authority under section 405(c)(2) of this title to establish and maintain records) on the basis of false information furnished to the Commissioner of Social Security by him or by any other person; or

(B) with intent to deceive, falsely represents a number to be the social security account number assigned by the Commissioner of Social Security to him or to another person, when in fact such number is not the social security account number assigned by the Commissioner of Social Security to him or to such other person; or

(C) knowingly alters a social security card issued by the Commissioner of Social Security, buys or sells a card that is, or purports to be, a card so issued, counterfeits a social security card, or possesses a social security card or counterfeit social security card with intent to sell or alter it;

(8) discloses, uses, or compels the disclosure of the social security number of any person in violation of the laws of the United States; or

(9) conspires to commit any offense described in any of paragraphs (1) through (4),

shall be guilty of a felony and upon conviction thereof shall be fined under Title 18 or imprisoned for not more than five years, or both, except that in the case of a person who receives a fee or other income for services performed in connection with any determination with respect to benefits under this subchapter (including a claimant representative, translator, or current or former employee of the Social Security Administration), or who is a physician or other health care provider who submits, or causes the submission of, medical or other evidence in connection with any such determination, such person shall be guilty of a felony and upon conviction thereof shall be fined under Title 18, or imprisoned for not more than ten years, or both.

(b) Restitution

(1) Any Federal court, when sentencing a defendant convicted of an offense under subsection (a), may order, in addition to or in lieu of any other penalty authorized by law, that the defendant make restitution to the victims of such offense specified in paragraph (4).

(2) Sections 3612, 3663, and 3664 of Title 18 shall apply with respect to the issuance and enforcement of orders of restitution to victims of such offense under this subsection.

(3) If the court does not order restitution, or orders only partial restitution, under this subsection, the court shall state on the record the reasons therefor.

(4) For purposes of paragraphs (1) and (2), the victims of an offense under subsection (a) are the following:

(A) Any individual who suffers a financial loss as a result of the defendant's violation of subsection (a).

(B) The Commissioner of Social Security, to the extent that the defendant's violation of subsection (a) results in—

(i) the Commissioner of Social Security making a benefit payment that should not have been made; or

(ii) an individual suffering a financial loss due to the defendant's violation of subsection (a) in his or her capacity as the individual's representative payee appointed pursuant to section 405(j) of this title.

(5)(A) Except as provided in subparagraph (B), funds paid to the Commissioner of Social Security as restitution pursuant to a court order shall be deposited in the Federal Old-Age and Survivors Insurance Trust Fund, or the Federal Disability Insurance Trust Fund, as appropriate.

(B) In the case of funds paid to the Commissioner of Social Security pursuant to paragraph (4)(B)(ii), the Commissioner of Social Security shall certify for payment to the individual described in such paragraph an amount equal to the lesser of the amount of the funds so paid or the individual's outstanding financial loss, except that such amount may be reduced by the amount of any overpayments of benefits owed under this subchapter, subchapter VIII, or subchapter XVI by the individual.

(c) Violations by certified payees

Any person or other entity who is convicted of a violation of any of the provisions of this section, if such violation is committed by such person or entity in his role as, or in applying to become, a certified payee under section 405(j) of this title on behalf of another individual (other than such person's spouse), upon his second or any subsequent such conviction shall, in lieu of the penalty set forth in the preceding provisions of this section, be guilty of a felony and shall be fined under Title 18 or imprisoned for not more than five years, or both.

(d) Effect upon certification as payee; definitions

Any individual or entity convicted of a felony under this section or under section 1383a(b) of this title may not be certified as a payee under section 405(j) of this title. For the purpose of subsection (a)(7), the terms "social security number" and "social security account number" mean such numbers as are assigned by the Commissioner of Social Security under section 405(c)(2) of this title whether or not, in actual use, such numbers are called social security numbers.

(e) Application of subsection (a)(6) and (7) to certain aliens

(1) Except as provided in paragraph (2), an alien—

(A) whose status is adjusted to that of lawful temporary resident under section 1160 or 1255a of Title 8 or under section 902 of the Foreign Relations Authorization Act, Fiscal Years 1988 and 1989,

(B) whose status is adjusted to that of permanent resident—

(i) under section 202 of the Immigration Reform and Control Act of 1986, or

(ii) pursuant to section 1259 of Title 8, or

(C) who is granted special immigrant status under section 1101(a)(27)(I) of Title 8,

shall not be subject to prosecution for any alleged conduct described in paragraph (6) or (7) of subsection (a) if such conduct is alleged to have occurred prior to 60 days after November 5, 1990.

(2) Paragraph (1) shall not apply with respect to conduct (described in subsection (a)(7)(C)) consisting of—

(A) selling a card that is, or purports to be, a social security card issued by the Commissioner of Social Security,

(B) possessing a social security card with intent to sell it, or

(C) counterfeiting a social security card with intent to sell it.

(3) Paragraph (1) shall not apply with respect to any criminal conduct involving both the conduct described in subsection (a)(7) to which paragraph (1) applies and any other criminal conduct if such other conduct would be criminal conduct if the conduct described in subsection (a)(7) were not committed.

(Aug. 14, 1935, c. 531, Title II, § 208, 49 Stat. 625; Aug. 10, 1939, c. 666, Title II, § 201, 53 Stat. 1372; Aug. 28, 1950, c. 809, Title I, § 109(c), 64 Stat. 523; Sept. 1, 1954, c. 1206, Title I, § 111(b), 68 Stat. 1085; Pub.L. 85–840, Title III, § 310, Aug. 28, 1958, 72 Stat. 1034; Pub.L. 86–778, Title II, § 211(m), Sept. 13, 1960, 74 Stat. 958; Pub.L. 92–603, Title I, § 130(a), Oct. 30, 1972, 86 Stat. 1359; Pub.L. 94–455, Title XII, § 1211(a), (d), Oct. 4, 1976, 90 Stat. 1711, 1712; Pub.L. 97–123, § 4(a), (b), Dec. 29, 1981, 95 Stat. 1663; Pub.L. 98–369, Div. B, Title VI, § 2663(a)(5), July 18, 1984, 98 Stat. 1162; Pub.L. 98–460, § 16(c)(2), Oct. 9, 1984, 98 Stat. 1811; Pub.L. 100–690, Title VII, § 7088, Nov. 18, 1988, 102 Stat. 4409; Pub.L. 101–508, Title V, §§ 5121, 5130(a)(1), Nov. 5, 1990, 104 Stat. 1388–283, 1388–289; Pub.L. 103–296, Title I, § 107(a)(4), Title III, § 321(a)(12), Aug. 15, 1994, 108 Stat. 1478, 1536; Pub.L. 106–553, § 1(a)(2) [Title VI, § 635(c)(2)(1), (2)], Dec. 21, 2000, 114 Stat. 2762, 2762A–117; Pub.L. 106–554, § 1(a)(4) [Div. A, § 213(a)(6)], Dec. 21, 2000, 114 Stat. 2763, 2763A–180; Pub.L. 108–203, Title II, § 209(a), Mar. 2, 2004, 118 Stat. 513; Pub.L. 114–74, Title VIII, § 813(a)(1), (b)(1), Nov. 2, 2015, 129 Stat. 602, 603.)

HISTORICAL AND STATUTORY NOTES

References in Text

For provision deeming a reference in other laws to a provision of the 1939 Code as a reference to the corresponding provisions of Title 26, see section 7852(b) of Title 26. For tables of comparisons of the 1939 Code to the 1986 Code, see Tables. The Internal Revenue Code of 1986 is classified generally to Title 26.

Subchapter E of chapter 1 and subchapters A and E of chapter 9 of the Internal Revenue Code of 1939, referred to in subsec. (a)(1), were comprised of sections 480 to 482, 1400 to 1432, and 1630 to 1636, respectively, and were repealed (subject to certain exceptions) by section 7851(a)(1)(A), (3) of Title 26, Internal Revenue Code of 1954 (Act Aug. 16, 1954, c. 736, 68A Stat. 3). The I.R.C. 1954 was redesignated I.R.C. 1986 by Pub.L. 99–514, § 2, Oct. 22, 1986, 100 Stat. 2095.

Chapters 2 and 21 and subtitle F of the Internal Revenue Code of 1954, referred to in subsec. (a)(1), were redesignated Chapters 2 and 21 and Subtitle F of the Internal Revenue Code of 1986, and are classified to 26 U.S.C.A. §§ 1401 et seq., 3101 et seq., and 6001 et seq., respectively.

This subchapter, referred to in text, originally read "this title", meaning the Social Security Act, Act Aug. 14, 1935, c. 531, Title II, 49 Stat. 622, as amended, which is classified as this subchapter, 42 U.S.C.A. § 401 et seq.

Subchapter VIII, referred to in subsec. (b)(5)(B), originally read "title VIII", meaning the Social Security Act, Act Aug. 14, 1935, c. 531, Title VIII, as added Dec. 14, 1999, Pub.L. 106–169, Title II, § 251(a), 113 Stat. 1844, as amended, which is classified as subchapter VIII of this chapter, 42 U.S.C.A. § 1001 et seq.

Subchapter XVI, referred to in subsec. (b)(5)(B), originally read "title XVI", meaning the Social Security Act, Act Aug. 14, 1935, c. 531, Title XVI, as added Oct. 30, 1972, Pub.L. 92–603, Title III, § 301, 86 Stat. 1465, as amended, which is classified as subchapter XVI of this chapter, 42 U.S.C.A. § 1381 et seq.

Section 1383a(b) of this title, referred to in subsec. (d), was redesignated section 1383a(c) of this title and amended by Pub.L. 108–203, Title II, § 209(c), Mar. 2, 2004, 118 Stat. 515.

Section 902 of the Foreign Relations Authorization Act, Fiscal Years 1988 and 1989, referred to in subsec. (e)(1)(A), is section 902 of Pub.L. 100–204, Dec. 22, 1987, 101 Stat. 1331, 1400, which is set out as a note under section 1255a of Title 8, Aliens and Nationality. For complete classification of this Act to the Code, see Short Title note set out under 22 U.S.C.A. § 2651 and Tables.

Section 202 of the Immigration Reform and Control Act of 1986, referred to in subsec. (e)(1)(B)(i), means section 202 of Pub.L. 99–603, Nov. 6, 1986, 100 Stat. 3359, 3404, which is set out as a note under section 1255a of Title 8, Aliens and Nationality. For complete classification of this Act to the Code, see Short Title note set out under 8 U.S.C.A. § 1101 and Tables.

Codifications

Amendment by section 5130(a)(1) of Pub.L. 101–508, which directed the substitution of "section 205(c)(2)" for "section 405(c)(2) of this title" required no change in text as section 205(c)(2) was editorially translated as section 405(c)(2) for codification purposes.

Effective and Applicability Provisions

2004 Acts. Pub.L. 108–203, Title II, § 209(d), Mar. 2, 2004, 118 Stat. 516, provided that: "The amendments made by subsections (a), (b), and (c) [amending this section, and 42 U.S.C.A. §§ 1011 and 1383] shall apply with respect to violations occurring on or after the date of enactment of this Act [Mar. 2, 2004]."

2000 Acts. Pub.L. 106–553, § 1(a)(2) [Title VI, § 635(c)(2)(3)], Dec. 21, 2000, 114 Stat. 2762, 2762A–117, which provided that the amendments made by such section 635(c) of Pub.L. 106–553 [amending this section and enacting section 1320b–23 of this title] apply with respect to violations occurring on and after the date that is 2 years after Dec. 21, 2000, was repealed by Pub.L. 106–554, § 1(a)(4) [Div. A,

§ 213(a)(6)], Dec. 21, 2000, 114 Stat. 2763, 2763A–180, which repealed Pub.L. 106–553, § 1(a)(2) [Title VI, § 635].

Pub.L. 106–554, § 1(a)(4) [Div. A, § 213(b)], Dec. 21, 2000, 114 Stat. 2763, 2763A–180, provided that: "The amendments made by this section [which amended certain provisions of Pub.L. 106–553, § 1(a)(2), Dec. 21, 2000, 114 Stat. 2762, 2762A–117, which affected this section and sections 1320b–23 and 10601 of this title, section 2709 of Title 22, and section 524 of Title 28, and provisions set out as notes under this section and sections 1305 and 1320b–23 of this title, and sections 4001 and 4013 of Title 18] shall take effect as if included in H.R. 4942 of the 106th Congress [Pub.L. 106–553, Dec. 21, 2000, 114 Stat. 2762] on the date of its enactment [Dec. 21, 2000]."

1994 Acts. Amendment by section 107(a)(4) of Pub.L. 103–296 effective Mar. 31, 1995, see section 110 of Pub.L. 103–296, set out as a note under section 401 of this title.

1990 Acts. Amendment by section 5130 of Pub.L. 101–508 effective as if included in the enactment of Pub.L. 100–690 [probably meaning the date of the enactment of Pub.L. 100–690] which was approved November 18, 1988, see section 5130(b) of Pub.L. 101–508, set out as a note under section 1402 of Title 26, Internal Revenue Code.

1984 Acts. Amendment by Pub.L. 98–460 effective Oct. 9, 1984, see section 16(d) of Pub. L. 98–460, set out as a note under section 405 of this title.

Amendment by Pub.L. 98–369 effective July 18, 1984, but not to be construed as changing or affecting any right, liability, status or interpretation which existed (under the provisions of law involved) before that date, see section 2664(b) of Pub.L. 98–369, set out as a note under section 401 of this title.

1981 Acts. Section 4(c) of Pub.L. 97–123 provided that: "The amendments made by subsections (a) and (b) [amending this section] shall be effective with respect to violations committed after the date of the enactment of this Act [Dec. 29, 1981]."

1972 Acts. Section 130(b) of Pub.L. 92–603 provided that: "The amendments made by subsection (a) [adding subsecs. (f) and (g) of this section] shall apply with respect to information furnished to the Secretary after the date of the enactment of this Act [Oct. 30, 1972]."

1960 Acts. Amendment by Pub.L. 86–778 effective in the manner provided in section 211(p) and (q) of Pub.L. 86–778, see section 211(s) of Pub.L. 88–778, set out as a note under section 403 of this title.

1939 Acts. Amendment by Act Aug. 10, 1939 effective Jan. 1, 1940, see section 201 of Act Aug. 10, 1939.

§ 409. "Wages" defined

(a) In general

For the purposes of this subchapter, the term "wages" means remuneration paid prior to 1951 which was wages for the purposes of this subchapter under the law applicable to the payment of such remuneration, and remuneration paid after 1950 for employment, including the cash value of all remuneration (including benefits) paid in any medium other than cash; except that, in the case of remuneration paid after 1950, such term shall not include—

(1)(A) That part of remuneration which, after remuneration (other than remuneration referred to in the succeeding subsections of this section) equal to $3,600 with respect to employment has been paid to an individual during any calendar year prior to 1955, is paid to such individual during such calendar year;

(B) That part of remuneration which, after remuneration (other than remuneration referred to in the succeeding subsections of this section) equal to $4,200 with respect to employment has been paid to an individual during any calendar year after 1954 and prior to 1959, is paid to such individual during such calendar year;

(C) That part of remuneration which, after remuneration (other than remuneration referred to in the succeeding subsections of this section) equal to $4,800 with respect to employment has been paid to an individual during any calendar year after 1958 and prior to 1966, is paid to such individual during such calendar year;

(D) That part of remuneration which, after remuneration (other than remuneration referred to in the succeeding subsections of this section) equal to $6,600 with respect to employment has been paid to an individual during any calendar year after 1965 and prior to 1968, is paid to such individual during such calendar year;

(E) That part of remuneration which, after remuneration (other than remuneration referred to in the succeeding subsections of this section) equal to $7,800 with respect to employment has been paid to an individual during any calendar year after 1967 and prior to 1972, is paid to such individual during such calendar year;

(F) That part of remuneration which, after remuneration (other than remuneration referred to in the succeeding subsections of this section) equal to $9,000 with respect to employment has been paid to an individual during any calendar year after 1971 and prior to 1973, is paid to such individual during any such calendar year;

(G) That part of remuneration which, after remuneration (other than remuneration referred to in the succeeding subsections of this section) equal to $10,800 with respect to employment has been paid to an individual during any calendar year after 1972 and prior to 1974, is paid to such individual during such calendar year;

(H) That part of remuneration which, after remuneration (other than remuneration referred to in the succeeding subsections of this section) equal to $13,200 with respect to employment has been paid to an individual during any calendar year after 1973 and prior to 1975, is paid to such individual during such calendar year;

(I) That part of remuneration which, after remuneration (other than remuneration referred to in the succeeding subsections of this section) equal to the contribution and benefit base (determined under section 430 of this title) with respect to employment has been paid to an individual during any calendar year after 1974 with respect to which such contribution and benefit base is effective, is paid to such individual during such calendar year;

(2) The amount of any payment (including any amount paid by an employer for insurance or annuities, or into a fund, to provide for any such payment) made to, or on behalf of, an employee or any of his dependents under a plan or system established by an employer which makes provision for his employees generally (or for his employees generally and their dependents) or for a class or classes of his employees (or for a class or classes of his employees and their dependents), on account of (A) sickness or accident disability (but, in the case of payments made to an employee or any of his dependents, this clause shall exclude from the term "wages" only payments which are received under a workmen's compensation law), or (B) medical or hospitalization expenses in connection with sickness or accident disability, or (C) death, except that this subsection does not apply to a payment for group-term life insurance to the extent that such payment is includible in the gross income of the employee under the Internal Revenue Code of 1986;

(3) Any payment on account of sickness or accident disability, or medical or hospitalization expenses in connection with sickness or accident disability, made by an employer to, or on behalf of, an employee after the expiration of six calendar months following the last calendar month in which the employee worked for such employer;

(4) Any payment made to, or on behalf of, an employee or his beneficiary (A) from or to a trust exempt from tax under section 165(a) of the Internal Revenue Code of 1939 at the time of such payment or, in the case of a payment after 1954, under sections 401 and 501(a) of the Internal Revenue Code of 1954 or the Internal Revenue Code of 1986, unless such payment is made to an employee of the trust as remuneration for services rendered as such employee and not as a beneficiary of the trust, or (B) under or to an annuity plan which, at the time of such payment, meets the requirements of section 165(a)(3), (4), (5), and (6) of the Internal Revenue Code of 1939 or, in the case of a payment after 1954 and prior to 1963, the requirements of section 401(a)(3), (4), (5), and (6) of the Internal Revenue Code of 1954, or (C) under or to an annuity plan which, at the time of any such payment after 1962, is a plan described in section 403(a) of the Internal Revenue Code of 1986, or (D) under or to a bond purchase plan which, at the time of any such payment after 1962, is a qualified bond purchase plan described in section 405(a) of the Internal Revenue Code of 1954 (as in effect before July 18, 1984), or (E) under or to an annuity contract described in section 403(b) of the Internal Revenue Code of 1986, other than a payment for the purchase of such contract which is made by reason of a salary reduction agreement (whether evidenced by a written instrument or otherwise), or (F) under or to an exempt governmental deferred compensation plan (as defined in section 3121(v)(3) of such Code), or (G) to supplement pension benefits under a plan or trust described in any of the foregoing provisions of this subsection to take into account some portion or all of the increase in the cost of living (as determined by the Secretary of Labor) since retirement but only if such supplemental payments are under a plan which is treated as a welfare plan under section 3(2)(B)(ii) of the Employee Retirement Income Security Act of 1974, or (H) under a simplified employee pension (as defined in section 408(k)(1) of such Code), other than any contributions described in section 408(k)(6) of such Code, or (I) under a cafeteria plan (within the meaning of section 125 of the Internal Revenue Code of 1986) if such payment would not be treated as wages without regard to such plan and it is reasonable to believe that (if section 125 applied for purposes of this section) section 125 would not treat any wages as constructively received; or (J) under an arrangement to which section 408(p) of such Code applies, other than any elective contributions under paragraph (2)(A)(i) thereof; or (K) under a plan described in section 457(e)(11)(A)(ii) of the Internal Revenue Code of 1986 and maintained by an eligible employer (as defined in section 457(e)(1) of such Code);

(5) The payment by an employer (without deduction from the remuneration of the employee)—

(A) of the tax imposed upon an employee under section 3101 of the Internal Revenue Code of 1986, or

(B) of any payment required from an employee under a State unemployment compensation law,

with respect to remuneration paid to an employee for domestic service in a private home of the employer or for agricultural labor;

(6)(A) Remuneration paid in any medium other than cash to an employee for service not in the course of the employer's trade or business or for domestic service in a private home of the employer;

(B) Cash remuneration paid by an employer in any calendar year to an employee for domestic service in a private home of the employer (including domestic service on a farm operated for profit), if the cash remuneration paid in such year by the employer to the employee for such service is less than the applicable dollar threshold (as defined in section 3121(x) of the Internal Revenue Code of 1986) for such year;

(C) Cash remuneration paid by an employer in any calendar year to an employee for service not in the course of the employer's trade or business, if the cash remuneration paid in such year by the employer to the employee for such service is less than $100. As used in this paragraph, the term "service not in the course of the employer's trade or business" does not include domestic service in a private home of the employer and does not include service described in section 410(f)(5) of this title;

(7)(A) Remuneration paid in any medium other than cash for agricultural labor;

(B) Cash remuneration paid by an employer in any calendar year to an employee for agricultural labor unless—

(i) the cash remuneration paid in such year by the employer to the employee for such labor is $150 or more, or

(ii) the employer's expenditures for agricultural labor in such year equal or exceed $2,500,

except that clause (ii) shall not apply in determining whether remuneration paid to an employee constitutes "wages" under this section if such employee (I) is employed as a hand harvest laborer and is paid on a piece rate basis in an operation which has been, and is customarily and generally recognized as having been, paid on a piece rate basis in the region of employment, (II) commutes daily from his permanent residence to the farm on which he is so employed, and (III) has been employed in agriculture less than 13 weeks during the preceding calendar year;

(8) Remuneration paid by an employer in any year to an employee for service described in section 410(j)(3)(C) of this title (relating to home workers), if the cash remuneration paid in such year by the employer to the employee for such service is less than $100;

(9) Remuneration paid to or on behalf of an employee if (and to the extent that) at the time of the payment of such remuneration it is reasonable to believe that a corresponding deduction is allowable under section 217 of the Internal Revenue Code of 1986 (determined without regard to section 274(n) of such Code);

(10)(A) Tips paid in any medium other than cash;

(B) Cash tips received by an employee in any calendar month in the course of his employment by an employer unless the amount of such cash tips is $20 or more;

(11) Any payment or series of payments by an employer to an employee or any of his dependents which is paid—

(A) upon or after the termination of an employee's employment relationship because of (A) [1] death, or (B) [1] retirement for disability, and

(B) under a plan established by the employer which makes provision for his employees generally or a class or classes of his employees (or for such employees or class or classes of employees and their dependents),

other than any such payment or series of payments which would have been paid if the employee's employment relationship had not been so terminated;

(12) Any payment made by an employer to a survivor or the estate of a former employee after the calendar year in which such employee died;

(13) Any payment made by an employer to an employee, if at the time such payment is made such employee is entitled to disability insurance benefits under section 423(a) of this title and such entitlement commenced prior to the calendar year in which such payment is made, and if such employee did not perform any services for such employer during the period for which such payment is made;

(14) Remuneration paid by an organization exempt from income tax under section 501 of the Internal Revenue Code of 1986 in any calendar year to an employee for service rendered in the employ of such organization, if the remuneration paid in such year by the organization to the employee for such service is less than $100;

(15) Any payment made, or benefit furnished, to or for the benefit of an employee if at the time of such payment or such furnishing it is reasonable to believe that the employee will be able to exclude such payment or benefit from income under section 127 or 129 of the Internal Revenue Code of 1986;

(16) The value of any meals or lodging furnished by or on behalf of the employer if at the time of such furnishing it is reasonable to believe that the employee will be able to exclude such items from income under section 119 of the Internal Revenue Code of 1986;

(17) Any benefit provided to or on behalf of an employee if at the time such benefit is provided it is reasonable to believe that the employee will be able to exclude such benefit from income under section 74(c), 108(f)(4), 117, or 132 of the Internal Revenue Code of 1986;

(18) Remuneration consisting of income excluded from taxation under section 7873 of the Internal Revenue Code of 1986 (relating to income derived by Indians from exercise of fishing rights);

(19) Remuneration on account of—

(A) a transfer of a share of stock to any individual pursuant to an exercise of an incentive stock option (as defined in section 422(b) of the Internal Revenue Code of 1986) or under an employee stock purchase plan (as defined in section 423(b) of such Code), or

(B) any disposition by the individual of such stock; or

(20) Any benefit or payment which is excludable from the gross income of the employee under section 139B(b) of the Internal Revenue Code of 1986)[2].

(b) Regulations providing exclusions from term

Nothing in the regulations prescribed for purposes of chapter 24 of the Internal Revenue Code of 1986 (relating to income tax withholding) which provides an exclusion from "wages" as used in such chapter shall be construed to require a similar exclusion from "wages" in the regulations prescribed for purposes of this subchapter.

(c) Individuals performing domestic services

For purposes of this subchapter, in the case of domestic service described in subsection (a)(6)(B), any payment of cash remuneration for such service which is more or less than a whole-dollar amount shall, under such conditions and to such extent as may be prescribed by regulations made under this subchapter, be computed to the nearest dollar. For the purpose of the computation to the nearest dollar, the payment of a fractional part of a dollar shall be disregarded unless it amounts to one-half dollar or more, in which case it shall be increased to $1. The amount of any payment of cash remuneration so computed to the nearest dollar shall, in lieu of the amount actually paid, be deemed to constitute the amount of cash remuneration for purposes of subsection (a)(6)(B).

(d) Members of uniformed services

For purposes of this subchapter, in the case of an individual performing service, as a member of a uniformed service, to which the provisions of section 410(*l*)(1) of this title are applicable, the term "wages" shall, subject to the provisions of subsection (a)(1) of this section, include as such individual's remuneration for such service only (1) his basic pay as described in chapter 3 and section 1009 of Title 37 in the case of an individual performing service to which subparagraph (A) of such section 410(*l*)(1) of this title applies, or (2) his compensation for such service as determined under section 206(a) of Title 37 in the case of an individual performing service to which subparagraph (B) of such section 410 (*l*)(1) of this title applies.

(e) Peace Corps volunteers

For purposes of this subchapter, in the case of an individual performing service, as a volunteer or volunteer leader within the meaning of the Peace Corps Act, to which the provisions of section 410(*o*) of this title are applicable, (1) the term "wages" shall, subject to the provisions of subsection (a) of this section, include as such individual's remuneration for such service only amounts certified as payable pursuant to section 5(c) or 6(1) of the Peace Corps Act, and (2) any such amount shall be deemed to have been paid to such individual at the time the service, with respect to which it is paid, is performed.

(f) Tips

For purposes of this subchapter, tips received by an employee in the course of his employment shall be considered remuneration for employment. Such remuneration shall be deemed to be paid at the time a written statement including such tips is furnished to the employer pursuant to section 6053(a) of the Internal Revenue Code of 1986 or (if no statement including such tips is so furnished) at the time received.

(g) Members of religious orders

For purposes of this subchapter, in any case where an individual is a member of a religious order (as defined in section 3121(r)(2) of the Internal Revenue Code of 1986) performing service in the exercise of duties required by such order, and an election of coverage under section 3121(r) of such Code is in effect with respect to such order or with respect to the autonomous subdivision thereof to which such member belongs, the term "wages" shall, subject to the provisions of subsection (a) of this section, include as such individual's remuneration for such service the fair market value of any board, lodging, clothing, and other perquisites furnished to such member by such order or subdivision thereof or by any other person or organization pursuant to an agreement with such order or subdivision, except that the amount included as such individual's remuneration under this paragraph shall not be less than $100 a month.

(h) Retired justices and judges

For purposes of this subchapter, in the case of an individual performing service under the provisions of section 294 of Title 28 (relating to assignment of retired justices and judges to active duty), the term "wages" shall not include any payment under section 371(b) of such Title 28 which is received during the period of such service.

(i) Employer contributions under sections 401(k) and 414(h)(2) of Internal Revenue Code

Nothing in any of the foregoing provisions of this section (other than subsection (a)) shall exclude from the term "wages"—

(1) Any employer contribution under a qualified cash or deferred arrangement (as defined in section 401(k) of the Internal Revenue Code of 1986) to the extent not included in gross income by reason of section 402(a)(8) of such Code, or

(2) Any amount which is treated as an employer contribution under section 414(h)(2) of such Code where the pickup referred to in such section is pursuant to a salary reduction agreement (whether evidenced by a written instrument or otherwise).

(j) Amounts deferred under nonqualified deferred compensation plans

Any amount deferred under a nonqualified deferred compensation plan (within the meaning of section

3121(v)(2)(C) of the Internal Revenue Code of 1986) shall be taken into account for purposes of this subchapter as of the later of when the services are performed, or when there is no substantial risk of forfeiture of the rights to such amount. Any amount taken into account as wages by reason of the preceding sentence (and the income attributable thereto) shall not thereafter be treated as wages for purposes of this subchapter.

(k) "National average wage index" and "deferred compensation amount" defined

(1) For purposes of sections 403(f)(8)(B)(ii), 413(d)(2)(B), 415(a)(1)(B)(ii), 415(a)(1)(C)(ii), 415(a)(1)(D), 415(b)(3)(A)(ii), 415(i)(1)(E), 415(i)(2)(C)(ii), 424a(f)(2)(B), and 430(b)(2) (and 430(b)(2) of this title as in effect immediately prior to the enactment of the Social Security Amendments of 1977), the term "national average wage index" for any particular calendar year means, subject to regulations of the Commissioner of Social Security under paragraph (2), the average of the total wages for such particular calendar year.

(2) The Commissioner of Social Security shall prescribe regulations under which the national average wage index for any calendar year shall be computed—

(A) on the basis of amounts reported to the Secretary of the Treasury or his delegate for such year,

(B) by disregarding the limitation on wages specified in subsection (a)(1),

(C) with respect to calendar years after 1990, by incorporating deferred compensation amounts and factoring in for such years the rate of change from year to year in such amounts, in a manner consistent with the requirements of section 10208 of the Omnibus Budget Reconciliation Act of 1989, and

(D) with respect to calendar years before 1978, in a manner consistent with the manner in which the average of the total wages for each of such calendar years was determined as provided by applicable law as in effect for such years.

(3) For purposes of this subsection, the term "deferred compensation amount" means—

(A) any amount excluded from gross income under chapter 1 of the Internal Revenue Code of 1986 by reason of section 402(a)(8), 402(h)(1)(B), or 457(a) of such Code or by reason of a salary reduction agreement under section 403(b) of such Code,

(B) any amount with respect to which a deduction is allowable under chapter 1 of such Code by reason of a contribution to a plan described in section 501(c)(18) of such Code, and

(C) to the extent provided in regulations of the Commissioner of Social Security, deferred compensation provided under any arrangement, agreement, or plan referred to in subsection (i) or (j).

(Aug. 14, 1935, c. 531, Title II, § 209, 49 Stat. 625; Aug. 10, 1939, c. 666, Title II, § 201, 53 Stat. 1373; Mar. 24, 1943, c. 26, § 1(b)(2), 57 Stat. 47; Apr. 4, 1944, c. 161, § 2, 58 Stat. 188; Oct. 23, 1945, c. 433, § 7(b), 59 Stat. 548; Dec. 29, 1945, c. 652, Title I, § 5(a), 59 Stat. 671; Aug. 10, 1946, c. 951, Title IV, §§ 407(a), 408(a), 409(a), 410, 411, 414, 60 Stat. 988, 989, 990; Apr. 20, 1948, c. 222, § 1(a), 62 Stat. 195; Aug. 28, 1950, c. 809, Title I, § 104(a), 64 Stat. 492; Sept. 1, 1954, c. 1206, Title I, §§ 101(a)(1)-(3), 104(a), 68 Stat. 1052, 1078; Aug. 1, 1956, c. 836, Title I, § 105(a), 70 Stat. 828; Aug. 1, 1956, c. 837, Title IV, § 401, 70 Stat. 869; Pub.L. 85–786, § 1, Aug. 27, 1958, 72 Stat. 938; Pub.L. 85–840, Title I, § 102(a), Aug. 28, 1958, 72 Stat. 1019; Pub.L. 86–778, Title I, § 103(j)(2)(C), (F), Sept. 13, 1960, 74 Stat. 937, 938; Pub.L. 87–64, Title I, § 102(c)(3)(A), June 30, 1961, 75 Stat. 134; Pub.L. 87–293, Title II, § 202(b)(2), Sept. 22, 1961, 75 Stat. 626; Pub.L. 88–272, Title II, § 220(c)(3), Feb. 26, 1964, 78 Stat. 63; Pub.L. 88–650, § 4(a), Oct. 13, 1964, 78 Stat. 1077; Pub.L. 89–97, Title III, §§ 313(a), 320(a)(1), July 30, 1965, 79 Stat. 382, 393; Pub.L. 90–248, Title I, § 108(a)(1), Title V, § 504(c), Jan. 2, 1968, 81 Stat. 834, 935; Pub.L. 92–5, Title II, § 203(a)(1), Mar. 17, 1971, 85 Stat. 10; Pub.L. 92–336, Title II, § 203(a)(1), July 1, 1972, 86 Stat. 417; Pub.L. 92–603, Title I, §§ 104(g), 122(a), 123(c)(1), 138(a), Oct. 30, 1972, 86 Stat. 1341, 1354, 1356, 1365; Pub.L. 93–66, Title II, § 203(a)(1), July 9, 1973, 87 Stat. 153; Pub.L. 93–233, § 5(a)(1), Dec. 31, 1973, 87 Stat. 953; Pub.L. 95–216, Title III, § 351(a)(1)-(3)(A), Dec. 20, 1977, 91 Stat. 1549; Pub.L. 95–472, § 3(c), Oct. 17, 1978, 92 Stat. 1333; Pub.L. 95–600, Title I, § 164(b)(4), Nov. 6, 1978, 92 Stat. 2814; Pub.L. 96–499, Title XI, § 1141(a)(2), Dec. 5, 1980, 94 Stat. 2693; Pub.L. 97–34, Title I, § 124(e)(2)(B), Aug. 13, 1981, 95 Stat. 201; Pub.L. 97–123, § 3(a), Dec. 29, 1981, 95 Stat. 1662; Pub.L. 98–21, Title I, § 101(c)(1), Title III, §§ 324(c)(1)-(3), 327(a)(2), (b)(2), 328(b), Apr. 20, 1983, 97 Stat. 70, 124, 125, 127, 128; Pub.L. 98–369, Div. A, Title IV, § 491(d)(39), Title V, § 531(d)(1)(B), Div. B, Title VI, §§ 2661(i), 2663(a)(6), July 18, 1984, 98 Stat. 851, 884, 1157, 1162; Pub.L. 99–272, Title XII, § 12112(a), Apr. 7, 1986, 100 Stat. 288; Pub.L. 99–514, Title I, § 122(e)(5), Title XI, § 1151(d)(2)(C), Oct. 22, 1986, 100 Stat. 2112, 2505; Pub.L. 100–203, Title IX, §§ 9001(a)(2), 9002(a), 9003(a)(1), Dec. 22, 1987, 101 Stat. 1330–286, 1330–287; Pub.L 100–647, Title I, §§ 1001(g)(4)(C), 1011(f)(8), 1011B(a)(22)(E), (23)(B), Title III, § 3043(a), Title VIII, § 8017(a), Nov. 10, 1988, 102 Stat. 3352, 3463, 3486, 3641, 3793; Pub.L. 101–140, Title II, § 203(a)(2), Nov. 8, 1989, 103 Stat. 830; Pub.L. 101–239, Title X, § 10208(a), (d)(1), Dec. 19, 1989, 103 Stat. 2476, 2479; Pub.L. 101–508, Title V, § 5130(a)(5), Nov. 5, 1990, 104 Stat. 1388–289; Pub.L. 103–296, Title I, § 107(a)(4), Title III, § 321(c)(4), (e)(1), Aug. 15, 1994, 108 Stat. 1478, 1538, 1539; Pub.L. 103–387, § 2(a)(2)(A), Oct. 22, 1994, 108 Stat. 4072; Pub.L. 104–188, Title I, §§ 1421(b)(8)(B), 1458(b)(2), Aug. 20, 1996, 110 Stat. 1798, 1820; Pub.L. 108–203, Title IV, § 423(b), Mar. 2, 2004, 118 Stat. 536; Pub.L. 108–357, Title II, § 251(a)(1)(B), Title III, § 320(b)(5), Oct. 22, 2004, 118 Stat. 1458, 1473; Pub.L. 110–245, Title I, § 115(a)(2), June 17, 2008, 122 Stat. 1636; Pub.L. 113–295, Div. A, Title II, § 221(a)(19)(B)(viii), Dec. 19, 2014, 128 Stat. 4040.)

[1] So in original. Probably should be "(i)" and "(ii)", respectively.

[2] So in original. The closing parenthesis probably should not appear.

HISTORICAL AND STATUTORY NOTES

References in Text

The Internal Revenue Code of 1986, referred to in text, is classified to Title 26.

Section 165 of the Internal Revenue Code of 1939, referred to in subsec. (a)(4), was a part of chapter 1 of the 1939 Code, and was repealed by section 7851(a)(1)(A) of Title 26, Internal Revenue Code of 1954; the 1954 Internal Revenue Code was redesignated the Internal Revenue Code of 1986 by Pub.L. 99–514, § 2, Oct. 22, 1986, 100 Stat. 2095.

For provision deeming a reference in other laws to a provision of the 1939 Code as a reference to the corresponding provisions of the 1986 Code, see section 7852(b) of the 1986 Code. For tables of comparisons of the 1939 Code to the 1986 Code, see tables at end of Title 26, Internal Revenue Code.

Sections 401 and 501(a) of the Internal Revenue Code of 1954 or the Internal Revenue Code of 1986, referred to in subsec. (a)(4), are classified to sections 401 and 501(a), respectively, of Title 26.

Section 405(a) of Title 26, referred to in subsec. (a)(4), was repealed by Pub.L. 98–369, Div. A, Title IV, § 491(a), July 18, 1984, 98 Stat. 848.

The Employee Retirement Income Security Act of 1974, referred to in subsec. (a)(4), is Pub.L. 93–406, Sept. 2, 1974, 88 Stat. 829, as amended, also known as ERISA, which is classified principally to chapter 18 of Title 29, 29 U.S.C.A. § 1001 et seq. Section 3(2)(B)(ii) of the Act is classified to 29 U.S.C.A. § 1002(2)(B)(ii). For complete classification, see Short Title note set out under 29 U.S.C.A. § 1001 and Tables.

The Peace Corps Act, referred to in subsec. (e), is Pub.L. 87–293, Sept. 22, 1961, 75 Stat. 612, which is classified principally to chapter 34 of Title 22, 22 U.S.C.A. § 2501 et seq. Sections 5 and 6 of that Act are classified to 22 U.S.C.A. §§ 2504 and 2505, respectively. For complete classification, see Short Title note set out under 22 U.S.C.A. § 2501 and Tables.

The enactment of the Social Security Amendments of 1977, referred to in subsec. (k)(1), means the enactment of Pub.L. 95–216, which was approved Dec. 20, 1977.

Section 10208 of the Omnibus Budget Reconciliation Act of 1989, referred to in subsec. (k)(2), is section 10208 of Pub.L. 101–239, Title X, Dec. 19, 1989, 103 Stat. 2476, which amended this section and sections 403, 413, 415, 417, 418, 424a, and 430 of this title, section 206 of Title 29, Labor, and section 231 of Title 45, Railroads, and enacted provisions set out as a note under section 430 of this title. For complete classification of this Act to the Code, see Tables.

Section 402 of the Internal Revenue Code of 1986, referred to in subsec. (k)(3)(A), was amended by Pub.L. 102–318, § 521, and, as so amended, provisions formerly contained in section 402(a)(8) are contained in 26 U.S.C.A. § 402(e)(3).

Codifications

"Sections 401(1) and 403 of Title 38" was substituted for "section 102(10) of the Servicemen's and Veterans' Survivor Benefit Act" on authority of section 5(a) of Pub.L. 85–857, Sept. 2, 1958, 72 Stat. 1262, § 1 of which enacted Title 38, Veterans' Benefits. Section 403 of Title 38 was repealed by Pub.L. 97–306, Title I, § 113(b)(1), Oct. 14, 1982, 96 Stat. 1432.

Effective and Applicability Provisions

2014 Acts. For effective date and savings provisions of amendments made by Pub.L. 113–295, Div. A, Title II, § 221, which, except as otherwise provided, shall take effect on Dec. 19, 2014, see Pub.L. 113–295, Div. A, Title II, § 221(b), set out as a note under 26 U.S.C.A. § 1.

2008 Acts. Amendments by Pub.L. 110–245, § 115 effective as if included in Pub.L. 110–142, § 5, Dec. 20, 2007, 121 Stat. 1805, see Pub.L. 110–245, § 115(d), set out as a note under 26 U.S.C.A. § 3121.

2004 Acts. Amendments to this section by Pub.L. 108–357, § 251, applicable to stock acquired pursuant to options exercised after Oct. 22, 2004, see Pub.L. 108–357, § 251(d), set out as a note under 26 U.S.C.A. § 421.

Amendments to subsec. (a)(17) of this section by Pub.L. 108–357, § 320, applicable to amounts received by an individual in taxable years beginning after Dec. 31, 2003, see Pub.L. 108–357, § 320(c), set out as a note under 26 U.S.C.A. § 108.

1996 Acts. Amendment by section 1421 of Pub.L. 104–188 applicable to taxable years beginning after Dec. 31, 1996, see section 1421(e) of Pub.L. 104–188, set out as a note under section 72 of Title 26, Internal Revenue Code.

Amendment by section 1458(b)(2) of Pub.L. 104–188 applicable to remuneration paid after Dec. 31, 1996, see section 1458(c)(2) of Pub.L. 104–188, set out as a note under section 3121 of Title 26, Internal Revenue Code.

1994 Acts. Amendment by Pub.L. 103–387 applicable to remuneration paid after December 31, 1993, see section 2(a)(3)(A) of Pub.L. 103–387, set out as a note under section 3102 of Title 26, Internal Revenue Code.

Amendment by section 107(a)(4) of Pub.L. 103–296 effective Mar. 31, 1995, see section 110 of Pub.L. 103–296, set out as a note under section 401 of this title.

1990 Acts. Amendment by section 5130 of Pub.L. 101–508 effective as if included in the enactment of Pub.L. 101–239 [probably meaning the date of the enactment of Pub.L. 101–239] which was approved December 19, 1989, see section 5130(b) of Pub.L. 101–508, set out as a note under section 1402 of Title 26, Internal Revenue Code.

1989 Acts. Amendment by Pub.L. 101–239 applicable with respect to computation of average total wage amounts for calendar years after 1990, including transitional rule, see section 10208(c) of Pub.L. 101–239, set out as a note under section 430 of this title.

Amendment by section 203 of Pub.L. 101–140 effective as if included in section 1151 of Pub.L. 99–514, see section 203(c) of Pub.L. 101–140, set out as a note under section 79 of Title 26, Internal Revenue Code.

1988 Acts. Amendment by sections 1001(g)(4)(C), 1011(f)(8) and 1011B(a)(23)(B) of Pub.L. 100–647 effective except as otherwise provided, as if included in the provision of the Tax Reform Act of 1986, Pub.L. 99–514, to which such amendment relates, see section 1019(a) of Pub.L. 100–647, set out as a note under section 1 of Title 26, Internal Revenue Code.

Section 1011B(a)(22)(F) of Pub.L. 100–647, which had provided that the amendments made by par. (22) of section 1011B of Pub.L. 100–647 did not apply to any individual who separated from service with the employer before January 1, 1989, was repealed by Pub.L. 101–140, Title II, § 203(a)(2), Nov. 8, 1989, 103 Stat. 830, effective as if such repeal were included in section 1151 of Pub.L. 99–514. See section 203(c) of Pub.L. 101–140, set out as a note under section 79 of Title 26, Internal Revenue Code.

Amendment by section 3043(a) of Pub.L. 100–647 applicable to all periods beginning before, on, or after Nov. 10, 1988, with no inference created as to existence or non-existence or scope of any exemption from tax for income derived from fishing rights secured as of Mar. 17, 1988, by any treaty, law, or Executive Order, see section 3044 of Pub.L. 100–647, set out as a note under section 7873 of Title 26.

Amendment by section 8017(a) of Pub.L. 100–647 effective as if included in amendments made by section 9002 of Omnibus Budget Reconciliation Act of 1987, Pub.L. 100–203, see section 8017(c) of Pub.L. 100–647, set out as a note under section 3121 of Title 26.

1987 Acts. Amendment by section 9001(a)(2) of Pub.L. 100–203 applicable with respect to remuneration paid after Dec. 31, 1987, see section 9001(d) of Pub.L. 100–203, set out as a note under section 3121 of Title 26, Internal Revenue Code.

Amendment of subsec. (h)(2) by section 9002(a) of Pub.L. 100–203 applicable with respect to remuneration for agricultural labor paid after Dec. 31, 1987, see section 9002(c) of Pub.L. 100–203, set out as a note under section 3121 of Title 26.

Amendment of subsec. (b)(3) by section 9003(a)(1) of Pub.L. 100–203 applicable with respect to group-term life insurance coverage in effect after Dec. 31, 1987, with exception for employer's group-term life insurance payments for certain former employees, see section 9003(b) of Pub.L. 100–203, as amended, set out as a note under section 3121 of Title 26.

1986 Acts. Amendment by section 122(e)(5) of Pub.L. 99–514 applicable to prizes and awards granted after Dec. 31, 1986, see section 151(c) of Pub.L. 99–514, set out as a note under section 1 of Title 26, Internal Revenue Code.

Amendment by section 1151(d)(2)(C) of Pub.L. 99–514 applicable to taxable years beginning after Dec. 31, 1983, see section 1151(k)(5) of Pub.L. 99–514, set out as a note under section 79 of Title 26.

Section 12112(c) of Pub.L. 99–272 provided that: "The amendments made by this section [amending this section and section 3121(i)(5) of Title 26, Internal Revenue Code] shall be effective with respect to service performed after December 31, 1983."

1984 Acts. Amendment by section 491(d)(39) of Pub.L. 98–369 applicable to obligations issued after Dec. 31, 1983, see section 491(f)(1) of Pub.L. 98–369, set out as a note under section 62 of Title 26, Internal Revenue Code.

Amendment of text prec. subsec. (a) and enactment of subsec. (s) by Pub.L. 98–369 effective Jan. 1, 1985, see section 531(i), formerly 531(h) of Pub.L. 98–369, set out as a note under section 132 of Title 26.

Amendment to subsec. (e) and par. (2) in unenumerated provisions following subsec. (r) by section 2661(i) of Pub.L. 98–369 effective as though included in the enactment of the Social Security Amendments of 1983 [Pub.L. 98–21], see section 2664(a) of Pub.L. 98–369, set out as a note under section 401 of this title.

Amendment to subsecs. (a), (e), (f), (k) to (r), and the seventh unenumerated paragraph from the end, by section 2663(a)(6) of Pub.L. 98–369 effective July 18, 1984, but not to be construed as changing or affecting any right, liability, status or interpretation which existed (under the provisions of law involved) before that date, see section 2664(b) of Pub.L. 98–369, set out as a note under section 401 of this title.

1983 Acts. Amendment by section 101(c)(1) of Pub.L. 98–21 effective with respect to service performed after Dec. 31, 1983, see section 101(d) of Pub.L. 98–21, as amended, set out as a note under section 3121 of Title 26, Internal Revenue Code.

Amendment by section 324(c)(1)–(3) of Pub.L. 98–21 applicable to remuneration paid after Dec. 31, 1983, except for certain employer contributions made during 1984 under a qualified cash or deferred arrangement, and except in the case of an agreement with certain nonqualified deferred compensation plans in existence on Mar. 24, 1983, see section 324(d) of Pub.L. 98–21, set out as a note under section 3121 of Title 26.

Amendment by section 327(a)(2) of Pub.L. 98–21 applicable to remuneration paid after Dec. 31, 1983, see section 327(d)(1) of Pub.L. 98–21, as amended, set out as a note under section 3121 of Title 26.

Amendment by section 327(b)(2) of Pub.L. 98–21 applicable to remuneration (other than amounts excluded under 26 U.S.C. 119) paid after Mar. 4, 1983, and to any such remuneration paid on or before such date which the employer treated as wages when paid, see section 327(d)(2) of Pub.L. 98–21, as amended, set out as a note under section 3121 of Title 26.

Amendment by section 328(b) of Pub.L. 98–21 applicable to remuneration paid after Dec. 31, 1983, see section 328(d)(1) of Pub.L. 98–21, set out as a note under section 3121 of Title 26.

1981 Acts. Amendment by Pub.L. 97–123 applicable, except as otherwise provided, to remuneration paid after Dec. 31, 1981, see section 3(g) of Pub.L. 97–123, set out as a note under section 3121 of Title 26, Internal Revenue Code.

Amendment by Pub.L. 97–34 applicable to remuneration paid after Dec. 31, 1981, see section 124(f) of Pub.L. 97–34, set out as a note under section 21 of Title 26.

1980 Acts. For effective date of amendment by Pub.L. 96–499, see section 1141(c) of Pub.L. 96–499, set out as a note under section 3121 of Title 26, Internal Revenue Code.

1978 Acts. Amendment by Pub.L. 95–600 applicable with respect to taxable years beginning after Dec. 31, 1978, see section 164(d) of Pub.L. 95–600, set out as a note under section 127 of Title 26, Internal Revenue Code.

Amendment by Pub.L. 95–472 applicable with respect to taxable years beginning after Dec. 31, 1976, see section 3(d) of Pub.L. 95–472, set out as a note under section 3121 of Title 26.

1977 Acts. Section 351(d) of Pub.L. 95–216 provided that: "The amendments made by subsection (a) [amending subsecs. (g)(3), (j), and (n) to (p) of this section and section 410(a)(10), (17)(A), and (f)(4)(B) of this title] shall apply with respect to remuneration paid and services rendered after December 31, 1977. The amendments made by subsections (b) [amending section 412 of this title] and (c) [amending section 413(a)(2) of this title] shall be effective January 1, 1978."

1973 Acts. Section 5(e) of Pub.L. 93–233 provided that: "The amendments made by this section [to sections 409(a)(8), 411(b)(1)(H), 413(a)(2)(ii), (iii), and 430(c) of this title and sections 3121(a), 3122, 3125(a) to (c), 6413(c)(1), (2)(A), and 6654(d)(2)(B)(ii) of Title 26, Internal Revenue Code], except subsection (a)(4), shall apply only with respect to remuneration paid after, and taxable years beginning after, 1973. The amendments made by subsection (a)(4) [to section 415(e)(1) of this title] shall apply with respect to calendar years after 1973."

Section 203(e) of Pub.L. 93–66 provided that: "The amendments made by this section [to sections 409(a)(8), 411(b)(1)(H), 413(a)(2)(ii), (iii), and 430(c) of this title and sections 3121(a), 3122, 3125(a) to (c), 6413(c)(1), (2)(A), and 6654(d)(2)(B)(ii) of Title 26, Internal Revenue Code], except subsection (a)(4), shall apply only with respect to remuneration paid after, and taxable years beginning after, 1973. The amendments made by subsection (a)(4) [to section 415(e)(1) of this title] shall apply with respect to calendar years after 1973."

1972 Acts. Amendment of subsec. (i) of this section by section 104(g) of Pub.L. 92–603 applicable only with respect to payments after 1974, see section 104(j) of Pub.L. 92–603, set out as a note under section 414 of this title.

Section 122(c) of Pub.L. 92–603 provided that: "The amendments made by this section [enacting subsec. (n) of this section and section 3121(a)(14) of Title 26, Internal Revenue Code] shall apply in the case of any payment made after December 1972."

Section 138(c) of Pub.L. 92–603 provided that: "The amendments made by this section [amending subsec. (*o*) of this section and section 3121 of Title 26, Internal Revenue Code] shall apply in the case of any payment made after December 1972."

Section 203(c) of Pub.L. 92–336 provided that: "The amendments made by subsections (a)(1) [amending subsec. (a)(6) to (9) of this section] and (a)(3)(A) [amending section 413(a)(2)(ii) of this title], and the amendments made by subsection (b) [amending sections 3121(a)(1), 3122, 3125, 6413(c)(1), and 6413(c)(2)(A) of Title 26, Internal Revenue Code] (except paragraphs (1) and (7) thereof), shall apply only with respect to remuneration paid after December 1972. The amendments made by subsections (a)(2) [section 411(b)(1)(F) to (I) of this title], (a)(3)(B) [section 413(a)(2)(iii) of this title], (b)(1) [section 1402(b)(1)(F) to (I) of Title 26], and (b)(7) [section 6654(d)(2)(B)(ii) of Title 26], shall apply only with respect to taxable years beginning after 1972. The amendment made by subsection (a)(4) [section 415(e)(1) of this title] shall apply only with respect to calendar years after 1972."

1971 Acts. Section 203(c) of Pub.L. 92–5 provided that: "The amendments made by subsections (a)(1) [amending this section] and (a)(3)(A) [amending section 413(a)(2)(ii) of this title], and the amendments made by subsection (b) (except paragraphs (1) and (7) thereof) [amending sections 3121, 3122, 3125, and 6413 of Title 26, Internal Revenue Code], shall apply only with respect to remuneration paid after December 1971. The amendments made by subsections (a)(2), (a)(3)(B), (b)(1), and (b)(7) [amending sections 411 and 413(a)(2)(iii) of this title and sections 1402 and 6654 of Title 26] shall apply only with respect to taxable years beginning after 1971. The amendment made by subsection (a)(4) [amending section 415 of this title] shall apply only with respect to calendar years after 1971."

1968 Acts. Section 108(c) of Pub.L. 90–248 provided that: "The amendments made by subsections (a)(1) [to subsecs. (a)(4), (5) of this section] and (a)(3)(A) [to section 423(a)(2)(ii) of this title], and the amendments made by subsection (b) (except paragraph (1) thereof) [to sections 1402(b)(1)(E), 3121(a)(1), 3122, 3125, and 6413(c)(1), (2)(A) of Title 26, Internal Revenue Code], shall apply only with respect to remuneration paid after December 1967. The amendments made by subsections (a)(2) [to section 411(b)(1)(D), (E) of this title], (a)(3)(B) [to section 413(a)(2)(iii) of this title], and (b)(1) [to section 1402(b)(1)(D) of Title 26] shall apply only with respect to taxable years ending after 1967. The amendment made by subsection (a)(4) [to section 415(e)(1) of this title] shall apply only with respect to calendar years after 1967."

Subsec. (m) of this section applicable with respect to remuneration paid after Jan. 2, 1968, see section 504(d) of Pub.L. 90–248, set out as a note under section 3121 of Title 26, Internal Revenue Code.

1965 Acts. Amendment by section 313(a) of Pub.L. 89–97 applicable only with respect to tips received by employees after 1965, see section 313(f) of Pub.L. 89–97, set out as a note under section 6053 of Title 26, Internal Revenue Code.

Amendment by section 320(a)(1) of Pub.L. 89–97 applicable with respect to remuneration paid after December, 1965, see section 320(c) of Pub.L. 89–97, set out as a note under section 3121 of Title 26.

1964 Acts. Subsec. (k) of this section applicable with respect to remuneration paid on or after the first day of the first calendar month which begins more than ten days after Oct. 13, 1964, see section 4(d) of Pub.L. 88–650, set out as a note under section 3121 of Title 26, Internal Revenue Code.

Amendment of subsec. (e) by Pub.L. 88–272 applicable to remuneration paid after Dec. 31, 1962, see section 220(d) of Pub.L. 88–272, set out as a note under section 406 of Title 26.

1961 Acts. Amendment by Pub.L. 87–293 applicable with respect to service performed after Sept. 22, 1961, but in the case of persons serving under the Peace Corps agency established by executive order applicable with respect to service performed on or after the effective date of enrollment, see section 202(c) of Pub.L. 87–293, set out as a note under section 3121 of Title 26, Internal Revenue Code.

Amendment of subsec. (i) of this section by Pub.L. 87–64 applicable with respect to monthly benefits for months beginning on or after Aug. 1, 1961, based on applications filed in or after March, 1961, and with respect to lump-sum death payments under this subchapter in the case of deaths on or after Aug. 1, 1961, see sections 102(f) and 109 of Pub.L. 87–64, set out as 1961 Increase in Monthly Benefits; Effective Date, and Effective Date of 1961 Amendment notes, respectively, under section 402 of this title.

1960 Acts. Amendment of subsec. (j) and the last paragraph of this section by Pub.L. 86–778 effective on Sept. 13, 1960, see section 103(v)(1) of Pub.L. 86–778, set out as a note under section 402 of this title.

1958 Acts. Section 2 of Pub.L. 85–786 provided that: "The amendment made by section 1 [amending subsec. (i) of this section] shall be applicable to remuneration paid after the enactment of this Act [Aug. 27, 1958], except that, in the case of any coverage group which is included under the agreement of a State under section 218 of the Social Security Act [section 418 of this title], the amendment made by section 1 [amending subsec. (i) of this section] shall also be applicable to remuneration for any member of such coverage group with respect to services performed after the effective date, specified in such agreement, for such coverage group, if such State has paid or agrees, prior to January 1, 1959, to pay, prior to such date, the amounts which under section 218(e) [section 418(e) of this title] would have been payable with respect to remuneration of all members of such coverage group had the amendment made by section 1 [amending subsec. (i) of this section] been in effect on and after January 1, 1951. Failure by a State to make such payments prior to January 1, 1959, shall be treated the same as failure to make payments when due under section 218(e) [section 418(e) of this title]."

1956 Acts. Amendment by Act Aug. 1, 1956, c. 837, effective Jan. 1, 1957, see section 603(a) of Act Aug. 1, 1956.

Section 105(d) of Act Aug. 1, 1956, c. 836, provided that: "The amendment made by subsection (a) of this section [to subsec. (h)(2) of this section] shall apply with respect to remuneration paid after 1956, and the amendment made by subsection (b) of this section [to section 410(*o*) of this title] shall apply with respect to service performed after 1956."

1954 Acts. Section 101(n) of Act Sept. 1, 1954 provided in part that the amendments to subsecs. (g)(2), (3), and (h)(1), (2) by § 101(a)(1), (2), (3), of Act Sept. 1, 1954, shall be applicable only with respect to remuneration paid after 1954, see section 101(n) of Act Sept. 1, 1954, set out as a note under section 405 of this title.

1950 Acts. Section 104(b) of Act Aug. 28, 1950 provided that: "The amendment made by subsection (a) [amending this section] shall take effect January 1, 1951, except that sections 214, 215, and 216 of the Social Security Act [sections 414 to 416 of this title] shall be applicable (1) in the case of monthly benefits for months after August 1950, and (2) in the case of lump-sum death payments with respect to deaths after August 1950."

1948 Acts. Section 1(b) of Act Apr. 20, 1948 provided in part that: "The amendment made by subsection (a) to section 209(b)(15) of the Social Security Act [former subsec. (b)(15) of this section] shall be applicable with respect to services performed after the date of the enactment of this Act [Apr. 20, 1948]."

1946 Acts. Sections 407(b), 408(b), and 409(b) of Act Aug. 10 1946 each provided that: "The amendment made by subsection (a) of this section [amending this section] shall be applicable only in cases of applications for benefits under this title [this subchapter] filed after December 31, 1946."

1945 Acts. Amendment of former subsec. (b) by Act Dec. 29, 1945 was made effective Jan. 1, 1946 by section 5(a) thereof.

1939 Acts. Amendment by Act Aug. 10, 1939 was made effective Jan. 1, 1940 by section 201 of such Act.

Transfer of Functions

"Administrator" was substituted for "Board" and "Federal Security Administrator" for "Social Security Board" and for "Board" by section 4 of 1946 Reorg. Plan No. 2. See note under section 902 of this title.

Repeals; Amendments and Application of Amendments Unaffected

Section 202(b)(2) of Pub.L. 87–293, cited as a credit to this section, was repealed by Pub.L. 89–572, § 5(a), Sept. 13, 1966, 80 Stat. 765. Such repeal not deemed to affect amendments to this section contained in such provisions, and continuation in full force and effect until modified by appropriate authority of all determinations, authorization, regulations, orders, contracts, agreements, and other actions issued, undertaken, or entered into under authority of the repealed provisions, see section 5(b) of Pub.L. 89–572, set out as a note under former section 2515 of Title 22, Foreign Relations and Intercourse.

Exclusion From Wages and Compensation of Refunds Required From Employers to Compensate for Duplication of Medicare Benefits by Health Care Benefits Provided by Employers

See section 10202 of Pub.L. 101–239 set out as a note under section 1395b of this title.

Non-Enforcement of Amendment Made by Section 1151 of Pub.L. 99–514; Monies Appropriated for Fiscal Year 1990 Not to be Used for Enforcement or Implementation of Amendment

No monies appropriated by the Treasury, Postal Service and General Government Appropriations Act, 1990, to be used to implement or enforce section 1151 of the Tax Reform Act of 1986 [Pub.L. 99–514] or the amendments made by such section, see section 528 of Pub.L. 101–136, set out as a note under former section 89 of Title 26, Internal Revenue Code.

Payments Under State Temporary Disability Law to be Treated as Remuneration for Service

For purposes of applying this section with respect to the parenthetical matter contained in subsec. (b)(2) of this section, payments under a state temporary disability law shall be treated as remuneration for service, see section 3(e) of Pub.L. 97–123, set out as a note under section 3121 of Title 26, Internal Revenue Code.

Plan Amendments Not Required Until January 1, 1998

For provisions directing that if any amendments made by sections 1401 to 1465 of Pub.L. 104–188 require an amendment to any plan or annuity contract, such amendment shall not be required to be made before the first day of the first plan year beginning on or after Jan. 1, 1998, see section 1465 of Pub.L. 104–188, set out as a note under section 401 of Title 26, Internal Revenue Code.

Refunds or Credits for Overpayments

Section 3 of Act Apr. 20, 1948, provided that: "If any amount paid prior to the date of the enactment of this Act [Apr. 20, 1948] constitutes an overpayment of tax solely by reason of an amendment made by this Act [to this section], no refund or credit shall be made or allowed with respect to the amount of such overpayment."

Services for Cooperatives Prior to 1951

Section 110 of Act Aug. 28, 1950, provided that: "In any case in which—

"(1) an individual has been employed at any time prior to 1951 by organizations enumerated in the first sentence of section 101(12) of the Internal Revenue Code [1939],

"(2) the service performed by such individual during the time he was so employed constituted agricultural labor as defined in section 209(*l*) of the Social Security Act [former subsec. (*l*) of this section] and section 1426(h) of the Internal Revenue Code [1939], as in effect prior to the enactment of this Act [Aug. 28, 1950], and such service would, but for the provisions of such sections, have constituted employment for the purposes of Title II of the Social Security Act [this subchapter] and subchapter A of chapter 9 of such Code [1939],

"(3) the taxes imposed by sections 1400 and 1410 of the Internal Revenue Code [1939] have been paid with respect to any part of the remuneration paid to such individual by such organization for such service and the payment of such taxes by such organization has been made in good faith upon the assumption that such service did not constitute agricultural labor as so defined, and

"(4) no refund of such taxes has been obtained,

the amount of such remuneration with respect to which such taxes have been paid shall be deemed to constitute remuneration for employment as defined in section 209(b) of the Social Security Act [former subsec. (b) of this section] as in effect prior to the enactment of this Act [Aug. 28, 1950] (but it shall not constitute wages for purposes of deductions under section 203 of such Act [section 403 of this title] for months for which benefits under Title II of such Act [this subchapter] have been certified and paid prior to the enactment of this Act [Aug. 28, 1950])."

Social Security Coverage of Retired Federal Judges on Active Duty

Amendment of subsec. (s) by section 101(c)(1) of Pub.L. 98–21 [defining wages for purposes of this subchapter in the case of individuals performing service under section 294 of Title 28 (relating to assignment of retired justices and judges to active duty) to include payments under section 371(b) of Title 28 received during the period of such service] to apply only with respect to remuneration paid after Dec. 31, 1985, with remuneration paid prior to Jan. 1, 1986, under section 371(b) of Title 28 to an individual performing service under section 294 of Title 28 not to be included in the term "wages" for purposes of this section or section 3121(a) of Title 26, Internal Revenue Code, notwithstanding section 101(d) of Pub.L. 98–21, see section 4 of Pub.L. 98–118, set out as a note under section 3121 of Title 26, Internal Revenue Code.

§ 410. Definitions relating to employment

For the purposes of this subchapter—

(a) Employment

The term "employment" means any service performed after 1936 and prior to 1951 which was employment for the purposes of this subchapter under the law applicable to the period in which such service was performed, and any service, of whatever nature, performed after 1950 (A) by an employee for the person employing him, irrespective of the citizenship or residence of either, (i) within the United States, or (ii) on or in connection with an American vessel or American aircraft under a contract of service which is entered into within the United States or during the performance of which and while the employee is employed on the vessel or aircraft it touches at a port in the United States, if the employee is employed on and in connection with such vessel or aircraft when outside the United States, or (B) outside the United States by a citizen or resident of the United States as an employee (i) of an American employer (as defined in subsection (e) of this section), or (ii) of a foreign affiliate (as defined in section 3121(l)(6) of the Internal Revenue Code of 1986) of an American employer during any period for which there is in effect an agreement, entered into pursuant to section 3121(l) of such Code, with respect to such affiliate, or (C) if it is service, regardless of where or by whom performed, which is designated as employment or recognized as equivalent to employment under an agreement entered into under section 433 of this title; except that, in the case of service performed after 1950, such term shall not include—

(1) Service performed by foreign agricultural workers lawfully admitted to the United States from the Bahamas, Jamaica, and the other British West Indies, or from any other foreign country or possession thereof, on a temporary basis to perform agricultural labor;

(2) Domestic service performed in a local college club, or local chapter of a college fraternity or sorority, by a student who is enrolled and is regularly attending classes at a school, college, or university;

(3)(A) Service performed by a child under the age of 18 in the employ of his father or mother;

(B) Service not in the course of the employer's trade or business, or domestic service in a private home of the employer, performed by an individual under the age of 21 in the employ of his father or mother, or performed by an individual in the employ of his spouse or son or daughter; except that the provisions of this subparagraph shall not be applicable to such domestic service performed by an individual in the employ of his son or daughter if—

(i) the employer is a surviving spouse or a divorced individual and has not remarried, or has a spouse living in the home who has a mental or physical condition which results in such spouse's being incapable of caring for a son, daughter, stepson, or stepdaughter (referred to in clause (ii)) for at least 4 continuous weeks in the calendar quarter in which the service is rendered, and

(ii) a son, daughter, stepson, or stepdaughter of such employer is living in the home, and

(iii) the son, daughter, stepson, or stepdaughter (referred to in clause (ii)) has not attained age 18 or has a mental or physical condition which requires the personal care and supervision of an adult for at least 4 continuous weeks in the calendar quarter in which the service is rendered;

(4) Service performed by an individual on or in connection with a vessel not an American vessel, or on or in connection with an aircraft not an American aircraft, if (A) the individual is employed on and in connection with such vessel or aircraft when outside the United States and (B)(i) such individual is not a citizen of the United States or (ii) the employer is not an American employer;

(5) Service performed in the employ of the United States or any instrumentality of the United States, if such service—

(A) would be excluded from the term "employment" for purposes of this subchapter if the provisions of paragraphs (5) and (6) of this subsection as in effect in January 1983 had remained in effect, and

(B) is performed by an individual who—

(i) has been continuously performing service described in subparagraph (A) since December 31, 1983, and for purposes of this clause—

(I) if an individual performing service described in subparagraph (A) returns to the performance of such service after being separated therefrom for a period of less than 366 consecutive days, regardless of whether the period began before, on, or after December 31, 1983, then such service shall be considered continuous,

(II) if an individual performing service described in subparagraph (A) returns to the performance of such service after being detailed or transferred to an international organization as described under section 3343 of subchapter III of chapter 33 of Title 5 or under section 3581 of chapter 35 of such Title, then the service performed for that organization shall be considered service described in subparagraph (A),

(III) if an individual performing service described in subparagraph (A) is reemployed or reinstated after being separated from such service for the purpose of accepting employment with the American Institute of Taiwan as provided under section 3310 of Title 22, then the service performed for that Institute shall be considered service described in subparagraph (A),

(IV) if an individual performing service described in subparagraph (A) returns to the performance of such service after performing service as a member of a uniformed service (including, for purposes of this clause, service in the National Guard and temporary service in the Coast Guard Reserve) and after exercising restoration or reemployment rights as provided under chapter 43 of Title 38, then the service so performed as a member of a uniformed service shall be considered service described in subparagraph (A), and

(V) if an individual performing service described in subparagraph (A) returns to the performance of such service after employment (by a tribal organization) to which section 5323(e)(2) of Title 25 applies, then the service performed for that tribal organization shall be considered service described in subparagraph (A); or

(ii) is receiving an annuity from the Civil Service Retirement and Disability Fund, or benefits (for service as an employee) under another retirement system established by a law of the United States for employees of the Federal Government (other than for members of the uniformed services);

except that this paragraph shall not apply with respect to any such service performed on or after any date on which such individual performs—

(C) service performed as the President or Vice President of the United States,

(D) service performed—

(i) in a position placed in the Executive Schedule under sections 5312 through 5317 of Title 5,

(ii) as a noncareer appointee in the Senior Executive Service or a noncareer member of the Senior Foreign Service, or

(iii) in a position to which the individual is appointed by the President (or his designee) or the Vice President under section 105(a)(1), 106(a)(1), or 107(a)(1) or (b)(1) of Title 3, if the maximum rate of basic pay for such position is at or above the rate for level V of the Executive Schedule,

(E) service performed as the Chief Justice of the United States, an Associate Justice of the Supreme Court, a judge of a United States court of appeals, a judge of a United States district court (including the district court of a territory), a judge of the United States Court of Federal Claims, a judge of the United States Court of International Trade, a judge of the United States Tax Court, a United States magistrate judge, or a referee in bankruptcy or United States bankruptcy judge,

(F) service performed as a Member, Delegate, or Resident Commissioner of or to the Congress,

(G) any other service in the legislative branch of the Federal Government if such service—

(i) is performed by an individual who was not subject to subchapter III of chapter 83 of Title 5 or to another retirement system established by a law of the United States for employees of the Federal Government (other than for members of the uniformed services), on December 31, 1983, or

(ii) is performed by an individual who has, at any time after December 31, 1983, received a lump-sum payment under section 8342(a) of Title 5 or under the corresponding provision of the law establishing the other retirement system described in clause (i), or

(iii) is performed by an individual after such individual has otherwise ceased to be subject to subchapter III of chapter 83 of Title 5 (without having an application pending for coverage under such subchapter), while performing service in the legislative branch (determined without regard to the provisions of subparagraph (B) relating to continuity of employment), for any period of time after December 31, 1983,

and for purposes of this subparagraph (G) an individual is subject to such subchapter III or to any such other retirement system at any time only if (a) such individual's pay is subject to deductions, contributions, or similar payments (concurrent with the service being performed at that time) under section 8334(a) of such Title 5 or the corresponding provision of the law establishing such other system, or (in a case to which section 8332(k)(1) of such Title applies) such individual is making payments of amounts equivalent to such deductions, contributions, or similar payments while on leave without pay, or (b) such individual is receiving an annuity from the Civil Service Retirement and Disability Fund, or is receiving benefits (for service as an employee) under another retirement system established by a law of the United States for employees of the Federal Government (other than for members of the uniformed services), or

(H) service performed by an individual—

(i) on or after the effective date of an election by such individual, under section 301 of the Federal Employees' Retirement System Act of 1986, section 2157 of Title 50, or the Federal Employees' Retirement System Open Enrollment Act of 1997[1] to become subject to the Federal Employees' Retirement System provided in chapter 84 of Title 5, or

(ii) on or after the effective date of an election by such individual, under regulations issued under section 860 of the Foreign Service Act of 1980, to become subject to the Foreign Service Pension System provided in subchapter II of chapter 8 of title I of such Act;

(6) Service performed in the employ of the United States or any instrumentality of the United States if such service is performed—

(A) in a penal institution of the United States by an inmate thereof;

(B) by any individual as an employee included under section 5351(2) of Title 5 (relating to certain interns, student nurses, and other student employees of hospitals of the Federal Government), other than as a medical or dental intern or a medical or dental resident in training; or

(C) by any individual as an employee serving on a temporary basis in case of fire, storm, earthquake, flood, or other similar emergency;

(7) Service performed in the employ of a State, or any political subdivision thereof, or any instrumentality of any one or more of the foregoing which is wholly owned thereby, except that this paragraph shall not apply in the case of—

(A) service included under an agreement under section 418 of this title,

(B) service which, under subsection (k), constitutes covered transportation service,

(C) service in the employ of the Government of Guam or the Government of American Samoa or any political subdivision thereof, or of any instrumentality of any one or more of the foregoing which is wholly owned thereby, performed by an officer or employee thereof (including a member of the legislature of any such Government or political subdivision), and, for purposes of this subchapter—

(i) any person whose service as such an officer or employee is not covered by a retirement system established by a law of the United States shall not, with respect to such service, be regarded as an officer or employee of the United States or any agency or instrumentality thereof, and

(ii) the remuneration for service described in clause (i) (including fees paid to a public official) shall be deemed to have been paid by the Government of Guam or the Government of American Samoa or by a political subdivision thereof or an instrumentality of any one or more of the foregoing which is wholly owned thereby, whichever is appropriate,

(D) service performed in the employ of the District of Columbia or any instrumentality which is wholly owned thereby, if such service is not covered by a retirement system established by a law of the United States (other than the Federal Employees Retirement System provided in chapter 84 of Title 5); except that the provisions of this subparagraph shall not be applicable to service performed—

(i) in a hospital or penal institution by a patient or inmate thereof;

(ii) by any individual as an employee included under section 5351(2) of Title 5 (relating to certain interns, student nurses, and other student employees of hospitals of the District of Columbia Government), other than as a medical or dental intern or as a medical or dental resident in training;

(iii) by any individual as an employee serving on a temporary basis in case of fire, storm, snow, earthquake, flood, or other similar emergency; or

(iv) by a member of a board, committee, or council of the District of Columbia, paid on a per diem, meeting, or other fee basis,

(E) service performed in the employ of the Government of Guam (or any instrumentality which is wholly owned by such Government) by an employee properly classified as a temporary or intermittent employee, if such service is not covered by a retirement system established by a law of Guam; except that (i) the provisions of this subparagraph shall not be applicable to services performed by an elected official or a member of the legislature or in a hospital or penal institution by a patient or inmate thereof, and (ii) for purposes of this subparagraph, clauses (i) and (ii) of subparagraph (C) shall apply, or

(F) service in the employ of a State (other than the District of Columbia, Guam, or American Samoa), of any political subdivision thereof, or of any instrumentality of any one or more of the foregoing which is wholly owned thereby, by an individual who is not a member of a retirement system of such State, political subdivision, or instrumentality, except that the provisions of this subparagraph shall not be applicable to service performed—

(i) by an individual who is employed to relieve such individual from unemployment;

(ii) in a hospital, home, or other institution by a patient or inmate thereof;

(iii) by any individual as an employee serving on a temporary basis in case of fire, storm, snow, earthquake, flood, or other similar emergency;

(iv) by an election official or election worker if the remuneration paid in a calendar year for such service is less than $1,000 with respect to service performed during any calendar year commencing on or after January 1, 1995, ending on or before December 31, 1999, and the adjusted amount determined under section 418(c)(8)(B) of this title for any calendar year commencing on or after January 1, 2000, with respect to service performed during such calendar year; or

(v) by an employee in a position compensated solely on a fee basis which is treated pursuant to section 411(c)(2)(E) of this title as a trade or business for purposes of inclusion of such fees in net earnings from self employment;

for purposes of this subparagraph, except as provided in regulations prescribed by the Secretary of the Treasury, the term "retirement system" has the meaning given such term by section 418(b)(4) of this title;

(8)(A) Service performed by a duly ordained, commissioned, or licensed minister of a church in the exercise of his ministry or by a member of a religious order in the exercise of duties required by such order, except that this subparagraph shall not apply to service performed by a member of such an order in the exercise of such duties, if an election of coverage under section 3121(r) of the Internal Revenue Code of 1986 is in effect with respect to such order, or with respect to the autonomous subdivision thereof to which such member belongs;

(B) Service performed in the employ of a church or qualified church-controlled organization if such church or organization has in effect an election under section 3121(w) of the Internal Revenue Code of 1986, other than service in an unrelated trade or business (within the meaning of section 513(a) of such Code);

(9) Service performed by an individual as an employee or employee representative as defined in section 3231 of the Internal Revenue Code of 1986;

(10) Service performed in the employ of—

(A) a school, college, or university, or

(B) an organization described in section 509(a)(3) of the Internal Revenue Code of 1986 if the organization is organized, and at all times thereafter is operated, exclusively for the benefit of, to perform the functions of, or to carry out the purposes of a school, college, or university and is operated, supervised, or controlled by or in connection with such school, college, or university, unless it is a school, college, or university of a State or a political subdivision thereof and the services in its employ performed by a student referred to in section 418(c)(5) of this title are covered under the agreement between the Commissioner of Social Security and such State entered into pursuant to section 418 of this title;

if such service is performed by a student who is enrolled and regularly attending classes at such school, college, or university;

(11) Service performed in the employ of a foreign government (including service as a consular or other officer or employee or a nondiplomatic representative);

(12) Service performed in the employ of an instrumentality wholly owned by a foreign government—

(A) If the service is of a character similar to that performed in foreign countries by employees of the United States Government or of an instrumentality thereof; and

(B) If the Secretary of State shall certify to the Secretary of the Treasury that the foreign government, with respect to whose instrumentality and employees thereof exemption is claimed, grants an equivalent exemption with respect to similar service performed in the foreign country by employees of the United States Government and of instrumentalities thereof;

(13) Service performed as a student nurse in the employ of a hospital or a nurses' training school by an individual who is enrolled and is regularly attending classes in a nurses' training school chartered or approved pursuant to State law;

(14)(A) Service performed by an individual under the age of eighteen in the delivery or distribution of newspapers or shopping news, not including delivery or distribution to any point for subsequent delivery or distribution;

(B) Service performed by an individual in, and at the time of, the sale of newspapers or magazines to ultimate consumers, under an arrangement under which the newspapers or magazines are to be sold by him at a fixed price, his compensation being based on the retention of the excess of such price over the amount at which the newspapers or magazines are charged to him, whether or not he is guaranteed a minimum amount of compensation for such service, or is entitled to be credited with the unsold newspapers or magazines turned back;

(15) Service performed in the employ of an international organization entitled to enjoy privileges, exemptions, and immunities as an international organization under the International Organizations Immunities Act (59 Stat. 669), except service which constitutes "employment" under subsection (r);

(16) Service performed by an individual under an arrangement with the owner or tenant of land pursuant to which—

(A) such individual undertakes to produce agricultural or horticultural commodities (including livestock, bees, poultry, and fur-bearing animals and wildlife) on such land,

(B) the agricultural or horticultural commodities produced by such individual, or the proceeds therefrom, are to be divided between such individual and such owner or tenant, and

(C) the amount of such individual's share depends on the amount of the agricultural or horticultural commodities produced;

(17) Repealed. Pub.L. 113–295, Div. A, Title II, § 221(a)(99)(C)(ii), Dec. 19, 2014, 128 Stat. 4052

(18) Service performed in Guam by a resident of the Republic of the Philippines while in Guam on a temporary basis as a nonimmigrant alien admitted to Guam pursuant to section 1101(a)(15)(H)(ii) of Title 8;

(19) Service which is performed by a nonresident alien individual for the period he is temporarily present in the United States as a nonimmigrant under subparagraph (F), (J), (M), or (Q) of section 1101(a)(15) of Title 8, and which is performed to carry out the purpose specified in subparagraph (F), (J), (M), or (Q) as the case may be;

(20) Service (other than service described in paragraph (3)(A)) performed by an individual on a boat engaged in catching fish or other forms of aquatic animal life under an arrangement with the owner or operator of such boat pursuant to which—

(A) such individual does not receive any additional compensation other than as provided in subparagraph (B) and other than cash remuneration—

(i) which does not exceed $100 per trip;

(ii) which is contingent on a minimum catch; and

(iii) which is paid solely for additional duties (such as mate, engineer, or cook) for which additional cash remuneration is traditional in the industry,

(B) such individual receives a share of the boat's (or the boats' in the case of a fishing operation involving more than one boat) catch of fish or other forms of aquatic animal life or a share of the proceeds from the sale of such catch, and

(C) the amount of such individual's share depends on the amount of the boat's (or boats' in the case of a fishing operation involving more than one boat) catch of fish or other forms of aquatic animal life,

but only if the operating crew of such boat (or each boat from which the individual receives a share in the case of a fishing operation involving more than one boat) is normally made up of fewer than 10 individuals;

(21) Domestic service in a private home of the employer which—

(A) is performed in any year by an individual under the age of 18 during any portion of such year; and

(B) is not the principal occupation of such employee; or

(22) Service performed by members of Indian tribal councils as tribal council members in the employ of an Indian tribal government, except that this paragraph shall not apply in the case of service included under an agreement under section 418a of this title.

For purposes of paragraph (20), the operating crew of a boat shall be treated as normally made up of fewer than 10 individuals if the average size of the operating crew on trips made during the preceding 4 calendar quarters consisted of fewer than 10 individuals.

(b) Included and excluded service

If the services performed during one-half or more of any pay period by an employee for the person employing him constitute employment, all the services of such employee for such period shall be deemed to be employment; but if the services performed during more than one-half of any such pay period by an employee for the person employing him do not constitute employment, then none of the services of such employee for such period shall be deemed to be employment. As used in this subsection, the term "pay period" means a period (of not more than thirty-one consecutive days) for which a payment of remuneration is ordinarily made to the employee by the person employing him. This subsection shall not be applicable with respect to services performed in a pay period by an employee for the person employing him, where any of such service is excepted by paragraph (9) of subsection (a).

(c) American vessel

The term "American vessel" means any vessel documented or numbered under the laws of the United States; and includes any vessel which is neither documented or numbered under the laws of the United States nor documented under the laws of any foreign country, if its crew is employed solely by one or more citizens or residents of the United States or corporations organized under the laws of the United States or of any State.

(d) American aircraft

The term "American aircraft" means an aircraft registered under the laws of the United States.

(e) American employer

(1) The term "American employer" means an employer which is (A) the United States or any instrumentality thereof, (B) a State or any political subdivision thereof, or any instrumentality of any one or more of the foregoing, (C) an individual who is a resident of the United States, (D) a partnership, if two-thirds or more of the partners are residents of the United States, (E) a trust, if all of the trustees are residents of the United States, or (F) a corporation organized under the laws of the United States or of any State.

(2)(A) If any employee of a foreign person is performing services in connection with a contract between the United States Government (or any instrumentality thereof) and any member of any domestically controlled group of entities which includes such foreign person, such foreign person shall be treated as an American employer with respect to such services performed by such employee.

(B) For purposes of this paragraph—

(i) The term "domestically controlled group of entities" means a controlled group of entities the common parent of which is a domestic corporation.

(ii) The term "controlled group of entities" means a controlled group of corporations as defined in section 1563(a)(1) of the Internal Revenue Code of 1986, except that—

(I) "more than 50 percent" shall be substituted for "at least 80 percent" each place it appears therein, and

(II) the determination shall be made without regard to subsections (a)(4) and (b)(2) of section 1563 of such Code.

A partnership or any other entity (other than a corporation) shall be treated as a member of a controlled group of entities if such entity is controlled (within the meaning of section 954(d)(3) of such Code) by members of such group (including any entity treated as a member of such group by reason of this sentence).

(C) Subparagraph (A) shall not apply to any services to which paragraph (1) of section 3121(z) of the Internal Revenue Code of 1986 does not apply by reason of paragraph (4) of such section.

(f) Agricultural labor

The term "agricultural labor" includes all service performed—

(1) On a farm, in the employ of any person, in connection with cultivating the soil, or in connection with raising or harvesting any agricultural or horticultural commodity, including the raising, shearing, feeding, caring for, training, and management of livestock, bees, poultry, and fur-bearing animals and wildlife.

(2) In the employ of the owner or tenant or other operator of a farm, in connection with the operation, management, conservation, improvement, or maintenance of such farm and its tools and equipment, or in salvaging timber or clearing land of brush and other debris left by a hurricane, if the major part of such service is performed on a farm.

(3) In connection with the production or harvesting of any commodity defined as an agricultural commodity in section 1141j(g) of Title 12, or in connection with the ginning of cotton, or in connection with the operation or maintenance of ditches, canals, reservoirs, or waterways, not owned or operated for profit, used exclusively for supplying and storing water for farming purposes.

(4)(A) In the employ of the operator of a farm in handling, planting, drying, packing, packaging, processing, freezing, grading, storing, or delivering to storage or to market or to a carrier for transportation to market, in its unmanufactured state, any agricultural or horticultural commodity; but only if such operator produced more than one-half of the commodity with respect to which such service is performed.

(B) In the employ of a group of operators of farms (other than a cooperative organization) in the performance of service described in subparagraph (A) of this paragraph, but only if such operators produced all of the commodity with respect to which such service is performed. For the purposes of this subparagraph, any unincorporated group of operators shall be deemed a cooperative organization if the number of operators comprising such group is more than twenty at any time during the calendar year in which such service is performed.

(5) On a farm operated for profit if such service is not in the course of the employer's trade or business.

The provisions of subparagraphs (A) and (B) of paragraph (4) of this subsection shall not be deemed to be applicable with respect to service performed in connection with commercial canning or commercial freezing or in connection with any agricultural or horticultural commodity after its delivery to a terminal market for distribution for consumption.

(g) Farm

The term "farm" includes stock, dairy, poultry, fruit, fur-bearing animal, and truck farms, plantations, ranches, nurseries, ranges, greenhouses or other similar structures used primarily for the raising of agricultural or horticultural commodities, and orchards.

(h) State

The term "State" includes the District of Columbia, the Commonwealth of Puerto Rico, the Virgin Islands, Guam, and American Samoa.

(i) United States

The term "United States" when used in a geographical sense means the States, the District of Columbia, the Commonwealth of Puerto Rico, the Virgin Islands, Guam, and American Samoa.

(j) Employee

The term "employee" means—

(1) any officer of a corporation; or

(2) any individual who, under the usual common law rules applicable in determining the employer-employee relationship, has the status of an employee; or

(3) any individual (other than an individual who is an employee under paragraph (1) or (2) of this subsection) who performs services for remuneration for any person—

(A) as an agent-driver or commission-driver engaged in distributing meat products, vegetable products, fruit products, bakery products, beverages (other than milk), or laundry or dry-cleaning services, for his principal;

(B) as a full-time life insurance salesman;

(C) as a home worker performing work, according to specifications furnished by the person for whom the services are performed, on materials or goods furnished by such person which are required to be returned to such person or a person designated by him; or

(D) as a traveling or city salesman, other than as an agent-driver or commission-driver, engaged upon a full-time basis in the solicitation on behalf of, and the transmission to, his principal (except for side-line sales activities on behalf of some other person) of orders from wholesalers, retailers, contractors, or operators of hotels, restaurants, or other similar establishments for merchandise for resale or supplies for use in their business operations;

if the contract of service contemplates that substantially all of such services are to be performed personally by such individual; except that an individual shall not be included in the term "employee" under the provisions of this paragraph if such individual has a substantial investment in facilities used in connection with the performance of such services (other than in facilities for transportation), or if the services are in the nature of a single transaction not part of a continuing relationship with the person for whom the services are performed.

(k) Covered transportation service

(1) Except as provided in paragraph (2) of this subsection, all service performed in the employ of a State or political subdivision in connection with its operation of a public transportation system shall constitute covered transportation service if any part of the transportation system was acquired from private ownership after 1936 and prior to 1951.

(2) Service performed in the employ of a State or political subdivision in connection with the operation of its public transportation system shall not constitute covered transportation service if—

(A) any part of the transportation system was acquired from private ownership after 1936 and prior to 1951, and substantially all service in connection with the operation of the transportation system is, on December 31, 1950, covered under a general retirement system providing benefits which, by reason of a provision of the State constitution dealing specifically with retirement systems of the State or political subdivisions thereof, cannot be diminished or impaired; or

(B) no part of the transportation system operated by the State or political subdivision on December 31, 1950, was acquired from private ownership after 1936 and prior to 1951;

except that if such State or political subdivision makes an acquisition after 1950 from private ownership of any part of its transportation system, then, in the case of any employee who—

(C) became an employee of such State or political subdivision in connection with and at the time of its acquisition after 1950 of such part, and

(D) prior to such acquisition rendered service in employment in connection with the operation of such part of the transportation system acquired by the State or political subdivision,

the service of such employee in connection with the operation of the transportation system shall constitute covered transportation service, commencing with the first day of the third calendar quarter following the calendar quarter in which the acquisition of such part took place, unless on such first day such service of such employee is covered by a general retirement system which does not, with respect to such employee, contain special provisions applicable only to employees described in subparagraph (C) of this paragraph.

(3) All service performed in the employ of a State or political subdivision thereof in connection with its operation of a public transportation system shall constitute covered transportation service if the transportation system was not operated by the State or political subdivision prior to 1951 and, at the time of its first acquisition (after 1950) from private ownership of any part of its transportation system, the State or political subdivision did not have a general retirement system covering substantially all service performed in connection with the operation of the transportation system.

(4) For the purposes of this subsection—

(A) The term "general retirement system" means any pension, annuity, retirement, or similar fund or system established by a State or by a political subdivision thereof for employees of the State, political subdivision, or both; but such term shall not include such a fund or system which covers only service performed in positions connected with the operation of its public transportation system.

(B) A transportation system or a part thereof shall be considered to have been acquired by a State or political subdivision from private ownership if prior to the acquisition service performed by employees in connection with the operation of the system or part thereof acquired constituted employment under this subchapter, and some of such employees became employees of the State or political subdivision in connection with and at the time of such acquisition.

(C) The term "political subdivision" includes an instrumentality of (i) a State, (ii) one or more political subdivisions of a State, or (iii) a State and one or more of its political subdivisions.

(*l*) Service in uniformed services

(1) Except as provided in paragraph (4), the term "employment" shall, notwithstanding the provisions of subsection (a) of this section, include—

(A) service performed after December 1956 by an individual as a member of a uniformed service on active duty, but such term shall not include any such service which is performed while on leave without pay, and

(B) service performed after December 1987 by an individual as a member of a uniformed service on inactive duty training.

(2) The term "active duty" means "active duty" as described in paragraph (21) of section 101 of Title 38, except that it shall also include "active duty for training" as described in paragraph (22) of such section.

(3) The term "inactive duty training" means "inactive duty training" as described in paragraph (23) of such section 101.

(4)(A) Paragraph (1) of this subsection shall not apply in the case of any service, performed by an individual as a member of a uniformed service, which is creditable under section 231b(i) of Title 45. The Railroad Retirement Board shall notify the Commissioner of Social Security,[2] with respect to all such service which is so creditable.

(B) In any case where benefits under this subchapter are already payable on the basis of such individual's wages and self-employment income at the time such notification (with respect to such individual) is received by the Commissioner of Social Security, the Commissioner of Social Security shall certify no further benefits for payment under this subchapter on the basis of such individual's wages and self-employment income, or shall recompute the amount of any further benefits payable on the basis of such wages and self-employment income, as may be required as a consequence of subparagraph (A) of this paragraph. No payment of a benefit to any person on the basis of such individual's wages and self-employment income, certified by the Commissioner of Social Security prior to the end of the month in which the Commissioner receives such notification from the Railroad Retirement Board, shall be deemed by reason of this subparagraph to have been an erroneous payment or a payment to which such person was not entitled. The Commissioner of Social Security shall, as soon as possible after the receipt of such notification from the Railroad Retirement Board, advise such Board whether or not any such benefit will be reduced or terminated by reason of subparagraph (A) of this paragraph, and if any such benefit will be so reduced or terminated, specify the first month with respect to which such reduction or termination will be effective.

(m) Member of a uniformed service

The term "member of a uniformed service" means any person appointed, enlisted, or inducted in a component of the Army, Navy, Air Force, Marine Corps, or Coast Guard (including a reserve component as defined in section 101(27) of Title 38), or in one of those services without specification of component, or as a commissioned officer of the Coast and Geodetic Survey, the National Oceanic and Atmospheric Administration Corps, or the Regular or Reserve Corps of the Public Health Service, and any person serving in the Army or Air Force under call or conscription. The term includes—

(1) a retired member of any of those services;

(2) a member of the Fleet Reserve or Fleet Marine Corps Reserve;

(3) a cadet at the United States Military Academy, a midshipman at the United States Naval Academy, and a cadet at the United States Coast Guard Academy or United States Air Force Academy;

(4) a member of the Reserve Officers' Training Corps, the Naval Reserve Officers' Training Corps, or the Air Force Reserve Officers' Training Corps, when ordered to annual training duty for fourteen days or more, and while performing authorized travel to and from that duty; and

(5) any person while en route to or from, or at, a place for final acceptance or for entry upon active duty in the military, naval, or air service—

(A) who has been provisionally accepted for such duty; or

(B) who, under the Military Selective Service Act, has been selected for active military, naval, or air service;

and has been ordered or directed to proceed to such place.

The term does not include a temporary member of the Coast Guard Reserve.

(n) Crew leader

The term "crew leader" means an individual who furnishes individuals to perform agricultural labor for another person, if such individual pays (either on his own behalf or on behalf of such person) the individuals so furnished by him for the agricultural labor performed by them and if such individual has not entered into a written agreement with such person whereby such individual has been designated as an employee of such person; and such individuals furnished by the crew leader to perform agricultural labor for another person shall be deemed to be the employees of such crew leader. A crew leader shall, with respect to services performed in furnishing individuals to perform agricultural labor for another person and service performed as a member of the crew, be deemed not to be an employee of such other person.

(*o*) Peace Corps volunteer service

The term "employment" shall, notwithstanding the provisions of subsection (a), include service performed by an individual as a volunteer or volunteer leader within the meaning of the Peace Corps Act.

(p) Medicare qualified government employment

(1) For purposes of sections 426 and 426-1 of this title, the term "medicare qualified government employment" means any service which would constitute "employment" as defined in subsection (a) of this section but for the application of the provisions of—

(A) subsection (a)(5), or

(B) subsection (a)(7), except as provided in paragraphs (2) and (3).

(2) Service shall not be treated as employment by reason of paragraph (1)(B) if the service is performed—

(A) by an individual who is employed by a State or political subdivision thereof to relieve him from unemployment,

(B) in a hospital, home, or other institution by a patient or inmate thereof as an employee of a State or political subdivision thereof or of the District of Columbia,

(C) by an individual, as an employee of a State or political subdivision thereof or of the District of Columbia, serving on a temporary basis in case of fire, storm, snow, earthquake, flood or other similar emergency,

(D) by any individual as an employee included under section 5351(2) of Title 5 (relating to certain interns, student nurses, and other student employees of hospitals of the District of Columbia Government), other than as a medical or dental intern or a medical or dental resident in training, or

(E) by an election official or election worker if the remuneration paid in a calendar year for such service is less than $1,000 with respect to service performed during any calendar year commencing on or after January 1, 1995, ending on or before December 31, 1999, and the adjusted amount determined under section 418(c)(8)(B) of this title for any calendar year commencing on or after January 1, 2000, with respect to service performed during such calendar year.

As used in this paragraph, the terms "State" and "political subdivision" have the meanings given those terms in section 418(b) of this title.

(3) Service performed for an employer shall not be treated as employment by reason of paragraph (1)(B) if—

(A) such service would be excluded from the term "employment" for purposes of this section if paragraph (1)(B) did not apply;

(B) such service is performed by an individual—

(i) who was performing substantial and regular service for remuneration for that employer before April 1, 1986,

(ii) who is a bona fide employee of that employer on March 31, 1986, and

(iii) whose employment relationship with that employer was not entered into for purposes of meeting the requirements of this subparagraph; and

(C) the employment relationship with that employer has not been terminated after March 31, 1986.

(4) For purposes of paragraph (3), under regulations (consistent with regulations established under section 3121(u)(2)(D) of the Internal Revenue Code of 1986)—

(A) all agencies and instrumentalities of a State (as defined in section 418(b) of this title) or of the District of Columbia shall be treated as a single employer, and

(B) all agencies and instrumentalities of a political subdivision of a State (as so defined) shall be treated as a single employer and shall not be treated as described in subparagraph (A).

(q) Treatment of real estate agents and direct sellers

Notwithstanding any other provision of this subchapter, the rules of section 3508 of the Internal Revenue Code of 1986 shall apply for purposes of this subchapter.

(r) Service in employ of international organizations by certain transferred Federal employees

(1) For purposes of this subchapter, service performed in the employ of an international organization by an individual pursuant to a transfer of such individual to such international organization pursuant to section 3582 of Title 5 shall constitute "employment" if—

(A) immediately before such transfer, such individual performed service with a Federal agency which constituted "employment" as defined in subsection (a), and

(B) such individual would be entitled, upon separation from such international organization and proper application, to reemployment with such Federal agency under such section 3582.

(2) For purposes of this subsection:

(A) The term "Federal agency" means an agency, as defined in section 3581(1) of Title 5.

(B) The term "international organization" has the meaning provided such term by section 3581(3) of Title 5.

(Aug. 14, 1935, c. 531, Title II, § 210, as added Aug. 10, 1946, c. 951, Title II, § 201, 60 Stat. 979; amended Aug. 28, 1950, c. 809, Title I, § 104(a), 64 Stat. 494; Oct. 31, 1949, c. 792, Title V, § 506(a), formerly § 505(a), as added July 12, 1951, c. 223, 65 Stat. 120; renumbered Pub.L. 87–345, § 3, Oct. 3, 1961, 75 Stat. 761; amended Sept. 1, 1954, c. 1206, Title I, § 101(a)(4), (5), (b), (c)(1), (2), (e), (f), (m), 68 Stat. 1052, 1054, 1061; Aug. 1, 1956, c. 836, Title I, §§ 104(a), (b), (c)(1), 105(b), 121 (c), 70 Stat. 824, 828, 839; Aug. 1, 1956, c. 837, Title IV, § 402(a), 70 Stat. 870; Pub.L. 85–840, Title III, §§ 311(a), 312(a), Aug. 28, 1958, 72 Stat. 1035; Pub.L. 86–70, § 32(c)(2), June 25, 1959, 73 Stat. 149; Pub.L. 86–168, Title I, § 104(h), Title II, § 202(a), Aug. 18, 1959, 73 Stat. 387, 389; Pub.L. 86–624, § 30(c)(2), July 12, 1960, 74 Stat. 420; Pub.L. 86–778, Title I, §§ 103(c) to (f), (j)(2)(A), (B), 104(a), Sept. 13, 1960, 74 Stat. 936, 937, 942; Pub.L. 87–256, § 110(e)(2), Sept. 21, 1961, 75 Stat. 537; Pub.L. 87–293, Title II, § 202(b)(1), Sept. 22, 1961, 75 Stat. 626; Pub.L. 89–97, Title III, §§ 311(a)(3), (4), 317(a), July 30, 1965, 79 Stat. 380, 381, 388; Pub.L. 90–248, Title I, § 123(a), Title IV, § 403(a), Jan. 2, 1968, 81 Stat. 844, 931; Pub.L. 92–603, Title I, §§ 123(a)(1), 128(a), 129(a)(1), Oct. 30, 1972, 86 Stat. 1354, 1358, 1359; Pub.L. 93–445, Title III, § 311, Oct. 16, 1974, 88 Stat. 1359; Pub.L. 94–455, Title XII, § 1207(e)(2)(A), Oct. 4, 1976, 90 Stat. 1707; Pub.L. 94–563, § 1(a), Oct. 19, 1976, 90 Stat. 2655; Pub.L. 95–216, Title III, § 351(a)(1), (3)(B), Dec. 20, 1977, 91 Stat. 1549; Pub.L. 95–600, Title VII, § 703(j)(14)(C), Nov. 6, 1978, 92 Stat. 2942; Pub.L. 97–248, Title II, §§ 269(b), 278(b)(1), Sept. 3, 1982, 96 Stat. 552, 560; Pub.L. 97–448, Title III, § 309(b)(23), Jan. 12, 1983, 96 Stat. 2410; Pub.L. 98–21, Title I, §§ 101(a), 102(a), Title III, §§ 321(b), 322(a)(1), 323(a)(2), Apr. 20, 1983, 97 Stat. 67, 70, 118, 120, 121; Pub.L. 98–369, Div. B, Title VI, §§ 2601(a), 2603(a)(1), 2661(j), 2663(a)(7), (j)(3)(A)(i), July 18, 1984, 98 Stat. 1122, 1128, 1157, 1162, 1170; Pub.L. 99–221, § 3(b), Dec. 26, 1985, 99 Stat. 1735; Pub.L. 99–272, Title XIII, §§ 13205(b)(1), 13303(c)(2), Apr. 7, 1986, 100 Stat. 316, 327; Pub.L. 99–335, Title III, § 304(a), June 6, 1986, 100 Stat. 606; Pub.L. 99–514, Title XVIII, §§ 1883(a)(4), 1895(b)(18)(B), (19), Oct. 22, 1986, 100 Stat. 2916, 2935; Pub.L. 100–203, Title IX, §§ 9001(a)(1), 9004(a), 9005(a), 9023(a), Dec. 22, 1987, 101 Stat. 1330–286 to 1330–288, 1330–295; Pub.L. 100–647, Title I, § 1001(d)(2)(E), Title VIII, §§ 8015(b)(1), (c)(1), 8016(a)(4)(B), (C), Nov. 10, 1988, 102 Stat. 3351, 3791–3793; Pub.L. 101–239, Title X, § 10201(b)(1), Dec. 19, 1989, 103 Stat. 2472; Pub.L. 101–508, Title XI, § 11332(a), Nov. 5, 1990, 104 Stat. 1388–469; Pub.L. 101–650, Title III, § 321, Dec. 1, 1990, 104 Stat. 5117; Pub.L. 102–572, Title IX, § 902(b)(1), Oct. 29, 1992, 106 Stat. 4516; Pub.L. 103–178, Title II, § 204(d), Dec. 3, 1993, 107 Stat. 2033; Pub.L. 103–296, Title I, § 107(a)(4), Title III, §§ 303(a)(1), (b)(1), 319(b)(1), (3), 320(b), 321(a)(13), (c)(6)(C), (D), Aug. 15, 1994, 108 Stat. 1478, 1518, 1519, 1534, 1535, 1536, 1538; Pub.L. 103–387, § 2(a)(2)(B), Oct. 22, 1994, 108 Stat. 4072; Pub.L. 104–188, Title I, § 1116(a)(2), Aug. 20, 1996, 110 Stat. 1762; Pub.L. 105–61, Title VI, § 642(d)(1), Oct. 10, 1997, 111 Stat. 1319; Pub.L. 105–33, Title XI, § 11246(b)(2)(B), as added Pub.L. 105–277, Div. A, § 101(h) [Title VIII, § 802(a)(2)], Oct. 21, 1998, 112 Stat. 2681–480, 2681–532; Pub.L. 108–203, Title IV, § 423(c), Mar. 2, 2004, 118 Stat. 536; Pub.L. 109–280, Title VIII, § 854(c)(9), Aug. 17, 2006, 120 Stat. 1019; Pub.L. 110–245, Title III, § 302(b), June 17, 2008, 122 Stat. 1648; Pub.L. 110–458, Title I, § 108(k)(2), Dec. 23, 2008, 122 Stat. 5110; Pub.L. 113–295, Div. A, Title II, § 221(a)(99)(C)(ii), Dec. 19, 2014, 128 Stat. 4052; Pub.L. 115–243, § 2(b)(1), Sept. 20, 2018, 132 Stat. 2895.)

[1] So in original. Probably should be followed by a comma.

[2] So in original. Comma probably should not appear.

HISTORICAL AND STATUTORY NOTES

References in Text

The Internal Revenue Code of 1986, referred to in text, is classified to Title 26.

Section 5323(e)(2) of Title 25, referred to in subsec. (a)(5)(B)(i)(V), was in the original a reference to section 105(e)(2) of the Indian Self-Determination Act. Section 105 of that Act was renumbered section 104 by Pub.L. 100–472, Title II, § 203(a), Oct. 5, 1988, 102 Stat. 2290, without a corresponding amendment to this section. Section 104 of the Indian Self-Determination Act is classified to 25 U.S.C.A. § 5323. Section 105 of that Act is classified to 25 U.S.C.A. § 5324.

The Civil Service Retirement and Disability Fund, referred to in subsec. (a)(5)(B)(ii), (G), is provided for in 5 U.S.C.A. § 8348.

Section 301 of the Federal Employees' Retirement Act of 1986, referred to in subsec. (a)(5)(H)(i), is section 301 of Pub.L. 99–335, Title III, June 6, 1986, 100 Stat. 599, which is set out as a note under 5 U.S.C.A. § 8331.

The Federal Employees' Retirement System Open Enrollment Act, referred to in subsec. (a)(5)(H)(i), is Pub.L. 105–61, Title VI, § 642, Oct. 10, 1997, 111 Stat. 1318, which amended this section and 26 U.S.C.A. § 3121, and enacted provisions set out as a note under 5 U.S.C.A. § 8331. For complete classification, see Tables.

The Foreign Service Act of 1980, referred to in subsec. (a)(5)(H)(ii), is Pub.L. 96–465, Oct. 17, 1980, 94 Stat. 2071, as amended. Subchapter II of chapter 8 of title I of the Act is classified generally to part II of subchapter VIII of chapter 52 of Title 22, 22 U.S.C.A. § 4071 et seq. Section 860 of the Act is classified to 22 U.S.C.A. § 4071i. For complete classification, see Short Title note set out under 22 U.S.C.A. § 3901 and Tables.

Chapter 84 of Title 5, referred to in subsec. (a)(7)(D), is 5 U.S.C.A. § 8401 et seq.

The International Organizations Immunities Act, referred to in subsec. (a)(15), is Act Dec. 29, 1945, c. 652, Title I, 59 Stat. 669, as amended, which is classified principally to subchapter XVIII of chapter 7 of Title 22, 22 U.S.C.A. § 288 et seq. For complete classification, see Short Title note set out under 22 U.S.C.A. § 288 and Tables.

Section 1141j(g) of Title 12, referred to in subsec. (f)(3), was redesignated section 1141j(f) by Pub.L. 110–246, Title I, § 1610, June 18, 2008, 122 Stat. 1746.

The Military Selective Service Act, referred to in subsec. (m)(5)(B), is Act June 24, 1948, c. 625, 62 Stat. 604, as amended, which is classified principally to chapter 49 of Title 50, 50 U.S.C.A. § 3801 et seq. For complete classification, see Tables.

The Peace Corps Act, referred to in subsec. (*o*), is Pub.L. 87–293, Sept. 22, 1961, 75 Stat. 612, which is classified principally to chapter 34 of Title 22, 22 U.S.C.A. § 2501 et seq. For complete classification, see Short Title note set out under 22 U.S.C.A. § 2501 and Tables.

Codifications

Pub.L. 105–277, § 101(h) [Title VIII, § 802(a)(1)], amended Pub.L. 105–33, § 11246(b), by redesignating par. (2) thereof, which was not classified to the Code, as par. (3).

Pub.L.105–61, Title VI, § 642(d)(1), Oct. 10, 1997, 111 Stat. 1319, amending subsec. (a)(5)(H)(i) of this section, was the subject of a line item veto contained in Cancellation No. 97–56, dated Oct. 16, 1997. The United States Supreme Court, in Clinton v. City of New York, U.S.Dist.Col.1998, 118 S.Ct. 2091, found that the Line Item Veto Act of 1996, Pub.L. 104–130, April 9, 1996, 110 Stat. 1200, which is classified generally to Subchapter III of Chapter 17B (section 691 et seq.) of Title 2 was unconstitutional as a violation of the Presentment Clause of the United States Constitution (U.S.C.A. Const. Art. I, § 7, cl. 2).

"Section 101 of Title 38" was substituted for "section 102 of the Servicemen's and Veterans' Survivor Benefits Act" and for "such section 102" in subsec. (*l*)(2) and (3), respectively, and "section 101(27) of Title 38" was substituted for "section 102(3) of the Servicemen's and Veterans' Survivor Benefits Act" in subsec. (m) on authority of section 5(a) of Pub.L. 85–857, Sept. 2, 1958, 72 Stat. 1261, section 1 of which enacted Title 38, Veterans' Benefits.

Effective and Applicability Provisions

2014 Acts. For effective date and savings provisions of amendments made by Pub.L. 113–295, Div. A, Title II, § 221, which, except as otherwise provided, shall take effect on Dec. 19, 2014, see Pub.L. 113–295, Div. A, Title II, § 221(b), set out as a note under 26 U.S.C.A. § 1.

2008 Acts. Except as otherwise provided in §§ 101 to 111 of Pub.L. 110–458, amendments by §§ 101 to 111 of Pub.L. 110–458 shall take effect as if included in the provisions of Pub.L. 109–280 to which the amendments relate, see Pub.L. 110-458, § 112, set out as a note under 26 U.S.C.A. § 72.

Amendments by Pub.L. 110–245, § 302 applicable to services performed in calendar months beginning more than 30 days after June 17, 2008, see Pub.L. 110–245, § 302(c), set out as a note under 26 U.S.C.A. § 3121.

1998 Acts. Pub.L. 105–277, Div. A, § 101(h) [Title VIII, § 805], provided that except as otherwise specifically provided, amendments to this section by section 802 of Pub.L. 105–277 shall take effect as if included in the enactment of Title XI of the Balanced Budget Act of 1997 [Title XI of Pub.L. 105–33, Aug. 5, 1997, 111 Stat. 251, 712. For complete classification of Pub.L. 105–33 to the Code, see Tables]. See section 805 of Pub.L. 105–277, set out as a note under section 3121 of Title 26.

1997 Acts. Amendment by Pub.L. 105–33 applicable with respect to all months beginning after the date on which the Director of the Office of Personnel Management issues regulations to carry out section 11–1726, District of Columbia Code, see section 11246(b)(4) of Pub.L. 105–33, set out as a note under 26 U.S.C.A. § 3121.

1996 Acts. Amendments by section 1116 of Pub.L. 104–188 applicable to remuneration paid after Dec. 31, 1994, and after Dec. 31, 1984, and before Jan. 1, 1995, unless the payor treated such remuneration (when paid) as being subject to tax under chapter 21 (section 3101 et seq.) of Title 26, Internal Revenue Code, see section 1116(a)(3) of Pub.L. 104–188, set out as a note under section 3121 of Title 26.

1994 Acts. Amendment by Pub.L. 103–387 applicable to services performed after December 31, 1994, see section 2(a)(3)(B) of Pub.L. 103–387, set out as a note under section 3102 of Title 26, Internal Revenue Code.

Amendment by section 107(a)(4) of Pub.L. 103–296 effective Mar. 31, 1995, see section 110 of Pub.L. 103–296, set out as a note under section 401 of this title.

Section 303(e) of Pub.L. 103–296 provided that: "The amendments made by subsections (a), (b), and (c) [amending subsecs. (a)(7)(F)(iv) and (p)(2)(E) of this section, section 418 of this title, and section 3121 of Title 26, Internal Revenue Code] shall apply with respect to service performed on or after January 1, 1995."

Enactment of subsec. (r) and amendment of subsec. (a)(15) of this section by section 319(b)(1), (3) of Pub.L. 103–296 applicable with respect to service performed after the calendar quarter following the calendar quarter in which Aug. 15, 1994, occurs, see section 319(c) of Pub.L. 103–296, set out as a note under section 1402 of Title 26, Internal Revenue Code.

Amendment of subsec. (a)(19) of this section by section 320(b) of Pub.L. 103–296 effective with the calendar quarter following Aug. 15, 1994, see section 320(c) of Pub.L. 103–296, set out as a note under section 871 of Title 26.

1992 Acts. Amendment by Title IX of Pub.L. 102–572 effective Oct. 29, 1992, see section 911 of Pub.L. 102–572, set out as a note under section 171 of Title 28, Judiciary and Judicial Procedure.

1990 Acts. Amendment by section 11332 of Pub.L. 101–508 applicable with respect to service performed after July 1, 1991, see section 11332(d) of Pub.L. 101–508, set out as a note under section 3121 of Title 26, Internal Revenue Code.

1989 Acts. Amendment by section 10201 of Pub.L. 101–239 applicable to any agreement in effect under section 3121(*l*) of Title 26 on or after June 15, 1989, with respect to which no notice of termination is in effect on such date, see section 10201(c) of Pub.L. 101–239, set out as a note under section 406 of Title 26, Internal Revenue Code.

1988 Acts. Amendment by section 1001(d)(2)(E) of Pub.L. 100–647 effective, except as otherwise provided, as if included in the provision of the Tax Reform Act of 1986, Pub.L. 99–514, to which such amendment relates, see section 1019(a) of Pub.L. 100–647, set out as a note under section 1 of Title 26, Internal Revenue Code.

Amendment by section 8015(b)(1) of Pub.L. 100–647 applicable as if such amendment had been included or reflected in section 304 of Federal Employees' Retirement System Act of 1986, Pub.L. 99–335, at the time of its enactment (June 6, 1986), see section 8015(b)(3) of Pub.L. 100–647, set out as a note under section 3121 of Title 26.

Amendment by section 8015(c)(1) of Pub.L. 100–647 applicable to any individual only upon the performance by such individual of service described in subpar. (C), (D), (E), (F), (G), or (H) of subsec. (a)(5) of this section on or after Nov. 10, 1988, see section 8015(c)(3) of Pub.L. 100–647, set out as a note under section 3121 of Title 26.

Amendment by section 8016(a)(4)(B), (C) of Pub.L. 100–647 effective Nov. 10, 1988, except that any amendment to a provision of a particular Public Law which is referred to by its number, or to a provision of the Social Security Act [42 U.S.C. 301 et seq.], or to Title 26, as added or amended by a provision of a particular Public Law which is so referred to, effective as though included or reflected in the relevant provisions of that Public Law at the time of its enactment, see section 8016(b) of Pub.L. 100–647, set out as a note under section 3111 of Title 26.

1987 Acts. Amendment of subsec. (e)(i) by section 9001(a)(1) of Pub.L. 100–203 applicable with respect to remuneration paid after Dec. 31, 1987, see section 9001(d) of Pub.L. 100–203, set out as a note under section 3121 of Title 26, Internal Revenue Code.

Amendment of subsec. (a)(3)(A), (B) by section 9004(a)(1), (2) of Pub.L. 100–203 applicable with respect to remuneration paid after Dec. 31, 1987, see section 9004(c) of Pub.L. 100–203, set out as a note under section 3121 of Title 26, Internal Revenue Code.

Amendment of subsec. (a)(3)(A), (B) by section 9005(a)(1), (2) of Pub.L. 100–203 applicable with respect to remuneration paid after Dec. 31, 1987, see section 9005(c) of Pub.L. 100–203, set out as a note under section 3121 of Title 26, Internal Revenue Code.

1986 Acts. Amendment by section 1883(a)(4) of Pub.L. 99–514 effective Oct. 22, 1986, see section 1883(f) of Pub.L. 99–514, set out as a note under section 402 of this title.

Amendment by section 1895(b)(19) of Pub.L. 99–514 to be effective, unless otherwise provided, as if included in the enactment of the Consolidated Omnibus Budget Reconciliation Act of 1985, Pub.L. 99–272, which was approved Apr. 7, 1986, see section 1895(e) of Pub.L. 99–514, set out as a note under section 162 of Title 26, Internal Revenue Code.

Amendment to subsec. (p)(2) by section 1895(b)(18)(B) of Pub.L. 99–514 to apply to services performed after Mar. 31, 1986, see section 1895(b)(18)(C) of Pub.L. 99–514, set out as a note under section 3121 of Title 26, Internal Revenue Code.

Section 13205(d)(2) of Pub.L. 99–272 provided that:

"(A) In general.—The amendments made by subsection (b) [amending this section and sections 426, 426–1, and 1395c of this title] shall be effective after March 31, 1986, and the amendments made by paragraph (3) of that subsection [subsection does not contain a paragraph (3)] shall apply to services performed (for medicare qualified government employment) after that date.

"(B) Treatment of certain disabilities.—For purposes of establishing entitlement to hospital insurance benefits under part A of title XVIII of the Social Security Act [section 1395c et seq. of this title] pursuant to the amendments made by subsection (b), no individual may be considered to be under a disability for any period beginning before April 1, 1986."

1985 Acts. Section 3(c) of Pub.L. 99–221 provided that: "The amendments made by subsection (b) [enacting subsec. (a)(5)(B)(i)(V) of this section and section 3121(b)(5)(B)(i)(V) of Title 26, Internal Revenue Code] apply to any return to the performance of service in the employ of the United States, or of an instrumentality thereof, after 1983."

1984 Acts. Section 2601(f) of Pub.L. 98–369 provided that: "Except as provided in subsection (d) [set out as a note under this section], the amendments made by subsections (a) and (b) [amending subsec. (a)(5) of this section and section 3121(b)(5) of Title 26, Internal Revenue Code] (and the provisions of subsection (e) [set out as a note under this section] shall be effective with respect to service performed after December 31, 1983."

Section 2603(e) of Pub.L. 98–369 provided that: "The amendments made by this section [enacting subsec. (a)(8)(B) of this section, section 411(a)(13) and (c)(2)(G) of this title, and 1402(a)(14) and (c)(2)(G) and 3121(b)(8)(B) and (w) of Title 26, Internal Revenue Code] shall apply to service performed after December 31, 1983."

Amendment to subsec. (a) by section 2661(j) of Pub.L. 98–369 effective as though included in the enactment of the Social Security Amendments of 1983 [Pub.L. 98–21], see section 2664(a) of Pub.L. 98–369, set out as a note under section 401 of this title.

Amendment to subsecs. (a)(1), (7)(D), (9), (10), (19), (*l*), and (m) by section 2663 (a)(7), (j)(3)(A)(i) of Pub.L. 98–369 effective July 18, 1984, but not to be construed as changing or affecting any right, liability, status or interpretation which existed (under the provisions of law involved) before that date, see section 2664(b) of Pub.L. 98–369, set out as a note under section 401 of this title.

Amendment by section 102(a) of Pub.L. 98–21 effective with respect to service performed after Dec. 31, 1983, see section 102(c) of Pub.L. 98–21, set out as a note under section 3121 of Title 26.

Amendment by section 321(b) of Pub.L. 98–21 applicable to agreements entered into after Apr. 20, 1983, except that at the election of any American employer such amendment shall also apply to any agreement entered into on or before Apr. 20, 1983, see section 321(f) of Pub.L. 98–21, set out as a note under section 406 of Title 26.

Amendment by section 322(a)(1) of Pub.L. 98–21 effective in taxable years beginning on or after Apr. 20, 1983, see section 322(c) of Pub.L. 98–21, set out as a note under section 3121 of Title 26.

Amendment by section 323(a)(2) of Pub.L. 98–21 applicable to remuneration paid after Dec. 31, 1983, see section 323(c)(1) of Pub.L. 98–21, set out as a note under section 3121 of Title 26.

1983 Acts. Amendment by section 101(a) of Pub.L. 98–21 effective with respect to service performed after Dec. 31, 1983, see section 101(d) of Pub.L. 98–21, as amended, set out as a note under section 3121 of Title 26, Internal Revenue Code.

1982 Acts. Amendment by section 269(6) of Pub.L. 97–248 applicable to services performed after Dec. 31, 1982, see section 269(e)(1) of Pub.L. 97–248, set out as a note under section 3508 of Title 26, Internal Revenue Code.

Enactment of subsec. (p) by section 278(b)(1) of Pub.L. 97–248 effective on and after Jan. 1, 1983, see section 278(c)(2)(A) of Pub.L. 97–248, set out as a note under section 426 of this title.

1978 Acts. Amendment by Pub.L. 95–600 effective Oct. 4, 1976, see section 703(r) of Pub.L. 95–600, set out as a note under section 46 of Title 26, Internal Revenue Code.

1977 Acts. Amendment by Pub.L. 95–216 applicable with respect to remuneration paid and services rendered after Dec. 31, 1977, see section 351(d) of Pub.L. 95–216, set out as a note under section 409 of this title.

1976 Acts. Amendment by Pub.L. 94–563 applicable with respect to services performed after 1950, to the extent covered by waiver certificates filed or deemed to have been filed under section 3121(k)(4) or (5) of Title 26, see section 1(d) of Pub.L. 94–563, set out as a note under section 3121 of Title 26, Internal Revenue Code.

1974 Acts. Amendment by Pub.L. 93–445 effective Jan. 1, 1975, see section 603 of Pub.L. 93–445, set out as a note under section 402 of this title.

1972 Acts. Section 128(c) of Pub.L. 92–603 provided that: "The amendments made by this section [enacting subsec. (a)(7)(E) of this section and section 3121(b)(7)(D) of Title 26] shall apply with respect to service performed on and after the first day of the first calendar quarter which begins on or after the date of the enactment of this Act [Oct. 30, 1972]."

Section 129(b) of Pub.L. 92–603 provided that: "The amendments made by subsection (a) [amending subsec. (a)(10)(B) of this section and section 3121(b)(10)(B) of Title 26] shall apply to services performed after December 31, 1972."

1968 Acts. Section 123(c) of Pub.L. 90–248 provided that: "The amendments made by this section [to subsec. (a)(3)(B) of this section and section 3121(b)(3)(B) of Title 26, Internal Revenue Code] shall apply with respect to services performed after December 31, 1967."

1965 Acts. Section 311(c) of Pub.L. 89–97 provided that: "The amendments made by paragraphs (1) and (2) of subsection (a) [to section 411(c) of this title], and by paragraphs (1), (2), and (3) of subsection (b) [to section 1402(c), (e)(1), (e)(2)(A) of Title 26], shall apply only with respect to taxable years ending on or after December 31, 1965. The amendments made by paragraphs (3) and (4) of subsection (a) [to subsec. (a)(6)(C)(iv) and (a)(13) of this section], and by paragraphs (4) and (5) of subsection (b) [to section 3121(b)(6)(C)(iv), (b)(13) of Title 26], shall apply only with respect to services performed after 1965."

Section 317(g) of Pub.L. 89–97 provided that: "The amendments made by this section [to subsec. (a)(7) of this section and sections 3121(b)(7), 3125, 6205(a)(4) and 6413(a)(4), (c)(2) of Title 26, Internal Revenue Code] shall apply with respect to service performed after the calendar quarter in which this section is enacted [quarter ending Sept. 30, 1965] and after the calendar quarter in which the Secretary of the Treasury receives a certification from the Commissioners of the District of Columbia expressing their desire to have the insurance system established by Title II (and part A of Title XVIII) of the Social Security Act [this subchapter and part A of subchapter XVIII of this chapter] extended to the officers and employees coming under the provisions of such amendments."

1961 Acts. Amendment by Pub.L. 87–293 applicable with respect to service performed after Sept. 22, 1961, but in the case of persons serving under the Peace Corps agency established by executive order applicable with respect to service performed on or after the effective date of enrollment, see section 202(c) of Pub.L. 87–293, set out as a note under section 3121 of Title 26, Internal Revenue Code.

Amendment by Pub.L. 87–256 applicable with respect to service performed after Dec. 31, 1961, see section 110(h)(3) of Pub.L. 87–256, set out as a note under section 3121 of Title 26.

1960 Acts. Section 104(c) of Pub.L. 86–778 provided that: "The amendments made by subsections (a) and (b) [to subsec. (a)(3) of this section and section 3121(b)(3) of Title 26, Internal Revenue Code] shall apply only with respect to services performed after 1960."

Amendment of subsec. (a)(7) by Pub.L. 86–778 applicable only with respect to (1) service in the employ of the Government of Guam or any political subdivision thereof, or any instrumentality of any one or more of the foregoing wholly owned thereby, which is performed after 1960 and after the calendar quarter in which the Secretary of the Treasury receives a certification by the Governor of Guam that legislation has been enacted by the Government of Guam expressing its desire to have the insurance system established by this subchapter extended to the officers and employees of such Government and such political subdivisions and instrumentalities, and (2) service in the employ of the Government of American Samoa or any political subdivision thereof or any instrumentality of any one or more of the foregoing wholly owned thereby, which is performed after 1960 and after the calendar quarter in which the Secretary of the Treasury receives a certification by the Governor of American Samoa that the Government of American Samoa desires to have the insurance system established by this subchapter extended to the officers and employees of such Government and such political subdivisions and instrumentalities, see section 103(v)(1), (2) of Pub.L. 86–778, set out as a note under section 402 of this title.

Subsec. (a)(18) of this section applicable only with respect to service performed after 1960, see section 103(v)(1) of Pub.L. 86–778, set out as a note under section 402 of this title.

Amendment of subsecs. (h) and (i) by Pub.L. 86–778 applicable only with respect to service performed after 1960, except that insofar as the carrying on of a trade or business (other than performance of service as an employee) is concerned, the amendment shall be applicable only in the case of taxable years beginning after 1960, with exception relating to Puerto Rico, see section 103(v)(1), (3), of Pub.L. 86–778, set out as a note under section 402 of this title.

Amendment of subsecs. (h) and (i) by Pub.L. 86–624 effective Aug. 21, 1959, see section 47(f) of Pub.L. 86–624, set out as a note under section 645 of Title 20, Education.

Repeal of former subsec. (j) and redesignation of subsecs. (k) to (*o*) of this section as subsecs. (j) to (n) by Pub.L. 86–778 effective Sept. 13, 1960, with exception relating to Puerto Rico, see section 103(v)(1), (3) of Pub.L. 86–778, set out as a note under section 402 of this title.

1959 Acts. Amendment by Pub.L. 86–168 effective Jan. 1, 1960, see section 203(c) of Pub.L. 86–168.

Amendment by Pub.L. 86–70 effective Jan. 3, 1959, see section 47(d) of Pub.L. 86–70.

1958 Acts. Section 311(b) of Pub.L. 85–840 provided that: "The amendment made by subsection (a) [to subsec. (a)(1) of this section] shall apply with respect to service performed after 1958."

Section 312(b) of Pub.L. 85–840 provided that: "The amendment made by subsection (a) [to subsec. (a)(8)(B) of this section] shall apply with respect to certificates filed under section 3121(k)(1) of the Internal Revenue Code of 1954 [section 312(k)(1) of Title 26, Internal Revenue Code] after the date of enactment of this Act [Aug. 28, 1958]."

1956 Acts. Section 104(i) of Act Aug. 1, 1956, c. 836, as amended by Pub.L. 92–603, Title I, § 125(b), Oct. 30, 1972, 86 Stat. 1357, provided that:

"**(1)** The amendment made by subsection (a) [to subsec. (a)(1)(B) of this section] shall apply with respect to service performed after 1956. The amendments made by paragraph (1) of subsection (c) [to subsec. (a)(16) of this section] shall apply with respect to service performed after 1954. The amendment made by paragraph (2) of subsection (c) [to section 411(a)(1) of this title] shall apply with respect to taxable years ending after 1955. The amendment made by paragraph (3) of subsection (c) [to section 411(c)(2) of this title] shall apply with respect to taxable years ending after 1954. The amendment made by subsection (d) [to section 411(c)(5) of this title] shall apply with respect to taxable years ending after 1955. The amendment made by subsection (h) [to section 411(a)(7)(B) of this title] shall apply with respect to the same taxable years with respect to which the amendment made by section 201(g) of this Act [to section 1402(a)(8)(B) of Title 26] applies.

"**(2)(A)** Except as provided in subparagraphs (B) and (C), the amendments made by subsection (b) [to subsec. (a)(6)(B)(ii) and (a)(6)(C)(vi) of this section] shall apply only with respect to service performed after June 30, 1957, and only if—

"**(i)** [Repealed. Pub.L. 92–603, Title I, § 125(b), Oct. 30, 1972, 86 Stat. 1357]

"**(ii)** in the case of the amendment made by paragraph (2) of such subsection [to subsec. (a)(6)(C)(vi) of this section], the conditions prescribed in subparagraph (C) are met.

"**(B)** [Repealed. Pub.L. 92–603, Title I, § 125(b), Oct. 30, 1972, 86 Stat. 1357]

"**(C)** The amendment made by paragraph (2) of subsection (b) [to subsec. (a)(6)(C)(vi) of this section] shall be effective only if—

"**(i)** the Board of Directors of the Tennessee Valley Authority submits to the Secretary of Health, Education, and Welfare, and the Secretary approves, before July 1, 1957, a plan, with respect to employees of the Tennessee Valley Authority, for the coordination, on an equitable basis, of the benefits provided by the retirement system applicable to such employees with the benefits provided by Title II of the Social Security Act [this subchapter]; and

"**(ii)** such plan specifies, as the effective date of the plan, July 1, 1957, or the first day of a prior calendar quarter beginning not earlier than January 1, 1956. If the plan specifies as the effective date of the plan a day before July 1, 1957, the amendment made by paragraph (2) of subsection (b) [to subsec. (a)(6)(C)(vi) of this section] shall apply with respect to service performed on or after such effective date; except that, if such effective date is prior to the day on which the Secretary approves the plan, such amendment shall not apply with respect to service performed, prior to the day on which the Secretary approves the plan, by an individual who is not an employee of the Tennessee Valley Authority on such day.

"**(D)** The Secretary of Health, Education, and Welfare shall, on or before July 31, 1957, submit a report to the Congress setting forth the details of any plan approved by him under subparagraph (B) or (C)."

Subsecs. (m) and (n) effective Jan. 1, 1957, see section 603(a) of Act Aug. 1, 1956, c. 837.

Subsec. (*o*) of this section, added by section 105(b) of Act Aug. 1, 1956, c. 836, as applicable with respect to service performed after 1956, see section 105(d) of Act Aug. 1, 1956, set out as a note under section 409 of this title.

1954 Acts. Section 101(n) of Act Sept. 1, 1954 provided in part that the amendments to subsec. (a) by section 101(a)(4), (5) of Act Sept. 1, 1954 shall be applicable only with respect to services (whether performed after 1954 or prior to 1955) for which the remuneration is paid after 1954, see section 101(n) of Act Sept. 1, 1954, set out as a note under section 405 of this title.

Section 101(n) of Act Sept. 1, 1954 provided in part that the amendments to subsecs. (a)(4), (6)(B) and (C), (14) and (15), and (k)(3)(C) made by section 101(b), (c)(1) and (2), (e) and (f) of Act Sept. 1, 1954 shall be applicable only with respect to services performed after 1954, see section 101(n) of Act Sept. 1, 1954, set out as a note under section 405 of this title.

1950 Acts. Section as added by section 104(a) effective Jan. 1, 1951, see note set out under section 409 of this title. Section 410 was stricken out effective Sept. 1, 1950 by section 105 of Act Aug. 28, 1950.

Change of Name

"United States magistrate judge" substituted for "United States magistrate" in text pursuant to section 321 of Pub.L. 101–650, set out as a note under 28 U.S.C.A. § 631.

"Secretary of Health and Human Services" was substituted for "Secretary of Health, Education, and Welfare" in subsecs. (a)(10)(B) and (*l*)(4)(A), pursuant to section 509(b) of Pub.L. 96–88, which is classified to section 3508(b) of Title 20, Education.

The Coast and Geodetic Survey was consolidated with the National Weather Bureau in 1965 to form the Environmental Science Services Administration by Reorg. Plan No. 2, of 1965, eff. July 13, 1965, 30 F.R. 8819, 79 Stat. 1318, set out in the Appendix to Title 5, Government Organization and Employees. The Commissioned Officer Corps of the Environmental Science Services Administration was changed to the Commissioned Officer Corps of the National Oceanic and Atmospheric Administration, see Reorg. Plan No. 4 of 1970, § 4(d), eff. Oct. 3, 1970, 35 F.R. 15627, 84 Stat. 2090, set out in Appendix 1 to Title 5.

Transfer of Functions

For transfer of authorities, functions, personnel, and assets of the Coast Guard, including the authorities and functions of the Secretary of Transportation relating thereto, to the Department of Homeland Security, and for treatment of related references, see 6 U.S.C.A. §§ 468(b), 551(d), 552(d) and 557, and the Department of Homeland Security Reorganization Plan of November 25, 2002, as modified, set out as a note under 6 U.S.C.A. § 542.

Rules of Construction

Nothing in Pub.L. 115–243, or the amendments made by that Act, shall be construed to affect application of any Federal income tax withholding requirements under Title 26, see Pub.L. 115–243, § 2(c), set out as a note under 26 U.S.C.A. § 3121.

Line Item Veto

Section 642(d)(1) of Pub.L. 105–61, amending this section, was subject to line item veto by the President, Cancellation No. 97–56, signed Oct. 16, 1997, 62 F.R. 54338, Oct. 17, 1997. For decision holding line item veto unconstitutional, see Clinton v. City of New York, 524 U.S. 417, 118 S.Ct. 2091, 141 L.Ed.2d 393 (1998).

Repeal of Law; Amendments and Application of Amendments Unaffected

Section 202(b)(1) of Pub.L. 87–293, cited as a credit to this section, was repealed by Pub.L. 89–572, § 5(a), Sept. 13, 1966, 80 Stat. 765. Such repeal not deemed to affect amendments to this section contained in such provisions, and continuation in full force and effect until modified by appropriate authority of all determinations, authorization, regulations, orders, contracts, agreements, and other actions issued, undertaken, or entered into under authority of the repealed provisions, see section 5(b) of Pub.L. 89–572, set out as a note under former section 2515 of Title 22, Foreign Relations and Intercourse.

Accrued Federal Retirement Entitlements; Reduction Prohibited

Section 101(e) of Pub.L. 98–21 provided that: "Nothing in this Act [see Short Title of 1983 Amendment note under section 1305 of this title] shall reduce the accrued entitlements to future benefits under the Federal Retirement System of current and retired Federal employees and their families."

Coverage of Federal Home Loan Bank Employees

Section 125(a) of Pub.L. 92–603 provided that: "The provisions of section 210(a)(6)(B)(ii) of the Social Security Act [subsec. (a)(6)(B)(ii) of this section] and section 3121(b)(6)(B)(ii) of the Internal Revenue Code of 1954 [section 3121(b)(6)(B)(ii) of Title 26, Internal Revenue Code], insofar as they relate to service performed in the employ of a Federal home loan bank, shall be effective—

"(1) with respect to all service performed in the employ of a Federal home loan bank on and after the first day of the first calendar quarter which begins on or after the date of the enactment of this Act [Oct. 30, 1972]; and

"(2) in the case of individuals who are in the employ of a Federal home loan bank on such first day, with respect to any service performed in the employ of a Federal home loan bank after the last day of the sixth calendar year preceding the year in which this Act is enacted [1972]; but this paragraph shall be effective only if an amount equal to the taxes imposed by sections 3101 and 3111 of such Code [sections 3101 and 3111 of Title 26, Internal Revenue Code] with respect to the services of all such individuals performed in the employ of Federal home loan banks after the last day of the sixth calendar year preceding the year in which this Act is enacted [1972] are paid under the provisions of section 3122 of such Code [section 3122 of Title 26] by July 1, 1973, or by such later date as may be provided in an agreement entered into before such date with the Secretary of the Treasury or his delegate for purposes of this paragraph."

Covered Employment Not Counted Under Other Federal Retirement Systems

Section 115 of Act Sept. 1, 1954, which prohibited counting employment under other Federal retirement systems in determining eligibility for benefits under this subchapter, was repealed by Pub.L. 91–630, § 1, Dec. 31, 1970, 84 Stat. 1875. Section 2 of Pub.L. 91–630 provided that such repeal shall not apply in the case of a person who, on Dec. 31, 1970, is receiving or is entitled to receive benefits under any retirement system established by the United States or any instrumentality thereof unless he requests, in writing, the office which administers his retirement system to apply it in his case, and that any additional benefits payable pursuant to such request shall commence on January 1, 1971.

Federal Legislative Branch Employees Who Contribute Reduced Amounts by Reason of Federal Employees' Retirement Contribution Temporary Adjustment Act of 1983

Section 2601(c) of Pub.L. 98–369 provided that: "For purposes of section 210(a)(5)(G) of the Social Security Act [subsec. (a)(5)(G) of this section] and section 3121(b)(5)(G) of the Internal Revenue Code of 1954 [section 3121(b)(5)(G) of Title 26, Internal Revenue Code], an individual shall not be considered to be subject to subchapter III of chapter 83 of title 5, United States Code [section 8331 et seq. of Title 5, Government Organization and Employees], or to another retirement system established by a law of the United States for employees of the Federal Government (other than for members of the uniformed services), if he is contributing a reduced amount by reason of the Federal Employees' Retirement Contribution Temporary Adjustment Act of 1983 [Pub.L. 98–168, Title II, § 201 et seq., Nov. 29, 1983, 97 Stat. 1106, set out as a note under section 8331 of Title 5]."

Plan Amendments Not Required Until January 1, 1989

For provisions directing that if any amendments made by subtitle A or subtitle C of title XI [§§ 1101–1147 and 1171–1177] or title XVIII [§§ 1800–1899A] of Pub.L. 99–514 require an amendment to any plan, such plan amendment shall not be required to be made before the first plan year beginning on or after Jan. 1, 1989, see section 1140 of Pub.L. 99–514, as amended, set out as a note under section 401 of Title 26, Internal Revenue Code.

Qualification and Requalification of Federal Employees for Benefits

Section 2601(d) of Pub.L. 98–369, as amended Pub.L. 99–514, Title XVIII, § 1883(a)(5)(A), Oct. 22, 1986, 100 Stat. 2916, provided that:

"(1) Any individual who—

"(A) was subject to subchapter III of chapter 83 of title 5, United States Code [section 8331 et seq. of Title 5, Government Organization and Employees], or to another retirement system established by a law of the United States for employees of the Federal Government (other than for members of the uniformed services), on December 31, 1983 (as determined for purposes of section 210(a)(5)(G) of the Social Security Act) [subsec. (a)(5)(G) of this section], and

"(B)(i) received a lump-sum payment under section 8342(a) of such title 5 [section 8342(a) of Title 5], or under the corresponding provision of the law establishing the other retirement system described in subparagraph (A), after December 31, 1983, and prior to June 15, 1984, or received such a payment on or after June 15, 1984, pursuant to an application which was filed in accordance with such section 8342(a) [section 8342(a) of Title 5] or the corresponding provision of the law establishing such other retirement system prior to that date, or

"(ii) otherwise ceased to be subject to subchapter III of chapter 83 of title 5, United States Code, for a period after December 31, 1983, to which section 210(a)(5)(G)(iii) of the Social Security Act [subsec. (a)(5)(G)(iii) of this section] applies,

shall, if such individual again becomes subject to subchapter III of chapter 83 of title 5 (or effectively applies for coverage under such subchapter) after the date on which he last ceased to be subject to such subchapter but prior to, or within 30 days after, the date of the enactment of this Act [July 18, 1984], requalify for the exemption from social security coverage and taxes under section 210(a)(5) of the Social Security Act [subsec. (a)(5) of this section] and section 3121(b)(5) of the Internal Revenue Code of 1954 [section 3121(b)(5) of Title 26, Internal Revenue Code] as if the cessation of coverage under title 5 had not occurred.

"(2) An individual meeting the requirements of subparagraphs (A) and (B) of paragraph (1) who is not in the employ of the United States or an instrumentality thereof on the date of the enactment of this Act [July 18, 1984] may requalify for such exemptions in the same manner as under paragraph (1) if such individual again becomes subject to subchapter III of chapter 83 of title 5 [section 8331 et seq. of Title 5] (or effectively applies for coverage under such subchapter) within 30 days after the date on which he first returns to service in the legislative branch after such date of enactment, if such date (on which he returns to service) is within 365 days after he was last in the employ of the United States or an instrumentality thereof.

"(3) If an individual meeting the requirements of subparagraphs (A) and (B) of paragraph (1) does not again become subject to subchapter III of chapter 83 of title 5 [section 8331 et seq. of Title 5] (or effectively apply for coverage under such subchapter) prior to the date of the enactment of this Act [July 18, 1984] or within the relevant 30-day period as provided in paragraph (1) or (2), social security coverage and taxes by reason of section 210(a)(5)(G) of the Social Security Act [subsec. (a)(5)(G) of this section] and section 3121(b)(5)(G) of the Internal Revenue Code of 1954 [section 3121(b)(5)(G) of Title 26] shall, with respect to such individual's service in the legislative branch of the Federal Government, become effective with the first month beginning after such 30-day period.

"(4) The provisions of paragraphs (1) and (2) shall apply only for purposes of reestablishing an exemption from social security coverage and taxes, and do not affect the amount of service to be credited to an individual for purposes of title 5, United States Code."

Services Performed for Nonprofit Organizations by Federal Employees

Section 2601(e) of Pub.L. 98-369 provided that:

"(1) For purposes of section 210(a)(5) of the Social Security Act [subsec. (a)(5) of this section] (as in effect in January 1983 and as in effect on and after January 1, 1984) and section 3121(b)(5) of the Internal Revenue Code of 1954 [section 3121(b)(5) of Title 26, Internal Revenue Code] (as so in effect), service performed in the employ of a nonprofit organization described in section 501(c)(3) of the Internal Revenue Code of 1954 [section 501(c)(3) of Title 26] by an employee who is required by law to be subject to subchapter III of chapter 83 of title 5, United States Code [section 8331 et seq. of Title 5, Government Organization and Employees], with respect to such service, shall be considered to be service performed in the employ of an instrumentality of the United States.

"(2) For purposes of section 203 of the Federal Employees' Retirement Contribution Temporary Adjustment Act of 1983 [section 203 of Pub.L. 98-168, set out as a note under section 8331 of Title 5], service described in paragraph (1) which is also 'employment' for purposes of title II of the Social Security Act [this subchapter], shall be considered to be 'covered service'."

Termination of War and Emergencies

Joint Res. July 25, 1947, c. 327, § 3, 61 Stat. 451, provided that in the interpretation of former § 410 of this title, the date July 25, 1947, shall be deemed to be the date of termination of any state of war theretofore declared by Congress and of the national emergencies proclaimed by the President on Sept. 8, 1939, and May 27, 1941.

§ 410a. Transferred

HISTORICAL AND STATUTORY NOTES

Codifications

Section, Act Aug. 29, 1935, c. 812, § 17, as added June 24, 1937, c. 382, Part I, § 1, 50 Stat. 317, and amended Oct. 30, 1951, c. 632, § 24, 65 Stat. 690, was transferred to section 228q of Title 45, Railroads, and was subsequently superseded. See section 231q of Title 45.

§ 411. Definitions relating to self-employment

For the purposes of this subchapter—

(a) Net earnings from self-employment

The term "net earnings from self-employment" means the gross income, as computed under subtitle A of the Internal Revenue Code of 1986, derived by an individual from any trade or business carried on by such individual, less the deductions allowed under such subtitle which are attributable to such trade or business, plus his distributive share (whether or not distributed) of the ordinary net income or loss, as computed under section 702(a)(8) of such Code, from any trade or business carried on by a partnership of which he is a member; except that in computing such gross income and deductions and such distributive share of partnership ordinary net income or loss—

(1) There shall be excluded rentals from real estate and from personal property leased with the real estate (including such rentals paid in crop shares, and including payments under section 3833(2) of Title 16 to individuals receiving benefits under section 402 or 423 of this title), together with the

deductions attributable thereto, unless such rentals are received in the course of a trade or business as a real estate dealer; except that the preceding provisions of this paragraph shall not apply to any income derived by the owner or tenant of land if (A) such income is derived under an arrangement, between the owner or tenant and another individual, which provides that such other individual shall produce agricultural or horticultural commodities (including livestock, bees, poultry, and fur-bearing animals and wildlife) on such land, and that there shall be material participation by the owner or tenant (as determined without regard to any activities of an agent of such owner or tenant) in the production or the management of the production of such agricultural or horticultural commodities, and (B) there is material participation by the owner or tenant (as determined without regard to any activities of an agent of such owner or tenant) with respect to any such agricultural or horticultural commodity;

(2) There shall be excluded dividends on any share of stock, and interest on any bond, debenture, note, or certificate, or other evidence of indebtedness, issued with interest benefits [1] or in registered form by any corporation (including one issued by a government or political subdivision thereof), unless such dividends and interest are received in the course of a trade or business as a dealer in stocks or securities;

(3) There shall be excluded any gain or loss (A) which is considered under subtitle A of the Internal Revenue Code of 1986 as gain or loss from the sale or exchange of a capital asset, (B) from the cutting of timber, or the disposal of timber, coal, or iron ore, if section 631 of the Internal Revenue Code of 1986 applies to such gain or loss, or (C) from the sale, exchange, involuntary conversion, or other disposition of property if such property is neither (i) stock in trade or other property of a kind which would properly be includible in inventory if on hand at the close of the taxable year, nor (ii) property held primarily for sale to customers in the ordinary course of the trade or business;

(4) The deduction for net operating losses provided in section 172 of the Internal Revenue Code of 1986 shall not be allowed;

(5)(A) If any of the income derived from a trade or business (other than a trade or business carried on by a partnership) is community income under community property laws applicable to such income, the gross income and deductions attributable to such trade or business shall be treated as the gross income and deductions of the spouse carrying on such trade or business or, if such trade or business is jointly operated, treated as the gross income and deductions of each spouse on the basis of their respective distributive share of the gross income and deductions;

(B) If any portion of a partner's distributive share of the ordinary net income or loss from a trade or business carried on by a partnership is community income or loss under the community property laws applicable to such share, all of such distributive share shall be included in computing the net earnings from self-employment of such partner, and no part of such share shall be taken into account in computing the net earnings from self-employment of the spouse of such partner;

(6) A resident of the Commonwealth of Puerto Rico shall compute his net earnings from self-employment in the same manner as a citizen of the United States but without regard to the provisions of section 933 of the Internal Revenue Code of 1986;

(7) An individual who is a duly ordained, commissioned, or licensed minister of a church or a member of a religious order shall compute his net earnings from self-employment derived from the performance of service described in subsection (c)(4) without regard to section 107 (relating to rental value of parsonages), section 119 (relating to meals and lodging furnished for the convenience of the employer), and section 911 (relating to earned income from sources without the United States) of the Internal Revenue Code of 1986, but shall not include in any such net earnings from self-employment the rental value of any parsonage or any parsonage allowance (whether or not excluded under section 107 of the Internal Revenue Code of 1986) provided after the individual retires, or any other retirement benefit received by such individual from a church plan (as defined in section 414(e) of such Code) after the individual retires;

(8) The exclusion from gross income provided by section 931 of the Internal Revenue Code of 1986 shall not apply;

(9) There shall be excluded amounts received by a partner pursuant to a written plan of the partnership, which meets such requirements as are prescribed by the Secretary of the Treasury or his delegate, and which provides for payments on account of retirement, on a periodic basis, to partners generally or to a class or classes of partners, such payments to continue at least until such partner's death, if—

(A) such partner rendered no services with respect to any trade or business carried on by such partnership (or its successors) during the taxable year of such partnership (or its successors), ending within or with his taxable year, in which such amounts were received, and

(B) no obligation exists (as of the close of the partnership's taxable year referred to in subparagraph (A)) from the other partners to such partner except with respect to retirement payments under such plan, and

(C) such partner's share, if any, of the capital of the partnership has been paid to him in full before the close of the partnership's taxable year referred to in subparagraph (A);

(10) The exclusion from gross income provided by section 911(a)(1) of the Internal Revenue Code of 1986 shall not apply;

(11) In lieu of the deduction provided by section 164(f) of the Internal Revenue Code of 1986 (relating to deduction for one-half of self-employment taxes), there shall be allowed a deduction equal to the product of—

(A) the taxpayer's net earnings from self-employment for the taxable year (determined without regard to this paragraph), and

(B) one-half of the sum of the rates imposed by subsections (a) and (b) of section 1401 of such Code for such year;

(12) There shall be excluded the distributive share of any item of income or loss of a limited partner, as such, other than guaranteed payments described in section 707(c) of the Internal Revenue Code of 1986 to that partner for services actually rendered to or on behalf of the partnership to the extent that those payments are established to be in the nature of remuneration for those services;

(13) In the case of church employee income, the special rules of subsection (i)(1) shall apply;

(14) There shall be excluded income excluded from taxation under section 7873 of the Internal Revenue Code of 1986 (relating to income derived by Indians from exercise of fishing rights);

(15) The deduction under section 162(*l*) of the Internal Revenue Code of 1986 (relating to health insurance costs of self-employed individuals) shall not be allowed; and

(16) Notwithstanding the preceding provisions of this subsection, each spouse's share of income or loss from a qualified joint venture shall be taken into account as provided in section 761(f) of the Internal Revenue Code of 1986 in determining net earnings from self-employment of such spouse.

If the taxable year of a partner is different from that of the partnership, the distributive share which he is required to include in computing his net earnings from self-employment shall be based upon the ordinary net income or loss of the partnership for any taxable year of the partnership (even though beginning prior to 1951) ending within or with his taxable year. In the case of any trade or business which is carried on by an individual or by a partnership and in which, if such trade or business were carried on exclusively by employees, the major portion of the services would constitute agricultural labor as defined in section 410(f) of this title—

(i) in the case of an individual, if the gross income derived by him from such trade or business is not more than the upper limit, the net earnings from self-employment derived by him from such trade or business may, at his option, be deemed to be 66⅔ percent of such gross income; or

(ii) in the case of an individual, if the gross income derived by him from such trade or business is more than the upper limit and the net earnings from self-employment derived by him from such trade or business (computed under this subsection without regard to this sentence) are less than the lower limit, the net earnings from self-employment derived by him from such trade or business may, at his option, be deemed to be the lower limit; and

(iii) in the case of a member of a partnership, if his distributive share of the gross income of the partnership derived from such trade or business (after such gross income has been reduced by the sum of all payments to which section 707(c) of the Internal Revenue Code of 1986 applies) is not more than the upper limit, his distributive share of income described in section 702(a)(8) of such Code derived from such trade or business may, at his option, be deemed to be an amount equal to 66⅔ percent of his distributive share of such gross income (after such gross income has been so reduced); or

(iv) in the case of a member of a partnership, if his distributive share of the gross income of the partnership derived from such trade or business (after such gross income has been reduced by the sum of all payments to which section 707(c) of the Internal Revenue Code of 1986 applies) is more than the upper limit and his distributive share (whether or not distributed) of income described in section 702(a)(8) of such Code derived from such trade or business (computed under this subsection without regard to this sentence) is less than the lower limit, his distributive share of income described in such section 702(a)(8) derived from such trade or business may, at his option, be deemed to be the lower limit.

For purposes of the preceding sentence, gross income means—

(v) in the case of any such trade or business in which the income is computed under a cash receipts and disbursements method, the gross receipts from such trade or business reduced by the cost or other basis of property which was purchased and sold in carrying on such trade or business, adjusted (after such reduction) in accordance with the provisions of paragraphs (1) through (6) and paragraph (8) of this subsection; and

(vi) in the case of any such trade or business in which the income is computed under an accrual method, the gross income from such trade or business, adjusted in accordance with the provisions of paragraphs (1) through (6) and paragraph (8) of this subsection;

and, for purposes of such sentence, if an individual (including a member of a partnership) derives gross income from more than one such trade or business, such gross income (including his distributive share of the gross income of any partnership derived from any such trade or business) shall be deemed to have been derived from one trade or business.

The preceding sentence and clauses (i) through (iv) of the second preceding sentence shall also apply in the case of any trade or business (other than a trade or business specified in such second preceding sentence) which is carried on by an individual who is self-employed on a regular basis as defined in subsection (g), or by a partnership of which an individual is a member on a regular basis as defined in subsection (g), but only if such individual's net earnings from self-employment in the taxable year as determined without regard to this sentence are less than the lower limit and less than 66⅔ percent of the sum (in such taxable year) of such individual's gross income derived from all trades or businesses carried on by him and his distributive share of the income or loss from all trades or businesses carried on by all the partnerships of which he is a member; except that this sentence shall not apply to more than 5 taxable years in the case of any individual, and in no case in which an individual elects to determine the amount of his net earnings from self-employment for a taxable year under the provisions of the two preceding sentences with respect to a trade or business to which the second preceding sentence applies and with respect to a trade or business to which this sentence applies shall such net earnings for such year exceed the lower limit.

(b) Self-employment income

The term "self-employment income" means the net earnings from self-employment derived by an individual (other than a nonresident alien individual, except as provided by an agreement under section 433 of this title) during any taxable year beginning after 1950; except that such term shall not include—

(1) That part of the net earnings from self-employment which is in excess of—

(A) For any taxable year ending prior to 1955, (i) $3,600, minus (ii) the amount of the wages paid to such individual during the taxable year; and

(B) For any taxable year ending after 1954 and prior to 1959, (i) $4,200, minus (ii) the amount of the wages paid to such individual during the taxable year; and

(C) For any taxable year ending after 1958 and prior to 1966, (i) $4,800, minus (ii) the amount of the wages paid to such individual during the taxable year; and

(D) For any taxable year ending after 1965 and prior to 1968, (i) $6,600, minus (ii) the amount of the wages paid to such individual during the taxable year; and

(E) For any taxable year ending after 1967 and beginning prior to 1972, (i) $7,800, minus (ii) the amount of the wages paid to such individual during the taxable year; and

(F) For any taxable year beginning after 1971 and prior to 1973, (i) $9,000, minus (ii) the amount of the wages paid to such individual during the taxable year; and

(G) For any taxable year beginning after 1972 and prior to 1974, (i) $10,800, minus (ii) the amount of the wages paid to such individual during the taxable year; and

(H) For any taxable year beginning after 1973 and prior to 1975, (i) $13,200, minus (ii) the amount of the wages paid to such individual during the taxable year; and

(I) For any taxable year beginning in any calendar year after 1974, (i) an amount equal to the contribution and benefit base (as determined under section 430 of this title) which is effective for such calendar year, minus (ii) the amount of the wages paid to such individual during such taxable year; or

(2) The net earnings from self-employment, if such net earnings for the taxable year are less than $400.

An individual who is not a citizen of the United States but who is a resident of the Commonwealth of Puerto Rico, the Virgin Islands, Guam, or American Samoa shall not, for the purpose of this subsection, be considered to be a nonresident alien individual. In the case of church employee income, the special rules of subsection (i)(2) shall apply for purposes of paragraph (2).

(c) Trade or business

The term "trade or business", when used with reference to self-employment income or net earnings from self-employment, shall have the same meaning as when used in section 162 of the Internal Revenue Code of 1986, except that such term shall not include—

(1) The performance of the functions of a public office, other than the functions of a public office of a State or a political subdivision thereof with respect to fees received in any period in which the functions are performed in a position compensated solely on a fee basis and in which such functions are not covered under an agreement entered into by such State and the Commissioner of Social Security pursuant to section 418 of this title;

(2) The performance of service by an individual as an employee, other than—

(A) service described in section 410(a)(14)(B) of this title performed by an individual who has attained the age of eighteen,

(B) service described in section 410(a)(16) of this title,

(C) service described in section 410(a)(11), (12), or (15) of this title performed in the United States by a citizen of the United States, except service which constitutes "employment" under section 410(r) of this title,

(D) service described in paragraph (4) of this subsection,

(E) service performed by an individual as an employee of a State or a political subdivision thereof in a position compensated solely on a fee basis with respect to fees received in any period in which such service is not covered under an agreement entered into by such State and the Commissioner of Social Security pursuant to section 418 of this title,

(F) service described in section 410(a)(20) of this title, and

(G) service described in section 410(a)(8)(B) of this title;

(3) The performance of service by an individual as an employee or employee representative as defined in section 3231 of the Internal Revenue Code of 1986;

(4) The performance of service by a duly ordained, commissioned, or licensed minister of a church in the exercise of his ministry or by a member of a religious order in the exercise of duties required by such order;

(5) The performance of service by an individual in the exercise of his profession as a Christian Science practitioner; or

(6) The performance of service by an individual during the period for which an exemption under section 1402(g) of the Internal Revenue Code of 1986 is effective with respect to him.

The provisions of paragraph (4) or (5) shall not apply to service (other than service performed by a member of a religious order who has taken a vow of poverty as a member of such order) performed by an individual unless an exemption under section 1402(e) of the Internal Revenue Code of 1986 is effective with respect to him.

(d) Partnership and partner

The term "partnership" and the term "partner" shall have the same meaning as when used in subchapter K of chapter 1 of the Internal Revenue Code of 1986.

(e) Taxable year

The term "taxable year" shall have the same meaning as when used in subtitle A of the Internal Revenue Code of 1986; and the taxable year of any individual shall be a calendar year unless he has a different taxable year for the purposes of subtitle A of such Code, in which case his taxable year for the purposes of this subchapter shall be the same as his taxable year under such subtitle A.

(f) Partner's taxable year ending as result of death

In computing a partner's net earnings from self-employment for his taxable year which ends as a result of his death (but only if such taxable year ends within, and not with, the taxable year of the partnership), there shall be included so much of the deceased partner's distributive share of the partnership's ordinary income or loss for the partnership taxable year as is not attributable to an interest in the partnership during any period beginning on or after the first day of the first calendar month following the month in which such partner died. For purposes of this subsection—

(1) in determining the portion of the distributive share which is attributable to any period specified in the preceding sentence, the ordinary income or loss of the partnership shall be treated as having been realized or sustained ratably over the partnership taxable year; and

(2) the term "deceased partner's distributive share" includes the share of his estate or of any other person succeeding, by reason of his death, to rights with respect to his partnership interest.

(g) Regular basis

An individual shall be deemed to be self-employed on a regular basis in a taxable year, or to be a member of a partnership on a regular basis in such year, if he had net earnings from self-employment, as defined in the first sentence of subsection (a), of not less than $400 in at least two of the three consecutive taxable years immediately preceding such taxable year from trades or businesses carried on by such individual or such partnership.

(h) Option dealers and commodity dealers

(1) In determining the net earnings from self-employment of any options dealer or commodities dealer—

(A) notwithstanding subsection (a)(3)(A), there shall not be excluded any gain or loss (in the normal course of the taxpayer's activity of dealing in or trading section 1256 contracts) from section 1256 contracts or property related to such contracts, and

(B) the deduction provided by section 1202 of the Internal Revenue Code of 1986 shall not apply.

(2) For purposes of this subsection—

(A) The term "options dealer" has the meaning given such term by section 1256(g)(8) of such Code.

(B) The term "commodities dealer" means a person who is actively engaged in trading section 1256 contracts and is registered with a domestic board of trade which is designated as a contract market by the Commodities Futures Trading Commission.

(C) The term "section 1256 contracts" has the meaning given to such term by section 1256(b) of such Code.

(i) Church employee income

(1) In applying subsection (a)—

(A) church employee income shall not be reduced by any deduction;

(B) church employee income and deductions attributable to such income shall not be taken into account in determining the amount of other net earnings from self-employment.

(2)(A) Subsection (b)(2) shall be applied separately—

(i) to church employee income, and

(ii) to other net earnings from self-employment.

(B) In applying subsection (b)(2) to church employee income, "$100" shall be substituted for "$400".

(3) Paragraph (1) shall not apply to any amount allowable as a deduction under subsection (a)(11), and paragraph (1) shall be applied before determining the amount so allowable.

(4) For purposes of this section, the term "church employee income" means gross income for services which are described in section 410(a)(8)(B) of this title (and are not described in section 410(a)(8)(A) of this title).

(j) Codification of treatment of certain termination payments received by former insurance salesmen

Nothing in subsection (a) shall be construed as including in the net earnings from self-employment of an individual any amount received during the taxable year from an insurance company on account of services performed by such individual as an insurance salesman for such company if—

(1) such amount is received after termination of such individual's agreement to perform such services for such company,

(2) such individual performs no services for such company after such termination and before the close of such taxable year,

(3) such individual enters into a covenant not to compete against such company which applies to at least the 1–year period beginning on the date of such termination, and

(4) the amount of such payment—

(A) depends primarily on policies sold by or credited to the account of such individual during the last year of such agreement or the extent to which such policies remain in force for some period after such termination, or both, and

(B) does not depend to any extent on length of service or overall earnings from services performed for such company (without regard to whether eligibility for payment depends on length of service).

(k) Upper and lower limits

For purposes of subsection (a)—

(1) The lower limit for any taxable year is the sum of the amounts required under section 413(d) of this title for a quarter of coverage in effect with respect to each calendar quarter ending with or within such taxable year.

(2) The upper limit for any taxable year is the amount equal to 150 percent of the lower limit for such taxable year.

(Aug. 14, 1935, c. 531, Title II, § 211, as added Aug. 28, 1950, c. 809, Title I, § 104(a), 64 Stat. 492, 502; amended Sept. 23, 1950, c. 994, Title II, § 221(j)(2), 64 Stat. 947; Sept. 1, 1954, c. 1206, Title I, §§ 101(d), (g), 104(b), 68 Stat. 1054, 1078; Aug. 1, 1956, c. 836, Title I, §§ 104(c)(2), (3), (d), (h), 106(a), 70 Stat. 824 to 826, 828; Pub.L. 85–239, § 5(a), Aug. 30, 1957, 71 Stat. 523; Pub.L. 85–840, Title I, § 102(b), Title III, § 313(a), Aug. 28, 1958, 72 Stat. 1019, 1036; Pub.L. 86–778, Title I, §§ 103(g), (h), (j)(3), 106(a), Sept. 13, 1960, 74 Stat. 937, 938, 945; Pub.L. 88–272, Title II, § 227(b)(7), Feb. 26, 1964, 78 Stat. 98; Pub.L. 89–97, Title III, §§ 311(a)(1), (2), 312(a), 319(b), 320(a)(2), July 30, 1965, 79 Stat. 380, 381, 391, 393; Pub.L. 90–248, Title I, §§ 108(a)(2), 115(a), 118(b), 122(a), Jan. 2, 1968, 81 Stat. 834, 839, 841, 843; Pub.L. 92–5, Title II, § 203(a)(2), Mar. 17, 1971, 85 Stat. 10; Pub.L. 92–336, Title II, § 203(a)(2), July 1, 1972, 86 Stat. 418; Pub.L. 92–603, Title I, §§ 121(a), 124(a), 140(a), Oct. 30, 1972, 86 Stat. 1353, 1357, 1366; Pub.L. 93–66, Title II, § 203(a)(2), July 9, 1973, 87 Stat. 153; Pub.L. 93–233, § 5(a)(2), Dec. 31, 1973, 87 Stat. 953; Pub.L. 93–368, § 10(a), Aug. 7, 1974, 88 Stat. 422; Pub.L. 94–455, Title XII, § 1207(e)(2)(B), Oct. 4, 1976, 90 Stat. 1707; Pub.L. 95–216, Title III, § 313(a), Dec. 20, 1977, 91 Stat. 1535; Pub.L. 95–600, Title VII, § 703(j)(14)(D), (E), Nov. 6, 1978, 92 Stat. 2942; Pub.L. 98–21, Title I, § 124(c)(3), Title III, §§ 322(b)(1), 323(b)(2), Apr. 20, 1983, 97 Stat. 90, 121; Pub.L. 98–369, Div. A, Title I, § 102(c)(2), Div. B, Title VI, §§ 2603(c)(1), (d)(1), 2663(a)(8), July 18, 1984, 98 Stat. 622, 1129, 1163; Pub.L. 99–514, Title XVIII, §§ 1882(b)(2), 1883(a)(6), Oct. 22, 1986, 100 Stat. 2915, 2916; Pub.L. 100–203, Title IX, §§ 9022(a), 9023(b), Dec. 22, 1987, 101 Stat. 1330–295, 1330–296; Pub.L. 100–647, Title I, § 1011B(b)(4), Title III, § 3043(b), Title VIII, § 8016(a)(2), Nov. 10, 1988, 102 Stat. 3488, 3642, 3792; Pub.L. 101–508, Title V, §§ 5123(a)(1), 5130(a)(2), (3), Nov. 5, 1990, 104 Stat. 1388–284, 1388–289; Pub.L. 103–296, Title I, § 107(a)(4), Title III, §§ 319(b)(2), 321(a)(14), (c)(5), (6)(E) to (G), Aug. 15, 1994, 108 Stat. 1478, 1535, 1536, 1538; Pub.L. 105–34, Title IX, § 922(b), Aug. 5, 1997, 111 Stat. 880; Pub.L. 108–203, Title IV, §§ 422(a), 424(a), 425(a), Mar. 2, 2004, 118 Stat. 536; Pub.L. 110–28, Title VIII, § 8215(b)(2), May 25, 2007, 121 Stat. 194; Pub.L. 110–234, Title IV, § 4115(c)(1)(A)(i), (B)(iii), Title XV, §§ 15301(b), 15352(b)(1), (2), May 22, 2008, 122 Stat. 1109, 1501, 1526; Pub.L. 110–246, § 4(a), Title IV, § 4115(c)(1)(A)(i), (B)(iii), Title XV, §§ 15301(b), 15352(b)(1), (2), June 18, 2008, 122 Stat. 1664, 1870, 2263, 2288.)

[1] So in original. Probably should be "coupons". See 2008 Amendments note set out under this section.

HISTORICAL AND STATUTORY NOTES

References in Text

The Internal Revenue Code of 1986, referred to in text, is classified to Title 26, 26 U.S.C.A. § 1 et seq.

Section 3833(2) of Title 16, referred to in subsec. (a)(1), was in the original a reference to "section 1233(2) of the Food Security Act of 1985 (16 U.S.C. 3833(2))", which is section 1233(2) of Pub.L. 99–198, and which was classified to 16 U.S.C.A. § 3833(2), prior to the general amendment of section 1233 by Pub.L. 113–79, Title II, § 2004, Feb. 7, 2014, 128 Stat. 715. As so amended, the substance of former section 1233(2) now appears in section 1233(a)(2), which is classified to 16 U.S.C.A. § 3833(a)(2).

Codifications

The authorities provided by each provision of, and each amendment made by, Pub.L. 110–246, as in effect on Sept. 30, 2012, to continue, and the Secretary of Agriculture to carry out the authorities, until the later of Sept. 30, 2013, or the date specified in the provision of, or amendment made by, Pub.L. 110–246, see section 701(a) of Pub.L. 112–240, set out in a note under 7 U.S.C.A. § 8701.

Amendment by section 3043(b)(1) of Pub.L. 100–647, directing that subsec. (a) of this section be amended by striking "and" at the end of par. (12) could not be executed in view of the amendment by section 124(c)(3) of Pub.L. 98–21.

Section 703(j)(14)(D) of Pub.L. 95–600 directed that "(other than interest described in section 35 of the Internal Revenue Code of 1954)" be deleted from subsec. (a)(2) of this section. Since this phrase did not appear in subsec. (a)(2) of this section, "(other than interest described in section 25(a) of the Internal Revenue Code of 1939)" has been deleted as the probable intent of Congress.

Directory language of section 322(b)(1) of Pub.L. 98–21 which directed that reference to agreements under section 433 of this title be inserted in subsec. (b) of this section after "nonresident alien individual" and which failed to specify which of the two possible places in subsec. (b) the new reference was to be inserted was corrected by Pub.L. 101–508, § 5130(a)(2), and required no change in text.

Effective and Applicability Provisions

2008 Acts. Amendments by Pub.L. 110–246, except as otherwise provided, shall take effect on the earlier of June 18, 2008 or May 22, 2008, see Pub.L. 110–246, § 4(b), set out in a Repeal of Duplicative Enactment note under 7 U.S.C.A. § 8701.

Amendments by Title IV of Pub.L. 110–246, except as otherwise provided, take effect on October 1, 2008, see Pub.L. 110–246, § 4407, set out as a note under 2 U.S.C.A. § 1161.

Amendments made by Pub.L. 110–234, § 15301 and Pub.L. 110–246, § 15301, shall apply to payments made after December 31, 2007, see Pub.L. 110–234, § 15301(c) and Pub.L. 110–246, § 15301(c), set out as Effective and Applicability Provisions notes under 26 U.S.C.A. § 1402.

Amendments made by Pub.L. 110–234, § 15352 and Pub.L. 110–246, § 15352, shall apply to taxable years beginning after December 31, 2007, see Pub.L. 110–234, § 15352(c) and Pub.L. 110–246, § 15352(c), set out as Effective and Applicability Provisions notes under 26 U.S.C.A. § 1402.

2007 Acts. Amendments by Pub.L. 110–28, § 8215, applicable to taxable years beginning after Dec. 31, 2006, see Pub.L. 110–28, § 8215(c), set out as a note under 26 U.S.C.A. § 761.

2004 Acts. Pub.L. 108–203, Title IV, § 422(b), Mar. 2, 2004, 118 Stat. 536, provided that: "The amendment made by this section [amending subsec. (a)(7) of this section] shall apply to years beginning before, on, or after December 31, 1994."

1997 Acts. Amendment by section 922(b) of Pub.L. 105–34 applicable to payments after December 31, 1997, see section 922(c) of Pub.L. 105–34, set out as a note under section 1402 of Title 26, Internal Revenue Code.

1994 Acts. Amendment by section 107(a)(4) of Pub.L. 103–296 effective Mar. 31, 1995, see section 110 of Pub.L. 103–296, set out as a note under section 401 of this title.

Amendment by section 319(b)(2) of Pub.L. 103–296 applicable with respect to service performed after the calendar quarter following the calendar quarter in which Aug. 15, 1994, occurs, see section 319(c) of Pub.L. 103–296, set out as a note under section 1402 of Title 26, Internal Revenue Code.

1990 Acts. Amendment by section 5130(a)(3) of Pub.L. 101–508 effective as if included in the enactment of Pub.L. 100–647 [probably meaning the date of the enactment of Pub.L. 100–647] which was approved November 10, 1988, and amendment to subsection (b) by section 5130(a)(2) of Pub.L. 101–508, effective as if included in the enactment of Pub.L. 98–21 [probably meaning the date of the enactment of Pub.L. 98–21] which was approved April 20, 1983, see section 5130(b) of Pub.L. 101–508, set out as a note under section 1402 of Title 26, Internal Revenue Code.

1987 Acts. Amendment by section 9022(a) of Pub.L. 100–203 applicable with respect to services performed in taxable years beginning on or after Jan. 1, 1988, see section 9022(c) of Pub.L. 100–203, set out as a note under section 1402 of Title 26, Internal Revenue Code.

1986 Acts. Amendment by section 1882(b)(2) of Pub.L. 99–514 applicable to remuneration paid or derived in taxable years beginning after Dec. 31, 1985, see section 1882(b)(3) of Pub.L. 99–514, set out as a note under section 1402 of Title 26, Internal Revenue Code.

Amendment by section 1883(a)(6) of Pub.L. 99–514 effective Oct. 22, 1986, see section 1883(f) of Pub.L. 99–514, set out as a note under section 402 of this title.

1984 Acts. Enactment by section 102(c)(2) of Pub.L. 98–369 applicable to taxable years beginning after July 18, 1984, except as otherwise provided, see section 102(f)(3), (g) of Pub.L. 98–369, set out as a note under section 1256 of Title 26, Internal Revenue Code.

Amendment by section 2603(c)(1), (d)(1) of Pub.L. 98–369 applicable to services performed after December 31, 1983, see section 2603(e) of Pub.L. 98–369, set out as a note under section 410 of this title.

Amendment by section 2663(a)(8) of Pub.L. 98–369 effective July 18, 1984, but not to be construed as changing or affecting any right, liability, status or interpretation which existed (under the provisions of law involved) before that date, see section 2664(b) of Pub.L. 98–369, set out as a note under section 401 of this title.

1983 Acts. Enactment by Pub.L. 98–21 applicable to taxable years beginning after Dec. 31, 1989, see section 124(d)(2) of Pub.L. 98–21, set out as a note under section 1401 of Title 26, Internal Revenue Code.

Amendment by section 322(b)(2) of Pub.L. 98–21 effective in taxable years beginning on or after Apr. 20, 1983, see section 322(c) of Pub.L. 98–21, set out as a note under section 3121 of Title 26, Internal Revenue Code.

Amendment by section 323(b)(2)(A) of Pub.L. 98–21 applicable to taxable years beginning after Dec. 31, 1983, see section 323(c)(2) of Pub.L. 98–21, set out as a note under section 1402 of Title 26.

Section 323(b)(2)(B) of Pub.L. 98–21 provided in part that amendment by section 323(b)(2)(B) of Pub.L. 98–21 is effective with respect to taxable years beginning after Dec. 31, 1981, and before Jan. 1, 1984.

1978 Acts. Amendment by Pub.L. 95–600 effective Oct. 4, 1976, see section 703(r) of Pub.L. 95–600, set out as a note under section 46 of Title 26, Internal Revenue Code.

1977 Acts. Section 313(c) of Pub.L. 95–216 provided that: "The amendments made by this section [amending subsec. (a) of this section and section 1402 of Title 26, Internal Revenue Code] shall apply with respect to taxable years beginning after December 31, 1977."

1974 Acts. Section 10(c) of Pub.L. 93–368 provided that: "The amendments made by this section [to subsec. (a)(1) of this section and section 1402(a)(1) of Title 26, Internal Revenue Code] shall apply with respect to taxable years beginning after December 31, 1973."

1973 Acts. Amendment by Pub.L. 93–233 applicable only with respect to remuneration paid after, and taxable years beginning after, 1973, see section 5(e) of Pub.L. 93–233, set out as a note under section 409 of this title.

Amendment by Pub.L. 93–66 applicable only with respect to remuneration paid after, and taxable years beginning after, 1973, see section 203(e) of Pub.L. 93–66, set out as a note under section 409 of this title.

1972 Acts. Section 121(c) of Pub.L. 92–603 provided that: "The amendments made by this section [enacting subsec. (g) of this section and amending subsecs. (a) of this section and section 1402 of Title 26, Internal Revenue Code] shall apply with respect to taxable years beginning after December 31, 1972."

Section 124(c) of Pub.L. 92–603 provided that: "The amendments made by this section [enacting subsec. (a)(10) of this section and section 1402(a)(11) of Title 26] shall apply only with respect to taxable years beginning after December 31, 1972."

Section 140(c) of Pub.L. 92–603 provided that: "The amendments made by this section [amending subsec. (a)(7) of this section and section 1402(a)(8) of Title 26, Internal Revenue Code] shall apply with respect to taxable years beginning after December 31, 1972."

Amendment by Pub.L. 92–336 applicable only with respect to taxable years beginning after 1972, see section 203(c) of Pub.L. 92–336, set out as a note under section 409 of this title.

1971 Acts. Amendment by Pub.L. 92–5 applicable only with respect to taxable years beginning after 1971, see section 203(c) of Pub.L. 92–5, set out as a note under section 409 of this title.

1968 Acts. Enactment by section 118(b) of Pub.L. 90–248 applicable only with respect to taxable years ending on or after Dec. 31, 1967, see section 118(c) of Pub.L. 90–248, set out as a note under section 1402 of Title 26, Internal Revenue Code.

Amendment by section 108(a)(2) of Pub.L. 90–248 applicable only with respect to taxable years ending after 1967, see section 108(c) of Pub.L. 90–248, set out as a note under section 409 of this title.

Amendment by section 115(a) of Pub.L. 90–248 applicable only with respect to taxable years ending after 1967, see section 115(c) of Pub.L. 90–248, set out as a note under section 1402 of Title 26, Internal Revenue Code.

Amendment by section 122(a)(1), (2) of Pub.L. 90–248 applicable with respect to fees received after 1967 and with respect to election to exempt fees from coverage as self-employment income, see section 122(c) of Pub.L. 90–248, set out as a note under section 1402 of Title 26.

1965 Acts. Amendment by Pub.L. 89–97 applicable only with respect to taxable years ending on or after Dec. 31, 1965, see section 311(c) of Pub.L. 89–97, set out as a note under section 410 of this title.

Section 312(c) of Pub.L. 89–97 provided that: "The amendments made by this section [amending subsec. (a) of this section and subsec. (a) of section 1402 of Title 26, Internal Revenue Code] shall apply only with respect to taxable years beginning after December 31, 1965."

Amendment by section 319 of Pub.L. 89–97 applicable with respect to taxable years beginning after Dec. 31, 1950, see section 319(e) of Pub.L. 89–97, set out as a note under section 1402 of Title 26.

Amendment by section 320 of Pub.L. 89–97 applicable with respect to taxable years ending after 1965, see section 320(c) of Pub.L. 89–97, set out as a note under section 3121 of Title 26.

1964 Acts. Amendment by Pub.L. 88–272 applicable with respect to amounts received or accrued in taxable years beginning after Dec. 31, 1963, attributable to iron ore mined in such years, see section 227(c) of Pub.L. 88–272, set out as a note under section 272 of Title 26, Internal Revenue Code.

1960 Acts. Amendment by Pub.L. 86–778 effective Sept. 13, 1960, see section 103(v)(1), (3) of Pub.L. 86–778, set out as a note under section 402 of this title.

Enactment of subsec. (a)(8) applicable only in the case of taxable years beginning after 1960, except that, insofar as such enactment involves the nonapplication of section 932 of Title 26, Internal Revenue Code, to the Virgin Islands for purposes of sections 1401 et seq. of Title 26 and this section, such enactment shall be effective in the case of all taxable years with respect to which such sections 1401 et seq. (and corresponding provisions of prior law) and this section are applicable, see section 103(v)(1) of Pub.L. 86–778, set out as a note under section 402 of this title.

Amendment by Pub.L. 86–778 applicable only in the case of taxable years beginning after 1960, see section 103(v)(1), (3) of Pub.L. 86–778, set out as a note under section 402 of this title.

Section 106(c) of Pub.L. 86–778 provided that: "The amendments made by this section [to subsec. (c)(2) of this section and section 1402(c)(2) of Title 26, Internal Revenue Code] shall apply only with respect to taxable years ending on or after December 31, 1960; except that for purposes of section 203 of the Social Security Act [section 403 of this title], the amendment made by subsection (a) [to subsec. (c)(2) of this section] shall apply only with respect to taxable years (of the individual performing the service involved) beginning after the date of the enactment of this Act [Sept. 13, 1960]."

1958 Acts. Section 313(b) of Pub.L. 85–840 provided that: "The amendment made by subsection (a) [adding subsec. (f) of this section] shall apply—

"(1) with respect to individuals who die after the date of the enactment of this Act [Aug. 28, 1958], and

"(2) with respect to any individual who died after 1955 and on or before the date of the enactment of this Act [Aug. 28, 1958], but only if the requirements of section 403(b)(2) of this Act [section 603(b)(2) of this title] are met."

1957 Acts. Amendment by Pub.L. 85–239 applicable, except for purposes of section 403 of this title, only with respect to taxable years ending on or after Dec. 31, 1957, see section 5(c) of Pub.L. 85–239, set out as a note under section 1402 of Title 26, Internal Revenue Code.

1956 Acts. Amendment by section 104(c)(2), (d) of Act Aug. 1, 1956 applicable with respect to taxable years ending after 1955, see section 104(i) of Act Aug. 1, 1956, set out as a note under section 410 of this title.

Amendment by section 104(h) of Act Aug. 1, 1956 applicable with respect to the same taxable years with respect to which the amendment to section 3121(k)(1) of Title 26, Internal Revenue Code, applies, see section 104(i) of Act Aug. 1, 1956, set out as a note under section 410 of this title, and section 201(m)(2) of Act Aug. 1, 1956, set out as a note under section 3121 of Title 26.

Amendment by section 104(c)(3) of Act Aug. 1, 1956 applicable with respect to taxable years ending after 1954, see section 104(i) of Act Aug. 1, 1956, set out as a note under section 410 of this title.

Section 106(b) of Act Aug. 1, 1956 provided that: "The amendment made by subsection (a) [to the last two sentences of subsec. (a) of this section] shall be effective with respect to taxable years ending on or after December 31, 1956."

1954 Acts. Section 101(n) of Act Sept. 1, 1954 provided in part that the amendment by section 101(g)(3) of Act Sept. 1, 1954, shall be applicable only with respect to taxable years beginning after 1950 and that the amendments by section 101(d), (g)(1), (2), (4), of Act Sept. 1, 1954, should be applicable only with respect to taxable years ending after 1954. See section 101(h) of Act Sept. 1, 1954, set out as a note under section 405 of this title.

1950 Acts. Amendment by Act Sept. 23, 1950 applicable with respect to taxable years beginning after Dec. 31, 1950, see section 221(k) of Act Sept. 23, 1950.

Repeals

Pub.L. 110–234 repealed effective May 22, 2008, see Repeal of Duplicative Enactment by Pub.L. 110–246, § 4(a), set out in a note under 7 U.S.C.A. § 8701.

Plan Amendments Not Required Until January 1, 1989

For provisions directing that if any amendments made by subtitle A or subtitle C of title XI [sections 1101 to 1147 and 1171 to 1177] or title XVIII [sections 1800 to 1899A] of Pub.L. 99–514 require an amendment to any plan, such plan amendment shall not be required to be made before the first plan year beginning on or after Jan. 1, 1989, see section 1140 of Pub.L. 99–514, as amended, set out as a note under section 401 of Title 26, Internal Revenue Code.

Treaty Obligations

Section 214 of Act Sept. 23, 1950 provided that: "No amendment made by this Act [see Tables for classification] shall apply in any case where its application would be contrary to any treaty obligation of the United States."

§ 412. Self-employment income credited to calendar years

(a) Taxable years prior to 1978

For the purposes of determining average monthly wage and quarters of coverage the amount of self-employment income derived during any taxable year which begins before 1978 shall—

(1) in the case of a taxable year which is a calendar year, be credited equally to each quarter of such calendar year; and

(2) in the case of any other taxable year, be credited equally to the calendar quarter in which such taxable year ends and to each of the next three or fewer preceding quarters any part of which is in such taxable year.

(b) Taxable years after 1977

Except as provided in subsection (c), for the purposes of determining average indexed monthly earnings, average monthly wage, and quarters of coverage the amount of self-employment income derived during any taxable year which begins after 1977 shall—

(1) in the case of a taxable year which is a calendar year or which begins with or during a calendar year and ends with or during such year, be credited to such calendar year; and

(2) in the case of any other taxable year, be allocated proportionately to the two calendar years, portions of which are included within such taxable year, on the basis of the number of months in each such calendar year which are included completely within the taxable year.

For purposes of clause (2), the calendar month in which a taxable year ends shall be treated as included completely within that taxable year.

(c) Proportional allocation

For the purpose of determining average indexed monthly earnings, average monthly wage, and quarters of coverage in the case of any individual who elects the option described in clause (ii) or (iv) in the matter following section 411(a)(16) of this title for any taxable year that does not begin with or during a particular calendar year and end with or during such year, the self-employment income of such individual deemed to be derived during such taxable year shall be allocated to the two calendar years, portions of which are included within such taxable year, in the same proportion to the total of such deemed self-employment income as the sum of the amounts applicable under section 413(d) of this title for the calendar quarters ending with or within each such calendar year bears to the lower limit for such taxable year specified in section 411(k)(1) of this title.

(Aug. 14, 1935, c. 531, Title II, § 212, as added Aug. 28, 1950, c. 809, Title I, § 104(a), 64 Stat. 492, 504; amended Pub.L. 95–216, Title III, § 351(b), Dec. 20, 1977, 91 Stat. 1549, Pub.L. 110–234, Title XV, § 15352(b)(3), May 22, 2008, 122 Stat. 1526; Pub.L. 110–246, § 4(a), Title XV, § 15352(b)(3), June 18, 2008, 122 Stat. 1664, 2288.)

HISTORICAL AND STATUTORY NOTES

Codifications

The authorities provided by each provision of, and each amendment made by, Pub.L. 110–246, as in effect on Sept. 30, 2012, to continue, and the Secretary of Agriculture to carry out the authorities, until the later of Sept. 30, 2013, or the date specified in the provision of, or amendment made by, Pub.L. 110–246, see section 701(a) of Pub.L. 112–240, set out in a note under 7 U.S.C.A. § 8701.

Effective and Applicability Provisions

2008 Acts. Amendments by Pub.L. 110–246, except as otherwise provided, shall take effect on the earlier of June 18, 2008 or May 22, 2008, see Pub.L. 110–246, § 4(b), set out in a Repeal of Duplicative Enactment note under 7 U.S.C.A. § 8701.

Amendments made by Pub.L. 110–234, § 15352 and Pub.L. 110–246, § 15352, shall apply to taxable years beginning after December 31, 2007, see Pub.L. 110–234, § 15352(c) and Pub.L. 110–246, § 15352(c), set out as Effective and Applicability Provisions notes under 26 U.S.C.A. § 1402.

1977 Acts. Amendment by Pub.L. 95–216 effective Jan. 1, 1978, see section 351(d) of Pub.L. 95–216, set out as a note under section 409 of this title.

Repeals

Pub.L. 110–234 repealed effective May 22, 2008, see Repeal of Duplicative Enactment by Pub.L. 110–246, § 4(a), set out in a note under 7 U.S.C.A. § 8701.

§ 413. Quarter and quarter of coverage

(a) Definitions

For the purposes of this subchapter—

(1) The term "quarter", and the term "calendar quarter", mean a period of three calendar months ending on March 31, June 30, September 30, or December 31.

(2)(A) The term "quarter of coverage" means—

(i) for calendar years before 1978, and subject to the provisions of subparagraph (B), a quarter in which an individual has been paid $50 or more in wages (except wages for agricultural labor paid after 1954) or for which he has been credited (as determined under section 412 of this title) with $100 or more of self-employment income; and

(ii) for calendar years after 1977, and subject to the provisions of subparagraph (B), each portion of the total of the wages paid and the self-employment income credited (pursuant to section 412 of this title) to an individual in a calendar year which equals the amount required for a quarter of coverage in that calendar year (as determined under subsection (d)), with such quarter of coverage being assigned to a specific calendar quarter in such calendar year only if necessary in the case of any individual who has attained age 62 or died or is under a disability and the requirements for insured status in subsection (a) or (b) of section 414 of this title, the requirements for entitlement to a computation or recomputation of his primary insurance amount, or the requirements of paragraph (3) of section 416(i) of this title would not otherwise be met.

(B) Notwithstanding the provisions of subparagraph (A)—

(i) no quarter after the quarter in which an individual dies shall be a quarter of coverage, and no quarter any part of which is included in a period of disability (other than the initial quarter and the last quarter of such period) shall be a quarter of coverage;

(ii) if the wages paid to an individual in any calendar year equal $3,000 in the case of a calendar year before 1951, or $3,600 in the case of a calendar year after 1950 and before 1955, or $4,200 in the case of a calendar year after 1954 and before 1959, or $4,800 in the case of a calendar year after 1958 and before 1966, or $6,600 in the case of a calendar year after 1965 and before 1968, or $7,800 in the case of a calendar year after 1967 and before 1972, or $9,000 in the case of the calendar year 1972, or $10,800 in the case of the calendar year 1973, or $13,200 in the case of the calendar year 1974, or an amount equal to the contribution and benefit base (as determined under section 430 of this title) in the case of any calendar year after 1974 and before 1978 with respect to which such contribution and benefit base is effective, each quarter of such year shall (subject to clauses (i) and (v)) be a quarter of coverage;

(iii) if an individual has self-employment income for a taxable year, and if the sum of such income and the wages paid to him during such year equals $3,600 in the case of a taxable year beginning after 1950 and ending before 1955, or $4,200 in the case of a taxable year ending after 1954 and before 1959, or $4,800 in the case of a taxable year ending after 1958 and before 1966, or $6,600 in the case of a taxable year ending after 1965 and before 1968, or $7,800 in the case of a taxable year ending after 1967 and before 1972, or $9,000 in the case of a taxable year beginning after 1971 and before 1973, or $10,800 in the case of a taxable year beginning after 1972 and before 1974, or $13,200 in the case of a taxable year beginning after 1973 and before 1975, or an amount equal to the contribution and benefit base (as determined under section 430 of this title) which is effective for the calendar year in the case of any taxable year beginning in any calendar year after 1974 and before 1978, each quarter any part of which falls in such year shall (subject to clauses (i) and (v)) be a quarter of coverage;

(iv) if an individual is paid wages for agricultural labor in a calendar year after 1954 and before 1978, then, subject to clauses (i) and (v), (I) the last quarter of such year which can be but is not otherwise a quarter of coverage shall be a quarter of coverage if such wages equal or exceed $100 but are less than $200; (II) the last two quarters of such year which can be but are not otherwise quarters of coverage shall be quarters of coverage if such wages equal or exceed $200 but are less than $300; (III) the last three quarters of such year which can be but are not otherwise quarters of coverage shall be quarters of coverage if such wages equal or exceed $300 but are less than $400; and (IV) each quarter of such year which is not otherwise a quarter of coverage shall be a quarter of coverage if such wages are $400 or more;

(v) no quarter shall be counted as a quarter of coverage prior to the beginning of such quarter;

(vi) not more than one quarter of coverage may be credited to a calendar quarter; and

(vii) no more than four quarters of coverage may be credited to any calendar year after 1977.

If in the case of an individual who has attained age 62 or died or is under a disability and who has been paid wages for agricultural labor in a calendar year after 1954 and before 1978, the requirements for insured status in subsection (a) or (b) of section 414 of this title, the requirements for entitlement to a computation or recomputation of his primary insurance amount, or the requirements of paragraph (3) of section 416(i) of this title are not met after assignment of quarters of coverage to quarters in such year as provided in clause (iv) of the preceding sentence, but would be met if such quarters of coverage were assigned to different quarters in such year, then such quarters of coverage shall instead be assigned, for purposes only of determining compliance with such requirements, to such different quarters. If, in the case of an individual who did not die prior to January 1, 1955, and who attained age 62 (if a woman) or age 65 (if a man) or died before July 1, 1957, the requirements for insured status in section 414(a)(3) of this title are not met because of his having too few quarters of coverage but would be met if his quarters of coverage in the first calendar year in which he had any covered employment had been determined on the basis of the period during which wages were earned rather than on the basis of the period during which wages were paid (any such wages paid that are reallocated on an earned basis shall not be used in determining quarters of coverage for subsequent calendar years), then upon application filed by the individual or his survivors and satisfactory proof of his record of wages earned being furnished by such individual or his survivors, the quarters of coverage in such calendar year may be determined on the basis of the periods during which wages were earned.

(b) Crediting of wages paid in 1937

With respect to wages paid to an individual in the six-month periods commencing either January 1, 1937, or July 1, 1937; (A) if wages of not less than $100 were paid in any such period, one-half of the total amount thereof shall be deemed to have been paid in each of the calendar quarters in such period; and (B) if wages of less than $100 were paid in any such period, the total amount thereof shall be deemed to have been paid in the latter quarter of such period, except that if in any such period, the individual attained age sixty-five, all of the wages paid in such period shall be deemed to have been paid before such age was attained.

(c) Alternative method for determining quarters of coverage with respect to wages in period from 1937 to 1950

For purposes of sections 414(a) and 415(d) of this title, an individual shall be deemed to have one quarter of coverage for each $400 of his total wages prior to 1951 (as defined in section 415(d)(1)(C) of this title), except where such individual is not a fully insured individual on the basis of the number of quarters of coverage so derived plus the number of quarters of coverage derived from the wages and self-employment income credited to such individual for periods after 1950.

(d) Amount required for a quarter of coverage

(1) The amount of wages and self-employment income which an individual must have in order to be credited with a quarter of coverage in any year under subsection (a)(2)(A)(ii) shall be $250 in the calendar year 1978 and the amount determined under paragraph (2) of this subsection for years after 1978.

(2) The Commissioner of Social Security shall, on or before November 1 of 1978 and of every year thereafter, determine and publish in the Federal Register the amount of wages and self-employment income which an individual must have in order to be credited with a quarter of coverage in the succeeding calendar year. The amount required for a quarter of coverage shall be the larger of—

(A) the amount in effect in the calendar year in which the determination under this subsection is made, or

(B) the product of the amount prescribed in paragraph (1) which is required for a quarter of coverage in 1978 and the ratio of the national average wage index (as defined in section 409(k)(1) of this title) for the calendar year before the year in which the determination under this paragraph is made to the national average wage index (as so defined) for 1976,

with such product, if not a multiple of $10, being rounded to the next higher multiple of $10 where such amount is a multiple of $5 but not of $10 and to the nearest multiple of $10 in any other case.

(Aug. 14, 1935, c. 531, Title II, § 213, as added Aug. 28, 1950, c. 809, Title I, § 104(a), 64 Stat. 492, 504; amended July 18, 1952, c. 945, § 3(a), 66 Stat. 770; Sept. 1, 1954, c. 1206, Title I, §§ 104(c), 106(a), 108(b), 68 Stat. 1078, 1084; Aug. 1, 1956, c. 836, Title I, § 105(c), 70 Stat. 828; Pub.L. 85–840, Title I, § 102(c), Aug. 28, 1958, 72 Stat. 1019; Pub.L. 86–442, § 3, Apr. 22, 1960, 74 Stat. 82; Pub.L. 86–778, Title II, § 206(a), Sept. 13, 1960, 74 Stat. 949; Pub.L. 87–64, Title I,

§ 102(c)(2)(A), (3)(B), June 30, 1961, 75 Stat. 134, 135; Pub.L. 89–97, Title III, § 320(a)(3), July 30, 1965, 79 Stat. 393; Pub.L. 90–248, Title I, §§ 108(a)(3), 155(b)(1), Jan. 2, 1968, 81 Stat. 834, 865; Pub.L. 92–5, Title II, § 203(a)(3), Mar. 17, 1971, 85 Stat. 10; Pub.L. 92–336, Title II, § 203(a)(3), July 1, 1972, 86 Stat. 418; Pub.L. 93–66, Title II, § 203(a)(3), July 9, 1973, 87 Stat. 153; Pub.L. 93–233, § 5(a)(3), Dec. 31, 1973, 87 Stat. 953; Pub.L. 95–216, Title III, §§ 351(c), 352(a), (b), Dec. 20, 1977, 91 Stat. 1550, 1552; Pub.L. 96–473, § 6(c), Oct. 19, 1980, 94 Stat. 2265; Pub.L. 98–369, Div. B, Title VI, § 2663(a)(9), July 18, 1984, 98 Stat. 1164; Pub.L. 101–239, Title X, § 10208(b)(2)(A), (B), (d)(2)(A)(i), Dec. 19, 1989, 103 Stat. 2477, 2478, 2480; Pub.L. 101–508, Title V, § 5117(c)(1), Nov. 5, 1990, 104 Stat. 1388–278; Pub.L. 103–296, Title I, § 107(a)(4), Title III, § 321(a)(15), (e)(2)(A), Aug. 15, 1994, 108 Stat. 1478, 1536, 1539.)

HISTORICAL AND STATUTORY NOTES

Effective and Applicability Provisions

1994 Acts. Amendment by section 107(a)(4) of Pub.L. 103–296 effective Mar. 31, 1995, see section 110 of Pub.L. 103–296, set out as a note under section 401 of this title.

1990 Acts. Section 5117(c)(3) of Pub.L. 101–508, provided that: "The amendments made by this subsection [amending this section and provisions set out as a note under this section] shall apply only with respect to individuals who—

"**(A)** make application for benefits under section 202 of the Social Security Act [section 402 of this title] after the 18–month period following the month in which this Act is enacted [Nov. 1990], and

"**(B)** are not entitled to benefits under section 227 or 228 of such Act [section 427 or 428 of this title] for the month in which such application is made."

1989 Acts. Amendment by section 10208(b)(2)(A), (B) of Pub.L. 101–239 applicable with respect to computation of average total wage amounts (under amended provisions) for calendar years after 1990, including transitional rule, see section 10208(c) of Pub.L. 101–239, set out as a note under section 430 of this title.

1984 Acts. Amendment by section 2663 of Pub.L. 98–369 effective July 18, 1984, but not to be construed as changing or affecting any right, liability, status or interpretation which existed (under the provisions of law involved) before that date, see section 2664(b) of Pub.L. 98–369, set out as a note under section 401 of this title.

1977 Acts. Amendment of subsec. (a)(2) by Pub.L. 95–216 effective Jan. 1, 1978, see section 351(d) of Pub.L. 95–216, set out as a note under section 409 of this title.

Section 352(c) of Pub.L. 95–216 provided that: "The amendments made by this section [amending subsec. (a)(2)(A)(ii), relating to determinations under subsec. (d) of this section of amounts for quarters of coverage, and adding subsec. (d) of this section] shall be effective January 1, 1978."

1973 Acts. Amendment by Pub.L. 93–233 applicable only with respect to remuneration paid after, and taxable years beginning after, 1973, see section 5(e) of Pub.L. 93–233, set out as a note under section 409 of this title.

Amendment by Pub.L. 93–66 applicable only with respect to remuneration paid after, and taxable years beginning after, 1973, see section 203(e) of Pub.L. 93–66, set out as a note under section 409 of this title.

1972 Acts. Amendment of subsec. (a)(2)(ii) by section 203(a)(3)(A) of Pub.L. 92–336 applicable only with respect to remuneration paid after December, 1972, see section 203(c) of Pub.L. 92–336, set out as a note under section 409 of this title.

Amendment of subsec. (a)(2)(iii) of this section by section 203(a)(3)(B) of Pub.L. 92–336 applicable only with respect to taxable years beginning after 1972, see section 203(c) of Pub.L. 92–336, set out as a note under section 409 of this title.

1971 Acts. Amendment of subsec. (a)(2)(ii) of this section by section 203(a)(3)(A) of Pub.L. 92–5 applicable only with respect to remuneration paid after December, 1971, see section 203(c) of Pub.L. 92–5, set out as a note under section 409 of this title.

Amendment of subsec. (a)(2)(iii) by section 203(a)(3)(B) of Pub.L. 92–5 applicable only with respect to taxable years beginning after 1971, see section 203(c) of Pub.L. 92–5, set out as a note under section 409 of this title.

1968 Acts. Amendment of subsec. (a)(2)(ii) by section 108(a)(3)(A) of Pub.L. 90–248 applicable only with respect to remuneration paid after December, 1967, and amendment of subsec. (a)(2)(iii) of this section by section 108(a)(3)(B) applicable only with respect to taxable years ending after 1967, see section 108(c) of Pub.L. 90–248, set out as a note under section 409 of this title.

Section 155(b)(2) of Pub.L. 90–248, as amended Pub.L. 101–508, Title V, § 5117(c)(2), Nov. 5, 1990, 104 Stat. 1388–278, provided that: "The amendment made by paragraph (1) [enacting subsec. (c) of this section] shall apply only in the case of an individual who applies for benefits under section 202(a) of the Social Security Act [section 402(a) of this title] after the date of the enactment of this Act [Jan. 2, 1968], or who dies without being entitled to benefits under section 202(a) or 223 of the Social Security Act [section 402(a) or 423 of this title]."

1965 Acts. Amendment of subsec. (a)(2)(ii) by section 320(a)(3)(A) of Pub.L. 89–97 applicable with respect to remuneration paid after December, 1965, see section 320(c) of Pub.L. 89–97, set out as a note under section 3121 of Title 26, Internal Revenue Code.

Amendment of subsec. (a)(2)(iii) by section 320(a)(3)(B) of Pub.L. 89–97 applicable with respect to taxable years ending after 1965, see section 320(c) of Pub.L. 89–97, set out as a note under section 3121 of Title 26.

1961 Acts. Amendment of subsec. (a) by Pub.L. 87–64 applicable with respect to monthly benefits for months beginning on or after Aug. 1, 1961, based on applications filed in or after March, 1961, and with respect to lump-sum death payments under this subchapter in the case of deaths on or after Aug. 1, 1961, see sections 102(f) and 109 of Pub.L. 87–64, set out as notes under section 402 of this title.

1960 Acts. Section 206(b) of Pub.L. 86–778 provided that:

"**(1)** Except as provided in paragraph (2), the amendment made by subsection (a) [to subsec. (a)(2) of this section] shall apply only in the case of monthly benefits under Title II of the Social Security Act [this subchapter], and the lump-sum death payment under section 202 of such Act [section 402 of this title], based on the wages and self-employment income of an individual—

"**(A)** who becomes entitled to benefits under section 202(a) or 223 of such Act [section 402(a) or 423 of this title] on the basis of an application filed in or after the month in which this Act is enacted [September, 1960]; or

"**(B)** who is (or would, but for the provisions of section 215(f)(6) of the Social Security Act [section 415(f)(6) of this title], be) entitled to a recomputation of his primary insurance amount under section 215(f)(2)(A) of such Act [section 415(f)(2)(A) of this title] on the basis of an application filed in or after the month in which this Act is enacted [September, 1960]; or

"(C) who dies without becoming entitled to benefits under section 202(a) or 223 of the Social Security Act [section 402(a) or 423 of this title], and (unless he dies a currently insured individual but not a fully insured individual (as those terms are defined in section 214 of such Act [section 414 of this title])) without leaving any individual entitled (on the basis of his wages and self-employment income) to survivor's benefits or a lump-sum death payment under section 202 of such Act [section 402 of this title] on the basis of an application filed prior to the month in which this Act is enacted [September, 1960]; or

"(D) who dies in or after the month in which this Act is enacted [September, 1960] and whose survivors are (or would, but for the provisions of section 215(f)(6) of the Social Security Act [section 415(f)(6) of this title], be) entitled to a recomputation of his primary insurance amount under section 215(f)(4)(A) of such Act [section 415(f)(4)(A) of this title]; or

"(E) who dies prior to the month in which this Act is enacted [September, 1960] and (i) whose survivors are (or would, but for the provisions of section 215(f)(6) of the Social Security Act [section 415(f)(6) of this title], be) entitled to a recomputation of his primary insurance amount under section 215(f)(4)(A) of such Act [section 415(f)(4)(A) of this title], and (ii) on the basis of whose wages and self-employment income no individual was entitled to survivor's benefits or a lump-sum death payment under section 202 of such Act [section 402 of this title] on the basis of an application filed prior to the month in which this Act is enacted [September, 1960] (and no individual was entitled to such a benefit, without the filing of an application, for any month prior to the month in which this Act is enacted [September 1960]); or

"(F) who files an application for a recomputation under section 102(f)(2)(B) of the Social Security Amendments of 1954 [formerly set out as a note under section 415 of this title] in or after the month in which this Act is enacted [September, 1960] and is (or would, but for the fact that such recomputation would not result in a higher primary insurance amount, be) entitled to have his primary insurance amount recomputed under such subparagraph; or

"(G) who dies and whose survivors are (or would, but for the fact that such recomputation would not result in a higher primary insurance amount for such individual, be) entitled, on the basis of an application filed in or after the month in which this Act [September, 1960] is enacted, to have his primary insurance amount recomputed under section 102(f)(2)(B) of the Social Security Amendments of 1954 [set out as a note under section 415 of this title].

"(2) The amendment made by subsection (a) [to subsec. (a)(2) of this section] shall also be applicable in the case of applications for disability determination under section 216(i) of the Social Security Act [section 416(i) of this title] filed in or after the month in which this Act is enacted [September, 1960].

"(3) Notwithstanding any other provision of this subsection, in the case of any individual who would not be a fully insured individual under section 214(a) of the Social Security Act [section 414(a) of this title] except for the enactment of this section, no benefits shall be payable on the basis of his wages and self-employment income for any month prior to the month in which this Act is enacted [September, 1960]."

Section 3 of Pub.L. 86–442 provided in part that: "This amendment [to subsec. (a)(2)(B)] shall be applicable in the case of monthly benefits under Title II of the Social Security Act [this subchapter] for months after June 1957, and in the case of the lump-sum death payments under such title, with respect to deaths occurring after such month; the requirements for filing applications for such benefits and payments within certain time limits, as prescribed in sections 202(i) and 202(j) of such title [sections 402(i) and 402(j) of this title], shall not apply if an application is filed within the one-year period beginning with the first day of the month after the month in which this Act is enacted [April, 1960]."

1954 Acts. Section 106(h) of Act Sept. 1, 1954 provided that: "Notwithstanding the provisions of section 215(f)(1) of the Social Security Act [section 415(f) of this title], the amendments made by subsections (a), (b), (c), (d), (e), and (f) of this section [amending this section and sections 414 to 417 of this title and section 228e of Title 45, Railroads] shall apply with respect to monthly benefits under title II of the Social Security Act [subchapter II of this chapter] for months after June 1955, and with respect to lump-sum death payments under such title in the case of deaths occurring after June 1955; but no recomputation of benefits by reason of such amendments shall be regarded as a recomputation for purposes of section 215(f) of the Social Security Act [section 415(f) of this title]."

1952 Acts. Section 3(f) of Act July 18, 1952 provided that: "Notwithstanding the provisions of section 215(f)(1) of the Social Security Act [section 415(f)(1) of this title], the amendments made by subsections (a), (b), (c), and (d) of this section [to sections 413 to 416, 420 and 421 of this title] shall apply to monthly benefits under Title II of the Social Security Act [this subchapter] for months after June 1953, and to lump-sum death payments under such title in the case of deaths occurring after June 1953; but no recomputation of benefits by reason of such amendments shall be regarded as a recomputation for purposes of section 215(f) of the Social Security Act [section 415(f) of this title]."

Section 3(g) of Act July 18, 1952 provided that: "Notwithstanding the preceding provisions of this section and the amendments made thereby [to sections 413 to 416, 420, and 421 of this title], such provisions and amendments shall cease to be in effect at the close of June 30, 1953, and after such amendments cease to be in effect any provision of law amended thereby shall be in full force and effect as though this Act [Act July 18, 1952] had not been enacted."

Quarter of Coverage Amount for 1986

By notice of the Secretary of Health and Human Services, Oct. 29, 1985, published in the Federal Register on Oct. 31, 1985, at 50 F.R. 45560, it was determined and announced, pursuant to the authority contained in subsec. (d)(2) of this section, that the 1986 amount of earnings required for a quarter of coverage is $440.

§ 414. Insured status for purposes of old-age and survivors insurance benefits

For the purposes of this subchapter—

(a) "Fully insured individual" defined

The term "fully insured individual" means any individual who had not less than—

(1) one quarter of coverage (whenever acquired) for each calendar year elapsing after 1950 (or, if later, the year in which he attained age 21) and before the year in which he died or (if earlier) the year in which he attained age 62, except that in no case shall an individual be a fully insured individual unless he has at least 6 quarters of coverage; or

(2) 40 quarters of coverage; or

(3) in the case of an individual who died before 1951, 6 quarters of coverage;

not counting as an elapsed year for purposes of paragraph (1) any year any part of which was included in a period of disability (as defined in section 416(i) of this title), and who satisfies the criterion specified in subsection (c).

(b) "Currently insured individual" defined

The term "currently insured individual" means any individual who had not less than six quarters of coverage during the thirteen-quarter period ending with (1) the quarter in which he died, (2) the quarter in which he became entitled to old-age insurance benefits, (3) the quarter in which he became entitled to primary insurance benefits under this subchapter as in effect prior to August 28, 1950, or (4) in the case of any individual entitled to disability insurance benefits, the quarter in which he most recently became entitled to disability insurance benefits, not counting as part of such thirteen-quarter period any quarter any part of which was included in a period of disability unless such quarter was a quarter of coverage, and who satisfies the criterion specified in subsection (c).

(c) Criterion described

For purposes of subsections (a) and (b), the criterion specified in this subsection is that the individual, if not a United States citizen or national—

(1) has been assigned a social security account number that was, at the time of assignment, or at any later time, consistent with the requirements of subclause (I) or (III) of section 405(c)(2)(B)(i) of this title; or

(2) at the time any such quarters of coverage are earned—

(A) is described in subparagraph (B) or (D) of section 1101(a)(15) of Title 8,

(B) is lawfully admitted temporarily to the United States for business (in the case of an individual described in such subparagraph (B)) or the performance as a crewman (in the case of an individual described in such subparagraph (D)), and

(C) the business engaged in or service as a crewman performed is within the scope of the terms of such individual's admission to the United States.

(Aug. 14, 1935, c. 531, Title II, § 214, as added Aug. 28, 1950, c. 809, Title I, § 104(a), 64 Stat. 492, 505; amended July 18, 1952, c. 945, § 3(b), 66 Stat. 770; Sept. 1, 1954, c. 1206, Title I, §§ 106(b), 108(a), 68 Stat. 1079, 1083; Aug. 1, 1956, c. 836, Title I, § 108, 70 Stat. 830; Pub.L. 85–840, Title II, § 205(*l*), Aug. 28, 1958, 72 Stat. 1025; Pub.L. 86–778, Title II, § 204(a), Sept. 13, 1960, 74 Stat. 948; Pub.L. 87–64, Title I, § 103(a), June 30, 1961, 75 Stat. 137; Pub.L. 92–603, Title I, § 104(a), Oct. 30, 1972, 86 Stat. 1340; Pub.L. 108–203, Title II, § 211(a), Mar. 2, 2004, 118 Stat. 518.)

HISTORICAL AND STATUTORY NOTES

Codifications

Amendment by Pub.L. 108–203, § 211(a), to an unidentified "Section 214" was executed to this section, which was enacted by section 214 of the Social Security Act, as the probable intent of Congress.

Effective and Applicability Provisions

2004 Acts. Pub.L. 108–203, Title II, § 211(c), Mar. 2, 2004, 118 Stat. 518, provided that: "The amendments made by this section [amending this section and 42 U.S.C.A. § 423] apply to benefit applications based on social security account numbers issued on or after January 1, 2004."

1972 Acts. Section 104(j) of Pub.L. 92–603 provided that:

"(1) The amendments made by this section [amending subsec. (a)(1) of this section, sections 415(b)(3), 416(i)(3)(A), 423(a)(2), (c)(1)(A), and 427(a)(1), (b)(1) of this title and provisions set out as a note under section 415 of this title] (except the amendment made by subsection (i), and the amendment made by subsection (g) to section 209(i) of the Social Security Act) shall apply only in the case of a man who attains (or would attain) age 62 after December 1974. The amendment made by subsection (i), and the amendment made by subsection (g) to section 209(i) of the Social Security Act [amending section 409(i) of this title and section 3121(a)(9) of Title 26, Internal Revenue Code], shall apply only with respect to payments after 1974.

"(2) In the case of a man who attains age 62 prior to 1975, the number of his elapsed years for purposes of section 215(b)(3) of the Social Security Act [section 415(b)(3) of this title] shall be equal to (A) the number determined under such section as in effect on September 1, 1972, or (B) if less, the number determined as though he attained age 65 in 1975, except that monthly benefits under Title II of the Social Security Act [this subchapter] for months prior to January 1973 payable on the basis of his wages and self-employment income shall be determined as though this section had not been enacted.

"(3)(A) In the case of a man who attains or will attain age 62 in 1973, the figure '65' in sections 214(a)(1), 223(c)(1)(A), and 216(i)(3)(A) of the Social Security Act [subsec. (a)(1) of this section and sections 423(c)(1)(A) and 416(i)(3)(A) of this title] shall be deemed to read '64'.

"(B) In the case of a man who attains or will attain age 62 in 1974, the figure '65' in sections 214(a)(1), 223(c)(1)(A), and 216(i)(3)(A) of the Social Security Act [subsec. (a)(1) of this section and sections 423(c)(1)(A) and 416(i)(3)(A) of this title] shall be deemed to read '63'."

1961 Acts. Section 103(b) of Pub.L. 87–64 provided that:

"The amendment made by subsection (a) [to subsec. (a) of this section] shall apply—

"(1) in the case of monthly benefits under Title II of the Social Security Act [this subchapter] for months beginning on or after the effective date of this title [see Effective Date of 1961 Amendment note under section 402 of this title], based on applications filed in or after March 1961,

"(2) in the case of lump-sum death payments under such title [this subchapter] with respect to deaths on or after the effective date of this title [see note under section 402 of this title], and

"(3) in the case of an application for a disability determination (with respect to a period of disability, as defined in section 216(i) of such Act [section 416(i) of this title]) filed in or after March 1961."

1960 Acts. Section 204(d)(1) of Pub.L. 86–778 provided that: "The amendments made by subsections (a) and (b) of this section [amending subsec. (a) of this section and enacting provisions set out as a note under section 415 of this title] shall be applicable (A) in the case of monthly benefits under Title II of the Social Security Act [this subchapter] for months after the month in which this Act is enacted [September, 1960], on the basis of applications filed in or after such month, (B) in the case of lump-sum death payments under such title with respect to deaths occurring after such month, and (C) in the case of an application for a disability determination with respect to a period of disability (as defined in section 216(i) of the Social Security Act [section 416(i) of this title]) filed after such month."

1958 Acts. Amendment of subsec. (b) of this section by section 205(*l*) of Pub.L. 85–840 applicable with respect to monthly benefits under this subchapter for months after August, 1958, but only if an application for such benefits is filed on or after Aug. 28, 1958, see section 207(a) of Pub.L. 85–840, set out as a note under section 416 of this title.

1954 Acts. Amendment by section 106(b) of Act Sept. 1, 1954 applicable with respect to monthly benefits under this sub-chapter for months after June 1955, and with respect to lump-sum death payments under such subchapter in the case of deaths occurring after June 1955; but that no recomputation of benefits by reason of such amendments shall be regarded as a recomputation for purposes of section 415(f) of this title, see section 106(h) of Act Sept. 1, 1954, set out as a note under section 413 of this title.

1952 Acts. For effective and termination dates of amendment by Act July 18, 1952, see sections 3(f) and 3(g) of Act July 18, 1952, set out as a note under section 413 of this title.

1950 Acts. Section applicable (1) in case of monthly benefits for months after August, 1950, and (2) in the case of lump-sum death payments with respect to deaths after August, 1950, see section 104(b) of Act Aug. 28, 1950, set out as a note under section 409 of this title.

Determination of Entitlement to Monthly Benefits for September 1960 and Prior Months and Individual's Closing Date Prior to 1960

Section 204(d)(2) of Pub.L. 86–778 provided that the provisions of subsec. (a) of this section in effect prior to Sept. 13, 1960, and the provisions of section 109 of Act Sept. 1, 1954, c. 1206, 68 Stat. 1084, set out as a note under section 415 of this title, as in effect prior to such date were to apply for purposes of determining entitlement to monthly benefits under this subchapter for September, 1960, and prior months with respect to wages and self-employment income of an individual and for purposes of determining an individual's closing date prior to 1960 under section 415(b)(3)(B) of this title.

Employees of Nonprofit Organizations as Fully Insured Individuals

Pub.L. 98–21, Title I, § 102(e), Apr. 20, 1983, 97 Stat. 71, provided that:

"(1) If any individual—

"(A) On January 1, 1984, is age 55 or over, and is an employee of an organization described in section 210(a)(8)(B) of the Social Security Act [section 410(a)(8)(B) of this title] (A) which does not have in effect (on that date) a waiver certificate under section 3121(k) of the Internal Revenue Code of 1954 [section 3121(k) of Title 26, Internal Revenue Code] and (B) to the employees of which social security coverage is extended on January 1, 1984, solely by reason of the enactment of this section [amending section 410 of this title and section 3121 of Title 26 and enacting provisions set out as notes under section 3121 of Title 26], and

"(B) after December 31, 1983, acquires the number of quarters of coverage (within the meaning of section 213 of the Social Security Act [section 413 of this title]) which is required for purposes of this subparagraph under paragraph (2),

then such individual shall be deemed to be a fully insured individual (as defined in section 214 of the Social Security Act [this section]) for all of the purposes of Title II of such Act [this subchapter].

"(2) The number of quarters of coverage which is required for purposes of subparagraph (B) of paragraph (1) shall be determined as follows:

"In the case of an individual who on January 1, 1984, is—	"The number of quarters of coverage so required shall be—
"age 59 or over but less than age 60	8
"age 60 or over	6
"age 58 or over but less than age 59	12
"age 57 or over but less than age 58	16
"age 55 or over but less than age 57	20."

§ 415. Computation of primary insurance amount

For the purposes of this subchapter—

(a) Primary insurance amount

(1)(A) The primary insurance amount of an individual shall (except as otherwise provided in this section) be equal to the sum of—

(i) 90 percent of the individual's average indexed monthly earnings (determined under subsection (b)) to the extent that such earnings do not exceed the amount established for purposes of this clause by subparagraph (B),

(ii) 32 percent of the individual's average indexed monthly earnings to the extent that such earnings exceed the amount established for purposes of clause (i) but do not exceed the amount established for purposes of this clause by subparagraph (B), and

(iii) 15 percent of the individual's average indexed monthly earnings to the extent that such earnings exceed the amount established for purposes of clause (ii),

rounded, if not a multiple of $0.10, to the next lower multiple of $0.10, and thereafter increased as provided in subsection (i).

(B)(i) For individuals who initially become eligible for old-age or disability insurance benefits, or who die (before becoming eligible for such benefits), in the calendar year 1979, the amount established for purposes of clause (i) and (ii) of subparagraph (A) shall be $180 and $1,085, respectively.

(ii) For individuals who initially become eligible for old-age or disability insurance benefits, or who die (before becoming eligible for such benefits), in any calendar year after 1979, each of the amounts so established shall equal the product of the corresponding amount established with respect to the calendar year 1979 under clause (i) of this subparagraph and the quotient obtained by dividing—

(I) the national average wage index (as defined in section 409(k)(1) of this title) for the second calendar year preceding the calendar year for which the determination is made, by

(II) the national average wage index (as so defined) for 1977.

(iii) Each amount established under clause (ii) for any calendar year shall be rounded to the nearest $1, except that any amount so established which is a multiple of $0.50 but not of $1 shall be rounded to the next higher $1.

(C)(i) No primary insurance amount computed under subparagraph (A) may be less than an amount equal to $11.50 multiplied by the individual's years of coverage in excess of 10, or the increased amount determined for purposes of this clause under subsection (i).

(ii) For purposes of clause (i), the term "years of coverage" with respect to any individual means the number (not exceeding 30) equal to the sum of (I) the number (not exceeding 14 and disregarding any fraction) determined by dividing (a) the total of the wages credited to such individual (including wages deemed to be paid prior to 1951 to such individual under section 417 of this title, compensation under the Railroad Retirement Act of 1937 prior to 1951 which is creditable to such individual pursuant to this subchapter, and wages deemed to be paid prior to 1951 to such individual under section 431 of this title) for years after 1936 and before 1951 by (b) $900, plus (II) the number equal to the number of years after 1950 each of which is a computation base year (within the meaning of subsection (b)(2)(B)(ii)) and in each of which he is credited with wages (including wages deemed to be paid to such individual under section 417 of this title, compensation under the Railroad Retirement Act of 1937 or 1974 which is creditable to such individual pursuant to this subchapter, and wages deemed to be paid to such individual under section 429 of this title) and self-employment income of not less than 25 percent (in the case of a year after 1950 and before 1978) of the maximum amount which (pursuant to subsection (e)) may be counted for such year, or 25 percent (in the case of a year after 1977 and before 1991) or 15 percent (in the case of a year after 1990) of the maximum amount which (pursuant to subsection (e)) could be counted for such year if section 430 of this title as in effect immediately prior to December 20, 1977, had remained in effect without change (except that, for purposes of subsection (b) of such section 430 of this title as so in effect, the reference to the contribution and benefit base in paragraph (1) of such subsection (b) shall be deemed a reference to an amount equal to $45,000, each reference in paragraph (2) of such subsection (b) to the average of the wages of all employees as reported to the Secretary of the Treasury shall be deemed a reference to the national average wage index (as defined in section 409(k)(1) of this title), the reference to a preceding calendar year in paragraph (2)(A) of such subsection (b) shall be deemed a reference to the calendar year before the calendar year in which the determination under subsection (a) of such section 430 of this title is made, and the reference to a calendar year in paragraph (2)(B) of such subsection (b) shall be deemed a reference to 1992).

(D) In each calendar year the Commissioner of Social Security shall publish in the Federal Register, on or before November 1, the formula for computing benefits under this paragraph and for adjusting wages and self-employment income under subsection (b)(3) in the case of an individual who becomes eligible for an old-age insurance benefit, or (if earlier) becomes eligible for a disability insurance benefit or dies, in the following year, and the national average wage index (as defined in section 409(k)(1) of this title) on which that formula is based.

(2)(A) A year shall not be counted as the year of an individual's death or eligibility for purposes of this subsection or subsection (i) in any case where such individual was entitled to a disability insurance benefit for any of the 12 months immediately preceding the month of such death or eligibility (but there shall be counted instead the year of the individual's eligibility for the disability insurance benefit or benefits to which he was entitled during such 12 months).

(B) In the case of an individual who was entitled to a disability insurance benefit for any of the 12 months before the month in which he became entitled to an old-age insurance benefit, became reentitled to a disability insurance benefit, or died, the primary insurance amount for determining any benefit attributable to that entitlement, reentitlement, or death is the greater of—

(i) the primary insurance amount upon which such disability insurance benefit was based, increased by the amount of each general benefit increase (as defined in subsection (i)(3)), and each increase provided under subsection (i)(2), that would have applied to such primary insurance amount had the individual remained entitled to such disability insurance benefit until the month in which he became so entitled or reentitled or died, or

(ii) the amount computed under paragraph (1)(C).

(C) In the case of an individual who was entitled to a disability insurance benefit for any month, and with respect to whom a primary insurance amount is required to be computed at any time after the close of the period of the individual's disability (whether because of such individual's subsequent entitlement to old-age insurance benefits or to a disability insurance benefit based upon a subsequent period of disability, or because of such individual's death), the primary insurance amount so computed may in no case be less than the primary insurance amount with respect to which such former disability insurance benefit was most recently determined.

(3)(A) Paragraph (1) applies only to an individual who was not eligible for an old-age insurance benefit prior to January 1979 and who in that or any succeeding month—

(i) becomes eligible for such a benefit,

(ii) becomes eligible for a disability insurance benefit, or

(iii) dies,

and (except for subparagraph (C)(i) thereof) it applies to every such individual except to the extent otherwise provided by paragraph (4).

(B) For purposes of this subchapter, an individual is deemed to be eligible—

(i) for old-age insurance benefits, for months beginning with the month in which he attains age 62, or

(ii) for disability insurance benefits, for months beginning with the month in which his period of disability began as provided under section 416(i)(2)(C) of this title,

except as provided in paragraph (2)(A) in cases where fewer than 12 months have elapsed since the termination of a prior period of disability.

(4) Paragraph (1) (except for subparagraph (C)(i) thereof) does not apply to the computation or recomputation of a primary insurance amount for—

(A) an individual who was eligible for a disability insurance benefit for a month prior to January 1979 unless, prior to the month in which occurs the event described in clause (i), (ii), or (iii) of paragraph (3)(A), there occurs a period of at least 12 consecutive months for which he was not entitled to a disability insurance benefit, or

(B) an individual who had wages or self-employment income credited for one or more years prior to 1979, and who was not eligible for an old-age or disability insurance benefit, and did not die, prior to January 1979, if in the year for which the computation or recomputation would be made the individual's primary insurance amount would be greater if computed or recomputed—

(i) under this subsection as in effect in December 1978, for purposes of old-age insurance benefits in the case of an individual who becomes eligible for such benefits prior to 1984, or

(ii) as provided by subsection (d), in the case of an individual to whom such section applies.

In determining whether an individual's primary insurance amount would be greater if computed or recomputed as provided in subparagraph (B), (I) the table of benefits in effect in December 1978, as modified by paragraph (6), shall be applied without regard to any increases in that table which may become effective (in accordance with subsection (i)(4)) for years after 1978 (subject to clause (iii) of subsection (i)(2)(A)) and (II) such individual's average monthly wage shall be computed as provided by subsection (b)(4).

(5)(A) Subject to subparagraphs (B), (C), (D) and (E), for purposes of computing the primary insurance amount (after December 1978) of an individual to whom paragraph (1) does not apply (other than an individual described in paragraph (4)(B)), this section as in effect in December 1978 shall remain in effect, except that, effective for January 1979, the dollar amount specified in paragraph (3) of this subsection shall be increased to $11.50.

(B)(i) Subject to clauses (ii), (iii), and (iv), and notwithstanding any other provision of law, the primary insurance amount of any individual described in subparagraph (C) shall be, in lieu of the primary insurance amount as computed pursuant to any of the provisions referred to in subparagraph (D), the primary insurance amount computed under subsection (a) of this section as in effect in December 1978, without regard to subsections (b)(4) and (c) of this section as so in effect.

(ii) The computation of a primary insurance amount under this subparagraph shall be subject to section 104(j)(2) of the Social Security Amendments of 1972 (relating to the number of elapsed years under subsection (b)).

(iii) In computing a primary insurance amount under this subparagraph, the dollar amount specified in paragraph (3) of subsection (a) (as in effect in December 1978) shall be increased to $11.50.

(iv) In the case of an individual to whom subsection (d) applies, the primary insurance amount of such individual shall be the greater of—

(I) the primary insurance amount computed under the preceding clauses of this subparagraph, or

(II) the primary insurance amount computed under subsection (d).

(C) An individual is described in this subparagraph if—

(i) paragraph (1) does not apply to such individual by reason of such individual's eligibility for an old-age or disability insurance benefit, or the individual's death, prior to 1979, and

(ii) such individual's primary insurance amount computed under this section as in effect immediately before November 5, 1990, would have been computed under the provisions described in subparagraph (D).

(D) The provisions described in this subparagraph are—

(i) the provisions of this subsection as in effect prior to July 30, 1965, if such provisions would preclude the use of wages prior to 1951 in the computation of the primary insurance amount,

(ii) the provisions of section 409 of this title as in effect prior to August 28, 1950, and

(iii) the provisions of subsection (d) as in effect prior to December 20, 1977.

(E) For purposes of this paragraph, the table for determining primary insurance amounts and maximum family benefits contained in this section in December 1978 shall be revised as provided by subsection (i) for each year after 1978.

(6)(A) In applying the table of benefits in effect in December 1978 under this section for purposes of the last sentence of paragraph (4), such table, revised as provided by subsection (i), as applicable, shall be extended for average monthly wages of less than $76.00 and primary insurance benefits (as determined under subsection (d)) of less than $16.20.

(B) The Commissioner of Social Security shall determine and promulgate in regulations the methodology for extending the table under subparagraph (A).

(7)(A) In the case of an individual whose primary insurance amount would be computed under paragraph (1) of this subsection, who—

(i) attains age 62 after 1985 (except where he or she became entitled to a disability insurance benefit before 1986 and remained so entitled in any of the 12 months immediately preceding his or her attainment of age 62), or

(ii) would attain age 62 after 1985 and becomes eligible for a disability insurance benefit after 1985,

and who first becomes eligible after 1985 for a monthly periodic payment (including a payment determined under subparagraph (C), but excluding (I) a payment under the Railroad Retirement Act of 1974 or 1937, (II) a payment by a social security system of a foreign country based on an agreement concluded between the United States and such foreign country pursuant to section 433 of this title, and (III) a payment based wholly on service as a member of a uniformed service (as defined in section 410(m) of this title)) which is based in whole or in part upon his or her earnings for service which did not constitute "employment" as defined in section 410 of this title for purposes of this subchapter (hereafter in this paragraph and in subsection (d)(3) referred to as "noncovered service"), the primary insurance amount of that individual during his or her concurrent entitlement to such monthly periodic payment and to old-age or disability insurance benefits shall be computed or recomputed under subparagraph (B).

(B)(i) If paragraph (1) of this subsection would apply to such an individual (except for subparagraph (A) of this paragraph), there shall first be computed an amount equal to the individual's primary insurance amount under paragraph (1) of this subsection, except that for purposes of such computation the percentage of the individual's average indexed monthly earnings established by subparagraph (A)(i) of paragraph (1) shall be the percent specified in clause (ii). There shall then be computed (without regard to this paragraph) a second amount, which shall be equal to the individual's primary insurance amount under paragraph (1) of this subsection, except that such second amount shall be reduced by an amount equal to one-half of the portion of the monthly periodic payment which is attributable to noncovered service performed after 1956 (with such attribution being based on the proportionate number of years of such noncovered service) and to which the individual is entitled (or is deemed to be entitled) for the initial month of his or her concurrent entitlement to such monthly periodic payment and old-age or disability insurance benefits. The individual's primary insurance amount shall be the larger of the two amounts computed under this subparagraph (before the application of subsection (i)) and shall be deemed to be computed under paragraph (1) of this subsection for the purpose of applying other provisions of this subchapter.

(ii) For purposes of clause (i), the percent specified in this clause is—

(I) 80.0 percent with respect to individuals who become eligible (as defined in paragraph (3)(B)) for old-age insurance benefits (or became eligible as so defined for disability insurance benefits before attaining age 62) in 1986;

(II) 70.0 percent with respect to individuals who so become eligible in 1987;

(III) 60.0 percent with respect to individuals who so become eligible in 1988;

(IV) 50.0 percent with respect to individuals who so become eligible in 1989; and

(V) 40.0 percent with respect to individuals who so become eligible in 1990 or thereafter.

(C)(i) Any periodic payment which otherwise meets the requirements of subparagraph (A), but which is paid on other than a monthly basis, shall be allocated on a basis equivalent to a monthly payment (as determined by the Commissioner of Social Security), and such equivalent monthly payment shall constitute a monthly periodic payment for purposes of this paragraph.

(ii) In the case of an individual who has elected to receive a periodic payment that has been reduced so as to provide a survivor's benefit to any other individual, the payment shall be deemed to be increased (for purposes of any computation under this paragraph or subsection (d)(3)) by the amount of such reduction.

(iii) For purposes of this paragraph, the term "periodic payment" includes a payment payable in a lump sum if it is a commutation of, or a substitute for, periodic payments.

(D) This paragraph shall not apply in the case of an individual who has 30 years or more of coverage. In the case of an individual who has more than 20 years of coverage but less than 30 years of coverage (as so defined), the percent specified in the applicable subdivision of subparagraph (B)(ii) shall (if such percent is smaller than the applicable percent specified in the following table) be deemed to be the applicable percent specified in the following table:

If the number of such individual's years of coverage (as so defined) is:	The applicable percent is:
29	85 percent
28	80 percent
27	75 percent
26	70 percent
25	65 percent
24	60 percent
23	55 percent
22	50 percent
21	45 percent.

For purposes of this subparagraph, the term "year of coverage" shall have the meaning provided in paragraph (1)(C)(ii), except that the reference to "15 percent" therein shall be deemed to be a reference to "25 percent".

(E) This paragraph shall not apply in the case of an individual whose eligibility for old-age or disability insurance benefits is based on an agreement concluded pursuant to section 433 of this title or an individual who on January 1, 1984—

(i) is an employee performing service to which social security coverage is extended on that date solely by reason of the amendments made by section 101 of the Social Security Amendments of 1983; or

(ii) is an employee of a nonprofit organization which (on December 31, 1983) did not have in effect a waiver certificate under section 3121(k) of the Internal Revenue Code of 1954 and to the employees of which social security coverage is extended on that date solely by reason of the amendments made by section 102 of that Act, unless social security coverage had previously extended to service performed by such individual as an employee of that organization under a waiver certificate which was subsequently (prior to December 31, 1983) terminated.

(b) Average indexed monthly earnings; average monthly wage

(1) An individual's average indexed monthly earnings shall be equal to the quotient obtained by dividing—

(A) the total (after adjustment under paragraph (3)) of his wages paid in and self-employment income credited to his benefit computation years (determined under paragraph (2)), by

(B) the number of months in those years.

(2)(A) The number of an individual's benefit computation years equals the number of elapsed years reduced—

(i) in the case of an individual who is entitled to old-age insurance benefits (except as provided in the second sentence of this subparagraph), or who has died, by 5 years, and

(ii) in the case of an individual who is entitled to disability insurance benefits, by the number of years equal to one-fifth of such individual's elapsed years (disregarding any resulting fractional part of a year), but not by more than 5 years.

Clause (ii), once applicable with respect to any individual, shall continue to apply for purposes of determining such individual's primary insurance amount for purposes of any subsequent eligibility for disability or old-age insurance benefits unless prior to the month in which such eligibility begins there occurs a period of at least 12 consecutive months for which he was not entitled to a disability or an old-age insurance benefit. If an individual described in clause (ii) is living with a child (of such individual or his or her spouse) under the age of 3 in any calendar year which is included in such individual's computation base years, but which is not disregarded pursuant to clause (ii) or to subparagraph (B) (in determining such individual's benefit computation years) by reason of the reduction in the number of such individual's elapsed years under clause (ii), the number by which such elapsed years are reduced under this subparagraph pursuant to clause (ii) shall be increased by one (up to a combined total not exceeding 3) for each such calendar year; except that (I) no calendar year shall be disregarded by reason of this sentence (in determining such individual's benefit computation years) unless the individual was living with such child substantially throughout the period in which the child was alive and under the age of 3 in such year and the individual had no earnings as described in section 403(f)(5) of this title in such year, (II) the particular calendar years to be disregarded under this sentence (in determining such benefit computation years) shall be those years (not otherwise disregarded under clause (ii)) which, before the application of subsection (f), meet the conditions of subclause (I), and (III) this sentence shall apply only to the extent that its application would not result in a lower primary insurance amount. The number of an individual's benefit computation years as determined under this subparagraph shall in no case be less than 2.

(B) For purposes of this subsection with respect to any individual—

(i) the term "benefit computation years" means those computation base years, equal in number to the number determined under subparagraph (A), for which the total of such individual's wages and self-employment income, after adjustment under paragraph (3), is the largest;

(ii) the term "computation base years" means the calendar years after 1950 and before—

(I) in the case of an individual entitled to old-age insurance benefits, the year in which occurred (whether by reason of section 402(j)(1) of this title or otherwise) the first month of that entitlement; or

(II) in the case of an individual who has died (without having become entitled to old-age insurance benefits), the year succeeding the year of his death;

except that such term excludes any calendar year entirely included in a period of disability; and

(iii) the term "number of elapsed years" means (except as otherwise provided by section 104(j)(2) of the Social Security Amendments of 1972) the number of calendar years after 1950 (or, if later, the year in which the individual attained age 21) and before the year in which the individual died, or, if it occurred earlier (but after 1960), the year in which he attained age 62; except that such term excludes any calendar year any part of which is included in a period of disability.

(3)(A) Except as provided by subparagraph (B), the wages paid in and self-employment income credited to each of an individual's computation base years for purposes of the selection therefrom of benefit computation years under paragraph (2) shall be deemed to be equal to the product of—

(i) the wages and self-employment income paid in or credited to such year (as determined without regard to this subparagraph), and

(ii) the quotient obtained by dividing—

(I) the national average wage index (as defined in section 409(k)(1) of this title) for the second calendar year preceding the earliest of the year of the individual's death, eligibility for an old-age insurance benefit, or eligibility for a disability insurance benefit (except that the year in which the individual dies, or becomes eligible, shall not be considered as such year if the individual was entitled to disability insurance benefits for any month in the 12–month period immediately preceding such death or eligibility, but there shall be counted instead the year of the individual's eligibility for the disability insurance benefit to which he was entitled in such 12–month period), by

(II) the national average wage index (as so defined) for the computation base year for which the determination is made.

(B) Wages paid in or self-employment income credited to an individual's computation base year which—

(i) occurs after the second calendar year specified in subparagraph (A)(ii)(I), or

(ii) is a year treated under subsection (f)(2)(C) as though it were the last year of the period specified in paragraph (2)(B)(ii),

shall be available for use in determining an individual's benefit computation years, but without applying subparagraph (A) of this paragraph.

(4) For purposes of determining the average monthly wage of an individual whose primary insurance amount is computed (after 1978) under subsection (a) or (d) as in effect (except with respect to the table contained therein) in December 1978, by reason of subsection (a)(4)(B), this subsection as in effect in December 1978 shall remain in effect, except that paragraph (2)(C) (as then in effect) shall be deemed to provide that "computation base years" include only calendar years in the period after 1950 (or 1936, if applicable) and prior to the year in which occurred the first month for which the individual was eligible (as defined in subsection (a)(3)(B) as in effect in January 1979) for an old-age or disability insurance benefit, or, if earlier, the year in which he died. Any calendar year all of which is included in a period of disability shall not be included as a computation base year for such purposes.

(c) Application of prior provisions in certain cases

Subject to the amendments made by section 5117 of the Omnibus Budget Reconciliation Act of 1990, this subsection as in effect in December 1978 shall remain in effect with respect to an individual to whom subsection (a)(1) does not apply by reason of the individual's eligibility for an old-age or disability insurance benefit, or the individual's death, prior to 1979.

(d) Primary insurance amount under 1939 Act

(1) For purposes of column I of the table appearing in subsection (a), as that subsection was in effect in December 1977, an individual's primary insurance benefit shall be computed as follows:

(A) The individual's average monthly wage shall be determined as provided in subsection (b), as in effect in December 1977 (but without regard to paragraph (4) thereof and subject to section 104(j)(2) of the Social Security Amendments of 1972), except that for purposes of paragraphs (2)(C) and (3) of that subsection (as so in effect) 1936 shall be used instead of 1950.

(B) For purposes of subparagraphs (B) and (C) of subsection (b)(2) (as so in effect)—

(i) the total wages prior to 1951 (as defined in subparagraph (C) of this paragraph) of an individual—

(I) shall, in the case of an individual who attained age 21 prior to 1950, be divided by the number of years (hereinafter in this subparagraph referred to as the "divisor") elapsing after the year in which the individual attained age 20, or 1936 if later, and prior to the earlier of the year of death or 1951, except that such divisor shall not include any calendar year entirely included in a period of disability, and in no case shall the divisor be less than one, and

(II) shall, in the case of an individual who died before 1950 and before attaining age 21, be divided by the number of years (hereinafter in this subparagraph referred to as the "divisor") elapsing after the second year prior to the year of death, or 1936 if later, and prior to the year of death, and in no case shall the divisor be less than one; and

(ii) the total wages prior to 1951 (as defined in subparagraph (C) of this paragraph) of an individual who either attained age 21 after 1949 or died after 1949 before attaining age 21, shall be divided by the number of years (hereinafter in this subparagraph referred to as the "divisor") elapsing after 1949 and prior to 1951.

The quotient so obtained shall be deemed to be the individual's wages credited to each of the years which were used in computing the amount of the divisor, except that—

(iii) if the quotient exceeds $3,000, only $3,000 shall be deemed to be the individual's wages for each of the years which were used in computing the amount of the divisor, and the remainder of the individual's total wages prior to 1951 (I) if less than $3,000, shall be deemed credited to the computation base year (as defined in subsection (b)(2) as in effect in December 1977) immediately preceding the earliest year used in computing the amount of the divisor, or (II) if $3,000 or more, shall be deemed credited, in $3,000 increments, to the computation base year (as so defined) immediately preceding the earliest year used in computing the amount of the divisor and to each of the computation base years (as so defined) consecutively preceding that year, with any remainder less than $3,000 being credited to the computation base year (as so defined) immediately preceding the earliest year to which a full $3,000 increment was credited; and

(iv) no more than $42,000 may be taken into account, for purposes of this subparagraph, as total wages after 1936 and prior to 1951.

(C) For the purposes of subparagraph (B), "total wages prior to 1951" with respect to an individual means the sum of (i) remuneration credited to such individual prior to 1951 on the records of the Commissioner of Social Security, (ii) wages deemed paid prior to 1951 to such individual under section 417 of this title, (iii) compensation under the Railroad Retirement Act of 1937 prior to 1951 creditable to him pursuant to this subchapter, and (iv) wages deemed paid prior to 1951 to such individual under section 431 of this title.

(D) The individual's primary insurance benefit shall be 40 percent of the first $50 of his average monthly wage as computed under this subsection, plus 10 percent of the next $200 of his average monthly wage, increased by 1 percent for each increment year. The number of increment years is the number, not more than 14 nor less than 4, that is equal to the individual's total wages prior to 1951 divided by $1,650 (disregarding any fraction).

(2) The provisions of this subsection shall be applicable only in the case of an individual—

(A) with respect to whom at least one of the quarters elapsing prior to 1951 is a quarter of coverage;

(B) who attained age 22 after 1950 and with respect to whom less than six of the quarters elapsing after 1950 are quarters of coverage, or who attained such age before 1951; and

(C)(i) who becomes entitled to benefits under section 402(a) or 423 of this title or who dies, or

(ii) whose primary insurance amount is required to be recomputed under paragraph (2), (6), or (7) of subsection (f) or under section 431 of this title.

(3) In the case of an individual whose primary insurance amount is not computed under paragraph (1) of subsection (a) by reason of paragraph (4)(B)(ii) of that subsection, who—

(A) attains age 62 after 1985 (except where he or she became entitled to a disability insurance benefit before 1986, and remained so entitled in any of the 12 months immediately preceding his or her attainment of age 62), or

(B) would attain age 62 after 1985 and becomes eligible for a disability insurance benefit after 1985,

and who first becomes eligible after 1985 for a monthly periodic payment (including a payment determined under subsection (a)(7)(C), but excluding (I) a payment under the Railroad Retirement Act of 1974 or 1937, (II) a payment by a social security system of a foreign country based on an agreement concluded between the United States and such foreign country pursuant to section 433 of this title, and (III) a payment based wholly on service as a member of a uniformed service (as defined in section 410(m) of this title)) which is based (in whole or in part) upon his or her earnings in noncovered service, the primary insurance amount of such individual during his or her concurrent entitlement to such monthly periodic payment and to old-age or disability insurance benefits shall be the primary insurance amount computed or recomputed under this subsection (without regard to this paragraph and before the application of subsection (i)) reduced by an amount equal to the smaller of—

(i) one-half of the primary insurance amount (computed without regard to this paragraph and before the application of subsection (i)), or

(ii) one-half of the portion of the monthly periodic payment (or payment determined under subsection (a)(7)(C)) which is attributable to noncovered service performed after 1956 (with such attribution being based on the proportionate number of years of such noncovered service) and to which that individual is entitled (or is deemed to be entitled) for the initial month of such concurrent entitlement.

This paragraph shall not apply in the case of any individual to whom subsection (a)(7) would not apply by reason of subparagraph (E) or the first sentence of subparagraph (D) thereof.

(e) Certain wages and self-employment income not to be counted

For the purposes of subsections (b) and (d)—

(1) in computing an individual's average indexed monthly earnings or, in the case of an individual whose primary insurance amount is computed under subsection (a) as in effect prior to January 1979, average monthly wage, there shall not be counted the excess over $3,600 in the case of any calendar year after 1950 and before 1955, the excess over $4,200 in the case of any calendar year after 1954 and before 1959, the excess over $4,800 in the case of any calendar year after 1958 and before 1966, the excess over $6,600 in the case of any calendar year after 1965 and before 1968, the excess over $7,800 in the case of any calendar year after 1967 and before 1972, the excess over $9,000 in the case of any calendar year after 1971 and before 1973, the excess over $10,800 in the case of any calendar year after 1972 and before 1974, the excess over $13,200 in the case of any calendar year after 1973 and before 1975, and the excess over an amount equal to the contribution and benefit base (as determined under section 430 of this title) in the case of any calendar year after 1974 with respect to which such contribution and benefit base is effective, (before the application, in the case of average indexed monthly earnings, of subsection (b)(3)(A)) of (A) the wages paid to him in such year, plus (B) the self-employment income credited to such year (as determined under section 412 of this title); and

(2) if an individual's average indexed monthly earnings or, in the case of an individual whose primary insurance amount is computed under subsection (a) as in effect prior to January 1979, average monthly wage, computed under subsection (b) or for the purposes of subsection (d) is not a multiple of $1, it shall be reduced to the next lower multiple of $1.

(f) Recomputation of benefits

(1) After an individual's primary insurance amount has been determined under this section, there shall be no recomputation of such individual's primary insurance amount except as provided in this subsection or, in the case of a World War II veteran who died prior to July 27, 1954, as provided in section 417(b) of this title.

(2)(A) If an individual has wages or self-employment income for a year after 1978 for any part of which he is entitled to old-age or disability insurance benefits, the Commissioner of Social Security shall, at such time or times and within such period as the Commissioner may by regulation prescribe, recompute the individual's primary insurance amount for that year.

(B) For the purpose of applying subparagraph (A) of subsection (a)(1) to the average indexed monthly earnings of an individual to whom that subsection applies and who receives a recomputation under this paragraph, there shall be used, in lieu of the amounts established by subsection (a)(1)(B) for purposes of clauses (i) and (ii) of subsection (a)(1)(A), the amounts so established that were (or, in the case of an individual described in subsection (a)(4)(B), would have been) used in the computation of such individual's primary insurance amount prior to the application of this subsection.

(C) A recomputation of any individual's primary insurance amount under this paragraph shall be made as provided in subsection (a)(1) as though the year with respect to which it is made is the last year of the period specified in subsection (b)(2)(B)(ii); and subsection (b)(3)(A) shall apply with respect to any such recomputation as it applied in the computation of such individual's primary insurance amount prior to the application of this subsection.

(D) A recomputation under this paragraph with respect to any year shall be effective—

(i) in the case of an individual who did not die in that year, for monthly benefits beginning with benefits for January of the following year; or

(ii) in the case of an individual who died in that year, for monthly benefits beginning with benefits for the month in which he died.

(3) Repealed. Pub.L. 95–216, Title II, § 201(f)(2), Dec. 20, 1977, 91 Stat. 1521

(4) A recomputation shall be effective under this subsection only if it increases the primary insurance amount by at least $1.

(5) In the case of a man who became entitled to old-age insurance benefits and died before the month in which he attained retirement age (as defined in section 416(*l*) of this title), the Commissioner of Social Security shall recompute his primary insurance amount as provided in subsection (a) as though he became entitled to old-age insurance benefits in the month in which he died; except that (i) his computation base years referred to in subsection (b)(2) shall include the year in which he died, and (ii) his elapsed years referred to in subsection (b)(3) shall not include the year in which he died or any year thereafter. Such recomputation of such primary insurance amount shall be effective for and after the month in which he died.

(6) Upon the death after 1967 of an individual entitled to benefits under section 402(a) or section 423 of this title, if any person is entitled to monthly benefits or a lump-sum death payment, on the wages and self-employment income of such individual, the Commissioner of Social Security shall recompute the decedent's primary insurance amount, but only if the decedent during his lifetime was paid compensation which was treated under section 405(*o*) of this title as remuneration for employment.

(7) This subsection as in effect in December 1978 shall continue to apply to the recomputation of a primary insurance amount computed under subsection (a) or (d) as in effect (without regard to the table in subsection (a)) in that month, and, where appropriate, under subsection (d) as in effect in December 1977, including a primary insurance amount computed under any such subsection whose operation is modified as a result of the amendments made by section 5117 of the Omnibus Budget Reconciliation Act of 1990. For purposes of recomputing a primary insurance amount determined under subsection (a) or (d) (as so in effect) in the case of an individual to whom those subsections apply by reason of subsection (a)(4)(B) as in effect after December 1978, no remuneration shall be taken into account for the year in which the individual initially became eligible for an old-age or disability insurance benefit or died, or for any year thereafter, and (effective January 1982) the recomputation shall be modified by the application of subsection (a)(6) where applicable.

(8) The Commissioner of Social Security shall recompute the primary insurance amounts applicable to beneficiaries whose benefits are based on a primary insurance amount which was computed under subsection (a)(3) effective prior to January 1979, or would have been so computed if the dollar amount specified therein were $11.50. Such recomputation shall be effective January 1979, and shall include the effect of the increase in the dollar amount provided by subsection (a)(1)(C)(i). Such primary insurance amount shall be deemed to be provided under such section for purposes of subsection (i).

(9)(A) In the case of an individual who becomes entitled to a periodic payment determined under subsection (a)(7)(A) (including a payment determined under subsection (a)(7)(C)) in a month subsequent to the first month in which he or she becomes entitled to an old-age or disability insurance benefit, and whose primary insurance amount has been computed without regard to either such subsection or subsection (d)(3), such individual's primary insurance amount shall be recomputed (notwithstanding paragraph (4)), in accordance with either such subsection or subsection (d)(3), as may be applicable, effective with the first month of his or her concurrent entitlement to such benefit and such periodic payment.

(B) If an individual's primary insurance amount has been computed under subsection (a)(7) or (d)(3), and it becomes necessary to recompute that primary insurance amount under this subsection—

(i) so as to increase the monthly benefit amount payable with respect to such primary insurance amount (except in the case of the individual's death), such increase shall be determined as though the recomputed primary insurance amount were being computed under subsection (a)(7) or (d)(3), or

(ii) by reason of the individual's death, such primary insurance amount shall be recomputed without regard to (and as though it had never been computed with regard to) subsection (a)(7) or (d)(3).

(g) Rounding of benefits

The amount of any monthly benefit computed under section 402 or 423 of this title which (after any reduction under sections 403(a) and 424a of this title and any deduction under section 403(b) of this title, and after any deduction under section 1395s(a)(1) of this title) is not a multiple of $1 shall be rounded to the next lower multiple of $1.

(h) Service of certain Public Health Service officers

(1) Notwithstanding the provisions of subchapter III of chapter 83 of Title 5, remuneration paid for service to which the provisions of section 410(*l*)(1) of this title are applicable and which is performed by an individual as a commissioned officer of the Reserve Corps of the Public Health Service prior to July 1, 1960, shall not be included in computing entitlement to or the amount of any monthly benefit under this subchapter, on the basis of his wages and self-employment income, for any month after June 1960 and prior to the first month with respect to which the Director of the Office of Personnel Management certifies to the Commissioner of Social Security that, by reason of a waiver filed as provided in paragraph (2), no further annuity will be paid to him, his wife, and his children, or, if he has died, to his widow and children, under subchapter III of chapter 83 of Title 5 on the basis of such service.

(2) In the case of a monthly benefit for a month prior to that in which the individual, on whose wages and self-employment income such benefit is based, dies, the waiver must be filed by such individual; and such waiver shall be irrevocable and shall constitute a waiver on behalf of himself, his wife, and his children. If such individual did not file such a waiver before he died, then in the case of a benefit for the month in which he died or any month thereafter, such waiver must be filed by his widow, if any, and by or on behalf of all his children, if any; and such waivers shall be irrevocable. Such a waiver by a child shall be filed by his legal guardian or guardians, or, in the absence thereof, by the person (or persons) who has the child in his care.

(i) Cost-of-living increases in benefits

(1) For purposes of this subsection—

(A) the term "base quarter" means (i) the calendar quarter ending on September 30 in each year after 1982, or (ii) any other calendar quarter in which occurs the effective month of a general benefit increase under this subchapter;

(B) the term "cost-of-living computation quarter" means a base quarter, as defined in subparagraph (A)(i), with respect to which the applicable increase percentage is greater than zero; except that there shall be no cost-of-living computation quarter in any calendar year if in the year prior to such year a law has been enacted providing a general benefit increase under this subchapter or if in such prior year such a general benefit increase becomes effective;

(C) the term "applicable increase percentage" means—

(i) with respect to a base quarter or cost-of-living computation quarter in any calendar year before 1984, or in any calendar year after 1983 and before 1989 for which the OASDI fund ratio is 15.0 percent or more, or in any calendar year after 1988 for which the OASDI fund ratio is 20.0 percent or more, the CPI increase percentage; and

(ii) with respect to a base quarter or cost-of-living computation quarter in any calendar year after 1983 and before 1989 for which the OASDI fund ratio is less than 15.0 percent, or in any calendar year after 1988 for which the OASDI fund ratio is less than 20.0 percent, the CPI increase percentage or the wage increase percentage, whichever (with respect to that quarter) is the lower;

(D) the term "CPI increase percentage", with respect to a base quarter or cost-of-living computation quarter in any calendar year, means the percentage (rounded to the nearest one-tenth of 1 percent) by which the Consumer Price Index for that quarter (as prepared by the Department of Labor) exceeds such index for the most recent prior calendar quarter which was a base quarter under subparagraph (A)(ii) or, if later, the most recent cost-of-living computation quarter under subparagraph (B);

(E) the term "wage increase percentage", with respect to a base quarter or cost-of-living computation quarter in any calendar year, means the percentage (rounded to the nearest one-tenth of 1 percent) by which the national average wage index (as defined in section 409(k)(1) of this title) for the year immediately preceding such calendar year exceeds such index for the year immediately preceding the most recent prior calendar year which included a base quarter under subparagraph (A)(ii) or, if later, which included a cost-of-living computation quarter;

(F) the term "OASDI fund ratio", with respect to any calendar year, means the ratio of—

(i) the combined balance in the Federal Old-Age and Survivors Insurance Trust Fund and the Federal Disability Insurance Trust Fund as of the beginning of such year, including the taxes transferred under section 401(a) of this title on the first day of such year and reduced by the outstanding amount of any loan (including interest thereon) theretofore made to either such Fund from the Federal Hospital Insurance Trust Fund under section 401(*l*) of this title, to

(ii) the total amount which (as estimated by the Commissioner of Social Security) will be paid from the Federal Old-Age and Survivors Insurance Trust Fund and the Federal Disability Insurance Trust Fund during such calendar year for all purposes authorized by section 401 of this title (other than payments of interest on, or repayments of, loans from the Federal Hospital Insurance Trust Fund under section 401(*l*) of this title), but excluding any transfer payments between such trust funds and reducing the amount of any transfers to the Railroad Retirement Account by the amount of any transfers into either such trust fund from that Account;[1]

(G) the Consumer Price Index for a base quarter, a cost-of-living computation quarter, or any other calendar quarter shall be the arithmetical mean of such index for the 3 months in such quarter.

(2)(A)(i) The Commissioner of Social Security shall determine each year beginning with 1975 (subject to the limitation in paragraph (1)(B)) whether the base quarter (as defined in paragraph (1)(A)(i)) in such year is a cost-of-living computation quarter.

(ii) If the Commissioner of Social Security determines that the base quarter in any year is a cost-of-living computation quarter, the Commissioner shall, effective with the month of December of that year as provided in subparagraph (B), increase—

(I) the benefit amount to which individuals are entitled for that month under section 427 or 428 of this title,

(II) the primary insurance amount of each other individual on which benefit entitlement is based under this subchapter, and

(III) the amount of total monthly benefits based on any primary insurance amount which is permitted under section 403 of this title (and such total shall be increased, unless otherwise so increased under another provision of this subchapter, at the same time as such primary insurance amount) or, in the case of a primary insurance amount computed under subsection (a) as in effect (without regard to the table contained therein) prior to January 1979, the amount to which the beneficiaries may be entitled under section 403 of this title as in effect in December 1978, except as provided by section 403(a)(7) and (8) of this title as in effect after December 1978.

The increase shall be derived by multiplying each of the amounts described in subdivisions (I), (II), and (III) (including each of those amounts as previously increased under this subparagraph) by the applicable increase percentage; and any amount so increased that is not a multiple of $0.10 shall be decreased to the next lower multiple of $0.10. Any increase under this subsection in a primary insurance amount determined under subparagraph (C)(i) of subsection (a)(1) shall be applied after the initial determination of such primary insurance amount under that subparagraph (with the amount of such increase, in the case of an individual who becomes eligible for old-age or disability insurance benefits or dies in a calendar year after 1979, being determined from the range of possible primary insurance amounts published by the Commissioner of Social Security under the last sentence of subparagraph (D)).

(iii) In the case of an individual who becomes eligible for an old-age or disability insurance benefit, or who dies prior to becoming so eligible, in a year in which there occurs an increase provided under clause (ii), the individual's primary insurance amount (without regard to the time of entitlement to that benefit) shall be increased (unless otherwise so increased under another provision of this subchapter and, with respect to a primary insurance amount determined under subsection (a)(1)(C)(i)(I) in the case of an individual to whom that subsection (as in effect in December 1981) applied, subject to the provisions of subsection (a)(1)(C)(i) and clauses (iv) and (v) of this subparagraph (as then in effect)) by the amount of that increase and subsequent applicable increases, but only with respect to benefits payable for months after November of that year.

(B) The increase provided by subparagraph (A) with respect to a particular cost-of-living computation quarter shall apply in the case of monthly benefits under this subchapter for months after November of the calendar year in which occurred such cost-of-living computation quarter, and in the case of lump-sum death payments with respect to deaths occurring after November of such calendar year.

(C)(i) Whenever the Commissioner of Social Security determines that a base quarter in a calendar year is also a cost-of-living computation quarter, the Commissioner shall notify the House Committee on Ways and Means and the Senate Committee on Finance of such determination within 30 days after the close of such quarter, indicating the amount of the benefit increase to be provided, the Commissioner's estimate of the extent to which the cost of such increase would be met by an increase in the contribution and benefit base under section 430 of this title and the estimated amount of the increase in such base, the actuarial estimates of the effect of such increase, and the actuarial assumptions and methodology used in preparing such estimates.

(ii) The Commissioner of Social Security shall determine and promulgate the OASDI fund ratio for the current calendar year on or before November 1 of the current calendar year, based upon the most recent data then available. The Commissioner of Social Security shall include a statement of the fund ratio and the national average wage index (as defined in section 409(k)(1) of this title) and a statement of the effect such ratio and the level of such index may have upon benefit increases under this subsection in any notification made under clause (i) and any determination published under subparagraph (D).

(D) If the Commissioner of Social Security determines that a base quarter in a calendar year is also a cost-of-living computation quarter, the Commissioner shall publish in the Federal Register within 45 days after the close of such quarter a determination that a benefit increase is resultantly required and the percentage thereof. The Commissioner shall also publish in the Federal Register at that time (i) a revision of the range of the primary insurance amounts which are possible after the application of this subsection based on the dollar amount specified in subparagraph (C)(i) of subsection (a)(1) (with such revised primary insurance amounts constituting the increased amounts determined for purposes of such subparagraph (C)(i) under this subsection), or specified in subsection (a)(3) as in effect prior to 1979, and (ii) a revision of the range of maximum family benefits which correspond to such primary insurance amounts (with such maximum benefits being effective notwithstanding section 403(a) of this title except for paragraph (3)(B) thereof (or paragraph (2) thereof as in effect prior to 1979)). Notwithstanding the preceding sentence, such revision of maximum family benefits shall be subject to paragraph (6) of section 403(a) of this title (as added by section 101(a)(3) of the Social Security Disability Amendments of 1980).

(3) As used in this subsection, the term "general benefit increase under this subchapter" means an increase (other than an increase under this subsection) in all primary insurance amounts on which monthly insurance benefits under this subchapter are based.

(4) This subsection as in effect in December 1978, and as amended by sections 111(a)(6), 111(b)(2), and 112 of the Social Security Amendments of 1983 and by section 9001 of the Omnibus Budget Reconciliation Act of 1986, shall continue to apply to subsections (a) and (d), as then in effect and as amended by section 5117 of the Omnibus Budget Reconciliation Act of 1990, for purposes of computing the primary insurance amount of an individual to whom subsection (a), as in effect after December 1978, does not apply (including an individual to whom subsection (a) does not apply in any year by reason of paragraph (4)(B) of that subsection (but the application of this subsection in such cases shall be modified by the application of subdivision (I) in the last sentence of paragraph (4) of that subsection)), except that for this purpose, in applying paragraphs (2)(A)(ii), (2)(D)(iv), and (2)(D)(v) of this subsection as in effect in December 1978, the phrase "increased to the next higher multiple of $0.10" shall be deemed to read "decreased to the next lower multiple of $0.10". For purposes of computing primary insurance amounts and maximum family benefits (other than primary insurance amounts and maximum family benefits for individuals to whom such paragraph (4)(B) applies), the Commissioner of Social Security shall revise the table of benefits contained in subsection (a), as in effect in December 1978, in accordance with the requirements of paragraph (2)(D) of this subsection as then in effect, except that the requirement in such paragraph (2)(D) that the Commissioner of Social Security publish such revision of the table of benefits in the Federal Register shall not apply.

(5)(A) If—

(i) with respect to any calendar year the "applicable increase percentage" was determined under clause (ii) of paragraph (1)(C) rather than under clause (i) of such paragraph, and the increase becoming effective under paragraph (2) in such year was accordingly determined on the basis of the wage increase percentage rather than the CPI increase percentage (or there was no such increase becoming effective under paragraph (2) in that year because there was no wage increase percentage greater than zero), and

(ii) for any subsequent calendar year in which an increase under paragraph (2) becomes effective the OASDI fund ratio is greater than 32.0 percent,

then each of the amounts described in subdivisions (I), (II), and (III) of paragraph (2)(A)(ii), as increased under paragraph (2) effective with the month of December in such subsequent calendar year, shall be further increased (effective with such month) by an additional percentage, which shall be determined under subparagraph (B) and shall apply as provided in subparagraph (C). Any amount so increased that is not a multiple of $0.10 shall be decreased to the next lower multiple of $0.10.

(B) The applicable additional percentage by which the amounts described in subdivisions (I), (II), and (III) of paragraph (2)(A)(ii) are to be further increased under subparagraph (A) in the subsequent calendar year involved shall be the amount derived by—

(i) subtracting (I) the compounded percentage benefit increases that were actually paid under paragraph (2) and this paragraph from (II) the compounded percentage benefit increases that would have been paid if all increases under paragraph (2) had been made on the basis of the CPI increase percentage,

(ii) dividing the difference by the sum of the compounded percentage in clause (i)(I) and 100 percent, and

(iii) multiplying such quotient by 100 so as to yield such applicable additional percentage (which shall be rounded to the nearest one-tenth of 1 percent),

with the compounded increases referred to in clause (i) being measured—

(iv) in the case of amounts described in subdivision (I) of paragraph (2)(A)(ii), over the period beginning with the calendar year in which monthly benefits described in such subdivision were first increased on the basis of the wage increase percentage and ending with the year before such subsequent calendar year, and

(v) in the case of amounts described in subdivisions (II) and (III) of paragraph (2)(A)(ii), over the period beginning with the calendar year in which the individual whose primary insurance amount is increased under such subdivision (II) became eligible (as defined in subsection (a)(3)(B)) for the old-age or disability insurance benefit that is being increased under this subsection, or died before becoming so eligible, and ending with the year before such subsequent calendar year;

except that if the Commissioner of Social Security determines in any case that the application (in accordance with subparagraph (C)) of the additional percentage as computed under the preceding provisions of this subparagraph would cause the OASDI fund ratio to fall below 32.0 percent in the calendar year immediately following such subsequent year, the Commissioner shall reduce such applicable additional percentage to the extent necessary to ensure that the OASDI fund ratio will remain at or above 32.0 percent through the end of such following year.

(C) Any applicable additional percentage increase in an amount described in subdivision (I), (II), or (III) of paragraph (2)(A)(ii), made under this paragraph in any calendar year, shall thereafter be treated for all the purposes of this chapter as a part of the increase made in such amount under paragraph (2) for that year.

(Aug. 14, 1935, c. 531, Title II, § 215, as added Aug. 28, 1950, c. 809, Title I, § 104(a), 64 Stat. 492, 506; amended July 18, 1952, c. 945, §§ 2(a), (b)(1), 3(c), 6(a), (b), 66 Stat. 767, 768, 770, 776; Sept. 1, 1954, c. 1206, Title I, §§ 102(a)-(d), (e)(1)-(4), 104(d), 106(c), 68 Stat. 1062, 1078, 1079; Aug. 1, 1956, c. 836, Title I, §§ 103(c)(4), (5), 109(a), 115(a) to (c), 70 Stat. 818, 830, 832, 833; Pub.L. 85–840, Title I, §§ 101(a)-(d), 102(d), Title II, § 205(m), Aug. 28, 1958, 72 Stat. 1013, 1020, 1025; Pub.L. 86–415, § 7, Apr. 8, 1960, 74 Stat. 35; Pub.L. 86–778, Title I, § 103(j)(2)(C), Title II, § 211(n), Title III, §§ 303(a)-(e), 304(a), Sept. 13, 1960, 74 Stat. 937, 958, 960, 966; Pub.L. 87–64, Title I, §§ 101(a), 102(d), June 30, 1961, 75 Stat. 131, 135; Pub.L. 89–97, Title III, §§ 301(a), (b), 302(a)-(d), 303(e), 304(k), 320(a)(4), July 30, 1965, 79 Stat. 361, 363–365, 367, 370, 393; Pub.L. 90–248, Title I, §§ 101(a), (c), (d), 108(a)(4), 155(a)(1)-(6), Title IV, § 403(b), Jan. 2, 1968, 81 Stat. 824, 827, 834, 864, 865, 931; Pub.L. 91–172, Title X, § 1002(a), (c), (d), Dec. 30, 1969, 83 Stat. 737, 740; Pub.L. 92–5, Title II, §§ 201(a), (c), (d), 203(a)(4), Mar. 17, 1971, 85 Stat. 6, 9, 10; Pub.L. 92–336, Title II, §§ 201(a), (c)-(f), 202(a)(1), (3), 203(a)(4), July 1, 1972, 86 Stat. 406, 410–412, 416, 418; Pub.L. 92–603, Title I, §§ 101(a), (c)-(e), 104(b), 134, 142(b), (c), 144(a)(1), Oct. 30, 1972, 86 Stat. 1333, 1334, 1340, 1362, 1368, 1369; Pub.L. 93–66, Title II, § 203(a)(4), July 9, 1973, 87 Stat. 153; Pub.L. 93–233, §§ 1(h)(1), 2(a), (d), 3(a)-(h), 5(a)(4), Dec. 31, 1973, 87 Stat. 948, 952, 953; Pub.L. 95–216, Title I, § 103(d), Title II, § 201, Dec. 20, 1977, 91 Stat. 1514, 1519; Pub.L. 96–265, Title I, §§ 101(b)(3), (4), 102(a), June 9, 1980, 94 Stat. 442, 443; Pub.L. 96–473, § 6(d), Oct. 19, 1980, 94 Stat. 2265; Pub.L. 97–35, Title XXII, §§ 2201(a), (b)(1)-(9), (c)(1)-(5), 2206(a), (b)(5)-(7), Aug. 13, 1981, 95 Stat. 830, 831, 838; Pub.L. 97–123, § 2(a)-(d), Dec. 29, 1981, 95 Stat. 1660; Pub.L. 98–21, Title I, §§ 111(a)(1)-(3), (6), (b)(1), (2), (c), 112(a)-(d), 113(a)-(c), Title II, § 201(c)(1)(C), Apr. 20, 1983, 97 Stat. 72–76, 78, 109; Pub.L. 98–369, Div. B., Title VI, §§ 2661(k), 2662(c)(1), 2663(a)(10), July 18, 1984, 98 Stat. 1157, 1159, 1164; Pub.L. 99–272, Title XII, § 12105, Apr. 7, 1986, 100 Stat. 286; Pub.L. 99–509, Title IX, § 9001(a), (b), Oct. 21, 1986, 100 Stat. 1969, 1970; Pub.L. 99–514, Title XVIII, § 1883(a)(7), Oct. 22, 1986, 100 Stat. 2916; Pub.L. 100–647, Title VIII, §§ 8003(a), 8011(a), (b), Nov. 10, 1988, 102 Stat. 3780, 3789; Pub.L. 101–239, Title X, § 10208(b)(1), (2)(A), (B), (3), (4), (d)(2)(A)(i), Dec. 19, 1989, 103 Stat. 2477, 2478, 2480; Pub.L. 101–508, Title V, §§ 5117(a)(1)-(3)(A), (C)-(E), 5122, Nov. 5, 1990, 104 Stat. 1388–274, 1388–277, 1388–283; Pub.L. 103–296, Title I, § 107(a)(4), Title III, §§ 307(a),(b), 308(b), 321(a)(16), (17), (e)(2)(B)-(G), (g)(1)(C), Aug. 15, 1994, 108 Stat. 1478, 1522, 1536, 1539, 1543.)

[1] So in original. Probably should be followed by "and".

HISTORICAL AND STATUTORY NOTES

References in Text

The Railroad Retirement Act of 1937, referred in subsecs. (a)(1)(C)(ii), (7)(A), (d)(1)(C), (3), is Act Aug. 29, 1935, c. 812, 49 Stat. 867, as amended generally. See paragraph immediately following for Railroad Retirement Act of 1974.

The Railroad Retirement Act of 1974, referred to in subsecs. (a)(1)(C)(ii), (7)(A), (d)(3), is Title I of Pub.L. 93–445, Oct. 16, 1974, 88 Stat. 1305, and is classified generally to subchapter IV (section 231 et seq.) of chapter 9 of Title 45, Railroads. Such Title I completely amended and revised the Railroad Retirement Act of 1937 (approved June 24, 1937, c. 382, 50 Stat. 307), and as thus amended and revised, the 1937 Act was redesignated the Railroad Retirement Act of 1974. Previously, the 1937 Act had completely amended and revised the Railroad Retirement Act of 1935 (approved Aug. 29, 1935, c. 812, 49 Stat. 967). Section 201 of the 1937 Act provided that the 1935 Act, as in force prior to amendment by the 1937 Act, may be cited as the Railroad Retirement Act of 1935; and that the 1935 Act, as amended by the 1937 Act may be cited as the Railroad Retirement Act of 1937. The Railroad Retirement Acts of 1935 and 1937 were classified to subchapter II (section 215 et seq.) and subchapter III (section 228a et seq.), respectively, of chapter 9 of Title 45.

Section 104(j)(2) of the Social Security Amendments of 1972, referred to in subsecs. (a)(5)(B)(ii), (b)(2)(B)(iii), (d)(1)(A), means section 104(j)(2) of Pub.L. 92–603, Oct. 30, 1972, 86 Stat. 1329, which is set out as a note under section 414 of this title.

Section 101 of the Social Security Amendments of 1983, referred to in subsec. (a)(7)(E)(i), is section 101 of Pub.L. 98–21, Title I, Apr. 20, 1983, 97 Stat. 67, which amended sections 409 and 410 of this title and section 3121 of Title 26, Internal Revenue Code, and enacted provisions set out as notes under section 410 of this title and section 3121 of Title 26.

Section 3121(k) of the Internal Revenue Code of 1954, referred to in subsec. (a)(7)(E)(ii), was classified to 26 U.S.C.A. § 3121(k), and was repealed by Pub.L. 98–21, Title I, § 102(b)(2), Apr. 20, 1983, 97 Stat. 71.

Section 102 of that Act, referred to in subsec. (a)(7)(E)(ii), is section 102 of Pub.L. 98–21, Title I, Apr. 20, 1983, 97 Stat. 70, which amended section 410 of this title and section 3121 of Title 26 and enacted provisions set out as notes under section 414 of this title and section 3121 of Title 26.

Section 5117 of the Omnibus Budget Reconciliation Act of 1990, referred to in subsecs. (c), (f)(7), (i)(4), means section 5117 of Pub.L. 101–508, Nov. 5, 1990, 104 Stat. 1388–277, which in addition to amending this section, amended sections 403, 413 and 417 of this title. For complete classification of this Act to the Code, see Tables.

The 1939 Act, referred to in subsec. (d), probably means Act Aug. 10, 1939, c. 666, 53 Stat. 1360, known as the Social Security Act Amendments of 1939, which enacted sections 901a, 1306 and 1307 of this title, amended sections 302, 303, 306, 401, 402 to 409, 502, 503, 602, 603, 606, 701, 702, 703, 711, 712, 713, 714, 721, 801, 1011, 1202, 1203, 1206, 1301, of this title, section 642 of Title 7, Agriculture, section 1464 of Title 12, Banks and Banking, section 1601 of former Title 26, Internal Revenue Code of 1939, section 45b of Title 29, Labor, and enacted provisions set out as notes under section 363 of Title 45, Railroads. For complete classification of this Act to the Code, see Tables.

Section 101(a)(3) of the Social Security Disability Amendments of 1980, referred to in subsec. (i)(2)(D), is section 101(a)(3) of Pub.L. 96–265, Title I, June 9, 1980, 94 Stat. 442, which enacted section 403(a)(6) of this title.

The amendments by sections 111(a)(6), 111(b)(2), and 112 of the Social Security Amendments of 1983, referred to in subsec. (i)(4), are the amendments of subsec. (i)(1), (2), and (5) of this section by sections 111(a)(6), 111(b)(2), and 112 of Pub.L. 98–21, which amended subsec. (i) of this section and enacted provisions set out as notes under this section. For descriptions of those amendments see 1983 Amendment note under this section.

Section 9001 of the Omnibus Budget Reconciliation Act of 1986, referred to in subsec. (i)(4), is section 9001 of Pub.L. 99–509, Title IX, Oct. 21, 1986, 100 Stat. 1969, which amended 42 U.S.C.A. §§ 415 and 1395r and enacted provisions set out as a note below.

Codifications

Quotation mark at the beginning of the directory language of section 5117(a)(3)(E)(iii) of Pub.L. 101–508, amending subsec. (f)(9)(B) of this section, was deleted as the probable intent of Congress.

Section 201(c) of Pub.L. 98–21, set out in the credit of this section, was amended by section 2662(c)(1) of Pub.L. 98–369 to correct an error in the directory language of Pub.L. 98–21 under which the article "the" had been left out in the direction to strike out references to the age of 65.

Effective and Applicability Provisions

1994 Acts. Amendment by section 107(a)(4) of Pub.L. 103–296 effective Mar. 31, 1995, see section 110 of Pub.L. 103–296, set out as a note under section 401 of this title.

Section 307(c) of Pub.L. 103–296 provided that: "The amendments made by this section [amending subsecs. (a) and (d) of this section] shall apply (notwithstanding section 215(f)(1) of the Social Security Act (42 U.S.C. 415(f)(1))) with respect to benefits payable for months after December 1994."

Amendment of subsecs. (a)(7)(A) and (d)(3) by section 308(b) of Pub.L. 103–296, applicable (notwithstanding subsec. (f) of this section) with respect to benefits payable for months after Dec. 1994, see section 308(c) of Pub.L. 103–296, set out as a note under section 402 of this title.

Section 321(g)(3)(A) of Pub.L. 103–296 provided that: "The amendments made by paragraph (1) [amending subsec. (a)(1)(C)(ii) of this section and section 430(b)(1), (2), (d) of this title] shall be effective with respect to the determination of the contribution and benefit base for years after 1994."

1990 Acts. Amendment by Pub.L. 101–508 applicable to computation of primary insurance in cases of entitlement to benefits under section 402 or 423 of this title on the basis of the insured's wages and self employment income for months after an 18 month period following Nov. 1990, except in cases where entitlement, based on wages and self employment income of the insured, accrues the month preceding the initial month of entitlement to benefits under section 402 or 423 of this title, and applicable to primary insurance amounts upon recomputation, if such recomputation is effective for months after the 18 month period after Nov. 1990, see section 5117(a)(4) of Pub.L. 101–508, set out as a note under section 403 of this title.

1989 Acts. Amendment by Pub.L. 101–239 applicable with respect to computation of average total wage amounts for calendar years after 1990, including transitional rule, see section 10208(c) of Pub.L. 101–239, set out as a note under section 430 of this title.

1988 Acts. Section 8003(b) of Pub.L. 100–647 provided that: "The amendments made by subsection (a) [amending subsec. (a)(7)(D) of this section] shall apply to benefits payable for months after December 1988."

Section 8011(c) of Pub.L. 100–647 provided that: "The amendments made by this section [amending subsecs. (a)(7)(A), (B)(i), (C) and (d)(5)(ii) of this section] shall apply to benefits based on applications filed after the month [November] in which this Act is enacted [Nov. 10, 1988]."

1986 Acts. Amendment by Pub.L. 99–514 effective Oct. 22, 1986, see section 1883(f) of Pub.L. 99–514, set out as a note under section 402 of this title.

Section 9001(d) of Pub.L. 99–509 provided that:

"(1) Except as provided in paragraphs (2) and (3), the amendments made by this section [amending this section and section 1395r of this title] shall apply with respect to cost-of-living increases determined under section 215(i) of the Social Security Act [subsec. (i) of this section] (as currently in effect, and as in effect in December 1978 and applied in certain cases under the provisions of such Act [this chapter] in effect after December 1978) in 1986 and subsequent years.

"(2) The amendments made by paragraphs (1)(A) [amending subsec. (i)(2)(C)(i), (ii)] and (2)(B) [see Italicized note] of subsection (b)] shall apply with respect to months after September 1986."

"(3) The amendment made by subsection (c) [amending section 1395r of this title] shall apply with respect to monthly premiums (under section 1839 of the Social Security Act) [section 1395r of this title] for months after December 1986."

Section 12115 of Pub.L. 99–272 provided that: "Except as otherwise specifically provided, the preceding provisions of this subtitle, including the amendments made thereby [amending this section and sections 402, 403, 404, 409, 415, 418, 423, 424a, 907, 909, 910, 1310 and 1383 of this title and sections 86, 871, 932, and 3121 of Title 26, Internal Revenue Code, enacting provisions set out as notes under sections 402, 403, 404, 409, 418, 424a, 907, 909 of this title and section 932 of Title 26, and amending provisions set out as notes under section 1310 of this title, and repealing provisions set out as a note under section 907 of this title], shall take effect on the first day of the month following the month in which this Act is enacted [Apr.1986]."

1984 Acts. Amendment to subsecs. (a)(7)(B)(ii)(I), (C)(ii), (f), (i)(5) by sections 2661(k), 2662(c)(1) of Pub.L. 98–369 effective as though included in the enactment of the Social Security Amendments of 1983 [Pub.L. 98–21], see section 2664(a) of Pub.L. 98–369, set out as a note under section 401 of this title.

Amendment to subsecs. (a)(1), (4), (f)(2), (h)(1) by section 2663(a)(10) of Pub.L. 98–369 effective July 19, 1984, but not to be construed as changing or affecting any right, liability, status or interpretation which existed (under the provisions of law involved) before that date, see section 2664(b) of Pub.L. 98–369, set out as a note under section 401 of this title.

1983 Acts. Section 111(a)(6) of Pub.L. 98–21 provided in part that the substitution by section 111(a)(6) of Pub.L. 98–21 of "December" for "June" in subsec. (i)(2)(A)(ii) of this section and the substitution of "November" for "May" in subsec. (i)(2)(B) of this section is effective as this section was in effect in December 1978 and as this section is applied in certain cases under the provisions of this chapter as in effect after December 1978.

Amendment of subsec. (i)(2)(A)(ii), (iii), and (B) by section 111(a) of Pub.L. 98–21 applicable with respect to cost-of-living increases determined under subsec. (i) of this section for years after 1982, see section 111(a)(8) of Pub.L. 98–21, set out as a note under section 402 of this title.

Section 111(b)(2) of Pub.L. 98–21 provided in part that the substitution by section 111(b)(2) of Pub.L. 98–21 of "September 30" for "March 31" and "1982" for "1974" in subsec. (i)(1)(A) of this section is effective as this section was in effect in December 1978 and as applied in certain cases under the provisions of this chapter as in effect after December 1978.

Section 111(b)(3) of Pub.L. 98–21 provided that: "The amendments made by this subsection [amending subsec. (i)(1)(A) of this section] shall apply with respect to cost-of-living increases determined under section 215(i) of the Social Security Act [subsec. (i) of this section] for years after 1983."

Section 112(e) of Pub.L. 98–21 provided that: "The amendments made by the preceding provisions of this section [amending subsec. (i) of this section so as to base cost-of-living increases on the lower of either wages or prices when the balance of OASDI funds falls below a specified level] shall apply with respect to monthly benefits under Title II of the Social Security Act [this subchapter] for months after December 1983."

1981 Acts. Section 2(j)(2) to (4) of Pub.L. 97–123 provided that:

"(2) Except as provided in paragraphs (3) and (4), the amendments made by section 2201 of the Omnibus Budget Reconciliation Act of 1981 [enacting section 1382k of this title, amending subsecs. (a)(1)(C)(i), (ii), (3)(A), (4) to (6), (f)(7), (8), (i)(2)(A)(ii) to (v), (D), and (4) of this section and sections 402(m), (q)(4), (10), (w)(1), (5), 403(a)(8), 417(b)(1), and 433(c)(2) of this title] (other than subsection (f) thereof [amending section 402(i) of this title]), together with the amendments made by the preceding subsections of this section [repealing section 1382k of this title and a provision set out as a note under section 1382k of this title and amending subsecs. (a)(5), (6)(A), (f)(7), (i)(2)(A)(iii), and (4) of this section and sections 402(q)(4) and (10), 403(a)(8), and 417(b)(1) of this title], shall apply with respect to benefits for months after December 1981; and the amendment made by subsection (f) [amending section 402(i) of this title] of such section 2201 shall apply with respect to deaths occurring after December 1981.

"(3) Such amendments shall not apply—

"(A) in the case of an old-age insurance benefit, if the individual who is entitled to such benefit first became eligible (as defined in section 215(a)(3)(B) of the Social Security Act [subsec. (a)(3)(B) of this section]) for such benefit before January 1982,

"(B) in the case of a disability insurance benefit, if the individual who is entitled to such benefit first became eligible (as so defined) for such benefit before January 1982, or attained age sixty-two before January 1982,

"(C) in the case of a wife's or husband's insurance benefit, or a child's insurance benefit based on the wages and self-employment income of a living individual, if the individual on whose wages and self-employment income such benefit is based is entitled to an old-age or disability insurance benefit with respect to which such amendments do not apply, or

"(D) in the case of a survivors insurance benefit, if the individual on whose wages and self-employment income such benefit is based died before January 1982, or dies in or after January 1982 and at the time of his death is eligible (as so defined) for an old-age or disability insurance benefit with respect to which such amendments do not apply.

"(4) In the case of an individual who is a member of a religious order (within the meaning of section 3121(r)(2) of Title 26, or an autonomous subdivision of such order, whose members are required to take a vow of poverty, and which order or subdivision elected coverage under Title II of the Social Security Act [this subchapter] before the date of the enactment of this Act [Dec. 29, 1981], or who would be such a member except that such individual is considered retired because of old age or total disability, paragraphs (2) and (3) shall apply, except that each reference therein to 'December 1981' or 'January 1982' shall be considered a reference to 'December 1991' or 'January 1992', respectively."

Amendment of subsec. (g) by section 2206(a) of Pub.L. 97–35, and amendment of subsec. (a)(1)(A), (i)(2)(A)(ii), and (i)(4) by section 2206(b)(5)–(7) of Pub.L. 97–35, respectively, applicable only with respect to initial calculations and adjustments of primary insurance amounts and benefit amounts which are attributable to periods after August, 1981, see section 2206(c) of Pub.L. 97–35, set out as a note under 402 of this title.

1980 Acts. Section 102(c) of Pub.L. 96–265 provided that: "The amendments made by this section [amending sections 415(b)(2)(A) and 423 of this title] shall apply only with respect to monthly benefits payable on the basis of the wages and self-employment income of an individual who first becomes entitled to disability insurance benefits on or after July 1, 1980; except that the third sentence of section 215(b)(2)(A) of the Social Security Act (as added by such amendments) [subsec. (b)(2)(A) of this section] shall apply only with respect to monthly benefits payable for months beginning on or after July 1, 1981."

For effective date of amendment of subsec. (i)(2)(A)(ii)(III) and (D) of this section by Pub.L. 96–265, see section 101(c) of Pub.L. 96–265, set out as a note under section 403 of this title.

Amendment by section 201 of Pub.L. 95–216 effective only with respect to monthly benefits under this subchapter payable for months after December, 1978, and with respect to lump-sum death payments with respect to deaths occurring after December, 1978, except that the amendments made by Section 201(d) of Pub.L. 95–216 [amending subsec. (d) of this section] shall be effective with respect to monthly benefits of an individual who becomes eligible for an old-age or disability insurance benefit, or dies after December, 1977, see section 206 of Pub.L. 95–216, set out as a note under section 402 of this title.

1977 Acts. Amendment by section 103(d) of Pub.L. 95–216 [which amended the second and third sentences of cl. (v) of subsec. (i)(2)(D)] applicable with respect to remuneration paid or received, and taxable years beginning, after 1977, see section 104 of Pub.L. 95–216, set out as a note under section 1401 of Title 26, Internal Revenue Code.

1973 Acts. Section 1(h)(2) of Pub.L. 93–233 provided that: "The amendment made by paragraph (1) [to subsec. (a)(3) of this section] shall be effective with respect to benefits payable for months after February 1974."

Section 2(c) of Pub.L. 93–233 provided that: "The amendment made by subsections (a) and (b) [revising subsec. (a) benefits table of this section, amending sections 427(a), (b) and 428(b)(1), (2), (c)(3)(A), (B) of this title, and repealing section 202(a)(4) of Pub.L. 92–336. Title II, July 1, 1972, 86 Stat. 416] shall apply with respect to monthly benefits under Title II of the Social Security Act [this subchapter] for months after May 1974, and with respect to lump-sum death payments under section 202(i) of such Act [section 402(i) of this title] in the case of deaths occurring after such month."

Amendment by section 5(a)(4) of Pub.L. 93–233 applicable with respect to calendar years after 1973, see section 5(e) of Pub.L. 93–233, set out as a note under section 409 of this title.

Amendment by Pub.L. 93–66 applicable with respect to calendar years after 1973, see section 203(e) of Pub.L. 93–66, set out as a note under section 409 of this title.

1972 Acts. Section 101(g) of Pub.L. 92–603 provided that: "The amendments made by this section [amending subsecs. (a), (f), and (i) of this section and section 403(a) of this title] shall apply with respect to monthly insurance benefits under Title II of the Social Security Act [this subchapter] for months after December 1972 (without regard to when the insured individual became entitled to such benefits or when he died) and with respect to lump-sum death payments under such title in the case of deaths occurring after such month."

Amendment of subsec. (b)(3) by section 104(b) of Pub.L. 92–603 applicable only in the case of a man who attains (or would attain) age 62 after December, 1974, with provision for the determination of the number of elapsed years for purposes of subsec. (b)(3) of this section in the case of a man who attains age 62 prior to 1975, see section 104(j) of Pub.L. 92–603, set out as a note under section 414 of this title.

Amendment by section 144(a)(1) of Pub.L. 92–603 effective in like manner as if such amendment had been included in Title II of Pub.L. 92–336, see section 144(b) of Pub.L. 92–603, set out as a note under section 403 of this title.

Section 201(i) of Pub.L. 92–336 provided that: "The amendments made by this section [amending subsecs. (a), (b)(4), (c) and (f)(2) of this section and section 403(a)(2) of this title] (other than the amendments made by subsections (g) and (h)) shall apply with respect to monthly benefits under title II of the Social Security Act [this subchapter] for months after August 1972 and with respect to lump-sum death payments under such title in the case of deaths occurring after such month. The amendments made by subsection (g) [amending sections 427 and 428 of this title] shall apply with respect to monthly benefits under title II of such Act for months after August 1972. The amendments made by subsection (h)(1) [amending section 403(a)(4) of this title] shall apply with respect to monthly benefits under Title II of such Act for months after December 1971."

Section 202(a)(3)(A) to (C) of Pub.L. 92–336, as amended by Pub.L. 93–233, § 2(d), Dec. 31, 1973, 87 Stat. 952, provided in part that amendment of subsecs. (a)(1)(A), (2), (b)(4), and (c) by section 202(a)(3)(A)(i), (ii), (B), (C), of Pub.L. 92–336 shall be effective June 1, 1974.

Amendment of subsec. (e)(1) by section 203(a)(4) of Pub.L. 92–336 applicable only with respect to calendar years after 1972, see section 203(c) of Pub.L. 92–336, set out as a note under section 409 of this title.

1971 Acts. Section 201(e) of Pub.L. 92–5 provided that: "The amendments made by this section [amending subsecs. (a), (b)(4), and (c) of this section and section 403 of this title] shall apply with respect to monthly benefits under Title II of the Social Security Act [this subchapter] for months after December 1970 and with respect to lump-sum death payments under such title in the case of deaths occurring in and after the month in which this Act is enacted [March, 1971]."

Amendment of subsec. (e)(1) by Pub.L. 92–5 applicable only with respect to calendar years after 1971, see section 203(c) of Pub.L. 92–5, set out as a note under section 409 of this title.

1969 Acts. Section 1002(e) of Pub.L. 91–172 provided that: "The amendments made by this section [amending this section and section 403(a)(2) of this title] shall apply with respect to monthly benefits under title II of the Social Security Act [this subchapter] for months after December 1969 and with respect to lump-sum death payments under such title in the case of deaths occurring after December 1969."

1968 Acts. Section 101(e) of Pub.L. 90–248 provided that: "The amendments made by this section [to subsecs. (a), (b)(4) and (5), and (c) of this section and to section 403(a)(2) of this title] shall apply with respect to monthly benefits under title II of the Social Security Act [this subchapter] for months after January 1968 and with respect to lump-sum death payments under such title [this subchapter] in the case of deaths occurring after January 1968."

Amendment of subsec. (e)(1) by section 108(a)(4) of Pub.L. 90–248 applicable only with respect to calendar years after 1967, see section 108(c) of Pub.L. 90–248, set out as a note under section 409 of this title.

Section 155(a)(7), (9) of Pub.L. 90–248 provided that:

"(7)(A) The amendments made by paragraphs (4) and (5) [to subsec. (f)(2) of this section] shall apply with respect to recomputations made under section 215(f)(2) of the Social Security Act [subsec. (f)(2) of this section] after the date of the enactment of this Act [Jan. 2, 1968].

"(B) The amendment made by paragraph (6) [enacting subsec. (f)(5) of this section] shall apply with respect to individuals who die after the date of enactment of this Act [Jan. 2, 1968].

"(9) The amendment made by paragraphs (1) and (2) [amending subsecs. (d)(1) and (2) of this section] shall not apply with respect to monthly benefits for any month prior to January 1967."

1965 Acts. Section 301(d) of Pub.L. 89–97 provided that: "The amendments made by subsections (a), (b), and (c) of this section [to subsecs. (a) and (c) of this section and section 403(a) of this title] shall apply with respect to monthly benefits under Title II of the Social Security Act [this subchapter] for months after December 1964 and with respect to lump-sum death payments under such title [this subchapter] in the case of deaths occurring in or after the month in which this Act is enacted [July, 1965]."

Section 302(d)(2) of Pub.L. 89–97 provided in part that the repeal of former pars. (3), (4), and (7) of subsec. (f) and the redesignation of pars. (5) and (6) as (3) and (4) of such subsec. (f) shall be effective Jan. 2, 1966.

Section 302(f)(1) to (5) of Pub.L. 89–97 provided that:

"(1) The amendments made by subsection (c) [repealing subsec. (e)(3) of this section] shall apply only to individuals who become entitled to old-age insurance benefits under section 202(a) of the Social Security Act [section 402(a) of this title] after 1965.

"(2) Any individual who would, upon filing an application prior to January 2, 1966, be entitled to a recomputation of his monthly benefit amount for purposes of Title II of the Social Security Act [this subchapter] shall be deemed to have filed such application on the earliest date on which such application could have been filed, or on the day on which this Act is enacted [July 30, 1965], whichever is the later.

"(3) In the case of an individual who died after 1960 and prior to 1966 and who was entitled to old-age insurance benefits under section 202(a) of the Social Security Act [section 402(a) of this title] at the time of his death, the provisions of sections 215(f)(3)(B) and 215(f)(4) of such Act [subsec. (f)(3)(B) and (f)(4) of this section] as in effect before the enactment of this Act [July 30, 1965] shall apply.

"(4) In the case of a man who attains age 65 prior to 1966, or dies before such year, the provisions of section 215(f)(7) of the Social Security Act [subsec. (f)(7) of this section] as in effect before the enactment of this Act [July 30, 1965] shall apply.

"(5) The amendments made by subsection (e) of this section [to section 423(a)(2) of this title] shall apply in the case of individuals who become entitled to disability insurance benefits under section 223 of the Social Security Act [section 423 of this title] after December 1965."

Section 303(f)(2) of Pub.L. 89–97 provided that: "The amendment made by subsection (e) [to subsec. (a)(4) of this section] shall apply in the case of the primary insurance amounts of individuals who attain age 65 after the date of enactment of this Act [July 30, 1965]."

Amendment of subsec. (a)(4) by section 304 of Pub.L. 89–97 applicable with respect to monthly insurance benefits under this subchapter for and after the second month following July 1965, but only on the basis of applications filed in or after July, 1965, see section 304(*o*) of Pub.L. 89–97, set out as a note under section 402 of this title.

Amendment by section 320 of Pub.L. 89–97 applicable only with respect to calendar years after 1965, see section 320(c) of Pub.L. 89–97, set out as a note under section 3121 of Title 26, Internal Revenue Code.

1961 Acts. Section 101(b) of Pub.L. 87–64 provided that: "The amendment made by subsection (a) [amending subsec. (a) of this section] shall apply only in the case of monthly insurance benefits under title II of the Social Security Act [this subchapter] for months beginning on or after the effective date of this title [see note under section 402 of this title], and in the case of lump-sum death payments under such title [this subchapter] with respect to deaths on or after such effective date."

Amendment of subsecs. (a)(4) and (b)(3) by Pub.L. 87–64 applicable with respect to monthly benefits for months beginning on or after Aug. 1, 1961, based on applications filed in or after March, 1961, and with respect to lump-sum death payments under this subchapter in the case of deaths on or after Aug. 1, 1961, see sections 102(f) and 109 of Pub.L. 87–64, set out as notes under section 402 of this title.

1960 Acts. Amendment of subsec. (h)(1) by Pub.L. 86–778 effective Sept. 13, 1960, see a section 103(v)(1) of Pub.L. 86–778, set out as a note under section 402 of this title.

Amendment of subsec. (g) by Pub.L. 86–778 effective in the manner provided in section 211(p) and (q) of Pub.L. 86–778, see section 211(p) to (s) of Pub.L. 86–778, set out as a note under section 403 of this title.

Section 303(d)(1) of Pub.L. 86–778 provided in part that the amendment of subsec. (e)(3) by such section 303(d)(1) of Pub.L. 86–778 shall be effective with respect to individuals who become entitled to benefits under section 402(a) of this title after 1960.

Section 303(d)(2) of Pub.L. 86–778 provided in part that the elimination of par. (4) of subsec. (e) by such section 303(d)(2) shall be effective with respect to individuals who meet any of the subparagraphs of par. (4) of subsec. (b) of this section, as amended by Pub.L. 86–778.

Section 303(e)(1) of Pub.L. 86–778 provided in part that the amendment of subsec. (f)(2)(A) by such section 303(e)(1) of Pub.L. 86–778, which substituted "1960" for "1954" in the opening provisions, and "filed such application after such calendar year" for "filed such application no earlier than six months after such calendar year" in cl. (iii) shall be effective with respect to applications for recomputation under subsec. (f)(2) of this section filed after 1960.

Section 303(e)(4)(B) of Pub.L. 86–778 provided in part that the amendment of subsec. (f)(4) by such section 303(e)(4)(B) of Pub.L. 86–778, which eliminated words "(without the application of clause (iii) thereof)" following "paragraph (2)(A)" in cl. (A), shall be effective in the case of deaths occurring on or after Sept. 13, 1960.

1958 Acts. Section 101(g) of Pub.L. 85–840 provided that: "The amendments made by this section [to subsecs. (a), (b)(1), (b)(5), (c), and (d) of this section, and sections 402(m) and 403(a) of this title] shall be applicable in the case of monthly benefits under Title II of the Social Security Act [this subchapter], for months after December 1958, and in the case of the lump-sum death payments under such title, with respect to deaths occurring after such month."

Amendment of subsec. (g) by section 205(m) of Pub.L. 85–840 applicable with respect to monthly benefits under this subchapter for August 1958 and succeeding months, see section 207(a) of Pub.L. 85–840, set out as a note under section 416 of this title.

1956 Acts. Section 109(b) of Act Aug. 1, 1956 provided that: "The amendment made by subsection (a) [to subsec. (b)(4) of this section] shall apply in the case of monthly benefits under section 202 of the Social Security Act [section 402 of this title], and the lump-sum death payment under such section, based on the wages and self-employment income of an individual—

"(1) who becomes entitled to benefits under subsection (a) of such section on the basis of an application filed on or after the date of enactment of this Act [Aug. 1, 1956]; or

"(2) who is (but for the provisions of subsection (f)(6) of section 215 of the Social Security Act [subsec. (f)(6) of this section]) entitled to a recomputation of his primary insurance amount under subsection (f)(2)(A) of such section 215 [subsec. (f)(2)(A) of this section] based on an application filed on or after the date of enactment of this Act [Aug. 1, 1956]; or

"(3) who dies without becoming entitled to benefits under subsection (a) of such section 202 [section 402(a) of this title] and no individual was entitled to survivor's benefits and no lump-sum death payment was payable under such section 202 [section 402 of this title] on the basis of an application filed prior to such date of enactment [Aug. 1, 1956]; or

"(4) who dies on or after such date of enactment [Aug. 1, 1956] and whose survivors are (but for the provisions of subsection (f)(6) of such section 215 [subsec. (f)(6) of this section]) entitled to a recomputation of his primary insurance amount under subsection (f)(4)(A) of such section 215 [subsec. (f)(4)(A) of this section]; or

"(5) who dies prior to such date of enactment [Aug. 1, 1956] and (A) whose survivors are (but for the provisions of subsection (f)(6) of such section 215 [subsec. (f)(6) of this section]) entitled to a recomputation of his primary insurance amount under subsection (f)(4)(A) of such section 215 [subsec. (f)(4)(A) of this section], and (B) on the basis of whose wages and self-employment income no individual was entitled to survivor's benefits under such section 202 [section 402 of this title], and no lump-sum death payment was payable under such section, on the basis of an application filed prior to such date of enactment [Aug. 1, 1956] and no individual was entitled to such a benefit, without the filing of an application for the month in which this Act is enacted [August, 1956] or any month prior thereto."

Section 115(d) of Act Aug. 1, 1956 provided that: "The amendments made by this section [to subsecs. (b)(1), (d)(5), and (e)(4) of this section] shall apply in the case of an individual (1) who becomes entitled (without the application of section 202(j)(1) of the Social Security Act [section 402(j)(1) of this title]) to benefits under section 202(a) of such Act [section 402(a) of this title] after the date of enactment of this Act [Aug. 1, 1956], or (2) who dies without becoming entitled to benefits under such section 202(a) [section 402(a) of this title] and on the basis of whose wages and self-employment income an application for benefits or a lump-sum death payment under section 202 of such Act [section 402 of this title] is filed after the date of enactment of this Act [Aug. 1, 1956], or (3) who becomes entitled to benefits under section 223 of such Act [section 423 of this title], or (4) who files, after the date of enactment of this Act [Aug. 1, 1956], an application for a disability determination which is accepted as an application for purposes of section 216(i) of such Act [section 416(i) of this title]."

1954 Acts. Section 102(f) of Act Sept. 1, 1954, as amended by Pub.L. 86–778, Title III, § 303(k), Sept. 13, 1960, 74 Stat. 966; Pub.L. 89–97, Title III, § 302(f)(7), July 30, 1965, 79 Stat. 366, provided that:

"**(1)** The amendments [to subsecs. (a), (c), and (d) and to section 403(a) of this title] made by the preceding subsections, other than subsection (b) and paragraphs (1), (2), (3), and (4) of subsection (e), shall (subject to the provisions of paragraph (2) and notwithstanding the provisions of section 215(f)(1) of the Social Security Act [subsec. (f)(1) of this section]) apply in the case of lump-sum death payments under section 202 of such Act [section 402 of this title] with respect to deaths occurring after, and in the case of monthly benefits under such section for months after, August 1954.

"**(2)(A)** The amendment [to subsec. (b)(4) of this section] made by subsection (b)(2) shall be applicable only in the case of monthly benefits for months after August 1954, and the lump-sum death payment in the case of death after August 1954, based on the wages and self-employment income of an individual (i) who does not become eligible for benefits under section 202(a) of the Social Security Act [section 402(a) of this title] until after August 1954, or (ii) who dies after August 1954, and without becoming eligible for benefits under such section 202(a) [section 402(a) of this title], or (iii) who is or has been entitled to have his primary insurance amount recomputed under section 215(f)(2) of the Social Security Act, as amended by subsection (e)(2) of this section [subsec. (f)(2) of this section], or under subsection (e)(5)(B) of this section [set out as a note under this section], or (iv) with respect to whom not less than six of the quarters elapsing after June 1953 are quarters of coverage (as defined in such Act), or (v) who files an application for a disability determination which is accepted as an application for purposes of section 216(i) of such Act [section 416(i) of this title], or (vi) who dies after August 1954, and whose survivors are (or would, but for the provisions of section 215(f)(6) of such Act [subsec. (f)(6) of this section], be) entitled to a recomputation of his primary insurance amount under section 215(f)(4)(A) of such Act, as amended by this Act [subsec. (f)(4)(A) of this section]. For purposes of the preceding sentence an individual shall be deemed eligible for benefits under section 202(a) of the Social Security Act [section 402(a) of this title] for any month if he was, or would upon filing application therefor in such month have been, entitled to such benefits for such month.

"**(B)** [Repealed. Pub.L. 89–97, Title III, § 302(f)(7), July 30, 1965, 79 Stat. 366, eff. Jan. 2, 1966.]

"**(3)** The amendments [to subsecs. (b)(1) to (3), (e), (f)(3)(B)] made by subsections (b)(1), (e)(1), and (e)(3)(B) shall be applicable only in the case of monthly benefits based on the wages and self-employment income of an individual who does not become entitled to old-age insurance benefits under section 202(a) of the Social Security Act [section 402(a) of this title] until after August 1954, or who dies after August 1954 without becoming entitled to such benefits, or who files an application after August 1954 and is entitled to a recomputation under paragraph (2) or (4) of section 215(f) of the Social Security Act, as amended by this Act [subsec. (f)(2) or (4) of this section], or who is entitled to a recomputation under paragraph (2)(B) of this subsection, or who is entitled to a recomputation under paragraph (5) of subsection (e) [set out as a note under this section].

"**(4)** The amendments [to subsec. (f)(2) of this section] made by subsection (e)(2) shall be applicable only in the case of applications for recomputation filed after 1954. The amendment to subsec. (f)(4) made by subsection (e)(4) shall be applicable only in the case of deaths after 1954.

"**(5)** The amendments [to subsec. (f)(3)(A), (B) of this section] made by subparagraph (A) of subsection (e)(3) shall be applicable only in the case of applications for recomputation filed, or deaths occurring, after August 1954.

"**(6)** No increase in any benefit by reason of the amendments made by this section (other than subsection (e)) or by reason of subparagraph (B) of paragraph (2) of this subsection shall be regarded as a recomputation for purposes of section 215(f) of the Social Security Act [subsec. (f) of this section]."

Amendment by section 106(c) of Act Sept. 1, 1954 applicable with respect to monthly benefits under this subchapter for months after June 1955, and with respect to lump-sum death payments under such subchapter in the case of deaths occurring after June 1955; but that no recomputation of benefits by reason of such amendments shall be regarded as a recomputation for purposes of subsec. (f) of this section, see section 106(h) of Act Sept. 1, 1954, set out as a note under section 413 of this title.

1952 Acts. For effective and termination dates of amendment by Act July 18, 1952, see section 3(f) and 3(g) of Act July 18, 1952, set out as a note under section 413 of this title.

Section 2(c)(1), (3) of Act July 18, 1952 provided that: "(1) The amendments made by subsection (a) [to subsec. (c)(1), (2), (4) of this section] shall, subject to the provisions of paragraph (2) of this subsection and notwithstanding the provisions of section 215(f)(1) of the Social Security Act [subsec. (f)(1) of this section], apply in the case of lump-sum death payments under section 202 of such Act [section 402 of this title] with respect to deaths occurring after, and in the case of monthly benefits under such section for any month after, August 1952.

"(3) The amendments made by subsection (b) [to sections 403(a) and 415(a)(1) of this title] shall (notwithstanding the provisions of section 215(f)(1) of the Social Security Act [subsec. (f)(1) of this section]) apply in the case of lump-sum death payments under section 202 of such Act [section 402 of this title] with respect to deaths occurring after August 1952, and in the case of monthly benefits under such section for months after August 1952."

1950 Acts. Section applicable (1) in case of monthly benefits for months after August, 1950, and (2) in the case of lump-sum death payments with respect to deaths after August, 1950, see section 104(b) of Act Aug. 28, 1950, set out as a note under section 409 of this title.

Termination of Reporting Requirements

For termination of reporting provisions of subsec. (i)(2)(C)(i) of this section, effective May 15, 2000, see Pub.L. 104–66, § 3003, as amended, set out as a note under 31 U.S.C.A. § 1113, and page 99 of House Document No. 103–7.

Transfer of Functions

All functions of Public Health Service, of the Surgeon General of the Public Health Service, and of all other officers and employees of the Public Health Service, and all functions of all agencies of or in the Public Health Service transferred to Secretary of Health, Education, and Welfare by Reorg. Plan No. 3 of 1966, 31 F.R. 8855, 80 Stat. 1610, effective June 25, 1966, set out in the Appendix to Title 5, Government Organization and Employees. The Secretary and Department of Health, Education and Welfare were redesignated the Secretary and Department of Health and Human Services by section 509(b) of Pub.L. 96–88 which is classified to section 3508(b) of Title 20, Education.

Savings Provisions

1960. —Section 303(i) of Pub.L. 86–778 provided that in the case of an application for recomputation under subsec. (f)(2) of this section, the provisions of subsec. (f)(2) as in effect prior to Sept. 13, 1960, were to apply where the application was filed after 1954 and before 1961, and that in the case of an individual who died after 1954 and before 1961 and who was entitled to an old-age insurance benefit under section 402(a) of this title, the provisions of subsec. (f)(4) as in effect prior to Sept. 13, 1960 were to apply.

1958. —Section 101(i) of Pub.L. 85–840 provided that: "In the case of any individual to whom the provisions of subsection (b)(5) of section 215 of the Social Security Act [subsec. (b)(5) of this section], as amended by this Act, are applicable and on the basis of whose wages and self-employment income benefits are payable for months prior to January 1959, his primary insurance amount for purposes of benefits for such prior months shall, if based on an application for such benefits or for a recomputation of such amount, as the case may be, filed after December 1958, be determined under such section 215 [this section], as in effect prior to the enactment of this Act [Aug. 28, 1958], and, if such individual's primary insurance amount as so determined is larger than the primary insurance amount determined for him under section 215 [this section] as amended by this Act, such larger primary insurance amount (increased to the next higher dollar if it is not a multiple of a dollar) shall, for months after December 1958, be his primary insurance amount for purposes of such section 215 (and of the other provisions) of the Social Security Act [this section] as amended by this Act in lieu of the amount determined without regard to this subsection."

1952. —Subsec. (d) of section 2 of Act July 18, 1952, provided that:

"(1) Where—

"(A) an individual was entitled (without the application of section 202(j)(1) of the Social Security Act [section 402(j)(1) of this title]) to an old-age insurance benefit under Title II of such Act [this subchapter] for August 1952;

"(B) two or more other persons were entitled (without the application of such section 202(j)(1) [section 402(j)(1) of this title]) to monthly benefits under such title [this subchapter] for such month on the basis of the wages and self-employment income of such individual; and

"(C) the total of the benefits to which all persons are entitled under such title [this subchapter] on the basis of such individual's wages and self-employment income for any subsequent month for which he is entitled to an old-age insurance benefit under such title [this subchapter], would (but for the provisions of this paragraph) be reduced by reason of the application of section 203(a) of the Social Security Act, as amended by this Act [section 403(a) of this title],

then the total of benefits, referred to in clause (C), for such subsequent month shall be reduced to whichever of the following is the larger:

"(D) the amount determined pursuant to section 203(a) of the Social Security Act, as amended by this Act [section 403(a) of this title]; or

"(E) the amount determined pursuant to such section, as in effect prior to the enactment of this Act [July 18, 1952], for August 1952 plus the excess of (i) the amount of his old-age insurance benefit for August 1952 computed as if the amendments made by the preceding subsections of this section had been applicable in the case of such benefit for August 1952, over (ii) the amount of his old-age insurance benefit for August 1952.

"(2) No increase in any benefit by reason of the amendments made by this section or by reason of paragraph (2) of subsection (c) of this section shall be regarded as a recomputation for purposes of section 215(f) of the Social Security Act [subsec. (f) of this section]."

Termination of Reporting Requirements

Reporting requirement of subsec. (i)(2)(C)(i) of this section excepted from termination under Pub.L. 104–66, § 3003(a)(1), as amended, set out as a note under 31 U.S.C.A. § 1113, see Pub.L. 106–554, § 1(a)(7) [Title III, § 301], set out as a note under 31 U.S.C.A. § 1113.

Average Monthly Wage for Certain Individuals Entitled to Monthly Benefits or to Recomputation of Primary Insurance Amount for Months Prior to January 1961

Section 303(j) of Pub.L. 86–778 provided that:

"In the case of an individual whose average monthly wage is computed under the provisions of section 215(b) of the Social Security Act [former provisions of subsec. (b) of this section], as amended by this Act, and—

"(1) who is entitled, by reason of the provisions of section 202(j)(1) or section 223(b) of the Social Security Act [former provisions of section 402(j)(1) or section 423(b) of this title], to a monthly benefit for any month prior to January 1961, or

"(2) who is (or would, but for the fact that such recomputation would not result in a higher primary insurance amount for such individual, be) entitled, by reason of section 215(f) of the Social Security Act [subsec. (f) of this section], to have his primary insurance amount recomputed effective for a month prior to January 1961,

his average monthly wage as determined under the provisions of such section 215(b) [subsec. (b) of this section] shall be his average monthly wage for the purposes of determining his primary insurance amount for such prior month."

"Base Quarter" in Calendar Year 1983

Section 111(d) of Pub.L. 98–21 provided that: "Notwithstanding any provision to the contrary in section 215(i) of the Social Security Act [subsec. (i) of this section], the 'base quarter' (as defined in paragraph (1)(A)(i) of such section) in the calendar year 1983 shall be a 'cost-of-living computation quarter' within the meaning of paragraph (1)(B) of such section (and shall be deemed to have been determined by the Secretary of Health and Human Services to be a 'cost-of-living computation quarter' under paragraph (2)(A) of such section) for all of the purposes of such Act [this chapter] as amended by this section and by other provisions of this Act [Social Security Amendments of 1983], without regard to the extent by which the Consumer Price Index has increased since the last prior cost-of-living computation quarter which was established under such paragraph (1)(B)."

Benefits in Certain Cases of Deaths Before September 1950

Section 109 of Act Sept. 1, 1954, as amended by Pub.L. 86–778, Title II, § 204(c), Sept. 13, 1960, 74 Stat. 948, provided that in the case of an individual who died prior to Sept. 1, 1950, and was not a fully insured individual when he died and who had at least six quarters of coverage under this subchapter, such individual was generally to be deemed to have died fully insured, his primary insurance amount was to be deemed to be computed under former provisions of subsec. (a)(2) of this section, the proof of support requirement in former provisions of section 402(h) of this title was not to be applicable where such proof was filed before September, 1956, and that the provisions of this section were to apply to monthly benefits under section 402 of this title for months after August, 1954, and in or prior to September, 1960.

Change of Wage Closing Date of Certain Individuals Dead or Eligible in 1952 to First Day of Quarter of Death or Entitlement

Section 6(c) of Act July 18, 1952 provided that: "In the case of an individual who died or became (without the application of section 202(j)(1) of the Social Security Act [former provisions of section 402(j)(1) of this title]) entitled to old-age insurance benefits in 1952 and with respect to whom not less than six of the quarters elapsing after 1950 and prior to the quarter following the quarter in which he died or became entitled to old-age insurance benefits, whichever first occurred, are quarters of coverage, his wage closing date shall be the first day of such quarter of death or entitlement instead of the day specified in section 215(b)(3) of such Act [former provisions of subsec. (b)(3) of this section], but only if it would result in a higher primary insurance amount for such individual. The terms used in this paragraph shall have the same meaning as when used in title II of the Social Security Act [this subchapter]."

Combined Balance in Trust Funds Used in Determining OASDI Fund Ratio With Respect to Calendar Year 1984

Section 112(f) of Pub.L. 98–21, as amended Pub.L. 98–369, Div. B, Title VI, § 2662(b), July 18, 1984, 98 Stat. 1159, provided that: "Notwithstanding anything to the contrary in section 215(i)(1)(F) of the Social Security Act [subsec. (i)(1)(F) of this section] (as added by subsection (a)(4) of this section), the combined balance in the Trust Funds which is to be used in determining the 'OASDI fund ratio' with respect to the calendar year 1984 under such section shall be the estimated combined balance in such Funds as of the close of that year (rather than as of its beginning), including the taxes transferred under section 201(a) of such Act [section 401(a) of this title] on the first day of the year following that year."

Commission on the Social Security "Notch" Issue

Pub.L. 102–393, Title VI, § 635, Oct. 6, 1992, 106 Stat. 1777, as amended Pub.L. 103–123, Title VI, § 627, Oct. 28, 1993, 107 Stat. 1266, provided that:

"(a) **Establishment.**—There is established a Commission on the Social Security 'Notch' Issue (in this section referred to as the 'Commission').

"(b) **Membership.**—The Commission shall be composed of 12 members as follows:

"(1) 4 members appointed by the President from among officers or employees of the executive branch, private citizens of the United States, or both. Not more than 2 of the members appointed by the President shall be members of the same political party.

"(2) 2 members appointed by the Majority Leader of the United States Senate, in consultation with the Chairman of the Committee on Finance of the United States Senate, from among members of the Senate, private citizens of the United States, or both.

"(3) 2 members appointed by the Minority Leader of the United States Senate, in consultation with the Ranking Member of the Committee on Finance of the United States Senate, from among members of the Senate, private citizens of the United States, or both.

"(4) 2 members appointed by the Speaker of the House of Representatives, in consultation with the Chairman of the Committee on Ways and Means of the House of Representatives, from among members of the House of Representatives, private citizens of the United States, or both.

"(5) 2 members appointed by the Minority Leader of the House of Representatives, in consultation with the Ranking Member of the Committee on Ways and Means of the House of Representatives, from among members of the House of Representatives, private citizens of the United States, or both.

"(c) **Functions of the Commission.**—

"(1) **Study.**—The Commission shall conduct a comprehensive study of what has come to be known as the 'notch' issue. The study shall examine the causes of the controversy, whether there are inequities in the treatment of social security beneficiaries born in different years, whether legislative action should be taken, and the effect on social security trust funds of such legislative action.

"(2) **Findings and conclusions.**—The Commission shall transmit a report to the Congress not later than December 31, 1994. The report shall contain a detailed statement of the findings and conclusions of the Commission, together with any recommendations the Commission considers appropriate. Any recommendations which would increase social security expenditures would have to be accompanied by cost estimates and options for financing such recommendations.

"(d) **Chairperson; meetings.**—The President shall designate a Chairperson from among the membership. The Commission shall meet at the call of the Chairperson or a majority of its members.

"(e) **Pay.**—Members of the Commission shall serve without compensation, except that members of the Commission who are private citizens of the United States shall be reimbursed for travel, subsistence, and other necessary expenses incurred in the performance of their duties as members of the Commission.

"(f) **Staff.**—

"(1) **Staff.**—Subject to rules prescribed by the Commission, the Chairperson may appoint and fix the pay of such personnel as the Chairperson considers appropriate.

"(2) **Staff of Department of Health and Human Services.**—Upon request of the Commission, the Secretary of Health and Human Services may detail, on a reimbursable basis, any of the personnel of the Department of Health and Human Services to the Commission to assist it in carrying out its duties under this section.

"(g) **Obtaining official data.**—The Commission may secure directly from any department or agency of the United States such information as is necessary and appropriate to enable it to carry out this section. Upon request of the Chairperson of the Commission, the head of that department or agency shall, to the extent permitted by law, furnish that information to the Commission.

"(h) **Termination.**—The Commission shall terminate 30 days after transmittal of its report to the Congress.

"(i) **Authorization of appropriations.**—There is authorized to be appropriated $2,000,000 for purposes of this section, to remain available until expended, but in no event beyond the date of termination provided in subsection (h)."

Computation of Average Monthly Wage for Certain Individuals Entitled to Disability Insurance Benefits Prior to 1961

Section 303(g)(2) of Pub.L. 86–778 provided that: "Notwithstanding the amendments made by the preceding subsections of this section [to subsecs. (b), (d)(1), (3), (e)(2), and (f)(2), (4) of this section, former subsecs. (c)(2), (e)(3)(4), and (f)(3) of this section, and section 423(a)(2) of this title], in the case of any individual who was entitled (without regard to the provisions of section 223(b) of the Social Security Act [section 423(b) of this title]) to a disability insurance benefit under such section 223 [section 423 of this title] for the month before the month in which he became entitled to an old-age insurance benefit under section 202(a) of such Act [section 402(a) of this title], or in which he died, and such disability insurance benefit was based upon a primary insurance amount determined under the provisions of section 215 of the Social Security Act [this section] in effect prior to the enactment of this Act [Sept. 13, 1960], the Secretary shall, in applying the provisions of such section 215(a) [subsec. (a) of this section] (except paragraph (4) thereof) [former provisions of subsec. (a)(4) of this section], for purposes of determining benefits payable under section 202 of such Act [section 402 of this title] on the basis of such individual's wages and self-employment income, determine such individual's average monthly wage under the provisions of section 215 of the Social Security Act [this section] in effect prior to the enactment of this Act [Sept. 13, 1960]. The provisions of this paragraph shall not apply with respect to any such individual, entitled to such old-age insurance benefits, (i) who applies, after 1960, for a recomputation (to which he is entitled) of his primary insurance amount under section 215(f)(2) of such Act [former provisions of subsec. (f)(2) of this section] or (ii) who dies after 1960 and meets the conditions for a recomputation of his primary insurance amount under section 215(f)(4) of such Act [former provisions of subsec. (f)(4) of this section]."

Computation of Increased Benefits for Dependents and Survivors on Benefit Rolls for August 1952

Section 2(c)(2) of Act July 18, 1952, as amended by Act Sept. 1, 1954, § 102(g), eff. Sept. 1, 1954, provided that:

"(A) In the case of any individual who is (without the application of section 202(j)(1) of the Social Security Act) [former provisions of section 402(j)(1) of this title] entitled to a monthly benefit under subsection (b), (c), (d), (e), (f), (g), or (h) of such section 202 [section 402 of this title], for August 1952, whose benefit for such month is computed through use of a primary insurance amount determined under paragraph (1) or (2) of section 215(c) of such Act [former provisions of subsec. (c) of this section], and who is entitled to such benefit for any succeeding month on the basis of the same wages and self-employment income, the amendments made by this section shall not (subject to the provisions of subparagraph (B) of this paragraph) apply for purposes of computing the amount of such benefit for such succeeding month. The amount of such benefit for such succeeding month shall instead be equal to the larger of (i) 112½ per centum of the amount of such benefit (after the application of sections 203(a) and 215(g) of the Social Security Act [former provisions of sections 403(a) and 415(g) of this title] as in effect prior to the enactment of this Act [July 18, 1952]) for August 1952, increased, if it is not a multiple of $0.10, to the next higher multiple of $0.10, or (ii) the amount of such benefit (after the application of sections 203(a) and 215(g) of the Social Security Act [former provisions of sections 403(a) and 415(g) of this title] as in effect prior to the enactment of this Act [July 18, 1952]) for August 1952, increased by an amount equal to the product obtained by multiplying $5 by the fraction applied to the primary insurance amount which was used in determining such benefit, and further increased, if such product is not a multiple of $0.10, to the next higher multiple of $0.10. The provisions of section 203(a) of the Social Security Act, as amended by this section (and, for purposes of such section 203(a) [former provisions of section 403(a) of this title], the provisions of section 215(c)(4) of the Social Security Act, as amended by this section [former subsec. (c)(4) of this section]), shall apply to such benefit as computed under the preceding sentence of this subparagraph, and the resulting amount, if not a multiple of $0.10, shall be increased to the next higher multiple of $0.10.

"(B) The provisions of subparagraph (A) shall cease to apply to the benefit of any individual under title II of the Social Security Act [this subchapter] for any month after August 1954."

Computation of Increased Benefits to Individuals Entitled Thereto for August 1952

Section 6(e) of Act July 18, 1952, provided that: "In case the benefit of any individual for any month after August 1952 is computed under section 2(c)(2)(A) of this Act [set out as a note under this section] through use of a benefit (after the application of sections 203 and 215(g) of the Social Security Act [section 403 and former provisions of section 415(g) of this title] as in effect prior to the enactment of this Act [July 18, 1952]) for August 1952 which could have been derived from either of two (and not more than two) primary insurance amounts, and such primary insurance amounts differ from each other by not more than $0.10, then the benefit of such individual for such month of August 1952 shall, for the purposes of the last sentence of such section 2(c)(2)(A) [set out as a note under this section], be deemed to have been derived from the larger of such two primary insurance amounts."

Computation of Primary Insurance Amount for Certain Individuals Who Were Fully Insured and Had Attained Retirement Age Prior to 1961

Section 303(g)(1) of Pub.L. 86–778, as amended by Pub.L. 87–64, Title I, § 103(d), June 30, 1961, 75 Stat. 138; Pub.L. 89–97, Title III, § 302(f)(6), July 30, 1965, 79 Stat. 366; Pub.L. 90–248, Title I, § 155(c), Jan. 2, 1968, 81 Stat. 866; Pub.L. 92–603, Title I, § 104(h), Oct. 30, 1972, 86 Stat. 1341, provided that: "In the case of any individual who both was fully insured and had attained retirement age prior to 1961 and (A) who becomes entitled to old-age insurance benefits after 1960, or (B) who dies after 1960 without being entitled to such benefits, then, notwithstanding the amendments made by the preceding subsections of this section [to subsecs. (b), (d)(1), (3), (e)(2), and (f)(2), (4) of this section, former subsecs. (c)(2), (e)(3), (4), and (f)(3) of this section, and section 423(a)(2) of this title], or the amendments made by the Social Security Amendments of 1965, 1967, 1969, and 1972 (and by Public Law 92–5) [See Tables for classification of Pub.L. 89–97, July 30, 1965, 79 Stat. 286, Pub.L. 90–248, Jan. 2, 1968, 81 Stat. 821, Pub.L. 91–172, Title X, Dec. 30, 1969, 83 Stat. 737, Pub.L. 92–603, Oct. 30, 1972, 86 Stat. 1329, Pub.L. 92–5, Mar. 17, 1971, 85 Stat. 5] the Secretary shall also compute such individual's primary insurance amount on the basis of such individual's average monthly wage determined under the provisions of section 215 of the Social Security Act [this section] in effect prior to the enactment of this Act with a closing date determined under section 215(b)(3)(B) of such Act [former subsec. (b)(3)(B) of this section] as then in effect, but only if such closing date would have been applicable to such computation had this section not been enacted. If the primary insurance amount resulting from the use of such an average monthly wage is higher than the primary insurance amount resulting from the use of an average monthly wage determined pursuant to the provisions of section 215 of the Social Security Act [this section], as amended by the Social Security Amendments of 1960 [Pub.L. 86–778], or (if such individual becomes entitled to old-age insurance benefits after the date of enactment of the Social Security Amendments of 1972 [Oct. 30, 1972], or dies after such date without becoming so entitled) as amended by the Social Security Amendments of 1972 [Pub.L. 92–603], such higher primary insurance amount shall be the individual's primary insurance amount for purposes of such section 215 [this section]. The terms used in this subsection shall have the meaning assigned to them by title II of the Social Security Act [this subchapter]; except that the terms 'fully insured' and 'retirement age' shall have the meaning assigned to them by such title II [this subchapter] as in effect on September 13, 1960."

Computation of Primary Insurance Amount for Persons Entitled to Benefits After January 2 and Before February 1968

Section 155(a)(8) of Pub.L. 90–248 provided that:

"In any case in which—

"(A) any person became entitled to a monthly benefit under section 202 or 223 of the Social Security Act [section 402 or 423 of this title] after the date of enactment of this Act [Jan. 2, 1968] and before February 1968, and

"(B) the primary insurance amount on which the amount of such benefit is based was determined by applying section 215(d) of the Social Security Act [subsec. (d) of this section] as amended by this Act,

such primary insurance amount shall, for purposes of section 215(c) of the Social Security Act [subsec. (c) of this section], as amended by this Act, be deemed to have been computed on the basis of the Social Security Act [this chapter] in effect prior to the enactment of this Act [Jan. 2, 1968]."

Computation of Primary Insurance Amount of Individuals Who Died Prior to 1940

Section 205(c) of Pub.L. 86–778 provided that: "The primary insurance amount (for purposes of Title II of the Social Security Act [this subchapter]) of any individual who died prior to 1940, and who had not less than six quarters of coverage (as defined in section 213 of such Act [section 413 of this title]), shall be computed under section 215(a)(2) of such Act [former provisions of subsec. (a)(2) of this section]."

[Section 205(c) of Pub.L. 86–778 as applicable only in the case of monthly benefits under this subchapter for months after September, 1960, on the basis of applications filed in or after such month, see section 205(d) of Pub.L. 86–778, set out as an Effective Date of 1960 Amendments note under section 402 of this title.]

Conversion of Disability Insurance Benefits to Old-Age Insurance Benefits

Section 201(f) of Pub.L. 92–5 provided that: "If an individual was entitled to a disability insurance benefit under section 223 of the Social Security Act [section 423 of this title] for December 1970 on the basis of an application filed in or after the month in which this Act is enacted [March, 1971], and became entitled to old-age insurance benefits under section 202(a) of such Act [section 402(a) of this title] for January 1971, then, for purposes of section 215(a)(4) of the Social Security Act [former provisions of subsec. (a)(4) of this section] (if applicable), the amount in column IV of the table appearing in such section 215(c) [probably means section 215(a) which is subsec. (a) of this section] for such individual shall be the amount in such column on the line on which in column II appears his primary insurance amount (as determined under section 215(c) of such Act [subsec. (c) of this section]) instead of the amount in column IV equal to the primary insurance amount on which his disability insurance benefit is based."

Section 1002(f) of Pub.L. 91–172 provided that: "If an individual was entitled to a disability insurance benefit under section 223 of the Social Security Act [section 423 of this title] for December 1969 and became entitled to old-age insurance benefits under section 202(a) of such Act [section 402(a) of this title] for January 1970, or he died in such month, then, for purposes of section 215(a)(4) of the Social Security Act [former provisions of subsec. (a)(4) of this section] (if applicable), the amount in column IV of the table appearing in such section 215(a) [subsec. (a) of this section] for such individual shall be the amount in such column on the line on which in column II appears his primary insurance amount (as determined under section 215(c) of such Act [subsec. (c) of this section]) instead of the amount in column IV equal to the primary insurance amount on which his disability insurance benefit is based."

Section 101(f) of Pub.L. 90–248 provided that: "If an individual was entitled to a disability insurance benefit under section 223 of the Social Security Act [section 423 of this title] for the month of January 1968 and became entitled to old-age insurance benefits under section 202(a) of such Act [section 402(a) of this title] for the month of February 1968, or who died in such month, then, for purposes of section 215(a)(4) of the Social Security Act [subsec. (a)(4) of this section] (if applicable) the amount in column IV of the table appearing in such section 215(a) [former provisions of subsec. (a) of this section] for such individual shall be the amount in such column on the line on which in column II appears his primary insurance amount (as determined under section 215(c) of such Act [subsec. (c) of this section]) instead of the amount in column IV equal to the primary insurance amount on which his disability insurance benefit is based."

Section 301(e) of Pub.L. 89–97 provided that: "If an individual is entitled to a disability insurance benefit under section 223 of the Social Security Act [section 423 of this title] for December 1964 on the basis of an application filed after enactment of this Act [July 30, 1965] and is entitled to old-age insurance benefits under section 202(a) of such Act [section 402(a) of this title] for January 1965, then, for purposes of section 215(a)(4) of the Social Security Act [former provisions of subsec. (a)(4) of this section] (if applicable) the amount in column IV of the table appearing in such section 215(a) [subsec. (a) of this section] for such individual shall be the amount in such column on the line on which in column II appears his primary insurance amount (as determined under section 215(c) of such Act [subsec. (c) of this section]) instead of the amount in column IV equal to his disability insurance benefit."

Section 101(h) of Pub.L. 85–840 provided that: "If an individual was entitled to a disability insurance benefit under section 223 of the Social Security Act [section 423 of this title] for December 1958, and became entitled to old-age insurance benefits under section 202(a) of such Act [section 402(a) of this title], or died, in January 1959, then, for purposes of paragraph (4) of section 215(a) of the Social Security Act [former provisions of subsec. (a)(4) of this section], as amended by this Act, the amount in column IV of the table appearing in such section 215(a) [subsec. (a) of this section] for such individual shall be the amount in such column on the line on which in column II appears his primary insurance amount (as determined under subsection (c) of such section 215 [subsec. (c) of this section]) instead of the amount in column IV equal to his disability insurance benefit."

Cost-of-Living Increase in Benefits

Section 3(i) of Pub.L. 93–233 provided that; "For purposes of section 203(f)(8) [section 403(f)(8) of this title], so much of section 215(i)(1)(B) [subsec. (i)(1)(B) of this section] as follows the semicolon, and section 230(a) of the Social Security Act [section 430(a) of this title], the increase in benefits provided by section 2 of this Act [revising benefits table of subsec. (a) of this section and amending sections 427(a), (b) and 428(b)(1), (2), (c)(3)(A), (B) of this title] shall be considered an increase under section 215(i) of the Social Security Act [subsec. (i) of this section]."

Cost-of-Living Increases; Cost-of-Living Computation Quarter Determinations

Pub.L. 98–604, § 1, Oct. 30, 1984, 98 Stat. 3161, provided: "That (a) in determining whether the base quarter ending on September 30, 1984, is a cost-of-living computation quarter for the purposes of the cost-of-living increases under sections 215(i) and 1617 of the Social Security Act [subsec. (i) of this section and section 1382f of this title], the phrase 'is 3 percent or more' appearing in section 215(i)(1)(B) of such Act [subsec. (i)(1)(B) of this section] shall be deemed to read 'is greater than zero' (and the phrase 'exceeds, by not less than 3 per centum, such Index' appearing in section 215(i)(1)(B) of such Act [subsec. (i)(1)(B) of this section] as in effect in December 1978 shall be deemed to read 'exceeds such Index').

"(b) For purposes of section 215(i) of such Act [subsec. (i) of this section], the provisions of subsection (a) shall not constitute a 'general benefit increase'."

Determination of Primary Insurance Amount of Individuals Who Died After 1939 and Prior to 1951

Section 204(b) of Pub.L. 86–778 provided that: "The primary insurance amount (for purposes of title II of the Social Security Act [this subchapter]) of any individual who died after 1939 and prior to 1951 shall be determined as provided in section 215(a)(2) of such Act [former provisions of subsec. (a)(2) of this section]."

Disregarding OASDI Benefit Increases and Child's Insurance Benefit Payments Beyond Age 18 to Extent Attributable to Retroactive Effective Date of 1965 Amendments

Section 406 of Pub.L. 89–97 authorized a State to disregard, in determining the need for aid or assistance under State plans approved under subchapter I, IV, X, XIV, or XVI of this chapter, any amount paid to an individual under subchapter II of this chapter or the Railroad Retirement Act of 1937, former section 228a et seq. of Title 45, Railroads, by reason of the amendments made by section 326(a) of Pub.L. 89–97 to former sections 228a(q) and 228e(*l*)(9) of Title 45, for months occurring after December, 1964, and before the third month following July, 1965, in certain instances.

Disregarding of Income of OASDI Recipients and Railroad Retirement Recipients in Determining Need for Public Assistance

Section 1007 of Pub.L. 91–172, as amended by Pub.L. 91–306, § 2(b)(1), July 6, 1970, 84 Stat. 408; Pub.L. 91–669, Jan. 11, 1971, 84 Stat. 2038; Pub.L. 92–223 § 5, Dec. 28, 1971, 85 Stat. 810; Pub.L. 92–603, Title III, § 304, Oct. 30, 1972, 86 Stat. 1484, eff. Oct. 30, 1972, provided a minimum aid requirement in addition to the requirements imposed by law as conditions of approval of State plans for aid to individuals under subchapters I, X, XIV, or XVI of this chapter, in the case of any individual found eligible for aid for any month after March, 1970 and before January, 1974 who also received a monthly insurance benefit under this subchapter, and in the case of such an individual who also received a monthly annuity or pension under the Railroad Retirement Acts of 1935 or

1937, set out in former sections 215 et seq. and 228a et seq., respectively, of Title 45, Railroads.

Disregarding of Retroactive Payment of OASDI Benefit Increase and of Railroad Retirement Benefit Increase

Section 201(g) of Pub.L. 92–5 provided that: "Notwithstanding the provisions of sections 2(a)(10), 402(a)(7), 1002(a)(8), 1402(a)(8), and 1602(a)(13) and (14) of the Social Security Act [sections 302(a)(10), 602(a)(7), 1202(a)(8), 1352(a)(8), and 1382(a)(13) and (14) of this title], each State, in determining need for aid or assistance under a State plan approved under Title I, X, XIV, or XVI, or part A of Title IV, of such Act [subchapters I, X, XIV, or XVI, or part A of subchapter IV of this chapter], may disregard (and the plan may be deemed to require the State to disregard), in addition to any other amounts which the State is required or permitted to disregard in determining such need, any amount paid to an individual under Title II of such Act [subchapter II of this chapter] (or under the Railroad Retirement Act of 1937 [former section 228a et seq. of Title 45, Railroads] by reason of the first proviso in section 3(e) thereof [former section 228c(e) of Title 45]), in any month after the month in which this Act is enacted [March, 1971], to the extent that (1) such payment is attributable to the increase in monthly benefits under the old-age survivors, and disability insurance system for January, February, March, or April 1971 resulting from the enactment of this title, and (2) the amount of such increase is paid separately from the rest of the monthly benefit of such individual for January, February, March, or April 1971."

Section 1006 of Title X of Pub.L. 91–172, as amended by Pub.L. 91–306, § 2(a)(1), July 6, 1970, 84 Stat. 407, provided that: "Notwithstanding the provisions of sections 2(a)(10) [section 302(a)(10) of this title], 402(a)(7) [section 602(a)(7) of this title], 1002(a)(8) [section 1202(a)(8) of this title], 1402(a)(8) [section 1352(a)(8) of this title], and 1602(a)(13) and (14) of the Social Security Act [subsecs. (a)(13) and (14) of section 1382 of this title], each State, in determining need for aid or assistance under a State plan approved under Title I, X, XIV, or XVI [subchapters I, X, XIV, or XVI of this chapter], or part A of Title IV, of such Act [part A of subchapter IV of this chapter], shall disregard (and the plan shall be deemed to require the State to disregard), in addition to any other amounts which the State is required or permitted to disregard in determining such need, any amount paid to an individual (1) under title II of such Act [this subchapter] (or under the Railroad Retirement Act of 1937 [former section 228a et seq. of Title 45, Railroads] by reason of the first proviso in section 3(e) thereof [former section 228c(e) of Title 45]), in any month after December 1969, to the extent that (A) such payment is attributable to the increase in monthly benefits under the old-age, survivors, and disability insurance system for January or February 1970 resulting from the enactment of this title [this chapter], and (B) the amount of such increase is paid separately from the rest of the monthly benefit of such individual for January or February 1970; or (2) as annuity or pension under the Railroad Retirement Act of 1937 or the Railroad Retirement Act of 1935, if such amount is paid in a lump-sum to carry out any retroactive increase in annuities or pensions payable under the Railroad Retirement Act of 1937 or the Railroad Retirement Act of 1935 [former section 215 et seq. of Title 45] brought about by reason of the enactment (after May 30, 1970 and prior to December 31, 1970) of any Act which increases, retroactively, the amount of such annuities or pensions."

Increase of Old-Age or Disability Insurance Benefits Following Increase in Primary Insurance Amount or Entitlement to Benefits on Higher Amount

Section 101(f) of Pub.L. 92–603 provided that: "Whenever an insured individual is entitled to benefits for a month which are based on a primary insurance amount under paragraph (1) or paragraph (3) of section 215(a) of the Social Security Act [subsec. (a)(1) or (3) of this section] and for the following month such primary insurance amount is increased or such individual becomes entitled to benefits on a higher primary insurance amount under a different paragraph of such section 215(a) [subsec. (a) of this section], such individual's old-age or disability insurance benefit (beginning with the effective month of the increased primary insurance amount) shall be increased by an amount equal to the difference between the higher primary insurance amount and the primary insurance amount on which such benefit was based for the month prior to such effective month, after the application of section 202(q) of such Act [section 402(q) of this title] where applicable, to such difference."

Lag Recomputation Preserved for Certain Individuals Eligible or Dead Prior to September 1954

Section 102(e)(8) of Act Sept. 1, 1954, as amended by Pub.L. 86–778, Title III, § 304(c), Sept. 13, 1960, 74 Stat. 966, provided that: "In the case of an individual who became (without the application of section 202(j)(1) [former provisions of section 402(j)(1) of this title]) entitled to old-age insurance benefits or died prior to September 1954, the provisions of section 215(f)(3) [former subsec. (f)(3) of this section] as in effect prior to the enactment of this Act [Sept. 1, 1954] shall be applicable as though this Act had not been enacted but only if such individual files the application referred to in subparagraph (A) of such section prior to January 1961 or (if he dies without filing such application) his death occurred prior to January 1961."

Recalculation of Primary Insurance Amounts Applicable to Certain Beneficiaries

Section 2201(e) of Pub.L. 97–35, which provided for recalculation of primary insurance amounts for certain beneficiaries and which was formerly set out as a note under this section, was repealed by Pub.L. 97–123, § 2(i), Dec. 29, 1981, 95 Stat. 1661.

Recomputation of Primary Insurance Amount in Certain Cases Where Application for Recomputation is Filed On or After September 13, 1960

Section 303(h) of Pub.L. 86–778 provided that:

"In any case where application for recomputation under section 215(f)(3) of the Social Security Act [former subsec. (f)(3) of this section] is filed on or after the date of the enactment of this Act [Sept. 13, 1960) with respect to an individual for whom the last previous computation of the primary insurance amount was based on an application filed prior to 1961, or who died before 1961, the provisions of section 215 of such Act [this section] as in effect prior to the enactment of this Act shall apply except that—

"(1) such recomputation shall be made as provided in section 215(a) of the Social Security Act [subsec. (a) of this section] (as in effect prior to the enactment of this Act) and as though such individual first became entitled to old-age insurance benefits in the month in which he filed his application for such recomputation or died without filing such an application, and his closing date for such purposes shall be as specified in such section 215(f)(3) [former subsec. (f)(3) of this section]; and

"(2) the provisions of section 215(b)(4) of the Social Security Act [former provisions of subsec. (b)(4) of this section] (as in effect prior to the enactment of this Act) shall apply only if they were applicable to the last previous computation of such individual's primary insurance amount, or would have been applicable to such computation if there had been taken into account—

"(A) his wages and self-employment income in the year in which he became entitled to old-age insurance benefits or filed application for the last previous recomputation of his primary insurance amount, where he is living at the time of the application for recomputation under this subsection, or

"(B) his wages and self-employment income in the year in which he died without becoming entitled to old-age insurance benefits, or (if he was entitled to such benefits) the year in which application was filed for the last previous computation of his primary insurance amount or in which he died, whichever first occurred, where he has died at the time of the application for such recomputation.

If the primary insurance amount of an individual was recomputed under section 215(f)(3) of the Social Security Act [former subsec. (f)(3) of this section] as in effect prior to the enactment of this Act, and such amount would have been larger if the recomputation had been made under such section as modified by this subsection, then the Secretary shall recompute such primary insurance amount under such section as so modified, but only if an application for such recomputation is filed on or after the date of the enactment of this Act [Sept. 13, 1960]. A recomputation under the preceding sentence shall be effective for and after the first month for which the last previous recomputation of such individual's primary insurance amount under such section 215 [this section] was effective, but in no event for any month prior to the twenty-fourth month before the month in which the application for a recomputation is filed under the preceding sentence."

Right to Recomputation Under Law Prior to Enactment of Act September 1, 1954

Section 102(e)(5) of Act Sept. 1, 1954, as amended by Pub.L. 86–778, Title III, § 304(b), Sept. 13, 1960, 74 Stat. 966, provided that:

"(A) In the case of any individual who upon filing application therefor before September 1954, would (but for the provisions of section 215(f)(6) of the Social Security Act [former provisions of subsec. (f)(6) of this section]) have been entitled to a recomputation under subparagraph (A) or (B) of section 215(f)(2) of such Act [former provisions of subsec. (f)(2)(A) or (B) of this section] as in effect prior to the enactment of this Act [Sept. 1, 1954], the Secretary shall recompute such individual's primary insurance amount, but only if he files an application therefor or, in case he died before filing such application, an application for monthly manner as for an individual to whom subsection (a)(1) of such section, as in effect prior to the enactment of this Act [Sept. 1, 1954], is applicable; and such recomputation shall take into account only such wages and self-employment income as would be taken into account under section 215(b) of the Social Security Act [section 415(b) of this title] if the month in which the application for recomputation is filed, or if the individual died without filing the application for recomputation, the month in which he died, were deemed to be the month in which he became entitled to old-age insurance benefits. In the case of monthly benefits, such recomputation shall be effective for and after the month in which such application for recomputation is filed or, if the individual has died without filing the application, for and after the month in which the person filing the application for monthly survivor benefits becomes entitled to such benefits.

"(B) In the case of—

"(i) any individual who is entitled to a recomputation under subparagraph (A) of section 215(f)(2) of the Social Security Act [former provisions of subsec. (f)(2)(A) of this section] as in effect prior to the enactment of this Act [Sept. 1, 1954] on the basis of an application filed after August 1954, or who died after such month leaving any survivors entitled to a recomputation under section 215(f)(4) of the Social Security Act [former provisions of subsec. (f)(4) of this section] as in effect prior to the enactment of this Act [Sept. 1, 1954] on the basis of his wages and self-employment income, and whose sixth quarter of coverage after 1950 was acquired after August 1954 or with respect to whom the twelfth month referred to in such subparagraph (A) occurred after such month, and

"(ii) any individual who is entitled to a recomputation under section 215(f)(2)(B) of the Social Security Act [former provisions of subsec. (f)(2)(B) of this section] as in effect prior to the enactment of this Act [Sept. 1, 1954] on the basis of an application filed after August 1954, or who died after August 1954 leaving any survivors entitled to a recomputation under section 215(f)(4) of the Social Security Act [former provisions of subsec. (f)(4) of this section] as in effect prior to the enactment of this Act [Sept. 1, 1954] on the basis of his wages and self-employment income, and whose sixth quarter of coverage after 1950 was acquired after August 1954 or who did not attain the age of seventy-five prior to September, 1954, the recomputation of his primary insurance amount shall be made in the manner provided in section 215 of the Social Security Act, as amended by this Act [this section], for computation of such amount, except that his closing date, for purposes of subsection (b) of such section 215, shall be determined as though he became entitled to old-age insurance benefits in the month in which he filed such application for or, if he has died, in the month in which he died. In the case of monthly benefits, such recomputation shall be effective for and after the month in which such application for recomputation is filed or, if the individual has died without filing the application, for and after the month in which the person filing the application for monthly survivors benefits becomes entitled to such benefits.

"(C) An individual or, in case of his death, his survivors entitled to a lump-sum death payment or to monthly benefits under section 202 of the Social Security Act [section 402 of this title] on the basis of his wages and self-employment income shall be entitled to a recomputation of his primary insurance amount under section 215(f)(2) or section 215(f)(4) of the Social Security Act [former provisions of subsec. (f)(2), (4) of this section] as in effect prior to the date of enactment of this Act [Sept. 1, 1954] only if (i) he had not less than six quarters of coverage in the period after 1950 and prior to January 1, 1955, and (ii) either the twelfth month referred to in subparagraph (A) of such section 215(f)(2) occurred prior to January 1, 1955, or he attained the age of 75 prior to 1955, and (iii) he meets the other conditions of entitlement to such a recomputation. No individual shall be entitled to a computation under subparagraph (A) or (B) of this paragraph if his primary insurance amount has previously been recomputed under either of such subparagraphs.

"(D) Notwithstanding the provisions of subparagraphs (A), (B), and (C), the primary insurance amount of an individual shall not be recomputed under such provisions unless such individual files the application referred to in subparagraph (A) or (B) prior to January 1961 or, if he dies without filing such application, his death occurred prior to January 1961."

Special Starting and Closing Dates for Certain Individuals for Computation of 1957 Benefit Amounts

Section 110 of Act Aug. 1, 1956 provided that: "In the case of an individual who died or became (without the application of section 202(j)(1) of the Social Security Act [former provisions of section 402(j)(1) of this title]) entitled to old-age insurance benefits in 1957 and with respect to whom not less than six of the quarters elapsing after 1955 and prior to the quarter following the quarter in which he died or became entitled to old-age insurance benefits, whichever first occurred, are quarters of coverage, his primary insurance amount shall be computed under section 215(a)(1)(A) of such Act [former provisions of subsec. (a)(1)(A) of this section], with a starting date of December 31, 1955, and a closing date of July 1, 1957, but only if it would result in a higher primary insurance amount. For the purposes of section 215(f)(3)(C) of such Act [former subsec. (f)(3)(C) of this section], the determination of an individual's closing date under the preceding sentence shall be considered as a determination of the individual's closing date under section 215(b)(3)(A) of such Act [former provisions of subsec. (b)(3)(A) of this section], and the recomputation provided for by such section 215(f)(3)(C) [former subsec. (f)(3)(C) of this section] shall be made using July 1, 1957, as the closing date, but only if it would result in a higher primary insurance amount. In any such computation on the basis of a July 1, 1957, closing date, the total of his wages and self-employment income after December 31, 1956, shall, if it is in excess of $2,100, be reduced to such amount."

Special Starting and Closing Dates for Certain Individuals for Computation of 1956 Benefit Amounts

Section 102(e)(6) of Act Sept. 1, 1954 provided that: "In the case of an individual who died or became (without the application of section 202(j)(1) of the Social Security Act [former provisions of section 402(j)(1) of this title]) entitled to old-age insurance benefits in 1956 and with respect to whom not less than six of the quarters elapsing after 1954 and prior to the quarter following the quarter in which he died or became entitled to old-age insurance benefits, whichever first occurred, are quarters of coverage, his primary insurance amount shall be computed under section 215(a)(1)(A) of such Act, as amended by this Act [former provisions of subsec. (a)(1)(A) of this section], with a starting date of December 31, 1954, and a closing date of July 1, 1956, but only if it would result in a higher primary insurance amount. For the purposes of section 215(f)(3)(C) of such Act [former subsec. (f)(3)(C) of this section], the determination of an individual's closing date under the preceding sentence shall be considered as a determination of the individual's closing date under section 215(b)(3)(A) of such Act [former provisions of subsec. (b)(3)(A) of this section], and the recomputation provided for by such section 215(f)(3)(C) [former subsec. (f)(3)(C) of this section] shall be made using July 1, 1956, as the closing date, but only if it would result in a higher primary insurance amount. In any such computation on the basis of a July 1, 1956 closing date, the total of his wages and self-employment income after December 31, 1955, shall, if it is in excess of $2,100, be reduced to such amount."

Study of Feasibility of Increasing Benefits

Section 404 of Act Sept. 1, 1954 authorized the Secretary of Health, Education, and Welfare [now Secretary of Health and Human Services] to conduct a feasibility study with a view toward increasing the minimum old-age insurance benefit under this subchapter to $55, $60, or $75 per month and required him to report the results of his study to the Congress at the earliest practicable date.

Table Modification and Extension; Effective Date; Publication in Federal Register

Section 203(f) of Pub.L. 93–66 provided that effective June 1, 1974, the Secretary of Health, Education, and Welfare [now Secretary of Health and Human Services] would prescribe and publish in the Federal Register all necessary modifications and extensions in the table formerly contained in subsec. (a) of this section.

§ 416. Additional definitions

For the purposes of this subchapter—

(a) Spouse; surviving spouse

(1) The term "spouse" means a wife as defined in subsection (b) or a husband as defined in subsection (f).

(2) The term "surviving spouse" means a widow as defined in subsection (c) or a widower as defined in subsection (g).

(b) Wife

The term "wife" means the wife of an individual, but only if she (1) is the mother of his son or daughter, (2) was married to him for a period of not less than one year immediately preceding the day on which her application is filed, or (3) in the month prior to the month of her marriage to him (A) was entitled to, or on application therefor and attainment of age 62 in such prior month would have been entitled to, benefits under subsection (b), (e), or (h) of section 402 of this title, (B) had attained age eighteen and was entitled to, or on application therefor would have been entitled to, benefits under subsection (d) of such section (subject, however, to section 402(s) of this title), or (C) was entitled to, or upon application therefor and attainment of the required age (if any) would have been entitled to, a widow's, child's (after attainment of age 18), or parent's insurance annuity under section 231a of Title 45. For purposes of clause (2), a wife shall be deemed to have been married to an individual for a period of one year throughout the month in which occurs the first anniversary of her marriage to such individual. For purposes of subparagraph (C) of section 402(b)(1) of this title, a divorced wife shall be deemed not to be married throughout the month in which she becomes divorced.

(c) Widow

(1) The term "widow" (except when used in the first sentence of section 402(i) of this title) means the surviving wife of an individual, but only if (A) she is the mother of his son or daughter, (B) she legally adopted his son or daughter while she was married to him and while such son or daughter was under the age of eighteen, (C) he legally adopted her son or daughter while she was married to him and while such son or daughter was under the age of eighteen, (D) she was married to him at the time both of them legally adopted a child under the age of eighteen, (E) except as provided in paragraph (2), she was married to him for a period of not less than nine months immediately prior to the day on which he died, or (F) in the month prior to the month of her marriage to him (i) she was entitled to, or on application therefor and attainment of age 62 in such prior month would have been entitled to, benefits under subsection (b), (e), or (h) of section 402 of this title, (ii) she had attained age eighteen and was entitled to, or on application therefor would have been entitled to, benefits under subsection (d) of such section (subject, however, to section 402(s) of this title), or (iii) she was entitled to, or upon application therefor and attainment of the required age (if any) would have been entitled to, a widow's, child's (after attainment of age 18), or parent's insurance annuity under section 231a of Title 45.

(2) The requirements of paragraph (1)(E) in connection with the surviving wife of an individual shall be treated as satisfied if—

(A) the individual had been married prior to the individual's marriage to the surviving wife,

(B) the prior wife was institutionalized during the individual's marriage to the prior wife due to mental incompetence or similar incapacity,

(C) during the period of the prior wife's institutionalization, the individual would have divorced the prior wife and married the surviving wife, but the individual did not do so because such divorce would have been unlawful, by reason of the prior wife's institutionalization, under the laws of the State in which the individual was domiciled at the time (as determined based on evidence satisfactory to the Commissioner of Social Security),

(D) the prior wife continued to remain institutionalized up to the time of her death, and

(E) the individual married the surviving wife within 60 days after the prior wife's death.

(d) Divorced spouses; divorce

(1) The term "divorced wife" means a woman divorced from an individual, but only if she had been married to such individual for a period of 10 years immediately before the date the divorce became effective.

(2) The term "surviving divorced wife" means a woman divorced from an individual who has died, but only if she had been married to the individual for a period of 10 years immediately before the date the divorce became effective.

(3) The term "surviving divorced mother" means a woman divorced from an individual who has died, but only if (A) she is the mother of his son or daughter, (B) she legally adopted his son or daughter while she was married to him and while such son or daughter was under the age of 18, (C) he legally adopted her son or daughter while she was married to him and while such son or daughter was under the age of 18, or (D) she was married to him at the time both of them legally adopted a child under the age of 18.

(4) The term "divorced husband" means a man divorced from an individual, but only if he had been married to such individual for a period of 10 years immediately before the date the divorce became effective.

(5) The term "surviving divorced husband" means a man divorced from an individual who has died, but only if he had been married to the individual for a period of 10 years immediately before the divorce became effective.

(6) The term "surviving divorced father" means a man divorced from an individual who has died, but only if (A) he is the father of her son or daughter, (B) he legally adopted her son or daughter while he was married to her and while such son or daughter was under the age of 18, (C) she legally adopted his son or daughter while he was married to her and while such son or daughter was under the age of 18, or (D) he was married to her at the time both of them legally adopted a child under the age of 18.

(7) The term "surviving divorced parent" means a surviving divorced mother as defined in paragraph (3) of this subsection or a surviving divorced father as defined in paragraph (6).

(8) The terms "divorce" and "divorced" refer to a divorce a vinculo matrimonii.

(e) Child

The term "child" means (1) the child or legally adopted child of an individual, (2) a stepchild who has been such stepchild for not less than one year immediately preceding the day on which application for child's insurance benefits is filed or (if the insured individual is deceased) not less than nine months immediately preceding the day on which such individual died, and (3) a person who is the grandchild or stepgrandchild of an individual or his spouse, but only if (A) there was no natural or adoptive parent (other than such a parent who was under a disability, as defined in section 423(d) of this title) of such person living at the time (i) such individual became entitled to old-age insurance benefits or disability insurance benefits or died, or (ii) if such individual had a period of disability which continued until such individual became entitled to old-age insurance benefits or disability insurance benefits, or died, at the time such period of disability began, or (B) such person was legally adopted after the death of such individual by such individual's surviving spouse in an adoption that was decreed by a court of competent jurisdiction within the United States and such person's natural or adopting parent or stepparent was not living in such individual's household and making regular contributions toward such person's support at the time such individual died. For purposes of clause (1), a person shall be deemed, as of the date of death of an individual, to be the legally adopted child of such individual if such person was either living with or receiving at least one-half of his support from such individual at the time of such individual's death and was legally adopted by such individual's surviving spouse after such individual's death but only if (A) proceedings for the adoption of the child had been instituted by such individual before his death, or (B) such child was adopted by such individual's surviving spouse before the end of two years after (i) the day on which such individual died or (ii) August 28, 1958. For purposes of clause (2), a person who is not the stepchild of an individual shall be deemed the stepchild of such individual if such individual was not the mother or adopting mother or the father or adopting father of such person and such individual and the mother or adopting mother, or the father or adopting father, as the case may be, of such person went through a marriage ceremony resulting in a purported marriage between them which, but for a legal impediment described in the last sentence of subsection (h)(1)(B), would have been a valid marriage. For purposes of clause (2), a child shall be deemed to have been the stepchild of an individual for a period of one year throughout the month in which occurs the expiration of such one year. For purposes of clause (3), a person shall be deemed to have no natural or adoptive parent living (other than a parent who was under a disability) throughout the most recent month in which a natural or adoptive parent (not under a disability) dies.

(f) Husband

The term "husband" means the husband of an individual, but only if (1) he is the father of her son or daughter, (2) he was married to her for a period of not less than one year immediately preceding the day on which his application is filed, or (3) in the month prior to the month of his marriage to her (A) he was entitled to, or on application therefor and attainment of age 62 in such prior month would have been entitled to, benefits under subsection (c), (f) or (h) of section 402 of this title, (B) he had attained age eighteen and was entitled to, or on application therefor would have been entitled to, benefits under subsection (d) of such section (subject, however, to section 402(s) of this title), or (C) he was entitled to, or upon application therefor and attainment of the required age (if any) he would have been entitled to, a widower's, child's (after attainment of age 18), or parent's insurance annuity under section 231a of Title 45. For purposes of clause (2), a husband shall be deemed to have been married to an individual for a period of one year throughout the month in which occurs the first anniversary of his marriage to her. For purposes of subparagraph (C) of section 402(c)(1) of this title, a divorced husband shall be deemed not to be married throughout the month which he becomes divorced.

(g) Widower

(1) The term "widower" (except when used in the first sentence of section 402(i) of this title) means the surviving husband of an individual, but only if (A) he is the father of her son or daughter, (B) he legally adopted her son or daughter while he was married to her and while such son or daughter was under the age of eighteen, (C) she legally adopted his son or daughter while he was married to her and while such son or daughter was under the age of eighteen, (D) he was married to her at the time both of them legally adopted a child under the age of eighteen, (E) except as provided in paragraph (2), he was married to her for a period of not less than nine months immediately prior to the day on which she died, or (F) in the month before the month of his marriage to her (i) he was entitled to, or on application therefor and attainment of age 62 in such prior month would have been entitled to, benefits under subsection (c), (f) or (h) of section 402 of this title, (ii) he had attained age eighteen and was entitled to, or on application therefor would have been entitled to, benefits under subsection (d) of such section (subject, however, to section 402(s) of this title), or (iii) he was entitled to, or on application therefor and attainment of the required age (if any) he would have been entitled to, a widower's, child's (after attainment of age 18), or parent's insurance annuity under section 231a of Title 45.

(2) The requirements of paragraph (1)(E) in connection with the surviving husband of an individual shall be treated as satisfied if—

(A) the individual had been married prior to the individual's marriage to the surviving husband,

(B) the prior husband was institutionalized during the individual's marriage to the prior husband due to mental incompetence or similar incapacity,

(C) during the period of the prior husband's institutionalization, the individual would have divorced the prior husband and married the surviving husband, but the individual did not do so because such divorce would have been unlawful, by reason of the prior husband's institutionalization, under the laws of the State in which the individual was domiciled at the time (as determined based on evidence satisfactory to the Commissioner of Social Security),

(D) the prior husband continued to remain institutionalized up to the time of his death, and

(E) the individual married the surviving husband within 60 days after the prior husband's death.

(h) Determination of family status

(1)(A)(i) An applicant is the wife, husband, widow, or widower of a fully or currently insured individual for purposes of this subchapter if the courts of the State in which such insured individual is domiciled at the time such applicant files an application, or, if such insured individual is dead, the courts of the State in which he was domiciled at the time of death, or, if such insured individual is or was not so domiciled in any State, the courts of the District of Columbia, would find that such applicant and such insured individual were validly married at the time such applicant files such application or, if such insured individual is dead, at the time he died.

(ii) If such courts would not find that such applicant and such insured individual were validly married at such time, such applicant shall, nevertheless be deemed to be the wife, husband, widow, or widower, as the case may be, of such insured individual if such applicant would, under the laws applied by such courts in determining the devolution of intestate personal property, have the same status with respect to the taking of such property as a wife, husband, widow, or widower of such insured individual.

(B)(i) In any case where under subparagraph (A) an applicant is not (and is not deemed to be) the wife, widow, husband, or widower of a fully or currently insured individual, or where under subsection (b), (c), (d), (f), or (g) such applicant is not the wife, divorced wife, widow, surviving divorced wife, husband, divorced husband, widower, or surviving divorced husband of such individual, but it is established to the satisfaction of the Commissioner of Social Security that such applicant in good faith went through a marriage ceremony with such individual resulting in a purported marriage between them which, but for a legal impediment not known to the applicant at the time of such ceremony, would have been a valid marriage, then, for purposes of subparagraph (A) and subsections (b), (c), (d), (f), and (g), such purported marriage shall be deemed to be a valid marriage. Notwithstanding the preceding sentence, in the case of any person who would be deemed under the preceding sentence a wife, widow, husband, or widower of the insured individual, such marriage shall not be deemed to be a valid marriage unless the applicant and the insured individual were living in the same household at the time of the death of the insured individual or (if the insured individual is living) at the time the applicant files the application. A marriage that is deemed to be a valid marriage by reason of the preceding sentence shall continue to be deemed a valid marriage if the insured individual and the person entitled to benefits as the wife or husband of the insured individual are no longer living in the same household at the time of the death of such insured individual.

(ii) The provisions of clause (i) shall not apply if the Commissioner of Social Security determines, on the basis of information brought to the Commissioner's attention, that such applicant entered into such purported marriage with such insured individual with knowledge that it would not be a valid marriage.

(iii) The entitlement to a monthly benefit under subsection (b) or (c) of section 402 of this title, based on the wages and self-employment income of such insured individual, of a person who would not be deemed to be a wife or husband of such insured individual but for this subparagraph, shall end with the month before the month in which such person enters into a marriage, valid without regard to this subparagraph, with a person other than such insured individual.

(iv) For purposes of this subparagraph, a legal impediment to the validity of a purported marriage includes only an impediment (I) resulting from the lack of dissolution of a previous marriage or otherwise arising out of such previous marriage or its dissolution, or (II) resulting from a defect in the procedure followed in connection with such purported marriage.

(2)(A) In determining whether an applicant is the child or parent of a fully or currently insured individual for purposes of this subchapter, the Commissioner of Social Security shall apply such law as would be applied in determining the devolution of intestate personal property by the courts of the State in which such insured individual is domiciled at the time such applicant files application, or, if such insured individual is dead, by the courts of the State in which he was domiciled at the time of his death, or, if such insured individual is or was not so domiciled in any State, by the courts of the District of Columbia. Applicants who according to such law would have the same status relative to taking intestate personal property as a child or parent shall be deemed such.

(B) If an applicant is a son or daughter of a fully or currently insured individual but is not (and is not deemed to be) the child of such insured individual under subparagraph (A), such applicant shall nevertheless be deemed to be the child of such insured individual if such insured individual and the mother or father, as the case may be, of such applicant went through a marriage ceremony resulting in a purported marriage between them which, but for a legal impediment described in the last sentence of paragraph (1)(B), would have been a valid marriage.

(3) An applicant who is the son or daughter of a fully or currently insured individual, but who is not (and is not deemed to be) the child of such insured individual under paragraph (2) of this subsection, shall nevertheless be deemed to be the child of such insured individual if:

(A) in the case of an insured individual entitled to old-age insurance benefits (who was not, in the month preceding such entitlement, entitled to disability insurance benefits)—

(i) such insured individual—

(I) has acknowledged in writing that the applicant is his or her son or daughter,

(II) has been decreed by a court to be the mother or father of the applicant, or

(III) has been ordered by a court to contribute to the support of the applicant because the applicant is his or her son or daughter,

and such acknowledgment, court decree, or court order was made not less than one year before such insured individual became entitled to old-age insurance benefits or attained retirement age (as defined in subsection (l)), whichever is earlier; or

(ii) such insured individual is shown by evidence satisfactory to the Commissioner of Social Security to be the mother or father of the applicant and was living with or contributing to the support of the applicant at the time such applicant's application for benefits was filed;

(B) in the case of an insured individual entitled to disability insurance benefits, or who was entitled to such benefits in the month preceding the first month for which he or she was entitled to old-age insurance benefits—

(i) such insured individual—

(I) has acknowledged in writing that the applicant is his or her son or daughter,

(II) has been decreed by a court to be the mother or father of the applicant, or

(III) has been ordered by a court to contribute to the support of the applicant because the applicant is his or her son or daughter,

and such acknowledgment, court decree, or court order was made before such insured individual's most recent period of disability began; or

(ii) such insured individual is shown by evidence satisfactory to the Commissioner of Social Security to be the mother or father of the applicant and was living with or contributing to the support of that applicant at the time such applicant's application for benefits was filed;

(C) in the case of a deceased individual—

(i) such insured individual—

(I) had acknowledged in writing that the applicant is his or her son or daughter,

(II) had been decreed by a court to be the mother or father of the applicant, or

(III) had been ordered by a court to contribute to the support of the applicant because the applicant was his or her son or daughter,

and such acknowledgment, court decree, or court order was made before the death of such insured individual, or

(ii) such insured individual is shown by evidence satisfactory to the Commissioner of Social Security to have been the mother or father of the applicant, and such insured individual was living with or contributing to the support of the applicant at the time such insured individual died.

For purposes of subparagraphs (A)(i) and (B)(i), an acknowledgement, court decree, or court order shall be deemed to have occurred on the first day of the month in which it actually occurred.

(i) Disability; period of disability

(1) Except for purposes of sections 402(d), 402(e), 402(f), 423, and 425 of this title, the term "disability" means (A) inability to engage in any substantial gainful activity by reason of any medically determinable physical or mental impairment which can be expected to result in death or has lasted or can be expected to last for a continuous period of not less than 12 months, or (B) blindness; and the term "blindness" means central visual acuity of 20/200 or less in the better eye with the use of a correcting lens. An eye which is accompanied by a limitation in the fields of vision such that the widest diameter of the visual field subtends an angle no greater than 20 degrees shall be considered for purposes of this paragraph as having a central visual acuity of 20/200 or less. The provisions of paragraphs (2)(A), (2)(B), (3), (4), (5), and (6) of section 423(d) of this title shall be applied for purposes of determining whether an individual is under a disability within the meaning of the first sentence of this paragraph in the same manner as they are applied for purposes of paragraph (1) of such section. Nothing in this subchapter shall be construed as authorizing the Commissioner of Social Security or any other officer or employee of the United States to interfere in any way with the practice of medicine or with relationships between practitioners of medicine and their patients, or to exercise any supervision or control over the administration or operation of any hospital.

(2)(A) The term "period of disability" means a continuous period (beginning and ending as hereinafter provided in this subsection) during which an individual was under a disability (as defined in paragraph (1)), but only if such period is of not less than five full calendar months' duration or such individual was entitled to benefits under section 423 of this title for one or more months in such period.

(B) No period of disability shall begin as to any individual unless such individual files an application for a disability determination with respect to such period; and no such period shall begin as to any individual after such individual attains retirement age (as defined in subsection (*l*)). In the case of a deceased individual, the requirement of an application under the preceding sentence may be satisfied by an application for a disability determination filed with respect to such individual within 3 months after the month in which he died.

(C) A period of disability shall begin—

(i) on the day the disability began, but only if the individual satisfies the requirements of paragraph (3) on such day; or

(ii) if such individual does not satisfy the requirements of paragraph (3) on such day, then on the first day of the first quarter thereafter in which he satisfies such requirements.

(D) A period of disability shall end with the close of whichever of the following months is the earlier: (i) the month preceding the month in which the individual attains retirement age (as defined in subsection (*l*)), or (ii) the month preceding (I) the termination month (as defined in section 423(a)(1) of this title), or, if earlier (II) the first month for which no benefit is payable by reason of section 423(e) of this title, where no benefit is payable for any of the succeeding months during the 36-month period referred to in such section. The provisions set forth in section 423(f) of this title with respect to determinations of whether entitlement to benefits under this subchapter or subchapter XVIII based on the disability of any individual is terminated (on the basis of a finding that the physical or mental impairment on the basis of which such benefits are provided has ceased, does not exist, or is not disabling) shall apply in the same manner and to the same extent with respect to determinations of whether a period of disability has ended (on the basis of a finding that the physical or mental impairment on the basis of which the finding of disability was made has ceased, does not exist, or is not disabling).

(E) Except as is otherwise provided in subparagraph (F), no application for a disability determination which is filed more than 12 months after the month prescribed by subparagraph (D) as the month in which the period of disability ends (determined without regard to subparagraph (B) and this subparagraph) shall be accepted as an application for purposes of this paragraph.

(F) An application for a disability determination which is filed more than 12 months after the month prescribed by subparagraph (D) as the month in which the period of disability ends (determined without regard to subparagraphs (B) and (E)) shall be accepted as an application for purposes of this paragraph if—

(i) in the case of an application filed by or on behalf of an individual with respect to a disability which ends after January 1968, such application is filed not more than 36 months after the month in which such disability ended, such individual is alive at the time the application is filed, and the Commissioner of Social Security finds in accordance with regulations prescribed by the Commissioner that the failure of such individual to file an application for a disability determination within the time specified in subparagraph (E) was attributable to a physical or mental condition of such individual which rendered him incapable of executing such an application, and

(ii) in the case of an application filed by or on behalf of an individual with respect to a period of disability which ends in or before January 1968—

(I) such application is filed not more than 12 months after January 1968,

(II) a previous application for a disability determination has been filed by or on behalf of such individual (1) in or before January 1968, and (2) not more than 36 months after the month in which his disability ended, and

(III) the Commissioner of Social Security finds in accordance with regulations prescribed by the Commissioner, that the failure of such individual to file an application within the then specified time period was attributable to a physical or mental condition of such individual which rendered him incapable of executing such an application.

In making a determination under this subsection, with respect to the disability or period of disability of any individual whose application for a determination thereof is accepted solely by reason of the provisions of this subparagraph (F), the provisions of this subsection (other than the provisions of this subparagraph) shall be applied as such provisions are in effect at the time such determination is made.

(G) An application for a disability determination filed before the first day on which the applicant satisfies the requirements for a period of disability under this subsection shall be deemed a valid application (and shall be deemed to have been filed on such first day) only if the applicant satisfies the requirements for a period of disability before the Commissioner of Social Security makes a final decision on the application and no request under section

405(b) of this title for notice and opportunity for a hearing thereon is made or, if such a request is made, before a decision based upon the evidence adduced at the hearing is made (regardless of whether such decision becomes the final decision of the Commissioner of Social Security).

(3) The requirements referred to in clauses (i) and (ii) of paragraph (2)(C) of this subsection are satisfied by an individual with respect to any quarter only if—

(A) he would have been a fully insured individual (as defined in section 414 of this title) had he attained age 62 and filed application for benefits under section 402(a) of this title on the first day of such quarter; and

(B)(i) he had not less than 20 quarters of coverage during the 40-quarter period which ends with such quarter, or

(ii) if such quarter ends before he attains (or would attain) age 31, not less than one-half (and not less than 6) of the quarters during the period ending with such quarter and beginning after he attained the age of 21 were quarters of coverage, or (if the number of quarters in such period is less than 12) not less than 6 of the quarters in the 12-quarter period ending with such quarter were quarters of coverage, or

(iii) in the case of an individual (not otherwise insured under clause (i)) who, by reason of clause (ii), had a prior period of disability that began during a period before the quarter in which he or she attained age 31, not less than one-half of the quarters beginning after such individual attained age 21 and ending with such quarter are quarters of coverage, or (if the number of quarters in such period is less than 12) not less than 6 of the quarters in the 12-quarter period ending with such quarter are quarters of coverage;

except that the provisions of subparagraph (B) of this paragraph shall not apply in the case of an individual who is blind (within the meaning of "blindness" as defined in paragraph (1)). For purposes of subparagraph (B) of this paragraph, when the number of quarters in any period is an odd number, such number shall be reduced by one, and a quarter shall not be counted as part of any period if any part of such quarter was included in a prior period of disability unless such quarter was a quarter of coverage.

(j) Periods of limitation ending on nonwork days

Where this subchapter, any provision of another law of the United States (other than the Internal Revenue Code of 1986) relating to or changing the effect of this subchapter, or any regulation issued by the Commissioner of Social Security pursuant thereto provides for a period within which an act is required to be done which affects eligibility for or the amount of any benefit or payment under this subchapter or is necessary to establish or protect any rights under this subchapter, and such period ends on a Saturday, Sunday, or legal holiday, or on any other day all or part of which is declared to be a nonwork day for Federal employees by statute or Executive order, then such act shall be considered as done within such period if it is done on the first day thereafter which is not a Saturday, Sunday, or legal holiday or any other day all or part of which is declared to be a nonwork day for Federal employees by statute or Executive order. For purposes of this subsection, the day on which a period ends shall include the day on which an extension of such period, as authorized by law or by the Commissioner of Social Security pursuant to law, ends. The provisions of this subsection shall not extend the period during which benefits under this subchapter may (pursuant to section 402(j)(1) or 423(b) of this title) be paid for months prior to the day application for such benefits is filed, or during which an application for benefits under this subchapter may (pursuant to section 402(j)(2) or 423(b) of this title) be accepted as such.

(k) Waiver of nine-month requirement for widow, stepchild, or widower in case of accidental death or in case of serviceman dying in line of duty, or in case of remarriage to same individual

The requirement in clause (E) of subsection (c)(1) or clause (E) of subsection (g)(1) that the surviving spouse of an individual have been married to such individual for a period of not less than nine months immediately prior to the day on which such individual died in order to qualify as such individual's widow or widower, and the requirement in subsection (e) that the stepchild of a deceased individual have been such stepchild for not less than nine months immediately preceding the day on which such individual died in order to qualify as such individual's child, shall be deemed to be satisfied, where such individual dies within the applicable nine-month period, if—

(1) his death—

(A) is accidental, or

(B) occurs in line of duty while he is a member of a uniformed service serving on active duty (as defined in section 410(*l*)(2) of this title),

unless the Commissioner of Social Security determines that at the time of the marriage involved the individual could not have reasonably been expected to live for nine months, or

(2)(A) the widow or widower of such individual had been previously married to such individual and subsequently divorced and such requirement would have been satisfied at the time of such divorce if such previous marriage had been terminated by the death of such individual at such time instead of by divorce; or

(B) the stepchild of such individual had been the stepchild of such individual during a previous marriage of such stepchild's parent to such individual which ended in divorce and such requirement would have been satisfied at the time of such divorce if such previous marriage had been terminated by the death of such individual at such time instead of by divorce;

except that paragraph (2) of this subsection shall not apply if the Commissioner of Social Security determines that at the time of the marriage involved the individual could not have reasonably been expected to live for nine months. For purposes of paragraph (1)(A) of this subsection, the death of an individual is accidental if he receives bodily injuries solely through violent, external, and accidental means and, as a direct result of the bodily injuries and independently of all other causes, loses his life not later than three months after the day on which he receives such bodily injuries.

(*l*) Retirement age

(1) The term "retirement age" means—

(A) with respect to an individual who attains early retirement age (as defined in paragraph (2)) before January 1, 2000, 65 years of age;

(B) with respect to an individual who attains early retirement age after December 31, 1999, and before January 1, 2005, 65 years of age plus the number of months in the age increase factor (as determined under paragraph (3)) for the calendar year in which such individual attains early retirement age;

(C) with respect to an individual who attains early retirement age after December 31, 2004, and before January 1, 2017, 66 years of age;

(D) with respect to an individual who attains early retirement age after December 31, 2016, and before January 1, 2022, 66 years of age plus the number of months in the age increase factor (as determined under paragraph (3)) for the calendar year in which such individual attains early retirement age; and

(E) with respect to an individual who attains early retirement age after December 31, 2021, 67 years of age.

(2) The term "early retirement age" means age 62 in the case of an old-age, wife's, or husband's insurance benefit, and age 60 in the case of a widow's or widower's insurance benefit.

(3) The age increase factor for any individual who attains early retirement age in a calendar year within the period to which subparagraph (B) or (D) of paragraph (1) applies shall be determined as follows:

(A) With respect to an individual who attains early retirement age in the 5-year period consisting of the calendar years 2000 through 2004, the age increase factor shall be equal to two-twelfths of the number of months in the period beginning with January 2000 and ending with December of the year in which the individual attains early retirement age.

(B) With respect to an individual who attains early retirement age in the 5-year period consisting of the calendar years 2017 through 2021, the age increase factor shall be equal to two-twelfths of the number of months in the period beginning with January 2017 and ending with December of the year in which the individual attains early retirement age.

(Aug. 14, 1935, c. 531, Title II, § 216, as added Aug. 28, 1950, c. 809, Title I, § 104(a), 64 Stat. 492, 510; amended July 18, 1952, c. 945, § 3(d), 66 Stat. 771; Sept. 1, 1954, c. 1206, Title I, § 106(d), 68 Stat. 1080; Aug. 1, 1956, c. 836, Title I, §§ 102(a), (d)(12), 103(c)(6), 70 Stat. 809, 815, 818; Pub.L. 85–109, § 1, July 17, 1957, 71 Stat. 308; Pub.L. 85–238, § 3(h), Aug. 30, 1957, 71 Stat. 519; Pub.L. 85–840, Title II, §§ 201, 203, 204(a), Title III, §§ 301(a)(2), (b)(2), (c)(2), (d), (e), 302(a), 305(b), Aug. 28, 1958, 72 Stat. 1020, 1021, 1026–1028, 1030; Pub.L. 86–778, Title II, §§ 207(a)–(c), 208(a)–(c), Title IV, §§ 402(e), 403(c), Title VII, § 703, Sept. 13, 1960, 74 Stat. 950–952, 968, 969, 994; Pub.L. 87–64, Title I, §§ 102(b)(2)(D), (c)(1), (2)(B), (3)(C), 105, June 30, 1961, 75 Stat. 134, 135, 139; Pub.L. 88–650, § 1(a) to (c), Oct. 13, 1964, 78 Stat. 1075; Pub.L. 89–97, Title III, §§ 303(a)(1), (b)(1), (2), 304(*l*), 306(c)(13), 308(c), (d)(2)(B), 328(b), 334(a) to (d), 339(a), 344(a), July 30, 1965, 79 Stat. 366, 367, 370, 373, 377, 378, 400, 404, 405, 409, 412; Pub.L. 90–248, Title I, §§ 104(d)(2), 105(a), 111(a), 150(a), 156(a) to (d), 158(d), 172(a), (b), Jan. 2, 1968, 81 Stat. 832, 833, 837, 860, 866, 869, 877; Pub.L. 92–603, Title I, §§ 104(g), 113(a), 115(b), 116(d), 117(a), 118(b), 145(a), Oct. 30, 1972, 86 Stat. 1341, 1347, 1349 to 1351, 1370; Pub.L. 93–445, Title III, § 304, Oct. 16, 1974, 88 Stat. 1358; Pub.L. 95–216, Title III, § 337(a), Dec. 20, 1977, 91 Stat. 1548; Pub.L. 96–265, Title III, §§ 303(b)(2)(B), 306(b), June 9, 1980, 94 Stat. 453, 457; Pub.L. 96–473, § 5(a)(2), Oct. 19, 1980, 94 Stat. 2265; Pub.L. 97–35, Title XXII, §§ 2202(a)(2), 2203(b)(2), (c)(2), (d)(3), (4), Aug. 13, 1981, 95 Stat. 835–837; Pub.L. 98–21, Title II, § 201(a), (c)(1)(D), Title III, §§ 301(c), 303, 304(c), 306(c), 309(j), (k), 332(a), 333(a), Apr. 20, 1983, 97 Stat. 107, 109, 111, 112, 114, 117, 129; Pub.L. 98–369, Div. B, Title VI, §§ 2661(*l*), 2662(c)(1), 2663(a)(11), July 18, 1984, 98 Stat. 1158, 1159, 1164; Pub.L. 98–460, §§ 2(b), 4(a)(2), Oct. 9, 1984, 98 Stat. 1796, 1800; Pub.L. 100–203, Title IX, § 9010(e)(1), Dec. 22, 1987, 101 Stat. 1330–294; Pub.L. 101–508, Title V, §§ 5103(b)(1), 5104(a), 5119(a), (b), Nov. 5, 1990, 104 Stat. 1388–251, 1388–254, 1388–278, 1388–279; Pub.L. 103–296, Title I, § 107(a)(4), Title III, § 321(c)(6)(H), Aug. 15, 1994, 108 Stat. 1478, 1538; Pub.L. 108–203, Title IV, § 414(a) to (c), Mar. 2, 2004, 118 Stat. 529, 530.)

Validity

The United States Supreme Court has held that certain provisions of the Social Security Act, as amended (section 339(a) of Pub.L. 89–97; 42 U.S.C.A. § 416(h)(3)), prohibiting eligibility for disability benefits for certain nonlegitimated illegitimates born after onset of disability, violates the equal protection of the law guaranteed by the due process provisions of U.S.C.A.Const. Amend. 5. Jimenez v. Weinberger, U.S.Ill.1974, 417 U.S. 628, 94 S.Ct. 2496, 41 L.Ed.2d 363.

HISTORICAL AND STATUTORY NOTES

References in Text

The Internal Revenue Code of 1986, referred to in subsec. (j), is classified to Title 26, 26 U.S.C.A. § 1 et seq.

This subchapter, referred to in text, originally read "this title", meaning the Social Security Act, Act Aug. 14, 1935, c. 531, Title II, 49 Stat. 622, as amended, which is classified as this subchapter, 42 U.S.C.A. § 401 et seq.

Codifications

Section 2203(d)(4) of Pub.L. 97–35, set out in the credit of this section, was amended by section 2663(a)(11)(A) of Pub.L. 98–369, to add "(after and below subparagraph (C)(ii))" in the directory language of section 2203(d)(4) of Pub.L. 97–35 in describing the placement of the sentence in subsec. (h) of this section which was added by section 2203(d)(4) of Pub.L. 97–35.

Section 201(c) of Pub.L. 98–21, set out in the credit of this section, was amended by section 2662(c)(1) of Pub.L. 98–369 to correct an error in the directory language of Pub.L. 98–21 under which the article "the" had been left out in the direction to strike out references to the age of 65.

Effective and Applicability Provisions

2004 Acts. Pub.L. 108–203, Title IV, § 414(d), Mar. 2, 2004, 118 Stat. 530, provided that: "The amendments made by this section [amending this section] shall be effective with respect to applications for benefits under title II of the Social Security Act [this subchapter] filed during months ending after the date of the enactment of this Act [Mar. 2, 2004]."

1994 Acts. Amendment by section 107(a)(4) of Pub.L. 103–296 effective Mar. 31, 1995, see section 110 of Pub.L. 103–296, set out as a note under section 401 of this title.

1990 Acts. Amendment by section 5103(b)(1) of Pub.L. 101–508 applicable with respect to monthly insurance benefits for months after Dec., 1990 for which applications are filed on or after Jan. 1, 1991, or are pending on such date, see section 5103(e)(1) of Pub.L. 101–508, set out as a note under section 402 of this title.

Section 5104(b) of Pub.L. 101–508 provided that: "The amendments made by this section [amending subsec. (e) of this section] shall apply with respect to benefits payable for months after December 1990, but only on the basis of applications filed after December 31, 1990."

Amendment by section 5119 of Pub.L. 101–508 applicable with respect to benefits for months after Dec. 1990, providing an application for such benefits is filed after Dec. 31, 1990, and excluding from the application requirement benefits to individuals if they are entitled to benefits under section 402(b), (c), (e) or (f) of this title for Dec. 1990 and the individual on whose wages and self employment income such benefit for Dec. 1990 is based is the same individual on the basis of whose wages and self employment income application would otherwise be required, see section 5119(e) of Pub.L. 101–508, set out as a note under section 403 of this title.

1987 Acts. Amendment of subsec. (i)(2)(D)(II) by section 9010(e)(1) of Pub.L. 100–203 effective Jan. 1, 1988 and applicable with respect to individuals entitled to benefits under specific provisions of sections 402 and 423 of this title for any month after Dec. 1987, and individuals entitled to benefits payable under specific provisions of sections 402 and 423 of this title for any month before Jan. 1988 and with respect to whom the 15-month period described in the applicable provision amended by section 9010 of Pub.L. 100–203 has not elapsed as of Jan. 1, 1988, see section 9010(f) of Pub.L. 100–203, set out as a note under section 402 of this title.

1984 Acts. Amendment to subsec. (i)(2)(D) by section 2(b) of Pub.L. 98–460 applicable to determinations made by the Secretary on or after Oct. 9, 1984, with certain enumerated exceptions and qualifications, see section 2(d) of Pub.L. 98–460, set out as a note under section 423 of this title.

Amendment of subsec. (i)(1) by section 4(a)(2) of Pub.L. 98–460 applicable with respect to determinations made on or after Dec. 1, 1984, see section 4(c) of Pub.L. 98–460, set out as a note under section 423 of this title.

Amendment to subsecs. (f), (h), (i) by sections 2661(*l*), 2662(c)(1), Pub.L. 98–369 effective as though included in the enactment of the Social Security Amendments of 1983 [Pub.L. 98–21], see section 2664(a) of Pub.L. 98–369, set out as a note under section 401 of this title.

Amendment by section 2663(a)(11) of Pub.L. 98–369 effective July 18, 1984, but not to be construed as changing or affecting any right, liability, status or interpretation which existed (under the provisions of law involved) before that date, see section 2664(b) of Pub.L. 98–369, set out as a note under section 401 of this title.

1983 Acts. Amendment by sections 301(c), 303, 304(c), 306(c), and 309(j), (k) of Pub.L. 98–21 applicable only with respect to monthly payments payable under this subchapter for months after April, 1983, except as otherwise specifically provided, see section 310 of Pub.L. 98–21, set out as a note under section 402 of this title.

Section 332(c) of Pub.L. 98–21 provided that: "The amendments made by this section [adding subsec. (i)(3)(B)(iii) of this section and subsec. (c)(1)(B)(iii) of section 423 of this title] shall be effective with respect to applications for disability insurance benefits under section 223 of the Social Security Act [section 423 of this title], and for disability determinations under section 216(i) of such Act [subsec. (i) of this section], filed after the date of the enactment of this Act [Apr. 20, 1983], except that no monthly benefits under Title II of the Social Security Act [this subchapter] shall be payable or increased by reason of the amendments made by this section for months before the month following the month of enactment of this Act [April, 1983]."

Section 333(b) of Pub.L. 98–21 provided that: "The amendment made by subsection (a) [amending subsec. (h)(3) of this section] shall be effective on the date of the enactment of this Act [Apr. 20, 1983]."

1981 Acts. Amendment of subsecs. (c) and (g) by section 2202(a)(2) of Pub.L. 97–35 applicable only with respect to deaths occurring after August, 1981, see section 2202(b) of Pub.L. 97–35, set out as a note under section 402 of this title.

Amendment of subsecs. (b) and (f) by section 2203(b)(2) and (c)(2) of Pub.L. 97–35, respectively, applicable only to monthly insurance benefits payable to individuals who attain age 62 after August, 1981, see section 2203(f)(1) of Pub.L. 97–35, set out as a note under section 402 of this title.

Amendment of subsecs. (e) and (h) by section 2203(d)(3) and (4) of Pub.L. 97–35, respectively, applicable to monthly insurance benefits for months after August, 1981, and only in the case of individuals who were not entitled to such insurance benefits for August, 1981, or any preceding month, see section 2203(f)(2) of Pub.L. 97–35, set out as a note under section 402 of this title.

1980 Acts. Amendment by Pub.L. 96–473 effective with respect to benefits payable for months beginning on or after Oct. 1, 1980, see section 5(d) of Pub.L. 96–473, set out as a note under section 402 of this title.

Amendment by section 303(b)(2)(B) of Pub.L. 96–265 effective the first day of the sixth month which begins after June 9, 1980, to apply with respect to any individual whose disability has not been determined to have ceased prior to such first day, see section 303(d) of Pub.L. 96–265, set out as a note under section 402 of this title.

Amendment by section 306(b) of Pub.L. 96–265 applicable to applications filed after June, 1980, see section 306(d) of Pub.L. 96–265, set out as a note under section 402 of this title.

1977 Acts. Amendment by Pub.L. 95–216 effective with respect to monthly benefits after December, 1978, and applications filed on or after Jan. 1, 1979, see section 337(c) of Pub.L. 95–216, set out as a note under section 402 of this title.

1974 Acts. Amendment by Pub.L. 93–445 effective Jan. 1, 1975, see section 603 of Pub.L. 93–445, set out as a note under section 402 of this title.

1972 Acts. Amendment of subsec. (i)(3)(A) by section 104(g) of Pub.L. 92–603 applicable only in the case of a man who attains (or would attain) age 62 after December, 1974, with the figure "65" in subsec. (i)(3)(A) of this section to be deemed to read "64" in the case of a man who attains age 62 in 1973, and deemed to read "63" in the case of a man who attains age 62 in 1974, see section 104(j) of Pub.L. 92–603, set out as a note under section 414 of this title.

Amendment of subsec. (e) by section 113(a) of Pub.L. 92–603 applicable with respect to monthly benefits payable under this subchapter for months after December, 1972, but only on the basis of applications filed on or after Oct. 30, 1972, see section 113(c) of Pub.L. 92–603, set out as a note under section 402 of this title.

Section 115(c) of Pub.L. 92–603 provided that: "The amendments made by this section [amending subsec. (k) of this section] shall apply only with respect to benefits payable under title II of the Social Security Act [this subchapter] for months after December 1972 on the basis of applications filed in or after the month in which this Act is enacted [October, 1972]."

Amendment of subsec. (i)(2)(A) by section 116(d) of Pub.L. 92–603 effective with respect to applications for disability determinations under subsec. (i) of this section filed in or after October, 1972, or before October, 1972, under specified conditions, see section 116(e) of Pub.L. 92–603, set out as a note under section 423 of this title.

Amendment of subsec. (i)(3) by section 117(a) of Pub.L. 92–603 effective with respect to applications for disability determinations under subsec. (i) of this section filed in or after October, 1972, or before October, 1972, under specified conditions, see section 117(c) of Pub.L. 92–603, set out as a note under section 423 of this title.

Section 118(c) of Pub.L. 92–603 provided that: "The amendments made by this section [amending subsec. (i)(2)(B) of this section and section 423(a)(1), (a)(2), (b), and (c)(2)(A) of this title] shall apply in the case of deaths occurring after December 31, 1969. For purposes of such amendments (and for purposes of sections 202(j)(1) and 223(b) of the Social Security Act [sections 402(j)(1) and 423(b) of this title]), any application with respect to an individual whose death occurred after December 31, 1969, but before the date of the enactment of this Act [Oct. 30, 1972] which is filed in, or within 3 months after the month in which this Act is enacted [October, 1972] shall be deemed to have been filed in the month in which such death occurred."

Section 145(b) of Pub.L. 92–603 provided that: "The amendments made by this section [amending subsec. (k) of this section] shall apply only with respect to benefits payable under title II of the Social Security Act [this subchapter] for months after December 1972 on the basis of applications filed in or after the month in which this Act is enacted [October, 1972]."

1968 Acts. Amendment of subsec. (i)(1) by section 104 of Pub.L. 90–248 applicable with respect to monthly benefits under this subchapter for and after the month of February, 1968, but only on the basis of applications for such benefits filed in or after January, 1968, see section 104(e) of Pub.L. 90–248, set out as a note under section 402 of this title.

Section 105(c) of Pub.L. 90–248 provided that: "The amendment made by subsection (a) [which deleted "and he is under a disability by reason of blindness (as defined in paragraph (1))" from subsec. (i)(3)(B)(ii) of this section] shall apply only with respect to applications for disability determinations filed under section 216(i) of the Social Security Act [subsec. (i) of this section] in or after the month in which this Act is enacted [January, 1968]. The amendments made by subsection (b) [to section 423(c)(1)(B)(ii) of this title] shall apply with respect to monthly benefits under title II of such Act [this subchapter] for months after January 1968, but only on the basis of applications for such benefits filed in or after the month in which this Act is enacted [January, 1968]."

Section 111(b) of Pub.L. 90–248 provided that: "No monthly insurance benefits under title II of the Social Security Act [this subchapter] shall be payable or increased for any month before the month in which this Act is enacted [January, 1968] by reason of amendments made by subsection (a) [to subsec. (i)(2) of this section]."

Section 150(b) of Pub.L. 90–248 provided that: "The amendment made by subsection (a) [to subsec. (e) of this section] shall apply with respect to monthly benefits payable under title II of the Social Security Act [this subchapter] for months after January 1968, but only on the basis of an application filed in or after the month in which this Act is enacted [January, 1968]."

Section 156(e) of Pub.L. 90–248 provided that: "The amendments made by this section [enacting subsec. (k) of this section and amending subsecs. (c)(5), (e) and (g) of this section] shall apply with respect to monthly benefits under title II of the Social Security Act [this subchapter] for months after January 1968, but only on the basis of applications filed in or after the month in which this Act is enacted [January, 1968]."

Amendment by section 158 of Pub.L. 90–248 applicable with respect to applications for disability insurance benefits under section 423 of this title and to disability determinations under section 416(i) of this title, filed in or after Jan. 1968, or before Jan. 1968, if the applicant has not died before such month and if (A) notice of the final decision of the Secretary of Health, Education, and Welfare has not been given to the applicant before such month; or (B) the notice referred to in subparagraph (A) has been so given before such month but a civil action with respect to such final decision is commenced under section 205(g) of the Social Security Act [section 405(g) of this title] (whether before, in, or after such month) and the decision in such civil action has not become final before such month, see section 158(e) of Pub.L. 90–248, set out as a note under section 423 of this title.

Section 172(c) of Pub.L. 90–248 provided that: "The amendments made by this section [to subsec. (i)(1) of this section] shall be effective with respect to benefits under section 223 of the Social Security Act [section 423 of this title] for months after January 1968 based on applications filed after the date of enactment of this Act [Jan. 2, 1968] and with respect to disability determinations under section 216(i) of the Social Security Act [subsec. (i) of this section] based on applications filed after the date of enactment of this Act [Jan. 2, 1968]."

1965 Acts. Amendment of subsec. (i)(1)(A), (2) by section 303(a)(1), (b)(1), (2) of Pub.L. 89–97 effective with respect to applications for disability insurance benefits under section 423 of this title, and for disability determinations under subsec. (i) of this section, filed in or after July, 1965, or before July, 1965, if the applicant has not died before such month, and notice of final administrative decision has not been given to the applicant before such month, unless a civil action has been commenced; except that monthly insurance benefits under this subchapter shall not be payable or increased by reason of amendments to subsecs. (i)(1)(A), (2), (3), of this section for months before the second month following July, 1965, see section 303(f)(1) of Pub.L. 89–97, set out as a note under section 423 of this title.

Amendment of subsec. (i)(2) by section 304 of Pub.L. 89–97 applicable with respect to monthly insurance benefits under this subchapter for and after the second month following July, 1965, but only on the basis of applications filed in or after July, 1965, see section 304(*o*) of Pub.L. 89–97, set out as a note under section 402 of this title.

Amendment of subsecs. (b) to (d) by Pub.L. 89–97 applicable with respect to monthly insurance benefits under this subchapter beginning with the second month following July, 1965, but, in the case of an individual who was not entitled to a monthly insurance benefit under section 402 of this title for the first month following July, 1965, only on the basis of an application filed in or after July, 1965, see section 308(e) of Pub.L. 89–97, set out as a note under section 402 of this title.

Section 328(d) of Pub.L. 89–97 provided that: "The amendments made by this section [subsec. (i)(2)(F) of this section and sections 402(j)(2) and 423(b) of this title] shall apply with respect to (1) applications filed on or after the date of enactment of this Act [July 30, 1965], (2) applications as to which the Secretary has not made a final decision before the date of enactment of this Act [July 30, 1965], and (3) if a civil action with respect to final decision by the Secretary has been commenced under section 205(g) of the Social Security Act [section 405(g) of this title] before the date of enactment of this Act [July 30, 1965], applications as to which there has been no final judicial decision before the date of enactment of this Act [July 30, 1965]."

Amendment of subsecs. (b), (c), (f), and (g) by section 334 of Pub.L. 89–97 applicable only with respect to monthly insurance benefits under this subchapter beginning with September, 1965, but only on the basis of applications filed in or after July, 1965, see section 334(g) of Pub.L. 89–97, set out as a note under section 402 of this title.

Section 339(c) of Pub.L. 89–97 provided that: "The amendments made by subsections (a) and (b) [to subsec. (h)(3) of this section and section 402(d)(3) of this title] shall be applicable with respect to monthly insurance benefits under title II of the Social Security Act [this subchapter] beginning with the second month following the month in which this Act is enacted [July, 1965] but only on the basis of an application filed in or after the month in which this Act is enacted [July, 1965]."

Section 344(e) of Pub.L. 89–97 provided that: "The amendments made by this section [to subsec. (i)(3) of this section and section 423(a)(1), (c)(1), and (c)(2)(B) of this title] shall apply only with respect to monthly benefits under title II of the Social Security Act [this subchapter] for months after the first month following the month in which this Act is enacted [July, 1965], on the basis of applications for such benefits filed in or after the month in which this Act is enacted [July, 1965]."

1964 Acts. Section 1(d) of Pub.L. 88–650 provided that:

"**(1)** The amendments made by subsections (a), (b), and (c) [to subsec. (i) of this section] shall apply in the case of applications for disability determinations under section 216(i) of the Social Security Act [subsec. (i) of this section] filed after the month following the month in which this Act is enacted [October, 1964].

"**(2)** Except as provided in the succeeding paragraphs, such amendments shall also apply, and as though such amendments had been enacted on July 1, 1962, in the case of applications for disability determinations filed under section 216(i) of the Social Security Act [subsec. (i) of this section] during the period beginning July 1, 1962, and ending with the close of the month following the month in which this Act is enacted [October, 1964], by an individual who—

"**(A)** has been under a disability (as defined in such section 216(i) [subsec. (i) of this section]) continuously since he filed such application and up to (i) the first day of the second month following the month in which this Act is enacted [October, 1964] or (ii) if earlier, the first day of the month in which he attained the age of 65, and

"**(B)** is living on the day specified in subparagraph (A)(i).

"**(3)** In the case of an individual to whom paragraph (2) applies and who filed an application for disability insurance benefits under section 223 of the Social Security Act [section 423 of this title] during the period specified in such paragraph—

"**(A)** if such individual was under a disability (as defined in section 223(c) of such Act [section 423(c) of this title]) throughout such period and was not entitled to disability insurance benefits under such section 223 [section 423 of this title] for any month in such period (except for the amendments made by this section), such application and any application filed during such period for benefits under section 202 of the Social Security Act [section 402 of this title] on the basis of the wages and self-employment income of such individual shall, notwithstanding section 202(j)(2) [section 402(j)(2) of this title] and the first sentence of section 223(b) [section 423(b) of this title], be deemed an effective application, or

"**(B)** if such individual was entitled (without the application of this section) to disability insurance benefits under section 223 [section 423 of this title] for a continuous period of months immediately preceding—

"**(i)** the second month following the month in which this Act was enacted [October, 1964], or

"**(ii)** if earlier, the month in which he became entitled to benefits under section 202(a) [section 402(a) of this title],

his primary insurance amount shall be recomputed, but only if such amount would be increased solely by reason of the enactment of this section.

"(4) No monthly insurance benefits, and no increase in monthly insurance benefits, may be paid under title II of the Social Security Act [this subchapter] by reason of the enactment of this section for any month before the eleventh month before the month in which this Act is enacted [October, 1964].

"(5) In the case of an individual (A) who is entitled under section 202 of the Social Security Act [section 402 of this title] (but without the application of subsection (j)(1) of such section) to a widow's, widower's, or parent's insurance benefit, or to an old-age, wife's, or husband's insurance benefit which is reduced under section 202(q) of such Act [section 402(q) of this title], for any month in the period referred to in paragraph (2) of this subsection, (B) who was under a disability (as defined in section 223(c) of the Social Security Act [section 423(c) of this title]) which began prior to the sixth month before the first month for which the benefits referred to in clause (A) are payable and which continued through the month following the month in which this Act is enacted [October, 1964], and (C) who files an application for disability insurance benefits under section 223(a)(1) of the Social Security Act [section 423(a)(1) of this title]—

"(i) subsection (a)(3) of section 223 of the Social Security Act [section 423(a)(3) of this title] shall not prevent him from being entitled to such disability insurance benefits;

"(ii) the provisions of subsection (a)(1) of such section 223 [section 423(a)(1) of this title] terminating entitlement to disability insurance benefits by reason of entitlement to old-age insurance benefits shall not apply with respect to him unless and until he again becomes entitled to such old-age insurance benefits under the provisions of section 202 of such Act [section 402 of this title];

"(iii) such individual shall, for any month for which he is thereby entitled to both old-age insurance benefits and disability insurance benefits, be entitled only to such disability insurance benefits; and

"(iv) in case the benefits reduced under subsection (q) of section 202 of such Act [section 402(q) of this title] are old-age insurance benefits (I) such old-age insurance benefits for the months in the period referred to in paragraph (2) of this subsection shall not be recomputed solely by reason of the enactment of this section, and, if otherwise recomputed, the provisions of and amendments made by this section shall not apply to such recomputation; and (II) the months for which he received such old-age insurance benefits before or during the period for which he becomes entitled, by reason of such enactment, to disability insurance benefits under such section 223 [section 423 of this title] and the months for which he received such disability insurance benefits shall be excluded from the 'reduction period' and the 'adjusted reduction period', as defined in paragraphs (5) and (6), respectively, of such subsection (q) for purposes of determining the amount of the old-age insurance benefits to which he may subsequently become entitled.

"(6) The entitlement of any individual to benefits under section 202 of the Social Security Act [section 402 of this title] shall not be terminated solely by reason of the enactment of this section, except where such individual is entitled to benefits under section 202(a) or 223 of such Act [section 402(a) or 423 of this title] in an amount which (but for this subsection) would have required termination of such benefits under such section 202 [section 402 of this title]."

1961 Acts. Amendment of subsecs. (b), (c), (f), (g), and (i)(3)(A) and repeal of subsec. (a) applicable with respect to monthly benefits for months beginning on or after Aug. 1, 1961, based on applications filed in or after March, 1961, and with respect to lump-sum death payments under this subchapter in the case of deaths on or after Aug. 1, 1961, see sections 102(f)(4), (6), and 109 of Pub.L. 87–64, set out as notes under section 402 of this title.

Amendment of subsec. (i)(2) by Pub.L. 87–64 effective Aug. 1, 1961, see sections 102(f)(4), (6), and 109 of Pub.L. 87–64, set out as notes under section 402 of this title.

Section 105 of Pub.L. 87–64 provided in part that the amendment of subsec. (i)(4) of this section by Pub.L. 87–64 shall be effective with respect to applications for disability determinations filed on or after July 1, 1961.

1960 Acts. Section 207(d) of Pub.L. 86–778 provided that: "The amendments made by this section [to subsecs. (b) and (f) of this section and to the first sentence of subsec. (e) of this section] shall apply only with respect to monthly benefits under section 202 of the Social Security Act [section 402 of this title] for months beginning with the month in which this Act is enacted [September, 1960], on the basis of applications filed in or after such month."

Section 208(f) of Pub.L. 86–778 provided that: "The amendments made by the preceding provisions of this section [amending subsecs. (h)(1) and (h)(2) of this section, adding sentence following section 402(d)(3)(B) of this title, and adding the last sentence to subsec. (e) of this section] shall be applicable (1) with respect to monthly benefits under title II of the Social Security Act [this subchapter] for months beginning with the month in which this Act is enacted [September, 1960] on the basis of an application filed in or after such month, and (2) in the case of a lump-sum death payment under such title [this subchapter] based on an application filed in or after such month, but only if no person, other than the person filing such application, has filed an application for a lump-sum death payment under such title [this subchapter] prior to the date of the enactment of this Act [Sept. 13, 1960] with respect to the death of the same individual."

Amendment of subsec. (i)(2) by section 402(e) of Pub.L. 86–778, which redefined the term "period of disability" and inserted provisions relating to the acceptance of applications and providing that any application for a disability determination which is filed within the three months' period or six months' period shall be deemed to have been filed on such first day or in such first month, applicable only in the case of individuals who become entitled to benefits under section 423 of this title in or after September, 1960, see section 402(f) of Pub.L. 86–778 set out as a note under section 423 of this title.

Amendment of subsec. (i)(2) by section 403(c) of Pub.L. 86–778, which required a period of disability to end with the close of the last day of the month preceding whichever of the following months is the earlier: the month in which the individual attains age sixty-five or the third month following the month in which the disability ceases, applicable only in the case of individuals who have a period of disability (as defined in subsec. (i) of this section) beginning on or after Sept. 13, 1960, or beginning before Sept. 13, 1960, and continuing, without regard to such amendment, beyond the end of September, 1960, see section 403(e) of Pub.L. 86–778, set out as a note under section 422 of this title.

1958 Acts. Section 207(a) of Pub.L. 85–840 provided that: "The amendments made by section 201 [to subsec. (i)(2) of this section] shall apply with respect to applications for a disability determination under section 216(i) of the Social Security Act [subsec. (i) of this section] filed after June 1961. The amendments made by section 202 [to subsecs. (b) and (c)(3) of section 423 of this title] shall apply with respect to applications for disability insurance benefits under section 223 of such Act [section 423 of this title] filed after December 1957. The amendments made by section 203 [to subsec. (i)(4) of this section] shall apply with respect to applications for a disability determination under such section 216(i) [subsec. (i) of this section] filed after June 1958. The amendments made by section 204 [to subsec. (i)(3) of this section and section 423(c)(1)(A) of this title] shall apply with respect to (1) applications for disability insurance benefits under such section 223 [section 423 of this title] or for a disability determination under such section 216(i) [subsec. (i) of this section] filed on or after the date of enactment of this Act [Aug. 28, 1958], and (2) applications for such benefits or for such a determination filed after 1957 and prior to such date of enactment [Aug. 28, 1958] if the applicant has not died prior to such date of enactment [Aug. 28, 1958] and if notice to the applicant of the Secretary's decision with respect thereto has not been given to him on or prior to such date, except that (A) no benefits under title II of the Social Security Act [this subchapter] for the month in which this Act is enacted [August, 1958] or any prior month shall be payable or increased by reason of the amendments made by section 204 of this Act, and (B) the provisions of section 215(f)(1) of the Social Security Act [section 415(f)(1) of this title] shall not prevent recomputation of monthly benefits under section 202 of such Act [section 402 of this title] (but no such recomputation shall be regarded as a recomputation for purposes of section 215(f) of such Act [section 415(f) of this title]). The amendments made by section 205 (other than by subsections (k) and (m)) [to sections 401(h), 402(b), (c)(1), (d)(1), (f)(1)(D), (g)(1)(F), (h)(1)(B), (k), (q)(5), (6), 403(3), 414(b), 422(b)(3), and 425 of this title] shall apply with respect to monthly benefits under title II of the Social Security Act [this subchapter] for months after the month in which this Act is enacted [August, 1958], but only if an application for such benefits is filed on or after the date of enactment of this Act [Aug. 28, 1958]. The amendments made by section 206 [repealing section 424 of this title] and by subsections (k) and (m) of section 205 [to sections 403(h) and 415(g) of this title] shall apply with respect to monthly benefits under title II of the Social Security Act [this subchapter] for the month in which this Act is enacted [August, 1958] and succeeding months."

Amendment of subsecs. (b) to (d), (f), and (g) by section 301 of Pub.L. 85–840 applicable with respect to monthly benefits under section 402 of this title for months beginning after Aug. 28, 1958, but only if an application for such benefits is filed on or after such date, see section 301(f) of Pub.L. 85–840, set out as a note under section 402 of this title.

Section 302(b) of Pub.L. 85–840 provided that: "The amendment made by this section [to subsec. (e) of this section] shall apply with respect to monthly benefits under section 202 of the Social Security Act [section 402 of this title] for months beginning after the date of enactment of this Act [Aug. 28, 1958], but only if an application for such benefits is filed on or after such date."

Repeal of subsec. (h)(3) by section 305(b) of Pub.L. 85–840 applicable in the case of lump-sum death payments under section 402(i) of this title on the basis of the wages and self-employment income of any individual who dies after August, 1958, see section 305(c) of Pub.L. 85–840, set out as a note under section 402 of this title.

1957 Acts. Amendment by Pub.L. 85–238 applicable to monthly benefits under section 402 of this title for months after August 1957, but not to operate to deprive any such parent of benefits to which he would otherwise be entitled under section 402(h) of this title, see section 3(i) of Pub.L. 85–238, set out as a note under section 402 of this title.

1956 Acts. Section 102(b) of Act Aug. 1, 1956 provided that:

"(1) The amendment made by subsection (a) [to subsec. (a) of this section] shall apply in the case of benefits under subsection (e) of section 202 of the Social Security Act [section 402(e) of this title] for months after October 1956, but only, except in the case of an individual who was entitled to wife's or mother's insurance benefits under such section 202 [section 402 of this title] for October 1956, or any month thereafter, on the basis of applications filed after the date of enactment of this Act [Aug. 1, 1956]. The amendment made by subsection (a) shall apply in the case of benefits under subsection (h) of such section 202 [section 402(h) of this title] for months after October 1956 on the basis of applications filed after the date of enactment of this Act [Aug. 1, 1956].

"(2) Except as provided in paragraphs (1) and (4), the amendment made by subsection (a) shall apply in the case of lump-sum death payments under section 202(i) of the Social Security Act [section 402(i) of this title] with respect to deaths after October 1956, and in the case of monthly benefits under Title II of such Act [this subchapter] for months after October 1956 on the basis of applications filed after the date of enactment of this Act [Aug. 1, 1956].

"(3) For the purposes of section 215(b)(3)(B) of the Social Security Act [section 415(b)(3)(B) of this title] (but subject to paragraphs (1) and (2) of this subsection)—

"(A) a woman who attains the age of sixty-two prior to November 1956 and who was not eligible for old-age insurance benefits under section 202 of such Act [section 402 of this title] (as in effect prior to the enactment of this Act [Aug. 1, 1956]) for any month prior to November 1956 shall be deemed to have attained the age of sixty-two in 1956 or, if earlier, the year in which she died;

"(B) a woman shall not, by reason of the amendment made by subsection (a), be deemed to be a fully insured individual before November 1956 or the month in which she died, whichever month is the earlier; and

"(C) the amendment made by subsection (a) shall not be applicable in the case of any woman who was eligible for old-age insurance benefits under such section 202 [section 402 of this title] for any month prior to November 1956.

A woman shall, for purposes of this paragraph, be deemed eligible for old-age insurance benefits under section 202 of the Social Security Act [section 402 of this title] for any month if she was or would have been, upon filing application therefor in such month, entitled to such benefits for such month.

"(4) For purposes of section 209(i) of such Act [section 409(i) of this title], the amendment made by subsection (a) shall apply only with respect to remuneration paid after October 1956."

1954 Acts. Amendment by section 106(d) of Act Sept. 1, 1954 applicable with respect to monthly benefits under this subchapter for months after June 1955, and with respect to lump-sum death payments under such subchapter in the case of deaths occurring after June 1955; but that no recomputation of benefits by reason of such amendments shall be regarded as a recomputation for purposes of section 415(f) of this title, see section 106(h) of Act Sept. 1, 1954, set out as a note under section 413 of this title.

1952 Acts. For effective and termination dates of amendment by Act July 18, 1952, see section 3(f) and 3(g) of Act July 18, 1952, set out as a note under section 413 of this title.

1950 Acts. Section applicable (1) in case of monthly benefits for months after August, 1950, and (2) in the case of lump-sum death payments with respect to deaths after August 1950, see section 104(b) of Act Aug. 28, 1950, set out as a note under section 409 of this title.

Regulations

For provisions requiring the Secretary of Health and Human Services to prescribe regulations necessary to implement amendment to subsec. (i)(2)(D) by Pub.L. 98–460 not later than 180 days after Oct. 9, 1984, see section 2(g) of Pub.L. 98–460, set out as a note under section 423 of this title.

Retroactive Benefits

For provisions relating to entitlement to retroactive benefits under section 2 of Pub.L. 98–460, see section 2(f) of Pub.L. 98–460, set out as a note under section 423 of this title.

Special Insured Status Test in Certain Cases for Disability Purposes

Section 404 of Pub.L. 86–778 provided that:

"**(a)** In the case of any individual who does not meet the requirements of section 216(i)(3) of the Social Security Act [former provisions of subsec. (i)(3) of this section] with respect to any quarter, or who is not insured for disability insurance benefits as determined under section 223(c)(1) of such Act [former provisions of section 423(c)(1) of this title] with respect to any month in a quarter, such individual shall be deemed to have met such requirements with respect to such quarter or to be so insured with respect to such month of such quarter, as the case may be, if—

"(1) he had a total of not less than twenty quarters of coverage (as defined in section 213 of such Act [section 413 of this title]) during the period ending with the close of such quarter, and

"(2) all of the quarters elapsing after 1950 and up to but excluding such quarter were quarters of coverage with respect to him and there were not fewer than six such quarters of coverage.

"**(b)** Subsection (a) shall apply only in the case of applications for disability insurance benefits under section 223 of the Social Security Act [section 423 of this title], or for disability determinations under section 216(i) of such Act [subsec. (i) of this section], filed in or after the month in which this Act is enacted [September, 1960], and then only with respect to an individual who, but for such subsection (a), would not meet the requirements for a period of disability under section 216(i) [subsec. (i) of this section] with respect to the quarter in which this Act is enacted or any prior quarter and would not meet the requirements for benefits under section 223 [section 423 of this title] with respect to the month in which this Act is enacted [September, 1960] or any prior month. No benefits under title II of the Social Security Act [this subchapter] for the month in which this Act is enacted [September, 1960] or any prior month shall be payable or increased by reason of the amendment made by such subsection."

Study of Effect of Raising Retirement Age on Those Unlikely to Benefit From Improvements in Longevity

Section 201(d) of Pub.L. 98–21 required the Secretary to conduct a comprehensive study and analysis of the implications of the changes made by this section (amending sections 402, 403, 415, 416, and 423 of this title) in retirement age in the case of certain individuals and submit to Congress no later than January 1, 1986, a full report on the study and analysis, including any recommendations for legislative changes.

§ 417. Benefits for veterans

(a) Determination of benefits

(1) For purposes of determining entitlement to and the amount of any monthly benefit for any month after August 1950, or entitlement to and the amount of any lump-sum death payment in case of a death after such month, payable under this subchapter on the basis of the wages and self-employment income of any World War II veteran, and for purposes of section 416(i)(3) of this title, such veteran shall be deemed to have been paid wages (in addition to the wages, if any, actually paid to him) of $160 in each month during any part of which he served in the active military or naval service of the United States during World War II. This subsection shall not be applicable in the case of any monthly benefit or lump-sum death payment if—

(A) a larger such benefit or payment, as the case may be, would be payable without its application; or

(B) a benefit (other than a benefit payable in a lump sum unless it is a commutation of, or a substitute for, periodic payments) which is based, in whole or in part, upon the active military or naval service of such veteran during World War II is determined by any agency or wholly owned instrumentality of the United States (other than the Department of Veterans Affairs) to be payable by it under any other law of the United States or under a system established by such agency or instrumentality.

The provisions of clause (B) of this paragraph shall not apply in the case of any monthly benefit or lump-sum death payment under this subchapter if its application would reduce by $0.50 or less the primary insurance amount (as computed under section 415 of this title prior to any recomputation thereof pursuant to section 415(f) of this title) of the individual on whose wages and self-employment income such benefit or payment is based. The provisions of clause (B) of this paragraph shall also not apply for purposes of section 416(i)(3) of this title.

(2) Upon application for benefits or a lump-sum death payment on the basis of the wages and self-employment income of any World War II veteran, the Commissioner of Social Security shall make a decision without regard to clause (B) of paragraph (1) of this subsection unless the Commissioner has been notified by some other agency or instrumentality of the United States that, on the basis of the military or naval service of such veteran during World War II, a benefit described in clause (B) of paragraph (1) of this subsection has been determined by such agency or instrumentality to be payable by it. If the Commissioner has not been so notified, the Commissioner of Social Security shall then ascertain whether some other agency or wholly owned instrumentality of the United States has decided that a benefit described in clause (B) of paragraph (1) of this subsection is payable by it. If any such agency or instrumentality has decided, or thereafter decides, that such a benefit is payable by it, it shall so notify the Commissioner of Social Security, and the Commissioner of Social Security shall certify no further benefits for payment or shall recompute the amount of any further benefits payable, as may be required by paragraph (1) of this subsection.

(3) Any agency or wholly owned instrumentality of the United States which is authorized by any law of the United States to pay benefits, or has a system of benefits which are based, in whole or in part, on military or naval service during World War II shall, at the request of the Commissioner of Social Security, certify to the Commissioner, with respect to any veteran, such information as the Commissioner of Social Security deems necessary to carry out the Commissioner's functions under paragraph (2) of this subsection.

(b) Determination of insurance status

(1) Subject to paragraph (3), any World War II veteran who died during the period of three years immediately following his separation from the active military or naval service of the United States shall be deemed to have died a fully insured individual whose primary insurance amount is the amount determined under section 415(c) of this title as in effect in December 1978. Notwithstanding section 415(d) of this title as in effect in December 1978, the primary insurance benefit (for purposes of section 415(c) of this title as in effect in December 1978) of such veteran shall be determined as provided in this subchapter as in effect prior to August 28, 1950, except that the 1 per centum addition provided for in section 409(a)(4)(B) of this title as in effect prior to August 28, 1950, shall be applicable only with respect to calendar years prior to 1951. This subsection shall not be applicable in the case of any monthly benefit or lump-sum death payment if—

(A) a larger such benefit or payment, as the case may be, would be payable without its application;

(B) any pension or compensation is determined by the Secretary of Veterans Affairs to be payable by him on the basis of the death of such veteran;

(C) the death of the veteran occurred while he was in the active military or naval service of the United States; or

(D) such veteran has been discharged or released from the active military or naval service of the United States subsequent to July 26, 1951.

(2) Upon an application for benefits or a lump-sum death payment on the basis of the wages and self-employment income of any World War II veteran, the Commissioner of Social Security shall make a decision without regard to paragraph (1)(B) of this subsection unless the Commissioner has been notified by the Secretary of Veterans Affairs that pension or compensation is determined to be payable by that Secretary by reason of the death of such veteran. The Commissioner of Social Security shall thereupon report such decision to the Secretary of Veterans Affairs. If the Secretary of Veterans Affairs in any such case has made an adjudication or thereafter makes an adjudication that any pension or compensation is payable under any law administered by it, the Secretary of Veterans Affairs shall notify the Commissioner of Social Security, and the Commissioner of Social Security shall certify no further benefits for payment, or shall recompute the amount of any further benefits payable, as may be required by paragraph (1) of this subsection. Any payments theretofore certified by the Commissioner of Social Security on the basis of paragraph (1) of this subsection to any individual, not exceeding the amount of any accrued pension or compensation payable to him by the Secretary of Veterans Affairs, shall (notwithstanding the provisions of section 5301 of Title 38) be deemed to have been paid to him by that Secretary on account of such accrued pension or compensation. No such payment certified by the Commissioner of Social Security, and no payment certified by the Commissioner for any month prior to the first month for which any pension or compensation is paid by the Secretary of Veterans Affairs shall be deemed by reason of this subsection to have been an erroneous payment.

(3)(A) The preceding provisions of this subsection shall apply for purposes of determining the entitlement to benefits under section 402 of this title, based on the primary insurance amount of the deceased World War II veteran, of any surviving individual only if such surviving individual makes application for such benefits before the end of the 18–month period after November 1990.

(B) Subparagraph (A) shall not apply if any person is entitled to benefits under section 402 of this title based on the primary insurance amount of such veteran for the month preceding the month in which such application is made.

(c) Filing proof of support

In the case of any World War II veteran to whom subsection (a) is applicable, proof of support required under section 402(h) of this title may be filed by a parent at any time prior to July 1951 or prior to the expiration of two years after the date of the death of such veteran, whichever is the later.

(d) Definitions

For the purposes of this section—

(1) The term "World War II" means the period beginning with September 16, 1940, and ending at the close of July 24, 1947.

(2) The term "World War II veteran" means any individual who served in the active military or naval

service of the United States at any time during World War II and who, if discharged or released therefrom, was so discharged or released under conditions other than dishonorable after active service of ninety days or more or by reason of a disability or injury incurred or aggravated in service in line of duty; but such term shall not include any individual who died while in the active military or naval service of the United States if his death was inflicted (other than by an enemy of the United States) as lawful punishment for a military or naval offense.

(e) Determination based on wages and self-employment

(1) For purposes of determining entitlement to and the amount of any monthly benefit or lump-sum death payment payable under this subchapter on the basis of wages and self-employment income of any veteran (as defined in paragraph (4) of this subsection), and for purposes of section 416(i)(3) of this title, such veteran shall be deemed to have been paid wages (in addition to the wages, if any, actually paid to him) of $160 in each month during any part of which he served in the active military or naval service of the United States on or after July 25, 1947, and prior to January 1, 1957. This subsection shall not be applicable in the case of any monthly benefit or lump-sum death payment if—

(A) a larger such benefit or payment, as the case may be, would be payable without its application; or

(B) a benefit (other than a benefit payable in a lump sum unless it is a commutation of, or a substitute for, periodic payments) which is based, in whole or in part, upon the active military or naval service of such veteran on or after July 25, 1947, and prior to January 1, 1957, is determined by any agency or wholly owned instrumentality of the United States (other than the Department of Veterans Affairs) to be payable by it under any other law of the United States or under a system established by such agency or instrumentality.

The provisions of clause (B) of this paragraph shall not apply in the case of any monthly benefit or lump-sum death payment under this subchapter if its application would reduce by $0.50 or less the primary insurance amount (as computed under section 415 of this title prior to any recomputation thereof pursuant to subsection (f) of section 415 of this title) of the individual on whose wages and self-employment income such benefit or payment is based. The provisions of clause (B) of this paragraph shall also not apply for purposes of section 416(i)(3) of this title. In the case of monthly benefits under this subchapter for months after December 1956 (and any lump-sum death payment under this subchapter with respect to a death occurring after December 1956) based on the wages and self-employment income of a veteran who performed service (as a member of a uniformed service) to which the provisions of section 410(*l*)(1) of this title are applicable, wages which would, but for the provisions of clause (B) of this paragraph, be deemed under this subsection to have been paid to such veteran with respect to his active military or naval service performed after December 1950 shall be deemed to have been paid to him with respect to such service notwithstanding the provisions of such clause, but only if the benefits referred to in such clause which are based (in whole or in part) on such service are payable solely by the Army, Navy, Air Force, Marine Corps, Coast Guard, Coast and Geodetic Survey, National Oceanic and Atmospheric Administration Corps, or Public Health Service.

(2) Upon application for benefits or a lump-sum death payment on the basis of the wages and self-employment income of any veteran, the Commissioner of Social Security shall make a decision without regard to clause (B) of paragraph (1) of this subsection unless the Commissioner has been notified by some other agency or instrumentality of the United States that, on the basis of the military or naval service of such veteran on or after July 25, 1947, and prior to January 1, 1957, a benefit described in clause (B) of paragraph (1) of this subsection has been determined by such agency or instrumentality to be payable by it. If the Commissioner has not been so notified, the Commissioner of Social Security shall then ascertain whether some other agency or wholly owned instrumentality of the United States has decided that a benefit described in clause (B) of paragraph (1) of this subsection is payable by it. If any such agency or instrumentality has decided, or thereafter decides, that such a benefit is payable by it, it shall so notify the Commissioner of Social Security, and the Commissioner of Social Security shall certify no further benefits for payment or shall recompute the amount of any further benefits payable, as may be required by paragraph (1) of this subsection.

(3) Any agency or wholly owned instrumentality of the United States which is authorized by any law of the United States to pay benefits, or has a system of benefits which are based, in whole or in part, on military or naval service on or after July 25, 1947, and prior to January 1, 1957, shall, at the request of the Commissioner of Social Security, certify to the Commissioner, with respect to any veteran, such information as the Commissioner of Social Security deems necessary to carry out the Commissioner's functions under paragraph (2) of this subsection.

(4) For the purposes of this subsection, the term "veteran" means any individual who served in the active military or naval service of the United States at any time on or after July 25, 1947, and prior to January 1, 1957, and who, if discharged or released therefrom, was so discharged or released under conditions other than dishonorable after active service of ninety days or more or by reason of a disability or injury incurred or aggravated in service in line of duty; but such term shall not include any individual who died while in the active military or naval service of the

United States if his death was inflicted (other than by an enemy of the United States) as lawful punishment for a military or naval offense.

(f) Right to annuity; waiver

(1) In any case where a World War II veteran (as defined in subsection (d)(2)) or a veteran (as defined in subsection (e)(4)) has died or shall hereafter die, and his or her surviving spouse or child is entitled under subchapter III of chapter 83 of Title 5 to an annuity in the computation of which his or her active military or naval service was included, clause (B) of subsection (a)(1) or clause (B) of subsection (e)(1) shall not operate (solely by reason of such annuity) to make such subsection inapplicable in the case of any monthly benefit under section 402 of this title which is based on his or her wages and self-employment income; except that no such surviving spouse or child shall be entitled under section 402 of this title to any monthly benefit in the computation of which such service is included by reason of this subsection (A) unless such surviving spouse or child after December 1956 waives his or her right to receive such annuity, or (B) for any month prior to the first month with respect to which the Director of the Office of Personnel Management certifies to the Commissioner of Social Security that (by reason of such waiver) no further annuity will be paid to such surviving spouse or child under such subchapter III on the basis of such veteran's military or civilian service. Any such waiver shall be irrevocable.

(2) Whenever a surviving spouse waives his or her right to receive such annuity such waiver shall constitute a waiver on his or her own behalf; a waiver by a legal guardian or guardians, or, in the absence of a legal guardian, the person (or persons) who has the child in his or her care, of the child's right to receive such annuity shall constitute a waiver on behalf of such child. Such a waiver with respect to an annuity based on a veteran's service shall be valid only if the surviving spouse and all children, or, if there is no surviving spouse, all the children, waive their rights to receive annuities under subchapter III of chapter 83 of Title 5 based on such veteran's military or civilian service.

(g) Appropriation to trust funds

(1) Within thirty days after April 20, 1983, the Commissioner of Social Security shall determine the amount equal to the excess of—

(A) the actuarial present value as of April 20, 1983, of the past and future benefit payments from the Federal Old-Age and Survivors Insurance Trust Fund, the Federal Disability Insurance Trust Fund, and the Federal Hospital Insurance Trust Fund under this subchapter and subchapter XVIII, together with associated administrative costs, resulting from the operation of this section (other than this subsection) and section 410 of this title as in effect before the enactment of the Social Security Amendments of 1950, over

(B) any amounts previously transferred from the general fund of the Treasury to such Trust Funds pursuant to the provisions of this subsection as in effect immediately before April 20, 1983.

Such actuarial present value shall be based on the relevant actuarial assumptions set forth in the report of the Board of Trustees of each such Trust Fund for 1983 under sections 401(c) and 1395i(b) of this title. Within thirty days after April 20, 1983, the Secretary of the Treasury shall transfer the amount determined under this paragraph with respect to each such Trust Fund to such Trust Fund from amounts in the general fund of the Treasury not otherwise appropriated.

(2) The Commissioner of Social Security shall revise the amount determined under paragraph (1) with respect to each such Trust Fund in 1985 and each fifth year thereafter through 2010, as determined appropriate by the Commissioner of Social Security from data which becomes available to the Commissioner after the date of the determination under paragraph (1) on the basis of the amount of benefits and administrative expenses actually paid from such Trust Fund under this subchapter or subchapter XVIII and the relevant actuarial assumptions set forth in the report of the Board of Trustees of such Trust Fund for such year under section 401(c) or 1395i(b) of this title. The Secretary of Health and Human Services shall revise the amount determined under paragraph (1) with respect to the Federal Hospital Insurance Trust Fund under subchapter XVIII in 2015 and each fifth year thereafter through such date, and using such data, as the Secretary determines appropriate on the basis of the amount of benefits and administrative expenses actually paid from such Trust Fund under subchapter XVIII and the relevant actuarial assumptions set forth in the report of the Board of Trustees of such Trust Fund for such year under section 1395i(b) of this title. Within 30 days after any such revision, the Secretary of the Treasury, to the extent provided in advance in appropriation Acts, shall transfer to such Trust Fund, from amounts in the general fund of the Treasury not otherwise appropriated, or from such Trust Fund to the general fund of the Treasury, such amounts as the Secretary of the Treasury determines necessary to take into account such revision.

(h) Determination of veterans status

(1) For the purposes of this section, any individual who the Commissioner of Social Security finds—

(A) served during World War II (as defined in subsection (d)(1)) in the active military or naval service of a country which was on September 16, 1940, at war with a country with which the United States was at war during World War II;

(B) entered into such active service on or before December 8, 1941;

(C) was a citizen of the United States throughout such period of service or lost his United States citizenship solely because of his entrance into such service;

(D) had resided in the United States for a period or periods aggregating four years during the five-year period ending on the day of, and was domiciled in the United States on the day of, such entrance into such active service; and

(E)(i) was discharged or released from such service under conditions other than dishonorable after active service of ninety days or more or by reason of a disability or injury incurred or aggravated in service in line of duty, or

(ii) died while in such service,

shall be considered a World War II veteran (as defined in subsection (d)(2)) and such service shall be considered to have been performed in the active military or naval service of the United States.

(2) In the case of any individual to whom paragraph (1) applies, proof of support required under section 402(f) or (h) of this title may be filed at any time prior to the expiration of two years after the date of such individual's death or August 28, 1958, whichever is the later.

(Aug. 14, 1935, c. 531, Title II, § 217, as added Aug. 28, 1950, c. 809, Title I, § 105, 64 Stat. 512; amended July 18, 1952, c. 945, § 5(a), (d)(1), 66 Stat. 773, 775; Aug. 14, 1953, c. 483, § 1, 67 Stat. 580; Sept. 1, 1954, c. 1206, Title I, § 106(e), 68 Stat. 1081; Aug. 9, 1955, c. 685, § 1, 69 Stat. 621; Aug. 1, 1956, c. 837, Title IV, §§ 404(a), (b), 406, 70 Stat. 872, 875; Pub.L. 85–840, Title III, § 314(a), (b), Aug. 28, 1958, 72 Stat. 1036; Pub.L. 85–857, § 13(i)(2), Sept. 2, 1958, 72 Stat. 1265; Pub.L. 86–778, Title I, § 103(j)(2)(C), Sept. 13, 1960, 74 Stat. 937; Pub.L. 89–97, Title III, § 322, July 30, 1965, 79 Stat. 396; Pub.L. 90–248, Title IV, § 403(c), Jan. 2, 1968, 81 Stat. 932; Pub.L. 94–273, §§ 2(23), 16, Apr. 21, 1976, 90 Stat. 376, 379; Pub.L. 95–216, Title II, § 205(c), Dec. 20, 1977, 91 Stat. 1529; Pub.L. 97–35, Title XXII, § 2201(c)(7), Aug. 13, 1981, 95 Stat. 832; Pub.L. 97–123, § 2(g), Dec. 29, 1981, 95 Stat. 1661; Pub.L. 98–21, Title I, § 151(a), Title III, § 308, Apr. 20, 1983, 97 Stat. 103, 115; Pub.L. 98–369, Div. B, Title VI, § 2663(a)(12), (j)(3)(A)(ii), July 18, 1984, 98 Stat. 1164, 1170; Pub.L. 101–239, Title X, § 10208(d)(2)(A)(iv), Dec. 19, 1989, 103 Stat. 2481; Pub.L. 101–508, Title V, § 5117(b), Nov. 5, 1990, 104 Stat. 1388–277; Pub.L. 102–40, Title IV, § 402(d)(2), May 7, 1991, 105 Stat. 239; Pub.L. 102–54, § 13(q)(3)(A)(i), (D), (E), June 13, 1991, 105 Stat. 279; Pub.L. 103–296, Title I, § 107(a)(4), Aug. 15, 1994, 108 Stat. 1478; Pub.L. 114–74, Title VIII, § 842, Nov. 2, 2015, 129 Stat. 617.)

HISTORICAL AND STATUTORY NOTES

References in Text

This subchapter, referred to in text, originally read "this title", meaning Title II of the Social Security Act, Act Aug. 14, 1935, c. 531, 49 Stat. 620, as amended, which is principally classified to subchapter II of this chapter, 42 U.S.C.A. § 401 et seq.

The Social Security Act Amendments of 1950, referred to in subsec. (g)(1)(A), probably means Act Aug. 28, 1950, c. 809, 64 Stat. 477, known as the Social Security Act Amendments of 1950. For complete classification of this Act to the Code, see Short Title of 1950 Amendment note set out under 42 U.S.C.A. § 1305 and Tables.

Subchapter XVIII, referred to in subsec. (g)(2), originally read "title XVIII", meaning Title XVIII of the Social Security Act, Aug. 14, 1935, c. 531, Title XVIII, § 1801 et seq., as added and amended, which is principally classified to subchapter XVIII of this chapter, 42 U.S.C.A. § 1395 et seq.

Effective and Applicability Provisions

1994 Acts. Amendment by section 107(a)(4) of Pub.L. 103–296 effective Mar. 31, 1995, see section 110 of Pub.L. 103–296, set out as a note under section 401 of this title.

1984 Acts. Amendment by Pub.L. 98–369 effective July 18, 1984, but not to be construed as changing or affecting any right, liability, status or interpretation which existed (under the provisions of law involved) before that date, see section 2664(b) of Pub.L. 98–369, set out as a note under section 401 of this title.

1983 Acts. Amendment by section 308 of Pub.L. 98–21 applicable only with respect to monthly payments payable under this subchapter for months after April, 1983, except as otherwise specifically provided, see section 310 of Pub.L. 98–21 set out as a note under section 402 of this title.

1981 Acts. Amendment by section 2201(c)(7) of Pub.L. 97–35 and by section 2(g) of Pub.L. 97–123 applicable with respect to benefits for months after December 1981 with certain exceptions, see section 2(j)(2) to (4) of Pub.L. 97–123, set out as a note under section 415 of this title.

1977 Acts. Amendment by Pub.L. 95–216 effective with respect to monthly benefits and lump-sum death payments for deaths occurring after Dec., 1978, see section 206 of Pub.L. 95–216, set out as a note under section 402 of this title.

1960 Acts. Amendment of subsec. (e)(1) by Pub.L. 86–778 effective Sept. 13, 1960, see section 103(v)(1) of Pub.L. 86–778, set out as a note under section 402 of this title.

1958 Acts. Amendment of subsec. (b)(2) by Pub.L. 85–857 effective Jan. 1, 1959, see section 2 of Pub.L. 85–857, set out as a note preceding Part I of Title 38, Veterans' Benefits.

Section 314(c)(1) of Pub.L. 85–840 provided that: "The amendment made by subsection (a) [adding subsec. (h) of this section] shall apply only with respect to (A) monthly benefits under sections 202 and 223 of the Social Security Act [sections 402 and 423 of this title] for months after the month in which this Act is enacted [August 1958], (B) lump-sum death payments under such section 202 [section 402 of this title] in the case of deaths occurring after the month in which this Act is enacted [August 1958], and (C) periods of disability under section 216(i) [section 416(i) of this title] in the case of applications for a disability determination filed after the month in which this Act is enacted [August 1958]."

1956 Acts. Section 404(d) of Act Aug. 1, 1956 provided that: "Except for the last sentence of section 217(e)(1) of the Social Security Act as amended by subsection (a) of this section [subsec. (e)(1) of this section], the amendments made by such subsection (a) [to subsec. (e) and (f) of this section] shall be effective as though they had been enacted on March 31, 1956. Such last sentence of section 217(e)(1) of the Social Security Act shall become effective January 1, 1957."

Subsec. (g), as added by Act Aug. 1, 1956, effective Jan. 1, 1957, pursuant to the provisions of section 603(a) of Act Aug. 1, 1956.

1954 Acts. Amendment by section 106(e) of Act Sept. 1, 1954 applicable with respect to monthly benefits under this subchapter for months after June 1955, and with respect to lump-sum death payments under such subchapter in the case of deaths occurring after June 1955; but that no recomputation of benefits by reason of such amendments shall be regarded as a recomputation for purposes of section 415(f) of this title, see section 106(h) of Act Sept. 1, 1954, set out as a note under section 413 of this title.

1952 Acts. Section 5(c) of Act July 18, 1952, as amended by Pub.L. 86–778, Title III, § 304(d), Sept. 13, 1960, 74 Stat. 966, provided that:

"(1) The amendments made by subsections (a) and (b) [to sections 417(e) and 405(*o*) of this title] shall apply with respect to monthly benefits under section 202 of the Social Security Act [section 402 of this title] for months after August 1952, and with respect to lump-sum death payments in the case of deaths occurring after August, 1952, except that, in the case of any individual who is entitled, on the basis of the wages and self-employment income of any individual to whom section 217(e) of the Social Security Act [subsec. (e) of this section] applies, to monthly benefits under such section 202 for August 1952 [section 402 of this title], such amendments shall apply (A) only if an application for recomputation by reason of such amendments is filed by such individual, or any other individual, entitled to benefits under such section 202 [section 402 of this title] on the basis of such wages and self-employment income, and (B) only with respect to such benefits for months after whichever of the following is the later: August 1952 or the seventh month before the month in which such application was filed. Recomputations of benefits as required to carry out the provisions of this paragraph shall be made notwithstanding the provisions of section 215(f)(1) of the Social Security Act [section 415(f)(1) of this title]; but no such recomputation shall be regarded as a recomputation for purposes of section 215(f) of such Act [section 415(f) of this title]. Notwithstanding the preceding provisions of this paragraph, the primary insurance amount of an individual shall not be recomputed under such provisions unless such individual files the application referred to in clause (A) of the first sentence of this paragraph prior to January 1961 or, if he dies without filing such application, his death occurred prior to January 1961.

"(2) In the case of any veteran (as defined in section 217(e)(4) of the Social Security Act [subsec. (e)(4) of this section]) who died prior to September 1952, the requirement in subsections (f) and (h) of section 202 of the Social Security Act [section 402(f), (h) of this title] that proof of support be filed within two years of the date of such death shall not apply if such proof is filed prior to September 1954."

Section 5(d)(2) of Act July 18, 1952 provided that: "The amendment made by paragraph (1) of this subsection [to subsec. (a)(1)(B) of this section] shall apply only in the case of applications for benefits under section 202 of the Social Security Act [section 402 of this title] filed after August 1952."

1950 Acts. Section 105 of Act Aug. 28, 1950 provided in part that this section shall be effective Sept. 1, 1950.

Change of Name

The Coast and Geodetic Survey was consolidated with the Weather Bureau to form a new agency in the Department of Commerce to be known as the Environmental Science Services Administration, and the commissioned officers of the Survey were transferred to ESSA, by Reorg. Plan No. 2 of 1965, eff. July 13, 1965, 30 F.R. 8819, 79 Stat. 1318, set out in Appendix 1 to Title 5, Government Organization and Employees. Reorg. Plan No. 4 of 1970, eff. Oct. 3, 1970, 35 F.R. 15627, 84 Stat. 2090, abolished the Environmental Science Services Administration, established the National Oceanic and Atmospheric Administration, and redesignated the Commissioned Officer Corps of ESSA as the Commissioned Officer Corps of NOAA. For further details, see Transfer of Functions note set out under section 851 of Title 33, Navigation and Navigable Waters.

Transfer of Functions

"Director of the Office of Personnel Management" was substituted for "Civil Service Commission" pursuant to Reorg. Plan No. 2 of 1978, § 102, 43 F.R. 36037, 92 Stat. 3784, set out under section 1101 of Title 5, Government Organization and Employees, which transferred all functions vested by statute in the United States Civil Service Commission to the Director of the Office of Personnel Management (except as otherwise specified), effective Jan. 1, 1979, as provided by section 1–102 of Ex. Ord. No. 12107, Dec. 28, 1978, 44 F.R. 1055, set out under section 1101 of Title 5.

The Coast Guard was transferred to the Department of Transportation, and all functions, powers, and duties relating to the Coast Guard of the Secretary of the Treasury and of other officers and offices of the Department of the Treasury were transferred to the Secretary of Transportation by Pub.L. 89–670, § 6(b)(1), Oct. 15, 1966, 80 Stat. 938. Section 6(b)(2) of Pub.L. 89–670, however, provided that notwithstanding such transfer of functions, the Coast Guard shall operate as part of the Navy in time of war or when the President directs as provided in section 3 [now section 103] of Title 14, Coast Guard. See section 108 of Title 49, Transportation.

For transfer of authorities, functions, personnel, and assets of the Coast Guard, including the authorities and functions of the Secretary of Transportation relating thereto, to the Department of Homeland Security, and for treatment of related references, see 6 U.S.C.A. §§ 468(b), 551(d), 552(d) and 557, and the Department of Homeland Security Reorganization Plan of November 25, 2002, as modified, set out as a note under 6 U.S.C.A. § 542.

All functions of the Federal Security Administrator were transferred to the Secretary of Health, Education, and Welfare [now the Secretary of Health and Human Services] and all agencies of the Federal Security Agency were transferred to the Department of Health, Education, and Welfare [now the Department of Health and Human Services] by section 5 of Reorg. Plan No. 1 of 1953, set out as a note under section 3501 of this title. The Federal Security Agency and the office of Administrator were abolished by section 8 of Reorg. Plan No. 1 of 1953. The Secretary and Department of Health, Education, and Welfare were redesignated the Secretary and Department of Health and Human Services by section 509(b) of Pub.L. 96–88 which is classified to section 3508(b) of Title 20, Education.

Recomputation of Primary Insurance Amount of Certain Individuals

Section 314(c)(2) of Pub.L. 85–840 provided that:

"In the case of any individual—

"(A) who is a World War II veteran (as defined in section 217(d)(2) of the Social Security Act [subsec. (d)(2) of this section]) wholly or partly by reason of service described in section 217(h)(1)(A) of such Act [subsec. (h)(1)(A) of this section]; and

"(B) who (i) became entitled to old-age insurance benefits under section 202(a) of the Social Security Act [section 402(a) of this title] or to disability insurance benefits under section 223 of such Act [section 423 of this title] prior to the first day of the month following the month in which this Act is enacted [August 1958], or (ii) died prior to such first day, and whose widow, former wife divorced, widower, child, or parent is entitled for the month in which this Act is enacted [August 1958], on the basis of his wages and self-employment income, to a monthly benefit under section 202 of such Act [section 402 of this title]; and

"(C) any part of whose service described in section 217(h)(1)(A) of the Social Security Act [subsec. (h)(1)(A) of this section] was not included in the computation of his primary insurance amount under section 215 of such Act [section 415 of this title] but would have been included in such computation if the amendment made by subsection (a) of this section had been effective prior to the date of such computation,

the Secretary of Health, Education, and Welfare [now Secretary of Health and Human Services] shall, notwithstanding the provisions of section 215(f)(1) of the Social Security Act [section 415(f)(1) of this title], recompute the primary insurance amount of such individual upon the filing of an application, after the month in which this Act is enacted [August 1958], by him or (if he has died without filing such an application) by any person entitled to monthly benefits under section 202 of the Social Security Act [section 402 of this title] on the basis of his wages and self-employment income. Such recomputation shall be made only in the manner provided in title II of the Social Security Act [this subchapter] as in effect at the time of the last previous computation or recomputation of such individual's primary insurance amount, and as though application therefor was filed in the month in which application for such last previous computation or recomputation was filed. No recomputation made under this subsection shall be regarded as a recomputation under section 215(f) of the Social Security Act [section 415(f) of this title]. Any such recomputation shall be effective for and after the twelfth month before the month in which the application is filed, but in no case for the month in which this Act is enacted [August 1958] or any prior month."

Recomputation of Social Security Benefits of Widows and Children Who Waive Right to Annuity Under Civil Service Retirement Act

Section 404(c) of Act Aug. 1, 1956, c. 837, provided that:

"In the case of any deceased individual—

"(1) who is a World War II veteran (as defined in section 217(d)(2) of the Social Security Act [subsec. (d)(2) of this section]) or a veteran (as defined in section 217(e)(4) of such Act [subsec. (d)(4) of this section]); and

"(2) whose widow or child is entitled under the Civil Service Retirement Act of May 29, 1930, as amended [see section 8301 et seq. of Title 5, Government Organization and Employees], to an annuity in the computation of which his active military or naval service after September 15, 1940 and before January 1, 1957, was included; and

"(3) whose widow or child is entitled under section 202 of the Social Security Act [section 402 of this title], on the basis of his wages and self-employment income, to a monthly benefit in the computation of which such active military or naval service was excluded (under clause (B) of subsection (a)(1) or (e)(1) of section 217 of such Act [this section]) solely by reason of the annuity described in the preceding paragraph; and

"(4) whose widow or child is entitled by reason of section 217(f) of the Social Security Act [subsec. (f) of this section] to have such active military or naval service included in the computation of such monthly benefit,

the Secretary of Health, Education, and Welfare [now Secretary of Health and Human Services] shall, notwithstanding the provisions of section 215(f)(1) of the Social Security Act [section 415(f)(1) of this title], recompute the primary insurance amount of such individual upon the filing of an application, after December 1956, by or on behalf of such widow or child. Such recomputation shall be made only in the manner provided in title II of the Social Security Act [this subchapter] as in effect at the time of such individual's death, and as though application therefor was filed in the month in which he died. No recomputation made under this subsection shall be regarded as a recomputation under section 215(f) of the Social Security Act [section 415(f) this title]. Any such recomputation shall be effective for and after the twelfth month before the month in which the application is filed, but in no case for any month before the first month with respect to which such widow or child is entitled by reason of section 217(f) of the Social Security Act [subsec. (f) of this section] to have such active military or naval service included in the computation of such monthly benefits. The terms used in this subsection shall have the same meaning as when used in title II of the Social Security Act [this subchapter]."

§ 418. Voluntary agreements for coverage of State and local employees

(a) Purpose of agreement

(1) The Commissioner of Social Security shall, at the request of any State, enter into an agreement with such State for the purpose of extending the insurance system established by this subchapter to services performed by individuals as employees of such State or any political subdivision thereof. Each such agreement shall contain such provisions, not inconsistent with the provisions of this section, as the State may request.

(2) Notwithstanding section 410(a) of this title, for the purposes of this subchapter the term "employment" includes any service included under an agreement entered into under this section.

(b) Definitions

For the purposes of this section—

(1) The term "State" does not include the District of Columbia, Guam, or American Samoa.

(2) The term "political subdivision" includes an instrumentality of (A) a State, (B) one or more political subdivisions of a State, or (C) a State and one or more of its political subdivisions.

(3) The term "employee" includes an officer of a State or political subdivision.

(4) The term "retirement system" means a pension, annuity, retirement, or similar fund or system established by a State or by a political subdivision thereof.

(5) The term "coverage group" means (A) employees of the State other than those engaged in performing service in connection with a proprietary function; (B) employees of a political subdivision of a State other than those engaged in performing service in connection with a proprietary function; (C) employees of a State engaged in performing service in connection with a single proprietary function; or (D) employees of a political subdivision of a State engaged in performing service in connection with a single proprietary function. If under the preceding sentence an employee would be included in more than one coverage group by reason of the fact that he performs service in connection with two or more proprietary functions or in connection with both a proprietary function and a nonproprietary function, he shall be included in only one such coverage group. The determination of the coverage group in which such employee shall be included shall be made in such manner as may be specified in the agreement. Persons employed under section 709 of Title 32, who elected under section 6 of the National Guard Technicians Act of 1968 to remain covered by an employee retirement system of, or plan sponsored by, a State or the Commonwealth of Puerto Rico, shall, for the purposes of this chapter, be employees of the State or the Commonwealth of Puerto Rico and (notwithstanding the preceding provisions of this paragraph), shall be deemed to be a separate coverage group. For purposes of this section, individuals employed pursuant to an agreement, entered into pursuant to section 1624 of Title 7 or section 499n of Title 7, between a State and the United States Department of Agriculture to perform services as inspectors of agricultural products may be deemed, at the option of the State, to be employees of the State and (notwithstanding the preceding provisions of this paragraph) shall be deemed to be a separate coverage group.

(c) Services covered

(1) An agreement under this section shall be applicable to any one or more coverage groups designated by the State.

(2) In the case of each coverage group to which the agreement applies, the agreement must include all services (other than services excluded by or pursuant to subsection (d) or paragraph (3), (5), or (6) of this subsection) performed by individuals as members of such group.

(3) Such agreement shall, if the State requests it, exclude (in the case of any coverage group) any one or more of the following:

(A) All services in any class or classes of (i) elective positions, (ii) part-time positions, or (iii) positions the compensation for which is on a fee basis;

(B) All services performed by individuals as members of a coverage group in positions covered by a retirement system on the date such agreement is made applicable to such coverage group, but only in the case of individuals who, on such date (or, if later, the date on which they first occupy such positions), are not eligible to become members of such system and whose services in such positions have not already been included under such agreement pursuant to subsection (d)(3).

(4) The Commissioner of Social Security shall, at the request of any State, modify the agreement with such State so as to (A) include any coverage group to which the agreement did not previously apply, or (B) include, in the case of any coverage group to which the agreement applies, services previously excluded from the agreement; but the agreement as so modified may not be inconsistent with the provisions of this section applicable in the case of an original agreement with a State. A modification of an agreement pursuant to clause (B) of the preceding sentence may apply to individuals to whom paragraph (3)(B) of this subsection is applicable (whether or not the previous exclusion of the service of such individuals was pursuant to such paragraph), but only if such individuals are, on the effective date specified in such modification, ineligible to be members of any retirement system or if the modification with respect to such individuals is pursuant to subsection (d)(3).

(5) Such agreement shall, if the State requests it, exclude (in the case of any coverage group) any agricultural labor, or service performed by a student, designated by the State. This paragraph shall apply only with respect to service which is excluded from employment by any provision of section 410(a) of this title other than paragraph (7) of such section and service the remuneration for which is excluded from wages by subparagraph (B) of section 409(a)(7) of this title.

(6) Such agreement shall exclude—

(A) service performed by an individual who is employed to relieve him from unemployment,

(B) service performed in a hospital, home, or other institution by a patient or inmate thereof,

(C) covered transportation service (as determined under section 410(k) of this title),

(D) service (other than agricultural labor or service performed by a student) which is excluded from employment by any provision of section 410(a) of this title other than paragraph (7) of such section,

(E) service performed by an individual as an employee serving on a temporary basis in case of fire, storm, snow, earthquake, flood, or other similar emergency, and

(F) service described in section 410(a)(7)(F) of this title which is included as "employment" under section 410(a) of this title.

(7) No agreement may be made applicable (either in the original agreement or by any modification thereof) to service performed by any individual to whom paragraph (3)(B) of this subsection is applicable unless such agreement provides (in the case of each coverage group involved) either that the service of any individual to whom such paragraph is applicable and who is a member of such coverage group shall continue to be covered by such agreement in case he thereafter becomes eligible to be a member of a retirement system, or that such service shall cease to be so covered when he becomes eligible to be a member of such a system (but only if the agreement is not already applicable to such system pursuant to subsection (d)(3)), whichever may be desired by the State.

(8)(A) Notwithstanding any other provision of this section, the agreement with any State entered into under this section may at the option of the State be modified at any time to exclude service performed by election officials or election workers if the remuneration paid in a calendar year for such service is less than $1,000 with respect to service performed during any calendar year commencing on or after January 1, 1995, ending on or before December 31, 1999, and the adjusted amount determined under subparagraph (B) for any calendar year commencing on or after January 1, 2000, with respect to service performed during such calendar year. Any modification of an agreement pursuant to this paragraph shall be effective with respect to services performed in and after the calendar year in which the modification is mailed or delivered by other means to the Commissioner of Social Security.

(B) For each year after 1999, the Commissioner of Social Security shall adjust the amount referred to in subparagraph (A) at the same time and in the same manner as is provided under section 415(a)(1)(B)(ii) of this title with respect to the amounts referred to in section 415(a)(1)(B)(i) of this title, except that—

(i) for purposes of this subparagraph, 1997 shall be substituted for the calendar year referred to in section 415(a)(1)(B)(ii)(II) of this title, and

(ii) such amount as so adjusted, if not a multiple of $100, shall be rounded to the next higher multiple of $100 where such amount is a multiple of $50 and to the nearest multiple of $100 in any other case.

The Commissioner of Social Security shall determine and publish in the Federal Register each adjusted amount determined under this subparagraph not later than November 1 preceding the year for which the adjustment is made.

(d) Positions covered by retirement systems

(1) No agreement with any State may be made applicable (either in the original agreement or by any modification thereof) to any service performed by employees as members of any coverage group in positions covered by a retirement system either (A) on the date such agreement is made applicable to such coverage group, or (B) on September 1, 1954 (except in the case of positions which are, by reason of action by such State or political subdivision thereof, as may be appropriate, taken prior to September 1, 1954, no longer covered by a retirement system on the date referred to in clause (A), and except in the case of positions excluded by paragraph (5)(A) of this subsection). The preceding sentence shall not be applicable to any service performed by an employee as a member of any coverage group in a position (other than a position excluded by paragraph (5)(A) of this subsection) covered by a retirement system on the date an agreement is made applicable to such coverage group if, on such date (or, if later, the date on which such individual first occupies such position), such individual is ineligible to be a member of such system.

(2) It is declared to be the policy of the Congress in enacting the succeeding paragraphs of this subsection that the protection afforded employees in positions covered by a retirement system on the date an agreement under this section is made applicable to service performed in such positions, or receiving periodic benefits under such retirement system at such time, will not be impaired as a result of making the agreement so applicable or as a result of legislative enactment in anticipation thereof.

(3) Notwithstanding paragraph (1) of this subsection, an agreement with a State may be made applicable (either in the original agreement or by any modification thereof) to service performed by employees in positions covered by a retirement system (including positions specified in paragraph (4) of this subsection but not including positions excluded by or pursuant to paragraph (5)), if the governor of the State, or an official of the State designated by him for the purpose, certifies to the Commissioner of Social Security that the following conditions have been met:

(A) A referendum by secret written ballot was held on the question of whether service in positions covered by such retirement system should be excluded from or included under an agreement under this section;

(B) An opportunity to vote in such referendum was given (and was limited) to eligible employees;

(C) Not less than ninety days' notice of such referendum was given to all such employees;

(D) Such referendum was conducted under the supervision of the governor or an agency or individual designated by him; and

(E) A majority of the eligible employees voted in favor of including service in such positions under an agreement under this section.

An employee shall be deemed an "eligible employee" for purposes of any referendum with respect to any retirement system if, at the time such referendum was held, he was in a position covered by such retirement system and was a member of such system, and if he was in such a position at the time notice of such referendum was given as required by clause (C) of the preceding sentence; except that he shall not be deemed an "eligible employee" if, at the time the referendum was held, he was in a position to which the State agreement already applied, or if he was in a position excluded by or pursuant to paragraph (5). No referendum with respect to a retirement system shall be valid for purposes of this paragraph unless held within the two-year period which ends on the date of execution of the agreement or modification which extends the insurance system established by this subchapter to such retirement system, nor shall any referendum with respect to a retirement system be valid for purposes of this paragraph if held less than one year after the last previous referendum held with respect to such retirement system.

(4) For the purposes of subsection (c) of this section, the following employees shall be deemed to be a separate coverage group—

(A) all employees in positions which were covered by the same retirement system on the date the agreement was made applicable to such system (other than employees to whose services the agreement already applied on such date);

(B) all employees in positions which became covered by such system at any time after such date; and

(C) all employees in positions which were covered by such system at any time before such date and to whose services the insurance system established by this subchapter has not been extended before such date because the positions were covered by such retirement system (including employees to whose services the agreement was not applicable on such date because such services were excluded pursuant to subsection (c)(3)(B)).

(5)(A) Nothing in paragraph (3) of this subsection shall authorize the extension of the insurance system established by this subchapter to service in any policeman's or fireman's position.

(B) At the request of the State, any class or classes of positions covered by a retirement system which may be excluded from the agreement pursuant to paragraph (3) or (5) of subsection (c), and to which the agreement does not already apply, may be excluded from the agreement at the time it is made applicable to such retirement system; except that, notwithstanding the provisions of paragraph (3)(B) of such subsection, such exclusion may not include any services to which such paragraph (3)(B) is applicable. In the case of any such exclusion, each such class so excluded shall, for purposes of this subsection, constitute a separate retirement system in case of any modification of the agreement thereafter agreed to.

(6)(A) If a retirement system covers positions of employees of the State and positions of employees of one or more political subdivisions of the State, or covers positions of employees of two or more political subdivisions of the State, then, for purposes of the preceding paragraphs of this subsection, there shall, if the State so desires, be deemed to be a separate retirement system with respect to any one or more of the political subdivisions concerned and, where the retirement system covers positions of employees of the State, a separate retirement system with respect to the State or with respect to the State and any one or more of the political subdivisions concerned. Where a retirement system covering positions of employees of a State and positions of employees of one or more political subdivisions of the State, or covering positions of employees of two or more political subdivisions of the State, is not divided into separate retirement systems pursuant to the preceding sentence or pursuant to subparagraph (C), then the State may, for purposes of subsection (e) only, deem the system to be a separate retirement system with respect to any one or more of the political subdivisions concerned and, where the retirement system covers positions of employees of the State, a separate retirement system with respect to the State or with respect to the State and any one or more of the political subdivisions concerned.

(B) If a retirement system covers positions of employees of one or more institutions of higher learning, then, for purposes of such preceding paragraphs there shall, if the State so desires, be deemed to be a separate retirement system for the employees of each such institution of higher learning. For the purposes of this subparagraph, the term "institutions of higher learning" includes junior colleges and teachers colleges. If a retirement system covers positions of employees of a hospital which is an integral part of a political subdivision, then, for purposes of the preceding paragraphs there shall, if the State so desires, be deemed to be a separate retirement system for the employees of such hospital.

(C) For the purposes of this subsection, any retirement system established by the State of Alaska, California, Connecticut, Florida, Georgia, Illinois, Kentucky, Louisiana, Massachusetts, Minnesota, Nevada, New Jersey, New Mexico, New York, North Dakota, Pennsylvania, Rhode Island, Tennessee, Texas, Vermont, Washington, Wisconsin, or Hawaii, or any political subdivision of any such State, which, on, before, or after August 1, 1956, is divided into two divisions or parts, one of which is composed of positions of members of such system who desire coverage under an agreement under this section and the other of which is composed of positions of members of such system who do not desire such coverage, shall, if the State so desires and if it is provided that there shall be included in such division or part composed of members desiring such coverage the positions of individuals who become members of such system after such coverage is extended, be deemed to be a separate retirement system with respect to each such division or part. If, in the case of a separate retirement system which is deemed to exist by reason of subparagraph (A) and which has been divided into two divisions or parts pursuant to the first sentence of this subparagraph, individuals become members of such system by reason of action taken by a political subdivision after coverage under an agreement under this section has been extended to the division or part thereof composed of positions of individuals who desire such coverage, the positions of such individuals who become members of such retirement system by reason of the action so taken shall be included in the division or part of such system composed of positions of members who do not desire such coverage if (i) such individuals, on the day before becoming such members, were in the division or part of another separate retirement system (deemed to exist by reason of subparagraph (A)) composed of positions of members of such system who do not desire coverage under an agreement under this section, and (ii) all of the positions in the separate retirement system of which such individuals so become members and all of the positions in the separate retirement system referred to in clause (i) would have been covered by a single retirement system if the State had not taken action to provide for separate retirement systems under this paragraph.

(D)(i) The position of any individual which is covered by any retirement system to which subparagraph (C) is applicable shall, if such individual is ineligible to become a member of such system on August 1, 1956, or, if later, the day he first occupies such position, be deemed to be covered by the separate retirement system consisting of the positions of members of the division or part who do not desire coverage under the insurance system established under this subchapter.

(ii) Notwithstanding clause (i), the State may, pursuant to subsection (c)(4)(B) and subject to the conditions of continuation or termination of coverage provided for in subsection (c)(7), modify its agreement under this section to include services performed by all individuals described in clause (i) other than those individuals to whose services the agreement already applies. Such individuals shall be deemed (on and after the effective date of the modification) to be in positions covered by the separate retirement system consisting of the positions of members of the division or part who desire coverage under the insurance system established under this subchapter.

(E) An individual who is in a position covered by a retirement system to which subparagraph (C) is applicable and who is not a member of such system but is eligible to become a member thereof shall, for purposes of this subsection (other than paragraph (8) of this subsection), be regarded as a member of such system; except that, in the case of any retirement system a division or part of which is covered under the agreement (either in the original agreement or by a modification thereof), which coverage is agreed to prior to 1960, the preceding provisions of this subparagraph shall apply only if the State so requests and any such individual referred to in such preceding provisions shall, if the State so requests, be treated, after division of the retirement system pursuant to such subparagraph (C), the same as individuals in positions referred to in subparagraph (F).

(F) In the case of any retirement system divided pursuant to subparagraph (C), the position of any member of the division or part composed of positions of members who do not desire coverage may be transferred to the separate retirement system composed of positions of members who desire such coverage if it is so provided in a modification of such agreement which is mailed, or delivered by other means, to the Commissioner of Social Security prior to 1970 or, if later, the expiration of two years after the date on which such agreement, or the modification thereof making the agreement applicable to such separate retirement system, as the case may be, is agreed to, but only if, prior to such modification or such later modification, as the case may be, the individual occupying such position files with the State a written request for such transfer. Notwithstanding subsection (e)(1), any such modification or later modification, providing for the transfer of additional positions within a retirement system previously divided pursuant to subparagraph (C) to the separate retirement system composed of positions of members who desire coverage, shall be effective with respect to services performed after the same effective date as that which was specified in the case of such previous division.

(G) For the purposes of this subsection, in the case of any retirement system of the State of Florida, Georgia, Minnesota, North Dakota, Pennsylvania, Washington, or Hawaii which covers positions of employees of such State who are compensated in whole or in part from grants made to such State under subchapter III, there shall be deemed to be, if such State so desires, a separate retirement system with respect to any of the following:

(i) the positions of such employees;

(ii) the positions of all employees of such State covered by such retirement system who are employed in the department of such State in which the employees referred to in clause (i) are employed; or

(iii) employees of such State covered by such retirement system who are employed in such department of such State in positions other than those referred to in clause (i).

(7) The certification by the governor (or an official of the State designated by him for the purpose) required under paragraph (3) of this subsection shall be deemed to have been made, in the case of a division or part (created under subparagraph (C) of paragraph (6) of this subsection or the corresponding provision of prior law) consisting of the positions of members of a retirement system who desire coverage under the agreement under this section, if the governor (or the official so designated) certifies to the Commissioner of Social Security that—

(A) an opportunity to vote by written ballot on the question of whether they wish to be covered under an agreement under this section was given to all individuals who were members of such system at the time the vote was held;

(B) not less than ninety days' notice of such vote was given to all individuals who were members of such system on the date the notice was issued;

(C) the vote was conducted under the supervision of the governor or an agency or individual designated by him; and

(D) such system was divided into two parts or divisions in accordance with the provisions of subparagraphs (C) and (D) of paragraph (6) of this subsection or the corresponding provision of prior law.

For purposes of this paragraph, an individual in a position to which the State agreement already applied or in a position excluded by or pursuant to paragraph (5) of this subsection shall not be considered a member of the retirement system.

(8)(A) Notwithstanding paragraph (1) of this subsection, if under the provisions of this subsection an agreement is, after December 31, 1958, made applicable to service performed in positions covered by a retirement system, service performed by an individual in a position covered by such a system may not be excluded from the agreement because such position is also covered under another retirement system.

(B) Subparagraph (A) shall not apply to service performed by an individual in a position covered under a retirement system if such individual, on the day the agreement is made applicable to service performed in positions covered by such retirement system, is not a member of such system and is a member of another system.

(C) If an agreement is made applicable, prior to 1959, to service in positions covered by any retirement system, the preceding provisions of this paragraph shall be applicable in the case of such system if the agreement is modified to so provide.

(D) Except in the case of State agreements modified as provided in subsection (*l*) and agreements with interstate instrumentalities, nothing in this paragraph shall authorize the application of an agreement to service in any policeman's or fireman's position.

(e) Effective date of agreement; retroactive coverage

(1) Any agreement or modification of an agreement under this section shall be effective with respect to services performed after an effective date specified in such agreement or modification; except that such date may not be earlier than the last day of the sixth calendar year preceding the year in which such agreement or modification, as the case may be, is mailed or delivered by other means to the Commissioner of Social Security.

(2) In the case of service performed by members of any coverage group—

(A) to which an agreement under this section is made applicable, and

(B) with respect to which the agreement, or modification thereof making the agreement so applicable, specifies an effective date earlier than the date of execution of such agreement and such modification, respectively,

the agreement shall, if so requested by the State, be applicable to such services (to the extent the agreement was not already applicable) performed before such date of execution and after such effective date by any individual as a member of such coverage group if he is such a member on a date, specified by the State, which is earlier than such date of execution, except that in no case may the date so specified be earlier than the date such agreement or such modification, as the case may be, is mailed, or delivered by other means, to the Commissioner of Social Security.

(3) Notwithstanding the provisions of paragraph (2) of this subsection, in the case of services performed by individuals as members of any coverage group to which an agreement under this section is made applicable, and with respect to which there were timely paid in good faith to the Secretary of the Treasury amounts equivalent to the sum of the taxes which would have been imposed by sections 3101 and 3111 of the Internal Revenue Code of 1986 had such services constituted employment for purposes of chapter 21 of such Code at the time they were performed, and with respect to which refunds were not obtained, such individuals may, if so requested by the State, be deemed to be members of such coverage group on the date designated pursuant to paragraph (2).

(f) Duration of agreement

No agreement under this section may be terminated, either in its entirety or with respect to any coverage group, on or after April 20, 1983.

(g) Instrumentalities of two or more States

(1) The Commissioner of Social Security may, at the request of any instrumentality of two or more States, enter into an agreement with such instrumentality for the purpose of extending the insurance system established by this subchapter to services performed by individuals as employees of such instrumentality. Such agreement, to the extent practicable, shall be governed by the provisions of this section applicable in the case of an agreement with a State.

(2) In the case of any instrumentality of two or more States, if—

(A) employees of such instrumentality are in positions covered by a retirement system of such instrumentality or of any of such States or any of the political subdivisions thereof, and

(B) such retirement system is (on, before, or after August 30, 1957) divided into two divisions or parts, one of which is composed of positions of members of such system who are employees of such instrumentality and who desire coverage under an agreement under this section and the other of which is composed of positions of members of such system who are employees of such instrumentality and who do not desire such coverage, and

(C) it is provided that there shall be included in such division or part composed of the positions of members desiring such coverage the positions of employees of such instrumentality who become members of such system after such coverage is extended,

then such retirement system shall, if such instrumentality so desires, be deemed to be a separate retirement system with respect to each such division or part. An individual who is in a position covered by a retirement system divided pursuant to the preceding sentence and who is not a member of such system but is eligible to become a member thereof shall, for purposes of this subsection, be regarded as a member of such system. Coverage under the agreement of any such individual shall be provided under the same conditions, to the extent practicable, as are applicable in the case of the States to which the provisions of subsection (d)(6)(C) apply. The position of any employee of any such instrumentality which is covered by any retirement system to which the first sentence of this paragraph is applicable shall, if such individual is ineligible to become a member of such system on August 30, 1957, or, if later, the day he first occupies such position, be deemed to be covered by the separate retirement system consisting of the positions of members of the division or part who do not desire coverage under the insurance system established under this subchapter. Services in positions covered by a separate retirement system created pursuant to this subsection (and consisting of the positions of members who desire coverage under an agreement under this section) shall be covered under such agreement on compliance, to the extent practicable, with the same conditions as are applicable to coverage under an agreement under this section of services in positions covered by a separate retirement system created pursuant to subparagraph (C) of subsection (d)(6) or the corresponding provision of prior law (and consisting of the positions of members who desire coverage under such agreement).

(3) Any agreement with any instrumentality of two or more States entered into pursuant to this chapter may, notwithstanding the provisions of subsection (d)(5)(A) and the references thereto in subsections (d)(1) and (d)(3), apply to service performed by employees of such instrumentality in any policeman's or fireman's position covered by a retirement system, but only upon compliance, to the extent practicable, with the requirements of subsection (d)(3). For the purpose of the preceding sentence, a retirement system which covers positions of policemen or firemen or both, and other positions shall, if the instrumentality concerned so desires, be deemed to be a separate retirement system with respect to the positions of such policemen or firemen, or both, as the case may be.

(h) Delegation of functions

The Commissioner of Social Security is authorized, pursuant to agreement with the head of any Federal agency, to delegate any of the Commissioner's functions under this section to any officer or employee of such agency and otherwise to utilize the services and facilities of such agency in carrying out such functions, and payment therefor shall be in advance or by way of reimbursement, as may be provided in such agreement.

(i) Wisconsin retirement fund

(1) Notwithstanding paragraph (1) of subsection (d), the agreement with the State of Wisconsin may, subject to the provisions of this subsection, be modified so as to apply to service performed by employees in positions covered by the Wisconsin retirement fund or any successor system.

(2) All employees in positions covered by the Wisconsin retirement fund at any time on or after January 1, 1951, shall, for the purposes of subsection (c) only, be deemed to be a separate coverage group; except that there shall be excluded from such separate coverage group all employees in positions to which the agreement applies without regard to this subsection.

(3) The modification pursuant to this subsection shall exclude (in the case of employees in the coverage group established by paragraph (2) of this subsection) service performed by any individual during any period before he is included under the Wisconsin retirement fund.

(4) The modification pursuant to this subsection shall, if the State of Wisconsin requests it, exclude (in the case of employees in the coverage group established by paragraph (2) of this subsection) all service

performed in policemen's positions, all service performed in firemen's positions, or both.

(j) Certain positions no longer covered by retirement systems

Notwithstanding subsection (d), an agreement with any State entered into under this section prior to September 1, 1954 may, prior to January 1, 1958, be modified pursuant to subsection (c)(4) so as to apply to services performed by employees, as members of any coverage group to which such agreement already applies (and to which such agreement applied on September 1, 1954), in positions (1) to which such agreement does not already apply, (2) which were covered by a retirement system on the date such agreement was made applicable to such coverage group, and (3) which, by reason of action by such State or political subdivision thereof, as may be appropriate, taken prior to September 1, 1954, are no longer covered by a retirement system on the date such agreement is made applicable to such services.

(k) Certain employees of State of Utah

Notwithstanding the provisions of subsection (d), the agreement with the State of Utah entered into pursuant to this section may be modified pursuant to subsection (c)(4) so as to apply to services performed for any of the following, the employees performing services for each of which shall constitute a separate coverage group: Weber Junior College, Carbon Junior College, Dixie Junior College, Central Utah Vocational School, Salt Lake Area Vocational School, Center for the Adult Blind, Union High School (Roosevelt, Utah), Utah High School Activities Association, State Industrial School, State Training School, State Board of Education, and Utah School Employees Retirement Board. Any modification agreed to prior to January 1, 1955, may be made effective with respect to services performed by employees as members of any of such coverage groups after an effective date specified therein, except that in no case may any such date be earlier than December 31, 1950. Coverage provided for in this subsection shall not be affected by a subsequent change in the name of a group.

(*l*) Policemen and firemen in certain States

Any agreement with a State entered into pursuant to this section may, notwithstanding the provisions of subsection (d)(5)(A) and the references thereto in subsections (d)(1) and (d)(3), be modified pursuant to subsection (c)(4) to apply to service performed by employees of such State or any political subdivision thereof in any policeman's or fireman's position covered by a retirement system in effect on or after August 1, 1956, but only upon compliance with the requirements of subsection (d)(3). For the purposes of the preceding sentence, a retirement system which covers positions of policemen or firemen, or both, and other positions shall, if the State concerned so desires, be deemed to be a separate retirement system with respect to the positions of such policemen or firemen, or both, as the case may be.

(m) Positions compensated solely on a fee basis

(1) Notwithstanding any other provision in this section, an agreement entered into under this section may be made applicable to service performed after 1967 in any class or classes of positions compensated solely on a fee basis to which such agreement did not apply prior to 1968 only if the State specifically requests that its agreement be made applicable to such service in such class or classes of positions.

(2) Notwithstanding any other provision in this section, an agreement entered into under this section may be modified, at the option of the State, at any time after 1967, so as to exclude services performed in any class or classes of positions compensation for which is solely on a fee basis.

(3) Any modification made under this subsection shall be effective with respect to services performed after the last day of the calendar year in which the modification is mailed or delivered by other means to the Commissioner of Social Security.

(4) If any class or classes of positions have been excluded from coverage under the State agreement by a modification agreed to under this subsection, the Commissioner of Social Security and the State may not thereafter modify such agreement so as to again make the agreement applicable with respect to such class or classes of positions.

(n) Optional medicare coverage of current employees

(1) The Commissioner of Social Security shall, at the request of any State, enter into or modify an agreement with such State under this section for the purpose of extending the provisions of subchapter XVIII, and sections 426 and 426–1 of this title, to services performed by employees of such State or any political subdivision thereof who are described in paragraph (2).

(2) This subsection shall apply only with respect to employees—

(A) whose services are not treated as employment as that term applies under section 410(p) of this title by reason of paragraph (3) of such section; and

(B) who are not otherwise covered under the State's agreement under this section.

(3) For purposes of sections 426 and 426–1 of this title, services covered under an agreement pursuant to this subsection shall be treated as "medicare qualified government employment".

(4) Except as otherwise provided in this subsection, the provisions of this section shall apply with respect to services covered under the agreement pursuant to this subsection.

(Aug. 14, 1935, c. 531, Title II, § 218, as added Aug. 28, 1950, c. 809, Title I, § 106, 64 Stat. 514; amended June 28, 1952, c. 483, 66 Stat. 285; Aug. 15, 1953, c. 504, § 1, 67 Stat. 587; Sept. 1, 1954, c. 1206, Title I, § 101(a)(5), (6), (h)(1) to (8), (i)(1), (2), (j), 68 Stat. 1055 to 1059; Aug. 1, 1956, c. 836, Title I, §§ 103(f), (g), 104(e), (g), 70 Stat. 823, 825, 826; Pub.L. 85–226, Aug. 30, 1957, 71 Stat. 511; Pub.L. 85–227, § 1, Aug. 30, 1957, 71 Stat. 512; Pub.L. 85–229, Aug. 30, 1957, 71 Stat. 513; Pub.L. 85–787, §§ 1, 2, Aug. 27, 1958, 72 Stat. 939; Pub.L. 85–798, §§ 2, 3, Aug. 28, 1958, 72 Stat. 964, 965; Pub.L. 85–840, Title III, § 315(a) to (c)(1), Aug. 28, 1958, 72 Stat. 1038 to 1040; Pub.L. 86–284, § 2, Sept. 16, 1959, 73 Stat. 566; Pub.L. 86–624, § 30(e), (f), July 12, 1960, 74 Stat. 420; Pub.L. 86–778, Title I, §§ 102(a), (b)(1), (c)(1), (2), (d), (e), (f)(1), (g), (*l*), 103(i), (j)(2)(G), Sept. 13, 1960, 74 Stat. 928 to 930, 934, 936 to 938; Pub.L. 87–64, Title I, §§ 106, 107, June 30, 1961, 75 Stat. 139, 140; Pub.L. 87–878, § 2, Oct. 24, 1962, 76 Stat. 1202; Pub.L. 88–350, § 2, July 2, 1964, 78 Stat. 240; Pub.L. 88–382, July 23, 1964, 78 Stat. 335; Pub.L. 89–97, Title I, § 108(b), Title III, §§ 314, 315, July 30, 1965, 79 Stat. 338, 385; Pub.L. 90–248, Title I, §§ 116(a) to (b)(2), (c), (d), 117, 119(a), 120(a), 121, 122(d), Jan. 2, 1968, 81 Stat. 840 to 844; Pub.L. 90–486, § 7, Aug. 13, 1968, 82 Stat. 759; Pub.L. 92–603, Title I, § 126, Oct. 30, 1972, 86 Stat. 1358; Priv.L. 93–107, § 2, Dec. 31, 1974, 88 Stat. 2386; Pub.L. 95–216, Title III, §§ 319 to 321, 353(b), Dec. 20, 1977, 91 Stat. 1541, 1553; Pub.L. 96–265, Title V, § 503(a), June 9, 1980, 94 Stat. 470; Pub.L. 98–21, Title I, § 103(a), Title III, §§ 325(a), 342(a), Apr. 20, 1983, 97 Stat. 71, 126, 136; Pub.L. 98–369, Div. B, Title VI, § 2663(a)(13), (j)(2)(A)(ii), (3)(A)(iii), July 18, 1984, 98 Stat. 1164, 1170; Pub.L. 99–272, Title XII, § 12110(a), (b), Title XIII, § 13205(c), Apr. 7, 1986, 100 Stat. 287, 317; Pub.L. 99–509, Title IX, § 9002(c)(1), (2)(C) to (E), Oct. 21, 1986, 100 Stat. 1971, 1972; Pub.L. 99–514, Title XVIII, § 1883(a)(8), Oct. 22, 1986, 100 Stat. 2916; Pub.L. 100–203, Title IV, § 4009(j)(7), Title IX, § 9023(c), Dec. 22, 1987, 101 Stat. 1330–59, 1330–296; Pub.L. 101–239, Title X, § 10208(d)(2)(A)(v), Dec. 19, 1989, 103 Stat. 2481; Pub.L. 101–508, Title XI, § 11332(c), Nov. 5, 1990, 104 Stat. 1388–470; Pub.L. 103–296, Title I, § 107(a)(4), Title III, §§ 303(c), (d), 305(a), (b), 321(a)(18), (c)(6)(I), Aug. 15, 1994, 108 Stat. 1478, 1519, 1521, 1537, 1538; Pub.L. 108–203, Title IV, § 416(a), Mar. 2, 2004, 118 Stat. 530.)

HISTORICAL AND STATUTORY NOTES

References in Text

This subchapter, referred to in text, originally read "this title", meaning the Social Security Act, Aug. 14, 1935, c. 531, Title II, 49 Stat. 622, as amended, which is classified as this subchapter, 42 U.S.C.A. § 401 et seq.

Section 6 of the National Guard Technicians Act of 1968, referred to in subsec. (b)(5), is section 6 of Pub.L. 90–486, which is set out as a note under section 709 of Title 32, National Guard.

The Internal Revenue Code of 1986, referred to in subsec. (e)(3), is classified to 26 U.S.C.A. § 1 et seq.

Codifications

Amendment by Pub.L. 100–203, Title IV, § 4009(j)(7), repealed par. (3) of subsec. (v) without reference to subsequent transfer of subsec. (v) to subsec. (n) and accompanying repeal of par. (3).

Effective and Applicability Provisions

2004 Acts. Pub.L. 108–203, Title IV, § 416(b), Mar. 2, 2004, 118 Stat. 530, provided that: "The amendment made by subsection (a) [amending this section] takes effect on January 1, 2003."

1994 Acts. Amendment by section 107(a)(4) of Pub.L. 103–296 effective Mar. 31, 1995, see section 110 of Pub.L. 103–296, set out as a note under section 401 of this title.

Amendment of subsec. (c)(8) by section 303(c) of Pub.L. 103–296, applicable with respect to service performed on or after Jan. 1, 1995, see section 303(e) of Pub.L. 103–296, set out as a note under section 410 of this title.

Section 305(c) of Pub.L. 103–296 provided that: "The amendments made by this section [amending subsecs. (d) and (*l*) of this section] shall apply with respect to modifications filed by States after the date of the enactment of this Act [Aug. 15, 1994]."

1990 Acts. Amendment by Pub.L. 101–508 applicable with respect to service performed after July 1, 1991, see section 11332(d) of Pub.L. 101–508, set out as a note under section 3121 of Title 26, Internal Revenue Code.

1986 Acts. Amendment by Pub.L. 99–514 effective Oct. 22, 1986, see section 1883(f) of Pub.L. 99–514, set out as a note under section 402 of this title.

Section 9002(d) of Pub.L. 99–509 provided that: "The amendments made by this section [enacting section 3126 of Title 26, Internal Revenue Code; amending this section and sections 405 and 424a of this title, and sections 1402, 3121, 3128, and 3306 of Title 26] are effective with respect to payments due with respect to wages paid after December 31, 1986, including wages paid after such date by a State (or political subdivision thereof) that modified its agreement pursuant to the provisions of section 218(e)(2) of the Social Security Act [subsec. (e)(2) of this section] prior to the date of the enactment of this Act [Oct. 21, 1986]; except that in cases where, in accordance with the currently applicable schedule, deposits of taxes due under an agreement entered into pursuant to section 218 of the Social Security Act [this section] would be required within 3 days after the close of an eighth-monthly period, such 3-day requirement shall be changed to a 7-day requirement for wages paid prior to October 1, 1987, and to a 5-day requirement for wages paid after September 30, 1987, and prior to October 1, 1988. For wages paid prior to October 1, 1988, the deposit schedule for taxes imposed under sections 3101 and 3111 shall be determined separately from the deposit schedule for taxes withheld under section 3402 [section 3402 of Title 26] if the taxes imposed under sections 3101 and 3111 [sections 3101 and 3111 of Title 26] are due with respect to service included under an agreement entered into pursuant to section 218 of the Social Security Act [this section]."

Section 12110(c) of Pub.L. 99–272 provided that: "The amendments made by this section [amending subsecs. (f)(1), (v)(3) of this section] shall apply with respect to agreements and modifications of agreements which are mailed or delivered to the Secretary of Health and Human Services (under section 218 of the Social Security Act [this section] on or after the date of the enactment of this Act [Apr. 7, 1986]."

Section 13205(d)(3) of Pub.L. 99–272 provided that: "The amendment made by subsection (c) [amending this section] shall apply to services performed after March 31, 1986."

1984 Acts. Amendment by Pub.L. 98–369 effective July 18, 1984, but not to be construed as changing or affecting any right, liability, status or interpretation which existed (under the provisions of law involved) before that date, see section 2664(b) of Pub.L. 98–369, set out as a note under section 401 of this title.

1983 Acts. Section 103(b) of Pub.L. 98–21 provided that: "The amendment made by subsection (a) [amending subsec. (g) of this section] shall apply to any agreement in effect under section 218 of the Social Security Act [this section] on the date of the enactment of this Act [April 20, 1983], without regard to whether a notice of termination is in effect on such date, and to any agreement or modification thereof which may become effective under such section 218 [this section] after that date."

Section 325(b) of Pub.L. 98–21 provided that: "The amendment made by subsection (a) [amending subsec. (*o*) of this section] shall apply with respect to name changes made before, on, or after the date of the enactment of this section [Apr. 20, 1983]."

Section 342(b) of Pub.L. 98–21 provided that: "The amendments made by this section [amending subsec. (e)(1)(A) of this section] shall apply to calendar months beginning after December 31, 1983."

1980 Acts. Section 503(b) of Pub.L. 96–265 provided that: "The amendment made by subsection (a) [amending this section] shall be effective with respect to the payment of taxes (referred to in section 218(e)(1)(A) of the Social Security Act [subsec. (e)(1)(A) of this section], as amended by subsection (a)) on account of wages paid on or after July 1, 1980."

1977 Acts. Section 353(g) of Pub.L. 95–216 provided that: "The amendments made by subsection (b) of this section [amending subsecs. (c)(8), (q)(4)(B), (6)(B) and (r)(1) of this section] shall apply with respect to remuneration paid after December 31, 1977, except that the amendment made by subsection (b)(2) [amending subsec. (g)(1) of this section] shall apply with respect to notices submitted by the States to the Secretary after the date of the enactment of this Act [Dec. 20, 1977]. The amendments made by subsections (d) [amending section 429(a) of this title] and (f)(2) [amending section 405(c)(1) of this title] shall be effective January 1, 1978. Except as otherwise specifically provided, the remaining amendments made by this section [amending sections 403(f)(8)(B)(i), (ii), 424a(f)(2), and 430(b) of this title] shall be effective January 1, 1979."

1968 Acts. Amendment by Pub.L. 90–486 effective Jan. 1, 1969, except that no deductions or withholding from salary which result therefrom shall commence before the first day of the first pay period that begins on or after Jan. 1, 1969, see section 11 of Pub.L. 90–486, set out as a note under section 709 of Title 32, National Guard.

Section 116(b)(3) of Pub.L. 90–248 provided that: "The amendments made by this subsection [to subsecs. (c)(3), (4), (6), (7), (d)(4)(C), (5)(B) of this section] shall be effective with respect to services performed on or after January 1, 1968."

Section 120(c) of Pub.L. 90–248 provided that: "The amendment made by this section [to subsec. (p) of this section] shall apply in the case of any State with respect to modifications of such State agreement under section 218 of the Social Security Act [this section] made after the date of enactment of this Act [Jan. 2, 1968]."

1961 Acts. Amendment by Pub.L. 87–64 effective Aug. 1, 1961, see section 109 of Pub.L. 87–64, set out as a note under section 402 of this title.

1960 Acts. Section 102(b)(2) of Pub.L. 86–778 provided that: "The amendment made by paragraph (1) [to subsec. (d)(6)(C) of this section] shall apply in the case of transfers of positions (as described therein) which occur on or after the date of enactment of this Act [Sept. 13, 1960]. Such amendment shall also apply in the case of such transfers in any State which occurred prior to such date, but only upon request of the Governor (or other official designated by him for the purpose) filed with the Secretary of Health, Education, and Welfare [now Secretary of Health and Human Services] before July 1, 1961; and, in the case of any such request, such amendment shall apply only with respect to wages paid on and after the date on which such request is filed."

Section 102(c)(3) of Pub.L. 86–778 provided that: "The amendment made by paragraph (1) [to subsec. (f)(1) of this section] shall apply in the case of any agreement or modification of an agreement under section 218 of the Social Security Act [this section] which is agreed to on or after January 1, 1960; except that in the case of any such agreement or modification agreed to before January 1, 1961, the effective date specified therein shall not be earlier than December 31, 1955. The amendment made by paragraph (2) [to subsec. (d)(6)(A) of this section] shall apply in the case of any such agreement or modification which is agreed to on or after the date of the enactment of this Act [Sept. 13, 1960]."

Section 102(f)(3) of Pub.L. 86–778 provided that:

"**(A)** The amendments made by paragraphs (1) and (2) [adding subsecs. (q) to (t) of this section and amending subsec. (c)(5)(F) of section 405 of this title] shall become effective on the first day of the second calendar year following the year in which this Act is enacted [1960].

"**(B)** In any case in which the Secretary of Health, Education, and Welfare [now Secretary of Health and Human Services] has notified a State prior to the beginning of such second calendar year that there is an amount due by such State, that such State's claim for a credit or refund of an overpayment is disallowed, or that such State has been allowed a credit or refund of an overpayment, under an agreement pursuant to section 218 of the Social Security Act [this section], then the Secretary shall be deemed to have made an assessment of such amount due as provided in section 218(q) of such Act [subsec. (q) of this section] or notified the State of such allowance or disallowance, as the case may be, on the first day of such second calendar year. In such a case the 90-day limitation in section 218(s) of such Act [subsec. (s) of this section] shall not be applicable with respect to the assessment so deemed to have been made or the notification of allowance or disallowance so deemed to have been given the State. However, the preceding sentences of this subparagraph shall not apply if the Secretary makes an assessment of such amount due or notifies the State of such allowance or disallowance on or after the first day of the second calendar year following the year in which this Act is enacted [1960] and within the period specified in section 218(q) of the Social Security Act [subsec. (q) of this section] or the period specified in section 218(r) of such Act [subsec. (r) of this section], as the case may be."

Amendment of subsec. (b)(1) by Pub.L. 86–778 applicable only with respect to service performed after 1960, see section 103(v)(1) of Pub.L. 86–778, set out as a note under section 402 of this title.

Amendment of subsec. (c)(6)(C) by Pub.L. 86–778 effective Sept. 13, 1960, see section 103(v)(1) of Pub.L. 86–778, set out as a note under section 402 of this title.

1958 Acts. Section 315(c)(2) of Pub.L. 85–840 provided that: "The amendment made by this subsection [to subsec. (f) of this section] shall apply in the case of any agreement, or modification of an agreement, under section 218 of the Social Security Act [this section], which is executed after the date of enactment of this Act [August 28, 1958]."

1954 Acts. Section 101(h)(9) of Act Sept. 1, 1954 provided that: "The amendments made by this subsection, other than paragraph (1)(B) [amending this section], shall take effect January 1, 1955."

Section 101(i)(1) of Act Sept. 1, 1954, which added a new sentence, relating to civilian employees of State National Guard units, to subsec. (b)(5) provided that the amendment shall be effective as of Jan. 1, 1951.

Section 101(i)(2) of Act Sept. 1, 1954, which added to subsec. (b)(5) provisions relating to certain State inspectors of agricultural products, provided in part that the amendment shall be effective as of Jan. 1, 1955.

Section 101(i)(3) of Act Sept. 1, 1954 provided that: "In the case of any coverage group to which the amendment made by paragraph (1) [to subsec. (b)(5) of this section] is applicable, any agreement or modification of an agreement agreed to prior to January 1, 1956, may, notwithstanding section 218(f) of the Social Security Act [subsec. (f) of this section], be made effective with respect to services performed by employees as members of such coverage group after any effective date specified therein, but in no case may such effective date be earlier than December 31, 1950."

Section 101(j) of Act Sept. 1, 1954, which added subsec. (*o*), provided in part that it shall be effective Jan. 1, 1951.

Section 101(n) of Act Sept. 1, 1954 provided in part that the amendments to subsecs. (c)(5) and (c)(6)(D) by section 101(a)(5), (6) of Act Sept. 1, 1954 shall be applicable only with respect to services (whether performed after 1954 or prior to 1955) for which the remuneration is paid after 1954, see section 101(n) of Act Sept. 1, 1954, set out as a note under section 405 of this title.

1953 Acts. Section 2 of Act Aug. 15, 1953 provided that: "For the purposes of section 418(f) of the Social Security Act (relating to effective date of agreements) [subsec. (f) of this section], the amendment made by the first section of this Act [amending this section] shall take effect as of January 1, 1951."

Transfer of Functions

All functions of the Federal Security Administrator were transferred to the Secretary of Health, Education, and Welfare [now Secretary of Health and Human Services] and all agencies of the Federal Security Agency were transferred to the Department of Health, Education and Welfare [now Department of Health and Human Services] by section 5 of Reorg. Plan No. 1 of 1953, set out as a note under section 3501 of this title. The Federal Security Agency and the office of Administrator were abolished by section 8 of Reorg. Plan No. 1 of 1953. The Secretary and Department of Health, Education, and Welfare were redesignated the Secretary and Department of Health and Human Services by section 509(b) of Pub.L. 96–88 which is classified to section 3508(b) of Title 20, Education.

Exemption for Students Employed by State Schools, Colleges, or Universities

Pub.L. 105–277, Div. J, Title II, § 2023, Oct. 21, 1998, 112 Stat. 2681–904, provided that:

"(a) In general.—Notwithstanding section 218 of the Social Security Act [this section], any agreement with a State (or any modification thereof) entered into pursuant to such section may, at the option of such State, be modified at any time on or after January 1, 1999, and on or before March 31, 1999, so as to exclude service performed in the employ of a school, college, or university if such service is performed by a student who is enrolled and is regularly attending classes at such school, college, or university.

"(b) Effective date of modification.—Any modification of an agreement pursuant to subsection (a) [of this note] shall be effective with respect to services performed after June 30, 2000.

"(c) Irrevocability of modification.—If any modification of an agreement pursuant to subsection (a) [of this note] terminates coverage with respect to service performed in the employ of a school, college, or university, by a student who is enrolled and regularly attending classes at such school, college, or university, the Commissioner of Social Security and the State may not thereafter modify such agreement so as to again make the agreement applicable to such service performed in the employ of such school, college, or university."

Extension of Coverage to Service in Firemen's Position

Section 120(b) of Pub.L. 90–248 provided that: "Nothing in the amendments made by subsection (a) [to subsec. (p) of this section] shall authorize the extension of the insurance system established by title II of the Social Security Act [this subchapter] under the provisions of section 218(d)(6)(C) of such Act [subsec. (d)(6)(C) of this section] to service in any fireman's position."

Modification of Agreement With Connecticut to Provide Coverage for Connecticut State Police

Section 12114 of Pub.L. 99–272 provided that: "Notwithstanding any provision of section 218 of the Social Security Act [this section], the Secretary of Health and Human Services shall, upon the request of the Governor of Connecticut, modify the agreement under such section between the Secretary and the State of Connecticut to provide that service performed after the date of the enactment of this Act [Apr. 7, 1986] by members of the Division of the State Police within the Connecticut Department of Public Safety, who are hired on or after May 8, 1984, and who are members of the tier II plan of the Connecticut State Employees Retirement System, shall be covered under such agreement."

Modification of Agreement With Illinois to Provide Coverage for Certain Policemen and Firemen

Section 318 of Pub.L. 95–216 provided that the agreement with the State of Illinois entered into pursuant to this section could, at any time prior to Jan. 1, 1979, be modified pursuant to subsec. (c)(4) of this section so as to apply to services performed in the policemen's or firemen's positions covered by the Illinois Municipal Retirement Fund on Dec. 20, 1977, if the State of Illinois had prior to such date paid to the Secretary of the Treasury, with respect to any of the services performed in such positions, the sums prescribed pursuant to subsec. (e)(1) of this section.

Modification of Agreement With Iowa to Provide Coverage for Certain Policemen and Firemen

Section 9008 of Pub.L. 100–203 provided that:

"(a) In general.—Notwithstanding subsection (d)(5)(A) of section 218 of the Social Security Act [subsec. (d)(5)(A) of this section] and the references thereto in subsections (d)(1) and (d)(3) of such section 218 [subsecs. (d)(1) and (d)(3) of this section], the agreement with the State of Iowa heretofore entered into pursuant to such section 218 [this section] may, at any time prior to January 1, 1989, be modified pursuant to subsection (c)(4) of such section 218 [subsec. (c)(4) of this section] so as to apply to services performed in policemen's or firemen's positions required to be covered by a retirement system pursuant to section 410.1 of the Iowa Code as in effect on July 1, 1953, if the State of Iowa has at any time prior to the date of the enactment of this Act paid to the Secretary of the Treasury, with respect to any of the services performed in such positions, the sums prescribed pursuant to subsection (e)(1) of such section 218 [subsec. (e)(1) of this section] (as in effect on December 31, 1986, with respect to payments due with respect to wages paid on or before such date).

"**(b) Service to be covered.**—Notwithstanding the provisions of subsection (e) of section 218 of the Social Security Act (as so redesignated by section 9002(c)(1) of the Omnibus Budget Reconciliation Act of 1986)) [subsec. (e) of this section], any modification in the agreement with the State of Iowa under subsection (a) shall be made effective with respect to—

"**(1)** all services performed in any policemen's or firemen's position to which the modification relates on or after January 1, 1987, and

"**(2)** all services performed in such a position before January 1, 1987, with respect to which the State of Iowa has paid to the Secretary of the Treasury the sums prescribed pursuant to subsection (e)(1) of such section 218 [subsec. (e)(1) of this section] (as in effect on December 31, 1986, with respect to payments due with respect to wages paid on or before such date) at the time or times established pursuant to such subsection (e)(1) [subsec. (e)(1) of this section], if and to the extent that—

"**(A)** no refund of the sums so paid has been obtained, or

"**(B)** a refund of part or all of the sums so paid has been obtained but the State of Iowa repays to the Secretary of the Treasury the amount of such refund within 90 days after the date on which the modification is agreed to by the State and the Secretary of Health and Human Services."

Modification of Agreement With Louisiana With Respect to Voter Registrars

Section 139 of Pub.L. 92–603 provided that:

"**(a)** Notwithstanding the provisions of section 218(g)(1) of the Social Security Act [subsec. (g)(1) of this section], the Secretary may, under such conditions as he deems appropriate, permit the State of Louisiana to modify its agreement entered into under section 218 of such Act [this section] so as to terminate the coverage of all employees who are in positions under the Registrars of Voters Employees' Retirement System, effective after December 1975, but only if such State files with him notice of termination on or before December 31, 1973.

"**(b)** If the coverage of such employees in positions under such retirement system is terminated pursuant to subsection (a), coverage cannot later be extended to employees in positions under such retirement system."

Modification of Agreement With Massachusetts With Respect to Employees of Massachusetts Turnpike Authority

Section 124 of Pub.L. 90–248 provided that:

"**(a)** Notwithstanding the provisions of section 218(g)(1) of the Social Security Act [subsec. (g)(1) of this section] the Secretary may, under such conditions as he deems appropriate, permit the State of Massachusetts to modify its agreement entered into under section 218 of such Act [this section] so as to terminate the coverage of the employees of the Massachusetts Turnpike Authority effective at the end of any calendar quarter within the two years next following the date on which such agreement is so modified.

"**(b)** If the coverage of employees of the Massachusetts Turnpike Authority is terminated pursuant to subsection (a), coverage cannot later be extended to the employees of such Authority."

Modification of Agreements With North Dakota and Iowa With Respect to Certain Students

Section 338 of Pub.L. 89–97 provided that: "Notwithstanding any provision of section 218 of the Social Security Act [this section], the agreements with the States of North Dakota and Iowa entered into pursuant to such section may, at the option of the State, be modified so as to exclude service performed in any calendar quarter in the employ of a school, college, or university if such service is performed by a student who is enrolled and is regularly attending classes at such school, college, or university and if the remuneration for such service is less than $50. Any modification of either of such agreements pursuant to this Act shall be effective with respect to services performed after an effective date specified in such modification, except that such date shall not be earlier than the date of enactment of this Act [July 30, 1965]."

Modification of Agreement With State of Nebraska for Exclusion of Services Performed by Justices of the Peace and Constables

Section 102(i) of Pub.L. 86–778 provided that: "Notwithstanding any provision of section 218 of the Social Security Act [this section], the agreement with the State of Nebraska entered into pursuant to such section may, at the option of such State, be modified so as to exclude services performed within such State by individuals as justices of the peace or constables, if such individuals are compensated for such services on a fee basis. Any modification of such agreement pursuant to this subsection shall be effective with respect to services performed after an effective date specified in such modification, except that such date shall not be earlier than the date of enactment of this Act [Sept. 13, 1960]."

Modification of Agreements With States With Respect to Certain Students and Part-Time Employees

Section 141 of Pub.L. 92–603 provided that:

"**(a)** Notwithstanding any provision of section 218 of the Social Security Act [this section], the agreement with any State (or any modifications thereof) entered into pursuant to such section may, at the option of such State, be modified at any time prior to January 1, 1974, so as to exclude either or both of the following:

"**(1)** service in any class or classes of part-time positions; or

"**(2)** service performed in the employ of a school, college, or university if such service is performed by a student who is enrolled and is regularly attending classes at such school, college, or university.

"(b) Any modification of such agreement pursuant to this section shall be effective with respect to services performed after the end of the calendar quarter following the calendar quarter in which such agreement is modified.

"(c) If any such modification terminates coverage with respect to service in any class or classes of part-time positions in any coverage group, the Secretary of Health, Education, and Welfare [now Secretary of Health and Human Services] and the State may not thereafter modify such agreement so as to again make the agreement applicable to service in such positions in such coverage group; if such modification terminates coverage with respect to service performed in the employ of a school, college, or university, by a student who is enrolled and regularly attending classes at such school, college, or university, the Secretary of Health, Education, and Welfare [now Secretary of Health and Human Services] and the State may not thereafter modify such agreement so as to again make the agreement applicable to such service performed in the employ of such school, college, or university."

Modification of Agreement With West Virginia With Respect to Certain Policemen and Firemen

Pub.L. 94–202, § 6, Jan. 2, 1976, 89 Stat. 1136, provided that:

"(a) Notwithstanding the provisions of subsection (d)(5)(A) of section 218 of the Social Security Act [subsec. (d)(5)(A) of this section] and the references thereto in subsections (d)(1) and (d)(3) of such section 218 [subsec. (d)(1) and (d)(3) of this section], the agreement with the State of West Virginia heretofore entered into pursuant to such section 218 [this section] may, at any time prior to 1977, be modified pursuant to subsection (c)(4) of such section 218 [subsec. (c)(4) of this section] so as to apply to services performed in policemen's or firemen's positions covered by a retirement system on the date of the enactment of this Act [Jan. 2, 1976] by individuals as employees of any class III or class IV municipal corporation (as defined in or under the laws of the State) if the State of West Virginia has at any time prior to the date of the enactment of this Act [Jan. 2, 1976] paid to the Secretary of the Treasury, with respect to any of the services performed in such positions by individuals as employees of such municipal corporation, the sums prescribed pursuant to subsection (e)(1) of such section 218 [subsec. (e)(1) of this section]. For purposes of this subsection, a retirement system which covers positions of policemen or firemen, or both, and other positions, shall, if the State of West Virginia so desires, be deemed to be a separate retirement system with respect to the positions of such policemen or firemen, or both, as the case may be.

"(b) Notwithstanding the provisions of subsection (f) of section 218 of the Social Security Act [subsec. (f) of this section], any modification in the agreement with the State of West Virginia under subsection (a) of this section, to the extent it involves services performed by individuals as employees of any class III or class IV municipal corporation, may be made effective with respect to—

"(1) all services performed by such individual, in any policemen's or firemen's position to which the modification relates, on or after the date of the enactment of this Act [Jan. 2, 1976]; and

"(2) all services performed by such individual in such a position before such date of enactment [Jan. 2, 1976] with respect to which the State of West Virginia has paid to the Secretary of the Treasury the sums prescribed pursuant to subsection (e)(1) of such section 218 [subsec. (e)(1) of this section] at the time or times established pursuant to such subsection (e)(1) [subsec. (e)(1) of this section], if and to the extent that—

"(A) no refund of the sums so paid has been obtained, or

"(B) a refund of part or all of the sums so paid has been obtained but the State of West Virginia repays to the Secretary of the Treasury the amount of such refund within ninety days after the date that the modification is agreed to by the State and the Secretary of Health, Education, and Welfare [now Secretary of Health and Human Services]."

Section 143 of Pub.L. 92–603 provided that:

"(a) Notwithstanding the provisions of subsection (d)(5)(A) of section 218 of the Social Security Act [subsec. (d)(5)(A) of this section] and the references thereto in subsections (d)(1) and (d)(3) of such section 218 [subsecs. (d)(1) and (d)(3) of this section], the agreement with the State of West Virginia heretofore entered into pursuant to such section 218 [this section] may, at any time prior to 1974, be modified pursuant to subsection (c)(4) of such section 218 [subsec. (c)(4) of this section] so as to apply to services performed in policemen's or firemen's positions covered by a retirement system on the date of the enactment of this Act [Oct. 30, 1972] by individuals as employees of any class III or class IV municipal corporation (as defined in or under the laws of the State) if the State of West Virginia has at any time prior to the date of the enactment of this Act [Oct. 30, 1972] paid to the Secretary of the Treasury, with respect to any of the services performed in such positions by individuals as employees of such municipal corporation, the sums prescribed pursuant to subsection (e)(1) of such section 218 [subsec. (e)(1) of this section]. For purposes of this subsection, a retirement system which covers positions of policemen or firemen, or both, and other positions, shall, if the State of West Virginia so desires, be deemed to be a separate retirement system with respect to the positions of such policemen or firemen, or both, as the case may be.

"(b) Notwithstanding the provisions of subsection (f) of section 218 of the Social Security Act [subsec. (f) of this section], any modification in the agreement with the State of West Virginia under subsection (a) of this section, to the extent it involves services performed by individuals as employees of any class III or class IV municipal corporation, may be made effective with respect to—

"(1) all services performed by such individual, in any policeman's or fireman's position to which the modification relates, on or after the date of the enactment of this Act [Oct. 30, 1972]; and

"(2) all services performed by such individual in such a position before such date of enactment [Oct. 30, 1972] with respect to which the State of West Virginia has paid to the Secretary of the Treasury the sums prescribed pursuant to subsection (e)(1) of such section 218 [subsec. (e)(1) of this section] at the time or times established pursuant to such subsection (e)(1), if and to the extent that—

"(A) no refund of the sums so paid has been obtained, or

"(B) a refund of part or all of the sums so paid has been obtained but the State of West Virginia repays to the Secretary of the Treasury the amount of such refund within ninety days after the date that the modification is agreed to by the State and the Secretary of Health,

Education, and Welfare [now Secretary of Health and Human Services]."

Modification of Existing Agreement With New Mexico to Cover Certain Hospital Employees

Section 127 of Pub.L. 92–603 provided that: "Notwithstanding any provisions of section 218 of the Social Security Act [this section], the Agreement with the State of New Mexico heretofore entered into pursuant to such section may at the option of such State be modified at any time prior to the first day of the fourth month after the month in which this Act is enacted [Oct. 1972], so as to apply to the services of employees of a hospital which is an integral part of a political subdivision to which an agreement under this section has not been made applicable, as a separate coverage group within the meaning of section 218(b)(5) of such Act [subsec. (b)(5) of this section], but only if such hospital has prior to 1966 withdrawn from a retirement system which had been applicable to the employees of such hospital."

Modification of Existing Agreement With State of Arizona Prior to January 1, 1956

Section 101(k) of Act Sept. 1, 1954, provided that: "If, prior to January 1, 1956, the agreement with the State of Arizona entered into pursuant to section 218 of the Social Security Act [this section] is modified pursuant to subsection (d)(3) of such section so as to apply to service performed by employees in positions covered by the Arizona Teachers' Retirement System the modification may, notwithstanding section 218(f) of the Social Security Act [subsec. (f) of this section], be made effective with respect to service performed in such positions after an effective date specified in the modification, but in no case may such effective date be earlier than December 31, 1950. For the purposes of any such modification, all employees in positions covered by the Arizona Teachers' Retirement System shall be deemed, notwithstanding the provisions of section 218(d)(6) of such Act [subsec. (d)(6) of this section], to constitute a separate coverage group."

Modification of Existing Agreement With State of California Prior to February 1966

Section 102(k) of Pub.L. 86–778, as amended by Pub.L. 89–97, Title III, § 318, July 30, 1965, 79 Stat. 390, provided that:

"(1) Notwithstanding any provision of section 218 of the Social Security Act [this section], the agreement with the State of California heretofore entered into pursuant to such section may at the option of such State be modified, at any time prior to 1962, pursuant to subsection (c)(4) of such section 218 [subsec. (c)(4) of this section], so as to apply to services performed by any individual who, on or after January 1, 1957, and on or before December 31, 1959, was employed by such State (or any political subdivision thereof) in any hospital employee's position which, on September 1, 1954, was covered by a retirement system, but which, prior to 1960, was removed from coverage by such retirement system if, prior to July 1, 1960, there have been paid in good faith to the Secretary of the Treasury, with respect to any of the services performed by such individual in any such position, amounts equivalent to the sum of the taxes which would have been imposed by sections 3101 and 3111 of the Internal Revenue Code of 1954 (now 1986) [sections 3101 and 3111 of Title 26, Internal Revenue Code] if such services had constituted employment for purposes of chapter 21 of such Code [section 3101 et seq. of Title 26] at the time they were performed. Notwithstanding the provisions of subsection (f) of such section 218 [subsec. (f) of this section] such modification shall be effective with respect to (1) all services performed by such individual in any such position on or after January 1, 1960, and (2) all such services, performed before such date, with respect to which amounts equivalent to such taxes have, prior to the date of enactment of this subsection [Sept. 13, 1960], been paid.

"(2) Such agreement, as modified pursuant to paragraph (1), may at the option of such State be further modified, at any time prior to the seventh month after the month [July, 1965] in which this paragraph is enacted, so as to apply to services performed for any hospital affected by such earlier modification by any individual who after December 31, 1959, is or was employed by such State (or any political subdivision thereof) in any position described in paragraph (1). Such modification shall be effective with respect to (A) all services performed by such individual in any such position on or after January 1, 1962, and (B) all such services, performed before such date, with respect to which amounts equivalent to the sum of the taxes which would have been imposed by sections 3101 and 3111 of the Internal Revenue Code of 1954 (now 1986) [sections 3101 and 3111 of Title 26] if such services had constituted employment for purposes of chapter 21 of such Code at the time they were performed have, prior to the date of the enactment of this paragraph [July 30, 1965], been paid."

Modification of Existing Agreements With States of California, Connecticut, Minnesota, or Rhode Island Prior to 1960

Section 2 of Pub.L. 85–227 provided that: "Notwithstanding subsection (f) of section 218 of the Social Security Act [subsec. (f) of this section], any modification of the agreement with the State of California, Connecticut, Minnesota, or Rhode Island under such section which makes such agreement applicable to services performed in positions covered by a separate retirement system created pursuant to the fourth sentence of subsection (d)(6) of such section (and consisting of the positions of members who desire coverage under the agreement) may, if such modification is agreed to prior to 1960, be made effective with respect to services performed in such positions after an effective date specified in such modification, except that in no case may such date be earlier than December 31, 1955."

Modification of Existing Agreements With States of Florida, Nevada, New Mexico, Minnesota, Oklahoma, Pennsylvania, Texas, Washington, or Hawaii prior to July 1, 1962

Section 104(f) of Act Aug. 1, 1956, as amended by Pub.L. 86–284, § 1, provided that: "Notwithstanding the provisions of subsection (d) of section 218 of the Social Security Act [subsec. (d) of this section], any agreement under such section entered into prior to the date of enactment of this Act [August 1, 1956] by the State of Florida, Nevada, New Mexico, Minnesota, Oklahoma, Pennsylvania, Texas, Washington, or the Territory of Hawaii shall if the State or Territory concerned so requests, be modified prior to January 1, 1962, so as to apply to services performed by employees of the respective public school districts of such State or Territory who, on the date such agreement is made applicable to such services, are not in positions the incumbents of which are required by State or Territorial law or regulation to have valid State or Territorial teachers' or administrators' certificates in order to receive pay for their services. The provisions of this subsection shall not apply to services of any such employees to which any such agreement applies without regard to this subsection."

Modification of Existing Agreement With State of Maine Prior to July 1, 1967

Section 316 of Pub.L. 85–840, as amended by Pub.L. 86–778, Title I, § 102(j), Sept. 13, 1960, 74 Stat. 935; Pub.L. 88–350, § 1, July 2, 1964, 78 Stat. 240; Pub.L. 89–97, Title III, § 337, July 30, 1965, 79 Stat. 409, eff. July 1, 1965, provided that: "For the purposes of any modification which might be made after the date of enactment of this Act [August 28, 1958] and prior to July 1, 1967, by the State of Maine of its existing agreement made under section 218 of the Social Security Act [this section] any retirement system of such State which covers positions of teachers and positions of other employees shall, if such State so desires, be deemed (notwithstanding the provisions of subsection (d) of such section [subsec. (d) of this section]) to consist of a separate retirement system with respect to the positions of such teachers and a separate retirement system with respect to the positions of such other employees; and for the purposes of this sentence, the term 'teacher' shall mean any teacher, principal, supervisor, school nurse, school dietitian, school secretary or superintendent employed in any public school, including teachers in unorganized territory."

Modification of Existing Agreement With State of Oklahoma Prior to 1962

Section 3 of Pub.L. 86–284 provided that: "Notwithstanding the provisions of subsection (d)(5)(A) of section 218 of the Social Security Act [subsec. (d)(5)(A) of this section] and the references thereto in subsections (d)(1) and (d)(3) of such section 218 [subsecs. (d)(1) and (d)(3) of this section], the agreement with the State of Oklahoma heretofore entered into pursuant to such section 218 [this section] may, at any time prior to 1962, be modified pursuant to subsection (c)(4) of such section 218 [subsec. (c)(4) of this section] so as to apply to services performed by any individual employed by such State (or any political subdivision thereof) in any policeman's position covered by a retirement system in effect on the date of enactment of this Act [Sept. 16, 1959] if (1) in the case of an individual performing such services on such date, such individual is ineligible to become a member of such retirement system, or, in the case of an individual who prior to such date has ceased to perform such services, such individual was, on the last day he did perform such services, ineligible to become a member of such retirement system, and (2) such State has, prior to 1959, paid to the Secretary of the Treasury, with respect to any of the services performed by such individual in any such position, the sums prescribed pursuant to subsection (e)(1) of such section 218 [subsec. (e)(1) of this section]. Notwithstanding the provisions of subsection (f) of such section 218 [subsec. (f) of this section] such modification shall be effective with respect to (i) all services performed by such individual in any such position on or after the date of enactment of this Act [Sept. 16, 1959], and (ii) all such services, performed before such date, with respect to which such State has paid to the Secretary of the Treasury the sums prescribed pursuant to subsection (e) of such section 218 [subsec. (e) of this section], at the time or times established pursuant to such subsection."

Modification of Reporting Procedures in Effect December 1, 1975, Under Federal-State Agreements

Pub.L. 94–202, § 8(k), Jan. 2, 1976, 89 Stat. 1140, provided that: "Notwithstanding the provisions of section 218(i) of the Social Security Act [subsec. (i) of this section], nothing contained in the amendments made by the preceding provisions of this section [enacting section 432 of this title, and amending sections 401, 403, 424a, and 430 of this title and section 6103 of Title 26, Internal Revenue Code, and enacting provisions set out as notes under sections 401 and 432 of this title] shall be construed to authorize or require the Secretary, in promulgating regulations or amendments thereto under such section 218(i) [subsec. (i) of this section], substantially to modify the procedures, as in effect on December 1, 1975, for the reporting by States to the Secretary of the wages of individuals covered by social security pursuant to Federal-State agreements entered into pursuant to section 218 of the Social Security Act [this section]."

Presumptions of Work Deductions for Services Performed Prior to 1955 in Case of Certain Retroactive State Agreements; Recomputation

Section 101(*l*) of Act Sept. 1, 1954, provided that:

"**(1)** In the case of any services performed prior to 1955 to which an agreement under section 218 of the Social Security Act [this section] was made applicable, deductions which—

"**(A)** were not imposed under section 203 of such Act [section 403 of this title] with respect to such services performed prior to the date the agreement was agreed to or, if the original agreement was not applicable to such services, performed prior to the date the modification making such agreement applicable to such services was agreed to, and

"**(B)** would have been imposed under such section 203 [section 403 of this title] had such agreement, or modification, as the case may be, been agreed to on the date it became effective,

shall be deemed to have been imposed but only for purposes of section 215(f)(2)(A) or section 215(f)(4)(A) of such Act [section 415(f)(2)(A) or section 415(f)(4)(A) of this title] as in effect prior to the enactment of this Act. An individual with respect to whose services the preceding sentence is applicable, or in the case of his death, his survivors entitled to monthly benefits under section 202 of the Social Security Act [section 402 of this title] on the basis of his wages and self-employment income, shall be entitled to a recomputation of his primary insurance amount under such section 215(f)(2)(A) or section 215(f)(4)(A) [section 415(f)(2)(A) or section 415(f)(4)(A) of this title], as the case may be, if the conditions specified therein are met and if, with respect to a recomputation under such section 215(f)(2)(A) [section 415(f)(2)(A) of this title], such individual files the application referred to in such section after August 1954 and prior to January 1956 or, with respect to a recomputation under such section 215(f)(4)(A) [section 415(f)(4)(A) of this title], such individual died prior to January 1956 and any of such survivors entitled to monthly benefits files an application, in addition to the application filed for such monthly benefits, for a recomputation under such section 215(f)(4)(A) [section 415(f)(4)(A) of this title].

"**(2)** For purposes of a recomputation made by reason of paragraph (1) of this subsection, the primary insurance amount of the individual who performed the services referred to in such paragraph shall be computed under subsection (a)(2) of section 215 of the Social Security Act, as amended by this Act [section 415(a)(2) of this title] (but, for such purposes, without application of subsection (d)(4) of such section, as in effect prior to the enactment of this Act or as amended by this Act [section 415(d)(4) of this title]) and as though he became entitled to old-age insurance benefits in whichever of the following months yields the highest primary insurance amount:

"(A) the month following the last month for which deductions are deemed, pursuant to paragraph (1) of this subsection, to have been made; or

"(B) the first month after the month determined under subparagraph (A) (and prior to September 1954) in which his benefits under section 202(a) of the Social Security Act [section 402(a) of this title] were no longer subject to deductions under section 203(b) of such Act [section 403(b) of this title]; or

"(C) the first month after the last month (and prior to September 1954) in which his benefits under section 202(a) of the Social Security Act [section 402(a) of this title] were subject to deductions under section 203(b) of such Act [section 403(b) of this title]; or

"(D) the month in which such individual filed his application for recomputation referred to in paragraph (1) of this subsection or, if he died without filing such application and prior to January 1, 1956, the month in which he died, and in any such case (but, if the individual is deceased, only if death occurred after August 1954) the amendments made by subsections (b)(1), (e)(1) and (e)(3)(B) of section 102 of this Act [to section 415(b), (e) and (f)(3) of this title] shall be applicable.

Such recomputation shall be effective for and after the month in which the application required by paragraph (1) of this subsection is filed. The provisions of this subsection shall not be applicable in the case of any individual if his primary insurance amount has been recomputed under section 215(f)(2) of the Social Security Act [section 415(f)(2) of this title] on the basis of an application filed prior to September 1954.

"(3) If any recomputation under section 215(f) of the Social Security Act [section 415(f) of this title] is made by reason of deductions deemed pursuant to paragraph (1) of this subsection to have been imposed with respect to benefits based on the wages and self-employment income of any individual, the total of the benefits based on such wages and self-employment income for months for which such deductions are so deemed to have been imposed shall be recovered by making, in addition to any other deductions under section 203 of such Act [section 403 of this title], deductions from any increase in benefits, based on such wages and self-employment income, resulting from such recomputation."

Treatment of Certain Credits as Amounts Deposited in Social Security Trust Funds Pursuant to Agreement

Section 123(b)(4) of Pub.L. 98–21 provided that: "For purposes of subsection (h) of section 218 of the Social Security Act [subsec. (h) of this section] (relating to deposits in social security trust funds of amounts received under section 218 agreements), amounts allowed as a credit pursuant to subsection (d) of section 3510 of the Internal Revenue Code of 1954 [now 1986] [section 3510(d) of Title 26] (relating to credit for remuneration paid during 1984 which is covered under an agreement under section 218 of the Social Security Act [this section]) shall be treated as amounts received under such an agreement."

Validation of Coverage for Certain Employees of Integral Unit of Political Subdivision of Alaska

Section 342 of Pub.L. 89–97 provided that: "For purposes of the agreement under section 218 of the Social Security Act [this section] entered into by the State of Alaska, or its predecessor the Territory of Alaska, where employees of an integral unit of a political subdivision of the State or Territory of Alaska have in good faith been included under the State or Territory's agreement as a coverage group on the basis that such integral unit of a political subdivision was a political subdivision, then such unit of the political subdivision shall, for purposes of section 218(b)(2) of such Act [subsec. (b)(2) of this section], be deemed to be a political subdivision, and employees performing services within such unit shall be deemed to be a coverage group, effective with the effective date specified in such agreement or modification of such agreement with respect to such coverage group and ending with the last day of the year in which this Act is enacted [1965]."

Validation of Coverage for Certain Employees of Integral Unit of Political Subdivision of Arkansas

Section 1 of Pub.L. 87–878 provided: "That, for purposes of the agreement under section 218 of the Social Security Act [this section] entered into by the State of Arkansas, where employees of an integral unit of a political subdivision of the State of Arkansas have in good faith been included under the State's agreement as a coverage group on the basis that such integral unit of a political subdivision was a political subdivision, then such unit of the political subdivision shall, for purposes of section 218(b)(2) of such Act [subsec. (b)(2) of this section], be deemed to be a political subdivision, and employees performing services within such unit shall be deemed to be a coverage group, effective with the effective date specified in such agreement or modification of such agreement with respect to such coverage group and ending with the last day of the year in which this Act is enacted [1962]."

Validation of Coverage for Certain Firemen in State of Nebraska

Section 119(b) of Pub.L. 90–248 provided that: "In any case in which—

"(1) an individual has performed services prior to the enactment of this Act [Jan. 2, 1968] in the employ of a political subdivision of the State of Nebraska in a fireman's position, and

"(2) amounts, equivalent to the sum of the taxes which would have been imposed by sections 3101 and 3111 of the Internal Revenue Code of 1954 [now 1988] [sections 3101 and 3111 of Title 26, Internal Revenue Code] had such services constituted employment for purposes of section 21 of such Code [section 21 of Title 26] at the time they were performed, were timely paid in good faith to the Secretary of the Treasury, and

"(3) no refunds of such amounts paid in lieu of taxes have been obtained,

the amount of the remuneration of such services with respect to which such amounts have been paid shall be deemed to constitute remuneration for employment as defined in section 209 of the Social Security Act [section 409 of this title]."

Validation of Coverage for Certain Mississippi Teachers

Section 102(h) of Pub.L. 86–778 provided that: "For purposes of the Agreement under section 218 of the Social Security Act [this section] entered into by the State of Mississippi, services of teachers in such State performed after February 28, 1951, and prior to October 1, 1959, shall be deemed to have been performed by such teachers as employees of the State. The term 'teacher' as used in the preceding sentence means—

"(1) any individual who is licensed to serve in the capacity of teacher, librarian, registrar, supervisor, principal, or superintendent and who is principally engaged in the public elementary or secondary school system of the State in any one or more of such capacities;

"(2) any employee in the office of the county superintendent of education or the county school supervisor, or in the office of the principal of any county or municipal public elementary or secondary school in the State; and

"(3) any individual licensed to serve in the capacity of teacher who is engaged in any educational capacity in any day or night school conducted under the supervision of the State department of education as a part of the adult education program provided for under the laws of Mississippi or under the laws of the United States."

Validation of Coverage for District Engineering Aides of Soil and Water Conservation Districts of Oklahoma

Pub.L. 88–650, § 3, Oct. 13, 1964, 78 Stat. 1077, provided that: "For purposes of the agreement under section 218 of the Social Security Act [this section] entered into by the State of Oklahoma, remuneration paid to district engineering aides of soil and water conservation districts of the State of Oklahoma which was reported by the State as amounts paid to such aides as employees of the State for services performed by them during the period beginning January 1, 1951, and ending with the close of June 30, 1962, shall be deemed to have been paid to such aides for services performed by them in the employ of the State."

§ 418a. Voluntary agreements for coverage of Indian tribal council members

(a) Purpose of agreement

(1) The Commissioner of Social Security shall, at the request of any Indian tribe, enter into an agreement with such Indian tribe for the purpose of extending the insurance system established by this subchapter to services performed by individuals as members of such Indian tribe's tribal council. Any agreement with an Indian tribe under this section applies to all members of the tribal council, and shall include all services performed by individuals in their capacity as council members.

(2) Notwithstanding section 410(a) of this title, for the purposes of this subchapter, the term "employment" includes any service included under an agreement entered into under this section.

(b) Definitions

For the purposes of this section:

(1) The term "member" means, with respect to a tribal council, an individual appointed or elected to serve as a member or the head of the tribal council.

(2) The term "tribal council" means the appointed or elected governing body of a federally recognized Indian tribe.

(c) Effective date of agreement

(1) Any agreement under this section shall be effective with respect to services performed after an effective date specified in such agreement, provided that such date may not be earlier than the first day of the next calendar month after the month in which the agreement is executed by both parties.

(2) At the request of the Indian tribe at the time of the agreement, such agreement may apply with respect to services performed before such effective date for which there were timely paid in good faith (and not subsequently refunded) to the Secretary of the Treasury amounts equivalent to the sum of the taxes which would have been imposed by sections 3101 and 3111 of the Internal Revenue Code of 1986 had such services constituted employment for purposes of chapter 21 of such Code. No agreement under this section may require payment to be made after the effective date specified in such agreement of any taxes with respect to services performed before such effective date.

(d) Duration of agreement

No agreement under this section may be terminated on or after the effective date of the agreement.

(Aug. 14, 1935, c. 531, Title II, § 218A, as added Pub.L. 115–243, § 2(a), Sept. 20, 2018, 132 Stat. 2894.)

HISTORICAL AND STATUTORY NOTES

References in Text

This subchapter, referred to in subsec. (a), originally read "this title", meaning Title II of the Social Security Act, Act Aug. 14, 1935, c. 531, 49 Stat. 622, as amended, which is classified to this subchapter, 42 U.S.C.A. § 401 et seq.

Chapter 21 of such Code, referred to in subsec. (c)(2), probably means the Internal Revenue Code of 1986, which is classified to 26 U.S.C.A. § 3101 et seq.

Rules of Construction

Nothing in Pub.L. 115–243, or the amendments made by that Act, shall be construed to affect application of any Federal income tax withholding requirements under Title 26, see Pub.L. 115–243, § 2(c), set out as a note under 26 U.S.C.A. § 3121.

§ 419. Repealed. Pub.L. 86–778, Title I, § 103(j)(1), Sept. 13, 1960, 74 Stat. 937

HISTORICAL AND STATUTORY NOTES

Section, Act Aug. 14, 1935, c. 531, Title II, § 219, as added Aug. 28, 1950, c. 809, Title I, § 107, 64 Stat. 517, prescribed the effective date of this subchapter in Puerto Rico as January 1 of the first calendar year which begins more than 90 days after the date on which the President received a certification from the Governor of Puerto Rico.

Effective Date of Repeal

Section repealed effective Sept. 13, 1960, with exceptions and qualifications, see Section 103(v)(1), (3), of Pub.L. 86–778, set out as an Effective Date of 1960 Amendment note under section 402 of this title.

§ 420. Disability provisions inapplicable if benefit rights impaired

None of the provisions of this subchapter relating to periods of disability shall apply in any case in which their application would result in the denial of monthly benefits or a lump-sum death payment which would otherwise be payable under this subchapter; nor shall they apply in the case of any monthly benefit or lump-sum death payment under this subchapter if such benefit or payment would be greater without their application.

(Aug. 14, 1935, c. 531, Title II, § 220, as added Sept. 1, 1954, c. 1206, Title I, § 106(g), 68 Stat. 1081.)

HISTORICAL AND STATUTORY NOTES

Prior Provisions

A prior section 420, Act Aug. 14, 1935, c. 531, Title II, § 220, as added July 18, 1952, c. 945, § 3(e), 66 Stat. 772, relating to the inapplicability of the disability provisions if benefits were reduced, ceased to be in effect at the close of June 30, 1953. See section 3(g) of Act July 18, 1952, set out as an Effective and Termination Date of 1952 Amendment note under section 413 of this title.

§ 421. Disability determinations

(a) State agencies

(1) In the case of any individual, the determination of whether or not he is under a disability (as defined in section 416(i) or 423(d) of this title) and of the day such disability began, and the determination of the day on which such disability ceases, shall be made by a State agency, notwithstanding any other provision of law, in any State that notifies the Commissioner of Social Security in writing that it wishes to make such disability determinations commencing with such month as the Commissioner of Social Security and the State agree upon, but only if (A) the Commissioner of Social Security has not found, under subsection (b)(1), that the State agency has substantially failed to make disability determinations in accordance with the applicable provisions of this section or rules issued thereunder, and (B) the State has not notified the Commissioner of Social Security, under subsection (b)(2), that it does not wish to make such determinations. If the Commissioner of Social Security once makes the finding described in clause (A) of the preceding sentence, or the State gives the notice referred to in clause (B) of such sentence, the Commissioner of Social Security may thereafter determine whether (and, if so, beginning with which month and under what conditions) the State may again make disability determinations under this paragraph.

(2) The disability determinations described in paragraph (1) made by a State agency shall be made in accordance with the pertinent provisions of this subchapter and the standards and criteria contained in regulations or other written guidelines of the Commissioner of Social Security pertaining to matters such as disability determinations, the class or classes of individuals with respect to which a State may make disability determinations (if it does not wish to do so with respect to all individuals in the State), and the conditions under which it may choose not to make all such determinations. In addition, the Commissioner of Social Security shall promulgate regulations specifying, in such detail as the Commissioner deems appropriate, performance standards and administrative requirements and procedures to be followed in performing the disability determination function in order to assure effective and uniform administration of the disability insurance program throughout the United States. The regulations may, for example, specify matters such as—

(A) the administrative structure and the relationship between various units of the State agency responsible for disability determinations,

(B) the physical location of and relationship among agency staff units, and other individuals or organizations performing tasks for the State agency, and standards for the availability to applicants and beneficiaries of facilities for making disability determinations,

(C) State agency performance criteria, including the rate of accuracy of decisions, the time periods within which determinations must be made, the procedures for and the scope of review by the Commissioner of Social Security, and, as the Commissioner finds appropriate, by the State, of its performance in individual cases and in classes of cases, and rules governing access of appropriate Federal officials to State offices and to State records relating to its administration of the disability determination function,

(D) fiscal control procedures that the State agency may be required to adopt, and

(E) the submission of reports and other data, in such form and at such time as the Commissioner of Social Security may require, concerning the State agency's activities relating to the disability determination.

Nothing in this section shall be construed to authorize the Commissioner of Social Security to take any action except pursuant to law or to regulations promulgated pursuant to law.

(b) Determinations by Commissioner

(1) If the Commissioner of Social Security finds, after notice and opportunity for a hearing, that a State agency is substantially failing to make disability determinations in a manner consistent with the Commissioner's regulations and other written guidelines, the Commissioner of Social Security shall, not earlier than 180 days following the Commissioner's finding, and after the Commissioner has complied with the requirements of paragraph (3), make the disability determinations referred to in subsection (a)(1).

(2) If a State, having notified the Commissioner of Social Security of its intent to make disability determinations under subsection (a)(1), no longer wishes to make such determinations, it shall notify the Commissioner of Social Security in writing of that fact, and, if

an agency of the State is making disability determinations at the time such notice is given, it shall continue to do so for not less than 180 days, or (if later) until the Commissioner of Social Security has complied with the requirements of paragraph (3). Thereafter, the Commissioner of Social Security shall make the disability determinations referred to in subsection (a)(1).

(3)(A) The Commissioner of Social Security shall develop and initiate all appropriate procedures to implement a plan with respect to any partial or complete assumption by the Commissioner of Social Security of the disability determination function from a State agency, as provided in this section, under which employees of the affected State agency who are capable of performing duties in the disability determination process for the Commissioner of Social Security shall, notwithstanding any other provision of law, have a preference over any other individual in filling an appropriate employment position with the Commissioner of Social Security (subject to any system established by the Commissioner of Social Security for determining hiring priority among such employees of the State agency) unless any such employee is the administrator, the deputy administrator, or assistant administrator (or his equivalent) of the State agency, in which case the Commissioner of Social Security may accord such priority to such employee.

(B) The Commissioner of Social Security shall not make such assumption of the disability determination function until such time as the Secretary of Labor determines that, with respect to employees of such State agency who will be displaced from their employment on account of such assumption by the Commissioner of Social Security and who will not be hired by the Commissioner of Social Security to perform duties in the disability determination process, the State has made fair and equitable arrangements to protect the interests of employees so displaced. Such protective arrangements shall include only those provisions which are provided under all applicable Federal, State and local statutes including, but not limited to, (i) the preservation of rights, privileges, and benefits (including continuation of pension rights and benefits) under existing collective-bargaining agreements; (ii) the continuation of collective-bargaining rights; (iii) the assignment of affected employees to other jobs or to retraining programs; (iv) the protection of individual employees against a worsening of their positions with respect to their employment; (v) the protection of health benefits and other fringe benefits; and (vi) the provision of severance pay, as may be necessary.

(c) Review of determination by Commissioner

(1) The Commissioner of Social Security may on the Commissioner's own motion or as required under paragraphs (2) and (3) review a determination, made by a State agency under this section, that an individual is or is not under a disability (as defined in section 416(i) or 423(d) of this title) and, as a result of such review, may modify such agency's determination and determine that such individual either is or is not under a disability (as so defined) or that such individual's disability began on a day earlier or later than that determined by such agency, or that such disability ceased on a day earlier or later than that determined by such agency. A review by the Commissioner of Social Security on the Commissioner's own motion of a State agency determination under this paragraph may be made before or after any action is taken to implement such determination.

(2) The Commissioner of Social Security (in accordance with paragraph (3)) shall review determinations, made by State agencies pursuant to this section, that individuals are under disabilities (as defined in section 416(i) or 423(d) of this title). Any review by the Commissioner of Social Security of a State agency determination under this paragraph shall be made before any action is taken to implement such determination.

(3)(A) In carrying out the provisions of paragraph (2) with respect to the review of determinations made by State agencies pursuant to this section that individuals are under disabilities (as defined in section 416(i) or 423(d) of this title), the Commissioner of Social Security shall review—

(i) at least 50 percent of all such determinations made by State agencies on applications for benefits under this subchapter, and

(ii) other determinations made by State agencies pursuant to this section to the extent necessary to assure a high level of accuracy in such other determinations.

(B) In conducting reviews pursuant to subparagraph (A), the Commissioner of Social Security shall, to the extent feasible, select for review those determinations which the Commissioner of Social Security identifies as being the most likely to be incorrect.

(C) Not later than April 1, 1992, and annually thereafter, the Commissioner of Social Security shall submit to the Committee on Ways and Means of the House of Representatives and the Committee on Finance of the Senate a written report setting forth the number of reviews conducted under subparagraph (A)(ii) during the preceding fiscal year and the findings of the Commissioner of Social Security based on such reviews of the accuracy of the determinations made by State agencies pursuant to this section.

(d) Hearings and judicial review

Any individual dissatisfied with any determination under subsection (a), (b), (c), or (g) shall be entitled to a hearing thereon by the Commissioner of Social Security to the same extent as is provided in section 405(b) of this title with respect to decisions of the Commissioner of Social Security, and to judicial review of the

Commissioner's final decision after such hearing as is provided in section 405(g) of this title.

(e) State's right to cost from Trust Funds

Each State which is making disability determinations under subsection (a)(1) shall be entitled to receive from the Trust Funds, in advance or by way of reimbursement, as determined by the Commissioner of Social Security, the cost to the State of making disability determinations under subsection (a)(1). The Commissioner of Social Security shall from time to time certify such amount as is necessary for this purpose to the Managing Trustee, reduced or increased, as the case may be, by any sum (for which adjustment hereunder has not previously been made) by which the amount certified for any prior period was greater or less than the amount which should have been paid to the State under this subsection for such period; and the Managing Trustee, prior to audit or settlement by the Government Accountability Office, shall make payment from the Trust Funds at the time or times fixed by the Commissioner of Social Security, in accordance with such certification. Appropriate adjustments between the Federal Old-Age and Survivors Insurance Trust Fund and the Federal Disability Insurance Trust Fund with respect to the payments made under this subsection shall be made in accordance with paragraph (1) of subsection (g) of section 401 of this title (but taking into account any refunds under subsection (f) of this section) to insure that the Federal Disability Insurance Trust Fund is charged with all expenses incurred which are attributable to the administration of section 423 of this title and the Federal Old-Age and Survivors Insurance Trust Fund is charged with all other expenses.

(f) Use of funds

All money paid to a State under this section shall be used solely for the purposes for which it is paid; and any money so paid which is not used for such purposes shall be returned to the Treasury of the United States for deposit in the Trust Funds.

(g) Regulations governing determinations in certain cases

In the case of individuals in a State which does not undertake to perform disability determinations under subsection (a)(1), or which has been found by the Commissioner of Social Security to have substantially failed to make disability determinations in a manner consistent with the Commissioner's regulations and guidelines, in the case of individuals outside the United States, and in the case of any class or classes of individuals for whom no State undertakes to make disability determinations, the determinations referred to in subsection (a) shall be made by the Commissioner of Social Security in accordance with regulations prescribed by the Commissioner.

(h) Evaluation of impairments by qualified medical professionals

An initial determination under subsection (a), (c), (g), or (i) shall not be made until the Commissioner of Social Security has made every reasonable effort to ensure—

(1) in any case where there is evidence which indicates the existence of a mental impairment, that a qualified psychiatrist or psychologist has completed the medical portion of the case review and any applicable residual functional capacity assessment; and

(2) in any case where there is evidence which indicates the existence of a physical impairment, that a qualified physician has completed the medical portion of the case review and any applicable residual functional capacity assessment.

(i) Review of disability cases to determine continuing eligibility; permanent disability cases; appropriate number of cases reviewed; reporting requirements

(1) In any case where an individual is or has been determined to be under a disability, the case shall be reviewed by the applicable State agency or the Commissioner of Social Security (as may be appropriate), for purposes of continuing eligibility, at least once every 3 years, subject to paragraph (2); except that where a finding has been made that such disability is permanent, such reviews shall be made at such times as the Commissioner of Social Security determines to be appropriate. Reviews of cases under the preceding sentence shall be in addition to, and shall not be considered as a substitute for, any other reviews which are required or provided for under or in the administration of this subchapter.

(2) The requirement of paragraph (1) that cases be reviewed at least every 3 years shall not apply to the extent that the Commissioner of Social Security determines, on a State-by-State basis, that such requirement should be waived to insure that only the appropriate number of such cases are reviewed. The Commissioner of Social Security shall determine the appropriate number of cases to be reviewed in each State after consultation with the State agency performing such reviews, based upon the backlog of pending reviews, the projected number of new applications for disability insurance benefits, and the current and projected staffing levels of the State agency, but the Commissioner of Social Security shall provide for a waiver of such requirement only in the case of a State which makes a good faith effort to meet proper staffing requirements for the State agency and to process case reviews in a timely fashion. The Commissioner of Social Security shall report annually to the Committee on Finance of the Senate and the Committee on Ways and Means of the House of Representatives with respect to the determinations made

by the Commissioner of Social Security under the preceding sentence.

(3) The Commissioner of Social Security shall report annually to the Committee on Finance of the Senate and the Committee on Ways and Means of the House of Representatives with respect to the number of reviews of continuing disability carried out under paragraph (1), the number of such reviews which result in an initial termination of benefits, the number of requests for reconsideration of such initial termination or for a hearing with respect to such termination under subsection (d), or both, and the number of such initial terminations which are overturned as the result of a reconsideration or hearing.

(4) In any case in which the Commissioner of Social Security initiates a review under this subsection of the case of an individual who has been determined to be under a disability, the Commissioner of Social Security shall notify such individual of the nature of the review to be carried out, the possibility that such review could result in the termination of benefits, and the right of the individual to provide medical evidence with respect to such review.

(5) For suspension of reviews under this subsection in the case of an individual using a ticket to work and self-sufficiency, see section 1320b–19(i) of this title.

(j) Rules and regulations; consultative examinations

The Commissioner of Social Security shall prescribe regulations which set forth, in detail—

(1) the standards to be utilized by State disability determination services and Federal personnel in determining when a consultative examination should be obtained in connection with disability determinations;

(2) standards for the type of referral to be made; and

(3) procedures by which the Commissioner of Social Security will monitor both the referral processes used and the product of professionals to whom cases are referred.

Nothing in this subsection shall be construed to preclude the issuance, in accordance with section 553(b)(A) of Title 5, of interpretive rules, general statements of policy, and rules of agency organization relating to consultative examinations if such rules and statements are consistent with such regulations.

(k) Establishment of uniform standards for determination of disability

(1) The Commissioner of Social Security shall establish by regulation uniform standards which shall be applied at all levels of determination, review, and adjudication in determining whether individuals are under disabilities as defined in section 416(i) or 423(d) of this title.

(2) Regulations promulgated under paragraph (1) shall be subject to the rulemaking procedures established under section 553 of Title 5.

(*l*) Special notice to blind individuals with respect to hearings and other official actions

(1) In any case where an individual who is applying for or receiving benefits under this subchapter on the basis of disability by reason of blindness is entitled to receive notice from the Commissioner of Social Security of any decision or determination made or other action taken or proposed to be taken with respect to his or her rights under this subchapter, such individual shall at his or her election be entitled either (A) to receive a supplementary notice of such decision, determination, or action, by telephone, within 5 working days after the initial notice is mailed, (B) to receive the initial notice in the form of a certified letter, or (C) to receive notification by some alternative procedure established by the Commissioner of Social Security and agreed to by the individual.

(2) The election under paragraph (1) may be made at any time, but an opportunity to make such an election shall in any event be given, to every individual who is an applicant for benefits under this subchapter on the basis of disability by reason of blindness, at the time of his or her application. Such an election, once made by an individual, shall apply with respect to all notices of decisions, determinations, and actions which such individual may thereafter be entitled to receive under this subchapter until such time as it is revoked or changed.

(m) Work activity as basis for review

(1) In any case where an individual entitled to disability insurance benefits under section 423 of this title or to monthly insurance benefits under section 402 of this title based on such individual's disability (as defined in section 423(d) of this title) has received such benefits for at least 24 months

(A) no continuing disability review conducted by the Commissioner may be scheduled for the individual solely as a result of the individual's work activity;

(B) no work activity engaged in by the individual may be used as evidence that the individual is no longer disabled; and

(C) no cessation of work activity by the individual may give rise to a presumption that the individual is unable to engage in work.

(2) An individual to which paragraph (1) applies shall continue to be subject to

(A) continuing disability reviews on a regularly scheduled basis that is not triggered by work; and

(B) termination of benefits under this subchapter in the event that the individual has earnings that exceed the level of earnings established by the Commissioner to represent substantial gainful activity.

(Aug. 14, 1935, c. 531, Title II, § 221, as added Sept. 1, 1954, c. 1206, Title I, § 106(g), 68 Stat. 1081; amended Aug. 1, 1956, c. 836, Title I, § 103(c)(7), (8), (h), 70 Stat. 818, 823; Pub.L. 90–248, Title I, § 158(c)(3), (4), Jan. 2, 1968, 81 Stat. 869; Pub.L. 96–265, Title III, §§ 304(a) to (f), 311(a), June 9, 1980, 94 Stat. 453 to 456, 460; Pub.L. 97–455, §§ 3, 6, Jan. 12, 1983, 96 Stat. 2499, 2500; Pub.L. 98–369, Div. B, Title VI, § 2663(a)(14), July 18, 1984, 98 Stat. 1164; Pub.L. 98–460, §§ 6(a), 8(a), 9(a)(1), 10(a), 17(a), Oct. 9, 1984, 98 Stat. 1802, 1804, 1805, 1811; Pub.L. 99–514, Title XVIII, § 1883(a)(9), Oct. 22, 1986, 100 Stat. 2916; Pub.L. 100–647, Title VIII, § 8012(a), Nov. 10, 1988, 102 Stat. 3789; Pub.L. 101–239, Title X, § 10306(a)(1), Dec. 19, 1989, 103 Stat. 2484; Pub.L. 101–508, Title V, § 5128(a), Nov. 5, 1990, 104 Stat. 1388–286; Pub.L. 103–296, Title I, § 107(a)(4), Aug. 15, 1994, 108 Stat. 1478; Pub.L. 106–170, Title I, §§ 101(b)(1)(A), 111(a), Dec. 17, 1999, 113 Stat. 1873, 1881; Pub.L. 108–271, § 8(b), July 7, 2004, 118 Stat. 814; Pub.L. 114–74, Title VIII, § 832(a), Nov. 2, 2015, 129 Stat. 613.)

HISTORICAL AND STATUTORY NOTES

Codifications

Amendment of subsec. (e) by section 1883(a)(9) of Pub.L. 99–514, directing the deletion of "under this section" to avoid the appearance in text of "subsection (a)(1) of this section under this section" resulting from amendment of subsec. (e) by section 304(e)(1) of Pub.L. 96–265, had been previously editorially executed, thus requiring no further change in text.

In subsec. (e), amendment by section 304(e)(1) of Pub.L. 96–265, which directed that "which is making disability determinations under subsection (a)(1) of this section" be substituted for "which has an agreement with the Secretary" was executed by striking out "under this section" following "Secretary" as the probable intent of Congress, to avoid "subsection (a)(1) of this section under this section" from appearing in text.

Effective and Applicability Provisions

2015 Acts. Pub.L. 114–74, Title VIII, § 832(b), Nov. 2, 2015, 129 Stat. 613, provided that: "The amendment made by subsection (a) [amending this section] shall apply with respect to determinations of disability made on or after the date that is 1 year after the date of the enactment of this Act [Nov. 2, 2015]."

1999 Acts. Amendment by Pub.L. 106–170, § 101(b)(1)(A) shall take effect with the first month following 1 year after December 17, 1999, subject to graduated implementation of program provisions of section 101(d) of Pub.L. 106–170 [set out as a note under section 1320b–19 of this title], see section 101(c) of Pub.L. 106–170, set out as a note under section 1320b–19 of this title.

Pub.L. 106–170, Title I, § 111(b), Dec. 17, 1999, 113 Stat. 1881, provided that: "The amendment made by subsection (a) [amending this section] shall take effect on January 1, 2002."

1994 Acts. Amendment by section 107(a)(4) of Pub.L. 103–296 effective Mar. 31, 1995, see section 110 of Pub.L. 103–296, set out as a note under section 401 of this title.

1990 Acts. Section 5128(b) of Pub.L. 101–508 provided that: "The amendment made by subsection (a) [amending subsec. (c) of this section] shall apply with respect to determinations made by State agencies in fiscal years after fiscal year 1990."

1989 Acts. Section 10306(a)(3) of Pub.L. 101–239 provided that: "The amendment made by this section [amending this section] shall apply with respect to notices issued on or after July 1, 1990."

1988 Acts. Section 8012(b) of Pub.L. 100–647 provided that: "The amendment made by this section [amending subsec. (i)(3) of this section] shall apply to reports required to be submitted after the date of the enactment of this Act [Nov. 10, 1988]."

1986 Acts. Amendment by section 1883(a)(9) of Pub.L. 99–514 effective Oct. 22, 1986, see section 1883(f) of Pub.L. 99–514, set out as a note under section 402 of this title.

1984 Acts. Section 8(c) of Pub.L. 98–460 provided that: "The amendments made by this section [enacting subsec. (h) of this section and section 1382c(a)(3)(H) of this title] shall apply to determinations made after 60 days after the date of the enactment of this Act. [Oct. 9, 1984]."

Section 17(b) of Pub.L. 98–460 provided that: "The amendments made by subsection (a) of this section [amending subsecs. (a)(1), (b)(1), (3) and (d) of this section] shall become effective on the date of the enactment of this Act [Oct. 9, 1984] and shall expire on December 31, 1987. The provisions of the Social Security Act amended by subsection (a) of this section (as such provisions were in effect immediately before the date of the enactment of this Act) shall be effective after December 31, 1987."

Amendment by section 2663 of Pub.L. 98–369 effective July 18, 1984, but not to be construed as changing or affecting any right, liability, status or interpretation which existed (under the provisions of law involved) before that date, see section 2664(b) of Pub.L. 98–369, set out as a note under section 401 of this title.

1983 Acts. Section 3(b) of Pub.L. 97–455 provided that: "The amendments made by subsection (a) [amending pars. (1) and (2) of subsec. (h) of this section] shall become effective on the date of the enactment of this Act [Jan. 12, 1983]."

1980 Acts. Section 304(h) of Pub.L. 96–265 provided that: "The amendments made by subsections (a), (b), (d), (e), and (f) [amending subsecs. (a), (b), (d), (e), and (g) of this section] shall be effective beginning with the twelfth month following the month in which this Act is enacted [June 1980]. Any State that, on the effective date of the amendments made by this section, has in effect an agreement with the Secretary of Health and Human Services under section 221(a) of the Social Security Act [subsec. (a) of this section] (as in effect prior to such amendments) will be deemed to have given to the Secretary the notice specified in section 221(a)(1) of such Act as amended by this section, in lieu of continuing such agreement in effect after the effective date of such amendments. Thereafter, a State may notify the Secretary in writing that it no longer wishes to make disability determinations, effective not less than 180 days after the notification is given."

Section 311(b) of Pub.L. 96–265 provided that: "The amendment made by subsection (a) [enacting subsec. (h) of this section] shall become effective on January 1, 1982."

1968 Acts. Amendment by section 158 of Pub.L. 90–248 applicable with respect to applications for disability insurance benefits under section 423 of this title and to disability determinations under section 416(i) of this title, filed in or after Jan., 1968, or before Jan. 1968 if the applicant has not died before such month and if (A) notice of the final decision of the Secretary of Health, Education, and Welfare has not been given to the applicant before such month; or (B) the notice referred to in subparagraph (A) has been so given before such month but a civil action with respect to such final decision is commenced under section 205(g) of the Social Security Act [section 405(g) of this title] (whether before, in, or after such month) and the decision in such civil action has not become final before such month, see section 158(e) of Pub.L. 90–248, set out as a note under section 423 of this title.

Termination of Reporting Requirements

For termination of reporting provisions of subsec. (i)(2) and (3) of this section, effective May 15, 2000, see Pub.L. 104-66, § 3003, as amended, set out as a note under 31 U.S.C.A. § 1113, and the 2nd and 3rd items on page 99 of House Document No. 103–7.

Prior Provisions

A prior section 421, Act Aug. 14, 1935, c. 531, Title II, § 221, as added July 18, 1952, c. 945, § 3(e), 66 Stat. 772, and amended by 1953 Reorg. Plan No. 1, § 5, eff. Apr. 11, 1953, 18 F.R. 2053, 67 Stat. 631, relating to disability determinations, ceased to be in effect at the close of June 30, 1953. See section 3(g) of Act July 18, 1952, set out as a note under section 413 of this title.

Termination of Reporting Requirements

Reporting requirements of subsecs. (c)(3)(C) and (i)(3) of this section excepted from termination under Pub.L. 104-66, § 3003(a)(1), as amended, set out as a note under 31 U.S.C.A. § 1113, see Pub.L. 108–203, § 413, set out as a note under 31 U.S.C.A. § 1113.

Reporting requirement of subsec. (i)(2) and (3) of this section excepted from termination under Pub.L. 104–66, § 3003(a)(1), as amended, set out as a note under 31 U.S.C.A. § 1113, see Pub.L. 106–554, § 1(a)(7) [Title III, § 301], set out as a note under 31 U.S.C.A. § 1113.

Annual Report on Work-Related Continuing Disability Reviews

Pub.L. 114–74, Title VIII, § 845(b), Nov. 2, 2015, 129 Stat. 618, provided that:

"The Commissioner of Social Security shall annually submit to the Committee on Ways and Means of the House of Representatives and the Committee on Finance of the Senate a report on the number of work-related continuing disability reviews conducted each year to determine whether earnings derived from services demonstrate an individual's ability to engage in substantial gainful activity. Such report shall include—

"(1) the number of individuals receiving benefits based on disability under title II of such Act [probably means Title II of Act Aug. 14, 1935, c. 531, which is classified to 42 U.S.C.A. § 401 et seq.] for whom reports of earnings were received from any source by the Commissioner in the previous calendar year, reported as a total number and separately by the source of the report;

"(2) the number of individuals for whom such reports resulted in a determination to conduct a work-related continuing disability review, and the basis on which such determinations were made;

"(3) in the case of a beneficiary selected for a work-related continuing disability review on the basis of a report of earnings from any source—

"(A) the average number of days—

"(i) between the receipt of the report and the initiation of the review;

"(ii) between the initiation and the completion of the review; and

"(iii) the average amount of overpayment, if any;

"(B) the number of such reviews completed during such calendar year, and the number of such reviews that resulted in a suspension or termination of benefits;

"(C) the number of such reviews initiated in the current year that had not been completed as of the end of such calendar year;

"(D) the number of such reviews initiated in a prior year that had not been completed as of the end of such calendar year;

"(4) the total savings to the Trust Funds and the Treasury generated from benefits suspended or terminated as a result of such reviews; and

"(5) with respect to individuals for whom a work-related continuing disability review was completed during such calendar year—

"(A) the number who participated in the Ticket to Work program under section 1148 [probably means section 1148 of Act Aug. 14, 1935, c. 531, which is classified to 42 U.S.C.A. § 1320b–19] during such calendar year;

"(B) the number who used any program work incentives during such calendar year; and

"(C) the number who received vocational rehabilitation services during such calendar year with respect to which the Commissioner of Social Security reimbursed a State agency under section 222(d) [probably means section 222(d) of Act Aug. 14, 1935, c. 531, which is classified to 42 U.S.C.A. § 422(d)]."

Expansion of Cooperative Disability Investigations Units

Pub.L. 114–74, Title VIII, § 811, Nov. 2, 2015, 129 Stat. 601, provided that:

"(a) **In general.**—Not later than October 1, 2022, the Commissioner of Social Security shall take any necessary actions, subject to the availability of appropriations, to ensure that cooperative disability investigations units have been established, in areas where there is cooperation with local law enforcement agencies, that would cover each of the 50 States, the District of Columbia, Puerto Rico, Guam, the Northern Mariana Islands, the Virgin Islands, and American Samoa.

"(b) **Report.**—Not later than 90 days after the date of the enactment of this Act [Nov. 2, 2015] and annually thereafter until the earlier of 2022 or the date on which nationwide coverage is achieved, the Commissioner of Social Security shall submit to the Committee on Ways and Means of the House of Representatives and the Committee on Finance of the Senate a report describing a plan to implement the nationwide coverage described in subsection (a) and outlining areas where the Social Security Administration did not receive the cooperation of local law enforcement agencies."

Assumption by Secretary of Functions and Operations of State Disability Determination Units

Section 304(i) of Pub.L. 96–265 provided that: "The Secretary of Health and Human Services shall submit to the Congress by July 1, 1980, a detailed plan on how he expects to assume the functions and operations of a State disability determination unit when this becomes necessary under the amendments made by this section [amending subsecs. (a) to (e) and (g) of this section], and how he intends to meet the requirements of section 221(b)(3) of the Social Security Act [subsec. (b)(3) of this section]. Such plan should assume the uninterrupted operation of the disability determination function and the utilization of the best qualified personnel to carry out such function. If any amendment of Federal law or regulation is required to carry out such plan, recommendations for such amendment should be included in the report."

Demonstration Projects; Opportunity for Personal Appearance Prior to Disability Determinations; Report to Congressional Committees

Section (6)(d), (e) of Pub. L. 98–460 provided that:

"**(d)** The Secretary of Health and Human Services shall, as soon as practicable after the date of the enactment of this Act [Oct. 9, 1984], implement demonstration projects in which the opportunity for a personal appearance prior to a determination of ineligibility for persons reviewed under section 221(i) of the Social Security Act [subsec. (i) of this section] is substituted for the face to face evidentiary hearing required by section 205(b)(2) of such Act [405(b)(2) of this title]. Such demonstration projects shall be conducted in not fewer than five States, and shall also include disability determinations with respect to individuals reviewed under title XVI of such Act [subchapter XVI of this chapter]. The Secretary shall report to the Committee on Ways and Means of the House of Representatives and the Committee on Finance of the Senate concerning such demonstration projects, together with any recommendations, not later than December 31, 1986.

"**(e)** The Secretary of Health and Human Services shall, as soon as practicable after the date of the enactment of this Act [Oct. 9, 1984], implement demonstration projects in which the opportunity for a personal appearance is provided the applicant prior to initial disability determinations under subsections (a), (c), and (g) of section 221 of the Social Security Act [subsecs. (a), (c), and (g) of this section], and prior to initial disability determinations on applications for benefits under title XVI of such Act [subchapter XVI of this chapter]. Such demonstration projects shall be conducted in not fewer than five States. The Secretary shall report to the Committee on Ways and Means of the House of Representatives and the Committee on Finance of the Senate concerning such demonstration projects, together with any recommendations, not later than December 31, 1986."

Election by Current Recipients of Form of Notification

Section 10306(a)(2) of Pub.L. 101–239 provided that: "Not later than July 1, 1990, the Secretary of Health and Human Services shall provide every individual receiving benefits under title II of the Social Security Act [this subchapter] on the basis of disability by reason of blindness an opportunity to make an election under section 221(*l*)(1) of such Act [subsec. (*l*)(1) of this section] (as added by paragraph (1))."

Frequency of Continuing Eligibility Reviews

Section 15 of Pub.L. 98–460 provided that: "The Secretary of Health and Human Services shall promulgate final regulations, within 180 days after the date of the enactment of this Act [Oct. 9, 1984], which establish the standards to be used by the Secretary in determining the frequency of reviews under section 221(i) of the Social Security Act [subsec. (i) of this section]. Until such regulations have been issued as final regulations, no individual may be reviewed more than once under section 221(i) of the Social Security Act [subsec. (i) of this section]."

Institution of Notification System

Section 6(c) of Pub.L. 98–460 provided that: "(c) The Secretary shall institute a system of notification required by the amendments made by subsections (a) and (b) [enacting subsec. (i)(4) of this section and section 1383b(c) of this title] as soon as is practicable after the date of the enactment of this Act [Oct. 9, 1984]."

Moratorium on Mental Impairment Reviews

Section 5 of Pub.L. 98–460 provided that:

"**(a)** The Secretary of Health and Human Services (hereafter in this section referred to as the 'Secretary') shall revise the criteria embodied under the category 'Mental Disorders' in the 'Listing of Impairments' in effect on the date of the enactment of this Act [Oct. 9, 1984] under appendix 1 to subpart P of part 404 of title 20 of the Code of Federal Regulations. The revised criteria and listings, alone and in combination with assessments of the residual functional capacity of the individuals involved, shall be designed to realistically evaluate the ability of a mentally impaired individual to engage in substantial gainful activity in a competitive workplace environment. Regulations establishing such revised criteria and listings shall be published no later than 120 days after the date of the enactment of this Act [Oct. 9, 1984].

"**(b)(1)** Until such time as revised criteria have been established by regulation in accordance with subsection (a), no continuing eligibility review shall be carried out under section 221(i) of the Social Security Act [subsec. (i) of this section], or under the corresponding requirements established for disability determinations and reviews under title XVI of such Act [subchapter XVI of this chapter], with respect to any individual previously determined to be under a disability by reason of a mental impairment, if—

"**(A)** no initial decision on such review has been rendered with respect to such individual prior to the date of the enactment of this Act [Oct. 9, 1984], or

"**(B)** an initial decision on such review was rendered with respect to such individual prior to the date of the enactment of this Act but a timely appeal from such decision was filed or was pending on or after June 7, 1983.

For purposes of this paragraph and subsection (c)(1) the term 'continuing eligibility review', when used to refer to a review of a previous determination of disability, includes any reconsideration of or hearing on the initial decision rendered in such review as well as such initial decision itself, and any review by the Appeals Council of the hearing decision.

"(2) Paragraph (1) shall not apply in any case where the Secretary determines that fraud was involved in the prior determination, or where an individual (other than an individual eligible to receive benefits under section 1619 of the Social Security Act [section 1382h of this title]) is determined by the Secretary to be engaged in substantial gainful activity (or gainful activity, in the case of a widow, surviving divorced wife, widower, or surviving divorced husband for purposes of section 202(e) and (f) of such Act [section 402(e), (f) of this title]).

"**(c)(1)** Any initial determination that an individual is not under a disability by reason of a mental impairment and any determination that an individual is not under a disability by reason of a mental impairment in a reconsideration of or hearing on an initial disability determination, made or held under title II or XVI [this subchapter or subchapter XVI of this chapter] of the Social Security Act after the date of the enactment of this Act [Oct. 9, 1984] and prior to the date on which revised criteria are established by regulation in accordance with subsection (a), and any determination that an individual is not under a disability by reason of a mental impairment made under or in accordance with title II or XVI of such Act in a reconsideration of, hearing on, review by the Appeals Council of, or judicial review of a decision rendered in any continuing eligibility review to which subsection (b)(1) applies, shall be redetermined by the Secretary as soon as feasible after the date on which such criteria are so established, applying such revised criteria.

"(2) In the case of a redetermination under paragraph (1) of a prior action which found that an individual was not under a disability, if such individual is found on redetermination to be under a disability, such redetermination shall be applied as though it had been made at the time of such prior action.

"(3) Any individual with a mental impairment who was found to be not disabled pursuant to an initial disability determination or a continuing eligibility review between March 1, 1981, and the date of the enactment of this Act [Oct. 9, 1984], and who reapplies for benefits under title II or XVI of the Social Security Act [this subchapter or subchapter XVI of this chapter], may be determined to be under a disability during the period considered in the most recent prior determination. Any reapplication under this paragraph must be filed within one year after the date of the enactment of this Act, and benefits payable as a result of the preceding sentence shall be paid only on the basis of the reapplication."

Regulations

Section 9(a)(2) of Pub.L. 98–460 provided that: "The Secretary of Health and Human Services shall prescribe regulations required under section 221(j) of the Social Security Act [subsec. (j) of this section] not later than 180 days after the date of the enactment of this Act [Oct. 9, 1984]."

Review of Decisions Rendered by Administrative Law Judges as Result of Disability Hearings; Report to Congress

Section 304(g) of Pub.L. 96–265 provided that: "The Secretary of Health and Human Services shall implement a program of reviewing, on his own motion, decisions rendered by administrative law judges as a result of hearings under section 221(d) of the Social Security Act [subsec. (d) of this section], and shall report to the Congress by January 1, 1982, on his progress."

Travel Expenses for Medical Examinations, Reconsideration Interviews, and Proceedings Before Administrative Law Judges

Provisions authorizing payment of travel expenses either on an actual cost or commuted basis, to an individual for travel incident to medical examinations, and to parties, their representatives and all reasonably necessary witnesses for travel within the United States, Puerto Rico, and the Virgin Islands, to reconsider interviews and to proceedings before administrative law judges under subchapters II, XVI, and XVIII of this chapter were contained in the following appropriation Acts:

Oct. 18, 1978, Pub.L. 95–480, Title II, 92 Stat. 1582.
Sept. 30, 1976, Pub.L. 94–439, Title II, 90 Stat. 1432.
Jan. 28, 1976, Pub.L. 94–206, Title II, 90 Stat. 17.
Dec. 7, 1974, Pub.L. 93–517, Title II, 88 Stat. 1645.
Dec. 18, 1973, Pub.L. 93–192, Title II, 87 Stat. 759.
Aug. 10, 1971, Pub.L. 92–80, Title II, 85 Stat. 296.
Jan. 11, 1971, Pub.L. 91–667, Title II, 84 Stat. 2013.
Mar. 5, 1970, Pub.L. 91–204, Title II, 84 Stat. 41.
Oct. 11, 1968, Pub.L. 90–557, Title II, 82 Stat. 988.
Nov. 8, 1967, Pub.L. 90–132, Title II, 81 Stat. 402.
Nov. 7, 1966, Pub.L. 89–787, Title II, 80 Stat. 1395.
Aug. 31, 1965, Pub.L. 89–156, Title II, 79 Stat. 604.
Sept. 19, 1964, Pub.L. 88–605, Title II, 78 Stat. 974.
Oct. 11, 1963, Pub.L. 88–136, Title II, 77 Stat. 239.
Aug. 14, 1962, Pub.L. 87–582, Title II, 76 Stat. 375.
Sept. 22, 1961, Pub.L. 87–290, Title II, 75 Stat. 604.
Sept. 2, 1960, Pub.L. 86–703, Title II, 74 Stat. 769.
Aug. 14, 1959, Pub.L. 86–158, Title II, 73 Stat. 352.
Aug. 1, 1958, Pub.L. 85–580, Title II, 72 Stat. 471.
June 29, 1957, Pub.L. 85–67, Title II, 71 Stat. 221.
June 29, 1956, c. 477, Title II, 70 Stat. 434.
Aug. 1, 1955, c. 437, Title II, 69 Stat. 408.

§ 422. Rehabilitation services

(a) Repealed. Pub.L. 106–170, Title I, § 101(b)(1)(B), Dec. 17, 1999, 113 Stat. 1873

(b) Repealed. Pub.L. 106–170, Title I, § 101(b)(1)(C), Dec. 17, 1999, 113 Stat. 1873

(c) "Period of trial work" defined

(1) The term "period of trial work", with respect to an individual entitled to benefits under section 423, 402(d), 402(e), or 402(f) of this title, means a period of months beginning and ending as provided in paragraphs (3) and (4).

(2) For purposes of sections 416(i) and 423 of this title, any services rendered by an individual during a period of trial work shall be deemed not to have been rendered by such individual in determining whether his disability has ceased in a month during such period. For purposes of this subsection the term "services" means activity (whether legal or illegal) which is performed for remuneration or gain or is determined by the Commissioner of Social Security to be of a type normally performed for remuneration or gain.

(3) A period of trial work for any individual shall begin with the month in which he becomes entitled to disability insurance benefits, or, in the case of an individual entitled to benefits under section 402(d) of this title who has attained the age of eighteen, with the month in which he becomes entitled to such benefits or the month in which he attains the age of eighteen, whichever is later, or, in the case of an individual entitled to widow's or widower's insurance benefits under section 402(e) or (f) of this title who became entitled to such benefits prior to attaining age 60, with the month in which such individual becomes so entitled. Notwithstanding the preceding sentence, no period of trial work may begin for any individual prior to the beginning of the month following September 1960; and no such period may begin for an individual in a period of disability of such individual in which he had a previous period of trial work.

(4) A period of trial work for any individual shall end with the close of whichever of the following months is the earlier:

(A) the ninth month, in any period of 60 consecutive months, in which the individual renders services (whether or not such nine months are consecutive); or

(B) the month in which his disability (as defined in section 423(d) of this title) ceases (as determined after application of paragraph (2) of this subsection).

(5) Upon conviction by a Federal court, or the imposition of a civil monetary penalty under section 1320a–8 of this title, that an individual has fraudulently concealed work activity during a period of trial work from the Commissioner of Social Security by—

(A) providing false information to the Commissioner of Social Security as to whether the individual had earnings in or for a particular period, or as to the amount thereof;

(B) receiving disability insurance benefits under this subchapter while engaging in work activity under another identity, including under another social security account number or a number purporting to be a social security account number; or

(C) taking other actions to conceal work activity with an intent fraudulently to secure payment in a greater amount than is due or when no payment is authorized,

no benefit shall be payable to such individual under this subchapter with respect to a period of disability for any month before such conviction during which the individual rendered services during the period of trial work with respect to which the fraudulently concealed work activity occurred, and amounts otherwise due under this subchapter as restitution, penalties, assessments, fines, or other repayments shall in all cases be in addition to any amounts for which such individual is liable as overpayments by reason of such concealment.

(d) Cost of rehabilitation services from trust funds

(1) For purposes of making vocational rehabilitation services more readily available to disabled individuals who are—

(A) entitled to disability insurance benefits under section 423 of this title,

(B) entitled to child's insurance benefits under section 402(d) of this title after having attained age 18 (and are under a disability),

(C) entitled to widow's insurance benefits under section 402(e) of this title prior to attaining age 60, or

(D) entitled to widower's insurance benefits under section 402(f) of this title prior to attaining age 60,

to the end that savings will accrue to the Trust Funds as a result of rehabilitating such individuals, there are authorized to be transferred from the Federal Old-Age and Survivors Insurance Trust Fund and the Federal Disability Insurance Trust Fund each fiscal year such sums as may be necessary to enable the Commissioner of Social Security to reimburse the State for the reasonable and necessary costs of vocational rehabilitation services furnished such individuals (including services during their waiting periods), under a State plan for vocational rehabilitation services approved under title I of the Rehabilitation Act of 1973, **(i)** in cases where the furnishing of such services results in the performance by such individuals of substantial gainful activity for a continuous period of nine months, **(ii)** in cases where such individuals receive benefits as a result of section 425(b) of this title (except that no reimbursement under this paragraph shall be made for services furnished to any individual receiving such benefits for any period after the close of such individual's ninth consecutive month of substantial gainful activity or the close of the month in which his or her entitlement to such benefits ceases, whichever first occurs), and **(iii)** in cases where such individuals, without good cause, refuse to continue to accept vocational rehabilitation services or fail to cooperate in such a manner as to preclude their successful rehabilitation. The determination that the vocational rehabilitation services contributed to the successful return of an individual to substantial gainful activity, the determination that an individual, without good cause, refused to continue to accept vocational rehabilitation services or failed to cooperate in such a manner as to preclude successful rehabilitation, and the determination of the amount of costs to be reimbursed under this subsection shall be made by the Commissioner of Social Security in accordance with criteria formulated by the Commissioner.

(2) In the case of any State which is unwilling to participate or does not have a plan which meets the requirements of paragraph (1), the Commissioner of Social Security may provide such services in such State by agreement or contract with other public or private agencies, organizations, institutions, or individuals. The provision of such services shall be subject to the same conditions as otherwise apply under paragraph (1).

(3) Payments under this subsection shall be made in advance or by way of reimbursement, with necessary adjustments for overpayments and underpayments.

(4) Money paid from the Trust Funds under this subsection for the reimbursement of the costs of providing services to individuals who are entitled to benefits under section 423 of this title (including services during their waiting periods), or who are entitled to benefits under section 402(d) of this title on the basis of the wages and self-employment income of such individuals, shall be charged to the Federal Disability Insurance Trust Fund, and all other money paid from the Trust Funds under this subsection shall be charged to the Federal Old-Age and Survivors Insurance Trust

Fund. The Commissioner of Social Security shall determine according to such methods and procedures as the Commissioner may deem appropriate—

(A) the total amount to be reimbursed for the cost of services under this subsection, and

(B) subject to the provisions of the preceding sentence, the amount which should be charged to each of the Trust Funds.

(5) For purposes of this subsection the term "vocational rehabilitation services" shall have the meaning assigned to it in title I of the Rehabilitation Act of 1973, except that such services may be limited in type, scope, or amount in accordance with regulations of the Commissioner of Social Security designed to achieve the purpose of this subsection.

(e) Treatment referrals for individuals with alcoholism or drug addiction condition

In the case of any individual whose benefits under this subchapter are paid to a representative payee pursuant to section 405(j)(1)(B) of this title, the Commissioner of Social Security shall refer such individual to the appropriate State agency administering the State plan for substance abuse treatment services approved under subpart II of part B of title XIX of the Public Health Service Act (42 U.S.C. 300x–21 et seq.).

(Aug. 14, 1935, c. 531, Title II, § 222, as added Sept. 1, 1954, c. 1206, Title I, § 106(g), 68 Stat. 1081; amended Aug. 1, 1956, c. 836, Title I, § 103(b), 70 Stat. 817; Pub.L. 85–840, Title II, § 205(n), Title III, § 307(g), Aug. 28, 1958, 72 Stat. 1025, 1032; Pub.L. 86–778, Title IV, § 403(a), Sept. 13, 1960, 74 Stat. 968; Pub.L. 89–97, Title III, §§ 306(c)(14), 308(d)(11), 336, July 30, 1965, 79 Stat. 373, 379, 408; Pub.L. 90–248, Title I, §§ 104(d)(3), (4), 158(c)(5), Jan. 2, 1968, 81 Stat. 832, 869; Pub.L. 92–603, Title I, §§ 107(b)(3), (4), 131, Oct. 30, 1972, 86 Stat. 1343, 1360; Pub.L. 96–265, Title III, § 303(a), June 9, 1980, 94 Stat. 451; Pub.L. 97–35, Title XXII, § 2209(a), Aug. 13, 1981, 95 Stat. 840; Pub.L. 98–21, Title III, § 309(*l*) to (n), Apr. 20, 1983, 97 Stat. 117; Pub.L. 98–369, Div. B, Title VI, § 2663(a)(15), July 18, 1984, 98 Stat. 1165; Pub.L. 98–460, § 11(a), Oct. 9, 1984, 98 Stat. 1805; Pub.L. 101–508, Title V, § 5112(a), Nov. 5, 1990, 104 Stat. 1388–273; Pub.L. 103–296, Title I, § 107(a)(4), Title II, § 201(a)(4)(B), Aug. 15, 1994, 108 Stat. 1478, 1499; Pub.L. 104–121, Title I, § 105(a)(3), Mar. 29, 1996, 110 Stat. 852; Pub.L. 106–170, Title I, § 101(b)(1)(B), (C), Dec. 17, 1999, 113 Stat. 1873; Pub.L. 108–203, Title II, § 208(a), Mar. 2, 2004, 118 Stat. 513; Pub.L. 114–74, Title VIII, § 813(d), Nov. 2, 2015, 129 Stat. 604.)

HISTORICAL AND STATUTORY NOTES

References in Text

This subchapter, referred to in text, originally read "this title", meaning the Social Security Act, Aug. 14, 1935, c. 531, Title II, 49 Stat. 622, as amended, which is classified as this subchapter, 42 U.S.C.A. § 401 et seq.

The Rehabilitation Act of 1973, referred to in subsec. (d)(1), (5), is Pub.L. 93–112, Sept. 26, 1973, 87 Stat. 355, as amended, which is classified principally to chapter 16 of Title 29, 29 U.S.C.A. § 701 et seq. Title I of the Act is classified generally to subchapter I of chapter 16 of Title 29, 29 U.S.C.A. § 720 et seq. Pursuant to 29 U.S.C.A. § 3361(c), references to a provision of the Rehabilitation Act of 1973 are deemed to refer to the corresponding provision of such Act, as amended by the Workforce Innovation and Opportunity Act, Pub.L. 113–128, July 22, 2014, 128 Stat. 1425. For complete classification, see Short Title note set out under 29 U.S.C.A. § 701 and Tables.

The Public Health Service Act, referred to in subsec. (e), is Act July 1, 1944, c. 373, 58 Stat. 682, as amended. Subpart II of part B of title XIX of that Act is classified generally to subpart II of part B of subchapter XVII of chapter 6A of this title (section 300x–21 et seq.). For complete classification of this Act to the Code, see Short Title note set out under section 201 of this title and Tables.

Effective and Applicability Provisions

2004 Acts. Pub.L. 108–203, Title II, § 208(b), Mar. 2, 2004, 118 Stat. 513, provided that: "The amendment made by subsection (a) [amending this section] shall apply with respect to work activity performed after the date of the enactment of this Act [Mar. 2, 2004]."

1999 Acts. Amendment by section 101(b) of Pub.L. 106–170 effective with the first month following 1 year after December 17, 1999, subject to graduated implementation of program provisions of section 101(d) of Pub.L. 106–170 [set out as a note under section 1320b–19 of this title], see section 101(c) of Pub.L. 106–170, set out as a note under section 1320b–19 of this title.

1996 Acts. Amendment by section 105(a)(3) of Pub.L. 104–121 applicable to benefits for which applications are filed after third month following March, 1996, see section 105(a)(5) of Pub.L. 104–121, set out as a note under section 405 of this title.

1994 Acts. Amendment by section 107(a)(4) of Pub.L. 103–296 effective Mar. 31, 1995, see section 110 of Pub.L. 103–296, set out as a note under section 401 of this title.

Section 201(a)(4)(C) of Pub.L. 103–296 provided that: "The amendments made by this paragraph [amending subsec. (c)(2) of this section and section 423 (d)(4) of this title] shall take effect on the date of the enactment of this Act [Aug. 15, 1994]."

1990 Acts. Section 5112(b) of Pub.L. 101–508 provided that: "The amendments made by subsection (a) [amending this section] shall take effect on January 1, 1992."

1984 Acts. Section 11(c) of Pub.L. 98–460 provided that: "The amendments made by this section [amending subsec. (d)(1) of this section and section 1382d(d) of this title] shall apply with respect to individuals who receive benefits as a result of section 225(b) or section 1631(a)(6) of the Social Security Act [section 425(b) or section 1383(a)(6) of this title], or who refuse to continue to accept rehabilitation services or fail to cooperate in an approved vocational rehabilitation program, in or after the first month following the month in which this Act is enacted [Oct., 1984]."

Amendment by Pub.L. 98–369 effective July 18, 1984, but not to be construed as changing or affecting any right, liability, status or interpretation which existed (under the provisions of law involved) before that date, see section 2664(b) of Pub.L. 98–369, set out as a note under section 401 of this title.

1983 Acts. Amendment by section 422(*l*)–(n) of Pub.L. 98–21 applicable only with respect to monthly payments payable under this subchapter for months after April 1983, except as otherwise specifically provided, see section 310 of Pub.L. 98–21, set out as a note under section 402 of this title.

1981 Acts. Section 2209(b) of Pub.L. 97–35 provided that: "The amendment made by subsection (a) [amending subsec. (d) of this section] shall apply with respect to services rendered on or after October 1, 1981."

1980 Acts. Amendment by Pub.L. 96–265 effective the first day of the sixth month which begins after June 9, 1980, and applicable to any individual whose disability has not been determined to have ceased prior to such first day, see section 303(d) of Pub.L. 96–265, set out as a note under section 402 of this title.

1972 Acts. Amendment of subsec. (b)(1) and (d)(1)(D) by sections 107(b)(3), (4) of Pub.L. 92–603 applicable with respect to monthly benefits under this subchapter for months after Dec. 1972, with specified exceptions, see section 107(c) of Pub.L. 92–603, set out as a note under section 402 of this title.

1968 Acts. Amendment of subsecs. (a), (b)(1), (d)(1) by section 104 of Pub.L. 90–248 applicable with respect to monthly benefits under this subchapter for and after the month of February 1968, but only on the basis of applications for such benefits filed in or after January 1968, see section 104(e) of Pub.L. 90–248, set out as a note under section 402 of this title.

Amendment by section 158 of Pub.L. 90–248 applicable with respect to applications for disability insurance benefits under section 423 of this title and to disability determinations under section 416(i) of this title, filed in or after Jan. 1968, or before Jan. 1968 if the applicant has not died before such month and if (A) notice of the final decision of the Secretary of Health, Education, and Welfare has not been given to the applicant before such month; or (B) the notice referred to in subparagraph (A) has been so given before such month but a civil action with respect to such final decision is commenced under section 205(g) of the Social Security Act [section 405(g) of this title] (whether before, in, or after such month) and the decision in such civil action has not become final before such month, see section 158(e) of Pub.L. 90–248, set out as a note under section 423 of this title.

1965 Acts. Amendment of subsec. (b)(3) by Pub.L. 89–97 applicable with respect to monthly insurance benefits under this subchapter beginning with the second month following July 1965, but, in the case of an individual who was not entitled to a monthly insurance benefit under section 402 of this title for the first month following July 1965, only on the basis of an application filed in or after July 1965, see section 308(e) of Pub.L. 89–97, set out as a note under section 402 of this title.

1960 Acts. Section 403(e) of Pub.L. 86–778 provided that:

"(1) The amendment made by subsection (a) [to subsec. (c) of this section] shall be effective only with respect to months beginning after the month in which this Act is enacted [Sept. 1960].

"(2) The amendments made by subsections (b) and (d) [to sections 423(a)(1) and 402(d)(1) of this title] shall apply only with respect to benefits under section 223(a) or 202(d) of the Social Security Act [section 423(a) or 402(d) of this title] for months after the month in which this Act is enacted [Sept. 1960] in the case of individuals who, without regard to such amendments, would have been entitled to such benefits for the month in which this Act is enacted [Sept. 1960] or for any succeeding month.

"(3) The amendment made by subsection (c) [to section 416(i)(2) of this title] shall apply only in the case of individuals who have a period of disability (as defined in section 216(i) of the Social Security Act [section 416(i) of this title]) beginning on or after the date of the enactment of this Act [Sept. 13, 1960], or beginning before such date and continuing, without regard to such amendment, beyond the end of the month in which this Act is enacted [Sept. 1960]."

1958 Acts. Amendment of subsec. (b)(3) by section 205 of Pub.L. 85–840 applicable with respect to monthly benefits under this subchapter for months after Aug., 1958, but only if an application for such benefits is filed on or after Aug. 28, 1958, see section 207(a) of Pub.L. 85–840, set out as a note under section 416 of this title.

Section 307(h)(3) of Pub.L. 85–840 provided that: "The amendments made by subsection (g) [adding subsec. (b)(2) of this section] shall apply with respect to monthly benefits under section 202 of the Social Security Act [section 402 of this title] for months, occurring after the month in which this Act is enacted [August 1958], in which a deduction is incurred under paragraph (1) of section 222(b) of the Social Security Act [par. (1) of subsec. (b) of this section]."

Continuation of Federal Programs and Activities During Fiscal Year Transition Period From July l, 1976, Through September 30, 1976

Pub.L. 94–274, Title I, § 101(a), Apr. 21, 1976, 90 Stat. 383, provided that:

"**(a)** For the purposes of sections 222(d)(1), 421, 506(d), 516, 705, 901(e)(2) and (f), 902, 905(b)(2), 1108, 1115, and 2002(a)(2) of the Social Security Act [subsec. (d)(1) of this section, and sections 621, 706(d), 716, 906(b), 1101(e)(2) and (f)(3)(A), 1102(a), 1105(b)(2)(B), 1308, 1315, and 1397a(a)(2) of this title, respectively] the term 'fiscal year' includes the period of July 1, 1976, through September 30, 1976, and the exercise of authority pursuant to these provisions for that period shall be subject to the conditions stated in the following paragraphs:

"(1) notwithstanding the provisions of section 222(d)(1) (42 U.S.C. 422(d)(1)) [subsec. (d)(1) of this section], the amount authorized to be transferred from the trust funds pursuant to that section in the period beginning July 1, 1976, and ending September 30, 1976, may not exceed 1.5 per centum of the total of the benefits certified for payment in the first quarter of the fiscal year beginning July 1, 1975, and the amount authorized to be transferred from the Trust Funds in the fiscal year beginning October 1, 1976, may not exceed 1.5 per centum of the total of the benefits certified for payment in the preceding twelve months:

"(2) the fixed dollar allotment to each State under section 421 (42 U.S.C. 621) [section 621 of this title] shall be $17,500;

"(3) the reduction required by section 506(d) (42 U.S.C. 706(d)) [section 706(d) of this title] shall be the amount by which the sum expended from non-Federal sources for that period is less than one-fourth the sum expended from such sources for the fiscal year ending June 30, 1968;

"(4) the amount allotted to each State under section 516 (42 U.S.C. 716) [section 716 of this title] shall be the excess of one-fourth the amount of the allotment for the State under sections 503 and 504 of the Social Security Act (42 U.S.C. 703 and 704) [sections 703 and 704 of this title], for the fiscal year ending June 30, 1973, plus the amount of any grants to the State under sections 508, 509, and 510 of that Act (42 U.S.C. 708, 709, and 710) [sections 708 to 710 of this title], over the amount of the allotment of the State under sections 503 and 504 of that Act for the period;

"(5) the limitation imposed by section 705(b) (42 U.S.C. 906(b)) [section 906(b) of this title] on the amount that may be available for carrying out section 705(f) [section 906(f) of this title] shall be $500,000 for that period;

"(6) the percentage referenced in the second sentence of section 901(e)(2) (42 U.S.C. 1101(e)(2)) [section 1101(e)(2) of this title] shall be reduced to 10 per centum for the purpose of advances to be made in that period;

"(7) notwithstanding the provisions of section 901(f)(3)(A) (42 U.S.C. 1101(f)(3)(A)) [section 1101(f)(3)(A) of this title], for the fiscal year beginning October 1, 1976, the excess in the employment administration account shall be retained until the amount in such account is equal to 160 per centum of the amount of the total appropriation by the Congress out of the account for the period July 1, 1976, through September 30, 1976, and $37,500,000 or three thirty-seconds of the amount in the employment security administration account, whichever is the lesser, is authorized to be made available for that period under the conditions provided therein;

"(8) the determinative calendar year for the purpose of a transfer to the unemployment account pursuant to section 902(a) (42 U.S.C. 1102(a)) [section 1102(a) of this title], at the beginning of the fiscal year beginning October 1, 1976, shall be calendar year 1975;

"(9) the determinative calendar year for the purposes of a transfer to the extended unemployment compensation account pursuant to section 905(b)(2)(B) (42 U.S.C. 1105(b)(2)(B)) [section 1105(b)(2)(B) of this title], at the beginning of the fiscal year beginning October 1, 1976, shall be calendar year 1975;

"(10) the limitations imposed by section 1108 (42 U.S.C. 1308) [section 1308 of this title] on amounts certified by the Secretary shall be one-fourth of the limitations imposed by that section with respect to the fiscal year ending June 30, 1976;

"(11) the dollar limitation imposed by section 1115 (42 U.S.C. 1315) [section 1315 of this title] on the amount available for payments to the States for the cost of projects under that section shall be $1,000,000 of the aggregate amount appropriated for payments to the States for the period; and

"(12) notwithstanding the provisions of subparagraph (A) of section 2002(a)(2) (42 U.S.C. 1397a(a)(2)) [section 1397a(a)(2)(A) of this title], the limitation imposed by that subparagraph on payments with respect to expenditures by a State for the period shall be one-fourth of the limitation imposed on such payments with respect to expenditures by the State for the fiscal year beginning July 1, 1975; and notwithstanding the provisions of subparagraph (D) of section 2002(a)(2) [section 1397a(a)(2)(D) of this title], the maximum allotments under that subparagraph for the period shall be $3,750,000 for Puerto Rico, $125,000 for Guam, and $125,000 for the Virgin Islands, but nothing in this Act shall apply to the second sentence of section 2002(a)(2)(A)."

§ 423. Disability insurance benefit payments

(a) Disability insurance benefits

(1) Every individual who—

(A) is insured for disability insurance benefits (as determined under subsection (c)(1)),

(B) has not attained retirement age (as defined in section 416(*l*) of this title),

(C) if not a United States citizen or national—

(i) has been assigned a social security account number that was, at the time of assignment, or at any later time, consistent with the requirements of subclause (I) or (III) of section 405(c)(2)(B)(i) of this title; or

(ii) at the time any quarters of coverage are earned—

(I) is described in subparagraph (B) or (D) of section 1101(a)(15) of Title 8,

(II) is lawfully admitted temporarily to the United States for business (in the case of an individual described in such subparagraph (B)) or the performance as a crewman (in the case of an individual described in such subparagraph (D)), and

(III) the business engaged in or service as a crewman performed is within the scope of the terms of such individual's admission to the United States.[1]

(D) has filed application for disability insurance benefits, and

(E) is under a disability (as defined in subsection (d))

shall be entitled to a disability insurance benefit (i) for each month beginning with the first month after his waiting period (as defined in subsection (c)(2)) in which he becomes so entitled to such insurance benefits, or (ii) for each month beginning with the first month during all of which he is under a disability and in which he becomes so entitled to such insurance benefits, but only if he was entitled to disability insurance benefits which terminated, or had a period of disability (as defined in section 416(i) of this title) which ceased, within the 60-month period preceding the first month in which he is under such disability, and ending with the month preceding whichever of the following months is the earliest: the month in which he dies, the month in which he attains retirement age (as defined in section 416(*l*) of this title), or, subject to subsection (e), the termination month. For purposes of the preceding sentence, the termination month for any individual shall be the third month following the month in which his disability ceases; except that, in the case of an individual who has a period of trial work which ends as determined by application of section 422(c)(4)(A) of this title, the termination month shall be the earlier of (I) the third month following the earliest month after the end of such period of trial work with respect to which such individual is determined to no longer be suffering from a disabling physical or mental impairment, or (II) the third month following the earliest month in which such individual engages or is determined able to engage in substantial gainful activity, but in no event earlier than the first month occurring after the 36 months following such period of trial work in which he engages or is determined able to engage in substantial gainful activity. No payment under this paragraph may be made to an individual who would not meet the definition of disability in subsection (d) except for paragraph (1)(B) thereof for any month in which he engages in substantial gainful activity, and no payment may be made for such month under subsection (b), (c), or (d) of section 402 of this title to any person on the basis of the wages and self-employment income of such individual. In the case of a deceased individual, the requirement of subparagraph (C) may be satisfied by an application for benefits filed with respect to such individual within 3 months after the month in which he died.

(2) Except as provided in section 402(q) of this title and section 415(b)(2)(A)(ii) of this title, such individual's disability insurance benefit for any month shall be equal to his primary insurance amount for such month determined under section 415 of this title as though he had attained age 62 in—

(A) the first month of his waiting period, or

(B) in any case in which clause (ii) of paragraph (1) of this subsection is applicable, the first month for which he becomes entitled to such disability insurance benefits,

and as though he had become entitled to old-age insurance benefits in the month in which the application for disability insurance benefits was filed and he was entitled to an old-age insurance benefit for each month for which (pursuant to subsection (b)) he was entitled to a disability insurance benefit. For the purposes of the preceding sentence, in the case of an individual who attained age 62 in or before the first month referred to in subparagraph (A) or (B) of such sentence, as the case may be, the elapsed years referred to in section 415(b)(3) of this title shall not include the year in which he attained age 62, or any year thereafter.

(b) Filing application

An application for disability insurance benefits filed before the first month in which the applicant satisfies the requirements for such benefits (as prescribed in subsection (a)(1)) shall be deemed a valid application (and shall be deemed to have been filed in such first month) only if the applicant satisfies the requirements for such benefits before the Commissioner of Social Security makes a final decision on the application and no request under section 405(b) of this title for notice and opportunity for a hearing thereon is made, or if such a request is made, before a decision based upon the evidence adduced at the hearing is made (regardless of whether such decision becomes the final decision of the Commissioner of Social Security). An individual who would have been entitled to a disability insurance benefit for any month had he filed application therefor before the end of such month shall be entitled to such benefit for such month if such application is filed before the end of the 12th month immediately succeeding such month.

(c) Definitions; insured status; waiting period

For purposes of this section—

(1) An individual shall be insured for disability insurance benefits in any month if—

(A) he would have been a fully insured individual (as defined in section 414 of this title) had he attained age 62 and filed application for benefits under section 402(a) of this title on the first day of such month, and

(B)(i) he had not less than 20 quarters of coverage during the 40-quarter period which ends with the quarter in which such month occurred, or

(ii) if such month ends before the quarter in which he attains (or would attain) age 31, not less than one-half (and not less than 6) of the quarters during the period ending with the quarter in which such month occurred and beginning after he attained the age of 21 were quarters of coverage, or (if the number of quarters in such period is less than 12) not less than 6 of the quarters in the 12-quarter period ending with such quarter were quarters of coverage, or

(iii) in the case of an individual (not otherwise insured under clause (i)) who, by reason of section 416(i)(3)(B)(ii) of this title, had a prior period of disability that began during a period before the quarter in which he or she attained age 31, not less than one-half of the quarters beginning after such individual attained age 21 and ending with the quarter in which such month occurs are quarters of coverage, or (if the number of quarters in such period is less than 12) not less than 6 of the quarters in the 12-quarter period ending with such quarter are quarters of coverage;

except that the provisions of subparagraph (B) of this paragraph shall not apply in the case of an individual who is blind (within the meaning of "blindness" as defined in section 416(i)(1) of this title). For purposes of subparagraph (B) of this paragraph, when the number of quarters in any period is an odd number, such number shall be reduced by one, and a quarter shall not be counted as part of any period if any part of such quarter was included in a period of disability unless such quarter was a quarter of coverage.

(2) The term "waiting period" means, in the case of any application for disability insurance benefits, the earliest period of five consecutive calendar months—

(A) throughout which the individual with respect to whom such application is filed has been under a disability, and

(B) (i) which begins not earlier than with the first day of the seventeenth month before the month in which such application is filed if such individual is insured for disability insurance benefits in such seventeenth month, or (ii) if he is not so insured in such month, which begins not earlier than with the first day of the first month after such seventeenth month in which he is so insured.

Notwithstanding the preceding provisions of this paragraph, no waiting period may begin for any individual before January 1, 1957.

(d) "Disability" defined

(1) The term "disability" means—

(A) inability to engage in any substantial gainful activity by reason of any medically determinable physical or mental impairment which can be expected to result in death or which has lasted or can be expected to last for a continuous period of not less than 12 months; or

(B) in the case of an individual who has attained the age of 55 and is blind (within the meaning of "blindness" as defined in section 416(i)(1) of this title), inability by reason of such blindness to engage in substantial gainful activity requiring skills or abilities comparable to those of any gainful activity in which he has previously engaged with some regularity and over a substantial period of time.

(2) For purposes of paragraph (1)(A)—

(A) An individual shall be determined to be under a disability only if his physical or mental impairment or impairments are of such severity that he is not only unable to do his previous work but cannot, considering his age, education, and work experience, engage in any other kind of substantial gainful work which exists in the national economy, regardless of whether such work exists in the immediate area in which he lives, or whether a specific job vacancy exists for him, or whether he would be hired if he applied for work. For purposes of the preceding sentence (with respect to any individual), "work which exists in the national economy" means work which exists in significant numbers either in the region where such individual lives or in several regions of the country.

(B) In determining whether an individual's physical or mental impairment or impairments are of a sufficient medical severity that such impairment or impairments could be the basis of eligibility under this section, the Commissioner of Social Security shall consider the combined effect of all of the individual's impairments without regard to whether any such impairment, if considered separately, would be of such severity. If the Commissioner of Social Security does find a medically severe combination of impairments, the combined impact of the impairments shall be considered throughout the disability determination process.

(C) An individual shall not be considered to be disabled for purposes of this subchapter if alcoholism or drug addiction would (but for this subparagraph) be a contributing factor material to the Commissioner's determination that the individual is disabled.

(3) For purposes of this subsection, a "physical or mental impairment" is an impairment that results from anatomical, physiological, or psychological abnormalities which are demonstrable by medically acceptable clinical and laboratory diagnostic techniques.

(4)**(A)** The Commissioner of Social Security shall by regulations prescribe the criteria for determining when services performed or earnings derived from services demonstrate an individual's ability to engage in substantial gainful activity. No individual who is blind shall be regarded as having demonstrated an ability to engage in substantial gainful activity on the basis of earnings that do not exceed an amount equal to the exempt amount which would be applicable under section 403(f)(8) of this title, to individuals described in subparagraph (D) thereof, if section 102 of the Senior Citizens' Right to Work Act of 1996 had not been enacted. Notwithstanding the provisions of paragraph (2), an individual whose services or earnings meet such criteria shall, except for purposes of section 422(c) of this title, be found not to be disabled. In determining whether an individual is able to engage in substantial gainful activity by reason of his earnings, where his disability is sufficiently severe to result in a functional limitation requiring assistance in order for him to work, there shall be excluded from such earnings an amount equal to the cost (to such individual) of any attendant care services, medical devices, equipment, prostheses, and similar items and services (not including routine drugs or routine medical services unless such drugs or services are necessary for the control of the disabling condition) which are necessary (as determined by the Commissioner of Social Security in regulations) for that purpose, whether or not such assistance is also needed to enable him to carry out his normal daily functions; except that the amounts to be excluded shall be subject to such reasonable limits as the Commissioner of Social Security may prescribe.

(B) In determining under subparagraph (A) when services performed or earnings derived from services demonstrate an individual's ability to engage in substantial gainful activity, the Commissioner of Social Security shall apply the criteria described in subparagraph (A) with respect to services performed by any individual without regard to the legality of such services.

(C)(i) Subject to clause (ii), in determining when earnings derived from services demonstrate an individual's ability to engage in substantial gainful activity, such earnings shall be presumed to have been earned—

(I) in making a determination of initial entitlement on the basis of disability, in the month in which the services were performed from which such earnings were derived; and

(II) in any other case, in the month in which such earnings were paid.

(ii) A presumption made under clause (i) shall not apply to a determination described in such clause if—

(I) the Commissioner can reasonably establish, based on evidence readily available at the time of such determination, that the earnings were earned in a different month than when paid; or

(II) in any case in which there is a determination that no benefit is payable due to earnings, after the individual is notified of the presumption made and provided with an opportunity to submit additional information along with an explanation of what additional information is needed, the individual shows to the satisfaction of the Commissioner that such earnings were earned in another month.

(5)(A) An individual shall not be considered to be under a disability unless he furnishes such medical and other evidence of the existence thereof as the Commissioner of Social Security may require. An individual's statement as to pain or other symptoms shall not alone be conclusive evidence of disability as defined in this section; there must be medical signs and findings, established by medically acceptable clinical or laboratory diagnostic techniques, which show the existence of a medical impairment that results from anatomical, physiological, or psychological abnormalities which could reasonably be expected to produce the pain or other symptoms alleged and which, when considered with all evidence required to be furnished under this paragraph (including statements of the individual or his physician as to the intensity and persistence of such pain or other symptoms which may reasonably be accepted as consistent with the medical signs and findings), would lead to a conclusion that the individual is under a disability. Objective medical evidence of pain or other symptoms established by medically acceptable clinical or laboratory techniques (for example, deteriorating nerve or muscle tissue) must be considered in reaching a conclusion as to whether the individual is under a disability. Any non-Federal hospital, clinic, laboratory, or other provider of medical services, or physician not in the employ of the Federal Government, which supplies medical evidence required and requested by the Commissioner of Social Security under this paragraph shall be entitled to payment from the Commissioner of Social Security for the reasonable cost of providing such evidence.

(B) In making any determination with respect to whether an individual is under a disability or continues to be under a disability, the Commissioner of Social Security shall consider all evidence available in such individual's case record, and shall develop a complete medical history of at least the preceding twelve months for any case in which a determination is made that the individual is not under a disability. In making any determination the Commissioner of Social Security shall make every reasonable effort to obtain from the individual's treating physician (or other treating health care provider) all medical evidence, including diagnostic tests, necessary in order to properly make such determination, prior to evaluating medical evidence obtained from any other source on a consultative basis.

(C)(i) In making any determination with respect to whether an individual is under a disability or continues to be under a disability, the Commissioner of Social Security may not consider (except for good cause as determined by the Commissioner) any evidence furnished by—

(I) any individual or entity who has been convicted of a felony under section 408 of this title or under section 1383a of this title;

(II) any individual or entity who has been excluded from participation in any Federal health care program under section 1320a–7 of this title; or

(III) any person with respect to whom a civil money penalty or assessment has been imposed under section 1320a–8 of this title for the submission of false evidence.

(ii) To the extent and at such times as is necessary for the effective implementation of clause (i) of this subparagraph—

(I) the Inspector General of the Social Security Administration shall transmit to the Commissioner information relating to persons described in subclause (I) or (III) of clause (i);[2]

(II) the Secretary of Health and Human Services shall transmit to the Commissioner information relating to persons described in subclause (II) of clause (i); and[3]

(6)(A) Notwithstanding any other provision of this subchapter, any physical or mental impairment which arises in connection with the commission by an individual (after October 19, 1980) of an offense which constitutes a felony under applicable law and for which such individual is subsequently convicted, or which is aggravated in connection with such an offense (but only to the extent so aggravated), shall not be considered in determining whether an individual is under a disability.

(B) Notwithstanding any other provision of this subchapter, any physical or mental impairment which arises in connection with an individual's confinement in a jail, prison, or other penal institution or correctional facility pursuant to such individual's conviction of an offense (committed after October 19, 1980) constituting a felony under applicable law, or which is aggravated in connection with such a confinement (but only to the extent so aggravated), shall not be considered in determining whether such individual is under a disability for purposes of benefits payable for any month during which such individual is so confined.

(e) Engaging in substantial gainful activity

(1) No benefit shall be payable under subsection (d)(1)(B)(ii), (d)(6)(A)(ii), (d)(6)(B), (e)(1)(B)(ii), or (f)(1)(B)(ii) of section 402 of this title or under subsection (a)(1) of this section to an individual for any month, after the third month, in which he engages in substantial gainful activity during the 36–month period following the end of his trial work period determined by application of section 422(c)(4)(A) of this title.

(2) No benefit shall be payable under section 402 of this title on the basis of the wages and self-employment income of an individual entitled to a benefit under subsection (a)(1) of this section for any month for which the benefit of such individual under subsection (a)(1) is not payable under paragraph (1).

(f) Standard of review for termination of disability benefits

A recipient of benefits under this subchapter or subchapter XVIII based on the disability of any individual may be determined not to be entitled to such benefits on the basis of a finding that the physical or mental impairment on the basis of which such benefits are provided has ceased, does not exist, or is not disabling only if such finding is supported by—

(1) substantial evidence which demonstrates that—

(A) there has been any medical improvement in the individual's impairment or combination of impairments (other than medical improvement which is not related to the individual's ability to work), and

(B) the individual is now able to engage in substantial gainful activity; or

(2) substantial evidence which—

(A) consists of new medical evidence and a new assessment of the individual's residual functional capacity, and demonstrates that—

(i) although the individual has not improved medically, he or she is nonetheless a beneficiary of advances in medical or vocational therapy or technology (related to the individual's ability to work), and

(ii) the individual is now able to engage in substantial gainful activity, or

(B) demonstrates that—

(i) although the individual has not improved medically, he or she has undergone vocational therapy (related to the individual's ability to work), and

(ii) the individual is now able to engage in substantial gainful activity; or.

(3) substantial evidence which demonstrates that, as determined on the basis of new or improved diagnostic techniques or evaluations, the individual's impairment or combination of impairments is not as disabling as it was considered to be at the time of the most recent prior decision that he or she was under a disability or continued to be under a disability, and that therefore the individual is able to engage in substantial gainful activity; or

(4) substantial evidence (which may be evidence on the record at the time any prior determination of the entitlement to benefits based on disability was made, or newly obtained evidence which relates to that determination) which demonstrates that a prior determination was in error.

Nothing in this subsection shall be construed to require a determination that a recipient of benefits under this subchapter or subchapter XVIII based on an individual's disability is entitled to such benefits if the prior determination was fraudulently obtained or if the individual is engaged in substantial gainful activity, cannot be located, or fails, without good cause, to cooperate in a review of the entitlement to such benefits or to follow prescribed treatment which would be expected to restore his or her ability to engage in substantial gainful activity. In making for purposes of the preceding sentence any determination relating to fraudulent behavior by any individual or failure by any individual without good cause to cooperate or to take any required action, the Commissioner of Social Security shall specifically take into account any physical, mental, educational, or linguistic limitation such individual may have (including any lack of facility with the English language). Any determination under this section shall be made on the basis of all the evidence available in the individual's case file, including new evidence concerning the individual's prior or current condition which is presented by the individual or secured by the Commissioner of Social Security. Any determination made under this section shall be made on the basis of the weight of the evidence and on a neutral basis with regard to the individual's condition, without any initial inference as to the presence or absence of disability being drawn from the fact that the individual has previously been determined to be disabled. For purposes of this subsection, a benefit under this subchapter is based on an individual's disability if it is a disability insurance benefit, a child's, widow's, or widower's insurance benefit based on disability, or a mother's or father's insurance benefit based on the disability of the mother's or father's child who has attained age 16.

(g) Continued payment of disability benefits during appeal

(1) In any case where—

(A) an individual is a recipient of disability insurance benefits, or of child's, widow's, or widower's insurance benefits based on disability,

(B) the physical or mental impairment on the basis of which such benefits are payable is found to have ceased, not to have existed, or to no longer be disabling, and as a consequence such individual is determined not to be entitled to such benefits, and

(C) a timely request for a hearing under section 421(d) of this title, or for an administrative review prior to such hearing, is pending with respect to the determination that he is not so entitled,

such individual may elect (in such manner and form and within such time as the Commissioner of Social Security shall by regulations prescribe) to have the payment of such benefits, the payment of any other benefits under this subchapter based on such individual's wages and self-employment income, the payment of mother's or father's insurance benefits to such individual's mother or father based on the disability of such individual as a child who has attained age 16, and the payment of benefits under subchapter XVIII based on such individual's disability, continued for an additional period beginning with the first month beginning after January 12, 1983, for which (under such determination) such benefits are no longer otherwise payable, and ending with the earlier of (i) the month preceding the month in which a decision is made after such a hearing, or (ii) the month preceding the month in which no such request for a hearing or an administrative review is pending.

(2)(A) If an individual elects to have the payment of his benefits continued for an additional period under paragraph (1), and the final decision of the Commissioner of Social Security affirms the determination that he is not entitled to such benefits, any benefits paid under this subchapter pursuant to such election (for months in such additional period) shall be considered overpayments for all purposes of this subchapter, except as otherwise provided in subparagraph (B).

(B) If the Commissioner of Social Security determines that the individual's appeal of his termination of benefits was made in good faith, all of the benefits paid pursuant to such individual's election under paragraph (1) shall be subject to waiver consideration under the provisions of section 404 of this title. In making for purposes of this subparagraph any determination of whether any individual's appeal is made in good faith, the Commissioner of Social Security shall specifically take into account any physical, mental, educational, or linguistic limitation such individual may have (including any lack of facility with the English language).

(h) Interim benefits in cases of delayed final decisions

(1) In any case in which an administrative law judge has determined after a hearing as provided under section 405(b) of this title that an individual is entitled to disability insurance benefits or child's, widow's, or widower's insurance benefits based on disability and the Commissioner of Social Security has not issued the Commissioner's final decision in such case within 110 days after the date of the administrative law judge's determination, such benefits shall be currently paid for the months during the period beginning with the month preceding the month in which such 110-day period expires and ending with the month preceding the month in which such final decision is issued.

(2) For purposes of paragraph (1), in determining whether the 110-day period referred to in paragraph (1) has elapsed, any period of time for which the action or inaction of such individual or such individual's representative without good cause results in the delay in the issuance of the Commissioner's final decision shall not be taken into account to the extent that such period of time exceeds 20 calendar days.

(3) Any benefits currently paid under this subchapter pursuant to this subsection (for the months described in paragraph (1)) shall not be considered overpayments for any purpose of this subchapter (unless payment of such benefits was fraudulently obtained), and such benefits shall not be treated as past-due benefits for purposes of section 406(b)(1) of this title.

(i) Reinstatement of entitlement

(1)(A) Entitlement to benefits described in subparagraph (B)(i)(I) shall be reinstated in any case where the Commissioner determines that an individual described in subparagraph (B) has filed a request for reinstatement meeting the requirements of paragraph (2)(A) during the period prescribed in subparagraph (C). Reinstatement of such entitlement shall be in accordance with the terms of this subsection.

(B) An individual is described in this subparagraph if

(i) prior to the month in which the individual files a request for reinstatement—

(I) the individual was entitled to benefits under this section or section 402 of this title on the basis of disability pursuant to an application filed therefor; and

(II) such entitlement terminated due to the performance of substantial gainful activity;

(ii) the individual is under a disability and the physical or mental impairment that is the basis for the finding of disability is the same as (or related to) the physical or mental impairment that was the basis for the finding of disability that gave rise to the entitlement described in clause (i); and

(iii) the individual's disability renders the individual unable to perform substantial gainful activity.

(C)(i) Except as provided in clause (ii), the period prescribed in this subparagraph with respect to an individual is 60 consecutive months beginning with the month following the most recent month for which the individual was entitled to a benefit described in subparagraph (B)(i)(I) prior to the entitlement termination described in subparagraph (B)(i)(II).

(ii) In the case of an individual who fails to file a reinstatement request within the period prescribed in clause (i), the Commissioner may extend the period if the Commissioner determines that the individual had good cause for the failure to so file.

(2)(A)(i) A request for reinstatement shall be filed in such form, and containing such information, as the Commissioner may prescribe.

(ii) A request for reinstatement shall include express declarations by the individual that the individual meets the requirements specified in clauses (ii) and (iii) of paragraph (1)(B).

(B) A request for reinstatement filed in accordance with subparagraph (A) may constitute an application for benefits in the case of any individual who the Commissioner determines is not entitled to reinstated benefits under this subsection.

(3) In determining whether an individual meets the requirements of paragraph (1)(B)(ii), the provisions of subsection (f) shall apply.

(4)(A)(i) Subject to clause (ii), entitlement to benefits reinstated under this subsection shall commence with the benefit payable for the month in which a request for reinstatement is filed.

(ii) An individual whose entitlement to a benefit for any month would have been reinstated under this subsection had the individual filed a request for reinstatement before the end of such month shall be entitled to such benefit for such month if such request for reinstatement is filed before the end of the twelfth month immediately succeeding such month.

(B)(i) Subject to clauses (ii) and (iii), the amount of the benefit payable for any month pursuant to the reinstatement of entitlement under this subsection shall be determined in accordance with the provisions of this subchapter.

(ii) For purposes of computing the primary insurance amount of an individual whose entitlement to benefits under this section is reinstated under this subsection, the date of onset of the individual's disability shall be the date of onset used in determining the individual's most recent period of disability arising in connection with such benefits payable on the basis of an application.

(iii) Benefits under this section or section 402 of this title payable for any month pursuant to a request for reinstatement filed in accordance with paragraph (2) shall be reduced by the amount of any provisional benefit paid to such individual for such month under paragraph (7).

(C) No benefit shall be payable pursuant to an entitlement reinstated under this subsection to an individual for any month in which the individual engages in substantial gainful activity.

(D) The entitlement of any individual that is reinstated under this subsection shall end with the benefits payable for the month preceding whichever of the following months is the earliest:

(i) The month in which the individual dies.

(ii) The month in which the individual attains retirement age.

(iii) The third month following the month in which the individual's disability ceases.

(5) Whenever an individual's entitlement to benefits under this section is reinstated under this subsection, entitlement to benefits payable on the basis of such individual's wages and self-employment income may be reinstated with respect to any person previously entitled to such benefits on the basis of an application if the Commissioner determines that such person satisfies all the requirements for entitlement to such benefits except requirements related to the filing of an application. The provisions of paragraph (4) shall apply to the reinstated entitlement of any such person to the same extent that they apply to the reinstated entitlement of such individual.

(6) An individual to whom benefits are payable under this section or section 402 of this title pursuant to a reinstatement of entitlement under this subsection for 24 months (whether or not consecutive) shall, with respect to benefits so payable after such twenty-fourth month, be deemed for purposes of paragraph (1)(B)(i)(I) and the determination, if appropriate, of the termination month in accordance with subsection (a)(1) of this section, or subsection (d)(1), (e)(1), or (f)(1) of section 402 of this title, to be entitled to such benefits on the basis of an application filed therefor.

(7)(A) An individual described in paragraph (1)(B) who files a request for reinstatement in accordance with the provisions of paragraph (2)(A) shall be entitled to provisional benefits payable in accordance with this paragraph, unless the Commissioner determines that the individual does not meet the requirements of paragraph (1)(B)(i) or that the individual's declaration under paragraph (2)(A)(ii) is false. Any such determination by the Commissioner shall be final and not subject to review under subsection (b) or (g) of section 405 of this title.

(B) The amount of a provisional benefit for a month shall equal the amount of the last monthly benefit payable to the individual under this subchapter on the basis of an application increased by an amount equal to the amount, if any, by which such last monthly benefit would have been increased as a result of the operation of section 415(i) of this title.

(C)(i) Provisional benefits shall begin with the month in which a request for reinstatement is filed in accordance with paragraph (2)(A).

(ii) Provisional benefits shall end with the earliest of

(I) the month in which the Commissioner makes a determination regarding the individual's entitlement to reinstated benefits;

(II) the fifth month following the month described in clause (i);

(III) the month in which the individual performs substantial gainful activity; or

(IV) the month in which the Commissioner determines that the individual does not meet the requirements of paragraph (1)(B)(i) or that the individual's declaration made in accordance with paragraph (2)(A)(ii) is false.

(D) In any case in which the Commissioner determines that an individual is not entitled to reinstated benefits, any provisional benefits paid to the individual under this paragraph shall not be subject to recovery as an overpayment unless the Commissioner determines that the individual knew or should have known that the individual did not meet the requirements of paragraph (1)(B).

(j) Limitation on payments to prisoners

For provisions relating to limitation on payments to prisoners, see section 402(x) of this title.

(Aug. 14, 1935, c. 531, Title II, § 223, as added Aug. 1, 1956, c. 836, Title I, § 103(a), 70 Stat. 815; amended Pub.L. 85–840, Title II, §§ 202, 204(b), Aug. 28, 1958, 72 Stat. 1020, 1021; Pub.L. 86–778, Title III, § 303(f), Title IV, §§ 401(a), (b), 402(a) to (d), 403(b), Sept. 13, 1960, 74 Stat. 964, 967, 969; Pub.L. 87–64, Title I, § 102(b)(2)(B), (C), (c)(2)(C), (3)(D), (E), June 30, 1961, 75 Stat. 134, 135; Pub.L. 89–97, Title III, §§ 302(e), 303(a)(2), (b)(3), (4), (c), 304(m), (n), 328(c), 344(b) to (d), July 30, 1965, 79 Stat. 366, 367, 370, 400, 413; Pub.L. 90–248, Title I, §§ 105(b), 158(a), (b), (c)(6) to (8), Jan. 2, 1968, 81 Stat. 833, 867–869; Pub.L. 92–603, Title I, §§ 104(c), (d), 116(a), 117(b), 118(a), Oct. 30, 1972, 86 Stat. 1340, 1350, 1351; Pub.L. 95–216, Title III, § 335, Dec. 20, 1977, 91 Stat. 1547; Pub.L. 96–265, Title I, § 102(b), Title III, §§ 302(a)(1), 303(b)(1)(A), (2)(A), 306(c), 309(a), June 9, 1980, 94 Stat. 443, 450, 451, 453, 458, 459; Pub.L. 96–473, § 5(a)(1), (c), Oct. 19, 1980, 94 Stat. 2264, 2265; Pub.L. 97–123, § 6, Dec. 29, 1981, 95 Stat. 1664; Pub.L. 97–455, § 2, Jan. 12, 1983, 96 Stat. 2498; Pub.L. 98–21, Title II, § 201(c)(1)(E), (3), Title III, §§ 309(*o*), 332(b), 339(b), Apr. 20, 1983, 97 Stat. 109, 117, 129, 134; Pub.L. 98–118, § 2, Oct. 11, 1983, 97 Stat. 803; Pub.L. 98–369, Div. B, Title VI, §§ 2661(m), 2662(c)(2), (i), 2663(a)(16), July 18, 1984, 98 Stat. 1158–1160, 1165; Pub.L. 98–460, §§ 2(a), 3(a)(1), 4(a)(1), 7(a), 9(b)(1), Oct. 9, 1984, 98 Stat. 1794, 1799, 1800, 1803, 1805; Pub.L. 99–272, Title XII, § 12107(b), Apr. 7, 1986, 100 Stat. 286; Pub.L. 99–514, Title XVIII, § 1883(a)(10), Oct. 22, 1986, 100 Stat. 2916; Pub.L. 100–203, Title IX, §§ 9009, 9010(a), (e)(2), Dec. 22, 1987, 101 Stat. 1330–293, 1330–294; Pub.L. 100–647, Title VIII, §§ 8001(a), 8006, Nov. 10, 1988, 102 Stat. 3778, 3781; Pub.L. 101–239, Title X, §§ 10101, 10305(c), (d), Dec. 19, 1989, 103 Stat. 2471, 2483; Pub.L. 101–508, Title V, §§ 5102, 5103(a), (b)(2) to (5), 5118(a), Nov. 5, 1990, 104 Stat. 1388–250, 1388–251, 1388–278; Pub.L. 103–296, Title I, § 107(a)(4), Title II, § 201(a)(4)(A), Title III, § 321(a)(19), (f)(1), Aug. 15, 1994, 108 Stat. 1478, 1499, 1537, 1540; Pub.L. 104–121, Title I, §§ 102(b)(2), 105(a)(1), Mar. 29, 1996, 110 Stat. 848, 852; Pub.L. 106–170, Title I, § 112(a), Dec. 17, 1999, 113 Stat. 1881; Pub.L. 108–203, Title II, § 211(b), Mar. 2, 2004, 118 Stat. 518; Pub.L. 114–74, Title VIII, §§ 812(a), 825(a), Nov. 2, 2015, 129 Stat. 602, 610.)

1 So in original. The period probably should be a comma.

2 So in original. Probably should be followed by "and".

3 So in original. The "; and" probably should be a period.

HISTORICAL AND STATUTORY NOTES

References in Text

This subchapter, referred to in text, originally read "this title", meaning the Social Security Act, Aug. 14, 1935, c. 531, Title II, 49 Stat. 622, as amended, which is classified as this subchapter, 42 U.S.C.A. § 401 et seq.

The Senior Citizens' Right to Work Act of 1996, referred to in subsec. (d)(4)(A), is Title I of Pub.L. 104–121, Mar. 29, 1996, 110 Stat. 847. Section 102 of such Act amended this section and section 403 of this title, and enacted provisions set out as a note under section 403 of this title. For complete classification of such Act to the Code, see Short Title note set out under section 1305 of this title and Tables.

Codifications

Section 5118(a) of Pub.L. 101–508, which directed that section 223(e) (42 U.S.C. 623(e)) be amended, was executed to this section as the probable intent of Congress.

Amendment by section 1883(a)(10) of Pub.L. 99–514 to subsec. (g)(1) directing that the second comma following the term "benefits" be struck out where such term appears in the matter following subpar. (C) was not executed in view of previous editorial deletion.

Section 201(c)(1), (3) of Pub.L. 98–21, set out in the credit of this section, was amended by section 2662(c)(1), (2), of Pub.L. 98–369 to correct an error in the directory language of Pub.L. 98–21 under which the article "the" had been left out in the direction to strike out references to the age of 65.

Effective and Applicability Provisions

2015 Acts. Pub.L. 114–74, Title VIII, § 812(c), Nov. 2, 2015, 129 Stat. 602, provided that: "The amendment made by subsection (a) [enacting subsec. (d)(5)(C) of this section] shall apply with respect to determinations of disability made on or after the earlier of—

"(1) the effective date of the regulations issued by the Commissioner under subsection (b) [Pub.L. 114–74, § 812(b), set out as a note under this section]; or

"(2) one year after the date of the enactment of this Act [Nov. 2, 2015]."

Pub.L. 114–74, Title VIII, § 825(b), Nov. 2, 2015, 129 Stat. 611, provided that: "The amendment made by subsection (a) [amending this section] shall take effect upon the date of the enactment of this Act [Nov. 2, 2015], or as soon as practicable thereafter."

2004 Acts. Amendments made by Pub.L. 108–203, § 211, amending this section, applicable to benefit applications based on social security account numbers issued on or after Jan. 1, 2004, see Pub.L. 108–203, § 211(c), set out as a note under 42 U.S.C.A. § 414.

1999 Acts. Pub.L. 106–170, Title I, § 112(c), Dec. 17, 1999, 113 Stat. 1886, provided that:

"(1) **In general.**—The amendments made by this section [amending this section and section 1383 of this title] shall take effect on the first day of the thirteenth month beginning after the date of the enactment of this Act [Dec. 17, 1999].

"(2) **Limitation.**—No benefit shall be payable under title II or XVI [probably means Title II or XVI of the Social Security Act, which are principally classified to this subchapter (42 U.S.C.A. § 401 et seq.) and subchapter XVI of this chapter (42 U.S.C.A. § 1381 et seq.)] on the basis of a request for reinstatement filed under section 223(i) or 1631(p) of the

Social Security Act (42 U.S.C. 423(i), 1383(p)) before the effective date described in paragraph (1)."

1996 Acts. Amendment by section 102(b)(2) of Pub.L. 104–121 applicable with respect to taxable years ending after 1995, see section 102(c) of Pub.L. 104–121, set out as a note under section 403 of this title.

Amendment by section 105(a)(1) of Pub.L. 104–121 applicable to individual who applies for, or whose claim is adjudicated with respect to, benefits under this subchapter based on disability on or after Mar. 29, 1996, with certain conditions applying for benefits before Mar. 29, 1996, see section 105(a)(5) of Pub.L. 104–121, set out as a note under section 405 of this title.

1994 Acts. Amendment by section 107(a)(4) of Pub.L. 103–296 effective Mar. 31, 1995, see section 110 of Pub.L. 103–296, set out as a note under section 401 of this title.

Amendment to subsec. (d)(4) of this section by section 201(a)(4)(A) of Pub.L. 103–296 to take effect on Aug. 15, 1994, see section 201(a)(4)(C) of Pub.L. 103–296, set out as a note under section 422 of this title.

Amendments to subsec. (f)(2) of this section by section 321(f)(1) of Pub.L. 103–296 effective as if included in the provisions of Pub.L. 101–508 to which they relate, see section 321(f)(5) of Pub.L. 103–296, set out as a note under section 405 of this title.

1990 Acts. Amendment by section 5103(a) and (b)(2) through (5) of Pub.L. 101–508 applicable with respect to monthly insurance benefits for months after Dec., 1990 for which applications are filed on or after Jan. 1, 1991, or are pending on such date, see section 5103(e)(1) of Pub.L. 101–508, set out as a note under section 402 of this title.

Section 5118(b) of Pub.L. 101–508 provided that: "The amendments made by subsection (a) [amending subsec. (e) of this section] shall apply with respect to benefits for months after the date of the enactment of this Act [Nov. 5, 1990]."

1989 Acts. Amendment of subsecs. (f) foll. par. (4) and (g)(2)(B) by Pub.L. 101–239 applicable with respect to determinations made on or after July 1, 1990, see section 10305(f) of Pub.L. 101–239, set out as a note under section 403 of this title.

1988 Acts. Section 8001(c) of Pub.L. 100–647 provided that: "The amendments made by this section [enacting subsec. (h) and redesignating as subsec. (i) former subsec. (h) of this section and enacting section 1383(a)(8) of this title] shall apply to determinations by administrative law judges of entitlement to benefits made after 180 days after the date of the enactment of this Act [Nov. 10, 1988]."

1987 Acts. Amendment of subsecs. (a)(1) and (e) by section 9010(a), (e)(2) of Pub.L. 100–203 effective Jan. 1, 1988 and applicable with respect to individuals entitled to benefits under specific provisions of this section and section 402 of this title for any month after Dec. 1987 and individuals entitled to benefits payable under specific provisions of this section and section 402 of this title for any month before Jan. 1988 and with respect to whom the 15-month period described in the applicable provision amended by section 9010 of Pub.L. 100–203 has not elapsed as of Jan. 1, 1988, see section 9010(f) of Pub.L. 100–203, set out as a note under section 402 of this title.

1986 Acts. Amendment by section 1883(a)(10) of Pub.L. 99–514 effective Oct. 22, 1986, see section 1883(f) of Pub.L. 99–514, set out as a note under section 402 of this title.

Amendment by Pub.L. 99–272 effective Dec. 1, 1980, and applicable with respect to any individual who is under a disability (as defined in subsection (d) of this section) on or after that date, see section 12107(c) of Pub.L. 99–272, set out as a note under section 402 of this title.

1984 Acts. Section 2(d) of Pub.L. 98–460 provided that:

"(1) The amendments made by this section [enacting subsec. (f) of this section and amending sections 416(i)(2)(D) and 1382c(a) of this title and enacting provisions set out as notes under this section] shall apply only as provided in this subsection.

"(2) The amendments made by this section shall apply to—

"(A) determinations made by the Secretary on or after the date of the enactment of this Act [Oct. 9, 1984];

"(B) determinations with respect to which a final decision of the Secretary has not yet been made as of the date of the enactment of this Act and with respect to which a request for administrative review is made in conformity with the time limits, exhaustion requirements, and other provisions of section 205 of the Social Security Act [section 405 of this title] and regulations of the Secretary;

"(C) determinations with respect to which a request for judicial review was pending on September 19, 1984, and which involve an individual litigant or a member of a class in a class action who is identified by name in such pending action on such date; and

"(D) determinations with respect to which a timely request for judicial review is or has been made by an individual litigant of a final decision of the Secretary made within 60 days prior to the date of the enactment of this Act [Oct. 9, 1984].

In the case of determinations described in subparagraphs (C) and (D) in actions relating to medical improvement, the court shall remand such cases to the Secretary for review in accordance with the provisions of the Social Security Act [this chapter] as amended by this section.

"(3) In the case of a recipient of benefits under title II, XVI, or XVIII [this subchapter, subchapter XVI, or subchapter XVIII of this chapter] of the Social Security Act—

"(A) who has been determined not to be entitled to such benefits on the basis of a finding that the physical or mental impairment on the basis of which such benefits were provided has ceased, does not exist, or is not disabling, and

"(B) who was a member of a class certified on or before September 19, 1984, in a class action relating to medical improvement pending on September 19, 1984, but was not identified by name as a member of the class of such date,

the court shall remand such case to the Secretary. The Secretary shall notify such individual by certified mail that he may request a review of the determination described in subparagraph (A) based on the provisions of this section and the provisions of the Social Security Act [this chapter] as amended by this section. Such notification shall specify that the individual must request such review within 120 days after the date on which such notification is received. If such request is made in a timely manner, the Secretary shall make a review of the determination described in subparagraph (A) in accordance with the provisions of this section and the provisions of the Social Security Act [this chapter] as amended by this section. The amendments made by this section [enacting subsec. (f) of this section and amending sections 416(i)(2)(D) and 1382c(a) of this title and enacting provisions set out as notes under this section] shall apply with respect to such review, and the determination described in subparagraph

(A) (and any redetermination resulting from such review) shall be subject to further administrative and judicial review, only if such request is made in a timely manner.

"(4) The decision by the Secretary on a case remanded by a court pursuant to this subsection shall be regarded as a new decision on the individual's claim for benefits, which supersedes the final decision of the Secretary. The new decision shall be subject to further administrative review and to judicial review only in conformity with the time limits, exhaustion requirements, and other provisions of section 205 of the Social Security Act [section 405 of this title] and regulations issued by the Secretary in conformity with such section.

"(5) No class in a class action relating to medical improvement may be certified after September 19, 1984, if the class action seeks judicial review of a decision terminating entitlement (or a period of disability) made by the Secretary of Health and Human Services prior to September 19, 1984.

"(6) For purposes of this subsection, the term 'action relating to medical improvement' means an action raising the issue of whether an individual who has had his entitlement to benefits under title II, XVI, or XVIII [this subchapter, subchapter XVI, or subchapter XVIII of this title] of the Social Security Act based on disability terminated (or period of disability ended) should not have had such entitlement terminated (or period of disability ended) without consideration of whether there has been medical improvement in the condition of such individual (or another individual on whose disability such entitlement is based) since the time of a prior determination that the individual was under a disability."

Section 3(a)(3) of Pub.L. 98–460 provided that: "The amendments made by paragraphs (1) and (2) [amending subsec. (d)(5) of this section and inserting reference to section 423(d)(5) of this title in section 1382c(a)(3)(H) of this title] shall apply to determinations made prior to January 1, 1987."

Section 4(c) of Pub.L. 98–460 provided that: "The amendments made by this section [enacting subsec. (d)(2)(C) of this section and section 1382c(a)(3)(G) of this title and amending section 416(i)(1) of this title] shall apply with respect to determinations made on or after the first day of the first month beginning after 30 days after the date of the enactment of this Act [Oct. 9, 1984]."

Section 9(b)(2) of Pub.L. 98–460, provided that: "The amendments made by this subsection [designating existing provisions of par. (5) as (5)(A), and adding subpar. (B)] shall apply to determinations made on or after the date of the enactment of this Act [Oct. 9, 1984]."

Enactment of subsec. (h) by section 2662(i) of Pub.L. 98–369 and amendment to subsecs. (a) and (c) by sections 2662(c), 2661(m), respectively, of Pub.L. 98–369 effective as though included in the enactment of the Social Security Amendments of 1983 [Pub.L. 98–21], see section 2664(a) of Pub.L. 98–369, set out as a note under section 401 of this title.

Amendment to subsec. (d)(2)(A) by section 2663(a)(16) of Pub.L. 98–369 effective July 18, 1984, but not to be construed as changing or affecting any right, liability, status or interpretation which existed (under the provisions of law involved) before that date, see section 2664(b) of Pub.L. 98–369, set out as a note under section 401 of this title.

1983 Acts. Amendment by section 309(*o*) of Pub.L. 98–21 applicable only with respect to monthly payments payable under this subchapter for months after April, 1983, except as otherwise specifically provided, see section 310 of Pub.L. 98–21, set out as a note under section 402 of this title.

Amendment by section 332(b) of Pub.L. 98–21 effective with respect to applications for disability insurance benefits under this section filed after Apr. 20, 1983, except that no monthly benefits under this subchapter shall be payable or increased by reason of such amendment for months before the month following April, 1983, see section 332(c) of Pub.L. 98–21, set out as a note under section 416 of this title.

Repeal of subsec. (f) by section 339(b) of Pub.L. 98–21 applicable with respect to monthly benefits payable for months beginning on or after April 20, 1983, see section 339(c) of Pub.L. 98–21, set out as a note under section 402 of this title.

1980 Acts. Amendment by Pub.L. 96–473 effective with respect to benefits payable for months beginning on or after Oct. 1, 1980, see section 5(d) of Pub.L. 96–473, set out as a note under section 402 of this title.

For effective date of amendment of subsec. (a)(2) of this section by Pub.L. 96–265, see section 102(c) of Pub.L. 96–265, set out as a note under section 415 of this title.

Section 302(c) of Pub.L. 96–265 provided that: "The amendments made by this section [amending sections 423(d)(4), 1382a, and 1382c of this title] shall apply with respect to expenses incurred on or after the first day of the sixth month which begins after the date of the enactment of this Act [June 9, 1980]."

For effective date of amendment of subsec. (a)(1) and (e) by Pub.L. 96–265, see section 303(d) of Pub.L. 96–265, set out as a note under section 402 of this title.

Amendment of subsec. (b) by Pub.L. 96–265 applicable to applications filed after June 1980, see section 306(d) of Pub.L. 96–265, set out as a note under section 402 of this title.

Section 309(b) of Pub.L. 96–265 provided that: "The amendment made by subsection (a) [amending subsec. (d)(5) of this section] shall apply with respect to evidence requested on or after the first day of the sixth month which begins after the date of the enactment of this Act [June 9, 1980]."

1972 Acts. Amendment of subsecs. (a)(2) and (c)(1)(A) of this section by section 104(c), (d) of Pub.L. 92–603 applicable only in the case of a man who attains (or would attain) age 62 after Dec. 1974, with the figure "65" in subsec. (c)(1)(A) of this section to be deemed to read "64" in the case of a man who attains age 62 in 1973, and deemed to read "63" in the case of a man who attains age 62 in 1974, see section 104(j) of Pub.L. 92–603, set out as a note under section 414 of this title.

Section 116(e) of Pub.L. 92–603 provided that: "The amendments made by this section [amending subsec. (c)(2) of this section and sections 402(e)(6), (b)(7), and 416(i)(2)(A) of this title] shall be effective with respect to applications for disability insurance benefits under section 223 of the Social Security Act [this section], applications for widow's and widower's insurance benefits based on disability under section 202 of such Act [section 402 of this title], and applications for disability determinations under section 216(i) of such Act [section 416(i) of this title], filed—

"(1) in or after the month in which this Act is enacted [Oct. 1972], or

"(2) before the month in which this Act is enacted [Oct. 1972] if—

"(A) notice of the final decision of the Secretary of Health, Education, and Welfare has not been given to the applicant before such month, or

"(B) the notice referred to in subparagraph (A) has been so given before such month but a civil action with respect to such final decision is commenced under section 205(g) of the Social Security Act [section 405(g) of this title] (whether before, in, or after such month) and the decision in such civil action has not become final before such month;

except that no monthly benefits under title II of the Social Security Act [this subchapter] shall be payable or increased by reason of the amendments made by this section for any month before January 1973."

[The Secretary of Health, Education, and Welfare was redesignated the Secretary of Health and Human Services by section 3508(b) of Title 20, Education.]

Section 117(c) of Pub.L. 92–603 provided that: "The amendments made by this section [amending subsec. (c)(1) of this section and section 416(i)(3) of this title] shall be effective with respect to applications for disability insurance benefits under section 223 of the Social Security Act [this section], and for disability determinations under section 216(i) of such Act [section 416(i) of this title], filed—

"(1) in or after the month in which this Act is enacted [Oct. 1972], or

"(2) before the month in which this Act [Oct. 1972] is enacted if—

"(A) notice of the final decision of the Secretary of Health, Education, and Welfare has not been given to the applicant before such month; or

"(B) the notice referred to in subparagraph (A) has been so given before such month but a civil action with respect to such final decision is commenced under section 205(g) of the Social Security Act [section 405(g) of this title] (whether before, in, or after such month) and the decision in such civil action has not become final before such month;

except that no monthly benefits under title II of the Social Security Act [this subchapter] shall be payable or increased by reason of the amendments made by this section for months before January 1973."

[The Secretary of Health, Education, and Welfare was redesignated the Secretary of Health and Human Services by § 3508(b) of Title 20, Education.]

Amendment of subsecs. (a)(1), (a)(2), (b), and (c)(2)(A) of this section by section 118(a) of Pub.L. 92–603 applicable in the case of deaths occurring after Dec. 31, 1969, with any applications with respect to an individual whose death occurred after Dec. 31, 1969, but before Oct. 30, 1972, to be deemed to have been filed in the month in which death occurred if filed in or within three months after Oct. 1972, see section 118(c) of Pub.L. 92–603, set out as a note under section 416 of this title.

1968 Acts. Amendment of subsec. (c)(1)(B) by section 105(b) of Pub.L. 90–248 applicable with respect to monthly benefits under this subchapter for months after January 1968, but only on the basis of applications for such benefits filed in or after January 1968, see section 105(c) of Pub.L. 90–248 set out as a note under section 416 of this title.

Section 158(e) of Pub.L. 90–248 provided that: "The amendments made by this section [enacting subsec. (d) of this section and amending subsecs. (a)(1) and (c) of this section, and sections 402(d)(2), (s)(1) to (3), 416(i)(1), 421(a), (c), 422(c)(4) and 425 of this title] shall be effective with respect to applications for disability insurance benefits under section 223 of the Social Security Act [this section], and for disability determinations under section 216(i) of such Act [section 416(i) of this title], filed—

"(1) in or after the month in which this Act is enacted [Jan. 1968], or

"(2) before the month in which this Act is enacted [Jan. 1968] if the applicant has not died before such month and if—

"(A) notice of the final decision of the Secretary of Health, Education, and Welfare has not been given to the applicant before such month; or

"(B) the notice referred to in subparagraph (A) has been so given before such month but a civil action with respect to such final decision is commenced under section 205(g) of the Social Security Act [section 405(g) of this title] (whether before, in, or after such month) and the decision in such civil action has not become final before such month."

[The Secretary of Health, Education, and Welfare was redesignated the Secretary of Health and Human Services by section 3508(b) of Title 20, Education.]

1965 Acts. Amendment of subsec. (a)(2) by Pub.L. 89–97 applicable in the case of individuals who become entitled to disability insurance benefits under this section after December 1965, see section 302(f)(5) of Pub.L. 89–97, set out as a note under section 415 of this title.

Section 303(f)(1) of Pub.L. 89–97 provided that: "The amendments made by subsection (a) [to subsec. (c)(2)(A) of this section and section 416(i)(1)(A) of this title], paragraphs (3) and (4) of subsection (b) [to subsec. (a)(1) and (c)(3)(A) of this section] and subsections (c) and (d) [to subsec. (b) of this section and section 402(j)(1) of this title], and the provisions of subparagraphs (B) and (E) of section 216(i)(2) of the Social Security Act [section 416(i)(2) of this title] (as amended by subsection (b)(1) of this section), shall be effective with respect to applications for disability insurance benefits under section 223 [this section], and for disability determinations under section 216(i) [section 416(i) of this title], of the Social Security Act filed—

"(A) in or after the month in which this Act is enacted [July 1965], or

"(B) before the month in which this Act is enacted [July 1965], if the applicant has not died before such month and if—

"(i) notice of the final decision of the Secretary of Health, Education, and Welfare has not been given to the applicant before such month; or

"(ii) the notice referred to in subparagraph (i) has been so given before such month but a civil action with respect to such final decision is commenced under section 205(g) of the Social Security Act [section 405(g) of this title] (whether before, in, or after such month) and the decision in such civil action has not become final before such month;

except that no monthly insurance benefits under title II of the Social Security Act [this subchapter] shall be payable or increased by reason of the amendments made by subsections (a) [to subsec. (c)(2)(A) of this section and section 416(i)(1)(A) of this title] and (b) [to subsecs. (a)(1) and (c)(3)(A) of this section and section 416(i)(2), (3) of this title] for months before the second month following the month in which this Act is enacted [July 1965]. The preceding sentence shall also be applicable in the case of applications for monthly insurance benefits under title II of the Social Security Act [this subchapter] based on the wages and self-employment income of an applicant with respect to whose application for disability insurance benefits under section 223 of such Act [this section] such preceding sentence is applicable."

[The Secretary of Health, Education, and Welfare was redesignated the Secretary of Health and Human Services by § 3508(b) of Title 20, Education.]

Amendment of subsec. (a)(2), (3) by section 304 of Pub.L. 89–97 applicable with respect to monthly insurance benefits under this subchapter for and after the second month following July 1965 but only on the basis of applications filed in or after July 1965, see section 304(*o*) of Pub.L. 89–97, set out as a note under section 402 of this title.

Amendment of subsec. (b) by section 328 of Pub.L. 89–97 applicable with respect to applications filed on or after July 30, 1965, applications as to which the Secretary has not made a final decision before July 30, 1965, and, if a civil action with respect to a final decision of the Secretary has been commenced under section 405(g) of this title before July 30, 1965, applications as to which there has been no final judicial decision before July 30, 1965, see section 328(d) of Pub.L. 89–97, set out as a note under section 416 of this title.

Amendment of subsecs. (a)(1), (c)(1), and (c)(2)(B) by section 344 of Pub.L. 89–97 applicable only with respect to monthly benefits under this subchapter for months after Aug. 1965 on the basis of applications for such benefits filed in or after July 1965, see section 344(e) of Pub.L. 89–97, set out as a note under section 416 of this title.

1961 Acts. Amendment by section 102(b)(2)(B), (C) of Pub.L. 87–64 effective Aug. 1, 1961, and amendment by section 102(c)(2)(C), (3)(D), (E) of Pub.L. 87–64 applicable with respect to monthly benefits for months beginning on or after August 1, 1961, based on applications filed in or after March 1961, and with respect to lump-sum death payments under this subchapter in the case of deaths on or after August 1, 1961, see sections 102(f)(4), (6) and 109 of Pub.L. 87–64, set out as notes under section 402 of this title.

1960 Acts. Section 303(f) of Pub.L. 86–778 provided in part that the amendment of subsec. (a)(2) by section 303(f) of Pub.L. 86–778 shall be effective with respect to individuals who become entitled to benefits under this section after 1960.

Section 401(c) of Pub.L. 86–778 provided that: "The amendments made by this section [to subsecs. (a)(1)(B) and (c)(3) of this section] shall apply only with respect to monthly benefits under sections 202 and 223 of the Social Security Act [this section and section 402 of this title] for months after the month following the month in which this Act is enacted [Sept. 1960] which are based on the wages and self-employment income of an individual who did not attain the age of fifty in or prior to the month following the month in which this Act is enacted [Sept. 1960], but only where applications for such benefits are filed in or after the month in which this Act is enacted [Sept. 1960]."

Section 402(f) of Pub.L. 86–778 provided that: "The amendments made by subsections (a) and (b) [which inserted provisions in subsec. (a)(1) of this section authorizing payment of benefits to an individual for each month beginning with the first month during all of which he is under a disability and in which he becomes so entitled to such insurance benefits, but only if he was entitled to disability insurance benefits which terminated, or had a period of disability which ceased, within the 60-month period preceding the first month in which he is under such disability, and amended subsec. (a)(2) of this section as set out in the note under this section] shall apply only with respect to benefits under section 223 of the Social Security Act [this section] for the month in which this Act is enacted [Sept. 1960] and subsequent months. The amendment made by subsection (c) [to the first sentence of subsec. (b) of this section] shall apply only in the case of applications for benefits under such section 223 [this section] filed after the seventh month before the month in which this Act is enacted [Sept. 1960]. The amendment made by subsection (d) [to the second sentence of subsec. (b) of this section] shall apply only in the case of applications for benefits under such section 223 [this section] filed in or after the month in which this Act is enacted [Sept. 1960]. The amendment made by subsection (e) [which redefined the term period of disability in section 416(i)(2) of this title and inserted provisions in section 416(i)(2) of this title prohibiting acceptance of an application, in any case in which section 423(a)(ii) of this title is applicable, filed more than six months before the first month for which the applicant becomes entitled to benefits under this section and providing that any application for a disability determination which is filed within such three months' period or six months' period shall be deemed to have been filed on such first day or in such first month, as the case may be] shall apply only in the case of individuals who become entitled to benefits under such section 223 [this section] in or after the month in which this Act is enacted [Sept. 1960]."

Amendment of subsec. (a)(1) by section 403(b) of Pub.L. 86–778, which substituted "whichever of the following months is the earliest: the month in which he dies, the month in which he attains the age of sixty-five, or the third month following the month in which his disability ceases" for "the first month in which any of the following occurs: his disability ceases, he dies, or he attains the age of sixty-five", applicable only with respect to benefits under subsec. (a) of this section or section 402(d) of this title for months after Sept. 1960, in the case of individuals who, without regard to such amendment would have been entitled to such benefits for Sept. 1960, or for any succeeding month, see section 403(e) of Pub.L. 86–778, set out as a note under section 422 of this title.

1958 Acts. Amendment of subsecs. (b) and (c)(3) by section 202 of Pub.L. 85–840 applicable with respect to applications for disability insurance benefits under this section filed after Dec. 1957, see section 207(a) of Pub.L. 85–840, set out as a note section 416 of this title.

For applicability of subsec. (c)(1)(A) as amended by section 204 of Pub.L. 85–840, see section 207(a) of Pub.L. 85–840, set out as a note under section 416 of this title.

1950 Acts. Section 103(d) of Act Aug. 1, 1956 provided that:

"(1) The amendment made by subsection (a) [adding sections 423 to 425 of this title] shall apply only with respect to monthly benefits under title II of the Social Security Act [this subchapter] for months after June 1957.

"(2) For purposes of determining entitlement to a disability insurance benefit for any month after June 1957 and before December 1957, an application for disability insurance benefits filed by any individual after July 1957 and before January 1958 shall be deemed to have been filed during the first month after June 1957 for which such individual would (without regard to this paragraph) have been entitled to a disability insurance benefit had he filed application before the end of such month."

Electronic Reporting of Earnings

Pub.L. 114–74, Title VIII, § 826, Nov. 2, 2015, 129 Stat. 611, provided that:

"**(a) In general.**—Not later than September 30, 2017, the Commissioner of Social Security shall establish and implement a system that—

"(1) allows an individual entitled to a monthly insurance benefit based on disability under title II of the Social Security Act [this subchapter] (or a representative of the individual) to report to the Commissioner the individual's earnings derived from services through electronic means, including by telephone and Internet; and

"(2) automatically issues a receipt to the individual (or representative) after receiving each such report.

"**(b) Supplemental Security Income reporting system as model.**—The Commissioner shall model the system established under subsection (a) on the electronic wage reporting systems for recipients of supplemental security income under title XVI of such Act [subchapter XVI of this chapter, 42 U.S.C.A. § 1381 et seq.]."

Commission on Evaluation of Pain

Section 3(b) of Pub.L. 98–460 provided that:

"(1) The Secretary of Health and Human Services shall appoint a Commission on the Evaluation of Pain (hereafter in this section referred to as the "Commission") to conduct a study concerning the evaluation of pain in determining under titles II and XVI [this subchapter and subchapter XVI of this chapter] of the Social Security Act whether an individual is under a disability. Such study shall be conducted in consultation with the National Academy of Sciences.

"(2) The Commission shall consist of at least twelve experts, including a significant representation from the field of medicine who are involved in the study of pain, and representation from the fields of law, administration of disability insurance programs, and other appropriate fields of expertise.

"(3) The Commission shall be appointed by the Secretary of Health and Human Services (without regard to the requirements of the Federal Advisory Committee Act [5 U.S.C.A. App. 2 § 1 et seq.]) within 60 days after the date of the enactment of this Act [Oct. 9, 1984]. The Secretary shall from time to time appoint one of the members to serve as Chairman. The Commission shall meet as often as the Secretary deems necessary.

"(4) Members of the Commission shall be appointed without regard to the provisions of title 5, United States Code, governing appointments in the competitive service. Members who are not employees of the United States, while attending meetings of the Commission or otherwise serving on the business of the Commission, shall be paid at a rate equal to the per diem equivalent of the rate provided for level IV of the Executive Schedule under section 5315 of title 5, United States Code [section 5315 of Title 5, Government Organization and Employees], for each day, including traveltime, during which they are engaged in the actual performance of duties vested in the Commission. While engaged in the performance of such duties away from their homes or regular places of business they may be allowed travel expenses, including per diem in lieu of subsistence, as authorized by section 5703 of title 5, United States Code [section 5703 of Title 5], for persons in the Government service employed intermittently.

"(5) The Commission may engage such technical assistance from individuals skilled in medical and other aspects of pain as may be necessary to carry out its functions. The Secretary shall make available to the Commission such secretarial, clerical, and other assistance and any pertinent data prepared by the Department of Health and Human Services as the Commission may require to carry out its functions.

"(6) The Secretary shall submit the results of the study under paragraph (1), together with any recommendations, to the Committee on Ways and Means of the House of Representatives and the Committee on Finance of the Senate not later than December 31, 1985. The Commission shall terminate at the time such results are submitted."

Election of Payments

Section 2(e) of Pub.L. 98–460 provided that: "Any individual whose case is remanded to the Secretary pursuant to subsection (d) or whose request for a review is made in a timely manner pursuant to subsection (d), may elect, in accordance with section 223(g) or 1631(a)(7) of the Social Security Act [subsec. (g) of this section or section 1383(a)(7) of this title], to have payments made beginning with the month in which he makes such election, and ending as under such section 223(g) or 1631(a)(7). Notwithstanding such section 223(g) or 1631(a)(7), such payments (if elected)—

"(1) shall be made at least until an initial redetermination is made by the Secretary; and

"(2) shall begin with the payment for the month in which such individual makes such election."

Lump Sum Payment of Disability Insurance Benefits for Period Beginning After 1959 and Ending Prior to 1964; Filing of Application

Section 133 of Pub.L. 92–603 provided that:

"**(a)** If an individual would (upon the timely filing of an application for a disability determination under section 216(i) of the Social Security Act [section 416(i) of this title] and of an application for disability insurance benefits under section 223 of such Act [this section]) have been entitled to disability insurance benefits under such section 223 for a period which began after 1959 and ended prior to 1964, such individual shall, upon filing application for disability insurance benefits under such section 223 with respect to such period not later than 6 months after the date of enactment of this section [Oct. 30, 1972], be entitled, notwithstanding any other provision of title II of the Social Security Act [this subchapter], to receive in a lump sum, as disability insurance benefits payable under section 223, an amount equal to the total amounts of disability insurance benefits which would have been payable to him for such period if he had timely filed such an application for a disability determination and such an application for disability insurance benefits with respect to such period; but only if—

"(1) prior to the date of enactment of this section [Oct. 30, 1972] and after the date of enactment of the Social Security Amendments of 1967 [Jan. 2, 1968], such period was determined (under section 216(i) of the Social Security Act) [section 416(i) of this title] to be a period of disability as to such individual; and

"(2) the application giving rise to the determination (under such section 216(i) [section 416(i) of this title] that such period is a period of disability as to such individual would not have been accepted as an application for such a determination except for the provisions of section 216(i)(2)(F) [section 416(i)(2)(F) of this title].

"**(b)** No payment shall be made to any individual by reason of the provisions of subsection (a) except upon the basis of an application filed after the date of enactment of this section [Oct. 30, 1972]."

Regulations

Pub.L. 114–74, Title VIII, § 812(b), Nov. 2, 2015, 129 Stat. 602, provided that: "Not later than 1 year after the date of the enactment of this Act [Nov. 2, 2015], the Commissioner of Social Security shall issue regulations to carry out the amendment made by subsection (a) [enacting subsec. (d)(5)(C) of this section]."

Section 2(g) of Pub.L. 98–460 provided that: "The Secretary of Health and Human Services shall prescribe regulations necessary to implement the amendments made by this section [enacting subsec. (f) of this section and amending sections 416(i)(2)(D) and 1382c(a) of this title and enacting provisions set out as notes under this section] not later than 180 days after the date of the enactment of this Act [Oct. 9, 1984]."

Retroactive Benefits

Section 2(f) of Pub.L. 98–460 provided that: "In the case of any individual who is found to be under a disability after a review required under this section, such individual shall be entitled to retroactive benefits beginning with benefits payable for the first month to which the most recent termination of benefits applied."

Special Insured Status Test in Certain Cases for Disability Purposes

Individuals not insured for disability benefits as determined under subsec. (c)(1) of this section with respect to any month in a quarter deemed to have met such requirements in certain cases, see section 404 of Pub.L. 86–778, set out as a note under section 416 of this title.

Study and Report to Congressional Committees on Effect of Continued Payment of Disability Benefits During Appeal on Trust Fund Expenditures and Rate of Appeals

Section 7(c) of Pub.L. 98–460 provided that:

"(1) The Secretary of Health and Human Services shall, as soon as practicable after the date of the enactment of this Act [Oct. 9, 1984], conduct a study concerning the effect which the enactment and continued operation of section 223(g) of the Social Security Act [subsec. (g) of this section] is having on expenditures from the Federal Old-Age and Survivors Insurance Trust Fund, the Federal Disability Insurance Trust Fund, the Federal Hospital Insurance Trust Fund, and the Federal Supplementary Medical Insurance Trust Fund, and the rate of appeals to administrative law judges of unfavorable determinations relating to disability or periods of disability.

"(2) The Secretary shall submit the results of the study under paragraph (1), together with any recommendations, to the Committee on Ways and Means of the House of Representatives and the Committee on Finance of the Senate not later than July 1, 1986."

Termination of Special $50 Payment Under Tax Reduction Act of 1975

Special payment of $50, pursuant to section 702 of Pub.L. 94–12, as soon as practicable after Mar. 29, 1975, by the Secretary of the Treasury to each individual who, for the month of March, 1975, was entitled to a monthly insurance benefit payable under this subchapter, but no payments to be made under that section after May 23, 1997, see section 406 of Pub.L. 95–30, set out as a note under section 402 of this title.

§ 424. Repealed. Pub.L. 85–840, Title II, § 206, Aug. 28, 1958, 72 Stat. 1025

HISTORICAL AND STATUTORY NOTES

Section, Act Aug. 14, 1935, c. 531, Title II, § 224, as added Aug. 1, 1956, c. 836, Title I, § 103(a), 70 Stat. 816, and amended July 17, 1957, Pub.L. 85–109, § 2(a), 71 Stat. 308, related to reduction of benefits based on disability.

Effective Date of Repeal

Repeal of this section applicable with respect to monthly benefits under this subchapter for Aug. 1958 and succeeding months, see section 207(a) of Pub.L. 85–840, set out as an Effective Date of 1958 Amendment note under section 416 of this title.

§ 424a. Reduction of disability benefits

(a) Conditions for reduction; computation

If for any month prior to the month in which an individual attains retirement age (as defined in section 416(*l*)(1) of this title)

(1) such individual is entitled to benefits under section 423 of this title, and

(2) such individual is entitled for such month to—

(A) periodic benefits on account of his or her total or partial disability (whether or not permanent) under a workmen's compensation law or plan of the United States or a State, or

(B) periodic benefits on account of his or her total or partial disability (whether or not permanent) under any other law or plan of the United States, a State, a political subdivision (as that term is used in section 418(b)(2) of this title), or an instrumentality of two or more States (as that term is used in section 418(g) of this title), other than (i) benefits payable under Title 38, (ii) benefits payable under a program of assistance which is based on need, (iii) benefits based on service all or substantially all of which was included under an agreement entered into by a State and the Commissioner of Social Security under section 418 of this title, and (iv) benefits under a law or plan of the United States based on service all or substantially all of which is employment as defined in section 410 of this title,

the total of his benefits under section 423 of this title for such month and of any benefits under section 402 of this title for such month based on his wages and self-employment income shall be reduced (but not below zero) by the amount by which the sum of—

(3) such total of benefits under sections 423 and 402 of this title for such month, and

(4) such periodic benefits payable (and actually paid) for such month to such individual under such laws or plans,

exceeds the higher of—

(5) 80 per centum of his "average current earnings", or

(6) the total of such individual's disability insurance benefits under section 423 of this title for such month and of any monthly insurance benefits under section 402 of this title for such month based on his wages and self-employment income, prior to reduction under this section.

In no case shall the reduction in the total of such benefits under sections 423 and 402 of this title for a month (in a continuous period of months) reduce such total below the sum of—

(7) the total of the benefits under sections 423 and 402 of this title, after reduction under this section, with respect to all persons entitled to benefits on the basis of such individual's wages and self-employment income for such month which were determined for such individual and such persons for the first month for which reduction under this section was made (or which would have been so determined if all of them had been so entitled in such first month), and

(8) any increase in such benefits with respect to such individual and such persons, before reduction under this section, which is made effective for months after the first month for which reduction under this section is made.

For purposes of clause (5), an individual's average current earnings means the largest of (A) the average monthly wage (determined under section 415(b) of this title as in effect prior to January 1979) used for purposes of computing his benefits under section 423 of this title, (B) one-sixtieth of the total of his wages and self-employment income (computed without regard to the limitations specified in sections 409(a)(1) and 411(b)(1) of this title) for the five consecutive calendar years after 1950 for which such wages and self-employment income were highest, or (C) one-twelfth of the total of his wages and self-employment income (computed without regard to the limitations specified in sections 409(a)(1) and 411(b)(1) of this title) for the calendar year in which he had the highest such wages and income during the period consisting of the calendar year in which he became disabled (as defined in section 423(d) of this title) and the five years preceding that year.

(b) Reduction where benefits payable on other than monthly basis

If any periodic benefit for a total or partial disability under a law or plan described in subsection (a)(2) is payable on other than a monthly basis (excluding a benefit payable as a lump sum except to the extent that it is a commutation of, or a substitute for, periodic payments), the reduction under this section shall be made at such time or times and in such amounts as the Commissioner of Social Security finds will approximate as nearly as practicable the reduction prescribed by subsection (a).

(c) Reductions and deductions under other provisions

Reduction of benefits under this section shall be made after any reduction under subsection (a) of section 403 of this title, but before deductions under such section and under section 422(b) of this title.

(d) Exception

The reduction of benefits required by this section shall not be made if the law or plan described in subsection (a)(2) under which a periodic benefit is payable provides for the reduction thereof when anyone is entitled to benefits under this subchapter on the basis of the wages and self-employment income of an individual entitled to benefits under section 423 of this title, and such law or plan so provided on February 18, 1981.

(e) Conditions for payment

If it appears to the Commissioner of Social Security that an individual may be eligible for periodic benefits under a law or plan which would give rise to reduction under this section, the Commissioner may require, as a condition of certification for payment of any benefits under section 423 of this title to any individual for any month and of any benefits under section 402 of this title for such month based on such individual's wages and self-employment income, that such individual certify (i) whether he has filed or intends to file any claim for such periodic benefits, and (ii) if he has so filed, whether there has been a decision on such claim. The Commissioner of Social Security may, in the absence of evidence to the contrary, rely upon such a certification by such individual that he has not filed and does not intend to file such a claim, or that he has so filed and no final decision thereon has been made, in certifying benefits for payment pursuant to section 405(i) of this title.

(f) Redetermination of reduction

(1) In the second calendar year after the year in which reduction under this section in the total of an individual's benefits under section 423 of this title and any benefits under section 402 of this title based on his wages and self-employment income was first required (in a continuous period of months), and in each third year thereafter, the Commissioner of Social Security shall redetermine the amount of such benefits which are still subject to reduction under this section; but such redetermination shall not result in any decrease in the total amount of benefits payable under this subchapter on the basis of such individual's wages and self-employment income. Such redetermined benefit shall be determined as of, and shall become effective with, the January following the year in which such redetermination was made.

(2) In making the redetermination required by paragraph (1), the individual's average current earnings (as defined in subsection (a)) shall be deemed to be the product of—

(A) his average current earnings as initially determined under subsection (a); and

(B) the ratio of (i) the national average wage index (as defined in section 409(k)(1) of this title) for the calendar year before the year in which such redetermination is made to (ii) the national average wage index (as so defined) for the calendar year before the year in which the reduction was first computed (but not counting any reduction made in benefits for a previous period of disability).

Any amount determined under this paragraph which is not a multiple of $1 shall be reduced to the next lower multiple of $1.

(g) Proportionate reduction; application of excess

Whenever a reduction in the total of benefits for any month based on an individual's wages and self-employment income is made under this section, each benefit, except the disability insurance benefit, shall first be proportionately decreased, and any excess of such reduction over the sum of all such benefits other than the disability insurance benefit shall then be applied to such disability insurance benefit.

(h) Furnishing of information

(1) Notwithstanding any other provision of law, the head of any Federal agency shall provide such information within its possession as the Commissioner of Social Security may require for purposes of making a timely determination of the amount of the reduction, if any, required by this section in benefits payable under this subchapter, or verifying other information necessary in carrying out the provisions of this section.

(2) The Commissioner of Social Security is authorized to enter into agreements with States, political subdivisions, and other organizations that administer a law or plan subject to the provisions of this section, in order to obtain such information as the Commissioner may require to carry out the provisions of this section.

(Aug. 14, 1935, c. 531, Title II, § 224, as added Pub.L. 89–97, Title III, § 335, July 30, 1965, 79 Stat. 406; amended Pub.L. 90–248, Title I, § 159(a), Jan. 2, 1968, 81 Stat. 869; Pub.L. 92–603, Title I, § 119(a), (b), Oct. 30, 1972, 86 Stat. 1352; Pub.L. 94–202, § 8(j), Jan. 2, 1976, 89 Stat. 1140; Pub.L. 95–216, Title II, § 205(d), Title III, § 353(c), Dec. 20, 1977, 91 Stat. 1529, 1553; Pub.L. 97–35, Title XXII, § 2208(a), Aug. 13, 1981, 95 Stat. 839; Pub.L. 99–272, Title XII, § 12109(a), Apr. 7, 1986, 100 Stat. 286; Pub.L. 99–509, Title IX, § 9002(c)(2)(F), Oct. 21, 1986, 100 Stat. 1972; Pub.L. 101–239, Title X, § 10208(b)(2)(A), (C), (d)(2)(A)(i), (iii), Dec. 19, 1989, 103 Stat. 2477, 2478, 2480, 2481; Pub.L. 103–296, Title I, § 107(a)(4), Title III, § 321(e)(2)(H), Aug. 15, 1994, 108 Stat. 1478, 1540; Pub.L. 113–295, Div. B, Title II, § 201(a), Dec. 19, 2014, 128 Stat. 4064.)

HISTORICAL AND STATUTORY NOTES

References in Text

Section 422(b) of this title, referred to in subsec. (c), was repealed by Pub.L. 106–170, Title I, § 101(b)(1)(C), Dec. 17, 1999, 113 Stat. 1873.

Effective and Applicability Provisions

2014 Acts. Pub.L. 113–295, Div. B, Title II, § 201(b), Dec. 19, 2014, 128 Stat. 4064, provided that: "The amendment made by subsection (a) [amending this section] shall apply with respect to any individual who attains 65 years of age on or after the date that is 12 months after the date of the enactment of this Act [Dec. 19, 2014]."

1994 Acts. Amendment by section 107(a)(4) of Pub.L. 103–296 effective Mar. 31, 1995, see section 110 of Pub.L. 103–296, set out as a note under section 401 of this title.

1989 Acts. Amendment by Pub.L. 101–239, § 10208, applicable with respect to computation of average total wage amounts for calendar years after 1990, including transitional rule, see section 10208(c) of Pub.L. 101–239, set out as a note under section 430 of this title.

1986 Acts. Amendment by Pub.L. 99–509 effective with respect to payments due with respect to wages paid after Dec. 31, 1986, including wages paid after such date by a State (or political subdivision thereof) that modified its agreement pursuant to section 418(e)(2) of this title prior to Oct. 21, 1986, with certain exceptions, see section 9002(d) of Pub.L. 99–509 set out as a note under section 418 of this title.

Section 12109(b) of Pub.L. 99–272 provided that:

"(1) The amendment made by subsection (a)(1) [amending subsec. (a)(2) of this section] shall be effective as though it had been included or reflected in the amendment made by section 2208(a)(3) of the Omnibus Budget Reconciliation Act of 1981. [See Effective Date of 1981 Amendment set out under this section].

"(2) The amendment made by subsection (a)(2) [amending subsec. (a)(2)(B) of this section by substituting 'all or substantially all of which' for 'all or part of which' in cl. (iv)] shall apply only with respect to monthly benefits payable on the basis of the wages and self-employment income of individuals who become disabled (within the meaning of section 223(d) of the Social Security Act [section 423(d) of this title]) after the month in which this Act is enacted [April, 1986]."

1981 Acts. Section 2208(b) of Pub.L. 97–35 provided that: "The amendments made by subsection (a) [amending this section] shall be effective with respect to individuals who first become entitled to benefits under section 223(a) of the Social Security Act [section 423(a) of this title] for months beginning after the month in which this Act is enacted [August, 1981], but only in the case of an individual who became disabled within the meaning of section 223(d) of such Act [section 423(d) of this title] after the sixth month preceding the month in which this Act is enacted [August 1981]."

1977 Acts. Amendment by section 205(d) of Pub.L. 95–216 [adding "(determined under section 415(b) of this title as in effect prior to January 1979)" following "(A) the average monthly wage" in the provisions following par. (8) of subsec. (a) of this section] effective with respect to monthly benefits under this subchapter payable for months after Dec. 1978 and with respect to lump-sum death payments with respect to deaths occurring after Dec. 1978, see section 206 of Pub.L. 95–216, set out as a note under section 402 of this title.

Section 353(c)(1) of Pub.L. 95–216 provided in part that the amendment by section 353(c)(1) of Pub.L. 95–216 [which struck out requirement in the provisions following par. (8) of subsec. (a) of this section that the Secretary estimate the total of wages and self-employment income in those cases where an individual's reported wages and self-employment income for the calendar year reached the limitations specified in sections 409(a) and 411(b)(1) of this title] is effective with respect to the estimates for calendar years beginning after Dec. 31, 1977.

Amendment of subsec. (f)(2) by section 353(c)(2) of Pub.L. 95–216 effective Jan. 1, 1979, see section 353(g) of Pub.L. 95–216, set out as a note under section 418 of this title.

1972 Acts. Section 119(c) of Pub.L. 92–603 provided that: "The amendments made by subsections (a) and (b) [amending subsec. (a) of this section] shall apply with respect to monthly benefits under title II of the Social Security Act [this subchapter] for months after December 1972."

1968 Acts. Section 159(b) of Pub.L. 90–248 provided that:

"(1) The amendments made by subsection (a) [to subsec. (a) of this section] shall apply only with respect to monthly benefits under title II of the Social Security Act [this subchapter] for months after January 1968.

"(2) For purposes of any redetermination which is made under section 224(f) of the Social Security Act [subsec. (f) of this section] in the case of benefits, subject to reduction under section 224 of such Act [this section], where such reduction as first computed was effective with respect to benefits for the month in which this Act is enacted [Jan. 1968] or a prior month, the amendments made by subsection (a) of this section [to subsec. (a) of this section] shall also be deemed to have applied in the initial determination of the 'average current earnings' of the individual whose wages and self-employment income are involved."

1965 Acts. Section 335 of Pub.L. 89–97 made this section effective with respect to benefits under this subchapter for months after Dec. 1965 based on the wages and self-employment income of individuals entitled to benefits, under section 423 of this title whose period of disability (as defined in this subchapter) began after June 1, 1965.

Prior Provisions

A prior section 224 of Act Aug. 14, 1935, was classified to section 424 of this title and was repealed by Pub.L. 85–840, Title II, § 206, Aug. 28, 1958, 72 Stat. 1025.

§ 425. Additional rules relating to benefits based on disability

(a) Suspension of benefits

If the Commissioner of Social Security, on the basis of information obtained by or submitted to the Commissioner, believes that an individual entitled to benefits under section 423 of this title, or that a child who has attained the age of eighteen and is entitled to benefits under section 402(d) of this title, or that a widow or surviving divorced wife who has not attained age 60 and is entitled to benefits under section 402(e) of this title, or that a widower or surviving divorced husband who has not attained age 60 and is entitled to benefits under section 402(f) of this title, may have ceased to be under a disability, the Commissioner of Social Security may suspend the payment of benefits under such section 402(d), 402(e), 402(f), or 423 of this title until it is determined (as provided in section 421 of this title) whether or not such individual's disability has ceased or until the Commissioner of Social Security believes that such disability has not ceased. In the case of any individual whose disability is subject to determination under an agreement with a State under section 421(b) of this title, the Commissioner of Social Security shall promptly notify the appropriate State of the Commissioner's action under this subsection and shall request a prompt determination of whether such individual's disability has ceased. For purposes of this subsection, the term "disability" has the meaning assigned to such term in section 423(d) of this title. Whenever the benefits of an individual entitled to a disability insurance benefit are suspended for any month, the benefits of any individual entitled thereto under subsection (b), (c), or (d) of section 402 of this title, on the basis of the wages and self-employment income of such individual, shall be suspended for such month. The first sentence of this subsection shall not apply to any child entitled to benefits under section 402(d) of this title, if he has attained the age of 18 but has not attained the age of 22, for any month during which he is a full-time student (as defined and determined under section 402(d) of this title).

(b) Continued payments during rehabilitation program

Notwithstanding any other provision of this subchapter, payment to an individual of benefits based on disability (as described in the first sentence of subsection (a)) shall not be terminated or suspended because the physical or mental impairment, on which the individual's entitlement to such benefits is based, has or may have ceased, if—

(1) such individual is participating in a program consisting of the Ticket to Work and Self-Sufficiency Program under section 1320b–19 of this title or another program of vocational rehabilitation services, employment services, or other support services, approved by the Commissioner of Social Security, and

(2) the Commissioner of Social Security determines that the completion of such program, or its continuation for a specified period of time, will increase the likelihood that such individual may (following his participation in such program) be permanently removed from the disability benefit rolls.

(c) Access to information held by payroll data providers

(1) The Commissioner of Social Security may require each individual who applies for or is entitled to monthly insurance benefits under subsections (d)(1)(B)(ii), (d)(6)(A)(ii), (d)(6)(B), (e)(1)(B)(ii), and (f)(1)(B)(ii) of section 402 of this title and subsection (a)(1) of section 423 of this title to provide authorization by the individual for the Commissioner to obtain from any payroll data provider (as defined in section 1320e–3(c)(1) of this title) any record held by the payroll data provider with respect to the individual whenever the Commissioner determines the record is needed in connection with a determination of initial or ongoing entitlement to such benefits.

(2) An authorization provided by an individual under this subsection shall remain effective until the earliest of—

(A) the rendering of a final adverse decision on the individual's application or entitlement to benefits under this subchapter;

(B) the termination of the individual's entitlement to benefits under this subchapter; or

(C) the express revocation by the individual of the authorization, in a written notification to the Commissioner.

(3) The Commissioner of Social Security is not required to furnish any authorization obtained pursuant to this subsection to the payroll data provider.

(4) The Commissioner shall inform any person who provides authorization pursuant to this clause of the duration and scope of the authorization.

(5) If an individual who applies for or is entitled to benefits under this subchapter refuses to provide, or revokes, any authorization under this subsection, subsection (d) shall not apply to such individual beginning with the first day of the first month in which he or she refuses or revokes such authorization.

(d) Reporting responsibilities for beneficiaries subject to information exchange with payroll data provider

An individual who has authorized the Commissioner of Social Security to obtain records from a payroll data provider under subsection (c) shall not be subject to a penalty under section 1320a–8a of this title for any omission or error with respect to such individual's wages as reported by the payroll data provider.

(Aug. 14, 1935, c. 531, Title II, § 225, as added Aug. 1, 1956, c. 836, Title I, § 103(a), 70 Stat. 817; amended Pub.L. 85–840, Title II, § 205(*o*), Aug. 28, 1958, 72 Stat. 1025; Pub.L. 89–97, Title III, § 306(c)(15), July 30, 1965, 79 Stat. 373; Pub.L. 90–248, Title I, §§ 104(d)(5), 158(c)(9), Jan. 2, 1968, 81 Stat. 833, 869; Pub.L. 92–603, Title I, § 107(b)(5), Oct. 30, 1972, 86 Stat. 1343; Pub.L. 96–265, Title III, § 301(a), June 9, 1980, 94 Stat. 449; Pub.L. 98–21, Title III, § 309(p), Apr. 20, 1983, 97 Stat. 117; Pub.L. 101–508, Title V, § 5113(a), Nov. 5, 1990, 104 Stat. 1388–273; Pub.L. 103–296, Title I, § 107(a)(4), Title II, § 201(a)(3)(A), Aug. 15, 1994, 108 Stat. 1478, 1494; Pub.L. 104–121, Title I, § 105(a)(4), Mar. 29, 1996, 110 Stat. 853; Pub.L. 106–170, Title I, § 101(b)(1)(D), Dec. 17, 1999, 113 Stat. 1873; Pub.L. 114–74, Title VIII, § 824(b)(1), (c)(1), Nov. 2, 2015, 129 Stat. 608, 609.)

HISTORICAL AND STATUTORY NOTES

References in Text

This subchapter, referred to in text, originally read "this title", meaning Title II of the Social Security Act, Act Aug. 14, 1935, c. 531, 49 Stat. 620, as amended, which is principally classified to subchapter II of this chapter, 42 U.S.C.A. § 401 et seq.

Effective and Applicability Provisions

2015 Acts. Pub.L. 114–74, Title VIII, § 824(e), Nov. 2, 2015, 129 Stat. 610, provided that: "The amendments made by this section [enacting 42 U.S.C.A. § 1320e–3, amending this section and 42 U.S.C.A. § 1383] shall take effect on the date that is 1 year after the date of the enactment of this Act [Nov. 2, 2015]."

1999 Acts. Amendment by section 101(b) of Pub.L. 106–170 effective with the first month following 1 year after December 17, 1999, subject to graduated implementation of program provisions of section 101(d) of Pub.L. 106–170 [set out as a note under section 1320b–19 of this title], see section 101(c) of Pub.L. 106–170, set out as a note under section 1320b–19 of this title.

1996 Acts. Amendment by section 105(a)(4) of Pub.L. 104–121 applicable to individual who applies for, or whose claim is adjudicated with respect to, benefits under this subchapter based on disability on or after Mar. 29, 1996, with certain conditions applying for benefits before Mar. 29, 1996, see section 105(a)(5) of Pub.L. 104–121, set out as a note under section 405 of this title.

1994 Acts. Amendment by section 107(a)(4) of Pub.L. 103–296 effective Mar. 31, 1995, see section 110 of Pub.L. 103–296, set out as a note under section 401 of this title.

Section 201(a)(3)(E) of Pub.L. 103–296 provided that:

"(i) In general.—Except as otherwise provided in this paragraph, the amendments made by this paragraph [amending section heading and subsecs. (a), (b), and (c) of this section and sections 426 and 426–1 of this title and enacting provisions set out as notes under this section] shall apply with respect to benefits based on disability (as defined in section 225(c)(9) of the Social Security Act, added by this section) [subsec. (c)(9) of this section] which are otherwise payable in months beginning after 180 days after the date of the enactment of this Act [Aug. 15, 1994]. The Secretary of Health and Human Services shall issue regulations necessary to carry out the amendments made by this paragraph not later than 180 days after the date of the enactment of this Act [Aug. 15, 1994].

"(ii) Referral and monitoring agencies.—Section 225(c)(5) of the Social Security Act (added by this subsection) [subsec. (c)(5) of this section] shall take effect 180 days after the date of the enactment of this Act [Aug. 15, 1994].

"(iii) Termination after 36 months.—Section 225(c)(7) of the Social Security Act (added by this subsection) [subsec. (c)(7) of this section] shall apply with respect to benefits based on disability (as so defined) for months beginning after 180 days after the date of the enactment of this Act [Aug. 15, 1994]."

1990 Acts. Section 5113(c) of Pub.L. 101–508 provided that: "The amendments made by this section [amending this section and section 1383 of this title] shall be effective with respect to benefits payable for months after the eleventh month following the month in which this Act is enacted [Pub.L. 101–508 was approved Nov. 5, 1990] and shall apply only with respect to individuals whose blindness or disability has or may have ceased after such eleventh month."

1984 Acts. Amendment of sections 422 and 1382d of this title by section 11(a), (b) of Pub.L. 98–460 applicable with respect to individuals who receive benefits as a result of section 425(b) or section 1383(a)(6) of this title, or who refuse to continue to accept rehabilitation services or fail to cooperate in an approved vocational rehabilitation program, in or after the first month following October 1984, see section 11(c) of Pub.L. 98–460, set out as a note under section 422 of this title.

1983 Acts. Amendment by section 309(p) of Pub.L. 98–21 applicable only with respect to monthly payments payable under this subchapter for months after April, 1983, except as otherwise specifically provided, see section 310 of Pub.L. 98–21, set out as a note under section 402 of this title.

1980 Acts. Section 301(c) of Pub.L. 96–265 provided that: "The amendments made by this section [amending sections 425 and 1383 of this title] shall become effective on the first day of the sixth month which begins after the date of the enactment of this Act [June 9, 1980], and shall apply with respect to individuals whose disability has not been determined to have ceased prior to such first day."

1972 Acts. Amendment by Pub.L. 92–603 applicable with respect to monthly benefits under this subchapter for months after Dec. 1972, with specified exceptions, see section 107(c) of Pub.L. 92–603, set out as a note under section 402 of this title.

1968 Acts. Amendment by section 104 of Pub.L. 90–248 applicable with respect to monthly benefits under this subchapter for and after the month of Feb. 1968, but only on the basis of applications for such benefits filed in or after January 1968, see section 104(e) of Pub.L. 90–248 set out as a note under section 402 of this title.

Amendment by section 158 of Pub.L. 90–248 applicable with respect to applications for disability insurance benefits under section 423 of this title and to disability determinations under section 416(i) of this title, filed in or after Jan. 1968, or before Jan. 1968 if the applicant has not died before such month and if (A) notice of the final decision of the Secretary of Health, Education, and Welfare has not been given to the applicant before such month; or (B) the notice referred to in subparagraph (A) has been so given before such month but a civil action with respect to such final decision is commenced under section 205(g) of the Social Security Act [section 405(g) of this title] (whether before, in, or after such month) and the decision in such civil action has not become final before such month; see section 158(e) of Pub.L. 90–248, set out as a note under section 423 of this title.

1958 Acts. Amendment by section 205 of Pub.L. 85–840 applicable with respect to monthly benefits under this subchapter for months after Aug. 1958 but only if an application for such benefits is filed on or after Aug. 28, 1958, see section 207(a) of Pub.L. 85–840, set out as a note under section 416 of this title.

1956 Acts. Section applicable only with respect to monthly benefits under this subchapter for months after June 1957, with qualifications, see section 103(d) of Act Aug. 1, 1956, set out as a note under section 423 of this title.

Sunset Provisions

Section 201(a)(3)(C) of Pub.L. 103–296 provided that: "Section 225(c)(7) of the Social Security Act [subsec. (c)(7) of this section] (added by subparagraph (A)) shall cease to be effective with respect to benefits for months after September 2004."

Demonstration Projects Relating to Referral, Monitoring, and Treatment for Alcoholics or Drug Addicts

Section 201(c) of Pub.L. 103–296, which related to demonstration projects relating to referral, monitoring, and treatment for alcoholics or drug addicts, was repealed by Pub.L. 104–121, Title I, § 105(c), Mar. 29, 1996, 110 Stat. 855.

Report on Referral, Monitoring, Testing, and Treatment of Individuals Where Entitlement to or Termination of Benefits Involves Alcoholism or Drug Addiction

Section 201(a)(3)(B) of Pub.L. 103–296, requiring the Secretary of Health and Human Services to submit a report to Congress on referral, monitoring, testing, and treatment of individuals whose entitlement or termination of benefits involves alcoholism or drug addiction, was repealed by Pub.L. 105–33, Title V, § 5525(c), Aug. 5, 1997, 111 Stat. 625.

[Repeal of the above note by section 5525(c) of Pub.L. 105–33 effective August 5, 1997, see section 5528(c)(2) of Pub.L. 105–33, set out as a note under section 903 of this title.]

Transition Rules for Current Beneficiaries

Section 201(a)(3)(F) of Pub.L. 103–296 provided that: "In any case in which an individual is entitled to benefits based on disability, the determination of disability was made by the Secretary of Health and Human services during or before the 180–day period following the date of the enactment of this Act [Aug. 15, 1994], and alcoholism or drug addiction is a contributing factor material to the Secretary's determination that the individual is under a disability—

"(i) Treatment requirement.—Paragraphs (1) through (4) of section 225(c) of the Social Security Act [subsec. (c)(1) to (4) of this section] (added by this subsection) shall apply only with respect to benefits paid in months after the month in which such individual is notified by the Secretary in writing that alcoholism or drug addiction is a contributing factor material to the Secretary's determination and that such individual is therefore required to comply with the provisions of section 225(c) of such Act [subsec. (c) of this section].

"(ii) Termination after 36 months.—

"(I) In general.—For purposes of section 225(c)(7) of the Social Security Act [subsec. (c)(7) of this section] (added by this subsection), the first month of entitlement beginning after 180 days after the date of the enactment of this Act [Aug. 15, 1994] shall be treated as the individual's first month of entitlement to such benefits.

"(II) Concurrent beneficiaries currently under treatment.—In any case in which the individual is also entitled to benefits under title XVI [42 U.S.C.A. § 1381 et seq.] and, as of 180 days after the date of the enactment of this Act [Aug. 15, 1994], such individual is undergoing treatment required under section 1611(e)(3) of the Social Security Act [42 U.S.C.A. § 1382(e)(3)] (as in effect immediately before the date of the enactment of this Act [Aug. 15, 1994]), the Secretary of Health and Human Services shall notify such individual of the provisions of section 225(c)(7) of the Social Security Act [subsec. (c)(7) of this section] (added by this subsection) not later than 180 days after the date of the enactment of this Act [Aug. 15, 1994].

"(III) Concurrent beneficiaries not currently under treatment.—In any case in which the individual is also entitled to benefits under title XVI [42 U.S.C.A. § 1381 et seq.] but, as of 180 days after the date of the enactment of this Act [Aug. 15, 1994], such individual is not undergoing treatment described in subclause (II), section 225(c)(7) [subsec. (c)(7) of this section] (added by this subsection) shall apply only with respect to benefits for months after the month in which treatment required under section 1611(e)(3) of the Social Security Act [42 U.S.C.A. § 1382(e)(3)] (as amended by subsection (b)) is available, as determined under regulations of the Secretary of Health and Human

Services, and the Secretary notifies such individual of the availability of such treatment and describes in such notification the provisions of section 225(c)(7) of the Social Security Act [subsec. (c)(7) of this section] (added by this subsection)."

Payment of Costs of Rehabilitation Services

Amendment of section 422 and 1382d of this title by section 11(a), (b) of Pub.L. 98–460 applicable with respect to individuals who receive benefits as a result of section 425(b) or section 1383(a)(6) of this title, or who refuse to continue to accept rehabilitation services or fail to cooperate in an approved vocational rehabilitation program, in or after the first month following October 1984, see section 11(c) of Pub. L. 98–460, set out as a note under 42 U.S.C.A. § 422.

§ 426. Entitlement to hospital insurance benefits

(a) Individuals over 65 years

Every individual who—

(1) has attained age 65, and

(2)(A) is entitled to monthly insurance benefits under section 402 of this title, would be entitled to those benefits except that he has not filed an application therefor (or application has not been made for a benefit the entitlement to which for any individual is a condition of entitlement therefor), or would be entitled to such benefits but for the failure of another individual, who meets all the criteria of entitlement to monthly insurance benefits, to meet such criteria throughout a month, and, in conformity with regulations of the Secretary, files an application for hospital insurance benefits under part A of subchapter XVIII,

(B) is a qualified railroad retirement beneficiary, or

(C) (i) would meet the requirements of subparagraph (A) upon filing application for the monthly insurance benefits involved if medicare qualified government employment (as defined in section 410(p) of this title) were treated as employment (as defined in section 410(a) of this title) for purposes of this subchapter, and (ii) files an application, in conformity with regulations of the Secretary, for hospital insurance benefits under part A of subchapter XVIII,

shall be entitled to hospital insurance benefits under part A of subchapter XVIII for each month for which he meets the condition specified in paragraph (2), beginning with the first month after June 1966 for which he meets the conditions specified in paragraphs (1) and (2).

(b) Individuals under 65 years

Every individual who—

(1) has not attained age 65, and

(2)(A) is entitled to, and has for 24 calendar months been entitled to, **(i)** disability insurance benefits under section 423 of this title or **(ii)** child's insurance benefits under section 402(d) of this title by reason of a disability (as defined in section 423(d) of this title) or **(iii)** widow's insurance benefits under section 402(e) of this title or widower's insurance benefits under section 402(f) of this title by reason of a disability (as defined in section 423(d) of this title), or

(B) is, and has been for not less than 24 months, a disabled qualified railroad retirement beneficiary, within the meaning of section 231f(d) of Title 45, or

(C)(i) has filed an application, in conformity with regulations of the Secretary, for hospital insurance benefits under part A of subchapter XVIII pursuant to this subparagraph, and

(ii) would meet the requirements of subparagraph (A) (as determined under the disability criteria, including reviews, applied under this subchapter), including the requirement that he has been entitled to the specified benefits for 24 months, if—

(I) medicare qualified government employment (as defined in section 410(p) of this title) were treated as employment (as defined in section 410(a) of this title) for purposes of this subchapter, and

(II) the filing of the application under clause (i) of this subparagraph were deemed to be the filing of an application for the disability-related benefits referred to in clause (i), (ii), or (iii) of subparagraph (A),

shall be entitled to hospital insurance benefits under part A of subchapter XVIII for each month beginning with the later of (I) July 1973 or (II) the twenty-fifth month of his entitlement or status as a qualified railroad retirement beneficiary described in paragraph (2), and ending (subject to the last sentence of this subsection) with the month following the month in which notice of termination of such entitlement to benefits or status as a qualified railroad retirement beneficiary described in paragraph (2) is mailed to him, or if earlier, with the month before the month in which he attains age 65. In applying the previous sentence in the case of an individual described in paragraph (2)(C), the "twenty-fifth month of his entitlement" refers to the first month after the twenty-fourth month of entitlement to specified benefits referred to in paragraph (2)(C) and "notice of termination of such entitlement" refers to a notice that the individual would no longer be determined to be entitled to such specified benefits under the conditions described in that paragraph. For purposes of this subsection, an individual who has had a period of trial work which ended as provided in section 422(c)(4)(A) of this title, and whose entitlement to benefits or status as a qualified railroad retirement beneficiary as described in paragraph (2) has subsequently terminated, shall be deemed to be entitled to such benefits or to occupy such status (notwithstanding the termination of such entitlement or status) for the period of consecutive months throughout all of which the physical or mental impairment, on which such entitlement or status was based, continues, and throughout all of which such individual would have been entitled to monthly insurance benefits under this subchapter or as a qualified railroad retirement beneficiary had such individual been unable to engage in substantial gainful activity, but not in excess of 78 such months. In determining when an individual's entitlement or status terminates for purposes of the preceding sentence, the term "36 months" in the second sentence of section 423(a)(1) of this title, in section 402(d)(1)(G)(i) of this title, in the last sentence of section 402(e)(1) of this title, and in the last sentence of section 402(f)(1) of this title shall be applied as though it read "15 months".

(c) Conditions

For purposes of subsection (a)—

(1) entitlement of an individual to hospital insurance benefits for a month shall consist of entitlement to have payment made under, and subject to the limitations in, part A of subchapter XVIII on his behalf for inpatient hospital services, post-hospital extended care services, and home health services (as such terms are defined in part E of subchapter XVIII) furnished him in the United States (or outside the United States in the case of inpatient hospital services furnished under the conditions described in section 1395f(f) of this title) during such month; except that (A) no such payment may be made for post-hospital extended care services furnished before January 1967, and (B) no such payment may be made for post-hospital extended care services unless the discharge from the hospital required to qualify such services for payment under part A of subchapter XVIII occurred (i) after June 30, 1966, or on or after the first day of the month in which he attains age 65, whichever is later, or (ii) if he was entitled to hospital insurance benefits pursuant to subsection (b), at a time when he was so entitled; and

(2) an individual shall be deemed entitled to monthly insurance benefits under section 402 or section 423 of this title, or to be a qualified railroad retirement beneficiary, for the month in which he died if he would have been entitled to such benefits, or would have been a qualified railroad retirement beneficiary, for such month had he died in the next month.

(d) "Qualified railroad retirement beneficiary" defined

For purposes of this section, the term "qualified railroad retirement beneficiary" means an individual whose name has been certified to the Secretary by the Railroad Retirement Board under section 231f(d) of Title 45. An individual shall cease to be a qualified railroad retirement beneficiary at the close of the month preceding the month which is certified by the Railroad Retirement Board as the month in which he ceased to meet the requirements of section 231f(d) of Title 45.

(e) Benefits for widows and widowers

(1)(A) For purposes of determining entitlement to hospital insurance benefits under subsection (b) in the case of widows and widowers described in paragraph (2)(A)(iii) thereof—

(i) the term "age 60" in sections 402(e)(1)(B)(ii), 402(e)(4), 402(f)(1)(B)(ii), and 402(f)(4) of this title shall be deemed to read "age 65"; and

(ii) the phrase "before she attained age 60" in the matter following subparagraph (F) of section 402(e)(1) of this title and the phrase "before he attained age 60" in the matter following subparagraph (F) of section 402(f)(1) of this title shall each be deemed to read "based on a disability".

(B) For purposes of subsection (b)(2)(A)(iii), each month in the period commencing with the first month for which an individual is first eligible for supplemental security income benefits under subchapter XVI, or State supplementary payments of the type referred to in section 1382e(a) of this title (or payments of the type described in section 212(a) of Public Law 93–66) which are paid by the Secretary under an agreement referred to in section 1382e(a) of this title (or in section 212(b) of Public Law 93–66), shall be included as one of the 24 months for which such individual must have been entitled to widow's or widower's insurance benefits on the basis of disability in order to become entitled to hospital insurance benefits on that basis.

(2) For purposes of determining entitlement to hospital insurance benefits under subsection (b) in the case of an individual under age 65 who is entitled to benefits under section 402 of this title, and who was entitled to widow's insurance benefits or widower's insurance benefits based on disability for the month before the first month in which such individual was so entitled to old-age insurance benefits (but ceased to be entitled to such widow's or widower's insurance benefits upon becoming entitled to such old-age insurance benefits), such individual shall be deemed to have continued to be entitled to such widow's insurance benefits or widower's insurance benefits for and after such first month.

(3) For purposes of determining entitlement to hospital insurance benefits under subsection (b), any disabled widow aged 50 or older who is entitled to mother's insurance benefits (and who would have been entitled to widow's insurance benefits by reason of disability if she had filed for such widow's benefits), and any disabled widower aged 50 or older who is entitled to father's insurance benefits (and who would have been entitled to widower's insurance benefits by reason of disability if he had filed for such widower's benefits), shall, upon application for such hospital insurance benefits be deemed to have filed for such widow's or widower's insurance benefits.

(4) For purposes of determining entitlement to hospital insurance benefits under subsection (b) in the case of an individual described in clause (iii) of subsection (b)(2)(A), the entitlement of such individual to widow's or widower's insurance benefits under section 402(e) or (f) of this title by reason of a disability shall be deemed to be the entitlement to such benefits that would result if such entitlement were determined without regard to the provisions of section 402(j)(4) of this title.

(f) Medicare waiting period for recipients of disability benefits

For purposes of subsection (b) (and for purposes of section 1395p(g)(1) of this title and section 231f(d)(2)(ii) of Title 45), the 24 months for which an individual has to have been entitled to specified monthly benefits on the basis of disability in order to become entitled to hospital insurance benefits on such basis effective with any particular month (or to be deemed to have enrolled in the supplementary medical insurance program, on the basis of such entitlement, by reason of section 1395p(f) of this title), where such individual had been entitled to specified monthly benefits of the same type during a previous period which terminated—

(1) more than 60 months before the month in which his current disability began in any case where such monthly benefits were of the type specified in clause (A)(i) or (B) of subsection (b)(2), or

(2) more than 84 months before the month in which his current disability began in any case where such monthly benefits were of the type specified in clause (A)(ii) or (A)(iii) of such subsection,

shall not include any month which occurred during such previous period, unless the physical or mental impairment which is the basis for disability is the same as (or directly related to) the physical or mental impairment which served as the basis for disability in such previous period.

(g) Information regarding eligibility of Federal employees

The Secretary and Director of the Office of Personnel Management shall jointly prescribe and carry out procedures designed to assure that all individuals who perform medicare qualified government employment by virtue of service described in section 410(a)(5) of this title are fully informed with respect to (1) their eligibility or potential eligibility for hospital insurance benefits (based on such employment) under part A of subchapter XVIII, (2) the requirements for and conditions of such eligibility, and (3) the necessity of timely application as a condition of entitlement under subsection (b)(2)(C), giving particular attention to individuals who apply for an annuity under chapter 83[1] of Title 5 or under another similar Federal retirement program, and whose eligibility for such an annuity is or would be based on a disability.

(h) Waiver of waiting period for individuals with ALS

For purposes of applying this section in the case of an individual medically determined to have amyotrophic lateral sclerosis (ALS), the following special rules apply:

(1) Subsection (b) shall be applied as if there were no requirement for any entitlement to benefits, or status, for a period longer than 1 month.

(2) The entitlement under such subsection shall begin with the first month (rather than twenty-fifth month) of entitlement or status.

(3) Subsection (f) shall not be applied.

(i) Certain uninsured individuals

For entitlement to hospital insurance benefits in the case of certain uninsured individuals, see section 426a of this title.

(j) Redesignated (i)

(Aug. 14, 1935, c. 531, Title II, § 226, as added Pub.L. 89–97, Title I, § 101, July 30, 1965, 79 Stat. 290; amended Pub.L. 90–248, Title I, § 129(c)(1), Jan. 2, 1968, 81 Stat. 847; Pub.L. 92–603, Title II, §§ 201(b), 299I, Oct. 30, 1972, 86 Stat. 1371, 1463; Pub.L. 93–58, § 3, July 6, 1973, 87 Stat. 142; Pub.L. 93–233, § 18(f), Dec. 31, 1973, 87 Stat. 969; Pub.L. 93–445, Title III, § 305, Oct. 16, 1974, 88 Stat. 1358; Pub.L. 95–216, Title III, §§ 332(a)(3), 334(d)(4)(B), Dec. 20, 1977, 91 Stat. 1543, 1546; Pub.L. 95–292, §§ 1(b), 3, June 13, 1978, 92 Stat. 308, 315; Pub.L. 96–265, Title I, §§ 103(a)(1), (b), 104(a), June 9, 1980, 94 Stat. 444; Pub.L. 96–473, § 2(a), Oct. 19, 1980, 94 Stat. 2263; Pub.L. 96–499, Title IX, § 930(q), Dec. 5, 1980, 94 Stat. 2633; Pub.L. 97–35, Title XXII, § 2203(e), Aug. 13, 1981, 95 Stat. 837; Pub.L. 97–248, Title II, § 278(b)(2)(A), (B), (4), Sept. 3, 1982, 96 Stat. 560, 561; Pub.L. 98–21, Title I, § 131(a)(3)(H), (b)(3)(G), Title III, § 309(q)(1), Apr. 20, 1983, 97 Stat. 93, 117; Pub.L. 98–369, Div.B, Title VI, § 2663(a)(17), July 18, 1984, 98 Stat. 1165; Pub.L. 99–272, Title XIII, § 13205(b)(2)(A), (C)(ii), Apr. 7, 1986, 100 Stat. 317; Pub.L. 100–203, Title IV, § 4033(a) [formerly § 4033(a)(1)], Title IX, § 9010(e)(3), Dec. 22, 1987, 101 Stat. 1330–77, 1330–294; Pub.L. 100–360, Title IV, § 411(e)(2), (n)(1), July 1, 1988, 102 Stat. 775, 807; Pub.L. 100–485, Title VI, § 608(f)(5), Oct. 13, 1988, 102 Stat. 2424; Pub.L. 101–508, Title V, § 5103(c)(2)(C), Nov. 5, 1990, 104 Stat. 1388–252; Pub.L. 103–296, Title II, § 201(a)(3)(D)(i), Aug. 15, 1994, 108 Stat. 1497; Pub.L. 105–33, Title IV, § 4002(f)(1), Aug. 5, 1997, 111 Stat. 329; Pub.L. 106–170, Title II, § 202(a), Dec. 17, 1999, 113 Stat. 1894; Pub.L. 106–554, § 1(a)(6) [Title I, § 115(a)], Dec. 21, 2000, 114 Stat. 2763, 2763A–474; Pub.L. 108–173, Title I, § 101(e)(1), Dec. 8, 2003, 117 Stat. 2150; Pub.L. 108–203, Title IV, § 418(b)(4)(B)(vii), Mar. 2, 2004, 118 Stat. 533; Pub.L. 114–74, Title VIII, § 844(a), Nov. 2, 2015, 129 Stat. 617.)

[1] So in original. Probably should be "subchapter III of chapter 83".

HISTORICAL AND STATUTORY NOTES

References in Text

Parts A and E of subchapter XVIII of this chapter, referred to in text, are classified to 42 U.S.C.A. § 1395c et seq. and 42 U.S.C.A. § 1395x et seq., respectively.

This subchapter, referred to in text, originally read "this title", meaning the Social Security Act, Aug. 14, 1935, c. 531, Title II, 49 Stat. 622, as amended, which is classified as this subchapter, 42 U.S.C.A. § 401 et seq.

Section 212 of Pub.L. 93–66, referred to in subsec. (e)(1)(B), is set out as a note under section 1382 of this title.

Reference in subsec. (g) to an annuity under "chapter 83 of Title 5" was probably intended to be a reference to Subchapter III of chapter 83 of Title 5, which contains provisions relating to civil service retirement.

Section 425(c) of this title, referred to in subsec. (i), was repealed by Pub.L. 104–121, title I, § 105(a)(4), Mar. 29, 1996, 110 Stat. 853.

Effective and Applicability Provisions

2004 Amendments. Amendment made by Pub.L. 108–203, § 418, amending this section, to apply with respect to applications for benefits under this subchapter filed on or after the first day of the first month that begins after Mar. 2, 2004, with exceptions and transition rule, see Pub.L. 108–203, § 418(c), set out as a note under 42 U.S.C.A. § 402.

2000 Acts. Pub.L. 106–554, § 1(a)(6) [Title I, § 115(c)], Dec. 21, 2000, 114 Stat. 2763, 2763A–474, provided that: "The amendments made by this section [amending this section and section 1395p of this title] shall apply to benefits for months beginning July 1, 2001."

1999 Acts. Pub.L. 106–170, Title II, § 202(b), Dec. 17, 1999, 113 Stat. 1894, provided that: "The amendment made by subsection (a) [amending this section] shall be effective on and after October 1, 2000."

1994 Acts. Amendment to this section by section 201(a)(3)(D)(i) of Pub.L. 103–296, enacting subsec. (i), to apply with respect to benefits based on disability (as defined in section 425(c)(9) of this title) which are otherwise payable in months beginning after 180 days after Aug. 15, 1994, with the Secretary of Health and Human Services to issue regulations necessary to carry out such amendment not later than 180 days after Aug. 15, 1994, see section 201(a)(3)(E)(i) of Pub.L. 103–296, set out as a note under section 425 of this title.

1990 Acts. Amendment by section 5103(c)(2)(C) of Pub.L. 101–508 applicable with respect to items and services furnished after Dec. 1990, see section 5103(e)(1) of Pub.L. 101–508, set out as a note under section 402 of this title.

1988 Acts. Section 608(f)(5) of Pub.L. 100–485 provided in part that the amendment to subsec. (a) of this section by section 608(f)(5) of Pub.L. 100–485 is effective as of the date of the enactment of Pub.L. 95–292, which was approved June 13, 1978.

Except as specifically provided in section 411 of Pub.L. 100–360, amendment by section 411 of Pub.L. 100–360, as it relates to a provision in the Omnibus Budget Reconciliation Act of 1987, Pub.L. 100–203, effective as if included in the enactment of that provision of Pub.L. 100–203, see section 411(a)(2) of Pub.L. 100–360, set out as a note under section 106 of Title 1, General Provisions.

1987 Acts. Section 4033(b), formerly section 4033(a)(2), of Pub.L. 100–203, as renumbered and amended by Pub.L. 100–360, Title IV, § 411(e)(2)(B), (C), July 1, 1988, 102 Stat. 775, provided that:

"(1) The amendment made by subsection (a) [amending subsec. (f) of this section] shall apply to months beginning after the end of the 60–day period beginning on the date of enactment of this Act [Dec. 22, 1987].

"(2) The amendment made by subsection (a) [amending subsec. (f) of this section] shall not apply so as to include (for the purposes described in section 226(f) of the Social Security Act [subsec. (f) of this section]) monthly benefits paid for any month in a previous period (described in that section) that terminated before the end of the 60–day period described in paragraph (1)."

Amendment of subsec. (b) by section 9010(e)(3) of Pub.L. 100–203 effective Jan. 1, 1988 and applicable with respect to individuals entitled to benefits under specific provisions of sections 402 and 423 of this title for any month after Dec. 1987 and individuals entitled to benefits payable under specific provisions of sections 402 and 423 of this title for any month before Jan. 1988 and with respect to whom the 15–month period described in the applicable provision amended by section 9010 of Pub.L. 100–203 has not elapsed as of Jan. 1, 1988, see section 9010(f) of Pub.L. 100–203, set out as a note under section 402 of this title.

1986 Acts. Amendment by section 13205(b) of Pub.L. 99–272 effective after Mar. 31, 1986, with no individual to be considered under disability for any period beginning before Apr. 1, 1986 for purposes of hospital insurance benefits, see section 13205(d)(2) of Pub.L. 99–272, set out as a note under section 410 of this title.

1984 Acts. Amendment by Pub.L. 98–369 effective July 18, 1984, but not to be construed as changing or affecting any right, liability, status, or interpretation which existed (under the provisions of law involved) before that date, see section 2664(b) of Pub.L. 98–369, set out as a note under section 401 of this title.

1983 Acts. Amendment of subsec. (e)(1)(A) by section 131 of Pub.L. 98–21 effective with respect to monthly benefits payable under this subchapter for months after December 1983, and in the case of an individual who was not entitled to a monthly benefit of the type involved under this subchapter for December 1983, no benefit shall be paid under this subchapter by reason of such amendments unless proper application for such benefit is made, see section 131(d) of Pub.L. 98–21, set out as a note under section 402 of this title.

Amendment by section 309(q)(1) of Pub.L. 98–21 applicable only with respect to monthly payments payable under this subchapter for months after April, 1983, except as otherwise specifically provided, see section 310 of Pub.L. 98–21, set out as a note under section 402 of this title.

Pub.L. 97–448, Title III, § 309(c)(1), Jan. 12, 1983, 96 Stat. 2410, provided that: "Any amendment to the Tax Equity and Fiscal Responsibility Act of 1982 [Pub.L. 97–248, Sept. 3, 1982, 96 Stat. 324] made by this section [amending sections 1395x, 1395cc, and 1396a of this title and amending provisions set out as notes under this section and sections 1320c, 1395b–1, 1395f, 1395u, 1395xx, 1395ww, and 1396*o* of this title] shall be effective as if it had been originally included in the provision of such Act to which such amendment relates."

1981 Acts. Section 2203(f)(3) of Pub.L. 97–35, as amended Pub.L. 97–248, Title I, § 128(c)(2), Sept. 3, 1982, 96 Stat. 367, provided that: "The amendments made by subsection (e) of this section [amending subsec. (a)(2) of this title] shall apply only to individuals aged 65 and over whose insured spouse attains age 62 after August 1981."

1980 Acts. Amendment by Pub.L. 96–499 effective with respect to services furnished on or after July 1, 1981, see section 930(s)(1) of Pub.L. 96–499, set out as a note under section 1395x of this title.

Section 2(d) of Pub.L. 96–473 provided that: "The amendments made by subsections (a) and (b) [amending sections 426 and 1395c of this title] shall be effective after the second month beginning after the date on which this Act is enacted [Oct. 19, 1980]."

Section 103(c) of Pub.L. 96–265 provided that: "The amendments made by this section [amending sections 426, 1395c and 1395p of this title and section 231f of Title 45] shall apply with respect to hospital insurance or supplementary medical insurance benefits for services provided on or after the first day of the sixth month which begins after the date of the enactment of this Act [June 9, 1980]."

Section 104(b) of Pub.L. 96–265 provided that: "The amendments made by subsection (a) [amending subsec. (b) of this section] shall become effective on the first day of the sixth month which begins after the date of the enactment of this Act [June 9, 1980], and shall apply with respect to any individual whose disability has not been determined to have ceased prior to such first day."

1978 Acts. Section 6 of Pub.L. 95–292 provided that: "The amendments made by the preceding sections of this Act [enacting sections 426–1 and 1395rr of this title and amending sections 426, 1395c, 1395i, 1395*l*, 1395t, 1395x, 1395cc, and 1395mm of this title] shall become effective with respect to services, supplies, and equipment furnished after the third calendar month which begins after the date of the enactment of this Act [June 13, 1978], except that those amendments providing for the implementation of an incentive reimbursement system for dialysis services furnished in facilities and providers shall become effective with respect to a facility's or provider's first accounting period which begins after the last day of the twelfth month following the month of the enactment of this Act [June 1978], and those amendments providing for reimbursement rates for home dialysis shall become effective on April 1, 1979."

1977 Acts. Amendment of subsec. (h)(4) by Pub.L. 95–216 effective with respect to monthly insurance benefits under this subchapter to which an individual becomes entitled on the basis of an application filed on or after Jan. 1, 1978, see section 332(b) of Pub.L. 95–216, set out as a note under section 402 of this title.

Amendment of subsec. (h)(1)(B) by Pub.L. 95–216 applicable with respect to monthly insurance benefits payable under this subchapter for months beginning with December, 1977, on the basis of applications filed in or after December, 1977, see section 334(f) of Pub.L. 95–216, set out as a note under section 402 of this title.

1974 Acts. Amendment by Pub.L. 93–445 effective Jan. 1, 1975, see section 603 of Pub.L. 93–445, set out as a note under section 402 of this title.

1973 Acts. Section 4(a) of Pub.L. 93–58 provided that: "The provisions of this Act [amending this section and sections 228c and 228e of Title 45], except the provisions of section 1, shall be effective as of the date the corresponding provisions of Public Law 92–603 are effective as follows: clause (xi) [45 U.S.C.A. § 228c(e)(xi)] effective with respect to services provided on and after July 1, 1973. The provisions of clauses (xi) and (xii), which are added by section 1 of this Act, shall be effective as follows: clause (xi) [45 U.S.C.A. § 228c(e)(xi)] shall be effective with respect to calendar years after 1971 for annuities accruing after December 1972; and clause (xii) [45 U.S.C.A. § 228c(e)(xii)] shall be effective as of the date the delayed retirement provision of Public Law 92–603 is effective [section 402(w) of this title applicable with respect to old-age insurance benefits payable under this subchapter for months beginning after 1972]."

1972 Acts. Section 299I of Pub.L. 92–603 provided in part that enactment of subsecs. (e) to (g) by section 299I of Pub.L. 92–603, is effective with respect to services provided on and after July 1, 1973.

1968 Acts. Amendment by Pub.L. 90–248 applicable with respect to services furnished after Mar. 31, 1968, see section 129(d) of Pub.L. 90–248, set out as a note under section 1395d of this title.

Effective Date of 1982 Acts; Transitional Provisions

Section 278(c)(2) and (d) of Pub.L. 97–248, as amended Pub.L. 97–448, Title III, § 309(a)(10), (11), Jan. 12, 1983, 96 Stat. 2408, provided that:

"**(c) Effective dates.**—

"(1) Omitted [See Effective Date of 1982 Acts note set out under section 3121 of Title 26, Internal Revenue Code]

"**(2) Medicare coverage.**—

"**(A) In general.**—The amendments made by subsection (b) [amending this section and sections 410, 426–1, and 1395c of this title] are effective on and after January 1, 1983, and the amendments made by paragraph (2) of that subsection [amending subsecs. (a) and (b) of this section and section 426–1 of this title] apply to remuneration (for medicare qualified Federal employment) paid after December 31, 1982.

"**(B) Treatment of current disabilities.**—For purposes of establishing entitlement to hospital insurance benefits under part A of title XVIII of the Social Security Act [part A of subchapter XVIII of this chapter] pursuant to the amendments made by subsection (b) or the provisions of subsection (d), no individual may be considered to be under a disability for any period before January 1, 1983.

"**(d) Transitional provisions.**—

"**(1) In general.**—For purposes of sections 226, 226A, and 1811 of the Social Security Act [this section and sections 426–1 and 1395c of this title], in the case of any individual who performs service both during January 1983, and before January 1, 1983, which constitutes medicare qualified Federal employment (as defined in section 210(p) of such Act [section 410(p) of this title]), the individual's medicare qualified Federal employment (as so defined) performed before January 1, 1983, for which remuneration was paid before such date, shall be considered to be 'employment' (as defined for purposes of title II of such Act [this subchapter]), but only for the purpose of providing the individual (or another person) with entitlement to hospital insurance benefits under part A of title XVIII of such Act [part A of subchapter XVIII of this chapter].

"**(2) Appropriations.**—There are authorized to be appropriated to the Federal Hospital Insurance Trust Fund from time to time such sums as the Secretary of Health and Human Services deems necessary for any fiscal year, on account of—

"(A) payments made or to be made during such fiscal year from such Trust Fund with respect to individuals who are entitled to benefits under title XVIII of the Social Security Act [subchapter XVIII of this chapter] solely by reason of paragraph (1) of this subsection,

"(B) the additional administrative expenses resulting or expected to result therefrom, and

"(C) any loss in interest to such Trust Fund resulting from the payment of those amounts,

in order to place such Trust Fund in the same position at the end of such fiscal year as it would have been in if this subsection had not been enacted."

Conforming References to Previous Part D

Any reference in law in effect before Dec. 8, 2003 to part D of title XVIII of the Social Security Act [part D of subchapter XVIII of this chapter] is deemed a reference to part E of such title [part E of subchapter XVIII of this chapter], see Pub.L. 107-173, § 101(e)(1), set out as a note under 42 U.S.C.A. § 1395x.

GAO Report

Pub.L. 106-170, Title II, § 202(c), Dec. 17, 1999, 113 Stat. 1894, provided that: "Not later than 5 years after the date of the enactment of this Act [Dec. 17, 1999], the Comptroller General of the United States shall submit a report to the Congress that—

"(1) examines the effectiveness and cost of the amendment made by subsection (a) [amending this section];

"(2) examines the necessity and effectiveness of providing continuation of medicare coverage under section 226(b) of the Social Security Act (42 U.S.C. 426(b)) to individuals whose annual income exceeds the contribution and benefit base (as determined under section 230 of such Act (42 U.S.C. 430));

"(3) examines the viability of providing the continuation of medicare coverage under such section 226(b) [subsec. (b) of this section] based on a sliding scale premium for individuals whose annual income exceeds such contribution and benefit base;

"(4) examines the viability of providing the continuation of medicare coverage under such section 226(b) [subsec. (b) of this section] based on a premium buy-in by the beneficiary's employer in lieu of coverage under private health insurance;

"(5) examines the interrelation between the use of the continuation of medicare coverage under such section 226(b) [subsec. (b) of this section] and the use of private health insurance coverage by individuals during the extended period; and

"(6) recommends such legislative or administrative changes relating to the continuation of medicare coverage for recipients of social security disability benefits as the Comptroller General determines are appropriate."

Adopted Child's Reenlistment to Annuity

Section 4(b) of Pub.L. 93-58 provided that: "Any child (1) whose entitlement to an annuity under section 5(c) of the Railroad Retirement Act [45 U.S.C.A. § 228e(c)] was terminated by reason of his adoption prior to the enactment of this Act [July 6, 1973], and (2) who, except for such adoption, would be entitled to an annuity under such section for a month after the month in which this Act is enacted [July 1973], may, upon filing application for an annuity under the Railroad Retirement Act [45 U.S.C.A. § 228a et seq.] after the date of enactment of this Act [July 6, 1973], become reentitled to such annuity; except that no child shall, by reason of the enactment of this Act [amending this section and sections 228c, 228e of Title 45] become reentitled to such annuity for any month prior to the effective date of the relevant amendments made by this Act to section 5(*l*)(1)(ii) of the Railroad Retirement Act [45 U.S.C.A. § 228e(*l*)(1)(ii)]."

Applicability of Pub.L. 96-473 to Applications for Hospital Insurance Benefits

Section 2(c) of Pub.L. 96-473 provided that: "For purposes of section 226 of such Act as amended by subsection (a) of this section [subsec. (a)(2) of this section], an individual who filed an application for monthly insurance benefits under section 202 of such Act [42 U.S.C.A. § 402] prior to the effective date of the amendment made by subsection (a) [see section 2(d) of Pub.L. 96-473, set out as a note under this section] shall be deemed to have filed an application for hospital insurance benefits under part A of title XVIII of such Act [part A of subchapter XVIII of this chapter], at the time he applied for such benefits under section 202 [42 U.S.C.A. § 402] regardless of the continuing status or effect of the application for benefits under section 202, if he would have been entitled to benefits under that section had such application remained in effect."

Conforming References to Previous Part C

Any reference in law to part C of title XVIII of the Social Security Act [part C of subchapter XVIII of this chapter] is deemed a reference to part D of such title [part D of subchapter XVIII of this chapter], see section 4002(f)(1) of Pub.L. 105-33, set out as a note under section 1395x of this title.

Termination of Special $50 Payment Under Tax Reduction Act of 1975

Special payment of $50, pursuant to section 702 of Pub.L. 94-12, as soon as practicable after Mar. 29, 1975, by the Secretary of the Treasury to each individual who, for the month of March, 1975, was entitled to a monthly insurance benefit payable under this subchapter, but no payments to be made under that section after May 23, 1977, see section 406 of Pub.L. 95-30, set out as a note under section 402 of this title.

Time in Which to Furnish Proof of Disability for Hospital Benefits

Section 309(q)(2) of Pub.L. 98-21 provided that: "For purposes of determining entitlement to hospital insurance benefits under section 226(e)(3) of such Act [subsec. (e)(3) of this section], as amended by paragraph (1), an individual becoming entitled to such hospital insurance benefits as a result of the amendment made by such paragraph shall, upon furnishing proof of his or her disability within twelve months after the month in which this Act is enacted [April, 1983], under such procedures as the Secretary of Health and Human Services may prescribe, be deemed to have been entitled to the widow's or widower's benefits referred to in such section 226(e)(3) [subsec. (e)(3) of this section], as so amended, as of the time such individual would have been entitled to such widow's or widower's benefits if he or she had filed a timely application therefor."

§ 426-1. End stage renal disease program

(a) Entitlement to benefits

Notwithstanding any provision to the contrary in section 426 of this title or subchapter XVIII, every individual who—

(1)(A) is fully or currently insured (as such terms are defined in section 414 of this title), or would be fully or currently insured if (i) his service as an employee (as defined in the Railroad Retirement Act of 1974) after December 31, 1936, were included within the meaning of the term "employment" for purposes of this subchapter, and (ii) his medicare qualified government employment (as defined in section 410(p) of this title) were included within the meaning of the term "employment" for purposes of this subchapter;

(B)(i) is entitled to monthly insurance benefits under this subchapter, (ii) is entitled to an annuity under the Railroad Retirement Act of 1974, or (iii) would be entitled to a monthly insurance benefit under this subchapter if medicare qualified government employment (as defined in section 410(p) of this title) were included within the meaning of the term "employment" for purposes of this subchapter; or

(C) is the spouse or dependent child (as defined in regulations) of an individual described in subparagraph (A) or (B);

(2) is medically determined to have end stage renal disease; and

(3) has filed an application for benefits under this section;

shall, in accordance with the succeeding provisions of this section, be entitled to benefits under part A and eligible to enroll under part B of subchapter XVIII, subject to the deductible, premium, and coinsurance provisions of that subchapter.

(b) Duration of period of entitlement

Subject to subsection (c), entitlement of an individual to benefits under part A and eligibility to enroll under part B of subchapter XVIII by reasons of this section on the basis of end stage renal disease—

(1) shall begin with—

(A) the third month after the month in which a regular course of renal dialysis is initiated, or

(B) the month in which such individual receives a kidney transplant, or (if earlier) the first month in which such individual is admitted as an inpatient to an institution which is a hospital meeting the requirements of section 1395x(e) of this title (and such additional requirements as the Secretary may prescribe under section 1395rr(b) of this title for such institutions) in preparation for or anticipation of kidney transplantation, but only if such transplantation occurs in that month or in either of the next two months,

whichever first occurs (but no earlier than one year preceding the month of the filing of an application for benefits under this section); and

(2) shall end, in the case of an individual who receives a kidney transplant, with the thirty-sixth month after the month in which such individual receives such transplant or, in the case of an individual who has not received a kidney transplant and no longer requires a regular course of dialysis, with the twelfth month after the month in which such course of dialysis is terminated.

(c) Individuals participating in self-care dialysis training programs; kidney transplant failures; resumption of previously terminated regular course of dialysis

Notwithstanding the provisions of subsection (b)—

(1) in the case of any individual who participates in a self-care dialysis training program prior to the third month after the month in which such individual initiates a regular course of renal dialysis in a renal dialysis facility or provider of services meeting the requirements of section 1395rr(b) of this title, entitlement to benefits under part A and eligibility to enroll under part B of subchapter XVIII shall begin with the month in which such regular course of renal dialysis is initiated;

(2) in any case in which a kidney transplant fails (whether during or after the thirty-six-month period specified in subsection (b)(2)) and as a result the individual who received such transplant initiates or resumes a regular course of renal dialysis, entitlement to benefits under part A and eligibility to enroll under part B of subchapter XVIII shall begin with the month in which such course is initiated or resumed; and

(3) in any case in which a regular course of renal dialysis is resumed subsequent to the termination of an earlier course, entitlement to benefits under part A and eligibility to enroll under part B of subchapter XVIII shall begin with the month in which such regular course of renal dialysis is resumed.

(Aug. 14, 1935, c. 531, Title II, § 226A, as added Pub.L. 95–292, § 1(a), June 13, 1978, 92 Stat. 307; amended Pub.L. 97–248, Title II, § 278(b)(2)(C), Sept. 3, 1982, 96 Stat. 561; Pub.L. 97–448, Title III, § 309(b)(1), Jan. 12, 1983, 96 Stat. 2408; Pub.L. 99–272, Title XIII, § 13205(b)(2)(B), Apr. 7, 1986, 100 Stat. 317; Pub.L. 103–296, Title II, § 201(a)(3)(D)(ii), Aug. 15, 1994, 108 Stat. 1497; Pub.L. 114–74, Title VIII, § 844(b), Nov. 2, 2015, 129 Stat. 617.)

HISTORICAL AND STATUTORY NOTES

References in Text

Parts A and B of subchapter XVIII, referred to in text, are classified to 42 U.S.C.A. §§ 1395c et seq. and 1395j et seq., respectively.

The Railroad Retirement Act of 1974, referred to in subsec. (a)(1)(A) and (B), is Title I of Pub.L. 93–445, Oct. 16, 1974, 88 Stat. 1305, and is classified generally to subchapter IV (section 231 et seq.) of chapter 9 of Title 45, Railroads. Such Title I completely amended and revised the Railroad Retirement Act of 1937 (approved June 24, 1937, c. 382, 50 Stat. 307), and as thus amended and revised, the 1937 Act was redesignated the Railroad Retirement Act of 1974. Previously, the 1937 Act had completely amended and revised the Railroad Retirement Act of 1935 (approved Aug. 29, 1935, c. 812, 49 Stat. 967). Section 201 of the 1937 Act provided that the 1935 Act, as in force prior to amendment by the 1937 Act, may be cited as the Railroad Retirement Act of 1935; and that the 1935 Act, as amended by the 1937 Act may be cited as the Railroad Retirement Act of 1937. The Railroad Retirement Acts of 1935 and 1937 were classified to subchapter II (section 215 et seq.) and subchapter III (section 228a et seq.), respectively, of chapter 9 of Title 45.

Effective and Applicability Provisions

1994 Acts. Amendment to this section by section 201(a)(3)(D)(ii) of Pub.L. 103–296, adding subsec. (c) relating to continuing eligibility of certain terminated individuals, to apply with respect to benefits based on disability (as defined in section 425(c)(9) of this title) which are otherwise payable in months beginning after 180 days after Aug. 15, 1994, with the Secretary of Health and Human Services to issue regulations necessary to carry out such amendment not later than 180 days after Aug. 15, 1994, see section 201(a)(3)(E)(i) of Pub.L. 103–296, set out as a note under section 425 of this title.

1986 Acts. Amendment by section 13205(b) of Pub.L. 99–272 effective after Mar. 31, 1986, with no individual to be considered under disability for any period beginning before Apr. 1, 1986 for purposes of hospital insurance benefits, see section 13205(d)(2) of Pub.L. 99–272, set out as a note under section 410 of this title.

1983 Acts. Section 309(c)(2) of Pub.L. 97–448 provided that: "Any amendment to the Social Security Act [this chapter] made by this section [amending sections 410, 426–1, 1320c–2, 1320c–3, 1395d, 1395f; 1395r, 1395y, 1395cc, 1395mm, 1395ww, 1396b, 1396n, 1396o, and 1396p of this title] shall be effective as if it had been originally included as a part of that provision of the Social Security Act [this chapter] to which it relates, as such provision of such Act was amended or added by the Tax Equity and Fiscal Responsibility Act of 1982 [Pub.L. 97–248, Sept. 3, 1982, 96 Stat. 324]."

1982 Acts. Amendment of subsec. (a)(1) by Pub.L. 97–248 effective on and after Jan. 1, 1983, applicable to remuneration (for medicare qualified Federal employment) paid after Dec. 31, 1982, see section 278(c)(2)(A) of Pub.L. 97–248, set out as a note under section 426 of this title.

1978 Acts. Section effective with respect to services, supplies, and equipment furnished after the third calendar month beginning after June 13, 1978, except that provisions for the implementation of an incentive reimbursement system for dialysis services furnished in facilities and providers to become effective with respect to a facility's or provider's first accounting period beginning after the last day of the twelfth month following the month of June 1978, and except that provisions for reimbursement rates for home dialysis to become effective on Apr. 1, 1979, see section 6 of Pub.L. 95–292, set out as a note under section 426 of this title.

§ 426a. Transitional provision on eligibility of uninsured individuals for hospital insurance benefits

(a) Entitlement to benefits

Anyone who—

(1) has attained the age of 65,

(2)(A) attained such age before 1968, or **(B)** has not less than 3 quarters of coverage (as defined in this subchapter or section 228e(*l*) of Title 45), whenever acquired, for each calendar year elapsing after 1966 and before the year in which he attained such age,

(3) is not, and upon filing application for monthly insurance benefits under section 402 of this title would not be, entitled to hospital insurance benefits under section 426 of this title, and is not certifiable as a qualified railroad retirement beneficiary under section 228s–2 of Title 45,

(4) is a resident of the United States (as defined in section 410(i) of this title), and is **(A)** a citizen of the United States or **(B)** an alien lawfully admitted for permanent residence who has resided in the United States (as so defined) continuously during the 5 years immediately preceding the month in which he files application under this section, and

(5) has filed an application under this section in such manner and in accordance with such other requirements as may be prescribed in regulations of the Secretary,

shall (subject to the limitations in this section) be deemed, solely for purposes of section 426 of this title, to be entitled to monthly insurance benefits under such section 402 for each month, beginning with the first month in which he meets the requirements of this subsection and ending with the month in which he dies, or, if earlier, the month before the month in which he becomes (or upon filing application for monthly insurance benefits under section 402 of this title would become) entitled to hospital insurance benefits under section 426 of this title or becomes certifiable as a qualified railroad retirement beneficiary. An individual who would have met the preceding requirements of this subsection in any month had he filed application under paragraph (5) hereof before the end of such month shall be deemed to have met such requirements in such month if he files such application before the end of the twelfth month following such month. No application under this section which is filed by an individual more than 3 months before the first month in which he meets the requirements of paragraphs (1), (2), (3), and (4) shall be accepted as an application for purposes of this section.

(b) Persons ineligible

The provisions of subsection (a) shall not apply to any individual who—

(1) is, at the beginning of the first month in which he meets the requirements of subsection (a), a member of any organization referred to in section 410(a)(17)[1] of this title,

(2) has, prior to the beginning of such first month, been convicted of any offense listed in section 402(u) of this title, or

(3)(A) at the beginning of such first month is covered by an enrollment in a health benefits plan under chapter 89 of Title 5,

(B) was so covered on February 16, 1965, or

(C) could have been so covered for such first month if he or some other person had availed himself of opportunities to enroll in a health benefits plan under such chapter and to continue such enrollment (but this subparagraph shall not apply unless he or such other person was a Federal employee at any time after February 15, 1965).

Paragraph (3) shall not apply in the case of any individual for the month (or any month thereafter) in which coverage under such a health benefits plan ceases (or would have ceased if he had had such coverage) by reason of his or some other person's separation from Federal service, if he or such other person was not (or would not have been) eligible to continue such coverage after such separation.

(c) Authorization of appropriations

There are authorized to be appropriated to the Federal Hospital Insurance Trust Fund (established by section 1395i of this title) from time to time such sums as the Secretary deems necessary for any fiscal year, on account of—

(1) payments made or to be made during such fiscal year from such Trust Fund under part A of subchapter XVIII of this chapter with respect to individuals who are entitled to hospital insurance benefits under section 426 of this title solely by reason of this section,

(2) the additional administrative expenses resulting or expected to result therefrom, and

(3) any loss in interest to such Trust Fund resulting from the payment of such amounts,

in order to place such Trust Fund in the same position at the end of such fiscal year in which it would have been if the preceding subsections of this section had not been enacted.

(Pub.L. 89–97, Title I, § 103, July 30, 1965, 79 Stat. 333; Pub.L. 90–248, Title I, § 139, Title IV, § 403(h), Jan. 2, 1968, 81 Stat. 854, 932.)

1 Repealed by Pub.L. 113–295, Div. A, Title II, § 221(a)(99)(C)(ii), Dec. 19, 2014, 128 Stat. 4052.

HISTORICAL AND STATUTORY NOTES

References in Text

Sections 228e(*l*) and 228s–2 of Title 45, referred to in subsec. (a)(2) and (3), are references to sections 5(*l*) and 21 of the Railroad Retirement Act of 1937. That Act was amended in its entirety and completely revised by Pub.L. 93–445, Oct. 16, 1974, 88 Stat. 1305. That Act, as thus amended and revised, was redesignated the Railroad Retirement Act of 1974, and is classified generally to subchapter IV (section 231 et seq.) of chapter 9 of Title 45, Railroads. Sections 228e and 228s–2 of Title 45 are now covered by sections 231e, and 231f of Title 45, respectively.

Section 410(a)(17) of this title, referred to in subsec. (b)(1), was repealed by Pub.L. 113–295, Div. A, Title II, § 221(a)(99)(C)(ii), Dec. 19, 2014, 128 Stat. 4052.

Part A of subchapter XVIII of this chapter, referred to in subsec. (c)(1), is classified to 42 U.S.C.A § 1395c et seq.

Codifications

Section was not enacted as part of the Social Security Act, which comprises this chapter.

§ 427. Transitional insured status for purposes of old-age and survivors benefits

(a) Determination of entitlement to benefits under section 402(a) to (c) of this title

In the case of any individual who attains the age of 72 before 1969 but who does not meet the requirements of section 414(a) of this title, the 6 quarters of coverage referred to in paragraph (1) of section 414(a) of this title shall, instead, be 3 quarters of coverage for purposes of determining entitlement of such individual to benefits under section 402(a) of this title, and of the spouse to benefits under section 402(b) or section 402(c) of this title, but, in the case of such spouse, only if he or she attains the age of 72 before 1969 and only with respect to spouse's insurance benefits under section 402(b) or section 402(c) of this title for and after the month in which he or she attains such age. For each month before the month in which any such individual meets the requirements of section 414(a) of this title, the amount of the old-age insurance benefit shall, notwithstanding the provisions of section 402(a) of this title, be the larger of $64.40 or the amount most recently established in lieu thereof under section 415(i) of this title and the amount of the spouse's insurance benefit of the spouse shall, notwithstanding the provisions of section 402(b) or section 402(c) of this title, be the larger of $32.20 or the amount most recently established in lieu thereof under section 415(i) of this title.

(b) Determination of entitlement to surviving spouse's benefits under section 402(e) or (f) of this title

In the case of any individual who has died, who does not meet the requirements of section 414(a) of this title, and whose surviving spouse attains age 72 before 1969, the 6 quarters of coverage referred to in paragraph (3) of section 414(a) of this title and in paragraph (1) thereof shall, for purposes of determining the entitlement to surviving spouse's insurance benefits under section 402(e) or section 402(f) of this title, instead be—

(1) 3 quarters of coverage if such surviving spouse attains the age of 72 in or before 1966,

(2) 4 quarters of coverage if such surviving spouse attains the age of 72 in 1967, or

(3) 5 quarters of coverage if such surviving spouse attains the age of 72 in 1968.

The amount of the surviving spouse's insurance benefit for each month shall, notwithstanding the provisions of section 402(e) or section 402(f) of this title (and section 402(m)[1] of this title), be the larger of $64.40 or the amount most recently established in lieu thereof under section 415(i) of this title.

(c) Deceased individual entitled to benefits by reason of subsection (a) deemed to meet requirements of subsection (b)

In the case of any individual who becomes, or upon filing application therefor would become, entitled to benefits under section 402(a) of this title by reason of the application of subsection (a) of this section, who dies, and whose surviving spouse attains the age of 72 before 1969, such deceased individual shall be deemed to meet the requirements of subsection (b) of this section for purposes of determining entitlement of such surviving spouse to surviving spouse's insurance benefits under section 402(e) or section 402(f) of this title.

(Aug. 14, 1935, c. 531, Title II, § 227, as added Pub.L. 89–97, Title III, § 309(a), July 30, 1965, 79 Stat. 379; amended Pub.L. 90–248, Title I, § 102(a), Jan. 2, 1968, 81 Stat. 827; Pub.L. 91–172, Title X, § 1003(a), Dec. 30, 1969, 83 Stat. 740; Pub.L. 92–5, Title II, § 202(a), Mar. 17, 1971, 85 Stat. 10; Pub.L. 92–336, Title II, § 201(g)(1), July 1, 1972, 86 Stat. 411; Pub.L. 92–603, Title I, § 104(e), (f), Oct. 30, 1972, 86 Stat. 1340; Pub.L. 93–233, § 2(b)(1), Dec. 31, 1973, 87 Stat. 952; Pub.L. 98–21, Title III, § 304(a), (b), Apr. 20, 1983, 97 Stat. 112.)

[1] Repealed by Pub.L. 97–35, Title XXII, § 2201(b)(10). See References in Text note set out under this section.

HISTORICAL AND STATUTORY NOTES

References in Text

Section 402(m) of this title, referred to in subsec. (b), was repealed by Pub.L. 97–35, Title XXII, § 2201(b)(10), Aug. 13, 1981, 95 Stat. 831, applicable with respect to benefits for months after December 1981.

Effective and Applicability Provisions

1983 Acts. Amendment by section 304(a), (b) of Pub.L. 98–21 applicable only with respect to monthly payments payable under this subchapter for months after April, 1983, except as otherwise specifically provided, see section 310 of Pub.L. 98–21, set out as a note under section 402 of this title.

1973 Acts. Section 2(b)(1) of Pub.L. 93–233 provided in part that amendment of subsecs. (a) and (b) of this section and section 428(b)(1), (2), (c)(3)(A), (B) of this title shall be effective June 1, 1974.

Amendment of subsecs. (a) and (b) by section 2(b)(1) of Pub.L. 93–233 applicable with respect to monthly benefits under this subchapter for months after May 1974, and with respect to lump-sum death payments under section 402(i) of this title, see section 2(c) of Pub.L. 93–233, set out as a note under section 415 of this title.

1972 Acts. Amendment of subsecs. (a)(1) and (b)(1) by section 104(e), (f) of Pub.L. 92–603 applicable only in the case of a man who attains (or would attain) age 62 after December 1974, see section 104(j) of Pub.L. 92–603, set out as a note under section 414 of this title.

Amendment by Pub.L. 92–336 applicable with respect to monthly benefits under this subchapter for months after August 1972, see section 201(i) of Pub.L. 92–336, set out as a note under section 415 of this title.

1971 Acts. Section 202(c) of Pub.L. 92–5 provided that: "The amendments made by subsections (a) and (b) [amending this section and section 428 of this title] shall apply with respect to monthly benefits under title II of the Social Security Act [this subchapter] for months after December 1970."

1969 Acts. Section 1003(c) of Pub.L. 91–172 provided that: "The amendments made by subsections (a) and (b) [amending this section and section 428 of this title] shall apply with respect to monthly benefits under title II of the Social Security Act [this subchapter] for months after December 1969."

1968 Acts. Section 102(c) of Pub.L. 90–248 provided that: "The amendments made by subsections (a) and (b) [to subsecs. (a) and (b) of this section and to section 428(b)(1), (2), (c)(2), (3)(A), and (3)(B) of this title] shall apply with respect to monthly benefits under title II of the Social Security Act [this subchapter] for months after January 1968."

1965 Acts. Section 309(b) of Pub.L. 89–97 provided that: "The amendment made by subsection (a) [adding this section] shall apply in the case of monthly benefits under title II of the Social Security Act [this subchapter] for and after the second month following the month [July 1965] in which this Act [Pub.L. 89–97] is enacted on the basis of applications filed in or after the month [July 1965] in which this Act [Pub.L. 89–97] is enacted."

Repeal of Amendment of Subsections (a) and (b) Prior to Effective Date

Section 202(a)(4) of Pub.L. 92–336, Title II, July 1, 1972, 86 Stat. 416, which, effective Jan. 1, 1975, substituted "the larger of $58.00 or the amount most recently established in lieu thereof under section 415(i) of this title" for "$58.00" and "the larger of $29.00 or the amount most recently established in lieu thereof under section 415(i) of this title" for "$29.00", was repealed prior to its effective date by Pub.L. 93–233, § 2(b)(2), Dec. 31, 1973, 87 Stat. 952, applicable with respect to monthly benefits under this subchapter for months after May 1974, and with respect to lump-sum death payments under section 402(i) of this title. See section 2(c) of Pub.L. 93–233, set out as a note under section 415 of this title.

§ 428. Benefits at age 72 for certain uninsured individuals

(a) Eligibility

Every individual who—

(1) has attained the age of 72,

(2) (A) attained such age before 1968, or (B)(i) attained such age after 1967 and before 1972, and (ii) has not less than 3 quarters of coverage, whenever acquired, for each calendar year elapsing after 1966 and before the year in which he or she attained such age,

(3) is a resident of the United States (as defined in subsection (e)), and is (A) a citizen of the United

States or (B) an alien lawfully admitted for permanent residence who has resided in the United States (as defined in section 410(i) of this title) continuously during the 5 years immediately preceding the month in which he or she files application under this section, and

(4) has filed application for benefits under this section,

shall (subject to the limitations in this section) be entitled to a benefit under this section for each month beginning with the first month after September 1966 in which he or she becomes so entitled to such benefits and ending with the month preceding the month in which he or she dies. No application under this section which is filed by an individual more than 3 months before the first month in which he or she meets the requirements of paragraphs (1), (2), and (3) shall be accepted as an application for purposes of this section.

(b) Amount of benefits

The benefit amount to which an individual is entitled under this section for any month shall be the larger of $64.40 or the amount most recently established in lieu thereof under section 415(i) of this title.

(c) Reduction for government pension system benefits

(1) The benefit amount of any individual under this section for any month shall be reduced (but not below zero) by the amount of any periodic benefit under a governmental pension system for which he or she is eligible for such month.

(2) In the case of a husband and wife only one of whom is entitled to benefits under this section for any month, the benefit amount, after any reduction under paragraph (1), shall be further reduced (but not below zero) by the excess (if any) of (A) the total amount of any periodic benefits under governmental pension systems for which the spouse who is not entitled to benefits under this section is eligible for such month, over (B) the benefit amount as determined without regard to this subsection.

(3) In the case of a husband or wife both of whom are entitled to benefits under this section for any month, the benefit amount of each spouse, after any reduction under paragraph (1), shall be further reduced (but not below zero) by the excess (if any) of (A) the total amount of any periodic benefits under governmental pension systems for which the other spouse is eligible for such month, over (B) the benefit amount of such other spouse as determined without regard to this subsection.

(4) For purposes of this subsection, in determining whether an individual is eligible for periodic benefits under a governmental pension system—

(A) such individual shall be deemed to have filed application for such benefits,

(B) to the extent that entitlement depends on an application by such individual's spouse, such spouse shall be deemed to have filed application, and

(C) to the extent that entitlement depends on such individual or his or her spouse having retired, such individual and his or her spouse shall be deemed to have retired before the month for which the determination of eligibility is being made.

(5) For purposes of this subsection, if any periodic benefit is payable on any basis other than a calendar month, the Commissioner of Social Security shall allocate the amount of such benefit to the appropriate calendar months.

(6) If, under the foregoing provisions of this section, the amount payable for any month would be less than $1, such amount shall be reduced to zero. In the case of a husband and wife both of whom are entitled to benefits under this section for the month, the preceding sentence shall be applied with respect to the aggregate amount so payable for such month.

(7) If any benefit amount computed under the foregoing provisions of this section is not a multiple of $0.10, it shall be raised to the next higher multiple of $0.10.

(8) Under regulations prescribed by the Commissioner of Social Security, benefit payments under this section to an individual (or aggregate benefit payments under this section in the case of a husband and wife) of less than $5 may be accumulated until they equal or exceed $5.

(d) Suspension for months in which cash payments are made under public assistance or in which supplemental security income benefits are payable

The benefit to which any individual is entitled under this section for any month shall not be paid for such month if—

(1) such individual receives aid or assistance in the form of money payments in such month under a State plan approved under subchapter I, X, XIV, or XVI, or under a State program funded under part A of subchapter IV, or

(2) such individual's husband or wife receives such aid or assistance in such month, and under the State plan the needs of such individual were taken into account in determining eligibility for (or amount of) such aid or assistance,

unless the State agency administering or supervising the administration of such plan notifies the Commissioner of Social Security, at such time and in such manner as may be prescribed in accordance with regulations of the Commissioner of Social Security, that such payments to such individual (or such individual's husband or wife) under such plan are being terminated with the payment or payments made in such month and such individual is not an individual with respect to whom supplemental security income benefits are payable pursuant to subchapter XVI or section 211 of Public Law 93–66 for the following month, nor shall such benefit be paid for such month if such individual is an individual with respect to whom supplemental security income benefits are payable pursuant to subchapter XVI or section 211 of Public Law 93–66 for such month, unless the Commissioner of Social Security determines that such benefits are not payable with respect to such individual for the month following such month.

(e) Suspension where individual is residing outside United States

The benefit to which any individual is entitled under this section for any month shall not be paid if, during such month, such individual is not a resident of the United States. For purposes of this subsection, the term "United States" means the 50 States and the District of Columbia.

(f) Treatment as monthly insurance benefits

For purposes of subsections (t) and (u) of section 402 of this title, and of section 1395s of this title, a monthly benefit under this section shall be treated as a monthly insurance benefit payable under section 402 of this title.

(g) Annual reimbursement of Federal Old-Age and Survivors Insurance Trust Fund

There are authorized to be appropriated to the Federal Old-Age and Survivors Insurance Trust Fund for the fiscal year ending June 30, 1969, and for each fiscal year thereafter, such sums as the Commissioner of Social Security deems necessary on account of—

(1) payments made under this section during the second preceding fiscal year and all fiscal years prior thereto to individuals who, as of the beginning of the calendar year in which falls the month for which payment was made, had less than 3 quarters of coverage,

(2) the additional administrative expenses resulting from the payments described in paragraph (1), and

(3) any loss in interest to such Trust Fund resulting from such payments and expenses,

in order to place such Trust Fund in the same position at the end of such fiscal year as it would have been in if such payments had not been made.

(h) Definitions

For purposes of this section—

(1) The term "quarter of coverage" includes a quarter of coverage as defined in section 228e(*l*) of Title 45.

(2) The term "governmental pension system" means the insurance system established by this subchapter or any other system or fund established by the United States, a State, any political subdivision of a State, or any wholly owned instrumentality of any one or more of the foregoing which provides for payment of (A) pensions, (B) retirement or retired pay, or (C) annuities or similar amounts payable on account of personal services performed by any individual (not including any payment under any workmen's compensation law or any payment by the Secretary of Veterans Affairs as compensation for service-connected disability or death).

(3) The term "periodic benefit" includes a benefit payable in a lump sum if it is a commutation of, or a substitute for, periodic payments.

(4) The determination of whether an individual is a husband or wife for any month shall be made under subsection (h) of section 416 of this title without regard to subsections (b) and (f) of section 416 of this title.

(Aug. 14, 1935, c. 531, Title II, § 228, as added Pub.L. 89–368, Title III, § 302(a), Mar. 15, 1966, 80 Stat. 67; amended Pub.L. 90–248, Title I, § 102(b), Title II, § 241(a), Jan. 2, 1968, 81 Stat. 827, 916; Pub.L. 91–172, Title X, § 1003(b), Dec. 30, 1969, 83 Stat. 740; Pub.L. 92–5, Title II, § 202(b), Mar. 17, 1971, 85 Stat. 10; Pub.L. 92–336, Title II, § 201(g)(2), July 1, 1972, 86 Stat. 411; Pub.L. 93–233, §§ 2(b)(1), 18(c), Dec. 31, 1973, 87 Stat. 952, 968; Pub.L. 98–21, Title III, § 305(a) to (d), Apr. 20, 1983, 97 Stat. 113; Pub.L. 98–369, Div. B, Title VI, §§ 2662(e), 2663(j)(3)(A)(iv), July 18, 1984, 98 Stat. 1159, 1170; Pub.L. 101–508, Title V, § 5114(a), Nov. 5, 1990, 104 Stat. 1388–273; Pub.L. 102–54, § 13(q)(3)(B)(i), June 13, 1991, 105 Stat. 279; Pub.L. 103–296, Title I, § 107(a)(4), Aug. 15, 1994, 108 Stat. 1478; Pub.L. 104–193, Title I, § 108(a)(2), Aug. 22, 1996, 110 Stat. 2165.)

HISTORICAL AND STATUTORY NOTES

References in Text

Section 211 of Pub.L. 93–66, referred to in subsec. (d), is set out as a note under section 1382 of this title.

Part A of subchapter IV, referred to in subsec. (d)(1), is classified to 42 U.S.C.A. § 601 et seq.

Section 228e(*l*) of Title 45, referred to in subsec. (h)(1), is a reference to § 5(*l*) of the Railroad Retirement Act of 1937. That Act was amended in its entirety and completely revised by Pub.L. 93–445, Oct. 16, 1974, 88 Stat. 1305. The Act, as thus amended and revised, was redesignated the Railroad Retirement Act of 1974, and is classified generally to subchapter IV (section 231 et seq.) of chapter 9 of Title 45, Railroads. Section 228e of Title 45 is now covered by section 231e of Title 45.

Effective and Applicability Provisions

1996 Acts. Amendment by Pub.L. 104–193 effective July 1, 1997, with transition rules relating to State options to accelerate such date, rules relating to claims, actions, and proceedings commenced before such date, rules relating to closing out of accounts for terminated or substantially modified programs and continuance in office of Assistant Secretary for Family Support, and provisions relating to termination of entitlement under AFDC program, see section 116 of Pub.L. 104–193, set out as a note under section 601 of this title.

1994 Acts. Amendment by section 107(a)(4) of Pub.L. 103–296 effective Mar. 31, 1995, see section 110 of Pub.L. 103–296, set out as a note under section 401 of this title.

1990 Acts. Section 5114(b) of Pub.L. 101–508 provided that: "The amendment made by subsection (a) [amending subsec. (a) of this section] shall apply with respect [to] benefits payable on the basis of applications filed after the date of the enactment of this Act [Nov. 5, 1990]."

1984 Acts. Amendment by section 2662(e) of Pub.L. 98–369 effective as though included in the enactment of the Social Security Amendments of 1983 [Pub.L. 98–21], see section 2664(a) of Pub.L. 98–369, set out as a note under section 401 of this title.

Amendment by section 2663(j)(3)(A)(iv) of Pub.L. 98–369 effective July 18, 1984, but not to be construed as changing or affecting any right, liability, status or interpretation which existed (under the provisions of law involved) before that date, see section 2664(b) of Pub.L. 98–369, set out as a note under section 401 of this title.

1983 Acts. Amendment by Pub.L. 98–21 applicable only with respect to monthly payments payable under this subchapter for months after April, 1983, except as otherwise specifically provided, see section 310 of Pub.L. 98–21, set out as a note under section 402 of this title.

1973 Acts. Amendment by section 2(b)(1) of Pub.L. 93–233 effective June 1, 1974, see section 2(b)(1) of Pub.L. 93–233, set out in part as a note under section 427 of this title.

Amendment by section 2(b)(1) of Pub.L. 93–233 applicable with respect to monthly benefits under this subchapter for months after May 1974, and with respect to lump-sum death payments under section 402(i) of this title, see section 2(c) of Pub.L. 93–233, set out as a note under section 415 of this title.

1972 Acts. Amendment by Pub.L. 92–336 applicable with respect to monthly benefits under this subchapter for months after August 1972, see section 201(i) of Pub.L. 92–336, set out as a note under section 415 of this title.

1971 Acts. Amendment by Pub.L. 92–5 applicable with respect to monthly benefits under this subchapter for months after December 1970, see section 202(c) of Pub.L. 92–5, set out as a note under section 427 of this title.

1969 Acts. Amendment by Pub.L. 91–172 applicable for months after December 1969, see section 1003(c) of Pub.L. 91–172, set out as a note under section 427 of this title.

1968 Acts. Amendment by section 102(b) of Pub.L. 90–248 applicable with respect to monthly benefits under this subchapter for months after Jan. 1968, see section 102(c) of Pub.L. 90–248, set out a note under section 427 of this title.

Application to Northern Mariana Islands

For applicability of this section to the Northern Mariana Islands, see section 502(a)(1) of the Covenant to Establish a Commonwealth of the Northern Mariana Islands in Political Union with the United States of America, as set forth in Pub.L. 94–241, Mar. 24, 1976, 90 Stat. 263, eff. Jan. 9, 1978, pursuant to Proc. No. 4534, Oct. 24, 1977, 42 F.R. 56593, set out as notes under section 1681 of Title 48, Territories and Insular Possessions.

Applications for Transitional Coverage of Uninsured Individuals for Hospital Insurance Benefits

Section 302(b) of Pub.L. 89–368 provided that: "For purposes of paragraph (4) of section 228(a) of the Social Security Act (added by subsection (a) of this section) [subsec. (a)(4) of this section], an application filed under section 103 of the Social Security Amendments of 1965 [section 426a of this title] before July 1966 shall be regarded as an application under such section 228 [this section] and shall, for purposes of such paragraph and of the last sentence of such section 228(a) [subsec. (a) of this section], be deemed to have been filed in July 1966, unless the person by whom or on whose behalf such application was filed notifies the Secretary that he does not want such application so regarded."

Increases to Take Into Account General Benefit Increases

Section 305(e) of Pub.L. 98–21 provided that: "The Secretary shall increase the amounts specified in section 228 of the Social Security Act [this section], as amended by this section, to take into account any general benefit increases (as referred to in section 215(i)(3) of such Act [section 415(i)(3) of this title]), and any increases under section 215(i) of such Act [section 415(i) of this title], which have occurred after June 1974 or may hereafter occur."

Repeal of Amendment of Subsections (b)(1), (2) and (c)(3)(A), (B) Prior to Effective Date

Section 202(a)(4) of Pub.L. 92–336, Title II, July 1, 1972, 86 Stat. 416, which, effective Jan. 1, 1975, substituted "the larger of $58.00 or the amount most recently established in lieu thereof under section 415(i) of this title" for "$58.00" and "the larger of $29.00 or the amount most recently established in lieu thereof under section 415(i) of this title" for "$29.00", was repealed prior to its effective date by Pub.L. 93–233, § 2(b)(2), Dec. 31, 1973, 87 Stat. 952, applicable with respect to monthly benefits under this subchapter for months after May 1974, and with respect to lump-sum death payments under section 402(i) of this title. See section 2(c) of Pub.L. 93–233, set out as an Effective Date of 1973 Amendment note under section 415 of this title.

Special $50 Payment Under Tax Reduction Act of 1975

Special payment of $50 as soon as practicable after Mar. 29, 1975, by the Secretary of the Treasury to each individual who, for the month of March, 1975, was entitled to a monthly insurance benefit payable under this subchapter, see section 702 of Pub.L. 94–12, set out as a note under section 402 of this title.

§ 429. Benefits in case of members of uniformed services

For purposes of determining entitlement to and the amount of any monthly benefit for any month after December 1972, or entitlement to and the amount of any lump-sum death payment in case of a death after such month, payable under this subchapter on the basis of the wages and self-employment income of any individual, and for purposes of section 416(i)(3) of this title, such individual, if he was paid wages for service as a member of a uniformed service (as defined in section 410(m) of this title) which was included in the term "employment" as defined in section 410(a) of this title as a result of the provisions of section 410(*l*)(1)(A) of this title, shall be deemed to have been paid—

(1) in each calendar quarter occurring after 1956 and before 1978 in which he was paid such wages, additional wages of $300, and

(2) in each calendar year occurring after 1977 and before 2002 in which he was paid such wages, additional wages of $100 for each $300 of such wages, up to a maximum of $1,200 of additional wages for any calendar year.

(Aug. 14, 1935, c. 531, Title II, § 229, as added Pub.L. 90–248, Title I, § 106, Jan. 2, 1968, 81 Stat. 833; amended Pub.L. 92–603, Title I, § 120(a), Oct. 30, 1972, 86 Stat. 1352; Pub.L. 95–216, Title III, § 353(d), Dec. 20, 1977, 91 Stat. 1554; Pub.L. 98–21, Title I, § 151(b)(1), Apr. 20, 1983, 97 Stat. 104; Pub.L. 98–369, Div. B, Title VI, § 2661(n), July 18, 1984, 98 Stat. 1158; Pub.L. 100–203, Title IX, § 9001(c), Dec. 22, 1987, 101 Stat. 1330–286; Pub.L. 103–296, Title I, § 107(a)(4), Title III, § 321(c)(6)(J), Aug. 15, 1994, 108 Stat. 1478, 1538; Pub.L. 108–203, Title IV, § 420(b), Mar. 2, 2004, 118 Stat. 535.)

HISTORICAL AND STATUTORY NOTES

Effective and Applicability Provisions

1994 Acts. Amendment by section 107(a)(4) of Pub.L. 103–296 effective Mar. 31, 1995, see section 110 of Pub.L. 103–296, set out as a note under section 401 of this title.

1987 Acts. Amendment by Pub.L. 100–203 applicable with respect to remuneration paid after Dec. 31, 1987, see section 9001(d) of Pub.L. 100–203, set out as a note under section 3121 of Title 26, Internal Revenue Code.

1984 Acts. Amendment by Pub.L. 98–369 effective as though included in the enactment of the Social Security Amendments of 1983 [Pub.L. 98–21], see section 2664(a) of Pub.L. 98–369, set out as a note under section 401 of this title.

1983 Acts. Section 151(b)(2) of Pub.L. 98–21 provided that: "The amendment made by paragraph (1) [amending subsec. (b) of this section] shall be effective with respect to wages deemed to have been paid for calendar years after 1983."

1977 Acts. Amendment by Pub.L. 95–216 effective Jan. 1, 1978, see section 353(g) of Pub.L. 95–216, set out as a note under section 418 of this title.

1972 Acts. Section 120(b) of Pub.L. 92–603 provided that: "The amendments made by subsection (a) [amending subsec. (a) of this section] shall apply with respect to monthly benefits under title II of the Social Security Act [this subchapter] for months after December 1972 and with respect to lump-sum death payments under such title [this subchapter] in the case of deaths occurring after December 1972 except that, in the case of any individual who is entitled, on the basis of the wages and self-employment income of any individual to whom section 229 of such Act [this section] applies, to monthly benefits under title II of such Act [this subchapter] for the month in which this Act is enacted [Oct. 1972], such amendments shall apply (1) only if a written request for a recalculation of such benefits (by reason of such amendments) under the provisions of section 215(b) and (d) of such Act [section 415(b) and (d) of this title], as in effect at the time such request is filed, is filed by such individual, or any other individual, entitled to benefits under such title II [this subchapter] on the basis of such wages and self-employment income, and (2) only with respect to such benefits for months beginning with whichever of the following is later: January 1973 or the twelfth month before the month in which such request was filed. Recalculations of benefits as required to carry out the provisions of this section shall be made notwithstanding the provisions of section 215(f)(1) of the Social Security Act [section 415(f)(1) of this title], and no such recalculation shall be regarded as a recomputation for purposes of section 215(f) of such Act [section 415(f) of this title]."

Payment of Wages

Pub.L. 107–117, Div. A, Title VIII, § 8134, Jan. 10, 2002, 115 Stat. 2278, provided that: " Notwithstanding section 229(a) of the Social Security Act [subsec. (a) of this section], no wages shall be deemed to have been paid to any individual pursuant to that section in any calendar year after 2001."

Compensatory Payments to Trust Funds

Section 151(b)(3) of Pub.L. 98–21 provided that:

"(A) Within thirty days after the date of the enactment of this Act [Apr. 20, 1983], the Secretary of Health and Human Services shall determine the additional amounts which would have been appropriated to the Federal Old-Age and Survivors Insurance Trust Fund, the Federal Disability Insurance Trust Fund, and the Federal Hospital Insurance Trust Fund under sections 201 and 1817 of the Social Security Act [sections 401 and 1395i of this title] if the additional wages deemed to have been paid under section 229(a) of the Social Security Act [subsec. (a) of this section] prior to 1984 had constituted remuneration for employment (as defined in section 3121(b) of the Internal Revenue Code of 1954 [section 3121(b) of Title 26]) for purposes of the taxes imposed by sections 3101 and 3111 of the Internal Revenue Code of 1954 [sections 3101 and 3111 of Title 26], and the amount of interest which would have been earned on such amounts if they had been so appropriated.

"(B)(i) Within thirty days after the date of the enactment of this Act [Apr. 20, 1983], the Secretary of the Treasury shall transfer to each such Trust Fund, from amounts in the general fund of the Treasury not otherwise appropriated, an amount equal to the amount determined with respect to such Trust Fund under subparagraph (A), less any amount appropriated to such Trust Fund pursuant to the provisions of section 229(b) of the Social Security Act [subsec. (b) of this section] prior to the date of the determination made under subparagraph (A) with respect to wages deemed to have been paid for calendar years prior to 1984.

"(ii) The Secretary of Health and Human Services shall revise the amount determined under clause (i) with respect to each such Trust Fund within one year after the date of the transfer made to such Trust Fund under clause (i), as determined appropriate by such Secretary from data which becomes available to him after the date of the transfer under clause (i). Within 30 days after any such revision, the Secretary of the Treasury shall transfer to such Trust Fund, from amounts in the general fund of the Treasury not otherwise appropriated, or from such Trust Fund to the general fund of the Treasury, such amounts as the Secretary of Health and Human Services certifies as necessary to take into account such revision."

§ 430. Adjustment of contribution and benefit base

(a) Determination and publication by Commissioner in Federal Register subsequent to cost-of-living benefit increase; effective date

Whenever the Commissioner of Social Security pursuant to section 415(i) of this title increases benefits effective with the December following a cost-of-living computation quarter, the Commissioner shall also determine and publish in the Federal Register on or before November 1 of the calendar year in which such quarter occurs the contribution and benefit base determined under subsection (b) or (c) which shall be effective with respect to remuneration paid after the calendar year in which such quarter occurs and taxable years beginning after such year.

(b) Determination of amount

The amount of such contribution and benefit base shall (subject to subsection (c)) be the amount of the contribution and benefit base in effect in the year in which the determination is made or, if larger, the product of—

(1) $60,600, and

(2) the ratio of (A) the national average wage index (as defined in section 409(k)(1) of this title) for the calendar year before the calendar year in which the determination under subsection (a) is made to (B) the national average wage index (as so defined) for 1992,

with such product, if not a multiple of $300, being rounded to the next higher multiple of $300 where such product is a multiple of $150 but not of $300 and to the nearest multiple of $300 in any other case.

(c) Amount of base for period prior to initial cost-of-living benefit increase

For purposes of this section, and for purposes of determining wages and self-employment income under sections 409, 411, 413, and 415 of this title and sections 1402, 3121, 3122, 3125, 6413, and 6654 of the Internal Revenue Code of 1986, (1) the "contribution and benefit base" with respect to remuneration paid in (and taxable years beginning in) any calendar year after 1973 and prior to the calendar year with the June of which the first increase in benefits pursuant to section 415(i) of this title becomes effective shall be $13,200 or (if applicable) such other amount as may be specified in a law enacted subsequent to the law which added this section, and (2) the "contribution and benefit base" with respect to remuneration paid (and taxable years beginning)—

(A) in 1978 shall be $17,700,

(B) in 1979 shall be $22,900,

(C) in 1980 shall be $25,900, and

(D) in 1981 shall be $29,700.

For purposes of determining under subsection (b) the "contribution and benefit base" with respect to remuneration paid (and taxable years beginning) in 1982 and subsequent years, the dollar amounts specified in clause (2) of the preceding sentence shall be considered to have resulted from the application of such subsection (b) and to be the amount determined (with respect to the years involved) under that subsection.

(d) Determinations for calendar years after 1976 for purposes of retirement benefit plans

Notwithstanding any other provision of law, the contribution and benefit base determined under this section for any calendar year after 1976 for purposes of section 1322(b)(3)(B) of Title 29, with respect to any plan, shall be the contribution and benefit base that would have been determined for such year if this section as in effect immediately prior to the enactment of the Social Security Amendments of 1977 had remained in effect without change (except that, for purposes of subsection (b) of such section 430 of this title as so in effect, the reference to the contribution and benefit base in paragraph (1) of such subsection (b) shall be deemed a reference to an amount equal to $45,000, each reference in paragraph (2) of such subsection (b) to the average of the wages of all employees as reported to the Secretary of the Treasury shall be deemed a reference to the national average wage index (as defined in section 409(k)(1) of this title), the reference to a preceding calendar year in paragraph (2)(A) of such subsection (b) shall be deemed a reference to the calendar year before the calendar year in which the determination under subsection (a) of such section 430 of this title is made, and the reference to a calendar year in paragraph (2)(B) of such subsection (b) shall be deemed a reference to 1992).

(Aug. 14, 1935, c. 531, Title II, § 230, as added Pub.L. 92–336, Title II, § 202(b)(1), July 1, 1972, 86 Stat. 416; amended Pub.L. 92–603, Title I, § 144(a)(4), Oct. 30, 1972, 86 Stat. 1370; Pub.L. 93–66, Title II, § 203(c), July 9, 1973, 87 Stat. 153; Pub.L. 93–233, §§ 3(j), 5(c), Dec. 31, 1973, 87 Stat. 952, 954; Pub.L. 94–202, § 8(h), Jan. 2, 1976, 89 Stat. 1139; Pub.L. 95–216, Title I, § 103(a) to (c)(1), Title III, § 353(e), Dec. 20, 1977, 91 Stat. 1513, 1514, 1554; Pub.L. 97–34, Title VII, § 741(d)(1), Aug. 13, 1981, 95 Stat. 347; Pub.L. 98–21, Title I, § 111(a)(5), Apr. 20, 1983, 97 Stat. 72; Pub.L. 98–76, Title II, §§ 211(d), 225(a)(4), Aug. 12, 1983, 97 Stat. 419, 425; Pub.L. 98–369, Div. B, Title VI, § 2663(a)(18), July 18, 1984, 98 Stat. 1165; Pub.L. 101–239, Title X, § 10208(b)(1)(A), (B), (5), (d)(2)(A)(i), Dec. 19, 1989, 103 Stat. 2477, 2478, 2480; Pub.L. 103–296, Title I, § 107(a)(4), Title III, § 321(b)(2), (c)(6)(K), (g)(1)(A), (B), Aug. 15, 1994, 108 Stat. 1478, 1537, 1538, 1542.)

Maximum Contribution of Social Security Employment Taxes Paid By Employee

The following table indicates, pursuant to published notice, maximum wages subject to social security employment taxes and maximum annual contribution by employee:

Year	Tax Rate	Maximum Wages Taxable	Maximum Annual Contributions
2018:			
OASDI	6.2	$ 128,400.00	$7,960.80
Health Ins.	1.45	All	
2017:			
OASDI	6.2	$ 127,200.00	$7,886.40

Year	Tax Rate	Maximum Wages Taxable	Maximum Annual Contributions
Health Ins.	1.45	All	
2016:			
OASDI	6.2	$ 118,500.00	$7,347.00
Health Ins.	1.45	All	
2015:			
OASDI	6.2	$ 118,500.00	$7,347.00
Health Ins.	1.45	All	
2014:			
OASDI	6.2	$ 117,000.00	$7,254.00
Health Ins.	1.45	All	
2013:			
OASDI	6.2	$ 113,700.00	$7,049.40
Health Ins.	1.45	All	
2012:			
OASDI	4.2	$ 110,100.00	$6,826.20
Health Ins.	1.45	All	
2011:			
OASDI	4.2	$ 106,800.00	$6,621.60
Health Ins.	1.45	All	
2010:			
OASDI	6.2	$ 106,800.00	$6,621.60
Health Ins.	1.45	All	
2009:			
OASDI	6.2	$ 106,800.00	$6,621.60
Health Ins.	1.45	All	
2008:			
OASDI	6.2	$ 102,000.00	$6,324.00
Health Ins.	1.45	All	
2007:			
OASDI	6.2	$ 97,500.00	$6,045.00
Health Ins.	1.45	All	
2006:			
OASDI	6.2	$ 94,200.00	$5,840.40
Health Ins.	1.45	All	
2005:			
OASDI	6.2	$ 90,000.00	$5,580.00
Health Ins.	1.45	All	
2004:			
OASDI	6.2	$ 87,900.00	$5,449.80
Health Ins.	1.45	All	
2003:			
OASDI	6.2	$ 87,000.00	$5,394.00
Health Ins.	1.45	All	
2002:			
OASDI	6.2	$ 84,900.00	$5,263.80
Health Ins.	1.45	All	
2001:			
OASDI	6.2	$ 80,400.00	$4,984.80
Health Ins.	1.45	All	
2000:			
OASDI	6.2	$ 76,200.00	$4,724.40
Health Ins.	1.45	All	
1999:			
OASDI	6.2	$ 72,600.00	$4,501.20
Health Ins.	1.45	All	
1998:			
OASDI	6.2	$ 68,400.00	$4,240.80
Health Ins.	1.45	All	
1997:			
OASDI	6.2	$ 65,400.00	$4,054.80
Health Ins.	1.45	All	
1996:			
OASDI	6.2	$ 62,700.00	$3,887.40
Health Ins.	1.45	All	
1995:			
OASDI	6.2	$ 61,200.00	$3,794.40
Health Ins.	1.45	All	
1994:			
OASDI	6.2	$ 60,600.00	$3,757.20
Health Ins.	1.45	All	
1993:			
OASDI	6.2	$ 57,600.00	$3,571.20
Health Ins.	1.45	135,000.00	1,957.50
1992:			
OASDI	6.2	$55,500.00	3,441.00
Health Ins.	1.45	130,200.00	1,887.90
1991:			
OASDI	6.2	53,400.00	3,310.80
Health Ins.	1.45	125,000.00	1,812.50
1990	7.65	51,300.00	3,924.45
1989	7.51	48,000.00	3,604.80
1988	7.51	45,000.00	3,379.50
1987	7.15	43,800.00	3,131.70
1986	7.15	42,000.00	3,003.00
1985	7.05	39,600.00	2,791.80
1984	6.70	37,800.00	2,532.60
1983	6.70	35,700.00	2,391.90
1982	6.70	32,400.00	2,170.80
1981	6.65	29,700.00	1,975.05
1980	6.13	25,900.00	1,587.67
1979	6.13	22,900.00	1,403.77
1978	6.05	17,700.00	1,070.85
1977	5.85	16,500.00	965.25
1976	5.85	15,300.00	895.05
1975	5.85	14,100.00	824.85
1974	5.85	13,200.00	772.20
1973	5.85	10,800.00	631.80

Year	Tax Rate	Maximum Wages Taxable	Maximum Annual Contributions
1972	5.2	9,000.00	468.00
1971	5.2	7,800.00	405.60
1970	4.8	7,800.00	374.40
1969	4.8	7,800.00	374.40
1968	4.4	7,800.00	343.20
1967	4.4	6,600.00	290.40
1966	4.2	6,600.00	277.20
1965	3.625	4,800.00	174.00
1964	3.625	4,800.00	174.00
1963	3.625	4,800.00	174.00
1962	3.125	4,800.00	150.00
1961	3.0	4,800.00	144.00
1960	3.0	4,800.00	144.00
1959	2.5	4,800.00	120.00
1958	2.25	4,200.00	94.50
1957	2.25	4,200.00	94.50
1956	2.0	4,200.00	84.00
1955	2.0	4,200.00	84.00
1954	2.0	3,600.00	72.00
1953	1.5	3,600.00	54.00
1952	1.5	3,600.00	54.00
1951	1.5	3,600.00	54.00
1950	1.5	3,000.00	45.00
1949	1.0	3,000.00	30.00
1948	1.0	3,000.00	30.00
1947	1.0	3,000.00	30.00
1946	1.0	3,000.00	30.00
1945	1.0	3,000.00	30.00
1944	1.0	3,000.00	30.00
1943	1.0	3,000.00	30.00
1942	1.0	3,000.00	30.00
1941	1.0	3,000.00	30.00
1940	1.0	3,000.00	30.00
1939	1.0	3,000.00	30.00
1938	1.0	3,000.00	30.00
1937	1.0	3,000.00	30.00

HISTORICAL AND STATUTORY NOTES

References in Text

The Internal Revenue Code of 1986, referred to in subsec. (c), is classified to Title 26.

"Subsequent to the law which added this section", referred to in subsec. (c), means subsequent to the enactment of Pub.L. 92–336, which was approved July 1, 1972.

This section "as in effect immediately prior to the enactment of the Social Security Amendments of 1977", referred to in subsec. (d), means this section as in effect prior to the enactment of Pub.L. 95–216 which was approved Dec. 20, 1977.

The enactment of the Social Security Amendments of 1977, referred to in subsec. (d), means the enactment of Pub.L. 95–216 which was approved Dec. 20, 1977.

Effective and Applicability Provisions

1994 Acts. Amendment by section 107(a)(4) of Pub.L. 103–296 effective Mar. 31, 1995, see section 110 of Pub.L. 103–296, set out as a note under section 401 of this title.

Section 321(b)(2) of Pub.L. 103–296 provided in part that the amendment by section 321(b)(2) of Pub.L. 103–296 of faulty directory language in section 10208(b)(1) of Pub.L. 101–239 (which had amended subsec. (b)(2) of this section in 1989) is effective as if the correcting language of Pub.L. 103–296 had been included as part of the original directory language of Pub.L. 101–239.

Amendment of subsecs. (b)(1), (2) and (d) of this section by section 321(g)(1)(A), (B) of Pub.L. 103–296 effective with respect to the determination of the contribution and benefit base for years after 1994, see section 321(g)(3)(A) of Pub.L. 103–296, set out as a note under section 415 of this title.

1989 Acts. Section 10208(c) of Pub.L. 101–239 provided that:

"(1) In general.—The amendments made by subsections (a) [enacting section 409(k) of this title] and (b) [amending sections 413(d)(2)(B), 415(a)(1)(B)(ii), (B)(ii)(II), (a)(1)(C)(ii), (i)(1)(G), 424a(f)(2)(B), (B)(ii), and 430(d) of this title] shall apply with respect to the computation of average total wage amounts (under the amended provisions) for calendar years after 1990.

"(2) Transitional rule.—For purposes of determining the contribution and benefit base for 1990, 1991, and 1992 under section 230(b) of the Social Security Act [subsec. (b) of this section] (and section 230(b) of such Act [subsec. (b) of this section] as in effect immediately prior to enactment of the Social Security Amendments of 1977 [Pub.L. 95–216, approved Dec. 20, 1977.])—

"(A) the average of total wages for 1988 shall be deemed to be equal to the amount which would have been determined without regard to this paragraph, plus 2 percent of the amount which has been determined to the average of total wages for 1987,

"(B) the average of total wages for 1989 shall be deemed to be equal to the amount which would have been determined without regard to this paragraph, plus 2 percent of the amount which would have been determined to the average of total wages for 1988 without regard to subparagraph (A), and

"(C) the average of total wages reported to the Secretary of the Treasury for 1990 shall be deemed to be equal to the product of—

"(i) the SSA average wage index (as defined in section 215(i)(1)(G) of the Social Security Act [section 415(i)(1)(G) of this title] and promulgated by the Secretary) for 1989, and

"(ii) the quotient obtained by dividing—

"(I) the average of total wages (as defined in regulations of the Secretary and computed without regard to the limitations of section 209(a)(1) of the Social Security Act [section 409(a)(1) of this title] and by including deferred compensation amounts, within the meaning of section 209(k)(2) of such Act [section 409(k)(2) of this title] as added by this section) reported to the Secretary of the Treasury or his delegate for 1990, by

"(II) the average of total wages (as so defined and computed without regard to the limitations specified in such section 209(a)(1) [section 409(a)(1) of this title] and by excluding deferred compensation amounts within the meaning of such section 209(k)(2) [section 409(k)(2) of this title]) reported to the Secretary of the Treasury or his delegate for 1989.

"(3) Determination of contribution and benefit base for 1993.—For purposes of determining the contribution and benefit base for 1993 under section 230(b) of the Social Security Act [subsec. (b) of this section] (and section 230(b) of such Act [subsec. (b) of this section] as in effect immediately prior to enactment of the Social Security Amendments of 1977), the average of total wages for 1990 shall be determined without regard to subparagraph (C) of paragraph (2).

"(4) **Revised determination under section 230 of the Social Security Act [this section].**—As soon as possible after the enactment of this Act [Dec. 19, 1989], the Secretary of Health and Human Services shall revise and publish, in accordance with the provisions of this Act [Pub.L. 101–239] and the amendments made thereby, the contribution and benefit base under section 230 of the Social Security Act [this section] with respect to remuneration paid after 1989 and taxable years beginning after calendar year 1989."

1984 Acts. Amendment by Pub.L. 98–369 effective July 18, 1984, but not to be construed as changing or affecting any right, liability, status or interpretation which existed (under the provisions of law involved) before that date, see section 2664(b) of Pub.L. 98–369, set out as a note under section 401 of this title.

1983 Acts. Amendment by section 211(d) of Pub.L. 98–76 applicable to compensation paid for services rendered after Dec. 31, 1983, and before Jan. 1, 1985, see section 212 of Pub.L. 98–76, set out as a note under section 3201 of Title 26, Internal Revenue Code.

Amendment by section 225(a)(4) of Pub.L. 98–76 applicable to remuneration paid after Dec. 31, 1984, see section 227(a) of Pub.L. 98–76, set out as a note under section 3201 of Title 26.

Amendment by Pub.L. 98–21 applicable with respect to cost-of-living increases determined under section 415(i) of this title for years after 1982, see section 111(a)(8) of Pub.L. 98–21, set out as a note under section 402 of this title.

1981 Acts. Amendment by Pub.L. 97–34 applicable to compensation paid for services rendered after Sept. 30, 1981, see section 741(e) of Pub.L. 97–34, set out as a note under section 3201 of Title 26, Internal Revenue Code.

1977 Acts. Amendment by section 103(a) and (b) of Pub.L. 95–216 [amending subsecs. (a), (c), and the provisions preceding par. (1) of subsec. (b) of this section] applicable with respect to remunerations paid or received, and taxable years beginning, after 1977, see section 104 of Pub.L. 95–216, set out as a note under section 1401 of Title 26, Internal Revenue Code.

Section 103(c)(2) of Pub.L. 95–216, provided that: "The amendment made by paragraph (1) [adding subsec. (d) of this section] shall apply with respect to plan terminations occurring after the date of the enactment of this Act [Dec. 20, 1977]."

Amendment by section 353(e) of Pub.L. 95–216 [amending pars. (1) and (2) of subsec. (b) and the provisions following par. (2) of subsec. (b) of this section] effective Jan. 1, 1979, see section 353(g) of Pub.L. 95–216, set out as a note under section 418 of this title.

1973 Acts. Amendment by Pub.L. 93–233 applicable only with respect to remuneration paid after, and taxable years beginning after, 1973, see section 5(e) of Pub.L. 93–233, set out as a note under section 409 of this title.

Amendment by Pub.L. 93–66 applicable only with respect to remuneration paid after, and taxable years beginning after, 1973, see section 203(e) of Pub.L. 93–66, set out as a note under section 409 of this title.

1972 Acts. Amendment by Pub.L. 92–603 effective in like manner as if such amendment had been included in Title II of Pub.L. 92–336, see section 144(b) of Pub.L. 92–603, set out as a note under section 403 of this title.

Cost-of-Living Increase in Benefits

For purposes of subsec. (a) of this section, the increase in benefits provided by section 2 of Pub.L. 93–233, revising benefits table of section 415(a) of this title and amending sections 427(a), (b) and 428(b)(1), (2), (c)(3)(A), (B) of this title considered an increase under section 415(i) of this title, see section 3(i) of Pub.L. 93–233, set out as a note under section 415 of this title.

§ 431. Benefits for certain individuals interned by United States during World War II

(a) "Internee" defined

For the purposes of this section the term "internee" means an individual who was interned during any period of time from December 7, 1941, through December 31, 1946, at a place within the United States operated by the Government of the United States for the internment of United States citizens of Japanese ancestry.

(b) Applicability in determining entitlement to and amount of monthly benefits and lump-sum death payments, and period of disability; effect of payment of benefits by other agency or instrumentality of United States

(1) For purposes of determining entitlement to and the amount of any monthly benefit for any month after December 1972, or entitlement to and the amount of any lump-sum death payment in the case of a death after such month, payable under this subchapter on the basis of the wages and self-employment income of any individual, and for purposes of section 416(i)(3) of this title, such individual shall be deemed to have been paid during any period after he attained age 18 and for which he was an internee, wages (in addition to any wages actually paid to him) at a weekly rate of basic pay during such period as follows—

(A) in the case such individual was not employed prior to the beginning of such period, 40 multiplied by the minimum hourly rate or rates in effect at any such time under section 206(a)(1) of Title 29, for each full week during such period; and

(B) in the case such individual who [1] was employed prior to the beginning of such period, 40 multiplied by the greater of (i) the highest hourly rate received during any such employment, or (ii) the minimum hourly rate or rates in effect at any such time under section 206(a)(1) of Title 29, for each full week during such period.

(2) This subsection shall not be applicable in the case of any monthly benefit or lump-sum death payment if—

(A) a larger such benefit or payment, as the case may be, would be payable without its application; or

(B) a benefit (other than a benefit payable in a lump-sum unless it is a commutation of, or a substitute for, periodic payments) which is based, in whole or in part, upon internment during any period from

December 7, 1941, through December 31, 1946, at a place within the United States operated by the Government of the United States for the internment of United States citizens of Japanese ancestry, is determined by any agency or wholly owned instrumentality of the United States to be payable by it under any other law of the United States or under a system established by such agency or instrumentality.

The provisions of clause (B) shall not apply in the case of any monthly benefit or lump-sum death payment under this subchapter if its application would reduce by $0.50 or less the primary insurance amount (as computed under section 415 of this title prior to any recomputation thereof pursuant to subsection (f) of such section) of the individual on whose wages and self-employment income such benefit or payment is based. The provisions of clause (B) shall also not apply for purposes of section 416(i)(3) of this title.

(3) Upon application for benefits, a recalculation of benefits (by reason of this section), or a lump-sum death payment on the basis of the wages and self-employment income of any individual who was an internee, the Commissioner of Social Security shall accept the certification of the Secretary of Defense or his designee concerning any period of time for which an internee is to receive credit under paragraph (1) and shall make a decision without regard to clause (B) of paragraph (2) of this subsection unless the Commissioner has been notified by some other agency or instrumentality of the United States that, on the basis of the period for which such individual was an internee, a benefit described in clause (B) of paragraph (2) has been determined by such agency or instrumentality to be payable by it. If the Commissioner of Social Security has not been so notified, the Commissioner shall then ascertain whether some other agency or wholly owned instrumentality of the United States has decided that a benefit described in clause (B) of paragraph (2) is payable by it. If any such agency or instrumentality has decided, or thereafter decides, that such a benefit is payable by it, it shall so notify the Commissioner of Social Security, and the Commissioner of Social Security shall certify no further benefits for payment or shall recompute the amount of any further benefits payable, as may be required by this section.

(4) Any agency or wholly owned instrumentality of the United States which is authorized by any law of the United States to pay benefits, or has a system of benefits which are based, in whole or in part, on any period for which any individual was an internee shall, at the request of the Commissioner of Social Security, certify to the Commissioner, with respect to any individual who was an internee, such information as the Commissioner of Social Security deems necessary to carry out the Commissioner's functions under paragraph (3) of this subsection.

(c) Authorization of appropriations

There are authorized to be appropriated to the Trust Funds and the Federal Hospital Insurance Trust Fund for the fiscal year ending June 30, 1978, such sums as the Commissioner of Social Security and the Secretary jointly determine would place the Trust Funds and the Federal Hospital Insurance Trust Fund in the position in which they would have been if the preceding provisions of this section had not been enacted.

(Aug. 14, 1935, c. 531, Title II, § 231, as added Pub.L. 92–603, Title I, § 142(a), Oct. 30, 1972, 86 Stat. 1367; amended Pub.L. 98–369, Div. B, Title VI, § 2663(j)(2)(A)(iii), July 18, 1984, 98 Stat. 1170; Pub.L. 103–296, Title I, § 107(a)(1), (4), (c), Aug. 15, 1994, 108 Stat. 1477, 1478, 1481.)

[1] So in original.

HISTORICAL AND STATUTORY NOTES

Effective and Applicability Provisions

1994 Acts. Amendment by section 107(a)(1), (4), and (c) of Pub.L. 103–296 effective Mar. 31, 1995, see section 110 of Pub.L. 103–296, set out as a note under section 401 of this title.

1984 Acts. Amendment by Pub.L. 98–369 effective July 18, 1984, but not to be construed as changing or affecting any right, liability, status or interpretation which existed (under the provisions of law involved) before that date, see section 2664(b) of Pub.L. 98–369, set out as a note under section 401 of this title.

Change of Name

"Secretary of Health and Human Services" was substituted for "Secretary of Health, Education, and Welfare" in subsec. (b), pursuant to section 509(b) of Pub.L. 96–88, which is classified to section 3508(b) of Title 20, Education.

Special $50 Payment Under Tax Reduction Act of 1975

Special payment of $50 as soon as practicable after Mar. 29, 1975, by the Secretary of the Treasury to each individual who, for the month of March, 1975, was entitled to a monthly insurance benefit payable under this subchapter, see section 702 of Pub.L. 94–12, set out as a note under section 402 of this title.

§ 432. Processing of tax data

The Secretary of the Treasury shall make available information returns filed pursuant to part III of subchapter A of chapter 61 of subtitle F of the Internal Revenue Code of 1986, to the Commissioner of Social Security for the purposes of this subchapter and subchapter XI. The Commissioner of Social Security and the Secretary of the Treasury are authorized to enter into an agreement for the processing by the Commissioner of Social Security of information contained in returns filed pursuant to part III of subchapter A of chapter 61 of subtitle F of the Internal Revenue Code of 1986. Notwithstanding the provisions of section 6103(a) of the Internal Revenue Code of 1986, the Secretary of the Treasury shall make available to the Commissioner of Social Security such documents as may be agreed upon as being necessary for purposes of such processing. The Commissioner of Social Security shall process any withholding tax statements or other documents made available to the Commissioner by the

Secretary of the Treasury pursuant to this section. Any agreement made pursuant to this section shall remain in full force and effect until modified or otherwise changed by mutual agreement of the Commissioner of Social Security and the Secretary of the Treasury.

(Aug. 14, 1935, c. 531, Title II, § 232, as added Pub.L. 94–202, § 8(b), Jan. 2, 1976, 89 Stat. 1137; amended Pub.L. 103–296, Title I, § 107(a)(4), Title III, § 321(c)(6)(L), Aug. 15, 1994, 108 Stat. 1478, 1538.)

HISTORICAL AND STATUTORY NOTES

References in Text

Part III of subchapter A of chapter 61 of subtitle F of the Internal Revenue Code of 1986, referred to in text, is classified to 26 U.S.C.A. § 6031 et seq.

Effective and Applicability Provisions

1994 Acts. Amendment by section 107(a)(4) of Pub.L. 103–296 effective Mar. 31, 1995, see section 110 of Pub.L. 103–296, set out as a note under section 401 of this title.

1976 Acts. Section 8(c) of Pub.L. 94–202 provided that: "Section 232 of the Social Security Act [this section], as added by subsection (b) of this section, shall be effective with respect to statements reporting income received after 1977."

§ 433. International agreements

(a) Purpose of agreement

The President is authorized (subject to the succeeding provisions of this section) to enter into agreements establishing totalization arrangements between the social security system established by this subchapter and the social security system of any foreign country, for the purposes of establishing entitlement to and the amount of old-age, survivors, disability, or derivative benefits based on a combination of an individual's periods of coverage under the social security system established by this subchapter and the social security system of such foreign country.

(b) Definitions

For the purposes of this section—

(1) the term "social security system" means, with respect to a foreign country, a social insurance or pension system which is of general application in the country and under which periodic benefits, or the actuarial equivalent thereof, are paid on account of old age, death, or disability; and

(2) the term "period of coverage" means a period of payment of contributions or a period of earnings based on wages for employment or on self-employment income, or any similar period recognized as equivalent thereto under this subchapter or under the social security system of a country which is a party to an agreement entered into under this section.

(c) Crediting periods of coverage; conditions of payment of benefits

(1) Any agreement establishing a totalization arrangement pursuant to this section shall provide—

(A) that in the case of an individual who has at least 6 quarters of coverage as defined in section 413 of this title and periods of coverage under the social security system of a foreign country which is a party to such agreement, periods of coverage of such individual under such social security system of such foreign country may be combined with periods of coverage under this subchapter and otherwise considered for the purposes of establishing entitlement to and the amount of old-age, survivors, and disability insurance benefits under this subchapter;

(B) (i) that employment or self-employment, or any service which is recognized as equivalent to employment or self-employment under this subchapter or the social security system of a foreign country which is a party to such agreement, shall, on or after the effective date of such agreement, result in a period of coverage under the system established under this subchapter or under the system established under the laws of such foreign country, but not under both, and (ii) the methods and conditions for determining under which system employment, self-employment, or other service shall result in a period of coverage; and

(C) that where an individual's periods of coverage are combined, the benefit amount payable under this subchapter shall be based on the proportion of such individual's periods of coverage which was completed under this subchapter.

(2) Any such agreement may provide that an individual who is entitled to cash benefits under this subchapter shall, notwithstanding the provisions of section 402(t) of this title, receive such benefits while he resides in a foreign country which is a party to such agreement.

(3) Section 426 of this title shall not apply in the case of any individual to whom it would not be applicable but for this section or any agreement or regulation under this section.

(4) Any such agreement may contain other provisions which are not inconsistent with the other provisions of this subchapter and which the President deems appropriate to carry out the purposes of this section.

(d) Regulations

The Commissioner of Social Security shall make rules and regulations and establish procedures which are reasonable and necessary to implement and administer any agreement which has been entered into in accordance with this section.

(e) Reports to Congress; effective date of agreements

(1) Any agreement to establish a totalization arrangement entered into pursuant to this section shall be transmitted by the President to the Congress together with a report on the estimated number of individuals who will be affected by the agreement and the effect of the agreement on the estimated income and expenditures of the programs established by this chapter.

(2) Such an agreement shall become effective on any date, provided in the agreement, which occurs after the expiration of the period (following the date on which the agreement is transmitted in accordance with paragraph (1)) during which at least one House of the Congress has been in session on each of 60 days; except that such agreement shall not become effective if, during such period, either House of the Congress adopts a resolution of disapproval of the agreement.

(Aug. 14, 1935, c. 531, Title II, § 233, as added Pub.L. 95–216, Title III, § 317(a), Dec. 20, 1977, 91 Stat. 1538; amended Pub.L. 97–35, Title XXII, § 2201(b)(12), Aug. 13, 1981, 95 Stat. 831; Pub.L. 98–21, Title III, § 326(a), Apr. 20, 1983, 97 Stat. 126; Pub.L. 98–369, Div. B, Title VI, § 2663(j)(3)(A)(v), July 18, 1984, 98 Stat. 1170; Pub.L. 103–296, Title I, § 107(a)(4), Aug. 15, 1994, 108 Stat. 1478.)

HISTORICAL AND STATUTORY NOTES

Effective and Applicability Provisions

1994 Acts. Amendment by section 107(a)(4) of Pub.L. 103–296 effective Mar. 31, 1995, see section 110 of Pub.L. 103–296, set out as a note under section 401 of this title.

1984 Acts. Amendment by Pub.L. 98–369 effective July 18, 1984, but not to be construed as changing or affecting any right, liability, status or interpretation which existed (under the provisions of law involved) before that date, see section 2664(b) of Pub.L. 98–369, set out as a note under section 401 of this title.

1983 Acts. Section 326(b) of Pub.L. 98–21 provided that: "The amendment made by subsection (a) [amending subsec. (e)(2) of this section] shall be effective on the date of the enactment of this Act [Apr. 20, 1983]."

1981 Acts. Amendment by Pub.L. 97–35 applicable with respect to benefits for months after December 1981, with certain exceptions, see section 2(j)(2) to (4) of Pub.L. 97–123, set out as a note under section 415 of this title.

Change of Name

"Secretary of Health and Human Services" was substituted for "Secretary of Health, Education, and Welfare" in subsec. (d), pursuant to section 509(b) of Pub.L. 96–88, which is classified to section 3508(b) of Title 20, Education.

Termination of Reporting Requirements

Reporting requirement of subsec. (e)(1) of this section excepted from termination under Pub.L. 104–66, § 3003(a)(1), as amended, set out as a note under 31 U.S.C.A. § 1113, see Pub.L. 106–554, § 1(a)(7) [Title III, § 301], set out as a note under 31 U.S.C.A. § 1113.

§ 434. Demonstration project authority

(a) Authority

(1) In general

The Commissioner of Social Security (in this section referred to as the "Commissioner") shall develop and carry out experiments and demonstration projects designed to promote attachment to the labor force and to determine the relative advantages and disadvantages of—

(A) various alternative methods of treating the work activity of individuals entitled to disability insurance benefits under section 423 of this title or to monthly insurance benefits under section 402 of this title based on such individual's disability (as defined in section 423(d) of this title), including such methods as a reduction in benefits based on earnings, designed to encourage the return to work of such individuals;

(B) altering other limitations and conditions applicable to such individuals (including lengthening the trial work period (as defined in section 422(c) of this title), altering the 24–month waiting period for hospital insurance benefits under section 426 of this title, altering the manner in which the program under this subchapter is administered, earlier referral of such individuals for rehabilitation, and greater use of employers and others to develop, perform, and otherwise stimulate new forms of rehabilitation); and

(C) implementing sliding scale benefit offsets using variations in—

(i) the amount of the offset as a proportion of earned income;

(ii) the duration of the offset period; and

(iii) the method of determining the amount of income earned by such individuals,

to the end that savings will accrue to the Trust Funds, or to otherwise promote the objectives or facilitate the administration of this subchapter.

(2) Authority for expansion of scope

The Commissioner may expand the scope of any such experiment or demonstration project to include any group of applicants for benefits under the program established under this subchapter with impairments that reasonably may be presumed to be disabling for purposes of such demonstration project, and may limit any such demonstration project to any such group of applicants, subject to the terms of such demonstration project which shall define the extent of any such presumption.

(b) Requirements

The experiments and demonstration projects developed under subsection (a) shall be of sufficient scope and shall be carried out on a wide enough scale to permit a thorough evaluation of the alternative methods under consideration while giving assurance that the results derived from the experiments and projects will obtain generally in the operation of the disability insurance program under this subchapter without committing such program to the adoption of any particular system either locally or nationally.

(c) Authority to waive compliance with benefits requirements

In the case of any experiment or demonstration project initiated under subsection (a) on or before December 30, 2021, the Commissioner may waive compliance with the benefit requirements of this subchapter and the requirements of section 1320b–19 of this title as they relate to the program established under this subchapter, and the Secretary may (upon the request of the Commissioner) waive compliance with the benefits requirements of subchapter XVIII, insofar as is necessary for a thorough evaluation of the alternative methods under consideration. No such experiment or project shall be actually placed in operation unless at least 90 days prior thereto a written report, prepared for purposes of notification and information only and containing a full and complete description thereof, including the objectives of the experiment or demonstration project, the expected annual and total costs, and the dates on which the experiment or demonstration project is expected to start and finish, has been transmitted by the Commissioner to the Committee on Ways and Means of the House of Representatives and to the Committee on Finance of the Senate. Periodic reports on the progress of such experiments and demonstration projects shall be submitted by the Commissioner to such committees. When appropriate, such reports shall include detailed recommendations for changes in administration or law, or both, to carry out the objectives stated in subsection (a).

(d) Reports

(1) Interim reports

On or before September 30 of each year, the Commissioner shall submit to the Committee on Ways and Means of the House of Representatives and to the Committee on Finance of the Senate an annual interim report on the progress of the experiments and demonstration projects carried out under this subsection [1] together with any related data and materials that the Commissioner may consider appropriate.

(2) Termination and final report

The authority to initiate projects under the preceding provisions of this section shall terminate on December 31, 2021, and the authority to carry out such projects shall terminate on December 31, 2022. Not later than 90 days after the termination of any experiment or demonstration project carried out under this section, the Commissioner shall submit to the Committee on Ways and Means of the House of Representatives and to the Committee on Finance of the Senate a final report with respect to that experiment or demonstration project.

(e) Additional requirements

In developing and carrying out any experiment or demonstration project under this section, the Commissioner may not require any individual to participate in such experiment or demonstration project and shall ensure—

(1) that the voluntary participation of individuals in such experiment or demonstration project is obtained through informed written consent which satisfies the requirements for informed consent established by the Commissioner for use in such experiment or demonstration project in which human subjects are at risk;

(2) that any individual's voluntary agreement to participate in any such experiment or demonstration project may be revoked by such individual at any time; and

(3) that such experiment or demonstration project is expected to yield statistically significant results.

(f) Promoting opportunity demonstration project

(1) In general

The Commissioner shall carry out a demonstration project under this subsection as described in paragraph (2) during a 5-year period beginning not later than January 1, 2017.

(2) Benefit offset

Under the demonstration project described in this paragraph, with respect to any individual participating in the project who is otherwise entitled to a benefit under section 423(a)(1) of this title for a month—

(A) any such benefit otherwise payable to the individual for such month (other than a benefit payable for any month prior to the 1st month beginning after the date on which the individual's entitlement to such benefit is determined) shall be reduced by $1 for each $2 by which the individual's earnings derived from services paid during such month exceeds an amount equal to the individual's impairment-related work expenses for such month (as determined under paragraph (3)), except that such benefit may not be reduced below $0;

(B) no benefit shall be payable under section 402 of this title on the basis of the wages and self-employment income of the individual for any month for which the benefit of such individual under section 423(a)(1) of this title is reduced to $0 pursuant to subparagraph (A);

(C) entitlement to any benefit described in subparagraph (A) or (B) shall not terminate due to earnings derived from services except following the first month for which such benefit has been reduced to $0 pursuant to subparagraph (A) (and the trial work period (as defined in section 422(c) of this title) and extended period of eligibility shall not apply to any such individual for any such month); and

(D) in any case in which such an individual is entitled to hospital insurance benefits under part A of subchapter XVIII by reason of section 426(b) of this title and such individual's entitlement to a benefit described in subparagraph (A) or (B) or status as a qualified railroad retirement beneficiary is terminated pursuant to subparagraph (C), such individual shall be deemed to be entitled to such benefits or to occupy such status (notwithstanding the termination of such entitlement or status) for the period of consecutive months throughout all of which the physical or mental impairment, on which such entitlement or status was based, continues, and throughout all of which such individual would have been entitled to monthly insurance benefits under subchapter II or as a qualified railroad retirement beneficiary had such termination of entitlement or status not occurred, but not in excess of 93 such months.

(3) Impairment-related work expenses

(A) In general

For purposes of paragraph (2)(A) and except as provided in subparagraph (C), the amount of an individual's impairment-related work expenses for a month is deemed to be the minimum threshold amount.

(B) Minimum threshold amount

In this paragraph, the term "minimum threshold amount" means an amount, to be determined by the Commissioner, which shall not exceed the amount sufficient to demonstrate that an individual has rendered services in a month, as determined by the Commissioner under section 422(c)(4)(A) of this title. The Commissioner may test multiple minimum threshold amounts.

(C) Exception for itemized impairment-related work expenses

(i) In general

Notwithstanding subparagraph (A), in any case in which the amount of such an individual's itemized impairment-related work expenses (as defined in clause (ii)) for a month is greater than the minimum threshold amount, the amount of the individual's impairment-related work expenses for the month shall be equal to the amount of the individual's itemized impairment-related work expenses (as so defined) for the month.

(ii) Definition

In this subparagraph, the term "itemized impairment-related work expenses" means the amount excluded under section 423(d)(4)(A) of this title from an individual's earnings for a month in determining whether an individual is able to engage in substantial gainful activity by reason of such earnings in such month, except that such amount does not include the cost to the individual of any item or service for which the individual does not provide to the Commissioner a satisfactory itemized accounting.

(D) Limitation

Notwithstanding the other provisions of this paragraph, for purposes of paragraph (2)(A), the amount of an individual's impairment-related work expenses for a month shall not exceed the amount of earnings derived from services, prescribed by the Commissioner under regulations issued pursuant to section 423(d)(4)(A) of this title, sufficient to demonstrate an individual's ability to engage in substantial gainful activity.

(Aug. 14, 1935, c. 531, Title II, § 234, as added Pub.L. 106–170, Title III, § 301(a), Dec. 17, 1999, 113 Stat. 1900; amended Pub.L. 108–203, Title IV, § 401, Mar. 2, 2004, 118 Stat. 525; Pub.L. 114–74, Title VIII, §§ 821, 822, 823, Nov. 2, 2015, 129 Stat. 605.)

1 So in original. Probably should be "section".

HISTORICAL AND STATUTORY NOTES

References in Text

This subchapter, referred to in text, was in the original "this title", meaning Title II of the Social Security Act, Act Aug. 14, 1935, c. 531, Title II, 49 Stat. 622, as amended, which enacted this subchapter. For complete classification of this Act to the Code, see Tables.

Subchapter XVIII of this chapter, referred to in subsec. (c), originally read "title XVIII", meaning Title XVIII of the Social Security Act, Aug. 14, 1935, c. 531, Title XVIII, § 1801 et seq., as added and amended, which is principally classified to subchapter XVIII of this chapter, 42 U.S.C.A. § 1395 et seq.

Part A of subchapter XVIII of this chapter, referred to in subsec. (f)(2)(D), originally read "part A of title XVIII", meaning part A of Title XVIII of the Social Security Act, Aug. 14, 1935, c. 531, Title XVIII, § 1811 et seq., as added and amended, which is principally classified to part A of subchapter XVIII of this chapter, 42 U.S.C.A. § 1395c et seq.

Demonstration Projects Providing for Reductions in Disability Insurance Benefits Based on Earnings

Pub.L. 106–170, Title III, § 302, Dec. 17, 1999, 113 Stat. 1902, as amended Pub.L. 108–203, Title IV, §§ 402, 403, Mar. 2, 2004, 118 Stat. 525, provided that:

"(a) **Authority.**—The Commissioner of Social Security shall conduct demonstration projects for the purpose of evaluating, through the collection of data, a program for title II disability beneficiaries (as defined in section 1148(k)(3) of the Social Security Act [42 U.S.C.A. § 1320b–19(k)(3)]) under which benefits payable under section 223 of such Act [42 U.S.C.A. § 423], or under section 202 of such Act [42 U.S.C.A. § 402] based on the beneficiary's disability, are reduced by $1 for each $2 of the beneficiary's earnings that is above a level to be determined by the Commissioner. Such projects shall be conducted at a number of localities which the Commissioner shall determine is sufficient to adequately evaluate the appropriateness of national implementation of such a program. Such projects shall identify reductions in Federal expenditures that may result from the permanent implementation of such a program.

"(b) Scope and scale and matters to be determined.—

"(1) In general.—The demonstration projects developed under subsection (a) shall be of sufficient duration, shall be of sufficient scope, and shall be carried out on a wide enough scale to permit a thorough evaluation of the project to determine—

"(A) the effects, if any, of induced entry into the project and reduced exit from the project;

"(B) the extent, if any, to which the project being tested is affected by whether it is in operation in a locality within an area under the administration of the Ticket to Work and Self-Sufficiency Program established under section 1148 of the Social Security Act [42 U.S.C.A. § 1320b–19]; and

"(C) the savings that accrue to the Federal Old-Age and Survivors Insurance Trust Fund, the Federal Disability Insurance Trust Fund, and other Federal programs under the project being tested.

The Commissioner shall take into account advice provided by the Ticket to Work and Work Incentives Advisory Panel pursuant to section 101(f)(2)(B)(ii) of this Act [42 U.S.C.A. § 1320b–19 note].

"(2) Additional matters.—The Commissioner shall also determine with respect to each project—

"(A) the annual cost (including net cost) of the project and the annual cost (including net cost) that would have been incurred in the absence of the project;

"(B) the determinants of return to work, including the characteristics of the beneficiaries who participate in the project; and

"(C) the employment outcomes, including wages, occupations, benefits, and hours worked, of beneficiaries who return to work as a result of participation in the project.

The Commissioner may include within the matters evaluated under the project the merits of trial work periods and periods of extended eligibility.

"(c) Waivers.—The Commissioner may waive compliance with the benefit provisions of title II of the Social Security Act [this subchapter] (42 U.S.C. 401 et seq.) and the requirements of section 1148 of such Act (42 U.S.C. 1320b–19) as they relate to the program established under title II of such Act [this subchapter], and the Secretary of Health and Human Services may waive compliance with the benefit requirements of title XVIII of such Act [subchapter XVIII of this chapter] (42 U.S.C. 1395 et seq.), insofar as is necessary for a thorough evaluation of the alternative methods under consideration. No such project shall be actually placed in operation unless at least 90 days prior thereto a written report, prepared for purposes of notification and information only and containing a full and complete description thereof, has been transmitted by the Commissioner to the Committee on Ways and Means of the House of Representatives and to the Committee on Finance of the Senate. Periodic reports on the progress of such projects shall be submitted by the Commissioner to such committees. When appropriate, such reports shall include detailed recommendations for changes in administration or law, or both, to carry out the objectives stated in subsection (a) [of this note].

"(d) Interim reports.—Not later than 2 years after the date of the enactment of this Act [Dec. 17, 1999], and annually thereafter, the Commissioner of Social Security shall submit to the Congress an interim report on the progress of the demonstration projects carried out under this subsection together with any related data and materials that the Commissioner of Social Security may consider appropriate.

"(e) Final report.—The Commissioner of Social Security shall submit to the Congress a final report with respect to all demonstration projects carried out under this section not later than 1 year after their completion.

"(f) Expenditures.—Administrative expenses for demonstration projects under this section shall be paid from funds available for the administration of title II or XVIII of the Social Security Act [this subchapter or subchapter XVIII of this chapter, 42 U.S.C.A. § 1395 et seq.], as appropriate. Benefits payable to or on behalf of individuals by reason of participation in projects under this section [this note] shall be made from the Federal Disability Insurance Trust Fund and the Federal Old-Age and Survivors Insurance Trust Fund, as determined appropriate by the Commissioner of Social Security, and from the Federal Hospital Insurance Trust Fund and the Federal Supplementary Medical Insurance Trust Fund, as determined appropriate by the Secretary of Health and Human Services, from funds available for benefits under such title II or XVIII [this subchapter or subchapter XVIII of this chapter, 42 U.S.C.A. § 1395 et seq.]."

Study by General Accounting Office [now Government Accountability Office] of the Impact of the Substantial Gainful Activity Limit on Return to Work

Pub.L. 106–170, Title III, § 303(c), Dec. 17, 1999, 113 Stat. 1904, provided that:

"(1) Study.—As soon as practicable after the date of the enactment of this Act [Dec. 17, 1999], the Comptroller General of the United States shall undertake a study of the substantial gainful activity level applicable as of that date to recipients of benefits under section 223 of the Social Security Act (42 U.S.C. 423) and under section 202 of such Act (42 U.S.C. 402) on the basis of a recipient having a disability, and the effect of such level as a disincentive for those recipients to return to work. In the study, the Comptroller General also shall address the merits of increasing the substantial gainful activity level applicable to such recipients of benefits and the rationale for not yearly indexing that level to inflation.

"(2) Report.—Not later than 2 years after the date of the enactment of this Act [Dec. 17, 1999], the Comptroller General shall transmit to the Committee on Ways and Means of the House of Representatives and the Committee on Finance of the Senate a written report presenting the results of the Comptroller General's study conducted pursuant to this subsection, together with such recommendations for legislative or administrative changes as the Comptroller General determines are appropriate."

Study by the General Accounting Office [now Government Accountability Office] of Social Security Administration's Disability Insurance Program Demonstration Authority

Pub.L. 106–170, Title III, § 303(e), Dec. 17, 1999, 113 Stat. 1905, provided that:

"(1) Study.—As soon as practicable after the date of the enactment of this Act [Dec. 17, 1999], the Comptroller General of the United States shall undertake a study to assess the results of the Social Security Administration's efforts to conduct disability demonstrations authorized under prior law as well as under section 234 of the Social Security Act [this section] (as added by section 301 of this Act).

"(2) **Report.**—Not later than 5 years after the date of the enactment of this Act [Dec. 17, 1999], the Comptroller General shall transmit to the Committee on Ways and Means of the House of Representatives and the Committee on Finance of the Senate a written report presenting the results of the Comptroller General's study conducted pursuant to this section, together with a recommendation as to whether the demonstration authority authorized under section 234 of the Social Security Act [this section] (as added by section 301 of this Act) should be made permanent."

SUBCHAPTER XVI—SUPPLEMENTAL SECURITY INCOME FOR AGED, BLIND, AND DISABLED

§ 1381. Statement of purpose; authorization of appropriations

For the purpose of establishing a national program to provide supplemental security income to individuals who have attained age 65 or are blind or disabled, there are authorized to be appropriated sums sufficient to carry out this subchapter.

(Aug. 14, 1935, c. 531, Title XVI, § 1601, as added Pub.L. 92–603, Title III, § 301, Oct. 30, 1972, 86 Stat. 1465.)

HISTORICAL AND STATUTORY NOTES

Effective and Applicability Provisions

1972 Acts. Section 301 of Pub.L. 92–603 provided that this section is effective Jan. 1, 1974.

Prior Provisions

A prior section 1381, Act Aug. 14, 1935, c. 531, Title XVI, § 1601, as added July 25, 1962, Pub.L. 87–543, Title I, § 141(a), 76 Stat. 197, authorized appropriations for grants to States for aid to the aged, blind, or disabled, and for medical assistance for the aged, prior to the general amendment of Title XVI of the Social Security Act by Pub.L. 92–603, § 301, but is set out as a note under this section in view of its continued applicability to Puerto Rico, Guam, and the Virgin Islands.

Continuation of Federal Financial Participation in Experimental, Pilot, or Demonstration Projects Approved Before October 1973, for Period On-and-After December 31, 1973, Without Denial or Reduction on Account of Subchapter XVI Provisions; Waiver of Subchapter XVI Restrictions for Individuals; Federal Payments of Non-Federal Share as Supplementary Payments

Subchapter provisions without effect on Federal Financial Participation in Experimental, Pilot, or Demonstration Projects approved before Oct. 1, 1973, for period on-and-after Dec. 31, 1973, see section 11 of Pub.L. 93–233, Dec. 31, 1973, 87 Stat. 958, set out as a note under section 1315 of this title.

Northern Mariana Islands

For applicability of this section to the Northern Mariana Islands, see section 502(a)(1) of the Covenant to Establish a Commonwealth of the Northern Mariana Islands in Political Union with the United States of America, as set forth in Pub.L. 94–241, Mar. 24, 1976, 90 Stat. 263, eff. Jan. 9, 1978, pursuant to Proc. No. 4534, Oct. 24, 1977, 42 F.R. 6593, set out as notes under section 1681 of Title 48, Territories and Insular Possessions.

Payments Under Chapter Provisions in Effect Before January 1, 1974, for: Activities Carried Out Through December 31, 1973, Under State Plans Approved Under Subchapter I, X, XIV, or XVI Provisions; and for Administrative Activities After January 1, 1974, Closing Out Such Activities

Pub.L. 93–233, § 19(b), Dec. 31, 1973, 87 Stat. 974, provided that: "Notwithstanding the provisions of section 301 of the Social Security Amendments of 1972 [enacting this subchapter], the Secretary of Health, Education, and Welfare [now Secretary of Health and Human Services] shall make payments to the 50 States and the District of Columbia after December 31, 1973, in accordance with the provisions of the Social Security Act [this chapter] as in effect prior to January 1, 1974, for (1) activities carried out through the close of December 31, 1973, under State plans approved under title [subchapter] I, X, XIV, or XVI, of such Act [this chapter], and (2) administrative activities carried out after December 31, 1973, which such Secretary determines are necessary to bring to a close activities carried out under such State plans."

Puerto Rico, Guam, and Virgin Islands

Enactment of section 1601 of the Social Security Act [this section] by Pub.L. 92–603, eff. Jan. 1, 1974, was not applicable to Puerto Rico, Guam, and the Virgin Islands. See section 303(b) of Pub.L. 92–603 set out as a note under section 301 of this title. Therefore, as to Puerto Rico, Guam, and the Virgin Islands, section 1601 of the Social Security Act [this section] as it existed prior to reenactment by Pub.L. 92–603, and as amended, continues to apply and reads as follows:

§ 1381. Authorization of appropriations

For the purpose of enabling each State, as far as practicable under the conditions in such State, to furnish financial assistance to needy individuals who are 65 years of age or over, are blind, or are 18 years of age or over and permanently and totally disabled, there is hereby authorized to be appropriated for each fiscal year a sum sufficient to carry out the purposes of this subchapter. The sums made available under this section shall be used for making payments to States which have submitted, and had approved, by the Commissioner of Social Security, State plans for aid to the aged, blind, or disabled.

(Aug. 14, 1935, c. 531, Title XVI, § 1601, as added July 25, 1962, Pub.L. 87–543, Title I, § 141(a), 76 Stat. 197, and amended Oct. 17, 1979, Pub.L. 96–88, Title V, § 509(b), 93 Stat. 695; Aug. 13, 1981, Pub.L. 97–35, Title XXI, § 2184(d)(3), Title XXIII, § 2353(m)(1), 95 Stat. 817, 873; Aug. 15, 1994, Pub.L. 103–296, Title I, § 107(a), 108 Stat. 1477.)

§ 1381a. Basic entitlement to benefits

Every aged, blind, or disabled individual who is determined under part A to be eligible on the basis of his income and resources shall, in accordance with and subject to the provisions of this subchapter, be paid benefits by the Commissioner of Social Security.

(Aug. 14, 1935, c. 531, Title XVI, § 1602, as added Pub.L. 92–603, Title III, § 301, Oct. 30, 1972, 86 Stat. 1465; amended Pub.L. 98–369, Div. B, Title VI, § 2663(j)(2)(E), July 18, 1984, 98 Stat. 1170; Pub.L. 103–296, Title I, § 107(a)(1), Aug. 15, 1994, 108 Stat. 1478.)

HISTORICAL AND STATUTORY NOTES

Effective and Applicability Provisions

1994 Acts. Amendment by section 107(a)(1) of Pub.L. 103–296 effective Mar. 31, 1995, see section 110 of Pub.L. 103–296, set out as a note under section 401 of this title.

1984 Acts. Amendment by Pub.L. 98–369, effective July 18, 1984, but not to be construed as changing or affecting any right, liability, status or interpretation which existed (under the provisions of law involved) before that date, see section

2664(b) of Pub.L. 98–369, set out as a note under section 401 of this title.

1972 Acts. Section 301 of Pub.L. 92–603 provided that this section is effective Jan. 1, 1974.

Prior Provisions

A prior section 1602 of Act Aug. 14, 1935, c. 531, Title XVI, as added July 25, 1962, Pub.L. 87–543, Title I, § 141(a), 76 Stat. 198, and amended Oct. 13, 1964, Pub.L. 88–650, § 5(b), 78 Stat. 1078; July 30, 1965, Pub.L. 89–97, Title II, § 221(d)(3), Title IV, § 403(e), 79 Stat. 358, 418; Jan. 2, 1968, Pub.L. 90–248, Title II, §§ 210(a)(5), 213(a)(4), 241(d), 81 Stat. 896, 898, 917, formerly classified to section 1382 of this title, set forth the required contents of State plans for aid to the aged, blind, or disabled, and for medical assistance for the aged, prior to the general amendment of Title XVI of the Social Security Act by Pub.L. 92–603, § 301.

Northern Mariana Islands

For applicability of this section to the Northern Mariana Islands, see section 502(a)(1) of the Covenant to Establish a Commonwealth of the Northern Mariana Islands in Political Union with the United States of America, as set forth in Pub.L. 94–241, Mar. 24, 1976, 90 Stat. 263, eff. Jan. 9, 1978, pursuant to Proc. No. 4534, Oct. 24, 1977, 42 F.R. 6593 set out as notes under section 1681 of Title 48, Territories and Insular Possessions.

Puerto Rico, Guam, and Virgin Islands

Enactment of provisions of Pub.L. 92–603, eff. Jan. 1, 1974, not applicable to Puerto Rico, Guam, and the Virgin Islands, see section 303(b) of Pub.L. 92–603, set out as a note under section 301 of this title.

PART A—DETERMINATION OF BENEFITS

§ 1382. Eligibility for benefits

(a) "Eligible individual" defined

(1) Each aged, blind, or disabled individual who does not have an eligible spouse and—

(A) whose income, other than income excluded pursuant to section 1382a(b) of this title, is at a rate of not more than $1,752 (or, if greater, the amount determined under section 1382f of this title) for the calendar year 1974 or any calendar year thereafter, and

(B) whose resources, other than resources excluded pursuant to section 1382b(a) of this title, are not more than (i) in case such individual has a spouse with whom he is living, the applicable amount determined under paragraph (3)(A), or (ii) in case such individual has no spouse with whom he is living, the applicable amount determined under paragraph (3)(B),

shall be an eligible individual for purposes of this subchapter.

(2) Each aged, blind, or disabled individual who has an eligible spouse and—

(A) whose income (together with the income of such spouse), other than income excluded pursuant to section 1382a(b) of this title, is at a rate of not more than $2,628 (or, if greater, the amount determined under section 1382f of this title) for the calendar year 1974, or any calendar year thereafter, and

(B) whose resources (together with the resources of such spouse), other than resources excluded pursuant to section 1382b(a) of this title, are not more than the applicable amount determined under paragraph (3)(A),

shall be an eligible individual for purposes of this subchapter.

(3)(A) The dollar amount referred to in clause (i) of paragraph (1)(B), and in paragraph (2)(B), shall be $2,250 prior to January 1, 1985, and shall be increased to $2,400 on January 1, 1985, to $2,550 on January 1, 1986, to $2,700 on January 1, 1987, to $2,850 on January 1, 1988, and to $3,000 on January 1, 1989.

(B) The dollar amount referred to in clause (ii) of paragraph (1)(B), shall be $1,500 prior to January 1, 1985, and shall be increased to $1,600 on January 1, 1985, to $1,700 on January 1, 1986, to $1,800 on January 1, 1987, to $1,900 on January 1, 1988, and to $2,000 on January 1, 1989.

(b) Amount of benefits

(1) The benefit under this subchapter for an individual who does not have an eligible spouse shall be payable at the rate of $1,752 (or, if greater, the amount determined under section 1382f of this title) for the calendar year 1974 and any calendar year thereafter, reduced by the amount of income, not excluded pursuant to section 1382a(b) of this title, of such individual.

(2) The benefit under this subchapter for an individual who has an eligible spouse shall be payable at the rate of $2,628 (or, if greater, the amount determined under section 1382f of this title) for the calendar year 1974 and any calendar year thereafter, reduced by the amount of income, not excluded pursuant to section 1382a(b) of this title, of such individual and spouse.

(c) Period for determination of benefits

(1) An individual's eligibility for a benefit under this subchapter for a month shall be determined on the basis of the individual's (and eligible spouse's, if any) income, resources, and other relevant characteristics in such month, and, except as provided in paragraphs (2), (3), (4), (5), and (6), the amount of such benefit shall be determined for such month on the basis of income and other characteristics in the first or, if the Commissioner of Social Security so determines, second month preceding such month. Eligibility for and the amount of such benefits shall be redetermined at such time or times as may be provided by the Commissioner of Social Security.

(2) The amount of such benefit for the month in which an application for benefits becomes effective (or, if the Commissioner of Social Security so determines, for such month and the following month) and for any

month immediately following a month of ineligibility for such benefits (or, if the Commissioner of Social Security so determines, for such month and the following month) shall—

(A) be determined on the basis of the income of the individual and the eligible spouse, if any, of such individual and other relevant circumstances in such month; and

(B) in the case of the first month following a period of ineligibility in which eligibility is restored after the first day of such month, bear the same ratio to the amount of the benefit which would have been payable to such individual if eligibility had been restored on the first day of such month as the number of days in such month including and following the date of restoration of eligibility bears to the total number of days in such month.

(3) For purposes of this subsection, an increase in the benefit amount payable under subchapter II (over the amount payable in the preceding month, or, at the election of the Commissioner of Social Security, the second preceding month) to an individual receiving benefits under this subchapter shall be included in the income used to determine the benefit under this subchapter of such individual for any month which is—

(A) the first month in which the benefit amount payable to such individual under this title is increased pursuant to section 1382f of this title, or

(B) at the election of the Commissioner of Social Security, the month immediately following such month.

(4)(A) Notwithstanding paragraph (3), if the Commissioner of Social Security determines that reliable information is currently available with respect to the income and other circumstances of an individual for a month (including information with respect to a class of which such individual is a member and information with respect to scheduled cost-of-living adjustments under other benefit programs), the benefit amount of such individual under this subchapter for such month may be determined on the basis of such information.

(B) The Commissioner of Social Security shall prescribe by regulation the circumstances in which information with respect to an event may be taken into account pursuant to subparagraph (A) in determining benefit amounts under this subchapter.

(5) Notwithstanding paragraphs (1) and (2), any income which is paid to or on behalf of an individual in any month pursuant to (A) a State program funded under part A of subchapter IV, (B) section 672 of this title (relating to foster care assistance), (C) section 1522(e) of Title 8 (relating to assistance for refugees), (D) section 501(a) of Public Law 96–422 (relating to assistance for Cuban and Haitian entrants), or (E) section 13 of Title 25 (relating to assistance furnished by the Bureau of Indian Affairs), shall be taken into account in determining the amount of the benefit under this subchapter of such individual (and his eligible spouse, if any) only for that month, and shall not be taken into account in determining the amount of the benefit for any other month.

(6) The dollar amount in effect under subsection (b) as a result of any increase in benefits under this subchapter by reason of section 1382f of this title shall be used to determine the value of any in-kind support and maintenance required to be taken into account in determining the benefit payable under this subchapter to an individual (and the eligible spouse, if any, of the individual) for the 1st 2 months for which the increase in benefits applies.

(7) For purposes of this subsection, an application of an individual for benefits under this subchapter shall be effective on the later of—

(A) the first day of the month following the date such application is filed, or

(B) the first day of the month following the date such individual becomes eligible for such benefits with respect to such application.

(8) The Commissioner of Social Security may waive the limitations specified in subparagraphs (A) and (B) of subsection (e)(1) on an individual's eligibility and benefit amount for a month (to the extent either such limitation is applicable by reason of such individual's presence throughout such month in a hospital, extended care facility, nursing home, or intermediate care facility) if such waiver would promote the individual's removal from such institution or facility. Upon waiver of such limitations, the Commissioner of Social Security shall apply, to the month preceding the month of removal, or, if the Commissioner of Social Security so determines, the two months preceding the month of removal, the benefit rate that is appropriate to such individual's living arrangement subsequent to his removal from such institution or facility.

(9)(A) Notwithstanding paragraphs (1) and (2), any nonrecurring income which is paid to an individual in the first month of any period of eligibility shall be taken into account in determining the amount of the benefit under this subchapter of such individual (and his eligible spouse, if any) only for that month, and shall not be taken into account in determining the amount of the benefit for any other month.

(B) For purposes of subparagraph (A), payments to an individual in varying amounts from the same or similar source for the same or similar purpose shall not be considered to be nonrecurring income.

(10) For purposes of this subsection, remuneration for service performed as a member of a uniformed service may be treated as received in the month in which it was earned, if the Commissioner of Social Security determines that such treatment would promote the economical and efficient administration of the program authorized by this subchapter.

(d) Limitation on amount of gross income earned; "gross income" defined

The Commissioner of Social Security may prescribe the circumstances under which, consistently with the purposes of this subchapter, the gross income from a trade or business (including farming) will be considered sufficiently large to make an individual ineligible for benefits under this subchapter. For purposes of this subsection, the term "gross income" has the same meaning as when used in chapter 1 of the Internal Revenue Code of 1986.

(e) Limitation on eligibility of certain individuals

(1)(A) Except as provided in subparagraphs (B), (C), (D), (E), and (G), no person shall be an eligible individual or eligible spouse for purposes of this subchapter with respect to any month if throughout such month he is an inmate of a public institution.

(B) In any case where an eligible individual or his eligible spouse (if any) is, throughout any month (subject to subparagraph (G)), in a medical treatment facility receiving payments (with respect to such individual or spouse) under a State plan approved under subchapter XIX, or an eligible individual is a child described in section 1382c(f)(2)(B) of this title, or, in the case of an eligible individual who is a child under the age of 18, receiving payments (with respect to such individual) under any health insurance policy issued by a private provider of such insurance the benefit under this subchapter for such individual for such month shall be payable (subject to subparagraph (E))—

(i) at a rate not in excess of $360 per year (reduced by the amount of any income not excluded pursuant to section 1382a(b) of this title) in the case of an individual who does not have an eligible spouse;

(ii) in the case of an individual who has an eligible spouse, if only one of them is in such a facility throughout such month, at a rate not in excess of the sum of—

(I) the rate of $360 per year (reduced by the amount of any income, not excluded pursuant to section 1382a(b) of this title, of the one who is in such facility), and

(II) the applicable rate specified in subsection (b)(1) (reduced by the amount of any income, not excluded pursuant to section 1382a(b) of this title, of the other); and

(iii) at a rate not in excess of $720 per year (reduced by the amount of any income not excluded pursuant to section 1382a(b) of this title) in the case of an individual who has an eligible spouse, if both of them are in such a facility throughout such month.

For purposes of this subsection, a medical treatment facility that provides services described in section 1396p(c)(1)(C) of this title shall be considered to be receiving payments with respect to an individual under a State plan approved under subchapter XIX during any period of ineligibility of such individual provided for under the State plan pursuant to section 1396p(c) of this title.

(C) As used in subparagraph (A), the term "public institution" does not include a publicly operated community residence which serves no more than 16 residents.

(D) A person may be an eligible individual or eligible spouse for purposes of this subchapter with respect to any month throughout which he is a resident of a public emergency shelter for the homeless (as defined in regulations which shall be prescribed by the Commissioner of Social Security); except that no person shall be an eligible individual or eligible spouse by reason of this subparagraph more than 6 months in any 9–month period.

(E) Notwithstanding subparagraphs (A) and (B), any individual who—

(i)(I) is an inmate of a public institution, the primary purpose of which is the provision of medical or psychiatric care, throughout any month as described in subparagraph (A), or

(II) is in a medical treatment facility throughout any month as described in subparagraph (B),

(ii) was eligible under section 1382h(a) or (b) of this title for the month preceding such month, and

(iii) under an agreement of the public institution or the medical treatment facility is permitted to retain any benefit payable by reason of this subparagraph,

may be an eligible individual or eligible spouse for purposes of this subchapter (and entitled to a benefit determined on the basis of the rate applicable under subsection (b)) for the month referred to in subclause (I) or (II) of clause (i) and, if such subclause still applies, for the succeeding month.

(F) An individual who is an eligible individual or an eligible spouse for a month by reason of subparagraph (E) shall not be treated as being eligible under section 1382h(a) or (b) of this title for such month for purposes of clause (ii) of such subparagraph.

(G) A person may be an eligible individual or eligible spouse for purposes of this subchapter, and subparagraphs (A) and (B) shall not apply, with respect to any particular month throughout which he or she is an inmate of a public institution the primary purpose of which is the provision of medical or psychiatric care, or is in a medical treatment facility receiving payments (with respect to such individual or spouse) under a State plan approved under subchapter XIX or, in the case of an individual who is a child under the age of 18, under any health insurance policy issued by a private provider of such insurance, if it is determined in accordance with subparagraph (H) or (J) that—

(i) such person's stay in that institution or facility (or in that institution or facility and one or more other such institutions or facilities during a continuous period of institutionalization) is likely (as certified by a physician) not to exceed 3 months, and the particular month involved is one of the first 3 months throughout which such person is in such an institution or facility during a continuous period of institutionalization; and

(ii) such person needs to continue to maintain and provide for the expenses of the home or living arrangement to which he or she may return upon leaving the institution or facility.

The benefit of any person under this subchapter (including State supplementation if any) for each month to which this subparagraph applies shall be payable, without interruption of benefit payments and on the date the benefit involved is regularly due, at the rate that was applicable to such person in the month prior to the first month throughout which he or she is in the institution or facility.

(H) The Commissioner of Social Security shall establish procedures for the determinations required by clauses (i) and (ii) of subparagraph (G), and may enter into agreements for making such determinations (or for providing information or assistance in connection with the making of such determinations) with appropriate State and local public and private agencies and organizations. Such procedures and agreements shall include the provision of appropriate assistance to individuals who, because of their physical or mental condition, are limited in their ability to furnish the information needed in connection with the making of such determinations.

(I)(i) The Commissioner shall enter into an agreement, with any interested State or local institution comprising a jail, prison, penal institution, or correctional facility, or with any other interested State or local institution a purpose of which is to confine individuals as described in section 402(x)(1)(A)(ii) of this title, under which—

(I) the institution shall provide to the Commissioner, on a monthly basis and in a manner specified by the Commissioner, the first, middle, and last names, social security account numbers or taxpayer identification numbers, prison assigned inmate numbers, last known addresses, dates of birth, confinement commencement dates, dates of release or anticipated dates of release, dates of work release, and, to the extent available to the institution, such other identifying information concerning the inmates of the institution as the Commissioner may require for the purpose of carrying out this paragraph and clause (iv)[1] of this subparagraph and the other provisions of this subchapter; and

(II) the Commissioner shall pay to any such institution, with respect to each individual who receives in the month preceding the first month throughout which such individual is an inmate of the jail, prison, penal institution, or correctional facility that furnishes information respecting such individual pursuant to subclause (I), or is confined in the institution (that so furnishes such information) as described in section 402(x)(1)(A)(ii) of this title, a benefit under this subchapter for such preceding month, and who is determined by the Commissioner to be ineligible for benefits under this subchapter by reason of confinement based on the information provided by such institution, $400 (subject to reduction under clause (ii)) if the institution furnishes the information described in subclause (I) to the Commissioner within 15 days after the date such individual becomes an inmate of such institution, or $200 (subject to reduction under clause (ii)) if the institution furnishes such information after 15 days after such date but within 90 days after such date.

(ii) The dollar amounts specified in clause (i)(II) shall be reduced by 50 percent if the Commissioner is also required to make a payment to the institution with respect to the same individual under an agreement entered into under section 402(x)(3)(B) of this title.

(iii) The Commissioner shall maintain, and shall provide on a reimbursable basis, information obtained pursuant to agreements entered into under clause (i) to any Federal or federally-assisted cash, food, or medical assistance program for eligibility and other administrative purposes under such program, for statistical and research activities conducted by Federal and State agencies, and to the Secretary of the Treasury for the purposes of tax administration, debt collection, and identifying, preventing, and recovering improper payments under federally funded programs.

(iv) Payments to institutions required by clause (i)(II) shall be made from funds otherwise available for the payment of benefits under this subchapter and shall be treated as direct spending for purposes of the Balanced Budget and Emergency Deficit Control Act of 1985.

(v)(I) The Commissioner may disclose information received pursuant to this paragraph to any officer, employee, agent, or contractor of the Department of the Treasury whose official duties require such information to assist in the identification, prevention, and recovery of improper payments or in the collection of delinquent debts owed to the United States, including payments certified by the head of an executive, judicial, or legislative paying agency, and payments made to individuals whose eligibility, or continuing eligibility, to participate in a Federal program (including those administered by a State or political subdivision thereof) is being reviewed.

(II) Notwithstanding the provisions of section 552a of Title 5 or any other provision of Federal or State law, the Secretary of the Treasury may compare information disclosed under subclause (I) with any other personally identifiable information derived from a Federal system of records or similar records maintained by a Federal contractor, a Federal grantee, or an entity administering a Federal program or activity and may redisclose such comparison of information to any paying or administering agency and to the head of the Federal Bureau of Prisons and the head of any State agency charged with the administration of prisons with respect to inmates whom the Secretary of the Treasury has determined may have been issued, or facilitated in the issuance of, an improper payment.

(III) The comparison of information disclosed under subclause (I) shall not be considered a matching program for purposes of section 552a of Title 5.

(J) For the purpose of carrying out this paragraph, the Commissioner of Social Security shall conduct periodic computer matches with data maintained by the Secretary of Health and Human Services under subchapter XVIII or XIX. The Secretary shall furnish to the Commissioner, in such form and manner and under such terms as the Commissioner and the Secretary shall mutually agree, such information as the Commissioner may request for this purpose. Information obtained pursuant to such a match may be substituted for the physician's certification otherwise required under subparagraph (G)(i).

(2) No person shall be an eligible individual or eligible spouse for purposes of this subchapter if, after notice to such person by the Commissioner of Social Security that it is likely that such person is eligible for any payments of the type enumerated in section 1382a(a)(2)(B) of this title, such person fails within 30 days to take all appropriate steps to apply for and (if eligible) obtain any such payments.

(3) Notwithstanding anything to the contrary in the criteria being used by the Commissioner of Social Security in determining when a husband and wife are to be considered two eligible individuals for purposes of this subchapter and when they are to be considered an eligible individual with an eligible spouse, the State agency administering or supervising the administration of a State plan under any other program under this chapter may (in the administration of such plan) treat a husband and wife living in the same medical treatment facility described in paragraph (1)(B) as though they were an eligible individual with his or her eligible spouse for purposes of this subchapter (rather than two eligible individuals), after they have continuously lived in the same such facility for 6 months, if treating such husband and wife as two eligible individuals would prevent either of them from receiving benefits or assistance under such plan or reduce the amount thereof.

(4)(A) No person shall be considered an eligible individual or eligible spouse for purposes of this subchapter with respect to any month if during such month the person is—

(i) fleeing to avoid prosecution, or custody or confinement after conviction, under the laws of the place from which the person flees, for a crime, or an attempt to commit a crime, which is a felony under the laws of the place from which the person flees, or, in jurisdictions that do not define crimes as felonies, is punishable by death or imprisonment for a term exceeding 1 year regardless of the actual sentence imposed; or

(ii) violating a condition of probation or parole imposed under Federal or State law.

(B) Notwithstanding subparagraph (A), the Commissioner shall, for good cause shown, treat the person referred to in subparagraph (A) as an eligible individual or eligible spouse if the Commissioner determines that—

(i) a court of competent jurisdiction has found the person not guilty of the criminal offense, dismissed the charges relating to the criminal offense, vacated the warrant for arrest of the person for the criminal offense, or issued any similar exonerating order (or taken similar exonerating action), or

(ii) the person was erroneously implicated in connection with the criminal offense by reason of identity fraud.

(C) Notwithstanding subparagraph (A), the Commissioner may, for good cause shown based on mitigating circumstances, treat the person referred to in subparagraph (A) as an eligible individual or eligible spouse if the Commissioner determines that—

(i) the offense described in subparagraph (A)(i) or underlying the imposition of the probation or parole described in subparagraph (A)(ii) was nonviolent and not drug-related, and

(ii) in the case of a person who is not considered an eligible individual or eligible spouse pursuant to subparagraph (A)(ii), the action that resulted in the violation of a condition of probation or parole was nonviolent and not drug-related.

(5) Notwithstanding any other provision of law (other than section 6103 of the Internal Revenue Code of 1986 and section 1306(c) of this title), the Commissioner shall furnish any Federal, State, or local law enforcement officer, upon the written request of the officer, with the current address, Social Security number, and photograph (if applicable) of any recipient of benefits under this subchapter, if the officer furnishes the Commissioner with the name of the recipient, and other identifying information as reasonably required by the Commissioner to establish the unique identity of the recipient, and notifies the Commissioner that—

(A) the recipient is described in clause (i) or (ii) of paragraph (4)(A); and

(B) the location or apprehension of the recipient is within the officer's official duties.

(f) Individuals outside United States; determination of status

(1) Notwithstanding any other provision of this subchapter, no individual (other than a child described in section 1382c(a)(1)(B)(ii) of this title) shall be considered an eligible individual for purposes of this subchapter for any month during all of which such individual is outside the United States (and no person shall be considered the eligible spouse of an individual for purposes of this subchapter with respect to any month during all of which such person is outside the United States). For purposes of the preceding sentence, after an individual has been outside the United States for any period of 30 consecutive days, he shall be treated as remaining outside the United States until he has been in the United States for a period of 30 consecutive days.

(2) For a period of not more than 1 year, the first sentence of paragraph (1) shall not apply to any individual who—

(A) was eligible to receive a benefit under this subchapter for the month immediately preceding the first month during all of which the individual was outside the United States; and

(B) demonstrates to the satisfaction of the Commissioner of Social Security that the absence of the individual from the United States will be—

(i) for not more than 1 year; and

(ii) for the purpose of conducting studies as part of an educational program that is—

(I) designed to substantially enhance the ability of the individual to engage in gainful employment;

(II) sponsored by a school, college, or university in the United States; and

(III) not available to the individual in the United States.

(g) Individuals deemed to meet resources test

In the case of any individual or any individual and his spouse (as the case may be) who—

(1) received aid or assistance for December 1973 under a plan of a State approved under subchapter I, X, XIV, or XVI,

(2) has, since December 31, 1973, continuously resided in the State under the plan of which he or they received such aid or assistance for December 1973, and

(3) has, since December 31, 1973, continuously been (except for periods not in excess of six consecutive months) an eligible individual or eligible spouse with respect to whom supplemental security income benefits are payable,

the resources of such individual or such individual and his spouse (as the case may be) shall be deemed not to exceed the amount specified in subsections (a)(1)(B) and (a)(2)(B) during any period that the resources of such individual or such individual and his spouse (as the case may be) does not exceed the maximum amount of resources specified in the State plan, as in effect for October 1972, under which he or they received such aid or assistance for December 1973.

(h) Individuals deemed to meet income test

In determining eligibility for, and the amount of, benefits payable under this section in the case of any individual or any individual and his spouse (as the case may be) who—

(1) received aid or assistance for December 1973 under a plan of a State approved under subchapter X or XVI,

(2) is blind under the definition of that term in the plan, as in effect for October 1972, under which he or they received such aid or assistance for December 1973,

(3) has, since December 31, 1973, continuously resided in the State under the plan of which he or they received such aid or assistance for December 1973, and

(4) has, since December 31, 1973, continuously been (except for periods not in excess of six consecutive months) an eligible individual or an eligible spouse with respect to whom supplemental security income benefits are payable,

there shall be disregarded an amount equal to the greater of (A) the maximum amount of any earned or unearned income which could have been disregarded under the State plan, as in effect for October 1972, under which he or they received such aid or assistance for December 1973, and (B) the amount which would be required to be disregarded under section 1382a of this title without application of this subsection.

(i) Application and review requirements for certain individuals

For application and review requirements affecting the eligibility of certain individuals, see section 1383(j) of this title.

(Aug. 14, 1935, c. 531, Title XVI, § 1611, as added Pub.L. 92–603, Title III, § 301, Oct. 30, 1972, 86 Stat. 1466; amended Pub.L. 93–66, Title II, § 210(a), (b), July 9, 1973, 87 Stat. 154; Pub.L. 93–233, §§ 4(b)(1), (2), 18(d), (e), Dec. 31, 1973, 87 Stat. 953, 968; Pub.L. 93–368, § 6(a), Aug. 7, 1974, 88 Stat. 421; Pub.L. 94–566, Title V, §§ 502, 505(a), Oct. 20, 1976, 90 Stat. 2685, 2686; Pub.L. 96–265, Title III, § 303(c)(2), June 9, 1980, 94 Stat. 453; Pub.L. 97–35, Title XXIII, § 2341(a), Aug. 13, 1981, 95 Stat. 865; Pub.L. 97–248, Title I, §§ 181(a), 183(a), Sept. 3, 1982, 96 Stat. 404, 405; Pub.L. 98–21, Title IV, § 403(a), Apr. 20, 1983, 97 Stat. 140; Pub.L. 98–369, Div. B,

Title VI, §§ 2611(a) to (c), 2663(g)(1), (2), July 18, 1984, 98 Stat. 1130, 1168; Pub.L. 99–514, § 2, Oct. 22, 1986, 100 Stat. 2095; Pub.L. 99–643, §§ 3(a), 4(c)(3), (d)(1), 9(a), Nov. 10, 1986, 100 Stat. 3574, 3577, 3579; Pub.L. 100–203, Title IX, §§ 9106(a), 9107, 9113(a), 9115(a), 9119(a), Dec. 22, 1987, 101 Stat. 1330–301, 1330–302, 1330–304, 1330–305, 1330–308; Pub.L. 100–360, Title III, § 303(c)(2), July 1, 1988, 102 Stat. 762; Pub.L. 101–239, Title VIII, §§ 8009(a), 8010(b), Dec. 19, 1989, 103 Stat. 2463, 2464; Pub.L. 103–66, Title XIII, § 13735(a), Aug. 10, 1993, 107 Stat. 662; Pub.L. 103–296, Title I, § 107(a)(4), Title II, §§ 201(b)(3)(A), (B)(i), 204(a), Aug. 15, 1994, 108 Stat. 1478, 1502, 1504, 1508; Pub.L. 104–121, Title I, § 105(b)(4)(A), Mar. 29, 1996, 110 Stat. 854; Pub.L. 104–193, Title I, § 108(j), Title II, §§ 201(a), 202(a), (b), 203(a)(1), 204(a), 214(a), Aug. 22, 1996, 110 Stat. 2169, 2185 to 2187, 2195; Pub.L. 105–33, Title V, §§ 5521, 5522(c), Aug. 5, 1997, 111 Stat. 621, 623; Pub.L. 106–169, Title II, §§ 204, 207(c), 212, Dec. 14, 1999, 113 Stat. 1833, 1838, 1843; Pub.L. 106–170, Title IV, § 402(a)(3), (c)(1) to (3), Dec. 17, 1999, 113 Stat. 1908; Pub.L. 108–203, Title II, § 203(b), Title IV, §§ 433(a), (b), 436(a), Mar. 2, 2004, 118 Stat. 510, 539 to 541; Pub.L. 113–67, Div. A, Title II, § 204(a)(2), (b)(2), Dec. 26, 2013, 127 Stat. 1179, 1180; Pub.L. 115–123, Div. E, Title XII, § 53118(a), Feb. 9, 2018, 132 Stat. 307.)

[1] So in original. Probably should refer to cl. (iii).

HISTORICAL AND STATUTORY NOTES

References in Text

Part A of subchapter IV, referred to in subsec. (c)(5), is classified to 42 U.S.C.A. § 601 et seq.

Section 501(a) of Public Law 96–422, referred to in subsec. (c)(5), is section 501(a) of Pub.L. 96–422, Title V, Oct. 10, 1980, 94 Stat. 1799, as amended, which is set out as a note under 8 U.S.C.A. § 1522.

This subchapter, referred to in subsec. (c)(9), (10), originally read "this title", meaning the Social Security Act, Act Aug. 14, 1935, c. 531, Title XVI, as added Oct. 30, 1972, Pub.L. 92–603, Title III, § 301, 86 Stat. 1465, as amended, which is classified as this subchapter, 42 U.S.C.A. § 1381 et seq.

The Internal Revenue Code of 1986, referred to in subsecs. (d) and (e)(5), is classified generally to Title 26, 26 U.S.C.A. § 1 et seq.

The Balanced Budget and Emergency Deficit Control Act of 1985, referred to in subsec. (e)(1)(I)(iv), is Title II of Pub.L. 99-177, Dec. 12, 1985, 99 Stat. 1038, as amended, which enacted chapter 20 of Title 2, 2 U.S.C.A. § 900 et seq., and 2 U.S.C.A. §§ 654 to 656, amended 2 U.S.C.A. §§ 602, 622, 631 to 642, and 651 to 653, 31 U.S.C.A. §§ 1104 to 1106, and 1109, and 42 U.S.C.A. § 911, repealed 2 U.S.C.A. § 661, enacted provisions set out as notes under 2 U.S.C.A. § 900 and 42 U.S.C.A. § 911, and amended provisions set out as a note under 2 U.S.C.A. § 621. For complete classification, see Short Title note set out under 2 U.S.C.A. § 900 and Tables.

Codifications

Amendment by section 201(b)(3)(C) of Pub.L. 103–296, which provided that subsec. (e)(3)(A)(v) of this section, as added by section 201(b)(3)(A) of Pub.L. 103–296, shall cease to be effective with respect to benefits for months after Sept. 2004, was incapable of execution due to repeal of such subsec. (e)(3) by section 105(b)(b)(4)(A) of Pub.L. 104–121. See 1996 Amendments and Sunset Provisions notes set out under this section.

Effective and Applicability Provisions

2018 Acts. Pub.L. 115–123, Div. E, Title XII, § 53118(b), Feb. 9, 2018, 132 Stat. 307, provided that: "The amendments made by subsection (a) [amending subsec. (e)(1)(I)(i)(II) of this section] shall apply with respect to any payment made by the Commissioner of Social Security pursuant to section 1611(e)(1)(I)(i)(II) of the Social Security Act (42 U.S.C. 1382(e)(1)(I)(i)(II)) (as amended by such subsection) [subsec. (e)(1)(I)(i)(II) of this section] on or after the date that is 6 months after the date of enactment of this Act [Feb. 9, 2018]."

2004 Acts. Amendments made by Pub.L. 108–203, § 203(b), amending subsec. (e)(4) and (5) of this section, to take effect on the first day of the first month that begins on or after the date that is 9 months after Mar. 2, 2004, see Pub.L. 108–203, § 203(d), set out as a note under 42 U.S.C.A. § 402.

Pub.L. 108–203, Title IV, § 433(c), Mar. 2, 2004, 118 Stat. 540, provided that: "The amendments made by this section [enacting subsec. (c)(9) of this section and amending subsec. (c)(2)(B) of this section] shall be effective with respect to benefits payable for months that begin on or after 1 year after the date of enactment of this Act [Mar. 2, 2004]."

Pub.L. 108–203, Title IV, § 436(b), Mar. 2, 2004, 118 Stat. 541, provided that: "The amendments made by this section [enacting subsec. (c)(10) of this section] shall apply to benefits payable for months that begin more than 90 days after the date of enactment of this Act [Mar. 2, 2004]."

1999 Acts. Pub.L. 106–170, Title IV, § 402(c)(4), Dec. 17, 1999, 113 Stat. 1909, provided that: "The amendments made by this subsection [amending this section] shall take effect as if included in the enactment of section 203(a) of the Personal Responsibility and Work Opportunity Reconciliation Act of 1996 (Public Law 104–193; 110 Stat. 2186) [amending this section and enacting a note set out under this section]. The reference to section 202(x)(1)(A)(ii) of the Social Security Act [42 U.S.C.A. § 402(x)(1)(A)(ii)] in section 1611(e)(1)(I)(i) of the Social Security Act [subsec. (e)(1)(I)(i) of this section], as amended by paragraph (2) of this subsection, shall be deemed a reference to such section 202(x)(1)(A)(ii) of such Act as amended by subsection (b)(1)(C) of this section."

Amendment by section 402(a)(3) of Pub.L. 106–170 to apply to individuals whose period of confinement in an institution commences on or after the first day of the fourth month beginning after December 1999, see section 402(a)(4) of Pub.L. 106–170, set out as a note under section 402 of this title.

Amendment by section 207(c) of Pub.L. 106–169 applicable to statements and representations made on or after Dec. 14, 1999, see section 207(e) of Pub.L. 106–169, set out as a note under section 402 of this title.

1997 Acts. Amendments by sections 5521 and 5522(c) of Pub.L. 105–33 effective as if included in enactment of Title II of Pub.L. 104–193, see section 5528(a) of Title V of Pub.L. 105–33, set out as a note under section 903 of this title.

1996 Acts. Amendment by section 108(j) of Pub.L. 104–193 effective July 1, 1997, with transition rules relating to State options to accelerate such date, rules relating to claims, actions, and proceedings commenced before such date, rules relating to closing out of accounts for terminated or substantially modified programs and continuance in office of Assistant Secretary for Family Support, and provisions relating to termination of entitlement under AFDC program, see section 116 of Pub.L. 104–193, set out as a note under section 601 of this title.

Section 201(b) of Pub.L. 104–193 provided that: "The amendment made by this section [amending this section] shall take effect on the date of the enactment of this Act [Aug. 22, 1996]."

Section 202(c) of Pub.L. 104–193 provided that: "The amendments made by this section [amending this section] shall take effect on the date of the enactment of this Act [Aug. 22, 1996]."

Section 203(a)(2) of Pub.L. 104–193 provided that: "The amendment made by this subsection [amending this section] shall apply to individuals whose period of confinement in an institution commences on or after the first day of the seventh month beginning after the month in which this Act is enacted [Aug. 1996]."

Section 204(d) of Pub.L. 104–193 provided that:

"**(1) In general.**—The amendments made by this section [amending this section and sections 1382c and 1383 of this title] shall apply to applications for benefits under title XVI of the Social Security Act [this subchapter] filed on or after the date of the enactment of this Act [Aug. 22, 1996], without regard to whether regulations have been issued to implement such amendments.

"**(2) Benefits under Title XVI.**—For purposes of this subsection, the term 'benefits under title XVI of the Social Security Act' includes supplementary payments pursuant to an agreement for Federal administration under section 1616(a) of the Social Security Act [section 1382e(a) of this title], and payments pursuant to an agreement entered into under section 212(b) of Public Law 93–66 [set out as a note under this section]."

Section 214(b) of Pub.L. 104–193 provided that: "The amendment made by this section [amending this section] shall apply to benefits for months beginning 90 or more days after the date of the enactment of this Act [Aug. 22, 1996], without regard to whether regulations have been issued to implement such amendments."

Section 105(b)(5) of Pub.L. 104–121, as amended Pub.L. 105–33, § 5525(a), (b), Aug. 5, 1997, 111 Stat. 624, provided that:

"**(A)** The amendments made by paragraphs (1) [amending section 1382c of this title] and (4) [amending this section and section 1383c of this title] shall apply to any individual who applies for, or whose claim is finally adjudicated with respect to, supplemental security income benefits under title XVI of the Social Security Act [this subchapter] based on disability on or after the date of the enactment of this Act [Mar. 29, 1996], and, in the case of any individual who has applied for, and whose claim has been finally adjudicated with respect to, such benefits before such date of enactment, such amendments shall apply only with respect to such benefits for months beginning on or after January 1, 1997.

"**(B)** The amendments made by paragraphs (2) [amending section 1383 of this title] and (3) [enacting section 1383e of this title] shall take effect on July 1, 1996, with respect to any individual—

"**(i)** whose claim for benefits is finally adjudicated on or after the date of the enactment of this Act [March 29, 1996], or

"**(ii)** whose eligibility for benefits is based upon an eligibility redetermination made pursuant to subparagraph (C).

"**(C)** Within 90 days after the date of the enactment of this Act [Mar. 29, 1996], the Commissioner of Social Security shall notify each individual who is eligible for supplemental security income benefits under title XVI of the Social Security Act [this subchapter] for the month in which this Act is enacted [March, 1996] and whose eligibility for such benefits would terminate by reason of the amendments made by this subsection [enacting section 1383e of this title, and amending this section and section 1382c, 1383 and 1383c of this title]. If such an individual reapplies for supplemental security income benefits under title XVI of such Act (as amended by this Act) [this subchapter as amended by Pub.L. 104–121] within 120 days after the date of the enactment of this Act [Mar. 29, 1996], the Commissioner of Social Security shall, not later than January 1, 1997, complete the eligibility redetermination (including a new medical determination) with respect to such individual pursuant to the procedures of such title.

"**(D)** For purposes of this paragraph, an individual's claim, with respect to supplemental security income benefits under title XVI of the Social Security Act [this subchapter] based on disability, which has been denied in whole before the date of the enactment of this Act [March 29, 1996], may not be considered to be finally adjudicated before such date if, on or after such date—

"**(i)** there is pending a request for either administrative or judicial review with respect to such claim, or

"**(ii)** there is pending, with respect to such claim, a readjudication by the Commissioner of Social Security pursuant to relief in a class action or implementation by the Commissioner of a court remand order.

"**(E)** Notwithstanding the provisions of this paragraph, with respect to any individual for whom the Commissioner does not perform the eligibility redetermination before the date prescribed in subparagraph (C), the Commissioner shall perform such eligibility redetermination in lieu of a continuing disability review whenever the Commissioner determines that the individual's eligibility is subject to redetermination based on the preceding provisions of this paragraph, and the provisions of section 1614(a)(4) of the Social Security Act [section 1382c(a)(4) of this title] shall not apply to such redetermination.

"**(F)** For purposes of this paragraph, the phrase 'supplemental security income benefits under title XVI of the Social Security Act' includes supplementary payments pursuant to an agreement for Federal administration under section 1616(a) of the Social Security Act [section 1382e(a) of this title] and payments pursuant to an agreement entered into under section 212(b) of Public Law 93–66 [set out as a note under this section]."

[Amendments to above note by Pub.L. 105–33 effective as if included in enactment of section 105 of Pub.L. 104–121, see section 5528(c)(1) of Pub.L. 105–33, set out as a note under section 903 of this title.]

1994 Acts. Amendment by section 107(a)(4) of Pub.L. 103–296 effective Mar. 31, 1995, see section 110 of Pub.L. 103–296, set out as a note under section 401 of this title.

Section 201(b)(3)(E) of Pub.L. 103–296 provided that:

"**(i) In general.**—Except as otherwise provided in this paragraph, the amendments made by this paragraph [amending subsec. (e) of this section and section 1383c of this title and enacting provisions set out as notes under this section] shall apply with respect to supplemental security income benefits under title XVI of the Social Security Act [this subchapter] by reason of disability which are otherwise payable in months beginning after 180 days after the date of the enactment of this Act [Aug. 15, 1994]. The Secretary of Health and Human Services shall issue regulations necessary to carry out the amendments made by this paragraph not later than 180 days after such date of enactment.

"(ii) Referral and monitoring agencies.—The amendments made by subparagraph (B) [amending this section and enacting provisions set out as a note under this section] shall take effect 180 days after the date of the enactment of this Act [Aug. 15, 1994].

"(iii) Termination after 36 months.—Clause (v) of section 1611(e)(3)(A) of the Social Security Act [subsec. (e)(3)(A) of this section] (added by the amendment made by subparagraph (A) of this paragraph) shall apply with respect to supplemental security income benefits under title XVI of the Social Security Act [this subchapter] by reason of disability for months beginning after 180 days after the date of the enactment of this Act [Aug. 15, 1994]."

Section 204(b) of Pub.L. 103–296 provided that: "The amendment made by subsection (a) [amending this section] shall take effect on January 1, 1995."

1993 Acts. Section 13735(b) of Pub.L. 103–66, provided that: "The amendments made by subsection (a) [amending this section] shall apply to benefits paid for months after the calendar year 1994."

1989 Acts. Section 8009(c) of Pub.L. 101–239 provided that: "The amendments made by subsections (a) [amending this section] and (b) [amending section 1382c of this title] shall apply with respect to benefits for months after March 1990."

Section 8010(c) of Pub.L. 101–239 provided that: "The amendments made by subsections (a) [amending section 1382c of this title] and (b) [amending this section] shall take effect on the 1st day of the 6th calendar month beginning after the date of the enactment of this Act [Dec. 19, 1989]."

1988 Acts. Amendment by Pub.L. 100–360 applicable to transfers occurring on or after July 1, 1988, without regard to whether or not final regulations to carry out such amendment have been promulgated by such date, see section 303(g)(3) of Pub.L. 100–360, set out as a note under section 1396r–5 of this title.

1987 Acts. Section 9106(b) of Pub.L. 100–203 provided that: "The amendments made by subsection (a) [amending this section] shall become effective April 1, 1988."

Section 9107 of Pub.L. 100–203 provided that amendment by such section is effective Nov. 10, 1986.

Section 9113(b) of Pub.L. 100–203 provided that:

"(1) The amendment made by subsection (a) [amending this section] shall become effective January 1, 1988.

"(2) In the application of section 1611(e)(1)(D) of the Social Security Act [subsec. (e)(1)(D) of this section] on and after the effective date of such amendment, months before January 1988 in which a person was an eligible individual or eligible spouse by reason of such section shall not be taken into account."

Section 9115(c) of Pub.L. 100–203 provided that: "The amendments made by this section [amending this section and section 1396a of this title] shall become effective July 1, 1988."

Section 9119(c) of Pub.L. 100–203 provided that: "The amendments made by subsections (a) and (b) [amending this section and section 1382g of this title, respectively] shall become effective July 1, 1988."

1986 Acts. Section 9(b) of Pub.L. 99–643 provided that: "The amendment made by subsection (a) [amending this section] shall take effect on the date of the enactment of this Act [Nov. 10, 1986]."

Amendment by sections 3(a) and 4(c)(3), (d)(1) of Pub.L. 99–643 effective July 1, 1987, except as otherwise provided (State plans requiring State legislation), see section 10(b) of Pub.L. 99–643, set out as a note under section 1396a of this title.

1984 Acts. Amendment by section 2611(a) to (c) of Pub.L. 98–369 effective Oct. 1, 1984, except as otherwise specially provided, see section 2646 of Pub.L. 98–369, set out as a note under section 602 of this title.

Amendment by section 2663(g)(1), (2) of Pub.L. 98–369 effective July 18, 1984, but not to be construed as changing or affecting any right, liability, status or interpretation which existed (under the provisions of law involved) before that date, see section 2664(b) of Pub.L. 98–369, set out as a note under section 401 of this title.

1983 Acts. Section 403(b) of Pub.L. 98–21 provided that: "The amendments made by subsection (a) [amending this section] shall be effective with respect to months after the month in which this Act is enacted [April, 1983]."

1982 Acts. Section 181(b) of Pub.L. 97–248 provided that: "The amendment made by this section [amending this section] shall become effective on October 1, 1982."

Section 183(b) of Pub.L. 97–248 provided that: "The amendment made by subsection (a) [amending this section] shall become effective October 1, 1982."

1981 Acts. Section 2341(c) of Pub.L. 97–35 provided that:

"(1) The amendments made by this section [amending this section and section 1382a of this title] shall be effective with respect to months after the first calendar quarter which ends more than five months after the month in which this Act is enacted [August, 1981].

"(2) The Secretary of Health and Human Services [now Commissioner of Social Security] may, under conditions determined by him to be necessary and appropriate, make a transitional payment or payments during the first two months for which the amendments made by this section are effective. A transitional payment made under this section shall be deemed to be a payment of supplemental security income benefits."

1980 Acts. Enactment by Pub.L. 96–265 effective the first day of sixth month which begins after June 9, 1980, and applicable with respect to any individual whose disability has not been determined to have ceased prior to such first day, see section 303(d) of Pub.L. 96–265, set out as a note under section 402 of this title.

1976 Acts. Section 505(e) of Pub.L. 94–566 provided that: "The amendments [amending this section and section 1382a of this title] and repeals [repealing section 1382e(e) of this title] made by this section, unless otherwise specified therein, shall take effect on October 1, 1976."

1973 Acts. Section 4(b) of Pub.L. 93–233 provided that amendments by section 4(b) of Pub.L. 93–233 shall be effective with respect to payments for months after June 1974.

Section 210(c) of Pub.L. 93–66, as amended Pub.L. 93–233, § 4(a)(1), Dec. 30, 1973, 87 Stat. 953, provided that: "The amendments made by this section [amending this section] shall apply with respect to payments for months after December 1973."

1972 Acts. Section 301 of Pub.L. 92–603 provided that this section is effective Jan. 1, 1974.

Sunset Provisions

Section 201(b)(3)(C) of Pub.L. 103–296 provided that: "Section 1611(e)(3)(A)(v) of the Social Security Act [subsec. (e)(3)(A)(v) of this section] (added by subparagraph (A) of this paragraph) shall cease to be effective with respect to benefits for months after September 2004." See Codifications note under this section.

Prior Provisions

A prior section 1382, Act Aug. 14, 1935, c. 531, Title XVI, § 1602, as added July 25, 1962, Pub.L. 87–543, Title I, § 141(a), 76 Stat. 198, and amended Oct. 13, 1964, Pub.L. 88–650, § 5(b), 78 Stat. 1078; July 30, 1965, Pub.L. 89–97, Title II, § 221(d)(3), Title IV, § 403(e), 79 Stat. 358, 418; Jan. 2, 1968, Pub.L. 90–248, Title II, §§ 210(a)(5), 213(a)(4), 241(d), 81 Stat. 896, 898, 917; Oct. 30, 1972, Pub.L. 92–603, Title IV, §§ 405(d), 406(d), 407(d), 410(d), 413(d), 86 Stat. 1488, 1489, 1491, 1492, set forth required contents of State plans for aid to aged, blind, or disabled, and for medical assistance for aged, prior to the general amendment of Title XVI of the Social Security Act by Pub.L. 92–603, § 301, but is set out as a note under this section in view of its continued applicability to Puerto Rico, Guam, and the Virgin Islands.

Study of Denial of SSI Benefits for Family Farmers

Pub.L. 106–169, Title II, § 261, Dec. 14, 1999, 113 Stat. 1856, provided that:

"**(a) In general.**—The Commissioner of Social Security shall conduct a study of the reasons why family farmers with resources of less than $100,000 are denied supplemental security income benefits under title XVI of the Social Security Act [subchapter XVI of this chapter 42 U.S.C.A. § 1381 et seq.], including whether the deeming process unduly burdens and discriminates against family farmers who do not institutionalize a disabled dependent, and shall determine the number of such farmers who have been denied such benefits during each of the preceding 10 years.

"**(b) Report to the Congress.**—Within 1 year after the date of the enactment of this Act [Dec. 14, 1999], the Commissioner of Social Security shall prepare and submit to the Committee on Ways and Means of the House of Representatives and the Committee on Finance of the Senate a report that contains the results of the study, and the determination, required by subsection (a)."

Additional Report to Congress

Section 203(c) of Pub.L. 104–193 provided that: "Not later than October 1, 1998, the Commissioner of Social Security shall provide to the Committee on Finance of the Senate and the Committee on Ways and Means of the House of Representatives a list of the institutions that are and are not providing information to the Commissioner under section 1611(e)(1)(I) of the Social Security Act (as added by this section) [subsec. (e)(1)(I) of this section]."

Adjustment of Individual's Monthly Supplemental Security Income Payments; Regulations; Limitations

Pub.L. 93–335, § 2(b)(2), July 8, 1974, 88 Stat. 291, authorized the Secretary of Health, Education, and Welfare [now Commissioner of Social Security] to prescribe regulations for the adjustment of an individual's monthly supplemental security income payment in accordance with any increase to which such individual may be entitled under the amendment made by subsection (a) of this section [amending section 212(a)(3)(B)(i) of Pub.L. 93–66, set out as a note below]; provided, That such adjustment in monthly payment, together with remittance of any prior unpaid increments to which such individual might be entitled under such amendment, was to be made no later than the first day of the first month beginning more than sixty days after July 8, 1974.

Annual Reports on Reviews of OASDI and SSI Cases

Secretary of Health and Human Services to annually submit to Committee on Ways and Means of the House of Representatives and Committee on Finance of the Senate a report on extent to which Secretary has exercised his authority to review cases of entitlement to monthly insurance benefits under subchapter II of this chapter and supplemental security income cases under this subchapter, and extent to which the cases reviewed were those that involved a high likelihood or probability of fraud, pursuant to section 206(g) of Pub.L. 103–296, set out as a note under section 405 of this title.

Application to Northern Mariana Islands

For applicability of this section to the Northern Mariana Islands, see section 502(a)(1) of the Covenant to Establish a Commonwealth of the Northern Mariana Islands in Political Union with the United States of America, as set forth in Pub.L. 94–241, Mar. 24, 1976, 90 Stat. 263, eff. Jan. 9, 1978, pursuant to Proc. No. 4534, Oct. 24, 1977, 42 F.R. 6593, set out as notes under section 1681 of Title 48, Territories and Insular Possessions.

Assistance Paid Under Certain Housing Acts Not Considered in Determining Eligibility for Benefits Under This Subchapter; Effective Date

Pub.L. 94–375, § 2(h), Aug. 3, 1976, 90 Stat. 1068, provided that: "Notwithstanding any other provision of law, the value of any assistance paid with respect to a dwelling unit under the United States Housing Act of 1937 [section 1437 et seq. of this title], the National Housing Act [section 1701 et seq. of Title 12, Banks and Banking], section 101 of the Housing and Urban Development Act of 1965 [section 1701s of Title 12 and section 1451 and former section 1465 of this title], or title V of the Housing Act of 1949 [section 1471 et seq. of this title] may not be considered as income or a resource for the purpose of determining the eligibility of, or the amount of the benefits payable to, any person living in such unit for assistance under title XVI of the Social Security Act [this subchapter]. This subsection shall become effective on October 1, 1976."

Commission on Childhood Disability

Section 202 of Pub.L. 103–296 provided for establishment of a Commission on the Evaluation of Disability in Children for the purpose of conducting a study, in consultation with the National Academy of Sciences, of the effects of the definition of "disability" under this subchapter in effect on Aug. 15, 1994, as such definition applied to determining whether a child under the age of 18 was eligible to receive benefits under this subchapter, the appropriateness of such definition, and the advantages and disadvantages of using any alternative definition of disability in determining whether a child under age 18 is eligible to receive benefits under this subchapter, and provided for appointment and qualifications of members, administration of Commission, issues to be included in study, and for a report to be submitted to Congress not later than Nov. 30, 1995.

Continuing Disability Reviews

Section 208 of Pub.L. 103–296 provided that:

"(a) Temporary annual minimum number of reviews.—During each year of the 3–year period that begins on October 1, 1995, the Secretary of Health and Human Services shall apply section 221(i) of the Social Security Act [section 421(i) of this title] in making disability determinations under title XVI of such Act [this subchapter] with respect to at least 100,000 recipients of supplemental security income benefits under such title [this subchapter].

"(b) Report to the Congress.—Not later than October 1, 1998, the Secretary of Health and Human Services shall submit to the Committee on Ways and Means of the House of Representatives and the Committee on Finance of the Senate a report on the activities conducted under subsection (a)."

Disability Review Required for SSI Recipients Who Are 18 Years of Age

Section 207 of Pub.L. 103–296, which required applicable State agency or Secretary of Health and Human Services to redetermine eligibility of qualified individual for supplemental security income benefits under this subchapter by reason of disability, by applying criteria used in determining eligibility for such benefits of applicants who have attained 18 years of age during 1–year period beginning on date qualified individual attains 18 years of age, and Secretary to conduct such redeterminations with respect to not less than ⅓ of qualified individuals in each of fiscal years 1996 through 1998, defined term "qualified individual", and provided that such redetermination was to be considered substitute for review required under section 1382c(a)(3)(G) of this title, that redetermination requirement was to have no force or effect after Oct. 1, 1998, and that not later than Oct. 1, 1998, Secretary was to submit to House Ways and Means and Senate Finance Committees report on such activities, was repealed by Pub.L. 104–193, Title II, § 212(b)(2), (d), Aug. 22, 1996, 110 Stat. 2193, 2194, with repeal applicable to benefits for months beginning on or after Aug. 22, 1996, without regard to whether regulations have been issued to implement such repeal.

Federal Program of Supplemental Security Income; Supplemental Security Income Benefits for Essential Persons; Definitions of Qualified Individual and Essential Person

Section 211 of Pub.L. 93–66, as amended Pub.L. 93–233, § 4(a)(2), (b)(3), Dec. 31, 1973, 87 Stat. 953, provided that:

"(a)(1) In determining (for purposes of title XVI of the Social Security Act [this subchapter], as in effect after December 1973) the eligibility for and the amount of the supplemental security income benefit payable to any qualified individual (as defined in subsection (b)), with respect to any period for which such individual has in his home an essential person (as defined in subsection (c))—

"(A) the dollar amounts specified in subsection (a)(1)(A) and (2)(A), and subsection (b)(1) and (2), of section 1611 of such Act [this section], shall each be increased by $876 for each such essential person, and

"(B) the income and resources of such individual shall (for purposes of such title XVI [this subchapter]) be deemed to include the income and resources of such essential person;

except that the provisions of this subsection shall not, in the case of any individual, be applicable for any period which begins in or after the first month that such individual—

"(C) does not but would (except for the provisions of subparagraph (B)) meet—

"(i) the criteria established with respect to income in section 1611(a) of such Act [subsec. (a) of this section], or

"(ii) the criteria established with respect to resources by such section 1611(a) [subsec. (a) of this section] (or, if applicable, by section 1611(g) of such Act [subsec. (g) of this section]).

"(2) The provisions of section 1611(g) of the Social Security Act [subsec. (g) of this section] (as in effect after December 1973) shall, in the case of any qualified individual (as defined in subsection (b)), be applied so as to include, in the resources of such individual, the resources of any person (describe in subsection (b)(2)) whose needs were taken into account in determining the need of such individual for the aid or assistance referred to in subsection (b)(1).

"(b) For purposes of this section, an individual shall be a 'qualified individual' only if—

"(1) for the month of December 1973 such individual was a recipient of aid or assistance under a State plan approved under title [subchapter] I, X, XIV, or XVI of the Social Security Act [this chapter], and

"(2) in determining the need of such individual for such aid or assistance for such month under such State plan, there were taken into account the needs of a person (other than such individual) who—

"(A) was living in the home of such individual, and

"(B) was not eligible (in his or her own right) for aid or assistance under such State plan for such month.

"(c) The term 'essential person', when used in connection with any qualified individual, means a person who—

"(1) for the month of December 1973 was a person (described in subsection (b)(2)) whose needs were taken into account in determining the need of such individual for aid or assistance under a State plan referred to in subsection (b)(1) as such State plan was in effect for June 1973,

"(2) lives in the home of such individual,

"(3) is not eligible (in his or her own right) for supplemental security income benefits under title XVI of the Social Security Act [this subchapter] (as in effect after December 1973), and

"(4) is not the eligible spouse (as that term is used in such title XVI [this subchapter]) of such individual or any other individual.

If for any month after December 1973 any person fails to meet the criteria specified in paragraph (2), (3), or (4) of the preceding sentence, such person shall not, for such month or any month thereafter be considered to be an essential person."

[Amendment of section 211(a)(1)(A) of Pub.L. 93–66, set out above, by Pub.L. 93–233 effective with respect to payments for months after June 1974, see section 4(b) of Pub.L. 93–233.]

Mandatory Minimum State Supplementation of Supplemental Security Income Benefits Program; December 1973 Income; Title XVI Benefit Plus Other Income; Reduction of Amount; Administration Agreement; Payments to Secretary [now Commissioner of Social Security]; State Constitutional Restriction

Section 212 of Pub.L. 93–66, as amended Pub.L. 93–233, § 10, Dec. 31, 1973, 87 Stat. 957; Pub.L. 93–335, § 2(a), July 8, 1974, 88 Stat. 291; Pub.L. 96–265, Title II, § 201(b)(2), June 9, 1980, 94 Stat. 446; Pub.L. 103–66, Title XIII, § 13731(a)(2), Aug. 10, 1993, 107 Stat. 661; Pub.L. 105–33, Title V, § 5102(a)(2), Aug. 5, 1997, 111 Stat. 596, Pub.L.

105–78, Title V, § 516(a)(2), (b)(1)(B), Nov. 13, 1997, 111 Stat. 1518, 1519, provided that:

"(a)(1) In order for any State (other than the Commonwealth of Puerto Rico, Guam, or the Virgin Islands) to be eligible for payments pursuant to title XIX [subchapter XIX of this chapter], with respect to expenditures for any quarter beginning after December 1973, such State must have in effect an agreement with the Secretary of Health, Education, and Welfare [now Commissioner of Social Security] (hereinafter in this section referred to as the 'Secretary') whereby the State will provide to individuals residing in the State supplementary payments as required under paragraph (2).

"(2) Any agreement entered into by a State pursuant to paragraph (1) shall provide that each individual who—

"(A) is an aged, blind, or disabled individual (within the meaning of section 1614(a) of the Social Security Act, as enacted by section 301 of the Social Security Amendments of 1972 [section 1382c(a) of this title]), and

"(B) for the month of December 1973 was a recipient of (and was eligible to receive) aid or assistance (in the form of money payments) under a State plan of such State (approved under title I, X, XIV, or XVI, of the Social Security Act [subchapter I, X, XIV, or XVI, of this chapter]),

shall be entitled to receive, from the State, the supplementary payment described in paragraph (3) for each month, beginning with January 1974, and ending with whichever of the following first occurs:

"(C) the month in which such individual dies, or

"(D) the first month in which such individual ceases to meet the condition specified in subparagraph (A);

except that no individual shall be entitled to receive such supplementary payment for any month, if, for such month, such individual was ineligible to receive supplemental income benefits under title XVI of the Social Security Act [this chapter] by reason of the provisions of § 1611(e)(1)(A), (2), or (3), 1611(f), or 1615(c) of such Act [subsections (e)(1)(A), (2), or (3), (f) of this section or section 1382d(c) of this title].

"(3)(A) The supplementary payment referred to in paragraph (2) which shall be paid for any month to any individual who is entitled thereto under an agreement entered into pursuant to this subsection shall (except as provided in subparagraphs (D) and (E)) be an amount equal to (i) the amount by which such individual's 'December 1973 income' (as determined under subparagraph (B)) exceeds the amount of such individual's 'title XVI benefit plus other income' (as determined under subparagraph (C)) for such month, or (ii) if greater, such amount as the State may specify.

"(B) For purposes of subparagraph (A), an individual's 'December 1973 income' means an amount equal to the aggregate of—

"(i) the amount of the aid or assistance (in the form of money payments) which such individual would have received (including any part of such amount which is attributable to meeting the needs of any other person whose presence in such individual's home is essential to such individual's well-being) for the month of December 1973 under a plan (approved under title I, X, XIV, or XVI, of the Social Security Act [subchapter I, X, XIV, or XVI, of this chapter]) of the State entering into an agreement under this subsection, if the terms and conditions of such plan (relating to eligibility for an amount of such aid or assistance payable thereunder) were, for the month of December 1973, the same as those in effect, under such plan, for the month of June 1973, together with the bonus value of food stamps for January 1972, as defined in section 401(b)(3) of Public Law 92–603 [set out as a note under section 1382e of this title], if, for such month, such individual resides in a State which provides State supplementary payments (I) of the type described in section 1616(a) of the Social Security Act [section 1382e(a) of this title], and (II) the level of which has been found by the Secretary [now Commissioner of Social Security] pursuant to section 8 of Public Law 93–233 [set out as notes under section 1382e of this title and sections 612c, 1431 and 2012 of Title 7, Agriculture] to have been specifically increased so as to include the bonus value of food stamps, and

"(ii) the amount of the income of such individual (other than the aid or assistance described in clause (i)) received by such individual in December 1973, minus any such income which did not result, but which if properly reported would have resulted in a reduction in the amount of such aid or assistance.

"(C) For purposes of subparagraph (A), the amount of an individual's 'title XVI benefit plus other income' for any month means an amount equal to the aggregate of—

"(i) the amount (if any) of the supplemental security income benefit to which such individual is entitled for such month under title XVI of the Social Security Act [this subchapter], and

"(ii) the amount of any income of such individual for such month (other than income in the form of a benefit described in clause (i)).

"(D) If the amount determined under subparagraph (B)(i) includes, in the case of any individual, an amount which was payable to such individual solely because of—

"(i) a special need of such individual (including any special allowance for housing, or the rental value of housing furnished in kind to such individual in lieu of a rental allowance) which existed in December 1973, or

"(ii) any special circumstance (such as the recognition of the needs of a person whose presence in such individual's home, in December 1973, was essential to such individual's well-being),

and, if for any month after December 1973 there is a change with respect to such special need or circumstance which, if such change had existed in December 1973, the amount described in subparagraph (B)(i) with respect to such individual would have been reduced on account of such change, then, for such month and for each month thereafter the amount of the supplementary payment payable under the agreement entered into under this subsection to such individual shall (unless the State, at its option, otherwise specifies) be reduced by an amount equal to the amount by which the amount (described in subparagraph (B)(i)) would have been so reduced.

"(E)(i) In the case of an individual who, for December 1973 lived as a member of a family unit other members of which received aid (in the form of money payments) under a State plan of a State approved under part A of title IV of the Social Security Act [part A of subchapter IV of this chapter], such State at its option, may (subject to clause (ii)) reduce such individual's December 1973 income (as determined under subparagraph (B)) to such extent as may be necessary to cause the supplementary payment (referred to in paragraph (2)) payable to such individual for January 1974 or any month thereafter to be reduced to a level designed to assure that the total income of such individual (and of the members of such family unit) for any month after December 1973 does not exceed the total income of such individual (and of the members of such family unit) for December 1973.

"(ii) The amount of the reduction (under clause (i)) of any individual's December 1973 income shall not be in an amount which would cause the supplementary payment (referred to in paragraph (2)) payable to such individual to be reduced below the amount of such supplementary payment which would be payable to such individual if he had, for the month of December 1973 not lived in a family, members of which were receiving aid under part A of title IV of the Social Security Act [part A of subchapter IV of this chapter], and had had no income for such month other than that received as aid or assistance under a State plan approved under title I, X, XIV, or XVI of the Social Security Act [subchapter I, X, XIV, or XVI of this chapter].

"(4) Any State having an agreement with the Secretary [now Commissioner of Social Security] under paragraph (1) may, at its option, include individuals receiving benefits under section 1619 of the Social Security Act [section 1382h of this title], or who would be eligible to receive such benefits but for their income, under the agreement as though they are aged, blind, or disabled individuals as specified in paragraph (2)(A).

"(b)(1) Any State having an agreement with the Secretary [now Commissioner of Social Security] under subsection (a) may enter into an administration agreement with the Secretary whereby the Secretary will, on behalf of such State, make the supplementary payments required under the agreement entered into under subsection (a).

"(2) Any such administration agreement between the Secretary [now Commissioner of Social Security] and a State entered into under this subsection shall provide that the State will (A) certify to the Secretary the names of each individual who, for December 1973, was a recipient of aid or assistance (in the form of money payments) under a plan of such State approved under title I, X, XIV, or XVI of the Social Security Act [subchapter I, X, XIV, or XVI of this chapter], together with the amount of such assistance payable to each such individual and the amount of such individual's December 1973 income (as defined in subsection (a)(3)(B)), and (B) provide the Secretary with such additional data at such times as the Secretary may reasonably require in order properly, economically, and efficiently to carry out such administration agreement.

"(3)(A) Any State which has entered into an administration agreement under this subsection shall, at such times and in such installments as may be agreed upon between the Secretary [now Commissioner of Social Security] and the State, pay to the Secretary an amount equal to the expenditures made by the Secretary as supplementary payments to individuals entitled thereto under the agreement entered into with such State under subsection (a), plus an administration fee assessed in accordance with subparagraph (B) and any additional services fee charged in accordance with subparagraph (C).

"(B)(i) The Secretary [now Commissioner of Social Security] shall assess each State an administration fee in an amount equal to—

"(I) the number of supplementary payments made by the Secretary [now Commissioner of Social Security] on behalf of the State under this subsection for any month in a fiscal year; multiplied by

"(II) the applicable rate for the fiscal year.

"(ii) As used in clause (i), the term 'applicable rate' means—

"(I) for fiscal year 1994, $1.67;

"(II) for fiscal year 1995, $3.33;

"(III) for fiscal year 1996, $5.00;

"(IV) for fiscal year 1997, $5.00;

"(V) for fiscal year 1998, $6.20;

"(VI) for fiscal year 1999, $7.60;

"(VII) for fiscal year 2000, $7.80;

"(VIII) for fiscal year 2001, $8.10;

"(IX) for fiscal year 2002, $8.50; and

"(X) for fiscal year 2003 and each succeeding fiscal year—

"(aa) the applicable rate in the preceding fiscal year, increased by the percentage, if any, by which the Consumer Price Index for the month of June of the calendar year of the increase exceeds the Consumer Price Index for the month of June of the calendar year preceding the calendar year of the increase, and rounded to the nearest whole cent; or

"(bb) such different rate as the Commissioner determines is appropriate for the State.

"(iii) Upon making a determination under clause (ii)(X)(bb), the Secretary [now Commissioner of Social Security] shall promulgate the determination in regulations, which may take into account the complexity of administering the State's supplementary payment program.

"(iv) All fees assessed pursuant to this subparagraph shall be transferred to the Secretary [now Commissioner of Social Security] at the same time that amounts for such supplementary payments are required to be so transferred.

"(C)(i) The Secretary [now Commissioner of Social Security] may charge a State an additional services fee if, at the request of the State, the Secretary provides additional services beyond the level customarily provided, in the administration of State supplementary payments pursuant to this subsection.

"(ii) The additional services fee shall be in an amount that the Secretary determines is necessary to cover all costs (including indirect costs) incurred by the Federal Government in furnishing the additional services referred to in clause (i).

"(D)(i) The first $5 of each administration fee assessed pursuant to subparagraph (B), upon collection, shall be deposited in the general fund of the Treasury of the United States as miscellaneous receipts.

"(ii) The portion of each administration fee in excess of $5, and 100 percent of each additional services fee charged pursuant to subparagraph (C), upon collection for fiscal year 1998 and each subsequent fiscal year, shall be credited to a special fund established in the Treasury of the United States for State supplementary payment fees. The amounts so credited, to the extent and in the amounts provided in advance in appropriations Acts, shall be available to defray expenses incurred in carrying out this section and title XVI of the Social Security Act [this subchapter] and related laws.

"(c)(1) Supplementary payments made pursuant to an agreement entered into under subsection (a) shall be excluded under section 1612(b)(6) of the Social Security Act [section 1382a(b)(6) of this title] (as in effect after December 1973) in determining income of individuals for purposes of title XVI of such Act [this subchapter] (as so in effect).

"(2) Supplementary payments made by the Secretary [now Commissioner of Social Security] (pursuant to an administration agreement entered into under subsection (b)) shall, for purposes of section 401 of the Social Security Amendments of 1972 [set out as a note under section 1382e of this title], be considered to be payments made under an agreement entered into under section 1616 of the Social Security Act (as enacted by section 301 of the Social Security Amendments of 1972 [section 1382e of this title]); except that nothing in this paragraph shall be construed to waive, with respect to the payments so made by the Secretary, the provisions of subsection (b) of such section 401 [set out as a note under section 1382e of this title].

"**(d)** For purposes of subsection (a)(1), a State shall be deemed to have entered into an agreement under subsection (a) of this section if such State has entered into an agreement with the Secretary [now Commissioner of Social Security] under section 1616 of the Social Security Act [section 1382e of this title] under which—

"**(1)** individuals, other than individuals described in subsection (a)(2)(A) and (B), are entitled to receive supplementary payments, and

"**(2)** supplementary benefits are payable, to individuals described in subsection (a)(2)(A) and (B) at a level and under terms and conditions which meet the minimum requirements specified in subsection (a).

"**(e)** Except as the Secretary [now Commissioner of Social Security] may by regulations otherwise provide, the provisions of title XVI of the Social Security Act [this subchapter] (as enacted by section 301 of the Social Security Amendments of 1972), including the provisions of part B of such title [section 1383 et seq. of this title], relating to the terms and conditions under which the benefits authorized by such title [this subchapter] are payable shall, where not inconsistent with the purposes of this section, be applicable to the payments made under an agreement under subsection (b) of this section; and the authority conferred upon the Secretary by such title may, where appropriate, be exercised by him in the administration of this section.

"**(f)** The provisions of subsection (a)(1) shall not be applicable in the case of any State—

"**(1)** the Constitution of which contains provisions which make it impossible for such State to enter into and commence carrying out (on January 1, 1974) an agreement referred to in subsection (a), and

"**(2)** the Attorney General (or other appropriate State official) of which has, prior to July 1, 1973, made a finding that the State Constitution of such State contains limitations which prevent such State from making supplemental payments of the type described in section 1616 of the Social Security Act [section 1382e of this title]."

[Amendments by Pub.L. 103–66 applicable to supplementary payments made pursuant to this note for any calendar month beginning after Sept. 30, 1993, and to services furnished after such date, regardless of whether implementing regulations have been promulgated by such date or whether any agreement entered into under this note has been modified, see section 13731(b) of Pub.L. 103–66, set out as a note under section 1382e of this title.]

[Section 2(b)(1) of Pub.L. 93–335, July 8, 1974, 88 Stat. 291, provided that amendment of section 212(a)(3)(B)(i) of Pub.L. 93–66 by section 2(a) of Pub.L. 93–335 is effective Jan. 1, 1974.]

[Enactment of subsec. (a)(4) of section 212 of Pub.L. 93–66 effective Jan. 1, 1981, see section 201(d) of Pub.L. 96–265, as amended, set out as a note under section 1382h of this title.]

[Pub.L. 106–170, Title IV, § 410(a)(2), (b), Dec. 17, 1999, 113 Stat. 1916, 1917, provided that, applicable to payments and fees arising under an agreement between a State and the Commissioner of Social Security under section 1382e of this title or under this note with respect to monthly benefits paid to individuals under this subchapter for months after September 2009 (October 2009 in the case of a State with a fiscal year that coincides with the Federal fiscal year), without regard to whether the agreement has been modified to reflect such amendments or the Commissioner has promulgated regulations implementing such amendments, section 212 of Public Law 93–66 (this note) is amended—

(a) in subsection (b)(3)(A), by striking "at such times and in such installments as may be agreed upon between the Secretary and the State" and inserting "in accordance with subparagraph (E)";

(b) by adding at the end of subsection (b)(3) the following new subparagraph:

"**(E)(i)** Any State which has entered into an agreement with the Commissioner of social security under this section shall remit the payments and fees required under this paragraph with respect to monthly benefits paid to individuals under title XVI of the Social Security Act [this subchapter] no later than—

"**(I)** the business day preceding the date that the Commissioner pays such monthly benefits; or

"**(II)** with respect to such monthly benefits paid for the month that is the last month of the State's fiscal year, the fifth business day following such date.

"**(ii)** The Cash Management Improvement Act of 1990 [Pub.L. 101–453, Oct. 24, 1990, 104 Stat. 1058; see Tables for complete classification] shall not apply to any payments or fees required under this paragraph that are paid by a State before the date required by clause (i).

"**(iii)** Notwithstanding clause (i), the Commissioner may make supplementary payments on behalf of a State with funds appropriated for payment of supplemental security income benefits under title XVI of the Social Security Act [this subchapter], and subsequently to be reimbursed for such payments by the State at such times as the Commissioner and State may agree. Such authority may be exercised only if extraordinary circumstances affecting a State's ability to make payment when required by clause (i) are determined by the Commissioner to exist."; and

(c) by striking "Secretary of Health, Education, and Welfare" and "Secretary" each place such term appear and inserting "Commissioner of Social Security".]

Medicaid Eligibility for Individuals Receiving Mandatory State Supplementary Payments; Effective Date

Additional requirement for approval of subchapter XIX State plan for medical assistance respecting medicaid eligibility for individuals receiving mandatory State supplementary payments, see section 13(c) of Pub.L. 93–233, set out as a note under section 1396(a) of this title.

Notification of Possible Benefit Availability to Potential Supplemental Security Income Recipients

Section 405 of Pub.L. 98–21 provided that: "Prior to July 1, 1984, the Secretary of Health and Human Services shall notify all elderly recipients of benefits under title II of the Social Security Act [subchapter II of this chapter] who may be eligible for supplemental security income benefits under title XVI of such Act [this subchapter] of the availability of the supplemental security income program, and shall encourage such recipients to contact the Social Security district office. Such notification shall also be made to all recipients prior to attainment of age 65, with the notification made with respect to eligibility for supplementary medical insurance."

Puerto Rico, Guam, and Virgin Islands

Enactment of section 1602 of the Social Security Act [this section] by Pub.L. 92–603, eff. Jan. 1, 1974, was not applicable to Puerto Rico, Guam, and the Virgin Islands. See section 303(b) of Pub.L. 92–603, set out as a note under section 301 of this title. Therefore, as to Puerto Rico, Guam, and the Virgin Islands, section 1602 of the Social Security Act [this section] as it existed prior to reenactment by Pub.L. 92–603, and as amended, continues to apply and reads as follows:

"§ 1382. State plans for aid to aged, blind, or disabled

"(a) Contents

"A state plan for aid to the aged, blind, or disabled, must—

"(1) except to the extent permitted by the Commissioner of Social Security with respect to services, provide that it shall be in effect in all political subdivisions of the State, and, if administered by them, be mandatory upon them;

"(2) provide for financial participation by the State;

"(3) either provide for the establishment or designation of a single State agency to administer the plan, or provide for the establishment or designation of a single State agency to supervise the administration of the plan;

"(4) provide (A) for granting an opportunity for a fair hearing before the State agency to any individual whose claim for aid or assistance under the plan is denied or is not acted upon with reasonable promptness, and (B) that if the State plan is administered in each of the political subdivisions of the State by a local agency and such local agency provides a hearing at which evidence may be presented prior to a hearing before the State agency, such local agency may put into effect immediately upon issuance its decision upon the matter considered at such hearing.

"(5) provide (A) such methods of administration (including methods relating to the establishment and maintenance of personnel standards on a merit basis, except that the Commissioner of Social Security shall exercise no authority with respect to the selection, tenure of office, and compensation of any individual employed in accordance with such methods) as are found by the Commissioner of Social Security to be necessary for the proper and efficient operation of the plan, and (B) for the training and effective use of paid subprofessional staff, with particular emphasis on the full-time or part-time employment of recipients and other persons of low income, as community service aides, in the administration of the plan and for the use of nonpaid or partially paid volunteers in a social service volunteer program in providing services to applicants and recipients and in assisting any advisory committees established by the State agency;

"(6) provide that the State agency will make such reports, in such form and containing such information, as the Commissioner of Social Security may from time to time require, and comply with such provisions as the Commissioner of Social Security may from time to time find necessary to assure the correctness and verification of such reports;

"(7) provide safeguards which permit the use or disclosure of information concerning applicants or recipients only (A) to public officials who require such information in connection with their official duties, or (B) to other persons for purposes directly connected with the administration of the State plan;

"(8) provide that all individuals wishing to make application for aid or assistance under the plan shall have opportunity to do so, and that such aid or assistance shall be furnished with reasonable promptness to all eligible individuals;

"(9) provide, if the plan includes aid or assistance to or on behalf of individuals in private or public institutions, for the establishment or designation of a State authority or authorities which shall be responsible for establishing and maintaining standards for such institutions;

"(10) provide a description of the services (if any) which the State agency makes available (using whatever internal organizational arrangement it finds appropriate for this purpose) to applicants for or recipients of aid or assistance under the plan to help them attain self-support or self-care, including a description of the steps taken to assure, in the provision of such services, maximum utilization of other agencies providing similar or related services;

"(11) provide that no aid or assistance will be furnished any individual under the plan with respect to any period with respect to which he is receiving assistance under the State plan approved under subchapter I of this chapter or assistance under a State program funded under part A of subchapter IV of this chapter or under subchapter X or XIV of this chapter;

"(12) provide that, in determining whether an individual is blind, there shall be an examination by a physician skilled in the diseases of the eye or by an optometrist, whichever the individual may select;

"(13) include reasonable standards, consistent with the objectives of this subchapter, for determining eligibility for and the extent of aid or assistance under the plan;

"(14) provide that the State agency shall, in determining need for aid to the aged, blind, or disabled, take into consideration any other income and resources of an individual claiming such aid, as well as any expenses reasonably attributable to the earning of any such income; except that, in making such determination with respect to any individual—

"(A) if such individual is blind, the State agency (i) shall disregard the first $85 per month of earned income plus one-half of earned income in excess of $85 per month, and (ii) shall, for a period not in excess of 12 months, and may, for a period not in excess of 36 months, disregard such additional amounts of other income and resources, in the case of any such individual who has a plan for achieving self-support approved by the State agency, as may be necessary for the fulfillment of such plan,

"(B) if such individual is not blind but is permanently and totally disabled, (i) of the first $80 per month of earned income, the State agency may disregard not more than the first $20 thereof plus one-half of the remainder, and (ii) the State agency may, for a period not in excess of 36 months, disregard such additional amounts of other income and resources, in the case of any such individual who has a plan for achieving self-support approved by the State agency, as may be necessary for the fulfillment of such plan, but only with respect to the part or parts of such period during substantially all of which he is actually undergoing vocational rehabilitation,

"(C) if such individual has attained age 65 and is neither blind nor permanently and totally disabled, of the first $80 per month of earned income the State agency may disregard not more than the first $20 thereof plus one-half of the remainder, and

"(D) the State agency may, before disregarding the amounts referred to above in this paragraph (14), disregard not more than $7.50 of any income; and

"(15) provide that information is requested and exchanged for purposes of income and eligibility verification in accordance with a State system which meets the requirements of section 1320b–7 of this title.

Notwithstanding paragraph (3), if on January 1, 1962, and on the date on which a State submits its plan for approval under this subchapter, the State agency which administered or supervised the administration of the plan of such State approved under subchapter X of this chapter was different from the State agency which administered or supervised the administration of the plan of such State approved under subchapter I of this chapter and the State agency which administered or supervised the administration of the plan of such State approved under subchapter XIV of this chapter, the State agency which administered or supervised the administration of such plan approved under subchapter X of this chapter may be designated to administer or supervise the administration of the portion of the State plan for aid to the aged, blind, or disabled which relates to blind individuals and a separate State agency may be established or designated to administer or supervise the administration of the rest of such plan; and in such case the part of the plan which each such agency administers, or the administration of which each such agency supervises, shall be regarded as a separate plan for purposes of this subchapter.

"(b) Approval by Commissioner of Social Security

"The Commissioner of Social Security shall approve any plan which fulfills the conditions specified in subsection (a) of this section, except that the Commissioner shall not approve any plan which imposes, as a condition of eligibility for aid or assistance under the plan—

"(1) an age requirement of more than sixty-five years; or

"(2) any residence requirement which excludes any resident of the State who has resided therein five years during the nine years immediately preceding the application for such aid and has resided therein continuously for one year immediately preceding the application; or

"(3) any citizenship requirement which excludes any citizen of the United States.

At the option of the State, the plan may provide that manuals and other policy issuances will be furnished to persons without charge for the reasonable cost of such materials, but such provision shall not be required by the Commissioner of Social Security as a condition for the approval of such plan under this subchapter. In the case of any State to which the provisions of § 344 of the Social Security Act Amendments of 1950 were applicable on January 1, 1962, and to which the sentence of § 1202(b) of this title following paragraph (2) thereof is applicable on the date on which its State plan for aid to the aged, blind, or disabled was submitted for approval under this subchapter, the Commissioner of Social Security shall approve the plan of such State for aid to the aged, blind, or disabled for purposes of this subchapter, even though it does not meet the requirements of paragraph (14) of subsection (a) of this section, if it meets all other requirements of this subchapter for an approved plan for aid to the aged, blind, or disabled; but payments under § 1383 of this title shall be made, in the case of any such plan, only with respect to expenditures thereunder which would be included as expenditures for the purposes of § 1383 of this title under a plan approved under this section without regard to the provisions of this sentence.

"(c) Limitation on number of plans

"Subject to the last sentence of subsection (a) of this section, nothing in this subchapter shall be construed to permit a State to have in effect with respect to any period more than one State plan approved under this subchapter. (Aug. 14, 1935, c. 531, Title XVI, § 1602, as added July 25, 1962, Pub.L. 87–543, Title I, § 141(a), 76 Stat. 198, and amended Oct. 13, 1964, Pub.L. 88–650, § 5(b), 78 Stat. 1078; July 30, 1965, Pub.L. 89–97, Title II, § 221(d)(3), Title IV, § 403(e), 79 Stat. 358, 418; Jan. 2, 1968, Pub.L. 90–248, Title II, §§ 210(a)(5), 213(a)(4), 241(d), 81 Stat. 896, 898, 917; Oct. 30, 1972, Pub.L. 92–603, Title IV, §§ 405(d), 406(d), 407(d), 410(d), 413(d), 86 Stat. 1488, 1489, 1491, 1492; Aug. 13, 1981, Pub.L. 97–35, Title XXI, § 2184(d)(4), 95 Stat. 817; July 18, 1984, Pub.L. 98–369, Div. B, Title VI, § 2651(h), 98 Stat. 1150; Aug. 15, 1994, Pub.L. 103–296, Title I, § 107(a)(4), 108 Stat. 1478; Aug. 22, 1996, Pub.L. 104–193, Title I, § 108(i), 110 Stat. 2169.)."

[Amendment by section 107(a)(4) of Pub.L. 103–296 effective Mar. 31, 1995, see section 110 of Pub.L. 103–296, set out as a note under section 401 of this title.]

[Functions of the Secretary of Health and Human Services under this subchapter and subchapter II of this chapter transferred to the Commissioner of Social Security, effective Mar. 31, 1995, pursuant to Pub.L. 103–296, Title II, §§ 105(a), 110(a), Aug. 15, 1994, 108 Stat. 1472, 1490.]

[Amendment by section 108(i) of Pub.L. 104–193 effective July 1, 1997, with transition rules relating to State options to accelerate such date, rules relating to claims, actions, and proceedings commenced before such date, rules relating to closing out of accounts for terminated or substantially modified programs and continuance in office of Assistant Secretary for Family Support, and provisions relating to termination of entitlement under AFDC program, see section 116 of Pub.L. 104–193, set out as a note under section 601 of this title.]

Regulations

Section 215 of Pub.L. 104–193 provided that: "Within 3 months after the date of the enactment of this Act [Aug. 22, 1996], the Commissioner of Social Security shall prescribe such regulations as may be necessary to implement the amendments made by this subtitle [Pub.L. 104–193, Title II, Subtitle B, §§ 211 to 215, Aug. 22, 1966, 110 Stat. 2188 to 2196, amending this section, sections 1382a, 1382b, 1382c, and 1383 of this title, and sections 665e and 901 of Title 2, The Congress, enacting provisions set out as notes under this section and sections 1382a and 1382c of this title, amending provisions set out as a note under section 401 of this title, and repealing provisions set out as a note under this section]."

Report to Congress on Referral, Monitoring and Treatment Activities Relating to Alcoholics and Drug Addicts

Section 201(b)(3)(B)(ii) of Pub.L. 103–296, requiring the Secretary of Health and Human Services to submit a report to Congress on referral, monitoring and treatment activities relating to alcoholics and drug addicts, was repealed by Pub.L. 105–33, Title V, § 5525(c), Aug. 5, 1997, 111 Stat. 625, effective Aug. 5, 1997, see section 5528(c)(2) of Pub.L. 105–33, set out as a note under section 903 of this title.

Study by General Accounting Office [now Government Accountability Office]

Section 232 of Pub.L. 104–193 provided that: "Not later than January 1, 1999, the Comptroller General of the United States shall study and report on—

"(1) the impact of the amendments made by, and the provisions of, this title [Pub.L. 104–193, Title II, §§ 201 to 232, Aug. 22, 1996, 110 Stat. 2185 to 2198, which enacted section 1383f of this title, amended this section, sections 1382a, 1382b, 1382c, and 1383 of this title, and sections 665e and 901 of Title 2, The Congress, enacted provisions set out as notes under this section and sections 1382a, 1382c, and 1383 of this title, amended provisions set out as a note under section 401 of this title, and repealed provisions set out as a note under this section] on the supplemental security income program under title XVI of the Social Security Act [this subchapter]; and

"(2) extra expenses incurred by families of children receiving benefits under such title [this subchapter] that are not covered by other Federal, State, or local programs."

Study of Other Potential Improvements in the Collection of Information Respecting Public Inmates

Section 203(b) of Pub.L. 104–193 provided that:

"(1) **Study.**—The Commissioner of Social Security shall conduct a study of the desirability, feasibility, and cost of—

"(A) establishing a system under which Federal, State, and local courts would furnish to the Commissioner such information respecting court orders by which individuals are confined in jails, prisons, or other public penal, correctional, or medical facilities as the Commissioner may require for the purpose of carrying out section 1611(e)(1) of the Social Security Act [subsec. (e)(1) of this section]; and

"(B) requiring that State and local jails, prisons, and other institutions that enter into agreements with the Commissioner under section 1611(e)(1)(I) of the Social Security Act [subsec. (e)(1)(I) of this section] furnish the information required by such agreements to the Commissioner by means of an electronic or other sophisticated data exchange system.

"(2) **Report.**—Not later than 1 year after the date of the enactment of this Act [Aug. 22, 1996], the Commissioner of Social Security shall submit a report on the results of the study conducted pursuant to this subsection to the Committee on Finance of the Senate and the Committee on Ways and Means of the House of Representatives."

Termination of Special $50 Payment Under Tax Reduction Act of 1975

Special payment of $50, pursuant to section 702 of Pub.L. 94–12, as soon as practicable after Mar. 29, 1975, by the Secretary of the Treasury to each individual who, for the month of March, 1975, was entitled to a monthly insurance benefit payable under this subchapter, but no payments to be made under that section after May 23, 1997, see section 406 of Pub.L. 95–30, set out as a note under section 402 of this title.

Transition Rules for Current Beneficiaries

Section 201(b)(3)(F) of Pub.L. 103–296 provided that: "In any case in which an individual is eligible for supplemental security income benefits under title XVI of the Social Security Act [this subchapter] by reason of disability, the determination of disability was made by the Secretary of Health and Human Services during or before the 180–day period following the date of the enactment of this Act [Aug. 15, 1994], and alcoholism or drug addiction is a contributing factor material to the Secretary's determination that the individual is disabled, for purposes of section 1611(e)(3)(A)(v) of the Social Security Act [subsec. (e)(3)(A)(v) of this section] (added by the amendment made by subparagraph (A) of this paragraph)—

"(i) the first month of such eligibility beginning after 180 days after the date of the enactment of this Act [Aug. 15, 1994] shall be treated as the individual's first month of such eligibility; and

"(ii) the Secretary shall notify the individual of the requirements of the amendments made by this paragraph no later than 180 days after the date of the enactment of this Act [Aug. 15, 1994]."

§ 1382a. Income; earned and unearned income defined; exclusions from income

(a) For purposes of this subchapter, income means both earned income and unearned income; and—

(1) earned income means only—

(A) wages as determined under section 403(f)(5)(C) of this title but without the application of section 410(j)(3) of this title (and, in the case of cash remuneration paid for service as a member of a uniformed service (other than payments described in paragraph (2)(H) of this subsection or subsection (b)(20)), without regard to the limitations contained in section 409(d) of this title);

(B) net earnings from self-employment, as defined in section 411 of this title (without the application of the second and third sentences following subsection (a)(11),[1] the last paragraph of subsection (a), and section 410(j)(3) of this title), including earnings for services described in paragraphs (4), (5), and (6) of subsection (c);

(C) remuneration received for services performed in a sheltered workshop or work activities center; and

(D) any royalty earned by an individual in connection with any publication of the work of the individual, and that portion of any honorarium which is received for services rendered; and

(2) unearned income means all other income, including—

(A) support and maintenance furnished in cash or kind; except that (i) in the case of any individual (and his eligible spouse, if any) living in another person's household and receiving support and maintenance in kind from such person, the dollar amounts otherwise applicable to such individual (and spouse) as specified in subsections (a) and (b) of section 1382 of this title shall be reduced by 33⅓ percent in lieu of including such support and maintenance in the unearned income of such individual (and spouse) as otherwise required by this subparagraph, (ii) in the case of any individual or his eligible spouse who resides in a nonprofit retirement home or similar nonprofit institution, support and maintenance shall not be included to the extent that it is furnished to such individual or such spouse without such institution receiving payment therefor (unless such institution has expressly undertaken an obligation to furnish full support and maintenance to such individual or spouse without any current or future payment therefor) or payment therefor is made by another nonprofit organization, and (iii) support and maintenance shall not be included and the provisions of clause (i) shall not be applicable in the case of any individual (and his eligible spouse, if any) for the period which begins with the month in which such individual (or such individual and his eligible spouse) began to receive support and maintenance while living in a residential facility (including a private household) maintained by another person and ends with the close of the month in which such individual (or such individual and his eligible spouse) ceases to receive support and maintenance while living in such a residential facility (or, if earlier, with the close of the seventeenth month following the month in which such period began), if, not more than 30 days prior to the date on which such individual (or such individual and his eligible spouse) began to receive support and maintenance while living in such a residential facility, (I) such individual (or such individual and his eligible spouse) were residing in a household maintained by such individual (or by such individual and others) as his or their own home, (II) there occurred within the area in which such household is located (and while such individual, or such individual and his spouse, were residing in the household referred to in subclause (I)) a catastrophe on account of which the President declared a major disaster to exist therein for purposes of the Disaster Relief and Emergency Assistance Act, and (III) such individual declares that he (or he and his eligible spouse) ceased to continue living in the household referred to in subclause (II) because of such catastrophe;

(B) any payments received as an annuity, pension, retirement, or disability benefit, including veterans' compensation and pensions, workmen's compensation payments, old-age, survivors, and disability insurance benefits, railroad retirement annuities and pensions, and unemployment insurance benefits;

(C) prizes and awards;

(D) payments to the individual occasioned by the death of another person, to the extent that the total of such payments exceeds the amount expended by such individual for purposes of the deceased person's last illness and burial;

(E) support and alimony payments, and (subject to the provisions of subparagraph (D) excluding certain amounts expended for purposes of a last illness and burial) gifts (cash or otherwise) and inheritances;

(F) rents, dividends, interest, and royalties not described in paragraph (1)(E);

(G) any earnings of, and additions to, the corpus of a trust established by an individual (within the meaning of section 1382b(e) of this title), of which the individual is a beneficiary, to which section 1382b(e) of this title applies, and, in the case of an irrevocable trust, with respect to which circumstances exist under which a payment from the earnings or additions could be made to or for the benefit of the individual; and

(H) payments to or on behalf of a member of a uniformed service for housing of the member (and his or her dependents, if any) on a facility of a uniformed service, including payments provided under section 403 of Title 37 for housing that is acquired or constructed under subchapter IV of chapter 169 of Title 10, or any related provision of law, and any such payments shall be treated as support and maintenance in kind subject to subparagraph (A) of this paragraph.

(b) In determining the income of an individual (and his eligible spouse) there shall be excluded—

(1) subject to limitations (as to amount or otherwise) prescribed by the Commissioner of Social Security, if such individual is under the age of 22 and is, as determined by the Commissioner of Social Security, a student regularly attending a school, college, or university, or a course of vocational or technical training designed to prepare him for gainful employment, the earned income of such individual;

(2)(A) the first $240 per year (or proportionately smaller amounts for shorter periods) of income (whether earned or unearned) other than income which is paid on the basis of the need of the eligible individual, and

(B) monthly (or other periodic) payments received by any individual, under a program established prior to July 1, 1973 (or any program established prior to such date but subsequently amended so as to conform to State or Federal constitutional standards), if (i) such payments are made by the State of which the individual receiving such payments is a resident, (ii) eligibility of any individual for such payments is not based on need and is based solely on attainment of age 65 or any other age set by the State and residency in such State by such individual, and (iii) on or before September 30, 1985, such individual (I) first becomes an eligible individual or an eligible spouse under this title, and (II) satisfies the twenty-five-year residency requirement of such program as such program was in effect prior to January 1, 1983;

(3) in any calendar quarter, the first—

(A) $60 of unearned income, and

(B) $30 of earned income,

of such individual (and such spouse, if any) which, as determined in accordance with criteria prescribed by the Commissioner of Social Security, is received too infrequently or irregularly to be included;

(4)(A) if such individual (or such spouse) is blind (and has not attained age 65, or received benefits under this subchapter (or aid under a State plan approved under section 1202 or 1382 of this title) for the month before the month in which he attained age 65), (i) the first $780 per year (or proportionately smaller amounts for shorter periods) of earned income not excluded by the preceding paragraphs of this subsection, plus one-half of the remainder thereof, (ii) an amount equal to any expenses reasonably attributable to the earning of any income, and (iii) such additional amounts of other income, where such individual has a plan for achieving self-support approved by the Commissioner of Social Security, as may be necessary for the fulfillment of such plan,

(B) if such individual (or such spouse) is disabled but not blind (and has not attained age 65, or received benefits under this subchapter (or aid under a State plan approved under section 1352 or 1382 of this title) for the month before the month in which he attained age 65), (i) the first $780 per year (or proportionately smaller amounts for shorter periods) of earned income not excluded by the preceding paragraphs of this subsection, (ii) such additional amounts of earned income of such individual, if such individual's disability is sufficiently severe to result in a functional limitation requiring assistance in order for him to work, as may be necessary to pay the costs (to such individual) of attendant care services, medical devices, equipment, prostheses, and similar items and services (not including routine drugs or routine medical services unless such drugs or services are necessary for the control of the disabling condition) which are necessary (as determined by the Commissioner of Social Security in regulations) for that purpose, whether or not such assistance is also needed to enable him to carry out his normal daily functions, except that the amounts to be excluded shall be subject to such reasonable limits as the Commissioner of Social Security may prescribe, (iii) one-half of the amount of earned income not excluded after the application of the preceding provisions of this subparagraph, and (iv) such additional amounts of other income, where such individual has a plan for achieving self-support approved by the Commissioner of Social Security, as may be necessary for the fulfillment of such plan, or

(C) if such individual (or such spouse) has attained age 65 and is not included under subparagraph (A) or (B), the first $780 per year (or proportionately smaller amounts for shorter periods) of earned income not excluded by the preceding paragraphs of this subsection, plus one-half of the remainder thereof;

(5) any amount received from any public agency as a return or refund of taxes paid on real property or on food purchased by such individual (or such spouse);

(6) assistance, furnished to or on behalf of such individual (and spouse), which is based on need and furnished by any State or political subdivision of a State;

(7) any portion of any grant, scholarship, fellowship, or gift (or portion of a gift) used to pay the cost of tuition and fees at any educational (including technical or vocational education) institution;

(8) home produce of such individual (or spouse) utilized by the household for its own consumption;

(9) if such individual is a child, one-third of any payment for his support received from an absent parent;

(10) any amounts received for the foster care of a child who is not an eligible individual but who is living in the same home as such individual and was placed in such home by a public or nonprofit private child-placement or child-care agency;

(11) assistance received under the Disaster Relief and Emergency Assistance Act or other assistance provided pursuant to a Federal statute on account of a catastrophe which is declared to be a major disaster by the President;

(12) interest income received on assistance funds referred to in paragraph (11) within the 9–month period beginning on the date such funds are received (or such longer periods as the Commissioner of Social Security shall by regulations prescribe in cases where good cause is shown by the individual concerned for extending such period);

(13) any support or maintenance assistance furnished to or on behalf of such individual (and spouse if any) which (as determined under regulations of the Commissioner of Social Security by such State agency as the chief executive officer of the State may designate) is based on need for such support or maintenance, including assistance received to assist in meeting the costs of home energy (including both heating and cooling), and which is (A) assistance furnished in kind by a private nonprofit agency, or (B) assistance furnished by a supplier of home heating oil or gas, by an entity providing home energy whose revenues are primarily derived on a rate-of-return basis regulated by a State or Federal governmental entity, or by a municipal utility providing home energy;

(14) assistance paid, with respect to the dwelling unit occupied by such individual (or such individual and spouse), under the United States Housing Act of 1937, the National Housing Act, section 101 of the

Housing and Urban Development Act of 1965, title V of the Housing Act of 1949, or section 202(h) of the Housing Act of 1959;

(15) the value of any commercial transportation ticket, for travel by such individual (or spouse) among the 50 States, the District of Columbia, the Commonwealth of Puerto Rico, the Virgin Islands, Guam, American Samoa, and the Northern Mariana Islands, which is received as a gift by such individual (or such spouse) and is not converted to cash;

(16) interest accrued on the value of an agreement entered into by such individual (or such spouse) representing the purchase of a burial space excluded under section 1382b(a)(2)(B) of this title, and left to accumulate;

(17) any amount received by such individual (or such spouse) from a fund established by a State to aid victims of crime;

(18) relocation assistance provided by a State or local government to such individual (or such spouse), comparable to assistance provided under title II of the Uniform Relocation Assistance and Real Property Acquisitions [2] Policies Act of 1970 which is subject to the treatment required by section 216 of such Act;

(19) any refund of Federal income taxes made to such individual (or such spouse) by reason of section 32 of the Internal Revenue Code of 1986 (relating to earned income tax credit), and any payment made to such individual (or such spouse) by an employer under section 3507 of such Code (relating to advance payment of earned income credit);

(20) special pay received pursuant to section 310, or paragraph (1) or (3) of section 351(a), of Title 37;

(21) the interest or other earnings on any account established and maintained in accordance with section 1383(a)(2)(F) of this title;

(22) any gift to, or for the benefit of, an individual who has not attained 18 years of age and who has a life-threatening condition, from an organization described in section 501(c)(3) of the Internal Revenue Code of 1986 which is exempt from taxation under section 501(a) of such Code—

(A) in the case of an in-kind gift, if the gift is not converted to cash; or

(B) in the case of a cash gift, only to the extent that the total amount excluded from the income of the individual pursuant to this paragraph in the calendar year in which the gift is made does not exceed $2,000;

(23) interest or dividend income from resources—

(A) not excluded under section 1382b(a) of this title, or

(B) excluded pursuant to Federal law other than section 1382b(a) of this title;

(24) any annuity paid by a State to the individual (or such spouse) on the basis of the individual's being a veteran (as defined in section 101 of Title 38), and blind, disabled, or aged;

(25) any benefit (whether cash or in-kind) conferred upon (or paid on behalf of) a participant in an AmeriCorps position approved by the Corporation for National and Community Service under section 12573 of this title; and

(26) the first $2,000 received during a calendar year by such individual (or such spouse) as compensation for participation in a clinical trial involving research and testing of treatments for a rare disease or condition (as defined in section 360ee(b)(2) of Title 21), but only if the clinical trial—

(A) has been reviewed and approved by an institutional review board that is established—

(i) to protect the rights and welfare of human subjects participating in scientific research; and

(ii) in accord with the requirements under part 46 of title 45, Code of Federal Regulations; and

(B) meets the standards for protection of human subjects as provided under part 46 of title 45, Code of Federal Regulations.

(Aug. 14, 1935, c. 531, Title XVI, § 1612, as added Pub.L. 92–603, Title III, § 301, Oct. 30, 1972, 86 Stat. 1468; amended Pub.L. 93–484, § 4, Oct. 26, 1974, 88 Stat. 1460; Pub.L. 94–202, § 9, Jan. 2, 1976, 89 Stat. 1140; Pub.L. 94–331, §§ 2(a), 4(a), June 30, 1976, 90 Stat. 781, 782; Pub.L. 94–455, Title XXI, § 2125, Oct. 4, 1976, 90 Stat. 1920; Pub.L. 94–566, Title V, § 505(b), Oct. 20, 1976, 90 Stat. 2686; Pub.L. 95–171, § 8(a), Nov. 12, 1977, 91 Stat. 1355; Pub.L. 96–222, Title I, § 101(a)(2)(B), Apr. 1, 1980, 94 Stat. 195; Pub.L. 96–265, Title II, § 202(a), Title III, § 302(b), June 9, 1980, 94 Stat. 449, 451; Pub.L. 96–473, § 6(g), Oct. 19, 1980, 94 Stat. 2266; Pub.L. 97–35, Title XXIII, § 2341(b), Aug. 13, 1981, 95 Stat. 865; Pub.L. 97–424, Title V, § 545(a), Jan. 6, 1983, 96 Stat. 2198; Pub.L. 98–21, Title IV, § 404(a), Apr. 20, 1983, 97 Stat. 140; Pub.L. 98–369, Div. B, Title VI, §§ 2616(a), 2639(b), (c), 2663(g)(3), (4), July 18, 1984, 98 Stat. 1133, 1144, 1145, 1168; Pub.L. 99–514, § 2, Title XVIII, § 1883(d)(2), (3), Oct. 22, 1986, 100 Stat. 2095, 2918; Pub.L. 100–203, Title IX, § 9120(a), Dec. 22, 1987, 101 Stat. 1330–309; Pub.L. 100–647, Title VIII, § 8103(a), Nov. 10, 1988, 102 Stat. 3795; Pub.L. 100–707, Title I, § 109(p), Nov. 23, 1988, 102 Stat. 4709; Pub.L. 101–239, Title VIII, §§ 8011(a), 8013(a), Dec. 19, 1989, 103 Stat. 2464; Pub.L. 101–508, Title V, §§ 5031(a), 5033(a), 5034(a), 5035(a), Title XI, 11115(b)(1), Nov. 5, 1990, 104 Stat. 1388–224, 1388–225, 1388–414; Pub.L. 103–66, Title XIII, § 13733(b), Aug. 10, 1993, 107 Stat. 662; Pub.L. 103–296, Title I, § 107(a)(4), Aug. 15, 1994, 108 Stat. 1478; Pub.L. 103–432, Title II, §§ 264(a), 267(a), Oct. 31, 1994, 108 Stat. 4467, 4469; Pub.L. 104–193, Title II, § 213(c), Aug. 22, 1996, 110 Stat. 2195; Pub.L. 105–306, § 7(a), Oct. 28, 1998, 112 Stat. 2928; Pub.L. 106–169, Title II, § 205(b), Dec. 14, 1999, 113 Stat. 1834; Pub.L. 106–554, § 1(a)(1) [Title V, § 519], Dec. 21, 2000, 114 Stat. 2763, 2763A–74; Pub.L. 108–203, Title IV, §§ 430(a), (b), 432(a), 435(a), Mar. 2, 2004, 118 Stat. 538 to 540; Pub.L. 110–245, Title II, §§ 201, 202(a), 203, June 17, 2008, 122 Stat. 1637, 1638; Pub.L. 111–255, § 3(a), (e), Oct. 5, 2010, 124 Stat. 2641; Pub.L. 114–63, § 2, Oct. 7, 2015, 129 Stat. 549; Pub.L. 114–328, Div. A, Title VI, § 618(i), Dec. 23, 2016, 130 Stat. 2161.)

[1] So in original. Probably should be subsection "(a)(15),".
[2] So in original. Probably should be "Acquisition".

HISTORICAL AND STATUTORY NOTES

References in Text

The Internal Revenue Code of 1986, referred to in text, is classified generally to Title 26, 26 U.S.C.A. § 1 et seq.

Section 1382 of this title, referred to in subsecs. (a)(2)(A), (b)(4)(A), (B), is a reference to § 1382 of this title as it existed prior to the general revision of this subchapter by Pub.L. 92–603, Title III, § 301, Oct. 30, 1972, 86 Stat. 1465, eff. Jan. 1, 1974. The prior section (which is set out as a note under section 1382 of this title) continues in effect for Puerto Rico, Guam, and the Virgin Islands.

The [Robert T. Stafford] Disaster Relief and Emergency Assistance Act, referred to in subsec. (a)(2)(A), (b)(11), is Pub.L. 93–288, May 22, 1974, 88 Stat. 143, as amended, which is classified principally to chapter 68 (section 5121 et seq.) of this title. For complete classification of this Act to the Code, see Short Title note set out under section 5121 of this title and Tables.

Subchapter IV of chapter 169 of Title 10, referred to in subsec. (a)(2)(H), is 10 U.S.C.A. § 2871 et seq.

The United States Housing Act of 1937, referred to in subsec. (b)(14), is Act Sept. 1, 1937, c. 896, as revised generally by Pub.L. 93–383, Title II, § 201(a), Aug. 22, 1974, 88 Stat. 653, and amended, which is classified generally to chapter 8 of this title (42 U.S.C.A. § 1437 et seq.). For complete classification of this Act to the Code, see Short Title note set out under section 1437 of this title and Tables.

The National Housing Act, referred to in subsec. (b)(14), is Act June 27, 1934, c. 847, 48 Stat. 1246, as amended, which is classified principally to chapter 13 of Title 12, Banks and Banking (12 U.S.C.A. § 1701 et seq.). For complete classification of this Act to the Code, see section 1701 of Title 12 and Tables.

The Housing and Urban Development Act of 1965, referred to in subsec. (b)(14), is Pub.L. 89–117, Aug. 10, 1965, 79 Stat. 451, as amended. Section 101 of the Housing and Urban Development Act of 1965 enacted section 1701s of Title 12, Banks and Banking and amended section 1451 and former section 1465 of this title. For complete classification of this Act to the Code, see Short Title of 1965 Amendment note set out under section 1701 of Title 12 and Tables.

The Housing Act of 1949, referred to in subsec. (b)(14), is Act July 15, 1949, c. 338, 63 Stat. 413, as amended. Title V of the Housing Act of 1949 is classified generally to subchapter III (section 1471 et seq.) of chapter 8A of this title. For complete classification of this Act to the Code, see Short Title note set out under section 1441 of this title and Tables.

The Housing Act of 1959, referred to in subsec. (b)(14), is Pub.L. 86–372, Sept. 23, 1959, 73 Stat. 654, as amended. Section 202(h) of the Housing Act of 1959 is classified to section 1701q(h) of Title 12, Banks and Banking. For complete classification of this Act to the Code, see Short Title of 1959 Amendment note set out under section 1701 of Title 12 and Tables.

Title II of the Uniform Relocation Assistance and Real Property Acquisitions Policies Act of 1970, referred to in subsec. (b)(18), means title II of Pub.L. 91–646, Jan. 2, 1971, 84 Stat. 1895, which enacted sections 4621 to 4638 of this title, amended sections 1415, 2473, and 3307 of this title and section 1606 of Title 49, Appendix, Transportation, repealed sections 1465 and 3074 of this title, section 2680 of Title 10, Armed Forces, sections 501 to 512 of Title 23, Highways, sections 1231 to 1234 of Title 43, Public Lands, and enacted provisions set out as notes under sections 4601 and 4621 of this title and under sections 501 to 512 of Title 23. Section 216 of the Act is classified to section 4636 of this title. For complete classification of title II to the Code, see Tables.

Effective and Applicability Provisions

2015 Acts. Pub.L. 114–63, § 2, Oct. 7, 2015, 129 Stat. 549, provided in part that Pub.L. 111–255, § 3(e) is repealed, effective as if included in the enactment of Pub.L. 111–255. See Sunset Provisions note set out under this section.

2010 Acts. Pub.L. 111–255, § 3(d), Oct. 5, 2010, 124 Stat. 2641, as amended by Pub.L. 111–255, § 3(e), Oct. 5, 2010, 124 Stat. 2641; Pub.L. 114–63, § 2, Oct. 7, 2015, 129 Stat. 549, provided that: "The amendments made by this section [amending this section and 42 U.S.C.A. §§ 1382b and 1396a] shall take effect on the date that is the earlier of—

"(1) the effective date of final regulations promulgated by the Commissioner of Social Security to carry out this section and such amendments; or

"(2) 180 days after the date of enactment of this Act [Oct. 5, 2010]."

[Pub.L. 111–255, § 3(e), which provided that Pub.L. 111–255 and the amendments made by Pub.L. 111–255 were repealed on the date that was 5 years after Oct. 5, 2010, was subsequently repealed by Pub.L. 114–63, § 2, effective as if included in the enactment of Pub.L. 111–255, see Pub.L. 111–255, § 3(e), set out as a Sunset Provisions note under this section.]

2008 Acts. Pub.L. 110–245, Title II, § 204, June 17, 2008, 122 Stat. 1638, provided that: "The amendments made by this title [Pub.L. 110–245, Title II, §§ 201 to 204, June 17, 2008, 122 Stat. 1637, amending this section and 42 U.S.C.A. § 1382b] shall be effective with respect to benefits payable for months beginning after 60 days after the date of the enactment of this Act [June 17, 2008]."

2004 Acts. Pub.L. 108–203, Title IV, § 430(c), Mar. 2, 2004, 118 Stat. 538, provided that: "The amendments made by this section [enacting subsec. (b)(23) of this section and amending subsec. (b)(3), (21), and (22) of this section] shall be effective with respect to benefits payable for months in calendar quarters that begin more than 90 days after the date of the enactment of this Act [Mar. 2, 2004]."

Pub.L. 108–203, Title IV, § 432(b), Mar. 2, 2004, 118 Stat. 539, provided that: "The amendment made by this section [amending subsec. (b)(1) of this section] shall be effective with respect to benefits payable for months that begin on or after 1 year after the date of enactment of this Act [Mar. 2, 2004]."

Pub.L. 108–203, Title IV, § 435(c), Mar. 2, 2004, 118 Stat. 540, provided that: "The amendments made by this section [enacting 42 U.S.C.A. § 1382b(a)(15) and amending this section and 42 U.S.C.A. § 1382b(a)(13), (14)] shall apply to benefits payable for months that begin more than 90 days after the date of enactment of this Act [Mar. 2, 2004]."

1999 Acts. Pub.L. 106–169, Title II, § 205(d), Dec. 14, 1999, 113 Stat. 1834, provided that: "The amendments made by this section [amending subsec. (a)(2) of this section and sections 1382b and 1396a of this title] shall take effect on January 1, 2000, and shall apply to trusts established on or after such date."

1998 Acts. Pub.L. 105–306, § 7(c), Oct. 28, 1998, 112 Stat. 2928, provided that: "The amendments made by this section [amending this section and section 1382b of this title] shall apply to gifts made on or after the date that is 2 years before the date of the enactment of this Act [Oct. 28, 1998]."

1996 Acts. Section 213(d) of Pub.L. 104–193 provided that: "The amendments made by this section [amending this section and sections 1382b and 1383 of this title] shall apply to payments made after the date of the enactment of this Act [Aug. 22, 1996]."

1994 Acts. Amendments by section 264 of Pub.L. 103–432 effective as if included in provisions of Pub.L. 101–508, 104 Stat. 1388, which was approved Nov. 5, 1990, to which such amendments relate at the time such provisions were enacted into law, see section 264(h) of Pub.L. 103–432, set out as a note under section 602 of this title.

Amendment by section 107(a)(4) of Pub.L. 103–296 effective Mar. 31, 1995, see section 110 of Pub.L. 103–296, set out as a note under section 401 of this title.

1993 Acts. Section 13733(c) of Pub.L. 103–66, provided that: "The amendments made by this section [amending subsec. (b)(18) to (20) and section 1382c(f)(4) of this title] shall take effect on the 1st day of the 2nd month that begins after the date of the enactment of this Act [Aug. 10, 1993]."

1990 Acts. Section 5031(d) of Pub.L. 101–508 provided that: "The amendments made by this section [amending this section and sections 1382b and 1383 of this title] shall apply with respect to benefits for months beginning on or after the first day of the 6th calendar month following the month in which this Act is enacted [Nov. 1990]."

Section 5033(b) of Pub.L. 101–508 provided that: "The amendment made by subsection (a) [amending subsec. (b) of this section] shall apply to benefits payable for calendar months beginning after the date of the enactment of this Act [Nov. 1990]."

Section 5034(b) of Pub.L. 101–508 provided that: "The amendments made by subsection (a) [amending subsec. (a) of this section] shall apply with respect to benefits for months beginning on or after the first day of the 13th calendar month following the month in which this Act is enacted [Nov. 1990]."

Section 5035(c) of Pub.L. 101–508, as amended Pub.L. 103–66, Title XIII, § 13732, Aug. 10, 1993, 107 Stat. 662, provided that: "The amendments made by this section [amending subsec. (b) of this section and section 1382b(a) of this title] shall apply with respect to benefits for calendar months beginning on or after the first day of the 6th calendar month following the month in which this Act is enacted [Nov. 1990]."

Amendment by section 11115(b) of Pub.L. 101–508 applicable to determinations of income or resources made for any period after Dec. 31, 1990, see section 11115(e) of Pub.L. 101–508, set out as a note under section 602 of this title.

1989 Acts. Section 8011(b) of Pub.L. 101–239 provided that: "The amendments made by subsection (a) [enacting subsec. (b)(15) of this section] shall take effect on the 1st day of the 3rd calendar month beginning after the date of the enactment of this Act [Dec. 19, 1989]."

Section 8013(c) of Pub.L. 101–239 provided that: "The amendments made by subsections (a) [enacting subsec. (b)(16) of this section] and (b) [amending section 1382b(a)(2)(B) of this title] shall take effect on the 1st day of the 4th month beginning after the date of the enactment of this Act [Dec. 19, 1989]."

1988 Acts. Section 8103(c) of Pub.L. 100–647 provided that: "The amendments made by this section [enacting subsec. (b)(14) of this section and section 1382b(a)(8) of this title] shall be effective as though they had been included in section 162 of the Housing and Community Development Act of 1987 [Pub.L. 100–242, see Effective Date of 1988 Amendment note set out under 12 U.S.C.A. § 1701q] at the time of its enactment [Feb. 5, 1988]."

1987 Acts. Section 9120(b) of Pub.L. 100–203 provided that: "The amendments made by subsection (a) [amending subsec. (a)(2)(D), (E) of this section] shall become effective April 1, 1988."

1986 Acts. Amendment by Pub.L. 99–514 effective Oct. 22, 1986, see section 1883(f) of Pub.L. 99–514, set out as a note under section 402 of this title.

1984 Acts. Section 2616(b) of Pub.L. 98–369 provided that: "The amendment made by subsection (a) [amending subsec. (b)(2)(B) of this section] shall become effective on the date of the enactment of this Act [July 18, 1984]."

Amendment by section 2639(b) of Pub.L. 98–369 effective with respect to months which begin after Sept. 30, 1984, see section 2639(d) of Pub.L. 98–369, as amended, set out as a note under section 602 of this title.

Amendment by section 2663(g)(3), (4) of Pub.L. 98–369 effective July 18, 1984, but not to be construed as changing or affecting any right, liability, status, or interpretation which existed (under the provisions of law involved) before that date, see section 2664(b) of Pub.L. 98–369, set out as a note under section 401 of this title.

1983 Acts. Section 545(c) of Pub.L. 97–424 and section 404(c) of Pub.L. 98–21, which had provided for the effective and termination dates covering the enactment and subsequent amendment of subsec. (b)(13) of this section by section 545(a) of Pub.L. 98–424 and section 404(a) of Pub.L. 98–21, were repealed by section 2639(c), (d) of Pub.L. 98–369, effective with respect to months beginning after Sept. 30, 1984, see note set out under section 602 of this title.

1981 Acts. Amendment by Pub.L. 97–35 effective with respect to months after the first calendar quarter which ends more than five months after August, 1981, with provision for transitional payments, see section 2341(c) of Pub.L. 97–35, set out as an Effective Date of 1981 Act and Transitional Provisions note under section 1382 of this title.

1980 Acts. Section 202(b) of Pub.L. 96–265 provided that: "The amendments made by subsection (a) [enacting subsec. (a)(1)(D) of this section] shall apply only with respect to remuneration received in months after September 1980."

Amendment by section 302(b) of Pub.L. 96–265 applicable with respect to expenses incurred on or after first day of sixth month which begins after June 9, 1980, see section 302(c) of Pub.L. 96–265, set out as a note under section 423 of this title.

Amendment by Pub.L. 96–222 applicable to payments for months beginning after Dec. 31, 1979, see section 101(b)(1)(B) of Pub.L. 96–222, set out as a note under section 602 of this title.

1977 Acts. Section 8(b) of Pub.L. 95–171 provided that: "The amendment made by this section [enacting subsec. (b)(12) of this section] shall be effective July 1, 1976, with respect to catastrophes which occurred on or after June 1, 1976, and before December 31, 1976. With respect to catastrophes which occurred on or after December 31, 1976, the amendment made by this section [enacting subsec. (b)(12) of this section] shall be effective the first day of the calendar quarter following enactment of this Act [Nov. 12, 1977]."

1976 Acts. Amendment by Pub.L. 94–566 effective Oct. 1, 1976, see section 505(e) of Pub.L. 94–566, set out as a note under section 1382 of this title.

Section 2(b) of Pub.L. 94–331, as amended by Pub.L. 95–171, § 6(a), Nov. 12, 1977, 91 Stat. 1355, effective the first day of calendar quarter following Nov. 12, 1977, provided that: "The amendments made by this Act [amending subsec. (b)(11) of this section and sections 815, 3402, 6153, and 6154 of Title 26, Internal Revenue Code, and enacting provisions set out as notes under sections 815 and 3402 of Title 26] shall be applicable only in the case of catastrophes which occur on or after June 1, 1976."

Section 4(b) of Pub.L. 94–331, as amended by Pub.L. 95–171, § 7(a), Nov. 12, 1977, 91 Stat. 1355, effective the first day of calendar quarter following Nov. 12, 1977, provided that: "The amendments made by this Act [see section 2(b) of Pub.L. 94–331, set out hereunder] shall be applicable only in the case of catastrophes which occur on or after June 1, 1976."

1974 Acts. Section 4 of Pub.L. 93–484 provided that amendment of subsec. (a)(2)(A) by Pub.L. 93–484 is effective Jan. 1, 1974.

1972 Acts. Section 301 of Pub.L. 92–603 provided that this section is effective Jan. 1, 1974.

Sunset Provisions

Pub.L. 111–255, § 3(e), Oct. 5, 2010, 124 Stat. 2641, which provided that Pub.L. 111–255 and the amendments made by Pub.L. 111–255, which amended this section and 42 U.S.C.A. §§ 1382b, and 1396a, and enacted provisions set out as notes under this section and 42 U.S.C.A. § 1305, were repealed on the date that was 5 years after Oct. 5, 2010, was subsequently repealed by Pub.L. 114–63, § 2, Oct. 7, 2015, 129 Stat. 549, effective as if included in the enactment of Pub.L. 111–255.

Findings

Pub.L. 111–255, § 2, Oct. 5, 2010, 124 Stat. 2640, as amended by Pub.L. 111–255, § 3(e), Oct. 5, 2010, 124 Stat. 2641; Pub. L. 114–63, § 2, Oct. 7, 2015, 129 Stat. 549, provided that: "Congress finds the following:

"(1) Advances in medicine depend on clinical trial research conducted at public and private research institutions across the United States.

"(2) The challenges associated with enrolling participants in clinical research studies are especially difficult for studies that evaluate treatments for rare diseases and conditions (defined by the Orphan Drug Act as a disease or condition affecting fewer than 200,000 Americans), where the available number of willing and able research participants may be very small.

"(3) In accordance with ethical standards established by the National Institutes of Health, sponsors of clinical research may provide payments to trial participants for out-of-pocket costs associated with trial enrollment and for the time and commitment demanded by those who participate in a study. When offering compensation, clinical trial sponsors are required to provide such payments to all participants.

"(4) The offer of payment for research participation may pose a barrier to trial enrollment when such payments threaten the eligibility of clinical trial participants for Supplemental Security Income and Medicaid benefits.

"(5) With a small number of potential trial participants and the possible loss of Supplemental Security Income and Medicaid benefits for many who wish to participate, clinical trial research for rare diseases and conditions becomes exceptionally difficult and may hinder research on new treatments and potential cures for these rare diseases and conditions."

[Pub.L. 111–255, § 3(e), which provided that Pub.L. 111–255 and the amendments made by Pub.L. 111–255 were repealed on the date that was 5 years after Oct. 5, 2010, was subsequently repealed by Pub.L. 114–63, § 2, effective as if included in the enactment of Pub.L. 111–255, see Pub.L. 111–255, § 3(e), set out as a Sunset Provisions note under this section.]

Application to Northern Mariana Islands

For inapplicability of this section to the Northern Mariana Islands, see section 502(a)(1) of the Covenant to Establish a Commonwealth of the Northern Mariana Islands in Political Union with the United States of America, as set forth in Pub.L. 94–241, Mar. 24, 1976, 90 Stat. 263, eff. Jan. 9, 1978, pursuant to Proc. No. 4534, Oct. 24, 1977, 42 F.R. 6593, set out as notes under section 1681 of Title 48, Territories and Insular Possessions.

Puerto Rico, Guam, and Virgin Islands

Enactment of provisions of Pub.L. 92–603, eff. Jan. 1, 1974, not applicable to Puerto Rico, Guam, and the Virgin Islands, see section 303(b) of Pub.L. 92–603, set out as a note under section 301 of this title.

§ 1382b. Resources

(a) Exclusions from resources

In determining the resources of an individual (and his eligible spouse, if any) there shall be excluded—

(1) the home (including the land that appertains thereto);

(2)(A) household goods, personal effects, and an automobile, to the extent that their total value does not exceed such amount as the Commissioner of Social Security determines to be reasonable; and

(B) the value of any burial space or agreement (including any interest accumulated thereon) representing the purchase of a burial space (subject to such limits as to size or value as the Commissioner of Social Security may by regulation prescribe) held for the purpose of providing a place for the burial of the individual, his spouse, or any other member of his immediate family;

(3) other property which is so essential to the means of self-support of such individual (and such spouse) as to warrant its exclusion, as determined in accordance with and subject to limitations prescribed by the Commissioner of Social Security, except that the Commissioner of Social Security shall not establish a limitation on property (including the tools of a tradesperson and the machinery and livestock of a farmer) that is used in a trade or business or by such individual as an employee;

(4) such resources of an individual who is blind or disabled and who has a plan for achieving self-

support approved by the Commissioner of Social Security, as may be necessary for the fulfillment of such plan;

(5) in the case of Natives of Alaska, shares of stock held in a Regional or a Village Corporation, during the period of twenty years in which such stock is inalienable, as provided in section 1606(h) and section 1607(c) of Title 43;

(6) assistance referred to in section 1382a(b)(11) of this title for the 9-month period beginning on the date such funds are received (or for such longer period as the Commissioner of Social Security shall by regulations prescribe in cases where good cause is shown by the individual concerned for extending such period); and, for purposes of this paragraph, the term "assistance" includes interest thereon which is excluded from income under section 1382a(b)(12) of this title;

(7) any amount received from the United States which is attributable to underpayments of benefits due for one or more prior months, under this subchapter or subchapter II, to such individual (or spouse) or to any other person whose income is deemed to be included in such individual's (or spouse's) income for purposes of this subchapter; but the application of this paragraph in the case of any such individual (and eligible spouse if any), with respect to any amount so received from the United States, shall be limited to the first 9 months following the month in which such amount is received, and written notice of this limitation shall be given to the recipient concurrently with the payment of such amount;

(8) the value of assistance referred to in section 1382a(b)(14) of this title, paid with respect to the dwelling unit occupied by such individual (or such individual and spouse);

(9) for the 9-month period beginning after the month in which received, any amount received by such individual (or such spouse) from a fund established by a State to aid victims of crime, to the extent that such individual (or such spouse) demonstrates that such amount was paid as compensation for expenses incurred or losses suffered as a result of a crime;

(10) for the 9-month period beginning after the month in which received, relocation assistance provided by a State or local government to such individual (or such spouse), comparable to assistance provided under title II of the Uniform Relocation Assistance and Real Property Acquisitions [1] Policies Act of 1970 which is subject to the treatment required by section 216 of such Act;

(11) for the 9-month period beginning after the month in which received—

(A) notwithstanding section 203 of the Economic Growth and Tax Relief Reconciliation Act of 2001, any refund of Federal income taxes made to such individual (or such spouse) under section 24 of the Internal Revenue Code of 1986 (relating to child tax credit) by reason of subsection (d) thereof; and

(B) any refund of Federal income taxes made to such individual (or such spouse) by reason of section 32 of the Internal Revenue Code of 1986 (relating to earned income tax credit), and any payment made to such individual (or such spouse) by an employer under section 3507 of such Code (relating to advance payment of earned income credit);

(12) any account, including accrued interest or other earnings thereon, established and maintained in accordance with section 1383(a)(2)(F) of this title;

(13) any gift to, or for the benefit of, an individual who has not attained 18 years of age and who has a life-threatening condition, from an organization described in section 501(c)(3) of the Internal Revenue Code of 1986 which is exempt from taxation under section 501(a) of such Code—

(A) in the case of an in-kind gift, if the gift is not converted to cash; or

(B) in the case of a cash gift, only to the extent that the total amount excluded from the resources of the individual pursuant to this paragraph in the calendar year in which the gift is made does not exceed $2,000;

(14) for the 9-month period beginning after the month in which received, any amount received by such individual (or spouse) or any other person whose income is deemed to be included in such individual's (or spouse's) income for purposes of this subchapter as restitution for benefits under this subchapter, subchapter II, or subchapter VIII that a representative payee of such individual (or spouse) or such other person under section 405(j), 1007, or 1383(a)(2) of this title has misused;

(15) for the 9-month period beginning after the month in which received, any grant, scholarship, fellowship, or gift (or portion of a gift) used to pay the cost of tuition and fees at any educational (including technical or vocational education) institution;

(16) for the month of receipt and every month thereafter, any annuity paid by a State to the individual (or such spouse) on the basis of the individual's being a veteran (as defined in section 101 of Title 38), and blind, disabled, or aged; and

(17) any amount received by such individual (or such spouse) which is excluded from income under section 1382a(b)(26) of this title (relating to compensation for participation in a clinical trial involving research and testing of treatments for a rare disease or condition).

In determining the resources of an individual (or eligible spouse) an insurance policy shall be taken into account only to the extent of its cash surrender value; except that if the total face value of all life insurance policies on any person is $1,500 or less, no part of the value of any such policy shall be taken into account.

(b) Disposition of resources; grounds for exemption from disposition requirements

(1) The Commissioner of Social Security shall prescribe the period or periods of time within which, and the manner in which, various kinds of property must be disposed of in order not to be included in determining an individual's eligibility for benefits. Any portion of the individual's benefits paid for any such period shall be conditioned upon such disposal; and any benefits so paid shall (at the time of the disposal) be considered overpayments to the extent they would not have been paid had the disposal occurred at the beginning of the period for which such benefits were paid.

(2) Notwithstanding the provisions of paragraph (1), the Commissioner of Social Security shall not require the disposition of any real property for so long as it cannot be sold because (A) it is jointly owned (and its sale would cause undue hardship, due to loss of housing, for the other owner or owners), (B) its sale is barred by a legal impediment, or (C) as determined under regulations issued by the Commissioner of Social Security, the owner's reasonable efforts to sell it have been unsuccessful.

(c) Disposal of resources for less than fair market value

(1)(A)(i) If an individual or the spouse of an individual disposes of resources for less than fair market value on or after the look-back date described in clause (ii)(I), the individual is ineligible for benefits under this subchapter for months during the period beginning on the date described in clause (iii) and equal to the number of months calculated as provided in clause (iv).

(ii)(I) The look-back date described in this subclause is a date that is 36 months before the date described in subclause (II).

(II) The date described in this subclause is the date on which the individual applies for benefits under this subchapter or, if later, the date on which the individual (or the spouse of the individual) disposes of resources for less than fair market value.

(iii) The date described in this clause is the first day of the first month in or after which resources were disposed of for less than fair market value and which does not occur in any other period of ineligibility under this paragraph.

(iv) The number of months calculated under this clause shall be equal to—

(I) the total, cumulative uncompensated value of all resources so disposed of by the individual (or the spouse of the individual) on or after the look-back date described in clause (ii)(I); divided by

(II) the amount of the maximum monthly benefit payable under section 1382(b) of this title, plus the amount (if any) of the maximum State supplementary payment corresponding to the State's payment level applicable to the individual's living arrangement and eligibility category that would otherwise be payable to the individual by the Commissioner pursuant to an agreement under section 1382e(a) of this title or section 212(b) of Public Law 93–66, for the month in which occurs the date described in clause (ii)(II),

rounded, in the case of any fraction, to the nearest whole number, but shall not in any case exceed 36 months.

(B)(i) Notwithstanding subparagraph (A), this subsection shall not apply to a transfer of a resource to a trust if the portion of the trust attributable to the resource is considered a resource available to the individual pursuant to subsection (e)(3) (or would be so considered but for the application of subsection (e)(4)).

(ii) In the case of a trust established by an individual or an individual's spouse (within the meaning of subsection (e)), if from such portion of the trust, if any, that is considered a resource available to the individual pursuant to subsection (e)(3) (or would be so considered but for the application of subsection (e)(4)) or the residue of the portion on the termination of the trust—

(I) there is made a payment other than to or for the benefit of the individual; or

(II) no payment could under any circumstance be made to the individual,

then, for purposes of this subsection, the payment described in clause (I) or the foreclosure of payment described in clause (II) shall be considered a transfer of resources by the individual or the individual's spouse as of the date of the payment or foreclosure, as the case may be.

(C) An individual shall not be ineligible for benefits under this subchapter by reason of the application of this paragraph to a disposal of resources by the individual or the spouse of the individual, to the extent that—

(i) the resources are a home and title to the home was transferred to—

(I) the spouse of the transferor;

(II) a child of the transferor who has not attained 21 years of age, or is blind or disabled;

(III) a sibling of the transferor who has an equity interest in such home and who was residing in the transferor's home for a period of at least 1 year immediately before the date the transferor becomes an institutionalized individual; or

(IV) a son or daughter of the transferor (other than a child described in subclause (II)) who was residing in the transferor's home for a period of at least 2 years immediately before the date the transferor becomes an institutionalized individual, and who provided care to the transferor which permitted the transferor to reside at home rather than in such an institution or facility;

(ii) the resources—

(I) were transferred to the transferor's spouse or to another for the sole benefit of the transferor's spouse;

(II) were transferred from the transferor's spouse to another for the sole benefit of the transferor's spouse;

(III) were transferred to, or to a trust (including a trust described in section 1396p(d)(4) of this title) established solely for the benefit of, the transferor's child who is blind or disabled; or

(IV) were transferred to a trust (including a trust described in section 1396p(d)(4) of this title) established solely for the benefit of an individual who has not attained 65 years of age and who is disabled;

(iii) a satisfactory showing is made to the Commissioner of Social Security (in accordance with regulations promulgated by the Commissioner) that—

(I) the individual who disposed of the resources intended to dispose of the resources either at fair market value, or for other valuable consideration;

(II) the resources were transferred exclusively for a purpose other than to qualify for benefits under this subchapter; or

(III) all resources transferred for less than fair market value have been returned to the transferor; or

(iv) the Commissioner determines, under procedures established by the Commissioner, that the denial of eligibility would work an undue hardship as determined on the basis of criteria established by the Commissioner.

(D) For purposes of this subsection, in the case of a resource held by an individual in common with another person or persons in a joint tenancy, tenancy in common, or similar arrangement, the resource (or the affected portion of such resource) shall be considered to be disposed of by the individual when any action is taken, either by the individual or by any other person, that reduces or eliminates the individual's ownership or control of such resource.

(E) In the case of a transfer by the spouse of an individual that results in a period of ineligibility for the individual under this subsection, the Commissioner shall apportion the period (or any portion of the period) among the individual and the individual's spouse if the spouse becomes eligible for benefits under this subchapter.

(F) For purposes of this paragraph—

(i) the term "benefits under this subchapter" includes payments of the type described in section 1382e(a) of this title and of the type described in section 212(b) of Public Law 93–66;

(ii) the term "institutionalized individual" has the meaning given such term in section 1396p(e)(3) of this title; and

(iii) the term "trust" has the meaning given such term in subsection (e)(6)(A) of this section.

(2)(A) At the time an individual (and the individual's eligible spouse, if any) applies for benefits under this subchapter, and at the time the eligibility of an individual (and such spouse, if any) for such benefits is redetermined, the Commissioner of Social Security shall—

(i) inform such individual of the provisions of paragraph (1) and section 1396p(c) of this title providing for a period of ineligibility for benefits under this subchapter and subchapter XIX, respectively, for individuals who make certain dispositions of resources for less than fair market value, and inform such individual that information obtained pursuant to clause (ii) will be made available to the State agency administering a State plan under subchapter XIX (as provided in subparagraph (B)); and

(ii) obtain from such individual information which may be used in determining whether or not a period of ineligibility for such benefits would be required by reason of paragraph (1) or section 1396p(c) of this title.

(B) The Commissioner of Social Security shall make the information obtained under subparagraph (A)(ii) available, on request, to any State agency administering a State plan approved under subchapter XIX.

(d) Funds set aside for burial expenses

(1) In determining the resources of an individual, there shall be excluded an amount, not in excess of $1,500 each with respect to such individual and his spouse (if any), that is separately identifiable and has been set aside to meet the burial and related expenses of such individual or spouse.

(2) The amount of $1,500, referred to in paragraph (1), with respect to an individual shall be reduced by an amount equal to (A) the total face value of all insurance policies on his life which are owned by him or his spouse and the cash surrender value of which has been excluded in determining the resources of such individual or of such individual and his spouse, and (B) the total of any amounts in an irrevocable trust (or other irrevocable arrangement) available to meet the burial and related expenses of such individual or his spouse.

(3) If the Commissioner of Social Security finds that any part of the amount excluded under paragraph (1) was used for purposes other than those for which it was set aside in cases where the inclusion of any portion of the amount would cause the resources of such individual, or of such individual and spouse, to

exceed the limits specified in paragraph (1) or (2) (whichever may be applicable) of section 1382(a) of this title, the Commissioner shall reduce any future benefits payable to the eligible individual (or to such individual and his spouse) by an amount equal to such part.

(4) The Commissioner of Social Security may provide by regulations that whenever an amount set aside to meet burial and related expenses is excluded under paragraph (1) in determining the resources of an individual, any interest earned or accrued on such amount (and left to accumulate), and any appreciation in the value of prepaid burial arrangements for which such amount was set aside, shall also be excluded (to such extent and subject to such conditions or limitations as such regulations may prescribe) in determining the resources (and the income) of such individual.

(e) Trusts

(1) In determining the resources of an individual, paragraph (3) shall apply to a trust (other than a trust described in paragraph (5)) established by the individual.

(2)(A) For purposes of this subsection, an individual shall be considered to have established a trust if any assets of the individual (or of the individual's spouse) are transferred to the trust other than by will.

(B) In the case of an irrevocable trust to which are transferred the assets of an individual (or of the individual's spouse) and the assets of any other person, this subsection shall apply to the portion of the trust attributable to the assets of the individual (or of the individual's spouse).

(C) This subsection shall apply to a trust without regard to—

(i) the purposes for which the trust is established;

(ii) whether the trustees have or exercise any discretion under the trust;

(iii) any restrictions on when or whether distributions may be made from the trust; or

(iv) any restrictions on the use of distributions from the trust.

(3)(A) In the case of a revocable trust established by an individual, the corpus of the trust shall be considered a resource available to the individual.

(B) In the case of an irrevocable trust established by an individual, if there are any circumstances under which payment from the trust could be made to or for the benefit of the individual (or of the individual's spouse), the portion of the corpus from which payment to or for the benefit of the individual (or of the individual's spouse) could be made shall be considered a resource available to the individual.

(4) The Commissioner of Social Security may waive the application of this subsection with respect to an individual if the Commissioner determines that such application would work an undue hardship (as determined on the basis of criteria established by the Commissioner) on the individual.

(5) This subsection shall not apply to a trust described in subparagraph (A) or (C) of section 1396p(d)(4) of this title.

(6) For purposes of this subsection—

(A) the term "trust" includes any legal instrument or device that is similar to a trust;

(B) the term "corpus" means, with respect to a trust, all property and other interests held by the trust, including accumulated earnings and any other addition to the trust after its establishment (except that such term does not include any such earnings or addition in the month in which the earnings or addition is credited or otherwise transferred to the trust); and

(C) the term "asset" includes any income or resource of the individual (or of the individual's spouse), including—

(i) any income excluded by section 1382a(b) of this title;

(ii) any resource otherwise excluded by this section; and

(iii) any other payment or property to which the individual (or of the individual's spouse) is entitled but does not receive or have access to because of action by—

(I) the individual or spouse;

(II) a person or entity (including a court) with legal authority to act in place of, or on behalf of, the individual or spouse; or

(III) a person or entity (including a court) acting at the direction of, or on the request of, the individual or spouse.

(Aug. 14, 1935, c. 531, Title XVI, § 1613, as added Pub.L. 92–603, Title III, § 301, Oct. 30, 1972, 86 Stat. 1470; amended Pub.L. 94–569, § 5, Oct. 20, 1976, 90 Stat. 2700; Pub.L. 95–171, § 9(a), Nov. 12, 1977, 91 Stat. 1355; Pub.L. 96–611, § 5(a), Dec. 28, 1980, 94 Stat. 3567; Pub.L. 97–248, Title I, § 185(a), (b), Sept. 3, 1982, 96 Stat. 406; Pub.L. 98–369, Div. B, Title VI, §§ 2614, 2663(g)(5), July 18, 1984, 98 Stat. 1132, 1168; Pub.L. 100–203, Title IX, §§ 9103(a), 9104(a), 9105(a), 9114(a), Dec. 22, 1987, 101 Stat. 1330–301, 1330–304; Pub.L. 100–360, Title III, § 303(c)(1), July 1, 1988, 102 Stat. 762; Pub.L. 100–647, Title VIII, § 8103(b), Nov. 10, 1988, 102 Stat. 3795; Pub.L. 101–239, Title VIII, §§ 8013(b), 8014(a), Dec. 19, 1989, 103 Stat. 2465; Pub.L. 101–508, Title V, §§ 5031(b), 5035(b), Title XI, § 11115(b)(2), Nov. 5, 1990, 104 Stat. 1388–224, 1388–225, 1388–414; Pub.L. 103–296, Title I, § 107(a)(4), Title III, § 321(h)(2), Aug. 15, 1994, 108 Stat. 1478, 1544; Pub.L. 104–193, Title II, § 213(b), Aug. 22, 1996, 110 Stat. 2195; Pub.L. 105–306, § 7(b), Oct. 28, 1998, 112 Stat. 2928; Pub.L. 106–169, Title II, §§ 205(a), 206(a), Dec. 14, 1999, 113 Stat. 1833, 1834; Pub.L. 108–203, Title I, § 101(c)(2), Title IV, §§ 431(a), (b), 435(b), Mar. 2, 2004, 118 Stat. 496, 539, 540; Pub.L. 110–245, Title II, § 202(b), June 17, 2008, 122 Stat. 1638; Pub.L. 111–255, § 3(b), (e), Oct. 5,

2010, 124 Stat. 2641; Pub.L. 114–63, § 2, Oct. 7, 2015, 129 Stat. 549.)

[1] So in original. Probably should be "Acquisition".

HISTORICAL AND STATUTORY NOTES

References in Text

The Internal Revenue Code of 1986, referred to in text, is classified generally to Title 26, 26 U.S.C.A. § 1 et seq.

Title II of the Uniform Relocation Assistance and Real Property Acquisitions Policies Act of 1970, referred to in subsec. (a)(10) means title II of Pub.L. 91–646, Jan. 2, 1971, 84 Stat. 1895, which enacted sections 4621 to 4638 of this title, amended sections 1415, 2473, and 3307 of this title and section 1606 of Title 49, Appendix, Transportation, repealed sections 1465 and 3074 of this title, section 2680 of Title 10, Armed Forces, sections 501 to 512 of Title 23, Highways, sections 1231 to 1234 of Title 43, Public Lands, and enacted provisions set out as notes under sections 4601 and 4621 of this title and under sections 50 to 512 of Title 23. Section 216 of the Act is classified to section 4636 of this title. For complete classification of Title II to the Code, see Tables.

Section 203 of the Economic Growth and Tax Relief Reconciliation Act of 2001, referred to in subsec. (a)(11)(A), is Pub.L. 107–16, Title II, § 203, June 7, 2001, 115 Stat. 49, which is set out as a note under 26 U.S.C.A. § 24.

This subchapter, referred to in subsec. (a)(14), originally read "this title", meaning the Social Security Act, Act Aug. 14, 1935, c. 531, Title XVI, as added Oct. 30, 1972, Pub.L. 92–603, Title III, § 301, 86 Stat. 1465, as amended, which is classified as this subchapter, 42 U.S.C.A. § 1381 et seq.

Subchapter II of this chapter, referred to in subsec. (a)(14), originally read "title II", meaning the Social Security Act, Act Aug. 14, 1935, c. 531, Title II, 49 Stat. 622, as amended, which is classified as subchapter II of this chapter, 42 U.S.C.A. § 401 et seq.

Subchapter VIII of this chapter, referred to in subsec. (a)(14), originally read "title VIII", meaning the Social Security Act, Act Aug. 14, 1935, c. 531, Title VIII, as added Dec. 14, 1999, Pub.L. 106–169, Title II, § 251(a), 113 Stat. 1844, as amended, which is classified as subchapter VIII of this chapter, 42 U.S.C.A. § 1001 et seq.

Section 212(b) of Public Law 93–66, referred to in subsec. (c)(1)(A)(iv)(II) and (c)(1)(F), is classified to 42 U.S.C.A. § 1382 note.

Section 1396p(e)(3) of this title, referred to in subsec. (c)(1)(F)(ii), was redesignated section 1396p(h)(3) of this title by Pub.L. 109–171, Title VI, §§ 6012(a), 6014(a), 6015(b), Feb. 8, 2006, 120 Stat. 62, 64, 65.

Effective and Applicability Provisions

2010 Acts. Amendments made by Pub.L. 111–255, § 3, effective on the earlier of the effective date of final regulations promulgated to carry out amendment by Pub.L. 111–255, § 3, or 180 days after Oct. 5, 2010, see Pub.L. 111–255, § 3(d), set out as a note under 42 U.S.C.A. § 1382a.

2008 Acts. Amendments by Pub.L. 110–245, § 202 effective with respect to benefits payable for months beginning after 60 days after June 17, 2008, see Pub.L. 110–245, § 204, set out as a note under 42 U.S.C.A. § 1382a.

2004 Acts. Amendments made by Pub.L. 108–203, § 101, enacting subsec. (a)(14) of this section and amending subsec. (a)(12) and (13) of this section, to apply to any case of benefit misuse by a representative payee with respect to which the Commissioner of Social Security makes the determination of misuse on or after Jan. 1, 1995, see Pub.L. 108–203, § 101(d), set out as a note under 42 U.S.C.A. § 405.

Pub.L. 108–203, Title IV, § 431(c), Mar. 2, 2004, 118 Stat. 539, provided that: "The amendments made by this section [amending subsec. (a)(7), (11) of this section] shall take effect on the date of enactment of this Act [Mar. 2, 2004], and shall apply to amounts described in paragraph (7) of section 1613(a) of the Social Security Act [subsec. (a)(7) of this section] and refunds of Federal income taxes described in paragraph (11) of such section [subsec. (a)(11) of this section], that are received by an eligible individual or eligible spouse on or after such date."

Amendments by section 435(b) of Pub.L. 108–203, enacting subsec. (a)(15) of this section and amending subsec. (a)(13) and (14) of this section, shall apply to benefits payable for months that begin more than 90 days after Mar. 2, 2004, see Pub.L. 108–203, § 435(c), set out as a note under 42 U.S.C.A. § 1382a.

1999 Acts. Pub.L. 106–169, Title II, § 206(c), Dec. 14, 1999, 113 Stat. 1837, provided that: "The amendments made by this section [amending subsec. (c) of this section and section 1396a of this title] shall be effective with respect to disposals made on or after the date of the enactment of this Act [Dec. 14, 1999]."

Amendment by section 205(a) of Pub.L. 106–169 effective Jan. 1, 2000, and applicable to trusts established on or after such date, see section 205(d) of Pub.L. 106–169, set out a note under section 1382a of this title.

1998 Acts. Amendment by section 7(b) of Pub.L. 105–306 applicable to gifts made on or after the date that is 2 years before Oct. 28, 1998, see section 7(c) of Pub.L. 105–306, set out as a note under section 1382a of this title.

1996 Acts. Amendment by section 213(b) of Pub.L. 104–193 applicable to payments made after Aug. 22, 1996, see section 213(d) of Pub.L. 104–193, set out as a note under section 1382a of this title.

1994 Acts. Amendment by section 107(a)(4) of Pub.L. 103–296 effective Mar. 31, 1995, see section 110 of Pub.L. 103–296, set out as a note under section 401 of this title.

Section 321(h)(3) of Pub.L. 103–296 provided that: "The amendments made by this subsection [amending this section and section 1383 of this title] shall take effect on the date of the enactment of this Act [Aug. 15, 1994]."

1990 Acts. Amendment by section 5031(b) of Pub.L. 101–508 applicable with respect to benefits for months beginning on or after first day of sixth calendar month following Nov., 1990, see section 5031(d) of Pub.L. 101–508, set out as a note under section 1382a of this title.

Amendment by section 5035(b) of Pub.L. 101–508 applicable with respect to benefits for calendar months beginning in 3-year period which begins on first day of sixth calendar month following Nov., 1990, see section 5035(c) of Pub.L. 101–508, set out as a note under section 1382a of this title.

Amendment by section 11115(b)(2) of Pub.L. 101–508 applicable to determinations of income or resources made for any period after Dec. 31, 1990, see section 11115(e) of Pub.L. 101–508, set out as a note under section 602 of this title.

1989 Acts. Amendment of subsec. (a)(2)(B) by section 8013(b) of Pub.L. 101–239 effective the 1st day of 4th month beginning after Dec. 19, 1989, see section 8013(c) of Pub.L. 101–239, set out as a note under section 1382a of this title.

Section 8014(b) of Pub.L. 101–239 provided that: "The amendment made by subsection (a) [amending subsec. (a)(3) of this section] shall take effect on the 1st day of the 5th calendar month beginning after the date of the enactment of this Act [Dec. 19, 1989]."

1988 Acts. Amendment by Pub.L. 100–647 effective as though included in section 162 of Housing and Community Development Act of 1987, Pub.L. 100–242, at time of its enactment on Feb. 5, 1988, see section 8103(c) of Pub.L. 100–647, set out as a note under section 1382a of this title.

Amendment by Pub.L. 100–360 applicable to transfers occurring on or after July 1, 1988, without regard to whether or not final regulations to carry out such amendment have been promulgated by such date, see section 303(g)(3) of Pub.L. 100–360, set out as a note under section 1396r–5 of this title.

1987 Acts. Section 9103(b) of Pub.L. 100–203 provided that: "The amendments made by subsection (a) [amending subsec. (b) of this section] shall become effective April 1, 1988."

Section 9104(b) of Pub.L. 100–203 provided that: "The amendments made by subsection (a) [amending subsecs. (c)(1), (4) of this section] shall become effective April 1, 1988."

Section 9105(b) of Pub.L. 100–203 provided that: "The amendments made by subsection (a) [amending subsec. (d)(1), (2) of this section] shall become effective April 1, 1988."

Section 9114(b) of Pub.L. 100–203 provided that: "The amendment made by subsection (a) [amending subsec. (a)(7) of this section] shall become effective January 1, 1988."

1984 Acts. Amendment by section 2614 of Pub.L. 98–369 effective Oct. 1, 1984, except as otherwise specially provided, see section 2646 of Pub.L. 98–369, set out as a note under section 602 of this title.

Amendment by section 2663(g)(5) of Pub.L. 98–369 effective July 18, 1984, but not to be construed as changing or affecting any right, liability, status, or interpretation which existed (under the provisions of law involved) before that date, see section 2664(b) of Pub.L. 98–369, set out as a note under section 401 of this title.

1982 Acts. Section 185(c) of Pub.L. 97–248 provided that: "The amendment made by this section [amending this section] shall take effect on the first day of the second month after the month in which this Act is enacted [September 1982]."

1980 Acts. Section 5(c) of Pub.L. 96–611 provided that: "The amendment made by subsection (a) [enacting subsec. (c) of this section] shall be effective with respect to applications for benefits under title XVI of the Social Security Act [this subchapter] filed on or after the first day of the first month which begins at least 60 days after the date of enactment of this Act [Dec. 28, 1980]."

1977 Acts. Section 9(b) of Pub.L. 95–171 provided that: "The amendment made by this section [enacting subsec. (a)(6) of this section] shall be effective July 1, 1976, with respect to catastrophes which occurred on or after June 1, 1976, and before December 31, 1976. With respect to catastrophes which occurred on or after December 1, 1976, the amendment made by this section [enacting subsec. (a)(6) of this section] shall be effective the first day of the calendar quarter following enactment of this Act [Nov. 12, 1977]."

1972 Acts. Section 301 of Pub.L. 92–603 provided that this section is effective Jan. 1, 1974.

Sunset Provisions

Pub.L. 111–255, § 3(e), Oct. 5, 2010, 124 Stat. 2641, which provided that Pub.L. 111–255 and the amendments made by Pub.L. 111–255 were repealed on the date that was 5 years after Oct. 5, 2010, was subsequently repealed by Pub.L. 114–63, § 2, effective as if included in the enactment of Pub.L. 111–255; see Pub.L. 111–255, § 3(e), set out as a note under 42 U.S.C.A. § 1382a.

Application to Northern Mariana Islands

For applicability of this section to the Northern Mariana Islands, see section 502(a)(1) of the Covenant to Establish a Commonwealth of the Northern Mariana Islands in Political Union with the United States of America, as set forth in Pub.L. 94–241, Mar. 24, 1976, 90 Stat. 263, eff. Jan. 9, 1978, pursuant to Proc. No. 4534, Oct. 24, 1977, 42 F.R. 6593, set out as notes under section 1681 of Title 48, Territories and Insular Possessions.

Puerto Rico, Guam, and Virgin Islands

Enactment of provisions of Pub.L. 92–603, eff. Jan. 1, 1974, not applicable to Puerto Rico, Guam, and the Virgin Islands, see section 303(b) of Pub.L. 92–603, set out as a note under section 301 of this title.

§ 1382c. Definitions

(a)(1) For purposes of this subchapter, the term "aged, blind, or disabled individual" means an individual who—

(A) is 65 years of age or older, is blind (as determined under paragraph (2)), or is disabled (as determined under paragraph (3)), and

(B)(i) is a resident of the United States, and is either (I) a citizen or (II) an alien lawfully admitted for permanent residence or otherwise permanently residing in the United States under color of law (including any alien who is lawfully present in the United States as a result of the application of the provisions of section 1182(d)(5) of Title 8), or

(ii) is a child who is a citizen of the United States, and who is living with a parent of the child who is a member of the Armed Forces of the United States assigned to permanent duty ashore outside the United States.

(2) An individual shall be considered to be blind for purposes of this subchapter if he has central visual acuity of 20/200 or less in the better eye with the use of a correcting lens. An eye which is accompanied by a limitation in the fields of vision such that the widest diameter of the visual field subtends an angle no greater than 20 degrees shall be considered for purposes of the first sentence of this subsection as having a central visual acuity of 20/200 or less. An individual shall also be considered to be blind for purposes of this subchapter if he is blind as defined under a State plan approved under subchapter X or XVI as in effect for October 1972 and received aid under such plan (on the basis of blindness) for December 1973, so long as he is continuously blind as so defined.

(3)(A) Except as provided in subparagraph (C), an individual shall be considered to be disabled for purposes of this subchapter if he is unable to engage in any substantial gainful activity by reason of any medically determinable physical or mental impairment which can be expected to result in death or which has lasted or can be expected to last for a continuous period of not less than twelve months.

(B) For purposes of subparagraph (A), an individual shall be determined to be under a disability only if his physical or mental impairment or impairments are of such severity that he is not only unable to do his previous work but cannot, considering his age, education, and work experience, engage in any other kind of substantial gainful work which exists in the national economy, regardless of whether such work exists in the immediate area in which he lives, or whether a specific job vacancy exists for him, or whether he would be hired if he applied for work. For purposes of the preceding sentence (with respect to any individual), "work which exists in the national economy" means work which exists in significant numbers either in the region where such individual lives or in several regions of the country.

(C)(i) An individual under the age of 18 shall be considered disabled for the purposes of this subchapter if that individual has a medically determinable physical or mental impairment, which results in marked and severe functional limitations, and which can be expected to result in death or which has lasted or can be expected to last for a continuous period of not less than 12 months.

(ii) Notwithstanding clause (i), no individual under the age of 18 who engages in substantial gainful activity (determined in accordance with regulations prescribed pursuant to subparagraph (E)) may be considered to be disabled.

(D) For purposes of this paragraph, a physical or mental impairment is an impairment that results from anatomical, physiological, or psychological abnormalities which are demonstrable by medically acceptable clinical and laboratory diagnostic techniques.

(E) The Commissioner of Social Security shall by regulations prescribe the criteria for determining when services performed or earnings derived from services demonstrate an individual's ability to engage in substantial gainful activity. In determining whether an individual is able to engage in substantial gainful activity by reason of his earnings, where his disability is sufficiently severe to result in a functional limitation requiring assistance in order for him to work, there shall be excluded from such earnings an amount equal to the cost (to such individual) of any attendant care services, medical devices, equipment, prostheses, and similar items and services (not including routine drugs or routine medical services unless such drugs or services are necessary for the control of the disabling condition) which are necessary (as determined by the Commissioner of Social Security in regulations) for that purpose, whether or not such assistance is also needed to enable him to carry out his normal daily functions; except that the amounts to be excluded shall be subject to such reasonable limits as the Commissioner of Social Security may prescribe. Notwithstanding the provisions of subparagraph (B), an individual whose services or earnings meet such criteria shall be found not to be disabled. The Commissioner of Social Security shall make determinations under this subchapter with respect to substantial gainful activity, without regard to the legality of the activity.

(F) Notwithstanding the provisions of subparagraphs (A) through (E), an individual shall also be considered to be disabled for purposes of this subchapter if he is permanently and totally disabled as defined under a State plan approved under subchapter XIV or XVI as in effect for October 1972 and received aid under such plan (on the basis of disability) for December 1973 (and for at least one month prior to July 1973), so long as he is continuously disabled as so defined.

(G) In determining whether an individual's physical or mental impairment or impairments are of a sufficient medical severity that such impairment or impairments could be the basis of eligibility under this section, the Commissioner of Social Security shall consider the combined effect of all of the individual's impairments without regard to whether any such impairment, if considered separately, would be of such severity. If the Commissioner of Social Security does find a medically severe combination of impairments, the combined impact of the impairments shall be considered throughout the disability determination process.

(H)(i) In making determinations with respect to disability under this subchapter, the provisions of sections 421(h), 421(k), and 423(d)(5) of this title shall apply in the same manner as they apply to determinations of disability under subchapter II.

(ii)(I) Not less frequently than once every 3 years, the Commissioner shall review in accordance with paragraph (4) the continued eligibility for benefits under this subchapter of each individual who has not attained 18 years of age and is eligible for such benefits by reason of an impairment (or combination of impairments) which is likely to improve (or, at the option of the Commissioner, which is unlikely to improve).

(II) A representative payee of a recipient whose case is reviewed under this clause shall present, at the time of review, evidence demonstrating that the recipient is, and has been, receiving treatment, to the extent considered medically necessary and available, of the condition which was the basis for providing benefits under this subchapter.

(III) If the representative payee refuses to comply without good cause with the requirements of subclause (II), the Commissioner of Social Security shall, if the Commissioner determines it is in the best interest of the individual, promptly suspend payment of benefits to the representative payee, and provide for payment of benefits to an alternative representative payee of the individual or, if the interest of the individual under this subchapter would be served thereby, to the individual.

(IV) Subclause (II) shall not apply to the representative payee of any individual with respect to whom the Commissioner determines such application would be inappropriate or unnecessary. In making such determination, the Commissioner shall take into consideration the nature of the individual's impairment (or combination of impairments). Section 1383(c) of this title shall not apply to a finding by the Commissioner that the requirements of subclause (II) should not apply to an individual's representative payee.

(iii) If an individual is eligible for benefits under this subchapter by reason of disability for the month preceding the month in which the individual attains the age of 18 years, the Commissioner shall redetermine such eligibility—

(I) by applying the criteria used in determining initial eligibility for individuals who are age 18 or older; and

(II) either during the 1–year period beginning on the individual's 18th birthday or, in lieu of a continuing disability review, whenever the Commissioner determines that an individual's case is subject to a redetermination under this clause.

With respect to any redetermination under this clause, paragraph (4) shall not apply.

(iv)(I) Except as provided in subclause (VI), not later than 12 months after the birth of an individual, the Commissioner shall review in accordance with paragraph (4) the continuing eligibility for benefits under this subchapter by reason of disability of such individual whose low birth weight is a contributing factor material to the Commissioner's determination that the individual is disabled.

(II) A review under subclause (I) shall be considered a substitute for a review otherwise required under any other provision of this subparagraph during that 12–month period.

(III) A representative payee of a recipient whose case is reviewed under this clause shall present, at the time of review, evidence demonstrating that the recipient is, and has been, receiving treatment, to the extent considered medically necessary and available, of the condition which was the basis for providing benefits under this subchapter.

(IV) If the representative payee refuses to comply without good cause with the requirements of subclause (III), the Commissioner of Social Security shall, if the Commissioner determines it is in the best interest of the individual, promptly suspend payment of benefits to the representative payee, and provide for payment of benefits to an alternative representative payee of the individual or, if the interest of the individual under this subchapter would be served thereby, to the individual.

(V) Subclause (III) shall not apply to the representative payee of any individual with respect to whom the Commissioner determines such application would be inappropriate or unnecessary. In making such determination, the Commissioner shall take into consideration the nature of the individual's impairment (or combination of impairments). Section 1383(c) of this title shall not apply to a finding by the Commissioner that the requirements of subclause (III) should not apply to an individual's representative payee.

(VI) Subclause (I) shall not apply in the case of an individual described in that subclause who, at the time of the individual's initial disability determination, the Commissioner determines has an impairment that is not expected to improve within 12 months after the birth of that individual, and who the Commissioner schedules for a continuing disability review at a date that is after the individual attains 1 year of age.

(I) In making any determination under this subchapter with respect to the disability of an individual who has not attained the age of 18 years and to whom section 421(h) of this title does not apply, the Commissioner of Social Security shall make reasonable efforts to ensure that a qualified pediatrician or other individual who specializes in a field of medicine appropriate to the disability of the individual (as determined by the Commissioner of Social Security) evaluates the case of such individual.

(J) Notwithstanding subparagraph (A), an individual shall not be considered to be disabled for purposes of this subchapter if alcoholism or drug addiction would (but for this subparagraph) be a contributing factor material to the Commissioner's determination that the individual is disabled.

(4) A recipient of benefits based on disability under this subchapter may be determined not to be entitled to such benefits on the basis of a finding that the physical or mental impairment on the basis of which such benefits are provided has ceased, does not exist, or is not disabling only if such finding is supported by—

(A) in the case of an individual who is age 18 or older—

(i) substantial evidence which demonstrates that—

(I) there has been any medical improvement in the individual's impairment or combination of impairments (other than medical improvement which is not related to the individual's ability to work), and

(II) the individual is now able to engage in substantial gainful activity; or

(ii) substantial evidence (except in the case of an individual eligible to receive benefits under section 1382h of this title) which—

(I) consists of new medical evidence and a new assessment of the individual's residual functional capacity, and demonstrates that—

(aa) although the individual has not improved medically, he or she is nonetheless a beneficiary of advances in medical or vocational therapy or technology (related to the individual's ability to work), and

(bb) the individual is now able to engage in substantial gainful activity, or

(II) demonstrates that—

(aa) although the individual has not improved medically, he or she has undergone vocational therapy (related to the individual's ability to work), and

(bb) the individual is now able to engage in substantial gainful activity; or

(iii) substantial evidence which demonstrates that, as determined on the basis of new or improved diagnostic techniques or evaluations, the individual's impairment or combination of impairments is not as disabling as it was considered to be at the time of the most recent prior decision that he or she was under a disability or continued to be under a disability, and that therefore the individual is able to engage in substantial gainful activity; or

(B) in the case of an individual who is under the age of 18—

(i) substantial evidence which demonstrates that there has been medical improvement in the individual's impairment or combination of impairments, and that such impairment or combination of impairments no longer results in marked and severe functional limitations; or

(ii) substantial evidence which demonstrates that, as determined on the basis of new or improved diagnostic techniques or evaluations, the individual's impairment or combination of impairments, is not as disabling as it was considered to be at the time of the most recent prior decision that the individual was under a disability or continued to be under a disability, and such impairment or combination of impairments does not result in marked and severe functional limitations; or

(C) in the case of any individual, substantial evidence (which may be evidence on the record at the time any prior determination of the entitlement to benefits based on disability was made, or newly obtained evidence which relates to that determination) which demonstrates that a prior determination was in error.

Nothing in this paragraph shall be construed to require a determination that an individual receiving benefits based on disability under this subchapter is entitled to such benefits if the prior determination was fraudulently obtained or if the individual is engaged in substantial gainful activity, cannot be located, or fails, without good cause, to cooperate in a review of his or her entitlement or to follow prescribed treatment which would be expected (i) to restore his or her ability to engage in substantial gainful activity, or (ii) in the case of an individual under the age of 18, to eliminate or improve the individual's impairment or combination of impairments so that it no longer results in marked and severe functional limitations. Any determination under this paragraph shall be made on the basis of all the evidence available in the individual's case file, including new evidence concerning the individual's prior or current condition which is presented by the individual or secured by the Commissioner of Social Security. Any determination made under this paragraph shall be made on the basis of the weight of the evidence and on a neutral basis with regard to the individual's condition, without any initial inference as to the presence or absence of disability being drawn from the fact that the individual has previously been determined to be disabled.

(b) For purposes of this subchapter, the term "eligible spouse" means an aged, blind, or disabled individual who is the husband or wife of another aged, blind, or disabled individual, and who, in a month, is living with such aged, blind, or disabled individual on the first day of the month or, in any case in which either spouse files an application for benefits, on the first day of the month following the date the application is filed, or, in any case in which either spouse requests restoration of eligibility under this subchapter during the month, at the time the request is filed. If two aged, blind, or disabled individuals are husband and wife as described in the preceding sentence, only one of them may be an "eligible individual" within the meaning of section 1382(a) of this title.

(c) For purposes of this subchapter, the term "child" means an individual who is neither married nor (as determined by the Commissioner of Social Security) the head of a household, and who is (1) under the age of eighteen, or (2) under the age of twenty-two and (as determined by the Commissioner of Social Security) a student regularly attending a school, college, or university, or a course of vocational or technical training designed to prepare him for gainful employment.

(d) In determining whether two individuals are husband and wife for purposes of this subchapter, appropriate State law shall be applied; except that—

(1) if a man and woman have been determined to be husband and wife under section 416(h)(1) of this title for purposes of subchapter II they shall be considered (from and after the date of such determination or the date of their application for benefits

under this subchapter, whichever is later) to be husband and wife for purposes of this subchapter, or

(2) if a man and woman are found to be holding themselves out to the community in which they reside as husband and wife, they shall be so considered for purposes of this subchapter notwithstanding any other provision of this section.

(e) For purposes of this subchapter, the term "United States", when used in a geographical sense, means the 50 States and the District of Columbia.

(f)(1) For purposes of determining eligibility for and the amount of benefits for any individual who is married and whose spouse is living with him in the same household but is not an eligible spouse, such individual's income and resources shall be deemed to include any income and resources of such spouse, whether or not available to such individual, except to the extent determined by the Commissioner of Social Security to be inequitable under the circumstances.

(2)(A) For purposes of determining eligibility for and the amount of benefits for any individual who is a child under age 18, such individual's income and resources shall be deemed to include any income and resources of a parent of such individual (or the spouse of such a parent) who is living in the same household as such individual, whether or not available to such individual, except to the extent determined by the Commissioner of Social Security to be inequitable under the circumstances.

(B) Subparagraph (A) shall not apply in the case of any child who has not attained the age of 18 years who—

(i) is disabled;

(ii) received benefits under this subchapter, pursuant to section 1382(e)(1)(B) of this title, while in an institution described in section 1382(e)(1)(B) of this title;

(iii) is eligible for medical assistance under a State home care plan approved by the Secretary under the provisions of section 1396n(c) of this title relating to waivers, or authorized under section 1396a(e)(3) of this title; and

(iv) but for this subparagraph, would not be eligible for benefits under this subchapter.

(3) For purposes of determining eligibility for and the amount of benefits for any individual who is an alien, such individual's income and resources shall be deemed to include the income and resources of his sponsor and such sponsor's spouse (if such alien has a sponsor) as provided in section 1382j of this title. Any such income deemed to be income of such individual shall be treated as unearned income of such individual.

(4) For purposes of paragraphs (1) and (2), a spouse or parent (or spouse of such a parent) who is absent from the household in which the individual lives due solely to a duty assignment as a member of the Armed Forces on active duty shall, in the absence of evidence to the contrary, be deemed to be living in the same household as the individual.

(Aug. 14, 1935, c. 531, Title XVI, § 1614, as added Pub.L. 92–603, Title III, § 301, Oct. 30, 1972, 86 Stat. 1471; amended Pub.L. 93–233, § 9, Dec. 31, 1973, 87 Stat. 957; Pub.L. 96–265, Title II, § 203(a), Title III, §§ 302(a)(2), 303(c)(1), Title V, § 504(a), June 9, 1980, 94 Stat. 449, 450, 453, 471; Pub.L. 98–369, Div. B, Title VI, § 2663(g)(6), (7), July 18, 1984, 98 Stat. 1168, 1169; Pub.L. 98–460, §§ 2(c), 3(a)(2), 4(b), 8(b), 10(b), Oct. 9, 1984, 98 Stat. 1796, 1799, 1800, 1804, 1805; Pub.L. 99–643, § 4(d)(2), (3)(A), Nov. 10, 1986, 100 Stat. 3577; Pub.L. 101–239, Title VIII, §§ 8009(b), 8010(a), 8012(a), Dec. 19, 1989, 103 Stat. 2463, 2464; Pub.L. 101–508, Title V, § 5036(a), Nov. 5, 1990, 104 Stat. 1388–225; Pub.L. 101–649, Title I, § 162(e)(5), Nov. 29, 1990, 104 Stat. 5011; Pub.L. 103–66, Title XIII, §§ 13733(a), 13734(a), Aug. 10, 1993, 107 Stat. 662; Pub.L. 103–296, Title I, § 107(a)(4), Title II, § 201(b)(4)(A), Aug. 15, 1994, 108 Stat. 1478, 1505; Pub.L. 103–432, Title II, § 221(a), Oct. 31, 1994, 108 Stat. 4462; Pub.L. 104–121, Title I, § 105(b)(1), Mar. 29, 1996, 110 Stat. 853; Pub.L. 104–193, Title II, §§ 204(c)(1), 211(a), (c), 212(a), (b)(1), (c), Aug. 22, 1996, 110 Stat. 2188, 2189, 2192, 2193; Pub.L. 105–33, Title V, § 5522(a), (d), Aug. 5, 1997, 111 Stat. 622, 623; Pub.L. 108–203, Title IV, § 434(a), Mar. 2, 2004, 118 Stat. 540.)

HISTORICAL AND STATUTORY NOTES

Effective and Applicability Provisions

2004 Acts. Pub.L. 108–203, Title IV, § 434(b), Mar. 2, 2004, 118 Stat. 540, provided that: "The amendments made by this section [amending this section] shall be effective with respect to benefits payable for months beginning after the date of enactment of this Act [Mar. 2, 2004], but only on the basis of an application filed after such date."

1997 Acts. Amendments by section 5522 of Pub.L. 105–33 effective as if included in enactment of Pub.L. 104–193, see section 5528(a) of Pub.L. 105–33, set out as a note under section 903 of this title.

1996 Acts. Amendment by section 204(c)(1) of Pub.L. 104–193 applicable to applications for benefits under this subchapter filed on or after Aug. 22, 1996, without regard to whether regulations have been issued to implement such amendment, except as otherwise provided, see section 204(d) of Pub.L. 104–193, set out as a note under section 1382 of this title.

Section 211(d) of Pub.L. 104–193, as amended Pub.L. 105–33, § 5101, 111 Stat. 595, provided that:

"(1) Effective dates.—

"(A) Subsections (a) and (b).—

"(i) In general.—The provisions of, and amendments made by, subsections (a) and (b) of this section [subsec. (a) of section 211 of Pub.L.104–193 amended subsec. (a)(3) of this section; subsec. (b) of section 211 of Pub.L. 104–193 was not classified to the Code] shall apply to any individual who applies for, or whose claim is finally adjudicated with respect to, benefits under title XVI of the Social Security Act [this subchapter] on or after the date of the enactment of this Act [Aug. 22, 1996], without regard to whether regulations have been issued to implement such provisions and amendments.

"(ii) Determination of final adjudication.—For purposes of clause (i), no individual's claim with respect to such benefits may be considered to be finally adjudicated before such date of enactment [Aug. 22, 1996] if, on or after such date, there is pending a request for either administrative or judicial review with respect to such claim that has been denied in whole, or there is pending, with respect to such claim, readjudication by the Commissioner of Social Security pursuant to relief in a class action or implementation by the Commissioner of a court remand order.

"(B) Subsection (c).—The amendments made by subsection (c) of this section [amending subsec. (a)(4) of this section] shall apply with respect to benefits under title XVI of the Social Security Act [this subchapter] for months beginning on or after the date of the enactment of this Act [Aug. 22, 1996], without regard to whether regulations have been issued to implement such amendments.

"(2) Application to current recipients.—

"(A) Eligibility redeterminations.—During the period beginning on the date of the enactment of this Act [Aug. 22, 1996] and ending on the date which is 18 months after such date of enactment, the Commissioner of Social Security shall redetermine the eligibility of any individual under age 18 who is eligible for supplemental security income benefits by reason of disability under title XVI of the Social Security Act [this subchapter] as of the date of the enactment of this Act [Aug. 22, 1996] and whose eligibility for such benefits may terminate by reason of the provisions of, or amendments made by, subsections (a) and (b) of this section [subsec. (a) of section 211 of Pub.L. 104–193 amended subsec. (a)(3) of this section; subsec. (b) of section 211 of Pub.L. 104–193 was not classified to the Code]. Any redetermination required by the preceding sentence that is not performed before the end of the period described in the preceding sentence shall be performed as soon as is practicable thereafter. With respect to any redetermination under this subparagraph—

"(i) section 1614(a)(4) of the Social Security Act (42 U.S.C. 1382c(a)(4)) [subsec. (a)(4) of this section] shall not apply;

"(ii) the Commissioner of Social Security shall apply the eligibility criteria for new applicants for benefits under title XVI of such Act [this subchapter];

"(iii) the Commissioner shall give such redetermination priority over all continuing eligibility reviews and other reviews under such title [this subchapter]; and

"(iv) such redetermination shall be counted as a review or redetermination otherwise required to be made under section 208 of the Social Security Independence and Program Improvements Act of 1994 [section 208 of Pub.L.103–296, set out as a note under section 1382 of this title] or any other provision of title XVI of the Social Security Act [this subchapter].

"(B) Grandfather provision.—The provisions of, and amendments made by, subsections (a) and (b) of this section [subsec. (a) of section 211 of Pub.L. 104–193 amended subsec. (a)(3) of this section; subsec. (b) of section 211 of Pub.L. 104–193 was not classified to the Code], and the redetermination under subparagraph (A), shall only apply with respect to the benefits of an individual described in subparagraph (A) for months beginning on or after the later of July 1, 1997, or the date of the redetermination with respect to such individual.

"(C) Notice.—Not later than January 1, 1997, the Commissioner of Social Security shall notify an individual described in subparagraph (A) of the provisions of this paragraph. Before commencing a redetermination under the 2nd sentence of subparagraph (A), in any case in which the individual involved has not already been notified of the provisions of this paragraph, the Commissioner of Social Security shall notify the individual involved of the provisions of this paragraph.

"(3) Report.—The Commissioner of Social Security shall report to the Congress regarding the progress made in implementing the provisions of, and amendments made by, this section [amending this section, sections 665e and 901 of Title 2, The Congress, and provisions set out as a note under section 401 of this title] on child disability evaluations not later than 180 days after the date of the enactment of this Act [Aug. 22, 1996].

"(4) Regulations.—Notwithstanding any other provision of law, the Commissioner of Social Security shall submit for review to the committees of jurisdiction in the Congress any final regulation pertaining to the eligibility of individuals under age 18 for benefits under title XVI of the Social Security Act [this subchapter] at least 45 days before the effective date of such regulation. The submission under this paragraph shall include supporting documentation providing a cost analysis, workload impact, and projections as to how the regulation will effect the future number of recipients under such title.

"(5) Cap adjustment for SSI administrative work required by welfare reform.—

"(A) Authorization.—For the additional costs of continuing disability reviews and redeterminations under title XVI of the Social Security Act [this subchapter], there is hereby authorized to be appropriated to the Social Security Administration, in addition to amounts authorized under section 201(g)(1)(A) of the Social Security Act [section 401(g)(1)(A) of this title], $150,000,000 in fiscal year 1997 and $100,000,000 in fiscal year 1998.

"(B) to (D) [Omitted]

"(6) Benefits under Title XVI.—For purposes of this subsection, the term 'benefits under title XVI of the Social Security Act' includes supplementary payments pursuant to an agreement for Federal administration under section 1616(a) of the Social Security Act [section 1382e(a) of this title], and payments pursuant to an agreement entered into under section 212(b) of Public Law 93–66 [set out as a note under section 1382 of this title]."

Section 212(d) of Pub.L. 104–193 provided that: "The amendments made by this section [amending this section and repealing provisions set out as a note under section 1382 of this title] shall apply to benefits for months beginning on or after the date of the enactment of this Act [Aug. 22, 1996], without regard to whether regulations have been issued to implement such amendments."

Amendment by section 105(b)(1) of Pub.L. 104–121 applicable to individual who applies for, or whose claim is adjudicated with respect to, benefits under this subchapter based on disability on or after Mar. 29, 1996, with certain conditions applying for benefits before Mar. 29, 1996, see section 105(b)(5) of Pub.L. 104–121, set out as a note under section 1382 of this title.

1994 Acts. Amendment by section 107(a)(4) of Pub.L. 103–296 effective Mar. 31, 1995, see section 110 of Pub.L. 103–296, set out as a note under section 401 of this title.

Section 201(b)(4)(B) of Pub.L. 103–296 provided that: "The amendment made by subparagraph (A) [amending subsec. (a)(3)(D) of this section] shall take effect on the date of the enactment of this Act [Aug. 15, 1994]."

Section 221(b) of Pub.L. 103–432 provided that: "The amendments made by subsection (a) [amending subsec. (a)(3)(A) and (H) of this section] shall apply to determinations made on or after the date of the enactment of this Act [Oct. 31, 1994]."

1993 Acts. Amendment of subsec. (f)(4) by section 13733(a) of Pub.L. 103–66 effective on the 1st day of the 2nd month that begins after Aug. 10, 1993, see section 13733(c) of Pub.L. 103–66 set out as an Effective Date note under section 1382a of this title.

Section 13734(b) of Pub.L. 103–66, provided that: "The amendment made by subsection (a) [amending subsec. (a)(1)(B)(ii) of this section] shall take effect on the 1st day of the 3rd month that begins after the date of the enactment of this Act [Aug. 10, 1993]."

1990 Acts. Amendment by section 162(e)(5) of Pub.L. 101–649 effective Oct. 1, 1991, and applicable beginning with fiscal year 1992, with general transition provisions, admissibility standards, and construction provisions, see section 161 of Pub.L. 101–649, set out as a note under section 1101 of this title.

Section 5036(b) of Pub.L. 101–508 provided that: "The amendment made by subsection (a) [amending subsec. (a) of this section] shall apply to determinations made 6 or more months after the date of the enactment of this Act [Nov. 5, 1990]."

1989 Acts. Amendment by section 8009(b) of Pub.L. 101–239 applicable with respect to benefits for months after Mar. 1990, see section 8009(c) of Pub.L. 101–239, set out as a note under section 1382 of this title.

Amendment by section 8010(a) of Pub.L. 101–239 effective the 1st day of 6th calendar month beginning after Dec. 19, 1989, see section 8010(c) of Pub.L. 101–239, set out as a note under section 1382 of this title.

Section 8012(b) of Pub.L. 101–239 provided that: "The amendment made by subsection (a) [amending subsec. (b) of this section] shall take effect on October 1, 1990."

1986 Acts. Amendment by Pub.L. 99–643 effective July 1, 1987, except for State plans requiring State legislation, see section 10(b) of Pub.L. 99–643, set out as a note under section 1396a of this title.

1984 Acts. Amendment by section 2(c) of Pub.L. 98–460 applicable to determinations made by the Secretary on or after Oct. 9, 1984, with certain enumerated exceptions and qualifications, see section 2(d) of Pub.L. 98–460, set out as a note under section 423 of this title.

Amendment by section 3(a)(2) of Pub.L. 98–460 applicable to determinations made prior to Jan. 1, 1987, see section 3(a)(3) of Pub.L. 98–460, set out as a note under section 423 of this title.

Amendment by section 4(b) of Pub.L. 98–460 applicable with respect to determinations made on or after Dec. 1, 1984, see section 4(c) of Pub.L. 98–460, set out as a note under section 423 of this title.

Amendment by section 8(b) of Pub.L. 98–460 applicable to determinations made after 60 days after Oct. 9, 1984, see section 8(c) of Pub.L. 98–460, set out as a note under section 421 of this title.

Amendment by Pub.L. 98–369 effective July 18, 1984, but not to be construed as changing or affecting any right, liability, status, or interpretation which existed (under the provisions of law involved) before that date, see section 2664(b) of Pub.L. 98–369, set out as a note under section 401 of this title.

1980 Acts. Section 203(b) of Pub.L. 96–265 provided that: "The amendment made by subsection (a) [amending subsec. (f)(2) of this section] shall become effective on October 1, 1980; except that the amendment made by such subsection shall not apply, in the case of any child who, in September 1980, was 18 or over and received a supplemental security income benefit for such month, during any period for which such benefit would be greater without the application of such amendment."

Amendment by section 302(a)(2) of Pub.L. 96–265 applicable with respect to expenses incurred on or after the first day of the sixth month which begins after June 9, 1980, see section 302(c) of Pub.L. 96–265, set out as a note under section 423 of this title.

Amendment by section 303(c)(1) of Pub.L. 96–265 effective on first day of sixth month which begins after June 9, 1980, and applicable with respect to any individual whose disability has not been determined to have ceased prior to such first day, see section 303(d) of Pub.L. 96–265, set out as a note under section 402 of this title.

Amendment by section 504(a) of Pub.L. 96–265 effective with respect to individuals applying for supplemental security income benefits under this subchapter for the first time after Sept. 30, 1980, see section 504(c) of Pub.L. 96–265, set out as a note under section 1382j of this title.

1972 Acts. Section 301 of Pub.L. 92–603 provided that this section is effective Jan. 1, 1974.

Application to Northern Mariana Islands

For applicability of this section to the Northern Mariana Islands, see section 502(a)(1) of the Covenant to Establish a Commonwealth of the Northern Mariana Islands in Political Union with the United States of America, as set forth in Pub.L. 94–241, Mar. 24, 1976, 90 Stat. 263, eff. Jan. 9, 1978, pursuant to Proc. No. 4534, Oct. 24, 1977, 42 F.R. 6593, set out as notes under section 1681 of Title 48, Territories and Insular Possessions.

Regulations

For provisions requiring the Secretary of Health and Human Services to prescribe regulations necessary to implement enactment of subsec. (a)(5) by Pub.L. 98–460, § 2(c), not later than 180 days after Oct. 9, 1984, see section 2(g) of Pub.L. 98–460, set out as a note under section 423 of this title.

Puerto Rico, Guam, and Virgin Islands

Enactment of provisions of Pub.L. 92–603, eff. Jan. 1, 1974, not applicable to Puerto Rico, Guam, and the Virgin Islands, see section 303(b) of Pub.L. 92–603, set out as a note under section 301 of this title.

Retroactive Benefits

For provisions relating to entitlement to retroactive benefits under section 2 of Pub.L. 98–460, see section 2(f) of Pub.L. 98–460, set out as a note under section 423 of this title.

§ 1382d. Rehabilitation services for blind and disabled individuals

(a) Referral by Commissioner of eligible individuals to appropriate State agency

In the case of any blind or disabled individual who—

(1) has not attained age 16; and

(2) with respect to whom benefits are paid under this subchapter,

the Commissioner of Social Security shall make provision for referral of such individual to the appropriate State agency administering the State program under subchapter V.

(b) Repealed. Pub.L. 97–35, Title XXI, § 2193(c)(8)(B), Aug. 13, 1981, 95 Stat. 828

(c) Repealed. Pub.L. 106–170, Title I, § 101(b)(2)(B), Dec. 17, 1999, 113 Stat. 1874

(d) Reimbursement by Commissioner to State agency of costs of providing services to referred individuals

The Commissioner of Social Security is authorized to reimburse the State agency administering or supervising the administration of a State plan for vocational rehabilitation services approved under title I of the Rehabilitation Act of 1973 for the costs incurred under such plan in the provision of rehabilitation services to individuals who are referred for such services pursuant to subsection (a), (1) in cases where the furnishing of such services results in the performance by such individuals of substantial gainful activity for a continuous period of nine months, (2) in cases where such individuals receive benefits as a result of section 1383(a)(6) of this title (except that no reimbursement under this subsection shall be made for services furnished to any individual receiving such benefits for any period after the close of such individual's ninth consecutive month of substantial gainful activity or the close of the month with which his or her entitlement to such benefits ceases, whichever first occurs), and (3) in cases where such individuals, without good cause, refuse to continue to accept vocational rehabilitation services or fail to cooperate in such a manner as to preclude their successful rehabilitation. The determination that the vocational rehabilitation services contributed to the successful return of an individual to substantial gainful activity, the determination that an individual, without good cause, refused to continue to accept vocational rehabilitation services or failed to cooperate in such a manner as to preclude successful rehabilitation, and the determination of the amount of costs to be reimbursed under this subsection shall be made by the Commissioner of Social Security in accordance with criteria determined by the Commissioner in the same manner as under section 422(d)(1) of this title.

(e) Reimbursement for vocational rehabilitation services furnished during certain months of nonpayment of insurance benefits

The Commissioner of Social Security may reimburse the State agency described in subsection (d) for the costs described therein incurred in the provision of rehabilitation services—

(1) for any month for which an individual received—

(A) benefits under section 1382 or 1382h(a) of this title;

(B) assistance under section 1382h(b) of this title; or

(C) a federally administered State supplementary payment under section 1382e of this title or section 212(b) of Public Law 93–66; and

(2) for any month before the 13th consecutive month for which an individual, for a reason other than cessation of disability or blindness, was ineligible for—

(A) benefits under section 1382 or 1382h(a) of this title;

(B) assistance under section 1382h(b) of this title; or

(C) a federally administered State supplementary payment under section 1382e of this title or section 212(b) of Public Law 93–66.

(Aug. 14, 1935, c. 531, Title XVI, § 1615, as added Pub.L. 92–603, Title III, § 301, Oct. 30, 1972, 86 Stat. 1474; amended Pub.L. 94–566, Title V, § 501(a), Oct. 20, 1976, 90 Stat. 2683; Pub.L. 96–272, Title III, § 304, June 17, 1980, 94 Stat. 529; Pub.L. 97–35, Title XXI, § 2193(a)(4), (c)(8), Title XXIII, § 2344, Aug. 13, 1981, 95 Stat. 827, 828, 867; Pub.L. 98–369, Div. B, Title VI, § 2663(g)(8), July 18, 1984, 98 Stat. 1169; Pub.L. 98–460, § 11(b), Oct. 9, 1984, 98 Stat. 1806; Pub.L. 101–508, Title V, § 5037(a), Nov. 5, 1990, 104 Stat. 1388–226; Pub.L. 103–296, Title I, § 107(a)(4), Aug. 15, 1994, 108 Stat. 1478; Pub.L. 105–33, Title V, § 5523, Aug. 5, 1997, 111 Stat. 623; Pub.L. 106–170, Title I, § 101(b)(2)(A), (B), Dec. 17, 1999, 113 Stat. 1874.)

HISTORICAL AND STATUTORY NOTES

References in Text

The Rehabilitation Act of 1973, referred to in subsec. (d), is Pub.L. 93–112, Sept. 26, 1973, 87 Stat. 355, as amended, which is classified principally to chapter 16 of Title 29, 29 U.S.C.A. § 701 et seq. Title I of the Act is classified generally to subchapter I of chapter 16 of Title 29, 29 U.S.C.A. § 720 et seq. Pursuant to 29 U.S.C.A. § 3361(c), references to a provision of the Rehabilitation Act of 1973 are deemed to refer to the corresponding provision of such Act, as amended by the Workforce Innovation and Opportunity Act, Pub.L. 113–128, July 22, 2014, 128 Stat. 1425. For complete classification, see Short Title note set out under 29 U.S.C.A. § 701 and Tables.

Section 212(b) of Public Law 93–66, referred to in subsecs. (e)(1)(C), (2)(C), means section 212(b) of Pub.L. 93–66, July 9, 1973, 87 Stat. 155 to 158, which is set out as a note under section 1382 of this title.

Codifications

Pub.L. 105–33, Title V, § 5523(1), Aug. 5, 1997, 111 Stat. 623, which directed that the first sentence in subsec. (d) of this section be amended by inserting a comma after "subsection (a)(1) of this section" was executed by inserting a comma after "subsection (a) of this section", as the probable intent of Congress.

Pub.L. 105–33, § 5523(2), which directed that the last sentence in subsec. (d) of this section be amended by substituting "the Commissioner" for "him", was not executed since such change was already made by Pub.L. 103–296, § 107(a)(4).

Effective and Applicability Provisions

1999 Acts. Amendment by section 101(b) of Pub.L. 106–170 effective with the first month following 1 year after December 17, 1999, subject to graduated implementation of program provisions of section 101(d) of Pub.L. 106–170 [set out as a note under section 1320b–19 of this title], see section 101(c) of Pub.L. 106–170, set out as a note under section 1320b–19 of this title.

1997 Acts. Amendments by section 5523 of Pub.L. 105–33 effective as if included in enactment of Pub.L. 104–193, see section 5528(a) of Pub.L. 105–33, set out as a note under section 903 of this title.

1994 Acts. Amendment by section 107(a)(4) of Pub.L. 103–296 effective Mar. 31, 1995, see section 110 of Pub.L. 103–296, set out as a note under section 401 of this title.

1990 Acts. Section 5037(b) of Pub.L. 101–508 provided that: "The amendment made by subsection (a) [enacting subsec. (e) of this section] shall take effect on the date of the enactment of this Act [Nov. 5, 1990] and shall apply to claims for reimbursement pending on or after such date."

1984 Acts. Amendment by Pub.L. 98–369 effective July 18, 1984, but not to be construed as changing or affecting any right, liability, status, or interpretation which existed (under the provisions of law involved) before that date, see section 2664(b) of Pub.L. 98–369, set out as a note under section 401 of this title.

Amendment by Pub.L. 98–360 applicable with respect to individuals who receive benefits as a result of section 425(b) or section 1383(a)(6) of this title, or who refuse to continue to accept rehabilitation services or fail to cooperate in an approved vocational rehabilitation program, in or after Nov. 1984, see section 11(c) of Pub.L. 98–460, set out as a note under section 422 of this title.

1981 Acts. Section 2193(a)(4)(B), of Pub.L. 97–35 provided that amendment by section 2193(a)(4)(B) is effective for fiscal year 1982.

For effective date, savings, and transitional provisions relating to amendments by section 2193(a)(4)(A) and (c)(8) of Pub.L. 97–35, see section 2194 of Pub.L. 97–35, set out as a note under section 701 of this title.

Section 2344 of Pub.L. 97–35 provided in part that amendment by section 2344 of Pub.L. 97–35 is effective Oct. 1, 1981.

1972 Acts. Section 301 of Pub.L. 92–603 provided in part that this section is to take effect Jan. 1, 1974.

Application to Northern Mariana Islands

For applicability of this section to the Northern Mariana Islands, see section 502(a)(1) of the Covenant to Establish a Commonwealth of the Northern Mariana Islands in Political Union with the United States of America, as set forth in Pub.L. 94–241, Mar. 24, 1976, 90 Stat. 263, eff. Jan. 9, 1978, pursuant to Proc. No. 4534, Oct. 24, 1977, 42 F.R. 6593, set out as notes under section 1681 of Title 48, Territories and Insular Possessions.

Publication of Criteria

Section 501(b) of Pub.L. 94–566 provided that: "The Secretary shall, within 120 days after the enactment of this subsection [Oct. 20, 1976], publish criteria to be employed to determine disability (as defined in section 1614(a)(3) of the Social Security Act [section 1382c(a)(3) of this title]) in the case of persons who have not attained the age of 18."

Puerto Rico, Guam, and Virgin Islands

Enactment of provisions of Pub.L. 92–603, eff. Jan. 1, 1974, not applicable to Puerto Rico, Guam, and the Virgin Islands, see section 303(b) of Pub.L. 92–603, set out as a note under section 301 of this title.

§ 1382e. Supplementary assistance by State or subdivision to needy individuals

(a) Exclusion of cash payments in determination of income of individuals for purposes of eligibility for benefits; agreement by Commissioner and State for Commissioner to make supplementary payments on behalf of State or subdivision

Any cash payments which are made by a State (or political subdivision thereof) on a regular basis to individuals who are receiving benefits under this subchapter or who would but for their income be eligible to receive benefits under this subchapter, as assistance based on need in supplementation of such benefits (as determined by the Commissioner of Social Security), shall be excluded under section 1382a(b)(6) of this title in determining the income of such individuals for purposes of this subchapter and the Commissioner of Social Security and such State may enter into an agreement which satisfies subsection (b) under which the Commissioner of Social Security will, on behalf of such State (or subdivision) make such supplementary payments to all such individuals.

(b) Agreement between Commissioner and State; contents

Any agreement between the Commissioner of Social Security and a State entered into under subsection (a) shall provide—

(1) that such payments will be made (subject to subsection (c)) to all individuals residing in such State (or subdivision) who are receiving benefits under this subchapter, and

(2) such other rules with respect to eligibility for or amount of the supplementary payments, and such procedural or other general administrative provisions, as the Commissioner of Social Security finds necessary (subject to subsection (c)) to achieve efficient and effective administration of both the program which the Commissioner conducts under this subchapter and the optional State supplementation.

At the option of the State (but subject to paragraph (2) of this subsection), the agreement between the Commissioner of Social Security and such State entered into under subsection (a) shall be modified to provide that the Commissioner of Social Security will make supplementary payments, on and after an effective date to be specified in the agreement as so modified, to individuals receiving benefits determined under section 1382(e)(1)(B) of this title.

(c) Residence requirement by State or subdivision for supplementary payments; disregarding amounts of certain income by State or subdivision in determining eligibility for supplementary payments

(1) Any State (or political subdivision) making supplementary payments described in subsection (a) may at its option impose as a condition of eligibility for such payments, and include in the State's agreement with the Commissioner of Social Security under such subsection, a residence requirement which excludes individuals who have resided in the State (or political subdivision) for less than a minimum period prior to application for such payments.

(2) Any State (or political subdivision), in determining the eligibility of any individual for supplementary payments described in subsection (a), may disregard amounts of earned and unearned income in addition to other amounts which it is required or permitted to disregard under this section in determining such eligibility, and shall include a provision specifying the amount of any such income that will be disregarded, if any.

(3) Any State (or political subdivision) making supplementary payments described in subsection (a) shall have the option of making such payments to individuals who receive benefits under this subchapter under the provisions of section 1382h of this title, or who would be eligible to receive such benefits but for their income.

(d) Payment to Commissioner by State of amount equal to expenditures by Commissioner as supplementary payments; time and manner of payment by State; fees for Federal administration of State supplementary payments

(1) Any State which has entered into an agreement with the Commissioner of Social Security under this section which provides that the Commissioner of Social Security will, on behalf of the State (or political subdivision), make the supplementary payments to individuals who are receiving benefits under this subchapter (or who would but for their income be eligible to receive such benefits), shall, in accordance with paragraph (5), pay to the Commissioner of Social Security an amount equal to the expenditures made by the Commissioner of Social Security as such supplementary payments, plus an administration fee assessed in accordance with paragraph (2) and any additional services fee charged in accordance with paragraph (3).

(2)(A) The Commissioner of Social Security shall assess each State an administration fee in an amount equal to—

(i) the number of supplementary payments made by the Commissioner of Social Security on behalf of the State under this section for any month in a fiscal year; multiplied by

(ii) the applicable rate for the fiscal year.

(B) As used in subparagraph (A), the term "applicable rate" means—

(i) for fiscal year 1994, $1.67;

(ii) for fiscal year 1995, $3.33;

(iii) for fiscal year 1996, $5.00;

(iv) for fiscal year 1997, $5.00;

(v) for fiscal year 1998, $6.20;

(vi) for fiscal year 1999, $7.60;

(vii) for fiscal year 2000, $7.80;

(viii) for fiscal year 2001, $8.10;

(ix) for fiscal year 2002, $8.50; and

(x) for fiscal year 2003 and each succeeding fiscal year—

(I) the applicable rate in the preceding fiscal year, increased by the percentage, if any, by which the Consumer Price Index for the month of June of the calendar year of the increase exceeds the Consumer Price Index for the month of June of the calendar year preceding the calendar year of the increase, and rounded to the nearest whole cent; or

(II) such different rate as the Commissioner determines is appropriate for the State.

(C) Upon making a determination under subparagraph (B)(x)(II), the Commissioner of Social Security shall promulgate the determination in regulations, which may take into account the complexity of administering the State's supplementary payment program.

(D) All fees assessed pursuant to this paragraph shall be transferred to the Commissioner of Social Security at the same time that amounts for such supplementary payments are required to be so transferred.

(3)(A) The Commissioner of Social Security may charge a State an additional services fee if, at the request of the State, the Commissioner of Social Security provides additional services beyond the level customarily provided, in the administration of State supplementary payments pursuant to this section.

(B) The additional services fee shall be in an amount that the Commissioner of Social Security determines is necessary to cover all costs (including indirect costs) incurred by the Federal Government in furnishing the additional services referred to in subparagraph (A).

(4)(A) The first $5 of each administration fee assessed pursuant to paragraph (2), upon collection, shall be deposited in the general fund of the Treasury of the United States as miscellaneous receipts.

(B) That portion of each administration fee in excess of $5, and 100 percent of each additional services fee charged pursuant to paragraph (3), upon collection for fiscal year 1998 and each subsequent fiscal year, shall be credited to a special fund established in the Treasury of the United States for State supplementary payment fees. The amounts so credited, to the extent and in the amounts provided in advance in appropriations Acts, shall be available to defray expenses incurred in carrying out this subchapter and related laws.

(5)(A)(i) Any State which has entered into an agreement with the Commissioner of Social Security under this section shall remit the payments and fees required under this subsection with respect to monthly benefits paid to individuals under this subchapter no later than

(I) the business day preceding the date that the Commissioner pays such monthly benefits; or

(II) with respect to such monthly benefits paid for the month that is the last month of the State's fiscal year, the fifth business day following such date.

(ii) The Commissioner may charge States a penalty in an amount equal to 5 percent of the payment and the fees due if the remittance is received after the date required by clause (i).

(B) The Cash Management Improvement Act of 1990 shall not apply to any payments or fees required under this subsection that are paid by a State before the date required by subparagraph (A)(i).

(C) Notwithstanding subparagraph (A)(i), the Commissioner may make supplementary payments on behalf of a State with funds appropriated for payment of benefits under this subchapter, and subsequently to be reimbursed for such payments by the State at such times as the Commissioner and State may agree. Such authority may be exercised only if extraordinary circumstances affecting a State's ability to make payment when required by subparagraph (A)(i) are determined by the Commissioner to exist.

(e) State standards; establishment; annual public review; annual certification; payments to individuals

(1) Each State shall establish or designate one or more State or local authorities which shall establish, maintain, and insure the enforcement of standards for any category of institutions, foster homes, or group living arrangements in which (as determined by the State) a significant number of recipients of supplemental security income benefits is residing or is likely to reside. Such standards shall be appropriate to the needs of such recipients and the character of the facilities involved, and shall govern such matters as admission policies, safety, sanitation, and protection of civil rights.

(2) Each State shall annually make available for public review a summary of the standards established pursuant to paragraph (1), and shall make available to any interested individual a copy of such standards, along with the procedures available in the State to insure the enforcement of such standards and a list of any waivers of such standards and any violations of such standards which have come to the attention of the authority responsible for their enforcement.

(3) Each State shall certify annually to the Commissioner of Social Security that it is in compliance with the requirements of this subsection.

(4) Payments made under this subchapter with respect to an individual shall be reduced by an amount equal to the amount of any supplementary payment (as described in subsection (a)) or other payment made by a State (or political subdivision thereof) which is made for or on account of any medical or any other type of remedial care provided by an institution of the type described in paragraph (1) to such individual as a resident or an inpatient of such institution if such institution is not approved as meeting the standards described in such paragraph by the appropriate State or local authorities.

(Aug. 14, 1935, c. 531, Title XVI, § 1616, as added Pub.L. 92–603, Title III, § 301, Oct. 30, 1972, 86 Stat. 1474; amended Pub.L. 93–233, § 14, Dec. 31, 1973, 87 Stat. 965; Pub.L. 94–566, Title V, § 505(c), (d), Oct. 20, 1976, 90 Stat. 2687; Pub.L. 96–265, Title II, § 201(b)(1), June 9, 1980, 94 Stat. 446; Pub.L. 97–35, Title XXIII, § 2353(n), Aug. 13, 1981, 95 Stat. 873; Pub.L. 99–272, Title XII, § 12201(b), Apr. 7, 1986, 100 Stat. 290; Pub.L. 103–66, Title XIII, § 13731(a)(1), Aug. 10, 1993, 107 Stat. 660; Pub.L. 103–296, Title I, § 107(a)(4), Aug. 15, 1994, 108 Stat. 1478; Pub.L. 105–33, Title V, § 5102(a)(1), (b)(1)(A), Aug. 5, 1997, 111 Stat. 595, 596; Pub.L. 105–78, Title V, § 516(a)(1), (b)(1)(A), Nov. 13, 1997, 111 Stat. 1517, 1518; Pub.L. 106–170, Title IV, § 410(a)(1), Dec. 17, 1999, 113 Stat. 1916).

HISTORICAL AND STATUTORY NOTES

References in Text

The Cash Management Improvement Act of 1990, referred to in subsec. (d)(5)(B), enacted section 3335 of Title 31, amended sections 6501 and 6503 of Title 31, and enacted provisions set out as notes under those sections. See Tables for complete classification.

Codifications

The authorities provided by each provision of, and each amendment made by, Pub.L. 110–246, as in effect on Sept. 30, 2012, to continue, and the Secretary of Agriculture to carry out the authorities, until the later of Sept. 30, 2013, or the date specified in the provision of, or amendment made by, Pub.L. 110–246, see section 701(a) of Pub.L. 112–240, set out in a note under 7 U.S.C.A. § 8701.

Section 516(a)(1) and (b)(1)(A) of Pub.L. 105–78 made identical amendments to this section as section 5102(a)(1) and (b)(1)(A) of Pub.L. 105–33 without any reference to such amendments by Pub.L. 105–33.

Effective and Applicability Provisions

1999 Acts. Pub.L. 106–170, Title IV, § 410(b), Dec. 17, 1999, 113 Stat. 1917, as amended Pub.L. 106–554, § 1(a)(1) [Title V, § 515], Dec. 21, 2000, 114 Stat. 2763, 2763A–72, provided that: "The amendments made by subsection (a) [amending this section and a note set out under section 1382 of this title] shall apply to payments and fees arising under an agreement between a State and the Commissioner of Social Security under section 1616 of the Social Security Act (42 U.S.C. 1382e) [this section] or under section 212 of Public Law 93–66 (42 U.S.C. 1382 note) with respect to monthly benefits paid to individuals under title XVI of the Social Security Act [this subchapter] for months after September 2001 (October 2001 in the case of a State with a fiscal year that coincides with the Federal fiscal year), without regard to whether the agreement has been modified to reflect such amendments or the Commissioner has promulgated regulations implementing such amendments."

1994 Acts. Amendment by section 107(a)(4) of Pub.L. 103–296 effective Mar. 31, 1995, see section 110 of Pub.L. 103–296, set out as a note under section 401 of this title.

1993 Acts. Section 13731(b) of Pub.L. 103–66, provided that: "The amendments made by this section [amending this section and provisions set out as notes under section 1382 of this title] shall apply to supplementary payments made pursuant to section 1616(a) of the Social Security Act [subsec. (a) of this section] or section 212(a) of Public Law 93–66 [set out as a note under section 1382 of this title] for any calendar month beginning after September 30, 1993, and to services furnished after such date, regardless of whether regulations to implement such amendments have been promulgated by such date, or whether any agreement entered into under such section 1616(a) or such section 212(a) has been modified."

1981 Acts. Amendment by Pub.L. 97–35 effective Oct. 1, 1981, except as otherwise explicitly provided, see section 2354 of Pub.L. 97–35, set out as a note under section 1397 of this title.

1980 Acts. Amendment by Pub.L. 96–265 effective Jan. 1, 1981, see section 201(d) of Pub.L. 96–265, as amended, set out as a note under section 1382h of this title.

1976 Acts. Amendment by section 505(c) of Pub.L. 94–566 effective Oct. 1, 1976, see section 505(e) of Pub.L. 94–566, set out as a note under section 1382 of this title.

Section 505(d) of Pub.L. 94–566 provided that amendment made by such section 505(d) is effective Oct. 1, 1977.

1972 Acts. Section 301 of Pub.L. 92–603 provided that this section is effective Jan. 1, 1974.

Adjusted Payment Level; Payment Level Modification

Section 8(e), formerly 8(d), of Pub.L. 93–233, as renumbered Pub.L. 94–379, § 1(a), Aug. 10, 1976, 90 Stat. 1111, provided that: "Section 401(b)(1) of the Social Security Amendments of 1972 [set out as a note under this section] is amended by striking out everything after the word 'exceed' and inserting in lieu thereof: 'a payment level modification (as defined in paragraph (2) of this subsection) with respect to such plans'."

Section 8(f), formerly 8(e), of Pub.L. 93–233, as amended Pub.L. 93–335, § 1(b), July 8, 1974, 88 Stat. 291; Pub.L. 94–44, § 3(b), June 28, 1975, 89 Stat. 235; Pub.L. 94–365, § 2(2), July 14, 1976, 90 Stat. 990; renumbered § 8(f) and amended Pub.L. 94–379, § 1(a), (b), Aug. 10, 1976, 90 Stat. 1111; Pub.L. 95–59, § 3(2), June 30, 1977, 91 Stat. 255; Pub.L. 95–113, Title XIII, § 1302(a)(4), Sept. 29, 1977, 91 Stat. 979, provided that: "The amendment made by subsection (e) [set out as a note under this section] shall not be effective in any State which provides supplementary payments of the type described in section 1616(a) of the Social Security Act [subsec. (a) of this section] the level of which has been found by the Secretary to have been specifically increased so as to include the bonus value of food stamps."

[Amendment of section 8(f) [formerly 8(e)] of Pub.L. 93–233 by section 1(b) of Pub.L. 93–335, effective July 1, 1974, see section 1(c) of Pub.L. 93–335, set out as a note under this section.]

[Section 1(c) of Pub.L. 93–335 provided that amendments by section 1(a) and (b) of Pub.L. 93–335 to section 8(a)(1), (2), (b)(1) to (3) and (f) [formerly (e)] of Pub.L. 93–233, Dec. 31, 1973, 87 Stat. 956, set out as notes under this section and sections 612c, 1431 and 2012 of Title 7, Agriculture, shall take effect July 1, 1974.]

[Section 3 of Pub.L. 95–59 provided that amendment of section 8(f) [formerly 8(e)] of Pub.L. 93–233, set out under this section, by section 3(2) of Pub.L. 95–59 was effective July 1, 1977.]

[Section 1302(b) of Pub.L. 95–113 provided that amendment of section 8(f) [formerly 8(e)] of Pub.L. 93–233, set out under this section, by section 1302(a)(4) of Pub.L. 95–113 was effective Oct. 1, 1977.]

Application to Northern Mariana Islands

For applicability of this section to the Northern Mariana Islands, see section 502(a)(1) of the Covenant to Establish a Commonwealth of the Northern Mariana Islands in Political Union with the United States of America, as set forth in Pub.L. 94–241, Mar. 24, 1976, 90 Stat. 263, eff. Jan. 9, 1978, pursuant to Proc. No. 4534, Oct. 24, 1977, 42 F.R. 6593, set out as notes under section 1681 of Title 48, Territories and Insular Possessions.

Commodity Distribution Program; Individual Receiving Supplemental Security Income Benefits as Member of Household for any Purpose of Program

Individual receiving supplemental security income benefits or payments as part of benefits or payments described in subsec. (a) of this section as member of a household for any purpose of the food distribution program, see section 4(c) of Pub.L. 93–86, set out as a note under section 612c of Title 7, Agriculture.

Election of Payments Under Combined State Plan Rather Than Separate Plans

Pub.L. 87–543, § 141(b), July 25, 1962, 76 Stat. 205, provided that: "No payment may be made to a State under title I, X, or XIV of the Social Security Act [subchapter I, X, or XIV of this chapter] for any period for which such State receives any payments under title XVI of such Act [this subchapter] or any period thereafter."

Eligibility of Supplemental Security Income Recipients for Food Stamps

Section 8(c) of Pub.L. 93–233, as amended Pub.L. 95–113, Title XIII, § 1302(a)(3), Sept. 29, 1977, 91 Stat. 979, provided that: "For purposes of section 6(g) of the Food Stamp Act of

1977 [section 2015(g) of Title 7, Agriculture] and subsections (b)(3) [set out as a note under section 612c of Title 7] and (f) [set out as a note under this section] of this section, the level of State supplementary payment under section 1616(a) [subsec. (a) of this section] shall be found by the Secretary to have been specifically increased so as to include the bonus value of food stamps (1) only if, prior to October 1, 1973, the State has entered into an agreement with the Secretary or taken other positive steps which demonstrate its intention to provide supplementary payments under section 1616(a) [subsec. (a) of this section] at a level which is at least equal to the maximum level which can be determined under section 401(b)(1) of the Social Security Amendments of 1972 [set out as a note under this section] and which is such that the limitation on State fiscal liability under section 401 [set out as a note under this section] does result in a reduction in the amount which would otherwise be payable to the Secretary by the State, and (2) only with respect to such months as the State may, at its option, elect."

[Section 1302(b) of Pub.L. 95–113 provided that amendment of section 8(c) of Pub.L. 93–233 by section 1302(a)(3) of Pub.L. 95–113 was effective Oct. 1, 1977.]

Section 8(d) of Pub.L. 93–233, as added Pub.L. 94–379, § 1(a), Aug. 10, 1976, 90 Stat. 1111, and amended Pub.L. 95–458, § 5(a), Oct. 14, 1978, 92 Stat. 1260; Pub.L. 97–18, § 2, June 30, 1981, 95 Stat. 102; Pub.L. 97–35, Title XXIII, § 2342(a), Aug. 13, 1981, 95 Stat. 866, provided that: "Upon the request of a State, the Secretary shall find, for purposes of the provisions specified in subsection (c) [set out as a note under this section] that the level of such State's supplementary payments of the type described in section 1616(a) of the Social Security Act [subsec. (a) of this section] has been specifically increased for any month so as to include the bonus value of food stamps (and that such State meets the applicable requirements of subsection (c)(1) if—

"**(1)** the Secretary has found (under this subsection or subsection (d), as in effect in December 1980) that such State's supplementary payments in December 1980 were increased to include the bonus value of food stamps; and

"**(2)** such State continues without interruption to meet the requirements of section 1618 of such Act [section 1382g of this title] for each month after the month referred to in paragraph (1) and up to and including the month for which the Secretary is making the determination."

[Section 2 of Pub.L. 97–18 provided that amendment of section 8(d) of Pub.L. 93–233, set out as a note under this section, by section 2 of Pub.L. 97–18 was effective for the period July 1, 1981 to Aug. 1, 1981.]

[Section 2342(b) of Pub.L. 97–35 provided that amendment of section 8(d) of Pub.L. 93–233, set out as a note under this section, by section 2342(a) of Pub.L. 97–35 was effective July 1, 1981.]

Limitations on Authorization of Appropriations

Section 516(b)(2) of Pub.L. 105–78 provided that: "From amounts credited pursuant to section 1616(d)(4)(B) of the Social Security Act [subsection (d)(4)(B) of this section] and section 212(b)(3)(D)(ii) of Public Law 93–66 [set out as a note under section 1382 of this title] to the special fund established in the Treasury of the United States for State supplementary payment fees, there is authorized to be appropriated an amount not to exceed $35,000,000 for fiscal year 1998, and such sums as may be necessary for each fiscal year thereafter, for administrative expenses in carrying out the supplemental security income program under title XVI of the Social Security Act [this subchapter] and related laws."

Section 5102(b)(2) of Pub.L. 105–33 provided that: "From amounts credited pursuant to section 1616(d)(4)(B) of the Social Security Act [subsection (d)(4)(B) of this section] and section 212(b)(3)(D)(ii) of Public Law 93–66 [set out as a note under section 1382 of this title] to the special fund established in the Treasury of the United States for State supplementary payment fees, there is authorized to be appropriated an amount not to exceed $35,000,000 for fiscal year 1998, and such sums as may be necessary for each fiscal year thereafter."

Limitation on Fiscal Liability of States for Payment to Secretary of Supplementary Payments Made by Secretary Pursuant to Agreement

Section 401 of Pub.L. 92–603, as amended Pub.L. 93–233, § 18(h), Dec. 31, 1973, 87 Stat. 969; Pub.L. 94–566, Title V, § 504(a), Oct. 20, 1976, 90 Stat. 2686; Pub.L. 94–585 § 2(b), Oct. 21, 1976, 90 Stat. 2902; Pub.L. 97–248, Title I, § 184(a), Sept. 3, 1982, 96 Stat. 406; Pub.L. 110–234, Title IV, § 4115(c)(1)(A)(ii), (vi), (B)(iv), May 22, 2008, 122 Stat. 1109, and Pub.L. 110–246, Title IV, § 4115(c)(1)(A)(ii), (vi), (B)(iv), June 18, 2008, 122 Stat. 1870, 1871, provided that:

"**(a)(1)** The amount payable to the Secretary by a State for any fiscal year, other than fiscal year 1974, pursuant to its agreement or agreements under section 1616 of the Social Security Act [this section] shall not exceed the non-Federal share of expenditures as aid or assistance for quarters in the calendar year 1972 under the plans of the State approved under titles I, X, XIV, and XVI of the Social Security Act [subchapters I, X, XIV, and XVI of this chapter] (as defined in subsection (c) of this section), and the amount payable for fiscal year 1974 pursuant to such agreement or agreements shall not exceed one-half of the non-Federal share of such expenditures.

"**(2)** Paragraph (1) of this subsection shall only apply with respect to that portion of the supplementary payments made by the Secretary on behalf of the State under such agreements in any fiscal year which does not exceed in the case of any individual the difference between—

"**(A)** the adjusted payment level under the appropriate approved plan of such State as in effect for January 1972 (as defined in subsection (b) of this section), and

"**(B)** the benefits under title XVI of the Social Security Act [this subchapter] (subject to the second sentence of this paragraph), plus income not excluded under section 1612(b) of such Act [section 1382a(b) of this title] in determining such benefits, paid to such individual in such fiscal year,

"and shall not apply with respect to supplementary payments to any individual who (i) is not required by section 1616 of such Act [this section] to be included in any such agreement administered by the Secretary and (ii) would have been ineligible (for reasons other than income) for payments under the appropriate approved State plan as in effect for January 1972. In determining the difference between the level specified in subparagraph (A) and the benefits and income described in subparagraph (B) there shall be excluded any part of any such benefit which results from (and would not be payable but for) any cost-of-living increase in such benefits under section 1617 of such Act [section 1382f of this title] (or any general increase enacted by law in the dollar amounts referred to in such section) becoming effective after June 30, 1977.

"(b)(1) For purposes of subsection (a), the term 'adjusted payment level under the appropriate approved plan of a State as in effect for January 1972' means the amount of the money payment which an individual with no other income would have received under the plan of such State approved under title I, X, XIV, or XVI of the Social Security Act [subchapters I, X, XIV, or XVI of this chapter], as may be appropriate, and in effect for January 1972; except that the State may, as its option, increase such payment level with respect to any such plan by an amount which does not exceed the sum of—

"(A) a payment level modification (as defined in paragraph (2) of this subsection) with respect to such plan, and

"(B) the bonus value of benefits in such State for January 1972 (as defined in paragraph (3) of this subsection).

"(2) For purposes of paragraph (1), the term 'payment level modification' with respect to any State plan means that amount by which a State which for January 1972 made money payments under such plan to individuals with no other income which were less than 100 per centum of its standard of need could have increased such money payments without increasing (if it reduced its standard of need under such plan so that such increased money payments equaled 100 per centum of such standard of need) the non-Federal share of expenditures as aid or assistance for quarters in calendar year 1972 under the plans of such State approved under titles I, X, XIV, and XVI of the Social Security Act [subchapters I, X, XIV, and XVI of this chapter].

"(3) For purposes of paragraph (1), the term 'bonus value of food stamps in a State for January 1972' with respect to an individual means—

"(A) the face value of the benefit allotment which would have been provided to such an individual under the Food Stamp Act of 1964 [chapter 51 (section 2011 et seq.) of Title 7, Agriculture] for January 1972, reduced by

"(B) the charge which such an individual would have paid for such benefit allotment.

"if the income of such individual, for purposes of determining the charge it would have been paid for its benefit allotment, had been equal to the adjusted payment level under the State plan (including any payment level modification with respect to the plan adopted pursuant to paragraph (2) (but not including any amount under this paragraph)). The total face value of benefits and the cost thereof in January 1972 shall be determined in accordance with the rules prescribed by the Secretary of Agriculture in effect in such month.

"(c) For purposes of this section, the term 'non-Federal share of expenditures as aid or assistance for quarters in the calendar year 1972 under the plans of a State approved under titles I, X, XIV, and XVI of the Social Security Act' [subchapters I, X, XIV, and XVI of this chapter] means the difference between]—

"(1) the total expenditures in such quarters under such plans for aid or assistance (excluding expenditures authorized under section 1119 of such Act [section 1319 of this title] for repairing the home of an individual who was receiving aid or assistance under one of such plans (as such section was in effect prior to the enactment of this Act)), and

"(2) the total of the amounts determined under sections 3, 1003, 1403, and 1603 of the Social Security Act [sections 303, 1203, 1353, and 1383 of this title], under section 1118 of such Act [section 1318 of this title] and under section 9 of the Act of April 19, 1950 [former section 639 of Title 25], for such State with respect to such expenditures in such quarters.

"(d) In addition to the amount which a State must pay to the Secretary for the fiscal year 1983 or the fiscal year 1984, as determined under subsection (a), the State shall also pay, for the fiscal year 1983, 60 percent of the further amount that would be payable but for the limit specified in subsection (a), and, for the fiscal year 1984, 80 percent of such further amount. For each fiscal year thereafter, the limit prescribed in subsection (a) shall be inapplicable and a State shall pay to the Secretary the full amount of any supplementary payments he makes on behalf of such State."

[References in any Federal, State, tribal, or local law to a "coupon", "authorization card", or other access device provided under the Food and Nutrition Act of 2008, 7 U.S.C.A. § 2011 et seq., considered to be a reference to a "benefit" provided under that Act, see Pub.L. 110–234, § 4115(d), and Pub.L. 110–246, § 4115(d), set out as a note under 7 U.S.C.A. § 2012.]

[Amendments by Pub.L. 110–246, except as otherwise provided, shall take effect on the earlier of June 18, 2008, or May 22, 2008, see Pub.L. 110–246, § 4(b), set out in a Repeal of Duplicative Enactment note under 7 U.S.C.A. § 8701; Pub.L. 110–234 repealed effective May 22, 2008, see Repeal of Duplicative Enactment by Pub.L. 110–246, § 4(a), set out in a note under 7 U.S.C.A. § 8701.]

[Amendments by Title IV of Pub.L. 110–246, except as otherwise provided, take effect on October 1, 2008, see Pub.L. 110–246, § 4407, set out as a note under 2 U.S.C.A. § 1161.]

[Section 184(b) of Pub.L. 97–248 provided that enactment of section 401(d) of Pub.L. 92–603 by section 184(a) of Pub.L. 97–248 was effective Sept. 3, 1982.]

[Amendment of section 401(a)(2) of Pub.L. 92–603 by Pub.L. 94–585, identical to amendments by Pub.L. 94–566 less the words "and before July 1, 1979" following "June 30, 1977", effective with respect to benefits payable for months after June 1977, see section 2(c) of Pub.L. 94–585, set out as a note under section 1382g of this title.]

[Amendment of section 401(a)(2) of Pub.L. 92–603 by Pub.L. 94–566 inserting parenthetical text in subpar. (B) and enacting last sentence effective under provisions of Pub.L. 94–566, Title V, § 504(b), Oct. 20, 1976, 90 Stat. 2686, with respect to benefits payable for months after June 1977.]

[Amendment of section 401 of Pub.L. 92–603 by section 18(h) of Pub.L. 93–233 effective Jan. 1, 1974, see section 18(z–3)(1) of Pub.L. 93–233.]

Overpayment or Underpayment Adjustments

Pub.L. 87–543, § 141(f), July 25, 1962, 76 Stat. 205, provided that: "In the case of any State which has a State plan approved under title XVI of the Social Security Act [this subchapter], any overpayment or underpayment which the Secretary determines was made to such State under section 3, 1003, or 1403 of such Act [section 303, 1203, or 1353 of this title] with respect to a period before the approval of the plan under such title XVI [this subchapter], and with respect to which adjustment has not been already made under subsection (b) of such section 3, 1003, or 1403 [subsec. (b) of section 303, 1203, or 1353 of this title], shall, for purposes of section 1603(b) of such Act [section 1383(b) of this title prior to its omission on Oct. 30, 1972], be considered an overpayment or underpayment (as the case may be) made under section 1603 of such Act [section 1383 of this title as its existed prior to Oct. 30, 1972]."

Period Within Which California May Make Cash Payments in Lieu of Food Stamps to Recipients of Supplemental Security Income Benefits

Pub.L. 95–458, § 5(b), Oct. 14, 1978, 92 Stat. 1261, provided that: "No additional cash payment under title XVI of the Social Security Act [this subchapter] may be made pursuant to the third sentence of section 8(d) of Public Law 93–233 (as added by subsection (a) of this section) [amending a note under this section] for any month beginning before October 1, 1978, or ending after September 30, 1979."

Puerto Rico, Guam, and Virgin Islands

Enactment of provisions of Pub.L. 92–603, eff. Jan. 1, 1974, not applicable to Puerto Rico, Guam, and the Virgin Islands, see section 303(b) of Pub.L. 92–603, set out as a note under section 301 of this title.

Transitional Administration of Programs by State Pursuant to Agreement Between State and Secretary

Section 402 of Pub.L. 92–603, as amended Pub.L. 93–233, § 18(i), Dec. 31, 1973, 87 Stat. 970, provided that: "In order for a State to be eligible for any payments pursuant to title IV, V, VI, or XIX of the Social Security Act [subchapters IV, V, XVI, or XIX of this chapter] with respect to expenditures for the third and fourth quarters in the fiscal year ending June 30, 1974, and any quarter in the fiscal year ending June 30, 1975, and for the purpose of providing an orderly transition from State to Federal administration of the Supplemental Security Income Program, such State shall enter into an agreement with the Secretary of Health, Education, and Welfare under which the State agencies responsible for administering or for supervising the administration of the plans approved under titles I, X, XIV, and XVI of the Social Security Act [subchapters I, X, XIX, and XVI of this chapter] will, on behalf of the Secretary, administer all or such part or parts of the program established by section 301 of this Act [enacting this subchapter], during such portion of the third and fourth quarters of the fiscal year ending June 30, 1974, and any quarter of the fiscal year ending June 30, 1975, as may be provided in such agreement."

§ 1382f. Cost-of-living adjustments in benefits

(a) Increase of dollar amounts

Whenever benefit amounts under subchapter II are increased by any percentage effective with any month as a result of a determination made under section 415(i) of this title—

(1) each of the dollar amounts in effect for such month under subsections (a)(1)(A), (a)(2)(A), (b)(1), and (b)(2) of section 1382 of this title, and subsection (a)(1)(A) of section 211 of Public Law 93–66, as specified in such subsections or as previously increased under this section, shall be increased by the amount (if any) by which—

(A) the amount which would have been in effect for such month under such subsection but for the rounding of such amount pursuant to paragraph (2), exceeds

(B) the amount in effect for such month under such subsection; and

(2) the amount obtained under paragraph (1) with respect to each subsection shall be further increased by the same percentage by which benefit amounts under subchapter II are increased for such month, or, if greater (in any case where the increase under subchapter II was determined on the basis of the wage increase percentage rather than the CPI increase percentage), the percentage by which benefit amounts under subchapter II would be increased for such month if the increase had been determined on the basis of the CPI increase percentage, (and rounded, when not a multiple of $12, to the next lower multiple of $12), effective with respect to benefits for months after such month.

(b) Publication in Federal Register of new dollar amounts

The new dollar amounts to be in effect under section 1382 of this title and under section 211 of Public Law 93–66 by reason of subsection (a) of this section shall be published in the Federal Register together with, and at the same time as, the material required by section 415(i)(2)(D) of this title to be published therein by reason of the determination involved.

(c) Additional increases

Effective July 1, 1983—

(1) each of the dollar amounts in effect under subsections (a)(1)(A) and (b)(1) of section 1382 of this title, as previously increased under this section, shall be increased by $240 (and the dollar amount in effect under subsection (a)(1)(A) of section 211 of Public Law 93–66, as previously so increased, shall be increased by $120); and

(2) each of the dollar amounts in effect under subsections (a)(2)(A) and (b)(2) of section 1382 of this title, as previously increased under this section, shall be increased by $360.

(Aug. 14, 1935, c. 531, Title XVI, § 1617, as added Pub.L. 93–368, § 6(b), Aug. 7, 1974, 88 Stat. 421; amended Pub.L. 97–248, Title I, § 182(a), Sept. 3, 1982, 96 Stat. 404; Pub.L. 98–21, Title IV, § 401, Apr. 20, 1983, 97 Stat. 138.)

HISTORICAL AND STATUTORY NOTES

References in Text

Section 211 of Public Law 93–66, referred to in subsecs. (a)(1), (b), and (c)(1), is set out as section 211 of Pub.L. 93–66, Title II, July 9, 1973, 87 Stat. 154, as amended, which is a note under section 1382 of this title.

Effective and Applicability Provisions

1982 Acts. Section 182(b) of Pub.L. 97–248 provided that: "The amendment made by this section [amending this section] shall become effective on October 1, 1982."

Application to Northern Mariana Islands

For applicability of sections to the Northern Mariana Islands, see section 502(a)(1) of the Covenant to Establish a Commonwealth of the Northern Mariana Islands in Political Union with the United States of America, as set forth in Pub.L. 94–241, Mar. 24, 1976, 90 Stat. 263, eff. Jan. 9, 1978, pursuant to Proc. No. 4534, Oct. 24, 1977, 42 F.R. 6593, set out as notes under section 1681 of Title 48, Territories and Insular Possessions.

Cost-of-Living Increases; Cost-of-Living Computation Quarter Determinations

Payment of increased benefits under program covered in subchapter II of this chapter, see Pub.L. 98–604, § 1, Oct. 30, 1984, 98 Stat. 3161, set out as a note under section 415 of this title.

§ 1382g. Payments to State for operation of supplementation program

(a) Eligibility; agreement with Commissioner

In order for any State which makes supplementary payments of the type described in section 1382e(a) of this title (including payments pursuant to an agreement entered into under section 212(a) of Public Law 93–66), on or after June 30, 1977, to be eligible for payments pursuant to subchapter XIX with respect to expenditures for any calendar quarter which begins—

(1) after June 30, 1977, or, if later,

(2) after the calendar quarter in which it first makes such supplementary payments,

such State must have in effect an agreement with the Commissioner of Social Security whereby the State will—

(3) continue to make such supplementary payments, and

(4) maintain such supplementary payments at levels which are not lower than the levels of such payments in effect in December 1976, or, if no such payments were made in that month, the levels for the first subsequent month in which such payments were made.

(b) Levels of supplementary payments

(1) The Commissioner of Social Security shall not find that a State has failed to meet the requirements imposed by paragraph (4) of subsection (a) with respect to the levels of its supplementary payments for a particular month or months if the State's expenditures for such payments in the twelve-month period (within which such month or months fall) beginning on the effective date of any increase in the level of supplemental security income benefits pursuant to section 1382f of this title are not less than its expenditures for such payments in the preceding twelve-month period.

(2) For purposes of determining under paragraph (1) whether a State's expenditures for supplementary payments in the 12–month period beginning on the effective date of any increase in the level of supplemental security income benefits are not less than the State's expenditures for such payments in the preceding 12–month period, the Commissioner of Social Security, in computing the State's expenditures, shall disregard, pursuant to a 1–time election of the State, all expenditures by the State for retroactive supplementary payments that are required to be made in connection with the retroactive supplemental security income benefits referred to in section 5041 of the Omnibus Budget Reconciliation Act of 1990.

(c) Election to apply subsection (a)(4)

Any State which satisfies the requirements of this section solely by reason of subsection (b) for a particular month or months in any 12-month period (described in such subsection) ending on or after June 30, 1982, may elect, with respect to any month in any subsequent 12-month period (so described), to apply subsection (a)(4) as though the reference to December 1976 in such subsection were a reference to the month of December which occurred in the 12-month period immediately preceding such subsequent period.

(d) Determinations respecting any portion of period July 1, 1980, through June 30, 1981

The Commissioner of Social Security shall not find that a State has failed to meet the requirements imposed by paragraph (4) of subsection (a) with respect to the levels of its supplementary payments for any portion of the period July 1, 1980, through June 30, 1981, if the State's expenditures for such payments in that twelve-month period were not less than its expenditures for such payments for the period July 1, 1976, through June 30, 1977 (or, if the State made no supplementary payments in the period July 1, 1976, through June 30, 1977, the expenditures for the first twelve-month period extending from July 1 through June 30 in which the State made such payments).

(e) Meeting subsection (a)(4) requirements for any month after March 1983

(1) For any particular month after March 1983, a State which is not treated as meeting the requirements imposed by paragraph (4) of subsection (a) by reason of subsection (b) shall be treated as meeting such requirements if and only if—

(A) the combined level of its supplementary payments (to recipients of the type involved) and the amounts payable (to or on behalf of such recipients) under section 1382(b) of this title and section 211(a)(1)(A) of Public Law 93–66, for that particular month,

is not less than—

(B) the combined level of its supplementary payments (to recipients of the type involved) and the amounts payable (to or on behalf of such recipients) under section 1382(b) of this title and section 211(a)(1)(A) of Public Law 93–66, for March 1983, increased by the amount of all cost-of-living adjustments under section 1382f of this title (and any other benefit increases under this subchapter) which have occurred after March 1983 and before that particular month.

(2) In determining the amount of any increase in the combined level involved under paragraph (1)(B) of this

subsection, any portion of such amount which would otherwise be attributable to the increase under section 1382f(c) of this title shall be deemed instead to be equal to the amount of the cost-of-living adjustment which would have occurred in July 1983 (without regard to the 3-percent limitation contained in section 415(i)(1)(B) of this title) if section 111 of the Social Security Amendments of 1983 had not been enacted.

(f) Passthrough relating to optional State supplementation

The Commissioner of Social Security shall not find that a State has failed to meet the requirements imposed by subsection (a) with respect to the levels of its supplementary payments for the period January 1, 1984, through December 31, 1985, if in the period January 1, 1986, through December 31, 1986, its supplementary payment levels (other than to recipients of benefits determined under section 1382(e)(1)(B) of this title) are not less than those in effect in December 1976, increased by a percentage equal to the percentage by which payments under section 1382(b) of this title and section 211(a)(1)(A) of Public Law 93–66 have been increased as a result of all adjustments under section 1382f(a) and (c) of this title which have occurred after December 1976 and before February 1986.

(g) Mandatory pass-through of increased personal needs allowance

In order for any State which makes supplementary payments of the type described in section 1382e(a) of this title (including payments pursuant to an agreement entered into under section 212(a) of Public Law 93–66) to recipients of benefits determined under section 1382(e)(1)(B) of this title, on or after October 1, 1987, to be eligible for payments pursuant to subchapter XIX with respect to any calendar quarter which begins—

(1) after October 1, 1987, or, if later

(2) after the calendar quarter in which it first makes such supplementary payments to recipients of benefits so determined,

such State must have in effect an agreement with the Commissioner of Social Security whereby the State will—

(3) continue to make such supplementary payments to recipients of benefits so determined, and

(4) maintain such supplementary payments to recipients of benefits so determined at levels which assure (with respect to any particular month beginning with July 1988) that—

(A) the combined level of such supplementary payments and the amounts payable to or on behalf of such recipients under section 1382(e)(1)(B) of this title for that particular month,

is not less than—

(B) the combined level of such supplementary payments and the amounts payable to or on behalf of such recipients under section 1382(e)(1)(B) of this title for October 1987 (or, if no such supplementary payments were made for that month, the combined level for the first subsequent month for which such payments were made), increased—

(i) in a case to which clause (i) of such section 1382(e)(1)(B) of this title applies or (with respect to the individual or spouse who is in the hospital, home, or facility involved) to which clause (ii) of such section applies, by $5, and

(ii) in a case to which clause (iii) of such section 1382(e)(1)(B) of this title applies, by $10.

(Aug. 14, 1935, c. 531, Title XVI, § 1618, as added Pub.L. 94–585, § 2(a), Oct. 21, 1976, 90 Stat. 2901; amended Pub.L. 97–248, Title I, § 186, Sept. 3, 1982, 96 Stat. 407; Pub.L. 97–377, Title I, § 147, Dec. 21, 1982, 96 Stat. 1917; Pub.L. 98–21, Title IV, § 402, Apr. 20, 1983, 97 Stat. 139; Pub.L. 98–369, Div. B, Title VI, § 2663(g)(9), July 18, 1984, 98 Stat. 1169; Pub.L. 99–272, Title XII, § 12201(a), Apr. 7, 1986, 100 Stat. 289; Pub.L. 100–203, Title IX, § 9119(b), Dec. 22, 1987, 101 Stat. 1330–309; Pub.L. 103–296, Title I, § 107(a)(4), Title II, § 209(a), Aug. 15, 1994, 108 Stat. 1478, 1517.)

HISTORICAL AND STATUTORY NOTES

References in Text

Sections 211(a)(1)(A) and 212(a) of Public Law 93–66, referred to in subsecs. (a), (e)(1), (f), and (g), are sections 211(a)(1)(A) and 212(a) of Pub.L. 93–66, Title II, July 9, 1973, 87 Stat. 154, 155, as amended, which are set out as notes under section 1382 of this title.

Section 5041 of the Omnibus Budget Reconciliation Act of 1990, referred to in subsec. (b)(2), is Pub.L. 101–508, Title V, § 5041, Nov. 5, 1990, 104 Stat. 1388-227, which provided for notification to certain individuals of their eligibility to receive retroactive SSI benefits as a result of the 1990 United States Supreme Court decision in Sullivan v. Zebley (110 S.Ct. 2658). Section 5041 of Pub.L. 101–508 was not classified to the Code.

Section 111 of the Social Security Amendments of 1983, referred to in subsec. (e)(2), is section 111 of Pub.L. 98–21, Title I, Apr. 20, 1983, 97 Stat. 72, which amended sections 402, 403, 415, and 430 of this title and enacted provisions set out as notes under sections 402 and 415 of this title and section 3023 of Title 38, Veterans' Benefits.

Effective and Applicability Provisions

1994 Acts. Amendment by section 107(a)(4) of Pub.L. 103–296 effective Mar. 31, 1995, see section 110 of Pub.L. 103–296, set out as a note under section 401 of this title.

Section 209(b) of Pub.L. 103–296 provided that: "The amendments made by subsection (a) [amending this section] shall apply with respect to increases in the level of supplemental security income benefits under title XVI of the Social Security Act [this subchapter] whether occurring before, on, or after the date of the enactment of this Act [Aug. 15, 1994]."

1987 Acts. Amendment by Pub.L. 100–203 effective July 1, 1988, see section 9119(c) of Pub.L. 100–203, set out as a note under section 1382 of this title.

1984 Acts. Amendment by Pub.L. 98–369 effective July 18, 1984, but not to be construed as changing or affecting any right, liability, status or interpretation which existed (under the provisions of law involved) before that date, see section 2664(b) of Pub.L. 98–369, set out as a note under section 401 of this title.

1976 Acts. Section 2(c) of Pub.L. 94–585 provided that: "The provisions of this section [enacting this section and provision set out as a note under section 1382e of this title] shall be effective with respect to benefits payable for months after June 1977."

Application to Northern Mariana Islands

For applicability of this section to the Northern Mariana Islands, see section 502(a)(1) of the Covenant to Establish a Commonwealth of the Northern Mariana Islands in Political Union with the United States of America, as set forth in Pub.L. 94–241, Mar. 24, 1976, 90 Stat. 263, eff. Jan. 9, 1978, pursuant to Proc. No. 4534, Oct. 24, 1977, 42 F.R. 6593, set out as notes under section 1681 of Title 48, Territories and Insular Possessions.

§ 1382h. Benefits for individuals who perform substantial gainful activity despite severe medical impairment

(a) Eligible individuals

(1) Except as provided in section 1383(j) of this title, any individual who was determined to be an eligible individual (or eligible spouse) by reason of being under a disability and was eligible to receive benefits under section 1382 of this title (or a federally administered State supplementary payment) for a month and whose earnings in a subsequent month exceed the amount designated by the Commissioner of Social Security ordinarily to represent substantial gainful activity shall qualify for a monthly benefit under this subsection for such subsequent month (which shall be in lieu of any benefit under section 1382 of this title) equal to an amount determined under section 1382(b)(1) of this title (or, in the case of an individual who has an eligible spouse, under section 1382(b)(2) of this title), and for purposes of subchapter XIX shall be considered to be receiving supplemental security income benefits under this subchapter, for so long as—

(A) such individual continues to have the disabling physical or mental impairment on the basis of which such individual was found to be under a disability; and

(B) the income of such individual, other than income excluded pursuant to section 1382a(b) of this title, is not equal to or in excess of the amount which would cause him to be ineligible for payments under section 1382 of this title and such individual meets all other non-disability-related requirements for eligibility for benefits under this subchapter.

(2) The Commissioner of Social Security shall make a determination under paragraph (1)(A) with respect to an individual not later than 12 months after the first month for which the individual qualifies for a benefit under this subsection.

(b) Blind or disabled individuals receiving supplemental security income benefits

(1) Except as provided in section 1383(j) of this title, for purposes of subchapter XIX, any individual who was determined to be a blind or disabled individual eligible to receive a benefit under section 1382 of this title or any federally administered State supplementary payment for a month and who in a subsequent month is ineligible for benefits under this subchapter (and for any federally administered State supplementary payments) because of his or her income shall, nevertheless, be considered to be receiving supplemental security income benefits for such subsequent month provided that the Commissioner of Social Security determines under regulations that—

(A) such individual continues to be blind or continues to have the disabling physical or mental impairment on the basis of which he was found to be under a disability and, except for his earnings, meets all non-disability-related requirements for eligibility for benefits under this subchapter;

(B) the income of such individual would not, except for his earnings and increases pursuant to section 415(i) of this title in the level of monthly insurance benefits to which the individual is entitled under subchapter II that occur while such individual is considered to be receiving supplemental security income benefits by reason of this subsection, be equal to or in excess of the amount which would cause him to be ineligible for payments under section 1382(b) of this title (if he were otherwise eligible for such payments);

(C) the termination of eligibility for benefits under subchapter XIX would seriously inhibit his ability to continue his employment; and

(D) such individual's earnings are not sufficient to allow him to provide for himself a reasonable equivalent of the benefits under this subchapter (including any federally administered State supplementary payments), benefits under subchapter XIX, and publicly funded attendant care services (including personal care assistance), which would be available to him in the absence of such earnings.

(2)(A) Determinations made under paragraph (1)(D) shall be based on information and data updated no less frequently than annually.

(B) In determining an individual's earnings for purposes of paragraph (1)(D), there shall be excluded from such earnings an amount equal to the sum of any amounts which are or would be excluded under clauses (ii) and (iv) of section 1382a(b)(4)(B) of this title (or under clauses (ii) and (iii) of section 1382a(b)(4)(A) of this title) in determining his or her income.

(3) In the case of a State that exercises the option under section 1396a(f) of this title, any individual who—

(A)(i) qualifies for a benefit under subsection (a), or

(ii) meets the requirements of paragraph (1); and

(B) was eligible for medical assistance under the State plan approved under subchapter XIX in the month immediately preceding the first month in which the individual qualified for a benefit under such subsection or met such requirements,

shall remain eligible for medical assistance under such plan for so long as the individual qualifies for a benefit under such subsection or meets such requirements.

(c) Continuing disability or blindness reviews; limitation

Subsection (a)(2) and section 1383(j)(2)(A) of this title shall not be construed, singly or jointly, to require more than 1 determination during any 12–month period with respect to the continuing disability or blindness of an individual.

(d) Information and training programs

The Commissioner of Social Security and the Secretary of Education shall jointly develop and disseminate information, and establish training programs for staff personnel, with respect to the potential availability of benefits and services for disabled individuals under the provisions of this section. The Commissioner of Social Security shall provide such information to individuals who are applicants for and recipients of benefits based on disability under this subchapter and shall conduct such programs for the staffs of the district offices of the Social Security Administration. The Secretary of Education shall conduct such programs for the staffs of the State Vocational Rehabilitation agencies, and in cooperation with such agencies shall also provide such information to other appropriate individuals and to public and private organizations and agencies which are concerned with rehabilitation and social services or which represent the disabled.

(Aug. 14, 1935, c. 531, Title XVI, § 1619, as added Pub.L. 96–265, Title II, § 201(a), June 9, 1980, 94 Stat. 445; amended Pub.L. 97–35, Title XXIII, § 2353(*o*), Aug. 13, 1981, 95 Stat. 873; Pub.L. 98–460, § 14(b), Oct. 9, 1984, 98 Stat. 1808; Pub.L. 99–643, §§ 4(a), (b), (c)(2), 7(a), Nov. 10, 1986, 100 Stat. 3575, 3577, 3579; Pub.L. 101–508, Title V, §§ 5032(a), 5039(a), Nov. 5, 1990, 104 Stat. 1388–224, 1388–226; Pub.L. 103–296, Title I, § 107(a)(1), (4), Title II, § 205(a), Aug. 15, 1994, 108 Stat. 1477, 1478, 1509.)

HISTORICAL AND STATUTORY NOTES

Codifications

Amendment by section 5032(a) of Pub.L. 101–508, directed that section 1619(b)(1) (42 U.S.C. 1392h(b)(1)) be amended. The amendment was executed to this section as the probable intent of Congress.

Effective and Applicability Provisions

1994 Acts. Amendment by section 107(a)(1) and (4) of Pub.L. 103–296 effective Mar. 31, 1995, see section 110 of Pub.L. 103–296, set out as a note under section 410 of this title.

Section 205(b) of Pub.L. 103–296 provided that: "The amendment made by subsection (a) [amending subsec. (b)(1)(B) of this section] shall apply to eligibility determinations for months after December 1994."

1990 Acts. Section 5032(b) of Pub.L. 101–508 provided that: "The amendment made by subsection (a) [amending subsec. (b)(1) of this section] shall apply with respect to benefits for months beginning on or after the first day of the 6th calendar month following the month in which this Act is enacted [Nov. 1990]."

Section 5039(c) of Pub.L. 101–508 provided that: "The amendments made by this section [enacting subsec. (c) and redesignating as subsec. (d) former subsec. (c) of this section and amending section 1383(j)(2)(A) of this title] shall take effect on the date of the enactment of this Act [Nov. 5, 1990]."

1986 Acts. Amendment by Pub.L. 99–643 effective July 1, 1987, except for State plans requiring State legislation, see section 10(b) of Pub.L. 99–643, set out as a note under section 1396a of this title.

1981 Acts. Amendment by Pub.L. 97–35 effective Oct. 1, 1981, except as otherwise explicitly provided, see section 2354 of Pub.L. 97–35, set out as a note under section 1397 of this title.

1980 Acts. Section 201(d) of Pub.L. 96–265, as amended Pub.L. 98–460, § 14(a), Oct. 9, 1984, 98 Stat. 1808; Pub.L. 99–643, § 2, Nov. 10, 1986, 100 Stat. 3574, provided that: "The amendments made by subsections (a) and (b) [enacting this section and amending section 1382e of this title and provisions set out as a note under section 1382 of this title] shall become effective on January 1, 1981.

Section 10(a) of Pub.L. 99–643 provided that: "The amendment made by section 2 [amending section 201(d) of Pub.L. 96–265, set out hereunder] shall become effective on the date of the enactment of this Act [Nov. 10, 1986]."

Separate Accounts With Respect to Benefits Payable; Evaluation of Program

Section 201(e) of Pub.L. 96–265 provided that: "The Secretary shall provide for separate accounts with respect to the benefits payable by reason of the amendments made by subsections (a) and (b) [enacting this section and section 1382e(c)(3) of this title and amending provisions set out as a note under section 1382 of this title] so as to provide for evaluation of the effects of such amendments on the programs established by titles II, XVI, XIX, and XX of the Social Security Act [subchapters II, XVI, XIX, and XX of this chapter]."

§ 1382i. Medical and social services for certain handicapped persons

(a) Authorization of appropriations for pilot program

There are authorized to be appropriated such sums as may be necessary to establish and carry out a 3-year Federal-State pilot program to provide medical and social services for certain handicapped individuals in accordance with this section.

(b) State allotments

(1) The total sum of $18,000,000 shall be allotted to the States for such program by the Commissioner of

Social Security, during the period beginning September 1, 1981, and ending September 30, 1984, as follows:

(A) The total sum of $6,000,000 shall be allotted to the States for the fiscal year ending September 30, 1982 (which for purposes of this section shall include the month of September 1981).

(B) The total sum of $6,000,000, plus any amount remaining available (after the application of paragraph (4)) from the allotment made under subparagraph (A), shall be allotted to the States for the fiscal year ending September 30, 1983.

(C) The total sum of $6,000,000, plus any amount remaining available (after the application of paragraph (4)) from the allotments made under subparagraphs (A) and (B), shall be allotted to the States for the fiscal year ending September 30, 1984.

(2) The allotment to each State from the total sum allotted under paragraph (1) for any fiscal year shall bear the same ratio to such total sum as the number of individuals in such State who are over age 17 and under age 65 and are receiving supplemental security income benefits as disabled individuals in such year (as determined by the Commissioner of Social Security on the basis of the most recent data available) bears to the total number of such individuals in all the States. For purposes of the preceding sentence, the term "supplemental security income benefits" includes payments made pursuant to an agreement under section 1382e(a) of this title or under section 212(b) of Public Law 93–66.

(3) At the beginning of each fiscal year in which the pilot program under this section is in effect, each State that does not intend to use the allotment to which it is entitled for such year (or any allotment which was made to it for a prior fiscal year), or that does not intend to use the full amount of any such allotment, shall certify to the Commissioner of Social Security the amount of such allotment which it does not intend to use, and the State's allotment for the fiscal year (or years) involved shall thereupon be reduced by the amount so certified.

(4) The portion of the total amount available for allotment for any particular fiscal year under paragraph (1) which is not allotted to States for that year by reason of paragraph (3) (plus the amount of any reductions made at the beginning of such year in the allotments of States for prior fiscal years under paragraph (3)) shall be reallocated in such manner as the Commissioner of Social Security may determine to be appropriate to States which need, and will use, additional assistance in providing services to severely handicapped individuals in that particular year under their approved plans. Any amount reallocated to a State under this paragraph for use in a particular fiscal year shall be treated for purposes of this section as increasing such State's allotment for that year by an equivalent amount.

(c) Requisite features of State plans

In order to participate in the pilot program and be eligible to receive payments for any period under subsection (d), a State (during such period) must have a plan, approved by the Commissioner of Social Security as meeting the requirements of this section, which provides medical and social services for severely handicapped individuals whose earnings are above the level which ordinarily demonstrates an ability to engage in substantial gainful activity and who are not receiving benefits under section 1382 or 1382h of this title or assistance under a State plan approved under section 1396a of this title, and which—

(1) declares the intent of the State to participate in the pilot program;

(2) designates an appropriate State agency to administer or supervise the administration of the program in the State;

(3) describes the criteria to be applied by the State in determining the eligibility of any individual for assistance under the plan and in any event requires a determination by the State agency to the effect that (A) such individual's ability to continue his employment would be significantly inhibited without such assistance and (B) such individual's earnings are not sufficient to allow him to provide for himself a reasonable equivalent of the cash and other benefits that would be available to him under this subchapter and subchapters XIX and XX in the absence of those earnings;

(4) describes the process by which the eligibility of individuals for such assistance is to be determined (and such process may not involve the performance of functions by any State agency or entity which is engaged in making determinations of disability for purposes of disability insurance or supplemental security income benefits except when the use of a different agency or entity to perform those functions would not be feasible);

(5) describes the medical and social services to be provided under the plan;

(6) describes the manner in which the medical and social services involved are to be provided and, if they are not to be provided through the State's medical assistance and social services programs under subchapters XIX and XX (with the Federal payments being made under subsection (d) of this section rather than under those subchapters), specifies the particular mechanisms and procedures to be used in providing such services; and

(7) contains such other provisions as the Commissioner of Social Security may find to be necessary or appropriate to meet the requirements of this section or otherwise carry out its purpose.

(d) Payments to States; computation of payments

(1) From its allotment under subsection (b) for any fiscal year (and any amounts remaining available from allotments made to it for prior fiscal years), the Commissioner of Social Security shall from time to time pay to each State which has a plan approved under subsection (c) an amount equal to 75 per centum of the total sum expended under such plan (including the cost of administration of such plan) in providing medical and social services to severely handicapped individuals who are eligible for such services under the plan.

(2) The method of computing and making payments under this section shall be as follows:

(A) The Commissioner of Social Security shall, prior to each period for which a payment is to be made to a State, estimate the amount to be paid to the State for such period under the provisions of this section.

(B) From the allotment available therefor, the Commissioner of Social Security shall pay the amount so estimated, reduced or increased, as the case may be, by any sum (not previously adjusted under this subsection) by which the Commissioner finds that the Commissioner's estimate of the amount to be paid the State for any prior period under this section was greater or less than the amount which should have been paid to the State for such period under this section.

(e) Rules and regulations

Within nine months after June 9, 1980, the Commissioner of Social Security shall prescribe and publish such regulations as may be necessary or appropriate to carry out the pilot program and otherwise implement this section.

(f) Reports

Each State participating in the pilot program under this section shall from time to time report to the Commissioner of Social Security on the operation and results of such program in that State, with particular emphasis upon the work incentive effects of the program. On or before October 1, 1983, the Commissioner of Social Security shall submit to the Congress a report on the program, incorporating the information contained in the State reports along with the Commissioner's findings and recommendations.

(Aug. 14, 1935, c. 531, Title XVI, § 1620, as added Pub.L. 96–265, Title II, § 201(c), June 9, 1980, 94 Stat. 446; amended Pub.L. 97–35, Title XXIII, § 2353(p), Aug. 13, 1981, 95 Stat. 874; Pub.L. 103–296, Title I, § 107(a)(4), Aug. 15, 1994, 108 Stat. 1478.)

HISTORICAL AND STATUTORY NOTES

References in Text

Section 212(b) of Pub.L. 93–66, referred to in subsec. (b)(2), is section 212(b) of Pub.L. 93–66, Title II, July 9, 1973, 87 Stat. 155, as amended, which is set out as a note under section 1382 of this title.

Effective and Applicability Provisions

1994 Acts. Amendment by section 107(a)(4) of Pub.L. 103–296 effective Mar. 31, 1995, see section 110 of Pub.L. 103–296, set out as a note under section 401 of this title.

1981 Acts. Amendment by Pub.L. 97–35 effective Oct. 1, 1981, except as otherwise explicitly provided, see section 2354 of Pub.L. 97–35, set out as a note under section 1397 of this title.

§ 1382j. Attribution of sponsor's income and resources to aliens

(a) Attribution as unearned income

For purposes of determining eligibility for and the amount of benefits under this subchapter for an individual who is an alien, the income and resources of any person who (as a sponsor of such individual's entry into the United States) executed an affidavit of support or similar agreement with respect to such individual, and the income and resources of the sponsor's spouse, shall be deemed to be the income and resources of such individual (in accordance with subsections (b) and (c)) for a period of 3 years after the individual's entry into the United States. Any such income deemed to be income of such individual shall be treated as unearned income of such individual.

(b) Determination of amount and resources

(1) The amount of income of a sponsor (and his spouse) which shall be deemed to be the unearned income of an alien for any year shall be determined as follows:

(A) The total yearly rate of earned and unearned income (as determined under section 1382a(a) of this title) of such sponsor and such sponsor's spouse (if such spouse is living with the sponsor) shall be determined for such year.

(B) The amount determined under subparagraph (A) shall be reduced by an amount equal to (i) the maximum amount of the Federal benefit under this subchapter for such year which would be payable to an eligible individual who has no other income and who does not have an eligible spouse (as determined under section 1382(b)(1) of this title), plus (ii) one-half of the amount determined under clause (i) multiplied by the number of individuals who are dependents of such sponsor (or such sponsor's spouse if such spouse is living with the sponsor), other than such alien and such alien's spouse.

(C) The amount of income which shall be deemed to be unearned income of such alien shall be at a yearly rate equal to the amount determined under subparagraph (B). The period for determination of such amount shall be the same as the period for determination of benefits under section 1382(c) of this title.

(2) The amount of resources of a sponsor (and his spouse) which shall be deemed to be the resources of an alien for any year shall be determined as follows:

(A) The total amount of the resources (as determined under section 1382b of this title) of such sponsor and such sponsor's spouse (if such spouse is living with the sponsor) shall be determined.

(B) The amount determined under subparagraph (A) shall be reduced by an amount equal to (i) the applicable amount determined under section 1382(a)(3)(B) of this title in the case of a sponsor who has no spouse with whom he is living, or (ii) the applicable amount determined under section 1382(a)(3)(A) of this title in the case of a sponsor who has a spouse with whom he is living.

(C) The resources of such sponsor (and spouse) as determined under subparagraphs (A) and (B) shall be deemed to be resources of such alien in addition to any resources of such alien.

(c) Support and maintenance

In determining the amount of income of an alien during the period of 3 years after such alien's entry into the United States, the reduction in dollar amounts otherwise required under section 1382a(a)(2)(A)(i) of this title shall not be applicable if such alien is living in the household of a person who is a sponsor (or such sponsor's spouse) of such alien, and is receiving support and maintenance in kind from such sponsor (or spouse), nor shall support or maintenance furnished in cash or kind to an alien by such alien's sponsor (to the extent that it reflects income or resources which were taken into account in determining the amount of income and resources to be deemed to the alien under subsection (a) or (b)) be considered to be income of such alien under section 1382a(a)(2)(A) of this title.

(d) Information and documentation; agreements with Secretary of State and Attorney General

(1) Any individual who is an alien shall, during the period of 3 years after entry into the United States, in order to be an eligible individual or eligible spouse for purposes of this subchapter, be required to provide to the Commissioner of Social Security such information and documentation with respect to his sponsor as may be necessary in order for the Commissioner of Social Security to make any determination required under this section, and to obtain any cooperation from such sponsor necessary for any such determination. Such alien shall also be required to provide to the Commissioner of Social Security such information and documentation as the Commissioner of Social Security may request and which such alien or his sponsor provided in support of such alien's immigration application.

(2) The Commissioner of Social Security shall enter into agreements with the Secretary of State and the Attorney General whereby any information available to such persons and required in order to make any determination under this section will be provided by such persons to the Commissioner of Social Security, and whereby such persons shall inform any sponsor of an alien, at the time such sponsor executes an affidavit of support or similar agreement, of the requirements imposed by this section.

(e) Joint and several liability of alien and sponsor for overpayments

Any sponsor of an alien, and such alien, shall be jointly and severally liable for an amount equal to any overpayment made to such alien during the period of 3 years after such alien's entry into the United States, on account of such sponsor's failure to provide correct information under the provisions of this section, except where such sponsor was without fault, or where good cause for such failure existed. Any such overpayment which is not repaid to the Commissioner of Social Security or recovered in accordance with section 1383(b) of this title shall be withheld from any subsequent payment to which such alien or such sponsor is entitled under any provision of this chapter.

(f) Exemptions

(1) The provisions of this section shall not apply with respect to any individual who is an "aged, blind, or disabled individual" for purposes of this subchapter by reason of blindness (as determined under section 1382c(a)(2) of this title) or disability (as determined under section 1382c(a)(3) of this title), from and after the onset of the impairment, if such blindness or disability commenced after the date of such individual's admission into the United States for permanent residence.

(2) The provisions of this section shall not apply with respect to any alien who is—

(A) admitted to the United States as a result of the application, prior to April 1, 1980, of the provisions of section 1153(a)(7) of Title 8;

(B) admitted to the United States as a result of the application, after March 31, 1980, of the provisions of section 1157(c)(1) of Title 8;

(C) paroled into the United States as a refugee under section 1182(d)(5) of Title 8; or

(D) granted political asylum by the Attorney General.

(Aug. 14, 1935, c. 531, Title XVI, § 1621, as added Pub.L. 96–265, Title V, § 504(b), June 9, 1980, 94 Stat. 471; amended Pub.L. 98–369, Div. B, Title VI, §§ 2611(d), 2663(g)(10), July 18, 1984, 98 Stat. 1131, 1169; Pub.L. 103–152, § 7(a)(1), (b)(1), Nov. 24, 1993, 107 Stat. 1519; Pub.L. 103–296, Title I, § 107(a)(4), Aug. 15, 1994, 108 Stat. 1478.)

HISTORICAL AND STATUTORY NOTES

References in Text

Section 1153(a)(7) of Title 8, referred to in subsec. (f)(2)(A), to be deemed a reference to such section as in effect prior to Apr. 1, 1980, and to sections 1157 and 1158 of Title 8, Aliens and Nationality. See section 203(h) of Pub.L. 96–212, set out as a note under section 1153 of Title 8.

Effective and Applicability Provisions

1994 Acts. Amendment by section 107(a)(4) of Pub.L. 103–296 effective Mar. 31, 1995, see section 110 of Pub.L. 103–296, set out as a note under section 401 of this title.

1993 Acts. Section 7(a)(2) of Pub.L. 103–152 provided that: "The amendments made by paragraph (1) [amending subsecs. (a), (c), (d)(1), and (e) of this section] shall take effect on January 1, 1994."

Section 7(b)(2) of Pub.L. 103–152 provided that: "The amendments made by paragraph (1) [amending subsecs. (a), (c), (d)(1), and (e) of this section] shall take effect on October 1, 1996."

1984 Acts. Amendment by section 2611(d) of Pub.L. 98–369 effective Oct. 1, 1984, except as otherwise specifically provided, see section 2646 of Pub.L. 98–369, set out as a note under section 602 of this title.

Amendment by section 2663(g)(10) of Pub.L. 98–369 effective July 18, 1984, but not to be construed as changing or affecting any right, liability, status or interpretation which existed (under the provisions of law involved) before that date, see section 2664(b) of Pub.L. 98–369, set out as a note under section 401 of this title.

1980 Acts. Section 504(c) of Pub.L. 96–265 provided that: "The amendments made by this section [enacting this section and section 1382c(f)(3) of this title] shall be effective with respect to individuals applying for supplemental security income benefits under title XVI of the Social Security Act [this subchapter] for the first time after September 30, 1980."

Transfer of Functions

For abolition of Immigration and Naturalization Service (INS), transfer of functions, and treatment of related references, see note set out under 8 U.S.C.A. § 1551.

§ 1382k. Repealed. Pub.L. 97–123, § 2(h), Dec. 29, 1981, 95 Stat. 1661

HISTORICAL AND STATUTORY NOTES

Section, Act Aug. 14, 1935, c. 531, Title XVI, § 1622, as added Aug. 13, 1981, Pub.L. 97–35, Title XXII, § 2201(g), 95 Stat. 833, related to benefits for individuals formerly receiving minimum benefits.

Effective Date of Repeal

Repeal effective with respect to benefits for months after December 1981, see section 2(j)(2) of Pub.L. 97–123, set out as a note under section 415 of this title.

Pub.L. 97–35, Title XXII, § 2201(h), Aug. 13, 1981, 95 Stat. 834, which provided for the effective date of this section and the other enactments and amendments made by section 2201 of Pub.L. 97–35, was repealed by Pub.L. 97–123, § 2(j)(1), Dec. 29, 1981, 95 Stat. 1661.

PART B—PROCEDURAL AND GENERAL PROVISIONS

§ 1383. Procedure for payment of benefits

(a) Time, manner, form, and duration of payments; representative payees; promulgation of regulations

(1) Benefits under this subchapter shall be paid at such time or times and (subject to paragraph (10)) in such installments as will best effectuate the purposes of this subchapter, as determined under regulations (and may in any case be paid less frequently than monthly where the amount of the monthly benefit would not exceed $10).

(2)(A)(i) Payments of the benefit of any individual may be made to any such individual or to the eligible spouse (if any) of such individual or partly to each.

(ii)(I) Upon a determination by the Commissioner of Social Security that the interest of such individual would be served thereby, such payments shall be made, regardless of the legal competency or incompetency of the individual or eligible spouse, to another individual, or an organization, with respect to whom the requirements of subparagraph (B) have been met (in this paragraph referred to as such individual's "representative payee") for the use and benefit of the individual or eligible spouse.

(II) In the case of an individual eligible for benefits under this subchapter by reason of disability, the payment of such benefits shall be made to a representative payee if the Commissioner of Social Security determines that such payment would serve the interest of the individual because the individual also has an alcoholism or drug addiction condition (as determined by the Commissioner) and the individual is incapable of managing such benefits.

(iii) If the Commissioner of Social Security or a court of competent jurisdiction determines that the representative payee of an individual or eligible spouse has misused any benefits which have been paid to the representative payee pursuant to clause (ii) or section 405(j)(1) or 1007 of this title, the Commissioner of Social Security shall promptly terminate payment of benefits to the representative payee pursuant to this subparagraph, and provide for payment of benefits to an alternative representative payee of the individual or eligible spouse or, if the interest of the individual under this subchapter would be served thereby, to the individual or eligible spouse.

(iv) For purposes of this paragraph, misuse of benefits by a representative payee occurs in any case in which the representative payee receives payment under this subchapter for the use and benefit of another person and converts such payment, or any part thereof, to a use other than for the use and benefit of such other person. The Commissioner of Social Security may prescribe by regulation the meaning of the term "use and benefit" for purposes of this clause.

(B)(i) Any determination made under subparagraph (A) for payment of benefits to the representative payee of an individual or eligible spouse shall be made on the basis of—

(I) an investigation by the Commissioner of Social Security of the person to serve as representative payee, which shall be conducted in advance of such payment, and shall, to the extent practicable, include a face-to-face interview with such person; and

(II) adequate evidence that such payment is in the interest of the individual or eligible spouse (as determined by the Commissioner of Social Security in regulations).

(ii) As part of the investigation referred to in clause (i)(I), the Commissioner of Social Security shall—

(I) require the person being investigated to submit documented proof of the identity of such person, unless information establishing such identity was submitted with an application for benefits under subchapter II, subchapter VIII, or this subchapter;

(II) verify the social security account number (or employer identification number) of such person;

(III) determine whether such person has been convicted of a violation of section 408, 1011, or 1383a of this title;

(IV) obtain information concerning whether the person has been convicted of any other offense under Federal or State law which resulted in imprisonment for more than 1 year;

(V) obtain information concerning whether such person is a person described in section 1382(e)(4)(A) of this title;

(VI) determine whether payment of benefits to such person has been terminated pursuant to subparagraph (A)(iii), whether the designation of such person as a representative payee has been revoked pursuant to section 1007(a) of this title, and whether certification of payment of benefits to such person has been revoked pursuant to section 405(j) of this title, by reason of misuse of funds paid as benefits under subchapter II, subchapter VIII, or this subchapter,[1] and

(VII) determine whether such person has been convicted (and not subsequently exonerated), under Federal or State law, of a felony provided under clause (xv), or of an attempt or a conspiracy to commit such a felony.

(iii) Benefits of an individual may not be paid to any other person pursuant to subparagraph (A)(ii) if—

(I) such person has previously been convicted as described in clause (ii)(III);

(II) except as provided in clause (iv), payment of benefits to such person pursuant to subparagraph (A)(ii) has previously been terminated as described in clause (ii)(VI), the designation of such person as a representative payee has been revoked pursuant to section 1007(a) of this title, or certification of payment of benefits to such person under section 405(j) of this title has previously been revoked as described in section 405(j)(2)(B)(i)(VI) of this title;

(III) except as provided in clause (v), such person is a creditor of such individual who provides such individual with goods or services for consideration;

(IV) the person has previously been convicted as described in clause (ii)(IV) of this subparagraph, unless the Commissioner determines that the payment would be appropriate notwithstanding the conviction;

(V) such person is a person described in section 1382(e)(4)(A) of this title,

(VI) except as provided in clause (xvii), such person has previously been convicted (and not subsequently exonerated) as described in clause (ii)(VII),[1] or

(VII) such person's benefits under this subchapter, subchapter II, or subchapter VIII are certified for payment to a representative payee during the period for which the individual's benefits would be certified for payment to another person.

(iv) The Commissioner of Social Security shall prescribe regulations under which the Commissioner of Social Security may grant an exemption from clause (iii)(II) to any person on a case-by-case basis if such exemption would be in the best interest of the individual or eligible spouse whose benefits under this subchapter would be paid to such person pursuant to subparagraph (A)(ii).

(v) Clause (iii)(III) shall not apply with respect to any person who is a creditor referred to therein if such creditor is—

(I) a relative of such individual if such relative resides in the same household as such individual;

(II) a legal guardian or legal representative of such individual;

(III) a facility that is licensed or certified as a care facility under the law of a State or a political subdivision of a State;

(IV) a person who is an administrator, owner, or employee of a facility referred to in subclause (III) if such individual resides in such facility, and the payment of benefits under this subchapter to such facility or such person is made only after good faith efforts have been made by the local servicing office of the Social Security Administration to locate an alternative representative payee to whom the payment of such benefits would serve the best interests of such individual; or

(V) an individual who is determined by the Commissioner of Social Security, on the basis of written findings and under procedures which the Commissioner of Social Security shall prescribe by regulation, to be acceptable to serve as a representative payee.

(vi) The procedures referred to in clause (v)(V) shall require the individual who will serve as representative payee to establish, to the satisfaction of the Commissioner of Social Security, that—

(I) such individual poses no risk to the beneficiary;

(II) the financial relationship of such individual to the beneficiary poses no substantial conflict of interest; and

(III) no other more suitable representative payee can be found.

(vii) In the case of an individual described in subparagraph (A)(ii)(II), when selecting such individual's representative payee, preference shall be given to—

(I) a certified community-based nonprofit social service agency (as defined in subparagraph (I));

(II) a Federal, State, or local government agency whose mission is to carry out income maintenance, social service, or health care-related activities;

(III) a State or local government agency with fiduciary responsibilities; or

(IV) a designee of an agency (other than of a Federal agency) referred to in the preceding subclauses of this clause, if the Commissioner of Social Security deems it appropriate,

unless the Commissioner of Social Security determines that selection of a family member would be appropriate.

(viii) Subject to clause (ix), if the Commissioner of Social Security makes a determination described in subparagraph (A)(ii) with respect to any individual's benefit and determines that direct payment of the benefit to the individual would cause substantial harm to the individual, the Commissioner of Social Security may defer (in the case of initial entitlement) or suspend (in the case of existing entitlement) direct payment of such benefit to the individual, until such time as the selection of a representative payee is made pursuant to this subparagraph.

(ix)(I) Except as provided in subclause (II), any deferral or suspension of direct payment of a benefit pursuant to clause (viii) shall be for a period of not more than 1 month.

(II) Subclause (I) shall not apply in any case in which the individual or eligible spouse is, as of the date of the Commissioner's determination, legally incompetent, under the age of 15 years, or described in subparagraph (A)(ii)(II).

(x) Payment pursuant to this subparagraph of any benefits which are deferred or suspended pending the selection of a representative payee shall be made to the individual, or to the representative payee upon such selection, as a single sum or over such period of time as the Commissioner of Social Security determines is in the best interests of the individual entitled to such benefits.

(xi) Any individual who is dissatisfied with a determination by the Commissioner of Social Security to pay such individual's benefits to a representative payee under this subchapter, or with the designation of a particular person to serve as representative payee, shall be entitled to a hearing by the Commissioner of Social Security, and to judicial review of the Commissioner's final decision, to the same extent as is provided in subsection (c).

(xii) In advance of the first payment of an individual's benefit to a representative payee under subparagraph (A)(ii), the Commissioner of Social Security shall provide written notice of the Commissioner's initial determination to make any such payment. Such notice shall be provided to such individual, except that, if such individual—

(I) is under the age of 15,

(II) is an unemancipated minor under the age of 18, or

(III) is legally incompetent,

then such notice shall be provided solely to the legal guardian or legal representative of such individual.

(xiii) Any notice described in clause (xii) shall be clearly written in language that is easily understandable to the reader, shall identify the person to be designated as such individual's representative payee, and shall explain to the reader the right under clause (xi) of such individual or of such individual's legal guardian or legal representative—

(I) to appeal a determination that a representative payee is necessary for such individual,

(II) to appeal the designation of a particular person to serve as the representative payee of such individual, and

(III) to review the evidence upon which such designation is based and submit additional evidence.

(xiv) Notwithstanding the provisions of section 552a of Title 5 or any other provision of Federal or State law (other than section 6103 of the Internal Revenue Code of 1986 and section 1306(c) of this title), the Commissioner shall furnish any Federal, State, or local law enforcement officer, upon the written request of the officer, with the current address, social security account number, and photograph (if applicable) of any person investigated under this subparagraph, if the officer furnishes the Commissioner with the name of such person and such other identifying information as may reasonably be required by the Commissioner to establish the unique identity of such person, and notifies the Commissioner that—

(I) such person is described in section 1382(e)(4)(A) of this title,

(II) such person has information that is necessary for the officer to conduct the officer's official duties, and

(III) the location or apprehension of such person is within the officer's official duties.

(xv) The felony crimes provided under this clause, whether an offense under State or Federal law, are the following:

(I) Human trafficking, including as prohibited under sections 1590 and 1591 of Title 18.

(II) False imprisonment, including as prohibited under section 1201 of Title 18.

(III) Kidnapping, including as prohibited under section 1201 of Title 18.

(IV) Rape and sexual assault, including as prohibited under sections 2241, 2242, 2243, and 2244 of Title 18.

(V) First-degree homicide, including as prohibited under section 1111 of Title 18.

(VI) Robbery, including as prohibited under section 2111 of Title 18.

(VII) Fraud to obtain access to government assistance, including as prohibited under sections 287, 1001, and 1343 of Title 18.

(VIII) Fraud by scheme, including as prohibited under section 1343 of Title 18.

(IX) Theft of government funds or property, including as prohibited under section 641 of Title 18.

(X) Abuse or neglect, including as prohibited under sections 111, 113, 114, 115, 116, or 117 of Title 18.

(XI) Forgery, including as prohibited under section 642 and chapter 25 (except section 512) of Title 18.

(XII) Identity theft or identity fraud, including as prohibited under sections 1028 and 1028A of Title 18.

The Commissioner of Social Security may promulgate regulations to provide for additional felony crimes under this clause.

(xvi)(I) For the purpose of carrying out the activities required under clause (ii) as part of the investigation under clause (i)(I), the Commissioner may conduct a background check of any individual seeking to serve as a representative payee under this subsection and may disqualify from service as a representative payee any such individual who fails to grant permission for the Commissioner to conduct such a background check.

(II) The Commissioner may revoke certification of payment of benefits under this subsection to any individual serving as a representative payee on or after January 1, 2019 who fails to grant permission for the Commissioner to conduct such a background check.

(xvii)(I) With respect to any person described in subclause (II)—

(aa) clause (ii)(VII) shall not apply; and

(bb) the Commissioner may grant an exemption from the provisions of clause (iii)(VI) if the Commissioner determines that such exemption is in the best interest of the individual entitled to benefits.

(II) A person is described in this subclause if the person—

(aa) is the custodial parent of a minor child for whom the person applies to serve;

(bb) is the custodial spouse of the beneficiary for whom the person applies to serve;

(cc) is the custodial parent of a beneficiary who is under a disability which began before the beneficiary attained the age of 22, for whom the person applies to serve;

(dd) is the custodial court appointed guardian of the beneficiary for whom the person applies to serve;

(ee) is the custodial grandparent of a minor grandchild for whom the person applies to serve;

(ff) is the parent who was previously representative payee for his or her minor child who has since turned 18 and continues to be eligible for such benefit; or

(gg) received a presidential or gubernatorial pardon for the relevant conviction.

(C)(i) In any case where payment is made under this subchapter to a representative payee of an individual or spouse, the Commissioner of Social Security shall establish a system of accountability monitoring whereby such person shall report not less often than annually with respect to the use of such payments. The Commissioner of Social Security shall establish and implement statistically valid procedures for reviewing such reports in order to identify instances in which such persons are not properly using such payments.

(ii) Clause (i) shall not apply in any case where the representative payee is a State institution. In such cases, the Commissioner of Social Security shall establish a system of accountability monitoring for institutions in each State.

(iii) Clause (i) shall not apply in any case where the individual entitled to such payment is a resident of a Federal institution and the representative payee is the institution.

(iv)(I) Clause (i) shall not apply in any case where the representative payee is—

(aa) a parent, or other individual who is a legal guardian of, a minor child entitled to such payment who primarily resides in the same household;

(bb) a parent of an individual entitled to such payment who is under a disability who primarily resides in the same household; or

(cc) the spouse of the individual entitled to such payment.

(II) The Commissioner of Social Security shall establish and implement procedures as necessary for the

Commissioner to determine the eligibility of such parties for the exemption provided in subclause (I). The Commissioner shall prescribe such regulations as may be necessary to determine eligibility for such exemption.

(v) Notwithstanding clauses (i), (ii), (iii), and (iv), the Commissioner of Social Security may require a report at any time from any representative payee, if the Commissioner of Social Security has reason to believe that the representative payee is misusing such payments.

(vi) In any case in which the person described in clause (i) or (v) receiving payments on behalf of another fails to submit a report required by the Commissioner of Social Security under clause (i) or (v), the Commissioner may, after furnishing notice to the person and the individual entitled to the payment, require that such person appear in person at a field office of the Social Security Administration serving the area in which the individual resides in order to receive such payments.

(D)(i) Except as provided in the next sentence, a qualified organization may collect from an individual a monthly fee for expenses (including overhead) incurred by such organization in providing services performed as such individual's representative payee pursuant to subparagraph (A)(ii) if the fee does not exceed the lesser of—

(I) 10 percent of the monthly benefit involved, or

(II) $25.00 per month ($50.00 per month in any case in which an individual is described in subparagraph (A)(ii)(II)).

A qualified organization may not collect a fee from an individual for any month with respect to which the Commissioner of Social Security or a court of competent jurisdiction has determined that the organization misused all or part of the individual's benefit, and any amount so collected by the qualified organization for such month shall be treated as a misused part of the individual's benefit for purposes of subparagraphs (E) and (F). The Commissioner of Social Security shall adjust annually (after 1995) each dollar amount set forth in subclause (II) of this clause under procedures providing for adjustments in the same manner and to the same extent as adjustments are provided for under the procedures used to adjust benefit amounts under section 415(i)(2)(A) of this title, except that any amount so adjusted that is not a multiple of $1.00 shall be rounded to the nearest multiple of $1.00. Any agreement providing for a fee in excess of the amount permitted under this clause shall be void and shall be treated as misuse by the organization of such individual's benefits.

(ii) For purposes of this subparagraph, the term "qualified organization" means any State or local government agency whose mission is to carry out income maintenance, social service, or health care-related activities, any State or local government agency with fiduciary responsibilities, or any certified community-based nonprofit social service agency (as defined in subparagraph (I)), if the agency, in accordance with any applicable regulations of the Commissioner of Social Security—

(I) regularly provides services as a representative payee pursuant to subparagraph (A)(ii) or section 405(j)(4) or 1007 of this title concurrently to 5 or more individuals; and

(II) demonstrates to the satisfaction of the Commissioner of Social Security that such agency is not otherwise a creditor of any such individual.

The Commissioner of Social Security shall prescribe regulations under which the Commissioner of Social Security may grant an exception from subclause (II) for any individual on a case-by-case basis if such exception is in the best interests of such individual.

(iii) Any qualified organization which knowingly charges or collects, directly or indirectly, any fee in excess of the maximum fee prescribed under clause (i) or makes any agreement, directly or indirectly, to charge or collect any fee in excess of such maximum fee, shall be fined in accordance with Title 18, or imprisoned not more than 6 months, or both.

(iv) In the case of an individual who is no longer eligible for benefits under this subchapter but to whom any amount of past-due benefits under this subchapter has not been paid, for purposes of clause (i), any amount of such past-due benefits payable in any month shall be treated as a monthly benefit referred to in clause (i)(I).

(E) Restitution

In cases where the negligent failure of the Commissioner of Social Security to investigate or monitor a representative payee results in misuse of benefits by the representative payee, the Commissioner of Social Security shall make payment to the beneficiary or the beneficiary's representative payee of an amount equal to such misused benefits. In any case in which a representative payee that—

(i) is not an individual (regardless of whether it is a "qualified organization" within the meaning of subparagraph (D)(ii)); or

(ii) is an individual who, for any month during a period when misuse occurs, serves 15 or more individuals who are beneficiaries under this subchapter, subchapter II, subchapter VIII, or any combination of such subchapters;

misuses all or part of an individual's benefit paid to such representative payee, the Commissioner of Social Security shall pay to the beneficiary or the beneficiary's alternative representative payee an amount equal to the amount of such benefit so misused. The provisions of this subparagraph are subject to the limitations of subparagraph (H)(ii). The Commissioner of

Social Security shall make a good faith effort to obtain restitution from the terminated representative payee.

(F)(i)(I) Each representative payee of an eligible individual under the age of 18 who is eligible for the payment of benefits described in subclause (II) shall establish on behalf of such individual an account in a financial institution into which such benefits shall be paid, and shall thereafter maintain such account for use in accordance with clause (ii).

(II) Benefits described in this subclause are past-due monthly benefits under this subchapter (which, for purposes of this subclause, include State supplementary payments made by the Commissioner pursuant to an agreement under section 1382e of this title or section 212(b) of Public Law 93–66) in an amount (after any withholding by the Commissioner for reimbursement to a State for interim assistance under subsection (g) and payment of attorney fees under subsection (d)(2)(B)) that exceeds the product of—

(aa) 6, and

(bb) the maximum monthly benefit payable under this subchapter to an eligible individual.

(ii)(I) A representative payee shall use funds in the account established under clause (i) to pay for allowable expenses described in subclause (II).

(II) An allowable expense described in this subclause is an expense for—

(aa) education or job skills training;

(bb) personal needs assistance;

(cc) special equipment;

(dd) housing modification;

(ee) medical treatment;

(ff) therapy or rehabilitation; or

(gg) any other item or service that the Commissioner determines to be appropriate;

provided that such expense benefits such individual and, in the case of an expense described in item (bb), (cc), (dd), (ff), or (gg), is related to the impairment (or combination of impairments) of such individual.

(III) The use of funds from an account established under clause (i) in any manner not authorized by this clause—

(aa) by a representative payee shall be considered a misapplication of benefits for all purposes of this paragraph, and any representative payee who knowingly misapplies benefits from such an account shall be liable to the Commissioner in an amount equal to the total amount of such benefits; and

(bb) by an eligible individual who is his or her own payee shall be considered a misapplication of benefits for all purposes of this paragraph and in any case in which the individual knowingly misapplies benefits from such an account, the Commissioner shall reduce future benefits payable to such individual (or to such individual and his spouse) by an amount equal to the total amount of such benefits so misapplied.

(IV) This clause shall continue to apply to funds in the account after the child has reached age 18, regardless of whether benefits are paid directly to the beneficiary or through a representative payee.

(iii) The representative payee may deposit into the account established under clause (i) any other funds representing past due benefits under this subchapter to the eligible individual, provided that the amount of such past due benefits is equal to or exceeds the maximum monthly benefit payable under this subchapter to an eligible individual (including State supplementary payments made by the Commissioner pursuant to an agreement under section 1382e of this title or section 212(b) of Public Law 93–66).

(iv) The Commissioner of Social Security shall establish a system for accountability monitoring whereby such representative payee shall report, at such time and in such manner as the Commissioner shall require, on activity respecting funds in the account established pursuant to clause (i).

(G)(i) In addition to such other reviews of representative payees as the Commissioner of Social Security may otherwise conduct, the Commissioner shall provide for the periodic onsite review of any person or agency that receives the benefits payable under this subchapter (alone or in combination with benefits payable under subchapter II or subchapter VIII) to another individual pursuant to the appointment of the person or agency as a representative payee under this paragraph, section 405(j) of this title, or section 1007 of this title in any case in which—

(I) the representative payee is a person who serves in that capacity with respect to 15 or more such individuals;

(II) the representative payee is a certified community-based nonprofit social service agency (as defined in subparagraph (I) of this paragraph or section 405(j)(10) of this title); or

(III) the representative payee is an agency (other than an agency described in subclause (II)) that serves in that capacity with respect to 50 or more such individuals.

(ii) Within 120 days after the end of each fiscal year, the Commissioner shall submit to the Committee on Ways and Means of the House of Representatives and the Committee on Finance of the Senate a report on the results of periodic onsite reviews conducted during the fiscal year pursuant to clause (i) and of any other reviews of representative payees conducted during such fiscal year in connection with benefits under this subchapter. Each such report shall describe in detail all problems identified in the reviews and any corrective action taken or planned to be taken to correct the problems, and shall include—

(I) the number of the reviews;

(II) the results of such reviews;

(III) the number of cases in which the representative payee was changed and why;

(IV) the number of cases involving the exercise of expedited, targeted oversight of the representative payee by the Commissioner conducted upon receipt of an allegation of misuse of funds, failure to pay a vendor, or a similar irregularity;

(V) the number of cases discovered in which there was a misuse of funds;

(VI) how any such cases of misuse of funds were dealt with by the Commissioner;

(VII) the final disposition of such cases of misuse of funds, including any criminal penalties imposed; and

(VIII) such other information as the Commissioner deems appropriate.

(H)(i) If the Commissioner of Social Security or a court of competent jurisdiction determines that a representative payee that is not a Federal, State, or local government agency has misused all or part of an individual's benefit that was paid to the representative payee under this paragraph, the representative payee shall be liable for the amount misused, and the amount (to the extent not repaid by the representative payee) shall be treated as an overpayment of benefits under this subchapter to the representative payee for all purposes of this chapter and related laws pertaining to the recovery of the overpayments. Subject to clause (ii), upon recovering all or any part of the amount, the Commissioner shall make payment of an amount equal to the recovered amount to such individual or such individual's alternative representative payee.

(ii) The total of the amount paid to such individual or such individual's alternative representative payee under clause (i) and the amount paid under subparagraph (E) may not exceed the total benefit amount misused by the representative payee with respect to such individual.

(I) For purposes of this paragraph, the term "certified community-based nonprofit social service agency" means a community-based nonprofit social service agency which is in compliance with requirements, under regulations which shall be prescribed by the Commissioner, for annual certification to the Commissioner that it is bonded in accordance with requirements specified by the Commissioner and that it is licensed in each State in which it serves as a representative payee (if licensing is available in the State) in accordance with requirements specified by the Commissioner. Any such annual certification shall include a copy of any independent audit on the agency which may have been performed since the previous certification.

(3) The Commissioner of Social Security may by regulation establish ranges of incomes within which a single amount of benefits under this subchapter shall apply.

(4) The Commissioner of Social Security—

(A) may make to any individual initially applying for benefits under this subchapter who is presumptively eligible for such benefits for the month following the date the application is filed and who is faced with financial emergency a cash advance against such benefits, including any federally-administered State supplementary payments, in an amount not exceeding the monthly amount that would be payable to an eligible individual with no other income for the first month of such presumptive eligibility, which shall be repaid through proportionate reductions in such benefits over a period of not more than 6 months; and

(B) may pay benefits under this subchapter to an individual applying for such benefits on the basis of disability or blindness for a period not exceeding 6 months prior to the determination of such individual's disability or blindness, if such individual is presumptively disabled or blind and is determined to be otherwise eligible for such benefits, and any benefits so paid prior to such determination shall in no event be considered overpayments for purposes of subsection (b) solely because such individual is determined not to be disabled or blind.

(5) Payment of the benefit of any individual who is an aged, blind, or disabled individual solely by reason of blindness (as determined under section 1382c(a)(2) of this title) or disability (as determined under section 1382c(a)(3) of this title), and who ceases to be blind or to be under such disability, shall continue (so long as such individual is otherwise eligible) through the second month following the month in which such blindness or disability ceases.

(6) Notwithstanding any other provision of this subchapter, payment of the benefit of any individual who is an aged, blind, or disabled individual solely by reason of blindness (as determined under section 1382c(a)(2) of this title) or disability (as determined under section 1382c(a)(3) of this title) shall not be terminated or suspended because the blindness or other physical or mental impairment, on which the individual's eligibility for such benefit is based, has or may have ceased, if—

(A) such individual is participating in a program consisting of the Ticket to Work and Self-Sufficiency Program under section 1320b–19 of this title or another program of vocational rehabilitation services, employment services, or other support services approved by the Commissioner of Social Security, and

(B) the Commissioner of Social Security determines that the completion of such program, or its continuation for a specified period of time, will increase the likelihood that such individual may (following his participation in such program) be permanently removed from the blindness and disability benefit rolls.

(7)(A) In any case where—

(i) an individual is a recipient of benefits based on disability or blindness under this subchapter,

(ii) the physical or mental impairment on the basis of which such benefits are payable is found to have ceased, not to have existed, or to no longer be disabling, and as a consequence such individual is determined not to be entitled to such benefits, and

(iii) a timely request for review or for a hearing is pending with respect to the determination that he is not so entitled,

such individual may elect (in such manner and form and within such time as the Commissioner of Social Security shall by regulations prescribe) to have the payment of such benefits continued for an additional period beginning with the first month beginning after October 9, 1984, for which (under such determination) such benefits are no longer otherwise payable, and ending with the earlier of (I) the month preceding the month in which a decision is made after such a hearing, or (II) the month preceding the month in which no such request for review or a hearing is pending.

(B)(i) If an individual elects to have the payment of his benefits continued for an additional period under subparagraph (A), and the final decision of the Commissioner of Social Security affirms the determination that he is not entitled to such benefits, any benefits paid under this subchapter pursuant to such election (for months in such additional period) shall be considered overpayments for all purposes of this subchapter, except as otherwise provided in clause (ii).

(ii) If the Commissioner of Social Security determines that the individual's appeal of his termination of benefits was made in good faith, all of the benefits paid pursuant to such individual's election under subparagraph (A) shall be subject to waiver consideration under the provisions of subsection (b)(1).

(C) The provisions of subparagraphs (A) and (B) shall apply with respect to determinations (that individuals are not entitled to benefits) which are made on or after October 9, 1984, or prior to such date but only on the basis of a timely request for review or for a hearing.

(8)(A) In any case in which an administrative law judge has determined after a hearing as provided in subsection (c) that an individual is entitled to benefits based on disability or blindness under this subchapter and the Commissioner of Social Security has not issued the Commissioner's final decision in such case within 110 days after the date of the administrative law judge's determination, such benefits shall be currently paid for the months during the period beginning with the month in which such 110–day period expires and ending with the month in which such final decision is issued.

(B) For purposes of subparagraph (A), in determining whether the 110–day period referred to in subparagraph (A) has elapsed, any period of time for which the action or inaction of such individual or such individual's representative without good cause results in the delay in the issuance of the Commissioner's final decision shall not be taken into account to the extent that such period of time exceeds 20 calendar days.

(C) Any benefits currently paid under this subchapter pursuant to this paragraph (for the months described in subparagraph (A)) shall not be considered overpayments for any purposes of this subchapter, unless payment of such benefits was fraudulently obtained.

(9) Benefits under this subchapter shall not be denied to any individual solely by reason of the refusal of the individual to accept an amount offered as compensation for a crime of which the individual was a victim.

(10)(A) If an individual is eligible for past-due monthly benefits under this subchapter in an amount that (after any withholding for reimbursement to a State for interim assistance under subsection (g) and payment of attorney fees under subsection (d)(2)(B)) equals or exceeds the product of—

(i) 3, and

(ii) the maximum monthly benefit payable under this subchapter to an eligible individual (or, if appropriate, to an eligible individual and eligible spouse),

then the payment of such past-due benefits (after any such reimbursement to a State and payment of attorney fees under subsection (d)(2)(B)) shall be made in installments as provided in subparagraph (B).

(B)(i) The payment of past-due benefits subject to this subparagraph shall be made in not to exceed 3 installments that are made at 6–month intervals.

(ii) Except as provided in clause (iii), the amount of each of the first and second installments may not exceed an amount equal to the product of clauses (i) and (ii) of subparagraph (A).

(iii) In the case of an individual who has—

(I) outstanding debt attributable to—

(aa) food,

(bb) clothing,

(cc) shelter, or

(dd) medically necessary services, supplies or equipment, or medicine; or

(II) current expenses or expenses anticipated in the near term attributable to—

(aa) medically necessary services, supplies or equipment, or medicine, or

(bb) the purchase of a home, and

such debt or expenses are not subject to reimbursement by a public assistance program, the Secretary under subchapter XVIII, a State plan approved under subchapter XIX, or any private entity legally liable to provide payment pursuant to an insurance policy, prepaid plan, or other arrangement, the limitation specified in clause (ii) may be exceeded by an amount equal to the total of such debt and expenses.

(C) This paragraph shall not apply to any individual who, at the time of the Commissioner's determination that such individual is eligible for the payment of past-due monthly benefits under this subchapter—

(i) is afflicted with a medically determinable impairment that is expected to result in death within 12 months; or

(ii) is ineligible for benefits under this subchapter and the Commissioner determines that such individual is likely to remain ineligible for the next 12 months.

(D) For purposes of this paragraph, the term "benefits under this subchapter" includes supplementary payments pursuant to an agreement for Federal administration under section 1382e(a) of this title, and payments pursuant to an agreement entered into under section 212(b) of Public Law 93–66.

(b) Overpayments and underpayments; adjustment, recovery, or payment of amounts by Commissioner

(1)(A) Whenever the Commissioner of Social Security finds that more or less than the correct amount of benefits has been paid with respect to any individual, proper adjustment or recovery shall, subject to the succeeding provisions of this subsection, be made by appropriate adjustments in future payments to such individual or by recovery from such individual or his eligible spouse (or from the estate of either) or by payment to such individual or his eligible spouse, or, if such individual is deceased, by payment—

(i) to any surviving spouse of such individual, whether or not the individual's eligible spouse, if (within the meaning of the first sentence of section 402(i) of this title) such surviving husband or wife was living in the same household with the individual at the time of his death or within the 6 months immediately preceding the month of such death, or

(ii) if such individual was a disabled or blind child who was living with his parent or parents at the time of his death or within the 6 months immediately preceding the month of such death, to such parent or parents.

(B) The Commissioner of Social Security (i) shall make such provision as the Commissioner finds appropriate in the case of payment of more than the correct amount of benefits with respect to an individual with a view to avoiding penalizing such individual or his eligible spouse who was without fault in connection with the overpayment, if adjustment or recovery on account of such overpayment in such case would defeat the purposes of this subchapter, or be against equity and good conscience, or (because of the small amount involved) impede efficient or effective administration of this subchapter, and (ii) shall in any event make the adjustment or recovery (in the case of payment of more than the correct amount of benefits), in the case of an individual or eligible spouse receiving monthly benefit payments under this subchapter (including supplementary payments of the type described in section 1382e(a) of this title and payments pursuant to an agreement entered into under section 212(a) of Public Law 93–66), in amounts which in the aggregate do not exceed (for any month) the lesser of (I) the amount of his or their benefit under this subchapter for that month or (II) an amount equal to 10 percent of his or their income for that month (including such benefit but excluding payments under subchapter II when recovery is made from subchapter II payments pursuant to section 1320b–17 of this title and excluding income excluded pursuant to section 1382a(b) of this title), and in the case of an individual or eligible spouse to whom a lump sum is payable under this subchapter (including under section 1382e(a) of this title or under an agreement entered into under section 212(a) of Public Law 93–66) shall, as at least one means of recovering such overpayment, make the adjustment or recovery from the lump sum payment in an amount equal to not less than the lesser of the amount of the overpayment or the lump sum payment, unless fraud, willful misrepresentation, or concealment of material information was involved on the part of the individual or spouse in connection with the overpayment, or unless the individual requests that such adjustment or recovery be made at a higher or lower rate and the Commissioner of Social Security determines that adjustment or recovery at such rate is justified and appropriate. The availability (in the case of an individual who has been paid more than the correct amount of benefits) of procedures for adjustment or recovery at a limited rate under clause (ii) of the preceding sentence shall not, in and of itself, prevent or restrict the provision (in such case) of more substantial relief under clause (i) of such sentence. In making for purposes of this subparagraph a determination of whether an adjustment or recovery would defeat the purpose of this subchapter, the Commissioner of Social Security shall require an individual to provide authorization for the Commissioner to obtain (subject to the cost reimbursement requirements of section 1115(a) of the Right to Financial Privacy Act) from any financial institution (within the meaning of section 1101(1) of such Act) any financial record (within the meaning of section 1101(2) of such Act) held by the institution with respect to such individual whenever the Commissioner determines that the record is needed in connection with a determination with respect to such adjustment or recovery, under the terms and conditions established under subsection (e)(1)(B).

(2) Notwithstanding any other provision of this section, when any payment of more than the correct amount is made to or on behalf of an individual who has died, and such payment—

(A) is made by direct deposit to a financial institution;

(B) is credited by the financial institution to a joint account of the deceased individual and another person; and

(C) such other person is the surviving spouse of the deceased individual, and was eligible for a payment under this subchapter (including any State supplementation payment paid by the Commissioner of Social Security) as an eligible spouse (or as either member of an eligible couple) for the month in which the deceased individual died,

the amount of such payment in excess of the correct amount shall be treated as a payment of more than the correct amount to such other person. If any payment of more than the correct amount is made to a representative payee on behalf of an individual after the individual's death, the representative payee shall be liable for the repayment of the overpayment, and the Commissioner of Social Security shall establish an overpayment control record under the social security account number of the representative payee.

(3)(A) When any payment of more than the correct amount is made on behalf of an individual who is a represented minor beneficiary for a month in which such individual is in foster care under the responsibility of a State and the State is the representative payee of such individual, the State shall be liable for the repayment of the overpayment, and there shall be no adjustment of payments to, or recovery by the United States from, such individual.

(B) For purposes of this paragraph, the term "represented minor beneficiary", with respect to an individual for a month, means a child (as defined for purposes of section 675(8) of this title) entitled to benefits under this subchapter for such month whose benefits are certified for payment to a representative payee.

(4) If any overpayment with respect to an individual (or an individual and his or her spouse) is attributable solely to the ownership or possession by such individual (and spouse if any) of resources having a value which exceeds the applicable dollar figure specified in paragraph (1)(B) or (2)(B) of section 1382(a) of this title by $50 or less, such individual (and spouse if any) shall be deemed for purposes of the second sentence of paragraph (1) to have been without fault in connection with the overpayment, and no adjustment or recovery shall be made under the first sentence of such paragraph, unless the Commissioner of Social Security finds that the failure of such individual (and spouse if any) to report such value correctly and in a timely manner was knowing and willful.

(5)(A) With respect to any delinquent amount, the Commissioner of Social Security may use the collection practices described in sections 3711(f), 3716, 3717, and 3718 of Title 31 and in section 5514 of Title 5, all as in effect immediately after April 26, 1996.

(B) For purposes of subparagraph (A), the term "delinquent amount" means an amount

(i) in excess of the correct amount of payment under this subchapter;

(ii) paid to a person after such person has attained 18 years of age; and

(iii) determined by the Commissioner of Social Security, under regulations, to be otherwise unrecoverable under this section after such person ceases to be a beneficiary under this subchapter.

(6) For payments for which adjustments are made by reason of a retroactive payment of benefits under subchapter II, see section 1320a–6 of this title.

(7) For provisions relating to the cross-program recovery of overpayments made under programs administered by the Commissioner of Social Security, see section 1320b–17 of this title.

(8)(A) In the case of payment of less than the correct amount of benefits to or on behalf of any individual, no payment shall be made to such individual pursuant to this subsection during any period for which such individual—

(i) is not an eligible individual or eligible spouse under section 1382(e)(1) of this title because such individual is an inmate of a public institution that is a jail, prison, or other penal institution or correctional facility the purpose of which is to confine individuals as described in clause (ii) or (iii) of section 402(x)(1)(A) of this title, or

(ii) is not an eligible individual or eligible spouse under section 1382(e)(4) of this title,

until such person is no longer considered an ineligible individual or ineligible spouse under section 1382(e)(1) or 1382(e)(4) of this title.

(B) Nothing in subparagraph (A) shall be construed to limit the Commissioner's authority to withhold amounts, make adjustments, or recover amounts due under this subchapter, subchapter II, or subchapter VIII that would be deducted from a payment that would otherwise be payable to such individual but for such subparagraph.

(c) Hearing to determine eligibility or amount of benefits; subsequent application; time within which to request hearing; time for determinations of Commissioner pursuant to hearing; judicial review

(1)(A) The Commissioner of Social Security is directed to make findings of fact, and decisions as to the rights of any individual applying for payment under this subchapter. Any such decision by the Commissioner of Social Security which involves a determination of disability and which is in whole or in part unfavorable to such individual shall contain a statement of the case, in understandable language, setting forth a discussion of the evidence, and stating the Commissioner's determination and the reason or reasons upon which it is based. The Commissioner of Social Security shall provide reasonable notice and opportunity for a hearing to any individual who is or claims to be an eligible individual or eligible spouse and is in disagreement with any determination under this subchapter with respect to eligibility of such individual for benefits, or the amount of such individual's benefits, if such individual requests a hearing on the matter in disagreement within sixty days after notice of such determination is received, and, if a hearing is held, shall, on the basis of evidence adduced at the hearing affirm, modify, or reverse the Commissioner's findings of fact and such decision. The Commissioner of Social Security is further authorized, on the Commissioner's own motion, to hold such hearings and to conduct such investigations and other proceedings as the Commissioner may deem necessary or proper for the administration of this subchapter. In the course of any hearing, investigation, or other proceeding, the Commissioner may administer oaths and affirmations, examine witnesses, and receive evidence. Evidence may be received at any hearing before the Commissioner of Social Security even though inadmissible under the rules of evidence applicable to court procedure. The Commissioner of Social Security shall specifically take into account any physical, mental, educational, or linguistic limitation of such individual (including any lack of facility with the English language) in determining, with respect to the eligibility of such individual for benefits under this subchapter, whether such individual acted in good faith or was at fault, and in determining fraud, deception, or intent.

(B)(i) A failure to timely request review of an initial adverse determination with respect to an application for any payment under this subchapter or an adverse determination on reconsideration of such an initial determination shall not serve as a basis for denial of a subsequent application for any payment under this subchapter if the applicant demonstrates that the applicant, or any other individual referred to in subparagraph (A), failed to so request such a review acting in good faith reliance upon incorrect, incomplete, or misleading information, relating to the consequences of reapplying for payments in lieu of seeking review of an adverse determination, provided by any officer or employee of the Social Security Administration or any State agency acting under section 421 of this title.

(ii) In any notice of an adverse determination with respect to which a review may be requested under subparagraph (A), the Commissioner of Social Security shall describe in clear and specific language the effect on possible eligibility to receive payments under this subchapter of choosing to reapply in lieu of requesting review of the determination.

(2) Determination on the basis of such hearing, except to the extent that the matter in disagreement involves a disability (within the meaning of section 1382c(a)(3) of this title), shall be made within ninety days after the individual requests the hearing as provided in paragraph (1).

(3) The final determination of the Commissioner of Social Security after a hearing under paragraph (1) shall be subject to judicial review as provided in section 405(g) of this title to the same extent as the Commissioner's final determinations under section 405 of this title.

(d) Procedures applicable; prohibition on assignment of payments; representation of claimants; maximum fees; penalties for violations

(1) The provisions of section 407 of this title and subsections (a), (d), and (e) of section 405 of this title shall apply with respect to this part to the same extent as they apply in the case of subchapter II.

(2)(A) The provisions of section 406 of this title (other than subsections (a)(4) and (d) thereof) shall apply to this part to the same extent as they apply in the case of subchapter II, except that such section shall be applied—

(i) by substituting, in subparagraphs (A)(ii)(I) and (D)(i) of subsection (a)(2)[2] the phrase "(as determined before any applicable reduction under section 1383(g) of this title, and reduced by the amount of any reduction in benefits under this subchapter or subchapter II made pursuant to section 1320a–6(a) of this title)" for the parenthetical phrase contained therein;

(ii) by substituting, in subsections (a)(2)(B) and (b)(1)(B)(i), the phrase "paragraph (7)(A) or (8)(A) of section 1383(a) of this title or the requirements of due process of law" for the phrase "subsection (g) or (h) of section 423 of this title";

(iii) by substituting, in subsection (a)(2)(C)(i), the phrase "under subchapter II" for the phrase "under subchapter XVI";

(iv) by substituting, in subsection (b)(1)(A), the phrase "pay the amount of such fee" for the phrase "certify the amount of such fee for payment" and by striking, in subsection (b)(1)(A), the phrase "or certified for payment";

(v) by substituting, in subsection (b)(1)(B)(ii), the phrase "deemed to be such amounts as determined before any applicable reduction under section 1383(g) of this title, and reduced by the amount of any reduction in benefits under this subchapter or subchapter II made pursuant to section 1320a–6(a) of this title" for the phrase "determined before any applicable reduction under section 1320a–6(a) of this title)"; [3] and

(vi) by substituting, in subsection (e)(1)—

(I) "subparagraphs (B) and (C) of section 1383(d)(2) of this title" for "the preceding provisions of this section"; and

(II) "subchapter XVI" for "this subchapter".

(B) Subject to subparagraph (C), if the claimant is determined to be entitled to past-due benefits under this subchapter and the person representing the claimant is an attorney, the Commissioner of Social Security shall pay out of such past-due benefits to such attorney an amount equal to the lesser of—

(i) so much of the maximum fee as does not exceed 25 percent of such past-due benefits (as determined before any applicable reduction under subsection (g) and reduced by the amount of any reduction in benefits under this subchapter or subchapter II pursuant to section 1320a–6(a) of this title), or

(ii) the amount of past-due benefits available after any applicable reductions under subsection (g) and section 1320a–6(a) of this title.

(C)(i) Whenever a fee for services is required to be paid to an attorney from a claimant's past-due benefits pursuant to subparagraph (B), the Commissioner shall impose on the attorney an assessment calculated in accordance with clause (ii).

(ii)(I) The amount of an assessment under clause (i) shall be equal to the product obtained by multiplying the amount of the representative's fee that would be required to be paid by subparagraph (B) before the application of this subparagraph, by the percentage specified in subclause (II), except that the maximum amount of the assessment may not exceed $75. In the case of any calendar year beginning after the amendments made by section 302 of the Social Security Protection Act of 2003 take effect, the dollar amount specified in the preceding sentence (including a previously adjusted amount) shall be adjusted annually under the procedures used to adjust benefit amounts under section 415(i)(2)(A)(ii) of this title, except such adjustment shall be based on the higher of $75 or the previously adjusted amount that would have been in effect for December of the preceding year, but for the rounding of such amount pursuant to the following sentence. Any amount so adjusted that is not a multiple of $1 shall be rounded to the next lowest multiple of $1, but in no case less than $75.

(II) The percentage specified in this subclause is such percentage rate as the Commissioner determines is necessary in order to achieve full recovery of the costs of determining and approving fees to attorneys from the past-due benefits of claimants, but not in excess of 6.3 percent.

(iii) The Commissioner may collect the assessment imposed on an attorney under clause (i) by offset from the amount of the fee otherwise required by subparagraph (B) to be paid to the attorney from a claimant's past-due benefits.

(iv) An attorney subject to an assessment under clause (i) may not, directly or indirectly, request or otherwise obtain reimbursement for such assessment from the claimant whose claim gave rise to the assessment.

(v) Assessments on attorneys collected under this subparagraph shall be deposited as miscellaneous receipts in the general fund of the Treasury.

(vi) The assessments authorized under this subparagraph shall be collected and available for obligation only to the extent and in the amount provided in advance in appropriations Acts. Amounts so appropriated are authorized to remain available until expended, for administrative expenses in carrying out this subchapter and related laws.

(D) The Commissioner of Social Security shall notify each claimant in writing, together with the notice to such claimant of an adverse determination, of the options for obtaining attorneys to represent individuals in presenting their cases before the Commissioner of Social Security. Such notification shall also advise the claimant of the availability to qualifying claimants of legal services organizations which provide legal services free of charge.

(e) Administrative requirements prescribed by Commissioner; criteria; reduction of benefits to individual for noncompliance with requirements; payment to homeless

(1)(A) The Commissioner of Social Security shall, subject to subparagraph (B) and subsection (j), prescribe such requirements with respect to the filing of applications, the suspension or termination of assistance, the furnishing of other data and material, and the reporting of events and changes in circumstances, as may be necessary for the effective and efficient administration of this subchapter.

(B)(i) The requirements prescribed by the Commissioner of Social Security pursuant to subparagraph (A) shall require that eligibility for benefits under this subchapter will not be determined solely on the basis of declarations by the applicant concerning eligibility factors or other relevant facts, and that relevant information will be verified from independent or collateral sources and additional information obtained as necessary in order to assure that such benefits are only provided to eligible individuals (or eligible spouses) and that the amounts of such benefits are correct. For this purpose and for purposes of federally administered supplementary payments of the type described in section 1382e(a) of this title (including payments pursuant to an agreement entered into under section 212(a) of

Public Law 93–66), the Commissioner of Social Security shall, as may be necessary, request and utilize information available pursuant to section 6103(*l*)(7) of the Internal Revenue Code of 1986, and any information which may be available from State systems under section 1320b–7 of this title, and shall comply with the requirements applicable to States (with respect to information available pursuant to section 6103(*l*)(7)(B) of such Code) under subsections (a)(6) and (c) of such section 1320b–7 of this title.

(ii)(I) The Commissioner of Social Security may require each applicant for, or recipient of, benefits under this subchapter to provide authorization by the applicant or recipient (or by any other person whose income or resources are material to the determination of the eligibility of the applicant or recipient for such benefits) for the Commissioner to obtain (subject to the cost reimbursement requirements of section 1115(a) of the Right to Financial Privacy Act) from any financial institution (within the meaning of section 1101(1) of such Act) any financial record (within the meaning of section 1101(2) of such Act) held by the institution with respect to the applicant or recipient (or any such other person) whenever the Commissioner determines the record is needed in connection with a determination with respect to such eligibility or the amount of such benefits.

(II) Notwithstanding section 1104(a)(1) of the Right to Financial Privacy Act, an authorization provided by an applicant or recipient (or any other person whose income or resources are material to the determination of the eligibility of the applicant or recipient) pursuant to subclause (I) of this clause shall remain effective until the earliest of

(aa) the rendering of a final adverse decision on the applicant's application for eligibility for benefits under this subchapter;

(bb) the cessation of the recipient's eligibility for benefits under this subchapter; or

(cc) the express revocation by the applicant or recipient (or such other person referred to in subclause (I)) of the authorization, in a written notification to the Commissioner.

(III)(aa) An authorization obtained by the Commissioner of Social Security pursuant to this clause shall be considered to meet the requirements of the Right to Financial Privacy Act for purposes of section 1103(a) of such Act, and need not be furnished to the financial institution, notwithstanding section 1104(a) of such Act.

(bb) The certification requirements of section 1103(b) of the Right to Financial Privacy Act shall not apply to requests by the Commissioner of Social Security pursuant to an authorization provided under this clause.

(cc) A request by the Commissioner pursuant to an authorization provided under this clause is deemed to meet the requirements of section 1104(a)(3) of the Right to Financial Privacy Act and the flush language of section 1102 of such Act.

(IV) The Commissioner shall inform any person who provides authorization pursuant to this clause of the duration and scope of the authorization.

(V) If an applicant for, or recipient of, benefits under this subchapter (or any such other person referred to in subclause (I)) refuses to provide, or revokes, any authorization made by the applicant or recipient for the Commissioner of Social Security to obtain from any financial institution any financial record, the Commissioner may, on that basis, determine that the applicant or recipient is ineligible for benefits under this subchapter, determine that adjustment or recovery on account of an overpayment with respect to the applicant or recipient would not defeat the purpose of this subchapter, or both.

(iii)(I) The Commissioner of Social Security may require each applicant for, or recipient of, benefits under this subchapter to provide authorization by the applicant, recipient or legal guardian (or by any other person whose income or resources are material to the determination of the eligibility of the applicant or recipient for such benefits) for the Commissioner to obtain from any payroll data provider (as defined in section 1320e–3(c)(1) of this title) any record held by the payroll data provider with respect to the applicant or recipient (or any such other person) whenever the Commissioner determines the record is needed in connection with a determination of initial or ongoing eligibility or the amount of such benefits.

(II) An authorization provided by an applicant, recipient or legal guardian (or any other person whose income or resources are material to the determination of the eligibility of the applicant or recipient) under this clause shall remain effective until the earliest of—

(aa) the rendering of a final adverse decision on the applicant's application for eligibility for benefits under this subchapter;

(bb) the cessation of the recipient's eligibility for benefits under this subchapter;

(cc) the express revocation by the applicant, or recipient (or such other person referred to in subclause (I)) of the authorization, in a written notification to the Commissioner; or

(dd) the termination of the basis upon which the Commissioner considers another person's income and resources available to the applicant or recipient.

(III) The Commissioner of Social Security is not required to furnish any authorization obtained pursuant to this clause to the payroll data provider.

(IV) The Commissioner shall inform any person who provides authorization pursuant to this clause of the duration and scope of the authorization.

(V) If an applicant for, or recipient of, benefits under this subchapter (or any such other person referred to in subclause (I)) refuses to provide, or revokes, any authorization required by subclause (I), paragraph (2)(B) and paragraph (10) shall not apply to such applicant or recipient beginning with the first day of the first month in which he or she refuses or revokes such authorization.

(C) For purposes of making determinations under section 1382(e) of this title, the requirements prescribed by the Commissioner of Social Security pursuant to subparagraph (A) of this paragraph shall require each administrator of a nursing home, extended care facility, or intermediate care facility, within 2 weeks after the admission of any eligible individual or eligible spouse receiving benefits under this subchapter, to transmit to the Commissioner a report of the admission.

(2)(A) In the case of the failure by any individual to submit a report of events and changes in circumstances relevant to eligibility for or amount of benefits under this subchapter as required by the Commissioner of Social Security under paragraph (1), or delay by any individual in submitting a report as so required, the Commissioner of Social Security (in addition to taking any other action the Commissioner may consider appropriate under paragraph (1)) shall reduce any benefits which may subsequently become payable to such individual under this subchapter by—

(i) $25 in the case of the first such failure or delay,

(ii) $50 in the case of the second such failure or delay, and

(iii) $100 in the case of the third or a subsequent such failure or delay,

except where the individual was without fault or good cause for such failure or delay existed.

(B) For purposes of subparagraph (A), the Commissioner of Social Security shall find that good cause exists for the failure of, or delay by, an individual in submitting a report of an event or change in circumstances relevant to eligibility for or amount of benefits under this subchapter in any case where—

(i) the individual (or another person referred to in paragraph (1)(B)(iii)(I)) has provided authorization to the Commissioner to access payroll data records related to the individual; and

(ii) the event or change in circumstance is a change in the individual's employer.

(3) The Commissioner of Social Security shall provide a method of making payments under this subchapter to an eligible individual who does not reside in a permanent dwelling or does not have a fixed home or mailing address.

(4) A translation into English by a third party of a statement made in a foreign language by an applicant for or recipient of benefits under this subchapter shall not be regarded as reliable for any purpose under this subchapter unless the third party, under penalty of perjury—

(A) certifies that the translation is accurate; and

(B) discloses the nature and scope of the relationship between the third party and the applicant or recipient, as the case may be.

(5) In any case in which it is determined to the satisfaction of the Commissioner of Social Security that an individual failed as of any date to apply for benefits under this subchapter by reason of misinformation provided to such individual by any officer or employee of the Social Security Administration relating to such individual's eligibility for benefits under this subchapter, such individual shall be deemed to have applied for such benefits on the later of—

(A) the date on which such misinformation was provided to such individual, or

(B) the date on which such individual met all requirements for entitlement to such benefits (other than application therefor).

(6) In any case in which an individual visits a field office of the Social Security Administration and represents during the visit to an officer or employee of the Social Security Administration in the office that the individual's visit is occasioned by—

(A) the receipt of a notice from the Social Security Administration indicating a time limit for response by the individual, or

(B) the theft, loss, or nonreceipt of a benefit payment under this subchapter,

the Commissioner of Social Security shall ensure that the individual is granted a face-to-face interview at the office with an officer or employee of the Social Security Administration before the close of business on the day of the visit.

(7)(A)(i) The Commissioner of Social Security shall immediately redetermine the eligibility of an individual for benefits under this subchapter if there is reason to believe that fraud or similar fault was involved in the application of the individual for such benefits, unless a United States attorney, or equivalent State prosecutor, with jurisdiction over potential or actual related criminal cases, certifies, in writing, that there is a substantial risk that such action by the Commissioner of Social Security with regard to recipients in a particular investigation would jeopardize the criminal prosecution of a person involved in a suspected fraud.

(ii) When redetermining the eligibility, or making an initial determination of eligibility, of an individual for benefits under this subchapter, the Commissioner of Social Security shall disregard any evidence if there is reason to believe that fraud or similar fault was involved in the providing of such evidence.

(B) For purposes of subparagraph (A), similar fault is involved with respect to a determination if—

(i) an incorrect or incomplete statement that is material to the determination is knowingly made; or

(ii) information that is material to the determination is knowingly concealed.

(C) If, after redetermining the eligibility of an individual for benefits under this subchapter, the Commissioner of Social Security determines that there is insufficient evidence to support such eligibility, the Commissioner of Social Security may terminate such eligibility and may treat benefits paid on the basis of such insufficient evidence as overpayments.

(8)(A) The Commissioner of Social Security shall request the Immigration and Naturalization Service or the Centers for Disease Control to provide the Commissioner of Social Security with whatever medical information, identification information, and employment history either such entity has with respect to any alien who has applied for benefits under this subchapter to the extent that the information is relevant to any determination relating to eligibility for such benefits under this subchapter.

(B) Subparagraph (A) shall not be construed to prevent the Commissioner of Social Security from adjudicating the case before receiving such information.

(9) Notwithstanding any other provision of law, the Commissioner shall, at least 4 times annually and upon request of the Immigration and Naturalization Service (hereafter in this paragraph referred to as the "Service"), furnish the Service with the name and address of, and other identifying information on, any individual who the Commissioner knows is not lawfully present in the United States, and shall ensure that each agreement entered into under section 1382e(a) of this title with a State provides that the State shall furnish such information at such times with respect to any individual who the State knows is not lawfully present in the United States.

(10) An individual who has authorized the Commissioner of Social Security to obtain records from a payroll data provider under paragraph (1)(B)(iii) (or on whose behalf another person described in subclause (I) of such paragraph has provided such authorization) shall not be subject to a penalty under section 1320a–8a of this title for any omission or error with respect to such individual's wages as reported by the payroll data provider.

(f) Furnishing of information by Federal agencies

The head of any Federal agency shall provide such information as the Commissioner of Social Security needs for purposes of determining eligibility for or amount of benefits, or verifying other information with respect thereto.

(g) Reimbursement to States for interim assistance payments

(1) Notwithstanding subsection (d)(1) and subsection (b) as it relates to the payment of less than the correct amount of benefits, the Commissioner of Social Security may, upon written authorization by an individual, withhold benefits due with respect to that individual and may pay to a State (or a political subdivision thereof if agreed to by the Commissioner of Social Security and the State) from the benefits withheld an amount sufficient to reimburse the State (or political subdivision) for interim assistance furnished on behalf of the individual by the State (or political subdivision).

(2) For purposes of this subsection, the term "benefits" with respect to any individual means supplemental security income benefits under this subchapter, and any State supplementary payments under section 1382e of this title or under section 212 of Public Law 93–66 which the Commissioner of Social Security makes on behalf of a State (or political subdivision thereof), that the Commissioner of Social Security has determined to be due with respect to the individual at the time the Commissioner of Social Security makes the first payment of benefits with respect to the period described in clause (A) or (B) of paragraph (3). A cash advance made pursuant to subsection (a)(4)(A) shall not be considered as the first payment of benefits for purposes of the preceding sentence.

(3) For purposes of this subsection, the term "interim assistance" with respect to any individual means assistance financed from State or local funds and furnished for meeting basic needs (A) during the period, beginning with the month following the month in which the individual filed an application for benefits (as defined in paragraph (2)), for which he was eligible for such benefits, or (B) during the period beginning with the first month for which the individual's benefits (as defined in paragraph (2)) have been terminated or suspended if the individual was subsequently found to have been eligible for such benefits.

(4) In order for a State to receive reimbursement under the provisions of paragraph (1), the State shall have in effect an agreement with the Commissioner of Social Security which shall provide—

(A) that if the Commissioner of Social Security makes payment to the State (or a political subdivision of the State as provided for under the agreement) in reimbursement for interim assistance (as defined in paragraph (3)) for any individual in an amount greater than the reimbursable amount authorized by paragraph (1), the State (or political subdivision) shall pay to the individual the balance of such payment in excess of the reimbursable amount as expeditiously as possible, but in any event within ten working days or a shorter period specified in the agreement; and

(B) that the State will comply with such other rules as the Commissioner of Social Security finds necessary to achieve efficient and effective administration of this subsection and to carry out the purposes of the program established by this subchapter, including protection of hearing rights for any individual aggrieved by action taken by the State (or political subdivision) pursuant to this subsection.

(5) The provisions of subsection (c) shall not be applicable to any disagreement concerning payment by the Commissioner of Social Security to a State pursuant to the preceding provisions of this subsection nor the amount retained by the State (or political subdivision).

(h) Payment of certain travel expenses

The Commissioner of Social Security shall pay travel expenses, either on an actual cost or commuted basis, to individuals for travel incident to medical examinations requested by the Commissioner of Social Security in connection with disability determinations under this subchapter, and to parties, their representatives, and all reasonably necessary witnesses for travel within the United States (as defined in section 1382c(e) of this title) to attend reconsideration interviews and proceedings before administrative law judges with respect to any determination under this subchapter. The amount available under the preceding sentence for payment for air travel by any person shall not exceed the coach fare for air travel between the points involved unless the use of first-class accommodations is required (as determined under regulations of the Commissioner of Social Security) because of such person's health condition or the unavailability of alternative accommodations; and the amount available for payment for other travel by any person shall not exceed the cost of travel (between the points involved) by the most economical and expeditious means of transportation appropriate to such person's health condition, as specified in such regulations. The amount available for payment under this subsection for travel by a representative to attend an administrative proceeding before an administrative law judge or other adjudicator shall not exceed the maximum amount allowable under this subsection for such travel originating within the geographic area of the office having jurisdiction over such proceeding.

(i) Unnegotiated checks; notice to Commissioner; payment to States; notice to States; investigation of payees

(1) The Secretary of the Treasury shall, on a monthly basis, notify the Commissioner of Social Security of all benefit checks issued under this subchapter which include amounts representing State supplementary payments as described in paragraph (2) and which have not been presented for payment within one hundred and eighty days after the day on which they were issued.

(2) The Commissioner of Social Security shall from time to time determine the amount representing the total of the State supplementary payments made pursuant to agreements under section 1382e(a) of this title and under section 212(b) of Public Law 93–66 which is included in all such benefit checks not presented for payment within one hundred and eighty days after the day on which they were issued, and shall pay each State (or credit each State with) an amount equal to that State's share of all such amount. Amounts not paid to the States shall be returned to the appropriation from which they were originally paid.

(3) The Commissioner of Social Security, upon notice from the Secretary of the Treasury under paragraph (1), shall notify any State having an agreement described in paragraph (2) of all such benefit checks issued under that State's agreement which were not presented for payment within one hundred and eighty days after the day on which they were issued.

(4) The Commissioner of Social Security shall, to the maximum extent feasible, investigate the whereabouts and eligibility of the individuals whose benefit checks were not presented for payment within one hundred and eighty days after the day on which they were issued.

(j) Application and review requirements for certain individuals

(1) Notwithstanding any provision of section 1382 or 1382h of this title, any individual who—

(A) was an eligible individual (or eligible spouse) under section 1382 of this title or was eligible for benefits under or pursuant to section 1382h of this title, and

(B) who, after such eligibility, is ineligible for benefits under or pursuant to both such sections for a period of 12 consecutive months (or 24 consecutive months, in the case of such an individual whose ineligibility for benefits under or pursuant to both such sections is a result of being called to active duty pursuant to section 12301(d) or 12302 of Title 10 or section 502(f) of Title 32),

may not thereafter become eligible for benefits under or pursuant to either such section until the individual has reapplied for benefits under section 1382 of this title and been determined to be eligible for benefits under such section, or has filed a request for reinstatement of eligibility under subsection (p)(2) and been determined to be eligible for reinstatement.

(2)(A) Notwithstanding any provision of section 1382 of this title or section 1382h of this title (other than subsection (c) thereof), any individual who was eligible for benefits pursuant to section 1382h(b) of this title, and who—

(i)(I) on the basis of the same impairment on which his or her eligibility under such section 1382h(b) of this title was based becomes eligible (other than pursuant to a request for reinstatement under subsection (p)) for benefits under section 1382 or 1382h(a) of this title for a month that follows a period during which the individual was ineligible for benefits under sections 1382 and 1382h(a) of this title, and

(II) has earned income (other than income excluded pursuant to section 1382a(b) of this title) for any month in the 12–month period preceding such month that is equal to or in excess of the amount that would cause him or her to be ineligible for payments under section 1382(b) of this title for that month (if he or she were otherwise eligible for such payments); or

(ii)(I) on the basis of the same impairment on which his or her eligibility under such section 1382h(b) of this title was based becomes eligible under section 1382h(b) of this title for a month that follows a period during which the individual was ineligible under section 1382 of this title and section 1382h of this title, and

(II) has earned income (other than income excluded pursuant to section 1382a(b) of this title) for such month or for any month in the 12–month period preceding such month that is equal to or in excess of the amount that would cause him or her to be ineligible for payments under section 1382(b) of this title for that month (if he or she were otherwise eligible for such payments);

shall, upon becoming eligible (as described in clause (i)(I) or (ii)(I)), be subject to a prompt review of the type described in section 1382c(a)(4) of this title.

(B) If the Commissioner of Social Security determines pursuant to a review required by subparagraph (A) that the impairment upon which the eligibility of an individual is based has ceased, does not exist, or is not disabling, such individual may not thereafter become eligible for a benefit under or pursuant to section 1382 of this title or section 1382h of this title until the individual has reapplied for benefits under section 1382 of this title and been determined to be eligible for benefits under such section.

(k) Notifications to applicants and recipients

The Commissioner of Social Security shall notify an individual receiving benefits under section 1382 of this title on the basis of disability or blindness of his or her potential eligibility for benefits under or pursuant to section 1382h of this title—

(1) at the time of the initial award of benefits to the individual under section 1382 of this title (if the individual has attained the age of 18 at the time of such initial award), and

(2) at the earliest time after an initial award of benefits to an individual under section 1382 of this title that the individual's earned income for a month (other than income excluded pursuant to section 1382a(b) of this title) is $200 or more, and periodically thereafter so long as such individual has earned income (other than income so excluded) of $200 or more per month.

(*l*) Special notice to blind individuals with respect to hearings and other official actions

(1) In any case where an individual who is applying for or receiving benefits under this subchapter on the basis of blindness is entitled (under subsection (c) or otherwise) to receive notice from the Commissioner of Social Security of any decision or determination made or other action taken or proposed to be taken with respect to his or her rights under this subchapter, such individual shall at his or her election be entitled either (A) to receive a supplementary notice of such decision, determination, or action, by telephone, within 5 working days after the initial notice is mailed, (B) to receive the initial notice in the form of a certified letter, or (C) to receive notification by some alternative procedure established by the Commissioner of Social Security and agreed to by the individual.

(2) The election under paragraph (1) may be made at any time; but an opportunity to make such an election shall in any event be given (A) to every individual who is an applicant for benefits under this subchapter on the basis of blindness, at the time of his or her application, and (B) to every individual who is a recipient of such benefits on the basis of blindness, at the time of each redetermination of his or her eligibility. Such an election, once made by an individual, shall apply with respect to all notices of decisions, determinations, and actions which such individual may thereafter be entitled to receive under this subchapter until such time as it is revoked or changed.

(m) Pre-release procedures for institutionalized persons

The Commissioner of Social Security shall develop a system under which an individual can apply for supplemental security income benefits under this subchapter prior to the discharge or release of the individual from a public institution.

(n) Concurrent SSI and supplemental nutrition assistance applications by institutionalized individuals

The Commissioner of Social Security and the Secretary of Agriculture shall develop a procedure under which an individual who applies for supplemental security income benefits under this subchapter shall also be permitted to apply at the same time for participation in the supplemental nutrition assistance program authorized under the Food and Nutrition Act of 2008 (7 U.S.C. 2011 et seq.).

(*o*) Notice requirements

The Commissioner of Social Security shall take such actions as are necessary to ensure that any notice to one or more individuals issued pursuant to this subchapter by the Commissioner of Social Security or by a State agency—

(1) is written in simple and clear language, and

(2) includes the address and telephone number of the local office of the Social Security Administration which serves the recipient.

In the case of any such notice which is not generated by a local servicing office, the requirements of paragraph (2) shall be treated as satisfied if such notice includes the address of the local office of the Social Security Administration which services the recipient of the notice and a telephone number through which such office can be reached.

(p) Reinstatement of eligibility on the basis of blindness or disability

(1)(A) Eligibility for benefits under this subchapter shall be reinstated in any case where the Commissioner determines that an individual described in subparagraph (B) has filed a request for reinstatement meeting the requirements of paragraph (2)(A) during the period prescribed in subparagraph (C). Reinstatement of eligibility shall be in accordance with the terms of this subsection.

(B) An individual is described in this subparagraph if

(i) prior to the month in which the individual files a request for reinstatement—

(I) the individual was eligible for benefits under this subchapter on the basis of blindness or disability pursuant to an application filed therefor; and

(II) the individual thereafter was ineligible for such benefits due to earned income (or earned and unearned income) for a period of 12 or more consecutive months;

(ii) the individual is blind or disabled and the physical or mental impairment that is the basis for the finding of blindness or disability is the same as (or related to) the physical or mental impairment that was the basis for the finding of blindness or disability that gave rise to the eligibility described in clause (i);

(iii) the individual's blindness or disability renders the individual unable to perform substantial gainful activity; and

(iv) the individual satisfies the nonmedical requirements for eligibility for benefits under this subchapter.

(C)(i) Except as provided in clause (ii), the period prescribed in this subparagraph with respect to an individual is 60 consecutive months beginning with the month following the most recent month for which the individual was eligible for a benefit under this subchapter (including section 1382h of this title) prior to the period of ineligibility described in subparagraph (B)(i)(II).

(ii) In the case of an individual who fails to file a reinstatement request within the period prescribed in clause (i), the Commissioner may extend the period if the Commissioner determines that the individual had good cause for the failure to so file.

(2)(A)(i) A request for reinstatement shall be filed in such form, and containing such information, as the Commissioner may prescribe.

(ii) A request for reinstatement shall include express declarations by the individual that the individual meets the requirements specified in clauses (ii) through (iv) of paragraph (1)(B).

(B) A request for reinstatement filed in accordance with subparagraph (A) may constitute an application for benefits in the case of any individual who the Commissioner determines is not eligible for reinstated benefits under this subsection.

(3) In determining whether an individual meets the requirements of paragraph (1)(B)(ii), the provisions of section 1382c(a)(4) of this title shall apply.

(4)(A) Eligibility for benefits reinstated under this subsection shall commence with the benefit payable for the month following the month in which a request for reinstatement is filed.

(B)(i) Subject to clause (ii), the amount of the benefit payable for any month pursuant to the reinstatement of eligibility under this subsection shall be determined in accordance with the provisions of this subchapter.

(ii) The benefit under this subchapter payable for any month pursuant to a request for reinstatement filed in accordance with paragraph (2) shall be reduced by the amount of any provisional benefit paid to such individual for such month under paragraph (7).

(C) Except as otherwise provided in this subsection, eligibility for benefits under this subchapter reinstated pursuant to a request filed under paragraph (2) shall be subject to the same terms and conditions as eligibility established pursuant to an application filed therefor.

(5) Whenever an individual's eligibility for benefits under this subchapter is reinstated under this subsection, eligibility for such benefits shall be reinstated with respect to the individual's spouse if such spouse was previously an eligible spouse of the individual under this subchapter and the Commissioner determines that such spouse satisfies all the requirements for eligibility for such benefits except requirements related to the filing of an application. The provisions of paragraph (4) shall apply to the reinstated eligibility of the spouse to the same extent that they apply to the reinstated eligibility of such individual.

(6) An individual to whom benefits are payable under this subchapter pursuant to a reinstatement of eligibility under this subsection for twenty-four months

(whether or not consecutive) shall, with respect to benefits so payable after such twenty-fourth month, be deemed for purposes of paragraph (1)(B)(i)(I) to be eligible for such benefits on the basis of an application filed therefor.

(7)(A) An individual described in paragraph (1)(B) who files a request for reinstatement in accordance with the provisions of paragraph (2)(A) shall be eligible for provisional benefits payable in accordance with this paragraph, unless the Commissioner determines that the individual does not meet the requirements of paragraph (1)(B)(i) or that the individual's declaration under paragraph (2)(A)(ii) is false. Any such determination by the Commissioner shall be final and not subject to review under paragraph (1) or (3) of subsection (c).

(B)(i) Except as otherwise provided in clause (ii), the amount of a provisional benefit for a month shall equal the amount of the monthly benefit that would be payable to an eligible individual under this subchapter with the same kind and amount of income.

(ii) If the individual has a spouse who was previously an eligible spouse of the individual under this subchapter and the Commissioner determines that such spouse satisfies all the requirements of section 1382c(b) of this title except requirements related to the filing of an application, the amount of a provisional benefit for a month shall equal the amount of the monthly benefit that would be payable to an eligible individual and eligible spouse under this subchapter with the same kind and amount of income.

(C)(i) Provisional benefits shall begin with the month following the month in which a request for reinstatement is filed in accordance with paragraph (2)(A).

(ii) Provisional benefits shall end with the earliest of

(I) the month in which the Commissioner makes a determination regarding the individual's eligibility for reinstated benefits;

(II) the fifth month following the month for which provisional benefits are first payable under clause (i); or

(III) the month in which the Commissioner determines that the individual does not meet the requirements of paragraph (1)(B)(i) or that the individual's declaration made in accordance with paragraph (2)(A)(ii) is false.

(D) In any case in which the Commissioner determines that an individual is not eligible for reinstated benefits, any provisional benefits paid to the individual under this paragraph shall not be subject to recovery as an overpayment unless the Commissioner determines that the individual knew or should have known that the individual did not meet the requirements of paragraph (1)(B).

(8) For purposes of this subsection other than paragraph (7), the term "benefits under this subchapter" includes State supplementary payments made pursuant to an agreement under section 1382e(a) of this title or section 212(b) of Public Law 93–66.

(Aug. 14, 1935, c. 531, Title XVI, § 1631, as added Pub.L. 92–603, Title III, § 301, Oct. 30, 1972, 86 Stat. 1475; amended Pub.L. 93–233, § 18(g), Dec. 31, 1973, 87 Stat. 969; Pub.L. 93–368, § 5, Aug. 7, 1974, 88 Stat. 420; Pub.L. 94–202, §§ 1, 2, Jan. 2, 1976, 89 Stat. 1135; Pub.L. 94–365, § 1, July 14, 1976, 90 Stat. 990; Pub.L. 94–569, § 4(a), Oct. 20, 1976, 90 Stat. 2700; Pub.L. 96–222, Title I, § 101(a)(2)(C), Apr. 1, 1980, 94 Stat. 195; Pub.L. 96–265, Title III, §§ 301(b), 305(b), 310(b), Title V, § 501(c), June 9, 1980, 94 Stat. 450, 457, 459, 470; Pub.L. 96–473, § 6(h), Oct. 19, 1980, 94 Stat. 2266; Pub.L. 97–35, Title XXIII, § 2343(a), Aug. 13, 1981, 95 Stat. 866; Pub.L. 97–248, Title I, § 187(a), Sept. 3, 1982, 96 Stat. 407; Pub.L. 98–369, Div. B, Title VI, §§ 2612(a), 2613, 2651(j), 2663(g)(11), (12), July 18, 1984, 98 Stat. 1131, 1150, 1169; Pub.L. 98–460, §§ 7(b), 16(b), Oct. 9, 1984, 98 Stat. 1803, 1809; Pub.L. 99–272, Title XII, § 12113(b), Apr. 7, 1986, 100 Stat. 288; Pub.L. 99–514, § 2, Title XVIII, § 1883(d)(1), Oct. 22, 1986, 100 Stat. 2095, 2918; Pub.L. 99–570, Title XI, §§ 11005(a), 11006, Oct. 27, 1986, 100 Stat. 3207–169; Pub.L. 99–643, §§ 4(c)(1), (d)(3)(B), 5, 8(a), Nov. 10, 1986, 100 Stat. 3576 to 3579; Pub.L. 100–203, Title IX, §§ 9109(a), 9110(a), (b), 9111(a)(1), 9112(a), 9123, Dec. 22, 1987, 101 Stat. 1330–302 to 1330–304, 1330–313; Pub.L. 100–647, Title VIII, § 8001(b), Nov. 10, 1988, 102 Stat. 3779; Pub.L. 101–239, Title X, §§ 10302(b)(1), 10303(b), 10305(e), 10307(a)(2), (b)(2), Dec. 19, 1989, 103 Stat. 2482, 2483, 2485; Pub.L. 101–508, Title V, §§ 5031(c), 5038(a), 5039(b), 5040, 5105(a)(1)(B), (2)(A)(ii), (3)(A)(ii), (c)(2), (d)(1)(B), 5106(a)(2), (c), 5107(a)(2), 5109(a)(2), 5113(b), Nov. 5, 1990, 104 Stat. 1388–224, 1388–226, 1388–227, 1388–255, 1388–258, 1388–261, 1388–265, 1388–266, 1388–268, 1388–269, 1388–271, 1388–273; Pub.L. 103–296, Title I, § 107(a)(4), Title II, §§ 201(b)(1)(A), (B), (2)(A), (B), 206(a)(2), (d)(2), (f)(1), Title III, § 321(f)(2)(B), (3)(A), (h)(1), Aug. 15, 1994, 108 Stat. 1478, 1499, 1500, 1501, 1509, 1514, 1515, 1541, 1544; Pub.L. 103–387, § 6(a), Oct. 22, 1994, 108 Stat. 4077; Pub.L. 103–432, Title II, §§ 264(b), (e) to (g), 267(b), 268, Oct. 31, 1994, 108 Stat. 4468 to 4470; Pub.L. 104–121, Title I, § 105(b)(2), Mar. 29, 1996, 110 Stat. 853; Pub.L. 104–193, Title II, §§ 204(b), (c)(2), 213(a), 221(a), (b), Title IV, § 404(c), Aug. 22, 1996, 110 Stat. 2188, 2194, 2196, 2197, 2267; Pub.L. 105–33, Title V, §§ 5522(b), 5564, Aug. 5, 1997, 111 Stat. 622, 639; Pub.L. 105–306, § 8(b)(2), Oct. 28, 1998, 112 Stat. 2929; Pub.L. 106–169, Title II, §§ 201(b), 202(a), 203(a), 213, 251(b)(9), Dec. 14, 1999, 113 Stat. 1831, 1832, 1843, 1856; Pub.L. 106–170, Title I, §§ 101(b)(2)(C), 112(b), Dec. 17, 1999, 113 Stat. 1874, 1884; Pub.L. 108–203, Title I, §§ 101(c)(1), (3), 102(a)(2), (b)(3), 103(c), 104(b), 105(c), 106(c), Title II, § 210(b)(4), Title III, § 302(a), (b), Mar. 2, 2004, 118 Stat. 496, 497, 500, 502, 503, 505, 506, 517, 519, 521; Pub.L. 109–163, Div. A, Title VI, § 689, Jan. 6, 2006, 119 Stat. 3337; Pub.L. 109–171, Title VII, § 7502(a), Feb. 8, 2006, 120 Stat. 154; Pub.L. 110–234, Title IV, § 4002(b)(1)(A), (B), (2)(V), May 22, 2008, 122 Stat. 1095, 1097; Pub.L. 110–246, § 4(a), Title IV, § 4002(b)(1)(A), (B), (2)(V), June 18, 2008, 122 Stat. 1664, 1857, 1858; Pub.L. 111–115, § 2(b), Dec. 15, 2009, 123 Stat. 3029; Pub.L. 111–142, § 3(b)(1), Feb. 27, 2010, 124 Stat. 39; Pub.L. 113–79, Title IV, § 4030(r), Feb. 7, 2014, 128 Stat. 815; Pub.L. 114–74, Title VIII, §§ 824(b)(2), (c)(2), 834(b), Nov. 2, 2015, 129 Stat. 609, 615; Pub. L. 115–165, Title I, §§ 102(c), 104(b), Title II, §§ 202(c), 203(c), Apr. 13, 2018, 132 Stat. 1261, 1264, 1270, 1272.)

[1] So in original. Probably should be a semicolon instead of a comma.

[2] So in original. Probably should be followed by a comma.

[3] So in original. The closing parenthesis after "title" probably should not appear.

HISTORICAL AND STATUTORY NOTES

References in Text

The Right to Financial Privacy Act, referred to in text, probably means the Right to Financial Privacy Act of 1978, Title XI of Pub.L. 95–630, Nov. 10, 1978, 92 Stat. 3697, which is classified generally to chapter 35 of Title 12, 12 U.S.C.A. § 3401 et seq. Sections 1101, 1102, 1103, 1104, and 1115 of the Act are classified to 12 U.S.C.A. §§ 3401, 3402, 3403, 3404, and 3415, respectively. For complete classification, see Short Title note set out under 12 U.S.C.A. § 3401 and Tables.

This subchapter, referred to in text, originally read "this title", meaning the Social Security Act, Act Aug. 14, 1935, c. 531, Title XVI, as added Oct. 30, 1972, Pub.L. 92–603, Title III, § 301, 86 Stat. 1465, as amended, which is classified as this subchapter, 42 U.S.C.A. § 1381 et seq.

Subchapter II, referred to in text, originally read "title II", meaning the Social Security Act, Act Aug. 14, 1935, c. 531, Title II, 49 Stat. 622, as amended, which is classified as subchapter II, 42 U.S.C.A. § 401 et seq.

Subchapter VIII, referred to in text, originally read "title VIII", meaning the Social Security Act, Act Aug. 14, 1935, c. 531, Title VIII, as added Dec. 14, 1999, Pub.L. 106–169, Title II, § 251(a), 113 Stat. 1844, as amended, which is classified as subchapter VIII, 42 U.S.C.A. § 1001 et seq.

Subchapter XVI, referred to in text, originally read "title XVI", meaning Title XVI of the Social Security Act, Act, Aug. 14, 1935, c. 531, 49 Stat. 622, as amended, which is principally classified to this subchapter, 42 U.S.C.A. § 1381 et seq.

The Internal Revenue Code of 1986, referred to in subsecs. (a)(2)(B)(xiv) and (e)(1)(B)(i), is classified generally to Title 26.

Section 212 of Public Law 93–66, referred to in subsecs. (a)(2)(F), (10)(D), (b)(1)(B), (e)(1)(B), (g)(2), and (i)(2), is section 212 of Pub.L. 93–66, Title II, July 9, 1973, 87 Stat. 155, as amended, which is set out as a note under section 1382 of this title.

This chapter, referred to in subsec. (a)(2)(H)(i), originally read "this Act", meaning the Social Security Act, Act Aug. 14, 1935, c. 531, 49 Stat. 620, as amended, which is classified generally to this chapter, 42 U.S.C.A. § 301 et seq.

Section 302 of the Social Security Protection Act of 2003, referred to in subsec. (d)(2)(C)(ii)(I), probably means Section 302 of the Social Security Protection Act of 2004, which is Pub.L. 108–203, Title III, § 302, Mar. 2, 2004, 118 Stat. 519, which amended this section and enacted provisions set out as an Effective and Applicability Provisions note under this section.

The Food and Nutrition Act of 2008, referred to in subsec. (n), is Pub.L. 88–525, Aug. 31, 1964, 78 Stat. 703, as amended, formerly known as the Food Stamp Act of 1977, which principally enacted chapter 51 of Title 7, Agriculture. For complete classification, see Short Title note set out under 7 U.S.C.A. § 2011 and Tables.

Codifications

The authorities provided by each provision of, and each amendment made by, Pub.L. 110–246, as in effect on Sept. 30, 2012, to continue, and the Secretary of Agriculture to carry out the authorities, until the later of Sept. 30, 2013, or the date specified in the provision of, or amendment made by, Pub.L. 110–246, see section 701(a) of Pub.L. 112–240, set out in a note under 7 U.S.C.A. § 8701.

Pub.L. 101–239, Title X, § 10307(a)(2), (3), Dec. 19, 1989, 103 Stat. 2485, amended subsec. (d)(2), effective June 1, 1991, by adding at the end the following sentence: "The Secretary shall maintain in the electronic information retrieval system used by the Social Security Administration a current record, with respect to any claimant before the Secretary, of the identity of any person representing such claimant in accordance with this paragraph.". Such amendment could not be executed to the present text in view of complete revision of the subsection.

Section 204(c)(2) of Pub.L. 104–193, directing amendment of section 1631(g)(3) of the Social Security Act (subsec. (g)(3) of this section), was executed to subsec. (g)(3) of this section, despite parenthetical reference to "42 U.S.C. 1382j(g)(3)", as the probable intent of Congress.

Effective and Applicability Provisions

2018 Acts. Amendments by section 102 of Pub.L. 115–165 shall take effect on April 13, 2018, see Pub.L. 115–165, § 102(d), set out as a note under 42 U.S.C.A. § 405.

Amendments by section 202(c) of Pub.L. 115–165, applicable with respect to any individual appointed to serve as a representative payee on or after Jan. 1, 2019, see Pub.L. 115–165 § 202(d), set out as a note under 42 U.S.C.A. § 405.

Except as otherwise provided for prior appointments, amendments by section 203(c) of Pub.L. 115–165, applicable with respect to any individual appointed to serve as a representative payee on or after Jan. 1, 2019, see Pub.L. 115–165 § 203(d), set out as a note under 42 U.S.C.A. § 405.

2015 Acts. Amendments by Pub.L. 114–74, § 824, shall take effect on the date that is 1 year after Nov. 2, 2015, see Pub.L. 114–74, § 824(e), set out as a note under 42 U.S.C.A. § 425.

Amendments made by Pub.L. 114–74, § 834, shall apply with respect to determinations made on or after the date that is 3 months after Nov. 2, 2015, see Pub.L. 114–74, § 834(c), set out as a note under 42 U.S.C.A. § 404.

2009 Acts. Amendments by Pub.L. 111–115, § 2, shall be effective for payments that would otherwise be made on or after December 15, 2009, see Pub.L. 111–115, § 2(c), set out as a note under 42 U.S.C.A. § 404.

2008 Acts. Amendments by Pub.L. 110–246, except as otherwise provided, shall take effect on the earlier of June 18, 2008, or May 22, 2008, see Pub.L. 110–246, § 4(b), set out in a Repeal of Duplicative Enactment note under 7 U.S.C.A. § 8701.

Amendments by Title IV of Pub.L. 110–246, except as otherwise provided, take effect on October 1, 2008, see Pub.L. 110–246, § 4407, set out as a note under 2 U.S.C.A. § 1161.

2006 Acts. Pub.L. 109–171, Title VII, § 7502(b), Feb. 8, 2006, 120 Stat. 154, provided that: "The amendment made by subsection (a) [amending this section] shall take effect 3 months after the date of the enactment of this Act [Feb. 8, 2006].

Except as otherwise provided in Title VII of Pub.L. 109–171, amendments by Title VII of Pub.L. 109–171 effective as if enacted on Oct. 1, 2005, see Pub.L. 109–171, § 7701, set out as a note under 42 U.S.C.A. § 603.

2004 Acts. Amendments made by Pub.L. 108–203, § 101, enacting subsec. (a)(2)(A)(iv) of this section and amending subsec. (a)(2)(E) of this section, to apply to any case of benefit misuse by a representative payee with respect to which the Commissioner of Social Security makes the determination of misuse on or after Jan. 1, 1995, see Pub.L. 108–203, § 101(d), set out as a note under 42 U.S.C.A. § 405.

Amendments made by Pub.L. 108–203, § 102(a), enacting subsec. (a)(2)(I) of this section and amending subsec. (a)(2)(B)(vii) and (D)(ii) of this section, to take effect on the first day of the thirteenth month beginning after Mar. 2, 2004, see Pub.L. 108–203, § 102(a)(3), set out as a note under 42 U.S.C.A. § 405.

Amendments made by Pub.L. 108–203, § 103, enacting subsec. (a)(2)(B)(iii)(IV) and (V) and (a)(2)(B)(xiv) of this section and amending subsec. (a)(2)(B) of this section, to take effect on the first day of the thirteenth month beginning after Mar. 2, 2004, see Pub.L. 108–203, § 103(d), set out as a note under 42 U.S.C.A. § 405.

Amendments made by Pub.L. 108–203, § 104, amending subsec. (a)(2)(D)(i) of this section, to apply to any month involving benefit misuse by a representative payee in any case with respect to which the Commissioner of Social Security or a court of competent jurisdiction makes the determination of misuse after 180 days after Mar. 2, 2004, see Pub.L. 108–203, § 104(c), set out as a note under 42 U.S.C.A. § 405.

Amendments made by Pub.L. 108–203, § 105, amending subsec. (a)(2)(G)(i)(II) and (H) of this section, to apply to benefit misuse by a representative payee in any case with respect to which the Commissioner of Social Security or a court of competent jurisdiction makes the determination of misuse after 180 days after Mar. 2, 2004, see Pub.L. 108–203, § 105(d), set out as a note under 42 U.S.C.A. § 405.

Amendments made by Pub.L. 108–203, § 106, enacting subsec. (a)(2)(C)(v) of this section, to take effect 180 days after Mar. 2, 2004, see Pub.L. 108–203, § 106(d), set out as a note under 42 U.S.C.A. § 405.

Amendments made by Pub.L. 108–203, § 210, amending subsec. (b)(1)(B) and (6) of this section, to take effect on Mar. 2, 2004, and to be effective with respect to overpayments under this subchapter and subchapters II and VIII of this chapter, 42 U.S.C.A. §§ 401 et seq. and 1001 et seq., respectively, that are outstanding on or after Mar. 2, 2004, see Pub.L. 108–203, § 210(c), set out as a note under 42 U.S.C.A. § 404.

Pub.L. 108–203, Title II, § 302(c), Mar. 2, 2004, 118 Stat. 521, as amended Pub.L. 111–142, § 2(a)(2), Feb. 27, 2010, 124 Stat. 38, provided that: "The amendments made by this section [amending subsecs. (a)(2)(F)(i)(II), (10)(A) and (d)(2)(A) to (D) of this section] shall apply with respect to fees for representation of claimants which are first required to be paid under section 1631(d)(2) of the Social Security Act [subsec. (d)(2) of this section] on or after the date of the submission by the Commissioner of Social Security to each House of Congress pursuant to section 303(d) of this Act [Pub.L. 108–203, Title III, § 303(d), Mar. 2, 2004, 118 Stat. 522, which requires such submission not later than 1 year after Mar. 2, 2004, and which is set out in a note under 42 U.S.C.A. § 406] of written notice of completion of full implementation of the requirements for operation of the demonstration project under section 303 of this Act [Pub.L. 108–203, Title III, § 303, Mar. 2, 2004, 118 Stat. 521, which is set out as a note under 42 U.S.C.A. § 406]."

1999 Acts. Amendment by section 112 of Pub.L. 106–170 effective on the first day of the thirteenth month beginning after Dec. 17, 1999, see section 112(c) of Pub.L. 106–170, set out as a note under section 423 of this title.

Amendment by section 101(b) of Pub.L. 106–170 effective with the first month following 1 year after December 17, 1999, subject to graduated implementation of program provisions of section 101(d) of Pub.L. 106–170 [set out as a note under section 1320b–19 of this title], see section 101(c) of Pub.L. 106–170, set out as a note under section 1320b–19 of this title.

Amendment by section 203(a) of Pub.L. 106–169 applicable to debt outstanding on or after Dec. 14, 1999, see section 203(d) of Pub.L. 106–169, set out as a note under section 3701 of Title 31.

Pub.L. 106–169, Title II, § 202(b), Dec. 14, 1999, 113 Stat. 1832, provided that: "The amendments made by this section [amending subsec. (b) of this section] shall take effect 12 months after the date of the enactment of this Act [Dec. 14, 1999] and shall apply to amounts incorrectly paid which remain outstanding on or after such date."

Amendment by section 201(b) of Pub.L. 106–169 applicable to overpayments made 12 months or more after Dec. 14, 1999, see section 201(c) of Pub.L. 106–169, set out as a note under section 404 of this title.

1998 Acts. Amendment by section 8(b) of Pub.L. 105–306 effective Oct. 28, 1998 and applicable to amounts incorrectly paid which remain outstanding on or after Oct. 28, 1998, see section 8(c) of Pub.L. 105–306, set out as a note under section 404 of this title.

1997 Acts. Amendments by Chapter 2 of Subtitle F of Title V (§§ 5521 to 5528) of Pub.L. 105–33 effective as if included in enactment of Pub.L. 104–193, see section 5528(a) of Pub.L. 105–33, set out as a note under section 903 of this title.

Amendments by sections 5561 and 5565 of Pub.L. 105–33 effective as if included in the enactment of Title IV of the Personal Responsibility and Work Opportunity Reconciliation Act of 1996 [Pub.L. 104–193, Title IV, Aug. 22, 1996, 110 Stat. 2260], see section 5582 of Pub.L. 105–33, set out as a note under section 1367 of Title 8, Aliens and Nationality.

1996 Acts. Amendment by section 204(b) and (c)(2) of Pub.L. 104–193 applicable to applications for benefits under this subchapter filed on or after Aug. 22, 1996, without regard to whether regulations have been issued to implement such amendment, except as otherwise provided, see section 204(d) of Pub.L. 104–193, set out as a note under section 1382 of this title.

Amendment by section 213(a) of Pub.L. 104–193 applicable to payments made after Aug. 22, 1996, see section 213(d) of Pub.L. 104–193, set out as a note under section 1382a of this title.

Section 221(c) of Pub.L. 104–193 provided that:

"(1) **In general.**—The amendments made by this section [amending this section] are effective with respect to past-due benefits payable under title XVI of the Social Security Act [this subchapter] after the third month following the month in which this Act is enacted [Aug. 1996].

"(2) **Benefits payable under title XVI.**—For purposes of this subsection, the term 'benefits payable under title XVI of the Social Security Act' includes supplementary payments pursuant to an agreement for Federal administration under section 1616(a) of the Social Security Act [section 1382e(a) of this title], and payments pursuant to an agreement entered into under section 212(b) of Public Law 93–66 [set out as a note under section 1382 of this title]."

Amendment by section 105(b)(2) of Pub.L. 104–121 applicable to benefits for which applications are filed after third month following March, 1996, see section 105(b)(5) of Pub.L. 104–121, set out as a note under section 1382 of this title.

1994 Acts. Amendments by section 264 of Pub.L. 103–432 effective as if included in provisions of Pub.L. 101–508, 104 Stat. 1388, which was approved Nov. 5, 1990, to which such amendments relate at the time such provisions were enacted into law, see section 264(h) of Pub.L. 103–432, set out as a note under section 602 of this title.

Section 6(b) of Pub.L. 103–387 provided that: "The amendment made by subsection (a) [amending this section] shall apply to admissions occurring on or after October 1, 1995."

Amendment by section 107(a)(4) of Pub.L. 103–296 effective Mar. 31, 1995, see section 110 of Pub.L. 103–296, set out as a note under section 401 of this title.

Section 201(b)(1)(C) of Pub.L. 103–296 provided that: "The amendments made by this paragraph [amending subsec. (a)(2)(A) and (B)(viii) of this section] shall apply with respect to months beginning after 180 days after the date of the enactment of this Act [Aug. 15, 1994]."

Section 201(b)(2)(B)(iii)(I) of Pub.L. 103–296 provided in part that the repeal by that section of former subsec. (a)(2)(D)(iv) of this section is effective July 1, 1994.

Section 201(b)(2)(C) of Pub.L. 103–296 provided that: "Except as provided in subparagraph (B)(iii)(I), the amendments made by this paragraph [amending subsec. (a)(2)(B) and (D) of this section and enacting provisions set out as a note under this section] shall apply with respect to months beginning after 90 days after the date of the enactment of this Act [Aug. 15, 1994]."

Subsec. (e)(4) of this section applicable to transactions made on or after Oct. 1, 1994, see section 206(a)(3) of Pub.L. 103–296, set out as a note under section 405 of this title.

Subsec. (e)(6) of this section to take effect on Oct. 1, 1994, and to apply to determinations made before, on, or after Oct. 1, 1994, see section 206(d)(3) of Pub.L. 103–296, set out as a note under section 405 of this title.

Section 206(f)(2) of Pub.L. 103–296 provided that: "The amendment made by paragraph (1) [enacting subsec. (e)(7) of this section] shall take effect on October 1, 1994."

Amendments of subsec. (a)(2)(E) to (G) and (d)(2)(A)(i) by section 321(f)(2)(B) and (3)(A), respectively, of Pub.L. 103–296 effective as if included in the provisions of Pub.L. 101–508 to which they relate, see section 321(f)(5) of Pub.L. 103–296, set out as a note under section 405 of this title.

Amendment of subsecs. (n) and (*o*) of this section by section 321(h)(1) of Pub.L. 103–321 effective Aug. 15, 1994, see section 321(h)(3) of Pub.L. 103–296, set out as a note under section 1382b of this title.

1990 Acts. Amendment by section 5031 of Pub.L. 101–508 applicable with respect to benefits for months beginning on or after the first day of the sixth calendar month following Nov., 1990, see section 5031(d) of Pub.L. 101–508, set out as a note under section 1382a of this title.

Section 5038(b) of Pub.L. 101–508 provided that: "The amendment made by subsection (a) [amending subsec. (a) of this section] shall apply with respect to benefits for months beginning on or after the first day of the 6th calendar month following the month in which this Act is enacted [Nov. 1990]."

Amendment by section 5039 of Pub.L. 101–508 effective Nov. 5, 1990, see section 5039(c) of Pub.L. 101–508, set out as a note under section 1382h of this title.

Amendment by section 5105(a)(1)(B), (C), (2)(A)(ii), (3)(A)(ii) of Pub.L. 101–508 effective July 1, 1991, except as provided for, see section 5105(a)(5) of Pub.L. 101–508, set out as a note under section 405 of this title.

Amendment by section 5106 of Pub.L. 101–508 applicable with respect to determinations made on or after July 1, 1991, and to reimbursements for travel expenses incurred on or after April 1, 1991, see section 5106(d) of Pub.L. 101–508, set out as a note under section 401 of this title.

Amendment by section 5107 of Pub.L. 101–508 applicable with respect to adverse determinations made on or after July 1, 1991, see section 5107(b) of Pub.L. 101–508, set out as a note under section 405 of this title.

Amendment by section 5109 of Pub.L. 101–508 applicable with respect to notices issued on or after July 1, 1991, see section 5109(b) of Pub.L. 101–508, set out as a note under section 405 of this title.

Amendment by section 5113(b)(2) of Pub.L. 101–508 effective with respect to benefits payable for months after the eleventh month following November 1990, and applicable only with respect to individuals whose blindness or disability has or may have ceased after such eleventh month, see section 5113(c) of Pub.L. 101–508, set out as a note under section 425 of this title.

1989 Acts. Section 10302(b)(2) of Pub.L. 101–239 provided that: "The amendment made by paragraph (1) [enacting subsec. (e)(5) of this section] shall apply with respect to misinformation furnished on or after the date of the enactment of this Act [Dec. 19, 1989] and to benefits for months after the month [December 1989] in which this Act is enacted."

Amendment by section 10303(b) of Pub.L. 101–239 applicable to visits to field offices of the Social Security Administration on or after Jan. 1, 1990, see section 10303(c) of Pub.L. 101–239, set out as a note under section 405 of this title.

Amendment by section 10305(e) of Pub.L. 101–239 applicable with respect to determinations made on or after July 1, 1990, see section 10305(f) of Pub.L. 101–239, set out as a note under section 403 of this title.

Amendment by section 10307(a)(2) of Pub.L. 101–239 effective June 1, 1991, see section 10307(a)(3) of Pub.L. 101–239, set out as a note under section 406 of this title.

Amendment by section 10307(b)(2) of Pub.L. 101–239 applicable to adverse determinations made on or after Jan. 1, 1991, see section 10307(b)(3) of Pub.L. 101–239, set out as a note under section 406 of this title.

1988 Acts. Amendment by Pub.L. 100–647 applicable to determinations by administrative law judges of entitlement to benefits made after 180 days after Nov. 10, 1988, see section 8001(c) of Pub.L. 100–647, set out as a note under section 423 of this title.

1987 Acts. Section 9109(b) of Pub.L. 100–203 provided that: "The amendment made by subsection (a) [amending subsec. (a)(4)(A) of this section] shall become effective on the date of the enactment of this Act [Dec. 22, 1987]."

Section 9110(c) of Pub.L. 100–203 provided that: "The amendments made by this section [amending subsecs. (g)(2), (3) of this section] shall become effective with the 13th month following the month in which this Act is enacted [Dec. 22,

1987], or, if sooner, with the first month for which the Secretary of Health and Human Services determines that it is administratively feasible."

Section 9111(c) of Pub.L. 100–203 provided that: "The amendment made by subsection (a) [enacting subsec. (l) of this section] shall become effective July 1, 1988."

Section 9112(b) of Pub.L. 100–203 provided that: "The amendments made by subsection (a) [amending subsec. (a)(6) of this section] shall become effective April 1, 1988."

1986 Acts. Amendment by sections 4(c)(1), (d)(3)(B), and 5 of Pub.L. 99–643 effective July 1, 1987, except for State plans requiring State legislation, see section 10(b) of Pub.L. 99–643, set out as a note under section 1396a of this title.

Section 8(b) of Pub.L. 99–643 provided that: "The amendments made by subsection (a) [amending subsec. (b) of this section] shall apply with respect to benefits payable for months after May 1986."

Section 11005(c)(1) of Pub.L. 99–570 provided that: "The amendment made by subsection (a) [enacting subsec. (e)(3)] shall become effective on the date of the enactment of this Act [Oct. 27, 1986]."

Amendment by Pub.L. 99–514 effective Oct. 22, 1986, see section 1883(f) of Pub.L. 99–514, set out as a note under section 602 of this title.

Amendment by Pub.L. 99–272 applicable only in the case of deaths of which the Secretary is first notified on or after Apr. 7, 1986, see section 12113(c) of Pub.L. 99–272, set out as a note under section 404 of this Title.

1984 Acts. Amendment by section 16(b) of Pub.L. 98–460 effective Oct. 9, 1984, see section 16(d) of Pub.L. 98–460, set out as a note under section 405 of this title.

Amendment by sections 2612 and 2613 of Pub.L. 98–369 effective October 1, 1984, except as otherwise specifically provided, see section 2646 of Pub.L. 98–369, set out as a note under section 602 of this title.

Amendment by section 2651(j) of Pub.L. 98–369 effective July 18, 1984, see section 2651(*l*)(1) of Pub.L. 98–369, set out as a note under section 1320b–7 of this title.

Amendment by section 2663(g)(11), (12) of Pub.L. 98–369 effective July 18, 1984, but not to be construed as changing or affecting any right, liability, status or interpretation which existed (under the provisions of law involved) before that date, see section 2664(b) of Pub.L. 98–369, set out as a note under section 401 of this title.

1982 Acts. Section 187(b) of Pub.L. 97–248 provided that: "The amendment made by subsection (a) [amending subsec. (i)(2) of this section] shall become effective October 1, 1982."

1981 Acts. Section 2343(b) of Pub.L. 97–35 provided that: "The amendment made by subsection (a) [adding subsec. (i) of this section] shall become effective October 1, 1982."

1980 Acts. Amendment by section 301(b) of Pub.L. 96–265 effective the first day of sixth month which begins after June 9, 1980, and applicable with respect to individuals whose disability has not been determined to have ceased prior to such first day, see section 301(c) of Pub.L. 96–265, set out as a note under section 425 of this title.

Amendment by section 305(b) of Pub.L. 96–265 applicable with respect to decisions made on or after first day of 13th month following June 1980, see section 305(c) of Pub.L. 96–265, set out as a note under section 405 of this title.

Amendment by section 501(c) of Pub.L. 96–265 applicable in the case of payments of monthly insurance benefits under subchapter II of this chapter [42 U.S.C.A. § 401 et seq.] entitlement for which is determined on or after July 1, 1981, see section 501(d) of Pub.L. 96–265, set out as a note under section 1320a–6 of this title.

1976 Acts. Section 4(b) of Pub.L. 94–569 provided that: "The amendments made by this section [amending subsec. (a)(4)(B) of this section] shall apply with respect to months after the month following the month in which this Act is enacted [Oct. 1976]."

Amendment by sections 1 and 2 of Pub.L. 94–202 effective Jan. 2, 1976, with the amendment by section 2 of Pub.L. 94–202, to the extent that it changes the period within which a hearing must be requested, applicable to any decision or determination which is received on or after Jan. 2, 1976, see section 5 of Pub.L. 94–202, set out as a note under section 405 of this title.

1973 Acts. Amendment by Pub.L. 93–233 effective Jan. 1, 1974, see section 18(z–3)(1) of Pub.L. 93–233.

1972 Acts. Section 301 of Pub.L. 92–603 provided that this section is effective Jan. 1, 1974.

Repeals

Pub.L. 110–234 repealed effective May 22, 2008, see Repeal of Duplicative Enactment by Pub.L. 110–246, § 4(a), set out in a note under 7 U.S.C.A. § 8701.

Prior Provisions

A prior section 1383, Act Aug. 14, 1935, c. 531, Title XVI, § 1603, as added July 25, 1962, Pub.L. 87–543, Title I, § 141(a), 76 Stat. 200, and amended July 30, 1965, Pub.L. 89–97, Title I, § 122, Title II, § 221(d)(4), Title IV, § 401(b), 79 Stat. 353, 359, 414; Jan. 2, 1968, Pub.L. 90–248, Title II, § 212(d), 81 Stat. 898; Oct. 20, 1972, Pub.L. 92–512, Title III, § 301(b), (d), 86 Stat. 946, 947, which, prior to the general revision of Title XVI of the Social Security Act by Pub.L. 92–603, § 301, related to the determination of amounts payable to the States, is now set out as a note under this section in view of its continued applicability to Puerto Rico, Guam, and the Virgin Islands.

Transfer of Functions

For abolition of Immigration and Naturalization Service (INS), transfer of functions, and treatment of related references, see note set out under 8 U.S.C.A. § 1551.

Application to Northern Mariana Islands

For applicability of this section to the Northern Mariana Islands, see section 502(a)(1) of the Covenant to Establish a Commonwealth of the Northern Mariana Islands in Political Union with the United States of America, as set forth in Pub.L. 94–241, Mar. 24, 1976, 90 Stat. 263, eff. Jan. 9, 1978, pursuant to Proc. No. 4534, Oct. 24, 1977, 42 F.R. 6593, set out as notes under section 1681 of Title 48, Territories and Insular Possessions.

Demonstration Program to Assist Homeless Individuals

Section 9117 of Pub.L. 100–203, as amended Pub.L. 104–66, Title I, § 1061(e), Dec. 21, 1995, 109 Stat. 720, provided that:

"(a) In general.—The Secretary of Health and Human Services (in this section referred to as the 'Secretary') is authorized to make grants to States for projects designed to demonstrate and test the feasibility of special procedures and services to ensure that homeless individuals are provided SSI and other benefits under the Social Security Act [this chapter] to which they are entitled and receive assistance in using such benefits to obtain permanent housing, food, and health care. Each project approved under this section shall meet such conditions and requirements, consistent with this section, as the Secretary shall prescribe.

"(b) **Scope of projects.**—Projects for which grants are made under this section shall include, more specifically, procedures and services to overcome barriers which prevent homeless individuals (particularly the chronically mentally ill) from receiving and appropriately using benefits, including—

"(1) the creation of cooperative approaches between the Social Security Administration, State and local governments, shelters for the homeless, and other providers of services to the homeless;

"(2) the establishment, where appropriate, of multi-agency SSI Outreach Teams (as described in subsection (c)) to facilitate communication between the agencies and staff involved in taking and processing claims for SSI and other benefits by the homeless who use shelters;

"(3) special efforts to identify homeless individuals who are potentially eligible for SSI or other benefits under the Social Security Act [this chapter];

"(4) the provision of special assistance to the homeless in applying for benefits, including assistance in obtaining and developing evidence of disability and supporting documentation for nondisability-related eligibility requirements;

"(5) the provision of special training and assistance to public and private agency staff, including shelter employees, on disability eligibility procedures and evidentiary requirements;

"(6) the provision of ongoing assistance to formerly homeless individuals to ensure their responding to information requests related to periodic redeterminations of eligibility for SSI and other benefits;

"(7) the provision of assistance in ensuring appropriate use of benefit funds for the purpose of enabling homeless individuals to obtain permanent housing, nutrition, and physical and mental health care, including the use, where appropriate, of the disabled individual's representative payee for case management services; and

"(8) such other procedures and services as the Secretary may approve.

"(c) **SSI outreach team projects.**—(1) If a State applies for funds under this section for the purpose of establishing a multi-agency SSI Outreach Team, the membership and functions of such Team shall be as follows (except as provided in paragraph (2)):

"(A) The membership of the Team shall include a social services case worker (or case workers, if necessary); a consultative medical examiner who is qualified to provide consultative examinations for the Disability Determination Service of the State; a disability examiner, from the State Disability Determination Service; and a claims representative from an office of the Social Security Administration.

"(B) The Team shall have designated members responsible for—

"(i) identification of homeless individuals who are potentially eligible for SSI or other benefits under the Social Security Act [this chapter];

"(ii) ensuring that such individuals understand their rights under the programs;

"(iii) assisting such individuals in applying for benefits, including assistance in obtaining and developing evidence and supporting documentation relating to disability- and nondisability-related eligibility requirements;

"(iv) arranging transportation and accompanying applicants to necessary examinations, if needed; and

"(v) providing for the tracking and monitoring of all claims for benefits by individuals under the project.

"(2) If the Secretary determines that an application by a State for an SSI Outreach Team Project under this section which proposes a membership and functions for such Team different from those prescribed in paragraph (1) but which is expected to be as effective, the Secretary [Commissioner of Social Security] may waive the requirements of such paragraph.

["(d) Repealed. Pub.L. 104–66, Title I, § 1061(e), Dec. 21, 1995, 109 Stat. 720]

"(e) **Authorization of appropriations.**—To carry out this section, there are authorized to be appropriated to the Secretary—

"(A) the sum of $1,250,000 for the fiscal year 1988;

"(B) the sum of $2,500,000 for the fiscal year 1989; and

"(C) such sums as may be necessary for each fiscal year thereafter."

[Functions of the Secretary of Health and Human Services under this subchapter and subchapter II of this chapter [42 U.S.C.A. § 401 et seq.] transferred to the Commissioner of Social Security, effective Mar. 31, 1995, pursuant to Pub.L. 103–296, Title II, §§ 105(a), 110(a), Aug. 15, 1994, 108 Stat. 1472, 1490.]

Deposit of Overpayments in General Fund of Treasury

Pub.L. 102–170, Title II, Nov. 26, 1991, 105 Stat. 1122, provided in part: "That for fiscal year 1992 and thereafter, all collections from repayments of overpayments shall be deposited in the general fund of the Treasury."

Hearing Examiners Appointed Prior to January 2, 1976

Pub.L. 95–216, Title III, § 371, Dec. 20, 1977, 91 Stat. 1559, provided that: "The persons who were appointed to serve as hearing examiners under section 1631(d)(2) of the Social Security Act [subsec. (d)(2) of this section] (as in effect prior to January 2, 1976), and who by section 3 of Public Law 94–202 [set out as a note hereunder] were deemed to be appointed under section 3105 of title 5, United States Code [section 3105 of Title 5, Government Organization and Employees] (with such appointments terminating no later than at the close of the period ending December 31, 1978), shall be deemed appointed to career-absolute positions as hearing examiners under and in accordance with section 3105 of title 5, United States Code, with the same authority and tenure (without regard to the expiration of such period) as hearing examiners appointed directly under such section 3105, and shall receive compensation at the same rate as hearing examiners appointed by the Secretary of Health, Education, and Welfare [now Secretary of Health and Human Services] directly under such section 3105. All of the provisions of title 5, United States Code [Title 5, Government Organization and Employees], and the regulations promulgated pursuant thereto, which are applicable to hearing examiners appointed under such section 3105, shall apply to the persons described in the preceding sentence."

[Functions of the Secretary of Health and Human Services under this subchapter and subchapter II of this chapter [42 U.S.C.A. § 401 et seq.] transferred to the Commissioner of Social Security, effective Mar. 31, 1995, pursuant to Pub.L.

103–296, Title II, §§ 105(a), 110(a), Aug. 15, 1994, 108 Stat. 1472, 1490.]

Section 3 of Pub.L. 94–202 provided that: "The persons appointed under section 1631(d)(2) of the Social Security Act [subsec. (d)(2) of this section] (as in effect prior to the enactment of this Act) to serve as hearing examiners in hearings under section 1631(c) of such Act [subsec. (c) of this section] may conduct hearings under titles II, XVI, and XVIII of the Social Security Act [subchapters II, XVI, and XVIII of this chapter] if the Secretary of Health, Education, and Welfare [now Secretary of Health and Human Services] finds it will promote the achievement of the objectives of such titles [subchapters], notwithstanding the fact that their appointments were made without meeting the requirements for hearing examiners appointed under section 3105 of title 5, United States Code but their appointments shall terminate not later than at the close of the period ending December 31, 1978, and during that period they shall be deemed to be hearing examiners appointed under such section 3105 and subject as such to subchapter II of chapter 5 of title 5, United States Code, to the second sentence of such section 3105, and to all of the other provisions of such title 5 which apply to hearing examiners appointed under such section 3105."

[Functions of the Secretary of Health and Human Services under this subchapter and subchapter II of this chapter [42 U.S.C.A. § 401 et seq.] transferred to the Commissioner of Social Security, effective Mar. 31, 1995, pursuant to Pub.L. 103–296, Title II, §§ 105(a), 110(a), Aug. 15, 1994, 108 Stat. 1472, 1490.]

Institution of Notification System

For provisions requiring the Secretary to institute the system of notification required by subsec. (c) as soon as practicable after Oct. 9, 1984, see section 6(c) of Pub.L. 98–460, set out as a note under section 1383b of this title.

[Functions of the Secretary of Health and Human Services under this subchapter and subchapter II of this chapter transferred to the Commissioner of Social Security, effective Mar. 31, 1995, pursuant to Pub.L. 103–296, Title II, §§ 105(a), 110(a), Aug. 15, 1994, 108 Stat. 1472, 1490.]

Notification of Adjustment of Benefits by Secretary [Commissioner of Social Security]

Section 2612(b) of Pub.L. 98–369 provided that: "If an adjustment referred to in section 1631(b)(1) of the Social Security Act [subsec. (b)(1) of this section] is in effect with respect to an individual or eligible spouse on the effective date of this subsection [July 18, 1984], and the amount of such adjustment for a month is greater than the amount described in section 1631(b)(1)(B)(ii) of such Act [subsec. (b)(1)(B)(ii) of this section] as added by subsection (a), the Secretary shall notify the individual whose benefits are being adjusted, in writing, of his or her right to have the adjustment reduced to the amount described in such section 1631(b)(1)(B)(ii)."

[Functions of the Secretary of Health and Human Services under this subchapter and subchapter II of this chapter [42 U.S.C.A. § 401 et seq.] transferred to the Commissioner of Social Security, effective Mar. 31, 1995, pursuant to Pub.L. 103–296, Title II, §§ 105(a), 110(a), Aug. 15, 1994, 108 Stat. 1472, 1490.]

Opportunity for Individuals Receiving Benefits to Make Election for Type of Notice of Hearing or Other Official Action

Section 9111(a)(2) of Pub.L. 100–203 provided that: "Not later than one year after the date on which the amendment made by paragraph (1) [adding subsec. (*l*) of this section] becomes effective [July 1, 1988], the Secretary of Health and Human Services shall provide every individual receiving benefits under title XVI of the Social Security Act [this subchapter] on the basis of blindness an opportunity to make an election under section 1631(*l*)(1) of such Act [subsec. (*l*) of this section] (as added by such amendment)."

[Functions of the Secretary of Health and Human Services under this subchapter and subchapter II of this chapter [42 U.S.C.A. § 401 et seq.] transferred to the Commissioner of Social Security, effective Mar. 31, 1995, pursuant to Pub.L. 103–296, Title II, §§ 105(a), 110(a), Aug. 15, 1994, 108 Stat. 1472, 1490.]

Payment of Costs of Rehabilitation Services

Amendment to sections 422 and 1382d of this title by section 11(a), (b) of Pub.L. 98–360 to apply with respect to individuals receiving benefits as a result of subsec. (a)(6) of this section, see section 11(c) of Pub.L. 98–360, set out as a note under section 422 of this title.

Payment of Travel Expenses

Pub.L. 102–394, Title II, Oct. 6, 1992, 106 Stat. 1807, provided in part: "That for fiscal year 1993 and thereafter, travel expense payments under section 1631(h) of such Act [subsec. (h) of this section] for travel to hearings may be made only when travel of more than seventy-five miles is required [.]"

Similar provisions were contained in the following prior appropriation Acts:

Pub.L. 102–170, Title II, Nov. 26, 1991, 105 Stat. 1122.

Pub.L. 101–517, Title II, Nov. 5, 1990, 104 Stat. 2204.

Pub.L. 101–166, Title II, Nov. 21, 1989, 103 Stat. 1173.

Pub.L. 100–436, Title II, Sept. 20, 1988, 102 Stat. 1695.

Pub.L. 100–202, § 101(h) [Title II], Dec. 22, 1987, 101 Stat. 1329–270.

Pub.L. 99–591, § 101(i) [H.R. 5233, Title II], Oct. 30, 1986, 100 Stat. 3341—287.

Pub.L. 99–500, § 101(i) [H.R. 5233, Title II], Oct. 18, 1986, 100 Stat. 1783—287.

Pub.L. 99–178, Title II, § 200, Dec. 12, 1985, 99 Stat. 1116.

Pub.L. 98–619, Title II, § 200, Nov. 8, 1984, 98 Stat. 1891.

Pub.L. 98–139, Title II, § 200, Oct. 31, 1983, 97 Stat. 884.

Pub.L. 97–377, Title I, § 101(e)(1), Dec. 21, 1982, 96 Stat. 1891.

Pub.L. 97–92, § 101(a) [H.R. 4560, Title II], Dec. 15, 1981, 95 Stat. 1183.

Presumptive Disability Benefits; Time Extension

Pub.L. 93–256, § 1, Mar. 28, 1974, 88 Stat. 52, provided: "That any individual who would be considered disabled under section 1614(a)(3)(E) of the Social Security Act [section 1382c(a)(3)(E) of this title] except that he did not receive aid under the appropriate State plan for at least one month prior to July 1973 may be considered to be presumptively disabled under section 1631(a)(4)(B) of that Act [subsec. (a)(4)(B) of this section] and may be paid supplemental security income benefits under title XVI of that Act [this subchapter] on the basis of such presumptive disability, and State supplementary payments under section 212 of Public Law 93–66 [set out as a note under section 1382 of this title] as though he had been determined to be disabled within the meaning of section 1614(a)(3) of the Social Security Act [section 1382c(a)(3) of this title], for any month in calendar year 1974 for which it has been determined that he is otherwise eligible for such benefits, without regard to the three-month limitation in section 1631(a)(4)(B) of that Act [subsec. (a)(4)(B) of this section] on the period for which benefits may be paid to presumptively disabled individuals, except that no such benefits may be paid on the basis of such presumptive disability for any month after the month in which the Secretary of Health, Education, and Welfare [now Secretary of Health and Human Services] has made a determination as to whether such individual is disabled, as defined in section 1614(a)(3)(A) of that Act [section 1382c(a)(3)(A) of this title]."

[Functions of the Secretary of Health and Human Services under this subchapter and subchapter II of this chapter [42 U.S.C.A. § 401 et seq.] transferred to the Commissioner of Social Security, effective Mar. 31, 1995, pursuant to Pub.L. 103–296, Title II, §§ 105(a), 110(a), Aug. 15, 1994, 108 Stat. 1472, 1490.]

Puerto Rico, Guam, and Virgin Islands

Enactment of section 1603 of the Social Security Act [this section] by Pub.L. 92–603, eff. Jan. 1, 1974, was not applicable to Puerto Rico, Guam and the Virgin Islands. See section 303(b) of Pub.L. 92–603, set out as a note under section 301 of this title. Therefore, as to Puerto Rico, Guam, and the Virgin Islands, section 1603 of the Social Security Act [this section] as it existed prior to reenactment by Pub.L. 92–603, and as amended, continues to apply and reads as follows:

§ 1383. Payments to States; quarterly expenditures to exceed average of total expenditures for each quarter of fiscal year ending June 30, 1965

(a) From the sums appropriated therefor, the Commissioner of Social Security shall pay to each State which has a plan approved under this subchapter for each quarter, beginning with the quarter commencing October 1, 1962—

(1) Repealed. Pub.L. 97–35, Title XXI, § 2184(d)(5)(A), Aug. 13, 1981, 95 Stat. 818

(2) In the case of Puerto Rico, the Virgin Islands, and Guam, an amount equal to—

(A) one-half of the total of the sums expended during such quarter as aid to the aged, blind, or disabled under the State plan, not counting so much of any expenditure with respect to any month as exceeds $37.50 multiplied by the total number of recipients of aid to the aged, blind, or disabled for such month; plus

(B) one-half of the amount by which such expenditures exceed the maximum which may be counted under clause (A), not counting so much of any expenditure with respect to any month as exceeds the product of $45 multiplied by the total number of such recipients of aid to the aged, blind, or disabled for such month; and

(3) Repealed. Pub.L. 97–35, Title XXI, § 2184(d)(5)(A), Aug. 13, 1981, 95 Stat. 818

(4) In the case of any State, an amount equal to 50 percent of the total amounts expended during such quarter as found necessary by the Commissioner of Social Security for the proper and efficient administration of the State plan.

(b)(1) Prior to the beginning of each quarter, the Commissioner of Social Security shall estimate the amount to which a State will be entitled under subsection (a) of this section for such quarter, such estimates to be based on (A) a report filed by the State containing its estimate of the total sum to be expended in such quarter in accordance with the provisions of such subsection, and stating the amount appropriated or made available by the State and its political subdivisions for such expenditures in such quarter, and if such amount is less than the State's proportionate share of the total sum of such estimated expenditures, the source or sources from which the different is expected to be derived, and (B) such other investigation as the Commissioner of Social Security may find necessary.

(2) The Commissioner of Social Security shall then pay, in such installments as the Commissioner may determine, to the State the amount so estimated, reduced or increased to the extent of any overpayment or underpayment which the Commissioner of Social Security determines was made under this section to such State for any prior quarter and with respect to which adjustment has not already been made under this subsection.

(3) The pro rata share to which the United States is equitably entitled, as determined by the Commissioner of Social Security, of the net amount recovered during any quarter by the State or any political subdivision thereof with respect to aid or assistance furnished under the State plan, but excluding any amount of such aid or assistance recovered from the estate of a deceased recipient which is not in excess of the amount expended by the State or any political subdivision thereof for the funeral expenses of the deceased, shall be considered an overpayment to be adjusted under this subsection.

(4) Upon the making of any estimate by the Commissioner of Social Security under this subsection, any appropriations available for payments under this section shall be deemed obligated.

(Aug. 14, 1935, c. 531, Title XVI, § 1603, as added July 25, 1962, Pub.L. 87–543, Title I, § 141(a), 76 Stat. 200, and amended July 30, 1965, Pub.L. 89–97, Title I, § 122, Title II, § 221(d)(4), Title IV, § 401(b), 79 Stat. 353, 359, 414; Jan. 2, 1968, Pub.L. 90–248, Title II, § 212(d), 81 Stat. 898; Oct. 20, 1972, Pub.L. 92–512, Title III, § 301(b), (d), 86 Stat. 946, 947; Jan. 4, 1975, Pub.L. 93–647, §§ 3(e)(2), 5(e), 88 Stat. 2349, 2350; Aug. 13 1981, Pub.L. 97–35, Title XXI, § 2184(d)(5), Title XXIII, § 2353(m)(2), (3), 95 Stat. 818, 873; Title I, § 121(b)(4), Nov. 6, 1986, Pub.L. 99–603, 100 Stat. 3391; Aug. 10, 1993, Pub.L. 103–66, Title XIII, § 13741(b), 107 Stat. 663; Aug. 15, 1994, Pub.L. 103–296, Title I, § 107(a)(4), 108 Stat. 1478.)

[Amendment by section 107(a)(4) of Pub.L. 103–296 effective Mar. 31, 1995, see section 110 of Pub.L. 103–296, set out as a note under section 401 of this title.]

[Amendment by Pub.L. 103–66 effective with respect to calendar quarters beginning on or after Apr. 1, 1994, with special rule in the case of States whose legislatures meet biennially and do not have regular sessions scheduled in calendar year 1994, see section 13741(c) of Pub.L. 103–66, set out as a note under section 303 of this title.]

[Amendment by Pub.L. 99–603 effective Oct. 1, 1987, see section 121(c)(2) of Pub.L. 92–603, set out as a note under section 502 of this title.]

[Functions of the Secretary of Health and Human Services under this subchapter and subchapter II of this chapter [42 U.S.C.A. § 401 et seq.] transferred to the Commissioner of Social Security, effective Mar. 31, 1995, pursuant to Pub.L. 103–296, Title II, §§ 105(a), 110(a), Aug. 15, 1994, 108 Stat. 1472, 1490.]

Regulations

Section 222 of Pub.L. 104–193 provided that: "Within 3 months after the date of the enactment of this Act [Aug. 22, 1996], the Commissioner of Social Security shall prescribe such regulations as may be necessary to implement the amendments made by this subtitle [Pub.L. 104–193, Title II, Subtitle C, §§ 221, 222, Aug. 22, 1996, 110 Stat. 2196, 2197, amending this section and enacting provisions set out as notes under this section]."

Reimbursement for Erroneous State Supplementary Payments; Authorization of Appropriations

Pub.L. 95–216, Title IV, § 405, Dec. 20, 1977, 91 Stat. 1564, provided that:

"(a) Notwithstanding any other provision of law, the Secretary of Health, Education, and Welfare [now Secretary of Health and Human Services] is authorized and directed to pay to each State an amount equal to the amount expended by such State for erroneous supplementary payments to aged, blind, or disabled individuals whenever, and to the extent to which, the Secretary through an audit by the Department of Health, Education, and Welfare [now Department of Health and Human Services] which has been reviewed and concurred in by the Inspector General of such department [Administration] determines that—

"(1) such amount was paid by such State as a supplementary payment during the calendar year 1974 pursuant to an agreement between the State and the Secretary required by section 212 of the Act entitled 'An Act to extend the Renegotiation Act of 1951 for one year, and for other purposes', approved July 9, 1973 [set out as a note under § 1382 of this title], or such amount was paid by such State as an optional State supplementation, as defined in § 1616 of the Social Security Act [§ 1382 of this title], during the calendar year 1974,

"(2) the erroneous payments were the result of good faith reliance by such State upon erroneous or incomplete information supplied by the Department of Health, Education, and Welfare [now Department of Health and Human Services], through the State data exchange, or good faith reliance upon incorrect supplemental security income benefit payments made by such department, and

"(3) recovery of the erroneous payments by such State would be impossible or unreasonable.

"(b) There are authorized to be appropriated such sums as are necessary to carry out the provisions of this section."

[Functions of the Secretary of Health and Human Services under this subchapter and subchapter II of this chapter [42 U.S.C.A. § 401 et seq.] transferred to the Commissioner of Social Security, effective Mar. 31, 1995, pursuant to Pub.L. 103–296, Title II, §§ 105(a), 110(a), Aug. 15, 1994, 108 Stat. 1472, 1490.]

Study of Desirability and Feasibility of Special Notices of Hearings and Other Actions to Other Individuals Unable to Read

Section 9111(b) of Pub.L. 100–203, provided that: "The Secretary of Health and Human Services shall study the desirability and feasibility of extending special or supplementary notices of the type provided to blind individuals by section 1631(*l*) of the Social Security Act [subsec. (*l*) of this section] (as added by subsection (a) of this section) to other individuals who may lack the ability to read and comprehend regular written notices, and shall report the results of such study to the Congress, along with such recommendations as may be appropriate, within 12 months after the date of the enactment of this Act [Dec. 22, 1987]."

[Functions of the Secretary of Health and Human Services under this subchapter and subchapter II of this chapter [42 U.S.C.A. § 401 et seq.] transferred to the Commissioner of Social Security, effective Mar. 31, 1995, pursuant to Pub.L. 103–296, Title II, §§ 105(a), 110(a), Aug. 15, 1994, 108 Stat. 1472, 1490.]

§ 1383a. Penalties for fraud

(a) In general

Whoever—

(1) knowingly and willfully makes or causes to be made any false statement or representation of a material fact in any application for any benefit under this subchapter,

(2) at any time knowingly and willfully makes or causes to be made any false statement or representation of a material fact for use in determining rights to any such benefit,

(3) having knowledge of the occurrence of any event affecting (A) his initial or continued right to any such benefit, or (B) the initial or continued right to any such benefit of any other individual in whose behalf he has applied for or is receiving such benefit, conceals or fails to disclose such event with an intent fraudulently to secure such benefit either in a greater amount or quantity than is due or when no such benefit is authorized,

(4) having made application to receive any such benefit for the use and benefit of another and having received it, knowingly and willfully converts such benefit or any part thereof to a use other than for the use and benefit of such other person, or

(5) conspires to commit any offense described in any of paragraphs (1) through (3),

shall be fined under Title 18, imprisoned not more than 5 years, or both, except that in the case of a person who receives a fee or other income for services performed in connection with any determination with respect to benefits under this subchapter (including a claimant representative, translator, or current or former employee of the Social Security Administration), or who is a physician or other health care provider who submits, or causes the submission of, medical or other evidence in connection with any such determination, such person shall be guilty of a felony and upon conviction thereof shall be fined under Title 18, or imprisoned for not more than ten years, or both.

(b) Restitution

(1) Any Federal court, when sentencing a defendant convicted of an offense under subsection (a), may order, in addition to or in lieu of any other penalty authorized by law, that the defendant make restitution

to the Commissioner of Social Security, in any case in which such offense results in—

(A) the Commissioner of Social Security making a benefit payment that should not have been made, or

(B) an individual suffering a financial loss due to the defendant's violation of subsection (a) in his or her capacity as the individual's representative payee appointed pursuant to section 1383(a)(2) of this title.

(2) Sections 3612, 3663, and 3664 of Title 18 shall apply with respect to the issuance and enforcement of orders of restitution under this subsection. In so applying such sections, the Commissioner of Social Security shall be considered the victim.

(3) If the court does not order restitution, or orders only partial restitution, under this subsection, the court shall state on the record the reasons therefor.

(4)(A) Except as provided in subparagraph (B), funds paid to the Commissioner of Social Security as restitution pursuant to a court order shall be deposited as miscellaneous receipts in the general fund of the Treasury.

(B) In the case of funds paid to the Commissioner of Social Security pursuant to paragraph (1)(B), the Commissioner of Social Security shall certify for payment to the individual described in such paragraph an amount equal to the lesser of the amount of the funds so paid or the individual's outstanding financial loss as described in such paragraph, except that such amount may be reduced by any overpayment of benefits owed under this subchapter, subchapter II, or subchapter VIII by the individual.

(c) Prohibition on certification as representative payee

Any person or entity convicted of a violation of subsection (a) of this section or of section 408 of this title may not be certified as a representative payee under section 1383(a)(2) of this title.

(Aug. 14, 1935, c. 531, Title XVI, § 1632, as added Pub.L. 92–603, Title III, § 301, Oct. 30, 1972, 86 Stat. 1478; amended Pub.L. 98–460, § 16(c)(1), Oct. 9, 1984, 98 Stat. 1810; Pub.L. 103–296, Title II, § 206(c)(1), (2), Aug. 15, 1994, 108 Stat. 1513; Pub.L. 108–203, Title II, § 209(c), Mar. 2, 2004, 118 Stat. 515; Pub.L. 114–74, Title VIII, § 813(a)(3), (b)(3), Nov. 2, 2015, 129 Stat. 603.)

HISTORICAL AND STATUTORY NOTES

References in Text

This subchapter, referred to in text, originally read "this title", meaning the Social Security Act, Act Aug. 14, 1935, c. 531, Title XVI, as added Oct. 30, 1972, Pub.L. 92–603, Title III, § 301, 86 Stat. 1465, as amended, which is classified as this subchapter, 42 U.S.C.A. § 1381 et seq.

Subchapter II of this chapter, referred to in subsec. (b)(4)(B), originally read "title II", meaning the Social Security Act, Act Aug. 14, 1935, c. 531, Title II, 49 Stat. 622, as amended, which is classified as subchapter II of this chapter, 42 U.S.C.A. § 401 et seq.

Subchapter VIII of this chapter, referred to in subsec. (b)(4)(B), originally read "title VIII", meaning the Social Security Act, Act Aug. 14, 1935, c. 531, Title VIII, as added Dec. 14, 1999, Pub.L. 106–169, Title II, § 251(a), 113 Stat. 1844, as amended, which is classified as subchapter VIII of this chapter, 42 U.S.C.A. § 1001 et seq.

Effective and Applicability Provisions

2004 Acts. The amendments made by section 209(c) of Pub.L. 108–203 applicable with respect to violations occurring on or after Mar. 2, 2004, see Pub.L. 108–203, § 209(d), set out as a note under 42 U.S.C.A. § 408.

1994 Acts. Section 206(c)(3) of Pub.L. 103–296 provided that: "The amendments made by this subsection [amending this section] shall apply to conduct occurring on or after October 1, 1994."

1984 Acts. Amendment by Pub. L. 98–460 effective Oct. 9, 1984, and applicable with respect to violations occurring on or after such date, see section 16(d) of Pub. L. 98–460, set out as a note under section 405 of this title.

1972 Acts. Section 301 of Pub.L. 92–603 provided that this section is effective Jan. 1, 1974.

Application to Northern Mariana Islands

For applicability of this section to the Northern Mariana Islands, see section 502(a)(1) of the Covenant to Establish a Commonwealth of the Northern Mariana Islands in Political Union with the United States of America, as set forth in Pub.L. 94–241, Mar. 24, 1976, 90 Stat. 263, eff. Jan. 9, 1978, pursuant to Proc. No. 4534, Oct. 24, 1977, 42 F.R. 6593, set out as notes under section 1681 of Title 48, Territories and Insular Possessions.

Puerto Rico, Guam, and Virgin Islands

Enactment of provisions of Pub.L. 92–603, eff. Jan. 1, 1974, not applicable to Puerto Rico, Guam, and the Virgin Islands, see section 303(b) of Pub.L. 92–603, set out as a note under section 301 of this title.

§ 1383b. Administration

(a) Authority of Commissioner

Subject to subsection (b), the Commissioner of Social Security may make such administrative and other arrangements (including arrangements for the determination of blindness and disability under section 1382c(a)(2) and (3) of this title in the same manner and subject to the same conditions as provided with respect to disability determinations under section 421 of this title) as may be necessary or appropriate to carry out the Commissioner's functions under this subchapter.

(b) Examination to determine blindness

In determining, for purposes of this subchapter, whether an individual is blind, there shall be an examination of such individual by a physician skilled in the diseases of the eye or by an optometrist, whichever the individual may select.

(c) Notification of review

(1) In any case in which the Commissioner of Social Security initiates a review under this subchapter, similar to the continuing disability reviews authorized for purposes of subchapter II under section 421(i) of this title, the Commissioner of Social Security shall notify the individual whose case is to be reviewed in the same manner as required under section 421(i)(4) of this title.

(2) For suspension of continuing disability reviews and other reviews under this subchapter similar to reviews under section 421 of this title in the case of an individual using a ticket to work and self-sufficiency, see section 1320b–19(i) of this title.

(d) Regulations regarding completion of plans for achieving self-support

The Commissioner of Social Security shall establish by regulation criteria for time limits and other criteria related to individuals' plans for achieving self-support, that take into account—

(1) the length of time that the individual will need to achieve the individual's employment goal (within such reasonable period as the Commissioner of Social Security may establish); and

(2) other factors determined by the Commissioner of Social Security to be appropriate.

(e) Review of State agency blindness and disability determinations

(1) The Commissioner of Social Security shall review determinations, made by State agencies pursuant to subsection (a) in connection with applications for benefits under this subchapter on the basis of blindness or disability, that individuals who have attained 18 years of age are blind or disabled as of a specified onset date. The Commissioner of Social Security shall review such a determination before any action is taken to implement the determination.

(2)(A) In carrying out paragraph (1), the Commissioner of Social Security shall review—

(i) at least 20 percent of all determinations referred to in paragraph (1) that are made in fiscal year 2006;

(ii) at least 40 percent of all such determinations that are made in fiscal year 2007; and

(iii) at least 50 percent of all such determinations that are made in fiscal year 2008 or thereafter.

(B) In carrying out subparagraph (A), the Commissioner of Social Security shall, to the extent feasible, select for review the determinations which the Commissioner of Social Security identifies as being the most likely to be incorrect.

(Aug. 14, 1935, c. 531, Title XVI, § 1633, as added Pub.L. 92–603, Title III, § 301, Oct. 30, 1972, 86 Stat. 1478; amended Pub.L. 93–66, Title II, § 214, July 9, 1973, 87 Stat. 158; Pub.L. 98–460, § 6(b), Oct. 9, 1984, 98 Stat. 1802; Pub.L. 103–296, Title I, § 107(a)(4), Title II, § 203(a), Aug. 15, 1994, 108 Stat. 1478, 1508; Pub.L. 106–170, Title I, § 101(b)(2)(D), Dec. 17, 1999, 113 Stat. 1874; Pub.L. 109–171, Title VII, § 7501, Feb. 8, 2006, 120 Stat. 154.)

HISTORICAL AND STATUTORY NOTES

Effective and Applicability Provisions

2006 Acts. Except as otherwise provided in Title VII of Pub.L. 109–171, amendments by Title VII of Pub.L. 109–171 effective as if enacted on Oct. 1, 2005, see Pub.L. 109–171, § 7701, set out as a note under 42 U.S.C.A. § 603.

1999 Acts. Amendment by section 101(b) of Pub.L. 106–170 effective with the first month following 1 year after December 17, 1999, subject to graduated implementation of program provisions of section 101(d) of Pub.L. 106–170 [set out as a note under section 1320b–19 of this title], see section 101(c) of Pub.L. 106–170, set out as a note under section 1320b–19 of this title.

1994 Acts. Amendment by section 107(a)(4) of Pub.L. 103–296 effective Mar. 31, 1995, see section 110 of Pub.L. 103–296, set out as a note under section 401 of this title.

Section 203(b) of Pub.L. 103–296 provided that: "The amendment made by subsection (a) [amending this section] shall take effect on January 1, 1995."

1972 Acts. Section 301 of Pub.L. 92–603 provided that this section is effective Jan. 1, 1974.

Application to Northern Mariana Islands

For applicability of this section to the Northern Mariana Islands, see section 502(a)(1) of the Covenant to Establish a Commonwealth of the Northern Mariana Islands in Political Union with the United States of America, as set forth in Pub.L. 94–241, Mar. 24, 1976, 90 Stat. 263, eff. Jan. 9, 1978, pursuant to Proc. No. 4534, Oct. 24, 1977, 42 F.R. 6593, set out as notes under section 1681 of Title 48, Territories and Insular Possessions.

Federal Program of Supplemental Security Income; Preference for Present State and Local Employees

Section 213 of Pub.L. 93–66 provided that: "The Secretary of Health, Education, and Welfare [now Secretary of Health and Human Services], in the recruitment and selection for employment of personnel whose services will be utilized in the administration of the Federal program of supplemental security income for the aged, blind, and disabled (established by title XVI of the Social Security Act [this subchapter]), shall give a preference, as among applicants whose qualifications are reasonably equal (subject to any preferences conferred by law or regulation on individuals who have been Federal employees and have been displaced from such employment), to applicants for employment who are or were employed in the administration of any State program approved under title I, X, XIV, or XVI of such Act [subchapter I, X, XIV, or XVI of this chapter] and are or were involuntarily displaced from their employment as a result of the displacement of such State program by such Federal program."

Institution of Notification System

For provisions requiring the Secretary to institute the system of notification required by subsec. (c) of this section as soon as practicable after Oct. 9, 1984, see section 6(c) of Pub.L. 98–460, set out as a note under section 421 of this title.

Puerto Rico, Guam, and Virgin Islands

Enactment of provisions of Pub.L. 92–603, eff. Jan. 1, 1974, not applicable to Puerto Rico, Guam, and the Virgin Islands, see section 303(b) of Pub.L. 92–603, set out as a note under section 301 of this title.

§ 1383c. Eligibility for medical assistance of aged, blind, or disabled individuals under State's medical assistance plan

(a) Determination by Commissioner pursuant to agreement between Commissioner and State; costs

The Commissioner of Social Security may enter into an agreement with any State which wishes to do so under which the Commissioner will determine eligibility for medical assistance in the case of aged, blind, or disabled individuals under such State's plan approved under subchapter XIX. Any such agreement shall provide for payments by the State, for use by the Commissioner of Social Security in carrying out the agreement, of an amount equal to one-half of the cost of carrying out the agreement, but in computing such cost with respect to individuals eligible for benefits under this subchapter, the Commissioner of Social Security shall include only those costs which are additional to the costs incurred in carrying out this subchapter.

(b) Preservation of benefit status for certain disabled widows and widowers

(1) An eligible disabled widow or widower (described in paragraph (2)) who is entitled to a widow's or widower's insurance benefit based on a disability for any month under section 402(e) or (f) of this title but is not eligible for benefits under this subchapter in that month, and who applies for the protection of this subsection under paragraph (3), shall be deemed for purposes of subchapter XIX to be an individual with respect to whom benefits under this subchapter are paid in that month if he or she—

(A) has been continuously entitled to such widow's or widower's insurance benefits from the first month for which the increase described in paragraph (2)(C) was reflected in such benefits through the month involved, and

(B) would be eligible for benefits under this subchapter in the month involved if the amount of the increase described in paragraph (2)(C) in his or her widow's or widower's insurance benefits, and any subsequent cost-of-living adjustments in such benefits under section 415(i) of this title, were disregarded.

(2) For purposes of paragraph (1), the term "eligible disabled widow or widower" means an individual who—

(A) was entitled to a monthly insurance benefit under subchapter II for December 1983,

(B) was entitled to a widow's or widower's insurance benefit based on a disability under section 402(e) or (f) of this title for January 1984 and with respect to whom a benefit under this subchapter was paid in that month, and

(C) because of the increase in the amount of his or her widow's or widower's insurance benefits which resulted from the amendments made by section 134 of the Social Security Amendments of 1983 (Public Law 98–21) (eliminating the additional reduction factor for disabled widows and widowers under age 60), was ineligible for benefits under this subchapter in the first month in which such increase was paid to him or her (and in which a retroactive payment of such increase for prior months was not made).

(3) This subsection shall only apply to an individual who files a written application for protection under this subsection, in such manner and form as the Commissioner of Social Security may prescribe, no later than July 1, 1988.

(4) For purposes of this subsection, the term "benefits under this subchapter" includes payments of the type described in section 1382e(a) of this title or of the type described in section 212(a) of Public Law 93–66.

(c) Loss of benefits upon entitlement to child's insurance benefits based on disability

If any individual who has attained the age of 18 and is receiving benefits under this subchapter on the basis of blindness or a disability which began before he or she attained the age of 22—

(1) becomes entitled, on or after the effective date of this subsection, to child's insurance benefits which are payable under section 402(d) of this title on the basis of such disability or to an increase in the amount of the child's insurance benefits which are so payable, and

(2) ceases to be eligible for benefits under this subchapter because of such child's insurance benefits or because of the increase in such child's insurance benefits,

such individual shall be treated for purposes of subchapter XIX as receiving benefits under this subchapter so long as he or she would be eligible for benefits under this subchapter in the absence of such child's insurance benefits or such increase.

(d) Retention of medicaid when SSI benefits are lost upon entitlement to early widow's or widower's insurance benefits

(1) This subsection applies with respect to any person who—

(A) applies for and obtains benefits under subsection (e) or (f) of section 402 of this title (or under any other subsection of section 402 of this title if such person is also eligible for benefits under such subsection (e) or (f)) being then not entitled to hospital insurance benefits under part A of subchapter XVIII, and

(B) is determined to be ineligible (by reason of the receipt of such benefits under section 402 of this title) for supplemental security income benefits under this subchapter or for State supplementary payments of the type described in section 1382e(a) of this title (or payments of the type described in section 212(a) of Public Law 93–66).

(2) For purposes of subchapter XIX, each person with respect to whom this subsection applies—

(A) shall be deemed to be a recipient of supplemental security income benefits under this subchapter if such person received such a benefit for the month before the month in which such person began to receive a benefit described in paragraph (1)(A), and

(B) shall be deemed to be a recipient of State supplementary payments of the type referred to in section 1382e(a) of this title (or payments of the type described in section 212(a) of Public Law 93–66) if such person received such a payment for the month before the month in which such person began to receive a benefit described in paragraph (1)(A),

for so long as such person (i) would be eligible for such supplemental security income benefits, or such State supplementary payments (or payments of the type described in section 212(a) of Public Law 93–66), in the absence of benefits described in paragraph (1)(A), and (ii) is not entitled to hospital insurance benefits under part A of subchapter XVIII.

(Aug. 14, 1935, c. 531, Title XVI, § 1634, as added Pub.L. 92–603, Title III, § 301, Oct. 30, 1972, 86 Stat. 1478; amended Pub.L. 99–272, Title XII, § 12202(a), Apr. 7, 1986, 100 Stat. 290; Pub.L. 99–643, § 6(a), Nov. 10, 1986, 100 Stat. 3578; Pub.L. 100–203, Title IX, §§ 9108, 9116(a), Dec. 22, 1987, 101 Stat. 1330–302, 1330–305; Pub.L. 101–508, Title V, § 5103(c)(1), Nov. 5, 1990, 104 Stat. 1388–251; Pub.L. 103–296, Title I, § 107(a)(4), Title II, § 201(b)(3)(D), Aug. 15, 1994, 108 Stat. 1478, 1504; Pub.L. 104–121, Title I, § 105(b)(4)(B), Mar. 29, 1996, 110 Stat. 854.)

HISTORICAL AND STATUTORY NOTES

References in Text

Section 134 of the Social Security Amendments of 1983 (Public Law 98–21), referred to in subsec. (b)(2)(C), is section 134 of Pub.L. 98–21, Title I, Apr. 20, 1983, 97 Stat. 97. Section 134(a), (b) of Pub.L. 98–21 amended section 402 of this title. Section 134(c) of Pub.L. 98–21 is set out as a note under section 402 of this title.

Section 212(a) of Public Law 93–66, referred to in subsecs. (b)(4), (d)(1)(B), and (2)(B), is section 212(a) of Pub.L. 93–66, Title II, July 9, 1973, 87 Stat. 155, as amended, which is set out as a note under section 1382 of this title.

The effective date of this subsection, referred to in subsec. (c)(1), is July 1, 1987, with an exception for State plans requiring State legislation. See section 10(b) of Pub.L. 99–643, set out as a note under section 1396a of this title.

Part A of subchapter XVIII of this chapter, referred to in subsec. (d), is classified to section 1395c et seq. of this title.

Codifications

Amendment by section 201(b)(3)(D) of Pub.L. 103–296 has been executed to this section as the probable intent of Congress notwithstanding directory language purporting to require the amendment of "(42 U.S.C. 13283c)".

Effective and Applicability Provisions

1996 Acts. Amendment by section 105(b)(4)(B) of Pub.L. 104–121 applicable to individual who applies for, or whose claim is adjudicated with respect to, benefits under this subchapter based on disability on or after Mar. 29, 1996, with certain conditions applying for benefits before Mar. 29, 1996, see section 105(b)(5) of Pub.L. 104–121, set out as a note under section 1382 of this title.

1994 Acts. Amendment by section 107(a)(4) of Pub.L. 103–296 effective Mar. 31, 1995, see section 110 of Pub.L. 103–296, set out as a note under section 401 of this title.

Amendment to this section by section 201(b)(3)(D) of Pub.L. 103–296 to apply with respect to supplemental security income benefits under this subchapter by reason of disability which are otherwise payable in months beginning after 180 days after Aug. 15, 1994, with the Secretary of Health and Human Services to issue regulations necessary to carry out such amendment not later than 180 days after Aug. 15, 1994, see section 201(b)(3)(E)(i) of Pub.L. 103–296, set out as a note under section 1382 of this title.

1990 Acts. Amendment by Pub.L. 101–508 applicable with respect to medical assistance provided after Dec. 1990, see section 5103(e)(1) of Pub.L. 101–508, set out as a note under section 402 of this title.

1987 Acts. Section 9108 of Pub.L. 100–203 provided that amendment of subsec. (b)(3) by section 9108 is effective July 1, 1987.

Section 9116(e) of Pub.L. 100–203 provided that: "The amendments made by subsection (a) [adding subsec. (d) of this section] shall apply with respect to any individual without regard to whether the determination of his or her ineligibility for supplemental security income benefits by reason of the receipt of benefits under section 202 of the Social Security Act [section 402 of this title] (as described in section 1634(d)(2) of such Act [subsec. (d)(2) of this section]) occurred before, on, or after the date of the enactment of this Act [Dec. 22, 1987]; but no individual shall be eligible for assistance under title XIX of such Act [subchapter XIX of this chapter] by reason of such amendments for any period before July 1, 1988."

1986 Acts. Amendment by Pub.L. 99–643 effective July 1, 1987, except for State plans requiring State legislation, see section 10(b) of Pub.L. 99–643, set out as a note under section 1396a of this title.

Section 12202(c) of Pub.L. 99–272 provided that: "The amendment made by subsection (a)(2) [adding subsec. (b) of this section] shall not have the effect of deeming an individual eligible for medical assistance for any month which begins less than two months after the date of the enactment of this Act [Apr. 7, 1986]."

1972 Acts. Section 301 of Pub.L. 92–603 provided that this section is effective Jan. 1, 1974.

Application to Northern Mariana Islands

For applicability of this section to the Northern Mariana Islands, see section 502(a)(1) of the Covenant to Establish a Commonwealth of the Northern Mariana Islands in Political Union with the United States of America, as set forth in Pub.L. 94–241, Mar. 24, 1976, 90 Stat. 263, eff. Jan. 9, 1978, pursuant to Proc. No. 4534, Oct. 24, 1977, 42 F.R. 6593, set out as notes under section 1681 of Title 48, Territories and Insular Possessions.

Identification of Potential Beneficiaries Under Subsection (b) of This Section

Section 12202(b) of Pub.L. 99–272 provided that:

"(1) As soon as possible after the date of the enactment of this Act [Apr. 7, 1986], the Secretary of Health and Human Services shall provide each State with the names of all individuals receiving widow's or widower's insurance benefits under subsection (e) or (f) of section 202 of the Social Security Act [section 402 of this title] based on a disability who might qualify for medical assistance under the plan of that State approved under title XIX of such Act [subchapter XIX of this chapter] by reason of the application of section 1634(b) of the Social Security Act [subsec. (b) of this section].

"(2) Each State shall—

"(A) using the information so provided and any other information it may have, promptly notify all individuals who may qualify for medical assistance under its plan by reason of such section 1634(b) [subsec. (b) of this section] of their right to make application for such assistance,

"(B) solicit their applications for such assistance, and

"(C) make the necessary determination of such individuals' eligibility for such assistance under such section and under such title XIX [subchapter XIX of this chapter]."

Notice of Possible Eligibility for Medicaid Assistance

Section 9116(b) of Pub.L. 100–203 provided that: "The Secretary of Health and Human Services, acting through the Social Security Administration, shall (within 3 months after the date of the enactment of this Act [Dec. 22, 1987]) issue a notice to all individuals who will have attained age 60 but not age 65 as of April 1, 1988, and who received supplemental security income benefits under title XVI of the Social Security Act [this subchapter] prior to attaining age 60 but lost those benefits by reason of the receipt of widow's or widower's insurance benefits (or other benefits as described in section 1634(d)(1) of that Act [subsec. (d)(1) of this section] as added by subsection (a) of this section) under title II of that Act [subchapter II of this chapter]. Each such notice shall set forth and explain the provisions of section 1634(d) of the Social Security Act (as so added) [subsec. (d) of this section] and shall inform the individual that he or she should contact the Secretary or the appropriate State agency concerning his or her possible eligibility for medical assistance benefits under such title XIX [subchapter XIX of this chapter]."

Puerto Rico, Guam, and Virgin Islands

Enactment of provisions of Pub.L. 92–603, eff. Jan. 1, 1974, not applicable to Puerto Rico, Guam, and the Virgin Islands, see section 303(b) of Pub.L. 92–603, set out as a note under section 301 of this title.

State determinations

Section 9116(c) of Pub.L. 100–203 provided that: "Any determination required under section 1634(d) of the Social Security Act [subsec. (d) of this section] with respect to whether an individual would be eligible for benefits under title XVI of such Act [this subchapter] (or State supplementary payments) in the absence of benefits under section 202 [section 402 of this title] shall be made by the appropriate State agency."

Section 6(b) of Pub.L. 99–643 provided that: "Any determination required under section 1634(c) of the Social Security Act [subsec. (c) of this section] with respect to whether an individual would be eligible for benefits under title XVI of such Act [this subchapter] in the absence of children's benefits (or an increase thereof) shall be made by the appropriate State agency."

§ 1383d. Outreach program for children

(a) Establishment

The Commissioner of Social Security shall establish and conduct an ongoing program of outreach to children who are potentially eligible for benefits under this subchapter by reason of disability or blindness.

(b) Requirements

Under this program, the Commissioner of Social Security shall—

(1) aim outreach efforts at populations for whom such efforts would be most effective; and

(2) work in cooperation with other Federal, State, and private agencies, and nonprofit organizations, which serve blind or disabled individuals and have knowledge of potential recipients of supplemental security income benefits, and with agencies and organizations (including school systems and public and private social service agencies) which focus on the needs of children.

(Aug. 14, 1935, c. 531, Title XVI, § 1635, as added Pub.L. 101–239, Title VIII, § 8008(a), Dec. 19, 1989, 103 Stat. 2463; amended Pub.L. 103–296, Title I, § 107(a)(4), Aug. 15, 1994, 108 Stat. 1478.)

HISTORICAL AND STATUTORY NOTES

Effective and Applicability Provisions

1994 Acts. Amendment by section 107(a)(4) of Pub.L. 103–296 effective Mar. 31, 1995, see section 110 of Pub.L. 103–296, set out as a note under section 401 of this title.

1989 Acts. Section 8008(b) of Pub.L. 101–239 provided that: "The amendment made by subsection (a) [enacting this section] shall take effect 3 months after the date of the enactment of this Act [Dec. 19, 1989]."

Application to Northern Mariana Islands

For applicability of this section to the Northern Mariana Islands, see section 502(a)(1) of the Covenant to Establish a Commonwealth of the Northern Mariana Islands in Political Union with the United States of America and Proc. No. 4534, Oct. 24, 1977, 42 F.R. 6593, set out as notes under 48 U.S.C.A. § 1801.

§ 1383e. Treatment referrals for individuals with alcoholism or drug addiction condition

In the case of any individual whose benefits under this subchapter are paid to a representative payee pursuant to section 1383(a)(2)(A)(ii)(II) of this title, the Commissioner of Social Security shall refer such individual to the appropriate State agency administering the State plan for substance abuse treatment services approved under subpart II of part B of title XIX of the Public Health Service Act (42 U.S.C. 300x–21 et seq.).

(Aug. 14, 1935, c. 531, Title XVI, § 1636, as added Pub.L. 104–121, Title I, § 105(b)(3), Mar. 29, 1996, 110 Stat. 854.)

HISTORICAL AND STATUTORY NOTES

References in Text

The Public Health Service Act, referred to in text, is Act July 1, 1944, c. 373, 58 Stat. 682, as amended. Subpart II of part B of title XIX of that Act is classified generally to subpart II of part B of subchapter XVII of chapter 6A of this title (section 300x–21 et seq.). For complete classification of this Act to the Code, see Short Title note set out under section 201 of this title and Tables.

Effective and Applicability Provisions

1996 Acts. Enactment by Pub.L. 104–121 applicable to benefits for which applications are filed after third month following March, 1996, see section 105(b)(5) of Pub.L. 104–121, set out as a note under section 1382 of this title.

§ 1383f. Annual report on program

(a) In general

Not later than May 30 of each year, the Commissioner of Social Security shall prepare and deliver a report annually to the President and the Congress regarding the program under this subchapter, including—

(1) a comprehensive description of the program;

(2) historical and current data on allowances and denials, including number of applications and allowance rates for initial determinations, reconsideration determinations, administrative law judge hearings, appeals council reviews, and Federal court decisions;

(3) historical and current data on characteristics of recipients and program costs, by recipient group (aged, blind, disabled adults, and disabled children);

(4) historical and current data on prior enrollment by recipients in public benefit programs, including State programs funded under part A of subchapter IV of this chapter and State general assistance programs;

(5) projections of future number of recipients and program costs, through at least 25 years;

(6) number of redeterminations and continuing disability reviews, and the outcomes of such redeterminations and reviews;

(7) data on the utilization of work incentives;

(8) detailed information on administrative and other program operation costs;

(9) summaries of relevant research undertaken by the Social Security Administration, or by other researchers;

(10) State supplementation program operations;

(11) a historical summary of statutory changes to this subchapter; and

(12) such other information as the Commissioner deems useful.

(b) Views of individual members of Social Security Advisory Board

Each member of the Social Security Advisory Board shall be permitted to provide an individual report, or a joint report if agreed, of views of the program under this subchapter, to be included in the annual report required under this section.

(Aug. 14, 1935, c. 531, Title XVI, § 1637, as added Pub.L. 104–193, Title II, § 231, Aug. 22, 1996, 110 Stat. 2197.)

HISTORICAL AND STATUTORY NOTES

References in Text

Part A of subchapter IV of this chapter, referred to in subsec. (a)(4), is classified to 42 U.S.C.A. § 601 et seq.

§ 1384. Omitted

HISTORICAL AND STATUTORY NOTES

Codifications

Section, Act Aug. 14, 1935, c. 531, Title XVI, § 1604, as added July 25, 1962, Pub.L. 87–543, Title I, § 141(a), 76 Stat. 204, related to operation of State plans, prior to the general revision of this subchapter by Pub.L. 92–603, Oct. 30, 1972, 86 Stat. 1465, eff. Jan. 1, 1974.

Puerto Rico, Guam, and Virgin Islands

Enactment of subchapter XVI of the Social Security Act [this subchapter] by section 301 of Pub.L. 92–603, eff. Jan. 1, 1974, was not applicable to Puerto Rico, Guam, and the Virgin Islands. See section 303(b) of Pub.L. 92–603, set out as a note under section 301 of this title. Therefore, as to Puerto Rico, Guam, and the Virgin Islands, section 1604 of the Social Security Act [this section] as it existed prior to reenactment of this subchapter by Pub.L. 92–603 continues to apply and reads as follows:

§ 1384. Operation of State plans

If the Commissioner of Social Security, after reasonable notice and opportunity for hearing to the State agency administering or supervising the administration of the State plan approved under this subchapter, finds—

(1) that the plan has been so changed that it no longer complies with the provisions of § 1382 of this title; or

(2) that in the administration of the plan there is a failure to comply substantially with any such provision;

the Commissioner of Social Security shall notify such State agency that further payments will not be made to the State (or, in the Commissioner's discretion, that payments will be limited to categories under or parts of the State plan not affected by such failure), until the Commissioner of Social Security is satisfied that there will no longer be any such failure to comply. Until the Commissioner is so satisfied the Commissioner shall make no further payments to such State (or shall limit payments to categories under or parts of the State plan not affected by such failure).

(Aug. 14, 1935, c. 531, Title XVI, § 1604, as added July 25, 1962, Pub.L. 87–543, Title I, § 141(a), 76 Stat. 204, and amended Pub.L. 103–296, Aug. 15, 1994, Title I, § 107(a)(4), 108 Stat. 1478.)

[Pub.L. 103–296, Title I, §§ 107(a)(4), 110(a), Aug. 15, 1994, 108 Stat. 1478, 1490, effective Mar. 31, 1995, substituted "Commissioner of Social Security" for "Secretary", "the Commissioner's" for "his", and "the Commissioner" for "he", wherever appearing.]

§ 1385. Omitted

HISTORICAL AND STATUTORY NOTES

Codifications

Section, Act Aug. 14, 1935, c. 531, Title XVI, § 1605, as added July 25, 1962, Pub.L. 87–543, Title I, § 141(a), 76 Stat. 204, and amended July 30, 1965, Pub.L. 89–97, Title II, §§ 221(d)(1), (2), 222(b), Title IV, § 402(b), 79 Stat. 358, 360, 416; Oct. 30, 1972, Pub.L. 92–603, Title IV, §§ 408(d), 409(d), 86 Stat. 1490, 1491, defined "aid to the aged, blind, or disabled" and "medical assistance for the aged", prior to general revision of this subchapter by Pub.L. 92–603, Oct. 30, 1972, 86 Stat. 1465, eff. Jan. 1, 1974.

Puerto Rico, Guam, and Virgin Islands

Enactment of subchapter XVI of the Social Security Act [this subchapter] by section 301 of Pub.L. 92–603, eff. Jan. 1, 1974, was not applicable to Puerto Rico, Guam, and the Virgin Islands. See section 303(b) of Pub.L. 92–603, set out as a note under section 301 of this title. Therefore, as to Puerto Rico, Guam, and the Virgin Islands, section 1605 of the Social Security Act [this section] as it existed prior to reenactment of this subchapter by Pub.L. 92–603, and as amended, continues to apply and to read as follows:

§ 1385. Definitions

(a) For purposes of this subchapter, the term "aid to the aged, blind, or disabled" means money payments to needy individuals who are 65 years of age or older, are blind, or are 18 years of age or over and permanently and totally disabled, but such term does not include—

(1) any such payments to or care in behalf of any individual who is an inmate of a public institution (except as a patient in a medical institution); or

(2) any such payments to or care in behalf of any individual who has not attained 65 years of age and who is a patient in an institution for tuberculosis or mental diseases.

Such term also includes payments which are not included within the meaning of such term under the preceding sentence, but which would be so included except that they are made on behalf of such a needy individual to another individual who (as determined in accordance with standards prescribed by the Commissioner of Social Security) is interested in or concerned with the welfare of such needy individual, but only with respect to a State whose State plan approved under § 1382 of this title includes provision for—

(A) determination by the State agency that such needy individual has, by reason of his physical or mental condition, such inability to manage funds that making payments to him would be contrary to his welfare and, therefore, it is necessary to provide such aid through payments described in this sentence;

(B) making such payments only in cases in which such payments will, under the rules otherwise applicable under the State plan for determining need and the amount of aid to the aged, blind, or disabled to be paid (and in conjunction with other income and resources), meet all the need [*sic*] of the individuals with respect to whom such payments are made;

(C) undertaking and continuing special efforts to protect the welfare of such individual and to improve, to the extent possible, his capacity for self-care and to manage funds;

(D) periodic review by such State agency of the determination under clause (A) of this subsection to ascertain whether conditions justifying such determination still exist, with provision for termination of such payments if they do not and for seeking judicial appointment of a guardian or other legal representative, as described in § 1311 of this title, if and when it appears that such action will best serve the interests of such needy individual; and

(E) opportunity for a fair hearing before the State agency on the determination referred to in clause (A) of this subsection for any individual with respect to whom it is made.

At the option of a State (if its plan approved under this subchapter so provides), such term (i) need not include money payments to an individual who has been absent from such State for a period in excess of ninety consecutive days (regardless of whether he has maintained his residence in such State during such period) until he has been present in such State for thirty consecutive days in the case of such an individual who has maintained his residence in such State during such period or ninety consecutive days in the case of any other such individual, and (ii) may include rent payments made directly to a public housing agency on behalf of a recipient or a group or groups of recipients of aid under such plan.

(b) Repealed. Pub.L. 97–35, Title XXI, § 2184(d)(6)(B), Aug. 13, 1981, 95 Stat. 818

(Aug. 14, 1935, c. 531, Title XVI, § 1605, as added July 25, 1962, Pub.L. 87–543, Title I, § 141(a), 76 Stat. 204, and amended July 30, 1965, Pub.L. 89–97, Title II, §§ 221(d)(1), (2), 222(b), Title IV, § 402(b), 79 Stat. 358, 360, 416; Oct. 30, 1972, Pub.L. 92–603, Title IV, §§ 408(d), 409(d), 86 Stat. 1490, 1491; Aug. 13, 1981, Pub.L. 97–35, Title XXI, § 2184(d)(6), 95 Stat. 818; Aug. 15, 1994, Pub.L. 103–296, Title I, § 107(a)(4), 108 Stat. 1478.)

[Pub.L. 103–296, Title I, §§ 107(a)(4), 110(a), Aug. 15, 1994, 108 Stat. 1478, 1490, effective Mar. 31, 1995, substituted "Commissioner of Social Security" for "Secretary".]

SUBCHAPTER XVIII—HEALTH INSURANCE FOR AGED AND DISABLED

PART D—VOLUNTARY PRESCRIPTION DRUG BENEFIT PROGRAM

Subpart 1—Part D Eligible Individuals and Prescription Drug Benefits

§ 1395w–101. Eligibility, enrollment, and information

(a) Provision of qualified prescription drug coverage through enrollment in plans—

(1) In general

Subject to the succeeding provisions of this part, each part D eligible individual (as defined in paragraph (3)(A)) is entitled to obtain qualified prescription drug coverage (described in section 1395w–102(a) of this title) as follows:

(A) Fee-for-service enrollees may receive coverage through a prescription drug plan

A part D eligible individual who is not enrolled in an MA plan may obtain qualified prescription drug coverage through enrollment in a prescription drug plan (as defined in section 1395w–151(a)(14) of this title).

(B) Medicare Advantage enrollees

(i) Enrollees in a plan providing qualified prescription drug coverage receive coverage through the plan

A part D eligible individual who is enrolled in an MA–PD plan obtains such coverage through such plan.

(ii) Limitation on enrollment of MA plan enrollees in prescription drug plans

Except as provided in clauses (iii) and (iv), a part D eligible individual who is enrolled in an MA plan may not enroll in a prescription drug plan under this part.

(iii) Private fee-for-service enrollees in MA plans not providing qualified prescription drug coverage permitted to enroll in a prescription drug plan

A part D eligible individual who is enrolled in an MA private fee-for-service plan (as defined in section 1395w–28(b)(2) of this title) that does not provide qualified prescription drug coverage may obtain qualified prescription drug coverage through enrollment in a prescription drug plan.

(iv) Enrollees in MSA plans permitted to enroll in a prescription drug plan

A part D eligible individual who is enrolled in an MSA plan (as defined in section 1395w–28(b)(3) of this title) may obtain qualified prescription drug coverage through enrollment in a prescription drug plan.

(2) Coverage first effective January 1, 2006

Coverage under prescription drug plans and MA–PD plans shall first be effective on January 1, 2006.

(3) Definitions

For purposes of this part:

(A) Part D eligible individual

The term "part D eligible individual" means an individual who is entitled to benefits under part A or enrolled under part B.

(B) MA plan

The term "MA plan" has the meaning given such term in section 1395w–28(b)(1) of this title.

(C) MA-PD plan

The term "MA-PD plan" means an MA plan that provides qualified prescription drug coverage.

(b) Enrollment process for prescription drug plans

(1) Establishment of process

(A) In general

The Secretary shall establish a process for the enrollment, disenrollment, termination, and change of enrollment of part D eligible individuals in prescription drug plans consistent with this subsection.

(B) Application of MA rules

In establishing such process, the Secretary shall use rules similar to (and coordinated with) the rules for enrollment, disenrollment, termination, and change of enrollment with an MA–PD plan under the following provisions of section 1395w–21 of this title:

(i) Residence requirements

Section 1395w–21(b)(1)(A) of this title, relating to residence requirements.

(ii) Exercise of choice

Section 1395w–21(c) of this title (other than paragraph (3)(A) and paragraph (4) of such section), relating to exercise of choice.

(iii) Coverage election periods

Subject to paragraphs (2) and (3) of this subsection, section 1395w–21(e) of this title (other than subparagraphs (B), (C), (E), and (F) of paragraph (2) and the second sentence of paragraph (4) of such section), relating to coverage election periods, including initial periods, annual coordinated election periods, special election periods, and election periods for exceptional circumstances.

(iv) Coverage periods

Section 1395w–21(f) of this title, relating to effectiveness of elections and changes of elections.

(v) Guaranteed issue and renewal

Section 1395w–21(g) of this title (other than paragraph (2) of such section and clause (i) and the second sentence of clause (ii) of paragraph (3)(C) of such section), relating to guaranteed issue and renewal.

(vi) Marketing material and application forms

Section 1395w–21(h) of this title, relating to approval of marketing material and application forms.

In applying clauses (ii), (iv), and (v) of this subparagraph, any reference to section 1395w–21(e) of this title shall be treated as a reference to such section as applied pursuant to clause (iii) of this subparagraph.

(C) Special rule

The process established under subparagraph (A) shall include, except as provided in subparagraph (D), in the case of a part D eligible individual who is a full-benefit dual eligible individual (as defined in section 1396u–5(c)(6) of this title) who has failed to enroll in a prescription drug plan or an MA–PD plan, for the enrollment in a prescription drug plan that has a monthly beneficiary premium that does not exceed the premium assistance available under section 1395w–114(a)(1)(A) of this title).[1] If there is more than one such plan available, the Secretary shall enroll such an individual on a random basis among all such plans in the PDP region. Nothing in the previous sentence shall prevent such an individual from declining or changing such enrollment.

(D) Special rule for plans that waive de minimis premiums

The process established under subparagraph (A) may include, in the case of a part D eligible individual who is a subsidy eligible individual (as defined in section 1395w–114(a)(3) of this title) who has failed to enroll in a prescription drug plan or an MA–PD plan, for the enrollment in a prescription drug plan or MA–PD plan that has waived the monthly beneficiary premium for such subsidy eligible individual under section 1395w–114(a)(5) of this title. If there is more than one such plan available, the Secretary shall enroll such an individual under the preceding sentence on a random basis among all such plans in the PDP region. Nothing in the previous sentence shall prevent such an individual from declining or changing such enrollment.

(2) Initial enrollment period

(A) Program initiation

In the case of an individual who is a part D eligible individual as of November 15, 2005, there shall be an initial enrollment period that shall be the same as the annual, coordinated open election period described in section 1395w–21(e)(3)(B)(iii) of this title, as applied under paragraph (1)(B)(iii).

(B) Continuing periods

In the case of an individual who becomes a part D eligible individual after November 15, 2005, there shall be an initial enrollment period which is the period under section 1395w–21(e)(1) of this title, as applied under paragraph (1)(B)(iii) of this section,[2] as if "entitled to benefits under part A or enrolled under part B" were substituted for "entitled to benefits under part A and enrolled under part B", but in no case shall such period end before the period described in subparagraph (A).

(3) Additional special enrollment periods

The Secretary shall establish special enrollment periods, including the following:

(A) Involuntary loss of creditable prescription drug coverage

(i) In general

In the case of a part D eligible individual who involuntarily loses creditable prescription drug coverage (as defined in section 1395w–113(b)(4) of this title).

(ii) Notice

In establishing special enrollment periods under clause (i), the Secretary shall take into account when the part D eligible individuals are provided notice of the loss of creditable prescription drug coverage.

(iii) Failure to pay premium

For purposes of clause (i), a loss of coverage shall be treated as voluntary if the coverage is terminated because of failure to pay a required beneficiary premium.

(iv) **Reduction in coverage**

For purposes of clause (i), a reduction in coverage so that the coverage no longer meets the requirements under section 1395w–113(b)(5) of this title (relating to actuarial equivalence) shall be treated as an involuntary loss of coverage.

(B) **Errors in enrollment**

In the case described in section 1395p(h) of this title (relating to errors in enrollment), in the same manner as such section applies to part B.

(C) **Exceptional circumstances**

In the case of part D eligible individuals who meet such exceptional conditions (in addition to those conditions applied under paragraph (1)(B)(iii)) as the Secretary may provide.

(D) **Medicaid coverage**

In the case of an individual (as determined by the Secretary, subject to such limits as the Secretary may establish for individuals identified pursuant to section 1395w–104(c)(5) of this title) who is a full-benefit dual eligible individual (as defined in section 1396u–5(c)(6) of this title).

(E) **Discontinuance of MA–PD election during first year of eligibility**

In the case of a part D eligible individual who discontinues enrollment in an MA–PD plan under the second sentence of section 1395w–21(e)(4) of this title at the time of the election of coverage under such sentence under the original medicare fee-for-service program.

(4) **Information to facilitate enrollment**

(A) **In general**

Notwithstanding any other provision of law but subject to subparagraph (B), the Secretary may provide to each PDP sponsor and MA organization such identifying information about part D eligible individuals as the Secretary determines to be necessary to facilitate efficient marketing of prescription drug plans and MA–PD plans to such individuals and enrollment of such individuals in such plans.

(B) **Limitation**

(i) **Provision of information**

The Secretary may provide the information under subparagraph (A) only to the extent necessary to carry out such subparagraph.

(ii) **Use of information**

Such information provided by the Secretary to a PDP sponsor or an MA organization may be used by such sponsor or organization only to facilitate marketing of, and enrollment of part D eligible individuals in, prescription drug plans and MA–PD plans.

(5) **Reference to enrollment procedures for MA–PD plans**

For rules applicable to enrollment, disenrollment, termination, and change of enrollment of part D eligible individuals in MA–PD plans, see section 1395w–21 of this title.

(6) **Reference to penalties for late enrollment**

Section 1395w–113(b) of this title imposes a late enrollment penalty for part D eligible individuals who—

(A) enroll in a prescription drug plan or an MA–PD plan after the initial enrollment period described in paragraph (2); and

(B) fail to maintain continuous creditable prescription drug coverage during the period of non-enrollment.

(c) **Providing information to beneficiaries**

(1) **Activities**

The Secretary shall conduct activities that are designed to broadly disseminate information to part D eligible individuals (and prospective part D eligible individuals) regarding the coverage provided under this part. Such activities shall ensure that such information is first made available at least 30 days prior to the initial enrollment period described in subsection (b)(2)(A).

(2) **Requirements**

The activities described in paragraph (1) shall—

(A) be similar to the activities performed by the Secretary under section 1395w–21(d) of this title, including dissemination (including through the toll-free telephone number 1–800–MEDICARE) of comparative information for prescription drug plans and MA–PD plans; and

(B) be coordinated with the activities performed by the Secretary under such section and under section 1395b–2 of this title.

(3) **Comparative information**

(A) **In general**

Subject to subparagraph (B), the comparative information referred to in paragraph (2)(A) shall include a comparison of the following with respect to qualified prescription drug coverage:

(i) **Benefits**

The benefits provided under the plan.

(ii) **Monthly beneficiary premium**

The monthly beneficiary premium under the plan.

(iii) **Quality and performance**

The quality and performance under the plan.

(iv) **Beneficiary cost-sharing**

The cost-sharing required of part D eligible individuals under the plan.

(v) **Consumer satisfaction surveys**

The results of consumer satisfaction surveys regarding the plan conducted pursuant to section 1395w–104(d) of this title.

(B) **Exception for unavailability of information**

The Secretary is not required to provide comparative information under clauses (iii) and (v) of subparagraph (A) with respect to a plan—

(i) for the first plan year in which it is offered; and

(ii) for the next plan year if it is impracticable or the information is otherwise unavailable.

(4) **Information on late enrollment penalty**

The information disseminated under paragraph (1) shall include information concerning the methodology for determining the late enrollment penalty under section 1395w–113(b) of this title.

(Aug. 14, 1935, c. 531, Title XVIII, § 1860D–1, as added Pub.L. 108–173, Title I, § 101(a)(2), Dec. 8, 2003, 117 Stat. 2071; amended Pub.L. 109–432, Div. B, Title II, § 206(b), Dec. 20, 2006, 120 Stat. 2990; Pub.L. 111–148, Title III, § 3303(b), Mar. 23, 2010, 124 Stat. 469; Pub.L. 114–10, Title II, § 209(b)(2)(B)(ii), Apr. 16, 2015, 129 Stat. 149; Pub.L. 114–198, Title VII, § 704(a)(3), July 22, 2016, 130 Stat. 748.)

[1] So in original. The closing parenthesis probably should not appear.

[2] So in original. Probably should read "of this subsection,".

HISTORICAL AND STATUTORY NOTES

Revision Notes and Legislative Reports

2003 Acts. House Conference Report No. 108–391 and Statement by President, see 2003 U.S. Code Cong. and Adm. News, p. 1808.

2006 Acts. Statement by President, see 2006 U.S. Code Cong. and Adm. News, p. S73.

References in Text

Part D, referred to in text, means Part D of Title XVIII of the Social Security Act, Act Aug. 14, 1935, c. 531, Title XVIII, § 1860D–1 et seq., as added, Pub.L. 108–173, Title I, § 101(a)(2), Dec. 8, 2003, 117 Stat. 2071, which is classified to this part, 42 U.S.C.A. 1395w–101 et seq.

Part A, referred to in text, means Part A of Title XVIII of the Social Security Act, Act Aug. 14, 1935, c. 531, Title XVIII, § 1811 et seq., as added July 30, 1965, Pub.L. 89–97, Title I, § 102(a), 79 Stat. 291, and amended, which is classified to part A of this subchapter, 42 U.S.C.A. § 1395c et seq.

Part B, referred to in text, means Part B of Title XVIII of the Social Security Act, Act Aug. 14, 1935, c. 531, Title XVIII, § 1831 et seq., as added July 30, 1965, Pub.L. 89–97, Title I, § 102(a), 79 Stat. 301, and amended, which is classified to part B of this subchapter, 42 U.S.C.A. § 1395j et seq.

Amendments

2006 Amendments. Subsec. (b)(1)(B)(iii). Pub.L. 109–432, Div. B, Title II, § 206(b), struck out "subparagraphs (B) and (C)" and inserted "subparagraphs (B), (C), and (E)".

Effective and Applicability Provisions

2016 Acts. Pub.L. 114–198, Title VII, § 704(g)(1), July 22, 2016, 130 Stat. 751, provided that: "The amendments made by this section [amending this section and 42 U.S.C.A. §§ 1395w–104, 1395w–152, 1395ddd, and 1395iii] shall apply to prescription drug plans (and MA–PD plans) for plan years beginning on or after January 1, 2019."

2010 Acts. Pub.L. 111–148, Title III, § 3303(c), Mar. 23, 2010, 124 Stat. 469, provided that: "The amendments made by this subsection [sic; probably should be 'section'; amending subsec. (b)(1) of this section and 42 U.S.C.A. § 1395w–114] shall apply to premiums for months, and enrollments for plan years, beginning on or after January 1, 2011."

Stakeholder Meetings Prior to Effective Date; Rulemaking

Pub.L. 114–198, Title VII, § 704(g)(2), (3), July 22, 2016, 130 Stat. 751, provided that:

"(2) Stakeholder meetings prior to effective date.—

"(A) In general.—Not later than January 1, 2017, the Secretary of Health and Human Services shall convene stakeholders, including individuals entitled to benefits under part A of title XVIII of the Social Security Act [42 U.S.C.A. § 1395c et seq.] or enrolled under part B of such title [42 U.S.C.A. § 1395j et seq.], advocacy groups representing such individuals, physicians, pharmacists, and other clinicians, retail pharmacies, plan sponsors, entities delegated by plan sponsors, and biopharmaceutical manufacturers for input regarding the topics described in subparagraph (B). The input described in the preceding sentence shall be provided to the Secretary in sufficient time in order for the Secretary to take such input into account in promulgating the regulations pursuant to paragraph (3).

"(B) Topics described.—The topics described in this subparagraph are the topics of—

"(i) the anticipated impact of drug management programs for at-risk beneficiaries under paragraph (5) of section 1860D–4(c) of the Social Security Act (42 U.S.C. 1395w–104(c)) on cost-sharing and ensuring accessibility to prescription drugs for enrollees in prescription drug plans of PDP sponsors, and enrollees in MA–PD plans, who are at-risk beneficiaries for prescription drug abuse (as defined in subparagraph (C) of such paragraph);

"(ii) the use of an expedited appeals process under which such an enrollee may appeal an identification of such enrollee as an at-risk beneficiary for prescription drug abuse under such paragraph (similar to the processes established under the Medicare Advantage program under part C of title XVIII of the Social Security Act [42 U.S.C.A. § 1395w–21 et seq.] that allow an automatic escalation to external review of claims submitted under such part);

"(iii) the types of enrollees that should be treated as exempted individuals, as described in subparagraph (C)(ii) of such paragraph;

"(iv) the manner in which terms and definitions in such paragraph should be applied, such as the use of clinical appropriateness in determining whether an enrollee is an at-risk beneficiary for prescription drug abuse as defined in subparagraph (C) of such paragraph;

"(v) the information to be included in the notices described in subparagraph (B) of such paragraph and the standardization of such notices;

"(vi) with respect to a PDP sponsor (or Medicare Advantage organization) that establishes a drug management program for at-risk beneficiaries under such paragraph, the responsibilities of such PDP sponsor (or organization) with respect to the implementation of such program;

"(vii) notices for plan enrollees at the point of sale that would explain why an at-risk beneficiary has been prohibited from receiving a prescription at a location outside of the designated pharmacy;

"(viii) evidence-based prescribing guidelines for opiates; and

"(ix) the sharing of claims data under parts A and B of title XVIII of the Social Security Act [42 U.S.C.A. § 1395c et seq., 42 U.S.C.A. § 1395j et seq.] with PDP sponsors.

"(3) **Rulemaking.**—Not later than one year after the date of the enactment of this Act [July 22, 2016], the Secretary of Health and Human Services shall, taking into account the input gathered pursuant to paragraph (2)(A) and after providing notice and an opportunity to comment, promulgate regulations to carry out the provisions of, and amendments made by[,] this section [amending this section and 42 U.S.C.A. §§ 1395w-104, 1395w-152, 1395ddd, and 1395iii and enacting provisions set out as a note above]."

Office of the Inspector General Studies and Reports

Pub.L. 111-148, Title III, § 3313, Mar. 23, 2010, 124 Stat. 477, provided that:

"(a) **Study and annual report on part D [this part] formularies' inclusion of drugs commonly used by dual eligibles.**—

"(1) **Study.**—The Inspector General of the Department of Health and Human Services shall conduct a study of the extent to which formularies used by prescription drug plans and MA-PD plans under part D [this part] include drugs commonly used by full-benefit dual eligible individuals (as defined in section 1935(c)(6) of the Social Security Act (42 U.S.C. 1396u-5(c)(6))).

"(2) **Annual reports.**—Not later than July 1 of each year (beginning with 2011), the Inspector General shall submit to Congress a report on the study conducted under paragraph (1), together with such recommendations as the Inspector General determines appropriate.

"(b) **Study and report on prescription drug prices under Medicare part D and Medicaid.**—

"(1) **Study.**—

"(A) **In general.**—The Inspector General of the Department of Health and Human Services shall conduct a study on prices for covered part D [this part] drugs under the Medicare prescription drug program under part D [this part] of title XVIII of the Social Security Act [this part, 42 U.S.C.A. § 1395w-101 et seq.] and for covered outpatient drugs under title XIX [subchapter XIX of this chapter, 42 U.S.C.A. § 1396 et seq.]. Such study shall include the following:

"(i) A comparison, with respect to the 200 most frequently dispensed covered part D [this part] drugs under such program and covered outpatient drugs under such title (as determined by the Inspector General based on volume and expenditures), of—

"(I) the prices paid for covered part D [this part] drugs by PDP sponsors of prescription drug plans and Medicare Advantage organizations offering MA-PD plans; and

"(II) the prices paid for covered outpatient drugs by a State plan under title XIX [subchapter XIX of this chapter, 42 U.S.C.A. § 1396 et seq.].

"(ii) An assessment of—

"(I) the financial impact of any discrepancies in such prices on the Federal Government; and

"(II) the financial impact of any such discrepancies on enrollees under part D [this part] or individuals eligible for medical assistance under a State plan under title XIX [subchapter XIX of this chapter, 42 U.S.C.A. § 1396 et seq.].

"(B) **Price.**—For purposes of subparagraph (A), the price of a covered part D [this part] drug or a covered outpatient drug shall include any rebate or discount under such program or such title, respectively, including any negotiated price concession described in section 1860D-2(d)(1)(B) of the Social Security Act (42 U.S.C. 1395w-102(d)(1)(B)) or rebate under an agreement under section 1927 of the Social Security Act (42 U.S.C. 1396r-8).

"(C) **Authority to collect any necessary information.**—Notwithstanding any other provision of law, the Inspector General of the Department of Health and Human Services shall be able to collect any information related to the prices of covered part D [this part] drugs under such program and covered outpatient drugs under such title XIX [subchapter XIX of this chapter, 42 U.S.C.A. § 1396 et seq.] necessary to carry out the comparison under subparagraph (A).

"(2) **Report.**—

"(A) **In general.**—Not later than October 1, 2011, subject to subparagraph (B), the Inspector General shall submit to Congress a report containing the results of the study conducted under paragraph (1), together with recommendations for such legislation and administrative action as the Inspector General determines appropriate.

"(B) **Limitation on information contained in report.**—The report submitted under subparagraph (A) shall not include any information that the Inspector General determines is proprietary or is likely to negatively impact the ability of a PDP sponsor or a State plan under title XIX [subchapter XIX of this chapter, 42 U.S.C.A. § 1396 et seq.] to negotiate prices for covered part D [this part] drugs or covered outpatient drugs, respectively.

"(3) **Definitions.**—In this section:

"(A) **Covered part D [this part] drug.**—The term 'covered part D [this part] drug' has the meaning given such term in section 1860D-2(e) of the Social Security Act (42 U.S.C. 1395w-102(e)).

"(B) Covered outpatient drug.—The term 'covered outpatient drug' has the meaning given such term in section 1927(k) of such Act (42 U.S.C. 1396r(k) [so in original; probably should read '42 U.S.C. 1396r–8(k)']).

"(C) MA–PD plan.—The term 'MA–PD plan' has the meaning given such term in section 1860D–41(a)(9) of such Act (42 U.S.C. 1395w–151(a)(9)).

"(D) Medicare Advantage organization.—The term 'Medicare Advantage organization' has the meaning given such term in section 1859(a)(1) of such Act (42 U.S.C. 1395w–28)(a)(1)).

"(E) PDP sponsor.—The term 'PDP sponsor' has the meaning given such term in section 1860D–41(a)(13) of such Act (42 U.S.C. 1395w–151(a)(13)).

"(F) Prescription drug plan.—The term 'prescription drug plan' has the meaning given such term in section 1860D–41(a)(14) of such Act (42 U.S.C. 1395w–151(a)(14))."

Submission of Legislative Proposal

Pub.L. 108–173, Title I, § 101(b), Dec. 8, 2003, 117 Stat. 2150, provided that: "Not later than 6 months after the date of the enactment of this Act [Dec. 8, 2003], the Secretary shall submit to the appropriate committees of Congress a legislative proposal providing for such technical and conforming amendments in the law as are required by the provisions of this title [this subchapter] and title II [subchapter II of this chapter, 42 U.S.C.A. § 401 et seq.]."

Study on Transitioning Part B Prescription Drug Coverage

Pub.L. 108–173, Title I, § 101(c), Dec. 8, 2003, 117 Stat. 2150, provided that: "Not later than January 1, 2005, the Secretary shall submit a report to Congress that makes recommendations regarding methods for providing benefits under subpart 1 of part D of title XVIII of the Social Security Act [42 U.S.C.A. § 1395w–101 et seq.] for outpatient prescription drugs for which benefits are provided under part B of such title [42 U.S.C.A. § 1395j et seq.]."

Report on Progress in Implementation of Prescription Drug Benefit

Pub.L. 108–173, Title I, § 101(d), Dec. 8, 2003, 117 Stat. 2150, provided that: "Not later than March 1, 2005, the Secretary shall submit a report to Congress on the progress that has been made in implementing the prescription drug benefit under this title. The Secretary shall include in the report specific steps that have been taken, and that need to be taken, to ensure a timely start of the program on January 1, 2006. The report shall include recommendations regarding an appropriate transition from the program under section 1860D–31 of the Social Security Act [42 U.S.C.A. § 1395w–141] to prescription drug benefits under subpart 1 of part D of title XVIII of such Act [42 U.S.C.A. § 1395w–101 et seq.]."

Rules of Construction

Provisions of Pub.L. 108–173 not to be construed to require an issuer of a medicare supplemental policy under this section to participate as a PDP sponsor under part D of this subchapter [42 U.S.C.A. § 1395w–101 et seq.], as a condition for issuing such policy, and a State may not require an issuer of a medicare supplemental policy under this section to participate as a PDP sponsor under part D of this subchapter [42 U.S.C.A. § 1395w–101 et seq.] as a condition for issuing such policy, see Pub.L. 108–173, Title I, § 104(c), Dec. 8, 2003, 117 Stat. 2165, set out as a note under 42 U.S.C.A. § 1395ss.

State Pharmaceutical Assistance Transition Commission

Pub.L. 108–173, Title I, § 106, Dec. 8, 2003, 117 Stat. 2168, provided that:

"(a) Establishment.—

"(1) In general.—There is established, as of the first day of the third month beginning after the date of the enactment of this Act [Dec. 8, 2003], a State Pharmaceutical Assistance Transition Commission (in this section [this note] referred to as the 'Commission') to develop a proposal for addressing the unique transitional issues facing State pharmaceutical assistance programs, and program participants, due to the implementation of the voluntary prescription drug benefit program under part D of title XVIII of the Social Security Act, as added by section 101 [the Medicare Prescription Drug, Improvement, and Modernization Act of 2003, Pub.L. 108–173, Title I, § 101, Dec. 8, 2003, 117 Stat. 2071, which enacted this part].

"(2) Definitions.—For purposes of this section [this note]:

"(A) State pharmaceutical assistance program defined.—The term 'State pharmaceutical assistance program' means a program (other than the medicaid program) operated by a State (or under contract with a State) that provides as of the date of the enactment of this Act [Dec. 8, 2003] financial assistance to medicare beneficiaries for the purchase of prescription drugs.

"(B) Program participant.—The term 'program participant' means a low-income medicare beneficiary who is a participant in a State pharmaceutical assistance program.

"(b) Composition.—The Commission shall include the following:

"(1) A representative of each Governor of each State that the Secretary identifies as operating on a statewide basis a State pharmaceutical assistance program that provides for eligibility and benefits that are comparable or more generous than the low-income assistance eligibility and benefits offered under section 1860D–14 of the Social Security Act [42 U.S.C.A. § 1395w–114].

"(2) Representatives from other States that the Secretary identifies have in operation other State pharmaceutical assistance programs, as appointed by the Secretary.

"(3) Representatives of organizations that have an inherent interest in program participants or the program itself, as appointed by the Secretary but not to exceed the number of representatives under paragraphs (1) and (2).

"(4) Representatives of Medicare Advantage organizations, pharmaceutical benefit managers, and other private health insurance plans, as appointed by the Secretary.

"(5) The Secretary (or the Secretary's designee) and such other members as the Secretary may specify.

"The Secretary shall designate a member to serve as Chair of the Commission and the Commission shall meet at the call of the Chair.

"(c) Development of proposal.—The Commission shall develop the proposal described in subsection (a) [of this note] in a manner consistent with the following principles:

"(1) Protection of the interests of program participants in a manner that is the least disruptive to such participants and that includes a single point of contact for enrollment and processing of benefits.

"(2) Protection of the financial and flexibility interests of States so that States are not financially worse off as a result of the enactment of this title [Pub.L. 108–173, Title I, Dec. 8, 2003, 117 Stat. 2071, which, inter alia, enacted this part; see Tables for complete classification].

"(3) Principles of medicare modernization under this Act [Pub.L. 108–173, Dec. 8, 2003, 117 Stat. 2066; see Tables for complete classification].

"**(d) Report.**—By not later than January 1, 2005, the Commission shall submit to the President and Congress a report that contains a detailed proposal (including specific legislative or administrative recommendations, if any) and such other recommendations as the Commission deems appropriate.

"**(e) Support.**—The Secretary shall provide the Commission with the administrative support services necessary for the Commission to carry out its responsibilities under this section [this note].

"**(f) Termination.**—The Commission shall terminate 30 days after the date of submission of the report under subsection (d) [of this section]."

Conflict of Interest Study

Pub.L. 108–173, Title I, § 110, Dec. 8, 2003, 117 Stat. 2174, provided that:

"**(a) Study.**—The Federal Trade Commission shall conduct a study of differences in payment amounts for pharmacy services provided to enrollees in group health plans that utilize pharmacy benefit managers. Such study shall include the following:

"(1) An assessment of the differences in costs incurred by such enrollees and plans for prescription drugs dispensed by mail-order pharmacies owned by pharmaceutical benefit managers compared to mail-order pharmacies not owned by pharmaceutical benefit managers, and community pharmacies.

"(2) Whether such plans are acting in a manner that maximizes competition and results in lower prescription drug prices for enrollees.

"**(b) Report.**—Not later than 18 months after the date of the enactment of this Act [Dec. 8, 2003], the Commission shall submit to Congress a report on the study conducted under subsection (a) [of this note]. Such report shall include recommendations regarding any need for legislation to ensure the fiscal integrity of the voluntary prescription drug benefit program under part D of title XVIII [this part], as added by section 101, that may be appropriated as the result of such study.

"**(c) Exemption from paperwork reduction act.**—Chapter 35 of title 44, United States Code [44 U.S.C.A. § 3501 et seq.], shall not apply to the collection of information under subsection (a) [of this note]."

§ 1395w–102. Prescription drug benefits

(a) Requirements

(1) In general

For purposes of this part and part C, the term "qualified prescription drug coverage" means either of the following:

(A) Standard prescription drug coverage with access to negotiated prices

Standard prescription drug coverage (as defined in subsection (b)) and access to negotiated prices under subsection (d).

(B) Alternative prescription drug coverage with at least actuarially equivalent benefits and access to negotiated prices

Coverage of covered part D drugs which meets the alternative prescription drug coverage requirements of subsection (c) and access to negotiated prices under subsection (d), but only if the benefit design of such coverage is approved by the Secretary, as provided under subsection (c).

(2) Permitting supplemental prescription drug coverage

(A) In general

Subject to subparagraph (B), qualified prescription drug coverage may include supplemental prescription drug coverage consisting of either or both of the following:

(i) Certain reductions in cost-sharing

(I) In general

A reduction in the annual deductible, a reduction in the coinsurance percentage, or an increase in the initial coverage limit with respect to covered part D drugs, or any combination thereof, insofar as such a reduction or increase increases the actuarial value of benefits above the actuarial value of basic prescription drug coverage.

(II) Construction

Nothing in this paragraph shall be construed as affecting the application of subsection (c)(3).

(ii) Optional drugs

Coverage of any product that would be a covered part D drug but for the application of subsection (e)(2)(A).

(B) Requirement

A PDP sponsor may not offer a prescription drug plan that provides supplemental prescription drug coverage pursuant to subparagraph (A) in an area unless the sponsor also offers a prescription drug plan in the area that only provides basic prescription drug coverage.

(3) Basic prescription drug coverage

For purposes of this part and part C, the term "basic prescription drug coverage" means either of the following:

(A) Coverage that meets the requirements of paragraph (1)(A).

(B) Coverage that meets the requirements of paragraph (1)(B) but does not have any supplemental prescription drug coverage described in paragraph (2)(A).

(4) Application of secondary payor provisions

The provisions of section 1395w–22(a)(4) of this title shall apply under this part in the same manner as they apply under part C.

(5) Construction

Nothing in this subsection shall be construed as changing the computation of incurred costs under subsection (b)(4).

(b) Standard prescription drug coverage

For purposes of this part and part C, the term "standard prescription drug coverage" means coverage of covered part D drugs that meets the following requirements:

(1) Deductible

(A) In general

The coverage has an annual deductible—

(i) for 2006, that is equal to $250; or

(ii) for a subsequent year, that is equal to the amount specified under this paragraph for the previous year increased by the percentage specified in paragraph (6) for the year involved.

(B) Rounding

Any amount determined under subparagraph (A)(ii) that is not a multiple of $5 shall be rounded to the nearest multiple of $5.

(2) Benefit structure

(A) 25 percent coinsurance

Subject to subparagraphs (C) and (D), the coverage has coinsurance (for costs above the annual deductible specified in paragraph (1) and up to the initial coverage limit under paragraph (3)) that is—

(i) equal to 25 percent; or

(ii) actuarially equivalent (using processes and methods established under section 1395w–111(c) of this title) to an average expected payment of 25 percent of such costs.

(B) Use of tiers

Nothing in this part shall be construed as preventing a PDP sponsor or an MA organization from applying tiered copayments under a plan, so long as such tiered copayments are consistent with subparagraphs (A)(ii), (C), and (D).

(C) Coverage for generic drugs in coverage gap

(i) In general

Except as provided in paragraph (4), the coverage for an applicable beneficiary (as defined in section 1395w–114a(g)(1) of this title) has coinsurance (for costs above the initial coverage limit under paragraph (3) and below the out-of-pocket threshold) for covered part D drugs that are not applicable drugs under section 1395w–114a(g)(2) of this title that is—

(I) equal to the generic-gap coinsurance percentage (specified in clause (ii)) for the year; or

(II) actuarially equivalent (using processes and methods established under section 1395w–111(c) of this title) to an average expected payment of such percentage of such costs for covered part D drugs that are not applicable drugs under section 1395w–114a(g)(2) of this title.

(ii) Generic-gap coinsurance percentage

The generic-gap coinsurance percentage specified in this clause for—

(I) 2011 is 93 percent;

(II) 2012 and each succeeding year before 2020 is the generic-gap coinsurance percentage under this clause for the previous year decreased by 7 percentage points; and

(III) 2020 and each subsequent year is 25 percent.

(D) Coverage for applicable drugs in coverage gap

(i) In general

Except as provided in paragraph (4), the coverage for an applicable beneficiary (as defined in section 1395w–114a(g)(1) of this title) has coinsurance (for costs above the initial coverage limit under paragraph (3) and below the out-of-pocket threshold) for the negotiated price (as defined in section 1395w–114a(g)(6) of this title) of covered part D drugs that are applicable drugs under section 1395w–114a(g)(2) of this title that is—

(I) equal to the difference between—

(aa) the applicable gap percentage (specified in clause (ii) for the year); and

(bb) the discount percentage specified in section 1395w–114a(g)(4)(A) of this title for such applicable drugs (or, in the case of a year after 2018, 50 percent); or

(II) actuarially equivalent (using processes and methods established under section 1395w–111(c) of this title) to an average expected payment of such percentage of such costs, for covered part D drugs that are applicable drugs under section 1395w–114a(g)(2) of this title.

(ii) **Applicable gap percentage**

The applicable gap percentage specified in this clause for—

(I) 2013 and 2014 is 97.5 percent;

(II) 2015 and 2016 is 95 percent;

(III) 2017 is 90 percent;

(IV) 2018 is 85 percent; and

(V) 2019 and each subsequent year is 75 percent.

(VI) Redesignated (V)

(3) Initial coverage limit

(A) In general

Except as provided in paragraphs (2)(C), (2)(D), and (4), the coverage has an initial coverage limit on the maximum costs that may be recognized for payment purposes (including the annual deductible)—

(i) for 2006, that is equal to $2,250; or

(ii) for a subsequent year, that is equal to the amount specified in this paragraph for the previous year, increased by the annual percentage increase described in paragraph (6) for the year involved.

(B) Rounding

Any amount determined under subparagraph (A)(ii) that is not a multiple of $10 shall be rounded to the nearest multiple of $10.

(4) Protection against high out-of-pocket expenditures

(A) In general

(i) In general

The coverage provides benefits, after the part D eligible individual has incurred costs (as described in subparagraph (C)) for covered part D drugs in a year equal to the annual out-of-pocket threshold specified in subparagraph (B), with cost-sharing that is equal to the greater of—

(I) a copayment of $2 for a generic drug or a preferred drug that is a multiple source drug (as defined in section 1396r–8(k)(7)(A)(i) of this title) and $5 for any other drug; or

(II) coinsurance that is equal to 5 percent.

(ii) Adjustment of amount

For a year after 2006, the dollar amounts specified in clause (i)(I) shall be equal to the dollar amounts specified in this subparagraph for the previous year, increased by the annual percentage increase described in paragraph (6) for the year involved. Any amount established under this clause that is not a multiple of a 5 cents shall be rounded to the nearest multiple of 5 cents.

(B) Annual out-of-pocket threshold

(i) In general

For purposes of this part, the "annual out-of-pocket threshold" specified in this subparagraph—

(I) for 2006, is equal to $3,600;

(II) for each of years 2007 through 2013, is equal to the amount specified in this subparagraph for the previous year, increased by the annual percentage increase described in paragraph (6) for the year involved;

(III) for 2014 and 2015, is equal to the amount specified in this subparagraph for the previous year, increased by the annual percentage increase described in paragraph (6) for the year involved, minus 0.25 percentage point;

(IV) for each of years 2016 through 2019, is equal to the amount specified in this subparagraph for the previous year, increased by the lesser of—

(aa) the annual percentage increase described in paragraph (7) for the year involved, plus 2 percentage points; or

(bb) the annual percentage increase described in paragraph (6) for the year;

(V) for 2020, is equal to the amount that would have been applied under this subparagraph for 2020 if the amendments made by section 1101(d)(1) of the Health Care and Education Reconciliation Act of 2010 had not been enacted; or

(VI) for a subsequent year, is equal to the amount specified in this subparagraph for the previous year, increased by the annual percentage increase described in paragraph (6) for the year involved.

(ii) Rounding

Any amount determined under clause (i)(II) that is not a multiple of $50 shall be rounded to the nearest multiple of $50.

(C) Application

Except as provided in subparagraph (E), in applying subparagraph (A)—

(i) incurred costs shall only include costs incurred with respect to covered part D drugs for the annual deductible described in paragraph

(1), for cost-sharing described in paragraph (2), and for amounts for which benefits are not provided because of the application of the initial coverage limit described in paragraph (3), but does not include any costs incurred for covered part D drugs which are not included (or treated as being included) in the plan's formulary;

(ii) subject to clause (iii), such costs shall be treated as incurred only if they are paid by the part D eligible individual (or by another person, such as a family member, on behalf of the individual) and the part D eligible individual (or other person) is not reimbursed through insurance or otherwise, a group health plan, or other third-party payment arrangement (other than under such section or such a Program) for such costs; and

(iii) such costs shall be treated as incurred and shall not be considered to be reimbursed under clause (ii) if such costs are borne or paid—

(I) under section 1395w–114 of this title;

(II) under a State Pharmaceutical Assistance Program;

(III) by the Indian Health Service, an Indian tribe or tribal organization, or an urban Indian organization (as defined in section 1603 of Title 25); or

(IV) under an AIDS Drug Assistance Program under part B of title XXVI of the Public Health Service Act.

(D) Information regarding third-party reimbursement

(i) Procedures for exchanging information

In order to accurately apply the requirements of subparagraph (C)(ii), the Secretary is authorized to establish procedures, in coordination with the Secretary of the Treasury and the Secretary of Labor—

(I) for determining whether costs for part D eligible individuals are being reimbursed through insurance or otherwise, a group health plan, or other third-party payment arrangement; and

(II) for alerting the PDP sponsors and MA organizations that offer the prescription drug plans and MA–PD plans in which such individuals are enrolled about such reimbursement arrangements.

(ii) Authority to request information from enrollees

A PDP sponsor or an MA organization may periodically ask part D eligible individuals enrolled in a prescription drug plan or an MA–PD plan offered by the sponsor or organization whether such individuals have or expect to receive such third-party reimbursement. A material misrepresentation of the information described in the preceding sentence by an individual (as defined in standards set by the Secretary and determined through a process established by the Secretary) shall constitute grounds for termination of enrollment in any plan under section 1395w–21(g)(3)(B) of this title (and as applied under this part under section 1395w–101(b)(1)(B)(v) of this title) for a period specified by the Secretary.

(E) Inclusion of costs of applicable drugs under Medicare coverage gap discount program

In applying subparagraph (A), incurred costs shall include the negotiated price (as defined in paragraph (6) of section 1395w–114a(g) of this title) of an applicable drug (as defined in paragraph (2) of such section) of a manufacturer that is furnished to an applicable beneficiary (as defined in paragraph (1) of such section) under the Medicare coverage gap discount program under section 1395w–114a of this title, regardless of whether part of such costs were paid by a manufacturer under such program, except that incurred costs shall not include the portion of the negotiated price that represents the reduction in coinsurance resulting from the application of paragraph (2)(D).

(5) Construction

Nothing in this part shall be construed as preventing a PDP sponsor or an MA organization offering an MA–PD plan from reducing to zero the cost-sharing otherwise applicable to preferred or generic drugs.

(6) Annual percentage increase

The annual percentage increase specified in this paragraph for a year is equal to the annual percentage increase in average per capita aggregate expenditures for covered part D drugs in the United States for part D eligible individuals, as determined by the Secretary for the 12–month period ending in July of the previous year using such methods as the Secretary shall specify.

(7) Additional annual percentage increase

The annual percentage increase specified in this paragraph for a year is equal to the annual percentage increase in the consumer price index for all urban consumers (United States city average) for the 12–month period ending in July of the previous year.

(c) Alternative prescription drug coverage requirements

A prescription drug plan or an MA–PD plan may provide a different prescription drug benefit design from standard prescription drug coverage so long as the Secretary determines (consistent with section 1395w–111(c) of this title) that the following requirements are met and the plan applies for, and receives, the approval of the Secretary for such benefit design:

(1) Assuring at least actuarially equivalent coverage

(A) Assuring equivalent value of total coverage

The actuarial value of the total coverage is at least equal to the actuarial value of standard prescription drug coverage.

(B) Assuring equivalent unsubsidized value of coverage

The unsubsidized value of the coverage is at least equal to the unsubsidized value of standard prescription drug coverage. For purposes of this subparagraph, the unsubsidized value of coverage is the amount by which the actuarial value of the coverage exceeds the actuarial value of the subsidy payments under section 1395w–115 of this title with respect to such coverage.

(C) Assuring standard payment for costs at initial coverage limit

The coverage is designed, based upon an actuarially representative pattern of utilization, to provide for the payment, with respect to costs incurred that are equal to the initial coverage limit under subsection (b)(3) for the year, of an amount equal to at least the product of—

(i) the amount by which the initial coverage limit described in subsection (b)(3) for the year exceeds the deductible described in subsection (b)(1) for the year; and

(ii) 100 percent minus the coinsurance percentage specified in subsection (b)(2)(A)(i).

(2) Maximum required deductible

The deductible under the coverage shall not exceed the deductible amount specified under subsection (b)(1) for the year.

(3) Same protection against high out-of-pocket expenditures

The coverage provides the coverage required under subsection (b)(4).

(d) Access to negotiated prices

(1) Access

(A) In general

Under qualified prescription drug coverage offered by a PDP sponsor offering a prescription drug plan or an MA organization offering an MA–PD plan, the sponsor or organization shall provide enrollees with access to negotiated prices used for payment for covered part D drugs, regardless of the fact that no benefits may be payable under the coverage with respect to such drugs because of the application of a deductible or other cost-sharing or an initial coverage limit (described in subsection (b)(3)).

(B) Negotiated prices

For purposes of this part, negotiated prices shall take into account negotiated price concessions, such as discounts, direct or indirect subsidies, rebates, and direct or indirect remunerations, for covered part D drugs, and include any dispensing fees for such drugs.

(C) Medicaid-related provisions

The prices negotiated by a prescription drug plan, by an MA–PD plan with respect to covered part D drugs, or by a qualified retiree prescription drug plan (as defined in section 1395w–132(a)(2) of this title) with respect to such drugs on behalf of part D eligible individuals, shall (notwithstanding any other provision of law) not be taken into account for the purposes of establishing the best price under section 1396r–8(c)(1)(C) of this title.

(2) Disclosure

A PDP sponsor offering a prescription drug plan or an MA organization offering an MA–PD plan shall disclose to the Secretary (in a manner specified by the Secretary) the aggregate negotiated price concessions described in paragraph (1)(B) made available to the sponsor or organization by a manufacturer which are passed through in the form of lower subsidies, lower monthly beneficiary prescription drug premiums, and lower prices through pharmacies and other dispensers. The provisions of section 1396r–8(b)(3)(D) of this title apply to information disclosed to the Secretary under this paragraph.

(3) Audits

To protect against fraud and abuse and to ensure proper disclosures and accounting under this part and in accordance with section 1395w–27(d)(2)(B) of this title (as applied under section 1395w–112(b)(3)(C) of this title), the Secretary may conduct periodic audits, directly or through contracts, of the financial statements and records of PDP sponsors with respect to prescription drug plans and MA organizations with respect to MA–PD plans.

(e) Covered part D drug defined

(1) In general

Except as provided in this subsection, for purposes of this part, the term "covered part D drug" means—

(A) a drug that may be dispensed only upon a prescription and that is described in subparagraph (A)(i), (A)(ii), or (A)(iii) of section 1396r–8(k)(2) of this title; or

(B) a biological product described in clauses (i) through (iii) of subparagraph (B) of such section or insulin described in subparagraph (C) of such section and medical supplies associated with the injection of insulin (as defined in regulations of the Secretary),

and such term includes a vaccine licensed under section 262 of this title (and, for vaccines administered on or after January 1, 2008, its administration) and any use of a covered part D drug for a medically accepted indication (as defined in paragraph (4)).

(2) Exclusions

(A) In general

Such term does not include drugs or classes of drugs, or their medical uses, which may be excluded from coverage or otherwise restricted under section 1396r–8(d)(2) of this title, other than subparagraph (E) of such section (relating to smoking cessation agents), other than subparagraph (I) of such section (relating to barbiturates) if the barbiturate is used in the treatment of epilepsy, cancer, or a chronic mental health disorder, and other than subparagraph (J) of such section (relating to benzodiazepines), or under section 1396r–8(d)(3) of this title, as such sections were in effect on December 8, 2003. Such term also does not include a drug when used for the treatment of sexual or erectile dysfunction, unless such drug were used to treat a condition, other than sexual or erectile dysfunction, for which the drug has been approved by the Food and Drug Administration.

(B) Medicare covered drugs

A drug prescribed for a part D eligible individual that would otherwise be a covered part D drug under this part shall not be so considered if payment for such drug as so prescribed and dispensed or administered with respect to that individual is available (or would be available but for the application of a deductible) under part A or B for that individual.

(3) Application of general exclusion provisions

A prescription drug plan or an MA–PD plan may exclude from qualified prescription drug coverage any covered part D drug—

(A) for which payment would not be made if section 1395y(a) of this title applied to this part; or

(B) which is not prescribed in accordance with the plan or this part.

Such exclusions are determinations subject to reconsideration and appeal pursuant to subsections (g) and (h), respectively, of section 1395w–104 of this title.

(4) Medically accepted indication defined

(A) In general

For purposes of paragraph (1), the term "medically accepted indication" has the meaning given that term—

(i) in the case of a covered part D drug used in an anticancer chemotherapeutic regimen, in section 1395x(t)(2)(B) of this title, except that in applying such section—

(I) "prescription drug plan or MA–PD plan" shall be substituted for "carrier" each place it appears; and

(II) subject to subparagraph (B), the compendia described in section 1396r–8(g)(1)(B)(i)(III) of this title shall be included in the list of compendia described in clause (ii)(I) section 1395x(t)(2)(B) of this title; and

(ii) in the case of any other covered part D drug, in section 1396r–8(k)(6) of this title.

(B) Conflict of interest

On and after January 1, 2010, subparagraph (A)(i)(II) shall not apply unless the compendia described in section 1396r–8(g)(1)(B)(i)(III) of this title meets [1] the requirement in the third sentence of section 1395x(t)(2)(B) of this title.

(C) Update

For purposes of applying subparagraph (A)(ii), the Secretary shall revise the list of compendia described in section 1396r–8(g)(1)(B)(i) of this title as is appropriate for identifying medically accepted indications for drugs. Any such revision shall be done in a manner consistent with the process for revising compendia under section 1395x(t)(2)(B) of this title.

(Aug. 14, 1935, c. 531, Title XVIII, § 1860D–2, as added Pub.L. 108–173, Title I, § 101(a)(2), Dec. 8, 2003, 117 Stat. 2075; amended Pub.L. 109–91, Title I, § 103(a), Oct. 20, 2005, 119 Stat. 2092; Pub.L. 109–432, Div. B, Title II, § 202(b), Dec. 20, 2006, 120 Stat. 2986; Pub.L. 110–275, Title I, §§ 175(a), 182(a)(1), July 15, 2008, 122 Stat. 2581, 2583; Pub.L. 111–148, Title III, §§ 3301(c)(1), 3314(a), 3315, Mar. 23, 2010, 124 Stat. 467, 478, 479; Pub.L. 111–152, Title I, § 1101(a)(2), (b)(3), (d), Mar. 30, 2010, 124 Stat. 1037, 1038, 1039; Pub.L. 115–123, Div. E, Title XII, § 53116(a), Feb. 9, 2018, 132 Stat. 306.)

[1] So in original. Probably should be "meet".

HISTORICAL AND STATUTORY NOTES

Revision Notes and Legislative Reports

2003 Acts. House Conference Report No. 108–391 and Statement by President, see 2003 U.S. Code Cong. and Adm. News, p. 1808.

2006 Acts. Statement by President, see 2006 U.S. Code Cong. and Adm. News, p. S73.

References in Text

Part C, referred to in text, means Part C of Title XVIII of the Social Security Act, Act Aug. 14, 1935, c. 531, Title XVIII, § 1851 et seq., as added Aug. 5, 1997, Pub.L. 105–33, Title IV, § 4001, 111 Stat. 276, and amended, which is classified to part C of this subchapter, 42 U.S.C.A. § 1395w–21 et seq.

Part D, referred to in text, means Part D of Title XVIII of the Social Security Act, Act Aug. 14, 1935, c. 531, Title XVIII, § 1860D–1 et seq., as added, Pub.L. 108–173, Title I, § 101(a)(2), Dec. 8, 2003, 117 Stat. 2071, which is classified to this part, 42 U.S.C.A. § 1395w–101 et seq.

Section 1101(d)(1) of the Health Care and Education Reconciliation Act of 2010, referred to in subsec. (b)(4)(B)(i)(V), is Pub.L. 111–152, Title I, § 1101(d)(1), Mar. 30, 2010, 124 Stat. 1039, which amended this section.

The Public Health Service Act, referred to in subsec. (b)(4)(C)(iii)(IV), is Act July 1, 1944, c. 373, 58 Stat. 682. Part B of title XXVI of the Act is classified generally to part B of subchapter XXIV of chapter 6A of this title, 42 U.S.C.A. § 300ff-21 et seq. For complete classification, see Short Title note set out under 42 U.S.C.A. § 201 and Tables.

Part A, referred to in subsec. (e)(2)(B), means Part A of Title XVIII of the Social Security Act, Act Aug. 14, 1935, c. 531, Title XVIII, § 1811 et seq., as added July 30, 1965, Pub.L. 89–97, Title I, § 102(a), 79 Stat. 291, and amended, which is classified to part A of this subchapter, 42 U.S.C.A. § 1395c et seq.

Part B, referred to in subsec. (e)(2)(B), means Part B of Title XVIII of the Social Security Act, Act Aug. 14, 1935, c. 531, Title XVIII, § 1831 et seq., as added July 30, 1965, Pub.L. 89–97, Title I, § 102(a), 79 Stat. 301, and amended, which is classified to part B of this subchapter, 42 U.S.C.A. § 1395j et seq.

Codifications

Pub.L. 110–275, Title I, § 182(a)(1)(B), July 15, 2008, 122 Stat. 2583, which directed the addition of par. (4) at the end of subsec. (e)(1), was executed by adding par. (4) to the end of subsec. (e) as the probable intent of Congress.

Amendments

2008 Amendments. Subsec. (e)(1). Pub.L. 110–275, § 182(a)(1)(A), in the matter following subpar. (B), struck out "(as defined in section 1396r–8(k)(6) of this title)" and inserted "(as defined in paragraph (4))".

2006 Amendments. Subsec. (e)(1). Pub.L. 109–432, Div. B, Title II, § 202(b), inserted "(and, for vaccines administered on or after January 1, 2008, its administration)" after "section 262 of this title".

2005 Amendments. Subsec. (e)(2)(A). Pub.L. 109–91, § 103(a)(1), struck out the period at the end and inserted ", as such sections were in effect on the date of the enactment of this part."

Pub.L. 109–91, § 103(a)(2), added at the end the following: "Such term also does not include a drug when used for the treatment of sexual or erectile dysfunction, unless such drug were used to treat a condition, other than sexual or erectile dysfunction, for which the drug has been approved by the Food and Drug Administration."

Effective and Applicability Provisions

2010 Acts. Pub.L. 111–148, Title III, § 3301(c)(2), Mar. 23, 2010, 124 Stat. 468, provided that: "The amendments made by this subsection [amending subsec. (b)(4)(C) and (E) of this section] shall apply to costs incurred on or after July 1, 2010."

Pub.L. 111–148, Title III, § 3314(b), Mar. 23, 2010, 124 Stat. 479, provided that: "The amendments made by subsection (a) [amending subsec. (b)(4)(C)(i) to (iii) of this section] shall apply to costs incurred on or after January 1, 2011."

2008 Acts. Pub.L. 110–275, Title I, § 175(b), July 15, 2008, 122 Stat. 2581, provided that: "The amendments made by subsection (a) [amending this section] shall apply to prescriptions dispensed on or after January 1, 2013."

Pub.L. 110–275, Title I, § 182(a)(2), July 15, 2008, 122 Stat. 2583, provided that: "The amendments made by this subsection [amending this section] shall apply to plan years beginning on or after January 1, 2009."

2005 Acts. Pub.L. 109–91, Title I, § 103(c), Oct. 20, 2005, 119 Stat. 2092, provided that: "The amendment made by subsection (a)(1) [amending subsec. (e)(2)(A) of this section by adding a reference to the date of enactment of this part] shall take effect as if included in the enactment of the Medicare Prescription Drug, Improvement, and Modernization Act of 2003 (Public Law 108–173 [Pub.L. 108–173, Dec. 8, 2003, 117 Stat. 2066]) and the amendment made by subsection (a)(2) [amending subsec. (e)(2)(A) of this section by adding provisions relating to treatment of sexual or erectile dysfunction] shall apply to coverage for drugs dispensed on or after January 1, 2007."

Repeal of Section 3315 of Pub.L. 111–148

Pub.L. 111–152, Title I, § 1101(a)(2), Mar. 30, 2010, 124 Stat. 1037, provided that: "Section 3315 of the Patient Protection and Affordable Care Act (including the amendments made by such section) [Pub.L. 111–148, Title III, § 3315, Mar. 23, 2010, 124 Stat. 479, amending subsec. (b)(3)(A) and (7) of this section] is repealed, and any provision of law amended or repealed by such sections is hereby restored or revived as if such section had not been enacted into law."

Transition for 2007

Pub.L. 109–432, Div. B, Title II, § 202(a), Dec. 20, 2006, 120 Stat. 2986, provided that: "Notwithstanding any other provision of law, in the case of a vaccine that is a covered part D drug under section 1860D–2(e) of the Social Security Act (42 U.S.C. 1395w–102(e)) [subsec. (e) of this section] and that is administered during 2007, the administration of such vaccine shall be paid under part B of title XVIII of such Act [42 U.S.C.A. § 1395j et seq.] as if it were the administration of a vaccine described in section 1861(s)(10)(B) of such Act (42 U.S.C. 1395w(s)(10)(B)) [sic; probably should be '42 U.S.C. 1395x(s)(10)(B)']."

Construction

Pub.L. 109–91, Title I, § 103(b), Oct. 20, 2005, 119 Stat. 2092, provided that: "Nothing in this section [Pub.L. 109–91, Title I, § 103, Oct. 20, 2005, 119 Stat. 2092, which amended this section and enacted provisions set out as notes under this section] shall be construed as preventing a prescription drug plan or an MA–PD plan from providing coverage of drugs for the treatment of sexual or erectile dysfunction as supplemental prescription drug coverage under section 1860D–2(a)(2)(A)(ii) of the Social Security Act (42 U.S.C. 1395w–102(a)(2)(A)(ii)) [subsec. (a)(2)(A)(ii) of this section]."

§ 1395w–103. Access to a choice of qualified prescription drug coverage

(a) Assuring access to a choice of coverage

(1) Choice of at least two plans in each area

The Secretary shall ensure that each part D eligible individual has available, consistent with paragraph (2), a choice of enrollment in at least 2 qualifying plans (as defined in paragraph (3)) in the area in which the individual resides, at least one of which is a prescription drug plan. In any such case in which such plans are not available, the part D eligible individual shall be given the opportunity to enroll in a fallback prescription drug plan.

(2) Requirement for different plan sponsors

The requirement in paragraph (1) is not satisfied with respect to an area if only one entity offers all the qualifying plans in the area.

(3) Qualifying plan defined

For purposes of this section, the term "qualifying plan" means—

(A) a prescription drug plan; or

(B) an MA–PD plan described in section 1395w–21(a)(2)(A)(i) of this title that provides—

(i) basic prescription drug coverage; or

(ii) qualified prescription drug coverage that provides supplemental prescription drug coverage so long as there is no MA monthly supplemental beneficiary premium applied under the plan, due to the application of a credit against such premium of a rebate under section 1395w–24(b)(1)(C) of this title.

(b) Flexibility in risk assumed and application of fallback plan

In order to ensure access pursuant to subsection (a) in an area—

(1) the Secretary may approve limited risk plans under section 1395w–111(f) of this title for the area; and

(2) only if such access is still not provided in the area after applying paragraph (1), the Secretary shall provide for the offering of a fallback prescription drug plan for that area under section 1395w–111(g) of this title.

(Aug. 14, 1935, c. 531, Title XVIII, § 1860D–3, as added Pub.L. 108–173, Title I, § 101(a)(2), Dec. 8, 2003, 117 Stat. 2081.)

HISTORICAL AND STATUTORY NOTES

Revision Notes and Legislative Reports

2003 Acts. House Conference Report No. 108–391 and Statement by President, see 2003 U.S. Code Cong. and Adm. News, p. 1808.

References in Text

Part D, referred to in subsec. (a)(1), means Part D of Title XVIII of the Social Security Act, Act Aug. 14, 1935, c. 531, Title XVIII, § 1860D–1 et seq., as added, Pub.L. 108–173, Title I, § 101(a)(2), Dec. 8, 2003, 117 Stat. 2071, which is classified to this part, 42 U.S.C.A. § 1395w–101 et seq.

§ 1395w–104. Beneficiary protections for qualified prescription drug coverage

(a) Dissemination of information—

(1) General information

(A) Application of MA information

A PDP sponsor shall disclose, in a clear, accurate, and standardized form to each enrollee with a prescription drug plan offered by the sponsor under this part at the time of enrollment and at least annually thereafter, the information described in section 1395w–22(c)(1) of this title relating to such plan, insofar as the Secretary determines appropriate with respect to benefits provided under this part, and, subject to subparagraph (C), including the information described in subparagraph (B).

(B) Drug specific information

The information described in this subparagraph is information concerning the following:

(i) Access to specific covered part D drugs, including access through pharmacy networks.

(ii) How any formulary (including any tiered formulary structure) used by the sponsor functions, including a description of how a part D eligible individual may obtain information on the formulary consistent with paragraph (3).

(iii) Beneficiary cost-sharing requirements and how a part D eligible individual may obtain information on such requirements, including tiered or other copayment level applicable to each drug (or class of drugs), consistent with paragraph (3).

(iv) The medication therapy management program required under subsection (c).

(v) The drug management program for at-risk beneficiaries under subsection (c)(5).

(vi) For plan year 2021 and each subsequent plan year, subject to subparagraph (C), with respect to the treatment of pain—

(I) the risks associated with prolonged opioid use; and

(II) coverage of nonpharmacological therapies, devices, and nonopioid medications—

(aa) in the case of an MA–PD plan under part C, under such plan; and

(bb) in the case of a prescription drug plan, under such plan and under parts A and B.

(C) Targeted provision of information

A PDP sponsor of a prescription drug plan may, in lieu of disclosing the information described in subparagraph (B)(vi) to each enrollee under the plan, disclose such information through mail or electronic communications to a subset of enrollees under the plan, such as enrollees who have been prescribed an opioid in the previous 2-year period.

(2) Disclosure upon request of general coverage, utilization, and grievance information

Upon request of a part D eligible individual who is eligible to enroll in a prescription drug plan, the PDP sponsor offering such plan shall provide information similar (as determined by the Secretary) to the information described in subparagraphs (A), (B), and (C) of section 1395w–22(c)(2) of this title to such individual.

(3) Provision of specific information

(A) Response to beneficiary questions

Each PDP sponsor offering a prescription drug plan shall have a mechanism for providing specific information on a timely basis to enrollees upon request. Such mechanism shall include access to information through the use of a toll-free telephone number and, upon request, the provision of such information in writing.

(B) Availability of information on changes in formulary through the Internet

A PDP sponsor offering a prescription drug plan shall make available on a timely basis through an Internet website information on specific changes in the formulary under the plan (including changes to tiered or preferred status of covered part D drugs).

(4) Claims information

A PDP sponsor offering a prescription drug plan must furnish to each enrollee in a form easily understandable to such enrollees—

(A) an explanation of benefits (in accordance with section 1395b–7(a) of this title or in a comparable manner); and

(B) when prescription drug benefits are provided under this part, a notice of the benefits in relation to—

(i) the initial coverage limit for the current year; and

(ii) the annual out-of-pocket threshold for the current year.

Notices under subparagraph (B) need not be provided more often than as specified by the Secretary and notices under subparagraph (B)(ii) shall take into account the application of section 1395w–102(b)(4)(C) of this title to the extent practicable, as specified by the Secretary.

(b) Access to covered part D drugs

(1) Assuring pharmacy access

(A) Participation of any willing pharmacy

A prescription drug plan shall permit the participation of any pharmacy that meets the terms and conditions under the plan.

(B) Discounts allowed for network pharmacies

For covered part D drugs dispensed through in-network pharmacies, a prescription drug plan may, notwithstanding subparagraph (A), reduce coinsurance or copayments for part D eligible individuals enrolled in the plan below the level otherwise required. In no case shall such a reduction result in an increase in payments made by the Secretary under section 1395w–115 of this title to a plan.

(C) Convenient access for network pharmacies

(i) In general

The PDP sponsor of the prescription drug plan shall secure the participation in its network of a sufficient number of pharmacies that dispense (other than by mail order) drugs directly to patients to ensure convenient access (consistent with rules established by the Secretary).

(ii) Application of TRICARE standards

The Secretary shall establish rules for convenient access to in-network pharmacies under this subparagraph that are no less favorable to enrollees than the rules for convenient access to pharmacies included in the statement of work of solicitation (#MDA906–03–R–0002) of the Department of Defense under the TRICARE Retail Pharmacy (TRRx) as of March 13, 2003.

(iii) Adequate emergency access

Such rules shall include adequate emergency access for enrollees.

(iv) Convenient access in long-term care facilities

Such rules may include standards with respect to access for enrollees who are residing in long-term care facilities and for pharmacies operated by the Indian Health Service, Indian tribes and tribal organizations, and urban Indian organizations (as defined in section 1603 of Title 25).

(D) Level playing field

Such a sponsor shall permit enrollees to receive benefits (which may include a 90–day supply of drugs or biologicals) through a pharmacy (other than a mail order pharmacy), with any differential in charge paid by such enrollees.

(E) Not required to accept insurance risk

The terms and conditions under subparagraph (A) may not require participating pharmacies to accept insurance risk as a condition of participation.

(2) Use of standardized technology

(A) In general

The PDP sponsor of a prescription drug plan shall issue (and reissue, as appropriate) such a card (or other technology) that may be used by an enrollee to assure access to negotiated prices under section 1395w–102(d) of this title.

(B) Standards

(i) In general

The Secretary shall provide for the development, adoption, or recognition of standards relating to a standardized format for the card or other technology required under subparagraph (A). Such standards shall be compatible with part C of subchapter XI and may be based on standards developed by an appropriate standard setting organization.

(ii) Consultation

In developing the standards under clause (i), the Secretary shall consult with the National Council for Prescription Drug Programs and other standard setting organizations determined appropriate by the Secretary.

(iii) Implementation

The Secretary shall develop, adopt, or recognize the standards under clause (i) by such date as the Secretary determines shall be sufficient to ensure that PDP sponsors utilize such standards beginning January 1, 2006.

(3) Requirements on development and application of formularies

If a PDP sponsor of a prescription drug plan uses a formulary (including the use of tiered cost–sharing), the following requirements must be met:

(A) Development and revision by a pharmacy and therapeutic (P&T) committee

(i) In general

The formulary must be developed and reviewed by a pharmacy and therapeutic committee. A majority of the members of such committee shall consist of individuals who are practicing physicians or practicing pharmacists (or both).

(ii) Inclusion of independent experts

Such committee shall include at least one practicing physician and at least one practicing pharmacist, each of whom—

(I) is independent and free of conflict with respect to the sponsor and plan; and

(II) has expertise in the care of elderly or disabled persons.

(B) Formulary development

In developing and reviewing the formulary, the committee shall—

(i) base clinical decisions on the strength of scientific evidence and standards of practice, including assessing peer-reviewed medical literature, such as randomized clinical trials, pharmacoeconomic studies, outcomes research data, and on such other information as the committee determines to be appropriate; and

(ii) take into account whether including in the formulary (or in a tier in such formulary) particular covered part D drugs has therapeutic advantages in terms of safety and efficacy.

(C) Inclusion of drugs in all therapeutic categories and classes

(i) In general

Subject to subparagraph (G), the formulary must include drugs within each therapeutic category and class of covered part D drugs, although not necessarily all drugs within such categories and classes.

(ii) Model guidelines

The Secretary shall request the United States Pharmacopeia to develop, in consultation with pharmaceutical benefit managers and other interested parties, a list of categories and classes that may be used by prescription drug plans under this paragraph and to revise such classification from time to time to reflect changes in therapeutic uses of covered part D drugs and the additions of new covered part D drugs.

(iii) Limitation on changes in therapeutic classification

The PDP sponsor of a prescription drug plan may not change the therapeutic categories and classes in a formulary other than at the beginning of each plan year except as the Secretary may permit to take into account new therapeutic uses and newly approved covered part D drugs.

(D) Provider and patient education

The PDP sponsor shall establish policies and procedures to educate and inform health care providers and enrollees concerning the formulary.

(E) Notice before removing drug from formulary or changing preferred or tier status of drug

Any removal of a covered part D drug from a formulary and any change in the preferred or tiered cost-sharing status of such a drug shall take effect only after appropriate notice is made available (such as under subsection (a)(3)) to the Secretary, affected enrollees, physicians, pharmacies, and pharmacists.

(F) Periodic evaluation of protocols

In connection with the formulary, the sponsor of a prescription drug plan shall provide for the periodic evaluation and analysis of treatment protocols and procedures.

(G) Required inclusion of drugs in certain categories and classes

(i) Formulary requirements

(I) In general

Subject to subclause (II), a PDP sponsor offering a prescription drug plan shall be required to include all covered part D drugs in the categories and classes identified by the Secretary under clause (ii)(I).

(II) Exceptions

The Secretary may establish exceptions that permit a PDP sponsor offering a prescription drug plan to exclude from its formulary a particular covered part D drug in a category or class that is otherwise required to be included in the formulary under subclause (I) (or to otherwise limit access to such a drug, including through prior authorization or utilization management).

(ii) Identification of drugs in certain categories and classes

(I) In general

Subject to clause (iv), the Secretary shall identify, as appropriate, categories and classes of drugs for which the Secretary determines are of clinical concern.

(II) Criteria

The Secretary shall use criteria established by the Secretary in making any determination under subclause (I).

(iii) Implementation

The Secretary shall establish the criteria under clause (ii)(II) and any exceptions under clause (i)(II) through the promulgation of a regulation which includes a public notice and comment period.

(iv) Requirement for certain categories and classes until criteria established

Until such time as the Secretary establishes the criteria under clause (ii)(II) the following categories and classes of drugs shall be identified under clause (ii)(I):

(I) Anticonvulsants.

(II) Antidepressants.

(III) Antineoplastics.

(IV) Antipsychotics.

(V) Antiretrovirals.

(VI) Immunosuppressants for the treatment of transplant rejection.

(H) Use of single, uniform exceptions and appeals process

Notwithstanding any other provision of this part, each PDP sponsor of a prescription drug plan shall—

(i) use a single, uniform exceptions and appeals process (including, to the extent the Secretary determines feasible, a single, uniform model form for use under such process) with respect to the determination of prescription drug coverage for an enrollee under the plan; and

(ii) provide instant access to such process by enrollees through a toll-free telephone number and an Internet website.

(c) Cost and utilization management; quality assurance; medication therapy management program

(1) In general

The PDP sponsor shall have in place, directly or through appropriate arrangements, with respect to covered part D drugs, the following:

(A) A cost-effective drug utilization management program, including incentives to reduce costs when medically appropriate, such as through the use of multiple source drugs (as defined in section 1396r–8(k)(7)(A)(i) of this title).

(B) Quality assurance measures and systems to reduce medication errors and adverse drug interactions and improve medication use.

(C) A medication therapy management program described in paragraph (2).

(D) A program to control fraud, abuse, and waste.

(E) A utilization management tool to prevent drug abuse (as described in paragraph (6)(A)).[1]

(F) With respect to plan years beginning on or after January 1, 2022, a drug management program for at-risk beneficiaries described in paragraph (5).

Nothing in this section shall be construed as impairing a PDP sponsor from utilizing cost management tools (including differential payments) under all methods of operation.

(2) Medication therapy management program

(A) Description

(i) In general

A medication therapy management program described in this paragraph is a program of drug therapy management that may be furnished by a pharmacist and that is designed to assure, with respect to targeted beneficiaries described in clause (ii), that covered part D drugs under the prescription drug plan are appropriately used to optimize therapeutic outcomes through improved medication use, and to reduce the risk of adverse events, including adverse drug interactions. Such a program may distinguish between services in ambulatory and institutional settings.

(ii) Targeted beneficiaries described

Targeted beneficiaries described in this clause are the following:

(I) Part D eligible individuals who—

(aa) have multiple chronic diseases (such as diabetes, asthma, hypertension, hyperlipidemia, and congestive heart failure);

(bb) are taking multiple covered part D drugs; and

(cc) are identified as likely to incur annual costs for covered part D drugs that exceed a level specified by the Secretary.

(II) Beginning January 1, 2021, at-risk beneficiaries for prescription drug abuse (as defined in paragraph (5)(C)).

(B) Elements

Such program—

(i) may include elements that promote—

(I) enhanced enrollee understanding to promote the appropriate use of medications by enrollees and to reduce the risk of potential adverse events associated with medications, through beneficiary education, counseling, and other appropriate means;

(II) increased enrollee adherence with prescription medication regimens through medication refill reminders, special packaging, and other compliance programs and other appropriate means; and

(III) detection of adverse drug events and patterns of overuse and underuse of prescription drugs; and

(ii) with respect to plan years beginning on or after January 1, 2021, shall provide for—

(I) the provision of information to the enrollee on the safe disposal of prescription drugs that are controlled substances that meets the criteria established under section 1395w–22 of this title, including information on drug takeback programs that meet such requirements determined appropriate by the Secretary and information on in-home disposal; and

(II) cost-effective means by which an enrollee may so safely dispose of such drugs.

(C) Required interventions

For plan years beginning on or after the date that is 2 years after March 23, 2010, prescription drug plan sponsors shall offer medication therapy management services to targeted beneficiaries described in subparagraph (A)(ii) that include, at a minimum, the following to increase adherence to prescription medications or other goals deemed necessary by the Secretary:

(i) An annual comprehensive medication review furnished person-to-person or using telehealth technologies (as defined by the Secretary) by a licensed pharmacist or other qualified provider. The comprehensive medication review—

(I) shall include a review of the individual's medications and may result in the creation of a recommended medication action plan or other actions in consultation with the individual and with input from the prescriber to the extent necessary and practicable; and

(II) shall include providing the individual with a written or printed summary of the results of the review.

The Secretary, in consultation with relevant stakeholders, shall develop a standardized format for the action plan under subclause (I) and the summary under subclause (II).

(ii) Follow-up interventions as warranted based on the findings of the annual medication review or the targeted medication enrollment and which may be provided person-to-person or using telehealth technologies (as defined by the Secretary).

(D) Assessment

The prescription drug plan sponsor shall have in place a process to assess, at least on a quarterly basis, the medication use of individuals who are at risk but not enrolled in the medication therapy management program, including individuals who have experienced a transition in care, if the prescription drug plan sponsor has access to that information.

(E) [2] **Automatic enrollment with ability to opt-out**

The prescription drug plan sponsor shall have in place a process to—

(i) subject to clause (ii), automatically enroll targeted beneficiaries described in subparagraph (A)(ii), including beneficiaries identified under subparagraph (D), in the medication therapy management program required under this subsection; and

(ii) permit such beneficiaries to opt-out of enrollment in such program.

(E) [2] **Development of program in cooperation with licensed pharmacists**

Such program shall be developed in cooperation with licensed and practicing pharmacists and physicians.

(F) Coordination with care management plans

The Secretary shall establish guidelines for the coordination of any medication therapy management program under this paragraph with respect to a targeted beneficiary with any care management plan established with respect to such beneficiary under a chronic care improvement program under section 1395b–8 of this title.

(G) Considerations in pharmacy fees

The PDP sponsor of a prescription drug plan shall take into account, in establishing fees for pharmacists and others providing services under such plan, the resources used, and time required to, implement the medication therapy management program under this paragraph. Each such sponsor shall disclose to the Secretary upon request the amount of any such management or dispensing fees. The provisions of section 1396r–8(b)(3)(D) of this title apply to information disclosed under this subparagraph.

(3) Reducing wasteful dispensing of outpatient prescription drugs in long-term care facilities

The Secretary shall require PDP sponsors of prescription drug plans to utilize specific, uniform dispensing techniques, as determined by the Secretary, in consultation with relevant stakeholders (including representatives of nursing facilities, residents of nursing facilities, pharmacists, the pharmacy industry (including retail and long-term care pharmacy), prescription drug plans, MA–PD plans, and any other stakeholders the Secretary determines appropriate), such as weekly, daily, or automated dose dispensing, when dispensing covered part D drugs to enrollees who reside in a long-term care facility in order to reduce waste associated with 30–day fills.

(4) Requiring valid prescriber National Provider Identifiers on pharmacy claims

(A) In general

For plan year 2016 and subsequent plan years, the Secretary shall require a claim for a covered part D drug for a part D eligible individual enrolled in a prescription drug plan under this part or an MA–PD plan under part C to include a prescriber National Provider Identifier that is determined to be valid under the procedures established under subparagraph (B)(i).

(B) Procedures

(i) Validity of prescriber National Provider Identifiers

The Secretary, in consultation with appropriate stakeholders, shall establish procedures for determining the validity of prescriber National Provider Identifiers under subparagraph (A).

(ii) Informing beneficiaries of reason for denial

The Secretary shall establish procedures to ensure that, in the case that a claim for a covered part D drug of an individual described in subparagraph (A) is denied because the claim does not meet the requirements of this paragraph, the individual is properly informed at the point of service of the reason for the denial.

(C) Report

Not later than January 1, 2018, the Inspector General of the Department of Health and Human Services shall submit to Congress a report on the effectiveness of the procedures established under subparagraph (B)(i).

(D) Notification and additional requirements with respect to outlier prescribers of opioids

(i) Notification

Not later than January 1, 2021, the Secretary shall, in the case of a prescriber identified by the Secretary under clause (ii) to be an outlier prescriber of opioids, provide, subject to clause (iv), an annual notification to such prescriber that such prescriber has been so identified and that includes resources on proper prescribing methods and other information as specified in accordance with clause (iii).

(ii) Identification of outlier prescribers of opioids

(I) In general

The Secretary shall, subject to subclause (III), using the valid prescriber National Provider Identifiers included pursuant to subparagraph (A) on claims for covered part D drugs for part D eligible individuals enrolled in prescription drug plans under this part or MA–PD plans under part C and based on the thresholds established under subclause (II), identify prescribers that are outlier opioids prescribers for a period of time specified by the Secretary.

(II) Establishment of thresholds

For purposes of subclause (I) and subject to subclause (III), the Secretary shall, after consultation with stakeholders, establish thresholds, based on prescriber specialty and geographic area, for identifying whether a prescriber in a specialty and geographic area is an outlier prescriber of opioids as compared to other prescribers of opioids within such specialty and area.

(III) Exclusions

The following shall not be included in the analysis for identifying outlier prescribers of opioids under this clause:

(aa) Claims for covered part D drugs for part D eligible individuals who are receiving hospice care under this subchapter.

(bb) Claims for covered part D drugs for part D eligible individuals who are receiving oncology services under this subchapter.

(cc) Prescribers who are the subject of an investigation by the Centers for Medicare & Medicaid Services or the Inspector General of the Department of Health and Human Services.

(iii) Contents of notification

The Secretary shall include the following information in the notifications provided under clause (i):

(I) Information on how such prescriber compares to other prescribers within the same specialty and geographic area.

(II) Information on opioid prescribing guidelines, based on input from stakeholders, that may include the Centers for Disease Control and Prevention guidelines for prescribing opioids for chronic pain and guidelines developed by physician organizations.

(III) Other information determined appropriate by the Secretary.

(iv) Modifications and expansions

(I) Frequency

Beginning 5 years after October 24, 2018, the Secretary may change the frequency of the notifications described in clause (i) based on stakeholder input and changes in opioid prescribing utilization and trends.

(II) Expansion to other prescriptions

The Secretary may expand notifications under this subparagraph to include identifications and notifications with respect to concurrent prescriptions of covered Part D drugs used in combination with opioids that are considered to have adverse side effects when so used in such combination, as determined by the Secretary.

(v) Additional requirements for persistent outlier prescribers

In the case of a prescriber who the Secretary determines is persistently identified under clause (ii) as an outlier prescriber of opioids, the following shall apply:

(I) Such prescriber may be required to enroll in the program under this title under section 1396cc(j) of this title if such prescriber is not otherwise required to enroll, but only after other appropriate remedies have been provided, such as the provision of education funded through section 6052 of the SUPPORT for Patients and Communities Act, for a period determined by the Secretary as sufficient to correct the prescribing patterns that lead to identification of such prescriber as a persistent outlier prescriber of opioids. The Secretary shall determine the length of the period for which such prescriber is required to maintain such enrollment, which shall be the minimum period necessary to correct such prescribing patterns.

(II) Not less frequently than annually (and in a form and manner determined appropriate by the Secretary), the Secretary, consistent with clause(iv)(I), shall communicate information on such prescribers to sponsors of a prescription drug plan and Medicare Advantage organizations offering an MA–PD plan.

(vi) Public availability of information

The Secretary shall make aggregate information under this subparagraph available on the internet website of the Centers for Medicare & Medicaid Services. Such information shall be in a form and manner determined appropriate by the Secretary and shall not identify any specific prescriber. In carrying out this clause, the Secretary shall consult with interested stakeholders.

(vii) Opioids defined

For purposes of this subparagraph, the term "opioids" has such meaning as specified by the Secretary.

(viii) Other activities

Nothing in this subparagraph shall preclude the Secretary from conducting activities that provide prescribers with information as to how they compare to other prescribers that are in addition to the activities under this subparagraph, including activities that were being conducted as of October 24, 2018.

(5) Drug management program for at-risk beneficiaries

(A) Authority to establish

A PDP sponsor may (and for plan years beginning on or after January 1, 2022, a PDP sponsor shall) establish a drug management program for at-risk beneficiaries under which, subject to subparagraph (B), the PDP sponsor may, in the case of an at-risk beneficiary for prescription drug abuse who is an enrollee in a prescription drug plan of such PDP sponsor, limit such beneficiary's access to coverage for frequently abused drugs under such plan to frequently abused drugs that are prescribed for such beneficiary by one or more prescribers selected under subparagraph (D), and dispensed for such beneficiary by one or more pharmacies selected under such subparagraph.

(B) Requirement for notices

(i) In general

A PDP sponsor may not limit the access of an at-risk beneficiary for prescription drug abuse to coverage for frequently abused drugs under a prescription drug plan until such sponsor—

(I) provides to the beneficiary an initial notice described in clause (ii) and a second notice described in clause (iii); and

(II) verifies with the providers of the beneficiary that the beneficiary is an at-risk beneficiary for prescription drug abuse.

(ii) Initial notice

An initial notice described in this clause is a notice that provides to the beneficiary—

(I) notice that the PDP sponsor has identified the beneficiary as potentially being an at-risk beneficiary for prescription drug abuse;

(II) information describing all State and Federal public health resources that are designed to address prescription drug abuse to which the beneficiary has access, including mental health services and other counseling services;

(III) notice of, and information about, the right of the beneficiary to appeal such identification under subsection (h), including notice that if on reconsideration a PDP sponsor affirms its denial, in whole or in part, the case shall be automatically forwarded to the independent, outside entity contracted with the Secretary for review and resolution;

(IV) a request for the beneficiary to submit to the PDP sponsor preferences for which prescribers and pharmacies the beneficiary would prefer the PDP sponsor to select under subparagraph (D) in the case that the beneficiary is identified as an at-risk beneficiary for prescription drug abuse as described in clause (iii)(I);

(V) an explanation of the meaning and consequences of the identification of the beneficiary as potentially being an at-risk beneficiary for prescription drug abuse, including an explanation of the drug management program established by the PDP sponsor pursuant to subparagraph (A);

(VI) clear instructions that explain how the beneficiary can contact the PDP sponsor in order to submit to the PDP sponsor the preferences described in subclause (IV) and any other communications relating to the drug management program for at-risk beneficiaries established by the PDP sponsor; and

(VII) contact information for other organizations that can provide the beneficiary with assistance regarding such drug management program (similar to the information provided by the Secretary in other standardized notices provided to part D eligible individuals enrolled in prescription drug plans under this part).

(iii) Second notice

A second notice described in this clause is a notice that provides to the beneficiary notice—

(I) that the PDP sponsor has identified the beneficiary as an at-risk beneficiary for prescription drug abuse;

(II) that such beneficiary is subject to the requirements of the drug management program for at-risk beneficiaries established by such PDP sponsor for such plan;

(III) of the prescriber (or prescribers) and pharmacy (or pharmacies) selected for such individual under subparagraph (D);

(IV) of, and information about, the beneficiary's right to appeal such identification under subsection (h), including notice that if on reconsideration a PDP sponsor affirms its denial, in whole or in part, the case shall be automatically forwarded to the independent, outside entity contracted with the Secretary for review and resolution;

(V) that the beneficiary can, in the case that the beneficiary has not previously submitted to the PDP sponsor preferences for which prescribers and pharmacies the beneficiary would prefer the PDP sponsor select under subparagraph (D), submit such preferences to the PDP sponsor; and

(VI) that includes clear instructions that explain how the beneficiary can contact the PDP sponsor.

(iv) Timing of notices

(I) In general

Subject to subclause (II), a second notice described in clause (iii) shall be provided to the beneficiary on a date that is not less than 30 days after an initial notice described in clause (ii) is provided to the beneficiary.

(II) Exception

In the case that the PDP sponsor, in conjunction with the Secretary, determines that concerns identified through rulemaking by the Secretary regarding the health or safety of the beneficiary or regarding significant drug diversion activities require the PDP sponsor to provide a second notice described in clause (iii) to the beneficiary on a date that is earlier than the date described in subclause (I), the PDP sponsor may provide such second notice on such earlier date.

(C) At-risk beneficiary for prescription drug abuse

(i) In general

Except as provided in clause (v), for purposes of this paragraph, the term "at-risk beneficiary for prescription drug abuse" means a part D eligible individual who is not an exempted individual described in clause (ii) and—

(I) who is identified as such an at-risk beneficiary through the use of clinical guidelines that indicate misuse or abuse of prescription drugs described in subparagraph (G) and that are developed by the Secretary in consultation with PDP sponsors and other stakeholders, including individuals entitled to benefits under part A or enrolled under part B, advocacy groups representing such individuals, physicians, pharmacists, and other clinicians, retail pharmacies, plan sponsors, entities delegated by plan sponsors, and biopharmaceutical manufacturers; or

(II) with respect to whom the PDP sponsor of a prescription drug plan, upon enrolling such individual in such plan, received notice from the Secretary that such individual was identified under this paragraph to be an at-risk beneficiary for prescription drug abuse under the prescription drug plan in which such individual was most recently previously enrolled and such identification has not been terminated under subparagraph (F).

(ii) Exempted individual described

An exempted individual described in this clause is an individual who—

(I) receives hospice care under this subchapter;

(II) is a resident of a long-term care facility, of a facility described in section 1396d(d) of this title, or of another facility for which frequently abused drugs are dispensed for residents through a contract with a single pharmacy; or

(III) the Secretary elects to treat as an exempted individual for purposes of clause (i).

(iii) Program size

The Secretary shall establish policies, including the guidelines developed under clause (i)(I) and the exemptions under clause (ii)(III), to ensure that the population of enrollees in a drug management program for at-risk beneficiaries operated by a prescription drug plan can be effectively managed by such plans.

(iv) Clinical contact

With respect to each at-risk beneficiary for prescription drug abuse enrolled in a prescription drug plan offered by a PDP sponsor, the PDP sponsor shall contact the beneficiary's providers who have prescribed frequently abused drugs regarding whether prescribed medications are appropriate for such beneficiary's medical conditions.

(v) Treatment of enrollees with a history of opioid-related overdose

(I) In general

For plan years beginning not later than January 1, 2021, a part D eligible individual who is not an exempted individual described in clause (ii) and who is identified under this clause as a part D eligible individual with a history of opioid-related overdose (as defined by the Secretary) shall be included as a potentially at-risk beneficiary for prescription drug abuse under the drug management program under this paragraph.

(II) **Identification and notice**

For purposes of this clause, the Secretary shall—

(aa) identify part D eligible individuals with a history of opioid-related overdose (as so defined); and

(bb) notify the PDP sponsor of the prescription drug plan in which such an individual is enrolled of such identification.

(D) **Selection of prescribers and pharmacies**

(i) **In general**

With respect to each at-risk beneficiary for prescription drug abuse enrolled in a prescription drug plan offered by such sponsor, a PDP sponsor shall, based on the preferences submitted to the PDP sponsor by the beneficiary pursuant to clauses (ii)(IV) and (iii)(V) of subparagraph (B) (except as otherwise provided in this subparagraph) select—

(I) one, or, if the PDP sponsor reasonably determines it necessary to provide the beneficiary with reasonable access under clause (ii), more than one, individual who is authorized to prescribe frequently abused drugs (referred to in this paragraph as a "prescriber") who may write prescriptions for such drugs for such beneficiary; and

(II) one, or, if the PDP sponsor reasonably determines it necessary to provide the beneficiary with reasonable access under clause (ii), more than one, pharmacy that may dispense such drugs to such beneficiary.

For purposes of subclause (II), in the case of a pharmacy that has multiple locations that share real-time electronic data, all such locations of the pharmacy shall collectively be treated as one pharmacy.

(ii) **Reasonable access**

In making the selections under this subparagraph—

(I) a PDP sponsor shall ensure that the beneficiary continues to have reasonable access to frequently abused drugs (as defined in subparagraph (G)), taking into account geographic location, beneficiary preference, impact on costsharing, and reasonable travel time; and

(II) a PDP sponsor shall ensure such access (including access to prescribers and pharmacies with respect to frequently abused drugs) in the case of individuals with multiple residences, in the case of natural disasters and similar situations, and in the case of the provision of emergency services.

(iii) **Beneficiary preferences**

If an at-risk beneficiary for prescription drug abuse submits preferences for which in-network prescribers and pharmacies the beneficiary would prefer the PDP sponsor select in response to a notice under subparagraph (B), the PDP sponsor shall—

(I) review such preferences;

(II) select or change the selection of prescribers and pharmacies for the beneficiary based on such preferences; and

(III) inform the beneficiary of such selection or change of selection.

(iv) **Exception regarding beneficiary preferences**

In the case that the PDP sponsor determines that a change to the selection of prescriber or pharmacy under clause (iii)(II) by the PDP sponsor is contributing or would contribute to prescription drug abuse or drug diversion by the beneficiary, the PDP sponsor may change the selection of prescriber or pharmacy for the beneficiary without regard to the preferences of the beneficiary described in clause (iii). If the PDP sponsor changes the selection pursuant to the preceding sentence, the PDP sponsor shall provide the beneficiary with—

(I) at least 30 days written notice of the change of selection; and

(II) a rationale for the change.

(v) **Confirmation**

Before selecting a prescriber or pharmacy under this subparagraph, a PDP sponsor must notify the prescriber and pharmacy that the beneficiary involved has been identified for inclusion in the drug management program for at-risk beneficiaries and that the prescriber and pharmacy has been selected as the beneficiary's designated prescriber and pharmacy.

(E) **Terminations and appeals**

The identification of an individual as an at-risk beneficiary for prescription drug abuse under this paragraph, a coverage determination made under a drug management program for at-risk beneficiaries, the selection of prescriber or pharmacy under subparagraph (D), and information to be shared under subparagraph (I), with respect to such individual, shall be subject to reconsideration and appeal under subsection (h) and if on reconsideration a PDP sponsor affirms its denial, in whole or in part, the case shall be automatically forwarded to the independent, outside entity contracted with the Secretary for review and resolution.

(F) **Termination of identification**

(i) **In general**

The Secretary shall develop standards for the termination of identification of an individual as an at-risk beneficiary for prescription drug abuse under this paragraph. Under such standards such identification shall terminate as of the earlier of—

(I) the date the individual demonstrates that the individual is no longer likely, in the absence of the restrictions under this paragraph, to be an at-risk beneficiary for prescription drug abuse described in subparagraph (C)(i); and

(II) the end of such maximum period of identification as the Secretary may specify.

(ii) **Rule of construction**

Nothing in clause (i) shall be construed as preventing a plan from identifying an individual as an at-risk beneficiary for prescription drug abuse under subparagraph (C)(i) after such termination on the basis of additional information on drug use occurring after the date of notice of such termination.

(G) **Frequently abused drug**

For purposes of this subsection, the term "frequently abused drug" means a drug that is a controlled substance that the Secretary determines to be frequently abused or diverted.

(H) **Data disclosure**

(i) **Data on decision to impose limitation**

In the case of an at-risk beneficiary for prescription drug abuse (or an individual who is a potentially at-risk beneficiary for prescription drug abuse) whose access to coverage for frequently abused drugs under a prescription drug plan has been limited by a PDP sponsor under this paragraph, the Secretary shall establish rules and procedures to require the PDP sponsor to disclose data, including any necessary individually identifiable health information, in a form and manner specified by the Secretary, about the decision to impose such limitations and the limitations imposed by the sponsor under this part.

(ii) **Data to reduce fraud, abuse, and waste**

The Secretary shall establish rules and procedures to require PDP sponsors operating a drug management program for at-risk beneficiaries under this paragraph to provide the Secretary with such data as the Secretary determines appropriate for purposes of identifying patterns of prescription drug utilization for plan enrollees that are outside normal patterns and that may indicate fraudulent, medically unnecessary, or unsafe use.

(I) **Sharing of information for subsequent plan enrollments**

The Secretary shall establish procedures under which PDP sponsors who offer prescription drug plans shall share information with respect to individuals who are at-risk beneficiaries for prescription drug abuse (or individuals who are potentially at-risk beneficiaries for prescription drug abuse) and enrolled in a prescription drug plan and who subsequently disenroll from such plan and enroll in another prescription drug plan offered by another PDP sponsor.

(J) **Privacy issues**

Prior to the implementation of the rules and procedures under this paragraph, the Secretary shall clarify privacy requirements, including requirements under the regulations promulgated pursuant to section 264(c) of the Health Insurance Portability and Accountability Act of 1996 (42 U.S.C. 1320d–2 note), related to the sharing of data under subparagraphs (H) and (I) by PDP sponsors. Such clarification shall provide that the sharing of such data shall be considered to be protected health information in accordance with the requirements of the regulations promulgated pursuant to such section 264(c).

(K) **Education**

The Secretary shall provide education to enrollees in prescription drug plans of PDP sponsors and providers regarding the drug management program for at-risk beneficiaries described in this paragraph, including education—

(i) provided by Medicare administrative contractors through the improper payment outreach and education program described in section 1395kk–1(h) of this title; and

(ii) through current education efforts (such as State health insurance assistance programs described in subsection (a)(1)(A) of section 119 of the Medicare Improvements for Patients and Providers Act of 2008 (42 U.S.C. 1395b–3 note)) and materials directed toward such enrollees.

(L) **Application under MA–PD plans**

Pursuant to section 1395w–131(c)(1) of this title, the provisions of this paragraph apply under part D to MA organizations offering MA–PD plans to MA eligible individuals in the same manner as such provisions apply under this part to a PDP sponsor offering a prescription drug plan to a part D eligible individual.

(M) CMS compliance review

The Secretary shall ensure that existing plan sponsor compliance reviews and audit processes include the drug management programs for at-risk beneficiaries under this paragraph, including appeals processes under such programs.

(6) [3] Utilization management tool to prevent drug abuse

(A) In general

A tool described in this paragraph is any of the following:

(i) A utilization tool designed to prevent the abuse of frequently abused drugs by individuals and to prevent the diversion of such drugs at pharmacies.

(ii) Retrospective utilization review to identify—

(I) individuals that receive frequently abused drugs at a frequency or in amounts that are not clinically appropriate; and

(II) providers of services or suppliers that may facilitate the abuse or diversion of frequently abused drugs by beneficiaries.

(iii) Consultation with the contractor described in subparagraph (B) to verify if an individual enrolling in a prescription drug plan offered by a PDP sponsor has been previously identified by another PDP sponsor as an individual described in clause (ii)(I).

(B) Reporting

A PDP sponsor offering a prescription drug plan (and an MA organization offering an MA–PD plan) in a State shall submit to the Secretary and the Medicare drug integrity contractor with which the Secretary has entered into a contract under section 1395ddd of this title with respect to such State a report, on a monthly basis, containing information on—

(i) any provider of services or supplier described in subparagraph (A)(ii)(II) that is identified by such plan sponsor (or organization) during the 30-day period before such report is submitted; and

(ii) the name and prescription records of individuals described in paragraph (5)(C).

(C) CMS compliance review

The Secretary shall ensure that plan sponsor compliance reviews and program audits biennially include a certification that utilization management tools under this paragraph are in compliance with the requirements for such tools.

(6) [3] Providing prescription drug plans with parts A and B claims data to promote the appropriate use of medications and improve health outcomes

(A) Process

Subject to subparagraph (B), the Secretary shall establish a process under which a PDP sponsor of a prescription drug plan may submit a request for the Secretary to provide the sponsor, on a periodic basis and in an electronic format, beginning in plan year 2020, data described in subparagraph (D) with respect to enrollees in such plan. Such data shall be provided without regard to whether such enrollees are described in clause (ii) of paragraph (2)(A).

(B) Purposes

A PDP sponsor may use the data provided to the sponsor pursuant to subparagraph (A) for any of the following purposes:

(i) To optimize therapeutic outcomes through improved medication use, as such phrase is used in clause (i) of paragraph (2)(A).

(ii) To improving care coordination so as to prevent adverse health outcomes, such as preventable emergency department visits and hospital readmissions.

(iii) For any other purpose determined appropriate by the Secretary.

(C) Limitations on data use

A PDP sponsor shall not use data provided to the sponsor pursuant to subparagraph (A) for any of the following purposes:

(i) To inform coverage determinations under this part.

(ii) To conduct retroactive reviews of medically accepted indications determinations.

(iii) To facilitate enrollment changes to a different prescription drug plan or an MA–PD plan offered by the same parent organization.

(iv) To inform marketing of benefits.

(v) For any other purpose that the Secretary determines is necessary to include in order to protect the identity of individuals entitled to, or enrolled for, benefits under this subchapter and to protect the security of personal health information.

(D) Data described

The data described in this clause are standardized extracts (as determined by the Secretary) of claims data under parts A and B for items and services furnished under such parts for time periods specified by the Secretary. Such data shall include data as current as practicable.

(d) Consumer satisfaction surveys

In order to provide for comparative information under section 1395w–101(c)(3)(A)(v) of this title, the Secretary shall conduct consumer satisfaction surveys with respect to PDP sponsors and prescription drug plans in a manner similar to the manner such surveys are conducted for MA organizations and MA plans under part C.

(e) Electronic prescription program

(1) Application of standards

As of such date as the Secretary may specify, but not later than 1 year after the date of promulgation of final standards under paragraph (4)(D), prescriptions and other information described in paragraph (2)(A) for covered part D drugs prescribed for part D eligible individuals that are transmitted electronically shall be transmitted only in accordance with such standards under an electronic prescription drug program that meets the requirements of paragraph (2).

(2) Program requirements

Consistent with uniform standards established under paragraph (3)—

(A) Provision of information to prescribing health care professional and dispensing pharmacies and pharmacists

An electronic prescription drug program shall provide for the electronic transmittal to the prescribing health care professional and to the dispensing pharmacy and pharmacist of the prescription and information on eligibility and benefits (including the drugs included in the applicable formulary, any tiered formulary structure, and any requirements for prior authorization) and of the following information with respect to the prescribing and dispensing of a covered part D drug:

(i) Information on the drug being prescribed or dispensed and other drugs listed on the medication history, including information on drug-drug interactions, warnings or cautions, and, when indicated, dosage adjustments.

(ii) Information on the availability of lower cost, therapeutically appropriate alternatives (if any) for the drug prescribed.

(B) Application to medical history information

Effective on and after such date as the Secretary specifies and after the establishment of appropriate standards to carry out this subparagraph, the program shall provide for the electronic transmittal in a manner similar to the manner under subparagraph (A) of information that relates to the medical history concerning the individual and related to a covered part D drug being prescribed or dispensed, upon request of the professional or pharmacist involved.

(C) Limitations

Information shall only be disclosed under subparagraph (A) or (B) if the disclosure of such information is permitted under the Federal regulations (concerning the privacy of individually identifiable health information) promulgated under section 264(c) of the Health Insurance Portability and Accountability Act of 1996.

(D) Timing

To the extent feasible, the information exchanged under this paragraph shall be on an interactive, real-time basis.

(E) Electronic prior authorization

(i) In general

Not later than January 1, 2021, the program shall provide for the secure electronic transmission of—

(I) a prior authorization request from the prescribing health care professional for coverage of a covered part D drug for a part D eligible individual enrolled in a part D plan (as defined in section 1395w–133(a)(5) of this title) to the PDP sponsor or Medicare Advantage organization offering such plan; and

(II) a response, in accordance with this subparagraph, from such PDP sponsor or Medicare Advantage organization, respectively, to such professional.

(ii) Electronic transmission

(I) Exclusions

For purposes of this subparagraph, a facsimile, a proprietary payer portal that does not meet standards specified by the Secretary, or an electronic form shall not be treated as an electronic transmission described in clause (i).

(II) Standards

In order to be treated, for purposes of this subparagraph, as an electronic transmission described in clause (i), such transmission shall comply with technical standards adopted by the Secretary in consultation with the National Council for Prescription Drug Programs, other standard setting organizations determined appropriate by the Secretary, and stakeholders including PDP sponsors, Medicare Advantage organizations, health care professionals, and health information technology software vendors.

(III) Application

Notwithstanding any other provision of law, for purposes of this subparagraph, the Secretary may require the use of such standards adopted under subclause (II) in lieu of any other applicable standards for an electronic transmission described in clause (i) for a covered part D drug for a part D eligible individual.

(3) **Standards**

(A) **In general**

The Secretary shall provide consistent with this subsection for the promulgation of uniform standards relating to the requirements for electronic prescription drug programs under paragraph (2).

(B) **Objectives**

Such standards shall be consistent with the objectives of improving—

(i) patient safety;

(ii) the quality of care provided to patients; and

(iii) efficiencies, including cost savings, in the delivery of care.

(C) **Design criteria**

Such standards shall—

(i) be designed so that, to the extent practicable, the standards do not impose an undue administrative burden on prescribing health care professionals and dispensing pharmacies and pharmacists;

(ii) be compatible with standards established under part C of subchapter XI, standards established under subsection (b)(2)(B)(i), and with general health information technology standards; and

(iii) be designed so that they permit electronic exchange of drug labeling and drug listing information maintained by the Food and Drug Administration and the National Library of Medicine.

(D) **Permitting use of appropriate messaging**

Such standards shall allow for the messaging of information only if it relates to the appropriate prescribing of drugs, including quality assurance measures and systems referred to in subsection (c)(1)(B).

(E) **Permitting patient designation of dispensing pharmacy**

(i) **In general**

Consistent with clause (ii), such standards shall permit a part D eligible individual to designate a particular pharmacy to dispense a prescribed drug.

(ii) **No change in benefits**

Clause (i) shall not be construed as affecting—

(I) the access required to be provided to pharmacies by a prescription drug plan; or

(II) the application of any differences in benefits or payments under such a plan based on the pharmacy dispensing a covered part D drug.

(4) **Development, promulgation, and modification of standards**

(A) **Initial standards**

Not later than September 1, 2005, the Secretary shall develop, adopt, recognize, or modify initial uniform standards relating to the requirements for electronic prescription drug programs described in paragraph (2) taking into consideration the recommendations (if any) from the National Committee on Vital and Health Statistics (as established under section 242k(k) of this title) under subparagraph (B).

(B) **Role of NCVHS**

The National Committee on Vital and Health Statistics shall develop recommendations for uniform standards relating to such requirements in consultation with the following:

(i) Standard setting organizations (as defined in section 1320d(8) of this title) [4]

(ii) Practicing physicians.

(iii) Hospitals.

(iv) Pharmacies.

(v) Practicing pharmacists.

(vi) Pharmacy benefit managers.

(vii) State boards of pharmacy.

(viii) State boards of medicine.

(ix) Experts on electronic prescribing.

(x) Other appropriate Federal agencies.

(C) **Pilot project to test initial standards**

(i) **In general**

During the 1-year period that begins on January 1, 2006, the Secretary shall conduct a pilot project to test the initial standards developed under subparagraph (A) prior to the promulgation of the final uniform standards under subparagraph (D) in order to provide for the efficient implementation of the requirements described in paragraph (2).

(ii) **Exception**

Pilot testing of standards is not required under clause (i) where there already is adequate industry experience with such standards, as determined by the Secretary after consultation with effected standard setting organizations and industry users.

(iii) **Voluntary participation of physicians and pharmacies**

In order to conduct the pilot project under clause (i), the Secretary shall enter into agreements with physicians, physician groups, pharmacies, hospitals, PDP sponsors, MA organizations, and other appropriate entities under which health care professionals electronically transmit prescriptions to dispensing pharmacies and pharmacists in accordance with such standards.

(iv) **Evaluation and report**

(I) **Evaluation**

The Secretary shall conduct an evaluation of the pilot project conducted under clause (i).

(II) **Report to Congress**

Not later than April 1, 2007, the Secretary shall submit to Congress a report on the evaluation conducted under subclause (I).

(D) **Final standards**

Based upon the evaluation of the pilot project under subparagraph (C)(iv)(I) and not later than April 1, 2008, the Secretary shall promulgate uniform standards relating to the requirements described in paragraph (2).

(5) **Relation to State laws**

The standards promulgated under this subsection shall supersede any State law or regulation that—

(A) is contrary to the standards or restricts the ability to carry out this part; and

(B) pertains to the electronic transmission of medication history and of information on eligibility, benefits, and prescriptions with respect to covered part D drugs under this part.

(6) **Establishment of safe harbor**

The Secretary, in consultation with the Attorney General, shall promulgate regulations that provide for a safe harbor from sanctions under paragraphs (1) and (2) of section 1320a–7b(b) of this title and an exception to the prohibition under subsection (a)(1) of section 1395nn of this title with respect to the provision of nonmonetary remuneration (in the form of hardware, software, or information technology and training services) necessary and used solely to receive and transmit electronic prescription information in accordance with the standards promulgated under this subsection—

(A) in the case of a hospital, by the hospital to members of its medical staff;

(B) in the case of a group practice (as defined in section 1395nn(h)(4) of this title), by the practice to prescribing health care professionals who are members of such practice; and

(C) in the case of a PDP sponsor or MA organization, by the sponsor or organization to pharmacists and pharmacies participating in the network of such sponsor or organization, and to prescribing health care professionals.

(7) **Requirement of e-prescribing for controlled substances**

(A) **In general**

Subject to subparagraph (B), a prescription for a covered part D drug under a prescription drug plan (or under an MA–PD plan) for a schedule II, III, IV, or V controlled substance shall be transmitted by a health care practitioner electronically in accordance with an electronic prescription drug program that meets the requirements of paragraph (2).

(B) **Exception for certain circumstances**

The Secretary shall, through rulemaking, specify circumstances and processes by which the Secretary may waive the requirement under subparagraph (A), with respect to a covered part D drug, including in the case of—

(i) a prescription issued when the practitioner and dispensing pharmacy are the same entity;

(ii) a prescription issued that cannot be transmitted electronically under the most recently implemented version of the National Council for Prescription Drug Programs SCRIPT Standard;

(iii) a prescription issued by a practitioner who received a waiver or a renewal thereof for a period of time as determined by the Secretary, not to exceed one year, from the requirement to use electronic prescribing due to demonstrated economic hardship, technological limitations that are not reasonably within the control of the practitioner, or other exceptional circumstance demonstrated by the practitioner;

(iv) a prescription issued by a practitioner under circumstances in which, notwithstanding the practitioner's ability to submit a prescription electronically as required by this subsection, such practitioner reasonably determines that it would be impractical for the individual involved to obtain substances prescribed by electronic prescription in a timely manner, and such delay would adversely impact the individual's medical condition involved;

(v) a prescription issued by a practitioner prescribing a drug under a research protocol;

(vi) a prescription issued by a practitioner for a drug for which the Food and Drug Administration requires a prescription to contain elements that are not able to be included in electronic prescribing, such as a drug with risk evaluation and mitigation strategies that include elements to assure safe use;

(vii) a prescription issued by a practitioner—

(I) for an individual who receives hospice care under this subchapter; and

(II) that is not covered under the hospice benefit under this subchapter; and

(viii) a prescription issued by a practitioner for an individual who is—

(I) a resident of a nursing facility (as defined in section 1396r(a) of this title); and

(II) dually eligible for benefits under this subchapter and subchapter XIX.

(C) Dispensing

(i) Nothing in this paragraph shall be construed as requiring a sponsor of a prescription drug plan under this part, MA organization offering an MA–PD plan under part C, or a pharmacist to verify that a practitioner, with respect to a prescription for a covered part D drug, has a waiver (or is otherwise exempt) under subparagraph (B) from the requirement under subparagraph (A).

(ii) Nothing in this paragraph shall be construed as affecting the ability of the plan to cover or the pharmacists' ability to continue to dispense covered part D drugs from otherwise valid written, oral, or fax prescriptions that are consistent with laws and regulations.

(iii) Nothing in this paragraph shall be construed as affecting the ability of an individual who is being prescribed a covered part D drug to designate a particular pharmacy to dispense the covered part D drug to the extent consistent with the requirements under subsection (b)(1) and under this paragraph.

(D) Enforcement

The Secretary shall, through rulemaking, have authority to enforce and specify appropriate penalties for non-compliance with the requirement under subparagraph (A).

(f) Grievance mechanism

Each PDP sponsor shall provide meaningful procedures for hearing and resolving grievances between the sponsor (including any entity or individual through which the sponsor provides covered benefits) and enrollees with prescription drug plans of the sponsor under this part in accordance with section 1395w–22(f) of this title.

(g) Coverage determinations and reconsiderations

(1) Application of coverage determination and reconsideration provisions

A PDP sponsor shall meet the requirements of paragraphs (1) through (3) of section 1395w–22(g) of this title with respect to covered benefits under the prescription drug plan it offers under this part in the same manner as such requirements apply to an MA organization with respect to benefits it offers under an MA plan under part C.

(2) Request for a determination for the treatment of tiered formulary drug

In the case of a prescription drug plan offered by a PDP sponsor that provides for tiered cost-sharing for drugs included within a formulary and provides lower cost-sharing for preferred drugs included within the formulary, a part D eligible individual who is enrolled in the plan may request an exception to the tiered cost-sharing structure. Under such an exception, a nonpreferred drug could be covered under the terms applicable for preferred drugs if the prescribing physician determines that the preferred drug for treatment of the same condition either would not be as effective for the individual or would have adverse effects for the individual or both. A PDP sponsor shall have an exceptions process under this paragraph consistent with guidelines established by the Secretary for making a determination with respect to such a request. Denial of such an exception shall be treated as a coverage denial for purposes of applying subsection (h).

(h) Appeals

(1) In general

Subject to paragraph (2), a PDP sponsor shall meet the requirements of paragraphs (4) and (5) of section 1395w–22(g) of this title with respect to benefits (including a determination related to the application of tiered cost-sharing described in subsection (g)(2)) in a manner similar (as determined by the Secretary) to the manner such requirements apply to an MA organization with respect to benefits under the original medicare fee-for-service program option it offers under an MA plan under part C. In applying this paragraph only the part D eligible individual shall be entitled to bring such an appeal.

(2) Limitation in cases on nonformulary determinations

A part D eligible individual who is enrolled in a prescription drug plan offered by a PDP sponsor may appeal under paragraph (1) a determination not to provide for coverage of a covered part D drug that is not on the formulary under the plan only if the prescribing physician determines that all covered part D drugs on any tier of the formulary for treatment of the same condition would not be as effective for the individual as the nonformulary drug, would have adverse effects for the individual, or both.

(3) Treatment of nonformulary determinations

If a PDP sponsor determines that a plan provides coverage for a covered part D drug that is not on the formulary of the plan, the drug shall be treated as being included on the formulary for purposes of section 1395w–102(b)(4)(C)(i) of this title.

(i) Privacy, confidentiality, and accuracy of enrollee records

The provisions of section 1395w–22(h) of this title shall apply to a PDP sponsor and prescription drug plan in the same manner as it applies to an MA organization and an MA plan.

(j) Treatment of accreditation

Subparagraph (A) of section 1395w–22(e)(4) of this title (relating to treatment of accreditation) shall apply to a PDP sponsor under this part with respect to the following requirements, in the same manner as it applies to an MA organization with respect to the requirements in subparagraph (B) (other than clause (vii) thereof) of such section:

(1) Subsection (b) of this section (relating to access to covered part D drugs).

(2) Subsection (c) of this section (including quality assurance and medication therapy management).

(3) Subsection (i) of this section (relating to confidentiality and accuracy of enrollee records).

(k) Public disclosure of pharmaceutical prices for equivalent drugs

(1) In general

A PDP sponsor offering a prescription drug plan shall provide that each pharmacy that dispenses a covered part D drug shall inform an enrollee of any differential between the price of the drug to the enrollee and the price of the lowest priced generic covered part D drug under the plan that is therapeutically equivalent and bioequivalent and available at such pharmacy.

(2) Timing of notice

(A) In general

Subject to subparagraph (B), the information under paragraph (1) shall be provided at the time of purchase of the drug involved, or, in the case of dispensing by mail order, at the time of delivery of such drug.

(B) Waiver

The Secretary may waive subparagraph (A) in such circumstances as the Secretary may specify.

(*l*) Requirements with respect to sales and marketing activities

The following provisions shall apply to a PDP sponsor (and the agents, brokers, and other third parties representing such sponsor) in the same manner as such provisions apply to a Medicare Advantage organization (and the agents, brokers, and other third parties representing such organization):

(1) The prohibition under section 1395w–21(h)(4)(C) of this title on conducting activities described in section 1395w–21(j)(1) of this title.

(2) The requirement under section 1395w–21(h)(4)(D) of this title to conduct activities described in section 1395w–21(j)(2) of this title in accordance with the limitations established under such subsection.

(3) The inclusion of the plan type in the plan name under section 1395w–21(h)(6) of this title.

(4) The requirements regarding the appointment of agents and brokers and compliance with State information requests under subparagraphs (A) and (B), respectively, of section 1395w–21(h)(7) of this title.

(m) [5]Prohibition on limiting certain information on drug prices

A PDP sponsor and a Medicare Advantage organization shall ensure that each prescription drug plan or MA–PD plan offered by the sponsor or organization does not restrict a pharmacy that dispenses a prescription drug or biological from informing, nor penalize such pharmacy for informing, an enrollee in such plan of any differential between the negotiated price of, or copayment or coinsurance for, the drug or biological to the enrollee under the plan and a lower price the individual would pay for the drug or biological if the enrollee obtained the drug without using any health insurance coverage.

(m) [5]Program integrity transparency measures

For program integrity transparency measures applied with respect to prescription drug plan and MA plans, see section 1395w–28(i) of this title.

(Aug. 14, 1935, c. 531, Title XVIII, § 1860D–4, as added Pub.L. 108–173, Title I, § 101(a)(2), Dec. 8, 2003, 117 Stat. 2082; amended Pub.L. 110–275, Title I, §§ 103(a)(2), (b)(2), (c)(2), (d)(2), 176, July 15, 2008, 122 Stat. 2499, 2500, 2501, 2581; Pub.L. 111–148, Title III, §§ 3307(a), 3310(a), 3312(a), Title X, § 10328(a), Mar. 23, 2010, 124 Stat. 471, 475, 476, 965; Pub.L. 114–10, Title V, § 507, Apr. 16, 2015, 129 Stat. 168; Pub.L. 114–198, Title VII, § 704(a)(1), (2), (b), July 22, 2016, 130 Stat. 742, 748; Pub.L. 115–123, Div. E, Title III, § 50354, Feb. 9, 2018, 132 Stat. 213; Pub.L. 115–262, § 2(a), Oct. 10, 2018, 132 Stat. 3670; Pub.L. 115–271, Title II, §§ 2003(a), 2004, 2006, 2007(a), Title VI, §§ 6062, 6063(c), 6064, 6065, 6102, 6103(b), Oct. 24, 2018, 132 Stat. 3926, 3928, 3930, 3986, 3989, 4004, 4005.)

1 So in original. Probably refers to subpar. (A) of the first par. (6).

2 So in original. Two subpars. (E) have been enacted.

3 So in original. Two pars. (6) have been enacted.

4 So in original. Probably should be followed by a period.

5 So in original. Two subsecs. (m) have been enacted.

HISTORICAL AND STATUTORY NOTES

Revision Notes and Legislative Reports

2003 Acts. House Conference Report No. 108–391 and Statement by President, see 2003 U.S. Code Cong. and Adm. News, p. 1808.

References in Text

This subchapter, referred to in text, originally read "this title", meaning Title XVIII of the Social Security Act, which is principally classified to this subchapter, 42 U.S.C.A. § 1395 et seq.

Part A, referred to in text, is part A of Title XVIII of the Social Security Act, which is principally classified to part A of this subchapter, 42 U.S.C.A. § 1395c et seq.

Part B, referred to in text, is part B of Title XVIII of the Social Security Act, which is principally classified to part B of this subchapter, 42 U.S.C.A. § 1395j et seq.

Part C, referred to in text, means Part C of Title XVIII of the Social Security Act, Act Aug. 14, 1935, c. 531, Title XVIII, § 1851 et seq., as added Aug. 5, 1997, Pub.L. 105–33, Title IV, § 4001, 111 Stat. 276, and amended, which is classified to part C of this subchapter, 42 U.S.C.A. § 1395w–21 et seq.

Part D, referred to in text, means Part D of Title XVIII of the Social Security Act, Act Aug. 14, 1935, c. 531, Title XVIII, § 1860D–1 et seq., as added, Pub.L. 108–173, Title I, § 101(a)(2), Dec. 8, 2003, 117 Stat. 2071, which is classified to this part, 42 U.S.C.A. § 1395w–101 et seq.

Part C of subchapter XI, referred to in subsecs. (b)(2)(B)(i) and (e)(3)(C)(ii), originally read "part C of title XI", meaning part C of Title XI of the Social Security Act, Act Aug. 14, 1935, c. 531, Title XI, § 1171 et seq., as added Aug. 21, 1996, Pub.L. 104–191, Title II, § 262(a), 110 Stat. 2021, as amended, which is principally classified to part C of subchapter XI of this chapter, 42 U.S.C.A. § 1320d et seq.

Section 6052 of the SUPPORT for Patients and Communities Act, referred to in subsec. (c)(4)(D)(v)(I), is Pub.L. 115–271, Title VI, § 6052, Oct. 24, 2018, 132 Stat. 3985, which is set out as a note under this section.

The Health Insurance Portability and Accountability Act of 1996, referred to in subsec. (c)(5)(J), is Pub.L. 104–191, Aug. 21, 1996, 110 Stat. 1936, also known as HIPPA and HIPAA. Section 264 of the Act is set out in a note under 42 U.S.C.A. § 1320d–2. For complete classification, see Short Title note set out under 42 U.S.C.A. § 201 and Tables.

The Medicare Improvements for Patients and Providers Act of 2008, referred to in subsec. (c)(5)(K)(ii), is Pub.L. 110–275, July 15, 2008, 122 Stat. 2494. Section 119 of the Act is set out as a note under 42 U.S.C.A. § 1395b–3. See Tables for classifications.

Section 264(c) of the Health Insurance Portability and Accountability Act of 1996, referred to in subsec. (e)(2)(C), is section 264(c) of Pub.L. 104–191, Title II, § 264(c), Aug. 21, 1996, 110 Stat. 2033, which was formerly set out as a note under 42 U.S.C.A. § 1320d–2.

Subchapter XIX, referred to in subsec. (w)(2), originally read "title XIX", meaning Title XIX of the Social Security Act, Act Aug. 14, 1935, c. 531, 49 Stat. 620, as amended, which is principally classified to subchapter XIX of chapter 7 of Title 42, 42 U.S.C.A. § 1396 et seq.

Effective and Applicability Provisions

2018 Acts. Pub.L. 115–271, Title II, § 2003(b), Oct. 24, 2018, 132 Stat. 3928, provided that: "The amendment made by subsection (a) [adding subsec. (e)(7) of this section] shall apply to coverage of drugs prescribed on or after January 1, 2021."

Pub.L. 115–271, Title II, § 2007(b), Oct. 24, 2018, 132 Stat. 3931, provided that: "The amendments made by subsection (a) [amending subsec. (c)(5)(B) of this section] shall apply beginning not later January 1, 2021."

Pub.L. 115–262, § 2(b), Oct. 10, 2018, 132 Stat. 3671, provided that: "The amendment made by subsection (a) [enacting subsec. (m) of this section] shall apply to plan years beginning on or after January 1, 2020."

2016 Acts. Amendments made by Pub.L. 114–198, § 704, shall apply to prescription drug plans and MA–PD plans for plan years beginning on or after Jan. 1, 2019, see Pub.L. 114–198, § 704(g)(1), set out as a note under 42 U.S.C.A. § 1395w–101.

2010 Acts. Pub.L. 111–148, Title III, § 3307(b), Mar. 23, 2010, 124 Stat. 472, provided that: "The amendments made by this section [amending subsec. (b)(3)(G) of this section] shall apply to plan year 2011 and subsequent plan years."

Pub.L. 111–148, Title III, § 3310(b), Mar. 23, 2010, 124 Stat. 475, provided that: "The amendment made by subsection (a) [enacting subsec. (c)(3) of this section] shall apply to plan years beginning on or after January 1, 2012."

Pub.L. 111–148, Title III, § 3312(b), Mar. 23, 2010, 124 Stat. 476, provided that: "The amendment made by subsection (a) [enacting subsec. (b)(3)(H) of this section] shall apply to exceptions and appeals on or after January 1, 2012."

2008 Acts. Amendments by Pub.L. 110–275, Title I, § 103(a), applicable to plan years beginning on or after January 1, 2009, see Pub.L. 110–275, Title I, § 103(a)(3), set out as a note under 42 U.S.C.A. § 1395w–21.

Amendments by Pub.L. 110–275, Title I, § 103(b), shall take effect on a date specified by the Secretary (but in no case later than November 15, 2008), see Pub.L. 110–275, Title I, § 103(b)(3), set out as a note under 42 U.S.C.A. § 1395w–21.

Amendments by Pub.L. 110–275, Title I, § 103(d), applicable to plan years beginning on or after January 1, 2009, see Pub.L. 110–275, Title I, § 103(d)(3), set out as a note under 42 U.S.C.A. § 1395w–21.

Rules of Construction

Except as provided in subtitle A of Title V [§§ 501 to 519] of Pub.L. 114–10, nothing in that subtitle shall be construed as preventing the use of notice and comment rulemaking in the implementation of the provisions of, and the amendments made by, that subtitle, see Pub.L. 114–10, § 519, set out as a note under 42 U.S.C.A. § 405.

Pub.L. 111–148, Title X, § 10328(b), Mar. 23, 2010, 124 Stat. 965, provided that: "Nothing in this section [amending subsec. (c)(2) of this section] shall limit the authority of the Secretary of Health and Human Services to modify or broaden requirements for a medication therapy management program under part D of title XVIII of the Social Security Act [this part] or to study new models for medication therapy management through the Center for Medicare and Medicaid Innovation under section 1115A of such Act, as added by section 3021 [42 U.S.C.A. § 1315a]."

Update of Biometric Component of Multifactor Authentication

Pub.L. 115–271, Title II, § 2003(c), Oct. 24, 2018, 132 Stat. 3928, provided that: "Not later than 1 year after the date of enactment of this Act [Oct. 24, 2018], the Attorney General shall update the requirements for the biometric component of multifactor authentication with respect to electronic prescriptions of controlled substances."

Grants to Provide Technical Assistance to Outlier Prescribers of Opioids

Pub.L. 115–271, Title VI, § 6052, Oct. 24, 2018, 132 Stat. 3985, provided that:

"**(a) Grants authorized.**—The Secretary of Health and Human Services (in this section referred to as the 'Secretary') shall, through the Centers for Medicare & Medicaid Services, award grants, contracts, or cooperative agreements to eligible entities for the purposes described in subsection (b).

"**(b) Use of funds.**—Grants, contracts, and cooperative agreements awarded under subsection (a) shall be used to support eligible entities through technical assistance—

"(1) to educate and provide outreach to outlier prescribers of opioids about best practices for prescribing opioids;

"(2) to educate and provide outreach to outlier prescribers of opioids about non-opioid pain management therapies; and

"(3) to reduce the amount of opioid prescriptions prescribed by outlier prescribers of opioids.

"**(c) Application.**—Each eligible entity seeking to receive a grant, contract, or cooperative agreement under subsection (a) shall submit to the Secretary an application, at such time, in such manner, and containing such information as the Secretary may require.

"**(d) Geographic distribution.**—In awarding grants, contracts, and cooperative agreements under this section, the Secretary shall prioritize establishing technical assistance resources in each State.

"**(e) Definitions.**—In this section:

"**(1) Eligible entity.**—The term 'eligible entity' means—

"(A) an organization—

"(i) that has demonstrated experience providing technical assistance to health care professionals on a State or regional basis; and

"(ii) that has at least—

"(I) one individual who is a representative of consumers on its governing body; and

"(II) one individual who is a representative of health care providers on its governing body; or

"(B) an entity that is a quality improvement entity with a contract under part B of title XI of the Social Security Act (42 U.S.C. 1320c et seq.) [part b of subchapter XI].

"**(2) Outlier prescriber of opioids.**—The term 'outlier prescriber of opioids' means, with respect to a period, a prescriber identified by the Secretary under subparagraph (D)(ii) of section 1860D–4(c)(4) of the Social Security Act (42 U.S.C. 1395w–104(c)(4)), as added by section 6065 of this Act [Pub.L. 115–271, Title VI, § 6065, Oct. 24, 2018, 132 Stat. 3989], to be an outlier prescriber of opioids for such period.

"**(3) Prescribers.**—The term 'prescriber' means any health care professional, including a nurse practitioner or physician assistant, who is licensed to prescribe opioids by the State or territory in which such professional practices.

"**(f) Funding.**—For purposes of implementing this section, $75,000,000 shall be available from the Federal Supplementary Medical Insurance Trust Fund under section 1841 of the Social Security Act (42 U.S.C. 1395t), to remain available until expended."

Grants to Physicians to Implement Electronic Prescription Drug Programs

Pub.L. 108–173, Title I, § 108, Dec. 8, 2003, 117 Stat. 2172, provided that:

"**(a) In general.**—The Secretary is authorized to make grants to physicians for the purpose of assisting such physicians to implement electronic prescription drug programs that comply with the standards promulgated or modified under section 1860D–4(e) of the Social Security Act, as inserted by section 101(a) [subsec. (e) of this section].

"**(b) Awarding of grants.**—

"**(1) Application.**—No grant may be made under this section [this note] except pursuant to a grant application that is submitted and approved in a time, manner, and form specified by the Secretary.

"**(2) Considerations and preferences.**—In awarding grants under this section [this note], the Secretary shall—

"(A) give special consideration to physicians who serve a disproportionate number of medicare patients; and

"(B) give preference to physicians who serve a rural or underserved area.

"**(3) Limitation on grants.**—Only 1 grant may be awarded under this section [this note] with respect to any physician or group practice of physicians.

"**(c) Terms and conditions.**—

"**(1) In general.**—Grants under this section [this note] shall be made under such terms and conditions as the Secretary specifies consistent with this section.

"**(2) Use of grant funds.**—Funds provided under grants under this section [this note] may be used for any of the following:

"(A) For purchasing, leasing, and installing computer software and hardware, including handheld computer technologies.

"(B) Making upgrades and other improvements to existing computer software and hardware to enable e-prescribing.

"(C) Providing education and training to eligible physician staff on the use of technology to implement the electronic transmission of prescription and patient information.

"**(3) Provision of information.**—As a condition for the awarding of a grant under this section [this note], an applicant shall provide to the Secretary such information as the Secretary may require in order to—

"(A) evaluate the project for which the grant is made; and

"(B) ensure that funding provided under the grant is expended only for the purposes for which it is made.

"**(4) Audit.**—The Secretary shall conduct appropriate audits of grants under this section [this note].

"**(5) Matching requirement.**—The applicant for a grant under this section [this note] shall agree, with respect to the costs to be incurred by the applicant in implementing an electronic prescription drug program, to make available (directly or through donations from public or private entities) non-Federal contributions toward such costs in an amount that is not less than 50 percent of such costs.

Non–Federal contributions under the previous sentence may be in cash or in kind, fairly evaluated, including plant, equipment, or services. Amounts provided by the Federal Government, or services assisted or subsidized to any significant extent by the Federal Government, may not be included in determining the amount of such contributions.

"(d) Authorization of appropriations.—There are authorized to be appropriated to carry out this section [this note] $50,000,000 for fiscal year 2007 and such sums as may be necessary for each of fiscal years 2008 and 2009."

CROSS REFERENCES

Patient safety improvement, network of patient safety databases, patient safety organization certification and listing, see 42 USCA § 299b–21 et seq.

Subpart 2—Prescription Drug Plans; PDP Sponsors; Financing

§ 1395w–111. PDP regions; submission of bids; plan approval

(a) Establishment of PDP regions; service areas—

(1) Coverage of entire PDP region

The service area for a prescription drug plan shall consist of an entire PDP region established under paragraph (2).

(2) Establishment of PDP regions

(A) In general

The Secretary shall establish, and may revise, PDP regions in a manner that is consistent with the requirements for the establishment and revision of MA regions under subparagraphs (B) and (C) of section 1395w–27a(a)(2) of this title.

(B) Relation to MA regions

To the extent practicable, PDP regions shall be the same as MA regions under section 1395w–27a(a)(2) of this title. The Secretary may establish PDP regions which are not the same as MA regions if the Secretary determines that the establishment of different regions under this part would improve access to benefits under this part.

(C) Authority for territories

The Secretary shall establish, and may revise, PDP regions for areas in States that are not within the 50 States or the District of Columbia.

(3) National plan

Nothing in this subsection shall be construed as preventing a prescription drug plan from being offered in more than one PDP region (including all PDP regions).

(b) Submission of bids, premiums, and related information

(1) In general

A PDP sponsor shall submit to the Secretary information described in paragraph (2) with respect to each prescription drug plan it offers. Such information shall be submitted at the same time and in a similar manner to the manner in which information described in paragraph (6) of section 1395w–24(a) of this title is submitted by an MA organization under paragraph (1) of such section.

(2) Information described

The information described in this paragraph is information on the following:

(A) Coverage provided

The prescription drug coverage provided under the plan, including the deductible and other cost-sharing.

(B) Actuarial value

The actuarial value of the qualified prescription drug coverage in the region for a part D eligible individual with a national average risk profile for the factors described in section 1395w–115(c)(1)(A) of this title (as specified by the Secretary).

(C) Bid

Information on the bid, including an actuarial certification of—

(i) the basis for the actuarial value described in subparagraph (B) assumed in such bid;

(ii) the portion of such bid attributable to basic prescription drug coverage and, if applicable, the portion of such bid attributable to supplemental benefits;

(iii) assumptions regarding the reinsurance subsidy payments provided under section 1395w–115(b) of this title subtracted from the actuarial value to produce such bid; and

(iv) administrative expenses assumed in the bid.

(D) Service area

The service area for the plan.

(E) Level of risk assumed

(i) In general

Whether the PDP sponsor requires a modification of risk level under clause (ii) and, if so, the extent of such modification. Any such modification shall apply with respect to all prescription drug plans offered by a PDP sponsor in a PDP region. This subparagraph shall not apply to an MA–PD plan.

(ii) **Risk levels described**

A modification of risk level under this clause may consist of one or more of the following:

(I) **Increase in Federal percentage assumed in initial risk corridor**

An equal percentage point increase in the percents applied under subparagraphs (B)(i), (B)(ii)(I), (C)(i), and (C)(ii)(I) of section 1395w–115(e)(2) of this title. In no case shall the application of previous sentence prevent the application of a higher percentage under section 1395w–115(e)(2)(B)(iii) of this title.

(II) **Increase in Federal percentage assumed in second risk corridor**

An equal percentage point increase in the percents applied under subparagraphs (B)(ii)(II) and (C)(ii)(II) of section 1395w–115(e)(2) of this title.

(III) **Decrease in size of risk corridors**

A decrease in the threshold risk percentages specified in section 1395w–115(e)(3)(C) of this title.

(F) **Additional information**

Such other information as the Secretary may require to carry out this part.

(3) **Paperwork reduction for offering of prescription drug plans nationally or in multi-region areas**

The Secretary shall establish requirements for information submission under this subsection in a manner that promotes the offering of such plans in more than one PDP region (including all regions) through the filing of consolidated information.

(c) **Actuarial valuation**

(1) **Processes**

For purposes of this part, the Secretary shall establish processes and methods for determining the actuarial valuation of prescription drug coverage, including—

(A) an actuarial valuation of standard prescription drug coverage under section 1395w–102(b) of this title;

(B) actuarial valuations relating to alternative prescription drug coverage under section 1395w–102(c)(1) of this title;

(C) an actuarial valuation of the reinsurance subsidy payments under section 1395w–115(b) of this title;

(D) the use of generally accepted actuarial principles and methodologies; and

(E) applying the same methodology for determinations of actuarial valuations under subparagraphs (A) and (B).

(2) **Accounting for drug utilization**

Such processes and methods for determining actuarial valuation shall take into account the effect that providing alternative prescription drug coverage (rather than standard prescription drug coverage) has on drug utilization.

(3) **Responsibilities**

(A) **Plan responsibilities**

PDP sponsors and MA organizations are responsible for the preparation and submission of actuarial valuations required under this part for prescription drug plans and MA–PD plans they offer.

(B) **Use of outside actuaries**

Under the processes and methods established under paragraph (1), PDP sponsors offering prescription drug plans and MA organizations offering MA–PD plans may use actuarial opinions certified by independent, qualified actuaries to establish actuarial values.

(d) **Review of information and negotiation**

(1) **Review of information**

The Secretary shall review the information filed under subsection (b) for the purpose of conducting negotiations under paragraph (2).

(2) **Negotiation regarding terms and conditions**

Subject to subsection (i), in exercising the authority under paragraph (1), the Secretary—

(A) has the authority to negotiate the terms and conditions of the proposed bid submitted and other terms and conditions of a proposed plan; and

(B) has authority similar to the authority of the Director of the Office of Personnel Management with respect to health benefits plans under chapter 89 of Title 5.

(3) **Rejection of bids**

Paragraph (5)(C) of section 1395w–24(a) of this title shall apply with respect to bids submitted by a PDP sponsor under subsection (b) in the same manner as such paragraph applies to bids submitted by an MA organization under such section 1395w–24(a) of this title.

(e) **Approval of proposed plans**

(1) **In general**

After review and negotiation under subsection (d), the Secretary shall approve or disapprove the prescription drug plan.

(2) **Requirements for approval**

The Secretary may approve a prescription drug plan only if the following requirements are met:

(A) Compliance with requirements

The plan and the PDP sponsor offering the plan comply with the requirements under this part, including the provision of qualified prescription drug coverage.

(B) Actuarial determinations

The Secretary determines that the plan and PDP sponsor meet the requirements under this part relating to actuarial determinations, including such requirements under section 1395w–102(c) of this title.

(C) Application of FEHBP standard

(i) In general

The Secretary determines that the portion of the bid submitted under subsection (b) that is attributable to basic prescription drug coverage is supported by the actuarial bases provided under such subsection and reasonably and equitably reflects the revenue requirements (as used for purposes of section 300e–1(8)(C) of this title) for benefits provided under that plan, less the sum (determined on a monthly per capita basis) of the actuarial value of the reinsurance payments under section 1395w–115(b) of this title.

(ii) Supplemental coverage

The Secretary determines that the portion of the bid submitted under subsection (b) that is attributable to supplemental prescription drug coverage pursuant to section 1395w–102(a)(2) of this title is supported by the actuarial bases provided under such subsection and reasonably and equitably reflects the revenue requirements (as used for purposes of section 300e–1(8)(C) of this title) for such coverage under the plan.

(D) Plan design

(i) In general

The Secretary does not find that the design of the plan and its benefits (including any formulary and tiered formulary structure) are likely to substantially discourage enrollment by certain part D eligible individuals under the plan.

(ii) Use of categories and classes in formularies

The Secretary may not find that the design of categories and classes within a formulary violates clause (i) if such categories and classes are consistent with guidelines (if any) for such categories and classes established by the United States Pharmacopeia.

(f) Application of limited risk plans

(1) Conditions for approval of limited risk plans

The Secretary may only approve a limited risk plan (as defined in paragraph (4)(A)) for a PDP region if the access requirements under section 1395w–103(a) of this title would not be met for the region but for the approval of such a plan (or a fallback prescription drug plan under subsection (g)).

(2) Rules

The following rules shall apply with respect to the approval of a limited risk plan in a PDP region:

(A) Limited exercise of authority

Only the minimum number of such plans may be approved in order to meet the access requirements under section 1395w–103(a) of this title.

(B) Maximizing assumption of risk

The Secretary shall provide priority in approval for those plans bearing the highest level of risk (as computed by the Secretary), but the Secretary may take into account the level of the bids submitted by such plans.

(C) No full underwriting for limited risk plans

In no case may the Secretary approve a limited risk plan under which the modification of risk level provides for no (or a de minimis) level of financial risk.

(3) Acceptance of all full risk contracts

There shall be no limit on the number of full risk plans that are approved under subsection (e).

(4) Risk-plans defined

For purposes of this subsection:

(A) Limited risk plan

The term "limited risk plan" means a prescription drug plan that provides basic prescription drug coverage and for which the PDP sponsor includes a modification of risk level described in subparagraph (E) of subsection (b)(2) in its bid submitted for the plan under such subsection. Such term does not include a fallback prescription drug plan.

(B) Full risk plan

The term "full risk plan" means a prescription drug plan that is not a limited risk plan or a fallback prescription drug plan.

(g) Guaranteeing access to coverage

(1) Solicitation of bids

(A) In general

Separate from the bidding process under subsection (b), the Secretary shall provide for a process for the solicitation of bids from eligible fallback entities (as defined in paragraph (2)) for the offering in all fallback service areas (as defined in paragraph (3)) in one or more PDP regions of a fallback prescription drug plan (as defined in paragraph (4)) during the contract period specified in paragraph (5).

(B) Acceptance of bids

(i) In general

Except as provided in this subparagraph, the provisions of subsection (e) shall apply with respect to the approval or disapproval of fallback prescription drug plans. The Secretary shall enter into contracts under this subsection with eligible fallback entities for the offering of fallback prescription drug plans so approved in fallback service areas.

(ii) Limitation of 1 plan for all fallback service areas in a PDP region

With respect to all fallback service areas in any PDP region for a contract period, the Secretary shall approve the offering of only 1 fallback prescription drug plan.

(iii) Competitive procedures

Competitive procedures (as defined in section 132 of Title 41) shall be used to enter into a contract under this subsection. The provisions of subsection (d) of section 1395kk–1 of this title shall apply to a contract under this section in the same manner as they apply to a contract under such section.

(iv) Timing

The Secretary shall approve a fallback prescription drug plan for a PDP region in a manner so that, if there are any fallback service areas in the region for a year, the fallback prescription drug plan is offered at the same time as prescription drug plans would otherwise be offered.

(V) [1] No national fallback plan

The Secretary shall not enter into a contract with a single fallback entity for the offering of fallback plans throughout the United States.

(2) Eligible fallback entity

For purposes of this section, the term "eligible fallback entity" means, with respect to all fallback service areas in a PDP region for a contract period, an entity that—

(A) meets the requirements to be a PDP sponsor (or would meet such requirements but for the fact that the entity is not a risk-bearing entity); and

(B) does not submit a bid under subsection (b) for any prescription drug plan for any PDP region for the first year of such contract period.

For purposes of subparagraph (B), an entity shall be treated as submitting a bid with respect to a prescription drug plan if the entity is acting as a subcontractor of a PDP sponsor that is offering such a plan. The previous sentence shall not apply to entities that are subcontractors of an MA organization except insofar as such organization is acting as a PDP sponsor with respect to a prescription drug plan.

(3) Fallback service area

For purposes of this subsection, the term "fallback service area" means, for a PDP region with respect to a year, any area within such region for which the Secretary determines before the beginning of the year that the access requirements of the first sentence of section 1395w–103(a) of this title will not be met for part D eligible individuals residing in the area for the year.

(4) Fallback prescription drug plan

For purposes of this part, the term "fallback prescription drug plan" means a prescription drug plan that—

(A) only offers the standard prescription drug coverage and access to negotiated prices described in section 1395w–102(a)(1)(A) of this title and does not include any supplemental prescription drug coverage; and

(B) meets such other requirements as the Secretary may specify.

(5) Payments under the contract

(A) In general

A contract entered into under this subsection shall provide for—

(i) payment for the actual costs (taking into account negotiated price concessions described in section 1395w–102(d)(1)(B) of this title) of covered part D drugs provided to part D eligible individuals enrolled in a fallback prescription drug plan offered by the entity; and

(ii) payment of management fees that are tied to performance measures established by the Secretary for the management, administration, and delivery of the benefits under the contract.

(B) Performance measures

The performance measures established by the Secretary pursuant to subparagraph (A)(ii) shall include at least measures for each of the following:

(i) **Costs**

The entity contains costs to the Medicare Prescription Drug Account and to part D eligible individuals enrolled in a fallback prescription drug plan offered by the entity through mechanisms such as generic substitution and price discounts.

(ii) **Quality programs**

The entity provides such enrollees with quality programs that avoid adverse drug reactions and overutilization and reduce medical errors.

(iii) **Customer service**

The entity provides timely and accurate delivery of services and pharmacy and beneficiary support services.

(iv) **Benefit administration and claims adjudication**

The entity provides efficient and effective benefit administration and claims adjudication.

(6) Monthly beneficiary premium

Except as provided in section 1395w–113(b) of this title (relating to late enrollment penalty) and subject to section 1395w–114 of this title (relating to low-income assistance), the monthly beneficiary premium to be charged under a fallback prescription drug plan offered in all fallback service areas in a PDP region shall be uniform and shall be equal to 25.5 percent of an amount equal to the Secretary's estimate of the average monthly per capita actuarial cost, including administrative expenses, under the fallback prescription drug plan of providing coverage in the region, as calculated by the Chief Actuary of the Centers for Medicare & Medicaid Services. In calculating such administrative expenses, the Chief Actuary shall use a factor that is based on similar expenses of prescription drug plans that are not fallback prescription drug plans.

(7) General contract terms and conditions

(A) In general

Except as may be appropriate to carry out this section, the terms and conditions of contracts with eligible fallback entities offering fallback prescription drug plans under this subsection shall be the same as the terms and conditions of contracts under this part for prescription drug plans.

(B) Period of contract

(i) In general

Subject to clause (ii), a contract approved for a fallback prescription drug plan for fallback service areas for a PDP region under this section shall be for a period of 3 years (except as may be renewed after a subsequent bidding process).

(ii) Limitation

A fallback prescription drug plan may be offered under a contract in an area for a year only if that area is a fallback service area for that year.

(C) Entity not permitted to market or brand fallback prescription drug plans

An eligible fallback entity with a contract under this subsection may not engage in any marketing or branding of a fallback prescription drug plan.

(h) Annual report on use of limited risk plans and fallback plans

The Secretary shall submit to Congress an annual report that describes instances in which limited risk plans and fallback prescription drug plans were offered under subsections (f) and (g). The Secretary shall include in such report such recommendations as may be appropriate to limit the need for the provision of such plans and to maximize the assumption of financial risk under section [2] subsection (f).

(i) Noninterference

In order to promote competition under this part and in carrying out this part, the Secretary—

(1) may not interfere with the negotiations between drug manufacturers and pharmacies and PDP sponsors; and

(2) may not require a particular formulary or institute a price structure for the reimbursement of covered part D drugs.

(j) Coordination of benefits

A PDP sponsor offering a prescription drug plan shall permit State Pharmaceutical Assistance Programs and Rx plans under sections 1395w–133 and 1395w–134 of this title to coordinate benefits with the plan and, in connection with such coordination with such a Program, not to impose fees that are unrelated to the cost of coordination.

(Aug. 14, 1935, c. 531, Title XVIII, § 1860D–11, as added Pub.L. 108–173, Title I, § 101(a)(2), Dec. 8, 2003, 117 Stat. 2092; amended Pub.L. 111–148, Title III, § 3209(b), Mar. 23, 2010, 124 Stat. 460.)

[1] So in original. Probably should read "(v)".

[2] So in original.

HISTORICAL AND STATUTORY NOTES

Revision Notes and Legislative Reports

2003 Acts. House Conference Report No. 108–391 and Statement by President, see 2003 U.S. Code Cong. and Adm. News, p. 1808.

References in Text

Part D, referred to in text, means Part D of Title XVIII of the Social Security Act, Act Aug. 14, 1935, c. 531, Title XVIII, § 1860D–1 et seq., as added, Pub.L. 108–173, Title I, § 101(a)(2), Dec. 8, 2003, 117 Stat. 2071, which is classified to this part, 42 U.S.C.A. 1395w–101 et seq.

Section 1395w–115(e)(2)(B)(iii) of this title, referred to in subsec. (b)(2)(E)(ii)(I), was in the original "section 1869D–15(e)(2)(B)(iii)", and was translated as reading "section 1860D–15(e)(2)(B)(iii)", meaning section 1860D–15(e)(2)(B)(iii) of the Social Security Act, to reflect the probable intent of Congress. The Social Security Act does not contain a section 1869D–15 and section 1395w–115(e)(2)(B)(iii) of this title provides for an application of a higher percentage for years 2006 and 2007.

Chapter 89 of Title 5, referred to in subsec. (d)(2)(B), is 5 U.S.C.A. § 8901 et seq.

Codifications

In subsec. (g)(1)(B)(iii), "section 132 of Title 41" substituted for "section 4(5) of the Office of Federal Procurement Policy Act (41 U.S.C. 403(5)" on authority of Pub.L. 111–350, § 6(c), Jan. 4, 2011, 124 Stat. 3854, which Act enacted Title 41, Public Contracts.

Effective and Applicability Provisions

2010 Acts. Amendments by Pub.L. 111–148, § 3209, applicable to bids submitted for contract years beginning on or after January 1, 2011, see Pub.L. 111–148, § 3209(c), set out as a note under 42 U.S.C.A. § 1395w–24.

Study Regarding Regional Variations in Prescription Drug Spending

Pub.L. 108–173, Title I, § 107(a), Dec. 8, 2003, 117 Stat. 2169, provided that:

"**(1) In general.**—The Secretary shall conduct a study that examines variations in per capita spending for covered part D drugs under part D of title XVIII of the Social Security Act [this part] among PDP regions and, with respect to such spending, the amount of such variation that is attributable to—

"(A) price variations (described in section 1860D–15(c)(2) of such Act [42 U.S.C.A. § 1395w–115(c)(2)]); and

"(B) differences in per capita utilization that is not taken into account in the health status risk adjustment provided under section 1860D–15(c)(1) of such Act [42 U.S.C.A. § 1395w–115(c)(1)].

"**(2) Report and recommendations.**—Not later than January 1, 2009, the Secretary shall submit to Congress a report on the study conducted under paragraph (1). Such report shall include—

"(A) information regarding the extent of geographic variation described in paragraph (1)(B);

"(B) an analysis of the impact on direct subsidies under section 1860D–15(a)(1) of the Social Security Act [42 U.S.C.A. § 1395w–115(a)(1)] in different PDP regions if such subsidies were adjusted to take into account the variation described in subparagraph (A); and

"(C) recommendations regarding the appropriateness of applying an additional geographic adjustment factor under section 1860D–15(c)(2) [42 U.S.C.A. § 1395w–115(c)(2)] that reflects some or all of the variation described in subparagraph (A)."

§ 1395w–112. Requirements for and contracts with prescription drug plan (PDP) sponsors

(a) General requirements

Each PDP sponsor of a prescription drug plan shall meet the following requirements:

(1) Licensure

Subject to subsection (c), the sponsor is organized and licensed under State law as a risk-bearing entity eligible to offer health insurance or health benefits coverage in each State in which it offers a prescription drug plan.

(2) Assumption of financial risk for unsubsidized coverage

(A) In general

Subject to subparagraph (B), to the extent that the entity is at risk the entity assumes financial risk on a prospective basis for benefits that it offers under a prescription drug plan and that is not covered under section 1395w–115(b) of this title.

(B) Reinsurance permitted

The plan sponsor may obtain insurance or make other arrangements for the cost of coverage provided to any enrollee to the extent that the sponsor is at risk for providing such coverage.

(3) Solvency for unlicensed sponsors

In the case of a PDP sponsor that is not described in paragraph (1) and for which a waiver has been approved under subsection (c), such sponsor shall meet solvency standards established by the Secretary under subsection (d).

(b) Contract requirements

(1) In general

The Secretary shall not permit the enrollment under section 1395w–101 of this title in a prescription drug plan offered by a PDP sponsor under this part, and the sponsor shall not be eligible for payments under section 1395w–114 or 1395w–115 of this title, unless the Secretary has entered into a contract under this subsection with the sponsor with respect to the offering of such plan. Such a contract with a sponsor may cover more than one prescription drug plan. Such contract shall provide that the sponsor agrees to comply with the applicable requirements and standards of this part and the terms and conditions of payment as provided for in this part.

(2) Limitation on entities offering fallback prescription drug plans

The Secretary shall not enter into a contract with a PDP sponsor for the offering of a prescription drug plan (other than a fallback prescription drug plan) in a PDP region for a year if the sponsor—

(A) submitted a bid under section 1395w–111(g) of this title for such year (as the first year of a contract period under such section) to offer a fallback prescription drug plan in any PDP region;

(B) offers a fallback prescription drug plan in any PDP region during the year; or

(C) offered a fallback prescription drug plan in that PDP region during the previous year.

For purposes of this paragraph, an entity shall be treated as submitting a bid with respect to a prescription drug plan or offering a fallback prescription drug plan if the entity is acting as a subcontractor of a PDP sponsor that is offering such a plan. The previous sentence shall not apply to entities that are subcontractors of an MA organization except insofar as such organization is acting as a PDP sponsor with respect to a prescription drug plan.

(3) Incorporation of certain medicare advantage contract requirements

Except as otherwise provided, the following provisions of section 1395w–27 of this title shall apply to contracts under this section in the same manner as they apply to contracts under section 1395w–27(a) of this title:

(A) Minimum enrollment

Paragraphs (1) and (3) of section 1395w–27(b) of this title, except that—

(i) the Secretary may increase the minimum number of enrollees required under such paragraph (1) as the Secretary determines appropriate; and

(ii) the requirement of such paragraph (1) shall be waived during the first contract year with respect to an organization in a region.

(B) Contract period and effectiveness

Section 1395w–27(c) of this title, except that in applying paragraph (4)(B) of such section any reference to payment amounts under section 1395w–23 of this title shall be deemed payment amounts under section 1395w–115 of this title.

(C) Protections against fraud and beneficiary protections

Section 1395w–27(d) of this title.

(D) Additional contract terms

Section 1395w–27(e) of this title; except that section 1395w–27(e)(2) of this title shall apply as specified to PDP sponsors and payments under this part to an MA–PD plan shall be treated as expenditures made under part D. Notwithstanding any other provision of law, information provided to the Secretary under the application of section 1395w–27(e)(1) of this title to contracts under this section under the preceding sentence—

(i) may be used for the purposes of carrying out this part, improving public health through research on the utilization, safety, effectiveness, quality, and efficiency of health care services (as the Secretary determines appropriate); and

(ii) shall be made available to Congressional [1] support agencies (in accordance with their obligations to support Congress as set out in their authorizing statutes) for the purposes of conducting Congressional [1] oversight, monitoring, making recommendations, and analysis of the program under this subchapter.

(E) Intermediate sanctions

Section 1395w–27(g) of this title (other than paragraph (1)(F) of such section), except that in applying such section the reference in section 1395w–27(g)(1)(B) of this title to section 1395w–24 of this title is deemed a reference to this part.

(F) Procedures for termination

Section 1395w–27(h) of this title.

(4) Prompt payment of clean claims

(A) Prompt payment

(i) In general

Each contract entered into with a PDP sponsor under this part with respect to a prescription drug plan offered by such sponsor shall provide that payment shall be issued, mailed, or otherwise transmitted with respect to all clean claims submitted by pharmacies (other than pharmacies that dispense drugs by mail order only or are located in, or contract with, a long-term care facility) under this part within the applicable number of calendar days after the date on which the claim is received.

(ii) Clean claim defined

In this paragraph, the term "clean claim" means a claim that has no defect or impropriety (including any lack of any required substantiating documentation) or particular circumstance requiring special treatment that prevents timely payment from being made on the claim under this part.

(iii) Date of receipt of claim

In this paragraph, a claim is considered to have been received—

(I) with respect to claims submitted electronically, on the date on which the claim is transferred; and

(II) with respect to claims submitted otherwise, on the 5th day after the postmark date of the claim or the date specified in the time stamp of the transmission.

(B) Applicable number of calendar days defined

In this paragraph, the term "applicable number of calendar days" means—

(i) with respect to claims submitted electronically, 14 days; and

(ii) with respect to claims submitted otherwise, 30 days.

(C) Interest payment

(i) In general

Subject to clause (ii), if payment is not issued, mailed, or otherwise transmitted within the applicable number of calendar days (as defined in subparagraph (B)) after a clean claim is received, the PDP sponsor shall pay interest to the pharmacy that submitted the claim at a rate equal to the weighted average of interest on 3–month marketable Treasury securities determined for such period, increased by 0.1 percentage point for the period beginning on the day after the required payment date and ending on the date on which payment is made (as determined under subparagraph (D)(iv)). Interest amounts paid under this subparagraph shall not be counted against the administrative costs of a prescription drug plan or treated as allowable risk corridor costs under section 1395w–115(e) of this title.

(ii) Authority not to charge interest

The Secretary may provide that a PDP sponsor is not charged interest under clause (i) in the case where there are exigent circumstances, including natural disasters and other unique and unexpected events, that prevent the timely processing of claims.

(D) Procedures involving claims

(i) Claim deemed to be clean

A claim is deemed to be a clean claim if the PDP sponsor involved does not provide notice to the claimant of any deficiency in the claim—

(I) with respect to claims submitted electronically, within 10 days after the date on which the claim is received; and

(II) with respect to claims submitted otherwise, within 15 days after the date on which the claim is received.

(ii) Claim determined to not be a clean claim

(I) In general

If a PDP sponsor determines that a submitted claim is not a clean claim, the PDP sponsor shall, not later than the end of the period described in clause (i), notify the claimant of such determination. Such notification shall specify all defects or improprieties in the claim and shall list all additional information or documents necessary for the proper processing and payment of the claim.

(II) Determination after submission of additional information

A claim is deemed to be a clean claim under this paragraph if the PDP sponsor involved does not provide notice to the claimant of any defect or impropriety in the claim within 10 days of the date on which additional information is received under subclause (I).

(iii) Obligation to pay

A claim submitted to a PDP sponsor that is not paid or contested by the sponsor within the applicable number of days (as defined in subparagraph (B)) after the date on which the claim is received shall be deemed to be a clean claim and shall be paid by the PDP sponsor in accordance with subparagraph (A).

(iv) Date of payment of claim

Payment of a clean claim under such subparagraph is considered to have been made on the date on which—

(I) with respect to claims paid electronically, the payment is transferred; and

(II) with respect to claims paid otherwise, the payment is submitted to the United States Postal Service or common carrier for delivery.

(E) Electronic transfer of funds

A PDP sponsor shall pay all clean claims submitted electronically by electronic transfer of funds if the pharmacy so requests or has so requested previously. In the case where such payment is made electronically, remittance may be made by the PDP sponsor electronically as well.

(F) Protecting the rights of claimants

(i) In general

Nothing in this paragraph shall be construed to prohibit or limit a claim or action not covered by the subject matter of this section that any individual or organization has against a provider or a PDP sponsor.

(ii) Anti-retaliation

Consistent with applicable Federal or State law, a PDP sponsor shall not retaliate against an individual or provider for exercising a right of action under this subparagraph.

(G) Rule of construction

A determination under this paragraph that a claim submitted by a pharmacy is a clean claim shall not be construed as a positive determination regarding eligibility for payment under this subchapter, nor is it an indication of government approval of, or acquiescence regarding, the claim submitted. The determination shall not relieve any party of civil or criminal liability with respect to the claim, nor does it offer a defense to any administrative, civil, or criminal action with respect to the claim.

(5) Submission of claims by pharmacies located in or contracting with long-term care facilities

Each contract entered into with a PDP sponsor under this part with respect to a prescription drug plan offered by such sponsor shall provide that a pharmacy located in, or having a contract with, a long-term care facility shall have not less than 30 days (but not more than 90 days) to submit claims to the sponsor for reimbursement under the plan.

(6) Regular update of prescription drug pricing standard

If the PDP sponsor of a prescription drug plan uses a standard for reimbursement of pharmacies based on the cost of a drug, each contract entered into with such sponsor under this part with respect to the plan shall provide that the sponsor shall update such standard not less frequently than once every 7 days, beginning with an initial update on January 1 of each year, to accurately reflect the market price of acquiring the drug.

(7) Suspension of payments pending investigation of credible allegations of fraud by pharmacies

(A) In general

Section 1395y(*o*)(1) of this title shall apply with respect to a PDP sponsor with a contract under this part, a pharmacy, and payments to such pharmacy under this part in the same manner as such section applies with respect to the Secretary, a provider of services or supplier, and payments to such provider of services or supplier under this subchapter. A PDP sponsor shall notify the Secretary regarding the imposition of any payment suspension pursuant to the previous sentence, such as through the secure internet website portal (or other successor technology) established under section 1395w-28(i) of this title.

(B) Rule of construction

Nothing in this paragraph shall be construed as limiting the authority of a PDP sponsor to conduct postpayment review.

(c) Waiver of certain requirements to expand choice

(1) Authorizing waiver

(A) In general

In the case of an entity that seeks to offer a prescription drug plan in a State, the Secretary shall waive the requirement of subsection (a)(1) that the entity be licensed in that State if the Secretary determines, based on the application and other evidence presented to the Secretary, that any of the grounds for approval of the application described in paragraph (2) have been met.

(B) Application of regional plan waiver rule

In addition to the waiver available under subparagraph (A), the provisions of section 1395w-27a(d) of this title shall apply to PDP sponsors under this part in a manner similar to the manner in which such provisions apply to MA organizations under part C, except that no application shall be required under paragraph (1)(B) of such section in the case of a State that does not provide a licensing process for such a sponsor.

(2) Grounds for approval

(A) In general

The grounds for approval under this paragraph are—

(i) subject to subparagraph (B), the grounds for approval described in subparagraphs (B), (C), and (D) of section 1395w-25(a)(2) of this title; and

(ii) the application by a State of any grounds other than those required under Federal law.

(B) Special rules

In applying subparagraph (A)(i)—

(i) the ground of approval described in section 1395w-25(a)(2)(B) of this title is deemed to have been met if the State does not have a licensing process in effect with respect to the PDP sponsor; and

(ii) for plan years beginning before January 1, 2008, if the State does have such a licensing process in effect, such ground for approval described in such section is deemed to have been met upon submission of an application described in such section.

(3) Application of waiver procedures

With respect to an application for a waiver (or a waiver granted) under paragraph (1)(A) of this subsection, the provisions of subparagraphs (E), (F), and (G) of section 1395w–25(a)(2) of this title shall apply, except that clauses (i) and (ii) of such subparagraph (E) shall not apply in the case of a State that does not have a licensing process described in paragraph (2)(B)(i) in effect.

(4) References to certain provisions

In applying provisions of section 1395w–25(a)(2) of this title under paragraphs (2) and (3) of this subsection to prescription drug plans and PDP sponsors—

(A) any reference to a waiver application under section 1395w–25 of this title shall be treated as a reference to a waiver application under paragraph (1)(A) of this subsection; and

(B) any reference to solvency standards shall be treated as a reference to solvency standards established under subsection (d) of this section.

(d) Solvency standards for non-licensed entities

(1) Establishment and publication

The Secretary, in consultation with the National Association of Insurance Commissioners, shall establish and publish, by not later than January 1, 2005, financial solvency and capital adequacy standards for entities described in paragraph (2).

(2) Compliance with standards

A PDP sponsor that is not licensed by a State under subsection (a)(1) and for which a waiver application has been approved under subsection (c) shall meet solvency and capital adequacy standards established under paragraph (1). The Secretary shall establish certification procedures for such sponsors with respect to such solvency standards in the manner described in section 1395w–25(c)(2) of this title.

(e) Licensure does not substitute for or constitute certification

The fact that a PDP sponsor is licensed in accordance with subsection (a)(1) or has a waiver application approved under subsection (c) does not deem the sponsor to meet other requirements imposed under this part for a sponsor.

(f) Periodic review and revision of standards

(1) In general

Subject to paragraph (2), the Secretary may periodically review the standards established under this section and, based on such review, may revise such standards if the Secretary determines such revision to be appropriate.

(2) Prohibition of midyear implementation of significant new regulatory requirements

The Secretary may not implement, other than at the beginning of a calendar year, regulations under this section that impose new, significant regulatory requirements on a PDP sponsor or a prescription drug plan.

(g) Prohibition of State imposition of premium taxes; relation to State laws

The provisions of sections 1395w–24(g) and 1395w–26(b)(3) of this title shall apply with respect to PDP sponsors and prescription drug plans under this part in the same manner as such sections apply to MA organizations and MA plans under part C.

(Aug. 14, 1935, c. 531, Title XVIII, § 1860D–12, as added Pub.L. 108–173, Title I, § 101(a)(2), Dec. 8, 2003, 117 Stat. 2099; amended Pub.L. 110–275, Title I, §§ 171(a), 172(a)(1), 173(a), 181, July 15, 2008, 122 Stat. 2578, 2580, 2581, 2582; Pub.L. 115–271, Title II, § 2008(a), Oct. 24, 2018, 132 Stat. 3931.)

[1] So in original. Probably should not be capitalized.

HISTORICAL AND STATUTORY NOTES

Revision Notes and Legislative Reports

2003 Acts. House Conference Report No. 108–391 and Statement by President, see 2003 U.S. Code Cong. and Adm. News, p. 1808.

References in Text

This subchapter, referred to in text, originally read "this title", meaning Title XVIII of the Social Security Act, Act Aug. 14, 1935, c.531, 49 Stat. 620, as amended, which is principally classified to this subchapter, 42 U.S.C.A. § 1395 et seq.

Part D, referred to in subsec. (b)(3)(D), means Part D of Title XVIII of the Social Security Act, Act Aug. 14, 1935, c. 531, Title XVIII, § 1860D–1 et seq., as added, Pub.L. 108–173, Title I, § 101(a)(2), Dec. 8, 2003, 117 Stat. 2071, which is classified to this part, 42 U.S.C.A. § 1395w–101 et seq.

Part C, referred to in subsecs. (c)(1)(B) and (g), means Part C of Title XVIII of the Social Security Act, Act Aug. 14, 1935, c. 531, Title XVIII, § 1851 et seq., as added Aug. 5, 1997, Pub.L. 105–33, Title IV, § 4001, 111 Stat. 276, and amended, which is classified to part C of this subchapter, 42 U.S.C.A. § 1395w–21 et seq.

Effective and Applicability Provisions

2008 Acts. Amendments by Pub.L. 110–275, § 171, applicable to plan years beginning on or after Jan. 1, 2010, see Pub.L. 110–275, § 171(c), set out as a note under 42 U.S.C.A. § 1395w–27.

Amendments by Pub.L. 110–275, § 172, applicable to plan years beginning on or after Jan. 1, 2010, see Pub.L. 110–275, § 172(b), set out as a note under 42 U.S.C.A. § 1395w–27.

Amendments by Pub.L. 110–275, § 173, applicable to plan years beginning on or after Jan. 1, 2009, see Pub.L. 110–275, § 173(c), set out as a note under 42 U.S.C.A. § 1395w–27.

§ 1395w–113. Premiums; late enrollment penalty

(a) Monthly beneficiary premium

(1) Computation

(A) In general

The monthly beneficiary premium for a prescription drug plan is the base beneficiary premium computed under paragraph (2) as adjusted under this paragraph.

(B) Adjustment to reflect difference between bid and national average bid

(i) Above average bid

If for a month the amount of the standardized bid amount (as defined in paragraph (5)) exceeds the amount of the adjusted national average monthly bid amount (as defined in clause (iii)), the base beneficiary premium for the month shall be increased by the amount of such excess.

(ii) Below average bid

If for a month the amount of the adjusted national average monthly bid amount for the month exceeds the standardized bid amount, the base beneficiary premium for the month shall be decreased by the amount of such excess.

(iii) Adjusted national average monthly bid amount defined

For purposes of this subparagraph, the term "adjusted national average monthly bid amount" means the national average monthly bid amount computed under paragraph (4), as adjusted under section 1395w–115(c)(2) of this title.

(C) Increase for supplemental prescription drug benefits

The base beneficiary premium shall be increased by the portion of the PDP approved bid that is attributable to supplemental prescription drug benefits.

(D) Increase for late enrollment penalty

The base beneficiary premium shall be increased by the amount of any late enrollment penalty under subsection (b).

(E) Decrease for low-income assistance

The monthly beneficiary premium is subject to decrease in the case of a subsidy eligible individual under section 1395w–114 of this title.

(F) Increase based on income

The monthly beneficiary premium shall be increased pursuant to paragraph (7).

(G) Uniform premium

Except as provided in subparagraphs (D), (E), and (F), the monthly beneficiary premium for a prescription drug plan in a PDP region is the same for all part D eligible individuals enrolled in the plan.

(2) Base beneficiary premium

The base beneficiary premium under this paragraph for a prescription drug plan for a month is equal to the product [1]—

(A) the beneficiary premium percentage (as specified in paragraph (3)); and

(B) the national average monthly bid amount (computed under paragraph (4)) for the month.

(3) Beneficiary premium percentage

For purposes of this subsection, the beneficiary premium percentage for any year is the percentage equal to a fraction—

(A) the numerator of which is 25.5 percent; and

(B) the denominator of which is 100 percent minus a percentage equal to—

(i) the total reinsurance payments which the Secretary estimates are payable under section 1395w–115(b) of this title with respect to the coverage year; divided by

(ii) the sum of—

(I) the amount estimated under clause (i) for the year; and

(II) the total payments which the Secretary estimates will be paid to prescription drug plans and MA–PD plans that are attributable to the standardized bid amount during the year, taking into account amounts paid by the Secretary and enrollees.

(4) Computation of national average monthly bid amount

(A) In general

For each year (beginning with 2006) the Secretary shall compute a national average monthly bid amount equal to the average of the standardized bid amounts (as defined in paragraph (5)) for each prescription drug plan and for each MA–PD plan described in section 1395w–21(a)(2)(A)(i) of this title. Such average does not take into account the bids submitted for MSA plans, MA private fee-for-service plan, and specialized MA plans for special needs individuals, PACE programs under section 1395eee of this title (pursuant to section 1395w–131(f) of this title), and under reasonable cost reimbursement contracts under section 1395mm(h) of this title (pursuant to section 1395w–131(e) of this title).

(B) Weighted average

(i) In general

The monthly national average monthly bid amount computed under subparagraph (A) for a year shall be a weighted average, with the weight for each plan being equal to the average number of part D eligible individuals enrolled in such plan in the reference month (as defined in section 1395w–27a(f)(4) of this title).

(ii) **Special rule for 2006**

For purposes of applying this paragraph for 2006, the Secretary shall establish procedures for determining the weighted average under clause (i) for 2005.

(5) Standardized bid amount defined

For purposes of this subsection, the term "standardized bid amount" means the following:

(A) Prescription drug plans

(i) Basic coverage

In the case of a prescription drug plan that provides basic prescription drug coverage, the PDP approved bid (as defined in paragraph (6)).

(ii) Supplemental coverage

In the case of a prescription drug plan that provides supplemental prescription drug coverage, the portion of the PDP approved bid that is attributable to basic prescription drug coverage.

(B) MA–PD plans

In the case of an MA–PD plan, the portion of the accepted bid amount that is attributable to basic prescription drug coverage.

(6) PDP approved bid defined

For purposes of this part, the term "PDP approved bid" means, with respect to a prescription drug plan, the bid amount approved for the plan under this part.

(7) Increase in base beneficiary premium based on income

(A) In general

In the case of an individual whose modified adjusted gross income exceeds the threshold amount applicable under paragraph (2) of section 1395r(i) of this title (including application of paragraph (5) of such section) for the calendar year, the monthly amount of the beneficiary premium applicable under this section for a month after December 2010 shall be increased by the monthly adjustment amount specified in subparagraph (B).

(B) Monthly adjustment amount

The monthly adjustment amount specified in this subparagraph for an individual for a month in a year is equal to the product of—

(i) the quotient obtained by dividing—

(I) the applicable percentage determined under paragraph (3)(C) of section 1395r(i) of this title (including application of paragraph (5) of such section) for the individual for the calendar year reduced by 25.5 percent; by

(II) 25.5 percent; and

(ii) the base beneficiary premium (as computed under paragraph (2)).

(C) Modified adjusted gross income

For purposes of this paragraph, the term "modified adjusted gross income" has the meaning given such term in subparagraph (A) of section 1395r(i)(4) of this title, determined for the taxable year applicable under subparagraphs (B) and (C) of such section.

(D) Determination by Commissioner of Social Security

The Commissioner of Social Security shall make any determination necessary to carry out the income-related increase in the base beneficiary premium under this paragraph.

(E) Procedures to assure correct income-related increase in base beneficiary premium

(i) Disclosure of base beneficiary premium

Not later than September 15 of each year beginning with 2010, the Secretary shall disclose to the Commissioner of Social Security the amount of the base beneficiary premium (as computed under paragraph (2)) for the purpose of carrying out the income-related increase in the base beneficiary premium under this paragraph with respect to the following year.

(ii) Additional disclosure

Not later than October 15 of each year beginning with 2010, the Secretary shall disclose to the Commissioner of Social Security the following information for the purpose of carrying out the income-related increase in the base beneficiary premium under this paragraph with respect to the following year:

(I) The modified adjusted gross income threshold applicable under paragraph (2) of section 1395r(i) of this title (including application of paragraph (5) of such section).

(II) The applicable percentage determined under paragraph (3)(C) of section 1395r(i) of this title (including application of paragraph (5) of such section).

(III) The monthly adjustment amount specified in subparagraph (B).

(IV) Any other information the Commissioner of Social Security determines necessary to carry out the income-related increase in the base beneficiary premium under this paragraph.

(F) Rule of construction

The formula used to determine the monthly adjustment amount specified under subparagraph (B) shall only be used for the purpose of determining such monthly adjustment amount under such subparagraph.

(b) Late enrollment penalty

(1) In general

Subject to the succeeding provisions of this subsection, in the case of a part D eligible individual described in paragraph (2) with respect to a continuous period of eligibility, there shall be an increase in the monthly beneficiary premium established under subsection (a) in an amount determined under paragraph (3).

(2) Individuals subject to penalty

A part D eligible individual described in this paragraph is, with respect to a continuous period of eligibility, an individual for whom there is a continuous period of 63 days or longer (all of which in such continuous period of eligibility) beginning on the day after the last date of the individual's initial enrollment period under section 1395w–101(b)(2) of this title and ending on the date of enrollment under a prescription drug plan or MA–PD plan during all of which the individual was not covered under any creditable prescription drug coverage.

(3) Amount of penalty

(A) In general

The amount determined under this paragraph for a part D eligible individual for a continuous period of eligibility is the greater of—

(i) an amount that the Secretary determines is actuarially sound for each uncovered month (as defined in subparagraph (B)) in the same continuous period of eligibility; or

(ii) 1 percent of the base beneficiary premium (computed under subsection (a)(2)) for each such uncovered month in such period.

(B) Uncovered month defined

For purposes of this subsection, the term "uncovered month" means, with respect to a part D eligible individual, any month beginning after the end of the initial enrollment period under section 1395w–101(b)(2) of this title unless the individual can demonstrate that the individual had creditable prescription drug coverage (as defined in paragraph (4)) for any portion of such month.

(4) Creditable prescription drug coverage defined

For purposes of this part, the term "creditable prescription drug coverage" means any of the following coverage, but only if the coverage meets the requirement of paragraph (5):

(A) Coverage under prescription drug plan or MA–PD plan

Coverage under a prescription drug plan or under an MA–PD plan.

(B) Medicaid

Coverage under a medicaid plan under subchapter XIX or under a waiver under section 1315 of this title.

(C) Group health plan

Coverage under a group health plan, including a health benefits plan under chapter 89 of Title 5, (commonly known as the Federal employees health benefits program), and a qualified retiree prescription drug plan (as defined in section 1395w–132(a)(2) of this title).

(D) State pharmaceutical assistance program

Coverage under a State pharmaceutical assistance program described in section 1395w–133(b)(1) of this title.

(E) Veterans' coverage of prescription drugs

Coverage for veterans, and survivors and dependents of veterans, under chapter 17 of Title 38.

(F) Prescription drug coverage under medigap policies

Coverage under a medicare supplemental policy under section 1395ss of this title that provides benefits for prescription drugs (whether or not such coverage conforms to the standards for packages of benefits under section 1395ss(p)(1) of this title).

(G) Military coverage (including TRICARE)

Coverage under chapter 55 of Title 10.

(H) Other coverage

Such other coverage as the Secretary determines appropriate.

(5) Actuarial equivalence requirement

Coverage meets the requirement of this paragraph only if the coverage is determined (in a manner specified by the Secretary) to provide coverage of the cost of prescription drugs the actuarial value of which (as defined by the Secretary) to the individual equals or exceeds the actuarial value of standard prescription drug coverage (as determined under section 1395w–111(c) of this title).

(6) Procedures to document creditable prescription drug coverage

(A) In general

The Secretary shall establish procedures (including the form, manner, and time) for the documentation of creditable prescription drug coverage, including procedures to assist in determining whether coverage meets the requirement of paragraph (5).

(B) Disclosure by entities offering creditable prescription drug coverage

(i) In general

Each entity that offers prescription drug coverage of the type described in subparagraphs (B) through (H) of paragraph (4) shall provide for disclosure, in a form, manner, and time consistent with standards established by the Secretary, to the Secretary and part D eligible individuals of whether the coverage meets the requirement of paragraph (5) or whether such coverage is changed so it no longer meets such requirement.

(ii) Disclosure of non-creditable coverage

In the case of such coverage that does not meet such requirement, the disclosure to part D eligible individuals under this subparagraph shall include information regarding the fact that because such coverage does not meet such requirement there are limitations on the periods in a year in which the individuals may enroll under a prescription drug plan or an MA–PD plan and that any such enrollment is subject to a late enrollment penalty under this subsection.

(C) Waiver of requirement

In the case of a part D eligible individual who was enrolled in prescription drug coverage of the type described in subparagraphs (B) through (H) of paragraph (4) which is not creditable prescription drug coverage because it does not meet the requirement of paragraph (5), the individual may apply to the Secretary to have such coverage treated as creditable prescription drug coverage if the individual establishes that the individual was not adequately informed that such coverage did not meet such requirement.

(7) Continuous period of eligibility

(A) In general

Subject to subparagraph (B), for purposes of this subsection, the term "continuous period of eligibility" means, with respect to a part D eligible individual, the period that begins with the first day on which the individual is eligible to enroll in a prescription drug plan under this part and ends with the individual's death.

(B) Separate period

Any period during all of which a part D eligible individual is entitled to hospital insurance benefits under part A and—

(i) which terminated in or before the month preceding the month in which the individual attained age 65; or

(ii) for which the basis for eligibility for such entitlement changed between section 426(b) of this title and section 426(a) of this title, between 426(b) [2] of this title and section 426–1 of this title, or between section 426–1 of this title and section 426(a) of this title,

shall be a separate continuous period of eligibility with respect to the individual (and each such period which terminates shall be deemed not to have existed for purposes of subsequently applying this paragraph).

(8) Waiver of penalty for subsidy-eligible individuals

In no case shall a part D eligible individual who is determined to be a subsidy eligible individual (as defined in section 1395w–114(a)(3) of this title) be subject to an increase in the monthly beneficiary premium established under subsection (a).

(c) Collection of monthly beneficiary premiums

(1) In general

Subject to paragraphs (2), (3), and (4), the provisions of section 1395w–24(d) of this title shall apply to PDP sponsors and premiums (and any late enrollment penalty) under this part in the same manner as they apply to MA organizations and beneficiary premiums under part C, except that any reference to a Trust Fund is deemed for this purpose a reference to the Medicare Prescription Drug Account.

(2) Crediting of late enrollment penalty

(A) Portion attributable to increased actuarial costs

With respect to late enrollment penalties imposed under subsection (b), the Secretary shall specify the portion of such a penalty that the Secretary estimates is attributable to increased actuarial costs assumed by the PDP sponsor or MA organization (and not taken into account through risk adjustment provided under section 1395w–115(c)(1) of this title or through reinsurance payments under section 1395w–115(b) of this title) as a result of such late enrollment.

(B) Collection through withholding

In the case of a late enrollment penalty that is collected from a part D eligible individual in the manner described in section 1395w–24(d)(2)(A) of this title, the Secretary shall provide that only the portion of such penalty estimated under subparagraph (A) shall be paid to the PDP sponsor or MA organization offering the part D plan in which the individual is enrolled.

(C) Collection by plan

In the case of a late enrollment penalty that is collected from a part D eligible individual in a manner other than the manner described in section 1395w–24(d)(2)(A) of this title, the Secretary shall establish procedures for reducing payments otherwise made to the PDP sponsor or MA organization by an amount equal to the amount of such penalty less the portion of such penalty estimated under subparagraph (A).

(3) Fallback plans

In applying this subsection in the case of a fallback prescription drug plan, paragraph (2) shall not apply and the monthly beneficiary premium shall be collected in the manner specified in section 1395w–24(d)(2)(A) of this title (or such other manner as may be provided under section 1395s of this title in the case of monthly premiums under section 1395r of this title).

(4) Collection of monthly adjustment amount

(A) In general

Notwithstanding any provision of this subsection or section 1395w–24(d)(2) of this title, subject to subparagraph (B), the amount of the income-related increase in the base beneficiary premium for an individual for a month (as determined under subsection (a)(7)) shall be paid through withholding from benefit payments in the manner provided under section 1395s of this title.

(B) Agreements

In the case where the monthly benefit payments of an individual that are withheld under subparagraph (A) are insufficient to pay the amount described in such subparagraph, the Commissioner of Social Security shall enter into agreements with the Secretary, the Director of the Office of Personnel Management, and the Railroad Retirement Board as necessary in order to allow other agencies to collect the amount described in subparagraph (A) that was not withheld under such subparagraph.

(Aug. 14, 1935, c. 531, Title XVIII, § 1860D–13, as added Pub.L. 108–173, Title I, § 101(a)(2), Dec. 8, 2003, 117 Stat. 2102; amended Pub.L. 110–275, Title I, § 114(a)(1), July 15, 2008, 122 Stat. 2506; Pub.L. 111–148, Title III, § 3308(a), (b)(1), Mar. 23, 2010, 124 Stat. 472, 474.)

1 So in original. The word "of" probably should be appear after the word "product".

2 So in original. Probably should be "section 426(b)".

HISTORICAL AND STATUTORY NOTES

Revision Notes and Legislative Reports

2003 Acts. House Conference Report No. 108–391 and Statement by President, see 2003 U.S. Code Cong. and Adm. News, p. 1808.

References in Text

Part D, referred to in text, means Part D of Title XVIII of the Social Security Act, Act Aug. 14, 1935, c. 531, Title XVIII, § 1860D–1 et seq., as added, Pub.L. 108–173, Title I, § 101(a)(2), Dec. 8, 2003, 117 Stat. 2071, which is classified to this part, 42 U.S.C.A. § 1395w–101 et seq.

Subchapter XIX, referred to in subsec. (b)(4)(B), originally read "title XIX", meaning Title XIX of the Social Security Act, Aug. 14, 1935, c. 531, Title XIX, § 1901 et seq., as added July 30, 1965, Pub.L. 89–97, Title I, § 121(a), 79 Stat. 343, and amended, which is principally classified to subchapter XIX of this chapter, 42 U.S.C.A. § 1396 et seq.

Chapter 89 of Title 5, referred to in subsec. (b)(4)(C), is 5 U.S.C.A. § 8901 et seq.

Chapter 17 of Title 38, referred to in subsec. (b)(4)(E), is 38 U.S.C.A. § 1700 et seq.

Chapter 55 of Title 10, referred to in subsec. (b)(4)(G), is 10 U.S.C.A. § 1071 et seq.

Part A, referred to in subsec. (b)(7)(B), means Part A of Title XVIII of the Social Security Act, Act Aug. 14, 1935, c. 531, Title XVIII, § 1811 et seq., as added July 30, 1965, Pub.L. 89–97, Title I, § 102(a), 79 Stat. 291, and amended, which is classified to part A of this subchapter, 42 U.S.C.A. § 1395c et seq.

Part C, referred to in subsec. (c)(1), means Part C of Title XVIII of the Social Security Act, Act Aug. 14, 1935, c. 531, Title XVIII, § 1851 et seq., as added Aug. 5, 1997, Pub.L. 105–33, Title IV, § 4001, 111 Stat. 276, and amended, which is classified to part C of this subchapter, 42 U.S.C.A. § 1395w–21 et seq.

Effective and Applicability Provisions

2008 Acts. Pub.L. 110–275, Title I, § 114(b), July 15, 2008, 122 Stat. 2507, provided that: "The amendments made by this section [amending this section and 42 U.S.C.A. § 1395w–114] shall apply to subsidies for months beginning with January 2009."

§ 1395w–114. Premium and cost-sharing subsidies for low-income individuals

(a) Income-related subsidies for individuals with income up to 150 percent of poverty line

(1) Individuals with income below 135 percent of poverty line

In the case of a subsidy eligible individual (as defined in paragraph (3)) who is determined to have income that is below 135 percent of the poverty line applicable to a family of the size involved and who meets the resources requirement described in paragraph (3)(D) or who is covered under this paragraph under paragraph (3)(B)(i), the individual is entitled under this section to the following:

(A) Full premium subsidy

An income-related premium subsidy equal to 100 percent of the amount described in subsection (b)(1), but not to exceed the premium amount specified in subsection (b)(2)(B).

(B) Elimination of deductible

A reduction in the annual deductible applicable under section 1395w–102(b)(1) of this title to $0.

(C) Continuation of coverage above the initial coverage limit

The continuation of coverage from the initial coverage limit (under paragraph (3) of section 1395w–102(b) of this title) for expenditures incurred through the total amount of expenditures at which benefits are available under paragraph (4) of such section, subject to the reduced cost-sharing described in subparagraph (D).

(D) Reduction in cost-sharing below out-of-pocket threshold

(i) Institutionalized individuals

In the case of an individual who is a full-benefit dual eligible individual and who is an institutionalized individual or couple (as defined in section 1396a(q)(1)(B) of this title) or, effective on a date specified by the Secretary (but in no case earlier than January 1, 2012), who would be such an institutionalized individual or couple, if the full-benefit dual eligible individual were not receiving services under a home and community-based waiver authorized for a State under section 1315 of this title or subsection (c) or (d) of section 1396n of this title or under a State plan amendment under subsection (i) of such section or services provided through enrollment in a medicaid managed care organization with a contract under section 1396b(m) of this title or under section 1396u–2 of this title, the elimination of any beneficiary coinsurance described in section 1395w–102(b)(2) of this title (for all amounts through the total amount of expenditures at which benefits are available under section 1395w–102(b)(4) of this title).

(ii) Lowest income dual eligible individuals

In the case of an individual not described in clause (i) who is a full-benefit dual eligible individual and whose income does not exceed 100 percent of the poverty line applicable to a family of the size involved, the substitution for the beneficiary coinsurance described in section 1395w–102(b)(2) of this title (for all amounts through the total amount of expenditures at which benefits are available under section 1395w–102(b)(4) of this title) of a copayment amount that does not exceed $1 for a generic drug or a preferred drug that is a multiple source drug (as defined in section 1396r–8(k)(7)(A)(i) of this title) and $3 for any other drug, or, if less, the copayment amount applicable to an individual under clause (iii).

(iii) Other individuals

In the case of an individual not described in clause (i) or (ii), the substitution for the beneficiary coinsurance described in section 1395w–102(b)(2) of this title (for all amounts through the total amount of expenditures at which benefits are available under section 1395w–102(b)(4) of this title) of a copayment amount that does not exceed the copayment amount specified under section 1395w–102(b)(4)(A)(i)(I) of this title for the drug and year involved.

(E) Elimination of cost-sharing above annual out-of-pocket threshold

The elimination of any cost-sharing imposed under section 1395w–102(b)(4)(A) of this title.

(2) Other individuals with income below 150 percent of poverty line

In the case of a subsidy eligible individual who is not described in paragraph (1), the individual is entitled under this section to the following:

(A) Sliding scale premium subsidy

An income-related premium subsidy determined on a linear sliding scale ranging from 100 percent of the amount described in paragraph (1)(A) for individuals with incomes at or below 135 percent of such level to 0 percent of such amount for individuals with incomes at 150 percent of such level.

(B) Reduction of deductible

A reduction in the annual deductible applicable under section 1395w–102(b)(1) of this title to $50.

(C) Continuation of coverage above the initial coverage limit

The continuation of coverage from the initial coverage limit (under paragraph (3) of section 1395w–102(b) of this title) for expenditures incurred through the total amount of expenditures at which benefits are available under paragraph (4) of such section, subject to the reduced coinsurance described in subparagraph (D).

(D) Reduction in cost-sharing below out-of-pocket threshold

The substitution for the beneficiary coinsurance described in section 1395w–102(b)(2) of this title (for all amounts above the deductible under subparagraph (B) through the total amount of expenditures at which benefits are available under section 1395w–102(b)(4) of this title) of coinsurance of "15 percent" instead of coinsurance of "25 percent" in section 1395w–102(b)(2) of this title.

(E) Reduction of cost-sharing above annual out-of-pocket threshold

Subject to subsection (c), the substitution for the cost-sharing imposed under section 1395w–102(b)(4)(A) of this title of a copayment or coinsurance not to exceed the copayment or coinsurance amount specified under section 1395w–102(b)(4)(A)(i)(I) of this title for the drug and year involved.

(3) Determination of eligibility

(A) Subsidy eligible individual defined

For purposes of this part, subject to subparagraph (F), the term "subsidy eligible individual" means a part D eligible individual who—

(i) is enrolled in a prescription drug plan or MA–PD plan;

(ii) has income below 150 percent of the poverty line applicable to a family of the size involved; and

(iii) meets the resources requirement described in subparagraph (D) or (E).

(B) Determinations

(i) In general

The determination of whether a part D eligible individual residing in a State is a subsidy eligible individual and whether the individual is described in paragraph (1) shall be determined under the State plan under subchapter XIX for the State under section 1396u–5(a) of this title or by the Commissioner of Social Security. There are authorized to be appropriated to the Social Security Administration such sums as may be necessary for the determination of eligibility under this subparagraph.

(ii) Effective period

Determinations under this subparagraph shall be effective beginning with the month in which the individual applies for a determination that the individual is a subsidy eligible individual and shall remain in effect for a period specified by the Secretary, but not to exceed 1 year.

(iii) Redeterminations and appeals through medicaid

Redeterminations and appeals, with respect to eligibility determinations under clause (i) made under a State plan under subchapter XIX, shall be made in accordance with the frequency of, and manner in which, redeterminations and appeals of eligibility are made under such plan for purposes of medical assistance under such subchapter.

(iv) Redeterminations and appeals through Commissioner

With respect to eligibility determinations under clause (i) made by the Commissioner of Social Security—

(I) redeterminations shall be made at such time or times as may be provided by the Commissioner;

(II) the Commissioner shall establish procedures for appeals of such determinations that are similar to the procedures described in the third sentence of section 1383(c)(1)(A) of this title; and

(III) judicial review of the final decision of the Commissioner made after a hearing shall be available to the same extent, and with the same limitations, as provided in subsections (g) and (h) of section 405 of this title.

(v) Treatment of medicaid beneficiaries

Subject to subparagraph (F), the Secretary—

(I) shall provide that part D eligible individuals who are full- benefit dual eligible individuals (as defined in section 1396u–5(c)(6) of this title) or who are recipients of supplemental security income benefits under subchapter XVI shall be treated as subsidy eligible individuals described in paragraph (1); and

(II) may provide that part D eligible individuals not described in subclause (I) who are determined for purposes of the State plan under subchapter XIX to be eligible for medical assistance under clause (i), (iii), or (iv) of section 1396a(a)(10)(E) of this title are treated as being determined to be subsidy eligible individuals described in paragraph (1).

Insofar as the Secretary determines that the eligibility requirements under the State plan for medical assistance referred to in subclause (II) are substantially the same as the requirements for being treated as a subsidy eligible individual described in paragraph (1), the Secretary shall provide for the treatment described in such subclause.

(vi) Special rule for widows and widowers

Notwithstanding the preceding provisions of this subparagraph, in the case of an individual whose spouse dies during the effective period for a determination or redetermination that has been made under this subparagraph, such effective period shall be extended through the date that is 1 year after the date on which the determination or redetermination would (but for the application of this clause) otherwise cease to be effective.

(C) **Income determinations**

For purposes of applying this section—

(i) in the case of a part D eligible individual who is not treated as a subsidy eligible individual under subparagraph (B)(v), income shall be determined in the manner described in section 1396d(p)(1)(B) of this title, without regard to the application of section 1396a(r)(2) of this title and except that support and maintenance furnished in kind shall not be counted as income; and

(ii) the term "poverty line" has the meaning given such term in section 9902(2) of this title, including any revision required by such section.

Nothing in clause (i) shall be construed to affect the application of section 1396a(r)(2) of this title for the determination of eligibility for medical assistance under subchapter XIX.

(D) **Resource standard applied to full low-income subsidy to be based on three times SSI resource standard**

The resources requirement of this subparagraph is that an individual's resources (as determined under section 1382b of this title for purposes of the supplemental security income program subject to the life insurance policy exclusion provided under subparagraph (G)) do not exceed—

(i) for 2006 three times the maximum amount of resources that an individual may have and obtain benefits under that program; and

(ii) for a subsequent year the resource limitation established under this clause for the previous year increased by the annual percentage increase in the consumer price index (all items; U.S. city average) as of September of such previous year.

Any resource limitation established under clause (ii) that is not a multiple of $10 shall be rounded to the nearest multiple of $10.

(E) **Alternative resource standard**

(i) **In general**

The resources requirement of this subparagraph is that an individual's resources (as determined under section 1382b of this title for purposes of the supplemental security income program subject to the life insurance policy exclusion provided under subparagraph (G)) do not exceed—

(I) for 2006, $10,000 (or $20,000 in the case of the combined value of the individual's assets or resources and the assets or resources of the individual's spouse); and

(II) for a subsequent year the dollar amounts specified in this subclause (or subclause (I)) for the previous year increased by the annual percentage increase in the consumer price index (all items; U.S. city average) as of September of such previous year.

Any dollar amount established under subclause (II) that is not a multiple of $10 shall be rounded to the nearest multiple of $10.

(ii) **Use of simplified application form and process**

The Secretary, jointly with the Commissioner of Social Security, shall—

(I) develop a model, simplified application form and process consistent with clause (iii) for the determination and verification of a part D eligible individual's assets or resources under this subparagraph; and

(II) provide such form to States.

(iii) **Documentation and safeguards**

Under such process—

(I) the application form shall consist of an attestation under penalty of perjury regarding the level of assets or resources (or combined assets and resources in the case of a married part D eligible individual) and valuations of general classes of assets or resources;

(II) such form shall be accompanied by copies of recent statements (if any) from financial institutions in support of the application; and

(III) matters attested to in the application shall be subject to appropriate methods of verification.

(iv) **Methodology flexibility**

The Secretary may permit a State in making eligibility determinations for premium and cost-sharing subsidies under this section to use the same asset or resource methodologies that are used with respect to eligibility for medical assistance for medicare cost-sharing described in section 1396d(p) of this title so long as the Secretary determines that the use of such methodologies will not result in any significant differences in the number of individuals determined to be subsidy eligible individuals.

(F) **Treatment of territorial residents**

In the case of a part D eligible individual who is not a resident of the 50 States or the District of Columbia, the individual is not eligible to be a subsidy eligible individual under this section but may be eligible for financial assistance with prescription drug expenses under section 1396u–5(e) of this title.

(G) Life insurance policy exclusion

In determining the resources of an individual (and the eligible spouse of the individual, if any) under section 1382b of this title for purposes of subparagraphs (D) and (E) no part of the value of any life insurance policy shall be taken into account.

(4) Indexing dollar amounts

(A) Copayment for lowest income dual eligible individuals

The dollar amounts applied under paragraph (1)(D)(ii)—

(i) for 2007 shall be the dollar amounts specified in such paragraph increased by the annual percentage increase in the consumer price index (all items; U.S. city average) as of September of such previous year; or

(ii) for a subsequent year shall be the dollar amounts specified in this clause (or clause (i)) for the previous year increased by the annual percentage increase in the consumer price index (all items; U.S. city average) as of September of such previous year.

Any amount established under clause (i) or (ii), that is based on an increase of $1 or $3, that is not a multiple of 5 cents or 10 cents, respectively, shall be rounded to the nearest multiple of 5 cents or 10 cents, respectively.

(B) Reduced deductible

The dollar amount applied under paragraph (2)(B)—

(i) for 2007 shall be the dollar amount specified in such paragraph increased by the annual percentage increase described in section 1395w–102(b)(6) of this title for 2007; or

(ii) for a subsequent year shall be the dollar amount specified in this clause (or clause (i)) for the previous year increased by the annual percentage increase described in section 1395w–102(b)(6) of this title for the year involved.

Any amount established under clause (i) or (ii) that is not a multiple of $1 shall be rounded to the nearest multiple of $1.

(5) Waiver of de minimis premiums

The Secretary shall, under procedures established by the Secretary, permit a prescription drug plan or an MA–PD plan to waive the monthly beneficiary premium for a subsidy eligible individual if the amount of such premium is de minimis. If such premium is waived under the plan, the Secretary shall not reassign subsidy eligible individuals enrolled in the plan to other plans based on the fact that the monthly beneficiary premium under the plan was greater than the low-income benchmark premium amount.

(b) Premium subsidy amount

(1) In general

The premium subsidy amount described in this subsection for a subsidy eligible individual residing in a PDP region and enrolled in a prescription drug plan or MA–PD plan is the low-income benchmark premium amount (as defined in paragraph (2)) for the PDP region in which the individual resides or, if greater, the amount specified in paragraph (3).

(2) Low-income benchmark premium amount defined

(A) In general

For purposes of this subsection, the term "low-income benchmark premium amount" means, with respect to a PDP region in which—

(i) all prescription drug plans are offered by the same PDP sponsor, the weighted average of the amounts described in subparagraph (B)(i) for such plans; or

(ii) there are prescription drug plans offered by more than one PDP sponsor, the weighted average of amounts described in subparagraph (B) for prescription drug plans and MA–PD plans described in section 1395w–21(a)(2)(A)(i) of this title offered in such region.

(B) Premium amounts described

The premium amounts described in this subparagraph are, in the case of—

(i) a prescription drug plan that is a basic prescription drug plan, the monthly beneficiary premium for such plan;

(ii) a prescription drug plan that provides alternative prescription drug coverage the actuarial value of which is greater than that of standard prescription drug coverage, the portion of the monthly beneficiary premium that is attributable to basic prescription drug coverage; and

(iii) an MA–PD plan, the portion of the MA monthly prescription drug beneficiary premium that is attributable to basic prescription drug benefits (described in section 1395w–22(a)(6)(B)(ii) of this title [1]) and determined before the application of the monthly rebate computed under section 1395w–24(b)(1)(C)(i) of this title for that plan and year involved and, in the case of a qualifying plan, before the application of the increase under section 1395w–23(*o*) of this title for that plan and year involved.

The premium amounts described in this subparagraph do not include any amounts attributable to late enrollment penalties under section 1395w–113(b) of this title.

(3) **Access to 0 premium plan**

In no case shall the premium subsidy amount under this subsection for a PDP region be less than the lowest monthly beneficiary premium for a prescription drug plan that offers basic prescription drug coverage in the region.

(c) **Administration of subsidy program**

(1) **In general**

The Secretary shall provide a process whereby, in the case of a part D eligible individual who is determined to be a subsidy eligible individual and who is enrolled in a prescription drug plan or is enrolled in an MA–PD plan—

(A) the Secretary provides for a notification of the PDP sponsor or the MA organization offering the plan involved that the individual is eligible for a subsidy and the amount of the subsidy under subsection (a);

(B) the sponsor or organization involved reduces the premiums or cost-sharing otherwise imposed by the amount of the applicable subsidy and submits to the Secretary information on the amount of such reduction;

(C) the Secretary periodically and on a timely basis reimburses the sponsor or organization for the amount of such reductions; and

(D) the Secretary ensures the confidentiality of individually identifiable information.

In applying subparagraph (C), the Secretary shall compute reductions based upon imposition under subsections (a)(1)(D) and (a)(2)(E) of unreduced copayment amounts applied under such subsections.

(2) **Use of capitated form of payment**

The reimbursement under this section with respect to cost-sharing subsidies may be computed on a capitated basis, taking into account the actuarial value of the subsidies and with appropriate adjustments to reflect differences in the risks actually involved.

(d) **Facilitation of reassignments**

Beginning not later than January 1, 2011, the Secretary shall, in the case of a subsidy eligible individual who is enrolled in one prescription drug plan and is subsequently reassigned by the Secretary to a new prescription drug plan, provide the individual, within 30 days of such reassignment, with—

(1) information on formulary differences between the individual's former plan and the plan to which the individual is reassigned with respect to the individual's drug regimens; and

(2) a description of the individual's right to request a coverage determination, exception, or reconsideration under section 1395w–104(g) of this title, bring an appeal under section 1395w–104(h) of this title, or resolve a grievance under section 1395w–104(f) of this title.

(e) **Relation to medicaid program**

For special provisions under the medicaid program relating to medicare prescription drug benefits, see section 1396u–5 of this title.

(Aug. 14, 1935, c. 531, Title XVIII, § 1860D–14, as added Pub.L. 108–173, Title I, § 101(a)(2), Dec. 8, 2003, 117 Stat. 2107; amended Pub.L. 110–275, Title I, §§ 114(a)(2), 116(a), 117(a), July 15, 2008, 122 Stat. 2506, 2507; Pub.L. 111–148, Title III, §§ 3302(a), 3303(a), 3304(a), 3305, 3309, Mar. 23, 2010, 124 Stat. 468, 469, 470, 475; Pub.L. 111–152, Title I, § 1102(c)(4), Mar. 30, 2010, 124 Stat. 1045.)

[1] So in original. Section 1395w–22(a)(6) of this title does not contain a subpar. (B).

HISTORICAL AND STATUTORY NOTES

Revision Notes and Legislative Reports

2003 Acts. House Conference Report No. 108–391 and Statement by President, see 2003 U.S. Code Cong. and Adm. News, p. 1808.

References in Text

Part D, referred to in text, means Part D of Title XVIII of the Social Security Act, Act Aug. 14, 1935, c. 531, Title XVIII, § 1860D–1 et seq., as added, Pub.L. 108–173, Title I, § 101(a)(2), Dec. 8, 2003, 117 Stat. 2071, which is classified to this part, 42 U.S.C.A. § 1395w–101 et seq.

Subchapter XIX, referred to in text, originally read "title XIX", meaning Title XIX of the Social Security Act, Aug. 14, 1935, c. 531, Title XIX, § 1901 et seq., as added July 30, 1965, Pub.L. 89–97, Title I, § 121(a), 79 Stat. 343, and amended, which is principally classified to subchapter XIX of this chapter, 42 U.S.C.A. § 1396 et seq.

Subchapter XVI, referred to in subsec. (a)(3)(B)(v)(I), originally read "title XVI", meaning Title XVI of the Social Security Act, Act Aug. 14, 1935, c. 531, Title XVI, § 1601 et seq., as added Oct. 30, 1972, Pub.L. 92–603, Title III, § 301, 86 Stat. 1465, and amended, which is principally classified to subchapter XVI of this chapter 7, 42 U.S.C.A. § 1396 et seq.

Effective and Applicability Provisions

2010 Acts. Pub.L. 111–148, Title III, § 3302(b), Mar. 23, 2010, 124 Stat. 468, provided that: "The amendment made by subsection (a) [amending subsec. (b)(2)(B)(iii) of this section] shall apply to premiums for months beginning on or after January 1, 2011."

Amendments by Pub.L. 111–148, § 3303, applicable to premiums for months, and enrollments for plan years, beginning on or after January 1, 2011, see Pub.L. 111–148, § 3303(c), set out as a note under 42 U.S.C.A. § 1395w–101.

Pub.L. 111–148, Title III, § 3304(b), Mar. 23, 2010, 124 Stat. 470, provided that: "The amendment made by subsection (a) [enacting subsec. (a)(3)(B)(vi) of this section] shall take effect on January 1, 2011."

2008 Acts. Amendments by Pub.L. 110–275, Title I, § 114(a)(2), applicable to subsidies for months beginning with January 2009, see Pub.L. 110–275, Title I, § 114(b), set out as a note under 42 U.S.C.A. § 1395w–113.

Pub.L. 110–275, Title I, § 116(b), July 15, 2008, 122 Stat. 2507, provided that: "The amendments made by this section [amending subsec. (a)(3)(C)(i), (D), (E)(i) and adding (a)(3)(G) of this section] shall take effect with respect to applications filed on or after January 1, 2010."

Pub.L. 110–275, Title I, § 117(b), July 15, 2008, 122 Stat. 2507, provided that: "The amendments made by subsection (a) [amending subsec. (a)(3)(B)(iv) of this section] shall take effect as if included in the enactment of section 101 of the Medicare Prescription Drug, Improvement, and Modernization Act of 2003 [Pub.L. 108–173, Title I, § 101, Dec. 8, 2003, 117 Stat. 2071, which principally enacted this part, 42 U.S.C.A. § 1395w–101 et seq.; see Tables for complete classification]".

GAO Study Regarding Impact of Assets Test for Subsidy Eligible Individuals

Pub.L. 108–173, Title I, § 107(e), Dec. 8, 2003, 117 Stat. 2171, provided that:

"(1) **Study.**—The Comptroller General of the United States shall conduct a study to determine the extent to which drug utilization and access to covered part D drugs under part D of title XVIII of the Social Security Act [this part] by subsidy eligible individuals differs from such utilization and access for individuals who would qualify as such subsidy eligible individuals but for the application of section 1860D–14(a)(3)(A)(iii) of such Act [subsec. (a)(3)(A)(iii) of this section].

"(2) **Report.**—Not later than September 30, 2007, the Comptroller General shall submit a report to Congress on the study conducted under paragraph (1) that includes such recommendations for legislation as the Comptroller General determines are appropriate."

§ 1395w–114a. Medicare coverage gap discount program

(a) Establishment

The Secretary shall establish a Medicare coverage gap discount program (in this section referred to as the "program") by not later than January 1, 2011. Under the program, the Secretary shall enter into agreements described in subsection (b) with manufacturers and provide for the performance of the duties described in subsection (c)(1). The Secretary shall establish a model agreement for use under the program by not later than 180 days after March 23, 2010, in consultation with manufacturers, and allow for comment on such model agreement.

(b) Terms of agreement

(1) In general

(A) Agreement

An agreement under this section shall require the manufacturer to provide applicable beneficiaries access to discounted prices for applicable drugs of the manufacturer.

(B) Provision of discounted prices at the point-of-sale

Except as provided in subsection (c)(1)(A)(iii), such discounted prices shall be provided to the applicable beneficiary at the pharmacy or by the mail order service at the point-of-sale of an applicable drug.

(C) Timing of agreement

(i) Special rule for 2011

In order for an agreement with a manufacturer to be in effect under this section with respect to the period beginning on January 1, 2011, and ending on December 31, 2011, the manufacturer shall enter into such agreement not later than not later than[1] 30 days after the date of the establishment of a model agreement under subsection (a).

(ii) 2012 and subsequent years

In order for an agreement with a manufacturer to be in effect under this section with respect to plan year 2012 or a subsequent plan year, the manufacturer shall enter into such agreement (or such agreement shall be renewed under paragraph (4)(A)) not later than January 30 of the preceding year.

(2) Provision of appropriate data

Each manufacturer with an agreement in effect under this section shall collect and have available appropriate data, as determined by the Secretary, to ensure that it can demonstrate to the Secretary compliance with the requirements under the program.

(3) Compliance with requirements for administration of program

Each manufacturer with an agreement in effect under this section shall comply with requirements imposed by the Secretary or a third party with a contract under subsection (d)(3), as applicable, for purposes of administering the program, including any determination under clause (i) of subsection (c)(1)(A) or procedures established under such subsection (c)(1)(A).

(4) Length of agreement

(A) In general

An agreement under this section shall be effective for an initial period of not less than 18 months and shall be automatically renewed for a period of not less than 1 year unless terminated under subparagraph (B).

(B) Termination

(i) By the Secretary

The Secretary may provide for termination of an agreement under this section for a knowing and willful violation of the requirements of the agreement or other good cause shown. Such termination shall not be effective earlier than 30 days after the date of notice to the manufacturer of such termination. The Secretary shall provide, upon request, a manufacturer with a hearing concerning such a termination, and such hearing shall take place prior to the effective date of the termination with sufficient time for such effective date to be repealed if the Secretary determines appropriate.

(ii) By a manufacturer

A manufacturer may terminate an agreement under this section for any reason. Any such termination shall be effective, with respect to a plan year—

(I) if the termination occurs before January 30 of a plan year, as of the day after the end of the plan year; and

(II) if the termination occurs on or after January 30 of a plan year, as of the day after the end of the succeeding plan year.

(iii) Effectiveness of termination

Any termination under this subparagraph shall not affect discounts for applicable drugs of the manufacturer that are due under the agreement before the effective date of its termination.

(iv) Notice to third party

The Secretary shall provide notice of such termination to a third party with a contract under subsection (d)(3) within not less than 30 days before the effective date of such termination.

(c) Duties described and special rule for supplemental benefits

(1) Duties described

The duties described in this subsection are the following:

(A) Administration of program

Administering the program, including—

(i) the determination of the amount of the discounted price of an applicable drug of a manufacturer;

(ii) except as provided in clause (iii), the establishment of procedures under which discounted prices are provided to applicable beneficiaries at pharmacies or by mail order service at the point-of-sale of an applicable drug;

(iii) in the case where, during the period beginning on January 1, 2011, and ending on December 31, 2011, it is not practicable to provide such discounted prices at the point-of-sale (as described in clause (ii)), the establishment of procedures to provide such discounted prices as soon as practicable after the point-of-sale;

(iv) the establishment of procedures to ensure that, not later than the applicable number of calendar days after the dispensing of an applicable drug by a pharmacy or mail order service, the pharmacy or mail order service is reimbursed for an amount equal to the difference between—

(I) the negotiated price of the applicable drug; and

(II) the discounted price of the applicable drug;

(v) the establishment of procedures to ensure that the discounted price for an applicable drug under this section is applied before any coverage or financial assistance under other health benefit plans or programs that provide coverage or financial assistance for the purchase or provision of prescription drug coverage on behalf of applicable beneficiaries as the Secretary may specify;

(vi) the establishment of procedures to implement the special rule for supplemental benefits under paragraph (2); and

(vii) providing a reasonable dispute resolution mechanism to resolve disagreements between manufacturers, applicable beneficiaries, and the third party with a contract under subsection (d)(3).

(B) Monitoring compliance

(i) In general

The Secretary shall monitor compliance by a manufacturer with the terms of an agreement under this section.

(ii) Notification

If a third party with a contract under subsection (d)(3) determines that the manufacturer is not in compliance with such agreement, the third party shall notify the Secretary of such noncompliance for appropriate enforcement under subsection (e).

(C) Collection of data from prescription drug plans and MA–PD plans

The Secretary may collect appropriate data from prescription drug plans and MA–PD plans in a timeframe that allows for discounted prices to be provided for applicable drugs under this section.

(2) Special rule for supplemental benefits

For plan year 2011 and each subsequent plan year, in the case where an applicable beneficiary has supplemental benefits with respect to applicable drugs under the prescription drug plan or MA–PD plan that the applicable beneficiary is enrolled in, the applicable beneficiary shall not be provided a discounted price for an applicable drug under this section until after such supplemental benefits have been applied with respect to the applicable drug.

(d) Administration

(1) In general

Subject to paragraph (2), the Secretary shall provide for the implementation of this section, including the performance of the duties described in subsection (c)(1).

(2) Limitation

(A) In general

Subject to subparagraph (B), in providing for such implementation, the Secretary shall not receive or distribute any funds of a manufacturer under the program.

(B) Exception

The limitation under subparagraph (A) shall not apply to the Secretary with respect to drugs dispensed during the period beginning on January 1, 2011, and ending on December 31, 2011, but only if the Secretary determines that the exception to such limitation under this subparagraph is necessary in order for the Secretary to begin implementation of this section and provide applicable beneficiaries timely access to discounted prices during such period.

(3) Contract with third parties

The Secretary shall enter into a contract with 1 or more third parties to administer the requirements established by the Secretary in order to carry out this section. At a minimum, the contract with a third party under the preceding sentence shall require that the third party—

(A) receive and transmit information between the Secretary, manufacturers, and other individuals or entities the Secretary determines appropriate;

(B) receive, distribute, or facilitate the distribution of funds of manufacturers to appropriate individuals or entities in order to meet the obligations of manufacturers under agreements under this section;

(C) provide adequate and timely information to manufacturers, consistent with the agreement with the manufacturer under this section, as necessary for the manufacturer to fulfill its obligations under this section; and

(D) permit manufacturers to conduct periodic audits, directly or through contracts, of the data and information used by the third party to determine discounts for applicable drugs of the manufacturer under the program.

(4) Performance requirements

The Secretary shall establish performance requirements for a third party with a contract under paragraph (3) and safeguards to protect the independence and integrity of the activities carried out by the third party under the program under this section.

(5) Implementation

The Secretary may implement the program under this section by program instruction or otherwise.

(6) Administration

Chapter 35 of Title 44 shall not apply to the program under this section.

(e) Enforcement

(1) Audits

Each manufacturer with an agreement in effect under this section shall be subject to periodic audit by the Secretary.

(2) Civil money penalty

(A) In general

The Secretary shall impose a civil money penalty on a manufacturer that fails to provide applicable beneficiaries discounts for applicable drugs of the manufacturer in accordance with such agreement for each such failure in an amount the Secretary determines is commensurate with the sum of—

(i) the amount that the manufacturer would have paid with respect to such discounts under the agreement, which will then be used to pay the discounts which the manufacturer had failed to provide; and

(ii) 25 percent of such amount.

(B) Application

The provisions of section 1320a–7a of this title (other than subsections (a) and (b)) shall apply to a civil money penalty under this paragraph in the same manner as such provisions apply to a penalty or proceeding under section 1320a–7a(a) of this title.

(f) Clarification regarding availability of other covered part D drugs

Nothing in this section shall prevent an applicable beneficiary from purchasing a covered part D drug that is not an applicable drug (including a generic drug or a drug that is not on the formulary of the prescription drug plan or MA–PD plan that the applicable beneficiary is enrolled in).

(g) Definitions

In this section:

(1) Applicable beneficiary

The term "applicable beneficiary" means an individual who, on the date of dispensing a covered part D drug—

(A) is enrolled in a prescription drug plan or an MA–PD plan;

(B) is not enrolled in a qualified retiree prescription drug plan;

(C) is not entitled to an income-related subsidy under section 1395w–114(a) of this title; and

(D) who—

(i) has reached or exceeded the initial coverage limit under section 1395w–102(b)(3) of this title during the year; and

(ii) has not incurred costs for covered part D drugs in the year equal to the annual out-of-pocket threshold specified in section 1395w–102(b)(4)(B) of this title.

(E) Redesignated (D)

(2) Applicable drug

The term "applicable drug" means, with respect to an applicable beneficiary, a covered part D drug—

(A) approved under a new drug application under section 355(b) of Title 21 or, in the case of a biologic product, licensed under section 262 of this title (other than, with respect to a plan year before 2019, a product licensed under subsection (k) of such section 262 of this title); and

(B)(i) if the PDP sponsor of the prescription drug plan or the MA organization offering the MA–PD plan uses a formulary, which is on the formulary of the prescription drug plan or MA–PD plan that the applicable beneficiary is enrolled in;

(ii) if the PDP sponsor of the prescription drug plan or the MA organization offering the MA–PD plan does not use a formulary, for which benefits are available under the prescription drug plan or MA–PD plan that the applicable beneficiary is enrolled in; or

(iii) is provided through an exception or appeal.

(3) Applicable number of calendar days

The term "applicable number of calendar days" means—

(A) with respect to claims for reimbursement submitted electronically, 14 days; and

(B) with respect to claims for reimbursement submitted otherwise, 30 days.

(4) Discounted price

(A) In general

The term "discounted price" means 50 percent (or, with respect to a plan year after plan year 2018, 30 percent) of the negotiated price of the applicable drug of a manufacturer.

(B) Clarification

Nothing in this section shall be construed as affecting the responsibility of an applicable beneficiary for payment of a dispensing fee for an applicable drug.

(C) Special case for certain claims

In the case where the entire amount of the negotiated price of an individual claim for an applicable drug with respect to an applicable beneficiary does not fall at or above the initial coverage limit under section 1395w–102(b)(3) of this title and below the annual out-of-pocket threshold specified in section 1395w–102(b)(4)(B) of this title for the year, the manufacturer of the applicable drug shall provide the discounted price under this section on only the portion of the negotiated price of the applicable drug that falls at or above such initial coverage limit and below such annual out-of-pocket threshold.

(5) Manufacturer

The term "manufacturer" means any entity which is engaged in the production, preparation, propagation, compounding, conversion, or processing of prescription drug products, either directly or indirectly by extraction from substances of natural origin, or independently by means of chemical synthesis, or by a combination of extraction and chemical synthesis. Such term does not include a wholesale distributor of drugs or a retail pharmacy licensed under State law.

(6) Negotiated price

The term "negotiated price" has the meaning given such term in section 423.100 of title 42, Code of Federal Regulations (as in effect on March 23, 2010), except that such negotiated price shall not include any dispensing fee for the applicable drug.

(7) Qualified retiree prescription drug plan

The term "qualified retiree prescription drug plan" has the meaning given such term in section 1395w–132(a)(2) of this title.

(Aug. 14, 1935, c. 531, Title XVIII, § 1860D–14A, as added Pub.L. 111–148, Title III, § 3301(b), Mar. 23, 2010, 124 Stat. 462; amended Pub.L. 111–152, Title I, § 1101(b)(2), Mar. 30, 2010, 124 Stat. 1037; Pub.L. 115–123, Div. E, Title XII, §§ 53113, 53116(b), Feb. 9, 2018, 132 Stat. 305, 307.)

[1] So in original.

HISTORICAL AND STATUTORY NOTES

References in Text

Part D, referred to in text, is part D of Title XVIII of the Social Security Act, Act Aug. 14, 1935, c. 531, Title XVIII, § 1860D–1 et seq., as added and amended, which is principally classified to this part D, 42 U.S.C.A. § 1395w–101 et seq.

Chapter 35 of Title 44, referred to in subsec. (d)(6), is 44 U.S.C.A. § 3501 et seq.

Codifications

Pub.L. 111–152, Title I, § 1101(b)(2)(B), Mar. 30, 2010, 124 Stat. 1037, which directed amendment of subsec. (b)(1)(C), was executed to subsec. (b)(1)(C)(i) as the probable intent of Congress. See 2010 Amendments notes set out under this section.

§ 1395w–115. Subsidies for part D eligible individuals for qualified prescription drug coverage

(a) Subsidy payment

In order to reduce premium levels applicable to qualified prescription drug coverage for part D eligible individuals consistent with an overall subsidy level of 74.5 percent for basic prescription drug coverage, to reduce adverse selection among prescription drug plans and MA–PD plans, and to promote the participation of PDP sponsors under this part and MA organizations under part C of this subchapter, the Secretary shall provide for payment to a PDP sponsor that offers a prescription drug plan and an MA organization that offers an MA–PD plan of the following subsidies in accordance with this section:

(1) Direct subsidy

A direct subsidy for each part D eligible individual enrolled in a prescription drug plan or MA–PD plan for a month equal to—

(A) the amount of the plan's standardized bid amount (as defined in section 1395w–113(a)(5) of this title), adjusted under subsection (c)(1) of this section, reduced by

(B) the base beneficiary premium (as computed under paragraph (2) of section 1395w–113(a) of this title and as adjusted under paragraph (1)(B) of such section).

(2) Subsidy through reinsurance

The reinsurance payment amount (as defined in subsection (b) of this section).

This section constitutes budget authority in advance of appropriations Acts and represents the obligation of the Secretary to provide for the payment of amounts provided under this section.

(b) Reinsurance payment amount

(1) In general

The reinsurance payment amount under this subsection for a part D eligible individual enrolled in a prescription drug plan or MA–PD plan for a coverage year is an amount equal to 80 percent of the allowable reinsurance costs (as specified in paragraph (2)) attributable to that portion of gross covered prescription drug costs as specified in paragraph (3) incurred in the coverage year after such individual has incurred costs that exceed the annual out-of-pocket threshold specified in section 1395w–102(b)(4)(B) of this title.

(2) Allowable reinsurance costs

For purposes of this section, the term "allowable reinsurance costs" means, with respect to gross covered prescription drug costs under a prescription drug plan offered by a PDP sponsor or an MA–PD plan offered by an MA organization, the part of such costs that are actually paid (net of discounts, chargebacks, and average percentage rebates) by the sponsor or organization or by (or on behalf of) an enrollee under the plan, but in no case more than the part of such costs that would have been paid under the plan if the prescription drug coverage under the plan were basic prescription drug coverage, or, in the case of a plan providing supplemental prescription drug coverage, if such coverage were standard prescription drug coverage.

(3) Gross covered prescription drug costs

For purposes of this section, the term "gross covered prescription drug costs" means, with respect to a part D eligible individual enrolled in a prescription drug plan or MA–PD plan during a coverage year, the costs incurred under the plan, not including administrative costs, but including costs directly related to the dispensing of covered part D drugs during the year and costs relating to the deductible. Such costs shall be determined whether they are paid by the individual or under the plan, regardless of whether the coverage under the plan exceeds basic prescription drug coverage.

(4) Coverage year defined

For purposes of this section, the term "coverage year" means a calendar year in which covered part D drugs are dispensed if the claim for such drugs (and payment on such claim) is made not later than such period after the end of such year as the Secretary specifies.

(c) Adjustments relating to bids

(1) Health status risk adjustment

(A) Establishment of risk adjustors

The Secretary shall establish an appropriate methodology for adjusting the standardized bid amount under subsection (a)(1)(A) of this section to take into account variation in costs for basic prescription drug coverage among prescription drug plans and MA–PD plans based on the differences in actuarial risk of different enrollees being served. Any such risk adjustment shall be designed in a manner so as not to result in a change in the aggregate amounts payable to such plans under subsection (a)(1) of this section and through that portion of the monthly beneficiary prescription drug premiums described in subsection (a)(1)(B) of this section and MA monthly prescription drug beneficiary premiums.

(B) Considerations

In establishing the methodology under subparagraph (A), the Secretary may take into account the similar methodologies used under section 1395w–23(a)(3) of this title to adjust payments to MA organizations for benefits under the original medicare fee-for-service program option.

(C) Data collection

In order to carry out this paragraph, the Secretary shall require—

(i) PDP sponsors to submit data regarding drug claims that can be linked at the individual level to part A and part B of this subchapter data and such other information as the Secretary determines necessary; and

(ii) MA organizations that offer MA–PD plans to submit data regarding drug claims that can be linked at the individual level to other data that such organizations are required to submit to the Secretary and such other information as the Secretary determines necessary.

(D) Publication

At the time of publication of risk adjustment factors under section 1395w–23(b)(1)(B)(i)(II) of this title, the Secretary shall publish the risk adjusters established under this paragraph for the succeeding year.

(2) Geographic adjustment

(A) In general

Subject to subparagraph (B), for purposes of section 1395w–113(a)(1)(B)(iii) of this title, the Secretary shall establish an appropriate methodology for adjusting the national average monthly bid amount (computed under section 1395w–113(a)(4) of this title) to take into account differences in prices for covered part D drugs among PDP regions.

(B) De minimis rule

If the Secretary determines that the price variations described in subparagraph (A) among PDP regions are de minimis, the Secretary shall not provide for adjustment under this paragraph.

(C) Budget neutral adjustment

Any adjustment under this paragraph shall be applied in a manner so as to not result in a change in the aggregate payments made under this part that would have been made if the Secretary had not applied such adjustment.

(d) Payment methods

(1) In general

Payments under this section shall be based on such a method as the Secretary determines. The Secretary may establish a payment method by which interim payments of amounts under this section are made during a year based on the Secretary's best estimate of amounts that will be payable after obtaining all of the information.

(2) Requirement for provision of information

(A) Requirement

Payments under this section to a PDP sponsor or MA organization are conditioned upon the furnishing to the Secretary, in a form and manner specified by the Secretary, of such information as may be required to carry out this section.

(B) Restriction on use of information

Information disclosed or obtained pursuant to subparagraph (A) may be used by officers, employees, and contractors of the Department of Health and Human Services only for the purposes of, and to the extent necessary in, carrying out this section.

(3) Source of payments

Payments under this section shall be made from the Medicare Prescription Drug Account.

(4) Application of enrollee adjustment

The provisions of section 1395w–23(a)(2) of this title shall apply to payments to PDP sponsors under this section in the same manner as they apply to payments to MA organizations under section 1395w–23(a) of this title.

(e) Portion of total payments to a sponsor or organization subject to risk (application of risk corridors)

(1) Computation of adjusted allowable risk corridor costs

(A) In general

For purposes of this subsection, the term "adjusted allowable risk corridor costs" means, for a plan for a coverage year (as defined in subsection (b)(4) of this section)—

(i) the allowable risk corridor costs (as defined in subparagraph (B)) for the plan for the year, reduced by

(ii) the sum of (I) the total reinsurance payments made under subsection (b) of this section to the sponsor of the plan for the year, and (II) the total subsidy payments made under section 1395w–114 of this title to the sponsor of the plan for the year.

(B) Allowable risk corridor costs

For purposes of this subsection, the term "allowable risk corridor costs" means, with respect to a prescription drug plan offered by a PDP sponsor or an MA–PD plan offered by an MA organization, the part of costs (not including administrative costs, but including costs directly related to the dispensing of covered part D drugs during the year) incurred by the sponsor or organization under the plan that are actually paid (net of discounts, chargebacks, and average percentage rebates) by the sponsor or organization under the plan, but in no case more than the part of such costs that would have been paid under the plan if the prescription drug coverage under the plan were basic prescription drug coverage, or, in the case of a plan providing supplemental prescription drug coverage, if such coverage were basic prescription drug coverage taking into account the adjustment under section 1395w–111(c)(2) of this title. In computing allowable costs under this paragraph, the Secretary shall compute such costs based upon imposition under paragraphs (1)(D) and (2)(E) of section 1395w–114(a) of this title of the maximum amount of copayments permitted under such paragraphs.

(2) Adjustment of payment

(A) No adjustment if adjusted allowable risk corridor costs within risk corridor

If the adjusted allowable risk corridor costs (as defined in paragraph (1)) for the plan for the year are at least equal to the first threshold lower limit of the risk corridor (specified in paragraph (3)(A)(i)), but not greater than the first threshold upper limit of the risk corridor (specified in paragraph (3)(A)(iii)) for the plan for the year, then no payment adjustment shall be made under this subsection.

(B) Increase in payment if adjusted allowable risk corridor costs above upper limit of risk corridor

(i) Costs between first and second threshold upper limits

If the adjusted allowable risk corridor costs for the plan for the year are greater than the first threshold upper limit, but not greater than the second threshold upper limit, of the risk corridor for the plan for the year, the Secretary shall increase the total of the payments made to the sponsor or organization offering the plan for the year under this section by an amount equal to 50 percent (or, for 2006 and 2007, 75 percent or 90 percent if the conditions described in clause (iii) are met for the year) of the difference between such adjusted allowable risk corridor costs and the first threshold upper limit of the risk corridor.

(ii) Costs above second threshold upper limits

If the adjusted allowable risk corridor costs for the plan for the year are greater than the second threshold upper limit of the risk corridor for the plan for the year, the Secretary shall increase the total of the payments made to the sponsor or organization offering the plan for the year under this section by an amount equal to the sum of—

(I) 50 percent (or, for 2006 and 2007, 75 percent or 90 percent if the conditions described in clause (iii) are met for the year) of the difference between the second threshold upper limit and the first threshold upper limit; and

(II) 80 percent of the difference between such adjusted allowable risk corridor costs and the second threshold upper limit of the risk corridor.

(iii) Conditions for application of higher percentage for 2006 and 2007

The conditions described in this clause are met for 2006 or 2007 if the Secretary determines with respect to such year that—

(I) at least 60 percent of prescription drug plans and MA–PD plans to which this subsection applies have adjusted allowable risk corridor costs for the plan for the year that are more than the first threshold upper limit of the risk corridor for the plan for the year; and

(II) such plans represent at least 60 percent of part D eligible individuals enrolled in any prescription drug plan or MA–PD plan.

(C) Reduction in payment if adjusted allowable risk corridor costs below lower limit of risk corridor

(i) Costs between first and second threshold lower limits

If the adjusted allowable risk corridor costs for the plan for the year are less than the first threshold lower limit, but not less than the second threshold lower limit, of the risk corridor for the plan for the year, the Secretary shall reduce the total of the payments made to the sponsor or organization offering the plan for the year under this section by an amount (or otherwise recover from the sponsor or organization an amount) equal to 50 percent (or, for 2006 and 2007, 75 percent) of the difference between the first threshold lower limit of the risk corridor and such adjusted allowable risk corridor costs.

(ii) Costs below second threshold lower limit

If the adjusted allowable risk corridor costs for the plan for the year are less the second threshold lower limit of the risk corridor for the plan for the year, the Secretary shall reduce the total of the payments made to the sponsor or organization offering the plan for the year under this section by an amount (or otherwise recover from the sponsor or organization an amount) equal to the sum of—

(I) 50 percent (or, for 2006 and 2007, 75 percent) of the difference between the first threshold lower limit and the second threshold lower limit; and

(II) 80 percent of the difference between the second threshold upper limit of the risk corridor and such adjusted allowable risk corridor costs.

(3) Establishment of risk corridors

(A) In general

For each plan year the Secretary shall establish a risk corridor for each prescription drug plan and each MA–PD plan. The risk corridor for a plan for a year shall be equal to a range as follows:

(i) First threshold lower limit

The first threshold lower limit of such corridor shall be equal to—

(I) the target amount described in subparagraph (B) for the plan; minus

(II) an amount equal to the first threshold risk percentage for the plan (as determined under subparagraph (C)(i)) of such target amount.

(ii) Second threshold lower limit

The second threshold lower limit of such corridor shall be equal to—

(I) the target amount described in subparagraph (B) for the plan; minus

(II) an amount equal to the second threshold risk percentage for the plan (as determined under subparagraph (C)(ii)) of such target amount.

(iii) First threshold upper limit

The first threshold upper limit of such corridor shall be equal to the sum of—

(I) such target amount; and

(II) the amount described in clause (i)(II).

(iv) Second threshold upper limit

The second threshold upper limit of such corridor shall be equal to the sum of—

(I) such target amount; and

(II) the amount described in clause (ii)(II).

(B) Target amount described

The target amount described in this paragraph is, with respect to a prescription drug plan or an MA–PD plan in a year, the total amount of payments paid to the PDP sponsor or MA–PD organization for the plan for the year, taking into account amounts paid by the Secretary and enrollees, based upon the standardized bid amount (as defined in section 1395w–113(a)(5) of this title and as risk adjusted under subsection (c)(1) of this section), reduced by the total amount of administrative expenses for the year assumed in such standardized bid.

(C) First and second threshold risk percentage defined

(i) First threshold risk percentage

Subject to clause (iii), for purposes of this section, the first threshold risk percentage is—

(I) for 2006 and 2007, and [1] 2.5 percent;

(II) for 2008 through 2011, 5 percent; and

(III) for 2012 and subsequent years, a percentage established by the Secretary, but in no case less than 5 percent.

(ii) Second threshold risk percentage

Subject to clause (iii), for purposes of this section, the second threshold risk percentage is—

(I) for 2006 and 2007, 5 percent;

(II) for 2008 through 2011, 10 percent; and

(III) for 2012 and subsequent years, a percentage established by the Secretary that is greater than the percent established for the year under clause (i)(III), but in no case less than 10 percent.

(iii) Reduction of risk percentage to ensure 2 plans in an area

Pursuant to section 1395w–111(b)(2)(E)(ii) of this title, a PDP sponsor may submit a bid that requests a decrease in the applicable first or second threshold risk percentages or an increase in the percents applied under paragraph (2).

(4) Plans at risk for entire amount of supplemental prescription drug coverage

A PDP sponsor and MA organization that offers a plan that provides supplemental prescription drug benefits shall be at full financial risk for the provision of such supplemental benefits.

(5) No effect on monthly premium

No adjustment in payments made by reason of this subsection shall affect the monthly beneficiary premium or the MA monthly prescription drug beneficiary premium.

(f) Disclosure of information

(1) In general

Each contract under this part and under part C of this subchapter shall provide that—

(A) the PDP sponsor offering a prescription drug plan or an MA organization offering an MA–PD plan shall provide the Secretary with such information as the Secretary determines is necessary to carry out this section; and

(B) the Secretary shall have the right in accordance with section 1395w–27(d)(2)(B) of this title (as applied under section 1395w–112(b)(3)(C) of this title) to inspect and audit any books and records of a PDP sponsor or MA organization that pertain to the information regarding costs provided to the Secretary under subparagraph (A).

(2) Restriction on use of information

Information disclosed or obtained pursuant to the provisions of this section may be used—

(A) by officers, employees, and contractors of the Department of Health and Human Services for the purposes of, and to the extent necessary in—

(i) carrying out this section; and

(ii) conducting oversight, evaluation, and enforcement under this subchapter; and

(B) by the Attorney General and the Comptroller General of the United States for the purposes of, and to the extent necessary in, carrying out health oversight activities.

(g) Payment for fallback prescription drug plans

In lieu of the amounts otherwise payable under this section to a PDP sponsor offering a fallback prescription drug plan (as defined in section 1395w–111(g)(4) of this title), the amount payable shall be the amounts determined under the contract for such plan pursuant to section 1395w–111(g)(5) of this title.

(Aug. 14, 1935, c. 531, Title XVIII, § 1860D–15, as added Pub.L. 108–173, Title I, § 101(a)(2), Dec. 8, 2003, 117 Stat. 2113; amended Pub.L. 111–148, Title VI, § 6402(b)(1), Mar. 23, 2010, 124 Stat. 756.)

[1] So in original. The word "and" probably should not appear.

HISTORICAL AND STATUTORY NOTES

Revision Notes and Legislative Reports

2003 Acts. House Conference Report No. 108–391 and Statement by President, see 2003 U.S. Code Cong. and Adm. News, p. 1808.

References in Text

Part D, referred to in text, means Part D of Title XVIII of the Social Security Act, Act Aug. 14, 1935, c. 531, Title XVIII, § 1860D–1 et seq., as added, Pub.L. 108–173, Title I, § 101(a)(2), Dec. 8, 2003, 117 Stat. 2071, which is classified to this part, 42 U.S.C.A. § 1395w–101 et seq.

This subchapter, referred to in text, originally read "this title", meaning Title XVIII of the Social Security Act, Act Aug. 14, 1935, c. 531, Title XVIII, § 1801 et seq., as added and amended, which is classified to this subchapter, 42 U.S.C.A. § 1395 et seq.

Part C, referred to in subsecs. (a) and (f)(1), means Part C of Title XVIII of the Social Security Act, Act Aug. 14, 1935, c. 531, Title XVIII, § 1851 et seq., as added Aug. 5, 1997, Pub.L. 105–33, Title IV, § 4001, 111 Stat. 276, and amended, which is classified to part C of this subchapter, 42 U.S.C.A. § 1395w–21 et seq.

Part A, referred to in subsec. (c)(1), means Part A of Title XVIII of the Social Security Act, Act Aug. 14, 1935, c. 531, Title XVIII, § 1811 et seq., as added July 30, 1965, Pub.L. 89–97, Title I, § 102(a), 79 Stat. 291, and amended, which is classified to part A of this subchapter, 42 U.S.C.A. § 1395c et seq.

Part B, referred to in subsec. (c)(1), means Part B of Title XVIII of the Social Security Act, Act Aug. 14, 1935, c. 531, Title XVIII, § 1831 et seq., as added July 30, 1965, Pub.L. 89–97, Title I, § 102(a), 79 Stat. 301, and amended, which is classified to part B of this subchapter, 42 U.S.C.A. § 1395j et seq.

Section 1395w–111(g)(4) of this title, referred to in subsec. (g), was in the original "section 1860D–3(c)(4)", and was translated as reading "section 1860D–11(g)(4)", meaning section 1860D–11(g)(4) of the Social Security Act, which is classified to 42 U.S.C.A. § 1395w–111(g)(4), to reflect the probable intent of Congress. Section 1860D–3, which is classified to section 1395w–103 of this title, does not contain a subsec. (c), and section 1395w–111(g)(4) of this title defines "fallback prescription drug plan" for purposes of this part.

§ 1395w–116. Medicare Prescription Drug Account in the Federal Supplementary Medical Insurance Trust Fund

(a) Establishment and operation of account—

(1) Establishment

There is created within the Federal Supplementary Medical Insurance Trust Fund established by section 1395t of this title an account to be known as the "Medicare Prescription Drug Account" (in this section referred to as the "Account").

(2) Funding

The Account shall consist of such gifts and bequests as may be made as provided in section 401(i)(1) of this title, accrued interest on balances in the Account, and such amounts as may be deposited in, or appropriated to, such Account as provided in this part.

(3) Separate from rest of Trust Fund

Funds provided under this part to the Account shall be kept separate from all other funds within the Federal Supplementary Medical Insurance Trust Fund, but shall be invested, and such investments redeemed, in the same manner as all other funds and investments within such Trust Fund.

(b) Payments from Account

(1) In general

The Managing Trustee shall pay from time to time from the Account such amounts as the Secretary certifies are necessary to make payments to operate the program under this part, including—

(A) payments under section 1395w–114 of this title (relating to low-income subsidy payments);

(B) payments under section 1395w–115 of this title (relating to subsidy payments and payments for fallback plans);

(C) payments to sponsors of qualified retiree prescription drug plans under section 1395w–132(a) of this title; and

(D) payments with respect to administrative expenses under this part in accordance with section 401(g) of this title.

(2) Transfers to Medicaid account for increased administrative costs

The Managing Trustee shall transfer from time to time from the Account to the Grants to States for Medicaid account amounts the Secretary certifies are attributable to increases in payment resulting from the application of section 1396u–5(b) of this title.

(3) Payments of premiums withheld

The Managing Trustee shall make payment to the PDP sponsor or MA organization involved of the premiums (and the portion of late enrollment penalties) that are collected in the manner described in section 1395w–24(d)(2)(A) of this title and that are payable under a prescription drug plan or MA–PD plan offered by such sponsor or organization.

(4) Treatment in relation to part B premium

Amounts payable from the Account shall not be taken into account in computing actuarial rates or premium amounts under section 1395r of this title.

(c) Deposits into account

(1) Low-income transfer

Amounts paid under section 1396u–5(c) of this title (and any amounts collected or offset under paragraph (1)(C) of such section) are deposited into the Account.

(2) Amounts withheld

Pursuant to sections 1395w–113(c) and 1395w–24(d) of this title (as applied under this part), amounts that are withheld (and allocated) to the Account are deposited into the Account.

(3) Appropriations to cover Government contributions

There are authorized to be appropriated from time to time, out of any moneys in the Treasury not otherwise appropriated, to the Account, an amount equivalent to the amount of payments made from the Account under subsection (b) of this section plus such amounts as the Managing Trustee certifies is necessary to maintain an appropriate contingency margin, reduced by the amounts deposited under paragraph (1) or subsection (a)(2) of this section.

(4) Initial funding and reserve

In order to assure prompt payment of benefits provided under this part and the administrative expenses thereunder during the early months of the program established by this part and to provide an initial contingency reserve, there are authorized to be appropriated to the Account, out of any moneys in the Treasury not otherwise appropriated, such amount as the Secretary certifies are required, but not to exceed 10 percent of the estimated total expenditures from such Account in 2006.

(5) Transfer of any remaining balance from Transitional Assistance Account

Any balance in the Transitional Assistance Account that is transferred under section 1395w–141(k)(5) of this title shall be deposited into the Account.

(Aug. 14, 1935, c. 531, Title XVIII, § 1860D–16, as added Pub.L. 108–173, Title I, § 101(a)(2), Dec. 8, 2003, 117 Stat. 2120.)

HISTORICAL AND STATUTORY NOTES

Revision Notes and Legislative Reports

2003 Acts. House Conference Report No. 108–391 and Statement by President, see 2003 U.S. Code Cong. and Adm. News, p. 1808.

References in Text

Part B, referred to in subsec. (b)(4), means Part B of Title XVIII of the Social Security Act, Act Aug. 14, 1935, c. 531, Title XVIII, § 1831 et seq., as added July 30, 1965, Pub.L. 89–97, Title I, § 102(a), 79 Stat. 301, and amended, which is classified to part B of this subchapter, 42 U.S.C.A. § 1395j et seq.

Subpart 3—Application to Medicare Advantage Program and Treatment of Employer–Sponsored Programs and Other Prescription Drug Plans

§ 1395w–131. Application to Medicare Advantage program and related managed care programs

(a) Special rules relating to offering of qualified prescription drug coverage

(1) **In general**

An MA organization on and after January 1, 2006—

(A) may not offer an MA plan described in section 1395w–21(a)(2)(A) of this title in an area unless either that plan (or another MA plan offered by the organization in that same service area) includes required prescription drug coverage (as defined in paragraph (2)); and

(B) may not offer prescription drug coverage (other than that required under parts A and B of this subchapter) to an enrollee—

(i) under an MSA plan; or

(ii) under another MA plan unless such drug coverage under such other plan provides qualified prescription drug coverage and unless the requirements of this section with respect to such coverage are met.

(2) **Qualifying coverage**

For purposes of paragraph (1)(A), the term "required coverage" means with respect to an MA–PD plan—

(A) basic prescription drug coverage; or

(B) qualified prescription drug coverage that provides supplemental prescription drug coverage, so long as there is no MA monthly supplemental beneficiary premium applied under the plan (due to the application of a credit against such premium of a rebate under section 1395w–24(b)(1)(C) of this title).

(b) Application of default enrollment rules

(1) **Seamless continuation**

In applying section 1395w–21(c)(3)(A)(ii) of this title, an individual who is enrolled in a health benefits plan shall not be considered to have been deemed to make an election into an MA–PD plan unless such health benefits plan provides any prescription drug coverage.

(2) **MA continuation**

In applying section 1395w–21(c)(3)(B) of this title, an individual who is enrolled in an MA plan shall not be considered to have been deemed to make an election into an MA–PD plan unless—

(A) for purposes of the election as of January 1, 2006, the MA plan provided as of December 31, 2005, any prescription drug coverage; or

(B) for periods after January 1, 2006, such MA plan is an MA–PD plan.

(3) **Discontinuance of MA–PD election during first year of eligibility**

In applying the second sentence of section 1395w–21(e)(4) of this title in the case of an individual who is electing to discontinue enrollment in an MA–PD plan, the individual shall be permitted to enroll in a prescription drug plan under part D of this subchapter at the time of the election of coverage under the original medicare fee-for-service program.

(4) **Rules regarding enrollees in MA plans not providing qualified prescription drug coverage**

In the case of an individual who is enrolled in an MA plan (other than an MSA plan) that does not provide qualified prescription drug coverage, if the organization offering such coverage discontinues the offering with respect to the individual of all MA plans that do not provide such coverage—

(i) the individual is deemed to have elected the original medicare fee-for-service program option, unless the individual affirmatively elects to enroll in an MA–PD plan; and

(ii) in the case of such a deemed election, the disenrollment shall be treated as an involuntary termination of the MA plan described in subparagraph (B)(ii) of section 1395ss(s)(3) of this title for purposes of applying such section.

The information disclosed under section 1395w–22(c)(1) of this title for individuals who are enrolled in such an MA plan shall include information regarding such rules.

(c) Application of part D rules for prescription drug coverage

With respect to the offering of qualified prescription drug coverage by an MA organization under this part on and after January 1, 2006—

(1) **In general**

Except as otherwise provided, the provisions of this part shall apply under part C of this subchapter with respect to prescription drug coverage provided under MA–PD plans in lieu of the other provisions of part C of this subchapter that would apply to such coverage under such plans.

(2) **Waiver**

The Secretary shall waive the provisions referred to in paragraph (1) to the extent the Secretary determines that such provisions duplicate, or are in conflict with, provisions otherwise applicable to the organization or plan under part C of this subchapter or as may be necessary in order to improve coordination of this part with the benefits under this part.

(3) **Treatment of MA owned and operated pharmacies**

The Secretary may waive the requirement of section 1395w–104(b)(1)(C) of this title in the case of an MA–PD plan that provides access (other than mail order) to qualified prescription drug coverage through pharmacies owned and operated by the MA organization, if the Secretary determines that the organization's pharmacy network is sufficient to provide comparable access for enrollees under the plan.

(d) Special rules for private fee-for-service plans that offer prescription drug coverage

With respect to an MA plan described in section 1395w–21(a)(2)(C) of this title that offers qualified prescription drug coverage, on and after January 1, 2006, the following rules apply:

(1) Requirements regarding negotiated prices

Subsections (a)(1) and (d)(1) of section 1395w–102 of this title and section 1395w–104(b)(2)(A) of this title shall not be construed to require the plan to provide negotiated prices (described in subsection (d)(1)(B) of such section), but shall apply to the extent the plan does so.

(2) Modification of pharmacy access standard and disclosure requirement

If the plan provides coverage for drugs purchased from all pharmacies, without charging additional cost-sharing, and without regard to whether they are participating pharmacies in a network or have entered into contracts or agreements with pharmacies to provide drugs to enrollees covered by the plan, subsections (b)(1)(C) and (k) of section 1395w–104 of this title shall not apply to the plan.

(3) Drug utilization management program and medication therapy management program not required

The requirements of subparagraphs (A) and (C) of section 1395w–104(c)(1) of this title shall not apply to the plan.

(4) Application of reinsurance

The Secretary shall determine the amount of reinsurance payments under section 1395w–115(b) of this title using a methodology that—

(A) bases such amount on the Secretary's estimate of the amount of such payments that would be payable if the plan were an MA–PD plan described in section 1395w–21(a)(2)(A)(i) of this title and the previous provisions of this subsection did not apply; and

(B) takes into account the average reinsurance payments made under section 1395w–115(b) of this title for populations of similar risk under MA–PD plans described in such section.

(5) Exemption from risk corridor provisions

The provisions of section 1395w–115(e) of this title shall not apply.

(6) Exemption from negotiations

Subsections (d) and (e)(2)(C) of section 1395w–111 of this title shall not apply and the provisions of section 1395w–24(a)(5)(B) of this title prohibiting the review, approval, or disapproval of amounts described in such section shall apply to the proposed bid and terms and conditions described in section 1395w–111(d) of this title.

(7) Treatment of incurred costs without regard to formulary

The exclusion of costs incurred for covered part D drugs which are not included (or treated as being included) in a plan's formulary under section 1395w–102(b)(4)(B)(i) of this title shall not apply insofar as the plan does not utilize a formulary.

(e) Application to reasonable cost reimbursement contractors

(1) In general

Subject to paragraphs (2) and (3) and rules established by the Secretary, in the case of an organization that is providing benefits under a reasonable cost reimbursement contract under section 1395mm(h) of this title and that elects to provide qualified prescription drug coverage to a part D eligible individual who is enrolled under such a contract, the provisions of this part (and related provisions of part C of this subchapter) shall apply to the provision of such coverage to such enrollee in the same manner as such provisions apply to the provision of such coverage under an MA–PD local plan described in section 1395w–21(a)(2)(A)(i) of this title and coverage under such a contract that so provides qualified prescription drug coverage shall be deemed to be an MA–PD local plan.

(2) Limitation on enrollment

In applying paragraph (1), the organization may not enroll part D eligible individuals who are not enrolled under the reasonable cost reimbursement contract involved.

(3) Bids not included in determining national average monthly bid amount

The bid of an organization offering prescription drug coverage under this subsection shall not be taken into account in computing the national average monthly bid amount and low-income benchmark premium amount under this part.

(f) Application to PACE

(1) In general

Subject to paragraphs (2) and (3) and rules established by the Secretary, in the case of a PACE program under section 1395eee of this title that elects to provide qualified prescription drug coverage to a part D eligible individual who is enrolled under such program, the provisions of this part (and related provisions of part C of this subchapter) shall apply to the provision of such coverage to such enrollee in a manner that is similar to the manner in which such provisions apply to the provision of such coverage under an MA–PD local plan described in section 1395w–21(a)(2)(A)(ii) of this title and a PACE program that so provides such coverage may be deemed to be an MA–PD local plan.

(2) Limitation on enrollment

In applying paragraph (1), the organization may not enroll part D eligible individuals who are not enrolled under the PACE program involved.

(3) Bids not included in determining standardized bid amount

The bid of an organization offering prescription drug coverage under this subsection is not be taken into account in computing any average benchmark bid amount and low-income benchmark premium amount under this part.

(Aug. 14, 1935, c. 531, Title XVIII, § 1860D–21, as added Pub.L. 108–173, Title I, § 101(a)(2), Dec. 8, 2003, 117 Stat. 2122.)

HISTORICAL AND STATUTORY NOTES

Revision Notes and Legislative Reports

2003 Acts. House Conference Report No. 108–391 and Statement by President, see 2003 U.S. Code Cong. and Adm. News, p. 1808.

References in Text

Part A, referred to in subsec. (a)(1)(B), means Part A of Title XVIII of the Social Security Act, Act Aug. 14, 1935, c. 531, Title XVIII, § 1811 et seq., as added July 30, 1965, Pub.L. 89–97, Title I, § 102(a), 79 Stat. 291, and amended, which is classified to part A of this subchapter, 42 U.S.C.A. § 1395c et seq.

Part B, referred to in subsec. (a)(1)(B), means Part B of Title XVIII of the Social Security Act, Act Aug. 14, 1935, c. 531, Title XVIII, § 1831 et seq., as added July 30, 1965, Pub.L. 89–97, Title I, § 102(a), 79 Stat. 301, and amended, which is classified to part B of this subchapter, 42 U.S.C.A. § 1395j et seq.

Part D, referred to in text, means Part D of Title XVIII of the Social Security Act, Act Aug. 14, 1935, c. 531, Title XVIII, § 1860D–1 et seq., as added, Pub.L. 108–173, Title I, § 101(a)(2), Dec. 8, 2003, 117 Stat. 2071, which is classified to this part, 42 U.S.C.A. § 1395w–101 et seq.

Part C, referred to in text, means Part C of Title XVIII of the Social Security Act, Act Aug. 14, 1935, c. 531, Title XVIII, § 1851 et seq., as added Aug. 5, 1997, Pub.L. 105–33, Title IV, § 4001, 111 Stat. 276, and amended, which is classified to part C of this subchapter, 42 U.S.C.A. § 1395w–21 et seq.

§ 1395w–132. Special rules for employer-sponsored programs

(a) Subsidy payment—

(1) In general

The Secretary shall provide in accordance with this subsection for payment to the sponsor of a qualified retiree prescription drug plan (as defined in paragraph (2)) of a special subsidy payment equal to the amount specified in paragraph (3) for each qualified covered retiree under the plan (as defined in paragraph (4)). This subsection constitutes budget authority in advance of appropriations Acts and represents the obligation of the Secretary to provide for the payment of amounts provided under this section.

(2) Qualified retiree prescription drug plan defined

For purposes of this subsection, the term "qualified retiree prescription drug plan" means employment-based retiree health coverage (as defined in subsection (c)(1) of this section) if, with respect to a part D eligible individual who is a participant or beneficiary under such coverage, the following requirements are met:

(A) Attestation of actuarial equivalence to standard coverage

The sponsor of the plan provides the Secretary, annually or at such other time as the Secretary may require, with an attestation that the actuarial value of prescription drug coverage under the plan (as determined using the processes and methods described in section 1395w–111(c) of this title) is at least equal to the actuarial value of standard prescription drug coverage, not taking into account the value of any discount or coverage provided during the gap in prescription drug coverage that occurs between the initial coverage limit under section 1395w–102(b)(3) of this title during the year and the out-of-pocket threshold specified in section 1395w–102(b)(4)(B) of this title.

(B) Audits

The sponsor of the plan, or an administrator of the plan designated by the sponsor, shall maintain (and afford the Secretary access to) such records as the Secretary may require for purposes of audits and other oversight activities necessary to ensure the adequacy of prescription drug coverage and the accuracy of payments made under this section. The provisions of section 1395w–102(d)(3) of this title shall apply to such information under this section (including such actuarial value and attestation) in a manner similar to the manner in which they apply to financial records of PDP sponsors and MA organizations.

(C) Provision of disclosure regarding prescription drug coverage

The sponsor of the plan shall provide for disclosure of information regarding prescription drug coverage in accordance with section 1395w–113(b)(6)(B) of this title.

(3) Employer and union special subsidy amounts

(A) In general

For purposes of this subsection, the special subsidy payment amount under this paragraph for a qualifying covered retiree for a coverage year enrolled with the sponsor of a qualified retiree prescription drug plan is, for the portion of the retiree's gross covered retiree plan-related prescription drug costs (as defined in subparagraph (C)(ii)) for such year that exceeds the cost threshold amount specified in subparagraph (B) and does not exceed the cost limit under such subparagraph, an amount equal to 28 percent of the allowable retiree costs (as defined in subparagraph (C)(i)) attributable to such gross covered prescription drug costs.

(B) Cost threshold and cost limit applicable

(i) In general

Subject to clause (ii)—

(I) the cost threshold under this subparagraph is equal to $250 for plan years that end in 2006; and

(II) the cost limit under this subparagraph is equal to $5,000 for plan years that end in 2006.

(ii) Indexing

The cost threshold and cost limit amounts specified in subclauses (I) and (II) of clause (i) for a plan year that ends after 2006 shall be adjusted in the same manner as the annual deductible and the annual out-of-pocket threshold, respectively, are annually adjusted under paragraphs (1) and (4)(B) of section 1395w–102(b) of this title.

(C) Definitions

For purposes of this paragraph:

(i) Allowable retiree costs

The term "allowable retiree costs" means, with respect to gross covered prescription drug costs under a qualified retiree prescription drug plan by a plan sponsor, the part of such costs that are actually paid (net of discounts, chargebacks, and average percentage rebates) by the sponsor or by or on behalf of a qualifying covered retiree under the plan.

(ii) Gross covered retiree plan-related prescription drug costs

For purposes of this section, the term "gross covered retiree plan-related prescription drug costs" means, with respect to a qualifying covered retiree enrolled in a qualified retiree prescription drug plan during a coverage year, the costs incurred under the plan, not including administrative costs, but including costs directly related to the dispensing of covered part D drugs during the year. Such costs shall be determined whether they are paid by the retiree or under the plan.

(iii) Coverage year

The term "coverage year" has the meaning given such term in section 1395w–115(b)(4) of this title.

(4) Qualifying covered retiree defined

For purposes of this subsection, the term "qualifying covered retiree" means a part D eligible individual who is not enrolled in a prescription drug plan or an MA–PD plan but is covered under a qualified retiree prescription drug plan.

(5) Payment methods, including provision of necessary information

The provisions of section 1395w–115(d) of this title (including paragraph (2), relating to requirement for provision of information) shall apply to payments under this subsection in a manner similar to the manner in which they apply to payment under section 1395w–115(b) of this title.

(6) Construction

Nothing in this subsection shall be construed as—

(A) precluding a part D eligible individual who is covered under employment-based retiree health coverage from enrolling in a prescription drug plan or in an MA–PD plan;

(B) precluding such employment-based retiree health coverage or an employer or other person from paying all or any portion of any premium required for coverage under a prescription drug plan or MA–PD plan on behalf of such an individual;

(C) preventing such employment-based retiree health coverage from providing coverage—

(i) that is better than standard prescription drug coverage to retirees who are covered under a qualified retiree prescription drug plan; or

(ii) that is supplemental to the benefits provided under a prescription drug plan or an MA–PD plan, including benefits to retirees who are not covered under a qualified retiree prescription drug plan but who are enrolled in such a prescription drug plan or MA–PD plan; or

(D) preventing employers to provide for flexibility in benefit design and pharmacy access provisions, without regard to the requirements for basic prescription drug coverage, so long as the actuarial equivalence requirement of paragraph (2)(A) is met.

(b) Application of MA waiver authority

The provisions of section 1395w–27(i) of this title shall apply with respect to prescription drug plans in relation to employment-based retiree health coverage in a manner similar to the manner in which they apply to an MA plan in relation to employers, including authorizing the establishment of separate premium amounts for enrollees in a prescription drug plan by reason of such coverage and limitations on enrollment to part D eligible individuals enrolled under such coverage.

(c) Definitions

For purposes of this section:

(1) Employment-based retiree health coverage

The term "employment-based retiree health coverage" means health insurance or other coverage of health care costs (whether provided by voluntary insurance coverage or pursuant to statutory or contractual obligation) for part D eligible individuals (or for such individuals and their spouses and dependents) under a group health plan based on their status as retired participants in such plan.

(2) Sponsor

The term "sponsor" means a plan sponsor, as defined in section 1002(16)(B) of Title 29, in relation to a group health plan, except that, in the case of a plan maintained jointly by one employer and an employee organization and with respect to which the employer is the primary source of financing, such term means such employer.

(3) Group health plan

The term "group health plan" includes such a plan as defined in section 1167(1) of Title 29 and also includes the following:

(A) Federal and State Governmental plans

Such a plan established or maintained for its employees by the Government of the United States, by the government of any State or political subdivision thereof, or by any agency or instrumentality of any of the foregoing, including a health benefits plan offered under chapter 89 of Title 5.

(B) Collectively bargained plans

Such a plan established or maintained under or pursuant to one or more collective bargaining agreements.

(C) Church plans

Such a plan established and maintained for its employees (or their beneficiaries) by a church or by a convention or association of churches which is exempt from tax under section 501 of the Internal Revenue Code of 1986.

(Aug. 14, 1935, c. 531, Title XVIII, § 1860D–22, as added Pub.L. 108–173, Title I, § 101(a)(2), Dec. 8, 2003, 117 Stat. 2125; amended Pub.L. 111–152, Title I, § 1101(b)(4), Mar. 30, 2010, 124 Stat. 1039.)

HISTORICAL AND STATUTORY NOTES

Revision Notes and Legislative Reports

2003 Acts. House Conference Report No. 108–391 and Statement by President, see 2003 U.S. Code Cong. and Adm. News, p. 1808.

References in Text

Part D, referred to in text, means Part D of Title XVIII of the Social Security Act, Act Aug. 14, 1935, c. 531, Title XVIII, § 1860D–1 et seq., as added, Pub.L. 108–173, Title I, § 101(a)(2), Dec. 8, 2003, 117 Stat. 2071, which is classified to this part, 42 U.S.C.A. § 1395w–101 et seq.

Chapter 89 of Title 5, referred to in subsec. (c)(3)(A), is 5 U.S.C.A. § 8901 et seq.

The Internal Revenue Code of 1986, referred to in subsec. (c)(3)(C), is classified generally to Title 26, 26 U.S.C.A. § 1 et seq. Section 501 of the Code is classified to 26 U.S.C.A. § 501.

Study on Employment–Based Retiree Health Coverage

Pub.L. 108–173, Title I, § 111, Dec. 8, 2003, 117 Stat. 2174, provided that:

"**(a) Study.**—The Comptroller General of the United States shall conduct an initial and final study under this subsection to examine trends in employment-based retiree health coverage (as defined in 1860D–22(c)(1) of the Social Security Act [subsec. (c)(1) of this section], as added by section 101), including coverage under the Federal Employees Health Benefits Program (FEHBP), and the options and incentives available under this Act which may have an effect on the voluntary provision of such coverage.

"**(b) Content of initial study.**—The initial study under this section shall consider the following:

"(1) Trends in employment-based retiree health coverage prior to the date of the enactment of this Act [Dec. 8, 2003].

"(2) The opinions of sponsors of employment-based retiree health coverage concerning which of the options available under this Act [the Medicare, Prescription Drug, Improvement, and Modernization Act of 2003, Pub.L. 108–173, Dec. 8, 2003, 117 Stat. 2006; see Tables for complete classification] they are most likely to utilize for the provision of health coverage to their medicare-eligible retirees, including an assessment of the administrative burdens associated with the available options.

"(3) The likelihood of sponsors of employment-based retiree health coverage to maintain or adjust their levels of retiree health benefits beyond coordination with medicare, including for prescription drug coverage, provided to medicare-eligible retirees after the date of the enactment of this Act [Dec. 8, 2003].

"(4) The factors that sponsors of employment-based retiree health coverage expect to consider in making decisions about any changes they may make in the health coverage provided to medicare-eligible retirees.

"(5) Whether the prescription drug plan options available, or the health plan options available under the Medicare Advantage program, are likely to cause employers and other entities that did not provide health coverage to retirees prior to the date of the enactment of this Act [Dec. 8, 2003] to provide supplemental coverage or contributions toward premium expenses for medicare-eligible retirees who may enroll in such options in the future.

"(c) **Contents of final study.**—The final study under this section [this note] shall consider the following:

"(1) Changes in the trends in employment-based retiree health coverage since the completion of the initial study by the Comptroller General.

"(2) Factors contributing to any changes in coverage levels.

"(3) The number and characteristics of sponsors of employment-based retiree health coverage who receive the special subsidy payments under section 1860D–22 of the Social Security Act, as added by section 101 [this section], for the provision of prescription drug coverage to their medicare-eligible retirees that is the same or greater actuarial value as the prescription drug coverage available to other medicare beneficiaries without employment-based retiree health coverage.

"(4) The extent to which sponsors of employment-based retiree health coverage provide supplemental health coverage or contribute to the premiums for medicare-eligible retirees who enroll in a prescription drug plan or an MA–PD plan.

"(5) Other coverage options, including tax-preferred retirement or health savings accounts, consumer-directed health plans, or other vehicles that sponsors of employment-based retiree health coverage believe would assist retirees with their future health care needs and their willingness to sponsor such alternative plan designs.

"(6) The extent to which employers or other entities that did not provide employment-based retiree health coverage prior to the date of the enactment of this Act [Dec. 8, 2003] provided some form of coverage or financial assistance for retiree health care needs after the date of the enactment of this Act [Dec. 8, 2003].

"(7) Recommendations by employers, benefits experts, academics, and others on ways that the voluntary provision of employment-based retiree health coverage may be improved and expanded.

"(d) **Reports.**—The Comptroller General shall submit a report to Congress on—

"(1) the initial study under subsection (b) [of this note] not later than 1 year after the date of the enactment of this Act [Dec. 8, 2003]; and

"(2) the final study under subsection (c) [of this note] not later than January 1, 2007.

"(e) **Consultation.**—The Comptroller General shall consult with sponsors of employment-based retiree health coverage, benefits experts, human resources professionals, employee benefits consultants, and academics with experience in health benefits and survey research in the development and design of the initial and final studies under this section [this note]."

§ 1395w–133. State Pharmaceutical Assistance Programs

(a) Requirements for benefit coordination—

(1) In general

Before July 1, 2005, the Secretary shall establish consistent with this section requirements for prescription drug plans to ensure the effective coordination between a part D plan (as defined in paragraph (5)) and a State Pharmaceutical Assistance Program (as defined in subsection (b) of this section) with respect to—

(A) payment of premiums and coverage; and

(B) payment for supplemental prescription drug benefits,

for part D eligible individuals enrolled under both types of plans.

(2) Coordination elements

The requirements under paragraph (1) shall include requirements relating to coordination of each of the following:

(A) Enrollment file sharing.

(B) The processing of claims, including electronic processing.

(C) Claims payment.

(D) Claims reconciliation reports.

(E) Application of the protection against high out-of-pocket expenditures under section 1395w–102(b)(4) of this title.

(F) Other administrative processes specified by the Secretary.

Such requirements shall be consistent with applicable law to safeguard the privacy of any individually identifiable beneficiary information.

(3) Use of lump sum per capita method

Such requirements shall include a method for the application by a part D plan of specified funding amounts from a State Pharmaceutical Assistance Program for enrolled individuals for supplemental prescription drug benefits.

(4) Consultation

In establishing requirements under this subsection, the Secretary shall consult with State Pharmaceutical Assistance Programs, MA organizations, States, pharmaceutical benefit managers, employers, representatives of part D eligible individuals, the data processing experts, pharmacists, pharmaceutical manufacturers, and other experts.

(5) Part D plan defined

For purposes of this section and section 1395w–134 of this title, the term "part D plan" means a prescription drug plan and an MA–PD plan.

(b) State Pharmaceutical Assistance Program

For purposes of this part, the term "State Pharmaceutical Assistance Program" means a State program—

(1) which provides financial assistance for the purchase or provision of supplemental prescription drug coverage or benefits on behalf of part D eligible individuals;

(2) which, in determining eligibility and the amount of assistance to part D eligible individuals under the Program, provides assistance to such individuals in all part D plans and does not discriminate

based upon the part D plan in which the individual is enrolled; and

(3) which satisfies the requirements of subsections (a) and (c) of this section.

(c) Relation to other provisions

(1) Medicare as primary payor

The requirements of this section shall not change or affect the primary payor status of a part D plan.

(2) Use of a single card

A card that is issued under section 1395w–104(b)(2)(A) of this title for use under a part D plan may also be used in connection with coverage of benefits provided under a State Pharmaceutical Assistance Program and, in such case, may contain an emblem or symbol indicating such connection.

(3) Other provisions

The provisions of section 1395w–134(c) of this title shall apply to the requirements under this section.

(4) Special treatment under out-of-pocket rule

In applying section 1395w–102(b)(4)(C)(ii) of this title, expenses incurred under a State Pharmaceutical Assistance Program may be counted toward the annual out-of-pocket threshold.

(5) Construction

Nothing in this section shall be construed as requiring a State Pharmaceutical Assistance Program to coordinate or provide financial assistance with respect to any part D plan.

(d) Facilitation of transition and coordination with State Pharmaceutical Assistance Programs

(1) Transitional grant program

The Secretary shall provide payments to State Pharmaceutical Assistance Programs with an application approved under this subsection.

(2) Use of funds

Payments under this section may be used by a Program for any of the following:

(A) Educating part D eligible individuals enrolled in the Program about the prescription drug coverage available through part D plans under this part.

(B) Providing technical assistance, phone support, and counseling for such enrollees to facilitate selection and enrollment in such plans.

(C) Other activities designed to promote the effective coordination of enrollment, coverage, and payment between such Program and such plans.

(3) Allocation of funds

Of the amount appropriated to carry out this subsection for a fiscal year, the Secretary shall allocate payments among Programs that have applications approved under paragraph (4) for such fiscal year in proportion to the number of enrollees enrolled in each such Program as of October 1, 2003.

(4) Application

No payments may be made under this subsection except pursuant to an application that is submitted and approved in a time, manner, and form specified by the Secretary.

(5) Funding

Out of any funds in the Treasury not otherwise appropriated, there are appropriated for each of fiscal years 2005 and 2006, $62,500,000 to carry out this subsection.

(Aug. 14, 1935, c. 531, Title XVIII, § 1860D–23, as added Pub.L. 108–173, Title I, § 101(a)(2), Dec. 8, 2003, 117 Stat. 2128.)

HISTORICAL AND STATUTORY NOTES

Revision Notes and Legislative Reports

2003 Acts. House Conference Report No. 108–391 and Statement by President, see 2003 U.S. Code Cong. and Adm. News, p. 1808.

References in Text

Part D, referred to in text, means Part D of Title XVIII of the Social Security Act, Act Aug. 14, 1935, c. 531, Title XVIII, § 1860D–1 et seq., as added, Pub.L. 108–173, Title I, § 101(a)(2), Dec. 8, 2003, 117 Stat. 2071, which is classified to this part, 42 U.S.C.A. § 1395w–101 et seq.

§ 1395w–134. Coordination requirements for plans providing prescription drug coverage

(a) Application of benefit coordination requirements to additional plans—

(1) In general

The Secretary shall apply the coordination requirements established under section 1395w–133(a) of this title to Rx plans described in subsection (b) of this section in the same manner as such requirements apply to a State Pharmaceutical Assistance Program.

(2) Application to treatment of certain out-of-pocket expenditures

To the extent specified by the Secretary, the requirements referred to in paragraph (1) shall apply to procedures established under section 1395w–102(b)(4)(D) of this title.

(3) User fees

(A) In general

The Secretary may impose user fees for the transmittal of information necessary for benefit coordination under section 1395w–102(b)(4)(D) of this title in a manner similar to the manner in which user fees are imposed under section

1395u(h)(3)(B) of this title, except that the Secretary may retain a portion of such fees to defray the Secretary's costs in carrying out procedures under section 1395w–102(b)(4)(D) of this title.

(B) Application

A user fee may not be imposed under subparagraph (A) with respect to a State Pharmaceutical Assistance Program.

(b) Rx plan

An Rx plan described in this subsection is any of the following:

(1) Medicaid programs

A State plan under subchapter XIX of this chapter, including such a plan operating under a waiver under section 1315 of this title, if it meets the requirements of section 1395w–133(b)(2) of this title.

(2) Group health plans

An employer group health plan.

(3) FEHBP

The Federal employees health benefits plan under chapter 89 of Title 5.

(4) Military coverage (including TRICARE)

Coverage under chapter 55 of Title 10.

(5) Other prescription drug coverage

Such other health benefit plans or programs that provide coverage or financial assistance for the purchase or provision of prescription drug coverage on behalf of part D eligible individuals as the Secretary may specify.

(c) Relation to other provisions

(1) Use of cost management tools

The requirements of this section shall not impair or prevent a PDP sponsor or MA organization from applying cost management tools (including differential payments) under all methods of operation.

(2) No affect[1] on treatment of certain out-of-pocket expenditures

The requirements of this section shall not affect the application of the procedures established under section 1395w–102(b)(4)(D) of this title.

(Aug. 14, 1935, c. 531, Title XVIII, § 1860D–24, as added Pub.L. 108–173, Title I, § 101(a)(2), Dec. 8, 2003, 117 Stat. 2130.)

[1] So in original. Probably should be "effect".

HISTORICAL AND STATUTORY NOTES

Revision Notes and Legislative Reports

2003 Acts. House Conference Report No. 108–391 and Statement by President, see 2003 U.S. Code Cong. and Adm. News, p. 1808.

References in Text

Subchapter XIX of this chapter, referred to in text, originally read "title XIX", meaning Title XIX of the Social Security Act, Aug. 14, 1935, c. 531, Title XIX, § 1901 et seq., as added July 30, 1965, Pub.L. 89–97, Title I, § 121(a), 79 Stat. 343, and amended, which is principally classified to subchapter XIX of this chapter, 42 U.S.C.A. § 1396 et seq.

Chapter 89 of Title 5, referred to in subsec. (b)(3), is 5 U.S.C.A. § 8901 et seq.

Chapter 55 of Title 10, referred to in subsec. (b)(4) is 10 U.S.C.A. § 1071 et seq.

Part D, referred to in subsec. (b)(5), means Part D of Title XVIII of the Social Security Act, Act Aug. 14, 1935, c. 531, Title XVIII, § 1860D–1 et seq., as added, Pub.L. 108–173, Title I, § 101(a)(2), Dec. 8, 2003, 117 Stat. 2071, which is classified to this part, 42 U.S.C.A. § 1395w–101 et seq.

Subpart 4—Medicare Prescription Drug Discount Card and Transitional Assistance Program

§ 1395w–141. Medicare prescription drug discount card and transitional assistance program

(a) Establishment of program—

(1) In general

The Secretary shall establish a program under this section—

(A) to endorse prescription drug discount card programs that meet the requirements of this section in order to provide access to prescription drug discounts through prescription drug card sponsors for discount card eligible individuals throughout the United States; and

(B) to provide for transitional assistance for transitional assistance eligible individuals enrolled in such endorsed programs.

(2) Period of operation

(A) Implementation deadline

The Secretary shall implement the program under this section so that discount cards and transitional assistance are first available by not later than 6 months after December 8, 2003.

(B) Expediting implementation

The Secretary shall promulgate regulations to carry out the program under this section which may be effective and final immediately on an interim basis as of the date of publication of the interim final regulation. If the Secretary provides for an interim final regulation, the Secretary shall provide for a period of public comments on such regulation after the date of publication. The Secretary may change or revise such regulation after completion of the period of public comment.

(C) Termination and transition

(i) In general

Subject to clause (ii)—

(I) the program under this section shall not apply to covered discount card drugs dispensed after December 31, 2005; and

(II) transitional assistance shall be available after such date to the extent the assistance relates to drugs dispensed on or before such date.

(ii) Transition

In the case of an individual who is enrolled in an endorsed discount card program as of December 31, 2005, during the individual's transition period (if any) under clause (iii), in accordance with transition rules specified by the Secretary—

(I) such endorsed program may continue to apply to covered discount card drugs dispensed to the individual under the program during such transition period;

(II) no annual enrollment fee shall be applicable during the transition period;

(III) during such period the individual may not change the endorsed program plan in which the individual is enrolled; and

(IV) the balance of any transitional assistance remaining on January 1, 2006, shall remain available for drugs dispensed during the individual's transition period.

(iii) Transition period

The transition period under this clause for an individual is the period beginning on January 1, 2006, and ending in the case of an individual who—

(I) is enrolled in a prescription drug plan or an MA–PD plan before the last date of the initial enrollment period under section 1395w–101(b)(2)(A) of this title, on the effective date of the individual's coverage under such part; or

(II) is not so enrolled, on the last day of such initial period.

(3) Voluntary nature of program

Nothing in this section shall be construed as requiring a discount card eligible individual to enroll in an endorsed discount card program under this section.

(4) Glossary and definitions of terms

For purposes of this section:

(A) Covered discount card drug

The term "covered discount card drug" has the meaning given the term "covered part D drug" in section 1395w–102(e) of this title.

(B) Discount card eligible individual

The term "discount card eligible individual" is defined in subsection (b)(1)(A) of this section.

(C) Endorsed discount card program; endorsed program

The terms "endorsed discount card program" and "endorsed program" mean a prescription drug discount card program that is endorsed (and for which the sponsor has a contract with the Secretary) under this section.

(D) Negotiated price

Negotiated prices are described in subsection (e)(1)(A)(ii) of this section.

(E) Prescription drug card sponsor; sponsor

The terms "prescription drug card sponsor" and "sponsor" are defined in subsection (h)(1)(A) of this section.

(F) State

The term "State" has the meaning given such term for purposes of subchapter XIX of this chapter.

(G) Transitional assistance eligible individual

The term "transitional assistance eligible individual" is defined in subsection (b)(2) of this section.

(b) Eligibility for discount card and for transitional assistance

For purposes of this section:

(1) Discount card eligible individual

(A) In general

The term "discount card eligible individual" means an individual who—

(i) is entitled to benefits, or enrolled, under part A of this subchapter or enrolled under part B of this subchapter; and

(ii) subject to paragraph (4), is not an individual described in subparagraph (B).

(B) Individual described

An individual described in this subparagraph is an individual described in subparagraph (A)(i) who is enrolled under subchapter XIX of this chapter (or under a waiver under section 1315 of this title of the requirements of such subchapter) and is entitled to any medical assistance for outpatient prescribed drugs described in section 1396d(a)(12) of this title.

(2) **Transitional assistance eligible individual**

(A) **In general**

Subject to subparagraph (B), the term "transitional assistance eligible individual" means a discount card eligible individual who resides in one of the 50 States or the District of Columbia and whose income (as determined under subsection (f)(1)(B) of this section) is not more than 135 percent of the poverty line (as defined in section 9902(2) of this title, including any revision required by such section) applicable to the family size involved (as determined under subsection (f)(1)(B) of this section).

(B) **Exclusion of individuals with certain prescription drug coverage**

Such term does not include an individual who has coverage of, or assistance for, covered discount card drugs under any of the following:

(i) A group health plan or health insurance coverage (as such terms are defined in section 300gg–91 of this title), other than coverage under a plan under part C of this subchapter and other than coverage consisting only of excepted benefits (as defined in such section).

(ii) Chapter 55 of Title 10 (relating to medical and dental care for members of the uniformed services).

(iii) A plan under chapter 89 of Title 5 (relating to the Federal employees' health benefits program).

(3) **Special transitional assistance eligible individual**

The term "special transitional assistance eligible individual" means a transitional assistance eligible individual whose income (as determined under subsection (f)(1)(B) of this section) is not more than 100 percent of the poverty line (as defined in section 9902(2) of this title, including any revision required by such section) applicable to the family size involved (as determined under subsection (f)(1)(B) of this section).

(4) **Treatment of medicaid medically needy**

For purposes of this section, the Secretary shall provide for appropriate rules for the treatment of medically needy individuals described in section 1396a(a)(10)(C) of this title as discount card eligible individuals and as transitional assistance eligible individuals.

(c) **Enrollment and enrollment fees**

(1) **Enrollment process**

The Secretary shall establish a process through which a discount card eligible individual is enrolled and disenrolled in an endorsed discount card program under this section consistent with the following:

(A) **Continuous open enrollment**

Subject to the succeeding provisions of this paragraph and subsection (h)(9) of this section, a discount card eligible individual who is not enrolled in an endorsed discount card program and is residing in a State may enroll in any such endorsed program—

(i) that serves residents of the State; and

(ii) at any time beginning on the initial enrollment date, specified by the Secretary, and before January 1, 2006.

(B) **Use of standard enrollment form**

An enrollment in an endorsed program shall only be effected through completion of a standard enrollment form specified by the Secretary. Each sponsor of an endorsed program shall transmit to the Secretary (in a form and manner specified by the Secretary) information on individuals who complete such enrollment forms and, to the extent provided under subsection (f) of this section, information regarding certification as a transitional assistance eligible individual.

(C) **Enrollment only in one program**

(i) **In general**

Subject to clauses (ii) and (iii), a discount card eligible individual may be enrolled in only one endorsed discount card program under this section.

(ii) **Change in endorsed program permitted for 2005**

The Secretary shall establish a process, similar to (and coordinated with) the process for annual, coordinated elections under section 1395w–21(e)(3) of this title during 2004, under which an individual enrolled in an endorsed discount card program may change the endorsed program in which the individual is enrolled for 2005.

(iii) **Additional exceptions**

The Secretary shall permit an individual to change the endorsed discount card program in which the individual is enrolled in the case of an individual who changes residence to be outside the service area of such program and in such other exceptional cases as the Secretary may provide (taking into account the circumstances for special election periods under section 1395w–21(e)(4) of this title). Under the previous sentence, the Secretary may consider a change in residential setting (such as placement in a nursing facility) or enrollment in or disenrollment from a plan under part C of this subchapter through which the individual was enrolled in an endorsed program to be an exceptional circumstance.

(D) Disenrollment

(i) Voluntary

An individual may voluntarily disenroll from an endorsed discount card program at any time. In the case of such a voluntary disenrollment, the individual may not enroll in another endorsed program, except under such exceptional circumstances as the Secretary may recognize under subparagraph (C)(iii) or during the annual coordinated enrollment period provided under subparagraph (C)(ii).

(ii) Involuntary

An individual who is enrolled in an endorsed discount card program and not a transitional assistance eligible individual may be disenrolled by the sponsor of the program if the individual fails to pay any annual enrollment fee required under the program.

(E) Application to certain enrollees

In the case of a discount card eligible individual who is enrolled in a plan described in section 1395w–21(a)(2)(A) of this title or under a reasonable cost reimbursement contract under section 1395mm(h) of this title that is offered by an organization that also is a prescription discount card sponsor that offers an endorsed discount card program under which the individual may be enrolled and that has made an election to apply the special rules under subsection (h)(9)(B) of this section for such an endorsed program, the individual may only enroll in such an endorsed discount card program offered by that sponsor.

(2) Enrollment fees

(A) In general

Subject to the succeeding provisions of this paragraph, a prescription drug card sponsor may charge an annual enrollment fee for each discount card eligible individual enrolled in an endorsed discount card program offered by such sponsor. The annual enrollment fee for either 2004 or 2005 shall not be prorated for portions of a year. There shall be no annual enrollment fee for a year after 2005.

(B) Amount

No annual enrollment fee charged under subparagraph (A) may exceed $30.

(C) Uniform enrollment fee

A prescription drug card sponsor shall ensure that the annual enrollment fee (if any) for an endorsed discount card program is the same for all discount card eligible individuals enrolled in the program and residing in the State.

(D) Collection

The annual enrollment fee (if any) charged for enrollment in an endorsed program shall be collected by the sponsor of the program.

(E) Payment of fee for transitional assistance eligible individuals

Under subsection (g)(1)(A) of this section, the annual enrollment fee (if any) otherwise charged under this paragraph with respect to a transitional assistance eligible individual shall be paid by the Secretary on behalf of such individual.

(F) Optional payment of fee by State

(i) In general

The Secretary shall establish an arrangement under which a State may provide for payment of some or all of the enrollment fee for some or all enrollees who are not transitional assistance eligible individuals in the State, as specified by the State under the arrangement. Insofar as such a payment arrangement is made with respect to an enrollee, the amount of the enrollment fee shall be paid directly by the State to the sponsor.

(ii) No Federal matching available under medicaid or SCHIP

Expenditures made by a State for enrollment fees described in clause (i) shall not be treated as State expenditures for purposes of Federal matching payments under subchapter XIX or XXI of this chapter.

(G) Rules in case of changes in program enrollment during a year

The Secretary shall provide special rules in the case of payment of an annual enrollment fee for a discount card eligible individual who changes the endorsed program in which the individual is enrolled during a year.

(3) Issuance of discount card

Each prescription drug card sponsor of an endorsed discount card program shall issue, in a standard format specified by the Secretary, to each discount card eligible individual enrolled in such program a card that establishes proof of enrollment and that can be used in a coordinated manner to identify the sponsor, program, and individual for purposes of the program under this section.

(4) Period of access

In the case of a discount card eligible individual who enrolls in an endorsed program, access to negotiated prices and transitional assistance, if any, under such endorsed program shall take effect on such date as the Secretary shall specify.

(d) Provision of information on enrollment and program features

(1) Secretarial responsibilities

(A) In general

The Secretary shall provide for activities under this subsection to broadly disseminate information to discount card eligible individuals (and prospective eligible individuals) regarding—

(i) enrollment in endorsed discount card programs; and

(ii) the features of the program under this section, including the availability of transitional assistance.

(B) Promotion of informed choice

In order to promote informed choice among endorsed prescription drug discount card programs, the Secretary shall provide for the dissemination of information which—

(i) compares the annual enrollment fee and other features of such programs, which may include comparative prices for covered discount card drugs; and

(ii) includes educational materials on the variability of discounts on prices of covered discount card drugs under an endorsed program.

The dissemination of information under clause (i) shall, to the extent practicable, be coordinated with the dissemination of educational information on other medicare options.

(C) Special rule for initial enrollment date under the program

To the extent practicable, the Secretary shall ensure, through the activities described in subparagraphs (A) and (B), that discount card eligible individuals are provided with such information at least 30 days prior to the initial enrollment date specified under subsection (c)(1)(A)(ii) of this section.

(D) Use of medicare toll-free number

The Secretary shall provide through the toll-free telephone number 1–800–MEDICARE for the receipt and response to inquiries and complaints concerning the program under this section and endorsed programs.

(2) Prescription drug card sponsor responsibilities

(A) In general

Each prescription drug card sponsor that offers an endorsed discount card program shall make available to discount card eligible individuals (through the Internet and otherwise) information that the Secretary identifies as being necessary to promote informed choice among endorsed discount card programs by such individuals, including information on enrollment fees and negotiated prices for covered discount card drugs charged to such individuals.

(B) Response to enrollee questions

Each sponsor offering an endorsed discount card program shall have a mechanism (including a toll-free telephone number) for providing upon request specific information (such as negotiated prices and the amount of transitional assistance remaining available through the program) to discount card eligible individuals enrolled in the program. The sponsor shall inform transitional assistance eligible individuals enrolled in the program of the availability of such toll-free telephone number to provide information on the amount of available transitional assistance.

(C) Information on balance of transitional assistance available at point-of-sale

Each sponsor offering an endorsed discount card program shall have a mechanism so that information on the amount of transitional assistance remaining under subsection (g)(1)(B) of this section is available (electronically or by telephone) at the point-of-sale of covered discount card drugs.

(3) Public disclosure of pharmaceutical prices for equivalent drugs

(A) In general

A prescription drug card sponsor offering an endorsed discount card program shall provide that each pharmacy that dispenses a covered discount card drug shall inform a discount card eligible individual enrolled in the program of any differential between the price of the drug to the enrollee and the price of the lowest priced generic covered discount card drug under the program that is therapeutically equivalent and bioequivalent and available at such pharmacy.

(B) Timing of notice

(i) In general

Subject to clause (ii), the information under subparagraph (A) shall be provided at the time of purchase of the drug involved, or, in the case of dispensing by mail order, at the time of delivery of such drug.

(ii) Waiver

The Secretary may waive clause (i) in such circumstances as the Secretary may specify.

(e) Discount card features

(1) Savings to enrollees through negotiated prices

(A) Access to negotiated prices

(i) In general

Each prescription drug card sponsor that offers an endorsed discount card program shall provide each discount card eligible individual enrolled in the program with access to negotiated prices.

(ii) Negotiated prices

For purposes of this section, negotiated prices shall take into account negotiated price concessions, such as discounts, direct or indirect subsidies, rebates, and direct or indirect remunerations, for covered discount card drugs, and include any dispensing fees for such drugs.

(B) Ensuring pharmacy access

Each prescription drug card sponsor offering an endorsed discount card program shall secure the participation in its network of a sufficient number of pharmacies that dispense (other than solely by mail order) drugs directly to enrollees to ensure convenient access to covered discount card drugs at negotiated prices (consistent with rules established by the Secretary). The Secretary shall establish convenient access rules under this clause that are no less favorable to enrollees than the standards for convenient access to pharmacies included in the statement of work of solicitation (#MDA906–03–R–0002) of the Department of Defense under the TRICARE Retail Pharmacy (TRRx) as of March 13, 2003.

(C) Prohibition on charges for required services

(i) In general

Subject to clause (ii), a prescription drug card sponsor (and any pharmacy contracting with such sponsor for the provision of covered discount card drugs to individuals enrolled in such sponsor's endorsed discount card program) may not charge an enrollee any amount for any items and services required to be provided by the sponsor under this section.

(ii) Construction

Nothing in clause (i) shall be construed to prevent—

(I) the sponsor from charging the annual enrollment fee (except in the case of a transitional assistance eligible individual); and

(II) the pharmacy dispensing the covered discount card drug, from imposing a charge (consistent with the negotiated price) for the covered discount card drug dispensed, reduced by the amount of any transitional assistance made available.

(D) Inapplicability of medicaid best price rules

The prices negotiated from drug manufacturers for covered discount card drugs under an endorsed discount card program under this section shall (notwithstanding any other provision of law) not be taken into account for the purposes of establishing the best price under section 1396r–8(c)(1)(C) of this title.

(2) Reduction of medication errors and adverse drug interactions

Each endorsed discount card program shall implement a system to reduce the likelihood of medication errors and adverse drug interactions and to improve medication use.

(f) Eligibility procedures for endorsed programs and transitional assistance

(1) Determinations

(A) Procedures

The determination of whether an individual is a discount card eligible individual or a transitional assistance eligible individual or a special transitional assistance eligible individual (as defined in subsection (b) of this section) shall be determined under procedures specified by the Secretary consistent with this subsection.

(B) Income and family size determinations

For purposes of this section, the Secretary shall define the terms "income" and "family size" and shall specify the methods and period for which they are determined. If under such methods income or family size is determined based on the income or family size for prior periods of time, the Secretary shall permit (whether through a process of reconsideration or otherwise) an individual whose income or family size has changed to elect to have eligibility for transitional assistance determined based on income or family size for a more recent period.

(2) Use of self-certification for transitional assistance

(A) In general

Under the procedures specified under paragraph (1)(A) an individual who wishes to be treated as a transitional assistance eligible individual or a special transitional assistance eligible individual under this section (or another qualified person on such individual's behalf) shall certify on the enrollment form under subsection (c)(1)(B) of this section (or similar form specified by the Secretary), through a simplified means specified by the Secretary and under penalty of perjury or similar sanction for false statements, as to the amount of the individual's income, family size, and individual's prescription drug coverage (if any) insofar as they relate to eligibility to be a transitional assistance eligible individual or a special transitional assistance eligible individual. Such certification shall be deemed as consent to verification of respective eligibility under paragraph (3). A certification under this paragraph may be provided before, on, or after the time of enrollment under an endorsed program.

(B) Treatment of self-certification

The Secretary shall treat a certification under subparagraph (A) that is verified under paragraph (3) as a determination that the individual involved is a transitional assistance eligible individual or special transitional assistance eligible individual (as the case may be) for the entire period of the enrollment of the individual in any endorsed program.

(3) Verification

(A) In general

The Secretary shall establish methods (which may include the use of sampling and the use of information described in subparagraph (B)) to verify eligibility for individuals who seek to enroll in an endorsed program and for individuals who provide a certification under paragraph (2).

(B) Information described

The information described in this subparagraph is as follows:

(i) Medicaid-related information

Information on eligibility under subchapter XIX of this chapter and provided to the Secretary under arrangements between the Secretary and States in order to verify the eligibility of individuals who seek to enroll in an endorsed program and of individuals who provide certification under paragraph (2).

(ii) Social Security information

Financial information made available to the Secretary under arrangements between the Secretary and the Commissioner of Social Security in order to verify the eligibility of individuals who provide such certification.

(iii) Information from Secretary of the Treasury

Financial information made available to the Secretary under section 6103(*l*)(19) of the Internal Revenue Code of 1986 in order to verify the eligibility of individuals who provide such certification.

(C) Verification in cases of medicaid enrollees

(i) In general

Nothing in this section shall be construed as preventing the Secretary from finding that a discount card eligible individual meets the income requirements under subsection (b)(2)(A) of this section if the individual is within a category of discount card eligible individuals who are enrolled under subchapter XIX of this chapter (such as qualified medicare beneficiaries (QMBs), specified low-income medicare beneficiaries (SLMBs), and certain qualified individuals (QI–1s)).

(ii) Availability of information for verification purposes

As a condition of provision of Federal financial participation to a State that is one of the 50 States or the District of Columbia under subchapter XIX of this chapter, for purposes of carrying out this section, the State shall provide the information it submits to the Secretary relating to such subchapter in a manner specified by the Secretary that permits the Secretary to identify individuals who are described in subsection (b)(1)(B) of this section or are transitional assistance eligible individuals or special transitional assistance eligible individuals.

(4) Reconsideration

(A) In general

The Secretary shall establish a process under which a discount card eligible individual, who is determined through the certification and verification methods under paragraphs (2) and (3) not to be a transitional assistance eligible individual or a special transitional assistance eligible individual, may request a reconsideration of the determination.

(B) Contract authority

The Secretary may enter into a contract to perform the reconsiderations requested under subparagraph (A).

(C) Communication of results

Under the process under subparagraph (A) the results of such reconsideration shall be communicated to the individual and the prescription drug card sponsor involved.

(g) Transitional assistance

(1) Provision of transitional assistance

An individual who is a transitional assistance eligible individual (as determined under this section) and who is enrolled with an endorsed program is entitled—

(A) to have payment made of any annual enrollment fee charged under subsection (c)(2) of this section for enrollment under the program; and

(B) to have payment made, up to the amount specified in paragraph (2), under such endorsed program of 90 percent (or 95 percent in the case of a special transitional assistance eligible individual) of the costs incurred for covered discount card drugs obtained through the program taking into account the negotiated price (if any) for the drug under the program.

(2) Limitation on dollar amount

(A) In general

Subject to subparagraph (B), the amount specified in this paragraph for a transitional assistance eligible individual—

(i) for costs incurred during 2004, is $600; or

(ii) for costs incurred during 2005, is—

(I) $600, plus

(II) except as provided in subparagraph (E), the amount by which the amount available under this paragraph for 2004 for that individual exceeds the amount of payment made under paragraph (1)(B) for that individual for costs incurred during 2004.

(B) Proration

(i) In general

In the case of an individual not described in clause (ii) with respect to a year, the Secretary may prorate the amount specified in subparagraph (A) for the balance of the year involved in a manner specified by the Secretary.

(ii) Individual described

An individual described in this clause is a transitional assistance eligible individual who—

(I) with respect to 2004, enrolls in an endorsed program, and provides a certification under subsection (f)(2) of this section, before the initial implementation date of the program under this section; and

(II) with respect to 2005, is enrolled in an endorsed program, and has provided such a certification, before February 1, 2005.

(C) Accounting for available balances in cases of changes in program enrollment

In the case of a transitional assistance eligible individual who changes the endorsed discount card program in which the individual is enrolled under this section, the Secretary shall provide a process under which the Secretary provides to the sponsor of the endorsed program in which the individual enrolls information concerning the balance of amounts available on behalf of the individual under this paragraph.

(D) Limitation on use of funds

Pursuant to subsection (a)(2)(C) of this section, no assistance shall be provided under paragraph (1)(B) with respect to covered discount card drugs dispensed after December 31, 2005.

(E) No rollover permitted in case of voluntary disenrollment

Except in such exceptional cases as the Secretary may provide, in the case of a transitional assistance eligible individual who voluntarily disenrolls from an endorsed plan, the provisions of subclause (II) of subparagraph (A)(ii) shall not apply.

(3) Payment

The Secretary shall provide a method for the reimbursement of prescription drug card sponsors for assistance provided under this subsection.

(4) Coverage of coinsurance

(A) Waiver permitted by pharmacy

Nothing in this section shall be construed as precluding a pharmacy from reducing or waiving the application of coinsurance imposed under paragraph (1)(B) in accordance with section 1320a–7b(b)(3)(G) of this title.

(B) Optional payment of coinsurance by State

(i) In general

The Secretary shall establish an arrangement under which a State may provide for payment of some or all of the coinsurance under paragraph (1)(B) for some or all enrollees in the State, as specified by the State under the arrangement. Insofar as such a payment arrangement is made with respect to an enrollee, the amount of the coinsurance shall be paid directly by the State to the pharmacy involved.

(ii) No Federal matching available under medicaid or SCHIP

Expenditures made by a State for coinsurance described in clause (i) shall not be treated as State expenditures for purposes of Federal matching payments under subchapter XIX or XXI of this chapter.

(iii) Not treated as medicare cost-sharing

Coinsurance described in paragraph (1)(B) shall not be treated as coinsurance under this subchapter for purposes of section 1396d(p)(3)(B) of this title.

(C) Treatment of coinsurance

The amount of any coinsurance imposed under paragraph (1)(B), whether paid or waived under this paragraph, shall not be taken into account in applying the limitation in dollar amount under paragraph (2).

(5) Ensuring access to transitional assistance for qualified residents of long-term care facilities and American Indians

(A) Residents of long-term care facilities

The Secretary shall establish procedures and may waive requirements of this section as necessary to negotiate arrangements with sponsors to provide arrangements with pharmacies that support long-term care facilities in order to ensure access to transitional assistance for transitional assistance eligible individuals who reside in long-term care facilities.

(B) American Indians

The Secretary shall establish procedures and may waive requirements of this section to ensure that, for purposes of providing transitional assistance, pharmacies operated by the Indian Health Service, Indian tribes and tribal organizations, and urban Indian organizations (as defined in section 1603 of Title 25) have the opportunity to participate in the pharmacy networks of at least two endorsed programs in each of the 50 States and the District of Columbia where such a pharmacy operates.

(6) No impact on benefits under other programs

The availability of negotiated prices or transitional assistance under this section shall not be treated as benefits or otherwise taken into account in determining an individual's eligibility for, or the amount of benefits under, any other Federal program.

(7) Disregard for purposes of part C

Nonuniformity of benefits resulting from the implementation of this section (including the provision or nonprovision of transitional assistance and the payment or waiver of any enrollment fee under this section) shall not be taken into account in applying section 1395w–24(f) of this title.

(h) Qualification of prescription drug card sponsors and endorsement of discount card programs; beneficiary protections

(1) Prescription drug card sponsor and qualifications

(A) Prescription drug card sponsor and sponsor defined

For purposes of this section, the terms "prescription drug card sponsor" and "sponsor" mean any nongovernmental entity that the Secretary determines to be appropriate to offer an endorsed discount card program under this section, which may include—

(i) a pharmaceutical benefit management company;

(ii) a wholesale or retail pharmacy delivery system;

(iii) an insurer (including an insurer that offers medicare supplemental policies under section 1395ss of this title);

(iv) an organization offering a plan under part C of this subchapter; or

(v) any combination of the entities described in clauses (i) through (iv).

(B) Administrative qualifications

Each endorsed discount card program shall be operated directly, or through arrangements with an affiliated organization (or organizations), by one or more entities that have demonstrated experience and expertise in operating such a program or a similar program and that meets such business stability and integrity requirements as the Secretary may specify.

(C) Accounting for transitional assistance

The sponsor of an endorsed discount card program shall have arrangements satisfactory to the Secretary to account for the assistance provided under subsection (g) of this section on behalf of transitional assistance eligible individuals.

(2) Applications for program endorsement

(A) Submission

Each prescription drug card sponsor that seeks endorsement of a prescription drug discount card program under this section shall submit to the Secretary, at such time and in such manner as the Secretary may specify, an application containing such information as the Secretary may require.

(B) Approval; compliance with applicable requirements

The Secretary shall review the application submitted under subparagraph (A) and shall determine whether to endorse the prescription drug discount card program. The Secretary may not endorse such a program unless—

(i) the program and prescription drug card sponsor offering the program comply with the applicable requirements under this section; and

(ii) the sponsor has entered into a contract with the Secretary to carry out such requirements.

(C) Termination of endorsement and contracts

An endorsement of an endorsed program and a contract under subparagraph (B) shall be for the duration of the program under this section (including any transition applicable under subsection (a)(2)(C)(ii) of this section), except that the Secretary may, with notice and for cause (as defined by the Secretary), terminate such endorsement and contract.

(D) Ensuring choice of programs

(i) In general

The Secretary shall ensure that there is available to each discount card eligible individual a choice of at least 2 endorsed programs (each offered by a different sponsor).

(ii) Limitation on number

The Secretary may limit (but not below 2) the number of sponsors in a State that are awarded contracts under this paragraph.

(3) Service area encompassing entire States

Except as provided in paragraph (9), if a prescription drug card sponsor that offers an endorsed program enrolls in the program individuals residing in any part of a State, the sponsor must permit any discount card eligible individual residing in any portion of the State to enroll in the program.

(4) Savings to medicare beneficiaries

Each prescription drug card sponsor that offers an endorsed discount card program shall pass on to discount card eligible individuals enrolled in the program negotiated prices on covered discount card drugs, including discounts negotiated with pharmacies and manufacturers, to the extent disclosed under subsection (i)(1) of this section.

(5) Grievance mechanism

Each prescription drug card sponsor shall provide meaningful procedures for hearing and resolving grievances between the sponsor (including any entity or individual through which the sponsor carries out the endorsed discount card program) and enrollees in endorsed discount card programs of the sponsor under this section in a manner similar to that required under section 1395w–22(f) of this title.

(6) Confidentiality of enrollee records

(A) In general

For purposes of the program under this section, the operations of an endorsed program are covered functions and a prescription drug card sponsor is a covered entity for purposes of applying part C of subchapter XI of this chapter and all regulatory provisions promulgated thereunder, including regulations (relating to privacy) adopted pursuant to the authority of the Secretary under section 264(c) of the Health Insurance Portability and Accountability Act of 1996 (42 U.S.C. 1320d–2 note).

(B) Waiver authority

In order to promote participation of sponsors in the program under this section, the Secretary may waive such relevant portions of regulations relating to privacy referred to in subparagraph (A), for such appropriate, limited period of time, as the Secretary specifies.

(7) Limitation on provision and marketing of products and services

The sponsor of an endorsed discount card program—

(A) may provide under the program—

(i) a product or service only if the product or service is directly related to a covered discount card drug; or

(ii) a discount price for nonprescription drugs; and

(B) may, to the extent otherwise permitted under paragraph (6) (relating to application of HIPAA requirements), market a product or service under the program only if the product or service is directly related to—

(i) a covered discount card drug; or

(ii) a drug described in subparagraph (A)(ii) and the marketing consists of information on the discounted price made available for the drug involved.

(8) Additional protections

Each endorsed discount card program shall meet such additional requirements as the Secretary identifies to protect and promote the interest of discount card eligible individuals, including requirements that ensure that discount card eligible individuals enrolled in endorsed discount card programs are not charged more than the lower of the price based on negotiated prices or the usual and customary price.

(9) Special rules for certain organizations

(A) In general

In the case of an organization that is offering a plan under part C of this subchapter or enrollment under a reasonable cost reimbursement contract under section 1395mm(h) of this title that is seeking to be a prescription drug card sponsor under this section, the organization may elect to apply the special rules under subparagraph (B) with respect to enrollees in any plan described in section 1395w–21(a)(2)(A) of this title that it offers or under such contract and an endorsed discount card program it offers, but only if it limits enrollment under such program to individuals enrolled in such plan or under such contract.

(B) Special rules

The special rules under this subparagraph are as follows:

(i) Limitation on enrollment

The sponsor limits enrollment under this section under the endorsed discount card program to discount card eligible individuals who are enrolled in the part C plan involved or under the reasonable cost reimbursement contract involved and is not required nor permitted to enroll other individuals under such program.

(ii) Pharmacy access

Pharmacy access requirements under subsection (e)(1)(B) of this section are deemed to be met if the access is made available through a pharmacy network (and not only through mail order) and the network used by the sponsor is approved by the Secretary.

(iii) Sponsor requirements

The Secretary may waive the application of such requirements for a sponsor as the Secretary determines to be duplicative or to conflict with a requirement of the organization under part C of this subchapter or section 1395mm of this title (as the case may be) or to be necessary in order to improve coordination of this section with the benefits under such part or section.

(i) Disclosure and oversight

(1) Disclosure

Each prescription drug card sponsor offering an endorsed discount card program shall disclose to the Secretary (in a manner specified by the Secretary) information relating to program performance, use of prescription drugs by discount card eligible individuals enrolled in the program, the extent to which negotiated price concessions described in subsection (e)(1)(A)(ii) of this section made available to the entity by a manufacturer are passed through to enrollees through pharmacies or otherwise, and such other information as the Secretary may specify. The provisions of section 1396r–8(b)(3)(D) of this title shall apply to drug pricing data reported under the previous sentence (other than data in aggregate form).

(2) Oversight; audit and inspection authority

The Secretary shall provide appropriate oversight to ensure compliance of endorsed discount card programs and their sponsors with the requirements of this section. The Secretary shall have the right to audit and inspect any books and records of a prescription discount card sponsor (and of any affiliated organization referred to in subsection (h)(1)(B) of this section) that pertain to the endorsed discount card program under this section, including amounts payable to the sponsor under this section.

(3) Sanctions for abusive practices

The Secretary may implement intermediate sanctions or may revoke the endorsement of a program offered by a sponsor under this section if the Secretary determines that the sponsor or the program no longer meets the applicable requirements of this section or that the sponsor has engaged in false or misleading marketing practices. The Secretary may impose a civil money penalty in an amount not to exceed $10,000 for conduct that a party knows or should know is a violation of this section. The provisions of section 1320a–7a of this title (other than subsections (a) and (b) and the second sentence of subsection (f)) shall apply to a civil money penalty under the previous sentence in the same manner as such provisions apply to a penalty or proceeding under section 1320a–7a(a) of this title.

(j) Treatment of territories

(1) In general

The Secretary may waive any provision of this section (including subsection (h)(2)(D) of this section) in the case of a resident of a State (other than the 50 States and the District of Columbia) insofar as the Secretary determines it is necessary to secure access to negotiated prices for discount card eligible individuals (or, at the option of the Secretary, individuals described in subsection (b)(1)(A)(i) of this section).

(2) Transitional assistance

(A) In general

In the case of a State, other than the 50 States and the District of Columbia, if the State establishes a plan described in subparagraph (B) (for providing transitional assistance with respect to the provision of prescription drugs to some or all individuals residing in the State who are described in subparagraph (B)(i)), the Secretary shall pay to the State for the entire period of the operation of this section an amount equal to the amount allotted to the State under subparagraph (C).

(B) Plan

The plan described in this subparagraph is a plan that—

(i) provides transitional assistance with respect to the provision of covered discount card drugs to some or all individuals who are entitled to benefits under part A of this subchapter or enrolled under part B of this subchapter, who reside in the State, and who have income below 135 percent of the poverty line; and

(ii) assures that amounts received by the State under this paragraph are used only for such assistance.

(C) Allotment limit

The amount described in this subparagraph for a State is equal to $35,000,000 multiplied by the ratio (as estimated by the Secretary) of—

(i) the number of individuals who are entitled to benefits under part A of this subchapter or enrolled under part B of this subchapter and who reside in the State (as determined by the Secretary as of July 1, 2003), to

(ii) the sum of such numbers for all States to which this paragraph applies.

(D) Continued availability of funds

Amounts made available to a State under this paragraph which are not used under this paragraph shall be added to the amount available to that State for purposes of carrying out section 1396u–5(e) of this title.

(k) Funding

(1) Establishment of Transitional Assistance Account

(A) In general

There is created within the Federal Supplementary Medical Insurance Trust Fund established by section 1395t of this title an account to be known as the "Transitional Assistance Account" (in this subsection referred to as the "Account").

(B) Funds

The Account shall consist of such gifts and bequests as may be made as provided in section 401(i)(1) of this title, accrued interest on balances in the Account, and such amounts as may be deposited in, or appropriated to, the Account as provided in this subsection.

(C) Separate from rest of Trust Fund

Funds provided under this subsection to the Account shall be kept separate from all other funds within the Federal Supplementary Medical Insurance Trust Fund, but shall be invested, and such investments redeemed, in the same manner as all other funds and investments within such Trust Fund.

(2) Payments from Account

(A) In general

The Managing Trustee shall pay from time to time from the Account such amounts as the Secretary certifies are necessary to make payments for transitional assistance provided under subsections (g) and (j)(2) of this section.

(B) Treatment in relation to part B premium

Amounts payable from the Account shall not be taken into account in computing actuarial rates or premium amounts under section 1395r of this title.

(3) Appropriations to cover benefits

There are appropriated to the Account in a fiscal year, out of any moneys in the Treasury not otherwise appropriated, an amount equal to the payments made from the Account in the year.

(4) For administrative expenses

There are authorized to be appropriated to the Secretary such sums as may be necessary to carry out the Secretary's responsibilities under this section.

(5) Transfer of any remaining balance to Medicare Prescription Drug Account

Any balance remaining in the Account after the Secretary determines that funds in the Account are no longer necessary to carry out the program under this section shall be transferred and deposited into the Medicare Prescription Drug Account under section 1395w–116 of this title.

(6) Construction

Nothing in this section shall be construed as authorizing the Secretary to provide for payment (other than payment of an enrollment fee on behalf of a transitional assistance eligible individual under subsection (g)(1)(A) of this section) to a sponsor for administrative expenses incurred by the sponsor in carrying out this section (including in administering the transitional assistance provisions of subsections (f) and (g) of this section).

(Aug. 14, 1935, c. 531, Title XVIII, § 1860D–31, as added Pub.L. 108–173, Title I, § 101(a)(2), Dec. 8, 2003, 117 Stat. 2131.)

HISTORICAL AND STATUTORY NOTES

Revision Notes and Legislative Reports

2003 Acts. House Conference Report No. 108–391 and Statement by President, see 2003 U.S. Code Cong. and Adm. News, p. 1808.

References in Text

Part A, referred to in text, means Part A of Title XVIII of the Social Security Act, Act Aug. 14, 1935, c. 531, Title XVIII, § 1811 et seq., as added July 30, 1965, Pub.L. 89–97, Title I, § 102(a), 79 Stat. 291, and amended, which is classified to part A of this subchapter, 42 U.S.C.A. § 1395c et seq.

Part B, referred to in text, means Part B of Title XVIII of the Social Security Act, Act Aug. 14, 1935, c. 531, Title XVIII, § 1831 et seq., as added July 30, 1965, Pub.L. 89–97, Title I, § 102(a), 79 Stat. 301, and amended, which is classified to part B of this subchapter, 42 U.S.C.A. § 1395j et seq.

Subchapter XIX of this chapter, referred to in text, originally read "title XIX", meaning Title XIX of the Social Security Act, Aug. 14, 1935, c. 531, Title XIX, § 1901 et seq., as added July 30, 1965, Pub.L. 89–97, Title I, § 121(a), 79 Stat. 343, and amended, which is principally classified to subchapter XIX of this chapter, 42 U.S.C.A. § 1396 et seq.

Subchapter XXI of this chapter, referred to in text, originally read "title XXI", meaning Title XXI of the Social Security Act, Aug. 14, 1935, c. 531, Title XXI, § 2101 et seq., as added, Aug. 5, 1997, Pub.L. 105–33, Title IV, § 4901(a), 111 Stat. 552, and amended, which is principally classified to subchapter XXI of this chapter, 42 U.S.C.A. § 1396 et seq., and 42 U.S.C.A. § 1397aa et seq., respectively.

December 8, 2003, referred to in subsec. (a)(2), originally read "the date of enactment of this section", meaning the date of enactment of Pub.L. 108–173, 117 Stat. 2066, which enacted this section, and was approved Dec. 8, 2003.

Part D, referred to in subsec. (a)(4)(A), means Part D of Title XVIII of the Social Security Act, Act Aug. 14, 1935, c. 531, Title XVIII, § 1860D–1 et seq., as added, Pub.L. 108–173, Title I, § 101(a)(2), Dec. 8, 2003, 117 Stat. 2071, which is classified to this part, 42 U.S.C.A. § 1395w–101 et seq.

Part C, referred to in subsecs. (b)(2)(B)(i) and (c)(1)(C)(iii), means Part C of Title XVIII of the Social Security Act, Act Aug. 14, 1935, c. 531, Title XVIII, § 1851 et seq., as added Aug. 5, 1997, Pub.L. 105–33, Title IV, § 4001, 111 Stat. 276, and amended, which is classified to part C of this subchapter, 42 U.S.C.A. § 1395w–21 et seq.

Chapter 55 of Title 10, referred to in subsec. (b)(2)(B)(ii) is 10 U.S.C.A. § 1071 et seq.

Chapter 89 of Title 5, referred to in subsec. (b)(2)(B)(iii), is 5 U.S.C.A. § 8901 et seq.

The Internal Revenue Code of 1986, referred to in subsec. (f)(3)(B)(iii), is classified generally to Title 26, 26 U.S.C.A. § 1 et seq. Section 6103 of the Code is classified to 26 U.S.C.A. § 6103.

Section 264(c) of the Health Insurance Portability and Accountability Act of 1996, referred to in subsec. (h)(6)(A), is section 264(c) of Pub.L. 104–191, Title II, § 264(c), August 21, 1996, 110 Stat. 2033, which is set out in a note under 42 U.S.C.A. § 1320d–2.

Part C of subchapter XI of this chapter, referred to in subsec. (h)(6)(A), originally read "part C of title XI", meaning Part C of Title XI of the Social Security Act, Aug. 14, 1935, c. 531, Title XI, § 1171, as added Aug. 21, 1996, Pub.L. 104–191, Title II, § 262(a), 110 Stat. 2021, and amended, which is principally classified to part C of subchapter XI of this chapter, 42 U.S.C.A. § 1320d et seq.

Rules for Implementation

Pub.L. 108–173, Title I, § 105(c), Dec. 8, 2003, 117 Stat. 2166 provided that:

"The following rules shall apply to the medicare prescription drug discount card and transitional assistance program under section 1860D–31 of the Social Security Act, as added by section 101(a) [this section]:

"(1) In promulgating regulations pursuant to subsection (a)(2)(B) of such section 1860D–31 [subsec. (a)(2)(B) of this section]—

"(A) section 1871(a)(3) of the Social Security Act (42 U.S.C. 1395hh(a)(3)), as added by section 902(a)(1), shall not apply;

"(B) chapter 35 of title 44, United States Code [44 U.S.C.A. § 3501 et seq.], shall not apply; and

"(C) sections 553(d) and 801(a)(3)(A) of title 5, United States Code [5 U.S.C.A. §§ 553(d) and 801(a)(3)(A)], shall not apply.

"(2) Section 1857(c)(5) of the Social Security Act (42 U.S.C. 1395w–27(c)(5)) shall apply with respect to section 1860D–31 of such Act, as added by section 101(a) [this section], in the same manner as it applies to part C of title XVIII of such Act [42 U.S.C.A. § 1395w–21 et seq.].

"(3) The administration of such program shall be made without regard to chapter 35 of title 44, United States Code [44 U.S.C.A. § 3501 et seq.].

"(4)(A) There shall be no judicial review of a determination not to endorse, or enter into a contract, with a prescription drug card sponsor under section 1860D–31 of the Social Security Act [this section].

"(B) In the case of any order issued to enjoin any provision of section 1860D–31 of the Social Security Act [this section] (or of any provision of this section [Pub.L. 108–173, Title I, § 105, enacting this note and amending 42 U.S.C.A. §§ 1395r and 1396r–8]), such order shall not affect any other provision of such section [this section] (or of this section [Pub.L. 108–173, Title I, § 105, enacting this note and amending 42 U.S.C.A. §§ 1395r and 1396r–8]) and all such provisions shall be treated as severable."

Subpart 5—Definitions and Miscellaneous Provisions

§ 1395w–151. Definitions; treatment of references to provisions in part C

(a) Definitions.—

For purposes of this part:

(1) Basic prescription drug coverage

The term "basic prescription drug coverage" is defined in section 1395w–102(a)(3) of this title.

(2) Covered part D drug

The term "covered part D drug" is defined in section 1395w–102(e) of this title.

(3) Creditable prescription drug coverage

The term "creditable prescription drug coverage" has the meaning given such term in section 1395w–113(b)(4) of this title.

(4) Part D eligible individual

The term "part D eligible individual" has the meaning given such term in section 1395w–101(a)(3)(A) of this title.

(5) Fallback prescription drug plan

The term "fallback prescription drug plan" has the meaning given such term in section 1395w–111(g)(4) of this title.

(6) Initial coverage limit

The term "initial coverage limit" means such limit as established under section 1395w–102(b)(3) of this title, or, in the case of coverage that is not standard prescription drug coverage, the comparable limit (if any) established under the coverage.

(7) Insurance risk

The term "insurance risk" means, with respect to a participating pharmacy, risk of the type commonly assumed only by insurers licensed by a State and does not include payment variations designed to reflect performance-based measures of activities within the control of the pharmacy, such as formulary compliance and generic drug substitution.

(8) MA plan

The term "MA plan" has the meaning given such term in section 1395w–101(a)(3)(B) of this title.

(9) MA–PD plan

The term "MA–PD plan" has the meaning given such term in section 1395w–101(a)(3)(C) of this title.

(10) Medicare Prescription Drug Account

The term "Medicare Prescription Drug Account" means the Account created under section 1395w–116(a) of this title.

(11) PDP approved bid

The term "PDP approved bid" has the meaning given such term in section 1395w–113(a)(6) of this title.

(12) PDP region

The term "PDP region" means such a region as provided under section 1395w–111(a)(2) of this title.

(13) PDP sponsor

The term "PDP sponsor" means a nongovernmental entity that is certified under this part as meeting the requirements and standards of this part for such a sponsor.

(14) Prescription drug plan

The term "prescription drug plan" means prescription drug coverage that is offered—

(A) under a policy, contract, or plan that has been approved under section 1395w–111(e) of this title; and

(B) by a PDP sponsor pursuant to, and in accordance with, a contract between the Secretary and the sponsor under section 1395w–112(b) of this title.

(15) Qualified prescription drug coverage

The term "qualified prescription drug coverage" is defined in section 1395w–102(a)(1) of this title.

(16) Standard prescription drug coverage

The term "standard prescription drug coverage" is defined in section 1395w–102(b) of this title.

(17) State Pharmaceutical Assistance Program

The term "State Pharmaceutical Assistance Program" has the meaning given such term in section 1395w–133(b) of this title.

(18) Subsidy eligible individual

The term "subsidy eligible individual" has the meaning given such term in section 1395w–114(a)(3)(A) of this title.

(b) Application of part C provisions under this part

For purposes of applying provisions of part C of this subchapter under this part with respect to a prescription drug plan and a PDP sponsor, unless otherwise provided in this part such provisions shall be applied as if—

(1) any reference to an MA plan included a reference to a prescription drug plan;

(2) any reference to an MA organization or a provider-sponsored organization included a reference to a PDP sponsor;

(3) any reference to a contract under section 1395w–27 of this title included a reference to a contract under section 1395w–112(b) of this title;

(4) any reference to part C of this subchapter included a reference to this part; and

(5) any reference to an election period under section 1395w–21 of this title were a reference to an enrollment period under section 1395w–101 of this title.

(Aug. 14, 1935, c. 531, Title XVIII, § 1860D–41, as added Pub.L. 108–173, Title I, § 101(a)(2), Dec. 8, 2003, 117 Stat. 2148.)

HISTORICAL AND STATUTORY NOTES

Revision Notes and Legislative Reports

2003 Acts. House Conference Report No. 108–391 and Statement by President, see 2003 U.S. Code Cong. and Adm. News, p. 1808.

References in Text

Part D, referred to in subsec. (a)(2) and (4), means Part D of Title XVIII of the Social Security Act, Act Aug. 14, 1935, c.

531, Title XVIII, § 1860D–1 et seq., as added, Pub.L. 108–173, Title I, § 101(a)(2), Dec. 8, 2003, 117 Stat. 2071, which is classified to this part, 42 U.S.C.A. § 1395w–101 et seq.

Section 1395w–101(a)(3) of this title, referred to in subsec. (a)(4), (8), (9), was in the original "section 1860D–1(a)(4)", and was translated as meaning section 1860D–1(a)(3) of the Social Security Act, which is classified to section 1395w–101(a)(3) of this title, to reflect the probable intent of Congress. Section 1395w–101(a) of this title does not contain a par. (4) and par. (3) defines terms for purposes of this part.

Part C, referred to in subsec. (b), means Part C of Title XVIII of the Social Security Act, Act Aug. 14, 1935, c. 531, Title XVIII, § 1851 et seq., as added Aug. 5, 1997, Pub.L. 105–33, Title IV, § 4001, 111 Stat. 276, and amended, which is classified to part C of this subchapter, 42 U.S.C.A. § 1395w–21 et seq.

§ 1395w–152. Miscellaneous provisions

(a) Access to coverage in territories

The Secretary may waive such requirements of this part, including section 1395w–103(a)(1) of this title, insofar as the Secretary determines it is necessary to secure access to qualified prescription drug coverage for part D eligible individuals residing in a State (other than the 50 States and the District of Columbia).

(b) Application of demonstration authority

The provisions of section 402 of the Social Security Amendments of 1967 (Public Law 90–248) shall apply with respect to this part and part C of this subchapter in the same manner it applies with respect to parts A and B of this subchapter, except that any reference with respect to a Trust Fund in relation to an experiment or demonstration project relating to prescription drug coverage under this part shall be deemed a reference to the Medicare Prescription Drug Account within the Federal Supplementary Medical Insurance Trust Fund.

(c) Coverage gap rebate for 2010

(1) In general

In the case of an individual described in subparagraphs (A) through (D) of section 1395w–114a(g)(1) of this title who as of the last day of a calendar quarter in 2010 has incurred costs for covered part D drugs so that the individual has exceeded the initial coverage limit under section 1395w–102(b)(3) of this title for 2010, the Secretary shall provide for payment from the Medicare Prescription Drug Account of $250 to the individual by not later than the 15th day of the third month following the end of such quarter.

(2) Limitation

The Secretary shall provide only 1 payment under this subsection with respect to any individual.

(d) Treatment of certain complaints for purposes of quality or performance assessment

In conducting a quality or performance assessment of a PDP sponsor, the Secretary shall develop or utilize existing screening methods for reviewing and considering complaints that are received from enrollees in a prescription drug plan offered by such PDP sponsor and that are complaints regarding the lack of access by the individual to prescription drugs due to a drug management program for at-risk beneficiaries.

(Aug. 14, 1935, c. 531, Title XVIII, § 1850D–42, as added Pub.L. 108–173, Title I, § 101(a)(2), Dec. 8, 2003, 117 Stat. 2149; amended Pub.L. 111–152, Title I, § 1101(a)(1), Mar. 30, 2010, 124 Stat. 1037; Pub.L. 114–198, Title VII, § 704(d), July 22, 2016, 130 Stat. 750.)

HISTORICAL AND STATUTORY NOTES

Revision Notes and Legislative Reports

2003 Acts. House Conference Report No. 108–391 and Statement by President, see 2003 U.S. Code Cong. and Adm. News, p. 1808.

References in Text

Part D, referred to in subsec. (a), means Part D of Title XVIII of the Social Security Act, Act Aug. 14, 1935, c. 531, Title XVIII, § 1860D–1 et seq., as added, Pub.L. 108–173, Title I, § 101(a)(2), Dec. 8, 2003, 117 Stat. 2071, which is classified to this part, 42 U.S.C.A. § 1395w–101 et seq.

Section 402 of the Social Security Amendments of 1967, referred to in subsec. (b), means section 402 of Pub.L. 90–248, which enacted 42 U.S.C.A. § 1395b–1 and amended 42 U.S.C.A. § 1395*ll*.

Part C, referred to in subsec. (b), means Part C of Title XVIII of the Social Security Act, Act Aug. 14, 1935, c. 531, Title XVIII, § 1851 et seq., as added Aug. 5, 1997, Pub.L. 105–33, Title IV, § 4001, 111 Stat. 276, and amended, which is classified to part C of this subchapter, 42 U.S.C.A. § 1395w–21 et seq.

Part A, referred to in subsec. (b), means Part A of Title XVIII of the Social Security Act, Act Aug. 14, 1935, c. 531, Title XVIII, § 1811 et seq., as added July 30, 1965, Pub.L. 89–97, Title I, § 102(a), 79 Stat. 291, and amended, which is classified to part A of this subchapter, 42 U.S.C.A. § 1395c et seq.

Part B, referred to in subsec. (b), means Part B of Title XVIII of the Social Security Act, Act Aug. 14, 1935, c. 531, Title XVIII, § 1831 et seq., as added July 30, 1965, Pub.L. 89–97, Title I, § 102(a), 79 Stat. 301, and amended, which is classified to part B of this subchapter, 42 U.S.C.A. § 1395j et seq.

Effective and Applicability Provisions

2016 Acts. Amendments made by Pub.L. 114–198, § 704, shall apply to prescription drug plans and MA–PD plans for plan years beginning on or after Jan. 1, 2019, see Pub.L. 114–198, § 704(g)(1), set out as a note under 42 U.S.C.A. § 1395w–101.

§ 1395w–153. Condition for coverage of drugs under this part

(a) In general

In order for coverage to be available under this part for covered part D drugs (as defined in section

1395w–102(e) of this title) of a manufacturer, the manufacturer must—

(1) participate in the Medicare coverage gap discount program under section 1395w–114a of this title;

(2) have entered into and have in effect an agreement described in subsection (b) of such section with the Secretary; and

(3) have entered into and have in effect, under terms and conditions specified by the Secretary, a contract with a third party that the Secretary has entered into a contract with under subsection (d)(3) of such section.

(b) Effective date

Subsection (a) shall apply to covered part D drugs dispensed under this part on or after January 1, 2011.

(c) Authorizing coverage for drugs not covered under agreements

Subsection (a) shall not apply to the dispensing of a covered part D drug if—

(1) the Secretary has made a determination that the availability of the drug is essential to the health of beneficiaries under this part; or

(2) the Secretary determines that in the period beginning on January 1, 2011, and [1] December 31, 2011, there were extenuating circumstances.

(d) Definition of manufacturer

In this section, the term "manufacturer" has the meaning given such term in section 1395w–114a(g)(5) of this title.

(Aug. 14, 1935, c. 531, Title XVIII, § 1860D–43, as added Pub.L. 111–148, Title III, § 3301(a), Mar. 23, 2010, 124 Stat. 461; amended Pub.L. 111–152, Title I, § 1101(b)(1), Mar. 30, 2010, 124 Stat. 1037.)

[1] So in original. Probably should be followed by "ending on".

HISTORICAL AND STATUTORY NOTES

References in Text

Part D, referred to in text, is part D of Title XVIII of the Social Security Act, Act Aug. 14, 1935, c. 531, Title XVIII, § 1860D–1 et seq., as added and amended, which is principally classified to this part D, 42 U.S.C.A. § 1395w–101 et seq.

§ 1395w–154. Improved Medicare prescription drug plan and MA-PD plan complaint system

(a) In general

The Secretary shall develop and maintain a complaint system, that is widely known and easy to use, to collect and maintain information on MA-PD plan and prescription drug plan complaints that are received (including by telephone, letter, e-mail, or any other means) by the Secretary (including by a regional office of the Department of Health and Human Services, the Medicare Beneficiary Ombudsman, a subcontractor, a carrier, a fiscal intermediary, and a Medicare administrative contractor under section 1395kk–1 of this title) through the date on which the complaint is resolved. The system shall be able to report and initiate appropriate interventions and monitoring based on substantial complaints and to guide quality improvement.

(b) Model electronic complaint form

The Secretary shall develop a model electronic complaint form to be used for reporting plan complaints under the system. Such form shall be prominently displayed on the front page of the Medicare.gov Internet website and on the Internet website of the Medicare Beneficiary Ombudsman.

(c) Annual reports by the Secretary

The Secretary shall submit to Congress annual reports on the system. Such reports shall include an analysis of the number and types of complaints reported in the system, geographic variations in such complaints, the timeliness of agency or plan responses to such complaints, and the resolution of such complaints.

(d) Definitions

In this section:

(1) MA-PD plan

The term "MA-PD plan" has the meaning given such term in section 1395w–151(a)(9) of this title.

(2) Prescription drug plan

The term "prescription drug plan" has the meaning given such term in section 1395w–151(a)(14) of this title.

(3) Secretary

The term "Secretary" means the Secretary of Health and Human Services.

(4) System

The term "system" means the plan complaint system developed and maintained under subsection (a).

(Pub.L. 111–148, Title III, § 3311, Mar. 23, 2010, 124 Stat. 475.)

HISTORICAL AND STATUTORY NOTES

Codifications

Section is enacted as part of the Patient Protection and Affordable Care Act, and not as part of the Social Security Act, which otherwise comprises this chapter.

TITLE 5

GOVERNMENT ORGANIZATION AND EMPLOYEES

EQUAL ACCESS TO JUSTICE ACT

Pub.L. 96–481, Title II, §§ 203(a)(1), 204(a), Oct. 21, 1980, 94 Stat. 2325, 2327

PART I—THE AGENCIES GENERALLY

CHAPTER 5—ADMINISTRATIVE PROCEDURE

SUBCHAPTER I—GENERAL PROVISIONS

§ 504. Costs and fees of parties

(a)(1) An agency that conducts an adversary adjudication shall award, to a prevailing party other than the United States, fees and other expenses incurred by that party in connection with that proceeding, unless the adjudicative officer of the agency finds that the position of the agency was substantially justified or that special circumstances make an award unjust. Whether or not the position of the agency was substantially justified shall be determined on the basis of the administrative record, as a whole, which is made in the adversary adjudication for which fees and other expenses are sought.

(2) A party seeking an award of fees and other expenses shall, within thirty days of a final disposition in the adversary adjudication, submit to the agency an application which shows that the party is a prevailing party and is eligible to receive an award under this section, and the amount sought, including an itemized statement from any attorney, agent, or expert witness representing or appearing in behalf of the party stating the actual time expended and the rate at which fees and other expenses were computed. The party shall also allege that the position of the agency was not substantially justified. When the United States appeals the underlying merits of an adversary adjudication, no decision on an application for fees and other expenses in connection with that adversary adjudication shall be made under this section until a final and unreviewable decision is rendered by the court on the appeal or until the underlying merits of the case have been finally determined pursuant to the appeal.

(3) The adjudicative officer of the agency may reduce the amount to be awarded, or deny an award, to the extent that the party during the course of the proceedings engaged in conduct which unduly and unreasonably protracted the final resolution of the matter in controversy. The decision of the adjudicative officer of the agency under this section shall be made a part of the record containing the final decision of the agency and shall include written findings and conclusions and the reason or basis therefor. The decision of the agency on the application for fees and other expenses shall be the final administrative decision under this section.

(4) If, in an adversary adjudication arising from an agency action to enforce a party's compliance with a statutory or regulatory requirement, the demand by the agency is substantially in excess of the decision of the adjudicative officer and is unreasonable when compared with such decision, under the facts and circumstances of the case, the adjudicative officer shall award to the party the fees and other expenses related to defending against the excessive demand, unless the party has committed a willful violation of law or otherwise acted in bad faith, or special circumstances make an award unjust. Fees and expenses awarded under this paragraph shall be paid only as a consequence of appropriations provided in advance.

(b)(1) For the purposes of this section—

(A) "fees and other expenses" includes the reasonable expenses of expert witnesses, the reasonable cost of any study, analysis, engineering report, test, or project which is found by the agency to be necessary for the preparation of the party's case, and reasonable attorney or agent fees (The amount of fees awarded under this section shall be based upon prevailing market rates for the kind and quality of the services furnished, except that (i) no expert witness shall be compensated at a rate in excess of the highest rate of compensation for expert witnesses paid by the agency involved, and (ii) attorney or agent fees shall not be awarded in excess of $125 per hour unless the agency determines by regulation that an increase in the cost of living or a special factor, such as the limited availability of qualified attorneys or agents for the proceedings involved, justifies a higher fee.);

(B) "party" means a party, as defined in section 551(3) of this title, who is (i) an individual whose net worth did not exceed $2,000,000 at the time the adversary adjudication was initiated, or (ii) any owner of an unincorporated business, or any partnership, corporation, association, unit of local government, or organization, the net worth of which did not exceed $7,000,000 at the time the adversary adjudication was initiated, and which had not more than 500 employees at the time the adversary adjudication was initiated; except that an organization described in section 501(c)(3) of the Internal Revenue Code of 1986 (26 U.S.C. 501(c)(3)) exempt from taxation under section 501(a) of such Code, or a cooperative association as defined in section 15(a) of the Agricultural Marketing Act (12 U.S.C. 1141j(a)), may be a party regardless of the net worth of such organization or cooperative association or for purposes of subsection (a)(4), a small entity as defined in section 601;

(C) "adversary adjudication" means (i) an adjudication under section 554 of this title in which the position of the United States is represented by counsel or otherwise, but excludes an adjudication for the purpose of establishing or fixing a rate or for the purpose of granting or renewing a license, (ii) any appeal of a decision made pursuant to section 7103 of title 41 before an agency board of contract appeals as provided in section 7105 of title 41, (iii) any hearing conducted under chapter 38 of title 31, and (iv) the Religious Freedom Restoration Act of 1993;

(D) "adjudicative officer" means the deciding official, without regard to whether the official is designated as an administrative law judge, a hearing officer or examiner, or otherwise, who presided at the adversary adjudication;

(E) "position of the agency" means, in addition to the position taken by the agency in the adversary adjudication, the action or failure to act by the agency upon which the adversary adjudication is based; except that fees and other expenses may not be awarded to a party for any portion of the adversary adjudication in which the party has unreasonably protracted the proceedings; and

(F) "demand" means the express demand of the agency which led to the adversary adjudication, but does not include a recitation by the agency of the maximum statutory penalty (i) in the administrative complaint, or (ii) elsewhere when accompanied by an express demand for a lesser amount.

(2) Except as otherwise provided in paragraph (1), the definitions provided in section 551 of this title apply to this section.

(c)(1) After consultation with the Chairman of the Administrative Conference of the United States, each agency shall by rule establish uniform procedures for the submission and consideration of applications for an award of fees and other expenses. If a court reviews the underlying decision of the adversary adjudication, an award for fees and other expenses may be made only pursuant to section 2412(d)(3) of title 28.

(2) If a party other than the United States is dissatisfied with a determination of fees and other expenses made under subsection (a), that party may, within 30 days after the determination is made, appeal the determination to the court of the United States having jurisdiction to review the merits of the underlying decision of the agency adversary adjudication. The court's determination on any appeal heard under this paragraph shall be based solely on the factual record made before the agency. The court may modify the determination of fees and other expenses only if the court finds that the failure to make an award of fees and other expenses, or the calculation of the amount of the award, was unsupported by substantial evidence.

(d) Fees and other expenses awarded under this subsection shall be paid by any agency over which the party prevails from any funds made available to the agency by appropriation or otherwise.

(e)(1) Not later than March 31 of the first fiscal year beginning after the date of enactment of the John D. Dingell, Jr. Conservation, Management, and Recreation Act, and every fiscal year thereafter, the Chairman of the Administrative Conference of the United States, after consultation with the Chief Counsel for Advocacy of the Small Business Administration, shall submit to Congress and make publicly available online a report on the amount of fees and other expenses awarded during the preceding fiscal year under this section.

(2) Each report under paragraph (1) shall describe the number, nature, and amount of the awards, the claims involved in the controversy, and any other relevant information that may aid Congress in evaluating the scope and impact of such awards.

(3)(A) Each report under paragraph (1) shall account for all payments of fees and other expenses awarded under this section that are made pursuant to a settlement agreement, regardless of whether the settlement agreement is sealed or otherwise subject to a nondisclosure provision.

(B) The disclosure of fees and other expenses required under subparagraph (A) shall not affect any other information that is subject to a nondisclosure provision in a settlement agreement.

(f) As soon as practicable, and in any event not later than the date on which the first report under subsection (e)(1) is required to be submitted, the Chairman of the Administrative Conference of the United States shall create and maintain online a searchable database containing, with respect to each award of fees and other expenses under this section made on or after the date of enactment of the John D. Dingell, Jr. Conservation, Management, and Recreation Act, the following information:

(1) The case name and number of the adversary adjudication, if available, hyperlinked to the case, if available.

(2) The name of the agency involved in the adversary adjudication.

(3) A description of the claims in the adversary adjudication.

(4) The name of each party to whom the award was made as such party is identified in the order or other court document making the award.

(5) The amount of the award.

(6) The basis for the finding that the position of the agency concerned was not substantially justified.

(g) The online searchable database described in subsection (f) may not reveal any information the disclosure of which is prohibited by law or a court order.

(h) The head of each agency shall provide to the Chairman of the Administrative Conference of the United States in a timely manner all information requested by the Chairman to comply with the requirements of subsections (e), (f), and (g).

(i) No award may be made under this section for costs, fees, or other expenses which may be awarded under section 7430 of the Internal Revenue Code of 1986.

(Added Pub.L. 96–481, Title II, § 203(a)(1), (c), Oct. 21, 1980, 94 Stat. 2325, 2327; revived and amended Pub.L. 99–80, §§ 1, 6, Aug. 5, 1985, 99 Stat. 183, 186; Pub.L. 99–509, Title VI, § 6103(c), Oct. 21, 1986, 100 Stat. 1948; Pub.L. 99–514, § 2, Oct. 22, 1986, 100 Stat. 2095; Pub.L. 100–647, Title VI, § 6239(b), Nov. 10, 1988, 102 Stat. 3746; Pub.L. 103–141, § 4(b), Nov. 16, 1993, 107 Stat. 1489; Pub.L. 104–121, Title II, § 231, Mar. 29, 1996, 110 Stat. 862; Pub.L. 111–350, § 5(a)(1), Jan. 4, 2011, 124 Stat. 3841; Pub.L. 116–9, Title IV, § 4201(a)(1), Mar. 12, 2019, 133 Stat. 762.)

HISTORICAL AND STATUTORY NOTES

References in Text

The Religious Freedom Restoration Act of 1993, referred to in subsec. (b)(1)(C)(iv), is Pub.L. 103–141, Nov. 16, 1993, 107 Stat. 1488, which is classified principally to chapter 21B (section 2000bb et seq.) of Title 42, The Public Health and Welfare. For complete classification of this Act to the Code, see Short Title of 1993 Acts note set out under 42 U.S.C.A. § 2000bb and Tables.

The date of enactment of the John D. Dingell, Jr. Conservation, Management, and Recreation Act, referred to in subsecs. (e)(1) and (f), is the date of enactment of Pub.L. 116–9, 133 Stat. 580, which was approved March 12, 2019.

Section 7430 of the Internal Revenue Code of 1986, referred to in subsec. (i), is classified to 26 U.S.C.A. § 7430.

Effective and Applicability Provisions

1996 Acts. Section 233 of Pub.L. 104–121 provided that: "The amendments made by sections 331 and 332 [probably should read 'sections 231 and 232', respectively, which amended this section and section 2412 of Title 28, Judiciary and Judicial Procedure, respectively] shall apply to civil actions and adversary adjudications commenced on or after the date of the enactment of this subtitle [Mar. 29, 1996]."

1988 Acts. Amendment by Pub.L. 100–647 applicable to proceedings commencing after Nov. 10, 1988, see section 6239(d) of Pub.L. 100–647, set out as a note under 26 U.S.C.A. § 7430.

1986 Acts. Amendment by Pub.L. 99–509 effective Oct. 21, 1986, and applicable to any claim or statement made, presented or submitted on or after such date, see section 6104 of Pub.L. 99–509, set out as a note under 31 U.S.C.A. § 3801.

1985 Acts. Section 7 of Pub.L. 99–80 provided that:

"(a) In general.—Except as otherwise provided in this section, the amendments made by this Act [reviving and amending this section and 28 U.S.C.A. § 2412(d), enacting and amending provisions set out as notes under this section and 28 U.S.C.A. § 2412, and repealing provisions set out as a note under this section] shall apply to cases pending on or commenced on or after the date of the enactment of this Act [Aug. 5, 1985].

"(b) Applicability of amendments to certain prior cases.—The amendments made by this Act shall apply to any case commenced on or after October 1, 1984, and finally disposed of before the date of the enactment of this Act [Aug. 5, 1985], except that in any such case, the 30–day period referred to in section 504(a)(2) of title 5, United States Code [subsec. (a)(2) of this section], or section 2412(d)(1)(B) of title 28, United States Code [28 U.S.C.A. § 2412(d)(1)(B)], as the case may be, shall be deemed to commence on the date of the enactment of this Act [Aug. 5, 1985].

"(c) Applicability of amendments to prior board of contracts appeals cases.—Section 504(b)(1)(C)(ii) of title 5, United States Code [subsec. (b)(1)(C)(ii) of this section], as added by section 1(c)(2) of this Act, and section 2412(d)(2)(E) of title 28, United States Code, [28 U.S.C.A. § 2412(d)(2)(E)], as added by section 2(c)(2) of this Act, shall apply to any adversary adjudication pending on or commenced on or after October 1, 1981, in which applications for fees and other expenses were timely filed and were dismissed for lack of jurisdiction."

1980 Acts. Section 208 of Title II of Pub.L. 96–481, as amended Pub.L. 99–80, § 5, Aug. 5, 1985, 99 Stat. 186, provided that: "This title and the amendments made by this title [see Short Title of 1980 Acts note under this section] shall take effect of [on] October 1, 1981, and shall apply to any adversary adjudication, as defined in section 504(b)(1)(C) of title 5, United States Code [subsec. (b)(1)(C) of this section], and any civil action or adversary adjudication described in section 2412 of title 28, United States Code [28 U.S.C.A. § 2412], which is pending on, or commenced on or after, such date. Awards may be made for fees and other expenses incurred before October 1, 1981, in any such adversary adjudication or civil action."

Section 203(c) of Pub.L. 96–481 which provided that effective Oct. 1, 1984, this section is repealed, except that the provisions of this section shall continue to apply through final disposition of any adversary adjudication initiated before the date of repeal, was itself repealed by Pub.L. 99–80, § 6(b)(1), Aug. 5, 1985, 99 Stat. 186.

Short Title

1980 Acts. Section 201 of Title II of Pub.L. 96–481 provided that: "This title [enacting this section, amending section 634b of Title 15, Commerce and Trade, section 2412 of Title 28, Judiciary and Judicial Procedure, Rule 37 of the Federal Rules of Civil Procedure, set out in Title 28, Appendix, and section 1988 of Title 42, The Public Health and Welfare, and enacting provisions set out as notes under this section and section 2412 of Title 28] may be cited as the 'Equal Access to Justice Act'."

Termination of Reporting Requirements

For termination, effective May 15, 2000, of provisions in subsec. (e) of this section relating to annual report to Congress on the amount of fees and other expenses, see Pub.L. 104–66, § 3003, as amended, set out as a note under 31 U.S.C.A. § 1113 and page 153 of House Document No. 103–7.

Termination of Administrative Conference of United States

For termination of Administrative Conference of United States, see provisions of title IV of Pub.L. 104–52, set out as a note preceding 5 U.S.C.A. § 591.

Congressional Findings and Purposes

Section 202 of Title II of Pub.L. 96–481 provided that:

"(a) The Congress finds that certain individuals, partnerships, corporations, and labor and other organizations may be deterred from seeking review of, or defending against, unreasonable governmental action because of the expense involved in securing the vindication of their rights in civil actions and in administrative proceedings.

"(b) The Congress further finds that because of the greater resources and expertise of the United States the standard for an award of fees against the United States should be different from the standard governing an award against a private litigant, in certain situations.

"(c) It is the purpose of this title [see Short Title of 1980 Acts note under this section]—

"(1) to diminish the deterrent effect of seeking review of, or defending against, governmental action by providing in specified situations an award of attorney fees, expert witness fees, and other costs against the United States; and

"(2) to insure the applicability in actions by or against the United States of the common law and statutory exceptions to the 'American rule' respecting the award of attorney fees."

Limitation on Payments

Section 207 of Title II of Pub.L. 96–481, which provided that the payment of judgments, fees and other expenses in the same manner as the payment of final judgments as provided in this Act [probably should be "this title", see Short Title of 1980 Acts note under this section] would be effective only to the extent and in such amounts as are provided in advance in appropriation Acts, was repealed by Pub.L. 99–80, § 4, Aug. 5, 1985, 99 Stat. 186.

Prohibition on Use of Energy and Water Development Appropriations to Pay Intervening Parties in Regulatory or Adjudicatory Proceedings

Pub.L. 102–377, Title V, § 502, Oct. 2, 1992, 106 Stat. 1342, provided that: "None of the funds in this Act [Pub. L. 102–377, Oct. 2, 1992, 106 Stat. 1315, for distribution of which, see Tables] or subsequent Energy and Water Development Appropriations Acts shall be used to pay the expenses of, or otherwise compensate, parties intervening in regulatory or adjudicatory proceedings funded in such Acts."

Revival of Previously Repealed Provisions

Section 6 of Pub.L. 99–80 provided that:

"**(a) Revival of certain expired provisions.**—Section 504 of title 5, United States Code [this section], and the item relating to that section in the table of sections of chapter 5 of title 5, United States Code [preceding section 500 of this title], and subsection (d) of section 2412 of title 28, United States Code [section 2412(d) of Title 28, Judiciary and Judicial Procedure], shall be effective on or after the date of the enactment of this Act [Aug. 5, 1985] as if they had not been repealed by sections 203(c) and 204(c) of the Equal Access to Justice Act [Pub.L. 96–481, Oct. 21, 1980, 94 Stat. 2325.]

"**(b) Repeals.**—

"(1) Section 203(c) of the Equal Access to Justice Act [which had repealed this section] is hereby repealed.

"(2) Section 204(c) of the Equal Access to Justice Act [which had repealed section 2412(d) of Title 28] is hereby repealed."

TITLE 28
JUDICIARY AND JUDICIAL PROCEDURE

PART VI—PARTICULAR PROCEEDINGS

CHAPTER 161—UNITED STATES AS PARTY GENERALLY

§ 2412. Costs and fees

(a)(1) Except as otherwise specifically provided by statute, a judgment for costs, as enumerated in section 1920 of this title, but not including the fees and expenses of attorneys, may be awarded to the prevailing party in any civil action brought by or against the United States or any agency or any official of the United States acting in his or her official capacity in any court having jurisdiction of such action. A judgment for costs when taxed against the United States shall, in an amount established by statute, court rule, or order, be limited to reimbursing in whole or in part the prevailing party for the costs incurred by such party in the litigation.

(2) A judgment for costs, when awarded in favor of the United States in an action brought by the United States, may include an amount equal to the filing fee prescribed under section 1914(a) of this title. The preceding sentence shall not be construed as requiring the United States to pay any filing fee.

(b) Unless expressly prohibited by statute, a court may award reasonable fees and expenses of attorneys, in addition to the costs which may be awarded pursuant to subsection (a), to the prevailing party in any civil action brought by or against the United States or any agency or any official of the United States acting in his or her official capacity in any court having jurisdiction of such action. The United States shall be liable for such fees and expenses to the same extent that any other party would be liable under the common law or under the terms of any statute which specifically provides for such an award.

(c)(1) Any judgment against the United States or any agency and any official of the United States acting in his or her official capacity for costs pursuant to subsection (a) shall be paid as provided in sections 2414 and 2517 of this title and shall be in addition to any relief provided in the judgment.

(2) Any judgment against the United States or any agency and any official of the United States acting in his or her official capacity for fees and expenses of attorneys pursuant to subsection (b) shall be paid as provided in sections 2414 and 2517 of this title, except that if the basis for the award is a finding that the United States acted in bad faith, then the award shall be paid by any agency found to have acted in bad faith and shall be in addition to any relief provided in the judgment.

(d)(1)(A) Except as otherwise specifically provided by statute, a court shall award to a prevailing party other than the United States fees and other expenses, in addition to any costs awarded pursuant to subsection (a), incurred by that party in any civil action (other than cases sounding in tort), including proceedings for judicial review of agency action, brought by or against the United States in any court having jurisdiction of that action, unless the court finds that the position of the United States was substantially justified or that special circumstances make an award unjust.

(B) A party seeking an award of fees and other expenses shall, within thirty days of final judgment in the action, submit to the court an application for fees and other expenses which shows that the party is a prevailing party and is eligible to receive an award under this subsection, and the amount sought, including an itemized statement from any attorney or expert witness representing or appearing in behalf of the party stating the actual time expended and the rate at which fees and other expenses were computed. The party shall also allege that the position of the United States was not substantially justified. Whether or not the position of the United States was substantially justified shall be determined on the basis of the record (including the record with respect to the action or failure to act by the agency upon which the civil action is based) which is made in the civil action for which fees and other expenses are sought.

(C) The court, in its discretion, may reduce the amount to be awarded pursuant to this subsection, or deny an award, to the extent that the prevailing party during the course of the proceedings engaged in conduct which unduly and unreasonably protracted the final resolution of the matter in controversy.

(D) If, in a civil action brought by the United States or a proceeding for judicial review of an adversary adjudication described in section 504(a)(4) of title 5, the demand by the United States is substantially in excess of the judgment finally obtained by the United States and is unreasonable when compared with such judgment, under the facts and circumstances of the case, the court shall award to the party the fees and other expenses related to defending against the excessive demand, unless the party has committed a willful violation of law or otherwise acted in bad faith, or special circumstances make an award unjust. Fees and expenses awarded under this subparagraph shall be paid only as a consequence of appropriations provided in advance.

(2) For the purposes of this subsection—

(A) "fees and other expenses" includes the reasonable expenses of expert witnesses, the reasonable cost of any study, analysis, engineering report, test, or project which is found by the court to be necessary for the preparation of the party's case, and reasonable attorney fees (The amount of fees awarded under this subsection shall be based upon prevailing market rates for the kind and quality of the services furnished, except that (i) no expert witness shall be compensated at a rate in excess of the highest rate of compensation for expert witnesses paid by the United States; and (ii) attorney fees shall not be awarded in excess of $125 per hour unless the court determines that an increase in the cost of living or a special factor, such as the limited availability of qualified attorneys for the proceedings involved, justifies a higher fee.);

(B) "party" means (i) an individual whose net worth did not exceed $2,000,000 at the time the civil action was filed, or (ii) any owner of an unincorporated business, or any partnership, corporation, association, unit of local government, or organization, the net worth of which did not exceed $7,000,000 at the time the civil action was filed, and which had not more than 500 employees at the time the civil action was filed; except that an organization described in section 501(c)(3) of the Internal Revenue Code of 1986 (26 U.S.C. 501(c)(3)) exempt from taxation under section 501(a) of such Code, or a cooperative association as defined in section 15(a) of the Agricultural Marketing Act (12 U.S.C. 1141j(a)), may be a party regardless of the net worth of such organization or cooperative association or for purposes of subsection (d)(1)(D), a small entity as defined in section 601 of title 5;

(C) "United States" includes any agency and any official of the United States acting in his or her official capacity;

(D) "position of the United States" means, in addition to the position taken by the United States in the civil action, the action or failure to act by the agency upon which the civil action is based; except that fees and expenses may not be awarded to a party for any portion of the litigation in which the party has unreasonably protracted the proceedings;

(E) "civil action brought by or against the United States" includes an appeal by a party, other than the United States, from a decision of a contracting officer rendered pursuant to a disputes clause in a contract with the Government or pursuant to chapter 71 of title 41;

(F) "court" includes the United States Court of Federal Claims and the United States Court of Appeals for Veterans Claims;

(G) "final judgment" means a judgment that is final and not appealable, and includes an order of settlement;

(H) "prevailing party", in the case of eminent domain proceedings, means a party who obtains a final judgment (other than by settlement), exclusive of interest, the amount of which is at least as close to the highest valuation of the property involved that is attested to at trial on behalf of the property owner as it is to the highest valuation of the property involved that is attested to at trial on behalf of the Government; and

(I) "demand" means the express demand of the United States which led to the adversary adjudication, but shall not include a recitation of the maximum statutory penalty (i) in the complaint, or (ii) elsewhere when accompanied by an express demand for a lesser amount.

(3) In awarding fees and other expenses under this subsection to a prevailing party in any action for judicial review of an adversary adjudication, as defined in subsection (b)(1)(C) of section 504 of title 5, or an adversary adjudication subject to chapter 71 of title 41, the court shall include in that award fees and other expenses to the same extent authorized in subsection (a) of such section, unless the court finds that during such adversary adjudication the position of the United States was substantially justified, or that special circumstances make an award unjust.

(4) Fees and other expenses awarded under this subsection to a party shall be paid by any agency over which the party prevails from any funds made available to the agency by appropriation or otherwise.

(5)(A) Not later than March 31 of the first fiscal year beginning after the date of enactment of the John D. Dingell, Jr. Conservation, Management, and Recreation Act, and every fiscal year thereafter, the Chairman of the Administrative Conference of the United States shall submit to Congress and make publicly available online a report on the amount of fees and other expenses awarded during the preceding fiscal year pursuant to this subsection.

(B) Each report under subparagraph (A) shall describe the number, nature, and amount of the awards, the claims involved in the controversy, and any other relevant information that may aid Congress in evaluating the scope and impact of such awards.

(C)(i) Each report under subparagraph (A) shall account for all payments of fees and other expenses awarded under this subsection that are made pursuant to a settlement agreement, regardless of whether the settlement agreement is sealed or otherwise subject to a nondisclosure provision.

(ii) The disclosure of fees and other expenses required under clause (i) shall not affect any other information that is subject to a nondisclosure provision in a settlement agreement.

(D) The Chairman of the Administrative Conference of the United States shall include and clearly identify in each annual report under subparagraph (A), for each case in which an award of fees and other expenses is included in the report—

(i) any amounts paid under section 1304 of title 31 for a judgment in the case;

(ii) the amount of the award of fees and other expenses; and

(iii) the statute under which the plaintiff filed suit.

(6) As soon as practicable, and in any event not later than the date on which the first report under paragraph (5)(A) is required to be submitted, the Chairman of the Administrative Conference of the United States shall create and maintain online a searchable database containing, with respect to each award of fees and other expenses under this subsection made on or after the date of enactment of the John D. Dingell, Jr. Conservation, Management, and Recreation Act, the following information:

(A) The case name and number, hyperlinked to the case, if available.

(B) The name of the agency involved in the case.

(C) The name of each party to whom the award was made as such party is identified in the order or other court document making the award.

(D) A description of the claims in the case.

(E) The amount of the award.

(F) The basis for the finding that the position of the agency concerned was not substantially justified.

(7) The online searchable database described in paragraph (6) may not reveal any information the disclosure of which is prohibited by law or a court order.

(8) The head of each agency (including the Attorney General of the United States) shall provide to the Chairman of the Administrative Conference of the United States in a timely manner all information requested by the Chairman to comply with the requirements of paragraphs (5), (6), and (7).

(e) The provisions of this section shall not apply to any costs, fees, and other expenses in connection with any proceeding to which section 7430 of the Internal Revenue Code of 1986 applies (determined without regard to subsections (b) and (f) of such section). Nothing in the preceding sentence shall prevent the awarding under subsection (a) of this section of costs enumerated in section 1920 of this title (as in effect on October 1, 1981).

(f) If the United States appeals an award of costs or fees and other expenses made against the United States under this section and the award is affirmed in whole or in part, interest shall be paid on the amount of the award as affirmed. Such interest shall be computed at the rate determined under section 1961(a) of this title, and shall run from the date of the award through the day before the date of the mandate of affirmance.

(June 25, 1948, c. 646, 62 Stat. 973; Pub.L. 89–507, § 1, July 18, 1966, 80 Stat. 308; Pub.L. 96–481, Title II, § 204(a), (c), Oct. 21, 1980, 94 Stat. 2327, 2329; Pub.L. 97–248, Title II, § 292(c), Sept. 3, 1982, 96 Stat. 574; Pub.L. 99–80, §§ 2, 6(a), (b)(2), Aug. 5, 1985, 99 Stat. 184, 186; Pub.L. 99–514, § 2, Oct. 22, 1986, 100 Stat. 2095; Pub.L. 102–572, Title III, § 301(a), Title V, §§ 502(b), 506(a), Title IX, § 902(b)(1), Oct. 29, 1992, 106 Stat. 4511–4513, 4516; Pub.L. 104–66, Title I, § 1091(b), Dec. 21, 1995, 109 Stat. 722; Pub.L. 104–121, Title II, § 232, Mar. 29, 1996, 110 Stat. 863; Pub.L. 105–368, Title V, § 512(b)(1)(B), Nov. 11, 1998, 112 Stat. 3342; Pub.L. 111–350, § 5(g)(9), Jan. 4, 2011, 124 Stat. 3848; Pub.L. 116–9, Title IV, § 4201(a)(2), (3), Mar. 12, 2019, 133 Stat. 763.)

HISTORICAL AND STATUTORY NOTES

References in Text

Chapter 71 of title 41, referred to in subsec. (d)(2)(E), (3), is classified to 41 U.S.C.A. § 7101 et seq.

The date of enactment of the John D. Dingell, Jr. Conservation, Management, and Recreation Act, referred to in subsec. (d)(5)(A) and (6), is the date of enactment of Pub.L. 116–9, 133 Stat. 580, which was approved March 12, 2019.

Section 7430 of the Internal Revenue Code of 1986, referred to in subsec. (e), is classified to 26 U.S.C.A. § 7430.

Effective and Applicability Provisions

1998 Acts. Amendment by Pub.L. 105–368 effective on the first day of the first month beginning more than 90 days after Nov. 11, 1998, see section 513 of Pub.L. 105–368, set out as a note under section 7251 of Title 38.

1996 Acts. Amendment by Pub.L. 104–121 applicable to civil actions and adversary adjudications commenced on or after March 29, 1996, see section 233 of Pub.L. 104–121, set out as a note under section 504 of Title 5, Government Organization and Employees.

1992 Acts. Section 506(b) of Pub.L. 102–572 provided that: "The amendment made by subsection (a) [amending subsec. (d)(2)(F) of this section] shall apply to any case pending before the United States Court of Veterans Appeals on the date of the enactment of this Act [Oct. 29, 1992], to any appeal filed in that court on or after such date, and to any appeal from that court that is pending on such date in the United States Court of Appeals for the Federal Circuit."

Section 506(d) of Pub.L. 102–572 provided that: "This section, and the amendment made by this section [amending subsec. (d)(2)(F) of this section and enacting provisions set out as notes under this section], shall take effect on the date of the enactment of this Act [Oct. 29, 1992]."

Amendment by section 902(b)(1) of Pub.L. 102–572 effective Oct. 29, 1992, see section 911 of Pub.L. 102–572, set out as a note under section 171 of this title.

Amendments by sections 301(a) and 502(b) of Pub.L. 102–572 effective Jan. 1, 1993, see section 1101(a) of Pub.L. 102–572, set out as a note under section 905 of Title 2, The Congress.

1985 Acts. Amendment by Pub. L. 99–80 applicable to cases pending on or commenced on or after Aug. 5, 1985, but with provision for additional applicability to certain prior cases and to prior board of contracts appeals cases, see section 7 of Pub. L. 99–80, set out as a note under section 504 of Title 5, Government Organization and Employees.

1982 Acts. Amendment by Pub.L. 97–248 applicable to civil actions or proceedings commenced after Feb. 28, 1983, see section 292(e)(1) of Pub.L. 97–248, as amended, set out as a note under section 7430 of Title 26, Internal Revenue Code.

1980 Acts. Amendment by section 204(a) of Pub.L. 96–481 to take effect on Oct. 1, 1981, and applicable to any adversary adjudication, as defined in section 504(b)(1)(C) of Title 5, and to civil actions and adversary adjudications described in this section, which are pending on, or commenced on or after, Oct. 1, 1981, see section 208 of Pub.L. 96–481, as amended, set out as a note under section 504 of Title 5, Government Organization and Employees.

Section 204(c) of Pub.L. 96–481 which provided in part that effective Oct. 1, 1984, subsec. (d) of this section is repealed, except that the provisions of subsec. (d) shall continue to apply through final disposition of any adversary adjudication initiated before the date of repeal, was repealed by Pub.L. 99–80, § 6(b)(2), Aug. 5, 1985, 99 Stat. 186.

1966 Acts. Section 3 of Pub.L. 89–507 provided that: "These amendments [to this section and section 2520 of this title] shall apply only to judgments entered in actions filed subsequent to the date of enactment of this Act [July 18, 1966]. These amendments [to this section and section 2520 of this title] shall not authorize the reopening or modification of judgments entered prior to the enactment of this Act [July 18, 1966]."

Savings Provisions

Section 206 of Pub.L. 96–481, as amended by Pub.L. 99–80, § 3, Aug. 5, 1985, 99 Stat. 186, provided that:

"(a) Except as provided in subsection (b), nothing in section 2412(d) of title 28, United States Code, as added by section 204(a) of this title [subsec. (d) of this section], alters, modifies, repeals, invalidates, or supersedes any other provision of Federal law which authorizes an award of such fees and other expenses to any party other than the United States that prevails in any civil action brought by or against the United States.

"(b) Section 206(b) of the Social Security Act (42 U.S.C. 406(b)(1)) [section 406(b) of Title 42, The Public Health and Welfare] shall not prevent an award of fees and other expenses under section 2412(d) of title 28, United States Code [subsec. (d) of this section]. Section 206(b)(2) of the Social Security Act [section 406(b)(2) of Title 42] shall not apply with respect to any such award but only if, where the claimant's attorney receives fees for the same work under both section 206(b) of that Act [section 406(b) of Title 42] and section 2412(d) of title 28, United States Code [subsec. (d) of this section], the claimant's attorney refunds to the claimant the amount of the smaller fee."

Congressional Findings and Purposes

For Congressional findings and purposes relating to 1980 amendment of this section, see section 202 of Pub.L. 96–481, set out as a note under section 504 of Title 5, Government Organization and Employees.

Fees Awarded to Non-attorney Practitioners

Pub.L. 107–330, Title IV, § 403, Dec. 6, 2002, 116 Stat. 2833, provided that: "The authority of the United States Court of Appeals for Veterans Claims to award reasonable fees and expenses of attorneys under section 2412(d) of title 28, United States Code [Subsec. (d) of this section], shall include authority to award fees and expenses, in an amount determined appropriate by the United States Court of Appeals for Veterans Claims, of individuals admitted to practice before the Court as non-attorney practitioners under subsection (b) or (c) of Rule 46 of the Rules of Practice and Procedure of the United States Court of Appeals for Veterans Claims."

Fee Agreements

Section 506(c) of Pub.L. 102–572 provided that: "Section 5904(d) of title 38, United States Code [section 5904(d) of Title 38, Veterans' Benefits], shall not prevent an award of fees and other expenses under section 2412(d) of title 28, United States Code [subsec. (d) of this section]. Section 5904(d) of title 38, United States Code, shall not apply with respect to any such award but only if, where the claimant's attorney receives fees for the same work under both section 5904 of title 38, United States Code, and section 2412(d) of title 28, United States Code, the claimant's attorney refunds to the claimant the amount of the smaller fee."

Nonliability of Judicial Officers for Costs

Pub.L. 104–317, Title III, § 309(a), Oct. 19, 1996, 110 Stat. 3853, provided that: "Notwithstanding any other provision of law, no judicial officer shall be held liable for any costs, including attorney's fees, in any action brought against such officer for an act or omission taken in such officer's judicial capacity, unless such action was clearly in excess of such officer's jurisdiction."

Revival of Previously Repealed Provisions

For revival of subsec. (d) of this section effective on or after Aug. 5, 1985, as if it had not been repealed by section 204(c) of Pub.L. 96–481, and repeal of section 204(c) of Pub.L. 96–481, see section 6 of Pub.L. 99–80, set out as a note under section 504 of Title 5, Government Organization and Employees.

CODE OF FEDERAL REGULATIONS

TITLE 20—EMPLOYEES' BENEFITS

CHAPTER III—SOCIAL SECURITY ADMINISTRATION

PART 401—PRIVACY AND DISCLOSURE OF OFFICIAL RECORDS AND INFORMATION

SUBPART A—GENERAL

SUBPART B—THE PRIVACY ACT

SUBPART C—DISCLOSURE OF OFFICIAL RECORDS AND INFORMATION

Authority: Secs. 205, 702(a)(5), 1106, and 1141 of the Social Security Act (42 U.S.C. 405, 902(a)(5), 1306, and 1320b–11); 5 U.S.C. 552 and 552a; 8 U.S.C. 1360; 26 U.S.C. 6103; 30 U.S.C. 923.

Source: 62 FR 4143, Jan. 29, 1997, unless otherwise noted.

SUBPART A—GENERAL

§ 401.5 Purpose of the regulations.

(a) General. The purpose of this part is to describe the Social Security Administration (SSA) policies and procedures for implementing the requirements of the Privacy Act of 1974, 5 U.S.C. 552a and section 1106 of the Social Security Act concerning disclosure of information about individuals, both with and without their consent. This part also complies with other applicable statutes.

(b) Privacy. This part implements the Privacy Act by establishing agency policies and procedures for the maintenance of records. This part also establishes agency policies and procedures under which you can ask us whether we maintain records about you or obtain access to your records. Additionally, this part establishes policies and procedures under which you may seek to have your record corrected or amended if you believe that your record is not accurate, timely, complete, or relevant.

(c) Disclosure. This part also sets out the general guidelines which we follow in deciding whether to make disclosures. However, we must examine the facts of each case separately to decide if we should disclose the information or keep it confidential.

§ 401.10 Applicability.

(a) SSA. All SSA employees and components are governed by this part. SSA employees governed by this part include all regular and special government employees of SSA; experts and consultants whose temporary (not in excess of 1 year) or intermittent services have been procured by SSA by contract pursuant to 5 U.S.C. 3109; volunteers where acceptance of their services are authorized by law; those individuals performing gratuitous services as permitted under conditions prescribed by the Office of Personnel Management; and, participants in work-study or training programs.

(b) Other entities. This part also applies to advisory committees and councils within the meaning of the Federal Advisory Committee Act which provide advice to: Any official or component of SSA; or the President and for which SSA has been delegated responsibility for providing services.

§ 401.15 Limitations on scope.

The regulations in this part do not—

(a) Make available to an individual records which are not retrieved by that individual's name or other personal identifier.

(b) Make available to the general public records which are retrieved by an individual's name or other personal identifier or make available to the general public records which would otherwise not be available to the general public under the Freedom of Information Act, 5 U.S.C. 552, and part 402 of this title.

(c) Govern the maintenance or disclosure of, notification about or access to, records in the possession of SSA which are subject to the regulations of another agency, such as personnel records which are part of a system of records administered by the Office of Personnel Management.

(d) Apply to grantees, including State and local governments or subdivisions thereof, administering federally funded programs.

(e) Make available records compiled by SSA in reasonable anticipation of court litigation or formal administrative proceedings. The availability of such records to the general public or to any subject individual or party to such litigation or proceedings shall be governed by applicable constitutional principles, rules of discovery, and applicable regulations of the agency.

§ 401.20 Scope.

(a) Access. Sections 401.30 through 401.95, which set out SSA's rules for implementing the Privacy Act, apply to records retrieved by an individual's name or personal identifier subject to the Privacy Act. The rules in §§ 401.30 through 401.95 also apply to information developed by medical sources for the Social Security program and shall not be accessed except as permitted by this part.

(b) Disclosure—

(1) Program records. Regulations that apply to the disclosure of information about an individual contained in SSA's program records are set out in §§ 401.100 through 401.200 of this part. These regulations also apply to the disclosure of other Federal program information which SSA maintains. That information includes:

(i) Health insurance records which SSA maintains for the Health Care Financing Administration's (HCFA) programs under title XVIII of the Social Security Act. We will disclose these records to HCFA. HCFA may redisclose these records under the regulations applying to records in HCFA's custody;

(ii) Black lung benefit records which SSA maintains for the administration of the Federal Coal Mine Health and Safety Act; (However, this information is not covered by section 1106 of the Social Security Act.) and

(iii) Information retained by medical sources pertaining to a consultative examination performed for the Social Security program shall not be disclosed except as permitted by this part.

(2) Nonprogram records. Section 401.110 sets out rules applicable to the disclosure of nonprogram records, e.g., SSA's administrative and personnel records.

[65 FR 16812, March 30, 2000; 72 FR 20939, April 27, 2007]

§ 401.25 Terms defined.

Access means making a record available to a subject individual.

Act means the Social Security Act.

Agency means the Social Security Administration.

Commissioner means the Commissioner of Social Security.

Disclosure means making a record about an individual available to or releasing it to another party.

FOIA means the Freedom of Information Act.

Individual when used in connection with the Privacy Act or for disclosure of nonprogram records, means a living person who is a citizen of the United States or an alien lawfully admitted for permanent residence. It does not include persons such as sole proprietorships, partnerships, or corporations. A business firm which is identified by the name of one or more persons is not an individual. When used in connection with the rules governing program information, individual means a living natural person; this does not include corporations, partnerships, and unincorporated business or professional groups of two or more persons.

Information means information about an individual, and includes, but is not limited to, vital statistics; race, sex, or other physical characteristics; earnings information; professional fees paid to an individual and other financial information; benefit data or other claims information; the social security number, employer identification number, or other individual identifier; address; phone number; medical information, including psychological or psychiatric information or lay information used in a medical determination; and information about marital and family relationships and other personal relationships.

Maintain means to establish, collect, use, or disseminate when used in connection with the term record; and, to have control over or responsibility for a system of records when used in connection with the term system of records.

Notification means communication to an individual whether he is a subject individual. (Subject individual is defined further on in this section.)

Program information means personal information and records collected and compiled by SSA in order to discharge its responsibilities under titles I, II, IV part A, X, XI, XIV, XVI and XVIII of the Act and parts B and C of the Federal Coal Mine Health and Safety Act.

Record means any item, collection, or grouping of information about an individual that is maintained by SSA including, but not limited to, information such as an individual's education, financial transactions, medical history, and criminal or employment history that contains the individual's name, or an identifying number, symbol, or any other means by which an individual can be identified. When used in this part, record means only a record which is in a system of records.

Routine use means the disclosure of a record outside SSA, without the consent of the subject individual, for a purpose which is compatible with the purpose for which the record was collected. It includes disclosures required to be made by statutes other than the Freedom of Information Act, 5 U.S.C. 552. It does not include disclosures which the Privacy Act otherwise permits without the consent of the subject individual and without regard to whether they are compatible with the purpose for which the information is collected, such as disclosures to the Bureau of the Census, the General Accounting Office, or to Congress.

Social Security Administration (SSA) means (1) that Federal agency which has administrative responsibilities under titles, I, II, X, XI, XIV, XVI, and XVIII of the Act; and (2) units of State governments which make determinations under agreements made under sections 221 and 1633 of the Act.

Social Security program means any program or provision of law which SSA is responsible for administering, including the Freedom of Information Act and Privacy Act. This includes our responsibilities under parts B and C of the Federal Coal Mine Health and Safety Act.

Statistical record means a record maintained for statistical research or reporting purposes only and not maintained to make determinations about a particular subject individual.

Subject individual means the person to whom a record pertains.

System of records means a group of records under our control from which information about an individual is retrieved by the name of the individual or by an identifying number, symbol, or other identifying particular. Single records or groups of records which are not retrieved by a personal identifier are not part of a system of records. Papers maintained by individual Agency employees which are prepared, maintained, or discarded at the discretion of the employee and which are not subject to the Federal Records Act, 44 U.S.C. 2901, are not part of a system of records; provided, that such personal papers are not used by the employee or the Agency to determine any rights, benefits, or privileges of individuals.

We and our mean the Social Security Administration.

SUBPART B—THE PRIVACY ACT

§ 401.30 Privacy Act and other responsibilities.

(a) Policy. Our policy is to protect the privacy of individuals to the fullest extent possible while nonetheless permitting the exchange of records required to fulfill our administrative and program responsibilities, and responsibilities for disclosing records which the general public is entitled to have under the Freedom of Information Act, 5 U.S.C. 552, and 20 CFR part 402.

(b) Maintenance of records. We will maintain no record unless:

(1) It is relevant and necessary to accomplish an SSA function which is required to be accomplished by statute or Executive Order;

(2) We obtain the information in the record, as much as it is practicable, from the subject individual if we may use the record to determine an individual's rights, benefits or privileges under Federal programs;

(3) We inform the individual providing the record to us of the authority for our asking him or her to provide the record (including whether providing the record is mandatory or voluntary, the principal purpose for maintaining the record, the routine uses for the record, and what effect his or her refusal to provide the record may have on him or her). Further, the individual agrees to provide the record, if the individual is not required by statute or Executive Order to do so.

(c) First Amendment rights. We will keep no record which describes how an individual exercises rights guaranteed by the First Amendment unless we are expressly authorized:

(1) By statute,

(2) By the subject individual, or

(3) Unless pertinent to and within the scope of an authorized law enforcement activity.

(d) Privacy Officer. The Privacy Officer is an advisor to the Agency on all privacy policy and disclosure matters. The Privacy Officer coordinates the development and implementation of Agency privacy policies and related legal requirements to ensure Privacy Act compliance, and monitors the coordination, collection, maintenance, use and disclosure of personal information. The Privacy Officer also ensures the integration of privacy principles into information technology systems architecture and technical designs, and generally provides to Agency officials policy guidance and directives in carrying out the privacy and disclosure policy.

(e) Senior Agency Official for Privacy. The Senior Agency Official for Privacy assumes overall responsibility and accountability for ensuring the agency's implementation of information privacy protections as well as agency compliance with federal laws, regulations, and policies relating to the privacy of information, such as the Privacy Act. The compliance efforts also include reviewing information privacy procedures to ensure that they are comprehensive and up-to-date and, where additional or revised procedures may be called for, working with the relevant agency offices in the consideration, adoption, and implementation of such procedures. The official also ensures that agency employees and contractors receive appropriate training and education programs regarding the information privacy laws, regulations, polices and procedures governing the agency's handling of personal information. In addition to the compliance role, the official has a central policy-making role in the agency's development and evaluation of legislative, regulatory and other policy proposals which might implicate information privacy issues, including those relating to the collection, use, sharing, and disclosure of personal information.

(f) Privacy Impact Assessment. In our comprehensive Privacy Impact Assessment (PIA) review process, we incorporate the tenets of privacy law, SSA privacy regulations, and privacy policy directly into the development of certain Information Technology projects. Our review examines the risks and ramifications of collecting, maintaining and disseminating information in identifiable form in an electronic information system and identifies and evaluates protections and alternate processes to reduce the risk of unauthorized disclosures. As we accomplish the PIA review, we ask systems personnel and program personnel to resolve questions on data needs and data protection prior to the development of the electronic system.

[72 FR 20939, April 27, 2007]

§ 401.35 Your right to request records.

The Privacy Act gives you the right to direct access to most records about yourself that are in our systems of records. Exceptions to this Privacy Act right include—

(a) Special procedures for access to certain medical records (see 5 U.S.C. 552a(f)(3) and § 401.55);

(b) Unavailability of certain criminal law enforcement records (see 5 U.S.C. 552a(k), and § 401.85); and

(c) Unavailability of records compiled in reasonable anticipation of a court action or formal administrative proceeding.

Note to § 401.35: The Freedom of Information Act (see 20 CFR part 402) allows you to request information from SSA whether or not it is in a system of records.

§ 401.40 How to get your own records.

(a) Your right to notification and access. Subject to the provisions governing medical records in § 401.55, you may ask for notification of or access to any record about yourself that is in an SSA system of records. If you are a minor, you may get information about yourself under the same rules as for an adult. Under the Privacy Act, if you are the parent or guardian of a minor, or the legal guardian of someone who has been declared legally incompetent, and you are acting on his or her behalf, you may ask for information about that individual. You may be accompanied by another individual of your choice when you request access to a record in person, provided that you affirmatively authorize the presence of such other individual during any discussion of a record to which you are requesting access.

(b) Identifying the records. At the time of your request, you must specify which systems of records you wish to have searched and the records to which you wish to have access. You may also request copies of all or any such records. Also, we may ask you to provide sufficient particulars to enable us to distinguish between records on individuals with the same name. The necessary particulars are set forth in the notices of systems of records which are published in the Federal Register.

(c) Requesting notification or access. To request notification of or access to a record, you may visit your local social security office or write to the manager of the SSA system of records. The name and address of the manager of the system is part of the notice of systems of records. Every local social security office keeps a copy of the Federal Register containing that notice. That office can also help you get access to your record. You do not need to use any special form to ask for a record about you in our files, but your request must give enough identifying information about the record you want to enable us to find your particular record. This identifying information should include the system of records in which the record is located and the name and social security number (or other identifier) under which the record is filed. We do not honor requests for all records, all information, or similar blanket requests. Before granting notification of or access to a record, we may, if you are making your request in person, require you to put your request in writing if you have not already done so.

§ 401.45 Verifying your identity.

(a) When required. Unless you are making a request for notification of or access to a record in person, and you are personally known to the SSA representative, you must verify your identity in accordance with paragraph (b) of this section if:

(1) You make a request for notification of a record and we determine that the mere notice of the existence of the record would be a clearly unwarranted invasion of privacy if disclosed to someone other than the subject individual; or,

(2) You make a request for access to a record which is not required to be disclosed to the general public under the Freedom of Information Act, 5 U.S.C. 552, and part 402 of this chapter.

(b) Manner of verifying identity—

(1) Request in person. If you make a request to us in person, you must provide at least one piece of tangible identification such as a driver's license, passport, alien or voter registration card, or union card to verify your identity. If you do not have identification papers to verify your identity, you must certify in writing that you are the individual who you claim to be and that you understand that the knowing and willful request for or acquisition of a record pertaining to an individual under false pretenses is a criminal offense.

(2) Request by telephone. If you make a request by telephone, you must verify your identity by providing identifying particulars which parallel the record to which notification or access is being sought. If we determine that the particulars provided by telephone are insufficient, you will be required to submit your request in writing or in person. We will not accept telephone requests where an individual is requesting notification of or access to sensitive records such as medical records.

(3) Electronic requests. If you make a request by computer or other electronic means, e.g., over the Internet, we require you to verify your identity by using identity confirmation procedures that are commensurate with the sensitivity of the information that you are requesting. If we cannot confirm your identity using our identity confirmation procedures, we will not process the electronic request. When you cannot verify your identity through our procedures, we will require you to submit your request in writing.

(4) Electronic disclosures. When we collect or provide personally identifiable information over open networks such as the Internet, we use encryption in all of our automated online transaction systems to protect the confidentiality of the information. When we provide an online access option, such as a standard e-mail comment form on our Web site, and encryption is not being used, we alert you that personally identifiable information (such as your social security number) should not be included in your message.

(5) Requests not made in person. Except as provided in paragraphs (b)(2) of this section, if you do not make a request in person, you must submit a written request to SSA to verify your identify or you must certify in your request that you are the individual you claim to be. You must also sign a statement that you understand that the knowing and willful request for or acquisition of a record pertaining to an individual under false pretenses is a criminal offense.

(6) Requests on behalf of another. If you make a request on behalf of a minor or legal incompetent as authorized under § 401.40, you must verify your relationship to the minor or legal incompetent, in addition to verifying your own identity, by providing a copy of the minor's birth certificate, a court order, or other competent evidence of guardianship to SSA; except that you are not required to verify your relationship to the minor or legal incompetent when you are not required to verify your own identity or when evidence of your relationship to the minor or legal incompetent has been previously given to SSA.

(7) Medical records—additional verification. You need to further verify your identity if you are requesting notification of or access to sensitive records such as medical records. Any information for further verification must parallel the information in the record to which notification or access is being sought. Such further verification may include such particulars as the date or place of birth, names of parents, name of employer or the specific times the individual received medical treatment.

[72 FR 20939, April 27, 2007]

§ 401.50 Granting notification of or access to a record.

(a) General. Subject to the provisions governing medical records in § 401.55 and the provisions governing exempt systems in § 401.85, upon receipt of your request for notification of or access to a record and verification of your identity, we will review your request and grant notification or access to a record, if you are the subject of the record.

(b) Our delay in responding. If we determine that we will have to delay responding to your request because of the number of requests we are processing, a breakdown of equipment, shortage of personnel, storage of records in other locations, etc., we will so inform you and tell you when notification or access will be granted.

§ 401.55 Access to medical records.

(a) General. You have a right to access your medical records, including any psychological information that we maintain.

(b) Medical records procedures—

(1) Notification of or access to medical records.

(i) You may request notification of or access to a medical record pertaining to you. Unless you are a parent or guardian requesting notification of or access to a minor's medical record, you must make a request for a medical record in accordance with this section and the procedures in §§ 401.45 through 401.50 of this part.

(ii) When you request medical information about yourself, you must also name a representative in writing. The representative may be a physician, other health professional, or other responsible individual who will be willing to review the record and inform you of its contents. Following the discussion, you are entitled to your records. The representative does not have the discretion to withhold any part of your record. If you do not designate a representative, we may decline to release the requested information. In some cases, it may be possible to release medical information directly to you rather than to your representative.

(2) Utilization of the designated representative. You will be granted direct access to your medical record if we can determine that direct access is not likely to have an adverse effect on you. If we believe that we are not qualified to determine, or if we do determine, that direct access to you is likely to have an adverse effect, the record will be sent to the designated representative. We will inform you in writing that the record has been sent.

(c) Medical records of minors—

(1) Request by the minor. You may request access to your own medical records in accordance with paragraph (b) of this section.

(2) Requests on a minor's behalf; notification of or access to medical records to an individual on a minor's behalf.

(i) To protect the privacy of a minor, we will not give to a parent or guardian direct notification of or access to a minor's record, even though the parent or guardian who requests such notification or access is authorized to act on a minor's behalf as provided in § 401.75 of this part.

(ii) A parent or guardian must make all requests for notification of or access to a minor's medical record in accordance with this paragraph and the procedures in §§ 401.45 through 401.50 of this part. A parent or guardian must at the time he or she makes a request designate a family physician or other health professional (other than a family member) to whom the record, if any, will be sent. If the parent or guardian will not designate a representative, we will decline to release the requested information.

(iii) Where a medical record on the minor exists, we will in all cases send it to the physician or health professional designated by the parent or guardian. The representative will review the record, discuss its contents with the parent or legal guardian, then release the entire record to the parent or legal guardian. The representative does not have the discretion to withhold any part of the minor's record. We will respond in the following similar manner to the parent or guardian making the request: "We have completed processing your request for notification of or access to ______'s (Name of minor) medical records. Please be informed that if any medical record was found pertaining to that individual, it has been sent to your designated physician or health professional."

(iv) In each case where we send a minor's medical record to a physician or health professional, we will make reasonable efforts to inform the minor that we have given the record to the representative.

(3) Requests on behalf of an incapacitated adult. If you are the legal guardian of an adult who has been declared legally incompetent, you may receive his or her records directly.

[72 FR 20939, April 27, 2007]

§ 401.60 Access to or notification of program records about more than one individual.

When information about more than one individual is in one record filed under your social security number, you may receive the information about you and the fact of entitlement and the amount of benefits payable to other persons based on your record. You may receive information about yourself or others, which is filed under someone else's social security number, if that information affects your entitlement to social security benefits or the amount of those benefits.

[72 FR 20940, April 27, 2007]

§ 401.65 How to correct your record.

(a) How to request a correction. This section applies to all records kept by SSA (as described in § 401.5) except for records of earnings. (20 CFR 422.125 describes how to request correction of your earnings record.) You may request that your record be corrected or amended if you believe that the record is not accurate, timely, complete, relevant, or necessary to the administration of a social security program. To amend or correct your record, you should write to the manager identified in the notice of systems of records which is published in the Federal Register (see § 401.40(c) on how to locate this information). The staff at any social security office can help you prepare the request. You should submit any available evidence to support your request. Your request should indicate—

(1) The system of records from which the record is retrieved;

(2) The particular record which you want to correct or amend;

(3) Whether you want to add, delete or substitute information in the record; and

(4) Your reasons for believing that your record should be corrected or amended.

(b) What we will not change. You cannot use the correction process to alter, delete, or amend information which is part of a determination of fact or which is evidence received in the record of a claim in the administrative appeal process. Disagreements with these determinations are to be resolved through the SSA appeal process. (See subparts I and J of part 404, and subpart N of part 416, of this chapter.) For example, you cannot use the correction process to alter or delete a document showing a birth date used in deciding your social security claim. However, you may submit a statement on why you think certain information should be altered, deleted, or amended, and we will make this statement part of your file.

(c) Acknowledgment of correction request. We will acknowledge receipt of a correction request within 10 working days, unless we can review and process the request and give an initial determination of denial or compliance before that time.

(d) Notice of error. If the record is wrong, we will correct it promptly. If wrong information was disclosed from the record, we will tell all those of whom we are aware received that information that it was wrong and will give them the correct information. This will not be necessary if the change is not due to an error, e.g., a change of name or address.

(e) Record found to be correct. If the record is correct, we will inform you in writing of the reason why we refuse to amend your record and we will also inform you of your right to seek a review of the refusal and the name and address of the official to whom you should send your request for review.

(f) Record of another government agency. If you request us to correct or amend a record governed by the regulation of another government agency, e.g., Office of Personnel Management, Federal Bureau of Investigation, we will forward your request to such government agency for processing and we will inform you in writing of the referral.

§ 401.70 Appeals of refusals to correct records or refusals to allow access to records.

(a) General. This section describes how to appeal decisions made by SSA under the Privacy Act concerning your request for correction of or access to your records, those of your minor child, or those of a person for whom you are the legal guardian. We generally handle a denial of your request for information about another person under the provisions of the Freedom of Information Act (see part 402 of this chapter). To appeal a decision under this section, your request must be in writing.

(b) Appeal of refusal to correct or amend records. If we deny your request to correct an SSA record, you may request a review of that decision. As discussed in § 401.65(e), our letter denying your request will tell you to whom to write.

(1) We will review your request within 30 working days from the date of the receipt. However, for a good reason and with the approval of the Executive Director for the Office of Public Disclosure, this time limit may be extended up to an additional 30 days. In that case, we will notify you about the delay, the reason for it and the date when the review is expected to be completed.

(2) If, after review, we determine that the record should be corrected, we will do so. However, if we refuse to amend the record as you requested, we will inform you that—

(i) Your request has been refused and the reason for refusing;

(ii) The refusal is SSA's final decision; and

(iii) You have a right to seek court review of SSA's final decision.

(3) We will also inform you that you have a right to file a statement of disagreement with the decision. Your statement should include the reason you disagree. We will make your statement available to anyone to whom the record is subsequently disclosed, together with a statement of our reasons for refusing to amend the record. Also, we will provide a copy of your statement to individuals whom we are aware received the record previously.

(c) Appeals after denial of access. If, under the Privacy Act, we deny your request for access to your own record, those of your minor child or those of a person to whom you are the legal guardian, we will advise you in writing of the reason for that denial, the name and title or position of the person responsible for the decision and your right to appeal that decision. You may appeal the denial decision to the Executive Director for the Office of Public Disclosure, 6401 Security Boulevard, Baltimore, MD 21235–6401, within 30 days after you receive notice denying all or part of your request, or, if later, within 30 days after you receive materials sent to you in partial compliance with your request.

(d) Filing your appeal. If you file an appeal, the Executive Director or his or her designee will review your request and any supporting information submitted and then send you a notice explaining the decision on your appeal. The time limit for making our decision after we receive your appeal is 30 working days. The Executive Director or his or her designee may extend this time limit up to 30 additional working days if one of the circumstances in 20 CFR 402.140 is met. We will notify you in writing of any extension, the reason for the extension and the date by which we will decide your appeal. The notice of the decision on your appeal will explain your right to have the matter reviewed in a Federal district court if you disagree with all or part of our decision.

[72 FR 20940, April 27, 2007]

§ 401.75 Rights of parents or legal guardians.

For purposes of this part, a parent or guardian of any minor or the legal guardian of any individual who has been declared incompetent due to physical or mental incapacity or age by a court of competent jurisdiction is authorized to act on behalf of a minor or incompetent individual. Except as provided in § 401.45, governing procedures for verifying an individual's identity, and § 401.55(c) governing special procedures for notification of or access to a minor's medical records, if you are authorized to act on behalf of a minor or legal incompetent, you will be viewed as if you were the individual or subject individual.

§ 401.80 Accounting for disclosures.

(a) We will maintain an accounting of all disclosures of a record for five years or for the life of the record, whichever is longer; except that, we will not make accounting for:

(1) Disclosures under paragraphs (a) and (b) of § 401.110; and,

(2) Disclosures of your record made with your written consent.

(b) The accounting will include:

(1) The date, nature, and purpose of each disclosure; and

(2) The name and address of the person or entity to whom the disclosure is made.

(c) You may request access to an accounting of disclosures of your record. You must request access to an accounting in accordance with the procedures in § 401.40. You will be granted access to an accounting of the disclosures of your record in accordance with the procedures of this part which govern access to the related record. We may, at our discretion, grant access to an accounting of a disclosure of a record made under paragraph (g) of § 401.110.

§ 401.85 Exempt systems.

(a) General policy. The Privacy Act permits certain types of specific systems of records to be exempt from some of its requirements. Our policy is to exercise authority to exempt systems of records only in compelling cases.

(b) Specific systems of records exempted.

(1) Those systems of records listed in paragraph (b)(2) of this section are exempt from the following provisions of the Act and this part:

(i) 5 U.S.C. 552a(c)(3) and paragraph (c) of § 401.80 of this part which require that you be granted access to an accounting of disclosures of your record.

(ii) 5 U.S.C. 552a(d)(1) through (4) and (f) and §§ 401.35 through 401.75 relating to notification of or access to records and correction or amendment of records.

(iii) 5 U.S.C. 552a(e)(4)(G) and (H) which require that we include information about SSA procedures for notification, access, and correction or amendment of records in the notice for the systems of records.

(iv) 5 U.S.C. 552a(e)(3) and § 401.30 which require that if we ask you to provide a record to us, we must inform you of the authority for our asking you to provide the record (including whether providing the record is mandatory or voluntary, the principal purposes for maintaining the record, the routine uses for the record, and what effect your refusal to provide the record may have on you), and if you are not required by statute or Executive Order to provide the record, that you agree to provide the record. This exemption applies only to an investigatory record compiled by SSA for criminal law enforcement purposes in a system of records exempt under subsection (j)(2) of the Privacy Act to the extent that these requirements would prejudice the conduct of the investigation.

(2) The following systems of records are exempt from those provisions of the Privacy Act and this part listed in paragraph (b)(1) of this section:

(i) Pursuant to subsection (j)(2) of the Privacy Act, the Investigatory Material Compiled for Law Enforcement Purposes System, SSA.

(ii) Pursuant to subsection (k)(2) of the Privacy Act:

(A) The General Criminal Investigation Files, SSA;

(B) The Criminal Investigations File, SSA; and,

(C) The Program Integrity Case Files, SSA.

(D) Civil and Administrative Investigative Files of the Inspector General, SSA/OIG.

(E) Complaint Files and Log. SSA/OGC.

(F) Anti–Harassment & Hostile Work Environment Case Tracking and Records System, SSA.

(G) Social Security Administration Violence Evaluation and Reporting System, SSA.

(iii) Pursuant to subsection (k)(5) of the Privacy Act:

(A) The Investigatory Material Compiled for Security and Suitability Purposes System, SSA; and,

(B) The Suitability for Employment Records, SSA.

(iv) Pursuant to subsection (k)(6) of the Privacy Act, the Personnel Research and Merit Promotion Test Records, SSA/DCHR/OPE.

(c) Notification of or access to records in exempt systems of records.

(1) Where a system of records is exempt as provided in paragraph (b) of this section, you may nonetheless request notification of or access to a record in that system. You should make requests for notification of

or access to a record in an exempt system of records in accordance with the procedures of §§ 401.35 through 401.55.

(2) We will grant you notification of or access to a record in an exempt system but only to the extent such notification or access would not reveal the identity of a source who furnished the record to us under an express promise, and prior to September 27, 1975, an implied promise, that his or her identity would be held in confidence, if:

(i) The record is in a system of records which is exempt under subsection (k)(2) of the Privacy Act and you have been, as a result of the maintenance of the record, denied a right, privilege, or benefit to which you would otherwise be eligible; or,

(ii) The record is in a system of records which is exempt under subsection (k)(5) of the Privacy Act.

(3) If we do not grant you notification of or access to a record in a system of records exempt under subsections (k)(2) and (5) of the Privacy Act in accordance with this paragraph, we will inform you that the identity of a confidential source would be revealed if we granted you notification of or access to the record.

(d) Discretionary actions by SSA. Unless disclosure of a record to the general public is otherwise prohibited by law, we may at our discretion grant notification of or access to a record in a system of records which is exempt under paragraph (b) of this section. Discretionary notification of or access to a record in accordance with this paragraph will not be a precedent for discretionary notification of or access to a similar or related record and will not obligate us to exercise discretion to grant notification of or access to any other record in a system of records which is exempt under paragraph (b) of this section.

[82 FR 16510, April 5, 2017; 83 FR 63416, Dec. 10, 2018]

§ 401.90 Contractors.

(a) All contracts which require a contractor to maintain, or on behalf of SSA to maintain, a system of records to accomplish an SSA function must contain a provision requiring the contractor to comply with the Privacy Act and this part.

(b) A contractor and any employee of such contractor will be considered employees of SSA only for the purposes of the criminal penalties of the Privacy Act, 5 U.S.C. 552a(i), and the employee standards of conduct (see appendix A of this part) where the contract contains a provision requiring the contractor to comply with the Privacy Act and this part.

(c) This section does not apply to systems of records maintained by a contractor as a result of his management discretion, e.g., the contractor's personnel records.

§ 401.95 Fees.

(a) Policy. Where applicable, we will charge fees for copying records in accordance with the schedule set forth in this section. We may only charge fees where you request that a copy be made of the record to which you are granted access. We will not charge a fee for searching a system of records, whether the search is manual, mechanical, or electronic. Where we must copy the record in order to provide access to the record (e.g., computer printout where no screen reading is available), we will provide the copy to you without cost. Where we make a medical record available to a representative designated by you or to a physician or health professional designated by a parent or guardian under § 401.55 of this part, we will not charge a fee.

(b) Fee schedule. Our Privacy Act fee schedule is as follows:

(1) Copying of records susceptible to photocopying—$.10 per page.

(2) Copying records not susceptible to photocopying (e.g., punch cards or magnetic tapes)—at actual cost to be determined on a case-by-case basis.

(3) We will not charge if the total amount of copying does not exceed $25.

(c) Other fees. We also follow §§ 402.155 through 402.165 of this chapter to determine the amount of fees, if any, we will charge for providing information under the FOIA and Privacy Act.

SUBPART C—DISCLOSURE OF OFFICIAL RECORDS AND INFORMATION

§ 401.100 Disclosure of records with the written consent of the subject of the record.

(a) General. Except as permitted by the Privacy Act and the regulations in this part, or when required by the FOIA, we will not disclose your records without your written consent.

(b) Disclosure with written consent. The written consent must clearly specify to whom the information may be disclosed, the information you want us to disclose (e.g., social security number, date and place of birth, monthly Social Security benefit amount, date of entitlement), and, where applicable, during which timeframe the information may be disclosed (e.g., during the school year, while the subject individual is out of the country, whenever the subject individual is receiving specific services).

(c) Disclosure of the entire record. We will not disclose your entire record. For example, we will not honor a blanket consent for all information in a system of records or any other record consisting of a variety of data elements. We will disclose only the information you specify in the consent. We will verify your identity and where applicable (e.g., where you consent to disclosure of a record to a specific individual), the identity of the individual to whom the record is to be disclosed.

(d) A parent or guardian of a minor is not authorized to give written consent to a disclosure of a minor's medical record. See § 401.55(c)(2) for the procedures for disclosure of or access to medical records of minors.

[72 FR 20940, April 27, 2007]

§ 401.105 Disclosure of personal information without the consent of the subject of the record.

(a) SSA maintains two categories of records which contain personal information:

(1) Nonprogram records, primarily administrative and personnel records which contain information about SSA's activities as a government agency and employer, and

(2) Program records which contain information about SSA's clients that it keeps to administer benefit programs under Federal law.

(b) We apply different levels of confidentiality to disclosures of information in the categories in paragraphs (a)(1) and (2) of this section. For administrative and personnel records, the Privacy Act applies. To the extent that SSA has physical custody of personnel records maintained as part of the Office of Personnel Management's (OPM) Privacy Act government-wide systems of records, these records are subject to OPM's rules on access and disclosure at 5 CFR parts 293 and 297. For program records, we apply somewhat more strict confidentiality standards than those found in the Privacy Act. The reason for this difference in treatment is that our program records include information about a much greater number of persons than our administrative records, the information we must collect for program purposes is often very sensitive, and claimants are required by statute and regulation to provide us with the information in order to establish entitlement for benefits.

[72 FR 20940, April 27, 2007]

§ 401.110 Disclosure of personal information in nonprogram records without the consent of the subject of the record.

The disclosures listed in this section may be made from our nonprogram records, e.g., administrative and personnel records, without your consent. Such disclosures are those:

(a) To officers and employees of SSA who have a need for the record in the performance of their duties. The SSA official who is responsible for the record may upon request of any officer or employee, or on his own initiative, determine what constitutes legitimate need.

(b) Required to be disclosed under the Freedom of Information Act, 5 U.S.C. 552, and 20 CFR part 402.

(c) For a routine use as defined in § 401.25 of this part. Routine uses will be listed in any notice of a system of records. SSA publishes notices of systems of records, including all pertinent routine uses, in the Federal Register.

(d) To the Bureau of the Census for purposes of planning or carrying out a census or survey or related activity pursuant to the provisions of Title 13 U.S.C.

(e) To a recipient who has provided us with advance written assurance that the record will be used solely as a statistical research or reporting record; Provided, that, the record is transferred in a form that does not identify the subject individual.

(f) To the National Archives of the United States as a record which has sufficient historical or other value to warrant its continued preservation by the United States Government, or for evaluation by the Administrator of General Services or his designee to determine whether the record has such value.

(g) To another government agency or to an instrumentality of any governmental jurisdiction within or under the control of the United States for a civil or criminal law enforcement activity if the activity is authorized by law, and if the head of such government agency or instrumentality has submitted a written request to us, specifying the record desired and the law enforcement activity for which the record is sought.

(h) To an individual pursuant to a showing of compelling circumstances affecting the health or safety of any individual if a notice of the disclosure is transmitted to the last known address of the subject individual.

(i) To either House of Congress, or to the extent of matter within its jurisdiction, any committee or subcommittee thereof, any joint committee of Congress or subcommittee of any such joint committee.

(j) To the Comptroller General, or any of his authorized representatives, in the course of the performance of duties of the Government Accountability Office.

(k) Pursuant to the order of a court of competent jurisdiction.

[72 FR 20940, April 27, 2007]

§ 401.115 Disclosure of personal information in program records without the consent of the subject of the record.

This section describes how various laws control the disclosure of personal information that we keep. We disclose information in the program records only when a legitimate need exists. For example, we disclose information to officers and employees of SSA who have a need for the record in the performance of their duties. We also must consider the laws identified below in the respective order when we disclose program information:

(a) Some laws require us to disclose information (§ 401.120); some laws require us to withhold information (§ 401.125). These laws control whenever they apply.

(b) If no law of this type applies in a given case, then we must look to FOIA principles. See § 401.130.

(c) When FOIA principles do not require disclosure, we may disclose information if both the Privacy Act and section 1106 of the Social Security Act permit the disclosure.

[72 FR 20940, April 27, 2007]

§ 401.120 Disclosures required by law.

We disclose information when a law specifically requires it. The Social Security Act requires us to disclose information for certain program purposes. These include disclosures to the SSA Office of Inspector General, the Federal Parent Locator Service, and to States pursuant to an arrangement regarding use of the Blood Donor Locator Service. Also, there are other laws which require that we furnish other agencies information which they need for their programs. These agencies include the Department of Veterans Affairs for its benefit programs, U.S. Citizenship and Immigration Services to carry out its duties regarding aliens, the Railroad Retirement Board for its benefit programs, and to Federal, State and local agencies administering Temporary Assistance for Needy Families, Medicaid, unemployment compensation, food stamps, and other programs.

[72 FR 20941, April 27, 2007]

§ 401.125 Disclosures prohibited by law.

We do not disclose information when a law specifically prohibits it. The Internal Revenue Code generally prohibits us from disclosing tax return information which we receive to maintain individual earnings records. This includes, for example, amounts of wages and contributions from employers. Other laws restrict our disclosure of certain information about drug and alcohol abuse which we collect to determine eligibility for social security benefits.

§ 401.130 Freedom of Information Act.

The FOIA requires us to disclose any information in our records upon request from the public, unless one of several exemptions in the FOIA applies. When the FOIA requires disclosure (see part 402 of this chapter), the Privacy Act permits it. The public does not include Federal agencies, courts, or the Congress, but does include State agencies, individuals, corporations, and most other parties. The FOIA does not apply to requests that are not from the public (e.g., from a Federal agency). However, we apply FOIA principles to requests from these other sources for disclosure of program information.

§ 401.135 Other laws.

When the FOIA does not apply, we may not disclose any personal information unless both the Privacy Act and section 1106 of the Social Security Act permit the disclosure. Section 1106 of the Social Security Act requires that disclosures which may be made must be set out in statute or regulations; therefore, any disclosure permitted by this part is permitted by section 1106.

§ 401.140 General principles.

When no law specifically requiring or prohibiting disclosure applies to a question of whether to disclose information, we follow FOIA principles to resolve that question. We do this to insure uniform treatment in all situations. The FOIA principle which most often applies to SSA disclosure questions is whether the disclosure would result in a "clearly unwarranted invasion of personal privacy." To decide whether a disclosure would be a clearly unwarranted invasion of personal privacy we consider—

(a) The sensitivity of the information (e.g., whether individuals would suffer harm or embarrassment as a result of the disclosure);

(b) The public interest in the disclosure;

(c) The rights and expectations of individuals to have their personal information kept confidential;

(d) The public's interest in maintaining general standards of confidentiality of personal information; and

(e) The existence of safeguards against unauthorized redisclosure or use.

§ 401.145 Safeguards against unauthorized redisclosure or use.

(a) The FOIA does not authorize us to impose any restrictions on how information is used after we disclose it under that law. In applying FOIA principles, we consider whether the information will be adequately safeguarded against improper use or redisclosure. We must consider all the ways in which the recipient might use the information and how likely the recipient is to redisclose the information to other parties. Thus, before we disclose personal information we may consider such factors as—

(1) Whether only those individuals who have a need to know the information will obtain it;

(2) Whether appropriate measures to safeguard the information to avoid unwarranted use or misuse will be taken; and

(3) Whether we would be permitted to conduct onsite inspections to see whether the safeguards are being met.

(b) We feel that there is a strong public interest in sharing information with other agencies with programs having the same or similar purposes, so we generally share information with those agencies. However, since there is usually little or no public interest in disclosing information for disputes between two private parties or for other private or commercial purposes, we generally do not share information for these purposes.

§ 401.150 Compatible purposes.

(a) General. The Privacy Act allows us to disclose information maintained in a system of records without your consent to any other party if such disclosure is pursuant to a routine use published in the system's notice of system of records. A "Routine use" must be compatible with the purpose for which SSA collected the information.

(b) Notice of routine use disclosures. A list of permissible routine use disclosures is included in every system of records notice published in the Federal Register.

(c) Determining compatibility—

(1) Disclosure to carry out SSA programs. We disclose information for published routine uses necessary to carry out SSA's programs.

(2) Disclosure to carry out programs similar to SSA programs. We may disclose information for the administration of other government programs. These disclosures are pursuant to published routine uses where the use is compatible with the purpose for which the information was collected. These programs generally meet the following conditions:

(i) The program is clearly identifiable as a Federal, State, or local government program.

(ii) The information requested concerns eligibility, benefit amounts, or other matters of benefit status in a Social Security program and is relevant to determining the same matters in the other program. For example, we disclose information to the Railroad Retirement Board for pension and unemployment compensation programs, to the Department of Veterans Affairs for its benefit programs, to worker's compensation programs, to State general assistance programs and to other income maintenance programs at all levels of government. We also disclose for health maintenance programs like Medicaid and Medicare.

(iii) The information will be used for appropriate epidemiological or similar research purposes.

[72 FR 20941, April 27, 2007]

§ 401.155 Law enforcement purposes.

(a) General. The Privacy Act allows us to disclose information for law enforcement purposes under certain conditions. Much of the information in our files is especially sensitive or very personal. Furthermore, participation in social security programs is mandatory, so people cannot limit what information is given to us. Therefore, we generally disclose information for law enforcement purposes only in limited situations. The Privacy Act allows us to disclose information if the head of the law enforcement agency makes a written request giving enough information to show that the conditions in paragraphs (b) or (c) of this section are met, what information is needed, and why it is needed. Paragraphs (b) and (c) of this section discuss the disclosures we generally make for these purposes.

(b) Serious crimes. SSA may disclose information for criminal law enforcement purposes where a violent crime such as murder or kidnapping has been committed and the individual about whom the information is being sought has been indicted or convicted of that crime.

(c) Criminal activity involving the social security program or another program with the same purposes. We disclose information when necessary to investigate or prosecute fraud or other criminal activity involving the social security program. We may also disclose information for investigation or prosecution of criminal activity in other income-maintenance or health-maintenance programs (e.g., other governmental pension programs, unemployment compensation, general assistance, Medicare or Medicaid) if the information concerns eligibility, benefit amounts, or other matters of benefit status in a social security program and is relevant to determining the same matters in the other program.

[72 FR 20941, April 27, 2007]

§ 401.160 Health or safety.

The Privacy Act allows us to disclose information in compelling circumstances where an individual's health or safety is affected. For example, if we learn that someone has been exposed to an excessive amount of radiation, we may notify that person and appropriate health officials. If we learn that someone has made a threat against someone else, we may notify that other person and law enforcement officials. When we make these disclosures, the Privacy Act requires us to send a notice of the disclosure to the last known address of the person whose record was disclosed.

§ 401.165 Statistical and research activities.

(a) General. Statistical and research activities often do not require information in a format that identifies specific individuals. Therefore, whenever possible, we release information for statistical or research purposes only in the form of aggregates or individual data that cannot be associated with a particular individual. The Privacy Act allows us to release records if there are safeguards that the record will be used solely as a statistical or research record and the individual cannot be identified from any information in the record.

(b) Safeguards for disclosure with identifiers. The Privacy Act also allows us to disclose data for statistical and research purposes in a form allowing individual identification, pursuant to published routine use, when the purpose is compatible with the purpose for which the record was collected. We will disclose personally identifiable information for statistical and research purposes if—

(1) We determine that the requestor needs the information in an identifiable form for a statistical or research activity, will use the information only for that purpose, and will protect individuals from unreasonable and unwanted contacts;

(2) The activity is designed to increase knowledge about present or alternative Social Security programs or other Federal or State income-maintenance or health-maintenance programs; or is used for research that is of importance to the Social Security program or the Social Security beneficiaries; or an epidemiological research project that relates to the Social Security program or beneficiaries; and

(3) The recipient will keep the information as a system of statistical records, will follow appropriate safeguards, and agrees to our on-site inspection of those safeguards so we can be sure the information is used or redisclosed only for statistical or research purposes. No redisclosure of the information may be made without SSA's approval.

(c) Statistical record. A statistical record is a record in a system of records which is maintained only for statistical and research purposes, and which is not used to make any determination about an individual. We maintain and use statistical records only for statistical and research purposes. We may disclose a statistical record if the conditions in paragraph (b) of this section are met.

(d) Compiling of records. Where a request for information for statistical and research purposes would require us to compile records, and doing that would be administratively burdensome to ongoing SSA operations, we may decline to furnish the information.

[72 FR 20941, April 27, 2007]

§ 401.170 Congress.

(a) We disclose information to either House of Congress. We also disclose information to any committee or subcommittee of either House, or to any joint committee of Congress or subcommittee of that committee, if the information is on a matter within the committee's or subcommittee's jurisdiction.

(b) We disclose to any member of Congress the information needed to respond to constituents' requests for information about themselves (including requests from parents of minors, or legal guardians). However, these disclosures are subject to the restrictions in §§ 401.35 through 401.60.

§ 401.175 Government Accountability Office.

We disclose information to the Government Accountability Office when that agency needs the information to carry out its duties.

[72 FR 20941, April 27, 2007]

§ 401.180 Disclosure under court order or other legal process.

(a) General. The Privacy Act permits us to disclose information when we are ordered to do so by a court of competent jurisdiction. When information is used in a court proceeding, it usually becomes part of the public record of the proceeding and its confidentiality often cannot be protected in that record. Much of the information that we collect and maintain in our records on individuals is especially sensitive. Therefore, we follow the rules in paragraph (d) of this section in deciding whether we may disclose information in response to an order from a court of competent jurisdiction. When we disclose pursuant to an order from a court of competent jurisdiction, and the order is a matter of public record, the Privacy Act requires us to send a notice of the disclosure to the last known address of the person whose record was disclosed.

(b) Court. For purposes of this section, a court is an institution of the judicial branch of the U.S. Federal government consisting of one or more judges who seek to adjudicate disputes and administer justice. (See 404.2(c)(6) of this chapter). Entities not in the judicial branch of the Federal government are not courts for purposes of this section.

(c) Court order. For purposes of this section, a court order is any legal process which satisfies all of the following conditions:

(1) It is issued under the authority of a Federal court;

(2) A judge or a magistrate judge of that court signs it;

(3) It commands SSA to disclose information; and

(4) The court is a court of competent jurisdiction.

(d) Court of competent jurisdiction. It is the view of SSA that under the Privacy Act the Federal Government has not waived sovereign immunity, which precludes state court jurisdiction over a Federal agency or official. Therefore, SSA will not honor state court orders as a basis for disclosure. State court orders will be treated in accordance with the other provisions of this part.

(e) Conditions for disclosure under a court order of competent jurisdiction. We disclose information in compliance with an order of a court of competent jurisdiction if—

(1) another section of this part specifically allows such disclosure, or

(2) SSA, the Commissioner of Social Security, or any officer or employee of SSA in his or her official capacity is properly a party in the proceeding, or

(3) disclosure of the information is necessary to ensure that an individual who is accused of criminal activity receives due process of law in a criminal

proceeding under the jurisdiction of the judicial branch of the Federal government.

(f) In other circumstances. We may disclose information to a court of competent jurisdiction in circumstances other than those stated in paragraph (e) of this section. We will make our decision regarding disclosure by balancing the needs of a court while preserving the confidentiality of information. For example, we may disclose information under a court order that restricts the use and redisclosure of the information by the participants in the proceeding; we may offer the information for inspection by the court in camera and under seal; or we may arrange for the court to exclude information identifying individuals from that portion of the record of the proceedings that is available to the public. We will make these determinations in accordance with § 401.140.

(g) Other regulations on request for testimony, subpoenas and production of records in legal proceedings. See 20 CFR part 403 of this chapter for additional rules covering disclosure of information and records governed by this part and requested in connection with legal proceedings.

[66 FR 2809, Jan. 12, 2001; 66 FR 9763, Feb. 12, 2001; 72 FR 20941, April 27, 2007]

§ 401.185 Other specific recipients.

In addition to disclosures we make under the routine use provision, we also release information to—

(a) The Bureau of the Census for purposes of planning or carrying out a census, survey, or related activity; and

(b) The National Archives of the United States if the record has sufficient historical or other value to warrant its continued preservation by the United States Government. We also disclose a record to the Administrator of General Services for a determination of whether the record has such a value.

§ 401.190 Deceased persons.

We do not consider the disclosure of information about a deceased person to be a clearly unwarranted invasion of that person's privacy. However, in disclosing information about a deceased person, we follow the principles in § 401.115 to insure that the privacy rights of a living person are not violated.

§ 401.195 Situations not specified in this part.

If no other provision in this part specifically allows SSA to disclose information, the Commissioner or designee may disclose this information if not prohibited by Federal law. For example, the Commissioner or designee may disclose information necessary to respond to life threatening situations.

§ 401.200 Blood donor locator service.

(a) General. We will enter into arrangements with State agencies under which we will furnish to them at their request the last known personal mailing addresses (residence or post office box) of blood donors whose blood donations show that they are or may be infected with the human immunodeficiency virus which causes acquired immune deficiency syndrome. The State agency or other authorized person, as defined in paragraph (b) of this section, will then inform the donors that they may need medical care and treatment. The safeguards that must be used by authorized persons as a condition to receiving address information from the Blood Donor Locator Service are in paragraph (g) of this section, and the requirements for a request for address information are in paragraph (d) of this section.

(b) Definitions. State means the 50 States, the District of Columbia, the Commonwealth of Puerto Rico, the Virgin Islands, Guam, the Commonwealth of Northern Marianas, and the Trust Territory of the Pacific Islands.

Authorized person means—

(1) Any agency of a State (or of a political subdivision of a State) which has duties or authority under State law relating to the public health or otherwise has the duty or authority under State law to regulate blood donations; and

(2) Any entity engaged in the acceptance of blood donations which is licensed or registered by the Food and Drug Administration in connection with the acceptance of such blood donations, and which provides for—

(i) The confidentiality of any address information received pursuant to the rules in this part and section 1141 of the Social Security Act and related blood donor records;

(ii) Blood donor notification procedures for individuals with respect to whom such information is requested and a finding has been made that they are or may be infected with the human immunodeficiency virus; and

(iii) Counseling services for such individuals who have been found to have such virus. New counseling programs are not required, and an entity may use existing counseling programs or referrals to provide these services.

Related blood donor records means any record, list, or compilation established in connection with a request for address information which indicates, directly or indirectly, the identity of any individual with respect to whom a request for address information has been made pursuant to the rules in this part.

(c) Use of social security number for identification. A State or an authorized person in the State may require a blood donor to furnish his or her social security number when donating blood. The number may then be used by an authorized person to identify and locate a donor whose blood donation indicates that he or she is or may be infected with the human immunodeficiency virus.

(d) Request for address of blood donor. An authorized person who has been unable to locate a blood donor at the address he or she may have given at the time of the blood donation may request assistance from the State agency which has arranged with us to participate in the Blood Donor Locator Service. The request to the Blood Donor Locator Service must—

(1) Be in writing;

(2) Be from a participating State agency either on its own behalf as an authorized person or on behalf of another authorized person;

(3) Indicate that the authorized person meets the confidentiality safeguards of paragraph (g) of this section; and

(4) Include the donor's name and social security number, the addresses at which the authorized person attempted without success to contact the donor, the date of the blood donation if available, a statement that the donor has tested positive for the human immunodeficiency virus according to the latest Food and Drug Administration standards or that the history of the subsequent use of the donated blood or blood products indicates that the donor has or may have the human immunodeficiency virus, and the name and address of the requesting blood donation facility.

(e) SSA response to request for address. After receiving a request that meets the requirements of paragraph (d) of this section, we will search our records for the donor's latest personal mailing address. If we do not find a current address, we will request that the Internal Revenue Service search its tax records and furnish us any personal mailing address information from its files, as required under section 6103(m)(6) of the Internal Revenue Code. After completing these searches, we will provide to the requesting State agency either the latest mailing address available for the donor or a response stating that we do not have this information. We will then destroy the records or delete all identifying donor information related to the request and maintain only the information that we will need to monitor the compliance of authorized persons with the confidentiality safeguards contained in paragraph (g) of this section.

(f) SSA refusal to furnish address. If we determine that an authorized person has not met the requirements of paragraphs (d) and (g) of this section, we will not furnish address information to the State agency. In that case, we will notify the State agency of our determination, explain the reasons for our determination, and explain that the State agency may request administrative review of our determination. The Commissioner of Social Security or a delegate of the Commissioner will conduct this review. The review will be based on the information of record and there will not be an opportunity for an oral hearing. A request for administrative review, which may be submitted only by a State agency, must be in writing. The State agency must send its request for administrative review to the Commissioner of Social Security, 6401 Security Boulevard, Baltimore, MD 21235, within 60 days after receiving our notice refusing to give the donor's address. The request for review must include supporting information or evidence that the requirements of the rules in this part have been met. If we do not furnish address information because an authorized person failed to comply with the confidentiality safeguards of paragraph (g) of this section, the State agency will have an opportunity to submit evidence that the authorized person is now in compliance. If we then determine, based on our review of the request for administrative review and the supporting evidence, that the authorized person meets the requirements of the rules in this part, we will respond to the address request as provided in paragraph (e) of this section. If we determine on administrative review that the requirements have not been met, we will notify the State agency in writing of our decision. We will make our determination within 30 days after receiving the request for administrative review, unless we notify the State agency within this 30–day time period that we will need additional time. Our determination on the request for administrative review will give the findings of fact, the reasons for the decision, and what actions the State agency should take to ensure that it or the blood donation facility is in compliance with the rules in this part.

(g) Safeguards to ensure confidentiality of blood donor records. We will require assurance that authorized persons have established and continue to maintain adequate safeguards to protect the confidentiality of both address information received from the Blood Donor Locator Service and related blood donor records. The authorized person must, to the satisfaction of the Secretary—

(1) Establish and maintain a system for standardizing records which includes the reasons for requesting the addresses of blood donors, dates of the requests, and any disclosures of address information;

(2) Store blood donors' addresses received from the Blood Donor Locator Service and all related blood donor records in a secure area or place that is physically safe from access by persons other than those whose duties and responsibilities require access;

(3) Restrict access to these records to authorized employees and officials who need them to perform their official duties related to notifying blood donors who are or may be infected with the human immunodeficiency virus that they may need medical care and treatment;

(4) Advise all personnel who will have access to the records of the confidential nature of the information, the safeguards required to protect the information, and

the civil and criminal sanctions for unauthorized use or disclosure of the information;

(5) Destroy the address information received from the Blood Donor Locator Service, as well as any records established in connection with the request which indicate directly or indirectly the identity of the individual, after notifying or attempting to notify the donor at the address obtained from the Blood Donor Locator Service; and

(6) Upon request, report to us the procedures established and utilized to ensure the confidentiality of address information and related blood donor records. We reserve the right to make onsite inspections to ensure that these procedures are adequate and are being followed and to request such information as we may need to ensure that the safeguards required in this section are being met.

(h) Unauthorized disclosure. Any official or employee of the Federal Government, a State, or a blood donation facility who discloses blood donor information, except as provided for in this section or under a provision of law, will be subject to the same criminal penalty as provided in section 7213(a) of the Internal Revenue Code of 1986 for the unauthorized disclosure of tax information.

APPENDIX A TO PART 401—EMPLOYEE STANDARDS OF CONDUCT

(a) General. All SSA employees are required to be aware of their responsibilities under the Privacy Act of 1974, 5 U.S.C. 552a. Regulations implementing the Privacy Act are set forth in this part. Instruction on the requirements of the Act and regulation shall be provided to all new employees of SSA. In addition, supervisors shall be responsible for assuring that employees who are working with systems of records or who undertake new duties which require the use of systems of records are informed of their responsibilities. Supervisors shall also be responsible for assuring that all employees who work with such systems of records are periodically reminded of the requirements of the Privacy Act and are advised of any new provisions or interpretations of the Act.

(b) Penalties. (1) All employees must guard against improper disclosure of records which are governed by the Privacy Act. Because of the serious consequences of improper invasions of personal privacy, employees may be subject to disciplinary action and criminal prosecution for knowing and willful violations of the Privacy Act and regulation. In addition, employees may also be subject to disciplinary action for unknowing or unwillful violations, where the employee had notice of the provisions of the Privacy Act and regulations and failed to inform himself or herself sufficiently or to conduct himself or herself in accordance with the requirements to avoid violations.

(2) SSA may be subjected to civil liability for the following actions undertaken by its employees:

(a) Making a determination under the Privacy Act and §§ 401.65 and 401.70 not to amend an individual's record in accordance with his or her request, or failing to make such review in conformity with those provisions;

(b) Refusing to comply with an individual's request for notification of or access to a record pertaining to him or her;

(c) Failing to maintain any record pertaining to any individual with such accuracy, relevance, timeliness, and completeness as is necessary to assure fairness in any determination relating to the qualifications, character, rights, or opportunities of, or benefits to the individual that may be made on the basis of such a record, and consequently makes a determination which is adverse to the individual; or

(d) Failing to comply with any other provision of the Act or any rule promulgated thereunder, in such a way as to have an adverse effect on an individual.

(3) An employee may be personally subject to criminal liability as set forth below and in 5 U.S.C. 552a(i):

(a) Willful disclosure. Any officer or employee of SSA, who by virtue of his employment or official position, has possession of, or access to, agency records which contain individually identifiable information the disclosure of which is prohibited by the Privacy Act or by rules or regulations established thereunder, and who, knowing that disclosure of the specific material is so prohibited, willfully discloses the material in any manner to any person or agency not entitled to receive it, shall be guilty of a misdemeanor and may be fined not more than $5,000.

(b) Notice requirements. Any officer or employee of SSA who willfully maintains a system of records without meeting the notice requirements [of the Privacy Act] shall be guilty of a misdemeanor and may be fined not more than $5,000.

(c) Rules governing employees not working with systems of records. Employees whose duties do not involve working with systems of records will not generally disclose to any one, without specific authorization from their supervisors, records pertaining to employees or other individuals which by reason of their official duties are available to them. Notwithstanding the above, the following records concerning Federal employees are a matter of public record and no further authorization is necessary for disclosure:

(1) Name and title of individual.

(2) Grade classification or equivalent and annual rate of salary.

(3) Position description.

(4) [Reserved by 72 FR 69617]

In addition, employees shall disclose records which are listed in SSA's Freedom of Information Regulation as being available to the public. Requests for other records will be referred to the responsible SSA Freedom of Information Officer. This does not preclude employees from discussing matters which are known to them personally, and without resort to a record, to official investigators of Federal agencies for official purposes such as suitability checks, Equal Employment Opportunity investigations, adverse action proceedings, grievance proceedings, etc.

(d) Rules governing employees whose duties require use or reference to systems of records. Employees whose official duties require that they refer to, maintain, service, or otherwise deal with systems of records (hereinafter referred to as "Systems Employees") are governed by the general provisions. In addition, extra precautions are required and systems employees are held to higher standards of conduct.

(1) Systems Employees shall:

(a) Be informed with respect to their responsibilities under the Privacy Act;

(b) Be alert to possible misuses of the system and report to their supervisors any potential or actual use of the system which they believe is not in compliance with the Privacy Act and regulation;

(c) Disclose records within SSA only to an employee who has a legitimate need to know the record in the course of his or her official duties;

(d) Maintain records as accurately as practicable.

(e) Consult with a supervisor prior to taking any action where they are in doubt whether such action is in conformance with the Act and regulation.

(2) Systems employees shall not:

(a) Disclose in any form records from a system of records except (1) with the consent or at the request of the subject individual; or (2) where its disclosure is permitted under § 401.110.

(b) Permit unauthorized individuals to be present in controlled areas. Any unauthorized individuals observed in controlled areas shall be reported to a supervisor or to the guard force.

(c) Knowingly or willfully take action which might subject SSA to civil liability.

(d) Make any arrangements for the design, development, or operation of any system of records without making reasonable effort to provide that the system can be maintained in accordance with the Act and regulation.

(e) Contracting officers. In addition to any applicable provisions set forth above, those employees whose official duties involve entering into contracts on behalf of SSA shall also be governed by the following provisions:

(1) Contracts for design, or development of systems and equipment. The contracting officer shall not enter into any contract for the design or development of a system of records, or for equipment to store, service or maintain a system of records unless the contracting officer has made reasonable effort to ensure that the product to be purchased is capable of being used without violation of the Privacy Act or the regulations in this part. He shall give special attention to provision of physical safeguards.

(2) Contracts for the operation of systems of records. The Contracting Officer, in conjunction with other officials whom he feels appropriate, shall review all proposed contracts providing for the operation of systems of records prior to execution of the contracts to determine whether operation of the system of records is for the purpose of accomplishing a Department function. If it is determined that the operation of the system is to accomplish an SSA function, the contracting officer shall be responsible for including in the contract appropriate provisions to apply the provisions of the Privacy Act and regulation to the system, including prohibitions against improper release by the contractor, his employees, agents, or subcontractors.

(3) Other service contracts. Contracting officers entering into general service contracts shall be responsible for determining the appropriateness of including provisions in the contract to prevent potential misuse (inadvertent or otherwise) by employees, agents, or subcontractors of the contractor.

(f) Rules governing SSA officials responsible for managing systems of records. In addition to the requirements for Systems Employees, SSA officials responsible for managing systems of records as described in § 401.40(c) (system managers) shall:

(1) Respond to all requests for notification of or access, disclosure, or amendment of records in a timely fashion in accordance with the Privacy Act and regulation;

(2) Make any amendment of records accurately and in a timely fashion;

(3) Inform all persons whom the accounting records show have received copies of the record prior to the amendments of the correction; and

(4) Associate any statement of disagreement with the disputed record, and

(a) Transmit a copy of the statement to all persons whom the accounting records show have received a copy of the disputed record, and

(b) Transmit that statement with any future disclosure.

[72 FR 69617, Dec. 10, 2007; 73 FR 25507, May 7, 2008]

PART 402—AVAILABILITY OF INFORMATION AND RECORDS TO THE PUBLIC

Authority: Secs. 205, 702(a)(5), and 1106 of the Social Security Act; (42 U.S.C. 405, 902(a)(5), and 1306); 5 U.S.C. 552 and 552a; 8 U.S.C. 1360; 18 U.S.C. 1905; 26 U.S.C. 6103; 30 U.S.C. 923b; 31 U.S.C. 9701; E.O. 12600, 52 FR 23781; 3 CFR, 1987 Comp., p. 235.

Source: 62 FR 4154, Jan. 29, 1997; 65 FR 16813, March 30, 2000, unless otherwise noted.

§ 402.5 Scope and purpose.

The rules in this part relate to the availability to the public, pursuant to the Freedom of Information Act (FOIA) 5 U.S.C. 552, of records of the Social Security Administration (SSA). They describe how to make a FOIA request; who can release records and who can decide not to release; how much time it should take to make a determination regarding release; what fees may be charged; what records are available for public inspection; why some records are not released; and your right to appeal and then go to court if we refuse to release records. The rules in this part do not revoke, modify, or supersede the regulations of SSA relating to disclosure of information in part 401 of this chapter.

§ 402.10 Policy.

As a general policy, SSA follows a balanced approach in administering FOIA. We not only recognize the right of public access to information in the possession of SSA, but also protect the integrity of internal processes. In addition, we recognize the legitimate interests of organizations or persons who have submitted records to SSA or who would otherwise be affected by release of records. For example, we have no discretion to release certain records, such as trade secrets and confidential commercial information, prohibited from release by law. This policy calls for the fullest responsible disclosure consistent with those requirements of administrative necessity and confidentiality which are recognized in the FOIA.

§ 402.15 Relationship between the FOIA and the Privacy Act of 1974.

(a) Coverage. The FOIA and the rules in this part apply to all SSA records. The Privacy Act, 5 U.S.C. 552a, applies to records that are about individuals, but only if the records are in a system of records. "Individuals" and "system of records" are defined in the Privacy Act and in 20 CFR 401.25.

(b) Requesting your own records. If you are an individual and request records, then to the extent you are requesting your own records in a system of records, we will handle your request under the Privacy Act. If there is any record that we need not release to you under those provisions, we will also consider your request under the FOIA and this rule, and we will release the record to you if the FOIA requires it.

(c) Requesting another individual's record. Whether or not you are an individual, if you request records that are about an individual (other than yourself) and that are in a system of records, we will handle your request under the FOIA and the rules in this part. However, if our disclosure in response to your request would be permitted by the Privacy Act's disclosure provision, (5 U.S.C. 552a(b)), for reasons other than the requirements of the FOIA, and if we decide to make the disclosure, then we will not handle your request under the FOIA and the rules in this part. For example, when we make routine use disclosures pursuant to requests, we do not handle them under the FOIA and the rules in this part. ("Routine use" is defined in the Privacy Act and in 20 CFR 401.25.) If we handle your request under the FOIA and the rules in this part and the FOIA does not require releasing the record to you, then the Privacy Act may prohibit the release and remove our discretion to release.

§ 402.20 Requests not handled under the FOIA.

(a) We will not handle your request under the FOIA and the regulations in this part to the extent it asks for records that are currently available, either from SSA or from another part of the Federal Government, under a separate statute that provides specific activity for charging fees for those records. For example, we will not handle your request under the FOIA and the regulations in this part to the extent it asks for detailed earnings statements under the Social Security program.

(b) We will not handle your request under the FOIA and the regulations in this part if you are seeking a record that is distributed by SSA as part of its regular program activity, for example, public information leaflets distributed by SSA.

§ 402.25 Referral of requests outside of SSA.

If you request records that were created by, or provided to us by, another Federal agency, and if that agency asserts control over the records, we may refer the records and your request to that agency. We may likewise refer requests for classified records to the agency that classified them. In these cases, the other agency will process and respond to your request, to the extent it concerns those records, under that agency's regulation, and you need not make a separate request to that agency. We will notify you when we refer your request to another agency.

§ 402.30 Definitions.

As used in this part,

Agency means any executive department, military department, government corporation, government controlled corporation, or other establishment in the executive branch of the Federal Government, or any independent regulatory agency. A private organization is not an agency even if it is performing work under contract with the Government or is receiving Federal financial assistance. Grantee and contractor records are not subject to the FOIA unless they are in the possession or under the control of SSA or its agents. Solely for the purpose of disclosure under the FOIA, we consider records of individual beneficiaries located in the State Disability Determination Services (DDS) to be agency records.

Commercial use means, when referring to a request, that the request is from or on behalf of one who seeks information for a use or purpose that furthers the commercial, trade, or profit interests of the requester or of a person on whose behalf the request is made. Whether a request is for a commercial use depends on the purpose of the request and the use to which the records will be put. The identity of the requester (individual, non-profit corporation, for-profit corporation) and the nature of the records, while in some cases indicative of that purpose or use, are not necessarily determinative. When a request is from a representative of the news media, a purpose or use supporting the requester's news dissemination function is not a commercial use.

Duplication means the process of making a copy of a record and sending it to the requester, to the extent necessary to respond to the request. Such copies include paper copy, microfilm, audio-visual materials, and magnetic tapes, cards, and discs.

Educational institution means a preschool, elementary or secondary school, institution of undergraduate or graduate higher education, or institution of professional or vocational education, which operates a program of scholarly research.

Freedom of Information Act or FOIA means 5 U.S.C. 552.

Freedom of Information Officer means an SSA official who has been delegated the authority to authorize disclosure of or withhold records and assess, waive, or reduce fees in response to FOIA requests.

Non-commercial scientific institution means an institution that is not operated substantially for purposes of furthering its own or someone else's business, trade, or profit interests, and that is operated for purposes of conducting scientific research whose results are not intended to promote any particular product or industry.

Records means any information maintained by an agency, regardless of forms or characteristics, that is made or received in connection with official business. This includes handwritten, typed, or printed documents (such as memoranda, books, brochures, studies, writings, drafts, letters, transcripts, and minutes) and material in other forms, such as punchcards; magnetic tapes; cards; computer discs or other electronic formats; paper tapes; audio or video recordings; maps; photographs; slides; microfilm; and motion pictures. It does not include objects or articles such as exhibits, models, equipment, and duplication machines, audiovisual processing materials, or computer software. It does not include personal records of an employee, or books, magazines, pamphlets, or other reference material in formally organized and officially designated SSA libraries, where such materials are available under the rules of the particular library.

Representative of the news media means a person actively gathering information for an entity organized and operated to publish or broadcast news to the public. News media entities include television and radio broadcasters, publishers of periodicals who distribute their products to the general public or who make their products available for purchase or subscription by the general public, and entities that may disseminate news through other media (e.g., electronic dissemination of text). We will treat freelance journalists as representatives of a news media entity if they can show a likelihood of publication through such an entity. A publication contract is such a basis, and the requester's past publication record may show such a basis.

Request means asking for records, whether or not you refer specifically to the FOIA. Requests from Federal agencies and court orders for documents are not included within this definition.

Review means, when used in connection with processing records for a commercial use request, examining the records to determine what portions, if any, may be withheld, and any other processing that is necessary to prepare the records for release. It includes only the examining and processing that are done the first time we analyze whether a specific exemption applies to a particular record or portion of a record. It does not include examination done in the appeal stage with respect to an exemption that was applied at the initial request stage. However, if we initially withhold a record under one exemption, and on appeal we determine that that exemption does not apply, then examining the record in the appeal stage for the purpose of determining whether a different exemption applies is included in review. It does not include the process of researching or resolving general legal or policy issues regarding exemptions.

Search means looking for records or portions of records responsive to a request. It includes reading and interpreting a request, and also page-by-page and line-by-line examination to identify responsive portions of a document. However, it does not include line-by-line examination where merely duplicating the entire page would be a less expensive and quicker way to comply with the request.

[63 FR 35132, June 29, 1998; 66 FR 2809, Jan. 12, 2001; 66 FR 9763, Feb. 12, 2001]

§ 402.35 Publication.

(a) Methods of publication. Materials we are required to publish pursuant to the provisions of 5 U.S.C. 552(a)(1) and (a)(2), we publish in one of the following ways:

(1) By publication in the Federal Register of Social Security Administration regulations, and by their subsequent inclusion in the Code of Federal Regulations;

(2) By publication in the Federal Register of appropriate general notices;

(3) By other forms of publication, when incorporated by reference in the Federal Register with the approval of the Director of the Federal Register; and

(4) By publication in the "Social Security Rulings" of indexes of precedential social security orders and opinions issued in the adjudication of claims, statements of policy and interpretations which have been adopted but have not been published in the Federal Register. The "Social Security Rulings" may be purchased through the Government Printing Office (See § 402.40).

(b) Publication of rulings. Although not required pursuant to 5 U.S.C. 552(a)(1) and (a)(2), we publish the following rulings in the Federal Register as well as by other forms of publication:

(1) We publish Social Security Rulings in the Federal Register under the authority of the Commissioner of Social Security. They are binding on all components of the Social Security Administration. These rulings represent precedent final opinions and orders and statements of policy and interpretations that we have adopted.

(2) We publish Social Security Acquiescence Rulings in the Federal Register under the authority of the Commissioner of Social Security. They are binding on all components of the Social Security Administration, except with respect to claims subject to the relitigation procedures established in 20 CFR 404.985(c), 410.670c, and 416.1485(c). For a description of Social Security Acquiescence Rulings, see 20 CFR 404.985(b), 410.670c(b), and 416.1485(b) of this title.

(c) Availability for inspection. To the extent practicable and to further assist the public, we make available for inspection at the address specified in § 402.135 those materials which are published in the Federal Register pursuant to 5 U.S.C. 552(a)(1).

(d) Availability by telecommunications. To the extent practicable, we will make available by means of computer telecommunications the indices and other records that are available for inspection.

[63 FR 35132, June 29, 1998; 65 FR 16813, March 30, 2000; 72 FR 14669, March 29, 2007; 72 FR 36360, July 3, 2007]

§ 402.40 Publications for sale.

The following publications containing information pertaining to the program, organization, functions, and procedures of the Social Security Administration may be purchased from the Superintendent of Documents, Government Printing Office, Washington, DC 20402:

(a) Title 20, parts 400–499 of the Code of Federal Regulations.

(b) Federal Register issues.

(c) Compilation of the Social Security Laws.

(d) Social Security Rulings.

(e) Social Security Handbook. The information in the Handbook is not of precedent or interpretative force.

(f) Social Security Bulletin.

(g) Social Security Acquiescence Rulings.

(h) SSA Publications on CD–ROM.

[63 FR 35132, June 29, 1998]

§ 402.45 Availability of records.

(a) What records are available. 5 U.S.C. 552, also known as the FOIA, permits any person to see, and get a copy of, any Federal agency's records unless the material is exempt from mandatory disclosure as described in § 402.70 of this part.

(b) FOIA. Under the FOIA, we are also required to make available to the public the instructional manuals issued to our employees, general statements of policy, and other materials which are used in processing claims and which are not published in the Federal Register, and an index of these manuals and materials.

(c) Record citation as precedent. We will not use or cite any record described in paragraph (b) of this section as a precedent for an action against a person unless we have indexed the record and published it or made it available, or unless the person has timely notice of the record.

(d) Electronic Reading Room. We will prepare an index of records which have become or are likely to become the subject of subsequent requests. The index, and, to the extent practicable, the records will be made available on the Internet or by other computer telecommunications means.

(e) Federal employees. We will not disclose information when the information sought is lists of telephone numbers and/or duty stations of one or more Federal employees if the disclosure, as determined at the discretion of the official responsible for custody of the information, would place employee(s) at risk of injury or other harm. Also, we will not disclose the requested information if the information is protected from mandatory disclosure under an exemption of the Freedom of Information Act.

[63 FR 35132, June 29, 1998; 72 FR 69617, Dec. 10, 2007; 73 FR 25507, May 7, 2008]

§ 402.50 Availability of administrative staff manuals.

All administrative staff manuals of the Social Security Administration and instructions to staff personnel which contain policies, procedures, or interpretations that affect the public are available for inspection and copying. A complete listing of such materials is published in the Index of Administrative Staff Manuals and Instructions. These manuals are generally not printed in a sufficient quantity to permit sale or other general distribution to the public. Selected material is maintained at district offices and field offices and may be inspected there. See §§ 402.55 and 402.60 for a listing of this material.

§ 402.55 Materials available at district offices and branch offices.

(a) Materials available for inspection. The following are available or will be made available for inspection at the district offices and branch offices:

(1) Compilation of the Social Security Laws.

(2) Social Security Administration regulations under the retirement, survivors, disability, and supplemental security income programs, i.e., 20 CFR parts 401, 402, 404, 416, and 422; and the Social Security Administration's regulations under part B of title IV (Black Lung Benefits) of the Federal Coal Mine Health and Safety Act of 1969, 20 CFR part 410.

(3) Social Security Rulings.

(4) Social Security Handbook.

(5) Social Security Acquiescence Rulings.

(b) Materials available for inspection and copying. The following materials are available or will be made available for inspection and copying at the district offices and branch offices (fees may be applicable per §§ 402.155 through 402.185):

(1) SSA Program Operations Manual System.

(2) SSA Organization Manual.

(3) Handbook for State Social Security Administrators.

(4) Indexes to the materials listed in paragraph (a) of this section and in this paragraph (b) and an index to the Hearings, Appeals and Litigation Law (HALLEX) manual.

(5) Index of Administrative Staff Manuals and Instructions.

§ 402.60 Materials in field offices of the Office of Hearings and Appeals.

(a) Materials available for inspection. The following materials are available for inspection in the field offices of the Office of Hearings and Appeals:

(1) Regulations of the Social Security Administration (see § 402.55(a)(2)).

(2) Title 5, United States Code.

(3) Compilation of the Social Security Laws.

(4) Social Security Rulings.

(5) Social Security Handbook.

(6) Social Security Acquiescence Rulings.

(b) The Hearings, Appeals and Litigation Law (HALLEX) manual is available for inspection and copying in the field offices of the Office of Hearings and Appeals (fees may be applicable per §§ 402.155 through 402.185).

§ 402.65 Health care information.

We have some information about health care programs under titles XVIII and XIX (Medicare and Medicaid) of the Social Security Act. We follow the rules in 42 CFR part 401 in determining whether to provide any portion of it to a requester.

§ 402.70 Reasons for withholding some records.

Section 552(b) of the Freedom of Information Act contains nine exemptions to the mandatory disclosure of records. We describe these exemptions in §§ 402.75 through 402.110 of this part and explain how we apply them to disclosure determinations. (In some cases more than one exemption may apply to the same document.) Information obtained by the agency from any individual or organization, furnished in reliance on a provision for confidentiality authorized by applicable statute or regulation, will not be disclosed, to the extent it can be withheld under one of these exemptions. This section does not itself authorize the giving of any pledge of confidentiality by any officer or employee of the agency.

§ 402.75 Exemption one for withholding records: National defense and foreign policy.

We are not required to release records that, as provided by FOIA, are "(a) specifically authorized under criteria established by an Executive Order to be kept secret in the interest of national defense or foreign policy and (b) are in fact properly classified pursuant to such Executive Order." Executive Order No. 12958 (1995) (3 CFR, 1987 Comp., p. 235) provides for such classification. When the release of certain records may adversely affect U.S. relations with foreign countries, we usually consult with officials of those countries or officials of the Department of State. Also, we may on occasion have in our possession records classified by some other agency. We may refer your request for such records to the agency that classified them and notify you that we have done so.

§ 402.80 Exemption two for withholding records: Internal personnel rules and practices.

We are not required to release records that are "related solely to the internal personnel rules and practices of an agency." Under this exemption, we may withhold routine internal agency practices and procedures. For example, we may withhold guard schedules and rules governing parking facilities or lunch periods. Also under this exemption, we may withhold internal records whose release would help some persons circumvent the law or agency regulations. For example, we ordinarily do not disclose manuals that instruct our investigators or auditors how to investigate possible violations of law, to the extent that this release would help some persons circumvent the law.

§ 402.85 Exemption three for withholding records: Records exempted by other statutes.

We are not required to release records if another statute specifically allows or requires us to withhold them. We may use another statute to justify withholding only if it absolutely prohibits disclosure or if it sets forth criteria to guide our decision on releasing or identifies particular types of material to be withheld. We often use this exemption to withhold information regarding a worker's earnings which is tax return information under section 6103 of the Internal Revenue Code.

§ 402.90 Exemption four for withholding records: Trade secrets and confidential commercial or financial information.

We will withhold trade secrets and commercial or financial information that is obtained from a person and is privileged or confidential.

(a) Trade secrets. A trade secret is a secret, commercially valuable plan, formula, process, or device that is used for the making, preparing, compounding, or processing of trade commodities and that can be said to be the end product of either innovation or substantial effort. There must be a direct relationship between the trade secret and the productive process.

(b) Commercial or financial information. We will not disclose records whose information is "commercial or financial," is obtained from a person, and is "privileged or confidential."

(1) Information is "commercial or financial" if it relates to businesses, commerce, trade, employment, profits, or finances (including personal finances). We interpret this category broadly.

(2) Information is "obtained from a person" if SSA or another agency has obtained it from someone outside the Federal Government or from someone within the Government who has a commercial or financial interest in the information. "Person" includes an individual, partnership, corporation, association, State or foreign government, or other organization. Information is not "obtained from a person" if it is generated by SSA or another Federal agency. However, infor-

mation is "obtained from a person" if it is provided by someone, including but not limited to an agency employee, who retains a commercial or financial interest in the information.

(3) Information is "privileged" if it would ordinarily be protected from disclosure in civil discovery by a recognized evidentiary privilege, such as the attorney-client privilege or the work product privilege. Information may be privileged for this purpose under a privilege belonging to a person outside the government, unless the providing of the information to the government rendered the information no longer protectable in civil discovery.

(4) Information is "confidential" if it meets one of the following tests:

(i) Disclosure may impair the government's ability to obtain necessary information in the future;

(ii) Disclosure would substantially harm the competitive position of the person who submitted the information;

(iii) Disclosure would impair other government interests, such as program effectiveness and compliance; or

(iv) Disclosure would impair other private interests, such as an interest in controlling availability of intrinsically valuable records, which are sold in the market by their owner.

(c) Analysis under tests in this section. The following questions may be relevant in analyzing whether a record meets one or more of the above tests:

(1) Is the information of a type customarily held in strict confidence and not disclosed to the public by the person to whom it belongs?

(2) What is the general custom or usage with respect to such information in the relevant occupation or business?

(3) How many, and what types of, individuals have access to the information?

(4) What kind and degree of financial injury can be expected if the information is disclosed?

(d) Designation of certain confidential information. A person who submits records to the government may designate part or all of the information in such records as exempt from disclosure under Exemption 4 of the FOIA. The person may make this designation either at the time the records are submitted to the government or within a reasonable time thereafter. The designation must be in writing. Where a legend is required by a request for proposals or request for quotations, pursuant to 48 CFR 352.215–12, then that legend is necessary for this purpose. Any such designation will expire ten years after the records were submitted to the government.

(e) Predisclosure notification. The procedures in this paragraph apply to records on which the submitter has designated information as provided in paragraph (d) of this section. They also apply to records that were submitted to the government where we have substantial reason to believe that information in the records could reasonably be considered exempt under Exemption 4. Certain exceptions to these procedures are stated in paragraph (f) of this section.

(1) When we receive a request for such records, and we determine that we may be required to disclose them, we will make reasonable efforts to notify the submitter about these facts. The notice will include a copy of the request, and it will inform the submitter about the procedures and time limits for submission and consideration of objections to disclosure. If we must notify a large number of submitters, we may do this by posting or publishing a notice in a place where the submitters are reasonably likely to become aware of it.

(2) The submitter has five working days from receipt of the notice to object to disclosure of any part of the records and to state all bases for its objections.

(3) We will give consideration to all bases that have been timely stated by the submitter. If we decide to disclose the records, we will notify the submitter in writing. This notice will briefly explain why we did not sustain its objections. We will include with the notice a copy of the records about which the submitter objected, as we propose to disclose them. The notice will state that we intend to disclose the records five working days after the submitter receives the notice unless we are ordered by a United States District Court not to release them.

(4) When a requester files suit under the FOIA to obtain records covered by this paragraph, we will promptly notify the submitter.

(5) Whenever we send a notice to a submitter under paragraph (e)(1) of this section, we will notify the requester that we are giving the submitter a notice and an opportunity to object. Whenever we send a notice to a submitter under paragraph (e)(3) of this section, we will notify the requester of this fact.

(f) Exceptions to predisclosure notification. The notice requirements in paragraph (e) of this section do not apply in the following situations:

(1) We decided not to disclose the records;

(2) The information has previously been published or made generally available;

(3) Disclosure is required by a regulation, issued after notice and opportunity for public comment, that specifies narrow categories of records that are to be disclosed under the FOIA, but in this case a submitter may still designate records as described in paragraph (d) of this section, and in exceptional cases, we may, at our discretion, follow the notice procedures in paragraph (e) of this section; or

(4) The designation appears to be obviously frivolous, but in this case we will still give the submitter the written notice required by paragraph (e)(3) of this section (although this notice need not explain our decision or include a copy of the records), and we will notify the requester as described in paragraph (e)(5) of this section.

§ 402.95 Exemption five for withholding records: Internal memoranda.

This exemption covers internal government communications and notes that fall within a generally recognized evidentiary privilege. Internal government communications include an agency's communications with an outside consultant or other outside person, with a court, or with Congress, when those communications are for a purpose similar to the purpose of privileged intra-agency communications. Some of the most-commonly applicable privileges are described in the following paragraphs:

(a) Deliberative process privilege. This privilege protects predecisional deliberative communications. A communication is protected under this privilege if it was made before a final decision was reached on some question of policy and if it expressed recommendations or opinions on that question. The purpose of the privilege is to prevent injury to the quality of the agency decisionmaking process by encouraging open and frank internal policy discussions, by avoiding premature disclosure of policies not yet adopted, and by avoiding the public confusion that might result from disclosing reasons that were not in fact the ultimate grounds for an agency's decision. Purely factual material in a deliberative document is within this privilege only if it is inextricably intertwined with the deliberative portions so that it cannot reasonably be segregated, if it would reveal the nature of the deliberative portions, or if its disclosure would in some other way make possible an intrusion into the decisionmaking process. We will release purely factual material in a deliberative document unless that material is otherwise exempt. The privilege continues to protect predecisional documents even after a decision is made.

(b) Attorney work product privilege. This privilege protects documents prepared by or for an agency, or by or for its representative (typically, our attorneys) in anticipation of litigation or for trial. It includes documents prepared for purposes of administrative adjudications as well as court litigation. It includes documents prepared by program offices as well as by attorneys. It includes factual material in such documents as well as material revealing opinions and tactics. Finally, the privilege continues to protect the documents even after the litigation is closed.

(c) Attorney-client communication privilege. This privilege protects confidential communications between a lawyer and an employee or agent of the Government where there is an attorney-client relationship between them (typically, where the lawyer is acting as attorney for the agency and the employee is communicating on behalf of the agency) and where the employee has communicated information to the attorney in confidence in order to obtain legal advice or assistance.

§ 402.100 Exemption six: Clearly unwarranted invasion of personal privacy.

(a) Documents affected. We may withhold records about individuals if disclosure would constitute a clearly unwarranted invasion of their personal privacy.

(b) Balancing test. In deciding whether to release records to you that contain personal or private information about someone else, we weigh the foreseeable harm of invading a person's privacy against the public interest in disclosure. In determining whether disclosure would be in the public interest, we will consider whether disclosure of the requested information would shed light on how a Government agency performs its statutory duties. However, in our evaluation of requests for records we attempt to guard against the release of information that might involve a violation of personal privacy because of a requester being able to "read between the lines" or piece together items that would constitute information that normally would be exempt from mandatory disclosure under Exemption Six.

(c) Examples. Some of the information that we frequently withhold under Exemption Six is: Home addresses, ages, and minority group status of our employees or former employees; social security numbers; medical information about individuals who have filed a claim for disability benefits; names and addresses of individual beneficiaries of our programs, or benefits such individuals receive; earnings records, claim files, and other personal information SSA maintains.

[63 FR 35132, June 29, 1998]

§ 402.105 Exemption seven for withholding records: Law enforcement.

We are not required to disclose information or records that the government has compiled for law enforcement purposes. The records may apply to actual or potential violations of either criminal or civil laws or regulations. We can withhold these records only to the extent that releasing them would cause harm in at least one of the following situations:

(a) Enforcement proceedings. We may withhold information whose release could reasonably be expected to interfere with prospective or ongoing law enforcement proceedings. Investigations of fraud and mismanagement, employee misconduct, and civil rights violations may fall into this category. In certain cases—such as when a fraud investigation is likely—we may refuse to confirm or deny the existence of records that relate to the violations in order not to disclose that an investigation is in progress, or may be conducted.

(b) Fair trial or impartial adjudication. We may withhold records whose release would deprive a person of a fair trial or an impartial adjudication because of prejudicial publicity.

(c) Personal privacy. We are careful not to disclose information that could reasonably be expected to constitute an unwarranted invasion of personal privacy. When a name surfaces in an investigation, that person is likely to be vulnerable to innuendo, rumor, harassment, and retaliation.

(d) Confidential sources and information. We may withhold records whose release could reasonably be expected to disclose the identity of a confidential source of information. A confidential source may be an individual; a State, local, or foreign government agency; or any private organization. The exemption applies whether the source provides information under an express promise of confidentiality or under circumstances from which such an assurance could be reasonably inferred. Also, where the record, or information in it, has been compiled by a law enforcement authority conducting a criminal investigation, or by an agency conducting a lawful national security investigation, the exemption also protects all information supplied by a confidential source. Also protected from mandatory disclosure is any information which, if disclosed, could reasonably be expected to jeopardize the system of confidentiality that assures a flow of information from sources to investigatory agencies.

(e) Techniques and procedures. We may withhold records reflecting special techniques or procedures of investigation or prosecution, not otherwise generally known to the public. In some cases, it is not possible to describe even in general terms those techniques without disclosing the very material to be withheld. We may also withhold records whose release would disclose guidelines for law enforcement investigations or prosecutions if this disclosure could reasonably be expected to create a risk that someone could circumvent requirements of law or of regulation.

(f) Life and physical safety. We may withhold records whose disclosure could reasonably be expected to endanger the life or physical safety of any individual. This protection extends to threats and harassment as well as to physical violence.

[63 FR 35132, June 29, 1998]

§ 402.110 Exemptions eight and nine for withholding records: Records on financial institutions; records on wells.

Exemption eight permits us to withhold records about regulation or supervision of financial institutions. Exemption nine permits the withholding of geological and geophysical information and data, including maps, concerning wells.

§ 402.115 [Reserved]

[63 FR 35132, June 29, 1998]

§ 402.120 [Reserved]

[63 FR 35132, June 29, 1998]

§ 402.125 Who may release a record.

Except as otherwise provided by regulation, only the Deputy Executive Director for the Office of Public Disclosure, Office of the General Counsel, SSA, or her or his designee may determine whether to release any record in SSA's control and possession. This official is SSA's Freedom of Information Officer. Sections 402.40, 402.55, and 402.60 list some of the materials which we have determined may be released.

[68 FR 60295, Oct. 22, 2003]

§ 402.130 How to request a record.

You may request a record in person or by mail or by electronic telecommunications. To the extent practicable, and in the future, we will attempt to provide access for requests by telephone, fax, Internet, and e-mail. Any request should reasonably describe the record you want. If you have detailed information which would assist us in identifying that record, please submit it with your request. We may charge fees for some requests (§§ 402.145–402.175 explain our fees). You should identify the request as a Freedom of Information Act request and mark the outside of any envelope used to submit your request as a "Freedom of Information Request." The staff at any Social Security office can help you prepare this request.

[63 FR 35132, June 29, 1998]

§ 402.135 Where to send a request.

You may send your request for a record to: The Deputy Executive Director for the Office of Public Disclosure, Office of the General Counsel, Social Security Administration, 6401 Security Boulevard, Baltimore, Maryland 21235.

[68 FR 60295, Oct. 22, 2003]

§ 402.140 How a request for a record is processed.

(a) In general, we will make a determination as to whether a requested record will be provided within 20 days (excepting Saturdays, Sundays, and legal public holidays) after receipt of a request by the appropriate official (see § 402.135). This 20–day period may be extended in unusual circumstances by written notice to you, explaining why we need additional time, and the extension may be for up to 10 additional working days when one or more of the following situations exist:

(1) The office processing the request needs to locate and then obtain the record from another facility;

(2) We need to locate, obtain, and appropriately examine a large number of records which are requested in a single request; or

(3) The office processing the request needs to consult with another agency which has a substantial interest in the subject matter of the request. This consultation shall be conducted with all practicable speed.

(b) If we cannot process your request within 10 additional days, we will notify you and provide you an opportunity to limit the scope of the request so that it may be processed within the additional 10 days, or we will provide you with an opportunity to arrange with us an alternative time frame for processing the request, or for processing a modified request.

(c) Multi-tracking procedures. We will establish four tracks for handling requests and the track to which a request is assigned will depend on the nature of the request and the estimated processing time:

(1) Track 1—Requests that can be answered with readily available records or information. These are the fastest to process.

(2) Track 2—Requests where we need records or information from other offices throughout the Agency but we do not expect that the decision on disclosure will be as time consuming as for requests in Track 3.

(3) Track 3—Requests which require a decision or input from another office or agency and a considerable amount of time will be needed for that, or the request is complicated or involves a large number of records. Usually, these cases will take the longest to process.

(4) Track 4—Requests that will be expedited.

(d) We will provide for expedited access for requesters who show a "compelling need" for a speedy response. The EFOIA describes compelling need as when the failure to obtain the records on an expedited basis could reasonably be expected to pose "an imminent threat to the life or physical safety of an individual," or when the request is from a person primarily engaged in disseminating information (such as a member of the news media), and there is an "urgency to inform the public concerning actual or alleged Federal Government activity." We also will expedite processing of a request if the requester explains in detail to our satisfaction that a prompt response is needed because the requester may be denied a legal right, benefit, or remedy without the requested information, and that it cannot be obtained elsewhere in a reasonable amount of time. We will respond within 10 days to a request for expedited processing and, if we decide to grant expedited processing, we will then notify you of our decision whether or not to disclose the records requested as soon as practicable.

[63 FR 35132, June 29, 1998]

§ 402.145 Responding to your request.

(a) Retrieving records. We are required to furnish copies of records only when they are in our possession or we can retrieve them from storage. We will make reasonable efforts to search for records manually or by automated means, including any information stored in an electronic form or format, except when such efforts would significantly interfere with the operation of our automated information system. If we have stored the records you want in the National Archives or another storage center, we will retrieve and review them for possible disclosure. However, the Federal Government destroys many old records, so sometimes it is impossible to fill requests. Various laws, regulations, and manuals give the time periods for keeping records before they may be destroyed. For example, there is information about retention of records in the Records Disposal Act of 1944, 44 U.S.C. 3301 through 3314; the Federal Property Management Regulations, 41 CFR 101–11.4; and the General Records Schedules of the National Archives and Records Administration.

(b) Furnishing records. We will furnish copies only of records that we have or can retrieve. We are not required to create new records or to perform research for you. We may decide to conserve Government resources and at the same time supply the records you need by consolidating information from various records rather than copying them all. For instance, we could extract sections from various similar records instead of providing repetitious information. We generally will furnish only one copy of a record. We will make reasonable efforts to provide the records in the form or format you request if the record is readily reproducible in that form or format.

(c) Deletions. When we publish or otherwise make available any record, we may delete information that is exempt from disclosure. For example, in an opinion or order, statement of policy, or other record which relates to a private party or parties, the name or names and other identifying details may be deleted. When technically feasible, we will indicate the extent of deletions on the portion of the record that is released or published at the place of the deletion unless including that indication would harm an interest protected by an exemption. If we deny a request, in whole or in part, we will make a reasonable effort to estimate the volume of any requested matter that is not disclosed, unless such an estimate would harm an interest protected by an exemption.

(d) Creation of records. We are not required to create new records merely to satisfy a request. However, we will search manually or by automated means to locate information that is responsive to the request. If extensive computer programming is needed to respond to a request, we may decline to commit such resources, or if we agree to do so, we may charge you for the reasonable cost of doing so. We do not mean that we will never help you get information that does not already exist in our records. However, diverting staff and equipment from our other responsibilities may not always be possible.

[63 FR 35133, June 29, 1998]

§ 402.150 Release of records.

(a) Records previously released. If we have released a record, or a part of a record, to others in the past, we will ordinarily release it to you also. However, we will not release it to you if a statute forbids this disclosure, and we will not necessarily release it to you if an exemption applies in your situation and it did not apply, or applied differently, in the previous situation(s) or if the previous release was unauthorized. See § 402.45(d) regarding records in electronic reading rooms.

(b) Poor copy. If we cannot make a legible copy of a record to be released, we do not attempt to reconstruct it. Instead, we furnish the best copy possible and note its poor quality in our reply.

[63 FR 35133, June 29, 1998]

§ 402.155 Fees to be charged—categories of requests.

Paragraphs (a) through (c) of this section state, for each category of request, the type of fees that we will generally charge. However, for each of these categories, the fees may be limited, waived, or reduced for the reasons given below or for other reasons.

(a) Commercial use request. If your request is for a commercial use, we will charge you the costs of search, review, and duplication.

(b) Educational and scientific institutions and news media. If you are an educational institution or a noncommercial scientific institution, operated primarily for scholarly or scientific research, or a representative of the news media, and your request is not for a commercial use, we will charge you only for the duplication of documents. Also, we will not charge you the copying costs for the first 100 pages of duplication.

(c) Other requesters. If your request is not the kind described by paragraph (a) or (b) of this section, then we will charge you only for the search and the duplication. Also, we will not charge you for the first two hours of search time or for the copying costs of the first 100 pages of duplication.

§ 402.160 Fees to be charged—general provisions.

(a) We may charge search fees even if the records we find are exempt from disclosure, or even if we do not find any records at all.

(b) If we are not charging you for the first two hours of search time, under paragraph (c) of § 402.155, and those two hours are spent on a computer search, then the two free hours are the first two hours of the time needed to access the information in the computer.

(c) If we are not charging you for the first 100 pages of duplication, under paragraph (b) or (c) of § 402.155, then those 100 pages are the first 100 pages of photocopies of standard size pages, or the first 100 pages of computer printout.

(d) We will charge interest on unpaid bills beginning on the 31st day following the day the bill was sent.

[63 FR 35133, June 29, 1998]

§ 402.165 Fee schedule.

The following is our fee schedule for providing records and related services under the FOIA:

(a) Manual searching for or reviewing of records. When the search or review is performed by employees at grade GS–1 through GS–8, we will charge an hourly rate based on the salary of a GS–5, step 7, employee; when done by a GS–9 through GS–14, an hourly rate based on the salary of a GS–12, step 4, employee; and when done by a GS–15 or above, an hourly rate based on the salary of a GS–15, step 7, employee. In each case, we will compute the hourly rate by taking the current hourly rate for the specified grade and step, adding 16% of that rate to cover benefits, and rounding to the nearest whole dollar. As of January 5, 1997, these rates were $14, $28, and $50 respectively. These rates are adjusted as Federal salaries change. When a search involves employees at more than one of these levels, we will charge the rate appropriate for each.

(b) Computer searching and printing. We will charge the actual cost of operating the computer plus charges for the time spent by the operator, at the rates given in paragraph (a) of this section.

(c) Photocopying standard size pages. We will charge $0.10 per page. The Freedom of Information (FOI) Officer may charge lower fees for particular documents where—

(1) The document has already been printed in large numbers;

(2) The program office determines that using existing stock to answer this request, and any other anticipated FOI requests, will not interfere with program requirements; and

(3) The FOI Officer determines that the lower fee is adequate to recover the prorated share of the original printing costs.

(d) Photocopying odd-size documents. For photocopying documents such as punchcards or blueprints, or reproducing other records such as tapes, we will charge the actual costs of operating the machine, plus the actual cost of the materials used, plus charges for the time spent by the operator, at the rates given in paragraph (a) of this section.

(e) Certifying that records are true copies. This service is not required by the FOIA. If we agree to provide it, we will charge $10 per certification.

(f) Sending records by express mail, certified mail, or other special methods. This service is not required by the FOIA. If we agree to provide it, we will charge our actual costs.

(g) Other special services. For performing any other special service that you request and we agree to, we will charge the actual costs of operating any machinery, plus actual cost of any materials used, plus charges for the time of our employees, at the rates given in paragraph (a) of this section.

(h) Billing exceeds cost of service. Generally we will not charge you a fee when the cost of the service is less than the cost of sending you a bill. However, where an individual, organization, or governmental unit makes multiple separate requests, we will total the costs incurred and periodically bill the requester for the services rendered.

(i) Fee for copies of printed materials. When extra copies of printed material are available, the charge is generally 1 cent per page. If the material may be purchased from the Superintendent of Documents, the charge is that set by the Superintendent. The Superintendent's address is in § 402.40.

(j) When not applicable. This fee schedule does not apply to requests for records of Social Security number holders, wage earners, employers, and claimants when the requests are governed by section 1106 of the Social Security Act and by §§ 402.170 and 402.175.

§ 402.170 Fees for providing records and related services for program purposes pursuant to section 1106 of the Social Security Act.

(a) Program purposes described.

(1) We consider a request to be program related if the information must be disclosed under the Social Security Act. For example, section 205(c)(2)(A) of the Act (42 U.S.C. 405(c)(2)(A)) requires that we provide certain information upon request to a worker, her or his legal representative, her or his survivor, or the legal representative of the worker's estate. That information is the amounts of the worker's wages and self-employment income and the periods during which they were paid or derived, as shown by our records.

(2) We also consider a request to be program related if the requester indicates the needed information will be used for a purpose which is directly related to the administration of a program under the Social Security Act.

(i) The major criteria we consider in deciding whether a proposed use is so related are:

(A) Is the information needed to pursue some benefit under the Act?

(B) Is the information needed solely to verify the accuracy of information obtained in connection with a program administered under the Act?

(C) Is the information needed in connection with an activity which has been authorized under the Act?

(D) Is the information needed by an employer to carry out her or his taxpaying responsibilities under the Federal Insurance Contributions Act or section 218 of the Act?

(ii) We will consider on a case by case basis those requests which do not meet these criteria but are claimed to be program related.

(b) When we charge. If we determine the request for information is program related, we may or may not charge for the information. For example, as stated in paragraph (a) of this section, we generally will not charge you for information needed to assure the accuracy of our records on which your present or future Social Security benefits depend. In addition, we generally will not charge for furnishing information under section 205(c)(2)(A) of the Act. However, if we do charge for a program related request (for example, if more detailed information or special services are requested) we will use the fee schedule in § 402.165 if information is being disclosed under the FOIA and the fee schedule in 20 CFR 401.95 if access to the information is being granted under the Privacy Act. (Exception: If the request is for purposes of administering employee benefits covered by the Employee Retirement Income Security Act of 1974 (ERISA), even if the request is covered by section 205(c)(2)(A) of the Act, we will charge under § 402.175.)

§ 402.175 Fees for providing information and related services for non-program purposes.

(a) General. Section 1106(c) of the Social Security Act permits the Commissioner to require requesters of information to pay the full cost of supplying the information where the information is requested to comply with the ERISA, or "* * * for any other purpose not directly related to the administration of the program or programs under * * *" the Social Security Act. This may be done notwithstanding the fee provisions of the FOIA and the Privacy Act or any other provision of law. As used in this section—

(1) Full cost includes the direct and indirect costs to SSA (including costs of duplication) of providing information and related services under section 1106(c) of the Act; and

(2) Full cost of an employee's time includes fringe benefits and overhead costs such as rent and utilities.

(b) Non-program related requests. We consider a request for information which does not meet or equal any of the criteria in § 402.170 to be non-program related. (Whether a request for information about an individual is made by that individual or by someone else is not a factor.) In responding to these requests, or requests for ERISA purposes, we will charge the full cost of our services as described in paragraph (c) of this section.

(c) Fee schedule. Our fee schedule for non-program related requests is:

(1) Manual searching for records. Full cost of the employee's time.

(2) Photocopying, or reproducing records such as magnetic tapes or punch cards. Full cost of the operator's time plus the full cost of the machine time and the materials used.

(3) Use of electronic data processing equipment to obtain records. Our full cost for the service, including computer search time, computer runs and printouts, and the time of computer programmers and operators and other employees.

(4) Certification or authentication of records. Full cost of certification or authentication.

(5) Forwarding materials to destination. If you request special arrangements for forwarding the material, we will charge you the full cost of this service (e.g., you request express mail or a commercial delivery service). If no special forwarding arrangements are requested, we will charge you the full cost of the service, including the U.S. Postal Service cost.

(6) Performing other special services. If we agree to provide any special services you request, we will charge you the full cost of the time of the employee who performs the service, plus the full cost of any machine time and materials that the employee uses.

(7) Billing exceeds cost of service. Generally we will not charge you a fee when the cost of the service is less than the cost of sending you a bill. However, where an individual, organization, or governmental unit makes multiple separate requests, we will total the costs incurred and bill the requester for the services rendered.

(d) Fee for copies of printed materials. When extra copies of printed material are available, the charge is generally 1 cent per page. If the material may be purchased from the Superintendent of Documents, the charge is that set by the Superintendent. The Superintendent's address is in § 402.40.

(e) Charging when requested record not found. We may charge you for search time, even though we fail to find the records. We may also charge you for search time if the records we locate are exempt from disclosure.

§ 402.180 Procedure on assessing and collecting fees for providing records.

(a) We will generally assume that when you send us a request, you agree to pay for the services needed to locate and send that record to you. You may specify in your request a limit on the amount you are willing to spend. If you do that or include with your request a payment that does not cover our fee, we will notify you if it appears that the fee will exceed that amount and ask whether you want us to continue to process your request. Also, before we start work on your request under § 402.140, we will generally notify you of our exact or estimated charge for the information, unless it is clear that you have a reasonable idea of the cost.

(b) If you have failed to pay previous bills in a timely fashion, or if our initial review of your request indicates that we will charge you fees exceeding $250, we will require you to pay your past due fees and/or the estimated fees, or a deposit, before we start searching for the records you want. If so, we will let you know promptly upon receiving your request. In such cases, administrative time limits (i.e., ten working days from receipt of initial requests and 20 working days from receipt of appeals from initial denials, plus permissible extensions of these time limits) will begin only after we come to an agreement with you over payment of fees, or decide that fee waiver or reduction is appropriate.

(c) We will normally require you to pay all fees before we furnish the records to you. We may, at our discretion, send you a bill along with or following the furnishing of the records. For example, we may do this if you have a history of prompt payment. We may also, at our discretion, aggregate the charges for certain time periods in order to avoid sending numerous small bills to frequent requesters, or to businesses or agents representing requesters. For example, we might send a bill to such a requester once a month. Fees should be paid in accordance with the instructions furnished by the person who responds to your requests.

(d) Payment of fees will be made by check or money order payable to "Social Security Administration".

[68 FR 60295, Oct. 22, 2003]

§ 402.185 Waiver or reduction of fees in the public interest.

(a) Standard. We will waive or reduce the fees we would otherwise charge if disclosure of the information meets both tests which are explained in paragraphs (b) and (c) of this section:

(1) It is in the public interest because it is likely to contribute significantly to public understanding of the operations or activities of the government; and

(2) It is not primarily in the commercial interest of the requester.

(b) Public interest. The disclosure passes the first test only if it furthers the specific public interest of being likely to contribute significantly to public understanding of government operations or activities, regardless of any other public interest it may further. In analyzing this question, we will consider the following factors:

(1) How, if at all, do the records to be disclosed pertain to the operations or activities of the Federal Government?

(2) Would disclosure of the records reveal any meaningful information about government operations or activities? Can one learn from these records anything about such operations that is not already public knowledge?

(3) Will the disclosure advance the understanding of the general public as distinguished from a narrow segment of interested persons? Under this factor we may consider whether the requester is in a position to contribute to public understanding. For example, we may consider whether the requester has such knowledge or expertise as may be necessary to understand the information, and whether the requester's intended use of the information would be likely to disseminate the information among the public. An unsupported claim to be doing research for a book or article does not demonstrate that likelihood, while such a claim by a representative of the news media is better evidence.

(4) Will the contribution to public understanding be a significant one? Will the public's understanding of the government's operations be substantially greater as a result of the disclosure?

(c) Not primarily in the requester's commercial interest. If the disclosure passes the test of furthering the specific public interest described in paragraph (b) of this section, we will determine whether it also furthers the requester's commercial interest and, if so, whether this effect outweighs the advancement of that public interest. In applying this second test, we will consider the following factors:

(1) Would the disclosure further a commercial interest of the requester, or of someone on whose behalf the requester is acting? "Commercial interests" include interests relating to business, trade, and profit. Not only profit-making corporations have commercial interests—so do nonprofit corporations, individuals, unions, and other associations. The interest of a representative of the news media in using the information for news dissemination purposes will not be considered a commercial interest.

(2) If disclosure would further a commercial interest of the requester, would that effect outweigh the advancement of the public interest defined in paragraph (b) of this section? Which effect is primary?

(d) Deciding between waiver and reduction. If the disclosure passes both tests, we will normally waive fees. However, in some cases we may decide only to reduce the fees. For example, we may do this when disclosure of some but not all of the requested records passes the tests.

(e) Procedure for requesting a waiver or reduction. You must make your request for a waiver or reduction at the same time you make your request for records. You should explain why you believe a waiver or reduction is proper under the analysis in paragraphs (a) through (d) of this section. Only FOI Officers may make the decision whether to waive, or reduce, the fees. If we do not completely grant your request for a waiver or reduction, the denial letter will designate a review official. You may appeal the denial to that official. In your appeal letter, you should discuss whatever reasons are given in our denial letter. The process prescribed in § 402.190 of this part will also apply to these appeals.

§ 402.190 Officials who may deny a request for records under FOIA.

Only the Deputy Executive Director for the Office of Public Disclosure, Office of the General Counsel, SSA, or her or his designee is authorized to deny a written request to obtain, inspect, or copy any social security record.

[68 FR 60295, Oct. 22, 2003]

§ 402.195 How a request is denied.

(a) Oral requests. If we cannot comply with your oral request because the Deputy Executive Director for the Office of Public Disclosure, Office of the General Counsel (or designee) has not previously made a determination to release the record you want, we will tell you that fact. If you still wish to pursue your request, you must put your request in writing.

(b) Written requests. If you make a written request and the information or record you requested will not be released, we will send you an official denial in writing. We will explain why the request was denied (for example, the reasons why the requested document is subject to one or more clearly described exemptions), will include the name and title or position of the person who made the decision, and what your appeal rights are.

(c) Unproductive searches. We make a diligent search for records to satisfy your request. Nevertheless, we may not be able always to find the records you want using the information you provided, or they may not exist. If we advise you that we have been unable to find the records despite a diligent search, this does not constitute a denial of your request.

[68 FR 60295, Oct. 22, 2003]

§ 402.200 How to appeal a decision denying all or part of a request.

(a) How to appeal. If all or part of your written request was denied, you may request that the Commissioner of Social Security, 6401 Security Boulevard, Baltimore, MD 21235 review that determination. Your request for review:

(1) Must be in writing;

(2) Must be mailed within 30 days after you received notification that all or part of your request was denied

or, if later, 30 days after you received materials in partial compliance with your request; and

(3) May include additional information or evidence to support your request.

(b) How the review is made. After reviewing the prior decision and after considering anything else you have submitted, the Commissioner or his or her designee will affirm or revise all or part of the prior decision. The Commissioner (or a designee) will affirm a denial only after consulting with the appropriate SSA official(s), including legal counsel. The decision must be made within 20 working days after your appeal is received. The Commissioner or a designee may extend this time limit up to 10 additional working days if one of the situations in § 402.140(a) exists, provided that, if a prior extension was used to process this request, the sum of the extensions may not exceed 10 working days. You will be notified in writing of any extension, the reason for the extension, and the date by which your appeal will be decided.

(c) How you are notified of the Commissioner's decision. The Commissioner or a designee will send you a written notice of the decision explaining the basis of the decision (for example, the reasons why an exemption applies) which will include the name and title or position of the person who made the decision. The notice will tell you that if any part of your request remains unsatisfied, you have the right to seek court review.

§ 402.205 U.S. District Court action.

If the Commissioner or a designee, upon review, affirms the denial of your request for records, in whole or in part, you may ask a U.S. District Court to review that denial. See 5 U.S.C. 552(a)(4)(B). If we fail to act on your request for a record or for review of a denial of such a request within the time limits in § 402.140(a) or in § 402.190(b), you may ask a U.S. District Court to treat this as if the Commissioner had denied your request.

PART 403—TESTIMONY BY EMPLOYEES AND THE PRODUCTION OF RECORDS AND INFORMATION IN LEGAL PROCEEDINGS

Authority: Secs. 702(a)(5) and 1106 of the Act, (42 U.S.C. 902(a)(5) and 1306); 5 U.S.C. 301; 31 U.S.C. 9701.

Source: 66 FR 2809, Jan. 12, 2001; 66 FR 9763, Feb. 12, 2001, unless otherwise noted.

§ 403.100 When can an SSA employee testify or produce information or records in legal proceedings?

An SSA employee can testify concerning any function of SSA or any information or record created or acquired by SSA as a result of the discharge of its official duties in any legal proceeding covered by this part only with the prior authorization of the Commissioner. An SSA employee can provide records or other information in a legal proceeding covered by this part only to the extent that doing so is consistent with 20 CFR parts 401 and 402. A request for both testimony and records or other information is considered two separate requests—one for testimony and one for records or other information. SSA maintains a policy of strict impartiality with respect to private litigants and seeks to minimize the disruption of official duties.

§ 403.105 What is the relationship between this part and 20 CFR parts 401 and 402?

(a) General. Disclosure of SSA's records and information contained in those records is governed by the regulations at 20 CFR parts 401 and 402. SSA employees will not disclose records or information in any legal proceeding covered by this part except as permitted by 20 CFR parts 401 and 402.

(b) Requests for information or records that do not include testimony.

(1) If you do not request testimony, §§ 403.120–403.140 do not apply.

(2) If 20 CFR part 401 or 402 permits disclosure to you of any requested record or information, we will make every reasonable effort to provide the disclosable information or record to you on or before the date specified in your request.

(3) If neither 20 CFR part 401 nor 402 permits disclosure of information or a record you request, we will notify you as provided in § 403.145. We will also send you any notices required by part 401 or 402.

§ 403.110 What special definitions apply to this part?

The following definitions apply:

(a) Application means a written request for testimony that conforms to the requirements of § 403.120.

(b)(1) Employee includes—

(i) Any person employed in any capacity by SSA, currently or in the past;

(ii) Any person appointed by, or subject to the supervision, jurisdiction, or control of SSA, the Commissioner of Social Security, or any other SSA official, currently or in the past; and

(iii) Any person who is not described elsewhere in this definition but whose disclosure of information is subject to the regulations at 20 CFR part 401, currently or in the past.

(2) For purposes of this paragraph (b), a person subject to SSA's jurisdiction or control includes any person hired as a contractor by SSA, any person performing services for SSA under an agreement (such as an officer or employee of a State agency involved in determining disability for SSA), and any consultant (including medical or vocational experts or medical services or consultative examination providers), contractor, or subcontractor of such person. Such a person would also include any person who has served or is serving in any advisory capacity, formal or informal.

(3) For purposes of this paragraph (b), a person employed by SSA in the past is considered an employee only when the matter about which the person would testify is one in which he or she was personally involved while at SSA; where the matter concerns official information that the employee acquired while working, such as sensitive or confidential agency information; where the person purports to speak for SSA; or where significant SSA resources would be required to prepare the person to testify. Such a person would not be considered an employee when the person will rely only on expertise or general knowledge he or she acquired while working at SSA.

(c) *Commissioner* means the Commissioner of Social Security or his or her designee(s).

(d) *Legal proceeding* includes any pretrial, trial, and post-trial stage of any existing or reasonably anticipated judicial or administrative action, hearing, investigation, or similar proceeding before a court, commission, board, agency, or other tribunal, authority or entity, foreign or domestic. *Legal proceeding* also includes any deposition or other pretrial proceeding, including a formal or informal request for testimony by an attorney or any other person.

(e) *Record* has the same meaning as "record" in 20 CFR 402.30.

(f) *Request* means any attempt to obtain the production, disclosure, or release of information, records, or the testimony of an SSA employee, including any order, subpoena, or other command issued in a legal proceeding as well as any informal or other attempt (by any method) by a party or a party's representative.

(g) *SSA* means the Social Security Administration.

(h) *Testimony* includes any sworn statement (oral or written), including (but not limited to)—

(1) Any statement provided through personal appearance; deposition; or recorded interview; or provided by telephone, television, or videotape;

(2) Any response during discovery or other similar proceedings that would involve more than the mere physical production of records; and

(3) Any declaration made under penalty of perjury or any affidavit.

(i) *We* or *our* means the Social Security Administration.

(j) *You* or *your* means an individual or entity that submits a request for records, information or testimony.

§ 403.115 When does this part apply?

(a) Except as specified in paragraph (b) of this section, this part applies to any request in connection with any legal proceeding for SSA records or other information or for testimony from SSA or its employees. This part applies to requests for testimony related to SSA's functions or to any information or record created or acquired by SSA as a result of the discharge of its official duties.

(b) This part does not apply to requests for testimony—

(1) In an SSA administrative proceeding;

(2) In a legal proceeding to which SSA is a party ("SSA" here includes the Commissioner and any employee acting in his or her official capacity);

(3) From the United States Department of Justice;

(4) In a criminal proceeding in which the United States is a party;

(5) In a legal proceeding initiated by state or local authorities arising from an investigation or audit initiated by, or conducted in cooperation with, SSA's Office of the Inspector General;

(6) From either house of Congress;

(7) In a law enforcement proceeding related to threats or acts against SSA, its employees, or its operations ("SSA" here includes the Commissioner and any employee acting in his or her official capacity); or

(8) Where Federal law or regulations expressly require a Federal employee to provide testimony.

§ 403.120 How do you request testimony?

(a) You must submit a written application for testimony of an SSA employee. Your application must—

(1) Describe in detail the nature and relevance of the testimony sought in the legal proceeding;

(2) Include a detailed explanation as to why you need the testimony, why you cannot obtain the information you need from an alternative source, and why providing it to you would be in SSA's interest; and

(3) Provide the date and time that you need the testimony and the place where SSA would present it.

(b) You must submit a complete application to SSA at least 30 days in advance of the date that you need the testimony. If your application is submitted fewer than 30 days before that date, you must provide, in addition to the requirements set out above, a detailed explanation as to why—

(1) You did not apply in a timely fashion; and

(2) It is in SSA's interest to review the untimely application.

(c) You must send your application for testimony to: Social Security Administration, Office of the General Counsel, Office of General Law, 6401 Security Boulevard, Room 617 Altmeyer Building, Baltimore, Maryland, 21235–6401, Attn: Touhy Officer. (If you are requesting testimony of an employee of the Office of the Inspector General, send your application to the address in § 403.125.)

(d) The Commissioner has the sole discretion to waive any requirement in this section.

(e) If your application does not include each of the items required by paragraph (a) of this section, we may return it to you for additional information. Unless the Commissioner waives one or more requirements, we will not process an incomplete or untimely application.

[66 FR 14316, March 12, 2001; 73 FR 26002, May 8, 2008; 74 FR 16327, April 10, 2009; 79 FR 7577, Feb. 10, 2014]

§ 403.125 How will we handle requests for records, information, or testimony involving SSA's Office of the Inspector General?

A request for records or information of the Office of the Inspector General or the testimony of an employee of the Office of the Inspector General will be handled in accordance with the provisions of this part, except that the Inspector General or the Inspector General's designee will make those determinations that the Commissioner otherwise would make. Send your request for records or information pertaining to the Office of the Inspector General or your application for testimony of an employee of the Office of the Inspector General to: Office of the Inspector General, Social Security Administration, 300 Altmeyer Building, 6401 Security Blvd., Baltimore, MD 21235–6401.

§ 403.130 What factors may the Commissioner consider in determining whether SSA will grant your application for testimony?

In deciding whether to authorize the testimony of an SSA employee, the Commissioner will consider applicable law and factors relating to your need and the burden to SSA. The considerations include, but are not limited to, the following:

(a) Risk of law violation or compromise of Government privilege.

(1) Would providing the testimony violate a statute (such as 26 U.S.C. 6103 or section 1106 of the Social Security Act, 42 U.S.C. 1306), Executive Order, or regulation (such as 20 CFR part 401)?

(2) Would providing the testimony put confidential, sensitive, or privileged information at risk?

(b) Burden on SSA.

(1) Would granting the application unduly expend for private purposes the resources of the United States (including the time of SSA employees needed for official duties)?

(2) Would the testimony be available in a less burdensome form or from another source?

(3) Would the testimony be limited to the purpose of the request?

(4) Did you previously request the same testimony in the same or a related proceeding?

(c) Interests served by allowing testimony.

(1) Would providing the testimony serve SSA's interest?

(2) Would providing the testimony maintain SSA's policy of impartiality among private litigants?

(3) Is another government agency involved in the proceeding?

(4) Do you need the testimony to prevent fraud or similar misconduct?

(5) Would providing the testimony be necessary to prevent a miscarriage of justice or to preserve the rights of an accused individual to due process in a criminal proceeding?

§ 403.135 What happens to your application for testimony?

(a) If 20 CFR part 401 or 402 does not permit disclosure of information about which you seek testimony from an SSA employee, we will notify you under § 403.145.

(b) If 20 CFR part 401 or 402 permits disclosure of the information about which you seek testimony,

(1) The Commissioner makes the final decision on your application;

(2) All final decisions are in the sole discretion of the Commissioner; and

(3) We will notify you of the final decision on your application.

§ 403.140 If the Commissioner authorizes testimony, what will be the scope and form of that testimony?

The employee's testimony must be limited to matters that were specifically approved. We will provide testimony in the form that is least burdensome to SSA unless you provide sufficient information in your application for SSA to justify a different form. For example, we will provide an affidavit or declaration rather than a deposition and a deposition rather than trial testimony.

§ 403.145 What will SSA do if you have not satisfied the conditions in this part or in 20 CFR part 401 or 402?

(a) We will provide the following information, as appropriate, to you or the court or other tribunal conducting the legal proceeding if your request states that a response is due on a particular date and the conditions prescribed in this part, or the conditions for disclosure in 20 CFR part 401 or 402, are not satisfied or we anticipate that they will not be satisfied by that date:

(1) A statement that compliance with the request is not authorized under 20 CFR part 401 or 402, or is prohibited without the Commissioner's approval;

(2) The requirements for obtaining the approval of the Commissioner for testimony or for obtaining information, records, or testimony under 20 CFR part 401 or 402; and

(3) If the request complies with § 403.120, the estimated time necessary for a decision. We will make every reasonable effort to provide this information in writing on or before the date specified in your request.

(b) Generally, if a response to a request for information, records, or testimony is due before the conditions of this part or the conditions for disclosure in 20 CFR part 401 or 402 are met, no SSA employee will appear.

(c) SSA will seek the advice and assistance of the Department of Justice when appropriate.

§ 403.150 Is there a fee for our services?

(a) General. Unless the Commissioner grants a waiver, you must pay fees for our services in providing information, records, or testimony. You must pay the fees as prescribed by the Commissioner. In addition, the Commissioner may require that you pay the fees in advance as a condition of providing the information, records, or testimony. Make fees payable to the Social Security Administration by check or money order.

(b) Records or information. Unless the Commissioner grants a waiver, you must pay the fees for production of records or information prescribed in 20 CFR §§ 401.95 and 402.155 through 402.185, as appropriate.

(c) Testimony. Unless the Commissioner grants a waiver, you must pay fees calculated to reimburse the United States Government for the full cost of providing the testimony. Those costs include, but are not limited to—

(1) The salary or wages of the witness and related costs for the time necessary to prepare for and provide the testimony and any travel time, and

(2) Other travel costs.

(d) Waiver or reduction of fees. The Commissioner may waive or reduce fees for providing information, records, or testimony under this part. The rules in 20 CFR § 402.185 apply in determining whether to waive fees for the production of records. In deciding whether to waive or reduce fees for testimony or for production of information that does not constitute a record, the Commissioner may consider other factors, including but not limited to—

(1) The ability of the party responsible for the application to pay the full amount of the chargeable fees;

(2) The public interest, as described in 20 CFR § 402.185, affected by complying with the application;

(3) The need for the testimony or information in order to prevent a miscarriage of justice;

(4) The extent to which providing the testimony or information serves SSA's interest; and

(5) The burden on SSA's resources required to provide the information or testimony.

§ 403.155 Does SSA certify records?

We can certify the authenticity of copies of records we disclose pursuant to 20 CFR parts 401 and 402, and this part. We will provide this service only in response to your written request. If we certify, we will do so at the time of the disclosure and will not certify copies of records that have left our custody. A request for certified copies of records previously released is considered a new request for records. Fees for this certification are set forth in 20 CFR 402.165(e).

PART 404—FEDERAL OLD-AGE, SURVIVORS AND DISABILITY INSURANCE (1950–)

SUBPART A—INTRODUCTION, GENERAL PROVISIONS AND DEFINITIONS

SUBPART B—INSURED STATUS AND QUARTERS OF COVERAGE

GENERAL

SUBPART C—COMPUTING PRIMARY INSURANCE AMOUNTS

GENERAL

SUBPART F—OVERPAYMENTS, UNDERPAYMENTS, WAIVER OF ADJUSTMENT OR RECOVERY OF OVERPAYMENTS, AND LIABILITY OF A CERTIFYING OFFICER

SUBPART G—FILING OF APPLICATIONS AND OTHER FORMS

GENERAL PROVISIONS

APPLICATIONS

SUBPART M—COVERAGE OF EMPLOYEES OF STATE AND LOCAL GOVERNMENTS

GENERAL

WHAT GROUPS OF EMPLOYEES MAY BE COVERED

HOW COVERAGE UNDER AGREEMENTS IS OBTAINED AND CONTINUES

HOW TO IDENTIFY COVERED EMPLOYEES

WHAT RECORDS OF COVERAGE MUST BE KEPT

REVIEW OF COMPLIANCE BY STATE WITH ITS AGREEMENT

HOW TO REPORT WAGES AND CONTRIBUTIONS—FOR WAGES PAID PRIOR TO 1987

WHAT IS A STATE'S LIABILITY FOR CONTRIBUTIONS—FOR WAGES PAID PRIOR TO 1987

FIGURING THE AMOUNT OF THE STATE'S CONTRIBUTIONS—FOR WAGES PAID PRIOR TO 1987

IF A STATE FAILS TO MAKE TIMELY PAYMENTS—FOR WAGES PAID PRIOR TO 1987

HOW ERRORS IN REPORTS AND CONTRIBUTIONS ARE ADJUSTED—FOR WAGES PAID PRIOR TO 1987

HOW OVERPAYMENTS OF CONTRIBUTIONS ARE CREDITED OR REFUNDED—FOR WAGES PAID PRIOR TO 1987

Authority: Secs. 202, 203, 204(a) and (e), 205(a) and (c), 216(*l*), 222(c), 223(e), 224, 225, 702(a)(5), and 1129A of the Social Security Act (42 U.S.C. 402, 403, 404(a) and (e), 405(a) and (c), 416(*l*), 422(c), 423(e), 424a, 425, 902(a)(5), and 1320a–8a); 48 U.S.C. 1801.

Source: 76 FR 65108, Oct. 20, 2011; 80 FR 34050, June 15, 2015, unless otherwise noted.

SUBPART A—INTRODUCTION, GENERAL PROVISIONS AND DEFINITIONS

Authority: Secs. 203, 205(a), 216(j), and 702(a)(5) of the Social Security Act (42 U.S.C. 403, 405(a), 416(j), and 902(a)(5)) and 48 U.S.C. 1801.

Source: 51 FR 11718, April 7, 1986; 52 FR 27540, July 22, 1987; 56 FR 60060, Nov. 27, 1991; 61 FR 5940, Feb. 15, 1996; 69 FR 51555, Aug. 20, 2004, unless otherwise noted.

§ 404.1 Introduction.

The regulations in this part 404 (Regulations No. 4 of the Social Security Administration) relate to the provisions of title II of the Social Security Act as amended on August 28, 1950, and as further amended thereafter. The regulations in this part are divided into 22 subparts:

(a) Subpart A contains provisions relating to general definitions and use of terms.

(b) Subpart B relates to quarters of coverage and insured status requirements.

(c) Subpart C relates to the computation and recomputation of the primary insurance amount.

(d) Subpart D relates to the requirements for entitlement to monthly benefits and to the lump-sum death payment duration of entitlement and benefit rates.

(e) Subpart E contains provisions relating to the reduction and increase of insurance benefits and to deductions from benefits and lump-sum death payments.

(f) Subpart F relates to overpayments, underpayments, waiver of adjustment or recovery of overpayments and liability of certifying officers.

(g) Subpart G relates to filing of applications and other forms.

(h) Subpart H relates to evidentiary requirements for establishing an initial and continuing right to monthly benefits and for establishing a right to lump-sum death payment. (Evidentiary requirements relating to disability are contained in subpart P.)

(i) Subpart I relates to maintenance and revision of records of wages and self-employment income.

(j) Subpart J relates to initial determinations, the administrative review process, and reopening of determinations and decisions.

(k) Subpart K relates to employment, wages, self-employment and self-employment income.

(*l*) Subpart L is reserved.

(m) Subpart M relates to coverage of employees of State and local Governments.

(n) Subpart N relates to benefits in cases involving veterans.

(*o*) Subpart O relates to the interrelationship of the old-age, survivors and disability insurance program with the railroad retirement program.

(p) Subpart P relates to the determination of disability or blindness.

(q) Subpart Q relates to standards, requirements and procedures for States making determinations of disability for the Commissioner. It also sets out the Commissioner's responsibilities in carrying out the disability determination function.

(r) Subpart R relates to the provisions applicable to attorneys and other individuals who represent applicants in connection with claims for benefits.

(s) Subpart S relates to the payment of benefits to individuals who are entitled to benefits.

(t) Subpart T relates to the negotiation and administration of totalization agreements between the United States and foreign countries.

(u) Subpart U relates to the selection of a representative payee to receive benefits on behalf of a beneficiary and to the duties and responsibilities of a representative payee.

(v) Subpart V relates to payments to State vocational rehabilitative agencies for vocational rehabilitation services.

[26 FR 7054, Aug. 5, 1961; 26 FR 7760, Aug. 19, 1961, as amended at 27 FR 4513, May 11, 1962; 28 FR 14492, Dec. 31, 1963; 51 FR 11718, April 7, 1986; 62 FR 38450, July 18, 1997; 83 FR 62456, Dec. 4, 2018]

§ 404.2 General definitions and use of terms.

(a) Terms relating to the Act and regulations.

(1) The Act means the Social Security Act, as amended (42 U.S.C. Chapter 7).

(2) Section means a section of the regulations in part 404 of this chapter unless the context indicates otherwise.

(b) Commissioner; Appeals Council; Administrative Law Judge defined.

(1) Commissioner means the Commissioner of Social Security.

(2) Appeals Council means the Appeals Council of the Office of Hearings and Appeals in the Social Security Administration or such member or members thereof as may be designated by the Chairman.

(3) Administrative Law Judge means an Administrative Law Judge in the Office of Hearings and Appeals in the Social Security Administration.

(c) Miscellaneous.

(1) Certify, when used in connection with the duty imposed on the Commissioner by section 205(i) of the act, means that action taken by the Administration in the form of a written statement addressed to the Managing Trustee, setting forth the name and address of the person to whom payment of a benefit or lump sum, or any part thereof, is to be made, the amount to be paid, and the time at which payment should be made.

(2) Benefit means an old-age insurance benefit, disability insurance benefit, wife's insurance benefit, husband's insurance benefit, child's insurance benefit, widow's insurance benefit, widower's insurance benefit, mother's insurance benefit, father's insurance benefit, or parent's insurance benefit under Title II of the Act. (Lump sums, which are death payments under title II of the Act, are excluded from the term benefit as defined in this part to permit greater clarity in the regulations.)

(3) Lump sum means a lump-sum death payment under title II of the act or any person's share of such a payment.

(4) Attainment of age. An individual attains a given age on the first moment of the day preceding the anniversary of his birth corresponding to such age.

(5) State, unless otherwise indicated, includes:

(i) The District of Columbia,

(ii) The Virgin Islands,

(iii) The Commonwealth of Puerto Rico effective January 1, 1951,

(iv) Guam and American Samoa, effective September 13, 1960, generally, and for purposes of sections 210(a) and 211 of the Act effective after 1960 with respect to service performed after 1960, and effective for taxable years beginning after 1960 with respect to crediting net earnings from self-employment and self-employment income,

(v) The Territories of Alaska and Hawaii prior to January 3, 1959, and August 21, 1959, respectively, when those territories acquired statehood, and

(vi) The Commonwealth of the Northern Mariana Islands (CNMI) effective January 1, 1987; Social Security coverage for affected temporary employees of the government of the CNMI is also effective on January 1, 1987, under section 210(a)(7)(E) of the Social Security Act. In addition, Social Security coverage for affected non-temporary employees of the government of the CNMI is effective on October 1, 2012, under section 210(a)(7)(C) of the Social Security Act.

(6) United States, when used in a geographical sense, includes, unless otherwise indicated:

(i) The States,

(ii) The Territories of Alaska and Hawaii prior to January 3, 1959, and August 21, 1959, respectively, when they acquired statehood,

(iii) The District of Columbia,

(iv) The Virgin Islands,

(v) The Commonwealth of Puerto Rico effective January 1, 1951,

(vi) Guam and American Samoa, effective September 13, 1960, generally, and for purposes of sections 210(a) and 211 of the Act, effective after 1960 with respect to service performed after 1960, and effective for taxable years beginning after 1960 with respect to crediting net earnings from self-employment and self-employment income, and

(vii) The Commonwealth of the Northern Mariana Islands effective January 1, 1987.

(7) Masculine gender includes the feminine, unless otherwise indicated.

(8) The terms defined in sections 209, 210, and 211 of the act shall have the meanings therein assigned to them.

[26 FR 7055, Aug. 5, 1961; 26 FR 7760, Aug. 19, 1961, as amended at 28 FR 1037, Feb. 2, 1963; 28 FR 14492, Dec. 31, 1963; 29 FR 15509, Nov. 19, 1964; 41 FR 32886, Aug. 6, 1976; 51 FR 11718, April 7, 1986; 61 FR 41330, Aug. 8, 1996; 62 FR 38450, July 18, 1997; 69 FR 51555, Aug. 20, 2004; 79 FR 33684, June 12, 2014; 83 FR 21708, May 10, 2018]

§ 404.3 General provisions.

(a) Effect of cross references. The cross references in the regulations in this part 404 to other portions of the regulations, when the word see is used, are made only for convenience and shall be given no legal effect.

(b) Periods of limitation ending on nonwork days. Pursuant to the provisions of section 216(j) of the act, effective September 13, 1960, where any provision of title II, or any provision of another law of the United States (other than the Internal Revenue Code of 1954) relating to or changing the effect of title II, or any regulation of the Commissioner issued under title II, provides for a period within which an act is required to be done which affects eligibility for or the amount of any benefit or payment under this title or is necessary to establish or protect any rights under this title, and such period ends on a Saturday, Sunday or Federal legal holiday or on any other day all or part of which is declared to be a nonwork day for Federal employees by statute or Executive Order, then such act shall be considered as done within such period if it is done on the first day thereafter which is not a Saturday, Sunday, or legal holiday or any other day all or part of which is declared to be a nonwork day for Federal employees either by statute or Executive Order. For purposes of this paragraph, the day on which a period ends shall include the final day of any extended period where such extension is authorized by law or by the Commissioner pursuant to law. Such extension of any period of limitation does not apply to periods during which benefits may be paid for months prior to the month an application for such benefits is filed pursuant to § 404.621, or to periods during which an application for benefits may be accepted as such pursuant to § 404.620.

[26 FR 7055, Aug. 5, 1961, as amended at 29 FR 15509, Nov. 19, 1964; 51 FR 11718, April 7, 1986; 61 FR 41330, Aug. 8, 1996; 62 FR 38450, July 18, 1997]

SUBPART B—INSURED STATUS AND QUARTERS OF COVERAGE

Authority: Secs. 205(a), 212, 213, 214, 216, 217, 223, and 702(a)(5) of the Social Security Act (42 U.S.C. 405(a), 412, 413, 414, 416, 417, 423, and 902(a)(5)).

Source: 45 FR 25384, Apr. 15, 1980; 52 FR 27540, July 22, 1987; 61 FR 5940, Feb. 15, 1996, unless otherwise noted.

GENERAL

§ 404.101 Introduction.

(a) Insured status. This subpart explains what we mean when we say that a person has insured status under the social security program. It also describes how a person may become fully insured, currently insured or insured for disability benefits. Your insured status is a basic factor in determining if you are entitled to old-age or disability insurance benefits or to a period of disability. It is also a basic factor in determining if dependents' or survivors' insurance benefits or a lump-sum death payment are payable based on your earnings record. If you are neither fully nor currently insured, no benefits are payable based on your earnings. (Subpart D of this part describes these benefits and the kind of insured status required for each.) In §§ 404.110 through 404.120 we tell how we determine if you are fully or currently insured. The rules for determining if you are insured for purposes of establishing a period of disability or becoming entitled to disability insurance benefits are in §§ 404.130 through 404.133. Whether you have the required insured status depends on the number of quarters of coverage (QCs) you have acquired.

(b) QCs. This subpart also sets out our rules on crediting you with QCs. QCs are used in determining insured status. In general, you are credited with QCs based on the wages you are paid and the self-employment income you derive during certain periods. (See subpart K of this part for a definition of wages and self-employment income.) Our rules on how and when you acquire a QC are contained in §§ 404.140 through 404.146.

§ 404.102 Definitions.

For the purpose of this subpart—

Act means the Social Security Act, as amended.

Age means how many years old you are. You reach a particular age on the day before your birthday. For example, if your sixty-second birthday is on July 1, 1979, you became age 62 on June 30, 1979.

Quarter or calendar quarter means a period of three calendar months ending March 31, June 30, September 30, or December 31 of any year.

We, our, or us means the Social Security Administration.

You or your means the worker whose insured status is being considered.

FULLY INSURED STATUS

§ 404.110 How we determine fully insured status.

(a) General. We describe how we determine the number of quarters of coverage (QCs) you need to be fully insured in paragraphs (b), (c), and (d) of this section. The table in § 404.115 may be used to determine the number of QCs you need to be fully insured under paragraph (b) of this section. We consider certain World War II veterans to have died fully insured (see § 404.111). We also consider certain employees of private nonprofit organizations to be fully insured if they meet special requirements (see § 404.112).

(b) How many QCs you need to be fully insured.

(1) You need at least 6 QCs but not more than 40 QCs to be fully insured. A person who died before 1951 with at least 6 QCs is fully insured.

(2) You are fully insured for old-age insurance benefits if you have one QC (whenever acquired) for each calendar year elapsing after 1950 or, if later, after the year in which you became age 21, and before the year you reach retirement age, that is, before—

(i) The year you become age 62, if you are a woman;

(ii) The year you become age 62, if you are a man who becomes age 62 after 1974;

(iii) The year 1975, if you are a man who became age 62 in 1973 or 1974; or

(iv) The year you became age 65, if you are a man who became age 62 before 1973.

(3) A person who is otherwise eligible for survivor's benefits and who files an application will be entitled to benefits based on your earnings if you die fully insured. You will be fully insured if you had one QC (whenever acquired) for each calendar year elapsing after 1950 or, if later, after the year you became age 21, and before the earlier of the following years:

(i) The year you die; or

(ii) The year you reach retirement age as shown in paragraph (b)(2) of this section.

(c) How a period of disability affects the number of QCs you need. In determining the number of elapsed years under paragraph (b) of this section, we do not count as an elapsed year any year which is wholly or partly in a period of disability we established for you. For example, if we established a period of disability for you from December 5, 1975 through January 31, 1977, the three years, 1975, 1976 and 1977, would not be counted as elapsed years.

(d) How we credit QCs for fully insured status based on your total wages before 1951—

(1) General. For purposes of paragraph (b) of this section, we may use the following rules in crediting QCs based on your wages before 1951 instead of the rule in § 404.141(b)(1).

(i) We may consider you to have one QC for each $400 of your total wages before 1951, as defined in paragraph (d)(2) of this section, if you have at least 7 elapsed years as determined under paragraph (b)(2) or (b)(3) of this section; and the number of QCs determined under this paragraph plus the number of QCs credited to you for periods after 1950 make you fully insured.

(ii) If you file an application in June 1992 or later and you are not entitled to a benefit under section 227 of the Act in the month the application is made, we may consider you to have at least one QC before 1951 if you have $400 or more total wages before 1951, as defined in paragraph (d)(2) of this section, provided that the number of QCs credited to you under this paragraph plus the number of QCs credited to you for periods after 1950 make you fully insured.

(2) What are total wages before 1951. For purposes of paragraph (d)(1) of this section, your total wages before 1951 include—

(i) Remuneration credited to you before 1951 on the records of the Secretary;

(ii) Wages considered paid to you before 1951 under section 217 of the Act (relating to benefits in case of veterans);

(iii) Compensation under the Railroad Retirement Act of 1937 before 1951 that can be credited to you under title II of the Social Security Act; and

(iv) Wages considered paid to you before 1951 under section 231 of the Act (relating to benefits in case of certain persons interned in the United States during World War II).

(e) When your fully insured status begins. You are fully insured as of the first day of the calendar quarter in which you acquire the last needed QC (see § 404.145).

[50 FR 36573, Sept. 9, 1985; 50 FR 38113, Sept. 20, 1985; 57 FR 23156, June 2, 1992; 83 FR 21708, May 10, 2018]

§ 404.111 When we consider a person fully insured based on World War II active military or naval service.

We consider that a person, who was not otherwise fully insured, died fully insured if—

(a) The person was in the active military or naval service of the United States during World War II;

(b) The person died within three years after separation from service and before July 27, 1954; and

(c) The conditions in § 404.1350 that permit us to consider the person fully insured are met.

(d) The provisions of this section do not apply to persons filing applications after May 31, 1992, unless a survivor is entitled to benefits under section 202 of the Act based on the primary insurance amount of the fully insured person for the month preceding the month in which the application is made.

[57 FR 23157, June 2, 1992]

§ 404.112 When we consider certain employees of private nonprofit organizations to be fully insured.

If you are age 55 or over on January 1, 1984, and are on that date an employee of an organization described in § 404.1025(a) which does not have in effect a waiver certificate under section 3121(k) of the Code on that date and whose employees are mandatorily covered as a result of section 102 of Pub.L. 98–21, we consider you to be fully insured if you meet the following requirements:

Your age on January 1, 1984 is–	QC's acquired after Dec. 31, 1983
60 or over	6
59 or over but less than age 60	8
58 or over but less than age 59	12
57 or over but less than age 58	16
55 or over but less than age 57	20

[50 FR 36573, Sept. 9, 1985; 50 FR 38113, Sept. 20, 1985]

§ 404.115 Table for determining the quarters of coverage you need to be fully insured.

(a) General. You may use the following table to determine the number of quarters of coverage (QCs) you need to be fully insured under § 404.110. Paragraphs (b) and (c) of this section tell you how to use this table.

Worker who reaches retirement age as described in § 404.110(b)(2)			Worker who dies before reaching retirement age as described in §404.110(b)(2)		
Col. I–Date of birth	Col. II[1] Men	Women	Col. III[2] Year of death	Col. IV[3]	Col. V[4] Age in year of death
Jan. 1, 1893 or earlier	6	6	[5] 1957	6	[6] 28
Jan. 2, 1893 to Jan. 1, 1894	7	6	1958	7	29
Jan. 2, 1894 to Jan. 1, 1895	8	6	1959	8	30
Jan. 2, 1895 to Jan. 1, 1896	9	6	1960	9	31
Jan. 2, 1896 to Jan. 1, 1897	10	7	1961	10	32
Jan. 2, 1897 to Jan. 1, 1898	11	8	1962	11	33
Jan. 2, 1898 to Jan. 1, 1899	12	9	1963	12	34
Jan. 2, 1899 to Jan. 1, 1900	13	10	1964	13	35
Jan. 2, 1900 to Jan. 1, 1901	14	11	1965	14	36
Jan. 2, 1901 to Jan. 1, 1902	15	12	1966	15	37
Jan. 2, 1902 to Jan. 1, 1903	16	13	1967	16	38
Jan. 2, 1903 to Jan. 1, 1904	17	14	1968	17	39
Jan. 2, 1904 to Jan. 1, 1905	18	15	1969	18	40
Jan. 2, 1905 to Jan. 1, 1906	19	16	1970	19	41
Jan. 2, 1906 to Jan. 1, 1907	20	17	1971	20	42
Jan. 2, 1907 to Jan. 1, 1908	21	18	1972	21	43
Jan. 2, 1908 to Jan. 1, 1909	22	19	1973	22	44
Jan. 2, 1909 to Jan. 1, 1910	23	20	1974	23	45
Jan. 2, 1910 to Jan. 1, 1911	24	21	1975	24	46
Jan. 2, 1911 to Jan. 1, 1912	24	22	1976	25	47
Jan. 2, 1912 to Jan. 1, 1913	24	23	1977	26	48
Jan. 2, 1913 to Jan. 1, 1914	24	24	1978	27	49

Worker who reaches retirement age as described in § 404.110(b)(2)			Worker who dies before reaching retirement age as described in §404.110(b)(2)		
Col. I–Date of birth	Col. II [1]		Col. III [2]	Col. IV [3]	Col. V [4]
	Men	Women	Year of death		Age in year of death
Jan. 2, 1914 to Jan. 1, 1915	25	25	1979	28	50
Jan. 2, 1915 to Jan. 1, 1916	26	26	1980	29	51
Jan. 2, 1916 to Jan. 1, 1917	27	27	1981	30	52
Jan. 2, 1917 to Jan. 1, 1918	28	28	1982	31	53
Jan. 2, 1918 to Jan. 1, 1919	29	29	1983	32	54
Jan. 2, 1919 to Jan. 1, 1920	30	30	1984	33	55
Jan. 2, 1920 to Jan. 1, 1921	31	31	1985	34	56
Jan. 2, 1921 to Jan. 1, 1922	32	32	1986	35	57
Jan. 2, 1922 to Jan. 1, 1923	33	33	1987	36	58
Jan. 2, 1923 to Jan. 1, 1924	34	34	1988	37	59
Jan. 2, 1924 to Jan. 1, 1925	35	35	1989	38	60
Jan. 2, 1925 to Jan. 1, 1926	36	36	1990	39	61
Jan. 2, 1926 to Jan. 1, 1927	37	37	[7]1991	40	62
Jan. 2, 1927 to Jan. 1, 1928	38	38	....	....	....
Jan. 2, 1928 to Jan. 1, 1929	39	39	....	....	....
Jan. 2, 1929 or later	40	....	....	....	....

[1] Number of QCs required for fully insured status; living worker or worker who dies after reaching retirement age.
[2] Worker born before Jan. 2, 1930 who dies before reaching retirement age.
[3] Number of QCs required for fully insured status.
[4] Worker born Jan. 2, 1930 or later, who dies before reaching retirement age.
[5] Or earlier.
[6] Or younger.
[7] Or later.

(b) Number of QCs you need. The QCs you need for fully insured status are in column II opposite your date of birth in column I. If a worker dies before reaching retirement age as described in § 404.110(b)(2), the QCs needed for fully insured status are shown in column IV opposite—

(1) The year of death in column III, if the worker was born before January 2, 1930; or

(2) The age in the year of death in column V, if the worker was born after January 1, 1930.

(c) How a period of disability affects the number of QCs you need. If you had a period of disability established for you, it affects the number of QCs you need to be fully insured (see § 404.110(c)). For each year which is wholly or partly in a period of disability, subtract one QC from the number of QCs shown in the appropriate line and column of the table as explained in paragraph (b) of this section.

CURRENTLY INSURED STATUS

§ 404.120 How we determine currently insured status.

(a) What the period is for determining currently insured status. You are currently insured if you have at least 6 quarters of coverage (QCs) during the 13–quarter period ending with the quarter in which you—

(1) Die;

(2) Most recently became entitled to disability insurance benefits; or

(3) Became entitled to old-age insurance benefits.

(b) What quarters are not counted as part of the 13–quarter period. We do not count as part of the 13–quarter period any quarter all or part of which is included in a period of disability established for you, except that the first and last quarters of the period of disability may be counted if they are QCs (see § 404.146(d)).

DISABILITY INSURED STATUS

§ 404.130 How we determine disability insured status.

(a) General. We have four different rules for determining if you are insured for purposes of establishing a period of disability or becoming entitled to disability insurance benefits. To have disability insured status, you must meet one of these rules and you must be fully insured (see § 404.132 which tells when the period ends for determining the number of quarters of coverage (QCs) you need to be fully insured).

(b) Rule I—You must meet the 20/40 requirement. You are insured in a quarter for purposes of establishing a period of disability or becoming entitled to disability insurance benefits if in that quarter—

(1) You are fully insured; and

(2) You have at least 20 QCs in the 40–quarter period (see paragraph (f) of this section) ending with that quarter.

(c) Rule II—You become disabled before age 31. You are insured in a quarter for purposes of establishing a period of disability or becoming entitled to disability insurance benefits if in that quarter—

(1) You have not become (or would not become) age 31;

(2) You are fully insured; and

(3) You have QCs in at least one-half of the quarters during the period ending with that quarter and begin-

ning with the quarter after the quarter you became age 21; however—

(i) If the number of quarters during this period is an odd number, we reduce the number by one; and

(ii) If the period has less than 12 quarters, you must have at least 6 QCs in the 12–quarter period ending with that quarter.

(d) Rule III—You had a period of disability before age 31. You are insured in a quarter for purposes of establishing a period of disability or becoming entitled to disability insurance benefits if in that quarter—

(1) You are disabled again at age 31 or later after having had a prior period of disability established which began before age 31 and for which you were only insured under paragraph (c) of this section; and

(2) You are fully insured and have QCs in at least one-half the calendar quarters in the period beginning with the quarter after the quarter you became age 21 and through the quarter in which the later period of disability begins, up to a maximum of 20 QCs out of 40 calendar quarters; however—

(i) If the number of quarters during this period is an odd number, we reduce the number by one;

(ii) If the period has less than 12 quarters, you must have at least 6 QCs in the 12–quarter period ending with that quarter; and

(iii) No monthly benefits may be paid or increased under Rule III before May 1983.

(e) Rule IV—You are statutorily blind. You are insured in a quarter for purposes of establishing a period of disability or becoming entitled to disability insurance benefits if in that quarter—

(1) You are disabled by blindness as defined in § 404.1581; and

(2) You are fully insured.

(f) How we determine the 40–quarter or other period. In determining the 40–quarter period or other period in paragraph (b), (c), or (d) of this section, we do not count any quarter all or part of which is in a prior period of disability established for you, unless the quarter is the first or last quarter of this period and the quarter is a QC. However, we will count all the quarters in the prior period of disability established for you if by doing so you would be entitled to benefits or the amount of the benefit would be larger.

[49 FR 28547, July 13, 1984; 55 FR 7313, March 1, 1990]

§ 404.131 When you must have disability insured status.

(a) For a period of disability. To establish a period of disability, you must have disability insured status in the quarter in which you become disabled or in a later quarter in which you are disabled.

(b) For disability insurance benefits.

(1) To become entitled to disability insurance benefits, you must have disability insured status in the first full month that you are disabled as described in § 404.1501(a), or if later—

(i) The 17th month (if you have to serve a waiting period described in § 404.315(d)) before the month in which you file an application for disability insurance benefits; or

(ii) The 12th month (if you do not have to serve a waiting period) before the month in which you file an application for disability insurance benefits.

(2) If you do not have disability insured status in a month specified in paragraph (b)(1) of this section, you will be insured for disability insurance benefits beginning with the first month after that month in which you do meet the insured status requirement and you also meet all other requirements for disability insurance benefits described in § 404.315.

§ 404.132 How we determine fully insured status for a period of disability or disability insurance benefits.

In determining if you are fully insured for purposes of paragraph (b), (c), (d), or (e) of § 404.130 on disability insured status, we use the fully insured status requirements in § 404.110, but apply the following rules in determining when the period of elapsed years ends:

(a) If you are a woman, or a man born after January 1, 1913, the period of elapsed years in § 404.110(b) used in determining the number of quarters of coverage (QCs) you need to be fully insured ends as of the earlier of—

(1) The year you become age 62; or

(2) The year in which—

(i) Your period of disability begins;

(ii) Your waiting period begins (see § 404.315(d)); or

(iii) You become entitled to disability insurance benefits (if you do not have to serve a waiting period).

(b) If you are a man born before January 2, 1913, the period of elapsed years in § 404.110(b) used in determining the number of QCs you need to be fully insured ends as of the earlier of—

(1) The year 1975; or

(2) The year specified in paragraph (a)(2) of this section.

[49 FR 28547, July 13, 1984]

§ 404.133 When we give you quarters of coverage based on military service to establish a period of disability.

For purposes of establishing a period of disability only, we give you quarters of coverage (QCs) for your military service before 1957 (see subpart N of this part). We do this even though we may not use that military service for other purposes of title II of the Act because a periodic benefit is payable from another Federal agency based in whole or in part on the same period of military service.

QUARTERS OF COVERAGE

§ 404.140 What is a quarter of coverage.

(a) General. A quarter of coverage (QC) is the basic unit of social security coverage used in determining a worker's insured status. We credit you with QCs based on your earnings covered under social security.

(b) How we credit QCs based on earnings before 1978 (General). Before 1978, wages were generally reported on a quarterly basis and self-employment income was reported on an annual basis. For the most part, we credit QCs for calendar years before 1978 based on your quarterly earnings. For these years, as explained in § 404.141, we generally credit you with a QC for each calendar quarter in which you were paid at least $50 in wages or were credited with at least $100 of self-employment income. Section 404.142 tells how self-employment income derived in a taxable year beginning before 1978 is credited to specific calendar quarters for purposes of § 404.141.

(c) How we credit QCs based on earnings after 1977 (General). After 1977, both wages and self-employment income are generally reported on an annual basis. For calendar years after 1977, as explained in § 404.143, we generally credit you with a QC for each part of your total covered earnings in a calendar year that equals the amount required for a QC in that year. Section 404.143 also tells how the amount required for a QC will be increased in the future as average wages increase. Section 404.144 tells how self-employment income derived in a taxable year beginning after 1977 is credited to specific calendar years for purposes of § 404.143.

(d) When a QC is acquired and when a calendar quarter is not a QC (general). Section 404.145 tells when a QC is acquired and § 404.146 tells when a calendar quarter cannot be a QC. These rules apply when we credit QCs under § 404.141 or § 404.143.

§ 404.141 How we credit quarters of coverage for calendar years before 1978.

(a) General. The rules in this section tell how we credit calendar quarters as quarters of coverage (QCs) for calendar years before 1978. We credit you with a QC for a calendar quarter based on the amount of wages you were paid and self-employment income you derived during certain periods. The rules in paragraphs (b), (c), and (d) of this section are subject to the limitations in § 404.146, which tells when a calendar quarter cannot be a QC.

(b) How we credit QCs based on wages paid in, or self-employment income credited to, a calendar quarter. We credit you with a QC for a calendar quarter in which—

(1) You were paid wages of $50 or more (see paragraph (c) of this section for an exception relating to wages paid for agricultural labor); or

(2) You were credited (under § 404.142) with self-employment income of $100 or more.

(c) How we credit QCs based on wages paid for agricultural labor in a calendar year after 1954.

(1) We credit QCs based on wages for agricultural labor depending on the amount of wages paid during a calendar year for that work. If you were paid wages for agricultural labor in a calendar year after 1954 and before 1978, we credit you with QCs for calendar quarters in that year which are not otherwise QCs according to the following table.

If the wages paid to you in a calendar year for agricultural labor were	We credit you with	And assign:[1]
$400 or more	4 QCs	All.
At least $300 but less than $400	3 QCs	Last 3.
At least $200 but less than $300	2 QCs	Last 2.
At least $100 but less than $200	1 QC	Last.
Less than $100	No QCs	

[1] One QC to each of the following calendar quarters in that year.

(2) When we assign QCs to calendar quarters in a year as shown in the table in paragraph (c)(1) of this section, you might not meet (or might not meet as early in the year as otherwise possible) the requirements to be fully or currently insured, to be entitled to a computation or recomputation of your primary insurance amount, or to establish a period of disability. If this happens, we assign the QCs to different quarters in that year than those shown in the table if this assignment permits you to meet these requirements (or meet them earlier in the year). We can only reassign QCs for purposes of meeting these requirements.

(d) How we credit QCs based on wages paid or self-employment income derived in a year.

(1) If you were paid wages in a calendar year after 1950 and before 1978 at least equal to the annual wage limitation in effect for that year as described in §§ 404.1047 and 404.1096, we credit you with a QC for each quarter in that calendar year. If you were paid at least $3,000 wages in a calendar year before 1951, we credit you with a QC for each quarter in that calendar year.

(2) If you derived self-employment income (or derived self-employment income and also were paid wages) during a taxable year beginning after 1950 and before 1978 at least equal to the self-employment

income and wage limitation in effect for that year as described in § 404.1068(b), we credit you with a QC for each calendar quarter wholly or partly in that taxable year.

[45 FR 25834, April 15, 1980; 45 FR 41931, June 3, 1980; 70 FR 14977, March 24, 2005]

§ 404.142 How we credit self-employment income to calendar quarters for taxable years beginning before 1978.

In crediting quarters of coverage under § 404.141(b)(2), we credit any self-employment income you derived during a taxable year that began before 1978 to calendar quarters as follows:

(a) If your taxable year was a calendar year, we credit your self-employment income equally to each quarter of that calendar year.

(b) If your taxable year was not a calendar year (that is, it began on a date other than January 1, or was less than a calendar year), we credit your self-employment income equally—

(1) To the calendar quarter in which your taxable year ended; and

(2) To each of the next three or fewer preceding quarters that were wholly or partly in your taxable year.

§ 404.143 How we credit quarters of coverage for calendar years after 1977.

(a) Crediting quarters of coverage (QCs). For calendar years after 1977, we credit you with a QC for each part of the total wages paid and self-employment income credited (under § 404.144) to you in a calendar year that equals the amount required for a QC in that year. For example, if the total of your wages and self-employment income for a calendar year is more than twice, but less than 3 times, the amount required for a QC in that year, we credit you with only 2 QCs for the year. The rules for crediting QCs in this section are subject to the limitations in § 404.146, which tells when a calendar quarter cannot be a QC. In addition, we cannot credit you with more than four QCs for any calendar year. The amount of wages and self-employment income that you must have for each QC is—

(1) $250 for calendar year 1978; and

(2) For each calendar year after 1978, an amount determined by the Commissioner for that year (on the basis of a formula in section 213(d)(2) of the Act which reflects national increases in average wages). The amount determined by the Commissioner is published in the Federal Register on or before November 1 of the preceding year and included in the appendix to this subpart.

(b) Assigning QCs. We assign a QC credited under paragraph (a) of this section to a specific calendar quarter in the calendar year only if the assignment is necessary to—

(1) Give you fully or currently insured status;

(2) Entitle you to a computation or recomputation of your primary insurance amount; or

(3) Permit you to establish a period of disability.

[62 FR 38450, July 18, 1997]

§ 404.144 How we credit self-employment income to calendar years for taxable years beginning after 1977.

In crediting quarters of coverage under § 404.143(a), we credit self-employment income you derived during a taxable year that begins after 1977 to calendar years as follows:

(a) If your taxable year is a calendar year or begins and ends within the same calendar year, we credit your self-employment income to that calendar year.

(b) If your taxable year begins in one calendar year and ends in the following calendar year, we allocate proportionately your self-employment income to the two calendar years on the basis of the number of months in each calendar year which are included completely within your taxable year. We consider the calendar month in which your taxable year ends as included completely within your taxable year.

Example: For the taxable year beginning May 15, 1978, and ending May 14, 1979, your self-employment income is $1200. We credit 7⁄12 ($700) of your self-employment income to calendar year 1978 and 5⁄12 ($500) of your self-employment income to calendar year 1979.

§ 404.145 When you acquire a quarter of coverage.

If we credit you with a quarter of coverage (QC) for a calendar quarter under paragraph (b), (c), or (d) of § 404.141 for calendar years before 1978 or assign it to a specific calendar quarter under paragraph (b) of § 404.143 for calendar years after 1977, you acquire the QC as of the first day of the calendar quarter.

§ 404.146 When a calendar quarter cannot be a quarter of coverage.

This section applies when we credit you with quarters of coverage (QCs) under § 404.141 for calendar years before 1978 and under § 404.143 for calendar years after 1977. We cannot credit you with a QC for—

(a) A calendar quarter that has not begun;

(b) A calendar quarter that begins after the quarter of your death;

(c) A calendar quarter that has already been counted as a QC; or

(d) A calendar quarter that is included in a period of disability established for you, unless—

(1) The quarter is the first or the last quarter of this period; or

(2) The period of disability is not taken into consideration (see § 404.320(a)).

APPENDIX TO SUBPART B OF PART 404—QUARTER OF COVERAGE AMOUNTS FOR CALENDAR YEARS AFTER 1978

This appendix shows the amount determined by the Commissioner that is needed for a quarter of coverage for each year after 1978 as explained in § 404.143. We publish the amount as a Notice in the Federal Register on or before November 1 of the preceding year. The amounts determined by the Commissioner are as follows:

Calendar year	Amount needed
1979	$260
1980	290
1981	310
1982	340
1983	370
1984	390
1985	410
1986	440
1987	460
1988	470
1989	500
1990	520
1991	540
1992	570

[52 FR 8247, March 17, 1987; 57 FR 44096, Sept. 24, 1992; 62 FR 38450, July 18, 1997]

SUBPART C—COMPUTING PRIMARY INSURANCE AMOUNTS

Authority: Secs. 202(a), 205(a), 215, and 702(a)(5) of the Social Security Act (42 U.S.C. 402(a), 405(a), 415, and 902(a)(5)).

Source: 61 FR 5940, Feb. 15, 1996, unless otherwise noted.

GENERAL

Authority: Secs. 202(a), 205(a), 215, and 1102 of the Social Security Act; 42 U.S.C. 402(a), 405(a), 415 and 1302.

Source: 41 FR 44363, Oct. 8, 1976; 47 FR 30734, July 15, 1982; 51 FR 4481, Feb. 5, 1986; 51 FR 12603, April 14, 1986; 52 FR 8247, March 17, 1987; 52 FR 27540, July 22, 1987, unless otherwise noted.

§ 404.201 What is included in this subpart?

In this subpart we describe how we compute your primary insurance amount (PIA), how and when we will recalculate or recompute your PIA to include credit for additional earnings, and how we automatically adjust your PIA to reflect changes in the cost of living.

(a) What is my primary insurance amount? Your primary insurance amount (PIA) is the basic figure we use to determine the monthly benefit amount payable to you and your family. For example, if you retire in the month you attain full retirement age (as defined in § 404.409) or if you become disabled, you will be entitled to a monthly benefit equal to your PIA. If you retire prior to full retirement age your monthly benefit will be reduced as explained in §§ 404.410—404.413. Benefits to other members of your family are a specified percentage of your PIA as explained in subpart D. Total benefits to your family are subject to a maximum as explained in § 404.403.

(b) How is this subpart organized?

(1) In §§ 404.201 through 404.204, we explain some introductory matters.

(2) In §§ 404.210 through 404.213, we describe the average-indexed-monthly-earnings method we use to compute the primary insurance amount (PIA) for workers who attain age 62 (or become disabled or die before age 62) after 1978.

(3) In §§ 404.220 through 404.222, we describe the average-monthly-wage method we use to compute the PIA for workers who attain age 62 (or become disabled or die before age 62) before 1979.

(4) In §§ 404.230 through 404.233, we describe the guaranteed alternative method we use to compute the PIA for people who attain age 62 after 1978 but before 1984.

(5) In §§ 404.240 through 404.243, we describe the old-start method we use to compute the PIA for those who had all or substantially all of their social security covered earnings before 1951.

(6) In §§ 404.250 through 404.252, we describe special rules we use to compute the PIA for a worker who previously had a period of disability.

(7) In §§ 404.260 through 404.261, we describe how we compute the special minimum PIA for long-term, low-paid workers.

(8) In §§ 404.270 through 404.278, we describe how we automatically increase your PIA because of increases in the cost of living.

(9) In §§ 404.280 through 404.288, we describe how and when we will recompute your PIA to include additional earnings which were not used in the original computation.

(10) In § 404.290 we describe how and when we will recalculate your PIA.

(11) Appendices I–VII contain material such as figures and formulas that we use to compute PIAs. [68 FR 4701, Jan. 30, 2003]

§ 404.202 Other regulations related to this subpart.

This subpart is related to several others. In subpart B of this part, we describe how you become insured for social security benefits as a result of your work in covered employment. In subpart D, we discuss the different kinds of social security benefits available—

old-age and disability benefits for you and benefits for your dependents and survivors—the amount of the benefits, and the requirements you and your family must meet to qualify for them; your work status, your age, the size of your family, and other factors may affect the amount of the benefits for you and your family. Rules relating to deductions, reductions, and nonpayment of benefits we describe in subpart E. In subpart F of this part, we describe what we do when a recalculation or recomputation of your primary insurance amount (as described in this subpart) results in our finding that you and your family have been overpaid or underpaid. In subparts G and H of this part, we tell how to apply for benefits and what evidence is needed to establish entitlement to them. In subpart J of this part, we describe how benefits are paid. Then in subparts I, K, N, and O of this part, we discuss your earnings that are taxable and creditable for social security purposes (and how we keep records of them), and deemed military wage credits which may be used in finding your primary insurance amount.

§ 404.203 Definitions.

(a) General definitions. As used in this subpart—

Ad hoc increase in primary insurance amounts means an increase in primary insurance amounts enacted by the Congress and signed into law by the President.

Entitled means that a person has applied for benefits and has proven his or her right to them for a given period of time.

We, us, or our means the Social Security Administration.

You or your means the insured worker who has applied for benefits or a deceased insured worker on whose social security earnings record someone else has applied.

(b) Other definitions. To make it easier to find them, we have placed other definitions in the sections of this subpart in which they are used.

[62 FR 38450, July 18, 1997]

§ 404.204 Methods of computing primary insurance amounts—general.

(a) General. We compute most workers' primary insurance amounts under one of two major methods. There are, in addition, several special methods of computing primary insurance amounts which we apply to some workers. Your primary insurance amount is the highest of all those computed under the methods for which you are eligible.

(b) Major methods.

(1) If after 1978 you reach age 62, or become disabled or die before age 62, we compute your primary insurance amount under what we call the average-indexed-monthly-earnings method, which is described in §§ 404.210 through 404.212. The earliest of the three dates determines the computation method we use.

(2) If before 1979 you reached age 62, became disabled, or died, we compute your primary insurance amount under what we call the average-monthly-wage method, described in §§ 404.220 through 404.222.

(c) Special methods.

(1) Your primary insurance amount, computed under any of the special methods for which you are eligible as described in this paragraph, may be substituted for your primary insurance amount computed under either major method described in paragraph (b) of this section.

(2) If you reach age 62 during the period 1979–1983, your primary insurance amount is guaranteed to be the highest of—

(i) The primary insurance amount we compute for you under the average-indexed-monthly-earnings method;

(ii) The primary insurance amount we compute for you under the average-monthly-wage method, as modified by the rules described in §§ 404.230 through 404.233; or

(iii) The primary insurance amount computed under what we call the old-start method; as described in §§ 404.240 through 404.242.

(3) If you had all or substantially all of your social security earnings before 1951, we will also compute your primary insurance amount under what we call the old-start method.

(4) We compute your primary insurance amount under the rules in §§ 404.250 through 404.252, if—

(i) You were disabled and received social security disability insurance benefits sometime in your life;

(ii) Your disability insurance benefits were terminated because of your recovery or because you engaged in substantial gainful activity; and

(iii) You are, after 1978, re-entitled to disability insurance benefits, or entitled to old-age insurance benefits, or have died.

(5) In some situations, we use what we call a special minimum computation, described in §§ 404.260 through 404.261, to find your primary insurance amount. Computations under this method reflect long-term, low-wage attachment to covered work.

AVERAGE–INDEXED–MONTHLY EARNINGS METHOD OF COMPUTING PRIMARY INSURANCE AMOUNTS

§ 404.210 Average-indexed-monthly-earnings method.

(a) Who is eligible for this method. If after 1978, you reach age 62, or become disabled or die before age

62, we will compute your primary insurance amount under the average-indexed-monthly-earnings method.

(b) Steps in computing your primary insurance amount under the average-indexed-monthly-earnings method. We follow these three major steps in computing your primary insurance amount:

(1) First, we find your average indexed monthly earnings, as described in § 404.211;

(2) Second, we find the benefit formula in effect for the year you reach age 62, or become disabled or die before age 62, as described in § 404.212; and

(3) Then, we apply that benefit formula to your average indexed monthly earnings to find your primary insurance amount, as described in § 404.212.

(4) Next, we apply any automatic cost-of-living or ad hoc increases in primary insurance amounts that became effective in or after the year you reached age 62, unless you are receiving benefits based on the minimum primary insurance amount, in which case not all the increases may be applied, as described in § 404.277.

§ 404.211 Computing your average indexed monthly earnings.

(a) General. In this method, your social security earnings after 1950 are indexed, as described in paragraph (d) of this section, then averaged over the period of time you can reasonably have been expected to have worked in employment or self-employment covered by social security. (Your earnings before 1951 are not used in finding your average indexed monthly earnings.)

(b) Which earnings may be used in computing your average indexed monthly earnings—

(1) Earnings. In computing your average indexed monthly earnings, we use wages, compensation, self-employment income, and deemed military wage credits (see §§ 404.1340 through 404.1343) that are creditable to you for social security purposes for years after 1950.

(2) Computation base years. We use your earnings in your computation base years in finding your average indexed monthly earnings. All years after 1950 up to (but not including) the year you become entitled to old-age or disability insurance benefits, and through the year you die if you had not been entitled to old-age or disability benefits, are computation base years for you. The year you become entitled to benefits and following years may be used as computation base years in a recomputation if their use would result in a higher primary insurance amount. (See §§ 404.280 through 404.287.) However, years after the year you die may not be used as computation base years even if you have earnings credited to you in those years. Computation base years do not include years wholly within a period of disability unless your primary insurance amount would be higher by using the disability years. In such situations, we count all the years during the period of disability, even if you had no earnings in some of them.

(c) Average of the total wages. Before we compute your average indexed monthly earnings, we must first know the "average of the total wages" of all workers for each year from 1951 until the second year before you become eligible. The average of the total wages for years after 1950 are shown in appendix I. Corresponding figures for more recent years which have not yet been incorporated into this appendix are published in the Federal Register on or before November 1 of the succeeding year. "Average of the total wages" (or "average wage") means:

(1) For the years 1951 through 1977, four times the amount of average taxable wages that were reported to the Social Security Administration for the first calendar quarter of each year for social security tax purposes. For years prior to 1973, these average wages were determined from a sampling of these reports.

(2) For the years 1978 through 1990, all remuneration reported as wages on Form W–2 to the Internal Revenue Service for all employees for income tax purposes, divided by the number of wage earners. We adjusted those averages to make them comparable to the averages for 1951–1977. For years after 1977, the term includes remuneration for services not covered by social security and remuneration for covered employment in excess of that which is subject to FICA contributions.

(3) For years after 1990, all remuneration reported as wages on Form W–2 to the Internal Revenue Service for all employees for income tax purposes, including remuneration described in paragraph (c)(2) of this section, plus contributions to certain deferred compensation plans described in section 209(k) of the Social Security Act (also reported on Form W–2), divided by the number of wage earners. If both distributions from and contributions to any such deferred compensation plan are reported on Form W–2, we will include only the contributions in the calculation of the average of the total wages. We will adjust those averages to make them comparable to the averages for 1951–1990.

(d) Indexing your earnings.

(1) The first step in indexing your social security earnings is to find the relationship (under paragraph (d)(2) of this section) between—

(i) The average wage of all workers in your computation base years; and

(ii) The average wage of all workers in your indexing year. As a general rule, your indexing year is the second year before the earliest of the year you reach age 62, or become disabled or die before age 62. However, your indexing year is determined under paragraph (d)(4) of this section if you die before age 62, your surviving spouse or surviving divorced spouse is first eligible for benefits after 1984, and the indexing year explained in paragraph (d)(4) results in a higher widow(er)'s benefit than results from determining the indexing year under the general rule.

(2) To find the relationship, we divide the average wages for your indexing year, in turn, by the average wages for each year beginning with 1951 and ending with your indexing year. We use the quotients found in these divisions to index your earnings as described in paragraph (d)(3) of this section.

(3) The second step in indexing your social security earnings is to multiply the actual year-by-year dollar amounts of your earnings (up to the maximum amounts creditable, as explained in §§ 404.1047 and 404.1096 of this part) by the quotients found in paragraph (d)(2) of this section for each of those years. We round the results to the nearer penny. (The quotient for your indexing year is 1.0; this means that your earnings in that year are used in their actual dollar amount; any earnings after your indexing year that may be used in computing your average indexed monthly earnings are also used in their actual dollar amount.)

Example: Ms. A reaches age 62 in July 1979. Her year-by-year social security earnings since 1950 are as follows:

Year	Earnings
1951	$3,200
1952	3,400
1953	3,300
1954	3,600
1955	3,700
1956	3,700
1957	4,000
1958	4,200
1959	4,400
1960	4,500
1961	2,800
1962	2,200
1963	0
1964	0
1965	3,700
1966	4,500
1967	5,400
1968	6,200
1969	6,900
1970	7,300
1971	7,500
1972	7,800
1973	8,200
1974	9,000
1975	9,900
1976	11,100
1977	9,900
1978	11,000

Step 1. The first step in indexing Ms. A's earnings is to find the relationship between the general wage level in Ms. A's indexing year (1977) and the general wage level in each of the years 1951–1976. We refer to appendix I for average wage figures, and perform the following computations:

Year	I. 1977 general wage level	II. Nation wide average of the total wages	III. Column I divided by column II equals relationship
1951	$9,779.44	$2,799.16	3.4937053
1952	9,779.44	2,973.32	3.2890641
1953	9,779.44	3,139.44	3.1150269
1954	9,779.44	3,155.64	3.0990354
1955	9,779.44	3,301.44	2.9621741
1956	9,779.44	3,532.36	2.7685287
1957	9,779.44	3,641.72	2.6853904
1958	9,779.44	3,673.80	2.6619413
1959	9,779.44	3,855.80	2.5362934
1960	9,779.44	4,007.12	2.4405159
1961	9,779.44	4,086.76	2.3929568
1962	9,779.44	4,291.40	2.2788461
1963	9,779.44	4,396.64	2.2242986
1964	9,779.44	4,576.32	2.1369659
1965	9,779.44	4,658.72	2.0991689
1966	9,779.44	4,938.36	1.9803012
1967	9,779.44	5,213.44	1.8758133
1968	9,779.44	5,571.76	1.7551797
1969	9,779.44	5,893.76	1.6592871
1970	9,779.44	6,186.24	1.5808375
1971	9,779.44	6,497.08	1.5052054
1972	9,779.44	7,133.80	1.3708599
1973	9,779.44	7,580.16	1.2901364
1974	9,779.44	8,030.76	1.2177478
1975	9,779.44	8,630.92	1.1330704
1976	9,779.44	9,226.48	1.0599318
1977	9,779.44	9,779.44	1.0000000

Step 2. After we have found these indexing quotients, we multiply Ms. A's actual year-by-year earnings by them to find her indexed earnings, as shown below:

Year	I. Actual earnings	II. Indexing quotient	III. Column I multiplied by column II equals indexed earnings
1951	$ 3,200	3.4937053	$11,179.86
1952	3,400	3.2890641	11,182.82
1953	3,300	3.1150269	10,279.59
1954	3,600	3.0990354	11,156.53
1955	3,700	2.9621741	10,960.04
1956	3,700	2.7685287	10,243.56
1957	4,000	2.6853904	10,741.56
1958	4,200	2.6619413	11,180.15
1959	4,400	2.5362934	11,159.69
1960	4,500	2.4405159	10,982.32
1961	2,800	2.3929568	6,700.28
1962	2,200	2.2788461	5,013.46
1963	0	2.2242986	0
1964	0	2.1369659	0
1965	3,700	2.0991689	7,766.92
1966	4,500	1.9803012	8,911.36
1967	5,400	1.8758133	10,129.39
1968	6,200	1.7551797	10,882.11
1969	6,900	1.6592871	11,449.08
1970	7,300	1.5808375	11,540.11
1971	7,500	1.5052054	11,289.04
1972	7,800	1.3708599	10,692.71
1973	8,200	1.2901364	10,579.12
1974	9,000	1.2177478	10,959.73
1975	9,900	1.1330704	11,217.40

Year	I. Actual earnings	II. Indexing quotient	III. Column I multiplied by column II equals indexed earnings
1976	11,100	1.0599318	11,765.24
1977	9,900	1.0000000	9,900.00
1978	11,000	0	11,000.00

(4) We calculate your indexing year under this paragraph if you, the insured worker, die before reaching age 62, your surviving spouse or surviving divorced spouse is first eligible after 1984, and the indexing year calculated under this paragraph results in a higher widow(er)'s benefit than results from the indexing year calculated under the general rule explained in paragraph (d)(1)(ii). For purposes of this paragraph, the indexing year is never earlier than the second year before the year of your death. Except for this limitation, the indexing year is the earlier of—

(i) The year in which you, the insured worker, attained age 60, or would have attained age 60 if you had lived, and

(ii) The second year before the year in which the surviving spouse or the surviving divorced spouse becomes eligible for widow(er)'s benefits, i.e., has attained age 60, or is age 50–59 and disabled.

(e) Number of years to be considered in finding your average indexed monthly earnings. To find the number of years to be used in computing your average indexed monthly earnings—

(1) We count the years beginning with 1951, or (if later) the year you reach age 22, and ending with the earliest of the year before you reach age 62, become disabled, or die. Years wholly or partially within a period of disability (as defined in § 404.1501(b) of subpart P of this part) are not counted unless your primary insurance amount would be higher. In that case, we count all the years during the period of disability, even though you had no earnings in some of those years. These are your elapsed years. From your elapsed years, we then subtract up to 5 years, the exact number depending on the kind of benefits to which you are entitled. You cannot, under this procedure, have fewer than 2 benefit computation years.

(2) For computing old-age insurance benefits and survivors insurance benefits, we subtract 5 from the number of your elapsed years. See paragraphs (e)(3) and (4) of this section for the dropout as applied to disability benefits. This is the number of your benefit computation years; we use the same number of your computation base years (see paragraph (b)(2) of this section) in computing your average indexed monthly earnings. For benefit computation years, we use the years with the highest amounts of earnings after indexing. They may include earnings from years that were not indexed, and must include years of no earnings if you do not have sufficient years with earnings. You cannot have fewer than 2 benefit computation years.

(3) Where the worker is first entitled to disability insurance benefits (DIB) after June 1980, there is an exception to the usual 5 year dropout provision explained in paragraph (e)(2) of this section. (For entitlement before July 1980, we use the usual dropout.) We call this exception the disability dropout. We divide the elapsed years by 5 and disregard any fraction. The result, which may not exceed 5, is the number of dropout years. We subtract that number from the number of elapsed years to get the number of benefit computation years, which may not be fewer than 2. After the worker dies, the disability dropout no longer applies and we use the basic 5 dropout years to compute benefits for survivors. We continue to apply the disability dropout when a person becomes entitled to old-age insurance benefits (OAIB), unless his or her entitlement to DIB ended at least 12 months before he or she became eligible for OAIB. For first DIB entitlement before July 1980, we use the rule in paragraph (e)(2) of this section.

(4) For benefits payable after June 1981, the disability dropout might be increased by the child care dropout. If the number of disability dropout years is fewer than 3, we will drop out a benefit computation year for each benefit computation year that the worker meets the child care requirement and had no earnings, until the total of all dropout years is 3. The child care requirement for any year is that the worker must have been living with his or her child (or his or her spouse's child) substantially throughout any part of any calendar year that the child was alive and under age 3. In actual practice, no more than 2 child care years may be dropped, because of the combined effect of the number of elapsed years, 1–for–5 dropout years (if any), and the computation years required for the computation.

Example: Ms. M., born August 4, 1953, became entitled to disability insurance benefits (DIB) beginning in July 1980 based on a disability which began January 15, 1980. In computing the DIB, we determined that the elapsed years are 1975 through 1979, the number of dropout years is 1 (5 elapsed years divided by 5), and the number of computation years is 4. Since Ms. M. had no earnings in 1975 and 1976, we drop out 1975 and use her earnings for the years 1977 through 1979.

Ms. M. lived with her child, who was born in 1972, in all months of 1973 and 1974 and did not have any earnings in those years. We, therefore, recompute Ms. M.'s DIB beginning with July 1981 to give her the advantage of the child care dropout. To do this, we reduce the 4 computation years by 1 child care year to get 3 computation years. Because the child care dropout cannot be applied to computation years in which the worker had earnings, we can drop only one of Ms. M.'s computation years, i.e., 1976, in addition to the year 1975 which we dropped in the initial computation.

(i) Living with means that you and the child ordinarily live in the same home and you exercise, or have the right to exercise, parental control. See § 404.366(c) for a further explanation.

(ii) Substantially throughout any part of any calendar year means that any period you were not living with the child during a calendar year did not exceed 3 months. If the child was either born or attained age 3 during the calendar year, the period of absence in the year cannot have exceeded the smaller period of 3 months, or one-half the time after the child's birth or before the child attained age 3.

(iii) Earnings means wages for services rendered and net earnings from self-employment minus any net loss for a taxable year. See § 404.429 for a further explanation.

(f) Your average indexed monthly earnings. After we have indexed your earnings and found your benefit computation years, we compute your average indexed monthly earnings by—

(1) Totalling your indexed earnings in your benefit computation years;

(2) Dividing the total by the number of months in your benefit computation years; and

(3) Rounding the quotient to the next lower whole dollar, if not already a multiple of $1.

Example: From the example in paragraph (d) of this section, we see that Ms. A reaches age 62 in 1979. Her elapsed years are 1951–1978 (28 years). We subtract 5 from her 28 elapsed years to find that we must use 23 benefit computation years. This means that we will use her 23 highest computation base years to find her average indexed monthly earnings. We exclude the 5 years 1961–1965 and total her indexed earnings for the remaining years, i.e., the benefit computation years (including her unindexed earnings in 1977 and 1978) and get $249,381.41. We then divide that amount by the 276 months in her 23 benefit computation years and find her average indexed monthly earnings to be $903.56, which is rounded down to $903.

[41 FR 44363, Oct. 8, 1976, as amended at 43 FR 8133, Feb. 28, 1978; 47 FR 30734, July 15, 1982; 47 FR 35479, Aug. 13, 1982; 48 FR 11695, March 21, 1983; 51 FR 4482, Feb. 5, 1986; 57 FR 1381, Jan. 14, 1992]

§ 404.212 Computing your primary insurance amount from your average indexed monthly earnings.

(a) General. We compute your primary insurance amount under the average-indexed-monthly-earnings method by applying a benefit formula to your average indexed monthly earnings.

(b) Benefit formula.

(1) We use the applicable benefit formula in appendix II for the year you reach age 62, become disabled, or die whichever occurs first. If you die before age 62, and your surviving spouse or surviving divorced spouse is first eligible after 1984, we may compute the primary insurance amount, for the purpose of paying benefits to your widow(er), as if you had not died but reached age 62 in the second year after the indexing year that we computed under the provisions of § 404.211(d)(4). We will not use this primary insurance amount for computing benefit amounts for your other survivors or for computing the maximum family benefits payable on your earnings record. Further, we will only use this primary insurance amount if it results in a higher widow(er)'s benefit than would result if we did not use this special computation.

(2) The dollar amounts in the benefit formula are automatically increased each year for persons who attain age 62, or who become disabled or die before age 62 in that year, by the same percentage as the increase in the average of the total wages (see appendix I).

(3) We will publish benefit formulas for years after 1979 in the Federal Register at the same time we publish the average of the total wage figures. We begin to use a new benefit formula as soon as it is applicable, even before we periodically update appendix II.

(4) We may use a modified formula, as explained in § 404.213, if you are entitled to a pension based on your employment which was not covered by Social Security.

(c) Computing your primary insurance amount from the benefit formula. We compute your primary insurance amount by applying the benefit formula to your average indexed monthly earnings and adding the results for each step of the formula. For computations using the benefit formulas in effect for 1979 through 1982, we round the total amount to the next higher multiple of $0.10 if it is not a multiple of $0.10 and for computations using the benefit formulas effective for 1983 and later years, we round to the next lower multiple of $0.10. (See paragraph (e) of this section for a discussion of the minimum primary insurance amount.)

(d) Adjustment of your primary insurance amount when entitlement to benefits occurs in a year after attainment of age 62, disability or death. If you (or your survivors) do not become entitled to benefits in the same year you reach age 62, become disabled, or die before age 62, we compute your primary insurance amount by—

(1) Computing your average indexed monthly earnings as described in § 404.211;

(2) Applying to your average indexed monthly earnings the benefit formula for the year in which you reach age 62, or become disabled or die before age 62; and

(3) Applying to the primary insurance amount all automatic cost-of-living and ad hoc increases in primary insurance amounts that have gone into effect in or after the year you reached age 62, became disabled, or died before age 62. (See § 404.277 for special rules on minimum benefits, and appendix VI for a table of percentage increases in primary insurance amounts since December 1978. Increases in primary insurance

amounts are published in the Federal Register and we periodically update appendix VI.)

(e) Minimum primary insurance amount. If you were eligible for benefits, or died without having been eligible, before 1982, your primary insurance amount computed under this method cannot be less than $122. This minimum benefit provision has been repealed effective with January 1982 for most workers and their families where the worker initially becomes eligible for benefits in that or a later month, or dies in January 1982 or a later month without having been eligible before January 1982. For members of a religious order who are required to take a vow of poverty, as explained in 20 CFR 404.1024, and which religious order elected Social Security coverage before December 29, 1981, the repeal is effective with January 1992 based on first eligibility or death in that month or later.

[48 FR 46142, Oct. 11, 1983; 51 FR 4482, Feb. 5, 1986; 52 FR 47916, Dec. 17, 1987]

§ 404.213 Computation where you are eligible for a pension based on your noncovered employment.

(a) When applicable. Except as provided in paragraph (d) of this section, we will modify the formula prescribed in § 404.212 and in appendix II of this subpart in the following situations:

(1) You become eligible for old-age insurance benefits after 1985; or

(2) You become eligible for disability insurance benefits after 1985; and

(3) For the same months after 1985 that you are entitled to old-age or disability benefits, you are also entitled to a monthly pension(s) for which you first became eligible after 1985 based in whole or part on your earnings in employment which was not covered under Social Security. We consider you to first become eligible for a monthly pension in the first month for which you met all requirements for the pension except that you were working or had not yet applied. In determining whether you are eligible for a pension before 1986, we consider all applicable service used by the pension-paying agency. (Noncovered employment includes employment outside the United States which is not covered under the United States Social Security system. Pensions from noncovered employment outside the United States include both pensions from social insurance systems that base benefits on earnings but not on residence or citizenship, and those from private employers. However, for benefits payable for months prior to January 1995, we will not modify the computation of a totalization benefit (see §§ 404.1908 and 404.1918) as a result of your entitlement to another pension based on employment covered by a totalization agreement. Beginning January 1995, we will not modify the computation of a totalization benefit in any case (see § 404.213(e)(8)).

(b) Amount of your monthly pension that we use. For purposes of computing your primary insurance amount, we consider the amount of your monthly pension(s) (or the amount prorated on a monthly basis) which is attributable to your noncovered work after 1956 that you are entitled to for the first month in which you are concurrently entitled to Social Security benefits. For applications filed before December 1988, we will use the month of earliest concurrent eligibility. In determining the amount of your monthly pension we will use, we will consider the following:

(1) If your pension is not paid on a monthly basis or is paid in a lump-sum, we will allocate it proportionately as if it were paid monthly. We will allocate this the same way we allocate lump-sum payments for a spouse or surviving spouse whose benefits are reduced because of entitlement to a Government pension. (See § 404.408a.)

(2) If your monthly pension is reduced to provide a survivor's benefit, we will use the unreduced amount.

(3) If the monthly pension amount which we will use in computing your primary insurance amount is not a multiple of $0.10, we will round it to the next lower multiple of $0.10.

(c) How we compute your primary insurance amount. When you become entitled to old-age or disability insurance benefits and to a monthly pension, we will compute your primary insurance amount under the average-indexed-monthly-earnings method (§ 404.212) as modified by paragraph (c)(1) and (2) of this section. Where applicable, we will also consider the 1977 simplified old-start method (§ 404.241) as modified by § 404.243 and a special minimum primary insurance amount as explained in §§ 404.260 and 404.261. We will use the highest result from these three methods as your primary insurance amount. We compute under the average-indexed-monthly-earnings method, and use the higher primary insurance amount resulting from the application of paragraphs (c) (1) and (2) of this section, as follows:

(1) The formula in appendix II, except that instead of the first percentage figure (i.e., 90 percent), we use—

(i) 80 percent if you initially become eligible for old-age or disability insurance benefits in 1986;

(ii) 70 percent for initial eligibility in 1987;

(iii) 60 percent for initial eligibility in 1988;

(iv) 50 percent for initial eligibility in 1989;

(v) 40 percent for initial eligibility in 1990 and later years, or

(2) The formula in appendix II minus one-half the portion of your monthly pension which is due to noncovered work after 1956 and for which you were entitled in the first month you were entitled to both Social Security benefits and the monthly pension. If the

monthly pension amount is not a multiple of $0.10, we will round to the next lower multiple of $0.10. To determine the portion of your pension which is due to noncovered work after 1956, we consider the total number of years of work used to compute your pension and the percentage of those years which are after 1956, and in which your employment was not covered. We take that percentage of your total pension as the amount which is due to your noncovered work after 1956.

(d) Alternate computation.

(1) If you have more than 20 but less than 30 years of coverage as defined in the column headed "Alternate Computation Under § 404.213(d)" in appendix IV of this subpart, we will compute your primary insurance amount using the applicable percentage given below instead of the first percentage in appendix II of this subpart if the applicable percentage below is larger than the percentage specified in paragraph (c) of this section:

(i) For benefits payable for months before January 1989—

Years of coverage	Percent
29	80
28	70
27	60
26	50

(ii) For benefits payable for months after December 1988—

Years of coverage	Percent
29	85
28	80
27	75
26	70
25	65
24	60
23	55
22	50
21	45

(2) If you later earn additional year(s) of coverage, we will recompute your primary insurance amount, effective with January of the following year.

(e) Exceptions. The computations in paragraph (c) of this section do not apply in the following situations:

(1) Payments made under the Railroad Retirement Act are not considered to be a pension from noncovered employment for the purposes of this section. See subpart O of this part for a discussion of railroad retirement benefits.

(2) You were entitled before 1986 to disability insurance benefits in any of the 12 months before you reach age 62 or again become disabled. (See § 404.251 for the appropriate computation.)

(3) You were a Federal employee performing service on January 1, 1984 to which Social Security coverage was extended on that date solely by reason of the amendments made by section 101 of the Social Security Amendments of 1983.

(4) You were an employee of a nonprofit organization who was exempt from Social Security coverage on December 31, 1983 unless you were previously covered under a waiver certificate which was terminated prior to that date.

(5) You have 30 years of coverage as defined in the column headed "Alternate Computation Under § 404.213(d)" in appendix IV of this subpart.

(6) Your survivors are entitled to benefits on your record of earnings. (After your death, we will recompute the primary insurance amount to nullify the effect of any monthly pension, based in whole or in part on noncovered employment, to which you had been entitled.)

(7) For benefits payable for months after December 1994, payments by the social security system of a foreign country which are based on a totalization agreement between the United States and that country are not considered to be a pension from noncovered employment for purposes of this section. See subpart T of this part for a discussion of totalization agreements.

(8) For benefits payable for months after December 1994, the computations in paragraph (c) do not apply in the case of an individual whose entitlement to U.S. social security benefits results from a totalization agreement between the United States and a foreign country.

(9) For benefits payable for months after December 1994, you are eligible after 1985 for monthly periodic benefits based wholly on service as a member of a uniformed service, including inactive duty training.

(f) Entitlement to a totalization benefit and a pension based on noncovered employment. If, before January 1995, you are entitled to a totalization benefit and to a pension based on noncovered employment that is not covered by a totalization agreement, we count your coverage from a foreign country with which the United States (U.S.) has a totalization agreement and your U.S. coverage to determine if you meet the requirements for the modified computation in paragraph (d) of this section or the exception in paragraph (e)(5) of this section.

(1) Where the amount of your totalization benefit will be determined using a computation method that does not consider foreign earnings (see § 404.1918), we will find your total years of coverage by adding your—

(i) Years of coverage from the agreement country (quarters of coverage credited under § 404.1908 divided by four) and

(ii) Years of U.S. coverage as defined for the purpose of computing the special minimum primary insurance amount under § 404.261.

(2) Where the amount of your totalization benefit will be determined using a computation method that does consider foreign earnings, we will credit your foreign earnings to your U.S. earnings record and then find your total years of coverage using the method described in § 404.261.

[52 FR 47916, Dec. 17, 1987; 55 FR 21382, May 24, 1990; 57 FR 22429, May 28, 1992; 60 FR 17444, April 6, 1995; 60 FR 56513, Nov. 9, 1995]

AVERAGE–MONTHLY–WAGE METHOD OF COMPUTING PRIMARY INSURANCE AMOUNTS

§ 404.220 Average-monthly-wage method.

(a) Who is eligible for this method. You must before 1979, reach age 62, become disabled or die to be eligible for us to compute your primary insurance amount under the average-monthly-wage method. Also, as explained in § 404.230, if you reach age 62 after 1978 but before 1984, you are eligible to have your primary insurance amount computed under a modified average-monthly-wage method if it is to your advantage. Being eligible for either the average-monthly-wage method or the modified average-monthly-wage method does not preclude your eligibility under the old-start method described in §§ 404.240 through 404.242.

(b) Steps in computing your primary insurance amount under the average-monthly-wage method. We follow these three major steps in computing your primary insurance amount under the average-monthly-wage method:

(1) First, we find your average monthly wage, as described in § 404.221;

(2) Second, we look at the benefit table in appendix III; and

(3) Then we find your primary insurance amount in the benefit table, as described in § 404.222.

(4) Finally, we apply any automatic cost-of-living or ad hoc increases that became effective in or after the year you reached age 62, or became disabled, or died before age 62, as explained in §§ 404.270 through 404.277.

§ 404.221 Computing your average monthly wage.

(a) General. Under the average-monthly-wage method, your social security earnings are averaged over the length of time you can reasonably have been expected to have worked under social security after 1950 (or after you reached age 21, if later).

(b) Which of your earnings may be used in computing your average monthly wage.

(1) In computing your average monthly wage, we consider all the wages, compensation, self-employment income, and deemed military wage credits that are creditable to you for social security purposes. (The maximum amounts creditable are explained in §§ 404.1047 and 404.1096 of this part.)

(2) We use your earnings in your computation base years in computing your average monthly wage. All years after 1950 up to (but not including) the year you become entitled to old-age or disability insurance benefits, or through the year you die if you had not been entitled to old-age or disability benefits, are computation base years for you. Years after the year you die may not be used as computation base years even if you have earnings credited to you in them. However, years beginning with the year you become entitled to benefits may be used for benefits beginning with the following year if using them would give you a higher primary insurance amount. Years wholly within a period of disability are not computation base years unless your primary insurance amount would be higher if they were. In such situations, we count all the years during the period of disability, even if you had no earnings in some of them.

(c) Number of years to be considered in computing your average monthly wage. To find the number of years to be used in computing your average monthly wage—

(1) We count the years beginning with 1951 or (if later) the year you reached age 22 and ending with the year before you reached age 62, or became disabled, or died before age 62. Any part of a year—or years—in which you were disabled, as defined in § 404.1505, is not counted unless doing so would give you a higher average monthly wage. In that case, we count all the years during the period of disability, even if you had no earnings in some of those years. These are your elapsed years. (If you are a male and you reached age 62 before 1975, see paragraph (c)(2) of this section for the rules on finding your elapsed years.)

(2) If you are a male and you reached age 62 in—

(i) 1972 or earlier, we count the years beginning with 1951 and ending with the year before you reached age 65, or became disabled or died before age 65 to find your elapsed years;

(ii) 1973, we count the years beginning with 1951 and ending with the year before you reached age 64, or became disabled or died before age 64 to find your elapsed years; or

(iii) 1974, we count the years beginning with 1951 and ending with the year before you reached age 63, became disabled, or died before age 63 to find your elapsed years.

(3) Then we subtract 5 from the number of your elapsed years. This is the number of your benefit computation years; we use the same number of your computation base years in computing your average monthly wage. For benefit computation years, we use the years with the highest amounts of earnings, but

they may include years of no earnings. You cannot have fewer than 2 benefit computation years.

(d) Your average monthly wage. After we find your benefit computation years, we compute your average monthly wage by—

(1) Totalling your creditable earnings in your benefit computation years;

(2) Dividing the total by the number of months in your benefit computation years; and

(3) Rounding the quotient to the next lower whole dollar if not already a multiple of $1.

Example: Mr. B reaches age 62 and becomes entitled to old-age insurance benefits in August 1978. He had no social security earnings before 1951 and his year-by-year social security earnings after 1950 are as follows:

Year	Earnings
1951	$2,700
1952	2,700
1953	3,400
1954	3,100
1955	4,000
1956	4,100
1957	4,000
1958	4,200
1959	4,800
1960	4,800
1961	4,800
1962	4,800
1963	4,800
1964	1,500
1965	0
1966	0
1967	0
1968	3,100
1969	5,200
1970	7,100
1971	7,800
1972	8,600
1973	8,900
1974	9,700
1975	10,100
1976	10,800
1977	11,900

We first find Mr. B's elapsed years, which are the 27 years 1951–1977. We subtract 5 from his 27 elapsed years to find that we must use 22 benefit computation years in computing his average monthly wage. His computation base years are 1951–1977, which are the years after 1950 and prior to the year he became entitled. This means that we will use his 22 computation base years with the highest earnings to compute his average monthly wage. Thus, we exclude the years 1964–1967 and 1951.

We total his earnings in his benefit computation years and get $132,700. We then divide that amount by the 264 months in his 22 benefit computation years and find his average monthly wage to be $502.65, which is rounded down to $502.

(e) "Deemed" average monthly wage for certain deceased veterans of World War II. Certain deceased veterans of World War II are "deemed" to have an average monthly wage of $160 (see §§ 404.1340 through 404.1343 of this part) unless their actual average monthly wage, as found in the method described in paragraphs (a) through (d) of this section is higher.

§ 404.222 Use of benefit table in finding your primary insurance amount from your average monthly wage.

(a) General. We find your primary insurance amount under the average-monthly-wage method in the benefit table in appendix III.

(b) Finding your primary insurance amount from benefit table. We find your average monthly wage in column III of the table. Your primary insurance amount appears on the same line in column IV (column II if you are entitled to benefits for any of the 12 months preceding the effective month in column IV). As explained in § 404.212(e), there is a minimum primary insurance amount of $122 payable for persons who became eligible or died after 1978 and before January 1982. There is also an alternative minimum of $121.80 (before the application of cost-of-living increases) for members of this group whose benefits were computed from the benefit table in effect in December 1978 on the basis of either the old-start computation method in §§ 404.240 through 404.242 or the guaranteed alternative computation method explained in §§ 404.230 through 404.233. However, as can be seen from the extended table in appendix III, the lowest primary insurance amount under this method is now $1.70 for individuals for whom the minimum benefit has been repealed.

Example: In the example in § 404.221(d), we computed Mr. B's average monthly wage to be $502. We refer to the December 1978 benefit table in appendix III. Then we find his average monthly wage in column III of the table. Reading across, his primary insurance amount is on the same line in column IV and is $390.50. A 9.9 percent automatic cost-of-living benefit increase was effective for June 1979, increasing Mr. B's primary insurance amount to $429.20, as explained in §§ 404.270 through 404.277. Then, we increase the $429.20 by the 14.3 percent June 1980 cost-of-living benefit increase and get $490.60, and by the 11.2 percent June 1981 increase to get $545.60.

[48 FR 46143, Oct. 13, 1983]

GUARANTEED ALTERNATIVE FOR PEOPLE REACHING AGE 62 AFTER 1978 BUT BEFORE 1984

§ 404.230 Guaranteed alternative.

(a) General. If you reach age 62 after 1978 but before 1984, we compute your primary insurance amount under a modified average-monthly-wage method as a guaranteed alternative to your primary insurance amount computed under the average-indexed-monthly-earnings method. We also compute your primary insurance amount under the old-start method (§§ 404.240 through 404.242) and under the special rules for a person who had a period of disability (§§ 404.250 through 404.252), if you are eligible. In

§§ 404.231 through 404.233, we explain the average-monthly-wage method as the alternative to the average-indexed-monthly-earnings method.

(b) Restrictions.

(1) To qualify for this guaranteed-alternative computation, you must have some creditable earnings before 1979.

(2) You or your survivors do not qualify for a guaranteed-alternative computation if you were eligible (you attained age 62, became disabled, or died before age 62) for social security benefits based on your own earnings at any time before 1979 unless—

(i) Those benefits were disability insurance benefits which were terminated because you recovered from your disability or you engaged in substantial gainful activity; and

(ii) You spent at least 12 months without being eligible for disability benefits again.

(3) This guaranteed alternative method applies only to old-age insurance benefits and to survivor benefits where the deceased worker reached the month of his or her 62nd birthday after 1978 but before 1984 and died after reaching age 62.

§ 404.231 Steps in computing your primary insurance amount under the guaranteed alternative—general.

If you reach age 62 after 1978 but before 1984, we follow three major steps in finding your guaranteed alternative:

(a) First, we compute your average monthly wage, as described in § 404.232;

(b) Second, we find the primary insurance amount that corresponds to your average monthly wage in the benefit table in appendix III.

(c) Then we apply any automatic cost-of-living or ad hoc increases in primary insurance amounts that have become effective in or after the year you reached age 62.

§ 404.232 Computing your average monthly wage under the guaranteed alternative.

(a) General. With the exception described in paragraph (b) of this section, we follow the rules in § 404.221 to compute your average monthly wage.

(b) Exception. We do not use any year after the year you reach age 61 as a computation base year in computing your average monthly wage for purposes of the guaranteed alternative.

§ 404.233 Adjustment of your guaranteed alternative when you become entitled after age 62.

(a) If you do not become entitled to benefits at the time you reach age 62, we adjust the guaranteed alternative computed for you under § 404.232 as described in paragraph (b) of this section.

(b) To the primary insurance amount computed under the guaranteed alternative, we apply any automatic cost-of-living or ad hoc increases in primary insurance amounts that go into effect in the year you reach age 62 and in years up through the year you become entitled to benefits. (See appendix VI for a list of the percentage increases in primary insurance amounts since December 1978.)

Example: Mr. C reaches age 62 in January 1981 and becomes entitled to old-age insurance benefits in April 1981. He had no social security earnings before 1951 and his year-by-year social security earnings after 1950 are as follows:

Year	Earnings
1951	$3,600
1952	3,600
1953	3,600
1954	3,600
1955	4,200
1956	4,200
1957	4,200
1958	4,200
1959	4,800
1960	4,800
1961	4,800
1962	4,800
1963	4,800
1964	4,800
1965	4,800
1966	6,600
1967	6,600
1968	7,800
1969	7,800
1970	7,800
1971	7,800
1972	9,000
1973	10,800
1974	13,200
1975	14,100
1976	15,300
1977	16,500
1978	17,700
1979	22,900
1980	25,900
1981	29,700

Mr. C's elapsed years are the 30 years 1951 through 1980. We subtract 5 from his 30 elapsed years to find that we must use 25 benefit computation years in computing his average monthly wage. His computation base years are 1951 through 1980 which are years after 1950 up to the year he reached age 62. We will use his 25 computation base years with the highest earnings to compute his average monthly wage. Thus, we exclude the years 1951–1955. The year 1981 is not a base year for this computation.

We total his earnings in his benefit computation years and get $236,000. We then divide by the 300 months in his 25 benefit computation years, and find his average monthly wage to be $786.66 which is rounded down to $786.

The primary insurance amount in the benefit table in appendix III that corresponds to Mr. C's average monthly wage is $521.70. The 9.9 percent and 14.3 percent cost of living increase for 1979 and 1980, respectively, are not applicable because Mr. C reached age 62 in 1981.

The average indexed monthly earnings method described in §§ 404.210 through 404.212 considers all of the earnings after 1950, including 1981 earnings which, in Mr. C's case cannot be used in the guaranteed alternative method. Mr. C's primary insurance amount under the average indexed earnings method is $548.40. Therefore, his benefit is based upon the $548.40 primary insurance amount. As in the guaranteed alternative method, Mr. C is not entitled to the cost of living increases for years before the year he reaches age 62.

OLD–START METHOD OF COMPUTING PRIMARY INSURANCE AMOUNTS

§ 404.240 Old-start method—general.

If you had all or substantially all your social security earnings before 1951, your primary insurance amount computed under the "1977 simplified old-start" method may be higher than any other primary insurance amount computed for you under any other method for which you are eligible. As explained in § 404.242, if you reach age 62 after 1978, your primary insurance amount computed under the old-start method is used, for purposes of the guaranteed alternative described in § 404.230, if the old-start primary insurance amount is higher than the one found under the average-monthly-wage method. We may use a modified computation, as explained in § 404.243, if you are entitled to a pension based on your employment which was not covered by Social Security.

[52 FR 47917, Dec. 17, 1987]

§ 404.241 1977 simplified old-start method.

(a) Who is qualified.

To qualify for the old-start computation, you must meet the conditions in paragraphs (a)(1), (2), or (3) of this section:

(1) You must—

(i) Have one "quarter of coverage" (see §§ 404.101 and 404.110 of this part) before 1951;

(ii) Have attained age 21 after 1936 and before 1950, or attained age 22 after 1950 and earned fewer than 6 quarters of coverage after 1950;

(iii) Have not had a period of disability which began before 1951, unless it can be disregarded, as explained in § 404.320 of this part; and,

(iv) Have attained age 62, become disabled, or died, after 1977.

(2)(i) You or your survivor becomes entitled to benefits for June 1992 or later;

(ii) You do not meet the conditions in paragraph (a)(1) of this section, and,

(iii) No person is entitled to benefits on your earnings record in the month before the month you or your survivor becomes entitled to benefits.

(3) A recomputation is first effective for June 1992 or later based on your earnings for 1992 or later.

(b) Steps in old-start computation.

(1) First, we allocate your earnings during the period 1937–1950 as described in paragraph (c) of this section.

(2) Next, we compute your average monthly wage, as described in paragraph (d) of this section.

(3) Next, we apply the old-start formula to your average monthly wage, as described in paragraph (e)(1) of this section.

(4) Next, we apply certain increments to the amount computed in step (3), as described in paragraph (e)(2) of this section.

(5) Next, we find your primary insurance amount in the benefit table in appendix III, as described in paragraph (f)(1) of this section.

(6) Then, we apply automatic cost-of-living or ad hoc increases in primary insurance amounts to the primary insurance amount found in step (5), as described in paragraph (f)(2) of this section.

(c) Finding your computation base years under the old-start method.

(1) Instead of using your actual year-by-year earnings before 1951, we find your computation base years for 1937–1950 (and the amount of earnings for each of them) by allocating your total 1937–1950 earnings among the years before 1951 under the following procedure:

(i) If you reached age 21 before 1950 and your total 1937–1950 earnings are not more than $3,000 times the number of years after the year you reached age 20 and before 1951 (a maximum of 14 years), we allocate your earnings equally among those years, and those years are your computation base years before 1951.

(ii) If you reached age 21 before 1950 and your total 1937–1950 earnings are more than $3,000 times the number of years after the year you reached age 20 and before 1951, we allocate your earnings at the rate of $3,000 per year for each year after you reached age 20 and before 1951 up to a maximum of 14 years. We credit any remainder in reverse order to years before age 21 in $3,000 increments and any amount left over of less than $3,000 to the year before the earliest year to which we credited $3,000. No more than $42,000 may be credited in this way and to no more than 14 years. Those years are your computation base years before 1951.

(iii) If you reached age 21 in 1950 or later and your total pre–1951 earnings are $3,000 or less, we credit the total to the year you reached age 20 and that year is your pre–1951 computation base year.

(iv) If you reached age 21 in 1950 or later and your total pre–1951 earnings are more than $3,000, we credit $3,000 to the year you reached age 20 and credit the remainder to earlier years (or year) in blocks of $3,000 in reverse order. We credit any remainder of less than $3,000 to the year before the earliest year to which we had credited $3,000. No more than $42,000 may be credited in this way and to no more than 14 years. Those years are your computation base years before 1951.

(v) If you die before 1951, we allocate your 1937–1950 earnings under paragraphs (c)(1)(i) through (iv), except that in determining the number of years, we will use the year of death instead of 1951. If you die before you attain age 21, the number of years in the period is equal to 1.

(vi) For purposes of paragraphs (c)(1)(i) through (v), if you had a period of disability which began before 1951, we will exclude the years wholly within a period of disability in determining the number of years.

(2)(i) All years after 1950 up to (but not including) the year you become entitled to old-age insurance or disability insurance benefits (or through the year you die if you had not become entitled to old-age or disability benefits) are also computation base years for you.

(ii) Years wholly within a period of disability are not computation base years unless your primary insurance amount would be higher if they were. In such situations, we count all the years during the period of disability, even if you had no earnings in some of them.

Example: Ms. D reaches age 62 in June 1979. Her total 1937–1950 social security earnings are $40,000 and she had social security earnings of $7,100 in 1976 and $6,300 in 1977. Since she reaches age 62 after 1978, we first compute her primary insurance amount under the average-indexed-monthly-earnings method (§§ 404.210 through 404.212). As of June 1981, it is $170.50, which is the minimum primary insurance amount applicable, because her average indexed monthly earnings of $50 would yield only $56.50 under the benefit formula. Ms. D reached age 62 after 1978 but before 1984 and her guaranteed alternative under the average-monthly-wage method as of June 1981 is $170.30, which is the minimum primary insurance amount based on average monthly wages of $48. (These amounts include the 9.9, the 14.3, and the 11.2 percent cost-of-living increases effective June 1979, June 1980, and June 1981 respectively.)

Ms. D is also eligible for the old-start method. We first allocate $3,000 of her 1937–1950 earnings to each of her 13 computation base years starting with the year she reached age 21 (1938) and ending with 1950. The remaining $1,000 is credited to the year she reached age 20. Ms. D, then, has 42 computation base years (14 before 1951 and 28 after 1950).

(d) Computing your average monthly wage under the old-start method.

(1) First, we count your elapsed years, which are the years beginning with 1937 (or the year you reach 22, if later) and ending with the year before you reach age 62, or become disabled or die before age 62. (See § 404.211(e)(1) for the rule on how we treat years wholly or partially within a period of disability.)

(2) Next, we subtract 5 from the number of your elapsed years, and this is the number of computation years we must use. We then choose this number of your computation base years in which you had the highest earnings. These years are your benefit computation years. You must have at least 2 benefit computation years.

(3) Then we compute your average monthly wage by dividing your total creditable earnings in your benefit computation years by the number of months in these years and rounding the quotient to the next lower dollar if not already a multiple of $1.

(e) Old-start computation formula. We use the following formula to compute your primary insurance benefit, which we will convert to your primary insurance amount:

(1) We take 40 percent of the first $50 of your average monthly wage, plus 10 percent of the next $200 of your average monthly wage up to a total average monthly wage of $250. (We do not use more than $250 of your average monthly wage.)

(2) We increase the amount found in paragraph (e)(1) of this section by 1 percent for each $1,650 in your pre–1951 earnings, disregarding any remainder less than $1,650. We always increase the amount by at least 4 of these 1 percent increments but may not increase it by more than 14 of them.

(f) Finding your primary insurance amount under the old-start method.

(1) In column I of the benefit table in appendix III we locate the amount (the primary insurance benefit) computed in paragraph (e) of this section and find the corresponding primary insurance amount on the same line in column IV of the table.

(2) We increase that amount by any automatic cost-of-living or ad hoc increases in primary insurance amounts effective since the beginning of the year in which you reached age 62, or became disabled or died before age 62. (See §§ 404.270 through 404.277.)

Example: From the example in paragraph (c)(2) of this section, we see that Ms. D's elapsed years total 40 (number of years at ages 22 to 61, both inclusive). Her benefit computation years, therefore, must total 35. Since she has only 16 years of actual earnings, we must include 19 years of zero earnings in this old-start computation to reach the required 35 benefit computation years.

We next divide her total social security earnings ($53,400) by the 420 months in her benefit computation years and find her average monthly wage to be $127.

We apply the old-start computation formula to Ms. D's average monthly wage as follows: 40 percent of the first $50 of her average monthly wage ($20.00), plus 10 percent of the remaining $77 of her average monthly wage ($7.70), for a total of $27.70.

We then apply 14 1–percent increments to that amount, increasing it by $3.88 to $31.58. We find $31.58 in column I of the December 1978 benefit table in appendix III and find her primary insurance amount of $195.90 on the same line in column IV. We apply the 9.9 percent automatic cost-of-living increase effective for June 1979 to $195.90 and get an old-start primary insurance amount of $215.30 which we then increase to $246.10 to reflect the 14.3 percent cost-of-living increase effective for June 1980, and to $273.70 to reflect the June 1981 increase. Since that primary insurance amount is higher than the $153.10 primary insurance amount computed under the average-monthly-wage method and the $153.30 primary insurance amount computed under the average-indexed-monthly-earnings method, we base Ms. D's benefits (and those of her family) on $215.30 (plus later cost-of-living increases), which is the highest primary insurance amount.

[55 FR 21382, May 24, 1990; 57 FR 23157, June 2, 1992]

§ 404.242 Use of old-start primary insurance amount as guaranteed alternative.

If your primary insurance amount as computed under the old-start method is higher than your primary insurance amount computed under the average-monthly-wage method, your old-start primary insurance amount will serve as the guaranteed alternative to your primary insurance amount computed under the average-indexed-monthly-earnings method, as described in § 404.230. However, earnings that you have in or after the year you reach age 62, or become disabled or die before age 62 are not used in an old-start computation in this situation.

§ 404.243 Computation where you are eligible for a pension based on noncovered employment.

The provisions of § 404.213 are applicable to computations under the old-start method, except for paragraphs (c)(1) and (2) and (d) of that section. Your primary insurance amount will be whichever of the following two amounts is larger:

(a) One-half the primary insurance amount computed according to § 404.241 (before application of the cost of living amount); or

(b) The primary insurance amount computed according to § 404.241 (before application of the cost of living amount), minus one-half the portion of your monthly pension which is due to noncovered work after 1956 and for which you were eligible in the first month you became eligible for Social Security benefits. If the result is not a multiple of $0.10, we will round to the next lower multiple of $0.10. (See § 404.213 (b)(3) if you are not eligible for a monthly pension in the first month you are entitled to Social Security benefits.) To determine the portion of your pension which is due to noncovered work after 1956, we consider the total number of years of work used to compute your pension and the percentage of those years which are after 1956 and in which your employment was not covered. We take that percentage of your total pension as the amount which is due to your noncovered work after 1956.

[52 FR 47918, Dec. 17, 1987]

SPECIAL COMPUTATION RULES FOR PEOPLE WHO HAD A PERIOD OF DISABILITY

§ 404.250 Special computation rules for people who had a period of disability.

If you were disabled at some time in your life, received disability insurance benefits, and those benefits were terminated because you recovered from your disability or because you engaged in substantial gainful activity, special rules apply in computing your primary insurance amount when you become eligible after 1978 for old-age insurance benefits or if you become re-entitled to disability insurance benefits or die. (For purposes of §§ 404.250 through 404.252, we use the term second entitlement to refer to this situation.) There are two sets of rules:

(a) Second entitlement within 12 months. If 12 months or fewer pass between the last month for which you received a disability insurance benefit and your second entitlement, see the rules in § 404.251; and

(b) Second entitlement after more than 12 months. If more than 12 months pass between the last month for which you received a disability insurance benefit and your second entitlement, see the rules in § 404.252.

§ 404.251 Subsequent entitlement to benefits less than [1] 12 months after entitlement to disability benefits ended.

(a) Disability before 1979; second entitlement after 1978. In this situation, we compute your second-entitlement primary insurance amount by selecting the highest of the following:

(1) The primary insurance amount to which you were entitled when you last received a benefit, increased by any automatic cost-of-living or ad hoc increases in primary insurance amounts that took effect since then;

[1] So in original; probably should read "within". See 52 FR 47914.

(2) The primary insurance amount resulting from a recomputation of your primary insurance amount, if one is possible; or

(3) The primary insurance amount computed for you as of the time of your second entitlement under any method for which you are qualified at that time, including the average-indexed-monthly-earnings method if the previous period of disability is disregarded.

(b) Disability and second entitlement after 1978. In this situation, we compute your second-entitlement primary insurance amount by selecting the highest of the following:

(1) The primary insurance amount to which you were entitled when you last received a benefit, increased by any automatic cost-of-living or ad hoc increases in primary insurance amount that took effect since then;

(2) The primary insurance amount resulting from a recomputation of your primary insurance amount, if one is possible (this recomputation may be under the average-indexed-monthly-earnings method only); or

(3) The primary insurance amount computed for you as of the time of your second entitlement under any method (including an old-start method) for which you are qualified at that time.

(c) Disability before 1986; second entitlement after 1985. When applying the rule in paragraph (b)(3) of this section, we must consider your receipt of a monthly pension based on noncovered employment. (See § 404.213). However, we will disregard your monthly pension if you were previously entitled to disability benefits before 1986 and in any of the 12 months before your second entitlement.

[52 FR 47918, Dec. 17, 1987]

§ 404.252 Subsequent entitlement to benefits 12 months or more after entitlement to disability benefits ended.

In this situation, we compute your second-entitlement primary insurance amount by selecting the higher of the following:

(a) New primary insurance amount. The primary insurance amount computed as of the time of your second entitlement under any of the computation methods for which you qualify at the time of your second entitlement; or

(b) Previous primary insurance amount. The primary insurance amount to which you were entitled in the last month for which you were entitled to a disability insurance benefit.

SPECIAL MINIMUM PRIMARY INSURANCE AMOUNTS

§ 404.260 Special minimum primary insurance amounts.

Regardless of the method we use to compute your primary insurance amount, if the special minimum primary insurance amount described in § 404.261 is higher, then your benefits (and those of your dependents or survivors) will be based on the special minimum primary insurance amount. Special minimum primary insurance amounts are not based on a worker's average earnings, as are primary insurance amounts computed under other methods. Rather, the special minimum primary insurance amount is designed to provide higher benefits to people who worked for long periods in low-paid jobs covered by social security.

§ 404.261 Computing your special minimum primary insurance amount.

(a) Years of coverage.

(1) The first step in computing your special minimum primary insurance amount is to find the number of your years of coverage, which is the sum of—

(i) The quotient found by dividing your total creditable social security earnings during the period 1937–1950 by $900, disregarding any fractional remainder; plus

(ii) The number of your computation base years after 1950 in which your social security earnings were at least the amounts shown in appendix IV. (Computation base years mean the same here as in other computation methods discussed in this subpart.)

(2) You must have at least 11 years of coverage to qualify for a special minimum primary insurance amount computation. However, special minimum primary insurance amounts based on little more than 10 years of coverage are usually lower than the regular minimum benefit that was in effect before 1982 (see §§ 404.212(e) and 404.222(b) of this part). In any situation where your primary insurance amount computed under another method is higher, we use that higher amount.

(b) Computing your special minimum primary insurance amount.

(1) First, we subtract 10 from your years of coverage and multiply the remainder (at least 1 and no more than 20) by $11.50;

(2) Then we increase the amount found in paragraph (b)(1) of this section by any automatic cost-of-living or ad hoc increases that have become effective since December 1978 to find your special minimum primary insurance amount. See appendix V for the applicable table, which includes the 9.9 percent cost-of-living increase that became effective June 1979, the 14.3 percent increase that became effective June 1980, and the 11.2 percent increase that became effective June 1981.

Example: Ms. F, who attained age 62 in January 1979, had $10,000 in total social security earnings before 1951 and her post–1950 earnings are as follows:

Year	Earnings
1951	$1,100
1952	950
1953	0
1954	1,000
1955	1,100
1956	1,200
1957	0
1958	1,300
1959	0
1960	1,300
1961	0
1962	1,400
1963	1,300
1964	0
1965	500
1966	700
1967	650
1968	900
1969	1,950
1970	2,100
1971	2,000
1972	1,500
1973	2,700
1974	2,100
1975	2,600
1976	3,850
1977	4,150
1978	0

Her primary insurance amount under the average-indexed-monthly-earnings method as of June 1981 is $240.40 (based on average indexed monthly earnings of $229). Her guaranteed-alternative primary insurance amount under the average-monthly-wage method as of June 1981 is $255.80 (based on average monthly wages of $131).

However, Ms. F has enough earnings before 1951 to allow her 11 years of coverage before 1951 ($10,000 ÷ $900 = 11, plus a remainder, which we drop). She has sufficient earnings in 1951–52, 1954–56, 1958, 1960, 1962–63, 1969–71, 1973, and 1976–77 to have a year of coverage for each of those years. She thus has 15 years of coverage after 1950 and a total of 26 years of coverage. We subtract 10 from her years of coverage, multiply the remainder (16) by $11.50 and get $184.00. We then apply the June 1979, June 1980, and June 1981 automatic cost-of-living increases (9.9 percent, 14.3 percent, and 11.2 percent, respectively) to that amount to find her special minimum primary insurance amount of $202.30 effective June 1979, $231.30 effective June 1980, and $257.30 effective June 1981. (See appendices V and VI.) Since her special minimum primary insurance amount is higher than the primary insurance amounts computed for her under the other methods described in this subpart for which she is eligible, her benefits (and those of her family) are based on the special minimum primary insurance amount.

[48 FR 46143, Oct. 11, 1983]

COST–OF–LIVING INCREASES

§ 404.270 Cost-of-living increases.

Your primary insurance amount may be automatically increased each December so it keeps up with rises in the cost of living. These automatic increases also apply to other benefit amounts, as described in § 404.271.

[51 FR 12603, April 14, 1986]

§ 404.271 When automatic cost-of-living increases apply.

Besides increases in the primary insurance amounts of current beneficiaries, automatic cost-of-living increases also apply to—

(a) The special minimum primary insurance amounts (described in §§ 404.260 through 404.261) of current and future beneficiaries;

(b) The primary insurance amounts of people who after 1978 become eligible for benefits or die before becoming eligible (beginning with December of the year they become eligible or die), although certain limitations are placed on the automatic adjustment of the frozen minimum primary insurance amount (as described in § 404.277); and

(c) The maximum family benefit amounts in column V of the benefit table in appendix III.

(d) [Redesignated as subsection (c) by 83 FR 21708]

[51 FR 12603, April 14, 1986; 83 FR 21708, May 10, 2018]

§ 404.272 Indexes we use to measure the rise in the cost-of-living.

(a) The bases. To measure increases in the cost-of-living for annual automatic increase purposes, we use either:

(1) The revised Consumer Price Index (CPI) for urban wage earners and clerical workers as published by the Department of Labor, or

(2) The average wage index (AWI), which is the average of the annual total wages that we use to index (i.e., update) a worker's past earnings when we compute his or her primary insurance amount (§ 404.211(c)).

(b) Effect of the OASDI fund ratio. Which of these indexes we use to measure increases in the cost-of-living depends on the Old–Age, Survivors, and Disability Insurance (OASDI) fund ratio.

(c) OASDI fund ratio for years after 1984. For purposes of cost-of-living increases, the OASDI fund ratio is the ratio of the combined assets in the Federal Old–Age and Survivors Insurance Trust Fund and the Federal Disability Insurance Trust Fund (see section 201 of the Social Security Act) on January 1 of a given year, to the estimated expenditures from the Funds in the same year. The January 1 balance consists of the assets (i.e., government bonds and cash) in the Federal Old–Age and Survivors Insurance Trust Fund and the Federal Disability Insurance Trust Fund, plus Federal Insurance Contributions Act (FICA) and Self–Employment Contributions Act (SECA) taxes transferred to these trust funds on January 1 of the given year, minus the outstanding amounts (principal and interest) owed to the Federal Hospital Insurance Trust Fund as a result of interfund loans. Estimated expenditures are amounts we expect to pay from the Old–Age and

Survivors Insurance and the Disability Insurance Trust Funds during the year, including the net amount that we pay into the Railroad Retirement Account, but excluding principal repayments and interest payments to the Hospital Insurance Trust Fund and transfer payments between the Old–Age and Survivors Insurance and the Disability Insurance Trust Funds. The ratio as calculated under this rule is rounded to the nearest 0.1 percent.

(d) Which index we use. We use the CPI if the OASDI fund ratio is 15.0 percent or more for any year from 1984 through 1988, and if the ratio is 20.0 percent or more for any year after 1988. We use either the CPI or the AWI, depending on which has the lower percentage increase in the applicable measuring period (see § 404.274), if the OASDI fund ratio is less than 15.0 percent for any year from 1984 through 1988, and if the ratio is less than 20.0 percent for any year after 1988. For example, if the OASDI fund ratio for a year is 17.0 percent, the cost-of-living increase effective December of that year will be based on the CPI.

[51 FR 12603, April 14, 1986]

§ 404.273 When are automatic cost-of-living increases effective?

We make automatic cost-of-living increases if the applicable index, either the CPI or the AWI, rises over a specified measuring period (see the rules on measuring periods in § 404.274). If the cost-of-living increase is to be based on an increase in the CPI, the increase is effective in December of the year in which the measuring period ends. If the increase is to be based on an increase in the AWI, the increase is effective in December of the year after the year in which the measuring period ends.

[51 FR 12603, April 14, 1986; 69 FR 19925, April 15, 2004]

§ 404.274 What are the measuring periods we use to calculate cost-of-living increases?

(a) General. Depending on the OASDI fund ratio, we measure the rise in one index or in both indexes during the applicable measuring period (described in paragraphs (b) and (c) of this section) to determine whether there will be an automatic cost-of-living increase and if so, its amount.

(b) Measuring period based on the CPI—

(1) When the period begins. The measuring period we use for finding the amount of the CPI increase begins with the later of—

(i) Any calendar quarter in which an ad hoc benefit increase is effective; or

(ii) The third calendar quarter of any year in which the last automatic increase became effective.

(2) When the period ends. The measuring period ends with the third calendar quarter of the following year. If this measuring period ends in a year after the year in which an ad hoc increase was enacted or took effect, there can be no cost-of-living increase at that time. We will extend the measuring period to the third calendar quarter of the next year.

(c) Measuring period based on the AWI—

(1) When the period begins. The measuring period we use for finding the amount of the AWI increase begins with the later of—

(i) The calendar year before the year in which an ad hoc benefit increase is effective; or

(ii) The calendar year before the year in which the last automatic increase became effective.

(2) When the period ends. The measuring period ends with the following year. If this measuring period ends in a year in which an ad hoc increase was enacted or took effect, there can be no cost-of-living increase at that time. We will extend the measuring period to the next calendar year.

[51 FR 12603, April 14, 1986; 69 FR 19925, April 15, 2004]

§ 404.275 How is an automatic cost-of-living increase calculated?

(a) Increase based on the CPI. We compute the average of the CPI for the quarters that begin and end the measuring period by adding the three monthly CPI figures, dividing the total by three, and rounding the result to the same number of decimal places as the published CPI figures. If the number of decimal places in the published CPI values differs between those used for the beginning and ending quarters, we use the number for the ending quarter. If the average for the ending quarter is higher than the average for the beginning quarter, we divide the average for the ending quarter by the average of the beginning quarter to determine the percentage increase in the CPI over the measuring period.

(b) Increase based on the AWI. If the AWI for the year that ends the measuring period is higher than the AWI for the year which begins the measuring period and all the other conditions for an AWI–based increase are met, we divide the higher AWI by the lower AWI to determine the percentage increase in the AWI.

(c) Rounding rules. We round the increase from the applicable paragraph (a) or (b) of this section to the nearest 0.1 percent by rounding 0.05 percent and above to the next higher 0.1 percent and otherwise rounding to the next lower 0.1 percent. For example, if the applicable index is the CPI and the increase in the CPI is 3.15 percent, we round the increase to 3.2 percent. We then apply this percentage increase to the amounts described in § 404.271 and round the resulting dollar amounts to the next lower multiple of $0.10 (if not already a multiple of $0.10).

(d) Additional increase. See § 404.278 for the additional increase that is possible.

[48 FR 46143, Oct. 11, 1983; 51 FR 12604, April 14, 1986; 69 FR 19925, April 15, 2004; 72 FR 2186, Jan. 18, 2007]

§ 404.276 Publication of notice of increase.

When we determine that an automatic cost-of-living increase is due, we publish in the Federal Register within 45 days of the end of the measuring period used in finding the amount of the increase—

(a) The fact that an increase is due;

(b) The amount of the increase;

(c) The increased special minimum primary insurance amounts; and

(d) The range of increased maximum family benefits that corresponds to the range of increased special minimum primary insurance amounts.

§ 404.277 When does the frozen minimum primary insurance amount increase because of cost-of-living adjustments?

(a) What is the frozen minimum primary insurance amount (PIA)? The frozen minimum is a minimum PIA for certain workers whose benefits are computed under the average-indexed-monthly-earnings method. Section 404.210(a) with § 404.212(e) explains when the frozen minimum applies.

(b) When does the frozen minimum primary insurance amount (PIA) increase automatically? The frozen minimum PIA increases automatically in every year in which you or your dependents or survivors are entitled to benefits and a cost-of-living increase applies.

(c) When are automatic increases effective for old-age or disability benefits based on a frozen minimum primary insurance amount (PIA)? Automatic cost-of-living increases apply to your frozen minimum PIA beginning with the earliest of:

(1) December of the year you become entitled to benefits and receive at least a partial benefit;

(2) December of the year you reach full retirement age (as defined in § 404.409) if you are entitled to benefits in or before the month you attain full retirement age, regardless of whether you receive at least a partial benefit; or

(3) December of the year you become entitled to benefits if that is after you attain full retirement age.

(d) When are automatic increases effective for survivor benefits based on a frozen minimum primary insurance amount (PIA)?

(1) Automatic cost-of-living increases apply to the frozen minimum PIA used to determine survivor benefits in December of any year in which your child(ren), your surviving spouse caring for your child(ren), or your parent(s), are entitled to survivor benefits for at least one month.

(2) Automatic cost-of-living increases apply beginning with December of the earlier of:

(i) The year in which your surviving spouse or surviving divorced spouse (as defined in §§ 404.335 and 404.336) has attained full retirement age (as defined in § 404.409) and receives at least a partial benefit, or

(ii) The year in which your surviving spouse or surviving disabled spouse becomes entitled to benefits and receives at least a partial benefit.

(3) Automatic cost-of-living increases are not applied to the frozen minimum PIA in any year in which no survivor of yours is entitled to benefits on your social security record.

[48 FR 46143, Oct. 11, 1983; 51 FR 12604, April 14, 1986; 68 FR 4702, Jan. 30, 2003]

§ 404.278 Additional cost-of-living increase.

(a) General. In addition to the cost-of-living increase explained in § 404.275 for a given year, we will further increase the amounts in § 404.271 if—

(1) The OASDI fund ratio is more than 32.0 percent in the given year in which a cost-of-living increase is due; and

(2) In any prior year, the cost-of-living increase was based on the AWI as the lower of the CPI and AWI.

(b) Measuring period for the additional increase—

(1) To compute the additional increase for all individuals and for maximum benefits payable to a family, we begin with the year in which the insured individual became eligible for old-age or disability benefits to which he or she is currently entitled, or died before becoming eligible.

(2) Ending. The end of the measuring period is the year before the first year in which a cost-of-living increase is due based on the CPI and in which the OASDI fund ratio is more than 32.0 percent.

(c) Compounded percentage benefit increase. To compute the additional cost-of-living increase, we must first compute the compounded percentage benefit increase (CPBI) for both the cost-of-living increases that were actually paid during the measuring period and for the increases that would have been paid if the CPI had been the basis for all the increases.

(d) Computing the CPBI. The computation of the CPBI is as follows—

(1) Obtain the sum of (i) 1.000 and (ii) the actual cost-of-living increase percentage (expressed as a decimal) for each year in the measuring period;

(2) Multiply the resulting amount for the first year by that for the second year, then multiply that product by the amount for the third year, and continue until the last amount has been multiplied by the product of the preceding amounts;

(3) Subtract 1 from the last product;

(4) Multiply the remaining product by 100. The result is what we call the actual CPBI.

(5) Substitute the cost-of-living increase percentage(s) that would have been used if the increase(s) had been based on the CPI (for some years, this will be the percentage that was used), and do the same computations as in paragraphs (d)(1) through (4) of this section. The result is what we call the assumed CPBI.

(e) Computing the additional cost-of-living increase. To compute the percentage increase, we—

(1) Subtract the actual CPBI from the assumed CPBI;

(2) Add 100 to the actual CPBI;

(3) Divide the answer from paragraph (e)(1) of this section by the answer from paragraph (e)(2) of this section, multiply the quotient by 100, and round to the nearest 0.1. The result is the additional increase percentage, which we apply to the appropriate amount described in § 404.271 after that amount has been increased under § 404.275 for a given year. If that increased amount is not a multiple of $0.10, we will decrease it to the next lower multiple of $0.10.

(f) Restrictions on paying an additional cost-of-living increase. We will pay the additional increase to the extent necessary to bring the benefits up to the level they would have been if they had been increased based on the CPI. However, we will pay the additional increase only to the extent payment will not cause the OASDI fund ratio to drop below 32.0 percent for the year after the year in which the increase is effective.

[51 FR 12604, April 14, 1986; 69 FR 19925, April 15, 2004; 83 FR 21708, May 10, 2018]

RECOMPUTING YOUR PRIMARY INSURANCE AMOUNT

§ 404.280 Recomputations.

At times after you or your survivors become entitled to benefits, we will recompute your primary insurance amount. Usually we will recompute only if doing so will increase your primary insurance amount. However, we will also recompute your primary insurance amount if you first became eligible for old-age or disability insurance benefits after 1985, and later become entitled to a pension based on your noncovered employment, as explained in § 404.213. There is no limit on the number of times your primary insurance amount may be recomputed, and we do most recomputations automatically. In the following sections, we explain:

(a) Why a recomputation is made (§ 404.281),

(b) When a recomputation takes effect (§ 404.282),

(c) Methods of recomputing (§§ 404.283 and 404.284),

(d) Automatic recomputations (§ 404.285),

(e) Requesting a recomputation (§ 404.286),

(f) Waiving a recomputation (§ 404.287), and

(g) Recomputing when you are entitled to a pension based on noncovered employment (§ 404.288).

[52 FR 47918, Dec. 17, 1987]

§ 404.281 Why your primary insurance amount may be recomputed.

(a) Earnings not included in earlier computation or recomputation. The most common reason for recomputing your primary insurance amount is to include earnings of yours that were not used in the first computation or in an earlier recomputation, as described in paragraphs (c) through (e) of this section. These earnings will result in a revised average monthly wage or revised average indexed monthly earnings.

(b) New computation method enacted. If a new method of computing or recomputing primary insurance amounts is enacted into law and you are eligible to have your primary insurance amount recomputed under the new method, we will recompute it under the new method if doing so would increase your primary insurance amount.

(c) Earnings in the year you reach age 62 or become disabled. In the initial computation of your primary insurance amount, we do not use your earnings in the year you become entitled to old-age insurance benefits or become disabled. However, we can use those earnings (called lag earnings) in a recomputation of your primary insurance amount. We recompute and begin paying you the higher benefits in the year after the year you become entitled to old-age benefits or become disabled.

(d) Earnings not reported to us in time to use them in the computation of your primary insurance amount. Because of the way reports of earnings are required to be submitted to us for years after 1977, the earnings you have in the year before you become entitled to old-age insurance benefits, or become disabled or in the year you die might not be reported to us in time to use them in computing your primary insurance amount. We recompute your primary insurance amount based on the new earnings information and begin paying you (or your survivors) the higher benefits based on the additional earnings, beginning with the month you became entitled or died.

(e) Earnings after entitlement that are used in a recomputation. Earnings that you have after you become entitled to benefits will be used in a recomputation of your primary insurance amount.

(f) Entitlement to a monthly pension. We will recompute your primary insurance amount if in a month after you became entitled to old-age or disability insurance benefits, you become entitled to a pension based on noncovered employment, as explained in § 404.213. Further, we will recompute your primary insurance amount after your death to disregard a monthly pension based on noncovered employment which affected your primary insurance amount.

[52 FR 47918, Dec. 17, 1987]

§ 404.282 Effective date of recomputations.

Most recomputations are effective beginning with January of the calendar year after the year in which the additional earnings used in the recomputation were paid. However, a recomputation to include earnings in the year of death (whether or not paid before death) is effective for the month of death. Additionally if you first became eligible for old-age or disability insurance benefits after 1985 and you later also become entitled to a monthly pension based on noncovered employment, we will recompute your primary insurance amount under the rules in § 404.213; this recomputed Social Security benefit amount is effective for the first month you are entitled to the pension. Finally, if your primary insurance amount was affected by your entitlement to a pension, we will recompute the amount to disregard the pension, effective with the month of your death.

[52 FR 47918, Dec. 17, 1987]

§ 404.283 Recomputation under method other than that used to find your primary insurance amount.

In some cases, we may recompute your primary insurance amount under a computation method different from the method used in the computation (or earlier recomputation) of your primary insurance amount, if you are eligible for a computation or recomputation under the different method.

§ 404.284 Recomputations for people who reach age 62, or become disabled, or die before age 62 after 1978.

(a) General. Years of your earnings after 1978 not used in the computation of your primary insurance amount (or in earlier recomputations) under the average-indexed-monthly-earnings method may be substituted for earlier years of your indexed earnings in a recomputation, but only under the average-indexed-monthly-earnings method. See § 404.288 for the rules on recomputing when you are entitled to a monthly pension based on noncovered employment.

(b) Substituting actual dollar amounts in earnings for earlier years of indexed earnings. When we recompute your primary insurance amount under the average-indexed-monthly earnings method, we use actual dollar amounts, i.e., no indexing, for earnings not included in the initial computation or earlier recomputation. These later earnings are substituted for earlier years of indexed or actual earnings that are lower.

(c) Benefit formula used in recomputation. The formula that was used in the first computation of your primary insurance amount is also used in recomputations of your primary insurance amount.

(d) Your recomputed primary insurance amount. We recompute your primary insurance amount by applying the benefit formula to your average indexed monthly earnings as revised to include additional earnings. See § 404.281. We then increase the recomputed PIA by the amounts of any automatic cost-of-living or ad hoc increases in primary insurance amounts that have become effective since you reached age 62, or became disabled or died before age 62.

(e) Minimum increase in primary insurance amounts. Your primary insurance amount may not be recomputed unless doing so would increase it by at least $1.

Example 1. Ms. A, whose primary insurance amount we computed to be $432.40 in June 1979 in §§ 404.210 through 404.212 (based on average indexed monthly earnings of $903), had earnings of $11,000 in 1979 which were not used in the initial computation of her primary insurance amount. We may recompute her primary insurance amount effective for January 1980. In this recomputation, her 1979 earnings may be substituted in their actual dollar amount for the lowest year of her indexed earnings that was used in the initial computation. In Ms. A's case, we substitute the $11,000 for her 1966 indexed earnings of $8,911.36. Her total indexed earnings are now $251,470.05 and her new average indexed monthly earnings are $911. We apply to Ms. A's new average indexed monthly earnings the same benefit formula we used in the initial computation. Doing so produces an amount of $396.00. An automatic cost-of-living increase of 9.9 percent was effective in June 1979. We increase the $396.00 amount by 9.9 percent to find Ms. A's recomputed primary insurance amount of $435.30. Later we increased the primary insurance amount to $497.60 to reflect the 14.3 percent cost-of-living increase beginning June 1980 and to $553.40 to reflect the 11.2 percent cost-of-living increase beginning June 1981.

Example 2. Mr. B, whose primary insurance amount we computed to be $429.20 (based on average monthly wages of $502) in June 1978 in §§ 404.220 through 404.222, had earnings of $12,000 in 1978 which were not used in the initial computation of his primary insurance amount. We may recompute his primary insurance amount effective for January 1979. In this recomputation, his 1978 earnings are substituted for the lowest year of earnings used in the initial computation ($2,700 in 1952). Mr. B's total earnings are now $142,000 and his new average monthly wage is $537.

We next find Mr. B's new average monthly wage in column III of the December 1978 benefit table in appendix III. Reading across, we find his recomputed primary insurance amount on the same line in column IV, which is $407.70. We then apply the 9.9 percent, the 14.3 percent and the 11.2 percent automatic cost-of-living increases for June 1979, June 1980, and June 1981, respectively, to compute Mr. B's primary insurance amount of $569.60.

(f) Guaranteed alternatives. We may recompute your primary insurance amount by any of the following methods for which you qualify, if doing so would result in a higher amount than the one computed under the average-indexed-monthly-earnings method. Earnings in or after the year you reach age 62 cannot be used.

(1) If you reached age 62 after 1978 and before 1984, we may recompute to include earnings for years before

the year you reached age 62 by using the guaranteed alternative (§ 404.231). We will increase the result by any cost-of-living or ad hoc increases in the primary insurance amounts that have become effective in and after the year you reached age 62.

(2) We will also recompute under the old-start guarantee (§ 404.242) and the prior-disability guarantee (§ 404.252) if you meet the requirements of either or both these methods.

[52 FR 47918, Dec. 17, 1987]

§ 404.285 Recomputations performed automatically.

Each year, we examine the earnings record of every retired, disabled, and deceased worker to see if the worker's primary insurance amount may be recomputed under any of the methods we have described. When a recomputation is called for, we perform it automatically and begin paying the higher benefits based on your recomputed primary insurance amount for the earliest possible month that the recomputation can be effective. You do not have to request this service, although you may request a recomputation at an earlier date than one would otherwise be performed (see § 404.286). Doing so, however, does not allow your increased primary insurance amount to be effective any sooner than it would be under an automatic recomputation. You may also waive a recomputation if one would disadvantage you or your family (see § 404.287).

§ 404.286 How to request an immediate recomputation.

You may request that your primary insurance amount be recomputed sooner than it would be recomputed automatically. To do so, you must make the request in writing to us and provide acceptable evidence of your earnings not included in the first computation or earlier recomputation of your primary insurance amount. If doing so will increase your primary insurance amount, we will recompute it. However, we cannot begin paying higher benefits on the recomputed primary insurance amount any sooner than we could under an automatic recomputation, i.e., for January of the year following the year in which the earnings were paid or derived.

§ 404.287 Waiver of recomputation.

If you or your family would be disadvantaged in some way by a recomputation of your primary insurance amount, or you and every member of your family do not want your primary insurance amount to be recomputed for any other reason, you may waive (that is, give up your right to) a recomputation, but you must do so in writing. That you waive one recomputation, however, does not mean that you also waive future recomputations for which you might be eligible.

§ 404.288 Recomputing when you are entitled to a monthly pension based on noncovered employment.

(a) After entitlement to old-age or disability insurance benefits. If you first become eligible for old-age or disability insurance benefits after 1985 and you later become entitled to a monthly pension based on noncovered employment, we may recompute your primary insurance amount under the rules in § 404.213. When recomputing, we will use the amount of the pension to which you are entitled or deemed entitled in the first month that you are concurrently eligible for both the pension and old-age or disability insurance benefits. We will disregard the rule in § 404.284(e) that the recomputation must increase your primary insurance amount by at least $1.

(b) Already entitled to benefits and to a pension based on noncovered employment. If we have already computed or recomputed your primary insurance amount to take into account your monthly pension, we may later recompute for one of the reasons explained in § 404.281. We will recompute your primary insurance amount under the rules in §§ 404.213 and 404.284. Any increase resulting from the recomputation under the rules of § 404.284 will be added to the most recent primary insurance amount which we had computed to take into account your monthly pension.

(c) After your death. If one or more survivors are entitled to benefits after your death, we will recompute the primary insurance amount as though it had never been affected by your entitlement to a monthly pension based in whole or in part on noncovered employment.

[52 FR 47918, Dec. 17, 1987]

RECALCULATIONS OF PRIMARY INSURANCE AMOUNTS

§ 404.290 Recalculations.

(a) Your primary insurance amount may be "recalculated" in certain instances. When we recalculate your primary amount, we refigure it under the same method we used in the first computation by taking into account—

(1) Earnings (including compensation for railroad service) incorrectly included or excluded in the first computation;

(2) Special deemed earnings credits including credits for military service (see subpart N of this part) and for individuals interned during World War II (see subpart K of this part), not available at the time of the first computation;

(3) Correction of clerical or mathematical errors; or

(4) Other miscellaneous changes in status.

(b) Unlike recomputations, which may only serve to increase your primary insurance amount, recalculations may serve to either increase or reduce it.

APPENDICES TO SUBPART C OF PART 404—NOTE

The following appendices contain data that are needed in computing primary insurance amounts. Appendix I contains average of the total wages figures, which we use to index a worker's earnings for purposes of computing his or her average indexed monthly earnings. Appendix II contains benefit formulas which we apply to a worker's average indexed monthly earnings to find his or her primary insurance amount. Appendix III contains the benefit table we use to find a worker's primary insurance amount from his or her average monthly wage. We use the figures in Appendix IV to find your years of coverage for years after 1950 for purposes of your special minimum primary insurance amount. Appendix V contains the table for computing the special minimum primary insurance amount. Appendix VI is a table of the percentage increases in primary insurance amounts since 1978. Appendix VII is a table of the old-law contribution and benefit base that would have been effective under the Social Security Act without enactment of the 1977 amendments.

The figures in the appendices are by law automatically adjusted each year. We are required to announce the changes through timely publication in the Federal Register. The only exception to the requirement of publication in the Federal Register is the update of benefit amounts shown in Appendix III. We update the benefit amounts for payment purposes but are not required by law to publish this extensive table in the Federal Register. We have not updated the table in Appendix III, but the introductory paragraphs at Appendix III explain how you can compute the current benefit amount.

When we publish the figures in the Federal Register, we do not change every one of these figures. Instead, we provide new ones for each year that passes. We continue to use the old ones for various computation purposes, as the regulations show. Most of the new figures for these appendices are required by law to be published by November 1 of each year. Notice of automatic cost-of-living increases in primary insurance amounts is required to be published within 45 days of the end of the applicable measuring period for the increase (see §§ 404.274 and 404.276). In effect, publication is required within 45 days of the end of the third calendar quarter of any year in which there is to be an automatic cost-of-living increase.

We begin to use the new data in computing primary insurance amounts as soon as required by law, even before we periodically update these appendices. If the data you need to find your primary insurance amount have not yet been included in the appendices, you may find the figures in the Federal Register on or about November 1.

[52 FR 8247, March 17, 1987]

APPENDIX I TO SUBPART C OF PART 404—AVERAGE OF THE TOTAL WAGES FOR YEARS AFTER 1950

Explanation: We use these figures to index your social security earnings (as described in § 404.211) for purposes of computing your average indexed monthly earnings.

Calendar year	Average of the total wages
1951	$ 2,799.16
1952	2,973.32
1953	3,139.44
1954	3,155.64
1955	3,301.44
1956	3,532.36
1957	3,641.72
1958	3,673.80
1959	3,855.80
1960	4,007.12
1961	4,086.76
1962	4,291.40
1963	4,396.64
1964	4,576.32
1965	4,658.72
1966	4,938.36
1967	5,213.44
1968	5,571.76
1969	5,893.76
1970	6,186.24
1971	6,497.08
1972	7,133.80
1973	7,580.16
1974	8,030.76
1975	8,630.92
1976	9,226.48
1977	9,779.44
1978	10,556.03
1979	11,479.46
1980	12,513.46
1981	13,773.10
1982	14,531.34
1983	15,239.24
1984	16,135.07
1985	16,822.51
1986	17,321.82
1987	18,426.51
1988	19,334.04
1989	20,099.55
1990	21,027.98

[52 FR 8247, March 17, 1987; 57 FR 44096, Sept. 24, 1992]

APPENDIX II TO SUBPART C OF PART 404—BENEFIT FORMULAS USED WITH AVERAGE INDEXED MONTHLY EARNINGS

As explained in § 404.212, we use one of the formulas below to compute your primary insurance amount from your average indexed monthly earnings (AIME). To select the appropriate formula, we find in the left-hand column the year after 1978 in which you reach age 62, or become disabled, or die before age 62. The benefit formula to be used in computing your primary insurance amount is on the same line in the right-hand columns. For example, if you reach age 62 or become disabled or die before age 62 in 1979, then we compute 90 percent of the first $180 of AIME, 32 percent of the next $905 of AIME, and 15 percent of AIME over $1,085. After we figure your amount for each step in the formula, we add the amounts. If the total is not already a multiple of $0.10, we round the total as follows:

(1) For computations using the benefit formulas in effect for 1979 through 1982, we round the total upward to the nearest $0.10, and

(2) For computations using the benefit formulas in effect for 1983 and later, we round the total downward to the nearest $0.10.

BENEFIT FORMULAS

Year you reach age 62 [1]	90 percent of the first—	plus 32 percent of the next—	plus 15 percent of AIME over—
1979	$180	$ 905	$1,085
1980	194	977	1,171
1981	211	1,063	1,274
1982	230	1,158	1,388
1983	254	1,274	1,528
1984	267	1,345	1,612
1985	280	1,411	1,691
1986	297	1,493	1,790
1987	310	1,556	1,866
1988	319	1,603	1,922
1989	339	1,705	2,044
1990	356	1,789	2,145
1991	370	1,860	2,230
1992	387	1,946	2,333

[1] Or become disabled or die before age 62.

[52 FR 8247, March 17, 1987; 55 FR 21382, May 24, 1990; 57 FR 44096, Sept. 24, 1992; 57 FR 45878, Oct. 5, 1992]

APPENDIX III TO SUBPART C OF PART 404—BENEFIT TABLE

This benefit table shows primary insurance amounts and maximum family benefits in effect in December 1978 based on cost-of-living increases which became effective for June 1978. (See § 404.403 for information on maximum family benefits.) You will also be able to find primary insurance amounts for an individual whose entitlement began in the period June 1977 through May 1978.

The benefit table in effect in December 1978 had a minimum primary insurance amount of $121.80. As explained in § 404.222(b), certain workers eligible, or who died without having been eligible, before 1982 had their benefit computed from this table. However, the minimum benefit provision was repealed for other workers by the 1981 amendments to the Act (the Omnibus Budget Reconciliation Act of 1981, Pub.L. 97–35 as modified by Pub.L. 97–123). As a result, this benefit table includes a downward extension from the former minimum of $121.80 to the lowest primary insurance amount now possible. The extension is calculated as follows. For each single dollar of average monthly wage in the benefit table, the primary insurance amount shown for December 1978 is $121.80 multiplied by the ratio of that average monthly wage to $76. The upper limit of each primary insurance benefit range in column I of the table is $16.20 multiplied by the ratio of the average monthly wage in column III of the table to $76. The maximum family benefit is 150 percent of the corresponding primary insurance amount.

The repeal of the minimum benefit provision is effective with January 1982 for most workers and their families where the worker initially becomes eligible for benefits after 1981 or dies after 1981 without having been eligible before January 1982. For members of a religious order who are required to take a vow of poverty, as explained in 20 CFR 404.1024, and which religious order elected Social Security coverage before December 29, 1981, the repeal is effective with January 1992 based on first eligibility or death in that month or later.

To use this table, you must first compute the primary insurance benefit (column I) or the average monthly wage (column III), then move across the same line to either column II or column IV as appropriate. To determine increases in primary insurance amounts since December 1978 you should see appendix VI. Appendix VI tells you, by year, the percentage of the increases. In applying each cost-of-living increase to primary insurance amounts, we round the increased primary insurance amount to the next lower multiple of $0.10 if not already a multiple of $0.10. (For cost-of-living increases which are effective before June 1982, we round to the next higher multiple of $0.10.)

EXTENDED DECEMBER 1978 TABLE OF BENEFITS EFFECTIVE JANUARY 1982
[In dollars]

I. Primary insurance benefit: If an individual's primary insurance benefit (as determined under § 404.241(e)) is– At least–	But not more than–	II. Primary insurance amount effective June 1977: Or his or her primary insurance amount is–	III. Average monthly wage: Or his or her average monthly wage (as determined under § 404.221) is– At least–	But not more than–	IV. Primary insurance amount effective January 1982: Then his or her primary insurance amount is–	V. Maximum family benefits: And the maximum amount of benefits payable on the basis of his or her wages and self-employment income is–
				1	1.70	2.60
	0.42		2	2	3.30	5.00
0.43	.63		3	3	4.90	7.40
.64	.85		4	4	6.50	9.80
.86	1.06		5	5	8.10	12.20
1.07	1.27		6	6	9.70	14.60
1.28	1.49		7	7	11.30	17.00
1.50	1.70		8	8	12.90	19.40
1.71	1.91		9	9	14.50	21.80
1.92	2.13		10	10	16.10	24.20
2.14	2.34		11	11	17.70	26.60
2.35	2.55		12	12	19.30	29.00
2.56	2.77		13	13	20.90	31.40
2.78	2.98		14	14	22.50	33.80
2.99	3.19		15	15	24.10	36.20
3.20	3.41		16	16	25.70	38.60
3.42	3.62		17	17	27.30	41.00
3.63	3.83		18	18	28.90	43.40
3.84	4.05		19	19	30.50	45.80
4.06	4.26		20	20	32.10	48.20
4.27	4.47		21	21	33.70	50.60
4.48	4.68		22	22	35.30	53.00
4.69	4.90		23	23	36.90	55.40
4.91	5.11		24	24	38.50	57.80
5.12	5.32		25	25	40.10	60.20
5.33	5.54		26	26	41.70	62.60
5.55	5.75		27	27	43.30	65.00
5.76	5.96		28	28	44.90	67.40
5.97	6.18		29	29	46.50	69.80
6.19	6.39		30	30	48.10	72.20
6.40	6.60		31	31	49.70	74.60
6.61	6.82		32	32	51.30	77.00
6.83	7.03		33	33	52.90	79.40
7.04	7.24		34	34	54.50	81.80
7.25	7.46		35	35	56.10	84.20
7.47	7.67		36	36	57.70	86.60
7.68	7.88		37	37	59.30	89.00
7.89	8.10		38	38	60.90	91.40
8.11	8.31		39	39	62.60	93.90
8.32	8.52		40	40	64.20	96.30
8.53	8.73		41	41	65.80	98.70
8.74	8.95		42	42	67.40	101.10
8.96	9.16		43	43	69.00	103.50
9.17	9.37		44	44	70.60	105.90
9.38	9.59		45	45	72.20	108.30
9.60	9.80		46	46	73.80	110.70
9.81	10.01		47	47	75.40	113.10
10.02	10.23		48	48	77.00	115.50
10.24	10.44		49	49	78.60	117.90
10.45	10.65		50	50	80.20	120.30
10.66	10.87		51	51	81.80	122.70
10.88	11.08		52	52	83.40	125.10
11.09	11.29		53	53	85.00	127.50
11.30	11.51		54	54	86.60	129.90
11.52	11.72		55	55	88.20	132.30
11.73	11.93		56	56	89.80	134.70
11.94	12.15		57	57	91.40	137.10
12.16	12.36		58	58	93.00	139.50
12.37	12.57		59	59	94.60	141.90
12.58	12.78		60	60	96.20	144.30
12.79	13.00		61	61	97.80	146.70
13.01	13.21		62	62	99.40	149.10
13.22	13.42		63	63	101.00	151.50
13.43	13.64		64	64	102.60	153.90
13.65	13.85		65	65	104.20	156.30
13.86	14.06		66	66	105.80	158.70
14.07	14.28		67	67	107.40	161.10
14.29	14.49		68	68	109.00	163.50
14.50	14.70		69	69	110.60	165.90
14.71	14.92		70	70	112.20	168.30

I. Primary insurance benefit: If an individual's primary insurance benefit (as determined under § 404.241(e)) is– At least–	But not more than–	II. Primary insurance amount effective June 1977: Or his or her primary insurance amount is–	III. Average monthly wage: Or his or her average monthly wage (as determined under § 404.221) is– At least–	But not more than–	IV. Primary insurance amount effective January 1982: Then his or her primary insurance amount is–	V. Maximum family benefits: And the maximum amount of benefits payable on the basis of his or her wages and self-employment income is–
14.93	15.13		71	71	113.80	170.70
15.14	15.34		72	72	115.40	173.10
15.35	15.56		73	73	117.00	175.50
15.57	15.77		74	74	118.60	177.90
15.78	15.98		75	75	120.20	180.30
15.99	16.20		76	76	121.80	182.70

TABLE OF BENEFITS IN EFFECT IN DECEMBER 1978
[In dollars]

I. Primary insurance benefit: If an individual's primary insurance benefit as determined under § 404.241(e)) is– At least–	But not more than–	II. Primary insurance amount effective June 1977: Or his or her primary insurance amount is–	III. Average monthly wage: Or his or her average monthly wage (as determined under § 404.221) is– At least–	But not more than–	IV. Primary insurance amount effective June 1978: Then his or her primary insurance amount is–	V. Maximum family benefits: And the maximum amount payable on the basis of his or her wages and self-employment income is–
	16.20	114.30		76	121.80	182.70
16.21	16.84	116.10	77	78	123.70	185.60
16.85	17.60	118.80	79	80	126.60	189.90
17.61	18.40	121.00	81	81	128.90	193.50
18.41	19.24	123.00	82	83	131.20	196.80
19.25	20.00	125.80	84	85	134.00	201.00
20.01	20.64	128.10	86	87	136.50	204.80
20.65	21.28	130.10	88	89	138.60	207.90
21.29	21.88	132.70	90	90	141.40	212.10
21.89	22.28	135.00	91	92	143.80	215.70
22.29	22.68	137.20	93	94	146.20	219.20
22.59	23.08	139.40	95	96	148.50	222.80
23.09	23.44	142.00	97	97	151.30	227.00
23.45	23.76	144.30	98	99	153.70	230.60
23.77	24.20	147.10	100	101	156.70	235.10
24.21	24.60	149.20	102	102	158.90	238.50
24.61	25.00	151.70	103	104	161.60	242.40
25.01	25.48	154.50	105	106	164.60	246.90
25.49	25.92	157.00	107	107	167.30	251.00
25.93	26.40	159.40	108	109	169.80	254.80
26.41	26.94	161.90	110	113	172.50	258.80
26.95	27.46	164.20	114	118	174.90	262.40
27.47	28.00	166.70	119	122	177.60	266.50
28.01	28.68	169.30	123	127	180.40	270.60
28.69	29.25	171.80	128	132	183.00	274.60
29.26	29.68	174.10	133	136	185.50	278.30
29.69	30.36	176.50	137	141	188.00	282.10
30.37	30.92	179.10	142	146	190.80	286.20
30.93	31.36	181.70	147	150	193.60	290.40
31.37	32.00	183.90	151	155	195.90	293.90
32.01	32.60	186.50	156	160	198.70	298.10
32.61	33.20	189.00	161	164	201.30	302.00
33.21	33.88	191.40	165	169	203.90	305.90
33.89	34.50	194.00	170	174	206.70	310.10
34.51	35.00	196.30	175	178	209.10	313.70
35.01	35.80	198.90	179	183	211.90	318.00
35.81	36.40	201.30	184	188	214.40	321.70
36.41	37.08	203.90	189	193	217.20	326.00
37.09	37.60	206.40	194	197	219.90	329.90
37.61	38.20	208.80	198	202	222.40	333.60
38.21	39.12	211.50	203	207	225.30	338.00
39.13	39.68	214.00	208	211	228.00	342.00
39.69	40.33	216.00	212	216	230.10	345.20
40.34	41.12	218.70	217	221	233.00	349.50
41.13	41.76	221.20	222	225	235.60	353.40
41.77	42.44	223.90	226	230	238.50	357.80
42.45	43.20	226.30	231	235	241.10	361.70
43.21	43.76	229.10	236	239	244.00	366.10
43.77	44.44	231.20	240	244	246.30	371.10
44.45	44.88	233.50	245	249	248.70	378.80
44.89	45.60	236.40	250	253	251.80	384.90
		238.70	254	258	254.30	392.50
		240.80	259	263	256.50	400.00
		243.70	264	267	259.60	206.00
		246.10	268	272	262.10	413.70
		248.70	273	277	264.90	421.20
		251.00	278	281	267.40	427.20

I. Primary insurance benefit: If an individual's primary insurance benefit as determined under § 404.241(e)) is– At least–	But not more than–	II. Primary insurance amount effective June 1977: Or his or her primary insurance amount is–	III. Average monthly wage: Or his or her average monthly wage (as determined under § 404.221) is– At least–	But not more than–	IV. Primary insurance amount effective June 1978: Then his or her primary insurance amount is–	V. Maximum family benefits: And the maximum amount payable on the basis of his or her wages and self-employment income is–
		253.50	282	286	270.00	434.90
		256.20	287	291	272.90	442.60
		258.30	292	295	275.10	448.50
		261.10	296	300	278.10	456.10
		263.50	301	305	280.70	463.80
		265.80	306	309	283.10	469.80
		268.50	310	314	286.00	477.40
		270.70	315	319	288.30	485.10
		273.20	320	323	291.00	491.10
		275.80	324	328	293.80	498.70
		278.10	329	333	296.20	506.20
		281.00	334	337	299.30	512.50
		283.00	338	342	301.40	519.90
		285.60	343	347	304.20	527.50
		288.30	348	351	307.10	533.60
		290.50	352	356	309.40	541.20
		293.30	357	361	312.40	548.80
		295.60	362	365	314.90	554.90
		297.90	366	370	317.30	562.50
		300.60	371	375	320.20	569.90
		303.10	376	379	322.90	576.30
		305.70	380	384	325.60	583.90
		307.90	385	389	328.00	591.30
		310.30	390	393	330.50	597.40
		313.00	394	398	333.40	605.10
		315.40	399	403	336.00	612.70
		318.20	404	407	338.90	618.60
		320.20	408	412	341.10	626.30
		322.50	413	417	343.50	633.80
		324.80	418	421	346.00	639.90
		327.40	422	426	348.70	647.50
		329.60	427	431	351.10	655.10
		331.60	432	436	353.20	662.70
		334.40	437	440	356.20	665.70
		336.50	441	445	358.40	669.70
		338.70	446	450	360.80	673.40
		341.30	451	454	363.50	676.30
		343.50	455	459	365.90	680.10
		345.80	460	464	368.30	683.80
		347.90	465	468	370.60	687.10
		350.70	469	473	373.50	690.80
		352.60	474	478	375.60	694.60
		354.90	479	482	378.00	697.70
		357.40	483	487	380.70	701.60
		359.70	488	492	383.10	705.40
		361.90	493	496	385.50	708.40
		364.50	497	501	388.20	712.10
		366.60	502	506	390.50	715.80
		368.90	507	510	392.90	719.00
		371.10	511	515	395.30	722.80
		373.70	516	520	398.00	726.70
		375.80	521	524	400.30	729.50
		378.10	525	529	402.70	733.40
		380.80	530	534	405.60	737.10
		382.80	535	538	407.70	740.20
		385.10	539	543	410.20	744.10
		387.60	544	548	412.80	747.80
		389.90	549	553	415.30	751.60
		392.10	554	556	417.60	753.90
		393.90	557	560	419.60	756.90
		396.10	561	563	421.90	759.30
		398.20	564	567	424.10	762.30
		400.40	568	570	426.50	764.50
		402.30	571	574	428.50	767.50
		404.40	575	577	430.70	769.90
		406.20	578	581	432.70	772.80
		408.40	582	584	435.00	775.20
		410.20	585	588	436.90	778.20
		412.60	589	591	439.50	780.50
		414.60	592	595	441.60	783.50
		416.70	596	598	443.80	785.60
		418.70	599	602	446.00	788.90
		420.70	603	605	448.10	791.10
		422.80	606	609	450.30	794.00
		424.90	610	612	452.60	796.50
		426.90	613	616	454.70	799.50
		428.90	617	620	456.80	802.50

I. Primary insurance benefit: If an individual's primary insurance benefit as determined under § 404.241(e)) is– At least–	But not more than–	II. Primary insurance amount effective June 1977: Or his or her primary insurance amount is–	III. Average monthly wage: Or his or her average monthly wage (as determined under § 404.221) is– At least–	But not more than–	IV. Primary insurance amount effective June 1978: Then his or her primary insurance amount is–	V. Maximum family benefits: And the maximum amount payable on the basis of his or her wages and self-employment income is–
		431.00	621	623	459.10	804.80
		433.00	624	627	461.20	807.90
		435.10	628	630	463.40	810.70
		437.10	631	634	465.60	814.70
		439.20	635	637	467.80	818.50
		441.40	638	641	470.10	822.40
		443.20	642	644	472.10	826.10
		445.40	645	648	474.40	830.10
		447.40	649	652	476.50	833.70
		448.60	653	656	477.80	836.10
		449.90	657	660	479.20	838.40
		451.50	661	665	480.90	841.50
		453.10	666	670	482.60	844.50
		454.80	671	675	484.40	847.40
		456.40	676	680	486.10	850.50
		458.00	681	685	487.80	853.50
		459.80	686	690	489.70	856.40
		461.20	691	695	491.20	859.60
		462.80	696	700	492.90	862.60
		464.50	701	705	494.70	865.60
		466.10	706	710	496.40	868.60
		467.70	711	715	498.20	871.50
		469.40	716	720	500.00	874.60
		471.00	721	725	501.70	877.60
		472.60	726	730	503.40	880.70
		474.20	731	735	505.10	883.80
		475.90	736	740	506.90	886.70
		477.40	741	745	508.50	889.90
		478.90	746	750	510.10	892.70
		480.40	751	755	511.70	896.40
		481.80	756	760	513.20	897.80
		483.20	761	765	514.70	900.40
		484.50	766	770	516.00	903.00
		485.80	771	775	517.40	905.40
		487.20	776	780	518.90	907.90
		488.60	781	785	520.40	910.40
		489.80	786	790	521.70	912.90
		491.10	791	795	523.10	915.40
		492.50	796	800	524.60	918.00
		494.00	801	805	526.20	920.50
		495.30	806	810	527.50	923.00
		496.70	811	815	529.00	925.60
		498.00	816	820	530.40	928.00
		499.40	821	825	531.90	930.60
		500.70	826	830	533.30	933.10
		502.00	831	835	534.70	935.70
		503.30	836	840	536.10	938.10
		504.70	841	845	537.60	940.80
		506.00	846	850	538.90	943.00
		507.50	851	855	540.50	945.70
		508.80	856	860	541.90	948.10
		510.20	861	865	543.40	950.70
		511.50	866	870	544.80	953.20
		512.90	871	875	546.30	955.70
		514.10	876	880	547.60	958.20
		515.50	881	885	549.10	960.80
		516.80	886	890	550.40	963.20
		518.20	891	895	551.90	966.00
		519.60	896	900	553.40	968.30
		521.00	901	905	554.90	970.90
		522.30	906	910	556.30	973.50
		523.70	911	915	557.80	976.00
		525.10	916	920	559.30	978.30
		526.30	921	925	560.60	961.00
		527.60	926	930	561.90	983.40
		529.00	931	935	563.40	985.90
		530.40	936	940	564.90	988.50
		531.70	941	945	566.30	991.00
		533.00	946	950	567.70	993.50
		534.50	951	955	569.30	996.10
		535.90	956	960	570.80	998.60
		537.30	961	965	572.30	1,001.00
		538.40	966	970	573.40	1,003.60
		539.80	971	975	574.90	1,006.20
		541.20	976	980	576.40	1,008.50
		542.60	981	985	577.90	1,011.10
		543.80	986	990	579.20	1,013.60

I. Primary insurance benefit: If an individual's primary insurance benefit as determined under § 404.241(e)) is– At least–	But not more than–	II. Primary insurance amount effective June 1977: Or his or her primary insurance amount is–	III. Average monthly wage: Or his or her average monthly wage (as determined under § 404.221) is– At least–	But not more than–	IV. Primary insurance amount effective June 1978: Then his or her primary insurance amount is–	V. Maximum family benefits: And the maximum amount payable on the basis of his or her wages and self-employment income is–
		545.20	991	995	580.70	1,016.20
		546.60	996	1,000	582.20	1,018.60
		547.80	1,001	1,005	583.50	1,020.70
		548.90	1,006	1,010	584.60	1,023.20
		550.20	1,011	1,015	586.00	1,025.30
		551.50	1,016	1,020	587.40	1,027.80
		552.60	1,021	1,025	588.60	1,029.90
		553.80	1,026	1,030	589.80	1,032.20
		555.10	1,031	1,035	591.20	1,034.50
		556.20	1,036	1,040	592.40	1,036.70
		557.50	1,041	1,045	593.80	1,039.10
		558.80	1,046	1,050	595.20	1,041.30
		559.80	1,051	1,055	596.20	1,043.40
		561.10	1,056	1,060	597.60	1,045.90
		562.40	1,061	1,065	599.00	1,048.00
		563.60	1,066	1,070	600.30	1,050.50
		564.80	1,071	1,075	601.60	1,052.60
		566.00	1,076	1,080	602.80	1,054.90
		567.30	1,081	1,085	604.20	1,057.10
		568.40	1,086	1,090	605.40	1,059.40
		569.70	1,091	1,095	606.80	1,061.70
		571.00	1,096	1,100	608.20	1,064.00
		572.00	1,101	1,105	609.20	1,066.10
		573.30	1,106	1,110	610.60	1,068.50
		574.60	1,111	1,115	612.00	1,070.70
		575.70	1,116	1,120	613.20	1,073.10
		577.00	1,121	1,125	614.60	1,075.30
		578.20	1,126	1,130	615.80	1,077.60
		579.40	1,131	1,135	617.10	1,079.70
		580.60	1,136	1,140	618.40	1,082.20
		581.90	1,141	1,145	619.80	1,084.40
		583.10	1,146	1,150	621.10	1,086.70
		584.20	1,151	1,555	622.20	1,088.80
		585.50	1,156	1,160	623.60	1,091.10
		586.70	1,161	1,165	624.90	1,093.40
		587.90	1,166	1,170	626.20	1,095.80
		589.20	1,171	1,175	627.50	1,098.00
		590.30	1,176	1,180	628.70	1,100.20
		591.40	1,181	1,185	629.90	1,102.20
		592.60	1,186	1,190	631.20	1,104.30
		593.70	1,191	1,195	632.30	1,106.50
		594.80	1,196	1,200	633.50	1,108.60
		595.90	1,201	1,205	634.70	1,110.60
		597.10	1,206	1,210	636.00	1,112.90
		598.20	1,211	1,215	637.10	1,114.90
		599.30	1,216	1,220	638.30	1,117.00
		600.40	1,221	1,225	639.50	1,119.00
		601.60	1,226	1,230	640.80	1,121.20
		602.70	1,231	1,235	641.90	1,123.30
		603.80	1,236	1,240	643.10	1,125.40
		605.00	1,241	1,245	644.40	1,127.50
		606.10	1,246	1,250	645.50	1,129.60
		607.20	1,251	1,255	646.70	1,131.60
		608.30	1,256	1,260	647.90	1,133.80
		609.50	1,261	1,265	649.20	1,135.90
		610.60	1,266	1,270	650.30	1,138.00
		611.70	1,271	1,275	651.50	1,140.00
		612.80	1,276	1,280	652.70	1,142.20
		613.80	1,281	1,285	653.70	1,144.10
		614.80	1,286	1,290	654.90	1,146.10
		616.00	1,291	1,295	656.10	1,148.00
		617.00	1,296	1,300	657.20	1,150.00
		618.10	1,301	1,305	658.30	1,152.00
		619.10	1,306	1,310	659.40	1,154.00
		620.20	1,311	1,315	660.60	1,155.90
		621.30	1,316	1,320	661.70	1,157.90
		622.30	1,321	1,325	662.80	1,159.80
		623.40	1,326	1,330	664.00	1,161.90
		624.40	1,331	1,335	665.00	1,163.80
		625.50	1,336	1,340	666.20	1,165.80
		626.60	1,341	1,345	667.40	1,167.70
		627.60	1,346	1,350	668.40	1,169.70
		628.70	1,351	1,355	669.60	1,171.70
		629.70	1,356	1,360	670.70	1,173.70
		630.80	1,361	1,365	671.90	1,175.60
		631.80	1,366	1,370	672.90	1,177.70
		632.90	1,371	1,375	674.10	1,179.60

I. Primary insurance benefit: If an individual's primary insurance benefit as determined under § 404.241(e)) is– At least–	But not more than–	II. Primary insurance amount effective June 1977: Or his or her primary insurance amount is–	III. Average monthly wage: Or his or her average monthly wage (as determined under § 404.221) is– At least–	But not more than–	IV. Primary insurance amount effective June 1978: Then his or her primary insurance amount is–	V. Maximum family benefits: And the maximum amount payable on the basis of his or her wages and self-employment income is–
		633.90	1,376	1,380	675.20	1,181.60
		634.90	1,381	1,385	676.20	1,183.40
		635.90	1,386	1,390	677.30	1,185.30
		636.90	1,391	1,395	678.30	1,187.10
		637.90	1,396	1,400	679.40	1,189.00
		638.90	1,401	1,405	680.50	1,190.80
		639.90	1,406	1,410	681.50	1,192.70
		640.90	1,411	1,415	682.60	1,194.60
		641.90	1,416	1,420	683.70	1,196.50
		642.90	1,421	1,425	685.70	1,198.30
		643.90	1,426	1,430	684.80	1,200.20
		644.90	1,431	1,435	686.90	1,202.00
		645.90	1,436	1,440	687.90	1,203.90
		646.90	1,441	1,445	689.00	1,205.70
		647.90	1,446	1,450	690.10	1,207.70
		648.90	1,451	1,455	691.10	1,209.50
		649.90	1,456	1,460	692.20	1,211.40
		650.90	1,461	1,465	693.30	1,213.20
		651.90	1,466	1,470	694.30	1,215.10
		652.90	1,471	1,475	695.40	1,216.90

[47 FR 30734, July 15, 1982; 47 FR 35479, Aug. 16, 1982; 48 FR 46143, Oct. 11, 1983; 48 FR 50076, Oct. 31, 1983]

APPENDIX IV TO SUBPART C OF PART 404—EARNINGS NEEDED FOR A YEAR OF COVERAGE AFTER 1950

MINIMUM SOCIAL SECURITY EARNINGS TO QUALIFY FOR A YEAR OF COVERAGE AFTER 1950 FOR PURPOSES OF THE—

Year	Special minimum primary insurance amount	Benefit computations described in section 404.213(d) [2]
1951-1954	$ 900	$ 900
1955-1958	1,050	1,050
1959-1965	1,200	1,200
1966-1967	1,650	1,650
1968-1971	1,950	1,950
1972	2,250	2,250
1973	2,700	2,700
1974	3,300	3,300
1975	3,525	3,525
1976	3,825	3,825
1977	4,125	4,125
1978	4,425	4,425
1979	4,725	4,725
1980	5,100	5,100
1981	5,550	5,550
1982	6,075	6,075
1983	6,675	6,675
1984	7,050	7,050
1985	7,425	7,425
1986	7,875	7,875
1987	8,175	8,175
1988	8,400	8,400
1989	8,925	8,925
1990	9,525	9,525
1991	5,940	9,900
1992	6,210	10,350

[2] Applies only to certain individuals with pensions from noncovered employment.

Note: For 1951–78, the amounts shown are 25 percent of the contribution and benefit base (the contribution and benefit base is the same as the annual wage limitation as shown in § 404.1047) in effect. For years after 1978, however, the amounts are 25 percent of what the contribution and benefit base would have been if the 1977 Social Security Amendments had not been enacted, except, for special minimum benefit purposes, the applicable percentage is 15 percent for years after 1990.

[52 FR 8247, March 17, 1987; 57 FR 22429, May 28, 1992; 57 FR 44096, Sept. 24, 1992]

APPENDIX V TO SUBPART C OF PART 404—COMPUTING THE SPECIAL MINIMUM PRIMARY INSURANCE AMOUNT AND RELATED MAXIMUM FAMILY BENEFITS

These tables are based on section 215(a)(1)(C)(i) of the Social Security Act, as amended. They include the percent cost-of-living increase shown in appendix VI for each effective date.

JUNE 1979

I. Years of coverage	II. Primary insurance amount	III. Maximum family benefit
11	$ 12.70	$ 19.10
12	25.30	38.00
13	38.00	57.00

14	50.60	75.90
15	63.20	94.90
16	75.90	113.90
17	88.50	132.80
18	101.20	151.80
19	113.80	170.70
20	126.40	189.60
21	139.10	208.70
22	151.70	227.60
23	164.40	246.60
24	177.00	265.50
25	189.60	284.50
26	202.30	303.50
27	214.90	322.40
28	227.50	341.30
29	240.20	360.30
30	252.80	379.20

JUNE 1980

I. Years of coverage	II. Primary insurance amount	III. Maximum family benefit
11	$ 14.60	$ 21.90
12	29.00	43.50
13	43.50	65.30
14	57.90	86.90
15	72.30	108.50
16	86.80	130.20
17	101.20	151.80
18	115.70	173.60
19	130.10	195.20
20	144.50	216.80
21	159.00	238.60
22	173.40	260.20
23	188.00	282.00
24	202.40	303.60
25	216.80	325.20
26	231.30	347.00
27	245.70	368.60
28	260.10	390.20
29	274.60	411.90
30	289.00	433.50

JUNE 1981

I. Years of coverage	II. Primary insurance amount	III. Maximum family benefit
11	$ 16.30	$ 24.50
12	32.30	48.50
13	48.40	72.70
14	64.40	96.70
15	80.40	120.70
16	96.60	144.90
17	112.60	168.90
18	128.70	193.10
19	144.70	217.10
20	160.70	241.10
21	176.90	265.40
22	192.90	289.40
23	209.10	313.70
24	225.10	337.70
25	241.10	361.70
26	257.30	386.00
27	273.30	410.00
28	289.30	434.00
29	305.40	458.10
30	321.40	482.10

JUNE 1982

I. Years of coverage	II. Primary insurance amount	III. Maximum family benefit
11	$ 17.50	$ 26.30
12	34.60	52.00
13	51.90	78.00
14	69.10	103.80
15	86.30	129.60
16	103.70	155.60
17	120.90	181.30
18	138.20	207.30
19	155.40	233.10
20	172.50	258.90
21	189.90	285.00
22	207.10	310.80
23	224.50	336.90
24	241.70	362.60
25	258.90	388.40
26	276.30	414.50
27	293.50	440.30
28	310.70	466.10
29	327.90	491.90
30	345.10	517.70

DECEMBER 1983

I. Years of coverage	II. Primary insurance amount	III. Maximum family benefit
11	$ 18.10	$ 27.20
12	35.80	53.80
13	53.70	80.70
14	71.50	107.40
15	89.30	134.10
16	107.30	161.00
17	125.10	187.60
18	143.00	214.50
19	160.80	241.20
20	178.50	267.90
21	196.50	294.90
22	214.30	321.60
23	232.30	348.60
24	250.10	375.20
25	267.90	401.90
26	285.90	429.00
27	303.70	455.70
28	321.50	482.40
29	339.30	509.10
30	357.10	535.80

DECEMBER 1984

I. Years of coverage	II. Primary insurance amount	III. Maximum family benefit
11	$ 18.70	$ 28.10
12	37.00	55.60
13	55.50	83.50
14	74.00	111.10
15	92.40	138.70
16	111.00	166.60
17	129.40	194.10
18	148.00	222.00
19	166.40	249.60
20	184.70	277.20
21	203.30	305.20
22	221.80	332.80
23	240.40	360.80
24	258.80	388.30
25	277.20	415.90
26	295.90	444.00
27	314.30	471.60
28	332.70	499.20
29	351.10	526.90

30	369.50	554.50

DECEMBER 1985

I. Years of coverage	II. Primary insurance amount	III. Maximum family benefit
11	$ 19.20	$ 28.90
12	38.10	57.30
13	57.20	86.00
14	76.20	114.50
15	95.20	142.90
16	114.40	171.70
17	133.40	200.10
18	152.50	228.80
19	171.50	257.30
20	190.40	285.70
21	209.60	314.60
22	228.60	343.10
23	247.80	371.90
24	266.80	400.30
25	285.70	428.70
26	305.00	457.70
27	324.00	486.20
28	343.00	514.60
29	361.90	543.20
30	380.90	571.60

DECEMBER 1986

I. Years of coverage	II. Primary insurance amount	III. Maximum family benefit
11	$ 19.40	$ 29.20
12	38.50	58.00
13	57.90	87.10
14	77.10	115.90
15	96.40	144.70
16	115.80	173.90
17	135.10	202.70
18	154.40	231.70
19	173.70	260.60
20	192.80	289.40
21	212.30	318.60
22	231.50	347.50
23	251.00	376.70
24	270.20	405.50
25	289.40	434.20
26	308.90	463.60
27	328.20	492.50
28	347.40	521.20
29	366.60	550.20
30	385.80	579.00

DECEMBER 1987

I. Years of coverage	II. Primary insurance amount	III. Maximum family benefit
11	$ 20.20	$ 30.40
12	40.10	60.40
13	60.30	90.70
14	80.30	120.70
15	100.40	150.70
16	120.60	181.20
17	140.70	211.20
18	160.80	241.40
19	180.90	271.50
20	200.80	301.50
21	221.20	331.90
22	241.20	362.00
23	261.50	392.50
24	281.50	422.50
25	301.50	452.40
26	321.80	483.00
27	341.90	513.10
28	361.90	543.00
29	381.90	573.30
30	402.00	603.30

DECEMBER 1988

I. Years of coverage	II. Primary insurance amount	III. Maximum family benefit
11	$ 21.00	$ 31.60
12	41.70	62.80
13	62.70	94.30
14	83.50	125.50
15	104.40	156.70
16	125.40	188.40
17	146.30	219.60
18	167.20	251.00
19	188.10	282.30
20	208.80	313.50
21	230.00	345.10
22	250.80	376.40
23	271.90	408.20
24	292.70	439.40
25	313.50	470.40
26	334.60	502.30
27	355.50	533.60
28	376.30	564.70
29	397.10	596.20
30	418.00	627.40

DECEMBER 1989

I. Years of coverage	II. Primary insurance amount	III. Maximum family benefit
11	$ 21.90	$ 33.00
12	43.60	65.70
13	65.60	98.70
14	87.40	131.30
15	109.30	164.00
16	131.20	197.20
17	153.10	229.90
18	175.00	262.70
19	196.90	295.50
20	218.60	328.20
21	240.80	361.30
22	262.50	394.00
23	284.60	427.30
24	306.40	460.00
25	328.20	492.50
26	350.30	525.90
27	372.20	558.60
28	393.90	591.20
29	415.70	624.20
30	437.60	656.80

DECEMBER 1990

I. Years of coverage	II. Primary insurance amount	III. Maximum family benefit
11	$ 23.00	$ 34.70
12	45.90	69.20
13	69.10	104.00
14	92.10	138.30
15	115.20	172.80
16	138.20	207.80
17	161.30	242.30
18	184.40	276.80
19	207.50	311.40

20	230.40	345.90
21	253.80	380.80
22	276.60	415.20
23	299.90	450.30
24	322.90	484.80
25	345.90	519.00
26	369.20	554.20
27	392.20	588.70
28	415.10	623.10
29	438.10	657.90
30	461.20	692.20

DECEMBER 1991

I. Years of coverage	II. Primary insurance amount	III. Maximum family benefit
11	$ 23.80	$ 35.90
12	47.50	71.70
13	71.60	107.80
14	95.50	143.40
15	119.40	179.10
16	143.30	215.40
17	167.20	251.20
18	191.20	287.00
19	215.10	322.90
20	238.90	358.60
21	263.10	394.80
22	286.80	430.50
23	310.90	466.90
24	334.80	502.70
25	358.60	538.20
26	382.80	574.70
27	406.70	610.40
28	430.40	646.10
29	454.30	682.20
30	478.20	717.80

Note: The amounts shown in the above table for years of coverage less than 19 are not payable for June 1981 through December 1981 because the corresponding values shown in column II are less than the $135.70 minimum primary insurance amount payable for that period. For months after December 1981, a special minimum primary insurance amount of $128.70 will be payable.

[52 FR 8247, March 17, 1987; 57 FR 44097, Sept. 24, 1992; 57 FR 45878, Oct. 5, 1992]

APPENDIX VI TO SUBPART C OF PART 404—PERCENTAGE OF AUTOMATIC INCREASES IN PRIMARY INSURANCE AMOUNTS SINCE 1978

Effective date	Percentage increase
06/79	9.9
06/80	14.3
06/81	11.2
06/82	7.4
12/83	3.5
12/84	3.5
12/85	3.1
12/86	1.3
12/87	4.2
12/88	4.0
12/89	4.7
12/90	5.4
12/91	3.7

[52 FR 8247, March 17, 1987; 57 FR 44097, Sept. 24, 1992]

APPENDIX VII TO SUBPART C OF PART 404—"OLD-LAW" CONTRIBUTION AND BENEFIT BASE

Explanation: We use these figures to determine the earnings needed for a year of coverage for years after 1978 (see § 404.261 and appendix IV). This is the contribution and benefit base that would have been effective under the Social Security Act without the enactment of the 1977 amendments.

Year	Amount
1979	$18,900
1980	20,400
1981	22,200
1982	24,300
1983	26,700
1984	28,200
1985	29,700
1986	31,500
1987	32,700
1988	33,600
1989	35,700
1990	38,100
1991	39,600
1992	41,400

[52 FR 8248, March 17, 1987; 57 FR 44097, Sept. 24, 1992; 57 FR 45878, Oct. 5, 1992]

SUBPART D—OLD-AGE, DISABILITY, DEPENDENTS' AND SURVIVORS' INSURANCE BENEFITS; PERIOD OF DISABILITY

Authority: Secs. 202, 203(a) and (b), 205(a), 216, 223, 225, and 702(a)(5) of the Social Security Act (42 U.S.C. 402, 403(a) and (b), 405(a), 416, 423, 425, and 902(a)(5)).

Source: 44 FR 34481, June 15, 1979; 51 FR 4482, Feb. 5, 1986; 51 FR 10615, March 28, 1986; 51 FR 12603, April 14, 1986; 51 FR 17617, May 14, 1986; 52 FR 19136, May 21, 1987; 52 FR 26955, July 17, 1987; 52 FR 27540, July 22, 1987; 57 FR 3938, Feb. 3, 1992; 57 FR 21598, May 21, 1992; 57 FR 30119, July 8, 1992; 60 FR 8145, Feb. 10, 1995; 61 FR 5941, Feb. 15, 1996; 70 FR 61365, Oct. 24, 2005; 83 FR 21708, May 10, 2018, unless otherwise noted.

GENERAL

§ 404.301 Introduction.

This subpart sets out what requirements you must meet to qualify for social security benefits, how your benefit amounts are figured, when your right to benefits begins and ends, and how family relationships are determined. These benefits are provided by title II of the Social Security Act. They include—

(a) For workers, old-age and disability benefits and benefit protection during periods of disability;

(b) For a worker's dependents, benefits for a worker's wife, divorced wife, husband, divorced husband, and child; and

(c) For a worker's survivors, benefits for a worker's widow, widower, divorced wife, child, and parent, and a lump-sum death payment.

(d) [Reserved by 83 FR 21708]

[83 FR 21708, May 10, 2018]

§ 404.302 Other regulations related to this subpart.

This subpart is related to several others. Subpart H sets out what evidence you need to prove you qualify for benefits. Subpart P describes what is needed to prove you are disabled. Subpart E describes when your benefits may be reduced or stopped for a time. Subpart G describes the need for and the effect of an application for benefits. Part 410 describes when you may qualify for black lung benefits. Part 416 describes when you may qualify for supplemental security income. Also 42 CFR part 405 describes when you may qualify for hospital and medical insurance if you are aged, disabled, or have chronic kidney disease.

§ 404.303 Definitions.

As used in this subpart:

Apply means to sign a form or statement that the Social Security Administration accepts as an application for benefits under the rules set out in subpart G.

Eligible means that a person would meet all the requirements for entitlement to benefits for a period of time but has not yet applied.

Entitled means that a person has applied and has proven his or her right to benefits for a period of time.

Insured person or the insured means someone who has enough earnings under social security to permit payment of benefits on his or her earnings record. The requirements for becoming insured are described in subpart B.

Permanent home means the true and fixed home (legal domicile) of a person. It is the place to which a person intends to return whenever he or she is absent.

Primary insurance amount means an amount that is determined from the average monthly earnings creditable to the insured person. This term and the manner in which it is computed are explained in subpart C.

We or Us means the Social Security Administration.

You means the person who has applied for benefits or the person for whom someone else has applied.

§ 404.304 What are the general rules on benefit amounts?

This subpart describes how we determine the highest monthly benefit amount you ordinarily could qualify for under each type of benefit. However, the highest monthly benefit amount you could qualify for may not be the amount you will be paid. In a particular month, your benefit amount may be reduced or not paid at all. Under some circumstances, your benefit amount may be increased. The most common reasons for a change in your benefit amount are listed below.

(a) Age. Sections 404.410 through 404.413 explain how your old-age, wife's or husband's, or widow's or widower's benefits may be reduced if you choose to receive them before you attain full retirement age (as defined in § 404.409).

(b) Earnings. Sections 404.415 through 404.418 explain how deductions will be made from your benefits if your earnings or the insured person's earnings go over certain limits.

(c) Overpayments and underpayments. Your benefits may be increased or decreased to make up for any previous overpayment or underpayment made on the insured person's record. For more information about this, see subpart F of this part.

(d) Family maximum. Sections 404.403 through 404.406 explain that there is a maximum amount payable on each insured person's earnings record. If you are entitled to benefits as the insured's dependent or survivor, your benefits may be reduced to keep total benefits payable to the insured's family within these limits.

(e) Government pension offset. If you are entitled to wife's, husband's, widow's, widower's, mother's, or father's benefits and receive a Government pension for work that was not covered under Social Security, your monthly benefits may be reduced because of that pension. For more information about this, see § 404.408a, which covers reductions for Government pensions.

(f) Rounding. After all other deductions or reductions, we reduce any monthly benefit that is not a multiple of $1 to the next lower multiple of $1.

[48 FR 46148, Oct. 11, 1983; 68 FR 4702, Jan. 30, 2003; 83 FR 21708, May 10, 2018]

§ 404.305 When you may not be entitled to benefits.

In addition to the situations described in § 404.304 when you may not receive a benefit payment, there are special circumstances when you may not be entitled to benefits. These circumstances are—

(a) Waiver of benefits. If you have waived benefits and been granted a tax exemption on religious grounds as described in §§ 404.1039 and 404.1075, no one may become entitled to any benefits or payments on your earnings record and you may not be entitled to benefits on anyone else's earnings record; and

(b) Person's death caused by an intentional act. You may not become entitled to or continue to receive any survivor's benefits or payments on the earnings record of any person, or receive any underpayment due a person, if you were convicted of a felony or an act in the nature of a felony of intentionally causing that person's death. If you were subject to the juvenile justice system, you may not become entitled to or continue to receive survivor's benefits or payments on the earnings record of any person, or receive any underpayment due a person, if you were found by a court of competent jurisdiction to have intentionally caused that person's death by committing an act which, if committed by an adult, would have been considered a felony or an act in the nature of a felony.

[44 FR 34481, June 15, 1981, as amended at 47 FR 13325, Mar. 30, 1982; 47 FR 42098, Sept. 24, 1982; 52 FR 19136, May 21, 1987; 52 FR 21410, June 5, 1987; 58 FR 64888, Dec. 10, 1993]

OLD–AGE AND DISABILITY BENEFITS

§ 404.310 When am I entitled to old-age benefits?

We will find you entitled to old-age benefits if you meet the following three conditions:

(a) You are at least 62 years old;

(b) You have enough social security earnings to be fully insured as defined in §§ 404.110 through 404.115; and

(c) You apply; or you are entitled to disability benefits up to the month you attain full retirement age (as defined in § 404.409). When you attain full retirement age, your disability benefits automatically become old-age benefits.

[51 FR 10616, March 28, 1986; 68 FR 4702, Jan. 30, 2003]

§ 404.311 When does my entitlement to old-age benefits begin and end?

(a) We will find you entitled to old-age benefits beginning with:

(1) If you have attained full retirement age (as defined in § 404.409), the first month covered by your application in which you meet all requirements for entitlement; or

(2) If you have attained age 62, but have not attained full retirement age (as defined in § 404.409), the first month covered by your application throughout which you meet all requirements for entitlement.

(b) We will find your entitlement to old-age benefits ends with the month before the month you die.

[48 FR 21926, May 16, 1983; 68 FR 4702, Jan. 30, 2003]

§ 404.312 How is my old-age benefit amount calculated?

(a) If your old-age benefits begin in the month you attain full retirement age (as defined in § 404.409), your monthly benefit is equal to the primary insurance amount (as explained in subpart C of this part).

(b) If your old-age benefits begin after the month you attain full retirement age, your monthly benefit is your primary insurance amount plus an increase for retiring after full retirement age. See § 404.313 for a description of these increases.

(c) If your old-age benefits begin before the month you attain full retirement age, your monthly benefit amount is the primary insurance amount minus a reduction for each month you are entitled before you attain full retirement age. These reductions are described in §§ 404.410 through 404.413.

[51 FR 12604, April 14, 1986; 68 FR 4702, Jan. 30, 2003]

§ 404.313 What are delayed retirement credits and how do they increase my old-age benefit amount?

(a) What are delayed retirement credits and how do I earn them? Delayed retirement credits (DRCs) are credits we use to increase the amount of your old-age benefit amount. You may earn a credit for each month during the period beginning with the month you attain full retirement age (as defined in § 404.409) and ending with the month you attain age 70 (72 before 1984). You earn a credit for each month for which you are fully insured and eligible but do not receive an old-age benefit either because you do not apply for benefits or because you elect to voluntarily suspend your benefits to earn DRCs. Even if you were entitled to old-age benefits before full retirement age you may still earn DRCs for months during the period from full retirement age to age 70, if you voluntarily elect to suspend those benefits. If we have determined that you are entitled to benefits, you may voluntarily suspend benefits for any month beginning with the month after the month in which you voluntarily request that we suspend your benefits. If you apply for benefits, and we have not made a determination that you are entitled to benefits, you may voluntarily have your benefits suspended for any month for which you have not received a payment.

(b) How is the amount of the increase because of delayed retirement credits computed?—

(1) Computation of the increase amount. The amount of the increase depends on your date of birth and the number of credits you earn. We total the number of credits (which need not be consecutive) and multiply that number by the applicable percentage from paragraph (b)(2) of this section. We then multiply the result by your benefit amount and round the answer to the next lower multiple of 10 cents (if the answer is not already a multiple of 10 cents). We add the result to your benefit amount. If a supplementary medical insurance premium is involved it is then deducted. The result is rounded to the next lower multiple of $1 (if the answer is not already a multiple of $1).

(2) Credit percentages. The applicable credit amount for each month of delayed retirement can be found in the table below.

If your date of birth is:	The credit for each month you delay retirement is:
Before 1/2/1917	1/12 of 1%

If your date of birth is:	The credit for each month you delay retirement is:
1/2/1917—1/1/1925	1/4 of 1%
1/2/1925—1/1/1927	7/24 of 1%
1/2/1927—1/1/1929	1/3 of 1%
1/2/1929—1/1/1931	3/8 of 1%
1/2/1931—1/1/1933	5/12 of 1%
1/2/1933—1/1/1935	11/24 of 1%
1/2/1935—1/1/1937	1/2 of 1%
1/2/1937—1/1/1939	13/24 of 1%
1/2/1939—1/1/1941	7/12 of 1%
1/2/1941—1/1/1943	5/8 of 1%
After 1/1/1943	2/3 of 1%

Example: Alan was qualified for old-age benefits when he reached age 65 on January 15, 1998. He decided not to apply for old-age benefits immediately because he was still working. When he became age 66 in January 1999, he stopped working and applied for benefits beginning with that month. Based on his earnings, his primary insurance amount was $782.60. However, because he did not receive benefits immediately upon attainment of full retirement age (65), he is due an increase based on his delayed retirement credits. He earned 12 credits, one for each month from January 1998 through December 1998. Based on his date of birth of 1/15/1933 he is entitled to a credit of 11/24 of one percent for each month of delayed retirement. 12 credits multiplied by 11/24 of one percent equals a credit of 5.5 percent. 5.5% of the primary insurance amount of $782.60 is $43.04 which is rounded to $43.00, the next lower multiple of 10 cents. $43.00 is added to the primary insurance amount, $782.60. The result, $825.60 is the monthly benefit amount. If a supplementary medical insurance premium is involved it is then deducted. The result is rounded to the next lower multiple of $1 (if the answer is not already a multiple of $1).

(c) When is the increase because of delayed retirement credits effective?—

(1) Credits earned after entitlement and before the year of attainment of age 70. If you are entitled to benefits, we examine our records after the end of each calendar year to determine whether you have earned delayed retirement credits during the previous year for months when you were at or over full retirement age and you were fully insured and eligible for benefits but did not receive them. Any increase in your benefit amount is effective beginning with January of the year after the year the credits were earned.

(2) Credits earned after entitlement in the year of attainment of age 70. If you are entitled to benefits in the month you attain age 70, we examine our records to determine if you earned any additional delayed retirement credits during the calendar year in which you attained age 70. Any increase in your benefit amount is effective beginning with the month you attained age 70.

(3) Credits earned prior to entitlement. If you are full retirement age or older and eligible for old-age benefits but do not apply for benefits, your delayed retirement credits for months from the month of attainment of full retirement age through the end of the year prior to the year of filing will be included in the computation of your initial benefit amount. Credits earned in the year you attain age 70 will be added in the month you attain age 70.

(d) How do delayed retirement credits affect the special minimum primary insurance amount? We do not add delayed retirement credits to your old-age benefit if your benefit is based on the special minimum primary insurance amount described in § 404.260. We add the delayed retirement credits only to your old-age benefit based on your regular primary insurance amount, i.e. as computed under one of the other provisions of subpart C of this part. If your benefit based on the regular primary insurance amount plus your delayed retirement credits is higher than the benefit based on your special minimum primary insurance amount, we will pay the higher amount to you. However, if the special minimum primary insurance amount is higher than the regular primary insurance amount without the delayed retirement credits, we will use the special minimum primary insurance amount to determine the family maximum and the benefits of others entitled on your earnings record.

(e) What is the effect of my delayed retirement credits on the benefit amount of others entitled on my earnings record?—

(1) Surviving spouse or surviving divorced spouse. If you earn delayed retirement credits during your lifetime, we will compute benefits for your surviving spouse or surviving divorced spouse based on your regular primary insurance amount plus the amount of those delayed retirement credits. All delayed retirement credits, including any earned during the year of death, can be used in computing the benefit amount for your surviving spouse or surviving divorced spouse beginning with the month of your death. We compute delayed retirement credits up to but not including the month of death.

(2) Other family member. We do not use your delayed retirement credits to increase the benefits of other family members entitled on your earnings record.

(3) Family maximum. We add delayed retirement credits to your benefit after we compute the family maximum. However, we add delayed retirement credits to your surviving spouse's or surviving divorced spouse's benefit before we reduce for the family maximum.

[51 FR 12605, April 14, 1986; 68 FR 4703, Jan. 30, 2003; 75 FR 76259, Dec. 8, 2010]

§ 404.315 Who is entitled to disability benefits?

(a) General. You are entitled to disability benefits while disabled before attaining full retirement age as defined in § 404.409 if—

(1) You have enough social security earnings to be insured for disability, as described in § 404.130;

(2) You apply;

(3) You have a disability, as defined in § 404.1505, or you are not disabled, but you had a disability that ended within the 12–month period before the month you applied; and

(4) You have been disabled for 5 full consecutive months. This 5–month waiting period begins with a month in which you were both insured for disability and disabled. Your waiting period can begin no earlier than the 17th month before the month you apply—no matter how long you were disabled before then. No waiting period is required if you were previously entitled to disability benefits or to a period of disability under § 404.320 any time within 5 years of the month you again became disabled.

(b) Prohibition against reentitlement to disability benefits if drug addiction or alcoholism is a contributing factor material to the determination of disability. You cannot be entitled to a period of disability payments if drug addiction or alcoholism is a contributing factor material to the determination of disability and your earlier entitlement to disability benefits on the same basis terminated after you received benefits for 36 months during which treatment was available.

[48 FR 21930, May 16, 1983; 51 FR 10616, March 28, 1986; 51 FR 16166, May 1, 1986; 53 FR 43681, Oct. 28, 1988; 57 FR 30119, July 8, 1992; 60 FR 8145, Feb. 10, 1995; 68 FR 4704, Jan. 30, 2003]

§ 404.316 When entitlement to disability benefits begins and ends.

(a) You are entitled to disability benefits beginning with the first month covered by your application in which you meet all the other requirements for entitlement. If a waiting period is required, your benefits cannot begin earlier than the first month following that period.

(b) Your entitlement to disability benefits ends with the earliest of these months:

(1) The month before the month of your death;

(2) The month before the month you attain full retirement age as defined in § 404.409 (at full retirement age your disability benefits will be automatically changed to old-age benefits);

(3) The second month after the month in which your disability ends as provided in § 404.1594(b)(1), unless continued subject to paragraph (c); or

(4) Subject to the provisions of paragraph (d) of this section, the month before your termination month (§ 404.325).

(c)(1) Your benefits, and those of your dependents, may be continued after your impairment is no longer disabling if—

(i) You are participating in an appropriate program of vocational rehabilitation services, employment services, or other support services, as described in § 404.327(a) and (b);

(ii) You began participating in the program before the date your disability ended; and

(iii) We have determined under § 404.328 that your completion of the program, or your continuation in the program for a specified period of time, will increase the likelihood that you will not have to return to the disability benefit rolls.

(2) We generally will stop your benefits with the earliest of these months—

(i) The month in which you complete the program; or

(ii) The month in which you stop participating in the program for any reason (see § 404.327(b) for what we mean by "participating" in the program); or

(iii) The month in which we determine under § 404.328 that your continuing participation in the program will no longer increase the likelihood that you will not have to return to the disability benefit rolls.

Exception to paragraph (c): In no case will we stop your benefits with a month earlier than the second month after the month your disability ends, provided that you meet all other requirements for entitlement to and payment of benefits through such month.

(d) If, after November 1980, you have a disabling impairment (§ 404.1511), you will be paid benefits for all months in which you do not do substantial gainful activity during the reentitlement period (§ 404.1592a) following the end of your trial work period (§ 404.1592). If you are unable to do substantial gainful activity in the first month following the reentitlement period, we will pay you benefits until you are able to do substantial gainful activity. (Earnings during your trial work period do not affect the payment of your benefit.) You will also be paid benefits for the first month after the trial work period in which you do substantial gainful activity and the two succeeding months, whether or not you do substantial gainful activity during those succeeding months. After those three months, you cannot be paid benefits for any months in which you do substantial gainful activity.

(e) If drug addiction or alcoholism is a contributing factor material to the determination of disability as described in § 404.1535, you may receive disability benefits on that basis for no more than 36 months regardless of the number of entitlement periods you may have. Not included in these 36 months are months in which treatment for your drug addiction or alcoholism is not available, months before March 1995, and months for which your benefit payments were suspended for any reason. Benefits to your dependents may continue after the 36 months of benefits if, but for the operation of this paragraph, you would otherwise be entitled to benefits based on disability.

The 36–month limit is no longer effective for benefits for months beginning after September 2004.

(f) If drug addiction or alcoholism is a contributing factor material to the determination of disability as described in § 404.1535 and your disability benefits are suspended for 12 consecutive months because of your failure to comply with treatment requirements, your disability benefits will be terminated effective the first month after such 12–month period. Benefits to your dependents may continue after the 12–month period if, but for the operation of this paragraph, you would otherwise be entitled to benefits based on disability.

[44 FR 34481, June 15, 1979, as amended at 47 FR 31542, July 21, 1982; 47 FR 52693, Nov. 23, 1982; 49 FR 22270, May 29, 1984; 51 FR 17616, May 14, 1986; 60 FR 8145, Feb. 10, 1995; 68 FR 4704, Jan. 30, 2003; 70 FR 36505, June 24, 2005]

§ 404.317 How is the amount of my disability benefit calculated?

Your monthly benefit is equal to the primary insurance amount (PIA). This amount is computed under the rules in subpart C of this part as if it was an old-age benefit, and as if you were 62 years of age at the beginning of the 5–month waiting period mentioned in § 404.315(a). If the 5–month waiting period is not required because of your previous entitlement, your PIA is figured as if you were 62 years old when you become entitled to benefits this time. Your monthly benefit amount may be reduced if you receive workers' compensation or public disability payments before you attain full retirement age (as defined in § 404.409) (see § 404.408). Your benefits may also be reduced if you were entitled to other retirement-age benefits before you attained full retirement age (as defined in § 404.409).

[68 FR 4704, Jan. 30, 2003; 81 FR 19033, April 4, 2016]

§ 404.320 Who is entitled to a period of disability.

(a) General. A period of disability is a continuous period of time during which you are disabled. If you become disabled, you may apply to have our records show how long your disability lasts. You may do this even if you do not qualify for disability benefits. If we establish a period of disability for you, the months in that period of time will not be counted in figuring your average earnings. If benefits payable on your earnings record would be denied or reduced because of a period of disability, the period of disability will not be taken into consideration.

(b) Who is entitled. You are entitled to a period of disability if you meet all the following conditions:

(1) You have or had a disability as defined in § 404.1505.

(2) You are insured for disability, as defined in § 404.130 in the calendar quarter in which you became disabled, or in a later calendar quarter in which you were disabled.

(3) You file an application while disabled, or no later than 12 months after the month in which your period of disability ended. If you were unable to apply within the 12–month period after your period of disability ended because of a physical or mental condition as described in § 404.322, you may apply not more than 36 months after the month your disability ended.

(4) At least 5 consecutive months go by from the month in which your period of disability begins and before the month in which it would end.

[48 FR 21930, May 16, 1983; 51 FR 10616, March 28, 1986]

§ 404.321 When a period of disability begins and ends.

(a) When a period of disability begins. Your period of disability begins on the day your disability begins if you are insured for disability on that day. If you are not insured for disability on that day, your period of disability will begin on the first day of the first calendar quarter after your disability began in which you become insured for disability. Your period of disability may not begin after you have attained full retirement age as defined in § 404.409.

(b) When disability ended before December 1, 1980. Your period of disability ends on the last day of the month before the month in which you become 65 years old or, if earlier, the last day of the second month following the month in which your disability ended.

(c) When disability ends after November 1980. Your period of disability ends with the close of whichever of the following is the earliest—

(1) The month before the month in which you attain full retirement age as defined in § 404.409.

(2) The month immediately preceding your termination month (§ 404.325); or

(3) If you perform substantial gainful activity during the reentitlement period described in § 404.1592a, the last month for which you received benefits.

(d) When drug addiction or alcoholism is a contributing factor material to the determination of disability.

(1) Your entitlement to receive disability benefit payments ends the month following the month in which, regardless of the number of entitlement periods you may have had based on disability where drug addiction or alcoholism is a contributing factor material to the determination of disability (as described in § 404.1535)—

(i) You have received a total of 36 months of disability benefits. Not included in these 36 months are months in which treatment for your drug addiction or alcoholism is not available, months before March 1995, and months for which your benefits were suspended for any reason; or

(ii) Your benefits have been suspended for 12 consecutive months because of your failure to comply with treatment requirements.

(2) For purposes other than payment of your disability benefits, your period of disability continues until the termination month as explained in § 404.325.

[44 FR 34481, June 15, 1979; 44 FR 73018, Dec. 17, 1979; 49 FR 22271, May 29, 1984; 60 FR 8145, Feb. 10, 1995; 65 FR 42782, July 11, 2000; 68 FR 4704, Jan. 30, 2003]

§ 404.322 When you may apply for a period of disability after a delay due to a physical or mental condition.

If because of a physical or mental condition you did not apply for a period of disability within 12 months after your period of disability ended, you may apply not more than 36 months after the month in which your disability ended. Your failure to apply within the 12–month time period will be considered due to a physical or mental condition if during this time—

(a) Your physical condition limited your activities to such an extent that you could not complete and sign an application; or

(b) You were mentally incompetent.

§ 404.325 The termination month.

If you do not have a disabling impairment, your termination month is the third month following the month in which your impairment is not disabling even if it occurs during the trial work period or the reentitlement period. If you continue to have a disabling impairment and complete 9 months of trial work, your termination month will be the third month following the earliest month you perform substantial gainful activity or are determined able to perform substantial gainful activity; however, in no event will the termination month under these circumstances be earlier than the first month after the end of the reentitlement period described in § 404.1592a.

Example 1: You complete your trial work period in December 1999. You then work at the substantial gainful activity level and continue to do so throughout the 36 months following completion of your trial work period and thereafter. Your termination month will be January 2003, which is the first month in which you performed substantial gainful activity after the end of your 36–month reentitlement period. This is because, for individuals who have disabling impairments (see § 404.1511) and who work, the termination month cannot occur before the first month after the end of the 36–month reentitlement period.

Example 2: You complete your trial work period in December 1999, but you do not do work showing your ability to do substantial gainful activity during your trial work period or throughout your 36–month reentitlement period. In April 2003, 4 months after your reentitlement period ends, you become employed at work that we determine is substantial gainful activity, considering all of our rules in §§ 404.1574 and 404.1574a. Your termination month will be July 2003; that is, the third month after the earliest month you performed substantial gainful activity.

[49 FR 22271, May 29, 1984; 65 FR 42782, July 11, 2000]

RULES RELATING TO CONTINUATION OF BENEFITS AFTER YOUR IMPAIRMENT IS NO LONGER DISABLING

Source: 70 FR 36505, June 24, 2005, unless otherwise noted.

§ 404.327 When you are participating in an appropriate program of vocational rehabilitation services, employment services, or other support services.

(a) What is an appropriate program of vocational rehabilitation services, employment services, or other support services? An appropriate program of vocational rehabilitation services, employment services, or other support services means—

(1) A program that is carried out under an individual work plan with an employment network under the Ticket to Work and Self–Sufficiency Program under part 411 of this chapter;

(2) A program that is carried out under an individualized plan for employment with—

(i) A State vocational rehabilitation agency (i.e., a State agency administering or supervising the administration of a State plan approved under title I of the Rehabilitation Act of 1973, as amended (29 U.S.C. 720–751) under 34 CFR part 361; or

(ii) An organization administering a Vocational Rehabilitation Services Project for American Indians with Disabilities authorized under section 121 of part C of title I of the Rehabilitation Act of 1973, as amended (29 U.S.C. 741);

(3) A program of vocational rehabilitation services, employment services, or other support services that is carried out under a similar, individualized written employment plan with—

(i) An agency of the Federal Government (for example, the Department of Veterans Affairs);

(ii) A one-stop delivery system or specialized one-stop center described in section 134(c) of the Workforce Investment Act of 1998 (29 U.S.C. 2864(c)); or

(iii) Another provider of services approved by us; providers we may approve include, but are not limited to—

(A) A public or private organization with expertise in the delivery or coordination of vocational rehabilitation services, employment services, or other support services; or

(B) A public, private or parochial school that provides or coordinates a program of vocational rehabilitation services, employment services, or other support services carried out under an individualized program or plan;

(4) An individualized education program developed under policies and procedures approved by the Secretary of Education for assistance to States for the education of individuals with disabilities under the Individuals with Disabilities Education Act, as amended (20 U.S.C. 1400 et seq.); you must be age 18 through age 21 for this provision to apply.

(b) When are you participating in the program?

(1) You are participating in a program described in paragraph (a)(1), (a)(2), or (a)(3) of this section when you are taking part in the activities and services outlined in your individual work plan, your individualized plan for employment, or your similar individualized written employment plan, as appropriate.

(2) If you are a student age 18 through 21 receiving services under an individualized education program described in paragraph (a)(4) of this section, you are participating in your program when you are taking part in the activities and services outlined in your program or plan.

(3) You are participating in your program under paragraph (b)(1) or (2) of this section during temporary interruptions in your program. For an interruption to be considered temporary, you must resume taking part in the activities and services outlined in your plan or program, as appropriate, no more than three months after the month the interruption occurred.

§ 404.328 When your completion of the program, or your continuation in the program for a specified period of time, will increase the likelihood that you will not have to return to the disability benefit rolls.

(a) We will determine that your completion of the program, or your continuation in the program for a specified period of time, will increase the likelihood that you will not have to return to the disability benefit rolls if your completion of or your continuation in the program will provide you with—

(1) Work experience (see § 404.1565) so that you would more likely be able to do past relevant work (see § 404.1560(b)), despite a possible future reduction in your residual functional capacity (see § 404.1545); or

(2) Education (see § 404.1564) and/or skilled or semi-skilled work experience (see § 404.1568) so that you would more likely be able to adjust to other work that exists in the national economy (see § 404.1560(c)), despite a possible future reduction in your residual functional capacity (see § 404.1545).

(b) If you are a student age 18 through age 21 participating in an individualized education program described in § 404.327(a)(4), we will find that your completion of or continuation in the program will increase the likelihood that you will not have to return to the disability benefit rolls.

(c) If you are receiving transition services after having completed an individualized education program as described in paragraph (b) of this section, we will determine that the transition services will increase the likelihood that you will not have to return to the disability benefit rolls if they meet the requirements in § 404.328(a).

BENEFITS FOR SPOUSES AND DIVORCED SPOUSES

§ 404.330 Who is entitled to wife's or husband's benefits.

You are entitled to benefits as the wife or husband of an insured person who is entitled to old-age or disability benefits if—

(a) You are the insured's wife or husband based upon a relationship described in §§ 404.345 through 404.346 and one of the following conditions is met:

(1) Your relationship to the insured as a wife or husband has lasted at least 1 year. (You will be considered to meet the 1-year duration requirement throughout the month in which the first anniversary of the marriage occurs.)

(2) You and the insured are the natural parents of a child; or

(3) In the month before you married the insured you were entitled to, or if you had applied and been old enough you could have been entitled to, any of these benefits or payments: Wife's, husband's, widow's, widower's, or parent's benefits; disabled child's benefits; or annuity payments under the Railroad Retirement Act for widows, widowers, parents, or children 18 years old or older;

(b) You apply;

(c) You are age 62 or older throughout a month and you meet all other conditions of entitlement, or you are the insured's wife or husband and have in your care (as defined in §§ 404.348 through 404.349), throughout a month in which all other conditions of entitlement are met, a child who is entitled to child's benefits on the insured's earnings record and the child is either under age 16 or disabled; and

(d) You are not entitled to an old-age or disability benefit based upon a primary insurance amount that is equal to or larger than the full wife's or husband's benefit.

[44 FR 34481, June 15, 1979; 44 FR 56691, Oct. 2, 1979, as amended at 45 FR 68932, Oct. 17, 1980; 48 FR 21926, May 16, 1983]

§ 404.331 Who is entitled to wife's or husband's benefits as a divorced spouse.

You are entitled to wife's or husband's benefits as the divorced wife or divorced husband of an insured person who is entitled to old-age or disability benefits if you meet the requirements of paragraphs (a) through (e). You are entitled to these benefits even though the insured person is not yet entitled to benefits, if the insured person is at least age 62 and if you meet the requirements of paragraphs (a) through (f). The requirements are that—

(a) You are the insured's divorced wife or divorced husband and—

(1) You were validly married to the insured under State law as described in § 404.345 or you were deemed to be validly married as described in § 404.346; and

(2) You were married to the insured for at least 10 years immediately before your divorce became final;

(b) You apply;

(c) You are not married. (For purposes of meeting this requirement, you will be considered not to be married throughout the month in which the divorce occurred);

(d) You are age 62 or older throughout a month in which all other conditions of entitlement are met; and

(e) You are not entitled to an old-age or disability benefit based upon a primary insurance amount that is equal to or larger than the full wife's or husband's benefit.

(f) You have been divorced from the insured person for at least 2 years.

[48 FR 21926, May 16, 1983; 51 FR 11911, April 8, 1986; 58 FR 64891, Dec. 10, 1993]

§ 404.332 When wife's and husband's benefits begin and end.

(a) You are entitled to wife's or husband's benefits beginning with the first month covered by your application in which you meet all the other requirements for entitlement under § 404.330 or § 404.331. However, if you are entitled as a divorced spouse before the insured person becomes entitled, your benefits cannot begin before January 1985 based on an application filed no earlier than that month.

(b) Your entitlement to benefits ends with the month before the month in which one of the following events first occurs:

(1) You become entitled to an old-age or disability benefit based upon a primary insurance amount that is equal to or larger than the full wife's or husband's benefit.

(2) You are the wife or husband and are divorced from the insured person unless you meet the requirements for benefits as a divorced wife or divorced husband as described in § 404.331.

(3) You are the divorced wife or divorced husband and you marry someone, other than the insured who is entitled to old-age benefits, unless that other person is someone entitled to benefits as a wife, husband, widow, widower, father, mother, parent or disabled child. Your benefits will end if you remarry the insured who is not yet entitled to old-age benefits.

(4) If you are under age 62, there is no longer a child of the insured who is under age 16 or disabled and entitled to child's benefits on the insured's earnings record. (See paragraph (c) of this section if you were entitled to wife's or husband's benefits for August 1981 on the basis of having a child in care.) (If you no longer have in your care a child who is under age 16 or disabled and entitled to child's benefits on the insured's earnings record, your benefits may be subject to deductions as provided in § 404.421.)

(5) The insured person dies or is no longer entitled to old age or disability benefits. Exception: Your benefits will continue if the insured person was entitled to disability benefits based on a finding that drug addiction or alcoholism was a contributing factor material to the determination of his or her disability (as described in § 404.1535), the insured person's benefits ended after 36 months of benefits (see § 404.316(e)) or 12 consecutive months of suspension for noncompliance with treatment (see § 404.316(f)), and but for the operation of these provisions, the insured person would remain entitled to benefits based on disability.

(6) If your benefits are based upon a deemed valid marriage and you have not divorced the insured, you marry someone other than the insured.

(7) You die.

(8) You became entitled as the divorced wife or the divorced husband before the insured person became entitled, but he or she is no longer insured.

(c) If you were entitled to wife's or husband's benefits for August 1981 on the basis of having a child in care, your entitlement will continue until September 1983, until the child reaches 18 (unless disabled) or is otherwise no longer entitled to child's benefits, or until one of the events described in paragraph (b)(1), (2), (3), (5), (6) or (7) of this section occurs, whichever is earliest.

[48 FR 21926, May 16, 1983; 49 FR 24115, June 12, 1984; 51 FR 11911, April 8, 1986; 58 FR 64891, Dec. 10, 1993; 60 FR 8145, Feb. 10, 1995; 64 FR 14608, March 26, 1999]

§ 404.333 Wife's and husband's benefit amounts.

Your wife's or husband's monthly benefit is equal to one-half the insured person's primary insurance amount. If you are entitled as a divorced wife or as a divorced husband before the insured person becomes entitled, we will compute the primary insurance amount as if he or she became entitled to old-age benefits in the first month you are entitled as a divorced wife or as a divorced husband. The amount of your monthly benefit may change as explained in § 404.304.

[51 FR 11912, April 8, 1986]

§ 404.335 How do I become entitled to widow's or widower's benefits?

We will find you entitled to benefits as the widow or widower of a person who died fully insured if you meet the requirements in paragraphs (a) through (e) of this section:

(a) You are the insured's widow or widower based upon a relationship described in §§ 404.345 through 404.346, and you meet one of the conditions in paragraphs (a)(1) through (4) of this section:

(1) Your relationship to the insured as a wife or husband lasted for at least 9 months immediately before the insured died.

(2) Your relationship to the insured as a wife or husband did not last 9 months before the insured died, but you meet one of the conditions in paragraphs (a)(2)(i) through (iv) of this section.

(i) At the time of your marriage the insured was reasonably expected to live for 9 months, and the death of the insured was accidental. The death is accidental if it was caused by an event that the insured did not expect, if it was the result of bodily injuries received from violent and external causes, and if, as a direct result of these injuries, death occurred not later than 3 months after the day on which the bodily injuries were received. An intentional and voluntary suicide will not be considered an accidental death.

(ii) At the time of your marriage the insured was reasonably expected to live for 9 months, and the death of the insured occurred in the line of duty while he or she was serving on active duty as a member of the uniformed services as defined in § 404.1019.

(iii) At the time of your marriage the insured was reasonably expected to live for 9 months, and you had been previously married to the insured for at least 9 months.

(iv) The insured had been married prior to his or her marriage to you and the prior spouse was institutionalized during the marriage to the insured due to mental incompetence or similar incapacity. During the period of the prior spouse's institutionalization, the insured, as determined based on evidence satisfactory to the Agency, would have divorced the prior spouse and married you, but the insured did not do so because the divorce would have been unlawful, by reason of the institutionalization, under the laws of the State in which the insured was domiciled at the time. Additionally, the prior spouse must have remained institutionalized up to the time of his or her death and the insured must have married you within 60 days after the prior spouse's death.

(3) You and the insured were the natural parents of a child; or you were married to the insured when either of you adopted the other's child or when both of you adopted a child who was then under 18 years old.

(4) In the month before you married the insured, you were entitled to or, if you had applied and had been old enough, could have been entitled to any of these benefits or payments: widow's, widower's, father's (based on the record of a fully insured individual), mother's (based on the record of a fully insured individual), wife's, husband's, parent's, or disabled child's benefits; or annuity payments under the Railroad Retirement Act for widows, widowers, parents, or children age 18 or older.

(b) You apply, except that you need not apply again if you meet one of the conditions in paragraphs (b)(1) through (4) of this section:

(1) You are entitled to wife's or husband's benefits for the month before the month in which the insured dies and you have attained full retirement age (as defined in § 404.409) or you are not entitled to either old-age or disability benefits.

(2) You are entitled to mother's or father's benefits for the month before the month in which you attained full retirement age (as defined in § 404.409).

(3) You are entitled to wife's or husband's benefits and to either old-age or disability benefits in the month before the month of the insured's death, you are under full retirement age (as defined in § 404.409) in the month of death, and you have filed a Certificate of Election in which you elect to receive reduced widow's or widower's benefits.

(4) You applied in 1990 for widow's or widower's benefits based on disability and you meet both of the conditions in paragraphs (b)(4)(i) and (ii) of this section:

(i) You were entitled to disability insurance benefits for December 1990, or eligible for supplemental security income or federally administered State supplementary payments, as specified in subparts B and T of part 416 of this chapter, respectively, for January 1991.

(ii) You were found not disabled for any month based on the definition of disability in §§ 404.1577 and 404.1578, as in effect prior to January 1991, but would have been entitled if the standard in § 404.1505(a) had applied. (This exception to the requirement for filing an application is effective only with respect to benefits payable for months after December 1990.)

(c) You are at least 60 years old; or you are at least 50 years old and have a disability as defined in § 404.1505 and you meet all of the conditions in paragraphs (c)(1) through (4) of this section:

(1) Your disability started not later than 7 years after the insured died or 7 years after you were last entitled to mother's or father's benefits or to widow's or widower's benefits based upon a disability, whichever occurred last.

(2) Your disability continued during a waiting period of 5 full consecutive months, unless months beginning

with the first month of eligibility for supplemental security income or federally administered State supplementary payments are counted, as explained in the Exception in paragraph (c)(3) of this section. The waiting period may begin no earlier than the 17th month before you applied; the fifth month before the insured died; or if you were previously entitled to mother's, father's, widow's, or widower's benefits, the 5th month before your entitlement to benefits ended. If you were previously entitled to widow's or widower's benefits based upon a disability, no waiting period is required.

(3) Exception: For monthly benefits payable for months after December 1990, if you were or have been eligible for supplemental security income or federally administered State supplementary payments, as specified in subparts B and T of part 416 of this chapter, respectively, your disability need not have continued through a separate, full 5–month waiting period before you may begin receiving benefits. We will include as months of the 5–month waiting period the months in a period beginning with the first month you received supplemental security income or a federally administered State supplementary payment and continuing through all succeeding months, regardless of whether the months in the period coincide with the months in which your waiting period would have occurred, or whether you continued to be eligible for supplemental security income or a federally administered State supplementary payment after the period began, or whether you met the nondisability requirements for entitlement to widow's or widower's benefits. However, we will not pay you benefits under this provision for any month prior to January 1991.

(4) You have not previously received 36 months of payments based on disability when drug addiction or alcoholism was a contributing factor material to the determination of disability (as described in § 404.1535), regardless of the number of entitlement periods you may have had, or your current application for widow's or widower's benefits is not based on a disability where drug addiction or alcoholism is a contributing factor material to the determination of disability.

(d) You are not entitled to an old-age benefit that is equal to or larger than the insured person's primary insurance amount.

(e) You are unmarried, unless for benefits for months after 1983 you meet one of the conditions in paragraphs (e)(1) through (3) of this section:

(1) You remarried after you became 60 years old.

(2) You are now age 60 or older and you meet both of the conditions in paragraphs (e)(2)(i) and (ii) of this section:

(i) You remarried after attaining age 50 but before attaining age 60.

(ii) At the time of the remarriage, you were entitled to widow's or widower's benefits as a disabled widow or widower.

(3) You are now at least age 50, but not yet age 60 and you meet both of the conditions in paragraphs (e)(3)(i) and (ii) of this section:

(i) You remarried after attaining age 50.

(ii) You met the disability requirements in paragraph (c) of this section at the time of your remarriage (i.e., your disability began within the specified time and before your remarriage).

[44 FR 34481, June 15, 1979, as amended at 47 FR 12162, March 22, 1982; 49 FR 24115, June 12, 1984; 51 FR 4482, Feb. 5, 1986; 51 FR 10616, March 28, 1986; 55 FR 25825, June 25, 1990; 57 FR 30119, July 8, 1992; 59 FR 14747, March 30, 1994; 60 FR 8145, Feb. 10, 1995; 68 FR 4704, Jan. 30, 2003; 70 FR 61365, Oct. 24, 2005]

§ 404.336 How do I become entitled to widow's or widower's benefits as a surviving divorced spouse?

We will find you entitled to widow's or widower's benefits as the surviving divorced wife or the surviving divorced husband of a person who died fully insured if you meet the requirements in paragraphs (a) through (e) of this section:

(a) You are the insured's surviving divorced wife or surviving divorced husband and you meet both of the conditions in paragraphs (a)(1) and (2) of this section:

(1) You were validly married to the insured under State law as described in § 404.345 or are deemed to have been validly married as described in § 404.346.

(2) You were married to the insured for at least 10 years immediately before your divorce became final.

(b) You apply, except that you need not apply again if you meet one of the conditions in paragraphs (b)(1) through (4) of this section:

(1) You are entitled to wife's or husband's benefits for the month before the month in which the insured dies and you have attained full retirement age (as defined in § 404.409) or you are not entitled to old-age or disability benefits.

(2) You are entitled to mother's or father's benefits for the month before the month in which you attain full retirement age (as defined in § 404.409).

(3) You are entitled to wife's or husband's benefits and to either old-age or disability benefits in the month before the month of the insured's death, you have not attained full retirement age (as defined in § 404.409) in the month of death, and you have filed a Certificate of Election in which you elect to receive reduced widow's or widower's benefits.

(4) You applied in 1990 for widow's or widower's benefits based on disability, and you meet the requirements in both paragraphs (b)(4)(i) and (ii) of this section:

(i) You were entitled to disability insurance benefits for December 1990 or eligible for supplemental security income or federally administered State supplementary payments, as specified in subparts B and T of part 416 of this chapter, respectively, for January 1991.

(ii) You were found not disabled for any month based on the definition of disability in §§ 404.1577 and 404.1578, as in effect prior to January 1991, but would have been entitled if the standard in § 404.1505(a) had applied. (This exception to the requirement for filing an application is effective only with respect to benefits payable for months after December 1990.)

(c) You are at least 60 years old; or you are at least 50 years old and have a disability as defined in § 404.1505 and you meet all of the conditions in paragraphs (c)(1) through (4) of this section:

(1) Your disability started not later than 7 years after the insured died or 7 years after you were last entitled to mother's or father's benefits or to widow's or widower's benefits based upon a disability, whichever occurred last.

(2) Your disability continued during a waiting period of 5 full consecutive months, unless months beginning with the first month of eligibility for supplemental security income or federally administered State supplementary payments are counted, as explained in the Exception in paragraph (c)(3) of this section. This waiting period may begin no earlier than the 17th month before you applied; the fifth month before the insured died; or if you were previously entitled to mother's, father's, widow's, or widower's benefits, the 5th month before your previous entitlement to benefits ended. If you were previously entitled to widow's or widower's benefits based upon a disability, no waiting period is required.

(3) Exception: For monthly benefits payable for months after December 1990, if you were or have been eligible for supplemental security income or federally administered State supplementary payments, as specified in subparts B and T of part 416 of this chapter, respectively, your disability does not have to have continued through a separate, full 5–month waiting period before you may begin receiving benefits. We will include as months of the 5–month waiting period the months in a period beginning with the first month you received supplemental security income or a federally administered State supplementary payment and continuing through all succeeding months, regardless of whether the months in the period coincide with the months in which your waiting period would have occurred, or whether you continued to be eligible for supplemental security income or a federally administered State supplementary payment after the period began, or whether you met the nondisability requirements for entitlement to widow's or widower's benefits. However, we will not pay you benefits under this provision for any month prior to January 1991.

(4) You have not previously received 36 months of payments based on disability when drug addiction or alcoholism was a contributing factor material to the determination of disability (as described in § 404.1535), regardless of the number of entitlement periods you may have had, or your current application for widow's or widower's benefits is not based on a disability where drug addiction or alcoholism is a contributing factor material to the determination of disability.

(d) You are not entitled to an old-age benefit that is equal to or larger than the insured person's primary insurance amount.

(e) You are unmarried, unless for benefits for months after 1983 you meet one of the conditions in paragraphs (e)(1) through (3) of this section:

(1) You remarried after you became 60 years old.

(2) You are now age 60 or older and you meet both of the conditions in paragraphs (e)(2)(i) and (ii) of this section:

(i) You remarried after attaining age 50 but before attaining age 60.

(ii) At the time of the remarriage, you were entitled to widow's or widower's benefits as a disabled widow or widower.

(3) You are now at least age 50 but not yet age 60 and you meet both of the conditions in paragraphs (e)(3)(i) and (ii) of this section:

(i) You remarried after attaining age 50.

(ii) You met the disability requirements in paragraph (c) of this section at the time of your remarriage (i.e., your disability began within the specified time and before your remarriage).

[44 FR 34481, June 15, 1979, as amended at 47 FR 12162, March 22, 1982; 51 FR 4482, Feb. 5, 1986; 55 FR 25300, June 21, 1990; 55 FR 25825, June 25, 1990; 57 FR 30119, July 8, 1992; 58 FR 64891, Dec. 10, 1993; 68 FR 4705, Jan. 30, 2003; 71 FR 24814, April 27, 2006]

§ 404.337 When does my entitlement to widow's and widower's benefits start and end?

(a) We will find you entitled to widow's or widower's benefits under § 404.335 or § 404.336 beginning with the first month covered by your application in which you meet all other requirements for entitlement.

(b) We will end your entitlement to widow's or widower's benefits at the earliest of the following times:

(1) The month before the month in which you become entitled to an old-age benefit that is equal to or larger than the insured's primary insurance amount.

(2) The second month after the month your disability ends or, where disability ends on or after December 1, 1980, the month before your termination month (§ 404.325). However your payments are subject to the provisions of paragraphs (c) and (d) of this section.

Note: You may remain eligible for payment of benefits if you attained full retirement age (as defined in § 404.409) before your termination month and you meet the other requirements for widow's or widower's benefits.

(3) If drug addiction or alcoholism is a contributing factor material to the determination of disability as described in § 404.1535, the month after the 12th consecutive month of suspension for noncompliance with treatment or after 36 months of benefits on that basis when treatment is available regardless of the number of entitlement periods you may have had, unless you are otherwise disabled without regard to drug addiction or alcoholism.

(4) The month before the month in which you die.

(c)(1) Your benefits may be continued after your impairment is no longer disabling if—

(i) You are participating in an appropriate program of vocational rehabilitation services, employment services, or other support services, as described in § 404.327(a) and (b);

(ii) You began participating in the program before the date your disability ended; and

(iii) We have determined under § 404.328 that your completion of the program, or your continuation in the program for a specified period of time, will increase the likelihood that you will not have to return to the disability benefit rolls.

(2) We generally will stop your benefits with the earliest of these months—

(i) The month in which you complete the program; or

(ii) The month in which you stop participating in the program for any reason (see § 404.327(b) for what we mean by "participating" in the program); or

(iii) The month in which we determine under § 404.328 that your continuing participation in the program will no longer increase the likelihood that you will not have to return to the disability benefit rolls.

Exception to paragraph (c): In no case will we stop your benefits with a month earlier than the second month after the month your disability ends, provided that you meet all other requirements for entitlement to and payment of benefits through such month.

(d) If, after November 1980, you have a disabling impairment (§ 404.1511), we will pay you benefits for all months in which you do not do substantial gainful activity during the reentitlement period (§ 404.1592a) following the end of your trial work period (§ 404.1592). If you are unable to do substantial gainful activity in the first month following the reentitlement period, we will pay you benefits until you are able to do substantial gainful activity. (Earnings during your trial work period do not affect the payment of your benefits.) We will also pay you benefits for the first month after the trial work period in which you do substantial gainful activity and the two succeeding months, whether or not you do substantial gainful activity during those succeeding months. After those three months, we cannot pay you benefits for any months in which you do substantial gainful activity.

[44 FR 34481, June 15, 1979, as amended at 47 FR 31542, July 21, 1982; 49 FR 22271, May 29, 1984; 51 FR 4482, Feb. 5, 1986; 51 FR 17617, May 14, 1986; 58 FR 64891, Dec. 10, 1993; 60 FR 8146, Feb. 10, 1995; 65 FR 16813, March 30, 2000; 68 FR 4706, Jan. 30, 2003; 70 FR 36506, June 24, 2005]

§ 404.338 Widow's and widower's benefits amounts.

(a) Your monthly benefit is equal to the insured person's primary insurance amount. If the insured person dies before reaching age 62 and you are first eligible after 1984, we may compute a special primary insurance amount to determine the amount of the monthly benefit (see § 404.212(b)).

(b) We may increase your monthly benefit amount if the insured person delays filing for benefits or requests voluntary suspension of benefits, and thereby earns delayed retirement credit (see § 404.313), and/or works before the year 2000 after reaching full retirement age (as defined in § 404.409(a)). The amount of your monthly benefit may change as explained in § 404.304.

(c) Your monthly benefit will be reduced if the insured person chooses to receive old-age benefits before reaching full retirement age. If so, your benefit will be reduced to the amount the insured person would be receiving if alive, or 82½ percent of his or her primary insurance amount, whichever is larger.

[51 FR 4482, Feb. 5, 1986; 68 FR 4706, Jan. 30, 2003; 70 FR 28811, May 19, 2005]

§ 404.339 How do I become entitled to mother's or father's benefits as a surviving spouse?

You may be entitled as the widow or widower to mother's or father's benefits on the earnings record of someone who was fully or currently insured when he or she died. You are entitled to these benefits if—

(a) You are the widow or widower of the insured and meet the conditions described in § 404.335(a);

(b) You apply for these benefits; or you were entitled to wife's benefits for the month before the insured died;

(c) You are unmarried;

(d) You are not entitled to widow's or widower's benefits, or to an old-age benefit that is equal to or larger than the full mother's or father's benefit; and

(e) You have in your care the insured's child who is entitled to child's benefits and he or she is under 16 years old or is disabled. Sections 404.348 and 404.349 describe when a child is in your care.

[48 FR 21927, May 16, 1983; 73 FR 40967, July 17, 2008]

§ 404.340 How do I become entitled to mother's or father's benefits as a surviving divorced spouse?

You may be entitled to mother's or father's benefits as the surviving divorced wife or the surviving divorced husband on the earnings record of someone who was fully or currently insured when she or he died. You are entitled to these benefits if—

(a) You were validly married to the insured under State law as described in § 404.345 or you were deemed to be validly married as described in § 404.346 but the marriage ended in a final divorce and—

(1) You are the mother or father of the insured's child; or

(2) You were married to the insured when either of you adopted the other's child or when both of you adopted a child and the child was then under 18 years old;

(b) You apply for these benefits; or you were entitled to wife's or husband's benefits for the month before the insured died;

(c) You are unmarried;

(d) You are not entitled to widow's or widower's benefits, or to an old-age benefit that is equal to or larger than the full mother's or father's benefit; and

(e) You have in your care the insured's child who is under age 16 or disabled, is your natural or adopted child, and is entitled to child's benefits on the insured person's record. Sections 404.348 and 404.349 describe when a child is in your care.

[44 FR 34481, June 15, 1979; 44 FR 73018, Dec. 17, 1979, as amended at 45 FR 68932, Oct. 17, 1980; 48 FR 21927, May 16, 1983; 58 FR 64891, Dec. 10, 1993; 73 FR 40967, July 17, 2008]

§ 404.341 When mother's and father's benefits begin and end.

(a) You are entitled to mother's or father's benefits beginning with the first month covered by your application in which you meet all the other requirements for entitlement.

(b) Your entitlement to benefits ends with the month before the month in which one of the following events first occurs:

(1) You become entitled to a widow's or widower's benefit or to an old-age benefit that is equal to or larger than the full mother's or father's benefit.

(2) There is no longer a child of the insured who is under age 16 or disabled and entitled to a child's benefit on the insured's earnings record. (See paragraph (c) of this section if you were entitled to mother's or father's benefits for August 1981.) (If you no longer have in your care a child who is under age 16 or disabled and entitled to child's benefits on the insured's earnings record, your benefits may be subject to deductions as provided in § 404.421.)

(3) You remarry. Your benefits will not end, however, if you marry someone entitled to old-age, disability, wife's, husband's, widow's, widower's, father's, mother's, parent's or disabled child's benefits.

(4) You die.

(c) If you were entitled to spouse's benefits on the basis of having a child in care, or to mother's or father's benefits for August 1981, your entitlement will continue until September 1983, until the child reaches 18 (unless disabled) or is otherwise no longer entitled to child's benefits, or until one of the events described in paragraph (b)(1), (3), or (4) of this section occurs, whichever is earliest.

[48 FR 21927, May 16, 1983; 49 FR 24115, June 12, 1984; 58 FR 64891, Dec. 10, 1993; 64 FR 14608, March 26, 1999]

§ 404.342 Mother's and father's benefit amounts.

Your mother's or father's monthly benefit is equal to 75 percent of the insured person's primary insurance amount. The amount of your monthly benefit may change as explained in § 404.304.

§ 404.344 Your relationship by marriage to the insured.

You may be eligible for benefits if you are related to the insured person as a wife, husband, widow, or widower. To decide your relationship to the insured, we look first to State laws. The State laws that we use are discussed in § 404.345. If your relationship cannot be established under State law, you may still be eligible for benefits if your relationship as the insured's wife, husband, widow, or widower is based upon a deemed valid marriage as described in § 404.346.

§ 404.345 Your relationship as wife, husband, widow, or widower under State law.

To decide your relationship as the insured's wife or husband, we look to the laws of the State where the insured had a permanent home when you applied for wife's or husband's benefits. To decide your relationship as the insured's widow or widower, we look to the laws of the State where the insured had a permanent home when he or she died. If the insured's permanent home is not or was not in one of the 50 States, the Commonwealth of Puerto Rico, the Virgin Islands, Guam, or American Samoa, we look to the laws of the District of Columbia. For a definition of permanent home, see § 404.303. If you and the insured were validly married under State law at the time you apply for wife's or husband's benefits or at the time the insured died if you apply for widow's, widower's, mother's, or father's benefits, the relationship requirement will be met. The relationship requirement will also be met if under State law you would be able to inherit a wife's, husband's, widow's, or widower's share of the insured's personal property if he or she were to die without leaving a will.

§ 404.346 Your relationship as wife, husband, widow, or widower based upon a deemed valid marriage.

(a) General. If your relationship as the insured's wife, husband, widow, or widower cannot be established under State law as explained in § 404.345, you may be eligible for benefits based upon a deemed valid marriage. You will be deemed to be the wife, husband, widow, or widower of the insured if, in good faith, you went through a marriage ceremony with the insured that would have resulted in a valid marriage except for a legal impediment. A legal impediment includes only an impediment which results because a previous marriage had not ended at the time of the ceremony or because there was a defect in the procedure followed in connection with the intended marriage. For example, a defect in the procedure may be found where a marriage was performed through a religious ceremony in a country that requires a civil ceremony for a valid marriage. Good faith means that at the time of the ceremony you did not know that a legal impediment existed, or if you did know, you thought that it would not prevent a valid marriage.

(b) Entitlement based upon a deemed valid marriage. To be entitled to benefits as a wife, husband, widow or widower as the result of a deemed valid marriage, you and the insured must have been living in the same household (see § 404.347) at the time the insured died or, if the insured is living, at the time you apply for benefits. However, a marriage that had been deemed valid, shall continue to be deemed valid if the insured individual and the person entitled to benefits as the wife or husband of the insured individual are no longer living in the same household at the time of death of the insured individual.

[44 FR 34481, June 15, 1979; 44 FR 56691, Oct. 2, 1979, as amended at 45 FR 65504, Oct. 3, 1980; 48 FR 21927, May 16, 1983; 58 FR 64892, Dec. 10, 1993]

§ 404.347 "Living in the same household" defined.

Living in the same household means that you and the insured customarily lived together as husband and wife in the same residence. You may be considered to be living in the same household although one of you is temporarily absent from the residence. An absence will be considered temporary if:

(a) It was due to service in the U.S. Armed Forces;

(b) It was 6 months or less and neither you nor the insured were outside of the United States during this time and the absence was due to business, employment, or confinement in a hospital, nursing home, other medical institution, or a penal institution;

(c) It was for an extended separation, regardless of the duration, due to the confinement of either you or the insured in a hospital, nursing home, or other medical institution, if the evidence indicates that you were separated solely for medical reasons and you otherwise would have resided together; or

(d) It was based on other circumstances, and it is shown that you and the insured reasonably could have expected to live together in the near future.

[61 FR 41330, Aug. 8, 1996]

§ 404.348 When is a child living with me in my care?

A child who has been living with you for at least 30 days is in your care unless—

(a) The child is in active military service;

(b) The child is 16 years old or older and not disabled;

(c) The child is 16 years old or older with a mental disability, but you do not actively supervise his or her activities and you do not make important decisions about his or her needs, either alone or with help from your spouse; or

(d) The child is 16 years old or older with a physical disability, but it is not necessary for you to perform personal services for him or her. Personal services are services such as dressing, feeding, and managing money that the child cannot do alone because of a disability.

[44 FR 34481, June 15, 1979; 44 FR 56691, Oct. 2, 1979; 48 FR 21927, May 16, 1983; 73 FR 40967, July 17, 2008]

§ 404.349 When is a child living apart from me in my care?

(a) In your care. A child living apart from you is in your care if—

(1) The child lived apart from you for not more than 6 months, or the child's current absence from you is not expected to last over 6 months;

(2) The child is under 16 years old, you supervise his or her activities and make important decisions about his or her needs, and one of the following circumstances exist:

(i) The child is living apart because of school but spends at least 30 days vacation with you each year unless some event makes having the vacation unreasonable; and if you and the child's other parent are separated, the school looks to you for decisions about the child's welfare;

(ii) The child is living apart because of your employment but you make regular and substantial contributions to his or her support; see § 404.366(a) for a definition of contributions for support;

(iii) The child is living apart because of a physical disability that the child has or that you have; or

(3) The child is 16 years old or older, is mentally disabled, and you supervise his or her activities, make important decisions about his or her needs, and help in his or her upbringing and development.

(b) Not in your care. A child living apart from you is not in your care if—

(1) The child is in active military service;

(2) The child is living with his or her other parent;

(3) The child is removed from your custody and control by a court order;

(4) The child is 16 years old or older, is mentally competent, and either has been living apart from you for 6 months or more or begins living apart from you and is expected to be away for more than 6 months;

(5) You gave your right to have custody and control of the child to someone else; or

(6) You are mentally disabled.

[48 FR 21927, May 16, 1983; 73 FR 40967, July 17, 2008]

CHILD'S BENEFITS

§ 404.350 Who is entitled to child's benefits?

(a) General. You are entitled to child's benefits on the earnings record of an insured person who is entitled to old-age or disability benefits or who has died if—

(1) You are the insured person's child, based upon a relationship described in §§ 404.355 through 404.359;

(2) You are dependent on the insured, as defined in §§ 404.360 through 404.365;

(3) You apply;

(4) You are unmarried; and

(5) You are under age 18; you are 18 years old or older and have a disability that began before you became 22 years old; or you are 18 years or older and qualify for benefits as a full-time student as described in § 404.367.

(b) Entitlement preclusion for certain disabled children. If you are a disabled child as referred to in paragraph (a)(5) of this section, and your disability was based on a finding that drug addiction or alcoholism was a contributing factor material to the determination of disability (as described in § 404.1535) and your benefits ended after your receipt of 36 months of benefits, you will not be entitled to benefits based on disability for any month following such 36 months regardless of the number of entitlement periods you have had if, in such following months, drug addiction or alcoholism is a contributing factor material to the later determination of disability (as described in § 404.1535).

[48 FR 21927, May 16, 1983; 60 FR 8146, Feb. 10, 1995; 61 FR 38363, July 24, 1996]

§ 404.351 Who may be reentitled to child's benefits?

If your entitlement to child's benefits has ended, you may be reentitled on the same earnings record if you have not married and if you apply for reentitlement. Your reentitlement may begin with—

(a) The first month in which you qualify as a full-time student. (See § 404.367.)

(b) The first month in which you are disabled, if your disability began before you became 22 years old.

(c) The first month you are under a disability that began before the end of the 84th month following the month in which your benefits had ended because an earlier disability had ended; or

(d) With respect to benefits payable for months beginning October 2004, you can be reentitled to childhood disability benefits at anytime if your prior entitlement terminated because you ceased to be under a disability due to the performance of substantial gainful activity and you meet the other requirements for reentitlement. The 84–month time limit in paragraph (c) in this section continues to apply if your previous entitlement to childhood disability benefits terminated because of medical improvement.

[48 FR 21927, May 16, 1983; 61 FR 38363, July 24, 1996; 71 FR 66865, Nov. 17, 2006]

§ 404.352 When does my entitlement to child's benefits begin and end?

(a) We will find your entitlement to child's benefits begins at the following times:

(1) If the insured is deceased, with the first month covered by your application in which you meet all other requirements for entitlement.

(2) If the insured is living and your first month of entitlement is September 1981 or later, with the first month covered by your application throughout which you meet all other requirements for entitlement.

(3) If the insured is living and your first month of entitlement is before September 1981, with the first month covered by your application in which you meet all other requirements for entitlement.

(b) We will find your entitlement to child's benefits ends at the earliest of the following times:

(1) With the month before the month in which you become 18 years old, if you are not disabled or a full-time student.

(2) With the second month following the month in which your disability ends, if you become 18 years old and you are disabled. If your disability ends on or after December 1, 1980, your entitlement to child's benefits continues, subject to the provisions of paragraphs (c) and (d) of this section, until the month before your termination month (§ 404.325).

(3) With the last month you are a full-time student or, if earlier, with the month before the month you become age 19, if you become 18 years old and you qualify as a full-time student who is not disabled. If you become age 19 in a month in which you have not completed the requirements for, or received, a diploma or equivalent certificate from an elementary or secondary school and you are required to enroll for each quarter or semester, we will find your entitlement ended with the month in which the quarter or semester in which you are enrolled ends. If the school you are attending does not have a quarter or semester system which requires reenrollment, we will find your entitlement to benefits ended with the month you complete the course or, if earlier, the first day of the third month following the month in which you become 19 years old.

(4) With the month before the month you marry. We will not find your benefits ended, however, if you are age 18 or older, disabled, and you marry a person entitled to child's benefits based on disability or person entitled to old-age, divorced wife's, divorced husband's, widow's, widower's, mother's, father's, parent's, or disability benefits.

(5) With the month before the month the insured's entitlement to old-age or disability benefits ends for a reason other than death or the attainment of full retirement age (as defined in § 404.409). Exception: We will continue your benefits if the insured person was entitled to disability benefits based on a finding that drug addiction or alcoholism was a contributing factor material to the determination of his or her disability (as described in § 404.1535), the insured person's benefits ended after 36 months of payment (see § 404.316(e)) or 12 consecutive months of suspension for noncompliance with treatment (see § 404.316(f)), and the insured person remains disabled.

(6) With the month before the month you die.

(7) With the month in which the divorce between your parent (including an adoptive parent) and the insured stepparent becomes final if you are entitled to benefits as a stepchild and the marriage between your parent (including an adoptive parent) and the insured stepparent ends in divorce.

(c) If you are entitled to benefits as a disabled child age 18 or over and your disability is based on a finding that drug addiction or alcoholism was a contributing factor material to the determination of disability (as described in § 404.1535), we will find your entitlement to benefits ended under the following conditions:

(1) If your benefits have been suspended for a period of 12 consecutive months for failure to comply with treatment, with the month following the 12 months unless you are otherwise disabled without regard to drug addiction or alcoholism (see § 404.470(c)).

(2) If you have received 36 months of benefits on that basis when treatment is available, regardless of the number of entitlement periods you may have had, with the month following such 36–month payment period unless you are otherwise disabled without regard to drug addiction or alcoholism.

(d)(1) Your benefits may be continued after your impairment is no longer disabling if—

(i) You are participating in an appropriate program of vocational rehabilitation services, employment services, or other support services, as described in § 404.327(a) and (b);

(ii) You began participating in the program before the date your disability ended; and

(iii) We have determined under § 404.328 that your completion of the program, or your continuation in the program for a specified period of time, will increase the likelihood that you will not have to return to the disability benefit rolls.

(2) We generally will stop your benefits with the earliest of these months—

(i) The month in which you complete the program; or

(ii) The month in which you stop participating in the program for any reason (see § 404.327(b) for what we mean by "participating" in the program); or

(iii) The month in which we determine under § 404.328 that your continuing participation in the program will no longer increase the likelihood that you will not have to return to the disability benefit rolls.

Exception to paragraph (d): In no case will we stop your benefits with a month earlier than the second month after the month your disability ends, provided that you meet all other requirements for entitlement to and payment of benefits through such month.

(e) If, after November 1980, you have a disabling impairment (§ 404.1511), we will pay you benefits for all months in which you do not do substantial gainful activity during the reentitlement period (§ 404.1592a) following the end of your trial work period (§ 404.1592). If you are unable to do substantial gainful activity in the first month following the reentitlement period, we will pay you benefits until you are able to do substantial gainful activity. (Earnings during your trial work period do not affect the payment of your benefits during that period.) We will also pay you benefits for the first month after the trial work period in which you do substantial gainful activity and the two succeeding months, whether or not you do substantial gainful activity during those succeeding months. After those three months, we cannot pay you benefits for any months in which you do substantial gainful activity.

[44 FR 34481, June 15, 1979; 44 FR 56691, Oct. 2, 1979, as amended at 47 FR 31543, July 21, 1982; 48 FR 21927, May 16, 1983; 49 FR 22271, May 29, 1984; 49 FR 24115, June 12, 1984; 51 FR 17617, May 14, 1986; 60 FR 8146, Feb. 10, 1995;

61 FR 38363, July 24, 1996; 68 FR 4707, Jan. 30, 2003; 70 FR 36506, June 24, 2005; 75 FR 52621, Aug. 27, 2010]

§ 404.353 Child's benefit amounts.

(a) General. Your child's monthly benefit is equal to one-half of the insured person's primary insurance amount if he or she is alive and three-fourths of the primary insurance amount if he or she has died. The amount of your monthly benefit may change as explained in § 404.304.

(b) Entitlement to more than one benefit. If you are entitled to a child's benefit on more than one person's earnings record, you will ordinarily receive only the benefit payable on the record with the highest primary insurance amount. If your benefit before any reduction would be larger on an earnings record with a lower primary insurance amount and no other person entitled to benefits on any earnings record would receive a smaller benefit as a result of your receiving benefits on the record with the lower primary insurance amount, you will receive benefits on that record. See § 404.407(d) for a further explanation. If you are entitled to a child's benefit and to other dependent's or survivor's benefits, you can receive only the highest of the benefits.

[44 FR 34481, June 15, 1979; 44 FR 56691, Oct. 2, 1979; 48 FR 21928, May 16, 1983; 51 FR 12606, April 14, 1986; 61 FR 38363, July 24, 1996]

§ 404.354 Your relationship to the insured.

You may be related to the insured person in one of several ways and be entitled to benefits as his or her child, i.e., as a natural child, legally adopted child, stepchild, grandchild, stepgrandchild, or equitably adopted child. For details on how we determine your relationship to the insured person, see §§ 404.355 through 404.359.

[49 FR 21513, May 22, 1984; 63 FR 57593, Oct. 28, 1998]

§ 404.355 Who is the insured's natural child?

(a) Eligibility as a natural child. You may be eligible for benefits as the insured's natural child if any of the following conditions is met:

(1) You could inherit the insured's personal property as his or her natural child under State inheritance laws, as described in paragraph (b) of this section.

(2) You are the insured's natural child and the insured and your mother or father went through a ceremony which would have resulted in a valid marriage between them except for a "legal impediment" as described in § 404.346(a).

(3) You are the insured's natural child and your mother or father has not married the insured, but the insured has either acknowledged in writing that you are his or her child, been decreed by a court to be your father or mother, or been ordered by a court to contribute to your support because you are his or her child. If the insured is deceased, the acknowledgment, court decree, or court order must have been made or issued before his or her death. To determine whether the conditions of entitlement are met throughout the first month as stated in § 404.352(a), the written acknowledgment, court decree, or court order will be considered to have occurred on the first day of the month in which it actually occurred.

(4) Your mother or father has not married the insured but you have evidence other than the evidence described in paragraph (a)(3) of this section to show that the insured is your natural father or mother. Additionally, you must have evidence to show that the insured was either living with you or contributing to your support at the time you applied for benefits. If the insured is not alive at the time of your application, you must have evidence to show that the insured was either living with you or contributing to your support when he or she died. See § 404.366 for an explanation of the terms "living with" and "contributions for support."

(b) Use of State Laws—

(1) General. To decide whether you have inheritance rights as the natural child of the insured, we use the law on inheritance rights that the State courts would use to decide whether you could inherit a child's share of the insured's personal property if the insured were to die without leaving a will. If the insured is living, we look to the laws of the State where the insured has his or her permanent home when you apply for benefits. If the insured is deceased, we look to the laws of the State where the insured had his or her permanent home when he or she died. If the insured's permanent home is not or was not in one of the 50 States, the Commonwealth of Puerto Rico, the Virgin Islands, Guam, American Samoa, or the Northern Mariana Islands, we will look to the laws of the District of Columbia. For a definition of permanent home, see § 404.303. For a further discussion of the State laws we use to determine whether you qualify as the insured's natural child, see paragraphs (b)(3) and (b)(4) of this section. If these laws would permit you to inherit the insured's personal property as his or her child, we will consider you the child of the insured.

(2) Standards. We will not apply any State inheritance law requirement that an action to establish paternity must be taken within a specified period of time measured from the worker's death or the child's birth, or that an action to establish paternity must have been started or completed before the worker's death. If applicable State inheritance law requires a court determination of paternity, we will not require that you obtain such a determination but will decide your paternity by using the standard of proof that the State court would use as the basis for a determination of paternity.

(3) Insured is living. If the insured is living, we apply the law of the State where the insured has his or her permanent home when you file your application for

benefits. We apply the version of State law in effect when we make our final decision on your application for benefits. If you do not qualify as a child of the insured under that version of State law, we look at all versions of State law that were in effect from the first month for which you could be entitled to benefits up until the time of our final decision and apply the version of State law that is most beneficial to you.

(4) Insured is deceased. If the insured is deceased, we apply the law of the State where the insured had his or her permanent home when he or she died. We apply the version of State law in effect when we make our final decision on your application for benefits. If you do not qualify as a child of the insured under that version of State law, we will apply the version of State law that was in effect at the time the insured died, or any version of State law in effect from the first month for which you could be entitled to benefits up until our final decision on your application. We will apply whichever version is most beneficial to you. We use the following rules to determine the law in effect as of the date of death:

(i) If a State inheritance law enacted after the insured's death indicates that the law would be retroactive to the time of death, we will apply that law; or

(ii) If the inheritance law in effect at the time of the insured's death was later declared unconstitutional, we will apply the State law which superseded the unconstitutional law.

[44 FR 34481, June 15, 1979, as amended at 45 FR 65540, Oct. 3, 1980; 48 FR 21928, May 16, 1983; 49 FR 24115, June 12, 1984; 63 FR 57593, Oct. 28, 1998]

§ 404.356 Who is the insured's legally adopted child?

You may be eligible for benefits as the insured's child if you were legally adopted by the insured. If you were legally adopted after the insured's death by his or her surviving spouse you may also be considered the insured's legally adopted child. We apply the adoption laws of the State or foreign country where the adoption took place, not the State inheritance laws described in § 404.355, to determine whether you are the insured's legally adopted child.

[63 FR 57594, Oct. 28, 1998]

§ 404.357 Who is the insured's stepchild?

You may be eligible for benefits as the insured's stepchild if, after your birth, your natural or adopting parent married the insured. You also may be eligible as a stepchild if you were conceived prior to the marriage of your natural parent to the insured but were born after the marriage and the insured is not your natural parent. The marriage between the insured and your parent must be a valid marriage under State law or a marriage which would be valid except for a legal impediment described in § 404.346(a). If the insured is alive when you apply, you must have been his or her stepchild for at least 1 year immediately preceding the day you apply. For purposes of determining whether the conditions of entitlement are met throughout the first month as stated in § 404.352(a)(2)(i), you will be considered to meet the one year duration requirement throughout the month in which the anniversary of the marriage occurs. If the insured is not alive when you apply, you must have been his or her stepchild for at least 9 months immediately preceding the day the insured died. This 9–month requirement will not have to be met if the marriage between the insured and your parent lasted less than 9 months under one of the conditions described in § 404.335(a)(2)(i)–(iii).

[44 FR 34481, June 15, 1979, as amended at 45 FR 65540, Oct. 3, 1980; 48 FR 21928, May 16, 1983; 64 FR 14608, March 26, 1999; 70 FR 61365, Oct. 24, 2005]

§ 404.358 Who is the insured's grandchild or stepgrandchild?

(a) Grandchild and stepgrandchild defined. You may be eligible for benefits as the insured's grandchild or stepgrandchild if you are the natural child, adopted child, or stepchild of a person who is the insured's child as defined in §§ 404.355 through 404.357, or § 404.359. Additionally, for you to be eligible as a grandchild or stepgrandchild, your natural or adoptive parents must have been either deceased or under a disability, as defined in § 404.1501(a), at the time your grandparent or stepgrandparent became entitled to old-age or disability benefits or died; or if your grandparent or stepgrandparent had a period of disability that continued until he or she became entitled to benefits or died, at the time the period of disability began. If your parent is deceased, for purposes of determining whether the conditions of entitlement are met throughout the first month as stated in § 404.352(a)(2)(i), your parent will be considered to be deceased as of the first day of the month of death.

(b) Legally adopted grandchild or stepgrandchild. If you are the insured's grandchild or stepgrandchild and you are legally adopted by the insured or by the insured's surviving spouse after his or her death, you are considered an adopted child and the dependency requirements of § 404.362 must be met.

[48 FR 21928, May 16, 1983]

§ 404.359 Who is the insured's equitably adopted child?

You may be eligible for benefits as an equitably adopted child if the insured had agreed to adopt you as his or her child but the adoption did not occur. The agreement to adopt you must be one that would be recognized under State law so that you would be able to inherit a child's share of the insured's personal property if he or she were to die without leaving a will. The agreement must be in whatever form, and you must meet whatever requirements for performance under the agreement, that State law directs. If you apply for child's benefits after the insured's death, the law of the State where the insured had his or her permanent home at the time of his or her death will be followed. If you apply for child's benefits during the insured's life, the law of the State where the insured has his or her permanent home at the time or your application will be followed.

§ 404.360 When a child is dependent upon the insured person.

One of the requirements for entitlement to child's benefits is that you be dependent upon the insured. The evidence you need to prove your dependency is determined by how you are related to the insured. To prove your dependency you may be asked to show that at a specific time you lived with the insured, that you received contributions for your support from the insured, or that the insured provided at least one-half of your support. These dependency requirements, and the time at which they must be met, are explained in §§ 404.361 through 404.365. The terms living with, contributions for support, and one-half support are defined in § 404.366.

§ 404.361 When a natural child is dependent.

(a) Dependency of natural child. If you are the insured's natural child, as defined in § 404.355, you are considered dependent upon him or her, except as stated in paragraph (b) of this section.

(b) Dependency of natural child legally adopted by someone other than the insured.

(1) Except as indicated in paragraph (b)(2) of this section, if you are legally adopted by someone other than the insured (your natural parent) during the insured's lifetime, you are considered dependent upon the insured only if the insured was either living with you or contributing to your support at one of the following times:

(i) When you applied;

(ii) When the insured died; or

(iii) If the insured had a period of disability that lasted until he or she became entitled to disability or old-age benefits or died, at the beginning of the period of disability or at the time he or she became entitled to disability or old-age benefits.

(2) You are considered dependent upon the insured (your natural parent) if:

(i) You were adopted by someone other than the insured after you applied for child's benefits; or

(ii) The insured had a period of disability that lasted until he or she became entitled to old-age or disability benefits or died, and you are adopted by someone other than the insured after the beginning of that period of disability.

[64 FR 14608, March 26, 1999]

§ 404.362 When a legally adopted child is dependent.

(a) General. If you were legally adopted by the insured before he or she became entitled to old-age or disability benefits, you are considered dependent upon him or her. If you were legally adopted by the insured after he or she became entitled to old-age or disability benefits and you apply for child's benefits during the life of the insured, you must meet the dependency requirements stated in paragraph (b) of this section. If you were legally adopted by the insured after he or she became entitled to old-age or disability benefits and you apply for child's benefits after the death of the insured, you are considered dependent upon him or her. If you were adopted after the insured's death by his or her surviving spouse, you may be considered dependent upon the insured only under the conditions described in paragraph (c) of this section.

(b) Adoption by the insured after he or she became entitled to benefits—

(1) General. If you are legally adopted by the insured after he or she became entitled to benefits and you are not the insured's natural child or stepchild, you are considered dependent on the insured during his or her lifetime only if—

(i) You had not attained age 18 when adoption proceedings were started, and your adoption was issued by a court of competent jurisdiction within the United States; or

(ii) You had attained age 18 before adoption proceedings were started; your adoption was issued by a court of competent jurisdiction within the United States; and you were living with or receiving at least one-half of your support from the insured for the year immediately preceding the month in which your adoption was issued.

(2) Natural child and stepchild. If you were legally adopted by the insured after he or she became entitled to benefits and you are the insured's natural child or stepchild, you are considered dependent upon the insured.

(c) Adoption by the insured's surviving spouse—

(1) General. If you are legally adopted by the insured's surviving spouse after the insured's death, you are considered dependent upon the insured as of the date of his or her death if—

(i) You were either living with or receiving at least one-half of your support from the insured at the time of his or her death; and,

(ii) The insured had started adoption proceedings before he or she died; or if the insured had not started the adoption proceedings before he or she died, his or her surviving spouse began and completed the adoption within 2 years of the insured's death.

(2) Grandchild or stepgrandchild adopted by the insured's surviving spouse. If you are the grandchild or stepgrandchild of the insured and any time after the death of the insured you are legally adopted by the insured's surviving spouse, you are considered the dependent child of the insured as of the date of his or her death if—

(i) Your adoption took place in the United States;

(ii) At the time of the insured's death, your natural, adopting or stepparent was not living in the insured's household and making regular contributions toward your support; and

(iii) You meet the dependency requirements stated in § 404.364.

[44 FR 34481, June 15, 1979; 44 FR 56691, Oct. 2, 1979; 52 FR 37604, Oct. 8, 1987; 56 FR 24000, May 28, 1991; 57 FR 3938, Feb. 3, 1992]

§ 404.363 When is a stepchild dependent?

If you are the insured's stepchild, as defined in § 404.357, we consider you dependent on him or her if you were receiving at least one-half of your support from him or her at one of these times—

(a) When you applied;

(b) When the insured died; or

(c) If the insured had a period of disability that lasted until his or her death or entitlement to disability or old-age benefits, at the beginning of the period of disability or at the time the insured became entitled to benefits.

[75 FR 52621, Aug. 27, 2010]

§ 404.364 When is a grandchild or stepgrandchild dependent?

If you are the insured's grandchild or stepgrandchild, as defined in § 404.358(a), you are considered dependent upon the insured if—

(a) You began living with the insured before you became 18 years old; and

(b) You were living with the insured in the United States and receiving at least one-half of your support from him or her for the year before he or she became entitled to old-age or disability benefits or died; or if the insured had a period of disability that lasted until he or she became entitled to benefits or died, for the year immediately before the month in which the period of disability began. If you were born during the 1-year period, the insured must have lived with you and provided at least one-half of your support for substantially all of the period that begins on the date of your birth. Paragraph (c) of this section explains when the substantially all requirement is met.

(c) The "substantially all" requirement will be met if, at one of the times described in paragraph (b) of this section, the insured was living with you and providing at least one-half of your support, and any period during which he or she was not living with you and providing one-half of your support did not exceed the lesser of 3 months or one-half of the period beginning with the month of your birth.

[73 FR 40967, July 17, 2008]

§ 404.365 When an equitably adopted child is dependent.

If you are the insured's equitably adopted child, as defined in § 404.359, you are considered dependent upon him or her if you were either living with or receiving contributions for your support from the insured at the time of his or her death. If your equitable adoption is found to have occurred after the insured became entitled to old-age or disability benefits, your dependency cannot be established during the insured's life. If your equitable adoption is found to have occurred before the insured became entitled to old-age or disability benefits, you are considered dependent upon him or her if you were either living with or receiving contributions for your support from the insured at one of these times—

(a) When you applied; or

(b) If the insured had a period of disability that lasted until he or she became entitled to old-age or disability benefits, at the beginning of the period of disability or at the time the insured became entitled to benefits.

§ 404.366 "Contributions for support," "one-half support," and "living with" the insured defined—determining first month of entitlement.

To be eligible for child's or parent's benefits, and in certain Government pension offset cases, you must be dependent upon the insured person at a particular time or be assumed dependent upon him or her. What it means to be a dependent child is explained in §§ 404.360 through 404.365; what it means to be a dependent parent is explained in § 404.370(f); and the Government pension offset is explained in § 404.408a. Your dependency upon the insured person may be based upon whether at a specified time you were receiving contributions for your support or one-half of your support from the insured person, or whether you were living with him or her. These terms are defined in paragraphs (a) through (c) of this section.

(a) Contributions for support. The insured makes a contribution for your support if the following conditions are met:

(1) The insured gives some of his or her own cash or goods to help support you. Support includes food, shelter, routine medical care, and other ordinary and customary items needed for your maintenance. The value of any goods the insured contributes is the same as the cost of the goods when he or she gave them for your support. If the insured provides services for you that would otherwise have to be paid for, the cash

value of his or her services may be considered a contribution for your support. An example of this would be work the insured does to repair your home. The insured person is making a contribution for your support if you receive an allotment, allowance, or benefit based upon his or her military pay, veterans' pension or compensation, or social security earnings.

(2) Contributions must be made regularly and must be large enough to meet an important part of your ordinary living costs. Ordinary living costs are the costs for your food, shelter, routine medical care, and similar necessities. If the insured person only provides gifts or donations once in a while for special purposes, they will not be considered contributions for your support. Although the insured's contributions must be made on a regular basis, temporary interruptions caused by circumstances beyond the insured person's control, such as illness or unemployment, will be disregarded unless during this interruption someone else takes over responsibility for supporting you on a permanent basis.

(b) One-half support. The insured person provides one-half of your support if he or she makes regular contributions for your ordinary living costs; the amount of these contributions equals or exceeds one-half of your ordinary living costs; and any income (from sources other than the insured person) you have available for support purposes is one-half or less of your ordinary living costs. We will consider any income which is available to you for your support whether or not that income is actually used for your ordinary living costs. Ordinary living costs are the costs for your food, shelter, routine medical care, and similar necessities. A contribution may be in cash, goods, or services. The insured is not providing at least one-half of your support unless he or she has done so for a reasonable period of time. Ordinarily we consider a reasonable period to be the 12–month period immediately preceding the time when the one-half support requirement must be met under the rules in §§ 404.362(c)(1) and 404.363 (for child's benefits), in § 404.370(f) (for parent's benefits) and in § 404.408a(c) (for benefits where the Government pension offset may be applied). A shorter period will be considered reasonable under the following circumstances:

(1) At some point within the 12–month period, the insured either begins or stops providing at least one-half of your support on a permanent basis and this is a change in the way you had been supported up to then. In these circumstances, the time from the change up to the end of the 12–month period will be considered a reasonable period, unless paragraph (b)(2) of this section applies. The change in your source of support must be permanent and not temporary. Changes caused by seasonal employment or customary visits to the insured's home are considered temporary.

(2) The insured provided one-half or more of your support for at least 3 months of the 12–month period, but was forced to stop or reduce contributions because of circumstances beyond his or her control, such as illness or unemployment, and no one else took over the responsibility for providing at least one-half of your support on a permanent basis. Any support you received from a public assistance program is not considered as a taking over of responsibility for your support by someone else. Under these circumstances, a reasonable period is that part of the 12–month period before the insured was forced to reduce or stop providing at least one-half of your support.

(c) "Living with" the insured. You are living with the insured if you ordinarily live in the same home with the insured and he or she is exercising, or has the right to exercise, parental control and authority over your activities. You are living with the insured during temporary separations if you and the insured expect to live together in the same place after the separation. Temporary separations may include the insured's absence because of active military service or imprisonment if he or she still exercises parental control and authority. However, you are not considered to be living with the insured if you are in active military service or in prison. If living with is used to establish dependency for your eligibility to child's benefits and the date your application is filed is used for establishing the point for determining dependency, you must have been living with the insured throughout the month your application is filed in order to be entitled to benefits for that month.

(d) Determining first month of entitlement. In evaluating whether dependency is established under paragraph (a), (b), or (c) of this section, for purposes of determining whether the conditions of entitlement are met throughout the first month as stated in § 404.352(a)(2)(i), we will not use the temporary separation or temporary interruption rules.

[44 FR 34481, June 15, 1979; 44 FR 56691, Oct. 2, 1979, as amended at 45 FR 65540, Oct. 3, 1980; 48 FR 21928, May 16, 1983; 52 FR 26955, July 17, 1987; 64 FR 14608, March 26, 1999]

§ 404.367 When you are a "full-time elementary or secondary school student".

You may be eligible for child's benefits if you are a full-time elementary or secondary school student. For the purposes of determining whether the conditions of entitlement are met throughout the first month as stated in § 404.352(a)(2)(i), if you are entitled as a student on the basis of attendance at an elementary or secondary school, you will be considered to be in full-time attendance for a month during any part of which you are in full-time attendance. You are a full-time elementary or secondary school student if you meet all the following conditions:

(a) You attend a school which provides elementary or secondary education as determined under the law of the State or other jurisdiction in which it is located. Participation in the following programs also meets the requirements of this paragraph:

(1) You are instructed in elementary or secondary education at home in accordance with a home school law of the State or other jurisdiction in which you reside; or

(2) You are in an independent study elementary or secondary education program in accordance with the law of the State or other jurisdiction in which you reside which is administered by the local school or school district/jurisdiction.

(b) You are in full-time attendance in a day or evening noncorrespondence course of at least 13 weeks duration and you are carrying a subject load which is considered full-time for day students under the institution's standards and practices. If you are in a home schooling program as described in paragraph (a)(1) of this section, you must be carrying a subject load which is considered full-time for day students under standards and practices set by the State or other jurisdiction in which you reside;

(c) To be considered in full-time attendance, your scheduled attendance must be at the rate of at least 20 hours per week unless one of the exceptions in paragraphs (c)(1) and (2) of this section applies. If you are in an independent study program as described in paragraph (a)(2) of this section, your number of hours spent in school attendance are determined by combining the number of hours of attendance at a school facility with the agreed upon number of hours spent in independent study. You may still be considered in full-time attendance if your scheduled rate of attendance is below 20 hours per week if we find that:

(1) The school attended does not schedule at least 20 hours per week and going to that particular school is your only reasonable alternative; or

(2) Your medical condition prevents you from having scheduled attendance of at least 20 hours per week. To prove that your medical condition prevents you from scheduling 20 hours per week, we may request that you provide appropriate medical evidence or a statement from the school.

(d) You are not being paid while attending the school by an employer who has requested or required that you attend the school;

(e) You are in grade 12 or below; and

(f) You are not subject to the provisions in § 404.468 for nonpayment of benefits to certain prisoners and certain other inmates of publicly funded institutions.

[44 FR 34481, June 15, 1979, as amended at 48 FR 5714, Feb. 8, 1983; 48 FR 21928, May 16, 1983; 48 FR 55452, Dec. 13, 1983; 56 FR 35999, July 30, 1991; 61 FR 38363, July 24, 1996]

§ 404.368 When you are considered a full-time student during a period of nonattendance.

If you are a full-time student, your eligibility may continue during a period of nonattendance (including part-time attendance) if all the following conditions are met:

(a) The period of nonattendance is 4 consecutive months or less;

(b) You show us that you intend to resume your studies as a full-time student at the end of the period or at the end of the period you are a full-time student; and

(c) The period of nonattendance is not due to your expulsion or suspension from the school.

[48 FR 21929, May 16, 1983]

§ 404.369 [Reserved]

[61 FR 38363, July 24, 1996]

PARENT'S BENEFITS

§ 404.370 Who is entitled to parent's benefits?

You may be entitled to parent's benefits on the earnings record of someone who has died and was fully insured. You are entitled to these benefits if all the following conditions are met:

(a) You are related to the insured person as his or her parent in one of the ways described in § 404.374.

(b) You are at least 62 years old.

(c) You have not married since the insured person died.

(d) You apply.

(e) You are not entitled to an old-age benefit equal to or larger than the parent's benefit amount.

(f) You were receiving at least one-half of your support from the insured at the time he or she died, or at the beginning of any period of disability he or she had that continued up to death. See § 404.366(b) for a definition of one-half support. If you were receiving one-half of your support from the insured at the time of the insured's death, you must give us proof of this support within 2 years of the insured's death. If you were receiving one-half of your support from the insured at the time his or her period of disability began, you must give us proof of this support within 2 years of the month in which the insured filed his or her application for the period of disability. You must file the evidence of support even though you may not be eligible for parent's benefits until a later time. There are two exceptions to the 2-year filing requirement:

(1) If there is a good cause for failure to provide proof of support within the 2-year period, we will consider the proof you give us as though it were provided within the 2-year period. Good cause does

not exist if you were informed of the need to provide the proof within the 2–year period and you neglected to do so or did not intend to do so. Good cause will be found to exist if you did not provide the proof within the time limit due to—

(i) Circumstances beyond your control, such as extended illness, mental or physical incapacity, or a language barrier;

(ii) Incorrect or incomplete information we furnished you;

(iii) Your efforts to get proof of the support without realizing that you could submit the proof after you gave us some other evidence of that support; or

(iv) Unusual or unavoidable circumstances that show you could not reasonably be expected to know of the 2–year time limit.

(2) The Soldiers' and Sailors' Civil Relief Act of 1940 provides for extending the filing time.

§ 404.371 When parent's benefits begin and end.

(a) You are entitled to parent's benefits beginning with the first month covered by your application in which you meet all the other requirements for entitlement.

(b) Your entitlement to benefits ends with the month before the month in which one of the following events first occurs:

(1) You become entitled to an old-age benefit equal to or larger than the parent's benefit.

(2) You marry, unless your marriage is to someone entitled to wife's, husband's, widow's, widower's, mother's, father's, parent's or disabled child's benefits. If you marry a person entitled to these benefits, the marriage does not affect your benefits.

(3) You die.

[49 FR 24116, June 12, 1984]

§ 404.373 Parent's benefit amounts.

Your parent's monthly benefit before any reduction that may be made as explained in § 404.304, is figured in one of the following ways:

(a) One parent entitled. Your parent's monthly benefit is equal to 82½ percent of the insured person's primary insurance amount if you are the only parent entitled to benefits on his or her earnings record.

(b) More than one parent entitled. Your parent's monthly benefit is equal to 75 percent of the insured person's primary insurance amount if there is another parent entitled to benefits on his or her earnings record.

§ 404.374 Parent's relationship to the insured.

You may be eligible for benefits as the insured person's parent if—

(a) You are the mother or father of the insured and would be considered his or her parent under the laws of the State where the insured had a permanent home when he or she died;

(b) You are the adoptive parent of the insured and legally adopted him or her before the insured person became 16 years old; or

(c) You are the stepparent of the insured and you married the insured's parent or adoptive parent before the insured became 16 years old. The marriage must be valid under the laws of the State where the insured had his or her permanent home when he or she died. See § 404.303 for a definition of permanent home.

SPECIAL PAYMENTS AT AGE 72 [RESERVED]

Source: 83 FR 21708, May 10, 2018, unless otherwise noted.

§§ 404.380 to 404.384 [Reserved by 83 FR 21708]

[83 FR 21708, May 10, 2018]

LUMP–SUM DEATH PAYMENT

§ 404.390 General.

If a person is fully or currently insured when he or she dies, a lump-sum death payment of $255 may be paid to the widow or widower of the deceased if he or she was living in the same household with the deceased at the time of his or her death. If the insured is not survived by a widow(er) who meets this requirement, all or part of the $255 payment may be made to someone else as described in § 404.392.

[48 FR 21929, May 16, 1983; 61 FR 41330, Aug. 8, 1996]

§ 404.391 Who is entitled to the lump-sum death payment as a widow or widower who was living in the same household?

You are entitled to the lump-sum death payment as a widow or widower who was living in the same household if—

(a) You are the widow or widower of the deceased insured individual based upon a relationship described in § 404.345 or § 404.346;

(b) You apply for this payment within two years after the date of the insured's death. You need not apply again if, in the month prior to the death of the insured, you were entitled to wife's or husband's benefits on his or her earnings record; and

(c) You were living in the same household with the insured at the time of his or her death. The term living in the same household is defined in § 404.347.

[48 FR 21929, May 16, 1983]

§ 404.392 Who is entitled to the lump-sum death payment when there is no widow(er) who was living in the same household?

(a) General. If the insured individual is not survived by a widow(er) who meets the requirements of § 404.391, the lump-sum death payment shall be paid as follows:

(1) To a person who is entitled (or would have been entitled had a timely application been filed) to widow's or widower's benefits (as described in § 404.335) or mother's or father's benefits (as described in § 404.339) on the work record of the deceased worker for the month of that worker's death; or

(2) If no person described in (1) survives, in equal shares to each person who is entitled (or would have been entitled had a timely application been filed) to child's benefits (as described in § 404.350) on the work record of the deceased worker for the month of that worker's death.

(b) Application requirement. A person who meets the requirements of paragraph (a)(1) of this section need not apply to receive the lump-sum death payment if, for the month prior to the death of the insured, that person was entitled to wife's or husband's benefits on the insured's earnings record. Otherwise, an application must be filed within 2 years of the insured's death.

[48 FR 21929, May 16, 1983; 61 FR 41330, Aug. 8, 1996]

§§ 404.393 to 404.395 [Reserved]

[61 FR 41330, Aug. 8, 1996]

SUBPART E—DEDUCTIONS; REDUCTIONS; AND NONPAYMENTS OF BENEFITS

Authority: Secs. 202, 203, 204(a) and (e), 205(a) and (c), 216(*l*), 222(c), 223(e), 224, 225, 702(a)(5), and 1129A of the Social Security Act (42 U.S.C. 402, 403, 404(a) and (e), 405(a) and (c), 416(*l*), 422(c), 423(e), 424a, 425, 902(a)(5), and 1320a–8a and 48 U.S.C. 1801.

Source: 32 FR 19159, Dec. 20, 1967; 51 FR 10616, March 28, 1986; 51 FR 11911, April 8, 1986; 51 FR 12603, April 14, 1986; 51 FR 23052, June 25, 1986; 52 FR 8249, March 17, 1987; 52 FR 26145, July 13, 1987; 52 FR 27540, July 22, 1987; 56 FR 41789, Aug. 23, 1991; 60 FR 8146, Feb. 10, 1995; 61 FR 5941, Feb. 15, 1996; 65 FR 42285, July 10, 2000; 66 FR 38906, July 26, 2001; 67 FR 20893, April 29, 2002; 68 FR 4707, Jan. 30, 2003; 68 FR 40122, July 7, 2003; 69 FR 25955, May 10, 2004; 69 FR 51555, Aug. 20, 2004; 70 FR 28811, May 19, 2005; 71 FR 66865, Nov. 17, 2006, unless otherwise noted.

§ 404.401 Deduction, reduction, and nonpayment of monthly benefits or lump-sum death payments.

Under certain conditions, the amount of a monthly insurance benefit or the lump-sum death payment as calculated under the pertinent provisions of sections 202 and 203 of the Act (including reduction for age under section 202(q) of a monthly benefit) must be increased or decreased to determine the amount to be actually paid to a beneficiary. Increases in the amount of a monthly benefit or lump-sum death payment are based upon recomputation and recalculations of the primary insurance amount (see subpart C of this part). A decrease in the amount of a monthly benefit or lump-sum death payment is required in the following instances:

(a) Reductions. A reduction of a person's monthly benefit is required where:

(1) The total amount of the monthly benefits payable on an earnings record exceeds the maximum that may be paid (see § 404.403);

(2) An application for monthly benefits is effective for a month during a retroactive period, and the maximum has already been paid for that month or would be exceeded if such benefit were paid for that month (see § 404.406);

(3) An individual is entitled to old-age or disability insurance benefits in addition to any other monthly benefit (see § 404.407);

(4) An individual under full retirement age (see § 404.409) is concurrently entitled to disability insurance benefits and to certain public disability benefits (see § 404.408);

(5) An individual is entitled in a month to a widow's or widower's insurance benefit that is reduced under section 202 (e)(4) or (f)(5) of the Act and to any other monthly insurance benefit other than an old-age insurance benefit (see § 404.407(b)); or

(6) An individual is entitled in a month to old-age, disability, wife's, husband's, widow's, or widower's insurance benefit and reduction is required under section 202(q) of the Act (see § 404.410).

(b) Deductions. A deduction from a monthly benefit or a lump-sum death payment may be required because of:

(1) An individual's earnings or work (see §§ 404.415 and 404.417);

(2) Failure of certain beneficiaries receiving wife's or mother's insurance benefits to have a child in her care (see § 404.421);

(3) The earnings or work of an old-age insurance beneficiary where a wife, husband, or child is also entitled to benefits (see §§ 404.415 and 404.417);

(4) Failure to report within the prescribed period either certain work outside the United States or not having the care of a child (see § 404.451);

(5) Failure to report within the prescribed period earnings from work in employment or self-employment (see § 404.453); or

(6) Certain taxes which were neither deducted from the wages of maritime employees nor paid to the Federal Government (see § 404.457).

(c) Adjustments. We may adjust your benefits to correct errors in payments under title II of the Act. We may also adjust your benefits if you received more than the correct amount due under titles VIII or XVI of the Act. For the title II rules on adjustment to your benefits, see subpart F of this part. For the rules on adjusting your benefits to recover title VIII overpayments, see § 408.930 of this chapter. For the rules on adjusting your benefits to recover title XVI overpayments, see § 416.572 of this chapter.

(d) Nonpayments. Nonpayment of monthly benefits may be required because:

(1) The individual is an alien who has been outside the United States for more than 6 months (see § 404.460);

(2) The individual on whose earnings record entitlement is based has been deported (see § 404.464);

(3) The individual is engaged in substantial gainful activity while entitled to disability insurance benefits based on "statutory blindness" (see § 404.467); or

(4) The individual has not provided satisfactory proof that he or she has a Social Security number or has not properly applied for a Social Security number (see § 404.469).

(e) Recalculation. A reduction by recalculation of a benefit amount may be prescribed because an individual has been convicted of certain offenses (see § 404.465) or because the primary insurance amount is recalculated (see subpart C of this part).

(f) Suspensions. Suspension of monthly benefits may be required pursuant to section 203(h)(3) of the Act (the Social Security Administration has information indicating that work deductions may reasonably be expected for the year), or pursuant to section 225 of the Act (the Social Security Administration has information indicating a beneficiary is no longer disabled).

[40 FR 30813, July 23, 1975; 48 FR 37016, Aug. 16, 1983; 56 FR 41789, Aug. 23, 1991; 65 FR 16813, March 30, 2000; 66 FR 38906, July 26, 2001; 68 FR 40122, July 7, 2003; 69 FR 25955, May 10, 2004; 81 FR 19033, April 4, 2016; 83 FR 21708, May 10, 2018]

§ 404.401a When we do not pay benefits because of a disability beneficiary's work activity.

If you are receiving benefits because you are disabled or blind as defined in title II of the Social Security Act, we will stop your monthly benefits even though you have a disabling impairment (§ 404.1511), if you engage in substantial gainful activity during the reentitlement period (§ 404.1592a) following completion of the trial work period (§ 404.1592). You will, however, be paid benefits for the first month after the trial work period in which you do substantial gainful activity and the two succeeding months, whether or not you do substantial gainful activity in those two months. If anyone else is receiving monthly benefits based on your earnings record, that individual will not be paid benefits for any month for which you cannot be paid benefits during the reentitlement period. Except as provided in § 404.471, earnings from work activity during a trial work period will not stop your benefits.

[49 FR 22271, May 29, 1984; 58 FR 64883, Dec. 10, 1993; 71 FR 66865, Nov. 17, 2006]

§ 404.402 Interrelationship of deductions, reductions, adjustments, and nonpayment of benefits.

(a) Deductions, reductions, adjustment. Deductions because of earnings or work (see §§ 404.415 and 404.417); failure to have a child "in his or her care" (see § 404.421); as a penalty for failure to timely report noncovered work outside the United States, failure to report that he or she no longer has a child "in his or her care," or failure to timely report earnings (see §§ 404.451 and 404.453); because of unpaid maritime taxes (see § 404.457); or nonpayments because of drug addiction and alcoholism to individuals other than an insured individual who are entitled to benefits on the insured individual's earnings record are made:

(1) Before making any reductions because of the maximum (see § 404.403),

(2) Before applying the benefit rounding provisions (see § 404.304(f)), and,

(3) Except for deductions imposed as a penalty (see §§ 404.451 and 404.453), before making any adjustment necessary because an error has been made in the payment of benefits (see subpart F). However, for purposes of charging excess earnings for taxable years beginning after December 1960 or ending after June 1961, see paragraph (b) of this section and § 404.437 for reductions that apply before such charging.

(b) Reductions, nonpayments.

(1) Reduction because of the maximum (see § 404.403) is made:

(i) Before reduction because of simultaneous entitlement to old-age or disability insurance benefits and to other benefits (see § 404.407);

(ii) Before reduction in benefits for age (see §§ 404.410 through 404.413);

(iii) Before adjustment necessary because an error has been made in the payment of benefits (see subpart F of this part);

(iv) Before reduction because of entitlement to certain public disability benefits provided under Federal, State, or local laws or plans (see § 404.408);

(v) Before nonpayment of an individual's benefits because he is an alien living outside the United States for 6 months (see § 404.460), or because of deportation (see § 404.464);

(vi) Before the redetermination of the amount of benefit payable to an individual who has been convicted of certain offenses (see § 404.465); and

(vii) Before suspension of benefits due to earnings (see § 404.456), for benefits payable or paid for months after December 1995 to a non-working auxiliary or survivor who resides in a different household than the working auxiliary or survivor whose benefits are suspended.

(2) Reduction of benefits because of entitlement to certain public disability benefits (see § 404.408) is made before deduction under section 203 of the Act relating to work (see §§ 404.415, 404.417, 404.451, and 404.453) and failure to have care of a child (see §§ 404.421 and 404.451).

(3) Reduction of the benefit of a spouse who is receiving a Government pension (see § 404.408(a)) is made after the withholding of payments as listed in paragraph (d)(1) of this section and after reduction because of receipt of certain public disability benefits (paragraph (b)(2) of this section).

(c) Alien outside the United States; deportation nonpayment—deduction. If an individual is subject to nonpayment of a benefit for a month under § 404.460 or § 404.464, no deduction is made from his benefit for that month under § 404.415, § 404.417, or § 404.421, and no deduction is made because of that individual's work from the benefit of any person entitled or deemed entitled to benefits under § 404.420, on his earnings record, for that month.

(d) Order of priority—deductions and other withholding provisions. Deductions and other withholding provisions are applied in accordance with the following order of priority:

(1) Current nonpayments under §§ 404.460, 404.464, 404.465, 404.467, and 404.469;

(2) Current reductions under § 404.408;

(3) Current reductions under § 404.408a;

(4) Current deductions under §§ 404.417 and 404.421;

(5) Current withholding of benefits under § 404.456;

(6) Unpaid maritime tax deductions (§ 404.457);

(7) Withholdings to recover overpayments (see subpart F of this part);

(8) Penalty deductions under §§ 404.451 and 404.453.

[40 FR 30813, July 23, 1975, as amended at 44 FR 29047, May 18, 1979; 48 FR 37016, Aug. 16, 1983; 48 FR 46148, Oct. 11, 1983; 56 FR 41789, Aug. 23, 1991; 60 FR 8146, Feb. 10, 1995; 68 FR 15659, April 1, 2003; 68 FR 40122, July 7, 2003]

§ 404.403 Reduction where total monthly benefits exceed maximum family benefits payable.

(a) General.

(1) The Social Security Act limits the amount of monthly benefits that can be paid for any month based on the earnings of an insured individual. If the total benefits to which all persons are entitled on one earnings record exceed a maximum amount prescribed by law, then those benefits must be reduced so that they do not exceed that maximum.

(2) The method of determining the total benefits payable (the family maximum) depends on when the insured individual died or became eligible, whichever is earlier. For purposes of this section, the year in which the insured individual becomes eligible refers generally to the year in which the individual attains age 62 or becomes disabled. However, where eligibility or death is in 1979 or later, the year of death, attainment of age 62, or beginning of current disability does not control if the insured individual was entitled to a disability benefit within the 12 month period preceding current eligibility or death. Instead the year in which the individual became eligible for the former disability insurance benefit is the year of eligibility.

(3) The benefits of an individual entitled as a divorced spouse or surviving divorced spouse will not be reduced pursuant to this section. The benefits of all other individuals entitled on the same record will be determined under this section as if no such divorced spouse or surviving divorced spouse were entitled to benefits.

(4) In any case where more than one individual is entitled to benefits as the spouse or surviving spouse of a worker for the same month, and at least one of those individuals is entitled based on a marriage not valid under State law (see §§ 404.345 and 404.346), the benefits of the individual whose entitlement is based on a valid marriage under State law will not be reduced pursuant to this section. The benefits of all other individuals entitled on the same record (unless excluded by paragraph (a)(3) of this section) will be determined under this section as if such validly married individual were not entitled to benefits.

(5) When a person entitled on a worker's earnings record is also entitled to benefits on another earnings record, we consider only the amount of benefits actually due or payable on the worker's record to the dually-entitled person when determining how much to reduce total monthly benefits payable on the worker's earnings record because of the maximum. We do not include, in total benefits payable, any amount not paid because of that person's entitlement on another earnings record (see § 404.407). The effect of this provision is to permit payment of up to the full maximum benefits to other beneficiaries who are not subject to a deduction or reduction. (See § 404.402 for other situations where we apply deductions or reductions before reducing total benefits for the maximum.)

Example 1: A wage earner, his wife and child are entitled to benefits. The wage earner's primary insurance amount is

$600.00. His maximum is $900.00. Due to the maximum limit, the monthly benefits for the wife and child must be reduced to $150.00 each. Their original benefit rates are $300.00 each.

Maximum—$900.00

Subtract primary insurance amount—$600.00

Amount available for wife and child—$300.00

Divide by 2—$150.00 each for wife and child

The wife is also entitled to benefits on her own record of $120.00 monthly. This reduces her wife's benefit to $30.00. The following table illustrates this calculation.

Wife's benefit, reduced for maximum—$150.00

Subtract reduction due to dual entitlement—$120.00

Wife's benefit—$30.00

In computing the total benefits payable on the record, we disregard the $120.00 we cannot pay the wife. This allows us to increase the amount payable to the child to $270.00. The table below shows the steps in our calculation.

Amount available under maximum—$300.00

Subtract amount due wife after reduction due to entitlement to her own benefit—$30.00

Child's benefit—$270.00

Example 2: A wage earner, his wife and 2 children are entitled to benefits. The wage earner's primary insurance amount is $1,250.00. His maximum is $2,180.00. Due to the maximum limit, the monthly benefits for the wife and children must be reduced to $310.00 each. Their original rates (50 percent of the worker's benefit) are $625.00 each. The following shows the calculation.

Maximum—$2,180.00

Subtract primary insurance amount—$1,250.00

Amount available for wife and children—$930.00

Divide by 3—$310 each for wife and children

The children are also entitled to benefits on their own records. Child one is entitled to $390.00 monthly and child two is entitled to $280.00 monthly. This causes a reduction in the benefit to child one to 0.00 and the benefit to child two to $30.00. Again, the following illustrates the calculation.

Benefit payable to child 1 reduced for maximum—$310.00

Subtract reduction due to dual entitlement—$390.00

Benefit payable to child 1—$0.00

Benefit payable to child 2, reduced for maximum—$310.00

Subtract reduction for dual entitlement—$280.00

Benefit payable to child 2—$30.00

In computing the total benefits payable on the record, we consider only the benefits actually paid to the children, or $30. This allows payment of an additional amount to the wife, increasing her benefit to $625.00. This is how the calculation works.

Amount available under maximum for wife and children—$930.00

Subtract amount due children after reduction due to entitlement to their own benefits—$30.00

Amount available for wife—$900.00

Amount payable to wife (original benefit)—$625.00

Example 3: A wage earner, his wife and 4 children are entitled to benefits. The wage earner's primary insurance amount is $1,250.00. His maximum is $2,180.00. Due to the maximum limit, the monthly benefits for the wife and children must be reduced to $186.00 each. Their original rates are $625.00 each. This is how the calculation works.

Maximum—$2,180.00

Subtract primary insurance amount—$1,250.00

Amount available for wife and children—$930.00

Divide by 5—$186.00 each for wife and four children

Two children are also entitled to benefits on their own records. Child one is entitled to $390.00 monthly and child two is entitled to $280.00 monthly. This causes a reduction in the benefit to child one to $0.00 and the benefit to child two to $0.00. This calculation is as follows.

Benefit to child 1, reduced for maximum—$186.00

Subtract reduction due to dual entitlement—$390.00

Benefit payable to child 1—$0.00

Benefit to child 2, reduced for maximum—$186.00

Subtract reduction for dual entitlement—$280.00

Benefit payable to child two—$0.00

In computing the total benefits payable on the record, we disregard the $372.00 we cannot pay the children. This allows payment of an additional amount to the wife, and the two remaining children as follows:

Amount available under maximum for wife and children—$930.00

Subtract amount due child one and child two after reduction due to entitlement to their own benefits—$0.00

Amount available for wife and the other two children—$930.00

Amount payable to the wife and each of the remaining two children—$310.00

(b) Eligibility or death before 1979. Where more than one individual is entitled to monthly benefits for the same month on the same earnings record, a reduction in the total benefits payable for that month may be required (except in cases involving a saving clause—see § 404.405) if the maximum family benefit is exceeded. The maximum is exceeded if the total of the monthly benefits exceeds the amount appearing in column V of the applicable table in section 215(a) of the Act on the line on which appears in column IV the primary insurance amount of the insured individual whose earnings record is the basis for the benefits payable. Where the maximum is exceeded, the total benefits for each month after 1964 are reduced to the amount appearing in column V. However, when any of the persons entitled to benefits on the insured individual's earnings would, except for the limitation described in § 404.353(b), be entitled to child's insurance benefits on the basis of the earnings record of one or more other insured individuals, the total benefits payable may not be reduced to less than the smaller of—

(1) The sum of the maximum amounts of benefits payable on the basis of the earnings records of all such insured individuals, or

(2) The last figure in column V of the applicable table in (or deemed to be in) section 215(a) of the Act. The applicable table refers to the table which is effective for the month the benefit is payable.

(c) Eligible for old-age insurance benefits or dies in 1979. If an insured individual becomes eligible for old-age insurance benefits or dies in 1979, the monthly maximum is as follows—

(1) 150 percent of the first $230 of the individual's primary insurance amount, plus

(2) 272 percent of the primary insurance amount over $230 but not over $332, plus

(3) 134 percent of the primary insurance amount over $332 but not over $433, plus

(4) 175 percent of the primary insurance amount over $433.

If the total of this computation is not a multiple of $0.10, it will be rounded to the next lower multiple of $0.10.

(d) Eligible for old-age insurance benefits or dies after 1979.

(1) If an insured individual becomes eligible for old-age insurance benefits or dies after 1979, the monthly maximum is computed as in paragraph (c) of this section. However, the dollar amounts shown there will be updated each year as average earnings rise. This updating is done by first dividing the average of the total wages (see § 404.203(m)) for the second year before the individual dies or becomes eligible, by the average of the total wages for 1977. The result of that computation is then multiplied by each dollar amount in the formula in paragraph (c) of this section. Each updated dollar amount will be rounded to the nearer dollar; if the amount is an exact multiple of $0.50 (but not of $1), it will be rounded to the next higher $1.

(2) Before November 2 of each calendar year after 1978, the Commissioner will publish in the Federal Register the formula and updated dollar amounts to be used for determining the monthly maximum for the following year.

(d–1) Entitled to disability insurance benefits after June 1980. If you first become eligible for old-age or disability insurance benefits after 1978 and first entitled to disability insurance benefits after June 1980, we compute the monthly family maximum under a formula which is different from that in paragraphs (c) and (d) of this section. The computation under the new formula is as follows:

(1) We take 85 percent of your average indexed monthly earnings and compare that figure with your primary insurance amount (see § 404.212 of this part). We work with the larger of these two amounts.

(2) We take 150 percent of your primary insurance amount.

(3) We compare the results of paragraphs (d–1)(1) and (2) of this section. The smaller amount is the monthly family maximum. As a result of this rule, the entitled spouse and children of some workers will not be paid any benefits because the family maximum does not exceed the primary insurance amount.

(e) Person entitled on more than one record during years after 1978 and before 1984.

(1) If any of the persons entitled to monthly benefits on the earnings record of an insured individual would, except for the limitation described in § 404.353(b), be entitled to child's insurance benefits on the earnings record of one or more other insured individuals, the total benefits payable may not be reduced to less than the smaller of—

(i) The sum of the maximum amounts of benefits payable on the earnings records of all the insured individuals, or

(ii) 1.75 times the highest primary insurance amount possible for that month based on the average indexed monthly earnings equal to one-twelfth of the contribution and benefit base determined for that year.

(2) If benefits are payable on the earnings of more than one individual and the primary insurance amount of one of the insured individuals was computed under the provisions in effect before 1979 and the primary insurance amount of the others was computed under the provisions in effect after 1978, the maximum monthly benefits cannot be more than the amount computed under paragraph (e)(1) of this section.

(f) Person entitled on more than one record for years after 1983.

(1) If any person for whom paragraphs (c) and (d) would apply is entitled to monthly benefits on the earnings record of an insured individual would, except for the limitation described in § 404.353(b), be entitled to child's insurance benefits on the earnings record of one or more other insured individuals, the total benefits payable to all persons on the earnings record of any of those insured individuals may not be reduced to less than the smaller of:

(i) The sum of the maximum amounts of benefits payable on the earnings records of all the insured individuals, or

(ii) 1.75 times the highest primary insurance amount possible for January 1983, or if later, January of the year that the person becomes entitled or reentitled on more than one record.

This highest primary insurance amount possible for that year will be based on the average indexed monthly earnings equal to one-twelfth of the contribution and benefit base determined for that year. Thereafter, the total monthly benefits payable to persons on the earnings record of those insured individuals will then be increased only when monthly benefits are increased because of cost-of-living adjustments (see § 404.270ff).

(2) If benefits are payable on the earnings of more than one individual and the primary insurance amount of one of the insured individuals was computed under

the provisions in effect before 1979 and the primary insurance amount of the other was computed under the provisions in effect after 1978, the maximum monthly benefits cannot be more than the amount computed under paragraph (f)(1) of this section.

(g) Person previously entitled to disability insurance benefits. If an insured individual who was previously entitled to disability insurance benefits becomes entitled to a "second entitlement" as defined in § 404.250, or dies, after 1995, and the insured individual's primary insurance amount is determined under §§ 404.251(a)(1), 404.251(b)(1), or 404.252(b), the monthly maximum during the second entitlement is determined under the following rules:

(1) If the primary insurance amount is determined under §§ 404.251(a)(1) or 404.251(b)(1), the monthly maximum equals the maximum in the last month of the insured individual's earlier entitlement to disability benefits, increased by any cost-of-living or ad hoc increases since then.

(2) If the primary insurance amount is determined under § 404.252(b), the monthly maximum equals the maximum in the last month of the insured individual's earlier entitlement to disability benefits.

(3) Notwithstanding paragraphs (g)(1) and (g)(2) of this section, if the second entitlement is due to the insured individual's retirement or death, and the monthly maximum in the last month of the insured individual's earlier entitlement to disability benefits was computed under paragraph (d–1) of this section, the monthly maximum is equal to the maximum that would have been determined for the last month of such earlier entitlement if computed without regard for paragraph (d–1) of this section.

[45 FR 1611, Jan. 8, 1980; 45 FR 6540, Jan. 29, 1980, as amended at 46 FR 25601, May 8, 1981; 48 FR 46148, Oct. 11, 1983; 51 FR 12606, April 14, 1986; 58 FR 64892, Dec. 10, 1993; 62 FR 38450, July 18, 1997; 64 FR 17101, April 8, 1999; 64 FR 57775, Oct. 27, 1999; 65 FR 16813, March 30, 2000; 65 FR 38426, June 21, 2000]

§ 404.404 How reduction for maximum affects insured individual and other persons entitled on his earnings record.

If a reduction of monthly benefits is required under the provisions of § 404.403, the monthly benefit amount of each of the persons entitled to a monthly benefits on the same earnings record (with the exception of the individual entitled to old-age or disability insurance benefits) is proportionately reduced so that the total benefits that can be paid in 1 month (including an amount equal to the primary insurance amount of the old-age or disability insurance beneficiary, when applicable) does not exceed the maximum family benefit (except as provided in § 404.405 where various savings clause provisions are described).

§ 404.405 Situations where total benefits can exceed maximum because of "savings clause."

The following provisions are savings clauses and describe exceptions to the rules concerning the maximum amount payable on an individual's earnings record in a month as described in § 404.403. The effect of a savings clause is to avoid lowering benefit amounts or to guarantee minimum increases to certain persons entitled on the earnings record of the insured individual when a statutory change has been made that would otherwise disadvantage them. The reduction described in § 404.403 does not apply in the following instances:

(a) to (m) [Reserved]

(n) Months after August 1972. The reduction described in § 404.403(a) shall not apply to benefits for months after August 1972 where two or more persons were entitled to benefits for August 1972 based upon the filing of an application in August 1972 or earlier and the total of such benefits was subject to reduction for the maximum under § 404.403 (or would have been subject to such reduction except for this paragraph) for January 1971. In such a case, maximum family benefits on the insured individual's earnings record for any month after August 1972 may not be less than the larger of:

(1) The maximum family benefits for such month determined under the applicable table in section 215(a) of the Act (the applicable table in section 215(a) is that table which is effective for the month the benefit is payable or in the case of a lump-sum payment, the month the individual died); or

(2) The total obtained by multiplying each benefit for August 1972 after reduction for the maximum but before deduction or reduction for age, by 120 percent and raising each such increased amount, if it is not a multiple of 10 cents, to the next higher multiple of 10 cents.

(*o*) Months after December 1972. The reduction described in § 404.403 shall not apply to benefits for months after December 1972 in the following cases:

(1) In the case of a redetermination of widow's or widower's benefits, the reduction described in § 404.403 shall not apply if:

(i) Two or more persons were entitled to benefits for December 1972 on the earnings records of a deceased individual and at least one such person is entitled to benefits as the deceased individual's widow or widower for December 1972 and for January 1973; and

(ii) The total of benefits to which all persons are entitled for January 1973 is reduced (or would be reduced if deductions were not applicable) for the maximum under § 404.403.

In such case, the benefit of each person referred to in paragraph (*o*)(1)(i) of this section for months after

December 1972 shall be no less than the amount it would have been if the widow's or widower's benefit had not been redetermined under the Social Security Amendments of 1972.

(2) In the case of entitlement to child's benefits based upon disability which began between ages 18 and 22 the reduction described in § 404.403 shall not apply if:

(i) One or more persons were entitled to benefits on the insured individual's earnings record for December 1972 based upon an application filed in that month or earlier; and

(ii) One or more persons not included in paragraph (*o*)(2)(i) of this section are entitled to child's benefits on that earnings record for January 1973 based upon disability which began in the period from ages 18 to 22; and

(iii) The total benefits to which all persons are entitled on that record for January 1973 is reduced (or would be reduced if deductions were not applicable) for the maximum under § 404.403.

In such case, the benefit of each person referred to in paragraph (*o*)(2)(i) of this section for months after December 1972 shall be no less than the amount it would have been if the person entitled to child's benefits based upon disability in the period from ages 18 to 22 were not so entitled.

(3) In the case of entitlement of certain surviving divorced mothers, the reduction described in § 404.403 shall not apply if:

(i) One or more persons were entitled to benefits on the insured individual's earnings record for December 1972 based upon an application filed in December 1972 or earlier; and

(ii) One or more persons not included in paragraph (*o*)(3)(i) of this section are entitled to benefits on that earnings record as a surviving divorced mother for a month after December 1972; and

(iii) The total of benefits to which all persons are entitled on that record for any month after December 1972 is reduced (or would be reduced if deductions were not applicable) for the maximum under § 404.403.

In such case, the benefit of each such person referred to in paragraph (*o*)(3)(i) of this section for months after December 1972 in which any person referred to in paragraph (*o*)(3)(ii) of this section is entitled shall be no less than it would have been if the person(s) referred to in paragraph (*o*)(3)(ii) of this section had not become entitled to benefits.

(p) Months after December 1973. The reduction described in § 404.403 shall not apply to benefits for months after December 1973 where two or more persons were entitled to monthly benefits for January 1971 or earlier based upon applications filed in January 1971 or earlier, and the total of such benefits was subject to reduction for the maximum under § 404.403 for January 1971 or earlier. In such a case, maximum family benefits payable on the insured individual's earnings record for any month after January 1971 may not be less than the larger of:

(1) The maximum family benefit for such month shown in the applicable table in section 215(a) of the Act (the applicable table in section 215(a) of the Act is that table which is effective for the month the benefit is payable or in the case of a lump-sum payment, the month the individual died); or

(2) The largest amount which has been determined payable for any month for persons entitled to benefits on the insured individual's earnings records; or

(3) In the case of persons entitled to benefits on the insured individual's earnings record for the month immediately preceding the month of a general benefit or cost-of-living increase after September 1972, an amount equal to the sum of the benefit amount for each person (excluding any part of an old-age insurance benefit increased because of delayed retirement under the provisions of § 404.305(a) for the month immediately before the month of increase in the primary insurance amount (after reduction for the family maximum but before deductions or reductions for age) multiplied by the percentage of increase. Any such increased amount, if it is not a multiple of $0.10, will be raised to the next higher multiple of $0.10 for months before June 1982 and reduced to the next lower multiple of $0.10 for months after May 1982.

(q) Months after May 1978. The family maximum for months after May 1978 is figured for all beneficiaries just as it would have been if none of them had gotten a benefit increase because of the retirement credit if:

(1) One or more persons were entitled (without the reduction required by § 404.406) to monthly benefits for May 1978 on the wages and self-employment income of a deceased wage earner;

(2) The benefit for June 1978 of at least one of those persons is increased by reason of a delayed retirement credit (see § 404.330(b)(4) or § 404.333(b)(4)); and

(3) The total amount of monthly benefits to which all those persons are entitled is reduced because of the maximum or would be so reduced except for certain restrictions (see § 404.403 and § 404.402(a)).

[32 FR 19159, Dec. 20, 1967, as amended at 40 FR 30814, July 23, 1975; 43 FR 8132, Feb. 28, 1978; 43 FR 29277, July 7, 1978; 48 FR 46148, Oct. 11, 1983]

§ 404.406 Reduction for maximum because of retroactive effect of application for monthly benefits.

Under the provisions described in § 404.403, beginning with the month in which a person files an application and becomes entitled to benefits on an insured individual's earnings record, the benefit rate of other persons entitled on the same earnings record (aside from the individual on whose earnings record entitlement is based) are adjusted downward, if necessary, so that the maximum benefits payable on one earnings record will not be exceeded. An application may also be effective (retroactively) for benefits for months before the month of filing (see § 404.603). For any month before the month of filing, however, benefits that have been previously certified by the Administration for payment to other persons (on the same earnings record) are not changed. Rather, the benefit payment of the person filing the application in the later month is reduced for each month of the retroactive period to the extent that may be necessary, so that no earlier payment to some other person is made erroneous. This means that for each month of the retroactive period the amount payable to the person filing the later application is the difference, if any, between (a) the total amount of benefits actually certified for payment to other persons for that month, and (b) the maximum amount of benefits payable for that month to all persons, including the person filing later.

[64 FR 14608, March 26, 1999]

§ 404.407 Reduction because of entitlement to other benefits.

(a) Entitlement to old-age or disability insurance benefit and other monthly benefit. If an individual is entitled to an old-age insurance benefit or disability insurance benefit for any month after August 1958 and to any other monthly benefit payable under the provisions of title II of the Act (see subpart D of this part) for the same month, such other benefit for the month, after any reduction under section 202(q) of the Act because of entitlement to such benefit for months before retirement age and any reduction under section 203(a) of the Act, is reduced (but not below zero) by an amount equal to such old-age insurance benefit (after reduction under section 202(q) of the Act) or such disability insurance benefit, as the case may be.

(b) Entitlement to widow's or widower's benefit and other monthly benefit. If an individual is entitled for any month after August 1965 to a widow's or widower's insurance benefit under the provisions of section 202 (e)(4) or (f)(5) of the Act and to any other monthly benefit payable under the provisions of title II of the Act (see subpart D) for the same month, except an old-age insurance benefit, such other insurance benefit for that month, after any reduction under paragraph (a) of this section, any reduction for age under section 202(q) of the Act, and any reduction under the provisions described in section 203(a) of the Act, shall be reduced, but not below zero, by an amount equal to such widow's or widower's insurance benefit after any reduction or reductions under paragraph (a) of this section or section 203(a) of the Act.

(c) Entitlement to old-age insurance benefit and disability insurance benefit. Any individual who is entitled for any month after August 1965 to both an old-age insurance benefit and a disability insurance benefit shall be entitled to only the larger of such benefits for such month, except that where the individual so elects, he or she shall instead be entitled to only the smaller of such benefits for such month. Only a person defined in § 404.612 (a), (c), or (d) may make the above described election.

(d) Child's insurance benefits. A child may, for any month, be simultaneously entitled to a child's insurance benefit on more than one individual's earnings if all the conditions for entitlement described in § 404.350 are met with respect to each claim. Where a child is simultaneously entitled to child's insurance benefits on more than one earnings record, the general rule is that the child will be paid an amount which is based on the record having the highest primary insurance amount. However, the child will be paid a higher amount which is based on the earnings record having a lower primary insurance amount if no other beneficiary entitled on any record would receive a lower benefit because the child is paid on the record with the lower primary insurance amount. (See § 404.353(b)).

(e) Entitlement to more than one benefit where not all benefits are child's insurance benefits and no benefit is an old-age or disability insurance benefit. If an individual (other than an individual to whom section 202 (e)(4) or (f)(5) of the Act applies) is entitled for any month to more than one monthly benefit payable under the provisions of this subpart, none of which is an old-age or disability insurance benefit and all of which are not child's insurance benefits, only the greater of the monthly benefits to which he would (but for the provisions of this paragraph) otherwise be entitled is payable for such month. For months after August 1965, an individual who is entitled for any month to more than one widow's or widower's insurance benefit to which section 202 (e)(4) or (f)(5) of the Act applies is entitled to only one such benefit for such month, such benefit to be the largest of such benefits.

[51 FR 12606, April 14, 1986; 54 FR 5603, Feb. 6, 1989]

§ 404.408 Reduction of benefits based on disability on account of receipt of certain other disability benefits provided under Federal, State, or local laws or plans.

(a) When reduction required. Under section 224 of the Act, a disability insurance benefit to which an individual is entitled under section 223 of the Act for a month (and any monthly benefit for the same month payable to others under section 202 on the basis of the same earnings record) is reduced (except as provided in paragraph (b) of this section) by an amount determined under paragraph (c) of this section if:

(1) The individual first became entitled to disability insurance benefits after 1965 but before September 1981 based on a period of disability that began after June 1, 1965, and before March 1981, and

(i) The individual entitled to the disability insurance benefit is also entitled to periodic benefits under a workers' compensation law or plan of the United States or a State for that month for a total or partial disability (whether or not permanent), and

(ii) The Commissioner has, in a month before that month, received a notice of the entitlement, and

(iii) The individual has not attained age 62, or

(2) The individual first became entitled to disability insurance benefits after August 1981 based on a disability that began after February 1981, and

(i) The individual entitled to the disability insurance benefit is also, for that month, concurrently entitled to a periodic benefit (including workers' compensation or any other payments based on a work relationship) on account of a total or partial disability (whether or not permanent) under a law or plan of the United States, a State, a political subdivision, or an instrumentality of two or more of these entities, and

(ii) The individual has not attained full retirement age as defined in § 404.409.

(b) When reduction not made.

(1) The reduction of a benefit otherwise required by paragraph (a)(1) of this section is not made if the workers' compensation law or plan under which the periodic benefit is payable provides for the reduction of such periodic benefit when anyone is entitled to a benefit under title II of the Act on the basis of the earnings record of an individual entitled to a disability insurance benefit under section 223 of the Act.

(2) The reduction of a benefit otherwise required by paragraph (a)(2) of this section is not to be made if:

(i) The law or plan under which the periodic public disability benefit is payable provides for the reduction of that benefit when anyone is entitled to a benefit under title II of the Act on the basis of the earnings record of an individual entitled to a disability insurance benefit under section 223 of the Act and that law or plan so provided on February 18, 1981. (The reduction required by paragraph (a)(2) of this section will not be affected by public disability reduction provisions not actually in effect on this date or by changes made after February 18, 1981, to provisions that were in effect on this date providing for the reduction of benefits previously not subject to a reduction); or

(ii) The benefit is a Veterans Administration benefit, a public disability benefit (except workers' compensation) payable to a public employee based on employment covered under Social Security, a public benefit based on need, or a wholly private pension or private insurance benefit.

(c) Amount of reduction—

(1) General. The total of benefits payable for a month under sections 223 and 202 of the Act to which paragraph (a) of this section applies is reduced monthly (but not below zero) by the amount by which the sum of the monthly disability insurance benefits payable on the disabled individual's earnings record and the other public disability benefits payable for that month exceeds the higher of:

(i) Eighty percent of his average current earnings, as defined in paragraph (c)(3) of this section, or

(ii) The total of such individual's disability insurance benefit for such month and all other benefits payable for such month based on such individual's earnings record, prior to reduction under this section.

(2) Limitation on reduction. In no case may the total of monthly benefits payable for a month to the disabled worker and to the persons entitled to benefits for such month on his earnings record be less than:

(i) The total of the benefits payable (after reduction under paragraph (a) of this section) to such beneficiaries for the first month for which reduction under this section is made, and

(ii) Any increase in such benefits which is made effective for months after the first month for which reduction under this section is made.

(3) Average current earnings defined.

(i) Beginning January 1, 1979, for purposes of this section, an individual's average current earnings is the largest of either paragraph (c)(3)(i) (a), (b) or (c) of this section (after reducing the amount to the next lower multiple of $1 when the amount is not a multiple of $1):

(A) The average monthly wage (determined under section 215(b) of the Act as in effect prior to January 1979) used for purposes of computing the individual's disability insurance benefit under section 223 of the Act;

(B) One-sixtieth of the total of the individual's wages and earnings from self-employment, without the limitations under sections 209(a) and 211(b)(1) of the Act (see paragraph (c)(3)(ii) of this section), for the 5 consecutive calendar years after 1950 for which the wages and earnings from self-employment were highest; or

(C) One-twelfth of the total of the individual's wages and earnings from self-employment, without the limitations under sections 209(a) and 211(b)(1) of the Act (see paragraph (c)(3)(ii) of this section), for the calendar year in which the individual had the highest wages and earnings from self-employment during the period consisting of the calendar year in which the individual became disabled and the 5 years immediately preceding that year. Any amount so computed which is not a multiple of $1 is reduced to the next lower multiple of $1.

(ii) Method of determining calendar year earnings in excess of the limitations under sections 209(a) and 211(b)(1) of the Act. For the purposes of paragraph (c)(3)(i) of this section, the extent by which the wages or earnings from self-employment of an individual exceed the maximum amount of earnings creditable under sections 209(a) and 211(b)(1) of the Act in any calendar year after 1950 and before 1978 will ordinarily be estimated on the basis of the earnings information available in the records of Administration. (See subpart I of this part.) If an individual provides satisfactory evidence of his actual earnings in any year, the extent, if any, by which his earnings exceed the limitations under sections 209(a) and 211(b)(1) of the Act shall be determined by the use of such evidence instead of by the use of estimates.

(4) Reentitlement to disability insurance benefits. If an individual's entitlement to disability insurance benefits terminates and such individual again becomes entitled to disability insurance benefits, the amount of the reduction is again computed based on the figures specified in this paragraph (c) applicable to the subsequent entitlement.

(5) Computing disability insurance benefits. When reduction is required, the total monthly Social Security disability insurance benefits payable after reduction can be more easily computed by subtracting the monthly amount of the other public disability benefit from the higher of paragraph (c)(1)(i) or (ii). This is the method employed in the examples used in this section.

(d) Items not counted for reduction. Amounts paid or incurred, or to be incurred, by the individual for medical, legal, or related expenses in connection with the claim for public disability payments (see § 404.408(a) and (b)) or the injury or occupational disease on which the public disability award or settlement agreement is based, are excluded in computing the reduction under paragraph (a) of this section to the extent they are consonant with the applicable Federal, State, or local law or plan and reflect either the actual amount of expenses already incurred or a reasonable estimate, given the circumstances in the individual's case, of future expenses. Any expenses not established by evidence required by the Administration or not reflecting a reasonable estimate of the individual's actual future expenses will not be excluded. These medical, legal, or related expenses may be evidenced by the public disability award, compromise agreement, a court order, or by other evidence as the Administration may require. This other evidence may consist of:

(1) A detailed statement by the individual's attorney, physician, or the employer's insurance carrier; or

(2) Bills, receipts, or canceled checks; or

(3) Other clear and convincing evidence indicating the amount of expenses; or

(4) Any combination of the foregoing evidence from which the amount of expenses may be determinable.

(e) Certification by individual concerning eligibility for public disability benefits. Where it appears that an individual may be eligible for a public disability benefit which would give rise to a reduction under paragraph (a) of this section, the individual may be required, as a condition of certification for payment of any benefit under section 223 of the Act to any individual for any month, and of any benefit under section 202 of the Act for any month based on such individual's earnings record, to furnish evidence as requested by the Administration and to certify as to:

(1) Whether he or she has filed or intends to file any claim for a public disability benefit, and

(2) If he or she has so filed, whether there has been a decision on the claim. The Commissioner may rely, in the absence of evidence to the contrary, upon a certification that he or she has not filed and does not intend to file such a claim, or that he or she has filed and no decision has been made, in certifying any benefit for payment pursuant to section 205(i) of the Act.

(f) Verification of eligibility or entitlement to a public disability benefit under paragraph (a). Section 224 of the Act requires the head of any Federal agency to furnish the Commissioner information from the Federal agency's records which is needed to determine the reduction amount, if any, or verify other information to carry out the provisions of this section. The Commissioner is authorized to enter into agreements with States, political subdivisions, and other organizations that administer a law or plan of public disability benefits in order to obtain information that may be required to carry out the provisions of this section.

(g) Public disability benefit payable on other than a monthly basis. Where public disability benefits are paid periodically but not monthly, or in a lump sum as a commutation of or a substitute for periodic benefits, such as a compromise and release settlement, the reduction under this section is made at the time or times and in the amounts that the Administration determines will approximate as nearly as practicable the reduction required under paragraph (a) of this section.

(h) Priorities.

(1) For an explanation of when a reduction is made under this section where other reductions, deductions, etc., are involved, see § 404.402.

(2) Whenever a reduction in the total of benefits for any month based on an individual's earnings record is made under paragraph (a) of this section, each benefit, except the disability insurance benefit, is first proportionately decreased. Any excess reduction over the sum of all the benefits, other than the disability insur-

ance benefit, is then applied to the disability insurance benefit.

Example 1: Effective September 1981, Harold is entitled to a monthly disability primary insurance amount of $507.90 and a monthly public disability benefit of $410.00 from the State. Eighty percent of Harold's average current earnings is $800.00. Because this amount ($800.00) is higher than Harold's disability insurance benefit ($507.90), we subtract Harold's monthly public disability benefit ($410.00) from eighty percent of his average current earnings ($800.00). This leaves Harold a reduced monthly disability benefit of $390.00.

Example 2: In September 1981, Tom is entitled to a monthly disability primary insurance amount of $559.30. His wife and two children are also entitled to monthly benefits of $93.20 each. The total family benefit is $838.90. Tom is also receiving a monthly workers' compensation benefit of $500.00 from the State. Eighty percent of Tom's average current earnings is $820.10. Because the total family benefit ($838.90) is higher than 80 percent of the average current earnings ($820.10), we subtract the monthly workers' compensation benefit ($500.00) from the total family benefit ($838.90), leaving $338.90 payable. This means the monthly benefits to Tom's wife and children are reduced to zero, and Tom's monthly disability benefit is reduced to $338.90.

(i) Effect of changes in family composition. The addition or subtraction in the number of beneficiaries in a family may cause the family benefit to become, or cease to be, the applicable limit for reduction purposes under this section. When the family composition changes, the amount of the reduction is recalculated as though the new number of beneficiaries were entitled for the first month the reduction was imposed. If the applicable limit both before and after the change is 80 percent of the average current earnings and the limitation on maximum family benefits is in effect both before and after the change, the amount payable remains the same and is simply redistributed among the beneficiaries entitled on the same earnings record.

Example 1: Frank is receiving $500.00 a month under the provisions of a State workers' compensation law. He had a prior period of disability which terminated in June 1978. In September 1981, Frank applies for a second period of disability and is awarded monthly disability insurance benefits with a primary insurance amount of $370.20. His child, Doug, qualifies for benefits of $135.10 a month on Frank's earnings record. The total family benefits is $505.30 monthly.

Frank's average monthly wage (as used to compute the primary insurance amount) is $400.00; eighty percent of his average current earnings (computed by using the 5 consecutive years in which his earnings were highest) is $428.80 (80% of $536.00); eighty percent of Frank's average current earnings (computed by using the 1 calendar year in which his earnings were highest) is $509.60 (80% of $637.00). The highest value for 80 percent of average current earnings is therefore $509.60 (80%). Since this is higher than the total family benefit ($505.30), the $509.60 is the applicable limit in determining the amount of the reduction (or offset). The amount payable after the reduction is—

80% of Frank's average current earnings	$509.60
Frank's monthly workers' compensation benefit	−500.00
Monthly benefit payable to Frank	9.60

No monthly benefits are payable to Doug because the reduction is applied to Doug's benefit first. In December 1981, another child, Mike, becomes entitled on Frank's earnings record. The monthly benefit to each child before reduction is now $109.10, the amount payable when there are two beneficiaries in addition to the wage earner. Thus, the total family benefit becomes $588.40. Because this is now higher than $509.60 (80% of Frank's average current earnings), $588.40 becomes the applicable limit in determining the amount of reduction. The amount payable after the increase in the total family benefit is—

The new total family benefit	$588.40
Frank's monthly workers' compensation rate	−500.00
Monthly benefit payable to Frank	88.40

No monthly benefits are payable to either child because the reduction (or offset) is applied to the family benefits first.

Example 2: Jack became entitled to disability insurance benefits in December 1973 (12/73), with a primary insurance amount (PIA) of $220.40. He was also receiving a workers' compensation benefit. An offset was imposed against the disability insurance benefit. By June 1977 (6/77), Jack's PIA had increased to $298.00 because of several statutory benefit increases. In December 1977 (12/77), his wife, Helen, attained age 65 and filed for unreduced wife's benefits. (She was not entitled to a benefit on her own earnings record.) This benefit was terminated in May 1978 (5/78), at her death. Helen's benefit was computed back to 12/73 as though she were entitled in the first month that offset was imposed against Jack. Since there were no other beneficiaries entitled and Helen's entire monthly benefit amount is subject to offset, the benefit payable to her for 12/77 through April 1978 (4/78), would be $38.80. This gives Helen the protected statutory benefit increases since 12/73. The table below shows how Helen's benefit was computed beginning with the first month offset was imposed.

Month of entitlement/ statutory increase	Jack's PIA	Helen's benefit prior to offset	Helen's statutory increase
December 1973	$220.40	$110.20	....
March 1974	236.00	118.00	$7.80
June 1974	244.80	122.40	+4.40
June 1975	264.40	132.20	+9.80
June 1976	281.40	140.70	+8.50
June 1977	298.00	149.00	+8.30
December 1977 through April 1978 [1]			38.80

[1] Monthly benefit payable to Helen.

(j) Effect of social security disability insurance benefit increases. Any increase in benefits due to a recomputation or a statutory increase in benefit rates is not subject to the reduction for public disability benefits under paragraph (a) and does not change the amount to be deducted from the family benefit. The increase is simply added to what amount, if any, is payable. If a new beneficiary becomes entitled to monthly benefits on the same earnings record after the increase, the amount of the reduction is redistributed among the new beneficiaries entitled under section 202 of the Act and deducted from their current benefit rate.

Example: In March 1981, Chuck became entitled to disability insurance benefits with a primary insurance amount of $362.40 a month. He has a wife and two children who are each entitled to a monthly benefit of $60.40. Chuck is receiving monthly disability compensation from a worker's compensation plan of $410.00. Eighty percent of his average current earnings is $800.00. Because this is higher than the total family benefit ($543.60), $800.00 is the applicable limit in computing the amount of reduction. The amount of monthly benefits payable after the reduction is—

Applicable limit	$800.00
Chuck's monthly disability compensation	−410.00
Total amount payable to Chuck and the family after reduction	$390.00
Amount payable to Chuck	−362.40
Total amount payable to the family	$27.60
$9.20 payable to each family member equals	$27.60 / 3

In June 1981, the disability benefit rates were raised to reflect an increase in the cost-of-living. Chuck is now entitled to $403.00 a month and each family member is entitled to $67.20 a month (an increase of $6.80 to each family member). The monthly amounts payable after the cost-of-living increase are now $403.00 to Chuck and $16.00 to each family member ($9.20 plus the $6.80 increase).

In September 1981, another child becomes entitled to benefits based on Chuck's earnings record. The monthly amount payable to the family (excluding Chuck) must now be divided by 4:

$6.90 payable to each family member equals	$27.60 / 4

The June 1981 cost-of-living increase is added to determine the amount payable. Chuck continues to receive $403.00 monthly. Each family member receives a cost-of-living increase of $5.10. Thus, the amount payable to each is $12.00 in September 1981 ($6.90 plus the $5.10 increase). (See Example 2 under (i).)

(k) Effect of changes in the amount of the public disability benefit. Any change in the amount of the public disability benefit received will result in a recalculation of the reduction under paragraph (a) and, potentially, an adjustment in the amount of such reduction. If the reduction is made under paragraph (a)(1) of this section, any increased reduction will be imposed effective with the month after the month the Commissioner received notice of the increase in the public disability benefit (it should be noted that only workers' compensation can cause this reduction). Adjustments due to a decrease in the amount of the public disability benefit will be effective with the actual date the decreased amount was effective. If the reduction is made under paragraph (a)(2) of this section, any increase or decrease in the reduction will be imposed effective with the actual date of entitlement to the new amount of the public disability benefit.

Example: In September 1981, based on a disability which began March 12, 1981, Theresa became entitled to Social Security disability insurance benefits with a primary insurance amount of $445.70 a month. She had previously been entitled to Social Security disability insurance benefits from March 1967 through July 1969. She is receiving a temporary total workers' compensation payment of $227.50 a month. Eighty percent of her average current earnings is $610.50. The amount of monthly disability insurance benefit payable after reduction is—

80 percent of Theresa's average current earnings	$610.50
Theresa's monthly workers' compensation payment	−227.50
Total amount payable to Theresa after reduction	383.00

On November 15, 1981, the Commissioner was notified that Theresa's workers' compensation rate was increased to $303.30 a month effective October 1, 1981. This increase reflected a cost-of-living adjustment granted to all workers' compensation recipients in her State. The reduction to her monthly disability insurance benefit is recomputed to take this increase into account—

80 percent of Theresa's average current earnings	$610.50
Theresa's monthly workers' compensation payment beginning October 1, 1981	−303.30
Total new amount payable to Theresa beginning October 1981 after recalculation of the reduction	$307.20

Effective January 1, 1982, Theresa's workers' compensation payment is decreased to $280.10 a month when she begins to receive a permanent partial payment. The reduction to her monthly disability insurance benefit is again recalculated to reflect her decreased workers' compensation amount—

80 percent of Theresa's average current earnings	$610.50
Theresa's monthly workers' compensation payment beginning January 1, 1982	−280.10
Total new amount payable to Theresa beginning January 1982 after recalculation of the reduction	$330.40

If, in the above example, Theresa had become entitled to disability insurance benefits in August 1981, the increased reduction to her benefit, due to the October 1, 1981 increase in her workers' compensation payment, would have been imposed beginning with December 1981, the month after the month she notified the Social Security Administration of the increase. The later decrease in her workers' compensation payment would still affect her disability insurance benefit beginning with January 1982.

(*l*) Redetermination of benefits—

(1) General. In the second calendar year after the year in which reduction under this section in the total of an individual's benefits under section 223 of the Act and any benefits under section 202 of the Act based on his or her wages and self-employment income is first required (in a continuous period of months), and in each third year thereafter, the amount of those benefits which are still subject to reduction under this section are redetermined, provided this redetermination does not result in any decrease in the total amount of benefits payable under title II of the Act on the basis of the workers' wages and self-employment income. The redetermined benefit is effective with the January following the year in which the redetermination is made.

(2) Average current earnings. In making the redetermination required by paragraph (*l*)(1) of this section, the individual's average current earnings (as defined in paragraph (c)(3) of this section) is deemed to be the product of his average current earnings as initially determined under paragraph (c)(3) of this section and:

(i) The ratio of the average of the total wages (as defined in § 404.1049) of all persons for whom wages were reported to the Secretary of the Treasury or his delegate for the calendar year before the year in which the redetermination is made, to the average of the total wages of all person reported to the Secretary of the Treasury or his delegate for calendar year 1977 or, if later, the calendar year before the year in which the reduction was first computed (but not counting any reduction made in benefits for a previous period of disability); and

(ii) In any case in which the reduction was first computed before 1978, the ratio of the average of the taxable wages reported to the Commissioner of Social Security for the first calendar quarter of 1977 to the average of the taxable wages reported to the Commissioner of Social Security for the first calendar quarter of the calendar year before the year in which the reduction was first computed (but not counting any reduction made in benefits for a previous period of disability). Any amount determined under the preceding two sentences which is not a multiple of $1 is reduced to the next lower multiple of $1.

(3) Effect of redetermination. Where the applicable limit on total benefits previously used was 80 percent of the average current earnings, a redetermination under this paragraph may cause an increase in the amount of benefits payable. Also, where the limit previously used was the total family benefit, the redetermination may cause the average current earnings to exceed the total family benefit and thus become the new applicable limit. If for some other reason (such as a statutory increase or recomputation) the benefit has already been increased to a level which equals or exceeds the benefit resulting from a redetermination under this paragraph, no additional increase is made.

A redetermination is designed to bring benefits into line with current wage levels when no other change in payments has done so.

Example: In October 1978, Alice became entitled to disability insurance benefits with a primary insurance amount of $505.10. Her two children were also entitled to monthly benefits of $189.40 each. Alice was also entitled to monthly disability compensation benefits of $667.30 from the State. Eighty percent of Alice's average current earnings is $1340.80, and that amount is the applicable limit. The amount of monthly benefits payable after the reduction is—

Applicable limit	$1,340.80
Alice's State disability compensation benefit	−667.30
Total benefits payable to Alice and both children after reduction	$673.50
Alice's disability insurance benefit	−505.10
Payable to the children	$168.40
$84.20 payable to each child after reduction equals	$168.40 / 2

In June 1979 and June 1980, cost-of-living increases in Social Security benefits raise Alice's benefit by $50.10 (to $555.20) and $79.40 (to $634.60) respectively. The children's benefits (before reduction) are each raised by $18.80 (to $208.20) and $29.80 (to $238.00). These increases in Social Security benefits are not subject to the reduction (i.e., offset).

In 1980, Alice's average current earnings are redetermined as required by law. The offset is recalculated, and if the amount payable to the family is higher than the current amount payable to the family, that higher amount becomes payable the following January (i.e., January 1981). The current amount payable to the family after the reduction is recalculated—

Alice's 1978 benefit after reduction	$505.10
Alice's cost-of-living increase in June 1979	+50.10
Alice's cost-of-living increase in June 1980	+79.40
One child's 1978 benefit after reduction	+84.20
That child's cost-of-living increase in June 1979	+18.70
That child's cost-of-living increase in June 1980	+29.70
The other child's 1978 benefit after reduction	+84.20
The other child's cost-of-living increase in June 1979	+18.70
The other child's cost-of-living increase in June 1980	+29.70
Total amount payable to the family after reduction in January 1981	899.80

The amount payable to the family after reduction is then recalculated using the redetermined average current earnings—

Average current earnings before redetermination	$1,676.00
Redetermination ratio effective for January 1981	×1.174
Redetermined average current earnings	$1,967.00
	×80%
80% of the redetermined average current earnings	$1,573.60

Alice's State disability compensation benefit	−667.30
Total benefits payable to the family after offset	$906.30

We then compare the total amount currently being paid to the family ($899.80) to the total amount payable after the redetermination ($906.30). In this example, the redetermination yields a higher amount and, therefore, becomes payable the following January (i.e., January 1981). Additional computations are required to determine the amount that will be paid to each family member—

Total benefits payable to the family using the redetermined average current earnings	$906.30
Total cost-of-living increases to both children ...	−96.80
Balance payable	809.50
Alice's current benefit amount before reduction	−634.60
Payable to the children	174.90
Total cost-of-living increases to both children ...	+96.80
Total payable to children after reduction	271.70
$135.90 (rounded from $135.85) payable to each child equals	$271.70 / 2

[32 FR 19159, Dec. 20, 1967; 33 FR 3060, Feb. 16, 1968, as amended at 37 FR 3425, Feb. 16, 1972; 43 FR 56037, Nov. 30, 1978; 48 FR 37017, Aug. 16, 1983; 48 FR 38814, Aug. 26, 1983; 49 FR 41245, Oct. 22, 1984; 62 FR 38450, July 18, 1997; 81 FR 19033, April 4, 2016]

§ 404.408a Reduction where spouse is receiving a Government pension.

(a) General—

(1) Terms used in this section.

(i) Government pension means any monthly periodic benefit (or equivalent) you receive that is based on your Federal, State, or local government employment.

(ii) Noncovered employment means Federal, State, or local government employment that Social Security did not cover and for which you did not pay Social Security taxes. For the purposes of this section, we consider your Federal, State, or local government employment to be noncovered employment if you pay only Medicare taxes.

(iii) Spouse's benefits are Social Security benefits you receive as a wife, husband, widow(er), mother, father, divorced spouse, or surviving divorced spouse.

(2) When reduction is required. We will reduce your spouse's benefit for each month that you receive a government pension based on noncovered employment, unless one of the exceptions in paragraph (b) of this section applies. When we consider whether you receive a government pension based on noncovered employment, we consider the entire month to be a month covered by Social Security if you worked for a Federal, State, or local government employer in a position covered by Social Security for at least 1 day in that month and there was no noncovered employment that month under the same pension plan.

(b) Exceptions. The reduction does not apply:

(1) If you are receiving a Government pension based on employment for an interstate instrumentality.

(2) If you received or are eligible to receive a Government pension for one or more months in the period December 1977 through November 1982 and you meet the requirements for Social Security benefits that were applied in January 1977, even though you don't claim benefits, and you don't actually meet the requirements for receiving benefits until a later month. The January 1977 requirements are, for a man, a one-half support test (see paragraph (c) of this section), and, for a woman claiming benefits as a divorced spouse, marriage for at least 20 years to the insured worker. You are considered eligible for a Government pension for any month in which you meet all the requirements for payment except that you are working or have not applied.

(3) If you were receiving or were eligible (as defined in paragraph (b)(2) of this section) to receive a Government pension for one or more months before July 1983, and you meet the dependency test of one-half support that was applied to claimants for husband's and widower's benefits in 1977, even though you don't claim benefits, and you don't actually meet the requirements for receiving benefits until a later month. If you meet the exception in this paragraph but you do not meet the exception in paragraph (b)(2), December 1982 is the earliest month for which the reduction will not affect your benefits.

(4) If you would have been eligible for a pension in a given month except for a requirement which delayed eligibility for such pension until the month following the month in which all other requirements were met, we will consider you to be eligible in that given month for the purpose of meeting one of the exceptions in paragraphs (b)(2) and (3) of this section. If you meet an exception solely because of this provision, your benefits will be unreduced for months after November 1984 only.

(5) If, with respect to monthly benefits payable for months after December 1994, you are receiving a Government pension based wholly upon service as a member of a uniformed service, regardless of whether on active or inactive duty and whether covered by social security. However, if the earnings on the last day of employment as a military reservist were not covered, January 1995 is the earliest month for which the reduction will not affect your benefits.

(6) If you are receiving a government pension and the last 60 months of your government employment were covered by both Social Security and the pension plan that provides your government pension.

(i) If the last day of your government employment was after June 30, 2004 and on or before March 2, 2009, we will apply a transitional rule to reduce the last 60–month requirement under the following conditions:

(A) You worked 60 months in Federal, State, or local government employment covered by Social Security before March 2, 2004, and you worked at least 1 month of covered government employment after March 2, 2004, or

(B) You worked fewer than 60 months in government employment covered by Social Security on or before March 2, 2004 and you worked the remaining number of months needed to total 60 months after March 2, 2004. The months that you worked before or after March 2, 2004 do not have to be consecutive.

(ii) We will always reduce your monthly spouse's benefit if you receive a government pension based on noncovered employment and you later go back to work for a Federal, State, or local government, unless:

(A) Your final 60 months of Federal, State, or local government employment were covered by Social Security; and

(B) Both your earlier and later Federal, State, or local government employment were under the same pension plan.

(7) If you are a former Federal employee and you receive a government pension based on work that included at least 60 months in employment covered by Social Security in the period beginning January 1, 1988 and ending with the first month you became entitled to spouse's benefits, whether or not the 60 months are consecutive), and:

(i) You worked in the Civil Service Retirement System (CSRS), but switched after 1987 to either the Federal Employees Retirement System (FERS) or the Foreign Service Pension System; or

(ii) You worked in the legislative branch and left CSRS after 1987 or received a lump sum payment from CSRS or another retirement system after 1987.

(8) You were a State or local government employee, or a Federal employee who worked in the CSRS but switched to the FERS before 1988, your last day of service was in covered employment, and

(i) You filed for spouse's benefits before April 1, 2004 and became entitled to benefits based on that filing, or

(ii) Your last day of service was before July 1, 2004,

(c) The one-half support test. For a man to meet the January 1977 requirement as provided in the exception in paragraph (b)(2) and for a man or a woman to meet the exception in paragraph (b)(3) of this section, he or she must meet a one-half support test. One-half support is defined in § 404.366 of this part. One-half support must be met at one of the following times:

(1) If the insured person had a period of disability which did not end before he or she became entitled to old-age or disability insurance benefits, or died, you must have been receiving at least one-half support from the insured either—

(i) At the beginning of his or her period of disability;

(ii) At the time he or she became entitled to old-age or disability insurance benefits; or

(iii) If deceased, at the time of his or her death.

(2) If the insured did not have a period of disability at the time of his or her entitlement or death, you must have been receiving at least one-half support from the insured either—

(i) At the time he or she became entitled to old-age insurance benefits; or

(ii) If deceased, at the time of his or her death.

(d) Amount and priority of reduction—

(1) Post–June 1983 government pensions.

(i) If you became eligible for a government pension after June 1983, and you do not meet one of the exceptions in paragraph (b) of this section, we will reduce (to zero, if necessary) your monthly Social Security spouse's benefits by two-thirds of the amount of your government pension.

(ii) If you earned part of your pension based on employment other than Federal, State, or local government employment, we will only use the part of your pension earned in government employment to compute the GPO.

(iii) If the reduction is not a multiple of 10 cents, we will round it to the next higher multiple of 10 cents.

(2) Pre–July 1983 government pensions.

(i) If you became eligible for a government pension before July 1983, and do not meet one of the exceptions in paragraph (b) of this section, we will reduce (to zero, if necessary) your monthly Social Security spouse's benefits as follows:

(A) By the full amount of your pension for months before December 1984; and

(B) By two-thirds the amount of your monthly pension for months after November 1984.

(ii) If the reduction is not a multiple of 10 cents, we will round it to the next higher multiple of 10 cents.

(3) Reductions for age and simultaneous entitlement. We will reduce your spouse's benefit, if necessary, for age and for simultaneous entitlement to other Social Security benefits before we reduce it because you are receiving a government pension. In addition, this reduction follows the order of priority stated in § 404.402(b).

(4) Reduction not a multiple of $1.00. If the monthly benefit payable to you after the required reduction(s) is not a multiple of $1.00, we will reduce it to the next lower multiple of $1.00 as required by § 404.304(f).

(5) Lump sum payments. If the government pension is not paid monthly or is paid in a lump sum, we will allocate the pension on a basis equivalent to a monthly benefit and then reduce the monthly Social Security benefit accordingly.

(i) We will generally obtain information about the number of years covered by a lump-sum payment from the pension plan.

(ii) If one of the alternatives to a lump-sum payment is a life annuity, and we can determine the amount of the monthly annuity, we will base the reduction on that monthly amount.

(iii) If the period or the equivalent monthly pension benefit is not clear, we may determine the reduction period and the equivalent monthly benefit on an individual basis.

(e) When effective. This reduction was put into the Social Security Act by the Social Security Amendments of 1977. It only applies to applications for benefits filed in or after December 1977 and only to benefits for December 1977 and later.

[44 FR 29047, May 18, 1979; 44 FR 36376, June 22, 1979; 49 FR 41245, Oct. 22, 1984; 49 FR 43951, Nov. 1, 1984; 49 FR 44458, Nov. 7, 1984; 49 FR 45420, Nov. 16, 1984; 50 FR 20902, May 21, 1985; 51 FR 23052, June 25, 1986; 60 FR 56513, Nov. 9, 1995; 80 FR 34050, June 15, 2015]

§ 404.408b Reduction of retroactive monthly social security benefits where supplemental security income (SSI) payments were received for the same period.

(a) When reduction is required. We will reduce your retroactive social security benefits if—

(1) You are entitled to monthly social security benefits for a month or months before the first month in which those benefits are paid; and

(2) SSI payments (including federally administered State supplementary payments) which were made to you for the same month or months would have been reduced or not made if your social security benefits had been paid when regularly due instead of retroactively.

(b) Amount of reduction. Your retroactive monthly social security benefits will be reduced by the amount of the SSI payments (including federally administered State supplementary payments) that would not have been paid to you, if you had received your monthly social security benefits when they were regularly due instead of retroactively.

(c) Benefits subject to reduction. The reduction described in this section applies only to monthly social security benefits. Social security benefits which we pay to you for any month after you have begun receiving recurring monthly social security benefits, and for which you did not have to file a new application, are not subject to reduction. The lump-sum death payment, which is not a monthly benefit, is not subject to reduction.

(d) Refiguring the amount of the reduction. We will refigure the amount of the reduction if there are subsequent changes affecting your claim which relate to the reduction period described in paragraph (a) of this section. Refiguring is generally required where there is a change in your month of entitlement or the amount of your social security benefits or SSI payments (including federally administered State supplementary payments) for the reduction period.

(e) Reimbursement of reduced retroactive monthly social security benefits. The amount of the reduction will be—

(1) First used to reimburse the States for the amount of any federally administered State supplementary payments that would not have been made to you if the monthly social security benefits had been paid when regularly due instead of retroactively; and

(2) The remainder, if any, shall be covered into the general fund of the U.S. Treasury for the amount of SSI benefits that would not have been paid to you if the monthly social security benefits had been paid to you when regularly due instead of retroactively.

[47 FR 4988, Feb. 3, 1982]

§ 404.409 What is full retirement age?

Full retirement age is the age at which you may receive unreduced old-age, wife's, husband's, widow's, or widower's benefits. Full retirement age has been 65 but is being gradually raised to age 67 beginning with people born after January 1, 1938. See § 404.102 regarding determination of age.

(a) What is my full retirement age for old-age benefits or wife's or husband's benefits? You may receive unreduced old-age, wife's, or husband's benefits beginning with the month you attain the age shown.

If your birth date is:	Full retirement age is:
Before 1/2/1938	65 years.
1/2/1938—1/1/1939	65 years and 2 months.
1/2/1939—1/1/1940	65 years and 4 months.
1/2/1940—1/1/1941	65 years and 6 months.
1/2/1941—1/1/1942	65 years and 8 months.
1/2/1942—1/1/1943	65 years and 10 months.
1/2/1943—1/1/1955	66 years.
1/2/1955—1/1/1956	66 years and 2 months.
1/2/1956—1/1/1957	66 years and 4 months.
1/2/1957—1/1/1958	66 years and 6 months.
1/2/1958—1/1/1959	66 years and 8 months.
1/2/1959—1/1/1960	66 years and 10 months.
1/2/1960 and later	67 years.

(b) What is my full retirement age for widow's or widower's benefits? You may receive unreduced widow's or widower's benefits beginning with the month you attain the age shown.

If your birth date is:	Full retirement age is:
Before 1/2/1912	62 years.
1/2/1912—1/1/1940	65 years.
1/2/1940—1/1/1941	65 years and 2 months.
1/2/1941—1/1/1942	65 years and 4 months.
1/2/1942—1/1/1943	65 years and 6 months.
1/2/1943—1/1/1944	65 years and 8 months.
1/2/1944—1/1/1945	65 years and 10 months.
1/2/1945—1/1/1957	66 years.
1/2/1957—1/1/1958	66 years and 2 months.
1/2/1958—1/1/1959	66 years and 4 months.
1/2/1959—1/1/1960	66 years and 6 months.
1/2/1960—1/1/1961	66 years and 8 months.
1/2/1961—1/1/1962	66 years and 10 months.
1/2/1962 and later	67 years.

(c) Can I still retire before full retirement age? You may still elect early retirement. You may receive old-age, wife's or husband's benefits at age 62. You may receive widow's or widower's benefits at age 60. Those benefits will be reduced as explained in § 404.410.

[68 FR 4707, Jan. 30, 2003]

§ 404.410 How does SSA reduce my benefits when my entitlement begins before full retirement age?

Generally your old-age, wife's, husband's, widow's, or widower's benefits are reduced if entitlement begins before the month you attain full retirement age (as defined in § 404.409). However, your benefits as a wife or husband are not reduced for any month in which you have in your care a child of the worker on whose earnings record you are entitled. The child must be entitled to child's benefits. Your benefits as a widow or widower are not reduced below the benefit amount you would receive as a mother or father for any month in which you have in your care a child of the worker on whose record you are entitled. The child must be entitled to child's benefits. Subject to §§ 404.411 through 404.413, reductions in benefits are made in the amounts described.

(a) How does SSA reduce my old-age benefits? The reduction in your primary insurance amount is based on the number of months of entitlement prior to the month you attain full retirement age. The reduction is 5/9 of 1 percent for each of the first 36 months and 5/12 of 1 percent for each month in excess of 36.

Example: Alex's full retirement age for unreduced benefits is 65 years and 8 months. She elects to begin receiving benefits at age 62. Her primary insurance amount of $980.50 must be reduced because of her entitlement to benefits 44 months prior to full retirement age. The reduction is 36 months at 5/9 of 1 percent and 8 months at 5/12 of 1 percent.

980.50 x 36 x 5/9 x .01 = $196.10

980.50 x 8 x 5/12 x .01 = $ 32.68

The two added together equal a total reduction of $228.78. This amount is rounded to $228.80 (the next higher multiple of 10 cents) and deducted from the primary insurance amount. The resulting $751.70 is the monthly benefit payable.

(b) How does SSA reduce my wife's or husband's benefits? Your wife's or husband's benefits before any reduction (see §§ 404.304 and 404.333) are reduced first (if necessary) for the family maximum under § 404.403. They are then reduced based on the number of months of entitlement prior to the month you attain full retirement age. This does not include any month in which you have a child of the worker on whose earnings record you are entitled in your care. The child must be entitled to child benefits. The reduction is 25/36 of 1 percent for each of the first 36 months and 5/12 of 1 percent for each month in excess of 36.

Example: Sam is entitled to old-age benefits. His spouse Ashley elects to begin receiving wife's benefits at age 63. Her full retirement age for unreduced benefits is 65 and 4 months. Her benefit will be reduced for 28 months of entitlement prior to full retirement age. If her unreduced benefit is $412.40 the reduction will be $412.40 x 28 x 25/36 x .01. The resulting $80.18 is rounded to $80.20 (the next higher multiple of 10 cents) and subtracted from $412.40 to determine the monthly benefit amount of $332.20.

(c) How does SSA reduce my widow's or widower's benefits?

Your entitlement to widow's or widower's benefits may begin at age 60 based on age or at age 50 based on disability. Refer to § 404.335 for more information on the requirements for entitlement. Both types are reduced if entitlement begins prior to attainment of full retirement age (as defined in § 404.409).

(1) Widow's or widower's benefits based on age. Your widow's or widower's unreduced benefit amount (the worker's primary insurance amount after any reduction for the family maximum under § 404.403), is reduced or further reduced based on the number of months of entitlement prior to the month you attain full retirement age. This does not include any month in which you have in your care a child of the worker on whose earnings record you are entitled. The child must be entitled to child's benefits. The number of months of entitlement prior to full retirement age is multiplied by .285 and then divided by the number of months in the period beginning with the month of attainment of age 60 and ending with the month immediately before the month of attainment of full retirement age.

Example: Ms. Bogle is entitled to an unreduced widow benefit of $785.70 beginning at age 64. Her full retirement age for unreduced old-age benefits is 65 years and 4 months. She will receive benefits for 16 months prior to attainment of full retirement age. The number of months in the period from age 60 through full retirement age of 65 and 4 months is 64. The reduction in her benefit is $785.70 x 16 x .285 divided by 64 or $55.98. $55.98 is rounded to the next higher multiple of 10 cents ($56.00) and subtracted from $785.70. The result is a monthly benefit of $729.70.

(2) Widow's or widower's benefits based on disability.

(i) For months after December 1983, your widow's or widower's benefits are not reduced for months of entitlement prior to age 60. You are deemed to be age 60 in your month of entitlement to disabled widow's or widower's benefits and your benefits are reduced only under paragraph (c)(1) of this section.

(ii) For months from January 1973 through December 1983, benefits as a disabled widow or widower were reduced under paragraph (c)(1) of this section. The benefits were then subject to an additional reduction of 43/240 of one percent for each month of entitlement prior to age 60 based on disability.

(3) Widow's or widower's benefits prior to 1973. For months prior to January 1973 benefits as a widow or widower were reduced only for months of entitlement prior to age 62. The reduction was 5/9 of one percent for each month of entitlement from the month of attainment of age 60 through the month prior to the month of attainment of age 62. There was an additional reduction of 43/198 of one percent for each month of entitlement prior to age 60 based on disability.

(d) If my benefits are reduced under this section does SSA ever change the reduction? The reduction computed under paragraphs (a), (b) or (c) of this section may later be adjusted to eliminate reduction for certain months of entitlement prior to full retirement age as provided in § 404.412. For special provisions on reducing benefits for months prior to full retirement age involving entitlement to two or more benefits, see § 404.411.

(e) Are my widow's or widower's benefits affected if the deceased worker was entitled to old-age benefits? If the deceased individual was entitled to old-age benefits, see § 404.338 for special rules that may affect your reduced widow's or widower's benefits.

[40 FR 30815, July 23, 1975; 48 FR 46149, Oct. 11, 1983; 49 FR 24116, June 12, 1984; 68 FR 4708, Jan. 30, 2003]

§ 404.411 How are benefits reduced for age when a person is entitled to two or more benefits?

(a) What is the general rule? Except as specifically provided in this section, benefits of an individual entitled to more than one benefit will be reduced for months of entitlement before full retirement age (as defined in § 404.409) according to the provisions of § 404.410. Such age reductions are made before any reduction under the provisions of § 404.407.

(b) How is my disability benefit reduced after entitlement to an old-age benefit or widow's or widower's benefit? A person's disability benefit is reduced following entitlement to an old-age or widow's or widower's benefit (or following the month in which all conditions for entitlement to the widow's or widower's benefit are met except that the individual is entitled to an old-age benefit which equals or exceeds the primary insurance amount on which the widow's or widower's benefit is based) in accordance with the following provisions:

(1) Individuals born January 2, 1928, or later whose disability began January 1, 1990, or later. When an individual is entitled to a disability benefit for a month after the month in which she or he becomes entitled to an old-age benefit which is reduced for age under § 404.410, the disability benefit is reduced by the amount by which the old-age benefit would be reduced under § 404.410 if she or he attained full retirement age in the first month of the most recent period of entitlement to the disability benefit.

(2) Individuals born January 2, 1928, or later whose disability began before January 1, 1990, and, all individuals born before January 2, 1928, regardless of when their disability began—

(i) First entitled to disability in or after the month of attainment of age 62. When an individual is first entitled to a disability benefit in or after the month in which she or he attains age 62 and for which she or he is first entitled to a widow's or widower's benefit (or would be so entitled except for entitlement to an equal or higher old-age benefit) before full retirement age, the disability benefit is reduced by the larger of:

(A) The amount the disability benefit would have been reduced under paragraph (b)(1) of this section; or

(B) The amount equal to the sum of the amount the widow's or widower's benefit would have been reduced under the provisions of § 404.410 if full retirement age for unreduced benefits were age 62 plus the amount by which the disability benefit would have been reduced under paragraph (b)(1) of this section if the benefit were equal to the excess of such benefit over the amount of the widow's or widower's benefit (without consideration of this paragraph).

(ii) First entitled to disability before age 62. When a person is first entitled to a disability benefit for a month before the month in which she or he attains age 62 and she or he is also entitled to a widow's or widower's benefit (or would be so entitled except for entitlement to an equal or higher old-age benefit), the disability benefit is reduced as if the widow or widower attained full retirement age in the first month of her or his most recent period of entitlement to the disability benefits.

(c) How is my old-age benefit reduced after entitlement to a widow's or widower's benefit?—

(1) Individual born after January 1, 1928. The old-age benefit is reduced in accordance with § 404.410(a). There is no further reduction.

(2) Individual born before January 2, 1928. The old-age benefit is reduced if, in the first month of entitlement, she or he is also entitled to a widow's or widower's benefit to which she or he was first entitled for a month before attainment of full retirement age or if, before attainment of full retirement age, she or he met

all conditions for entitlement to widow's or widower's benefits in or before the first month for which she or he was entitled to old-age benefits except that the old-age benefit equals or exceeds the primary insurance amount on which the widow's or widower's benefit would be based. Under these circumstances, the old-age benefit is reduced by the larger of the following:

(i) The amount by which the old-age benefit would be reduced under the regular age reduction provisions of § 404.410; or

(ii) An amount equal to the sum of:

(A) The amount by which the widow's or widower's benefit would be reduced under § 404.410 for months prior to age 62; and

(B) The amount by which the old-age benefit would be reduced under § 404.410 if it were equal to the excess of the individual's primary insurance amount over the widow's or widower's benefit before any reduction for age (but after any reduction for the family maximum under § 404.403).

(d) How is my wife's or husband's benefit reduced when I am entitled to a reduced old-age benefit in the same month? When a person is first entitled to a wife's or husband's benefit in or after the month of attainment of age 62, that benefit is reduced if, in the first month of entitlement, she or he is also entitled to an old-age benefit (but is not entitled to a disability benefit) to which she or he was first entitled before attainment of full retirement age. Under these circumstances, the wife's or husband's benefit is reduced by the sum of:

(1) The amount by which the old-age benefit would be reduced under the provisions of § 404.410; and

(2) The amount by which the spouse benefit would be reduced under the provisions of § 404.410 if it were equal to the excess of such benefit (before any reduction for age but after reduction for the family maximum under § 404.403) over the individual's own primary insurance amount.

(e) How is my wife's or husband's or widow's or widower's benefit reduced when I am entitled to a reduced disability benefit in the same month? When a person is first entitled to a spouse or widow's or widower's benefit in or after the month of attainment of age 62 (or in the case of widow's or widower's benefits, age 50) that benefit is reduced if, in the first month of entitlement to that benefit, he or she is also entitled to a reduced disability benefit. Under these circumstances, the wife's or husband's or widow's or widower's benefit is reduced by the sum of:

(1) The amount (if any) by which the disability benefit is reduced under paragraph (b)(1) of this section, and

(2) The amount by which the wife's or husband's or widow's or widower's benefit would be reduced under § 404.410 if it were equal to the excess of such benefit (before any reduction for age but after reduction for the family maximum under § 404.403) over the disability benefit (before any reduction under paragraph (b) of this section).

[40 FR 30816, July 23, 1975; 55 FR 50551, Dec. 7, 1990; 68 FR 4709, Jan. 30, 2003]

§ 404.412 After my benefits are reduced for age when and how will adjustments to that reduction be made?

(a) When may adjustment be necessary? The following months are not counted for purposes of reducing benefits in accordance with § 404.410;

(1) Months subject to deduction under § 404.415 or § 404.417;

(2) In the case of a wife's or husband's benefit, any month in which she or he had a child of the insured individual in her or his care and for which the child was entitled to child's benefits;

(3) In the case of a wife's or husband's benefit, any month for which entitlement to such benefits is precluded because the insured person's disability ceased (and, as a result, the insured individual's entitlement to disability benefits ended);

(4) In the case of a widow's or widower's benefit, any month in which she or he had in her or his care a child of the deceased insured individual and for which the child was entitled to child's benefits;

(5) In the case of a widow's or widower's benefit, any month before attainment of full retirement age for which she or he was not entitled to such benefits;

(6) In the case of an old-age benefit, any month for which the individual was entitled to disability benefits.

(b) When is the adjustment made? We make automatic adjustments in benefits to exclude the months of entitlement described in paragraphs (a)(1) through (6) of this section from consideration when determining the amount by which such benefits are reduced. Each year we examine beneficiary records to identify when an individual has attained full retirement age and one or more months described in paragraphs (a)(1) through (6) of this section occurred prior to such age during the period of entitlement to benefits reduced for age. Increases in benefit amounts based upon this adjustment are effective with the month of attainment of full retirement age. In the case of widow's or widower's benefits, this adjustment is made in the month of attainment of age 62 as well as the month of attainment of full retirement age.

[40 FR 30817, July 23, 1975; 49 FR 24117, June 12, 1984; 68 FR 4710, Jan. 30, 2003; 68 FR 40122, July 7, 2003]

§ 404.413 After my benefits are reduced for age what happens if there is an increase in my primary insurance amount?

(a) What is the general rule on reduction of increases? After an individual's benefits are reduced for age under §§ 404.410 through 404.411, the primary insurance amount on which such benefits are based may subsequently be increased because of a recomputation, a general benefit increase pursuant to an amendment of the Act, or increases based upon a rise in the cost-of-living under section 215(i) of the Social Security Act. When the primary insurance amount increases the monthly benefit amount also increases.

(b) How are subsequent increases in the primary insurance amount reduced after 1977? After 1977, when an individual's benefits have been reduced for age and the benefit is increased due to an increase in the primary insurance amount, the amount of the increase to which the individual is entitled is proportionately reduced as provided in paragraph (c) of this section. The method of reduction is determined by whether entitlement to reduced benefits began before 1978 or after 1977. When an individual is entitled to more than one benefit which is reduced for age, the rules for reducing the benefit increases apply to each reduced benefit.

(c) How is the reduction computed for increases after 1977?—

(1) Entitlement to reduced benefits after 1977. If an individual becomes entitled after 1977 to a benefit reduced for age, and the primary insurance amount on which the reduced benefit is based is increased, the amount of the increase payable to the individual is reduced by the same percentage as we use to reduce the benefit in the month of initial entitlement. Where the reduced benefit of an individual has been adjusted at full retirement age (age 62 and full retirement age for widows or widowers), any increase to which the individual becomes entitled thereafter is reduced by the adjusted percentage.

(2) Entitlement to reduced benefits before 1978. For an individual, who became entitled to a benefit reduced for age before 1978, whose benefit may be increased as a result of an increase in the primary insurance amount after 1977, we increase the amount of the benefit by the same percentage as the increase in the primary insurance amount.

(d) How was the reduction computed for increases prior to 1978? When the individual's primary insurance amount increased, the amount of the increase was reduced separately under §§ 404.410 and 404.411. The separate reduction was based on the number of months from the effective date of the increase through the month of attainment of age 65. This reduced increase amount was then added to the reduced benefit that was in effect in the month before the effective date of the increase. The result was the new monthly benefit amount.

[40 FR 30817, July 23, 1975, as amended at 43 FR 33706, Aug. 1, 1978; 68 FR 4710, Jan. 30, 2003]

§ 404.415 Deductions because of excess earnings.

(a) Deductions because of insured individual's earnings. Under the annual earnings test, we will reduce your monthly benefits (except disability insurance benefits based on the beneficiary's disability) by the amount of your excess earnings (as described in § 404.434), for each month in a taxable year (calendar year or fiscal year) in which you are under full retirement age (as defined in § 404.409(a)).

(b) Deductions from husband's, wife's, and child's benefits because of excess earnings of the insured individual. We will reduce husband's, wife's, and child's insurance benefits payable (or deemed payable—see § 404.420) on the insured individual's earnings record because of the excess earnings of the insured individual. However, beginning with January 1985, we will not reduce the benefits payable to a divorced wife or a divorced husband who has been divorced from the insured individual for at least 2 years.

(c) Deductions because of excess earnings of beneficiary other than the insured. If benefits are payable to you (or deemed payable—see § 404.420) on the earnings record of an insured individual and you have excess earnings (as described in § 404.430) charged to a month, we will reduce only your benefits for that month under the annual earnings test. Child's insurance benefits payable by reason of being disabled will be evaluated using Substantial Gainful Activity guidelines (as described in § 404.1574 or § 404.1575). This deduction equals the amount of the excess earnings. (See § 404.434 for charging of excess earnings where both the insured individual and you, a beneficiary, have excess earnings.)

[32 FR 19159, Dec. 20, 1967, as amended at 38 FR 9428, Apr. 16, 1973; 43 FR 8132, Feb. 28, 1978; 48 FR 4281, Jan. 31, 1983; 51 FR 11912, April 8, 1986; 70 FR 28811, May 19, 2005]

§ 404.416 [Reserved]

[70 FR 28811, May 19, 2005]

§ 404.417 Deductions because of noncovered remunerative activity outside the United States; 45 hour and 7–day work test.

(a) Deductions because of individual's activity—

(1) Prior to May 1983. For months prior to May 1983, a 7–day work test applies in a month before benefit deductions are made for noncovered remunerative activity outside the United States. A deduction is made from any monthly benefit (except disability insurance benefits, child's insurance benefits based on the child's disability, or widow's or widower's insurance benefits based on the widow's or widower's disability) payable to an individual for each month in a taxable year beginning after December 1954 in which the

beneficiary, while under age 72 (age 70 after December 1982), engages in noncovered remunerative activity (see § 404.418) outside the United States on 7 or more different calendar days. The deduction is for an amount equal to the benefit payable to the individual for that month.

(2) From May 1983 on. Effective May 1983, a 45–hour work test applies before a benefit deduction is made for the non-covered remunerative activity performed outside the United States in a month by the type of beneficiary described in paragraph (a)(1) of this section.

(b) Deductions from benefits because of the earnings or work of an insured individual—

(1) Prior to September 1984. Where the insured individual entitled to old-age benefits works on 7 or more days in a month prior to September 1984 while under age 72 (age 70 after December 1982), a deduction is made for that month from any:

(i) Wife's, husband's, or child's insurance benefit payable on the insured individual's earnings record; and

(ii) Mother's, father's, or child's insurance benefit based on child's disability, which under § 404.420 is deemed payable on the insured individual's earnings record because of the beneficiary's marriage to the insured individual.

(2) From September 1984 on. Effective September 1984, a benefit deduction is made for a month from the benefits described in paragraph (b)(1) of this section only if the insured individual, while under age 70, has worked in excess of 45 hours in that month.

(3) Amount of deduction. The amount of the deduction required by this paragraph (b) is equal to the wife's, husband's or child's benefit.

(4) From January 1985 on. Effective January 1985, no deduction will be made from the benefits payable to a divorced wife or a divorced husband who has been divorced from the insured individual for at least 2 years.

[32 FR 19159, Dec. 20, 1967, as amended at 38 FR 9429, April 16, 1973; 48 FR 4282, Jan. 31, 1983; 49 FR 24117, June 12, 1984; 51 FR 11912, April 8, 1986; 52 FR 26145, July 13, 1987]

§ 404.418 "Noncovered remunerative activity outside the United States," defined.

An individual is engaged in noncovered remunerative activity outside the United States for purposes of deductions described in § 404.417 if:

(a) He performs services outside the United States as an employee and the services do not constitute employment as defined in subpart K of this part and, for taxable years ending after 1955, the services are not performed in the active military or naval service of the United States; or

(b) He carries on a trade or business outside the United States (other than the performance of services as an employee) the net income or loss of which is not includable in computing his net earnings from self-employment (as defined in § 404.1050) for a taxable year and would not be excluded from net earnings from self-employment (see § 404.1052) if the trade or business were carried on in the United States. When used in the preceding sentence with respect to a trade or business, the term United States does not include the Commonwealth of Puerto Rico, the Virgin Islands and, with respect to taxable years beginning after 1960, Guam or American Samoa, in the case of an alien who is not a resident of the United States (including the Commonwealth of Puerto Rico, the Virgin Islands and, with respect to taxable years beginning after 1960, Guam and American Samoa), and the term trade or business shall have the same meaning as when used in section 162 of the Internal Revenue Code of 1954.

§ 404.420 Persons deemed entitled to benefits based on an individual's earnings record.

For purposes of imposing deductions under the annual earnings test (see § 404.415) and the foreign work test (see § 404.417), a person who is married to an old-age insurance beneficiary and who is entitled to a mother's or father's insurance benefit or a child's insurance benefit based on the child's disability (and all these benefits are based on the earnings record of some third person) is deemed entitled to such benefit based on the earnings record of the old-age insurance beneficiary to whom he or she is married. This section is effective for months in any taxable year of the old-age insurance beneficiary that begins after August 1958.

[49 FR 24117, June 12, 1984]

§ 404.421 How are deductions made when a beneficiary fails to have a child in his or her care?

Deductions for failure to have a child in care (as defined in subpart D of this part) are made as follows:

(a) Wife's or husband's benefit. A deduction is made from the wife's or husband's benefits to which he or she is entitled for any month if he or she is under full retirement age and does not have in his or her care a child of the insured entitled to child's benefits. However, a deduction is not made for any month in which he or she is age 62 or over, but under full retirement age, and there is in effect a certificate of election for him or her to receive actuarially reduced wife's or husband's benefits for such month (see subpart D of this part).

(b) Mother's or father's benefits—

(1) Widow or widower. A deduction is made from the mother's or father's benefits to which he or she is entitled as the widow or widower (see subpart D of this

part) of the deceased individual upon whose earnings such benefit is based, for any month in which he or she does not have in his or her care a child who is entitled to child's benefits based on the earnings of the deceased insured individual.

(2) Surviving divorced mother or father. A deduction is made from the mother's or father's benefits to which he or she is entitled as the surviving divorced mother or father (see subpart D of this part) of the deceased individual upon whose earnings record such benefit is based, for any month in which she or he does not have in care a child of the deceased individual who is her or his son, daughter, or legally adopted child and who is entitled to child's benefits based on the earnings of the deceased insured individual.

(c) Amount to be deducted. The amount deducted from the benefits, as described in paragraphs (a) and (b) of this section, is equal to the amount of the benefits which is otherwise payable for the month in which she or he does not have a child in his or her care.

(d) When a child is considered not entitled to benefits. For purposes of paragraphs (a) and (b) of this section, a person is considered not entitled to child's benefits for any month in which she or he is age 18 or over and is entitled to child's benefits because she or he is a full-time student at an educational institution. This paragraph applies to benefits for months after December 1964.

[49 FR 24117, June 12, 1984; 68 FR 4710, Jan. 30, 2003; 68 FR 40122, July 7, 2003]

§ 404.422 [Reserved]

[68 FR 40122, July 7, 2003]

§ 404.423 Manner of making deductions.

Deductions provided for in §§ 404.415, 404.417, and 404.421 (as modified in § 404.458) are made by withholding benefits (in whole or in part, depending upon the amount to be withheld) for each month in which an event causing a deduction occurred. If the amount to be deducted is not withheld from the benefits payable in the month in which the event causing the deduction occurred, such amount constitutes a deduction overpayment and is subject to adjustment or recovery in accordance with the provisions of subpart F of this part.

[68 FR 40122, July 7, 2003]

§ 404.424 Total amount of deductions where more than one deduction event occurs in a month.

If more than one of the deduction events specified in §§ 404.415, 404.417, and 404.421 occurred in any 1 month, each of which would occasion a deduction equal to the benefit for such month, only an amount equal to such benefit is deducted.

§ 404.425 Total amount of deductions where deduction events occur in more than 1 month.

If a deduction event described in §§ 404.415, 404.417, and 404.421 occurs in more than 1 month, the total amount deducted from an individual's benefits is equal to the sum of the deductions for all months in which any such event occurred.

[68 FR 40122, July 7, 2003]

§ 404.428 Earnings in a taxable year.

(a) When we apply the annual earnings test to your earnings as a beneficiary under this subpart (see § 404.415), we count all of your earnings (as defined in § 404.429) for all months of your taxable year even though you may not be entitled to benefits during all months of that year. (See § 404.430 for the rule that applies to the earnings of a beneficiary who attains full retirement age (as described in § 404.409(a))).

(b) Your taxable year is presumed to be a calendar year until you show to our satisfaction that you have a different taxable year. If you are self-employed, your taxable year is a calendar year unless you have a different taxable year for the purposes of subtitle A of the Internal Revenue Code of 1986. In either case, the number of months in a taxable year is not affected by:

(1) The date a claim for Social Security benefits is filed;

(2) Attainment of any particular age;

(3) Marriage or the termination of marriage; or

(4) Adoption.

(c) The month of death is counted as a month of the deceased beneficiary's taxable year in determining whether the beneficiary had excess earnings for the year under § 404.430. For beneficiaries who die after November 10, 1988, we use twelve as the number of months to determine whether the beneficiary had excess earnings for the year under § 404.430.

(d) Wages, as defined in § 404.429(c), are charged as earnings for the months and year in which you rendered the services. Net earnings or net losses from self-employment count as earnings or losses in the year for which such earnings or losses are reportable for Federal income tax purposes.

[32 FR 19159, Dec. 20, 1967, as amended at 43 FR 53714, Nov. 17, 1978; 45 FR 48116, July 18, 1980; 48 FR 4282, Jan. 31, 1983; 55 FR 37461, Sept. 12, 1990; 70 FR 28811, May 19, 2005]

§ 404.429 Earnings; defined.

(a) General. The term "earnings" as used in this subpart (other than as a part of the phrase "net earnings from self-employment") includes the sum of your wages for services rendered in a taxable year, plus your net earnings from self-employment for the taxable year, minus any net loss from self-employment for the same taxable year.

(b) Net earnings or net loss from self-employment. Your net earnings or net loss from self-employment are determined under the provisions in subpart K of this part, except that:

(1) In this section, the following occupations are included in the definition of "trade or business" (although they may be excluded in subpart K):

(i) The performance of the functions of a public office;

(ii) The performance of a service of a duly ordained, commissioned, or licensed minister of a church in the exercise of his or her ministry or by a member of a religious order in the exercise of duties required by the order;

(iii) The performance of service by an individual in the exercise of his or her profession as a Christian Science practitioner;

(iv) The performance by an individual in the exercise of his or her profession as a doctor of medicine, lawyer, dentist, osteopath, veterinarian, chiropractor, naturopath, or optometrist.

(2) For the sole purpose of the earnings test under this subpart:

(i) If you reach full retirement age, as defined in § 404.409(a), on or before the last day of your taxable year, you will have excluded from your gross earnings from self-employment, your royalties attributable to a copyright or patent obtained before the taxable year in which you reach full retirement age; and

(ii) If you are entitled to insurance benefits under title II of the Act, other than disability insurance benefits or child's insurance benefits payable by reason of being disabled, we will exclude from gross earnings any self-employment income you received in a year after your initial year of entitlement that is not attributable to services you performed after the first month you became entitled to benefits. In this section, services means any significant work activity you performed in the operation or management of a trade, profession, or business which can be related to the income received. If a part of the income you receive in a year is not related to any significant services you performed after the month of initial entitlement, only that part of your income may be excluded from gross earnings for deduction purposes. We count the balance of the income for deduction purposes. Your royalties or other self-employment income is presumed countable for purposes of the earnings test until it is shown to our satisfaction that such income may be excluded under this section.

(3) We do not count as significant services:

(i) Actions you take after the initial month of entitlement to sell a crop or product if it was completely produced in or before the month of entitlement. This rule does not apply to income you receive from a trade or business of buying and selling products produced or made by others; for example, a grain broker.

(ii) Your activities to protect an investment in a currently operating business or activities that are too irregular, occasional, or minor to be considered as having a bearing on the income you receive, such as—

(A) Hiring an agent, manager, or other employee to operate the business;

(B) Signing contracts where your signature is required, so long as the major contract negotiations were handled by others in running the business for you;

(C) Looking over the company's financial records to assess the effectiveness of those agents, managers, or employees in running the business for you;

(D) Personally contacting an old and valued customer solely for the purpose of maintaining good will when such contact has a minimal effect on the ongoing operation of the trade or business; or

(E) Occasionally filling in for an agent, manager, or other employee or partner in an emergency.

(4) In figuring your net earnings or net loss from self-employment, we count all net income or net loss even though:

(i) You did not perform personal services in carrying on the trade or business;

(ii) The net profit was less than $400;

(iii) The net profit was in excess of the maximum amount creditable to your earnings record; or

(iv) The net profit was not reportable for social security tax purposes.

(5) Your net earnings from self-employment is the excess of gross income over the allowable business deductions (allowed under the Internal Revenue Code). Net loss from self-employment is the excess of business deductions (that are allowed under the Internal Revenue Code) over gross income. You cannot deduct, from wages or net earnings from self-employment, expenses in connection with the production of income excluded from gross income under paragraph (b)(2)(ii) of this section.

(c) Wages. Wages include the gross amount of your wages rather than the net amount paid after deductions by your employer for items such as taxes and insurance. Wages are defined in subpart K of this part, except that we also include the following types of wages that are excluded in subpart K:

(1) Remuneration in excess of the amounts in the annual wage limitation table in § 404.1047;

(2) Wages of less than the amount stipulated in section § 404.1057 that you receive in a calendar year for domestic service in the private home of your em-

ployer, or service not in the course of your employer's trade or business;

(3) Payments for agricultural labor excluded under § 404.1055;

(4) Remuneration, cash and non-cash, for service as a home worker even though the cash remuneration you received is less than the amount stipulated in § 404.1058(a) in a calendar year;

(5) Services performed outside the United States in the Armed Forces of the United States.

(d) Presumptions concerning wages. For purposes of this section, when reports received by us show that you received wages (as defined in paragraph (c) of this section) during a taxable year, it is presumed that they were paid to you for services rendered in that year unless you present evidence to our satisfaction that the wages were paid for services you rendered in another taxable year. If a report of wages shows your wages for a calendar year, your taxable year is presumed to be a calendar year for purposes of this section unless you present evidence to our satisfaction that your taxable year is not a calendar year.

[32 FR 19159, Dec. 20, 1967, as amended at 41 FR 13912, Apr. 1, 1976; 47 FR 6001, Feb. 10, 1982; 47 FR 13792, Apr. 1, 1982; 47 FR 46690, Oct. 20, 1982; 52 FR 8249, March 17, 1987; 57 FR 44097, Sept. 24, 1992; 57 FR 59913, Dec. 17, 1992; 70 FR 28812, May 19, 2005]

§ 404.430 Monthly and annual exempt amounts defined; excess earnings defined.

(a) Monthly and annual exempt amounts.

(1) The earnings test monthly and annual exempt amounts are the amounts of wages and self-employment income which you, as a Social Security beneficiary, may earn in any month or year without part or all of your monthly benefit being deducted because of excess earnings. The monthly exempt amount, (which is 1/12 of the annual exempt amount), applies only in a beneficiary's grace year or years. (See § 404.435(a) and (b)). The annual exempt amount applies to the earnings of each non-grace taxable year prior to the year of full retirement age, as defined in § 404.409(a). A larger "annual" exempt amount applies to the total earnings of the months in the taxable year that precedes the month in which you attain full retirement age. The full annual exempt amount applies to the earnings of these pre-full retirement age months, even though they are earned in less than a year. For beneficiaries using a fiscal year as a taxable year, the exempt amounts applicable at the end of the fiscal year apply.

(2) We determine the monthly exempt amounts for each year by a method that depends on the type of exempt amount. In each case, the exempt amount so determined must be greater than or equal to the corresponding exempt amount in effect for months in the taxable year in which the exempt amount determination is being made.

(i) To calculate the lower exempt amount (the one applicable before the calendar year of attaining full retirement age) for any year after 1994, we multiply $670 (the lower exempt amount for 1994) by the ratio of the national average wage index for the second prior year to that index for 1992. If the amount so calculated is not a multiple of $10, we round it to the nearest multiple of $10 (i.e., if the amount ends in $5 or more, we round up, otherwise we round down). The annual exempt amount is then 12 times the rounded monthly exempt amount.

(ii) The higher exempt amount (the one applicable in months of the year of attaining full retirement age (as defined in section 404.409(a)) that precede such attainment) was set by legislation (Public Law 104–121) for years 1996–2002. To calculate the higher exempt amount for any year after 2002, we multiply $2,500 (the higher exempt amount for 2002) by the ratio of the national average wage index for the second prior year to that index for 2000. We round the result as described in paragraph (a)(2)(i) of this section for the lower exempt amount.

(iii) The following are the annual and monthly exempt amounts for taxable years 2000 through 2005.

Year	For years through taxable year preceding year of reaching full retirement age		Months of taxable year prior to month of full of retirement age	
	Reduction: $1 for every $2 over the exempt amount		Reduction: $1 for every $3 over the exempt amount	
	Annual	Monthly	Annual	Monthly
2000	$10,080	$840	$17,000	$1,417
2001	10,680	890	25,000	2,084
2002	11,280	940	30,000	2,500
2003	11,520	960	30,720	2,560
2004	11,640	970	31,080	2,590
2005	12,000	1,000	31,800	2,650

(b) Method of determining excess earnings for years after December 1999. If you have not yet reached your year of full retirement age, your excess earnings for a taxable year are 50 percent of your earnings (as described in § 404.429) that are above the exempt amount. After December 31, 1999, in the taxable year in which you will reach full retirement age (as defined in § 404.409(a)), the annual (and monthly, if applicable) earnings limit applies to the earnings of the months prior to the month in which you reach full retirement age. Excess earnings are 33 ⅓ percent of the earnings above the annual exempt amount. Your earnings after reaching the month of full retirement age are not subject to the earnings test.

[40 FR 42865, Sept. 17, 1975; 40 FR 45805, Oct. 3, 1975, as amended at 45 FR 48117, July 18, 1980; 45 FR 58107, Sept. 2, 1980; 48 FR 4282, Jan. 31, 1983; 55 FR 37461, Sept. 12, 1990; 62 FR 38450, July 18, 1997; 70 FR 28813, May 19, 2005]

§ 404.434 Excess earnings; method of charging.

(a) Months charged. If you have not yet reached your year of full retirement age, and if your estimated earnings for a year result in estimated excess earnings (as described in § 404.430), we will charge these excess earnings to your full benefit each month from the beginning of the year, until all of the estimated excess earnings have been charged. Excess earnings, however, are not charged to any month described in §§ 404.435 and 404.436.

(b) Amount of excess earnings charged—

(1) Insured individual's excess earnings. For each $1 of your excess earnings we will decrease by $1 the benefits to which you and all others are entitled (or deemed entitled—see § 404.420) on your earnings record. (See § 404.439 where the excess earnings for a month are less than the total benefits payable for that month.) (See 404.415(b) for the effect on divorced wife's and divorced husband's benefits.)

(2) Excess earnings of beneficiary other than insured individual. We will charge a beneficiary, other than the insured, $1 for each $1 of the beneficiary's excess earnings (see § 404.437). These excess earnings, however, are charged only against that beneficiary's own benefits.

(3) You, the insured individual, and a person entitled (or deemed entitled) on your earnings record both have excess earnings. If both you and a person entitled (or deemed entitled) on your earnings record have excess earnings (as described in § 404.430), your excess earnings are charged first against the total family benefits payable (or deemed payable) on your earnings record, as described in paragraph (b)(1) of this section. Next, the excess earnings of a person entitled on your earnings record are charged against his or her own benefits remaining after part of your excess earnings have been charged against his/her benefits (because of the reduction in the total family benefits payable). See § 404.441 for an example of this process and the manner in which partial monthly benefits are apportioned.

(c) Earnings test applicability. Public Law 106–182 eliminated the Social Security earnings test, beginning with the month in which a person attains full retirement age (as defined in § 404.409(a)), for taxable years after 1999. In the year that you reach full retirement age, the annual earnings test amount is applied to the earnings amounts of the months that precede your month of full retirement age. (See § 404.430). The reduction rate for these months is $1 of benefits for every $3 you earned above the earnings limit in these months. The earnings threshold amount will be increased in conjunction with increases in average wages.

[32 FR 19159, Dec. 20, 1967, as amended at 38 FR 17716, July 3, 1973; 43 FR 8133, Feb. 28, 1978; 70 FR 28813, May 19, 2005]

§ 404.435 Excess earnings; months to which excess earnings can or cannot be charged; grace year defined.

(a) Monthly benefits payable. We will not reduce your benefits on account of excess earnings for any month in which you, the beneficiary—

(1) Were not entitled to a monthly benefit;

(2) Were considered not entitled to benefits (due to non-covered work outside the United States or no child in care, as described in § 404.436);

(3) Were at full retirement age (as described in § 404.409(a));

(4) Were entitled to payment of a disability insurance benefit as defined in § 404.315; (see § 404.1592 and § 404.1592a(b) which describes the work test if you are entitled to disability benefits);

(5) Are age 18 or over and entitled to a child's insurance benefit based on disability;

(6) Are entitled to a widow's or widower's insurance benefit based on disability; or

(7) Had a non-service month in your grace year (see paragraph (b) of this section). A non-service month is any month in which you, while entitled to retirement or survivors benefits:

(i) Do not work in self-employment (see paragraphs (c) and (d) of this section);

(ii) Do not perform services for wages greater than the monthly exempt amount set for that month (see paragraph (e) of this section and § 404.430); and

(iii) Do not work in non-covered remunerative activity on 7 or more days in a month while outside the United States. A non-service month occurs even if there are no excess earnings in the year.

(b) Grace year defined.

(1) A beneficiary's initial grace year is the first taxable year in which the beneficiary has a non-service month (see paragraph (a)(7) of this section) in or after the month in which the beneficiary is entitled to a retirement, auxiliary, or survivor's benefit.

(2) A beneficiary may have another grace year each time his or her entitlement to one type of benefit ends and, after a break in entitlement of at least one month, the beneficiary becomes entitled to a different type of retirement or survivors benefit. The new grace year would then be the taxable year in which the first non-service month occurs after the break in entitlement.

(3) For purposes of determining whether a given year is a beneficiary's grace year, we will not count as a non-service month, a month that occurred while the beneficiary was entitled to disability benefits under section 223 of the Social Security Act or as a disabled widow, widower, or child under section 202.

(4) A beneficiary entitled to child's benefits, to spouse's benefits before age 62 (entitled only by reason of having a child in his or her care), or to mother's or father's benefits is entitled to a termination grace year in any year the beneficiary's entitlement to these types of benefits terminates. This provision does not apply if the termination is because of death or if the beneficiary is entitled to a Social Security benefit for the month following the month in which the entitlement ended. The beneficiary is entitled to a termination grace year in addition to any other grace year(s) available to him or her.

Example 1: Don, age 62, will retire from his regular job in April of next year. Although he will have earned $15,000 for January–April of that year and plans to work part time, he will not earn over the monthly exempt amount after April. Don's taxable year is the calendar year. Since next year will be the first year in which he has a non-service month while entitled to benefits, it will be his grace year and he will be entitled to the monthly earnings test for that year only. He will receive benefits for all months in which he does not earn over the monthly exempt amount (May–December) even though his earnings have substantially exceeded the annual exempt amount. However, in the years that follow, up to the year of full retirement age, only the annual earnings test will be applied if he has earnings that exceed the annual exempt amount, regardless of his monthly earnings amounts.

Example 2: Marion was entitled to mother's insurance benefits from 1998 because she had a child in her care. Because she had a non-service month in 1998, 1998 was her initial grace year. Marion's child turned 16 in May 2000, and the child's benefits terminated in April 2000. Marion's entitlement to mother's benefits also terminated in April 2000. Since Marion's entitlement did not terminate by reason of her death and she was not entitled to another type of Social Security benefit in the month after her entitlement to a mother's benefit ended, she is entitled to a termination grace year for 2000, the year in which her entitlement to mother's insurance benefits terminated. She applied for and became entitled to widow's insurance benefits effective February 2001. Because there was a break in entitlement to benefits of at least one month before entitlement to another type of benefit, 2001 will be a subsequent grace year if Marion has a non-service month in 2001.

(c) You worked in self-employment. You are considered to have worked in self-employment in any month in which you performed substantial services (see § 404.446) in the operation of a trade or business (or in a combination of trades and businesses if there are more than one), as an owner or partner even though you had no earnings or net earnings resulting from your services during the month.

(d) Presumption regarding work in self-employment. You are presumed to have worked in self-employment in each month of your taxable year until you show to our satisfaction that in a particular month you did not perform substantial services (see § 404.446(c)) in any trades and businesses from which you derived your annual net income or loss (see § 404.429).

(e) Presumption regarding services for wages. You are presumed to have performed services in any month for wages (as defined in § 404.429) of more than the applicable monthly exempt amount in each month of the year, until you show to our satisfaction that you did not perform services for wages in that month that exceeded the monthly exempt amount.

[45 FR 48117, July 18, 1980, as amended at 47 FR 6001, Feb. 10, 1982; 47 FR 46691, Oct. 20, 1982; 48 FR 4282, Jan. 31, 1983; 68 FR 40123, July 7, 2003; 70 FR 28814, May 19, 2005]

§ 404.436 Excess earnings; months to which excess earnings cannot be charged because individual is deemed not entitled to benefits.

Under the annual earnings test, excess earnings (as described in § 404.430) are not charged to any month in which an individual is deemed not entitled to a benefit. A beneficiary (i.e., the insured individual or any person entitled or deemed entitled on the individual's earnings record) is deemed not entitled to a benefit for a month if he is subject to a deduction for that month because of:

(a) Engaging in noncovered remunerative activity outside the United States (as described in §§ 404.417 and 404.418); or

(b) Failure to have a child in his or her care (as described in § 404.421).

[32 FR 19159, Dec. 20, 1967, as amended at 38 FR 9429, April 16, 1973; 38 FR 17716, July 3, 1973; 43 FR 8133, Feb. 28, 1978; 68 FR 40123, July 7, 2003]

§ 404.437 Excess earnings; benefit rate subject to deductions because of excess earnings.

We will further reduce your benefits (other than a disability insurance benefit) because of your excess earnings (see § 404.430), after your benefits may have been reduced because of the following:

(a) The family maximum (see §§ 404.403 and 404.404), which applies to entitled beneficiaries remaining after exclusion of beneficiaries deemed not entitled under § 404.436 (due to a deduction for engaging in non-covered remunerative activity outside the United States or failure to have a child in one's care);

(b) Your entitlement to benefits (see § 404.410) for months before you reach full retirement age (see § 404.409(a)) (this applies only to old-age, wife's, widow's, widower's or husband's benefits);

(c) Your receipt of benefits on your own earnings record, which reduces (see § 404.407) your entitlement (or deemed entitlement; see § 404.420) to benefits on another individual's earnings record; and

(d) Your entitlement to benefits payable (or deemed payable) to you based on the earnings record of an individual entitled to a disability insurance benefit because of that individual's entitlement to workers' compensation (see § 404.408).

[32 FR 19159, Dec. 20, 1967, as amended at 38 FR 17716, July 3, 1973; 43 FR 8133, Feb. 28, 1978; 68 FR 40123, July 7, 2003; 70 FR 28814, May 19, 2005]

§ 404.439 Partial monthly benefits; excess earnings of the individual charged against his benefits and the benefits of persons entitled (or deemed entitled) to benefits on his earnings record.

Deductions are made against the total family benefits where the excess earnings (as described in § 404.430) of an individual entitled to old-age insurance benefits are charged to a month and require deductions in an amount less than the total family benefits payable on his earnings record for that month (including the amount of a mother's or child's insurance benefit payable to a spouse who is deemed entitled on the individual's earnings record—see § 404.420). The difference between the total benefits payable and the deductions made under the annual earnings test for such month is paid (if otherwise payable under title II of the Act) to each person in the proportion that the benefit to which each is entitled (before the application of the reductions described in § 404.403 for the family maximum, § 404.407 for entitlement to more than one type of benefit, and section 202(q) of the Act for entitlement to benefits before retirement age) and before the application of § 404.304(f) to round to the next lower dollar bears to the total of the benefits to which all of them are entitled, except that the total amount payable to any such person may not exceed the benefits which would have been payable to that person if none of the insured individual's excess earnings had been charged to that month.

Example: A is entitled to an old-age insurance benefit of $165 and his wife is entitled to $82.50 before rounding, making a total of $247.50. After A's excess earnings have been charged to the appropriate months, there remains a partial benefit of $200 payable for October, which is apportioned as follows:

	Original benefit	Fraction of original	Benefit [1]
A.	$165	⅔	$133
Wife	82.50	⅓	66
Total	247.50	....	199

[1] After deductions for excess earnings and after rounding per § 404.304(f).

[38 FR 9429, Apr. 16, 1973, as amended at 38 FR 17717, July 3, 1973; 43 FR 8133, Feb. 28, 1978; 48 FR 46149, Oct. 11, 1983]

§ 404.440 Partial monthly benefits; pro-rated share of partial payment exceeds the benefit before deduction for excess earnings.

Where, under the apportionment described in § 404.439, a person's prorated share of the partial benefit exceeds the benefit rate to which he was entitled before excess earnings of the insured individual were charged, such person's share of the partial benefit is reduced to the amount he would have been paid had there been no deduction for excess earnings (see example). The remainder of the partial benefit is then paid to other persons eligible to receive benefits in the proportion that the benefit of each such other person bears to the total of the benefits to which all such other persons are entitled (before reduction for the family maximum). Thus, if only two beneficiaries are involved, payment is made to one as if no deduction had been imposed; and the balance of the partial benefit is paid to the other. If three or more beneficiaries are involved, however, reapportionment of the excess of the beneficiary's share of the partial benefit over the amount he would have been paid without the deduction is made in proportion to his original entitlement rate (before reduction for the family maximum). If the excess amount involved at any point totals less than $1, it is not reapportioned; instead, each beneficiary is paid on the basis of the last calculation.

Example: Family maximum is $150. Insured individual's excess earnings charged to the month are $25. The remaining $125 is prorated as partial payment.

	Original benefit	Fraction of original total benefit	Benefit after deductions for excess earnings but before reduction for family maximum	Benefit reduced for maximum but without deductions for excess earnings	Benefit payable after both deductions and reductions (and rounded)
Insured Individual	$100	⅖	50	100.00	75
Wife	50	⅕	25	16.60	16
Child	50	⅕	25	16.60	16
Child	50	⅕	25	16.60	16

[48 FR 46149, Oct. 11, 1983]

§ 404.441 Partial monthly benefits; insured individual and another person entitled (or deemed entitled) on the same earnings record both have excess earnings.

Where both the insured individual and another person entitled (or deemed entitled) on the same earnings record have excess earnings (as described in § 404.430), their excess earnings are charged, and their partial monthly benefit is apportioned, as follows:

Example: M and his wife are initially entitled to combined total benefits of $264 per month based on M's old-age insurance benefit of $176. For the taxable year in question, M's excess earnings were $1,599 and his wife's excess earnings were $265. Both were under age 65. M had wages of more than $340 in all months of the year except February, while his wife had wages of more than $340 in all months of the year. After M's excess earnings have been charged to the appropriate months (all months through July except February), there remains a partial benefit payment for August of $249, which is allocated to M and his wife in the ratio that the original benefit of each bears to the sum of their original benefits: $166 and $83. His wife's excess earnings are charged against her full benefit for February ($88), her partial benefit for August ($83), her full benefit for September, and from $6 of her October benefit, leaving an $82 benefit payable to her for that month.

[38 FR 9430, Apr. 16, 1973, as amended at 38 FR 17717, July 3, 1973; 43 FR 8133, Feb. 28, 1978; 48 FR 46149, Oct. 11, 1983]

§ 404.446 Definition of "substantial services" and "services."

(a) General. In general, the substantial services test will be applicable only in a grace year (including a termination grace year) as defined in § 404.435(c)(1). It is a test of whether, in view of all the services rendered by the individual and the surrounding circumstances, the individual reasonably can be considered retired in the month in question. In determining whether an individual has or has not performed substantial services in any month, the following factors are considered:

(1) The amount of time the individual devoted to all trades and businesses;

(2) The nature of the services rendered by the individual;

(3) The extent and nature of the activity performed by the individual before he allegedly retired as compared with that performed thereafter;

(4) The presence or absence of an adequately qualified paid manager, partner, or family member who manages the business;

(5) The type of business establishment involved;

(6) The amount of capital invested in the trade or business; and

(7) The seasonal nature of the trade or business.

(b) Individual engaged in more than one trade or business. When an individual, in any month, performs services in more than one trade or business, his services in all trades or businesses are considered together in determining whether he performed substantial services in self-employment in such month.

(c) Evidentiary requirements. An individual who alleges that he did not render substantial services in any month, or months, shall submit detailed information about the operation of the trades or businesses, including the individual's activities in connection therewith. When requested to do so by the Administration, the individual shall also submit such additional statements, information, and other evidence as the Administration may consider necessary for a proper determination of whether the individual rendered substantial services in self-employment. Failure of the individual to submit the requested statements, information, and other evidence is a sufficient basis for a determination that the individual rendered substantial services in self-employment during the period in question.

[32 FR 19159, Dec. 20, 1967, as amended at 47 FR 6002, Feb. 10, 1982; 47 FR 46691, Oct. 20, 1982]

§ 404.447 Evaluation of factors involved in substantial services test.

In determining whether an individual's services are substantial, consideration is given to the following factors:

(a) Amount of time devoted to trades or businesses. Consideration is first given to the amount of time the self-employed individual devotes to all trades or businesses, the net income or loss of which is includable in computing his earnings as defined in § 404.429. For the purposes of this paragraph, the time devoted to a trade or business includes all the time spent by the individual in any activity, whether physical or mental, at the place of business or elsewhere in furtherance of such trade or business. This includes the time spent in advising and planning the operation of the business, making business contacts, attending meetings, and preparing and maintaining the facilities and records of the business. All time spent at the place of business which cannot reasonably be considered unrelated to business activities is considered time devoted to the trade or business. In considering the weight to be given to the time devoted to trades or businesses the following rules are applied:

(1) Forty-five hours or less in a month devoted to trade or business. Where the individual establishes that the time devoted to his trades and businesses during a calendar month was not more than 45 hours, the individual's services in that month are not considered substantial unless other factors (see paragraphs (b), (c), and (d) of this section) make such a finding unreasonable. For example, an individual who worked only 15 hours in a month might nevertheless be found to have rendered substantial services if he was manag-

ing a sizable business or engaging in a highly skilled occupation. However, the services of less than 15 hours rendered in all trades and businesses during a calendar month are not substantial.

(2) More than 45 hours in a month devoted to trades and businesses. Where an individual devotes more than 45 hours to all trades and businesses during a calendar month, it will be found that the individual's services are substantial unless it is established that the individual could reasonably be considered retired in the month and, therefore, that such services were not, in fact, substantial.

(b) Nature of services rendered. Consideration is also given to the nature of the services rendered by the individual in any case where a finding that the individual was retired would be unreasonable if based on time alone (see paragraph (a) of this section). The more highly skilled and valuable his services in self-employment are, the more likely the individual rendering such services could not reasonably be considered retired. The performance of services regularly also tends to show that the individual has not retired. Services are considered in relation to the technical and management needs of the business in which they are rendered. Thus, skilled services of a managerial or technical nature may be so important to the conduct of a sizable business that such services would be substantial even though the time required to render the services is considerably less than 45 hours.

(c) Comparison of services rendered before and after retirement. Where consideration of the amount of time devoted to a trade or business (see paragraph (a) of this section) and the nature of services rendered (see paragraph (b) of this section) is not sufficient to establish whether an individual's services were substantial, consideration is given to the extent and nature of the services rendered by the individual before his retirement, as compared with the services performed during the period in question. A significant reduction in the amount or importance of services rendered in the business tends to show that the individual is retired; absence of such reduction tends to show that the individual is not retired.

(d) Setting in which services performed. Where consideration of the factors described in paragraphs (a), (b), and (c) of this section is not sufficient to establish that an individual's services in self-employment were or were not substantial, all other factors are considered. The presence or absence of a capable manager, the kind and size of the business, the amount of capital invested and whether the business is seasonal, as well as any other pertinent factors, are considered in determining whether the individual's services are such that he can reasonably be considered retired.

§ 404.450 Required reports of work outside the United States or failure to have care of a child.

(a) Beneficiary engaged in noncovered remunerative activity; report by beneficiary. Any individual entitled to a benefit which is subject to a deduction in that month because of noncovered remunerative activity outside the United States (see § 404.417) shall report the occurrence of such an event to the Social Security Administration before the receipt and acceptance of a benefit for the second month following the month in which such event occurred.

(b) Beneficiary receiving wife's, husband's, mother's or father's insurance benefits does not have care of a child; report by beneficiary. Any person receiving wife's, husband's, mother's, or father's insurance benefits which are subject to a deduction (as described in § 404.421) because he or she did not have a child in his or her care shall report the occurrence of such an event to the Social Security Administration before the receipt and acceptance of a benefit for the second month following the month in which the deduction event occurred.

(c) Report required by person receiving benefits on behalf of another. Where a person is receiving benefits on behalf of a beneficiary (see subpart U of this part) it is his duty to make the report to the Administration required by paragraph (a) or (b) of this section, on behalf of the beneficiary.

(d) Report; content and form. A report required under the provisions of this section shall be filed with the Social Security Administration. (See § 404.614 of this part for procedures concerning place of filing and date of receipt of such a report.) The report should be made on a form prescribed by the Administration and in accordance with instructions, printed thereon or attached thereto, as prescribed by the Administration. Prescribed forms may be obtained at any office of the Administration. If the prescribed form is not used, the report should be properly identified (e.g., show the name and social security claim number of the beneficiary about whom the report is made), describe the events being reported, tell when the events occurred, furnish any other pertinent data (e.g., who has care of the children), and be properly authenticated (e.g., bear the signature and address of the beneficiary making the report or the person reporting on his behalf). The report should contain all the information needed for a proper determination of whether a deduction applies and, if it does, the period for which such deductions should be made.

[49 FR 24117, June 12, 1984; 51 FR 10616, March 28, 1986; 65 FR 16813, March 30, 2000]

§ 404.451 Penalty deductions for failure to report within prescribed time limit noncovered remunerative activity outside the United States or not having care of a child.

(a) Penalty for failure to report. If an individual (or the person receiving benefits on his behalf) fails to comply with the reporting obligations of § 404.450 within the time specified in § 404.450 and it is found that good cause for such failure does not exist (see § 404.454), a penalty deduction is made from the individual's benefits in addition to the deduction described in § 404.417 (relating to noncovered remunerative activity outside the United States) or § 404.421 (relating to failure to have care of a child).

(b) Determining amount of penalty deduction. The amount of the penalty deduction for failure to report noncovered remunerative activity outside the United States or not having care of a child within the prescribed time is determined as follows:

(1) First failure to make timely report. The penalty deduction for the first failure to make a timely report is an amount equal to the individual's benefit or benefits for the first month for which the deduction event was not reported timely.

(2) Second failure to make timely report. The penalty deduction for the second failure to make a timely report is an amount equal to twice the amount of the individual's benefit or benefits for the first month for which the deduction event in the second failure period was not reported timely.

(3) Subsequent failures to make timely reports. The penalty deduction for the third or subsequent failure to file a timely report is an amount equal to three times the amount of the individual's benefit or benefits for the first month for which the deduction event in the third failure period was not reported timely.

(c) Determining whether a failure to file a timely report is first, second, third, or subsequent failure—

(1) Failure period. A failure period runs from the date of one delinquent report (but initially starting with the date of entitlement to monthly benefits) to the date of the next succeeding delinquent report, excluding the date of the earlier report and including the date of the later report. The failure period includes each month for which succeeding delinquent report, excluding a report becomes overdue during a failure period, but it does not include any month for which a report is not yet overdue on the ending date of such period. If good cause (see § 404.454) is found for the entire period, the period is not regarded as a failure period.

(2) First failure. When no penalty deduction under paragraph (b) of this section has previously been imposed against the beneficiary for failure to report noncovered remunerative activity outside the United States or for failure to report not having care of a child, the earliest month in the first failure period for which a report is delinquent and for which good cause (see § 404.454) for failure to make the required report is not found is considered to be the first failure.

(3) Second failure. After one penalty deduction under paragraph (b) of this section has been imposed against the beneficiary, the first month for which a report is delinquent in the second failure period is considered to be the second failure.

(4) Third and subsequent failures. After a second penalty deduction under paragraph (b) of this section has been imposed against the beneficiary, the first month for which a report is delinquent in the third failure period is considered to be the third failure. Subsequent failures will be determined in the same manner.

Example: M became entitled in January 1966 to mother's benefits; these benefits are not payable for any month in which the mother does not have a child in her care. M accepted benefits for each month from January 1966 through June 1967. In July 1967 she reported that she had not had a child in her care in January 1967. As she was not eligible for a benefit for any month in which she did not have a child in her care, M's July 1967 benefit was withheld to recover the overpayment she had received for January 1967, and the next payment she received was for August 1967. No penalty was imposed for her failure to make a timely report of the deduction event that occurred in January 1967 because it was determined that good cause existed.

In March 1968 M reported that she had not had a child in her care in September or October 1967; however, she had accepted benefit payments for each month from August 1967 through February 1968. Her benefits for March and April 1968 were withheld to recover the overpayment for September and October 1967. Also, it was determined that good cause was not present for M's failure to make a timely report of the deduction event that had occurred in September 1967. A penalty equal to her benefit for September 1967 was deducted from M's May 1968 payment since this was her first failure to report not having a child in her care. Payments to her then were continued.

On November 4, 1968, it was learned that M had not had a child in her care in November 1967 or in June, July, or August 1968 although she had accepted benefits for June through October 1968. Consequently, M's benefits for November 1968 through February 1969 were withheld to recover the 4 months' overpayment she received for months in which she did not have a child in her care. In addition, it was determined that good cause was not present for M's failure to report the deduction events, and a penalty was imposed equal to twice the amount of M's benefit for the month of June 1968. This was M's second failure to report not having a child in her care. No further penalty applied for November 1967 because that month was included in M's first-failure period.

(5) Penalty deductions imposed under § 404.453 not considered. A failure to make a timely report of earnings as required by § 404.452 for which a penalty deduction is imposed under § 404.453 is not counted as a failure to report in determining the first or subsequent failure to report noncovered remunerative activity outside the United States or not having care of a child.

(d) Limitation on amount of penalty deduction. Notwithstanding the provisions described in paragraph (b) of this section, the amount of the penalty deduction imposed for failure to make a timely report of noncovered remunerative activity outside the United States or for failure to report not having care of a child may not exceed the number of months in that failure period for which the individual received and accepted a benefit and for which a deduction is imposed by reason of his noncovered remunerative activity outside the United States or failure to have care of a child. (See § 404.458 for other limitations on the amount of the penalty deduction.)

[38 FR 3596, Feb. 8, 1973, as amended at 38 FR 9430, Apr. 16, 1973]

§ 404.452 Reports to Social Security Administration of earnings; wages; net earnings from self-employment.

(a) Reporting requirements and conditions under which a report of earnings, that is, wages and/or net earnings from self-employment, is required.

(1) If you have not reached full retirement age (see § 404.409(a)) and you are entitled to a monthly benefit, other than only a disability insurance benefit, you are required to report to us the total amount of your earnings (as defined in § 404.429) for each taxable year. This report will enable SSA to pay you accurate benefits and avoid both overpayments and underpayments.

(2) If your wages and/or net earnings from self-employment in any month(s) of the year are below the allowable amount (see §§ 404.446 and 404.447), your report should include this information in order to establish your grace year (see § 404.435) and possible eligibility for benefits for those months.

(3) Your report to us for a taxable year should be filed on or before the 15th day of the fourth month following the close of the taxable year; for example, April 15 when the beneficiary's taxable year is a calendar year. An income tax return or form W–2, filed timely with the Internal Revenue Service, may serve as the report required to be filed under the provisions of this section, where the income tax return or form W–2 shows the same wages and/or net earnings from self-employment that must be reported to us. Although we may accept W–2 information and special payment information from employers, you still have primary responsibility for making sure that the earnings we use for deduction purposes are correct. If there is a valid reason for a delay, we may grant you an extension of up to 4 months to file this report.

(4) You are not required to report to us if:

(i) You reached full retirement age before the first month of your entitlement to benefits; or

(ii) Your benefit payments were suspended under the provisions described in § 404.456 for all months of a taxable year before the year of full retirement age, or for all months prior to your full retirement age in the full retirement age year, unless you are entitled to benefits as an auxiliary or survivor and your benefits are reduced for any month in the taxable year because of earnings and there is another person entitled to auxiliary or survivor's benefits on the same record, but living in a different household.

(b) Report required by person receiving benefits on behalf of another. When you receive benefits as a representative payee on behalf of a beneficiary (see subpart U of this part), it is your duty to report any earnings of the beneficiary to us.

(c) Information required. If you are the beneficiary, your report should show your name, address, Social Security number, the taxable year for which the report is made, and the total amount of your wages and/or net earnings from self employment during the taxable year. If you are a representative payee, your report should show the name, address, and Social Security number of the beneficiary, the taxable year for which the report is made, and the total earnings of the beneficiary, as well as your name, address, and Social Security number.

(d) Requirement to furnish requested information. You, the beneficiary (or the person reporting on his/her behalf) are required to furnish any other information about earnings and services that we request for the purpose of determining the correct amount of benefits payable for a taxable year (see § 404.455).

(e) Extension of time for filing report—

(1) Request for extension to file report. Your request for an extension of time, or the request of your authorized agent, must be in writing and must be filed at a Social Security Administration office before your report is due. Your request must include the date, your name, the Social Security number of the beneficiary, the name and Social Security number of the person filing the request if other than the beneficiary, the year for which your report is due, the amount of additional time requested, the reason why you require this extension (see § 404.454), and your signature.

(2) Evidence that extension of time has been granted. If you do not receive written approval of an extension of time for making your report of earnings, it will be presumed that no extension of time was granted. In such case, if you do not file on time, you will need to establish that you had good cause (§ 404.454) for filing your report after the normal due date.

[32 FR 19159, Dec. 20, 1967, as amended at 38 FR 9430, April 16, 1973; 43 FR 8133, Feb. 28, 1978; 51 FR 10616, March 28, 1986; 60 FR 56513, Nov. 9, 1995; 62 FR 15610, April 2, 1997; 70 FR 28815, May 19, 2005]

§ 404.453 Penalty deductions for failure to report earnings timely.

(a) Penalty for failure to report earnings; general. Penalty deductions are imposed against an individual's benefits, in addition to the deductions required because of his excess earnings (see § 404.415), if:

(1) He fails to make a timely report of his earnings as specified in § 404.452 for a taxable year beginning after 1954;

(2) It is found that good cause for failure to report earnings timely (see § 404.454) does not exist;

(3) A deduction is imposed because of his earnings (see § 404.415) for that year; and

(4) He received and accepted any payment of benefits for that year.

(b) Determining amount of penalty deduction. The amount of the penalty deduction for failure to report earnings for a taxable year within the prescribed time is determined as follows:

(1) First failure to file timely report. The penalty deduction for the first failure to file a timely report is an amount equal to the individual's benefit or benefits for the last month for which he was entitled to such benefit or benefits during the taxable year, except that with respect to any deductions imposed on or after January 2, 1968, if the amount of the deduction imposed for the taxable year is less than the benefit or benefits for the last month of the taxable year for which he was entitled to a benefit under section 202 of the Act, the penalty deduction is an amount equal to the amount of the deduction imposed but not less than $10.

(2) Second failure to file timely report. The penalty deduction for the second failure to file a timely report is an amount equal to twice the amount of the individual's benefit or benefits for the last month for which he was entitled to such benefit or benefits during such taxable year.

(3) Subsequent failures to file timely reports. The penalty deduction for the third or subsequent failure to file a timely report is an amount equal to three times the amount of the individual's benefit or benefits for the last month for which he was entitled to such benefit or benefits during such taxable year.

(c) Determining whether a failure to file a timely report is first, second, or subsequent failure—

(1) No prior failure. Where no penalty deduction under this section has previously been imposed against the beneficiary for failure to make a timely report of his earnings, all taxable years (and this may include 2 or more years) for which a report of earnings is overdue as of the date the first delinquent report is made are included in the first failure. The latest of such years for which good cause for failure to make the required report (see § 404.454) is not found is considered the first failure to file a timely report.

Example: X became entitled to benefits in 1964 and had reportable earnings for 1964, 1965, and 1966. He did not make his annual reports for those years until July 1967. At that time it was found that 1966 was the only year for which he has good cause for not making a timely report of his earnings. Since all taxable years for which a report is overdue as of the date of the first delinquent report are included in the first failure period, it was found that his first failure to make a timely report was for 1965. The penalty is equal to his December 1965 benefit rate. If good cause had also been found for both 1965 and 1964, then X would have no prior failure within the meaning of this subsection.

(2) Second and subsequent failures. After one penalty deduction under paragraph (b) of this section has been imposed against an individual, each taxable year for which a timely report of earnings is not made (and the count commences with reports of earnings which become delinquent after the date the first delinquent report described in paragraph (c)(1) of this section was made), and for which good cause for failure to make the required report is not found, is considered separately in determining whether the failure is the second or subsequent failure to report timely.

Example: Y incurred a penalty deduction for not making his 1963 annual report until July 1964. In August 1966 it was found that he had not made a timely report of either his 1964 or 1965 earnings, and good cause was not present with respect to either year. The penalty for 1964 is equal to twice his benefit rate for December 1964. The penalty for 1965 is equal to three times his benefit rate for December 1965.

(3) Penalty deduction imposed under § 404.451 not considered. A failure to make a report as required by § 404.450, for which a penalty deduction is imposed under § 404.451, is not counted as a failure to report in determining, under this section, whether a failure to report earnings or wages is the first or subsequent failure to report.

(d) Limitation on amount of penalty deduction. Notwithstanding the provisions described in paragraph (b) of this section, the amount of the penalty deduction imposed for failure to file a timely report of earnings for a taxable year may not exceed the number of months in that year for which the individual received and accepted a benefit and for which deductions are imposed by reason of his earnings for such year. (See § 404.458 for other limitations on the amount of the penalty deduction.)

[32 FR 19159, Dec. 20, 1967, as amended at 38 FR 3597, Feb. 8, 1973; 38 FR 9431, Apr. 16, 1973]

§ 404.454 Good cause for failure to make required reports.

(a) General. The failure of an individual to make a timely report under the provisions described in §§ 404.450 and 404.452 will not result in a penalty deduction if the individual establishes to the satisfaction of the Administration that his failure to file a timely report was due to good cause. Before making any penalty determination as described in §§ 404.451 and 404.453, the individual shall be advised of the penalty and good cause provisions and afforded an opportunity to establish good cause for failure to report timely. The failure of the individual to submit evidence to establish good cause within a specified time may be considered a sufficient basis for a finding that good cause does not exist (see § 404.705). In determining whether good cause for failure to report timely has been established by the individual, consideration is given to whether the failure to report within the proper time limit was the result of untoward circumstances, misleading action of the Social Security Administration, confusion as to the requirements of the Act resulting from amendments to the Act or other legislation, or any physical, mental, educational, or linguistic limitations (including any lack of facility with the English language) the individual may have. For example, good cause may be found where failure to file a timely report was caused by:

(1) Serious illness of the individual, or death or serious illness in his immediate family;

(2) Inability of the individual to obtain, within the time required to file the report, earnings information from his employer because of death or serious illness of the employer or one in the employer's immediate family; or unavoidable absence of his employer; or destruction by fire or other damage of the employer's business records;

(3) Destruction by fire, or other damage, of the individual's business records;

(4) Transmittal of the required report within the time required to file the report, in good faith to another Government agency even though the report does not reach the Administration until after the period for reporting has expired;

(5) Unawareness of the statutory provision that an annual report of earnings is required for the taxable year in which the individual attained age 72 provided his earnings for such year exceeded the applicable amount, e.g., $1,680 for a 12-month taxable year ending after December 1967;

(6) Failure on the part of the Administration to furnish forms in sufficient time for an individual to complete and file the report on or before the date it was due, provided the individual made a timely request to the Administration for the forms;

(7) Belief that an extension of time for filing income tax returns granted by the Internal Revenue Service was also applicable to the annual report to be made to the Social Security Administration;

(8) Reliance upon a written report to the Social Security Administration made by, or on behalf of, the beneficiary before the close of the taxable year, if such report contained sufficient information about the beneficiary's earnings or work, to require suspension of his benefits (see § 404.456) and the report was not subsequently refuted or rescinded; or

(9) Failure of the individual to understand reporting responsibilities due to his or her physical, mental, educational, or linguistic limitation(s).

(b) Notice of determination. In every case in which it is determined that a penalty deduction should be imposed, the individual shall be advised of the penalty determination and of his reconsideration rights. If it is found that good cause for failure to file a timely report does not exist, the notice will include an explanation of the basis for this finding; the notice will also explain the right to partial adjustment of the overpayment, in accordance with the provisions of § 404.502(c).

(c) Good cause for subsequent failure. Where circumstances are similar and an individual fails on more than one occasion to make a timely report, good cause normally will not be found for the second or subsequent violation.

[38 FR 3597, Feb. 8, 1973, as amended at 43 FR 8133, Feb. 28, 1978; 59 FR 1634, Jan. 12, 1994]

§ 404.455 Request by Social Security Administration for reports of earnings and estimated earnings; effect of failure to comply with request.

(a) Request by Social Security Administration for report during taxable year; effect of failure to comply. The Social Security Administration may, during the course of a taxable year, request a beneficiary to estimate his or her earnings (as defined in § 404.429) for the current taxable year and for the next taxable year, and to furnish any other information about his or her earnings that the Social Security Administration may specify. If a beneficiary fails to comply with a request for an estimate of earnings for a taxable year, the beneficiary's failure, in itself, constitutes justification under section 203(h) of the Act for a determination that it may reasonably be expected that the beneficiary will have deductions imposed under the provisions described in § 404.415, due to his or her earnings for that taxable year. Furthermore, the failure of the beneficiary to comply with a request for an estimate of earnings for a taxable year will, in itself, constitute justification for the Social Security Administration to use the preceding taxable year's estimate of earnings (or, if available, reported earnings) to suspend payment of benefits for the current or next taxable year.

(b) Request by Social Security Administration for report after close of taxable year; failure to comply. After the close of his or her taxable year, the Social Security Administration may request a beneficiary to furnish a report of his or her earnings for the closed taxable year and to furnish any other information about his or her earnings for that year that the Social Security Administration may specify. If he or she fails to comply with this request, this failure shall, in itself, constitute justification under section 203(h) of the Act for a determination that the beneficiary's benefits are subject to deductions as described in § 404.415 for each month in the taxable year (or only for the months thereof specified by the Social Security Administration).

[56 FR 11373, March 18, 1991]

§ 404.456 Current suspension of benefits because an individual works or engages in self-employment.

(a) Circumstances under which benefit payments may be suspended. If, on the basis of information obtained by or submitted to the Administration, it is determined that an individual entitled to monthly benefits for any taxable year may reasonably be expected to have deductions imposed against his benefits (as described in § 404.415) by reason of his earnings for such year, the Administration may, before the close of the taxable year, suspend all or part, as the Administration may specify, of the benefits payable to the individual and to all other persons entitled (or deemed entitled—see § 404.420) to benefits on the basis of the individual's earnings record.

(b) Duration of suspension. The suspension described in paragraph (a) of this section shall remain in effect with respect to the benefits for each month until the Administration has determined whether or not any deduction under § 404.415 applies for such month.

(c) When suspension of benefits becomes final. For taxable years beginning after August 1958, if benefit payments were suspended (as described in paragraph (a) of this section) for all months of entitlement in an individual's taxable year, no benefit payment for any month in that year may be made after the expiration of the period of 3 years, 3 months, and 15 days following the close of the individual's taxable year unless, within that period, the individual, or any person entitled to benefits based on his earnings record, files with the Administration information showing that a benefit for a month is payable to the individual. Subject to the limitations of this paragraph, a determination about deductions may be reopened under the circumstances described in § 404.907.

[65 FR 16813, March 30, 2000]

§ 404.457 Deductions where taxes neither deducted from wages of certain maritime employees nor paid.

(a) When deduction is required. A deduction is required where:

(1) An individual performed services after September 1941 and before the termination of Title I of the First War Powers Act, 1941, on or in connection with any vessel as an officer or crew member; and

(2) The services were performed in the employ of the United States and employment was through the War Shipping Administration or, for services performed before February 11, 1942, through the United States Maritime Commission; and

(3) The services, under the provisions of § 404.1041 of this part, constituted employment for the purposes of title II of the Social Security Act; and

(4) The taxes imposed (by section 1400 of the Internal Revenue Code of 1939, as amended) with respect to such services were neither deducted from the individual's wages nor paid by the employer.

(b) Amount of deduction. The deduction required by paragraph (a) of this section is an amount equal to 1 percent of the wages with respect to which the taxes described in paragraph (a)(4) of this section were neither deducted nor paid by the employer.

(c) How deduction is made. The deduction required by paragraph (a) of this section is made by withholding an amount as determined under paragraph (b) of this section from any monthly benefit or lump-sum death payment based on the earnings record of the individual who performed the services described in paragraph (a) of this section.

[65 FR 16813, March 30, 2000]

§ 404.458 Limiting deductions where total family benefits payable would not be affected or would be only partly affected.

Notwithstanding the provisions described in §§ 404.415, 404.417, 404.421, 404.451, and 404.453 about the amount of the deduction to be imposed for a month, no such deduction is imposed for a month when the benefits payable for that month to all persons entitled to benefits on the same earnings record and living in the same household remain equal to the maximum benefits payable to them on that earnings record. Where making such deductions and increasing the benefits to others in the household (for the month in which the deduction event occurred) would give members of the household less than the maximum (as determined under § 404.404) payable to them, the amount of deduction imposed is reduced to the difference between the maximum amount of benefits payable to them and the total amount which would have been paid if the benefits of members of the household not subject to deductions were increased for that month. The individual subject to the deduction for such month may be paid the difference between the deduction so reduced and his benefit as adjusted under § 404.403 (without application of § 404.402(a)). All other persons in the household are paid, for such month, their benefits as adjusted under § 404.403 without application of § 404.402(a).

[32 FR 19159, Dec. 20, 1967, as amended at 47 FR 43673, Oct. 4, 1982; 68 FR 15659, April 1, 2003; 68 FR 40123, July 7, 2003]

§ 404.459 Penalty for making false or misleading statements or withholding information.

(a) Why would SSA penalize me? You will be subject to a penalty if:

(1) You make, or cause to be made, a statement or representation of a material fact, for use in determining any initial or continuing right to, or the amount of, monthly insurance benefits under title II or benefits or

payments under title XVI, that you know or should know is false or misleading; or

(2) You make a statement or representation of a material fact for use as described in paragraph (a)(1) of this section with knowing disregard for the truth; or

(3) You omit from a statement or representation made for use as described in paragraph (a)(1) of this section, or otherwise withhold disclosure (for example, fail to come forward to notify us) of, a fact which you know or should know is material to the determination of any initial or continuing right to, or the amount of, monthly insurance benefits under title II or benefits or payments under title XVI, if you know, or should know, that the statement or representation with such omission is false or misleading or that the withholding of such disclosure is misleading.

(b) *What is the penalty?* The penalty is nonpayment of benefits under title II that we would otherwise pay you and ineligibility for cash benefits under title XVI (including State supplementary payments made by SSA according to § 416.2005).

(c) *How long will the penalty last?* The penalty will last—

(1) Six consecutive months the first time we penalize you;

(2) Twelve consecutive months the second time we penalize you; and

(3) Twenty-four consecutive months the third or subsequent time we penalize you.

(d) *Will this penalty affect any of my other government benefits?* If we penalize you, the penalty will apply only to your eligibility for benefits under titles II and XVI (including State supplementary payments made by us according to § 416.2005). The penalty will not affect—

(1) Your eligibility for benefits that you would otherwise be eligible for under titles XVIII and XIX but for the imposition of the penalty; and

(2) The eligibility or amount of benefits payable under titles II or XVI to another person. For example, another person (such as your spouse or child) may be entitled to benefits under title II based on your earnings record. Benefits would still be payable to that person to the extent that you would be receiving such benefits but for the imposition of the penalty. As another example, if you are receiving title II benefits that are limited under the family maximum provision (§ 404.403) and we stop your benefits because we impose a penalty on you, we will not increase the benefits of other family members who are limited by the family maximum provision simply because you are not receiving benefits because of the penalty.

(e) *How will SSA make its decision to penalize me?* In order to impose a penalty on you, we must find that you knowingly (knew or should have known or acted with knowing disregard for the truth) made a false or misleading statement or omitted or failed to report a material fact if you knew, or should have known, that the omission or failure to disclose was misleading. We will base our decision to penalize you on the evidence and the reasonable inferences that can be drawn from that evidence, not on speculation or suspicion. Our decision to penalize you will be documented with the basis and rationale for that decision. In determining whether you knowingly made a false or misleading statement or omitted or failed to report a material fact so as to justify imposition of the penalty, we will consider all evidence in the record, including any physical, mental, educational, or linguistic limitations (including any lack of facility with the English language) which you may have had at the time. In determining whether you acted knowingly, we will also consider the significance of the false or misleading statement or omission or failure to disclose in terms of its likely impact on your benefits.

(f) *What should I do if I disagree with SSA's initial determination to penalize me?* If you disagree with our initial determination to impose a penalty, you have the right to request reconsideration of the penalty decision as explained in § 404.907. We will give you a chance to present your case, including the opportunity for a face-to-face conference. If you request reconsideration of our initial determination to penalize you, you have the choice of a case review, informal conference, or formal conference, as described in § 416.1413(a) through (c). If you disagree with our reconsidered determination you have the right to follow the normal administrative and judicial review process by requesting a hearing before an administrative law judge, Appeals Council review and Federal court review, as explained in § 404.900.

(g) *When will the penalty period begin and end?* Subject to the additional limitations noted in paragraphs (g)(1) and (g)(2) of this section, the penalty period will begin the first day of the month for which you would otherwise receive payment of benefits under title II or title XVI were it not for imposition of the penalty. Once a sanction begins, it will run continuously even if payments are intermittent. If more than one penalty has been imposed, but they have not yet run, the penalties will not run concurrently.

(1) If you do not request reconsideration of our initial determination to penalize you, the penalty period will begin no earlier than the first day of the second month following the month in which the time limit for requesting reconsideration ends. The penalty period will end on the last day of the final month of the penalty period. For example, if the time period for requesting reconsideration ends on January 10, a 6–month period of nonpayment begins on March 1 if you would otherwise be eligible to receive benefits for that month, and ends on August 31.

(2) If you request reconsideration of our initial determination to penalize you and the reconsidered determination does not change our original decision to penalize you, the penalty period will begin no earlier than the first day of the second month following the month we notify you of our reconsidered determination. The penalty period will end on the last day of the final month of the penalty period. For example, if we notify you of our reconsidered determination on August 31, 2001, and you are not otherwise eligible for payment of benefits at that time, but would again be eligible to receive payment of benefits on October 1, 2003, a 6–month period of nonpayment would begin on October 1, 2003 and end on March 31, 2004.

[65 FR 42283 on July 10, 2000; 67 FR 20893, April 29, 2002; 71 FR 61407, Oct. 18, 2006]

§ 404.460 Nonpayment of monthly benefits to aliens outside the United States.

(a) Nonpayment of monthly benefits to aliens outside the United States more than 6 months. Except as described in paragraph (b) and subject to the limitations in paragraph (c) of this section after December 1956 no monthly benefit may be paid to any individual who is not a citizen or national of the United States, for any month after the sixth consecutive calendar month during all of which he is outside the United States, and before the first calendar month for all of which he is in the United States after such absence.

(1) For nonpayment of benefits under this section, it is necessary that the beneficiary be an alien, and while an alien, be outside the United States for more than six full consecutive calendar months. In determining whether, at the time of a beneficiary's initial entitlement to benefits, he or she has been outside the United States for a period exceeding six full consecutive calendar months, not more than the six calendar months immediately preceding the month of initial entitlement may be considered. For the purposes of this section, outside the United States means outside the territorial boundaries of the 50 States, the District of Columbia, Puerto Rico, the Virgin Islands of the United States, Guam, American Samoa, and the Commonwealth of the Northern Mariana Islands.

(2) Effective with 6–month periods beginning after January 2, 1968, after an alien has been outside the United States for any period of 30 consecutive days, he is deemed to be outside the United States continuously until he has returned to the United States and remained in the United States for a period of 30 consecutive days.

(3) Payments which have been discontinued pursuant to the provisions of this section will not be resumed until the alien beneficiary has been in the United States for a full calendar month. A full calendar month includes 24 hours of each day of the calendar month.

(4) Nonpayment of benefits to an individual under this section does not cause nonpayment of benefits to other persons receiving benefits based on the individual's earnings record.

Example: R, an alien, leaves the United States on August 15, 1967, and returns on February 1, 1968. He leaves again on February 15, 1968, and does not return until May 15, 1968, when he spends 1 day in the United States. He has been receiving monthly benefits since July 1967.

R's first 6–month period of absence begins September 1, 1967. Since this period begins before January 2, 1968, his visit (Feb. 1, 1968, to Feb. 15, 1968) to the United States for less than 30 consecutive days is sufficient to break this 6–month period.

R's second 6–month period of absence begins March 1, 1968. Since this period begins after January 2, 1968, and he was outside the United States for 30 consecutive days, he must return and spend 30 consecutive days in the United States prior to September 1, 1968, to prevent nonpayment of benefits beginning September 1968. If R fails to return to the United States for 30 consecutive days prior to September 1, 1968, payments will be discontinued and will not be resumed until R spends at least 1 full calendar month in the United States.

(b) When nonpayment provisions do not apply. The provisions described in paragraph (a) of this section do not apply, subject to the limitations in paragraph (c) of this section, to a benefit for any month if:

(1) The individual was, or upon application would have been, entitled to a monthly benefit for December 1956, based upon the same earnings record; or

(2)(i) The individual upon whose earnings the benefit is based, before that month, has resided in the United States for a period or periods aggregating 10 years or more or has earned not less than 40 quarters of coverage;

(ii) Except that, effective with July 1968, § 404.460(b)(2)(i) does not apply if:

(A) The beneficiary is a citizen of a country with a social insurance or pension system meeting the conditions described in paragraphs (b)(7)(i), (ii), and (iii) of this section but does not meet the condition described in paragraph (b)(7)(iv) of this section; or

(B) The beneficiary is a citizen of a country with no social insurance or pension system of general application and at any time within 5 years before January 1968 (or the first month after December 1967 in which benefits are subject to suspension pursuant to paragraph (a) of this section) such beneficiary was residing in a country to which payments were withheld by the Treasury Department pursuant to Vol. II, 31 U.S.C. 3329. See § 404.460(c).

(iii) For purposes of this subparagraph a period of residence begins with the day the insured individual arrives in the United States with the intention of establishing at least a temporary home here; it continues so long as he maintains an attachment to an abode in the United States, accompanied by actual physical presence in the United States for a significant part of the period; and ends with the day of departure from the United States with the intention to reside elsewhere; or

(3) The individual is outside the United States while in the active military or naval service of the United States; or

(4) The individual on whose earnings the benefit is based died before that month and:

(i) Death occurred while the individual was on active duty or inactive duty training as a member of a uniformed service, or

(ii) Death occurred after the individual was discharged or released from a period of active duty or inactive duty training as a member of a uniformed service, and the Administrator of Veterans' Affairs determines, and certifies to the Commissioner, that the discharge or release was under conditions other than dishonorable and that death was as a result of a disease or injury incurred or aggravated in line of duty while on active duty or inactive duty training; or

(5) The individual on whose earnings record the benefit is based worked in service covered by the Railroad Retirement Act, and such work is treated as employment covered by the Social Security Act under the provisions described in subpart O of this part; or

(6) The nonpayment of monthly benefits under the provisions described in paragraph (a) of this section would be contrary to a treaty obligation of the United States in effect on August 1, 1956 (see § 404.463(b)); or

(7) The individual is a citizen of a foreign country that the Commissioner determines has in effect a social insurance or pension system (see § 404.463) which meets all of the following conditions:

(i) Such system pays periodic benefits or the actuarial equivalent thereof; and

(ii) The system is of general application; and

(iii) Benefits are paid in this system on account of old age, retirement, or death; and

(iv) Individuals who are citizens of the United States but not citizens of the foreign country and who qualify for such benefits are permitted to receive benefits without restriction or qualification, at their full rate, or the actuarial equivalent thereof, while outside of the foreign country and without regard to the duration of their absence therefrom.

(c) Nonpayment of monthly benefits to aliens residing in certain countries—

(1) Benefits for months after June 1968. Notwithstanding the provisions of paragraphs (a) and (b) of this section, we cannot pay monthly benefits for any month after June 1968 to anyone not a citizen or national of the United States for any month while residing in a country to which payments are being withheld by the Treasury Department pursuant to Vol. II, 31 U.S.C. 3329.

(2) Benefits for months before July 1968. If a person who is not a United States citizen or national is entitled to receive benefits under title II of the Social Security Act, and was residing in a country where the Treasury Department withheld benefits on June 30, 1968 pursuant to Vol. II, 31 U.S.C. 3329, benefits cannot be paid. However, if the Treasury Department subsequently removes that restriction, a person who is not a United States citizen or national may be able to be paid benefits to which they were entitled for months prior to July 1968. Benefits cannot be paid,—

(i) To any person other than such individual, or, if such individual dies before such benefits can be paid, to any person other than an individual who was entitled for the month in which the deceased individual died (with the application of section 202(j)(1) of the Social Security Act) to a monthly benefit under title II of such Act on the basis of the same wages and self-employment income as such deceased individual; or

(ii) In excess of an amount equal to the amount of the last 12 months' benefits that would have been payable to such individual.

(3) List of countries under Treasury Department alien payment restriction. The Treasury Department is currently withholding payments to persons residing in the following countries pursuant to Vol. II, 31 U.S.C. 3329. We will publish future additions to or deletions from the list of countries in the Federal Register: Cuba, North Korea.

(d) Nonpayment of monthly benefits to certain aliens entitled to benefits on a worker's earnings record. An individual who after December 31, 1984 becomes eligible for benefits on the earnings record of a worker for the first time, is an alien, has been outside the United States for more than 6 consecutive months, and is qualified to receive a monthly benefit by reason of the provisions of paragraphs (b)(2), (b)(3), (b)(5), or (b)(7) of this section, must also meet a U.S. residence requirement described in this section to receive benefits:

(1) An alien entitled to benefits as a child of a living or deceased worker—

(i) Must have resided in the U.S. for 5 or more years as the child of the parent on whose earnings record entitlement is based; or

(ii) The parent on whose earnings record the child is entitled and the other parent, if any, must each have either resided in the United States for 5 or more years or died while residing in the U.S.

(2) An alien who meets the requirements for child's benefits based on paragraph (d)(1) of this section above, whose status as a child is based on an adoptive relationship with the living or deceased worker, must also—

(i) Have been adopted within the United States by the worker on whose earnings record the child's entitlement is based; and

(ii) Have lived in the United States with, and received one-half support from, the worker for a period, beginning prior to the child's attainment of age 18, of

(A) At least one year immediately before the month in which the worker became eligible for old-age benefits or disability benefits or died (whichever occurred first), or

(B) If the worker had a period of disability which continued until the worker's entitlement to old-age or disability benefits or death, at least one year immediately before the month in which that period of disability began.

(3) An alien entitled to benefits as a spouse, surviving spouse, divorced spouse, surviving divorced spouse, or surviving divorced mother or father must have resided in the United States for 5 or more years while in a spousal relationship with the person on whose earnings record the entitlement is based. The spousal relationship over the required period can be that of wife, husband, widow, widower, divorced wife, divorced husband, surviving divorced wife, surviving divorced husband, surviving divorced mother, surviving divorced father, or a combination of two or more of these categories.

(4) An alien who is entitled to parent's benefits must have resided in the United States for 5 or more years as a parent of the person on whose earnings record the entitlement is based.

(5) Individuals eligible for benefits before January 1, 1985 (including those eligible for one category of benefits on a particular worker's earnings record after December 31, 1984, but also eligible for a different category of benefits on the same worker's earnings record before January 1, 1985), will not have to meet the residency requirement.

(6) Definitions applicable to paragraph (d) of this section are as follows:

Eligible for benefits means that an individual satisfies the criteria described in subpart D of this part for benefits at a particular time except that the person need not have applied for those benefits at that time.

Other parent for purposes of paragraph (d)(1)(ii) of this section means any other living parent who is of the opposite sex of the worker and who is the adoptive parent by whom the child was adopted before the child attained age 16 and who is or was the spouse of the person on whose earnings record the child is entitled; or the natural mother or natural father of the child; or the step-parent of the child by a marriage, contracted before the child attained age 16, to the natural or adopting parent on whose earnings record the child is entitled. (Note: Based on this definition, a child may have more than one living other parent. However, the child's benefit will be payable for a month if in that month he or she has one other parent who had resided in the U.S. for at least 5 years.)

Resided in the United States for satisfying the residency requirement means presence in the United States with the intention of establishing at least a temporary home. A period of residence begins upon arrival in the United States with that intention and continues so long as an attachment to an abode in the United States is maintained, accompanied by actual physical presence in the United States for a significant part of the period, and ending the day of departure from the United States with the intention to reside elsewhere. The period need not have been continuous and the requirement is satisfied if the periods of U.S. residence added together give a total of 5 full years.

(7) The provisions described in paragraph (d) of this section shall not apply if the beneficiary is a citizen or resident of a country with which the United States has a totalization agreement in force, except to the extent provided by that agreement.

[32 FR 19159, Dec. 20, 1967, as amended at 34 FR 13366, Aug. 19, 1969; 52 FR 8249, March 17, 1987; 52 FR 26145, July 13, 1987; 60 FR 17444, April 6, 1995; 62 FR 38450, July 18, 1997; 69 FR 51555, Aug. 20, 2004; 74 FR 48856, Sept. 25, 2009; 83 FR 21709, May 10, 2018]

§ 404.461 Nonpayment of lump sum after death of alien outside United States for more than 6 months.

Where an individual dies outside the United States after January 1957 and no monthly benefit was or could have been paid to him for the month preceding the month in which he died because of the provisions described in § 404.460, no lump-sum death payment may be made upon the basis of the individual's earnings record.

§ 404.462 Nonpayment of hospital and medical insurance benefits of alien outside United States for more than 6 months.

No payments may be made under part A (hospital insurance benefits) of title XVIII for items or services furnished to an individual in any month for which the prohibition described in § 404.460 against payment of benefits to an individual outside the United States for more than six full consecutive calendar months is applicable (or would be if he were entitled to any such benefits). Also, no payments may be made under part B (supplementary medical insurance benefits) of title XVIII for expenses incurred by an individual during any month the individual is not paid a monthly benefit by reason of the provisions described in § 404.460 or for which no monthly benefit would be paid if he were otherwise entitled thereto.

§ 404.463 Nonpayment of benefits of aliens outside the United States; "foreign social insurance system," and "treaty obligation" exceptions defined.

(a) Foreign social insurance system exception. The following criteria are used to evaluate the social insurance or pension system of a foreign country to determine whether the exception described in § 404.460(b) to the alien nonpayment provisions applies:

(1) Social insurance or pension system. A social insurance system means a governmental plan which pays benefits as an earned right, on the basis either of contributions or work in employment covered under the plan, without regard to the financial need of the beneficiary. However, a plan of this type may still be regarded as a social insurance system though it may provide, in a subordinate fashion, for a supplemental payment based on need. A pension system means a governmental plan which pays benefits based on residence or age, or a private employer's plan for which the government has set up uniform standards for coverage, contributions, eligibility, and benefit amounts provided that, in both of these types of plans, the financial need of the beneficiary is not a consideration.

(2) In effect. The social insurance or pension system of the foreign country must be in effect. This means that the foreign social insurance or pension system is in full operation with regard to taxes (or contributions) and benefits, or is in operation with regard to taxes (or contributions), and provision is made for payments to begin immediately upon the expiration of the period provided in the law for acquiring earliest eligibility. It is not in effect if the law leaves the beginning of operation to executive or other administrative action; nor is it in effect if the law has been temporarily suspended.

(3) General application. The term of general application means that the social insurance or pension system (or combination of systems) covers a substantial portion of the paid labor force in industry and commerce, taking into consideration the industrial classification and size of the paid labor force and the population of the country, as well as occupational, size of employer, and geographical limitations on coverage.

(4) Periodic benefit or actuarial equivalent. The term periodic benefit means a benefit payable at stated regular intervals of time such as weekly, biweekly, or monthly. Actuarial equivalent of a periodic benefit means the commutation of the value of the periodic benefit into a lump-sum payment, taking life expectancy and interest into account.

(5) Benefits payable on account of old age, retirement, or death. The requirement that benefits be payable on account of old age, retirement, or death, is satisfied if the foreign social insurance plan or system includes provision for payment of benefits to aged or retired persons and to dependents and survivors of covered workers. The requirement is also met where the system pays benefits based only on old age or retirement. The requirement is not met where the only benefits payable are workmen's compensation payments, cash sickness payments, unemployment compensation payments, or maternity insurance benefits.

(6) System under which U.S. citizens who qualify may receive payment while outside the foreign country. The foreign social insurance or pension system must permit payments to qualified U.S. citizens while outside such foreign country, regardless of the duration of their absence therefrom and must make the payments without restriction or qualification to these U.S. citizens at full rate, or at the full actuarial value. The foreign system is considered to pay benefits at the full rate if the U.S. citizen receives the full benefit rate in effect for qualified beneficiaries at the time of his award, whether he is then inside or outside the paying country; and he continues to receive the same benefit amount so long as he remains outside that country, even though he may not receive any increases going into effect after his award provided that in those other countries in which such increases are denied to beneficiaries, they are denied to all beneficiaries including nationals of the paying country.

(7) List of countries which meet the social insurance or pension system exception in section 202(t)(2) of the act. The following countries have been found to have in effect a social insurance or pension system which meets the requirements of section 202(t)(2) of the Act. Unless otherwise specified, each country meets such requirements effective January 1957. The effect of these findings is that beneficiaries who are citizens of such countries and not citizens of the United States may be paid benefits regardless of the duration of their absence from the United States unless for months beginning after June 1968 they are residing in a country to which payments to individuals are being withheld by the Treasury Department pursuant to the first section of the Act of October 9, 1940 (31 U.S.C. 123). Further additions to or deletions from the list of countries will be published in the Federal Register.

Antigua and Barbuda (effective November 1981)

Argentina (effective July 1968)

Austria (except from January 1958 through June 1961)

Bahamas, Commonwealth of the (effective October 1974)

Barbados (effective July 1968)

Belgium (effective July 1968)

Belize (effective September 1981)

Bolivia

Brazil

Burkina Faso, Republic of (formerly Upper Volta)

Canada (effective January 1966)

Chile

Colombia (effective January 1967)

Costa Rica (effective May 1962)

Cyprus (effective October 1964)

Czechoslovakia (effective July 1968)

Denmark (effective April 1964)

Dominica (effective November 1978)

Dominican Republic (effective November 1984)

Ecuador

El Salvador (effective January 1969)

Finland (effective May 1968)

France (effective June 1968)

Gabon (effective June 1964)

Grenada (effective April 1983)

Guatemala (effective October 1978)

Guyana (effective September 1969)

Iceland (effective December 1980)

Ivory Coast

Jamaica (effective July 1968)

Liechtenstein (effective July 1968)

Luxembourg

Malta (effective September 1964)

Mexico (effective March 1968)

Monaco

Netherlands (effective July 1968)

Nicaragua (effective May 1986)

Norway (effective June 1968)

Panama

Peru (effective February 1969)

Philippines (effective June 1960)

Poland (effective March 1957)

Portugal (effective May 1968)

San Marino (effective January 1965)

Spain (effective May 1966)

St. Christopher and Nevis (effective September 1983)

St. Lucia (effective August 1984)

Sweden (effective July 1966)

Switzerland (effective July 1968)

Trinidad and Tobago (effective July 1975)

Trust Territory of the Pacific Islands (Micronesia) (effective July 1976)

Turkey

United Kingdom

Western Samoa (effective August 1972)

Yugoslavia

Zaire (effective July 1961) (formerly Congo (Kinshasa))

(b) The "treaty obligation" exception. It is determined that the Treaties of Friendship, Commerce, and Navigation now in force between the United States and the Federal Republic of Germany, Greece, the Republic of Ireland, Israel, Italy, and Japan, respectively, create treaty obligations precluding the application of § 404.460(a) to citizens of such countries; and that the Treaty of Friendship, Commerce, and Navigation now in force between the United States and the Kingdom of the Netherlands creates treaty obligations precluding the application of § 404.460(a) to citizens of that country with respect to monthly survivors benefits only. There is no treaty obligation that would preclude the application of § 404.460(a) to citizens of any country other than those listed above.

[32 FR 19159, Dec. 20, 1967, as amended at 43 FR 2628, Jan. 18, 1978; 52 FR 8249, March 17, 1987]

§ 404.464 How does deportation or removal from the United States affect the receipt of benefits?

(a) Old-age or disability insurance benefits.

(1) You cannot receive an old-age or disability benefit for any month that occurs after the month we receive notice from the Secretary of Homeland Security or the Attorney General of the United States that you were:

(i) Deported under the provisions of section 241(a) of the Immigration and Nationality Act (INA) that were in effect before April 1, 1997, unless your deportation was under:

(A) Paragraph (1)(C) of that section; or

(B) Paragraph (1)(E) of that section and we received notice of your deportation under this paragraph before March 3, 2004;

(ii) Removed as deportable under the provisions of section 237(a) of the INA as in effect beginning April 1, 1997, unless your removal was under:

(A) Paragraph (1)(C) of that section; or

(B) Paragraph (1)(E) of that section and we received notice of your removal under this paragraph before March 3, 2004; or

(iii) Removed as inadmissible under the provisions of section 212(a)(6)(A) of the INA as in effect beginning April 1, 1997.

(2) Benefits that cannot be paid to you because of your deportation or removal under paragraph (a)(1) of

this section may again be payable for any month subsequent to your deportation or removal that you are lawfully admitted to the United States for permanent residence. You are considered lawfully admitted for permanent residence as of the month you enter the United States with permission to reside here permanently.

(b) Dependents or survivors benefits. If an insured person on whose record you are entitled cannot be paid (or could not have been paid while still alive) an old-age or disability benefit for a month(s) because of his or her deportation or removal under paragraph (a)(1) of this section, you cannot be paid a dependent or survivor benefit on the insured person's record for that month(s) unless:

(1) You are a U.S citizen; or

(2) You were present in the United States for the entire month. (This means you were not absent from the United States for any period during the month, no matter how short.)

(c) Lump sum death payment. A lump sum death payment cannot be paid on the record of a person who died:

(1) In or after the month we receive from the Secretary of Homeland Security or the Attorney General of the United States notice of his or her deportation or removal under the provisions of the INA specified in paragraph (a)(1) of this section (excluding the exceptions under paragraphs (a)(1)(i)(A) and (B) and (ii)(A) and (B) of this section); and

(2) Before the month in which the deceased person was thereafter lawfully admitted to the United States for permanent residence.

[58 FR 64889, Dec. 10, 1993; 62 FR 38450, July 18, 1997; 70 FR 16411, March 31, 2005]

§ 404.465 Conviction for subversive activities; effect on monthly benefits and entitlement to hospital insurance benefits.

(a) Effect of conviction. Where an individual is convicted of any offense (committed after August 1, 1956) under chapter 37 (relating to espionage and censorship), chapter 105 (relating to sabotage), or chapter 115 (relating to treason, sedition, and subversive activities) of title 18 U.S.C., or under section 4, 112, or 113 of the Internal Security Act of 1950, as amended, the court, in addition to all other penalties provided by law, may order that, in determining whether any monthly benefit is payable to the individual for the month in which he is convicted or for any month thereafter, and in determining whether the individual is entitled to hospital insurance benefits under part A of title XVIII for any such month, and in determining the amount of the benefit for that month, the following are not to be taken into account:

(1) Any wages paid to such individual, or to any other individual, in the calendar quarter in which such conviction occurred or in any prior calendar quarter, and

(2) Any net earnings from self-employment derived by the individual, or any other individual, during the taxable year in which the conviction occurred or during any prior taxable year.

(b) Recalculation of benefit. When notified by the Attorney General that the additional penalty as described in paragraph (a) of this section has been imposed against any individual entitled to benefits under section 202 or section 223 of the Act (see subpart D), the Administration, for the purposes of determining the individual's entitlement to such benefits as of the month in which convicted and the amount of the benefit, will exclude the applicable wages and net earnings in accordance with the order of the court.

(c) Effect of pardon. In the event that an individual, with respect to whom the additional penalty as described in paragraph (a) of this section has been imposed, is granted a pardon of the offense by the President of the United States, such penalty is not applied in determining such individual's entitlement to benefits, and the amount of such benefit, for any month beginning after the date on which the pardon is granted.

§ 404.466 Conviction for subversive activities; effect on enrollment for supplementary medical insurance benefits.

An individual may not enroll under part B (supplementary medical insurance benefits) of title XVIII if he has been convicted of any offense described in § 404.465.

§ 404.467 Nonpayment of benefits; individual entitled to disability insurance benefits or childhood disability benefits based on statutory blindness is engaging in substantial gainful activity.

(a) Disability insurance benefits. An individual who has attained age 55 and who meets the definition of disability for disability insurance benefits purposes based on statutory blindness, as defined in § 404.1581, may be entitled to disability insurance benefits for months in which he is engaged in certain types of substantial gainful activity. No payment, however, may be made to the individual or to beneficiaries entitled to benefits on his earnings record for any month in which such individual engages in any type of substantial gainful activity.

(b) Childhood disability benefits. An individual who has attained age 55 and who meets the definition of disability prescribed in § 404.1583 for childhood disability benefits on the basis of statutory blindness may be entitled to childhood disability benefits for months in which he engages in certain types of substantial gainful activity. However, no payment may be made to such individual for any month after December 1972 in which such individual engages in substantial gainful activity.

[39 FR 43715, Dec. 18, 1974; 51 FR 10616, March 28, 1986]

§ 404.468 Nonpayment of benefits to prisoners.

(a) General. No monthly benefits will be paid to any individual for any month any part of which the individual is confined in a jail, prison, or other penal institution or correctional facility for conviction of a felony. This rule applies to disability benefits (§ 404.315) and child's benefits based on disability (§ 404.350) effective with benefits payable for months beginning on or after October 1, 1980. For all other monthly benefits, this rule is effective with benefits payable for months beginning on or after May 1, 1983. However, it applies only to the prisoner; benefit payments to any other person who is entitled on the basis of the prisoner's wages and self-employment income are payable as though the prisoner were receiving benefits.

(b) Felonious offenses. An offense will be considered a felony if—

(1) It is a felony under applicable law: or

(2) In a jurisdiction which does not classify any crime as a felony, it is an offense punishable by death or imprisonment for a term exceeding one year.

(c) Confinement. In general, a jail, prison, or other penal institution or correctional facility is a facility which is under the control and jurisdiction of the agency in charge of the penal system or in which convicted criminals can be incarcerated. Confinement in such a facility continues as long as the individual is under a sentence of confinement and has not been released due to parole or pardon. An individual is considered confined even though he or she is temporarily or intermittently outside of that facility (e.g., on work release, attending school, or hospitalized).

(d) Vocational rehabilitation exception. The nonpayment provision of paragraph (a) of this section does not apply if a prisoner who is entitled to benefits on the basis of disability is actively and satisfactorily participating in a rehabilitation program which has been specifically approved for the individual by court of law. In addition, the Commissioner must determine that the program is expected to result in the individual being able to do substantial gainful activity upon release and within a reasonable time. No benefits will be paid to the prisoner for any month prior to the approval of the program.

[48 FR 5714, Feb. 8, 1983; 49 FR 48182, Dec. 11, 1984; 62 FR 38450, July 18, 1997]

§ 404.469 Nonpayment of benefits where individual has not furnished or applied for a Social Security number.

No monthly benefits will be paid to an entitled individual unless he or she either furnishes to the Social Security Administration (SSA) satisfactory proof of his or her Social Security number, or, if the individual has not been assigned a number, he or she makes a proper application for a number (see § 422.103). An individual submits satisfactory proof of his or her Social Security number by furnishing to SSA the number and sufficient additional information that can be used to determine whether that Social Security number or another number has been assigned to the individual. Sufficient additional information may include the entitled individual's date and place of birth, mother's maiden name, and father's name. If the individual does not know his or her Social Security number, SSA will use this additional information to determine the Social Security number, if any, that it assigned to the individual. This rule applies to individuals who become entitled to benefits beginning on or after June 1, 1989.

[56 FR 41789, Aug. 23, 1991]

§ 404.470 Nonpayment of disability benefits due to noncompliance with rules regarding treatment for drug addiction or alcoholism.

(a) Suspension of monthly benefits.

(1) For an individual entitled to benefits based on a disability (§ 404.1505) and for whom drug addiction or alcoholism is a contributing factor material to the determination of disability (as described in § 404.1535), monthly benefits will be suspended beginning with the first month after we notify the individual in writing that he or she has been determined not to be in compliance with the treatment requirements for such individuals (§ 404.1536).

(2) This rule applies to all individuals entitled to disability benefits (§ 404.315), widow(er)'s benefits (§ 404.335), and child's benefits based on a disability (§ 404.350) effective with benefits paid in months beginning on or after March 1, 1995.

(3) Benefit payments to any other person who is entitled on the basis of a disabled wage earner's entitlement to disability benefits are payable as though the disabled wage earner were receiving benefits.

(b) Resumption of monthly benefits. The payment of benefits may be resumed only after an individual demonstrates and maintains compliance with appropriate treatment requirements for:

(1) 2 consecutive months for the first determination of noncompliance;

(2) 3 consecutive months for the second determination of noncompliance; and

(3) 6 consecutive months for the third and all subsequent determinations of noncompliance.

(c) Termination of benefits.

(1) A suspension of benefit payments due to noncompliance with the treatment requirements for 12 consecutive months will result in termination of benefits effective with the first month following the 12th month of suspension of benefits.

(2) Benefit payments to any other person who is entitled on the basis of a disabled wage earner's entitlement to disability benefits are payable as though the disabled wage earner were receiving benefits.

[60 FR 8146, Feb. 10, 1995]

§ 404.471 Nonpayment of disability benefits for trial work period service months upon a conviction of fraudulently concealing work activity.

(a) Nonpayment of benefits during the trial work period. Beginning with work activity performed in March 2004 and thereafter, if you are convicted by a Federal court of fraudulently concealing your work activity and the concealment of the work activity occurred while you were in a trial work period, monthly disability benefits under title II of the Social Security Act are not payable for months in which you performed services during that trial work period prior to the conviction (see § 404.1592 for a definition of a trial work period and services). Benefits already received for months of work activity in the trial work period prior to the conviction and in the same period of disability during which the fraudulently concealed work activity occurred, will be considered an overpayment on the record.

(b) Concealment of work activity. You can be found to be fraudulently concealing work activity if—

(1) You provide false information to us concerning the amount of earnings you received or are receiving for a particular period;

(2) You received or are receiving disability benefits while engaging in work activity under another identity (this would include working under another social security number or a forged social security number); or

(3) You take other actions to conceal work activity with the intent of fraudulently obtaining benefits in excess of amounts that are due.

[71 FR 66866, Nov. 17, 2006]

§ 404.480 Paying benefits in installments: Drug addiction or alcoholism.

(a) General. For disabled beneficiaries who receive benefit payments through a representative payee because drug addiction or alcoholism is a contributing factor material to the determination of disability (as described in § 404.1535), certain amounts due the beneficiary for a past period will be paid in installments. The amounts subject to payment in installments include:

(1) Benefits due but unpaid which accrued prior to the month payment was effectuated;

(2) Benefits due but unpaid which accrued during a period of suspension for which the beneficiary was subsequently determined to have been eligible; and

(3) Any adjustment to benefits which results in an accrual of unpaid benefits.

(b) Installment formula. Except as provided in paragraph (c) of this section, the amount of the installment payment in any month is limited so that the sum of (1) the amount due for a past period (and payable under paragraph (a) of this section) paid in such month and (2) the amount of any benefit due for the preceding month under such entitlement which is payable in such month, does not exceed two times the amount of the beneficiary's benefit payment for the preceding month. In counting the amount of the beneficiary's benefit payment for the previous month, no reductions or deductions under this title are taken into account.

(c) Exception to installment limitation. An exception to the installment payment limitation in paragraph (b) of this section can be granted for the first month in which a beneficiary accrues benefit amounts subject to payment in installments if the beneficiary has unpaid housing expenses which result in a high risk of homelessness for the beneficiary. In that case, the benefit payment may be increased by the amount of the unpaid housing expenses so long as that increase does not exceed the amount of benefits which accrued during the most recent period of nonpayment. We consider a person to be at risk of homelessness if continued nonpayment of the outstanding housing expenses is likely to result in the person losing his or her place to live or if past nonpayment of housing expenses has resulted in the person having no appropriate personal place to live. In determining whether this exception applies, we will ask for evidence of outstanding housing expenses that shows that the person is likely to lose or has already lost his or her place to live. For purposes of this section, homelessness is the state of not being under the control of any public institution and having no appropriate personal place to live. Housing expenses include charges for all items required to maintain shelter (for example, mortgage payments, rent, heating fuel, and electricity).

(d) Payment through a representative payee. If the beneficiary does not have a representative payee, payment of amounts subject to installments cannot be made until a representative payee is selected.

(e) Underpaid beneficiary no longer entitled. In the case of a beneficiary who is no longer currently entitled to monthly payments, but to whom amounts defined in paragraph (a) of this section are still owing, we will treat such beneficiary's monthly benefit for the last month of entitlement as the beneficiary's benefit for the preceding month and continue to make installment payments of such benefits through a representative payee.

(f) Beneficiary currently not receiving Social Security benefits because of suspension for noncompliance with treatment. If a beneficiary is currently not receiving benefits because his or her benefits have been suspended for noncompliance with treatment (as defined in § 404.1536), the payment of amounts under paragraph (a) of this section will stop until the beneficiary has demonstrated compliance with treatment as described in § 404.470 and will again commence with the first month the beneficiary begins to receive benefit payments.

(g) Underpaid beneficiary deceased. Upon the death of a beneficiary, any remaining unpaid amounts as defined in paragraph (a) of this section will be treated as underpayments in accordance with § 404.503(b).

[60 FR 8146, Feb. 10, 1995]

SUBPART F—OVERPAYMENTS, UNDERPAYMENTS, WAIVER OF ADJUSTMENT OR RECOVERY OF OVERPAYMENTS, AND LIABILITY OF A CERTIFYING OFFICER

Authority: Secs. 204, 205(a), 702(a)(5), and 1147 of the Social Security Act (42 U.S.C. 404, 405(a), 902(a)(5), and 1320b–17); 31 U.S.C. 3711; 31 U.S.C. 3716; 31 U.S.C. 3720A.

Source: 52 FR 27540, July 22, 1987; 55 FR 1019, Jan. 11, 1990; 55 FR 7313, March 1, 1990; 56 FR 52468, Oct. 21, 1991; 61 FR 5941, Feb. 15, 1996; 62 FR 64277, Dec. 5, 1997; 70 FR 15, Jan. 3, 2005; 70 FR 16113, March 30, 2005; 76 FR 65108, Oct. 20, 2011; 79 FR 33684, June 12, 2014, unless otherwise noted.

§ 404.501 General applicability of section 204 of the Act.

(a) In general. Section 204 of the Act provides for adjustment as set forth in §§ 404.502 and 404.503, in cases where an individual has received more or less than the correct payment due under title II of the Act. As used in this subpart, the term overpayment includes a payment in excess of the amount due under title II of the Act, a payment resulting from the failure to impose deductions or to suspend or reduce benefits under sections 203, 222(b), 224, and 228(c), and (d), and (e) of the Act (see subpart E of this part), a payment pursuant to section 205(n) of the Act in an amount in excess of the amount to which the individual is entitled under section 202 or 223 of the Act, a payment resulting from the failure to terminate benefits, and a payment where no amount is payable under title II of the Act. The term underpayment as used in this subpart refers only to monthly insurance benefits and includes nonpayment where some amount of such benefits was payable. An underpayment may be in the form of an accrued unpaid benefit amount for which no check has been drawn or in the form of an unnegotiated check payable to a deceased individual. The provisions for adjustment also apply in cases where through error:

(1) A reduction required under section 202(j)(1), 202(k)(3), 203(a), or 205(n) of the Act is not made, or

(2) An increase or decrease required under section 202(d)(2), or 215 (f) or (g) of the Act is not made, or

(3) A deduction required under section 203(b)(as may be modified by the provisions of section 203(h)), 203(c), 203(d), 203(i), 222(b), or 223(a)(1)(D) of the Act or section 907 of the Social Security Amendments of 1939 is not made, or

(4) A suspension required under section 202(n) or 202(t) of the Act is not made, or

(5) A reduction under section 202(q) of the Act is not made, or

(6) A reduction, increase, deduction, or suspension is made which is either more or less than required, or

(7) A payment in excess of the amount due under title XVIII of the Act was made to or on behalf of an individual (see 42 CFR 405.350 through 405.351) entitled to benefits under title II of the Act, or

(8) A payment of past due benefits is made to an individual and such payment had not been reduced by the amount of attorney's fees payable directly to an attorney under section 206 of the Act (see § 404.977).

(9) A reduction under § 404.408b is made which is either more or less than required.

(b) Payments made on the basis of an erroneous report of death. Any monthly benefit or lump sum paid under title II of the Act on the basis of an erroneous report by the Department of Defense of the death of an individual in the line of duty while such individual was a member of the uniformed services (as defined in section 210(m) of the Act) on active duty (as defined in section 210(l) of the Act) is deemed a correct payment for any month prior to the month such Department notifies the Administration that such individual is alive.

(c) Payments made by direct deposit to a financial institution. When a payment in excess of the amount due under title II of the Act is made by direct deposit to a financial institution to or on behalf of an individual who has died, and the financial institution credits the payment to a joint account of the deceased individual and another person who was entitled to a monthly benefit on the basis of the same earnings record as the deceased individual for the month before the month in which the deceased individual died, the amount of the payment in excess of the correct amount will be an overpayment to the other person.

[34 FR 14887, Sept. 27, 1969, as amended at 44 FR 34942, June 18, 1979; 47 FR 4988, Feb. 3, 1982; 48 FR 46149, Oct. 11, 1983; 55 FR 7313, March 1, 1990]

§ 404.502 Overpayments.

Upon determination that an overpayment has been made, adjustments will be made against monthly benefits and lump sums as follows:

(a) Individual overpaid is living.

(1) If the individual to whom an overpayment was made is at the time of a determination of such overpayment entitled to a monthly benefit or a lump sum under title II of the Act, or at any time thereafter becomes so entitled, no benefit for any month and no lump sum is payable to such individual, except as provided in paragraphs (c) and (d) of this section, until an amount equal to the amount of the overpayment has been withheld or refunded. Such adjustments will be made against any monthly benefit or lump sum under title II of the Act to which such individual is entitled whether payable on the basis of such individual's earnings or the earnings of another individual.

(2) If any other individual is entitled to benefits for any month on the basis of the same earnings as the overpaid individual, except as adjustment is to be effected pursuant to paragraphs (c) and (d) of this section by withholding a part of the monthly benefit of either the overpaid individual or any other individual entitled to benefits on the basis of the same earnings, no benefit for any month will be paid on such earnings to such other individual until an amount equal to the amount of the overpayment has been withheld or refunded.

(3) If a representative payee receives a payment on behalf of a beneficiary after that beneficiary dies, the representative payee or his estate is solely liable for repaying the overpayment. If the representative payee is entitled to a monthly benefit or a lump sum under title II of the Act at the time we determine that an overpayment exists or at any time thereafter, except as provided in paragraphs (c) and (d) of this section, we will not pay the monthly benefits or the lump sum to the representative payee until the amount of the overpayment has been repaid. We will make such adjustments against any monthly benefit or lump sum under title II of the Act to which the representative payee is entitled whether payable on the basis of such representative payee's earnings or the earnings of another individual.

(b) Individual overpaid dies before adjustment. If an overpaid individual dies before adjustment is completed under the provisions of paragraph (a) of this section, no lump sum and no subsequent monthly benefit will be paid on the basis of earnings which were the basis of the overpayment to such deceased individual until full recovery of the overpayment has been effected, except as provided in paragraphs (c) and (d) of this section or under § 404.515. Such recovery may be effected through:

(1) Payment by the estate of the deceased overpaid individual,

(2) Withholding of amounts due the estate of such individual under title II of the Act,

(3) Withholding a lump sum or monthly benefits due any other individual on the basis of the same earnings which were the basis of the overpayment to the deceased overpaid individual, or

(4) Any combination of the amount above.

(5) The methods in paragraphs (b)(1) and (b)(2) of this section for overpayments owed by a representative payee for payments made after the beneficiary's death. We will not recover such overpayments from any person other than the individual who was representative payee or his estate, but we may recover these overpayments from such other person under § 404.503(b).

(c) Adjustment by withholding part of a monthly benefit.

(1) Where it is determined that withholding the full amount each month would defeat the purpose of title II, i.e., deprive the person of income required for ordinary and necessary living expenses (see § 404.508), adjustment under paragraphs (a) and (b) of this section may be effected by withholding an amount of not less than $10 of the monthly benefit payable to an individual.

(2) Adjustment as provided by this paragraph will not be available if the overpayment was caused by the individual's intentional false statement or representation, or willful concealment of, or deliberate failure to furnish, material information. In such cases, recovery of the overpayment will be accomplished as provided in paragraph (a) of this section.

(d) Individual overpaid enrolled under supplementary insurance plan. Notwithstanding the provisions of paragraphs (a), (b), and (c) of this section, if the individual liable for the overpayment is an enrollee under part B of title XVIII of the Act and the overpayment was not caused by such individual's intentional false statement or representation, or willful concealment of, or deliberate failure to furnish, material information, an amount of such individual's monthly benefit which is equal to his obligation for supplementary medical insurance premiums will be applied toward payment of such premiums, and the balance of the monthly benefit will be applied toward recovery of the overpayment. Further adjustment with respect to such balance may be made if the enrollee so requests and meets the conditions of paragraph (c) of this section.

[35 FR 5943, April 10, 1970, as amended at 43 FR 31318, July 21, 1978; 44 FR 20653, April 6, 1979; 73 FR 65542, Nov. 4, 2008]

§ 404.502a Notice of right to waiver consideration.

Whenever an initial determination is made that more than the correct amount of payment has been made, and we seek adjustment or recovery of the overpayment, the individual from whom we are seeking adjustment or recovery is immediately notified. The notice includes:

(a) The overpayment amount and how and when it occurred;

(b) A request for full, immediate refund, unless the overpayment can be withheld from the next month's benefit;

(c) The proposed adjustment of benefits if refund is not received within 30 days after the date of the notice and adjustment of benefits is available;

(d) An explanation of the availability of a different rate of withholding when full withholding is proposed, installment payments when refund is requested and adjustment is not currently available, and/or cross-program recovery when refund is requested and the individual is receiving another type of payment from SSA (language about cross-program recovery is not included in notices sent to individuals in jurisdictions where this recovery option is not available);

(e) An explanation of the right to request waiver of adjustment or recovery and the automatic scheduling of a file review and pre-recoupment hearing (commonly referred to as a personal conference) if a request for waiver cannot be approved after initial paper review;

(f) An explanation of the right to request reconsideration of the fact and/or amount of the overpayment determination;

(g) Instructions about the availability of forms for requesting reconsideration and waiver;

(h) An explanation that if the individual does not request waiver or reconsideration within 30 days of the date of the overpayment notice, adjustment or recovery of the overpayment will begin;

(i) A statement that an SSA office will help the individual complete and submit forms for appeal or waiver requests; and

(j) A statement that the individual receiving the notice should notify SSA promptly if reconsideration, waiver, a lesser rate of withholding, repayment by installments or cross-program adjustment is wanted.

[37 FR 10554, May 25, 1972; 61 FR 56131, Oct. 31, 1996]

§ 404.503 Underpayments.

Underpayments will be adjusted as follows:

(a) Individual underpaid is living. If an individual to whom an underpayment is due is living, the amount of such underpayment will be paid to such individual either in a single payment (if he is not entitled to a monthly benefit or a lump-sum death payment) or by increasing one or more monthly benefits or a lump-sum death payment to which such individual is or becomes entitled. However, if we determine that the individual to whom an underpayment is due also received an overpayment as defined in § 404.501(a) for a different period, we will apply any underpayment due the individual to reduce that overpayment, unless we have waived recovery of the overpayment under the provisions of §§ 404.506 through 404.512.

(b) Individual dies before adjustment of underpayment. If an individual who has been underpaid dies before receiving payment or negotiating a check or checks representing such payment, we first apply any amounts due the deceased individual against any overpayments as defined in § 404.501(a) owed by the deceased individual, unless we have waived recovery of such overpayment under the provisions of §§ 404.506 through 404.512. We then will distribute any remaining underpayment to the living person (or persons) in the highest order of priority as follows:

(1) The deceased individual's surviving spouse as defined in section 216(c), (g), or (h) of the Act who was either:

(i) Living in the same household (as defined in § 404.347) with the deceased individual at the time of such individual's death, or

(ii) Entitled to a monthly benefit on the basis of the same earnings record as was the deceased individual for the month in which such individual died.

(2) The child or children of the deceased individual (as defined in section 216(e) or (h) of the Act) entitled to a monthly benefit on the basis of the same earnings record as was the deceased individual for the month in which such individual died (if more than one such child, in equal shares to each such child).

(3) The parent or parents of the deceased individual, entitled to a monthly benefit on the basis of the same earnings record as was the deceased individual for the month in which such individual died (if more than one such parent, in equal shares to each such parent). For this purpose, the definition of "parent" in § 404.374 includes the parent(s) of any deceased individual who was entitled to benefits under title II of the Act.

(4) The surviving spouse of the deceased individual (as defined in section 216(c), (g), or (h) of the Act) who does not qualify under paragraph (b)(1) of this section.

(5) The child or children of the deceased individual (as defined in section 216(e) or (h) of the Act) who do not qualify under paragraph (b)(2) of this section (if more than one such child, in equal shares to each such child).

(6) The parent or parents of the deceased individual, who do not qualify under paragraph (b)(3) of this section (if more than one such parent, in equal shares to each such parent). For this purpose, the definition of "parent" in § 404.374 includes the parent(s) of any deceased individual who was entitled to benefits under title II of the Act.

(7) The legal representative of the estate of the deceased individual as defined in paragraph (d) of this section.

(c) In the event that a person who is otherwise qualified to receive an underpayment under the provisions of paragraph (b) of this section, dies before receiving payment or before negotiating the check or checks representing such payment, his share of the underpayment will be divided among the remaining living person(s) in the same order of priority. In the event that there is (are) no other such person(s), the underpayment will be paid to the living person(s) in the next lower order of priority under paragraph (b) of this section.

(d) Definition of legal representative. The term legal representative, for the purpose of qualifying to receive an underpayment, generally means the administrator or executor of the estate of the deceased individual. However, it may also include an individual, institution or organization acting on behalf of an unadministered estate, provided that such person can give the Administration good acquittance (as defined in paragraph (e) of this section). The following persons may qualify as legal representative for the purposes of this subpart, provided they can give the Administration good acquittance:

(1) A person who qualifies under a State's small estate statute,

(2) A person resident in a foreign country who, under the laws and customs of that country, has the right to receive assets of the estate,

(3) A public administrator, or

(4) A person who has the authority, under applicable law, to collect the assets of the estate of the deceased individual.

(e) Definition of "good acquittance." A person is considered to give the Administration good acquittance when payment to that person will release the Administration from further liability for such payment.

[34 FR 14487, Sept. 27, 1969, as amended at 35 FR 14129, Sept. 5, 1970; 55 FR 7313, March 1, 1990; 60 FR 17445, April 6, 1995; 73 FR 65543, Nov. 4, 2008]

§ 404.504 Relation to provisions for reductions and increases.

The amount of an overpayment or underpayment is the difference between the amount paid to the beneficiary and the amount of the payment to which the beneficiary was actually entitled. Such payment, for example, would be equal to the difference between the amount of a benefit in fact paid to the beneficiary and the amount of such benefit as reduced under section 202(j)(1), 202(k)(3), 203(a), or 224(a), or as increased under section 202(d)(2), 202(m), or 215(f) and (g). In effecting an adjustment with respect to an overpayment, no amount can be considered as having been withheld from a particular benefit which is in excess of the amount of such benefit as so decreased.

[34 FR 14888, Sept. 27, 1969]

§ 404.505 Relationship to provisions requiring deductions.

Adjustments required by any of the provisions in this subpart F are made in addition to, but after, any deductions required by section 202(t), 203(b), 203(c), 203(d), and 222(b) of the Act, or section 907 of the Social Security Act Amendments of 1939, and before any deductions required by section 203(g) or 203(h)(2) of the Act.

[34 FR 14888, Sept. 27, 1969]

§ 404.506 When waiver may be applied and how to process the request.

(a) Section 204(b) of the Act provides that there shall be no adjustment or recovery in any case where an overpayment under title II has been made to an individual who is without fault if adjustment or recovery would either defeat the purpose of title II of the Act, or be against equity and good conscience.

(b) If an individual requests waiver of adjustment or recovery of a title II overpayment within 30 days after receiving a notice of overpayment that contains the information in § 404.502a, no adjustment or recovery action will be taken until after the initial waiver determination is made. If the individual requests waiver more than 30 days after receiving the notice of overpayment, SSA will stop any adjustment or recovery actions until after the initial waiver determination is made.

(c) When waiver is requested, the individual gives SSA information to support his/her contention that he/she is without fault in causing the overpayment (see § 404.507) and that adjustment or recovery would either defeat the purpose of title II of the Act (see § 404.508) or be against equity and good conscience (see § 404.509). That information, along with supporting documentation, is reviewed to determine if waiver can be approved. If waiver cannot be approved after this review, the individual is notified in writing and given the dates, times and place of the file review and personal conference; the procedure for reviewing the claims file prior to the personal conference; the procedure for seeking a change in the scheduled dates, times, and/or place; and all other information necessary to fully inform the individual about the personal conference. The file review is always scheduled at least 5 days before the personal conference. We will offer to the individual the option of conducting the personal conference face-to-face at a place we designate, by telephone, or by video teleconference. The notice will advise the individual of the date and time of the personal conference.

(d) At the file review, the individual and the individual's representative have the right to review the claims file and applicable law and regulations with the decisionmaker or another SSA representative who is prepared to answer questions. We will provide copies of material related to the overpayment and/or waiver from the claims file or pertinent sections of the law or regulations that are requested by the individual or the individual's representative.

(e) At the personal conference, the individual is given the opportunity to:

(1) Appear personally, testify, cross-examine any witnesses, and make arguments;

(2) Be represented by an attorney or other representative (see § 404.1700), although the individual must be present at the conference; and

(3) Submit documents for consideration by the decisionmaker.

(f) At the personal conference, the decisionmaker:

(1) Tells the individual that the decisionmaker was not previously involved in the issue under review, that the waiver decision is solely the decisionmaker's, and that the waiver decision is based only on the evidence or information presented or reviewed at the conference;

(2) Ascertains the role and identity of everyone present;

(3) Indicates whether or not the individual reviewed the claims file;

(4) Explains the provisions of law and regulations applicable to the issue;

(5) Briefly summarizes the evidence already in file which will be considered;

(6) Ascertains from the individual whether the information presented is correct and whether he/she fully understands it;

(7) Allows the individual and the individual's representative, if any, to present the individual's case;

(8) Secures updated financial information and verification, if necessary;

(9) Allows each witness to present information and allows the individual and the individual's representative to question each witness;

(10) Ascertains whether there is any further evidence to be presented;

(11) Reminds the individual of any evidence promised by the individual which has not been presented;

(12) Lets the individual and the individual's representative, if any, present any proposed summary or closing statement;

(13) Explains that a decision will be made and the individual will be notified in writing; and

(14) Explains repayment options and further appeal rights in the event the decision is adverse to the individual.

(g) SSA issues a written decision to the individual (and his/her representative, if any) specifying the findings of fact and conclusions in support of the decision to approve or deny waiver and advising of the individual's right to appeal the decision. If waiver is denied, adjustment or recovery of the overpayment begins even if the individual appeals.

(h) If it appears that the waiver cannot be approved, and the individual declines a personal conference or fails to appear for a second scheduled personal conference, a decision regarding the waiver will be made based on the written evidence of record. Reconsideration is then the next step in the appeals process (but see § 404.930(a)(7)).

[32 FR 18026, Dec. 16, 1967; 61 FR 56131, Oct. 31, 1996; 73 FR 1973, Jan. 11, 2008]

§ 404.507 Fault.

Fault as used in without fault (see § 404.506 and 42 CFR 405.355) applies only to the individual. Although the Administration may have been at fault in making the overpayment, that fact does not relieve the overpaid individual or any other individual from whom the Administration seeks to recover the overpayment from liability for repayment if such individual is not without fault. In determining whether an individual is at fault, the Social Security Administration will consider all pertinent circumstances, including the individual's age and intelligence, and any physical, mental, educational, or linguistic limitations (including any lack of facility with the English language) the individual has. What constitutes fault (except for deduction overpayments—see § 404.510) on the part of the overpaid individual or on the part of any other individual from whom the Administration seeks to recover the overpayment depends upon whether the facts show that the incorrect payment to the individual or to a provider of services or other person, or an incorrect payment made under section 1814(e) of the Act, resulted from:

(a) An incorrect statement made by the individual which he knew or should have known to be incorrect; or

(b) Failure to furnish information which he knew or should have known to be material; or

(c) With respect to the overpaid individual only, acceptance of a payment which he either knew or could have been expected to know was incorrect.

[34 FR 14888, Sept. 27, 1969; 34 FR 15646, Oct. 9, 1969; as amended at 44 FR 34942, June 18, 1979; 59 FR 1634, Jan. 12, 1994]

§ 404.508 Defeat the purpose of Title II.

(a) General. Defeat the purpose of title II, for purposes of this subpart, means defeat the purpose of benefits under this title, i.e., to deprive a person of income required for ordinary and necessary living expenses. This depends upon whether the person has an income or financial resources sufficient for more than ordinary and necessary needs, or is dependent upon all of his current benefits for such needs. An individual's ordinary and necessary expenses include:

(1) Fixed living expenses, such as food and clothing, rent, mortgage payments, utilities, maintenance, insurance (e.g., life, accident, and health insurance including premiums for supplementary medical insurance benefits under title XVIII), taxes, installment payments, etc.;

(2) Medical, hospitalization, and other similar expenses;

(3) Expenses for the support of others for whom the individual is legally responsible; and

(4) Other miscellaneous expenses which may reasonably be considered as part of the individual's standard of living.

(b) When adjustment or recovery will defeat the purpose of title II. Adjustment or recovery will defeat the purposes of title II in (but is not limited to) situations where the person from whom recovery is sought needs substantially all of his current income (including social security monthly benefits) to meet current ordinary and necessary living expenses.

[32 FR 18026, Dec. 16, 1967, as amended at 34 FR 14888, Sept. 27, 1969]

§ 404.509 Against equity and good conscience; defined.

(a) Recovery of an overpayment is against equity and good conscience (under title II and title XVIII) if an individual—

(1) Changed his or her position for the worse (Example 1) or relinquished a valuable right (Example 2) because of reliance upon a notice that a payment would be made or because of the overpayment itself; or

(2) Was living in a separate household from the overpaid person at the time of the overpayment and did not receive the overpayment (Examples 3 and 4).

(b) The individual's financial circumstances are not material to a finding of against equity and good conscience.

Example 1. A widow, having been awarded benefits for herself and daughter, entered her daughter in private school because the monthly benefits made this possible. After the widow and her daughter received payments for almost a year, the deceased worker was found to be not insured and all payments to the widow and child were incorrect. The widow has no other funds with which to pay the daughter's private school expenses. Having entered the daughter in private school and thus incurred a financial obligation toward which the benefits had been applied, she was in a worse position financially than if she and her daughter had never been entitled to benefits. In this situation, the recovery of the payments would be against equity and good conscience.

Example 2. After being awarded old-age insurance benefits, an individual resigned from employment on the assumption he would receive regular monthly benefit payments. It was discovered 3 years later that (due to a Social Security Administration error) his award was erroneous because he did not have the required insured status. Due to his age, the individual was unable to get his job back and could not get any other employment. In this situation, recovery of the overpayments would be against equity and good conscience because the individual gave up a valuable right.

Example 3. M divorced K and married L. M died a few years later. When K files for benefits as a surviving divorced wife, she learns that L had been overpaid $3,200 on M's earnings record. Because K and L are both entitled to benefits on M's record of earnings and we could not recover the overpayment from L, we sought recovery from K. K was living in a separate household from L at the time of the overpayment and did not receive the overpayment. K requests waiver of recovery of the $3,200 overpayment from benefits due her as a surviving divorced wife of M. In this situation, it would be against equity and good conscience to recover the overpayment from K.

Example 4. G filed for and was awarded benefits. His daughter, T, also filed for student benefits on G's earnings record. Since T was an independent, full-time student living in another State, she filed for benefits on her own behalf. Later, after T received 12 monthly benefits, the school reported that T had been a full-time student only 2 months and had withdrawn from school. Since T was overpaid 10 monthly benefits, she was requested to return the overpayment to SSA. T did not return the overpayment and further attempts to collect the overpayment were unsuccessful. G was asked to repay the overpayment because he was receiving benefits on the same earnings record. G requested waiver. To support his waiver request G established that he was not at fault in causing the overpayment because he did not know that T was receiving benefits. Since G is without fault and, in addition, meets the requirements of not living in the same household at the time of the overpayment and did not receive the overpayment, it would be against equity and good conscience to recover the overpayment from G.

[27 FR 1162, Feb. 8, 1962, as amended at 28 FR 14492, Dec. 31, 1963; 32 FR 18026, Dec. 16, 1967; 43 FR 31318, July 21, 1978; 44 FR 20653, April 6, 1979; 53 FR 25483, July 7, 1988]

§ 404.510 When an individual is "without fault" in a deduction overpayment.

In determining whether an individual is "without fault" with respect to a deduction overpayment, the Social Security Administration will consider all pertinent circumstances, including the individual's age and intelligence, and any physical, mental, educational, or linguistic limitations (including any lack of facility with the English language) the individual has. Except as provided in § 404.511 or elsewhere in this subpart F, situations in which an individual will be considered to be "without fault" with respect to a deduction overpayment include, but are not limited to, those that are described in this section. An individual will be considered "without fault" in accepting a payment which is incorrect because he/she failed to report an event specified in sections 203 (b) and (c) of the Act, or an event specified in section 203(d) of the Act as in effect for monthly benefits for months after December 1960, or because a deduction is required under section 203 (b), (c), (d), or section 222(b) of the Act, or payments were not withheld as required by section 202(t) or section 228 of the Act, if it is shown that such failure to report or acceptance of the overpayment was due to one of the following circumstances:

(a) Reasonable belief that only his net cash earnings (take-home pay) are included in determining the annual earnings limitation or the monthly earnings limitation under section 203(f) of the Act.

(b) Reliance upon erroneous information from an official source within the Social Security Administration (or other governmental agency which the individual had reasonable cause to believe was connected with the administration of benefits under title II of the Act) with respect to the interpretation of a pertinent provision of the Social Security Act or regulations pertaining thereto. For example, this circumstance could occur where the individual is misinformed by such source as to the interpretation of a provision in the Act or regulations relating to deductions, or relating to the effect of residence of an alien outside the United States for more than 6 months.

(c) The beneficiary's death caused the earnings limit applicable to his earnings for purposes of deduction and the charging of excess earnings to be reduced below $1,680 for a taxable year ending after 1967.

(d) [Reserved]

(e) Reasonable belief that in determining, for deduction purposes, his earnings from employment and/or net earnings from self-employment in the taxable year in which he became entitled to benefits, earnings in such year prior to such entitlement would be excluded. However, this provision does not apply if his earnings in the taxable year, beginning with the first month of entitlement, exceeded the earnings limitation amount for such year.

(f) Unawareness that his earnings were in excess of the earnings limitation applicable to the imposition of deductions and the charging of excess earnings or that he should have reported such excess where these earnings were greater than anticipated because of:

(1) Retroactive increases in pay, including back-pay awards;

(2) Work at a higher pay rate than realized;

(3) Failure of the employer of an individual unable to keep accurate records to restrict the amount of earnings or the number of hours worked in accordance with a previous agreement with such individual;

(4) The occurrence of five Saturdays (or other work days, e.g., five Mondays) in a month and the earnings for the services on the fifth Saturday or other work day caused the deductions.

(g) The continued issuance of benefit checks to him after he sent notice to the Administration of the event which caused or should have caused the deductions provided that such continued issuance of checks led him to believe in good faith that he was entitled to checks subsequently received.

(h) Lack of knowledge that bonuses, vacation pay, or similar payments, constitute earnings for purposes of the annual earnings limitation.

(i) [Reserved]

(j) Reasonable belief that earnings in excess of the earnings limitation amount for the taxable year would subject him to deductions only for months beginning with the first month in which his earnings exceeded the earnings limitation amount. However, this provision is applicable only if he reported timely to the Administration during the taxable year when his earnings reached the applicable limitation amount for such year.

(k) Lack of knowledge by a wife, husband, or child entitled to wife's, husband's, or child's insurance benefits, as the case may be, that the individual entitled to old-age insurance benefits on the same earnings record has incurred or would incur deductions because of a violation of the annual earnings or 7–day foreign work test, whichever is applicable, provided the wife, husband, or child is not living with such old-age insurance beneficiary and did not know and had no reason to know that such beneficiary's earnings activity or the income derived therefrom has caused or would cause such deductions.

(*l*) Reasonable belief, with respect to earnings activity for months after December 1982, that net earnings from self-employment after attainment of age 70 (age 72 for months after December 1972 and before January 1983) in the taxable year in which such age was attained would not cause deductions (see § 404.430(a)) with respect to benefits payable for months in that taxable year prior to the attainment of such age.

(m) Reasonable belief by an individual entitled to child's, wife's, husband's, widow's, widower's, mother's, or parent's insurance benefits that earnings from employment and/or net earnings from self-employment after the termination of entitlement (other than termination by reason of entitlement to an old-age insurance benefit) in the taxable year in which the termination event occurred would not cause deductions with respect to benefits payable for months in that taxable year prior to the month in which the termination event occurred.

(n) Failure to understand the deduction provisions of the Act or the occurrence of unusual or unavoidable circumstances the nature of which clearly shows that the individual was unaware of a violation of such deduction provisions.

[27 FR 1162, Feb. 8, 1962, as amended at 28 FR 14492, Dec. 31, 1963; 34 FR 14888, Sept. 27, 1969; 36 FR 23361, Dec. 9, 1971; 43 FR 31318, July 21, 1978; 44 FR 20653, April 6, 1979; 59 FR 1634, Jan. 12, 1994; 60 FR 17445, April 6, 1995]

§ 404.510a When an individual is "without fault" in an entitlement overpayment.

A benefit payment under title II or title XVIII of the Act to or on behalf of an individual who fails to meet one or more requirements for entitlement to such payment or a benefit payment exceeding the amount to which he is entitled, constitutes an entitlement overpayment. Where an individual or other person on behalf of an individual accepts such overpayment because of reliance on erroneous information from an official source within the Social Security Administration (or other governmental agency which the individual had reasonable cause to believe was connected with the administration of benefits under title II or title XVIII of the Act) with respect to the interpretation of a pertinent provision of the Social Security Act or regulations pertaining thereto, or where an individual or other person on behalf of an individual is overpaid as a result of the adjustment upward (under the family maximum provision in section 203 of the Act) of the benefits of such individual at the time of the proper termination of one or more beneficiaries on the same social security record and the subsequent reduction of the benefits of such individual caused by the reentitlement of the terminated beneficiary(ies) pursuant to a change in a provision of the law, such individual, in accepting such overpayment, will be deemed to be without fault. For purposes of this section governmental agency includes intermediaries and carriers under contract pursuant to sections 1816 and 1842 of the Act.

[39 FR 43716, Dec. 18, 1974]

§ 404.511 When an individual is at "fault" in a deduction overpayment.

(a) Degree of care. An individual will not be without fault if the Administration has evidence in its possession which shows either a lack of good faith or failure to exercise a high degree of care in determining whether circumstances which may cause deductions from his benefits should be brought to the attention of the Administration by an immediate report or by return of a benefit check. The high degree of care expected of an individual may vary with the complexity of the circumstances giving rise to the overpayment and the capacity of the particular payee to realize that he is being overpaid. Accordingly, variances in the personal circumstances and situations of individual payees are to be considered in determining whether the necessary degree of care has been exercised by an individual to warrant a finding that he was without fault in accepting a deduction overpayment.

(b) Subsequent deduction overpayments. The Social Security Administration generally will not find an individual to be without fault where, after having been exonerated for a "deduction overpayment" and after having been advised of the correct interpretation of the deduction provision, the individual incurs another "deduction overpayment" under the same circumstances as the first overpayment. However, in determining whether the individual is without fault, the Social Security Administration will consider all of the pertinent circumstances surrounding the prior and subsequent "deduction overpayments," including any physical, mental, educational, or linguistic limitations (including any lack of facility with the English language) which the individual may have.

[16 FR 13054, Dec. 28, 1951; 59 FR 1634, Jan. 12, 1994]

§ 404.512 When adjustment or recovery of an overpayment will be waived.

(a) Adjustment or recovery deemed "against equity and good conscience." In the situations described in §§ 404.510(a), (b), and (c), and 404.510a, adjustment or recovery will be waived since it will be deemed such adjustment or recovery is against equity and good conscience. Adjustment or recovery will also be deemed against equity and good conscience in the situation described in § 404.510(e), but only as to a month in which the individual's earnings from wages do not exceed the total monthly benefits affected for that month.

(b) Adjustment or recovery considered to defeat the purpose of title II or be against equity and good conscience under certain circumstances. In the situation described in § 404.510(e)(except in the case of an individual whose monthly earnings from wages in employment do not exceed the total monthly benefits affected for a particular month), and in the situations described in § 404.510(f) through (n), adjustment or recovery shall be waived only where the evidence establishes that adjustment or recovery would work a financial hardship (see § 404.508) or would otherwise be inequitable (see § 404.509).

[27 FR 1163, Feb. 8, 1962, as amended at 35 FR 6321, April 18, 1970; 36 FR 23361, Dec. 9, 1971]

§ 404.513 Liability of a certifying officer.

No certifying or disbursing officer shall be held liable for any amount certified or paid by him to any individual.

(a) Where adjustment or recovery of such amount is waived under section 204(b) of the Act; or

(b) Where adjustment under section 204(a) of the Act is not completed prior to the death of all individuals against whose benefits or lump sums deductions are authorized; or

(c) Where a claim for recovery of an overpayment is compromised or collection or adjustment action is suspended or terminated pursuant to the Federal Claims Collection Act of 1966 (31 U.S.C. 951–953)(see § 404.515).

[34 FR 14889, Sept. 27, 1969]

§ 404.515 Collection and compromise of claims for overpayment.

(a) General effect of the Debt Collection Improvement Act of 1996. Claims by the Administration against an individual for recovery of overpayments under title II or title XVIII (not including title XVIII overpayments for which refund is requested from providers, physicians, or other suppliers of services) of the Act, not exceeding the sum of $100,000 or any higher amount authorized by the Attorney General, exclusive of interest, may be compromised, or collection suspended or terminated where such individual or his estate does not have the present or prospective ability to pay the full amount of the claim within a reasonable time (see paragraph (c) of this section) or the cost of collection is likely to exceed the amount of recovery (see paragraph (d) of this section) except as provided under paragraph (b) of this section.

(b) When there will be no compromise, suspension or termination of collection of a claim for overpayment—

(1) Overpaid individual alive. In any case where the overpaid individual is alive, a claim for overpayment will not be compromised, nor will there be suspension or termination of collection of the claim by the Administration if there is an indication of fraud, the filing of a false claim, or misrepresentation on the part of such individual or on the part of any other party having an interest in the claim.

(2) Overpaid individual deceased. In any case where the overpaid individual is deceased (i) a claim for overpayment in excess of $5,000 will not be compromised, nor will there be suspension or termination of collection of the claim by the Administration if there is an indication of fraud; the filing of a false claim, or misrepresentation on the part of such deceased individual, and (ii) a claim for overpayment regardless of the amount will not be compromised, nor will there be suspension or termination of collection of the claim by the Administration if there is an indication that any person other than the deceased overpaid individual had a part in the fraudulent action which resulted in the overpayment.

(c) Inability to pay claim for recovery of overpayment. In determining whether the overpaid individual is unable to pay a claim for recovery of an overpayment under title II or title XVIII of the Act, the Administration will consider such individual's age, health, present and potential income (including inheritance prospects), assets (e.g., real property, savings account), possible concealment or improper transfer of assets, and assets or income of such individual which may be available in enforced collection proceedings. The Administration will also consider exemptions available to such individual under the pertinent State or Federal law in such proceedings. In the event the overpaid individual is deceased, the Administration will consider the available assets of the estate, taking into account any liens or superior claims against the estate.

(d) Cost of collection or litigative probabilities. Where the probable costs of recovering an overpayment under title II or title XVIII of the Act would not justify enforced collection proceedings for the full amount of the claim or there is doubt concerning the Administration's ability to establish its claim as well as the time which it will take to effect such collection, a compromise or settlement for less than the full amount will be considered.

(e) Amount of compromise. The amount to be accepted in compromise of a claim for overpayment under title II or title XVIII of the Act shall bear a reasonable relationship to the amount which can be recovered by enforced collection proceedings giving due consideration to the exemptions available to the overpaid individual under State or Federal law and the time which such collection will take.

(f) Payment. Payment of the amount which the Administration has agreed to accept as a compromise in full settlement of a claim for recovery of an overpayment under title II or title XVIII of the Act must be made within the time and in the manner set by the Administration. A claim for such recovery of the overpayment shall not be considered compromised or settled until the full payment of the compromised amount has been made within the time and manner set by the Administration. Failure of the overpaid individual or his estate to make such payment as provided shall result in reinstatement of the full amount of the overpayment less any amounts paid prior to such default.

[34 FR 14889, Sept. 27, 1969; 34 FR 15413, Oct. 3, 1969; 79 FR 33684, June 12, 2014]

§ 404.520 Referral of overpayments to the Department of the Treasury for tax refund offset—General.

(a) The standards we will apply and the procedures we will follow before requesting the Department of the Treasury to offset income tax refunds due taxpayers who have an outstanding overpayment are set forth in §§ 404.520 through 404.526. These standards and procedures are authorized by 31 U.S.C. 3720A and are implemented through Department of the Treasury regulations at 31 CFR 285.2.

(b) We will use the Department of the Treasury tax refund offset procedure to collect overpayments that are certain in amount, past due and legally enforceable, and eligible for tax refund offset under regulations issued by the Department of the Treasury. We will use these procedures to collect overpayments only from persons who are not currently entitled to monthly Social Security benefits under title II of the Act. We will refer overpayments to the Department of the Treasury for offset against Federal tax refunds regardless of the length of time the debts have been outstanding.

[56 FR 52468, Oct. 21, 1991; 62 FR 38450, July 18, 1997; 62 FR 64277, Dec. 5, 1997; 76 FR 65108, Oct. 20, 2011]

§ 404.521 Notice to overpaid persons.

Before we request the collection of an overpayment by reduction of Federal and State income tax refunds, we will send a written notice of intent to the overpaid person. In our notice of intent to collect an overpayment through tax refund offset, we will state:

(a) The amount of the overpayment; and

(b) That we will collect the overpayment by requesting that the Department of the Treasury reduce any amounts payable to the overpaid person as refunds of Federal and State income taxes by an amount equal to the amount of the overpayment unless, within 60 calendar days from the date of our notice, the overpaid person:

(1) Repays the overpayment in full; or

(2) Provides evidence to us at the address given in our notice that the overpayment is not past due or legally enforceable; or

(3) Asks us to waive collection of the overpayment under section 204(b) of the Act.

(c) The conditions under which we will waive recovery of an overpayment under section 204(b) of the Act;

(d) That we will review any evidence presented that the overpayment is not past due or not legally enforceable;

(e) That the overpaid person has the right to inspect and copy our records related to the overpayment as determined by us and will be informed as to where and when the inspection and copying can be done after we receive notice from the overpaid person that inspection and copying are requested.

[56 FR 52468, Oct. 21, 1991; 62 FR 64278, Dec. 5, 1997; 76 FR 65108, Oct. 20, 2011]

§ 404.522 Review within SSA that an overpayment is past due and legally enforceable.

(a) Notification by overpaid individual. An overpaid individual who receives a notice as described in § 404.521 has the right to present evidence that all or part of the overpayment is not past due or not legally enforceable. To exercise this right, the individual must notify us and present evidence regarding the overpayment within 60 calendar days from the date of our notice.

(b) Submission of evidence. The overpaid individual may submit evidence showing that all or part of the debt is not past due or not legally enforceable as provided in paragraph (a) of this section. Failure to submit the notification and evidence within 60 calendar days will result in referral of the overpayment to the Department of the Treasury, unless the overpaid individual, within this 60–day time period, has asked us to waive collection of the overpayment under section 204(b) of the Act and we have not yet determined whether we can grant the waiver request. If the overpaid individual asks us to waive collection of the overpayment, we may ask that evidence to support the request be submitted to us.

(c) Review of the evidence. After a timely submission of evidence by the overpaid individual, we will consider all available evidence related to the overpayment. If the overpaid individual has not requested a waiver we will make findings based on a review of the written record, unless we determine that the question of indebtedness cannot be resolved by a review of the documentary evidence. If the overpaid individual has asked us to make a waiver determination and our records do not show that after an oral hearing we had previously determined that he was at "fault" in accepting the overpayment, we will not deny the waiver request without first scheduling an oral hearing.

[56 FR 52469, Oct. 21, 1991; 62 FR 64278, Dec. 5, 1997]

§ 404.523 Findings by SSA.

(a) Following the hearing or a review of the record, we will issue written findings which include supporting rationale for the findings. Issuance of these findings concerning whether the overpayment or part of the overpayment is past due and legally enforceable is the final Agency action with respect to the past-due status and enforceability of the overpayment. If we make a determination that a waiver request cannot be granted, we will issue a written notice of this determination in accordance with the regulations in subpart J of this part. Our referral of the overpayment to the Department of the Treasury will not be suspended under § 404.525 pending any further administrative review of the waiver request that the individual may seek.

(b) Copies of the findings described in paragraph (a) of this section will be distributed to the overpaid individual and the overpaid individual's attorney or other representative, if any.

(c) If the findings referred to in paragraph (a) of this section affirm that all or part of the overpayment is past due and legally enforceable and, if waiver is requested, we determine that the request cannot be granted, we will refer the overpayment to the Department of the Treasury. No referral will be made to the Department of the Treasury if, based on our review of the overpayment, we reverse our prior finding that the overpayment is past due and legally enforceable or, upon consideration of a waiver request, we determine that waiver of our collection of the overpayment is appropriate.

[56 FR 52469, Oct. 21, 1991; 62 FR 64278, Dec. 5, 1997]

§ 404.524 Review of our records related to the overpayment.

(a) Notification by the overpaid individual. An overpaid individual who intends to inspect or copy our records related to the overpayment as determined by us must notify us stating his or her intention to inspect or copy.

(b) Our response. In response to a notification by the overpaid individual as described in paragraph (a) of this section, we will notify the overpaid individual of the location and time when the overpaid individual may inspect or copy our records related to the overpayment. We may also, at our discretion, mail copies of the overpayment-related records to the overpaid individual.

[56 FR 52469, Oct. 21, 1991]

§ 404.525 Suspension of offset.

If, within 60 days of the date of the notice described in § 404.521, the overpaid individual notifies us that he or she is exercising a right described in § 404.522(a) and submits evidence pursuant to § 404.522(b) or requests a waiver under § 404.506, we will suspend any notice to the Department of the Treasury until we have issued written findings that affirm that an overpayment is past due and legally enforceable and, if applicable, make a determination that a waiver request cannot be granted.

[56 FR 52469, Oct. 21, 1991; 62 FR 64278, Dec. 5, 1997]

§ 404.526 Tax refund insufficient to cover amount of overpayment.

If a tax refund for a given taxable year is insufficient to recover an overpayment completely, the case will remain with the Department of the Treasury for offset, assuming that all criteria for offset continue to be met.

[56 FR 52469, Oct. 21, 1991; 62 FR 64278, Dec. 5, 1997]

§ 404.527 Additional methods for recovery of title II benefit overpayments.

(a) General. In addition to the methods specified in §§ 404.502 and 404.520, an overpayment under title II of the Act is also subject to recovery under the rules in subparts D and E of part 422 of this chapter. Subpart D of part 422 of this chapter applies only under the following conditions:

(1) The overpayment occurred after the individual has attained age 18;

(2) The overpaid individual is no longer entitled to benefits under title II of the Act; and

(3) Pursuant to paragraph (b) of this section, we have determined that the overpayment is otherwise unrecoverable under section 204 of the Act.

(b) When an overpayment is considered to be otherwise unrecoverable. An overpayment under title II of the Act is considered to be otherwise unrecoverable under section 204 of the Act if all of the following conditions are met:

(1) Our billing system sequence has been completed (i.e., we have sent the individual an initial notice of the overpayment, a reminder notice, and a past-due notice) or collection activity has been suspended or terminated in accordance with the Federal Claims Collection Standards in 31 CFR 903.2 or 903.3.

(2) We have not entered into an installment payment arrangement with the overpaid individual or, if we have entered into such an arrangement, the overpaid individual has failed to make any payment for two consecutive months.

(3) The overpaid individual has not requested waiver pursuant to § 404.506 or § 404.522 or, after a review conducted pursuant to those sections, we have determined that we will not waive collection of the overpayment.

(4) The overpaid individual has not requested reconsideration of the initial overpayment determination pursuant to §§ 404.907 and 404.909 or, after a review conducted pursuant to § 404.913, we have affirmed, in whole or in part, the initial overpayment determination.

(5) The overpayment cannot be recovered pursuant to § 404.502 by adjustment of benefits payable to any individual other than the overpaid individual. For purposes of this paragraph, an overpayment will be deemed to be unrecoverable from any individual who was living in a separate household from the overpaid person at the time of the overpayment and did not receive the overpayment.

[62 FR 64278, Dec. 5, 1997; 68 FR 74183, Dec. 23, 2003]

§ 404.530 Are title VIII and title XVI benefits subject to adjustment to recover title II overpayments?

(a) Definitions—

(1) Cross-program recovery. Cross-program recovery is the process that we will use to collect title II overpayments from benefits payable to you under title VIII and title XVI of the Act.

(2) Benefits payable. For purposes of this section, benefits payable means the amount of title VIII or title XVI benefits you actually would receive. For title VIII benefits, it includes your monthly benefit and any past-due benefits after any reduction by the amount of income for the month as described in §§ 408.505 through 408.515 of this chapter. For title XVI benefits, it includes your monthly benefit and any past-due benefits as described in § 416.420 of this chapter.

(b) When may we collect title II overpayments using cross-program recovery? We may use cross-program recovery to collect a title II overpayment you owe when benefits are payable to you under title VIII, title XVI, or both.

[70 FR 15, Jan. 3, 2005; 70 FR 16113, March 30, 2005]

§ 404.535 How much will we withhold from your title VIII and title XVI benefits to recover a title II overpayment?

(a) If past-due benefits are payable to you, we will withhold the lesser of the entire overpayment balance or the entire amount of past-due benefits.

(b)(1) We will collect the overpayment from current monthly benefits due in a month under title VIII and title XVI by withholding the lesser of the amount of the entire overpayment balance or:

(i) 10 percent of the monthly title VIII benefits payable for that month and

(ii) in the case of title XVI benefits, an amount no greater than the lesser of the benefit payable for that month or an amount equal to 10 percent of your income for that month (including such monthly benefit but excluding payments under title II when recovery is also made from title II benefits and excluding income excluded pursuant to §§ 416.1112 and 416.1124 of this chapter).

(2) Paragraph (b)(1) of this section does not apply if:

(i) You request and we approve a different rate of withholding, or

(ii) You or your spouse willfully misrepresented or concealed material information in connection with the overpayment.

(c) In determining whether to grant your request that we withhold less than the amount described in paragraph (b)(1) of this section, we will use the criteria applied under § 404.508 to similar requests about withholding from title II benefits.

(d) If you or your spouse willfully misrepresented or concealed material information in connection with the overpayment, we will collect the overpayment by withholding the lesser of the overpayment balance or the entire amount of title VIII and title XVI benefits payable to you. We will not collect at a lesser rate. (See § 416.571 of this chapter for what we mean by concealment of material information.)

[70 FR 15, Jan. 3, 2005; 70 FR 16113, March 30, 2005]

§ 404.540 Will you receive notice of our intention to apply cross-program recovery?

Before we collect an overpayment from you using cross-program recovery, we will send you a written notice that tells you the following information:

(a) We have determined that you owe a specific overpayment balance that can be collected by cross-program recovery;

(b) We will withhold a specific amount from the title VIII or title XVI benefits (see § 404.535);

(c) You may ask us to review this determination that you still owe this overpayment balance;

(d) You may request that we withhold a different amount from your current monthly benefits (the notice will not include this information if § 404.535(d) applies); and

(e) You may ask us to waive collection of this overpayment balance.

[70 FR 15, Jan. 3, 2005; 70 FR 16113, March 30, 2005]

§ 404.545 When will we begin cross-program recovery from current monthly benefits?

(a) We will begin collecting the overpayment balance from your title VIII or title XVI current monthly benefits or payments by cross-program recovery no sooner than 30 calendar days after the date of the notice described in § 404.540. If within that 30–day period you pay us the full overpayment balance stated in the notice, we will not begin cross-program recovery.

(b) If within that 30–day period you ask us to review our determination that you still owe us this overpayment balance, we will not begin cross-program recovery from your current monthly benefits before we review the matter and notify you of our decision in writing.

(c) If within that 30–day period you ask us to withhold a different amount than the amount stated in the notice, we will not begin cross-program recovery from your current monthly benefits until we determine the amount we will withhold. This paragraph does not apply when § 404.535(d) applies.

(d) If within that 30–day period you ask us to waive recovery of the overpayment balance, we will not begin cross-program recovery from your current monthly benefits before we review the matter and notify you of our decision in writing. See §§ 404.506 through 404.512.

[70 FR 15, Jan. 3, 2005; 70 FR 16113, March 30, 2005]

SUBPART G—FILING OF APPLICATIONS AND OTHER FORMS

Authority: Secs. 202(i), (j), (*o*), (p), and (r), 205(a), 216(i)(2), 223(b), 228(a), and 702(a)(5) of the Social Security Act (42 U.S.C. 402(i), (j), (*o*), (p), and (r), 405(a), 416(i)(2), 423(b), 428(a), and 902(a)(5)).

Source: 44 FR 37209, June 26, 1979; 51 FR 4482, Feb. 5, 1986; 51 FR 41951, Nov. 20, 1986; 52 FR 4003, Feb. 9, 1987; 52 FR 27540, July 22, 1987; 61 FR 5941, Feb. 15, 1996; 83 FR 21709, May 10, 2018, unless otherwise noted.

GENERAL PROVISIONS

§ 404.601 Introduction.

This subpart contains the Social Security Administration's rules for filing a claim for old-age, disability, dependents', and survivors' insurance benefits as described in subpart D of part 404. It tells what an application is, who may sign it, where and when it must be signed and filed, the period of time it is in effect and how it may be withdrawn. This subpart also explains when a written statement, request, or notice will be considered filed. Since the application form and procedures for filing a claim under this subpart are the same as those used to establish entitlement to Medicare benefits under 42 CFR part 405, persons who wish to become entitled to Medicare benefits should refer to the provisions of this subpart. Requirements concerning applications for the black lung benefits program are contained in part 410. Requirements concerning applications for the supplemental security income program are contained in part 416. Part 422 contains the requirements for applying for a social security number.

§ 404.602 Definitions.

For the purpose of this subpart—

Applicant means the person who files an application for benefits for himself or herself or for someone else. A person who files for himself or herself is both the applicant and the claimant.

Application refers only to an application on a form described in § 404.611.

Benefits means any old-age, disability, dependents', and survivors' insurance benefits described in subpart D, including a period of disability.

Claimant means the person who files an application for benefits for himself or herself or the person for whom an application is filed.

We, us, or *our* means the Social Security Administration (SSA).

You or *your* means, as appropriate, the person who applies for benefits, the person for whom an application is filed, or the person who may consider applying for benefits.

§ 404.603 You must file an application to receive benefits.

In addition to meeting other requirements, you must file an application to become entitled to benefits. If you believe you may be entitled to benefits, you should file an application. Filing an application will—

(a) Permit a formal decision to be made on your entitlement to benefits;

(b) Protect your entitlement to any benefits that may be payable for as many as 6 months or 12 months (depending on the type of benefit, as explained in § 404.621) before the application was filed; and

(c) Give you the right to appeal if you are dissatisfied with the decision.

[44 FR 37209, June 26, 1979, as amended at 46 FR 47444, Sept. 28, 1981]

APPLICATIONS

§ 404.610 What makes an application a claim for benefits?

We will consider your application a claim for benefits if it generally meets all of the following conditions:

(a) You must file on a prescribed form, as stated in § 404.611. See § 422.505(a) of this chapter for the types of prescribed applications you can file.

(b) You must complete and file the application with us as stated in § 404.611 and § 404.614.

(c) You, or someone described in § 404.612 who may sign an application for you, must sign the application.

(d) You must be alive at the time you file (unless one of the limited exceptions in § 404.615 applies).

[69 FR 498, Jan. 6, 2004]

§ 404.611 How do I file an application for Social Security benefits?

(a) *General rule.* You must apply for benefits on an application that we prescribe. See § 422.505(a) of this chapter for the types of applications we will accept. See § 404.614 for places where you can file your application for benefits.

(b) *What if I file a claim with the Railroad Retirement Board (RRB)?* If you file an application with the RRB on one of its forms for an annuity under section 2 of the Railroad Retirement Act, as amended, we will consider this an application for title II Social Security benefits, which you may be entitled to, unless you tell us otherwise.

(c) *What if I file a claim with the Department of Veterans Affairs (DVA)?* If you file an application with the DVA on one of its forms for survivors' dependency and indemnity compensation (see section 3005 of title 38 U.S.C.), we will consider this an application for Social Security survivors' benefits, except for the lump sum death payment.

[51 FR 41951, Nov. 20, 1986; 58 FR 60381, Nov. 16, 1993; 69 FR 498, Jan. 6, 2004]

§ 404.612 Who may sign an application.

We will determine who may sign an application according to the following rules:

(a) A claimant who is 18 years old or over, mentally competent, and physically able to do so, must sign his or her own application. If the claim is for child's benefits for a person who is not yet 22 years old, the application may be signed by a parent or a person standing in place of the parent.

(b) A claimant who is between 16 and 18 years old may sign his or her own application if he or she is mentally competent, has no court appointed representative, and is not in the care of any person.

(c) If the claimant is under age 18, or mentally incompetent, or physically unable to sign, the application may be signed by a court appointed representative or a person who is responsible for the care of the claimant, including a relative. If the claimant is in the care of an institution, the manager or principal officer of the institution may sign the application.

(d) If a person who could receive disability benefits or who could have a period of disability established dies before filing, an application for disability benefits or for a period of disability may be signed by a person who would be qualified to receive any benefits due the deceased.

(e) If a written statement showing an intent to claim benefits is filed with us, but the person for whom the benefits are claimed dies before an application is filed, an application may be filed as explained in § 404.630(d).

(f) If a person who could receive benefits on the basis of a "deemed" filing date of an application under § 404.633(b)(1)(i) or (b)(2)(i) dies before an application for the benefits is filed, the application may be signed by a person who would be qualified to receive any benefits due the deceased person as explained in § 404.633(b)(1)(ii) and (b)(2)(ii).

(g) If it is necessary to protect a claimant from losing benefits and there is good cause for the claimant not signing the application, we may accept an application signed by some one other than a person described in this section.

Example: Mr. Smith comes to a social security office a few days before the end of a month to file an application for old-age benefits for his neighbor, Mr. Jones. Mr. Jones, a 63 year old widower, just suffered a heart attack and is in the hospital. He asked Mr. Smith to file the application for him. We will accept an application signed by Mr. Smith since it would not be possible to have Mr. Jones sign and file the application until the next calendar month and a loss of one month's benefits would result.

[59 FR 44923, Aug. 31, 1994; 61 FR 41330, Aug. 8, 1996]

§ 404.613 Evidence of authority to sign an application for another.

(a) A person who signs an application for someone else will be required to provide evidence of his or her authority to sign the application for the person claiming benefits under the following rules:

(1) If the person who signs is a court appointed representative, he or she must submit a certificate issued by the court showing authority to act for the claimant.

(2) If the person who signs is not a court appointed representative, he or she must submit a statement describing his or her relationship to the claimant. The statement must also describe the extent to which the person is responsible for the care of the claimant. This latter information will not be requested if the application is signed by a parent for a child with whom he or she is living.

(3) If the person who signs is the manager or principal officer of an institution which is responsible for the care of the claimant, he or she must submit a statement indicating the person's position of responsibility at the institution.

(b) We may, at any time, require additional evidence to establish the authority of a person to sign an application for someone else.

§ 404.614 When an application or other form is considered filed.

(a) General rule. Except as otherwise provided in paragraph (b) of this section and in §§ 404.630 through 404.633 which relate to the filing date of an application, an application for benefits, or a written statement, request, or notice is filed on the day it is received by an SSA employee at one of our offices or by an SSA employee who is authorized to receive it at a place other than one of our offices.

(b) Other places and dates of filing. We will also accept as the date of filing—

(1) The date an application for benefits, or a written statement, request or notice is received by any office of the U.S. Foreign Service or by the Veterans Administration Regional Office in the Philippines;

(2) The date an application for benefits or a written statement, request or notice is mailed to us by the U.S. mail, if using the date we receive it would result in the loss or lessening of rights. The date shown by a U.S. postmark will be used as the date of mailing. If the postmark is unreadable, or there is no postmark, we will consider other evidence of when you mailed it to us; or

(3) The date an application for benefits is filed with the Railroad Retirement Board or the Veterans Administration. See § 404.611 (b) and (c) for an explanation of when an application for benefits filed with the Railroad Retirement Board or the Veterans Administration is considered an application for social security benefits.

[59 FR 44923, Aug. 31, 1994]

§ 404.615 Claimant must be alive when an application is filed.

A claimant must be alive at the time an application is filed. There are the following exceptions to this general rule:

(a) If a disabled person dies before filing an application for disability benefits or a period of disability, a person who would be qualified to receive any benefits due the deceased may file an application. The application must be filed within 3 months after the month in which the disabled person died.

(b) If a written statement showing an intent to claim benefits is filed with us, but the person for whom the benefits are claimed dies before an application is filed, an application may be filed as explained in § 404.630(d).

(c) If a person who could receive benefits on the basis of a "deemed" filing date of an application under § 404.633(b)(1)(i) or (b)(2)(i) dies before an application for the benefits is filed, the application may be signed by a person who would be qualified to receive any benefits due the deceased person as explained in § 404.633(b)(1)(ii) and (b)(2)(ii).

[59 FR 44923, Aug. 31, 1994; 61 FR 41330, Aug. 8, 1996]

§ 404.617 Pilot program for photographic identification of disability benefit applicants in designated geographic areas.

(a) To be eligible for Social Security disability insurance benefits in the designated pilot geographic areas during the time period of the pilot, you or a person acting on your behalf must give SSA permission to take your photograph and make this photograph a part of the claims folder. You must give us this permission when you apply for benefits and/or when we ask for it at a later time. Failure to cooperate will result in denial of benefits. We will permit an exception to the photograph requirement when an individual has a sincere religious objection. This pilot will be in effect for a six-month period after these final rules become effective.

(b) Designated pilot geographic areas means:

(1) All SSA field offices in the State of South Carolina.

(2) The Augusta, Georgia SSA field office.

(3) All SSA field offices in the State of Kansas.

(4) Selected SSA field offices located in New York City.

[68 FR 23194, May 1, 2003]

EFFECTIVE FILING PERIOD OF APPLICATION

§ 404.620 Filing before the first month you meet the requirements for benefits.

(a) General rule. If you file an application for benefits before the first month you meet all the other requirements for entitlement, the application will remain in effect until we make a final determination on your application unless there is an administrative law judge hearing decision on your application. If there is an administrative law judge hearing decision, your application will remain in effect until the administrative law judge hearing decision is issued.

(1) If you meet all the requirements for entitlement while your application is in effect, we may pay you benefits from the first month that you meet all the requirements.

(2) If you first meet all the requirements for entitlement after the period for which your application was in effect, you must file a new application for benefits. In this case, we may pay you benefits only from the first month that you meet all the requirements based on the new application.

(b) [Reserved by 83 FR 21709]

[52 FR 4003, Feb. 9, 1987; 83 FR 21709, May 10, 2018]

§ 404.621 What happens if I file after the first month I meet the requirements for benefits?

(a) Filing for disability benefits and for old-age, survivors', or dependents' benefits.

(1) If you file an application for disability benefits, widow's or widower's benefits based on disability, or wife's, husband's, or child's benefits based on the earnings record of a person entitled to disability benefits, after the first month you could have been entitled to them, you may receive benefits for up to 12 months immediately before the month in which your application is filed. Your benefits may begin with the first month in this 12–month period in which you meet all the requirements for entitlement. Your entitlement, however, to wife's or husband's benefits under this rule is limited by paragraph (a)(3) of this section.

(2) If you file an application for old-age benefits, widow's or widower's benefits not based on disability, wife's, husband's, or child's benefits based on the earnings record of a person not entitled to disability benefits, or mother's, father's, or parent's benefits, after the first month you could have been entitled to them, you may receive benefits for up to 6 months immediately before the month in which your application is filed. Your benefits may begin with the first month in this 6–month period in which you meet all the requirements for entitlement. Your entitlement, however, to old-age, wife's, husband's, widow's, or widower's benefits under this rule is limited by paragraph (a)(3) of this section.

(3) If the effect of the payment of benefits for a month before the month you file would be to reduce your benefits because of your age, you cannot be entitled to old-age, wife's, husband's, widow's, or widower's benefits for any month before the month in which your application is filed, unless you meet one of the conditions in paragraph (a)(4) of this section. (An explanation of the reduction that occurs because of age if you are entitled to these benefits for a month before you reach full retirement age, as defined in § 404.409, is in § 404.410.) An example follows that assumes you do not meet any of the conditions in paragraph (a)(4) of this section.

Example: You will attain full retirement age in March 2003. If you apply for old-age benefits in March, you cannot be entitled to benefits in the 6–month period before March because the payment of benefits for any of these months would result in your benefits being reduced for age. If you do not file your application until June 2003, you may be entitled to benefits for the month of March, April and May because the payment of benefits for these months would not result in your benefits being reduced for age. You will not, however, receive benefits for the 3 months before March.

(4) The limitation in paragraph (a)(3) of this section on your entitlement to old-age, wife's, husband's, widow's, or widower's benefits for months before you file an application does not apply if:

(i) You are a widow, widower, surviving divorced wife, or surviving divorced husband who is disabled and could be entitled to retroactive benefits for any month before age 60. If you could not be entitled before age 60, the limitation will prevent payment of benefits to you for past months, but it will not affect the month you become entitled to hospital insurance benefits.

(ii) You are a widow, widower, or surviving divorced spouse of the insured person who died in the month before you applied and you were at least age 60 in the month of death of the insured person on whose earnings record you are claiming benefits. In this case, you can be entitled beginning with the month the insured person died if you choose and if you file your application on or after July 1, 1983.

(b) Filing for lump-sum death payment. An application for a lump-sum death payment must be filed within 2 years after the death of the person on whose earnings record the claim is filed. There are two exceptions to the 2–year filing requirement:

(1) If there is a good cause for failure to file within the 2–year period, we will consider your application as though it were filed within the 2–year period. Good cause does not exist if you were informed of the need to file an application within the 2–year period and you neglected to do so or did not desire to make a claim. Good cause will be found to exist if you did not file within the time limit due to—

(i) Circumstances beyond your control, such as extended illness, mental or physical incapacity, or a language barrier;

(ii) Incorrect or incomplete information we furnished you;

(iii) Your efforts to get evidence to support your claim without realizing that you could submit the evidence after filing an application; or

(iv) Unusual or unavoidable circumstances which show that you could not reasonably be expected to know of the time limit.

(2) The Soldiers' and Sailors' Civil Relief Act of 1940 provides for extending the filing time.

(c) Filing for a period of disability. You must file an application for a period of disability while you are disabled or no later than 12 months after the month in which your period of disability ended. If you were unable to apply within the 12–month time period because of a physical or mental condition, you may apply not more than 36 months after your disability ended. The general rule we use to decide whether your failure to file was due to a physical or mental condition is stated in § 404.322.

(d) Filing after death of person eligible for disability benefits or period of disability. If you file for disability benefits or a period of disability for another person who died before filing an application and you would qualify under § 404.503(b) to receive any benefits due the deceased, you must file an application no later than the end of the third month following the month in which the disabled person died.

(e) [Redesignated as subsection (d) by 83 FR 21709]

[44 FR 37209, June 26, 1979, as amended at 46 FR 47444, Sept. 28, 1981; 51 FR 4482, Feb. 5, 1986; 56 FR 58846, Nov. 22, 1991; 68 FR 4711, Jan. 30, 2003; 83 FR 21709, May 10, 2018]

§ 404.622 Limiting an application.

Your application may entitle you to benefits for up to 6 months or 12 months (depending on the type of benefit, as explained in § 404.621) before the month in which it is filed. You may limit the number of months of your entitlement in the 6–month or 12–month period. You may state this choice any time before a decision is made on your claim by indicating, in writing, the month you want your benefits to begin. You may change the first month of entitlement in this 6–month or 12–month period after a decision has been made on your claim under the following conditions:

(a) You file the request in writing.

(b) If you are filing for the claimant, he or she is alive when the request is filed.

(c) If any other person who is entitled to benefits would lose some or all of those benefits because of the change, that person, or the person who filed for him or her, consents in writing.

(d) Any benefit payments that would become improper as a result of the change in entitlement month are repaid, or we are satisfied that they will be repaid.

[44 FR 37209, June 26, 1979, as amended at 46 FR 47445, Sept. 28, 1981]

§ 404.623 Am I required to file for all benefits if I am eligible for old-age and husband's or wife's benefits?

(a) Presumed filing for husband's or wife's benefits. If you file an application for old-age benefits, you are presumed to have filed an application for husband's or wife's benefits in the first month of your entitlement to old-age benefits, if—

(1) Your old-age benefits are reduced for age because you choose to receive them before you reach full retirement age (as defined in § 404.409); and

(2) You are eligible for either a husband's or a wife's benefit for the first month of your entitlement to old-age benefits.

(b) Presumed filing for old-age benefits. If you file an application for a husband's or a wife's benefit, you are presumed to have filed an application for old-age benefits in the first month of your entitlement to husband's or wife's benefits if—

(1) Your husband's or wife's benefits are reduced for age because you choose to receive them before you reach full retirement age (as defined in § 404.409); and

(2) You are eligible for old-age benefits for the first month of your entitlement to husband's or wife's benefits.

(c) Exception. Paragraph (b) of this section does not apply if you are also entitled to disability benefits in the first month of your entitlement to husband's or wife's benefits. In this event, you are presumed to have filed for old-age benefits only if your disability benefits end before you reach full retirement age (as defined in § 404.409).

[68 FR 4712, Jan. 30, 2003]

FILING DATE BASED ON WRITTEN STATEMENT

§ 404.630 Use of date of written statement as filing date.

If a written statement, such as a letter, indicating your intent to claim benefits either for yourself or for another person is filed with us under the rules stated in § 404.614, we will use the filing date of the written statement as the filing date of the application, if all of the following requirements are met:

(a) The statement indicates an intent to claim benefits.

(b) The statement is signed by the claimant, the claimant's spouse, or a person described in § 404.612. If the claimant, the claimant's spouse, or a person described in § 404.612 telephones us and advises us of his or her intent to file a claim but cannot file an application before the end of the month, we will prepare and sign a written statement if it is necessary to prevent the loss of benefits. If the claimant, the claimant's spouse, or a person described in § 404.612 contacts us through the Internet by completing and transmitting the Personal Identification Information data on the Internet Social Security Benefit Application to us, we will use the date of the transmission as the filing date if it is necessary to prevent the loss of benefits.

(c) The claimant files an application with us on an application form as described in § 404.611, or one is filed for the claimant by a person described in § 404.612, within 6 months after the date of a notice we will send advising of the need to file an application. We will send the notice to the claimant. However, if it is clear from the information we receive that the claimant is a minor or is mentally incompetent, we will send the notice to the person who submitted the written statement.

(d) The claimant is alive when the application is filed; or if the claimant has died after the written statement was filed, an application is filed—

(1) By or for a person who would be eligible to receive benefits on the deceased's earnings record;

(2) By a person acting for the deceased's estate; or

(3) If the statement was filed with a hospital under § 404.632, by the hospital if—

(i) No person described in paragraph (d)(1) or (2) of this section can be located; or

(ii) A person described in paragraphs (d)(1) or (2) of this section is located but refuses or fails to file the application unless the refusal or failure to file is because it would be harmful to the deceased person or the deceased's estate.

[71 FR 24814, April 27, 2006]

§ 404.631 Statements filed with the Railroad Retirement Board.

A written statement filed with the Railroad Retirement Board will be considered a written statement filed with us under the rules in § 404.630 if—

(a) The statement indicates an intent to claim any payments under the Railroad Retirement Act;

(b) It bears the signature of the person filing the statement;

(c) No application is filed with the Railroad Retirement Board on one of its forms. If an application has been filed, we will use the date of filing of that application as determined by the Railroad Retirement Board (see § 404.614(b)(3)); and

(d) The statement is sent to us by the Railroad Retirement Board.

§ 404.632 Statements filed with a hospital.

A statement (generally a hospital admission form) filed with a hospital may serve as a written statement under § 404.630 if the requirements of this section are met. The statement will be considered filed with us as of the date it was filed with the hospital and will serve to protect entitlement to benefits. A statement filed with a hospital by you or some other person for you requesting or indicating an intent to claim benefits will be considered a written statement filed with us and § 404.630 will apply to it if—

(a) You are a patient in the hospital;

(b) The hospital provides services covered by hospital insurance under the Medicare program;

(c) An application has not already been filed; and

(d) The statement is sent to us.

DEEMED FILING DATE BASED ON MISINFORMATION

§ 404.633 Deemed filing date in a case of misinformation.

(a) General. You may have considered applying for monthly benefits for yourself or for another person, and you may have contacted us in writing, by telephone or in person to inquire about filing an application for these benefits. It is possible that in responding to your inquiry, we may have given you misinformation about your eligibility for such benefits, or the eligibility of the person on whose behalf you were considering applying for benefits, which caused you not to file an application at that time. If this happened, and later an application for such benefits is filed with us, we may establish an earlier filing date under this section.

Example 1: Mrs. Smith, a widow of an insured individual, contacts a Social Security office when she reaches age 60 to inquire about applying for widow's insurance benefits. She is told by an SSA employee that she must be age 62 to be eligible for these benefits. This information, which was incorrect, causes Mrs. Smith not to file an application for benefits. When Mrs. Smith reaches age 62, she again contacts a Social Security office to ask about filing for widow's insurance benefits and learns that she could have received the benefits at age 60. She files an application for these benefits, provides the information required under paragraph (f) of this section to show that an SSA employee provided misinformation, and requests a deemed filing date based on the misinformation which she received from an SSA employee when she was age 60.

Example 2: Ms. Hill, a 22-year-old, is forced to stop work because of illness. When she contacts a Social Security office to inquire about applying for disability insurance benefits, she is told by an SSA employee that she must have 20 quarters of coverage out of the last 40 calendar quarters to be insured for disability insurance benefits. The employee fails to consider the special rules for insured status for persons who become disabled before age 31 and, consequently, tells Ms. Hill that she is not insured because she only has 16 quarters of coverage. The misinformation causes Ms. Hill not to file an application for disability insurance benefits. Because of her illness, she is unable to return to work. A year later, Ms. Hill reads an article that indicates that there are special rules for insured status for young workers who become disabled. She again contacts a Social Security office to inquire about benefits based on disability and learns that she was misinformed earlier about her insured status. She files an application for disability insurance benefits, provides the information required under paragraph (f) of this section to show that an SSA employee provided misinformation, and requests a deemed filing date based on the misinformation provided to her earlier.

(b) Deemed filing date of an application based on misinformation. Subject to the requirements and conditions in paragraphs (c) through (g) of this section, we may establish a deemed filing date of an application for monthly benefits under the following provisions.

(1)(i) If we determine that you failed to apply for monthly benefits for yourself because we gave you misinformation about your eligibility for such benefits, we will deem an application for such benefits to have been filed with us on the later of—

(A) The date on which the misinformation was provided to you; or

(B) The date on which you met all of the requirements for entitlement to such benefits, other than the requirement of filing an application.

(ii) Before we may establish a deemed filing date of an application for benefits for you under paragraph (b)(1)(i) of this section, you or a person described in § 404.612 must file an application for such benefits. If you die before an application for the benefits is filed with us, we will consider establishing a deemed filing date of an application for such benefits only if an application for the benefits is filed with us by a person who would be qualified to receive any benefits due you.

(2)(i) If you had authority under § 404.612 to sign an application for benefits for another person, and we determine that you failed to apply for monthly benefits for that person because we gave you misinformation about that person's eligibility for such benefits, we will deem an application for such benefits to have been filed with us on the later of—

(A) The date on which the misinformation was provided to you; or

(B) The date on which the person met all of the requirements for entitlement to such benefits, other than the requirement of filing an application.

(ii) Before we may establish a deemed filing date of an application for benefits for the person under paragraph (b)(2)(i) of this section, you, such person, or another person described in § 404.612 must file an application for such benefits. If the person referred to in paragraph (b)(2)(i) of this section dies before an application for the benefits is filed with us, we will consider establishing a deemed filing date of an application for such benefits only if an application for the benefits is filed with us by a person who would be qualified to receive any benefits due the deceased person.

(c) Requirements concerning the misinformation. We apply the following requirements for purposes of paragraph (b) of this section.

(1) The misinformation must have been provided to you by one of our employees while he or she was acting in his or her official capacity as our employee. For purposes of this section, an employee includes an officer of SSA.

(2) Misinformation is information which we consider to be incorrect, misleading, or incomplete in view of the facts which you gave to the employee, or of which the employee was aware or should have been aware, re-

garding your particular circumstances, or the particular circumstances of the person referred to in paragraph (b)(2)(i) of this section. In addition, for us to find that the information you received was incomplete, the employee must have failed to provide you with the appropriate, additional information which he or she would be required to provide in carrying out his or her official duties.

(3) The misinformation may have been provided to you orally or in writing.

(4) The misinformation must have been provided to you in response to a specific request by you to us for information about your eligibility for benefits or the eligibility for benefits of the person referred to in paragraph (b)(2)(i) of this section for which you were considering filing an application.

(d) Evidence that misinformation was provided. We will consider the following evidence in making a determination under paragraph (b) of this section.

(1) Preferred evidence. Preferred evidence is written evidence which relates directly to your inquiry about your eligibility for benefits or the eligibility of another person and which shows that we gave you misinformation which caused you not to file an application. Preferred evidence includes, but is not limited to, the following—

(i) A notice, letter or other document which was issued by us and addressed to you; or

(ii) Our record of your telephone call, letter or in-person contact.

(2) Other evidence. In the absence of preferred evidence, we will consider other evidence, including your statements about the alleged misinformation, to determine whether we gave you misinformation which caused you not to file an application. We will not find that we gave you misinformation, however, based solely on your statements. Other evidence which you provide or which we obtain must support your statements. Evidence which we will consider includes, but is not limited to, the following—

(i) Your statements about the alleged misinformation, including statements about—

(A) The date and time of the alleged contact(s);

(B) How the contact was made, e.g., by telephone or in person;

(C) The reason(s) the contact was made;

(D) Who gave the misinformation; and

(E) The questions you asked and the facts you gave us, and the questions we asked and the information we gave you, at the time of the contact;

(ii) Statements from others who were present when you were given the alleged misinformation, e.g., a neighbor who accompanied you to our office;

(iii) If you can identify the employee or the employee can recall your inquiry about benefits—

(A) Statements from the employee concerning the alleged contact, including statements about the questions you asked, the facts you gave, the questions the employee asked, and the information provided to you at the time of the alleged contact; and

(B) Our assessment of the likelihood that the employee provided the alleged misinformation;

(iv) An evaluation of the credibility and the validity of your allegations in conjunction with other relevant information; and

(v) Any other information regarding your alleged contact.

(e) Information which does not constitute satisfactory proof that misinformation was given. Certain kinds of information will not be considered satisfactory proof that we gave you misinformation which caused you not to file an application. Examples of such information include—

(1) General informational pamphlets that we issue to provide basic program information;

(2) The Personal Earnings and Benefit Estimate Statement that is based on an individual's reported and projected earnings and is an estimate which can be requested at any time;

(3) General information which we review or prepare but which is disseminated by the media, e.g., radio, television, magazines, and newspapers; and

(4) Information provided by other governmental agencies, e.g., the Department of Veterans Affairs, the Department of Defense, State unemployment agencies, and State and local governments.

(f) Claim for benefits based on misinformation. You may make a claim for benefits based on misinformation at any time. Your claim must contain information that will enable us to determine if we did provide misinformation to you about your eligibility for benefits, or the eligibility of a person on whose behalf you were considering applying for benefits, which caused you not to file an application for the benefits. Specifically, your claim must be in writing and it must explain what information was provided; how, when and where it was provided and by whom; and why the information caused you not to file an application. If you give us this information, we will make a determination on such a claim for benefits if all of the following conditions are also met.

(1) An application for the benefits described in paragraph (b)(1)(i) or (b)(2)(i) of this section is filed with us by someone described in paragraph (b)(1)(ii) or (b)(2)(ii) of this section, as appropriate. The application must be filed after the alleged misinformation was provided. This application may be—

(i) An application on which we have made a previous final determination or decision awarding the benefits, but only if the claimant continues to be entitled to benefits based on that application;

(ii) An application on which we have made a previous final determination or decision denying the benefits, but only if such determination or decision is reopened under § 404.988; or

(iii) A new application on which we have not made a final determination or decision.

(2) The establishment of a deemed filing date of an application for benefits based on misinformation could result in the claimant becoming entitled to benefits or to additional benefits.

(3) We have not made a previous final determination or decision to which you were a party on a claim for benefits based on alleged misinformation involving the same facts and issues. This provision does not apply, however, if the final determination or decision may be reopened under § 404.988.

(g) Effective date. This section applies only to misinformation which we provided after December 1982. In addition, this section is effective only for benefits payable for months after December 1982.

[59 FR 44924, Aug. 31, 1994]

WITHDRAWAL OF APPLICATION

§ 404.640 Withdrawal of an application.

(a) Request for withdrawal filed before a determination is made. An application may be withdrawn before we make a determination on it if—

(1) A written request for withdrawal is filed at a place described in § 404.614 by the claimant or a person who may sign an application for the claimant under § 404.612; and

(2) The claimant is alive at the time the request is filed.

(b) Request for withdrawal filed after a determination is made. An application may be withdrawn after we make a determination on it if—

(1) The conditions in paragraph (a) of this section are met;

(2) Any other person whose entitlement would be rendered erroneous because of the withdrawal consents in writing to it. Written consent for the person may be given by someone who could sign an application for him or her under § 404.612; and

(3) All benefits already paid based on the application being withdrawn are repaid or we are satisfied that they will be repaid.

(4) Old age benefits. An old age benefit application may be withdrawn if, in addition to the requirements of this section—

(i) The request for withdrawal is filed within 12 months of the first month of entitlement; and

(ii) The claimant has not previously withdrawn an application for old age benefits.

(c) Request for withdrawal filed after the claimant's death. An application may be withdrawn after the claimant's death, regardless of whether we have made a determination on it, if—

(1) The claimant's application was for old-age benefits that would be reduced because of his or her age;

(2) The claimant died before we certified his or her benefit entitlement to the Treasury Department for payment;

(3) A written request for withdrawal is filed at a place described in § 404.614 by or for the person eligible for widow's or widower's benefits based on the claimant's earnings; and

(4) The conditions in paragraphs (b)(2) and (3) of this section are met.

(d) Effect of withdrawal. If we approve a request to withdraw an application, the application will be considered as though it was never filed. If we disapprove a request for withdrawal, the application is treated as though the request was never filed.

[48 FR 21931, May 16, 1983; 51 FR 37720, Oct. 24, 1986; 75 FR 76259, Dec. 8, 2010]

§ 404.641 Cancellation of a request to withdraw.

A request to withdraw an application may be cancelled and the application reinstated if—

(a) A written request for cancellation is filed at a place described in § 404.614 by the claimant or someone who may sign an application for the claimant under § 404.612;

(b) The claimant is alive at the time the request for cancellation is filed; and

(c) For a cancellation request received after we have approved the withdrawal, the request is filed no later than 60 days after the date of the notice of approval.

SUBPART H—EVIDENCE

Authority: Secs. 205(a) and 702(a)(5) of the Social Security Act (42 U.S.C. 405(a) and 902(a)(5)).

Source: 43 FR 24795, June 7, 1978; 52 FR 27540, July 22, 1987; 61 FR 5941, Feb. 15, 1996, unless otherwise noted.

GENERAL

§ 404.701 Introduction.

This subpart contains the Social Security Administration's basic rules about what evidence is needed when a person claims old-age, disability, dependents' and survivors' insurance benefits as described in subpart D. In addition, there are special evidence requirements for disability benefits. These are contained in subpart P. Evidence of a person's earnings under social security is described in subpart I. Evidence needed to obtain a social security number card is described in part 422. Evidence requirements for the supplemental security income program are contained in part 416.

§ 404.702 Definitions.

As used in this subpart:

Apply means to sign a form or statement that the Social Security Administration accepts as an application for benefits under the rules set out in subpart G.

Benefits means any old-age, disability, dependents' and survivors' insurance benefits described in subpart D, including a period of disability.

Convincing evidence means one or more pieces of evidence that prove you meet a requirement for eligibility. See § 404.708 for the guides we use in deciding whether evidence is convincing.

Eligible means that a person would meet all the requirements for entitlement to benefits for a period of time but has not yet applied.

Entitled means that a person has applied and has proven his or her right to benefits for a period of time.

Evidence means any record, document, or signed statement that helps to show whether you are eligible for benefits or whether you are still entitled to benefits.

Insured person means someone who has enough earnings under social security to permit the payment of benefits on his or her earnings record. He or she is fully insured, transitionally insured, currently insured, or insured for disability as defined in subpart B.

We or Us refers to the Social Security Administration.

You refers to the person who has applied for benefits, or the person for whom someone else has applied.

§ 404.703 When evidence is needed.

When you apply for benefits, we will ask for evidence that you are eligible for them. After you become entitled to benefits, we may ask for evidence showing whether you continue to be entitled to benefits; or evidence showing whether your benefit payments should be reduced or stopped. See § 404.401 for a list showing when benefit payments must be reduced or stopped.

§ 404.704 Your responsibility for giving evidence.

When evidence is needed to prove your eligibility or your right to continue to receive benefit payments, you will be responsible for obtaining and giving the evidence to us. We will be glad to advise you what is needed and how to get it and we will consider any evidence you give us. If your evidence is a foreign-language record or document, we can have it translated for you. Evidence given to us will be kept confidential and not disclosed to anyone but you except under the rules set out in part 401. You should also be aware that Section 208 of the Social Security Act provides criminal penalties for misrepresenting the facts or for making false statements to obtain social security benefits for yourself or someone else.

§ 404.705 Failure to give requested evidence.

Generally, you will be asked to give us by a certain date specific kinds of evidence or information to prove you are eligible for benefits. If we do not receive the evidence or information by that date, we may decide you are not eligible for benefits. If you are already receiving benefits, you may be asked to give us by a certain date information needed to decide whether you continue to be entitled to benefits or whether your benefits should be stopped or reduced. If you do not give us the requested information by the date given, we may decide that you are no longer entitled to benefits or that your benefits should be stopped or reduced. You should let us know if you are unable to give us the requested evidence within the specified time and explain why there will be a delay. If this delay is due to illness, failure to receive timely evidence you have asked for from another source, or a similar circumstance, you will be given additional time to give us the evidence.

§ 404.706 Where to give evidence.

Evidence should be given to the people at a Social Security Administration office. In the Philippines evidence should be given to the people at the Veterans Administration Regional Office. Elsewhere outside the United States, evidence should be given to the people at a United States Foreign Service Office.

§ 404.707 Original records or copies as evidence.

(a) General. To prove your eligibility or continuing entitlement to benefits, you may be asked to show us an original document or record. These original records or documents will be returned to you after we have photocopied them. We will also accept copies of original records that are properly certified and some uncertified birth notifications. These types of records are described below in this section.

(b) Certified copies of original records. You may give us copies of original records or extracts from records if they are certified as true and exact copies by—

(1) The official custodian of the record;

(2) A Social Security Administration employee authorized to certify copies;

(3) A Veterans Administration employee if the evidence was given to that agency to obtain veteran's benefits;

(4) A U.S. Consular Officer or employee of the Department of State authorized to certify evidence received outside the United States; or

(5) An employee of a State Agency or State Welfare Office authorized to certify copies of original records in the agency's or office's files.

(c) Uncertified copies of original records. You may give us an uncertified photocopy of a birth registration notification as evidence where it is the practice of the local birth registrar to issue them in this way.

§ 404.708 How we decide what is enough evidence.

When you give us evidence, we examine it to see if it is convincing evidence. If it is, no other evidence is needed. In deciding if evidence is convincing, we consider whether—

(a) Information contained in the evidence was given by a person in a position to know the facts;

(b) There was any reason to give false information when the evidence was created;

(c) Information contained in the evidence was given under oath, or with witnesses present, or with the knowledge there was a penalty for giving false information;

(d) The evidence was created at the time the event took place or shortly thereafter;

(e) The evidence has been altered or has any erasures on it; and

(f) Information contained in the evidence agrees with other available evidence, including our records.

§ 404.709 Preferred evidence and other evidence.

If you give us the type of evidence we have shown as preferred in the following sections of this subpart, we will generally find it is convincing evidence. This means that unless we have information in our records that raises a doubt about the evidence, other evidence of the same fact will not be needed. If preferred evidence is not available, we will consider any other evidence you give us. If this other evidence is several different records or documents which all show the same information, we may decide it is convincing evidence even though it is not preferred evidence. If the other evidence is not convincing by itself, we will ask for additional evidence. If this additional evidence shows the same information, all the evidence considered together may be convincing. When we have convincing evidence of the facts that must be proven or it is clear that the evidence provided does not prove the necessary facts, we will make a formal decision about your benefit rights.

EVIDENCE OF AGE, MARRIAGE, AND DEATH

§ 404.715 When evidence of age is needed.

(a) If you apply for benefits, we will ask for evidence of age which shows your date of birth unless you are applying for—

(1) A lump-sum death payment;

(2) A wife's benefit and you have the insured person's child in your care;

(3) A mother's or father's benefit; or

(4) A disability benefit (or for a period of disability) and neither your eligibility nor benefit amount depends upon your age.

(b) If you apply for wife's benefits while under age 62 or if you apply for a mother's or father's benefit, you will be asked for evidence of the date of birth of the insured person's children in your care.

(c) If you apply for benefits on the earnings record of a deceased person, you may be asked for evidence of his or her age if this is needed to decide whether he or she was insured at the time of death or what benefit amount is payable to you.

§ 404.716 Type of evidence of age to be given.

(a) Preferred evidence. The best evidence of your age, if you can obtain it, is either: a birth certificate or hospital birth record recorded before age 5; or a religious record which shows your date of birth and was recorded before age 5.

(b) Other evidence of age. If you cannot obtain the preferred evidence of your age, you will be asked for other convincing evidence that shows your date of birth or age at a certain time such as: an original family bible or family record; school records; census records; a statement signed by the physician or midwife who was present at your birth; insurance policies; a marriage record; a passport; an employment record; a delayed birth certificate, your child's birth certificate; or an immigration or naturalization record.

§ 404.720 Evidence of a person's death.

(a) When evidence of death is required. If you apply for benefits on the record of a deceased person, we will ask for evidence of the date and place of his or her death. We may also ask for evidence of another person's death if this is needed to prove you are eligible for benefits.

(b) Preferred evidence of death. The best evidence of a person's death is—

(1) A certified copy or extract from the public record of death, coroner's report of death, or verdict of a coroner's jury; or a certificate by the custodian of the public record of death;

(2) A statement of the funeral director, attending physician, intern of the institution where death occurred;

(3) A certified copy of, or extract from an official report or finding of death made by an agency or department of the United States; or

(4) If death occurred outside the United States, an official report of death by a United States Consul or other employee of the State Department; or a copy of the public record of death in the foreign country.

(c) Other evidence of death. If you cannot obtain the preferred evidence of a person's death, you will be asked to explain why and to give us other convincing evidence such as: the signed statements of two or more people with personal knowledge of the death, giving the place, date, and cause of death.

§ 404.721 Evidence to presume a person is dead.

If you cannot prove the person is dead but evidence of death is needed, we will presume he or she died at a certain time if you give us the following evidence:

(a) A certified copy of, or extract from, an official report or finding by an agency or department of the United States that a missing person is presumed to be dead as set out in Federal law (5 U.S.C. 5565). Unless we have other evidence showing an actual date of death, we will use the date he or she was reported missing as the date of death.

(b) Signed statements by those in a position to know and other records which show that the person has been absent from his or her residence and has not been heard from for at least 7 years. If the presumption of death is not rebutted pursuant to § 404.722, we will use as the person's date of death either the date he or she left home, the date ending the 7 year period, or some other date depending upon what the evidence shows is the most likely date of death.

(c) If you are applying for benefits as the insured person's grandchild or stepgrandchild but the evidence does not identify a parent, we will presume the parent died in the first month in which the insured person became entitled to benefits.

[60 FR 19164, April 17, 1995]

§ 404.722 Rebuttal of a presumption of death.

A presumption of death made based on § 404.721(b) can be rebutted by evidence that establishes that the person is still alive or explains the individual's absence in a manner consistent with continued life rather than death.

Example 1: Evidence in a claim for surviving child's benefits showed that the worker had wages posted to his earnings record in the year following the disappearance. It was established that the wages belonged to the worker and were for work done after his "disappearance." In this situation, the presumption of death is rebutted by evidence (wages belonging to the worker) that the person is still alive after the disappearance.

Example 2: Evidence shows that the worker left the family home shortly after a woman, whom he had been seeing, also disappeared, and that the worker phoned his wife several days after the disappearance to state he intended to begin a new life in California. In this situation the presumption of death is rebutted because the evidence explains the worker's absence in a manner consistent with continued life.

[60 FR 19165, April 17, 1995]

§ 404.723 When evidence of marriage is required.

If you apply for benefits as the insured person's husband or wife, widow or widower, divorced wife or divorced husband, we will ask for evidence of the marriage and where and when it took place. We may also ask for this evidence if you apply for child's benefits or for the lump-sum death payment as the widow or widower. If you are a widow, widower, or divorced wife who remarried after your marriage to the insured person ended, we may also ask for evidence of the remarriage. You may be asked for evidence of someone else's marriage if this is necessary to prove your marriage to the insured person was valid. In deciding whether the marriage to the insured person is valid or not, we will follow the law of the State where the insured person had his or her permanent home when you applied or, if earlier, when he or she died—see § 404.770. What evidence we will ask for depends upon whether the insured person's marriage was a ceremonial marriage, a common-law marriage, or a marriage we will deem to be valid.

[43 FR 24795, June 7, 1978, as amended at 44 FR 34493, June 15, 1979]

§ 404.725 Evidence of a valid ceremonial marriage.

(a) General. A valid ceremonial marriage is one that follows procedures set by law in the State or foreign country where it takes place. These procedures cover who may perform the marriage ceremony, what licenses or witnesses are needed, and similar rules. A ceremonial marriage can be one that follows certain tribal Indian custom, Chinese custom, or similar traditional procedures. We will ask for the evidence described in this section.

(b) Preferred evidence. Preferred evidence of a ceremonial marriage is—

(1) If you are applying for wife's or husband's benefits, signed statements from you and the insured about when and where the marriage took place. If you are applying for the lump-sum death payment as the widow or widower, your signed statement about when and where the marriage took place; or

(2) If you are applying for any other benefits or there is evidence causing some doubt about whether there was a ceremonial marriage: a copy of the public record of marriage or a certified statement as to the marriage; a copy of the religious record of marriage or a certified statement as to what the record shows; or the original marriage certificate.

(c) Other evidence of a ceremonial marriage. If preferred evidence of a ceremonial marriage cannot be obtained, we will ask you to explain why and to give us a signed statement of the clergyman or official who held the marriage ceremony, or other convincing evidence of the marriage.

§ 404.726 Evidence of common-law marriage.

(a) General. A common-law marriage is one considered valid under certain State laws even though there was no formal ceremony. It is a marriage between two persons free to marry, who consider themselves married, live together as man and wife, and, in some States, meet certain other requirements. We will ask for the evidence described in this section.

(b) Preferred evidence. Preferred evidence of a common-law marriage is—

(1) If both the husband and wife are alive, their signed statements and those of two blood relatives;

(2) If either the husband or wife is dead, the signed statements of the one who is alive and those of two blood relatives of the deceased person; or

(3) If both the husband and wife are dead, the signed statements of one blood relative of each;

Note: All signed statements should show why the signer believes there was a marriage between the two persons. If a written statement cannot be gotten from a blood relative, one from another person can be used instead.

(c) Other evidence of common-law marriage. If you cannot get preferred evidence of a common-law marriage, we will ask you to explain why and to give us other convincing evidence of the marriage. We may not ask you for statements from a blood relative or other person if we believe other evidence presented to us proves the common-law marriage.

§ 404.727 Evidence of a deemed valid marriage.

(a) General. A deemed valid marriage is a ceremonial marriage we consider valid even though the correct procedures set by State law were not strictly followed or a former marriage had not yet ended. We will ask for the evidence described in this section.

(b) Preferred evidence. Preferred evidence of a deemed valid marriage is—

(1) Evidence of the ceremonial marriage as described in § 404.725(b)(2);

(2) If the insured person is alive, his or her signed statement that the other party to the marriage went through the ceremony in good faith and his or her reasons for believing the marriage was valid or believing the other party thought it was valid;

(3) The other party's signed statement that he or she went through the marriage ceremony in good faith and his or her reasons for believing it was valid;

(4) If needed to remove a reasonable doubt, the signed statements of others who might have information about what the other party knew about any previous marriage or other facts showing whether he or she went through the marriage in good faith; and

(5) Evidence the parties to the marriage were living in the same household when you applied for benefits or, if earlier, when the insured person died (see § 404.760).

(c) Other evidence of a deemed valid marriage. If you cannot obtain preferred evidence of a deemed valid marriage, we will ask you to explain why and to give us other convincing evidence of the marriage.

§ 404.728 Evidence a marriage has ended.

(a) When evidence is needed that a marriage has ended. If you apply for benefits as the insured person's divorced wife or divorced husband, you will be asked for evidence of your divorce. If you are the insured person's widow or divorced wife who had remarried but that husband died, we will ask you for evidence of his death. We may ask for evidence that a previous marriage you or the insured person had was ended before you married each other if this is needed to show the latter marriage was valid. If you apply for benefits as an unmarried person and you had a marriage which was annulled, we will ask for evidence of the annulment. We will ask for the evidence described in this section.

(b) Preferred evidence. Preferred evidence a marriage has ended is—

(1) A certified copy of the decree of divorce or annulment; or

(2) Evidence the person you married has died (see § 404.720).

(c) Other evidence a marriage has ended. If you cannot obtain preferred evidence the marriage has ended, we will ask you to explain why and to give us other convincing evidence the marriage has ended.

[43 FR 24795, June 7, 1978, as amended at 44 FR 34493, June 15, 1979]

EVIDENCE FOR CHILD'S AND PARENT'S BENEFITS

§ 404.730 When evidence of a parent or child relationship is needed.

If you apply for parent's or child's benefits, we will ask for evidence showing your relationship to the insured person. What evidence we will ask for depends on whether you are the insured person's natural parent or child; or whether you are the stepparent, stepchild, grandchild, stepgrandchild, adopting parent or adopted child.

§ 404.731 Evidence you are a natural parent or child.

If you are the natural parent of the insured person, we will ask for a copy of his or her public or religious birth record made before age 5. If you are the natural child of the insured person, we will ask for a copy of your public or religious birth record made before age 5. In either case, if this record shows the same last name for the insured and the parent or child, we will accept it as convincing evidence of the relationship. However, if other evidence raises some doubt about this record or if the record cannot be gotten, we will ask for other evidence of the relationship. We may also ask for evidence of marriage of the insured person or of his or her parent if this is needed to remove any reasonable doubt about the relationship. To show you are the child of the insured person, you may be asked for evidence you would be able to inherit his or her personal property under State law where he or she had a permanent home (see § 404.770). In addition, we may ask for the insured persons signed statement that you are his or her natural child, or for a copy of any court order showing the insured has been declared to be your natural parent or any court order requiring the insured to contribute to you support because you are his or her son or daughter.

§ 404.732 Evidence you are a stepparent or stepchild.

If you are the stepparent or stepchild of the insured person, we will ask for the evidence described in § 404.731 or § 404.733 that which shows your natural or adoptive relationship to the insured person's husband, wife, widow, or widower. We will also ask for evidence of the husband's, wife's, widow's, or widower's marriage to the insured person—see § 404.725.

§ 404.733 Evidence you are the legally adopting parent or legally adopted child.

If you are the adopting parent or adopted child, we will ask for the following evidence:

(a) A copy of the birth certificate made following the adoption; or if this cannot be gotten, other evidence of the adoption; and, if needed, evidence of the date of adoption;

(b) If the widow or widower adopted the child after the insured person died, the evidence described in paragraph (a) of this section; your written statement whether the insured person was living in the same household with the child when he or she died (see § 404.760); what support the child was getting from any other person or organization; and if the widow or widower had a deemed valid marriage with the insured person, evidence of that marriage—see § 404.727;

(c) If you are the insured's stepchild, grandchild, or stepgrandchild as well as his or her adopted child, we may also ask you for evidence to show how you were related to the insured before the adoption.

§ 404.734 Evidence you are an equitably adopted child.

In many States, the law will treat someone as a child of another if he or she agreed to adopt the child, the natural parents or the person caring for the child were parties to the agreement, he or she and the child then lived together as parent and child, and certain other requirements are met. If you are a child who had this kind or relationship to the insured person (or to the insured persons's wife, widow, or husband), we will ask for evidence of the agreement if it is in writing. If it is not in writing or cannot be gotten, other evidence may be accepted. Also, the following evidence will be asked for: Written statements of your natural parents and the adopting parents and other evidence of the child's relationship to the adopting parents.

§ 404.735 Evidence you are the grandchild or stepgrandchild.

If you are the grandchild or stepgrandchild of the insured person, we will ask you for the kind of evidence described in §§ 404.731 through 404.733 that shows your relationship to your parent and your parent's relationship to the insured.

§ 404.736 Evidence of a child's dependency.

(a) When evidence of a child's dependency is needed. If you apply for child's benefit's we may ask for evidence you were the insured person's dependent at a specific time—usually the time you applied or the time the insured died or became disabled. What evidence we ask for depends upon how you are related to the insured person.

(b) Natural or adopted child. If you are the insured person's natural or adopted child, we may ask for the following evidence:

(1) A signed statement by someone who knows the facts that confirms this relationship and which shows whether you were legally adopted by someone other than the insured. If you were adopted by someone else while the insured person was alive, but the adoption was annulled, we may ask for a certified copy of the annulment decree or other convincing evidence of the annulment.

(2) A signed statement by someone in a position to know showing when and where you lived with the insured and when and why you may have lived apart; and showing what contributions the insured made to your support and when and how they were made.

(c) Stepchild. If you are the insured person's stepchild, we will ask for the following evidence:

(1) A signed statement by someone in a position to know—showing when and where you lived with the insured and when and why you may have lived apart.

(2) A signed statement by someone in a position to know showing you received at least one-half of your support from the insured for the one-year period ending at one of the times mentioned in paragraph (a) of this section; and the income end support you had in this period from any other source.

(d) Grandchild or Stepgrandchild. If you are the insured person's grandchild or stepgrandchild, we will ask for evidence described in paragraph (c) of this section showing that you were living together with the insured and receiving one-half of your support from him or her for the year before the insured became entitled to benefits or to a period of disability, or died. We will also ask for evidence of your parent's death or disability.

§ 404.745 Evidence of school attendance for child age 18 or older.

If you apply for child's benefits as a student age 18 or over, we may ask for evidence you are attending school. We may also ask for evidence from the school you attend showing your status at the school. We will ask for the following evidence:

(a) Your signed statement that you are attending school full-time and are not being paid by an employer to attend school.

(b) If you apply before the school year has started and the school is not a high school, a letter of acceptance from the school, receipted bill, or other evidence showing you have enrolled or been accepted at that school.

§ 404.750 Evidence of a parent's support.

If you apply for parent's benefits, we will ask you for evidence to show that you received at least one-half of your support from the insured person in the one-year period before he or she died or became disabled. We may also ask others who know the facts for a signed statement about your sources of support. We will ask you for the following evidence:

(a) The parent's signed statement showing his or her income, any other sources of support, and the amount from each source over the one-year period.

(b) If the statement described in paragraph (a) of this section cannot be obtained, other convincing evidence that the parent received one-half of his or her support from the insured person.

OTHER EVIDENCE REQUIREMENTS

§ 404.760 Evidence of living in the same household with insured person.

If you apply for the lump-sum death payment as the insured person's widow or widower, or for wife's, husband's, widow's, or widower's benefits based upon a deemed valid marriage as described in § 404.727, we will ask for evidence you and the insured were living together in the same household when he or she died; or if the insured is alive, when you applied for benefits. We will ask for the following as evidence of this:

(a) If the insured person is living, his or her signed statement and yours showing whether you were living together when you applied for benefits.

(b) If the insured person is dead, your signed statement showing whether you were living together when he or she died.

(c) If you and the insured person were temporarily living apart, a signed statement explaining where each was living, how long the separation lasted, and why you were separated. If needed to remove any reasonable doubts about this, we may ask for the signed statements of others in a position to know, or for other convincing evidence you and the insured were living together in the same household.

§ 404.762 What is acceptable evidence of having a child in my care?

What evidence we will ask for depends upon whether the child is living with you or with someone else. You will be asked to give the following evidence:

(a) If the child is living with you, your signed statement showing that the child is living with you.

(b) If the child is living with someone else—

(1) Your signed statement showing with whom he or she is living and why he or she is living with someone else. We will also ask when he or she last lived with you and how long this separation will last, and what care and contributions you provide for the child;

(2) The signed statement of the one with whom the child is living showing what care you provide and the sources and amounts of support received for the child. If the child is in an institution, an official there should sign the statement. These statements are preferred evidence. If there is a court order or written agreement showing who has custody of the child, you may be asked to give us a copy; and

(3) If you cannot get the preferred evidence described in paragraph (b)(2) of this section, we will ask for other convincing evidence that the child is in your care.

[73 FR 40967, July 17, 2008]

§ 404.765 [Reserved]

[61 FR 41330, Aug. 8, 1996]

§ 404.770 Evidence of where the insured person had a permanent home.

(a) When evidence of the insured's permanent home is needed. We may ask for evidence of where the insured person's permanent home was at the time you applied or, if earlier, the time he or she died if—

(1) You apply for benefits as the insured's wife, husband, widow, widower, parent or child; and

(2) Your relationship to the insured depends upon the State law that would be followed in the place where the insured had his or her permanent home when you applied for benefits or when he or she died.

(b) What evidence is needed. We will ask for the following evidence of the insured person's permanent home:

(1) Your signed statement showing where the insured considered his permanent home to be.

(2) If the statement in paragraph (b)(1) of this section or other evidence we have raises a reasonable doubt about where the insured's permanent home was, evidence of where he or she paid personal, property, or income taxes, or voted; or other convincing evidence of where his or her permanent home was.

§ 404.780 Evidence of "good cause" for exceeding time limits on accepting proof of support or application for a lump-sum death payment.

(a) When evidence of good cause is needed. We may ask for evidence that you had good cause (as defined in § 404.370(f)) for not giving us sooner proof of the support you received from the insured as his or her parent. We may also ask for evidence that you had good cause (as defined in § 404.621(b)) for not applying sooner for the lump-sum death payment. You may be asked for evidence of good cause for these delays if—

(1) You are the insured person's parent giving us proof of support more than 2 years after he or she died, or became disabled; or

(2) You are applying for the lump-sum death payment more than 2 years after the insured died.

(b) What evidence of good cause is needed. We will ask for the following evidence of good cause:

(1) Your signed statement explaining why you did not give us the proof of support or the application for lump-sum death payment within the specified 2 year period.

(2) If the statement in paragraph (b)(1) of the section or other evidence raises a reasonable doubt whether there was good cause, other convincing evidence of this.

[43 FR 24795, June 7, 1978, as amended at 44 FR 34493, June 15, 1979]

SUBPART I—RECORDS OF EARNINGS

Authority: Secs. 205(a), (c)(1), (c)(2)(A), (c)(4), (c)(5), (c)(6), and (p), 702(a)(5), and 1143 of the Social Security Act (42 U.S.C. 405(a), (c)(1), (c)(2)(A), (c)(4), (c)(5), (c)(6), and (p), 902(a)(5), and 1320b–13).

Source: 44 FR 38454, July 2, 1979; 52 FR 27540, July 22, 1987; 57 FR 54919, Nov. 23, 1992; 61 FR 5941, Feb. 15, 1996, unless otherwise noted.

GENERAL PROVISIONS

§ 404.801 Introduction.

The Social Security Administration (SSA) keeps a record of the earnings of all persons who work in employment or self-employment covered under social security. We use these earnings records to determine entitlement to and the amount of benefits that may be payable based on a person's earnings under the retirement, survivors', disability and health insurance program. This subpart tells what is evidence of earnings, how you can find out what the record of your earnings shows, and how and under what circumstances the record of your earnings may be changed to correct errors.

§ 404.802 Definitions.

For the purpose of this subpart—

Earnings means wages and self-employment income earned by a person based on work covered by social security. (See subpart K for the rules about what constitutes wages and self-employment income for benefit purposes.)

Period means a taxable year when referring to self-employment income. When referring to wages it means a calendar quarter if the wages were reported or should have been reported quarterly by your employer or a calendar year if the wages were reported or should have been reported annually by your employer.

Record of earnings, earnings record, or record means SSA's records of the amounts of wages paid to you and the amounts of self-employment income you received, the periods in which the wages were paid and the self-employment income was received, and the quarters of coverage which you earned based on these earnings.

Survivor means your spouse, divorced wife, child, or parent, who survives you. Survivor also includes your surviving divorced wife who may be entitled to benefits as a surviving divorced mother.

Tax return means, as appropriate, a tax return of wages or a tax return of self-employment income (including information returns and other written statements filed with the Commissioner of Internal Revenue under chapter 2 or 21 of the Internal Revenue Code of 1954, as amended).

Time limit means a period of time 3 years, 3 months, and 15 days after any year in which you received earnings. The period may be extended by the Soldiers and Sailors Relief Act of 1940 because of your military service or the military service of certain relatives who survive you (50 U.S.C. App. 501 and following sections). Where the time limit ends on a Federal nonwork day, we will extend it to the next Federal work day.

Wage report means a statement filed by a State under section 218 of the Social Security Act or related regulations. This statement includes wage amounts for which a State is billed and wage amounts for which credits or refunds are made to a State according to an agreement under section 218 of the Act.

We, us, or our means the Social Security Administration (SSA).

Year means a calendar year when referring to wages and a taxable year when referring to self-employment income.

You or your means any person for whom we maintain a record of earnings.

§ 404.803 Conclusiveness of the record of your earnings.

(a) Generally. For social security purposes, SSA records are evidence of the amounts of your earnings and the periods in which they were received.

(b) Before time limit ends. Before the time limit ends for a year, SSA records are evidence, but not conclusive evidence, of the amounts and periods of your earnings in that year.

(c) After time limit ends. After the time limit ends for a year—

(1) If SSA records show an entry of self-employment income or wages for an employer for a period in that year, our records are conclusive evidence of your self-employment income in that year or the wages paid to you by that employer and the periods in which they were received unless one of the exceptions in § 404.822 applies;

(2) If SSA records show no entry of wages for an employer for a period in that year, our records are conclusive evidence that no wages were paid to you by that employer in that period unless one of the exceptions in § 404.822 applies; and

(3) If SSA records show no entry of self-employment income for that year, our records are conclusive evidence that you did not receive self-employment income in that year unless the exception in § 404.822(b)(2)(i) or (iii) applies.

OBTAINING EARNINGS INFORMATION

§ 404.810 How to obtain a statement of earnings and a benefit estimate statement.

(a) Right to a statement of earnings and a benefit estimate. You or your legal representative or, after your death, your survivor or the legal representative of your estate may obtain a statement of your earnings as shown on our records at the time of the request. If you have a social security number and have wages or net earnings from self-employment, you may also request and receive an earnings statement that will include an estimate of the monthly old-age, disability, dependents', and survivors' insurance benefits potentially payable on your earnings record, together with a description of the benefits payable under the medicare program. You may request these statements by writing, calling, or visiting a social security office.

(b) Contents of request. When you request a statement of your earnings, we will ask you to complete a prescribed form, giving us your name, social security number, date of birth, and sex. You, your authorized representative or, after your death, your survivor or the legal representative of your estate will be asked to sign and date the form. If you are requesting an estimate of the monthly benefits potentially payable on your earnings record, we will also ask you to give us the amount of your earnings for the last year, an estimate of your earnings for the current year, an estimate of your earnings for future years before your planned retirement, and the age at which you plan to retire, so that we can give you a more realistic estimate of the benefits that may be payable on your record. A request for a statement of earnings and a benefit estimate not made on the prescribed form will be accepted if the request is in writing, is signed and dated by the appropriate individual noted above, and contains all the information that is requested on the prescribed form.

[57 FR 54919, Nov. 23, 1992]

§ 404.811 The statement of earnings and benefit estimates you requested.

(a) General. After receiving a request for a statement of earnings and the information we need to comply with the request, we will provide you or your authorized representative a statement of the earnings we have credited to your record at the time of your request. With the statement of earnings, we will include estimates of the benefits potentially payable on your record, unless you do not have the required credits (quarters of coverage) for any kind of benefit(s). (However, see paragraph (b)(3) of this section regarding the possibility of our estimating up to eight additional credits on your record.) If we do not provide a statement of earnings and an estimate of all the benefits potentially payable, or any other information you requested, we will explain why.

(b) Contents of statement of earnings and benefit estimates. The statement of your earnings and benefit estimates will contain the following information:

(1) Your social security taxed earnings as shown by our records as of the date of your request;

(2) An estimate of the social security and medicare hospital insurance taxes paid on your earnings (although we do not maintain such tax information);

(3) The number of credits, i.e., quarters of coverage, not exceeding 40, you have for both social security and medicare hospital insurance purposes, and the number you need to be eligible for social security and also for medicare hospital insurance coverage. If you do not already have the required credits (quarters of coverage) to be eligible to receive social security benefits

and medicare hospital insurance coverage, we may include up to eight additional estimated credits (four per year) based on the earnings you told us you had for last year and this year that we have not yet entered on your record;

(4) A statement as to whether you meet the credits (quarters of coverage) requirements, as described in subpart B of this part, for each type of social security benefit when we prepare the benefit estimates, and also whether you are eligible for medicare hospital insurance coverage;

(5) Estimates of the monthly retirement (old-age), disability, dependents' and survivors' insurance benefits potentially payable on your record if you meet the credits (quarters of coverage) requirements. The benefit estimates we send you will be based partly on your stated earnings for last year (if not yet on your record), your estimate of your earnings for the current year and for future years before you plan to retire, and on the age at which you plan to retire. The estimate will include the retirement (old-age) insurance benefits you could receive at age 62 (or your current age if you are already over age 62), at full retirement age (currently age 65 to 67, depending on your year of birth) or at your current age if you are already over full retirement age, and at age 70;

(6) A description of the coverage under the medicare program;

(7) A reminder of your right to request a correction of your earnings record; and

(8) A remark that an annually updated statement is available on request.

[57 FR 54919, Nov. 23, 1992; 61 FR 18076, April 24, 1996]

§ 404.812 Statement of earnings and benefit estimates sent without request.

(a) Who will be sent a statement. Unless one of the conditions in paragraph (b) of this section applies to you, we will send you, without request, a statement of earnings and benefit estimates if:

(1) You have a social security account number;

(2) You have wages or net earnings from self-employment on your social security record;

(3) You have attained age 25 or older, as explained in paragraph (c)(3) of this section; and

(4) We can determine your current mailing address.

(b) Who will not be sent a statement. We will not send you an unrequested statement if any of the following conditions apply:

(1) You do not meet one or more of the conditions of paragraph (a) of this section;

(2) Our records contain a notation of your death;

(3) You are entitled to benefits under title II of the Act;

(4) We have already sent you a statement, based on your request, in the fiscal year we selected you to receive an unrequested statement;

(5) We cannot obtain your address (see paragraph (c)(2) of this section); or

(6) We are correcting your social security earnings record when we select you to receive a statement of earnings and benefit estimates.

(c) The selection and mailing process. Subject to the provisions of paragraphs (a) and (b) of this section, we will use the following process for sending statements without requests:

(1) Selection. We will use our records of assigned social security account numbers to identify individuals to whom we will send statements.

(2) Addresses. If you are living in one of the 50 States or the District of Columbia, our current procedure is to get your address from individual taxpayer files of the Internal Revenue Service, as authorized by section 6103(m)(7) of the Internal Revenue Code (26 U.S.C. 6103(m)(7)). If you live in Puerto Rico, the Virgin Islands, or Guam, we will get your address from the taxpayer records of the place in which you live.

(3) Age. If you have attained age 60 on or before September 30, 1995, we will send you a statement by that date. If you attain age 60 on or after October 1, 1995 but no later than September 30, 1999, we will send you a statement in the fiscal year in which you attain age 60, or in an earlier year as resources allow. Also, we will inform you that an annually updated statement is available on request. Beginning October 1, 1999, we will send you a statement each year in which you are age 25 or older.

(4) Ineligible. If we do not send you a statement because one or more conditions in paragraph (b) of this section apply when you are selected, we will send a statement in the first appropriate fiscal year thereafter in which you do qualify.

(5) Undeliverable. If the statement we send you is returned by the Post Office as undeliverable, we will not remail it.

(d) Contents of statement of earnings and benefit estimates. To prepare your statement and estimate your benefits, we will use the earnings in our records. If there are earnings recorded for you in either of the two years before the year in which you are selected to get a statement, we will use the later of these earnings as your earnings for the current year and future years when we estimate your benefits. In addition, if you do not already have the required credits (quarters of coverage) to be eligible to receive benefits, we will use that last recorded earnings amount to estimate up to eight additional credits (four per year) for last year and the current year if they are not yet entered on your record. If there are no earnings entered on your record in either of the two years preceding the year of selection, we will not estimate current and future earnings or additional credits for you. Your earnings and benefit estimates statement will contain the following information:

(1) Your social security taxed earnings as shown by our records as of the date we select you to receive a statement;

(2) An estimate of the social security and medicare hospital insurance taxes paid on your earnings (although we do not maintain such tax information);

(3) The number of credits, i.e., quarters of coverage, not exceeding 40 (as described in paragraph (d) of this section), that you have for both social security and medicare hospital insurance purposes, and the number you need to be eligible for social security benefits and also for medicare hospital insurance coverage;

(4) A statement as to whether you meet the credit (quarters of coverage) requirements, as described in subpart B of this part, for each type of social security benefit when we prepare the benefit estimates, and also whether you are eligible for medicare hospital insurance coverage;

(5) Estimates of the monthly retirement (old-age), disability, dependents' and survivors' insurance benefits potentially payable on your record if you meet the credits (quarters of coverage) requirements. If you are age 50 or older, the estimates will include the retirement (old-age) insurance benefits you could receive at age 62 (or your current age if you are already over age 62), at full retirement age (currently age 65 to 67, depending on your year of birth) or at your current age if you are already over full retirement age, and at age 70. If you are under age 50, instead of estimates, we may provide a general description of the benefits (including auxiliary benefits) that are available upon retirement;

(6) A description of the coverage provided under the medicare program;

(7) A reminder of your right to request a correction of your earnings record; and

(8) A remark that an annually updated statement is available on request.

[61 FR 18077, April 24, 1996]

CORRECTING THE EARNINGS RECORDS

§ 404.820 Filing a request for correction of the record of your earnings.

(a) When to file a request for correction. You or your survivor must file a request for correction of the record of your earnings within the time limit for the year being questioned unless one of the exceptions in § 404.822 applies.

(b) Contents of a request.

(1) A request for correction of an earnings record must be in writing and must state that the record is incorrect.

(2) A request must be signed by you or your survivor or by a person who may sign an application for benefits for you or for your survivor as described in § 404.612.

(3) A request should state the period being questioned.

(4) A request should describe, or have attached to it, any available evidence which shows that the record of earnings is incorrect.

(c) Where to file a request. A request may be filed with an SSA employee at one of our offices or with an SSA employee who is authorized to receive a request at a place other than one of our offices. A request may be filed with the Veterans Administration Regional Office in the Philippines or with any U.S. Foreign Service Office.

(d) When a request is considered filed. A request is considered filed on the day it is received by any of our offices, by an authorized SSA employee, by the Veterans Administration Regional Office in the Philippines, or by any U.S. Foreign Service Office. If using the date we receive a mailed request disadvantages the requester, we will use the date the request was mailed to us as shown by a U.S. postmark. If the postmark is unreadable or there is no postmark, we will consider other evidence of the date when the request was mailed.

(e) Withdrawal of a request for correction. A request for correction of SSA records of your earnings may be withdrawn as described in § 404.640.

(f) Cancellation of a request to withdraw. A request to withdraw a request for correction of SSA records of your earnings may be cancelled as described in § 404.641.

(g) Determinations on requests. When we receive a request described in this section, we will make a determination to grant or deny the request. If we deny the request, this determination may be appealed under the provisions of subpart J of this part.

§ 404.821 Correction of the record of your earnings before the time limit ends.

Before the time limit ends for any year, we will correct the record of your earnings for that year for any reason if satisfactory evidence shows SSA records are incorrect. We may correct the record as the result of a request filed under § 404.820 or we may correct it on our own.

§ 404.822 Correction of the record of your earnings after the time limit ends.

(a) Generally. After the time limit for any year ends, we may correct the record of your earnings for that year if satisfactory evidence shows SSA records are incorrect and any of the circumstances in paragraphs (b) through (e) of this section applies.

(b) Correcting SSA records to agree with tax returns. We will correct SSA records to agree with a tax return of wages or self-employment income to the extent that the amount of earnings shown in the return is correct.

(1) Tax returns of wages. We may correct the earnings record to agree with a tax return of wages or with a wage report of a State.

(2) Tax returns of self-employment income—

(i) Return filed before the time limit ended. We may correct the earnings record to agree with a tax return of self-employment income filed before the end of the time limit.

(ii) Return filed after time limit ended. We may remove or reduce, but not increase, the amount of self-employment income entered on the earnings record to agree with a tax return of self-employment income filed after the time limit ends.

(iii) Self-employment income entered in place of erroneously entered wages. We may enter self-employment income for any year up to an amount erroneously entered in SSA records as wages but which was later removed from the records. However, we may enter self-employment income under this paragraph only if—

(A) An amended tax return is filed before the time limit ends for the year in which the erroneously entered wages were removed; or

(B) Net earnings from self-employment, which are not already entered in the record of your earnings, were included in a tax return filed before the end of the time limit for the year in which the erroneously entered wages were removed.

(c) Written request for correction or application for benefits filed before the time limit ends—

(1) Written request for correction. We may correct an earnings record if you or your survivor files a request for correction before the time limit for that year ends. The request must state that the earnings record for that year is incorrect. However, we may not correct the record under this paragraph after our determination on the request becomes final.

(2) Application for benefits. We may correct an earnings record if an application is filed for monthly benefits or for a lump-sum death payment before the time limit for that year ends. However, we may not correct the record under this paragraph after our determination on the application becomes final.

(3) See subpart J for the rules on the finality of determinations.

(d) Transfer of wages to or from the Railroad Retirement Board—

(1) Wages erroneously reported. We may transfer to or from the records of the Railroad Retirement Board earnings which were erroneously reported to us or to the Railroad Retirement Board.

(2) Earnings certified by Railroad Retirement Board. We may enter earnings for railroad work under subpart O if the earnings are certified by the Railroad Retirement Board.

(e) Other circumstances permitting correction—

(1) Investigation started before time limit ends. We may correct an earnings record if the correction is made as the result of an investigation started before, but completed after the time limit ends. An investigation is started when we take an affirmative step leading to a decision on a question about the earnings record, for example, an investigation is started when one SSA unit asks another unit to obtain additional information or evidence. We will remove or reduce earnings on the record under this paragraph only if we carried out the investigation as promptly as circumstances permitted.

(2) Error apparent on face of records. We may correct an earnings record to correct errors, such as mechanical or clerical errors, which can be identified and corrected without going beyond any of the pertinent SSA records.

(3) Fraud. We may change any entry which was entered on the earnings record as the result of fraud.

(4) Entries for wrong person or period. We may correct errors in SSA records resulting from earnings being entered for the wrong person or period.

(5) Less than correct wages on SSA records. We may enter wages paid to you by an employer for a period if no part of those wages or less than the correct amount of those wages is entered on SSA records.

(6) Wage payments under a statute. We may enter and allocate wages awarded to you for a period as the result of a determination or agreement approved by a court or administrative agency that enforces Federal or State statutes protecting your right to employment or wages.

[57 FR 21600, May 21, 1992]

§ 404.823 Correction of the record of your earnings for work in the employ of the United States.

We may correct the record of your earnings to remove, reduce, or enter earnings for work in the employ of the United States only if—

(a) Correction is permitted under § 404.821 or § 404.822; and

(b) Any necessary determinations concerning the amount of remuneration paid for your work and the periods for which such remuneration was paid have been made as shown by—

(1) A tax return filed under section 3122 of the Internal Revenue Code (26 U.S.C. 3122); or

(2) A certification by the head of the Federal agency or instrumentality of which you have been an employee or his or her agent. A Federal instrumentality for these purposes includes a nonappropriated fund activity of the armed forces or Coast Guard.

[55 FR 24891, June 19, 1990]

NOTICE OF REMOVAL OR REDUCTION OF AN ENTRY OF EARNINGS

§ 404.830 Notice of removal or reduction of your wages.

If we remove or reduce an amount of wages entered on the record of your earnings, we will notify you of this correction if we previously notified you of the amount of your wages for the period involved. We will notify your survivor if we previously notified you or your survivor of the amount of your earnings for the period involved.

§ 404.831 Notice of removal or reduction of your self-employment income.

If we remove or reduce an amount of self-employment income entered on the record of your earnings, we will notify you of this correction. We will notify your survivor if we previously notified you or your survivor of the amount of your earnings for the period involved.

SUBPART J—DETERMINATIONS, ADMINISTRATIVE REVIEW PROCESS, AND REOPENING OF DETERMINATIONS AND DECISIONS

Authority: Secs. 201(j), 204(f), 205(a)-(b), (d)-(h), and (j), 221, 223(i), 225, and 702(a)(5) of the Social Security Act (42 U.S.C. 401(j), 404(f), 405(a)-(b), (d)-(h), and (j), 421, 423(i), 425, and 902(a)(5)); sec. 5, Pub.L. 97–455, 96 Stat. 2500 (42 U.S.C. 405 note); secs. 5, 6(c)-(e), and 15, Pub.L. 98–460, 98 Stat. 1802 (42 U.S.C. 421 note); sec. 202, Pub.L. 108–203, 118 Stat. 509 (42 U.S.C. 902 note).

Source: 45 FR 52081, Aug. 5, 1980; 50 FR 21437, May 24, 1985; 51 FR 8808, March 14, 1986; 51 FR 15471, April 24, 1986; 51 FR 28545, Aug. 8, 1986; 51 FR 44983, Dec. 16, 1986; 52 FR 4004, Feb. 9, 1987; 52 FR 27540, July 22, 1987; 56 FR 41790, Aug. 23, 1991; 56 FR 52469, Oct. 21, 1991; 57 FR 23056, June 1, 1992; 59 FR 1634, Jan. 12, 1994; 59 FR 44925, Aug. 31, 1994; 60 FR 8147, Feb. 10, 1995; 60 FR 34131, June 30, 1995; 61 FR 5941, Feb. 15, 1996; 62 FR 64278, Dec. 5, 1997; 68 FR 74183, Dec. 23, 2003; 70 FR 57142, Sept. 30, 2005; 71 FR 16443, March 31, 2006; 71 FR 66866, Nov. 17, 2006; 76 FR 24806, May 3, 2011, unless otherwise noted.

INTRODUCTION, DEFINITIONS, AND INITIAL DETERMINATIONS

§ 404.900 Introduction.

(a) Explanation of the administrative review process. This subpart explains the procedures we follow in determining your rights under title II of the Social Security Act. The regulations describe the process of administrative review and explain your right to judicial review after you have taken all the necessary administrative steps. These procedures apply also to persons claiming certain benefits under title XVIII of the Act (Medicare); see 42 CFR 405.904(a)(1). The administrative review process consists of several steps, which usually must be requested within certain time periods and in the following order:

(1) Initial determination. This is a determination we make about your entitlement or your continuing entitlement to benefits or about any other matter, as discussed in § 404.902, that gives you a right to further review.

(2) Reconsideration. If you are dissatisfied with an initial determination, you may ask us to reconsider it.

(3) Hearing before an administrative law judge. If you are dissatisfied with the reconsideration determination, you may request a hearing before an administrative law judge.

(4) Appeals Council review. If you are dissatisfied with the decision of the administrative law judge, you may request that the Appeals Council review the decision.

(5) Federal court review. When you have completed the steps of the administrative review process listed in paragraphs (a)(1) through (a)(4) of this section, we will have made our final decision. If you are dissatisfied with our final decision, you may request judicial review by filing an action in a Federal district court.

(6) Expedited appeals process. At some time after your initial determination has been reviewed, if you have no dispute with our findings of fact and our application and interpretation of the controlling laws, but you believe that a part of the law is unconstitutional, you may use the expedited appeals process. This process permits you to go directly to a Federal district court so that the constitutional issue may be resolved.

(b) Nature of the administrative review process. In making a determination or decision in your case, we conduct the administrative review process in an informal, non-adversarial manner. Subject to certain timeframes at the hearing level (see § 404.935) and the limitations on Appeals Council consideration of additional evidence (see § 404.970), we will consider at each step of the review process any information you present as well as all the information in our records. You may present the information yourself or have someone represent you, including an attorney. If you are dissatisfied with our decision in the review process, but do not take the next step within the stated time period, you will lose your right to further administrative review and your right to judicial review, unless you can show us that there was good cause for your failure to make a timely request for review.

[51 FR 300, Jan. 3, 1986; 51 FR 8808, March 14, 1986; 52 FR 4004, Feb. 9, 1987; 78 FR 57259, Sept. 18, 2013; 79 FR 11706, March 3, 2014; 80 FR 14835, March 20, 2015; 81 FR 90992, Dec. 16, 2016]

§ 404.901 Definitions.

As used in this subpart:

Date you receive notice means 5 days after the date on the notice, unless you show us that you did not receive it within the 5-day period.

Decision means the decision made by an administrative law judge or the Appeals Council.

Determination means the initial determination or the reconsidered determination.

Preponderance of the evidence means such relevant evidence that as a whole shows that the existence of the fact to be proven is more likely than not.

Remand means to return a case for further review.

Substantial evidence means such relevant evidence as a reasonable mind might accept as adequate to support a conclusion.

Vacate means to set aside a previous action.

Waive means to give up a right knowingly and voluntarily.

We, us, or our refers to the Social Security Administration.

You or your refers to any person claiming a right under the old age, disability, dependents' or survivors' benefits program.

[73 FR 76943, Dec. 18, 2008]

§ 404.902 Administrative actions that are initial determinations.

Initial determinations are the determinations we make that are subject to administrative and judicial review. We will base our initial determination on the preponderance of the evidence. We will state the important facts and give the reasons for our conclusions in the initial determination. In the old age, survivors' and disability insurance programs, initial determinations include, but are not limited to, determinations about—

(a) Your entitlement or your continuing entitlement to benefits;

(b) Your reentitlement to benefits;

(c) The amount of your benefit;

(d) A recomputation of your benefit;

(e) A reduction in your disability benefits because you also receive benefits under a workmen's compensation law;

(f) A deduction from your benefits on account of work;

(g) [Reserved]

(h) Termination of your benefits;

(i) Penalty deductions imposed because you failed to report certain events;

(j) Any overpayment or underpayment of your benefits;

(k) Whether an overpayment of benefits must be repaid to us;

(*l*) How an underpayment of benefits due a deceased person will be paid;

(m) The establishment or termination of a period of disability;

(n) A revision of your earnings record;

(*o*) Whether the payment of your benefits will be made, on your behalf, to a representative payee;

(p) Your drug addiction or alcoholism;

(q) Who will act as your payee if we determine that representative payment will be made;

(r) An offset of your benefits under § 404.408b because you previously received supplemental security income payments for the same period;

(s) Whether your completion of, or continuation for a specified period of time in, an appropriate program of vocational rehabilitation services, employment services, or other support services will increase the likelihood that you will not have to return to the disability benefit rolls, and thus, whether your benefits may be continued even though you are not disabled;

(t) Nonpayment of your benefits under § 404.468 because of your confinement in a jail, prison, or other penal institution or correctional facility for conviction of a felony;

(u) Whether or not you have a disabling impairment(s) as defined in § 404.1511;

(v) Nonpayment of your benefits under § 404.469 because you have not furnished us satisfactory proof of your Social Security number, or, if a Social Security number has not been assigned to you, you have not filed a proper application for one;

(w) A claim for benefits under § 404.633 based on alleged misinformation; and

(x) Whether we were negligent in investigating or monitoring or failing to investigate or monitor your representative payee, which resulted in the misuse of benefits by your representative payee.

[45 FR 52081, Aug. 5, 1980, as amended at 47 FR 4988, Feb. 3, 1982; 47 FR 31543, July 21, 1982; 48 FR 5714, Feb. 8, 1983; 49 FR 22272, May 29, 1984; 49 FR 38935, Oct. 2, 1984; 50 FR 20902, May 21, 1985; 51 FR 28545, Aug. 8, 1986; 56 FR 41790, Aug. 23, 1991; 59 FR 44925, Aug. 31, 1994; 60 FR 8147, Feb. 10, 1995; 68 FR 40123, July 7, 2003; 69 FR 60232, Oct. 7, 2004; 70 FR 36507, June 24, 2005; 73 FR 76943, Dec. 18, 2008]

§ 404.903 Administrative actions that are not initial determinations.

Administrative actions that are not initial determinations may be reviewed by us, but they are not subject to the administrative review process provided by this subpart, and they are not subject to judicial review. These actions include, but are not limited to, an action—

(a) Suspending benefits pending an investigation and determination of any factual issue relating to a deduction on account of work;

(b) Suspending benefits pending an investigation to determine if your disability has ceased;

(c) Denying a request to be made a representative payee;

(d) Certifying two or more family members for joint payment of benefits;

(e) Withholding less than the full amount of your monthly benefit to recover an overpayment;

(f) Determining the fee that may be charged or received by a person who has represented you in connection with a proceeding before us;

(g) Refusing to recognize, disqualifying, or suspending a person from acting as your representative in a proceeding before us (see §§ 404.1705 and 404.1745);

(h) Compromising, suspending or terminating collection of an overpayment under the Federal Claims Collection Act;

(i) Extending or not extending the time to file a report of earnings;

(j) Denying your request to extend the time period for requesting review of a determination or a decision;

(k) Denying your request to use the expedited appeals process;

(*l*) Denying your request to reopen a determination or a decision;

(m) Withholding temporarily benefits based on a wage earner's estimate of earnings to avoid creating an overpayment;

(n) Determining whether (and the amount of) travel expenses incurred are reimbursable in connection with proceedings before us;

(*o*) Denying your request to readjudicate your claim and apply an Acquiescence Ruling;

(p) Findings on whether we can collect an overpayment by using the Federal income tax refund offset procedure (see § 404.523);

(q) Determining whether an organization may collect a fee from you for expenses it incurred in serving as your representative payee (see § 404.2040a);

(r) Declining under § 404.633(f) to make a determination on a claim for benefits based on alleged misinformation because one or more of the conditions specified in § 404.633(f) are not met;

(s) The assignment of a monthly payment day (see § 404.1807);

(t) Determining whether we will refer information about your overpayment to a consumer reporting agency (see §§ 404.527 and 422.305 of this chapter);

(u) Determining whether we will refer your overpayment to the Department of the Treasury for collection by offset against Federal payments due you (see §§ 404.527 and 422.310 of this chapter);

(v) Determining whether we will order your employer to withhold from your disposable pay to collect an overpayment you received under title II of the Social Security Act (see part 422, subpart E, of this chapter);

(w) Determining whether provisional benefits are payable, the amount of the provisional benefits, and when provisional benefits terminate (see § 404.1592e);

(x) Determining whether to select your claim for the quick disability determination process under § 404.1619;

(y) The removal of your claim from the quick disability determination process under § 404.1619;

(z) Starting or discontinuing a continuing disability review;

(aa) Issuing a receipt in response to your report of a change in your work activity; and

(bb) Determining whether a non-attorney representative is eligible to receive direct fee payment as described in § 404.1717 of this part.

[51 FR 8808, March 14, 1986; 55 FR 1018, Jan. 11, 1990; 56 FR 52469, Oct. 21, 1991; 57 FR 23057, June 1, 1992; 59 FR 44925, Aug. 31, 1994; 62 FR 6120, Feb. 11, 1997; 62 FR 64278, Dec. 5, 1997; 68 FR 74183, Dec. 23, 2003; 70 FR 57142, Sept. 30, 2005; 71 FR 16443, March 31, 2006; 71 FR 66853, 66866, Nov. 17, 2006; 72 FR 51177, Sept. 6, 2007; 76 FR 45192, July 28, 2011; 76 FR 80245, Dec. 23, 2011; 80 FR 399, 400, Jan. 6, 2015]

§ 404.904 Notice of the initial determination.

We will mail a written notice of our initial determination to you at your last known address. The written notice will explain in simple and clear language what we have determined and the reasons for and the effect of our determination. If our determination involves a determination of disability that is in whole or in part unfavorable to you, our written notice also will contain in understandable language a statement of the case setting forth the evidence on which our determination is based. The notice also will inform you of your right to reconsideration. We will not mail a notice if the beneficiary's entitlement to benefits has ended because of his or her death.

[51 FR 300, Jan. 3, 1986; 72 FR 51177, Sept. 6, 2007]

§ 404.905 Effect of an initial determination.

An initial determination is binding unless you request a reconsideration within the stated time period, or we revise the initial determination.

[51 FR 300, Jan. 3, 1986]

§ 404.906 Testing modifications to the disability determination procedures.

(a) Applicability and scope. Notwithstanding any other provision in this part or part 422 of this chapter, we are establishing the procedures set out in this section to test modifications to our disability determination process. These modifications will enable us to test, either individually or in one or more combinations, the effect of: having disability claim managers assume primary responsibility for processing an application for disability benefits; providing persons who have applied for benefits based on disability with the opportunity for an interview with a decisionmaker when the decisionmaker finds that the evidence in the file is insufficient to make a fully favorable determination or requires an initial determination denying the claim; having a single decisionmaker make the initial determination with assistance from medical consultants, where appropriate; and eliminating the reconsideration step in the administrative review process and having a claimant who is dissatisfied with the initial determination request a hearing before an administrative law judge. The model procedures we test will be designed to provide us with information regarding the effect of these procedural modifications and enable us to decide whether and to what degree the disability determination process would be improved if they were implemented on a national level.

(b) Procedures for cases included in the tests. Prior to commencing each test or group of tests in selected site(s), we will publish a notice in the Federal Register. The notice will describe which model or combinations of models we intend to test, where the specific test site(s) will be, and the duration of the test(s). The individuals who participate in the test(s) will be randomly assigned to a test group in each site where the tests are conducted. Paragraphs (b)(1) through (4) of this section lists descriptions of each model.

(1) In the disability claim manager model, when you file an application for benefits based on disability, a disability claim manager will assume primary responsibility for the processing of your claim. The disability claim manager will be the focal point for your contacts with us during the claims intake process and until an initial determination on your claim is made. The disability claim manager will explain the disability programs to you, including the definition of disability and how we determine whether you meet all the requirements for benefits based on disability. The disability claim manager will explain what you will be asked to do throughout the claims process and how you can obtain information or assistance through him or her. The disability claim manager will also provide you with information regarding your right to representation, and he or she will provide you with appropriate referral sources for representation. The disability claim manager may be either a State agency employee or a Federal employee. In some instances, the disability claim manager may be assisted by other individuals.

(2) In the single decisionmaker model, the decisionmaker will make the disability determination and may also determine whether the other conditions for entitlement to benefits based on disability are met. The decisionmaker will make the disability determination after any appropriate consultation with a medical or psychological consultant. The medical or psychological consultant will not be required to sign the disability determination forms we use to have the State agency certify the determination of disability to us (see § 404.1615). However, before an initial determination is made in any case where there is evidence which indicates the existence of a mental impairment, the decisionmaker will make every reasonable effort to ensure that a qualified psychiatrist or psychologist has completed the medical portion of the case review and any applicable residual functional capacity assessment pursuant to our existing procedures (see § 404.1617). In some instances the decisionmaker may be the disability claim manager described in paragraph (b)(1) of this section. When the decisionmaker is a State agency employee, a team of individuals that includes a Federal employee will determine whether the other conditions for entitlement to benefits are met.

(3) In the predecision interview model, if the decisionmaker(s) finds that the evidence in your file is insufficient to make a fully favorable determination or requires an initial determination denying your claim, a predecision notice will be mailed to you. The notice will tell you that, before the decisionmaker(s) makes an initial determination about whether you are disabled, you may request a predecision interview with the decisionmaker(s). The notice will also tell you that you may submit additional evidence. You must request a predecision interview within 10 days after the date you receive the predecision notice. You must also submit any additional evidence within 10 days after you receive the predecision notice. If you request a predecision interview, the decisionmaker(s) will conduct the predecision interview in person, by videoconference, or by telephone as the decisionmaker(s) determines is appropriate under the circumstances. If you make a late request for a predecision interview, or submit additional evidence late, but show in writing that you had good cause under the standards in § 404.911 for missing the deadline, the decisionmaker(s) will extend the deadline. If you do not request the predecision interview, or if you do not appear for a scheduled predecision interview and do not submit additional evidence, or if you do not respond to our attempts to communicate with you, the decisionmaker(s) will make

an initial determination based upon the evidence in your file. If you identify additional evidence during the predecision interview, which was previously not available, the decisionmaker(s) will advise you to submit the evidence. If you are unable to do so, the decisionmaker(s) may assist you in obtaining it. The decisionmaker(s) also will advise you of the specific timeframes you have for submitting any additional evidence identified during the predecision interview. If you have no treating source(s) (see § 404.1502), or your treating source(s) is unable or unwilling to provide the necessary evidence, or there is a conflict in the evidence that cannot be resolved through evidence from your treating source(s), the decisionmaker(s) may arrange a consultative examination or resolve conflicts according to existing procedures (see § 404.1519a). If you attend the predecision interview, or do not attend the predecision interview but you submit additional evidence, the decisionmaker(s) will make an initial determination based on the evidence in your file, including the additional evidence you submit or the evidence obtained as a result of the predecision notice or interview, or both.

(4) In the reconsideration elimination model, we will modify the disability determination process by eliminating the reconsideration step of the administrative review process. If you receive an initial determination on your claim for benefits based on disability, and you are dissatisfied with the determination, we will notify you that you may request a hearing before an administrative law judge.

[51 FR 15471, April 24, 1986; 60 FR 20026, April 24, 1995; 73 FR 2415, Jan. 15, 2008; 73 FR 10381, Feb. 27, 2008; 76 FR 24806, May 3, 2011; 82 FR 5863, Jan. 18, 2017]

RECONSIDERATION

§ 404.907 Reconsideration—general.

If you are dissatisfied with the initial determination, reconsideration is the first step in the administrative review process that we provide, except that we provide the opportunity for a hearing before an administrative law judge as the first step for those situations described in §§ 404.930(a)(6) and (a)(7), where you appeal an initial determination denying your request for waiver of adjustment or recovery of an overpayment (see § 404.506). If you are dissatisfied with our reconsidered determination, you may request a hearing before an administrative law judge.

[51 FR 300, Jan. 3, 1986; 61 FR 56132, Oct. 31, 1996]

§ 404.908 Parties to a reconsideration.

(a) Who may request a reconsideration. If you are dissatisfied with the initial determination, you may request that we reconsider it. In addition, a person who shows in writing that his or her rights may be adversely affected by the initial determination may request a reconsideration.

(b) Who are parties to a reconsideration. After a request for the reconsideration, you and any person who shows in writing that his or her rights are adversely affected by the initial determination will be parties to the reconsideration.

§ 404.909 How to request reconsideration.

(a) We shall reconsider an initial determination if you or any other party to the reconsideration files a written request—

(1) Within 60 days after the date you receive notice of the initial determination (or within the extended time period if we extend the time as provided in paragraph (b) of this section);

(2) At one of our offices, the Veterans Administration Regional Office in the Philippines, or an office of the Railroad Retirement Board if you have 10 or more years of service in the railroad industry.

(b) Extension of time to request a reconsideration. If you want a reconsideration of the initial determination but do not request one in time, you may ask us for more time to request a reconsideration. Your request for an extension of time must be in writing and must give the reasons why the request for reconsideration was not filed within the stated time period. If you show us that you had good cause for missing the deadline, we will extend the time period. To determine whether good cause exists, we use the standards explained in § 404.911.

§ 404.911 Good cause for missing the deadline to request review.

(a) In determining whether you have shown that you had good cause for missing a deadline to request review we consider—

(1) What circumstances kept you from making the request on time;

(2) Whether our action misled you;

(3) Whether you did not understand the requirements of the Act resulting from amendments to the Act, other legislation, or court decisions; and

(4) Whether you had any physical, mental, educational, or linguistic limitations (including any lack of facility with the English language) which prevented you from filing a timely request or from understanding or knowing about the need to file a timely request for review.

(b) Examples of circumstances where good cause may exist include, but are not limited to, the following situations:

(1) You were seriously ill and were prevented from contacting us in person, in writing, or through a friend, relative, or other person.

(2) There was a death or serious illness in your immediate family.

(3) Important records were destroyed or damaged by fire or other accidental cause.

(4) You were trying very hard to find necessary information to support your claim but did not find the information within the stated time periods.

(5) You asked us for additional information explaining our action within the time limit, and within 60 days of receiving the explanation you requested reconsideration or a hearing, or within 30 days of receiving the explanation you requested Appeal Council review or filed a civil suit.

(6) We gave you incorrect or incomplete information about when and how to request administrative review or to file a civil suit.

(7) You did not receive notice of the determination or decision.

(8) You sent the request to another Government agency in good faith within the time limit and the request did not reach us until after the time period had expired.

(9) Unusual or unavoidable circumstances exist, including the circumstances described in paragraph (a)(4) of this section, which show that you could not have known of the need to file timely, or which prevented you from filing timely.

[59 FR 1634, Jan. 12, 1994]

§ 404.913 Reconsideration procedures.

(a) Case review. With the exception of the type of case described in paragraph (b) of this section, the reconsideration process consists of a case review. Under a case review procedure, we will give you and the other parties to the reconsideration an opportunity to present additional evidence to us. The official who reviews your case will then make a reconsidered determination based on all of this evidence.

(b) Disability hearing. If you have been receiving benefits based on disability and you request reconsideration of an initial or revised determination that, based on medical factors, you are not now disabled, we will give you and the other parties to the reconsideration an opportunity for a disability hearing. (See §§ 404.914 through 404.918.)

[51 FR 300, Jan. 3, 1986]

§ 404.914 Disability hearing—general.

(a) Availability. We will provide you with an opportunity for a disability hearing if:

(1) You have been receiving benefits based on a medical impairment that renders you disabled;

(2) We have made an initial or revised determination based on medical factors that you are not now disabled because your impairment:

(i) Has ceased;

(ii) Did not exist; or

(iii) Is no longer disabling; and

(3) You make a timely request for reconsideration of the initial or revised determination.

(b) Scope. The disability hearing will address only the initial or revised determination, based on medical factors, that you are not now disabled. Any other issues which arise in connection with your request for reconsideration will be reviewed in accordance with the reconsideration procedures described in § 404.913(a).

(c) Time and place—

(1) General. Either the State agency or the Associate Commissioner for Disability Determinations or his or her delegate, as appropriate, will set the time and place of your disability hearing. We will send you a notice of the time and place of your disability hearing at least 20 days before the date of the hearing. You may be expected to travel to your disability hearing. (See §§ 404.999 a–404.999 d regarding reimbursement for travel expenses.)

(2) Change of time or place. If you are unable to travel or have some other reason why you cannot attend your disability hearing at the scheduled time or place, you should request at the earliest possible date that the time or place of your hearing be changed. We will change the time or place if there is good cause for doing so under the standards in § 404.936 (c) and (d).

(d) Combined issues. If a disability hearing is available to you under paragraph (a) of this section, and you file a new application for benefits while your request for reconsideration is still pending, we may combine the issues on both claims for the purpose of the disability hearing and issue a combined initial/reconsidered determination which is binding with respect to the common issues on both claims.

(e) Definition. For purposes of the provisions regarding disability hearings (§§ 404.914 through 404.918) we, us or our means the Social Security Administration or the State agency.

[51 FR 300, Jan. 3, 1986; 51 FR 8808, March 14, 1986; 71 FR 10427, March 1, 2006]

§ 404.915 Disability hearing—disability hearing officers.

(a) General. Your disability hearing will be conducted by a disability hearing officer who was not involved in making the determination you are appealing. The disability hearing officer will be an experienced disability examiner, regardless of whether he or she is appointed by a State agency or by the Associate Commissioner for Disability Determinations or his or her delegate, as described in paragraphs (b) and (c) of this section.

(b) State agency hearing officers—

(1) Appointment of State agency hearing officers. If a State agency made the initial or revised determination that you are appealing, the disability hearing

officer who conducts your disability hearing may be appointed by a State agency. If the disability hearing officer is appointed by a State agency, that individual will be employed by an adjudicatory unit of the State agency other than the adjudicatory unit which made the determination you are appealing.

(2) State agency defined. For purposes of this subpart, State agency means the adjudicatory component in the State which issues disability determinations.

(c) Federal hearing officers. The disability hearing officer who conducts your disability hearing will be appointed by the Associate Commissioner for Disability Determinations or his or her delegate if:

(1) A component of our office other than a State agency made the determination you are appealing; or

(2) The State agency does not appoint a disability hearing officer to conduct your disability hearing under paragraph (b) of this section.

[51 FR 301, Jan. 3, 1986; 71 FR 10428, March 1, 2006]

§ 404.916 Disability hearing—procedures.

(a) General. The disability hearing will enable you to introduce evidence and present your views to a disability hearing officer if you are dissatisfied with an initial or revised initial determination, based on medical factors, that you are not now disabled as described in § 404.914(a)(2).

(b) Your procedural rights. We will advise you that you have the following procedural rights in connection with the disability hearing process:

(1) You may request that we assist you in obtaining pertinent evidence for your disability hearing and, if necessary, that we issue a subpoena to compel the production of certain evidence or testimony. We will follow subpoena procedures similar to those described in § 404.950(d) for the administrative law judge hearing process;

(2) You may have a representative at the hearing appointed under subpart R of this part, or you may represent yourself;

(3) You or your representative may review the evidence in your case file, either on the date of your hearing or at an earlier time at your request, and present additional evidence;

(4) You may present witnesses and question any witnesses at the hearing;

(5) You may waive your right to appear at the hearing. If you do not appear at the hearing, the disability hearing officer will prepare and issue a written reconsidered determination based on the information in your case file.

(c) Case preparation. After you request reconsideration, your case file will be reviewed and prepared for the hearing. This review will be conducted in the component of our office (including a State agency) that made the initial or revised determination, by personnel who were not involved in making the initial or revised determination. Any new evidence you submit in connection with your request for reconsideration will be included in this review. If necessary, further development of the evidence, including arrangements for medical examinations, will be undertaken by this component. After the case file is prepared for the hearing, it will be forwarded by this component to the disability hearing officer for a hearing. If necessary, the case file may be sent back to this component at any time prior to the issuance of the reconsidered determination for additional development. Under paragraph (d) of this section, this component has the authority to issue a favorable reconsidered determination at any time in its development process.

(d) Favorable reconsideration determination without a hearing. If all the evidence in your case file supports a finding that you are now disabled, either the component that prepares your case for hearing under paragraph (c) or the disability hearing officer will issue a written favorable reconsideration determination, even if a disability hearing has not yet been held.

(e) Opportunity to submit additional evidence after the hearing. At your request, the disability hearing officer may allow up to 15 days after your disability hearing for receipt of evidence which is not available at the hearing, if:

(1) The disability hearing officer determines that the evidence has a direct bearing on the outcome of the hearing; and

(2) The evidence could not have been obtained before the hearing.

(f) Opportunity to review and comment on evidence obtained or developed by us after the hearing. If, for any reason, additional evidence is obtained or developed by us after your disability hearing, and all evidence taken together can be used to support a reconsidered determination that is unfavorable to you with regard to the medical factors of eligibility, we will notify you, in writing, and give you an opportunity to review and comment on the additional evidence. You will be given 10 days from the date you receive our notice to submit your comments (in writing or, in appropriate cases, by telephone), unless there is good cause for granting you additional time, as illustrated by the examples in § 404.911(b). Your comments will be considered before a reconsidered determination is issued. If you believe that it is necessary to have further opportunity for a hearing with respect to the additional evidence, a supplementary hearing may be scheduled at your request. Otherwise, we will ask for your written comments on the additional evidence, or, in appropriate cases, for your telephone comments.

[51 FR 301, Jan. 3, 1986]

§ 404.917 Disability hearing—disability hearing officer's reconsidered determination.

(a) General. The disability hearing officer who conducts your disability hearing will prepare and will also issue a written reconsidered determination, unless:

(1) The disability hearing officer sends the case back for additional development by the component that prepared the case for the hearing, and that component issues a favorable determination, as permitted by § 404.916(c);

(2) It is determined that you are engaging in substantial gainful activity and that you are therefore not disabled; or

(3) The reconsidered determination prepared by the disability hearing officer is reviewed under § 404.918.

(b) Content. The disability hearing officer's reconsidered determination will give the findings of fact and the reasons for the reconsidered determination. The disability hearing officer must base the reconsidered determination on the preponderance of the evidence offered at the disability hearing or otherwise included in your case file.

(c) Notice. We will mail you and the other parties a notice of reconsidered determination in accordance with § 404.922.

(d) Effect. The disability hearing officer's reconsidered determination, or, if it is changed under § 404.918, the reconsidered determination that is issued by the Associate Commissioner for Disability Determinations or his or her delegate, is binding in accordance with § 404.921, subject to the exceptions specified in that section.

[51 FR 302, Jan. 3, 1986; 71 FR 10428, March 1, 2006; 73 FR 76943, Dec. 18, 2008]

§ 404.918 Disability hearing—review of the disability hearing officer's reconsidered determination before it is issued.

(a) General. The Associate Commissioner for Disability Determinations or his or her delegate may select a sample of disability hearing officers' reconsidered determinations, before they are issued, and review any such case to determine its correctness on any grounds he or she deems appropriate. The Associate Commissioner or his or her delegate shall review any case within the sample if:

(1) There appears to be an abuse of discretion by the hearing officer;

(2) There is an error of law; or

(3) The action, findings or conclusions of the disability hearing officer are not supported by substantial evidence.

Note to paragraph (a): If the review indicates that the reconsidered determination prepared by the disability hearing officer is correct, it will be dated and issued immediately upon completion of the review. If the reconsidered determination prepared by the disability hearing officer is found by the Associate Commissioner or his or her delegate to be deficient, it will be changed as described in paragraph (b) of this section.

(b) Methods of correcting deficiencies in the disability hearing officer's reconsidered determination. If the reconsidered determination prepared by the disability hearing officer is found by the Associate Commissioner for Disability Determinations or his or her delegate to be deficient, the Associate Commissioner or his or her delegate will take appropriate action to assure that the deficiency is corrected before a reconsidered determination is issued. The action taken by the Associate Commissioner or his or her delegate will take one of two forms:

(1) The Associate Commissioner or his or her delegate may return the case file either to the component responsible for preparing the case for hearing or to the disability hearing officer, for appropriate further action; or

(2) The Associate Commissioner or his or her delegate may issue a written reconsidered determination which corrects the deficiency.

(c) Further action on your case if it is sent back by the Associate Commissioner for Disability Determinations or his or her delegate either to the component that prepared your case for hearing or to the disability hearing officer. If the Associate Commissioner for Disability Determinations or his or her delegate sends your case back either to the component responsible for preparing the case for hearing or to the disability hearing officer for appropriate further action, as provided in paragraph (b)(1) of this section, any additional proceedings in your case will be governed by the disability hearing procedures described in § 404.916(f) or if your case is returned to the disability hearing officer and an unfavorable determination is indicated, a supplementary hearing may be scheduled for you before a reconsidered determination is reached in your case.

(d) Opportunity to comment before the Associate Commissioner for Disability Determinations or his or her delegate issues a reconsidered determination that is unfavorable to you. If the Associate Commissioner for Disability Determinations or his or her delegate proposes to issue a reconsidered determination as described in paragraph (b)(2) of this section, and that reconsidered determination is unfavorable to you, he or she will send you a copy of the proposed reconsidered determination with an explanation of the reasons for it, and will give you an opportunity to submit written comments before it is issued. At your request, you will also be given an opportunity to inspect the pertinent materials in your case file, including the reconsidered determination prepared by the disability hearing officer, before submitting your comments. You will be given 10 days from the date you receive the Associate Commissioner's notice of proposed action to submit your written comments, unless additional time is necessary to provide access to the pertinent file materials or there is good cause for providing more time, as illustrated by the examples in § 404.911(b). The Associate Commissioner or his or her delegate will consider your comments before taking any further action on your case.

[51 FR 302, Jan. 3, 1986; 71 FR 10428, March 1, 2006]

§ 404.919 Notice of another person's request for reconsideration.

If any other person files a request for reconsideration of the initial determination in your case, we shall notify you at your last known address before we reconsider the initial determination. We shall also give you an opportunity to present any evidence you think helpful to the reconsidered determination.

[51 FR 302, Jan. 3, 1986]

§ 404.920 Reconsidered determination.

After you or another person requests a reconsideration, we will review the evidence we considered in making the initial determination and any other evidence we receive. We will make our determination based on the preponderance of the evidence.

[51 FR 302, Jan. 3, 1986; 73 FR 76943, Dec. 18, 2008]

§ 404.921 Effect of a reconsidered determination.

The reconsidered determination is binding unless—

(a) You or any other party to the reconsideration requests a hearing before an administrative law judge within the stated time period and a decision is made;

(b) The expedited appeals process is used; or

(c) The reconsidered determination is revised.

[51 FR 302, Jan. 3, 1986]

§ 404.922 Notice of a reconsidered determination.

We shall mail a written notice of the reconsidered determination to the parties at their last known address. We shall state the specific reasons for the determination and tell you and any other parties of the right to a hearing. If it is appropriate, we will also tell you and any other parties how to use the expedited appeals process.

[51 FR 302, Jan. 3, 1986]

EXPEDITED APPEALS PROCESS

§ 404.923 Expedited appeals process—general.

By using the expedited appeals process you may go directly to a Federal district court without first completing the administrative review process that is generally required before the court will hear your case.

§ 404.924 When the expedited appeals process may be used.

You may use the expedited appeals process if all of the following requirements are met:

(a) We have made an initial and a reconsidered determination; an administrative law judge has made a hearing decision; or Appeals Council review has been requested, but a final decision has not been issued.

(b) You are a party to the reconsidered determination or the hearing decision.

(c) You have submitted a written request for the expedited appeals process.

(d) You have claimed, and we agree, that the only factor preventing a favorable determination or decision is a provision in the law that you believe is unconstitutional.

(e) If you are not the only party, all parties to the determination or decision agree to request the expedited appeals process.

§ 404.925 How to request expedited appeals process.

(a) Time of filing request. You may request the expedited appeals process—

(1) Within 60 days after the date you receive notice of the reconsidered determination (or within the extended time period if we extend the time as provided in paragraph (c) of this section);

(2) At any time after you have filed a timely request for a hearing but before you receive notice of the administrative law judge's decision;

(3) Within 60 days after the date you receive a notice of the administrative law judge's decision or dismissal (or within the extended time period if we extend the time as provided in paragraph (c) of this section); or

(4) At any time after you have filed a timely request for Appeals Council review, but before you receive notice of the Appeals Council's action.

(b) Place of filing request. You may file a written request for the expedited appeals process at one of our offices, the Veterans Administration Regional Office in the Philippines, or an office of the Railroad Retirement Board if you have 10 or more years of service in the railroad industry.

(c) Extension of time to request expedited appeals process. If you want to use the expedited appeals process but do not request it within the stated time period, you may ask for more time to submit your request. Your request for an extension of time must be in writing and must give the reasons why the request for the expedited appeals process was not filed within the stated time period. If you show that you had good cause for missing the deadline, the time period will be extended. To determine whether good cause exists, we use the standards explained in § 404.911.

§ 404.926 Agreement in expedited appeals process.

If you meet all the requirements necessary for the use of the expedited appeals process, our authorized representative shall prepare an agreement. The agreement must be signed by you, by every other party to the determination or decision and by our authorized representative. The agreement must provide that—

(a) The facts in your claim are not in dispute;

(b) The sole issue in dispute is whether a provision of the Act that applies to your case is unconstitutional;

(c) Except for your belief that a provision of the Act is unconstitutional, you agree with our interpretation of the law;

(d) If the provision of the Act that you believe is unconstitutional were not applied to your case, your claim would be allowed; and

(e) Our determination or the decision is final for the purpose of seeking judicial review.

§ 404.927 Effect of expedited appeals process agreement.

After an expedited appeals process agreement is signed, you will not need to complete the remaining steps of the administrative review process. Instead, you may file an action in a Federal district court within 60 days after the date you receive notice (a signed copy of the agreement will be mailed to you and will constitute notice) that the agreement has been signed by our authorized representative.

[49 FR 46369, Nov. 26, 1984]

§ 404.928 Expedited appeals process request that does not result in agreement.

If you do not meet all of the requirements necessary to use the expedited appeals process, we shall tell you that your request to use this process is denied and that your request will be considered as a request for a hearing or Appeals Council review, whichever is appropriate.

HEARING BEFORE AN ADMINISTRATIVE LAW JUDGE

§ 404.929 Hearing before an administrative law judge-general.

If you are dissatisfied with one of the determinations or decisions listed in § 404.930, you may request a hearing. The Deputy Commissioner for Disability Adjudication and Review, or his or her delegate, will appoint an administrative law judge to conduct the hearing. If circumstances warrant, the Deputy Commissioner, or his or her delegate, may assign your case to another administrative law judge. At the hearing, you may appear in person, by video teleconferencing, or, under certain extraordinary circumstances, by telephone. You may submit new evidence (subject to the provisions of § 404.935), examine the evidence used in making the determination or decision under review, and present and question witnesses. The administrative law judge who conducts the hearing may ask you questions. He or she will issue a decision based on the preponderance of the evidence in the hearing record. If you waive your right to appear at the hearing, in person, by video teleconferencing, or by telephone, the administrative law judge will make a decision based on the preponderance of the evidence that is in the file and, subject to the provisions of § 404.935, any new evidence that may have been submitted for consideration.

[51 FR 302, Jan. 3, 1986; 68 FR 5218, Feb. 3, 2003; 68 FR 69009, Dec. 11, 2003; 79 FR 35931, June 25, 2014; 81 FR 90992, Dec. 16, 2016]

§ 404.930 Availability of a hearing before an administrative law judge.

(a) You or another party may request a hearing before an administrative law judge if we have made—

(1) A reconsidered determination;

(2) A revised determination of an initial determination, unless the revised determination concerns the issue of whether, based on medical factors, you are disabled;

(3) A reconsideration of a revised initial determination concerning the issue of whether, based on medical factors, you are disabled;

(4) A revised reconsidered determination;

(5) A revised decision based on evidence not included in the record on which the prior decision was based;

(6) An initial determination denying waiver of adjustment or recovery of an overpayment based on a personal conference (see § 404.506); or

(7) An initial determination denying waiver of adjustment or recovery of an overpayment based on a review of the written evidence of record (see § 404.506), and the determination was made concurrent with, or subsequent to, our reconsideration determination regarding the underlying overpayment but before an administrative law judge holds a hearing.

(b) We will hold a hearing only if you or another party to the hearing file a written request for a hearing.

(c) [Reserved by 76 FR 24806]

[51 FR 303, Jan. 3, 1986; 61 FR 56132, Oct. 31, 1996; 73 FR 2415, Jan. 15, 2008; 73 FR 10381, Feb. 27, 2008; 76 FR 24806, May 3, 2011]

§ 404.932 Parties to a hearing before an administrative law judge.

(a) Who may request a hearing. You may request a hearing if a hearing is available under § 404.930. In addition, a person who shows in writing that his or her rights may be adversely affected by the decision may request a hearing.

(b) Who are parties to a hearing. After a request for a hearing is made, you, the other parties to the initial, reconsidered, or revised determination, and any other person who shows in writing that his or her rights may be adversely affected by the hearing, are parties to the hearing. In addition, any other person may be made a party to the hearing if his or her rights may be adversely affected by the decision, and we notify the person to appear at the hearing or to present evidence supporting his or her interest.

[51 FR 303, Jan. 3, 1986; 75 FR 39160, July 8, 2010]

§ 404.933 How to request a hearing before an administrative law judge.

(a) Written request. You may request a hearing by filing a written request. You should include in your request—

(1) The name and social security number of the wage earner;

(2) The reasons you disagree with the previous determination or decision;

(3) A statement of additional evidence to be submitted and the date you will submit it; and

(4) The name and address of any designated representative.

(b) When and where to file. The request must be filed—

(1) Within 60 days after the date you receive notice of the previous determination or decision (or within the extended time period if we extend the time as provided in paragraph (c) of this section);

(2) At one of our offices, the Veterans Administration Regional Office in the Philippines, or an office of the Railroad Retirement Board for persons having 10 or more years of service in the railroad industry.

(c) Extension of time to request a hearing. If you have a right to a hearing but do not request one in time, you may ask for more time to make your request. The request for an extension of time must be in writing and it must give the reasons why the request for a hearing was not filed within the stated time period. You may file your request for an extension of time at one of our offices. If you show that you had good cause for missing the deadline, the time period will be extended. To determine whether good cause exists, we use the standards explained in § 404.911.

[51 FR 303, Jan. 3, 1986]

§ 404.935 Submitting written evidence to an administrative law judge.

(a) When you submit your request for hearing, you should also submit information or evidence as required by § 404.1512 or any summary of the evidence to the administrative law judge. Each party must make every effort to ensure that the administrative law judge receives all of the evidence and must inform us about or submit any written evidence, as required in § 404.1512, no later than 5 business days before the date of the scheduled hearing. If you do not comply with this requirement, the administrative law judge may decline to consider or obtain the evidence, unless the circumstances described in paragraph (b) of this section apply.

(b) If you have evidence required under § 404.1512 but you have missed the deadline described in paragraph (a) of this section, the administrative law judge will accept the evidence if he or she has not yet issued a decision and you did not inform us about or submit the evidence before the deadline because:

(1) Our action misled you;

(2) You had a physical, mental, educational, or linguistic limitation(s) that prevented you from informing us about or submitting the evidence earlier; or

(3) Some other unusual, unexpected, or unavoidable circumstance beyond your control prevented you from informing us about or submitting the evidence earlier. Examples include, but are not limited to:

(i) You were seriously ill, and your illness prevented you from contacting us in person, in writing, or through a friend, relative, or other person;

(ii) There was a death or serious illness in your immediate family;

(iii) Important records were destroyed or damaged by fire or other accidental cause; or

(iv) You actively and diligently sought evidence from a source and the evidence was not received or was received less than 5 business days prior to the hearing.

[51 FR 303, Jan. 3, 1986; 80 FR 14835, March 20, 2015; 81 FR 90993, Dec. 16, 2016]

§ 404.936 Time and place for a hearing before an administrative law judge.

(a) General. We may set the time and place for any hearing. We may change the time and place, if it is necessary. After sending you reasonable notice of the proposed action, the administrative law judge may adjourn or postpone the hearing or reopen it to receive additional evidence any time before he or she notifies you of a hearing decision.

(b) Where we hold hearings. We hold hearings in the 50 States, the District of Columbia, American Samoa, Guam, the Northern Mariana Islands, the Commonwealth of Puerto Rico, and the United States Virgin Islands. The "place" of the hearing is the hearing office or other site(s) at which you and any other parties to the hearing are located when you make your appearance(s) before the administrative law judge, whether in person, by video teleconferencing, or by telephone.

(c) Determining how appearances will be made. In setting the time and place of the hearing, we will consider the following:

(1) We will consult with the administrative law judge to determine the status of case preparation and to determine whether your appearance, or the appearance of any other party to the hearing, will be made in person, by video teleconferencing or, under extraordinary circumstances, by telephone. The administrative law judge will determine that your appearance, or the appearance of any other party to the hearing, be conducted by video teleconferencing if video teleconferencing equipment is available to conduct the appearance, use of video teleconferencing to conduct the appearance would be more efficient than conducting the appearance in person, and the administrative law judge determines that there is no circumstance in the particular case that prevents the use of video teleconferencing to conduct the appearance. The administrative law judge will direct you or another party to the hearing to appear by telephone when:

(i) An appearance in person is not possible, such as if you are incarcerated, the facility will not allow a hearing to be held at the facility, and video teleconferencing is not available; or

(ii) The administrative law judge determines, either on his or her own, or at your request or at the request of any other party to the hearing, that extraordinary circumstances prevent you or another party to the hearing from appearing at the hearing in person or by video teleconferencing.

(2) The administrative law judge will determine whether any person other than you or any other party to the hearing, including a medical expert or a vocational expert, will appear at the hearing in person, by video teleconferencing, or by telephone. If you or any other party to the hearing objects to any other person appearing by video teleconferencing or by telephone, the administrative law judge will decide, either in writing or at the hearing, whether to have that person appear in person, by video teleconferencing, or by telephone. The administrative law judge will direct a person, other than you or any other party to the hearing if we are notified as provided in paragraph (e) of this section that you or any other party to the hearing objects to appearing by video teleconferencing, to appear by video teleconferencing or telephone when the administrative law judge determines:

(i) Video teleconferencing or telephone equipment is available;

(ii) Use of video teleconferencing or telephone equipment would be more efficient than conducting an examination of a witness in person, and;

(iii) The ALJ determines there is no other reason why video teleconferencing or telephone should not be used.

(d) Objecting to appearing by video teleconferencing. Prior to scheduling your hearing, we will notify you that we may schedule you to appear by video teleconferencing. If you object to appearing by video teleconferencing, you must notify us in writing within 30 days after the date you receive the notice. If you notify us within that time period and your residence does not change while your request for hearing is pending, we will set your hearing for a time and place at which you may make your appearance before the administrative law judge in person.

(1) Notwithstanding any objections you may have to appearing by video teleconferencing, if you change your residence while your request for hearing is pending, we may determine how you will appear, including by video teleconferencing, as provided in paragraph (c)(1) of this section. For us to consider your change of residence when we schedule your hearing, you must submit evidence verifying your new residence.

(2) If you notify us that you object to appearing by video teleconferencing more than 30 days after the date you receive our notice, we will extend the time period if you show you had good cause for missing the deadline. To determine whether good cause exists for extending the deadline, we use the standards explained in § 404.911.

(e) Objecting to the time or place of the hearing. If you object to the time or place of the hearing, you must:

(1) Notify us in writing at the earliest possible opportunity, but not later than 5 days before the date set for the hearing or 30 days after receiving notice of the hearing, whichever is earlier (or within the extended time period if we extend the time as provided in paragraph (e)(3) of this section); and

(2) State the reason(s) for your objection and state the time and place you want the hearing to be held. We will change the time or place of the hearing if the administrative law judge finds you have good cause, as determined under paragraph (f) of this section. Section 404.938 provides procedures we will follow when you do not respond to a notice of hearing.

(3) If you notify us that you object to the time or place of hearing less than 5 days before the date set for the hearing or, if earlier, more than 30 days after receiving notice of the hearing, we will extend the time period if you show you had good cause for missing the deadline. To determine whether good cause exists for extending the deadline, we use the standards explained in § 404.911.

(f) Good cause for changing the time or place. The administrative law judge will determine whether good cause exists for changing the time or place of your scheduled hearing. However, a finding that good cause exists to reschedule the time or place of your hearing will not change the assignment of the administrative law judge for your case, unless we determine reassignment will promote more efficient administration of the hearing process.

(1) We will reschedule your hearing, if your reason is one of the following circumstances and is supported by the evidence:

(i) A serious physical or mental condition or incapacitating injury makes it impossible for you or your representative to travel to the hearing, or a death in the family occurs; or

(ii) Severe weather conditions make it impossible for you or your representative to travel to the hearing.

(2) In determining whether good cause exists in circumstances other than those set out in paragraph (f)(1) of this section, the administrative law judge will consider your reason(s) for requesting the change, the facts supporting it, and the impact of the proposed change on the efficient administration of the hearing process. Factors affecting the impact of the change include, but are not limited to, the effect on the processing of other scheduled hearings, delays that might occur in rescheduling your hearing, and whether we previously granted you any changes in the time or place of your hearing. Examples of such other circumstances that you might give for requesting a change in the time or place of the hearing include, but are not limited to, the following:

(i) You unsuccessfully attempted to obtain a representative and need additional time to secure representation;

(ii) Your representative was appointed within 30 days of the scheduled hearing and needs additional time to prepare for the hearing;

(iii) Your representative has a prior commitment to be in court or at another administrative hearing on the date scheduled for the hearing;

(iv) A witness who will testify to facts material to your case would be unavailable to attend the scheduled hearing and the evidence cannot be otherwise obtained;

(v) Transportation is not readily available for you to travel to the hearing; or

(vi) You are unrepresented, and you are unable to respond to the notice of hearing because of any physical, mental, educational, or linguistic limitations (including any lack of facility with the English language) which you may have.

(g) Good cause in other circumstances. In determining whether good cause exists in circumstances other than those set out in paragraph (e) of this section, the administrative law judge will consider your reason for requesting the change, the facts supporting it, and the impact of the proposed change on the efficient administration of the hearing process. Factors affecting the impact of the change include, but are not limited to, the effect on the processing of other scheduled hearings, delays which might occur in rescheduling your hearing, and whether any prior changes were granted to you. Examples of such other circumstances, which you might give for requesting a change in the time or place of the hearing, include, but are not limited to, the following:

(1) You have attempted to obtain a representative but need additional time;

(2) Your representative was appointed within 30 days of the scheduled hearing and needs additional time to prepare for the hearing;

(3) Your representative has a prior commitment to be in court or at another administrative hearing on the date scheduled for the hearing;

(4) A witness who will testify to facts material to your case would be unavailable to attend the scheduled hearing and the evidence cannot be otherwise obtained;

(5) Transportation is not readily available for you to travel to the hearing;

(6) You live closer to another hearing site; or

(7) You are unrepresented, and you are unable to respond to the notice of hearing because of any physical, mental, educational, or linguistic limitations (including any lack of facility with the English language) which you may have.

(h) Consultation procedures. Before we exercise the authority to set the time and place for an administrative law judge's hearings, we will consult with the appropriate hearing office chief administrative law judge to determine if there are any reasons why we should not set the time and place of the administrative law judge's hearings. If the hearing office chief administrative law judge does not state a reason that we believe justifies the limited number of hearings scheduled by the administrative law judge, we will then consult with the administrative law judge before deciding whether to begin to exercise our authority to set the time and place for the administrative law judge's hearings. If the hearing office chief administrative law judge states a reason that we believe justifies the limited number of hearings scheduled by the administrative law judge, we will not exercise our authority to set the time and place for the administrative law judge's hearings. We will work with the hearing office chief administrative law judge to identify those circumstances where we can assist the administrative law judge and address any impediment that may affect the scheduling of hearings.

(i) Pilot program. The provisions of the first and second sentences of paragraph (a), the first sentence of paragraph (c)(1), and paragraph (g) of this section are a pilot program. These provisions will no longer be effective on August 11, 2017, unless we terminate them earlier or extend them beyond that date by notice of a final rule in the Federal Register.

[50 FR 21438, May 24, 1985; 51 FR 303, Jan. 3, 1986; 59 FR 1634, Jan. 12, 1994; 68 FR 5218, Feb. 3, 2003; 68 FR 69009, Dec. 11, 2003; 75 FR 39160, July 8, 2010; 78 FR 29626, May 21, 2013; 78 FR 45452, July 29, 2013; 79 FR 35931, June 25, 2014; 79 FR 41882, July 18, 2014; 80 FR 37971, July 2, 2015; 81 FR 41214, June 24, 2016]

§ 404.937 Protecting the safety of the public and our employees in our hearing process.

(a) Notwithstanding any other provision in this part or part 422 of this chapter, we are establishing the procedures set out in this section to ensure the safety of the public and our employees in our hearing process.

(b)(1) At the request of any hearing office employee, the Hearing Office Chief Administrative Law Judge will determine, after consultation with the presiding administrative law judge, whether a claimant or other individual poses a reasonable threat to the safety of our employees or other participants in the hearing. The Hearing Office Chief Administrative Law Judge will find that a claimant or other individual poses a threat to the safety of our employees or other participants in the hearing when he or she determines that the individual has made a threat and there is a reasonable likelihood that the claimant or other individual could act on the threat or when evidence suggests that a claimant or other individual poses a threat. In making a finding under this paragraph, the Hearing Office Chief Administrative Law Judge will consider all relevant evidence, including any information we have in the claimant's record and any information we have regarding the claimant's or other individual's past conduct.

(2) If the Hearing Office Chief Administrative Law Judge determines that the claimant or other individual poses a reasonable threat to the safety of our employees or other participants in the hearing, the Hearing Office Chief Administrative Law Judge will either:

(i) Require the presence of a security guard at the hearing; or

(ii) Require that the hearing be conducted by video teleconference or by telephone.

(c) If we have banned a claimant from any of our facilities, we will provide the claimant with the opportunity for a hearing that will be conducted by telephone.

(d) The actions of the Hearing Office Chief Administrative Law Judge taken under this section are final and not subject to further review.

[76 FR 13508, March 14, 2011; 77 FR 10658, Feb. 23, 2012]

§ 404.938 Notice of a hearing before an administrative law judge.

(a) Issuing the notice. After we set the time and place of the hearing, we will mail notice of the hearing to you at your last known address, or give the notice to you by personal service, unless you have indicated in writing that you do not wish to receive this notice. We will mail or serve the notice at least 75 days before the date of the hearing.

(b) Notice information. The notice of hearing will tell you:

(1) The specific issues to be decided in your case;

(2) That you may designate a person to represent you during the proceedings;

(3) How to request that we change the time or place of your hearing;

(4) That your hearing may be dismissed if neither you nor the person you designate to act as your representative appears at your scheduled hearing without good reason under § 404.957;

(5) Whether your appearance or that of any other party or witness is scheduled to be made in person, by video teleconferencing, or by telephone. If we have scheduled you to appear at the hearing by video teleconferencing, the notice of hearing will tell you that the scheduled place for the hearing is a video teleconferencing site and explain what it means to appear at your hearing by video teleconferencing;

(6) That you must make every effort to inform us about or submit all written evidence that is not already in the record no later than 5 business days before the date of the scheduled hearing, unless you show that your circumstances meet the conditions described in § 404.935(b); and

(7) Any other information about the scheduling and conduct of your hearing.

(c) Acknowledging the notice of hearing. The notice of hearing will ask you to return a form to let us know that you received the notice. If you or your representative do not acknowledge receipt of the notice of hearing, we will attempt to contact you for an explanation. If you tell us that you did not receive the notice of hearing, an amended notice will be sent to you by certified mail. See § 404.936 for the procedures we will follow in deciding whether the time or place of your scheduled hearing will be changed if you do not respond to the notice of hearing.

[50 FR 21438, May 24, 1985; 51 FR 303, Jan. 3, 1986; 68 FR 5219, Feb. 3, 2003; 68 FR 69009, Dec. 11, 2003; 75 FR 39160, July 8, 2010; 78 FR 29627, May 21, 2013; 79 FR 35932, June 25, 2014; 81 FR 90993, Dec. 16, 2016]

§ 404.939 Objections to the issues.

If you object to the issues to be decided at the hearing, you must notify the administrative law judge in writing at the earliest possible opportunity, but no later than 5 business days before the date set for the hearing, unless you show that your circumstances meet the conditions described in § 404.935(b). You must state the reason(s) for your objection(s). The administrative law judge will make a decision on your objection(s) either at the hearing or in writing before the hearing.

[81 FR 90993, Dec. 16, 2016]

§ 404.940 Disqualification of the administrative law judge.

An administrative law judge shall not conduct a hearing if he or she is prejudiced or partial with respect to any party or has any interest in the matter pending for decision. If you object to the administrative law judge who will conduct the hearing, you must notify the administrative law judge at your earliest opportunity. The administrative law judge shall consider your objections and shall decide whether to proceed with the hearing or withdraw. If he or she withdraws, the Associate Commissioner for Hearings and Appeals, or his or her delegate, will appoint another administrative law judge to conduct the hearing. If the administrative law judge does not withdraw, you may, after the hearing, present your objections to the Appeals Council as reasons why the hearing decision should be revised or a new hearing held before another administrative law judge.

§ 404.941 Prehearing case review.

(a) General. After a hearing is requested but before it is held, we may, for the purposes of a prehearing case review, forward the case to the component of our office (including a State agency) that issued the determination being reviewed. That component will decide whether it should revise the determination based on the preponderance of the evidence. A revised determination may be fully or partially favorable to you. A prehearing case review will not delay the scheduling of a hearing unless you agree to continue the review and delay the hearing. If the prehearing case review is not completed before the date of the hearing, the case will be sent to the administrative law judge unless a favorable revised determination is in process or you and the other parties to the hearing agree in writing to delay the hearing until the review is completed.

(b) When a prehearing case review may be conducted. We may conduct a prehearing case review if—

(1) Additional evidence is submitted;

(2) There is an indication that additional evidence is available;

(3) There is a change in the law or regulation; or

(4) There is an error in the file or some other indication that the prior determination may be revised.

(c) Notice of a prehearing revised determination. If we revise the determination in a prehearing case review, we will mail a written notice of the revised determination to all parties at their last known addresses. We will state the basis for the revised determination and advise all parties of the effect of the revised determination on the request for a hearing.

(d) Effect of a fully favorable revised determination. If the revised determination is fully favorable to you, we will tell you in the notice that an administrative law judge will dismiss the request for a hearing. We will also tell you that you or another party to the hearing may request that the administrative law judge vacate the dismissal and reinstate the request for a hearing if you or another party to the hearing disagrees with the revised determination for any reason. If you wish to make this request, you must do so in writing and send it to us within 60 days of the date you receive notice of the dismissal. If the request is timely, an administrative law judge will vacate the dismissal, reinstate the request for hearing, and offer you and all parties an opportunity for a hearing. The administrative law judge will extend the time limit if you show that you had good cause for missing the deadline. The administrative law judge will use the standards in § 404.911 to determine whether you had good cause.

(e) Effect of a partially favorable revised determination. If the revised determination is partially favorable to you, we will tell you in the notice what was not favorable. We will also tell you that an administrative law judge will hold the hearing you requested unless you and all other parties to the hearing agree in writing to dismiss the request for a hearing. An administrative law judge will dismiss the request for a hearing if we receive the written statement(s) agreeing to dismiss the request for a hearing before an administrative law judge mails a notice of his or her hearing decision.

[73 FR 76943, Dec. 18, 2008; 75 FR 33168, June 11, 2010; 76 FR 65369, Oct. 21, 2011]

§ 404.942 Prehearing proceedings and decisions by attorney advisors.

(a) General. After a hearing is requested but before it is held, an attorney advisor may conduct prehearing proceedings as set out in paragraph (c) of this section. If after the completion of these proceedings we can make a decision that is fully favorable to you and all other parties based on the preponderance of the evidence, an attorney advisor, instead of an administrative law judge, may issue the decision. The conduct of the prehearing proceedings by the attorney advisor will not delay the scheduling of a hearing. If the prehearing proceedings are not completed before the date of the hearing, the case will be sent to the administrative law judge unless a fully favorable decision is in process or you and all other parties to the hearing agree in writing to delay the hearing until the proceedings are completed.

(b) When prehearing proceedings may be conducted by an attorney advisor. An attorney advisor may conduct prehearing proceedings if you have filed a claim for benefits based on disability and—

(1) New and material evidence is submitted;

(2) There is an indication that additional evidence is available;

(3) There is a change in the law or regulations; or

(4) There is an error in the file or some other indication that a fully favorable decision may be issued.

(c) Nature of the prehearing proceedings that may be conducted by an attorney advisor. As part of the prehearing proceedings, the attorney advisor, in addition to reviewing the existing record, may—

(1) Request additional evidence that may be relevant to the claim, including medical evidence; and

(2) If necessary to clarify the record for the purpose of determining if a fully favorable decision is warranted, schedule a conference with the parties.

(d) Notice of a decision by an attorney advisor. If an attorney advisor issues a fully favorable decision under this section, we will mail a written notice of the decision to all parties at their last known addresses. We will state the basis for the decision and advise all parties that they may request that an administrative law judge reinstate the request for a hearing if they disagree with the decision for any reason. Any party who wants to make this request must do so in writing and send it to us within 60 days of the date he or she receives notice of the decision. The administrative law judge will extend the time limit if the requestor shows good cause for missing the deadline. The administrative law judge will use the standards in § 404.911 to determine whether there is good cause. If the request is timely, an administrative law judge will reinstate the request for a hearing and offer all parties an opportunity for a hearing.

(e) Effect of an attorney advisor's decision. An attorney advisor's decision under this section is binding unless—

(1) You or another party to the hearing submits a timely request that an administrative law judge reinstate the request for a hearing under paragraph (d) of this section;

(2) The Appeals Council reviews the decision on its own motion pursuant to § 404.969 as explained in paragraph (f)(3) of this section; or

(3) The decision of the attorney advisor is revised under the procedures explained in § 404.987.

(f) Ancillary provisions. For the purposes of the procedures authorized by this section, the regulations of part 404 shall apply to—

(1) Authorize an attorney advisor to exercise the functions performed by an administrative law judge under §§ 404.1513a, 404.1520a, 404.1526, and 404.1546.

(2) Define the term "decision" to include a decision made by an attorney advisor, as well as the decisions identified in § 404.901; and

(3) Make the decision of an attorney advisor under paragraph (d) of this section subject to review by the Appeals Council if the Appeals Council decides to review the decision of the attorney advisor anytime within 60 days after the date of the decision under § 404.969.

(g) [Reserved by 83 FR 40453]

[60 FR 34131, June 30, 1995; 62 FR 35074, June 30, 1997; 63 FR 35516, June 30, 1998; 64 FR 13678, March 22, 1999; 64 FR 51893, Sept. 27, 1999; 72 FR 44765, Aug. 9, 2007; 73 FR 11349, March 3, 2008; 73 FR 76944, Dec. 18, 2008; 74 FR 33328, July 13, 2009; 76 FR 18384, April 4, 2011; 76 FR 65370, Oct. 21, 2011; 78 FR 45460, July 29, 2013; 80 FR 31991, June 5, 2015; 82 FR 5863, Jan. 18, 2017; 82 FR 34401, July 25, 2017; 83 FR 712, Jan. 8, 2018; 83 FR 28993, June 22, 2018; 83 FR 40453, Aug. 15, 2018]

§ 404.943 Responsibilities of the adjudication officer.

(a)(1) General. Under the procedures set out in this section we will test modifications to the procedures we follow when you file a request for a hearing before an administrative law judge in connection with a claim for benefits based on disability where the question of whether you are under a disability as defined in § 404.1505 is at issue. These modifications will enable us to test the effect of having an adjudication officer be your primary point of contact after you file a hearing request and before you have a hearing with an administrative law judge. The tests may be conducted alone, or in combination with the tests of the modifications to the disability determination procedures which we conduct under § 404.906. The adjudication officer, working with you and your representative, if any, will identify issues in dispute, develop evidence, conduct informal conferences, and conduct any other prehearing proceeding as may be necessary. The adjudication officer has the authority to make a decision fully favorable to you if the evidence so warrants. If the adjudication officer does not make a decision on your claim, your hearing request will be assigned to an administrative law judge for further proceedings.

(2) Procedures for cases included in the tests. Prior to commencing tests of the adjudication officer position in selected site(s), we will publish a notice in the Federal Register. The notice will describe where the specific test site(s) will be and the duration of the test(s). We will also state whether the tests of the adjudication officer position in each site will be conducted alone, or in combination with the tests of the modifications to the disability determination procedures which we conduct under § 404.906. The individuals who participate in the test(s) will be assigned randomly to a test group in each site where the tests are conducted.

(b)(1) Prehearing procedures conducted by an Adjudication Officer. When you file a request for a hearing before an administrative law judge in connection with a claim for benefits based on disability where the question of whether you are under a disability as defined in § 404.1505 is at issue, the adjudication officer will conduct an interview with you. The interview may take place in person, by telephone, or by videoconference, as the adjudication officer determines is appropriate under the circumstances of your case. If you file a request for an extension of time to request a hearing in accordance with § 404.933(c), the adjudication officer may develop information on, and may decide where the adjudication officer issues a fully favorable decision to you that you had good cause for missing the deadline for requesting a hearing. To determine whether you had good cause for missing the deadline, the adjudication officer will use the standards contained in § 404.911.

(2) Representation. The adjudication officer will provide you with information regarding the hearing process, including your right to representation. As may be appropriate, the adjudication officer will provide you with referral sources for representation, and give you copies of necessary documents to facilitate the appointment of a representative. If you have a representative, the adjudication officer will conduct an informal conference with the representative, in person or by telephone, to identify the issues in dispute and prepare proposed written agreements for the approval of the administrative law judge regarding those issues which are not in dispute and those issues proposed for the hearing. If you decide to proceed without representation, the adjudication officer may hold an informal conference with you. If you obtain representation after the adjudication officer has concluded that your case is ready for a hearing, the administrative law judge will return your case to the adjudication officer who will conduct an informal conference with you and your representative.

(3) Evidence. You, or your representative, may submit, or may be asked to obtain and submit, additional evidence to the adjudication officer. As the adjudication officer determines is appropriate under the circumstances of your case, the adjudication officer may refer the claim for further medical or vocational evidence.

(4) Referral for a hearing. The adjudication officer will refer the claim to the administrative law judge for further proceedings when the development of evidence is complete, and you or your representative agree that a hearing is ready to be held. If you or your representative are unable to agree with the adjudication officer that the development of evidence is complete, the adjudication officer will note your disagreement and refer the claim to the administrative law judge for further proceedings. At this point, the administrative law judge conducts all further hearing proceedings, including scheduling and holding a hearing (§ 404.936), considering any additional evidence or arguments submitted (§§ 404.935, 404.944, 404.949, 404.950), and issuing a decision or dismissal of your request for a hearing, as may be appropriate (§§ 404.948, 404.953, 404.957). In addition, if the administrative law judge determines on or before the date of your hearing that the development of evidence is not complete, the administrative law judge may return the claim to the adjudication officer to complete the development of the evidence and for such other action as necessary.

(c)(1) Fully favorable decisions issued by an adjudication officer. If, after a hearing is requested but before it is held, the adjudication officer decides that the evidence in your case warrants a decision which is fully favorable to you, the adjudication officer may issue such a decision. For purposes of the tests authorized under this section, the adjudication officer's decision shall be considered to be a decision as defined in § 404.901. If the adjudication officer issues a decision under this section, it will be in writing and will give the findings of fact and the reasons for the decision. The adjudication officer will evaluate the issues relevant to determining whether or not you are disabled in accordance with the provisions of the Social Security Act, the rules in this part and part 422 of this chapter and applicable Social Security Rulings. For cases in which the adjudication officer issues a decision, he or she may determine your residual functional capacity in the same manner that an administrative law judge is authorized to do so in § 404.1546. The adjudication officer may also evaluate the severity of your mental impairments in the same manner that an administrative law judge is authorized to do so under § 404.1520a. The adjudication officer's decision will be based on the evidence which is included in the record and, subject to paragraph (c)(2) of this section, will complete the actions that will be taken on your request for hearing. A copy of the decision will be mailed to all parties at their last known address. We will tell you in the notice that the administrative law judge will not hold a hearing unless a party to the hearing requests that the hearing proceed. A request to proceed with the hearing must be made in writing within 30 days after the date the notice of the decision of the adjudication officer is mailed.

(2) Effect of a decision by an adjudication officer. A decision by an adjudication officer which is fully favorable to you under this section, and notification thereof, completes the administrative action on your request for hearing and is binding on all parties to the hearing and not subject to further review, unless—

(i) You or another party requests that the hearing continue, as provided in paragraph (c)(1) of this section;

(ii) The Appeals Council decides to review the decision on its own motion under the authority provided in § 404.969;

(iii) The decision is revised under the procedures explained in §§ 404.987 through 404.989; or

(iv) In a case remanded by a Federal court, the Appeals Council assumes jurisdiction under the procedures in § 404.984.

(3) Fee for a representative's services. The adjudication officer may authorize a fee for your representative's services if the adjudication officer makes a decision on your claim that is fully favorable to you, and you are represented. The actions of, and any fee authorization made by, the adjudication officer with respect to representation will be made in accordance with the provisions of subpart R of this part.

(d) Who may be an adjudication officer. The adjudication officer described in this section may be an employee of the Social Security Administration or a State agency that makes disability determinations for us.

[60 FR 47475, Sept. 13, 1995; 75 FR 33168, June 11, 2010]

ADMINISTRATIVE LAW JUDGE HEARING PROCEDURES

§ 404.944 Administrative law judge hearing procedures—general.

A hearing is open to the parties and to other persons the administrative law judge considers necessary and proper. At the hearing, the administrative law judge looks fully into the issues, questions you and the other witnesses, and, subject to the provisions of § 404.935: Accepts as evidence any documents that are material to the issues; may stop the hearing temporarily and continue it at a later date if he or she finds that there is material evidence missing at the hearing; and may reopen the hearing at any time before he or she mails a notice of the decision in order to receive new and material evidence. The administrative law judge may decide when the evidence will be presented and when the issues will be discussed.

[51 FR 303, Jan. 3, 1986; 81 FR 90993, Dec. 16, 2016]

§ 404.946 Issues before an administrative law judge.

(a) General. The issues before the administrative law judge include all the issues brought out in the initial, reconsidered or revised determination that were not decided entirely in your favor. However, if evidence presented before or during the hearing causes the administrative law judge to question a fully favorable determination, he or she will notify you and will consider it an issue at the hearing.

(b) New issues—

(1) General. The administrative law judge may consider a new issue at the hearing if he or she notifies you and all the parties about the new issue any time after receiving the hearing request and before mailing notice of the hearing decision. The administrative law judge or any party may raise a new issue; an issue may be raised even though it arose after the request for a hearing and even though it has not been considered in an initial or reconsidered determination. However, it may not be raised if it involves a claim that is within the jurisdiction of a State agency under a Federal–State agreement concerning the determination of disability.

(2) Notice of a new issue. The administrative law judge shall notify you and any other party if he or she will consider any new issue. Notice of the time and place of the hearing on any new issues will be given in the manner described in § 404.938, unless you have indicated in writing that you do not wish to receive the notice.

[51 FR 303, Jan. 3, 1986]

§ 404.948 Deciding a case without an oral hearing before an administrative law judge.

(a) Decision fully favorable. If the evidence in the hearing record supports a finding in favor of you and all the parties on every issue, the administrative law judge may issue a hearing decision based on a preponderance of the evidence without holding an oral hearing. The notice of the decision will state that you have the right to an oral hearing and to examine the evidence on which the administrative law judge based the decision.

(b) Parties do not wish to appear.

(1) The administrative law judge may decide a case on the record and not conduct an oral hearing if—

(i) You and all the parties indicate in writing that you do not wish to appear before the administrative law judge at an oral hearing; or

(ii) You live outside the United States, you do not inform us that you wish to appear, and there are no other parties who wish to appear.

(2) When an oral hearing is not held, the administrative law judge shall make a record of the material evidence. The record will include the applications, written statements, certificates, reports, affidavits, and other documents that were used in making the determination under review and any additional evidence you or any other party to the hearing present in writing. The decision of the administrative law judge must be based on this record.

(c) Case remanded for a revised determination.

(1) The administrative law judge may remand a case to the appropriate component of our office for a revised determination if there is reason to believe that the revised determination would be fully favorable to you. This could happen if the administrative law judge

receives new and material evidence or if there is a change in the law that permits the favorable determination.

(2) Unless you request the remand, the administrative law judge shall notify you that your case has been remanded and tell you that if you object, you must notify him or her of your objections within 10 days of the date the case is remanded or we will assume that you agree to the remand. If you object to the remand, the administrative law judge will consider the objection and rule on it in writing.

[51 FR 303, Jan. 3, 1986; 73 FR 76944, Dec. 18, 2008; 75 FR 33168, June 11, 2010; 76 FR 65370, Oct. 21, 2011]

§ 404.949 Presenting written statements and oral arguments.

You or a person you designate to act as your representative may appear before the administrative law judge to state your case, present a written summary of your case, or enter written statements about the facts and law material to your case in the record. If presenting written statements prior to hearing, you must provide a copy of your written statements for each party no later than 5 business days before the date set for the hearing, unless you show that your circumstances meet the conditions described in § 404.935(b).

[81 FR 90993, Dec. 16, 2016]

§ 404.950 Presenting evidence at a hearing before an administrative law judge.

(a) The right to appear and present evidence. Any party to a hearing has a right to appear before the administrative law judge, either in person, or, when the conditions in § 404.936(c)(1) exist, by video teleconferencing or telephone, to present evidence and to state his or her position. A party may also make his or her appearance by means of a designated representative, who may make the appearance in person, or, when the conditions in § 404.936(c)(1) exist, by video teleconferencing or telephone.

(b) Waiver of the right to appear. You may send the administrative law judge a waiver or a written statement indicating that you do not wish to appear at the hearing. You may withdraw this waiver any time before a notice of the hearing decision is mailed to you. Even if all of the parties waive their right to appear at a hearing, we may notify them of a time and a place for an oral hearing, if the administrative law judge believes that a personal appearance and testimony by you or any other party is necessary to decide the case.

(c) Admissible evidence. Subject to the provisions of § 404.935, the administrative law judge may receive any evidence at the hearing that he or she believes is material to the issues, even though the evidence would not be admissible in court under the rules of evidence used by the court.

(d) Subpoenas.

(1) When it is reasonably necessary for the full presentation of a case, an administrative law judge or a member of the Appeals Council may, on his or her own initiative or at the request of a party, issue subpoenas for the appearance and testimony of witnesses and for the production of books, records, correspondence, papers, or other documents that are material to an issue at the hearing.

(2) Parties to a hearing who wish to subpoena documents or witnesses must file a written request for the issuance of a subpoena with the administrative law judge or at one of our offices at least 10 business days before the hearing date, unless you show that your circumstances meet the conditions described in § 404.935(b). The written request must give the names of the witnesses or documents to be produced; describe the address or location of the witnesses or documents with sufficient detail to find them; state the important facts that the witness or document is expected to prove; and indicate why these facts could not be proven without issuing a subpoena.

(3) We will pay the cost of issuing the subpoena.

(4) We will pay subpoenaed witnesses the same fees and mileage they would receive if they had been subpoenaed by a Federal district court.

(e) Witnesses at a hearing. Witnesses may appear at a hearing in person or, when the conditions in § 404.936(c)(2) exist, by video teleconferencing or telephone. They will testify under oath or affirmation unless the administrative law judge finds an important reason to excuse them from taking an oath or affirmation. The administrative law judge may ask the witness any questions material to the issues and will allow the parties or their designated representatives to do so.

(f) Collateral estoppel—issues previously decided. An issue at your hearing may be a fact that has already been decided in one of our previous determinations or decisions in a claim involving the same parties, but arising under a different title of the Act or under the Federal Coal Mine Health and Safety Act. If this happens, the administrative law judge will not consider the issue again, but will accept the factual finding made in the previous determination or decision unless there are reasons to believe that it was wrong.

[51 FR 303, Jan. 3, 1986; 68 FR 5219, Feb. 3, 2003; 68 FR 69009, Dec. 11, 2003; 75 FR 39160, July 8, 2010; 78 FR 29627, May 21, 2013; 81 FR 90993, Dec. 16, 2016]

§ 404.951 Official record.

(a) Hearing recording. All hearings will be recorded. The hearing recording will be prepared as a typed copy of the proceedings if—

(1) The case is sent to the Appeals Council without a decision or with a recommended decision by the administrative law judge;

(2) You seek judicial review of your case by filing an action in a Federal district court within the stated time period, unless we request the court to remand the case; or

(3) An administrative law judge or the Appeals Council asks for a written record of the proceedings.

(b) Contents of the official record. All evidence upon which the administrative law judge relies for the decision must be contained in the record, either directly or by appropriate reference. The official record will include the applications, written statements, certificates, reports, affidavits, medical records, and other documents that were used in making the decision under review and any additional evidence or written statements that the administrative law judge admits into the record under §§ 404.929 and 404.935. All exhibits introduced as evidence must be marked for identification and incorporated into the record. The official record of your claim will contain all of the marked exhibits and a verbatim recording of all testimony offered at the hearing. It also will include any prior initial determinations or decisions on your claim.

[51 FR 303, Jan. 3, 1986; 81 FR 90994, Dec. 16, 2016]

§ 404.952 Consolidated hearing before an administrative law judge.

(a) General.

(1) A consolidated hearing may be held if—

(i) You have requested a hearing to decide your benefit rights under title II of the Act and you have also requested a hearing to decide your rights under another law we administer; and

(ii) One or more of the issues to be considered at the hearing you requested are the same issues that are involved in another claim you have pending before us.

(2) If the administrative law judge decides to hold the hearing on both claims, he or she decides both claims, even if we have not yet made an initial or reconsidered determination on the other claim.

(b) Record, evidence, and decision. There will be a single record at a consolidated hearing. This means that the evidence introduced in one case becomes evidence in the other(s). The administrative law judge may make either a separate or consolidated decision.

[51 FR 303, Jan. 3, 1986]

§ 404.953 The decision of an administrative law judge.

(a) General. The administrative law judge shall issue a written decision that gives the findings of fact and the reasons for the decision. The administrative law judge must base the decision on the preponderance of the evidence offered at the hearing or otherwise included in the record. The administrative law judge shall mail a copy of the decision to all the parties at their last known address. The Appeals Council may also receive a copy of the decision.

(b) Fully favorable oral decision entered into the record at the hearing. The administrative law judge may enter a fully favorable oral decision based on the preponderance of the evidence into the record of the hearing proceedings. If the administrative law judge enters a fully favorable oral decision into the record of the hearing proceedings, the administrative law judge may issue a written decision that incorporates the oral decision by reference. The administrative law judge may use this procedure only in those categories of cases that we identify in advance. The administrative law judge may only use this procedure in those cases where the administrative law judge determines that no changes are required in the findings of fact or the reasons for the decision as stated at the hearing. If a fully favorable decision is entered into the record at the hearing, the administrative law judge will also include in the record, as an exhibit entered into the record at the hearing, a document that sets forth the key data, findings of fact, and narrative rationale for the decision. If the decision incorporates by reference the findings and the reasons stated in an oral decision at the hearing, the parties shall also be provided, upon written request, a record of the oral decision.

(c) Recommended decision. Although an administrative law judge will usually make a decision, the administrative law judge may send the case to the Appeals Council with a recommended decision based on a preponderance of the evidence when appropriate. The administrative law judge will mail a copy of the recommended decision to the parties at their last known addresses and send the recommended decision to the Appeals Council.

[51 FR 303, Jan. 3, 1986; 54 FR 37792, Sept. 13, 1989; 69 FR 61597, Oct. 20, 2004; 73 FR 76944, Dec. 18, 2008; 75 FR 33168, June 11, 2010]

§ 404.955 The effect of an administrative law judge's decision.

The decision of the administrative law judge is binding on all parties to the hearing unless—

(a) You or another party request a review of the decision by the Appeals Council within the stated time period, and the Appeals Council reviews your case;

(b) You or another party requests a review of the decision by the Appeals Council within the stated time period, the Appeals Council denies your request for review, and you seek judicial review of your case by filing an action in a Federal district court;

(c) The decision is revised by an administrative law judge or the Appeals Council under the procedures explained in § 404.987;

(d) The expedited appeals process is used;

(e) The decision is a recommended decision directed to the Appeals Council; or

(f) In a case remanded by a Federal court, the Appeals Council assumes jurisdiction under the procedures in § 404.984.

[51 FR 303, Jan. 3, 1986; 54 FR 37792, Sept. 13, 1989]

§ 404.956 Removal of a hearing request from an administrative law judge to the Appeals Council.

If you have requested a hearing and the request is pending before an administrative law judge, the Appeals Council may assume responsibility for holding a hearing by requesting that the administrative law judge send the hearing request to it. If the Appeals Council holds a hearing, it shall conduct the hearing according to the rules for hearings before an administrative law judge. Notice shall be mailed to all parties at their last known address telling them that the Appeals Council has assumed responsibility for the case.

[51 FR 303, Jan. 3, 1986]

§ 404.957 Dismissal of a request for a hearing before an administrative law judge.

An administrative law judge may dismiss a request for a hearing under any of the following conditions:

(a) At any time before notice of the hearing decision is mailed, you or the party or parties that requested the hearing ask to withdraw the request. This request may be submitted in writing to the administrative law judge or made orally at the hearing.

(b)(1)(i) Neither you nor the person you designate to act as your representative appears at the time and place set for the hearing and you have been notified before the time set for the hearing that your request for hearing may be dismissed without further notice if you did not appear at the time and place of hearing, and good cause has not been found by the administrative law judge for your failure to appear; or

(ii) Neither you nor the person you designate to act as your representative appears at the time and place set for the hearing and within 10 days after the administrative law judge mails you a notice asking why you did not appear, you do not give a good reason for the failure to appear.

(2) In determining good cause or good reason under this paragraph, we will consider any physical, mental, educational, or linguistic limitations (including any lack of facility with the English language) which you may have.

(c) The administrative law judge decides that there is cause to dismiss a hearing request entirely or to refuse to consider any one or more of the issues because—

(1) The doctrine of res judicata applies in that we have made a previous determination or decision under this subpart about your rights on the same facts and on the same issue or issues, and this previous determination or decision has become final by either administrative or judicial action;

(2) The person requesting a hearing has no right to it under § 404.930;

(3) You did not request a hearing within the stated time period and we have not extended the time for requesting a hearing under § 404.933(c); or

(4) You die, there are no other parties, and we have no information to show that another person may be adversely affected by the determination that was to be reviewed at the hearing. However, dismissal of the hearing request will be vacated if, within 60 days after the date of the dismissal, another person submits a written request for a hearing on the claim and shows that he or she may be adversely affected by the determination that was to be reviewed at the hearing.

[50 FR 21438, May 24, 1985; 51 FR 303, Jan. 3, 1986; 59 FR 1634, Jan. 12, 1994]

§ 404.958 Notice of dismissal of a request for a hearing before an administrative law judge.

We shall mail a written notice of the dismissal of the hearing request to all parties at their last known address. The notice will state that there is a right to request that the Appeals Council vacate the dismissal action.

[51 FR 303, Jan. 3, 1986]

§ 404.959 Effect of dismissal of a request for a hearing before an administrative law judge.

The dismissal of a request for a hearing is binding, unless it is vacated by an administrative law judge or the Appeals Council.

[51 FR 303, Jan. 3, 1986]

§ 404.960 Vacating a dismissal of a request for a hearing before an administrative law judge.

(a) Except as provided in paragraph (b) of this section, an administrative law judge or the Appeals Council may vacate a dismissal of a request for a hearing if you request that we vacate the dismissal. If you or another party wish to make this request, you must do so within 60 days of the date you receive notice of the dismissal, and you must state why our dismissal of your request for a hearing was erroneous. The administrative law judge or Appeals Council will inform you in writing of the action taken on your request. The Appeals Council may also vacate a dismissal of a request for a hearing on its own motion. If the Appeals Council decides to vacate a dismissal on its own motion, it will do so within 60 days of the date we mail the notice of dismissal and will inform you in writing that it vacated the dismissal.

(b) If you wish to proceed with a hearing after you received a fully favorable revised determination under the prehearing case review process in § 404.941, you must follow the procedures in § 404.941(d) to request that an administrative law judge vacate his or her order dismissing your request for a hearing.

[51 FR 303, Jan. 3, 1986; 76 FR 65370, Oct. 21, 2011]

§ 404.961 Prehearing and posthearing conferences.

The administrative law judge may decide on his or her own, or at the request of any party to the hearing, to hold a prehearing or posthearing conference to facilitate the hearing or the hearing decision. The administrative law judge shall tell the parties of the time, place and purpose of the conference at least seven days before the conference date, unless the parties have indicated in writing that they do not wish to receive a written notice of the conference. At the conference, the administrative law judge may consider matters in addition to those stated in the notice, if the parties consent in writing. A record of the conference will be made. The administrative law judge shall issue an order stating all agreements and actions resulting from the conference. If the parties do not object, the agreements and actions become part of the hearing record and are binding on all parties.

§ 404.965 [Reserved]

APPEALS COUNCIL REVIEW

§ 404.966 Testing elimination of the request for Appeals Council review.

(a) Applicability and scope. Notwithstanding any other provision in this part or part 422 of this chapter, we are establishing the procedures set out in this section to test elimination of the request for review by the Appeals Council. These procedures will apply in randomly selected cases in which we have tested a combination of model procedures for modifying the disability claim process as authorized under §§ 404.906 and 404.943, and in which an administrative law judge has issued a decision (not including a recommended decision) that is less than fully favorable to you.

(b) Effect of an administrative law judge's decision. In a case to which the procedures of this section apply, the decision of an administrative law judge will be binding on all the parties to the hearing unless—

(1) You or another party file an action concerning the decision in Federal district court;

(2) The Appeals Council decides to review the decision on its own motion under the authority provided in § 404.969, and it issues a notice announcing its decision to review the case on its own motion no later than the day before the filing date of a civil action establishing the jurisdiction of a Federal district court; or

(3) The decision is revised by the administrative law judge or the Appeals Council under the procedures explained in § 404.987.

(c) Notice of the decision of an administrative law judge. The notice of decision the administrative law judge issues in a case processed under this section will advise you and any other parties to the decision that you may file an action in a Federal district court within 60 days after the date you receive notice of the decision.

(d) Extension of time to file action in Federal district court. Any party having a right to file a civil action under this section may request that the time for filing an action in Federal district court be extended. The request must be in writing and it must give the reasons why the action was not filed within the stated time period. The request must be filed with the Appeals Council. If you show that you had good cause for missing the deadline, the time period will be extended. To determine whether good cause exists, we will use the standards in § 404.911.

[62 FR 49602, Sept. 23, 1997; 75 FR 33168, June 11, 2010]

§ 404.967 Appeals Council review—general.

If you or any other party is dissatisfied with the hearing decision or with the dismissal of a hearing request, you may request that the Appeals Council review that action. The Appeals Council may deny or dismiss the request for review, or it may grant the request and either issue a decision or remand the case to an administrative law judge. The Appeals Council shall notify the parties at their last known address of the action it takes.

§ 404.968 How to request Appeals Council review.

(a) Time and place to request Appeals Council review. You may request Appeals Council review by filing a written request. You should submit any evidence you wish to have considered by the Appeals Council with your request for review, and the Appeals Council will consider the evidence in accordance with § 404.970. You may file your request—

(1) Within 60 days after the date you receive notice of the hearing decision or dismissal (or within the extended time period if we extend the time as provided in paragraph (b) of this section);

(2) At one of our offices, the Veterans Administration Regional Office in the Philippines, or an office of the Railroad Retirement Board if you have 10 or more years of service in the railroad industry.

(b) Extension of time to request review. You or any party to a hearing decision may ask that the time for filing a request for the review be extended. The request for an extension of time must be in writing. It must be filed with the Appeals Council, and it must give the reasons why the request for review was not filed within the stated time period. If you show that you had good cause for missing the deadline, the time period will be extended. To determine whether good cause exists, we use the standards explained in § 404.911.

[81 FR 90994, Dec. 16, 2016]

§ 404.969 Appeals Council initiates review.

(a) General. Anytime within 60 days after the date of a decision or dismissal that is subject to review under this section, the Appeals Council may decide on its own motion to review the action that was taken in your case. We may refer your case to the Appeals Council for it to consider reviewing under this authority.

(b) Identification of cases. We will identify a case for referral to the Appeals Council for possible review under its own-motion authority before we effectuate a decision in the case. We will identify cases for referral to the Appeals Council through random and selective sampling techniques, which we may use in association with examination of the cases identified by sampling. We will also identify cases for referral to the Appeals Council through the evaluation of cases we conduct in order to effectuate decisions.

(1) Random and selective sampling and case examinations. We may use random and selective sampling to identify cases involving any type of action (i.e., fully or partially favorable decisions, unfavorable decisions, or dismissals) and any type of benefits (i.e., benefits based on disability and benefits not based on disability). We will use selective sampling to identify cases that exhibit problematic issues or fact patterns that increase the likelihood of error. Neither our random sampling procedures nor our selective sampling procedures will identify cases based on the identity of the decisionmaker or the identity of the office issuing the decision. We may examine cases that have been identified through random or selective sampling to refine the identification of cases that may meet the criteria for review by the Appeals Council.

(2) Identification as a result of the effectuation process. We may refer a case requiring effectuation to the Appeals Council if, in the view of the effectuating component, the decision cannot be effectuated because it contains a clerical error affecting the outcome of the claim; the decision is clearly inconsistent with the Social Security Act, the regulations, or a published ruling; or the decision is unclear regarding a matter that affects the claim's outcome.

(c) Referral of cases. We will make referrals that occur as the result of a case examination or the effectuation process in writing. The written referral based on the results of such a case examination or the effectuation process will state the referring component's reasons for believing that the Appeals Council should review the case on its own motion. Referrals that result from selective sampling without a case examination may be accompanied by a written statement identifying the issue(s) or fact pattern that caused the referral. Referrals that result from random sampling without a case examination will only identify the case as a random sample case.

(d) Appeals Council's action. If the Appeals Council decides to review a decision or dismissal on its own motion, it will mail a notice of review to all the parties as provided in § 404.973. The Appeals Council will include with that notice a copy of any written referral it has received under paragraph (c) of this section. The Appeals Council's decision to review a case is established by its issuance of the notice of review. If it is unable to decide within the applicable 60–day period whether to review a decision or dismissal, the Appeals Council may consider the case to determine if the decision or dismissal should be reopened pursuant to §§ 404.987 and 404.988. If the Appeals Council decides to review a decision on its own motion or to reopen a decision as provided in §§ 404.987 and 404.988, the notice of review or the notice of reopening issued by the Appeals Council will advise, where appropriate, that interim benefits will be payable if a final decision has not been issued within 110 days after the date of the decision that is reviewed or reopened, and that any interim benefits paid will not be considered overpayments unless the benefits are fraudulently obtained.

[63 FR 36570, July 7, 1998; 75 FR 33168, June 11, 2010]

§ 404.970 Cases the Appeals Council will review.

(a) The Appeals Council will review a case if—

(1) There appears to be an abuse of discretion by the administrative law judge;

(2) There is an error of law;

(3) The action, findings or conclusions of the administrative law judge are not supported by substantial evidence;

(4) There is a broad policy or procedural issue that may affect the general public interest; or

(5) Subject to paragraph (b) of this section, the Appeals Council receives additional evidence that is new, material, and relates to the period on or before the date of the hearing decision, and there is a reasonable probability that the additional evidence would change the outcome of the decision.

(b) The Appeals Council will only consider additional evidence under paragraph (a)(5) of this section if you show good cause for not informing us about or submitting the evidence as described in § 404.935 because:

(1) Our action misled you;

(2) You had a physical, mental, educational, or linguistic limitation(s) that prevented you from informing us about or submitting the evidence earlier; or

(3) Some other unusual, unexpected, or unavoidable circumstance beyond your control prevented you from informing us about or submitting the evidence earlier. Examples include, but are not limited to:

(i) You were seriously ill, and your illness prevented you from contacting us in person, in writing, or through a friend, relative, or other person;

(ii) There was a death or serious illness in your immediate family;

(iii) Important records were destroyed or damaged by fire or other accidental cause;

(iv) You actively and diligently sought evidence from a source and the evidence was not received or was received less than 5 business days prior to the hearing; or

(v) You received a hearing level decision on the record and the Appeals Council reviewed your decision.

(c) If you submit additional evidence that does not relate to the period on or before the date of the administrative law judge hearing decision as required in paragraph (a)(5) of this section, or the Appeals Council does not find you had good cause for missing the deadline to submit the evidence in § 404.935, the Appeals Council will send you a notice that explains why it did not accept the additional evidence and advises you of your right to file a new application. The notice will also advise you that if you file a new application within 6 months after the date of the Appeals Council's notice, your request for review will constitute a written statement indicating an intent to claim benefits under § 404.630. If you file a new application within 6 months of the Appeals Council's notice, we will use the date you requested Appeals Council review as the filing date for your new application.

[52 FR 4004, Feb. 9, 1987; 81 FR 90994, Dec. 16, 2016]

§ 404.971 Dismissal by Appeals Council.

The Appeals Council will dismiss your request for review if you did not file your request within the stated period of time and the time for filing has not been extended. The Appeals Council may also dismiss any proceedings before it if—

(a) You and any other party to the proceedings files a written request for dismissal; or

(b) You or any other party to the proceedings dies and the record clearly shows that dismissal will not adversely affect any other person who wishes to continue the action.

§ 404.972 Effect of dismissal of request for Appeals Council review.

The dismissal of a request for Appeals Council review is binding and not subject to further review.

§ 404.973 Notice of Appeals Council review.

When the Appeals Council decides to review a case, it shall mail a notice to all parties at their last known address stating the reasons for the review and the issues to be considered.

§ 404.974 Obtaining evidence from Appeals Council.

You may request and receive copies or a statement of the documents or other written evidence upon which the hearing decision or dismissal was based and a copy or summary of the transcript of oral evidence. However, you will be asked to pay the costs of providing these copies unless there is a good reason why you should not pay.

§ 404.975 Filing briefs with the Appeals Council.

Upon request, the Appeals Council shall give you and all other parties a reasonable opportunity to file briefs or other written statements about the facts and law relevant to the case. A copy of each brief or statement should be filed for each party.

§ 404.976 Procedures before the Appeals Council on review.

(a) Limitation of issues. The Appeals Council may limit the issues it considers if it notifies you and the other parties of the issues it will review.

(b) Oral argument. You may request to appear before the Appeals Council to present oral argument. The Appeals Council will grant your request if it decides that your case raises an important question of law or policy or that oral argument would help to reach a proper decision. If your request to appear is granted, the Appeals Council will tell you the time and place of the oral argument at least 10 business days before the scheduled date. The Appeals Council will determine whether your appearance, or the appearance of any other person relevant to the proceeding, will be in person, by video teleconferencing, or by telephone.

[52 FR 4004, Feb. 9, 1987; 81 FR 6171, Feb. 5, 2016; 81 FR 90994, Dec. 16, 2016]

§ 404.977 Case remanded by Appeals Council.

(a) When the Appeals Council may remand a case. The Appeals Council may remand a case to an administrative law judge so that he or she may hold a hearing and issue a decision or a recommended decision. The Appeals Council may also remand a case in which additional evidence is needed or additional action by the administrative law judge is required.

(b) Action by administrative law judge on remand. The administrative law judge shall take any action that is ordered by the Appeals Council and may take any additional action that is not inconsistent with the Appeals Council's remand order.

(c) Notice when case is returned with a recommended decision. When the administrative law judge sends a case to the Appeals Council with a recommended decision, a notice is mailed to the parties at their last known address. The notice tells them that the case has been sent to the Appeals Council, explains the rules for filing briefs or other written statements with the Appeals Council, and includes a copy of the recommended decision.

(d) Filing briefs with and obtaining evidence from the Appeals Council.

(1) You may file briefs or other written statements about the facts and law relevant to your case with the Appeals Council within 20 days of the date that the recommended decision is mailed to you. Any party may ask the Appeals Council for additional time to file briefs or statements. The Appeals Council will extend this period, as appropriate, if you show that you had good cause for missing the deadline.

(2) All other rules for filing briefs with and obtaining evidence from the Appeals Council follow the procedures explained in this subpart.

(e) Procedures before the Appeals Council.

(1) The Appeals Council, after receiving a recommended decision, will conduct its proceedings and issue its decision according to the procedures explain in this subpart.

(2) If the Appeals Council believes that more evidence is required, it may again remand the case to an administrative law judge for further inquiry into the issues, rehearing, receipt of evidence, and another decision or recommended decision. However, if the Appeals Council decides that it can get the additional evidence more quickly, it will take appropriate action.

§ 404.979 Decision of Appeals Council.

After it has reviewed all the evidence in the administrative law judge hearing record and any additional evidence received, subject to the limitations on Appeals Council consideration of additional evidence in § 404.970, the Appeals Council will make a decision or remand the case to an administrative law judge. The Appeals Council may affirm, modify or reverse the administrative law judge hearing decision or it may adopt, modify or reject a recommended decision. If the Appeals Council issues its own decision, it will base its decision on the preponderance of the evidence. A copy of the Appeals Council's decision will be mailed to the parties at their last known address.

[52 FR 4004, Feb. 9, 1987; 73 FR 76944, Dec. 18, 2008; 81 FR 90994, Dec. 16, 2016]

§ 404.981 Effect of Appeals Council's decision or denial of review.

The Appeals Council may deny a party's request for review or it may decide to review a case and make a decision. The Appeals Council's decision, or the decision of the administrative law judge if the request for review is denied, is binding unless you or another party file an action in Federal district court, or the decision is revised. You may file an action in a Federal district court within 60 days after the date you receive notice of the Appeals Council's action.

§ 404.982 Extension of time to file action in Federal district court.

Any party to the Appeals Council's decision or denial of review, or to an expedited appeals process agreement, may request that the time for filing an action in a Federal district court be extended. The request must be in writing and it must give the reasons why the action was not filed within the stated time period. The request must be filed with the Appeals Council, or if it concerns an expedited appeals process agreement, with one of our offices. If you show that you had good cause for missing the deadline, the time period will be extended. To determine whether good cause exists, we use the standards explained in § 404.911.

COURT REMAND CASES

§ 404.983 Case remanded by a Federal court.

When a Federal court remands a case to the Commissioner for further consideration, the Appeals Council, acting on behalf of the Commissioner, may make a decision, or it may remand the case to an administrative law judge with instructions to take action and issue a decision or return the case to the Appeals Council with a recommended decision. If the case is remanded by the Appeals Council, the procedures explained in § 404.977 will be followed. Any issues relating to your claim may be considered by the administrative law judge whether or not they were raised in the administrative proceedings leading to the final decision in your case.

[54 FR 37792, Sept. 13, 1989; 62 FR 38450, July 18, 1997]

§ 404.984 Appeals Council review of administrative law judge decision in a case remanded by a Federal court.

(a) General. In accordance with § 404.983, when a case is remanded by a Federal court for further consideration, the decision of the administrative law judge will become the final decision of the Commissioner after remand on your case unless the Appeals Council assumes jurisdiction of the case. The Appeals Council may assume jurisdiction based on written exceptions to the decision of the administrative law judge which you file with the Appeals Council or based on its authority pursuant to paragraph (c) of this section. If the Appeals Council assumes jurisdiction of your case, any issues relating to your claim may be considered by the Appeals Council whether or not they were raised in the administrative proceedings leading to the final decision in your case or subsequently considered by the administrative law judge in the administrative proceedings following the court's remand order. The Appeals Council will either make a new, independent decision based on the preponderance of the evidence in the record that will be the final decision of the Commissioner after remand, or it will remand the case to an administrative law judge for further proceedings.

(b) You file exceptions disagreeing with the decision of the administrative law judge.

(1) If you disagree with the decision of the administrative law judge, in whole or in part, you may file exceptions to the decision with the Appeals Council. Exceptions may be filed by submitting a written statement to the Appeals Council setting forth your reasons for disagreeing with the decision of the administrative law judge. The exceptions must be filed within 30 days of the date you receive the decision of the administrative law judge or an extension of time in which to submit exceptions must be requested in writing within the 30–day period. A timely request for a 30–day extension will be granted by the Appeals Council. A request for an extension of more than 30 days should include a statement of reasons as to why you need the additional time.

(2) If written exceptions are timely filed, the Appeals Council will consider your reasons for disagreeing with the decision of the administrative law judge and all the issues presented by your case. If the Appeals Council concludes that there is no reason to change the decision of the administrative law judge, it will issue a notice to you addressing your exceptions and explaining why no change in the decision of the administrative law judge is warranted. In this instance, the decision of the administrative law judge is the final decision of the Commissioner after remand.

(3) When you file written exceptions to the decision of the administrative law judge, the Appeals Council may assume jurisdiction at any time, even after the 60–day time period which applies when you do not file exceptions. If the Appeals Council assumes jurisdiction, it will make a new, independent decision based on the preponderance of the evidence in the entire record affirming, modifying, or reversing the decision of the administrative law judge, or it will remand the case to an administrative law judge for further proceedings, including a new decision. The new decision of the Appeals Council is the final decision of the Commissioner after remand.

(c) Appeals Council assumes jurisdiction without exceptions being filed. Any time within 60 days after the date of the decision of the administrative law judge, the Appeals Council may decide to assume jurisdiction of your case even though no written exceptions have been filed. Notice of this action will be mailed to all parties at their last known address. You will be provided with the opportunity to file briefs or other written statements with the Appeals Council about the facts and law relevant to your case. After the Appeals Council receives the briefs or other written statements, or the time allowed (usually 30 days) for submitting them has expired, the Appeals Council will either issue a final decision of the Commissioner based on the preponderance of the evidence affirming, modifying, or reversing the decision of the administrative law judge, or remand the case to an administrative law judge for further proceedings, including a new decision.

(d) Exceptions are not filed and the Appeals Council does not otherwise assume jurisdiction. If no exceptions are filed and the Appeals Council does not assume jurisdiction of your case, the decision of the administrative law judge becomes the final decision of the Commissioner after remand.

[54 FR 37792, Sept. 13, 1989; 54 FR 40779, Oct. 3, 1989; 62 FR 38450, July 18, 1997; 73 FR 76944, Dec. 18, 2008]

§ 404.985 Application of circuit court law.

The procedures which follow apply to administrative determinations or decisions on claims involving the application of circuit court law.

(a) General. We will apply a holding in a United States Court of Appeals decision that we determine conflicts with our interpretation of a provision of the Social Security Act or regulations unless the Government seeks further judicial review of that decision or we relitigate the issue presented in the decision in accordance with paragraphs (c) and (d) of this section. We will apply the holding to claims at all levels of the administrative review process within the applicable circuit unless the holding, by its nature, applies only at certain levels of adjudication.

(b) Issuance of an Acquiescence Ruling. When we determine that a United States Court of Appeals holding conflicts with our interpretation of a provision of the Social Security Act or regulations and the Government does not seek further judicial review or is unsuccessful on further review, we will issue a Social Security Acquiescence Ruling. The Acquiescence Ruling will describe the administrative case and the court decision, identify the issue(s) involved, and explain how we will apply the holding, including, as necessary, how the holding relates to other decisions within the applicable circuit. These Acquiescence Rulings will generally be effective on the date of their publication in the Federal Register and will apply to all determinations and decisions made on or after that date unless an Acquiescence Ruling is rescinded as stated in paragraph (e) of this section. The process we will use when issuing an Acquiescence Ruling follows:

(1) We will release an Acquiescence Ruling for publication in the Federal Register for any precedential circuit court decision that we determine contains a holding that conflicts with our interpretation of a provision of the Social Security Act or regulations no later than 120 days from the receipt of the court's decision. This timeframe will not apply when we decide to seek

further judicial review of the circuit court decision or when coordination with the Department of Justice and/or other Federal agencies makes this timeframe no longer feasible.

(2) If we make a determination or decision on your claim between the date of a circuit court decision and the date we publish an Acquiescence Ruling, you may request application of the published Acquiescence Ruling to the prior determination or decision. You must demonstrate that application of the Acquiescence Ruling could change the prior determination or decision in your case. You may demonstrate this by submitting a statement that cites the Acquiescence Ruling or the holding or portion of a circuit court decision which could change the prior determination or decision in your case. If you can so demonstrate, we will readjudicate the claim in accordance with the Acquiescence Ruling at the level at which it was last adjudicated. Any readjudication will be limited to consideration of the issue(s) covered by the Acquiescence Ruling and any new determination or decision on readjudication will be subject to administrative and judicial review in accordance with this subpart. Our denial of a request for readjudication will not be subject to further administrative or judicial review. If you file a request for readjudication within the 60–day appeal period and we deny that request, we shall extend the time to file an appeal on the merits of the claim to 60 days after the date that we deny the request for readjudication.

(3) After we receive a precedential circuit court decision and determine that an Acquiescence Ruling may be required, we will begin to identify those claims that are pending before us within the circuit and that might be subject to readjudication if an Acquiescence Ruling is subsequently issued. When an Acquiescence Ruling is published, we will send a notice to those individuals whose cases we have identified which may be affected by the Acquiescence Ruling. The notice will provide information about the Acquiescence Ruling and the right to request readjudication under that Acquiescence Ruling, as described in paragraph (b)(2) of this section. It is not necessary for an individual to receive a notice in order to request application of an Acquiescence Ruling to his or her claim, as described in paragraph (b)(2) of this section.

(c) Relitigation of court's holding after publication of an Acquiescence Ruling. After we have published an Acquiescence Ruling to reflect a holding of a United States Court of Appeals on an issue, we may decide under certain conditions to relitigate that issue within the same circuit. We may relitigate only when the conditions specified in paragraphs (c)(2) and (3) of this section are met, and, in general, one of the events specified in paragraph (c)(1) of this section occurs.

(1) Activating events:

(i) An action by both Houses of Congress indicates that a circuit court decision on which an Acquiescence Ruling was based was decided inconsistently with congressional intent, such as may be expressed in a joint resolution, an appropriations restriction, or enactment of legislation which affects a closely analogous body of law;

(ii) A statement in a majority opinion of the same circuit indicates that the court might no longer follow its previous decision if a particular issue were presented again;

(iii) Subsequent circuit court precedent in other circuits supports our interpretation of the Social Security Act or regulations on the issue(s) in question; or

(iv) A subsequent Supreme Court decision presents a reasonable legal basis for questioning a circuit court holding upon which we base an Acquiescence Ruling.

(2) The General Counsel of the Social Security Administration, after consulting with the Department of Justice, concurs that relitigation of an issue and application of our interpretation of the Social Security Act or regulations to selected claims in the administrative review process within the circuit would be appropriate.

(3) We publish a notice in the Federal Register that we intend to relitigate an Acquiescence Ruling issue and that we will apply our interpretation of the Social Security Act or regulations within the circuit to claims in the administrative review process selected for relitigation. The notice will explain why we made this decision.

(d) Notice of relitigation. When we decide to relitigate an issue, we will provide a notice explaining our action to all affected claimants. In adjudicating claims subject to relitigation, decisionmakers throughout the SSA administrative review process will apply our interpretation of the Social Security Act and regulations, but will also state in written determinations or decisions how the claims would have been decided under the circuit standard. Claims not subject to relitigation will continue to be decided under the Acquiescence Ruling in accordance with the circuit standard. So that affected claimants can be readily identified and any subsequent decision of the circuit court or the Supreme Court can be implemented quickly and efficiently, we will maintain a listing of all claimants who receive this notice and will provide them with the relief ordered by the court.

(e) Rescission of an Acquiescence Ruling. We will rescind as obsolete an Acquiescence Ruling and apply our interpretation of the Social Security Act or regulations by publishing a notice in the Federal Register when any of the following events occurs:

(1) The Supreme Court overrules or limits a circuit court holding that was the basis of an Acquiescence Ruling;

(2) A circuit court overrules or limits itself on an issue that was the basis of an Acquiescence Ruling;

(3) A Federal law is enacted that removes the basis for the holding in a decision of a circuit court that was the subject of an Acquiescence Ruling; or

(4) We subsequently clarify, modify or revoke the regulation or ruling that was the subject of a circuit court holding that we determined conflicts with our interpretation of the Social Security Act or regulations, or we subsequently publish a new regulation(s) addressing an issue(s) not previously included in our regulations when that issue(s) was the subject of a circuit court holding that conflicted with our interpretation of the Social Security Act or regulations and that holding was not compelled by the statute or Constitution.

[55 FR 1018, Jan. 11, 1990; 62 FR 38450, July 18, 1997; 63 FR 24932, May 6, 1998]

REOPENING AND REVISING DETERMINATIONS AND DECISIONS

§ 404.987 Reopening and revising determinations and decisions.

(a) General. Generally, if you are dissatisfied with a determination or decision made in the administrative review process, but do not request further review within the stated time period, you lose your right to further review and that determination or decision becomes final. However, a determination or a decision made in your case which is otherwise final and binding may be reopened and revised by us.

(b) Procedure for reopening and revision. We may reopen a final determination or decision on our own initiative, or you may ask that a final determination or a decision to which you were a party be reopened. In either instance, if we reopen the determination or decision, we may revise that determination or decision. The conditions under which we may reopen a previous determination or decision, either on our own initiative or at your request, are explained in § 404.988.

[59 FR 8535, Feb. 23, 1994]

§ 404.988 Conditions for reopening.

A determination, revised determination, decision, or revised decision may be reopened—

(a) Within 12 months of the date of the notice of the initial determination, for any reason;

(b) Within four years of the date of the notice of the initial determination if we find good cause, as defined in § 404.989, to reopen the case; or

(c) At any time if—

(1) It was obtained by fraud or similar fault (see § 416.1488(c) of this chapter for factors which we take into account in determining fraud or similar fault);

(2) Another person files a claim on the same earnings record and allowance of the claim adversely affects your claim;

(3) A person previously determined to be dead, and on whose earnings record your entitlement is based, is later found to be alive;

(4) Your claim was denied because you did not prove that a person died, and the death is later established—

(i) By a presumption of death under § 404.721(b); or

(ii) By location or identification of his or her body;

(5) The Railroad Retirement Board has awarded duplicate benefits on the same earnings record;

(6) It either—

(i) Denies the person on whose earnings record your claim is based gratuitous wage credits for military or naval service because another Federal agency (other than the Veterans Administration) has erroneously certified that it has awarded benefits based on the service; or

(ii) Credits the earnings record of the person on which your claim is based with gratuitous wage credits and another Federal agency (other than the Veterans Administration) certifies that it has awarded a benefit based on the period of service for which the wage credits were granted;

(7) It finds that the claimant did not have insured status, but earnings were later credited to his or her earnings record to correct errors apparent on the face of the earnings record (section 205(c)(5)(C) of the Act), to enter items transferred by the Railroad Retirement Board, which were credited under the Railroad Retirement Act when they should have been credited to the claimant's Social Security earnings record (section 205(c)(5)(D) of the Act), or to correct errors made in the allocation of wages or self-employment income to individuals or periods (section 205(c)(5)(G) of the Act), which would have given him or her insured status at the time of the determination or decision if the earnings had been credited to his or her earnings record at that time, and the evidence of these earnings was in our possession or the possession of the Railroad Retirement Board at the time of the determination or decision;

(8) It is fully or partially unfavorable to a party, but only to correct clerical error or an error that appears on the face of the evidence that was considered when the determination or decision was made;

(9) It finds that you are entitled to monthly benefits or to a lump sum death payment based on the earnings of a deceased person, and it is later established that:

(i) You were convicted of a felony or an act in the nature of a felony for intentionally causing that person's death; or

(ii) If you were subject to the juvenile justice system, you were found by a court of competent jurisdiction to have intentionally caused that person's death by committing an act which, if committed by an adult, would have been considered a felony or an act in the nature of a felony;

(10) It either—

(i) Denies the person on whose earnings record your claim is based deemed wages for internment during World War II because of an erroneous finding that a benefit based upon the internment has been determined by an agency of the United States to be payable under another Federal law or under a system established by that agency; or

(ii) Awards the person on whose earnings record your claim is based deemed wages for internment during World War II and a benefit based upon the internment is determined by an agency of the United States to be payable under another Federal law or under a system established by that agency; or

(11) It is incorrect because—

(i) You were convicted of a crime that affected your right to receive benefits or your entitlement to a period of disability; or

(ii) Your conviction of a crime that affected your right to receive benefits or your entitlement to a period of disability is overturned.

[45 FR 52081, Aug. 5, 1980, as amended at 47 FR 13325, March 30, 1982; 47 FR 42098, Sept. 24, 1982; 49 FR 46369, Dec. 10, 1984; 51 FR 18313, May 19, 1986; 59 FR 1634, Jan. 12, 1994; 60 FR 19165, April 17, 1995; 75 FR 33168, June 11, 2010]

§ 404.989 Good cause for reopening.

(a) We will find that there is good cause to reopen a determination or decision if—

(1) New and material evidence is furnished;

(2) A clerical error in the computation or recomputation of benefits was made; or

(3) The evidence that was considered in making the determination or decision clearly shows on its face that an error was made.

(b) We will not find good cause to reopen your case if the only reason for reopening is a change of legal interpretation or administrative ruling upon which the determination or decision was made.

§ 404.990 Finality of determinations and decisions on revision of an earnings record.

A determination or a decision on a revision of an earnings record may be reopened only within the time period and under the conditions provided in section 205(c)(4) or (5) of the Act, or within 60 days after the date you receive notice of the determination or decision, whichever is later.

§ 404.991 Finality of determinations and decisions to suspend benefit payments for entire taxable year because of earnings.

A determination or decision to suspend benefit payments for an entire taxable year because of earnings may be reopened only within the time period and under the conditions provided in section 203(h)(1)(B) of the Act.

§ 404.991a Late completion of timely investigation.

We may revise a determination or decision after the applicable time period in § 404.988(a) or § 404.988(b) expires if we begin an investigation into whether to revise the determination or decision before the applicable time period expires. We may begin the investigation either based on a request by you or by an action on our part. The investigation is a process of gathering facts after a determination or decision has been reopened to determine if a revision of the determination or decision is applicable.

(a) If we have diligently pursued the investigation to its conclusion, we may revise the determination or decision. The revision may be favorable or unfavorable to you. "Diligently pursued" means that in light of the facts and circumstances of a particular case, the necessary action was undertaken and carried out as promptly as the circumstances permitted. Diligent pursuit will be presumed to have been met if we conclude the investigation and if necessary, revise the determination or decision within 6 months from the date we began the investigation.

(b) If we have not diligently pursued the investigation to its conclusion, we will revise the determination or decision if a revision is applicable and if it will be favorable to you. We will not revise the determination or decision if it will be unfavorable to you.

[49 FR 46369, Nov. 26, 1984; 49 FR 48036, Dec. 10, 1984]

§ 404.992 Notice of revised determination or decision.

(a) When a determination or decision is revised, notice of the revision will be mailed to the parties at their last known address. The notice will state the basis for the revised determination or decision and the effect of the revision. The notice will also inform the parties of the right to further review.

(b) If a reconsidered determination that you are disabled, based on medical factors, is reopened for the purpose of being revised, you will be notified, in writing, of the proposed revision and of your right to request that a disability hearing be held before a revised reconsidered determination is issued. If a revised reconsidered determination is issued, you may request a hearing before an administrative law judge.

(c) If an administrative law judge or the Appeals Council proposes to revise a decision, and the revision would be based on evidence not included in the record on which the prior decision was based, you and any other parties to the decision will be notified, in writing, of the proposed action and of your right to request that a hearing be held before any further action is taken. If a revised decision is issued by an administrative law judge, you and any other party may request that it be reviewed by the Appeals Council, or the Appeals Council may review the decision on its own initiative.

(d) If an administrative law judge or the Appeals Council proposes to revise a decision, and the revision would be based only on evidence included in the record on which the prior decision was based, you and any other parties to the decision will be notified, in writing, of the proposed action. If a revised decision is issued by an administrative law judge, you and any other party may request that it be reviewed by the Appeals Council, or the Appeals Council may review the decision on its own initiative.

[51 FR 303, Jan. 3, 1986]

§ 404.993 Effect of revised determination or decision.

A revised determination or decision is binding unless—

(a) You or another party to the revised determination file a written request for reconsideration or a hearing before an administrative law judge, as appropriate;

(b) You or another party to the revised decision file, as appropriate, a request for review by the Appeals Council or a hearing before an administrative law judge;

(c) The Appeals Council reviews the revised decision; or

(d) The revised determination or decision is further revised.

[51 FR 303, Jan. 3, 1986]

§ 404.994 Time and place to request a hearing on revised determination or decision.

You or another party to a revised determination or decision may request, as appropriate, further review or a hearing on the revision by filing a request in writing at one of our offices within 60 days after the date you receive notice of the revision. Further review or a hearing will be held on the revision according to the rules of this subpart.

§ 404.995 Finality of findings when later claim is filed on same earnings record.

If two claims for benefits are filed on the same earnings records, findings of fact made in a determination on the first claim may be revised in determining or deciding the second claim, even though the time limit for revising the findings made in the first claim has passed. However, a finding in connection with a claim that a person was fully or currently insured at the time of filing an application, at the time of death, or any other pertinent time, may be revised only under the conditions stated in § 404.988.

§ 404.996 Increase in future benefits where time period for reopening expires.

If, after the time period for reopening under § 404.988(b) has ended, new evidence is furnished showing a different date of birth or additional earnings for you (or for the person on whose earnings record your claim was based) which would otherwise increase the amount of your benefits, we will make the increase (subject to the limitations provided in section 205(c)(4) and (5) of the Act) but only for benefits payable after the time we received the new evidence. (If the new evidence we receive would lead to a decrease in your benefits, we will take no action if we cannot reopen under § 404.988.)

[49 FR 46369, Nov. 26, 1984]

PAYMENT OF CERTAIN TRAVEL EXPENSES

§ 404.999a Payment of certain travel expenses—general.

When you file a claim for Social Security benefits, you may incur certain travel expenses in pursuing your claim. Sections 404.999b–404.999d explain who may be reimbursed for travel expenses, the types of travel expenses that are reimbursable, and when and how to claim reimbursement. Generally, the agency that requests you to travel will be the agency that reimburses you. No later than when it notifies you of the examination or hearing described in § 404.999b(a), that agency will give you information about the right to travel reimbursement, the right to advance payment and how to request it, the rules on means of travel and unusual travel costs, and the need to submit receipts.

[51 FR 8808, March 14, 1986]

§ 404.999b Who may be reimbursed.

(a) The following individuals may be reimbursed for certain travel expenses—

(1) You, when you attend medical examinations upon request in connection with disability determinations; these are medical examinations requested by the State agency or by us when additional medical evidence is necessary to make a disability determination (also referred to as consultative examinations, see § 404.1517);

(2) You, your representative (see § 404.1705 (a) and (b)), and all unsubpoenaed witnesses we or the State agency determines to be reasonably necessary who attend disability hearings; and

(3) You, your representative, and all unsubpoenaed witnesses we determine to be reasonably necessary

who attend hearings on any claim for benefits before an administrative law judge.

(b) Sections 404.999a through 404.999d do not apply to subpoenaed witnesses. They are reimbursed under §§ 404.950(d) and 404.916(b)(1).

[51 FR 8808, March 14, 1986]

§ 404.999c What travel expenses are reimbursable.

Reimbursable travel expenses include the ordinary expenses of public or private transportation as well as unusual costs due to special circumstances.

(a) Reimbursement for ordinary travel expenses is limited—

(1) To the cost of travel by the most economical and expeditious means of transportation available and appropriate to the individual's condition of health as determined by the State agency or by us, considering the available means in the following order—

(i) Common carrier (air, rail, or bus);

(ii) Privately owned vehicles;

(iii) Commercially rented vehicles and other special conveyances;

(2) If air travel is necessary, to the coach fare for air travel between the specified travel points involved unless first-class air travel is authorized in advance by the State agency or by the Secretary in instances when—

(i) Space is not available in less-than-first-class accommodations on any scheduled flights in time to accomplish the purpose of the travel;

(ii) First-class accommodations are necessary because you, your representative, or reasonably necessary witness is so handicapped or otherwise impaired that other accommodations are not practical and the impairment is substantiated by competent medical authority;

(iii) Less-than-first-class accommodations on foreign carriers do not provide adequate sanitation or health standards; or

(iv) The use of first-class accommodations would result in an overall savings to the government based on economic considerations, such as the avoidance of additional subsistence costs that would be incurred while awaiting availability of less-than-first-class accommodations.

(b) Unusual travel costs may be reimbursed but must be authorized in advance and in writing by us or the appropriate State official, as applicable, unless they are unexpected or unavoidable; we or the State agency must determine their reasonableness and necessity and must approve them before payment can be made. Unusual expenses that may be covered in connection with travel include, but are not limited to—

(1) Ambulance services;

(2) Attendant services;

(3) Meals;

(4) Lodging; and

(5) Taxicabs.

(c) If we reimburse you for travel, we apply the rules in §§ 404.999b through 404.999d and the same rates and conditions of payment that govern travel expenses for Federal employees as authorized under 41 CFR chapter 301. If a State agency reimburses you, the reimbursement rates shall be determined by the rules in §§ 404.999b through 404.999d and that agency's rules and regulations and may differ from one agency to another and also may differ from the Federal reimbursement rates.

(1) When public transportation is used, reimbursement will be made for the actual costs incurred, subject to the restrictions in paragraph (a)(2) of this section on reimbursement for first-class air travel.

(2) When travel is by a privately owned vehicle, reimbursement will be made at the current Federal or State mileage rate specified for that geographic location plus the actual costs of tolls and parking, if travel by a privately owned vehicle is determined appropriate under paragraph (a)(1) of this section. Otherwise, the amount of reimbursement for travel by privately owned vehicle cannot exceed the total cost of the most economical public transportation available for travel between the same two points. Total cost includes the cost for all the authorized travelers who travel in the same privately owned vehicle. Advance approval of travel by privately owned vehicle is not required (but could give you assurance of its approval).

(3) Sometimes your health condition dictates a mode of transportation different from the most economical and expeditious. In order for your health to require a mode of transportation other than common carrier or passenger car, you must be so handicapped or otherwise impaired as to require special transportation arrangements and the conditions must be substantiated by competent medical authority.

(d) For travel to a hearing—

(1) Reimbursement is limited to travel within the U.S. For this purpose, the U.S. includes the U.S. as defined in § 404.2(c)(6) and the Northern Mariana Islands.

(2) We or the State agency will reimburse you, your representative, or an unsubpoenaed witness only if the distance from the person's residence or office (whichever he or she travels from) to the hearing site exceeds 75 miles.

(3) For travel expenses incurred on or after April 1, 1991, the amount of reimbursement under this section for travel by your representative to attend a disability hearing or a hearing before an administrative law judge shall not exceed the maximum amount allowable

under this section for travel to the hearing site from any point within the geographic area of the office having jurisdiction over the hearing.

(i) The geographic area of the office having jurisdiction over the hearing means, as appropriate—

(A) The designated geographic service area of the State agency adjudicatory unit having responsibility for providing the disability hearing;

(B) If a Federal disability hearing officer holds the disability hearing, the geographic area of the State (which includes a State as defined in § 404.2(c)(5) and also includes the Northern Mariana Islands) in which the claimant resides or, if the claimant is not a resident of a State, in which the hearing officer holds the disability hearing; or

(C) The designated geographic service area of the Office of Hearings and Appeals hearing office having responsibility for providing the hearing before an administrative law judge.

(ii) We or the State agency determine the maximum amount allowable for travel by a representative based on the distance to the hearing site from the farthest point within the appropriate geographic area. In determining the maximum amount allowable for travel between these two points, we or the State agency apply the rules in paragraphs (a) through (c) of this section and the limitations in paragraph (d)(1) and (4) of this section. If the distance between these two points does not exceed 75 miles, we or the State agency will not reimburse any of your representative's travel expenses.

(4) If a change in the location of the hearing is made at your request from the location we or the State agency selected to one farther from your residence or office, neither your additional travel expenses nor the additional travel expenses of your representative and witnesses will be reimbursed.

[51 FR 8808, March 14, 1986; 59 FR 8532, Feb. 23, 1994]

§ 404.999d When and how to claim reimbursement.

(a)(1) Generally, you will be reimbursed for your expenses after your trip. However, travel advances may be authorized if you request prepayment and show that the requested advance is reasonable and necessary.

(2) You must submit to us or the State agency, as appropriate, an itemized list of what you spent and supporting receipts to be reimbursed.

(3) Arrangements for special means of transportation and related unusual costs may be made only if we or the State agency authorizes the costs in writing in advance of travel, unless the costs are unexpected or unavoidable. If they are unexpected or unavoidable we or the State agency must determine their reasonableness and necessity and must approve them before payment may be made.

(4) If you receive prepayment, you must, within 20 days after your trip, provide to us or the State agency, as appropriate, an itemized list of your actual travel costs and submit supporting receipts. We or the State agency will require you to pay back any balance of the advanced amount that exceeds any approved travel expenses within 20 days after you are notified of the amount of that balance. (State agencies may have their own time limits in place of the 20–day periods in the preceding two sentences.)

(b) You may claim reimbursable travel expenses incurred by your representative for which you have been billed by your representative, except that if your representative makes a claim for them to us or the State, he or she will be reimbursed directly.

(Approved by the Office of Management and Budget under control number 0960–0434)

[51 FR 8809, March 14, 1986; 51 FR 28545, Aug. 8, 1986; 51 FR 44983, Dec. 16, 1986]

SUBPART K—EMPLOYMENT, WAGES, SELF–EMPLOYMENT, AND SELF–EMPLOYMENT INCOME

Authority: Secs. 202(v), 205(a), 209, 210, 211, 229(a), 230, 231, and 702(a)(5) of the Social Security Act (42 U.S.C. 402(v), 405(a), 409, 410, 411, 429(a), 430, 431, and 902(a)(5)) and 48 U.S.C.1801.

Source: 45 FR 20075, Mar. 27, 1980; 52 FR 8249, March 17, 1987; 52 FR 27541, July 22, 1987; 52 FR 29662, Aug. 11, 1987; 52 FR 39635, Oct. 23, 1987; 53 FR 38944, Oct. 4, 1988; 55 FR 7309, March 1, 1990; 57 FR 44098, Sept. 24, 1992; 57 FR 59910, Dec. 17, 1992; 58 FR 64889, Dec. 10, 1993; 61 FR 5941, Feb. 15, 1996; 69 FR 51555, Aug. 20, 2004; 70 FR 41955, July 21, 2005, unless otherwise noted.

§ 404.1001 Introduction.

(a)(1) In general, your social security benefits are based on your earnings that are on our records. (Subpart I of this part explains how we keep earnings records.) Basically, you receive credit only for earnings that are covered for social security purposes. The earnings are covered only if your work is covered. If you are an employee, your employer files a report of your covered earnings. If you are self-employed, you file a report of your covered earnings. Some work is covered by social security and some work is not. Also, some earnings are covered by social security and some are not. It is important that you are aware of what kinds of work and earnings are covered so that you will know whether your earnings should be on our records.

(2) If you are an employee, your covered work is called employment. This subpart explains our rules on the kinds of work that are covered as employment and the kinds that are not. We also explain who is an employee.

(3) If your work is employment, your covered earnings are called wages. This subpart explains our rules on the kinds of earnings that are covered as wages and the kinds that are not.

(4) If you work for yourself, you are self-employed. The subpart explains our rules on the kinds of self-employment that are covered and the kinds that are not.

(5) If you are self-employed, your covered earnings are called self-employment income which is based on your net earnings from self-employment during a taxable year. This subpart explains our rules on the kinds of earnings that are covered as net earnings from self-employment and the kinds that are not. We also explain how to figure your net earnings from self-employment and determine your self-employment income which is the amount that goes on our records.

(b) We include basically only the rules that apply to current work or that the law requires us to publish as regulations. We generally do not include rules that are seldom used or do not apply to current work because of changes in the law.

(c) The Social Security Act and the Internal Revenue Code (Code) have similar provisions on coverage of your earnings because the one law specifies the earnings for which you will receive credit for benefit purposes and the other the earnings on which you must pay social security taxes. Because the Code (title 26 U.S.C.) has some provisions that are not in the Act but which may affect you, you may need to refer to the Code or the Internal Revenue Service regulations (title 26 of the Code of Federal Regulations) to get complete information about your social security coverage.

(d) The rules are organized in the following manner:

(1) Sections 404.1003 through 404.1010 include the rules on employment. We discuss what we mean by employment, what work is covered as employment for social security purposes, and describe the kinds of workers who are considered employees.

(2) In §§ 404.1012 through 404.1038 we discuss various types of work that are not covered as employment for social security purposes.

(3) The rules on wages are found in §§ 404.1041 through 404.1059. We describe what is meant by the term wages, discuss the various types of pay that count as wages, and state when the pay counts for Social Security purposes. We include explanations of agriculture labor, domestic services, service not in the course of the employer's business, and home worker services under wages because special standards apply to these services.

(4) Our rules on self-employment and self-employment income are found in §§ 404.1065 through 404.1096. We discuss what we mean by self-employment, what we mean by a trade or business, what types of activities are considered self-employment, how to determine self-employment income, and how net earnings from self-employment are figured.

[55 FR 7309, March 1, 1990; 61 FR 38365, July 24, 1996]

§ 404.1002 Definitions.

(a) General definitions. As used in this subpart—

The Act means the Social Security Act, as amended.

The Code means the Internal Revenue Code of 1954, as amended.

We, our, or us means the Social Security Administration.

You or your means any person whose earnings from employment or self-employment are included or excluded under social security.

(b) Other definitions. For ease of reference, we have placed other definitions in the sections of this subpart in which they are used.

EMPLOYMENT

§ 404.1003 Employment.

Employment means, generally, any service covered by social security performed by an employee for his or her employer. The rules on who is an employee and who is an employer are contained in §§ 404.1005 through 404.1010. Section 404.1004 states the general rule on the kinds of work covered as employment. Exceptions to the general rule are contained in §§ 404.1012 through 404.1038 which explain the kinds of work excluded from employment. All of these rules apply to current work unless otherwise indicated.

[61 FR 38365, July 24, 1996]

§ 404.1004 What work is covered as employment?

(a) General requirements of employment. Unless otherwise excluded from coverage under §§ 404.1012 through 404.1038, the work you perform as an employee for your employer is covered as employment under social security if one of the following situations applies:

(1) You perform the work within the United States (whether or not you or your employer are a citizen or resident of the United States).

(2) You perform the work outside the United States and you are a citizen or resident of the United States working for—

(i) An American employer; or

(ii) A foreign affiliate of an American employer that has in effect an agreement covering your work under section 3121(*l*) of the Code.

(3) You perform the work on or in connection with an American vessel or American aircraft and the conditions in paragraphs (a)(3)(i) and (ii) are met. Your citizenship or residence does not matter. The citizen-

ship or residence of your employer matters only if it affects whether the vessel is an American vessel.

(i) You enter into the contract of employment within the United States or the vessel or aircraft touches at a port or airport within the United States during the performance of your contract of employment on the vessel or aircraft.

(ii) You are employed on and in connection with the vessel or aircraft when outside the United States.

(4) Your work is designated as employment or recognized as equivalent to employment under a totalization agreement. (See § 404.1913. An agreement may exempt work from coverage as well as extend coverage to work.)

(5) Your work performed after December 31, 1994, is in the employ of an international organization pursuant to a transfer from a Federal agency under section 3582 of title 5 of the United States Code and both the following are met:

(i) Immediately before the transfer, your work for the Federal agency was covered employment; and

(ii) You would be entitled, upon separation from the international organization and proper application, to reemployment with the Federal agency under section 3582.

(b) Explanation of terms used in this section—

(1) American employer means—

(i) The United States or any of its instrumentalities;

(ii) A State, a political subdivision of a State, or an instrumentality of any one or more States or political subdivisions of a State;

(iii) An individual who is a resident of the United States;

(iv) A partnership, if at least two-thirds of the partners are residents of the United States;

(v) A trust, if all of the trustees are residents of the United States; or

(vi) A corporation organized under the laws of the United States or of any State.

(2) American aircraft means an aircraft registered under the laws of the United States.

(3) American vessel means a vessel documented or numbered under the laws of the United States. It also includes a vessel neither documented nor numbered under the laws of the United States, nor documented under the laws of any foreign country, if its crew is employed solely by one or more citizens or residents of the United States, or corporations organized under the laws of the United States or of any State.

(4) Citizen of the United States includes a citizen of the Commonwealth of Puerto Rico, the Virgin Islands, Guam, American Samoa or the Commonwealth of the Northern Mariana Islands.

(5) Foreign affiliate refers to a foreign affiliate as defined in section 3121(*l*)(6) of the Code.

(6) On and in connection with refers to the performance of work on a vessel or aircraft which concerns the vessel or aircraft. Examples of this kind of work are the services performed on a vessel by employees as officers or crew members, or as employees of concessionaires, of the vessel.

(7) On or in connection with refers to work performed on the vessel or aircraft and to work which concerns the vessel or aircraft but not actually performed on it. For example, shore services in connection with repairing, loading, unloading, or provisioning a vessel performed by employees as officers or crew members, or as employees of concessionaires, of the vessel are included, since this work concerns the vessel though not performed on it.

(8) State refers to the 50 States, the District of Columbia, the Commonwealth of Puerto Rico, the Virgin Islands, Guam, American Samoa, and the Commonwealth of the Northern Mariana Islands.

(9) United States when used in a geographical sense means the 50 States, the District of Columbia, the Commonwealth of Puerto Rico, the Virgin Islands, Guam, American Samoa, and the Commonwealth of the Northern Mariana Islands.

[50 FR 36573, Sept. 9, 1985; 50 FR 38113, Sept. 20, 1985; 55 FR 51687, Dec. 17, 1990; 61 FR 38365, July 24, 1996; 69 FR 51555, Aug. 20, 2004]

§ 404.1005 Who is an employee.

You must be an employee for your work to be covered as employment for social security purposes. You are an employee if you are—

(a) A corporation officer as described in § 404.1006;

(b) A common-law employee as described in § 404.1007 (unless you are, after December 31, 1982, a qualified real estate agent or direct seller as described in § 404.1069); or

(c) An agent-driver or commission-driver, a full-time life insurance salesman, a home worker, or a traveling or city salesman as described in § 404.1008.

[48 FR 40515, Sept. 8, 1983]

§ 404.1006 Corporation officer.

If you are an officer of a corporation, you are an employee of the corporation if you are paid or you are entitled to be paid for holding office or performing services. However, if you are a director of a corporation, we consider you to be self-employed when you work as a director.

§ 404.1007 Common-law employee.

(a) General. The common-law rules on employer-employee status are the basic test for determining whether you and the person or firm you work for have the relationship of employee and employer. Even though you are considered self-employed under the common-law rules, you may still be an employee for social security purposes under § 404.1006 (relating to corporation officers) or § 404.1008 (relating to workers in four specific jobs). In general, you are a common-law employee if the person you work for may tell you what to do and how, when, and where to do it. The person or firm you work for does not have to give these orders, but needs only the right to do so. Whether or not you are a common-law employee is not always clear. Several aspects of your job arrangement are considered in determining whether you are an employee or are self-employed under the common-law rules.

(b) Factors that show employee status. Some aspects of a job arrangement that may show you are an employee are as follows:

(1) The person you work for may fire you.

(2) The person you work for furnishes you with tools or equipment and a place to work.

(3) You receive training from the person you work for or are required to follow that person's instructions.

(4) You must do the work yourself.

(5) You do not hire, supervise, or pay assistants (unless you are employed as a foreman, manager, or supervisor).

(6) The person you work for sets your hours of work, requires you to work full-time, or restricts you from doing work for others.

(7) The person you work for pays your business or traveling expenses.

(8) You are paid by the hour, week or month.

(c) Factors that show self-employed status. Some aspects of a job arrangement or business venture that may show you are self-employed are as follows:

(1) You make a profit or suffer a loss.

(2) You are hired to complete a certain job and if you quit before the job is completed you may be liable for damages.

(3) You work for a number of persons or firms at the same time.

(4) You advertise to the general public that you are available to perform services.

(5) You pay your own expenses and have your own equipment and work place.

(d) Questions about your status. If there is a question about whether you are working as an employee or are self-employed, we or the Internal Revenue Service will make a determination after examining all of the facts of your case.

§ 404.1008 Agent-driver or commission-driver, full-time life insurance salesman, home worker, or traveling or city salesman.

(a) General. In addition to common-law employees and corporation officers, we consider workers in the four types of jobs described in paragraphs (b) through (e) of this section to be employees if their services are performed under the following conditions:

(1) Under the work arrangement the worker is expected to do substantially all of the work personally.

(2) The worker must not have a substantial investment in the facilities used to do the work. Facilities include such things as a place to work, storage space, equipment, machinery and office furniture. However, facilities do not include tools, equipment or clothing of the kind usually provided by employees nor transportation such as a car or truck.

(3) The work must be performed as part of a continuing work relationship between the worker and the person for whom the work is done. The work performed must not be a single transaction. Part-time and regular seasonal work may be performed as part of a continuing work relationship.

(b) Agent-driver or commission-driver. This is a driver hired by another person to distribute meat products, vegetable products, fruit products, bakery products, beverages (other than milk), or laundry or dry-cleaning services. We consider you an agent-driver or commission-driver if you are paid a commission based on your sales or the difference between the price you charge your customers and the amount you pay for the goods or services. It makes no difference whether you drive your own truck or the company's truck or whether you solicit the customers you serve.

(c) Full-time life insurance salesman. A full-time life insurance salesman's main activity is selling life insurance or annuity contracts, or both, mostly for one life insurance company. If you are a full-time life insurance salesman, you are probably provided office space, stenographic help, telephone, forms, rate books and advertising materials by the company or general agent, without cost to you.

(d) Home worker. A home worker is a person who works away from the place of business of the person he or she works for, usually at home. If you are a home worker and you work according to the instructions of the person you work for, on material or goods furnished by that person, and are required to return the finished product to that person (or another person whom he or she designates), you are an employee.

(e) Traveling or city salesman. The main activity of a traveling or city salesman is taking orders for merchandise for another person or firm. The salesman gets orders from wholesalers, retailers, contractors, or operators of hotels, restaurants or other firms whose main business is furnishing food or lodging or both.

The salesman sells merchandise to others for resale or for use in their own business. We consider you a traveling or city salesman if most of your work is done for a single person or firm even though you have incidental sideline sales activities. However, you are not an employee under this paragraph as to those sideline sales. If you take orders for a number of persons or firms as a multiple line salesman, you are not a traveling or city salesman.

§ 404.1009 Who is an employer.

A person is an employer if he or she employs at least one employee. Sometimes it is not clear who a worker's employer is, since the employer does not always pay the worker's wages. When there is a question about who the employer is, we use the common-law rules to identify the employer (see § 404.1007).

§ 404.1010 Farm crew leader as employer.

A farm crew leader furnishes workers to do agricultural labor for another person, usually a farm operator. If the crew leader pays the workers (the money can be the crew leader's or the farm operator's), the crew leader is deemed to be the employer of the workers and is self-employed. However, the crew leader is not deemed the employer of the workers if there is a written agreement between the crew leader and the farm operator naming the crew leader as an employee. If the crew leader does not have this agreement and does not pay the workers, we use the common-law rules to determine the crew leader's status.

WORK EXCLUDED FROM EMPLOYMENT

§ 404.1012 Work excluded from employment.

Certain kinds of work performed by an employee are excluded from employment. They are described in §§ 404.1014 through 404.1038 and are exceptions to the general rule in § 404.1004 on the kinds of work that are covered as employment. In general, if the work performed by an employee is excluded from employment, the work is not covered under social security. However, certain kinds of work performed by an employee, even though excluded from employment, are covered as self-employment for social security purposes. In addition, if part of the work performed by an employee for the same employer is included as employment and part is excluded from employment, all the work may be included or all may be excluded as described in § 404.1013.

[61 FR 38365, July 24, 1996]

§ 404.1013 Included-excluded rule.

(a) If part of your work for an employer during a pay period is covered as employment and part excluded, all of your work during that period is considered covered if at least one-half of your time in the pay period is in covered work. If you spend most of your time in a pay period doing work that is excluded, all of your work in that period is excluded.

(b) A pay period is the period for which your employer ordinarily pays you. It cannot be more than 31 consecutive days. If the actual period is not always the same, your usual pay period will be used for applying the included-excluded rule.

(c) The included-excluded rule does not apply and your covered work will be counted if—

(1) Part of your work is covered by the Railroad Retirement Tax Act and part by the Social Security Act; or

(2) You have no usual pay period of 31 consecutive days or less, or you have separate pay periods for covered and excluded work.

§ 404.1014 Domestic service by a student for a local college club, fraternity or sorority.

(a) General. If you are a student and do work of a household nature in or about the club rooms or house of a local college club or local chapter of a college fraternity or sorority, and are enrolled and regularly attending classes at a school, college, or university, your work is not covered as employment.

(b) Explanation of terms—

(1) Work of a household nature means the type of work done by cooks, waiters, butlers, maids, janitors, laundresses, furnacemen, handymen, gardeners, housekeepers and housemothers.

(2) A local college club or local chapter of a college fraternity or sorority does not include an alumni club or chapter. Also, if the club rooms or house are used mostly for supplying board or lodging to students or nonstudents as a business, the work done is not excluded by this section.

§ 404.1015 Family services.

(a) General. If you work as an employee of a relative, the work is excluded from employment if—

(1) You work while under age 18 in the employ of your parent;

(2) You do nonbusiness work (see § 404.1058(a)(3) for an explanation of nonbusiness work) or perform domestic service (as described in § 404.1057(b)) as an employee of your parent while under age 21;

(3) You do nonbusiness work as an employee of your son, daughter, or spouse; or

(4) You perform domestic service in the private home of your son, daughter or spouse as an employee of that son, daughter or spouse unless—

(i) The son or daughter has a child (either natural, adopted or stepchild) living in the home who is under age 18 or, if older, has a mental or physical condition that requires the personal care and supervision of an adult for at least four continuous weeks in the calendar quarter in which the work is done; and

(ii) The son or daughter is a widower or widow, or is divorced and has not remarried, or has a spouse living in the home who, because of a physical or mental condition, is incapable of taking care of the child and the condition is present for at least four continuous weeks in the calendar quarter in which the work is done.

(b) Family work for other than sole proprietor. Work for a corporation is not excluded under this section, and work for a partnership is not excluded unless the required family relationship exists between the employee and each of the partners.

[57 FR 59913, Dec. 17, 1992]

§ 404.1016 Foreign agricultural workers.

Farm work done by foreign workers lawfully admitted to the United States on a temporary basis to do farm work is not covered as employment. The excluded work includes any services connected with farm operations.

§ 404.1017 Sharefarmers.

(a) If you are a sharefarmer, your services are not covered as employment, but as self-employment.

(b) You are a sharefarmer if you have an arrangement with the owner or tenant of the land and the arrangement provides for all of the following:

(1) You will produce agricultural or horticultural commodities on the land.

(2) The commodities you produce or the income from their sale will be divided between you and the person with whom you have the agreement.

(3) The amount of your share depends on the amount of commodities you produce.

(c) If under your agreement you are to receive a specific rate of pay, a fixed sum of money or a specific amount of the commodities not based on your production, you are not a sharefarmer for social security purposes.

§ 404.1018 Work by civilians for the United States Government or its instrumentalities—wages paid after 1983.

(a) General. If you are a civilian employee of the United States Government or an instrumentality of the United States, your employer will determine the amount of remuneration paid for your work and the periods in or for which such remuneration was paid. We will determine whether your employment is covered under Social Security, the periods of such covered employment, and whether remuneration paid for your work constitutes wages for purposes of Social Security. To make these determinations we will consider the date of your appointment to Federal service, your previous Federal employing agencies and positions (if any), whether you were covered under Social Security or a Federal civilian retirement system, and whether you made a timely election to join a retirement system established by the Federal Employees' Retirement System Act of 1986 or the Foreign Service Pension System Act of 1986. Using this information and the following rules, we will determine that your service is covered unless—

(1) The service would have been excluded if the rules in effect in January 1983 had remained in effect; and

(i) You have been continuously performing such service since December 31, 1983; or

(ii) You are receiving an annuity from the Civil Service Retirement and Disability Fund or benefits for service as an employee under another retirement system established by a law of the United States and in effect on December 31, 1983, for employees of the Federal Government other than a system for members of the uniformed services.

(2) The service is under the provisions of 28 U.S.C. 294, relating to the assignment of retired Federal justices and judges to active duty.

(b) Covered services—

(1) Federal officials. Any service for which you received remuneration after 1983 is covered if performed—

(i) As the President or the Vice President of the United States;

(ii) In a position placed in the Executive Schedule under 5 U.S.C. 5312 through 5317;

(iii) As a noncareer appointee in the Senior Executive Service or a noncareer member of the Senior Foreign Service;

(iv) In a position to which you are appointed by the President, or his designee, or the Vice President under 3 U.S.C. 105(a)(1), 106(a)(1), or 107(a)(1) or (b)(1) if the maximum rate of basic pay for such position is at or above the rate for level V of the Executive Schedule;

(v) As the Chief Justice of the United States, an Associate Justice of the Supreme Court, a judge of a United States court of appeals, a judge of a United States district court, including the district court of a territory, a judge of the United States Claims Court, a judge of the United States Court of International Trade, a judge of the United States Tax Court, a United States magistrate, or a referee in bankruptcy or United States bankruptcy judge; or

(vi) As a Member, Delegate, or Resident Commissioner of or to the Congress.

(2) Legislative Branch Employees. Service you perform for the legislative branch of the Federal Government for which you are paid remuneration after 1983 is

generally covered by Social Security if such service is not covered by the Civil Service Retirement System or by another retirement system established by a law of the United States and in effect on December 31, 1983, for employees of the Federal Government other than a system for members of the uniformed services.

(3) Election to become subject to the Federal Employees' Retirement System or the Foreign Service Pension System. Your service is covered if:

(i) You timely elect after June 30, 1987, under either the Federal Employees' Retirement System Act or the Central Intelligence Agency Retirement Act, to become subject to the Federal Employees Retirement System provided in 5 U.S.C. 8401 through 8479; or

(ii) You timely elect after June 30, 1987, to become subject to the Foreign Service Pension System provided in 22 U.S.C. 4071 through 4071(k).

(4) Subsequent Federal civilian service. If you perform Federal civilian service on or after November 10, 1988, which is described in paragraph (b)(1), (b)(2), or (b)(3) of this section you will continue to be covered for any subsequent Federal Civilian Service not excluded under paragraph (c) of this section.

(c) Excluded Service. Notwithstanding § 404.1018a and this section, your service is not covered if performed—

(1) In a penal institution of the United States as an inmate thereof;

(2) As an employee included under 5 U.S.C. 5351(2) relating to certain interns, student nurses, and other student employees of hospitals of the Federal Government, other than as a medical or dental intern or a medical or dental resident in training;

(3) As an employee serving on a temporary basis in case of fire, storm, earthquake, flood, or other similar emergency; or

(4) Under any other statutory provisions that would require exclusion for reasons other than being in the employ of the Federal Government or an instrumentality of such.

(d) Work as a Peace Corps Volunteer. Work performed as a volunteer or volunteer leader within the meaning of the Peace Corps Act, 22 U.S.C. 2501 through 2523, is covered as employment.

(e) Work as Job Corps Enrollee. Work performed as an enrollee in the Job Corps is considered to be performed in the employ of the United States.

(f) Work by Volunteer in Service to America. Work performed and training received as a Volunteer in Service to America is considered to be performed in the employ of the United States if the volunteer is enrolled for a period of service of at least 1 year. If the enrollment is for less than 1 year, we use the common-law rules in § 404.1007 to determine the volunteer's status.

(g) Work for international organizations. Work performed for an international organization by an employee who was transferred from a Federal agency is generally covered as employment if, immediately before the transfer, the employee's services for the Federal agency were covered. (See § 404.1004(a)(5) and § 404.1034(c).)

(h) Meaning of "continuously performing"—

(1) Absence of less than 366 days. You are considered to be continuously performing service described in paragraph (a)(1)(i) of this section if you return to the performance of such service after being separated from such service for a period of less than 366 consecutive days, regardless of whether the period began before, on, or after December 31, 1983.

(2) Other absences. You are considered to be continuously performing service described in paragraph (a)(1)(i) of this section regardless of the length of separation or whether the period of separation began before, on, or after December 31, 1983, if you—

(i) Return to the performance of such service after being detailed or transferred from such service to an international organization as described under 5 U.S.C. 3343 or under 5 U.S.C. 3581;

(ii) Are reemployed or reinstated after being separated from such service for the purpose of accepting employment with the American Institute of Taiwan as provided under 22 U.S.C. 3310;

(iii) Return to the performance of such service after performing service as a member of a uniformed service including service in the National Guard and temporary service in the Coast Guard Reserve and after exercising restoration or reemployment rights as provided under 38 U.S.C. chapter 43; or

(iv) Return to the performance of such service after employment by a tribal organization to which section 105(e)(2) of the Indian Self–Determination Act applies.

[53 FR 38944, Oct. 4, 1988; 53 FR 44551, Nov. 3, 1988; 55 FR 24891, June 19, 1990; 61 FR 38365, July 24, 1996; 79 FR 33684, June 12, 2014]

§ 404.1018a Work by civilians for the United States Government or its instrumentalities—remuneration paid prior to 1984.

(a) General—remuneration paid prior to 1984. If you worked as a civilian employee of the United States Government or an instrumentality of the United States, your work was excluded from employment if that work was covered by a retirement system established by law. Your work for an instrumentality that was exempt from Social Security tax was also excluded. Certain other work for the United States or an instrumentality of the United States was specifically excluded and is described in this section.

(b) Work covered by a retirement system—remuneration paid prior to 1984. Work you did as an employee of the United States or an instrumentality of the United States was excluded from employment if the work was covered by a retirement system established by a law of the United States. If you had a choice as to whether your work was covered by the retirement system, the work was not covered by that system until you chose that coverage. In order for the exclusion to apply, the work you did, rather than the position you held, must have been covered by the retirement system.

(c) Work that was specifically excluded—remuneration paid prior to 1984. Work performed by an employee of the United States or an instrumentality of the United States was excluded if it was done—

(1) As the President or Vice President of the United States;

(2) As a Member of the United States Congress, a Delegate to Congress, or a Resident Commissioner;

(3) In the legislative branch of the United States Government;

(4) By a student nurse, student dietitian, student physical therapist or student occupational therapist who was assigned or attached to a Federal hospital, clinic, or medical or dental laboratory;

(5) By a person designated as a student employee with the approval of the Office of Personnel Management who was assigned or attached primarily for training purposes to a Federal hospital, clinic, or medical or dental laboratory, other than a medical or dental intern or resident in training;

(6) By an employee who served on a temporary basis in case of fire, storm, earthquake, flood, or other similar emergency;

(7) By a person to whom the Civil Service Retirement Act did not apply because the person's services were subject to another retirement system established by a law of the United States or by the instrumentality of the United States for which the work was done, other than the retirement system established by the Tennessee Valley Authority under the plan approved by the Secretary of Health, Education, and Welfare on December 28, 1956; or

(8) By an inmate of a penal institution of the United States, if the work was done in the penal institution.

(d) Work for instrumentalities of the United States exempt from employer tax—remuneration paid prior to 1984.

(1) Work performed by an employee of an instrumentality of the United States was excluded if—

(i) The instrumentality was exempt from the employer tax imposed by section 3111 of the Code or by section 1410 of the Internal Revenue Code of 1939; and

(ii) The exemption was authorized by another law specifically referring to these sections.

(2) Work performed by an employee of an instrumentality of the United States was excluded if the instrumentality was not on December 31, 1950, subject to the employer tax imposed by section 1410 of the Internal Revenue Code of 1939 and the work was covered by a retirement system established by the instrumentality, unless—

(i) The work was for a corporation wholly owned by the United States;

(ii) The work was for a Federal land bank association, a production credit association, a Federal Reserve Bank, a Federal Credit Union, a Federal land bank, a Federal intermediate credit bank, a bank for cooperatives, or a Federal Home Loan Bank;

(iii) The work was for a State, county, or community committee under the Agriculture Marketing Service and the Commodity Stabilization Service, formerly the Production and Marketing Administration; or

(iv) The work was by a civilian, who was not paid from funds appropriated by the Congress, in activities conducted by an instrumentality of the United States subject to the jurisdiction of the Secretary of Defense or Secretary of Transportation at installations intended for the comfort, pleasure, contentment, and mental and physical improvement of personnel of the Defense Department or the Coast Guard, such as—

(A) Army and Air Force Exchange Service;

(B) Army and Air Force Motion Picture Service;

(C) Coast Guard Exchanges;

(D) Navy Ship's Service Stores; and

(E) Marine Corps Post Exchanges.

(3) For purposes of paragraph (d)(2) of this section, if an employee has a choice as to whether his or her work was covered by a retirement system, the work was not covered by that system until he or she chose that coverage. The work done, rather than the position held, must have been covered by the retirement system.

(e) Work as a Peace Corps Volunteer—remuneration paid prior to 1984. Work performed as a volunteer or volunteer leader within the meaning of the Peace Corps Act, 22 U.S.C. 2501 through 2523, was covered as employment.

(f) Work as Job Corps Enrollee—remuneration paid prior to 1984. Work performed as an enrollee in the Job Corps was considered to be performed in the employ of the United States.

(g) Work by Volunteer in Service to America—remuneration paid prior to 1984. Work performed and training received as a Volunteer in Service to America was considered to be performed in the employ of the United States if the volunteer was enrolled for a period of service of at least one year. If the enrollment was for less than one year, we used the common-law rules in § 404.1007 to determine the volunteer's status.

[53 FR 38945, Oct. 4, 1988]

§ 404.1018b Medicare qualified government employment.

(a) General. The work of a Federal, State, or local government employee not otherwise subject to Social Security coverage may constitute Medicare qualified government employment. Medicare qualified government employment means any service which in all ways meets the definition of "employment" for title II purposes of the Social Security Act, except for the fact that the service was performed by a Federal, State or local government employee. This employment is used solely in determining eligibility for protection under part A of title XVIII of the Social Security Act (Hospital Insurance) and for coverage under the Medicare program for end-stage renal disease.

(b) Federal employment. If, beginning with remuneration paid after 1982, your service as a Federal employee is not otherwise covered employment under the Social Security Act, it is Medicare qualified government employment unless excluded under § 404.1018(c).

(c) State and local government employment. If, beginning with service performed after March 31, 1986, your service as an employee of a State or political subdivision (as defined in § 404.1202(b)), Guam, American Samoa, the District of Columbia, or the Northern Mariana Islands is excluded from covered employment solely because of section 210(a)(7) of the Social Security Act which pertains to employees of State and local governments (note §§ 404.1020 through 404.1022), it is Medicare qualified government employment except as provided in paragraphs (c)(1) and (2) of this section.

(1) An individual's service shall not be treated as employment if performed—

(i) By an individual employed by a State or political subdivision for the purpose of relieving that individual from unemployment;

(ii) In a hospital, home, or other institution by a patient or inmate thereof as an employee of a State, political subdivision, or of the District of Columbia;

(iii) By an individual, as an employee of a State, political subdivision or the District of Columbia serving on a temporary basis in case of fire, storm, snow, earthquake, flood, or other similar emergency;

(iv) By an individual as an employee included under 5 U.S.C. 5351(2) (relating to certain interns, student nurses, and other student employees of hospitals of the District of Columbia government), other than as a medical or dental intern or a medical or dental resident in training; or

(v) By an election official or election worker paid less than $100 in a calendar year for such service prior to 1995, or less than $1,000 for service performed in any calendar year after 1994 and before 2000, or, for service performed in any calendar year after 1999, less than the $1,000 base amount, as adjusted pursuant to section 218(c)(8)(B) of the Social Security Act to reflect changes in wages in the economy. We will publish this adjustment of the $1,000 base amount in the Federal Register on or before November 1 preceding the year for which the adjustment is made.

(2) An individual's service performed for an employer shall not be treated as employment if—

(i) The service would be excluded from coverage under section 210(a)(7) of the Social Security Act which pertains to employees of State and local governments;

(ii) The service is performed by an individual who—

(A) Was performing substantial and regular service for remuneration for that employer before April 1, 1986;

(B) Was a bona fide employee of that employer on March 31, 1986; and

(C) Did not enter into the employment relationship with that employer for purposes of meeting the requirements of paragraphs (c)(2)(ii)(A) and (B) of this section; and

(iii) After March 31, 1986, but prior to the service being performed, the employment relationship with that employer had not been terminated.

[53 FR 38946, Oct. 4, 1988; 57 FR 59913, Dec. 17, 1992; 61 FR 38366, July 24, 1996]

§ 404.1019 Work as a member of a uniformed service of the United States.

(a) Your work as a member of a uniformed service of the United States is covered under Social Security (unless creditable under the Railroad Retirement Act), if—

(1) On or after January 1, 1957, the work is service on active duty or active duty for training but not including service performed while on leave without pay; or

(2) On or after January 1, 1988, the work is service on inactive duty training.

(b) You are a member of a uniformed service if—

(1) You are appointed, enlisted, or inducted into (or a retired member of)—

(i) One of the armed services (Army, Navy, Air Force, Marine Corps, or Coast Guard); or

(ii) A component of one of the armed services, including any reserve component as defined in Veterans' Benefits, 38 U.S.C. 101 (except the Coast Guard Reserve as a temporary member);

(2) You are a commissioned officer (including a retired commissioned officer) of the National Oceanic and Atmospheric Administration or the Regular or Reserve Corps of the Public Health Service;

(3) You are a member of the Fleet Reserve or Fleet Marine Corps Reserve;

(4) You are a cadet at the United States Military, Coast Guard, or Air Force Academy, or a midshipman at the United States Naval Academy;

(5) You are a member of the Reserve Officers Training Corps, the Naval Reserve Officers Training Corps, or the Air Force Reserve Officers Training Corps, when ordered to annual training duty for 14 days or more including periods of authorized travel to and from that duty; or

(6) You are selected for active military or naval training under the Military Selective Service Act or are provisionally accepted for active duty in the military or naval service and you are ordered or directed to a place for final acceptance or entry upon active duty and are on the way to or from, or at, that place.

[57 FR 59913, Dec. 17, 1992]

§ 404.1020 Work for States and their political subdivisions and instrumentalities.

(a) General. If you work as an employee of a State, a political subdivision of a State, or any wholly owned instrumentality of one or more of these, your work is excluded from employment unless—

(1) The work is covered under an agreement under section 218 of the Act (see subpart M of this part); or

(2) The work is covered transportation service as defined in section 210(k) of the Act (see paragraph (c) of this section).

(3) You perform services after July 1, 1991, as an employee of a State (other than the District of Columbia, Guam, the Commonwealth of the Northern Mariana Islands, or American Samoa), a political subdivision of a State, or any wholly owned instrumentality of one or more of the foregoing and you are not a member of a retirement system of such State, political subdivision, or instrumentality. Retirement system has the meaning given that term in section 218(b)(4) of the Act, except as provided in regulations prescribed by the Secretary of the Treasury. This paragraph does not apply to services performed—

(i) As an employee employed to relieve you from unemployment;

(ii) In a hospital, home, or other institution where you are a patient or inmate thereof;

(iii) As an employee serving on a temporary basis in case of fire, storm, snow, earthquake, flood, or other similar emergency;

(iv) As an election official or election worker if the remuneration paid in a calendar year for such service prior to 1995 is less than $100, or less than $1000 for service performed in any calendar year after 1994 and before 2000, or, for service performed in any calendar year after 1999, less than the $1000 base amount, as adjusted pursuant to section 218(c)(8)(B) of the Social Security Act to reflect changes in wages in the economy. We will publish this adjustment of the $1000 base amount in the Federal Register on or before November 1 preceding the year for which the adjustment is made.

(v) As an employee in a position compensated solely on a fee basis which is treated, pursuant to section 211(c)(2)(E) of the Act, as a trade or business for purposes of inclusion of the fees in net earnings from self-employment; or

(4) The work is covered under § 404.1021 or § 404.1022.

(b) Medicare qualified government employment. Notwithstanding the provisions of paragraph (a) of this section, your work may be covered as Medicare qualified government employment (see § 404.1018b(c) of this subpart).

(c) Covered transportation service—

(1) Work for a public transportation system. If you work for a public transportation system of a State or political subdivision of a State, your work may be covered transportation service if all or part of the system was acquired from private ownership. You must work as an employee of the State or political subdivision in connection with its operation of a public transportation system for your work to be covered transportation service. This paragraph sets out additional conditions that must be met for your work to be covered transportation service. If you work for a public transportation system but your work is not covered transportation service, your work may be covered for social security purposes under an agreement under section 218 of the Act (see subpart M of this part).

(2) Transportation system acquired in whole or in part after 1936 and before 1951. All work after 1950 for a public transportation system is covered transportation service if—

(i) Any part of the transportation system was acquired from private ownership after 1936 and before 1951; and

(ii) No general retirement system covering substantially all work in connection with the operation of the transportation system and guaranteed by the State constitution was in effect on December 31, 1950.

(3) Transportation system operated on December 31, 1950, no part of which was acquired after 1936 and before 1951. If no part of a transportation system operated by a State or political subdivision on December 31, 1950, was acquired from private ownership after 1936 and before 1951, work for that public transportation system is not covered transportation service unless performed under conditions described in paragraph (b)(4) of this section.

(4) Addition after 1950 to existing transportation system. Work for a public transportation system part of which was acquired from private ownership after 1950 as an addition to an existing transportation system is covered transportation service beginning with the first day of the third calendar quarter following the calendar quarter in which the addition was acquired if—

(i) The work is performed by an employee who—

(A) Worked in employment in connection with the operation of the addition before the addition was acquired by the State or political subdivision; and

(B) Became an employee of the State or political subdivision in connection with and at the time of its acquisition of the addition;

(ii) On that first day, work performed by that employee is—

(A) Not covered by a general retirement system; or

(B) Covered by a general retirement system which contains special provisions that apply only to employees described in paragraph (c)(4)(i)(B) of this section;

(iii) The existing transportation system was operated by the State or political subdivision on December 31, 1950; and

(iv) Work for the existing transportation system was not covered transportation service because—

(A) No part of the system was acquired from private ownership after 1936 and before 1951; or

(B) The general retirement system described in paragraph (c)(2)(ii) of this section was in effect on December 31, 1950.

(5) Transportation system acquired after 1950. All work for a public transportation system is covered transportation service if—

(i) The transportation system was not operated by the State or political subdivision before 1951;

(ii) All or part of the transportation system was first acquired from private ownership after 1950; and

(iii) At the time the State or political subdivision first acquired any part of its transportation system from private ownership, it did not have a general retirement system covering substantially all work performed in connection with the operation of the transportation system.

(6) Definitions.

(i) The term general retirement system means any pension, annuity, retirement, or similar fund or system established by a State or by a political subdivision of a State for employees of the State, the political subdivision, or both. The term does not include a fund or system which covers only work performed in positions connected with the operation of the public transportation system.

(ii) A transportation system (or part of a system) is considered to have been acquired from private ownership by a State or political subdivision if—

(A) Before the acquisition, work performed by employees in connection with the operation of the system (or an acquired part) constituted employment under the Act; and

(B) Some of these employees became employees of the State or political subdivision in connection with and at the time of the acquisition.

(iii) The term political subdivision includes an instrumentality of a State, of one or more political subdivisions of a State, or of a State and one or more of its political subdivisions.

[57 FR 59910, 59914, Dec. 17, 1992; 61 FR 38366, July 24, 1996; 69 FR 51556, Aug. 20, 2004]

§ 404.1021 Work for the District of Columbia.

If you work as an employee of the District of Columbia or a wholly owned instrumentality of the District of Columbia, your work is covered as employment unless—

(a) Your work is covered by a retirement system established by a law of the United States; or

(b) You are—

(1) A patient or inmate of a hospital or penal institution and your work is for that hospital or institution;

(2) A student employee (a student nurse, dietitian, or physical or occupational therapist, but not a medical or dental intern or resident in training) of a District of Columbia hospital, clinic, or medical or dental laboratory;

(3) An employee serving temporarily in case of fire, storm, snow, earthquake, flood, or other similar emergency; or

(4) A member of a board, committee, or council of the District of Columbia paid on a per diem, meeting, or other fee basis.

(c) Medicare qualified government employment. If your work is not covered under Social Security, it may be covered as Medicare qualified government employment (see § 404.1018b(c) of this subpart).

[57 FR 59914, Dec. 17, 1992]

§ 404.1022 American Samoa, Guam, or the Commonwealth of the Northern Mariana Islands.

(a) Work in American Samoa, Guam, or the Commonwealth of the Northern Mariana Islands. Work in American Samoa, Guam, or the Commonwealth of the Northern Mariana Islands for a private employer is covered as employment the same as in the 50 States. Work done by a resident of the Republic of the Philippines working in Guam on a temporary basis as a nonimmigrant alien admitted to Guam under section 101(a)(15)(H)(ii) of the Immigration and Nationality

Act is excluded from coverage regardless of the employer.

(b) Work for American Samoa or a political subdivision or wholly owned instrumentality of American Samoa. Work as an officer or employee (including a member of the legislature) of the government of American Samoa, its political subdivisions, or any wholly owned instrumentality of any one or more of these, is covered as employment (unless the work is covered by a retirement system established by a law of the United States). The officer or employee is not considered as an employee of the United States, an agency of the United States, or an instrumentality of the United States, for purposes of title II of the Act. We consider any pay for this work to have been paid by the government of American Samoa, or the political subdivision or the wholly owned instrumentality of American Samoa.

(c) Work for Guam, the Commonwealth of the Northern Mariana Islands (CNMI), or a political subdivision or wholly owned instrumentality of Guam or the CNMI. Work as an officer or employee (including a member of the legislature) of the government of the CNMI, its political subdivisions, or any wholly owned instrumentality of any one or more of these, is covered as employment beginning October 1, 2012. Work as an officer or employee (including a member of the legislature) of the government of Guam, its political subdivisions, or any wholly owned instrumentality of any one or more of these, is excluded from coverage as employment. However, the exclusion does not apply to employees classified as temporary or intermittent unless the work is—

(1) Covered by a retirement system established by a law of Guam or the CNMI;

(2) Done by an elected official;

(3) Done by a member of the legislature; or

(4) Done in a hospital or penal institution by a patient or inmate of the hospital or penal institution.

(d) Medicare qualified government employment. If your work is not covered under Social Security, it may be covered as Medicare qualified government employment (see § 404.1018b(c) of this subpart).

[57 FR 59914, Dec. 17, 1992; 69 FR 51556, Aug. 20, 2004; 79 FR 33684, June 12, 2014]

§ 404.1023 Ministers of churches and members of religious orders.

(a) General. If you are a duly ordained, commissioned, or licensed minister of a church, the work you do in the exercise of your ministry is excluded from employment. However, it is treated as self-employment for social security purposes. If you are a member of a religious order who has not taken a vow of poverty, the same rule applies to the work you do in the exercise of your duties required by that order. If you are a member of a religious order who has taken a vow of poverty, the work you do in the exercise of duties required by the order (the work may be done for the order or for another employer) is covered as employment only if the order or autonomous subdivision of the order to which you belong has filed an effective election of coverage. The election is made under section 3121(r) of the Code. For the rules on self-employment coverage of ministers and members of religious orders who have not taken vows of poverty, see § 404.1071.

(b) What is an ordained, commissioned, or licensed minister. The terms ordained, commissioned, or licensed describe the procedures followed by recognized churches or church denominations to vest ministerial status upon qualified individuals. If a church or church denomination has an ordination procedure, the commissioning or licensing of a person as a minister may not make him or her a commissioned or licensed minister for purposes of this subpart. Where there is an ordination procedure, the commissioning or licensing must be recognized as having the same effect as ordination and the person must be fully qualified to exercise all of the ecclesiastical duties of the church or church denomination.

(c) When is work by a minister in the exercise of the ministry.

(1) A minister is working in the exercise of the ministry when he or she is—

(i) Ministering sacerdotal functions or conducting religious worship (other than as described in paragraph (d)(2) of this section); or

(ii) Working in the control, conduct, and maintenance of a religious organization (including an integral agency of a religious organization) under the authority of a religious body constituting a church or church denomination.

(2) The following rules are used to decide whether a minister's work is in the exercise of the ministry:

(i) Whether the work is the conduct of religious worship or the ministration of sacerdotal functions depends on the tenets and practices of the religious body which is his or her church or church denomination.

(ii) Work in the control, conduct, and maintenance relates to directing, managing, or promoting the activities of the religious organization. Any religious organization is considered to be under the authority of a religious body constituting a church or church denomination if it is organized and dedicated to carrying out the tenets and principles of a faith according to either the requirements or sanctions governing the creation of institutions of the faith.

The term religious organization has the same meaning and application as is given to the term for income tax purposes under the Code.

(iii) If a minister is working in the conduct of religious worship or the ministration of sacerdotal functions, the work is in the exercise of the ministry whether or not it is performed for a religious organization. (See paragraph (d)(2) of this section for an exception to this rule.)

Example: M, a duly ordained minister, is engaged to work as chaplain at a privately owned university. M spends his entire time working as chaplain. This includes the conduct of religious worship, offering spiritual counsel to the university students, and teaching a class in religion. M is working in the exercise of the ministry.

(iv) If a minister is working for an organization which is operated as an integral agency of a religious organization under the authority of a religious body constituting a church or church denomination, all work by the minister in the conduct of religious worship, in the ministration of sacerdotal functions, or in the control, conduct, and maintenance of the organization is in the exercise of the ministry.

Example: M, a duly ordained minister, is engaged by the N Religious Board as director of one of its departments. M performs no other service. The N Religious Board is an integral agency of O, a religious organization operating under the authority of a religious body constituting a church denomination. M is working in the exercise of the ministry.

(v) If a minister, under an assignment or designation by a religious body constituting a church, works for an organization which is neither a religious organization nor operated as an integral agency of a religious organization, all service performed by him or her, even though the service may not involve the conduct of religious worship or the ministration of sacerdotal functions, is in the exercise of the ministry.

Example: M, a duly ordained minister, is assigned by X, the religious body constituting M's church, to perform advisory service to Y company in connection with the publication of a book dealing with the history of M's church denomination. Y is neither a religious organization nor operated as an integral agency of a religious organization. M performs no other service for X or Y. M is working in the exercise of the ministry.

(vi) If a minister is working for an organization which is neither a religious organization nor operated as an integral agency of a religious organization and the work is not performed under an assignment or designation by ecclesiastical superiors, then only the work done by the minister in the conduct of religious worship or the ministration of sacerdotal functions is in the exercise of the ministry. (See paragraph (d)(2) of this section for an exception to this rule.)

Example: M, a duly ordained minister, is engaged by N University to teach history and mathematics. M does no other work for N although from time to time M performs marriages and conducts funerals for relatives and friends. N University is neither a religious organization nor operated as an integral agency of a religious organization. M is not working for N under an assignment by his ecclesiastical superiors. The work performed by M for N University is not in the exercise of the ministry. However, service performed by M in performing marriages and conducting funerals is in the exercise of the ministry.

(d) When is work by a minister not in the exercise of the ministry.

(1) Work performed by a duly ordained, commissioned, or licensed minister of a church which is not in the exercise of the ministry is not excluded from employment.

(2) Work performed by a duly ordained, commissioned, or licensed minister of a church as an employee of the United States, or a State, territory, or possession of the United States, or the District of Columbia, or a foreign government, or a political subdivision of any of these, is not in the exercise of the ministry, even though the work may involve the ministration of sacerdotal functions or the conduct of religious worship. For example, we consider service performed as a chaplain in the Armed Forces of the United States to be work performed by a commissioned officer and not by a minister in the exercise of the ministry. Also, service performed by an employee of a State as a chaplain in a State prison is considered to be performed by a civil servant of the State and not by a minister in the exercise of the ministry.

(e) Work in the exercise of duties required by a religious order. Work performed by a member of a religious order in the exercise of duties required by the order includes all duties required of the member of the order. The nature or extent of the work is immaterial so long as it is service which the member is directed or required to perform by the member's ecclesiastical superiors.

§ 404.1024 Election of coverage by religious orders.

A religious order whose members are required to take a vow of poverty, or any autonomous subdivision of that religious order, may elect to have social security coverage extended to the work performed by its members in the exercise of duties required by that order or subdivision. The rules on the election of coverage by these religious orders are described in 26 CFR 31.3121(r). The rules on determining the wages of members of religious orders for which an election of coverage has been made are described in § 404.1046.

§ 404.1025 Work for religious, charitable, educational, or certain other organizations exempt from income tax.

(a) After 1983. Work done after 1983 by an employee in the employ of a religious, charitable, educational, or other organization described in section 501(c)(3) of the Code which is exempt from income tax under section 501(a) of the Code is covered as employment unless the work is for a church or church-controlled organization that has elected to have services performed by its employees excluded (see § 404.1026). (See § 404.1059(b) for special wage rule.)

(b) Before 1984. Work described in paragraph (a) of this section which was done before 1984 is excluded from employment. However, the exclusion does not apply to work done during the period for which a form SS–15, Certificate Waiving Exemption From Taxes Under the Federal Insurance Contributions Act, was filed (or was deemed to have been filed) with the Internal Revenue Service.

[50 FR 36573, Sept. 9, 1985; 50 FR 38113, Sept. 20, 1985]

§ 404.1026 Work for a church or qualified church-controlled organization.

(a) General. If you work for a church or qualified church-controlled organization, as described in this section, your employer may elect to have your services excluded from employment. You would then be considered to be self-employed and special conditions would apply to you. See § 404.1068(f) for those special conditions. The employer's election of the exclusion must be made with the Internal Revenue Service in accordance with Internal Revenue Service procedures and must state that the church or church-controlled organization is opposed for religious reasons to the payment of Social Security employment taxes. The exclusion applies to current and future employees. If you work in an unrelated trade or business (within the meaning of section 513(a) of the Code) of the church or church-controlled organization, the exclusion does not apply to your services.

(b) What is a church. For purposes of this section the term church means a church, a convention or association of churches, or an elementary or secondary school which is controlled, operated, or principally supported by a church or by a convention or association of churches.

(c) What is a qualified church-controlled organization. For purposes of this section the term qualified church-controlled organization means any church-controlled organization exempt from income tax under section 501(c)(3) of the Code but does not include an organization which:

(1) Offers goods, services, or facilities for sale to the general public, other than on an incidental basis, or for other than a nominal charge which is substantially less than the cost of providing such goods, services, or facilities; and

(2) Normally receives more than 25 percent of its support from either governmental sources or receipts from admissions, sales of merchandise, performance of services or furnishing of facilities other than in an unrelated trade or business, or both.

[50 FR 36573, Sept. 9, 1985; 50 FR 38113, Sept. 20, 1985; 55 FR 7309, March 1, 1990]

§ 404.1027 Railroad work.

We exclude from employment any work you do as an employee or employee representative as described in the Railroad Retirement Tax Act. However, railroad compensation can be counted for social security purposes under the conditions described in subpart O of this part.

§ 404.1028 Student working for a school, college, or university.

(a) For purposes of this section, a school, college, or university has its usual accepted meaning. It does not, however, include any school, college, or university that is an instrumentality or integral part of a State or a political subdivision of a State for which work can only be covered by an agreement under section 218 of the Act. (See subpart M of this part.)

(b) If you are a student, any work you do as an employee of a school, college or university is excluded from employment, if you are enrolled in and regularly attending classes at that school, college, or university. The exclusion also applies to work you do for a private nonprofit auxiliary organization of the school, college, or university if it is organized and operated exclusively for the benefit of, to perform functions of, or to carry out the purposes of the school, college, or university. The organization must be operated, supervised, or controlled by, or in connection with, the school, college, or university.

(c) Whether you are a student for purposes of this section depends on your relationship with your employer. If your main purpose is pursuing a course of study rather than earning a livelihood, we consider you to be a student and your work is not considered employment.

§ 404.1029 Student nurses.

If you are a student nurse, your work for a hospital or nurses training school is excluded from employment if you are enrolled and regularly attending classes in a nurses training school which is chartered or approved under State law.

§ 404.1030 Delivery and distribution or sale of newspapers, shopping news, and magazines.

(a) If you are under age 18. Work you do before you reach age 18 delivering or distributing newspapers or shopping news is excluded from employment. This does not include delivery or distribution to some point for further delivery or distribution by someone else. If you make house-to-house delivery or sale of newspapers or shopping news (including handbills and similar kinds of advertising material), your work is not covered while you are under age 18. Related work such as assembling newspapers is also excluded.

(b) If you are any age. No matter how old you are, work you do in connection with and at the time of the sale of newspapers or magazines to consumers is excluded from employment if there is an arrangement under which—

(1) You are to sell the newspapers or magazines at a fixed price; and

(2) Your pay is the difference between the fixed selling price and the amount you are charged for the newspapers or magazines (whether or not you are guaranteed a minimum amount of compensation or receive credit for unsold newspapers or magazines).

(c) If you are age 18 or older. If you have attained age 18, you are self-employed if you work under the arrangement described in paragraph (b) of this section. See § 404.1068(b).

§ 404.1031 Fishing.

(a) If you work on a boat engaged in catching fish or other forms of aquatic animal life, your work is not employment if you have an arrangement with the owner or operator of the boat which provides for all of the following:

(1) You do not receive any cash pay (other than as provided in paragraph (a)(2) of this section).

(2) You receive a share of the catch or a share of the proceeds from the sale of the catch.

(3) The amount of your share depends on the size of the catch.

(4) The operating crew of the boat (or each boat from which you receive a share if the fishing operation involves more than one boat) is normally made up of fewer than 10 individuals.

(b) Work excluded from employment under this section is considered to be self-employment (§ 404.1068(e)).

§ 404.1032 Work for a foreign government.

If you work as an employee of a foreign government in any capacity, your work is excluded from employment. If you are a citizen of the United States and work in the United States as an employee of a foreign government, you are considered to be self-employed (§ 404.1068(d)).

§ 404.1033 Work for a wholly owned instrumentality of a foreign government.

(a) If you work as an employee of an instrumentality of a foreign government, your work is excluded from employment if—

(1) The instrumentality is wholly owned by the foreign government;

(2) Your work is similar to work performed in foreign countries by employees of the United States Government or its instrumentalities; and

(3) The Secretary of State certifies to the Secretary of the Treasury that the foreign government grants an equivalent exemption for services performed in the foreign country by employees of the United States Government or its instrumentalities.

(b) Your work will not be excluded under this section if any of the conditions in paragraph (a) of this section are not met.

(c) If you are a citizen of the United States and work in the United States as an employee of an instrumentality of a foreign government and the conditions in paragraph (a) of this section are met, you are considered to be self-employed (§ 404.1068(d)).

§ 404.1034 Work for an international organization.

(a) If you work as an employee of an international organization entitled to enjoy privileges, exemptions, and immunities as an international organization under the International Organizations Immunities Act (59 Stat. 669), your work is excluded from employment except as described in paragraphs (b) and (c) of this section. The organization must meet the following conditions:

(1) It must be a public international organization in which the United States participates under a treaty or authority of an act of Congress authorizing, or making an appropriation for, participation.

(2) It must be designated by executive order to be entitled to enjoy the privileges, exemptions, and immunities provided in the International Organizations Immunities Act.

(3) The designation must be in effect, and all conditions and limitations in the designation must be met.

(b) Your work will not be excluded under this section if any of the conditions in paragraph (a) of this section are not met.

(c) Your work performed after December 31, 1994 will not be excluded under this section if you perform service in the employ of an international organization pursuant to a transfer from a Federal agency under section 3582 of title 5 of the United States Code and

(1) Immediately before such transfer you performed service with a Federal agency which was covered as employment; and

(2) You would be entitled, upon separation from the international organization and proper application, to reemployment with the Federal agency under section 3582.

(d) If you are a citizen of the United States and work in the United States as an employee of an international organization that meets the conditions in paragraph (a) of this section and you are not subject to coverage based on paragraph (c) of this section, you are considered to be self-employed (§ 404.1068(d)).

[61 FR 38366, July 24, 1996]

§ 404.1035 Work for a communist organization.

If you work as an employee of an organization which is registered, or which is required by a final order of the Subversive Activities Control Board to register under the Internal Security Act of 1950 as a communist action, communist-front, or communist-infiltrated organization, your work is excluded from employment. The exclusion is effective with the calendar year in which the organization is registered or the final order is in effect.

§ 404.1036 Certain nonresident aliens.

(a) Foreign students.

(1) Foreign students (nonimmigrant aliens) may be temporarily in the United States under subparagraph (F) of section 101(a)(15) of the Immigration and Nationality Act to attend a school or other recognized place of study approved by the Attorney General. On-campus work or work under permission granted by the Immigration and Naturalization Service which is done by these students is excluded from employment. Other work done by these foreign students is not excluded from employment under this section.

(2) Foreign students (nonimmigrant aliens) may be temporarily in the United States under subparagraph (M) of section 101(a)(15) of the Immigration and Nationality Act to pursue a vocational or nonacademic technical education approved by the Attorney General. Work done by these students to carry out the purpose for which they were admitted is excluded from employment. Other work done by these foreign students is not excluded from employment under this section.

(b) Exchange visitors.

(1) Exchange visitors (nonimmigrant aliens) may be temporarily in the United States under subparagraph (J) of section 101(a)(15) of the Immigration and Nationality Act to participate in exchange visitor programs designated by the Director of the United States Information Agency. Work done by these exchange visitors to carry out the purpose for which they were admitted and for which permission has been granted by the sponsor, is excluded from employment. Other work done by these exchange visitors is not excluded from employment under this section.

(2) Exchange visitors (nonimmigrant aliens) may be temporarily in the United States under subparagraph (Q) of section 101(a)(15) of the Immigration and Nationality Act to participate in an international cultural exchange program approved by the Attorney General. Effective October 1, 1994, work done by these exchange visitors to carry out the purpose for which they were admitted is excluded from employment. Other work done by these exchange visitors is not excluded from employment under this section.

(c) Spouse and children. Work done by a foreign student's or exchange visitor's alien spouse or minor child who is also temporarily in the United States under subparagraph (F), (J), (M), or (Q) of section 101(a)(15) of the Immigration and Nationality Act is not excluded from employment under this section unless that spouse or child and the work that is done meets the conditions of paragraph (a) or (b) of this section.

[61 FR 38366, July 24, 1996]

§ 404.1037 Work on or in connection with a non-American vessel or aircraft.

If you work as an employee within the United States on or in connection with (as explained in § 404.1004(b)(8)) a vessel or aircraft that is not an American vessel (as defined in § 404.1004(b)(3)) or American aircraft (as defined in § 404.1004(b)(2)), your work is excluded from employment if—

(a) You are not a citizen of the United States or your employer is not an American employer (as defined in § 404.1004(b)(1)); and

(b) You are employed on and in connection with (as explained in § 404.1004(b)(7)) the vessel or aircraft when outside the United States.

§ 404.1038 Domestic employees under age 18.

Domestic services you perform in a private home of your employer are excluded from employment, regardless of the amount earned, in any year in which you are under age 18 if domestic service is not your principal occupation. The exclusion applies to the entire year if you are under age 18 in any part of the year. See § 404.1057.

[61 FR 38366, July 24, 1996]

EXEMPTION FROM SOCIAL SECURITY BY REASON OF RELIGIOUS BELIEF

§ 404.1039 Employers (including partnerships) and employees who are both members of certain religious groups opposed to insurance.

(a) You and your employer (or, if the employer is a partnership, each of its partners) may file applications with the Internal Revenue Service for exemption from your respective shares of the Federal Insurance Contributions Act taxes on your wages paid by that employer if you and your employer (or, if the employer is a partnership, each of its partners)—

(1) Are members of a recognized religious sect or division of the sect; and

(2) Adhere to the tenets or teachings of the sect or division of the sect and for that reason are conscientiously opposed to receiving benefits from any private or public insurance that—

(i) Makes payment in the event of death, disability, old-age, or retirement; or

(ii) Makes payment for the cost of, or provides services for, medical care including the benefits of any insurance system established by the Act.

(b) Both your application and your employer's application (or, if your employer is a partnership, each partner's application) must be filed with and approved by the Internal Revenue Service pursuant to section 3127 of the Internal Revenue Code. An application must contain or be accompanied by the applicant's waiver of all benefits and payments under title II and part A of title XVIII of the Act. See § 404.305 for the effect of the filing of the waiver and the granting of the exemption.

(c) Regardless of whether the applicant meets all these conditions, the application will not be approved unless we find that—

(1) The sect or division of the sect has established tenets or teachings which cause the applicant to be conscientiously opposed to the types of insurance benefits described in paragraph (a)(2) of this section; and

(2) For a substantial period of time it has been the practice for members of the sect or division of the sect to make provision for their dependent members that is reasonable in view of their general level of living; and

(3) The sect or division of the sect has been in existence continuously since December 31, 1950.

(d) An application for exemption will be approved by the Internal Revenue Service only if no benefit or payment under title II or part A of title XVIII of the Act became payable (or, but for section 203 or section 222(b) of the Act, would have become payable) to the applicant at or before the time of the filing of the application for exemption.

(e) The tax exemption ceases to be effective with respect to wages paid beginning with the calendar quarter in which either the employer (or if the employer is a partnership, any of its partners) or the employee involved does not meet the requirements of paragraph (a) of this section or the religious sect or division of the sect is found by us to no longer meet the requirements of paragraph (c) of this section. If the tax exemption ceases to be effective, the waiver of the right to receive Social Security and Medicare Part A benefits will also no longer be effective. Benefits may be payable based upon the wages of the individual, whose exempt status was terminated, for and after the calendar year following the calendar year in which the event occurred upon which the cessation of the exemption is based. Benefits may be payable based upon the self-employment income of the individual whose exempt status was terminated for and after the taxable year in which the event occurred upon which the cessation of the exemption is based.

[58 FR 64889, Dec. 10, 1993]

WAGES

§ 404.1041 Wages.

(a) The term wages means remuneration paid to you as an employee for employment unless specifically excluded. Wages are counted in determining your entitlement to retirement, survivors', and disability insurance benefits.

(b) If you are paid wages, it is not important what they are called. Salaries, fees, bonuses and commissions on sales or on insurance premiums are wages if they are remuneration paid for employment.

(c) The way in which you are paid is unimportant. Wages may be paid on the basis of piecework or a percentage of the profits. Wages may be paid on an hourly, daily, weekly, monthly, or yearly basis. (See § 404.1056 for special rules for agricultural labor.)

(d) Your wages can be in any form. You can be paid in cash or something other than cash, for example, in goods or clothing. (See paragraphs (e) and (f) of this section for kinds of employment where cash payments alone are considered wages and § 404.1043(b) concerning the value of meals and lodging as wages.) If your employer pays you cash for your meals and lodging on a regular basis as part of your employment, these payments may be considered wages. Payments other than cash may be counted as wages on the basis of the fair value of the items when paid.

(e) In certain kinds of employment, cash payments alone count as wages. These types of employment are agricultural labor, domestic services, and services not in the course of the employer's trade or business.

(f) To count as wages, payments for services performed by home workers who are employees as described in § 404.1008(d) must be in cash and must amount to $100 or more in a calendar year. Once this cash pay test is met, all remuneration paid, whether in cash or kind, is also wages.

[55 FR 7309, March 1, 1990]

§ 404.1042 Wages when paid and received.

(a) In general. Wages are received by an employee at the time they are paid by the employer to the employee. Wages are paid by an employer at the time that they are actually or constructively paid unless they are deemed to be paid later (as described in paragraph (c)(3) of this section).

(b) Constructive payment. Wages are constructively paid when they are credited to the account of, or set aside for, an employee so that they may be drawn upon by the employee at any time although not then actually received. To be a payment—

(1) The wages must be credited to or set aside for the employee and must be made available without restriction so that they may be drawn upon at any time; or

(2) The employer must intend to pay or to set aside or credit, and have the ability to pay wages when due to the employee, and failure of the employer to credit or set aside the wages is due to clerical error or mistake in the mechanics of payment, and because of

the clerical error or mistake the wages are not actually available at that time.

(c) Deemed payment.

(1) The first $100 of cash paid, either actually or constructively, by an employer to an employee in a calendar year is considered paid at the time that the amount of the cash payment totals $100 for the year in the case of pay for—

(i) Work not in the course of the employer's trade or business (non-business work);

(ii) Work by certain home workers; and

(iii) Work for an organization exempt from income tax under section 501 of the Code.

(2) We also apply this rule to domestic work in a private home of the employer, except see § 404.1057(a)(1) for the applicable dollar amount.

(3) Cash of less than $150 that an employer pays to an employee in a calendar year, either actually or constructively, for agricultural labor is considered paid at the earliest of—

(i) The time in the calendar year that the employee's pay totals $150; or

(ii) The 20th day of the calendar year on which the employee works for cash pay computed on a time basis.

(4) If an employer pays cash to an employee for two or more of the kinds of work referred to in paragraph (c)(1) of this section, we apply the provisions of this paragraph to the pay for each kind of work.

(d) Employee tax deductions. We consider employee tax deductions under section 3101 of the Code to be part of the employee's wages and consider them to be paid at the time of the deduction. We consider other deductions from wages to be wages paid at the time of the deduction. It is immaterial that the deductions are required or permitted by an act of Congress or the law of any State.

(e) Tips.

(1) Tips received by an employee in the course of employment, that are considered to be wages, are deemed to be paid at the time the employee reports the tips to the employer in a written statement as provided under section 6053(a) of the Code. Tips that are not reported are deemed to be paid to the employee at the time they are received by the employee.

(2) We consider tips to be received in the course of employment whether they are received by the employee from the employer or from another person. Only tips employees receive and keep for themselves are considered to be the employees' pay. If employees split tips, each employee who receives part of the tip receives tips in the course of employment.

(f) Payments under nonqualified deferred compensation plans. Amounts that an employee is entitled to receive under nonqualified deferred compensation plans (plans that do not qualify for special tax treatment under the Code) are creditable as wages for Social Security purposes at the later of the following times:

(1) When the services are performed; or

(2) When there is no longer a substantial risk of forfeiture (as defined in section 83 of the Code) of the employee's rights to the deferred compensation.

Any amounts taken into account as wages by this paragraph (and the income attributable thereto) will not thereafter be treated as wages for Social Security purposes.

[55 FR 7309, March 1, 1990; 61 FR 38366, July 24, 1996]

§ 404.1043 Facilities or privileges—meals and lodging.

(a) Excluding the value of employer provided facilities or privileges from employee gross income prior to January 1, 1985.

(1) Generally, the facilities or privileges that an employer furnished an employee prior to January 1, 1985 are not wages if the facilities or privileges—

(i) Were of relatively small value; and

(ii) Were offered or furnished by the employer merely as a means of promoting the health, good will, contentment, or efficiency of the employees.

(2) The term facilities or privileges for the period prior to January 1, 1985 is intended to include such items as entertainment, medical services, and so-called courtesy discounts on purchases.

(b) Meals and lodging. The value of the meals and lodging furnished to an employee by an employer for reasons of the employer's convenience is not wages if—

(1) The meals are provided at the employer's place of business; and

(2) The employee, in the case of lodging, is required to accept lodging on the employer's business premises as a condition of employment.

[52 FR 29662, Aug. 11, 1987]

§ 404.1044 Vacation pay.

We consider your salary while on vacation, or a vacation allowance paid by your employer, to be wages.

§ 404.1045 Employee expenses.

Amounts that your employer pays you specifically—either as advances or reimbursements—for traveling or for other ordinary and necessary expenses incurred, or reasonably expected to be incurred, in your employer's business are not wages. The employer must identify these travel and other expenses either by making a separate payment or by specifically stating the separate amounts if both wages and expense allowances are combined in a single payment.

§ 404.1046 Pay for work by certain members of religious orders.

(a) If you are a member of a religious order who has taken a vow of poverty (§ 404.1023), and the order has elected Social Security coverage under section 3121(r) of the Code, your wages are figured in a special way. Your wages, for Social Security purposes, are the fair market value of any board, lodging, clothing, and other items of value furnished to you by the order, or furnished to the order on your behalf by another organization or person under an agreement with the order. See paragraph (b) of this section if you perform services for a third party. The order must report at least $100 a month for each active member. If the fair market value of items furnished to all members of a religious order does not vary significantly, the order may consider all members to have a uniform wage.

(b) If you perform services for a third party, the following rules apply:

(1) If you perform services for another agency of the supervising church or an associated institution, any amounts paid based on such services, whether paid directly to you or to the order, do not count on wages. Only wages figured under (a) above, are counted.

(2) If you perform services in a secular setting as an employee of a third party not affiliated or associated with the supervising church or an associated institution, any amounts paid based on such services, whether paid directly to you or to the order, count as wages paid to you by the third party. These wages are in addition to any wages counted under paragraph (a) of this section.

[55 FR 7309, March 1, 1990; 55 FR 17530, April 25, 1990]

§ 404.1047 Annual wage limitation.

Payments made by an employer to you as an employee in a calendar year that are more than the annual wage limitation are not wages. The annual wage limitation is:

Calendar year	Wage limitation
1951-54	$ 3,600
1955-58	4,200
1959-65	4,800
1966-67	6,600
1968-71	7,800
1972	9,000
1973	10,800
1974	13,200
1975	14,100
1976	15,300
1977	16,500
1978	17,700
1979	22,900
1980	25,900
1981	29,700
1982	32,400
1983	35,700
1984	37,800
1985	39,600
1986	42,000
1987	43,800
1988	45,000
1989	48,000
1990	51,300
1991	53,400
1992	55,500

[52 FR 8249, March 17, 1987; 57 FR 44098, Sept. 24, 1992]

§ 404.1048 Contribution and benefit base after 1992.

(a) General. The contribution and benefit base after 1992 is figured under the formula described in paragraph (b) of this section in any calendar year in which there is an automatic cost-of-living increase in old-age, survivors, and disability insurance benefits. For purposes of this section, the calendar year in which the contribution and benefit base is figured is called the determination year. The base figured in the determination year applies to wages paid after (and taxable years beginning after) the determination year.

(b) Formula for figuring the contribution and benefit base. For wages paid after (and taxable years beginning after) the determination year, the contribution and benefit base is the larger of—

(1) The contribution and benefit base in effect for the determination year; or

(2) The amount determined by—

(i) Multiplying the contribution and benefit base in effect for the determination year by the ratio of—

(A) The average of the total wages (as described in paragraph (c) of this section) reported to the Secretary of the Treasury for the calendar year before the determination year to;

(B) The average of the total wages reported to the Secretary of the Treasury for the calendar year before the most recent calendar year in which an increase in the contribution and benefit base was enacted or a determination under this section resulting in an increase of the base was made; and

(ii) Rounding the result of the multiplication, if not a multiple of $300, to—

(A) The nearest multiple of $300; or

(B) The next higher multiple of $300 if the result is a multiple of $150.

(c) Average of the total wages. The average of the total wages means the amount equal to all remuneration reported as wages on Form W–2 to the Internal Revenue Service for all employees for income tax purposes plus contributions to certain deferred compensation plans described in section 209(k) of the Social Security Act (also reported on Form W–2), divided by the number of wage earners. If both distributions from and contributions to any such deferred compensation plan are reported on Form W–2, we will include only the contributions in the calculation of the average of the total wages. The reported remuneration and deferred compensation contributions include earnings from work not covered under social security and earnings from work covered under social security that are more than the annual wage limitation described in § 404.1047.

[55 FR 7309, March 1, 1990; 57 FR 1382, Jan. 14, 1992]

§ 404.1049 Payments under an employer plan or system.

(a) Payments to, or on behalf of, you or any of your dependents under your employer's plan or system are excluded from wages if made because of your or your dependents'—

(1) Medical or hospitalization expenses connected with sickness or accident disability; or

(2) Death, except that the exclusion does not apply to payments for group-term life insurance to the extent that the payments are includible in the gross income of the employee under the Internal Revenue Code of 1986, effective with respect to group-term life insurance coverage in effect after 1987 for employees whose employment, for the employer (or successor of that employer) providing the insurance coverage, does not end prior to 1989. Such payments are wages, however, if they are for coverage for an employee who was separated from employment prior to January 1, 1989, if the payments are for any period for which the employee is reemployed by the employer (or successor of that employer) after the date of separation.

(b) Payments to you or your dependents under your employer's plan at or after the termination of your employment relationship because of your death or retirement for disability are excluded from wages.

(c) Payments made after 1983 to you or your dependents under your employer's plan at or after the termination of your employment relationship because of retirement after reaching an age specified in the plan or in a pension plan of the employer are not excluded from wages unless—

(1) The payments are to or from a trust or annuity plan of your employer as described in § 404.1052; or

(2) An agreement to retire was in effect on March 24, 1983, between you and your employer and the payments made after 1983 under a nonqualified deferred compensation plan (see § 404.1042(f)) are based on services performed for your employer before 1984.

(d) The plan or system established by the employer must provide for the employees generally or for a class or classes of employees. The plan or system may also provide for these employees' dependents. Payments under a plan or system established only for your dependents are not excluded from wages. The plan or system established by the employer can provide for payments on account of one or more of the items in paragraphs (a) and (b) of this section.

(e) For purposes of this section, your dependents include your husband or wife, children, and any other members of your immediate family.

(f) It does not make any difference that the benefit payments are considered in arriving at the amount of your pay or are required by the employment agreement.

[50 FR 1832, Jan. 14, 1985; 55 FR 7310, March 1, 1990; 55 FR 17530, April 25, 1990]

§ 404.1050 Retirement payments.

Payments made after 1983 to you (including any amount paid by an employer for insurance or annuities) on account of your retirement for age are not excluded from wages unless—

(a) The payments are to or from a trust or annuity plan of your employer as described in § 404.1052; or

(b) The payments satisfy the requirements described in § 404.1049(c)(2).

[55 FR 7310, March 1, 1990]

§ 404.1051 Payments on account of sickness or accident disability, or related medical or hospitalization expenses.

(a) We do not include as wages any payment that an employer makes to you, or on your behalf, on account of your sickness or accident disability, or related medical or hospitalization expenses, if the payment is made more than 6 consecutive calendar months following the last calendar month in which you worked for that employer. Payments made during the 6 consecutive months are included as wages.

(b) The exclusion in paragraph (a) of this section also applies to any such payment made by a third party (such as an insurance company). However, if you contributed to your employer's sick pay plan, that portion of the third party payments attributable to your contribution is not wages.

(c) Payments of medical or hospitalization expenses connected with sickness or accident disability are excluded from wages beginning with the first payment only if made under a plan or system of your employer as explained in § 404.1049(a)(1).

(d) Payments under a worker's compensation law are not wages.

[50 FR 1832, Jan. 14, 1985; 55 FR 7310, March 1, 1990]

§ 404.1051A [Reserved]

[50 FR 1832, Jan. 14, 1985; 55 FR 7310, March 1, 1990]

§ 404.1052 Payments from or to certain tax-exempt trusts or payments under or into certain annuity plans.

(a) We do not include as wages any payment made—

(1) Into a tax-exempt trust or annuity plan by your employer on behalf of you or your beneficiary; or

(2) From a tax-exempt trust or under an annuity plan to, or on behalf of, you or your beneficiary.

(b) The trust must be exempt from tax under sections 401 and 501(a) of the Code, and the annuity plan must be a plan described in section 403(a) of the Code when payment is made.

(c) The exclusion does not apply to payments to an employee of the trust for work done as an employee of the trust.

[55 FR 7310, March 1, 1990]

§ 404.1053 "Qualified benefits" under a cafeteria plan.

We do not include as wages any qualified benefits under a cafeteria plan as described in section 125 of the Code if such payment would not be treated as wages without regard to such plan and it is reasonable to believe that (if section 125 applied for purposes of this section) section 125 would not treat any wages as constructively received. This includes any qualified benefit made to you, or on your behalf, pursuant to a salary reduction agreement between you and your employer. The Internal Revenue Service decides whether any plan is a cafeteria plan under section 125 of the Code and whether any benefit under the plan is a qualified benefit.

[55 FR 7310, March 1, 1990]

§ 404.1054 Payments by an employer of employee's tax or employee's contribution under State law.

(a) We exclude as wages any payment by an employer (described in paragraph (b) of this section) that is not deducted from the employee's salary (or for which reimbursement is not made by the employee) of either—

(1) The tax imposed by section 3101 of the Code (employee's share of Social Security tax); or

(2) Any payment required from an employee under a State unemployment compensation law.

(b) The payments described in paragraph (a) of this section are not included as wages only if they are made by an employer on behalf of an employee employed in—

(1) Domestic service in the private home of the employer; or

(2) Agricultural labor.

[52 FR 29662, Aug. 11, 1987; 55 FR 7310, March 1, 1990]

§ 404.1055 Payments for agricultural labor.

(a) When cash payments are not wages. We do not include as wages your cash payments in a calendar year after 1987 from an employer for agricultural labor (see § 404.1056) if your employer's total expenditures for agricultural labor are less than $2500 in that year and your employer paid you less than $150 cash remuneration in that year for your agricultural labor.

(b) Exclusions for noncash payments and payments for seasonal agricultural labor.

(1) Noncash payments for agricultural labor are not wages.

(2) Your cash payments in a calendar year from an employer for agricultural labor are not wages, irrespective of your employer's total annual expenditures for agricultural labor, if you are a hand harvest laborer (i.e., seasonal agricultural labor), and—

(i) Your employer paid you less than $150 in that year;

(ii) You are paid on a piece rate basis in an operation which has been, and is customarily and generally recognized in the region of employment as paying on a piece rate basis;

(iii) You commute daily from your permanent residence to the farm on which you are so employed; and,

(iv) You were employed in agriculture less than 13 weeks during the previous calendar year.

Example: In 1988, A (not a hand harvest laborer) performs agricultural labor for X for cash pay of $144 in the year. X's total agricultural labor expenditures for 1988 are $2,450. Neither the $150 cash-pay test nor the $2,500 expenditures test is met. Therefore, X's payments to A are not wages.

(c) When cash-pay is creditable as wages.

(1) If you receive cash pay from an employer for services which are agricultural labor and for services which are not agricultural labor, we count only the amounts paid for agricultural labor in determining whether cash payments equal or exceed $150. If the amounts paid are less than $150, we count only those amounts paid for agricultural labor in determining if the $2500 expenditure test is met.

Example: Employer X operates a store and also operates a farm. Employee A, who regularly works in the store, works on X's farm when additional help is required for the farm activities. In calendar year 1988, X pays A $140 cash for agricultural labor performed in that year, and $2,260 for work in connection with the operation of the store. Additionally, X's total expenditures for agricultural labor in 1988 were $2,010. Since the cash payments by X to A in the calendar year 1988 for agricultural labor are less than $150, and total agricultural labor expenditures were under $2,500, the $140 paid by X to A for agricultural labor is not wages. The $2,260 paid for work in the store is wages.

(2) The amount of cash pay for agricultural labor that is creditable to an individual is based on cash paid in a calendar year rather than on amounts earned during a calendar year.

(3) If you receive cash pay for agricultural labor in any one calendar year from more than one employer, we apply the $150 cash-pay test and $2,500 total expenditures test to each employer.

(d) Application of the $150 cash-pay and 20–day tests prior to 1988.

(1) For the time period prior to 1988, we apply either the $150 a year cash-pay test or the 20–day test. Cash payments are wages if you receive $150 or more from an employer for agricultural labor or under the 20–day test if you perform agricultural labor for which cash pay is computed on a time basis on 20 or more days during a calendar year. For purposes of the 20–day test, the amount of the cash pay is immaterial, and it is immaterial whether you also receive payments other than cash or payments that are not computed on a time basis. If cash paid to you for agricultural labor is computed on a time basis, the payments are not wages unless they are paid in a calendar year in which either the 20–day test or the $150 cash-pay test is met.

(2) [Reserved]

[55 FR 7310, March 1, 1990; 57 FR 59914, Dec. 17, 1992; 61 FR 38366, July 24, 1996; 70 FR 41955, July 21, 2005]

§ 404.1056 Explanation of agricultural labor.

(a) What is agricultural labor.

(1) If you work on a farm as an employee of any person, you are doing agricultural labor if your work has to do with—

(i) Cultivating the soil;

(ii) Raising, shearing, feeding, caring for, training or managing livestock, bees, poultry, fur-bearing animals or wildlife; or

(iii) Raising or harvesting any other agricultural or horticultural commodity.

(2) If you work on a farm as an employee of any person in connection with the production or harvesting of maple sap, the raising or harvesting of mushrooms, or the hatching of poultry, you are doing agricultural labor. If you work in the processing of maple sap into maple syrup or maple sugar you are not doing agricultural labor even though you work on a farm. Work in a mushroom cave or poultry hatchery is agricultural labor only if the cave or hatchery is operated as part of a farm.

(3) If you work as an employee of the owner, tenant, or other operator of a farm, you are doing agricultural labor if most of your work is done on a farm and is involved with—

(i) The operation, management, conservation, improvement, or maintenance of the farm or its tools or equipment (this may include work by carpenters, painters, mechanics, farm supervisors, irrigation engineers, bookkeepers, and other skilled or semiskilled workers); or

(ii) Salvaging timber or clearing the land of brush and other debris left by a hurricane.

(4) You are doing agricultural labor no matter for whom or where you work, if your work involves—

(i) Cotton ginning;

(ii) Operating or maintaining ditches, canals, reservoirs, or waterways, if they are used only for supplying and storing water for farm purposes and are not owned or operated for profit; or

(iii) Producing or harvesting crude gum (oleoresin) from living trees or processing the crude gum into gum spirits of turpentine and gum resin (if the processing is done by the original producer).

(5) Your work as an employee in the handling, planting, drying, packing, packaging, processing, freezing, grading, storing, or delivering to storage, to a market or to a carrier for transportation to market, of any agricultural or horticultural commodity is agricultural labor if—

(i) You work for a farm operator or a group of farm operators (other than a cooperative organization);

(ii) Your work involves the commodity in its raw or unmanufactured state; and

(iii) The operator produced most of the commodity you work with during the period for which you are paid, or if you work for a group of operators, all of the commodity you work with during the pay period is produced by that group.

(6) If you do nonbusiness work, it is agricultural labor if you do the work on a farm operated for a profit. A farm is not operated for profit if the employer primarily uses it as a residence or for personal or family recreation or pleasure. (See § 404.1058(a) for an explanation of nonbusiness work.)

(7) The term farm operator means an owner, tenant, or other person, in possession of and operating a farm.

(8) Work is not agricultural labor if it is done in the employ of a cooperative organization, which includes corporations, joint-stock companies, and associations treated as corporations under the Code. Any unincorporated group of operators is considered to be a cooperative organization if more than 20 operators are in the group at any time during the calendar year in which the work is done.

(9) Processing work which changes the commodity from its raw or natural state is not agricultural labor. An example of this is the extraction of juices from fruits or vegetables. However, work in the cutting and drying of fruits or vegetables does not change the commodity from its raw or natural state and can be agricultural labor.

(10) The term commodity means a single agricultural or horticultural product. For example, all apples are a commodity, while apples and oranges are two commodities.

(11) Work connected with the commercial canning or freezing of a commodity is not agricultural labor nor is work done after the delivery of the commodity to a terminal market for distribution for consumption.

(b) What is a farm. For purposes of social security coverage, farm includes a stock, dairy, poultry, fruit, fur-bearing animal, or truck farm, plantation, ranch, nursery, range or orchard. A farm also includes a greenhouse or other similar structure used mostly for raising agricultural or horticultural products. A greenhouse or other similar structure used mostly for other purposes such as display, storage, making wreaths and bouquets is not a farm.

[55 FR 7310, March 1, 1990; 61 FR 38367, July 24, 1996; 70 FR 41955, July 21, 2005]

§ 404.1057 Domestic service in the employer's home.

(a) Payments for domestic service—

(1) The applicable dollar threshold. We do not include as wages cash payments that an employer makes to you in any calendar year for domestic service in the employer's private home if the cash pay in that calendar year is less than the applicable dollar threshold. The threshold per employer is $1000 in calendar year 1995. In calendar years after 1995, this amount will be subject to adjustment in $100 increments based on the formula in section 215(a)(1)(B)(i) of the Act to reflect changes in wages in the economy. Non-cash payments for domestic service are not counted as wages.

(2) How evaluation is made. We apply the applicable dollar threshold described in paragraph (a)(1) of this section based on when the payments are made to you rather than when the pay is earned. To count toward the applicable dollar threshold, payment must be made to you in cash (including checks or other forms of money). We apply the applicable dollar threshold only to services performed as a domestic employee. If an employer pays you for performing other work, the cash pay for the nondomestic work does not count toward the applicable dollar threshold domestic service pay required for the remuneration to count as wages.

(3) More than one domestic employer. The applicable dollar threshold as explained in paragraph (a)(1) of this section applies to each employer when you perform domestic services for more than one employer in a calendar year. The wages paid by more than one employer for domestic services may not be combined to decide whether you have been paid the applicable dollar threshold or more in a calendar year. The standard applies to each employee when an employer has two or more domestic employees during a calendar year.

(4) Rounding dollar amounts for reporting. For social security purposes, an employer has an option in the way he or she reports cash wages paid for domestic service in his or her private home. The employer may report the actual wages paid or may round the wages to the nearest dollar. For purposes of rounding to the nearest dollar the cents are disregarded unless it amounts to one-half dollar or more, in which case it will be raised to $1. If an employer uses this method to report a cash payment to you for domestic services in his or her private home in a calendar year, he or she must use the same method to report payments to other employees in that year for similar services.

(b) What is domestic service. Domestic service is work of a household nature done by you in or about a private home of the employer. A private home is a fixed place of residence of a person or family. A separate dwelling unit maintained by a person in an apartment house, hotel, or other similar establishment may be a private home. If a house is used primarily for supplying board or lodging to the public as a business enterprise, it is not a private home. In general, services of a household nature in or about a private home include services performed by cooks, waiters, butlers, housekeepers, governesses, maids, valets, baby sitters, janitors, laundresses, furnacemen, caretakers, handymen, gardeners, footmen, grooms, and chauffeurs of automobiles for family use. Pay for these services does not come under this provision unless the services are performed in or about a private home of the employer. Pay for services not of a household nature, such as services performed as a private secretary, tutor, or librarian, even though performed in the employer's home, does not come under this provision.

[45 FR 20075, March 27, 1980; 45 FR 25060, April 14, 1980; 55 FR 7310, March 1, 1990; 61 FR 38367, July 24, 1996]

§ 404.1058 Special situations.

(a) Payments for service not in course of employer's trade or business (nonbusiness work) and payments to certain home workers—

(1) The $100 standard. We do not include as wages cash pay of less than $100 paid to you in a calendar year by an employer for services not in the course of the employer's trade or business (nonbusiness work) and for services as a home worker as described in § 404.1008(d).

(2) How evaluation is made.

(i) We apply the $100 standard for a calendar year based on when the payments are made to you rather than when the pay is earned. To count toward the $100 amount, payment must be in cash (including checks or other forms of money). The $100 standard applies to each employer when you perform services not in the course of the employer's trade or business or as a homeworker for two or more employers.

(ii) If the employer has two or more employees, the standard applies to each employee. In applying the $100 standard, we disregard cash payments for any other type of services you perform for the employer.

(iii) The noncash payments an employer pays you for services not in the course of the employer's trade or business are not wages even if the employer has paid you cash wages of $100 or more in the calendar year for services of that type.

(iv) Amounts paid to you as a home worker as described in § 404.1008(d) are not wages unless you are paid $100 or more in cash in a calendar year. If you meet this test, any noncash payments you receive for your services also count as wages.

(v) Amounts paid to you as a home worker in a common-law employment relationship (see § 404.1007) count as wages regardless of amount or whether paid in cash or kind.

(3) Definitions. The term services not in the course of the employer's trade or business (also called non-business work) means services that do not promote or advance the trade or business of the employer. Services performed for a corporation do not come within this definition. A homeworker is described in § 404.1008(c).

(b) Nonprofit, income-tax exempt organizations—

(1) The $100 standard. We do not include as wages payments of less than $100 in a calendar year made by an employer that is an organization exempt from income tax under section 501 of the Code.

(2) How evaluation is made. We apply the $100 standard for a calendar year based on when the payments are made to you rather than when the pay is earned. To figure the $100 amount, both cash and noncash payments are counted. The $100 standard applies to each employer where you render services for two or more nonprofit, income-tax exempt organizations during a calendar year. The $100 standard also applies to each of you where a nonprofit, income-tax exempt organization has two or more employees. In applying the standard, the tax-exempt status of the employer and not the nature or place of your services is controlling.

(c) Payments to members of the uniformed services—

(1) The standard. We include as the wages of a member of the uniformed services—

(i) Basic pay, as explained in paragraph (c)(3) of this section, for performing the services described in paragraph (a)(1) of § 404.1019 of this subpart; or

(ii) Compensation, as explained in paragraph (c)(4) of this section, for performing the services described in paragraph (a)(2) of § 404.1019 of this subpart.

(2) Wages deemed paid. These following provisions apply to members of the uniformed services who perform services as described in paragraph (a)(1) of § 404.1019 of this subpart.

(i) After 1977, a member of the uniformed services is considered to have been paid additional wages of $100 for each $300 of basic pay paid to the individual in a calendar year. The amount of additional wages deemed paid cannot be more than $1,200 for any calendar year. No wages may be deemed paid for units of basic pay which are less than $300.

(ii) Before 1978, a member of the uniformed services is considered to have been paid additional wages of $300 for each calendar quarter after 1956 in which the individual is paid any amount of basic pay.

(3) Basic pay. Basic pay means the monthly pay prescribed by 37 U.S.C. 203 (Pay and Allowances for the Uniformed Services) for a member of the uniformed services on active duty or on active duty for training.

(4) Compensation. "Compensation" refers to the remuneration received for services as a member of a uniformed service, based on regulations issued by the Secretary concerned (as defined in 37 U.S.C. 101(5) under 37 U.S.C. 206(a), where such member is not entitled to the basic pay (as defined by paragraph (3) of this section).

(d) Payments to volunteers and volunteer leaders in the Peace Corps. If you are a volunteer or volunteer leader under the provisions of the Peace Corps Act (22 U.S.C. 2501ff), payments for your services are wages with the exception of amounts in excess of the amounts certified as payable under section 5(c) or 6(1) of the Peace Corps Act. Amounts certified under those sections are considered to have been paid to the individual at the time the service is performed. See § 404.1018(e) on coverage of these services.

(e) Moving expenses. We do not include as wages amounts paid to, or on behalf of, an employee for moving expenses if it is reasonable to believe that a similar deduction is allowable under section 217 of the Code.

(f) Payments by employer to survivor or estate of former employee. We do not include as wages any payment by an employer to a survivor or the estate of a former employee after the calendar year in which the employee died.

(g) Payments to an employee who is entitled to disability insurance benefits. We do not include as wages any payments made by an employer to an employee if at the time such payment is made—

(1) The employee is entitled to disability insurance benefits under the Act;

(2) The employee's entitlement to such benefits began before the calendar year in which the employer's payment is made; and

(3) The employee performed no work for the employer in the period in which the payments were paid by such employer (regardless of whether the employee worked in the period the payments were earned).

(h) Tips.

(1) We include as wages tips received by an employee if—

(i) The tips are paid in cash; and

(ii) The tips amount to $20 or more and are received in the course of employment by an employee in a calendar month.

(2) Cash tips include checks and other forms of money. Tips received in a form other than cash, such as passes, tickets, or other goods are not wages. If an employee works for more than one employer in a calendar month, we apply the $20 tip test to work done for each employer.

(i) Payments by employer under group legal services plan. We do not include as wages any contribution, payment, or service, provided by an employer under a qualified group legal services plan which is excludable from the gross income of an employee, or the employee's spouse or dependents, under section 120 of the Code.

[52 FR 29662, Aug. 11, 1987; 55 FR 7310, March 1, 1990; 57 FR 59914, Dec. 17, 1992]

§ 404.1059 Deemed wages for certain individuals interned during World War II.

(a) In general. Persons who were interned during any period of time from December 7, 1941, through December 31, 1946, by the United States Government at a place operated by the Government within the United States for the internment of United States citizens of Japanese ancestry are deemed to have been paid wages (in addition to wages actually paid) as provided in paragraph (c) of this section during any period after attaining age 18 while interned. This provision is effective for determining entitlement to, and the amount of, any monthly benefit for months after December 1972, for determining entitlement to, and the amount of, any lump-sum death payment in the case of a death after December 1972, and for establishing a period of disability.

(b) Information needed to process deemed wages. Unless we have already made a determination on deemed wages for a period of internment of an individual, any person applying for a monthly benefit, a recalculation of benefits by reason of this section, or a lump-sum death payment, must submit certain information before the benefit or payment may be computed on the basis of deemed wages. This information is—

(1) The place where the individual worked before internment;

(2) The highest hourly wage before internment;

(3) The place and date of internment;

(4) Date of birth (if not previously furnished);

(5) Whether or not another Federal benefit is being received based wholly or in part upon the period of internment; and

(6) In the case of a woman, her maiden name.

(c) Amount of deemed wages. The amount of wages which may be deemed is determined as follows:

(1) Employed prior to internment. If the individual was employed before being interned, the deemed wages are the greater of—

(i) The highest actual hourly rate of pay received for any employment before internment, multiplied by 40 for each full week during the period of internment; or

(ii) The Federal minimum hourly rate in effect for the period of internment, multiplied by 40 for each full week during that period.

(2) Self-employed or not employed prior to internment. If the individual was self-employed or was not employed before the period of internment, the deemed wages are the Federal minimum hourly rate in effect for that period, multiplied by 40 for each full week during the period.

(d) When wages are not deemed. Wages are not deemed under this section—

(1) For any period before the quarter in which the individual attained age 18; or

(2) If a larger benefit is payable without the deemed wages; or

(3) If a benefit based in whole or in part upon internment is determined by any agency of the United States to be payable under any other law of the United States or under a system set up by that agency. However, this exception does not apply in cases where the failure to receive deemed wages reduces the primary insurance amount by 50 cents or less.

(e) Certification of internment. The certification concerning the internment is made by the Archivist of the United States or his or her representative. After the internment has been verified, wages are deemed to have been paid to the internee.

[52 FR 29662, Aug. 11, 1987; 55 FR 7310, March 1, 1990]

§ 404.1060 [Reserved]

[55 FR 7310, March 1, 1990]

SELF-EMPLOYMENT

§ 404.1065 Self-employment coverage.

For an individual to have self-employment coverage under social security, the individual must be engaged in a trade or business and have net earnings from self-employment that can be counted as self-employment income for social security purposes. The rules explaining whether you are engaged in a trade or business are in §§ 404.1066 through 404.1077. What are net earnings from self-employment is discussed in §§ 404.1080 through 404.1095. Section 404.1096 describes the net earnings from self-employment that are counted as self-employment income for social security purposes. See § 404.1913 for the effect of a totalization agreement on self-employment coverage. An agreement may exempt an activity from coverage as well as extend coverage to an activity.

[50 FR 36574, Sept. 9, 1985; 50 FR 38113, Sept. 20, 1985]

§ 404.1066 Trade or business in general.

For you to be covered as a self-employed person for social security purposes, you must be engaged in a trade or business. You can carry on a trade or business as an individual or as a member of a partnership. With some exceptions, the term trade or business has the same meaning as it does when used in section 162 of the Code.

§ 404.1068 Employees who are considered self-employed.

(a) General. Although we generally exclude services performed by employees from the definition of trade or business, certain types of services are considered a trade or business even though performed by employees. If you perform any of the services described in paragraphs (b) through (f) of this section, you are self-employed for social security purposes. Certain other services described in § 404.1071 (relating to ministers and members of religious orders) and § 404.1073 (relating to certain public officers) may be considered a trade or business even though performed by employees.

(b) Newspaper vendors. If you have attained age 18 and perform services as a newspaper vendor that are described in § 404.1030(b), you are engaged in a trade or business.

(c) Sharefarmers. If you perform services as a sharefarmer that are described in § 404.1017, you are engaged in a trade or business.

(d) Employees of a foreign government, an instrumentality wholly owned by a foreign government, or an international organization. If you are a United States citizen and perform the services that are described in § 404.1032, § 404.1033(a), or § 404.1034(a), you are engaged in a trade or business if the services are performed in the United States and are not covered as employment based upon § 404.1034(c).

(e) Certain fishermen. If you perform services as a fisherman that are described in § 404.1031, you are engaged in a trade or business.

(f) Employees of a church or church-controlled organization that has elected to exclude employees from coverage as employment. If you perform services that are excluded from employment as described in § 404.1026, you are engaged in a trade or business. Special rules apply to your earnings from those services which are known as church employee income. If you are paid $100 or more in a taxable year by an employer who has elected to have its employees excluded, those earnings are self-employment income (see § 404.1096(c)(1)). In figuring your church employee income you may not reduce that income by any deductions attributable to your work. Your church employee income and deductions may not be taken into account in determining the amount of other net earnings from self-employment. Effective for taxable years beginning on or after January 1, 1990, your church employee income is exempt from self-employment tax under the conditions set forth for members of certain religious groups (see § 404.1075).

[50 FR 36574, Sept. 9, 1985; 50 FR 38113, Sept. 20, 1985; 55 FR 7311, March 1, 1990; 58 FR 64889, Dec. 10, 1993; 61 FR 38367, July 24, 1996]

§ 404.1069 Real estate agents and direct sellers.

(a) Trade or business. If you perform services after 1982 as a qualified real estate agent or as a direct seller, as defined in section 3508 of the Code, you are considered to be engaging in a trade or business.

(b) Who is a qualified real estate agent. You are a qualified real estate agent as defined in section 3508 of the Code if you are a salesperson and—

(1) You are a licensed real estate agent;

(2) Substantially all of the earnings (whether or not paid in cash) for the services you perform as a real estate agent are directly related to sales or other output (including the performance of services) rather than to the number of hours worked; and

(3) Your services are performed under a written contract between yourself and the person for whom the services are performed which provides you will not be treated as an employee with respect to these services for Federal tax purposes.

(c) Who is a direct seller. You are a direct seller as defined in section 3508 of the Code if—

(1) You are engaged in the trade or business of selling (or soliciting the sale of) consumer products—

(i) To any buyer on a buy-sell basis, a deposit-commission basis, or any similar basis which the Secretary of the Treasury prescribes by regulations, for resale (by the buyer or any other person) in the home or in other than a permanent retail establishment; or

(ii) In the home or in other than a permanent retail establishment; and

(2) Substantially all of your earnings (whether or not paid in cash) for the performance of these services are directly related to sales or other output (including the performance of services) rather than to the number of hours worked; and

(3) Your services are performed under a written contract between yourself and the person for whom the services are performed which provides you will not be treated as an employee with respect to these services for Federal tax purposes.

[48 FR 40515, Sept. 8, 1983]

§ 404.1070 Christian Science practitioners.

If you are a Christian Science practitioner, the services you perform in the exercise of your profession are a trade or business unless you were granted an exemption from coverage under section 1402(e) of the Code, and you did not revoke such exemption in accordance with section 1704(b) of the Tax Reform Act of 1986. An exemption cannot be granted if you filed a valid waiver certificate under the provisions that apply to taxable years ending before 1968.

[55 FR 7311, March 1, 1990]

§ 404.1071 Ministers and members of religious orders.

(a) If you are a duly ordained, commissioned, or licensed minister of a church, or a member of a religious order who has not taken a vow of poverty, the services you perform in the exercise of your ministry or in the exercise of duties required by the order (§ 404.1023(c) and (e)) are a trade or business unless you filed for and were granted an exemption from coverage under section 1402(e) of the Code, and you did not revoke such exemption in accordance with the Social Security Amendments of 1977, section 1704(b) of the Tax Reform Act of 1986, or section 403 of the Ticket to Work and Work Incentives Improvement Act of 1999. An exemption cannot be granted if you filed a valid waiver certificate under the provisions of section 1402(e) that apply to taxable years ending before 1968.

(b) If you are a member of a religious order and have taken a vow of poverty, the services you perform in the exercise of your duties required by the order may be covered as employment. (See § 404.1023 (a) and (e)).

[55 FR 7311, March 1, 1990; 69 FR 51556, Aug. 20, 2004]

§ 404.1073 Public office.

(a) General. The performance of the functions of a public office is not a trade or business except under the circumstances explained in paragraph (b) of this section. If you are an officer of a State or political subdivision, you are considered as employee of the State or political subdivision.

(b) State and local governmental employees paid by fees—

(1) Voluntary coverage under section 218 of the Act. The services of employees of States and political subdivisions, including those in positions paid solely on a fee-basis, may be covered as employment by a Federal–State agreement under section 218 of the Act (see subpart M of this part). States, when entering into these agreements, have the option of excluding under the agreement coverage of services in positions paid solely by fees. If you occupy a position paid solely on a fee-basis and the State has not covered your services under section 218 of the Act, you are considered to be engaged in a trade or business.

(2) Mandatory old-age, survivors, disability, and hospital insurance coverage. Beginning with services performed after July 1, 1991, Social Security coverage (old-age, survivors, disability, and hospital insurance) is mandatory, with certain exceptions, for services performed by employees of a State, a political subdivision of a State, or of a wholly owned instrumentality of one or more of the foregoing, if the employees are not members of a retirement system of the State, political subdivision, or instrumentality. Among the exclusions from such mandatory coverage is service performed by an employee in a position compensated solely on a fee-basis which is treated pursuant to section 211(c)(2)(E) of the Act as a trade or business for purposes of inclusion of such fees in the net earnings from self-employment.

(3) If you are a notary public, you are not a public officer even though you perform a public function. Your services as a notary public are not covered for social security purposes.

[57 FR 59910, Dec. 17, 1992]

§ 404.1074 Farm crew leader who is self-employed.

If you are a farm crew leader and are deemed the employer of the workers as described in § 404.1010, we consider you to be engaged in a trade or business. This includes services performed in furnishing workers to perform agricultural labor for others, as well as services performed as a member of the crew.

§ 404.1075 Members of certain religious groups opposed to insurance.

(a) You may file an application with the Internal Revenue Service for exemption from social security self-employment tax if—

(1) You are a member of a recognized religious sect or division of the sect; and

(2) You adhere to the tenets or teachings of the sect or division of the sect and for this reason are conscientiously opposed to receiving benefits from any private or public insurance that—

(i) Makes payments in the event of death, disability, old age, or retirement; or

(ii) Makes payments toward the cost of, or provides services for, medical care (including the benefits of any insurance system established by the Act).

(b) Your application must be filed under the rules described in 26 CFR 1.1402(h). An application must contain or be accompanied by the applicant's waiver of all benefits and payments under title II and part A of title XVIII of the Act. See § 404.305 for the effect of the filing of the waiver and the granting of the exemption.

(c) Regardless of whether you meet all these conditions, your application for exemption will not be approved unless we find that—

(1) The sect or division of the sect has established tenets or teachings which cause you to be conscientiously opposed to the types of insurance benefits described in paragraph (a)(2) of this section;

(2) For a substantial period of time it has been the practice for members of the sect or division of the sect to make provision for their dependent members which is reasonable in view of their general level of living; and

(3) The sect or division of the sect has been in existence continuously since December 31, 1950.

(d) Your application for exemption will be approved by the Internal Revenue Service only if no benefit or other payment under title II or part A of title XVIII of the Act became payable or, but for section 203 or section 222(b) of the Act, would have become payable, to you or on your behalf at or before the time of the filing of your application for exemption.

(e) The tax exemption ceases to be effective for any taxable year ending after the time you do not meet the requirements of paragraph (a) of this section or after the time we find the religious sect or division of the sect of which you are a member no longer meets the requirements of paragraph (c) of this section. If your tax exemption ceases to be effective, your waiver of the right to receive Social Security and Medicare part A benefits will also no longer be effective. Benefits may be payable based upon your wages for and after the calendar year following the calendar year in which the event occurred upon which the cessation of the exemption is based. Benefits may be payable based upon your self-employment income for and after the taxable year in which the event occurred upon which the cessation of the exemption is based.

[58 FR 64890, Dec. 10, 1993]

§ 404.1077 Individuals under railroad retirement system.

If you are an employee or employee representative as defined in section 3231(b) and (c) of the Code, your work is not a trade or business. Your services are covered under the railroad retirement system.

SELF-EMPLOYMENT INCOME

§ 404.1080 Net earnings from self-employment.

(a) Definition of net earnings from self-employment. If you are self-employed, you must first determine the amount of your net earnings from self-employment before figuring the amount of your earnings that count for social security purposes. Some of your earnings may not be included as net earnings from self-employment even though they are taxable for income tax purposes. If you are an employee but we consider you to be self-employed for social security purposes, you must figure your earnings as though you were actually self-employed unless you work for a church or church-controlled organization that has exempted its employees (see § 404.1068(f)). Subject to the special rules in §§ 404.1081 through 404.1095, the term net earnings from self-employment means—

(1) Your gross income, as figured under subtitle A of the Code, from any trade or business you carried on, less deductions attributed to your trade or business that are allowed by that subtitle; plus

(2) Your distributive share of income (or loss) from a trade or business carried on by a partnership of which you are a member, as described in paragraph (b) of this section.

(b) Income or loss from a partnership.

(1) Your distributive share (whether or not actually distributed) of the income or loss from any trade or business carried on by a partnership of which you are a member, other than as a limited partner, is determined under section 704 of the Code.

(2) If you are a limited partner, your distributive share is included in your net earnings from self-employment if—

(i) The amount is payable to you for services you render to or on behalf of the partnerships; and

(ii) It is a guaranteed payment described in section 707(c) of the Code.

(3) You are a limited partner if your financial liability for the obligations of the partnership is limited to the amount of your financial investment in the partnership. Generally, you will not have to perform services in the operation of, or participate in the control of, the business carried on by the partnership for the taxable year involved.

(c) Reporting methods. Your gross income from a trade or business includes the gross income you received (under the cash method) or that accrued to you (under the accrual method) from the trade or business in the taxable year. It is immaterial that the income may be attributable in whole or in part to services you rendered or other acts you performed in a prior taxable year.

(d) What is a taxable year.

(1) The term taxable year means—

(i) Your annual accounting period on which you regularly figure your income in keeping your books; or

(ii) A short period resulting from your death before the end of your annual accounting period or from a change of your annual accounting period.

(2) The term annual accounting period means—

(i) A calendar year, consisting of 12 months ending on December 31; or

(ii) A fiscal year, consisting of—

(A) 12 months ending on the last day of any month other than December; or

(B) A period, if elected under section 441 of the Code, that varies from 52 to 53 weeks and always ends on the same day of the week that occurs last in a calendar month or nearest to the last day of the calendar month.

(3) Your taxable year for figuring self-employment income is the same as your taxable year for the purposes of subtitle A of the Code. Your taxable year is a calendar year if—

(i) You keep no books;

(ii) You have no annual accounting period; or

(iii) You have an annual accounting period that differs from the definition of fiscal year as described in paragraph (d)(2)(ii) of this section.

[50 FR 36574, Sept. 9, 1985; 50 FR 38113, Sept. 20, 1985]

§ 404.1081 General rules for figuring net earnings from self-employment.

(a) Determining net earnings.

(1) In determining your gross income and the deductions attributable to your trade or business for the purpose of determining your net earnings from self-employment, the provisions that apply to the taxes imposed by sections 1 and 3 of the Code are used.

(2) If you use the accrual method of accounting to figure your taxable income from a trade or business, you must use the same method in determining your net earnings from self-employment.

(3) If you are engaged in a trade or business of selling property on the installment plan and elect, under the provisions of section 453 of the Code, to use the installment method of accounting in figuring your income, you must use the installment method in determining your net earnings from self-employment.

(4) Any income which can be excluded from gross income under any provision of subtitle A of the Code cannot be counted in determining your net earnings from self-employment, unless—

(i) You are a resident of Puerto Rico (see § 404.1089);

(ii) You are a minister or member of a religious order (see § 404.1091);

(iii) You are a United States citizen or resident engaged in a trade or business outside the United States (see § 404.1092); or

(iv) You are a citizen of, or have income from sources within, certain possessions of the United States (see § 404.1093).

(b) Trade or business carried on. You must carry on the trade or business either personally or through agents or employees. Income from a trade or business carried on by an estate or trust is not included in determining the net earnings from self-employment of the individual beneficiaries of the estate or trust.

(c) Aggregate net earnings. If you are engaged in more than one trade or business, your net earnings from self-employment consist of the total of the net income and losses of all the trades or businesses you carry on. A loss in one trade or business you carry on offsets the income from another trade or business.

(d) Partnerships. When you have net earnings from self-employment from a partnership as described in § 404.1080 (a) and (b), those net earnings are combined with your other net earnings from self-employment in determining your total net earnings from self-employment for the taxable year.

(e) Different taxable years. If you are a partner and your taxable year is different from that of the partnership, you must include, in figuring your net earnings from self-employment, your distributive share of the income or loss of the partnership for its taxable year ending with or within your taxable year. For the special rule in case of the termination of a partner's taxable year as a result of death, see § 404.1087.

(f) Meaning of partnerships. A partnership for social security purposes is one that is recognized as a partnership for income tax purposes. For income tax purposes, the term partnership includes not only a partnership as known under common law, but also a syndicate, group, pool, joint venture, or other unincorporated organization that carries on any trade or business, financial operation, or venture, and which is not a trust, estate, or a corporation.

(g) Proprietorship taxed as domestic corporation. If you are a proprietor of an unincorporated business enterprise and have elected to be taxed as a domestic corporation, you must figure your net earnings from self-employment without regard to the election you have made.

[50 FR 36574, Sept. 9, 1985; 50 FR 38113, Sept. 20, 1985]

§ 404.1082 Rentals from real estate; material participation.

(a) In general. Your rentals from real estate and from personal property leased with the real estate (including rentals paid in crop shares) and the deductions attributable to the rentals are excluded in figuring your net earnings from self-employment, unless you receive the rentals in the course of a trade or business as a real estate dealer. If you are an owner or lessee of land, rentals paid in crop shares include income you get under an agreement with another person if the arrangement provides for the following:

(1) The other person will produce agricultural or horticultural commodities on the land.

(2) The commodities produced, or the income from their sale, will be divided between you and the other person.

(3) The amount of your share depends on the amount of the commodities produced.

(b) Real estate dealers.

(1) You are a real estate dealer if you are engaged in the business of selling real estate to customers for profit.

(2) If you merely hold real estate for investment or speculation and receive rental income from it, you are not considered a real estate dealer.

(3) If you are a real estate dealer, but also hold real estate for investment or speculation in addition to real estate you hold for sale to customers, only the rental income from the real estate held for sale to customers and the deductions attributable to it are included in determining your net earnings from self-employment. The rental income from real estate you hold for investment or speculation and the deductions attributable to it are not counted in figuring your net earnings from self-employment.

(c) Special rule for farm rental income—

(1) In general. If you own or lease land, any income you derive from it is included in figuring your net earnings from self-employment if—

(i) The income results from an arrangement between you and another person which provides for the other person to produce agricultural or horticultural commodities on the land that you own or lease and for you to materially participate in the production or the management of the production of the agricultural or horticultural commodities; and

(ii) You actually do materially participate.

(2) Nature of arrangement.

(i) The arrangement between you and the other person may be either oral or written. It must provide that the other person will produce one or more agricultural or horticultural commodities and that you will materially participate in the production or the management of the production of the commodities.

(ii) The term production, refers to the physical work performed and the expenses incurred in producing a commodity. It includes activities like the actual work of planting, cultivating, and harvesting crops, and the furnishing of machinery, implements, seed, and livestock.

(iii) The term management of the production, refers to services performed in making managerial decisions about the production of the crop, such as when to plant, cultivate, dust, spray, or harvest, and includes advising and consulting, making inspections, and making decisions on matters, such as rotation of crops, the type of crops to be grown, the type of livestock to be raised, and the type of machinery and implements to be furnished.

(3) Material participation.

(i) If you show that you periodically advise or consult with the other person, who under the rental arrangement produces the agricultural or horticultural commodities, and also show that you periodically inspect the production activities on the land, you will have presented strong evidence that you are materially participating.

(ii) If you also show that you furnish a large portion of the machinery, tools, and livestock used in the production of the commodities, or that you furnish or advance monies, or assume financial responsibility, for a substantial part of the expense involved in the production of the commodities, you will have established that you are materially participating.

(4) Employees or agents. We consider any farm rental arrangement entered into by your employee or agent and another person to be an arrangement entered into by you. However, we do not consider the services of an employee or agent as your services in determining the extent to which you have participated in the production or management of production of a commodity.

(5) Examples.

Example 1. After the death of her husband, Ms. A rents her farm, together with its machinery and equipment, to B for one-half of the proceeds from the commodities produced on the farm by B. It is agreed that B will live in the tenant house on the farm and be responsible for the overall operation of the farm, such as planting, cultivating, and harvesting the field crops, caring for the orchard and harvesting the fruit and caring for the livestock and poultry. It also is agreed that Ms. A will continue to live in the farm residence and help B operate the farm. Under the agreement it is expected that Ms. A will regularly operate and clean the cream separator and feed the poultry flock and collect the eggs. When possible she will assist B in such work as spraying the fruit trees, penning livestock, culling the poultry, and controlling weeds. She will also assist in preparing the meals when B engages seasonal workers. The agreement between Ms. A and B clearly provides that she will materially participate in the overall production operations to be conducted on her farm by B. In actual practice, Ms. A regularly performs those services. The regularly performed services are material to the production of an agricultural commodity, and the services performed are material to the production operations to which they relate. The furnishing of a substantial portion of the farm machinery and equipment also supports the conclusion that Ms. A has materially participated. Accordingly, the rental income Ms. A receives from her farm should be included in her net earnings from self-employment.

Example 2. G owns a fully-equipped farm which he rents to H under an arrangement which provides that G will materially participate in the management of the production of crops raised on the farm under the arrangement. G lives in town about 5 miles from the farm. About twice a month he visits the farm and looks over the buildings and equipment. G may occasionally, in an emergency, discuss with H some phase of a crop production activity. In effect, H has complete charge of the management of farming operations regardless of the understanding between him and G. Although G pays one-half of the cost of the seed and fertilizer and is charged for the cost of materials purchased by H to make all necessary repairs, G's activities are not material in the crop production activities. Accordingly, G's income from the crops is not included in net earnings from self-employment.

(d) Rental income from living quarters—

(1) No services provided for occupants. Payments you receive for renting living quarters in a private residence, duplex, or multiple-housing unit are generally rental income from real estate. Except in the case of real estate dealers, these payments are excluded in determining net earnings from self-employment, even if the payments are in part attributable to personal property furnished under the lease.

(2) Services provided for occupants.

(i) Payments you receive for renting living quarters where services are also provided to the occupant, as in hotels, boarding houses, or apartment houses furnishing hotel services, or in tourist camps or tourist homes, are included in determining your net earnings from self-employment. Any payments you receive for the use of space in parking lots, warehouses, or storage garages are also included in determining your net earnings from self-employment.

(ii) Generally, we consider services to be provided to the occupant if they are primarily for the occupant's convenience and are other than those usually provided in connection with the rental of rooms or other space for occupancy only. We consider the supplying of maid service to be a service provided to the occupant. However, we do not consider the furnishing of heat and light, the cleaning of public entrances, exits, stairways, and lobbies and the collection of trash, as services provided to the occupant.

Example: A owns a building containing four apartments. During the taxable year, A received $1,400 from apartments numbered 1 and 2, which are rented without services provided to the occupants, and $3,600 from apartments numbered 3 and 4, which are rented with services provided. A's fixed expenses for the four apartments are $1,200 during the taxable year. In addition, A has $500 of expenses attributable to the services provided to the occupants of apartments 3 and 4. In determining his net earnings from self-employment, A includes the $3,600 received from apartments 3 and 4, and the expenses of $1,100 ($500 plus one-half of $1,200) attributable to them. The rentals and expenses attributable to apartments 1 and 2 are excluded. Therefore, A has $2,500 of net earnings from self-employment from the building for the taxable year.

(e) Treatment of business income which includes rentals from real estate. If an individual or a partnership is engaged in a trade or business other than real estate, and part of the income is rentals from real estate, only that part of the income which is not rentals and the expenses attributable to that portion are included in determining net earnings from self-employment.

§ 404.1083 Dividends and interest.

(a) The dividends you receive on shares of stock are excluded in determining your net earnings from self-employment, unless you are a dealer in stocks and securities and receive the dividends in the course of your trade or business.

(b) The interest you receive on a bond, debenture, note, certificate, or other evidence of indebtedness issued with interest coupons or in registered form by any corporation (including one issued by a government or political subdivision) is excluded in determining your net earnings from self-employment, unless you are a dealer in stocks and securities and receive the interest in the course of your trade or business.

(c) If you hold stocks or securities for investment or speculation purposes, any dividends and interest you receive that are excludable under paragraphs (a) and (b) of this section are excluded in determining your net earnings from self-employment, whether or not you are a dealer in stocks and securities.

(d) A dealer in stocks or securities is a merchant with an established place of business who is regularly engaged in the business of purchasing stocks or securities and reselling them to customers. The dealer, as a merchant, buys stocks or securities and sells them to customers with a view to making a profit. Persons who buy and sell or hold stocks or securities for investment or speculation, regardless of whether the buying or selling constitutes a trade or business, are not dealers in stocks or securities.

[45 FR 20075, Mar. 25, 1980; 45 FR 25060, Apr. 14, 1980]

§ 404.1084 Gain or loss from disposition of property; capital assets; timber, coal, and iron ore; involuntary conversion.

(a) If you are engaged in a trade or business, you must, in determining your net earnings from self-employment, exclude any gain or loss—

(1) That is considered a gain or loss from the sale or exchange of a capital asset;

(2) From the cutting of timber or from the disposal of timber or coal, even if held primarily for sale to customers, if section 631 of the Code applies to the gain or loss;

(3) From the disposal of iron ore mined in the United States, even if held primarily for sale to customers, if section 631 of the Code applies to the gain or loss; and

(4) From the sale, exchange, involuntary conversion, or other disposition of property that is not—

(i) Stock in trade or other property of a kind which would properly be included in inventory if on hand at the close of the taxable year; or

(ii) Property held primarily for sale to customers in the ordinary course of a trade or business;

(b) For purposes of paragraph (a)(4) of this section, it is immaterial whether a gain or loss is treated as a capital gain or as an ordinary gain or loss for purposes other than determining earnings from self-employment.

(c) For purposes of paragraph (a)(4) of this section—

(1) The term involuntary conversion means a compulsory or unintended change of property into other property or money as a result of such things as destruction, theft or seizure; and

(2) The term other disposition includes destruction or loss by fire, theft, storm, shipwreck, or other casualty, even though there is no change of the property into other property or money.

Example: During the taxable year 1976, A, who owns a grocery store, had a net profit of $1,500 from the sale of groceries and a gain of $350 from the sale of a refrigerator case. During the same year, he had a loss of $2,000 as a result of damage by fire to the store building. In figuring taxable income for income tax purposes, all of these items are considered. In determining net earnings from self-employment, however, only the $1,500 of profit derived from the sale of groceries is included. The $350 gain and the $2,000 loss are excluded.

§ 404.1085 Net operating loss deduction.

When determining your net earnings from self-employment, you disregard the deduction provided by section 172 of the Code that relates to net operating losses sustained in years other than the taxable year.

§ 404.1086 Community income.

If community property laws apply to income that an individual derives from a trade or business (other than a trade or business carried on by a partnership), the gross income and deductions attributable to such trade or business shall be treated as the gross income and deductions of the spouse carrying on such trade or business or, if such trade or business is jointly operated, treated as the gross income and deductions of each spouse on the basis of his or her respective distributive share of the gross income and deductions.

[70 FR 41955, July 21, 2005]

§ 404.1087 Figuring partner's net earnings from self-employment for taxable year which ends as a result of death.

(a) General. In the case of a deceased partner whose taxable year ends because of death, the deceased partner's net earnings from self-employment includes the amount of his or her distributive share of partnership ordinary income or loss for the partnership's taxable year that is attributable to an interest in the partnership through the month of death.

(b) Computation.

(1) The deceased partner's distributive share of partnership ordinary income or loss for the partnership taxable year in which death occurred is determined by applying the rules contained in paragraphs (d) and (f) of § 404.1081.

(2) The portion of the distributive share to be included in the deceased partner's net earnings from self-employment for his or her last taxable year is determined by treating the ordinary income or loss constituting the distributive share as having been realized or sustained ratably over the partnership taxable year during which the deceased partner had an interest in the partnership and during which the deceased partner's estate, or any other person succeeding by reason of the death to rights to his partnership interest, held an interest in the partnership.

(c) Deceased partner's distributive share. A deceased partner's distributive share includes the distributive share of the estate or of any other person succeeding to the interest of a deceased partner. It does not include any share attributable to a partnership interest that was not held by the deceased partner at the time of death. If a deceased partner's estate should acquire an interest in a partnership in addition to the interest to which it succeeded upon the death of the deceased partner, the amount of the distributive share attributable to the additional interest acquired by the estate is not included in computing the deceased partner's distributive share of the partnership's ordinary income or loss for the partnership taxable year.

(d) Options available to farmers. In determining the applicability of the optional method of figuring net earnings from self-employment to a member of a farm partnership it is necessary to determine the partner's distributive share of partnership gross income or distributive share of income described in section 702(a)(8) of the Code.

§ 404.1088 Retirement payment to retired partners.

(a) In general. If you are a retired partner, in figuring your net earnings from self-employment you must exclude payments made to you on a periodic basis by a partnership on account of your retirement and which are to continue until your death. This exclusion applies only if the payments are made under a written plan which meets the requirements set out in 26 CFR 1.1402(a)–(17) and the conditions in paragraph (b) of this section are met. The necessary requirements and conditions must be met throughout the entire partnership's taxable year for the payments to be excluded so that either all or none of the payments are excluded.

(b) Other conditions. You must have been paid your full share of the partnership's capital before the close of the partnership's taxable year in which retirement payments are made. Also, no member of the partnership can have any financial obligations to you (in his or her capacity as a partner) except to make the retirement payments. Lastly, you cannot perform any services for the partnership in the partnership's taxable year which falls wholly or partially in your taxable year in which you receive the retirement payments.

Example: D, a partner in the DEF partnership, retired from the partnership as of December 31, 1976. The taxable year of both D and the partnership is the calendar year. During the partnership's taxable year ending December 31, 1977, D rendered no service to any trade or business carried on by the partnership. On or before December 31, 1977, all obligations (other than retirement payments under the plan) from the other partners to D were liquidated, and D's share of the capital of the partnership was paid to him. Retirement payments received by D under the partnership's plan in his taxable year ending December 31, 1977, are excluded in determining net earnings from self-employment (if any) for that taxable year.

§ 404.1089 Figuring net earnings for residents and nonresidents of Puerto Rico.

(a) Residents. If you are a resident of Puerto Rico, whether or not you are an alien, a citizen of the United States, or a citizen of Puerto Rico, you must figure your net earnings from self-employment in the same manner as would a citizen of the United States residing in the United States. In figuring your net earnings from self-employment you must include your income from sources in Puerto Rico even though you are a resident of Puerto Rico during the entire taxable year.

(b) Nonresidents. A citizen of Puerto Rico, who is also a citizen of the United States and who is not a resident of Puerto Rico must figure net earnings from self-employment in the same manner as other citizens of the United States.

§ 404.1090 Personal exemption deduction.

The deduction provided by section 151 of the Code, relating to personal exemptions, is excluded in determining net earnings from self-employment.

§ 404.1091 Figuring net earnings for ministers and members of religious orders.

(a) General. If you are a duly ordained, commissioned, or licensed minister of a church or a member of a religious order who has not taken a vow of poverty, we consider you to be engaged in a trade or business under the conditions described in § 404.1071 with regard to services described in § 404.1023 (c) and (e). In figuring your net earnings from self-employment from performing these services, you must include certain income (described in paragraphs (b) and (c) of this section) that may be excluded from your gross income for income tax purposes.

(b) Housing and meals. You must include in figuring your net earnings from self-employment the rental value of a home furnished to you and any rental allowance paid to you as payment for services performed in the exercise of your ministry or in the exercise of duties required by your order even though the rental value or rental allowance may be excluded from gross income by section 107 of the Code. Also, the value of any meals or lodging furnished to you in connection with the performance of these services is included in figuring your net earnings from self-employment even though their value is excluded from gross income by section 119 of the Code.

(c) Housing allowance when included in retirement pay. You must exclude any parsonage or housing allowance included in your retirement pay or any other retirement benefit received after retirement pursuant to a church plan as defined in section 414(e) of the Internal Revenue Code when computing your net earnings from self-employment. For example, if a minister retires from Church A and the rental value of a parsonage or any other allowance is included in his/her retirement pay, the parsonage allowance must be excluded when determining net earnings from self-employment. However, if this same retired minister goes to work for Church B and is paid a parsonage allowance by Church B, this new income must be included when computing net earnings from self-employment.

(d) Services outside the United States. If you are a citizen or resident of the United States performing services outside the United States which are in the exercise of your ministry or in the exercise of duties required by your order, your net earnings from self-employment from the performance of these services are figured as described in paragraph (b) of this section. However, they are figured without regard to the exclusions from gross income provided in sections 911 and 931 of the Code relating to earned income from services performed outside the United States and from sources within possessions of the United States.

[50 FR 36574, Sept. 9, 1985; 50 FR 38113, Sept. 20, 1985; 70 FR 41955, July 21, 2005]

§ 404.1092 Figuring net earnings for U.S. citizens or residents living outside the United States.

(a) Taxable years beginning after December 31, 1983. If you are a citizen or resident of the United States and are engaged in a trade or business outside the United States, your net earnings from self-employment are figured without regard to the exclusion from gross income provided by section 911 (a)(1) of the Code.

(b) Taxable years beginning after December 31, 1981, and before January 1, 1984. If you are a citizen of the United States and were engaged in a trade or business outside the United States, your net earnings from self-employment are figured without regard to the exclusion from gross income provided by section 911(a)(1) of the Code unless you are a resident of a foreign country or countries for an uninterrupted period which includes an entire taxable year.

[50 FR 36574, Sept. 9, 1985; 50 FR 38113, Sept. 20, 1985]

§ 404.1093 Possession of the United States.

In using the exclusions from gross income provided under section 931 of the Code (relating to income from sources within possessions of the United States) and section 932 of the Code (relating to citizens of possessions of the United States) for purposes of figuring your net earnings from self-employment, the term possession of the United States shall be deemed not to include the Virgin Islands, Guam, the Commonwealth of the Northern Mariana Islands, or American Samoa.

[69 FR 51556, Aug. 20, 2004]

§ 404.1094 Options available for figuring net earnings from self-employment.

(a) General. If you have income from a trade or business in certain situations, you have options for figuring your net earnings from self-employment. The options available to you depend on whether you have income from an agricultural trade or business or a non-agricultural trade or business. For a definition of agricultural trade or business see § 404.1095.

(b) Agricultural trade or business. The net earnings from self-employment you derive from an agricultural trade or business may, at your option, be figured as follows:

(1) Gross income of $2,400 or less. If your gross income is $2,400 or less you may, at your option, report 66⅔ percent of the gross income as net earnings from self-employment instead of your actual net earnings from your business.

(2) Gross income of more than $2,400. If your gross income is more than $2,400 and your actual net earnings from your business are less than $1,600 you may, at your option, report $1,600 as net earnings from self-employment instead of your actual net earnings. If your actual net earnings are $1,600 or more you cannot use the optional method.

(3) Two or more agricultural trades or businesses. If you carry on more than one agricultural trade or business as a sole proprietor or as a partner, you must combine your gross income and net income from each trade or business to find out whether you may use the optional method of figuring net earnings.

(c) Non-agricultural trade or business.

(1) The net earnings from self-employment you derive from a non-agricultural trade or business may be reported under an optional method if you are self-employed on a regular basis (as defined in paragraph (c)(4) of this section). You cannot use the optional method of reporting for more than 5 taxable years, and you cannot report less than your actual net earnings from self-employment.

(2) Computation. If your actual net earnings from self-employment are less than $1,600 and less than 66⅔ percent of your gross income, you may, at your option, report 66⅔ percent of your gross income (but not more than $1,600) as your net earnings from self-employment.

Example: A operates a grocery store and files income tax returns on a calendar year basis. A meets the self-employed on a regular basis requirement because actual net earnings from self-employment were $400 or more in 1976 and in 1977. Gross income and net profit from operating the grocery store in 1978 through 1980 are as follows:

	1978	1979	1980
Gross income	$2,800	$1,200	$1,000
Net profit	300	400	800

For the year 1978, A may report as annual net earnings from self-employment either—

(i) None. (Actual net earnings from self-employment are less than $400); or

(ii) $1,600. (Non-agricultural option, 66⅔ percent of $2,800, but not to exceed the $1,600 maximum.)

For the year 1979, A may report as annual net earnings from self-employment either—

(i) $400. (Actual net earnings from self-employment); or

(ii) $800. (Non-agricultural option, 66⅔ percent of $1,200.)

For the year 1980, A must report $800, the actual net earnings from self-employment. The non-agricultural option is not available because A's actual net earnings are not less than 66⅔ percent of the gross income.

(3) Figuring net earnings from both non-agricultural and agricultural self-employment. If you are self-employed on a regular basis, you may use the non-agricultural optional method of reporting when you have both non-agricultural and agricultural trades or businesses. However, in order to use this method, your actual net earnings from non-agricultural self-employment combined with your actual net earnings from agricultural self-employment, or your optional net earnings from agricultural self-employment, must be less than $1,600, and the net non-agricultural earnings must be less than 66⅔ percent of your gross non-agricultural income. If you qualify for using both the non-agricultural and agricultural option, you may report less than your actual total net earnings, but not less than your actual net earnings from non-agricultural self-employment alone. If you elect to use both options in a given taxable year, the combined maximum reportable net earnings from self-employment may not exceed $1,600.

Example: C was regularly self-employed. She derived actual net earnings from self-employment of $400 or more in 1975 and in 1976. Her gross income and net profit from operating both a grocery store and a farm in 1978 are:

Grocery Store	
Gross income	$1,000
Net profit	800

Farm	
Gross income	$2,600
Net profit	400

For the year 1978, C may report $1,200 (actual net earnings from self-employment from both businesses), or $2,400 ($1,600 agricultural option (66⅔ percent of $2,600 farm gross income not to exceed $1,600) and $800 grocery store profit). C cannot use the non-agricultural option for 1978 because her actual grocery store net exceeds 66⅔ percent of her grocery store gross income.

(4) Self-employed on a regular basis. For any taxable year beginning after 1972, we consider you to be self-employed on a regular basis, or to be a member of a partnership on a regular basis, if, in at least 2 of the 3 taxable years immediately before that taxable year, you had actual net earnings from self-employment of not less than $400 from agricultural and non-agricultural trades or businesses (including your distributive share of the net income or loss from any partnership of which you are a member).

(d) Members of partnerships. If you are a member of a partnership you may use the optional method of reporting. Your gross income is your distributive share of the partnership's gross income (after all guaranteed payments to which section 707(c) of the Code applies have been deducted), plus your own guaranteed payment.

(e) Computing gross income. For purposes of this section gross income means—

(1) Under the cash method of computing, the gross receipts from the trade or business reduced by the cost or other basis of property that was purchased and sold, minus any income that is excluded in computing net earnings from self-employment; or

(2) Under the accrual method of computing, the gross income minus any income that is excluded in figuring net earnings from self-employment.

(f) Exercise of option. For each taxable year for which you are eligible to use the optional method and elect to use that method, you must figure your net earnings from self-employment in that manner on your tax return for that year. If you wish to change your method of reporting after your tax return is filed, you may change it by filing an amended tax return with the Internal Revenue Service or by filing with us Form 2190, Change in Method of Computing Net Earnings from Self–Employment.

§ 404.1095 Agricultural trade or business.

(a) An agricultural trade or business is one in which, if the trade or business were carried on entirely by employees, the major portion of the services would be agricultural labor (§ 404.1057).

(b)(1) If the services are partly agricultural and partly non-agricultural, the time devoted to the performance of each type of service is the test used to determine whether the major portion of the services is agricultural labor.

(2) If more than half of the time spent in performing all the services is spent in performing services that are agricultural labor, the trade or business is agricultural.

(3) If half or less of the time spent in performing all the services is spent in performing services that are agricultural labor, the trade or business is not agricultural. The time spent in performing the services is figured by adding the time spent in the trade or business during the taxable year by every individual (including the individual carrying on the trade or business and the members of that individual's family).

(c) We do not apply the rules in this section if the non-agricultural services are performed in connection with a trade or business separate and distinct from the agricultural trade or business. A roadside automobile service station on a farm is a trade or business separate and distinct from the agricultural trade or business, and the gross income from the service station, less the deductions attributable to it, is to be considered in determining net earnings from self-employment.

(d) We consider a sharefarmer (see § 404.1068(c)) or a materially participating owner or tenant (see § 404.1082(c)) to be engaged in an agricultural trade or business. We use the rules in this section to determine whether a farm crew leader who is self-employed (see § 404.1074) is engaged in an agricultural trade or business.

§ 404.1096 Self-employment income.

(a) General. Self-employment income is the amount of your net earnings from self-employment that is subject to social security tax and counted for social security benefit purposes. The term self-employment income means the net earnings from self-employment you derive in a taxable year, except as described in paragraphs (b), (c) and (d) of this section.

(b) Maximum self-employment income.

(1) The term self-employment income does not include that part of your net earnings from self-employment that exceeds (or that part of your net earnings from self-employment which, when added to the wages you received in that taxable year, exceeds)—

Taxable year	Amount
Ending before 1955	$ 3,600
Ending in 1955 through 1958	4,200
Ending in 1959 through 1965	4,800
Ending in 1966 and 1967	6,600
Ending after 1967 and beginning before 1972	7,800
Beginning in 1972	9,000
Beginning in 1973	10,800
Beginning in 1974	13,200
Beginning in 1975	14,100
Beginning in 1976	15,300
Beginning in 1977	16,500
Beginning in 1978	17,700
Beginning in 1979	22,900
Beginning in 1980	25,900

Taxable year	Amount
Beginning in 1981	29,700
Beginning in 1982	32,400
Beginning in 1983	35,700
Beginning in 1984	37,800
Beginning in 1985	39,600
Beginning in 1986	42,000
Beginning in 1987	43,800
Beginning in 1988	45,000
Beginning in 1989	48,000
Beginning in 1990	51,300
Beginning in 1991	53,400
Beginning in 1992	55,500

(2) For the purpose of this paragraph the term wages includes remuneration paid to an employee for services covered by an agreement entered into under section 218 of the Act, or an agreement entered into under section 3121(*l*) of the Code, which would be wages under section 209 of Act if the services were considered employment under section 210(a) of the Act.

(c) Minimum net earnings from self employment.

(1) Self-employment income does not include your net earnings from self-employment when the amount of those earnings for the taxable year is less than $400. If you have only $300 of net earnings from self-employment for the taxable year you would not have any self-employment income. (Special rules apply if you are paid $100 or more and work for a church or church-controlled organization that has exempted its employees (see § 404.1068(f)).)

(2) If you have net earnings from self-employment of $400 or more for the taxable year you may have less than $400 of creditable self-employment income. This occurs where your net earnings from self-employment is $400 or more for a taxable year and the amount of your net earnings from self-employment plus the amount of the wages paid to you during that taxable year exceed the maximum creditable earnings for a year. For example, if you had net earnings from self-employment of $1,000 for 1978, and were also paid wages of $17,500 during 1978, your creditable self-employment income for 1978 would be $200.

(d) Nonresident aliens. A nonresident alien has self-employment income only if coverage is provided under a totalization agreement [see § 404.1913]. We do not consider an individual who is a resident of the Commonwealth of Puerto Rico, the Virgin Islands, Guam, the Commonwealth of the Northern Mariana Islands, or American Samoa to be a nonresident alien.

[50 FR 36575, Sept. 9, 1985; 50 FR 38113, Sept. 20, 1985; 52 FR 8250, March 17, 1987; 57 FR 44098, Sept. 24, 1992; 69 FR 51556, Aug. 20, 2004]

SUBPART L—[RESERVED]

SUBPART M—COVERAGE OF EMPLOYEES OF STATE AND LOCAL GOVERNMENTS

Authority: Secs. 205, 210, 218, and 702(a)(5) of the Social Security Act (42 U.S.C. 405, 410, 418, and 902(a)(5)); sec. 12110, Pub.L. 99–272, 100 Stat. 287 (42 U.S.C. 418 note); sec. 9002, Pub.L. 99–509, 100 Stat. 1970.

Source: 53 FR 32976, Aug. 29, 1988; 57 FR 59911, Dec. 17, 1992; 61 FR 5941, Feb. 15, 1996; 69 FR 51556, Aug. 20, 2004, unless otherwise noted.

GENERAL

§ 404.1200 General.

(a) Coverage under section 218 of the Act. Under section 218 of the Social Security Act (the Act) a State may ask the Commissioner of Social Security to enter into an agreement to extend Federal old-age, survivors, disability and hospital insurance coverage to groups of employees of the State and its political subdivisions. The Commissioner shall enter into such an agreement. State and local government employees, after being covered under an agreement, have the same benefit rights and responsibilities as other employees who are mandatorily covered under the programs. For payments due on wages paid before 1987, the State assumes full financial and reporting responsibility for all groups covered under its agreement. The agreement may not be terminated in its entirety or with respect to any coverage group under that agreement. For payments due on wages paid in the year 1987 and years later, section 9002 of Pub.L. 99–509 amends section 218 of the Act by transferring responsibility for collecting contributions due and receiving wage reports from the Social Security Administration (SSA) to the Internal Revenue Service (IRS). Sections of the regulations wholly or partly affected by this amendment to the Act are appended with the phrase "—for wages paid prior to 1987."

(b) Mandatory old-age, survivors, disability, and hospital insurance coverage. Under section 210(a)(7)(F) of the Act, mandatory old-age, survivors, disability, and hospital insurance coverage is extended to certain services performed after July 1, 1991, by individuals who are employees of a State (other than the District of Columbia, Guam, the Commonwealth of the Northern Mariana Islands, or American Samoa), a political subdivision of the State, or any wholly owned instrumentality of one or more of the foregoing, and who are not members of the employer's retirement system. Certain services are excluded from such mandatory coverage (see § 404.1020(a)(3).

[57 FR 59911, Dec. 17, 1992; 62 FR 38450, July 18, 1997; 69 FR 51556, Aug. 20, 2004]

§ 404.1201 Scope of this subpart regarding coverage and wage reports and adjustments.

This subpart contains the rules of SSA about:

(a) Coverage under section 218 of the Act—

(1) How a State enters into and modifies an agreement; and

(2) What groups of employees a State can cover by agreement.

(b) Contributions, wage reports, and adjustments—for wages paid prior to 1987—

(1) How a State must identify covered employees and what records it must keep on those employees;

(2) Periodic reviews of the source records kept on covered employees;

(3) How and when a State must report wages and pay contributions;

(4) What the State's liability for contributions is and how SSA figures the amount of those contributions;

(5) What happens if a State fails to pay its contributions timely;

(6) How errors in reports and contribution payments are corrected;

(7) How overpayments of contributions are credited or refunded;

(8) How assessments are made if contributions are underpaid; and

(9) How a State can obtain administrative or judicial review of a decision on a credit, refund, or assessment.

[57 FR 59911, Dec. 17, 1992; 65 FR 16813, March 30, 2000]

§ 404.1202 Definitions.

(a) Terms which have special meaning in this subpart are described in this section. Where necessary, further explanation is included in the section where the term is used.

(b) Coverage terms:

Agreement—The agreement between the Commissioner of Social Security and the State containing the conditions under which retirement, survivors, disability and hospital insurance coverage is provided for State and local government employees.

Coverage—The extension of Social Security protection (retirement, survivors, disability, and hospital insurance) by agreement between the Commissioner of Social Security and a State to employees of the State and its political subdivisions or by agreement between the Commissioner of Social Security and an interstate instrumentality to employees of the interstate instrumentality.

Coverage group—The grouping by which employees are covered under an agreement.

Employee—An employee as defined in section 210(j) of the Act. Usually, the common-law control test is used in determining whether an employer-employee relationship exists. The term also includes an officer of a State or political subdivision.

Governmental function—The traditional functions of government: legislative, executive, and judicial.

Interstate instrumentality—An independent legal entity organized by two or more States to carry out one or more functions. For Social Security coverage purposes under section 218 of the Act, an interstate instrumentality is treated, to the extent practicable, as a "State."

Modification—A change to the agreement between the Commissioner of Social Security and a State which provides coverage of the services of employees not previously covered or which alters the agreement in some other respect.

Political subdivision—A separate legal entity of a State which usually has specific governmental functions. The term ordinarily includes a county, city, town, village, or school district, and in many States, a sanitation, utility, reclamation, drainage, flood control, or similar district. A political subdivision includes an instrumentality of a State, one or more political subdivisions of a State, or a State and one or more of its political subdivisions.

Proprietary function—A business engaged in by a State or political subdivision such as a public amusement park or public parking lot.

Retirement system—A pension, annuity, retirement, or similar fund or system established by a State or political subdivision.

SSA—The Social Security Administration.

State—Includes the fifty States, Puerto Rico, and the Virgin Islands. It does not include the District of Columbia, Guam, the Commonwealth of the Northern Mariana Islands, or American Samoa. "State" also refers to an interstate instrumentality where applicable.

We—The Social Security Administration.

(c) Contributions, wage reporting, and adjustment terms—for wages paid prior to 1987:

Allowance of a credit or refund—The written notice to a State of the determination by SSA of the amount owed to the State by SSA, the period involved, and the basis for the determination.

Assessment—The written notice to a State of the determination by SSA of the amount (contributions or accrued interest) owed to SSA by the State, the period involved, and the basis for the determination.

Contributions—Payments made under an agreement which the State deposits in a Federal Reserve bank. The amounts are based on the wages paid to employees whose services are covered under an agreement. These amounts are equal to the taxes imposed under the Internal Revenue Code on employers and employees in private employment.

Contribution return—Form used to identify and account for all contributions actions.

Disallowance of a State's claim for credit or refund—The written notice to a State of the determination by SSA that the State's claim for credit or refund is denied, the period involved, and the basis for the determination.

Overpayment—A payment of more than the correct amount of contributions or interest.

Underpayment—A payment of less than the correct amount of contributions or interest.

Wage reports—Forms used to identify employees who were paid wages for covered employment and the amounts of those wages paid. This includes corrective reports.

[62 FR 38450, July 18, 1997; 69 FR 51556, Aug. 20, 2004]

§ 404.1203 Evidence—for wages paid prior to 1987.

(a) State's responsibility for submitting evidence. The State, under the provisions of the agreement, is responsible for accurately reporting the wages paid employees for services covered by the agreement and for paying the correct amount of contributions due on those wages. This responsibility includes submitting evidence to verify the accuracy of the reports and payments.

(b) Failure to submit requested evidence. The State is required to submit information timely to SSA. If we request additional evidence to verify the accuracy of reports and payments, we specify when that evidence must be submitted. If we do not receive the evidence timely, and the State provides no satisfactory explanation for its failure to submit the evidence timely, we may proceed, if appropriate, on the basis of the information we have. Proceeding on the basis of the information we have permits us to credit the wage records of employees properly, where possible, while continuing to work with the State to resolve remaining discrepancies.

(Approved by the Office of Management and Budget under control number 0960–0425)

[66 FR 28836, May 25, 2001]

§ 404.1204 Designating officials to act on behalf of the State.

(a) Each State which enters into an agreement shall designate the official or officials authorized to act on the State's behalf in administering the agreement. Each State shall inform SSA of the name, title, and address of the designated official(s) and the extent of each official's authority. For example, a State may indicate that the State official is authorized:

(1) To enter into an agreement and execute modifications to the agreement; and

(2) To carry out the ministerial duties necessary to administer the agreement.

For wages paid prior to 1987:

(3) To enter into agreements to extend or re-extend the time limit for assessment or credit;

(4) To make arrangements in connection with onsite reviews; and

(5) To request administrative review of an assessment, an allowance of a credit or refund, or a disallowance of a credit or refund.

(b) Each State shall inform SSA timely of changes in designated officials or changes in their authority.

(Approved by the Office of Management and Budget under control number 0960–0425)

[66 FR 28836, May 25, 2001]

WHAT GROUPS OF EMPLOYEES MAY BE COVERED

§ 404.1205 Absolute coverage groups.

(a) General. An absolute coverage group is a permanent grouping of employees, e.g., all the employees of a city or town. It is a coverage group for coverage and reporting purposes. When used for coverage purposes, the term refers to groups of employees whose positions are not under a retirement system. An absolute coverage group may include positions which were formerly under a retirement system and, at the State's option, employees who are in positions under a retirement system but who are ineligible (see § 404.1208) to become members of that system.

(b) What an absolute coverage group consists of. An absolute coverage group consists of one of the following employee groups:

(1) State employees performing services in connection with the State's governmental functions;

(2) State employees performing services in connection with a single proprietary function of the State;

(3) Employees of a State's political subdivision performing services in connection with that subdivision's governmental functions;

(4) Employees of a State's political subdivision performing services in connection with a single proprietary function of the subdivision;

(5) Civilian employees of a State's National Guard units; and

(6) Individuals employed under an agreement between a State and the U.S. Department of Agriculture as agricultural products inspectors.

(c) Designated coverage groups. A State may provide coverage for designated (i.e., selected) absolute coverage groups of the State or a political subdivision. When coverage is extended to these designated groups, the State must specifically identify each group as a designated absolute coverage group and furnish the effective date of coverage and any optional exclusion(s) for each group. Where a State has provided coverage to designated absolute coverage groups, the State may, by modifying its agreement, extend that coverage to any absolute coverage group in the State.

§ 404.1206 Retirement system coverage groups.

(a) General. Section 218(d) of the Act authorizes coverage of services of employees in positions under a retirement system. For purposes of obtaining coverage, a system may be considered a separate retirement system authorized by sections 218(d)(6)(A) or (B) or 218(*l*) of the Act. Under these sections of the Act a State may designate the positions of any one of the following groupings of employees as a separate retirement system:

(1) The entire system;

(2) The employees of the State under the system;

(3) The employees of each political subdivision in the State under the system;

(4) The employees of the State and the employees of any one or more of the State's political subdivisions;

(5) The employees of any combination of the State's political subdivisions;

(6) The employees of each institution of higher learning, including junior colleges and teachers colleges;

(7) The employees of a hospital which is an integral part of a political subdivision; or

(8) The employees in police officers' positions or firefighters' positions, or both.

If State law requires a State or political subdivision to have a retirement system, it is considered established even though no action has been taken to establish the system.

(b) Retirement system coverage groups. A retirement system coverage group is a grouping of employees in positions under a retirement system. Employees in positions under the system have voted for coverage for the system by referendum and a State has provided coverage by agreement or modification of its agreement. It is not a permanent grouping. It exists only for referendum and coverage purposes and is not a separate group for reporting purposes. Once coverage has been obtained, the retirement system coverage group becomes part of one of the absolute coverage groups described in § 404.1205(b).

(c) What a retirement system coverage group consists of. A retirement system coverage group consists of:

(1) Current employees—all employees whose services are not already covered by the agreement, who are in positions covered by the same retirement system on the date an agreement or modification of the agreement is made applicable to the system;

(2) Future employees—all employees in positions brought under the system after an agreement or modification of the agreement is signed; and

(3) Other employees—all employees in positions which had been under the retirement system but which were not under the retirement system when the group was covered (including ineligibles who had been optionally excluded from coverage under section 218(c)(3)(B) of the Act).

(d) Referendum procedures. Prior to signing the agreement or modification, the governor or an official of the State named by the governor (for an interstate instrumentality, its chief executive officer) must certify to the Commissioner that:

(1) All eligible employees were given at least 90 days' notice of the referendum;

(2) All eligible employees were given an opportunity to vote in the referendum;

(3) Only eligible employees were permitted to vote in the referendum;

(4) Voting was by secret written ballot on the question of whether service in positions covered by the retirement system should be included under an agreement;

(5) The referendum was conducted under the supervision of the governor or agency or individual named by him; and

(6) A majority of the retirement system's eligible employees voted for coverage under an agreement.

The State has two years from the date of a favorable referendum to enter into an agreement or modification extending coverage to the retirement system coverage group. If the referendum is unfavorable, another referendum cannot be held until at least one year after that unfavorable referendum.

(e) Who is covered. If a majority of the eligible employees in a retirement system vote for coverage, all employees in positions in that retirement system become covered.

(f) Coverage of employees in positions under more than one retirement system.

(1) If an employee occupies two or more positions each of which is under a different retirement system, the employee's coverage in each position depends upon the coverage extended to each position under each system.

(2) If an employee is in a single position which is under more than one retirement system (because the employee's occupancy of that position permits her or him to become a member of more than one retirement system), the employee is covered when the retirement system coverage group including her or his position is covered under an agreement unless (A) he or she is not a member of the retirement system being covered and (B) he or she is a member of a retirement system which has not been covered. This rule also applies to the coverage of services in police officers' and firefight-

ers' positions in States and interstate instrumentalities as discussed in § 404.1212(c).

[61 FR 38367, July 24, 1996; 62 FR 38451, July 18, 1997]

§ 404.1207 Divided retirement system coverage groups.

(a) General. Under section 218(d)(6)(C) of the Act certain States and under section 218(g)(2) of the Act all interstate instrumentalities may divide a retirement system based on whether the employees in positions under that system want coverage. The States having this authority are Alaska, California, Connecticut, Florida, Georgia, Hawaii, Illinois, Kentucky, Louisiana, Massachusetts, Minnesota, Nevada, New Jersey, New Mexico, New York, North Dakota, Pennsylvania, Rhode Island, Tennessee, Texas, Vermont, Washington, and Wisconsin.

(b) Divided retirement system coverage group. A divided retirement system coverage group is a grouping under a retirement system of positions of members of the system who voted for coverage and positions of individuals who become members of the system (the "yes" group), and positions of members of the system who did not elect coverage (the "no" group) and ineligible employees (see § 404.1208). For purposes of this section for groups covered after 1959, the term "member" also includes individuals who have an option to become members of the retirement system but have not done so. The position of a member in the "no" group can be covered if, within two years after the agreement or modification extending coverage to the "yes" group is executed, the State provides an opportunity to transfer the position to the covered "yes" group and the individual occupying the position makes a written request for the transfer. The members of the "no" group can also be covered if, by referendum, a majority of them vote for coverage. If the majority votes for coverage, all positions of the members of the "no" group become covered. There is no further subdivision of the "no" group into those who voted for and those who voted against coverage. If the State requests, the ineligibles in the "no" group may become part of the "yes" group and have their services covered.

(c) Referendum procedures. To divide a retirement system, the State must conduct a referendum among the system's employees. If the system is to be divided, the governor or an individual named by him must certify to the Secretary that:

(1) The referendum was held by written ballot on the question of whether members of a retirement system wish coverage under an agreement;

(2) All members of the retirement system at the time the vote was held had the opportunity to vote;

(3) All members of the system on the date the notice of the referendum was issued were given at least 90 days' notice regarding the referendum;

(4) The referendum was conducted under the supervision of the governor or agency or person designated by him; and

(5) The retirement system was divided into two parts, one composed of positions of members of the system who voted for coverage and the other composed of the remaining positions under the retirement system.

After the referendum the State may include those members who chose coverage under its agreement as a retirement system coverage group. The State has two years from the date of the referendum to enter into an agreement or modification extending coverage to that group.

[70 FR 41956, July 21, 2005]

§ 404.1208 Ineligible employees.

(a) Definition. An ineligible is an employee who, on first occupying a position under a retirement system, is not eligible for membership in that system because of a personal disqualification like age, physical condition, or length of service.

(b) Coverage of ineligible employees. A State may, in its agreement or any modification to the agreement, provide coverage for the services of ineligible employees in one of three ways:

(1) As part of or as an addition to an absolute coverage group;

(2) As part of a retirement system coverage group covering all positions under the retirement system; or

(3) As part of or as an addition to a retirement system coverage group composed of those members in positions in a retirement system who chose coverage.

§ 404.1209 Mandatorily excluded services.

Some services are mandatorily excluded from coverage under a State's agreement. They are:

(a) Services of employees who are hired to relieve them from unemployment;

(b) Services performed in an institution by a patient or inmate of the institution;

(c) Transportation service subject to the Federal Insurance Contributions Act;

(d) Certain emergency services in case of fire, storm, snow, volcano, earthquake, flood or other similar emergency; and

(e) Services other than agricultural labor or student services which would be excluded from coverage if performed for a private employer.

(f) Services covered under section 210(a)(7)(F) of the Act. (See § 404.1200(b).)

[57 FR 59911, Dec. 17, 1992]

§ 404.1210 Optionally excluded services.

Certain services and positions may, if the State requests it, be excluded from coverage. These exclusions may be applied on a statewide basis or selectively by coverage groups. They are:

(a) Services in any class or classes of elective positions;

(b) Services in any class or classes of part-time positions;

(c) Services in any class or classes of positions where the pay is on a fee basis;

(d) Any agricultural labor or student services which would also be excluded if performed for a private employer; and

(e) For modifications executed after 1994, services performed by election officials or election workers if the payments for those services in a calendar year are less than $1000 for calendar years after 1994 and before 2000, or, for calendar years after 1999, are less than the $1000 base amount as adjusted pursuant to section 218(c)(8)(B) of the Act to reflect changes in wages in the economy. We will publish this adjustment of the $1000 base amount in the Federal Register on or before November 1 preceding the year for which the adjustment is made.

[61 FR 38367, July 24, 1996]

§ 404.1211 Interstate instrumentalities.

For Social Security coverage purposes under section 218 of the Act, interstate instrumentalities are treated, to the extent practicable, as States, that is:

(a) They must be legally authorized to enter into an agreement with the Commissioner;

(b) They are subject to the same rules that are applied to the States;

(c) They may divide retirement systems and cover only the positions of members who want coverage; and

(d) They may provide coverage for firefighters and police officers in positions under a retirement system.

[61 FR 38368, July 24, 1996; 62 FR 38451, July 18, 1997]

§ 404.1212 Police officers and firefighters.

(a) General. For Social Security coverage purposes under section 218 of the Act, a police officer's or firefighter's position is any position so classified under State statutes or court decisions. Generally, these positions are in the organized police and fire departments of incorporated cities, towns, and villages. In most States, a police officer is a member of the "police" which is an organized civil force for maintaining order, preventing and detecting crimes, and enforcing laws. The terms "police officer" and "firefighter" do not include services in positions which, although connected with police and firefighting functions, are not police officer or firefighter positions.

(b) Providing coverage. A State may provide coverage of:

(1) Police officers' and firefighters' positions not under a retirement system as part of an absolute coverage group; or

(2) Police officers' or firefighters' positions, or both, as part of a retirement system coverage group.

(c) Police officers and firefighters in positions under a retirement system. All States and interstate instrumentalities may provide coverage for employees in police officers' or firefighters' positions, or both, which are under a retirement system by following the majority vote referendum procedures in § 404.1206(d). In addition, all interstate instrumentalities and the States listed in § 404.1207 may use the desire for coverage procedures described in § 404.1207.

[61 FR 38368, July 24, 1996]

HOW COVERAGE UNDER AGREEMENTS IS OBTAINED AND CONTINUES

§ 404.1214 Agreement for coverage.

(a) General. A State may enter into a written agreement with the Commissioner to provide for Social Security coverage for its employees or the employees of one or more of its political subdivisions. An interstate instrumentality may enter into a similar agreement for its employees. These agreements cover employees in groups of positions or by types of services rather than the individual employees.

(b) Procedures. A State or interstate instrumentality may request coverage by submitting to SSA a proposed written agreement for the desired coverage.

(c) Authority to enter into an agreement for coverage—

(1) Federal law. Section 218(a) of the Act requires the Commissioner to enter into an agreement, at the request of the State, to extend Social Security coverage to the State's employees or those of its political subdivisions. Section 218(g) authorizes the Commissioner to enter into an agreement, at the request of an interstate instrumentality, to extend Social Security coverage to the employees of the interstate instrumentality.

(2) State law. State law must authorize a State or an interstate instrumentality to enter into an agreement with the Commissioner for Social Security coverage.

(d) Provisions of the agreement. The agreement must include:

(1) A description of the specific services to be covered and excluded;

(2) The State's promise to pay, to the Secretary of the Treasury, contributions equal to the sum of the taxes which would be required under the Federal Insurance Contributions Act from employers and employees if the employment were in the private sector;

(3) The State's promise to comply with the regulations the Commissioner prescribes for carrying out the provisions of section 218 of the Act; and

(4) Identification of the political subdivisions, coverage groups, or services being covered and the services that are excluded.

The agreement must be signed by the authorized State or interstate instrumentality official and the Commissioner or his or her designee.

(e) Effective date. The agreement must specify an effective date of coverage. However, the effective date cannot be earlier than the last day of the sixth calendar year preceding the year in which the agreement is mailed or delivered by other means to the Commissioner. The agreement is effective after the effective date.

(f) Applicability of agreement. The agreement establishes the continuing relationship between the Commissioner and the State or interstate instrumentality except as it is modified (see §§ 404.1215–404.1217).

(Approved by the Office of Management and Budget under control number 0960–0425)

[62 FR 38451, July 18, 1997; 66 FR 28836, May 25, 2001]

§ 404.1215 Modification of agreement.

(a) General. A State or interstate instrumentality may modify in writing its agreement, for example, to:

(1) Exclude, in limited situations, employee services or positions previously covered;

(2) Include additional coverage groups; or

(3) Include as covered services:

(i) Services of covered employees for additional retroactive periods of time; and

(ii) Services previously excluded from coverage.

(b) Controlling date for retroactive coverage. A State may specify in the modification a date to make all individuals in the coverage group who were in an employment relationship on that date eligible for retroactive coverage. This date is known as the controlling date for retroactive coverage. It can be no earlier than the date the modification is mailed or otherwise delivered to the Commissioner nor can it be later than the date the modification is signed by the Commissioner. If the State does not designate a controlling date, the date the modification is signed by the Commissioner is the controlling date.

(c) Conditions for modification. The provisions of section 218 of the Act which apply to the original agreement also apply to a modification to the agreement.

(d) Effective date. Generally, a modification must specify an effective date of coverage. However, the effective date cannot be earlier than the last day of the sixth calendar year preceding the year in which the modification is mailed or delivered by other means to the Commissioner. The modification is effective after the effective date.

(Approved by the Office of Management and Budget under control number 0960–0425)

[62 FR 38451, July 18, 1997; 66 FR 28836, May 25, 2001]

§ 404.1216 Modification of agreement to correct an error.

(a) General. If an agreement or modification contains an error, the State may correct the error by a subsequent modification to the agreement. For example, the agreement or modification incorrectly lists a covered service as an optionally excluded service or shows an improper effective date of coverage. In correcting this type of error, which affects the extent of coverage, the State must submit a modification along with evidence to establish that the error occurred. However, a modification is not needed to correct minor typographical or clerical errors. For example, an agreement or modification incorrectly lists School District No. 12 as School District No. 13. This type of error can be corrected based on a written request from the appropriate official of the State or interstate instrumentality.

(b) Correction of errors involving erroneous reporting to the IRS—for wages paid prior to 1987. Where a State or political subdivision makes reports and payments to the Internal Revenue Service under the provisions of the Federal Insurance Contributions Act which apply to employees in private employment in the mistaken belief that this action would provide coverage for its employees, the State may provide the desired coverage for those same periods of time by a subsequent modification to its agreement. If State law permits, the State may make that coverage effective with the first day of the first period for which the erroneous reports and payments were made. (In this instance, the limitation on retroactive coverage described in § 404.1215(d) is not applicable.) Where the State does not want to provide such retroactive coverage or is not permitted to do so by State law, the State may provide the coverage for the affected coverage group as of a specified date (§ 404.1215(b)). The coverage would then apply to the services performed by individuals as members of the coverage group

(1) Who were employees on that date, and

(2) Whose wages were erroneously reported to IRS, and

(3) For whom a refund of FICA taxes has not been obtained at the time the Commissioner.

(Approved by the Office of Management and Budget under control number 0960–0425)

[62 FR 38451, July 18, 1997; 66 FR 28836, May 25, 2001]

§ 404.1217 Continuation of coverage.

The coverage of State and local government employees continues as follows:

(a) Absolute coverage group. Generally, the services of an employee covered as a part of an absolute coverage group (see § 404.1205) continue to be covered indefinitely. A position covered as a part of an absolute coverage group continues to be covered even if the position later comes under a retirement system. This includes policemen's and firemen's positions which are covered with an absolute coverage group.

(b) Retirement system coverage group. Generally, the services of employees in positions covered as a part of a retirement system coverage group continue to be covered indefinitely. For a retirement system coverage group made up of members who chose coverage, a position continues to be covered until it is removed from the retirement system and is no longer occupied by a member who chose coverage or by a new member of the system. Coverage is not terminated because the positions are later covered under additional retirement systems or removed from coverage under a retirement system, or because the retirement system is abolished with respect to the positions. However, if the retirement system has been abolished, newly created or reclassified positions or positions in a newly created political subdivision cannot be covered as a part of the retirement system coverage group. If the retirement system is not abolished, a newly created or reclassified position is a part of the coverage group if the position would have been a part of the group had it existed earlier. If the retirement system coverage group is made up of members who chose coverage, the newly created or reclassified position is a part of the coverage group if it is occupied by a member who chose coverage or by a new member.

§ 404.1218 Resumption of coverage.

Before April 20, 1983, an agreement could be terminated in its entirety or with respect to one or more coverage groups designated by the State. Coverage of any coverage group which has been previously terminated may be resumed by a modification to the agreement.

§ 404.1219 Dissolution of political subdivision.

If a political subdivision whose employees are covered under the agreement is legally dissolved, the State shall give us satisfactory evidence of its dissolution or nonexistence. The evidence must establish that the entity is not merely inactive or dormant, but that it no longer legally exists. We will notify the State whether the evidence is satisfactory.

HOW TO IDENTIFY COVERED EMPLOYEES

§ 404.1220 Identification numbers.

(a) State and local governments. When a State submits a modification to its agreement under section 218 of the Act, which extends coverage to periods prior to 1987, SSA will assign a special identification number to each political subdivision included in that modification. SSA will send the State a Form SSA–214–CD, "Notice of Identifying Number," to inform the State of the special identification number(s). The special number will be used for reporting the pre–1987 wages to SSA. The special number will also be assigned to an interstate instrumentality if pre–1987 coverage is obtained and SSA will send a Form SSA–214–CD to the interstate instrumentality to notify it of the number assigned.

(b) Coverage group number for coverage groups. If a State's agreement provides coverage for a State or a political subdivision based on designated proprietary or governmental functions, the State shall furnish a list of those groups. The list shall identify each designated function and the title and business address of the official responsible for filing each designated group's wage report. SSA assigns a coverage group number to each designated group based on the information furnished in the list.

(c) Unit numbers for payroll record units. SSA assigns, at a State's request, unit numbers to payroll record units within a State or political subdivision. When a State requests separate payroll record unit numbers, it must furnish the following:

(1) The name of each payroll record unit for the coverage group; and

(2) The title and business address of the official responsible for each payroll unit.

(d) Unit numbers where contribution amounts are limited—for wages paid prior to 1987. An agreement, or modification of an agreement, may provide for the computation of contributions as prescribed in § 404.1256 for some employees of a political subdivision. In this situation, SSA assigns special unit numbers to the political subdivision to identify those employees. SSA does not assign a special unit number to a political subdivision in which the contributions for all employees are computed as prescribed in § 404.1256.

(e) Use. For wages paid prior to 1987, the employer shall show the appropriate SSA-issued identifying number, including any coverage group or payroll record unit number, on records, reports, returns, and claims to report wages, adjustments, and contributions.

(Approved by the Office of Management and Budget under control number 0960–0425)

[60 FR 42433, Aug. 16, 1995; 64 FR 33016, June 21, 1999; 66 FR 28836, May 25, 2001]

WHAT RECORDS OF COVERAGE MUST BE KEPT

§ 404.1225 Records—for wages paid prior to 1987.

(a) Who keeps the records. Every State which enters into an agreement shall keep, or require the political subdivisions whose employees are included under its agreement to keep, accurate records of all remuneration (whether in cash or in a medium other than cash) paid to employees performing services covered by that agreement. These records shall show for each employee:

(1) The employee's name, address, and Social Security number;

(2) The total amount of remuneration (including any amount withheld as contributions or for any other reason) and the date the remuneration was paid and the period of services covered by the payment;

(3) The amount of remuneration which constitutes wages (see § 404.1041 for wages and §§ 404.1047–404.1059 for exclusions from wages); and

(4) The amount of the employee's contribution, if any, withheld or collected, and if collected at a time other than the time such payment was made, the date collected. If the total remuneration (paragraph (a)(2) of this section) and the amount which is subject to contribution (paragraph (a)(3) of this section) are not equal, the reason shall be stated.

The State shall keep copies of all returns, reports, schedules, and statements required by this subpart, copies of claims for refund or credit, and copies of documents about each adjustment made under § 404.1265 or § 404.1271 as part of its records. These records may be maintained by the State or, for employees of a political subdivision, by the political subdivision. Each State shall use forms and systems of accounting as will enable the Commissioner to determine whether the contributions for which the State is liable are correctly figured and paid.

(b) Place and period of time for keeping records. All records required by this section shall:

(1) Be kept at one or more convenient and safe locations accessible to reviewing personnel (see § 404.1232(a));

(2) Be available for inspection by reviewing personnel at any time; and

(3) Be maintained for at least four years from the date of the event recorded. (This four-year requirement applies regardless of whether, in the meantime, the employing entity has been legally dissolved or, before April 20, 1983, the agreement was terminated in its entirety or in part.)

(Approved by the Office of Management and Budget under control number 0960–0425)

[62 FR 38451, July 18, 1997; 66 FR 28836, May 25, 2001]

REVIEW OF COMPLIANCE BY STATE WITH ITS AGREEMENT

§ 404.1230 Onsite review program.

To ensure that the services of employees covered by a State's agreement are reported and that those employees receive Social Security credit for their covered earnings, we periodically review the source records upon which a State's contribution returns and wage reports are based. These reviews are designed:

(a) To measure the effectiveness of the State's systems for ensuring that all wages for those employees covered by its agreement are reported and Social Security contributions on those wages are paid;

(b) To detect any misunderstanding of coverage or reporting errors and to advise the State of the corrective action it must take; and

(c) To find ways to improve a State's recordkeeping and reporting operations for the mutual benefit of the State and SSA.

§ 404.1231 Scope of review.

The onsite review focuses on four areas:

(a) State's controls and recordkeeping—to assess a State's systems for assuring timely receipt, correctness, and completeness of wage reports and contribution returns;

(b) Instruction, education, and guidance a State provides local reporting officials—to assess a State's systems for assuring on a continuing basis that all reporting officials and their staffs have the necessary instructions, guidelines, and training to meet the State's coverage, reporting and recordkeeping requirements;

(c) Compliance by reporting officials—to assess a State's systems for assuring that the reporting officials in the State have adequate recordkeeping procedures, are properly applying the appropriate provisions of the State's agreement, and are complying with reporting requirements; and

(d) Quality control with prompt corrective action—to assess a State's systems for assuring that its reports and those of its political subdivisions are correct, for identifying the causes and extent of any deficiencies, and for promptly correcting these deficiencies.

§ 404.1232 Conduct of review.

(a) Generally, SSA staff personnel conduct the onsite review. Occasionally, members of the Office of the Inspector General may conduct or participate in the review.

(b) The review is done when considered necessary by SSA or, if practicable, in response to a State's specific request for a review.

(c) All pertinent source records prepared by the State or its political subdivisions are reviewed, on site, to verify the wage reports and contribution returns. We may review with the appropriate employees in a subdivision those source records and how the information is gathered, processed, and maintained. We notify the State's Social Security Administrator when we plan to make the review and request her or him to make the necessary arrangements.

(d) The review is a cooperative effort between SSA and the States to improve the methods for reporting and maintaining wage data to carry out the provisions of the agreement.

[62 FR 38451, July 18, 1997]

§ 404.1234 Reports of review's findings.

We provide the State Social Security Administrator with reports of the review's findings. These reports may contain coverage questions which need development and resolution and reporting errors or omissions for the State to correct promptly. These reports may also recommend actions the State can take to improve its information gathering, recordkeeping, and wage reporting systems, and those of its political subdivisions.

HOW TO REPORT WAGES AND CONTRIBUTIONS—FOR WAGES PAID PRIOR TO 1987

§ 404.1237 Wage reports and contribution returns—general—for wages paid prior to 1987.

(a) Wage reports. Each State shall report each year the wages paid each covered employee during that year. With the wage report the State shall also identify, as prescribed by SSA, each political subdivision by its assigned identification number and, where appropriate, any coverage group or payroll record unit number assigned.

(b) Wage reports of remuneration for agricultural labor. A State may exclude from its agreement any services of employees the remuneration for which is not wages under section 209(h)(2) of the Act. Section 209(h)(2) excludes as wages the cash remuneration an employer pays employees for agricultural labor which is less than $150 in a calendar year, or, if the employee performs the agricultural labor for the employer on less than 20 days during a calendar year, the cash remuneration computed on a time basis. If a State does exclude the services and the individual meets the cash-pay or 20–day test described in § 404.1056, the State shall identify on the wage report and on any adjustment report each individual performing agricultural labor and the amount paid to her or him.

(c) Contribution returns. The State shall forward the contribution return as set out in § 404.1249(b). It shall make contribution payments under § 404.1262.

(Approved by the Office of Management and Budget under control number 0960–0425)

[66 FR 28836, May 25, 2001]

§ 404.1239 Wage reports for employees performing services in more than one coverage group—for wages paid prior to 1987.

(a) Employee of State in more than one coverage group. If a State employee is in more than one coverage group, the State shall report the employee's total wages, up to the annual wage limitations in § 404.1047, as though the wages were paid by only one of the coverage groups.

(b) Employee of political subdivision in more than one coverage group. If an employee of a political subdivision is in more than one coverage group, the State shall report the employee's total wages, up to the annual wage limitations in § 404.1047, as though the wages were paid by only one of the coverage groups.

(c) Employee of State and one or more political subdivisions. If an individual performs covered services as an employee of the State and an employee of one or more political subdivisions and the State agreement does not provide for limiting contributions under section 218(e)(2) of the Act as it read prior to the enactment of Pub.L. 99–509, the State and each political subdivision shall report the amount of covered wages it paid the employee up to the annual wage limitations in § 404.1047.

(d) Employee of more than one political subdivision. If an individual performs covered services as an employee of more than one political subdivision and the State agreement does not provide for limiting contributions under section 218(e)(2) of the Act as it read prior to the enactment of Pub.L. 99–509, each political subdivision shall report the covered wages it paid the employee up to the annual wage limitations in § 404.1047.

(e) Employee performing covered services for more than one political entity where section 218(e)(2) of the Act is applicable. If an agreement provides for limiting contributions under section 218(e)(2) of the Act as it read prior to the enactment of Pub.L. 99–509, the reporting officials compute the total amount of wages paid the employee by two or more political subdivisions of a State, or a State and one or more of its political subdivisions, which were subject to section 218(e)(2) of the Act. The State reports the amount of wages paid up to the annual wage limitations in § 404.1047. The employee is treated as having only one employer. If the employee also had wages not subject to section 218(e)(2) of the Act, the State shall report those wages separately.

(Approved by the Office of Management and Budget under control number 0960–0425)

[66 FR 28836, May 25, 2001]

§ 404.1242 Back pay.

(a) Back pay defined. Back pay is pay received in one period of time which would have been paid in a prior period of time except for a wrongful or improper action taken by an employer. It includes pay made under Federal or State laws intended to create an employment relationship (including situations where there is unlawful refusal to hire) or to protect an employee's right to wages.

(b) Back pay under a statute. Back pay under a statute is a payment by an employer following an award, determination or agreement approved or sanctioned by a court or administrative agency responsible for enforcing a Federal or State statute protecting an employee's right to employment or wages. Examples of these statutes are:

(1) National Labor Relations Act or a State labor relations act;

(2) Federal or State laws providing reemployment rights to veterans;

(3) State minimum wage laws; and

(4) Civil Rights Act of 1964.

Payments based on legislation comparable to and having a similar effect as those listed in this paragraph may also qualify as having been made under a statute. Back pay under a statute, excluding penalties, is wages if paid for covered employment. It is allocated to the periods of time in which it should have been paid if the employer had not violated the statute. For backpay awards affecting periods prior to 1987, a State must fill a wage report and pay the contributions due for all periods involved in the back pay award under the rules applicable to those periods.

(c) Back pay not under a statute. Where the employer and the employee agree on the amount payable without any award, determination or agreement approved or sanctioned by a court or administrative agency, the payment is not made under a statute. This back pay cannot be allocated to prior periods of time but must be reported by the employer for the period in which it is paid.

(Approved by the Office of Management and Budget under control number 0960–0425)

[66 FR 28836, May 25, 2001]

§ 404.1243 Use of reporting forms—for wages paid prior to 1987.

(a) Submitting wage reports. In the form and manner required by SSA, a State shall submit an annual report of the covered wages the State and its political subdivisions paid their employees. Any supplemental, adjustment, or correctional wage report filed is considered a part of the State's wage report.

(b) Correction of errors. If a State fails to report or incorrectly reports an employee's wages on its wage report, the State shall submit a corrective report as required by SSA.

(c) Reporting on magnetic tape or other media. After approval by SSA, a State may substitute magnetic tape or other media for any form required for submitting a report or reporting information.

(Approved by the Office of Management and Budget under control number 0960–0425)

[66 FR 28836, May 25, 2001]

§ 404.1247 When to report wages—for wages paid prior to 1987.

A State shall report wages for the calendar year in which they were actually paid. If the wages were constructively paid in a prior calendar year, the wages shall be reported for the prior year (see § 404.1042(b) regarding constructive payment of wages).

(Approved by the Office of Management and Budget under control number 0960–0425)

[66 FR 28836, May 25, 2001]

§ 404.1249 When and where to make deposits of contributions and to file contribution returns and wage reports—for wages paid prior to 1987.

(a) Deposits of contributions. The State shall pay contributions in the manner required in § 404.1262. (For failure to make deposits when due see § 404.1265.) The contribution payment is considered made when received by the appropriate Federal Reserve bank or branch (see § 404.1262). Except as provided in paragraphs (b)(2) and (3) and paragraph (c) of this section, contributions are due and payable as follows:

(1) For wages paid before July 1, 1980. Contribution payments for wages paid in a calendar quarter are due on the 15th day of the second month following the end of the calendar quarter during which the wages were paid.

(2) For wages paid beginning July 1, 1980, and before January 1984. Contribution payments for wages paid in a calendar month are due within the thirty day period following the last day of that month.

(3) For wages paid after December 1983 and prior to 1987. Contribution payments for wages paid in the first half of a calendar month are due on the last day of that month. Contribution payments for wages paid in the second half of that calendar month are due on the fifteenth day of the next month. (For purposes of this section, the first half of a calendar month is the first 15 days of that month and the second half is the remainder of that month.)

(b) Contribution returns and wage reports—

(1) Where to be filed. The State shall file the original copies of all contribution returns, wage reports, and adjustment reports with the SSA.

(2) When to be filed—

(i) For years prior to execution of agreement or modification. If an agreement or modification provides for the coverage of employees for periods prior to 1987, the State shall pay contributions due and shall file wage reports with SSA for these periods within 90 days after the date of the notice that the Commissioner has signed the agreement or modification.

(ii) For year of execution of agreement or modification. If the agreement or modification provides for the coverage of employees for the year of execution of the agreement or modification, the State may, within 90 days after the date of the notice that the Commissioner has signed the agreement or modification, submit a single contribution return and pay all contributions due for the following periods:

(A) The month in which the agreement or modification was signed;

(B) Any prior months in that year; and

(C) Any subsequent months before January 1984 (half-months after December 1983) whose contribution return and payment due date is within this 90 day period. The State shall file wage reports for that year by February 28 of the year following the date of execution or within 90 days of the date of the notice, whichever is later.

(iii) For years after execution of agreement or modification. Except as described in paragraph (b)(2)(ii) of this section, when the State pays its contributions under paragraph (a) of this section, it shall also file a contribution return. The State shall file the wage report for any calendar year after the year of execution of the agreement or modification by February 28 of the following calendar year.

(iv) For good cause shown, and upon written request by a State, the Commissioner may allow additional time for filing the reports and paying the related contributions described in paragraphs (b)(2)(i) and (b)(2)(ii) of this section.

(3) Due date is on a weekend, legal holiday or Federal nonworkday. If the last day for filing the wage report falls on a weekend, legal holiday or Federal nonworkday, the State may file the wage report on the next Federal workday. If the due date for paying contributions for the wages paid in a period (as specified in paragraph (a) of this section) falls on a weekend, legal holiday or Federal nonworkday, the State shall pay the contributions and shall file the contribution return no later than—

(i) The preceding Federal workday for wages paid in July 1980 through December 1983;

(ii) The next Federal workday for wages paid before July 1980 or after December 1983.

(4) Submitting reports and payments. When submitting the contribution returns or wage reports the State shall release them in time to reach SSA by the due date. When submitting contribution payments as described in § 404.1262, the State shall release the payments in time to reach the appropriate Federal Reserve bank or branch by the due date. In determining when to release any returns, reports, or payments the State shall provide sufficient time for them to timely reach their destination under the method of submission used, e.g., mail or electronic transfer of funds.

(c) Payments by third party on account of sickness or accident disability. Where a third party makes a payment to an employee on account of sickness or accident disability which constitutes wages for services covered under a State agreement, the wages will be considered, for purposes of the deposits required under this section, to have been paid to the employee on the date on which the employer receives notice from the third party of the amount of the payment. No interest will be assessed for failure to make a timely deposit of contributions due on such wages for which a deposit was made after December 1981 and before July 1982, to the extent that the failure to make the deposit timely is due to reasonable cause and not willful neglect.

[62 FR 38451, July 18, 1997; 66 FR 28836, May 25, 2001]

§ 404.1251 Final reports—for wages paid prior to 1987.

If a political subdivision is legally dissolved, the State shall file a final report on that entity. The report shall include each coverage group whose existence ceases with that of the entity. It shall:

(a) Be marked "final report";

(b) Cover the period during which final payment of wages subject to the agreement is made; and

(c) Indicate the last date wages were paid.

With the final report, the State shall submit a statement showing the title and business address of the State official responsible for keeping the State's records and of each State and local official responsible for keeping the records for each coverage group whose existence is ended. The State shall also identify, as prescribed by SSA, each political subdivision by its assigned number and, where applicable, any coverage group or payroll record unit number assigned.

(Approved by the Office of Management and Budget under control number 0960–0425)

[66 FR 28836, May 25, 2001]

WHAT IS A STATE'S LIABILITY FOR CONTRIBUTIONS—FOR WAGES PAID PRIOR TO 1987

§ 404.1255 State's liability for contributions—for wages paid prior to 1987.

A State's liability for contributions equals the sum of the taxes which would be imposed by sections 3101 and 3111 of the Internal Revenue Code of 1954, if the services of the employees covered by the State's agreement were employment as defined in section 3121 of the Code. The State's liability begins when those covered services are performed, for which wages are actually or constructively paid to those individuals, including wages paid in a form other than cash (see

§ 404.1041(d)). If an agreement is effective retroactively, the State's liability for contributions on wages paid during the retroactive period begins with the date of execution of the agreement or applicable modification. Where coverage of a coverage group has been terminated, the State is liable for contributions on wages paid for covered services even if the wages are paid after the effective date of termination of coverage.

§ 404.1256 Limitation on State's liability for contributions for multiple employment situations—for wages paid prior to 1987.

(a) Limitation due to multiple employment. Where an individual in any calendar year performs covered services as an employee of a State and as an employee of one or more political subdivisions of the State, or as an employee of more than one political subdivision; and the State provides all the funds for payment of the amounts which are equivalent to the taxes imposed on the employer under FICA on that individual's remuneration for those services; and no political subdivision reimburses the State for paying those amounts; the State's agreement or modification of an agreement may provide that the State's liability for the contributions on that individual's remuneration shall be computed as though the individual had performed services in employment for only one political subdivision. The State may then total the individual's covered wages from all these governmental employers and compute the contributions based on that total subject to the wage limitations in § 404.1047.

(b) Identification of employees in multiple employment. An agreement or modification of an agreement providing for the computation of contributions as described in paragraph (a) of this section shall identify the class or classes of employees to whose wages this method of computing contributions applies. For example, the State may provide that such computation shall apply to the wages paid to all individuals for services performed in positions covered by a particular retirement system, or to the wages paid to all individuals who are members of any two or more coverage groups designated in an agreement or modification. The State shall promptly notify SSA if the conditions in paragraph (a) of this section are no longer met by any class or classes of employees identified in an agreement or modification. In its notification, the State shall identify each class of employees and the date on which the conditions ceased to be met.

(c) Effective date. In the agreement or modification, the State shall provide that the computation of contributions shall apply to wages paid after the effective date stated in the agreement or modification. That date may be the last day of any calendar year; however, it may be no earlier than January 1 of the year in which the agreement or modification is submitted to SSA.

FIGURING THE AMOUNT OF THE STATE'S CONTRIBUTIONS—FOR WAGES PAID PRIOR TO 1987

§ 404.1260 Amount of contributions—for wages paid prior to 1987.

The State's contributions are equal to the product of the applicable contribution rate (which is equivalent to both the tax rates imposed under sections 3101 and 3111 of the Internal Revenue Code) times the amount of wages actually or constructively paid for covered services each year (subject to the wage limitations in § 404.1047) to the employee.

§ 404.1262 Manner of payment of contributions by State—for wages paid prior to 1987.

When paying its contributions, the State shall deposit its payment at the specific Federal Reserve bank or branch designated by SSA.

§ 404.1263 When fractional part of a cent may be disregarded—for wages paid prior to 1987.

In paying contributions to a Federal Reserve bank or branch, a State may disregard a fractional part of a cent unless it amounts to one-half cent or more, in which case it shall be increased to one cent. Fractional parts of a cent shall be used in computing the total of contributions.

IF A STATE FAILS TO MAKE TIMELY PAYMENTS—FOR WAGES PAID PRIOR TO 1987

§ 404.1265 Addition of interest to contributions—for wages paid prior to 1987.

(a) Contributions not paid timely. If a State fails to pay its contributions to the appropriate Federal Reserve bank or branch (see § 404.1262), when due under § 404.1249(a), we add interest on the unpaid amount of the contributions beginning with the date the payment was due, except as described in paragraphs (b) and (c) of this section. Interest, if charged, begins with the due date even if it is a weekend, legal holiday or Federal nonwork day. Interest is added at the rate prescribed in section 218(j) of the Act as it read prior to the enactment of Pub.L. 99–509.

(b) Method of making adjustment.

(1) If a State shall file a contribution return and shall accompany such return with payment of contributions due and payable as reported on such return in accordance with § 404.1249 but the amount of the contributions reported and paid is less than the correct amount of contributions due and payable and the un-

derpayment of contributions is attributable to an error in computing the contributions (other than an error in applying the rate of contributions in effect at the time the wages were paid), the State shall adjust the underpayment by reporting the additional amount due by reason of such underpayment either as an adjustment of total contributions due with the first wage report filed after notification of the underpayment by the Social Security Administration, or as a single adjustment of total contributions due with any contribution return filed prior to the filing of such wage report.

(2) If an underpayment of contributions is due to an underreporting of or a failure to report one or more employees:

(i) Where the underreporting or failure to report has been ascertained by the State, the State may cause an adjustment by filing a report within 30 days after ascertainment of the error by the State;

(ii) Where the underreporting or failure to report has been ascertained by the Social Security Administration, a notification of underpayment shall be forwarded to the State, and the State may cause an adjustment of the underpayment by returning to the Social Security Administration, within 30 days from the date of the notification, a copy of the notification of underpayment and the State's corrected report. The report shall show the amount of wages, if any, erroneously reported for the reporting period and the correct amount of wages that should have been reported and the identification number of the State or the political subdivision for each employee who was omitted or erroneously reported. The filing to correct an underreporting of or a failure to report one or more employees' wages shall not constitute an adjustment under this section unless the wages were erroneously omitted or erroneously reported.

(c) *Payment.* The amount of each underpayment adjusted in accordance with this section shall be paid to the Federal Reserve Bank, or branch thereof, serving the district in which the State is located, without interest, at the time of reporting the adjustment; except that where any amounts due with respect to such an adjustment had been paid in error to IRS and a refund thereof timely requested from, or instituted by, IRS, the amount of underpayment adjusted in accordance with this section, plus any interest paid by IRS on the amount of such underpayment, shall be paid to the Federal Reserve Bank, or branch thereof, serving the district in which the State is located, at the time of reporting the adjustment or within 30 days after the date of issuance by IRS of the refund of the erroneous payments, whichever is later. Except as provided in the preceding sentence of this paragraph, if an adjustment is reported pursuant to paragraph (b) of this section, but the amount thereof is not paid when due, interest thereafter accrues.

(d) *Verifying contributions paid against reported wages.* We check the computation of contributions to verify that a State has paid the correct amount of contributions on the wages it reports for a calendar year (see § 404.1249(b)(2)). If we determine that a State paid less than the amount of contributions due for that year, we add interest to the amount of the underpayment. We would add interest beginning with the date the unpaid contributions were initially due to the date those contributions are paid. However, if the total amount of the underpayment is 5 percent or less than 5 percent of the contributions due for a calendar year based upon the State's wage report and the State deposits the underpaid amount within 30 days after the date of our notification to the State of the amount due, the State may request that the interest on the underpaid amount be waived for good cause. This request must be made within 30 days of our notification to the State of the amount due. Such requests will be evaluated on an individual basis. The evaluation will include, but not be limited to, consideration of such factors as the circumstances causing the late payment, the State's past record of late payments and the amount involved.

Examples (1) The records of a political subdivision for the month of June are destroyed by fire. The State makes an estimated deposit of contributions for the month of June for that political subdivision and deposits contributions for the month of June for all other political subdivisions based on actual records. At the time SSA verifies contributions paid against reported wages, we discover that the State has paid only 97 percent of its total liability for the year. Within 30 days after we notify it of the amount due, the State asks that we waive the interest on the unpaid amount and the State deposits the unpaid amount. In this situation, we would waive the interest on the unpaid contributions.

(2) We would waive interest if:

(i) Some of the political subdivisions made small arithmetical errors in preparing their reports of wages,

(ii) After verification of the contributions paid against reported wages, SSA discovers that minimal additional contributions are due,

(iii) Within 30 days of our notice to the State regarding this underpayment the State, which usually makes its deposits timely, pays the amount due, and

(iv) Within that same 30 day period the State requests that we waive the interest due.

(3) We would not waive interest where a State frequently has problems depositing its contributions timely. Reasons given for the delays are, e.g., the computer was down, the 5 p.m. mail pickup was missed, one of the school district reports was misplaced. If requested we would not waive interest on this State's late payment of contributions based upon its past record of late payments and because of the circumstances cited.

(e) *Due date is on a weekend, legal holiday or Federal nonworkday.* If the last day of the 30–day periods specified in paragraphs (b) and (d) of this section is on a weekend, legal holiday or Federal nonworkday, the State shall make the required deposit or request for waiver of payment of interest on the next Federal workday.

(Approved by the Office of Management and Budget under control number 0960–0425)

[66 FR 28836, May 25, 2001]

§ 404.1267 Failure to make timely payments—for wages paid prior to 1987.

If a State does not pay its contributions when due, the Commissioner has the authority under section 218(j) of the Act as it read prior to the enactment of Pub.L. 99–509 to deduct the amounts of the unpaid contributions plus interest at the rate prescribed from any amounts certified by her or him to the Secretary of the Treasury for payments to the State under any other provision of the Social Security Act. The Commissioner notifies the Secretary of the Treasury of the amounts deducted and requests that the amount be credited to the Trust Funds. Amounts deducted are considered paid to the State under the other provision of the Social Security Act.

[62 FR 38451, July 18, 1997]

HOW ERRORS IN REPORTS AND CONTRIBUTIONS ARE ADJUSTED—FOR WAGES PAID PRIOR TO 1987

§ 404.1270 Adjustments in general—for wages paid prior to 1987.

States have the opportunity to adjust errors in the payment of contributions. A State but not its political subdivisions is authorized to adjust errors in the underpayment of contributions. Similarly, the State shall file all claims for credits or refunds and SSA makes the credits and refunds only to the State. Generally, we do not refund contributions in cash to a State unless the State is not expected to have future liability for contributions under section 218 of the Act.

§ 404.1271 Adjustment of overpayment of contributions—for wages paid prior to 1987.

(a) General. If a State pays more than the correct amount of contributions, the State shall adjust the overpayment with the next contribution return filed on which the amount owed equals or exceeds the amount of the overpayment.

(b) Overpayment due to overreporting of wages—

(1) Report to file. If the overpayment is due to the State's reporting more than the correct amount of wages paid to one or more employees during a reporting period and the overpayment is not adjusted under paragraph (a) of this section, the State shall file a report on the appropriate form showing:

(i) The corrected wage data as prescribed by SSA; and

(ii) The reason why the original reporting was incorrect.

(2) Refund or credit of overpayment where section 218(e)(2) of the Act not applicable. If:

(i) The State collected contributions from employees in excess of the amount of taxes that would have been required under section 3101 of the Internal Revenue Code; and

(ii) The State paid to the Secretary of the Treasury those contributions plus a matching amount in excess of the taxes which would have been required from an employer under section 3111 of the Code; and

(iii) The services of the employees in question would have constituted employment under section 3121(b) of the Code; and

(iv) Section 218(e)(2) of the Act as it read prior to the enactment of Pub.L. 99–509 does not apply (see § 404.1256(a)), then the State shall adjust the overpaid contributions under paragraph (b)(1) of this section. With its adjustment the State, where appropriate, shall include on the prescribed form a statement that the employees from whom the excess contributions were collected have not received nor expect to receive a refund of excess contributions under section 6413(c) of the Internal Revenue Code of 1954 (see § 404.1275(b)). Generally, if the State does not include this statement with its adjustment request, we only refund or credit the State for up to one-half of the overpaid amount.

(c) Refund or credit of overpayment where section 218(e)(2) of the Act applicable—

(1) General. If—

(i) The overreporting of the amount of wages paid to one or more employees during a reporting period(s) is due to a computation of contributions under § 404.1256 for a year or years prior to the year in which the agreement or modification providing for the computation is entered into, or

(ii) The overreporting is due to a failure to compute § 404.1256,

the State shall adjust the overpayment under paragraph (b)(1) of this section. An overpayment due to overreported wages which does not result from the computation of contributions or a failure to compute contributions under § 404.1256 shall also be adjusted by the State under paragraph (b)(1) of this section. If the adjustment of the overpayment results in an underreporting of wages for any employee by the State or any political subdivision, the State shall include with the report adjusting the overpayment a report adjusting each underreporting. If the adjustment of the overpayment does not result in an underreporting of wages for any employee by the State or any political subdivision, the State shall include with the report adjusting the overpayment a statement that the adjustment of the overpayment does not result in any underreporting.

(2) Amount of refund or credit. If the State collects excess contributions from employees, the State's claim for refund or credit is limited to the overpaid amounts. (See § 404.1275 relating to adjustment of employee contributions.) If—

(i) The State collected the correct amount of contributions from employees based on the amount of wages reported and the Forms W–2 issued to the employees show only the amount of contributions actually collected, but the amount of wages reported is being adjusted downward, or

(ii) The State collects excess contributions from employees but Forms W–2 have not been issued for an amount of wages which is being adjusted downward, the State may claim a refund or credit for the overpaid amounts. Where the State's claim for refund or credit is for the total overpaid amount, the adjustment report shall include a statement that excess contributions have not been collected from employees, or, where excess contributions have been collected, that Forms W–2 have not been issued and that, when issued, they will show the correct amount of employee contributions.

(Approved by the Office of Management and Budget under control number 0960–0425)

[66 FR 28836, May 25, 2001]

§ 404.1272 Refund or recomputation of overpayments which are not adjustable—for wages paid prior to 1987.

(a) General. If a State pays more than the correct amount of contributions or interest to the appropriate Federal Reserve bank or branch (see § 404.1262), and no adjustment in the amount of reported wages is necessary, that State may file a claim for refund or recomputation of the overpayment.

(b) Form of claim. No special form is required to make a claim for a refund or recomputation. If a credit is taken under § 404.1271, a claim is not required.

(c) Proof of representative capacity. If a report or return is made by an authorized official of the State who ceases to act in an official capacity and a claim for a refund is made by a successor official, the successor official must submit with the claim written evidence showing that he or she has the authority to make a claim for and receive a refund of any contributions paid by the former official. The written evidence is not necessary if the successor official has previously filed one or more reports or returns which contain her or his signature and official title.

(Approved by the Office of Management and Budget under control number 0960–0425)

[66 FR 28836, May 25, 2001]

§ 404.1275 Adjustment of employee contributions—for wages paid prior to 1987.

The amount of contributions a State deducts from an employee's remuneration for covered services, or any correction of that amount, is a matter between the employee and the State or political subdivision. The State shall show any correction of an employee's contribution on statements it furnishes the employee under § 404.1225 of this part. Where the State issues an employee a Form W–2 and then submits an overpayment adjustment but claims less than the total overpaid amount as a refund or credit, the State shall not correct the previously issued Form W–2 to reflect that adjustment.

[65 FR 16813, March 30, 2000]

§ 404.1276 Reports and payments erroneously made to Internal Revenue Service-transfer of funds—for wages paid prior to 1987.

(a) General. In some instances, State or local governmental entities not covered under an agreement make reports and pay contributions to IRS under the Federal Insurance Contributions Act (FICA) procedures applicable to private employers in the mistaken belief that this provides Social Security coverage under section 218 of the Act for their employees. In other instances, entities which are covered under an agreement erroneously report to IRS, or a State or local government employee reports other employees to IRS or reports to IRS as a self-employed individual. Where these reports and payments are erroneously made to IRS, the State may correct the error and obtain coverage under its agreement as described in paragraphs (b) through (f) of this section.

(b) Political subdivision not included in the State agreement. We notify the State that if it desires coverage, it may be provided by either a regular modification or an error modification, depending on the circumstances (§§ 404.1215 and 404.1216). In most cases, the State may obtain coverage by a regular modification. If a regular modification cannot be used (e.g., State law does not permit the retroactive effective date which would be desired), the State may use an error modification. The effective date of either modification depends on the facts of the situation being corrected.

(c) Political subdivision included in the agreement. If a political subdivision included in the agreement erroneously makes reports and payments under FICA procedures, the State must correct the reportings for periods not barred by the statute of limitations. If the covered entity reported both under the agreement and under FICA procedures, we notify IRS and make necessary corrections in the earnings records. We also advise the State that the entity which reported under FICA procedures should request a refund of payments erroneously made to IRS.

(d) State and local government employees erroneously reported as employees of individual or as self-employed—

(1) Covered entity. If employees of a covered entity are erroneously reported as employees of an individual or as self-employed, we advise the State that the individual who made the reports should request a refund from IRS for periods not barred by the statute of limitations. We require the State to file correctional reports and returns for any periods open under the State and local statute of limitations.

(2) Noncovered entity. We advise the State that the individual who made the reports should request a refund from IRS for the periods not barred by the statute of limitations. If the State wishes to provide coverage, it must submit a modification as discussed in paragraph (b) of this section. If the State does not wish to provide coverage, we void the reports. Amounts reported for periods barred by the statute of limitations remain on the earnings records.

(e) Filing wage reports and paying contributions. Generally, the entity or individual that makes the erroneous reports and payments requests the refund from IRS for periods not barred by the statute of limitations. The State files the necessary reports with SSA and pays any contributions due. The reports shall conform to the coverage provided by the agreement to the extent permitted by the statute of limitations. The due date for these reports depends on whether original reports or adjustment reports are involved. Reports and contribution returns for the entire retroactive period of coverage provided by a regular or error modification are due 90 days after the date of execution of the modification. The time limitations for issuing assessments and credits or refunds extend from this due date. Thus, SSA may issue assessments or credits or refunds for periods barred to refund by IRS. The State may request that reports and payments for the IRS barred periods be considered made under the agreement as described in paragraph (f) of this section.

(f) Use of transfer procedure. In limited situations, the State may request that reports and payments the State or a political subdivision (but not an individual) erroneously made under FICA procedures and which have been posted to the employee's earnings record be considered made under the State's agreement. We use a transfer procedure to do this. The transfer procedure may be used only where

(1) The periods are open to assessment under the State and local statute of limitations;

(2) The erroneous reports to be transferred are posted to SSA's records;

(3) The periods are barred to refund under the IRS statute of limitations; and

(4) A refund is not obtained from IRS by the reporting entity.

HOW OVERPAYMENTS OF CONTRIBUTIONS ARE CREDITED OR REFUNDED—FOR WAGES PAID PRIOR TO 1987

§ 404.1280 Allowance of credits or refunds—for wages paid prior to 1987.

If a State pays more than the amount of contributions due under an agreement, SSA may allow the State, subject to the time limitations in § 404.1282 and the exceptions to the time limitations in § 404.1283, a credit or refund of the overpayment.

§ 404.1281 Credits or refunds for periods of time during which no liability exists—for wages paid prior to 1987.

If a State pays contributions for any period of time for which contributions are not due, but the State is liable for contributions for another period, we credit the amount paid against the amount of contributions for which the State is liable. We refund any balance to the State.

§ 404.1282 Time limitations on credits or refunds—for wages paid prior to 1987.

(a) General. To get a credit or refund, a State must file a claim for a credit or refund of the overpaid amount with the Commissioner before the applicable time limitation expires. The State's claim for credit or refund is considered filed with the Commissioner when it is delivered or mailed to the Commissioner. Where the time limitation ends on a weekend, legal holiday or Federal nonworkday, we consider a claim timely filed if it is filed on the next Federal workday.

(b) Time limitation. Subject to the exceptions in § 404.1283, a State must file a claim for credit or refund of an overpayment before the end of the latest of the following time periods:

(1) 3 years, 3 months, and 15 days after the year in which the wages in question were paid or alleged to have been paid; or

(2) 3 years after the due date of the payment which included the overpayment; or

(3) 2 years after the overpayment was made to the Secretary of the Treasury.

[62 FR 38451, July 18, 1997]

§ 404.1283 Exceptions to the time limitations on credits or refunds—for wages paid prior to 1987.

(a)(1) Extension by agreement. The applicable time period described in § 404.1282 for filing a claim for credit for, or refund of, an overpayment may, before the expiration of such period, be extended for no more than 6 months by written agreement between the State and the Commissioner. The agreement must involve and identify a known issue or reporting error. It must also identify the periods involved, the time limitation which is being extended and the date to which it is being extended, and the coverage group(s) and position(s) or individual(s) to which the agreement applies. The extension of the period of limitation shall not become effective until the agreement is signed by the appropriate State official and the Commissioner. (See § 404.3(c) for the applicable rule where periods of limitation expire on nonwork days.) A claim for credit or refund filed by the State before the extended time limit ends shall be considered to have been filed within the time period limitation specified in section 218(r)(1) of the Act as it read prior to the enactment of Pub.L. 99–509. (See § 404.1282.)

(2) Reextension. An extension agreement provided for in paragraph (a)(1) of this section may be reextended by written agreement between the State and the Commissioner for no more than 6 months at a time beyond the expiration of the prior extension or reextension agreement, and only if one of the following conditions is met:

(i) Litigation (including intrastate litigation) or a review under §§ 404.1290 or 404.1297 involving wage reports or corrections on the same issue is pending; or

(ii) The State is actively pursuing corrections of a known error which require additional time to complete; or

(iii) The Social Security Administration is developing a coverage or wage issue which was being considered before the statute of limitations expired and additional time is needed to make a determination; or

(iv) The Social Security Administration has not issued to the State a final audit statement on the State's wage or correction reports; or

(v) There is pending Federal legislation which may substantially affect the issue in question, or the issue has national implications.

(b) Deletion of wage entry on employee's earnings record. If the Commissioner, under section 205(c)(5)(A), (B), or (E) of the Act, deletes a wage entry on an individual's earnings record, a claim for credit or refund of the overpayment resulting from the deletion is considered filed within the applicable time limitations in § 404.1282 if

(1) The State files the claim before the Commissioner's decision regarding the deletion of the wage entry from the individual's earnings record becomes final or

(2) The State files a claim regarding the deletion of the wage entry from the individual's earnings record which entry is erroneous because of fraud.

[62 FR 38451, July 18, 1997]

§ 404.1284 Offsetting underpayments against overpayments—for wages paid prior to 1987.

(a) State fails to make adjustment for allowance of credit. If SSA notifies a State that a credit is due the State, and the State does not make the adjustment for the allowance of the credit, SSA offsets the credit against any contributions or interest due. Before making the offset, SSA will give the State an opportunity to make the adjustment.

(b) State fails to make adjustment for underpayment of contributions or interest due. If SSA notifies a State that contributions or interest are due, and the State does not pay the contributions or interest, SSA offsets the contributions or interest due against any credit due the State. Before making the offset, SSA will give the State an opportunity to pay the underpayment or interest due.

HOW ASSESSMENTS FOR UNDERPAYMENTS OF CONTRIBUTIONS ARE MADE—FOR WAGES PAID PRIOR TO 1987

§ 404.1285 Assessments of amounts due—for wages paid prior to 1987.

(a) A State is liable for any amount due (which includes contributions or interest) under an agreement until the Commissioner is satisfied that the amount has been paid to the Secretary of the Treasury. If the Commissioner is not satisfied that a State has paid the amount due, the Commissioner issues an assessment for the amount due subject to the time limitations in § 404.1286 and the exceptions to the time limitations in §§ 404.1287 and 404.1289. If detailed wage information is not available, the assessment is issued based on the following:

(1) The largest number of individuals whose services are known to be covered under the agreement is used for computation purposes;

(2) The individuals are assumed to have maximum creditable earnings each year;

(3) The earnings are considered wages for covered services; and

(4) The amount computed is increased by twenty percent to insure that all covered wages are included in the assessment.

(b) If the State pays the amount assessed and the assessed amount is later determined to be more than the amount actually due, we issue a refund or credit to that State for the excess amount. When the assessment is issued within the applicable time limitation, there is no time limit on collecting the amount due. An assessment is issued on the date that it is mailed or otherwise delivered to the State.

[62 FR 38451, July 18, 1997]

§ 404.1286 Time limitations on assessments—for wages paid prior to 1987.

(a) Subject to the exceptions to the time limitations in §§ 404.1287 and 404.1289, a State is not liable for an amount due under an agreement unless the Commissioner makes an assessment for that amount before the later of the following periods ends:

(1) Three years, 3 months, and 15 days after the year in which the wages, upon which the amount is due, were paid; or

(2) Three years after the date the amount became due.

(b) Where the time limitation ends on a weekend, legal holiday or Federal nonworkday, an assessment is considered timely if the Commissioner makes the assessment on the next Federal workday.

[62 FR 38451, July 18, 1997]

§ 404.1287 Exceptions to the time limitations on assessments—for wages paid prior to 1987.

(a)(1) Extension by agreement. The applicable time period described in § 404.1286 for assessment of an amount due may, before the expiration of such period, be extended for no more than 6 months by written agreement between the State and the Commissioner. The agreement must involve and identify a known issue or reporting error. It must also identify the periods involved, the time limitation which is being extended and the date to which it is being extended, and the coverage group(s) and position(s) or individual(s) to which the agreement applies. The extension of the period of limitation shall not become effective until the agreement is signed by the appropriate State official and the Commissioner. (See § 404.3(c) for the applicable rule where periods of limitation expire on nonwork days.) An assessment made by the Commissioner before the extended time limit ends shall be considered to have been made within the time period limitation specified in section 218(q)(2) of the Act as it read prior to the enactment of Pub.L. 99–509. (See § 404.1286.)

(2) Reextension. An extension agreement provided for in paragraph (a)(1) of this section may be reextended by written agreement between the State and the Commissioner for no more than 6 months at a time beyond the expiration of the prior extension or reextension agreement, and only if one of the following conditions is met:

(i) Litigation (including intrastate litigation) or a review under § 404.1290 or § 404.1297 involving wage reports or corrections on the same issue is pending; or

(ii) The State is actively pursuing corrections of a known error which require additional time to complete; or

(iii) The Social Security Administration is developing a coverage or wage issue which was being considered before the statute of limitations expired and additional time is needed to make a determination; or

(iv) The Social Security Administration has not issued to the State a final audit statement on the State's wage or correction reports; or

(v) There is pending Federal legislation which may substantially affect the issue in question, or the issue has national implications.

(b) The 365–day period. If a State files a report before the applicable time limitation in § 404.1286 (or any extension under paragraph (a) of this section) ends and makes no payment or pays less than the correct amount due, the Commissioner may assess the State for the amount due after the applicable time limitation has ended. However, the Commissioner must make the assessment no later than the 365th day after the day the State makes payment to the Secretary of the Treasury. The Commissioner can only make this assessment on the wages paid to the reported individuals for the reported periods. The Commissioner, in making this assessment, credits the amount paid by the State on these individuals' wages for those reported periods.

(c) Revision of employee's earnings record. If, under section 205(c)(5)(A) or (B) of the Act, the Commissioner credits wages to an individual's earnings record, the Commissioner may make an assessment for any amount due on those wages before the Commissioner's decision on revising the individual's earnings record becomes final. (Sections 404.822(c)(1) and (2) describe the time limits for revising an earnings record where an individual has applied for monthly benefits or a lump-sum death payment or requested that we correct his earnings record.)

(d) Overpayment of contributions on wages of employee having other wages in a period barred to assessment. If the Commissioner allows a State a credit or refund of an overpayment for wages paid or alleged to have been paid an individual in a calendar year but the facts upon which the allowance is based establish that contributions are due on other wages paid that individual in that year which are barred to assessment, we may make an assessment notwithstanding the periods of limitation in § 404.1286. The assessment, however, must be made before or at the time we notify the State of the allowance of the credit or refund. In this situation, the Commissioner reduces the amount of the State's credit or refund by the assessed amount and notifies the State accordingly. For purposes of this paragraph, the assessment shall only include contributions and not interest as provided for in section 218(j) of the Act as it read prior to the enactment of Pub.L. 99–509.

Example: The State files an adjustment report timely to correct an error in the amount reported as wages for an employee. The correction reduces the employee's wages for the year to less than the maximum amount creditable. The employee has other earnings in the same year which were not reported because of the previously reported maximum amounts. The applicable time limitation for assessing contributions on wages for the year has expired before the credit was allowed. The Commissioner may assess for the underpaid contributions but no later than the date of the notice to the State that its claim for a credit had been allowed.

(e) Evasion of payment. The Commissioner may make an assessment of an amount due at any time where the State's failure to pay the amount due results from the fraudulent attempt of an officer or employee of the State or political subdivision to defeat or evade payment of that amount.

[62 FR 38451, July 18, 1997]

§ 404.1289 Payment after expiration of time limitation for assessment—for wages paid prior to 1987.

The Commissioner accepts wage reports filed by a State even though the applicable time limitation described in § 404.1286 (or as the time limitation is extended under § 404.1287) has expired, provided:

(a) The State pays to the Secretary of the Treasury the amount due on the wages paid to employees performing services in the coverage group in the calendar years for which the wage reports are being made; and

(b) The State agrees in writing with the Secretary to extend the time limitation for all employees in the coverage group in the calendar years for which the wage reports are being made.

In this situation, the time period for assessment is extended until the Commissioner notifies the State that the wage reports are accepted. Where the State pays the amount due within the time period as extended under this section, the amount shall not include interest as provided for in section 218(j) of the Act as it read prior to the enactment of Pub.L. 99–509.

[62 FR 38451, July 18, 1997]

SECRETARY'S REVIEW OF DECISIONS ON CREDITS, REFUNDS, OR ASSESSMENTS—FOR WAGES PAID PRIOR TO 1987

§ 404.1290 Review of decisions by the Secretary—for wages paid prior to 1987.

What decisions will be reviewed. A State, under section 218(s) of the Act as it read prior to the enactment of Pub.L. 99–509, may request review of an assessment of an amount due from the State, an allowance to the State of a credit or refund of an overpayment, or a disallowance of the State's claim for credit or refund of an overpayment. The Commissioner may review regardless of whether the amount assessed has been paid or whether the credit or refund has been accepted by the State. Prior to the Commissioner's review, however, an assessment, allowance or disallowance may be reconsidered under §§ 404.1291 through 404.1293.

[62 FR 38451, July 18, 1997]

§ 404.1291 Reconsideration—for wages paid prior to 1987.

After the State requests review of the assessment or allowance or disallowance of a credit or refund, and prior to the Commissioner's review, that decision may be reconsidered, and affirmed, modified, or reversed. We notify the State of the reconsidered determination and the basis for it. The State may request the Commissioner to review this reconsidered determination under § 404.1294(b). In limited situations, SSA and the State may agree that the reconsideration process should be waived, e.g., where major policy is at issue.

§ 404.1292 How to request review—for wages paid prior to 1987.

(a) Form of request. No particular form of request is required. However, a written request for review must:

(1) Identify the assessment, allowance or disallowance being questioned;

(2) Describe the specific issue on which the review is requested;

(3) Contain any additional information or argument relevant to that issue; and

(4) Be signed by an official authorized to request the review on behalf of the State.

(b) Submitting additional material. A State has 90 days from the date it requests review to submit additional evidence it wishes considered during the review process. The time limit for submitting additional evidence may be extended upon written request of the State and for good cause shown.

(Approved by the Office of Management and Budget under control number 0960–0425)

[66 FR 28836, May 25, 2001]

§ 404.1293 Time for filing request for review—for wages paid prior to 1987.

(a) Time for filing. The State must file its request for review within 90 days after the date of the notice of assessment, allowance, or disallowance. Usually, the date of the request for review is considered the filing date. Where the 90–day period ends on a weekend, legal holiday or Federal nonworkday, a request filed on the next Federal workday is considered as timely filed.

(b) Extension of time. For good cause shown, and upon written application by a State filed prior to the expiration of the time for filing a request for review, additional time for filing the request may be allowed.

§ 404.1294 Notification to State after reconsideration—for wages paid prior to 1987.

(a) The State will be notified in writing of the reconsidered determination on the assessment, allowance, or disallowance, and the basis for the determination.

(b) If the State does not agree with the reconsidered determination, it has 90 days from the date of notice of the reconsidered determination to request the Commissioner to review that determination. The rules on what the request should contain and the time for filing the request are the same as in §§ 404.1292 and 404.1293.

§ 404.1295 Commissioner's review—for wages paid prior to 1987.

Upon request by the State, the Commissioner will review the reconsidered determination (or the assessment, allowance or disallowance as initially issued if reconsideration is waived under § 404.1291). If necessary, the Commissioner may request the State to furnish additional evidence. Based upon the evidence considered in connection with the assessment, allowance or disallowance and any additional evidence submitted by the State or otherwise obtained by the Commissioner, the Commissioner affirms, modifies, or reverses the assessment, allowance or disallowance.

§ 404.1296 Commissioner's notification to the State—for wages paid prior to 1987.

The Commissioner notifies the State in writing of the decision on the assessment, allowance, or disallowance, and the basis for the decision.

HOW A STATE MAY SEEK COURT REVIEW OF COMMISSIONER'S DECISION—FOR WAGES PAID PRIOR TO 1987

§ 404.1297 Review by court—for wages paid prior to 1987.

(a) Who can file civil action in court. A State may file a civil action under section 218(t) of the Act as it read prior to the enactment of Pub.L. 99–509 requesting a district court of the United States to review any decision the Commissioner makes under section 218(s) of the Act as it read prior to the enactment of Pub.L. 99–509 concerning the assessment of an amount due, the allowance of a credit or refund, or the disallowance of a claim for credit or refund.

(b) Where the civil action must be filed. A State must file the civil action in the district court of the United States for the judicial district in which the State's capital is located. If the civil action is brought by an interstate instrumentality, it must file the civil action in the district court of the United States for the judicial district in which the instrumentality's principal office is located. The district court's judgment is final except that it is subject to review in the same manner as judgments of the court in other civil actions.

(c) No interest on credit or refund of overpayment. SSA has no authority to pay interest to a State after final judgment of a court involving a credit or refund of an overpayment made under section 218 of the Act.

[62 FR 38451, July 18, 1997]

§ 404.1298 Time for filing civil action—for wages paid prior to 1987.

(a) Time for filing. The State must file the civil action for a redetermination of the correctness of the assessment, allowance or disallowance within 2 years from the date the Commissioner mails to the State the notice of the decision under § 404.1296. Where the 2–year period ends on a Saturday, Sunday, legal holiday or Federal nonwork day, an action filed on the next Federal workday is considered timely filed.

(b) Extension of time for filing. The Commissioner, for good cause shown, may upon written application by a State filed prior to the end of the two-year period, extend the time for filing the civil action.

§ 404.1299 Final judgments—for wages paid prior to 1987.

(a) Overpayments. Payment of amounts due to a State required as the result of a final judgment of the court shall be adjusted under §§ 404.1271 and 404.1272.

(b) Underpayments. Wage reports and contribution returns required as the result of a final judgment of the court shall be filed under §§ 404.1237–404.1251. We will assess interest under § 404.1265 where, based upon a final judgment of the court, contributions are due from a State because the amount of contributions assessed was not paid by the State or the State had used an allowance of a credit or refund of an overpayment.

SUBPART N—WAGE CREDITS FOR VETERANS AND MEMBERS OF THE UNIFORMED SERVICES

Authority: Secs. 205(a) and (p), 210(*l*) and (m), 215(h), 217, 229, and 702(a)(5) of the Social Security Act (42 U.S.C. 405(a) and (p), 410(*l*) and (m), 415(h), 417, 429, and 902(a)(5)).

Source: 45 FR 16464, Mar. 14, 1980; 52 FR 27541, July 22, 1987; 52 FR 33316, Sept. 2, 1987; 61 FR 5941, Feb. 15, 1996, unless otherwise noted.

GENERAL

§ 404.1301 Introduction.

(a) The Social Security Act (Act), under section 217, provides for noncontributory wage credits to veterans who served in the active military or naval service of the United States from September 16, 1940, through December 31, 1956. These individuals are considered World War II or post-World War II veterans. The Act also provides for noncontributory wage credits to certain individuals who served in the active military or naval service of an allied country during World War II. These individuals are considered World War II veterans. In addition, certain individuals get wage credits, under section 229 of the Act, for service as members of the uniformed services on active duty or active duty for training beginning in 1957 when that service was first covered for social security purposes on a contributory basis through 2001. These individuals are considered members of the uniformed services.

(b) World War II or post-World War II veterans receive wage credits based on the length of active military or naval service, type of separation from service and, in some cases, whether the veteran is receiving another Federal benefit. However, a member of a uniformed service receives wage credits regardless of length of service, type of separation, or receipt of another Federal benefit.

(c) The Social Security Administration (SSA) uses these wage credits, along with any covered wages or self-employment income of the veteran or member of a uniformed service, to determine entitlement to, and the amount of, benefits and the lump-sum death payment that may be paid to them, their dependents or survivors under the old-age, survivors', and disability insurance programs. These wage credits can also be used by the veteran or member of the uniformed service to meet the insured status and quarters of coverage requirements for a period of disability.

(d) This subpart tells how veterans or members of the uniformed services obtain wage credits, what evidence of service SSA requires, how SSA uses the wage credits, and how the wage credits are affected by payment of other benefits.

(e) This subpart explains that certain World War II veterans who die are considered (deemed) fully insured. This gives those veterans' survivors the same benefit rights as if the veterans were actually fully insured when they died.

(f) The rules are organized in the following manner:

(1) Sections 404.1310 through 404.1313 contain the rules on World War II veterans. We discuss who may qualify as a World War II veteran, how we determine whether the 90–day active service requirement for a World War II veteran is met, what we consider to be World War II active military or naval service, and what we do not consider to be World War II active military or naval service.

(2) Sections 404.1320 through 404.1323 contain the rules on post-World War II veterans. We discuss who may qualify as a post-World War II veteran, how we determine whether the 90–day active service requirement for a post-World War II veteran is met, what we consider to be post-World War II active military or naval service, and what we do not consider to be post-World War II active military or naval service.

(3) In § 404.1325 we discuss what is a separation under conditions other than dishonorable. The law requires that a World War II or post-World War II veteran's separation from active military or naval service be other than dishonorable for the veteran to get wage credits.

(4) Section 404.1330 contains the rules on members of the uniformed services. We discuss who may qualify as a member of a uniformed service.

(5) In §§ 404.1340 through 404.1343, we discuss the amount of wage credits for veterans and members of the uniformed services, situations which may limit the use of wage credits for World War II and post-World War II veterans, and situations in which the limits do not apply.

(6) Sections 404.1350 through 404.1352 contain the rules on deemed insured status for World War II veterans. We discuss when deemed insured status applies, the amount of wage credits used for deemed insured World War II veterans, how the wage credits affect survivors' social security benefits, and when deemed insured status does not apply.

(7) Sections 404.1360 through 404.1363 contain the rules on the effect of other benefits on the payment of social security benefits and lump-sum death payments based on wage credits for veterans. We discuss what happens when we learn of a determination that a Veterans Administration pension or compensation is payable or that a Federal benefit is payable before or after we determine entitlement to a monthly benefit or lump-sum death payment based on the death of the veteran.

(8) Sections 404.1370 and 404.1371 contain the rules on what we accept as evidence of a World War II and post-World War II veteran's active military or naval service, including date and type of separation, and what we accept as evidence of entitlement to wage credits for membership in a uniformed service during the years 1957 through 1967.

[70 FR 11865, March 10, 2005]

§ 404.1302 Definitions.

As used in this subpart—

Act means the Social Security Act, as amended.

Active duty means periods of time an individual is on full-time duty in the active military or naval service after 1956 and includes active duty for training after 1956.

Active service means periods of time prior to 1957 an individual was on full-time duty in the active military or naval service. It does not include totaling periods of active duty for training purposes before 1957 which are less than 90 days.

Allied country means a country at war on September 16, 1940, with a country with which the United States was at war during the World War II period. Each of the following countries is considered an allied country: Australia, Belgium, Canada, Czechoslovakia, Denmark, France, India, Luxembourg, the Netherlands, New Zealand, Norway, Poland, Union of South Africa, and the United Kingdom.

Domiciled in the United States means an individual has a true, fixed, and permanent home in the United States to which the individual intends to return whenever he or she is absent.

Federal benefit means a benefit which is payable by another Federal agency (other than the Veterans Administration) or an instrumentality owned entirely by the United States under any law of the United States or under a program or pension system set up by the agency or instrumentality.

Post-World War II period means the time period July 25, 1947, through December 31, 1956.

Reserve component means Army Reserve, Naval Reserve, Marine Corps Reserve, Air Force Reserve, Coast Guard Reserve, National Guard of the United States or Air National Guard of the United States.

Resided in the United States means an individual had a place where he or she lived, whether permanently or temporarily, in the United States and was bodily present in that place.

Survivor means you are a parent, widow, divorced wife, widower, or child of a deceased veteran or member of a uniformed service.

United States means the 50 States, the District of Columbia, the Commonwealth of Puerto Rico, the Virgin Islands, Guam, and American Samoa.

Veteran means an individual who served in the active military or naval service of the United States and was discharged or released from that service under conditions other than dishonorable. For a more detailed definition of the World War II veteran and a post-World War II veteran, see §§ 404.1310 and 404.1320.

Wage credit means a dollar amount we add to the earnings record of a veteran of the World War II or the post-World War II period. It is also a dollar amount we add to the earnings record of a member of a uniformed service who was on active duty from 1957 through 2001. The amount is set out in the Act and is added for each month, calendar quarter, or calendar year of service as required by law.

We, us, or *our* means the Social Security Administration.

World War II period means the time period September 16, 1940, through July 24, 1947.

You or *your* means a veteran, a veteran's survivor or a member of a uniformed service applying for or entitled to a social security benefit or a lump-sum death payment.

[70 FR 11865, March 10, 2005]

WORLD WAR II VETERANS

§ 404.1310 Who is a World War II veteran.

You are a World War II veteran if you were in the active service of the United States during the World War II period and, if no longer in active service, you were separated from that service under conditions other than dishonorable after at least 90 days of active service. The 90-day active service requirement is discussed in § 404.1311.

§ 404.1311 Ninety-day active service requirement for World War II veterans.

(a) The 90 days of active service required for World War II veterans do not have to be consecutive if the 90 days were in the World War II period. The 90-day requirement cannot be met by totaling the periods of active duty for training purposes which were less than 90 days.

(b) If, however, all of the 90 days of active service required for World War II veterans were not in the World War II period, the 90 days must (only in those circumstances) be consecutive if the 90 days began before September 16, 1940, and ended on or after that date, or began before July 25, 1947, and ended on or after that date.

(c) The 90 days of active service is not required if the World War II veteran died in service or was separated from service under conditions other than dishonorable because of a disability or injury which began or worsened while performing service duties.

§ 404.1312 World War II service included.

Your service was in the active service of the United States during the World War II period if you were in the—

(a) Army, Navy, Marine Corps, or Coast Guard, or any part of them;

(b) Commissioned corps of the United States Public Health Service and were—

(1) On active commissioned service during the period beginning September 16, 1940, through July 28, 1945, and the active service was done while on detail to the Army, Navy, Marine Corps, or Coast Guard; or

(2) On active commissioned service during the period beginning July 29, 1945, through July 24, 1947, regardless of whether on detail to the Army, Navy, Marine Corps, or Coast Guard;

(c) Commissioned corps of the United States Coast and Geodetic Survey and were—

(1) During the World War II period—

(i) Transferred to active service with the Army, Navy, Marine Corps, or Coast Guard; or

(ii) Assigned to active service on military projects in areas determined by the Secretary of Defense to be areas of immediate military hazard; or

(2) On active service in the Philippine Islands on December 7, 1941; or

(3) On active service during the period beginning July 29, 1945, through July 24, 1947;

(d) Philippine Scouts and performed active service during the World War II period under the direct supervision of recognized military authority;

(e) Active service of an allied country during the World War II period and—

(1) Had entered into that active service before December 9, 1941;

(2) Were a citizen of the United States throughout that period of active service or lost your United States citizenship solely because of your entrance into that service;

(3) Had resided in the United States for a total of four years during the five-year period ending on the day you entered that active service; and

(4) Were domiciled in the United States on that day; or

(f) Women's Army Auxiliary Corps, during the period May 14, 1942, through September 29, 1943, and performed active service with the Army, Navy, Marine Corps, or Coast Guard after September 29, 1943.

§ 404.1313 World War II service excluded.

Your service was not in the active service of the United States during the World War II period if, for example, you were in the—

(a) Women's Army Auxiliary Corps, except as described in § 404.1312(f);

(b) Coast Guard Auxiliary;

(c) Coast Guard Reserve (Temporary) unless you served on active full-time service with military pay and allowances;

(d) Civil Air Patrol; or

(e) Civilian Auxiliary to the Military Police.

POST–WORLD WAR II VETERANS

§ 404.1320 Who is a post-World War II veteran.

You are a post-World War II veteran if you were in the active service of the United States during the post-World War II period and, if no longer in active service, you were separated from the service under conditions other than dishonorable after at least 90 days of active service. The 90–day active service requirement is discussed in § 404.1321.

§ 404.1321 Ninety-day active service requirement for post-World War II veterans.

(a) The 90 days of active service required for post-World War II veterans do not have to be consecutive if the 90 days were in the post-World War II period. The 90–day requirement cannot be met by totaling the periods of active duty for training purposes before 1957 which were less than 90 days.

(b) If, however, all of the 90 days of active service required for post-World War II veterans were not in the post-World War II period, the 90 days must (only in those circumstances) be consecutive if the 90 days began before July 25, 1947, and ended on or after that date, or began before January 1, 1957, and ended on or after that date.

(c) The 90 days of active service is not required if the post-World War II veteran died in service or was separated from service under conditions other than dishonorable because of a disability or injury which began or worsened while performing service duties.

§ 404.1322 Post–World War II service included.

Your service was in the active service of the United States during the post-World War II period if you were in the—

(a) Air Force, Army, Navy, Marine Corps, Coast Guard, or any part of them;

(b) Commissioned corps of the United States Public Health Service and were on active service during that period;

(c) Commissioned corps of the United States Coast and Geodetic Survey and were on active service during that period; or

(d) Philippine Scouts and performed active service during the post-World War II period under the direct supervision of recognized military authority.

§ 404.1323 Post–World War II service excluded.

Your service was not in the active service of the United States during the post-World War II period if, for example, you were in the—

(a) Coast Guard Auxiliary;

(b) Coast Guard Reserve (Temporary) unless you served on active full-time service with military pay and allowances;

(c) Civil Air Patrol; or

(d) Civilian Auxiliary to the Military Police.

SEPARATION FROM ACTIVE SERVICE

§ 404.1325 Separation from active service under conditions other than dishonorable.

Separation from active service under conditions other than dishonorable means any discharge or release from the active service except—

(a) A discharge or release for desertion, absence without leave, or fraudulent entry;

(b) A dishonorable or bad conduct discharge issued by a general court martial of the Army, Navy, Air Force, Marine Corps, or Coast Guard of the United States, or by the active service of an allied country during the World War II period;

(c) A dishonorable discharge issued by the United States Public Health Service or the United States Coast and Geodetic Survey;

(d) A resignation by an officer for the good of the service;

(e) A discharge or release because the individual was a conscientious objector; or

(f) A discharge or release because the individual was convicted by a civil court for treason, sabotage, espionage, murder, rape, arson, burglary, robbery, kidnapping, assault with intent to kill, assault with a deadly weapon, or because of an attempt to commit any of these crimes.

[45 FR 16464, March 14, 1980; 45 FR 22023, April 3, 1980]

MEMBERS OF THE UNIFORMED SERVICES

§ 404.1330 Who is a member of a uniformed service.

A member of a uniformed service is an individual who served on active duty after 1956. You are a member of a uniformed service if you—

(a) Are appointed, enlisted, or inducted into—

(1) The Air Force, Army, Navy, Coast Guard, or Marine Corps; or

(2) A reserve component of the uniformed services in paragraph (a)(1) of this section (except the Coast Guard Reserve as a temporary member);

(b) Served in the Army or Air Force under call or conscription;

(c) Are a commissioned officer of the National Oceanic and Atmospheric Administration or its predecessors, the Environmental Science Services Administration and the Coast and Geodetic Survey;

(d) Are a commissioned officer of the Regular or Reserve Corps of the Public Health Service;

(e) Are a retired member of any of the above services;

(f) Are a member of the Fleet Reserve or Fleet Marine Corps Reserve;

(g) Are a cadet at the United States Military Academy, Air Force Academy, or Coast Guard Academy, or a midshipman at the United States Naval Academy; or

(h) Are a member of the Reserve Officers Training Corps of the Army, Navy or Air Force, when ordered to annual training duty for at least 14 days and while performing official travel to and from that duty.

AMOUNTS OF WAGE CREDITS AND LIMITS ON THEIR USE

§ 404.1340 Wage credits for World War II and post-World War II veterans.

In determining your entitlement to, and the amount of, your monthly benefit or lump-sum death payment based on your active service during the World War II period or the post-World War II period, and for establishing a period of disability as discussed in §§ 404.132 and 404.133, we add the (deemed) amount of $160 for each month during a part of which you were in the active service as described in § 404.1312 or § 404.1322. For example, if you were in active service from October 11, 1942, through August 10, 1943, we add the (deemed) amount of $160 for October 1942 and August 1943 as well as November 1942 through July 1943. The amount of wage credits that are added in a calendar year cannot cause the total amount credited to your earnings record to exceed the annual earnings limitation explained in §§ 404.1047 and 404.1096(b).

§ 404.1341 Wage credits for a member of a uniformed service.

(a) General. In determining your entitlement to, and the amount of your monthly benefit (or lump sum death payment) based on your wages while on active duty as a member of the uniformed service from 1957 through 2001, and for establishing a period of disability as discussed in § 404.132, we add wage credits to the wages paid you as a member of that service. The amount of the wage credits, the applicable time periods, the wage credit amount limits, and the requirement of a minimum period of active duty service for granting these wage credits, are discussed in paragraphs (b), (c), and (d) of this section.

(b) Amount of wage credits. The amount of wage credits added is—

(1) $100 for each $300 in wages paid to you for your service in each calendar year from 1978 through 2001; and

(2) $300 for each calendar quarter in 1957 through 1977, regardless of the amount of wages actually paid you during that quarter for your service.

(c) Limits on wage credits. The amount of these wage credits cannot exceed—

(1) $1200 for any calendar year, or

(2) An amount which when added to other earnings causes the total earnings for the year to exceed the annual earnings limitation explained in §§ 404.1047 and 404.1096(b).

(d) Minimum active-duty service requirement.

(1) If you enlisted for the first time in a regular component of the Armed Forces on or after September 8, 1980, you must complete the shorter of 24 months of

continuous active duty or the full period that you were called to active duty to receive these wage credits, unless:

(i) You are discharged or released from active duty for the convenience of the government in accordance with section 1171 of title 10 U.S.C. or because of hardship as specified in section 1173 of title 10 U.S.C.;

(ii) You are discharged or released from active duty for a disability incurred or aggravated in line of duty;

(iii) You are entitled to compensation for service-connected disability or death under chapter 11 of title 38 U.S.C.;

(iv) You die during your period of enlistment; or

(v) You were discharged prior to October 14, 1982, and your discharge was—

(A) Under chapter 61 of title 10 U.S.C.; or

(B) Because of a disability which resulted from an injury or disease incurred in or aggravated during your enlistment which was not the result of your intentional misconduct and did not occur during a period of unauthorized absence.

(2) If you entered on active duty as a member of the uniformed services as defined in § 404.1330 on or after October 14, 1982, having neither previously completed a period of 24 months' active duty nor been discharged or released from this period of active duty under section 1171, title 10 U.S.C. (i.e., convenience of the government), you must complete the shorter of 24 months of continuous active duty or the full period you were called or ordered to active duty to receive these wage credits, unless:

(i) You are discharged or released from active duty for the convenience of the government in accordance with section 1171 of title 10 U.S.C. or because of hardship as specified in section 1173 of title 10 U.S.C.;

(ii) You are discharged or released from active duty for a disability incurred or aggravated in line of duty;

(iii) You are entitled to compensation for service-connected disability or death under chapter 11 of title 38 U.S.C.; or

(iv) You die during your period of active service.

[52 FR 29663, Aug. 11, 1987; 70 FR 11865, March 10, 2005]

§ 404.1342 Limits on granting World War II and post-World War II wage credits.

(a) You get wage credits for World War II or post-World War II active service only if the use of the wage credits results in entitlement to a monthly benefit, a higher monthly benefit, or a lump-sum death payment.

(b) You may get wage credits for active service in July 1947 for either the World War II period or the post-World War II period but not for both. If your active service is before and on or after July 25, 1947, we add the $160 wage credit to the period which is most advantageous to you.

(c) You do not get wage credits for the World War II period if another Federal benefit (other than one payable by the Veterans Administration) is determined by a Federal agency or an instrumentality owned entirely by the United States to be payable to you, even though the Federal benefit is not actually paid or is paid and then terminated, based in part on your active service during the World War II period except as explained in § 404.1343.

(d) You do not get wage credits for the post-World War II period if another Federal benefit (other than one payable by the Veterans Administration) is determined by a Federal agency or an instrumentality owned entirely by the United States to be payable to you, even though the Federal benefit is not actually paid or is paid and then terminated, based in part on your active service during the post-World War II period except as explained in § 404.1343.

§ 404.1343 When the limits on granting World War II and post-World War II wage credits do not apply.

The limits on granting wage credits described in § 404.1342 (c) and (d) do not apply—

(a) If the wage credits are used solely to meet the insured status and quarters of coverage requirements for a period of disability as described in §§ 404.132 and 404.133;

(b) If you are the surviving spouse or child of a veteran of the World War II period or post-World War II period and you are entitled under the Civil Service Retirement Act of 1930 to a survivor's annuity based on the veteran's active service and—

(1) You give up your right to receive the survivor's annuity;

(2) A benefit under the Civil Service Retirement Act of 1930 based on the veteran's active service was not payable to the veteran; and

(3) Another Federal benefit is not payable to the veteran or his or her survivors except as described in paragraph (c) of this section; or

(c) For the years 1951 through 1956, if another Federal benefit is payable by the Army, Navy, Air Force, Marine Corps, Coast Guard, Coast and Geodetic Survey, or the Public Health Service based on post-World War II active service but only if the veteran was also paid wages as a member of a uniformed service after 1956.

[49 FR 24118, June 12, 1984]

DEEMED INSURED STATUS FOR WORLD WAR II VETERANS

§ 404.1350 Deemed insured status.

(a) When deemed insured status applies. If you are the survivor of a World War II veteran, we consider the veteran to have died fully insured as discussed in § 404.111 and we include wage credits in determining your monthly benefit or lump-sum death payment if—

(1) The veteran was separated from active service of the United States before July 27, 1951; and

(2) The veteran died within 3 years after separation from active service and before July 27, 1954.

(b) Amount of credit given for deemed insured World War II veterans.

(1) When we compute a survivor's benefit or lump-sum death payment, we give credit for—

(i) $200 (for increment year purposes) for each calendar year in which the veteran had at least 30 days of active service beginning September 16, 1940, through 1950; and

(ii) An average monthly wage of $160.

(2) If the World War II veteran was fully or currently insured without the wage credits, we add increment years (years after 1936 and prior to 1951 in which the veteran had at least $200 in creditable earnings) to the increment years based on the veteran's wages.

§ 404.1351 When deemed insured status does not apply.

As a survivor of a World War II veteran, you cannot get a monthly benefit or lump-sum death payment based on the veteran's deemed insured status as explained in § 404.1350 if—

(a) Your monthly benefit or lump-sum death payment is larger without using the wage credits;

(b) The Veterans Administration has determined that a pension or compensation is payable to you based on the veteran's death;

(c) The veteran died while in the active service of the United States;

(d) The veteran was first separated from active service after July 26, 1951;

(e) The veteran died after July 26, 1954; or

(f) The veteran's only service during the World War II period was by enlistment in the Philippine Scouts as authorized by the Armed Forces Voluntary Recruitment Act of 1945 (Pub.L. 190 of the 79th Congress).

§ 404.1352 Benefits and payments based on deemed insured status.

(a) Our determination. We determine your monthly benefit or lump-sum death payment under the deemed insured status provisions in §§ 404.1350 and 404.1351 regardless of whether the Veterans Administration has determined that any pension or compensation is payable to you.

(b) Certification for payment. If we determine that you can be paid a monthly benefit or lump-sum death payment, we certify these benefits for payment. However, the amount of your monthly benefit or lump-sum death payment may be changed if we are informed by the Veterans Administration that a pension or compensation is payable because of the veteran's death as explained in § 404.1360.

(c) Payments not considered as pension or compensation. We do not consider as pension or compensation—

(1) National Service Life Insurance payments;

(2) United States Government Life Insurance payments; or

(3) Burial allowance payments made by the Veterans Administration.

EFFECT OF OTHER BENEFITS ON PAYMENT OF SOCIAL SECURITY BENEFITS AND PAYMENTS

§ 404.1360 Veterans Administration pension or compensation payable.

(a) Before we determine and certify payment. If we are informed by the Veterans Administration that a pension or compensation is payable to you before we determine and certify payment of benefits based on deemed insured status, we compute your monthly benefit or lump-sum death payment based on the death of the World War II veteran without using the wage credits discussed in § 404.1350.

(b) After we determine and certify payment. If we are informed by the Veterans Administration that a pension or compensation is payable to you after we determine and certify payment of benefits based on deemed insured status, we—

(1) Stop payment of your benefits or recompute the amount of any further benefits that can be paid to you; and

(2) Determine whether you were erroneously paid and the amount of any erroneous payment.

§ 404.1361 Federal benefit payable other than by Veterans Administration.

(a) Before we determine and certify payment. If we are informed by another Federal agency or instrumentality of the United States (other than the Veterans Administration) that a Federal benefit is payable to you by that agency or instrumentality based on the veteran's World War II or post-World War II active service before we determine and certify your monthly benefit or lump-sum death payment, we compute your monthly benefit or lump-sum death payment without using the wage credits discussed in § 404.1340.

(b) After we determine and certify payment. If we are informed by another Federal agency or instrumentality of the United States (other than the Veterans Administration) that a Federal benefit is payable to you by that agency or instrumentality based on the veteran's World War II or post-World War II active service after we determine and certify payment, we—

(1) Stop payment of your benefits or recompute the amount of any further benefits that can be paid to you; and

(2) Determine whether you were erroneously paid and the amount of any erroneous payment.

§ 404.1362 Treatment of social security benefits or payments where Veterans Administration pension or compensation payable.

(a) Before we receive notice from the Veterans Administration. If we certify your monthly benefit or a lump-sum death payment as determined under the deemed insured status provisions in § 404.1350 before we receive notice from the Veterans Administration that a pension or compensation is payable to you, our payments to you are erroneous only to the extent that they exceed the amount of the accrued pension or compensation payable.

(b) After we receive notice from the Veterans Administration. If we certify your monthly benefit or lump-sum death payment as determined under the deemed insured status provisions in § 404.1350 after we receive notice from the Veterans Administration that a pension or compensation is payable to you, our payments to you are erroneous whether or not they exceed the amount of the accrued pension or compensation payable.

§ 404.1363 Treatment of social security benefits or payments where Federal benefit payable other than by Veterans Administration.

If we certify your monthly benefit or lump-sum death payment based on World War II or post-World War II wage credits after we receive notice from another Federal agency or instrumentality of the United States (other than the Veterans Administration) that a Federal benefit is payable to you by that agency or instrumentality based on the veteran's World War II or post-World War II active service, our payments to you are erroneous to the extent the payments are based on the World War II or post-World War II wage credits. The payments are erroneous beginning with the first month you are eligible for the Federal benefit.

EVIDENCE OF ACTIVE SERVICE AND MEMBERSHIP IN A UNIFORMED SERVICE

§ 404.1370 Evidence of active service and separation from active service.

(a) General. When you file an application for a monthly benefit or lump-sum death payment based on the active service of a World War II or post-World War II veteran, you must submit evidence of—

(1) Your entitlement as required by subpart H of this part or other evidence that may be expressly required;

(2) The veteran's period in active service of the United States; and

(3) The veteran's type of separation from active service of the United States.

(b) Evidence we accept. We accept as proof of a veteran's active service and separation from active service—

(1) An original certificate of discharge, or an original certificate of service, from the appropriate military service, from the United States Public Health Service, or from the United States Coast and Geodetic Survey;

(2) A certified copy of the original certificate of discharge or service made by the State, county, city agency or department in which the original certificate is recorded;

(3) A certification from the appropriate military service, United States Public Health Service, or United States Coast and Geodetic Survey showing the veteran's period of active service and type of separation;

(4) A certification from a local selective service board showing the veteran's period of active service and type of separation; or

(5) Other evidence that proves the veteran's period of active service and type of separation.

§ 404.1371 Evidence of membership in a uniformed service during the years 1957 through 1967.

(a) General. When you file an application for a monthly benefit or lump-sum death payment based on the services of a member of a uniformed service during the years 1957 through 1967, you should submit evidence identifying the member's uniformed service and showing the period(s) he or she was on active duty during those years.

(b) Evidence we accept. The evidence we will accept includes any official correspondence showing the member's status as an active service member during the appropriate period, a certification of service by the uniformed service, official earnings statements, copies of the member's Form W–2, and military orders, for the appropriate period.

SUBPART O—INTERRELATIONSHIP OF OLD-AGE, SURVIVORS AND DISABILITY INSURANCE PROGRAM WITH THE RAILROAD RETIREMENT PROGRAM

Cross Reference: For regulations under the Railroad Retirement Act, see chapter II of this title.

Authority: Secs. 202(*l*), 205(a), (c)(5)(D), (i), and (*o*), 210(a)(9) and (*l*)(4), 211(c)(3), and 702(a)(5) of the Social Security Act (42 U.S.C. 402(*l*), 405(a), (c)(5)(D), (i), and (*o*), 410(a)(9) and (*l*)(4), 411(c)(3), and 902(a)(5)).

Source: 18 FR 8694, Dec. 24, 1953; 25 FR 5182, June 10, 1960; 52 FR 27541, July 22, 1987; 61 FR 5941, Feb. 15, 1996, unless otherwise noted.

§ 404.1401 What is the interrelationship between the Railroad Retirement Act and the Old-Age, Survivors and Disability Insurance Program of the Social Security Act?

(a) Background. The Railroad Retirement Act provides a system of benefits for railroad employees, their dependents and survivors, and is integrated with the Social Security Act to provide a coordinated system of retirement, survivor, dependent and disability benefits payable on the basis of an individual's work in the railroad industry and in employment and self-employment covered by the Social Security Act. With respect to the coordination between the two programs, the Railroad Retirement Act distinguishes between "career" or "vested" railroad workers and those individuals who may be considered "casual" or "non-vested" railroad workers based on the total amount of railroad service credited to the worker, as explained in paragraph (b) of this section. The Railroad Retirement Board transfers to the Social Security Administration (SSA) the compensation records of workers who at the time of retirement, onset of disability or death, are non-vested and meet certain other requirements. Any compensation paid to non-vested workers for service after 1936 becomes wages under the Social Security Act (to the extent they do not exceed the annual wage limitations described in § 404.1047). Any benefits payable to non-vested workers, their dependents, and their survivors, are computed on the basis of the combined compensation and social security covered earnings creditable to the workers' records. Once a railroad worker meets the vesting requirements, the record of the worker's railroad service and compensation generally may not be used for benefit purposes under the Social Security Act, but under certain circumstances may be transferred after the worker's death to SSA for use in determining social security benefit entitlement for the railroad worker's survivors (see § 404.1407). Under certain circumstances (see § 404.1413), certification of benefits payable under the provisions of the Social Security Act will be made to the Railroad Retirement Board. The Railroad Retirement Board will certify such benefits to the Secretary of the Treasury.

(b) Who is a vested railroad worker? You are a vested railroad worker if you have:

(1) Ten years or more of service in the railroad industry, or

(2) Effective January 1, 2002, you have at least 5 years of service in the railroad industry, all of which accrue after December 31, 1995.

(c) Definition of years of service. As used in paragraph (b) of this section, the term years of service has the same meaning as assigned to it by section 1(f) of the Railroad Retirement Act of 1974, as amended, (45 U.S.C. 231(f)).

[42 FR 18272, April 6, 1977; 69 FR 5692, Feb. 6, 2004]

§ 404.1402 When are railroad industry services by a non-vested worker covered under Social Security?

If you are a non-vested worker, we (the Social Security Administration) will consider your services in the railroad industry to be "employment" as defined in section 210 of the Social Security Act for the following purposes:

(a) To determine entitlement to, or the amount of, any monthly benefits or lump-sum death payment on the basis of your wages and self-employment income;

(b) To determine entitlement to, or the amount of, any survivor monthly benefit or any lump-sum death payment on the basis of your wages and self-employment income provided you did not have a "current connection" with the railroad industry, as defined in section 1(*o*) of the Railroad Retirement Act of 1974, as amended, (45 U.S.C. 231(*o*)), at the time of your death; (in such cases, survivor benefits are not payable under the Railroad Retirement Act);

(c) To determine entitlement to a period of disability (see subpart B of this part) on the basis of your wages and self-employment income; or

(d) To apply the provisions of section 203 of the Social Security Act concerning deductions from benefits under the annual earnings test (see subpart E of this part).

[42 FR 18273, Apr. 6, 1977; 69 FR 5693, Feb. 6, 2004]

§ 404.1403 [Reserved]

[69 FR 5693, Feb. 6, 2004]

§ 404.1404 Effective date of coverage of railroad services under the act.

Coverage under the act of services performed after 1936 by an individual in the railroad industry is effective as follows:

(a) The provisions of paragraphs (a) and (b) of § 404.1402 insofar as they relate to survivor monthly benefits are effective for months after December 1946 and insofar as they relate to lump-sum death payments are effective with respect to deaths after 1946;

(b) The provisions of paragraph (a) of § 404.1402 insofar as they relate to old-age insurance benefits or monthly benefits of dependents of old-age insurance beneficiaries are effective November 1, 1951; insofar as they relate to disability insurance benefits are effective for months after June 1957; and insofar as they relate to monthly benefits for dependents of disability insurance beneficiaries are effective for months after August 1958;

(c) The provisions of paragraph (c) of § 404.1402 are effective for benefits for months after June 1955; and

(d) The provisions of paragraph (d) of § 404.1402 are effective November 1, 1951.

[25 FR 5182, June 10, 1960]

§ 404.1405 If you have been considered a nonvested worker, what are the situations when your railroad industry work will not be covered under Social Security?

(a) Awards by the Railroad Retirement Board prior to October 30, 1951. The provisions of § 404.1402(a) shall not apply with respect to the wages and self-employment income of an individual if, prior to October 30, 1951, the Railroad Retirement Board has awarded under the Railroad Retirement Act a retirement annuity to such individual or a survivor annuity with respect to the death of such individual and such retirement or survivor annuity, as the case may be, was payable at the time an application for benefits is filed under the Social Security Act on the basis of the wages and self-employment income of such individual. A pension payable under section 6 of the Railroad Retirement Act of 1937 as in effect prior to the Railroad Retirement Act of 1974, or an annuity paid in a lump sum equal to its commuted value under section 3(i) of the Railroad Retirement Act in effect prior to the Social Security Act of October 30, 1951, is not a "retirement or survivor annuity" for the purpose of this paragraph.

(b) You continue to work in the railroad industry after establishing entitlement to old-age insurance benefits under section 202(a) of the Social Security Act. If your service in the railroad industry is used to establish your entitlement to, or to determine the amount of, your old-age insurance benefits under section 202(a) of the Social Security Act, but you become vested after the effective date of your benefits, your railroad service will no longer be deemed to be in "employment" as defined in section 210 of the Act. Your benefits and any benefits payable to your spouse or child under section 202(b), (c), or (d) of the Act will be terminated with the month preceding the month in which you become a vested worker. However, if you remain insured (see subpart B of this part) without the use of your railroad compensation, your benefits will instead be recalculated without using your railroad compensation. The recalculated benefits will be payable beginning with the month in which you become a vested worker. Any monthly benefits paid prior to the month you become a vested worker are deemed to be correct payments.

[18 FR 8694, Dec. 24, 1953; 25 FR 5182, June 10, 1960, as amended at 42 FR 18273, April 6, 1977; 69 FR 5693, Feb. 6, 2004]

§ 404.1406 Eligibility to railroad retirement benefits as a bar to payment of social security benefits.

Notwithstanding the fact that, pursuant to the preceding provisions of this subpart, services rendered by an individual in the railroad industry are in employment, no lump-sum death payment or survivor monthly benefits shall be paid (except as provided in § 404.1407) under the regulations in this part on the basis of such individual's wages and self-employment income if any person, upon filing application therefor, would be entitled to an annuity under section 2 of the Railroad Retirement Act of 1974 or a lump-sum payment under section 6(b) of such Act with respect to the death of that individual; or for periods prior to 1975, would have been entitled to an annuity under section 5 or a lump-sum payment under section 5(f)(1) of the Railroad Retirement Act of 1937 with respect to the death of that individual.

[42 FR 18273, Apr. 6, 1977]

§ 404.1407 When railroad retirement benefits do not bar payment of social security benefits.

The provisions of § 404.1406 shall not operate if:

(a) The survivor is, or upon filing application would be, entitled to a monthly benefit with respect to the death of an insured individual for a month prior to January 1947, if such monthly benefit is greater in amount than the survivor annuity payable to such survivor after 1946 under the Railroad Retirement Act; or

(b) The residual lump-sum payment provided by section 6(c) of the Railroad Retirement Act of 1974 (or section 5(f)(2) of the Railroad Retirement Act of 1937 prior to the 1974 Act) with respect to the death of an insured individual is paid by the Railroad Retirement Board pursuant to an irrevocable election filed with the Board by the widow, widower, or parent of such individual to waive all future annuities or benefits based on the combined record of earnings and compensation to which such widow, widower or parent might become entitled, but only to the extent that widow's, widower's or parent's benefits may be payable under the regulations of this part to such widow, widower or parent, as the case may be, solely on the basis of the wages and self-employment income of such deceased individual and without regard to any compensation which may be treated as wages pursuant to § 404.1408.

[42 FR 18273, Apr. 6, 1977]

§ 404.1408 Compensation to be treated as wages.

(a) General. Where pursuant to the preceding provisions of this subpart, services rendered by an individual in the railroad industry are considered to be employment as defined in section 210 of the Social Security Act (see § 404.1027 of this part). Thus, any compensation (as defined in section 1(h) of the Railroad Retirement Act of 1974 or prior to the 1974 Act, section 1(h) of the Railroad Retirement Act of 1937) received by such individual for such services shall constitute wages, provided that the provisions of § 404.1406 do not operate to bar the payments of benefits under title II of the Social Security Act.

(b) Military service exception. An exception to paragraph (a) of this section applies to any compensation attributable as having been paid during any month on account of military service creditable under section 1 of the Railroad Retirement Act of 1974 (or section 4 of the Railroad Retirement Act of 1937 prior to the 1974 Act). Such compensation shall not constitute wages for purposes of title II of the Social Security Act if, based on such services, wages are deemed to have been paid to such individual during such month under the provisions described in §§ 404.1350 through 404.1352 of this part.

[42 FR 18273, April 6, 1977; 65 FR 16813, March 30, 2000]

§ 404.1409 Purposes of using compensation.

Compensation which is treated as wages under § 404.1408 shall be used, together with wages (see subpart K of this part) and self-employment income (see subpart K of this part), for purposes of:

(a) Determining an individual's insured status for monthly benefits or the lump-sum death payment (see subpart B of this part);

(b) Computing such individual's primary insurance amount (see subpart C of this part);

(c) Determining an individual's entitlement to the establishment of a period of disability (see subpart B of this part for disability insured status requirements); and

(d) Applying the deduction provisions of section 203 of the act (see subpart E of this part).

[25 FR 5183, June 10, 1960]

§ 404.1410 Presumption on basis of certified compensation record.

(a) Years prior to 1975. Where the Railroad Retirement Board certifies to SSA a report of record of compensation, such compensation is treated as wages under § 404.1408. For periods of service which do not identify the months or quarters in which such compensation was paid, the sum of the compensation quarters of coverage (see § 404.1412) will be presumed, in the absence of evidence to the contrary, to represent an equivalent number of quarters of coverage (see § 404.101). No more than four quarters of coverage shall be credited to an individual in a single calendar year.

(b) Years after 1974. Compensation paid in a calendar year will, in the absence of evidence to the contrary, be presumed to have been paid in equal proportions with respect to all months in the year in which the employee will have been in railroad service. (For years prior to 1975, see § 404.1412.)

(c) Allocation of compensation to months of service. If by means of the presumptions in this section an individual does not have an insured status (see subpart B of this part) on the basis of quarters of coverage with which he is credited, or a deceased individual's primary insurance amount (see § 404.201) may be affected because he attained age 22 after 1936, the Administration may request the Railroad Retirement Board to furnish a report of the months in which such individual rendered service for compensation which is treated as wages under § 404.1408 if it appears the identification of such months may result in an insured status or if it will affect such primary insurance amount.

(d) Effect of self-employment income and maximum earnings. However, if such individual also had self-employment income for a taxable year and the sum of such income and wages (including compensation which is treated as wages under § 404.1408) paid to or received by him during such taxable year equals the following amounts, each calendar quarter any part of which falls in such taxable year, shall be a quarter of coverage:

(1) After 1950 and prior to 1955, equals $3,600 of remuneration;

(2) After 1954 and prior to 1959, equals $4,200 of remuneration;

(3) After 1958 and prior to 1966, equals $4,800 of remuneration;

(4) After 1965 and prior to 1968, equals $6,600 of remuneration;

(5) After 1967 and beginning prior to 1972, equals $7,800 of remuneration (including a fiscal year which began in 1971 and ended in 1972);

(6) Beginning after 1971 and prior to 1973, equals $9,000 of remuneration;

(7) Beginning after 1972 and prior to 1974, equals $10,800 of remuneration;

(8) Beginning after 1973 and prior to 1975, equals $13,200 of remuneration;

(9) Beginning after 1974 and prior to 1976, equals $14,100 of remuneration;

(10) Beginning after 1975 and prior to 1977, equals $15,300 of remuneration; or

(11) Beginning after 1976, and amount equal to the contribution and benefit base as determined under section 230 of the Social Security Act which is effective for such calendar year.

This subsection is an exception to the rule in paragraph (a) of this section concerning a presumption applicable to conversion of railroad compensation into quarters of coverage for years prior to 1975.

[42 FR 18273, April 6, 1977; 65 FR 16814, March 30, 2000]

§ 404.1412 Compensation quarters of coverage.

As used in this subpart, a compensation quarter of coverage is any quarter of coverage computed with respect to compensation paid to an individual for railroad employment after 1936 and prior to 1975 in accordance with the provisions for determining such quarters of coverage as contained in section 5(*l*)(4) of the Railroad Retirement Act of 1937. (For years beginning 1975, see § 404.1410(b)).

[42 FR 18274, Apr. 6, 1977]

§ 404.1413 When will we certify payment to the Railroad Retirement Board (RRB)?

(a) When we will certify payment to RRB. If we find that you are entitled to any payment under title II of the Social Security Act, we will certify payment to the Railroad Retirement Board if you meet any of the following requirements:

(1) You are a vested worker; or

(2) You are the wife or husband of a vested worker; or

(3) You are the survivor of a vested worker and you are entitled, or could upon application be entitled to, an annuity under section 2 of the Railroad Retirement Act of 1974, as amended, (45 U.S.C. 231(a)); or

(4) You are entitled to benefits under section 202 of the Social Security Act on the basis of the wages and self-employment income of a vested worker (unless you are the survivor of a vested worker who did not have a current connection, as defined in section 1(*o*) of the Railroad Retirement Act of 1974, as amended, (45 U.S.C. 231(*o*)) with the railroad industry at the time of his or her death).

(b) What information does certification include? The certification we make to the Railroad Retirement Board for individuals entitled to any payment(s) under title II will include your name, address, payment amount(s), and the date the payment(s) should begin.

(c) Applicability limitations. The applicability limitations in paragraphs (a)(1) through (4) of this section affect claimants who first become entitled to benefits under title II of the Social Security Act after 1974. (See also § 404.1810.)

[42 FR 18274, Apr. 6, 1977; 62 FR 38451, July 18, 1997; 69 FR 5693, Feb. 6, 2004]

SUBPART P—DETERMINING DISABILITY AND BLINDNESS

Authority: Secs. 202, 205(a)-(b) and (d)-(h), 216(i), 221(a) and (h)-(j), 222(c), 223, 225, and 702(a)(5) of the Social Security Act (42 U.S.C. 402, 405(a)-(b) and (d)-(h), 416(i), 421(a) and (h)-(j), 422(c), 423, 425, and 902(a)(5)); sec. 211(b), Pub.L. 104–193, 110 Stat. 2105, 2189; sec. 202, Pub.L. 108–203, 118 Stat. 509 (42 U.S.C. 902 note).

Source: 45 FR 55584, Aug. 20, 1980; 50 FR 50126, Dec. 6, 1985; 51 FR 10616, March 28, 1986; 51 FR 16824, May 7, 1986; 51 FR 17617, May 14, 1986; 52 FR 27541, July 22, 1987; 53 FR 29020, Aug. 2, 1988; 55 FR 2806, Jan. 29, 1990; 55 FR 35287, Aug. 28, 1990; 55 FR 35578, Aug. 31, 1990; 55 FR 51208, Dec. 12, 1990; 55 FR 51687, Dec. 17, 1990; 56 FR 26031, June 6, 1991; 56 FR 40781, Aug. 16, 1991; 56 FR 57941, Nov. 14, 1991; 57 FR 1383, Jan. 14, 1992; 57 FR 30120, July 8, 1992; 57 FR 61796, Dec. 29, 1992; 58 FR 44445, Aug. 23, 1993; 58 FR 64123, Dec. 6, 1993; 58 FR 64883, Dec. 10, 1993; 58 FR 65243, Dec. 13, 1993; 59 FR 671, Jan. 6, 1994; 59 FR 1635, Jan. 12, 1994; 59 FR 41975, Aug. 16, 1994; 60 FR 8147, Feb. 10, 1995; 60 FR 43710, Aug. 23, 1995; 61 FR 5941, Feb. 15, 1996; 62 FR 6418, Feb. 11, 1997; 71 FR 16443, March 31, 2006; 71 FR 66853, 66866, Nov. 17, 2006; 75 FR 32846, June 10, 2010; 75 FR 62680, Oct. 13, 2010; 77 FR 10655, Feb. 23, 2012; 77 FR 43494, July 25, 2012; 82 FR 5863, Jan. 18, 2017, unless otherwise noted.

GENERAL

§ 404.1501 Scope of subpart.

In order for you to become entitled to any benefits based upon disability or blindness or to have a period of disability established, you must be disabled or blind as defined in title II of the Social Security Act. This subpart explains how we determine whether you are disabled or blind. We discuss a period of disability in subpart D of this part. We have organized the rules in the following way.

(a) We define general terms, then discuss who makes our disability determinations and state that disability determinations made under other programs are not binding on our determinations.

(b) We explain the term disability and note some of the major factors that are considered in determining whether you are disabled in §§ 404.1505 through 404.1510.

(c) Sections 404.1512 through 404.1518 contain our rules on evidence. We explain your responsibilities for submitting evidence of your impairment, state what we consider to be acceptable sources of medical evidence, and describe what information should be included in medical reports.

(d) Our general rules on evaluating disability if you are filing a new application are stated in §§ 404.1520 through 404.1523. We describe the steps that we go through and the order in which they are considered.

(e) Our rules on medical considerations are found in §§ 404.1525 through 404.1530. We explain in these rules—

(1) The purpose of the Listing of Impairments found in appendix 1 of this subpart and how to use it;

(2) What we mean by the term medical equivalence and how we determine medical equivalence;

(3) The effect of a conclusion by your physician that you are disabled;

(4) What we mean by symptoms, signs, and laboratory findings;

(5) How we evaluate pain and other symptoms; and

(6) The effect on your benefits if you fail to follow treatment that is expected to restore your ability to work, and how we apply the rule.

(f) In §§ 404.1545 through 404.1546 we explain what we mean by the term residual functional capacity, state when an assessment of residual functional capacity is required, and who may make it.

(g) Our rules on vocational considerations are in §§ 404.1560 through 404.1569a. We explain in these rules—

(1) When we must consider vocational factors along with the medical evidence;

(2) How we use our residual functional capacity assessment to determine if you can still do your past relevant work or other work;

(3) How we consider the vocational factors of age, education, and work experience;

(4) What we mean by "work which exists in the national economy";

(5) How we consider the exertional, nonexertional, and skill requirements of work, and when we will consider the limitations or restrictions that result from your impairment(s) and related symptoms to be exertional, nonexertional, or a combination of both; and

(6) How we use the Medical–Vocational Guidelines in appendix 2 of this subpart.

(h) Our rules on substantial gainful activity are found in §§ 404.1571 through 404.1574. These explain what we mean by substantial gainful activity and how we evaluate your work activity.

(i) In §§ 404.1577, 404.1578, and 404.1579, we explain the special rules covering disability for widows, widowers, and surviving divorced spouses for monthly benefits payable for months prior to January 1991, and in §§ 404.1581 through 404.1587 we discuss disability due to blindness.

(j) Our rules on when disability continues and stops are contained in §§ 404.1579 and 404.1588 through 404.1598. We explain what your responsibilities are in telling us of any events that may cause a change in your disability status, when you may have a trial work period, and when we will review to see if you are still disabled. We also explain how we consider the issue of medical improvement (and the exceptions to medical improvement) in deciding whether you are still disabled.

[50 FR 50126, Dec. 6, 1985; 56 FR 57941, Nov. 14, 1991; 57 FR 30120, July 8, 1992; 68 FR 51161, Aug. 26, 2003]

§ 404.1502 Definitions for this subpart.

As used in the subpart—

(a) Acceptable medical source means a medical source who is a:

(1) Licensed physician (medical or osteopathic doctor);

(2) Licensed psychologist, which includes:

(i) A licensed or certified psychologist at the independent practice level; or

(ii) A licensed or certified school psychologist, or other licensed or certified individual with another title who performs the same function as a school psychologist in a school setting, for impairments of intellectual disability, learning disabilities, and borderline intellectual functioning only;

(3) Licensed optometrist for impairments of visual disorders, or measurement of visual acuity and visual fields only, depending on the scope of practice in the State in which the optometrist practices;

(4) Licensed podiatrist for impairments of the foot, or foot and ankle only, depending on whether the State in which the podiatrist practices permits the practice of podiatry on the foot only, or the foot and ankle;

(5) Qualified speech-language pathologist for speech or language impairments only. For this source, qualified means that the speech-language pathologist must be licensed by the State professional licensing agency, or be fully certified by the State education agency in the State in which he or she practices, or hold a Certificate of Clinical Competence in Speech–Language Pathology from the American Speech–Language–Hearing Association;

(6) Licensed audiologist for impairments of hearing loss, auditory processing disorders, and balance disorders within the licensed scope of practice only (with respect to claims filed (see § 404.614) on or after March 27, 2017);

(7) Licensed Advanced Practice Registered Nurse, or other licensed advanced practice nurse with another title, for impairments within his or her licensed scope of practice (only with respect to claims filed (see § 404.614) on or after March 27, 2017); or

(8) Licensed Physician Assistant for impairments within his or her licensed scope of practice (only with respect to claims filed (see § 404.614) on or after March 27, 2017).

(b) Commissioner means the Commissioner of Social Security or his or her authorized designee.

(c) Laboratory findings means one or more anatomical, physiological, or psychological phenomena that can be shown by the use of medically acceptable laboratory diagnostic techniques. Diagnostic techniques include chemical tests (such as blood tests), electrophysiological studies (such as electrocardiograms and electroencephalograms), medical imaging (such as X–rays), and psychological tests.

(d) Medical source means an individual who is licensed as a healthcare worker by a State and working within the scope of practice permitted under State or Federal law, or an individual who is certified by a State as a speech-language pathologist or a school psychologist and acting within the scope of practice permitted under State or Federal law.

(e) Nonmedical source means a source of evidence who is not a medical source. This includes, but is not limited to:

(1) You;

(2) Educational personnel (for example, school teachers, counselors, early intervention team members, developmental center workers, and daycare center workers);

(3) Public and private social welfare agency personnel; and

(4) Family members, caregivers, friends, neighbors, employers, and clergy.

(f) Objective medical evidence means signs, laboratory findings, or both.

(g) Signs means one or more anatomical, physiological, or psychological abnormalities that can be observed, apart from your statements (symptoms). Signs must be shown by medically acceptable clinical diagnostic techniques. Psychiatric signs are medically demonstrable phenomena that indicate specific psychological abnormalities, e.g., abnormalities of behavior, mood, thought, memory, orientation, development, or perception, and must also be shown by observable facts that can be medically described and evaluated.

(h) State agency means an agency of a State designated by that State to carry out the disability or blindness determination function.

(i) Symptoms means your own description of your physical or mental impairment.

(j) We or us means, as appropriate, either the Social Security Administration or the State agency making the disability or blindness determination.

(k) You or your means, as appropriate, the person who applies for benefits or for a period of disability, the person for whom an application is filed, or the person who is receiving benefits based on disability or blindness.

[46 FR 29204, May 29, 1981; 56 FR 36954, Aug. 1, 1991; 62 FR 38451, July 18, 1997; 65 FR 11875, March 7, 2000; 71 FR 16443, March 31, 2006; 76 FR 24806, May 3, 2011; 82 FR 5863, Jan. 18, 2017; 82 FR 15132, March 27, 2017]

DETERMINATIONS

§ 404.1503 Who makes disability and blindness determinations.

(a) State agencies. State agencies make disability and blindness determinations for the Commissioner for most persons living in the State. State agencies make these disability and blindness determinations under regulations containing performance standards and other administrative requirements relating to the disability and blindness determination function. States have the option of turning the function over to the Federal Government if they no longer want to make disability determinations. Also, the Commissioner may take the function away from any State which has substantially failed to make disability and blindness determinations in accordance with these regulations. Subpart Q of this part contains the rules the States must follow in making disability and blindness determinations.

(b) Social Security Administration. The Social Security Administration will make disability and blindness determinations for—

(1) Any person living in a State which is not making for the Commissioner any disability and blindness determinations or which is not making those determinations for the class of claimants to which that person belongs; and

(2) Any person living outside the United States.

(c) What determinations are authorized. The Commissioner has authorized the State agencies and the Social Security Administration to make determinations about—

(1) Whether you are disabled or blind;

(2) The date your disability or blindness began; and

(3) The date your disability or blindness stopped.

(d) Review of State Agency determinations. On review of a State agency determination or redetermination of disability or blindness we may find that—

(1) You are, or are not, disabled or blind, regardless of what the State agency found;

(2) Your disability or blindness began earlier or later than the date found by the State agency; and

(3) Your disability or blindness stopped earlier or later than the date found by the State agency.

(e) [Reserved by 82 FR 5864]

[46 FR 29204, May 29, 1981; 52 FR 33926, Sept. 9, 1987; 62 FR 38451, July 18, 1997; 65 FR 34957, June 1, 2000; 71 FR 16443, March 31, 2006; 72 FR 51177, Sept. 6, 2007; 82 FR 5864, Jan. 18, 2017]

§ 404.1503a Program integrity.

We will not use in our program any individual or entity, except to provide existing medical evidence, who is currently excluded, suspended, or otherwise barred from participation in the Medicare or Medicaid programs, or any other Federal or Federally-assisted program; whose license to provide health care services is currently revoked or suspended by any State licensing authority pursuant to adequate due process procedures for reasons bearing on professional competence, professional conduct, or financial integrity; or who, until a final determination is made, has surrendered such a license while formal disciplinary proceedings involving professional conduct are pending. By individual or entity we mean a medical or psychological consultant, consultative examination provider, or diagnostic test facility. Also see §§ 404.1519 and 404.1519g(b).

[56 FR 36954, Aug. 1, 1991]

§ 404.1503b Evidence from excluded medical sources of evidence.

(a) General. We will not consider evidence from the following medical sources excluded under section 223(d)(5)(C)(i) of the Social Security Act (Act), as amended, unless we find good cause under paragraph (b) of this section:

(1) Any medical source that has been convicted of a felony under section 208 or under section 1632 of the Act;

(2) Any medical source that has been excluded from participation in any Federal health care program under section 1128 of the Act; or

(3) Any medical source that has received a final decision imposing a civil monetary penalty or assessment, or both, for submitting false evidence under section 1129 of the Act.

(b) Good cause. We may find good cause to consider evidence from an excluded medical source of evidence under section 223(d)(5)(C)(i) of the Act, as amended, if:

(1) The evidence from the medical source consists of evidence of treatment that occurred before the date the source was convicted of a felony under section 208 or under section 1632 of the Act;

(2) The evidence from the medical source consists of evidence of treatment that occurred during a period in which the source was not excluded from participation in any Federal health care program under section 1128 of the Act;

(3) The evidence from the medical source consists of evidence of treatment that occurred before the date the source received a final decision imposing a civil monetary penalty or assessment, or both, for submitting false evidence under section 1129 of the Act;

(4) The sole basis for the medical source's exclusion under section 223(d)(5)(C)(i) of the Act, as amended, is that the source cannot participate in any Federal health care program under section 1128 of the Act, but the Office of Inspector General of the Department of Health and Human Services granted a waiver of the section 1128 exclusion; or

(5) The evidence is a laboratory finding about a physical impairment and there is no indication that the finding is unreliable.

(c) Reporting requirements for excluded medical sources of evidence. Excluded medical sources of evidence (as described in paragraph (a) of this section) must inform us in writing that they are excluded under section 223(d)(5)(C)(i) of the Act, as amended, each time they submit evidence related to a claim for initial or continuing benefits under titles II or XVI of the Act. This reporting requirement applies to evidence that excluded medical sources of evidence submit to us either directly or through a representative, claimant, or other individual or entity.

(1) Excluded medical sources of evidence must provide a written statement, which contains the following information:

(i) A heading stating: "WRITTEN STATEMENT REGARDING SECTION 223(d)(5)(C) OF THE SOCIAL SECURITY ACT—DO NOT REMOVE"

(ii) The name and title of the medical source;

(iii) The applicable excluding event(s) stated in paragraph (a)(1)-(a)(3) of this section;

(iv) The date of the medical source's felony conviction under sections 208 or 1632 of the Act, if applicable;

(v) The date of the imposition of a civil monetary penalty or assessment, or both, for the submission of false evidence, under section 1129 of the Act, if applicable; and

(vi) The basis, effective date, anticipated length of the exclusion, and whether the Office of the Inspector General of the Department of Health and Human Services waived the exclusion, if the excluding event was the medical source's exclusion from participation in any Federal health care program under section 1128 of the Act.

(2) The written statement provided by an excluded medical source of evidence may not be removed by any individual or entity prior to submitting evidence to us.

(3) We may request that the excluded medical source of evidence provide us with additional information or clarify any information submitted that bears on the medical source's exclusion(s) under section 223(d)(5)(C)(i) of the Act, as amended.

[81 FR 65540, Sept. 23, 2016]

§ 404.1504 Decisions by other governmental agencies and nongovernmental entities.

Other governmental agencies and nongovernmental entities—such as the Department of Veterans Affairs, the Department of Defense, the Department of Labor, the Office of Personnel Management, State agencies, and private insurers— make disability, blindness, employability, Medicaid, workers' compensation, and other benefits decisions for their own programs using their own rules. Because a decision by any other governmental agency or a nongovernmental entity about whether you are disabled, blind, employable, or entitled to any benefits is based on its rules, it is not binding on us and is not our decision about whether you are disabled or blind under our rules. Therefore, in claims filed (see § 404.614) on or after March 27, 2017, we will not provide any analysis in our determination or decision about a decision made by any other governmental agency or a nongovernmental entity about whether you are disabled, blind, employable, or entitled to any benefits. However, we will consider all of the supporting evidence underlying the other governmental agency or nongovernmental entity's decision that we receive as evidence in your claim in accordance with § 404.1513(a)(1) through (4).

[82 FR 5864, Jan. 18, 2017; 82 FR 15132, March 27, 2017]

DEFINITION OF DISABILITY

§ 404.1505 Basic definition of disability.

(a) The law defines disability as the inability to do any substantial gainful activity by reason of any medically determinable physical or mental impairment which can be expected to result in death or which has lasted or can be expected to last for a continuous period of not less than 12 months. To meet this definition, you must have a severe impairment(s) that makes you unable to do your past relevant work (see § 404.1560(b)) or any other substantial gainful work that exists in the national economy. If your severe impairment(s) does not meet or medically equal a listing in appendix 1, we will assess your residual functional capacity as provided in §§ 404.1520(e) and 404.1545. (See §§ 404.1520(g)(2) and 404.1562 for an exception to this rule.) We will use this residual functional capacity assessment to determine if you can do your past relevant work. If we find that you cannot do your past relevant work, we will use the same residual functional capacity assessment and your vocational factors of age, education, and work experience to determine if you can do other work. (See § 404.1520(h) for an exception to this rule.) We will use this definition of disability if you are applying for a period of disability, or disability insurance benefits as a disabled worker, or child's insurance benefits based on disability before age 22 or, with respect to disability benefits payable for months after December 1990, as a widow, widower, or surviving divorced spouse.

(b) There are different rules for determining disability for individuals who are statutorily blind. We discuss these in §§ 404.1581 through 404.1587. There are also different rules for determining disability for widows, widowers, and surviving divorced spouses for monthly benefits for months prior to January 1991. We discuss these rules in §§ 404.1577, 404.1578, and 404.1579.

[51 FR 10616, March 28, 1986; 57 FR 30120, July 8, 1992; 68 FR 51161, Aug. 26, 2003; 77 FR 43494, July 25, 2012]

§ 404.1506 When we will not consider your impairment.

(a) Permanent exclusion of felony-related impairment. In determining whether you are under a disability, we will not consider any physical or mental impairment, or any increase in severity (aggravation) of a preexisting impairment, which arises in connection with your commission of a felony after October 19, 1980, if you are subsequently convicted of this crime. Your subsequent conviction will invalidate any prior determination establishing disability if that determination was based upon any impairment, or aggravation, which we must exclude under this rule.

(b) Limited use of impairment arising in prison. In determining whether you are under a disability for purposes of benefit payments, we will not consider any physical or mental impairment, or any increase in severity (aggravation) of a preexisting impairment, which arises in connection with your confinement in a jail, prison, or other penal institution or correctional facility for conviction of a felony committed after October 19, 1980. The exclusion of the impairment, or aggravation, applies in determining disability for benefits payable for any month during which you are confined. This rule does not preclude the establishment of a period of disability based upon the impairment or aggravation. You may become entitled to benefits upon release from prison provided that you apply and are under a disability at the time.

(c) Felonious offenses. We will consider an offense a felony if—

(1) It is a felony under applicable law; or

(2) In a jurisdiction which does not classify any crime as a felony, it is an offense punishable by death or imprisonment for a term exceeding one year.

(d) Confinement. In general, a jail, prison, or other penal institution or correctional facility is a facility which is under the control and jurisdiction of the agency in charge of the penal system or in which convicted criminals can be incarcerated. Confinement in such a facility continues as long as you are under a sentence of confinement and have not been released due to parole or pardon. You are considered confined even though you are temporarily or intermittently outside of the facility (e.g., on work release, attending school, or hospitalized).

[48 FR 5714, Feb. 8, 1983]

§ 404.1508 [Reserved by 82 FR 5864]

[82 FR 5864, Jan. 18, 2017]

§ 404.1509 How long the impairment must last.

Unless your impairment is expected to result in death, it must have lasted or must be expected to last for a continuous period of at least 12 months. We call this the duration requirement.

§ 404.1510 Meaning of substantial gainful activity.

Substantial gainful activity means work that—

(a) Involves doing significant and productive physical or mental duties; and

(b) Is done (or intended) for pay or profit.

(See § 404.1572 for further details about what we mean by substantial gainful activity.)

§ 404.1511 Definition of a disabling impairment.

(a) Disabled workers, persons disabled since childhood and, for months after December 1990, disabled widows, widowers, and surviving divorced spouses. If you are entitled to disability cash benefits as a disabled worker, or to child's insurance benefits, or, for monthly benefits payable after December 1990, to widow's, widower's, or surviving divorced spouse's monthly benefits, a disabling impairment is an impairment (or combination of impairments) which, of itself, is so severe that it meets or equals a set of criteria in the Listing of Impairments in appendix 1 of this subpart or which, when considered with your age, education, and work experience, would result in a finding that you are disabled under § 404.1594. In determining whether you have a disabling impairment, earnings are not considered.

(b) Disabled widows, widowers, and surviving divorced spouses, for monthly benefits for months prior to January 1991. If you have been entitled to disability benefits as a disabled widow, widower, or surviving divorced spouse and we must decide whether you had a disabling impairment for any time prior to January 1991, a disabling impairment is an impairment (or combination of impairments) which, of itself, was so severe that it met or equaled a set of criteria in the Listing of Impairments in appendix 1 of this subpart, or results in a finding that you were disabled under § 404.1579. In determining whether you had a disabling impairment, earnings are not considered.

[49 FR 22272, May 29, 1984; 50 FR 50126, Dec. 6, 1985; 57 FR 30120, July 8, 1992]

EVIDENCE

§ 404.1512 Responsibility for evidence.

(a) Your responsibility.

(1) General. In general, you have to prove to us that you are blind or disabled. You must inform us about or submit all evidence known to you that relates to whether or not you are blind or disabled (see § 404.1513). This duty is ongoing and requires you to disclose any additional related evidence about which you become aware. This duty applies at each level of the administrative review process, including the Appeals Council level if the evidence relates to the period on or before the date of the administrative law judge hearing decision. We will consider only impairment(s) you say you have or about which we receive evidence. When you submit evidence received from another source, you must submit that evidence in its entirety, unless you previously submitted the same evidence to us or we instruct you otherwise. If we ask you, you must inform us about:

(i) Your medical source(s);

(ii) Your age;

(iii) Your education and training;

(iv) Your work experience;

(v) Your daily activities both before and after the date you say that you became disabled;

(vi) Your efforts to work; and

(vii) Any other factors showing how your impairment(s) affects your ability to work. In §§ 404.1560 through 404.1569, we discuss in more detail the evidence we need when we consider vocational factors.

(2) Completeness. The evidence in your case record must be complete and detailed enough to allow us to make a determination or decision about whether you are disabled or blind. It must allow us to determine—

(i) The nature and severity of your impairment(s) for any period in question;

(ii) Whether the duration requirement described in § 404.1509 is met; and

(iii) Your residual functional capacity to do work-related physical and mental activities, when the evaluation steps described in § 404.1520(e) or (f)(1) apply.

(b) Our responsibility.

(1) Development. Before we make a determination that you are not disabled, we will develop your complete medical history for at least the 12 months preceding the month in which you file your application unless there is a reason to believe that development of an earlier period is necessary or unless you say that your disability began less than 12 months before you filed your application. We will make every reasonable effort to help you get medical evidence from your own medical sources and entities that maintain your medical sources' evidence when you give us permission to request the reports.

(i) Every reasonable effort means that we will make an initial request for evidence from your medical source or entity that maintains your medical source's evidence, and, at any time between 10 and 20 calendar days after the initial request, if the evidence has not been received, we will make one follow-up request to obtain the medical evidence necessary to make a determination. The medical source or entity that maintains your medical source's evidence will have a minimum of 10 calendar days from the date of our follow-up request to reply, unless our experience with that source indicates that a longer period is advisable in a particular case.

(ii) Complete medical history means the records of your medical source(s) covering at least the 12 months preceding the month in which you file your application. If you say that your disability began less than 12 months before you filed your application, we will develop your complete medical history beginning with the month you say your disability began unless we have reason to believe your disability began earlier. If applicable, we will develop your complete medical history for the 12–month period prior to the month you were last insured for disability insurance benefits (see § 404.130), the month ending the 7–year period you may have to establish your disability and you are applying for widow's or widower's benefits based on disability (see § 404.335(c)(1)), or the month you attain age 22 and you are applying for child's benefits based on disability (see § 404.350).

(2) Obtaining a consultative examination. We may ask you to attend one or more consultative examinations at our expense. See §§ 404.1517 through 404.1519t for the rules governing the consultative examination process. Generally, we will not request a consultative examination until we have made every reasonable effort to obtain evidence from your own medical sources. We may order a consultative examination while awaiting receipt of medical source evidence in some instances, such as when we know a source is not productive, is uncooperative, or is unable to provide certain tests or procedures. We will not evaluate this evidence until we have made every reasonable effort to obtain evidence from your medical sources.

(3) Other work. In order to determine under § 404.1520(g) that you are able to adjust to other work, we must provide evidence about the existence of work in the national economy that you can do (see §§ 404.1560 through 404.1569a), given your residual functional capacity (which we have already assessed, as described in § 404.1520(e)), age, education, and work experience.

[56 FR 36954, Aug. 1, 1991; 65 FR 11875, March 7, 2000; 65 FR 34957, June 1, 2000; 68 FR 51161, Aug. 26, 2003; 71 FR 16444, March 31, 2006; 75 FR 62680, Oct. 13, 2010; 76 FR 24806, May 3, 2011; 77 FR 10655, Feb. 23, 2012; 79 FR 33685, June 12, 2014; 80 FR 14836, March 20, 2015; 82 FR 5864, Jan. 18, 2017]

§ 404.1513 Categories of evidence.

(a) What we mean by evidence. Subject to the provisions of paragraph (b), evidence is anything you or anyone else submits to us or that we obtain that relates to your claim. We consider evidence under §§ 404.1520b, 404.1520c (or under § 404.1527 for claims filed (see § 404.614) before March 27, 2017). We evaluate evidence we receive according to the rules pertaining to the relevant category of evidence. The categories of evidence are:

(1) Objective medical evidence. Objective medical evidence is medical signs, laboratory findings, or both, as defined in § 404.1502(f).

(2) Medical opinion. A medical opinion is a statement from a medical source about what you can still do despite your impairment(s) and whether you have one or more impairment-related limitations or restrictions in the following abilities: (For claims filed (see § 404.614) before March 27, 2017, see § 404.1527(a) for the definition of medical opinion.)

(i) Your ability to perform physical demands of work activities, such as sitting, standing, walking, lifting, carrying, pushing, pulling, or other physical functions (including manipulative or postural functions, such as reaching, handling, stooping, or crouching);

(ii) Your ability to perform mental demands of work activities, such as understanding; remembering; maintaining concentration, persistence, or pace; carrying out instructions; or responding appropriately to supervision, co-workers, or work pressures in a work setting;

(iii) Your ability to perform other demands of work, such as seeing, hearing, or using other senses; and

(iv) Your ability to adapt to environmental conditions, such as temperature extremes or fumes.

(3) Other medical evidence. Other medical evidence is evidence from a medical source that is not objective medical evidence or a medical opinion, including judgments about the nature and severity of your impairments, your medical history, clinical findings, diagnosis, treatment prescribed with response, or prognosis. (For claims filed (see § 404.614) before March 27, 2017, other medical evidence does not include a diagnosis, prognosis, or a statement that reflects a judgment(s) about the nature and severity of your impairment(s)).

(4) Evidence from nonmedical sources. Evidence from nonmedical sources is any information or statement(s) from a nonmedical source (including you) about any issue in your claim. We may receive evidence from nonmedical sources either directly from the nonmedical source or indirectly, such as from forms we receive and our administrative records.

(5) Prior administrative medical finding. A prior administrative medical finding is a finding, other than the ultimate determination about whether you are disabled, about a medical issue made by our Federal and State agency medical and psychological consultants at a prior level of review (see § 404.900) in your current claim based on their review of the evidence in your case record, such as:

(i) The existence and severity of your impairment(s);

(ii) The existence and severity of your symptoms;

(iii) Statements about whether your impairment(s) meets or medically equals any listing in the Listing of Impairments in Part 404, Subpart P, Appendix 1;

(iv) Your residual functional capacity;

(v) Whether your impairment(s) meets the duration requirement; and

(vi) How failure to follow prescribed treatment (see § 404.1530) and drug addiction and alcoholism (see § 404.1535) relate to your claim.

(b) Exceptions for privileged communications.

(1) The privileged communications listed in paragraphs (b)(1)(i) and (b)(1)(ii) of this section are not evidence, and we will neither consider nor provide any analysis about them in your determination or decision. This exception for privileged communications applies equally whether your representative is an attorney or a non-attorney.

(i) Oral or written communications between you and your representative that are subject to the attorney-client privilege, unless you voluntarily disclose the communication to us.

(ii) Your representative's analysis of your claim, unless he or she voluntarily discloses it to us. This analysis means information that is subject to the attorney work product doctrine, but it does not include medical evidence, medical opinions, or any other factual matter that we may consider in determining whether or not you are entitled to benefits (see paragraph (b)(2) of this section).

(2) The attorney-client privilege generally protects confidential communications between an attorney and his or her client that are related to providing or obtaining legal advice. The attorney work product doctrine generally protects an attorney's analyses, theories, mental impressions, and notes. In the context of your disability claim, neither the attorney-client privilege nor the attorney work product doctrine allow you to withhold factual information, medical opinions, or other medical evidence that we may consider in determining whether or not you are entitled to benefits. For example, if you tell your representative about the medical sources you have seen, your representative cannot refuse to disclose the identity of those medical sources to us based on the attorney-client privilege. As another example, if your representative asks a medical source to complete an opinion form related to your impairment(s), symptoms, or limitations, your representative cannot withhold the completed opinion form from us based on the attorney work product doctrine. The attorney work product doctrine would not protect the source's opinions on the completed form, regardless of whether or not your representative used the form in his or her analysis of your claim or made handwritten notes on the face of the report.

[56 FR 36955, Aug. 1, 1991; 65 FR 11875, March 7, 2000; 65 FR 34957, June 1, 2000; 71 FR 16444, March 31, 2006; 72 FR 9242, March 1, 2007; 76 FR 24806, May 3, 2011; 78 FR 46501, Aug. 1, 2013; 82 FR 5865, Jan. 18, 2017; 82 FR 15132, March 27, 2017]

§ 404.1513a Evidence from our Federal or State agency medical or psychological consultants.

The following rules apply to our Federal or State agency medical or psychological consultants that we consult in connection with administrative law judge hearings and Appeals Council reviews:

(a) In claims adjudicated by the State agency, a State agency medical or psychological consultant may make the determination of disability together with a State agency disability examiner or provide medical evidence to a State agency disability examiner when the disability examiner makes the initial or reconsideration determination alone (see § 404.1615(c)). The following rules apply:

(1) When a State agency medical or psychological consultant makes the determination together with a State agency disability examiner at the initial or reconsideration level of the administrative review process as provided in § 404.1615(c)(1), he or she will consider the evidence in your case record and make administrative findings about the medical issues, including, but not limited to, the existence and severity of your impairment(s), the existence and severity of your symptoms, whether your impairment(s) meets or medically equals the requirements for any impairment listed in appendix 1 to this subpart, and your residual functional capacity. These administrative medical findings are based on the evidence in your case but are not in themselves evidence at the level of the administrative review process at which they are made. See § 404.1513(a)(5).

(2) When a State agency disability examiner makes the initial determination alone as provided in § 404.1615(c)(3), he or she may obtain medical evidence from a State agency medical or psychological consultant about one or more of the medical issues listed in paragraph (a)(1) of this section. In these cases, the State agency disability examiner will consider the medical evidence of the State agency medical or psychological consultant under §§ 404.1520b, 404.1520c, and 404.1527.

(3) When a State agency disability examiner makes a reconsideration determination alone as provided in § 404.1615(c)(3), he or she will consider prior administrative medical findings made by a State agency medical or psychological consultant at the initial level of the administrative review process, and any medical evidence provided by such consultants at the initial and reconsideration levels, about one or more of the medi-

cal issues listed in paragraph (a)(1)(i) of this section under §§ 404.1520b, 404.1520c, and 404.1527.

(b) Administrative law judges are responsible for reviewing the evidence and making administrative findings of fact and conclusions of law. They will consider prior administrative medical findings and medical evidence from our Federal or State agency medical or psychological consultants as follows:

(1) Administrative law judges are not required to adopt any prior administrative medical findings, but they must consider this evidence according to §§ 404.1520b, 404.1520c, and 404.1527, as appropriate, because our Federal or State agency medical or psychological consultants are highly qualified and experts in Social Security disability evaluation.

(2) Administrative law judges may also ask for medical evidence from expert medical sources. Administrative law judges will consider this evidence under §§ 404.1520b, 404.1520c, and 404.1527, as appropriate.

(c) When the Appeals Council makes a decision, it will consider prior administrative medical findings according to the same rules for considering prior administrative medical findings as administrative law judges follow under paragraph (b) of this section.

[82 FR 5866, Jan. 18, 2017]

§ 404.1514 When we will purchase existing evidence.

We need specific medical evidence to determine whether you are disabled or blind. You are responsible for providing that evidence. However, we will pay physicians not employed by the Federal government and other non-Federal providers of medical services for the reasonable cost of providing us with existing medical evidence that we need and ask for after November 30, 1980.

[45 FR 71792, Oct. 30, 1980; 46 FR 45757, Sept. 15, 1981]

§ 404.1515 Where and how to submit evidence.

You may give us evidence about your impairment at any of our offices or at the office of any State agency authorized to make disability determinations. You may also give evidence to one of our employees authorized to accept evidence at another place. For more information about this, see subpart H of this part.

§ 404.1516 If you fail to submit medical and other evidence.

If you do not give us the medical and other evidence that we need and request, we will have to make a decision based on information available in your case. We will not excuse you from giving us evidence because you have religious or personal reasons against medical examinations, tests, or treatment.

§ 404.1517 Consultative examination at our expense.

If your medical sources cannot or will not give us sufficient medical evidence about your impairment for us to determine whether you are disabled or blind, we may ask you to have one or more physical or mental examinations or tests. We will pay for these examinations. However, we will not pay for any medical examination arranged by you or your representative without our advance approval. If we arrange for the examination or test, we will give you reasonable notice of the date, time, and place the examination or test will be given, and the name of the person or facility who will do it. We will also give the examiner any necessary background information about your condition.

[45 FR 55584, Aug. 20, 1980, as amended at 45 FR 71792, Oct. 30, 1980; 46 FR 45757, Sept. 15, 1981; 56 FR 36956, Aug. 1, 1991]

§ 404.1518 If you do not appear at a consultative examination.

(a) General. If you are applying for benefits and do not have a good reason for failing or refusing to take part in a consultative examination or test which we arrange for you to get information we need to determine your disability or blindness, we may find that you are not disabled or blind. If you are already receiving benefits and do not have a good reason for failing or refusing to take part in a consultative examination or test which we arranged for you, we may determine that your disability or blindness has stopped because of your failure or refusal. Therefore, if you have any reason why you cannot go for the scheduled appointment, you should tell us about this as soon as possible before the examination date. If you have a good reason, we will schedule another examination. We will consider your physical, mental, educational, and linguistic limitations (including any lack of facility with the English language) when determining if you have a good reason for failing to attend a consultative examination.

(b) Examples of good reasons for failure to appear. Some examples of what we consider good reasons for not going to a scheduled examination include—

(1) Illness on the date of the scheduled examination or test;

(2) Not receiving timely notice of the scheduled examination or test, or receiving no notice at all;

(3) Being furnished incorrect or incomplete information, or being given incorrect information about the physician involved or the time or place of the examination or test, or;

(4) Having had death or serious illness occur in your immediate family.

(c) Objections by your medical source(s). If any of your medical sources tell you that you should not take the examination or test, you should tell us at once. In many cases, we may be able to get the information we need in another way. Your medical source(s) may agree to another type of examination for the same purpose.

[59 FR 1635, Jan. 12, 1994; 82 FR 5866, Jan. 18, 2017]

STANDARDS TO BE USED IN DETERMINING WHEN A CONSULTATIVE EXAMINATION WILL BE OBTAINED IN CONNECTION WITH DISABILITY DETERMINATIONS

§ 404.1519 The consultative examination.

A consultative examination is a physical or mental examination or test purchased for you at our request and expense from a treating source or another medical source, including a pediatrician when appropriate. The decision to purchase a consultative examination will be made on an individual case basis in accordance with the provisions of §§ 404.1519a through 404.1519f. Selection of the source for the examination will be consistent with the provisions of § 404.1503a and §§ 404.1519g through 404.1519j. The rules and procedures for requesting consultative examinations set forth in §§ 404.1519a and 404.1519b are applicable at the reconsideration and hearing levels of review, as well as the initial level of determination.

[56 FR 36956, Aug. 1, 1991; 65 FR 11875, March 7, 2000]

§ 404.1519a When we will purchase a consultative examination and how we will use it.

(a) General. If we cannot get the information we need from your medical sources, we may decide to purchase a consultative examination. See § 404.1512 for the procedures we will follow to obtain evidence from your medical sources and § 404.1520b for how we consider evidence. Before purchasing a consultative examination, we will consider not only existing medical reports, but also the disability interview form containing your allegations as well as other pertinent evidence in your file.

(b) Situations that may require a consultative examination. We may purchase a consultative examination to try to resolve an inconsistency in the evidence, or when the evidence as a whole is insufficient to allow us to make a determination or decision on your claim. Some examples of when we might purchase a consultative examination to secure needed medical evidence, such as clinical findings, laboratory tests, a diagnosis, or prognosis, include but are not limited to:

(1) The additional evidence needed is not contained in the records of your medical sources;

(2) The evidence that may have been available from your treating or other medical sources cannot be obtained for reasons beyond your control, such as death or noncooperation of a medical source;

(3) Highly technical or specialized medical evidence that we need is not available from your treating or other medical sources; or

(4) There is an indication of a change in your condition that is likely to affect your ability to work, but the current severity of your impairment is not established.

[56 FR 36956, Aug. 1, 1991; 77 FR 10655, Feb. 23, 2012]

§ 404.1519b When we will not purchase a consultative examination.

We will not purchase a consultative examination in situations including, but not limited to, the following situations:

(a) In period of disability and disability insurance benefit claims, when you do not meet the insured status requirement in the calendar quarter you allege you became disabled or later and there is no possibility of establishing an earlier onset;

(b) In claims for widow's or widower's benefits based on disability, when your alleged month of disability is after the end of the 7–year period specified in § 404.335(c)(1) and there is no possibility of establishing an earlier onset date, or when the 7–year period expired in the past and there is no possibility of establishing an onset date prior to the date the 7–year period expired;

(c) In disability insurance benefit claims, when your insured status expired in the past and there is no possibility of establishing an onset date prior to the date your insured status expired;

(d) When any issues about your actual performance of substantial gainful activity or gainful activity have not been resolved;

(e) In claims for child's benefits based on disability, when it is determined that your alleged disability did not begin before the month you attained age 22, and there is no possibility of establishing an onset date earlier than the month in which you attained age 22;

(f) In claims for child's benefits based on disability that are filed concurrently with the insured individual's claim and entitlement cannot be established for the insured individual;

(g) In claims for child's benefits based on disability where entitlement is precluded based on other nondisability factors.

[56 FR 36956, Aug. 1, 1991]

STANDARDS FOR THE TYPE OF REFERRAL AND FOR REPORT CONTENT

§ 404.1519f Type of purchased examinations.

We will purchase only the specific examinations and tests we need to make a determination in your claim. For example, we will not authorize a comprehensive medical examination when the only evidence we need is a special test, such as an X-ray, blood studies, or an electrocardiogram.

[56 FR 36956, Aug. 1, 1991]

§ 404.1519g Who we will select to perform a consultative examination.

(a) We will purchase a consultative examination only from a qualified medical source. The medical source may be your own medical source or another medical source. If you are a child, the medical source we choose may be a pediatrician.

(b) By "qualified," we mean that the medical source must be currently licensed in the State and have the training and experience to perform the type of examination or test we will request; the medical source must not be barred from participation in our programs under the provisions of § 404.1503a. The medical source must also have the equipment required to provide an adequate assessment and record of the existence and level of severity of your alleged impairments.

(c) The medical source we choose may use support staff to help perform the consultative examination. Any such support staff (e.g., X–ray technician, nurse) must meet appropriate licensing or certification requirements of the State. See § 404.1503a.

[56 FR 36957, Aug. 1, 1991; 65 FR 11876, March 7, 2000; 82 FR 5866, Jan. 18, 2017]

§ 404.1519h Your medical source.

When, in our judgment, your medical source is qualified, equipped, and willing to perform the additional examination or test(s) for the fee schedule payment, and generally furnishes complete and timely reports, your medical source will be the preferred source for the purchased examination or test(s).

[56 FR 36957, Aug. 1, 1991; 65 FR 11876, March 7, 2000; 82 FR 5866, Jan. 18, 2017]

§ 404.1519i Other sources for consultative examinations.

We will use a different medical source than your medical source for a purchased examination or test in situations including, but not limited to, the following:

(a) Your medical source prefers not to perform such an examination or does not have the equipment to provide the specific data needed;

(b) There are conflicts or inconsistencies in your file that cannot be resolved by going back to your medical source;

(c) You prefer a source other than your medical source and have a good reason for your preference;

(d) We know from prior experience that your medical source may not be a productive source, such as when he or she has consistently failed to provide complete or timely reports; or

(e) Your medical source is not a qualified medical source as defined in § 404.1519g.

[56 FR 36957, Aug. 1, 1991; 65 FR 11876, March 7, 2000; 82 FR 5866, Jan. 18, 2017]

§ 404.1519j Objections to the medical source designated to perform the consultative examination.

You or your representative may object to your being examined by a medical source we have designated to perform a consultative examination. If there is a good reason for the objection, we will schedule the examination with another medical source. A good reason may be that the medical source we designated had previously represented an interest adverse to you. For example, the medical source may have represented your employer in a workers' compensation case or may have been involved in an insurance claim or legal action adverse to you. Other things we will consider include: The presence of a language barrier, the medical source's office location (e.g., 2nd floor, no elevator), travel restrictions, and whether the medical source had examined you in connection with a previous disability determination or decision that was unfavorable to you. If your objection is that a medical source allegedly "lacks objectivity" in general, but not in relation to you personally, we will review the allegations. See § 404.1519s. To avoid a delay in processing your claim, the consultative examination in your case will be changed to another medical source while a review is being conducted. We will handle any objection to use of the substitute medical source in the same manner. However, if we had previously conducted such a review and found that the reports of the medical source in question conformed to our guidelines, we will not change your examination.

[56 FR 36957, Aug. 1, 1991; 65 FR 11876, March 7, 2000]

§ 404.1519k Purchase of medical examinations, laboratory tests, and other services.

We may purchase medical examinations, including psychiatric and psychological examinations, X–rays and laboratory tests (including specialized tests, such as pulmonary function studies, electrocardiograms, and stress tests) from a medical source.

(a) The rate of payment for purchasing medical or other services necessary to make determinations of disability may not exceed the highest rate paid by Federal or public agencies in the State for the same or similar types of service. See §§ 404.1624 and 404.1626 of this part.

(b) If a physician's bill or a request for payment for a physician's services includes a charge for a laboratory test for which payment may be made under this part, the amount payable with respect to the test shall be determined as follows:

(1) If the bill or request for payment indicates that the test was personally performed or supervised by the physician who submitted the bill (or for whose services

the request for payment was made) or by another physician with whom that physician shares his or her practice, the payment will be based on the physician's usual and customary charge for the test or the rates of payment which the State uses for purchasing such services, whichever is the lesser amount.

(2) If the bill or request for payment indicates that the test was performed by an independent laboratory, the amount of reimbursement will not exceed the billed cost of the independent laboratory or the rate of payment which the State uses for purchasing such services, whichever is the lesser amount. A nominal payment may be made to the physician for collecting, handling and shipping a specimen to the laboratory if the physician bills for such a service. The total reimbursement may not exceed the rate of payment which the State uses for purchasing such services.

(c) The State will assure that it can support the rate of payment it uses. The State shall also be responsible for monitoring and overseeing the rate of payment it uses to ensure compliance with paragraphs (a) and (b) of this section.

[56 FR 36957, Aug. 1, 1991; 65 FR 11876, March 7, 2000; 71 FR 16444, March 31, 2006; 76 FR 24806, May 3, 2011]

§ 404.1519m Diagnostic tests or procedures.

We will request the results of any diagnostic tests or procedures that have been performed as part of a workup by your treating source or other medical source and will use the results to help us evaluate impairment severity or prognosis. However, we will not order diagnostic tests or procedures that involve significant risk to you, such as myelograms, arteriograms, or cardiac catheterizations for the evaluation of disability under the Social Security program. A State agency medical consultant must approve the ordering of any diagnostic test or procedure when there is a chance it may involve significant risk. The responsibility for deciding whether to perform the examination rests with the medical source designated to perform the consultative examination.

[56 FR 36957, Aug. 1, 1991; 65 FR 11876, March 7, 2000; 71 FR 16444, March 31, 2006; 76 FR 24806, May 3, 2011]

§ 404.1519n Informing the medical source of examination scheduling, report content, and signature requirements.

The medical sources who perform consultative examinations will have a good understanding of our disability programs and their evidentiary requirements. They will be made fully aware of their responsibilities and obligations regarding confidentiality as described in § 401.105(e). We will fully inform medical sources who perform consultative examinations at the time we first contact them, and at subsequent appropriate intervals, of the following obligations:

(a) Scheduling. In scheduling full consultative examinations, sufficient time should be allowed to permit the medical source to take a case history and perform the examination, including any needed tests. The following minimum scheduling intervals (i.e., time set aside for the individual, not the actual duration of the consultative examination) should be used.

(1) Comprehensive general medical examination—at least 30 minutes;

(2) Comprehensive musculoskeletal or neurological examination—at least 20 minutes;

(3) Comprehensive psychiatric examination—at least 40 minutes;

(4) Psychological examination—at least 60 minutes (Additional time may be required depending on types of psychological tests administered); and

(5) All others—at least 30 minutes, or in accordance with accepted medical practices.

We recognize that actual practice will dictate that some examinations may require longer scheduling intervals depending on the circumstances in a particular situation. We also recognize that these minimum intervals may have to be adjusted to allow for those claimants who do not attend their scheduled examination. The purpose of these minimum scheduling timeframes is to ensure that such examinations are complete and that sufficient time is made available to obtain the information needed to make an accurate determination in your case. State agencies will monitor the scheduling of examinations (through their normal consultative examination oversight activities) to ensure that any overscheduling is avoided, as overscheduling may lead to examinations that are not thorough.

(b) Report content. The reported results of your medical history, examination, requested laboratory findings, discussions and conclusions must conform to accepted professional standards and practices in the medical field for a complete and competent examination. The facts in a particular case and the information and findings already reported in the medical and other evidence of record will dictate the extent of detail needed in the consultative examination report for that case. Thus, the detail and format for reporting the results of a purchased examination will vary depending upon the type of examination or testing requested. The reporting of information will differ from one type of examination to another when the requested examination relates to the performance of tests such as ventilatory function tests, treadmill exercise tests, or audiological tests. The medical report must be complete enough to help us determine the nature, severity, and duration of the impairment, and residual functional capacity. The report should reflect your statement of your symptoms, not simply the medical source's statements or conclusions. The medical source's report of the consultative examination should include the objective medical facts as well as observations and opinions.

(c) Elements of a complete consultative examination. A complete consultative examination is one which involves all the elements of a standard examination in the applicable medical specialty. When the report of a complete consultative examination is involved, the report should include the following elements:

(1) Your major or chief complaint(s);

(2) A detailed description, within the area of specialty of the examination, of the history of your major complaint(s);

(3) A description, and disposition, of pertinent "positive" and "negative" detailed findings based on the history, examination and laboratory tests related to the major complaint(s), and any other abnormalities or lack thereof reported or found during examination or laboratory testing;

(4) The results of laboratory and other tests (e.g., X-rays) performed according to the requirements stated in the Listing of Impairments (see appendix 1 of this subpart P);

(5) The diagnosis and prognosis for your impairment(s);

(6) A medical opinion. Although we will ordinarily request a medical opinion as part of the consultative examination process, the absence of a medical opinion in a consultative examination report will not make the report incomplete. See § 404.1513(a)(3); and

(7) In addition, the medical source will consider, and provide some explanation or comment on, your major complaint(s) and any other abnormalities found during the history and examination or reported from the laboratory tests. The history, examination, evaluation of laboratory test results, and the conclusions will represent the information provided by the medical source who signs the report.

(d) When a complete consultative examination is not required. When the evidence we need does not require a complete consultative examination (for example, we need only a specific laboratory test result to complete the record), we may not require a report containing all of the elements in paragraph (c).

(e) Signature requirements. All consultative examination reports will be personally reviewed and signed by the medical source who actually performed the examination. This attests to the fact that the medical source doing the examination or testing is solely responsible for the report contents and for the conclusions, explanations or comments provided with respect to the history, examination and evaluation of laboratory test results. The signature of the medical source on a report annotated "not proofed" or "dictated but not read" is not acceptable. A rubber stamp signature of a medical source or the medical source's signature entered by any other person is not acceptable.

[56 FR 36958, Aug. 1, 1991; 65 FR 11876, March 7, 2000; 82 FR 5866, Jan. 18, 2017]

§ 404.1519o When a properly signed consultative examination report has not been received.

If a consultative examination report is received unsigned or improperly signed we will take the following action.

(a) When we will make determinations and decisions without a properly signed report. We will make a determination or decision in the circumstances specified in paragraphs (a)(1) and (a)(2) of this section without waiting for a properly signed consultative examination report. After we have made the determination or decision, we will obtain a properly signed report and include it in the file unless the medical source who performed the original consultative examination has died:

(1) Continuous period of disability allowance with an onset date as alleged or earlier than alleged; or

(2) Continuance of disability.

(b) When we will not make determinations and decisions without a properly signed report. We will not use an unsigned or improperly signed consultative examination report to make the determinations or decisions specified in paragraphs (b)(1), (b)(2), (b)(3), and (b)(4) of this section. When we need a properly signed consultative examination report to make these determinations or decisions, we must obtain such a report. If the signature of the medical source who performed the original examination cannot be obtained because the medical source is out of the country for an extended period of time, or on an extended vacation, seriously ill, deceased, or for any other reason, the consultative examination will be rescheduled with another medical source:

(1) Denial; or

(2) Cessation; or

(3) Allowance of a period of disability which has ended; or

(4) Allowance with an onset date later than alleged.

[56 FR 36958, Aug. 1, 1991; 65 FR 11877, March 7, 2000]

§ 404.1519p Reviewing reports of consultative examinations.

(a) We will review the report of the consultative examination to determine whether the specific information requested has been furnished. We will consider the following factors in reviewing the report:

(1) Whether the report provides evidence which serves as an adequate basis for decisionmaking in terms of the impairment it assesses;

(2) Whether the report is internally consistent; Whether all the diseases, impairments and complaints

described in the history are adequately assessed and reported in the clinical findings; Whether the conclusions correlate the findings from your medical history, clinical examination and laboratory tests and explain all abnormalities;

(3) Whether the report is consistent with the other information available to us within the specialty of the examination requested; Whether the report fails to mention an important or relevant complaint within that specialty that is noted in other evidence in the file (e.g., your blindness in one eye, amputations, pain, alcoholism, depression);

(4) Whether this is an adequate report of examination as compared to standards set out in the course of a medical education; and

(5) Whether the report is properly signed.

(b) If the report is inadequate or incomplete, we will contact the medical source who performed the consultative examination, give an explanation of our evidentiary needs, and ask that the medical source furnish the missing information or prepare a revised report.

(c) With your permission, or when the examination discloses new diagnostic information or test results that reveal a potentially life-threatening situation, we will refer the consultative examination report to your treating source. When we refer the consultative examination report to your treating source without your permission, we will notify you that we have done so.

(d) We will perform ongoing special management studies on the quality of consultative examinations purchased from major medical sources and the appropriateness of the examinations authorized.

(e) We will take steps to ensure that consultative examinations are scheduled only with medical sources who have access to the equipment required to provide an adequate assessment and record of the existence and level of severity of your alleged impairments.

[56 FR 36959, Aug. 1, 1991; 65 FR 11877, March 7, 2000]

§ 404.1519q Conflict of interest.

All implications of possible conflict of interest between medical or psychological consultants and their medical or psychological practices will be avoided. Such consultants are not only those physicians and psychologists who work for us directly but are also those who do review and adjudication work in the State agencies. Physicians and psychologists who work for us directly as employees or under contract will not work concurrently for a State agency. Physicians and psychologists who do review work for us will not perform consultative examinations for us without our prior approval. In such situations, the physician or psychologist will disassociate himself or herself from further involvement in the case and will not participate in the evaluation, decision, or appeal actions. In addition, neither they, nor any member of their families, will acquire or maintain, either directly or indirectly, any financial interest in a medical partnership, corporation, or similar relationship in which consultative examinations are provided. Sometimes physicians and psychologists who do review work for us will have prior knowledge of a case; for example, when the claimant was a patient. Where this is so, the physician or psychologist will not participate in the review or determination of the case. This does not preclude the physician or psychologist from submitting medical evidence based on treatment or examination of the claimant.

[56 FR 36959, Aug. 1, 1991]

AUTHORIZING AND MONITORING THE REFERRAL PROCESS

§ 404.1519s Authorizing and monitoring the consultative examination.

(a) Day-to-day responsibility for the consultative examination process rests with the State agencies that make disability determinations for us.

(b) The State agency will maintain a good working relationship with the medical community in order to recruit sufficient numbers of physicians and other providers of medical services to ensure ready availability of consultative examination providers.

(c) Consistent with Federal and State laws, the State agency administrator will work to achieve appropriate rates of payment for purchased medical services.

(d) Each State agency will be responsible for comprehensive oversight management of its consultative examination program, with special emphasis on key providers.

(e) A key consultative examination provider is a provider that meets at least one of the following conditions:

(1) Any consultative examination provider with an estimated annual billing to the disability programs we administer of at least $150,000; or

(2) Any consultative examination provider with a practice directed primarily towards evaluation examinations rather than the treatment of patients; or

(3) Any consultative examination provider that does not meet the above criteria, but is one of the top five consultative examination providers in the State by dollar volume, as evidenced by prior year data.

(f) State agencies have flexibility in managing their consultative examination programs, but at a minimum will provide:

(1) An ongoing active recruitment program for consultative examination providers;

(2) A process for orientation, training, and review of new consultative examination providers, with respect to SSA's program requirements involving consultative ex-

amination report content and not with respect to medical techniques;

(3) Procedures for control of scheduling consultative examinations;

(4) Procedures to ensure that close attention is given to specific evaluation issues involved in each case;

(5) Procedures to ensure that only required examinations and tests are authorized in accordance with the standards set forth in this subpart;

(6) Procedures for providing medical or supervisory approval for the authorization or purchase of consultative examinations and for additional tests or studies requested by consulting medical sources. This includes physician approval for the ordering of any diagnostic test or procedure where the question of significant risk to the claimant/beneficiary might be raised. See § 404.1519m.

(7) Procedures for the ongoing review of consultative examination results to ensure compliance with written guidelines;

(8) Procedures to encourage active participation by physicians in the consultative examination oversight program;

(9) Procedures for handling complaints;

(10) Procedures for evaluating claimant reactions to key providers; and

(11) A program of systematic, onsite reviews of key providers that will include annual onsite reviews of such providers when claimants are present for examinations. This provision does not contemplate that such reviews will involve participation in the actual examinations but, rather, offer an opportunity to talk with claimants at the provider's site before and after the examination and to review the provider's overall operation.

(g) The State agencies will cooperate with us when we conduct monitoring activities in connection with their oversight management of their consultative examination programs.

[56 FR 36959, Aug. 1, 1991; 65 FR 11877, March 7, 2000; 71 FR 16444, March 31, 2006; 75 FR 32846, June 10, 2010; 76 FR 24806, May 3, 2011]

PROCEDURES TO MONITOR THE CONSULTATIVE EXAMINATION

§ 404.1519t Consultative examination oversight.

(a) We will ensure that referrals for consultative examinations and purchases of consultative examinations are made in accordance with our policies. We will also monitor both the referral processes and the product of the consultative examinations obtained. This monitoring may include reviews by independent medical specialists under direct contract with SSA.

(b) Through our regional offices, we will undertake periodic comprehensive reviews of each State agency to evaluate each State's management of the consultative examination process. The review will involve visits to key providers, with State staff participating, including a program physician when the visit will deal with medical techniques or judgment, or factors that go to the core of medical professionalism.

(c) We will also perform ongoing special management studies of the quality of consultative examinations purchased from key providers and other sources and the appropriateness of the examinations authorized.

[56 FR 36960, Aug. 1, 1991]

EVALUATION OF DISABILITY

§ 404.1520 Evaluation of disability in general.

(a) General—

(1) Purpose of this section. This section explains the five-step sequential evaluation process we use to decide whether you are disabled, as defined in § 404.1505.

(2) Applicability of these rules. These rules apply to you if you file an application for a period of disability or disability insurance benefits (or both) or for child's insurance benefits based on disability. They also apply if you file an application for widow's or widower's benefits based on disability for months after December 1990. (See § 404.1505(a).)

(3) Evidence considered. We will consider all evidence in your case record when we make a determination or decision whether you are disabled. See § 404.1520b.

(4) The five-step sequential evaluation process. The sequential evaluation process is a series of five "steps" that we follow in a set order. See paragraph (h) of this section for an exception to this rule. If we can find that you are disabled or not disabled at a step, we make our determination or decision and we do not go on to the next step. If we cannot find that you are disabled or not disabled at a step, we go on to the next step. Before we go from step three to step four, we assess your residual functional capacity. (See paragraph (e) of this section.) We use this residual functional capacity assessment at both step four and step five when we evaluate your claim at these steps. These are the five steps we follow:

(i) At the first step, we consider your work activity, if any. If you are doing substantial gainful activity, we will find that you are not disabled. (See paragraph (b) of this section.)

(ii) At the second step, we consider the medical severity of your impairment(s). If you do not have a severe medically determinable physical or mental impairment that meets the duration requirement in § 404.1509, or a combination of impairments that is severe and meets the duration requirement, we will find that you are not disabled. (See paragraph (c) of this section.)

(iii) At the third step, we also consider the medical severity of your impairment(s). If you have an impairment(s) that meets or equals one of our listings in appendix 1 of this subpart and meets the duration requirement, we will find that you are disabled. (See paragraph (d) of this section.)

(iv) At the fourth step, we consider our assessment of your residual functional capacity and your past relevant work. If you can still do your past relevant work, we will find that you are not disabled. See paragraphs (f) and (h) of this section and § 404.1560(b).

(v) At the fifth and last step, we consider our assessment of your residual functional capacity and your age, education, and work experience to see if you can make an adjustment to other work. If you can make an adjustment to other work, we will find that you are not disabled. If you cannot make an adjustment to other work, we will find that you are disabled. See paragraphs (g) and (h) of this section and § 404.1560(c).

(5) When you are already receiving disability benefits. If you are already receiving disability benefits, we will use a different sequential evaluation process to decide whether you continue to be disabled. We explain this process in § 404.1594(f).

(b) If you are working. If you are working and the work you are doing is substantial gainful activity, we will find that you are not disabled regardless of your medical condition or your age, education, and work experience.

(c) You must have a severe impairment. If you do not have any impairment or combination of impairments which significantly limits your physical or mental ability to do basic work activities, we will find that you do not have a severe impairment and are, therefore, not disabled. We will not consider your age, education, and work experience. However, it is possible for you to have a period of disability for a time in the past even though you do not now have a severe impairment.

(d) When your impairment(s) meets or equals a listed impairment in appendix 1. If you have an impairment(s) which meets the duration requirement and is listed in appendix 1 or is equal to a listed impairment(s), we will find you disabled without considering your age, education, and work experience.

(e) When your impairment(s) does not meet or equal a listed impairment. If your impairment(s) does not meet or equal a listed impairment, we will assess and make a finding about your residual functional capacity based on all the relevant medical and other evidence in your case record, as explained in § 404.1545. (See paragraph (g)(2) of this section and § 404.1562 for an exception to this rule.) We use our residual functional capacity assessment at the fourth step of the sequential evaluation process to determine if you can do your past relevant work (paragraph (f) of this section) and at the fifth step of the sequential evaluation process (if the evaluation proceeds to this step) to determine if you can adjust to other work (paragraph (g) of this section).

(f) Your impairment(s) must prevent you from doing your past relevant work. If we cannot make a determination or decision at the first three steps of the sequential evaluation process, we will compare our residual functional capacity assessment, which we made under paragraph (e) of this section, with the physical and mental demands of your past relevant work. See paragraph (h) of this section and § 404.1560(b). If you can still do this kind of work, we will find that you are not disabled.

(g) Your impairment(s) must prevent you from making an adjustment to any other work.

(1) If we find that you cannot do your past relevant work because you have a severe impairment(s) (or you do not have any past relevant work), we will consider the same residual functional capacity assessment we made under paragraph (e) of this section, together with your vocational factors (your age, education, and work experience) to determine if you can make an adjustment to other work. (See § 404.1560(c).) If you can make an adjustment to other work, we will find you not disabled. If you cannot, we will find you disabled.

(2) We use different rules if you meet one of the two special medical-vocational profiles described in § 404.1562. If you meet one of those profiles, we will find that you cannot make an adjustment to other work, and that you are disabled.

(h) Expedited process. If we do not find you disabled at the third step, and we do not have sufficient evidence about your past relevant work to make a finding at the fourth step, we may proceed to the fifth step of the sequential evaluation process. If we find that you can adjust to other work based solely on your age, education, and the same residual functional capacity assessment we made under paragraph (e) of this section, we will find that you are not disabled and will not make a finding about whether you can do your past relevant work at the fourth step. If we find that you may be unable to adjust to other work or if § 404.1562 may apply, we will assess your claim at the fourth step and make a finding about whether you can perform your past relevant work. See paragraph (g) of this section and § 404.1560(c).

[50 FR 8727, March 5, 1985; 50 FR 19164, May 7, 1985; 56 FR 36960, Aug. 1, 1991; 65 FR 80308, Dec. 21, 2000; 68 FR 51161, Aug. 26, 2003; 77 FR 10655, Feb. 23, 2012; 77 FR 43494, July 25, 2012]

§ 404.1520a Evaluation of mental impairments.

(a) General. The steps outlined in § 404.1520 apply to the evaluation of physical and mental impairments. In addition, when we evaluate the severity of mental impairments for adults (persons age 18 and over) and in persons under age 18 when Part A of the Listing of Impairments is used, we must follow a special technique at each level in the administrative review process. We describe this special technique in paragraphs (b) through (e) of this section. Using the technique helps us:

(1) Identify the need for additional evidence to determine impairment severity;

(2) Consider and evaluate functional consequences of the mental disorder(s) relevant to your ability to work; and

(3) Organize and present our findings in a clear, concise, and consistent manner.

(b) Use of the technique.

(1) Under the special technique, we must first evaluate your pertinent symptoms, signs, and laboratory findings to determine whether you have a medically determinable mental impairment(s). See § 404.1521 for more information about what is needed to show a medically determinable impairment. If we determine that you have a medically determinable mental impairment(s), we must specify the symptoms, signs, and laboratory findings that substantiate the presence of the impairment(s) and document our findings in accordance with paragraph (e) of this section.

(2) We must then rate the degree of functional limitation resulting from the impairment(s) in accordance with paragraph (c) of this section and record our findings as set out in paragraph (e) of this section.

(c) Rating the degree of functional limitation.

(1) Assessment of functional limitations is a complex and highly individualized process that requires us to consider multiple issues and all relevant evidence to obtain a longitudinal picture of your overall degree of functional limitation. We will consider all relevant and available clinical signs and laboratory findings, the effects of your symptoms, and how your functioning may be affected by factors including, but not limited to, chronic mental disorders, structured settings, medication, and other treatment.

(2) We will rate the degree of your functional limitation based on the extent to which your impairment(s) interferes with your ability to function independently, appropriately, effectively, and on a sustained basis. Thus, we will consider such factors as the quality and level of your overall functional performance, any episodic limitations, the amount of supervision or assistance you require, and the settings in which you are able to function. See 12.00C through 12.00H of the Listing of Impairments in appendix 1 to this subpart for more information about the factors we consider when we rate the degree of your functional limitation.

(3) We have identified four broad functional areas in which we will rate the degree of your functional limitation: Understand, remember, or apply information; interact with others; concentrate, persist, or maintain pace; and adapt or manage oneself. See 12.00E of the Listing of Impairments in appendix 1 to this subpart.

(4) When we rate your degree of limitation in these areas (understand, remember, or apply information; interact with others; concentrate, persist, or maintain pace; and adapt or manage oneself), we will use the following five-point scale: None, mild, moderate, marked, and extreme. The last point on the scale represents a degree of limitation that is incompatible with the ability to do any gainful activity.

(d) Use of the technique to evaluate mental impairments. After we rate the degree of functional limitation resulting from your impairment(s), we will determine the severity of your mental impairment(s).

(1) If we rate the degrees of your limitation as "none" or "mild," we will generally conclude that your impairment(s) is not severe, unless the evidence otherwise indicates that there is more than a minimal limitation in your ability to do basic work activities (see § 404.1522).

(2) If your mental impairment(s) is severe, we will then determine if it meets or is equivalent in severity to a listed mental disorder. We do this by comparing the medical findings about your impairment(s) and the rating of the degree of functional limitation to the criteria of the appropriate listed mental disorder. We will record the presence or absence of the criteria and the rating of the degree of functional limitation on a standard document at the initial and reconsideration levels of the administrative review process, or in the decision at the administrative law judge hearing and Appeals Council levels (in cases in which the Appeals Council issues a decision). See paragraph (e) of this section.

(3) If we find that you have a severe mental impairment(s) that neither meets nor is equivalent in severity to any listing, we will then assess your residual functional capacity.

(e) Documenting application of the technique. At the initial and reconsideration levels of the administrative review process, we will complete a standard document to record how we applied the technique. At the administrative law judge hearing and Appeals Council levels (in cases in which the Appeals Council issues a decision), we will document application of the technique in the decision. The following rules apply:

(1) When a State agency medical or psychological consultant makes the determination together with a State agency disability examiner at the initial or reconsideration level of the administrative review process as

provided in § 404.1615(c)(1) of this part, the State agency medical or psychological consultant has overall responsibility for assessing medical severity. A State agency disability examiner may assist in preparing the standard document. However, our medical or psychological consultant must review and sign the document to attest that it is complete and that he or she is responsible for its content, including the findings of fact and any discussion of supporting evidence.

(2) When a State agency disability examiner makes the determination alone as provided in § 404.1615(c)(3), the State agency disability examiner has overall responsibility for assessing medical severity and for completing and signing the standard document.

(3) When a disability hearing officer makes a reconsideration determination as provided in § 404.1615(c)(4), the determination must document application of the technique, incorporating the disability hearing officer's pertinent findings and conclusions based on this technique.

(4) At the administrative law judge hearing and Appeals Council levels, the written decision must incorporate the pertinent findings and conclusions based on the technique. The decision must show the significant history, including examination and laboratory findings, and the functional limitations that were considered in reaching a conclusion about the severity of the mental impairment(s). The decision must include a specific finding as to the degree of limitation in each of the functional areas described in paragraph (c) of this section.

(5) If the administrative law judge requires the services of a medical expert to assist in applying the technique but such services are unavailable, the administrative law judge may return the case to the State agency or the appropriate Federal component, using the rules in § 404.941 of this part, for completion of the standard document. If, after reviewing the case file and completing the standard document, the State agency or Federal component concludes that a determination favorable to you is warranted, it will process the case using the rules found in § 404.941(d) or (e) of this part. If, after reviewing the case file and completing the standard document, the State agency or Federal component concludes that a determination favorable to you is not warranted, it will send the completed standard document and the case to the administrative law judge for further proceedings and a decision.

[50 FR 35065, Aug. 28, 1985; 55 FR 51229, Dec. 12, 1990; 57 FR 30120, July 8, 1992; 65 FR 50774, Aug. 21, 2000; 65 FR 60584, Oct. 12, 2000; 71 FR 16444, March 31, 2006; 75 FR 62680, Oct. 13, 2010; 76 FR 24806, May 3, 2011; 81 FR 66160, Sept. 26, 2016; 82 FR 5867, Jan. 18, 2017]

§ 404.1520b How we consider evidence.

After we review all of the evidence relevant to your claim, we make findings about what the evidence shows.

(a) Complete and consistent evidence. If all of the evidence we receive, including all medical opinion(s), is consistent and there is sufficient evidence for us to determine whether you are disabled, we will make our determination or decision based on that evidence.

(b) Incomplete or inconsistent evidence. In some situations, we may not be able to make our determination or decision because the evidence in your case record is insufficient or inconsistent. We consider evidence to be insufficient when it does not contain all the information we need to make our determination or decision. We consider evidence to be inconsistent when it conflicts with other evidence, contains an internal conflict, is ambiguous, or when the medical evidence does not appear to be based on medically acceptable clinical or laboratory diagnostic techniques. If the evidence in your case record is insufficient or inconsistent, we may need to take the additional actions in paragraphs (b)(1) through (4) of this section.

(1) If any of the evidence in your case record, including any medical opinion(s) and prior administrative medical findings, is inconsistent, we will consider the relevant evidence and see if we can determine whether you are disabled based on the evidence we have.

(2) If the evidence is consistent but we have insufficient evidence to determine whether you are disabled, or if after considering the evidence we determine we cannot reach a conclusion about whether you are disabled, we will determine the best way to resolve the inconsistency or insufficiency. The action(s) we take will depend on the nature of the inconsistency or insufficiency. We will try to resolve the inconsistency or insufficiency by taking any one or more of the actions listed in paragraphs (b)(2)(i) through (b)(2)(iv) of this section. We might not take all of the actions listed below. We will consider any additional evidence we receive together with the evidence we already have.

(i) We may recontact your medical source. We may choose not to seek additional evidence or clarification from a medical source if we know from experience that the source either cannot or will not provide the necessary evidence. If we obtain medical evidence over the telephone, we will send the telephone report to the source for review, signature, and return;

(ii) We may request additional existing evidence;

(iii) We may ask you to undergo a consultative examination at our expense (see §§ 404.1517 through 404.1519t); or

(iv) We may ask you or others for more information.

(3) When there are inconsistencies in the evidence that we cannot resolve or when, despite efforts to obtain additional evidence, the evidence is insufficient to determine whether you are disabled, we will make a determination or decision based on the evidence we have.

(c) Evidence that is inherently neither valuable nor persuasive. Paragraphs (c)(1) through (c)(3) apply in claims filed (see § 404.614) on or after March 27, 2017. Because the evidence listed in paragraphs (c)(1) through (c)(3) of this section is inherently neither valuable nor persuasive to the issue of whether you are disabled or blind under the Act, we will not provide any analysis about how we considered such evidence in our determination or decision, even under § 404.1520c:

(1) Decisions by other governmental agencies and nongovernmental entities. See § 404.1504.

(2) Disability examiner findings. Findings made by a State agency disability examiner made at a previous level of adjudication about a medical issue, vocational issue, or the ultimate determination about whether you are disabled.

(3) Statements on issues reserved to the Commissioner. The statements listed in paragraphs (c)(3)(i) through (c)(3)(viii) of this section would direct our determination or decision that you are or are not disabled or blind within the meaning of the Act, but we are responsible for making the determination or decision about whether you are disabled or blind:

(i) Statements that you are or are not disabled, blind, able to work, or able to perform regular or continuing work;

(ii) Statements about whether or not you have a severe impairment(s);

(iii) Statements about whether or not your impairment(s) meets the duration requirement (see § 404.1509);

(iv) Statements about whether or not your impairment(s) meets or medically equals any listing in the Listing of Impairments in Part 404, Subpart P, Appendix 1;

(v) Statements about what your residual functional capacity is using our programmatic terms about the functional exertional levels in Part 404, Subpart P, Appendix 2, Rule 200.00 instead of descriptions about your functional abilities and limitations (see § 404.1545);

(vi) Statements about whether or not your residual functional capacity prevents you from doing past relevant work (see § 404.1560);

(vii) Statements that you do or do not meet the requirements of a medical-vocational rule in Part 404, Subpart P, Appendix 2; and

(viii) Statements about whether or not your disability continues or ends when we conduct a continuing disability review (see § 404.1594).

[77 FR 10655, Feb. 23, 2012; 82 FR 5867, Jan. 18, 2017]

§ 404.1520c How we consider and articulate medical opinions and prior administrative medical findings for claims filed on or after March 27, 2017.

For claims filed (see § 404.614) on or after March 27, 2017, the rules in this section apply. For claims filed before March 27, 2017, the rules in § 404.1527 apply.

(a) How we consider medical opinions and prior administrative medical findings. We will not defer or give any specific evidentiary weight, including controlling weight, to any medical opinion(s) or prior administrative medical finding(s), including those from your medical sources. When a medical source provides one or more medical opinions or prior administrative medical findings, we will consider those medical opinions or prior administrative medical findings from that medical source together using the factors listed in paragraphs (c)(1) through (c)(5) of this section, as appropriate. The most important factors we consider when we evaluate the persuasiveness of medical opinions and prior administrative medical findings are supportability (paragraph (c)(1) of this section) and consistency (paragraph (c)(2) of this section). We will articulate how we considered the medical opinions and prior administrative medical findings in your claim according to paragraph (b) of this section.

(b) How we articulate our consideration of medical opinions and prior administrative medical findings. We will articulate in our determination or decision how persuasive we find all of the medical opinions and all of the prior administrative medical findings in your case record. Our articulation requirements are as follows:

(1) Source-level articulation. Because many claims have voluminous case records containing many types of evidence from different sources, it is not administratively feasible for us to articulate in each determination or decision how we considered all of the factors for all of the medical opinions and prior administrative medical findings in your case record. Instead, when a medical source provides multiple medical opinion(s) or prior administrative medical finding(s), we will articulate how we considered the medical opinions or prior administrative medical findings from that medical source together in a single analysis using the factors listed in paragraphs (c)(1) through (c)(5) of this section, as appropriate. We are not required to articulate how we considered each medical opinion or prior administrative medical finding from one medical source individually.

(2) Most important factors. The factors of supportability (paragraph (c)(1) of this section) and consistency (paragraph (c)(2) of this section) are the most important factors we consider when we determine how persuasive we find a medical source's medical opinions or prior administrative medical findings to be. Therefore, we will explain how we considered the supportability and consistency factors for a medical source's medical opinions or prior administrative medical findings in your determination or decision. We may, but are not required to, explain how we considered the factors in

paragraphs (c)(3) through (c)(5) of this section, as appropriate, when we articulate how we consider medical opinions and prior administrative medical findings in your case record.

(3) Equally persuasive medical opinions or prior administrative medical findings about the same issue. When we find that two or more medical opinions or prior administrative medical findings about the same issue are both equally well-supported (paragraph (c)(1) of this section) and consistent with the record (paragraph (c)(2) of this section) but are not exactly the same, we will articulate how we considered the other most persuasive factors in paragraphs (c)(3) through (c)(5) of this section for those medical opinions or prior administrative medical findings in your determination or decision.

(c) Factors. We will consider the following factors when we consider the medical opinion(s) and prior administrative medical finding(s) in your case:

(1) Supportability. The more relevant the objective medical evidence and supporting explanations presented by a medical source are to support his or her medical opinion(s) or prior administrative medical finding(s), the more persuasive the medical opinions or prior administrative medical finding(s) will be.

(2) Consistency. The more consistent a medical opinion(s) or prior administrative medical finding(s) is with the evidence from other medical sources and nonmedical sources in the claim, the more persuasive the medical opinion(s) or prior administrative medical finding(s) will be.

(3) Relationship with the claimant. This factor combines consideration of the issues in paragraphs (c)(3)(i) through (v) of this section.

(i) Length of the treatment relationship. The length of time a medical source has treated you may help demonstrate whether the medical source has a longitudinal understanding of your impairment(s).

(ii) Frequency of examinations. The frequency of your visits with the medical source may help demonstrate whether the medical source has a longitudinal understanding of your impairment(s).

(iii) Purpose of the treatment relationship. The purpose for treatment you received from the medical source may help demonstrate the level of knowledge the medical source has of your impairment(s).

(iv) Extent of the treatment relationship. The kinds and extent of examinations and testing the medical source has performed or ordered from specialists or independent laboratories may help demonstrate the level of knowledge the medical source has of your impairment(s).

(v) Examining relationship. A medical source may have a better understanding of your impairment(s) if he or she examines you than if the medical source only reviews evidence in your folder.

(4) Specialization. The medical opinion or prior administrative medical finding of a medical source who has received advanced education and training to become a specialist may be more persuasive about medical issues related to his or her area of specialty than the medical opinion or prior administrative medical finding of a medical source who is not a specialist in the relevant area of specialty.

(5) Other factors. We will consider other factors that tend to support or contradict a medical opinion or prior administrative medical finding. This includes, but is not limited to, evidence showing a medical source has familiarity with the other evidence in the claim or an understanding of our disability program's policies and evidentiary requirements. When we consider a medical source's familiarity with the other evidence in a claim, we will also consider whether new evidence we receive after the medical source made his or her medical opinion or prior administrative medical finding makes the medical opinion or prior administrative medical finding more or less persuasive.

(d) Evidence from nonmedical sources. We are not required to articulate how we considered evidence from nonmedical sources using the requirements in paragraphs (a)-(c) in this section.

[82 FR 5867, Jan. 18, 2017]

§ 404.1521 Establishing that you have a medically determinable impairment(s).

If you are not doing substantial gainful activity, we will then determine whether you have a medically determinable physical or mental impairment(s) (see § 404.1520(a)(4)(ii)). Your impairment(s) must result from anatomical, physiological, or psychological abnormalities that can be shown by medically acceptable clinical and laboratory diagnostic techniques. Therefore, a physical or mental impairment must be established by objective medical evidence from an acceptable medical source. We will not use your statement of symptoms, a diagnosis, or a medical opinion to establish the existence of an impairment(s). After we establish that you have a medically determinable impairment(s), then we determine whether your impairment(s) is severe.

[50 FR 8728, March 5, 1985; 82 FR 5868, Jan. 18, 2017]

§ 404.1522 What we mean by an impairment(s) that is not severe.

(a) Non-severe impairment(s). An impairment or combination of impairments is not severe if it does not significantly limit your physical or mental ability to do basic work activities.

(b) Basic work activities. When we talk about basic work activities, we mean the abilities and aptitudes necessary to do most jobs. Examples of these include—

(1) Physical functions such as walking, standing, sitting, lifting, pushing, pulling, reaching, carrying, or handling;

(2) Capacities for seeing, hearing, and speaking;

(3) Understanding, carrying out, and remembering simple instructions;

(4) Use of judgment;

(5) Responding appropriately to supervision, co-workers and usual work situations; and

(6) Dealing with changes in a routine work setting.

[50 FR 8728, March 5, 1985; 82 FR 5869, Jan. 18, 2017]

§ 404.1523 Multiple impairments.

(a) Unrelated severe impairments. We cannot combine two or more unrelated severe impairments to meet the 12–month duration test. If you have a severe impairment(s) and then develop another unrelated severe impairment(s) but neither one is expected to last for 12 months, we cannot find you disabled, even though the two impairments in combination last for 12 months.

(b) Concurrent impairments. If you have two or more concurrent impairments that, when considered in combination, are severe, we must determine whether the combined effect of your impairments can be expected to continue to be severe for 12 months. If one or more of your impairments improves or is expected to improve within 12 months, so that the combined effect of your remaining impairments is no longer severe, we will find that you do not meet the 12–month duration test.

(c) Combined effect. In determining whether your physical or mental impairment or impairments are of a sufficient medical severity that such impairment or impairments could be the basis of eligibility under the law, we will consider the combined effect of all of your impairments without regard to whether any such impairment, if considered separately, would be of sufficient severity. If we do find a medically severe combination of impairments, we will consider the combined impact of the impairments throughout the disability determination process. If we do not find that you have a medically severe combination of impairments, we will determine that you are not disabled (see § 404.1520).

[50 FR 8728, March 5, 1985; 82 FR 5869, Jan. 18, 2017]

MEDICAL CONSIDERATIONS

§ 404.1525 Listing of Impairments in appendix 1.

(a) What is the purpose of the Listing of Impairments? The Listing of Impairments (the listings) is in appendix 1 of this subpart. It describes for each of the major body systems impairments that we consider to be severe enough to prevent an individual from doing any gainful activity, regardless of his or her age, education, or work experience.

(b) How is appendix 1 organized? There are two parts in appendix 1:

(1) Part A contains criteria that apply to individuals age 18 and over. We may also use part A for individuals who are under age 18 if the disease processes have a similar effect on adults and children.

(2) Part B contains criteria that apply only to individuals who are under age 18; we never use the listings in part B to evaluate individuals who are age 18 or older. In evaluating disability for a person under age 18, we use part B first. If the criteria in part B do not apply, we may use the criteria in part A when those criteria give appropriate consideration to the effects of the impairment(s) in children. To the extent possible, we number the provisions in part B to maintain a relationship with their counterparts in part A.

(c) How do we use the listings?

(1) Most body system sections in parts A and B of appendix 1 are in two parts: an introduction, followed by the specific listings.

(2) The introduction to each body system contains information relevant to the use of the listings in that body system; for example, examples of common impairments in the body system and definitions used in the listings for that body system. We may also include specific criteria for establishing a diagnosis, confirming the existence of an impairment, or establishing that your impairment(s) satisfies the criteria of a particular listing in the body system. Even if we do not include specific criteria for establishing a diagnosis or confirming the existence of your impairment, you must still show that you have a severe medically determinable impairment(s), as defined in § 404.1521.

(3) In most cases, the specific listings follow the introduction in each body system, after the heading, Category of Impairments. Within each listing, we specify the objective medical and other findings needed to satisfy the criteria of that listing. We will find that your impairment(s) meets the requirements of a listing when it satisfies all of the criteria of that listing, including any relevant criteria in the introduction, and meets the duration requirement (see § 404.1509).

(4) Most of the listed impairments are permanent or expected to result in death. For some listings, we state a specific period of time for which your impairment(s) will meet the listing. For all others, the evidence must show that your impairment(s) has lasted or can be expected to last for a continuous period of at least 12 months.

(5) If your impairment(s) does not meet the criteria of a listing, it can medically equal the criteria of a listing. We explain our rules for medical equivalence in § 404.1526. We use the listings only to find that you are disabled or still disabled. If your impairment(s) does not meet or medically equal the criteria of

a listing, we may find that you are disabled or still disabled at a later step in the sequential evaluation process.

(d) Can your impairment(s) meet a listing based only on a diagnosis? No. Your impairment(s) cannot meet the criteria of a listing based only on a diagnosis. To meet the requirements of a listing, you must have a medically determinable impairment(s) that satisfies all of the criteria in the listing.

(e) How do we consider your symptoms when we determine whether your impairment(s) meets a listing? Some listed impairments include symptoms, such as pain, as criteria. Section 404.1529(d)(2) explains how we consider your symptoms when your symptoms are included as criteria in a listing.

[56 FR 57941, Nov. 14, 1991; 71 FR 10428, March 1, 2006; 76 FR 19696, April 8, 2011; 82 FR 5869, Jan. 18, 2017]

§ 404.1526 Medical equivalence.

(a) What is medical equivalence? Your impairment(s) is medically equivalent to a listed impairment in appendix 1 if it is at least equal in severity and duration to the criteria of any listed impairment.

(b) How do we determine medical equivalence? We can find medical equivalence in three ways.

(1)(i) If you have an impairment that is described in appendix 1, but—

(A) You do not exhibit one or more of the findings specified in the particular listing, or

(B) You exhibit all of the findings, but one or more of the findings is not as severe as specified in the particular listing,

(ii) We will find that your impairment is medically equivalent to that listing if you have other findings related to your impairment that are at least of equal medical significance to the required criteria.

(2) If you have an impairment(s) that is not described in appendix 1, we will compare your findings with those for closely analogous listed impairments. If the findings related to your impairment(s) are at least of equal medical significance to those of a listed impairment, we will find that your impairment(s) is medically equivalent to the analogous listing.

(3) If you have a combination of impairments, no one of which meets a listing (see § 404.1525(c)(3)), we will compare your findings with those for closely analogous listed impairments. If the findings related to your impairments are at least of equal medical significance to those of a listed impairment, we will find that your combination of impairments is medically equivalent to that listing.

(4) Section 404.1529(d)(3) explains how we consider your symptoms, such as pain, when we make findings about medical equivalence.

(c) What evidence do we consider when we determine if your impairment(s) medically equals a listing? When we determine if your impairment medically equals a listing, we consider all evidence in your case record about your impairment(s) and its effects on you that is relevant to this finding. We do not consider your vocational factors of age, education, and work experience (see, for example, § 404.1560(c)(1)). We also consider the opinion given by one or more medical or psychological consultants designated by the Commissioner. (See § 404.1616.)

(d) Who is a designated medical or psychological consultant? A medical or psychological consultant designated by the Commissioner includes any medical or psychological consultant employed or engaged to make medical judgments by the Social Security Administration, the Railroad Retirement Board, or a State agency authorized to make disability determinations. See § 404.1616 for the necessary qualifications for medical consultants and psychological consultants.

(e) Who is responsible for determining medical equivalence?

(1) In cases where the State agency or other designee of the Commissioner makes the initial or reconsideration disability determination, a State agency medical or psychological consultant or other designee of the Commissioner (see § 404.1616 of this part) has the overall responsibility for determining medical equivalence.

(2) For cases in the disability hearing process or otherwise decided by a disability hearing officer, the responsibility for determining medical equivalence rests with either the disability hearing officer or, if the disability hearing officer's reconsideration determination is changed under § 404.918 of this part, with the Associate Commissioner for Disability Policy or his or her delegate.

(3) For cases at the administrative law judge or Appeals Council level, the responsibility for deciding medical equivalence rests with the administrative law judge or Appeals Council.

[52 FR 33926, Sept. 9, 1987; 62 FR 38451, July 18, 1997; 65 FR 34957, June 1, 2000; 71 FR 10429, March 1, 2006; 71 FR 16445, March 31, 2006; 71 FR 57415, Sept. 29, 2006; 76 FR 24807, May 3, 2011; 82 FR 5869, Jan. 18, 2017; 82 FR 15132, March 27, 2017]

§ 404.1527 Evaluating opinion evidence for claims filed before March 27, 2017.

For claims filed (see § 404.614) before March 27, 2017, the rules in this section apply. For claims filed on or after March 27, 2017, the rules in § 404.1520c apply.

(a) Definitions.

(1) Medical opinions. Medical opinions are statements from acceptable medical sources that reflect judgments about the nature and severity of your im-

pairment(s), including your symptoms, diagnosis and prognosis, what you can still do despite impairment(s), and your physical or mental restrictions.

(2) Treating source. Treating source means your own acceptable medical source who provides you, or has provided you, with medical treatment or evaluation and who has, or has had, an ongoing treatment relationship with you. Generally, we will consider that you have an ongoing treatment relationship with an acceptable medical source when the medical evidence establishes that you see, or have seen, the source with a frequency consistent with accepted medical practice for the type of treatment and/or evaluation required for your medical condition(s). We may consider an acceptable medical source who has treated or evaluated you only a few times or only after long intervals (e.g., twice a year) to be your treating source if the nature and frequency of the treatment or evaluation is typical for your condition(s). We will not consider an acceptable medical source to be your treating source if your relationship with the source is not based on your medical need for treatment or evaluation, but solely on your need to obtain a report in support of your claim for disability. In such a case, we will consider the acceptable medical source to be a nontreating source.

(b) How we consider medical opinions. In determining whether you are disabled, we will always consider the medical opinions in your case record together with the rest of the relevant evidence we receive. See § 404.1520b.

(c) How we weigh medical opinions. Regardless of its source, we will evaluate every medical opinion we receive. Unless we give a treating source's medical opinion controlling weight under paragraph (c)(2) of this section, we consider all of the following factors in deciding the weight we give to any medical opinion.

(1) Examining relationship. Generally, we give more weight to the medical opinion of a source who has examined you than to the medical opinion of a medical source who has not examined you.

(2) Treatment relationship. Generally, we give more weight to medical opinions from your treating sources, since these sources are likely to be the medical professionals most able to provide a detailed, longitudinal picture of your medical impairment(s) and may bring a unique perspective to the medical evidence that cannot be obtained from the objective medical findings alone or from reports of individual examinations, such as consultative examinations or brief hospitalizations. If we find that a treating source's medical opinion on the issue(s) of the nature and severity of your impairment(s) is well-supported by medically acceptable clinical and laboratory diagnostic techniques and is not inconsistent with the other substantial evidence in your case record, we will give it controlling weight. When we do not give the treating source's medical opinion controlling weight, we apply the factors listed in paragraphs (c)(2)(i) and (c)(2)(ii) of this section, as well as the factors in paragraphs (c)(3) through (c)(6) of this section in determining the weight to give the medical opinion. We will always give good reasons in our notice of determination or decision for the weight we give your treating source's medical opinion.

(i) Length of the treatment relationship and the frequency of examination. Generally, the longer a treating source has treated you and the more times you have been seen by a treating source, the more weight we will give to the source's medical opinion. When the treating source has seen you a number of times and long enough to have obtained a longitudinal picture of your impairment, we will give the medical source's medical opinion more weight than we would give it if it were from a nontreating source.

(ii) Nature and extent of the treatment relationship. Generally, the more knowledge a treating source has about your impairment(s) the more weight we will give to the source's medical opinion. We will look at the treatment the source has provided and at the kinds and extent of examinations and testing the source has performed or ordered from specialists and independent laboratories. For example, if your ophthalmologist notices that you have complained of neck pain during your eye examinations, we will consider his or her medical opinion with respect to your neck pain, but we will give it less weight than that of another physician who has treated you for the neck pain. When the treating source has reasonable knowledge of your impairment(s), we will give the source's medical opinion more weight than we would give it if it were from a nontreating source.

(3) Supportability. The more a medical source presents relevant evidence to support a medical opinion, particularly medical signs and laboratory findings, the more weight we will give that medical opinion. The better an explanation a source provides for a medical opinion, the more weight we will give that medical opinion. Furthermore, because nonexamining sources have no examining or treating relationship with you, the weight we will give their medical opinions will depend on the degree to which they provide supporting explanations for their medical opinions. We will evaluate the degree to which these medical opinions consider all of the pertinent evidence in your claim, including medical opinions of treating and other examining sources.

(4) Consistency. Generally, the more consistent a medical opinion is with the record as a whole, the more weight we will give to that medical opinion.

(5) Specialization. We generally give more weight to the medical opinion of a specialist about medical issues related to his or her area of specialty than to the medical opinion of a source who is not a specialist.

(6) Other factors. When we consider how much weight to give to a medical opinion, we will also

consider any factors you or others bring to our attention, or of which we are aware, which tend to support or contradict the medical opinion. For example, the amount of understanding of our disability programs and their evidentiary requirements that a medical source has, regardless of the source of that understanding, and the extent to which a medical source is familiar with the other information in your case record are relevant factors that we will consider in deciding the weight to give to a medical opinion.

(d) Medical source opinions on issues reserved to the Commissioner. Opinions on some issues, such as the examples that follow, are not medical opinions, as described in paragraph (a)(1) of this section, but are, instead, opinions on issues reserved to the Commissioner because they are administrative findings that are dispositive of a case; i.e., that would direct the determination or decision of disability.

(1) Opinions that you are disabled. We are responsible for making the determination or decision about whether you meet the statutory definition of disability. In so doing, we review all of the medical findings and other evidence that support a medical source's statement that you are disabled. A statement by a medical source that you are "disabled" or "unable to work" does not mean that we will determine that you are disabled.

(2) Other opinions on issues reserved to the Commissioner. We use medical sources, including your treating source, to provide evidence, including opinions, on the nature and severity of your impairment(s). Although we consider opinions from medical sources on issues such as whether your impairment(s) meets or equals the requirements of any impairment(s) in the Listing of Impairments in appendix 1 to this subpart, your residual functional capacity (see §§ 404.1545 and 404.1546), or the application of vocational factors, the final responsibility for deciding these issues is reserved to the Commissioner.

(3) We will not give any special significance to the source of an opinion on issues reserved to the Commissioner described in paragraphs (d)(1) and (d)(2) of this section.

(e) Evidence from our Federal or State agency medical or psychological consultants. The rules in § 404.1513a apply except that when an administrative law judge gives controlling weight to a treating source's medical opinion, the administrative law judge is not required to explain in the decision the weight he or she gave to the prior administrative medical findings in the claim.

(f) Opinions from medical sources who are not acceptable medical sources and from nonmedical sources.

(1) Consideration. Opinions from medical sources who are not acceptable medical sources and from nonmedical sources may reflect the source's judgment about some of the same issues addressed in medical opinions from acceptable medical sources. Although we will consider these opinions using the same factors as listed in paragraph (c)(1) through (c)(6) in this section, not every factor for weighing opinion evidence will apply in every case because the evaluation of an opinion from a medical source who is not an acceptable medical source or from a nonmedical source depends on the particular facts in each case. Depending on the particular facts in a case, and after applying the factors for weighing opinion evidence, an opinion from a medical source who is not an acceptable medical source or from a nonmedical source may outweigh the medical opinion of an acceptable medical source, including the medical opinion of a treating source. For example, it may be appropriate to give more weight to the opinion of a medical source who is not an acceptable medical source if he or she has seen the individual more often than the treating source, has provided better supporting evidence and a better explanation for the opinion, and the opinion is more consistent with the evidence as a whole.

(2) Articulation. The adjudicator generally should explain the weight given to opinions from these sources or otherwise ensure that the discussion of the evidence in the determination or decision allows a claimant or subsequent reviewer to follow the adjudicator's reasoning, when such opinions may have an effect on the outcome of the case. In addition, when an adjudicator determines that an opinion from such a source is entitled to greater weight than a medical opinion from a treating source, the adjudicator must explain the reasons in the notice of decision in hearing cases and in the notice of determination (that is, in the personalized disability notice) at the initial and reconsideration levels, if the determination is less than fully favorable.

[[56 FR 36960, Aug. 1, 1991; 62 FR 38451, July 18, 1997; 65 FR 11877, March 7, 2000; 71 FR 16445, March 31, 2006; 75 FR 62681, Oct. 13, 2010; 76 FR 24807, May 3, 2011; 77 FR 10656, Feb. 23, 2012; 77 FR 43494, July 25, 2012; 82 FR 5869, Jan. 18, 2017; 82 FR 15132, March 27, 2017]

§ 404.1528 [Reserved by 82 FR 5871]

[82 FR 5871, Jan. 18, 2017]

§ 404.1529 How we evaluate symptoms, including pain.

(a) General. In determining whether you are disabled, we consider all your symptoms, including pain, and the extent to which your symptoms can reasonably be accepted as consistent with the objective medical evidence and other evidence. We will consider all of your statements about your symptoms, such as pain, and any description your medical sources or nonmedical sources may provide about how the symptoms affect your activities of daily living and your ability to work. However, statements about your pain or other symptoms will not alone establish that you are disabled. There must be objective medical evidence from an acceptable medical source that shows you have a medical impairment(s) which could reasonably be expected to produce the pain or other symptoms alleged and that, when considered with all of the other evidence (including statements about the intensity and persistence of your pain or other symptoms which may reasonably be accepted as consistent with the medical signs and laboratory findings), would lead to a conclusion that you are disabled. In evaluating the intensity and persistence of your symptoms, including pain, we will consider all of the available evidence, including your medical history, the medical signs and laboratory findings, and statements about how your symptoms affect you. We will then determine the extent to which your alleged functional limitations and restrictions due to pain or other symptoms can reasonably be accepted as consistent with the medical signs and laboratory findings and other evidence to decide how your symptoms affect your ability to work.

(b) Need for medically determinable impairment that could reasonably be expected to produce your symptoms, such as pain. Your symptoms, such as pain, fatigue, shortness of breath, weakness, or nervousness, will not be found to affect your ability to do basic work activities unless medical signs or laboratory findings show that a medically determinable impairment(s) is present. Medical signs and laboratory findings, established by medically acceptable clinical or laboratory diagnostic techniques, must show the existence of a medical impairment(s) which results from anatomical, physiological, or psychological abnormalities and which could reasonably be expected to produce the pain or other symptoms alleged. In cases decided by a State agency (except in disability hearings under §§ 404.914 through 404.918 of this part and in fully favorable determinations made by State agency disability examiners alone under § 404.1615(c)(3) of this part), a State agency medical or psychological consultant or other medical or psychological consultant designated by the Commissioner directly participates in determining whether your medically determinable impairment(s) could reasonably be expected to produce your alleged symptoms. In the disability hearing process, a medical or psychological consultant may provide an advisory assessment to assist a disability hearing officer in determining whether your impairment(s) could reasonably be expected to produce your alleged symptoms. At the administrative law judge hearing or Appeals Council level of the administrative review process, the adjudicator(s) may ask for and consider the opinion of a medical or psychological expert concerning whether your impairment(s) could reasonably be expected to produce your alleged symptoms. The finding that your impairment(s) could reasonably be expected to produce your pain or other symptoms does not involve a determination as to the intensity, persistence, or functionally limiting effects of your symptoms. We will develop evidence regarding the possibility of a medically determinable mental impairment when we have information to suggest that such an impairment exists, and you allege pain or other symptoms but the medical signs and laboratory findings do not substantiate any physical impairment(s) capable of producing the pain or other symptoms.

(c) Evaluating the intensity and persistence of your symptoms, such as pain, and determining the extent to which your symptoms limit your capacity for work—

(1) General. When the medical signs or laboratory findings show that you have a medically determinable impairment(s) that could reasonably be expected to produce your symptoms, such as pain, we must then evaluate the intensity and persistence of your symptoms so that we can determine how your symptoms limit your capacity for work. In evaluating the intensity and persistence of your symptoms, we consider all of the available evidence from your medical sources and nonmedical sources about how your symptoms affect you. We also consider the medical opinions as explained in § 404.1520c. Paragraphs (c)(2) through (c)(4) of this section explain further how we evaluate the intensity and persistence of your symptoms and how we determine the extent to which your symptoms limit your capacity for work, when the medical signs or laboratory findings show that you have a medically determinable impairment(s) that could reasonably be expected to produce your symptoms, such as pain.

(2) Consideration of objective medical evidence. Objective medical evidence is evidence obtained from the application of medically acceptable clinical and laboratory diagnostic techniques, such as evidence of reduced joint motion, muscle spasm, sensory deficit or motor disruption. Objective medical evidence of this type is a useful indicator to assist us in making reasonable conclusions about the intensity and persistence of your symptoms and the effect those symptoms, such as pain, may have on your ability to work. We must always attempt to obtain objective medical evidence and, when it is obtained, we will consider it in reaching a conclusion as to whether you are disabled. However, we will not reject your statements about the intensity and persistence of your pain or other symptoms or about the effect your symptoms have on your ability to work solely because the available objective medical evidence does not substantiate your statements.

(3) Consideration of other evidence. Because symptoms sometimes suggest a greater severity of impairment than can be shown by objective medical evidence alone, we will carefully consider any other information you may submit about your symptoms. The information that your medical sources or nonmedical sources provide about your pain or other symptoms (e.g., what may precipitate or aggravate your symptoms, what medications, treatments or other methods you use to alleviate them, and how the symptoms may affect your pattern of daily living) is also an important indicator of

the intensity and persistence of your symptoms. Because symptoms, such as pain, are subjective and difficult to quantify, any symptom-related functional limitations and restrictions that your medical sources or nonmedical sources report, which can reasonably be accepted as consistent with the objective medical evidence and other evidence, will be taken into account as explained in paragraph (c)(4) of this section in reaching a conclusion as to whether you are disabled. We will consider all of the evidence presented, including information about your prior work record, your statements about your symptoms, evidence submitted by your medical sources, and observations by our employees and other persons. Section 404.1520c explains in detail how we consider medical opinions and prior administrative medical findings about the nature and severity of your impairment(s) and any related symptoms, such as pain. Factors relevant to your symptoms, such as pain, which we will consider include:

(i) Your daily activities;

(ii) The location, duration, frequency, and intensity of your pain or other symptoms;

(iii) Precipitating and aggravating factors;

(iv) The type, dosage, effectiveness, and side effects of any medication you take or have taken to alleviate your pain or other symptoms;

(v) Treatment, other than medication, you receive or have received for relief of your pain or other symptoms;

(vi) Any measures you use or have used to relieve your pain or other symptoms (e.g., lying flat on your back, standing for 15 to 20 minutes every hour, sleeping on a board, etc.); and

(vii) Other factors concerning your functional limitations and restrictions due to pain or other symptoms.

(4) How we determine the extent to which symptoms, such as pain, affect your capacity to perform basic work activities. In determining the extent to which your symptoms, such as pain, affect your capacity to perform basic work activities, we consider all of the available evidence described in paragraphs (c)(1) through (c)(3) of this section. We will consider your statements about the intensity, persistence, and limiting effects of your symptoms, and we will evaluate your statements in relation to the objective medical evidence and other evidence, in reaching a conclusion as to whether you are disabled. We will consider whether there are any inconsistencies in the evidence and the extent to which there are any conflicts between your statements and the rest of the evidence, including your history, the signs and laboratory findings, and statements by your medical sources or other persons about how your symptoms affect you. Your symptoms, including pain, will be determined to diminish your capacity for basic work activities to the extent that your alleged functional limitations and restrictions due to symptoms, such as pain, can reasonably be accepted as consistent with the objective medical evidence and other evidence.

(d) Consideration of symptoms in the disability determination process. We follow a set order of steps to determine whether you are disabled. If you are not doing substantial gainful activity, we consider your symptoms, such as pain, to evaluate whether you have a severe physical or mental impairment(s), and at each of the remaining steps in the process. Sections 404.1520 and 404.1520a explain this process in detail. We also consider your symptoms, such as pain, at the appropriate steps in our review when we consider whether your disability continues. Sections 404.1579 and 404.1594 explain the procedure we follow in reviewing whether your disability continues.

(1) Need to establish a severe medically determinable impairment(s). Your symptoms, such as pain, fatigue, shortness of breath, weakness, or nervousness, are considered in making a determination as to whether your impairment or combination of impairment(s) is severe. (See § 404.1520(c).)

(2) Decision whether the Listing of Impairments is met. Some listed impairments include symptoms usually associated with those impairments as criteria. Generally, when a symptom is one of the criteria in a listing, it is only necessary that the symptom be present in combination with the other criteria. It is not necessary, unless the listing specifically states otherwise, to provide information about the intensity, persistence, or limiting effects of the symptom as long as all other findings required by the specific listing are present.

(3) Decision whether the Listing of Impairments is medically equaled. If your impairment is not the same as a listed impairment, we must determine whether your impairment(s) is medically equivalent to a listed impairment. Section 404.1526 explains how we make this determination. Under § 404.1526(b), we will consider medical equivalence based on all evidence in your case record about your impairment(s) and its effects on you that is relevant to this finding. In considering whether your symptoms, signs, and laboratory findings are medically equal to the symptoms, signs, and laboratory findings of a listed impairment, we will look to see whether your symptoms, signs, and laboratory findings are at least equal in severity to the listed criteria. However, we will not substitute your allegations of pain or other symptoms for a missing or deficient sign or laboratory finding to raise the severity of your impairment(s) to that of a listed impairment. If the symptoms, signs, and laboratory findings of your impairment(s) are equivalent in severity to those of a listed impairment, we will find you disabled. If it does not, we will consider the impact of your symptoms on your residual functional capacity. (See paragraph (d)(4) of this section.)

(4) Impact of symptoms (including pain) on residual functional capacity. If you have a medically determinable severe physical or mental impairment(s), but your impairment(s) does not meet or equal an impairment listed in appendix 1 of this subpart, we will consider the impact of your impairment(s) and any related symptoms, including pain, on your residual functional capacity. (See § 404.1545.)

[56 FR 57941, Nov. 14, 1991; 62 FR 38451, July 18, 1997; 71 FR 10429, March 1, 2006; 71 FR 16445, March 31, 2006; 75 FR 62681, Oct. 13, 2010; 76 FR 24807, May 3, 2011; 82 FR 5871, Jan. 18, 2017]

§ 404.1530 Need to follow prescribed treatment.

(a) What treatment you must follow. In order to get benefits, you must follow treatment prescribed by your medical source(s) if this treatment is expected to restore your ability to work.

(b) When you do not follow prescribed treatment. If you do not follow the prescribed treatment without a good reason, we will not find you disabled or, if you are already receiving benefits, we will stop paying you benefits.

(c) Acceptable reasons for failure to follow prescribed treatment. We will consider your physical, mental, educational, and linguistic limitations (including any lack of facility with the English language) when determining if you have an acceptable reason for failure to follow prescribed treatment. The following are examples of a good reason for not following treatment:

(1) The specific medical treatment is contrary to the established teaching and tenets of your religion.

(2) The prescribed treatment would be cataract surgery for one eye, when there is an impairment of the other eye resulting in a severe loss of vision and is not subject to improvement through treatment.

(3) Surgery was previously performed with unsuccessful results and the same surgery is again being recommended for the same impairment.

(4) The treatment because of its magnitude (e.g., open heart surgery), unusual nature (e.g., organ transplant), or other reason is very risky for you; or

(5) The treatment involves amputation of an extremity, or a major part of an extremity.

[59 FR 1635, Jan. 12, 1994; 82 FR 5871, Jan. 18, 2017]

§ 404.1535 How we will determine whether your drug addiction or alcoholism is a contributing factor material to the determination of disability.

(a) General. If we find that you are disabled and have medical evidence of your drug addiction or alcoholism, we must determine whether your drug addiction or alcoholism is a contributing factor material to the determination of disability.

(b) Process we will follow when we have medical evidence of your drug addiction or alcoholism.

(1) The key factor we will examine in determining whether drug addiction or alcoholism is a contributing factor material to the determination of disability is whether we would still find you disabled if you stopped using drugs or alcohol.

(2) In making this determination, we will evaluate which of your current physical and mental limitations, upon which we based our current disability determination, would remain if you stopped using drugs or alcohol and then determine whether any or all of your remaining limitations would be disabling.

(i) If we determine that your remaining limitations would not be disabling, we will find that your drug addiction or alcoholism is a contributing factor material to the determination of disability.

(ii) If we determine that your remaining limitations are disabling, you are disabled independent of your drug addiction or alcoholism and we will find that your drug addiction or alcoholism is not a contributing factor material to the determination of disability.

[60 FR 8147, Feb. 10, 1995]

§ 404.1536 Treatment required for individuals whose drug addiction or alcoholism is a contributing factor material to the determination of disability.

(a) If we determine that you are disabled and drug addiction or alcoholism is a contributing factor material to the determination of disability (as described in § 404.1535), you must avail yourself of appropriate treatment for your drug addiction or alcoholism at an institution or facility approved by us when this treatment is available and make progress in your treatment. Generally, you are not expected to pay for this treatment. You will not be paid benefits for any month after the month we have notified you in writing that—

(1) You did not comply with the terms, conditions and requirements of the treatment which has been made available to you; or

(2) You did not avail yourself of the treatment after you had been notified that it is available to you.

(b) If your benefits are suspended for failure to comply with treatment requirements, your benefits can be reinstated in accordance with the rules in § 404.470.

[60 FR 8147, Feb. 10, 1995]

§ 404.1537 What we mean by appropriate treatment.

By appropriate treatment, we mean treatment for drug addiction or alcoholism that serves the needs of the individual in the least restrictive setting possible consistent with your treatment plan. These settings range from outpatient counseling services through a variety of residential treatment settings including acute detoxification, short-term intensive residential treatment, long-term therapeutic residential treatment, and long-term recovery houses. Appropriate treatment is determined with the involvement of a State licensed or certified addiction professional on the basis of a detailed assessment of the individual's presenting symptomatology, psychosocial profile, and other relevant factors. This assessment may lead to a determination that more than one treatment modality is appropriate for the individual. The treatment will be provided or overseen by an approved institution or facility. This treatment may include (but is not limited to)—

(a) Medical examination and medical management;

(b) Detoxification;

(c) Medication management to include substitution therapy (e.g., methadone);

(d) Psychiatric, psychological, psychosocial, vocational, or other substance abuse counseling in a residential or outpatient treatment setting; or

(e) Relapse prevention.

[60 FR 8148, Feb. 10, 1995]

§ 404.1538 What we mean by approved institutions or facilities.

Institutions or facilities that we may approve include—

(a) An institution or facility that furnishes medically recognized treatment for drug addiction or alcoholism in conformity with applicable Federal or State laws and regulations;

(b) An institution or facility used by or licensed by an appropriate State agency which is authorized to refer persons for treatment of drug addiction or alcoholism;

(c) State licensed or certified care providers;

(d) Programs accredited by the Commission on Accreditation for Rehabilitation Facilities (CARF) and/or the Joint Commission for the Accreditation of Healthcare Organizations (JCAHO) for the treatment of drug addiction or alcoholism;

(e) Medicare or Medicaid certified care providers; or

(f) Nationally recognized self-help drug addiction or alcoholism recovery programs (e.g., Alcoholics Anonymous or Narcotics Anonymous) when participation in these programs is specifically prescribed by a treatment professional at an institution or facility described in paragraphs (a) through (e) of this section as part of an individual's treatment plan.

[60 FR 8148, Feb. 10, 1995]

§ 404.1539 How we consider whether treatment is available.

Our determination about whether treatment is available to you for your drug addiction or your alcoholism will depend upon—

(a) The capacity of an approved institution or facility to admit you for appropriate treatment;

(b) The location of the approved institution or facility, or the place where treatment, services or resources could be provided to you;

(c) The availability and cost of transportation for you to the place of treatment;

(d) Your general health, including your ability to travel and capacity to understand and follow the prescribed treatment;

(e) Your particular condition and circumstances; and

(f) The treatment that is prescribed for your drug addiction or alcoholism.

[60 FR 8148, Feb. 10, 1995]

§ 404.1540 Evaluating compliance with the treatment requirements.

(a) General. Generally, we will consider information from the treatment institution or facility to evaluate your compliance with your treatment plan. The treatment institution or facility will:

(1) Monitor your attendance at and participation in treatment sessions;

(2) Provide reports of the results of any clinical testing (such as, hematological or urinalysis studies for individuals with drug addiction and hematological studies and breath analysis for individuals with alcoholism) when such tests are likely to yield important information;

(3) Provide observational reports from the treatment professionals familiar with your individual case (subject to verification and Federal confidentiality requirements); or

(4) Provide their assessment or views on your noncompliance with treatment requirements.

(b) Measuring progress. Generally, we will consider information from the treatment institution or facility to evaluate your progress in completing your treatment plan. Examples of milestones for measuring your progress with the treatment which has been prescribed for your drug addiction or alcoholism may include (but are not limited to)—

(1) Abstinence from drug or alcohol use (initial progress may include significant reduction in use);

(2) Consistent attendance at and participation in treatment sessions;

(3) Improved social functioning and levels of gainful activity;

(4) Participation in vocational rehabilitation activities; or

(5) Avoidance of criminal activity.

[60 FR 8148, Feb. 10, 1995]

§ 404.1541 Establishment and use of referral and monitoring agencies.

We will contract with one or more agencies in each of the States, Puerto Rico and the District of Columbia to provide services to individuals whose disabilities are based on a determination that drug addiction or alcoholism is a contributing factor material to the determination of disability (as described in § 404.1535) and to submit information to us which we will use to make decisions about these individuals' benefits. These agencies will be known as referral and monitoring agencies. Their duties and responsibilities include (but are not limited to)–

(a) Identifying appropriate treatment placements for individuals we refer to them;

(b) Referring these individuals for treatment;

(c) Monitoring the compliance and progress with the appropriate treatment of these individuals; and

(d) Promptly reporting to us any individual's failure to comply with treatment requirements as well as failure to achieve progress through the treatment.

[60 FR 8148, Feb. 10, 1995]

RESIDUAL FUNCTIONAL CAPACITY

§ 404.1545 Your residual functional capacity.

(a) General—

(1) Residual functional capacity assessment. Your impairment(s), and any related symptoms, such as pain, may cause physical and mental limitations that affect what you can do in a work setting. Your residual functional capacity is the most you can still do despite your limitations. We will assess your residual functional capacity based on all the relevant evidence in your case record. (See § 404.1546.)

(2) If you have more than one impairment. We will consider all of your medically determinable impairments of which we are aware, including your medically determinable impairments that are not "severe," as explained in §§ 404.1520(c), 404.1521, and 404.1523, when we assess your residual functional capacity. (See paragraph (e) of this section.)

(3) Evidence we use to assess your residual functional capacity. We will assess your residual functional capacity based on all of the relevant medical and other evidence. In general, you are responsible for providing the evidence we will use to make a finding about your residual functional capacity. (See § 404.1512(c).) However, before we make a determination that you are not disabled, we are responsible for developing your complete medical history, including arranging for a consultative examination(s) if necessary, and making every reasonable effort to help you get medical reports from your own medical sources. (See §§ 404.1512(d) through (e).) We will consider any statements about what you can still do that have been provided by medical sources, whether or not they are based on formal medical examinations. (See § 404.1513.) We will also consider descriptions and observations of your limitations from your impairment(s), including limitations that result from your symptoms, such as pain, provided by you, your family, neighbors, friends, or other persons. (See paragraph (e) of this section and § 404.1529.)

(4) What we will consider in assessing residual functional capacity. When we assess your residual functional capacity, we will consider your ability to meet the physical, mental, sensory, and other requirements of work, as described in paragraphs (b), (c), and (d) of this section.

(5) How we will use our residual functional capacity assessment.

(i) We will first use our residual functional capacity assessment at step four of the sequential evaluation process to decide if you can do your past relevant work. (See §§ 404.1520(f) and 404.1560(b).)

(ii) If we find that you cannot do your past relevant work, you do not have any past relevant work, or if we use the procedures in § 404.1520(h) and § 404.1562 does not apply, we will use the same assessment of your residual functional capacity at step five of the sequential evaluation process to decide if you can adjust to any other work that exists in the national economy. (See §§ 404.1520(g) and 404.1566.) At this step, we will not use our assessment of your residual functional capacity alone to decide if you are disabled. We will use the guidelines in §§ 404.1560 through 404.1569a, and consider our residual functional capacity assessment together with the information about your vocational background to make our disability determination or decision. For our rules on residual functional capacity assessment in deciding whether your disability continues or ends, see § 404.1594.

(b) Physical abilities. When we assess your physical abilities, we first assess the nature and extent of your physical limitations and then determine your residual functional capacity for work activity on a regular and continuing basis. A limited ability to perform certain physical demands of work activity, such as sitting, standing, walking, lifting, carrying, pushing, pulling, or other physical functions (including manipulative or postural functions, such as reaching, handling, stooping or crouching), may reduce your ability to do past work and other work.

(c) Mental abilities. When we assess your mental abilities, we first assess the nature and extent of your mental limitations and restrictions and then determine your residual functional capacity for work activity on a regular and continuing basis. A limited ability to carry out certain mental activities, such as limitations in understanding, remembering, and carrying out instructions, and in responding appropriately to supervision, co-workers, and work pressures in a work setting, may reduce your ability to do past work and other work.

(d) Other abilities affected by impairment(s). Some medically determinable impairment(s), such as skin impairment(s), epilepsy, impairment(s) of vision, hearing or other senses, and impairment(s) which impose environmental restrictions, may cause limitations and restrictions which affect other work-related abilities. If you have this type of impairment(s), we consider any resulting limitations and restrictions which may reduce your ability to do past work and other work in deciding your residual functional capacity.

(e) Total limiting effects. When you have a severe impairment(s), but your symptoms, signs, and laboratory findings do not meet or equal those of a listed impairment in appendix 1 of this subpart, we will consider the limiting effects of all your impairment(s), even those that are not severe, in determining your residual functional capacity. Pain or other symptoms may cause a limitation of function beyond that which can be determined on the basis of the anatomical, physiological or psychological abnormalities considered alone; e.g., someone with a low back disorder may be fully capable of the physical demands consistent with those of sustained medium work activity, but another person with the same disorder, because of pain, may not be capable of more than the physical demands consistent with those of light work activity on a sustained basis. In assessing the total limiting effects of your impairment(s) and any related symptoms, we will consider all of the medical and nonmedical evidence, including the information described in § 404.1529(c).

[56 FR 36962, Aug. 1, 1991; 56 FR 57943, Nov. 14, 1991; 68 FR 51162, Aug. 26, 2003; 77 FR 10656, Feb. 23, 2012; 77 FR 43494, July 25, 2012]

§ 404.1546 Responsibility for assessing your residual functional capacity.

(a) Responsibility for assessing residual functional capacity at the State agency. When a State agency medical or psychological consultant and a State agency disability examiner make the disability determination as provided in § 404.1615(c)(1) of this part, a State agency medical or psychological consultant(s) is responsible for assessing your residual functional capacity. When a State agency disability examiner makes a disability determination alone as provided in § 404.1615(c)(3), the disability examiner is responsible for assessing your residual functional capacity.

(b) Responsibility for assessing residual functional capacity in the disability hearings process. If your case involves a disability hearing under § 404.914, a disability hearing officer is responsible for assessing your residual functional capacity. However, if the disability hearing officer's reconsidered determination is changed under § 404.918, the Associate Commissioner for the Office of Disability Determinations or his or her delegate is responsible for assessing your residual functional capacity.

(c) Responsibility for assessing residual functional capacity at the administrative law judge hearing or Appeals Council level. If your case is at the administrative law judge hearing level or at the Appeals Council review level, the administrative law judge or the administrative appeals judge at the Appeals Council (when the Appeals Council makes a decision) is responsible for assessing your residual functional capacity.

(d) [Reserved by 76 FR 24807]

[51 FR 304, Jan. 3, 1986; 52 FR 33926, Sept. 9, 1987; 56 FR 36962, Aug. 1, 1991; 62 FR 38451, July 18, 1997; 68 FR 51162, Aug. 26, 2003; 71 FR 16445, March 31, 2006; 75 FR 62681, Oct. 13, 2010; 76 FR 24807, May 3, 2011]

VOCATIONAL CONSIDERATIONS

§ 404.1560 When we will consider your vocational background.

(a) General. If you are applying for a period of disability, or disability insurance benefits as a disabled worker, or child's insurance benefits based on disability which began before age 22, or widow's or widower's benefits based on disability for months after December 1990, and we cannot decide whether you are disabled at one of the first three steps of the sequential evaluation process (see § 404.1520), we will consider your residual functional capacity together with your vocational background, as discussed in paragraphs (b) and (c) of this section.

(b) Past relevant work. We will first compare our assessment of your residual functional capacity with the physical and mental demands of your past relevant work. See § 404.1520(h) for an exception to this rule.

(1) Definition of past relevant work. Past relevant work is work that you have done within the past 15 years, that was substantial gainful activity, and that lasted long enough for you to learn to do it. (See § 404.1565(a).)

(2) Determining whether you can do your past relevant work. We will ask you for information about work you have done in the past. We may also ask other people who know about your work. (See § 404.1565(b).) We may use the services of vocational experts or vocational specialists, or other resources, such as the "Dictionary of Occupational Titles" and its companion volumes and supplements, published by the Department of Labor, to obtain evidence we need to help us determine whether you can do your past relevant work, given your residual functional capacity. A vocational expert or specialist may offer relevant evidence within his or her expertise or knowledge

concerning the physical and mental demands of a claimant's past relevant work, either as the claimant actually performed it or as generally performed in the national economy. Such evidence may be helpful in supplementing or evaluating the accuracy of the claimant's description of his past work. In addition, a vocational expert or specialist may offer expert opinion testimony in response to a hypothetical question about whether a person with the physical and mental limitations imposed by the claimant's medical impairment(s) can meet the demands of the claimant's previous work, either as the claimant actually performed it or as generally performed in the national economy.

(3) If you can do your past relevant work. If we find that you have the residual functional capacity to do your past relevant work, we will determine that you can still do your past work and are not disabled. We will not consider your vocational factors of age, education, and work experience or whether your past relevant work exists in significant numbers in the national economy.

(c) Other work.

(1) If we find that your residual functional capacity does not enable you to do any of your past relevant work or if we use the procedures in § 404.1520(h), we will use the same residual functional capacity assessment when we decide if you can adjust to any other work. We will look at your ability to adjust to other work by considering your residual functional capacity and the vocational factors of age, education, and work experience, as appropriate in your case. (See § 404.1520(h) for an exception to this rule.) Any other work (jobs) that you can adjust to must exist in significant numbers in the national economy (either in the region where you live or in several regions in the country).

(2) In order to support a finding that you are not disabled at this fifth step of the sequential evaluation process, we are responsible for providing evidence that demonstrates that other work exists in significant numbers in the national economy that you can do, given your residual functional capacity and vocational factors. We are not responsible for providing additional evidence about your residual functional capacity because we will use the same residual functional capacity assessment that we used to determine if you can do your past relevant work.

[55 FR 11011, March 26, 1990; 57 FR 30120, July 8, 1992; 68 FR 51163, Aug. 26, 2003; 77 FR 43494, July 25, 2012]

§ 404.1561 [Reserved]

[68 FR 51163, Aug. 26, 2003]

§ 404.1562 Medical-vocational profiles showing an inability to make an adjustment to other work.

(a) If you have done only arduous unskilled physical labor. If you have no more than a marginal education (see § 404.1564) and work experience of 35 years or more during which you did only arduous unskilled physical labor, and you are not working and are no longer able to do this kind of work because of a severe impairment(s) (see §§ 404.1520(c), 404.1521, and 404.1523), we will consider you unable to do lighter work, and therefore, disabled.

Example to paragraph (a): B is a 58–year-old miner's helper with a fourth grade education who has a lifelong history of unskilled arduous physical labor. B says that he is disabled because of arthritis of the spine, hips, and knees, and other impairments. Medical evidence shows a "severe" combination of impairments that prevents B from performing his past relevant work. Under these circumstances, we will find that B is disabled.

(b) If you are at least 55 years old, have no more than a limited education, and have no past relevant work experience. If you have a severe, medically determinable impairment(s) (see §§ 404.1520(c), 404.1521, and 404.1523), are of advanced age (age 55 or older, see § 404.1563), have a limited education or less (see § 404.1564), and have no past relevant work experience (see § 404.1565), we will find you disabled. If the evidence shows that you meet this profile, we will not need to assess your residual functional capacity or consider the rules in appendix 2 to this subpart.

[68 FR 51163, Aug. 26, 2003]

§ 404.1563 Your age as a vocational factor.

(a) General. "Age" means your chronological age. When we decide whether you are disabled under § 404.1520(g)(1), we will consider your chronological age in combination with your residual functional capacity, education, and work experience. We will not consider your ability to adjust to other work on the basis of your age alone. In determining the extent to which age affects a person's ability to adjust to other work, we consider advancing age to be an increasingly limiting factor in the person's ability to make such an adjustment, as we explain in paragraphs (c) through (e) of this section. If you are unemployed but you still have the ability to adjust to other work, we will find that you are not disabled. In paragraphs (b) through (e) of this section and in appendix 2 to this subpart, we explain in more detail how we consider your age as a vocational factor.

(b) How we apply the age categories. When we make a finding about your ability to do other work under § 404.1520(f)(1), we will use the age categories in paragraphs (c) through (e) of this section. We will use each of the age categories that applies to you during the period for which we must determine if you are disabled. We will not apply the age categories mechanically in a borderline situation. If you are within a few days to a few months of reaching an older age category, and using the older age category would result in a determination or decision that you are disabled, we will consider whether to use the older age category after evaluating the overall impact of all the factors of your case.

(c) Younger person. If you are a younger person (under age 50), we generally do not consider that your age will seriously affect your ability to adjust to other work. However, in some circumstances, we consider that persons age 45–49 are more limited in their ability to adjust to other work than persons who have not attained age 45. See Rule 201.17 in appendix 2.

(d) Person closely approaching advanced age. If you are closely approaching advanced age (age 50–54), we will consider that your age along with a severe impairment(s) and limited work experience may seriously affect your ability to adjust to other work.

(e) Person of advanced age. We consider that at advanced age (age 55 or older), age significantly affects a person's ability to adjust to other work. We have special rules for persons of advanced age and for persons in this category who are closely approaching retirement age (age 60 or older). See § 404.1568(d)(4).

(f) Information about your age. We will usually not ask you to prove your age. However, if we need to know your exact age to determine whether you get disability benefits or if the amount of your benefit will be affected, we will ask you for evidence of your age.

[65 FR 18000, April 6, 2000; 68 FR 51163, Aug. 26, 2003; 73 FR 64196, Oct. 29, 2008]

§ 404.1564 Your education as a vocational factor.

(a) General. Education is primarily used to mean formal schooling or other training which contributes to your ability to meet vocational requirements, for example, reasoning ability, communication skills, and arithmetical ability. However, if you do not have formal schooling, this does not necessarily mean that you are uneducated or lack these abilities. Past work experience and the kinds of responsibilities you had when you were working may show that you have intellectual abilities, although you may have little formal education. Your daily activities, hobbies, or the results of testing may also show that you have significant intellectual ability that can be used to work.

(b) How we evaluate your education. The importance of your educational background may depend upon how much time has passed between the completion of your formal education and the beginning of your physical or mental impairment(s) and by what you have done with your education in a work or other setting. Formal education that you completed many years before your impairment began, or unused skills and knowledge that were a part of your formal education, may no longer be useful or meaningful in terms of your ability to work. Therefore, the numerical grade level that you completed in school may not represent your actual educational abilities. These may be higher or lower. However, if there is no other evidence to contradict it, we will use your numerical grade level to determine your educational abilities. The term education also includes how well you are able to communicate in English since this ability is often acquired or improved by education. In evaluating your educational level, we use the following categories:

(1) Illiteracy. Illiteracy means the inability to read or write. We consider someone illiterate if the person cannot read or write a simple message such as instructions or inventory lists even though the person can sign his or her name. Generally, an illiterate person has had little or no formal schooling.

(2) Marginal education. Marginal education means ability in reasoning, arithmetic, and language skills which are needed to do simple, unskilled types of jobs. We generally consider that formal schooling at a 6th grade level or less is a marginal education.

(3) Limited education. Limited education means ability in reasoning, arithmetic, and language skills, but not enough to allow a person with these educational qualifications to do most of the more complex job duties needed in semi-skilled or skilled jobs. We generally consider that a 7th grade through the 11th grade level of formal education is a limited education.

(4) High school education and above. High school education and above means abilities in reasoning, arithmetic, and language skills acquired through formal schooling at a 12th grade level or above. We generally consider that someone with these educational abilities can do semi-skilled through skilled work.

(5) Inability to communicate in English. Since the ability to speak, read and understand English is generally learned or increased at school, we may consider this an educational factor. Because English is the dominant language of the country, it may be difficult for someone who doesn't speak and understand English to do a job, regardless of the amount of education the person may have in another language. Therefore, we consider a person's ability to communicate in English when we evaluate what work, if any, he or she can do. It generally doesn't matter what other language a person may be fluent in.

(6) Information about your education. We will ask you how long you attended school and whether you are able to speak, understand, read and write in English and do at least simple calculations in arithmetic. We will also consider other information about how much formal or informal education you may have had through your previous work, community projects, hobbies, and any other activities which might help you to work.

§ 404.1565 Your work experience as a vocational factor.

(a) General. Work experience means skills and abilities you have acquired through work you have done which show the type of work you may be expected to do. Work you have already been able to do shows the kind of work that you may be expected to do. We consider that your work experience applies when it was done within the last 15 years, lasted long enough for you to learn to do it, and was substantial gainful activity. We do not usually consider that work you did 15 years or more before the time we are deciding whether you are disabled (or when the disability insured status requirement was last met, if earlier) applies. A gradual change occurs in most jobs so that after 15 years it is no longer realistic to expect that skills and abilities acquired in a job done then continue to apply. The 15–year guide is intended to insure that remote work experience is not currently applied. If you have no work experience or worked only "off-and-on" or for brief periods of time during the 15–year period, we generally consider that these do not apply. If you have acquired skills through your past work, we consider you to have these work skills unless you cannot use them in other skilled or semi-skilled work that you can now do. If you cannot use your skills in other skilled or semi-skilled work, we will consider your work background the same as unskilled. However, even if you have no work experience, we may consider that you are able to do unskilled work because it requires little or no judgment and can be learned in a short period of time.

(b) Information about your work. Under certain circumstances, we will ask you about the work you have done in the past. If you cannot give us all of the information we need, we may try, with your permission, to get it from your employer or other person who knows about your work, such as a member of your family or a co-worker. When we need to consider your work experience to decide whether you are able to do work that is different from what you have done in the past, we will ask you to tell us about all of the jobs you have had in the last 15 years. You must tell us the dates you worked, all of the duties you did, and any tools, machinery, and equipment you used. We will need to know about the amount of walking, standing, sitting, lifting and carrying you did during the work day, as well as any other physical or mental duties of your job. If all of your work in the past 15 years has been arduous and unskilled, and you have very little education, we will ask you to tell us about all of your work from the time you first began working. This information could help you to get disability benefits.

[77 FR 43494, July 25, 2012]

§ 404.1566 Work which exists in the national economy.

(a) General. We consider that work exists in the national economy when it exists in significant numbers either in the region where you live or in several other regions of the country. It does not matter whether—

(1) Work exists in the immediate area in which you live;

(2) A specific job vacancy exists for you; or

(3) You would be hired if you applied for work.

(b) How we determine the existence of work. Work exists in the national economy when there is a significant number of jobs (in one or more occupations) having requirements which you are able to meet with your physical or mental abilities and vocational qualifications. Isolated jobs that exist only in very limited numbers in relatively few locations outside of the region where you live are not considered "work which exists in the national economy". We will not deny you disability benefits on the basis of the existence of these kinds of jobs. If work that you can do does not exist in the national economy, we will determine that you are disabled. However, if work that you can do does exist in the national economy, we will determine that you are not disabled.

(c) Inability to obtain work. We will determine that you are not disabled if your residual functional capacity and vocational abilities make it possible for you to do work which exists in the national economy, but you remain unemployed because of—

(1) Your inability to get work;

(2) Lack of work in your local area;

(3) The hiring practices of employers;

(4) Technological changes in the industry in which you have worked;

(5) Cyclical economic conditions;

(6) No job openings for you;

(7) You would not actually be hired to do work you could otherwise do; or

(8) You do not wish to do a particular type of work.

(d) Administrative notice of job data. When we determine that unskilled, sedentary, light, and medium jobs exist in the national economy (in significant numbers either in the region where you live or in several regions of the country), we will take administrative notice of reliable job information available from various governmental and other publications. For example, we will take notice of—

(1) Dictionary of Occupational Titles, published by the Department of Labor;

(2) County Business Patterns, published by the Bureau of the Census;

(3) Census Reports, also published by the Bureau of the Census;

(4) Occupational Analyses, prepared for the Social Security Administration by various State employment agencies; and

(5) Occupational Outlook Handbook, published by the Bureau of Labor Statistics.

(e) Use of vocational experts and other specialists. If the issue in determining whether you are disabled is whether your work skills can be used in other work and the specific occupations in which they can be used, or there is a similarly complex issue, we may use the services of a vocational expert or other specialist. We will decide whether to use a vocational expert or other specialist.

§ 404.1567 Physical exertion requirements.

To determine the physical exertion requirements of work in the national economy, we classify jobs as sedentary, light, medium, heavy, and very heavy. These terms have the same meaning as they have in the Dictionary of Occupational Titles, published by the Department of Labor. In making disability determinations under this subpart, we use the following definitions:

(a) Sedentary work. Sedentary work involves lifting no more than 10 pounds at a time and occasionally lifting or carrying articles like docket files, ledgers, and small tools. Although a sedentary job is defined as one which involves sitting, a certain amount of walking and standing is often necessary in carrying out job duties. Jobs are sedentary if walking and standing are required occasionally and other sedentary criteria are met.

(b) Light work. Light work involves lifting no more than 20 pounds at a time with frequent lifting or carrying of objects weighing up to 10 pounds. Even though the weight lifted may be very little, a job is in this category when it requires a good deal of walking or standing, or when it involves sitting most of the time with some pushing and pulling of arm or leg controls. To be considered capable of performing a full or wide range of light work, you must have the ability to do substantially all of these activities. If someone can do light work, we determine that he or she can also do sedentary work, unless there are additional limiting factors such as loss of fine dexterity or inability to sit for long periods of time.

(c) Medium work. Medium work involves lifting no more than 50 pounds at a time with frequent lifting or carrying of objects weighing up to 25 pounds. If someone can do medium work, we determine that he or she can also do sedentary and light work.

(d) Heavy work. Heavy work involves lifting no more than 100 pounds at a time with frequent lifting or carrying of objects weighing up to 50 pounds. If someone can do heavy work, we determine that he or she can also do medium, light, and sedentary work.

(e) Very heavy work. Very heavy work involves lifting objects weighing more than 100 pounds at a time with frequent lifting or carrying of objects weighing 50 pounds or more. If someone can do very heavy work, we determine that he or she can also do heavy, medium, light and sedentary work.

§ 404.1568 Skill requirements.

In order to evaluate your skills and to help determine the existence in the national economy of work you are able to do, occupations are classified as unskilled, semi-skilled, and skilled. In classifying these occupations, we use materials published by the Department of Labor. When we make disability determinations under this subpart, we use the following definitions:

(a) Unskilled work. Unskilled work is work which needs little or no judgment to do simple duties that can be learned on the job in a short period of time. The job may or may not require considerable strength. For example, we consider jobs unskilled if the primary work duties are handling, feeding and offbearing (that is, placing or removing materials from machines which are automatic or operated by others), or machine tending, and a person can usually learn to do the job in 30 days, and little specific vocational preparation and judgment are needed. A person does not gain work skills by doing unskilled jobs.

(b) Semi-skilled work. Semi-skilled work is work which needs some skills but does not require doing the more complex work duties. Semi-skilled jobs may require alertness and close attention to watching machine processes; or inspecting, testing or otherwise looking for irregularities; or tending or guarding equipment, property, materials, or persons against loss, damage or injury; or other types of activities which are similarly less complex than skilled work, but more complex than unskilled work. A job may be classified as semi-skilled where coordination and dexterity are necessary, as when hands or feet must be moved quickly to do repetitive tasks.

(c) Skilled work. Skilled work requires qualifications in which a person uses judgment to determine the machine and manual operations to be performed in order to obtain the proper form, quality, or quantity of material to be produced. Skilled work may require laying out work, estimating quality, determining the suitability and needed quantities of materials, making precise measurements, reading blueprints or other specifications, or making necessary computations or mechanical adjustments to control or regulate the work. Other skilled jobs may require dealing with people, facts, or figures or abstract ideas at a high level of complexity.

(d) Skills that can be used in other work (transferability)—

(1) What we mean by transferable skills. We consider you to have skills that can be used in other jobs, when the skilled or semi-skilled work activities you did in past work can be used to meet the requirements of skilled or semi-skilled work activities of other jobs or kinds of work. This depends largely on the similarity of occupationally significant work activities among different jobs.

(2) How we determine skills that can be transferred to other jobs. Transferability is most probable and meaningful among jobs in which—

(i) The same or a lesser degree of skill is required;

(ii) The same or similar tools and machines are used; and

(iii) The same or similar raw materials, products, processes, or services are involved.

(3) Degrees of transferability. There are degrees of transferability of skills ranging from very close similarities to remote and incidental similarities among jobs. A complete similarity of all three factors is not necessary for transferability. However, when skills are so specialized or have been acquired in such an isolated vocational setting (like many jobs in mining, agriculture, or fishing) that they are not readily usable in other industries, jobs, and work settings, we consider that they are not transferable.

(4) Transferability of skills for persons of advanced age. If you are of advanced age (age 55 or older), and you have a severe impairment(s) that limits you to sedentary or light work, we will find that you cannot make an adjustment to other work unless you have skills that you can transfer to other skilled or semiskilled work (or you have recently completed education which provides for direct entry into skilled work) that you can do despite your impairment(s). We will decide if you have transferable skills as follows. If you are of advanced age and you have a severe impairment(s) that limits you to no more than sedentary work, we will find that you have skills that are transferable to skilled or semiskilled sedentary work only if the sedentary work is so similar to your previous work that you would need to make very little, if any, vocational adjustment in terms of tools, work processes, work settings, or the industry. (See § 404.1567(a) and § 201.00(f) of appendix 2.) If you are of advanced age but have not attained age 60, and you have a severe impairment(s) that limits you to no more than light work, we will apply the rules in paragraphs (d)(1) through (d)(3) of this section to decide if you have skills that are transferable to skilled or semiskilled light work (see § 404.1567(b)). If you are closely approaching retirement age (age 60 or older) and you have a severe impairment(s) that limits you to no more than light work, we will find that you have skills that are transferable to skilled or semiskilled light work only if the light work is so similar to your previous work that you would need to make very little, if any, vocational adjustment in terms of tools, work processes, work settings, or the industry. (See § 404.1567(b) and Rule 202.00(f) of appendix 2 to this subpart.)

[65 FR 18000, April 6, 2000; 73 FR 64197, Oct. 29, 2008]

§ 404.1569 Listing of Medical–Vocational Guidelines in appendix 2.

The Dictionary of Occupational Titles includes information about jobs (classified by their exertional and skill requirements) that exist in the national economy. Appendix 2 provides rules using this data reflecting major functional and vocational patterns. We apply these rules in cases where a person is not doing substantial gainful activity and is prevented by a severe medically determinable impairment from doing vocationally relevant past work. (See § 404.1520(h) for an exception to this rule.) The rules in appendix 2 do not cover all possible variations of factors. Also, as we explain in § 200.00 of appendix 2, we do not apply these rules if one of the findings of fact about the person's vocational factors and residual functional capacity is not the same as the corresponding criterion of a rule. In these instances, we give full consideration to all relevant facts in accordance with the definitions and discussions under vocational considerations. However, if the findings of fact made about all factors are the same as the rule, we use that rule to decide whether a person is disabled.

[77 FR 43494, July 25, 2012]

§ 404.1569a Exertional and nonexertional limitations.

(a) General. Your impairment(s) and related symptoms, such as pain, may cause limitations of function or restrictions which limit your ability to meet certain demands of jobs. These limitations may be exertional, nonexertional, or a combination of both. Limitations are classified as exertional if they affect your ability to meet the strength demands of jobs. The classification of a limitation as exertional is related to the United States Department of Labor's classification of jobs by various exertional levels (sedentary, light, medium, heavy, and very heavy) in terms of the strength demands for sitting, standing, walking, lifting, carrying, pushing, and pulling. Sections 404.1567 and 404.1569 explain how we use the classification of jobs by exertional levels (strength demands) which is contained in the Dictionary of Occupational Titles published by the Department of Labor, to determine the exertional requirements of work which exists in the national economy. Limitations or restrictions which affect your ability to meet the demands of jobs other than the strength demands, that is, demands other than sitting, standing, walking, lifting, carrying, pushing or pulling, are considered nonexertional. When we decide whether you can do your past relevant work (see §§ 404.1520(f) and 404.1594(f)(7)), we will compare our assessment of your residual functional capacity with the demands of your past relevant work. If you cannot do your past relevant work, we will use the same residual functional capacity assessment along with your age, education, and work experience to decide if you can adjust to any other work which exists in the national economy. (See §§ 404.1520(g) and 404.1594(f)(8).) Paragraphs (b), (c), and (d) of this section explain how we apply the medical-vocational guidelines in appendix 2 of this subpart in making this determination, depending on whether the limitations or restrictions imposed by your impairment(s) and related symptoms, such as pain, are exertional, nonexertional, or a combination of both.

(b) Exertional limitations. When the limitations and restrictions imposed by your impairment(s) and related symptoms, such as pain, affect only your ability to meet the strength demands of jobs (sitting, standing, walking, lifting, carrying, pushing, and pulling), we consider that you have only exertional limitations. When your impairment(s) and related symptoms only impose exertional limitations and your specific vocational profile is listed in a rule contained in appendix 2 of this subpart, we will directly apply that rule to decide whether you are disabled.

(c) Nonexertional limitations.

(1) When the limitations and restrictions imposed by your impairment(s) and related symptoms, such as pain, affect only your ability to meet the demands of jobs other than the strength demands, we consider that you have only nonexertional limitations or restrictions. Some examples of nonexertional limitations or restrictions include the following:

(i) You have difficulty functioning because you are nervous, anxious, or depressed;

(ii) You have difficulty maintaining attention or concentrating;

(iii) You have difficulty understanding or remembering detailed instructions;

(iv) You have difficulty in seeing or hearing;

(v) You have difficulty tolerating some physical feature(s) of certain work settings, e.g., you cannot tolerate dust or fumes; or

(vi) You have difficulty performing the manipulative or postural functions of some work such as reaching, handling, stooping, climbing, crawling, or crouching.

(2) If your impairment(s) and related symptoms, such as pain, only affect your ability to perform the nonexertional aspects of work-related activities, the rules in appendix 2 do not direct factual conclusions of disabled or not disabled. The determination as to whether disability exists will be based on the principles in the appropriate sections of the regulations, giving consideration to the rules for specific case situations in appendix 2.

(d) Combined exertional and nonexertional limitations. When the limitations and restrictions imposed by your impairment(s) and related symptoms, such as pain, affect your ability to meet both the strength and demands of jobs other than the strength demands, we consider that you have a combination of exertional and nonexertional limitations or restrictions. If your impairment(s) and related symptoms, such as pain, affect your ability to meet both the strength and demands of jobs other than the strength demands, we will not directly apply the rules in appendix 2 unless there is a rule that directs a conclusion that you are disabled based upon your strength limitations; otherwise the rules provide a framework to guide our decision.

[56 FR 57943, Nov. 14, 1991; 68 FR 51163, Aug. 26, 2003]

SUBSTANTIAL GAINFUL ACTIVITY

§ 404.1571 General.

The work, without regard to legality, that you have done during any period in which you believe you are disabled may show that you are able to work at the substantial gainful activity level. If you are able to engage in substantial gainful activity, we will find that you are not disabled. (We explain the rules for persons who are statutorily blind in § 404.1584.) Even if the work you have done was not substantial gainful activity, it may show that you are able to do more work than you actually did. We will consider all of the medical and vocational evidence in your file to decide whether or not you have the ability to engage in substantial gainful activity.

[65 FR 42783, July 11, 2000]

§ 404.1572 What we mean by substantial gainful activity.

Substantial gainful activity is work activity that is both substantial and gainful:

(a) Substantial work activity. Substantial work activity is work activity that involves doing significant physical or mental activities. Your work may be substantial even if it is done on a part-time basis or if you do less, get paid less, or have less responsibility than when you worked before.

(b) Gainful work activity. Gainful work activity is work activity that you do for pay or profit. Work activity is gainful if it is the kind of work usually done for pay or profit, whether or not a profit is realized.

(c) Some other activities. Generally, we do not consider activities like taking care of yourself, household tasks, hobbies, therapy, school attendance, club activities, or social programs to be substantial gainful activity.

§ 404.1573 General information about work activity.

(a) The nature of your work. If your duties require use of your experience, skills, supervision and responsibilities, or contribute substantially to the operation of a business, this tends to show that you have the ability to work at the substantial gainful activity level.

(b) How well you perform. We consider how well you do your work when we determine whether or not you are doing substantial gainful activity. If you do your work satisfactorily, this may show that you are working at the substantial gainful activity level. If you are unable, because of your impairments, to do ordinary or simple tasks satisfactorily without more supervision or assistance than is usually given other people doing similar work, this may show that you are not working at the substantial gainful activity level. If you are doing work that involves minimal duties that make little or no demands on you and that are of little or no use to your employer, or to the operation of a business if you are self-employed, this does not show that you are working at the substantial gainful activity level.

(c) If your work is done under special conditions. The work you are doing may be done under special conditions that take into account your impairment, such as work done in a sheltered workshop or as a patient in a hospital. If your work is done under special conditions, we may find that it does not show that you have the ability to do substantial gainful activity. Also, if you are forced to stop or reduce your work because of the removal of special conditions that were related to your impairment and essential to your work, we may find that your work does not show that you are able to do substantial gainful activity. However, work done under special conditions may show that you have the necessary skills and ability to work at the substantial gainful activity level. Examples of the special conditions that may relate to your impairment include, but are not limited to, situations in which—

(1) You required and received special assistance from other employees in performing your work;

(2) You were allowed to work irregular hours or take frequent rest periods;

(3) You were provided with special equipment or were assigned work especially suited to your impairment;

(4) You were able to work only because of specially arranged circumstances, for example, other persons helped you prepare for or get to and from your work;

(5) You were permitted to work at a lower standard of productivity or efficiency than other employees; or

(6) You were given the opportunity to work despite your impairment because of family relationship, past association with your employer, or your employer's concern for your welfare.

(d) If you are self-employed. Supervisory, managerial, advisory or other significant personal services that you perform as a self-employed individual may show that you are able to do substantial gainful activity.

(e) Time spent in work. While the time you spend in work is important, we will not decide whether or not you are doing substantial gainful activity only on that basis. We will still evaluate the work to decide whether it is substantial and gainful regardless of whether you spend more time or less time at the job than workers who are not impaired and who are doing similar work as a regular means of their livelihood.

[65 FR 42783, July 11, 2000]

§ 404.1574 Evaluation guides if you are an employee.

(a) We use several guides to decide whether the work you have done shows that you are able to do substantial gainful activity. If you are working or have worked as an employee, we will use the provisions in paragraphs (a) through (d) of this section that are relevant to your work activity. We will use these provisions whenever they are appropriate, whether in connection with your application for disability benefits (when we make an initial determination on your application and throughout any appeals you may request), after you have become entitled to a period of disability or to disability benefits, or both.

(1) Your earnings may show you have done substantial gainful activity. Generally, in evaluating your work activity for substantial gainful activity purposes, our primary consideration will be the earnings you derive from the work activity. We will use your earnings to determine whether you have done substantial gainful activity unless we have information from you, your employer, or others that shows that we should not count all of your earnings. The amount of your earnings from work you have done (regardless of whether it is unsheltered or sheltered work) may show that you have engaged in substantial gainful activity. Generally, if you worked for substantial earnings, we will find that you are able to do substantial gainful activity. However, the fact that your earnings were not substantial will not necessarily show that you are not able to do substantial gainful activity. We generally consider work that you are forced to stop or to reduce below the substantial gainful activity level after a short time because of your impairment to be an unsuccessful work attempt. Your earnings from an unsuccessful work attempt will not show that you are able to do substantial gainful activity. We will use the criteria in paragraph (c) of this section to determine if the work you did was an unsuccessful work attempt.

(2) We consider only the amounts you earn. When we decide whether your earnings show that you have done substantial gainful activity, we do not consider any income that is not directly related to your productivity. When your earnings exceed the reasonable value of the work you perform, we consider only that part of your pay which you actually earn. If your earnings are being subsidized, we do not consider the amount of the subsidy when we determine if your earnings show that you have done substantial gainful activity. We consider your work to be subsidized if the true value of your work, when compared with the same or similar work done by unimpaired persons, is less than the actual amount of earnings paid to you for your work. For example, when a person with a serious impairment does simple tasks under close and continuous supervision, our determination of whether that person has done substantial gainful activity will not be based only on the amount of the wages paid. We will

first determine whether the person received a subsidy; that is, we will determine whether the person was being paid more than the reasonable value of the actual services performed. We will then subtract the value of the subsidy from the person's gross earnings to determine the earnings we will use to determine if he or she has done substantial gainful activity.

(3) If you are working in a sheltered or special environment. If you are working in a sheltered workshop, you may or may not be earning the amounts you are being paid. The fact that the sheltered workshop or similar facility is operating at a loss or is receiving some charitable contributions or governmental aid does not establish that you are not earning all you are being paid. Since persons in military service being treated for severe impairments usually continue to receive full pay, we evaluate work activity in a therapy program or while on limited duty by comparing it with similar work in the civilian work force or on the basis of reasonable worth of the work, rather than on the actual amount of the earnings.

(b) Earnings guidelines—

(1) General. If you are an employee, we first consider the criteria in paragraph (a) of this section and § 404.1576, and then the guides in paragraphs (b)(2) and (3) of this section. When we review your earnings to determine if you have been performing substantial gainful activity, we will subtract the value of any subsidized earnings (see paragraph (a)(2) of this section) and the reasonable cost of any impairment-related work expenses from your gross earnings (see § 404.1576). The resulting amount is the amount we use to determine if you have done substantial gainful activity. We will generally average your earnings for comparison with the earnings guidelines in paragraphs (b)(2) and (3) of this section. See § 404.1574a for our rules on averaging earnings.

(2) Earnings that will ordinarily show that you have engaged in substantial gainful activity. We will consider that your earnings from your work activity as an employee (including earnings from work in a sheltered workshop or a comparable facility especially set up for severely impaired persons) show that you engaged in substantial gainful activity if:

(i) Before January 1, 2001, they averaged more than the amount(s) in Table 1 of this section for the time(s) in which you worked.

(ii) Beginning January 1, 2001, and each year thereafter, they average more than the larger of:

(A) The amount for the previous year, or

(B) An amount adjusted for national wage growth, calculated by multiplying $700 by the ratio of the national average wage index for the year 2 calendar years before the year for which the amount is being calculated to the national average wage index for the year 1998. We will then round the resulting amount to the next higher multiple of $10 where such amount is a multiple of $5 but not of $10 and to the nearest multiple of $10 in any other case.

TABLE 1

For months:	Your monthly earnings averaged more than:
In calendar years before 1976	$200
In calendar year 1976	230
In calendar year 1977	240
In calendar year 1978	260
In calendar year 1979	280
In calendar years 1980–1989	300
January 1990–June 1999	500
July 1999–December 2000	700

(3) Earnings that will ordinarily show that you have not engaged in substantial gainful activity—

(i) General. If your average monthly earnings are equal to or less than the amount(s) determined under paragraph (b)(2) of this section for the year(s) in which you work, we will generally consider that the earnings from your work as an employee (including earnings from work in a sheltered workshop or comparable facility) will show that you have not engaged in substantial gainful activity. We will generally not consider other information in addition to your earnings except in the circumstances described in paragraph (b)(3)(ii) of this section.

(ii) When we will consider other information in addition to your earnings. We will generally consider other information in addition to your earnings if there is evidence indicating that you may be engaging in substantial gainful activity or that you are in a position to control when earnings are paid to you or the amount of wages paid to you (for example, if you are working for a small corporation owned by a relative). (See paragraph (b)(3)(iii) of this section for when we do not apply this rule.) Examples of other information we may consider include, whether—

(A) Your work is comparable to that of unimpaired people in your community who are doing the same or similar occupations as their means of livelihood, taking into account the time, energy, skill, and responsibility involved in the work; and

(B) Your work, although significantly less than that done by unimpaired people, is clearly worth the amounts shown in paragraph (b)(2) of this section, according to pay scales in your community.

(iii) Special rule for considering earnings alone when evaluating the work you do after you have received social security disability benefits for at least 24 months. Notwithstanding paragraph (b)(3)(ii) of this section, we will not consider other information in addition to your earnings to evaluate the work you are doing or have done if—

(A) At the time you do the work, you are entitled to social security disability benefits and you have received such benefits for at least 24 months (see paragraph (b)(3)(iv) of this section); and

(B) We are evaluating that work to consider whether you have engaged in substantial gainful activity or demonstrated the ability to engage in substantial gainful activity for the purpose of determining whether your disability has ceased because of your work activity (see §§ 404.1592a(a)(1) and (3)(ii) and 404.1594(d)(5) and (f)(1)).

(iv) When we consider you to have received social security disability benefits for at least 24 months. For purposes of paragraph (b)(3)(iii) of this section, social security disability benefits means disability insurance benefits for a disabled worker, child's insurance benefits based on disability, or widow's or widower's insurance benefits based on disability. We consider you to have received such benefits for at least 24 months beginning with the first day of the first month following the 24th month for which you actually received social security disability benefits that you were due or constructively received such benefits. The 24 months do not have to be consecutive. We will consider you to have constructively received a benefit for a month for purposes of the 24–month requirement if you were otherwise due a social security disability benefit for that month and your monthly benefit was withheld to recover an overpayment. Any months for which you were entitled to benefits but for which you did not actually or constructively receive a benefit payment will not be counted for the 24–month requirement. If you also receive supplemental security income payments based on disability or blindness under title XVI of the Social Security Act, months for which you received only supplemental security income payments will not be counted for the 24–month requirement.

(c) The unsuccessful work attempt—

(1) General. Ordinarily, work you have done will not show that you are able to do substantial gainful activity if, after you worked for a period of 6 months or less, your impairment forced you to stop working or to reduce the amount of work you do so that your earnings from such work fall below the substantial gainful activity earnings level in paragraph (b)(2) of this section, and you meet the conditions described in paragraphs (c)(2), (3), and (4) of this section. We will use the provisions of this paragraph when we make an initial determination on your application for disability benefits and throughout any appeal you may request. Except as set forth in § 404.1592a(a), we will also apply the provisions of this paragraph if you are already entitled to disability benefits, when you work and we consider whether the work you are doing is substantial gainful activity or demonstrates the ability to do substantial gainful activity.

(2) Event that must precede an unsuccessful work attempt. There must be a significant break in the continuity of your work before we will consider that you began a work attempt that later proved unsuccessful. You must have stopped working or reduced your work and earnings below the substantial gainful activity earnings level because of your impairment or because of the removal of special conditions that were essential to the further performance of your work. We explain what we mean by special conditions in § 404.1573(c). We will consider your prior work to be "discontinued" for a significant period if you were out of work at least 30 consecutive days. We will also consider your prior work to be "discontinued" if, because of your impairment, you were forced to change to another type of work or another employer.

(3) If you worked 6 months or less. We will consider work of 6 months or less to be an unsuccessful work attempt if you stopped working or you reduced your work and earnings below the substantial gainful activity earnings level because of your impairment or because of the removal of special conditions that took into account your impairment and permitted you to work.

(4) If you worked more than 6 months. We will not consider work you performed at the substantial gainful activity earnings level for more than 6 months to be an unsuccessful work attempt regardless of why it ended or was reduced below the substantial gainful activity earnings level.

(d) Work activity in certain volunteer programs. If you work as a volunteer in certain programs administered by the Federal government under the Domestic Volunteer Service Act of 1973 or the Small Business Act, we will not count any payments you receive from these programs as earnings when we determine whether you are engaging in substantial gainful activity. These payments may include a minimal stipend, payments for supportive services such as housing, supplies and equipment, an expense allowance, or reimbursement of out-of-pocket expenses. We will also disregard the services you perform as a volunteer in applying any of the substantial gainful activity tests discussed in paragraph (b)(6) of this section. This exclusion from the substantial gainful activity provisions will apply only if you are a volunteer in a program explicitly mentioned in the Domestic Volunteer Service Act of 1973 or the Small Business Act. Programs explicitly mentioned in those Acts include Volunteers in Service to America, University Year for ACTION, Special Volunteer Programs, Retired Senior Volunteer Program, Foster Grandparent Program, Service Corps of Retired Executives, and Active Corps of Executives. We will not exclude under this paragraph, volunteer work you perform in other programs or any nonvolunteer work you may perform, including nonvolunteer work under one of the specified programs. For civilians in certain government-sponsored job training and employment programs, we evaluate the work activity on a case-by-case basis under the substantial gainful activity earnings test. In programs such as these, subsidies often occur. We will subtract the value of any subsidy and use the remainder to determine if you have done substantial gainful activity. See paragraphs (a)(2)–(3) of this section.

(e) Work activity as a member or consultant of an advisory committee established under the Federal Advisory Committee Act (FACA), 5 U.S.C. App. 2. If you are serving as a member or consultant of an advisory committee, board, commission, council, or similar group established under FACA, we will not count any payments you receive from serving on such committees as earnings when we determine whether you are engaging in substantial gainful activity. These payments may include compensation, travel expenses, and special assistance. We also will exclude the services you perform as a member or consultant of an advisory committee established under FACA in applying any of the substantial gainful activity tests discussed in paragraph (b)(6) of this section. This exclusion from the substantial gainful activity provisions will apply only if you are a member or consultant of an advisory committee specifically authorized by statute, or by the President, or determined as a matter of formal record by the head of a federal government agency. This exclusion from the substantial gainful activity provisions will not apply if your service as a member or consultant of an advisory committee is part of your duties or is required as an employee of any governmental or non-governmental organization, agency, or business.

[46 FR 4869, Jan. 19, 1981; 48 FR 21936, May 16, 1983; 49 FR 22272, May 29, 1984; 54 FR 53605, Dec. 29, 1989; 64 FR 18570, April 15, 1999; 64 FR 22903, April 28, 1999; 65 FR 42783, July 11, 2000; 65 FR 82910, Dec. 29, 2000; 71 FR 3219, Jan. 20, 2006; 71 FR 66853, Nov. 17, 2006; 81 FR 71369, Oct. 17, 2016]

§ 404.1574a When and how we will average your earnings.

(a) If your work as an employee or as a self-employed person was continuous without significant change in work patterns or earnings, and there has been no change in the substantial gainful activity earnings levels, we will average your earnings over the entire period of work requiring evaluation to determine if you have done substantial gainful activity. See § 404.1592a for information on the reentitlement period.

(b) If you work over a period of time during which the substantial gainful activity earnings levels change, we will average your earnings separately for each period in which a different substantial gainful activity earnings level applies.

(c) If there is a significant change in your work pattern or earnings during the period of work requiring evaluation, we will average your earnings over each separate period of work to determine if any of your work efforts were substantial gainful activity.

(d) We will not average your earnings in determining whether benefits should be paid for any month(s) during or after the reentitlement period that occurs after the month disability has been determined to have ceased because of the performance of substantial gainful activity. See § 404.1592a for information on the reentitlement period. The following examples illustrate what we mean by a significant change in the work pattern of an employee and when we will average and will not average earnings.

Example 1: Mrs. H. began receiving disability insurance benefits in March 1993. In January 1995 she began selling magazines by telephone solicitation, expending a minimum of time, for which she received $225 monthly. As a result, Mrs. H. used up her trial work period during the months of January 1995 through September 1995. After the trial work period ended, we determined that Mrs. H. had not engaged in substantial gainful activity during her trial work period. Her reentitlement period began October 1995. In December 1995, Mrs. H. discontinued her telephone solicitation work to take a course in secretarial skills. In January 1997, she began work as a part-time temporary secretary in a banking firm. Mrs. H. worked 20 hours a week, without any subsidy or impairment-related work expenses, at beginner rates. She earned $285 per month in January 1997 and February 1997. In March 1997 she had increased her secretarial skills to journeyman level and was assigned as a part-time private secretary to one of the vice presidents of the banking firm. Mrs. H.'s earnings increased to $525 per month effective March 1997. We determined that Mrs. H. was engaging in substantial gainful activity beginning March 1997 and that her disability ceased that month, the first month of substantial gainful activity after the end of the trial work period. Mrs. H. is due payment for March 1997, the month of cessation, and the following 2 months (April 1997 and May 1997) because disability benefits terminate the third month following the earliest month in which she performed substantial gainful activity. We did not average earnings for the period January 1997 and February 1997 with the period beginning March 1997 because there was a significant change in earnings and work activity beginning March 1997. Thus, the earnings of January 1997 and February 1997 could not be averaged with those of March 1997 to reduce March 1997 earnings below the substantial gainful activity level. After we determine that Mrs. H.'s disability had ceased because of her performance of substantial gainful activity, we cannot average her earnings to determine whether she is due payment for any month during or after the reentitlement period. Beginning June 1997, the third month following the cessation month, we would evaluate all of Mrs. H.'s work activity on a month-by-month basis (see § 404.1592a(a)).

Example 2: Ms. M. began receiving disability insurance benefits in March 1992. In January 1995, she began selling cable television subscriptions by telephone solicitation, expending a minimum of time, for which she received $275 monthly. Ms. M. did not work in June 1995, and she resumed selling cable television subscriptions beginning July 1995. In this way, Ms. M. used up her 9–month trial work period during the months of January 1995 through May 1995 and July 1995 through October 1995. After Ms. M.'s trial work period ended, we determined that she had not engaged in substantial gainful activity during her trial work period. Ms. M.'s reentitlement period began November 1995. In December 1995, Ms. M. discontinued her telephone solicitation work to take a course in secretarial skills. In January 1997, she began work as a part-time temporary secretary in an accounting firm. Ms. M. worked, without any subsidy or impairment-related work expenses, at beginner rates. She earned $460 in January 1997, $420 in February 1997, and $510 in March 1997. In April 1997, she had increased her secretarial skills to journeyman level, and she was assigned as a part-time private secretary to one of the vice presidents of the firm. Ms. M.'s earnings increased to $860 per month effective April 1997. We determined that Ms. M. was engaging in substantial gainful activity beginning April 1997 and that her disability ceased that month, the first month of substantial gainful activity after the end of the trial work period. She is due payment for April 1997, May 1997 and June 1997, because disability benefits terminate the third month following the earliest month in which she performs substantial gainful activity (the month of cessation). We averaged her earnings for the period January 1997 through March 1997 and determined them to be about $467 per month for that period. We did not average earnings for the period January 1997 through March 1997 with earnings for the period beginning April 1997 because there was a significant change in work activity and earnings beginning April 1997. Therefore, we found that the earnings for January 1997 through March 1997 were under the substantial gainful activity level. After we determine that Ms M.'s disability has ceased because she performed substantial gainful activity, we cannot average her earnings in determining whether she is due payment for any month during or after the reentitlement period. In this example, beginning July 1997, the third month following the month of cessation, we would evaluate all of Ms. M.'s work activity on a month-by-month basis (see § 404.1592a(a)).

[65 FR 42784, July 11, 2000]

§ 404.1575 Evaluation guides if you are self-employed.

(a) If you are a self-employed person. If you are working or have worked as a self-employed person, we will use the provisions in paragraphs (a) through (e) of this section that are relevant to your work activity. We will use these provisions whenever they are appropriate, whether in connection with your application for disability benefits (when we make an initial determination on your application and throughout any appeals you may request), after you have become entitled to a period of disability or to disability benefits, or both.

(1) How we evaluate the work you do after you have become entitled to disability benefits. If you are entitled to social security disability benefits and you work as a self-employed person, the way we will evaluate your work activity will depend on whether the work activity occurs before or after you have received such benefits for at least 24 months and on the purpose of the evaluation. For purposes of paragraphs (a) and (e) of this section, social security disability benefits means disability insurance benefits for a disabled worker, child's insurance benefits based on disability, or widow's or widower's insurance benefits based on disability. We will use the rules in paragraph (e)(2) of this section to determine if you have received such benefits for at least 24 months.

(i) We will use the guides in paragraph (a)(2) of this section to evaluate any work activity you do before you have received social security disability benefits for at least 24 months to determine whether you have engaged in substantial gainful activity, regardless of the purpose of the evaluation.

(ii) We will use the guides in paragraph (e) of this section to evaluate any work activity you do after you have received social security disability benefits for at least 24 months to determine whether you have engaged in substantial gainful activity for the purpose of determining whether your disability has ceased because of your work activity.

(iii) If we have determined under § 404.1592a(a)(1) that your disability ceased in a month during the reentitlement period because you performed substantial gainful activity, and we need to decide under § 404.1592a(a)(2)(i) or (a)(3)(i) whether you are doing substantial gainful activity in a subsequent month in or after your reentitlement period, we will use the guides in paragraph (a)(2) of this section (subject to the limitations described in § 404.1592a(a)(2)(i) and (a)(3)(i)) to determine whether your work activity in that month is substantial gainful activity. We will use the guides in paragraph (a)(2) of this section for these purposes, regardless of whether your work activity in that month occurs before or after you have received social security disability benefits for at least 24 months.

(2) General rules for evaluating your work activity if you are self-employed. We will consider your activities and their value to your business to decide whether you have engaged in substantial gainful activity if you are self-employed. We will not consider your income alone because the amount of income you actually receive may depend on a number of different factors, such as capital investment and profit-sharing agreements. We will generally consider work that you were forced to stop or reduce to below substantial gainful activity after 6 months or less because of your impairment as an unsuccessful work attempt. See paragraph (d) of this section. We will evaluate your work activity based on the value of your services to the business regardless of whether you receive an immediate income for your services. We determine whether you have engaged in substantial gainful activity by applying three tests. If you have not engaged in substantial gainful activity under test one, then we will consider tests two and three. The tests are as follows:

(i) Test one: You have engaged in substantial gainful activity if you render services that are significant to the operation of the business and receive a substantial income from the business. Paragraphs (b) and (c) of this section explain what we mean by significant services and substantial income for purposes of this test.

(ii) Test Two: You have engaged in substantial gainful activity if your work activity, in terms of factors such as hours, skills, energy output, efficiency, duties, and responsibilities, is comparable to that of unimpaired individuals in your community who are in the same or similar businesses as their means of livelihood.

(iii) Test Three: You have engaged in substantial gainful activity if your work activity, although not comparable to that of unimpaired individuals, is clearly worth the amount shown in § 404.1574(b)(2) when considered in terms of its value to the business, or when compared to the salary that an owner would pay to an employee to do the work you are doing.

(b) What we mean by significant services.

(1) If you are not a farm landlord and you operate a business entirely by yourself, any services that you render are significant to the business. If your business involves the services of more than one person, we will consider you to be rendering significant services if you contribute more than half the total time required for the management of the business, or you render management services for more than 45 hours a month regardless of the total management time required by the business.

(2) If you are a farm landlord, that is, you rent farm land to another, we will consider you to be rendering significant services if you materially participate in the production or the management of the production of the things raised on the rented farm. (See § 404.1082 of this chapter for an explanation of material participation.) If you were given social security earnings credits because you materially participated in the activities of the farm and you continue these same activities, we will consider you to be rendering significant services.

(c) What we mean by substantial income—

(1) Determining countable income. We deduct your normal business expenses from your gross income to determine net income. Once we determine your net income, we deduct the reasonable value of any significant amount of unpaid help furnished by your spouse, children, or others. Miscellaneous duties that ordinarily would not have commercial value would not be considered significant. We deduct impairment-related work expenses that have not already been deducted in determining your net income. Impairment-related work expenses are explained in § 404.1576. We deduct unincurred business expenses paid for you by another individual or agency. An unincurred business expense occurs when a sponsoring agency or another person incurs responsibility for the payment of certain business expenses, e.g., rent, utilities, or purchases and repair of equipment, or provides you with equipment, stock, or other material for the operation of your business. We deduct soil bank payments if they were included as farm income. That part of your income remaining after we have made all applicable deductions represents the actual value of work performed. The resulting amount is the amount we use to determine if you have done substantial gainful activity. For purposes of this section, we refer to this amount as your countable income. We will generally average your countable income for comparison with the earnings guidelines in § 404.1574(b)(2). See § 404.1574a for our rules on averaging of earnings.

(2) When countable income is considered substantial. We will consider your countable income to be substantial if—

(i) It averages more than the amounts described in § 404.1574(b)(2); or

(ii) It averages less than the amounts described in § 404.1574(b)(2) but it is either comparable to what it was before you became seriously impaired if we had not considered your earnings or is comparable to that of unimpaired self-employed persons in your community who are in the same or a similar business as their means of livelihood.

(d) The unsuccessful work attempt—

(1) General. Ordinarily, work you have done will not show that you are able to do substantial gainful activity if, after working for a period of 6 months or less, you were forced by your impairment to stop working or to reduce the amount of work you do so that you are no longer performing substantial gainful activity and you meet the conditions described in paragraphs (d)(2), (3), and (4) of this section. We will use the provisions of this paragraph when we make an initial determination on your application for disability benefits and throughout any appeal you may request. Except as set forth in § 404.1592a(a), we will also apply the provisions of this paragraph if you are already entitled to disability benefits, when you work and we consider whether the work you are doing is substantial gainful activity or demonstrates the ability to do substantial gainful activity.

(2) Event that must precede an unsuccessful work attempt. There must be a significant break in the continuity of your work before we will consider you to have begun a work attempt that later proved unsuccessful. You must have stopped working or reduced your work and earnings below substantial gainful activity because of your impairment or because of the removal of special conditions which took into account your impairment and permitted you to work. Examples of such special conditions may include any significant amount of unpaid help furnished by your spouse, children, or others, or unincurred business expenses, as described in paragraph (c) of this section, paid for you by another individual or agency. We will consider your prior work to be "discontinued" for a significant period if you were out of work at least 30 consecutive days. We will also consider your prior work to be "discontinued" if, because of your impairment, you were forced to change to another type of work.

(3) If you worked 6 months or less. We will consider work of 6 months or less to be an unsuccessful work attempt if you stopped working or you reduced your work and earnings below the substantial gainful activity earnings level because of your impairment or because of the removal of special conditions that took into account your impairment and permitted you to work.

(4) If you worked more than 6 months. We will not consider work you performed at the substantial gainful activity level for more than 6 months to be an unsuccessful work attempt regardless of why it ended or was reduced below the substantial gainful activity earnings level.

(e) Special rules for evaluating the work you do after you have received social security disability benefits for at least 24 months—

(1) General. We will apply the provisions of this paragraph to evaluate the work you are doing or have done if, at the time you do the work, you are entitled to social security disability benefits and you have received such benefits for at least 24 months. We will apply the provisions of this paragraph only when we are evaluating that work to consider whether you have engaged in substantial gainful activity or demonstrated the ability to engage in substantial gainful activity for the purpose of determining whether your disability has ceased because of your work activity (see §§ 404.1592a(a)(1) and (3)(ii) and 404.1594(d)(5) and (f)(1)). We will use the countable income test described in paragraph (e)(3) of this section to determine whether the work you do after you have received such benefits for at least 24 months is substantial gainful activity or demonstrates the ability to do substantial gainful activity. We will not consider the services you perform in that work to determine that the work you are doing shows that you are able to engage in substantial gainful activity and are, therefore, no longer disabled. However, we may consider the services you perform to determine that you are not doing substantial gainful activity. We will generally consider work that you were forced to stop or reduce below substantial gainful activity after 6 months or less because of your impairment as an unsuccessful work attempt. See paragraph (d) of this section.

(2) The 24–month requirement. For purposes of paragraphs (a)(1) and (e) of this section, we consider you to have received social security disability benefits for at least 24 months beginning with the first day of the first month following the 24th month for which you actually received social security disability benefits that you were due or constructively received such benefits. The 24 months do not have to be consecutive. We will consider you to have constructively received a benefit for a month for purposes of the 24–month requirement if you were otherwise due a social security disability benefit for that month and your monthly benefit was withheld to recover an overpayment. Any months for which you were entitled to benefits but for which you did not actually or constructively receive a benefit payment will not be counted for the 24–month requirement. If you also receive supplemental security income payments based on disability or blindness under title XVI of the Social Security Act, months for which you received only supplemental security income payments will not be counted for the 24–month requirement.

(3) Countable income test. We will compare your countable income to the earnings guidelines in § 404.1574(b)(2) to determine if you have engaged in substantial gainful activity. See paragraph (c)(1) of this section for an explanation of countable income. We will consider that you have engaged in substantial gainful activity if your monthly countable income averages more than the amounts described in § 404.1574(b)(2) for the month(s) in which you work, unless the evidence shows that you did not render significant services in the month(s). See paragraph (b) of this section for what we mean by significant services. If your average monthly countable income is equal to or less than the amounts in § 404.1574(b)(2) for the month(s) in which you work, or if the evidence shows that you did not render significant services in the month(s), we will consider that your work as a self-employed person shows that you have not engaged in substantial gainful activity.

[46 FR 4870, Jan. 19, 1981; 48 FR 21936, May 16, 1983; 49 FR 22272, May 29, 1984; 65 FR 42785, July 11, 2000; 71 FR 66854, Nov. 17, 2006; 81 FR 71369, Oct. 17, 2016]

§ 404.1576 Impairment-related work expenses.

(a) General. When we figure your earnings in deciding if you have done substantial gainful activity, we will subtract the reasonable costs to you of certain items and services which, because of your impairment(s), you need and use to enable you to work. The costs are deductible even though you also need or use the items and services to carry out daily living functions unrelated to your work. Paragraph (b) of this section explains the conditions for deducting work expenses. Paragraph (c) of this section describes the expenses we will deduct. Paragraph (d) of this section explains when expenses may be deducted. Paragraph (e) of this section describes how expenses may be allocated. Paragraph (f) of this section explains the limitations on deducting expenses. Paragraph (g) of this section explains our verification procedures.

(b) Conditions for deducting impairment-related work expenses. We will deduct impairment-related work expenses if—

(1) You are otherwise disabled as defined in §§ 404.1505, 404.1577 and 404.1581–404.1583;

(2) The severity of your impairment(s) requires you to purchase (or rent) certain items and services in order to work;

(3) You pay the cost of the item or service. No deduction will be allowed to the extent that payment has been or will be made by another source. No deduction will be allowed to the extent that you have been, could be, or will be reimbursed for such cost by any other source (such as through a private insurance plan, Medicare or Medicaid, or other plan or agency). For example, if you purchase crutches for $80 but you were, could be, or will be reimbursed $64 by some agency, plan, or program, we will deduct only $16;

(4) You pay for the item or service in a month you are working (in accordance with paragraph (d) of this section); and

(5) Your payment is in cash (including checks or other forms of money). Payment in kind is not deductible.

(c) What expenses may be deducted—

(1) Payments for attendant care services.

(i) If because of your impairment(s) you need assistance in traveling to and from work, or while at work you need assistance with personal functions (e.g., eating, toileting) or with work-related functions (e.g., reading, communicating), the payments you make for those services may be deducted.

(ii) If because of your impairment(s) you need assistance with personal functions (e.g., dressing, administering medications) at home in preparation for going to and assistance in returning from work, the payments you make for those services may be deducted.

(iii)(A) We will deduct payments you make to a family member for attendant care services only if such person, in order to perform the services, suffers an economic loss by terminating his or her employment or by reducing the number of hours he or she worked.

(B) We consider a family member to be anyone who is related to you by blood, marriage or adoption, whether or not that person lives with you.

(iv) If only part of your payment to a person is for services that come under the provisions of paragraph (c)(1) of this section, we will only deduct that part of the payment which is attributable to those services. For example, an attendant gets you ready for work and helps you in returning from work, which takes about 2 hours a day. The rest of his or her 8 hour day is spent cleaning your house and doing your laundry, etc. We would only deduct one-fourth of the attendant's daily wages as an impairment-related work expense.

(2) Payments for medical devices. If your impairment(s) requires that you utilize medical devices in order to work, the payments you make for those devices may be deducted. As used in this subparagraph, medical devices include durable medical equipment which can withstand repeated use, is customarily used for medical purposes, and is generally not useful to a person in the absence of an illness or injury. Examples of durable medical equipment are wheelchairs, hemodialysis equipment, canes, crutches, inhalators and pacemakers.

(3) Payments for prosthetic devices. If your impairment(s) requires that you utilize a prosthetic device in order to work, the payments you make for that device may be deducted. A prosthetic device is that which replaces an internal body organ or external body part. Examples of prosthetic devices are artificial replacements of arms, legs and other parts of the body.

(4) Payments for equipment.

(i) Work-related equipment. If your impairment(s) requires that you utilize special equipment in order to do your job, the payments you make for that equipment may be deducted. Examples of work-related equipment are one-hand typewriters, vision aids, sensory aids for the blind, telecommunication devices for the deaf and tools specifically designed to accommodate a person's impairment(s).

(ii) Residential modifications. If your impairment(s) requires that you make modifications to your residence, the location of your place of work will determine if the cost of these modifications will be deducted. If you are employed away from home, only the cost of changes made outside of your home to permit you to get to your means of transportation (e.g., the installation of an exterior ramp for a wheelchair confined person or special exterior railings or pathways for someone who requires crutches) will be deducted. Costs relating to modifications of the inside of your home will not be deducted. If you work at home, the costs of modifying the inside of your home in order to create a working space to accommodate your impairment(s) will be deducted to the extent that the changes pertain specifically to the space in which you work. Examples of such changes are the enlargement of a doorway leading into the workspace or modification of the workspace to accommodate problems in dexterity. However, if you are self-employed at home, any cost deducted as a business expense cannot be deducted as an impairment-related work expense.

(iii) Nonmedical appliances and equipment. Expenses for appliances and equipment which you do not ordinarily use for medical purposes are generally not deductible. Examples of these items are portable room heaters, air conditioners, humidifiers, dehumidifiers, and electric air cleaners. However, expenses for such items may be deductible when unusual circumstances clearly establish an impairment-related and medically verified need for such an item because it is essential for the control of your disabling condition, thus enabling you to work. To be considered essential, the item must be of such a nature that if it were not available to you there would be an immediate adverse impact on your ability to function in your work activity. In this situation, the expense is deductible whether the item is used at home or in the working place. An example would be the need for an electric air cleaner by an individual with severe respiratory disease who cannot function in a non-purified air environment. An item such as an exercycle is not deductible if used for general physical fitness. If it is prescribed and used as necessary treatment of your impairment and necessary to enable you to work, we will deduct payments you make toward its cost.

(5) Payments for drugs and medical services.

(i) If you must use drugs or medical services (including diagnostic procedures) to control your impairment(s) the payments you make for them may be deducted. The drugs or services must be prescribed (or utilized) to reduce or eliminate symptoms of your impairment(s) or to slow down its progression. The diagnostic procedures must be performed to ascertain how the impairment(s) is progressing or to determine what type of treatment should be provided for the impairment(s).

(ii) Examples of deductible drugs and medical services are anticonvulsant drugs to control epilepsy or anticonvulsant blood level monitoring; antidepressant medication for mental disorders; medication used to allay the side effects of certain treatments; radiation treatment or chemotherapy for cancer patients; corrective surgery for spinal disorders; electroencephalograms and brain scans related to a disabling epileptic condition; tests to determine the efficacy of medication on a diabetic condition; and immunosuppressive medications that kidney transplant patients regularly take to protect against graft rejection.

(iii) We will only deduct the costs of drugs or services that are directly related to your impairment(s). Examples of non-deductible items are routine annual physical examinations, optician services (unrelated to a disabling visual impairment) and dental examinations.

(6) Payments for similar items and services—

(i) General. If you are required to utilize items and services not specified in paragraphs (c)(1) through (5) of this section but which are directly related to your impairment(s) and which you need to work, their costs are deductible. Examples of such items and services are medical supplies and services not discussed above, the purchase and maintenance of a dog guide which you need to work, and transportation.

(ii) Medical supplies and services not described above. We will deduct payments you make for expendable medical supplies, such as incontinence pads, catheters, bandages, elastic stockings, face masks, irrigating kits, and disposable sheets and bags. We will also deduct payments you make for physical therapy which you require because of your impairment(s) and which you need in order to work.

(iii) Payments for transportation costs. We will deduct transportation costs in these situations:

(A) Your impairment(s) requires that in order to get to work you need a vehicle that has structural or operational modifications. The modifications must be critical to your operation or use of the vehicle and directly related to your impairment(s). We will deduct the costs of the modifications, but not the cost of the vehicle. We will also deduct a mileage allowance for the trip to and from work. The allowance will be based on data compiled by the Federal Highway Administration relating to vehicle operating costs.

(B) Your impairment(s) requires you to use driver assistance, taxicabs or other hired vehicles in order to work. We will deduct amounts paid to the driver and, if your own vehicle is used, we will also deduct a mileage allowance, as provided in paragraph (c)(6)(iii)(A) of this section, for the trip to and from work.

(C) Your impairment(s) prevents your taking available public transportation to and from work and you must drive your (unmodified) vehicle to work. If we can verify through your physician or other sources that the need to drive is caused by your impairment(s) (and not due to the unavailability of public transportation), we will deduct a mileage allowance, as provided in paragraph (c)(6)(iii)(A) of this section, for the trip to and from work.

(7) Payments for installing, maintaining, and repairing deductible items. If the device, equipment, appliance, etc., that you utilize qualifies as a deductible item as described in paragraphs (c)(2), (3), (4) and (6) of this section, the costs directly related to installing, maintaining and repairing these items are also deductible. (The costs which are associated with modifications to a vehicle are deductible. Except for a mileage allowance, as provided for in paragraph (c)(6)(iii) of this section, the costs which are associated with the vehicle itself are not deductible.)

(d) When expenses may be deducted—

(1) Effective date. To be deductible an expense must be incurred after November 30, 1980. An expense may be considered incurred after that date if it is paid thereafter even though pursuant to a contract or other arrangement entered into before December 1, 1980.

(2) Payments for services. A payment you make for services may be deducted if the services are received while you are working and the payment is made in a month you are working. We consider you to be working even though you must leave work temporarily to receive the services.

(3) Payments for items. A payment you make toward the cost of a deductible item (regardless of when it is acquired) may be deducted if payment is made in a month you are working. See paragraph (e)(4) of this section when purchases are made in anticipation of work.

(e) How expenses are allocated—

(1) Recurring expenses. You may pay for services on a regular periodic basis, or you may purchase an item on credit and pay for it in regular periodic installments or you may rent an item. If so, each payment you make for the services and each payment you make toward the purchase or rental (including interest) is deductible in the month it is made.

Example: B starts work in October 1981 at which time she purchases a medical device at a cost of $4,800 plus interest charges of $720. Her monthly payments begin in October. She earns and receives $400 a month. The term of the installment contract is 48 months. No downpayment is made. The monthly allowable deduction for the item would be $115 ($5520 divided by 48) for each month of work during the 48 months.

(2) Nonrecurring expenses. Part or all of your expenses may not be recurring. For example, you may make a one-time payment in full for an item or service or make a downpayment. If you are working when you make the payment we will either deduct the entire amount in the month you pay it or allocate the amount over a 12 consecutive month period beginning with the month of payment, whichever you select.

Example: A begins working in October 1981 and earns $525 a month. In the same month he purchases and pays for a deductible item at a cost of $250. In this situation we could allow a $250 deduction for October 1981, reducing A's earnings below the SGA level for that month.

If A's earnings had been $15 above the SGA earnings amount, A probably would select the option of projecting the $250 payment over the 12-month period, October 1981–September 1982, giving A an allowable deduction of $20.83 a month for each month of work during that period. This deduction would reduce A's earnings below the SGA level for 12 months.

(3) Allocating downpayments. If you make a downpayment we will, if you choose, make a separate calculation for the downpayment in order to provide for uniform monthly deductions. In these situations we will determine the total payment that you will make over a 12 consecutive month period beginning with the month of the downpayment and allocate that amount over the 12 months. Beginning with the 13th month, the regular monthly payment will be deductible. This allocation process will be for a shorter period if your regular monthly payments will extend over a period of less than 12 months.

Example 1. C starts working in October 1981, at which time he purchases special equipment at a cost of $4,800, paying $1,200 down. The balance of $3,600, plus interest of $540, is to be repaid in 36 installments of $115 a month beginning November 1981. C earns $500 a month. He chooses to have the downpayment allocated. In this situation we would allow a deduction of $205.42 a month for each month of work during the period October 1981 through September 1982. After September 1982, the deduction amount would be the regular monthly payment of $115 for each month of work during the remaining installment period.

Explanation:

Downpayment in 10/81	$1,200	
Monthly payments 11/81 through 09/82..........................	1,265	
	12) 2,465	=$205.42

Example 2. D, while working, buys a deductible item in July 1981, paying $1,450 down. However, his first monthly payment of $125 is not due until September 1981. D chooses to have the downpayment allocated. In this situation we would allow a deduction of $225 a month for each month of work during the period July 1981 through June 1982. After June 1982, the deduction amount would be the regular monthly payment of $125 for each month of work.

Explanation:

Downpayment in 07/81	$1,450	
Monthly payments 09/81 through 06/82..........................	1,250	
	12) 2,700	=$225

(4) Payments made in anticipation of work. A payment toward the cost of a deductible item that you made in any of the 11 months preceding the month you started working will be taken into account in determining your impairment-related work expenses. When an item is paid for in full during the 11 months preceding the month you started working the payment will be allocated over the 12–consecutive month period beginning with the month of the payment. However, the only portion of the payment which may be deductible is the portion allocated to the month work begins and the following months. For example, if an item is purchased 3 months before the month work began and is paid for with a one-time payment of $600, the deductible amount would be $450 ($600 divided by 12, multiplied by 9). Installment payments (including a downpayment) that you made for a particular item during the 11 months preceding the month you started working will be totaled and considered to have been made in the month of your first payment for that item within this 11 month period. The sum of these payments will be allocated over the 12–consecutive month period beginning with the month of your first payment (but never earlier than 11 months before the month work began). However, the only portion of the total which may be deductible is the portion allocated to the month work begins and the following months. For example, if an item is purchased 3 months before the month work began and is paid for in 3 monthly installments of $200 each, the total payment of $600 will be considered to have been made in the month of the first payment, that is, 3 months before the month work began. The deductible amount would be $450 ($600 divided by 12, multiplied by 9). The amount, as determined by these formulas, will then be considered to have been paid in the first month of work. We will deduct either this entire amount in the first month of work or allocate it over a 12–consecutive month period beginning with the first month of work, whichever you select. In the

above examples, the individual would have the choice of having the entire $450 deducted in the first month of work or of having $37.50 a month ($450 divided by 12) deducted for each month that he works over a 12–consecutive month period, beginning with the first month of work. To be deductible the payments must be for durable items such as medical devices, prostheses, work-related equipment, residential modifications, non-medical appliances and vehicle modifications. Payments for services and expendable items such as drugs, oxygen, diagnostic procedures, medical supplies and vehicle operating costs are not deductible for purposes of this paragraph.

(f) Limits on deductions.

(1) We will deduct the actual amounts you pay towards your impairment-related work expenses unless the amounts are unreasonable. With respect to durable medical equipment, prosthetic devices, medical services, and similar medically-related items and services, we will apply the prevailing charges under Medicare (part B of title XVIII, Health Insurance for the Aged and Disabled) to the extent that this information is readily available. Where the Medicare guides are used, we will consider the amount that you pay to be reasonable if it is no more than the prevailing charge for the same item or service under the Medicare guidelines. If the amount you actually pay is more than the prevailing charge for the same item under the Medicare guidelines, we will deduct from your earnings the amount you paid to the extent you establish that the amount is consistent with the standard or normal charge for the same or similar item or service in your community. For items and services that are not listed in the Medicare guidelines, and for items and services that are listed in the Medicare guidelines but for which such guides cannot be used because the information is not readily available, we will consider the amount you pay to be reasonable if it does not exceed the standard or normal charge for the same or similar item(s) or service(s) in your community.

(2) Impairment-related work expenses are not deducted in computing your earnings for purposes of determining whether your work was "services" as described in § 404.1592(b).

(3) The decision as to whether you performed substantial gainful activity in a case involving impairment-related work expenses for items or services necessary for you to work generally will be based upon your "earnings" and not on the value of "services" you rendered. (See §§ 404.1574(b)(6)(i) and (ii), and 404.1575(a)). This is not necessarily so, however, if you are in a position to control or manipulate your earnings.

(4) The amount of the expenses to be deducted must be determined in a uniform manner in both the disability insurance and SSI programs.

(5) No deduction will be allowed to the extent that any other source has paid or will pay for an item or service. No deduction will be allowed to the extent that you have been, could be, or will be, reimbursed for payments you made. (See paragraph (b)(3) of this section.)

(6) The provisions described in the foregoing paragraphs of this section are effective with respect to expenses incurred on and after December 1, 1980, although expenses incurred after November 1980 as a result of contractual or other arrangements entered into before December 1980, are deductible. For months before December 1980 we will deduct impairment-related work expenses from your earnings only to the extent they exceeded the normal work-related expenses you would have had if you did not have your impairment(s). We will not deduct expenses, however, for those things which you needed even when you were not working.

(g) Verification. We will verify your need for items or services for which deductions are claimed, and the amount of the charges for those items or services. You will also be asked to provide proof that you paid for the items or services.

[48 FR 21936, May 16, 1983]

WIDOWS, WIDOWERS, AND SURVIVING DIVORCED SPOUSES

§ 404.1577 Disability defined for widows, widowers, and surviving divorced spouses for monthly benefits payable for months prior to January 1991.

For monthly benefits payable for months prior to January 1991, the law provides that to be entitled to a widow's or widower's benefit as a disabled widow, widower, or surviving divorced spouse, you must have a medically determinable physical or mental impairment which can be expected to result in death or has lasted or can be expected to last for a continuous period of not less than 12 months. The impairment(s) must have been of a level of severity to prevent a person from doing any gainful activity. To determine whether you were disabled, we consider only your physical or mental impairment(s). We do not consider your age, education, and work experience. We also do not consider certain felony-related and prison-related impairments, as explained in § 404.1506. (For monthly benefits payable for months after December 1990, see § 404.1505(a).)

[45 FR 55584, Aug. 20, 1980, as amended at 47 FR 12162, Mar. 22, 1982; 48 FR 5715, Feb. 8, 1983; 57 FR 30120, July 8, 1992]

§ 404.1578 How we determine disability for widows, widowers, and surviving divorced spouses for monthly benefits payable for months prior to January 1991.

(a) For monthly benefits payable for months prior to January 1991, we will find that you were disabled and pay you widow's or widower's benefits as a widow, widower, or surviving divorced spouse if—

(1) Your impairment(s) had specific clinical findings that were the same as those for any impairment in the Listing of Impairments in appendix 1 of this subpart or were medically equivalent to those for any impairment shown there;

(2) Your impairment(s) met the duration requirement.

(b) However, even if you met the requirements in paragraphs (a)(1) and (2) of this section, we will not find you disabled if you were doing substantial gainful activity.

[45 FR 55584, Aug. 20, 1980, as amended at 47 FR 12162, Mar. 22, 1982; 57 FR 30121, July 8, 1992]

§ 404.1579 How we will determine whether your disability continues or ends.

(a) General.

(1) The rules for determining whether disability continues for widow's or widower's monthly benefits for months after December 1990 are discussed in §§ 404.1594 through 404.1598. The rules for determining whether disability continues for monthly benefits for months prior to January 1991 are discussed in paragraph (a)(2) of this section and paragraphs (b) through (h) of this section.

(2) If you are entitled to disability benefits as a disabled widow, widower, or surviving divorced spouse, and we must decide whether your disability continued or ended for monthly benefits for months prior to January 1991, there are a number of factors we consider in deciding whether your disability continued. We must determine if there has been any medical improvement in your impairment(s) and, if so, whether this medical improvement is related to your ability to work. If your impairment(s) has not so medically improved, we must address whether one or more exceptions applies. If medical improvement related to your ability to work has not occurred and no exception applies, your benefits will continue. Even where medical improvement related to your ability to work has occurred or an exception applies, in most cases (see paragraph (e) of this section for exceptions) before we can find that you are no longer disabled, we must also show that your impairment(s), as shown by current medical evidence, is no longer deemed, under appendix 1 of this subpart, sufficient to preclude you from engaging in gainful activity.

(b) Terms and definitions. There are several terms and definitions which are important to know in order to understand how we review your claim to determine whether your disability continues.

(1) Medical improvement. Medical improvement is any decrease in the medical severity of your impairment(s) which was present at the time of the most recent favorable medical decision that you were disabled or continued to be disabled. A determination that there has been a decrease in medical severity must be based on improvement in the symptoms, signs, and/or laboratory findings associated with your impairment(s).

Example 1: You were awarded disability benefits due to a herniated nucleus pulposus which was determined to equal the level of severity contemplated by Listing 1.05.C. At the time of our prior favorable decision, you had had a laminectomy. Postoperatively, a myelogram still showed evidence of a persistent deficit in your lumbar spine. You had pain in your back, and pain and a burning sensation in your right foot and leg. There were no muscle weakness or neurological changes and a modest decrease in motion in your back and leg. When we reviewed your claim your treating physician reported that he had seen you regularly every 2 to 3 months for the past 2 years. No further myelograms had been done, complaints of pain in the back and right leg continued especially on sitting or standing for more than a short period of time. Your doctor further reported a moderately decreased range of motion in your back and right leg, but again no muscle atrophy or neurological changes were reported. Medical improvement has not occurred because there has been no decrease in the severity of your back impairment as shown by changes in symptoms, signs, or laboratory findings.

Example 2: You were awarded disability benefits due to rheumatoid arthritis of a severity as described in Listing 1.02 of appendix 1 of this subpart. At the time, laboratory findings were positive for this condition. Your doctor reported persistent swelling and tenderness of your fingers and wrists and that you complained of joint pain. Current medical evidence shows that while laboratory tests are still positive for rheumatoid arthritis, your impairment has responded favorably to therapy so that for the last year your fingers and wrists have not been significantly swollen or painful. Medical improvement has occurred because there has been a decrease in the severity of your impairment as documented by the current symptoms and signs reported by your physician. Although your impairment is subject to temporary remissions and exacerbations the improvement that has occurred has been sustained long enough to permit a finding of medical improvement. We would then determine if this medical improvement is related to your ability to work.

(2) Determining whether medical improvement is related to your ability to work. If medical improvement has occurred and the severity of the prior impairment(s) no longer meets or equals the listing section which was used in making our most recent favorable decision, we will find that the medical improvement was related to your ability to work. We make this finding because the criteria in appendix 1 of this subpart are related to ability to work because they reflect impairments which are considered severe enough to prevent a person from doing any gainful work. We must, of course, also establish that, considering all of your current impairments not just those which existed at the time of the most recent prior favorable medical decision, your condition does not meet or equal the requirements of appendix 1 before we could find that your disability has ended. If there has been any medical improvement in your impair-

ment(s), but it is not related to your ability to do work and none of the exceptions applies, your benefits will be continued.

(3) Determining whether your impairment(s) is deemed, under appendix 1 of this subpart, sufficient to preclude you from engaging in gainful activity. Even where medical improvement related to your ability to work has occurred or an exception applies, in most cases before we can find that you are no longer disabled, we must also show that your impairment(s) is no longer deemed, under appendix 1 of this subpart, sufficient to preclude you from engaging in gainful activity. All current impairments will be considered, not just the impairment(s) present at the time of our most recent favorable determination. Sections 404.1525, 404.1526, and 404.1578 set out how we will decide whether your impairment(s) meets or equals the requirements of appendix 1 of this subpart.

(4) Evidence and basis for our decision. Our decisions under this section will be made on a neutral basis without any initial inference as to the presence or absence of disability being drawn from the fact that you have previously been determined to be disabled. We will consider all evidence you submit and that we obtain from your medical sources and nonmedical sources. What constitutes "evidence" and our procedures for obtaining it are set out in §§ 404.1512 through 404.1518. Our determination regarding whether your disability continues will be made on the basis of the weight of the evidence.

(5) Point of comparison. For purposes of determining whether medical improvement has occurred, we will compare the current severity of that impairment(s) which was present at the time of the most recent favorable medical decision that you were disabled or continued to be disabled to the medical severity of that impairment(s) at that time. If medical improvement has occurred, we will determine whether the medical improvement is related to your ability to do work based on this previously existing impairment(s). The most recent favorable medical decision is the latest decision involving a consideration of the medical evidence and the issue of whether you were disabled or continued to be disabled which became final.

(c) Determining medical improvement and its relationship to your ability to do work. Paragraphs (b)(1) and (2) of this section discuss what we mean by medical improvement and how we determine whether medical improvement is related to your ability to work.

(1) Medical improvement. Medical improvement is any decrease in the medical severity of impairment(s) present at the time of the most recent favorable medical decision that you were disabled or continued to be disabled. Whether medical improvement has occurred is determined by a comparison of prior and current medical evidence which must show that there have been changes (improvement) in the symptoms, signs or laboratory findings associated with that impairment(s).

(2) Determining whether medical improvement is related to ability to work. If there is a decrease in medical severity as shown by the signs, symptoms and laboratory findings, we then must determine if it is related to your ability to do work, as explained in paragraph (b)(2) of this section. In determining if the medical improvement that has occurred is related to your ability to work, we will assess whether the previously existing impairments still meet or equal the level of severity contemplated by the same listing section in appendix 1 of this subpart which was used in making our most recent favorable decision. Appendix 1 of this subpart describes impairments which, if severe enough, affect a person's ability to work. If the appendix level of severity is met or equaled, the individual is deemed, in the absence of evidence of the contrary, to be unable to engage in gainful activity. If there has been medical improvement to the degree that the requirement of the listing section is no longer met or equaled, then the medical improvement is related to your ability to work. Unless an objective assessment shows that the listing requirement is no longer met or equaled based on actual changes shown by the medical evidence, the medical improvement that has occurred will not be considered to be related to your ability to work.

(3) Prior file cannot be located. If the prior file cannot be located, we will first determine whether your current impairment(s) is deemed, under appendix 1 of this subpart, sufficient to preclude you from engaging in gainful activity. (In this way, we will be able to determine that your disability continues at the earliest time without addressing the issue of reconstructing prior evidence which can be a lengthy process.) If so, your benefits will continue unless one of the second group of exceptions applies (see paragraph (e) of this section). If not, we will determine whether an attempt should be made to reconstruct those portions of the file that were relevant to our most recent favorable medical decision (e.g., medical evidence from treating sources and the results of consultative examinations). This determination will consider the potential availability of old records in light of their age, whether the source of the evidence is still in operation, etc.; and whether reconstruction efforts will yield a complete record of the basis for the most recent favorable medical decision. If relevant parts of the prior record are not reconstructed either because it is determined not to attempt reconstruction or because such efforts fail, medical improvement cannot be found. The documentation of your current impairments will provide a basis for any future reviews. If the missing file is later found, it may serve as a basis for reopening any decision under this section in accordance with the rules in § 404.988.

(4) Impairment(s) subject to temporary remission. In some cases the evidence shows that an individual's

impairment is subject to temporary remission. In assessing whether medical improvement has occurred in persons with this type of impairment, we will be careful to consider the longitudinal history of the impairment(s), including the occurrence of prior remissions, and prospects for future worsening of the impairment(s). Improvement in such impairments that is only temporary will not warrant a finding of medical improvement.

(5) Applicable listing has been revised since the most recent favorable medical decision. When determining whether any medical improvement is related to your ability to work, we use the same listing section in appendix 1 of this subpart which was used to make our prior favorable decision. We will use the listing as it appeared at the time of the prior decision, even where the requirement(s) of the listing was subsequently changed. The current revised listing requirement will be used if we determine that you have medically improved and it is necessary to determine whether you are now considered unable to engage in gainful activity.

(d) First group of exceptions to medical improvement. The law provides for certain limited situations when your disability can be found to have ended even though medical improvement has not occurred, if your impairment(s) is no longer considered, under appendix 1 of this subpart, sufficient to preclude you from engaging in gainful activity. These exceptions to medical improvement are intended to provide a way of finding that a person is no longer disabled in those limited situations where, even though there has been no decrease in severity of the impairment(s), evidence shows that the person should no longer be considered disabled or never should have been considered disabled. If one of these exceptions applies, before we can find you are no longer disabled, we must also show that, taking all your current impairment(s) into account, not just those that existed at the time of our most recent favorable medical decision, your impairment(s) is no longer deemed, under appendix 1 of this subpart, sufficient to preclude you from engaging in gainful activity. As part of the review process, you will be asked about any medical therapy you received or are receiving. Your answers and the evidence gathered as a result as well as all other evidence, will serve as the basis for the finding that an exception does or does not apply.

(1) Substantial evidence shows that you are the beneficiary of advances in medical therapy or technology (related to your ability to work). Advances in medical therapy or technology are improvements in treatment or rehabilitative methods which have favorably affected the severity of your impairment(s). We will apply this exception when substantial evidence shows that you have been the beneficiary of services which reflect these advances and they have favorably affected the severity of your impairment(s). This decision will be based on new medical evidence. In many instances, an advanced medical therapy or technology will result in a decrease in severity as shown by symptoms, signs and laboratory findings which will meet the definition of medical improvement. This exception will, therefore, see very limited application.

(2) Substantial evidence shows that based on new or improved diagnostic or evaluative techniques your impairment(s) is not as disabling as it was considered to be at the time of the most recent favorable decision. Changing methodologies and advances in medical and other diagnostic or evaluative techniques have given, and will continue to give, rise to improved methods for measuring and documenting the effect of various impairments on the ability to do work. Where, by such new or improved methods, substantial evidence shows that your impairment(s) is not as severe as was determined at the time of our most recent favorable medical decision, such evidence may serve as a basis for finding that you are no longer disabled, if your impairment(s) is no longer deemed, under appendix 1 of this subpart, sufficient to preclude you from engaging in gainful activity. In order to be used under this exception, however, the new or improved techniques must have become generally available after the date of our most recent favorable medical decision.

(i) How we will determine which methods are new or improved techniques and when they become generally available. New or improved diagnostic techniques or evaluations will come to our attention by several methods. In reviewing cases, we often become aware of new techniques when their results are presented as evidence. Such techniques and evaluations are also discussed and acknowledged in medical literature by medical professional groups and other governmental entities. Through these sources, we develop listings of new techniques and when they become generally available. For example, we will consult the Health Care Financing Administration for its experience regarding when a technique is recognized for payment under Medicare and when they began paying for the technique.

(ii) How you will know which methods are new or improved techniques and when they become generally available. We will let you know which methods we consider to be new or improved techniques and when they become available through two vehicles.

(A) Some of the future changes in the Listing of Impairments in appendix 1 of this subpart will be based on new or improved diagnostic or evaluative techniques. Such listing changes will clearly state this fact as they are published as Notices of Proposed Rulemaking and the new or improved technique will be considered generally available as of the date of the final publication of that particular listing in the Federal Register.

(B) A cumulative list since 1970 of new or improved diagnostic techniques or evaluations, how they changed the evaluation of the applicable impairment and the month and year they became generally available, will be published in the Notices section of the Federal Register. Included will be any changes in the Listing of Impairments published in the Code of Federal Regulations since 1970 which are reflective of new or improved techniques. No cases will be processed under this exception until this cumulative listing is so published. Subsequent changes to the list will be published periodically. The period will be determined by the volume of changes needed.

Example: The electrocardiographic exercise test has replaced the Master's 2–step test as a measurement of heart function since the time of your last favorable medical decision. Current evidence could show that your condition, which was previously evaluated based on the Master's 2–step test, is not now as disabling as was previously thought. If, taking all your current impairments into account, you are now able to engage in gainful activity, this exception would be used to find that you are no longer disabled even if medical improvement has not occurred.

(3) Substantial evidence demonstrates that any prior disability decision was in error. We will apply the exception to medical improvement based on error if substantial evidence (which may be evidence on the record at the time any prior determination of the entitlement to benefits based on disability was made, or newly obtained evidence which relates to that determination) demonstrates that a prior determination was in error. A prior determination will be found in error only if:

(i) Substantial evidence shows on its face that the decision in question should not have been made (e.g., the evidence in your file such as pulmonary function study values was misread or an adjudicative standard such as a listing in appendix 1 of this subpart was misapplied).

Example: You were granted benefits when it was determined that your epilepsy met Listing 11.02. This listing calls for a finding of major motor seizures more frequently than once a month as documented by EEG evidence and by a detailed description of a typical seizure pattern. A history of either diurnal episodes or nocturnal episodes with residuals interfering with daily activities is also required. On review, it is found that a history of the frequency of your seizures showed that they occurred only once or twice a year. The prior decision would be found to be in error, and whether you were still considered to be disabled would be based on whether your current impairment(s) meets or equals the requirements of appendix 1 of this subpart.

(ii) At the time of the prior evaluation, required and material evidence of the severity of your impairment(s) was missing. That evidence becomes available upon review, and substantial evidence demonstrates that had such evidence been present at the time of the prior determination, disability would not have been found.

(iii) Substantial evidence which is new evidence which relates to the prior determination (of allowance or continuance) refutes the conclusions that were based upon the prior evidence (e.g., a tumor thought to be malignant was later shown to have actually been benign). Substantial evidence must show that had the new evidence (which relates to the prior determination) been considered at the time of the prior decision, the claim would not have been allowed or continued. A substitution of current judgment for that used in the prior favorable decision will not be the basis for applying this exception.

Example: You were previously granted disability benefits on the basis of diabetes mellitus which the prior adjudicator believed was equivalent to the level of severity contemplated in the Listing of Impairments. The prior record shows that you had "brittle" diabetes for which you were taking insulin. Your urine was 3+ for sugar, and you alleged occasional hypoglycemic attacks caused by exertion. On review, symptoms, signs and laboratory findings are unchanged. The current adjudicator believes, however, that your impairment does not equal the severity contemplated by the listings. Error cannot be found because it would represent a substitution of current judgment for that of the prior adjudicator that your impairment equaled a listing.

(iv) The exception for error will not be applied retroactively under the conditions set out above unless the conditions for reopening the prior decision (see § 404.988) are met.

(4) You are currently engaging in substantial gainful activity. If you are currently engaging in substantial gainful activity before we determine whether you are no longer disabled because of your work activity, we will consider whether you are entitled to a trial work period as set out in § 404.1592. We will find that your disability has ended in the month in which you demonstrated your ability to engage in substantial gainful activity (following completion of a trial work period, where it applies). This exception does not apply in determining whether you continue to have a disabling impairment (§ 404.1511) for purposes of deciding your eligibility for a reentitlement period (§ 404.1592a).

(e) Second group of exceptions to medical improvement. In addition to the first group of exceptions to medical improvement, the following exceptions may result in a determination that you are no longer disabled. In these situations the decision will be made without a determination that you have medically improved or can engage in gainful activity.

(1) A prior determination or decision was fraudulently obtained. If we find that any prior favorable determination or decision was obtained by fraud, we may find that you are not disabled. In addition, we may reopen your claim under the rules in § 404.988. In determining whether a prior favorable determination or decision was fraudulently obtained, we will take into account any physical, mental, educational, or linguistic limitations (including any lack of facility with the English language) which you may have had at the time.

(2) You do not cooperate with us. If there is a question about whether you continue to be disabled and we ask you to give us medical or other evidence or to go for a physical or mental examination by a certain date, we will find that your disability has ended if you fail, without good cause, to do what we ask. Section 404.911 explains the factors we consider and how we will determine generally whether you have good cause for failure to cooperate. In addition, § 404.1518 discusses how we determine whether you have good cause for failing to attend a consultative examination. The month in which your disability ends will be the first month in which you failed to do what we asked.

(3) We are unable to find you. If there is a question about whether you continue to be disabled and we are unable to find you to resolve the question, we will determine that your disability has ended. The month your disability ends will be the first month in which the question arose and we could not find you.

(4) You fail to follow prescribed treatment which would be expected to restore your ability to engage in gainful activity. If treatment has been prescribed for you which would be expected to restore your ability to work, you must follow that treatment in order to be paid benefits. If you are not following that treatment and you do not have good cause for failing to follow that treatment, we will find that your disability has ended (see § 404.1530(c)). The month your disability ends will be the first month in which you failed to follow the prescribed treatment.

(f) Evaluation steps. To assure that disability reviews are carried out in a uniform manner, that decisions of continuing disability can be made in the most expeditious and administratively efficient way, and that any decisions to stop disability benefits are made objectively, neutrally and are fully documented, we will follow specific steps in reviewing the question of whether your disability continues. Our review may stop and benefits may be continued at any point if we determine there is sufficient evidence to find that you are still unable to engage in gainful activity. The steps are:

(1) Are you engaging in substantial gainful activity? If you are (and any applicable trial work period has been completed), we will find disability to have ended.

(2) If you are not, has there been medical improvement as defined in paragraph (b)(1) of this section? If there has been medical improvement as shown by a decrease in medical severity, see step (3). If there has been no decrease in medical severity, there has been no medical improvement. (see step (4).)

(3) If there has been medical improvement, we must determine (in accordance with paragraph (b)(2) of this section) whether it is related to your ability to work. If medical improvement is not related to your ability to do work, see step (4). If medical improvement is related to your ability to do work, see step (5).

(4) If we found at step (2) that there has been no medical improvement or if we found at step (3) that the medical improvement is not related to your ability to work, we consider whether any of the exceptions in paragraphs (d) and (e) of this section apply. If none of them apply, your disability will be found to continue. If one of the first group of exceptions to medical improvement (see paragraph (d) of this section) applies, we will proceed to step (5). If an exception from the second group of exceptions to medical improvement applies, your disability will be found to have ended. The second group of exceptions to medical improvement may be considered at any point in this process.

(5) If medical improvement is related to your ability to work or if one of the first group of exceptions to medical improvement applies, we will determine (considering all your impairments) whether the requirements of appendix 1 of this subpart are met or equaled. If your impairment(s) meets or equals the requirements of appendix 1 of this subpart, your disability will be found to continue. If not, your disability will be found to have ended.

(g) The month in which we will find you are no longer disabled. If the evidence shows that you are no longer disabled, we will find that your disability ended in the earliest of the following months—

(1) The month the evidence shows you are no longer disabled under the rules set out in this section, and you were disabled only for a specified period of time in the past;

(2) The month the evidence shows you are no longer disabled under the rules set out in this section, but not earlier than the month in which we mail you a notice saying that the information we have shows that you are not disabled;

(3) The month in which you demonstrated your ability to engage in substantial gainful activity (following completion of a trial work period); however, we may pay you benefits for certain months in and after the reentitlement period which follows the trial work period. (See § 404.1592 for a discussion of the trial work period, § 404.1592a for a discussion of the reentitlement period, and § 404.337 for when your benefits will end.);

(4) The month in which you return to full-time work, with no significant medical restrictions and acknowledge that medical improvement has occurred, as long as we expected your impairment(s) to improve (see § 404.1591);

(5) The first month in which you failed to do what we asked, without good cause when the rule set out in paragraph (e)(2) of this section applies;

(6) The first month in which the question of continuing disability arose and we could not find you, when the rule set out in paragraph (e)(3) of this section applies;

(7) The first month in which you failed to follow prescribed treatment without good cause, when the rule set out in paragraph (e)(4) of this section applies; or

(8) The first month you were told by your physician that you could return to work provided there is no substantial conflict between your physician's and your statements regarding your awareness of your capacity for work and the earlier date is supported by medical evidence.

(h) Before we stop your benefits. Before we determine you are no longer disabled, we will give you a chance to explain why we should not do so. Sections 404.1595 and 404.1597 describe your rights (including appeal rights) and the procedures we will follow.

[45 FR 55584, Aug. 20, 1980, as amended at 47 FR 12162, March 22, 1982; 49 FR 22272, May 29, 1984; 50 FR 50126, Dec. 6, 1985; 51 FR 7063, Feb. 28, 1986; 51 FR 16015, April 30, 1986; 57 FR 30121, July 8, 1992; 59 FR 1635, Jan. 12, 1994; 82 FR 5871, Jan. 18, 2017]

BLINDNESS

§ 404.1581 Meaning of blindness as defined in the law.

We will consider you blind under the law for a period of disability and for payment of disability insurance benefits if we determine that you are statutorily blind. Statutory blindness is defined in the law as central visual acuity of 20/200 or less in the better eye with the use of correcting lens. An eye which has a limitation in the field of vision so that the widest diameter of the visual field subtends an angle no greater than 20 degrees is considered to have a central visual acuity of 20/200 or less. Your blindness must meet the duration requirement in § 404.1509. We do not consider certain felony-related and prison-related impairments, as explained in § 404.1506.

[45 FR 55584, Aug. 20, 1980, as amended at 48 FR 5715, Feb. 8, 1983]

§ 404.1582 A period of disability based on blindness.

If we find that you are blind and you meet the insured status requirement, we may establish a period of disability for you regardless of whether you can do substantial gainful activity. A period of disability protects your earnings record under Social Security so that the time you are disabled will not count against you in determining whether you will have worked long enough to qualify for benefits and the amount of your benefits. However, you will not necessarily be entitled to receive disability insurance cash benefits even though you are blind. If you are a blind person under age 55, you must be unable to do any substantial gainful activity in order to be paid disability insurance cash benefits.

§ 404.1583 How we determine disability for blind persons who are age 55 or older.

We will find that you are eligible for disability insurance benefits even though you are still engaging in substantial gainful activity, if—

(a) You are blind;

(b) You are age 55 or older; and

(c) You are unable to use the skills or abilities like the ones you used in any substantial gainful activity which you did regularly and for a substantial period of time. (However, you will not be paid any cash benefits for any month in which you are doing substantial gainful activity.)

§ 404.1584 Evaluation of work activity of blind people.

(a) General. If you are blind (as explained in § 404.1581), we will consider the earnings from the work you are doing to determine whether or not you should be paid cash benefits.

(b) Under Age 55. If you are under age 55, we will evaluate the work you are doing using the guides in paragraph (d) of this section to determine whether or not your work shows that you are doing substantial gainful activity. If you are not doing substantial gainful activity, we will pay you cash benefits. If you are doing substantial gainful activity, we will not pay you cash benefits. However, you will be given a period of disability as described in subpart D of this part.

(c) Age 55 or older. If you are age 55 or older, we will evaluate your work using the guides in paragraph (d) of this section to determine whether or not your work shows that you are doing substantial gainful activity. If you have not shown this ability, we will pay you cash benefits. If you have shown an ability to do substantial gainful activity, we will evaluate your work activity to find out how your work compares with the work you did before. If the skills and abilities of your new work are about the same as those you used in the work you did before, we will not pay you cash benefits. However, if your new work requires skills and abilities which are less than or different than those you used in the work you did before, we will pay you cash benefits, but not for any month in which you actually perform substantial gainful activity.

(d) Evaluation of earnings—

(1) Earnings that will ordinarily show that you have engaged in substantial gainful activity. We will ordinarily consider that your earnings from your work activities show that you have engaged in substantial gainful activity if your monthly earnings average more than the amount(s) shown in paragraphs (d)(2) and (3) of this section. We will apply §§ 404.1574(a)(2), 404.1575(c), and 404.1576 in determining the amount of your average earnings.

(2) Substantial gainful activity guidelines for taxable years before 1978. For work activity performed in taxable years before 1978, the average earnings per month that we ordinarily consider enough to show that you have done substantial gainful activity are the same for blind people as for others. See § 404.1574(b)(2) for the earnings guidelines for other than blind individuals.

(3) Substantial gainful activity guidelines for taxable years beginning 1978. For taxable years beginning 1978, if you are blind, the law provides different earnings guidelines for determining if your earnings from your work activities are substantial gainful activity. Ordinarily, we consider your work to be substantial gainful activity, if your average monthly earnings are more than those shown in Table I. For years after 1977 and before 1996, increases in the substantial gainful activity guideline were linked to increases in the monthly exempt amount under the retirement earnings test for individuals aged 65 to 69. Beginning with 1996, increases in the substantial gainful activity amount have depended only on increases in the national average wage index.

TABLE I

Over	In year(s)
$ 334	1978
$ 375	1979
$ 417	1980
$ 459	1981
$ 500	1982
$ 550	1983
$ 580	1984
$ 610	1985
$ 650	1986
$ 680	1987
$ 700	1988
$ 740	1989
$ 780	1990
$ 810	1991
$ 850	1992
$ 880	1993
$ 930	1994
$ 940	1995
$ 960	1996
$1,000	1997
$1,050	1998
$1,110	1999
$1,170	2000

[48 FR 21939, May 16, 1983; 65 FR 42786, July 11, 2000]

§ 404.1585 Trial work period for persons age 55 or older who are blind.

If you become eligible for disability benefits even though you were doing substantial gainful activity because you are blind and age 55 or older, you are entitled to a trial work period if—

(a) You later return to substantial gainful activity that requires skills or abilities comparable to those required in the work you regularly did before you became blind or became 55 years old, whichever is later; or

(b) Your last previous work ended because of an impairment and the current work requires a significant vocational adjustment.

§ 404.1586 Why and when we will stop your cash benefits.

(a) When you are not entitled to benefits. If you become entitled to disability cash benefits as a statutorily blind person, we will find that you are no longer entitled to benefits beginning with the earliest of—

(1) The month your vision, based on current medical evidence, does not meet the definition of blindness and your disability does not continue under the rules in § 404.1594 and you were disabled only for a specified period of time in the past;

(2) The month your vision, based on current medical evidence, does not meet the definition of blindness and your disability does not continue under the rules in § 404.1594, but not earlier than the month in which we mail you a notice saying that the information we have shows that you are not disabled;

(3) If you are under age 55, the month in which you demonstrated your ability to engage in substantial gainful activity (following completion of a trial work period); however, we may pay you benefits for certain months in and after the reentitlement period which follows the trial work period. (See § 404.1592a for a discussion of the reentitlement period, and § 404.316 on when your benefits will end.); or

(4) If you are age 55 or older, the month (following completion of a trial work period) when your work activity shows you are able to use, in substantial gainful activity, skills and abilities comparable to those of some gainful activity which you did with some regularity and over a substantial period of time. The skills and abilities are compared to the activity you did prior to age 55 or prior to becoming blind, whichever is later.

(b) If we find that you are not entitled to disability cash benefits. If we find that you are not entitled to disability cash benefits on the basis of your work activity but your visual impairment is sufficiently severe to meet the definition of blindness, the period of disability that we established for you will continue.

(c) If you do not follow prescribed treatment. If treatment has been prescribed for you that can restore your ability to work, you must follow that treatment in order to be paid benefits. If you are not following that treatment and you do not have a good reason for failing to follow that treatment (see § 404.1530(c)), we will find that your disability has ended. The month in which your disability will be found to have ended will be the first month in which you failed to follow the prescribed treatment.

(d) If you do not cooperate with us. If we ask you to give us medical or other evidence or to go for a medical examination by a certain date, we will find that your disability has ended if you fail, without good cause, to do what we ask. Section 404.911 explains the factors we consider and how we will determine generally whether you have good cause for failure to cooperate. In addition, § 404.1518 discusses how we determine whether you have good cause for failing to attend a consultative examination. The month in which your disability will be found to have ended will be the month in which you failed to do what we asked.

(e) If we are unable to find you. If there is a question about whether you continue to be disabled by blindness and we are unable to find you to resolve the question, we will find that your disability, has ended. The month it ends will be the first month in which the question arose and we could not find you.

(f) Before we stop your benefits. Before we stop your benefits or period of disability, we will give you a chance to give us your reasons why we should not stop your benefits or your period of disability. Section 404.1595 describes your rights and the procedures we will follow.

(g) If you are in an appropriate program of vocational rehabilitation services, employment services, or other support services.

(1) Your benefits, and those of your dependents, may be continued after your impairment is no longer disabling if—

(i) You are participating in an appropriate program of vocational rehabilitation services, employment services, or other support services, as described in § 404.327(a) and (b);

(ii) You began participating in the program before the date your disability ended; and

(iii) We have determined under § 404.328 that your completion of the program, or your continuation in the program for a specified period of time, will increase the likelihood that you will not have to return to the disability benefit rolls.

(2) We generally will stop your benefits with the earliest of these months—

(i) The month in which you complete the program; or

(ii) The month in which you stop participating in the program for any reason (see § 404.327(b) for what we mean by "participating" in the program); or

(iii) The month in which we determine under § 404.328 that your continuing participation in the program will no longer increase the likelihood that you will not have to return to the disability benefit rolls.

Exception to paragraph (d): In no case will we stop your benefits with a month earlier than the second month after the month your disability ends, provided that you meet all other requirements for entitlement to and payment of benefits through such month.

[45 FR 55584, Aug. 20, 1980, as amended at 47 FR 31543, July 21, 1982; 47 FR 52693, Nov. 23, 1982; 49 FR 22272, May 29, 1984; 50 FR 50130, Dec. 6, 1985; 51 FR 17617, May 14, 1986; 59 FR 1635, Jan. 12, 1994; 70 FR 36507, June 24, 2005]

§ 404.1587 Circumstances under which we may suspend and terminate your benefits before we make a determination.

(a) We will suspend your benefits if you are not disabled. We will suspend your benefits if all of the information we have clearly shows that you are not disabled and we will be unable to complete a determination soon enough to prevent us from paying you more monthly benefits than you are entitled to. This may occur when you are blind as defined in the law and age 55 or older and you have returned to work similar to work you previously performed.

(b) We will suspend your benefits if you fail to comply with our request for necessary information. We will suspend your benefits effective with the month in which it is determined in accordance with § 404.1596(b)(2)(i) that your disability benefits should stop due to your failure, without good cause (see § 404.911), to comply with our request for necessary information. When we have received the information, we will reinstate your benefits for any previous month for which they are otherwise payable, and continue with the CDR process.

(c) We will terminate your benefits. We will terminate your benefits following 12 consecutive months of benefit suspension because you did not comply with our request for information in accordance with § 404.1596(b)(2)(i). We will count the 12–month suspension period from the start of the first month that you stopped receiving benefits (see paragraph (b) of this section). This termination is effective with the start of the 13th month after the suspension began because you failed to cooperate.

[71 FR 60822, Oct. 17, 2006]

CONTINUING OR STOPPING DISABILITY

§ 404.1588 Your responsibility to tell us of events that may change your disability status.

(a) Your responsibility to report changes to us. If you are entitled to cash benefits or to a period of disability because you are disabled, you should promptly tell us if—

(1) Your condition improves;

(2) You return to work;

(3) You increase the amount of your work; or

(4) Your earnings increase.

(b) Our responsibility when you report your work to us. When you or your representative report changes in your work activity to us under paragraphs (a)(2), (a)(3), and (a)(4) of this section, we will issue a receipt to you or your representative at least until a centralized computer file that records the information that you give us and the date that you make your report is in place. Once the centralized computer file is in place, we will continue to issue receipts to you or your representative if you request us to do so.

[71 FR 66866, Nov. 17, 2006]

§ 404.1589 We may conduct a review to find out whether you continue to be disabled.

After we find that you are disabled, we must evaluate your impairment(s) from time to time to determine if you are still eligible for disability cash benefits. We call this evaluation a continuing disability review. We may begin a continuing disability review for any number of reasons including your failure to follow the provisions of the Social Security Act or these regulations. When we begin such a review, we will notify you that we are reviewing your eligibility for disability benefits, why we are reviewing your eligibility, that in medical reviews the medical improvement review standard will apply, that our review could result in the termination of your benefits, and that you have the right to submit medical and other evidence for our consideration during the continuing disability review. In doing a medical review, we will develop a complete medical history of at least the preceding 12 months in any case in which a determination is made that you are no longer under a disability. If this review shows that we should stop payment of your benefits, we will notify you in writing and give you an opportunity to appeal. In § 404.1590 we describe those events that may prompt us to review whether you continue to be disabled.

[51 FR 16825, May 7, 1986]

§ 404.1590 When and how often we will conduct a continuing disability review.

(a) General. We conduct continuing disability reviews to determine whether or not you continue to meet the disability requirements of the law. Payment of cash benefits or a period of disability ends if the medical or other evidence shows that you are not disabled as determined under the standards set out in section 223(f) of the Social Security Act. In paragraphs (b) through (g) of this section, we explain when and how often we conduct continuing disability reviews for most individuals. In paragraph (h) of this section, we explain special rules for some individuals who are participating in the Ticket to Work program. In paragraph (i) of this section, we explain special rules for some individuals who work.

(b) When we will conduct a continuing disability review. Except as provided in paragraphs (h) and (i) of this section, we will start a continuing disability review if—

(1) You have been scheduled for a medical improvement expected diary review;

(2) You have been scheduled for a periodic review (medical improvement possible or medical improvement not expected) in accordance with the provisions of paragraph (d) of this section;

(3) We need a current medical or other report to see if your disability continues. (This could happen when, for example, an advance in medical technology, such as improved treatment for Alzheimer's disease or a change in vocational therapy or technology raises a disability issue.);

(4) You return to work and successfully complete a period of trial work;

(5) Substantial earnings are reported to your wage record;

(6) You tell us that—

(i) You have recovered from your disability; or

(ii) You have returned to work;

(7) Your State Vocational Rehabilitation Agency tells us that—

(i) The services have been completed; or

(ii) You are now working; or

(iii) You are able to work;

(8) Someone in a position to know of your physical or mental condition tells us any of the following, and it appears that the report could be substantially correct:

(i) You are not disabled; or

(ii) You are not following prescribed treatment; or

(iii) You have returned to work; or

(iv) You are failing to follow the provisions of the Social Security Act or these regulations;

(9) Evidence we receive raises a question as to whether your disability continues; or

(10) You have been scheduled for a vocational reexamination diary review.

(c) Definitions. As used in this section—

Medical improvement expected diary—refers to a case which is scheduled for review at a later date because the individual's impairment(s) is expected to improve. Generally, the diary period is set for not less than 6 months or for not more than 18 months. Examples of cases likely to be scheduled for medical improvement expected diary are fractures and cases in which corrective surgery is planned and recovery can be anticipated.

Permanent impairment—medical improvement not expected—refers to a case in which any medical improvement in the person's impairment(s) is not expected. This means an extremely severe condition determined on the basis of our experience in administering the disability programs to be at least static, but more likely to be progressively disabling either by itself or by reason of impairment complications, and unlikely to improve so as to permit the individual to engage in substantial gainful activity. The interaction of the individual's age, impairment consequences and lack of recent attachment to the labor market may also be considered in determining whether an impairment is permanent. Improvement which is considered temporary under § 404.1579(c)(4) or § 404.1594(c)(3)(iv), as appropriate, will not be considered in deciding if an impairment is permanent. Examples of permanent impairments taken from the list contained in our other written guidelines which are available for public review are as follows and are not intended to be all inclusive:

(1) Parkinsonian Syndrome which has reached the level of severity necessary to meet the Listing in appendix 1.

(2) Amyotrophic Lateral Sclerosis which has reached the level of severity necessary to meet the Listing in appendix 1.

(3) Diffuse pulmonary fibrosis in an individual age 55 or over which has reached the level of severity necessary to meet the Listing in appendix 1.

(4) Amputation of leg at hip.

Nonpermanent impairment—refers to a case in which any medical improvement in the person's impairment(s) is possible. This means an impairment for which improvement cannot be predicted based on current experience and the facts of the particular case but which is not at the level of severity of an impairment that is considered permanent. Examples of nonpermanent impairments are: regional enteritis, hyperthyroidism, and chronic ulcerative colitis.

Vocational reexamination diary—refers to a case which is scheduled for review at a later date because the individual is undergoing vocational therapy, training or an educational program which may improve his or her ability to work so that the disability requirement of the law is no longer met. Generally, the diary period will be set for the length of the training, therapy, or program of education.

(d) Frequency of review. If your impairment is expected to improve, generally we will review your continuing eligibility for disability benefits at intervals from 6 months to 18 months following our most recent decision. Our notice to you about the review of your case will tell you more precisely when the review will be conducted. If your disability is not considered permanent but is such that any medical improvement in your impairment(s) cannot be accurately predicted, we will review your continuing eligibility for disability benefits at least once every 3 years. If your disability is considered permanent, we will review your continuing eligibility for benefits no less frequently than once every 7 years but no more frequently than once every 5 years. Regardless of your classification, we will conduct an immediate continuing disability review if a question of continuing disability is raised pursuant to paragraph (b) of this section.

(e) Change in classification of impairment. If the evidence developed during a continuing disability review demonstrates that your impairment has improved, is expected to improve, or has worsened since the last review, we may reclassify your impairment to reflect this change in severity. A change in the classification of your impairment will change the frequency with which we will review your case. We may also reclassify certain impairments because of improved tests, treatment, and other technical advances concerning those impairments.

(f) Review after administrative appeal. If you were found eligible to receive or to continue to receive disability benefits on the basis of a decision by an administrative law judge, the Appeals Council or a Federal court, we will not conduct a continuing disability review earlier than 3 years after that decision unless your case should be scheduled for a medical improvement expected or vocational reexamination diary review or a question of continuing disability is raised pursuant to paragraph (b) of this section.

(g) Waiver of timeframes. All cases involving a nonpermanent impairment will be reviewed by us at least once every 3 years unless we, after consultation with the State agency, determine that the requirement should be waived to ensure that only the appropriate number of cases are reviewed. The appropriate number of cases to be reviewed is to be based on such considerations as the backlog of pending reviews, the projected number of new applications, and projected staffing levels. Such waiver shall be given only after good faith effort on the part of the State to meet staffing requirements and to process the reviews on a timely basis. Availability of independent medical resources may also be a factor. A waiver in this context refers to our administrative discretion to determine the appropriate number of cases to be reviewed on a State by State basis. Therefore, your continuing disability review may be delayed longer than 3 years following our original decision or other review under certain circumstances. Such a delay would be based on our need to ensure that backlogs, reviews required to be performed by the Social Security Disability Benefits Reform Act of 1984 (Pub.L. 98–460), and new disability claims workloads are accomplished within available medical and other resources in the State agency and that such reviews are done carefully and accurately.

(h) If you are participating in the Ticket to Work program. If you are participating in the Ticket to Work program, we will not start a continuing disability review during the period in which you are using a ticket. However, this provision does not apply to reviews we conduct using the rules in §§ 404.1571–404.1576 to determine whether the work you have done shows that you are able to do substantial gainful activity and are, therefore, no longer disabled. See subpart C of part 411 of this chapter.

(i) If you are working and have received social security disability benefits for at least 24 months—

(1) General. Notwithstanding the provisions in paragraphs (b)(4), (b)(5), (b)(6)(ii), (b)(7)(ii), and (b)(8)(iii) of this section, we will not start a continuing disability review based solely on your work activity if—

(i) You are currently entitled to disability insurance benefits as a disabled worker, child's insurance benefits based on disability, or widow's or widower's insurance benefits based on disability; and

(ii) You have received such benefits for at least 24 months (see paragraph (i)(2) of this section).

(2) The 24–month requirement.

(i) The months for which you have actually received disability insurance benefits as a disabled worker, child's insurance benefits based on disability, or widow's or widower's insurance benefits based on disability that you were due, or for which you have constructively received such benefits, will count for the 24–month requirement under paragraph (i)(1)(ii) of this section, regardless of whether the months were consecutive. We will consider you to have constructively received a benefit for a month for purposes of the 24–month requirement if you were otherwise due a social security disability benefit for that month and your monthly benefit was withheld to recover an overpayment. Any month for which you were entitled to benefits but for which you did not actually or constructively receive a benefit payment will not be counted for the 24–month requirement. Months for which your social security disability benefits are continued under § 404.1597a pending reconsideration and/or a hearing before an administrative law judge on a medical cessation determination will not be counted for the 24–month requirement. If you also receive supplemental security income payments based on disability or blindness under title XVI of the Social Security Act, months for which you received only supplemental security income payments will not be counted for the 24–month requirement.

(ii) In determining whether paragraph (i)(1) of this section applies, we consider whether you have received disability insurance benefits as a disabled worker, child's insurance benefits based on disability, or widow's or widower's insurance benefits based on disability for at least 24 months as of the date on which we start a continuing disability review. For purposes of this provision, the date on which we start a continuing disability review is the date on the notice we send you that tells you that we are beginning to review your disability case.

(3) When we may start a continuing disability review even if you have received social security disability benefits for at least 24 months. Even if you meet the requirements of paragraph (i)(1) of this section, we may still start a continuing disability review for a reason(s) other than your work activity. We may start a continuing disability review if we have scheduled you for a periodic review of your continuing disability, we need a current medical or other report to see if your disability continues, we receive evidence which raises a question as to whether your disability continues, or you fail to follow the provisions of the Social Security Act or these regulations. For example, we will start a continuing disability review when you have been scheduled for a medical improvement expected diary review, and we may start a continuing disability review if you failed to report your work to us.

(4) Reviews to determine whether the work you have done shows that you are able to do substantial gainful activity. Paragraph (i)(1) of this section does not apply to reviews we conduct using the rules in §§ 404.1571–404.1576 to determine whether the work you have done shows that you are able to do substantial gainful activity and are, therefore, no longer disabled.

(5) Erroneous start of the continuing disability review. If we start a continuing disability review based solely on your work activity that results in a medical cessation determination, we will vacate the medical cessation determination if—

(i) You provide us evidence that establishes that you met the requirements of paragraph (i)(1) of this section as of the date of the start of your continuing disability review and that the start of the review was erroneous; and

(ii) We receive the evidence within 12 months of the date of the notice of the initial determination of medical cessation.

[51 FR 16825, May 7, 1986; 71 FR 66856, Nov. 17, 2006]

§ 404.1591 If your medical recovery was expected and you returned to work.

If your impairment was expected to improve and you returned to full-time work with no significant medical limitations and acknowledge that medical improvement has occurred, we may find that your disability ended in the month you returned to work. Unless there is evidence showing that your disability has not ended, we will use the medical and other evidence already in your file and the fact that you returned to full-time work without significant limitations to determine that you are no longer disabled. (If your impairment is not expected to improve, we will not ordinarily review your claim until the end of the trial work period, as described in § 404.1592.)

Example: Evidence obtained during the processing of your claim showed that you had an impairment that was expected to improve about 18 months after your disability began. We, therefore, told you that your claim would be reviewed again at that time. However, before the time arrived for your scheduled medical re-examination, you told us that you had returned to work and your impairment had improved. We investigated immediately and found that, in the 16th month after your disability began, you returned to full-time work without any significant medical restrictions. Therefore, we would find that your disability ended in the first month you returned to full-time work.

[50 FR 50130, Dec. 6, 1985]

§ 404.1592 The trial work period.

(a) Definition of the trial work period. The trial work period is a period during which you may test your ability to work and still be considered disabled. It begins and ends as described in paragraph (e) of this section. During this period, you may perform services (see paragraph (b) of this section) in as many as 9 months, but these months do not have to be consecutive. We will not consider those services as showing that your disability has ended until you have performed services in at least 9 months. However, after the trial work period has ended we will consider the work you did during the trial work period in determining whether your disability ended at any time after the trial work period.

(b) What we mean by services. When used in this section, services means any activity (whether legal or illegal), even though it is not substantial gainful activity, which is done in employment or self-employment for pay or profit, or is the kind normally done for pay or profit. We generally do not consider work done without remuneration to be services if it is done merely as therapy or training or if it is work usually done in a daily routine around the house or in self-care. We will not consider work you have done as a volunteer in the federal programs described in section 404.1574(d) in determining whether you have performed services in the trial work period.

(1) If you are an employee. We will consider your work as an employee to be services if:

(i) Before January 1, 2002, your earnings in a month were more than the amount(s) indicated in Table 1 for the year(s) in which you worked.

(ii) Beginning January 1, 2002, your earnings in a month are more than an amount determined for each calendar year to be the larger of:

(A) Such amount for the previous year, or

(B) An amount adjusted for national wage growth, calculated by multiplying $530 by the ratio of the national average wage index for the year 2 calendar years before the year for which the amount is being calculated to the national average wage index for 1999. We will then round the resulting amount to the next higher multiple of $10 where such amount is a multiple of $5 but not of $10 and to the nearest multiple of $10 in any other case.

(2) If you are self-employed. We will consider your activities as a self-employed person to be services if:

(i) Before January 1, 2002, your net earnings in a month were more than the amount(s) indicated in Table 2 of this section for the year(s) in which you worked, or the hours you worked in the business in a month are more than the number of hours per month indicated in Table 2 for the years in which you worked.

(ii) Beginning January 1, 2002, you work more than 80 hours a month in the business, or your net earnings in a month are more than an amount determined for each calendar year to be the larger of:

(A) Such amount for the previous year, or

(B) An amount adjusted for national wage growth, calculated by multiplying $530 by the ratio of the national average wage index for the year 2 calendar years before the year for which the amount is being calculated to the national average wage index for 1999. We will then round the resulting amount to the next higher multiple of $10 where such amount is a multiple of $5 but not of $10 and to the nearest multiple of $10 in any other case.

TABLE 1—FOR EMPLOYEES

For months	You earn more than
In calendar years before 1979	$ 50
In calendar years 1979-1989	75
In calendar years 1990-2000	200
In calendar year 2001	530

TABLE 2—FOR THE SELF-EMPLOYED

For months	Your net earnings are more than	Or you work in the business more than
In calendar years before 1979	$ 50	15 hours.
In calendar years 1979-1989	75	15 hours.
In calendar years 1990-2000	200	40 hours.
In calendar year 2001	530	80 hours.

(c) Limitations on the number of trial work periods. You may have only one trial work period during a period of entitlement to cash benefits.

(d) Who is and is not entitled to a trial work period.

(1) You are generally entitled to a trial work period if you are entitled to disability insurance benefits, child's benefits based on disability, or widow's or widower's or surviving divorced spouse's benefits based on disability.

(2) You are not entitled to a trial work period—

(i) If you are entitled to a period of disability but not to disability insurance benefits, and you are not entitled to any other type of disability benefit under title II of the Social Security Act (i.e., child's benefits based on disability, or widow's or widower's benefits or surviving divorced spouse's benefits based on disability);

(ii) If you perform work demonstrating the ability to engage in substantial gainful activity during any required waiting period for benefits;

(iii) If you perform work demonstrating the ability to engage in substantial gainful activity within 12 months of the onset of the impairment(s) that prevented you from performing substantial gainful activity and before the date of any notice of determination or decision finding that you are disabled; or

(iv) For any month prior to the month of your application for disability benefits (see paragraph (e) of this section).

(e) When the trial work period begins and ends. The trial work period begins with the month in which you become entitled to disability insurance benefits, to child's benefits based on disability or to widow's, widower's, or surviving divorced spouse's benefits based on disability. It cannot begin before the month in which you file your application for benefits, and for widows, widowers, and surviving divorced spouses, it cannot begin before December 1, 1980. It ends with the close of whichever of the following calendar months is the earliest:

(1) The 9th month (whether or not the months have been consecutive) in which you have performed services if that 9th month is prior to January 1992;

(2) The 9th month (whether or not the months have been consecutive and whether or not the previous 8 months of services were prior to January 1992) in which you have performed services within a period of 60 consecutive months if that 9th month is after December 1991; or

(3) The month in which new evidence, other than evidence relating to any work you did during the trial work period, shows that you are not disabled, even though you have not worked a full 9 months. We may find that your disability has ended at any time during the trial work period if the medical or other evidence shows that you are no longer disabled. See § 404.1594 for information on how we decide whether your disability continues or ends.

(f) Nonpayment of benefits for trial work period service months. See § 404.471 for an explanation of when benefits for trial work period service months are not payable if you are convicted by a Federal court of fraudulently concealing your work activity.

[45 FR 55584, Aug. 20, 1980, as amended at 49 FR 22273, May 29, 1984; 50 FR 50130, Dec. 6, 1985; 54 FR 53605, Dec. 29, 1989; 65 FR 42787, July 11, 2000; 65 FR 82910, Dec. 29, 2000; 71 FR 66866, Nov. 17, 2006]

§ 404.1592a The reentitlement period.

(a) General. The reentitlement period is an additional period after 9 months of trial work during which you may continue to test your ability to work if you have a disabling impairment, as defined in § 404.1511. If you work during the reentitlement period, we may decide that your disability has ceased because your work is substantial gainful activity and stop your benefits. However, if, after the month for which we found that your disability ceased because you performed substantial gainful activity, you stop engaging in substantial gainful activity, we will start paying you benefits again; you will not have to file a new application. The following rules apply if you complete a trial work period and continue to have a disabling impairment:

(1) The first time you work after the end of your trial work period and engage in substantial gainful activity, we will find that your disability ceased. When we decide whether this work is substantial gainful activity, we will apply all of the relevant provisions of §§ 404.1571–404.1576 including, but not limited to, the provisions for averaging earnings, unsuccessful work attempts, and deducting impairment-related work expenses, as well as the special rules for evaluating the work you do after you have received disability benefits for at least 24 months. We will find that your disability ceased in the first month after the end of your trial work period in which you do substantial gainful activity, applying all the relevant provisions in §§ 404.1571–404.1576.

(2)(i) If we determine under paragraph (a)(1) of this section that your disability ceased during the reentitlement period because you perform substantial gainful activity, you will be paid benefits for the first month after the trial work period in which you do substantial gainful activity (i.e., the month your disability ceased) and the two succeeding months, whether or not you do substantial gainful activity in those succeeding months. After those three months, we will stop your benefits for any month in which you do substantial gainful activity. (See §§ 404.316, 404.337, 404.352 and 404.401a.) If your benefits are stopped because you do substantial gainful activity, they may be started again without a new application and a new determination of disability if you stop doing substantial gainful activity in a month during the reentitlement period. In determining whether you do substantial gainful activity in a month for purposes of stopping or starting benefits during the reentitlement period, we will consider only your work in, or earnings for, that month. Once we have determined that your disability has ceased during the reentitlement period because of the performance of substantial gainful activity as explained in paragraph (a)(1) of this section, we will not apply the provisions of §§ 404.1574(c) and 404.1575(d) regarding unsuccessful work attempts, the provisions of § 404.1574a regarding averaging of earnings, or the special rules in §§ 404.1574(b)(3)(iii) and 404.1575(e) for evaluating the work you do after you have received disability benefits for at least 24 months, to determine whether benefits should be paid for any particular month in the reentitlement period that occurs after the month your disability ceased.

(ii) If anyone else is receiving monthly benefits based on your earnings record, that individual will not be paid benefits for any month for which you cannot be paid benefits during the reentitlement period.

(3) The way we will consider your work activity after your reentitlement period ends (see paragraph (b)(2) of this section) will depend on whether you worked during the reentitlement period and if you did substantial gainful activity.

(i) If you worked during the reentitlement period and we decided that your disability ceased during the reentitlement period because of your work under paragraph (a)(1) of this section, we will find that your entitlement to disability benefits terminates in the first month in which you engaged in substantial gainful activity after the end of the reentitlement period (see § 404.325). (See § 404.321 for when entitlement to a period of disability ends.) When we make this determination, we will consider only your work in, or earnings for, that month; we will not apply the provisions of §§ 404.1574(c) and 404.1575(d) regarding unsuccessful work attempts, the provisions of § 404.1574a regarding averaging of earnings, or the special rules in §§ 404.1574(b)(3)(iii) and 404.1575(e) for evaluating the work you do after you have received disability benefits for at least 24 months.

(ii) If we did not find that your disability ceased because of work activity during the reentitlement period, we will apply all of the relevant provisions of §§ 404.1571–404.1576 including, but not limited to, the provisions for averaging earnings, unsuccessful work attempts, and deducting impairment-related work expenses, as well as the special rules for evaluating the work you do after you have received disability benefits for at least 24 months, to determine whether your disability ceased because you performed substantial gainful activity after the reentitlement period. If we find that your disability ceased because you performed substantial gainful activity in a month after your reentitlement period ended, you will be paid benefits for the month in which your disability ceased and the two succeeding months. After those three months, your entitlement to a period of disability or to disability benefits terminates (see §§ 404.321 and 404.325).

(b) When the reentitlement period begins and ends. The reentitlement period begins with the first month following completion of 9 months of trial work but cannot begin earlier than December 1, 1980. It ends with whichever is earlier—

(1) The month before the first month in which your impairment no longer exists or is not medically disabling; or

(2)(i) The last day of the 15th month following the end of your trial work period if you were not entitled to benefits after December 1987; or

(ii) The last day of the 36th month following the end of your trial work period if you were entitled to benefits after December 1987 or if the 15-month period described in paragraph (b)(2)(i) of this section had not ended as of January 1988. (See §§ 404.316, 404.337, and 404.352 for when your benefits end.)

(c) When you are not entitled to a reentitlement period. You are not entitled to a reentitlement period if:

(1) You are entitled to a period of disability, but not to disability insurance cash benefits;

(2) You are not entitled to a trial work period;

(3) Your entitlement to disability insurance benefits ended before you completed 9 months of trial work in that period of disability.

[49 FR 22273, May 29, 1984; 58 FR 64883, Dec. 10, 1993; 65 FR 42787, July 11, 2000; 71 FR 66856, Nov. 17, 2006]

§ 404.1592b What is expedited reinstatement?

The expedited reinstatement provision provides you another option for regaining entitlement to benefits when we previously terminated your entitlement to disability benefits due to your work activity. The expedited reinstatement provision provides you the option of requesting that your prior entitlement to disability benefits be reinstated, rather than filing a new application for a new period of entitlement. Since January 1, 2001, you can request to be reinstated to benefits if you stop doing substantial gainful activity within 60 months of your prior termination. You must not be able to do substantial gainful activity because of your medical condition. Your current impairment must be the same as or related to your prior impairment and you must be disabled. To determine if you are disabled, we will use our medical improvement review standard that we use in our continuing disability review process. The advantage of using the medical improvement review standard is that we will generally find that you are disabled unless your impairment has improved so that you are able to work or unless an exception under the medical improvement review standard process applies. We explain the rules for expedited reinstatement in §§ 404.1592c through 404.1592f.

[70 FR 57142, Sept. 30, 2005]

§ 404.1592c Who is entitled to expedited reinstatement?

(a) You can have your entitlement to benefits reinstated under expedited reinstatement if—

(1) You were previously entitled to a disability benefit on your own record of earnings as indicated in § 404.315, or as a disabled widow or widower as indicated in § 404.335, or as a disabled child as indicated in § 404.350, or to Medicare entitlement based on disability and Medicare qualified government employment as indicated in 42 CFR 406.15;

(2) Your disability entitlement referred to in paragraph (a)(1) of this section was terminated because you did substantial gainful activity;

(3) You file your request for reinstatement timely under § 404.1592d; and

(4) In the month you file your request for reinstatement—

(i) You are not able or become unable to do substantial gainful activity because of your medical condition as determined under paragraph (c) of this section;

(ii) Your current impairment is the same as or related to the impairment that we used as the basis for your previous entitlement referred to in paragraph (a)(2) of this section; and

(iii) You are disabled, as determined under the medical improvement review standard in §§ 404.1594(a) through (e).

(b) You are entitled to reinstatement on the record of an insured person who is or has been reinstated if—

(1) You were previously entitled to one of the following benefits on the record of the insured person—

(i) A spouse or divorced spouse benefit under §§ 404.330 and 404.331;

(ii) A child's benefit under § 404.350; or

(iii) A parent's benefit under § 404.370;

(2) You were entitled to benefits on the record when we terminated the insured person's entitlement;

(3) You meet the requirements for entitlement to the benefit described in the applicable paragraph (b)(1)(i) through (b)(1)(iii) of this section; and

(4) You request to be reinstated.

(c) We will determine that you are not able to do substantial gainful activity because of your medical condition, under paragraph (a)(4)(i) of this section, when:

(1) You certify under § 404.1592d(d)(2) that you are unable to do substantial gainful activity because of your medical condition;

(2) You are not able or become unable to do substantial gainful activity in the month you file your request for reinstatement; and

(3) We determine that you are disabled under paragraph (a)(4)(iii) of this section.

[70 FR 57142, Sept. 30, 2005; 81 FR 71369, Oct. 17, 2016]

§ 404.1592d How do I request reinstatement?

(a) You must make your request for reinstatement in writing.

(b) You must have filed your request on or after January 1, 2001.

(c) You must provide the information we request so that we can determine whether you meet the requirements for reinstatement as indicated in § 404.1592c.

(d) If you request reinstatement under § 404.1592c(a)—

(1) We must receive your request within the consecutive 60–month period that begins with the month in which your entitlement terminated due to doing substantial gainful activity. If we receive your request after the 60–month period we can grant you an extension if we determine you had good cause under the standards explained in § 404.911 for not filing the request timely; and

(2) You must certify that you are disabled, that your current impairment(s) is the same as or related to the impairment(s) that we used as the basis for the benefit you are requesting to be reinstated, and that you are unable to do substantial gainful activity because of your medical condition.

[70 FR 57142, Sept. 30, 2005]

§ 404.1592e How do we determine provisional benefits?

(a) You may receive up to 6 consecutive months of provisional cash benefits and Medicare during the provisional benefit period, while we determine whether we can reinstate your disability benefit entitlement under § 404.1592c—

(1) We will pay you provisional benefits, and reinstate your Medicare if you are not already entitled to Medicare, beginning with the month you file your request for reinstatement under § 404.1592c(a) if you do not perform substantial gainful activity in that month. We will pay you provisional benefits, and reinstate your Medicare if you are not already entitled to Medicare, beginning with the month after you file your request for reinstatement under § 404.1592c(a) if you perform substantial gainful activity in the month in which you file your request for reinstatement.

(2) We will pay you a monthly provisional benefit amount equal to the last monthly benefit payable to you during your prior entitlement, increased by any cost of living increases that would have been applicable to the prior benefit amount under § 404.270. The last monthly benefit payable is the amount of the monthly insurance benefit we determined that was actually paid to you for the month before the month in which your entitlement was terminated, after we applied the reduction, deduction and nonpayment provisions in § 404.401 through § 404.480.

(3) If you are entitled to another monthly benefit payable under the provisions of title II of the Act for the same month you can be paid a provisional benefit, we will pay you an amount equal to the higher of the benefits payable.

(4) If you request reinstatement for more than one benefit entitlement, we will pay you an amount equal to the higher of the provisional benefits payable.

(5) If you are eligible for Supplemental Security Income payments, including provisional payments, we will reduce your provisional benefits under § 404.408b if applicable.

(6) We will not reduce your provisional benefit, or the payable benefit to other individuals entitled on an earnings record, under § 404.403, when your provisional benefit causes the total benefits payable on the earnings record to exceed the family maximum.

(b) You cannot receive provisional cash benefits or Medicare a second time under this section when—

(1) You request reinstatement under § 404.1592c(a);

(2) You previously received provisional cash benefits or Medicare under this section based upon a prior request for reinstatement filed under § 404.1592c(a); and

(3) Your requests under paragraphs (b)(1) and (b)(2) are for the same previous disability entitlement referred to in § 404.1592c(a)(2).

(4) Examples:

Example 1: Mr. K files a request for reinstatement in April 2004. His disability benefit had previously terminated in January 2003. Since Mr. K meets other factors for possible reinstatement (i.e., his prior entitlement was terminated within the last 60 months because he was engaging in substantial gainful activity), we start paying him provisional benefits beginning April 2004 while we determine whether he is disabled and whether his current impairment(s) is the same as or related to the impairment(s) that we used as the basis for the benefit that was terminated in January 2003. In July 2004 we determine that Mr. K cannot be reinstated because he is not disabled under the medical improvement review standard; therefore we stop his provisional benefits. Mr. K does not request review of that determination. In January 2005 Mr. K again requests reinstatement on the entitlement that terminated in January 2003. Since this request meets all the factors for possible reinstatement, and his request is still within 60 months from January 2003, we will make a new determination on whether he is disabled and whether his current impairment(s) is the same as or related to the impairment(s) that we used as the basis for the benefit that was terminated in January 2003. Since the January 2005 request and the April 2004 request both request reinstatement on the same entitlement that terminated in January 2003, and since we already paid Mr. K provisional benefits based upon the April 2004 request, we will not pay additional provisional benefits on the January 2005 request for reinstatement.

Example 2: Assume the same facts as shown in Example 1 of this section, with the addition of these facts. We approve Mr. K's January 2005 request for reinstatement and start his reinstated benefits beginning January 2005. Mr. K subsequently returns to work and his benefits are again terminated due to engaging in substantial gainful activity in January 2012. Mr. K must again stop work and requests reinstatement in January 2015. Since Mr. K meets other factors for possible reinstatement (i.e., his prior entitlement was terminated within the last 60 months because he was engaging in substantial gainful activity) we start paying him provisional benefits beginning January 2015 while we determine whether he is disabled and whether his current impairment(s) is the same as or related to the impairment(s) that we used as the basis for the benefit that was terminated in January 2012.

(c) We will not pay you a provisional benefit for a month when an applicable nonpayment rule applies. Examples of when we will not pay a benefit include, but are not limited to—

(1) If you are a prisoner under § 404.468;

(2) If you have been removed/deported under § 404.464; or

(3) If you are an alien outside the United States under § 404.460.

(d) We will not pay you a provisional benefit for any month that is after the earliest of the following months—

(1) The month we send you a notice of our determination on your request for reinstatement;

(2) The month you do substantial gainful activity;

(3) The month before the month you attain full retirement age; or

(4) The fifth month following the month you requested expedited reinstatement.

(e) You are not entitled to provisional benefits if—

(1) Prior to starting your provisional benefits, we determine that you do not meet the requirements for reinstatement under §§ 404.1592c(a); or

(2) We determine that your statements on your request for reinstatement, made under § 404.1592d(d)(2), are false.

(f) Determinations we make regarding your provisional benefits under paragraphs (a) through (e) of this section are final and are not subject to administrative and judicial review under subpart J of part 404.

(g) If you were previously overpaid benefits under title II or title XVI of the Act, we will not recover the overpayment from your provisional benefits unless you give us permission. We can recover Medicare premiums you owe from your provisional benefits.

(h) If we determine you are not entitled to reinstated benefits, provisional benefits we have already paid you under this section that were made prior to the termination month under paragraph (d) of this section will not be subject to recovery as an overpayment unless we determine that you knew, or should have known, you did not meet the requirements for reinstatement in § 404.1592c. If we inadvertently pay you provisional benefits when you are not entitled to them because we have already made a determination described in paragraph (e) of this section, they will be subject to recover as an overpayment under subpart F of part 404.

[70 FR 57142, Sept. 30, 2005; 81 FR 71369, Oct. 17, 2016]

§ 404.1592f How do we determine reinstated benefits?

(a) If you meet the requirements for reinstatement under § 404.1592c(a), we will then consider in which month to reinstate your entitlement. We will reinstate your entitlement with the earliest month, in the 12–month period that ends with the month before you filed your request for reinstatement, that you would have met all of the requirements under § 404.1592c(a) if you had filed your request for reinstatement in that month. Otherwise, you will be entitled to reinstated benefits beginning with the month in which you filed your request for such benefits if you did not perform substantial gainful activity in that month. If you performed substantial gainful activity in the month of filing, but are no longer able to perform substantial gainful activity, we will reinstate your benefits with the month after the month you filed your request for reinstatement. We cannot reinstate your entitlement for any month prior to January 2001.

(b) When your entitlement is reinstated, you are also entitled to Medicare benefits under the provisions of 42 CFR part 406.

(c) We will compute your reinstated benefit amount and determine benefits payable under the applicable paragraphs of §§ 404.201 through 404.480 with certain exceptions—

(1) We will reduce your reinstated benefit due in a month by the amount of the provisional benefit we already paid you for that month. If your provisional benefit paid for a month exceeds the reinstated benefit, we will treat the difference as an overpayment under §§ 404.501 through 404.527.

(2) If you are reinstated on your own earnings record, we will compute your primary insurance amount with the same date of onset we used in your most recent period of disability on your earnings record.

(d) We will not pay you reinstated benefits for any months of substantial gainful activity during your initial reinstatement period. During the initial reinstatement period, the trial work period provisions of § 404.1592 and the reentitlement period provisions of § 404.1592a do not apply. The initial reinstatement period begins with the month your reinstated benefits begin under paragraph (a) of this section and ends when you have had 24 payable months of reinstated benefits. We consider you to have a payable month for the purposes of this paragraph when you do not do substantial gainful activity in that month and when the non-payment provisions in subpart E of part 404 also do not apply. If the amount of the provisional benefit already paid you for a month equals or exceeds the amount of the reinstated benefit payable for that month so that no additional payment is due, we will consider that month a payable month. When we determine if you have done substantial gainful activity in a month during the initial reinstatement period, we will consider only your work in, or earnings for, that month. We will not apply the unsuccessful work attempt provisions of §§ 404.1574(c) and 404.1575(d) or the averaging of earnings provisions in § 404.1574a.

(e) After you complete the 24–month initial reinstatement period as indicated in paragraph (d) of this section, your subsequent work will be evaluated under the trial work provisions in § 404.1592 and then the reentitlement period in § 404.1592a.

(f) Your entitlement to reinstated benefits ends with the month before the earliest of the following months—

(1) The month an applicable terminating event in § 404.301 through 404.389 occurs;

(2) The month in which you reach retirement age;

(3) The third month following the month in which your disability ceases; or

(4) The month in which you die.

(g) Determinations we make under §§ 404.1592f are initial determinations under § 404.902 and subject to review under subpart J of part 404.

(h) If we determine you are not entitled to reinstated benefits we will consider your request filed under § 404.1592c(a) your intent to claim benefits under § 404.630.

[70 FR 57142, Sept. 30, 2005; 82 FR 7648, Jan. 23, 2017]

§ 404.1593 Medical evidence in continuing disability review cases.

(a) General. If you are entitled to benefits or if a period of disability has been established for you because you are disabled, we will have your case file with the supporting medical evidence previously used to establish or continue your entitlement. Generally, therefore, the medical evidence we will need for a continuing disability review will be that required to make a current determination or decision as to whether you are still disabled, as defined under the medical improvement review standard. See §§ 404.1579 and 404.1594.

(b) Obtaining evidence from your medical sources. You must provide us with reports from your physician, psychologist, or others who have treated or evaluated you, as well as any other evidence that will help us determine if you are still disabled. See § 404.1512. You must have a good reason for not giving us this information or we may find that your disability has ended. See § 404.1594(e)(2). If we ask you, you must contact your medical sources to help us get the medical reports. We will make every reasonable effort to help you in getting medical reports when you give us permission to request them from your physician, psychologist, or other medical sources. See § 404.1512(d)(1) concerning what we mean by every reasonable effort. In some instances, such as when a source is known to be unable to provide certain tests or procedures or is known to be nonproductive or uncooperative, we may order a consultative examination while awaiting receipt of medical source evidence. Before deciding that your disability has ended, we will develop a complete medical history covering at least the 12 months preceding the date you sign a report about your continuing disability status. See § 404.1512(c).

(c) When we will purchase a consultative examination. A consultative examination may be purchased when we need additional evidence to determine whether or not your disability continues. As a result, we may ask you, upon our request and reasonable notice, to undergo consultative examinations and tests to help us determine if you are still disabled. See § 404.1517. We will decide whether or not to purchase a consultative examination in accordance with the standards in §§ 404.1519a through 404.1519b.

[50 FR 50130, Dec. 6, 1985; 56 FR 36962, Aug. 1, 1991]

§ 404.1594 How we will determine whether your disability continues or ends.

(a) General. There is a statutory requirement that, if you are entitled to disability benefits, your continued entitlement to such benefits must be reviewed periodically. If you are entitled to disability benefits as a disabled worker or as a person disabled since childhood, or, for monthly benefits payable for months after December 1990, as a disabled widow, widower, or surviving divorced spouse, there are a number of factors we consider in deciding whether your disability continues. We must determine if there has been any medical improvement in your impairment(s) and, if so, whether this medical improvement is related to your ability to work. If your impairment(s) has not medically improved we must consider whether one or more of the exceptions to medical improvement applies. If medical improvement related to your ability to work has not occurred and no exception applies, your benefits will continue. Even where medical improvement related to your ability to work has occurred or an exception applies, in most cases (see paragraph (e) of this section for exceptions), we must also show that you are currently able to engage in substantial gainful activity before we can find that you are no longer disabled.

(b) Terms and definitions. There are several terms and definitions which are important to know in order to understand how we review whether your disability continues. In addition, see paragraph (i) of this section if you work during your current period of entitlement based on disability or during certain other periods.

(1) Medical improvement. Medical improvement is any decrease in the medical severity of your impairment(s) which was present at the time of the most recent favorable medical decision that you were disabled or continued to be disabled. A determination that there has been a decrease in medical severity must be based on improvement in the symptoms, signs, and/or laboratory findings associated with your impairment(s).

Example 1: You were awarded disability benefits due to a herniated nucleus pulposus. At the time of our prior decision granting you benefits you had had a laminectomy. Postoperatively, a myelogram still shows evidence of a persistent deficit in your lumbar spine. You had pain in your back, and pain and a burning sensation in your right foot and leg. There were no muscle weakness or neurological changes and a modest decrease in motion in your back and leg. When we reviewed your claim, your medical source, who has treated you, reported that he or she had seen you regularly every 2 to 3 months for the past 2 years. No further myelograms had been done, complaints of pain in the back and right leg continued especially on sitting or standing for more than a short period of time. Your doctor further reported a moderately decreased range of motion in your back and right leg, but again no muscle atrophy or neurological changes were reported. Medical improvement has not occurred because there has been no decrease in the severity of your back impairment as shown by changes in symptoms, signs or laboratory findings.

Example 2: You were awarded disability benefits due to rheumatoid arthritis. At the time, laboratory findings were positive for this condition. Your doctor reported persistent swelling and tenderness of your fingers and wrists and that you complained of joint pain. Current medical evidence shows that while laboratory tests are still positive for rheumatoid arthritis, your impairment has responded favorably to therapy so that for the last year your fingers and wrists have not been significantly swollen or painful. Medical improvement has occurred because there has been a decrease in the severity of your impairment as documented by the current symptoms and signs reported by your physician. Although your impairment is subject to temporary remission and exacerbations, the improvement that has occurred has been sustained long enough to permit a finding of medical improvement. We would then determine if this medical improvement is related to your ability to work.

(2) Medical improvement not related to ability to do work. Medical improvement is not related to your ability to work if there has been a decrease in the severity of the impairment(s) as defined in paragraph (b)(1) of this section, present at the time of the most recent favorable medical decision, but no increase in your functional capacity to do basic work activities as defined in paragraph (b)(4) of this section. If there has been any medical improvement in your impairment(s), but it is not related to your ability to do work and none of the exceptions applies, your benefits will be continued.

Example: You are 65 inches tall and weighed 246 pounds at the time your disability was established. You had venous insufficiency and persistent edema in your legs. At the time, your ability to do basic work activities was affected because you were able to sit for 6 hours, but were able to stand or walk only occasionally. At the time of our continuing disability review, you had undergone a vein stripping operation. You now weigh 220 pounds and have intermittent edema. You are still able to sit for 6 hours at a time and to stand or walk only occasionally although you report less discomfort on walking.

Medical improvement has occurred because there has been a decrease in the severity of the existing impairment as shown by your weight loss and the improvement in your edema. This medical improvement is not related to your ability to work, however, because your functional capacity to do basic work activities (i.e., the ability to sit, stand and walk) has not increased.

(3) Medical improvement that is related to ability to do work. Medical improvement is related to your ability to work if there has been a decrease in the severity, as defined in paragraph (b)(1) of this section, of the impairment(s) present at the time of the most recent favorable medical decision and an increase in your functional capacity to do basic work activities as discussed in paragraph (b)(4) of this section. A determination that medical improvement related to your ability to do work has occurred does not, necessarily, mean that your disability will be found to have ended unless it is also shown that you are currently able to engage in substantial gainful activity as discussed in paragraph (b)(5) of this section.

Example 1: You have a back impairment and had a laminectomy to relieve the nerve root impingement and weakness in your left leg. At the time of our prior decision, basic work activities were affected because you were able to stand less than 6 hours, and sit no more than ½ hour at a time. You had a successful fusion operation on your back about 1 year before our review of your entitlement. At the time of our review, the weakness in your leg has decreased. Your functional capacity to perform basic work activities now is unimpaired because you now have no limitation on your ability to sit, walk, or stand. Medical improvement has occurred because there has been a decrease in the severity of your impairment as demonstrated by the decreased weakness in your leg. This medical improvement is related to your ability to work because there has also been an increase in your functional capacity to perform basic work activities (or residual functional capacity) as shown by the absence of limitation on your ability to sit, walk, or stand. Whether or not your disability is found to have ended, however, will depend on our determination as to whether you can currently engage in substantial gainful activity.

Example 2: You were injured in an automobile accident receiving a compound fracture to your right femur and a fractured pelvis. When you applied for disability benefits 10 months after the accident your doctor reported that neither fracture had yet achieved solid union based on his clinical examination. X-rays supported this finding. Your doctor estimated that solid union and a subsequent return to full weight bearing would not occur for at least 3 more months. At the time of our review 6 months later, solid union had occurred and you had been returned to full weight-bearing for over a month. Your doctor reported this and the fact that your prior fractures no longer placed any limitation on your ability to walk, stand, lift, etc., and, that in fact, you could return to fulltime work if you so desired.

Medical improvement has occurred because there has been a decrease in the severity of your impairments as shown by X-ray and clinical evidence of solid union and your return to full weight-bearing. This medical improvement is related to your ability to work because you no longer meet the same listed impairment in appendix 1 of this subpart (see paragraph (c)(3)(i) of this section). In fact, you no longer have an impairment which is severe (see § 404.1521) and your disability will be found to have ended.

(4) Functional capacity to do basic work activities. Under the law, disability is defined, in part, as the inability to do any substantial gainful activity by reason of any medically determinable physical or mental impairment(s). In determining whether you are disabled under the law, we must measure, therefore, how and to what extent your impairment(s) has affected your ability to do work. We do this by looking at how your functional capacity for doing basic work activities has been affected. Basic work activities means the abilities and aptitudes necessary to do most jobs. Included are exertional abilities such as walking, standing, pushing, pulling, reaching and carrying, and nonexertional abilities and aptitudes such as seeing, hearing, speaking, remembering, using judgment, dealing with changes and dealing with both supervisors and fellow workers. A person who has no impairment(s) would be able to do all basic work activities at normal levels; he or she would have an unlimited functional capacity to do basic work activities. Depending on its nature and severity, an impairment will result in some limitation to the functional capacity to do one or more of these basic work activities. Diabetes, for example, can result in circulatory problems which could limit the length of time a person could stand or walk and damage to his or her eyes as well, so that the person also had limited vision. What a person can still do despite an impairment, is called his or her residual functional capacity. How the residual functional capacity is assessed is discussed in more detail in § 404.1545. Unless an impairment is so severe that it is deemed to prevent you from doing substantial gainful activity (see §§ 404.1525 and 404.1526), it is this residual functional capacity that is used to determine whether you can still do your past work or, in conjunction with your age, education and work experience, any other work.

(i) A decrease in the severity of an impairment as measured by changes (improvement) in symptoms, signs or laboratory findings can, if great enough, result in an increase in the functional capacity to do work activities. Vascular surgery (e.g., femoropopliteal bypass) may sometimes reduce the severity of the circulatory complications of diabetes so that better circulation results and the person can stand or walk for longer periods. When new evidence showing a change in signs, symptoms and laboratory findings establishes that both medical improvement has occurred and your functional capacity to perform basic work activities, or residual functional capacity, has increased, we say that medical improvement which is related to your ability to do work has occurred. A residual functional capacity assessment is also used to determine whether you can engage in substantial gainful activity and, thus, whether you continue to be disabled (see paragraph (b)(5) of this section).

(ii) Many impairment-related factors must be considered in assessing your functional capacity for basic work activities. Age is one key factor. Medical literature shows that there is a gradual decrease in organ function with age; that major losses and deficits become irreversible over time and that maximum exercise performance diminishes with age. Other changes related to sustained periods of inactivity and the aging process include muscle atrophy, degenerative joint changes, decrease in range of motion, and changes in the cardiac and respiratory systems which limit the exertional range.

(iii) Studies have also shown that the longer an individual is away from the workplace and is inactive, the more difficult it becomes to return to ongoing gainful employment. In addition, a gradual change occurs in most jobs so that after about 15 years, it is no longer realistic to expect that skills and abilities acquired in these jobs will continue to apply to the current workplace. Thus, if you are age 50 or over and have been receiving disability benefits for a considerable period of time, we will consider this factor along with your age in assessing your residual functional capacity. This will ensure that the disadvantages resulting from inactivity and the aging process during a long period of disability will be considered. In some instances where available evidence does not resolve what you can or cannot do on a sustained basis, we will provide special work evaluations or other appropriate testing.

(5) Ability to engage in substantial gainful activity. In most instances, we must show that you are able to engage in substantial gainful activity before your benefits are stopped. When doing this, we will consider all your current impairments not just that impairment(s) present at the time of the most recent favorable determination. If we cannot determine that you are still disabled based on medical considerations alone (as discussed in §§ 404.1525 and 404.1526), we will use the new symptoms, signs and laboratory findings to make an objective assessment of your functional capacity to do basic work activities or residual functional capacity and we will consider your vocational factors. See §§ 404.1545 through 404.1569.

(6) Evidence and basis for our decision. Our decisions under this section will be made on a neutral basis without any initial inference as to the presence or absence of disability being drawn from the fact that you have previously been determined to be disabled. We will consider all evidence you submit and that we obtain from your medical sources and nonmedical sources. What constitutes evidence and our procedures for obtaining it are set out in §§ 404.1512 through 404.1518. Our determination regarding whether your disability continues will be made on the basis of the weight of the evidence.

(7) Point of comparison. For purposes of determining whether medical improvement has occurred, we will compare the current medical severity of that impairment(s) which was present at the time of the most recent favorable medical decision that you were disabled or continued to be disabled to the medical severity of that impairment(s) at that time. If medical improvement has occurred, we will compare your current functional capacity to do basic work activities (i.e., your residual functional capacity) based on this previously existing impairment(s) with your prior residual functional capacity in order to determine whether the medical improvement is related to your ability to do work. The most recent favorable medical decision is the latest decision involving a consideration of the medical evidence and the issue of whether you were disabled or continued to be disabled which became final.

(c) Determining medical improvement and its relationship to your abilities to do work. Paragraphs (b)(1) through (3) of this section discuss what we mean by medical improvement, medical improvement not related to your ability to work and medical improvement that is related to your ability to work. (In addition, see paragraph (i) of this section if you work during your current period of entitlement based on disability or during certain other periods.) How we will arrive at the decision that medical improvement has occurred and its relationship to the ability to do work, is discussed below.

(1) Medical improvement. Medical improvement is any decrease in the medical severity of impairment(s) present at the time of the most recent favorable medical decision that you were disabled or continued to be disabled and is determined by a comparison of prior and current medical evidence which must show that there have been changes (improvement) in the symptoms, signs or laboratory findings associated with that impairment(s).

(2) Determining if medical improvement is related to ability to work. If there is a decrease in medical severity as shown by the symptoms, signs and laboratory findings, we then must determine if it is related to your ability to do work. In paragraph (b)(4) of this section, we explain the relationship between medical severity and limitation on functional capacity to do basic work activities (or residual functional capacity) and how changes in medical severity can affect your residual functional capacity. In determining whether medical improvement that has occurred is related to your ability to do work, we will assess your residual functional capacity (in accordance with paragraph (b)(4) of this section) based on the current severity of the impairment(s) which was present at your last favorable medical decision. Your new residual functional capacity will then be compared to your residual functional capacity at the time of our most recent favorable medical decision. Unless an increase in the current residual functional capacity is based on changes in the

signs, symptoms, or laboratory findings, any medical improvement that has occurred will not be considered to be related to your ability to do work.

(3) Following are some additional factors and considerations which we will apply in making these determinations.

(i) Previous impairment met or equaled listings. If our most recent favorable decision was based on the fact that your impairment(s) at the time met or equaled the severity contemplated by the Listing of Impairments in appendix 1 of this subpart, an assessment of your residual functional capacity would not have been made. If medical improvement has occurred and the severity of the prior impairment(s) no longer meets or equals the same listing section used to make our most recent favorable decision, we will find that the medical improvement was related to your ability to work. Appendix 1 of this subpart describes impairments which, if severe enough, affect a person's ability to work. If the appendix level of severity is met or equaled, the individual is deemed, in the absence of evidence to the contrary, to be unable to engage in substantial gainful activity. If there has been medical improvement to the degree that the requirement of the listing section is no longer met or equaled, then the medical improvement is related to your ability to work. We must, of course, also establish that you can currently engage in gainful activity before finding that your disability has ended.

(ii) Prior residual functional capacity assessment made. The residual functional capacity assessment used in making the most recent favorable medical decision will be compared to the residual functional capacity assessment based on current evidence in order to determine if your functional capacity for basic work activities has increased. There will be no attempt made to reassess the prior residual functional capacity.

(iii) Prior residual functional capacity assessment should have been made, but was not. If the most recent favorable medical decision should have contained an assessment of your residual functional capacity (i.e., your impairments did not meet or equal the level of severity contemplated by the Listing of Impairments in appendix 1 of this subpart) but does not, either because this assessment is missing from your file or because it was not done, we will reconstruct the residual functional capacity. This reconstructed residual functional capacity will accurately and objectively assess your functional capacity to do basic work activities. We will assign the maximum functional capacity consistent with an allowance.

Example: You were previously found to be disabled on the basis that "while your impairment did not meet or equal a listing, it did prevent you from doing your past or any other work." The prior adjudicator did not, however, include a residual functional capacity assessment in the rationale of this decision and a review of the prior evidence does not show that such an assessment was ever made. If a decrease in medical severity, i.e., medical improvement, has occurred, the residual functional capacity based on the current level of severity of your impairment will have to be compared with your residual functional capacity based on its prior severity in order to determine if the medical improvement is related to your ability to do work. In order to make this comparison, we will review the prior evidence and make an objective assessment of your residual functional capacity at the time of our most recent favorable medical determination, based on the symptoms, signs and laboratory findings as they then existed.

(iv) Impairment subject to temporary remission. In some cases the evidence shows that an individual's impairments are subject to temporary remission. In assessing whether medical improvement has occurred in persons with this type of impairment, we will be careful to consider the longitudinal history of the impairments, including the occurrence of prior remission, and prospects for future worsenings. Improvement in such impairments that is only temporary will not warrant a finding of medical improvement.

(v) Prior file cannot be located. If the prior file cannot be located, we will first determine whether you are able to now engage in substantial gainful activity based on all your current impairments. (In this way, we will be able to determine that your disability continues at the earliest point without addressing the often lengthy process of reconstructing prior evidence.) If you cannot engage in substantial gainful activity currently, your benefits will continue unless one of the second group of exceptions applies (see paragraph (e) of this section). If you are able to engage in substantial gainful activity, we will determine whether an attempt should be made to reconstruct those portions of the missing file that were relevant to our most recent favorable medical decision (e.g., work history, medical evidence, and the results of consultative examinations). This determination will consider the potential availability of old records in light of their age, whether the source of the evidence is still in operation; and whether reconstruction efforts will yield a complete record of the basis for the most recent favorable medical decision. If relevant parts of the prior record are not reconstructed either because it is determined not to attempt reconstruction or because such efforts fail, medical improvement cannot be found. The documentation of your current impairments will provide a basis for any future reviews. If the missing file is later found, it may serve as a basis for reopening any decision under this section in accordance with the rules in § 404.988.

(d) First group of exceptions to medical improvement. The law provides for certain limited situations when your disability can be found to have ended even though medical improvement has not occurred, if you can engage in substantial gainful activity. These exceptions to medical improvement are intended to provide a way of finding that a person is no longer disabled in those limited situations where, even though there has been no decrease in severity of the impairment(s), evidence shows that the person should no longer be considered disabled or never should have been considered disabled. If one of these exceptions applies, we must also show that, taking all your current impairment(s) into account, not just those that existed at the time of our most recent favorable medical decision, you are now able to engage in substantial gainful activity before your disability can be found to have ended. As part of the review process, you will be asked about any medical or vocational therapy you received or are receiving. Your answers and the evidence gathered as a result as well as all other evidence, will serve as the basis for the finding that an exception applies.

(1) Substantial evidence shows that you are the beneficiary of advances in medical or vocational therapy or technology (related to your ability to work). Advances in medical or vocational therapy or technology are improvements in treatment or rehabilitative methods which have increased your ability to do basic work activities. We will apply this exception when substantial evidence shows that you have been the beneficiary of services which reflect these advances and they have favorably affected the severity of your impairment or your ability to do basic work activities. This decision will be based on new medical evidence and a new residual functional capacity assessment. (See § 404.1545.) In many instances, an advanced medical therapy or technology will result in a decrease in severity as shown by symptoms, signs and laboratory findings which will meet the definition of medical improvement. This exception will, therefore, see very limited application.

(2) Substantial evidence shows that you have undergone vocational therapy (related to your ability to work). Vocational therapy (related to your ability to work) may include, but is not limited to, additional education, training, or work experience that improves your ability to meet the vocational requirements of more jobs. This decision will be based on substantial evidence which includes new medical evidence and a new residual functional capacity assessment. (See § 404.1545.) If, at the time of our review you have not completed vocational therapy which could affect the continuance of your disability, we will review your claim upon completion of the therapy.

Example 1: You were found to be disabled because the limitations imposed on you by your impairment allowed you to only do work that was at a sedentary level of exertion. Your prior work experience was work that required a medium level of exertion. Your age and education at the time would not have qualified you for work that was below this medium level of exertion. You enrolled in and completed a specialized training course which qualifies you for a job in data processing as a computer programmer in the period since you were awarded benefits. On review of your claim, current evidence shows that there is no medical improvement and that you can still do only sedentary work. As the work of a computer programmer is sedentary in nature, you are now able to engage in substantial gainful activity when your new skills are considered.

Example 2: You were previously entitled to benefits because the medical evidence and assessment of your residual functional capacity showed you could only do light work. Your prior work was considered to be heavy in nature and your age, education and the nature of your prior work qualified you for work which was no less than medium in exertion. The current evidence and residual functional capacity show there has been no medical improvement and that you can still do only light work. Since you were originally entitled to benefits, your vocational rehabilitation agency enrolled you in and you successfully completed a trade school course so that you are now qualified to do small appliance repair. This work is light in nature, so when your new skills are considered, you are now able to engage in substantial gainful activity even though there has been no change in your residual functional capacity.

(3) Substantial evidence shows that based on new or improved diagnostic or evaluative techniques your impairment(s) is not as disabling as it was considered to be at the time of the most recent favorable decision. Changing methodologies and advances in medical and other diagnostic or evaluative techniques have given, and will continue to give, rise to improved methods for measuring and documenting the effect of various impairments on the ability to do work. Where, by such new or improved methods, substantial evidence shows that your impairment(s) is not as severe as was determined at the time of our most recent favorable medical decision, such evidence may serve as a basis for finding that you are no longer disabled, if you can currently engage in substantial gainful activity. In order to be used under this exception, however, the new or improved techniques must have become generally available after the date of our most recent favorable medical decision.

(i) How we will determine which methods are new or improved techniques and when they become generally available. New or improved diagnostic techniques or evaluations will come to our attention by several methods. In reviewing cases, we often become aware of new techniques when their results are presented as evidence. Such techniques and evaluations are also discussed and acknowledged in medical literature by medical professional groups and other governmental entities. Through these sources, we develop listings of new techniques and when they become generally available. For example, we will consult the Health Care Financing Administration for its experience regarding when a technique is recognized for payment under Medicare and when they began paying for the technique.

(ii) How you will know which methods are new or improved techniques and when they become generally available. We will let you know which methods we consider to be new or improved techniques and when they become available through two vehicles.

(A) Some of the future changes in the Listing of Impairments in appendix 1 of this subpart will be based on new or improved diagnostic or evaluative techniques. Such listings changes will clearly state this fact as they are published as Notices of Proposed Rulemaking and the new or improved technique will be considered generally available as of the date of the final publication of that particular listing in the Federal Register.

(B) A cumulative list since 1970 of new or improved diagnostic techniques or evaluations, how they changed the evaluation of the applicable impairment and the month and year they became generally available, will be published in the Notices section of the Federal Register. Included will be any changes in the Listing of Impairments published in the Code of Federal Regulations since 1970 which are reflective of new or improved techniques. No cases will be processed under this exception until this cumulative listing is so published. Subsequent changes to the list will be published periodically. The period will be determined by the volume of changes needed.

Example: The electrocardiographic exercise test has replaced the Master's 2–step test as a measurement of heart function since the time of your last favorable medical decision. Current evidence could show that your condition, which was previously evaluated based on the Master's 2–step test, is not now as disabling as was previously thought. If, taking all your current impairments into account, you are now able to engage in substantial gainful activity, this exception would be used to find that you are no longer disabled even if medical improvement has not occurred.

(4) Substantial evidence demonstrates that any prior disability decision was in error. We will apply the exception to medical improvement based on error if substantial evidence (which may be evidence on the record at the time any prior determination of the entitlement to benefits based on disability was made, or newly obtained evidence which relates to that determination) demonstrates that a prior determination was in error. A prior determination will be found in error only if:

(i) Substantial evidence shows on its face that the decision in question should not have been made (e.g., the evidence in your file such as pulmonary function study values was misread or an adjudicative standard such as a listing in appendix 1 or a medical/vocational rule in appendix 2 of this subpart was misapplied).

Example 1: You were granted benefits when it was determined that your epilepsy met Listing 11.02. This listing calls for a finding of major motor seizures more frequently than once a month as documented by EEG evidence and by a detailed description of a typical seizure pattern. A history of either diurnal episodes or nocturnal episodes with residuals interfering with daily activities is also required. On review, it is found that a history of the frequency of your seizures showed that they occurred only once or twice a year. The prior decision would be found to be in error, and whether you were still considered to be disabled would be based on whether you could currently engage in substantial gainful activity.

Example 2: Your prior award of benefits was based on vocational rule 201.12 in appendix 2 of this subpart. This rule applies to a person age 50–54 who has at least a high school education, whose previous work was entirely at a semiskilled level, and who can do only sedentary work. On review, it is found that at the time of the prior determination you were actually only age 46 and vocational rule 201.21 should have been used. This rule would have called for a denial of your claim and the prior decision is found to have been in error. Continuation of your disability would depend on a finding of your current ability to engage in substantial gainful activity.

(ii) At the time of the prior evaluation, required and material evidence of the severity of your impairment(s) was missing. That evidence becomes available upon review, and substantial evidence demonstrates that had such evidence been present at the time of the prior determination, disability would not have been found.

Example: You were found disabled on the basis of chronic obstructive pulmonary disease. The severity of your impairment was documented primarily by pulmonary function testing results. The evidence showed that you could do only light work. Spirometric tracings of this testing, although required, were not obtained, however. On review, the original report is resubmitted by the consultative examining physician along with the corresponding spirometric tracings. A review of the tracings shows that the test was invalid. Current pulmonary function testing supported by spirometric tracings reveals that your impairment does not limit your ability to perform basic work activities in any way. Error is found based on the fact that required, material evidence which was originally missing now becomes available and shows that if it had been available at the time of the prior determination, disability would not have been found.

(iii) Substantial evidence which is new evidence which relates to the prior determination (of allowance or continuance) refutes the conclusions that were based upon the prior evidence (e.g., a tumor thought to be malignant was later shown to have actually been benign). Substantial evidence must show that had the new evidence (which relates to the prior determination) been considered at the time of the prior decision, the claim would not have been allowed or continued. A substitution of current judgment for that used in the prior favorable decision will not be the basis for applying this exception.

Example: You were previously found entitled to benefits on the basis of diabetes mellitus which the prior adjudicator believed was equivalent to the level of severity contemplated in the Listing of Impairments. The prior record shows that you had "brittle" diabetes for which you were taking insulin. Your urine was 3+ for sugar, and you alleged occasional hypoglycemic attacks caused by exertion. On review, symptoms, signs and laboratory findings are unchanged. The current adjudicator feels, however, that your impairment clearly does not equal the severity contemplated by the listings. Error cannot be found because it would represent a substitution of current judgment for that of the prior adjudicator that your impairment equaled a listing.

(iv) The exception for error will not be applied retroactively under the conditions set out above unless the conditions for reopening the prior decision (see § 404.988) are met.

(5) You are currently engaging in substantial gainful activity. If you are currently engaging in substantial gainful activity before we determine whether you are no longer disabled because of your work activity, we will consider whether you are entitled to a trial work period as set out in § 404.1592. We will find that your disability has ended in the month in which you demonstrated your ability to engage in substantial gainful activity (following completion of a trial work period, where it applies). This exception does not apply in determining whether you continue to have a disabling impairment(s) (§ 404.1511) for purposes of deciding your eligibility for a reentitlement period (§ 404.1592a).

(e) *Second group of exceptions to medical improvement.* In addition to the first group of exceptions to medical improvement, the following exceptions may result in a determination that you are no longer disabled. In these situations the decision will be made without a determination that you have medically improved or can engage in substantial gainful activity.

(1) A prior determination or decision was fraudulently obtained. If we find that any prior favorable determination or decision was obtained by fraud, we may find that you are not disabled. In addition, we may reopen your claim under the rules in § 404.988. In determining whether a prior favorable determination or decision was fraudulently obtained, we will take into account any physical, mental, educational, or linguistic limitations (including any lack of facility with the English language) which you may have had at the time.

(2) You do not cooperate with us. If there is a question about whether you continue to be disabled and we ask you to give us medical or other evidence or to go for a physical or mental examination by a certain date, we will find that your disability has ended if you fail, without good cause, to do what we ask. Section 404.911 explains the factors we consider and how we will determine generally whether you have good cause for failure to cooperate. In addition, § 404.1518 discusses how we determine whether you have good cause for failing to attend a consultative examination. The month in which your disability ends will be the first month in which you failed to do what we asked.

(3) We are unable to find you. If there is a question about whether you continue to be disabled and we are unable to find you to resolve the question, we will determine that your disability has ended. The month your disability ends will be the first month in which the question arose and we could not find you.

(4) You fail to follow prescribed treatment which would be expected to restore your ability to engage in substantial gainful activity. If treatment has been prescribed for you which would be expected to restore your ability to work, you must follow that treatment in order to be paid benefits. If you are not following that treatment and you do not have good cause for failing to follow that treatment, we will find that your disability has ended (see § 404.1530(c)). The month your disability ends will be the first month in which you failed to follow the prescribed treatment.

(f) *Evaluation steps.* To assure that disability reviews are carried out in a uniform manner, that decisions of continuing disability can be made in the most expeditious and administratively efficient way, and that any decisions to stop disability benefits are made objectively, neutrally and are fully documented, we will follow specific steps in reviewing the question of whether your disability continues. Our review may cease and benefits may be continued at any point if we determine there is sufficient evidence to find that you are still unable to engage in substantial gainful activity. The steps are as follows. (See paragraph (i) of this section if you work during your current period of entitlement based on disability or during certain other periods.)

(1) Are you engaging in substantial gainful activity? If you are (and any applicable trial work period has been completed), we will find disability to have ended (see paragraph (d)(5) of this section).

(2) If you are not, do you have an impairment or combination of impairments which meets or equals the severity of an impairment listed in appendix 1 of this subpart? If you do, your disability will be found to continue.

(3) If you do not, has there been medical improvement as defined in paragraph (b)(1) of this section? If there has been medical improvement as shown by a decrease in medical severity, see step (4). If there has been no decrease in medical severity, there has been no medical improvement. (See step (5).)

(4) If there has been medical improvement, we must determine whether it is related to your ability to do work in accordance with paragraphs (b)(1) through (4) of this section; i.e., whether or not there has been an increase in the residual functional capacity based on the impairment(s) that was present at the time of the most recent favorable medical determination. If medical improvement is not related to your ability to do work, see step (5). If medical improvement is related to your ability to do work, see step (6).

(5) If we found at step (3) that there has been no medical improvement or if we found at step (4) that the medical improvement is not related to your ability to work, we consider whether any of the exceptions in paragraphs (d) and (e) of this section apply. If none of them apply, your disability will be found to continue. If one of the first group of exceptions to medical improvement applies, see step (6). If an exception from the second group of exceptions to medical improvement applies, your disability will be found to have

ended. The second group of exceptions to medical improvement may be considered at any point in this process.

(6) If medical improvement is shown to be related to your ability to do work or if one of the first group of exceptions to medical improvement applies, we will determine whether all your current impairments in combination are severe (see § 404.1521). This determination will consider all your current impairments and the impact of the combination of those impairments on your ability to function. If the residual functional capacity assessment in step (4) above shows significant limitation of your ability to do basic work activities, see step (7). When the evidence shows that all your current impairments in combination do not significantly limit your physical or mental abilities to do basic work activities, these impairments will not be considered severe in nature. If so, you will no longer be considered to be disabled.

(7) If your impairment(s) is severe, we will assess your current ability to do substantial gainful activity in accordance with § 404.1560. That is, we will assess your residual functional capacity based on all your current impairments and consider whether you can still do work you have done in the past. If you can do such work, disability will be found to have ended.

(8) If you are not able to do work you have done in the past, we will consider whether you can do other work given the residual functional capacity assessment made under paragraph (f)(7) of this section and your age, education, and past work experience (see paragraph (f)(9) of this section for an exception to this rule). If you can, we will find that your disability has ended. If you cannot, we will find that your disability continues.

(9) We may proceed to the final step, described in paragraph (f)(8) of this section, if the evidence in your file about your past relevant work is not sufficient for us to make a finding under paragraph (f)(7) of this section about whether you can perform your past relevant work. If we find that you can adjust to other work based solely on your age, education, and residual functional capacity, we will find that you are no longer disabled, and we will not make a finding about whether you can do your past relevant work under paragraph (f)(7) of this section. If we find that you may be unable to adjust to other work or if § 404.1562 may apply, we will assess your claim under paragraph (f)(7) of this section and make a finding about whether you can perform your past relevant work.

(g) The month in which we will find you are no longer disabled. If the evidence shows that you are no longer disabled, we will find that your disability ended in the earliest of the following months.

(1) The month the evidence shows you are no longer disabled under the rules set out in this section, and you were disabled only for a specified period of time in the past;

(2) The month the evidence shows you are no longer disabled under the rules set out in this section, but not earlier than the month in which we mail you a notice saying that the information we have shows that you are not disabled;

(3) The month in which you demonstrated your ability to engage in substantial gainful activity (following completion of a trial work period); however, we may pay you benefits for certain months in and after the reentitlement period which follows the trial work period. (See § 404.1592a for a discussion of the reentitlement period. If you are receiving benefits on your own earnings record, see § 404.316 for when your benefits will end. See § 404.352 if you are receiving benefits on a parent's earnings as a disabled adult child.);

(4) The month in which you actually do substantial gainful activity (where you are not entitled to a trial work period);

(5) The month in which you return to full-time work, with no significant medical restrictions and acknowledge that medical improvement has occurred, and we expected your impairment(s) to improve (see § 404.1591);

(6) The first month in which you failed without good cause to do what we asked, when the rule set out in paragraph (e)(2) of this section applies;

(7) The first month in which the question of continuing disability arose and we could not find you, when the rule set out in paragraph (e)(3) of this section applies;

(8) The first month in which you failed without good cause to follow prescribed treatment, when the rule set out in paragraph (e)(4) of this section applies; or

(9) The first month you were told by your physician that you could return to work, provided there is no substantial conflict between your physician's and your statements regarding your awareness of your capacity for work and the earlier date is supported by substantial evidence.

(h) Before we stop your benefits. Before we stop your benefits or a period of disability, we will give you a chance to explain why we should not do so. Sections 404.1595 and 404.1597 describe your rights (including appeal rights) and the procedures we will follow.

(i) If you work during your current period of entitlement based on disability or during certain other periods.

(1) We will not consider the work you are doing or have done during your current period of entitlement based on disability (or, when determining whether you are entitled to expedited reinstatement of benefits under section 223(i) of the Act, the work you are doing or have done during or after the previously terminated

period of entitlement referred to in section 223(i)(1)(B) of the Act) to be past relevant work under paragraph (f)(7) of this section or past work experience under paragraph (f)(8) of this section. In addition, if you are currently entitled to disability benefits under title II of the Social Security Act, we may or may not consider the physical and mental activities that you perform in the work you are doing or have done during your current period of entitlement based on disability, as explained in paragraphs (i)(2) and (3) of this section.

(2) If you are currently entitled to disability insurance benefits as a disabled worker, child's insurance benefits based on disability, or widow's or widower's insurance benefits based on disability under title II of the Social Security Act, and at the time we are making a determination on your case you have received such benefits for at least 24 months, we will not consider the activities you perform in the work you are doing or have done during your current period of entitlement based on disability if they support a finding that your disability has ended. (We will use the rules in § 404.1590(i)(2) to determine whether the 24–month requirement is met.) However, we will consider the activities you do in that work if they support a finding that your disability continues or they do not conflict with a finding that your disability continues. We will not presume that you are still disabled if you stop working.

(3) If you are not a person described in paragraph (i)(2) of this section, we will consider the activities you perform in your work at any of the evaluation steps in paragraph (f) of this section at which we need to assess your ability to function.

[49 FR 22273, May 29, 1984; 50 FR 50130, Dec. 6, 1985; 51 FR 7063, Feb. 28, 1986; 51 FR 16015, April 30, 1986; 52 FR 44971, Nov. 24, 1987; 57 FR 30121, July 8, 1992; 59 FR 1635, Jan. 12, 1994; 65 FR 42788, July 11, 2000; 68 FR 51163, Aug. 26, 2003; 71 FR 66857, Nov. 17, 2006; 77 FR 43495, July 25, 2012; 82 FR 5871, Jan. 18, 2017]

§ 404.1595 When we determine that you are not now disabled.

(a) When we will give you advance notice. Except in those circumstances described in paragraph (d) of this section, we will give you advance notice when we have determined that you are not now disabled because the information we have conflicts with what you have told us about your disability. If your dependents are receiving benefits on your Social Security number and do not live with you, we will also give them advance notice. To give you advance notice, we will contact you by mail, telephone or in person.

(b) What the advance notice will tell you. We will give you a summary of the information we have. We will also tell you why we have determined that you are not now disabled, and will give you a chance to reply. If it is because of—

(1) Medical reasons. The advance notice will tell you what the medical information in your file shows;

(2) Your work activity. The advance notice will tell you what information we have about the work you are doing or have done, and why this work shows that you are not disabled; or

(3) Your failure to give us information we need or do what we ask. The advance notice will tell you what information we need and why we need it or what you have to do and why.

(c) What you should do if you receive an advance notice. If you agree with the advance notice, you do not need to take any action. If you desire further information or disagree with what we have told you, you should immediately write or telephone the State agency or the social security office that gave you the advance notice or you may visit any social security office. If you believe you are now disabled, you should tell us why. You may give us any additional or new information, including reports from your doctors, hospitals, employers or others, that you believe we should have. You should send these as soon as possible to the local social security office or to the office that gave you the advance notice. We consider 10 days to be enough time for you to tell us, although we will allow you more time if you need it. You will have to ask for additional time beyond 10 days if you need it.

(d) When we will not give you advance notice. We will not give you advance notice when we determine that you are not disabled if—

(1) We recently told you that the information we have shows that you are not now disabled, that we were gathering more information, and that your benefits will stop; or

(2) We are stopping your benefits because you told us you are not now disabled; or

(3) We recently told you that continuing your benefits would probably cause us to overpay you and you asked us to stop your benefits.

§ 404.1596 Circumstances under which we may suspend and terminate your benefits before we make a determination.

(a) General. Under some circumstances, we may stop your benefits before we make a determination. Generally, we do this when the information we have clearly shows you are not now disabled but we cannot determine when your disability ended. These situations are described in paragraph (b)(1) and other reasons are given in paragraph (b)(2) of this section. We refer to this as a suspension of benefits. Your benefits, as well as those of your dependents (regardless of where they receive their benefits), may be suspended. When we do this we will give you advance notice. (See § 404.1595.) We will contact your spouse and children if they are receiving benefits on your Social Security number, and the benefits are being mailed to an address different from your own.

(b) When we will suspend your benefits—

(1) You are not now disabled. We will suspend your benefits if the information we have clearly shows that you are not disabled and we will be unable to complete a determination soon enough to prevent us from paying you more monthly benefits than you are entitled to. This may occur when—

(i) New medical or other information clearly shows that you are able to do substantial gainful activity and your benefits should have stopped more than 2 months ago;

(ii) You completed a 9–month period of trial work more than 2 months ago and you are still working;

(iii) At the time you filed for benefits your condition was expected to improve and you were expected to be able to return to work. You subsequently did return to work more than 2 months ago with no significant medical restrictions; or

(iv) You are not entitled to a trial work period and you are working.

(2) Other reasons. We will also suspend your benefits if—

(i) You have failed to respond to our request for additional medical or other evidence and we are satisfied that you received our request and our records show that you should be able to respond; or

(ii) We are unable to locate you and your checks have been returned by the Post Office as undeliverable.

(c) When we will not suspend your cash benefits. We will not suspend your cash benefits if—

(1) You have become disabled by another impairment; or

(2) Even though your impairment is no longer disabling,

(i) You are participating in an appropriate program of vocational rehabilitation services, employment services, or other support services, as described in § 404.327(a) and (b);

(ii) You began participating in the program before the date your disability ended; and

(iii) We have determined under § 404.328 that your completion of the program, or your continuation in the program for a specified period of time, will increase the likelihood that you will not have to return to the disability benefit rolls.

(d) When the suspension is effective. We will suspend your benefits effective with the month in which it is determined in accordance with paragraph (b)(2)(i) of this section that your disability benefits should stop due to your failure, without good cause (see § 404.911), to comply with our request for necessary information for your continuing disability review. This review is to determine whether or not you continue to meet the disability requirements of the law. When we have received the information, we will reinstate your benefits for any previous month for which they are otherwise payable, and continue with the CDR process.

(e) When we will terminate your benefits. We will terminate your benefits following 12 consecutive months of benefit suspension because you did not comply with our request for information in accordance with paragraph (b)(2)(i) of this section. We will count the 12–month suspension period from the start of the first month that you stopped receiving benefits (see paragraph (d) of this section). This termination is effective with the start of the 13th month after the suspension began because you failed to cooperate.

[45 FR 55584, Aug. 20, 1980, as amended at 47 FR 31543, July 21, 1982; 47 FR 52693, Nov. 23, 1982; 51 FR 17617, May 14, 1986; 68 FR 40123, July 7, 2003; 70 FR 36507, June 24, 2005; 71 FR 60822, Oct. 17, 2006]

§ 404.1597 After we make a determination that you are not now disabled.

(a) General. If we determine that you do not meet the disability requirements of the law, your benefits generally will stop. We will send you a formal written notice telling you why we believe you are not disabled and when your benefits should stop. If your spouse and children are receiving benefits on your social security number, we will also stop their benefits and tell them why. The notices will explain your right to reconsideration if you disagree with our determination. However, your benefits may continue even though your impairment is no longer disabling, if you are participating in an appropriate program of vocational rehabilitation services, employment services, or other support services (see § 404.327). You must have started participating in the program before the date your disability ended. In addition, we must have determined that your completion of the program, or your continuation in the program for a specified period of time, will increase the likelihood that you will not have to return to the disability benefit rolls. (See §§ 404.316(c), 404.328, 404.337(c), 404.352(d), and 404.1586(g).) You may still appeal our determination that you are not disabled even though your benefits are continuing because of your participation in an appropriate program of vocational rehabilitation services, employment services, or other support services. You may also appeal a determination that your completion of the program, or your continuation in the program for a specified period of time, will not increase the likelihood that you will not have to return to the disability benefit rolls and, therefore, you are not entitled to continue to receive benefits.

(b) If we make a determination that your physical or mental impairment(s) has ceased, did not exist, or is no longer disabling (Medical Cessation Determination). If we make a determination that the physical or mental impairment(s) on the basis of which benefits were payable has ceased, did not exist, or is no longer disabling (a medical cessation determination), your benefits will stop. As described in paragraph (a) of this section, you will receive a written notice explaining this determination and the month your benefits will stop. The written notice will also explain your right to appeal if you disagree with our determination and your right to request that your benefits and the benefits, if any, of your spouse or children, be continued under § 404.1597a. For the purpose of this section, benefits means disability cash payments and/or Medicare, if applicable. The continued benefit provisions of this section do not apply to an initial determination on an application for disability benefits, or to a determination that you were disabled only for a specified period of time.

[45 FR 55584, Aug. 20, 1980, as amended at 47 FR 31544, July 21, 1982; 51 FR 17618, May 14, 1986; 53 FR 29020, Aug. 2, 1988; 53 FR 39015, Oct. 4, 1988; 70 FR 36507, June 24, 2005]

§ 404.1597a Continued benefits pending appeal of a medical cessation determination.

(a) General. If we determine that you are not entitled to benefits because the physical or mental impairment(s) on the basis of which such benefits were payable is found to have ceased, not to have existed, or to no longer be disabling, and you appeal that determination, you may choose to have your benefits continued pending reconsideration and/or a hearing before an administrative law judge on the disability cessation determination. For the purpose of this entire section, the election of continued benefits means the election of disability cash payments and/or Medicare, if applicable. You can also choose to have the benefits continued for anyone else receiving benefits based on your wages and self-employment income (and anyone else receiving benefits because of your entitlement to benefits based on disability). If you appeal a medical cessation under both title II and title XVI (a concurrent case), the title II claim will be handled in accordance with title II regulations while the title XVI claim will be handled in accordance with the title XVI regulations.

(b) When the provisions of this section are available.

(1) Benefits may be continued under this section only if the determination that your physical or mental impairment(s) has ceased, has never existed, or is no longer disabling is made on or after January 12, 1983 (or before January 12, 1983, and a timely request for reconsideration or a hearing before an administrative law judge is pending on that date).

(2) Benefits may be continued under this section only for months beginning with January 1983, or the first month for which benefits are no longer otherwise payable following our determination that your physical or mental impairment(s) has ceased, has never existed, or is no longer disabling, whichever is later.

(3) Continued payment of benefits under this section will stop effective with the earlier of:

(i) The month before the month in which an administrative law judge's hearing decision finds that your physical or mental impairment(s) has ceased, has never existed, or is no longer disabling or the month before the month of a new administrative law judge decision (or final action by the Appeals Council on the administrative law judge's recommended decision) if your case was sent back to an administrative law judge for further action; or

(ii) The month before the month no timely request for a reconsideration or a hearing before an administrative law judge is pending. These continued benefits may be stopped or adjusted because of certain events (such as work and earnings or receipt of worker's compensation) which occur while you are receiving these continued benefits and affect your right to receive continued benefits.

(c) Continuation of benefits for anyone else pending your appeal.

(1) When you file a request for reconsideration or hearing before an administrative law judge on our determination that your physical or mental impairment(s) has ceased, has never existed, or is no longer disabling, or your case has been sent back (remanded) to an administrative law judge for further action, you may also choose to have benefits continue for anyone else who is receiving benefits based on your wages and self-employment income (and for anyone else receiving benefits because of your entitlement to benefits based on disability), pending the outcome of your appeal.

(2) If anyone else is receiving benefits based on your wages and self-employment income, we will notify him or her of the right to choose to have his or her benefits continue pending the outcome of your appeal. Such benefits can be continued for the time period in paragraph (b) of this section only if he or she chooses to have benefits continued and you also choose to have his or her benefits continued.

(d) Statement of choice. When you or another party request reconsideration under § 404.908(a) or a hearing before an administrative law judge under § 404.932(a) on our determination that your physical or mental impairment(s) has ceased, has never existed, or is no longer disabling, or if your case is sent back (remanded) to an administrative law judge for further action, we will explain your right to receive continued benefits and ask you to complete a statement specifying which benefits you wish to have continued pending the outcome of the reconsideration or hearing before an administrative law judge. You may elect to receive only Medicare benefits during appeal even if you do not want to receive continued disability benefits. If anyone else is receiving benefits based on your wages and self-employment income (or because of your entitlement to benefits based on disability), we will ask you to complete a statement specifying which benefits you wish to have continued for them, pending the outcome of the request for reconsideration or hearing before an administrative law judge. If you request appeal but you do not want to receive continued benefits, we will ask you to complete a statement declining continued benefits indicating that you do not want to have your benefits and those of your family, if any, continued during the appeal.

(e) Your spouse's or children's statement of choice. If you request, in accordance with paragraph (d) of this section, that benefits also be continued for anyone who had been receiving benefits based on your wages and self-employment, we will send them a written notice. The notice will explain their rights and ask them to complete a statement either declining continued benefits, or specifying which benefits they wish to have continued, pending the outcome of the request for reconsideration or a hearing before an administrative law judge.

(f) What you must do to receive continued benefits pending notice of our reconsideration determination.

(1) If you want to receive continued benefits pending the outcome of your request for reconsideration, you must request reconsideration and continuation of benefits no later than 10 days after the date you receive the notice of our initial determination that your physical or mental impairment(s) has ceased, has never existed, or is no longer disabling. Reconsideration must be requested as provided in § 404.909, and you must request continued benefits using a statement in accordance with paragraph (d) of this section.

(2) If you fail to request reconsideration and continued benefits within the 10–day period required by paragraph (f)(1) of this section, but later ask that we continue your benefits pending a reconsidered determination, we will use the rules in § 404.911 to determine whether good cause exists for your failing to request benefit continuation within 10 days after receipt of the notice of the initial cessation determination. If you request continued benefits after the 10–day period, we will consider the request to be timely and will pay continued benefits only if good cause for delay is established.

(g) What you must do to receive continued benefits pending an administrative law judge's decision.

(1) To receive continued benefits pending an administrative law judge's decision on our reconsideration determination, you must request a hearing and continuation of benefits no later than 10 days after the date you receive the notice of our reconsideration determination that your physical or mental impairment(s) has ceased, has never existed, or is no longer disabling. A hearing must be requested as provided in § 404.933, and you must request continued benefits using a statement in accordance with paragraph (d) of this section.

(2) If you request continued benefits pending an administrative law judge's decision but did not request continued benefits while we were reconsidering the initial cessation determination, your benefits will begin effective the month of the reconsideration determination.

(3) If you fail to request continued payment of benefits within the 10–day period required by paragraph (g)(1) of this section, but you later ask that we continue your benefits pending an administrative law judge's decision on our reconsidered determination, we will use the rules as provided in § 404.911 to determine whether good cause exists for your failing to request benefit continuation within 10 days after receipt of the reconsideration determination. If you request continued benefits after the 10–day period, we will consider the request to be timely and will pay continued benefits only if good cause for delay is established.

(h) What anyone else must do to receive continued benefits pending our reconsideration determination or an administrative law judge's decision.

(1) When you or another party (see §§ 404.908(a) and 404.932(a)) request a reconsideration or a hearing before an administrative law judge on our medical cessation determination or when your case is sent back (remanded) to an administrative law judge for further action, you may choose to have benefits continue for anyone else who is receiving benefits based on your wages and self-employment income. An eligible individual must also choose whether or not to have his or her benefits continue pending your appeal by completing a separate statement of election as described in paragraph (e) of this section.

(2) He or she must request continuation of benefits no later than 10 days after the date he or she receives notice of termination of benefits. He or she will then receive continued benefits beginning with the later of January 1983, or the first month for which benefits are no longer otherwise payable following our initial or reconsideration determination that your physical or mental impairment(s) has ceased, has never existed, or is no longer disabling. Continued benefits will continue until the earlier of:

(i) The month before the month in which an administrative law judge's hearing decision finds that your physical or mental impairment(s) has ceased, has never existed, or is no longer disabling or the month before the month of the new administrative law judge decision (or final action is taken by the Appeals Council on the administrative law judge's recommended decision) if your case was sent back to an administrative law judge for further action; or

(ii) The month before the month no timely request for a reconsideration or a hearing before an administrative law judge is pending. These continued benefits may be stopped or adjusted because of certain events (such as work and earnings or payment of worker's compensation) which occur while an eligible individual is receiving continued benefits and affect his or her right to receive continued benefits.

(3) If he or she fails to request continuation of benefits within the 10–day period required by this paragraph, but requests continuation of benefits at a later date, we will use the rules as provided in § 404.911 to determine whether good cause exists for his or her failure to request continuation of benefits within 10 days after receipt of the notice of termination of his or her benefits. His or her late request will be considered to be timely and we will pay him or her continued benefits only if good cause for delay is established.

(4) If you choose not to have benefits continued for anyone else who is receiving benefits based on your wages and self-employment income, pending the appeal on our determination, we will not continue benefits to him or her.

(i) What you must do when your case is remanded to an administrative law judge. If we send back (remand) your case to an administrative law judge for further action under the rules provided in § 404.977, and the administrative law judge's decision or dismissal order issued on your medical cessation appeal is vacated and is no longer in effect, continued benefits are payable pending a new decision by the administrative law judge or final action is taken by the Appeals Council on the administrative law judge's recommended decision.

(1) If you (and anyone else receiving benefits based on your wages and self-employment income or because of your disability) previously elected to receive continued benefits pending the administrative law judge's decision, we will automatically start these same continued benefits again. We will send you a notice telling you this, and that you do not have to do anything to have these same benefits continued until the month before the month the new decision of order of dismissal is issued by the administrative law judge or until the month before the month the Appeals Council takes final action on the administrative law judge's recommended decision. These benefits will begin again with the first month of nonpayment based on the prior administrative law judge hearing decision or dismissal order. Our notice explaining reinstatement of continued benefits will also tell you to report to us any changes or events that affect your receipt of benefits.

(2) After we automatically reinstate your continued benefits as described in paragraph (h)(1) of this section, we will contact you to determine if any adjustment is required to the amount of continued benefits payable due to events that affect the right to receive benefits involving you, your spouse and/or children. If you have returned to work, we will request additional information about this work activity. If you are working, your continued benefits will not be stopped while your appeal of the medical cessation of disability is still pending unless you have completed a trial work period and are engaging in substantial gainful activity. In this event, we will suspend your continued benefits. If any other changes have occurred which would require a reduction in benefit amounts, or nonpayment of benefits, we will send an advance notice to advise of any adverse change before the adjustment action is taken. The notice will also advise you of the right to explain why these benefits should not be adjusted or stopped. You will also receive a written notice of our determination. The notice will also explain your right to reconsideration if you disagree with this determination.

(3) If the final decision on your appeal of your medical cessation is a favorable one, we will send you a written notice in which we will advise you of your right to benefits, if any, before you engaged in substantial gainful activity and to reentitlement should you stop performing substantial gainful activity. If you disagree with our determination, you will have the right to appeal this decision.

(4) If the final decision on your appeal of your medical cessation is an unfavorable one (the cessation is affirmed), you will also be sent a written notice advising you of our determination, and your right to appeal if you think we are wrong.

(5) If you (or the others receiving benefits based on your wages and self-employment income or because of your disability) did not previously elect to have benefits continued pending an administrative law judge decision, and you now want to elect continued benefits, you must request to do so no later than 10 days after you receive our notice telling you about continued benefits. If you fail to request continued benefits within the 10–day period required by paragraph (f)(1) of this section, but later ask that we continue your benefits pending an administrative law judge remand decision, we will use the rules in § 404.911 to determine whether good cause exists for your failing to request benefit continuation within 10 days after receipt of the notice telling you about benefit continuation. We will consider the request to be timely and will pay continued benefits only if good cause for delay is established. If you make this new election, benefits may begin with the month of the order sending (remanding) your case back to the administrative law judge. Before we begin to pay you continued benefits as described in paragraph (h)(1) of this section we will contact you to determine if any adjustment is required to the amount of continued benefits payable due to events which may affect your right to benefits. If you have returned to work, we will request additional information about this work activity. If you are working, continued benefits may be started and will not be stopped because of your work while your appeal of the medical cessation of your

disability is still pending unless you have completed a trial work period and are engaging in substantial gainful activity. If any changes have occurred which establish a basis for not paying continued benefits or a reduction in benefit amount, we will send you a notice explaining the adjustment or the reason why we cannot pay continued benefits. The notice will also explain your right to reconsideration if you disagree with this determination. If the final decision on your appeal of your medical cessation is a favorable one, we will send you a written notice in which we will advise you of your right to benefits, if any, before you engaged in substantial gainful activity and to reentitlement should you stop performing substantial gainful activity. If you disagree with our determination, you will have the right to appeal this decision. If the final decision on your appeal of your medical cessation is an unfavorable one (the cessation is affirmed), you will also be sent a written notice advising you of our determination, and your right to appeal if you think we are wrong.

(6) If a court orders that your case be sent back to us (remanded) and your case is sent to an administrative law judge for further action under the rules provided in § 404.983, the administrative law judge's decision or dismissal order on your medical cessation appeal is vacated and is no longer in effect. Continued benefits are payable to you and anyone else receiving benefits based on your wages and self-employment income or because of your disability pending a new decision by the administrative law judge or final action is taken by the Appeals Council on the administrative law judge's recommended decision. In these court-remanded cases reaching the administrative law judge, we will follow the same rules provided in paragraphs (i)(1), (2), (3), (4) and (5) of this section.

(j) Responsibility to pay back continued benefits.

(1) If the final decision of the Commissioner affirms the determination that you are not entitled to benefits, you will be asked to pay back any continued benefits you receive. However, as described in the overpayment recovery and waiver provisions of subpart F of this part, you will have the right to ask that you not be required to pay back the benefits. You will not be asked to pay back any Medicare benefits you received during the appeal.

(2) Anyone else receiving benefits based on your wages and self-employment income (or because of your disability) will be asked to pay back any continued benefits he or she received if the determination that your physical or mental impairment(s) has ceased, has never existed, or is no longer disabling, is not changed by the final decision of the Commissioner. However, he or she will have the right to ask that he or she not be required to pay them back, as described in the overpayment recovery and waiver provisions of subpart F of this part. He or she will not be asked to pay back any Medicare benefits he or she received during the appeal.

(3) Waiver of recovery of an overpayment resulting from the continued benefits paid to you or anyone else receiving benefits based on your wages and self-employment income (or because of your disability) may be considered as long as the determination was appealed in good faith. It will be assumed that such appeal is made in good faith and, therefore, any overpaid individual has the right to waiver consideration unless such individual fails to cooperate in connection with the appeal, e.g., if the individual fails (without good reason) to give us medical or other evidence we request, or to go for a physical or mental examination when requested by us, in connection with the appeal. In determining whether an individual has good cause for failure to cooperate and, thus, whether an appeal was made in good faith, we will take into account any physical, mental, educational, or linguistic limitations (including any lack of facility with the English language) the individual may have which may have caused the individual's failure to cooperate.

[53 FR 29020, Aug. 2, 1988; 53 FR 39015, Oct. 4, 1988; 55 FR 2806, Jan. 29, 1990; 55 FR 35578, Aug. 31, 1990; 57 FR 1383, Jan. 14, 1992; 59 FR 1635, Jan. 12, 1994; 62 FR 38451, July 18, 1997; 65 FR 16814, March 30, 2000]

§ 404.1598 If you become disabled by another impairment(s).

If a new severe impairment(s) begins in or before the month in which your last impairment(s) ends, we will find that your disability is continuing. The new impairment(s) need not be expected to last 12 months or to result in death, but it must be severe enough to keep you from doing substantial gainful activity, or severe enough so that you are still disabled under § 404.1594.

[50 FR 50136, Dec. 6, 1985]

§ 404.1599 Work incentive experiments and rehabilitation demonstration projects in the disability program.

(a) Authority and purpose. Section 505(a) of the Social Security Disability Amendments of 1980, Pub.L. 96–265, directs the Commissioner to develop and conduct experiments and demonstration projects designed to provide more cost-effective ways of encouraging disabled beneficiaries to return to work and leave benefit rolls. These experiments and demonstration projects will test the advantages and disadvantages of altering certain limitations and conditions that apply to title II disabled beneficiaries. The objective of all work incentive experiments or rehabilitation demonstrations is to determine whether the alternative requirements will save Trust Fund monies or otherwise improve the administration of the disability program established under title II of the Act.

(b) Altering benefit requirements, limitations or conditions. Notwithstanding any other provision of this part, the Commissioner may waive compliance with the entitlement and payment requirements for disabled beneficiaries to carry our experiments and demonstration projects in the title II disability program. The projects involve altering certain limitations and conditions that currently apply to applicants and beneficiaries to test their effect on the program.

(c) Applicability and scope—

(1) Participants and nonparticipants. If you are selected to participate in an experiment or demonstration project, we may temporarily set aside one or more of the current benefit entitlement or payment requirements, limitations or conditions and apply alternative provisions to you. We may also modify current methods of administering the Act as part of a project and apply alternative procedures or policies to you. The alternative provisions or methods of administration used in the projects will not disadvantage you in contrast to current provisions, procedures or policies. If you are not selected to participate in the experiments or demonstration projects (or if you are placed in a control group which is not subject to alternative requirements and methods) we will continue to apply to you the current benefit entitlement and payment requirements, limitations and conditions and methods of administration in the title II disability program.

(2) Alternative provisions or methods of administration. The alternative provisions or methods of administration that apply to you in an experiment or demonstration project may include (but are not limited to) one or more of the following:

(i) Reducing your benefits (instead of not paying) on the basis of the amount of your earnings in excess of the SGA amount;

(ii) Extending your benefit eligibility period that follows 9 months of trial work, perhaps coupled with benefit reductions related to your earnings;

(iii) Extending your Medicare benefits if you are severely impaired and return to work even though you may not be entitled to monthly cash benefits;

(iv) Altering the 24–month waiting period for Medicare entitlement; and

(v) Stimulating new forms of rehabilitation.

(d) Selection of participants. We will select a probability sample of participants for the work incentive experiments and demonstration projects from newly awarded beneficiaries who meet certain pre-selection criteria (for example, individuals who are likely to be able to do substantial work despite continuing severe impairments). These criteria are designed to provide larger subsamples of beneficiaries who are not likely either to recover medically or die. Participants may also be selected from persons who have been receiving DI benefits for 6 months or more at the time of selection.

(e) Duration of experiments and demonstration projects. A notice describing each experiment or demonstration project will be published in the Federal Register before each experiment or project is placed in operation. The work incentive experiments and rehabilitation demonstrations will be activated in 1982. A final report on the results of the experiments and projects is to be completed and transmitted to Congress by June 9, 1993. However, the authority for the experiments and demonstration projects will not terminate at that time. Some of the alternative provisions or methods of administration may continue to apply to participants in an experiment or demonstration project beyond that date in order to assure the validity of the research. Each experiment and demonstration project will have a termination date (up to 10 years from the start of the experiment or demonstration project).

[48 FR 7575, Feb. 23, 1983; 52 FR 37605, Oct. 8, 1987; 55 FR 51687, Dec. 17, 1990; 62 FR 38451, July 18, 1997]

APPENDIX 1 TO SUBPART P OF PART 404—LISTING OF IMPAIRMENTS

Source: 50 FR 35066, Aug. 28, 1985; 50 FR 38113, Sept. 20, 1985; 51 FR 5989, Feb. 19, 1986; 51 FR 7933, March 7, 1986; 51 FR 16016, April 30, 1986; 53 FR 29879, Aug. 9, 1988; 54 FR 50235, Dec. 5, 1989; 55 FR 35287, Aug. 28, 1990; 55 FR 38190, Sept. 17, 1990; 55 FR 51101, 51208, 51229, 51230, Dec. 12, 1990; 56 FR 11304, 11305, March 15, 1991; 56 FR 26031, June 6, 1991; 56 FR 40781, Aug. 16, 1991; 56 FR 60060, Nov. 27, 1991; 57 FR 23946, 23947, June 5, 1992; 57 FR 24187, June 8, 1992; 57 FR 30121, July 8, 1992; 57 FR 57666, Dec. 7, 1992; 57 FR 61796, Dec. 29, 1992; 58 FR 31907, June 7, 1993; 58 FR 36051, 36052, 36056, July 2, 1993; 58 FR 36134, July 6, 1993; 58 FR 44445, Aug. 23, 1993; 58 FR 52359, Oct. 7, 1993; 58 FR 64123, Dec. 6, 1993; 59 FR 671, Jan. 6, 1994; 59 FR 1275, 1416, Jan. 10, 1994; 59 FR 6497, 6501, Feb. 10, 1994; 59 FR 30389, June 13, 1994; 59 FR 41975, Aug. 16, 1994; 60 FR 43710, Aug. 23, 1995; 60 FR 53267, Oct. 13, 1995; 60 FR 62330, Dec. 6, 1995; 61 FR 28047, June 4, 1996; 61 FR 64616, Dec. 6, 1996; 62 FR 6418, 6420, Feb. 11, 1997; 62 FR 13733, March 21, 1997; 62 FR 30747, June 5, 1997; 63 FR 4571, Jan. 30, 1998; 63 FR 30411, June 4, 1998; 64 FR 29788, June 3, 1999; 64 FR 46128, 46129, Aug. 24, 1999; 64 FR 67720, Dec. 3, 1999; 65 FR 31802, May 19, 2000; 65 FR 50775, 50780, Aug. 21, 2000; 65 FR 54776, Sept. 11, 2000; 65 FR 57947, Sept. 27, 2000; 66 FR 34362, June 28, 2001; 66 FR 58037, 58040, 58041, 58044, 58045, Nov. 19, 2001; 67 FR 20024, April 24, 2002; 67 FR 35723, May 21, 2002; 67 FR 43538, June 28, 2002; 68 FR 36912, June 20, 2003; 68 FR 51693, Aug. 28, 2003; 69 FR 32269, June 9, 2004; 69 FR 67032, Dec. 15, 2004; 70 FR 15227, March 25, 2005; 70 FR 35029, June 16, 2005; 70 FR 38590, July 5, 2005; 70 FR 51259–51261, Aug. 30, 2005; 71 FR 2325, 2335, Jan. 13, 2006; 71 FR 26412, May 5, 2006; 71 FR 67050, Nov. 20, 2006; 71 FR 77098, Dec. 22, 2006; 72 FR 33664, June 19, 2007; 72 FR 59422, 59426, Oct. 19, 2007; 73 FR 14601, March 18, 2008; 73 FR 31027, May 30, 2008; 74 FR 5808, Feb. 2, 2009; 74 FR 51232, Oct. 6, 2009; 75 FR 30701, June 2, 2010; 75 FR 33167, June 11, 2010; 76 FR 16532, March 24, 2011; 76 FR 19696, April 8, 2011; 77 FR 35265, June 13, 2012; 78 FR 7660, Feb. 4, 2013; 78 FR 18839, March 28, 2013; 78 FR 46501, Aug. 1, 2013; 78 FR 54757, Sept. 6, 2013; 78 FR 72572, Dec. 3, 2013; 79 FR 10662, Feb. 26, 2014; 79 FR 61224, Oct. 10, 2014; 79 FR 67350, Nov. 13, 2014; 80 FR 2, Jan. 2, 2015; 80 FR 19525, April 13, 2015; 80 FR 21165, April 17, 2015; 80 FR 28826, May 20, 2015; 80 FR

48248, Aug. 12, 2015; 81 FR 32645, May 24, 2016; 81 FR 37143, June 9, 2016; 81 FR 43052, July 1, 2016; 81 FR 51102, Aug. 3, 2016; 81 FR 66161, Sept. 26, 2016; 81 FR 86923, Dec. 2, 2016; 81 FR 86928, Dec. 2, 2016; 82 FR 5872, Jan. 18, 2017; 82 FR 39665, Aug. 22, 2017; 82 FR 59515, Dec. 15, 2017; 83 FR 11143, March 14, 2018; 83 FR 13863, April 2, 2018; 83 FR 23581, May 22, 2018, unless otherwise noted.

APPENDIX 1–PART–A1 TO SUBPART P OF PART 404—LISTING OF IMPAIRMENTS

The body system listings in parts A and B of the Listing of Impairments will no longer be effective on the following dates unless extended by the Commissioner or revised and promulgated again.

1. Low Birth Weight and Failure to Thrive (100.00): June 12, 2020.

2. Musculoskeletal System (1.00 and 101.00): January 27, 2020.

3. Special Senses and Speech (2.00 and 102.00): April 24, 2020.

4. Respiratory Disorders (3.00 and 103.00): October 7, 2019.

5. Cardiovascular System (4.00 and 104.00): January 27, 2020.

6. Digestive System (5.00 and 105.00): January 27, 2020.

7. Genitourinary Disorders (6.00 and 106.00): December 9, 2019.

8. Hematological Disorders (7.00 and 107.00): May 18, 2020.

9. Skin Disorders (8.00 and 108.00): January 27, 2020.

10. Endocrine Disorders (9.00 and 109.00): June 26, 2020.

11. Congenital Disorders That Affect Multiple Body Systems (10.00 and 110.00): April 3, 2020.

12. Neurological Disorders (11.00 and 111.00): September 29, 2021.

13. Mental Disorders (12.00 and 112.00): January 17, 2022.

14. Cancer (Malignant Neoplastic Diseases) (13.00 and 113.00): July 20, 2020.

15. Immune System Disorders (14.00 and 114.00): January 17, 2020.

Part A

Criteria applicable to individuals age 18 and over and to children under age 18 where criteria are appropriate.

Sec.

1.00 Musculoskeletal System.
2.00 Special Senses and Speech.
3.00 Respiratory Disorders
4.00 Cardiovascular System.
5.00 Digestive System.
6.00 Genitourinary Disorders.
7.00 Hematological Disorders.
8.00 Skin Disorders.
9.00 Endocrine Disorders.
10.00 Congenital Disorders That Affect Multiple Body Systems
11.00 Neurological Disorders
12.00 Mental Disorders.
13.00 Cancer (Malignant Neoplastic Diseases)
14.00 Immune System Disorders.

1.00 Musculoskeletal System

A. Disorders of the musculoskeletal system may result from hereditary, congenital, or acquired pathologic processes. Impairments may result from infectious, inflammatory, or degenerative processes, traumatic or developmental events, or neoplastic, vascular, or toxic/metabolic diseases.

B. Loss of function.

1. General. Under this section, loss of function may be due to bone or joint deformity or destruction from any cause; miscellaneous disorders of the spine with or without radiculopathy or other neurological deficits; amputation; or fractures or soft tissue injuries, including burns, requiring prolonged periods of immobility or convalescence. The provisions of 1.02 and 1.03 notwithstanding, inflammatory arthritis is evaluated under 14.09 (see 14.00D6). Impairments with neurological causes are to be evaluated under 11.00ff.

2. How We Define Loss of Function in These Listings

a. General. Regardless of the cause(s) of a musculoskeletal impairment, functional loss for purposes of these listings is defined as the inability to ambulate effectively on a sustained basis for any reason, including pain associated with the underlying musculoskeletal impairment, or the inability to perform fine and gross movements effectively on a sustained basis for any reason, including pain associated with the underlying musculoskeletal impairment. The inability to ambulate effectively or the inability to perform fine and gross movements effectively must have lasted, or be expected to last, for at least 12 months. For the purposes of these criteria, consideration of the ability to perform these activities must be from a physical standpoint alone. When there is an inability to perform these activities due to a mental impairment, the criteria in 12.00ff are to be used. We will determine whether an individual can ambulate effectively or can perform fine and gross movements effectively based on the medical and other evidence in the case record, generally without developing additional evidence about the individual's ability to perform the specific activities listed as examples in 1.00B2b(2) and 1.00B2c.

b. What We Mean by Inability To Ambulate Effectively

(1) Definition. Inability to ambulate effectively means an extreme limitation of the ability to walk; i.e., an impairment(s) that interferes very seriously with the individual's ability to independently initiate, sustain, or complete activities. Ineffective ambulation is defined generally as having insufficient lower extremity functioning (see 1.00J) to permit independent ambulation without the use of a hand-held assistive device(s) that limits the functioning of both upper extremities. (Listing 1.05C is an exception to this general definition because the individual has the use of only one upper extremity due to amputation of a hand.)

(2) To ambulate effectively, individuals must be capable of sustaining a reasonable walking pace over a sufficient distance to be able to carry out activities of daily living. They must have the ability to travel without companion assistance to and from a place of employment or school. Therefore, examples of ineffective ambulation include, but are not limited to, the inability to walk without the use of a walker, two crutches or two canes, the inability to walk a block at a reasonable pace on rough or uneven surfaces, the inability to use standard public transportation, the inability to carry out routine ambulatory activities, such as shopping and banking, and the inability to climb a few steps at a reasonable pace with the use of a single hand rail. The ability to walk independently about one's home without the use of assistive devices does not, in and of itself, constitute effective ambulation.

c. What we mean by inability to perform fine and gross movements effectively. Inability to perform fine and gross movements effectively means an extreme loss of function of both upper extremities; i.e., an impairment(s) that interferes very seriously with the individual's ability to independently initiate, sustain, or complete activities. To use their upper extremities effectively, individuals must be capable of sustaining such functions as reaching, pushing, pulling, grasping, and fingering to be able to carry out activities of daily living. Therefore, examples of inability to perform fine and gross movements effectively include, but are not limited to, the inability to prepare a simple meal and feed oneself, the inability to take care of personal hygiene, the inability to sort and handle papers or files, and the inability to place files in a file cabinet at or above waist level.

d. Pain or other symptoms. Pain or other symptoms may be an important factor contributing to functional loss. In order for pain or other symptoms to be found to affect an individual's ability to perform basic work activities, medical signs or laboratory findings must show the existence of a medically determinable impairment(s) that could reasonably be expected to produce the pain or other symptoms. The musculoskeletal listings that include pain or other symptoms among their criteria also include criteria for limitations in functioning as a result of the listed impairment, including limitations caused by pain. It is, therefore, important to evaluate the intensity and persistence of such pain or other symptoms carefully in order to determine their impact on the individual's functioning under these listings. See also §§ 404.1525(f) and 404.1529 of this part, and §§ 416.925(f) and 416.929 of part 416 of this chapter.

C. Diagnosis and Evaluation

1. General. Diagnosis and evaluation of musculoskeletal impairments should be supported, as applicable, by detailed descriptions of the joints, including ranges of motion, condition of the musculature (e.g., weakness, atrophy), sensory or reflex changes, circulatory deficits, and laboratory findings, including findings on x-ray or other appropriate medically acceptable imaging. Medically acceptable imaging includes, but is not limited to, x-ray imaging, computerized axial tomography (CAT scan) or magnetic resonance imaging (MRI), with or without contrast material, myelography, and radionuclear bone scans. "Appropriate" means that the technique used is the proper one to support the evaluation and diagnosis of the impairment.

2. Purchase of certain medically acceptable imaging. While any appropriate medically acceptable imaging is useful in establishing the diagnosis of musculoskeletal impairments, some tests, such as CAT scans and MRIs, are quite expensive, and we will not routinely purchase them. Some, such as myelograms, are invasive and may involve significant risk. We will not order such tests. However, when the results of any of these tests are part of the existing evidence in the case record we will consider them together with the other relevant evidence.

3. Consideration of electrodiagnostic procedures. Electrodiagnostic procedures may be useful in establishing the clinical diagnosis, but do not constitute alternative criteria to the requirements of 1.04.

D. The physical examination must include a detailed description of the rheumatological, orthopedic, neurological, and other findings appropriate to the specific impairment being evaluated. These physical findings must be determined on the basis of objective observation during the examination and not simply a report of the individual's allegation; e.g., "He says his leg is weak, numb." Alternative testing methods should be used to verify the abnormal findings; e.g., a seated straight-leg raising test in addition to a supine straight-leg raising test. Because abnormal physical findings may be intermittent, their presence over a period of time must be established by a record of ongoing management and evaluation. Care must be taken to ascertain that the reported examination findings are consistent with the individual's daily activities.

E. Examination of the Spine

1. General. Examination of the spine should include a detailed description of gait, range of motion of the spine given quantitatively in degrees from the vertical position (zero degrees) or, for straight-leg raising from the sitting and supine position (zero degrees), any other appropriate tension signs, motor and sensory abnormalities, muscle spasm, when present, and deep tendon reflexes. Observations of the individual during the examination should be reported; e.g., how he or she gets on and off the examination table. Inability to walk on the heels or toes, to squat, or to arise from a squatting position, when appropriate, may be considered evidence of significant motor loss. However, a report of atrophy is not acceptable as evidence of significant motor loss without circumferential measurements of both thighs and lower legs, or both upper and lower arms, as appropriate, at a stated point above and below the knee or elbow given in inches or centimeters. Additionally, a report of atrophy should be accompanied by measurement of the strength of the muscle(s) in question generally based on a grading system of 0 to 5, with 0 being complete loss of strength and 5 being maximum strength. A specific description of atrophy of hand muscles is acceptable without measurements of atrophy but should include measurements of grip and pinch strength.

2. When neurological abnormalities persist. Neurological abnormalities may not completely subside after treatment or with the passage of time. Therefore, residual neurological abnormalities that persist after it has been determined clinically or by direct surgical or other observation that the ongoing or progressive condition is no longer present will not satisfy the required findings in 1.04. More serious neurological deficits (paraparesis, paraplegia) are to be evaluated under the criteria in 11.00ff.

F. Major joints refers to the major peripheral joints, which are the hip, knee, shoulder, elbow, wrist-hand, and ankle-foot, as opposed to other peripheral joints (e.g., the joints of the hand or forefoot) or axial joints (i.e., the joints of the spine.) The wrist and hand are considered together as one major joint, as are the ankle and foot. Since only the ankle joint, which consists of the juncture of the bones of the lower leg (tibia and fibula) with the hindfoot (tarsal bones), but not the forefoot, is crucial to weight bearing, the ankle and foot are considered separately in evaluating weight bearing.

G. Measurements of joint motion are based on the techniques described in the chapter on the extremities, spine, and pelvis in the current edition of the "Guides to the Evaluation of Permanent Impairment" published by the American Medical Association.

H. Documentation

1. General. Musculoskeletal impairments frequently improve with time or respond to treatment. Therefore, a longitudinal clinical record is generally important for the assessment of severity and expected duration of an impairment unless the claim can be decided favorably on the basis of the current evidence.

2. Documentation of medically prescribed treatment and response. Many individuals, especially those who have listing-level impairments, will have received the benefit of medically prescribed treatment. Whenever evidence of such treatment is available it must be considered.

3. When there is no record of ongoing treatment. Some individuals will not have received ongoing treatment or have an ongoing relationship with the medical community despite the existence of a severe impairment(s). In such cases, evaluation will be made on the basis of the current objective medical evidence and other available evidence, taking into consideration the individual's medical history, symptoms, and medical source opinions. Even though an individual who does not receive treatment may not be able to show an impairment that meets the criteria of one of the musculoskeletal listings, the individual may have an impairment(s) equivalent in severity to one of the listed impairments or be disabled based on consideration of his or her residual functional capacity (RFC) and age, education and work experience.

4. Evaluation when the criteria of a musculoskeletal listing are not met. These listings are only examples of common musculoskeletal disorders that are severe enough to prevent a person from engaging in gainful activity. Therefore, in any case in which an individual has a medically determinable impairment that is not listed, an impairment that does not meet the requirements of a listing, or a combination of impairments no one of which meets the requirements of a listing, we will consider medical equivalence. (See §§ 404.1526 and 416.926.) Individuals who have an impairment(s) with a level of severity that does not meet or equal the criteria of the musculoskeletal listings may or may not have the RFC that would enable them to engage in substantial gainful activity. Evaluation of the impairment(s) of these individuals should proceed through the final steps of the sequential evaluation process in §§ 404.1520 and 416.920 (or, as appropriate, the steps in the medical improvement review standard in §§ 404.1594 and 416.994).

I. Effects of Treatment

1. General. Treatments for musculoskeletal disorders may have beneficial effects or adverse side effects. Therefore, medical treatment (including surgical treatment) must be considered in terms of its effectiveness in ameliorating the signs, symptoms, and laboratory

abnormalities of the disorder, and in terms of any side effects that may further limit the individual.

2. Response to treatment. Response to treatment and adverse consequences of treatment may vary widely. For example, a pain medication may relieve an individual's pain completely, partially, or not at all. It may also result in adverse effects, e.g., drowsiness, dizziness, or disorientation, that compromise the individual's ability to function. Therefore, each case must be considered on an individual basis, and include consideration of the effects of treatment on the individual's ability to function.

3. Documentation. A specific description of the drugs or treatment given (including surgery), dosage, frequency of administration, and a description of the complications or response to treatment should be obtained. The effects of treatment may be temporary or long-term. As such, the finding regarding the impact of treatment must be based on a sufficient period of treatment to permit proper consideration or judgment about future functioning.

J. Orthotic, Prosthetic, or Assistive Devices

1. General. Consistent with clinical practice, individuals with musculoskeletal impairments may be examined with and without the use of any orthotic, prosthetic, or assistive devices as explained in this section.

2. Orthotic devices. Examination should be with the orthotic device in place and should include an evaluation of the individual's maximum ability to function effectively with the orthosis. It is unnecessary to routinely evaluate the individual's ability to function without the orthosis in place. If the individual has difficulty with, or is unable to use, the orthotic device, the medical basis for the difficulty should be documented. In such cases, if the impairment involves a lower extremity or extremities, the examination should include information on the individual's ability to ambulate effectively without the device in place unless contraindicated by the medical judgment of a physician who has treated or examined the individual.

3. Prosthetic devices. Examination should be with the prosthetic device in place. In amputations involving a lower extremity or extremities, it is unnecessary to evaluate the individual's ability to walk without the prosthesis in place. However, the individual's medical ability to use a prosthesis to ambulate effectively, as defined in 1.00B2b, should be evaluated. The condition of the stump should be evaluated without the prosthesis in place.

4. Hand-held assistive devices. When an individual with an impairment involving a lower extremity or extremities uses a hand-held assistive device, such as a cane, crutch or walker, examination should be with and without the use of the assistive device unless contraindicated by the medical judgment of a physician who has treated or examined the individual. The individual's ability to ambulate with and without the device provides information as to whether, or the extent to which, the individual is able to ambulate without assistance. The medical basis for the use of any assistive device (e.g., instability, weakness) should be documented. The requirement to use a hand-held assistive device may also impact on the individual's functional capacity by virtue of the fact that one or both upper extremities are not available for such activities as lifting, carrying, pushing, and pulling.

K. Disorders of the spine, listed in 1.04, result in limitations because of distortion of the bony and ligamentous architecture of the spine and associated impingement on nerve roots (including the cauda equina) or spinal cord. Such impingement on nerve tissue may result from a herniated nucleus pulposus, spinal stenosis, arachnoiditis, or other miscellaneous conditions.

1. Herniated nucleus pulposus is a disorder frequently associated with the impingement of a nerve root. Nerve root compression results in a specific neuro-anatomic distribution of symptoms and signs depending upon the nerve root(s) compromised.

2. Spinal Arachnoiditis

a. General. Spinal arachnoiditis is a condition characterized by adhesive thickening of the arachnoid which may cause intermittent ill-defined burning pain and sensory dysesthesia, and may cause neurogenic bladder or bowel incontinence when the cauda equina is involved.

b. Documentation. Although the cause of spinal arachnoiditis is not always clear, it may be associated with chronic compression or irritation of nerve roots (including the cauda equina) or the spinal cord. For example, there may be evidence of spinal stenosis, or a history of spinal trauma or meningitis. Diagnosis must be confirmed at the time of surgery by gross description, microscopic examination of biopsied tissue, or by findings on appropriate medically acceptable imaging. Arachnoiditis is sometimes used as a diagnosis when such a diagnosis is unsupported by clinical or laboratory findings. Therefore, care must be taken to ensure that the diagnosis is documented as described in 1.04B. Individuals with arachnoiditis, particularly when it involves the lumbosacral spine, are generally unable to sustain any given position or posture for more than a short period of time due to pain.

3. Lumbar spinal stenosis is a condition that may occur in association with degenerative processes, or as a result of a congenital anomaly or trauma, or in association with Paget's disease of the bone. Pseudoclaudication, which may result from lumbar spinal stenosis, is manifested as pain and weakness, and may impair ambulation. Symptoms are usually bilateral, in the low back, buttocks, or thighs, although some individuals may experience only leg pain and, in a few cases, the leg pain may be unilateral. The pain gener-

ally does not follow a particular neuro-anatomical distribution, i.e., it is distinctly different from the radicular type of pain seen with a herniated intervertebral disc, is often of a dull, aching quality, which may be described as "discomfort" or an "unpleasant sensation," or may be of even greater severity, usually in the low back and radiating into the buttocks region bilaterally. The pain is provoked by extension of the spine, as in walking or merely standing, but is reduced by leaning forward. The distance the individual has to walk before the pain comes on may vary. Pseudoclaudication differs from peripheral vascular claudication in several ways. Pedal pulses and Doppler examinations are unaffected by pseudoclaudication. Leg pain resulting from peripheral vascular claudication involves the calves, and the leg pain in vascular claudication is ordinarily more severe than any back pain that may also be present. An individual with vascular claudication will experience pain after walking the same distance time after time, and the pain will be relieved quickly when walking stops.

4. Other miscellaneous conditions that may cause weakness of the lower extremities, sensory changes, areflexia, trophic ulceration, bladder or bowel incontinence, and that should be evaluated under 1.04 include, but are not limited to, osteoarthritis, degenerative disc disease, facet arthritis, and vertebral fracture. Disorders such as spinal dysrhaphism (e.g., spina bifida), diastematomyelia, and tethered cord syndrome may also cause such abnormalities. In these cases, there may be gait difficulty and deformity of the lower extremities based on neurological abnormalities, and the neurological effects are to be evaluated under the criteria in 11.00ff.

L. Abnormal curvatures of the spine. Abnormal curvatures of the spine (specifically, scoliosis, kyphosis and kyphoscoliosis) can result in impaired ambulation, but may also adversely affect functioning in body systems other than the musculoskeletal system. For example, an individual's ability to breathe may be affected; there may be cardiac difficulties (e.g., impaired myocardial function); or there may be disfigurement resulting in withdrawal or isolation. When there is impaired ambulation, evaluation of equivalence may be made by reference to 14.09A. When the abnormal curvature of the spine results in symptoms related to fixation of the dorsolumbar or cervical spine, evaluation of equivalence may be made by reference to 14.09C. When there is respiratory or cardiac involvement or an associated mental disorder, evaluation may be made under 3.00ff, 4.00ff, or 12.00ff, as appropriate. Other consequences should be evaluated according to the listing for the affected body system.

M. Under continuing surgical management, as used in 1.07 and 1.08, refers to surgical procedures and any other associated treatments related to the efforts directed toward the salvage or restoration of functional use of the affected part. It may include such factors as post-surgical procedures, surgical complications, infections, or other medical complications, related illnesses, or related treatments that delay the individual's attainment of maximum benefit from therapy. When burns are not under continuing surgical management, see 8.00F.

N. After maximum benefit from therapy has been achieved in situations involving fractures of an upper extremity (1.07), or soft tissue injuries (1.08), i.e., there have been no significant changes in physical findings or on appropriate medically acceptable imaging for any 6–month period after the last definitive surgical procedure or other medical intervention, evaluation must be made on the basis of the demonstrable residuals, if any. A finding that 1.07 or 1.08 is met must be based on a consideration of the symptoms, signs, and laboratory findings associated with recent or anticipated surgical procedures and the resulting recuperative periods, including any related medical complications, such as infections, illnesses, and therapies which impede or delay the efforts toward restoration of function. Generally, when there has been no surgical or medical intervention for 6 months after the last definitive surgical procedure, it can be concluded that maximum therapeutic benefit has been reached. Evaluation at this point must be made on the basis of the demonstrable residual limitations, if any, considering the individual's impairment-related symptoms, signs, and laboratory findings, any residual symptoms, signs, and laboratory findings associated with such surgeries, complications, and recuperative periods, and other relevant evidence.

O. Major function of the face and head, for purposes of listing 1.08, relates to impact on any or all of the activities involving vision, hearing, speech, mastication, and the initiation of the digestive process.

P. When surgical procedures have been performed, documentation should include a copy of the operative notes and available pathology reports.

Q. Effects of obesity. Obesity is a medically determinable impairment that is often associated with disturbance of the musculoskeletal system, and disturbance of this system can be a major cause of disability in individuals with obesity. The combined effects of obesity with musculoskeletal impairments can be greater than the effects of each of the impairments considered separately. Therefore, when determining whether an individual with obesity has a listing-level impairment or combination of impairments, and when assessing a claim at other steps of the sequential evaluation process, including when assessing an individual's residual functional capacity, adjudicators must consider any additional and cumulative effects of obesity.

1.01 Category of Impairments, Musculoskeletal

1.02 Major dysfunction of a joint(s) (due to any cause): Characterized by gross anatomical deformity (e.g., subluxation, contracture, bony or fibrous ankylosis, instability) and chronic joint pain and stiffness with signs of limitation of motion or other abnormal motion of the affected joint(s), and findings on appropriate medically acceptable imaging of joint space narrowing, bony destruction, or ankylosis of the affected joint(s). With:

A. Involvement of one major peripheral weight-bearing joint (i.e., hip, knee, or ankle), resulting in inability to ambulate effectively, as defined in 1.00B2b;

or

B. Involvement of one major peripheral joint in each upper extremity (i.e., shoulder, elbow, or wrist-hand), resulting in inability to perform fine and gross movements effectively, as defined in 1.00B2c.

1.03 Reconstructive surgery or surgical arthrodesis of a major weight-bearing joint, with inability to ambulate effectively, as defined in 1.00B2b, and return to effective ambulation did not occur, or is not expected to occur, within 12 months of onset.

1.04 Disorders of the spine (e.g., herniated nucleus pulposus, spinal arachnoiditis, spinal stenosis, osteoarthritis, degenerative disc disease, facet arthritis, vertebral fracture), resulting in compromise of a nerve root (including the cauda equina) or the spinal cord. With:

A. Evidence of nerve root compression characterized by neuro-anatomic distribution of pain, limitation of motion of the spine, motor loss (atrophy with associated muscle weakness or muscle weakness) accompanied by sensory or reflex loss and, if there is involvement of the lower back, positive straight-leg raising test (sitting and supine);

or

B. Spinal arachnoiditis, confirmed by an operative note or pathology report of tissue biopsy, or by appropriate medically acceptable imaging, manifested by severe burning or painful dysesthesia, resulting in the need for changes in position or posture more than once every 2 hours;

or

C. Lumbar spinal stenosis resulting in pseudoclaudication, established by findings on appropriate medically acceptable imaging, manifested by chronic nonradicular pain and weakness, and resulting in inability to ambulate effectively, as defined in 1.00B2b.

1.05 Amputation (due to any cause).

A. Both hands;

or

B. One or both lower extremities at or above the tarsal region, with stump complications resulting in medical inability to use a prosthetic device to ambulate effectively, as defined in 1.00B2b, which have lasted or are expected to last for at least 12 months;

or

C. One hand and one lower extremity at or above the tarsal region, with inability to ambulate effectively, as defined in 1.00B2b;

or

D. Hemipelvectomy or hip disarticulation.

1.06 Fracture of the femur, tibia, pelvis, or one or more of the tarsal bones. With:

A. Solid union not evident on appropriate medically acceptable imaging and not clinically solid;

and

B. Inability to ambulate effectively, as defined in 1.00B2b, and return to effective ambulation did not occur or is not expected to occur within 12 months of onset.

1.07 Fracture of an upper extremity with nonunion of a fracture of the shaft of the humerus, radius, or ulna, under continuing surgical management, as defined in 1.00M, directed toward restoration of functional use of the extremity, and such function was not restored or expected to be restored within 12 months of onset.

1.08 Soft tissue injury (e.g., burns) of an upper or lower extremity, trunk, or face and head, under continuing surgical management, as defined in 1.00M, directed toward the salvage or restoration of major function, and such major function was not restored or expected to be restored within 12 months of onset. Major function of the face and head is described in 1.00O.

2.00 Special Senses and Speech

A. How do we evaluate visual disorders?

1. What are visual disorders? Visual disorders are abnormalities of the eye, the optic nerve, the optic tracts, or the brain that may cause a loss of visual acuity or visual fields. A loss of visual acuity limits your ability to distinguish detail, read, or do fine work. A loss of visual fields limits your ability to perceive visual stimuli in the peripheral extent of vision.

2. How do we define statutory blindness? Statutory blindness is blindness as defined in sections 216(i)(1) and 1614(a)(2) of the Social Security Act (Act).

a. The Act defines blindness as central visual acuity of 20/200 or less in the better eye with the use of a correcting lens. We use your best-corrected central visual acuity for distance in the better eye when we determine if this definition is met. (For visual acuity testing requirements, see 2.00A5.)

b. The Act also provides that an eye that has a visual field limitation such that the widest diameter of the visual field subtends an angle no greater than 20 degrees is considered as having a central visual acuity of 20/200 or less. (For visual field testing requirements, see 2.00A6.)

c. You have statutory blindness only if your visual disorder meets the criteria of 2.02 or 2.03A. You do not have statutory blindness if your visual disorder medically equals the criteria of 2.02 or 2.03A or meets or medically equals the criteria of 2.03B, 2.03C, 2.04A, or 2.04B because your disability is based on criteria other than those in the statutory definition of blindness.

3. What evidence do we need to establish statutory blindness under title XVI? To establish that you have statutory blindness under title XVI, we need evidence showing only that your central visual acuity in your better eye or your visual field in your better eye meets the criteria in 2.00A2, provided that those measurements are consistent with the other evidence in your case record. We do not need documentation of the cause of your blindness. Also, there is no duration requirement for statutory blindness under title XVI (see §§ 416.981 and 416.983 of this chapter).

4. What evidence do we need to evaluate visual disorders, including those that result in statutory blindness under title II? To evaluate your visual disorder, we usually need a report of an eye examination that includes measurements of your best-corrected central visual acuity (see 2.00A5) or the extent of your visual fields (see 2.00A6), as appropriate. If you have visual acuity or visual field loss, we need documentation of the cause of the loss. A standard eye examination will usually indicate the cause of any visual acuity loss. A standard eye examination can also indicate the cause of some types of visual field deficits. Some disorders, such as cortical visual disorders, may result in abnormalities that do not appear on a standard eye examination. If the standard eye examination does not indicate the cause of your vision loss, we will request the information used to establish the presence of your visual disorder. If your visual disorder does not satisfy the criteria in 2.02, 2.03, or 2.04, we will request a description of how your visual disorder affects your ability to function.

5. How do we measure your best-corrected central visual acuity?

a. Visual acuity testing. When we need to measure your best-corrected central visual acuity (your optimal visual acuity attainable with the use of a corrective lens), we use visual acuity testing for distance that was carried out using Snellen methodology or any other testing methodology that is comparable to Snellen methodology.

(i) Your best-corrected central visual acuity for distance is usually measured by determining what you can see from 20 feet. If your visual acuity is measured for a distance other than 20 feet, we will convert it to a 20–foot measurement. For example, if your visual acuity is measured at 10 feet and is reported as 10/40, we will convert this measurement to 20/80.

(ii) A visual acuity recorded as CF (counts fingers), HM (hand motion only), LP or LPO (light perception or light perception only), or NLP (no light perception) indicates that no optical correction will improve your visual acuity. If your central visual acuity in an eye is recorded as CF, HM, LP or LPO, or NLP, we will determine that your best-corrected central visual acuity is 20/200 or less in that eye.

(iii) We will not use the results of pinhole testing or automated refraction acuity to determine your best-corrected central visual acuity. These tests provide an estimate of potential visual acuity but not an actual measurement of your best-corrected central visual acuity.

b. Other test charts. Most test charts that use Snellen methodology do not have lines that measure visual acuity between 20/100 and 20/200. Some test charts, such as the Bailey–Lovie or the Early Treatment Diabetic Retinopathy Study (ETDRS), used mostly in research settings, have such lines. If your visual acuity is measured with one of these charts, and you cannot read any of the letters on the 20/100 line, we will determine that you have statutory blindness based on a visual acuity of 20/200 or less. For example, if your best-corrected central visual acuity for distance in the better eye is 20/160 using an ETDRS chart, we will find that you have statutory blindness. Regardless of the type of test chart used, you do not have statutory blindness if you can read at least one letter on the 20/100 line. For example, if your best-corrected central visual acuity for distance in the better eye is 20/125+1 using an ETDRS chart, we will find that you do not have statutory blindness because you are able to read one letter on the 20/100 line.

c. Testing using a specialized lens. In some instances, you may have visual acuity testing performed using specialized lens, such as a contact lens. We will use the visual acuity measurements obtained with a specialized lens only if you have demonstrated the ability to use the specialized lens on a sustained basis. We will not use visual acuity measurements obtained with telescopic lenses.

d. Cycloplegic refraction is an examination of the eye performed after administering cycloplegic eye drops capable of relaxing the ability of the pupil to become smaller and temporarily paralyzing the focusing muscles. If your case record contains the results of cycloplegic refraction, we may use the results to determine your best-corrected central visual acuity. We will not purchase cycloplegic refraction.

e. Visual evoked response (VER) testing measures your response to visual events and can often detect dysfunction that is undetectable through other types of examinations. If you have an absent response to VER testing in your better eye, we will determine that your best-corrected central visual acuity is 20/200 or less in that eye and that your visual acuity loss satisfies the criterion in 2.02 when these test results are consistent with the other evidence in your case record. If you have a positive response to VER testing in an eye, we will not use that result to determine your best-corrected central visual acuity in that eye.

6. How do we measure your visual fields?

a. General. We generally need visual field testing when you have a visual disorder that could result in visual field loss, such as glaucoma, retinitis pigmentosa, or optic neuropathy, or when you display behaviors that suggest a visual field loss. When we need to measure the extent of your visual field loss, we use visual field testing (also referred to as perimetry) carried out using automated static threshold perimetry performed on an acceptable perimeter. (For perimeter requirements, see 2.00A9.)

b. Automated static threshold perimetry requirements.

(i) The test must use a white size III Goldmann stimulus and a 31.5 apostilb (asb) white background (or a 10 candela per square meter (cd/m^2) white background). The stimuli test locations must be no more than 6 degrees apart horizontally or vertically. Measurements must be reported on standard charts and include a description of the size and intensity of the test stimulus.

(ii) We measure the extent of your visual field loss by determining the portion of the visual field in which you can see a white III4e stimulus. The "III" refers to the standard Goldmann test stimulus size III (4 mm^2), and the "4e" refers to the standard Goldmann intensity filter (0 decibel (dB) attenuation, which allows presentation of the maximum luminance) used to determine the intensity of the stimulus.

(iii) In automated static threshold perimetry, the intensity of the stimulus varies. The intensity of the stimulus is expressed in decibels (dB). A perimeter's maximum stimulus luminance is usually assigned the value 0 dB. We need to determine the dB level that corresponds to a 4e intensity for the particular perimeter being used. We will then use the dB printout to determine which points you see at a 4e intensity level (a "seeing point"). For example:

A. When the maximum stimulus luminance (0 dB stimulus) on an acceptable perimeter is 10,000 asb, a 10 dB stimulus is equivalent to a 4e stimulus. Any point you see at 10 dB or greater is a seeing point.

B. When the maximum stimulus luminance (0 dB stimulus) on an acceptable perimeter is 4,000 asb, a 6 dB stimulus is equivalent to a 4e stimulus. Any point you see at 6 dB or greater is a seeing point.

C. When the maximum stimulus luminance (0 dB stimulus) on an acceptable perimeter is 1,000 asb, a 0 dB stimulus is equivalent to a 4e stimulus. Any point you see at 0 dB or greater is a seeing point.

c. Evaluation under 2.03A. To determine statutory blindness based on visual field loss in your better eye (2.03A), we need the results of a visual field test that measures the central 24 to 30 degrees of your visual field; that is, the area measuring 24 to 30 degrees from the point of fixation. Acceptable tests include the Humphrey Field Analyzer (HFA) 30–2, HFA 24–2, and Octopus 32.

d. Evaluation under 2.03B. To determine whether your visual field loss meets listing 2.03B, we use the mean deviation or defect (MD) from acceptable automated static threshold perimetry that measures the central 30 degrees of the visual field. MD is the average sensitivity deviation from normal values for all measured visual field locations. When using results from HFA tests, which report the MD as a negative number, we use the absolute value of the MD to determine whether your visual field loss meets listing 2.03B. We cannot use tests that do not measure the central 30 degrees of the visual field, such as the HFA 24–2, to determine if your impairment meets or medically equals 2.03B.

e. Other types of perimetry. If the evidence in your case contains visual field measurements obtained using manual or automated kinetic perimetry, such as Goldmann perimetry or the HFA "SSA Test Kinetic," we can generally use these results if the kinetic test was performed using a white III4e stimulus projected on a white 31.5 asb (10 cd/m^2) background. Automated kinetic perimetry, such as the HFA "SSA Test Kinetic," does not detect limitations in the central visual field because testing along a meridian stops when you see the stimulus. If your visual disorder has progressed to the point at which it is likely to result in a significant limitation in the central visual field, such as a scotoma (see 2.00A6h), we will not use automated kinetic perimetry to determine the extent of your visual field loss. Instead, we will determine the extent of your visual field loss using automated static threshold perimetry or manual kinetic perimetry.

f. Screening tests. We will not use the results of visual field screening tests, such as confrontation tests, tangent screen tests, or automated static screening tests, to determine that your impairment meets or medically equals a listing or to evaluate your residual functional capacity. We can consider normal results from visual field screening tests to determine whether your visual disorder is severe when these test results are consistent with the other evidence in your case record. (See §§ 404.1520(c), 404.1521, 416.920(c), and 416.921 of this chapter.) We will not consider normal test results to be consistent with the other evidence if the clinical findings indicate that your visual disorder has progressed to the point that it is likely to cause visual field loss, or you have a history of an operative procedure for retinal detachment.

g. Use of corrective lenses. You must not wear eyeglasses during visual field testing because they limit your field of vision. You may wear contact lenses to correct your visual acuity during the visual field test to obtain the most accurate visual field measurements. For this single purpose, you do not need to demonstrate that you have the ability to use the contact lenses on a sustained basis.

h. Scotoma. A scotoma is a field defect or nonseeing area (also referred to as a "blind spot") in the visual field surrounded by a normal field or seeing area. When we measure your visual field, we subtract the length of any scotoma, other than the normal blind spot, from the overall length of any diameter on which it falls.

7. How do we determine your visual acuity efficiency, visual field efficiency, and visual efficiency?

a. General. Visual efficiency, a calculated value of your remaining visual function, is the combination of your visual acuity efficiency and your visual field efficiency expressed as a percentage.

b. Visual acuity efficiency. Visual acuity efficiency is a percentage that corresponds to the best-corrected central visual acuity for distance in your better eye. See Table 1.

Table 1—Visual Acuity Efficiency

Snellen best-corrected central visual acuity for distance		Visual acuity efficiency (%) (2.04A)
English	Metric	
20/16	6/5	100
20/20	6/6	100
20/25	6/7.5	95
20/30	6/9	90
20/40	6/12	85
20/50	6/15	75
20/60	6/18	70
20/70	6/21	65
20/80	6/24	60
20/100	6/30	50

c. Visual field efficiency. Visual field efficiency is a percentage that corresponds to the visual field in your better eye. Under 2.03C, we require kinetic perimetry to determine your visual field efficiency percentage. We calculate the visual field efficiency percentage by adding the number of degrees you see along the eight principal meridians found on a visual field chart (0, 45, 90, 135, 180, 225, 270, and 315) in your better eye and dividing by 5. For example, in Figure 1:

A. The diagram of the left eye illustrates a visual field, as measured with a III4e stimulus, contracted to 30 degrees in two meridians (180 and 225) and to 20 degrees in the remaining six meridians. The visual efficiency percentage of this field is: ((2 x 30) + (6 x 20)) ÷ 5 = 36 percent.

B. The diagram of the right eye illustrates the extent of a normal visual field as measured with a III4e stimulus. The sum of the eight principal meridians of this field is 500 degrees. The visual efficiency percentage of this field is 500 ÷ 5 = 100 percent.

Figure 1:

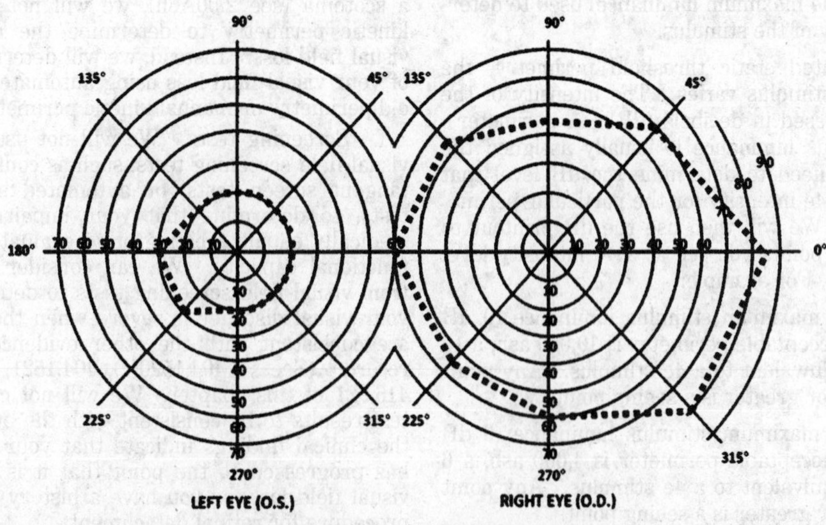

d. Visual efficiency. Under 2.04A, we calculate the visual efficiency percentage by multiplying your visual acuity efficiency percentage (see 2.00A7b) by your visual field efficiency percentage (see 2.00A7c) and dividing by 100. For example, if your visual acuity efficiency percentage is 75 and your visual field efficiency percentage is 36, your visual efficiency percentage is: (75 x 36) ÷ 100 = 27 percent.

8. How do we determine your visual acuity impairment value, visual field impairment value, and visual impairment value?

a. General. Visual impairment value, a calculated value of your loss of visual function, is the combination of your visual acuity impairment value and your visual field impairment value.

b. Visual acuity impairment value. Your visual acuity impairment value corresponds to the best-corrected central visual acuity for distance in your better eye. See Table 2.

Table 2—Visual Acuity Impairment Value

Snellen best-corrected central visual acuity for distance		Visual acuity impairment value (2.04B)
English	Metric	
20/16	6/5	0.00
20/20	6/6	0.00
20/25	6/7.5	0.10
20/30	6/9	0.18
20/40	6/12	0.30
20/50	6/15	0.40
20/60	6/18	0.48
20/70	6/21	0.54
20/80	6/24	0.60
20/100	6/30	0.70

c. Visual field impairment value. Your visual field impairment value corresponds to the visual field in your better eye. Using the MD from acceptable automated static threshold perimetry, we calculate the visual field impairment value by dividing the absolute value of the MD by 22. For example, if your MD on an HFA 30–2 is -16, your visual field impairment value is: $|-16| \div 22 = 0.73$.

d. Visual impairment value. Under 2.04B, we calculate the visual impairment value by adding your visual acuity impairment value (see 2.00A8b) and your visual field impairment value (see 2.00A8c). For example, if your visual acuity impairment value is 0.48 and your visual field impairment value is 0.73, your visual impairment value is: $0.48 + 0.73 = 1.21$.

9. What are our requirements for an acceptable perimeter? We will use results from automated static threshold perimetry performed on a perimeter that:

a. Uses optical projection to generate the test stimuli.

b. Has an internal normative database for automatically comparing your performance with that of the general population.

c. Has a statistical analysis package that is able to calculate visual field indices, particularly MD.

d. Demonstrates the ability to correctly detect visual field loss and correctly identify normal visual fields.

e. Demonstrates good test-retest reliability.

f. Has undergone clinical validation studies by three or more independent laboratories with results published in peer-reviewed ophthalmic journals.

B. How do we evaluate hearing loss?

1. What evidence do we need?

a. We need evidence showing that you have a medically determinable impairment that causes your hearing loss and audiometric measurements of the severity of your hearing loss. We generally require both an otologic examination and audiometric testing to establish that you have a medically determinable impairment that causes your hearing loss. You should have this audiometric testing within 2 months of the otologic examination. Once we have evidence that you have a medically determinable impairment, we can use the results of later audiometric testing to assess the severity of your hearing loss without another otologic examination. We will consider your test scores together with any other relevant information we have about your hearing, including information from outside of the test setting.

b. The otologic examination must be performed by a licensed physician (medical or osteopathic doctor) or audiologist. It must include your medical history, your description of how your hearing loss affects you, and the physician's or audiologist's description of the appearance of the external ears (pinnae and external ear canals), evaluation of the tympanic membranes, and assessment of any middle ear abnormalities.

c. Audiometric testing must be performed by, or under the direct supervision of, a licensed audiologist or an otolaryngologist.

2. What audiometric testing do we need when you do not have a cochlear implant?

a. We generally need pure tone air conduction and bone conduction testing, speech reception threshold (SRT) testing (also referred to as "spondee threshold" or "ST" testing), and word recognition testing (also referred to as "word discrimination" or "speech discrimination" testing). This testing must be conducted in a sound-treated booth or room and must be in accordance with the most recently published standards of the American National Standards Institute (ANSI). Each ear must be tested separately.

b. You must not wear hearing aids during the testing. Additionally, a person described in 2.00B1c must perform an otoscopic examination immediately before the audiometric testing. (An otoscopic examination provides a description of the appearance of your external ear canals and an evaluation of the tympanic membranes. In these rules, we use the term to include otoscopic examinations performed by physicians and otoscopic inspections performed by audiologists and others.) The otoscopic examination must show that there are no conditions that would prevent valid audiometric testing, such as fluid in the ear, ear infection, or obstruction in an ear canal. The person performing the test should also report on any other factors, such as your cooperation with the test, that can affect the interpretation of the test results.

c. To determine whether your hearing loss meets the air and bone conduction criteria in 2.10A, we will average your air and bone conduction hearing thresholds at 500, 1000, and 2000 Hertz (Hz). If you do not have a response at a particular frequency, we will use a threshold of 5 decibels (dB) over the limit of the audiometer.

d. The SRT is the minimum dB level required for you to recognize 50 percent of the words on a standard list of spondee words. (Spondee words are two-syllable words that have equal stress on each syllable.) The SRT is usually within 10 dB of the average pure tone air conduction hearing thresholds at 500, 1000, and 2000 Hz. If the SRT is not within 10 dB of the average pure tone air conduction threshold, the reason for the discrepancy must be documented. If we cannot determine that there is a medical basis for the discrepancy, we will not use the results of the testing to determine whether your hearing loss meets a listing.

e. Word recognition testing determines your ability to recognize a standardized list of phonetically balanced monosyllabic words in the absence of any visual cues. This testing must be performed in quiet. The list may be recorded or presented live, but in either case the words should be presented at a level of amplification that will measure your maximum ability to discriminate words, usually 35 to 40 dB above your SRT. However, the amplification level used in the testing must be medically appropriate, and you must be able to tolerate it. If you cannot be tested at 35 to 40 dB above your SRT, the person who performs the test should report your word recognition testing score at your highest comfortable level of amplification.

3. What audiometric testing do we need when you have a cochlear implant?

a. If you have a cochlear implant, we will consider you to be disabled until 1 year after initial implantation.

b. After that period, we need word recognition testing performed with any version of the Hearing in Noise Test (HINT) to determine whether your impairment meets 2.11B. This testing must be conducted in quiet in a sound field. Your implant must be functioning properly and adjusted to your normal settings. The sentences should be presented at 60 dB HL (Hearing Level) and without any visual cues.

4. How do we evaluate your word recognition ability if you are not fluent in English?

If you are not fluent in English, you should have word recognition testing using an appropriate word list for the language in which you are most fluent. The person conducting the test should be fluent in the language used for the test. If there is no appropriate word list or no person who is fluent in the language and qualified to perform the test, it may not be possible to measure your word recognition ability. If your word recognition ability cannot be measured, your hearing loss cannot meet 2.10B or 2.11B. Instead, we will consider the facts of your case to determine whether you have difficulty understanding words in the language in which you are most fluent, and if so, whether that degree of difficulty medically equals 2.10B or 2.11B. For example, we will consider how you interact with family members, interpreters, and other persons who speak the language in which you are most fluent.

C. How do we evaluate vertigo associated with disturbances of labyrinthine-vestibular function, including Meniere's disease?

1. These disturbances of balance are characterized by an hallucination of motion or loss of position sense and a sensation of dizziness which may be constant or may occur in paroxysmal attacks. Nausea, vomiting, ataxia, and incapacitation are frequently observed, particularly during the acute attack. It is important to differentiate the report of rotary vertigo from that of "dizziness" which is described as lightheadedness, unsteadiness, confusion, or syncope.

2. Ménière's disease is characterized by paroxysmal attacks of vertigo, tinnitus, and fluctuating hearing loss. Remissions are unpredictable and irregular, but may be longlasting; hence, the severity of impairment is best determined after prolonged observation and serial reexaminations.

3. The diagnosis of a vestibular disorder requires a comprehensive neuro-otolaryngologic examination with a detailed description of the vertiginous episodes, including notation of frequency, severity, and duration of the attacks. Pure tone and speech audiometry with the appropriate special examinations, such as Bekesy audiometry, are necessary. Vestibular functions is assessed by positional and caloric testing, preferably by electronystagmography. When polytomograms, contrast radiography, or other special tests have been performed, copies of the reports of these tests should be obtained in addition to appropriate medically acceptable imaging reports of the skull and temporal bone. Medically acceptable imaging includes, but is not limited to, x-ray imaging, computerized axial tomography (CAT scan) or magnetic resonance imaging

(MRI), with or without contrast material, myelography, and radionuclear bone scans. "Appropriate" means that the technique used is the proper one to support the evaluation and diagnosis of the impairment.

D. Loss of speech. In evaluating the loss of speech, the ability to produce speech by any means includes the use of mechanical or electronic devices that improve voice or articulation. Impairments of speech may also be evaluated under the body system for the underlying disorder, such as neurological disorders, 11.00ff.

E. How do we evaluate impairments that do not meet one of the special senses and speech listings?

1. These listings are only examples of common special senses and speech disorders that we consider severe enough to prevent an individual from doing any gainful activity. If your impairment(s) does not meet the criteria of any of these listings, we must also consider whether you have an impairment(s) that satisfies the criteria of a listing in another body system.

2. If you have a medically determinable impairment(s) that does not meet a listing, we will determine whether the impairment(s) medically equals a listing. (See §§ 404.1526 and 416.926.) If you have an impairment(s) that does not meet or medically equal a listing, you may or may not have the residual functional capacity to engage in substantial gainful activity. Therefore, we proceed to the fourth, and if necessary, the fifth steps of the sequential evaluation process in §§ 404.1520 and 416.920. When we decide whether you continue to be disabled, we use the rules in §§ 404.1594, 416.994, or 416.994a, as appropriate.

2.01 Category of Impairments, Special Senses and Speech

2.02 Loss of central visual acuity. Remaining vision in the better eye after best correction is 20/200 or less.

2.03 Contraction of the visual field in the better eye, with:

A. The widest diameter subtending an angle around the point of fixation no greater than 20 degrees.

OR

B. An MD of 22 decibels or greater, determined by automated static threshold perimetry that measures the central 30 degrees of the visual field (see 2.00A6d).

OR

C. A visual field efficiency of 20 percent or less, determined by kinetic perimetry (see 2.00A7c).

2.04 Loss of visual efficiency, or visual impairment, in the better eye:

A. A visual efficiency percentage of 20 or less after best correction (see 2.00A7d).

OR

B. A visual impairment value of 1.00 or greater after best correction (see 2.00A8d).

2.07 Disturbance of labyrinthine-vestibular function (including Ménière's disease), characterized by a history of frequent attacks of balance disturbance, tinnitus, and progressive loss of hearing. With both A and B:

A. Disturbed function of vestibular labyrinth demonstrated by caloric or other vestibular tests; and

B. Hearing loss established by audiometry.

2.09 Loss of speech due to any cause, with inability to produce by any means speech that can be heard, understood, or sustained.

Table 1.—Percentage of Visual Acuity Efficiency Corresponding to the Best-Corrected Visual Acuity Measurement for Distance in the Better Eye

Snellen		
English	Metric	Percent visual acuity efficiency
20/16	6/5	100
20/20	6/6	100
20/25	6/7.5	95
20/30	6/9	90
20/40	6/12	85
20/50	6/15	75
20/60	6/18	70
20/70	6/21	65
20/80	6/24	60
20/100	6/30	50

Table 2.—Chart of Visual Fields

Table 2.—Chart of Visual Fields

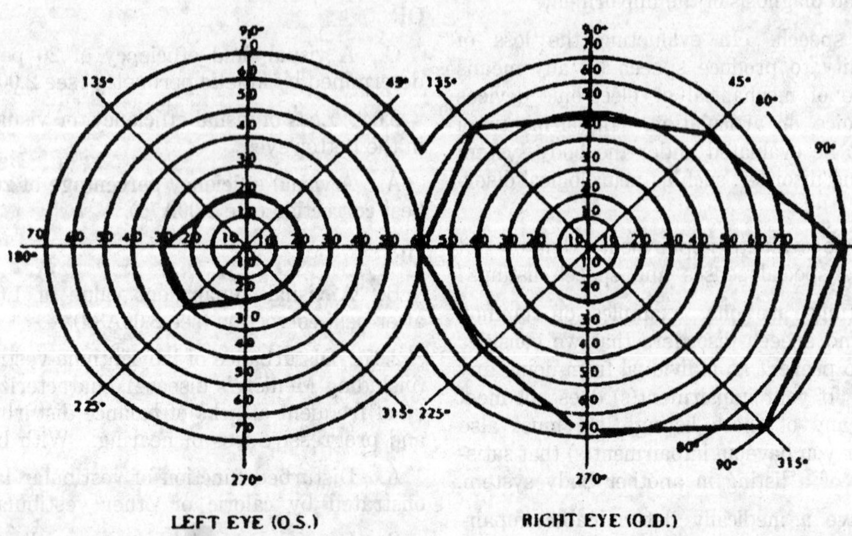

1. The diagram of the right eye illustrates the extent of a normal visual field as measured with a III4e stimulus. The sum of the eight principal meridians of this field is 500 degrees.

2. The diagram of the left eye illustrates a visual field contracted to 30 degrees in two meridians and to 20 degrees in the remaining six meridians. The percent of visual field efficiency of this field is: (2 x 30) + (6 x 20) = 180 ÷ 500 = 0.36 or 36 percent visual field efficiency.

2.10 Hearing Loss Not Treated With Cochlear Implantation

A. An average air conduction hearing threshold of 90 decibels or greater in the better ear and an average bone conduction hearing threshold of 60 decibels or greater in the better ear (see 2.00B2c).

OR

B. A word recognition score of 40 percent or less in the better ear determined using a standardized list of phonetically balanced monosyllabic words (see 2.00B2e).

2.11 Hearing loss treated with cochlear implantation

A. Consider under a disability for 1 year after initial implantation.

OR

B. If more than 1 year after initial implantation, a word recognition score of 60 percent or less determined using the HINT (see 2.00B3b).

3.00 RESPIRATORY DISORDERS

A. Which disorders do we evaluate in this body system?

1. We evaluate respiratory disorders that result in obstruction (difficulty moving air out of the lungs) or restriction (difficulty moving air into the lungs), or that interfere with diffusion (gas exchange) across cell membranes in the lungs. Examples of such disorders and the listings we use to evaluate them include chronic obstructive pulmonary disease (chronic bronchitis and emphysema, 3.02), pulmonary fibrosis and pneumoconiosis (3.02), asthma (3.02 or 3.03), cystic fibrosis (3.04), and bronchiectasis (3.02 or 3.07). We also use listings in this body system to evaluate respiratory failure (3.04D or 3.14), chronic pulmonary hypertension (3.09), and lung transplantation (3.11).

2. We evaluate cancers affecting the respiratory system under the listings in 13.00. We evaluate the pulmonary effects of neuromuscular and autoimmune disorders under these listings or under the listings in 11.00 or 14.00, respectively.

B. What are the symptoms and signs of respiratory disorders? Symptoms and signs of respiratory disorders include dyspnea (shortness of breath), chest pain, coughing, wheezing, sputum production, hemoptysis (coughing up blood from the respiratory tract), use of accessory muscles of respiration, and tachypnea (rapid rate of breathing).

C. What abbreviations do we use in this body system?

1. ABG means arterial blood gas.

2. BiPAP means bi-level positive airway pressure ventilation.

3. BTPS means body temperature and ambient pressure, saturated with water vapor.

4. CF means cystic fibrosis.

5. CFRD means CF–related diabetes.

6. CFTR means CF transmembrane conductance regulator.

7. CO means carbon monoxide.

8. COPD means chronic obstructive pulmonary disease.

9. DLCO means diffusing capacity of the lungs for carbon monoxide.

10. FEV_1 means forced expiratory volume in the first second of a forced expiratory maneuver.

11. FVC means forced vital capacity.

12. L means liter.

13. mL CO (STPD)/min/mmHg means milliliters of carbon monoxide at standard temperature and pressure, dry, per minute, per millimeter of mercury.

14. P_aO_2 means arterial blood partial pressure of oxygen.

15. $P_a CO_2$ means arterial blood partial pressure of carbon dioxide.

16. $S_p O_2$ means percentage of oxygen saturation of blood hemoglobin measured by pulse oximetry.

17. 6MWT means 6–minute walk test.

18. VI means volume of inhaled gas during a DLCO test.

D. What documentation do we need to evaluate your respiratory disorder?

1. We need medical evidence to document and assess the severity of your respiratory disorder. Medical evidence should include your medical history, physical examination findings, the results of imaging (see 3.00D3), pulmonary function tests (see 3.00D4), other relevant laboratory tests, and descriptions of any prescribed treatment and your response to it. We may not need all of this evidence depending on your particular respiratory disorder and its effects on you.

2. If you use supplemental oxygen, we still need medical evidence to establish the severity of your respiratory disorder.

3. Imaging refers to medical imaging techniques, such as x-ray and computerized tomography. The imaging must be consistent with the prevailing state of medical knowledge and clinical practice as the proper technique to support the evaluation of the disorder.

4. Pulmonary function tests include spirometry (which measures ventilation of the lungs), DLCO tests (which measure gas diffusion in the lungs), ABG tests (which measure the partial pressure of oxygen, P_aO_2, and carbon dioxide, P_aCO_2, in the arterial blood), and pulse oximetry (which measures oxygen saturation, S_pO_2, of peripheral blood hemoglobin).

E. What is spirometry and what are our requirements for an acceptable test and report?

1. Spirometry, which measures how well you move air into and out of your lungs, involves at least three forced expiratory maneuvers during the same test session. A forced expiratory maneuver is a maximum inhalation followed by a forced maximum exhalation, and measures exhaled volumes of air over time. The volume of air you exhale in the first second of the forced expiratory maneuver is the FEV_1. The total volume of air that you exhale during the entire forced expiratory maneuver is the FVC. We use your highest FEV_1 value to evaluate your respiratory disorder under 3.02A, 3.03A, and 3.04A, and your highest FVC value to evaluate your respiratory disorder under 3.02B, regardless of whether the values are from the same forced expiratory maneuver or different forced expiratory maneuvers.

2. We have the following requirements for spirometry under these listings:

a. You must be medically stable at the time of the test. Examples of when we would not consider you to be medically stable include when you are:

(i) Within 2 weeks of a change in your prescribed respiratory medication.

(ii) Experiencing, or within 30 days of completion of treatment for, a lower respiratory tract infection.

(iii) Experiencing, or within 30 days of completion of treatment for, an acute exacerbation (temporary worsening) of a chronic respiratory disorder. Wheezing by itself does not indicate that you are not medically stable.

(iv) Hospitalized, or within 30 days of a hospital discharge, for an acute myocardial infarction (heart attack).

b. During testing, if your FEV_1 is less than 70 percent of your predicted normal value, we require repeat spirometry after inhalation of a bronchodilator to evaluate your respiratory disorder under these listings, unless it is medically contraindicated. If you used a bronchodilator before the test and your FEV_1 is less than 70 percent of your predicted normal value, we still require repeat spirometry after inhalation of a bronchodilator unless the supervising physician determines that it is not safe for you to take a bronchodilator again (in which case we may need to reschedule the test). If you do not have post-bronchodilator spirometry, the test report must explain why. We can use the results of spirometry administered without bronchodilators when the use of bronchodilators is medically contraindicated.

c. Your forced expiratory maneuvers must be satisfactory. We consider a forced expiratory maneuver to be satisfactory when you exhale with maximum effort following a full inspiration, and when the test tracing has a sharp takeoff and rapid rise to peak flow, has a smooth contour, and either lasts for at least 6 seconds or maintains a plateau for at least 1 second.

3. The spirometry report must include the following information:

a. The date of the test and your name, age or date of birth, gender, and height without shoes. (We will assume that your recorded height on the date of the test is without shoes, unless we have evidence to the contrary.) If your spine is abnormally curved (for example, you have kyphoscoliosis), we will substitute the longest distance between your outstretched fingertips with your arms abducted 90 degrees in place of your height when this measurement is greater than your standing height without shoes.

b. Any factors, if applicable, that can affect the interpretation of the test results (for example, your cooperation or effort in doing the test).

c. Legible tracings of your forced expiratory maneuvers in a volume-time format showing your name and the date of the test for each maneuver.

4. If we purchase spirometry, the medical source we designate to administer the test is solely responsible for deciding whether it is safe for you to do the test and for how to administer it.

F. What is a DLCO test, and what are our requirements for an acceptable test and report?

1. A DLCO test measures the gas exchange across cell membranes in your lungs. It measures how well CO diffuses from the alveoli (air sacs) of your lungs into your blood. DLCO may be severely reduced in some disorders, such as interstitial lung disease (for example, idiopathic pulmonary fibrosis, asbestosis, and sarcoidosis) and COPD (particularly emphysema), even when the results of spirometry are not significantly reduced. We use the average of two of your unadjusted (that is, uncorrected for hemoglobin concentration) DLCO measurements reported in mL CO (STPD)/min/mmHg to evaluate your respiratory disorder under 3.02C1.

2. We have the following requirements for DLCO tests under these listings:

a. You must be medically stable at the time of the test. See 3.00E2a.

b. The test must use the single-breath technique.

(i) The VI during the DLCO maneuver must be at least 85 percent of your current FVC, and your time of inhalation must be less than 4 seconds. (See 3.00E for our rules for programmatically acceptable spirometry.) If you do not have an FVC measurement on the same day as the DLCO test, we may use your FVC from programmatically acceptable spirometry administered within 90 days of the DLCO test.

(ii) Your breath-hold time must be between 8 and 12 seconds.

(iii) Your total exhalation time must be less than or equal to 4 seconds, with a sample collection time of less than 3 seconds. If your FVC is at least 2.0 L, the washout volume must be between 0.75 L and 1.0 L. If your FVC is less than 2.0 L, the washout volume must be at least 0.5 L.

3. The DLCO test report must include the following information:

a. The date of the test and your name, age or date of birth, gender, and height without shoes. (We will assume that your recorded height on the date of the test is without shoes, unless we have evidence to the contrary.) If your spine is abnormally curved (for example, you have kyphoscoliosis), we will substitute the longest distance between your outstretched fingertips with your arms abducted 90 degrees in place of your height when this measurement is greater than your standing height without shoes.

b. Any factors, if applicable, that can affect the interpretation of the test results (for example, your cooperation or effort in doing the test).

c. Legible tracings of your VI, breath-hold maneuver, and volume of exhaled gas showing your name and the date of the test for each DLCO maneuver.

d. At least two acceptable (see 3.00F2) DLCO measurements within 3 mL CO (STPD)/min/mmHg of each other or within 10 percent of the highest value.

4. We may need to purchase a DLCO test to determine whether your disorder meets 3.02C1 when we have evidence showing that you have a chronic respiratory disorder that could result in impaired gas exchange, unless we can make a fully favorable determination or decision on another basis. Since the DLCO calculation requires a current FVC measurement, we may also purchase spirometry at the same time as the DLCO test, even if we already have programmatically acceptable spirometry.

5. Before we purchase a DLCO test, a medical consultant (see §§ 404.1616 and 416.1016 of this chapter), preferably one with experience in the care of people with respiratory disorders, must review your case record to determine if we need the test. The medical source we designate to administer the test is solely responsible for deciding whether it is safe for you to do the test and for how to administer it.

G. What is an ABG test, and what are our requirements for an acceptable test and report?

1. General. An ABG test measures P_a O_2, P_aCO_2, and the concentration of hydrogen ions in your arterial blood. We use a resting or an exercise ABG measurement to evaluate your respiratory disorder under 3.02C2.

2. Resting ABG tests.

a. We have the following requirements for resting ABG tests under these listings:

(i) You must be medically stable at the time of the test. See 3.00E2a.

(ii) The test must be administered while you are breathing room air; that is, without oxygen supplementation.

b. The resting ABG test report must include the following information:

(i) Your name, the date of the test, and either the altitude or both the city and State of the test site.

(ii) The P_a O_2 and P_aCO_2 values.

c. We may need to purchase a resting ABG test to determine whether your disorder meets 3.02C2 when we have evidence showing that you have a chronic respiratory disorder that could result in impaired gas exchange, unless we can make a fully favorable determination or decision on another basis.

d. Before we purchase a resting ABG test, a medical consultant (see §§ 404.1616 and 416.1016 of this chapter), preferably one with experience in the care of people with respiratory disorders, must review your case record to determine if we need the test. The medical source we designate to administer the test is solely responsible for deciding whether it is safe for you to do the test and for how to administer it.

3. Exercise ABG tests.

a. We will not purchase an exercise ABG test.

b. We have the following requirements for exercise ABG tests under these listings:

(i) You must have done the exercise under steady state conditions while breathing room air. If you were tested on a treadmill, you generally must have exercised for at least 4 minutes at a grade and speed providing oxygen (O_2) consumption of approximately 17.5 milliliters per kilogram per minute (mL/kg/min) or 5.0 metabolic equivalents (METs). If you were tested on a cycle ergometer, you generally must have exercised for at least 4 minutes at an exercise equivalent of 5.0 METs.

(ii) We may use a test in which you have not exercised for at least 4 minutes. If you were unable to complete at least 4 minutes of steady state exercise, we need a statement by the person administering the test about whether the results are a valid indication of your respiratory status. For example, this statement may include information about your cooperation or effort in doing the test and whether you were limited in completing the test because of your respiratory disorder or another impairment.

c. The exercise ABG test report must include the following information:

(i) Your name, the date of the test, and either the altitude or both the city and state of the test site.

(ii) The P_a O_2 and P_aCO_2 values.

H. What is pulse oximetry, and what are our requirements for an acceptable test and report?

1. Pulse oximetry measures S_pO_2, the percentage of oxygen saturation of blood hemoglobin. We use a pulse oximetry measurement (either at rest, during a 6MWT, or after a 6MWT) to evaluate your respiratory disorder under 3.02C3 or, if you have CF, to evaluate it under 3.04F.

2. We have the following requirements for pulse oximetry under 3.02C3:

a. You must be medically stable at the time of the test. See 3.00E2a.

b. Your pulse oximetry measurement must be recorded while you are breathing room air; that is, without oxygen supplementation.

c. Your pulse oximetry measurement must be stable. By "stable," we mean that the range of S_pO_2 values (that is, lowest to highest) during any 15-second interval cannot exceed 2 percentage points. For example:

(1) The measurement is stable if the lowest S_pO_2 value during a 15-second interval is 87 percent and the highest value is 89 percent—a range of 2 percentage points.

(2) The measurement is not stable if the lowest value is 86 percent and the highest value is 89 percent—a range of 3 percentage points.

d. If you have had more than one measurement (for example, at rest and after a 6MWT), we will use the measurement with the lowest S_pO_2 value.

e. The pulse oximetry report must include the following information:

(i) Your name, the date of the test, and either the altitude or both the city and State of the test site.

(ii) A graphical printout showing your S_pO_2 value and a concurrent, acceptable pulse wave. An acceptable pulse wave is one that shows the characteristic pulse wave; that is, sawtooth-shaped with a rapid systolic upstroke (nearly vertical) followed by a slower diastolic downstroke (angled downward).

f. We may need to purchase pulse oximetry at rest to determine whether your disorder meets 3.02C3 when we have evidence showing that you have a chronic respiratory disorder that could result in impaired gas exchange, unless we can make a fully favorable determination or decision on another basis. We may purchase pulse oximetry during and after a 6MWT if your S_pO_2 value at rest is greater than the value in Table V.

g. Before we purchase pulse oximetry, a medical consultant (see §§ 404.1616 and 416.1016 of this chapter), preferably one with experience in the care of people with respiratory disorders, must review your case record to determine if we need the test. The medical source we designate to administer the test is solely responsible for deciding whether it is safe for you to do the test and for how to administer it.

3. We have the following requirements for pulse oximetry under 3.04F:

a. You must be medically stable at the time of the test. See 3.00E2a.

b. Your pulse oximetry measurement must be recorded while you are breathing room air; that is, without oxygen supplementation.

c. If you have had more than one measurement (for example, at rest and after a 6MWT), we will use the measurement with the lowest S_pO_2 value.

d. The pulse oximetry report must include your name, the date of the test, and either the altitude or both the city and State of the test site. If you have CF, we do not require a graphical printout showing your S_pO_2 value and a concurrent, acceptable pulse wave.

I. What is asthma and how do we evaluate it?

1. Asthma is a chronic inflammatory disorder of the lung airways that we evaluate under 3.02 or 3.03. If you have respiratory failure resulting from chronic asthma (see 3.00N), we will evaluate it under 3.14.

2. For the purposes of 3.03:

a. We need evidence showing that you have listing-level (see Table VI in 3.03A) airflow obstruction at baseline while you are medically stable.

b. The phrase "consider under a disability for 1 year" in 3.03B does not refer to the date on which your disability began, only to the date on which we must reevaluate whether your asthma continues to meet a listing or is otherwise disabling.

c. We determine the onset of your disability based on the facts of your case, but it will be no later than the admission date of your first of three hospitalizations that satisfy the criteria of 3.03B.

J. What is CF and how do we evaluate it?

1. General. We evaluate CF, a genetic disorder that results in abnormal salt and water transport across cell membranes in the lungs, pancreas, and other body organs, under 3.04. We need the evidence described in 3.00J2 to establish that you have CF.

2. Documentation of CF. We need a report signed by a physician (see §§ 404.1513(a) and 416.913(a) of this chapter) showing both a and b:

a. One of the following:

(i) A positive newborn screen for CF; or

(ii) A history of CF in a sibling; or

(iii) Documentation of at least one specific CF phenotype or clinical criterion (for example, chronic sinopulmonary disease with persistent colonization or infections with typical CF pathogens, pancreatic insufficiency, or salt-loss syndromes); and

b. One of the following definitive laboratory tests:

(i) An elevated sweat chloride concentration equal to or greater than 60 millimoles per L; or

(ii) The identification of two CF gene mutations affecting the CFTR; or

(iii) Characteristic abnormalities in ion transport across the nasal epithelium.

c. When we have the report showing a and b, but it is not signed by a physician, we also need a report from a physician stating that you have CF.

d. When we do not have the report showing a and b, we need a report from a physician that is persuasive that a positive diagnosis of CF was confirmed by an appropriate definitive laboratory test. To be persuasive, this report must include a statement by the physician that you had the appropriate definitive laboratory test for diagnosing CF. The report must provide the test results or explain how your diagnosis was established that is consistent with the prevailing state of medical knowledge and clinical practice.

3. CF pulmonary exacerbations. Examples of CF pulmonary exacerbations include increased cough and sputum production, hemoptysis, increased shortness of breath, increased fatigue, and reduction in pulmonary function. Treatment usually includes intravenous antibiotics and intensified airway clearance therapy (for example, increased frequencies of chest percussion or increased use of inhaled nebulized therapies, such as bronchodilators or mucolytics).

4. For 3.04G, we require any two exacerbations or complications from the list in 3.04G1 through 3.04G4 within a 12–month period. You may have two of the same exacerbation or complication or two different ones.

a. If you have two of the acute exacerbations or complications we describe in 3.04G1 and 3.04G2, there must be at least 30 days between the two.

b. If you have one of the acute exacerbations or complications we describe in 3.04G1 and 3.04G2 and one of the chronic complications we describe in 3.04G3 and 3.04G4, the two can occur during the same time. For example, your CF meets 3.04G if you have the pulmonary hemorrhage we describe in 3.04G2 and the weight loss we describe in 3.04G3 even if the pulmonary hemorrhage occurs during the 90–day period in 3.04G3.

c. Your CF also meets 3.04G if you have both of the chronic complications in 3.04G3 and 3.04G4.

5. CF may also affect other body systems such as digestive or endocrine. If your CF, including pulmonary exacerbations and nonpulmonary complications, does not meet or medically equal a respiratory disorders listing, we may evaluate your CF–related impairments under the listings in the affected body system.

K. What is bronchiectasis and how do we evaluate it? Bronchiectasis is a chronic respiratory disorder that is characterized by abnormal and irreversible dilatation (enlargement) of the airways below the trachea, which may be associated with the accumulation of mucus, bacterial infections, and eventual airway scarring. We require imaging (see 3.00D3) to document this disorder. We evaluate your bronchiectasis under 3.02, or under 3.07 if you are having exacerbations or complications (for example, acute bacterial infections, increased shortness of breath, or coughing up blood) that require hospitalization.

L. What is chronic pulmonary hypertension and how do we evaluate it?

1. Chronic pulmonary hypertension is an increase in the blood pressure of the blood vessels of the lungs. If pulmonary hypertension is not adequately treated, it can eventually result in right heart failure. We evaluate chronic pulmonary hypertension due to any cause under 3.09.

2. Chronic pulmonary hypertension is usually diagnosed by catheterization of the pulmonary artery. We will not purchase cardiac catheterization.

M. How do we evaluate lung transplantation? If you receive a lung transplant (or a lung transplant simultaneously with other organs, such as the heart), we will consider you to be disabled under 3.11 for 3 years from the date of the transplant. After that, we evaluate your residual impairment(s) by considering the adequacy of your post-transplant function, the frequency and severity of any rejection episodes you have, complications in other body systems, and adverse treatment effects. People who receive organ transplants generally have impairments that meet our definition of disability before they undergo transplantation. The phrase "consider under a disability for 3 years" in 3.11 does not refer to the date on which your disability began, only to the date on which we must reevaluate whether your impairment(s) continues to meet a listing or is otherwise disabling. We determine the onset of your disability based on the facts of your case.

N. What is respiratory failure and how do we evaluate it? Respiratory failure is the inability of the lungs to perform their basic function of gas exchange. We evaluate respiratory failure under 3.04D if you have CF–related respiratory failure, or under 3.14 if you have respiratory failure due to any other chronic respiratory disorder. Continuous positive airway pressure does not satisfy the criterion in 3.04D or 3.14, and cannot be substituted as an equivalent finding, for invasive mechanical ventilation or noninvasive ventilation with BiPAP.

O. How do we consider the effects of obesity when we evaluate your respiratory disorder? Obesity is a medically determinable impairment that is often associated with respiratory disorders. Obesity makes it harder for the chest and lungs to expand, which can compromise the ability of the respiratory system to supply adequate oxygen to the body. The combined effects of obesity with a respiratory disorder can be greater than the effects of each of the impairments considered separately. We consider any additional and cumulative effects of your obesity when we determine whether you have a severe respiratory disorder, a listing-level respiratory disorder, a combination of impairments that medically equals the severity of a listed impairment, and when we assess your residual functional capacity.

P. What are sleep-related breathing disorders and how do we evaluate them?

1. Sleep-related breathing disorders (for example, sleep apnea) are characterized by transient episodes of interrupted breathing during sleep, which disrupt normal sleep patterns. Prolonged episodes can result in disorders such as hypoxemia (low blood oxygen) and pulmonary vasoconstriction (restricted blood flow in pulmonary blood vessels). Over time, these disorders may lead to chronic pulmonary hypertension or other complications.

2. We evaluate the complications of sleep-related breathing disorders under the listings in the affected body system(s). For example, we evaluate chronic pulmonary hypertension due to any cause under 3.09; chronic heart failure under 4.02; and disturbances in mood, cognition, and behavior under 12.02 or another appropriate mental disorders listing. We will not purchase polysomnography (sleep study).

Q. How do we evaluate mycobacterial, mycotic, and other chronic infections of the lungs? We evaluate chronic infections of the lungs that result in limitations in your respiratory function under 3.02.

R. How do we evaluate respiratory disorders that do not meet one of these listings?

1. These listings are only examples of common respiratory disorders that we consider severe enough to prevent you from doing any gainful activity. If your impairment(s) does not meet the criteria of any of these listings, we must also consider whether you have an impairment(s) that meets the criteria of a listing in another body system. For example, if your CF has resulted in chronic pancreatic or hepatobiliary disease, we evaluate your impairment under the listings in 5.00.

2. If you have a severe medically determinable impairment(s) that does not meet a listing, we will determine whether your impairment(s) medically equals a listing. See §§ 404.1526 and 416.926 of this chapter. Respiratory disorders may be associated with disorders in other body systems, and we consider the combined effects of multiple impairments when we determine whether they medically equal a listing. If your impairment(s) does not meet or medically equal a listing, you may or may not have the residual functional capacity to engage in substantial gainful activity. We proceed to the fourth step and, if necessary, the fifth step of the sequential evaluation process in §§ 404.1520 and 416.920 of this chapter. We use the rules in §§ 404.1594 and 416.994 of this chapter, as appropriate, when we decide whether you continue to be disabled.

3.01 Category of Impairments, Respiratory Disorders

3.02 Chronic respiratory disorders due to any cause except CF (for CF, see 3.04) with A, B, C, or D:

A. FEV_1 (see 3.00E) less than or equal to the value in Table I-A or I-B for your age, gender, and height without shoes (see 3.00E3a).

Table I—FEV1 Criteria for 3.02A

Height without shoes (centimeters) < means less than	Height without shoes (inches) < means less than	Table I-A Age 18 to attainment of age 20 Females FEV1 less than or equal to (L, BTPS)	Table I-A Age 18 to attainment of age 20 Males FEV1 less than or equal to (L, BTPS)	Table I-B Age 20 or older Females FEV1 less than or equal to (L, BTPS)	Table I-B Age 20 or older Males FEV1 less than or equal to (L, BTPS)
<153.0	<60.25	1.20	1.45	1.05	1.20
153.0 to <159.0	60.25 to <62.50	1.30	1.55	1.15	1.35
159.0 to <164.0	62.50 to <64.50	1.40	1.65	1.25	1.40
164.0 to <169.0	64.50 to <66.50	1.45	1.75	1.35	1.50
169.0 to <174.0	66.50 to <68.50	1.55	1.85	1.45	1.60
174.0 to <180.0	68.50 to <70.75	1.65	2.00	1.55	1.75
180.0 to <185.0	70.75 to <72.75	1.75	2.10	1.65	1.85
185.0 or more	72.75 or more	1.80	2.15	1.70	1.90

OR

B. FVC (see 3.00E) less than or equal to the value in Table II–A or II–B for your age, gender, and height without shoes (see 3.00E3a).

Table II—FVC Criteria for 3.02B

Height without shoes (centimeters) < means less than	Height without shoes (inches) < means less than	Table II-A Age 18 to attainment of age 20 Females FVC less than or equal to (L, BTPS)	Table II-A Age 18 to attainment of age 20 Males FVC less than or equal to (L, BTPS)	Table II-B Age 20 or older Females FVC less than or equal to (L, BTPS)	Table II-B Age 20 or older Males FVC less than or equal to (L, BTPS)
<153.0	<60.25	1.35	1.65	1.30	1.50
153.0 to <159.0	60.25 to <62.50	1.50	1.80	1.40	1.65
159.0 to <164.0	62.50 to <64.50	1.60	1.90	1.50	1.75
164.0 to <169.0	64.50 to <66.50	1.70	2.05	1.60	1.90
169.0 to <174.0	66.50 to <68.50	1.80	2.20	1.70	2.00
174.0 to <180.0	68.50 to <70.75	1.90	2.35	1.85	2.20
180.0 to <185.0	70.75 to <72.75	2.05	2.50	1.95	2.30
185.0 or more	72.75 or more	2.10	2.60	2.00	2.40

OR

C. Chronic impairment of gas exchange demonstrated by 1, 2, or 3:

1. Average of two unadjusted, single-breath DLCO measurements (see 3.00F) less than or equal to the value in Table III for your gender and height without shoes (see 3.00F3a); or

Table III—DLCO Criteria for 3.02C1

Height without shoes (centimeters) < means less than	Height without shoes (inches) < means less than	Females DLCO less than or equal to (mL CO (STPD)/min/mmHg)	Males DLCO less than or equal to (mL CO (STPD)/min/mmHg)
<153.0	< 60.25	8.0	9.0
153.0 to <159.0	60.25 to <62.50	8.5	9.5
159.0 to <164.0	62.50 to <64.50	9.0	10.0
164.0 to <169.0	64.50 to <66.50	9.5	10.5
169.0 to <174.0	66.50 to <68.50	10.0	11.0
174.0 to <180.0	68.50 to <70.75	10.5	11.5

180.0 to <185.0	70.75 to <72.75	11.0	12.0
185.0 or more	72.75 or more	11.5	12.5

2. Arterial P_aO_2 and P_aCO_2 measured concurrently by an ABG test, while at rest or during steady state exercise, breathing room air (see 3.00G3b), less than or equal to the applicable values in Table IV–A, IV–B, or IV–C; or

Tables IV–A, IV–B, and IV–C—ABG Criteria for 3.02C2

Table IV-A
[Applicable at test sites less than 3,000 feet above sea level]

Arterial P_aCO_2 (mm Hg) and	Arterial P_a O_2 less than or equal to (mm Hg)
30 or below	65
31	64
32	63
33	62
34	61
35	60
36	59
37	58
38	57
39	56
40 or above	55

Table IV-B
[Applicable at test sites from 3,000 through 6,000 feet above sea level]

Arterial P_aCO_2 (mm Hg) and	Arterial P_a O_2 less than or equal to (mm Hg)
30 or below	60
31	59
32	58
33	57
34	56
35	55
36	54
37	53
38	52
39	51
40 or above	50

Table IV-C
[Applicable at test sites over 6,000 feet above sea level]

Arterial P_aCO_2 (mm Hg) and	Arterial P_a O_2 less than or equal to (mm Hg)
30 or below	55
31	54
32	53
33	52
34	51
35	50
36	49
37	48
38	47
39	46
40 or above	45

3. S_pO_2 measured by pulse oximetry (see 3.00H2) either at rest, during a 6MWT, or after a 6MWT, less than or equal to the value in Table V.

Table V—S_pO_2 Criteria for 3.02C3

Test site altitude (feet above sea level)	S_pO_2 less than or equal to
Less than 3,000	87 percent.
3,000 through 6,000	85 percent.
Over 6,000	83 percent.

OR

D. Exacerbations or complications requiring three hospitalizations within a 12–month period and at least 30 days apart (the 12–month period must occur within the period we are considering in connection with your application or continuing disability review). Each hospitalization must last at least 48 hours, including hours in a hospital emergency department immediately before the hospitalization.

3.03 Asthma (see 3.00I), with both A and B:

A. FEV_1 (see 3.00E1) less than or equal to the value in Table VI–A or VI–B for your age, gender, and height without shoes (see 3.00E3a) measured within the same 12–month period as the hospitalizations in 3.03B.

Table VI—FEV1 Criteria for 3.03A

Height without shoes (centimeters) < means less than	Height without shoes (inches) < means less than	Table VI-A Age 18 to attainment of age 20 Females FEV1 less than or equal to (L, BTPS)	Table VI-A Age 18 to attainment of age 20 Males FEV1 less than or equal to (L, BTPS)	Table VI-B Age 20 or older Females FEV1 less than or equal to (L, BTPS)	Table VI-B Age 20 or older Males FEV1 less than or equal to (L, BTPS)
<153.0	<60.25	1.65	1.90	1.45	1.60
153.0 to <159.0	60.25 to <62.50	1.75	2.05	1.55	1.75
159.0 to <164.0	62.50 to <64.50	1.85	2.15	1.65	1.90
164.0 to <169.0	64.50 to <66.50	1.95	2.30	1.75	2.00
169.0 to <174.0	66.50 to <68.50	2.05	2.45	1.85	2.15
174.0 to <180.0	68.50 to <70.75	2.20	2.60	2.00	2.30

180.0 to <185.0	70.75 to <72.75	2.35	2.75	2.10	2.45
185.0 or more	72.75 or more	2.40	2.85	2.20	2.55

AND

B. Exacerbations or complications requiring three hospitalizations within a 12–month period and at least 30 days apart (the 12–month period must occur within the period we are considering in connection with your application or continuing disability review). Each hospitalization must last at least 48 hours, including hours in a hospital emergency department immediately before the hospitalization. Consider under a disability for 1 year from the discharge date of the last hospitalization; after that, evaluate the residual impairment(s) under 3.03 or another appropriate listing.

3.04 Cystic fibrosis (documented as described in 3.00J2) with A, B, C, D, E, F, or G:

A. FEV_1 (see 3.00E) less than or equal to the value in Table VII–A or VII–B for your age, gender, and height without shoes (see 3.00E3a).

Table VII—FEV1 Criteria for 3.04A

Height without shoes (centimeters) < means less than	Height without shoes (inches) < means less than	Table VII-A Age 18 to attainment of age 20		Table VII-B Age 20 or older	
		Females FEV1 less than or equal to (L, BTPS)	Males FEV1 less than or equal to (L, BTPS)	Females FEV1 less than or equal to (L, BTPS)	Males FEV1 less than or equal to (L, BTPS)
<153.0	<60.25	1.65	1.90	1.45	1.60
153.0 to <159.0	60.25 to <62.50	1.75	2.05	1.55	1.75
159.0 to <164.0	62.50 to <64.50	1.85	2.15	1.65	1.90
164.0 to <169.0	64.50 to <66.50	1.95	2.30	1.75	2.00
169.0 to <174.0	66.50 to <68.50	2.05	2.45	1.85	2.15
174.0 to <180.0	68.50 to <70.75	2.20	2.60	2.00	2.30
180.0 to <185.0	70.75 to <72.75	2.35	2.75	2.10	2.45
185.0 or more	72.75 or more	2.40	2.85	2.20	2.55

OR

B. Exacerbations or complications (see 3.00J3) requiring three hospitalizations of any length within a 12–month period and at least 30 days apart (the 12–month period must occur within the period we are considering in connection with your application or continuing disability review).

OR

C. Spontaneous pneumothorax, secondary to CF, requiring chest tube placement.

OR

D. Respiratory failure (see 3.00N) requiring invasive mechanical ventilation, noninvasive ventilation with BiPAP, or a combination of both treatments, for a continuous period of at least 48 hours, or for a continuous period of at least 72 hours if postoperatively.

OR

E. Pulmonary hemorrhage requiring vascular embolization to control bleeding.

OR

F. S_pO_2 measured by pulse oximetry (see 3.00H3) either at rest, during a 6MWT, or after a 6MWT, less than or equal to the value in Table VIII, twice within a 12–month period and at least 30 days apart (the 12–month period must occur within the period we are considering in connection with your application or continuing disability review).

Tables VIII—S_pO_2 Criteria for 3.04F

Test site altitude (feet above sea level)	S_pO_2 less than or equal to
Less than 3,000	89 percent.
3,000 through 6,000	87 percent.
Over 6,000	85 percent.

OR

G. Two of the following exacerbations or complications (either two of the same or two different, see 3.00J3 and 3.00J4) within a 12–month period (the 12–month period must occur within the period we are considering in connection with your application or continuing disability review):

1. Pulmonary exacerbation requiring 10 consecutive days of intravenous antibiotic treatment.

2. Pulmonary hemorrhage (hemoptysis with more than blood-streaked sputum but not requiring vascular embolization) requiring hospitalization of any length.

3. Weight loss requiring daily supplemental enteral nutrition via a gastrostomy for at least 90 consecutive days or parenteral nutrition via a central venous catheter for at least 90 consecutive days.

4. CFRD requiring daily insulin therapy for at least 90 consecutive days.

3.05 [Reserved]

3.06 [Reserved]

3.07 Bronchiectasis (see 3.00K), documented by imaging (see 3.00D3), with exacerbations or complications requiring three hospitalizations within a 12–month period and at least 30 days apart (the 12–month period must occur within the period we are considering in connection with your application or continuing disability review). Each hospitalization must last at least 48 hours, including hours in a hospital emergency department immediately before the hospitalization.

3.08 [Reserved]

3.09 Chronic pulmonary hypertension due to any cause (see 3.00L) documented by mean pulmonary artery pressure equal to or greater than 40 mm Hg as determined by cardiac catheterization while medically stable (see 3.00E2a).

3.10 [Reserved]

3.11 Lung transplantation (see 3.00M). Consider under a disability for 3 years from the date of the transplant; after that, evaluate the residual impairment(s).

3.12 [Reserved]

3.13 [Reserved]

3.14 Respiratory failure (see 3.00N) resulting from any underlying chronic respiratory disorder except CF (for CF, see 3.04D), requiring invasive mechanical ventilation, noninvasive ventilation with BiPAP, or a combination of both treatments, for a continuous period of at least 48 hours, or for a continuous period of at least 72 hours if postoperatively, twice within a 12–month period and at least 30 days apart (the 12–month period must occur within the period we are considering in connection with your application or continuing disability review).

4.00 Cardiovascular System

A. General

1. What do we mean by a cardiovascular impairment?

a. We mean any disorder that affects the proper functioning of the heart or the circulatory system (that is, arteries, veins, capillaries, and the lymphatic drainage). The disorder can be congenital or acquired.

b. Cardiovascular impairment results from one or more of four consequences of heart disease:

(i) Chronic heart failure or ventricular dysfunction.

(ii) Discomfort or pain due to myocardial ischemia, with or without necrosis of heart muscle.

(iii) Syncope, or near syncope, due to inadequate cerebral perfusion from any cardiac cause, such as obstruction of flow or disturbance in rhythm or conduction resulting in inadequate cardiac output.

(iv) Central cyanosis due to right-to-left shunt, reduced oxygen concentration in the arterial blood, or pulmonary vascular disease.

c. Disorders of the veins or arteries (for example, obstruction, rupture, or aneurysm) may cause impairments of the lower extremities (peripheral vascular disease), the central nervous system, the eyes, the kidneys, and other organs. We will evaluate peripheral vascular disease under 4.11 or 4.12 and impairments of another body system(s) under the listings for that body system(s).

2. What do we consider in evaluating cardiovascular impairments? The listings in this section describe cardiovascular impairments based on symptoms, signs, laboratory findings, response to a regimen of prescribed treatment, and functional limitations.

3. What do the following terms or phrases mean in these listings?

a. Medical consultant is an individual defined in §§ 404.1616(a) and 416.1016(a). This term does not include medical sources who provide consultative examinations for us. We use the abbreviation "MC" throughout this section to designate a medical consultant.

b. Persistent means that the longitudinal clinical record shows that, with few exceptions, the required finding(s) has been present, or is expected to be present, for a continuous period of at least 12 months, such that a pattern of continuing severity is established.

c. Recurrent means that the longitudinal clinical record shows that, within a consecutive 12–month period, the finding(s) occurs at least three times, with intervening periods of improvement of sufficient duration that it is clear that separate events are involved.

d. Appropriate medically acceptable imaging means that the technique used is the proper one to evaluate and diagnose the impairment and is commonly recognized as accurate for assessing the cited finding.

e. A consecutive 12–month period means a period of 12 consecutive months, all or part of which must occur within the period we are considering in connection with an application or continuing disability review.

f. Uncontrolled means the impairment does not adequately respond to standard prescribed medical treatment.

B. Documenting Cardiovascular Impairment

1. What basic documentation do we need? We need sufficiently detailed reports of history, physical examinations, laboratory studies, and any prescribed treatment and response to allow us to assess the severity and duration of your cardiovascular impairment. A longitudinal clinical record covering a period of not less than 3 months of observations and treatment is usually necessary, unless we can make a determination or decision based on the current evidence.

2. Why is a longitudinal clinical record important? We will usually need a longitudinal clinical record to assess the severity and expected duration of your impairment(s). If you have a listing-level impairment, you probably will have received medically prescribed treatment. Whenever there is evidence of such treatment, your longitudinal clinical record should include a description of the ongoing management and evaluation

provided by your treating or other medical source. It should also include your response to this medical management, as well as information about the nature and severity of your impairment. The record will provide us with information on your functional status over an extended period of time and show whether your ability to function is improving, worsening, or unchanging.

3. What if you have not received ongoing medical treatment?

a. You may not have received ongoing treatment or have an ongoing relationship with the medical community despite the existence of a severe impairment(s). In this situation, we will base our evaluation on the current objective medical evidence and the other evidence we have. If you do not receive treatment, you cannot show an impairment that meets the criteria of most of these listings. However, we may find you disabled because you have another impairment(s) that in combination with your cardiovascular impairment medically equals the severity of a listed impairment or based on consideration of your residual functional capacity and age, education, and work experience.

b. Unless we can decide your claim favorably on the basis of the current evidence, a longitudinal record is still important. In rare instances where there is no or insufficient longitudinal evidence, we may purchase a consultative examination(s) to help us establish the severity and duration of your impairment.

4. When will we wait before we ask for more evidence?

a. We will wait when we have information showing that your impairment is not yet stable and the expected change in your impairment might affect our determination or decision. In these situations, we need to wait to properly evaluate the severity and duration of your impairment during a stable period. Examples of when we might wait are:

(i) If you have had a recent acute event; for example, a myocardial infarction (heart attack).

(ii) If you have recently had a corrective cardiac procedure; for example, coronary artery bypass grafting.

(iii) If you have started new drug therapy and your response to this treatment has not yet been established; for example, beta-blocker therapy for dilated congestive cardiomyopathy.

b. In these situations, we will obtain more evidence 3 months following the event before we evaluate your impairment. However, we will not wait if we have enough information to make a determination or decision based on all of the relevant evidence in your case.

5. Will we purchase any studies? In appropriate situations, we will purchase studies necessary to substantiate the diagnosis or to document the severity of your impairment, generally after we have evaluated the medical and other evidence we already have. We will not purchase studies involving exercise testing if there is significant risk involved or if there is another medical reason not to perform the test. We will follow sections 4.00C6, 4.00C7, and 4.00C8 when we decide whether to purchase exercise testing.

6. What studies will we not purchase? We will not purchase any studies involving cardiac catheterization, such as coronary angiography, arteriograms, or electrophysiological studies. However, if the results of catheterization are part of the existing evidence we have, we will consider them together with the other relevant evidence. See 4.00C15a.

C. Using Cardiovascular Test Results

1. What is an ECG?

a. ECG stands for electrocardiograph or electrocardiogram. An electrocardiograph is a machine that records electrical impulses of your heart on a strip of paper called an electrocardiogram or a tracing. To record the ECG, a technician positions a number of small contacts (or leads) on your arms, legs, and across your chest to connect them to the ECG machine. An ECG may be done while you are resting or exercising.

b. The ECG tracing may indicate that you have a heart abnormality. It may indicate that your heart muscle is not getting as much oxygen as it needs (ischemia), that your heart rhythm is abnormal (arrhythmia), or that there are other abnormalities of your heart, such as left ventricular enlargement.

2. How do we evaluate ECG evidence? We consider a number of factors when we evaluate ECG evidence:

a. An original or legible copy of the 12–lead ECG obtained at rest must be appropriately dated and labeled, with the standardization inscribed on the tracing. Alteration in standardization of specific leads (such as to accommodate large QRS amplitudes) must be identified on those leads.

(i) Detailed descriptions or computer-averaged signals without original or legible copies of the ECG as described in listing 4.00C2a are not acceptable.

(ii) The effects of drugs or electrolyte abnormalities must be considered as possible noncardiac causes of ECG abnormalities of ventricular repolarization; that is, those involving the ST segment and T wave. If available, the predrug (especially digitalis glycosides) ECG should be submitted.

b. ECGs obtained in conjunction with treadmill, bicycle, or arm exercise tests should meet the following specifications:

(i) ECG reports must include the original calibrated ECG tracings or a legible copy.

(ii) A 12–lead baseline ECG must be recorded in the upright position before exercise.

(iii) A 12–lead ECG should be recorded at the end of each minute of exercise.

(iv) If ECG documentation of the effects of hyperventilation is obtained, the exercise test should be deferred for at least 10 minutes because metabolic changes of hyperventilation may alter the physiologic and ECG–recorded response to exercise.

(v) Post-exercise ECGs should be recorded using a generally accepted protocol consistent with the prevailing state of medical knowledge and clinical practice.

(vi) All resting, exercise, and recovery ECG strips must have the standardization inscribed on the tracing. The ECG strips should be labeled to indicate the date, the times recorded and the relationship to the stage of the exercise protocol. The speed and grade (treadmill test) or work rate (bicycle or arm ergometric test) should be recorded. The highest level of exercise achieved, heart rate and blood pressure levels during testing, and the reason(s) for terminating the test (including limiting signs or symptoms) must be recorded.

3. What are exercise tests and what are they used for?

a. Exercise tests have you perform physical activity and record how your cardiovascular system responds. Exercise tests usually involve walking on a treadmill, but other forms of exercise, such as an exercise bicycle or an arm exercise machine, may be used. Exercise testing may be done for various reasons; such as to evaluate the severity of your coronary artery disease or peripheral vascular disease or to evaluate your progress after a cardiac procedure or an acute event, like a myocardial infarction (heart attack). Exercise testing is the most widely used testing for identifying the presence of myocardial ischemia and for estimating maximal aerobic capacity (usually expressed in METs—metabolic equivalents) if you have heart disease.

b. We include exercise tolerance test (ETT) criteria in 4.02B3 (chronic heart failure) and 4.04A (ischemic heart disease). To meet the ETT criteria in these listings, the ETT must be a sign-or symptom-limited test in which you exercise while connected to an ECG until you develop a sign or symptom that indicates that you have exercised as much as is considered safe for you.

c. In 4.12B, we also refer to exercise testing for peripheral vascular disease. In this test, you walk on a treadmill, usually for a specified period of time, and the individual who administers the test measures the effect of exercise on the flow of blood in your legs, usually by using ultrasound. The test is also called an exercise Doppler test. Even though this test is intended to evaluate peripheral vascular disease, it will be stopped for your safety if you develop abnormal signs or symptoms because of heart disease.

d. Each type of test is done in a certain way following specific criteria, called a protocol. For our program, we also specify certain aspects of how any exercise test we purchase is to be done. See 4.00C10 and 4.00C17.

4. Do ETTs have limitations? An ETT provides an estimate of aerobic capacity for walking on a grade, bicycling, or moving one's arms in an environmentally controlled setting. Therefore, ETT results do not correlate with the ability to perform other types of exertional activities, such as lifting and carrying heavy loads, and do not provide an estimate of the ability to perform activities required for work in all possible work environments or throughout a workday. Also, certain medications (such as beta blockers) and conduction disorders (such as left or right bundle branch blocks) can cause false-negative or false-positive results. Therefore, we must consider the results of an ETT together with all the other relevant evidence in your case record.

5. How does an ETT with measurement of maximal or peak oxygen uptake VO_2) differ from other ETTs? Occasionally, medical evidence will include the results of an ETT with VO_2. While ETTs without measurement of VO_2 provide only an estimate of aerobic capacity, measured maximal or peak oxygen uptake provides an accurate measurement of aerobic capacity, which is often expressed in METs (metabolic equivalents). The MET level may not be indicated in the report of attained maximal or peak VO_2 testing, but can be calculated as follows: 1 MET = 3.5 milliliters (ml) of oxygen uptake per kilogram (kg) of body weight per minute. For example, a 70 kg (154 lb.) individual who achieves a maximal or peak VO_2 of 1225 ml in 1 minute has attained 5 METs (1225 ml/70 kg/1 min = 17.5 ml/kg/min. 17.5/3.5 = 5 METs).

6. When will we consider whether to purchase an exercise test?

a. We will consider whether to purchase an exercise test when:

(i) There is a question whether your cardiovascular impairment meets or medically equals the severity of one of the listings, or there is no timely test in the evidence we have (see 4.00C9), and we cannot find you disabled on some other basis; or

(ii) We need to assess your residual functional capacity and there is insufficient evidence in the record to make a determination or decision.

b. We will not purchase an exercise test when we can make our determination or decision based on the evidence we already have.

7. What must we do before purchasing an exercise test?

a. Before we purchase an exercise test, an MC, preferably one with experience in the care of patients with cardiovascular disease, must review the pertinent history, physical examinations, and laboratory tests that we have to determine whether the test would present a significant risk to you or if there is some other medical reason not to purchase the test (see 4.00C8).

b. If you are under the care of a treating source (see §§ 404.1502 and 416.902) for a cardiovascular impairment, this source has not performed an exercise test, and there are no reported significant risks to testing, we will request a statement from that source explaining why it was not done or should not be done before we decide whether we will purchase the test.

c. The MC, in accordance with the regulations and other instructions on consultative examinations, will generally give great weight to the treating source's opinion about the risk of exercise testing to you and will generally not override it. In the rare situation in which the MC does override the treating source's opinion, the MC must prepare a written rationale documenting the reasons for overriding the opinion.

d. If you do not have a treating source or we cannot obtain a statement from your treating source, the MC is responsible for assessing the risk to exercise testing based on a review of the records we have before purchasing an exercise test for you.

e. We must also provide your records to the medical source who performs the exercise test for review prior to conducting the test if the source does not already have them. The medical source who performs the exercise test has the ultimate responsibility for deciding whether you would be at risk.

8. When will we not purchase an exercise test or wait before we purchase an exercise test?

a. We will not purchase an exercise test when an MC finds that you have one of the following significant risk factors:

(i) Unstable angina not previously stabilized by medical treatment.

(ii) Uncontrolled cardiac arrhythmias causing symptoms or hemodynamic compromise.

(iii) An implanted cardiac defibrillator.

(iv) Symptomatic severe aortic stenosis.

(v) Uncontrolled symptomatic heart failure.

(vi) Aortic dissection.

(vii) Severe pulmonary hypertension (pulmonary artery systolic pressure greater than 60 mm Hg).

(viii) Left main coronary stenosis of 50 percent or greater that has not been bypassed.

(ix) Moderate stenotic valvular disease with a systolic gradient across the aortic valve of 50 mm Hg or greater.

(x) Severe arterial hypertension (systolic greater than 200 mm Hg or diastolic greater than 110 mm Hg).

(xi) Hypertrophic cardiomyopathy with a systolic gradient of 50 mm Hg or greater.

b. We also will not purchase an exercise test when you are prevented from performing exercise testing due to another impairment affecting your ability to use your arms and legs.

c. We will not purchase an ETT to document the presence of a cardiac arrhythmia.

d. We will wait to purchase an exercise test until 3 months after you have had one of the following events. This will allow for maximal, attainable restoration of functional capacity.

(i) Acute myocardial infarction.

(ii) Surgical myocardial revascularization (bypass surgery).

(iii) Other open-heart surgical procedures.

(iv) Percutaneous transluminal coronary angioplasty with or without stenting.

e. If you are deconditioned after an extended period of bedrest or inactivity and could improve with activity, or if you are in acute heart failure and are expected to improve with treatment, we will wait an appropriate period of time for you to recuperate before we purchase an exercise test.

9. What do we mean by a "timely" test?

a. We consider exercise test results to be timely for 12 months after the date they are performed, provided there has been no change in your clinical status that may alter the severity of your cardiovascular impairment.

b. However, an exercise test that is older than 12 months, especially an abnormal one, can still provide information important to our adjudication. For example, a test that is more than 12 months old can provide evidence of ischemic heart disease or peripheral vascular disease, information on decreased aerobic capacity, or information about the duration or onset of your impairment. Such tests can be an important component of the longitudinal record.

c. When we evaluate a test that is more than 12 months old, we must consider the results in the context of all the relevant evidence, including why the test was performed and whether there has been an intervening event or improvement or worsening of your impairment.

d. We will purchase a new exercise test only if we cannot make a determination or decision based on the evidence we have.

10. How must ETTs we purchase be performed?

a. The ETT must be a sign- or symptom-limited test characterized by a progressive multistage regimen. It must be performed using a generally accepted protocol consistent with the prevailing state of medical knowledge and clinical practice. A description of the protocol that was followed must be provided, and the test must meet the requirements of 4.00C2b and this section. A radionuclide perfusion scan may be useful for detecting or confirming ischemia when resting ECG abnormalities, medications, or other factors may decrease the accuracy of ECG interpretation of ischemia. (The perfusion imaging is done at the termination of exercise, which may be at a higher MET level than that at which ischemia first occurs. If the imaging confirms the presence of reversible ischemia, the exercise ECG may be useful for detecting the MET level at which ischemia initially appeared.) Exercise tests may also be performed using echocardiography to detect stress-induced ischemia and left ventricular dysfunction (see 4.00C12 and 4.00C13).

b. The exercise test must be paced to your capabilities and be performed following the generally accepted standards for adult exercise test laboratories. With a treadmill test, the speed, grade (incline), and duration of exercise must be recorded for each exercise test stage performed. Other exercise test protocols or techniques should use similar workloads. The exercise protocol may need to be modified in individual cases to allow for a lower initial workload with more slowly graded increments than the standard Bruce protocol.

c. Levels of exercise must be described in terms of workload and duration of each stage; for example, treadmill speed and grade, or bicycle ergometer work rate in kpm/min or watts.

d. The exercise laboratory's physical environment, staffing, and equipment must meet the generally accepted standards for adult exercise test laboratories.

11. How do we evaluate ETT results? We evaluate ETT results on the basis of the work level at which the test becomes abnormal, as documented by onset of signs or symptoms and any ECG or imaging abnormalities. The absence of an ischemic response on an ETT alone does not exclude the diagnosis of ischemic heart disease. We must consider the results of an ETT in the context of all of the other evidence in your case record.

12. When are ETTs done with imaging? When resting ECG abnormalities preclude interpretation of ETT tracings relative to ischemia, a radionuclide (for example, thallium–201 or technetium–99m) perfusion scan or echocardiography in conjunction with an ETT provides better results. You may have resting ECG abnormalities when you have a conduction defect—for example, Wolff–Parkinson–White syndrome, left bundle branch block, left ventricular hypertrophy—or when you are taking digitalis or other antiarrhythmic drugs, or when resting ST changes are present. Also, these techniques can provide a reliable estimate of ejection fraction.

13. Will we purchase ETTs with imaging? We may purchase an ETT with imaging in your case after an MC, preferably one with experience in the care of patients with cardiovascular disease, has reviewed your medical history and physical examination, any report(s) of appropriate medically acceptable imaging, ECGs, and other appropriate tests. We will consider purchasing an ETT with imaging when other information we have is not adequate for us to assess whether you have severe ventricular dysfunction or myocardial ischemia, there is no significant risk involved (see 4.00C8a), and we cannot make our determination or decision based on the evidence we already have.

14. What are drug-induced stress tests? These tests are designed primarily to provide evidence about myocardial ischemia or prior myocardial infarction, but do not require you to exercise. These tests are used when you cannot exercise or cannot exercise enough to achieve the desired cardiac stress. Drug-induced stress tests can also provide evidence about heart chamber dimensions and function; however, these tests do not provide information about your aerobic capacity and cannot be used to help us assess your ability to function. Some of these tests use agents, such as Persantine or adenosine, that dilate the coronary arteries and are used in combination with nuclear agents, such as thallium or technetium (for example, Cardiolyte or Myoview), and a myocardial scan. Other tests use agents, such as dobutamine, that stimulate the heart to contract more forcefully and faster to simulate exercise and are used in combination with a 2–dimensional echocardiogram. We may, when appropriate, purchase a drug-induced stress test to confirm the presence of myocardial ischemia after a review of the evidence in your file by an MC, preferably one with experience in the care of patients with cardiovascular disease.

15. How do we evaluate cardiac catheterization evidence?

a. We will not purchase cardiac catheterization; however, if you have had catheterization, we will make every reasonable effort to obtain the report and any ancillary studies. We will consider the quality and type of data provided and its relevance to the evaluation of your impairment. For adults, we generally see two types of catheterization reports: Coronary arteriography and left ventriculography.

b. For coronary arteriography, the report should provide information citing the method of assessing coronary arterial lumen diameter and the nature and location of obstructive lesions. Drug treatment at baseline and during the procedure should be reported. Some individuals with significant coronary atherosclerotic obstruction have collateral vessels that supply the myocardium distal to the arterial obstruction so that there is no evidence of myocardial damage or ischemia, even with exercise. When the results of quantitative computer measurements and analyses are included in your case record, we will consider them in interpreting the severity of stenotic lesions.

c. For left ventriculography, the report should describe the wall motion of the myocardium with regard to any areas of hypokinesis (abnormally decreased motion), akinesis (lack of motion), or dyskinesis (distortion of motion), and the overall contraction of the ventricle as measured by the ejection fraction. Measurement of chamber volumes and pressures may be useful. Quantitative computer analysis provides precise measurement of segmental left ventricular wall thickness and motion. There is often a poor correlation between left ventricular function at rest and functional capacity for physical activity.

16. What details should exercise Doppler test reports contain? The reports of exercise Doppler tests must describe the level of exercise; for example, the speed and grade of the treadmill settings, the duration of exercise, symptoms during exercise, and the reasons for stopping exercise if the expected level of exercise was not attained. They must also include the blood pressures at the ankle and other pertinent sites measured after exercise and the time required for the systolic blood pressure to return toward or to the pre-exercise level. The graphic tracings, if available, should also be included with the report. All tracings must be annotated with the standardization used by the testing facility.

17. How must exercise Doppler tests we purchase be performed? When we purchase an exercise Doppler test, you must exercise on a treadmill at 2 mph on a 12 percent grade for up to 5 minutes. The reports must include the information specified in 4.00C16. Because this is an exercise test, we must evaluate whether such testing would put you at significant risk, in accordance with the guidance found in 4.00C6, 4.00C7, and 4.00C8.

D. Evaluating Chronic Heart Failure

1. What is chronic heart failure (CHF)?

a. CHF is the inability of the heart to pump enough oxygenated blood to body tissues. This syndrome is characterized by symptoms and signs of pulmonary or systemic congestion (fluid retention) or limited cardiac output. Certain laboratory findings of cardiac functional and structural abnormality support the diagnosis of CHF. There are two main types of CHF:

(i) Predominant systolic dysfunction (the inability of the heart to contract normally and expel sufficient blood), which is characterized by a dilated, poorly contracting left ventricle and reduced ejection fraction (abbreviated EF, it represents the percentage of the blood in the ventricle actually pumped out with each contraction), and

(ii) Predominant diastolic dysfunction (the inability of the heart to relax and fill normally), which is characterized by a thickened ventricular muscle, poor ability of the left ventricle to distend, increased ventricular filling pressure, and a normal or increased EF.

b. CHF is considered in these listings as a single category whether due to atherosclerosis (narrowing of the arteries), cardiomyopathy, hypertension, or rheumatic, congenital, or other heart disease. However, if the CHF is the result of primary pulmonary hypertension secondary to disease of the lung (cor pulmonale), we will evaluate your impairment using 3.09, in the respiratory system listings.

2. What evidence of CHF do we need?

a. Cardiomegaly or ventricular dysfunction must be present and demonstrated by appropriate medically acceptable imaging, such as chest x-ray, echocardiography (M–Mode, 2–dimensional, and Doppler), radionuclide studies, or cardiac catheterization.

(i) Abnormal cardiac imaging showing increased left ventricular end diastolic diameter (LVEDD), decreased EF, increased left atrial chamber size, increased ventricular filling pressures measured at cardiac catheterization, or increased left ventricular wall or septum thickness, provides objective measures of both left ventricular function and structural abnormality in heart failure.

(ii) An LVEDD greater than 6.0 cm or an EF of 30 percent or less measured during a period of stability (that is, not during an episode of acute heart failure) may be associated clinically with systolic failure.

(iii) Left ventricular posterior wall thickness added to septal thickness totaling 2.5 cm or greater with left atrium enlarged to 4.5 cm or greater may be associated clinically with diastolic failure.

(iv) However, these measurements alone do not reflect your functional capacity, which we evaluate by considering all of the relevant evidence. In some situations, we may need to purchase an ETT to help us assess your functional capacity.

(v) Other findings on appropriate medically acceptable imaging may include increased pulmonary vascular markings, pleural effusion, and pulmonary edema. These findings need not be present on each report, since CHF may be controlled by prescribed treatment.

b. To establish that you have chronic heart failure, your medical history and physical examination should describe characteristic symptoms and signs of pulmonary or systemic congestion or of limited cardiac output associated with the abnormal findings on appropriate medically acceptable imaging. When an acute episode of heart failure is triggered by a remediable factor, such as an arrhythmia, dietary sodium overload, or high altitude, cardiac function may be restored and a chronic impairment may not be present.

(i) Symptoms of congestion or of limited cardiac output include easy fatigue, weakness, shortness of breath (dyspnea), cough, or chest discomfort at rest or with activity. Individuals with CHF may also experience shortness of breath on lying flat (orthopnea) or episodes of shortness of breath that wake them from sleep (paroxysmal nocturnal dyspnea). They may also experience cardiac arrhythmias resulting in palpitations, lightheadedness, or fainting.

(ii) Signs of congestion may include hepatomegaly, ascites, increased jugular venous distention or pressure, rales, peripheral edema, or rapid weight gain. However, these signs need not be found on all examinations because fluid retention may be controlled by prescribed treatment.

3. Is it safe for you to have an ETT, if you have CHF? The presence of CHF is not necessarily a contraindication to an ETT, unless you are having an acute episode of heart failure. Measures of cardiac performance are valuable in helping us evaluate your ability to do work-related activities. Exercise testing has been safely used in individuals with CHF; therefore, we may purchase an ETT for evaluation under 4.02B3 if an MC, preferably one experienced in the care of patients with cardiovascular disease, determines that there is no significant risk to you. (See 4.00C6 for when we will consider the purchase of an ETT. See 4.00C7–4.00C8 for what we must do before we purchase an ETT and when we will not purchase one.) ST segment changes from digitalis use in the treatment of CHF do not preclude the purchase of an ETT.

4. How do we evaluate CHF using 4.02?

a. We must have objective evidence, as described in 4.00D2, that you have chronic heart failure.

b. To meet the required level of severity for this listing, your impairment must satisfy the requirements of one of the criteria in A and one of the criteria in B.

c. In 4.02B2, the phrase periods of stabilization means that, for at least 2 weeks between episodes of acute heart failure, there must be objective evidence of clearing of the pulmonary edema or pleural effusions and evidence that you returned to, or you were medically considered able to return to, your prior level of activity.

d. Listing 4.02B3c requires a decrease in systolic blood pressure below the baseline level (taken in the standing position immediately prior to exercise) or below any systolic pressure reading recorded during exercise. This is because, normally, systolic blood pressure and heart rate increase gradually with exercise. Decreases in systolic blood pressure below the baseline level that occur during exercise are often associated with ischemia-induced left ventricular dysfunction resulting in decreased cardiac output. However, a blunted response (that is, failure of the systolic blood pressure to rise 10 mm Hg or more), particularly in the first 3 minutes of exercise, may be drug-related and is not necessarily associated with left ventricular dysfunction. Also, some individuals with increased sympathetic responses because of deconditioning or apprehension may increase their systolic blood pressure and heart rate above their baseline level just before and early into exercise. This can be associated with a drop in systolic pressure in early exercise that is not due to left ventricular dysfunction. Therefore, an early decrease in systolic blood pressure must be interpreted within the total context of the test; that is, the presence or absence of symptoms such as lightheadedness, ischemic changes, or arrhythmias on the ECG.

E. Evaluating Ischemic Heart Disease

1. What is ischemic heart disease (IHD)? IHD results when one or more of your coronary arteries is narrowed or obstructed or, in rare situations, constricted due to vasospasm, interfering with the normal flow of blood to your heart muscle (ischemia). The obstruction may be the result of an embolus, a thrombus, or plaque. When heart muscle tissue dies as a result of the reduced blood supply, it is called a myocardial infarction (heart attack).

2. What causes chest discomfort of myocardial origin?

a. Chest discomfort of myocardial ischemic origin, commonly known as angina pectoris, is usually caused by coronary artery disease (often abbreviated CAD). However, ischemic discomfort may be caused by a noncoronary artery impairment, such as aortic stenosis, hypertrophic cardiomyopathy, pulmonary hypertension, or anemia.

b. Instead of typical angina pectoris, some individuals with IHD experience atypical angina, anginal equivalent, variant angina, or silent ischemia, all of which we may evaluate using 4.04. We discuss the various manifestations of ischemia in 4.00E3–4.00E7.

3. What are the characteristics of typical angina pectoris? Discomfort of myocardial ischemic origin (angina pectoris) is discomfort that is precipitated by effort or emotion and promptly relieved by rest, sublingual nitroglycerin (that is, nitroglycerin tablets that are placed under the tongue), or other rapidly acting nitrates. Typically, the discomfort is located in the chest (usually substernal) and described as pressing, crushing, squeezing, burning, aching, or oppressive. Sharp, sticking, or cramping discomfort is less common. Discomfort occurring with activity or emotion should be described specifically as to timing and usual inciting factors (type and intensity), character, location, radiation, duration, and response to nitrate treatment or rest.

4. What is atypical angina? Atypical angina describes discomfort or pain from myocardial ischemia that is felt in places other than the chest. The common sites of cardiac pain are the inner aspect of the left arm, neck, jaw(s), upper abdomen, and back, but the discomfort or pain can be elsewhere. When pain of cardiac ischemic origin presents in an atypical site in the absence of chest discomfort, the source of the pain may be difficult to diagnose. To represent atypical

angina, your discomfort or pain should have precipitating and relieving factors similar to those of typical chest discomfort, and we must have objective medical evidence of myocardial ischemia; for example, ECG or ETT evidence or appropriate medically acceptable imaging.

5. What is anginal equivalent? Often, individuals with IHD will complain of shortness of breath (dyspnea) on exertion without chest pain or discomfort. In a minority of such situations, the shortness of breath is due to myocardial ischemia; this is called anginal equivalent. To represent anginal equivalent, your shortness of breath should have precipitating and relieving factors similar to those of typical chest discomfort, and we must have objective medical evidence of myocardial ischemia; for example, ECG or ETT evidence or appropriate medically acceptable imaging. In these situations, it is essential to establish objective evidence of myocardial ischemia to ensure that you do not have effort dyspnea due to non-ischemic or noncardiac causes.

6. What is variant angina?

a. Variant angina (Prinzmetal's angina, vasospastic angina) refers to the occurrence of anginal episodes at rest, especially at night, accompanied by transitory ST segment elevation (or, at times, ST depression) on an ECG. It is due to severe spasm of a coronary artery, causing ischemia of the heart wall, and is often accompanied by major ventricular arrhythmias, such as ventricular tachycardia. We will consider variant angina under 4.04 only if you have spasm of a coronary artery in relation to an obstructive lesion of the vessel. If you have an arrhythmia as a result of variant angina, we may consider your impairment under 4.05.

b. Variant angina may also occur in the absence of obstructive coronary disease. In this situation, an ETT will not demonstrate ischemia. The diagnosis will be established by showing the typical transitory ST segment changes during attacks of pain, and the absence of obstructive lesions shown by catheterization. Treatment in cases where there is no obstructive coronary disease is limited to medications that reduce coronary vasospasm, such as calcium channel blockers and nitrates. In such situations, we will consider the frequency of anginal episodes despite prescribed treatment when evaluating your residual functional capacity.

c. Vasospasm that is catheter-induced during coronary angiography is not variant angina.

7. What is silent ischemia?

a. Myocardial ischemia, and even myocardial infarction, can occur without perception of pain or any other symptoms; when this happens, we call it silent ischemia. Pain sensitivity may be altered by a variety of diseases, most notably diabetes mellitus and other neuropathic disorders. Individuals also vary in their threshold for pain.

b. Silent ischemia occurs most often in:

(i) Individuals with documented past myocardial infarction or established angina without prior infarction who do not have chest pain on ETT, but have a positive test with ischemic abnormality on ECG, perfusion scan, or other appropriate medically acceptable imaging.

(ii) Individuals with documented past myocardial infarction or angina who have ST segment changes on ambulatory monitoring (Holter monitoring) that are similar to those that occur during episodes of angina. ST depression shown on the ambulatory recording should not be interpreted as positive for ischemia unless similar depression is also seen during chest pain episodes annotated in the diary that the individual keeps while wearing the Holter monitor.

c. ST depression can result from a variety of factors, such as postural changes and variations in cardiac sympathetic tone. In addition, there are differences in how different Holter monitors record the electrical responses. Therefore, we do not consider the Holter monitor reliable for the diagnosis of silent ischemia except in the situation described in 4.00E7b(ii).

8. What other sources of chest discomfort are there? Chest discomfort of nonischemic origin may result from other cardiac impairments, such as pericarditis. Noncardiac impairments may also produce symptoms mimicking that of myocardial ischemia. These impairments include acute anxiety or panic attacks, gastrointestinal tract disorders, such as esophageal spasm, esophagitis, hiatal hernia, biliary tract disease, gastritis, peptic ulcer, and pancreatitis, and musculoskeletal syndromes, such as chest wall muscle spasm, chest wall syndrome (especially after coronary bypass surgery), costochondritis, and cervical or dorsal spine arthritis. Hyperventilation may also mimic ischemic discomfort. Thus, in the absence of documented myocardial ischemia, such disorders should be considered as possible causes of chest discomfort.

9. How do we evaluate IHD using 4.04?

a. We must have objective evidence, as described under 4.00C, that your symptoms are due to myocardial ischemia.

b. Listing-level changes on the ECG in 4.04A1 are the classically accepted changes of horizontal or downsloping ST depression occurring both during exercise and recovery. Although we recognize that ischemic changes may at times occur only during exercise or recovery, and may at times be upsloping with only junctional ST depression, such changes can be false positive; that is, occur in the absence of ischemia. Diagnosis of ischemia in this situation requires radionuclide or echocardiogram confirmation. See 4.00C12 and 4.00C13.

c. Also in 4.04A1, we require that the depression of the ST segment last for at least 1 minute of recovery because ST depression that occurs during exercise but that rapidly normalizes in recovery is a common false-positive response.

d. In 4.04A2, we specify that the ST elevation must be in non-infarct leads during both exercise and recovery. This is because, in the absence of ECG signs of prior infarction, ST elevation during exercise denotes ischemia, usually severe, requiring immediate termination of exercise. However, if there is baseline ST elevation in association with a prior infarction or ventricular aneurysm, further ST elevation during exercise does not necessarily denote ischemia and could be a false-positive ECG response. Diagnosis of ischemia in this situation requires radionuclide or echocardiogram confirmation. See 4.00C12 and 4.00C13.

e. Listing 4.04A3 requires a decrease in systolic blood pressure below the baseline level (taken in the standing position immediately prior to exercise) or below any systolic pressure reading recorded during exercise. This is the same finding required in 4.02B3c. See 4.00D4d for full details.

f. In 4.04B, each of the three ischemic episodes must require revascularization or be not amenable to treatment. Revascularization means angioplasty (with or without stent placement) or bypass surgery. However, reocclusion that occurs after a revascularization procedure but during the same hospitalization and that requires a second procedure during the same hospitalization will not be counted as another ischemic episode. Not amenable means that the revascularization procedure could not be done because of another medical impairment or because the vessel was not suitable for revascularization.

g. We will use 4.04C only when you have symptoms due to myocardial ischemia as described in 4.00E3–4.00E7 while on a regimen of prescribed treatment, you are at risk for exercise testing (see 4.00C8), and we do not have a timely ETT or a timely normal drug-induced stress test for you. See 4.00C9 for what we mean by a timely test.

h. In 4.04C1 the term nonbypassed means that the blockage is in a vessel that is potentially bypassable; that is, large enough to be bypassed and considered to be a cause of your ischemia. These vessels are usually major arteries or one of a major artery's major branches. A vessel that has become obstructed again after angioplasty or stent placement and has remained obstructed or is not amenable to another revascularization is considered a nonbypassed vessel for purposes of this listing. When you have had revascularization, we will not use the pre-operative findings to assess the current severity of your coronary artery disease under 4.04C, although we will consider the severity and duration of your impairment prior to your surgery in making our determination or decision.

F. Evaluating Arrhythmias

1. What is an arrhythmia? An arrhythmia is a change in the regular beat of the heart. Your heart may seem to skip a beat or beat irregularly, very quickly (tachycardia), or very slowly (bradycardia).

2. What are the different types of arrhythmias?

a. There are many types of arrhythmias. Arrhythmias are identified by where they occur in the heart (atria or ventricles) and by what happens to the heart's rhythm when they occur.

b. Arrhythmias arising in the cardiac atria (upper chambers of the heart) are called atrial or supraventricular arrhythmias. Ventricular arrhythmias begin in the ventricles (lower chambers). In general, ventricular arrhythmias caused by heart disease are the most serious.

3. How do we evaluate arrhythmias using 4.05?

a. We will use 4.05 when you have arrhythmias that are not fully controlled by medication, an implanted pacemaker, or an implanted cardiac defibrillator and you have uncontrolled recurrent episodes of syncope or near syncope. If your arrhythmias are controlled, we will evaluate your underlying heart disease using the appropriate listing. For other considerations when we evaluate arrhythmias in the presence of an implanted cardiac defibrillator, see 4.00F4.

b. We consider near syncope to be a period of altered consciousness, since syncope is a loss of consciousness or a faint. It is not merely a feeling of light-headedness, momentary weakness, or dizziness.

c. For purposes of 4.05, there must be a documented association between the syncope or near syncope and the recurrent arrhythmia. The recurrent arrhythmia, not some other cardiac or non-cardiac disorder, must be established as the cause of the associated symptom. This documentation of the association between the symptoms and the arrhythmia may come from the usual diagnostic methods, including Holter monitoring (also called ambulatory electrocardiography) and tilt-table testing with a concurrent ECG. Although an arrhythmia may be a coincidental finding on an ETT, we will not purchase an ETT to document the presence of a cardiac arrhythmia.

4. What will we consider when you have an implanted cardiac defibrillator and you do not have arrhythmias that meet the requirements of 4.05?

a. Implanted cardiac defibrillators are used to prevent sudden cardiac death in individuals who have had, or are at high risk for, cardiac arrest from life-threatening ventricular arrhythmias. The largest group at risk for sudden cardiac death consists of individuals with cardiomyopathy (ischemic or non-ischemic) and reduced ventricular function. However, life-threatening ventricular arrhythmias can also occur in individuals with little or no ventricular dysfunction. The shock from the implanted cardiac defibrillator is a unique form of treatment; it rescues an individual from what may have been cardiac arrest. However, as a consequence of the shock(s), individuals may experience psychological distress, which we may evaluate under the mental disorders listings in 12.00ff.

b. Most implantable cardiac defibrillators have rhythm-correcting and pacemaker capabilities. In some individuals, these functions may result in the termination of ventricular arrhythmias without an otherwise painful shock. (The shock is like being kicked in the chest.) Implanted cardiac defibrillators may deliver inappropriate shocks, often repeatedly, in response to benign arrhythmias or electrical malfunction. Also, exposure to strong electrical or magnetic fields, such as from MRI (magnetic resonance imaging), can trigger or reprogram an implanted cardiac defibrillator, resulting in inappropriate shocks. We must consider the frequency of, and the reason(s) for, the shocks when evaluating the severity and duration of your impairment.

c. In general, the exercise limitations imposed on individuals with an implanted cardiac defibrillator are those dictated by the underlying heart impairment. However, the exercise limitations may be greater when the implanted cardiac defibrillator delivers an inappropriate shock in response to the increase in heart rate with exercise, or when there is exercise-induced ventricular arrhythmia.

G. Evaluating Peripheral Vascular Disease

1. What is peripheral vascular disease (PVD)? Generally, PVD is any impairment that affects either the arteries (peripheral arterial disease) or the veins (venous insufficiency) in the extremities, particularly the lower extremities. The usual effect is blockage of the flow of blood either from the heart (arterial) or back to the heart (venous). If you have peripheral arterial disease, you may have pain in your calf after walking a distance that goes away when you rest (intermittent claudication); at more advanced stages, you may have pain in your calf at rest or you may develop ulceration or gangrene. If you have venous insufficiency, you may have swelling, varicose veins, skin pigmentation changes, or skin ulceration.

2. How do we assess limitations resulting from PVD? We will assess your limitations based on your symptoms together with physical findings, Doppler studies, other appropriate non-invasive studies, or angiographic findings. However, if the PVD has resulted in amputation, we will evaluate any limitations related to the amputation under the musculoskeletal listings, 1.00ff.

3. What is brawny edema? Brawny edema (4.11A) is swelling that is usually dense and feels firm due to the presence of increased connective tissue; it is also associated with characteristic skin pigmentation changes. It is not the same thing as pitting edema. Brawny edema generally does not pit (indent on pressure), and the terms are not interchangeable. Pitting edema does not satisfy the requirements of 4.11A.

4. What is lymphedema and how will we evaluate it?

a. Lymphedema is edema of the extremities due to a disorder of the lymphatic circulation; at its worst, it is called elephantiasis. Primary lymphedema is caused by abnormal development of lymph vessels and may be present at birth (congenital lymphedema), but more often develops during the teens (lymphedema praecox). It may also appear later, usually after age 35 (lymphedema tarda). Secondary lymphedema is due to obstruction or destruction of normal lymphatic channels due to tumor, surgery, repeated infections, or parasitic infection such as filariasis. Lymphedema most commonly affects one extremity.

b. Lymphedema does not meet the requirements of 4.11, although it may medically equal the severity of that listing. We will evaluate lymphedema by considering whether the underlying cause meets or medically equals any listing or whether the lymphedema medically equals a cardiovascular listing, such as 4.11, or a musculoskeletal listing, such as 1.02A or 1.03. If no listing is met or medically equaled, we will evaluate any functional limitations imposed by your lymphedema when we assess your residual functional capacity.

5. When will we purchase exercise Doppler studies for evaluating peripheral arterial disease (PAD)? If we need additional evidence of your PAD, we will generally purchase exercise Doppler studies (see 4.00C16 and 4.00C17) when your resting ankle/brachial systolic blood pressure ratio is at least 0.50 but less than 0.80, and only rarely when it is 0.80 or above. We will not purchase exercise Doppler testing if you have a disease that results in abnormal arterial calcification or small vessel disease, but will use your resting toe systolic blood pressure or resting toe/brachial systolic blood pressure ratio. (See 4.00G7c and 4.00G8.) There are no current medical standards for evaluating exercise toe pressures. Because any exercise test stresses your entire cardiovascular system, we will purchase exercise Doppler studies only after an MC, preferably one with experience in the care of patients with cardiovascular disease, has determined that the test would not present a significant risk to you and that there is no other medical reason not to purchase the test (see 4.00C6, 4.00C7, and 4.00C8).

6. Are there any other studies that are helpful in evaluating PAD? Doppler studies done using a recording ultrasonic Doppler unit and strain-gauge plethysmography are other useful tools for evaluating PAD. A recording Doppler, which prints a tracing of the arterial pulse wave in the femoral, popliteal, dorsalis pedis, and posterior tibial arteries, is an excellent evaluation tool to compare wave forms in normal and compromised peripheral blood flow. Qualitative analysis of the pulse wave is very helpful in the overall

assessment of the severity of the occlusive disease. Tracings are especially helpful in assessing severity if you have small vessel disease related to diabetes mellitus or other diseases with similar vascular changes, or diseases causing medial calcifications when ankle pressure is either normal or falsely high.

7. How do we evaluate PAD under 4.12?

a. The ankle blood pressure referred to in 4.12A and B is the higher of the pressures recorded from the posterior tibial and dorsalis pedis arteries in the affected leg. The higher pressure recorded from the two sites is the more significant measurement in assessing the extent of arterial insufficiency. Techniques for obtaining ankle systolic blood pressures include Doppler (See 4.00C16 and 4.00C17), plethysmographic studies, or other techniques. We will request any available tracings generated by these studies so that we can review them.

b. In 4.12A, the ankle/brachial systolic blood pressure ratio is the ratio of the systolic blood pressure at the ankle to the systolic blood pressure at the brachial artery; both taken at the same time while you are lying on your back. We do not require that the ankle and brachial pressures be taken on the same side of your body. This is because, as with the ankle pressure, we will use the higher brachial systolic pressure measured. Listing 4.12A is met when your resting ankle/brachial systolic blood pressure ratio is less than 0.50. If your resting ankle/brachial systolic blood pressure ratio is 0.50 or above, we will use 4.12B to evaluate the severity of your PAD, unless you also have a disease causing abnormal arterial calcification or small vessel disease, such as diabetes mellitus. See 4.00G7c and 4.00G8.

c. We will use resting toe systolic blood pressures or resting toe/brachial systolic blood pressure ratios (determined the same way as ankle/brachial ratios, see 4.00G7b) when you have intermittent claudication and a disease that results in abnormal arterial calcification (for example, Monckeberg's sclerosis or diabetes mellitus) or small vessel disease (for example, diabetes mellitus). These diseases may result in misleadingly high blood pressure readings at the ankle. However, high blood pressures due to vascular changes related to these diseases seldom occur at the toe level. While the criteria in 4.12C and 4.12D are intended primarily for individuals who have a disease causing abnormal arterial calcification or small vessel disease, we may also use them for evaluating anyone with PAD.

8. How are toe pressures measured? Toe pressures are measured routinely in most vascular laboratories through one of three methods: most frequently, photoplethysmography; less frequently, plethysmography using strain gauge cuffs; and Doppler ultrasound. Toe pressure can also be measured by using any blood pressure cuff that fits snugly around the big toe and is neither too tight nor too loose. A neonatal cuff or a cuff designed for use on fingers or toes can be used in the measurement of toe pressure.

9. How do we use listing 4.12 if you have had a peripheral graft? Peripheral grafting serves the same purpose as coronary grafting; that is, to bypass a narrow or obstructed arterial segment. If intermittent claudication recurs or persists after peripheral grafting, we may purchase Doppler studies to assess the flow of blood through the bypassed vessel and to establish the current severity of the peripheral arterial impairment. However, if you have had peripheral grafting done for your PAD, we will not use the findings from before the surgery to assess the current severity of your impairment, although we will consider the severity and duration of your impairment prior to your surgery in making our determination or decision.

H. Evaluating Other Cardiovascular Impairments

1. How will we evaluate hypertension? Because hypertension (high blood pressure) generally causes disability through its effects on other body systems, we will evaluate it by reference to the specific body system(s) affected (heart, brain, kidneys, or eyes) when we consider its effects under the listings. We will also consider any limitations imposed by your hypertension when we assess your residual functional capacity.

2. How will we evaluate symptomatic congenital heart disease? Congenital heart disease is any abnormality of the heart or the major blood vessels that is present at birth. Because of improved treatment methods, more children with congenital heart disease are living to adulthood. Although some types of congenital heart disease may be corrected by surgery, many individuals with treated congenital heart disease continue to have problems throughout their lives (symptomatic congenital heart disease). If you have congenital heart disease that results in chronic heart failure with evidence of ventricular dysfunction or in recurrent arrhythmias, we will evaluate your impairment under 4.02 or 4.05. Otherwise, we will evaluate your impairment under 4.06.

3. What is cardiomyopathy and how will we evaluate it? Cardiomyopathy is a disease of the heart muscle. The heart loses its ability to pump blood (heart failure), and in some instances, heart rhythm is disturbed, leading to irregular heartbeats (arrhythmias). Usually, the exact cause of the muscle damage is never found (idiopathic cardiomyopathy). There are various types of cardiomyopathy, which fall into two major categories: Ischemic and nonischemic cardiomyopathy. Ischemic cardiomyopathy typically refers to heart muscle damage that results from coronary artery disease, including heart attacks. Nonischemic cardiomyopathy includes several types: Dilated, hypertrophic, and restrictive. We will evaluate cardiomyopathy under 4.02, 4.04, 4.05, or 11.04, depending on its effects on you.

4. How will we evaluate valvular heart disease? We will evaluate valvular heart disease under the listing appropriate for its effect on you. Thus, we may use 4.02, 4.04, 4.05, 4.06, or an appropriate neurological listing in 11.00ff.

5. What do we consider when we evaluate heart transplant recipients?

a. After your heart transplant, we will consider you disabled for 1 year following the surgery because there is a greater likelihood of rejection of the organ and infection during the first year.

b. However, heart transplant patients generally meet our definition of disability before they undergo transplantation. We will determine the onset of your disability based on the facts in your case.

c. We will not assume that you became disabled when your name was placed on a transplant waiting list. This is because you may be placed on a waiting list soon after diagnosis of the cardiac disorder that may eventually require a transplant. Physicians recognize that candidates for transplantation often have to wait months or even years before a suitable donor heart is found, so they place their patients on the list as soon as permitted.

d. When we do a continuing disability review to determine whether you are still disabled, we will evaluate your residual impairment(s), as shown by symptoms, signs, and laboratory findings, including any side effects of medication. We will consider any remaining symptoms, signs, and laboratory findings indicative of cardiac dysfunction in deciding whether medical improvement (as defined in §§ 404.1594 and 416.994) has occurred.

6. When does an aneurysm have "dissection not controlled by prescribed treatment," as required under 4.10? An aneurysm (or bulge in the aorta or one of its major branches) is dissecting when the inner lining of the artery begins to separate from the arterial wall. We consider the dissection not controlled when you have persistence of chest pain due to progression of the dissection, an increase in the size of the aneurysm, or compression of one or more branches of the aorta supplying the heart, kidneys, brain, or other organs. An aneurysm with dissection can cause heart failure, renal (kidney) failure, or neurological complications. If you have an aneurysm that does not meet the requirements of 4.10 and you have one or more of these associated conditions, we will evaluate the condition(s) using the appropriate listing.

7. What is hyperlipidemia and how will we evaluate it? Hyperlipidemia is the general term for an elevation of any or all of the lipids (fats or cholesterol) in the blood; for example, hypertriglyceridemia, hypercholesterolemia, and hyperlipoproteinemia. These disorders of lipoprotein metabolism and transport can cause defects throughout the body. The effects most likely to interfere with function are those produced by atherosclerosis (narrowing of the arteries) and coronary artery disease. We will evaluate your lipoprotein disorder by considering its effects on you.

8. What is Marfan syndrome and how will we evaluate it?

a. Marfan syndrome is a genetic connective tissue disorder that affects multiple body systems, including the skeleton, eyes, heart, blood vessels, nervous system, skin, and lungs. There is no specific laboratory test to diagnose Marfan syndrome. The diagnosis is generally made by medical history, including family history, physical examination, including an evaluation of the ratio of arm/leg size to trunk size, a slit lamp eye examination, and a heart test(s), such as an echocardiogram. In some cases, a genetic analysis may be useful, but such analyses may not provide any additional helpful information.

b. The effects of Marfan syndrome can range from mild to severe. In most cases, the disorder progresses as you age. Most individuals with Marfan syndrome have abnormalities associated with the heart and blood vessels. Your heart's mitral valve may leak, causing a heart murmur. Small leaks may not cause symptoms, but larger ones may cause shortness of breath, fatigue, and palpitations. Another effect is that the wall of the aorta may be weakened and abnormally stretch (aortic dilation). This aortic dilation may tear, dissect, or rupture, causing serious heart problems or sometimes sudden death. We will evaluate the manifestations of your Marfan syndrome under the appropriate body system criteria, such as 4.10, or if necessary, consider the functional limitations imposed by your impairment.

I. Other Evaluation Issues

1. What effect does obesity have on the cardiovascular system and how will we evaluate it? Obesity is a medically determinable impairment that is often associated with disorders of the cardiovascular system. Disturbance of this system can be a major cause of disability if you have obesity. Obesity may affect the cardiovascular system because of the increased workload the additional body mass places on the heart. Obesity may make it harder for the chest and lungs to expand. This can mean that the respiratory system must work harder to provide needed oxygen. This in turn would make the heart work harder to pump blood to carry oxygen to the body. Because the body would be working harder at rest, its ability to perform additional work would be less than would otherwise be expected. Thus, the combined effects of obesity with cardiovascular impairments can be greater than the effects of each of the impairments considered separately. We must consider any additional and cumulative effects of obesity when we determine whether you have a severe cardiovascular impairment or a listing-level cardiovascular impairment (or a combination of impairments that medically equals the severity of a listed

impairment), and when we assess your residual functional capacity.

2. How do we relate treatment to functional status? In general, conclusions about the severity of a cardiovascular impairment cannot be made on the basis of type of treatment rendered or anticipated. The amount of function restored and the time required for improvement after treatment (medical, surgical, or a prescribed program of progressive physical activity) vary with the nature and extent of the disorder, the type of treatment, and other factors. Depending upon the timing of this treatment in relation to the alleged onset date of disability, we may need to defer evaluation of the impairment for a period of up to 3 months from the date treatment began to permit consideration of treatment effects, unless we can make a determination or decision using the evidence we have. See 4.00B4.

3. How do we evaluate impairments that do not meet one of the cardiovascular listings?

a. These listings are only examples of common cardiovascular impairments that we consider severe enough to prevent you from doing any gainful activity. If your severe impairment(s) does not meet the criteria of any of these listings, we must also consider whether you have an impairment(s) that satisfies the criteria of a listing in another body system.

b. If you have a severe medically determinable impairment(s) that does not meet a listing, we will determine whether your impairments(s) medically equals a listing. (See §§ 404.1526 and 416.926.) If you have a severe impairment(s) that does not meet or medically equal the criteria of a listing, you may or may not have the residual functional capacity to engage in substantial gainful activity. Therefore, we proceed to the fourth and, if necessary, the fifth steps of the sequential evaluation process in §§ 404.1520 and 416.920. If you are an adult, we use the rules in §§ 404.1594 or 416.994, as appropriate, when we decide whether you continue to be disabled.

4.01 Category of Impairments, Cardiovascular System

4.02 Chronic heart failure while on a regimen of prescribed treatment, with symptoms and signs described in 4.00D2. The required level of severity for this impairment is met when the requirements in both A and B are satisfied.

A. Medically documented presence of one of the following:

1. Systolic failure (see 4.00D1a(i)), with left ventricular end diastolic dimensions greater than 6.0 cm or ejection fraction of 30 percent or less during a period of stability (not during an episode of acute heart failure); or

2. Diastolic failure (see 4.00D1a(ii)), with left ventricular posterior wall plus septal thickness totaling 2.5 cm or greater on imaging, with an enlarged left atrium greater than or equal to 4.5 cm, with normal or elevated ejection fraction during a period of stability (not during an episode of acute heart failure);

AND

B. Resulting in one of the following:

1. Persistent symptoms of heart failure which very seriously limit the ability to independently initiate, sustain, or complete activities of daily living in an individual for whom an MC, preferably one experienced in the care of patients with cardiovascular disease, has concluded that the performance of an exercise test would present a significant risk to the individual; or

2. Three or more separate episodes of acute congestive heart failure within a consecutive 12–month period (see 4.00A3e), with evidence of fluid retention (see 4.00D2b(ii)) from clinical and imaging assessments at the time of the episodes, requiring acute extended physician intervention such as hospitalization or emergency room treatment for 12 hours or more, separated by periods of stabilization (see 4.00D4c); or

3. Inability to perform on an exercise tolerance test at a workload equivalent to 5 METs or less due to:

a. Dyspnea, fatigue, palpitations, or chest discomfort; or

b. Three or more consecutive premature ventricular contractions (ventricular tachycardia), or increasing frequency of ventricular ectopy with at least 6 premature ventricular contractions per minute; or

c. Decrease of 10 mm Hg or more in systolic pressure below the baseline systolic blood pressure or the preceding systolic pressure measured during exercise (see 4.00D4d) due to left ventricular dysfunction, despite an increase in workload; or

d. Signs attributable to inadequate cerebral perfusion, such as ataxic gait or mental confusion.

4.04 Ischemic heart disease, with symptoms due to myocardial ischemia, as described in 4.00E3–4.00E7, while on a regimen of prescribed treatment (see 4.00B3 if there is no regimen of prescribed treatment), with one of the following:

A. Sign-or symptom-limited exercise tolerance test demonstrating at least one of the following manifestations at a workload equivalent to 5 METs or less:

1. Horizontal or downsloping depression, in the absence of digitalis glycoside treatment or hypokalemia, of the ST segment of at least -0.10 millivolts (–1.0 mm) in at least 3 consecutive complexes that are on a level baseline in any lead other than aVR, and depression of at least -0.10 millivolts lasting for at least 1 minute of recovery; or

2. At least 0.1 millivolt (1 mm) ST elevation above resting baseline in non-infarct leads during both exercise and 1 or more minutes of recovery; or

3. Decrease of 10 mm Hg or more in systolic pressure below the baseline blood pressure or the preceding systolic pressure measured during exercise (see 4.00E9e) due to left ventricular dysfunction, despite an increase in workload; or

4. Documented ischemia at an exercise level equivalent to 5 METs or less on appropriate medically acceptable imaging, such as radionuclide perfusion scans or stress echocardiography.

OR

B. Three separate ischemic episodes, each requiring revascularization or not amenable to revascularization (see 4.00E9f), within a consecutive 12–month period (see 4.00A3e).

OR

C. Coronary artery disease, demonstrated by angiography (obtained independent of Social Security disability evaluation) or other appropriate medically acceptable imaging, and in the absence of a timely exercise tolerance test or a timely normal drug-induced stress test, an MC, preferably one experienced in the care of patients with cardiovascular disease, has concluded that performance of exercise tolerance testing would present a significant risk to the individual, with both 1 and 2:

1. Angiographic evidence showing:

a. 50 percent or more narrowing of a nonbypassed left main coronary artery; or

b. 70 percent or more narrowing of another nonbypassed coronary artery; or

c. 50 percent or more narrowing involving a long (greater than 1 cm) segment of a nonbypassed coronary artery; or

d. 50 percent or more narrowing of at least two nonbypassed coronary arteries; or

e. 70 percent or more narrowing of a bypass graft vessel; and

2. Resulting in very serious limitations in the ability to independently initiate, sustain, or complete activities of daily living.

4.05 Recurrent arrhythmias, not related to reversible causes, such as electrolyte abnormalities or digitalis glycoside or antiarrhythmic drug toxicity, resulting in uncontrolled (see 4.00A3f), recurrent (see 4.00A3c) episodes of cardiac syncope or near syncope (see 4.00F3b), despite prescribed treatment (see 4.00B3 if there is no prescribed treatment), and documented by resting or ambulatory (Holter) electrocardiography, or by other appropriate medically acceptable testing, coincident with the occurrence of syncope or near syncope (see 4.00F3c).

4.06 Symptomatic congenital heart disease (cyanotic or acyanotic), documented by appropriate medically acceptable imaging (see 4.00A3d) or cardiac catheterization, with one of the following:

A. Cyanosis at rest, and:

1. Hematocrit of 55 percent or greater; or

2. Arterial O_2 saturation of less than 90 percent in room air, or resting arterial PO_2 of 60 Torr or less.

OR

B. Intermittent right-to-left shunting resulting in cyanosis on exertion (e.g., Eisenmenger's physiology) and with arterial PO_2 of 60 Torr or less at a workload equivalent to 5 METs or less.

OR

C. Secondary pulmonary vascular obstructive disease with pulmonary arterial systolic pressure elevated to at least 70 percent of the systemic arterial systolic pressure.

4.09 Heart transplant. Consider under a disability for 1 year following surgery; thereafter, evaluate residual impairment under the appropriate listing.

4.10 Aneurysm of aorta or major branches, due to any cause (e.g., atherosclerosis, cystic medial necrosis, Marfan syndrome, trauma), demonstrated by appropriate medically acceptable imaging, with dissection not controlled by prescribed treatment (see 4.00H6).

4.11 Chronic venous insufficiency of a lower extremity with incompetency or obstruction of the deep venous system and one of the following:

A. Extensive brawny edema (see 4.00G3) involving at least two-thirds of the leg between the ankle and knee or the distal one-third of the lower extremity between the ankle and hip.

OR

B. Superficial varicosities, stasis dermatitis, and either recurrent ulceration or persistent ulceration that has not healed following at least 3 months of prescribed treatment.

4.12 Peripheral arterial disease, as determined by appropriate medically acceptable imaging (see 4.00A3d, 4.00G2, 4.00G5, and 4.00G6), causing intermittent claudication (see 4.00G1) and one of the following:

A. Resting ankle/brachial systolic blood pressure ratio of less than 0.50.

OR

B. Decrease in systolic blood pressure at the ankle on exercise (see 4.00G7a and 4.00C16–4.00C17) of 50 percent or more of pre-exercise level and requiring 10 minutes or more to return to pre-exercise level.

OR

C. Resting toe systolic pressure of less than 30 mm Hg (see 4.00G7c and 4.00G8).

OR

D. Resting toe/brachial systolic blood pressure ratio of less than 0.40 (see 4.00G7c).

5.00 Digestive System

A. What kinds of disorders do we consider in the digestive system? Disorders of the digestive system include gastrointestinal hemorrhage, hepatic (liver) dysfunction, inflammatory bowel disease, short bowel syndrome, and malnutrition. They may also lead to complications, such as obstruction, or be accompanied by manifestations in other body systems.

B. What documentation do we need? We need a record of your medical evidence, including clinical and laboratory findings. The documentation should include appropriate medically acceptable imaging studies and reports of endoscopy, operations, and pathology, as appropriate to each listing, to document the severity and duration of your digestive disorder. Medically acceptable imaging includes, but is not limited to, x-ray imaging, sonography, computerized axial tomography (CAT scan), magnetic resonance imaging (MRI), and radionuclide scans. Appropriate means that the technique used is the proper one to support the evaluation and diagnosis of the disorder. The findings required by these listings must occur within the period we are considering in connection with your application or continuing disability review.

C. How do we consider the effects of treatment?

1. Digestive disorders frequently respond to medical or surgical treatment; therefore, we generally consider the severity and duration of these disorders within the context of prescribed treatment.

2. We assess the effects of treatment, including medication, therapy, surgery, or any other form of treatment you receive, by determining if there are improvements in the symptoms, signs, and laboratory findings of your digestive disorder. We also assess any side effects of your treatment that may further limit your functioning.

3. To assess the effects of your treatment, we may need information about:

a. The treatment you have been prescribed (for example, the type of medication or therapy, or your use of parenteral (intravenous) nutrition or supplemental enteral nutrition via a gastrostomy);

b. The dosage, method, and frequency of administration;

c. Your response to the treatment;

d. Any adverse effects of such treatment; and

e. The expected duration of the treatment.

4. Because the effects of treatment may be temporary or long-term, in most cases we need information about the impact of your treatment, including its expected duration and side effects, over a sufficient period of time to help us assess its outcome. When adverse effects of treatment contribute to the severity of your impairment(s), we will consider the duration or expected duration of the treatment when we assess the duration of your impairment(s).

5. If you need parenteral (intravenous) nutrition or supplemental enteral nutrition via a gastrostomy to avoid debilitating complications of a digestive disorder, this treatment will not, in itself, indicate that you are unable to do any gainful activity, except under 5.07, short bowel syndrome (see 5.00F).

6. If you have not received ongoing treatment or have not had an ongoing relationship with the medical community despite the existence of a severe impairment(s), we will evaluate the severity and duration of your digestive impairment on the basis of the current medical and other evidence in your case record. If you have not received treatment, you may not be able to show an impairment that meets the criteria of one of the digestive system listings, but your digestive impairment may medically equal a listing or be disabling based on consideration of your residual functional capacity, age, education, and work experience.

D. How do we evaluate chronic liver disease?

1. General. Chronic liver disease is characterized by liver cell necrosis, inflammation, or scarring (fibrosis or cirrhosis), due to any cause, that persists for more than 6 months. Chronic liver disease may result in portal hypertension, cholestasis (suppression of bile flow), extrahepatic manifestations, or liver cancer. (We evaluate liver cancer under 13.19.) Significant loss of liver function may be manifested by hemorrhage from varices or portal hypertensive gastropathy, ascites (accumulation of fluid in the abdominal cavity), hydrothorax (ascitic fluid in the chest cavity), or encephalopathy. There can also be progressive deterioration of laboratory findings that are indicative of liver dysfunction. Liver transplantation is the only definitive cure for end stage liver disease (ESLD).

2. Examples of chronic liver disease include, but are not limited to, chronic hepatitis, alcoholic liver disease, non-alcoholic steatohepatitis (NASH), primary biliary cirrhosis (PBC), primary sclerosing cholangitis (PSC), autoimmune hepatitis, hemochromatosis, drug-induced liver disease, Wilson's disease, and serum alpha–1 antitrypsin deficiency. Acute hepatic injury is frequently reversible, as in viral, drug-induced, toxin-induced, alcoholic, and ischemic hepatitis. In the absence of evidence of a chronic impairment, episodes of acute liver disease do not meet 5.05.

3. Manifestations of chronic liver disease.

a. Symptoms may include, but are not limited to, pruritis (itching), fatigue, nausea, loss of appetite, or sleep disturbances. Symptoms of chronic liver disease may have a poor correlation with the severity of liver disease and functional ability.

b. Signs may include, but are not limited to, jaundice, enlargement of the liver and spleen, ascites, peripheral edema, and altered mental status.

c. Laboratory findings may include, but are not limited to, increased liver enzymes, increased serum total bilirubin, increased ammonia levels, decreased serum albumin, and abnormal coagulation studies, such as increased International Normalized Ratio (INR) or decreased platelet counts. Abnormally low serum albumin or elevated INR levels indicate loss of synthetic liver function, with increased likelihood of cirrhosis and associated complications. However, other abnormal lab tests, such as liver enzymes, serum total bilirubin, or ammonia levels, may have a poor correlation with the severity of liver disease and functional ability. A liver biopsy may demonstrate the degree of liver cell necrosis, inflammation, fibrosis, and cirrhosis. If you have had a liver biopsy, we will make every reasonable effort to obtain the results; however, we will not purchase a liver biopsy. Imaging studies (CAT scan, ultrasound, MRI) may show the size and consistency (fatty liver, scarring) of the liver and document ascites (see 5.00D6).

4. Chronic viral hepatitis infections.

a. General.

(i) Chronic viral hepatitis infections are commonly caused by hepatitis C virus (HCV), and to a lesser extent, hepatitis B virus (HBV). Usually, these are slowly progressive disorders that persist over many years during which the symptoms and signs are typically nonspecific, intermittent, and mild (for example, fatigue, difficulty with concentration, or right upper quadrant pain). Laboratory findings (liver enzymes, imaging studies, liver biopsy pathology) and complications are generally similar in HCV and HBV. The spectrum of these chronic viral hepatitis infections ranges widely and includes an asymptomatic state; insidious disease with mild to moderate symptoms associated with fluctuating liver tests; extrahepatic manifestations; cirrhosis, both compensated and decompensated; ESLD with the need for liver transplantation; and liver cancer. Treatment for chronic viral hepatitis infections varies considerably based on medication tolerance, treatment response, adverse effects of treatment, and duration of the treatment. Comorbid disorders, such as HIV infection, may accelerate the clinical course of viral hepatitis infection(s) or may result in a poorer response to medical treatment.

(ii) We evaluate all types of chronic viral hepatitis infections under 5.05 or any listing in an affected body system(s). If your impairment(s) does not meet or medically equal a listing, we will consider the effects of your hepatitis when we assess your residual functional capacity.

b. Chronic hepatitis B virus (HBV) infection.

(i) Chronic HBV infection can be diagnosed by the detection of hepatitis B surface antigen (HBsAg) or hepatitis B virus DNA (HBV DNA) in the blood for at least 6 months. In addition, detection of the hepatitis B e antigen (HBeAg) suggests an increased likelihood of progression to cirrhosis, ESLD, and hepatocellular carcinoma. (HBeAg may also be referred to as "hepatitis B early antigen" or "hepatitis B envelope antigen.")

(ii) The therapeutic goal of treatment is to suppress HBV replication and thereby prevent progression to cirrhosis, ESLD, and hepatocellular carcinoma. Treatment usually includes interferon injections, oral antiviral agents, or a combination of both. Common adverse effects of treatment are the same as noted in 5.00D4c(ii) for HCV, and generally end within a few days after treatment is discontinued.

c. Chronic hepatitis C virus (HCV) infection.

(i) Chronic HCV infection is diagnosed by the detection of hepatitis C viral RNA in the blood for at least 6 months. Documentation of the therapeutic response to treatment is also monitored by the quantitative assay of serum HCV RNA ("HCV viral load"). Treatment usually includes a combination of interferon injections and oral ribavirin; whether a therapeutic response has occurred is usually assessed after 12 weeks of treatment by checking the HCV viral load. If there has been a substantial reduction in HCV viral load (also known as early viral response, or EVR), this reduction is predictive of a sustained viral response with completion of treatment. Combined therapy is commonly discontinued after 12 weeks when there is no early viral response, since in that circumstance there is little chance of obtaining a sustained viral response (SVR). Otherwise, treatment is usually continued for a total of 48 weeks.

(ii) Combined interferon and ribavirin treatment may have significant adverse effects that may require dosing reduction, planned interruption of treatment, or discontinuation of treatment. Adverse effects may include: Anemia (ribavirin-induced hemolysis), neutropenia, thrombocytopenia, fever, cough, fatigue, myalgia, arthralgia, nausea, loss of appetite, pruritis, and insomnia. Behavioral side effects may also occur. Influenza-like symptoms are generally worse in the first 4 to 6 hours after each interferon injection and during the first weeks of treatment. Adverse effects generally end within a few days after treatment is discontinued.

d. Extrahepatic manifestations of HBV and HCV. In addition to their hepatic manifestations, both HBV and HCV may have significant extrahepatic manifestations in a variety of body systems. These include, but are not limited to: Keratoconjunctivitis (sicca syndrome), glomerulonephritis, skin disorders (for example, lichen planus, porphyria cutanea tarda), neuropathy, and immune dysfunction (for example, cryoglobulinemia, Sjögren's syndrome, and vasculitis). The extrahepatic manifestations of HBV and HCV may not correlate with the severity of your hepatic impairment. If your impairment(s) does not meet or medically equal a listing in an affected body system(s), we will consider the effects of your extrahepatic manifestations when we assess your residual functional capacity.

5. Gastrointestinal hemorrhage (5.02 and 5.05A). Gastrointestinal hemorrhaging can result in hematemesis (vomiting of blood), melena (tarry stools), or hematochezia (bloody stools). Under 5.02, the required transfusions of at least 2 units of blood must be at least 30 days apart and occur at least three times during a consecutive 6–month period. Under 5.05A, hemodynamic instability is diagnosed with signs such as pallor (pale skin), diaphoresis (profuse perspiration), rapid pulse, low blood pressure, postural hypotension (pronounced fall in blood pressure when arising to an upright position from lying down) or syncope (fainting). Hemorrhaging that results in hemodynamic instability is potentially life-threatening and therefore requires hospitalization for transfusion and supportive care. Under 5.05A, we require only one hospitalization for transfusion of at least 2 units of blood.

6. Ascites or hydrothorax (5.05B) indicates significant loss of liver function due to chronic liver disease. We evaluate ascites or hydrothorax that is not attributable to other causes under 5.05B. The required findings must be present on at least two evaluations at least 60 days apart within a consecutive 6–month period and despite continuing treatment as prescribed.

7. Spontaneous bacterial peritonitis (5.05C) is an infectious complication of chronic liver disease. It is diagnosed by ascitic peritoneal fluid that is documented to contain an absolute neutrophil count of at least 250 cells/mm^3. The required finding in 5.05C is satisfied with one evaluation documenting peritoneal fluid infection. We do not evaluate other causes of peritonitis that are unrelated to chronic liver disease, such as tuberculosis, malignancy, and perforated bowel, under this listing. We evaluate these other causes of peritonitis under the appropriate body system listings.

8. Hepatorenal syndrome (5.05D) is defined as functional renal failure associated with chronic liver disease in the absence of underlying kidney pathology. Hepatorenal syndrome is documented by elevation of serum creatinine, marked sodium retention, and oliguria (reduced urine output). The requirements of 5.05D are satisfied with documentation of any one of the three laboratory findings on one evaluation. We do not evaluate known causes of renal dysfunction, such as glomerulonephritis, tubular necrosis, drug-induced renal disease, and renal infections, under this listing. We evaluate these other renal impairments under 6.00ff.

9. Hepatopulmonary syndrome (5.05E) is defined as arterial deoxygenation (hypoxemia) that is associated with chronic liver disease due to intrapulmonary arteriovenous shunting and vasodilatation in the absence of other causes of arterial deoxygenation. Clinical manifestations usually include dyspnea, orthodeoxia (increasing hypoxemia with erect position), platypnea (improvement of dyspnea with flat position), cyanosis, and clubbing. The requirements of 5.05E are satisfied with documentation of any one of the findings on one evaluation. In 5.05E1, we require documentation of the altitude of the testing facility because altitude affects the measurement of arterial oxygenation. We will not purchase the specialized studies described in 5.05E2; however, if you have had these studies at a time relevant to your claim, we will make every reasonable effort to obtain the reports for the purpose of establishing whether your impairment meets 5.05E2.

10. Hepatic encephalopathy (5.05F).

a. General. Hepatic encephalopathy usually indicates severe loss of hepatocellular function. We define hepatic encephalopathy under 5.05F as a recurrent or chronic neuropsychiatric disorder, characterized by abnormal behavior, cognitive dysfunction, altered state of consciousness, and ultimately coma and death. The diagnosis is established by changes in mental status associated with fleeting neurological signs, including "flapping tremor" (asterixis), characteristic electroencephalographic (EEG) abnormalities, or abnormal laboratory values that indicate loss of synthetic liver function. We will not purchase the EEG testing described in 5.05F3b; however, if you have had this test at a time relevant to your claim, we will make every reasonable effort to obtain the report for the purpose of establishing whether your impairment meets 5.05F.

b. Acute encephalopathy. We will not evaluate your acute encephalopathy under 5.05F if it results from conditions other than chronic liver disease, such as vascular events and neoplastic diseases. We will evaluate these other causes of acute encephalopathy under the appropriate body system listings.

11. End stage liver disease (ESLD) documented by scores from the SSA Chronic Liver Disease (SSA CLD) calculation (5.05G).

a. We will use the SSA CLD score to evaluate your ESLD under 5.05G. We explain how we calculate the SSA CLD score in b. through g. of this section.

b. To calculate the SSA CLD score, we use a formula that includes three laboratory values: Serum total bilirubin (mg/dL), serum creatinine (mg/dL), and International Normalized Ratio (INR). The formula for the SSA CLD score calculation is:

9.57 x [Log$_e$(serum creatinine mg/dL)]

+ 3.78 x [Log$_e$(serum total bilirubin mg/dL)]

+ 11.2 x [Log$_e$(INR)]

+ 6.43

c. When we indicate "Log$_e$" in the formula for the SSA CLD score calculation, we mean the "base e logarithm" or "natural logarithm" (ln) of a numerical laboratory value, not the "base 10 logarithm" or "common logarithm" (log) of the laboratory value, and not the actual laboratory value. For example, if an individual has laboratory values of serum creatinine 1.2 mg/dL, serum total bilirubin 2.2 mg/dL, and INR 1.0, we would compute the SSA CLD score as follows:

9.57 x [Log_e(serum creatinine 1.2 mg/dL) = 0.182]

+3.78 x [Log_e(serum total bilirubin 2.2 mg/dL) = 0.788]

+11.2 x [Log_e(INR 1.0) = 0]

+6.43

= 1.74 + 2.98 + 0 + 6.43

= 11.15, which is then rounded to an SSA CLD score of 11.

d. For any SSA CLD score calculation, all of the required laboratory values must have been obtained within 30 days of each other. If there are multiple laboratory values within the 30–day interval for any given laboratory test (serum total bilirubin, serum creatinine, or INR), we will use the highest value for the SSA CLD score calculation. We will round all laboratory values less than 1.0 up to 1.0.

e. Listing 5.05G requires two SSA CLD scores. The laboratory values for the second SSA CLD score calculation must have been obtained at least 60 days after the latest laboratory value for the first SSA CLD score and within the required 6–month period. We will consider the date of each SSA CLD score to be the date of the first laboratory value used for its calculation.

f. If you are in renal failure or on dialysis within a week of any serum creatinine test in the period used for the SSA CLD calculation, we will use a serum creatinine of 4, which is the maximum serum creatinine level allowed in the calculation, to calculate your SSA CLD score.

g. If you have the two SSA CLD scores required by 5.05G, we will find that your impairment meets the criteria of the listing from at least the date of the first SSA CLD score.

12. Liver transplantation (5.09) may be performed for metabolic liver disease, progressive liver failure, life-threatening complications of liver disease, hepatic malignancy, and acute fulminant hepatitis (viral, drug-induced, or toxin-induced). We will consider you to be disabled for 1 year from the date of the transplantation. Thereafter, we will evaluate your residual impairment(s) by considering the adequacy of post-transplant liver function, the requirement for post-transplant antiviral therapy, the frequency and severity of rejection episodes, comorbid complications, and all adverse treatment effects.

E. How do we evaluate inflammatory bowel disease (IBD)?

1. Inflammatory bowel disease (5.06) includes, but is not limited to, Crohn's disease and ulcerative colitis. These disorders, while distinct entities, share many clinical, laboratory, and imaging findings, as well as similar treatment regimens. Remissions and exacerbations of variable duration are the hallmark of IBD. Crohn's disease may involve the entire alimentary tract from the mouth to the anus in a segmental, asymmetric fashion. Obstruction, stenosis, fistulization, perineal involvement, and extraintestinal manifestations are common. Crohn's disease is rarely curable and recurrence may be a lifelong problem, even after surgical resection. In contrast, ulcerative colitis only affects the colon. The inflammatory process may be limited to the rectum, extend proximally to include any contiguous segment, or involve the entire colon. Ulcerative colitis may be cured by total colectomy.

2. Symptoms and signs of IBD include diarrhea, fecal incontinence, rectal bleeding, abdominal pain, fatigue, fever, nausea, vomiting, arthralgia, abdominal tenderness, palpable abdominal mass (usually inflamed loops of bowel) and perineal disease. You may also have signs or laboratory findings indicating malnutrition, such as weight loss, edema, anemia, hypoalbuminemia, hypokalemia, hypocalcemia, or hypomagnesemia.

3. IBD may be associated with significant extraintestinal manifestations in a variety of body systems. These include, but are not limited to, involvement of the eye (for example, uveitis, episcleritis, iritis); hepatobiliary disease (for example, gallstones, primary sclerosing cholangitis); urologic disease (for example, kidney stones, obstructive hydronephrosis); skin involvement (for example, erythema nodosum, pyoderma gangrenosum); or non-destructive inflammatory arthritis. You may also have associated thromboembolic disorders or vascular disease. These manifestations may not correlate with the severity of your IBD. If your impairment does not meet any of the criteria of 5.06, we will consider the effects of your extraintestinal manifestations in determining whether you have an impairment(s) that meets or medically equals another listing, and we will also consider the effects of your extraintestinal manifestations when we assess your residual functional capacity.

4. Surgical diversion of the intestinal tract, including ileostomy and colostomy, does not preclude any gainful activity if you are able to maintain adequate nutrition and function of the stoma. However, if you are not able to maintain adequate nutrition, we will evaluate your impairment under 5.08.

F. How do we evaluate short bowel syndrome (SBS)?

1. Short bowel syndrome (5.07) is a disorder that occurs when ischemic vascular insults (for example,

volvulus), trauma, or IBD complications require surgical resection of more than one-half of the small intestine, resulting in the loss of intestinal absorptive surface and a state of chronic malnutrition. The management of SBS requires long-term parenteral nutrition via an indwelling central venous catheter (central line); the process is often referred to as hyperalimentation or total parenteral nutrition (TPN). Individuals with SBS can also feed orally, with variable amounts of nutrients being absorbed through their remaining intestine. Over time, some of these individuals can develop additional intestinal absorptive surface, and may ultimately be able to be weaned off their parenteral nutrition.

2. Your impairment will continue to meet 5.07 as long as you remain dependent on daily parenteral nutrition via a central venous catheter for most of your nutritional requirements. Long-term complications of SBS and parenteral nutrition include central line infections (with or without septicemia), thrombosis, hepatotoxicity, gallstones, and loss of venous access sites. Intestinal transplantation is the only definitive treatment for individuals with SBS who remain chronically dependent on parenteral nutrition.

3. To document SBS, we need a copy of the operative report of intestinal resection, the summary of the hospitalization(s) including: Details of the surgical findings, medically appropriate postoperative imaging studies that reflect the amount of your residual small intestine, or if we cannot get one of these reports, other medical reports that include details of the surgical findings. We also need medical documentation that you are dependent on daily parenteral nutrition to provide most of your nutritional requirements.

G. How do we evaluate weight loss due to any digestive disorder?

1. In addition to the impairments specifically mentioned in these listings, other digestive disorders, such as esophageal stricture, pancreatic insufficiency, and malabsorption, may result in significant weight loss. We evaluate weight loss due to any digestive disorder under 5.08 by using the Body Mass Index (BMI). We also provide a criterion in 5.06B for lesser weight loss resulting from IBD.

2. BMI is the ratio of your weight to the square of your height. Calculation and interpretation of the BMI are independent of gender in adults.

a. We calculate BMI using inches and pounds, meters and kilograms, or centimeters and kilograms. We must have measurements of your weight and height without shoes for these calculations.

b. We calculate BMI using one of the following formulas:

English Formula

$$\text{BMI} = \left(\frac{\text{Weight in Pounds}}{(\text{Height in Inches}) \times (\text{Height in Inches})} \right) \times 703$$

Metric Formula

$$\text{BMI} = \frac{\text{Weight in Kilograms}}{(\text{Height in Meters}) \times (\text{Height in Meters})}$$

Or

$$\text{BMI} = \left(\frac{\text{Weight in Kilograms}}{(\text{Height in Centimeters}) \times (\text{Height in Centimeters})} \right) \times 10{,}000$$

H. What do we mean by the phrase "consider under a disability for 1 year"? We use the phrase "consider under a disability for 1 year" following a specific event in 5.02, 5.05A, and 5.09 to explain how long your impairment can meet the requirements of those particular listings. This phrase does not refer to the date on which your disability began, only to the date on which we must reevaluate whether your impairment continues to meet a listing or is otherwise disabling. For example, if you have received a liver transplant, you may have become disabled before the transplant because of chronic liver disease. Therefore, we do not restrict our determination of the onset of disability to the date of the specified event. We will establish an onset date earlier than the date of the specified event if the evidence in your case record supports such a finding.

I. How do we evaluate impairments that do not meet one of the digestive disorder listings?

1. These listings are only examples of common digestive disorders that we consider severe enough to prevent you from doing any gainful activity. If your impairment(s) does not meet the criteria of any of these listings, we must also consider whether you have an impairment(s) that satisfies the criteria of a listing in another body system. For example, if you have hepatitis B or C and you are depressed, we will evaluate your impairment under 12.04.

2. If you have a severe medically determinable impairment(s) that does not meet a listing, we will determine whether your impairment(s) medically equals a listing. (See §§ 404.1526 and 416.926.) If your impairment(s) does not meet or medically equal a listing, you may or may not have the residual functional capacity to engage in substantial gainful activity. In this situation, we will proceed to the fourth, and if necessary, the fifth steps of the sequential evaluation process in §§ 404.1520 and 416.920. When we decide whether you continue to be disabled, we use the rules in §§ 404.1594, 416.994, and 416.994a as appropriate.

5.01 Category of Impairments, Digestive System

5.02 Gastrointestinal hemorrhaging from any cause, requiring blood transfusion (with or without hospitalization) of at least 2 units of blood per transfusion, and occurring at least three times during a consecutive 6–month period. The transfusions must be at least 30 days apart within the 6–month period. Consider under a disability for 1 year following the last documented transfusion; thereafter, evaluate the residual impairment(s).

5.03 [Reserved]

5.04 [Reserved]

5.05 Chronic liver disease, with:

A. Hemorrhaging from esophageal, gastric, or ectopic varices or from portal hypertensive gastropathy, demonstrated by endoscopy, x-ray, or other appropriate medically acceptable imaging, resulting in hemodynamic instability as defined in 5.00D5, and requiring hospitalization for transfusion of at least 2 units of blood. Consider under a disability for 1 year following the last documented transfusion; thereafter, evaluate the residual impairment(s).

OR

B. Ascites or hydrothorax not attributable to other causes, despite continuing treatment as prescribed, present on at least two evaluations at least 60 days apart within a consecutive 6–month period. Each evaluation must be documented by:

1. Paracentesis or thoracentesis; or

2. Appropriate medically acceptable imaging or physical examination and one of the following:

a. Serum albumin of 3.0 g/dL or less; or

b. International Normalized Ratio (INR) of at least 1.5.

OR

C. Spontaneous bacterial peritonitis with peritoneal fluid containing an absolute neutrophil count of at least 250 cells/mm^3.

OR

D. Hepatorenal syndrome as described in 5.00D8, with one of the following:

1. Serum creatinine elevation of at least 2 mg/dL; or

2. Oliguria with 24–hour urine output less than 500 mL; or

3. Sodium retention with urine sodium less than 10 mEq per liter.

OR

E. Hepatopulmonary syndrome as described in 5.00D9, with:

1. Arterial oxygenation (P_aO_2) on room air of:

a. 60 mm Hg or less, at test sites less than 3000 feet above sea level, or

b. 55 mm Hg or less, at test sites from 3000 to 6000 feet, or

c. 50 mm Hg or less, at test sites above 6000 feet; or

2. Documentation of intrapulmonary arteriovenous shunting by contrast-enhanced echocardiography or macroaggregated albumin lung perfusion scan.

OR

F. Hepatic encephalopathy as described in 5.00D10, with 1 and either 2 or 3:

1. Documentation of abnormal behavior, cognitive dysfunction, changes in mental status, or altered state of consciousness (for example, confusion, delirium, stupor, or coma), present on at least two evaluations at least 60 days apart within a consecutive 6–month period; and

2. History of transjugular intrahepatic portosystemic shunt (TIPS) or any surgical portosystemic shunt: or

3. One of the following occurring on at least two evaluations at least 60 days apart within the same consecutive 6–month period as in F1:

a. Asterixis or other fluctuating physical neurological abnormalities; or

b. Electroencephalogram (EEG) demonstrating triphasic slow wave activity; or

c. Serum albumin of 3.0 g/dL or less; or

d. International Normalized Ratio (INR) of 1.5 or greater.

OR

G. End stage liver disease with SSA CLD scores of 22 or greater calculated as described in 5.00D11. Consider under a disability from at least the date of the first score.

5.06 Inflammatory bowel disease (IBD) documented by endoscopy, biopsy, appropriate medically acceptable imaging, or operative findings with:

A. Obstruction of stenotic areas (not adhesions) in the small intestine or colon with proximal dilatation, confirmed by appropriate medically acceptable imaging or in surgery, requiring hospitalization for intestinal decompression or for surgery, and occurring on at least two occasions at least 60 days apart within a consecutive 6–month period;

OR

B. Two of the following despite continuing treatment as prescribed and occurring within the same consecutive 6–month period:

1. Anemia with hemoglobin of less than 10.0 g/dL, present on at least two evaluations at least 60 days apart; or

2. Serum albumin of 3.0 g/dL or less, present on at least two evaluations at least 60 days apart; or

3. Clinically documented tender abdominal mass palpable on physical examination with abdominal pain or cramping that is not completely controlled by prescribed narcotic medication, present on at least two evaluations at least 60 days apart; or

4. Perineal disease with a draining abscess or fistula, with pain that is not completely controlled by prescribed narcotic medication, present on at least two evaluations at least 60 days apart; or

5. Involuntary weight loss of at least 10 percent from baseline, as computed in pounds, kilograms, or BMI, present on at least two evaluations at least 60 days apart; or

6. Need for supplemental daily enteral nutrition via a gastrostomy or daily parenteral nutrition via a central venous catheter.

5.07 Short bowel syndrome (SBS), due to surgical resection of more than one-half of the small intestine, with dependence on daily parenteral nutrition via a central venous catheter (see 5.00F).

5.08 Weight loss due to any digestive disorder despite continuing treatment as prescribed, with BMI of less than 17.50 calculated on at least two evaluations at least 60 days apart within a consecutive 6–month period.

5.09 Liver transplantation. Consider under a disability for 1 year following the date of transplantation; thereafter, evaluate the residual impairment(s) (see 5.00D12 and 5.00H).

[50 FR 35066, Aug. 28, 1985; 50 FR 38113, Sept. 20, 1985; 51 FR 5989, Feb. 19, 1986; 51 FR 7933, March 7, 1986; 51 FR 16016, April 30, 1986; 53 FR 29879, Aug. 9, 1988; 54 FR 50235, Dec. 5, 1989; 55 FR 35287, Aug. 28, 1990; 55 FR 38190, Sept. 17, 1990; 55 FR 51101, 51208, 51229, 51230, Dec. 12, 1990; 56 FR 11304, 11305, March 15, 1991; 56 FR 26031, June 6, 1991; 56 FR 40781, Aug. 16, 1991; 56 FR 60060, Nov. 27, 1991; 57 FR 23946, 23947, June 5, 1992; 57 FR 24187, June 8, 1992; 57 FR 30121, July 8, 1992; 57 FR 57666, Dec. 7, 1992; 57 FR 61796, Dec. 29, 1992; 58 FR 31907, June 7, 1993; 58 FR 36051, 36052, 36056, July 2, 1993; 58 FR 36134, July 6, 1993; 58 FR 44445, Aug. 23, 1993; 58 FR 52359, Oct. 7, 1993; 58 FR 64123, Dec. 6, 1993; 59 FR 671, Jan. 6, 1994; 59 FR 1275, 1416, Jan. 10, 1994; 59 FR 6497, 6501, Feb. 10, 1994; 59 FR 30389, June 13, 1994; 59 FR 41975, Aug. 16, 1994; 60 FR 43710, Aug. 23, 1995; 60 FR 53267, Oct. 13, 1995; 60 FR 62330, Dec. 6, 1995; 61 FR 28047, June 4, 1996; 61 FR 64616, Dec. 6, 1996; 62 FR 6418, 6420, Feb. 11, 1997; 62 FR 13733, March 21, 1997; 62 FR 30747, June 5, 1997; 63 FR 4571, Jan. 30, 1998; 63 FR 30411, June 4, 1998; 64 FR 29788, June 3, 1999; 64 FR 46128, 46129, Aug. 24, 1999; 64 FR 67720, Dec. 3, 1999; 65 FR 31802, May 19, 2000; 65 FR 50775, 50780, Aug. 21, 2000; 65 FR 54776, Sept. 11, 2000; 65 FR 57947, Sept. 27, 2000; 66 FR 34362, June 28, 2001; 66 FR 58037, 58040, 58041, 58044, 58045, Nov. 19, 2001; 67 FR 20024, April 24, 2002; 67 FR 35723, May 21, 2002; 67 FR 43538, June 28, 2002; 68 FR 36912, June 20, 2003; 68 FR 51693, Aug. 28, 2003; 69 FR 32269, June 9, 2004; 69 FR 67032, Dec. 15, 2004; 70 FR 15227, March 25, 2005; 70 FR 35029, June 16, 2005; 70 FR 38590, July 5, 2005; 70 FR 51259–51261, Aug. 30, 2005; 71 FR 2325, 2335, Jan. 13, 2006; 71 FR 26412, May 5, 2006; 71 FR 67050, Nov. 20, 2006; 71 FR 77098, Dec. 22, 2006; 72 FR 33664, June 19, 2007; 72 FR 59422, 59426, Oct. 19, 2007; 73 FR 14601, March 18, 2008; 73 FR 31027, May 30, 2008; 74 FR 5808, Feb. 2, 2009; 74 FR 51232, Oct. 6, 2009; 75 FR 30701, June 2, 2010; 75 FR 33167, June 11, 2010; 76 FR 16532, March 24, 2011; 76 FR 19696, April 8, 2011; 77 FR 35265, June 13, 2012; 78 FR 7660, Feb. 4, 2013; 78 FR 18839, March 28, 2013; 78 FR 46501, Aug. 1, 2013; 78 FR 54757, Sept. 6, 2013; 78 FR 72572, Dec. 3, 2013; 79 FR 10662, Feb. 26, 2014; 79 FR 61224, Oct. 10, 2014; 79 FR 67350, Nov. 13, 2014; 80 FR 2, Jan. 2, 2015; 80 FR 19525, April 13, 2015; 80 FR 21165, April 17, 2015; 80 FR 28826, May 20, 2015; 80 FR 48248, Aug. 12, 2015; 81 FR 32645, May 24, 2016; 81 FR 37143, June 9, 2016; 81 FR 43052, July 1, 2016; 81 FR 51102, Aug. 3, 2016; 81 FR 64060, Sept. 19, 2016; 81 FR 66161, Sept. 26, 2016; 81 FR 86923, Dec. 2, 2016; 82 FR 5872, Jan. 18, 2017; 82 FR 59515, Dec. 15, 2017; 83 FR 13863, April 2, 2018; 83 FR 23581, May 22, 2018]

APPENDIX 1–PART–A2. TO SUBPART P OF PART 404—LISTING OF IMPAIRMENTS

6.00 GENITOURINARY DISORDERS

A. Which disorders do we evaluate under these listings?

We evaluate genitourinary disorders resulting in chronic kidney disease (CKD). Examples of such disorders include chronic glomerulonephritis, hypertensive nephropathy, diabetic nephropathy, chronic obstructive uropathy, and hereditary nephropathies. We also evaluate nephrotic syndrome due to glomerular dysfunction under these listings.

B. What evidence do we need?

1. We need evidence that documents the signs, symptoms, and laboratory findings of your CKD. This evidence should include reports of clinical examinations, treatment records, and documentation of your response to treatment. Laboratory findings, such as serum creatinine or serum albumin levels, may document your kidney function. We generally need evidence covering a period of at least 90 days unless we can make a fully favorable determination or decision without it.

2. Estimated glomerular filtration rate (eGFR). The eGFR is an estimate of the filtering capacity of the kidneys that takes into account serum creatinine concentration and other variables, such as your age, gender, and body size. If your medical evidence includes eGFR findings, we will consider them when we evaluate your CKD under 6.05.

3. Kidney or bone biopsy. If you have had a kidney or bone biopsy, we need a copy of the pathology report. When we cannot get a copy of the pathology report, we will accept a statement from an acceptable medical source verifying that a biopsy was performed and describing the results.

C. What other factors do we consider when we evaluate your genitourinary disorder?

1. Chronic hemodialysis or peritoneal dialysis.

a. Dialysis is a treatment for CKD that uses artificial means to remove toxic metabolic byproducts from the blood. Hemodialysis uses an artificial kidney machine to clean waste products from the blood; peritoneal dialysis uses a dialyzing solution that is introduced into and removed from the abdomen (peritoneal cavity) either continuously or intermittently. Under 6.03, your ongoing dialysis must have lasted or be expected to last for a continuous period of at least 12 months. To satisfy the requirements in 6.03, we will accept a report from an acceptable medical source that describes your CKD and your current dialysis, and indicates that your dialysis will be ongoing.

b. If you are undergoing chronic hemodialysis or peritoneal dialysis, your CKD may meet our definition of disability before you started dialysis. We will determine the onset of your disability based on the facts in your case record.

2. Kidney transplant.

a. If you receive a kidney transplant, we will consider you to be disabled under 6.04 for 1 year from the date of transplant. After that, we will evaluate your residual impairment(s) by considering your post-transplant function, any rejection episodes you have had, complications in other body systems, and any adverse effects related to ongoing treatment.

b. If you received a kidney transplant, your CKD may meet our definition of disability before you received the transplant. We will determine the onset of your disability based on the facts in your case record.

3. Renal osteodystrophy. This condition is the bone degeneration resulting from chronic kidney disease-mineral and bone disorder (CKD–MBD). CKD–MBD occurs when the kidneys are unable to maintain the necessary levels of minerals, hormones, and vitamins required for bone structure and function. Under 6.05B1, "severe bone pain" means frequent or intractable (resistant to treatment) bone pain that interferes with physical activity or mental functioning.

4. Peripheral neuropathy. This disorder results when the kidneys do not adequately filter toxic substances from the blood. These toxins can adversely affect nerve tissue. The resulting neuropathy may affect peripheral motor or sensory nerves, or both, causing pain, numbness, tingling, and muscle weakness in various parts of the body. Under 6.05B2, the peripheral neuropathy must be a severe impairment. (See §§ 404.1520(c), 404.1521, 416.920(c), and 416.921 of this chapter.) It must also have lasted or be expected to last for a continuous period of at least 12 months.

5. Fluid overload syndrome. This condition occurs when excess sodium and water retention in the body due to CKD results in vascular congestion. Under 6.05B3, we need a description of a physical examination that documents signs and symptoms of vascular congestion, such as congestive heart failure, pleural effusion (excess fluid in the chest), ascites (excess fluid in the abdomen), hypertension, fatigue, shortness of breath, or peripheral edema.

6. Anasarca (generalized massive edema or swelling). Under 6.05B3 and 6.06B, we need a description of the extent of edema, including pretibial (in front of the tibia), periorbital (around the eyes), or presacral (in front of the sacrum) edema. We also need a description of any ascites, pleural effusion, or pericardial effusion.

7. Anorexia (diminished appetite) with weight loss. Anorexia is a frequent sign of CKD and can result in weight loss. We will use body mass index (BMI) to determine the severity of your weight loss under 6.05B4. (BMI is the ratio of your measured weight to the square of your measured height.) The formula for calculating BMI is in section 5.00G.

8. Complications of CKD. The hospitalizations in 6.09 may be for different complications of CKD. Examples of complications from CKD that may result in hospitalization include stroke, congestive heart failure, hypertensive crisis, or acute kidney failure requiring a short course of hemodialysis. If the CKD complication occurs during a hospitalization that was initially for a co-occurring condition, we will evaluate it under our

rules for determining medical equivalence. (See §§ 404.1526 and 416.926 of this chapter.) We will evaluate co-occurring conditions, including those that result in hospitalizations, under the listings for the affected body system or under our rules for medical equivalence.

D. How do we evaluate disorders that do not meet one of the genitourinary listings?

1. The listed disorders are only examples of common genitourinary disorders that we consider severe enough to prevent you from doing any gainful activity. If your impairment(s) does not meet the criteria of any of these listings, we must also consider whether you have an impairment(s) that satisfies the criteria of a listing in another body system.

2. If you have a severe medically determinable impairment(s) that does not meet a listing, we will determine whether your impairment(s) medically equals a listing. (See §§ 404.1526 and 416.926 of this chapter.) Genitourinary disorders may be associated with disorders in other body systems, and we consider the combined effects of multiple impairments when we determine whether they medically equal a listing. If your impairment(s) does not meet or medically equal the criteria of a listing, you may or may not have the residual functional capacity to engage in substantial gainful activity. We proceed to the fourth and, if necessary, the fifth steps of the sequential evaluation process in §§ 404.1520 and 416.920 of this chapter. We use the rules in §§ 404.1594 and 416.994 of this chapter, as appropriate, when we decide whether you continue to be disabled.

6.01 Category of Impairments, Genitourinary Disorders

6.03 Chronic kidney disease, with chronic hemodialysis or peritoneal dialysis (see 6.00C1).

6.04 Chronic kidney disease, with kidney transplant. Consider under a disability for 1 year following the transplant; thereafter, evaluate the residual impairment (see 6.00C2).

6.05 Chronic kidney disease, with impairment of kidney function, with A and B:

A. Reduced glomerular filtration evidenced by one of the following laboratory findings documented on at least two occasions at least 90 days apart during a consecutive 12–month period:

1. Serum creatinine of 4 mg/dL or greater; or

2. Creatinine clearance of 20 ml/min. or less; or

3. Estimated glomerular filtration rate (eGFR) of 20 ml/min/1.73m^2 or less.

AND

B. One of the following:

1. Renal osteodystrophy (see 6.00C3) with severe bone pain and imaging studies documenting bone abnormalities, such as osteitis fibrosa, osteomalacia, or pathologic fractures; or

2. Peripheral neuropathy (see 6.00C4); or

3. Fluid overload syndrome (see 6.00C5) documented by one of the following:

a. Diastolic hypertension greater than or equal to diastolic blood pressure of 110 mm Hg despite at least 90 consecutive days of prescribed therapy, documented by at least two measurements of diastolic blood pressure at least 90 days apart during a consecutive 12–month period; or

b. Signs of vascular congestion or anasarca (see 6.00C6) despite at least 90 consecutive days of prescribed therapy, documented on at least two occasions at least 90 days apart during a consecutive 12–month period; or

4. Anorexia with weight loss (see 6.00C7) determined by body mass index (BMI) of 18.0 or less, calculated on at least two occasions at least 90 days apart during a consecutive 12–month period.

6.06 Nephrotic syndrome, with A and B:

A. Laboratory findings as described in 1 or 2, documented on at least two occasions at least 90 days apart during a consecutive 12–month period:

1. Proteinuria of 10.0 g or greater per 24 hours; or

2. Serum albumin of 3.0 g/dL or less, and

a. Proteinuria of 3.5 g or greater per 24 hours; or

b. Urine total-protein-to-creatinine ratio of 3.5 or greater.

AND

B. Anasarca (see 6.00C6) persisting for at least 90 days despite prescribed treatment.

6.09 Complications of chronic kidney disease (see 6.00C8) requiring at least three hospitalizations within a consecutive 12–month period and occurring at least 30 days apart. Each hospitalization must last at least 48 hours, including hours in a hospital emergency department immediately before the hospitalization.

7.00 HEMATOLOGICAL DISORDERS

A. What hematological disorders do we evaluate under these listings?

1. We evaluate non-malignant (non-cancerous) hematological disorders, such as hemolytic anemias (7.05), disorders of thrombosis and hemostasis (7.08), and disorders of bone marrow failure (7.10). These disorders disrupt the normal development and function of white blood cells, red blood cells, platelets, and clotting-factor proteins (factors).

2. We evaluate malignant (cancerous) hematological disorders, such as lymphoma, leukemia, and multiple myeloma, under the appropriate listings in 13.00, except for two lymphomas associated with human immunodeficiency virus (HIV) infection. We evaluate pri-

mary central nervous system lymphoma associated with HIV infection under 14.11B, and primary effusion lymphoma associated with HIV infection under 14.11C.

B. What evidence do we need to document that you have a hematological disorder?

We need the following evidence to document that you have a hematological disorder:

1. A laboratory report of a definitive test that establishes a hematological disorder, signed by a physician; or

2. A laboratory report of a definitive test that establishes a hematological disorder that is not signed by a physician and a report from a physician that states you have the disorder; or

3. When we do not have a laboratory report of a definitive test, a persuasive report from a physician that a diagnosis of your hematological disorder was confirmed by appropriate laboratory analysis or other diagnostic method(s). To be persuasive, this report must state that you had the appropriate definitive laboratory test or tests for diagnosing your disorder and provide the results, or explain how your diagnosis was established by other diagnostic method(s) consistent with the prevailing state of medical knowledge and clinical practice.

4. We will make every reasonable effort to obtain the results of appropriate laboratory testing you have had. We will not purchase complex, costly, or invasive tests, such as tests of clotting-factor proteins, and bone marrow aspirations.

C. What are hemolytic anemias, and how do we evaluate them under 7.05?

1. Hemolytic anemias, both congenital and acquired, are disorders that result in premature destruction of red blood cells (RBCs). Hemolytic disorders include abnormalities of hemoglobin structure (hemoglobinopathies), abnormal RBC enzyme content and function, and RBC membrane (envelope) defects that are congenital or acquired. The diagnosis of hemolytic anemia is based on hemoglobin electrophoresis or analysis of the contents of the RBC (enzymes) and membrane. Examples of congenital hemolytic anemias include sickle cell disease, thalassemia and their variants, and hereditary spherocytosis. Acquired hemolytic anemias may result from autoimmune disease (for example, systemic lupus erythematosus) or mechanical devices (for example, heart valves, intravascular patches).

2. The hospitalizations in 7.05B do not all have to be for the same complication of the hemolytic anemia. They may be for three different complications of the disorder. Examples of complications of hemolytic anemia that may result in hospitalization include osteomyelitis, painful (vaso-occlusive) crisis, pulmonary infections or infarctions, acute chest syndrome, pulmonary hypertension, chronic heart failure, gallbladder disease, hepatic (liver) failure, renal (kidney) failure, nephrotic syndrome, aplastic crisis, and stroke. We will count the hours you receive emergency treatment in a comprehensive sickle cell disease center immediately before the hospitalization if this treatment is comparable to the treatment provided in a hospital emergency department.

3. For 7.05C, we do not require hemoglobin to be measured during a period in which you are free of pain or other symptoms of your disorder. We will accept hemoglobin measurements made while you are experiencing complications of your hemolytic anemia.

4. 7.05D refers to the most serious type of beta thalassemia major in which the bone marrow cannot produce sufficient numbers of normal RBCs to maintain life. The only available treatments for beta thalassemia major are life-long RBC transfusions (sometimes called hypertransfusion) or bone marrow transplantation. For purposes of 7.05D, we do not consider prophylactic RBC transfusions to prevent strokes or other complications in sickle cell disease and its variants to be of equal significance to life-saving RBC transfusions for beta thalassemia major. However, we will consider the functional limitations associated with prophylactic RBC transfusions and any associated side effects (for example, iron overload) under 7.18 and any affected body system(s). We will also evaluate strokes and resulting complications under 11.00 and 12.00.

D. What are disorders of thrombosis and hemostasis, and how do we evaluate them under 7.08?

1. Disorders of thrombosis and hemostasis include both clotting and bleeding disorders, and may be congenital or acquired. These disorders are characterized by abnormalities in blood clotting that result in hypercoagulation (excessive blood clotting) or hypocoagulation (inadequate blood clotting). The diagnosis of a thrombosis or hemostasis disorder is based on evaluation of plasma clotting-factor proteins (factors) and platelets. Protein C or protein S deficiency and Factor V Leiden are examples of hypercoagulation disorders. Hemophilia, von Willebrand disease, and thrombocytopenia are examples of hypocoagulation disorders. Acquired excessive blood clotting may result from blood protein defects and acquired inadequate blood clotting (for example, acquired hemophilia A) may be associated with inhibitor autoantibodies.

2. The hospitalizations in 7.08 do not all have to be for the same complication of a disorder of thrombosis and hemostasis. They may be for three different complications of the disorder. Examples of complications that may result in hospitalization include anemias, thromboses, embolisms, and uncontrolled bleeding requiring multiple factor concentrate infusions or platelet transfusions. We will also consider any surgery that you have, even if it is not related to your hematological

disorder, to be a complication of your disorder of thrombosis and hemostasis if you require treatment with clotting-factor proteins (for example, factor VIII or factor IX) or anticoagulant medication to control bleeding or coagulation in connection with your surgery. We will count the hours you receive emergency treatment in a comprehensive hemophilia treatment center immediately before the hospitalization if this treatment is comparable to the treatment provided in a hospital emergency department.

E. What are disorders of bone marrow failure, and how do we evaluate them under 7.10?

1. Disorders of bone marrow failure may be congenital or acquired, characterized by bone marrow that does not make enough healthy RBCs, platelets, or granulocytes (specialized types of white blood cells); there may also be a combined failure of these bone marrow-produced cells. The diagnosis is based on peripheral blood smears and bone marrow aspiration or bone marrow biopsy, but not peripheral blood smears alone. Examples of these disorders are myelodysplastic syndromes, aplastic anemia, granulocytopenia, and myelofibrosis. Acquired disorders of bone marrow failure may result from viral infections, chemical exposure, or immunologic disorders.

2. The hospitalizations in 7.10A do not all have to be for the same complication of bone marrow failure. They may be for three different complications of the disorder. Examples of complications that may result in hospitalization include uncontrolled bleeding, anemia, and systemic bacterial, viral, or fungal infections.

3. For 7.10B, the requirement of life-long RBC transfusions to maintain life in myelodysplastic syndromes or aplastic anemias has the same meaning as it does for beta thalassemia major. (See 7.00C4.)

F. How do we evaluate bone marrow or stem cell transplantation under 7.17?

We will consider you to be disabled for 12 months from the date of bone marrow or stem cell transplantation, or we may consider you to be disabled for a longer period if you are experiencing any serious post-transplantation complications, such as graft-versus-host (GVH) disease, frequent infections after immunosuppressive therapy, or significant deterioration of organ systems. We do not restrict our determination of the onset of disability to the date of the transplantation in 7.17. We may establish an earlier onset date of disability due to your transplantation if evidence in your case record supports such a finding.

G. How do we use the functional criteria in 7.18?

1. When we use the functional criteria in 7.18, we consider all relevant information in your case record to determine the impact of your hematological disorder on your ability to function independently, appropriately, effectively, and on a sustained basis in a work setting. Factors we will consider when we evaluate your functioning under 7.18 include, but are not limited to: Your symptoms, the frequency and duration of complications of your hematological disorder, periods of exacerbation and remission, and the functional impact of your treatment, including the side effects of your medication.

2. Repeated complications means that the complications occur on an average of three times a year, or once every 4 months, each lasting 2 weeks or more; or the complications do not last for 2 weeks but occur substantially more frequently than three times in a year or once every 4 months; or they occur less frequently than an average of three times a year or once every 4 months but last substantially longer than 2 weeks. Your impairment will satisfy this criterion regardless of whether you have the same kind of complication repeatedly, all different complications, or any other combination of complications; for example, two of the same kind of complication and a different one. You must have the required number of complications with the frequency and duration required in this section. Additionally, the complications must occur within the period we are considering in connection with your application or continuing disability review.

3. To satisfy the functional criteria in 7.18, your hematological disorder must result in a "marked" level of limitation in one of three general areas of functioning: Activities of daily living, social functioning, or difficulties in completing tasks due to deficiencies in concentration, persistence, or pace. Functional limitations may result from the impact of the disease process itself on your mental functioning, physical functioning, or both your mental and physical functioning. This limitation could result from persistent or intermittent symptoms, such as pain, severe fatigue, or malaise, resulting in a limitation of your ability to do a task, to concentrate, to persevere at a task, or to perform the task at an acceptable rate of speed. (Severe fatigue means a frequent sense of exhaustion that results in significant reduced physical activity or mental function. Malaise means frequent feelings of illness, bodily discomfort, or lack of well-being that result in significantly reduced physical activity or mental function.) You may also have limitations because of your treatment and its side effects.

4. Marked limitation means that the symptoms and signs of your hematological disorder interfere seriously with your ability to function. Although we do not require the use of such a scale, "marked" would be the fourth point on a five-point scale consisting of no limitation, mild limitation, moderate limitation, marked limitation, and extreme limitation. We do not define "marked" by a specific number of different activities of daily living or different behaviors in which your social functioning is impaired, or a specific number of tasks that you are able to complete, but by the nature and overall degree of interference with your functioning. You may have a marked limitation when several activi-

ties or functions are impaired, or even when only one is impaired. Additionally, you need not be totally precluded from performing an activity to have a marked limitation, as long as the degree of limitation interferes seriously with your ability to function independently, appropriately, and effectively. The term "marked" does not imply that you must be confined to bed, hospitalized, or in a nursing home.

5. Activities of daily living include, but are not limited to, such activities as doing household chores, grooming and hygiene, using a post office, taking public transportation, or paying bills. We will find that you have a "marked" limitation in activities of daily living if you have a serious limitation in your ability to maintain a household or take public transportation because of symptoms such as pain, severe fatigue, anxiety, or difficulty concentrating, caused by your hematological disorder (including complications of the disorder) or its treatment, even if you are able to perform some self-care activities.

6. Social functioning includes the capacity to interact with others independently, appropriately, effectively, and on a sustained basis. It includes the ability to communicate effectively with others. We will find that you have a "marked" limitation in maintaining social functioning if you have a serious limitation in social interaction on a sustained basis because of symptoms such as pain, severe fatigue, anxiety, or difficulty concentrating, or a pattern of exacerbation and remission, caused by your hematological disorder (including complications of the disorder) or its treatment, even if you are able to communicate with close friends or relatives.

7. Completing tasks in a timely manner involves the ability to sustain concentration, persistence, or pace to permit timely completion of tasks commonly found in work settings. We will find that you have a "marked" limitation in completing tasks if you have a serious limitation in your ability to sustain concentration or pace adequate to complete work-related tasks because of symptoms, such as pain, severe fatigue, anxiety, or difficulty concentrating caused by your hematological disorder (including complications of the disorder) or its treatment, even if you are able to do some routine activities of daily living.

H. How do we consider your symptoms, including your pain, severe fatigue, and malaise?

Your symptoms, including pain, severe fatigue, and malaise, may be important factors in our determination whether your hematological disorder(s) meets or medically equals a listing, or in our determination whether you are otherwise able to work. We cannot consider your symptoms unless you have medical signs or laboratory findings showing the existence of a medically determinable impairment(s) that could reasonably be expected to produce the symptoms. If you have such an impairment(s), we will evaluate the intensity, persistence, and functional effects of your symptoms using the rules throughout 7.00 and in our other regulations. (See sections 404.1521, 404.1529, 416.921, and 416.929 of this chapter.) Additionally, when we assess the credibility of your complaints about your symptoms and their functional effects, we will not draw any inferences from the fact that you do not receive treatment or that you are not following treatment without considering all of the relevant evidence in your case record, including any explanations you provide that may explain why you are not receiving or following treatment.

I. How do we evaluate episodic events in hematological disorders?

Some of the listings in this body system require a specific number of events within a consecutive 12–month period. (See 7.05, 7.08, and 7.10A.) When we use such criteria, a consecutive 12–month period means a period of 12 consecutive months, all or part of which must occur within the period we are considering in connection with your application or continuing disability review. These events must occur at least 30 days apart to ensure that we are evaluating separate events.

J. How do we evaluate hematological disorders that do not meet one of these listings?

1. These listings are only common examples of hematological disorders that we consider severe enough to prevent a person from doing any gainful activity. If your disorder does not meet the criteria of any of these listings, we must consider whether you have a disorder that satisfies the criteria of a listing in another body system. For example, we will evaluate hemophilic joint deformity or bone or joint pain from myelofibrosis under 1.00; polycythemia vera under 3.00, 4.00, or 11.00; chronic iron overload resulting from repeated RBC transfusion (transfusion hemosiderosis) under 3.00, 4.00, or 5.00; and the effects of intracranial bleeding or stroke under 11.00 or 12.00.

2. If you have a severe medically determinable impairment(s) that does not meet a listing, we will determine whether your impairment(s) medically equals a listing. (See sections 404.1526 and 416.926 of this chapter.) Hematological disorders may be associated with disorders in other body systems, and we consider the combined effects of multiple impairments when we determine whether they medically equal a listing. If your impairment(s) does not medically equal a listing, you may or may not have the residual functional capacity to engage in substantial gainful activity. We proceed to the fourth, and, if necessary, the fifth steps of the sequential evaluation process in sections 404.1520 and 416.920. We use the rules in sections 404.1594, 416.994, and 416.994a of this chapter, as appropriate, when we decide whether you continue to be disabled.

7.01 Category of Impairments, Hematological Disorders

7.05 Hemolytic anemias, including sickle cell disease, thalassemia, and their variants (see 7.00C), with:

A. Documented painful (vaso-occlusive) crises requiring parenteral (intravenous or intramuscular) narcotic medication, occurring at least six times within a 12–month period with at least 30 days between crises.

OR

B. Complications of hemolytic anemia requiring at least three hospitalizations within a 12–month period and occurring at least 30 days apart. Each hospitalization must last at least 48 hours, which can include hours in a hospital emergency department or comprehensive sickle cell disease center immediately before the hospitalization (see 7.00C2).

OR

C. Hemoglobin measurements of 7.0 grams per deciliter (g/dL) or less, occurring at least three times within a 12–month period with at least 30 days between measurements.

OR

D. Beta thalassemia major requiring life-long RBC transfusions at least once every 6 weeks to maintain life (see 7.00C4).

7.08 Disorders of thrombosis and hemostasis, including hemophilia and thrombocytopenia (see 7.00D), with complications requiring at least three hospitalizations within a 12–month period and occurring at least 30 days apart. Each hospitalization must last at least 48 hours, which can include hours in a hospital emergency department or comprehensive hemophilia treatment center immediately before the hospitalization (see 7.00D2).

7.10 Disorders of bone marrow failure, including myelodysplastic syndromes, aplastic anemia, granulocytopenia, and myelofibrosis (see 7.00E), with:

A. Complications of bone marrow failure requiring at least three hospitalizations within a 12–month period and occurring at least 30 days apart. Each hospitalization must last at least 48 hours, which can include hours in a hospital emergency department immediately before the hospitalization (see 7.00E2).

OR

B. Myelodysplastic syndromes or aplastic anemias requiring life-long RBC transfusions at least once every 6 weeks to maintain life (see 7.00E3).

7.17 Hematological disorders treated by bone marrow or stem cell transplantation (see 7.00F). Consider under a disability for at least 12 consecutive months from the date of transplantation. After that, evaluate any residual impairment(s) under the criteria for the affected body system.

7.18 Repeated complications of hematological disorders (see 7.00G2), including those complications listed in 7.05, 7.08, and 7.10 but without the requisite findings for those listings, or other complications (for example, anemia, osteonecrosis, retinopathy, skin ulcers, silent central nervous system infarction, cognitive or other mental limitation, or limitation of joint movement), resulting in significant, documented symptoms or signs (for example, pain, severe fatigue, malaise, fever, night sweats, headaches, joint or muscle swelling, or shortness of breath), and one of the following at the marked level (see 7.00G4):

A. Limitation of activities of daily living (see 7.00G5).

B. Limitation in maintaining social functioning (see 7.00G6).

C. Limitation in completing tasks in a timely manner due to deficiencies in concentration, persistence, or pace (see 7.00G7).

8.00 Skin Disorders

A. What skin disorders do we evaluate with these listings? We use these listings to evaluate skin disorders that may result from hereditary, congenital, or acquired pathological processes. The kinds of impairments covered by these listings are: Ichthyosis, bullous diseases, chronic infections of the skin or mucous membranes, dermatitis, hidradenitis suppurativa, genetic photosensitivity disorders, and burns.

B. What documentation do we need? When we evaluate the existence and severity of your skin disorder, we generally need information about the onset, duration, frequency of flareups, and prognosis of your skin disorder; the location, size, and appearance of lesions; and, when applicable, history of exposure to toxins, allergens, or irritants, familial incidence, seasonal variation, stress factors, and your ability to function outside of a highly protective environment. To confirm the diagnosis, we may need laboratory findings (for example, results of a biopsy obtained independently of Social Security disability evaluation or blood tests) or evidence from other medically acceptable methods consistent with the prevailing state of medical knowledge and clinical practice.

C. How do we assess the severity of your skin disorder(s)? We generally base our assessment of severity on the extent of your skin lesions, the frequency of flareups of your skin lesions, how your symptoms (including pain) limit you, the extent of your treatment, and how your treatment affects you.

1. Extensive skin lesions. Extensive skin lesions are those that involve multiple body sites or critical body areas, and result in a very serious limitation. Examples of extensive skin lesions that result in a very serious limitation include but are not limited to:

a. Skin lesions that interfere with the motion of your joints and that very seriously limit your use of more than one extremity; that is, two upper extremities, two lower extremities, or one upper and one lower extremity.

b. Skin lesions on the palms of both hands that very seriously limit your ability to do fine and gross motor movements.

c. Skin lesions on the soles of both feet, the perineum, or both inguinal areas that very seriously limit your ability to ambulate.

2. Frequency of flareups. If you have skin lesions, but they do not meet the requirements of any of the listings in this body system, you may still have an impairment that prevents you from doing any gainful activity when we consider your condition over time, especially if your flareups result in extensive skin lesions, as defined in C1 of this section. Therefore, if you have frequent flareups, we may find that your impairment(s) is medically equal to one of these listings even though you have some periods during which your condition is in remission. We will consider how frequent and serious your flareups are, how quickly they resolve, and how you function between flareups to determine whether you have been unable to do any gainful activity for a continuous period of at least 12 months or can be expected to be unable to do any gainful activity for a continuous period of at least 12 months. We will also consider the frequency of your flareups when we determine whether you have a severe impairment and when we need to assess your residual functional capacity.

3. Symptoms (including pain). Symptoms (including pain) may be important factors contributing to the severity of your skin disorder(s). We assess the impact of symptoms as explained in §§ 404.1521, 404.1529, 416.921, and 416.929 of this chapter.

4. Treatment. We assess the effects of medication, therapy, surgery, and any other form of treatment you receive when we determine the severity and duration of your impairment(s). Skin disorders frequently respond to treatment; however, response to treatment can vary widely, with some impairments becoming resistant to treatment. Some treatments can have side effects that can in themselves result in limitations.

a. We assess the effects of continuing treatment as prescribed by determining if there is improvement in the symptoms, signs, and laboratory findings of your disorder, and if you experience side effects that result in functional limitations. To assess the effects of your treatment, we may need information about:

i. The treatment you have been prescribed (for example, the type, dosage, method, and frequency of administration of medication or therapy);

ii. Your response to the treatment;

iii. Any adverse effects of the treatment; and

iv. The expected duration of the treatment.

b. Because treatment itself or the effects of treatment may be temporary, in most cases sufficient time must elapse to allow us to evaluate the impact and expected duration of treatment and its side effects. Except under 8.07 and 8.08, you must follow continuing treatment as prescribed for at least 3 months before your impairment can be determined to meet the requirements of a skin disorder listing. (See 8.00H if you are not undergoing treatment or did not have treatment for 3 months.) We consider your specific response to treatment when we evaluate the overall severity of your impairment.

D. How do we assess impairments that may affect the skin and other body systems? When your impairment affects your skin and has effects in other body systems, we first evaluate the predominant feature of your impairment under the appropriate body system. Examples include, but are not limited to the following.

1. Tuberous sclerosis primarily affects the brain. The predominant features are seizures, which we evaluate under the neurological listings in 11.00, and developmental delays or other mental disorders, which we evaluate under the mental disorders listings in 12.00.

2. Malignant tumors of the skin (for example, malignant melanomas) are cancers, or neoplastic diseases, which we evaluate under the listings in 13.00.

3. Autoimmune disorders and other immune system disorders (for example, systemic lupus erythematosus (SLE), scleroderma, human immunodeficiency virus (HIV) infection, and Sjögren's syndrome) often involve more than one body system. We first evaluate these disorders under the immune system disorders listings in 14.00. We evaluate SLE under 14.02, scleroderma under 14.04, Sjögren's syndrome under 14.10, and HIV infection under 14.11.

4. Disfigurement or deformity resulting from skin lesions may result in loss of sight, hearing, speech, and the ability to chew (mastication). We evaluate these impairments and their effects under the special senses and speech listings in 2.00 and the digestive system listings in 5.00. Facial disfigurement or other physical deformities may also have effects we evaluate under the mental disorders listings in 12.00, such as when they affect mood or social functioning.

E. How do we evaluate genetic photosensitivity disorders?

1. Xeroderma pigmentosum (XP). When you have XP, your impairment meets the requirements of 8.07A if you have clinical and laboratory findings showing that you have the disorder. (See 8.00E3.) People who have XP have a lifelong hypersensitivity to all forms of ultraviolet light and generally lead extremely restricted lives in highly protective environments in order to prevent skin cancers from developing. Some people with XP also experience problems with their eyes, neurological problems, mental disorders, and problems in other body systems.

2. Other genetic photosensitivity disorders. Other genetic photosensitivity disorders may vary in their effects on different people, and may not result in an

inability to engage in any gainful activity for a continuous period of at least 12 months. Therefore, if you have a genetic photosensitivity disorder other than XP (established by clinical and laboratory findings as described in 8.00E3), you must show that you have either extensive skin lesions or an inability to function outside of a highly protective environment to meet the requirements of 8.07B. You must also show that your impairment meets the duration requirement. By inability to function outside of a highly protective environment we mean that you must avoid exposure to ultraviolet light (including sunlight passing through windows and light from unshielded fluorescent bulbs), wear protective clothing and eyeglasses, and use opaque broad-spectrum sunscreens in order to avoid skin cancer or other serious effects. Some genetic photosensitivity disorders can have very serious effects in other body systems, especially special senses and speech (2.00), neurological (11.00), mental (12.00), and neoplastic (13.00). We will evaluate the predominant feature of your impairment under the appropriate body system, as explained in 8.00D.

3. Clinical and laboratory findings.

a. General. We need documentation from an acceptable medical source to establish that you have a medically determinable impairment. In general, we must have evidence of appropriate laboratory testing showing that you have XP or another genetic photosensitivity disorder. We will find that you have XP or another genetic photosensitivity disorder based on a report from an acceptable medical source indicating that you have the impairment, supported by definitive genetic laboratory studies documenting appropriate chromosomal changes, including abnormal DNA repair or another DNA or genetic abnormality specific to your type of photosensitivity disorder.

b. What we will accept as medical evidence instead of the actual laboratory report. When we do not have the actual laboratory report, we need evidence from an acceptable medical source that includes appropriate clinical findings for your impairment and that is persuasive that a positive diagnosis has been confirmed by appropriate laboratory testing at some time prior to our evaluation. To be persuasive, the report must state that the appropriate definitive genetic laboratory study was conducted and that the results confirmed the diagnosis. The report must be consistent with other evidence in your case record.

F. How do we evaluate burns? Electrical, chemical, or thermal burns frequently affect other body systems; for example, musculoskeletal, special senses and speech, respiratory, cardiovascular, renal, neurological, or mental. Consequently, we evaluate burns the way we evaluate other disorders that can affect the skin and other body systems, using the listing for the predominant feature of your impairment. For example, if your soft tissue injuries are under continuing surgical management (as defined in 1.00M), we will evaluate your impairment under 1.08. However, if your burns do not meet the requirements of 1.08 and you have extensive skin lesions that result in a very serious limitation (as defined in 8.00C1) that has lasted or can be expected to last for a continuous period of at least 12 months, we will evaluate them under 8.08.

G. How do we determine if your skin disorder(s) will continue at a disabling level of severity in order to meet the duration requirement? For all of these skin disorder listings except 8.07 and 8.08, we will find that your impairment meets the duration requirement if your skin disorder results in extensive skin lesions that persist for at least 3 months despite continuing treatment as prescribed. By persist, we mean that the longitudinal clinical record shows that, with few exceptions, your lesions have been at the level of severity specified in the listing. For 8.07A, we will presume that you meet the duration requirement. For 8.07B and 8.08, we will consider all of the relevant medical and other information in your case record to determine whether your skin disorder meets the duration requirement.

H. How do we assess your skin disorder(s) if your impairment does not meet the requirements of one of these listings?

1. These listings are only examples of common skin disorders that we consider severe enough to prevent you from engaging in any gainful activity. For most of these listings, if you do not have continuing treatment as prescribed, if your treatment has not lasted for at least 3 months, or if you do not have extensive skin lesions that have persisted for at least 3 months, your impairment cannot meet the requirements of these skin disorder listings. (This provision does not apply to 8.07 and 8.08.) However, we may still find that you are disabled because your impairment(s) meets the requirements of a listing in another body system or medically equals the severity of a listing. (See §§ 404.1526 and 416.926 of this chapter.) We may also find you disabled at the last step of the sequential evaluation process.

2. If you have not received ongoing treatment or do not have an ongoing relationship with the medical community despite the existence of a severe impairment(s), or if your skin lesions have not persisted for at least 3 months but you are undergoing continuing treatment as prescribed, you may still have an impairment(s) that meets a listing in another body system or that medically equals a listing. If you do not have an impairment(s) that meets or medically equals a listing, we will assess your residual functional capacity and proceed to the fourth and, if necessary, the fifth step of the sequential evaluation process in §§ 404.1520 and 416.920 of this chapter. When we decide whether you continue to be disabled, we use the rules in §§ 404.1594 and 416.994 of this chapter.

8.01 Category of Impairments, Skin Disorders

8.02 Ichthyosis, with extensive skin lesions that persist for at least 3 months despite continuing treatment as prescribed.

8.03 Bullous disease (for example, pemphigus, erythema multiforme bullosum, epidermolysis bullosa, bullous pemphigoid, dermatitis herpetiformis), with extensive skin lesions that persist for at least 3 months despite continuing treatment as prescribed.

8.04 Chronic infections of the skin or mucous membranes, with extensive fungating or extensive ulcerating skin lesions that persist for at least 3 months despite continuing treatment as prescribed.

8.05 Dermatitis (for example, psoriasis, dyshidrosis, atopic dermatitis, exfoliative dermatitis, allergic contact dermatitis), with extensive skin lesions that persist for at least 3 months despite continuing treatment as prescribed.

8.06 Hidradenitis suppurativa, with extensive skin lesions involving both axillae, both inguinal areas or the perineum that persist for at least 3 months despite continuing treatment as prescribed.

8.07 Genetic photosensitivity disorders, established as described in 8.00E.

A. Xeroderma pigmentosum. Consider the individual disabled from birth.

B. Other genetic photosensitivity disorders, with:

1. Extensive skin lesions that have lasted or can be expected to last for a continuous period of at least 12 months, or

2. Inability to function outside of a highly protective environment for a continuous period of at least 12 months (see 8.00E2).

8.08 Burns, with extensive skin lesions that have lasted or can be expected to last for a continuous period of at least 12 months (see 8.00F).

9.00 Endocrine Disorders

A. What is an endocrine disorder?

An endocrine disorder is a medical condition that causes a hormonal imbalance. When an endocrine gland functions abnormally, producing either too much of a specific hormone (hyperfunction) or too little (hypofunction), the hormonal imbalance can cause various complications in the body. The major glands of the endocrine system are the pituitary, thyroid, parathyroid, adrenal, and pancreas.

B. How do we evaluate the effects of endocrine disorders? We evaluate impairments that result from endocrine disorders under the listings for other body systems. For example:

1. Pituitary gland disorders can disrupt hormone production and normal functioning in other endocrine glands and in many body systems. The effects of pituitary gland disorders vary depending on which hormones are involved. For example, when pituitary hypofunction affects water and electrolyte balance in the kidney and leads to diabetes insipidus, we evaluate the effects of recurrent dehydration under 6.00.

2. Thyroid gland disorders affect the sympathetic nervous system and normal metabolism. We evaluate thyroid-related changes in blood pressure and heart rate that cause arrhythmias or other cardiac dysfunction under 4.00; thyroid-related weight loss under 5.00; hypertensive cerebrovascular accidents (strokes) under 11.00; and cognitive limitations, mood disorders, and anxiety under 12.00.

3. Parathyroid gland disorders affect calcium levels in bone, blood, nerves, muscle, and other body tissues. We evaluate parathyroid-related osteoporosis and fractures under 1.00; abnormally elevated calcium levels in the blood (hypercalcemia) that lead to cataracts under 2.00; kidney failure under 6.00; and recurrent abnormally low blood calcium levels (hypocalcemia) that lead to increased excitability of nerves and muscles, such as tetany and muscle spasms, under 11.00.

4. Adrenal gland disorders affect bone calcium levels, blood pressure, metabolism, and mental status. We evaluate adrenal-related osteoporosis with fractures that compromises the ability to walk or to use the upper extremities under 1.00; adrenal-related hypertension that worsens heart failure or causes recurrent arrhythmias under 4.00; adrenal-related weight loss under 5.00; and mood disorders under 12.00.

5. Diabetes mellitus and other pancreatic gland disorders disrupt the production of several hormones, including insulin, that regulate metabolism and digestion. Insulin is essential to the absorption of glucose from the bloodstream into body cells for conversion into cellular energy. The most common pancreatic gland disorder is diabetes mellitus (DM). There are two major types of DM: type 1 and type 2. Both type 1 and type 2 DM are chronic disorders that can have serious disabling complications that meet the duration requirement. Type 1 DM—previously known as "juvenile diabetes" or "insulin-dependent diabetes mellitus" (IDDM)—is an absolute deficiency of insulin production that commonly begins in childhood and continues throughout adulthood. Treatment of type 1 DM always requires lifelong daily insulin. With type 2 DM—previously known as "adult-onset diabetes mellitus" or "non-insulin-dependent diabetes mellitus" (NIDDM)—the body's cells resist the effects of insulin, impairing glucose absorption and metabolism. Treatment of type 2 DM generally requires lifestyle changes, such as increased exercise and dietary modification, and sometimes insulin in addition to other medications. While both type 1 and type 2 DM are usually controlled, some persons do not achieve good control for a variety of reasons including, but not limited to, hypoglycemia unawareness, other disorders that can

affect blood glucose levels, inability to manage DM due to a mental disorder, or inadequate treatment.

a. Hyperglycemia. Both types of DM cause hyperglycemia, which is an abnormally high level of blood glucose that may produce acute and long-term complications. Acute complications of hyperglycemia include diabetic ketoacidosis. Long-term complications of chronic hyperglycemia include many conditions affecting various body systems.

(i) Diabetic ketoacidosis (DKA). DKA is an acute, potentially life-threatening complication of DM in which the chemical balance of the body becomes dangerously hyperglycemic and acidic. It results from a severe insulin deficiency, which can occur due to missed or inadequate daily insulin therapy or in association with an acute illness. It usually requires hospital treatment to correct the acute complications of dehydration, electrolyte imbalance, and insulin deficiency. You may have serious complications resulting from your treatment, which we evaluate under the affected body system. For example, we evaluate cardiac arrhythmias under 4.00, intestinal necrosis under 5.00, and cerebral edema and seizures under 11.00. Recurrent episodes of DKA may result from mood or eating disorders, which we evaluate under 12.00.

(ii) Chronic hyperglycemia. Chronic hyperglycemia, which is longstanding abnormally high levels of blood glucose, leads to long-term diabetic complications by disrupting nerve and blood vessel functioning. This disruption can have many different effects in other body systems. For example, we evaluate diabetic peripheral neurovascular disease that leads to gangrene and subsequent amputation of an extremity under 1.00; diabetic retinopathy under 2.00; coronary artery disease and peripheral vascular disease under 4.00; diabetic gastroparesis that results in abnormal gastrointestinal motility under 5.00; diabetic nephropathy under 6.00; poorly healing bacterial and fungal skin infections under 8.00; diabetic peripheral and sensory neuropathies under 11.00; and cognitive impairments, depression, and anxiety under 12.00.

b. Hypoglycemia. Persons with DM may experience episodes of hypoglycemia, which is an abnormally low level of blood glucose. Most adults recognize the symptoms of hypoglycemia and reverse them by consuming substances containing glucose; however, some do not take this step because of hypoglycemia unawareness. Severe hypoglycemia can lead to complications, including seizures or loss of consciousness, which we evaluate under 11.00, or altered mental status and cognitive deficits, which we evaluate under 12.00.

C. How do we evaluate endocrine disorders that do not have effects that meet or medically equal the criteria of any listing in other body systems? If your impairment(s) does not meet or medically equal a listing in another body system, you may or may not have the residual functional capacity to engage in substantial gainful activity. In this situation, we proceed to the fourth and, if necessary, the fifth steps of the sequential evaluation process in §§ 404.1520 and 416.920. When we decide whether you continue to be disabled, we use the rules in §§ 404.1594, 416.994, and 416.994a.

10.00 Congenital Disorders that Affect Multiple Body Systems

A. Which disorder do we evaluate under this body system? Although Down syndrome exists in non-mosaic and mosaic forms, we evaluate only non-mosaic Down syndrome under this body system.

B. What is non-mosaic Down syndrome? Non-mosaic Down syndrome is a genetic disorder. Most people with non-mosaic Down syndrome have three copies of chromosome 21 in all of their cells (chromosome 21 trisomy); some have an extra copy of chromosome 21 attached to a different chromosome in all of their cells (chromosome 21 translocation). Virtually all people with non-mosaic Down syndrome have characteristic facial or other physical features, delayed physical development, and intellectual disability. People with non-mosaic Down syndrome may also have congenital heart disease, impaired vision, hearing problems, and other disorders. We evaluate non-mosaic Down syndrome under 10.06. If you have non-mosaic Down syndrome documented as described in 10.00C, we consider you disabled from birth.

C. What evidence do we need to document non-mosaic Down syndrome under 10.06?

1. Under 10.06A, we will find you disabled based on laboratory findings.

a. To find that your disorder meets 10.06A, we need a copy of the laboratory report of karyotype analysis, which is the definitive test to establish non-mosaic Down syndrome. We will not purchase karyotype analysis. We will not accept a fluorescence in situ hybridization (FISH) test because it does not distinguish between the mosaic and non-mosaic forms of Down syndrome.

b. If a physician (see §§ 404.1513(a)(1) and 416.913(a)(1) of this chapter) has not signed the laboratory report of karyotype analysis, the evidence must also include a physician's statement that you have Down syndrome.

c. For purposes of 10.06A, we do not require additional evidence stating that you have the distinctive facial or other physical features of Down syndrome.

2. If we do not have a laboratory report of karyotype analysis showing that you have non-mosaic Down syndrome, we may find you disabled under 10.06B or 10.06C.

a. Under 10.06B, we need a physician's report stating: (i) your karyotype diagnosis or evidence that documents your type of Down syndrome is consistent with prior karyotype analysis (for example, reference to a diagnosis of "trisomy 21"), and (ii) that you have the distinctive facial or other physical features of Down syndrome. We do not require a detailed description of the facial or other physical features of the disorder. However, we will not find that your disorder meets 10.06B if we have evidence—such as evidence of functioning inconsistent with the diagnosis—that indicates that you do not have non-mosaic Down syndrome.

b. If we do not have evidence of prior karyotype analysis (you did not have testing, or you had testing but we do not have information from a physician about the test results), we will find that your disorder meets 10.06C if we have: (i) a physician's report stating that you have the distinctive facial or other physical features of Down syndrome, and (ii) evidence that your functioning is consistent with a diagnosis of non-mosaic Down syndrome. This evidence may include medical or nonmedical information about your physical and mental abilities, including information about your education, work history, or the results of psychological testing. However, we will not find that your disorder meets 10.06C if we have evidence—such as evidence of functioning inconsistent with the diagnosis—that indicates that you do not have non-mosaic Down syndrome.

D. How do we evaluate mosaic Down syndrome and other congenital disorders that affect multiple body systems?

1. Mosaic Down syndrome. Approximately 2 percent of people with Down syndrome have the mosaic form. In mosaic Down syndrome, there are some cells with an extra copy of chromosome 21 and other cells with the normal two copies of chromosome 21. Mosaic Down syndrome can be so slight as to be undetected clinically, but it can also be profound and disabling, affecting various body systems.

2. Other congenital disorders that affect multiple body systems. Other congenital disorders, such as congenital anomalies, chromosomal disorders, dysmorphic syndromes, inborn metabolic syndromes, and perinatal infectious diseases, can cause deviation from, or interruption of, the normal function of the body or can interfere with development. Examples of these disorders include both the juvenile and late-onset forms of Tay–Sachs disease, trisomy X syndrome (XXX syndrome), fragile X syndrome, phenylketonuria (PKU), caudal regression syndrome, and fetal alcohol syndrome. For these disorders and other disorders like them, the degree of deviation, interruption, or interference, as well as the resulting functional limitations and their progression, may vary widely from person to person and may affect different body systems.

3. Evaluating the effects of mosaic Down syndrome or another congenital disorder under the listings. When the effects of mosaic Down syndrome or another congenital disorder that affects multiple body systems are sufficiently severe we evaluate the disorder under the appropriate affected body system(s), such as musculoskeletal, special senses and speech, neurological, or mental disorders. Otherwise, we evaluate the specific functional limitations that result from the disorder under our other rules described in 10.00E.

E. What if your disorder does not meet a listing? If you have a severe medically determinable impairment(s) that does not meet a listing, we will consider whether your impairment(s) medically equals a listing. See §§ 404.1526 and 416.926 of this chapter. If your impairment(s) does not meet or medically equal a listing, you may or may not have the residual functional capacity to engage in substantial gainful activity. We proceed to the fourth, and if necessary, the fifth steps of the sequential evaluation process in §§ 404.1520 and 416.920 of this chapter. We use the rules in §§ 404.1594 and 416.994 of this chapter, as appropriate, when we decide whether you continue to be disabled.

10.01 Category of Impairments, Congenital Disorders That Affect Multiple Body Systems

10.06 Non-mosaic Down syndrome (chromosome 21 trisomy or chromosome 21 translocation), documented by:

A. A laboratory report of karyotype analysis signed by a physician, or both a laboratory report of karyotype analysis not signed by a physician and a statement by a physician that you have Down syndrome (see 10.00C1), or

B. A physician's report stating that you have chromosome 21 trisomy or chromosome 21 translocation consistent with prior karyotype analysis with the distinctive facial or other physical features of Down syndrome (see 10.00C2a), or

C. A physician's report stating that you have Down syndrome with the distinctive facial or other physical features and evidence demonstrating that you function at a level consistent with non-mosaic Down syndrome (see 10.00C2b).

11.00 NEUROLOGICAL DISORDERS

A. Which neurological disorders do we evaluate under these listings? We evaluate epilepsy, amyotrophic lateral sclerosis, coma or persistent vegetative state (PVS), and neurological disorders that cause disorganization of motor function, bulbar and neuromuscular dysfunction, communication impairment, or a combination of limitations in physical and mental functioning. We evaluate neurological disorders that may manifest in a combination of limitations in physical and mental functioning. For example, if you have a neurological disorder that causes mental limitations, such as Huntington's disease or early-onset Alzheimer's disease, which may limit executive functioning (e.g., regulating attention, planning, inhibiting responses, decision-making), we evaluate your limitations using the functional criteria under these listings (see 11.00G). Under this body system, we evaluate the limitations resulting from the impact of the neurological disease process itself. If your neurological disorder results in only mental impairment or if you have a co-occurring mental condition that is not caused by your neurological disorder (for example, dementia), we will evaluate your mental impairment under the mental disorders body system, 12.00.

B. What evidence do we need to document your neurological disorder?

1. We need both medical and non-medical evidence (signs, symptoms, and laboratory findings) to assess the effects of your neurological disorder. Medical evidence should include your medical history, examination findings, relevant laboratory tests, and the results of imaging. Imaging refers to medical imaging techniques, such as x-ray, computerized tomography (CT), magnetic resonance imaging (MRI), and electroencephalography (EEG). The imaging must be consistent with the prevailing state of medical knowledge and clinical practice as the proper technique to support the evaluation of the disorder. In addition, the medical evidence may include descriptions of any prescribed treatment and your response to it. We consider non-medical evidence such as statements you or others make about your impairments, your restrictions, your daily activities, or your efforts to work.

2. We will make every reasonable effort to obtain the results of your laboratory and imaging evidence. When the results of any of these tests are part of the existing evidence in your case record, we will evaluate the test results and all other relevant evidence. We will not purchase imaging, or other diagnostic tests, or laboratory tests that are complex, may involve significant risk, or that are invasive. We will not routinely purchase tests that are expensive or not readily available.

C. How do we consider adherence to prescribed treatment in neurological disorders? In 11.02 (Epilepsy), 11.06 (Parkinsonian syndrome), and 11.12 (Myasthenia gravis), we require that limitations from these neurological disorders exist despite adherence to prescribed treatment. "Despite adherence to prescribed treatment" means that you have taken medication(s) or followed other treatment procedures for your neurological disorder(s) as prescribed by a physician for three consecutive months but your impairment continues to meet the other listing requirements despite this treatment. You may receive your treatment at a health care facility that you visit regularly, even if you do not see the same physician on each visit.

D. What do we mean by disorganization of motor function?

1. Disorganization of motor function means interference, due to your neurological disorder, with movement of two extremities; i.e., the lower extremities, or upper extremities (including fingers, wrists, hands, arms, and shoulders). By two extremities we mean both lower extremities, or both upper extremities, or one upper extremity and one lower extremity. All listings in this body system, except for 11.02 (Epilepsy), 11.10 (Amyotrophic lateral sclerosis), and 11.20 (Coma and persistent vegetative state), include criteria for disorganization of motor function that results in an extreme limitation in your ability to:

a. Stand up from a seated position; or

b. Balance while standing or walking; or

c. Use the upper extremities (including fingers, wrists, hands, arms, and shoulders).

2. Extreme limitation means the inability to stand up from a seated position, maintain balance in a standing position and while walking, or use your upper extremities to independently initiate, sustain, and complete work-related activities. The assessment of motor function depends on the degree of interference with standing up; balancing while standing or walking; or using the upper extremities (including fingers, hands, arms, and shoulders).

a. Inability to stand up from a seated position means that once seated you are unable to stand and maintain an upright position without the assistance of another person or the use of an assistive device, such as a walker, two crutches, or two canes.

b. Inability to maintain balance in a standing position means that you are unable to maintain an upright position while standing or walking without the assistance of another person or an assistive device, such as a walker, two crutches, or two canes.

c. Inability to use your upper extremities means that you have a loss of function of both upper extremities (including fingers, wrists, hands, arms, and shoulders) that very seriously limits your ability to independently initiate, sustain, and complete work-related activities involving fine and gross motor movements. Inability to perform fine and gross motor movements could include not being able to pinch, manipulate, and use your fingers; or not being able to use your hands, arms, and shoulders to perform gross motor movements, such as handling, gripping, grasping, holding, turning, and reaching; or not being able to engage in exertional movements such a lifting, carrying, pushing, and pulling.

E. How do we evaluate communication impairments under these listings? We must have a description of a recent comprehensive evaluation including all areas of communication, performed by an acceptable medical source, to document a communication impairment associated with a neurological disorder. A communication impairment may occur when a medically determinable neurological impairment results in dysfunction in the parts of the brain responsible for speech and language. We evaluate communication impairments associated with neurological disorders under 11.04A, 11.07C, or 11.11B. We evaluate communication impairments due to non-neurological disorders under 2.09.

1. Under 11.04A, we need evidence documenting that your central nervous system vascular accident or insult (CVA) and sensory or motor aphasia have resulted in ineffective speech or communication. Ineffective speech or communication means there is an extreme limitation in your ability to understand or convey your message in simple spoken language resulting in your inability to demonstrate basic communication skills, such as following one-step commands or telling someone about your basic personal needs without assistance.

2. Under 11.07C, we need evidence documenting that your cerebral palsy has resulted in significant interference in your ability to speak, hear, or see. We will find you have "significant interference" in your ability to speak, hear, or see if your signs, such as aphasia, strabismus, or sensorineural hearing loss, seriously limit your ability to communicate on a sustained basis.

3. Under 11.11B, we need evidence documenting that your post-polio syndrome has resulted in the inability to produce intelligible speech.

F. What do we mean by bulbar and neuromuscular dysfunction? The bulbar region of the brain is responsible for controlling the bulbar muscles in the throat, tongue, jaw, and face. Bulbar and neuromuscular dysfunction refers to weakness in these muscles, resulting in breathing, swallowing, and speaking impairments. Listings 11.11 (Post-polio syndrome), 11.12 (Myasthenia gravis), and 11.22 (Motor neuron disorders other than ALS) include criteria for evaluating bulbar and neuromuscular dysfunction. If your neurological disorder has resulted in a breathing disorder, we may evaluate that condition under the respiratory system, 3.00.

G. How do we evaluate limitations in physical and mental functioning under these listings?

1. Neurological disorders may manifest in a combination of limitations in physical and mental functioning. We consider all relevant information in your case record to determine the effects of your neurological disorder on your physical and mental functioning. To satisfy the requirement described under 11.00G, your neurological disorder must result in a marked limitation in physical functioning and a marked limitation in at least one of four areas of mental functioning: Understanding, remembering, or applying information; interacting with others; concentrating, persisting, or maintaining pace; or adapting or managing oneself. If your neurological disorder results in an extreme limitation in at least one of the four areas of mental functioning, or results in marked limitation in at least two of the four areas of mental functioning, but you do not have at least a marked limitation in your physical functioning, we will consider whether your condition meets or medically equals one of the mental disorders body system listings, 12.00.

2. Marked Limitation. To satisfy the requirements of the functional criteria, your neurological disorder must result in a marked limitation in physical functioning and a marked limitation in one of the four areas of mental functioning (see 11.00G3). Although we do not require the use of such a scale, "marked" would be the fourth point on a five-point scale consisting of no limitation, mild limitation, moderate limitation, marked limitation, and extreme limitation. We consider the nature and overall degree of interference with your functioning. The term "marked" does not require that you must be confined to bed, hospitalized, or in a nursing home.

a. Marked limitation and physical functioning. For this criterion, a marked limitation means that, due to the signs and symptoms of your neurological disorder, you are seriously limited in the ability to independently initiate, sustain, and complete work-related physical activities (see 11.00G3). You may have a marked limitation in your physical functioning when your neurological disease process causes persistent or intermittent symptoms that affect your abilities to independently initiate, sustain, and complete work-related activities, such as standing, balancing, walking, using both upper extremities for fine and gross movements, or results in limitations in using one upper and one lower extremity. The persistent and intermittent symptoms must result in a serious limitation in your ability to do a task or activity on a sustained basis. We do not define "marked" by a specific number of different physical activities or tasks that demonstrate your ability, but by the overall effects of your neurological symptoms on your ability to perform such physical activities on a consistent and sustained basis. You need not be totally precluded from performing a function or activity to have a marked limitation, as long as the degree of limitation seriously limits your ability to independently initiate, sustain, and complete work-related physical activities.

b. Marked limitation and mental functioning. For this criterion, a marked limitation means that, due to the signs and symptoms of your neurological disorder, you are seriously limited in the ability to function independently, appropriately, effectively, and on a sustained basis in work settings (see 11.03G3). We do not define "marked" by a specific number of mental activities, such as: The number of activities that demonstrate your ability to understand, remember, and apply information; the number of tasks that demonstrate your ability to interact with others; a specific number of tasks that demonstrate you are able to concentrate, persist or maintain pace; or a specific number of tasks that demonstrate you are able to manage yourself.

You may have a marked limitation in your mental functioning when several activities or functions are impaired, or even when only one is impaired. You need not be totally precluded from performing an activity to have a marked limitation, as long as the degree of limitation seriously limits your ability to function independently, appropriately, and effectively on a sustained basis, and complete work-related mental activities.

3. Areas of physical and mental functioning.

a. Physical functioning. Examples of this criterion include specific motor abilities, such as independently initiating, sustaining, and completing the following activities: Standing up from a seated position, balancing while standing or walking, or using both your upper extremities for fine and gross movements (see 11.00D). Physical functioning may also include functions of the body that support motor abilities, such as the abilities to see, breathe, and swallow (see 11.00E and 11.00F). Examples of when your limitation in seeing, breathing, or swallowing may, on its own, rise to a "marked" limitation include: Prolonged and uncorrectable double vision causing difficulty with balance; prolonged difficulty breathing requiring the use of a prescribed assistive breathing device, such as a portable continuous positive airway pressure machine; or repeated instances, occurring at least weekly, of aspiration without causing aspiration pneumonia. Alternatively, you may have a combination of limitations due to your neurological disorder that together rise to a "marked" limitation in physical functioning. We may also find that you have a "marked" limitation in this area if, for example, your symptoms, such as pain or fatigue (see 11.00T), as documented in your medical record, and caused by your neurological disorder or its treatment, seriously limit your ability to independently initiate, sustain, and complete these work-related motor functions, or the other physical functions or physiological processes that support those motor functions. We may also find you seriously limited in an area if, while you retain some ability to perform the function, you are unable to do so consistently and on a sustained basis. The limitation in your physical functioning must last or be expected to last at least 12 months. These examples illustrate the nature of physical functioning. We do not require documentation of all of the examples.

b. Mental functioning.

(i) Understanding, remembering, or applying information. This area of mental functioning refers to the abilities to learn, recall, and use information to perform work activities. Examples include: Understanding and learning terms, instructions, procedures; following one- or two-step oral instructions to carry out a task; describing work activity to someone else; asking and answering questions and providing explanations; recognizing a mistake and correcting it; identifying and solving problems; sequencing multi-step activities; and using reason and judgment to make work-related decisions. These examples illustrate the nature of this area of mental functioning. We do not require documentation of all of the examples.

(ii) Interacting with others. This area of mental functioning refers to the abilities to relate to and work with supervisors, co-workers, and the public. Examples include: Cooperating with others; asking for help when needed; handling conflicts with others; stating your own point of view; initiating or sustaining conversation; understanding and responding to social cues (physical, verbal, emotional); responding to requests, suggestions, criticism, correction, and challenges; and keeping social interactions free of excessive irritability, sensitivity, argumentativeness, or suspiciousness. These examples illustrate the nature of this area of mental functioning. We do not require documentation of all of the examples.

(iii) Concentrating, persisting, or maintaining pace. This area of mental functioning refers to the abilities to focus attention on work activities and to stay on-task at a sustained rate. Examples include: Initiating and performing a task that you understand and know how to do; working at an appropriate and consistent pace; completing tasks in a timely manner; ignoring or avoiding distractions while working; changing activities or work settings without being disruptive; working close to or with others without interrupting or distracting them; sustaining an ordinary routine and regular attendance at work; and working a full day without needing more than the allotted number or length of rest periods during the day. These examples illustrate the nature of this area of mental functioning. We do not require documentation of all of the examples.

(iv) Adapting or managing oneself. This area of mental functioning refers to the abilities to regulate emotions, control behavior, and maintain well-being in a work setting. Examples include: Responding to demands; adapting to changes; managing your psychologically based symptoms; distinguishing between acceptable and unacceptable work performance; setting realistic goals; making plans for yourself independently of others; maintaining personal hygiene and attire appropriate to a work setting; and being aware of normal hazards and taking appropriate precautions. These examples illustrate the nature of this area of mental functioning. We do not require documentation of all of the examples.

4. Signs and symptoms of your disorder and the effects of treatment.

a. We will consider your signs and symptoms and how they affect your ability to function in the work place. When we evaluate your functioning, we will consider whether your signs and symptoms are persistent or intermittent, how frequently they occur and how long they last, their intensity, and whether you have periods of exacerbation and remission.

b. We will consider the effectiveness of treatment in improving the signs, symptoms, and laboratory findings related to your neurological disorder, as well as any aspects of treatment that may interfere with your ability to function. We will consider, for example: The effects of medications you take (including side effects); the time-limited efficacy of some medications; the intrusiveness, complexity, and duration of your treatment (for example, the dosing schedule or need for injections); the effects of treatment, including medications, therapy, and surgery, on your functioning; the variability of your response to treatment; and any drug interactions.

H. What is epilepsy, and how do we evaluate it under 11.02?

1. Epilepsy is a pattern of recurrent and unprovoked seizures that are manifestations of abnormal electrical activity in the brain. There are various types of generalized and "focal" or partial seizures. However, psychogenic nonepileptic seizures and pseudoseizures are not epileptic seizures for the purpose of 11.02. We evaluate psychogenic seizures and pseudoseizures under the mental disorders body system, 12.00. In adults, the most common potentially disabling seizure types are generalized tonic-clonic seizures and dyscognitive seizures (formerly complex partial seizures).

a. Generalized tonic-clonic seizures are characterized by loss of consciousness accompanied by a tonic phase (sudden muscle tensing causing the person to lose postural control) followed by a clonic phase (rapid cycles of muscle contraction and relaxation, also called convulsions). Tongue biting and incontinence may occur during generalized tonic-clonic seizures, and injuries may result from falling.

b. Dyscognitive seizures are characterized by alteration of consciousness without convulsions or loss of muscle control. During the seizure, blank staring, change of facial expression, and automatisms (such as lip smacking, chewing or swallowing, or repetitive simple actions, such as gestures or verbal utterances) may occur. During its course, a dyscognitive seizure may progress into a generalized tonic-clonic seizure (see 11.00H1a).

2. Description of seizure. We require at least one detailed description of your seizures from someone, preferably a medical professional, who has observed at least one of your typical seizures. If you experience more than one type of seizure, we require a description of each type.

3. Serum drug levels. We do not require serum drug levels; therefore, we will not purchase them. However, if serum drug levels are available in your medical records, we will evaluate them in the context of the other evidence in your case record.

4. Counting seizures. The period specified in 11.02A, B, C, or D cannot begin earlier than one month after you began prescribed treatment. The required number of seizures must occur within the period we are considering in connection with your application or continuing disability review. When we evaluate the frequency of your seizures, we also consider your adherence to prescribed treatment (see 11.00C). When we determine the number of seizures you have had in the specified period, we will:

a. Count multiple seizures occurring in a 24–hour period as one seizure.

b. Count status epilepticus (a continuous series of seizures without return to consciousness between seizures) as one seizure.

c. Count a dyscognitive seizure that progresses into a generalized tonic-clonic seizure as one generalized tonic-clonic seizure.

d. We do not count seizures that occur during a period when you are not adhering to prescribed treatment without good reason. When we determine that you had good reason for not adhering to prescribed treatment, we will consider your physical, mental, educational, and communicative limitations (including any language barriers). We will consider you to have good reason for not following prescribed treatment if, for example, the treatment is very risky for you due to its consequences or unusual nature, or if you are unable to afford prescribed treatment that you are willing to accept, but for which no free community resources are available. We will follow guidelines found in our policy, such as §§ 404.1530(c) and 416.930(c) of this chapter, when we determine whether you have a good reason for not adhering to prescribed treatment.

e. We do not count psychogenic nonepileptic seizures or pseudoseizures under 11.02. We evaluate these seizures under the mental disorders body system, 12.00.

5. Electroencephalography (EEG) testing. We do not require EEG test results; therefore, we will not purchase them. However, if EEG test results are available in your medical records, we will evaluate them in the context of the other evidence in your case record.

I. What is vascular insult to the brain, and how do we evaluate it under 11.04?

1. Vascular insult to the brain (cerebrum, cerebellum, or brainstem), commonly referred to as stroke or cerebrovascular accident (CVA), is brain cell death caused by an interruption of blood flow within or leading to the brain, or by a hemorrhage from a ruptured blood vessel or aneurysm in the brain. If you have a vision impairment resulting from your vascular insult, we may evaluate that impairment under the special senses body system, 2.00.

2. We need evidence of sensory or motor aphasia that results in ineffective speech or communication

under 11.04A (see 11.00E). We may evaluate your communication impairment under listing 11.04C if you have marked limitation in physical functioning and marked limitation in one of the four areas of mental functioning.

3. We generally need evidence from at least 3 months after the vascular insult to evaluate whether you have disorganization of motor functioning under 11.04B, or the impact that your disorder has on your physical and mental functioning under 11.04C. In some cases, evidence of your vascular insult is sufficient to allow your claim within 3 months post-vascular insult. If we are unable to allow your claim within 3 months after your vascular insult, we will defer adjudication of the claim until we obtain evidence of your neurological disorder at least 3 months post-vascular insult.

J. What are benign brain tumors, and how do we evaluate them under 11.05? Benign brain tumors are noncancerous (nonmalignant) abnormal growths of tissue in or on the brain that invade healthy brain tissue or apply pressure on the brain or cranial nerves. We evaluate their effects on your functioning as discussed in 11.00D and 11.00G. We evaluate malignant brain tumors under the cancer body system in 13.00. If you have a vision impairment resulting from your benign brain tumor, we may evaluate that impairment under the special senses body system, 2.00.

K. What is Parkinsonian syndrome, and how do we evaluate it under 11.06? Parkinsonian syndrome is a term that describes a group of chronic, progressive movement disorders resulting from loss or decline in the function of dopamine-producing brain cells. Dopamine is a neurotransmitter that regulates muscle movement throughout the body. When we evaluate your Parkinsonian syndrome, we will consider your adherence to prescribed treatment (see 11.00C).

L. What is cerebral palsy, and how do we evaluate it under 11.07?

1. Cerebral palsy (CP) is a term that describes a group of static, nonprogressive disorders caused by abnormalities within the brain that disrupt the brain's ability to control movement, muscle coordination, and posture. The resulting motor deficits manifest very early in a person's development, with delayed or abnormal progress in attaining developmental milestones. Deficits may become more obvious as the person grows and matures over time.

2. We evaluate your signs and symptoms, such as ataxia, spasticity, flaccidity, athetosis, chorea, and difficulty with precise movements when we determine your ability to stand up, balance, walk, or perform fine and gross motor movements. We will also evaluate your signs, such as dysarthria and apraxia of speech, and receptive and expressive language problems when we determine your ability to communicate.

3. We will consider your other impairments or signs and symptoms that develop secondary to the disorder, such as post-impairment syndrome (a combination of pain, fatigue, and weakness due to muscle abnormalities); overuse syndromes (repetitive motion injuries); arthritis; abnormalities of proprioception (perception of the movements and position of the body); abnormalities of stereognosis (perception and identification of objects by touch); learning problems; anxiety; and depression.

M. What are spinal cord disorders, and how do we evaluate them under 11.08?

1. Spinal cord disorders may be congenital or caused by injury to the spinal cord. Motor signs and symptoms of spinal cord disorders include paralysis, flaccidity, spasticity, and weakness.

2. Spinal cord disorders with complete loss of function (11.08A) addresses spinal cord disorders that result in a complete lack of motor, sensory, and autonomic function of the affected part(s) of the body.

3. Spinal cord disorders with disorganization of motor function (11.08B) addresses spinal cord disorders that result in less than a complete loss of function of the affected part(s) of the body, reducing, but not eliminating, motor, sensory, and autonomic function.

4. When we evaluate your spinal cord disorder, we generally need evidence from at least 3 months after your symptoms began in order to evaluate your disorganization of motor function. In some cases, evidence of your spinal cord disorder may be sufficient to allow your claim within 3 months after the spinal cord disorder. If the medical evidence demonstrates total cord transection causing a loss of motor and sensory functions below the level of injury, we will not wait 3 months but will make the allowance decision immediately.

N. What is multiple sclerosis, and how do we evaluate it under 11.09?

1. Multiple sclerosis (MS) is a chronic, inflammatory, degenerative disorder that damages the myelin sheath surrounding the nerve fibers in the brain and spinal cord. The damage disrupts the normal transmission of nerve impulses within the brain and between the brain and other parts of the body, causing impairment in muscle coordination, strength, balance, sensation, and vision. There are several forms of MS, ranging from mildly to highly aggressive. Milder forms generally involve acute attacks (exacerbations) with partial or complete recovery from signs and symptoms (remissions). Aggressive forms generally exhibit a steady progression of signs and symptoms with few or no remissions. The effects of all forms vary from person to person.

2. We evaluate your signs and symptoms, such as flaccidity, spasticity, spasms, incoordination, imbalance, tremor, physical fatigue, muscle weakness, dizziness,

tingling, and numbness when we determine your ability to stand up, balance, walk, or perform fine and gross motor movements. When determining whether you have limitations of physical and mental functioning, we will consider your other impairments or signs and symptoms that develop secondary to the disorder, such as fatigue; visual loss; trouble sleeping; impaired attention, concentration, memory, or judgment; mood swings; and depression. If you have a vision impairment resulting from your MS, we may evaluate that impairment under the special senses body system, 2.00.

O. What is amyotrophic lateral sclerosis, and how do we evaluate it under 11.10? Amyotrophic lateral sclerosis (ALS) is a type of motor neuron disorder that rapidly and progressively attacks the nerve cells responsible for controlling voluntary muscles. We establish ALS under 11.10 when you have a documented diagnosis of ALS. We require documentation based on generally accepted methods consistent with the prevailing state of medical knowledge and clinical practice. We require laboratory testing to establish the diagnosis when the clinical findings of upper and lower motor neuron disease are not present in three or more regions. Electrophysiological studies, such as nerve conduction velocity studies and electromyography (EMG), may support your diagnosis of ALS; however, we will not purchase these studies.

P. What are neurodegenerative disorders of the central nervous system, such as Huntington's disease, Friedreich's ataxia, and spinocerebellar degeneration, and how do we evaluate them under 11.17? Neurodegenerative disorders of the central nervous system are disorders characterized by progressive and irreversible degeneration of neurons or their supporting cells. Over time, these disorders impair many of the body's motor, cognitive, and other mental functions. We consider neurodegenerative disorders of the central nervous system under 11.17 that we do not evaluate elsewhere in section 11.00, such as Huntington's disease (HD), Friedreich's ataxia, spinocerebellar degeneration, Creutzfeldt–Jakob disease (CJD), progressive supranuclear palsy (PSP), early-onset Alzheimer's disease, and frontotemporal dementia (Pick's disease). When these disorders result in solely cognitive and other mental function effects, we will evaluate the disorder under the mental disorder listings.

Q. What is traumatic brain injury, and how do we evaluate it under 11.18?

1. Traumatic brain injury (TBI) is damage to the brain resulting from skull fracture, collision with an external force leading to a closed head injury, or penetration by an object that enters the skull and makes contact with brain tissue. We evaluate TBI that results in coma or persistent vegetative state (PVS) under 11.20.

2. We generally need evidence from at least 3 months after the TBI to evaluate whether you have disorganization of motor function under 11.18A or the impact that your disorder has on your physical and mental functioning under 11.18B. In some cases, evidence of your TBI is sufficient to determine disability within 3 months post–TBI. If we are unable to allow your claim within 3 months post–TBI, we will defer adjudication of the claim until we obtain evidence of your neurological disorder at least 3 months post–TBI. If a finding of disability still is not possible at that time, we will again defer adjudication of the claim until we obtain evidence at least 6 months after your TBI.

R. What are coma and persistent vegetative state, and how do we evaluate them under 11.20? Coma is a state of unconsciousness in which a person does not exhibit a sleep/wake cycle, and is unable to perceive or respond to external stimuli. People who do not fully emerge from coma may progress into a persistent vegetative state (PVS). PVS is a condition of partial arousal in which a person may have a low level of consciousness but is still unable to react to external stimuli. In contrast to coma, a person in a PVS retains sleep/wake cycles and may exhibit some key lower brain functions, such as spontaneous movement, opening and moving eyes, and grimacing. Coma or PVS may result from TBI, a nontraumatic insult to the brain (such as a vascular insult, infection, or brain tumor), or a neurodegenerative or metabolic disorder. Medically induced comas are not considered under 11.20 and should be considered under the section pertaining to the underlying reason the coma was medically induced and not under this section.

S. What are motor neuron disorders, other than ALS, and how do we evaluate them under 11.22? Motor neuron disorders such as progressive bulbar palsy, primary lateral sclerosis (PLS), and spinal muscular atrophy (SMA) are progressive neurological disorders that destroy the cells that control voluntary muscle activity, such as walking, breathing, swallowing, and speaking. We evaluate the effects of these disorders on motor functioning, bulbar and neuromuscular functioning, oral communication, or limitations in physical and mental functioning.

T. How do we consider symptoms of fatigue in these listings? Fatigue is one of the most common and limiting symptoms of some neurological disorders, such as multiple sclerosis, post-polio syndrome, and myasthenia gravis. These disorders may result in physical fatigue (lack of muscle strength) or mental fatigue (decreased awareness or attention). When we evaluate your fatigue, we will consider the intensity, persistence, and effects of fatigue on your functioning. This may include information such as the clinical and laboratory data and other objective evidence concerning your neurological deficit, a description of fatigue considered characteristic of your disorder, and information about your functioning. We consider the effects of physical fatigue on your ability to stand up, balance, walk, or perform fine and gross motor movements using the criteria described in 11.00D. We consider the effects of physical and mental fatigue when we evaluate your physical and mental functioning described in 11.00G.

U. How do we evaluate your neurological disorder when it does not meet one of these listings?

1. If your neurological disorder does not meet the criteria of any of these listings, we must also consider whether your impairment(s) meets the criteria of a listing in another body system. If you have a severe medically determinable impairment(s) that does not meet a listing, we will determine whether your impairment(s) medically equals a listing. See §§ 404.1526 and 416.926 of this chapter.

2. If your impairment(s) does not meet or medically equal the criteria of a listing, you may or may not have the residual functional capacity to perform your past relevant work or adjust to other work that exists in significant numbers in the national economy, which we determine at the fourth and, if necessary, the fifth steps of the sequential evaluation process in §§ 404.1520 and 416.920 of this chapter.

3. We use the rules in §§ 404.1594 and 416.994 of this chapter, as appropriate, when we decide whether you continue to be disabled.

11.01 Category of Impairments, Neurological Disorders

11.02 Epilepsy, documented by a detailed description of a typical seizure and characterized by A, B, C, or D:

A. Generalized tonic-clonic seizures (see 11.00H1a), occurring at least once a month for at least 3 consecutive months (see 11.00H4) despite adherence to prescribed treatment (see 11.00C); or

B. Dyscognitive seizures (see 11.00H1b), occurring at least once a week for at least 3 consecutive months (see 11.00H4) despite adherence to prescribed treatment (see 11.00C); or

C. Generalized tonic-clonic seizures (see 11.00H1a), occurring at least once every 2 months for at least 4 consecutive months (see 11.00H4) despite adherence to prescribed treatment (see 11.00C); and a marked limitation in one of the following:

1. Physical functioning (see 11.00G3a); or

2. Understanding, remembering, or applying information (see 11.00G3b(i)); or

3. Interacting with others (see 11.00G3b(ii)); or

4. Concentrating, persisting, or maintaining pace (see 11.00G3b(iii)); or

5. Adapting or managing oneself (see 11.00G3b(iv)); or

D. Dyscognitive seizures (see 11.00H1b), occurring at least once every 2 weeks for at least 3 consecutive months (see 11.00H4) despite adherence to prescribed treatment (see 11.00C); and a marked limitation in one of the following:

1. Physical functioning (see 11.00G3a); or

2. Understanding, remembering, or applying information (see 11.00G3b(i)); or

3. Interacting with others (see 11.00G3b(ii)); or

4. Concentrating, persisting, or maintaining pace (see 11.00G3b(iii)); or

5. Adapting or managing oneself (see 11.00G3b(iv)).

11.03 [Reserved]

11.04 Vascular insult to the brain, characterized by A, B, or C:

A. Sensory or motor aphasia resulting in ineffective speech or communication (see 11.00E1) persisting for at least 3 consecutive months after the insult; or

B. Disorganization of motor function in two extremities (see 11.00D1), resulting in an extreme limitation (see 11.00D2) in the ability to stand up from a seated position, balance while standing or walking, or use the upper extremities, persisting for at least 3 consecutive months after the insult; or

C. Marked limitation (see 11.00G2) in physical functioning (see 11.00G3a) and in one of the following areas of mental functioning, both persisting for at least 3 consecutive months after the insult:

1. Understanding, remembering, or applying information (see 11.00G3b(i)); or

2. Interacting with others (see 11.00G3b(ii)); or

3. Concentrating, persisting, or maintaining pace (see 11.00G3b(iii)); or

4. Adapting or managing oneself (see 11.00G3b(iv)).

11.05 Benign brain tumors, characterized by A or B:

A. Disorganization of motor function in two extremities (see 11.00D1), resulting in an extreme limitation (see 11.00D2) in the ability to stand up from a seated position, balance while standing or walking, or use the upper extremities; or

B. Marked limitation (see 11.00G2) in physical functioning (see 11.00G3a), and in one of the following:

1. Understanding, remembering, or applying information (see 11.00G3b(i)); or

2. Interacting with others (see 11.00G3b(ii)); or

3. Concentrating, persisting, or maintaining pace (see 11.00G3b(iii)); or

4. Adapting or managing oneself (see 11.00G3b(iv)).

11.06 Parkinsonian syndrome, characterized by A or B despite adherence to prescribed treatment for at least 3 consecutive months (see 11.00C):

A. Disorganization of motor function in two extremities (see 11.00D1), resulting in an extreme limitation (see 11.00D2) in the ability to stand up from a seated position, balance while standing or walking, or use the upper extremities; or

B. Marked limitation (see 11.00G2) in physical functioning (see 11.00G3a), and in one of the following:

1. Understanding, remembering, or applying information (see 11.00G3b(i)); or

2. Interacting with others (see 11.00G3b(ii)); or

3. Concentrating, persisting, or maintaining pace (see 11.00G3b(iii)); or

4. Adapting or managing oneself (see 11.00G3b(iv)).

11.07 Cerebral palsy, characterized by A, B, or C:

A. Disorganization of motor function in two extremities (see 11.00D1), resulting in an extreme limitation (see 11.00D2) in the ability to stand up from a seated position, balance while standing or walking, or use the upper extremities; or

B. Marked limitation (see 11.00G2) in physical functioning (see 11.00G3a), and in one of the following:

1. Understanding, remembering, or applying information (see 11.00G3b(i)); or

2. Interacting with others (see 11.00G3b(ii)); or

3. Concentrating, persisting, or maintaining pace (see 11.00G3b(iii)); or

4. Adapting or managing oneself (see 11.00G3b(iv)); or

C. Significant interference in communication due to speech, hearing, or visual deficit (see 11.00E2).

11.08 Spinal cord disorders, characterized by A, B, or C:

A. Complete loss of function, as described in 11.00M2, persisting for 3 consecutive months after the disorder (see 11.00M4); or

B. Disorganization of motor function in two extremities (see 11.00D1), resulting in an extreme limitation (see 11.00D2) in the ability to stand up from a seated position, balance while standing or walking, or use the upper extremities persisting for 3 consecutive months after the disorder (see 11.00M4); or

C. Marked limitation (see 11.00G2) in physical functioning (see 11.00G3a) and in one of the following areas of mental functioning, both persisting for 3 consecutive months after the disorder (see 11.00M4):

1. Understanding, remembering, or applying information (see 11.00G3b(i)); or

2. Interacting with others (see 11.00G3b(ii)); or

3. Concentrating, persisting, or maintaining pace (see 11.00G3b(iii)); or

4. Adapting or managing oneself (see 11.00G3b(iv)).

11.09 Multiple sclerosis, characterized by A or B:

A. Disorganization of motor function in two extremities (see 11.00D1), resulting in an extreme limitation (see 11.00D2) in the ability to stand up from a seated position, balance while standing or walking, or use the upper extremities; or

B. Marked limitation (see 11.00G2) in physical functioning (see 11.00G3a), and in one of the following:

1. Understanding, remembering, or applying information (see 11.00G3b(i)); or

2. Interacting with others (see 11.00G3b(ii)); or

3. Concentrating, persisting, or maintaining pace (see 11.00G3b(iii)); or

4. Adapting or managing oneself (see 11.00G3b(iv)).

11.10 Amyotrophic lateral sclerosis (ALS) established by clinical and laboratory findings (see 11.00O).

11.11 Post-polio syndrome, characterized by A, B, C, or D:

A. Disorganization of motor function in two extremities (see 11.00D1), resulting in an extreme limitation (see 11.00D2) in the ability to stand up from a seated position, balance while standing or walking, or use the upper extremities; or

B. Unintelligible speech (see 11.00E3); or

C. Bulbar and neuromuscular dysfunction (see 11.00F), resulting in:

1. Acute respiratory failure requiring mechanical ventilation; or

2. Need for supplemental enteral nutrition via a gastrostomy or parenteral nutrition via a central venous catheter; or

D. Marked limitation (see 11.00G2) in physical functioning (see 11.00G3a), and in one of the following:

1. Understanding, remembering, or applying information (see 11.00G3b(i)); or

2. Interacting with others (see 11.00G3b(ii)); or

3. Concentrating, persisting, or maintaining pace (see 11.00G3b(iii)); or

4. Adapting or managing oneself (see 11.00G3b(iv)).

11.12 Myasthenia gravis, characterized by A, B, or C despite adherence to prescribed treatment for at least 3 months (see 11.00C):

A. Disorganization of motor function in two extremities (see 11.00D1), resulting in an extreme limitation (see 11.00D2) in the ability to stand up from a seated position, balance while standing or walking, or use the upper extremities; or

B. Bulbar and neuromuscular dysfunction (see 11.00F), resulting in:

1. One myasthenic crisis requiring mechanical ventilation; or

2. Need for supplemental enteral nutrition via a gastrostomy or parenteral nutrition via a central venous catheter; or

C. Marked limitation (see 11.00G2) in physical functioning (see 11.00G3a), and in one of the following:

1. Understanding, remembering, or applying information (see 11.00G3b(i)); or

2. Interacting with others (see 11.00G3b(ii)); or

3. Concentrating, persisting, or maintaining pace (see 11.00G3b(iii)); or

4. Adapting or managing oneself (see 11.00G3b(iv)).

11.13 Muscular dystrophy, characterized by A or B:

A. Disorganization of motor function in two extremities (see 11.00D1), resulting in an extreme limitation (see 11.00D2) in the ability to stand up from a seated position, balance while standing or walking, or use the upper extremities; or

B. Marked limitation (see 11.00G2) in physical functioning (see 11.00G3a), and in one of the following:

1. Understanding, remembering, or applying information (see 11.00G3b(i)); or

2. Interacting with others (see 11.00G3b(ii)); or

3. Concentrating, persisting, or maintaining pace (see 11.00G3b(iii)); or

4. Adapting or managing oneself (see 11.00G3b(iv)).

11.14 Peripheral neuropathy, characterized by A or B:

A. Disorganization of motor function in two extremities (see 11.00D1), resulting in an extreme limitation (see 11.00D2) in the ability to stand up from a seated position, balance while standing or walking, or use the upper extremities; or

B. Marked limitation (see 11.00G2) in physical functioning (see 11.00G3a), and in one of the following:

1. Understanding, remembering, or applying information (see 11.00G3b(i)); or

2. Interacting with others (see 11.00G3b(ii)); or

3. Concentrating, persisting, or maintaining pace (see 11.00G3b(iii)); or

4. Adapting or managing oneself (see 11.00G3b(iv)).

11.15 [Reserved]

11.16 [Reserved]

11.17 Neurodegenerative disorders of the central nervous system, such as Huntington's disease, Friedreich's ataxia, and spinocerebellar degeneration, characterized by A or B:

A. Disorganization of motor function in two extremities (see 11.00D1), resulting in an extreme limitation (see 11.00D2) in the ability to stand up from a seated position, balance while standing or walking, or use the upper extremities; or

B. Marked limitation (see 11.00G2) in physical functioning (see 11.00G3a), and in one of the following:

1. Understanding, remembering, or applying information (see 11.00G3b(i)); or

2. Interacting with others (see 11.00G3b(ii)); or

3. Concentrating, persisting, or maintaining pace (see 11.00G3b(iii)); or

4. Adapting or managing oneself (see 11.00G3b(iv)).

11.18 Traumatic brain injury, characterized by A or B:

A. Disorganization of motor function in two extremities (see 11.00D1), resulting in an extreme limitation (see 11.00D2) in the ability to stand up from a seated position, balance while standing or walking, or use the upper extremities, persisting for at least 3 consecutive months after the injury; or

B. Marked limitation (see 11.00G2) in physical functioning (see 11.00G3a), and in one of the following areas of mental functioning, persisting for at least 3 consecutive months after the injury:

1. Understanding, remembering, or applying information (see 11.00G3b(i)); or

2. Interacting with others (see 11.00G3b(ii)); or

3. Concentrating, persisting, or maintaining pace (see 11.00G3b(iii)); or

4. Adapting or managing oneself (see 11.00G3b(iv)).

11.19 [Reserved]

11.20 Coma or persistent vegetative state, persisting for at least 1 month.

11.21 [Reserved]

11.22 Motor neuron disorders other than ALS, characterized by A, B, or C:

A. Disorganization of motor function in two extremities (see 11.00D1), resulting in an extreme limitation (see 11.00D2) in the ability to stand up from a seated position, balance while standing or walking, or use the upper extremities; or

B. Bulbar and neuromuscular dysfunction (see 11.00F), resulting in:

1. Acute respiratory failure requiring invasive mechanical ventilation; or

2. Need for supplemental enteral nutrition via a gastrostomy or parenteral nutrition via a central venous catheter; or

C. Marked limitation (see 11.00G2) in physical functioning (see 11.00G3a), and in one of the following:

1. Understanding, remembering, or applying information (see 11.00G3b(i)); or

2. Interacting with others (see 11.00G3b(ii)); or

3. Concentrating, persisting, or maintaining pace (see 11.00G3b(iii)); or

4. Adapting or managing oneself (see 11.00G3b(iv)).

12.00 Mental Disorders

A. How are the listings for mental disorders arranged, and what do they require?

1. The listings for mental disorders are arranged in 11 categories: Neurocognitive disorders (12.02); schizophrenia spectrum and other psychotic disorders (12.03); depressive, bipolar and related disorders (12.04); intellectual disorder (12.05); anxiety and obsessive-compulsive disorders (12.06); somatic symptom and related disorders (12.07); personality and impulse-control disorders (12.08); autism spectrum disorder (12.10); neurodevelopmental disorders (12.11); eating disorders (12.13); and trauma- and stressor-related disorders (12.15).

2. Listings 12.07, 12.08, 12.10, 12.11, and 12.13 have two paragraphs, designated A and B; your mental disorder must satisfy the requirements of both paragraphs A and B. Listings 12.02, 12.03, 12.04, 12.06, and 12.15 have three paragraphs, designated A, B, and C; your mental disorder must satisfy the requirements of both paragraphs A and B, or the requirements of both paragraphs A and C. Listing 12.05 has two paragraphs that are unique to that listing (see 12.00A3); your mental disorder must satisfy the requirements of either paragraph A or paragraph B.

a. Paragraph A of each listing (except 12.05) includes the medical criteria that must be present in your medical evidence.

b. Paragraph B of each listing (except 12.05) provides the functional criteria we assess, in conjunction with a rating scale (see 12.00E and 12.00F), to evaluate how your mental disorder limits your functioning. These criteria represent the areas of mental functioning a person uses in a work setting. They are: Understand, remember, or apply information; interact with others; concentrate, persist, or maintain pace; and adapt or manage oneself. We will determine the degree to which your medically determinable mental impairment affects the four areas of mental functioning and your ability to function independently, appropriately, effectively, and on a sustained basis (see §§ 404.1520a(c)(2) and 416.920a(c)(2) of this chapter). To satisfy the paragraph B criteria, your mental disorder must result in "extreme" limitation of one, or "marked" limitation of two, of the four areas of mental functioning. (When we refer to "paragraph B criteria" or "area[s] of mental functioning" in the introductory text of this body system, we mean the criteria in paragraph B of every listing except 12.05.)

c. Paragraph C of listings 12.02, 12.03, 12.04, 12.06, and 12.15 provides the criteria we use to evaluate "serious and persistent mental disorders." To satisfy the paragraph C criteria, your mental disorder must be "serious and persistent"; that is, there must be a medically documented history of the existence of the disorder over a period of at least 2 years, and evidence that satisfies the criteria in both C1 and C2 (see 12.00G). (When we refer to "paragraph C" or "the paragraph C criteria" in the introductory text of this body system, we mean the criteria in paragraph C of listings 12.02, 12.03, 12.04, 12.06, and 12.15.)

3. Listing 12.05 has two paragraphs, designated A and B, that apply to only intellectual disorder. Each paragraph requires that you have significantly subaverage general intellectual functioning; significant deficits in current adaptive functioning; and evidence that demonstrates or supports (is consistent with) the conclusion that your disorder began prior to age 22.

B. Which mental disorders do we evaluate under each listing category?

1. Neurocognitive disorders (12.02).

a. These disorders are characterized by a clinically significant decline in cognitive functioning. Symptoms and signs may include, but are not limited to, disturbances in memory, executive functioning (that is, higher-level cognitive processes; for example, regulating attention, planning, inhibiting responses, decision-making), visual-spatial functioning, language and speech, perception, insight, judgment, and insensitivity to social standards.

b. Examples of disorders that we evaluate in this category include major neurocognitive disorder; dementia of the Alzheimer type; vascular dementia; dementia due to a medical condition such as a metabolic disease (for example, late-onset Tay–Sachs disease), human immunodeficiency virus infection, vascular malformation, progressive brain tumor, neurological disease (for example, multiple sclerosis, Parkinsonian syndrome, Huntington disease), or traumatic brain injury; or substance-induced cognitive disorder associated with drugs of abuse, medications, or toxins. (We evaluate neurological disorders under that body system (see 11.00). We evaluate cognitive impairments that result from neurological disorders under 12.02 if they do not satisfy the requirements in 11.00 (see 11.00G).)

c. This category does not include the mental disorders that we evaluate under intellectual disorder (12.05), autism spectrum disorder (12.10), and neurodevelopmental disorders (12.11).

2. Schizophrenia spectrum and other psychotic disorders (12.03).

a. These disorders are characterized by delusions, hallucinations, disorganized speech, or grossly disorganized or catatonic behavior, causing a clinically significant decline in functioning. Symptoms and signs may include, but are not limited to, inability to initiate and persist in goal-directed activities, social withdrawal, flat or inappropriate affect, poverty of thought and speech, loss of interest or pleasure, disturbances of mood, odd beliefs and mannerisms, and paranoia.

b. Examples of disorders that we evaluate in this category include schizophrenia, schizoaffective disorder, delusional disorder, and psychotic disorder due to another medical condition.

3. Depressive, bipolar and related disorders (12.04).

a. These disorders are characterized by an irritable, depressed, elevated, or expansive mood, or by a loss of interest or pleasure in all or almost all activities, causing a clinically significant decline in functioning. Symptoms and signs may include, but are not limited to, feelings of hopelessness or guilt, suicidal ideation, a clinically significant change in body weight or appetite, sleep disturbances, an increase or decrease in energy, psychomotor abnormalities, disturbed concentration, pressured speech, grandiosity, reduced impulse control, sadness, euphoria, and social withdrawal.

b. Examples of disorders that we evaluate in this category include bipolar disorders (I or II), cyclothymic disorder, major depressive disorder, persistent depressive disorder (dysthymia), and bipolar or depressive disorder due to another medical condition.

4. Intellectual disorder (12.05).

a. This disorder is characterized by significantly subaverage general intellectual functioning, significant deficits in current adaptive functioning, and manifestation of the disorder before age 22. Signs may include, but are not limited to, poor conceptual, social, or practical skills evident in your adaptive functioning.

b. The disorder that we evaluate in this category may be described in the evidence as intellectual disability, intellectual developmental disorder, or historically used terms such as "mental retardation."

c. This category does not include the mental disorders that we evaluate under neurocognitive disorders (12.02), autism spectrum disorder (12.10), or neurodevelopmental disorders (12.11).

5. Anxiety and obsessive-compulsive disorders (12.06).

a. These disorders are characterized by excessive anxiety, worry, apprehension, and fear, or by avoidance of feelings, thoughts, activities, objects, places, or people. Symptoms and signs may include, but are not limited to, restlessness, difficulty concentrating, hypervigilance, muscle tension, sleep disturbance, fatigue, panic attacks, obsessions and compulsions, constant thoughts and fears about safety, and frequent physical complaints.

b. Examples of disorders that we evaluate in this category include social anxiety disorder, panic disorder, generalized anxiety disorder, agoraphobia, and obsessive-compulsive disorder.

c. This category does not include the mental disorders that we evaluate under trauma- and stressor-related disorders (12.15).

6. Somatic symptom and related disorders (12.07).

a. These disorders are characterized by physical symptoms or deficits that are not intentionally produced or feigned, and that, following clinical investigation, cannot be fully explained by a general medical condition, another mental disorder, the direct effects of a substance, or a culturally sanctioned behavior or experience. These disorders may also be characterized by a preoccupation with having or acquiring a serious medical condition that has not been identified or diagnosed. Symptoms and signs may include, but are not limited to, pain and other abnormalities of sensation, gastrointestinal symptoms, fatigue, a high level of anxiety about personal health status, abnormal motor movement, pseudoseizures, and pseudoneurological symptoms, such as blindness or deafness.

b. Examples of disorders that we evaluate in this category include somatic symptom disorder, illness anxiety disorder, and conversion disorder.

7. Personality and impulse-control disorders (12.08).

a. These disorders are characterized by enduring, inflexible, maladaptive, and pervasive patterns of behavior. Onset typically occurs in adolescence or young adulthood. Symptoms and signs may include, but are not limited to, patterns of distrust, suspiciousness, and odd beliefs; social detachment, discomfort, or avoidance; hypersensitivity to negative evaluation; an excessive need to be taken care of; difficulty making independent decisions; a preoccupation with orderliness, perfectionism, and control; and inappropriate, intense, impulsive anger and behavioral expression grossly out of proportion to any external provocation or psychosocial stressors.

b. Examples of disorders that we evaluate in this category include paranoid, schizoid, schizotypal, borderline, avoidant, dependent, obsessive-compulsive personality disorders, and intermittent explosive disorder.

8. Autism spectrum disorder (12.10).

a. These disorders are characterized by qualitative deficits in the development of reciprocal social interaction, verbal and nonverbal communication skills, and symbolic or imaginative activity; restricted repetitive and stereotyped patterns of behavior, interests, and activities; and stagnation of development or loss of acquired skills early in life. Symptoms and signs may include, but are not limited to, abnormalities and unevenness in the development of cognitive skills; unusual responses to sensory stimuli; and behavioral difficulties, including hyperactivity, short attention span, impulsivity, aggressiveness, or self-injurious actions.

b. Examples of disorders that we evaluate in this category include autism spectrum disorder with or without accompanying intellectual impairment, and autism spectrum disorder with or without accompanying language impairment.

c. This category does not include the mental disorders that we evaluate under neurocognitive disorders

(12.02), intellectual disorder (12.05), and neurodevelopmental disorders (12.11).

9. Neurodevelopmental disorders (12.11).

a. These disorders are characterized by onset during the developmental period, that is, during childhood or adolescence, although sometimes they are not diagnosed until adulthood. Symptoms and signs may include, but are not limited to, underlying abnormalities in cognitive processing (for example, deficits in learning and applying verbal or nonverbal information, visual perception, memory, or a combination of these); deficits in attention or impulse control; low frustration tolerance; excessive or poorly planned motor activity; difficulty with organizing (time, space, materials, or tasks); repeated accidental injury; and deficits in social skills. Symptoms and signs specific to tic disorders include sudden, rapid, recurrent, non-rhythmic, motor movement or vocalization.

b. Examples of disorders that we evaluate in this category include specific learning disorder, borderline intellectual functioning, and tic disorders (such as Tourette syndrome).

c. This category does not include the mental disorders that we evaluate under neurocognitive disorders (12.02), autism spectrum disorder (12.10), or personality and impulse-control disorders (12.08).

10. Eating disorders (12.13).

a. These disorders are characterized by disturbances in eating behavior and preoccupation with, and excessive self-evaluation of, body weight and shape. Symptoms and signs may include, but are not limited to, restriction of energy consumption when compared with individual requirements; recurrent episodes of binge eating or behavior intended to prevent weight gain, such as self-induced vomiting, excessive exercise, or misuse of laxatives; mood disturbances, social withdrawal, or irritability; amenorrhea; dental problems; abnormal laboratory findings; and cardiac abnormalities.

b. Examples of disorders that we evaluate in this category include anorexia nervosa, bulimia nervosa, binge-eating disorder, and avoidant/restrictive food disorder.

11. Trauma- and stressor-related disorders (12.15).

a. These disorders are characterized by experiencing or witnessing a traumatic or stressful event, or learning of a traumatic event occurring to a close family member or close friend, and the psychological aftermath of clinically significant effects on functioning. Symptoms and signs may include, but are not limited to, distressing memories, dreams, and flashbacks related to the trauma or stressor; avoidant behavior; diminished interest or participation in significant activities; persistent negative emotional states (for example, fear, anger) or persistent inability to experience positive emotions (for example, satisfaction, affection); anxiety; irritability; aggression; exaggerated startle response; difficulty concentrating; and sleep disturbance.

b. Examples of disorders that we evaluate in this category include posttraumatic stress disorder and other specified trauma- and stressor-related disorders (such as adjustment-like disorders with prolonged duration without prolonged duration of stressor).

c. This category does not include the mental disorders that we evaluate under anxiety and obsessive-compulsive disorders (12.06), and cognitive impairments that result from neurological disorders, such as a traumatic brain injury, which we evaluate under neurocognitive disorders (12.02).

C. What evidence do we need to evaluate your mental disorder?

1. General. We need objective medical evidence from an acceptable medical source to establish that you have a medically determinable mental disorder. We also need evidence to assess the severity of your mental disorder and its effects on your ability to function in a work setting. We will determine the extent and kinds of evidence we need from medical and nonmedical sources based on the individual facts about your disorder. For additional evidence requirements for intellectual disorder (12.05), see 12.00H. For our basic rules on evidence, see §§ 404.1512, 404.1513, 404.1520b, 416.912, 416.913, and 416.920b of this chapter. For our rules on evaluating medical opinions, see §§ 404.1520c, 404.1527, 416.920c, and 416.927 of this chapter. For our rules on evidence about your symptoms, see §§ 404.1529 and 416.929 of this chapter.

2. Evidence from medical sources. We will consider all relevant medical evidence about your disorder from your physician, psychologist, and other medical sources, which include health care providers such as physician assistants, psychiatric nurse practitioners, licensed clinical social workers, and clinical mental health counselors. Evidence from your medical sources may include:

a. Your reported symptoms.

b. Your medical, psychiatric, and psychological history.

c. The results of physical or mental status examinations, structured clinical interviews, psychiatric or psychological rating scales, measures of adaptive functioning, or other clinical findings.

d. Psychological testing, imaging results, or other laboratory findings.

e. Your diagnosis.

f. The type, dosage, and beneficial effects of medications you take.

g. The type, frequency, duration, and beneficial effects of therapy you receive.

h. Side effects of medication or other treatment that limit your ability to function.

i. Your clinical course, including changes in your medication, therapy, or other treatment, and the time required for therapeutic effectiveness.

j. Observations and descriptions of how you function during examinations or therapy.

k. Information about sensory, motor, or speech abnormalities, or about your cultural background (for example, language or customs) that may affect an evaluation of your mental disorder.

l. The expected duration of your symptoms and signs and their effects on your functioning, both currently and in the future.

3. Evidence from you and people who know you. We will consider all relevant evidence about your mental disorder and your daily functioning that we receive from you and from people who know you. We will ask about your symptoms, your daily functioning, and your medical treatment. We will ask for information from third parties who can tell us about your mental disorder, but you must give us permission to do so. This evidence may include information from your family, caregivers, friends, neighbors, clergy, case managers, social workers, shelter staff, or other community support and outreach workers. We will consider whether your statements and the statements from third parties are consistent with the medical and other evidence we have.

4. Evidence from school, vocational training, work, and work-related programs.

a. School. You may have recently attended or may still be attending school, and you may have received or may still be receiving special education services. If so, we will try to obtain information from your school sources when we need it to assess how your mental disorder affects your ability to function. Examples of this information include your Individualized Education Programs (IEPs), your Section 504 plans, comprehensive evaluation reports, school-related therapy progress notes, information from your teachers about how you function in a classroom setting, and information about any special services or accommodations you receive at school.

b. Vocational training, work, and work-related programs. You may have recently participated in or may still be participating in vocational training, work-related programs, or work activity. If so, we will try to obtain information from your training program or your employer when we need it to assess how your mental disorder affects your ability to function. Examples of this information include training or work evaluations, modifications to your work duties or work schedule, and any special supports or accommodations you have required or now require in order to work. If you have worked or are working through a community mental health program, sheltered or supported work program, rehabilitation program, or transitional employment program, we will consider the type and degree of support you have received or are receiving in order to work (see 12.00D).

5. Need for longitudinal evidence.

a. General. Longitudinal medical evidence can help us learn how you function over time, and help us evaluate any variations in the level of your functioning. We will request longitudinal evidence of your mental disorder when your medical providers have records concerning you and your mental disorder over a period of months or perhaps years (see §§ 404.1512(d) and 416.912(d) of this chapter).

b. Non-medical sources of longitudinal evidence. Certain situations, such as chronic homelessness, may make it difficult for you to provide longitudinal medical evidence. If you have a severe mental disorder, you will probably have evidence of its effects on your functioning over time, even if you have not had an ongoing relationship with the medical community or are not currently receiving treatment. For example, family members, friends, neighbors, former employers, social workers, case managers, community support staff, outreach workers, or government agencies may be familiar with your mental health history. We will ask for information from third parties who can tell us about your mental disorder, but you must give us permission to do so.

c. Absence of longitudinal evidence. In the absence of longitudinal evidence, we will use current objective medical evidence and all other relevant evidence available to us in your case record to evaluate your mental disorder. If we purchase a consultative examination to document your disorder, the record will include the results of that examination (see §§ 404.1514 and 416.914 of this chapter). We will take into consideration your medical history, symptoms, clinical and laboratory findings, and medical source opinions. If you do not have longitudinal evidence, the current evidence alone may not be sufficient or appropriate to show that you have a disorder that meets the criteria of one of the mental disorders listings. In that case, we will follow the rules in 12.00J.

6. Evidence of functioning in unfamiliar situations or supportive situations.

a. Unfamiliar situations. We recognize that evidence about your functioning in unfamiliar situations does not necessarily show how you would function on a sustained basis in a work setting. In one-time, time-limited, or other unfamiliar situations, you may function differently than you do in familiar situations. In unfamiliar situations, you may appear more, or less, limited than you do on a daily basis and over time.

b. Supportive situations. Your ability to complete tasks in settings that are highly structured, or that are less demanding or more supportive than typical work settings does not necessarily demonstrate your ability to complete tasks in the context of regular employment during a normal workday or work week.

c. Our assessment. We must assess your ability to complete tasks by evaluating all the evidence, such as reports about your functioning from you and third parties who are familiar with you, with an emphasis on how independently, appropriately, and effectively you are able to complete tasks on a sustained basis.

D. How do we consider psychosocial supports, structured settings, living arrangements, and treatment?

1. General. Psychosocial supports, structured settings, and living arrangements, including assistance from your family or others, may help you by reducing the demands made on you. In addition, treatment you receive may reduce your symptoms and signs and possibly improve your functioning, or may have side effects that limit your functioning. Therefore, when we evaluate the effects of your mental disorder and rate the limitation of your areas of mental functioning, we will consider the kind and extent of supports you receive, the characteristics of any structured setting in which you spend your time, and the effects of any treatment. This evidence may come from reports about your functioning from you or third parties who are familiar with you, and other third-party statements or information. Following are some examples of the supports you may receive:

a. You receive help from family members or other people who monitor your daily activities and help you to function. For example, family members administer your medications, remind you to eat, shop for you and pay your bills, or change their work hours so you are never home alone.

b. You participate in a special education or vocational training program, or a psychosocial rehabilitation day treatment or community support program, where you receive training in daily living and entry-level work skills.

c. You participate in a sheltered, supported, or transitional work program, or in a competitive employment setting with the help of a job coach or supervisor.

d. You receive comprehensive "24/7 wrap-around" mental health services while living in a group home or transitional housing, while participating in a semi-independent living program, or while living in individual housing (for example, your own home or apartment).

e. You live in a hospital or other institution with 24–hour care.

f. You receive assistance from a crisis response team, social workers, or community mental health workers who help you meet your physical needs, and who may also represent you in dealings with government or community social services.

g. You live alone and do not receive any psychosocial support(s); however, you have created a highly structured environment by eliminating all but minimally necessary contact with the world outside your living space.

2. How we consider different levels of support and structure in psychosocial rehabilitation programs.

a. Psychosocial rehabilitation programs are based on your specific needs. Therefore, we cannot make any assumptions about your mental disorder based solely on the fact that you are associated with such a program. We must know the details of the program(s) in which you are involved and the pattern(s) of your involvement over time.

b. The kinds and levels of supports and structures in psychosocial rehabilitation programs typically occur on a scale of "most restrictive" to "least restrictive." Participation in a psychosocial rehabilitation program at the most restrictive level would suggest greater limitation of your areas of mental functioning than would participation at a less restrictive level. The length of time you spend at different levels in a program also provides information about your functioning. For example, you could begin participation at the most restrictive crisis intervention level but gradually improve to the point of readiness for a lesser level of support and structure and possibly some form of employment.

3. How we consider the help or support you receive.

a. We will consider the complete picture of your daily functioning, including the kinds, extent, and frequency of help and support you receive, when we evaluate your mental disorder and determine whether you are able to use the four areas of mental functioning in a work setting. The fact that you have done, or currently do, some routine activities without help or support does not necessarily mean that you do not have a mental disorder or that you are not disabled. For example, you may be able to take care of your personal needs, cook, shop, pay your bills, live by yourself, and drive a car. You may demonstrate both strengths and deficits in your daily functioning.

b. You may receive various kinds of help and support from others that enable you to do many things that, because of your mental disorder, you might not be able to do independently. Your daily functioning may depend on the special contexts in which you function. For example, you may spend your time among only familiar people or surroundings, in a simple and steady routine or an unchanging environment, or in a highly structured setting. However, this does not necessarily show how you would function in a work setting on a sustained basis, throughout a normal workday and workweek. (See 12.00H for further discussion of these issues regarding significant deficits in adaptive functioning for the purpose of 12.05.)

4. How we consider treatment. We will consider the effect of any treatment on your functioning when we evaluate your mental disorder. Treatment may include medication(s), psychotherapy, or other forms of intervention, which you receive in a doctor's office, during a hospitalization, or in a day program at a hospital or outpatient treatment program. With treatment, you may not only have your symptoms and signs reduced, but may also be able to function in a work setting. However, treatment may not resolve all of the limitations that result from your mental disorder, and the medications you take or other treatment you receive for your disorder may cause side effects that limit your mental or physical functioning. For example, you may experience drowsiness, blunted affect, memory loss, or abnormal involuntary movements.

E. What are the paragraph B criteria?

1. Understand, remember, or apply information (paragraph B1). This area of mental functioning refers to the abilities to learn, recall, and use information to perform work activities. Examples include: Understanding and learning terms, instructions, procedures; following one- or two-step oral instructions to carry out a task; describing work activity to someone else; asking and answering questions and providing explanations; recognizing a mistake and correcting it; identifying and solving problems; sequencing multi-step activities; and using reason and judgment to make work-related decisions. These examples illustrate the nature of this area of mental functioning. We do not require documentation of all of the examples.

2. Interact with others (paragraph B2). This area of mental functioning refers to the abilities to relate to and work with supervisors, co-workers, and the public. Examples include: cooperating with others; asking for help when needed; handling conflicts with others; stating own point of view; initiating or sustaining conversation; understanding and responding to social cues (physical, verbal, emotional); responding to requests, suggestions, criticism, correction, and challenges; and keeping social interactions free of excessive irritability, sensitivity, argumentativeness, or suspiciousness. These examples illustrate the nature of this area of mental functioning. We do not require documentation of all of the examples.

3. Concentrate, persist, or maintain pace (paragraph B3). This area of mental functioning refers to the abilities to focus attention on work activities and stay on task at a sustained rate. Examples include: Initiating and performing a task that you understand and know how to do; working at an appropriate and consistent pace; completing tasks in a timely manner; ignoring or avoiding distractions while working; changing activities or work settings without being disruptive; working close to or with others without interrupting or distracting them; sustaining an ordinary routine and regular attendance at work; and working a full day without needing more than the allotted number or length of rest periods during the day. These examples illustrate the nature of this area of mental functioning. We do not require documentation of all of the examples.

4. Adapt or manage oneself (paragraph B4). This area of mental functioning refers to the abilities to regulate emotions, control behavior, and maintain well-being in a work setting. Examples include: Responding to demands; adapting to changes; managing your psychologically based symptoms; distinguishing between acceptable and unacceptable work performance; setting realistic goals; making plans for yourself independently of others; maintaining personal hygiene and attire appropriate to a work setting; and being aware of normal hazards and taking appropriate precautions. These examples illustrate the nature of this area of mental functioning. We do not require documentation of all of the examples.

F. How do we use the paragraph B criteria to evaluate your mental disorder?

1. General. We use the paragraph B criteria, in conjunction with a rating scale (see 12.00F2), to rate the degree of your limitations. We consider only the limitations that result from your mental disorder(s). We will determine whether you are able to use each of the paragraph B areas of mental functioning in a work setting. We will consider, for example, the kind, degree, and frequency of difficulty you would have; whether you could function without extra help, structure, or supervision; and whether you would require special conditions with regard to activities or other people (see 12.00D).

2. The five-point rating scale. We evaluate the effects of your mental disorder on each of the four areas of mental functioning based on a five-point rating scale consisting of none, mild, moderate, marked, and extreme limitation. To satisfy the paragraph B criteria, your mental disorder must result in extreme limitation of one, or marked limitation of two, paragraph B areas of mental functioning. Under these listings, the five rating points are defined as follows:

a. No limitation (or none). You are able to function in this area independently, appropriately, effectively, and on a sustained basis.

b. Mild limitation. Your functioning in this area independently, appropriately, effectively, and on a sustained basis is slightly limited.

c. Moderate limitation. Your functioning in this area independently, appropriately, effectively, and on a sustained basis is fair.

d. Marked limitation. Your functioning in this area independently, appropriately, effectively, and on a sustained basis is seriously limited.

e. Extreme limitation. You are not able to function in this area independently, appropriately, effectively, and on a sustained basis.

3. Rating the limitations of your areas of mental functioning.

a. General. We use all of the relevant medical and non-medical evidence in your case record to evaluate your mental disorder: The symptoms and signs of your disorder, the reported limitations in your activities, and any help and support you receive that is necessary for you to function. The medical evidence may include descriptors regarding the diagnostic stage or level of your disorder, such as "mild" or "moderate." Clinicians may use these terms to characterize your medical condition. However, these terms will not always be the same as the degree of your limitation in a paragraph B area of mental functioning.

b. Areas of mental functioning in daily activities. You use the same four areas of mental functioning in daily activities at home and in the community that you would use to function at work. With respect to a particular task or activity, you may have trouble using one or more of the areas. For example, you may have difficulty understanding and remembering what to do; or concentrating and staying on task long enough to do it; or engaging in the task or activity with other people; or trying to do the task without becoming frustrated and losing self-control. Information about your daily functioning can help us understand whether your mental disorder limits one or more of these areas; and, if so, whether it also affects your ability to function in a work setting.

c. Areas of mental functioning in work settings. If you have difficulty using an area of mental functioning from day-to-day at home or in your community, you may also have difficulty using that area to function in a work setting. On the other hand, if you are able to use an area of mental functioning at home or in your community, we will not necessarily assume that you would also be able to use that area to function in a work setting where the demands and stressors differ from those at home. We will consider all evidence about your mental disorder and daily functioning before we reach a conclusion about your ability to work.

d. Overall effect of limitations. Limitation of an area of mental functioning reflects the overall degree to which your mental disorder interferes with that area. The degree of limitation is how we document our assessment of your limitation when using the area of mental functioning independently, appropriately, effectively, and on a sustained basis. It does not necessarily reflect a specific type or number of activities, including activities of daily living, that you have difficulty doing. In addition, no single piece of information (including test results) can establish the degree of limitation of an area of mental functioning.

e. Effects of support, supervision, structure on functioning. The degree of limitation of an area of mental functioning also reflects the kind and extent of supports or supervision you receive and the characteristics of any structured setting where you spend your time, which enable you to function. The more extensive the support you need from others or the more structured the setting you need in order to function, the more limited we will find you to be (see 12.00D).

f. Specific instructions for paragraphs B1, B3, and B4. For paragraphs B1, B3, and B4, the greatest degree of limitation of any part of the area of mental functioning directs the rating of limitation of that whole area of mental functioning.

(i) To do a work-related task, you must be able to understand and remember and apply information required by the task. Similarly, you must be able to concentrate and persist and maintain pace in order to complete the task, and adapt and manage yourself in the workplace. Limitation in any one of these parts (understand or remember or apply; concentrate or persist or maintain pace; adapt or manage oneself) may prevent you from completing a work-related task.

(ii) We will document the rating of limitation of the whole area of mental functioning, not each individual part. We will not add ratings of the parts together. For example, with respect to paragraph B3, if you have marked limitation in maintaining pace, and mild or moderate limitations in concentrating and persisting, we will find that you have marked limitation in the whole paragraph B3 area of mental functioning.

(iii) Marked limitation in more than one part of the same paragraph B area of mental functioning does not satisfy the requirement to have marked limitation in two paragraph B areas of mental functioning.

4. How we evaluate mental disorders involving exacerbations and remissions.

a. When we evaluate the effects of your mental disorder, we will consider how often you have exacerbations and remissions, how long they last, what causes your mental disorder to worsen or improve, and any other relevant information. We will assess any limitation of the affected paragraph B area(s) of mental functioning using the rating scale for the paragraph B criteria. We will consider whether you can use the area of mental functioning on a regular and continuing basis (8 hours a day, 5 days a week, or an equivalent work schedule). We will not find that you are able to work solely because you have a period(s) of improvement (remission), or that you are disabled solely because you have a period of worsening (exacerbation), of your mental disorder.

b. If you have a mental disorder involving exacerbations and remissions, you may be able to use the four areas of mental functioning to work for a few weeks or months. Recurrence or worsening of symptoms and signs, however, can interfere enough to render you unable to sustain the work.

G. What are the paragraph C criteria, and how do we use them to evaluate your mental disorder?

1. General. The paragraph C criteria are an alternative to the paragraph B criteria under listings 12.02, 12.03, 12.04, 12.06, and 12.15. We use the paragraph C criteria to evaluate mental disorders that are "serious and persistent." In the paragraph C criteria, we recognize that mental health interventions may control the more obvious symptoms and signs of your mental disorder.

2. Paragraph C criteria.

a. We find a mental disorder to be "serious and persistent" when there is a medically documented history of the existence of the mental disorder in the listing category over a period of at least 2 years, and evidence shows that your disorder satisfies both C1 and C2.

b. The criterion in C1 is satisfied when the evidence shows that you rely, on an ongoing basis, upon medical treatment, mental health therapy, psychosocial support(s), or a highly structured setting(s), to diminish the symptoms and signs of your mental disorder (see 12.00D). We consider that you receive ongoing medical treatment when the medical evidence establishes that you obtain medical treatment with a frequency consistent with accepted medical practice for the type of treatment or evaluation required for your medical condition. We will consider periods of inconsistent treatment or lack of compliance with treatment that may result from your mental disorder. If the evidence indicates that the inconsistent treatment or lack of compliance is a feature of your mental disorder, and it has led to an exacerbation of your symptoms and signs, we will not use it as evidence to support a finding that you have not received ongoing medical treatment as required by this paragraph.

c. The criterion in C2 is satisfied when the evidence shows that, despite your diminished symptoms and signs, you have achieved only marginal adjustment. "Marginal adjustment" means that your adaptation to the requirements of daily life is fragile; that is, you have minimal capacity to adapt to changes in your environment or to demands that are not already part of your daily life. We will consider that you have achieved only marginal adjustment when the evidence shows that changes or increased demands have led to exacerbation of your symptoms and signs and to deterioration in your functioning; for example, you have become unable to function outside of your home or a more restrictive setting, without substantial psychosocial supports (see 12.00D). Such deterioration may have necessitated a significant change in medication or other treatment. Similarly, because of the nature of your mental disorder, evidence may document episodes of deterioration that have required you to be hospitalized or absent from work, making it difficult for you to sustain work activity over time.

H. How do we document and evaluate intellectual disorder under 12.05?

1. General. Listing 12.05 is based on the three elements that characterize intellectual disorder: Significantly subaverage general intellectual functioning; significant deficits in current adaptive functioning; and the disorder manifested before age 22.

2. Establishing significantly subaverage general intellectual functioning.

a. Definition. Intellectual functioning refers to the general mental capacity to learn, reason, plan, solve problems, and perform other cognitive functions. Under 12.05A, we identify significantly subaverage general intellectual functioning by the cognitive inability to function at a level required to participate in standardized intelligence testing. Our findings under 12.05A are based on evidence from an acceptable medical source. Under 12.05B, we identify significantly subaverage general intellectual functioning by an IQ score(s) on an individually administered standardized test of general intelligence that meets program requirements and has a mean of 100 and a standard deviation of 15. A qualified specialist (see 12.00H2c) must administer the standardized intelligence testing.

b. Psychometric standards. We will find standardized intelligence test results usable for the purposes of 12.05B1 when the measure employed meets contemporary psychometric standards for validity, reliability, normative data, and scope of measurement; and a qualified specialist has individually administered the test according to all pre-requisite testing conditions.

c. Qualified specialist. A "qualified specialist" is currently licensed or certified at the independent level of practice in the State where the test was performed, and has the training and experience to administer, score, and interpret intelligence tests. If a psychological assistant or paraprofessional administered the test, a supervisory qualified specialist must interpret the test findings and co-sign the examination report.

d. Responsibility for conclusions based on testing. We generally presume that your obtained IQ score(s) is an accurate reflection of your general intellectual functioning, unless evidence in the record suggests otherwise. Examples of this evidence include: a statement from the test administrator indicating that your obtained score is not an accurate reflection of your general intellectual functioning, prior or internally inconsistent IQ scores, or information about your daily functioning. Only qualified specialists, Federal and State agency medical and psychological consultants, and other contracted medical and psychological experts may conclude that your obtained IQ score(s) is not an accurate reflection of your general intellectual functioning. This conclusion must be well supported by appropriate clinical and laboratory diagnostic techniques and must be based on relevant evidence in the case record, such as:

(i) The data obtained in testing;

(ii) Your developmental history, including when your signs and symptoms began;

(iii) Information about how you function on a daily basis in a variety of settings; and

(iv) Clinical observations made during the testing period, such as your ability to sustain attention, concentration, and effort; to relate appropriately to the examiner; and to perform tasks independently without prompts or reminders.

3. Establishing significant deficits in adaptive functioning.

a. Definition. Adaptive functioning refers to how you learn and use conceptual, social, and practical skills in dealing with common life demands. It is your typical functioning at home and in the community, alone or among others. Under 12.05A, we identify significant deficits in adaptive functioning based on your dependence on others to care for your personal needs, such as eating and bathing. We will base our conclusions about your adaptive functioning on evidence from a variety of sources (see 12.00H3b) and not on your statements alone. Under 12.05B2, we identify significant deficits in adaptive functioning based on whether there is extreme limitation of one, or marked limitation of two, of the paragraph B criteria (see 12.00E; 12.00F).

b. Evidence. Evidence about your adaptive functioning may come from:

(i) Medical sources, including their clinical observations;

(ii) Standardized tests of adaptive functioning (see 12.00H3c);

(iii) Third party information, such as a report of your functioning from a family member or friend;

(iv) School records, if you were in school recently;

(v) Reports from employers or supervisors; and

(vi) Your own statements about how you handle all of your daily activities.

c. Standardized tests of adaptive functioning. We do not require the results of an individually administered standardized test of adaptive functioning. If your case record includes these test results, we will consider the results along with all other relevant evidence; however, we will use the guidelines in 12.00E and F to evaluate and determine the degree of your deficits in adaptive functioning, as required under 12.05B2.

d. How we consider common everyday activities.

(i) The fact that you engage in common everyday activities, such as caring for your personal needs, preparing simple meals, or driving a car, will not always mean that you do not have deficits in adaptive functioning as required by 12.05B2. You may demonstrate both strengths and deficits in your adaptive functioning. However, a lack of deficits in one area does not negate the presence of deficits in another area. When we assess your adaptive functioning, we will consider all of your activities and your performance of them.

(ii) Our conclusions about your adaptive functioning rest on whether you do your daily activities independently, appropriately, effectively, and on a sustained basis. If you receive help in performing your activities, we need to know the kind, extent, and frequency of help you receive in order to perform them. We will not assume that your ability to do some common everyday activities, or to do some things without help or support, demonstrates that your mental disorder does not meet the requirements of 12.05B2. (See 12.00D regarding the factors we consider when we evaluate your functioning, including how we consider any help or support you receive.)

e. How we consider work activity. The fact that you have engaged in work activity, or that you work intermittently or steadily in a job commensurate with your abilities, will not always mean that you do not have deficits in adaptive functioning as required by 12.05B2. When you have engaged in work activity, we need complete information about the work, and about your functioning in the work activity and work setting, before we reach any conclusions about your adaptive functioning. We will consider all factors involved in your work history before concluding whether your impairment satisfies the criteria for intellectual disorder under 12.05B. We will consider your prior and current work history, if any, and various other factors influencing how you function. For example, we consider whether the work was in a supported setting, whether you required more supervision than other employees, how your job duties compared to others in the same job, how much time it took you to learn the job duties, and the reason the work ended, if applicable.

4. Establishing that the disorder began before age 22. We require evidence that demonstrates or supports (is consistent with) the conclusion that your mental disorder began prior to age 22. We do not require evidence that your impairment met all of the requirements of 12.05A or 12.05B prior to age 22. Also, we do not require you to have met our statutory definition of disability prior to age 22. When we do not have evidence that was recorded before you attained age 22, we need evidence about your current intellectual and adaptive functioning and the history of your disorder that supports the conclusion that the disorder began before you attained age 22. Examples of evidence that can demonstrate or support this conclusion include:

a. Tests of intelligence or adaptive functioning;

b. School records indicating a history of special education services based on your intellectual functioning;

c. An Individualized Education Program (IEP), including your transition plan;

d. Reports of your academic performance and functioning at school;

e. Medical treatment records;

f. Interviews or reports from employers;

g. Statements from a supervisor in a group home or a sheltered workshop; and

h. Statements from people who have known you and can tell us about your functioning in the past and currently.

I. How do we evaluate substance use disorders? If we find that you are disabled and there is medical evidence in your case record establishing that you have a substance use disorder, we will determine whether your substance use disorder is a contributing factor material to the determination of disability (see §§ 404.1535 and 416.935 of this chapter).

J. How do we evaluate mental disorders that do not meet one of the mental disorders listings?

1. These listings include only examples of mental disorders that we consider serious enough to prevent you from doing any gainful activity. If your severe mental disorder does not meet the criteria of any of these listings, we will consider whether you have an impairment(s) that meets the criteria of a listing in another body system. You may have another impairment(s) that is secondary to your mental disorder. For example, if you have an eating disorder and develop a cardiovascular impairment because of it, we will evaluate your cardiovascular impairment under the listings for the cardiovascular body system.

2. If you have a severe medically determinable impairment(s) that does not meet a listing, we will determine whether your impairment(s) medically equals a listing (see §§ 404.1526 and 416.926 of this chapter).

3. If your impairment(s) does not meet or medically equal a listing, we will assess your residual functional capacity for engaging in substantial gainful activity (see §§ 404.1545 and 416.945 of this chapter). When we assess your residual functional capacity, we consider all of your impairment-related mental and physical limitations. For example, the side effects of some medications may reduce your general alertness, concentration, or physical stamina, affecting your residual functional capacity for non-exertional or exertional work activities. Once we have determined your residual functional capacity, we proceed to the fourth, and if necessary, the fifth steps of the sequential evaluation process in §§ 404.1520 and 416.920 of this chapter. We use the rules in §§ 404.1594 and 416.994 of this chapter, as appropriate, when we decide whether you continue to be disabled.

12.01 Category of Impairments, Mental Disorders

12.02 Neurocognitive disorders (see 12.00B1), satisfied by A and B, or A and C:

A. Medical documentation of a significant cognitive decline from a prior level of functioning in one or more of the cognitive areas:

1. Complex attention;

2. Executive function;

3. Learning and memory;

4. Language;

5. Perceptual-motor; or

6. Social cognition.

AND

B. Extreme limitation of one, or marked limitation of two, of the following areas of mental functioning (see 12.00F):

1. Understand, remember, or apply information (see 12.00E1).

2. Interact with others (see 12.00E2).

3. Concentrate, persist, or maintain pace (see 12.00E3).

4. Adapt or manage oneself (see 12.00E4).

OR

C. Your mental disorder in this listing category is "serious and persistent;" that is, you have a medically documented history of the existence of the disorder over a period of at least 2 years, and there is evidence of both:

1. Medical treatment, mental health therapy, psychosocial support(s), or a highly structured setting(s) that is ongoing and that diminishes the symptoms and signs of your mental disorder (see 12.00G2b); and

2. Marginal adjustment, that is, you have minimal capacity to adapt to changes in your environment or to demands that are not already part of your daily life (see 12.00G2c).

12.03 Schizophrenia spectrum and other psychotic disorders (see 12.00B2), satisfied by A and B, or A and C:

A. Medical documentation of one or more of the following:

1. Delusions or hallucinations;

2. Disorganized thinking (speech); or

3. Grossly disorganized behavior or catatonia.

AND

B. Extreme limitation of one, or marked limitation of two, of the following areas of mental functioning (see 12.00F):

1. Understand, remember, or apply information (see 12.00E1).

2. Interact with others (see 12.00E2).

3. Concentrate, persist, or maintain pace (see 12.00E3).

4. Adapt or manage oneself (see 12.00E4).

OR

C. Your mental disorder in this listing category is "serious and persistent;" that is, you have a medically documented history of the existence of the disorder over a period of at least 2 years, and there is evidence of both:

1. Medical treatment, mental health therapy, psychosocial support(s), or a highly structured setting(s) that is ongoing and that diminishes the symptoms and signs of your mental disorder (see 12.00G2b); and

2. Marginal adjustment, that is, you have minimal capacity to adapt to changes in your environment or to demands that are not already part of your daily life (see 12.00G2c).

12.04 Depressive, bipolar and related disorders (see 12.00B3), satisfied by A and B, or A and C:

A. Medical documentation of the requirements of paragraph 1 or 2:

1. Depressive disorder, characterized by five or more of the following:

a. Depressed mood;

b. Diminished interest in almost all activities;

c. Appetite disturbance with change in weight;

d. Sleep disturbance;

e. Observable psychomotor agitation or retardation;

f. Decreased energy;

g. Feelings of guilt or worthlessness;

h. Difficulty concentrating or thinking; or

i. Thoughts of death or suicide.

2. Bipolar disorder, characterized by three or more of the following:

a. Pressured speech;

b. Flight of ideas;

c. Inflated self-esteem;

d. Decreased need for sleep;

e. Distractibility;

f. Involvement in activities that have a high probability of painful consequences that are not recognized; or

g. Increase in goal-directed activity or psychomotor agitation.

AND

B. Extreme limitation of one, or marked limitation of two, of the following areas of mental functioning (see 12.00F):

1. Understand, remember, or apply information (see 12.00E1).

2. Interact with others (see 12.00E2).

3. Concentrate, persist, or maintain pace (see 12.00E3).

4. Adapt or manage oneself (see 12.00E4).

OR

C. Your mental disorder in this listing category is "serious and persistent;" that is, you have a medically documented history of the existence of the disorder over a period of at least 2 years, and there is evidence of both:

1. Medical treatment, mental health therapy, psychosocial support(s), or a highly structured setting(s) that is ongoing and that diminishes the symptoms and signs of your mental disorder (see 12.00G2b); and

2. Marginal adjustment, that is, you have minimal capacity to adapt to changes in your environment or to demands that are not already part of your daily life (see 12.00G2c).

12.05 Intellectual disorder (see 12.00B4), satisfied by A or B:

A. Satisfied by 1, 2, and 3 (see 12.00H):

1. Significantly subaverage general intellectual functioning evident in your cognitive inability to function at a level required to participate in standardized testing of intellectual functioning; and

2. Significant deficits in adaptive functioning currently manifested by your dependence upon others for personal needs (for example, toileting, eating, dressing, or bathing); and

3. The evidence about your current intellectual and adaptive functioning and about the history of your disorder demonstrates or supports the conclusion that the disorder began prior to your attainment of age 22.

OR

B. Satisfied by 1, 2, and 3 (see 12.00H):

1. Significantly subaverage general intellectual functioning evidenced by a or b:

a. A full scale (or comparable) IQ score of 70 or below on an individually administered standardized test of general intelligence; or

b. A full scale (or comparable) IQ score of 71–75 accompanied by a verbal or performance IQ score (or comparable part score) of 70 or below on an individually administered standardized test of general intelligence; and

2. Significant deficits in adaptive functioning currently manifested by extreme limitation of one, or marked limitation of two, of the following areas of mental functioning:

a. Understand, remember, or apply information (see 12.00E1); or

b. Interact with others (see 12.00E2); or

c. Concentrate, persist, or maintain pace (see 12.00E3); or

d. Adapt or manage oneself (see 12.00E4); and

3. The evidence about your current intellectual and adaptive functioning and about the history of your disorder demonstrates or supports the conclusion that the disorder began prior to your attainment of age 22.

12.06 Anxiety and obsessive-compulsive disorders (see 12.00B5), satisfied by A and B, or A and C:

A. Medical documentation of the requirements of paragraph 1, 2, or 3:

1. Anxiety disorder, characterized by three or more of the following;

a. Restlessness;

b. Easily fatigued;

c. Difficulty concentrating;

d. Irritability;

e. Muscle tension; or

f. Sleep disturbance.

2. Panic disorder or agoraphobia, characterized by one or both:

a. Panic attacks followed by a persistent concern or worry about additional panic attacks or their consequences; or

b. Disproportionate fear or anxiety about at least two different situations (for example, using public transportation, being in a crowd, being in a line, being outside of your home, being in open spaces).

3. Obsessive-compulsive disorder, characterized by one or both:

a. Involuntary, time-consuming preoccupation with intrusive, unwanted thoughts; or

b. Repetitive behaviors aimed at reducing anxiety.

AND

B. Extreme limitation of one, or marked limitation of two, of the following areas of mental functioning (see 12.00F):

1. Understand, remember, or apply information (see 12.00E1).

2. Interact with others (see 12.00E2).

3. Concentrate, persist, or maintain pace (see 12.00E3).

4. Adapt or manage oneself (see 12.00E4).

OR

C. Your mental disorder in this listing category is "serious and persistent;" that is, you have a medically documented history of the existence of the disorder over a period of at least 2 years, and there is evidence of both:

1. Medical treatment, mental health therapy, psychosocial support(s), or a highly structured setting(s) that is ongoing and that diminishes the symptoms and signs of your mental disorder (see 12.00G2b); and

2. Marginal adjustment, that is, you have minimal capacity to adapt to changes in your environment or to demands that are not already part of your daily life (see 12.00G2c).

12.07 Somatic symptom and related disorders (see 12.00B6), satisfied by A and B:

A. Medical documentation of one or more of the following:

1. Symptoms of altered voluntary motor or sensory function that are not better explained by another medical or mental disorder;

2. One or more somatic symptoms that are distressing, with excessive thoughts, feelings, or behaviors related to the symptoms; or

3. Preoccupation with having or acquiring a serious illness without significant symptoms present.

AND

B. Extreme limitation of one, or marked limitation of two, of the following areas of mental functioning (see 12.00F):

1. Understand, remember, or apply information (see 12.00E1).

2. Interact with others (see 12.00E2).

3. Concentrate, persist, or maintain pace (see 12.00E3).

4. Adapt or manage oneself (see 12.00E4).

12.08 Personality and impulse-control disorders (see 12.00B7), satisfied by A and B:

A. Medical documentation of a pervasive pattern of one or more of the following:

1. Distrust and suspiciousness of others;

2. Detachment from social relationships;

3. Disregard for and violation of the rights of others;

4. Instability of interpersonal relationships;

5. Excessive emotionality and attention seeking;

6. Feelings of inadequacy;

7. Excessive need to be taken care of;

8. Preoccupation with perfectionism and orderliness; or

9. Recurrent, impulsive, aggressive behavioral outbursts.

AND

B. Extreme limitation of one, or marked limitation of two, of the following areas of mental functioning (see 12.00F):

1. Understand, remember, or apply information (see 12.00E1).

2. Interact with others (see 12.00E2).

3. Concentrate, persist, or maintain pace (see 12.00E3).

4. Adapt or manage oneself (see 12.00E4).

12.09 [Reserved]

12.10 Autism spectrum disorder (see 12.00B8), satisfied by A and B:

A. Medical documentation of both of the following:

1. Qualitative deficits in verbal communication, nonverbal communication, and social interaction; and

2. Significantly restricted, repetitive patterns of behavior, interests, or activities.

AND

B. Extreme limitation of one, or marked limitation of two, of the following areas of mental functioning (see 12.00F):

1. Understand, remember, or apply information (see 12.00E1).

2. Interact with others (see 12.00E2).

3. Concentrate, persist, or maintain pace (see 12.00E3).

4. Adapt or manage oneself (see 12.00E4).

12.11 Neurodevelopmental disorders (see 12.00B9), satisfied by A and B:

A. Medical documentation of the requirements of paragraph 1, 2, or 3:

1. One or both of the following:

a. Frequent distractibility, difficulty sustaining attention, and difficulty organizing tasks; or

b. Hyperactive and impulsive behavior (for example, difficulty remaining seated, talking excessively, difficulty waiting, appearing restless, or behaving as if being "driven by a motor").

2. Significant difficulties learning and using academic skills; or

3. Recurrent motor movement or vocalization.

AND

B. Extreme limitation of one, or marked limitation of two, of the following areas of mental functioning (see 12.00F):

1. Understand, remember, or apply information (see 12.00E1).

2. Interact with others (see 12.00E2).

3. Concentrate, persist, or maintain pace (see 12.00E3).

4. Adapt or manage oneself (see 12.00E4).

12.12 [Reserved]

12.13 Eating disorders (see 12.00B10), satisfied by A and B:

A. Medical documentation of a persistent alteration in eating or eating-related behavior that results in a change in consumption or absorption of food and that significantly impairs physical or psychological health.

AND

B. Extreme limitation of one, or marked limitation of two, of the following areas of mental functioning (see 12.00F):

1. Understand, remember, or apply information (see 12.00E1).

2. Interact with others (see 12.00E2).

3. Concentrate, persist, or maintain pace (see 12.00E3).

4. Adapt or manage oneself (see 12.00E4).

12.15 Trauma- and stressor-related disorders (see 12.00B11), satisfied by A and B, or A and C:

A. Medical documentation of all of the following:

1. Exposure to actual or threatened death, serious injury, or violence;

2. Subsequent involuntary re-experiencing of the traumatic event (for example, intrusive memories, dreams, or flashbacks);

3. Avoidance of external reminders of the event;

4. Disturbance in mood and behavior; and

5. Increases in arousal and reactivity (for example, exaggerated startle response, sleep disturbance).

AND

B. Extreme limitation of one, or marked limitation of two, of the following areas of mental functioning (see 12.00F):

1. Understand, remember, or apply information (see 12.00E1).

2. Interact with others (see 12.00E2).

3. Concentrate, persist, or maintain pace (see 12.00E3).

4. Adapt or manage oneself (see 12.00E4).

OR

C. Your mental disorder in this listing category is "serious and persistent;" that is, you have a medically documented history of the existence of the disorder over a period of at least 2 years, and there is evidence of both:

1. Medical treatment, mental health therapy, psychosocial support(s), or a highly structured setting(s) that is ongoing and that diminishes the symptoms and signs of your mental disorder (see 12.00G2b); and

2. Marginal adjustment, that is, you have minimal capacity to adapt to changes in your environment or to demands that are not already part of your daily life (see 12.00G2c).

13.00 CANCER (MALIGNANT NEOPLASTIC DISEASES)

A. What impairments do these listings cover? We use these listings to evaluate all cancers (malignant neoplastic diseases) except certain cancers associated with human immunodeficiency virus (HIV) infection. We use the criteria in 14.11B to evaluate primary central nervous system lymphoma, 14.11C to evaluate primary effusion lymphoma, and 14.11E to evaluate pulmonary Kaposi sarcoma if you also have HIV infection. We evaluate all other cancers associated with HIV infection, for example, Hodgkin lymphoma or non-pulmonary Kaposi sarcoma, under this body system or under 14.11F–I in the immune system disorders body system.

B. What do we consider when we evaluate cancer under these listings? We will consider factors including:

1. Origin of the cancer.

2. Extent of involvement.

3. Duration, frequency, and response to anticancer therapy.

4. Effects of any post-therapeutic residuals.

C. How do we apply these listings? We apply the criteria in a specific listing to a cancer originating from that specific site.

D. What evidence do we need?

1. We need medical evidence that specifies the type, extent, and site of the primary, recurrent, or metastatic lesion. When the primary site cannot be identified, we will use evidence documenting the site(s) of metastasis to evaluate the impairment under 13.27.

2. For operative procedures, including a biopsy or a needle aspiration, we generally need a copy of both the:

a. Operative note, and

b. Pathology report.

3. When we cannot get these documents, we will accept the summary of hospitalization(s) or other medical reports. This evidence should include details of the findings at surgery and, whenever appropriate, the pathological findings.

4. In some situations, we may also need evidence about recurrence, persistence, or progression of the cancer, the response to therapy, and any significant residuals. (See 13.00G.)

E. When do we need longitudinal evidence?

1. Cancer with distant metastases. We generally do not need longitudinal evidence for cancer that has metastasized beyond the regional lymph nodes because this cancer usually meets the requirements of a listing. Exceptions are for cancer with distant metastases that we expect to respond to anticancer therapy. For these exceptions, we usually need a longitudinal record of 3 months after therapy starts to determine whether the therapy achieved its intended effect, and whether this effect is likely to persist.

2. Other cancers. When there are no distant metastases, many of the listings require that we consider your response to initial anticancer therapy; that is, the initial planned treatment regimen. This therapy may consist of a single modality or a combination of modalities; that is, multimodal therapy. (See 13.00I4.)

3. Types of treatment.

a. Whenever the initial planned therapy is a single modality, enough time must pass to allow a determination about whether the therapy will achieve its intended effect. If the treatment fails, the failure often happens within 6 months after treatment starts, and there will often be a change in the treatment regimen.

b. Whenever the initial planned therapy is multimodal, we usually cannot make a determination about the effectiveness of the therapy until we can determine the effects of all the planned modalities. In some cases, we may need to defer adjudication until we can assess the effectiveness of therapy. However, we do not need to defer adjudication to determine whether the therapy will achieve its intended effect if we can make a fully favorable determination or decision based on the length and effects of therapy, or the residuals of the cancer or therapy (see 13.00G).

c. We need evidence under 13.02E, 13.11D, and 13.14C to establish that your treating source initiated multimodal anticancer therapy. We do not need to make a determination about the length or effectiveness of your therapy. Multimodal therapy has been initiated, and satisfies the requirements in 13.02E, 13.11D, and 13.14C, when your treating source starts the first modality. We may defer adjudication if your treating source plans multimodal therapy and has not yet initiated it.

F. How do we evaluate impairments that do not meet one of the cancer listings?

1. These listings are only examples of cancer that we consider severe enough to prevent you from doing any gainful activity. If your severe impairment(s) does not meet the criteria of any of these listings, we must also consider whether you have an impairment(s) that meets the criteria of a listing in another body system.

2. If you have a severe medically determinable impairment(s) that does not meet a listing, we will determine whether your impairment(s) medically equals a listing. (See §§ 404.1526 and 416.926 of this chapter.) If your impairment(s) does not meet or medically equal a listing, you may or may not have the residual functional capacity to engage in substantial gainful activity. In that situation, we proceed to the fourth, and, if necessary, the fifth steps of the sequential evaluation process in §§ 404.1520 and 416.920 of this chapter. We use the rules in §§ 404.1594 and 416.994 of this chapter, as appropriate, when we decide whether you continue to be disabled.

G. How do we consider the effects of anticancer therapy?

1. How we consider the effects of anticancer therapy under the listings. In many cases, cancers meet listing criteria only if the therapy is not effective and the cancer persists, progresses, or recurs. However, as explained in the following paragraphs, we will not delay adjudication if we can make a fully favorable determination or decision based on the evidence in the case record.

2. Effects can vary widely.

a. We consider each case on an individual basis because the therapy and its toxicity may vary widely. We will request a specific description of the therapy, including these items:

i. Drugs given.

ii. Dosage.

iii. Frequency of drug administration.

iv. Plans for continued drug administration.

v. Extent of surgery.

vi. Schedule and fields of radiation therapy.

b. We will also request a description of the complications or adverse effects of therapy, such as the following:

i. Continuing gastrointestinal symptoms.

ii. Persistent weakness.

iii. Neurological complications.

iv. Cardiovascular complications.

v. Reactive mental disorders.

3. Effects of therapy may change. The severity of the adverse effects of anticancer therapy may change during treatment; therefore, enough time must pass to allow us to evaluate the therapy's effect. The residual effects of treatment are temporary in most instances; however, on occasion, the effects may be disabling for a consecutive period of at least 12 months. In some situations, very serious adverse effects may interrupt and prolong multimodal anticancer therapy for a continuous period of almost 12 months. In these situations, we may determine there is an expectation that your impairment will preclude you from engaging in any gainful activity for at least 12 months.

4. When the initial anticancer therapy is effective. We evaluate any post-therapeutic residual impairment(s) not included in these listings under the criteria for the affected body system. We must consider any complications of therapy. When the residual impairment(s) does not meet or medically equal a listing, we must consider its effect on your ability to do substantial gainful activity.

H. How long do we consider your impairment to be disabling?

1. In some listings, we specify that we will consider your impairment to be disabling until a particular point in time (for example, until at least 12 months from the date of transplantation). We may consider your impairment to be disabling beyond this point when the medical and other evidence justifies it.

2. When a listing does not contain such a specification, we will consider an impairment(s) that meets or medically equals a listing in this body system to be disabling until at least 3 years after onset of complete remission. When the impairment(s) has been in complete remission for at least 3 years, that is, the original tumor or a recurrence (or relapse) and any metastases have not been evident for at least 3 years, the impairment(s) will no longer meet or medically equal the criteria of a listing in this body system.

3. Following the appropriate period, we will consider any residuals, including residuals of the cancer or therapy (see 13.00G), in determining whether you are disabled. If you have a recurrence or relapse of your cancer, your impairment may meet or medically equal one of the listings in this body system again.

I. What do we mean by the following terms?

1. Anticancer therapy means surgery, radiation, chemotherapy, hormones, immunotherapy, or bone marrow or stem cell transplantation. When we refer to surgery as an anticancer treatment, we mean surgical excision for treatment, not for diagnostic purposes.

2. Inoperable means surgery is thought to be of no therapeutic value or the surgery cannot be performed; for example, when you cannot tolerate anesthesia or surgery because of another impairment(s), or you have a cancer that is too large or that has invaded crucial structures. This term does not include situations in which your cancer could have been surgically removed but another method of treatment was chosen; for example, an attempt at organ preservation. Your physician may determine whether the cancer is inoperable before or after you receive neoadjuvant therapy. Neoadjuvant therapy is anticancer therapy, such as chemotherapy or radiation, given before surgery in order to reduce the size of the cancer.

3. Metastases means the spread of cancer cells by blood, lymph, or other body fluid. This term does not

include the spread of cancer cells by direct extension of the cancer to other tissues or organs.

4. Multimodal therapy means anticancer therapy that is a combination of at least two types of treatment given in close proximity as a unified whole and usually planned before any treatment has begun. There are three types of treatment modalities: surgery, radiation, and systemic drug therapy (chemotherapy, hormone therapy, and immunotherapy or biological modifier therapy). Examples of multimodal therapy include:

a. Surgery followed by chemotherapy or radiation.

b. Chemotherapy followed by surgery.

c. Chemotherapy and concurrent radiation.

5. Persistent means the planned initial anticancer therapy failed to achieve a complete remission of your cancer; that is, your cancer is evident, even if smaller, after the therapy has ended.

6. Progressive means the cancer becomes more extensive after treatment; that is, there is evidence that your cancer is growing after you have completed at least half of your planned initial anticancer therapy.

7. Recurrent or relapse means the cancer that was in complete remission or entirely removed by surgery has returned.

8. Unresectable means surgery or surgeries did not completely remove the cancer. This term includes situations in which your cancer is incompletely resected or the surgical margins are positive. It does not include situations in which there is a finding of a positive margin(s) if additional surgery obtains a margin(s) that is clear. It also does not include situations in which the cancer is completely resected but you are receiving adjuvant therapy. Adjuvant therapy is anticancer therapy, such as chemotherapy or radiation, given after surgery in order to eliminate any remaining cancer cells or lessen the chance of recurrence.

J. Can we establish the existence of a disabling impairment prior to the date of the evidence that shows the cancer satisfies the criteria of a listing? Yes. We will consider factors such as:

1. The type of cancer and its location.

2. The extent of involvement when the cancer was first demonstrated.

3. Your symptoms.

K. How do we evaluate specific cancers?

1. Lymphoma.

a. Many indolent (non-aggressive) lymphomas are controlled by well-tolerated treatment modalities, although the lymphomas may produce intermittent symptoms and signs. We may defer adjudicating these cases for an appropriate period after therapy is initiated to determine whether the therapy will achieve its intended effect, which is usually to stabilize the disease process. (See 13.00E3.) Once your disease stabilizes, we will assess severity based on the extent of involvement of other organ systems and residuals from therapy.

b. A change in therapy for indolent lymphomas is usually an indicator that the therapy is not achieving its intended effect. However, your impairment will not meet the requirements of 13.05A2 if your therapy is changed solely because you or your physician chooses to change it and not because of a failure to achieve stability.

c. We consider Hodgkin lymphoma that recurs more than 12 months after completing initial anticancer therapy to be a new disease rather than a recurrence.

2. Leukemia.

a. Acute leukemia. The initial diagnosis of acute leukemia, including the accelerated or blast phase of chronic myelogenous (granulocytic) leukemia, is based on definitive bone marrow examination. Additional diagnostic information is based on chromosomal analysis, cytochemical and surface marker studies on the abnormal cells, or other methods consistent with the prevailing state of medical knowledge and clinical practice. Recurrent disease must be documented by peripheral blood, bone marrow, or cerebrospinal fluid examination, or by testicular biopsy. The initial and follow-up pathology reports should be included.

b. Chronic myelogenous leukemia (CML). We need a diagnosis of CML based on documented granulocytosis, including immature forms such as differentiated or undifferentiated myelocytes and myeloblasts, and a chromosomal analysis that demonstrates the Philadelphia chromosome. In the absence of a chromosomal analysis, or if the Philadelphia chromosome is not present, the diagnosis may be made by other methods consistent with the prevailing state of medical knowledge and clinical practice. The requirement for CML in the accelerated or blast phase is met in 13.06B if laboratory findings show the proportion of blast (immature) cells in the peripheral blood or bone marrow is 10 percent or greater.

c. Chronic lymphocytic leukemia.

i. We require the diagnosis of chronic lymphocytic leukemia (CLL) to be documented by evidence of a chronic lymphocytosis of at least 10,000 cells/mm^3 for 3 months or longer, or other acceptable diagnostic techniques consistent with the prevailing state of medical knowledge and clinical practice.

ii. We evaluate the complications and residual impairment(s) from CLL under the appropriate listings, such as 13.05A2 or the hematological listings (7.00).

d. Elevated white cell count. In cases of chronic leukemia (either myelogenous or lymphocytic), an elevated white cell count, in itself, is not a factor in determining the severity of the impairment.

3. Macroglobulinemia or heavy chain disease. We require the diagnosis of these diseases to be confirmed by protein electrophoresis or immunoelectrophoresis. We evaluate the resulting impairment(s) under the appropriate listings, such as 13.05A2 or the hematological listings (7.00).

4. Primary breast cancer.

a. We evaluate bilateral primary breast cancer (synchronous or metachronous) under 13.10A, which covers local primary disease, and not as a primary disease that has metastasized.

b. We evaluate secondary lymphedema that results from anticancer therapy for breast cancer under 13.10E if the lymphedema is treated by surgery to salvage or restore the functioning of an upper extremity. Secondary lymphedema is edema that results from obstruction or destruction of normal lymphatic channels. We may not restrict our determination of the onset of disability to the date of the surgery; we may establish an earlier onset date of disability if the evidence in your case record supports such a finding.

5. Carcinoma-in-situ. Carcinoma-in-situ, or preinvasive carcinoma, usually responds to treatment. When we use the term "carcinoma" in these listings, it does not include carcinoma-in-situ.

6. Primary central nervous system (CNS) cancers. We use the criteria in 13.13 to evaluate cancers that originate within the CNS (that is, brain and spinal cord cancers).

a. The CNS cancers listed in 13.13A1 are highly malignant and respond poorly to treatment, and therefore we do not require additional criteria to evaluate them. We do not list pituitary gland cancer (for example, pituitary gland carcinoma) in 13.13A1, although this CNS cancer is highly malignant and responds poorly to treatment. We evaluate pituitary gland cancer under 13.13A1 and do not require additional criteria to evaluate it.

b. We consider a CNS tumor to be malignant if it is classified as Grade II, Grade III, or Grade IV under the World Health Organization (WHO) classification of tumors of the CNS (WHO Classification of Tumours of the Central Nervous System, 2007).

c. We evaluate benign (for example, WHO Grade I) CNS tumors under 11.05. We evaluate metastasized CNS cancers from non–CNS sites under the primary cancers (see 13.00C). We evaluate any complications of CNS cancers, such as resultant neurological or psychological impairments, under the criteria for the affected body system.

7. Primary peritoneal carcinoma. We use the criteria in 13.23E to evaluate primary peritoneal carcinoma in women because this cancer is often indistinguishable from ovarian cancer and is generally treated the same way as ovarian cancer. We use the criteria in 13.15A to evaluate primary peritoneal carcinoma in men because many of these cases are similar to malignant mesothelioma.

8. Prostate cancer. We exclude "biochemical recurrence" in 13.24A, which is defined as an increase in the serum prostate-specific antigen (PSA) level following the completion of the hormonal intervention therapy. We need corroborating evidence to document recurrence, such as radiological studies or findings on physical examination.

9. Melanoma. We evaluate malignant melanoma that affects the skin (cutaneous melanoma), eye (ocular melanoma), or mucosal membranes (mucosal melanoma) under 13.29. We evaluate melanoma that is not malignant that affects the skin (benign melanocytic tumor) under the listings in 8.00 or other affected body systems.

L. How do we evaluate cancer treated by bone marrow or stem cell transplantation, including transplantation using stem cells from umbilical cord blood? Bone marrow or stem cell transplantation is performed for a variety of cancers. We require the transplantation to occur before we evaluate it under these listings. We do not need to restrict our determination of the onset of disability to the date of the transplantation (13.05, 13.06, or 13.07) or the date of first treatment under the treatment plan that includes transplantation (13.28). We may be able to establish an earlier onset date of disability due to your transplantation if the evidence in your case record supports such a finding.

1. Acute leukemia (including T–cell lymphoblastic lymphoma) or accelerated or blast phase of CML. If you undergo bone marrow or stem cell transplantation for any of these disorders, we will consider you to be disabled until at least 24 months from the date of diagnosis or relapse, or at least 12 months from the date of transplantation, whichever is later.

2. Lymphoma, multiple myeloma, or chronic phase of CML. If you undergo bone marrow or stem cell transplantation for any of these disorders, we will consider you to be disabled until at least 12 months from the date of transplantation.

3. Other cancers. We will evaluate any other cancer treated with bone marrow or stem cell transplantation under 13.28, regardless of whether there is another listing that addresses that impairment. The length of time we will consider you to be disabled depends on whether you undergo allogeneic or autologous transplantation.

a. Allogeneic bone marrow or stem cell transplantation. If you undergo allogeneic transplantation (transplantation from an unrelated donor or a related donor other than an identical twin), we will consider you to be disabled until at least 12 months from the date of transplantation.

b. Autologous bone marrow or stem cell transplantation. If you undergo autologous transplantation

(transplantation of your own cells or cells from your identical twin (syngeneic transplantation)), we will consider you to be disabled until at least 12 months from the date of the first treatment under the treatment plan that includes transplantation. The first treatment usually refers to the initial therapy given to prepare you for transplantation.

4. Evaluating disability after the appropriate time period has elapsed. We consider any residual impairment(s), such as complications arising from:

a. Graft-versus-host (GVH) disease.

b. Immunosuppressant therapy, such as frequent infections.

c. Significant deterioration of other organ systems.

13.01 Category of Impairments, Malignant Neoplastic Diseases

13.02 Soft tissue cancers of the head and neck (except salivary glands—13.08—and thyroid gland—13.09).

A. Inoperable or unresectable.

OR

B. Persistent or recurrent disease following initial anticancer therapy, except persistence or recurrence in the true vocal cord.

OR

C. With metastases beyond the regional lymph nodes.

OR

D. Small-cell (oat cell) carcinoma.

OR

E. Soft tissue cancers originating in the head and neck treated with multimodal anticancer therapy (see 13.00E3c). Consider under a disability until at least 18 months from the date of diagnosis. Thereafter, evaluate any residual impairment(s) under the criteria for the affected body system.

13.03 Skin.

A. Sarcoma or carcinoma with metastases to or beyond the regional lymph nodes.

OR

B. Carcinoma invading deep extradermal structures (for example, skeletal muscle, cartilage, or bone).

13.04 Soft tissue sarcoma.

A. With regional or distant metastases.

OR

B. Persistent or recurrent following initial anticancer therapy.

13.05 Lymphoma (including mycosis fungoides, but excluding T–cell lymphoblastic lymphoma—13.06). (See 13.00K1 and 13.00K2c.)

A. Non–Hodgkin's lymphoma, as described in 1 or 2:

1. Aggressive lymphoma (including diffuse large B–cell lymphoma) persistent or recurrent following initial anticancer therapy.

2. Indolent lymphoma (including mycosis fungoides and follicular small cleaved cell) requiring initiation of more than one (single mode or multimodal) anticancer treatment regimen within a period of 12 consecutive months. Consider under a disability from at least the date of initiation of the treatment regimen that failed within 12 months.

OR

B. Hodgkin lymphoma with failure to achieve clinically complete remission, or recurrent lymphoma within 12 months of completing initial anticancer therapy.

OR

C. With bone marrow or stem cell transplantation. Consider under a disability until at least 12 months from the date of transplantation. Thereafter, evaluate any residual impairment(s) under the criteria for the affected body system.

OR

D. Mantle cell lymphoma.

13.06 Leukemia. (See 13.00K2.)

A. Acute leukemia (including T–cell lymphoblastic lymphoma). Consider under a disability until at least 24 months from the date of diagnosis or relapse, or at least 12 months from the date of bone marrow or stem cell transplantation, whichever is later. Thereafter, evaluate any residual impairment(s) under the criteria for the affected body system.

OR

B. Chronic myelogenous leukemia, as described in 1 or 2:

1. Accelerated or blast phase (see 13.00K2b). Consider under a disability until at least 24 months from the date of diagnosis or relapse, or at least 12 months from the date of bone marrow or stem cell transplantation, whichever is later. Thereafter, evaluate any residual impairment(s) under the criteria for the affected body system.

2. Chronic phase, as described in a or b:

a. Consider under a disability until at least 12 months from the date of bone marrow or stem cell transplantation. Thereafter, evaluate any residual impairment(s) under the criteria for the affected body system.

b. Progressive disease following initial anticancer therapy.

13.07 Multiple myeloma (confirmed by appropriate serum or urine protein electrophoresis and bone marrow findings).

A. Failure to respond or progressive disease following initial anticancer therapy.

OR

B. With bone marrow or stem cell transplantation. Consider under a disability until at least 12 months from the date of transplantation. Thereafter, evaluate any residual impairment(s) under the criteria for the affected body system.

13.08 Salivary glands—carcinoma or sarcoma with metastases beyond the regional lymph nodes.

13.09 Thyroid gland.

A. Anaplastic (undifferentiated) carcinoma.

OR

B. Carcinoma with metastases beyond the regional lymph nodes progressive despite radioactive iodine therapy.

OR

C. Medullary carcinoma with metastases beyond the regional lymph nodes.

13.10 Breast (except sarcoma—13.04). (See 13.00K4.)

A. Locally advanced cancer (inflammatory carcinoma, cancer of any size with direct extension to the chest wall or skin, or cancer of any size with metastases to the ipsilateral internal mammary nodes).

OR

B. Carcinoma with metastases to the supraclavicular or infraclavicular nodes, to 10 or more axillary nodes, or with distant metastases.

OR

C. Recurrent carcinoma, except local recurrence that remits with anticancer therapy.

OR

D. Small-cell (oat cell) carcinoma.

OR

E. With secondary lymphedema that is caused by anticancer therapy and treated by surgery to salvage or restore the functioning of an upper extremity. (See 13.00K4b.) Consider under a disability until at least 12 months from the date of the surgery that treated the secondary lymphedema. Thereafter, evaluate any residual impairment(s) under the criteria for the affected body system.

13.11 Skeletal system—sarcoma.

A. Inoperable or unresectable.

OR

B. Recurrent cancer (except local recurrence) after initial anticancer therapy.

OR

C. With distant metastases.

OR

D. All other cancers originating in bone with multimodal anticancer therapy (see 13.00E3c). Consider under a disability for 12 months from the date of diagnosis. Thereafter, evaluate any residual impairment(s) under the criteria for the affected body system.

13.12 Maxilla, orbit, or temporal fossa.

A. Sarcoma or carcinoma of any type with regional or distant metastases.

OR

B. Carcinoma of the antrum with extension into the orbit or ethmoid or sphenoid sinus.

OR

C. Cancer with extension to the orbit, meninges, sinuses, or base of the skull.

13.13 Nervous system. (See 13.00K6.)

A. Primary central nervous system (CNS; that is, brain and spinal cord) cancers, as described in 1, 2, or 3:

1. Glioblastoma multiforme, ependymoblastoma, and diffuse intrinsic brain stem gliomas (see 13.00K6a).

2. Any Grade III or Grade IV CNS cancer (see 13.00K6b), including astrocytomas, sarcomas, and medulloblastoma and other primitive neuroectodermal tumors (PNETs).

3. Any primary CNS cancer, as described in a or b:

a. Metastatic.

b. Progressive or recurrent following initial anticancer therapy.

OR

B. Primary peripheral nerve or spinal root cancers, as described in 1 or 2:

1. Metastatic.

2. Progressive or recurrent following initial anticancer therapy.

13.14 Lungs.

A. Non-small-cell carcinoma—inoperable, unresectable, recurrent, or metastatic disease to or beyond the hilar nodes.

OR

B. Small-cell (oat cell) carcinoma.

OR

C. Carcinoma of the superior sulcus (including Pancoast tumors) with multimodal anticancer therapy (see 13.00E3c). Consider under a disability until at least 18 months from the date of diagnosis. Thereafter, evaluate any residual impairment(s) under the criteria for the affected body system.

13.15 Pleura or mediastinum.

A. Malignant mesothelioma of pleura.

OR

B. Tumors of the mediastinum, as described in 1 or 2:

1. With metastases to or beyond the regional lymph nodes.

2. Persistent or recurrent following initial anticancer therapy.

OR

C. Small-cell (oat cell) carcinoma.

13.16 Esophagus or stomach.

A. Carcinoma or sarcoma of the esophagus.

OR

B. Carcinoma or sarcoma of the stomach, as described in 1 or 2:

1. Inoperable, unresectable, extending to surrounding structures, or recurrent.

2. With metastases to or beyond the regional lymph nodes.

OR

C. Small-cell (oat cell) carcinoma.

13.17 Small intestine—carcinoma, sarcoma, or carcinoid.

A. Inoperable, unresectable, or recurrent.

OR

B. With metastases beyond the regional lymph nodes.

OR

C. Small-cell (oat cell) carcinoma.

13.18 Large intestine (from ileocecal valve to and including anal canal).

A. Adenocarcinoma that is inoperable, unresectable, or recurrent.

OR

B. Squamous cell carcinoma of the anus, recurrent after surgery.

OR

C. With metastases beyond the regional lymph nodes.

OR

D. Small-cell (oat cell) carcinoma.

13.19 Liver or gallbladder—cancer of the liver, gallbladder, or bile ducts.

13.20 Pancreas.

A. Carcinoma (except islet cell carcinoma).

OR

B. Islet cell carcinoma that is physiologically active and is either inoperable or unresectable.

13.21 Kidneys, adrenal glands, or ureters—carcinoma.

A. Inoperable, unresectable, or recurrent.

OR

B. With metastases to or beyond the regional lymph nodes.

13.22 Urinary bladder—carcinoma.

A. With infiltration beyond the bladder wall.

OR

B. Recurrent after total cystectomy.

OR

C. Inoperable or unresectable.

OR

D. With metastases to or beyond the regional lymph nodes.

OR

E. Small-cell (oat cell) carcinoma.

13.23 Cancers of the female genital tract—carcinoma or sarcoma (including primary peritoneal carcinoma).

A. Uterus (corpus), as described in 1, 2, or 3:

1. Invading adjoining organs.

2. With metastases to or beyond the regional lymph nodes.

3. Persistent or recurrent following initial anticancer therapy.

OR

B. Uterine cervix, as described in 1, 2, or 3:

1. Extending to the pelvic wall, lower portion of the vagina, or adjacent or distant organs.

2. Persistent or recurrent following initial anticancer therapy.

3. With metastases to distant (for example, para-aortic or supraclavicular) lymph nodes.

OR

C. Vulva or vagina, as described in 1, 2, or 3:

1. Invading adjoining organs.

2. With metastases to or beyond the regional lymph nodes.

3. Persistent or recurrent following initial anticancer therapy.

OR

D. Fallopian tubes, as described in 1 or 2:

1. Extending to the serosa or beyond.

2. Persistent or recurrent following initial anticancer therapy.

OR

E. Ovaries, as described in 1 or 2:

1. All cancers except germ-cell cancers, with at least one of the following:

a. Extension beyond the pelvis; for example, implants on, or direct extension to, peritoneal, omental, or bowel surfaces.

b. Metastases to or beyond the regional lymph nodes.

c. Recurrent following initial anticancer therapy.

2. Germ-cell cancers—progressive or recurrent following initial anticancer therapy.

OR

F. Small-cell (oat cell) carcinoma.

13.24 Prostate gland—carcinoma.

A. Progressive or recurrent (not including biochemical recurrence) despite initial hormonal intervention. (See 13.00K8.)

OR

B. With visceral metastases (metastases to internal organs).

OR

C. Small-cell (oat cell) carcinoma.

13.25 Testicles—cancer with metastatic disease progressive or recurrent following initial chemotherapy.

13.26 Penis—carcinoma with metastases to or beyond the regional lymph nodes.

13.27 Primary site unknown after appropriate search for primary—metastatic carcinoma or sarcoma, except for squamous cell carcinoma confined to the neck nodes.

13.28 Cancer treated by bone marrow or stem cell transplantation. (See 13.00L.)

A. Allogeneic transplantation. Consider under a disability until at least 12 months from the date of transplantation. Thereafter, evaluate any residual impairment(s) under the criteria for the affected body system.

OR

B. Autologous transplantation. Consider under a disability until at least 12 months from the date of the first treatment under the treatment plan that includes transplantation. Thereafter, evaluate any residual impairment(s) under the criteria for the affected body system.

13.29 Malignant melanoma (including skin, ocular, or mucosal melanomas), as described in either A, B, or C:

A. Recurrent (except an additional primary melanoma at a different site, which is not considered to be recurrent disease) following either 1 or 2:

1. Wide excision (skin melanoma).

2. Enucleation of the eye (ocular melanoma).

OR

B. With metastases as described in 1, 2, or 3:

1. Metastases to one or more clinically apparent nodes; that is, nodes that are detected by imaging studies (excluding lymphoscintigraphy) or by clinical evaluation (palpable).

2. If the nodes are not clinically apparent, with metastases to four or more nodes.

3. Metastases to adjacent skin (satellite lesions) or distant sites (for example, liver, lung, or brain).

OR

C. Mucosal melanoma.

14.00 Immune System Disorders

A. What disorders do we evaluate under the immune system disorders listings?

1. We evaluate immune system disorders that cause dysfunction in one or more components of your immune system.

a. The dysfunction may be due to problems in antibody production, impaired cell-mediated immunity, a combined type of antibody/cellular deficiency, impaired phagocytosis, or complement deficiency.

b. Immune system disorders may result in recurrent and unusual infections, or inflammation and dysfunction of the body's own tissues. Immune system disorders can cause a deficit in a single organ or body system that results in extreme (that is, very serious) loss of function. They can also cause lesser degrees of limitations in two or more organs or body systems, and when associated with symptoms or signs, such as severe fatigue, fever, malaise, diffuse musculoskeletal pain, or involuntary weight loss, can also result in extreme limitation.

c. We organize the discussions of immune system disorders in three categories: Autoimmune disorders; Immune deficiency disorders, excluding human immunodeficiency virus (HIV) infection; and HIV infection.

2. Autoimmune disorders (14.00D). Autoimmune disorders are caused by dysfunctional immune responses directed against the body's own tissues, resulting in chronic, multisystem impairments that differ in clinical

manifestations, course, and outcome. They are sometimes referred to as rheumatic diseases, connective tissue disorders, or collagen vascular disorders. Some of the features of autoimmune disorders in adults differ from the features of the same disorders in children.

3. Immune deficiency disorders, excluding HIV infection (14.00E). Immune deficiency disorders are characterized by recurrent or unusual infections that respond poorly to treatment, and are often associated with complications affecting other parts of the body. Immune deficiency disorders are classified as either primary (congenital) or acquired. Individuals with immune deficiency disorders also have an increased risk of malignancies and of having autoimmune disorders.

4. Human immunodeficiency virus (HIV) infection (14.00F). HIV infection may be characterized by increased susceptibility to common infections as well as opportunistic infections, cancers, or other conditions listed in 14.11.

B. What information do we need to show that you have an immune system disorder? Generally, we need your medical history, a report(s) of a physical examination, a report(s) of laboratory findings, and in some instances, appropriate medically acceptable imaging or tissue biopsy reports to show that you have an immune system disorder. Therefore, we will make every reasonable effort to obtain your medical history, medical findings, and results of laboratory tests. We explain the information we need in more detail in the sections below.

C. Definitions

1. Appropriate medically acceptable imaging includes, but is not limited to, angiography, x-ray imaging, computerized axial tomography (CAT scan) or magnetic resonance imaging (MRI), with or without contrast material, myelography, and radionuclear bone scans. "Appropriate" means that the technique used is the proper one to support the evaluation and diagnosis of the impairment.

2. Constitutional symptoms or signs, as used in these listings, means severe fatigue, fever, malaise, or involuntary weight loss. Severe fatigue means a frequent sense of exhaustion that results in significantly reduced physical activity or mental function. Malaise means frequent feelings of illness, bodily discomfort, or lack of well-being that result in significantly reduced physical activity or mental function.

3. Disseminated means that a condition is spread over a considerable area. The type and extent of the spread will depend on your specific disease.

4. Dysfunction means that one or more of the body regulatory mechanisms are impaired, causing either an excess or deficiency of immunocompetent cells or their products.

5. Extra-articular means "other than the joints"; for example, an organ(s) such as the heart, lungs, kidneys, or skin.

6. Inability to ambulate effectively has the same meaning as in 1.00B2b.

7. Inability to perform fine and gross movements effectively has the same meaning as in 1.00B2c.

8. Major peripheral joints has the same meaning as in 1.00F.

9. Persistent means that a sign(s) or symptom(s) has continued over time. The precise meaning will depend on the specific immune system disorder, the usual course of the disorder, and the other circumstances of your clinical course.

10. Recurrent means that a condition that previously responded adequately to an appropriate course of treatment returns after a period of remission or regression. The precise meaning, such as the extent of response or remission and the time periods involved, will depend on the specific disease or condition you have, the body system affected, the usual course of the disorder and its treatment, and the other facts of your particular case.

11. Resistant to treatment means that a condition did not respond adequately to an appropriate course of treatment. Whether a response is adequate or a course of treatment is appropriate will depend on the specific disease or condition you have, the body system affected, the usual course of the disorder and its treatment, and the other facts of your particular case.

12. Severe means medical severity as used by the medical community. The term does not have the same meaning as it does when we use it in connection with a finding at the second step of the sequential evaluation processes in §§ 404.1520, 416.920, and 416.924.

D. How do we document and evaluate the listed autoimmune disorders?

1. Systemic lupus erythematosus (14.02).

a. General. Systemic lupus erythematosus (SLE) is a chronic inflammatory disease that can affect any organ or body system. It is frequently, but not always, accompanied by constitutional symptoms or signs (severe fatigue, fever, malaise, involuntary weight loss). Major organ or body system involvement can include: Respiratory (pleuritis, pneumonitis), cardiovascular (endocarditis, myocarditis, pericarditis, vasculitis), renal (glomerulonephritis), hematologic (anemia, leukopenia, thrombocytopenia), skin (photosensitivity), neurologic (seizures), mental (anxiety, fluctuating cognition ("lupus fog"), mood disorders, organic brain syndrome, psychosis), or immune system disorders (inflammatory arthritis). Immunologically, there is an array of circulating serum auto-antibodies and pro- and anti-coagulant proteins that may occur in a highly variable pattern.

b. Documentation of SLE. Generally, but not always, the medical evidence will show that your SLE satisfies the criteria in the current "Criteria for the Classification of Systemic Lupus Erythematosus" by the American College of Rheumatology found in the most recent edition of the Primer on the Rheumatic Diseases published by the Arthritis Foundation.

2. Systemic vasculitis (14.03).

a. General.

(i) Vasculitis is an inflammation of blood vessels. It may occur acutely in association with adverse drug reactions, certain chronic infections, and occasionally, malignancies. More often, it is chronic and the cause is unknown. Symptoms vary depending on which blood vessels are involved. Systemic vasculitis may also be associated with other autoimmune disorders; for example, SLE or dermatomyositis.

(ii) There are several clinical patterns, including but not limited to polyarteritis nodosa, Takayasu's arteritis (aortic arch arteritis), giant cell arteritis (temporal arteritis), and Wegener's granulomatosis.

b. Documentation of systemic vasculitis. Angiography or tissue biopsy confirms a diagnosis of systemic vasculitis when the disease is suspected clinically. When you have had angiography or tissue biopsy for systemic vasculitis, we will make every reasonable effort to obtain reports of the results of that procedure. However, we will not purchase angiography or tissue biopsy.

3. Systemic sclerosis (scleroderma) (14.04).

a. General. Systemic sclerosis (scleroderma) constitutes a spectrum of disease in which thickening of the skin is the clinical hallmark. Raynaud's phenomenon, often medically severe and progressive, is present frequently and may be the peripheral manifestation of a vasospastic abnormality in the heart, lungs, and kidneys. The CREST syndrome (calcinosis, Raynaud's phenomenon, esophageal dysmotility, sclerodactyly, and telangiectasia) is a variant that may slowly progress over years to the generalized process, systemic sclerosis.

b. Diffuse cutaneous systemic sclerosis. In diffuse cutaneous systemic sclerosis (also known as diffuse scleroderma), major organ or systemic involvement can include the gastrointestinal tract, lungs, heart, kidneys, and muscle in addition to skin or blood vessels. Although arthritis can occur, joint dysfunction results primarily from soft tissue/cutaneous thickening, fibrosis, and contractures.

c. Localized scleroderma (linear scleroderma and morphea).

(i) Localized scleroderma (linear scleroderma and morphea) is more common in children than in adults. However, this type of scleroderma can persist into adulthood. To assess the severity of the impairment, we need a description of the extent of involvement of linear scleroderma and the location of the lesions. For example, linear scleroderma involving the arm but not crossing any joints is not as functionally limiting as sclerodactyly (scleroderma localized to the fingers). Linear scleroderma of a lower extremity involving skin thickening and atrophy of underlying muscle or bone can result in contractures and leg length discrepancy. In such cases, we may evaluate your impairment under the musculoskeletal listings (1.00).

(ii) When there is isolated morphea of the face causing facial disfigurement from unilateral hypoplasia of the mandible, maxilla, zygoma, or orbit, adjudication may be more appropriate under the criteria in the affected body system, such as special senses and speech (2.00) or mental disorders (12.00).

(iii) Chronic variants of these syndromes include disseminated morphea, Shulman's disease (diffuse fasciitis with eosinophilia), and eosinophilia-myalgia syndrome (often associated with toxins such as toxic oil or contaminated tryptophan), all of which can impose medically severe musculoskeletal dysfunction and may also lead to restrictive pulmonary disease. We evaluate these variants of the disease under the criteria in the musculoskeletal listings (1.00) or respiratory system listings (3.00).

d. Documentation of systemic sclerosis (scleroderma). Documentation involves differentiating the clinical features of systemic sclerosis (scleroderma) from other autoimmune disorders. However, there may be an overlap.

4. Polymyositis and dermatomyositis (14.05).

a. General. Polymyositis and dermatomyositis are related disorders that are characterized by an inflammatory process in striated muscle, occurring alone or in association with other autoimmune disorders or malignancy. The most common manifestations are symmetric weakness, and less frequently, pain and tenderness of the proximal limb-girdle (shoulder or pelvic) musculature. There may also be involvement of the cervical, cricopharyngeal, esophageal, intercostal, and diaphragmatic muscles.

b. Documentation of polymyositis and dermatomyositis. Generally, but not always, polymyositis is associated with elevated serum muscle enzymes (creatine phosphokinase (CPK), aminotransferases, and aldolase), and characteristic abnormalities on electromyography and muscle biopsy. In dermatomyositis there are characteristic skin findings in addition to the findings of polymyositis. When you have had electromyography or muscle biopsy for polymyositis or dermatomyositis, we will make every reasonable effort to obtain reports of the results of that procedure. However, we will not purchase electromyography or muscle biopsy.

c. Additional information about how we evaluate polymyositis and dermatomyositis under the listings.

(i) Weakness of your pelvic girdle muscles that results in your inability to rise independently from a squatting or sitting position or to climb stairs may be an indication that you are unable to ambulate effectively. Weakness of your shoulder girdle muscles may result in your inability to perform lifting, carrying, and reaching overhead, and also may seriously affect your ability to perform activities requiring fine movements. We evaluate these limitations under 14.05A.

(ii) We use the malignant neoplastic diseases listings (13.00) to evaluate malignancies associated with polymyositis or dermatomyositis. We evaluate the involvement of other organs/body systems under the criteria for the listings in the affected body system.

5. Undifferentiated and mixed connective tissue disease (14.06).

a. General. This listing includes syndromes with clinical and immunologic features of several autoimmune disorders, but which do not satisfy the criteria for any of the specific disorders described. For example, you may have clinical features of SLE and systemic vasculitis, and the serologic (blood test) findings of rheumatoid arthritis.

b. Documentation of undifferentiated and mixed connective tissue disease. Undifferentiated connective tissue disease is diagnosed when clinical features and serologic (blood test) findings, such as rheumatoid factor or antinuclear antibody (consistent with an autoimmune disorder) are present but do not satisfy the criteria for a specific disease. Mixed connective tissue disease (MCTD) is diagnosed when clinical features and serologic findings of two or more autoimmune diseases overlap.

6. Inflammatory arthritis (14.09).

a. General. The spectrum of inflammatory arthritis includes a vast array of disorders that differ in cause, course, and outcome. Clinically, inflammation of major peripheral joints may be the dominant manifestation causing difficulties with ambulation or fine and gross movements; there may be joint pain, swelling, and tenderness. The arthritis may affect other joints, or cause less limitation in ambulation or the performance of fine and gross movements. However, in combination with extra-articular features, including constitutional symptoms or signs (severe fatigue, fever, malaise, involuntary weight loss), inflammatory arthritis may result in an extreme limitation.

b. Inflammatory arthritis involving the axial spine (spondyloarthropathy). In adults, inflammatory arthritis involving the axial spine may be associated with disorders such as:

(i) Reiter's syndrome;

(ii) Ankylosing spondylitis;

(iii) Psoriatic arthritis;

(iv) Whipple's disease;

(v) Behçet's disease; and

(vi) Inflammatory bowel disease.

c. Inflammatory arthritis involving the peripheral joints. In adults, inflammatory arthritis involving peripheral joints may be associated with disorders such as:

(i) Rheumatoid arthritis;

(ii) Sjögren's syndrome;

(iii) Psoriatic arthritis;

(iv) Crystal deposition disorders (gout and pseudogout);

(v) Lyme disease; and

(vi) Inflammatory bowel disease.

d. Documentation of inflammatory arthritis. Generally, but not always, the diagnosis of inflammatory arthritis is based on the clinical features and serologic findings described in the most recent edition of the Primer on the Rheumatic Diseases published by the Arthritis Foundation.

e. How we evaluate inflammatory arthritis under the listings.

(i) Listing-level severity in 14.09A and 14.09C1 is shown by an impairment that results in an "extreme" (very serious) limitation. In 14.09A, the criterion is satisfied with persistent inflammation or deformity in one major peripheral weight-bearing joint resulting in the inability to ambulate effectively (as defined in 14.00C6) or one major peripheral joint in each upper extremity resulting in the inability to perform fine and gross movements effectively (as defined in 14.00C7). In 14.09C1, if you have the required ankylosis (fixation) of your cervical or dorsolumbar spine, we will find that you have an extreme limitation in your ability to see in front of you, above you, and to the side. Therefore, inability to ambulate effectively is implicit in 14.09C1, even though you might not require bilateral upper limb assistance.

(ii) Listing-level severity is shown in 14.09B, 14.09C2, and 14.09D by inflammatory arthritis that involves various combinations of complications of one or more major peripheral joints or other joints, such as inflammation or deformity, extra-articular features, repeated manifestations, and constitutional symptoms or signs. Extra-articular impairments may also meet listings in other body systems.

(iii) Extra-articular features of inflammatory arthritis may involve any body system; for example: Musculoskeletal (heel enthesopathy), ophthalmologic (iridocyclitis, keratoconjunctivitis sicca, uveitis), pulmonary (pleuritis, pulmonary fibrosis or nodules, restrictive lung disease), cardiovascular (aortic valve insufficiency, arrhythmias, coronary arteritis, myocarditis, pericarditis, Raynaud's phenomenon, systemic vasculitis), renal (amyloidosis of the kidney), hematologic (chronic anemia, thrombocytopenia), neurologic (peripheral neuropathy, radiculopathy, spinal cord or cauda equina compression with sensory and motor loss), mental (cognitive dysfunction, poor memory), and immune system (Felty's syndrome (hypersplenism with compromised immune competence)).

(iv) If both inflammation and chronic deformities are present, we evaluate your impairment under the criteria of any appropriate listing.

7. Sjögren's syndrome (14.10).

a. General.

(i) Sjögren's syndrome is an immune-mediated disorder of the exocrine glands. Involvement of the lacrimal and salivary glands is the hallmark feature, resulting in symptoms of dry eyes and dry mouth, and possible complications, such as corneal damage, blepharitis (eyelid inflammation), dysphagia (difficulty in swallowing), dental caries, and the inability to speak for extended periods of time. Involvement of the exocrine glands of the upper airways may result in persistent dry cough.

(ii) Many other organ systems may be involved, including musculoskeletal (arthritis, myositis), respiratory (interstitial fibrosis), gastrointestinal (dysmotility, dysphagia, involuntary weight loss), genitourinary (interstitial cystitis, renal tubular acidosis), skin (purpura, vasculitis), neurologic (central nervous system disorders, cranial and peripheral neuropathies), mental (cognitive dysfunction, poor memory), and neoplastic (lymphoma). Severe fatigue and malaise are frequently reported. Sjögren's syndrome may be associated with other autoimmune disorders (for example, rheumatoid arthritis or SLE); usually the clinical features of the associated disorder predominate.

b. Documentation of Sjögren's syndrome. If you have Sjögren's syndrome, the medical evidence will generally, but not always, show that your disease satisfies the criteria in the current "Criteria for the Classification of Sjögren's Syndrome" by the American College of Rheumatology found in the most recent edition of the Primer on the Rheumatic Diseases published by the Arthritis Foundation.

E. How do we document and evaluate immune deficiency disorders, excluding HIV infection?

1. General.

a. Immune deficiency disorders can be classified as:

(i) Primary (congenital); for example, X–linked agammaglobulinemia, thymic hypoplasia (DiGeorge syndrome), severe combined immunodeficiency (SCID), chronic granulomatous disease (CGD), C1 esterase inhibitor deficiency.

(ii) Acquired; for example, medication-related.

b. Primary immune deficiency disorders are seen mainly in children. However, recent advances in the treatment of these disorders have allowed many affected children to survive well into adulthood. Occasionally, these disorders are first diagnosed in adolescence or adulthood.

2. Documentation of immune deficiency disorders. The medical evidence must include documentation of the specific type of immune deficiency. Documentation may be by laboratory evidence or by other generally acceptable methods consistent with the prevailing state of medical knowledge and clinical practice.

3. Immune deficiency disorders treated by stem cell transplantation.

a. Evaluation in the first 12 months. If you undergo stem cell transplantation for your immune deficiency disorder, we will consider you disabled until at least 12 months from the date of the transplant.

b. Evaluation after the 12–month period has elapsed. After the 12–month period has elapsed, we will consider any residuals of your immune deficiency disorder as well as any residual impairment(s) resulting from the treatment, such as complications arising from:

(i) Graft-versus-host (GVH) disease.

(ii) Immunosuppressant therapy, such as frequent infections.

(iii) Significant deterioration of other organ systems.

4. Medication-induced immune suppression. Medication effects can result in varying degrees of immune suppression, but most resolve when the medication is ceased. However, if you are prescribed medication for long-term immune suppression, such as after an organ transplant, we will evaluate:

a. The frequency and severity of infections.

b. Residuals from the organ transplant itself, after the 12–month period has elapsed.

c. Significant deterioration of other organ systems.

F. How do we document and evaluate HIV infection? Any individual with HIV infection, including one with a diagnosis of acquired immune deficiency syndrome (AIDS), may be found disabled under 14.11 if his or her impairment meets the criteria in that listing or is medically equivalent to the criteria in that listing.

1. Documentation of HIV infection.

a. Definitive documentation of HIV infection. We may document a diagnosis of HIV infection by positive findings on one or more of the following definitive laboratory tests:

(i) HIV antibody screening test (for example, enzyme immunoassay, or EIA), confirmed by a supplemental HIV antibody test such as the Western blot (immunoblot), an immunofluorescence assay, or an HIV–1/HIV–2 antibody differentiation immunoassay.

(ii) HIV nucleic acid (DNA or RNA) detection test (for example, polymerase chain reaction, or PCR).

(iii) HIV p24 antigen (p24Ag) test.

(iv) Isolation of HIV in viral culture.

(v) Other tests that are highly specific for detection of HIV and that are consistent with the prevailing state of medical knowledge.

b. We will make every reasonable effort to obtain the results of your laboratory testing. Pursuant to §§ 404.1519f and 416.919f of this chapter, we will purchase examinations or tests necessary to make a determination in your claim if no other acceptable documentation exists.

c. Other acceptable documentation of HIV infection. We may also document HIV infection without definitive laboratory evidence.

(i) We will accept a persuasive report from a physician that a positive diagnosis of your HIV infection was confirmed by an appropriate laboratory test(s), such as those described in 14.00F1a. To be persuasive, this report must state that you had the appropriate definitive laboratory test(s) for diagnosing your HIV infection and provide the results. The report must also be consistent with the remaining evidence of record.

(ii) We may also document HIV infection by the medical history, clinical and laboratory findings, and diagnosis(es) indicated in the medical evidence, provided that such documentation is consistent with the prevailing state of medical knowledge and clinical practice and is consistent with the other evidence in your case record. For example, we will accept a diagnosis of HIV infection without definitive laboratory evidence of the HIV infection if you have an opportunistic disease that is predictive of a defect in cell-mediated immunity (for example, toxoplasmosis of the brain or Pneumocystis pneumonia (PCP)), and there is no other known cause of diminished resistance to that disease (for example, long-term steroid treatment or lymphoma). In such cases, we will make every reasonable effort to obtain full details of the history, medical findings, and results of testing.

2. Documentation of the manifestations of HIV infection.

a. Definitive documentation of manifestations of HIV infection. We may document manifestations of HIV infection by positive findings on definitive laboratory tests, such as culture, microscopic examination of biopsied tissue or other material (for example, bronchial washings), serologic tests, or on other generally acceptable definitive tests consistent with the prevailing state of medical knowledge and clinical practice.

b. We will make every reasonable effort to obtain the results of your laboratory testing. Pursuant to §§ 404.1519f and 416.919f of this chapter, we will purchase examinations or tests necessary to make a determination of your claim if no other acceptable documentation exists.

c. Other acceptable documentation of manifestations of HIV infection. We may also document manifestations of HIV infection without definitive laboratory evidence.

(i) We will accept a persuasive report from a physician that a positive diagnosis of your manifestation of HIV infection was confirmed by an appropriate laboratory test(s). To be persuasive, this report must state that you had the appropriate definitive laboratory test(s) for diagnosing your manifestation of HIV infection and provide the results. The report must also be consistent with the remaining evidence of record.

(ii) We may also document manifestations of HIV infection without the definitive laboratory evidence described in 14.00F2a, provided that such documentation is consistent with the prevailing state of medical knowledge and clinical practice and is consistent with the other evidence in your case record. For example, many conditions are now commonly diagnosed based on some or all of the following: Medical history, clinical manifestations, laboratory findings (including appropriate medically acceptable imaging), and treatment responses. In such cases, we will make every reasonable effort to obtain full details of the history, medical findings, and results of testing.

3. Disorders associated with HIV infection (14.11A–E).

a. Multicentric Castleman disease (MCD, 14.11A) affects multiple groups of lymph nodes and organs containing lymphoid tissue. This widespread involvement distinguishes MCD from localized (or unicentric) Castleman disease, which affects only a single set of lymph nodes. While not a cancer, MCD is known as a lymphoproliferative disorder. Its clinical presentation and progression is similar to that of lymphoma, and its treatment may include radiation or chemotherapy. We require characteristic findings on microscopic examination of the biopsied lymph nodes or other generally acceptable methods consistent with the prevailing state of medical knowledge and clinical practice to establish the diagnosis. Localized (or unicentric) Castleman disease does not meet or medically equal the criterion in 14.11A, but we may evaluate it under the criteria in 14.11H or 14.11I.

b. Primary central nervous system lymphoma (PCNSL, 14.11B) originates in the brain, spinal cord, meninges, or eye. Imaging tests (for example, MRI) of the brain, while not diagnostic, may show a single lesion or multiple lesions in the white matter of the brain. We require characteristic findings on microscopic examination of the cerebral spinal fluid or of the biopsied brain tissue, or other generally acceptable methods consistent with the prevailing state of medical knowledge and clinical practice to establish the diagnosis.

c. Primary effusion lymphoma (PEL, 14.11C) is also known as body cavity lymphoma. We require characteristic findings on microscopic examination of the effusion fluid or of the biopsied tissue from the affected internal organ, or other generally acceptable methods consistent with the prevailing state of medical knowledge and clinical practice to establish the diagnosis.

d. Progressive multifocal leukoencephalopathy (PML, 14.11D) is a progressive neurological degenerative syndrome caused by the John Cunningham (JC) virus in immunosuppressed individuals. Clinical findings of PML include clumsiness, progressive weakness, and visual and speech changes. Personality and cognitive changes may also occur. We require appropriate clinical findings, characteristic white matter lesions on MRI, and a positive PCR test for the JC virus in the cerebrospinal fluid to establish the diagnosis. We also accept a positive brain biopsy for JC virus or other generally acceptable methods consistent with the prevailing state of medical knowledge and clinical practice to establish the diagnosis.

e. Pulmonary Kaposi sarcoma (Kaposi sarcoma in the lung, 14.11E) is the most serious form of Kaposi sarcoma (KS). Other internal KS tumors (for example, tumors of the gastrointestinal tract) have a more variable prognosis. We require characteristic findings on microscopic examination of the induced sputum, bronchoalveolar lavage washings, or of the biopsied transbronchial tissue, or by other generally acceptable methods consistent with the prevailing state of medical knowledge and clinical practice to establish the diagnosis.

4. CD4 measurement (14.11F). To evaluate your HIV infection under 14.11F, we require one measurement of your absolute CD4 count (also known as CD4 count or CD4+ T-helper lymphocyte count). This measurement must occur within the period we are considering in connection with your application or continuing disability review. If you have more than one measurement of your absolute CD4 count within this period, we will use your lowest absolute CD4 count.

5. Measurement of CD4 and either body mass index or hemoglobin (14.11G). To evaluate your HIV infection under 14.11G, we require one measurement of your absolute CD4 count or your CD4 percentage, and either a measurement of your body mass index (BMI) or your hemoglobin. These measurements must occur within the period we are considering in connection with your application or continuing disability review. If you have more than one measurement of your CD4 (absolute count or percentage), BMI, or hemoglobin within this period, we will use the lowest of your CD4 (absolute count or percentage), BMI, or hemoglobin. The date of your lowest CD4 (absolute count or percentage) measurement may be different from the date of your lowest BMI or hemoglobin measurement. We calculate your BMI using the formulas in 5.00G2.

6. Complications of HIV infection requiring hospitalization (14.11H).

a. Complications of HIV infection may include infections (common or opportunistic), cancers, and other conditions. Examples of complications that may result in hospitalization include: Depression; diarrhea; immune reconstitution inflammatory syndrome; malnutrition; and PCP and other severe infections.

b. Under 14.11H, we require three hospitalizations within a 12-month period that are at least 30 days apart and that result from a complication(s) of HIV infection. The hospitalizations may be for the same complication or different complications of HIV infection and are not limited to the examples of complications that may result in hospitalization listed in 14.00F6a. All three hospitalizations must occur within the period we are considering in connection with your application or continuing disability review. Each hospitalization must last at least 48 hours, including hours in a hospital emergency department immediately before the hospitalization.

c. We will use the rules on medical equivalence in §§ 404.1526 and 416.926 of this chapter to evaluate your HIV infection if you have fewer, but longer, hospitalizations, or more frequent, but shorter, hospitalizations, or if you receive nursing, rehabilitation, or other care in alternative settings.

7. HIV infection manifestations specific to women.

a. General. Most women with severe immunosuppression secondary to HIV infection exhibit the typical opportunistic infections and other conditions, such as PCP, Candida esophagitis, wasting syndrome, cryptococcosis, and toxoplasmosis. However, HIV infection may have different manifestations in women than in men. Adjudicators must carefully scrutinize the medical evidence and be alert to the variety of medical conditions specific to, or common in, women with HIV infection that may affect their ability to function in the workplace.

b. Additional considerations for evaluating HIV infection in women. Many of these manifestations (for example, vulvovaginal candidiasis or pelvic inflammatory disease) occur in women with or without HIV infection, but can be more severe or resistant to treatment, or occur more frequently in a woman whose immune system is suppressed. Therefore, when evaluating the claim of a woman with HIV infection, it is important to consider gynecologic and other problems specific to women, including any associated symptoms (for example, pelvic pain), in assessing the severity of the impairment and resulting functional limitations. We may evaluate manifestations of HIV infection in women under 14.11H–I, or under the criteria for the appropriate body system (for example, cervical cancer under 13.23).

8. HIV-associated dementia (HAD). HAD is an advanced neurocognitive disorder, characterized by a significant decline in cognitive functioning. We evaluate HAD under 14.11I. Other names associated with

neurocognitive disorders due to HIV infection include: AIDS dementia complex, HIV dementia, HIV encephalopathy, and major neurocognitive disorder due to HIV infection.

G. How do we consider the effects of treatment in evaluating your autoimmune disorder, immune deficiency disorder, or HIV infection?

1. General. If your impairment does not otherwise meet the requirements of a listing, we will consider your medical treatment in terms of its effectiveness in improving the signs, symptoms, and laboratory abnormalities of your specific immune system disorder or its manifestations, and in terms of any side effects that limit your functioning. We will make every reasonable effort to obtain a specific description of the treatment you receive (including surgery) for your immune system disorder. We consider:

a. The effects of medications you take.

b. Adverse side effects (acute and chronic).

c. The intrusiveness and complexity of your treatment (for example, the dosing schedule, need for injections).

d. The effect of treatment on your mental functioning (for example, cognitive changes, mood disturbance).

e. Variability of your response to treatment (see 14.00G2).

f. The interactive and cumulative effects of your treatments. For example, many individuals with immune system disorders receive treatment both for their immune system disorders and for the manifestations of the disorders or co-occurring impairments, such as treatment for HIV infection and hepatitis C. The interactive and cumulative effects of these treatments may be greater than the effects of each treatment considered separately.

g. The duration of your treatment.

h. Any other aspects of treatment that may interfere with your ability to function.

2. Variability of your response to treatment. Your response to treatment and the adverse or beneficial consequences of your treatment may vary widely. The effects of your treatment may be temporary or long term. For example, some individuals may show an initial positive response to a drug or combination of drugs followed by a decrease in effectiveness. When we evaluate your response to treatment and how your treatment may affect you, we consider such factors as disease activity before treatment, requirements for changes in therapeutic regimens, the time required for therapeutic effectiveness of a particular drug or drugs, the limited number of drug combinations that may be available for your impairment(s), and the time-limited efficacy of some drugs. For example, an individual with HIV infection or another immune deficiency disorder who develops pneumonia or tuberculosis may not respond to the same antibiotic regimen used in treating individuals without HIV infection or another immune deficiency disorder, or may not respond to an antibiotic that he or she responded to before. Therefore, we must consider the effects of your treatment on an individual basis, including the effects of your treatment on your ability to function.

3. How we evaluate the effects of treatment for autoimmune disorders on your ability to function. Some medications may have acute or long-term side effects. When we consider the effects of corticosteroids or other treatments for autoimmune disorders on your ability to function, we consider the factors in 14.00G1 and 14.00G2. Long-term corticosteroid treatment can cause ischemic necrosis of bone, posterior subcapsular cataract, weight gain, glucose intolerance, increased susceptibility to infection, and osteoporosis that may result in a loss of function. In addition, medications used in the treatment of autoimmune disorders may also have effects on mental functioning, including cognition (for example, memory), concentration, and mood.

4. How we evaluate the effects of treatment for immune deficiency disorders, excluding HIV infection, on your ability to function. When we consider the effects of your treatment for your immune deficiency disorder on your ability to function, we consider the factors in 14.00G1 and 14.00G2. A frequent need for treatment such as intravenous immunoglobulin and gamma interferon therapy can be intrusive and interfere with your ability to work. We will also consider whether you have chronic side effects from these or other medications, including severe fatigue, fever, headaches, high blood pressure, joint swelling, muscle aches, nausea, shortness of breath, or limitations in mental function including cognition (for example, memory), concentration, and mood.

5. How we evaluate the effects of treatment for HIV infection on your ability to function.

a. General. When we consider the effects of antiretroviral drugs (including the effects of highly active antiretroviral therapy (HAART)) and the effects of treatments for the manifestations of HIV infection on your ability to function, we consider the factors in 14.00G1 and 14.00G2. Side effects of antiretroviral drugs include, but are not limited to: Bone marrow suppression, pancreatitis, gastrointestinal intolerance (nausea, vomiting, diarrhea), neuropathy, rash, hepatotoxicity, lipodystrophy (fat redistribution, such as "buffalo hump"), glucose intolerance, and lactic acidosis. In addition, medications used in the treatment of HIV infection may also have effects on mental functioning, including cognition (for example, memory), concentration, and mood, and may result in malaise, severe fatigue, joint and muscle pain, and insomnia. The symptoms of HIV infection and the side effects of medication may be indistinguishable from each other. We will consider all of your functional limitations, whether they result from your symptoms or signs of HIV infection or the side effects of your treatment.

b. Structured treatment interruptions. A structured treatment interruption (STI, also called a "drug holiday") is a treatment practice during which your treating source advises you to stop taking your medications temporarily. An STI in itself does not imply that your medical condition has improved; nor does it imply that you are noncompliant with your treatment because you are following your treating source's advice. Therefore, if you have stopped taking medication because your treating source prescribed or recommended an STI, we will not find that you are failing to follow treatment or draw inferences about the severity of your impairment on this fact alone. We will consider why your treating source has prescribed or recommended an STI and all the other information in your case record when we determine the severity of your impairment.

6. When there is no record of ongoing treatment. If you have not received ongoing treatment or have not had an ongoing relationship with the medical community despite the existence of a severe impairment(s), we will evaluate the medical severity and duration of your immune system disorder on the basis of the current objective medical evidence and other evidence in your case record, taking into consideration your medical history, symptoms, clinical and laboratory findings, and medical source opinions. If you have just begun treatment and we cannot determine whether you are disabled based on the evidence we have, we may need to wait to determine the effect of the treatment on your ability to function. The amount of time we need to wait will depend on the facts of your case. If you have not received treatment, you may not be able to show an impairment that meets the criteria of one of the immune system disorders listings, but your immune system disorder may medically equal a listing or be disabling based on a consideration of your residual functional capacity, age, education, and work experience.

H. How do we consider your symptoms, including your pain, severe fatigue, and malaise?

Your symptoms, including pain, severe fatigue, and malaise, may be important factors in our determination whether your immune system disorder(s) meets or medically equals a listing or in our determination whether you are otherwise able to work. In order for us to consider your symptoms, you must have medical signs or laboratory findings showing the existence of a medically determinable impairment(s) that could reasonably be expected to produce the symptoms. If you have such an impairment(s), we will evaluate the intensity, persistence, and functional effects of your symptoms using the rules throughout 14.00 and in our other regulations. See §§ 404.1521, 404.1529, 416.921, and 416.929. Additionally, when we assess the credibility of your complaints about your symptoms and their functional effects, we will not draw any inferences from the fact that you do not receive treatment or that you are not following treatment without considering all of the relevant evidence in your case record, including any explanations you provide that may explain why you are not receiving or following treatment.

I. How do we use the functional criteria in these listings?

1. The following listings in this body system include standards for evaluating the functional limitations resulting from immune system disorders: 14.02B, for systemic lupus erythematosus; 14.03B, for systemic vasculitis; 14.04D, for systemic sclerosis (scleroderma); 14.05E, for polymyositis and dermatomyositis; 14.06B, for undifferentiated and mixed connective tissue disease; 14.07C, for immune deficiency disorders, excluding HIV infection; 14.09D, for inflammatory arthritis; 14.10B, for Sjögren's syndrome; and 14.11I, for HIV infection.

2. When we use one of the listings cited in 14.00I1, we will consider all relevant information in your case record to determine the full impact of your immune system disorder on your ability to function on a sustained basis. Important factors we will consider when we evaluate your functioning under these listings include, but are not limited to: Your symptoms, the frequency and duration of manifestations of your immune system disorder, periods of exacerbation and remission, and the functional impact of your treatment, including the side effects of your medication.

3. As used in these listings, "repeated" means that the manifestations occur on an average of three times a year, or once every 4 months, each lasting 2 weeks or more; or the manifestations do not last for 2 weeks but occur substantially more frequently than three times in a year or once every 4 months; or they occur less frequently than an average of three times a year or once every 4 months but last substantially longer than 2 weeks. Your impairment will satisfy this criterion regardless of whether you have the same kind of manifestation repeatedly, all different manifestations, or any other combination of manifestations; for example, two of the same kind of manifestation and a different one. You must have the required number of manifestations with the frequency and duration required in this section. Also, the manifestations must occur within the period covered by your claim.

4. To satisfy the functional criterion in a listing, your immune system disorder must result in a "marked" level of limitation in one of three general areas of functioning: Activities of daily living, social functioning, or difficulties in completing tasks due to deficiencies in concentration, persistence, or pace. Functional limitation may result from the impact of the disease process itself on your mental functioning, physical functioning, or both your mental and physical functioning. This could result from persistent or inter-

mittent symptoms, such as depression, severe fatigue, or pain, resulting in a limitation of your ability to do a task, to concentrate, to persevere at a task, or to perform the task at an acceptable rate of speed. You may also have limitations because of your treatment and its side effects (see 14.00G).

5. Marked limitation means that the signs and symptoms of your immune system disorder interfere seriously with your ability to function. Although we do not require the use of such a scale, "marked" would be the fourth point on a five-point scale consisting of no limitation, mild limitation, moderate limitation, marked limitation, and extreme limitation. You may have a marked limitation when several activities or functions are impaired, or even when only one is impaired. Also, you need not be totally precluded from performing an activity to have a marked limitation, as long as the degree of limitation seriously interferes with your ability to function independently, appropriately, and effectively. The term "marked" does not imply that you must be confined to bed, hospitalized, or in a nursing home.

6. Activities of daily living include, but are not limited to, such activities as doing household chores, grooming and hygiene, using a post office, taking public transportation, or paying bills. We will find that you have a "marked" limitation of activities of daily living if you have a serious limitation in your ability to maintain a household or take public transportation because of symptoms, such as pain, severe fatigue, anxiety, or difficulty concentrating, caused by your immune system disorder (including manifestations of the disorder) or its treatment, even if you are able to perform some self-care activities.

7. Social functioning includes the capacity to interact independently, appropriately, effectively, and on a sustained basis with others. It includes the ability to communicate effectively with others. We will find that you have a "marked" limitation in maintaining social functioning if you have a serious limitation in social interaction on a sustained basis because of symptoms, such as pain, severe fatigue, anxiety, or difficulty concentrating, or a pattern of exacerbation and remission, caused by your immune system disorder (including manifestations of the disorder) or its treatment, even if you are able to communicate with close friends or relatives.

8. Completing tasks in a timely manner involves the ability to sustain concentration, persistence, or pace to permit timely completion of tasks commonly found in work settings. We will find that you have a "marked" limitation in completing tasks if you have a serious limitation in your ability to sustain concentration or pace adequate to complete work-related tasks because of symptoms, such as pain, severe fatigue, anxiety, or difficulty concentrating, caused by your immune system disorder (including manifestations of the disorder) or its treatment, even if you are able to do some routine activities of daily living.

J. How do we evaluate your immune system disorder when it does not meet one of these listings?

1. These listings are only examples of immune system disorders that we consider severe enough to prevent you from doing any gainful activity. If your impairment(s) does not meet the criteria of any of these listings, we must also consider whether you have an impairment(s) that satisfies the criteria of a listing in another body system.

2. Individuals with immune system disorders, including HIV infection, may manifest signs or symptoms of a mental impairment or of another physical impairment. For example, HIV infection may accelerate the onset of conditions such as diabetes or affect the course of or treatment options for diseases such as cardiovascular disease or hepatitis. We may evaluate these impairments under the affected body system. For example, we will evaluate:

a. Musculoskeletal involvement, such as surgical reconstruction of a joint, under 1.00.

b. Ocular involvement, such as dry eye, under 2.00.

c. Respiratory impairments, such as pleuritis, under 3.00.

d. Cardiovascular impairments, such as cardiomyopathy, under 4.00.

e. Digestive impairments, such as hepatitis (including hepatitis C) or weight loss as a result of HIV infection that affects the digestive system, under 5.00.

f. Genitourinary impairments, such as nephropathy, under 6.00.

g. Hematologic abnormalities, such as anemia, granulocytopenia, and thrombocytopenia, under 7.00.

h. Skin impairments, such as persistent fungal and other infectious skin eruptions, and photosensitivity, under 8.00.

i. Neurologic impairments, such as neuropathy or seizures, under 11.00.

j. Mental disorders, such as depression, anxiety, or cognitive deficits, under 12.00.

k. Allergic disorders, such as asthma or atopic dermatitis, under 3.00 or 8.00 or under the criteria in another affected body system.

l. Syphilis or neurosyphilis under the criteria for the affected body system; for example, 2.00 Special senses and speech, 4.00 Cardiovascular system, or 11.00 Neurological.

3. If you have a severe medically determinable impairment(s) that does not meet a listing, we will determine whether your impairment(s) medically equals a listing. (See §§ 404.1526 and 416.926.) If it does not, you may or may not have the residual functional capacity to engage in substantial gainful

activity. Therefore, we proceed to the fourth, and if necessary, the fifth steps of the sequential evaluation process in §§ 404.1520 and 416.920. We use the rules in §§ 404.1594, 416.994, and 416.994a as appropriate, when we decide whether you continue to be disabled.

14.01 Category of Impairments, Immune System Disorders.

14.02 Systemic lupus erythematosus. As described in 14.00D1. With:

A. Involvement of two or more organs/body systems, with:

1. One of the organs/body systems involved to at least a moderate level of severity; and

2. At least two of the constitutional symptoms or signs (severe fatigue, fever, malaise, or involuntary weight loss).

or

B. Repeated manifestations of SLE, with at least two of the constitutional symptoms or signs (severe fatigue, fever, malaise, or involuntary weight loss) and one of the following at the marked level:

1. Limitation of activities of daily living.

2. Limitation in maintaining social functioning.

3. Limitation in completing tasks in a timely manner due to deficiencies in concentration, persistence, or pace.

14.03 Systemic vasculitis. As described in 14.00D2. With:

A. Involvement of two or more organs/body systems, with:

1. One of the organs/body systems involved to at least a moderate level of severity; and

2. At least two of the constitutional symptoms or signs (severe fatigue, fever, malaise, or involuntary weight loss).

or

B. Repeated manifestations of systemic vasculitis, with at least two of the constitutional symptoms or signs (severe fatigue, fever, malaise, or involuntary weight loss) and one of the following at the marked level:

1. Limitation of activities of daily living.

2. Limitation in maintaining social functioning.

3. Limitation in completing tasks in a timely manner due to deficiencies in concentration, persistence, or pace.

14.04 Systemic sclerosis (scleroderma). As described in 14.00D3. With:

A. Involvement of two or more organs/body systems, with:

1. One of the organs/body systems involved to at least a moderate level of severity; and

2. At least two of the constitutional symptoms or signs (severe fatigue, fever, malaise, or involuntary weight loss).

or

B. With one of the following:

1. Toe contractures or fixed deformity of one or both feet, resulting in the inability to ambulate effectively as defined in 14.00C6; or

2. Finger contractures or fixed deformity in both hands, resulting in the inability to perform fine and gross movements effectively as defined in 14.00C7; or

3. Atrophy with irreversible damage in one or both lower extremities, resulting in the inability to ambulate effectively as defined in 14.00C6; or

4. Atrophy with irreversible damage in both upper extremities, resulting in the inability to perform fine and gross movements effectively as defined in 14.00C7.

or

C. Raynaud's phenomenon, characterized by:

1. Gangrene involving at least two extremities; or

2. Ischemia with ulcerations of toes or fingers, resulting in the inability to ambulate effectively or to perform fine and gross movements effectively as defined in 14.00C6 and 14.00C7;

or

D. Repeated manifestations of systemic sclerosis (scleroderma), with at least two of the constitutional symptoms or signs (severe fatigue, fever, malaise, or involuntary weight loss) and one of the following at the marked level:

1. Limitation of activities of daily living.

2. Limitation in maintaining social functioning.

3. Limitation in completing tasks in a timely manner due to deficiencies in concentration, persistence, or pace.

14.05 Polymyositis and dermatomyositis. As described in 14.00D4. With:

A. Proximal limb-girdle (pelvic or shoulder) muscle weakness, resulting in inability to ambulate effectively or inability to perform fine and gross movements effectively as defined in 14.00C6 and 14.00C7.

or

B. Impaired swallowing (dysphagia) with aspiration due to muscle weakness.

or

C. Impaired respiration due to intercostal and diaphragmatic muscle weakness.

or

D. Diffuse calcinosis with limitation of joint mobility or intestinal motility.

or

E. Repeated manifestations of polymyositis or dermatomyositis, with at least two of the constitutional symptoms or signs (severe fatigue, fever, malaise, or involuntary weight loss) and one of the following at the marked level:

1. Limitation of activities of daily living.
2. Limitation in maintaining social functioning.
3. Limitation in completing tasks in a timely manner due to deficiencies in concentration, persistence, or pace.

14.06 Undifferentiated and mixed connective tissue disease. As described in 14.00D5. With:

A. Involvement of two or more organs/body systems, with:

1. One of the organs/body systems involved to at least a moderate level of severity; and

2. At least two of the constitutional symptoms or signs (severe fatigue, fever, malaise, or involuntary weight loss).

or

B. Repeated manifestations of undifferentiated or mixed connective tissue disease, with at least two of the constitutional symptoms or signs (severe fatigue, fever, malaise, or involuntary weight loss) and one of the following at the marked level:

1. Limitation of activities of daily living.
2. Limitation in maintaining social functioning.
3. Limitation in completing tasks in a timely manner due to deficiencies in concentration, persistence, or pace.

14.07 Immune deficiency disorders, excluding HIV infection. As described in 14.00E. With:

A. One or more of the following infections. The infection(s) must either be resistant to treatment or require hospitalization or intravenous treatment three or more times in a 12–month period.

1. Sepsis; or
2. Meningitis; or
3. Pneumonia; or
4. Septic arthritis; or
5. Endocarditis; or
6. Sinusitis documented by appropriate medically acceptable imaging.

or

B. Stem cell transplantation as described under 14.00E3. Consider under a disability until at least 12 months from the date of transplantation. Thereafter, evaluate any residual impairment(s) under the criteria for the affected body system.

or

C. Repeated manifestations of an immune deficiency disorder, with at least two of the constitutional symptoms or signs (severe fatigue, fever, malaise, or involuntary weight loss) and one of the following at the marked level:

1. Limitation of activities of daily living.
2. Limitation in maintaining social function.
3. Limitation in completing tasks in a timely manner due to deficiencies in concentration, persistence, or pace.

14.08 [Reserved by 81 FR 86923]

14.09 Inflammatory arthritis. As described in 14.00D6. With:

A. Persistent inflammation or persistent deformity of:

1. One or more major peripheral weight-bearing joints resulting in the inability to ambulate effectively (as defined in 14.00C6); or

2. One or more major peripheral joints in each upper extremity resulting in the inability to perform fine and gross movements effectively (as defined in 14.00C7).

or

B. Inflammation or deformity in one or more major peripheral joints with:

1. Involvement of two or more organs/body systems with one of the organs/body systems involved to at least a moderate level of severity; and

2. At least two of the constitutional symptoms or signs (severe fatigue, fever, malaise, or involuntary weight loss).

or

C. Ankylosing spondylitis or other spondyloarthropathies, with:

1. Ankylosis (fixation) of the dorsolumbar or cervical spine as shown by appropriate medically acceptable imaging and measured on physical examination at 45° or more of flexion from the vertical position (zero degrees); or

2. Ankylosis (fixation) of the dorsolumbar or cervical spine as shown by appropriate medically acceptable imaging and measured on physical examination at 30° or more of flexion (but less than 45°) measured from the vertical position (zero degrees), and involvement of two or more organs/body systems with one of the organs/body systems involved to at least a moderate level of severity.

or

D. Repeated manifestations of inflammatory arthritis, with at least two of the constitutional symptoms or signs (severe fatigue, fever, malaise, or involuntary weight loss) and one of the following at the marked level:

1. Limitation of activities of daily living.

2. Limitation in maintaining social functioning.

3. Limitation in completing tasks in a timely manner due to deficiencies in concentration, persistence, or pace.

14.10 Sjögren's syndrome. As described in 14.00D7. With:

A. Involvement of two or more organs/body systems, with:

1. One of the organs/body systems involved to at least a moderate level of severity; and

2. At least two of the constitutional symptoms or signs (severe fatigue, fever, malaise, or involuntary weight loss).

or

B. Repeated manifestations of Sjögren's syndrome, with at least two of the constitutional symptoms or signs (severe fatigue, fever, malaise, or involuntary weight loss) and one of the following at the marked level:

1. Limitation of activities of daily living.

2. Limitation in maintaining social functioning.

3. Limitation in completing tasks in a timely manner due to deficiencies in concentration, persistence, or pace.

14.11 Human immunodeficiency virus (HIV) infection. With documentation as described in 14.00F1 and one of the following:

A. Multicentric (not localized or unicentric) Castleman disease affecting multiple groups of lymph nodes or organs containing lymphoid tissue (see 14.00F3a).

OR

B. Primary central nervous system lymphoma (see 14.00F3b).

OR

C. Primary effusion lymphoma (see 14.00F3c).

OR

D. Progressive multifocal leukoencephalopathy (see 14.00F3d).

OR

E. Pulmonary Kaposi sarcoma (see 14.00F3e).

OR

F. Absolute CD4 count of 50 cells/mm^3 or less (see 14.00F4).

OR

G. Absolute CD4 count of less than 200 cells/mm^3 or CD4 percentage of less than 14 percent, and one of the following (values do not have to be measured on the same date) (see 14.00F5):

1. BMI measurement of less than 18.5; or

2. Hemoglobin measurement of less than 8.0 grams per deciliter (g/dL).

OR

H. Complication(s) of HIV infection requiring at least three hospitalizations within a 12–month period and at least 30 days apart (see 14.00F6). Each hospitalization must last at least 48 hours, including hours in a hospital emergency department immediately before the hospitalization.

OR

I. Repeated (as defined in 14.00I3) manifestations of HIV infection, including those listed in 14.11A–H, but without the requisite findings for those listings (for example, Kaposi sarcoma not meeting the criteria in 14.11E), or other manifestations (including, but not limited to, cardiovascular disease (including myocarditis, pericardial effusion, pericarditis, endocarditis, or pulmonary arteritis), diarrhea, distal sensory polyneuropathy, glucose intolerance, gynecologic conditions (including cervical cancer or pelvic inflammatory disease, see 14.00F7), hepatitis, HIV–associated dementia, immune reconstitution inflammatory syndrome (IRIS), infections (bacterial, fungal, parasitic, or viral), lipodystrophy (lipoatrophy or lipohypertrophy), malnutrition, muscle weakness, myositis, neurocognitive or other mental limitations not meeting the criteria in 12.00, oral hairy leukoplakia, osteoporosis, pancreatitis, peripheral neuropathy) resulting in significant, documented symptoms or signs (for example, but not limited to, fever, headaches, insomnia, involuntary weight loss, malaise, nausea, night sweats, pain, severe fatigue, or vomiting) and one of the following at the marked level:

1. Limitation of activities of daily living.

2. Limitation in maintaining social functioning.

3. Limitation in completing tasks in a timely manner due to deficiencies in concentration, persistence, or pace.

[81 FR 66161, Sept. 26, 2016; 81 FR 86923, Dec. 2, 2016; 82 FR 5872, Jan. 18, 2017; 82 FR 39665, Aug. 22, 2017; 83 FR 11143, March 14, 2018]

APPENDIX 1–PART–B1. TO SUBPART P OF PART 404—LISTING OF IMPAIRMENTS

Part B

Medical criteria for the evaluation of impairments of children under age 18 (where criteria in part A do not give appropriate consideration to the particular disease process in childhood).

Sec.

100.00 Low Birth Weight and Failure to Thrive.

100.00 LOW BIRTH WEIGHT AND FAILURE TO THRIVE

A. What conditions do we evaluate under these listings? We evaluate low birth weight (LBW) in infants from birth to attainment of age 1 and failure to thrive (FTT) in infants and toddlers from birth to attainment of age 3.

B. How do we evaluate disability based on LBW under 100.04? In 100.04A and 100.04B, we use an infant's birth weight as documented by an original or certified copy of the infant's birth certificate or by a medical record signed by a physician. Birth weight means the first weight recorded after birth. In 100.04B, gestational age is the infant's age based on the date of conception as recorded in the medical record. If the infant's impairment meets the requirements for listing 100.04A or 100.04B, we will follow the rule in § 416.990(b)(11) of this chapter.

C. How do we evaluate disability based on FTT under 100.05?

1. General. We establish FTT with or without a known cause when we have documentation of an infant's or a toddler's growth failure and developmental delay from an acceptable medical source(s) as defined in § 416.913(a) of this chapter. We require documentation of growth measurements in 100.05A and developmental delay described in 100.05B or 100.05C within the same consecutive 12–month period. The dates of developmental testing and reports may be different from the dates of growth measurements. After the attainment of age 3, we evaluate growth failure under the affected body system(s).

2. Growth failure. Under 100.05A, we use the appropriate table(s) under 105.08B in the digestive system to determine whether a child's growth is less than the third percentile. The child does not need to have a digestive disorder for purposes of 100.05.

a. For children from birth to attainment of age 2, we use the weight-for-length table corresponding to the child's gender (Table I or Table II).

b. For children age 2 to attainment of age 3, we use the body mass index (BMI)-for-age table corresponding to the child's gender (Table III or Table IV).

c. BMI is the ratio of a child's weight to the square of his or her height. We calculate BMI using the formulas in 105.00G2c.

d. Growth measurements. The weight-for-length measurements for children from birth to the attainment of age 2 and BMI–for-age measurements for children age 2 to attainment of age 3 that are required for this listing must be obtained within a 12–month period and at least 60 days apart. If a child attains age 2 during the evaluation period, additional measurements are not needed. Any measurements taken before the child attains age 2 can be used to evaluate the impairment under the appropriate listing for the child's age. If the child attains age 3 during the evaluation period, the measurements can be used to evaluate the impairment in the affected body system.

3. Developmental delay.

a. Under 100.05B and C, we use reports from acceptable medical sources to establish delay in a child's development.

b. Under 100.05B, we document the severity of developmental delay with results from a standardized developmental assessment, which compares a child's level of development to the level typically expected for his or her chronological age. If the child was born prematurely, we may use the corrected chronological age (CCA) for comparison. (See § 416.924b(b) of this chapter.) CCA is the chronological age adjusted by a period of gestational prematurity. CCA = (chronological age)—(number of weeks premature). Acceptable medical sources or early intervention specialists, physical or occupational therapists, and other sources may conduct standardized developmental assessments and developmental screenings. The results of these tests and screenings must be accompanied by a statement or records from an acceptable medical source who established the child has a developmental delay.

c. Under 100.05C, when there are no results from a standardized developmental assessment in the case record, we need narrative developmental reports from the child's medical sources in sufficient detail to assess the severity of his or her developmental delay. A narrative developmental report is based on clinical observations, progress notes, and well-baby check-ups. To meet the requirements for 100.05C, the report must include: The child's developmental history; examination findings (with abnormal findings noted on repeated examinations); and an overall assessment of the child's development (that is, more than one or two isolated skills) by the medical source. Some narrative developmental reports may include results from developmental screening tests, which can identify a child who is not developing or achieving skills within expected timeframes. Although medical sources may refer to screening test results as supporting evidence in the narrative developmental report, screening test results alone cannot establish a diagnosis or the severity of developmental delay.

D. How do we evaluate disorders that do not meet one of these listings?

1. We may find infants disabled due to other disorders when their birth weights are greater than 1200 grams but less than 2000 grams and their weight and gestational age do not meet listing 100.04. The most common disorders of prematurity and LBW include retinopathy of prematurity (ROP), chronic lung disease of infancy (CLD, previously known as bronchopulmonary dysplasia, or BPD), intraventricular hemorrhage (IVH), necrotizing enterocolitis (NEC), and periventricular leukomalacia (PVL). Other disorders include poor nutrition and growth failure, hearing disorders, seizure disorders, cerebral palsy, and developmental disorders. We evaluate these disorders under the affected body systems.

2. We may evaluate infants and toddlers with growth failure that is associated with a known medical disorder under the body system of that medical disorder, for example, the respiratory or digestive body systems.

3. If an infant or toddler has a severe medically determinable impairment(s) that does not meet the criteria of any listing, we must also consider whether the child has an impairment(s) that medically equals a listing (see § 416.926 of this chapter). If the child's impairment(s) does not meet or medically equal a listing, we will determine whether the child's impairment(s) functionally equals the listings (see § 416.926a of this chapter) considering the factors in § 416.924a of this chapter. We use the rule in § 416.994a of this chapter when we decide whether a child continues to be disabled.

100.01 Category of Impairments, Low Birth Weight and Failure to Thrive

100.04 Low birth weight in infants from birth to attainment of age 1.

A. Birth weight (see 100.00B) of less than 1200 grams.

OR

B. The following gestational age and birth weight:

Gestational age (in weeks)	Birth weight
37-40	2000 grams or less.
36	1875 grams or less.
35	1700 grams or less.
34	1500 grams or less.
33	1325 grams or less.
32	1250 grams or less.

100.05 Failure to thrive in children from birth to attainment of age 3 (see 100.00C), documented by A and B, or A and C.

A. Growth failure as required in 1 or 2:

1. For children from birth to attainment of age 2, three weight-for-length measurements that are:

a. Within a consecutive 12–month period; and

b. At least 60 days apart; and

c. Less than the third percentile on the appropriate weight-for-length table in listing 105.08B1; or

2. For children age 2 to attainment of age 3, three BMI–for-age measurements that are:

a. Within a consecutive 12–month period; and

b. At least 60 days apart; and

c. Less than the third percentile on the appropriate BMI–for-age table in listing 105.08B2.

AND

B. Developmental delay (see 100.00C1 and C3), established by an acceptable medical source and documented by findings from one current report of a standardized developmental assessment (see 100.00C3b) that:

1. Shows development not more than two-thirds of the level typically expected for the child's age; or

2. Results in a valid score that is at least two standard deviations below the mean.

OR

C. Developmental delay (see 100.00C3), established by an acceptable medical source and documented by findings from two narrative developmental reports (see 100.00C3c) that:

1. Are dated at least 120 days apart (see 100.00C1); and

2. Indicate current development not more than two-thirds of the level typically expected for the child's age.

101.00 Musculoskeletal System

A. Disorders of the musculoskeletal system may result from hereditary, congenital, or acquired pathologic processes. Impairments may result from infectious, inflammatory, or degenerative processes, traumatic or developmental events, or neoplastic, vascular, or toxic/metabolic diseases.

B. Loss of Function

1. General. Under this section, loss of function may be due to bone or joint deformity or destruction from any cause; miscellaneous disorders of the spine

with or without radiculopathy or other neurological deficits; amputation; or fractures or soft tissue injuries, including burns, requiring prolonged periods of immobility or convalescence. The provisions of 101.02 and 101.03 notwithstanding, inflammatory arthritis is evaluated under 114.09 (see 114.00D6). We evaluate impairments with neurological causes under 111.00, as appropriate.

2. How We Define Loss of Function in These Listings

a. General. Regardless of the cause(s) of a musculoskeletal impairment, functional loss for purposes of these listings is defined as the inability to ambulate effectively on a sustained basis for any reason, including pain associated with the underlying musculoskeletal impairment, or the inability to perform fine and gross movements effectively on a sustained basis for any reason, including pain associated with the underlying musculoskeletal impairment. The inability to ambulate effectively or the inability to perform fine and gross movements effectively must have lasted, or be expected to last, for at least 12 months. For the purposes of these criteria, consideration of the ability to perform these activities must be from a physical standpoint alone. When there is an inability to perform these activities due to a mental impairment, the criteria in 112.00ff are to be used. We will determine whether a child can ambulate effectively or can perform fine and gross movements effectively based on the medical and other evidence in the case record, generally without developing additional evidence about the child's ability to perform the specific activities listed as examples in 101.00B2b(2) and (3) and 101.00B2c(2) and (3).

b. What We Mean by Inability To Ambulate Effectively

(1) Definition. Inability to ambulate effectively means an extreme limitation of the ability to walk; i.e., an impairment that interferes very seriously with the child's ability to independently initiate, sustain, or complete activities. Ineffective ambulation is defined generally as having insufficient lower extremity functioning (see 101.00J) to permit independent ambulation without the use of a hand-held assistive device(s) that limits the functioning of both upper extremities. (Listing 101.05C is an exception to this general definition because the child has the use of only one upper extremity due to amputation of a hand.)

(2) How we assess inability to ambulate effectively for children too young to be expected to walk independently. For children who are too young to be expected to walk independently, consideration of function must be based on assessment of limitations in the ability to perform comparable age-appropriate activities with the lower extremities, given normal developmental expectations. For such children, an extreme level of limitation means skills or performance at no greater than one-half of age-appropriate expectations based on an overall developmental assessment rather than on one or two isolated skills.

(3) How we assess inability to ambulate effectively for older children. Older children, who would be expected to be able to walk when compared to other children the same age who do not have impairments, must be capable of sustaining a reasonable walking pace over a sufficient distance to be able to carry out age-appropriate activities. They must have the ability to travel age-appropriately without extraordinary assistance to and from school or a place of employment. Therefore, examples of ineffective ambulation for older children include, but are not limited to, the inability to walk without the use of a walker, two crutches or two canes, the inability to walk a block at a reasonable pace on rough or uneven surfaces, the inability to use standard public transportation, the inability to carry out age-appropriate school activities independently, and the inability to climb a few steps at a reasonable pace with the use of a single hand rail. The ability to walk independently about the child's home or a short distance at school without the use of assistive devices does not, in and of itself, constitute effective ambulation.

c. What We Mean by Inability To Perform Fine and Gross Movements Effectively

(1) Definition. Inability to perform fine and gross movements effectively means an extreme loss of function of both upper extremities; i.e., an impairment that interferes very seriously with the child's ability to independently initiate, sustain, or complete activities. To use their upper extremities effectively, a child must be capable of sustaining such functions as reaching, pushing, pulling, grasping, and fingering in an age-appropriate manner to be able to carry out age-appropriate activities.

(2) How we assess inability to perform fine and gross movements in very young children. For very young children, we consider limitations in the ability to perform comparable age-appropriate activities involving the upper extremities compared to the ability of children the same age who do not have impairments. For such children, an extreme level of limitation means skills or performance at no greater than one-half of age-appropriate expectations based on an overall developmental assessment.

(3) How we assess inability to perform fine and gross movements in older children. For older children, examples of inability to perform fine and gross movements effectively include, but are not limited to, the inability to prepare a simple meal and feed oneself, the inability to take care of personal hygiene, or the inability to sort and handle papers or files, depending upon which activities are age-appropriate.

d. Pain or other symptoms. Pain or other symptoms may be an important factor contributing to functional loss. In order for pain or other symptoms to be found to affect a child's ability to function in an age-appropriate manner or to perform basic work activities, medical signs or laboratory findings must show the existence of a medically determinable impairment(s) that could reasonably be expected to produce the pain or other symptoms. The musculoskeletal listings that include pain or other symptoms among their criteria also include criteria for limitations in functioning as a result of the listed impairment, including limitations caused by pain. It is, therefore, important to evaluate the intensity and persistence of such pain or other symptoms carefully in order to determine their impact on the child's functioning under these listings. See also §§ 404.1525(f) and 404.1529 of this part, and §§ 416.925(f) and 416.929 of part 416 of this chapter.

C. Diagnosis and Evaluation

1. General. Diagnosis and evaluation of musculoskeletal impairments should be supported, as applicable, by detailed descriptions of the joints, including ranges of motion, condition of the musculature (e.g., weakness, atrophy), sensory or reflex changes, circulatory deficits, and laboratory findings, including findings on x-ray or other appropriate medically acceptable imaging. Medically acceptable imaging includes, but is not limited to, x-ray imaging, computerized axial tomography (CAT scan) or magnetic resonance imaging (MRI), with or without contrast material, myelography, and radionuclear bone scans. "Appropriate" means that the technique used is the proper one to support the evaluation and diagnosis of the impairment.

2. Purchase of certain medically acceptable imaging. While any appropriate medically acceptable imaging is useful in establishing the diagnosis of musculoskeletal impairments, some tests, such as CAT scans and MRIs, are quite expensive, and we will not routinely purchase them. Some, such as myelograms, are invasive and may involve significant risk. We will not order such tests. However, when the results of any of these tests are part of the existing evidence in the case record we will consider them together with the other relevant evidence.

3. Consideration of electrodiagnostic procedures. Electrodiagnostic procedures may be useful in establishing the clinical diagnosis, but do not constitute alternative criteria to the requirements of 101.04.

D. The physical examination must include a detailed description of the rheumatological, orthopedic, neurological, and other findings appropriate to the specific impairment being evaluated. These physical findings must be determined on the basis of objective observation during the examination and not simply a report of the child's allegation; e.g., "He says his leg is weak, numb." Alternative testing methods should be used to verify the abnormal findings; e.g., a seated straight-leg raising test in addition to a supine straight-leg raising test. Because abnormal physical findings may be intermittent, their presence over a period of time must be established by a record of ongoing management and evaluation. Care must be taken to ascertain that the reported examination findings are consistent with the child's age and activities.

E. Examination of the Spine

1. General. Examination of the spine should include a detailed description of gait, range of motion of the spine given quantitatively in degrees from the vertical position (zero degrees) or, for straight-leg raising from the sitting and supine position (zero degrees), any other appropriate tension signs, motor and sensory abnormalities, muscle spasm, when present, and deep tendon reflexes. Observations of the child during the examination should be reported; e.g., how he or she gets on and off the examination table. Inability to walk on the heels or toes, to squat, or to arise from a squatting position, when appropriate, may be considered evidence of significant motor loss. However, a report of atrophy is not acceptable as evidence of significant motor loss without circumferential measurements of both thighs and lower legs, or both upper and lower arms, as appropriate, at a stated point above and below the knee or elbow given in inches or centimeters. Additionally, a report of atrophy should be accompanied by measurement of the strength of the muscle(s) in question generally based on a grading system of 0 to 5, with 0 being complete loss of strength and 5 being maximum strength. A specific description of atrophy of hand muscles is acceptable without measurements of atrophy but should include measurements of grip and pinch strength. However, because of the unreliability of such measurement in younger children, these data are not applicable to children under 5 years of age.

2. When neurological abnormalities persist. Neurological abnormalities may not completely subside after treatment or with the passage of time. Therefore, residual neurological abnormalities that persist after it has been determined clinically or by direct surgical or other observation that the ongoing or progressive condition is no longer present will not satisfy the required findings in 101.04. More serious neurological deficits (paraparesis, paraplegia) are to be evaluated under the criteria in 111.00ff.

F. Major joints refers to the major peripheral joints, which are the hip, knee, shoulder, elbow, wrist-hand, and ankle-foot, as opposed to other peripheral joints (e.g., the joints of the hand or forefoot) or axial joints (i.e., the joints of the spine.) The wrist and hand are considered together as one major joint, as are the ankle and foot. Since only the ankle joint, which consists of the juncture of the bones of the lower leg (tibia and fibula) with the hindfoot (tarsal bones), but not the forefoot, is crucial to weight bearing, the ankle and foot are considered separately in evaluating weight bearing.

G. Measurements of joint motion are based on the techniques described in the chapter on the extremities, spine, and pelvis in the current edition of the "Guides to the Evaluation of Permanent Impairment" published by the American Medical Association.

H. Documentation.

1. General. Musculoskeletal impairments frequently improve with time or respond to treatment. Therefore, a longitudinal clinical record is generally important for the assessment of severity and expected duration of an impairment unless the child is a newborn or the claim can be decided favorably on the basis of the current evidence.

2. Documentation of medically prescribed treatment and response. Many children, especially those who have listing-level impairments, will have received the benefit of medically prescribed treatment. Whenever evidence of such treatment is available it must be considered.

3. When there is no record of ongoing treatment. Some children will not have received ongoing treatment or have an ongoing relationship with the medical community despite the existence of a severe impairment(s). In such cases, evaluation will be made on the basis of the current objective medical evidence and other available evidence, taking into consideration the child's medical history, symptoms, and medical source opinions. Even though a child who does not receive treatment may not be able to show an impairment that meets the criteria of one of the musculoskeletal listings, the child may have an impairment(s) that is either medically or, in the case of a claim for benefits under part 416 of this chapter, functionally equivalent in severity to one of the listed impairments.

4. Evaluation when the criteria of a musculoskeletal listing are not met. These listings are only examples of common musculoskeletal disorders that are severe enough to find a child disabled. Therefore, in any case in which a child has a medically determinable impairment that is not listed, an impairment that does not meet the requirements of a listing, or a combination of impairments no one of which meets the requirements of a listing, we will consider whether the child's impairment(s) is medically or, in the case of a claim for benefits under part 416 of this chapter, functionally equivalent in severity to the criteria of a listing. (See §§ 404.1526, 416.926, and 416.926a.) Individuals with claims for benefits under part 404, who have an impairment(s) with a level of severity that does not meet or equal the criteria of the musculoskeletal listings may or may not have the RFC that would enable them to engage in substantial gainful activity. Evaluation of the impairment(s) of these individuals should proceed through the final steps of the sequential evaluation process in § 404.1520 (or, as appropriate, the steps in the medical improvement review standard in § 404.1594).

I. Effects of Treatment

1. General. Treatments for musculoskeletal disorders may have beneficial effects or adverse side effects. Therefore, medical treatment (including surgical treatment) must be considered in terms of its effectiveness in ameliorating the signs, symptoms, and laboratory abnormalities of the disorder, and in terms of any side effects that may further limit the child.

2. Response to treatment. Response to treatment and adverse consequences of treatment may vary widely. For example, a pain medication may relieve a child's pain completely, partially, or not at all. It may also result in adverse effects, e.g., drowsiness, dizziness, or disorientation, that compromise the child's ability to function. Therefore, each case must be considered on an individual basis, and include consideration of the effects of treatment on the child's ability to function.

3. Documentation. A specific description of the drugs or treatment given (including surgery), dosage, frequency of administration, and a description of the complications or response to treatment should be obtained. The effects of treatment may be temporary or long-term. As such, the finding regarding the impact of treatment must be based on a sufficient period of treatment to permit proper consideration or judgment about future functioning.

J. Orthotic, Prosthetic, or Assistive Devices

1. General. Consistent with clinical practice, children with musculoskeletal impairments may be examined with and without the use of any orthotic, prosthetic, or assistive devices as explained in this section.

2. Orthotic devices. Examination should be with the orthotic device in place and should include an evaluation of the child's maximum ability to function effectively with the orthosis. It is unnecessary to routinely evaluate the child's ability to function without the orthosis in place. If the child has difficulty with, or is unable to use, the orthotic device, the medical basis for the difficulty should be documented. In such cases, if the impairment involves a lower extremity or extremities, the examination should include information on the child's ability to ambulate effectively without the device in place unless contraindicated by the medical judgment of a physician who has treated or examined the child.

3. Prosthetic devices. Examination should be with the prosthetic device in place. In amputations involving a lower extremity or extremities, it is unnecessary to evaluate the child's ability to walk without the prosthesis in place. However, the child's medical ability to use a prosthesis to ambulate effectively, as defined in 101.00B2b, should be evaluated. The condition of the stump should be evaluated without the prosthesis in place.

4. Hand-held assistive devices. When a child with an impairment involving a lower extremity or extremities uses a hand-held assistive device, such as a cane, crutch or walker, examination should be with and without the use of the assistive device unless contraindicated by the medical judgment of a physician who has treated or examined the child. The child's ability to ambulate with and without the device provides information as to whether, or the extent to which, the child is able to ambulate without assistance. The medical basis for the use of any assistive device (e.g., instability, weakness) should be documented. The requirement to use a hand-held assistive device may also impact on the child's functional capacity by virtue of the fact that one or both upper extremities are not available for such activities as lifting, carrying, pushing, and pulling.

K. Disorders of the spine, listed in 101.04, result in limitations because of distortion of the bony and ligamentous architecture of the spine and associated impingement on nerve roots (including the cauda equina) or spinal cord. Such impingement on nerve tissue may result from a herniated nucleus pulposus, spinal stenosis, arachnoiditis, or other miscellaneous conditions.

1. Herniated nucleus pulposus is a disorder frequently associated with the impingement of a nerve root, but occurs infrequently in children. Nerve root compression results in a specific neuro-anatomic distribution of symptoms and signs depending upon the nerve root(s) compromised.

2. Other miscellaneous conditions that may cause weakness of the lower extremities, sensory changes, areflexia, trophic ulceration, bladder or bowel incontinence, and that should be evaluated under 101.04 include, but are not limited to, lysosomal disorders, metabolic disorders, vertebral osteomyelitis, vertebral fractures and achondroplasia. Disorders such as spinal dysrhaphism, (e.g., spina bifida) diastematomyelia, and tethered cord syndrome may also cause such abnormalities. In these cases, there may be gait difficulty and deformity of the lower extremities based on neurological abnormalities, and the neurological effects are to be evaluated under the criteria in 111.00ff.

L. Abnormal curvatures of the spine. Abnormal curvatures of the spine (specifically, scoliosis, kyphosis and kyphoscoliosis) can result in impaired ambulation, but may also adversely affect functioning in body systems other than the musculoskeletal system. For example, a child's ability to breathe may be affected; there may be cardiac difficulties (e.g., impaired myocardial function); or there may be disfigurement resulting in withdrawal or isolation. When there is impaired ambulation, evaluation of equivalence may be made by reference to 114.09A. When the abnormal curvature of the spine results in symptoms related to fixation of the dorsolumbar or cervical spine, evaluation of equivalence may be made by reference to 114.09C. When there is respiratory or cardiac involvement or an associated mental disorder, evaluation may be made under 103.00ff, 104.00ff, or 112.00ff, as appropriate. Other consequences should be evaluated according to the listing for the affected body system.

M. Under continuing surgical management, as used in 101.07 and 101.08, refers to surgical procedures and any other associated treatments related to the efforts directed toward the salvage or restoration of functional use of the affected part. It may include such factors as post-surgical procedures, surgical complications, infections, or other medical complications, related illnesses, or related treatments that delay the child's attainment of maximum benefit from therapy. When burns are not under continuing surgical management, see 108.00F.

N. After maximum benefit from therapy has been achieved in situations involving fractures of an upper extremity (101.07), or soft tissue injuries (101.08), i.e., there have been no significant changes in physical findings or on appropriate medically acceptable imaging for any 6–month period after the last definitive surgical procedure or other medical intervention, evaluation must be made on the basis of the demonstrable residuals, if any. A finding that 101.07 or 101.08 is met must be based on a consideration of the symptoms, signs, and laboratory findings associated with recent or anticipated surgical procedures and the resulting recuperative periods, including any related medical complications, such as infections, illnesses, and therapies which impede or delay the efforts toward restoration of function. Generally, when there has been no surgical or medical intervention for 6 months after the last definitive surgical procedure, it can be concluded that maximum therapeutic benefit has been reached. Evaluation at this point must be made on the basis of the demonstrable residual limitations, if any, considering the child's impairment-related symptoms, signs, and laboratory findings, any residual symptoms, signs, and laboratory findings associated with such surgeries, complications, and recuperative periods, and other relevant evidence.

O. Major function of the face and head, for purposes of listing 101.08, relates to impact on any or all of the activities involving vision, hearing, speech, mastication, and the initiation of the digestive process.

P. When surgical procedures have been performed, documentation should include a copy of the operative notes and available pathology reports.

101.01 Category of Impairments, Musculoskeletal

101.02 Major dysfunction of a joint(s) (due to any cause): Characterized by gross anatomical deformity (e.g., subluxation, contracture, bony or fibrous ankylosis, instability) and chronic joint pain and stiffness with signs of limitation of motion or other abnormal motion of the affected joint(s), and findings on appropriate medically acceptable imaging of joint space narrowing, bony destruction, or ankylosis of the affected joint(s). With:

A. Involvement of one major peripheral weight-bearing joint (i.e., hip, knee, or ankle), resulting in inability to ambulate effectively, as defined in 101.00B2b;

or

B. Involvement of one major peripheral joint in each upper extremity (i.e., shoulder, elbow, or wrist-hand), resulting in inability to perform fine and gross movements effectively, as defined in 101.00B2c.

101.03 Reconstructive surgery or surgical arthrodesis of a major weight-bearing joint, with inability to ambulate effectively, as defined in 101.00B2b, and return to effective ambulation did not occur, or is not expected to occur, within 12 months of onset.

101.04 Disorders of the spine (e.g., lysosomal disorders, metabolic disorders, vertebral osteomyelitis, vertebral fracture, achondroplasia) resulting in compromise of a nerve root (including the cauda equina) or the spinal cord, with evidence of nerve root compression characterized by neuro-anatomic distribution of pain, limitation of motion of the spine, motor loss (atrophy with associated muscle weakness or muscle weakness) accompanied by sensory or reflex loss and, if there is involvement of the lower back, positive straight-leg raising test (sitting and supine).

101.05 Amputation (due to any cause).

A. Both hands;

or

B. One or both lower extremities at or above the tarsal region, with stump complications resulting in medical inability to use a prosthetic device to ambulate effectively, as defined in 101.00B2b, which have lasted or are expected to last for at least 12 months;

or

C. One hand and one lower extremity at or above the tarsal region, with inability to ambulate effectively, as defined in 101.00B2b;

or

D. Hemipelvectomy or hip disarticulation.

101.06 Fracture of the femur, tibia, pelvis, or one or more of the tarsal bones. With:

A. Solid union not evident on appropriate medically acceptable imaging, and not clinically solid;

and

B. Inability to ambulate effectively, as defined in 101.00B2b, and return to effective ambulation did not occur or is not expected to occur within 12 months of onset.

101.07 Fracture of an upper extremity with non-union of a fracture of the shaft of the humerus, radius, or ulna, under continuing surgical management, as defined in 101.00M, directed toward restoration of functional use of the extremity, and such function was not restored or expected to be restored within 12 months of onset.

101.08 Soft tissue injury (e.g., burns) of an upper or lower extremity, trunk, or face and head, under continuing surgical management, as defined in 101.00M, directed toward the salvage or restoration of major function, and such major function was not restored or expected to be restored within 12 months of onset. Major function of the face and head is described in 101.00O.

102.00 Special Senses and Speech

A. How do we evaluate visual disorders?

1. What are visual disorders? Visual disorders are abnormalities of the eye, the optic nerve, the optic tracts, or the brain that may cause a loss of visual acuity or visual fields. A loss of visual acuity limits your ability to distinguish detail, read, do fine work, or perform other age-appropriate activities. A loss of visual fields limits your ability to perceive visual stimuli in the peripheral extent of vision.

2. How do we define statutory blindness? Statutory blindness is blindness as defined in sections 216(i)(1) and 1614(a)(2) of the Social Security Act (Act).

a. The Act defines blindness as central visual acuity of 20/200 or less in the better eye with the use of a correcting lens. We use your best-corrected central visual acuity for distance in the better eye when we determine if this definition is met. (For visual acuity testing requirements, see 102.00A5.)

b. The Act also provides that an eye that has a visual field limitation such that the widest diameter of the visual field subtends an angle no greater than 20 degrees is considered as having a central visual acuity of 20/200 or less. (For visual field testing requirements, see 102.00A6.)

c. You have statutory blindness only if your visual disorder meets the criteria of 102.02A, 102.02B, or 102.03A. You do not have statutory blindness if your visual disorder medically equals the criteria of 102.02A, 102.02B, or 102.03A or meets or medically equals the criteria of 102.03B, 102.03C, 102.04A, or 102.04B because your disability is based on criteria other than those in the statutory definition of blindness.

3. What evidence do we need to establish statutory blindness under title XVI? To establish that you have statutory blindness under title XVI, we need evidence showing only that your central visual acuity in your better eye or your visual field in your better eye meets the criteria in 102.00A2, provided that those measurements are consistent with the other evidence in your case record. We do not need documentation of the cause of your blindness. Also, there is no duration

requirement for statutory blindness under title XVI (see §§ 416.981 and 416.983 of this chapter).

4. What evidence do we need to evaluate visual disorders, including those that result in statutory blindness under title II? To evaluate your visual disorder, we usually need a report of an eye examination that includes measurements of your best-corrected central visual acuity (see 102.00A5) or the extent of your visual fields (see 102.00A6), as appropriate. If you have visual acuity or visual field loss, we need documentation of the cause of the loss. A standard eye examination will usually indicate the cause of any visual acuity loss. A standard eye examination can also indicate the cause of some types of visual field deficits. Some disorders, such as cortical visual disorders, may result in abnormalities that do not appear on a standard eye examination. If the standard eye examination does not indicate the cause of your vision loss, we will request the information used to establish the presence of your visual disorder. If your visual disorder does not satisfy the criteria in 102.02, 102.03, or 102.04, we will request a description of how your visual disorder affects your ability to function.

5. How do we measure your best-corrected central visual acuity?

a. Visual acuity testing. When we need to measure your best-corrected central visual acuity, which is your optimal visual acuity attainable with the use of a corrective lens, we use visual acuity testing for distance that was carried out using Snellen methodology or any other testing methodology that is comparable to Snellen methodology.

(i) Your best-corrected central visual acuity for distance is usually measured by determining what you can see from 20 feet. If your visual acuity is measured for a distance other than 20 feet, we will convert it to a 20–foot measurement. For example, if your visual acuity is measured at 10 feet and is reported as 10/40, we will convert this measurement to 20/80.

(ii) A visual acuity recorded as CF (counts fingers), HM (hand motion only), LP or LPO (light perception or light perception only), or NLP (no light perception) indicates that no optical correction will improve your visual acuity. If your central visual acuity in an eye is recorded as CF, HM, LP or LPO, or NLP, we will determine that your best-corrected central visual acuity is 20/200 or less in that eye.

(iii) We will not use the results of pinhole testing or automated refraction acuity to determine your best-corrected central visual acuity. These tests provide an estimate of potential visual acuity but not an actual measurement of your best-corrected central visual acuity.

(iv) Very young children, such as infants and toddlers, cannot participate in testing using Snellen methodology or other comparable testing. If you are unable to participate in testing using Snellen methodology or other comparable testing due to your young age, we will consider clinical findings of your fixation and visual-following behavior. If both these behaviors are absent, we will consider the anatomical findings or the results of neuroimaging, electroretinogram, or visual evoked response (VER) testing when this testing has been performed.

b. Other test charts.

(i) Children between the ages of 3 and 5 often cannot identify the letters on a Snellen or other letter test chart. Specialists with expertise in assessment of childhood vision use alternate methods for measuring visual acuity in young children. We consider alternate methods, for example, the Landolt C test or the tumbling–E test, which are used to evaluate young children who are unable to participate in testing using Snellen methodology, to be comparable to testing using Snellen methodology.

(ii) Most test charts that use Snellen methodology do not have lines that measure visual acuity between 20/100 and 20/200. Some test charts, such as the Bailey–Lovie or the Early Treatment Diabetic Retinopathy Study (ETDRS), used mostly in research settings, have such lines. If your visual acuity is measured with one of these charts, and you cannot read any of the letters on the 20/100 line, we will determine that you have statutory blindness based on a visual acuity of 20/200 or less. For example, if your best-corrected central visual acuity for distance in the better eye is 20/160 using an ETDRS chart, we will find that you have statutory blindness. Regardless of the type of test chart used, you do not have statutory blindness if you can read at least one letter on the 20/100 line. For example, if your best-corrected central visual acuity for distance in the better eye is 20/125+1 using an ETDRS chart, we will find that you do not have statutory blindness because you are able to read one letter on the 20/100 line.

c. Testing using a specialized lens. In some instances, you may have visual acuity testing performed using a specialized lens, such as a contact lens. We will use the visual acuity measurements obtained with a specialized lens only if you have demonstrated the ability to use the specialized lens on a sustained basis. We will not use visual acuity measurements obtained with telescopic lenses.

d. Cycloplegic refraction is an examination of the eye performed after administering cycloplegic eye drops capable of relaxing the ability of the pupil to become smaller and temporarily paralyzing the focusing muscles. If your case record contains the results of cycloplegic refraction, we may use the results to determine your best-corrected central visual acuity. We will not purchase cycloplegic refraction.

e. VER testing measures your response to visual events and can often detect dysfunction that is undetectable through other types of examinations. If you have an absent response to VER testing in your better eye, we will determine that your best-corrected central visual acuity is 20/200 or less in that eye and that your visual acuity loss satisfies the criterion in 102.02A or 102.02B4, as appropriate, when these test results are consistent with the other evidence in your case record. If you have a positive response to VER testing in an eye, we will not use that result to determine your best-corrected central visual acuity in that eye.

6. How do we measure your visual fields?

a. General. We generally need visual field testing when you have a visual disorder that could result in visual field loss, such as glaucoma, retinitis pigmentosa, or optic neuropathy, or when you display behaviors that suggest a visual field loss. When we need to measure the extent of your visual field loss, we use visual field testing (also referred to as perimetry) carried out using automated static threshold perimetry performed on an acceptable perimeter. (For perimeter requirements, see 102.00A9.)

b. Automated static threshold perimetry requirements.

(i) The test must use a white size III Goldmann stimulus and a 31.5 apostilb (asb) white background (or a 10 candela per square meter (cd/m^2) white background). The stimuli test locations must be no more than 6 degrees apart horizontally or vertically. Measurements must be reported on standard charts and include a description of the size and intensity of the test stimulus.

(ii) We measure the extent of your visual field loss by determining the portion of the visual field in which you can see a white III4e stimulus. The "III" refers to the standard Goldmann test stimulus size III (4 mm^2), and the "4e" refers to the standard Goldmann intensity filter (0 decibel (dB) attenuation, which allows presentation of the maximum luminance) used to determine the intensity of the stimulus.

(iii) In automated static threshold perimetry, the intensity of the stimulus varies. The intensity of the stimulus is expressed in decibels (dB). A perimeter's maximum stimulus luminance is usually assigned the value 0 dB. We need to determine the dB level that corresponds to a 4e intensity for the particular perimeter being used. We will then use the dB printout to determine which points you see at a 4e intensity level (a "seeing point"). For example:

A. When the maximum stimulus luminance (0 dB stimulus) on an acceptable perimeter is 10,000 asb, a 10 dB stimulus is equivalent to a 4e stimulus. Any point you see at 10 dB or greater is a seeing point.

B. When the maximum stimulus luminance (0 dB stimulus) on an acceptable perimeter is 4,000 asb, a 6 dB stimulus is equivalent to a 4e stimulus. Any point you see at 6 dB or greater is a seeing point.

C. When the maximum stimulus luminance (0 dB stimulus) on an acceptable perimeter is 1,000 asb, a 0 dB stimulus is equivalent to a 4e stimulus. Any point you see at 0 dB or greater is a seeing point.

c. Evaluation under 102.03A. To determine statutory blindness based on visual field loss in your better eye (102.03A), we need the results of a visual field test that measures the central 24 to 30 degrees of your visual field; that is, the area measuring 24 to 30 degrees from the point of fixation. Acceptable tests include the Humphrey Field Analyzer (HFA) 30–2, HFA 24–2, and Octopus 32.

d. Evaluation under 102.03B. To determine whether your visual field loss meets listing 102.03B, we use the mean deviation or defect (MD) from acceptable automated static threshold perimetry that measures the central 30 degrees of the visual field. MD is the average sensitivity deviation from normal values for all measured visual field locations. When using results from HFA tests, which report the MD as a negative number, we use the absolute value of the MD to determine whether your visual field loss meets listing 102.03B. We cannot use tests that do not measure the central 30 degrees of the visual field, such as the HFA 24–2, to determine if your impairment meets or medically equals 102.03B.

e. Other types of perimetry. If your case record contains visual field measurements obtained using manual or automated kinetic perimetry, such as Goldmann perimetry or the HFA "SSA Test Kinetic," we can generally use these results if the kinetic test was performed using a white III4e stimulus projected on a white 31.5 asb (10 cd/m^2) background. Automated kinetic perimetry, such as the HFA "SSA Test Kinetic," does not detect limitations in the central visual field because testing along a meridian stops when you see the stimulus. If your visual disorder has progressed to the point at which it is likely to result in a significant limitation in the central visual field, such as a scotoma (see 102.00A6h), we will not use automated kinetic perimetry to determine the extent of your visual field loss. Instead, we will determine the extent of your visual field loss using automated static threshold perimetry or manual kinetic perimetry.

f. Screening tests. We will not use the results of visual field screening tests, such as confrontation tests, tangent screen tests, or automated static screening tests, to determine that your impairment meets or medically equals a listing, or functionally equals the listings. We can consider normal results from visual field screening tests to determine whether your visual disorder is severe when these test results are consistent with the other evidence in your case record. (See § 416.924(c) of this chapter.) We will not consider normal test results to be consistent with the other evidence if the clinical findings indicate that your visual disorder has progressed to the point that it is likely to cause visual field loss, or you have a history of an operative procedure for retinal detachment.

g. Use of corrective lenses. You must not wear eyeglasses during visual field testing because they limit your field of vision. You may wear contact lenses to correct your visual acuity during the visual field test to obtain the most accurate visual field measurements. For this single purpose, you do not need to demonstrate that you have the ability to use the contact lenses on a sustained basis.

h. Scotoma. A scotoma is a field defect or non-seeing area (also referred to as a "blind spot") in the visual field surrounded by a normal field or seeing area. When we measure your visual field, we subtract the length of any scotoma, other than the normal blind spot, from the overall length of any diameter on which it falls.

7. How do we determine your visual acuity efficiency, visual field efficiency, and visual efficiency?

a. General. Visual efficiency, a calculated value of your remaining visual function, is the combination of your visual acuity efficiency and your visual field efficiency expressed as a percentage.

b. Visual acuity efficiency. Visual acuity efficiency is a percentage that corresponds to the best-corrected central visual acuity for distance in your better eye. See Table 1.

Table 1—Visual Acuity Efficiency

Snellen best-corrected central visual acuity for distance		Visual acuity efficiency (%) (102.04A)
English	Metric	
20/16	6/5	100
20/20	6/6	100
20/25	6/7.5	95
20/30	6/9	90
20/40	6/12	85
20/50	6/15	75
20/60	6/18	70
20/70	6/21	65
20/80	6/24	60
20/100	6/30	50

c. Visual field efficiency. Visual field efficiency is a percentage that corresponds to the visual field in your better eye. Under 102.03C, we require kinetic perimetry to determine your visual field efficiency percentage. We calculate the visual field efficiency percentage by adding the number of degrees you see along the eight principal meridians found on a visual field chart (0, 45, 90, 135, 180, 225, 270, and 315) in your better eye and dividing by 5. For example, in Figure 1:

A. The diagram of the left eye illustrates a visual field, as measured with a III4e stimulus, contracted to 30 degrees in two meridians (180 and 225) and to 20 degrees in the remaining six meridians. The visual efficiency percentage of this field is: ((2 x 30) + (6 x 20)) ÷ 5 = 36 percent.

B. The diagram of the right eye illustrates the extent of a normal visual field as measured with a III4e stimulus. The sum of the eight principal meridians of this field is 500 degrees. The visual efficiency percentage of this field is 500 ÷ 5 = 100 percent.

Figure 1:

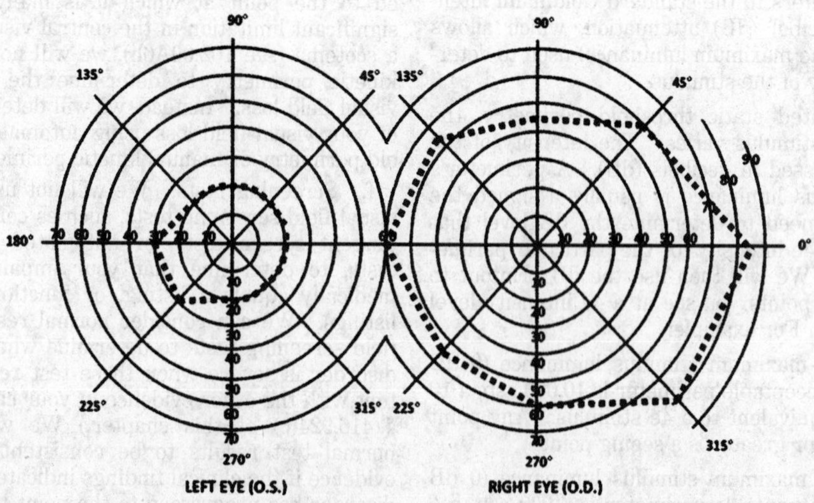

d. Visual efficiency. Under 102.04A, we calculate the visual efficiency percentage by multiplying your visual acuity efficiency percentage (see 102.00A7b) by your visual field efficiency percentage (see 102.00A7c) and dividing by 100. For example, if your visual acuity efficiency percentage is 75 and your visual field efficiency percentage is 36, your visual efficiency percentage is: (75 x 36) ÷ 100 = 27 percent.

8. How do we determine your visual acuity impairment value, visual field impairment value, and visual impairment value?

a. General. Visual impairment value, a calculated value of your loss of visual function, is the combination of your visual acuity impairment value and your visual field impairment value.

b. Visual acuity impairment value. Your visual acuity impairment value corresponds to the best-corrected central visual acuity for distance in your better eye. See Table 2.

Table 2—Visual Acuity Impairment Value

Snellen best-corrected central visual acuity for distance		Visual acuity impairment value (102.04B)
English	Metric	
20/16	6/5	0.00
20/20	6/6	0.00
20/25	6/7.5	0.10
20/30	6/9	0.18
20/40	6/12	0.30
20/50	6/15	0.40
20/60	6/18	0.48
20/70	6/21	0.54
20/80	6/24	0.60
20/100	6/30	0.70

c. Visual field impairment value. Your visual field impairment value corresponds to the visual field in your better eye. Using the MD from acceptable automated static threshold perimetry, we calculate the visual field impairment value by dividing the absolute value of the MD by 22. For example, if your MD on an HFA 30–2 is -16, your visual field impairment value is: |-16| ÷ 22 = 0.73.

d. Visual impairment value. Under 102.04B, we calculate the visual impairment value by adding your visual acuity impairment value (see 102.00A8b) and your visual field impairment value (see 102.00A8c). For example, if your visual acuity impairment value is 0.48 and your visual field impairment value is 0.73, your visual impairment value is: 0.48 + 0.73 = 1.21.

9. What are our requirements for an acceptable perimeter? We will use results from automated static threshold perimetry performed on a perimeter that:

a. Uses optical projection to generate the test stimuli.

b. Has an internal normative database for automatically comparing your performance with that of the general population.

c. Has a statistical analysis package that is able to calculate visual field indices, particularly mean deviation or mean defect.

d. Demonstrates the ability to correctly detect visual field loss and correctly identify normal visual fields.

e. Demonstrates good test-retest reliability.

f. Has undergone clinical validation studies by three or more independent laboratories with results published in peer-reviewed ophthalmic journals.

B. How do we evaluate hearing loss?

1. What evidence do we need?

a. We need evidence showing that you have a medically determinable impairment that causes your hearing loss and audiometric measurements of the severity of your hearing loss. We generally require both an otologic examination and audiometric testing to establish that you have a medically determinable impairment that causes your hearing loss. You should have this audiometric testing within 2 months of the otologic examination. Once we have evidence that you have a medically determinable impairment, we can use the results of later audiometric testing to assess the severity of your hearing loss without another otologic examination. We will consider your test scores together with any other relevant information we have about your hearing, including information from outside of the test setting.

b. The otologic examination must be performed by a licensed physician (medical or osteopathic doctor) or audiologist. It must include your medical history, your description of how your hearing loss affects you, and the physician's or audiologist's description of the appearance of the external ears (pinnae and external ear canals), evaluation of the tympanic membranes, and assessment of any middle ear abnormalities.

c. Audiometric testing must be performed by, or under the direct supervision of, a licensed audiologist or an otolaryngologist.

2. What audiometric testing do we need when you do not have a cochlear implant?

a. General. We need either physiologic or behavioral testing (other than screening testing, see 102.00B2g) that is appropriate for your age at the time of testing. See 102.00B2c–102.00B2f. We will make every reasonable effort to obtain the results of physiologic testing that has been done; however, we will not purchase such testing.

b. Testing requirements. The testing must be conducted in accordance with the most recently published standards of the American National Standards Institute (ANSI). You must not wear hearing aids during the testing. Additionally, a person described in 102.00B1c must perform an otoscopic examination immediately before the audiometric testing. (An otoscopic examination provides a description of the appearance of your external ear canals and an evaluation of the tympanic membranes. In these rules, we use the term to include otoscopic examinations performed by physicians and otoscopic inspections performed by audiologists and others.) The otoscopic examination must show that there are no conditions that would prevent valid audiometric testing, such as fluid in the ear, ear infection, or obstruction in an ear canal. The person performing the test should also report on any other factors, such as your ability to maintain attention, that can affect the interpretation of the test results.

c. Children from birth to the attainment of age 6 months.

(i) We need physiologic testing, such as auditory brainstem response (ABR) testing.

(ii) To determine whether your hearing loss meets 102.10A, we will average your hearing thresholds at 500, 1000, 2000, and 4000 Hertz (Hz). If you do not have a response at a particular frequency, we will use a threshold of 5 decibels (dB) over the limit of the audiometer.

d. Children from age 6 months to the attainment of age 2.

(i) We need air conduction thresholds determined by a behavioral assessment, usually visual reinforcement audiometry (VRA). We can use ABR testing if the behavioral assessment cannot be completed or if the results are inconclusive or unreliable.

(ii) To determine whether your hearing loss meets 102.10A, we will average your hearing thresholds at 500, 1000, 2000, and 4000 Hz. If you do not have a response at a particular frequency, we will use a threshold of 5 dB over the limit of the audiometer.

(iii) For this age group, behavioral assessments are often performed in a sound field, and each ear is not tested separately. If each ear is not tested separately, we will consider the test results to represent the hearing in the better ear.

e. Children from age 2 to the attainment of age 5.

(i) We need air conduction thresholds determined by a behavioral assessment, such as conditioned play audiometry (CPA), tangible or visually reinforced operant conditioning audiometry (TROCA, VROCA), or VRA. If you have had ABR testing, we can use the results of that testing if the behavioral assessment cannot be completed or the results are inconclusive or unreliable.

(ii) To determine whether your hearing loss meets 102.10A, we will average your hearing thresholds at 500, 1000, 2000, and 4000 Hz. If you do not have a response at a particular frequency, we will use a threshold of 5 dB over the limit of the audiometer.

(iii) For this age group, behavioral assessments are often performed in a sound field and each ear is not tested separately. If each ear is not tested separately, we will consider the test results to represent the hearing in the better ear.

f. Children from age 5 to the attainment of age 18.

(i) We generally need pure tone air conduction and bone conduction testing, speech reception threshold (SRT) testing (also referred to as "spondee threshold" or "ST" testing), and word recognition testing (also referred to as "word discrimination" or "speech discrimination" testing). This testing must be conducted in a sound-treated booth or room and must be in accordance with the most recently published ANSI standards. Each ear must be tested separately.

(ii) To determine whether your hearing loss meets the air and bone conduction criterion in 102.10B1 or 102.10B3, we will average your hearing thresholds at 500, 1000, 2000, and 4000 Hz. If you do not have a response at a particular frequency, we will use a threshold of 5 dB over the limit of the audiometer.

(iii) The SRT is the minimum dB level required for you to recognize 50 percent of the words on a standard list of spondee words. (Spondee words are two-syllable words that have equal stress on each syllable.) The SRT is usually within 10 dB of the average pure tone air conduction hearing thresholds at 500, 1000, and 2000 Hz. If the SRT is not within 10 dB of the average pure tone air conduction threshold, the reason for the discrepancy must be documented. If we cannot determine that there is a medical basis for the discrepancy, we will not use the results of the testing to determine whether your hearing loss meets a listing.

(iv) Word recognition testing determines your ability to recognize an age-appropriate, standardized list of phonetically balanced monosyllabic words in the absence of any visual cues. This testing must be performed in quiet. The list may be recorded or presented live, but in either case, the words should be presented at a level of amplification that will measure your maximum ability to discriminate words, usually 35 to 40 dB above your SRT. However, the amplification level used in the testing must be medically appropriate, and you must be able to tolerate it. If you cannot be tested at 35 to 40 dB above your SRT, the person who performs the test should report your word recognition testing score at your highest comfortable level of amplification.

g. Screening testing. Physiologic testing, such as ABR and otoacoustic emissions (OAE), and pure tone testing can be used as hearing screening tests. We will not use these tests to determine that your hearing loss meets or medically equals a listing, or to assess functional limitations due to your hearing loss, when they are used only as screening tests. We can consider normal results from hearing screening tests to determine that your hearing loss is not "severe" when these test results are consistent with the other evidence in your case record. See § 416.924(c).

3. What audiometric testing do we need when you have a cochlear implant?

a. If you have a cochlear implant, we will consider you to be disabled until age 5, or for 1 year after initial implantation, whichever is later.

b. After that period, we need word recognition testing performed with any age-appropriate version of the Hearing in Noise Test (HINT) or the Hearing in Noise Test for Children (HINT–C) to determine whether your impairment meets 102.11B. This testing must be conducted in quiet in a sound field. Your implant must be functioning properly and adjusted to your normal settings. The sentences should be presented at 60 dB HL (Hearing Level) and without any visual cues.

4. How do we evaluate your word recognition ability if you are not fluent in English?

If you are not fluent in English, you should have word recognition testing using an appropriate word list for the language in which you are most fluent. The person conducting the test should be fluent in the language used for the test. If there is no appropriate word list or no person who is fluent in the language and qualified to perform the test, it may not be possible to measure your word recognition ability. If your word recognition ability cannot be measured, your hearing loss cannot meet 102.10B2 or 102.11B. Instead, we will consider the facts of your case to determine whether you have difficulty understanding words in the language in which you are most fluent, and if so, whether that degree of difficulty medically equals 102.10B2 or 102.11B. For example, we will consider how you interact with family members, interpreters, and other persons who speak the language in which you are most fluent.

5. What do we mean by a marked limitation in speech or language as used in 102.10B3?

a. We will consider you to have a marked limitation in speech if:

(i) Entire phrases or sentences in your conversation are intelligible to unfamiliar listeners at least 50 percent (half) of the time but no more than 67 percent (two-thirds) of the time on your first attempt; and

(ii) Your sound production or phonological patterns (the ways in which you combine speech sounds) are atypical for your age.

b. We will consider you to have a marked limitation in language when your current and valid test score on an appropriate comprehensive, standardized test of overall language functioning is at least two standard deviations below the mean. In addition, the evidence of your daily communication functioning must be consistent with your test score. If you are not fluent in English, it may not be possible to test your language performance. If we cannot test your language performance, your hearing loss cannot meet 102.10B3. Instead, we will consider the facts of your case to determine whether your hearing loss medically equals 102.10B3.

C.[1] How do we evaluate impairments that do not meet one of the special senses and speech listings?

1. These listings are only examples of common special senses and speech disorders that we consider severe enough to result in marked and severe functional limitations. If your impairment(s) does not meet the criteria of any of these listings, we must also consider whether you have an impairment(s) that satisfies the criteria of a listing in another body system.

2. If you have a medically determinable impairment(s) that does not meet a listing, we will determine whether the impairment(s) medically equals a listing or functionally equals the listings. (See §§ 416.926 and 416.926a.) We use the rules in § 416.994a when we decide whether you continue to be disabled.

102.01 Category of Impairments, Special Senses and Speech

102.02 Loss of central visual acuity.

A. Remaining vision in the better eye after best correction is 20/200 or less.

OR

B. An inability to participate in visual acuity testing using Snellen methodology or other comparable testing, clinical findings that fixation and visual-following behavior are absent in the better eye, and one of the following:

1. Abnormal anatomical findings indicating a visual acuity of 20/200 or less in the better eye (such as the presence of Stage III or worse retinopathy of prematurity despite surgery, hypoplasia of the optic nerve, albinism with macular aplasia, or bilateral optic atrophy); or

2. Abnormal neuroimaging documenting damage to the cerebral cortex which would be expected to prevent the development of a visual acuity better than 20/200 in the better eye (such as neuroimaging showing bilateral encephalomyelitis or bilateral encephalomalacia); or

3. Abnormal electroretinogram documenting the presence of Leber's congenital amaurosis or achromatopsia in the better eye; or

4. An absent response to VER testing in the better eye.

102.03 Contraction of the visual field in the better eye, with:

A. The widest diameter subtending an angle around the point of fixation no greater than 20 degrees.

OR

[1] The official CFR appears to have inadvertently omitted section 102.00C of part B. See 75 FR 30693.

B. An MD of 22 decibels or greater, determined by automated static threshold perimetry that measures the central 30 degrees of the visual field (see 102.00A6d.).

OR

C. A visual field efficiency of 20 percent or less, determined by kinetic perimetry (see 102.00A7c).

102.04 Loss of visual efficiency, or visual impairment, in the better eye:

A. A visual efficiency percentage of 20 or less after best correction (see 102.00A7d.).

OR

B. A visual impairment value of 1.00 or greater after best correction (see 102.00A8d).

102.10 Hearing loss not treated with cochlear implantation.

A. For children from birth to the attainment of age 5, an average air conduction hearing threshold of 50 decibels or greater in the better ear (see 102.00B2).

OR

B. For children from age 5 to the attainment of age 18:

1. An average air conduction hearing threshold of 70 decibels or greater in the better ear and an average bone conduction hearing threshold of 40 decibels or greater in the better ear (see 102.00B2f); or

2. A word recognition score of 40 percent or less in the better ear determined using a standardized list of phonetically balanced monosyllabic words (see 102.00B2f); or

3. An average air conduction hearing threshold of 50 decibels or greater in the better ear and a marked limitation in speech or language (see 102.00B2f and 102.00B5).

102.11 Hearing loss treated with cochlear implantation.

A. Consider under a disability until the attainment of age 5 or for 1 year after initial implantation, whichever is later.

OR

B. Upon the attainment of age 5 or 1 year after initial implantation, whichever is later, a word recognition score of 60 percent or less determined using the HINT or the HINT–C (see 102.00B3b).

103.00 Respiratory Disorders

A. Which disorders do we evaluate in this body system?

1. We evaluate respiratory disorders that result in obstruction (difficulty moving air out of the lungs) or restriction (difficulty moving air into the lungs), or that interfere with diffusion (gas exchange) across cell membranes in the lungs. Examples of such disorders and the listings we use to evaluate them include chronic obstructive pulmonary disease (103.02), chronic lung disease of infancy (also known as bronchopulmonary dysplasia, 103.02C or 103.02E), pulmonary fibrosis (103.02), asthma (103.02 or 103.03), and cystic fibrosis (103.04). We also use listings in this body system to evaluate respiratory failure resulting from an underlying chronic respiratory disorder (103.04E or 103.14) and lung transplantation (103.11).

2. We evaluate cancers affecting the respiratory system under the listings in 113.00. We evaluate the pulmonary effects of neuromuscular and autoimmune disorders under these listings or under the listings in 111.00 or 114.00, respectively.

B. What are the symptoms and signs of respiratory disorders? Symptoms and signs of respiratory disorders include dyspnea (shortness of breath), chest pain, coughing, wheezing, sputum production, hemoptysis (coughing up blood from the respiratory tract), use of accessory muscles of respiration, and tachypnea (rapid rate of breathing).

C. What abbreviations do we use in this body system?

1. BiPAP means bi-level positive airway pressure ventilation.

2. BTPS means body temperature and ambient pressure, saturated with water vapor.

3. CF means cystic fibrosis.

4. CFRD means CF–related diabetes.

5. CFTR means CF transmembrane conductance regulator.

6. CLD means chronic lung disease of infancy.

7. FEV_1 means forced expiratory volume in the first second of a forced expiratory maneuver.

8. FVC means forced vital capacity.

9. L means liter.

D. What documentation do we need to evaluate your respiratory disorder?

1. We need medical evidence to document and assess the severity of your respiratory disorder. Medical evidence should include your medical history, physical examination findings, the results of imaging (see 103.00D3), spirometry (see 103.00E), other relevant laboratory tests, and descriptions of any prescribed treatment and your response to it. We may not need all of this evidence depending on your particular respiratory disorder and its effects on you.

2. If you use supplemental oxygen, we still need medical evidence to establish the severity of your respiratory disorder.

3. Imaging refers to medical imaging techniques, such as x-ray and computerized tomography. The imaging must be consistent with the prevailing state of

medical knowledge and clinical practice as the proper technique to support the evaluation of the disorder.

E. What is spirometry and what are our requirements for an acceptable test and report?

1. Spirometry, which measures how well you move air into and out of your lungs, involves at least three forced expiratory maneuvers during the same test session. A forced expiratory maneuver is a maximum inhalation followed by a forced maximum exhalation, and measures exhaled volumes of air over time. The volume of air you exhale in the first second of the forced expiratory maneuver is the FEV_1. The total volume of air that you exhale during the entire forced expiratory maneuver is the FVC. We use your highest FEV_1 value to evaluate your respiratory disorder under 103.02A and 103.04A, and your highest FVC value to evaluate your respiratory disorder under 103.02B, regardless of whether the values are from the same forced expiratory maneuver or different forced expiratory maneuvers. We will not purchase spirometry for children who have not attained age 6.

2. We have the following requirements for spirometry under these listings:

a. You must be medically stable at the time of the test. Examples of when we would not consider you to be medically stable include when you are:

(i) Within 2 weeks of a change in your prescribed respiratory medication.

(ii) Experiencing, or within 30 days of completion of treatment for, a lower respiratory tract infection.

(iii) Experiencing, or within 30 days of completion of treatment for, an acute exacerbation (temporary worsening) of a chronic respiratory disorder. Wheezing by itself does not indicate that you are not medically stable.

b. During testing, if your FEV_1 is less than 70 percent of your predicted normal value, we require repeat spirometry after inhalation of a bronchodilator to evaluate your respiratory disorder under these listings, unless it is medically contraindicated. If you used a bronchodilator before the test and your FEV_1 is less than 70 percent of your predicted normal value, we still require repeat spirometry after inhalation of a bronchodilator unless the supervising physician determines that it is not safe for you to take a bronchodilator again (in which case we may need to reschedule the test). If you do not have post-bronchodilator spirometry, the test report must explain why. We can use the results of spirometry administered without bronchodilators when the use of bronchodilators is medically contraindicated.

c. Your forced expiratory maneuvers must be satisfactory. We consider a forced expiratory maneuver to be satisfactory when you exhale with maximum effort following a full inspiration, and when the test tracing has a sharp takeoff and rapid rise to peak flow, has a smooth contour, and either lasts for at least 6 seconds (for children age 10 and older) or for at least 3 seconds (for children who have not attained age 10), or maintains a plateau for at least 1 second.

3. The spirometry report must include the following information:

a. The date of the test and your name, age or date of birth, gender, and height without shoes. (We will assume that your recorded height on the date of the test is without shoes, unless we have evidence to the contrary.) If your spine is abnormally curved (for example, you have kyphoscoliosis), we will substitute the longest distance between your outstretched fingertips with your arms abducted 90 degrees in place of your height when this measurement is greater than your standing height without shoes.

b. Any factors, if applicable, that can affect the interpretation of the test results (for example, your cooperation or effort in doing the test).

c. Legible tracings of your forced expiratory maneuvers in a volume-time format showing your name and the date of the test for each maneuver.

4. If you have attained age 6, we may need to purchase spirometry to determine whether your disorder meets a listing, unless we can make a fully favorable determination or decision on another basis.

5. Before we purchase spirometry for a child age 6 or older, a medical consultant (see § 416.1016 of this chapter), preferably one with experience in the care of children with respiratory disorders, must review your case record to determine if we need the test. If we purchase spirometry, the medical source we designate to administer the test is solely responsible for deciding whether it is safe for you to do the test and for how to administer it.

F. What is CLD and how do we evaluate it?

1. CLD, also known as bronchopulmonary dysplasia, or BPD, is scarring of the immature lung. CLD may develop as a complication of mechanical ventilation and oxygen therapy for infants with significant neonatal respiratory problems. Within the first 6 months of life, most infants with CLD are successfully weaned from mechanical ventilation, and then weaned from oxygen supplementation. We evaluate CLD under 103.02C, 103.02E, or if you are age 2 or older, under 103.03 or another appropriate listing.

2. If you have CLD, are not yet 6 months old, and need 24–hour-per-day oxygen supplementation, we will not evaluate your CLD under 103.02C until you are 6 months old. Depending on the evidence in your case record, we may make a fully favorable determination or decision under other rules before you are 6 months old.

3. We evaluate your CLD under 103.02C if you are at least 6 months old and you need 24–hour-per-day oxygen supplementation. (If you were born prema-

turely, we use your corrected chronological age. See § 416.924b(b) of this chapter.) We also evaluate your CLD under 103.02C if you were weaned off oxygen supplementation but needed it again by the time you were 6 months old or older.

4. We evaluate your CLD under 103.02E if you are any age from birth to the attainment of age 2 and have CLD exacerbations or complications (for example, wheezing, lower respiratory tract infections, or acute respiratory distress) that require hospitalization. For the purpose of 103.02E, we count your initial birth hospitalization as one hospitalization. The phrase "consider under a disability for 1 year from the discharge date of the last hospitalization or until the attainment of age 2, whichever is later" in 103.02E does not refer to the date on which your disability began, only to the date on which we must reevaluate whether your impairment(s) continues to meet a listing or is otherwise disabling.

G. What is asthma and how do we evaluate it?

1. Asthma is a chronic inflammatory disorder of the lung airways that we evaluate under 103.02 or 103.03. If you have respiratory failure resulting from chronic asthma (see 103.00J), we will evaluate it under 103.14.

2. For the purposes of 103.03:

a. The phrase "consider under a disability for 1 year" explains how long your asthma can meet the requirements of the listing. It does not refer to the date on which your disability began, only to the date on which we must reevaluate whether your asthma continues to meet a listing or is otherwise disabling.

b. We determine the onset of your disability based on the facts of your case, but it will be no later than the admission date of your first of three hospitalizations that satisfy the criteria of 103.03.

H. What is CF and how do we evaluate it?

1. General. We evaluate CF, a genetic disorder that results in abnormal salt and water transport across cell membranes in the lungs, pancreas, and other body organs, under 103.04. We need the evidence described in 103.00H2 to establish that you have CF.

2. Documentation of CF. We need a report signed by a physician (see § 416.913(a) of this chapter) showing both a and b:

a. One of the following:

(i) A positive newborn screen for CF; or

(ii) A history of CF in a sibling; or

(iii) Documentation of at least one specific CF phenotype or clinical criterion (for example, chronic sinopulmonary disease with persistent colonization or infections with typical CF pathogens, pancreatic insufficiency, or salt-loss syndromes); and

b. One of the following definitive laboratory tests:

(i) An elevated sweat chloride concentration equal to or greater than 60 millimoles per L; or

(ii) The identification of two CF gene mutations affecting the CFTR; or

(iii) Characteristic abnormalities in ion transport across the nasal epithelium.

c. When we have the report showing a and b, but it is not signed by a physician, we also need a report from a physician stating that you have CF.

d. When we do not have the report showing a and b, we need a report from a physician that is persuasive that a positive diagnosis of CF was confirmed by an appropriate definitive laboratory test. To be persuasive, this report must include a statement by the physician that you had the appropriate definitive laboratory test for diagnosing CF. The report must provide the test results or explain how your diagnosis was established that is consistent with the prevailing state of medical knowledge and clinical practice.

3. CF pulmonary exacerbations. Examples of CF pulmonary exacerbations include increased cough and sputum production, hemoptysis, increased shortness of breath, increased fatigue, and reduction in pulmonary function. Treatment usually includes intravenous antibiotics and intensified airway clearance therapy (for example, increased frequencies of chest percussion or increased use of inhaled nebulized therapies, such as bronchodilators or mucolytics).

4. For 103.04G, we require any two exacerbations or complications from the list in 103.04G1 through 103.04G4 within a 12–month period. You may have two of the same exacerbation or complication or two different ones.

a. If you have two of the acute exacerbations or complications we describe in 103.04G1 and 103.04G2, there must be at least 30 days between the two.

b. If you have one of the acute exacerbations or complications we describe in 103.04G1 and 103.04G2 and one of the chronic complications we describe in 103.04G3 and 103.04G4, the two can occur during the same time. For example, your CF meets 103.04G if you have the pulmonary hemorrhage we describe in 103.04G2 and the weight loss we describe in 103.04G3 even if the pulmonary hemorrhage occurs during the 90–day period in 103.04G3.

c. Your CF also meets 103.04G if you have both of the chronic complications in 103.04G3 and 103.04G4.

5. CF may also affect other body systems such as digestive or endocrine. If your CF, including pulmonary exacerbations and nonpulmonary complications, does not meet or medically equal a respiratory disorders listing, we may evaluate your CF–related impairments under the listings in the affected body system.

I. How do we evaluate lung transplantation? If you receive a lung transplant (or a lung transplant simultaneously with other organs, such as the heart), we will consider you to be disabled under 103.11 for 3 years from the date of the transplant. After that, we evaluate your residual impairment(s) by considering the adequacy of your post-transplant function, the frequency and severity of any rejection episodes you have, complications in other body systems, and adverse treatment effects. Children who receive organ transplants generally have impairments that meet our definition of disability before they undergo transplantation. The phrase "consider under a disability for 3 years" in 103.11 does not refer to the date on which your disability began, only to the date on which we must reevaluate whether your impairment(s) continues to meet a listing or is otherwise disabling. We determine the onset of your disability based on the facts of your case.

J. What is respiratory failure and how do we evaluate it? Respiratory failure is the inability of the lungs to perform their basic function of gas exchange. We evaluate respiratory failure under 103.04E if you have CF–related respiratory failure, or under 103.14 if you have respiratory failure due to any other chronic respiratory disorder. Continuous positive airway pressure does not satisfy the criterion in 103.04E or 103.14, and cannot be substituted as an equivalent finding, for invasive mechanical ventilation or noninvasive ventilation with BiPAP.

K. How do we evaluate growth failure due to any chronic respiratory disorder?

1. To evaluate growth failure due to any chronic respiratory disorder, we require documentation of the oxygen supplementation described in 103.06A and the growth measurements in 103.06B within the same consecutive 12–month period. The dates of oxygen supplementation may be different from the dates of growth measurements.

2. Under 103.06B, we use the appropriate table(s) under 105.08B in the digestive system to determine whether a child's growth is less than the third percentile.

a. For children from birth to attainment of age 2, we use the weight-for-length table corresponding to the child's gender (Table I or Table II).

b. For children age 2 to attainment of age 18, we use the body mass index (BMI)-for-age table corresponding to the child's gender (Table III or Table IV).

c. BMI is the ratio of a child's weight to the square of his or her height. We calculate BMI using the formulas in 105.00G2c.

L. How do we evaluate respiratory disorders that do not meet one of these listings?

1. These listings are only examples of common respiratory disorders that we consider severe enough to result in marked and severe functional limitations. If your impairment(s) does not meet the criteria of any of these listings, we must also consider whether you have an impairment(s) that meets the criteria of a listing in another body system. For example, if your CF has resulted in chronic pancreatic or hepatobiliary disease, we evaluate your impairment under the listings in 105.00.

2. If you have a severe medically determinable impairment(s) that does not meet a listing, we will determine whether your impairment(s) medically equals a listing. See § 416.926 of this chapter. Respiratory disorders may be associated with disorders in other body systems, and we consider the combined effects of multiple impairments when we determine whether they medically equal a listing. If your impairment(s) does not meet or medically equal a listing, we will also consider whether it functionally equals the listings. See § 416.926a of this chapter. We use the rules in § 416.994a of this chapter when we decide whether you continue to be disabled.

103.01 Category of Impairments, Respiratory Disorders

103.02 Chronic respiratory disorders due to any cause except CF (for CF, see 103.04), with A, B, C, D, or E:

A. FEV_1 (see 103.00E) less than or equal to the value in Table I–A or I–B for your age, gender, and height without shoes (see 103.00E3a).

Table I—FEV1 Criteria for 103.02A

Table I-A			Table I-B			
Age 6 to attainment of age 13 (for both females and males)			Age 13 to attainment of age 18			
Height without shoes (centimeters) < means less than	Height without shoes (inches) < means less than	FEV1 less than or equal to (L, BTPS)	Height without shoes (centimeters) < means less than	Height without shoes (inches) < means less than	Females FEV1 less than or equal to (L, BTPS)	Males FEV1 less than or equal to (L, BTPS)
<123.0	<48.50	0.80	<153.0	<60.25	1.35	1.40
123.0 to <129.0	48.50 to <50.75	0.90	153.0 to <159.0	60.25 to <62.50	1.45	1.50
129.0 to <134.0	50.75 to <52.75	1.00	159.0 to <164.0	62.50 to <64.50	1.55	1.60
134.0 to <139.0	52.75 to <54.75	1.10	164.0 to <169.0	64.50 to <66.50	1.65	1.70
139.0 to <144.0	54.75 to <56.75	1.20	169.0 to <174.0	66.50 to <68.50	1.75	1.85
144.0 to <149.0	56.75 to <58.75	1.30	174.0 to <180.0	68.50 to <70.75	1.85	2.00
149.0 or more	58.75 or more	1.40	180.0 or more	70.75 or more	1.95	2.10

OR

B. FVC (see 103.00E) less than or equal to the value in Table II–A or II–B for your age, gender, and height without shoes (see 103.00E3a).

Table II—FVC Criteria for 103.02B

Table II-A			Table II-B			
Age 6 to attainment of age 13 (for both females and males)			Age 13 to attainment of age 18			
Height without shoes (centimeters) < means less than	Height without shoes (inches) < means less than	FVC less than or equal to (L, BTPS)	Height without shoes (centimeters) < means less than	Height without shoes (inches) < means less than	Females FVC less than or equal to (L, BTPS)	Males FVC less than or equal to (L, BTPS)
<123.0	<48.50	0.85	<153.0	<60.25	1.65	1.65
123.0 to <129.0	48.50 to <50.75	1.00	153.0 to <159.0	60.25 to <62.50	1.70	1.80
129.0 to <134.0	50.75 to <52.75	1.10	159.0 to <164.0	62.50 to <64.50	1.80	1.95
134.0 to <139.0	52.75 to <54.75	1.30	164.0 to <169.0	64.50 to <66.50	1.95	2.10
139.0 to <144.0	54.75 to <56.75	1.40	169.0 to <174.0	66.50 to <68.50	2.05	2.25
144.0 to <149.0	56.75 to <58.75	1.55	174.0 to <180.0	68.50 to <70.75	2.20	2.45
149.0 or more	58.75 or more	1.70	180.0 or more	70.75 or more	2.30	2.55

OR

C. Hypoxemia with the need for at least 1.0 L per minute of continuous (24 hours per day) oxygen supplementation for at least 90 consecutive days.

OR

D. The presence of a tracheostomy.

1. Consider under a disability until the attainment of age 3; or

2. Upon the attainment of age 3, documented need for mechanical ventilation via a tracheostomy for at least 4 hours per day and for at least 90 consecutive days.

OR

E. For children who have not attained age 2, CLD (see 103.00F) with exacerbations or complications requiring three hospitalizations within a 12–month period and at least 30 days apart (the 12–month period must occur within the period we are considering in connection with your application or continuing disability review). Each hospitalization must last at least 48 hours, including hours in a hospital emergency department immediately before the hospitalization. (A child's initial birth hospitalization when CLD is first diagnosed counts as one hospitalization.) Consider under a disability for 1 year from the discharge date of the last hospitalization or until the attainment of age 2, whichever is later. After that, evaluate the impairment(s) under 103.03 or another appropriate listing.

103.03 Asthma (see 103.00G) with exacerbations or complications requiring three hospitalizations within a 12–month period and at least 30 days apart (the 12–month period must occur within the period we are considering in connection with your application or continuing disability review). Each hospitalization must last at least 48 hours, including hours in a hospital emergency department immediately before the hospitalization. Consider under a disability for 1 year from the discharge date of the last hospitalization; after that, evaluate the residual impairment(s) under 103.03 or another appropriate listing.

103.04 Cystic fibrosis (documented as described in 103.00H), with A, B, C, D, E, F, or G:

A. FEV_1 (see 103.00E) less than or equal to the value in Table III–A or Table III–B for your age, gender, and height without shoes (see 103.00E3a).

Table III—FEV1 Criteria for 103.04A

Table III-A			Table III-B			
Age 6 to attainment of age 13 (for both females and males)			Age 13 to attainment of age 18			
Height without shoes (centimeters) < means less than	Height without shoes (inches) < means less than	FEV1 less than or equal to (L, BTPS)	Height without shoes (centimeters) < means less than	Height without shoes (inches) < means less than	Females FEV1 less than or equal to (L, BTPS)	Males FEV1 less than or equal to (L, BTPS)
<123.0	<48.50	1.00	<153.0	<60.25	1.75	1.85
123.0 to <129.0	48.50 to <50.75	1.15	153.0 to <159.0	60.25 to <62.50	1.85	2.05
129.0 to <134.0	50.75 to <52.75	1.25	159.0 to <164.0	62.50 to <64.50	1.95	2.15
134.0 to <139.0	52.75 to <54.75	1.40	164.0 to <169.0	64.50 to <66.50	2.10	2.30
139.0 to <144.0	54.75 to <56.75	1.50	169.0 to <174.0	66.50 to <68.50	2.25	2.45
144.0 to <149.0	56.75 to <58.75	1.70	174.0 to <180.0	68.50 to <70.75	2.35	2.60
149.0 or more	58.75 or more	1.80	180.0 or more	70.75 or more	2.50	2.70

OR

B. For children who have not attained age 6, findings on imaging (see 103.00D3) of thickening of the proximal bronchial airways, nodular-cystic lesions, segmental or lobular atelectasis, or consolidation, and documentation of one of the following:

1. Shortness of breath with activity; or

2. Accumulation of secretions as manifested by repetitive coughing; or

3. Bilateral rales or rhonchi, or reduction of breath sounds.

OR

C. Exacerbations or complications (see 103.00H3) requiring three hospitalizations of any length within a 12–month period and at least 30 days apart (the 12–month period must occur within the period we are considering in connection with your application or continuing disability review).

OR

D. Spontaneous pneumothorax, secondary to CF, requiring chest tube placement.

OR

E. Respiratory failure (see 103.00J) requiring invasive mechanical ventilation, noninvasive ventilation with BiPAP, or a combination of both treatments, for a continuous period of at least 48 hours, or for a continuous period of at least 72 hours if postoperatively.

OR

F. Pulmonary hemorrhage requiring vascular embolization to control bleeding.

OR

G. Two of the following exacerbations or complications (either two of the same or two different, see 103.00H3 and 103.00H4) within a 12–month period (the 12–month period must occur within the period we are considering in connection with your application or continuing disability review):

1. Pulmonary exacerbation requiring 10 consecutive days of intravenous antibiotic treatment.

2. Pulmonary hemorrhage (hemoptysis with more than blood-streaked sputum but not requiring vascular embolization) requiring hospitalization of any length.

3. Weight loss requiring daily supplemental enteral nutrition via a gastrostomy for at least 90 consecutive days or parenteral nutrition via a central venous catheter for at least 90 consecutive days.

4. CFRD requiring daily insulin therapy for at least 90 consecutive days.

103.05 [Reserved]

103.06 Growth failure due to any chronic respiratory disorder (see 103.00K), documented by:

A. Hypoxemia with the need for at least 1.0 L per min of oxygen supplementation for at least 4 hours per day and for at least 90 consecutive days.

AND

B. Growth failure as required in 1 or 2:

1. For children from birth to attainment of age 2, three weight-for-length measurements that are:

a. Within a consecutive 12–month period; and

b. At least 60 days apart; and

c. Less than the third percentile on the appropriate weight-for-length table under 105.08B1; or

2. For children age 2 to attainment of age 18, three BMI–for-age measurements that are:

a. Within a consecutive 12–month period; and

b. At least 60 days apart; and

c. Less than the third percentile on the appropriate BMI–for-age table under 105.08B2.

103.07 [Reserved]

103.08 [Reserved]

103.09 [Reserved]

103.10 [Reserved]

103.11 Lung transplantation (see 103.00I). Consider under a disability for 3 years from the date of the transplant; after that, evaluate the residual impairment(s).

103.12 [Reserved]

103.13 [Reserved]

103.14 Respiratory failure (see 103.00J) resulting from any underlying chronic respiratory disorder except CF (for CF, see 103.04E), requiring invasive mechanical ventilation, noninvasive ventilation with BiPAP, or a combination of both treatments, for a continuous period of at least 48 hours, or for a continuous period of at least 72 hours if postoperatively, twice within a 12–month period and at least 30 days apart (the 12–month period must occur within the period we are considering in connection with your application or continuing disability review).

104.00 Cardiovascular System

A. General

1. What do we mean by a cardiovascular impairment?

a. We mean any disorder that affects the proper functioning of the heart or the circulatory system (that is, arteries, veins, capillaries, and the lymphatic drainage). The disorder can be congenital or acquired.

b. Cardiovascular impairment results from one or more of four consequences of heart disease:

(i) Chronic heart failure or ventricular dysfunction.

(ii) Discomfort or pain due to myocardial ischemia, with or without necrosis of heart muscle.

(iii) Syncope, or near syncope, due to inadequate cerebral perfusion from any cardiac cause, such as obstruction of flow or disturbance in rhythm or conduction resulting in inadequate cardiac output.

(iv) Central cyanosis due to right-to-left shunt, reduced oxygen concentration in the arterial blood, or pulmonary vascular disease.

c. Disorders of the veins or arteries (for example, obstruction, rupture, or aneurysm) may cause impairments of the lower extremities (peripheral vascular disease), the central nervous system, the eyes, the kidneys, and other organs. We will evaluate peripheral vascular disease under 4.11 or 4.12 in part A, and impairments of another body system(s) under the listings for that body system(s).

2. What do we consider in evaluating cardiovascular impairments? The listings in this section describe cardiovascular impairments based on symptoms, signs, laboratory findings, response to a regimen of prescribed treatment, and functional limitations.

3. What do the following terms or phrases mean in these listings?

a. Medical consultant is an individual defined in §§ 404.1616(a) and 416.1016(a). This term does not include medical sources who provide consultative examinations for us. We use the abbreviation "MC" throughout this section to designate a medical consultant.

b. Persistent means that the longitudinal clinical record shows that, with few exceptions, the required finding(s) has been present, or is expected to be present, for a continuous period of at least 12 months, such that a pattern of continuing severity is established.

c. Recurrent means that the longitudinal clinical record shows that, within a consecutive 12-month period, the finding(s) occurs at least three times, with intervening periods of improvement of sufficient duration that it is clear that separate events are involved.

d. Appropriate medically acceptable imaging means that the technique used is the proper one to evaluate and diagnose the impairment and is commonly recognized as accurate for assessing the cited finding.

e. A consecutive 12-month period means a period of 12 consecutive months, all or part of which must occur within the period we are considering in connection with an application or continuing disability review.

f. Currently present means that the finding is present at the time of adjudication.

g. Uncontrolled means the impairment does not respond adequately to standard prescribed medical treatment.

B. Documenting Cardiovascular Impairment

1. What basic documentation do we need? We need sufficiently detailed reports of history, physical examinations, laboratory studies, and any prescribed treatment and response to allow us to assess the severity and duration of your cardiovascular impairment. A longitudinal clinical record covering a period of not less than 3 months of observations and treatment is usually necessary, unless we can make a determination or decision based on the current evidence.

2. Why is a longitudinal clinical record important? We will usually need a longitudinal clinical record to assess the severity and expected duration of your impairment(s). If you have a listing-level impairment, you probably will have received medically prescribed treatment. Whenever there is evidence of such treatment, your longitudinal clinical record should include a description of the ongoing management and evaluation provided by your treating or other medical source. It should also include your response to this medical management, as well as information about the nature and severity of your impairment. The record will provide us with information on your functional status over an extended period of time and show whether your ability to function is improving, worsening, or unchanging.

3. What if you have not received ongoing medical treatment?

a. You may not have received ongoing treatment or have an ongoing relationship with the medical community despite the existence of a severe impairment(s). In this situation, we will base our evaluation on the current objective medical evidence and the other evidence we have. If you do not receive treatment, you cannot show an impairment that meets the criteria of these listings. However, we may find you disabled because you have another impairment(s) that in combination with your cardiovascular impairment medically equals the severity of a listed impairment or that functionally equals the listings.

b. Unless we can decide your claim favorably on the basis of the current evidence, a longitudinal record is still important. In rare instances where there is no or insufficient longitudinal evidence, we may purchase a consultative examination(s) to help us establish the severity and duration of your impairment.

4. When will we wait before we ask for more evidence?

a. We will wait when we have information showing that your impairment is not yet stable and the expected change in your impairment might affect our determination or decision. In these situations, we need to wait to properly evaluate the severity and duration of your impairment during a stable period. Examples of when we might wait are:

(i) If you have had a recent acute event; for example, acute rheumatic fever.

(ii) If you have recently had a corrective cardiac procedure; for example, open-heart surgery.

(iii) If you have started new drug therapy and your response to this treatment has not yet been established; for example, beta-blocker therapy for dilated congestive cardiomyopathy.

b. In these situations, we will obtain more evidence 3 months following the event before we evaluate your impairment. However, we will not wait if we have enough information to make a determination or decision based on all of the relevant evidence in your case.

5. Will we purchase any studies? In appropriate situations, we will purchase studies necessary to substantiate the diagnosis or to document the severity of your impairment, generally after we have evaluated the medical and other evidence we already have. We will not purchase studies involving exercise testing if there is significant risk involved or if there is another medical reason not to perform the test. We will follow sections 4.00C6, 4.00C7, 4.00C8, and 104.00B7 when we decide whether to purchase exercise testing. We will make a reasonable effort to obtain any additional studies from a qualified medical source in an office or center experienced in pediatric cardiac assessment. (See § 416.919g.)

6. What studies will we not purchase? We will not purchase any studies involving cardiac catheterization, such as coronary angiography, arteriograms, or electrophysiological studies. However, if the results of catheterization are part of the existing evidence we have, we will consider them together with the other relevant evidence. See 4.00C15a in part A.

7. Will we use exercise tolerance tests (ETTs) for evaluating children with cardiovascular impairment?

a. ETTs, though increasingly used, are still less frequently indicated in children than in adults, and can rarely be performed successfully by children under 6 years of age. An ETT may be of value in the assessment of some arrhythmias, in the assessment of the severity of chronic heart failure, and in the assessment of recovery of function following cardiac surgery or other treatment.

b. We will purchase an ETT in a childhood claim only if we cannot make a determination or decision based on the evidence we have and an MC, preferably one with experience in the care of children with cardiovascular impairments, has determined that an ETT is needed to evaluate your impairment. We will not purchase an ETT if you are less than 6 years of age. If we do purchase an ETT for a child age 12 or younger, it must be performed by a qualified medical source in a specialty center for pediatric cardiology or other facility qualified to perform exercise tests of children.

c. For full details on ETT requirements and usage, see 4.00C in part A.

C. Evaluating Chronic Heart Failure

1. What is chronic heart failure (CHF)?

a. CHF is the inability of the heart to pump enough oxygenated blood to body tissues. This syndrome is characterized by symptoms and signs of pulmonary or systemic congestion (fluid retention) or limited cardiac output. Certain laboratory findings of cardiac functional and structural abnormality support the diagnosis of CHF.

b. CHF is considered in these listings as a single category whether due to atherosclerosis (narrowing of the arteries), cardiomyopathy, hypertension, or rheumatic, congenital, or other heart disease. However, if the CHF is the result of primary pulmonary hypertension secondary to disease of the lung (cor pulmonale), we will evaluate your impairment using 3.09 in the respiratory system listings in part A.

2. What evidence of CHF do we need?

a. Cardiomegaly or ventricular dysfunction must be present and demonstrated by appropriate medically acceptable imaging, such as chest x-ray, echocardiography (M–Mode, 2–dimensional, and Doppler), radionuclide studies, or cardiac catheterization.

(i) Cardiomegaly is present when:

(A) Left ventricular diastolic dimension or systolic dimension is greater than 2 standard deviations above the mean for the child's body surface area;

(B) Left ventricular mass is greater than 2 standard deviations above the mean for the child's body surface area; or

(C) Chest x-ray (6 foot PA film) is indicative of cardiomegaly if the cardiothoracic ratio is over 60 percent at 1 year of age or less, or 55 percent or greater at more than 1 year of age.

(ii) Ventricular dysfunction is present when indices of left ventricular function, such as fractional shortening or ejection fraction (the percentage of the blood in the ventricle actually pumped out with each contraction), are greater than 2 standard deviations below the mean for the child's age. (Fractional shortening, also called shortening fraction, reflects the left ventricular systolic function in the absence of segmental wall motion abnormalities and has a linear correlation with ejection fraction. In children, fractional shortening is more commonly used than ejection fraction.)

(iii) However, these measurements alone do not reflect your functional capacity, which we evaluate by considering all of the relevant evidence.

(iv) Other findings on appropriate medically acceptable imaging may include increased pulmonary vascular markings, pleural effusion, and pulmonary edema. These findings need not be present on each report, since CHF may be controlled by prescribed treatment.

b. To establish that you have chronic heart failure, we require that your medical history and physical examination describe characteristic symptoms and signs of pulmonary or systemic congestion or of limited cardiac output associated with abnormal findings on appropriate medically acceptable imaging. When a remediable factor, such as arrhythmia, triggers an acute episode of heart failure, you may experience restored cardiac function, and a chronic impairment may not be present.

(i) Symptoms of congestion or of limited cardiac output include easy fatigue, weakness, shortness of breath (dyspnea), cough, or chest discomfort at rest or with activity. Children with CHF may also experience shortness of breath on lying flat (orthopnea) or episodes of shortness of breath that wake them from sleep (paroxysmal nocturnal dyspnea). They may also experience cardiac arrhythmias resulting in palpitations, lightheadedness, or fainting. Fatigue or exercise intolerance in an infant may be manifested by prolonged feeding time, often associated with excessive respiratory effort and sweating.

(ii) During infancy, other manifestations of chronic heart failure may include repeated lower respiratory tract infections.

(iii) Signs of congestion may include hepatomegaly, ascites, increased jugular venous distention or pressure, rales, peripheral edema, rapid shallow breathing (tachypnea), or rapid weight gain. However, these signs need not be found on all examinations because fluid retention may be controlled by prescribed treatment.

3. How do we evaluate growth failure due to CHF?

a. To evaluate growth failure due to CHF, we require documentation of the clinical findings of CHF described in 104.00C2 and the growth measurements in 104.02C within the same consecutive 12–month period. The dates of clinical findings may be different from the dates of growth measurements.

b. Under 104.02C, we use the appropriate table(s) under 105.08B in the digestive system to determine whether a child's growth is less than the third percentile.

(i) For children from birth to attainment of age 2, we use the weight-for-length table corresponding to the child's gender (Table I or Table II).

(ii) For children age 2 to attainment of age 18, we use the body mass index (BMI)-for-age table corresponding to the child's gender (Table III or Table IV).

(iii) BMI is the ratio of a child's weight to the square of his or her height. We calculate BMI using the formulas in 105.00G2c.

D. Evaluating Congenital Heart Disease

1. What is congenital heart disease? Congenital heart disease is any abnormality of the heart or the major blood vessels that is present at birth. Examples include:

a. Abnormalities of cardiac septation, including ventricular septal defect or atrioventricular canal;

b. Abnormalities resulting in cyanotic heart disease, including tetralogy of Fallot or transposition of the great arteries;

c. Valvular defects or obstructions to ventricular outflow, including pulmonary or aortic stenosis or coarctation of the aorta; and

d. Major abnormalities of ventricular development, including hypoplastic left heart syndrome or pulmonary tricuspid atresia with hypoplastic right ventricle.

2. How will we evaluate symptomatic congenital heart disease?

a. Because of improved treatment methods, more children with congenital heart disease are living longer. Although some types of congenital heart disease may be corrected by surgery, many children with treated congenital heart disease continue to have problems throughout their lives (symptomatic congenital heart disease). If you have congenital heart disease that results in chronic heart failure with evidence of ventricular dysfunction or in recurrent arrhythmias, we will evaluate your impairment under 104.02 or 104.05. Otherwise, we will evaluate your impairment under 104.06.

b. For 104.06A2, we will accept pulse oximetry measurements instead of arterial O_2, but the arterial O_2 values are preferred, if available.

c. For 104.06D, examples of impairments that in most instances will require life-saving surgery or a combination of surgery and other major interventional procedures (for example, multiple "balloon" catheter procedures) before age 1 include, but are not limited to, the following:

(i) Hypoplastic left heart syndrome,

(ii) Critical aortic stenosis with neonatal heart failure,

(iii) Critical coarctation of the aorta, with or without associated anomalies,

(iv) Complete atrioventricular canal defects,

(v) Transposition of the great arteries,

(vi) Tetralogy of Fallot,

(vii) Pulmonary atresia with intact ventricular septum,

(viii) Single ventricle,

(ix) Tricuspid atresia, and

(x) Multiple ventricular septal defects.

E. Evaluating Arrhythmias

1. What is an arrhythmia? An arrhythmia is a change in the regular beat of the heart. Your heart may seem to skip a beat or beat irregularly, very quickly (tachycardia), or very slowly (bradycardia).

2. What are the different types of arrhythmias?

a. There are many types of arrhythmias. Arrhythmias are identified by where they occur in the heart (atria or ventricles) and by what happens to the heart's rhythm when they occur.

b. Arrhythmias arising in the cardiac atria (upper chambers of the heart) are called atrial or supraventricular arrhythmias. Ventricular arrhythmias begin in the ventricles (lower chambers). In general, ventricular arrhythmias caused by heart disease are the most serious.

3. How do we evaluate arrhythmias using 104.05?

a. We will use 104.05 when you have arrhythmias that are not fully controlled by medication, an implanted pacemaker, or an implanted cardiac defibrillator and you have uncontrolled recurrent episodes of syncope or near syncope. If your arrhythmias are controlled, we will evaluate your underlying heart disease using the appropriate listing. For other considerations when we evaluate arrhythmias in the presence of an implanted cardiac defibrillator, see 104.00E4.

b. We consider near syncope to be a period of altered consciousness, since syncope is a loss of consciousness or a faint. It is not merely a feeling of light-headedness, momentary weakness, or dizziness.

c. For purposes of 104.05, there must be a documented association between the syncope or near syncope and the recurrent arrhythmia. The recurrent arrhythmia, not some other cardiac or non-cardiac disorder, must be established as the cause of the associated symptom. This documentation of the association between the symptoms and the arrhythmia may come from the usual diagnostic methods, including Holter monitoring (also called ambulatory electrocardiography) and tilt-table testing with a concurrent ECG. Although an arrhythmia may be a coincidental finding on an ETT, we will not purchase an ETT to document the presence of a cardiac arrhythmia.

4. What will we consider when you have an implanted cardiac defibrillator and you do not have arrhythmias that meet the requirements of 104.05?

a. Implanted cardiac defibrillators are used to prevent sudden cardiac death in children who have had, or are at high risk for, cardiac arrest from life-threatening ventricular arrhythmias. The largest group of children at risk for sudden cardiac death consists of children with cardiomyopathy (ischemic or non-ischemic) and reduced ventricular function. However, life-threatening ventricular arrhythmias can also occur in children with little or no ventricular dysfunction. The shock from the implanted cardiac defibrillator is a unique form of treatment; it rescues a child from what may have been cardiac arrest. However, as a consequence of the shock(s), children may experience psychological distress, which we may evaluate under the mental disorders listings in 112.00ff.

b. Most implantable cardiac defibrillators have rhythm-correcting and pacemaker capabilities. In some children, these functions may result in the termination of ventricular arrhythmias without an otherwise painful shock. (The shock is like being kicked in the chest.) Implanted cardiac defibrillators may deliver inappropriate shocks, often repeatedly, in response to benign arrhythmias or electrical malfunction. Also, exposure to strong electrical or magnetic fields, such as from MRI (magnetic resonance imaging), can trigger or reprogram an implanted cardiac defibrillator, resulting in inappropriate shocks. We must consider the frequency of, and the reason(s) for, the shocks when evaluating the severity and duration of your impairment.

c. In general, the exercise limitations imposed on children with an implanted cardiac defibrillator are those dictated by the underlying heart impairment. However, the exercise limitations may be greater when the implanted cardiac defibrillator delivers an inappropriate shock in response to the increase in heart rate with exercise, or when there is exercise-induced ventricular arrhythmia.

F. Evaluating Other Cardiovascular Impairments

1. What is ischemic heart disease (IHD) and how will we evaluate it in children? IHD results when one or more of your coronary arteries is narrowed or obstructed or, in rare situations, constricted due to vasospasm, interfering with the normal flow of blood to your heart muscle (ischemia). The obstruction may be the result of an embolus, a thrombus, or plaque. When heart muscle tissue dies as a result of the reduced blood supply, it is called a myocardial infarction (heart attack). Ischemia is rare in children, but when it occurs, its effects on children are the same as on adults. If you have IHD, we will evaluate it under 4.00E and 4.04 in part A.

2. How will we evaluate hypertension? Because hypertension (high blood pressure) generally causes disability through its effects on other body systems, we will evaluate it by reference to the specific body system(s) affected (heart, brain, kidneys, or eyes) when we consider its effects under the listings. We will also consider any limitations imposed by your hypertension when we consider whether you have an impairment that functionally equals the listings.

3. What is cardiomyopathy and how will we evaluate it? Cardiomyopathy is a disease of the heart muscle. The heart loses its ability to pump blood (heart failure), and in some instances, heart rhythm is disturbed, leading to irregular heartbeats (arrhythmias). Usually, the exact cause of the muscle damage is never found (idiopathic cardiomyopathy). There are various types of cardiomyopathy, which fall into two major categories: Ischemic and nonischemic cardiomyopathy. Ischemic cardiomyopathy typically refers to heart muscle damage that results from coronary artery disease, including heart attacks. Nonischemic cardiomyopathy includes several types: Dilated, hypertrophic, and restrictive. We will evaluate cardiomyopathy under 4.04 in part A, 104.02, 104.05, or 111.06, depending on its effects on you.

4. How will we evaluate valvular heart disease? We will evaluate valvular heart disease under the listing appropriate for its effect on you. Thus, we may use 4.04 in part A, 104.02, 104.05, 104.06, or an appropriate neurological listing in 111.00ff.

5. What do we consider when we evaluate heart transplant recipients?

a. After your heart transplant, we will consider you disabled for 1 year following the surgery because there is a greater likelihood of rejection of the organ and infection during the first year.

b. However, heart transplant patients generally meet our definition of disability before they undergo transplantation. We will determine the onset of your disability based on the facts in your case.

c. We will not assume that you became disabled when your name was placed on a transplant waiting list. This is because you may be placed on a waiting list soon after diagnosis of the cardiac disorder that may eventually require a transplant. Physicians recognize that candidates for transplantation often have to wait months or even years before a suitable donor heart is found, so they place their patients on the list as soon as permitted.

d. When we do a continuing disability review to determine whether you are still disabled, we will evaluate your residual impairment(s), as shown by symptoms, signs, and laboratory findings, including any side effects of medication. We will consider any remaining symptoms, signs, and laboratory findings indicative of cardiac dysfunction in deciding whether medical improvement (as defined in § 416.994a) has occurred.

6. How will we evaluate chronic rheumatic fever or rheumatic heart disease? The diagnosis should be made in accordance with the current revised Jones criteria for guidance in the diagnosis of rheumatic fever. We will evaluate persistence of rheumatic fever activity under 104.13. If you have evidence of chronic heart failure or recurrent arrhythmias associated with rheumatic heart disease, we will use 104.02 or 104.05.

7. What is hyperlipidemia and how will we evaluate it? Hyperlipidemia is the general term for an elevation of any or all of the lipids (fats or cholesterol) in the blood; for example, hypertriglyceridemia, hypercholesterolemia, and hyperlipoproteinemia. These disorders of lipoprotein metabolism and transport can cause defects throughout the body. The effects most likely to interfere with function are those produced by atherosclerosis (narrowing of the arteries) and coronary artery disease. We will evaluate your lipoprotein disorder by considering its effects on you.

8. How will we evaluate Kawasaki disease? We will evaluate Kawasaki disease under the listing appropriate to its effects on you, which may include major coronary artery aneurysm or heart failure. A major coronary artery aneurysm may cause ischemia or arrhythmia, which we will evaluate under 4.04 in part A or 104.05. We will evaluate chronic heart failure under 104.02.

9. What is lymphedema and how will we evaluate it?

a. Lymphedema is edema of the extremities due to a disorder of the lymphatic circulation; at its worst, it is called elephantiasis. Primary lymphedema is caused by abnormal development of lymph vessels and may be present at birth (congenital lymphedema), but more often develops during the teens (lymphedema praecox). Secondary lymphedema is due to obstruction or destruction of normal lymphatic channels due to tumor, surgery, repeated infections, or parasitic infection such as filariasis. Lymphedema most commonly affects one extremity.

b. Lymphedema does not meet the requirements of 4.11 in part A, although it may medically equal the severity of that listing. We will evaluate lymphedema by considering whether the underlying cause meets or medically equals any listing or whether the lymphedema medically equals a cardiovascular listing, such as 4.11, or a musculoskeletal listing, such as 101.02A or 101.03. If no listing is met or medically equaled, we will evaluate any functional limitations imposed by your lymphedema when we consider whether you have an impairment that functionally equals the listings.

10. What is Marfan syndrome and how will we evaluate it?

a. Marfan syndrome is a genetic connective tissue disorder that affects multiple body systems, including the skeleton, eyes, heart, blood vessels, nervous system, skin, and lungs. There is no specific laboratory test to diagnose Marfan syndrome. The diagnosis is generally made by medical history, including family history, physical examination, including an evaluation of the ratio of arm/leg size to trunk size, a slit lamp eye examination, and a heart test(s), such as an echocardiogram. In some cases, a genetic analysis may be useful, but such analyses may not provide any additional helpful information.

b. The effects of Marfan syndrome can range from mild to severe. In most cases, the disorder progresses as you age. Most individuals with Marfan syndrome have abnormalities associated with the heart and blood vessels. Your heart's mitral valve may leak, causing a heart murmur. Small leaks may not cause symptoms, but larger ones may cause shortness of breath, fatigue, and palpitations. Another effect is that the wall of the aorta may be weakened and stretch (aortic dilation). This aortic dilation may tear, dissect, or rupture, causing serious heart problems or sometimes sudden death. We will evaluate the manifestations of your Marfan syndrome under the appropriate body system criteria, such as 4.10 in part A, or if necessary consider the functional limitations imposed by your impairment.

G. Other Evaluation Issues

1. What effect does obesity have on the cardiovascular system and how will we evaluate it? Obesity is a medically determinable impairment that is often associated with disorders of the cardiovascular system. Disturbance of this system can be a major cause of disability in children with obesity. Obesity may affect the cardiovascular system because of the increased workload the additional body mass places on the heart. Obesity may make it harder for the chest and lungs to expand. This can mean that the respiratory system must work harder to provide needed oxygen. This in turn would make the heart work harder to pump blood to carry oxygen to the body. Because the body would be working harder at rest, its ability to perform additional work would be less than would otherwise be expected. Thus, the combined effects of obesity with cardiovascular impairments can be greater than the effects of each of the impairments considered separately. We must consider any additional and cumulative effects of obesity when we determine whether you have a severe cardiovascular impairment or a listing-level cardiovascular impairment (or a combination of impairments that medically equals a listing), and when we determine whether your impairment(s) functionally equals the listings.

2. How do we relate treatment to functional status? In general, conclusions about the severity of a cardiovascular impairment cannot be made on the basis of type of treatment rendered or anticipated. The amount of function restored and the time required for improvement after treatment (medical, surgical, or a prescribed program of progressive physical activity) vary with the nature and extent of the disorder, the type of treatment, and other factors. Depending upon the timing of this treatment in relation to the alleged onset date of disability, we may need to defer evaluation of the impairment for a period of up to 3 months from the date treatment began to permit consideration of treatment effects, unless we can make a determination or decision using the evidence we have. See 104.00B4.

3. How do we evaluate impairments that do not meet one of the cardiovascular listings?

a. These listings are only examples of common cardiovascular disorders that we consider severe enough to result in marked and severe functional limitations. If your severe impairment(s) does not meet the criteria of any of these listings, we must also consider whether you have an impairment(s) that satisfies the criteria of a listing in another body system.

b. If you have a severe medically determinable impairment(s) that does not meet a listing, we will determine whether your impairment(s) medically equals a listing. (See § 416.926.) If you have a severe impairment(s) that does not meet or medically equal the criteria of a listing, we will consider whether it functionally equals the listings. (See § 416.926a.) When we decide whether you continue to be disabled, we use the rules in § 416.994a.

104.01 Category of Impairments, Cardiovascular System

104.02. Chronic heart failure while on a regimen of prescribed treatment, with symptoms and signs described in 104.00C2, and with one of the following:

A. Persistent tachycardia at rest (see Table I);

OR

B. Persistent tachypnea at rest (see Table II) or markedly decreased exercise tolerance (see 104.00C2b);

OR

C. Growth failure as required in 1 or 2:

1. For children from birth to attainment of age 2, three weight-for-length measurements that are:

a. Within a consecutive 12–month period; and

b. At least 60 days apart; and

c. Less than the third percentile on the appropriate weight-for-length table under 105.08B1; or

2. For children age 2 to attainment of age 18, three BMI–for-age measurements that are:

a. Within a consecutive 12–month period; and

b. At least 60 days apart; and

c. Less than the third percentile on the appropriate BMI–for-age table under 105.08B2.

104.05 Recurrent arrhythmias, not related to reversible causes such as electrolyte abnormalities or digitalis glycoside or antiarrhythmic drug toxicity, resulting in uncontrolled (see 104.00A3g), recurrent (see 104.00A3c) episodes of cardiac syncope or near syncope (see 104.00E3b), despite prescribed treatment (see 104.00B3 if there is no prescribed treatment), and documented by resting or ambulatory (Holter) electrocardiography, or by other appropriate medically acceptable testing, coincident with the occurrence of syncope or near syncope (see 104.00E3c).

104.06 Congenital heart disease, documented by appropriate medically acceptable imaging (see 104.00A3d) or cardiac catheterization, with one of the following:

A. Cyanotic heart disease, with persistent, chronic hypoxemia as manifested by:

1. Hematocrit of 55 percent or greater on two evaluations 3 months or more apart within a consecutive 12–month period (see 104.00A3e); or

2. Arterial O_2 saturation of less than 90 percent in room air, or resting arterial PO_2 of 60 Torr or less; or

3. Hypercyanotic spells, syncope, characteristic squatting, or other incapacitating symptoms directly related to documented cyanotic heart disease; or

4. Exercise intolerance with increased hypoxemia on exertion.

OR

B. Secondary pulmonary vascular obstructive disease with pulmonary arterial systolic pressure elevated to at least 70 percent of the systemic arterial systolic pressure.

OR

C. Symptomatic acyanotic heart disease, with ventricular dysfunction interfering very seriously with the ability to independently initiate, sustain, or complete activities.

OR

D. For infants under 12 months of age at the time of filing, with life-threatening congenital heart impairment that will require or already has required surgical treatment in the first year of life, and the impairment is expected to be disabling (because of residual impairment following surgery, or the recovery time required, or both) until the attainment of at least 1 year of age, consider the infant to be under disability until the attainment of at least age 1; thereafter, evaluate impairment severity with reference to the appropriate listing.

104.09 Heart transplant. Consider under a disability for 1 year following surgery; thereafter, evaluate residual impairment under the appropriate listing.

104.13 Rheumatic heart disease, with persistence of rheumatic fever activity manifested by significant murmurs(s), cardiac enlargement or ventricular dysfunction (see 104.00C2a), and other associated abnormal laboratory findings; for example, an elevated sedimentation rate or ECG findings, for 6 months or more in a consecutive 12–month period (see 104.00A3e). Consider under a disability for 18 months from the established onset of impairment, then evaluate any residual impairment(s).

105.00 Digestive System

A. What kinds of disorders do we consider in the digestive system? Disorders of the digestive system include gastrointestinal hemorrhage, hepatic (liver) dysfunction, inflammatory bowel disease, short bowel syndrome, and malnutrition. They may also lead to complications, such as obstruction, or be accompanied by manifestations in other body systems. Congenital abnormalities involving the organs of the gastrointestinal system may interfere with the ability to maintain adequate nutrition, growth, and development.

B. What documentation do we need? We need a record of your medical evidence, including clinical and laboratory findings. The documentation should include appropriate medically acceptable imaging studies and reports of endoscopy, operations, and pathology, as appropriate to each listing, to document the severity and duration of your digestive disorder. We may also need assessments of your growth and development. Medically acceptable imaging includes, but is not limited to, x-ray imaging, sonography, computerized axial tomography (CAT scan), magnetic resonance imaging (MRI), and radionuclide scans. Appropriate means that the technique used is the proper one to support the evaluation and diagnosis of the disorder. The findings required by these listings must occur within the period we are considering in connection with your application or continuing disability review.

C. How do we consider the effects of treatment?

1. Digestive disorders frequently respond to medical or surgical treatment; therefore, we generally consider the severity and duration of these disorders within the context of the prescribed treatment.

2. We assess the effects of treatment, including medication, therapy, surgery, or any other form of treatment you receive, by determining if there are improvements in the symptoms, signs, and laboratory findings of your digestive disorder. We also assess any side effects of your treatment that may further limit your functioning.

3. To assess the effects of your treatment, we may need information about:

a. The treatment you have been prescribed (for example, the type of medication or therapy, or your use of parenteral (intravenous) nutrition or supplemental enteral nutrition via a gastrostomy);

b. The dosage, method, and frequency of administration;

c. Your response to the treatment;

d. Any adverse effects of such treatment; and

e. The expected duration of the treatment.

4. Because the effects of treatment may be temporary or long-term, in most cases we need information about the impact of your treatment, including its expected duration and side effects, over a sufficient period of time to help us assess its outcome. When adverse effects of treatment contribute to the severity of your impairment(s), we will consider the duration or expected duration of the treatment when we assess the duration of your impairment(s).

5. If you need parenteral (intravenous) nutrition or supplemental enteral nutrition via a gastrostomy to avoid debilitating complications of a digestive disorder, this treatment will not, in itself, indicate that you have marked and severe functional limitations. The exceptions are 105.07, short bowel syndrome, and 105.10, for children who have not attained age 3 and who require supplemental daily enteral feedings via a gastrostomy (see 105.00F and 105.00H).

6. If you have not received ongoing treatment or have not had an ongoing relationship with the medical community despite the existence of a severe impair-

ment(s), we will evaluate the severity and duration of your digestive impairment on the basis of current medical and other evidence in your case record. If you have not received treatment, you may not be able to show an impairment that meets the criteria of one of the digestive system listings, but your digestive impairment may medically equal a listing or functionally equal the listings.

D. How do we evaluate chronic liver disease?

1. General. Chronic liver disease is characterized by liver cell necrosis, inflammation, or scarring (fibrosis or cirrhosis), due to any cause, that persists for more than 6 months. Chronic liver disease may result in portal hypertension, cholestasis (suppression of bile flow), extrahepatic manifestations, or liver cancer. (We evaluate liver cancer under 113.03.) Significant loss of liver function may be manifested by hemorrhage from varices or portal hypertensive gastropathy, ascites (accumulation of fluid in the abdominal cavity), hydrothorax (ascitic fluid in the chest cavity), or encephalopathy. There can also be progressive deterioration of laboratory findings that are indicative of liver dysfunction. Liver transplantation is the only definitive cure for end stage liver disease (ESLD).

2. Examples of chronic liver disease include, but are not limited to, biliary atresia, chronic hepatitis, non-alcoholic steatohepatitis (NASH), primary biliary cirrhosis (PBC), primary sclerosing cholangitis (PSC), autoimmune hepatitis, hemochromatosis, drug-induced liver disease, Wilson's disease, and serum alpha-1 antitrypsin deficiency. Children can also have congenital abnormalities of abdominal organs or inborn metabolic disorders that result in chronic liver disease. Acute hepatic injury is frequently reversible as in viral, drug-induced, toxin-induced, and ischemic hepatitis. In the absence of evidence of a chronic impairment, episodes of acute liver disease do not meet 105.05.

3. Manifestations of chronic liver disease.

a. Symptoms may include, but are not limited to, pruritis (itching), fatigue, nausea, loss of appetite, or sleep disturbances. Children can also have associated developmental delays or poor school performance. Symptoms of chronic liver disease may have a poor correlation with the severity of liver disease and functional ability.

b. Signs may include, but are not limited to, jaundice, enlargement of the liver and spleen, ascites, peripheral edema, and altered mental status.

c. Laboratory findings may include, but are not limited to, increased liver enzymes, increased serum total bilirubin, increased ammonia levels, decreased serum albumin, and abnormal coagulation studies, such as increased International Normalized Ratio (INR) or decreased platelet counts. Abnormally low serum albumin or elevated INR levels indicate loss of synthetic liver function, with increased likelihood of cirrhosis and associated complications. However, other abnormal lab tests, such as liver enzymes, serum total bilirubin, or ammonia levels, may have a poor correlation with the severity of liver disease and functional ability. A liver biopsy may demonstrate the degree of liver cell necrosis, inflammation, fibrosis, and cirrhosis. If you have had a liver biopsy, we will make every reasonable effort to obtain the results; however, we will not purchase a liver biopsy. Imaging studies (CAT scan, ultrasound, MRI) may show the size and consistency (fatty liver, scarring) of the liver and document ascites (see 105.00D6).

4. Chronic viral hepatitis infections.

a. General.

(i) Chronic viral hepatitis infections are commonly caused by hepatitis C virus (HCV), and to a lesser extent, hepatitis B virus (HBV). Usually, these are slowly progressive disorders that persist over many years during which the symptoms and signs are typically nonspecific, intermittent, and mild (for example, fatigue, difficulty with concentration, or right upper quadrant pain). Laboratory findings (liver enzymes, imaging studies, liver biopsy pathology) and complications are generally similar in HCV and HBV. The spectrum of these chronic viral hepatitis infections ranges widely and includes an asymptomatic state; insidious disease with mild to moderate symptoms associated with fluctuating liver tests; extrahepatic manifestations; cirrhosis, both compensated and decompensated; ESLD with the need for liver transplantation; and liver cancer. Treatment for chronic viral hepatitis infections varies considerably based on age, medication tolerance, treatment response, adverse effects of treatment, and duration of the treatment. Comorbid disorders, such as HIV infection, may accelerate the clinical course of viral hepatitis infection(s) or may result in a poorer response to medical treatment.

(ii) We evaluate all types of chronic viral hepatitis infections under 105.05 or any listing in an affected body system(s). If your impairment(s) does not meet or medically equal a listing, we will consider the effects of your hepatitis when we assess whether your impairment(s) functionally equals the listings.

b. Chronic hepatitis B virus (HBV) infection.

(i) Chronic HBV infection can be diagnosed by the detection of hepatitis B surface antigen (HBsAg) or hepatitis B virus DNA (HBV DNA) in the blood for at least 6 months. In addition, detection of the hepatitis B e antigen (HBeAg) suggests an increased likelihood of progression to cirrhosis, ESLD, and hepatocellular carcinoma. (HBeAg may also be referred to as "hepatitis B early antigen" or "hepatitis B envelope antigen.")

(ii) The therapeutic goal of treatment is to suppress HBV replication and thereby prevent progression to cirrhosis, ESLD, and hepatocellular carcinoma. Treatment usually includes interferon injections, oral antiviral agents, or a combination of both. Common adverse effects of treatment are the same as noted in 105.00D4c(ii) for HCV, and generally end within a few days after treatment is discontinued.

c. Chronic hepatitis C virus (HCV) infection.

(i) Chronic HCV infection is diagnosed by the detection of hepatitis C viral RNA in the blood for at least 6 months. Documentation of the therapeutic response to treatment is also monitored by the quantitative assay of serum HCV RNA ("HCV viral load"). Treatment usually includes a combination of interferon injections and oral ribavirin; whether a therapeutic response has occurred is usually assessed after 12 weeks of treatment by checking the HCV viral load. If there has been a substantial reduction in HCV viral load (also known as early viral response, or EVR), this reduction is predictive of a sustained viral response with completion of treatment. Combined therapy is commonly discontinued after 12 weeks when there is no early viral response, since in that circumstance there is little chance of obtaining a sustained viral response (SVR). Otherwise, treatment is usually continued for a total of 48 weeks.

(ii) Combined interferon and ribavirin treatment may have significant adverse effects that may require dosing reduction, planned interruption of treatment, or discontinuation of treatment. Adverse effects may include: Anemia (ribavirin-induced hemolysis), neutropenia, thrombocytopenia, fever, cough, fatigue, myalgia, arthralgia, nausea, loss of appetite, pruritis, and insomnia. Behavioral side effects may also occur. Influenza-like symptoms are generally worse in the first 4 to 6 hours after each interferon injection and during the first weeks of treatment. Adverse effects generally end within a few days after treatment is discontinued.

d. Extrahepatic manifestations of HBV and HCV. In addition to their hepatic manifestations, both HBV and HCV may have significant extrahepatic manifestations in a variety of body systems. These include, but are not limited to: Keratoconjunctivitis (sicca syndrome), glomerulonephritis, skin disorders (for example, lichen planus, porphyria cutanea tarda), neuropathy, and immune dysfunction (for example, cryoglobulinemia, Sjögren's syndrome, and vasculitis). The extrahepatic manifestations of HBV and HCV may not correlate with the severity of your hepatic impairment. If your impairment(s) does not meet or medically equal a listing in an affected body system(s), we will consider the effects of your extrahepatic manifestations when we determine whether your impairment(s) functionally equals the listings.

5. Gastrointestinal hemorrhage (105.02 and 105.05A). Gastrointestinal hemorrhaging can result in hematemesis (vomiting of blood), melena (tarry stools), or hematochezia (bloody stools). Under 105.02, the required transfusions of at least 10 cc of blood/kg of body weight must be at least 30 days apart and occur at least three times during a consecutive 6–month period. Under 105.05A, hemodynamic instability is diagnosed with signs such as pallor (pale skin), diaphoresis (profuse perspiration), rapid pulse, low blood pressure, postural hypotension (pronounced fall in blood pressure when arising to an upright position from lying down) or syncope (fainting). Hemorrhaging that results in hemodynamic instability is potentially life-threatening and therefore requires hospitalization for transfusion and supportive care. Under 105.05A, we require only one hospitalization for transfusion of at least 10 cc of blood/kg of body weight.

6. Ascites or hydrothorax (105.05B) indicates significant loss of liver function due to chronic liver disease. We evaluate ascites or hydrothorax that is not attributable to other causes under 105.05B. The required findings must be present on at least two evaluations at least 60 days apart within a consecutive 6–month period and despite continuing treatment as prescribed.

7. Spontaneous bacterial peritonitis (105.05C) is an infectious complication of chronic liver disease. It is diagnosed by ascitic peritoneal fluid that is documented to contain an absolute neutrophil count of at least 250 cells/mm^3. The required finding in 105.05C is satisfied with one evaluation documenting peritoneal fluid infection. We do not evaluate other causes of peritonitis that are unrelated to chronic liver disease, such as tuberculosis, malignancy, and perforated bowel, under this listing. We evaluate these other causes of peritonitis under the appropriate body system listings.

8. Hepatorenal syndrome (105.05D) is defined as functional renal failure associated with chronic liver disease in the absence of underlying kidney pathology. Hepatorenal syndrome is documented by elevation of serum creatinine, marked sodium retention, and oliguria (reduced urine output). The requirements of 105.05D are satisfied with documentation of any one of the three laboratory findings on one evaluation. We do not evaluate known causes of renal dysfunction, such as glomerulonephritis, tubular necrosis, drug-induced renal disease, and renal infections, under this listing. We evaluate these other renal impairments under 106.00ff.

9. Hepatopulmonary syndrome (105.05E) is defined as arterial deoxygenation (hypoxemia) that is associated with chronic liver disease due to intrapulmonary arteriovenous shunting and vasodilatation, in the absence of other causes of arterial deoxygenation. Clinical manifestations usually include dyspnea, orthodeoxia (increasing hypoxemia with erect position), platypnea (improvement of dyspnea with flat position), cyanosis, and clubbing. The requirements of 105.05E are satisfied with documentation of any one of the findings on one evaluation. In 105.05E1, we require documentation of the altitude of the testing facility because altitude affects the measurement of arterial oxygenation. We will not purchase the specialized studies

described in 105.05E2; however, if you have had these studies at a time relevant to your claim, we will make every reasonable effort to obtain the reports for the purpose of establishing whether your impairment meets 105.05E2.

10. Hepatic encephalopathy (105.05F).

a. General. Hepatic encephalopathy usually indicates severe loss of hepatocellular function. We define hepatic encephalopathy under 105.05F as a recurrent or chronic neuropsychiatric disorder, characterized by abnormal behavior, cognitive dysfunction, altered state of consciousness, and ultimately coma and death. The diagnosis is established by changes in mental status associated with fleeting neurological signs, including "flapping tremor" (asterixis), characteristic electroencephalographic (EEG) abnormalities, or abnormal laboratory values that indicate loss of synthetic liver function. We will not purchase the EEG testing described in 105.05F3b. However, if you have had this test at a time relevant to your claim, we will make every reasonable effort to obtain the report for the purpose of establishing whether your impairment meets 105.05F.

b. Acute encephalopathy. We will not evaluate your acute encephalopathy under 105.05F if it results from conditions other than chronic liver disease, such as vascular events and neoplastic diseases. We will evaluate these other causes of acute encephalopathy under the appropriate body system listings.

11. End stage liver disease (ESLD) documented by scores from the SSA Chronic Liver Disease (SSA CLD) calculation (105.05G1) and SSA Chronic Liver Disease–Pediatric (SSA CLD–P) calculation (105.05G2).

a. SSA CLD score.

(i) If you are age 12 or older, we will use the SSA CLD score to evaluate your ESLD under 105.05G1. We explain how we calculate the SSA CLD score in a(ii) through a(vii) of this section.

(ii) To calculate the SSA CLD score, we use a formula that includes three laboratory values: Serum total bilirubin (mg/dL), serum creatinine (mg/dL), and International Normalized Ratio (INR). The formula for the SSA CLD score calculation is:

9.57 x [Log_e(serum creatinine mg/dL)]

+3.78 x [Log_e(serum total bilirubin mg/dL)]

+11.2 x [Log_e(INR)]

+6.43

(iii) When we indicate "Log_e" in the formula for the SSA CLD score calculation, we mean the "base e logarithm" or "natural logarithm" (ln) of a numerical laboratory value, not the "base 10 logarithm" or "common logarithm" (log) of the laboratory value, and not the actual laboratory value. For an example of SSA CLD calculation, see 5.00D11c.

(iv) For any SSA CLD score calculation, all of the required laboratory values must have been obtained within 30 days of each other. If there are multiple laboratory values within the 30–day interval for any given laboratory test (serum total bilirubin, serum creatinine, or INR), we will use the highest value for the SSA CLD score calculation. We will round all laboratory values less than 1.0 up to 1.0.

(v) Listing 105.05G requires two SSA CLD scores. The laboratory values for the second SSA CLD score calculation must have been obtained at least 60 days after the latest laboratory value for the first SSA CLD score and within the required 6–month period. We will consider the date of each SSA CLD score to be the date of the first laboratory value used for its calculation.

(vi) If you are in renal failure or on dialysis within a week of any serum creatinine test in the period used for the SSA CLD calculation, we will use a serum creatinine of 4, which is the maximum serum creatinine level allowed in the calculation, to calculate your SSA CLD score.

(vii) If you have the two SSA CLD scores required by 105.05G1, we will find that your impairment meets the criteria of the listing from at least the date of the first SSA CLD score.

b. SSA CLD–P score.

(i) If you have not attained age 12, we will use the SSA CLD–P score to evaluate your ESLD under 105.05G2. We explain how we calculate the SSA CLD–P score in b(ii) through b(vii) of this section.

(ii) To calculate the SSA CLD–P score, we use a formula that includes four parameters: Serum total bilirubin (mg/dL), International Normalized Ratio (INR), serum albumin (g/dL), and whether growth failure is occurring. The formula for the SSA CLD–P score calculation is:

4.80 x [Log_e(serum total bilirubin mg/dL)]

+18.57 x [Log_e(INR)]

–6.87 x [Log_e(serum albumin g/dL)]

+6.67 if the child has growth failure (<–2 standard deviations for weight or height)

(iii) When we indicate "Log_e" in the formula for the SSA CLD–P score calculation, we mean the "base e logarithm" or "natural logarithm" (ln) of a numerical laboratory value, not the "base 10 logarithm" or "common logarithm" (log) of the laboratory value, and not the actual laboratory value. For example, if a female child is 4.0 years old, has a current weight of 13.5 kg (10th percentile for age) and height of 92 cm (less than the third percentile for age), and has laboratory values of serum total bilirubin 2.2 mg/dL, INR 1.0, and serum albumin 3.5 g/dL, we will compute the SSA CLD–P score as follows:

4.80 x [Log_e + (serum total bilirubin 2.2 mg/dL) = 0.788]

+18.57 x [Log_e(INR 1.0) = 0]

–6.87 x [Log_e + (serum albumin 3.5 g/dL) = 1.253]

+6.67

= 3.78 + 0 -8.61 + 6.67

= 1.84, which is then rounded to an SSA CLD–P score of 2

(iv) For any SSA CLD–P score calculation, all of the required laboratory values (serum total bilirubin, INR, or serum albumin) must have been obtained within 30 days of each other. We will not purchase INR values for children who have not attained age 12. If there is no INR value for a child under 12 within the applicable time period, we will use an INR value of 1.1 to calculate the SSA CLD–P score. If there are multiple laboratory values within the 30–day interval for any given laboratory test, we will use the highest serum total bilirubin and INR values and the lowest serum albumin value for the SSA CLD–P score calculation. We will round all laboratory values less than 1.0 up to 1.0.

(v) The weight and length/height measurements used for the calculation must be obtained from one evaluation within the same 30–day period as in D11b(iv).

(vi) Listing 105.05G2 requires two SSA CLD–P scores. The laboratory values for the second SSA CLD–P score calculation must have been obtained at least 60 days after the latest laboratory value for the first SSA CLD–P score and within the required 6–month period. We will consider the date of each SSA CLD–P score to be the date of the first laboratory value used for its calculation.

(vii) If you have the two SSA CLD–P scores required by listing 105.05G2, we will find that your impairment meets the criteria of the listing from at least the date of the first SSA CLD–P score.

12. Extrahepatic biliary atresia (EBA) (105.05H) usually presents in the first 2 months of life with persistent jaundice. The impairment meets 105.05H if the diagnosis of EBA is confirmed by liver biopsy or intraoperative cholangiogram that shows obliteration of the extrahepatic biliary tree. EBA is usually surgically treated by portoenterostomy (for example, Kasai procedure). If this surgery is not performed in the first months of life or is not completely successful, liver transplantation is indicated. If you have had a liver transplant, we will evaluate your impairment under 105.09.

13. Liver transplantation (105.09) may be performed for metabolic liver disease, progressive liver failure, life-threatening complications of liver disease, hepatic malignancy, and acute fulminant hepatitis (viral, drug-induced, or toxin-induced). We will consider you to be disabled for 1 year from the date of the transplantation. Thereafter, we will evaluate your residual impairment(s) by considering the adequacy of post-transplant liver function, the requirement for post-transplant antiviral therapy, the frequency and severity of rejection episodes, comorbid complications, and all adverse treatment effects.

E. How do we evaluate inflammatory bowel disease (IBD)?

1. Inflammatory bowel disease (105.06) includes, but is not limited to, Crohn's disease and ulcerative colitis. These disorders, while distinct entities, share many clinical, laboratory, and imaging findings, as well as similar treatment regimens. Remissions and exacerbations of variable duration are the hallmark of IBD. Crohn's disease may involve the entire alimentary tract from the mouth to the anus in a segmental, asymmetric fashion. Obstruction, stenosis, fistulization, perineal involvement, and extraintestinal manifestations are common. Crohn's disease is rarely curable and recurrence may be a lifelong problem, even after surgical resection. In contrast, ulcerative colitis only affects the colon. The inflammatory process may be limited to the rectum, extend proximally to include any contiguous segment, or involve the entire colon. Ulcerative colitis may be cured by total colectomy.

2. Symptoms and signs of IBD include diarrhea, fecal incontinence, rectal bleeding, abdominal pain, fatigue, fever, nausea, vomiting, arthralgia, abdominal tenderness, palpable abdominal mass (usually inflamed loops of bowel) and perineal disease. You may also have signs or laboratory findings indicating malnutrition, such as weight loss, edema, anemia, hypoalbuminemia, hypokalemia, hypocalcemia, or hypomagnesemia.

3. IBD may be associated with significant extraintestinal manifestations in a variety of body systems. These include, but are not limited to, involvement of the eye (for example, uveitis, episcleritis, iritis); hepatobiliary disease (for example, gallstones, primary sclerosing cholangitis); urologic disease (for example, kidney stones, obstructive hydronephrosis); skin involvement (for example, erythema nodosum, pyoderma gangrenosum); or non-destructive inflammatory arthritis. You may also have associated thromboembolic disorders or vascular disease. These manifestations may not correlate with the severity of your IBD. If your impairment does not meet any of the criteria of 105.06, we will consider the effects of your extraintestinal manifestations in determining whether you have an impairment(s) that meets or medically equals another listing, and we will also consider the effects of your extraintestinal manifestations when we determine whether your impairment(s) functionally equals the listings.

4. Surgical diversion of the intestinal tract, including ileostomy and colostomy, does not very seriously interfere with age-appropriate functioning if you are able to maintain adequate nutrition and function of the stoma. However, if you are not able to maintain adequate nutrition, we will evaluate your impairment under 105.08.

F. How do we evaluate short bowel syndrome (SBS)?

1. Short bowel syndrome (105.07) is a disorder that occurs when congenital intestinal abnormalities, ischemic vascular insults (for example, necrotizing enterocolitis, volvulus), trauma, or IBD complications require surgical resection of more than one-half of the small intestine, resulting in the loss of intestinal absorptive surface and a state of chronic malnutrition. The management of SBS requires long-term parenteral nutrition via an indwelling central venous catheter (central line); the process is often referred to as hyperalimentation or total parenteral nutrition (TPN). Children with SBS can also feed orally, with variable amounts of nutrients being absorbed through their remaining intestine. Over time, some of these children can develop additional intestinal absorptive surface, and may ultimately be able to be weaned off their parenteral nutrition.

2. Your impairment will continue to meet 105.07 as long as you remain dependent on daily parenteral nutrition via a central venous catheter for most of your nutritional requirements. Long-term complications of SBS and parenteral nutrition include abnormal growth rates, central line infections (with or without septicemia), thrombosis, hepatotoxicity, gallstones, and loss of venous access sites. Intestinal transplantation is the only definitive treatment for children with SBS who remain chronically dependent on parenteral nutrition.

3. To document SBS, we need a copy of the operative report of intestinal resection, the summary of the hospitalization(s) including: Details of the surgical findings, medically appropriate postoperative imaging studies that reflect the amount of your residual small intestine, or if we cannot get one of these reports, other medical reports that include details of the surgical findings. We also need medical documentation that you are dependent on daily parenteral nutrition to provide most of your nutritional requirements.

G. How do we evaluate growth failure due to any digestive disorder?

1. To evaluate growth failure due to any digestive disorder, we require documentation of the laboratory findings of chronic nutritional deficiency described in 105.08A and the growth measurements in 105.08B within the same consecutive 12–month period. The dates of laboratory findings may be different from the dates of growth measurements.

2. Under 105.08B, we evaluate a child's growth failure by using the appropriate table for age and gender.

a. For children from birth to attainment of age 2, we use the weight-for-length table (see Table I or Table II).

b. For children age 2 to attainment of age 18, we use the body mass index (BMI)-for-age table (see Tables III or IV).

c. BMI is the ratio of a child's weight to the square of the child's height. We calculate BMI using one of the following formulas:

English Formula

BMI = [Weight in Pounds/(Height in Inches x Height in Inches)] x 703

Metric Formulas

BMI = Weight in Kilograms/(Height in Meters x Height in Meters)

BMI = [Weight in Kilograms/(Height in Centimeters x Height in Centimeters)] x 10,000

H. How do we evaluate the need for supplemental daily enteral feeding via a gastrostomy?

1. General. Infants and young children may have anatomical, neurological, or developmental disorders that interfere with their ability to feed by mouth, resulting in inadequate caloric intake to meet their growth needs. These disorders frequently result in the medical necessity to supplement caloric intake and to bypass the anatomical feeding route of mouth-throat-esophagus into the stomach.

2. Children who have not attained age 3 and who require supplemental daily enteral nutrition via a feeding gastrostomy meet 105.10 regardless of the medical reason for the gastrostomy. Thereafter, we evaluate growth impairment under 100.02, malnutrition under 105.08, or other medical or developmental disorder(s) (including the disorder(s) that necessitated gastrostomy placement) under the appropriate listing(s).

I. How do we evaluate esophageal stricture or stenosis? Esophageal stricture or stenosis (narrowing) from congenital atresia (absence or abnormal closure of a tubular body organ) or destructive esophagitis may result in malnutrition or the need for gastrostomy placement, which we evaluate under 105.08 or 105.10. Esophageal stricture or stenosis may also result in complications such as pneumonias due to frequent aspiration, or difficulty in maintaining nutritional status short of listing-level severity. While none of these complications may be of such severity that they would meet the criteria of another listing, the combination of impairments may medically equal the severity of a listing or functionally equal the listings.

J. What do we mean by the phrase "consider under a disability for 1 year"? We use the phrase "consider under a disability for 1 year" following a specific event in 105.02, 105.05A, and 105.09 to explain how long your impairment can meet the requirements of those particular listings. This phrase does not refer to the date on which your disability began, only to the date on which we must reevaluate whether your impairment continues to meet a listing or is otherwise disabling. For example, if you have received a liver transplant, you may have become disabled before the transplant because of chronic liver disease. Therefore, we do not restrict our determination of the onset of disability to the date of the specified event. We will establish an onset date earlier than the date of the specified event if the evidence in your case record supports such a finding.

K. How do we evaluate impairments that do not meet one of the digestive disorder listings?

1. These listings are only examples of common digestive disorders that we consider severe enough to result in marked and severe functional limitations. If your impairment(s) does not meet the criteria of any of these listings, we must also consider whether you have an impairment(s) that satisfies the criteria of a listing in another body system. For example:

a. If you have hepatitis B or C and you are depressed, we will evaluate your impairment under 112.04.

b. If you have multiple congenital abnormalities, we will evaluate your impairment(s) under the criteria in the listings for impairments that affect multiple body systems (110.00) or the criteria of listings in other affected body systems.

c. If you have digestive disorders that interfere with intake, digestion, or absorption of nutrition, and result in a reduction in your rate of growth, and your impairment does not satisfy the criteria in the malnutrition listing (105.08), we will evaluate your impairment under the growth impairment listings (100.00).

2. If you have a severe medically determinable impairment(s) that does not meet a listing, we will determine whether your impairment(s) medically equals a listing. (See § 416.926.) If your impairment(s) does not meet or medically equal a listing, you may or may not have an impairment(s) that functionally equals the listings. (See § 416.926a.) When we decide whether you continue to be disabled, we use the rules in § 416.994a.

105.01 Category of Impairments, Digestive System

105.02 Gastrointestinal hemorrhaging from any cause, requiring blood transfusion (with or without hospitalization) of at least 10 cc of blood/kg of body weight, and occurring at least three times during a consecutive 6–month period. The transfusions must be at least 30 days apart within the 6–month period. Consider under a disability for 1 year following the last documented transfusion; thereafter, evaluate the residual impairment(s).

105.03 [Reserved]

105.04 [Reserved]

105.05 Chronic liver disease, with:

A. Hemorrhaging from esophageal, gastric, or ectopic varices or from portal hypertensive gastropathy, demonstrated by endoscopy, x-ray, or other appropriate medically acceptable imaging, resulting in hemodynamic instability as defined in 105.00D5, and requiring hospitalization for transfusion of at least 10 cc of blood/kg of body weight. Consider under a disability for 1 year following the last documented transfusion; thereafter, evaluate the residual impairment(s).

OR

B. Ascites or hydrothorax not attributable to other causes, despite continuing treatment as prescribed, present on at least two evaluations at least 60 days apart within a consecutive 6–month period. Each evaluation must be documented by:

1. Paracentesis or thoracentesis; or

2. Appropriate medically acceptable imaging or physical examination and one of the following:

a. Serum albumin of 3.0 g/dL or less; or

b. International Normalized Ratio (INR) of at least 1.5.

OR

C. Spontaneous bacterial peritonitis with peritoneal fluid containing an absolute neutrophil count of at least 250 cells/mm^3.

OR

D. Hepatorenal syndrome as described in 105.00D8, with one of the following:

1. Serum creatinine elevation of at least 2 mg/dL; or

2. Oliguria with 24–hour urine output less than 1 mL/kg/hr; or

3. Sodium retention with urine sodium less than 10 mEq per liter.

OR

E. Hepatopulmonary syndrome as described in 105.00D9, with:

1. Arterial oxygenation (P_aO_2,) on room air of:

a. 60 mm Hg or less, at test sites less than 3000 feet above sea level, or

b. 55 mm Hg or less, at test sites from 3000 to 6000 feet, or

c. 50 mm Hg or less, at test sites above 6000 feet; or

2. Documentation of intrapulmonary arteriovenous shunting by contrast-enhanced echocardiography or macroaggregated albumin lung perfusion scan.

OR

F. Hepatic encephalopathy as described in 105.00D10, with 1 and either 2 or 3:

1. Documentation of abnormal behavior, cognitive dysfunction, changes in mental status, or altered state of consciousness (for example, confusion, delirium, stupor, or coma), present on at least two evaluations at least 60 days apart within a consecutive 6–month period; and

2. History of transjugular intrahepatic portosystemic shunt (TIPS) or any surgical portosystemic shunt; or

3. One of the following occurring on at least two evaluations at least 60 days apart within the same consecutive 6–month period as in F1:

a. Asterixis or other fluctuating physical neurological abnormalities; or

b. Electroencephalogram (EEG) demonstrating triphasic slow wave activity; or

c. Serum albumin of 3.0 g/dL or less; or

d. International Normalized Ratio (INR) of 1.5 or greater.

OR

G. End Stage Liver Disease, with:

1. For children 12 years of age or older, SSA CLD scores of 22 or greater calculated as described in 105.00D11a. Consider under a disability from at least the date of the first score.

2. For children who have not attained age 12, SSA CLD–P scores of 11 or greater calculated as described in 105.00D11b. Consider under a disability from at least the date of the first score.

OR

H. Extrahepatic biliary atresia as diagnosed on liver biopsy or intraoperative cholangiogram. Consider under a disability for 1 year following the diagnosis; thereafter, evaluate the residual liver function.

105.06 Inflammatory bowel disease (IBD) documented by endoscopy, biopsy, appropriate medically acceptable imaging, or operative findings with:

A. Obstruction of stenotic areas (not adhesions) in the small intestine or colon with proximal dilatation, confirmed by appropriate medically acceptable imaging or in surgery, requiring hospitalization for intestinal decompression or for surgery, and occurring on at least two occasions at least 60 days apart within a consecutive 6–month period;

OR

B. Two of the following despite continuing treatment as prescribed and occurring within the same consecutive 6–month period:

1. Anemia with hemoglobin less than 10.0 g/dL, present on at least two evaluations at least 60 days apart; or

2. Serum albumin of 3.0 g/dL or less, present on at least two evaluations at least 60 days apart; or

3. Clinically documented tender abdominal mass palpable on physical examination with abdominal pain or cramping that is not completely controlled by prescribed narcotic medication, present on at least two evaluations at least 60 days apart; or

4. Perineal disease with a draining abscess or fistula, with pain that is not completely controlled by prescribed narcotic medication, present on at least two evaluations at least 60 days apart; or

5. Need for supplemental daily enteral nutrition via a gastrostomy or daily parenteral nutrition via a central venous catheter. (See 105.10 for children who have not attained age 3.)

105.07 Short bowel syndrome (SBS), due to surgical resection of more than one-half of the small intestine, with dependence on daily parenteral nutrition via a central venous catheter (see 105.00F).

105.08 Growth failure due to any digestive disorder (see 105.00G), documented by A and B:

A. Chronic nutritional deficiency present on at least two evaluations at least 60 days apart within a consecutive 12–month period documented by one of the following:

1. Anemia with hemoglobin less than 10.0 g/dL; or

2. Serum albumin of 3.0 g/dL or less;

AND

B. Growth failure as required in 1 or 2:

1. For children from birth to attainment of age 2, three weight-for-length measurements that are:

a. Within a 12–month period; and

b. At least 60 days apart; and

c. Less than the third percentile on Table I or Table II; or

Table I—Males Birth to Attainment of Age 2
[Third Percentile Values for Weight-for-Length]

Length (centimeters)	Weight (kilograms)	Length (centimeters)	Weight (kilograms)	Length (centimeters)	Weight (kilograms)
45.0	1.597	64.5	6.132	84.5	10.301
45.5	1.703	65.5	6.359	85.5	10.499

Length (centimeters)	Weight (kilograms)	Length (centimeters)	Weight (kilograms)	Length (centimeters)	Weight (kilograms)
46.5	1.919	66.5	6.584	86.5	10.696
47.5	2.139	67.5	6.807	87.5	10.895
48.5	2.364	68.5	7.027	88.5	11.095
49.5	2.592	69.5	7.245	89.5	11.296
50.5	2.824	70.5	7.461	90.5	11.498
51.5	3.058	71.5	7.674	91.5	11.703
52.5	3.294	72.5	7.885	92.5	11.910
53.5	3.532	73.5	8.094	93.5	12.119
54.5	3.771	74.5	8.301	94.5	12.331
55.5	4.010	75.5	8.507	95.5	12.546
56.5	4.250	76.5	8.710	96.5	12.764
57.5	4.489	77.5	8.913	97.5	12.987
58.5	4.728	78.5	9.113	98.5	13.213
59.5	4.966	79.5	9.313	99.5	13.443
60.5	5.203	80.5	9.512	100.5	13.678
61.5	5.438	81.5	9.710	101.5	13.918
62.5	5.671	82.5	9.907	102.5	14.163
63.5	5.903	83.5	10.104	103.5	14.413

Table II—Females Birth to Attainment of Age 2
[Third percentile values for weight-for-length]

Length (centimeters)	Weight (kilograms)	Length (centimeters)	Weight (kilograms)	Length (centimeters)	Weight (kilograms)
45.0	1.613	64.5	5.985	84.5	10.071
45.5	1.724	65.5	6.200	85.5	10.270
46.5	1.946	66.5	6.413	86.5	10.469
47.5	2.171	67.5	6.625	87.5	10.670
48.5	2.397	68.5	6.836	88.5	10.871
49.5	2.624	69.5	7.046	89.5	11.074
50.5	2.852	70.5	7.254	90.5	11.278
51.5	3.081	71.5	7.461	91.5	11.484
52.5	3.310	72.5	7.667	92.5	11.691
53.5	3.538	73.5	7.871	93.5	11.901
54.5	3.767	74.5	8.075	94.5	12.112
55.5	3.994	75.5	8.277	95.5	12.326
56.5	4.220	76.5	8.479	96.5	12.541
57.5	4.445	77.5	8.679	97.5	12.760
58.5	4.669	78.5	8.879	98.5	12.981
59.5	4.892	79.5	9.078	99.5	13.205
60.5	5.113	80.5	9.277	100.5	13.431
61.5	5.333	81.5	9.476	101.5	13.661
62.5	5.552	82.5	9.674	102.5	13.895
63.5	5.769	83.5	9.872	103.5	14.132

2. For children age 2 to attainment of age 18, three BMI–for-age measurements that are:

a. Within a consecutive 12–month period; and

b. At least 60 days apart; and

c. Less than the third percentile on Table III or Table IV.

Table III—Males Age 2 to Attainment of Age 18
[Third Percentile Values for BMI-for-Age]

Age (yrs. and mos.)	BMI	Age (yrs. and mos.)	BMI	Age (yrs. and mos.)	BMI
2.0 to 2.1	14.5	10.11 to 11.2	14.3	14.9 to 14.10	16.1
2.2 to 2.4	14.4	11.3 to 11.5	14.4	14.11 to 15.0	16.2
2.5 to 2.7	14.3	11.6 to 11.8	14.5	15.1 to 15.3	16.3
2.8 to 2.11	14.2	11.9 to 11.11	14.6	15.4 to 15.5	16.4
3.0 to 3.2	14.1	12.0 to 12.1	14.7	15.6 to 15.7	16.5
3.3 to 3.6	14.0	12.2 to 12.4	14.8	15.8 to 15.9	16.6
3.7 to 3.11	13.9	12.5 to 12.7	14.9	15.10 to 15.11	16.7
4.0 to 4.5	13.8	12.8 to 12.9	15.0	16.0 to 16.1	16.8
4.6 to 5.0	13.7	12.10 to 13.0	15.1	16.2 to 16.3	16.9
5.1 to 6.0	13.6	13.1 to 13.2	15.2	16.4 to 16.5	17.0
6.1 to 7.6	13.5	13.3 to 13.4	15.3	16.6 to 16.8	17.1
7.7 to 8.6	13.6	13.5 to 13.7	15.4	16.9 to 16.10	17.2
8.7 to 9.1	13.7	13.8 to 13.9	15.5	16.11 to 17.0	17.3
9.2 to 9.6	13.8	13.10 to 13.11	15.6	17.1 to 17.2	17.4
9.7 to 9.11	13.9	14.0 to 14.1	15.7	17.3 to 17.5	17.5

Age (yrs. and mos.)	BMI	Age (yrs. and mos.)	BMI	Age (yrs. and mos.)	BMI
10.0 to 10.3........	14.0	14.2 to 14.4	15.8	17.6 to 17.7	17.6
10.4 to 10.7........	14.1	14.5 to 14.6	15.9	17.8 to 17.9	17.7
10.8 to 10.10......	14.2	14.7 to 14.8	16.0	17.10 to 17.11	17.8

Table IV—Females Age 2 to Attainment of Age 18
[Third Percentile Values for BMI-for-Age]

Age (yrs. and mos.)	BMI	Age (yrs. and mos.)	BMI	Age (yrs. and mos.)	BMI
2.0 to 2.2........	14.1	10.8 to 10.10	14.0	14.3 to 14.5	15.6
2.3 to 2.6........	14.0	10.11 to 11.2	14.1	14.6 to 14.7	15.7
2.7 to 2.10........	13.9	11.3 to 11.5	14.2	14.8 to 14.9	15.8
2.11 to 3.2........	13.8	11.6 to 11.7	14.3	14.10 to 15.0	15.9
3.3 to 3.6........	13.7	11.8 to 11.10	14.4	15.1 to 15.2	16.0
3.7 to 3.11........	13.6	11.11 to 12.1	14.5	15.3 to 15.5	16.1
4.0 to 4.4........	13.5	12.2 to 12.4	14.6	15.6 to 15.7	16.2
4.5 to 4.11........	13.4	12.5 to 12.6	14.7	15.8 to 15.10	16.3
5.0 to 5.9........	13.3	12.7 to 12.9	14.8	15.11 to 16.0	16.4
5.10 to 7.6........	13.2	12.10 to 12.11	14.9	16.1 to 16.3	16.5
7.7 to 8.4........	13.3	13.0 to 13.2	15.0	16.4 to 16.6	16.6
8.5 to 8.10........	13.4	13.3 to 13.4	15.1	16.7 to 16.9	16.7
8.11 to 9.3........	13.5	13.5 to 13.7	15.2	16.10 to 17.0	16.8
9.4 to 9.8........	13.6	13.8 to 13.9	15.3	17.1 to 17.3	16.9
9.9 to 10.0........	13.7	13.10 to 14.0	15.4	17.4 to 17.7	17.0
10.1 to 10.4........	13.8	14.1 to 14.2	15.5	17.8 to 17.11	17.1
10.5 to 10.7........	13.9				

105.09 Liver transplantation. Consider under a disability for 1 year following the date of transplantation; thereafter, evaluate the residual impairment(s) (see 105.00D13 and 105.00J).

105.10 Need for supplemental daily enteral feeding via a gastrostomy due to any cause, for children who have not attained age 3; thereafter, evaluate the residual impairment(s) (see 105.00H).

[81 FR 86923, Dec. 2, 2016; 82 FR 5872, Jan. 18, 2017]

APPENDIX 1–PART–B2. TO SUBPART P OF PART 404—LISTING OF IMPAIRMENTS

106.00 GENITOURINARY DISORDERS

A. Which disorders do we evaluate under these listings?

We evaluate genitourinary disorders resulting in chronic kidney disease (CKD). Examples of such disorders include chronic glomerulonephritis, hypertensive nephropathy, diabetic nephropathy, chronic obstructive uropathy, and hereditary nephropathies. We also evaluate nephrotic syndrome due to glomerular dysfunction, and congenital genitourinary disorders, such as ectopic ureter, exstrophic urinary bladder, urethral valves, and Eagle–Barrett syndrome (prune belly syndrome), under these listings.

B. What evidence do we need?

1. We need evidence that documents the signs, symptoms, and laboratory findings of your CKD. This evidence should include reports of clinical examinations, treatment records, and documentation of your response to treatment. Laboratory findings, such as serum creatinine or serum albumin levels, may document your kidney function. We generally need evidence covering a period of at least 90 days unless we can make a fully favorable determination or decision without it.

2. Estimated glomerular filtration rate (eGFR). The eGFR is an estimate of the filtering capacity of the kidneys that takes into account serum creatinine concentration and other variables, such as your age, gender, and body size. If your medical evidence includes eGFR findings, we will consider them when we evaluate your CKD under 106.05.

3. Kidney or bone biopsy. If you have had a kidney or bone biopsy, we need a copy of the pathology report. When we cannot get a copy of the pathology report, we will accept a statement from an acceptable medical source verifying that a biopsy was performed and describing the results.

C. What other factors do we consider when we evaluate your genitourinary disorder?

1. Chronic hemodialysis or peritoneal dialysis.

a. Dialysis is a treatment for CKD that uses artificial means to remove toxic metabolic byproducts from the blood. Hemodialysis uses an artificial kidney machine to clean waste products from the blood; peritoneal dialysis uses a dialyzing solution that is introduced into and removed from the abdomen (peritoneal cavity) either continuously or intermittently. Under 106.03, your ongoing dialysis must have lasted or be expected to last for a continuous period of at least 12 months. To satisfy the requirement in 106.03, we will accept a report from an acceptable medical source that describes your CKD and your current dialysis, and indicates that your dialysis will be ongoing.

b. If you are undergoing chronic hemodialysis or peritoneal dialysis, your CKD may meet our definition of disability before you started dialysis. We will determine the onset of your disability based on the facts in your case record.

2. Kidney transplant.

a. If you receive a kidney transplant, we will consider you to be disabled under 106.04 for 1 year from the date of transplant. After that, we will evaluate your residual impairment(s) by considering your post-transplant function, any rejection episodes you have had, complications in other body systems, and any adverse effects related to ongoing treatment.

b. If you received a kidney transplant, your CKD may meet our definition of disability before you received the transplant. We will determine the onset of your disability based on the facts in your case record.

3. Anasarca (generalized massive edema or swelling). Under 106.06B, we need a description of the extent of edema, including pretibial (in front of the tibia), periorbital (around the eyes), or presacral (in front of the sacrum) edema. We also need a description of any ascites, pleural effusion, or pericardial effusion.

4. Congenital genitourinary disorder. Procedures such as diagnostic cystoscopy or circumcision do not satisfy the requirement for urologic surgical procedures in 106.07.

5. Growth failure due to any chronic renal disease.

a. To evaluate growth failure due to any chronic renal disease, we require documentation of the laboratory findings described in 106.08A and the growth measurements in 106.08B within the same consecutive 12–month period. The dates of laboratory findings may be different from the dates of growth measurements.

b. Under 106.08B, we use the appropriate table(s) under 105.08B in the digestive system to determine whether a child's growth is less than the third percentile.

(i) For children from birth to attainment of age 2, we use the weight-for-length table corresponding to the child's gender (Table I or Table II).

(ii) For children age 2 to attainment of age 18, we use the body mass index (BMI)-for-age table corresponding to the child's gender (Table III or Table IV).

(iii) BMI is the ratio of a child's weight to the square of his or her height. We calculate BMI using the formulas in 105.00G2c.

6. Complications of CKD. The hospitalizations in 106.09 may be for different complications of CKD. Examples of complications from CKD that may result in hospitalization include stroke, congestive heart failure, hypertensive crisis, or acute kidney failure requiring a short course of hemodialysis. If the CKD complication occurs during a hospitalization that was initially for a co-occurring condition, we will evaluate it under our rules for determining medical equivalence. (See § 416.926 of this chapter.) We will evaluate co-occurring conditions, including those that result in hospitalizations, under the listings for the affected body system or under our rules for medical equivalence.

D. How do we evaluate disorders that do not meet one of the genitourinary listings?

1. The listed disorders are only examples of common genitourinary disorders that we consider severe enough to result in marked and severe functional limitations. If your impairment(s) does not meet the criteria of any of these listings, we must also consider whether you have an impairment(s) that satisfies the criteria of a listing in another body system.

2. If you have a severe medically determinable impairment(s) that does not meet a listing, we will determine whether your impairment(s) medically equals a listing. (See § 416.926 of this chapter.) Genitourinary disorders may be associated with disorders in other body systems, and we consider the combined effects of multiple impairments when we determine whether they medically equal a listing. If your impairment(s) does not medically equal a listing, we will also consider whether it functionally equals the listings. (See § 416.926a of this chapter.) We use the rules in § 416.994a of this chapter when we decide whether you continue to be disabled.

106.01 Category of Impairments, Genitourinary Disorders

106.03 Chronic kidney disease, with chronic hemodialysis or peritoneal dialysis (see 106.00C1).

106.04 Chronic kidney disease, with kidney transplant. Consider under a disability for 1 year following the transplant; thereafter, evaluate the residual impairment (see 106.00C2).

106.05 Chronic kidney disease, with impairment of kidney function, with one of the following documented on at least two occasions at least 90 days apart during a consecutive 12–month period:

A. Serum creatinine of 3 mg/dL or greater;

OR

B. Creatinine clearance of 30 ml/min/1.73m^2 or less;

OR

C. Estimated glomerular filtration rate (eGFR) of 30 ml/min/1.73m^2 or less.

106.06 Nephrotic syndrome, with A and B:

A. Laboratory findings as described in 1 or 2, documented on at least two occasions at least 90 days apart during a consecutive 12–month period:

1. Serum albumin of 3.0 g/dL or less, or

2. Proteinuria of 40 mg/m^2/hr or greater;

AND

B. Anasarca (see 106.00C3) persisting for at least 90 days despite prescribed treatment.

106.07 Congenital genitourinary disorder (see 106.00C4) requiring urologic surgical procedures at least three times in a consecutive 12–month period, with at least 30 days between procedures. Consider under a disability for 1 year following the date of the last surgery; thereafter, evaluate the residual impairment.

106.08 Growth failure due to any chronic renal disease (see 106.00C5), with:

A. Serum creatinine of 2 mg/dL or greater, documented at least two times within a consecutive 12–month period with at least 60 days between measurements.

AND

B. Growth failure as required in 1 or 2:

1. For children from birth to attainment of age 2, three weight-for-length measurements that are:

a. Within a consecutive 12–month period; and

b. At least 60 days apart; and

c. Less than the third percentile on the appropriate weight-for-length table under 105.08B1; or

2. For children age 2 to attainment of age 18, three BMI–for-age measurements that are:

a. Within a consecutive 12–month period; and

b. At least 60 days apart; and

c. Less than the third percentile on the appropriate BMI–for-age table under 105.08B2.

106.09 Complications of chronic kidney disease (see 106.00C5) requiring at least three hospitalizations within a consecutive 12–month period and occurring at least 30 days apart. Each hospitalization must last at least 48 hours, including hours in a hospital emergency department immediately before the hospitalization.

107.00 HEMATOLOGICAL DISORDERS

A. What hematological disorders do we evaluate under these listings?

1. We evaluate non-malignant (non-cancerous) hematological disorders, such as hemolytic anemias (107.05), disorders of thrombosis and hemostasis (107.08), and disorders of bone marrow failure (107.10). These disorders disrupt the normal development and function of white blood cells, red blood cells, platelets, and clotting-factor proteins (factors).

2. We evaluate malignant (cancerous) hematological disorders, such as lymphoma, leukemia, and multiple myeloma, under the appropriate listings in 113.00, except for two lymphomas associated with human immunodeficiency virus (HIV) infection. We evaluate primary central nervous system lymphoma associated with HIV infection under 114.11B, and primary effusion lymphoma associated with HIV infection under 114.11C.

B. What evidence do we need to document that you have a hematological disorder?

We need the following evidence to document that you have a hematological disorder:

1. A laboratory report of a definitive test that establishes a hematological disorder, signed by a physician; or

2. A laboratory report of a definitive test that establishes a hematological disorder that is not signed by a physician and a report from a physician that states you have the disorder; or

3. When we do not have a laboratory report of a definitive test, a persuasive report from a physician that a diagnosis of your hematological disorder was confirmed by appropriate laboratory analysis or other diagnostic method(s). To be persuasive, this report must state that you had the appropriate definitive laboratory test or tests for diagnosing your disorder and provide the results, or explain how your diagnosis was established by other diagnostic method(s) consistent with the prevailing state of medical knowledge and clinical practice.

4. We will make every reasonable effort to obtain the results of appropriate laboratory testing you have had. We will not purchase complex, costly, or invasive tests, such as tests of clotting-factor proteins, and bone marrow aspirations.

C. What are hemolytic anemias, and how do we evaluate them under 107.05?

1. Hemolytic anemias, both congenital and acquired, are disorders that result in premature destruction of red blood cells (RBCs). Hemolytic anemias include abnormalities of hemoglobin structure (hemoglobinopathies), abnormal RBC enzyme content and function, and RBC membrane (envelope) defects that are congenital or acquired. The diagnosis of hemolytic anemia is based on hemoglobin electrophoresis or analysis of the contents of the RBC (enzymes) and membrane. Examples of congenital hemolytic anemias include sickle cell disease, thalassemia, and their variants, and hereditary spherocytosis. Acquired hemolytic anemias may result from autoimmune disease (for example, systemic lupus erythematosus) or mechanical devices (for example, heart valves, intravascular patches).

2. The hospitalizations in 107.05B do not all have to be for the same complication of the hemolytic anemia. They may be for three different complications of the disorder. Examples of complications of hemolytic anemia that may result in hospitalization include dactylitis, osteomyelitis, painful (vaso-occlusive) crisis, pulmonary infections or infarctions, acute chest syndrome, pulmo-

nary hypertension, chronic heart failure, gallbladder disease, hepatic (liver) failure, renal (kidney) failure, nephrotic syndrome, aplastic crisis, and strokes. We will count the hours you receive emergency treatment in a comprehensive sickle cell disease center immediately before the hospitalization if this treatment is comparable to the treatment provided in a hospital emergency department.

3. For 107.05C, we do not require hemoglobin to be measured during a period in which you are free of pain or other symptoms of your disorder. We will accept hemoglobin measurements made while you are experiencing complications of your hemolytic anemia.

4. 107.05D refers to the most serious type of beta thalassemia major in which the bone marrow cannot produce sufficient numbers of normal RBCs to maintain life. The only available treatments for beta thalassemia major are life-long RBC transfusions (sometimes called hypertransfusion) or bone marrow transplantation. For purposes of 107.05D, we do not consider prophylactic RBC transfusions to prevent strokes or other complications in sickle cell disease and its variants to be of equal significance to life-saving RBC transfusions for beta thalassemia major. However, we will consider the functional limitations associated with prophylactic RBC transfusions and any associated side effects (for example, iron overload) under functional equivalence and any affected body system(s). We will also evaluate strokes and resulting complications under 111.00 and 112.00.

D. What are disorders of thrombosis and hemostasis, and how do we evaluate them under 107.08?

1. Disorders of thrombosis and hemostasis include both clotting and bleeding disorders, and may be congenital or acquired. These disorders are characterized by abnormalities in blood clotting that result in hypercoagulation (excessive blood clotting) or hypocoagulation (inadequate blood clotting). The diagnosis of a thrombosis or hemostasis disorder is based on evaluation of plasma clotting-factor proteins (factors) and platelets. Protein C or protein S deficiency and Factor V Leiden are examples of hypercoagulation disorders. Hemophilia, von Willebrand disease, and thrombocytopenia are examples of hypocoagulation disorders. Acquired excessive blood clotting may result from blood protein defects and acquired inadequate blood clotting (for example, acquired hemophilia A) may be associated with inhibitor autoantibodies.

2. The hospitalizations in 107.08 do not all have to be for the same complication of a disorder of thrombosis and hemostasis. They may be for three different complications of the disorder. Examples of complications that may result in hospitalization include anemias, thromboses, embolisms, and uncontrolled bleeding requiring multiple factor concentrate infusions or platelet transfusions. We will also consider any surgery that you have, even if it is not related to your hematological disorder, to be a complication of your disorder of thrombosis and hemostasis if you require treatment with clotting-factor proteins (for example, factor VIII or IX) or anticoagulant medication to control bleeding or coagulation in connection with your surgery. We will count the hours you receive emergency treatment in a comprehensive hemophilia treatment center immediately before the hospitalization if this treatment is comparable to the treatment provided in a hospital emergency department.

E. What are disorders of bone marrow failure, and how do we evaluate them under 107.10?

1. Disorders of bone marrow failure may be congenital or acquired, characterized by bone marrow that does not make enough healthy RBCs, platelets, or granulocytes (specialized types of white blood cells); there may also be a combined failure of these bone marrow-producing cells. The diagnosis is based on peripheral blood smears and bone marrow aspiration or bone marrow biopsy, but not peripheral blood smears alone. Examples of these disorders are myelodysplastic syndromes, aplastic anemia, granulocytopenia, and myelofibrosis. Acquired disorders of bone marrow failure may result from viral infections, chemical exposure, or immunologic disorders.

2. The hospitalizations in 107.10A do not all have to be for the same complication of bone marrow failure. They may be for three different complications of the disorder. Examples of complications that may result in hospitalization include uncontrolled bleeding, anemia, and systemic bacterial, viral, or fungal infections.

3. For 107.10B, the requirement of life-long RBC transfusions to maintain life in myelodysplastic syndromes or aplastic anemias has the same meaning as it does for beta thalassemia major. (See 107.00C4.)

F. How do we evaluate bone marrow or stem cell transplantation under 107.17?

We will consider you to be disabled for 12 months from the date of bone marrow or stem cell transplantation, or we may consider you to be disabled for a longer period if you are experiencing any serious post-transplantation complications, such as graft-versus-host (GVH) disease, frequent infections after immunosuppressive therapy, or significant deterioration of organ systems. We do not restrict our determination of the onset of disability to the date of the transplantation in 107.17. We may establish an earlier onset of disability due to your transplantation if evidence in your case record supports such a finding.

G. How do we consider your symptoms, including your pain, severe fatigue, and malaise?

Your symptoms, including pain, severe fatigue, and malaise, may be important factors in our determination whether your hematological disorder meets or medically equals a listing, or in our determination whether you otherwise have marked and severe functional limitations. We cannot consider your symptoms unless you have medical signs or laboratory findings showing the existence of a medically determinable impairment(s) that could reasonably be expected to produce the symptoms. If you have such an impairment(s), we will evaluate the intensity, persistence, and functional effects of your symptoms using the rules throughout 107.00 and in our other regulations. (See sections 416.921 and 416.929 of this chapter.) Additionally, when we assess the credibility of your complaints about your symptoms and their functional effects, we will not draw any inferences from the fact that you do not receive treatment or that you are not following treatment without considering all of the relevant evidence in your case record, including any explanations you provide on why you are not receiving or following treatment.

H. How do we evaluate episodic events in hematological disorders?

Some of the listings in this body system require a specific number of events within a consecutive 12–month period. (See 107.05, 107.08, and 107.10A.) When we use such criteria, a consecutive 12–month period means a period of 12 consecutive months, all or part of which must occur within the period we are considering in connection with your application or continuing disability review. These events must occur at least 30 days apart to ensure that we are evaluating separate events.

I. How do we evaluate hematological disorders that do not meet one of these listings?

1. These listings are only common examples of hematological disorders that we consider severe enough to result in marked and severe functional limitations. If your disorder does not meet the criteria of any of these listings, we must consider whether you have a disorder that satisfies the criteria of a listing in another body system. For example, we will evaluate hemophilic joint deformity under 101.00; polycythemia vera under 103.00, 104.00, or 111.00; chronic iron overload resulting from repeated RBC transfusion (transfusion hemosiderosis) under 103.00, 104.00, or 105.00; and the effects of intracranial bleeding or stroke under 111.00 or 112.00.

2. If you have a severe medically determinable impairment(s) that does not meet a listing, we will determine whether your impairment(s) medically equals a listing. (See section 416.926 of this chapter.) Hematological disorders may be associated with disorders in other body systems, and we consider the combined effects of multiple impairments when we determine whether they medically equal a listing. If your impairment(s) does not medically equal a listing, we will also consider whether it functionally equals the listings. (See section 416.926a of this chapter.) We use the rules in § 416.994a of this chapter when we decide whether you continue to be disabled.

107.01 Category of Impairments, Hematological Disorders

107.05 Hemolytic anemias, including sickle cell disease, thalassemia, and their variants (see 107.00C), with:

A. Documented painful (vaso-occlusive) crises requiring parenteral (intravenous or intramuscular) narcotic medication, occurring at least six times within a 12–month period with at least 30 days between crises.

OR

B. Complications of hemolytic anemia requiring at least three hospitalizations within a 12–month period and occurring at least 30 days apart. Each hospitalization must last at least 48 hours, which can include hours in a hospital emergency department or comprehensive sickle cell disease center immediately before the hospitalization (see 107.00C2).

OR

C. Hemoglobin measurements of 7.0 grams per deciliter (g/dL) or less, occurring at least three times within a 12–month period with at least 30 days between measurements.

OR

D. Beta thalassemia major requiring life-long RBC transfusions at least once every 6 weeks to maintain life (see 107.00C4).

107.08 Disorders of thrombosis and hemostasis, including hemophilia and thrombocytopenia (see 107.00D), with complications requiring at least three hospitalizations within a 12–month period and occurring at least 30 days apart. Each hospitalization must last at least 48 hours, which can include hours in a hospital emergency department or comprehensive hemophilia treatment center immediately before the hospitalization (see 107.00D2).

107.10 Disorders of bone marrow failure, including myelodysplastic syndromes, aplastic anemia, granulocytopenia, and myelofibrosis (see 107.00E), with:

A. Complications of bone marrow failure requiring at least three hospitalizations within a 12–month period and occurring at least 30 days apart. Each hospitalization must last at least 48 hours, which can include hours in a hospital emergency department immediately before the hospitalization (see 107.00E2).

OR

B. Myelodysplastic syndromes or aplastic anemias requiring life-long RBC transfusions at least once every 6 weeks to maintain life (see 107.00E3).

107.17 Hematological disorders treated by bone marrow or stem cell transplantation (see 107.00F). Consider under a disability for at least 12 consecutive months from the date of transplantation. After that, evaluate any residual impairment(s) under the criteria for the affected body system.

108.00 Skin Disorders

A. What skin disorders do we evaluate with these listings? We use these listings to evaluate skin disorders that may result from hereditary, congenital, or acquired pathological processes. The kinds of impairments covered by these listings are: Ichthyosis, bullous diseases, chronic infections of the skin or mucous membranes, dermatitis, hidradenitis suppurativa, genetic photosensitivity disorders, and burns.

B. What documentation do we need? When we evaluate the existence and severity of your skin disorder, we generally need information about the onset, duration, frequency of flareups, and prognosis of your skin disorder; the location, size, and appearance of lesions; and, when applicable, history of exposure to toxins, allergens, or irritants, familial incidence, seasonal variation, stress factors, and your ability to function outside of a highly protective environment. To confirm the diagnosis, we may need laboratory findings (for example, results of a biopsy obtained independently of Social Security disability evaluation or blood tests) or evidence from other medically acceptable methods consistent with the prevailing state of medical knowledge and clinical practice.

C. How do we assess the severity of your skin disorders(s)? We generally base our assessment of severity on the extent of your skin lesions, the frequency of flareups of your skin lesions, how your symptoms (including pain) limit you, the extent of your treatment, and how your treatment affects you.

1. Extensive skin lesions. Extensive skin lesions are those that involve multiple body sites or critical body areas, and result in a very serious limitation. Examples of extensive skin lesions that result in a very serious limitation include but are not limited to:

a. Skin lesions that interfere with the motion of your joints and that very seriously limit your use of more than one extremity; that is, two upper extremities, two lower extremities, or one upper and one lower extremity.

b. Skin lesions on the palms of both hands that very seriously limit your ability to do fine and gross motor movements.

c. Skin lesions on the soles of both feet, the perineum, or both inguinal areas that very seriously limit your ability to ambulate.

2. Frequency of flareups. If you have skin lesions, but they do not meet the requirements of any of the listings in this body system, you may still have an impairment that results in marked and severe functional limitations when we consider your condition over time, especially if your flareups result in extensive skin lesions, as defined in C1 of this section. Therefore, if you have frequent flareups, we may find that your impairment(s) is medically equal to one of these listings even though you have some periods during which your condition is in remission. We will consider how frequent and serious your flareups are, how quickly they resolve, and how you function between flareups to determine whether you have marked and severe functional limitations that have lasted for a continuous period of at least 12 months or that can be expected to last for a continuous period of at least 12 months. We will also consider the frequency of your flareups when we determine whether you have a severe impairment and when we need to assess functional equivalence.

3. Symptoms (including pain). Symptoms (including pain) may be important factors contributing to the severity of your skin disorder(s). We assess the impact of symptoms as explained in §§ 416.921 and 416.929 of this chapter.

4. Treatment. We assess the effects of medication, therapy, surgery, and any other form of treatment you receive when we determine the severity and duration of your impairment(s). Skin disorders frequently respond to treatment; however, response to treatment can vary widely, with some impairments becoming resistant to treatment. Some treatments can have side effects that can in themselves result in limitations.

a. We assess the effects of continuing treatment as prescribed by determining if there is improvement in the symptoms, signs, and laboratory findings of your disorder, and if you experience side effects that result in functional limitations. To assess the effects of your treatment, we may need information about:

i. The treatment you have been prescribed (for example, the type, dosage, method and frequency of administration of medication or therapy);

ii. Your response to the treatment;

iii. Any adverse effects of the treatment; and

iv. The expected duration of the treatment.

b. Because treatment itself or the effects of treatment may be temporary, in most cases sufficient time must elapse to allow us to evaluate the impact and expected duration of treatment and its side effects. Except under 108.07 and 108.08, you must follow continuing treatment as prescribed for at least 3 months before your impairment can be determined to meet the requirements of a skin disorder listing. (See 108.00H if you are not undergoing treatment or did not have treatment for 3 months.) We consider your specific response to treatment when we evaluate the overall severity of your impairment.

D. How do we assess impairments that may affect the skin and other body systems? When your impairment affects your skin and has effects in other body systems, we first evaluate the predominant feature of your impairment under the appropriate body system. Examples include, but are not limited to the following.

1. Tuberous sclerosis primarily affects the brain. The predominant features are seizures, which we evaluate under the neurological listings in 111.00, and developmental delays or other mental disorders, which we evaluate under the mental disorders listings in 112.00.

2. Malignant tumors of the skin (for example, malignant melanoma) are cancers, or neoplastic diseases, which we evaluate under the listings in 113.00.

3. Autoimmune disorders and other immune system disorders (for example, systemic lupus erythematosus (SLE), scleroderma, human immunodeficiency virus (HIV) infection, and Sjögren's syndrome) often involve more than one body system. We first evaluate these disorders under the immune system disorders listings in 114.00. We evaluate SLE under 114.02, scleroderma under 114.04, Sjögren's syndrome under 114.10, and HIV infection under 114.11.

4. Disfigurement or deformity resulting from skin lesions may result in loss of sight, hearing, speech, and the ability to chew (mastication). We evaluate these impairments and their effects under the special senses and speech listings in 102.00 and the digestive system listings in 105.00. Facial disfigurement or other physical deformities may also have effects we evaluate under the mental disorders listings in 112.00, such as when they affect mood or social functioning.

5. We evaluate erythropoietic porphyrias under the hemic and lymphatic listings in 107.00.

6. We evaluate hemangiomas associated with thrombocytopenia and hemorrhage (for example, Kasabach–Merritt syndrome) involving coagulation defects, under the hemic and lymphatic listings in 107.00. But, when hemangiomas impinge on vital structures or interfere with function, we evaluate their primary effects under the appropriate body system.

E. How do we evaluate genetic photosensitivity disorders?

1. Xeroderma pigmentosum (XP). When you have XP, your impairment meets the requirements of 108.07A if you have clinical and laboratory findings showing that you have the disorder. (See 108.00E3.) People who have XP have a lifelong hypersensitivity to all forms of ultraviolet light and generally lead extremely restricted lives in highly protective environments in order to prevent skin cancers from developing. Some people with XP also experience problems with their eyes, neurological problems, mental disorders, and problems in other body systems.

2. Other genetic photosensitivity disorders. Other genetic photosensitivity disorders may vary in their effects on different people, and may not result in marked and severe functional limitations for a continuous period of at least 12 months. Therefore, if you have a genetic photosensitivity disorder other than XP (established by clinical and laboratory findings as described in 108.00E3), you must show that you have either extensive skin lesions or an inability to function outside of a highly protective environment to meet the requirements of 108.07B. You must also show that your impairment meets the duration requirement. By inability to function outside of a highly protective environment we mean that you must avoid exposure to ultraviolet light (including sunlight passing through windows and light from unshielded fluorescent bulbs), wear protective clothing and eyeglasses, and use opaque broad-spectrum sunscreens in order to avoid skin cancer or other serious effects. Some genetic photosensitivity disorders can have very serious effects in other body systems, especially special senses and speech (102.00), neurological (111.00), mental (112.00), and neoplastic (113.00). We will evaluate the predominant feature of your impairment under the appropriate body system, as explained in 108.00D.

3. Clinical and laboratory findings.

a. General. We need documentation from an acceptable medical source to establish that you have a medically determinable impairment. In general, we must have evidence of appropriate laboratory testing showing that you have XP or another genetic photosensitivity disorder. We will find that you have XP or another genetic photosensitivity disorder based on a report from an acceptable medical source indicating that you have the impairment, supported by definitive genetic laboratory studies documenting appropriate chromosomal changes, including abnormal DNA repair or another DNA or genetic abnormality specific to your type of photosensitivity disorder.

b. What we will accept as medical evidence instead of the actual laboratory report. When we do not have the actual laboratory report, we need evidence from an acceptable medical source that includes appropriate clinical findings for your impairment and that is persuasive that a positive diagnosis has been confirmed by appropriate laboratory testing at some time prior to our evaluation. To be persuasive, the report must state that the appropriate definitive genetic laboratory study was conducted and that the results confirmed the diagnosis. The report must be consistent with other evidence in your case record.

F. How do we evaluate burns? Electrical, chemical, or thermal burns frequently affect other body systems; for example, musculoskeletal, special senses and speech, respiratory, cardiovascular, renal, neurological, or mental. Consequently, we evaluate burns the way we evaluate other disorders that can affect the skin and other body systems, using the listing for the predominant feature of your impairment. For example, if your soft tissue injuries are under continuing surgical management (as defined in 101.00M), we will evaluate your impairment under 101.08. However, if your burns do not meet the requirements of 101.08 and you have extensive skin lesions that result in a very serious limitation (as defined in 108.00C1) that has lasted or can be expected to last for a continuous period of at least 12 months, we will evaluate them under 108.08.

G. How do we determine if your skin disorder(s) will continue at a disabling level of severity in order to meet the duration requirement? For all of these skin disorder listings except 108.07 and 108.08, we will find that your impairment meets the duration requirement if your skin disorder results in extensive skin lesions that persist for at least 3 months despite continuing treatment as prescribed. By persist, we mean that the longitudinal clinical record shows that, with few exceptions, your lesions have been at the level of severity specified in the listing. For 108.07A, we will presume that you meet the duration requirement. For 108.07B and 108.08, we will consider all of the relevant medical and other information in your case record to determine whether your skin disorder meets the duration requirement.

H. How do we assess your skin disorder(s) if your impairment does not meet the requirements of one of these listings?

1. These listings are only examples of common skin disorders that we consider severe enough to result in marked and severe functional limitations. For most of these listings, if you do not have continuing treatment as prescribed, if your treatment has not lasted for at least 3 months, or if you do not have extensive skin lesions that have persisted for at least 3 months, your impairment cannot meet the requirements of these skin disorder listings. (This provision does not apply to 108.07 and 108.08.) However, we may still find that you are disabled because your impairment(s) meets the requirements of a listing in another body system, medically equals (see §§ 404.1526 and 416.926 of this chapter) the severity of a listing, or functionally equals the severity of the listings.

2. If you have not received ongoing treatment or do not have an ongoing relationship with the medical community despite the existence of a severe impairment(s), or if your skin lesions have not persisted for at least 3 months but you are undergoing continuing treatment as prescribed, you may still have an impairment(s) that meets a listing in another body system or that medically equals a listing. If you do not have an impairment(s) that meets or medically equals a listing, we will consider whether your impairment(s) functionally equals the listings. (See § 416.924 of this chapter.) When we decide whether you continue to be disabled, we use the rules in § 416.994a of this chapter.

108.01 Category of Impairments, Skin Disorders

108.02 Ichthyosis, with extensive skin lesions that persist for at least 3 months despite continuing treatment as prescribed.

108.03 Bullous disease (for example, pemphigus, erythema multiforme bullosum, epidermolysis bullosa, bullous pemphigoid, dermatitis herpetiformis), with extensive skin lesions that persist for at least 3 months despite continuing treatment as prescribed.

108.04 Chronic infections of the skin or mucous membranes, with extensive fungating or extensive ulcerating skin lesions that persist for at least 3 months despite continuing treatment as prescribed.

108.05 Dermatitis (for example, psoriasis, dyshidrosis, atopic dermatitis, exfoliative dermatitis, allergic contact dermatitis), with extensive skin lesions that persist for at least 3 months despite continuing treatment as prescribed.

108.06 Hidradenitis suppurativa, with extensive skin lesions involving both axillae, both inguinal areas, or the perineum that persist for at least 3 months despite continuing treatment as prescribed.

108.07 Genetic photosensitivity disorders, established as described in 108.00E.

A. Xeroderma pigmentosum. Consider the individual disabled from birth.

B. Other genetic photosensitivity disorders, with:

1. Extensive skin lesions that have lasted or can be expected to last for a continuous period of at least 12 months, or

2. Inability to function outside of a highly protective environment for a continuous period of at least 12 months (see 108.00E2).

108.08 Burns, with extensive skin lesions that have lasted or can be expected to last for a continuous period of at least 12 months. (See 108.00F).

109.00 Endocrine Disorders

A. What is an endocrine disorder?

An endocrine disorder is a medical condition that causes a hormonal imbalance. When an endocrine gland functions abnormally, producing either too much of a specific hormone (hyperfunction) or too little (hypofunction), the hormonal imbalance can cause various complications in the body. The major glands of the endocrine system are the pituitary, thyroid, parathyroid, adrenal, and pancreas.

B. How do we evaluate the effects of endocrine disorders? The only listing in this body system addresses children from birth to the attainment of age 6 who have diabetes mellitus (DM) and require daily insulin. We evaluate other impairments that result from endocrine disorders under the listings for other body systems. For example:

1. Pituitary gland disorders can disrupt hormone production and normal functioning in other endocrine glands and in many body systems. The effects of pituitary gland disorders vary depending on which hormones are involved. For example, when pituitary growth hormone deficiency in growing children limits bone maturation and results in pathological short stature, we evaluate this linear growth impairment under

100.00. When pituitary hypofunction affects water and electrolyte balance in the kidney and leads to diabetes insipidus, we evaluate the effects of recurrent dehydration under 106.00.

2. Thyroid gland disorders affect the sympathetic nervous system and normal metabolism. We evaluate thyroid-related changes in linear growth under 100.00; thyroid-related changes in blood pressure and heart rate that cause cardiac arrhythmias or other cardiac dysfunction under 104.00; thyroid-related weight loss under 105.00; and cognitive limitations, mood disorders, and anxiety under 112.00.

3. Parathyroid gland disorders affect calcium levels in bone, blood, nerves, muscle, and other body tissues. We evaluate parathyroid-related osteoporosis and fractures under 101.00; abnormally elevated calcium levels in the blood (hypercalcemia) that lead to cataracts under 102.00; kidney failure under 106.00; and recurrent abnormally low blood calcium levels (hypocalcemia) that lead to increased excitability of nerves and muscles, such as tetany and muscle spasms, under 111.00.

4. Adrenal gland disorders affect bone calcium levels, blood pressure, metabolism, and mental status. We evaluate adrenal-related linear growth impairments under 100.00; adrenal-related osteoporosis with fractures that compromises the ability to walk or to use the upper extremities under 101.00; adrenal-related hypertension that worsens heart failure or causes recurrent arrhythmias under 104.00; adrenal-related weight loss under 105.00; and mood disorders under 112.00.

5. Diabetes mellitus and other pancreatic gland disorders disrupt the production of several hormones, including insulin, that regulate metabolism and digestion. Insulin is essential to the absorption of glucose from the bloodstream into body cells for conversion into cellular energy. The most common pancreatic gland disorder is diabetes mellitus (DM). There are two major types of DM: type 1 and type 2. Both type 1 and type 2 DM are chronic disorders that can have serious, disabling complications that meet the duration requirement. Type 1 DM—previously known as "juvenile diabetes" or "insulin-dependent diabetes mellitus" (IDDM)—is an absolute deficiency of insulin secretion that commonly begins in childhood and continues throughout adulthood. Treatment of type 1 DM always requires lifelong daily insulin. With type 2 DM—previously known as "adult-onset diabetes mellitus" or "non-insulin-dependent diabetes mellitus" (NIDDM)—the body's cells resist the effects of insulin, impairing glucose absorption and metabolism. Type 2 is less common than type 1 DM in children, but physicians are increasingly diagnosing type 2 DM before age 18. Treatment of type 2 DM generally requires lifestyle changes, such as increased exercise and dietary modification, and sometimes insulin in addition to other medications. While both type 1 and type 2 DM are usually controlled, some children do not achieve good control for a variety of reasons including, but not limited to, hypoglycemia unawareness, other disorders that can affect blood glucose levels, inability to manage DM due to a mental disorder, or inadequate treatment.

a. Hyperglycemia. Both types of DM cause hyperglycemia, which is an abnormally high level of blood glucose that may produce acute and long-term complications. Acute complications of hyperglycemia include diabetic ketoacidosis. Long-term complications of chronic hyperglycemia include many conditions affecting various body systems but are rare in children.

b. Diabetic ketoacidosis (DKA). DKA is an acute, potentially life-threatening complication of DM in which the chemical balance of the body becomes dangerously hyperglycemic and acidic. It results from a severe insulin deficiency, which can occur due to missed or inadequate daily insulin therapy or in association with an acute illness. It usually requires hospital treatment to correct the acute complications of dehydration, electrolyte imbalance, and insulin deficiency. You may have serious complications resulting from your treatment, which we evaluate under the affected body system. For example, we evaluate cardiac arrhythmias under 104.00, intestinal necrosis under 105.00, and cerebral edema and seizures under 111.00. Recurrent episodes of DKA in adolescents may result from mood or eating disorders, which we evaluate under 112.00.

c. Hypoglycemia. Children with DM may experience episodes of hypoglycemia, which is an abnormally low level of blood glucose. Most children age 6 and older recognize the symptoms of hypoglycemia and reverse them by consuming substances containing glucose; however, some do not take this step because of hypoglycemia unawareness. Severe hypoglycemia can lead to complications, including seizures or loss of consciousness, which we evaluate under 111.00, or altered mental status, cognitive deficits, and permanent brain damage, which we evaluate under 112.00.

C. How do we evaluate DM in children?

Listing 109.08 is only for children with DM who have not attained age 6 and who require daily insulin. For all other children (that is, children with DM who are age 6 or older and require daily insulin, and children of any age with DM who do not require daily insulin), we follow our rules for determining whether the DM is severe, alone or in combination with another impairment, whether it meets or medically equals the criteria of a listing in another body system, or functionally equals the listings under the criteria in § 416.926a, considering the factors in § 416.924a. The management of DM in children can be complex and variable from day to day, and all children with DM require some level of adult supervision. For example, if a child age 6 or older has a medical need for 24–hour-a-day adult supervision of insulin treatment, food intake, and physical activity to ensure survival, we will find that the child's impairment functionally equals the listings based on the example in § 416.926a(m)(5).

D. How do we evaluate other endocrine disorders that do not have effects that meet or medically equal the criteria of any listing in other body systems? If your impairment(s) does not meet or medically equal a listing in another body system, we will consider whether your impairment(s) functionally equals the listings under the criteria in § 416.926a, considering the factors in § 416.924a. When we decide whether you continue to be disabled, we use the rules in § 416.994a.

109.01 Category of Impairments, Endocrine

109.08 Any type of diabetes mellitus in a child who requires daily insulin and has not attained age 6. Consider under a disability until the attainment of age 6. Thereafter, evaluate the diabetes mellitus according to the rules in 109.00B5 and C.

110.00 Congenital Disorders That Affect Multiple Body Systems

A. Which disorders do we evaluate under this body system? We evaluate non-mosaic Down syndrome and catastrophic congenital disorders under this body system.

B. What is non-mosaic Down syndrome? Non-mosaic Down syndrome is a genetic disorder. Most children with non-mosaic Down syndrome have three copies of chromosome 21 in all of their cells (chromosome 21 trisomy); some have an extra copy of chromosome 21 attached to a different chromosome in all of their cells (chromosome 21 translocation). Virtually all children with non-mosaic Down syndrome have characteristic facial or other physical features, delayed physical development, and intellectual disability. Children with non-mosaic Down syndrome may also have congenital heart disease, impaired vision, hearing problems, and other disorders. We evaluate non-mosaic Down syndrome under 110.06. If you have non-mosaic Down syndrome documented as described in 110.00C, we consider you disabled from birth.

C. What evidence do we need to document non-mosaic Down syndrome under 110.06?

1. Under 110.06A, we will find you disabled based on laboratory findings.

a. To find that your disorder meets 110.06A, we need a copy of the laboratory report of karyotype analysis, which is the definitive test to establish non-mosaic Down syndrome. We will not purchase karyotype analysis. We will not accept a fluorescence in situ hybridization (FISH) test because it does not distinguish between the mosaic and non-mosaic forms of Down syndrome.

b. If a physician (see §§ 404.1513(a)(1) and 416.913(a)(1) of this chapter) has not signed the laboratory report of karyotype analysis, the evidence must also include a physician's statement that you have Down syndrome.

c. For purposes of 110.06A, we do not require evidence stating that you have the distinctive facial or other physical features of Down syndrome.

2. If we do not have a laboratory report of karyotype analysis documenting that you have non-mosaic Down syndrome, we may find you disabled under 110.06B or 110.06C.

a. Under 110.06B, we need a physician's report stating: (i) your karyotype diagnosis or evidence that documents your type of Down syndrome that is consistent with prior karyotype analysis (for example, reference to a diagnosis of "trisomy 21") and (ii) that you have the distinctive facial or other physical features of Down syndrome. We do not require a detailed description of the facial or other physical features of the disorder. However, we will not find that your disorder meets 110.06B if we have evidence—such as evidence of functioning inconsistent with the diagnosis—that indicates that you do not have non-mosaic Down syndrome.

b. If we do not have evidence of prior karyotype analysis (you did not have testing, or you had testing but we do not have information from a physician about the test results), we will find that your disorder meets 110.06C if we have: (i) a physician's report stating that you have the distinctive facial or other physical features of Down syndrome and (ii) evidence that your functioning is consistent with a diagnosis of non-mosaic Down syndrome. This evidence may include medical or nonmedical information about your physical and mental abilities, including information about your development, education, work history, or the results of psychological testing. However, we will not find that your disorder meets 110.06C if we have evidence—such as evidence of functioning inconsistent with the diagnosis—that indicates that you do not have non-mosaic Down syndrome.

D. What are catastrophic congenital disorders? Some catastrophic congenital disorders, such as anencephaly, cyclopia, chromosome 13 trisomy (Patau syndrome or trisomy D), and chromosome 18 trisomy (Edwards' syndrome or trisomy E), are usually expected to result in early death. Others such as cri du chat syndrome (chromosome 5p deletion syndrome) and the infantile onset form of Tay–Sachs disease interfere very seriously with development. We evaluate catastrophic congenital disorders under 110.08. The term "very seriously" in 110.08 has the same meaning as in the term "extreme" in § 416.926a(e)(3) of this chapter.

E. What evidence do we need under 110.08?

We need one of the following to determine if your disorder meets 110.08A or B:

1. A laboratory report of the definitive test that documents your disorder (for example, genetic analysis or evidence of biochemical abnormalities) signed by a physician.

2. A laboratory report of the definitive test that documents your disorder that is not signed by a physician and a report from a physician stating that you have the disorder.

3. A report from a physician stating that you have the disorder with the typical clinical features of the disorder and that you had definitive testing that documented your disorder. In this case, we will find that your disorder meets 110.08A or B unless we have evidence that indicates that you do not have the disorder.

4. If we do not have the definitive laboratory evidence we need under E1, E2, or E3, we will find that your disorder meets 110.08A or B if we have: (i) a report from a physician stating that you have the disorder and that you have the typical clinical features of the disorder, and (ii) other evidence that supports the diagnosis. This evidence may include medical or nonmedical information about your development and functioning.

5. For obvious catastrophic congenital anomalies that are expected to result in early death, such as anencephaly and cyclopia, we need evidence from a physician that demonstrates that the infant has the characteristic physical features of the disorder. In these rare cases, we do not need laboratory testing or any other evidence that confirms the disorder.

F. How do we evaluate mosaic Down syndrome and other congenital disorders that affect multiple body systems?

1. Mosaic Down syndrome. Approximately 2 percent of children with Down syndrome have the mosaic form. In mosaic Down syndrome, there are some cells with an extra copy of chromosome 21 and other cells with the normal two copies of chromosome 21. Mosaic Down syndrome can be so slight as to be undetected clinically, but it can also be profound and disabling, affecting various body systems.

2. Other congenital disorders that affect multiple body systems. Other congenital disorders, such as congenital anomalies, chromosomal disorders, dysmorphic syndromes, inborn metabolic syndromes, and perinatal infectious diseases, can cause deviation from, or interruption of, the normal function of the body or can interfere with development. Examples of these disorders include both the juvenile and late-onset forms of Tay–Sachs disease, trisomy X syndrome (XXX syndrome), fragile X syndrome, phenylketonuria (PKU), caudal regression syndrome, and fetal alcohol syndrome. For these disorders and other disorders like them, the degree of deviation, interruption, or interference, as well as the resulting functional limitations and their progression, may vary widely from child to child and may affect different body systems.

3. Evaluating the effects of mosaic Down syndrome or another congenital disorder under the listings. When the effects of mosaic Down syndrome or another congenital disorder that affects multiple body systems are sufficiently severe we evaluate the disorder under the appropriate affected body system(s), such as musculoskeletal, special senses and speech, neurological, or mental disorders. Otherwise, we evaluate the specific functional limitations that result from the disorder under our other rules described in 110.00G.

G. What if your disorder does not meet a listing? If you have a severe medically determinable impairment(s) that does not meet a listing, we will consider whether your impairment(s) medically equals a listing. See § 416.926 of this chapter. If your impairment(s) does not meet or medically equal a listing, we will consider whether it functionally equals the listings. See §§ 416.924a and 416.926a of this chapter. We use the rules in § 416.994a of this chapter when we decide whether you continue to be disabled.

110.01 Category of Impairments, Congenital Disorders That Affect Multiple Body Systems

110.06 Non-mosaic Down syndrome (chromosome 21 trisomy or chromosome 21 translocation), documented by:

A. A laboratory report of karyotype analysis signed by a physician, or both a laboratory report of karyotype analysis not signed by a physician and a statement by a physician that the child has Down syndrome (see 110.00C1), or

B. A physician's report stating that the child has chromosome 21 trisomy or chromosome 21 translocation consistent with karyotype analysis with the distinctive facial or other physical features of Down syndrome (see 110.00C2a), or

C. A physician's report stating that the child has Down syndrome with the distinctive facial or other physical features and evidence demonstrating that the child is functioning at the level of a child with non-mosaic Down syndrome (see 110.00C2b).

110.08 A catastrophic congenital disorder (see 110.00D and 110.00E) with:

A. Death usually expected within the first months of life, or

B. Very serious interference with development or functioning.

111.00 NEUROLOGICAL DISORDERS

A. Which neurological disorders do we evaluate under these listings? We evaluate epilepsy, coma or persistent vegetative state (PVS), and neurological disorders that cause disorganization of motor function, bulbar and neuromuscular dysfunction, or communication impairment. Under this body system, we evaluate the limitations resulting from the impact of the neurological disease process itself. If you have a neurological disorder(s) that affects your physical and mental functioning, we will evaluate your impairments under the rules we use to determine functional equivalence. If your neurological disorder results in only mental impairment or if you have a co-occurring mental condition that is not caused by your neurological disorder (for example, Autism spectrum disorder), we will evaluate your mental impairment under the mental disorders body system, 112.00.

B. What evidence do we need to document your neurological disorder?

1. We need both medical and non-medical evidence (signs, symptoms, and laboratory findings) to assess the effects of your neurological disorder. Medical evidence should include your medical history, examination findings, relevant laboratory tests, and the results of imaging. Imaging refers to medical imaging techniques, such as x-ray, computerized tomography (CT), magnetic resonance imaging (MRI), and electroencephalography (EEG). The imaging must be consistent with the prevailing state of medical knowledge and clinical practice as the proper technique to support the evaluation of the disorder. In addition, the medical evidence may include descriptions of any prescribed treatment and your response to it. We consider non-medical evidence such as statements you or others make about your impairments, your restrictions, your daily activities, or, if you are an adolescent, your efforts to work.

2. We will make every reasonable effort to obtain the results of your laboratory and imaging evidence. When the results of any of these tests are part of the existing evidence in your case record, we will evaluate the test results and all other relevant evidence. We will not purchase imaging, or other diagnostic tests or laboratory tests that are complex, may involve significant risk, or that are invasive. We will not routinely purchase tests that are expensive or not readily available.

C. How do we consider adherence to prescribed treatment in neurological disorders? In 111.02 (Epilepsy) and 111.12 (Myasthenia gravis), we require that limitations from these neurological disorders exist despite adherence to prescribed treatment. "Despite adherence to prescribed treatment" means that you have taken medication(s) or followed other treatment procedures for your neurological disorder(s) as prescribed by a physician for three consecutive months but your impairment continues to meet the other listing requirements despite this treatment. You may receive your treatment at a health care facility that you visit regularly, even if you do not see the same physician on each visit.

D. What do we mean by disorganization of motor function?

1. Disorganization of motor function means interference, due to your neurological disorder, with movement of two extremities; i.e., the lower extremities, or upper extremities (including fingers, wrists, hands, arms, and shoulders). By two extremities we mean both lower extremities, or both upper extremities, or one upper extremity and one lower extremity. All listings in this body system, except for 111.02 (Epilepsy) and 111.20 (Coma and persistent vegetative state), include criteria for disorganization of motor function that results in an extreme limitation in your ability to:

a. Stand up from a seated position; or

b. Balance while standing or walking; or

c. Use the upper extremities (e.g., fingers, wrists, hands, arms, and shoulders).

2. Extreme limitation means the inability to stand up from a seated position, maintain balance in a standing position and while walking, or use your upper extremities to independently initiate, sustain, and complete age-appropriate activities. The assessment of motor function depends on the degree of interference with standing up; balancing while standing or walking; or using the upper extremities (including fingers, hands, arms, and shoulders).

a. Inability to stand up from a seated position means that once seated you are unable to stand and maintain an upright position without the assistance of another person or the use of an assistive device, such as a walker, two crutches, or two canes.

b. Inability to maintain balance in a standing position means that you are unable to maintain an upright position while standing or walking without the assistance of another person or an assistive device, such as a walker, two crutches, or two canes.

c. Inability to use your upper extremities means that you have a loss of function of both upper extremities (e.g., fingers, wrists, hands, arms, and shoulders) that very seriously limits your ability to independently initiate, sustain, and complete age- appropriate activities involving fine and gross motor movements. Inability to perform fine and gross motor movements could include not being able to pinch, manipulate, and use your fingers; or not being able to use your hands, arms, and shoulders to perform gross motor movements, such as handling, gripping, grasping, holding, turning, and reaching; or not being able to engage in exertional movements such a lifting, carrying, pushing, and pulling.

3. For children who are not yet able to balance, stand up, or walk independently, we consider their function based on assessments of limitations in the ability to perform comparable age-appropriate activities with the lower and upper extremities, given normal developmental milestones. For such children, an

extreme level of limitation means developmental milestones at less than one-half of the child's chronological age.

E. What do we mean by bulbar and neuromuscular dysfunction? The bulbar region of the brain is responsible for controlling the bulbar muscles in the throat, tongue, jaw, and face. Bulbar and neuromuscular dysfunction refers to weakness in these muscles, resulting in breathing, swallowing, and speaking impairments. Listings 111.12 (Myasthenia gravis) and 111.22 (Motor neuron disorders) include criteria for evaluating bulbar and neuromuscular dysfunction. If your neurological disorder has resulted in a breathing disorder, we may evaluate that condition under the respiratory system, 103.00.

F. What is epilepsy, and how do we evaluate it under 111.02?

1. Epilepsy is a pattern of recurrent and unprovoked seizures that are manifestations of abnormal electrical activity in the brain. There are various types of generalized and "focal" or partial seizures. In children, the most common potentially disabling seizure types are generalized tonic-clonic seizures, dyscognitive seizures (formerly complex partial seizures), and absence seizures. However, psychogenic nonepileptic seizures and pseudoseizures are not epileptic seizures for the purpose of 111.02. We evaluate psychogenic seizures and pseudoseizures under the mental disorders body system, 112.00.

a. Generalized tonic-clonic seizures are characterized by loss of consciousness accompanied by a tonic phase (sudden muscle tensing causing the child to lose postural control) followed by a clonic phase (rapid cycles of muscle contraction and relaxation, also called convulsions). Tongue biting and incontinence may occur during generalized tonic-clonic seizures, and injuries may result from falling.

b. Dyscognitive seizures are characterized by alteration of consciousness without convulsions or loss of muscle control. During the seizure, blank staring, change of facial expression, and automatisms (such as lip smacking, chewing or swallowing, or repetitive simple actions, such as gestures or verbal utterances) may occur. During its course, a dyscognitive seizure may progress into a generalized tonic-clonic seizure (see 111.00F1a).

c. Absence seizures (petit mal) are also characterized by an alteration in consciousness, but are shorter than other generalized seizures (e.g., tonic-clonic and dyscognitive) seizures, generally lasting for only a few seconds rather than minutes. They may present with blank staring, change of facial expression, lack of awareness and responsiveness, and a sense of lost time after the seizure. An aura never precedes absence seizures. Although absence seizures are brief, frequent occurrence may limit functioning. This type of seizure usually does not occur after adolescence.

d. Febrile seizures may occur in young children in association with febrile illnesses. We will consider seizures occurring during febrile illnesses. To meet 111.02, we require documentation of seizures during nonfebrile periods and epilepsy must be established.

2. Description of seizure. We require at least one detailed description of your seizures from someone, preferably a medical professional, who has observed at least one of your typical seizures. If you experience more than one type of seizure, we require a description of each type.

3. Serum drug levels. We do not require serum drug levels; therefore, we will not purchase them. However, if serum drug levels are available in your medical records, we will evaluate them in the context of the other evidence in your case record.

4. Counting seizures. The period specified in 111.02A or B cannot begin earlier than one month after you began prescribed treatment. The required number of seizures must occur within the period we are considering in connection with your application or continuing disability review. When we evaluate the frequency of your seizures, we also consider your adherence to prescribed treatment (see 111.00C). When we determine the number of seizures you have had in the specified period, we will:

a. Count multiple seizures occurring in a 24–hour period as one seizure.

b. Count status epilepticus (a continuous series of seizures without return to consciousness between seizures) as one seizure.

c. Count a dyscognitive seizure that progresses into a generalized tonic-clonic seizure as one generalized tonic-clonic seizure.

d. We do not count seizures that occur during a period when you are not adhering to prescribed treatment without good reason. When we determine that you had a good reason for not adhering to prescribed treatment, we will consider your physical, mental, educational, and communicative limitations (including any language barriers). We will consider you to have good reason for not following prescribed treatment if, for example, the treatment is very risky for you due to its consequences or unusual nature, or if you are unable to afford prescribed treatment that you are willing to accept, but for which no free community resources are available. We will follow guidelines found in our policy, such as § 416.930(c) of this chapter, when we determine whether you have a good reason for not adhering to prescribed treatment.

e. We do not count psychogenic nonepileptic seizures or pseudoseizures under 111.02.We evaluate these seizures under the mental disorders body system, 112.00.

5. Electroencephalography (EEG) testing. We do not require EEG test results; therefore, we will not purchase them. However, if EEG test results are available in your medical records, we will evaluate them in the context of the other evidence in your case record.

G. What is vascular insult to the brain, and how do we evaluate it under 111.04?

1. Vascular insult to the brain (cerebrum, cerebellum, or brainstem), commonly referred to as stroke or cerebrovascular accident (CVA), is brain cell death caused by an interruption of blood flow within or leading to the brain, or by a hemorrhage from a ruptured blood vessel or aneurysm in the brain. If you have a vision impairment resulting from your vascular insult, we may evaluate that impairment under the special senses body system, 102.00.

2. We generally need evidence from at least 3 months after the vascular insult to determine whether you have disorganization of motor function under 111.04. In some cases, evidence of your vascular insult is sufficient to allow your claim within 3 months post-vascular insult. If we are unable to allow your claim within 3 months after your vascular insult, we will defer adjudication of the claim until we obtain evidence of your neurological disorder at least 3 months post-vascular insult.

H. What are benign brain tumors, and how do we evaluate them under 111.05? Benign brain tumors are noncancerous (nonmalignant) abnormal growths of tissue in or on the brain that invade healthy brain tissue or apply pressure on the brain or cranial nerves. We evaluate their effects on your functioning as discussed in 111.00D. We evaluate malignant brain tumors under the cancer body system in 113.00. If you have a vision impairment resulting from your benign brain tumor, we may evaluate that impairment under the special senses body system, 102.00.

I. What is cerebral palsy, and how do we evaluate it under 111.07?

1. Cerebral palsy (CP) is a term that describes a group of static, nonprogressive disorders caused by abnormalities within the brain that disrupt the brain's ability to control movement, muscle coordination, and posture. The resulting motor deficits manifest very early in a child's development, with delayed or abnormal progress in attaining developmental milestones; deficits may become more obvious as the child grows and matures over time.

2. We evaluate your signs and symptoms, such as ataxia, spasticity, flaccidity, athetosis, chorea, and difficulty with precise movements when we determine your ability to stand up, balance, walk, or perform fine and gross motor movements. We will also evaluate your signs, such as dysarthria and apraxia of speech, and receptive and expressive language problems when we determine your ability to communicate.

3. We will consider your other impairments or signs and symptoms that develop secondary to the disorder, such as post-impairment syndrome (a combination of pain, fatigue, and weakness due to muscle abnormalities); overuse syndromes (repetitive motion injuries); arthritis; abnormalities of proprioception (perception of the movements and position of the body); abnormalities of stereognosis (perception and identification of objects by touch); learning problems; anxiety; and depression.

J. What are spinal cord disorders, and how do we evaluate them under 111.08?

1. Spinal cord disorders may be congenital or caused by injury to the spinal cord. Motor signs and symptoms of spinal cord disorders include paralysis, flaccidity, spasticity, and weakness.

2. Spinal cord disorders with complete loss of function (111.08A) addresses spinal cord disorders that result in complete lack of motor, sensory, and autonomic function of the affected part(s) of the body.

3. Spinal cord disorders with disorganization of motor function (111.08B) addresses spinal cord disorders that result in less than complete loss of function of the affected part(s) of the body, reducing, but not eliminating, motor, sensory, and autonomic function.

4. When we evaluate your spinal cord disorder, we generally need evidence from at least 3 months after your symptoms began in order to evaluate your disorganization of motor function. In some cases, evidence of your spinal cord disorder may be sufficient to allow your claim within 3 months after the spinal cord disorder. If the medical evidence demonstrates total cord transection causing a loss of motor and sensory functions below the level of injury, we will not wait 3 months but will make the allowance decision immediately.

K. What are communication impairments associated with neurological disorders, and how do we evaluate them under 111.09?

1. Communication impairments result from medically determinable neurological disorders that cause dysfunction in the parts of the brain responsible for speech and language. Under 111.09, we must have recent comprehensive evaluation including all areas of affective and effective communication, performed by a qualified professional, to document a communication impairment associated with a neurological disorder.

2. Under 111.09A, we need documentation from a qualified professional that your neurological disorder has resulted in a speech deficit that significantly affects your ability to communicate. Significantly affects means that you demonstrate a serious limitation in communicating, and a person who is unfamiliar with you cannot easily understand or interpret your speech.

3. Under 111.09B, we need documentation from a qualified professional that shows that your neurological disorder has resulted in a comprehension deficit that results in ineffective verbal communication for your age. For the purposes of 111.09B, comprehension deficit means a deficit in receptive language. Ineffective verbal communication means that you demonstrate serious limitation in your ability to communicate orally on the same level as other children of the same age and level of development.

4. Under 111.09C, we need documentation of a neurological disorder that has resulted in hearing loss. Your hearing loss will be evaluated under listing 102.10 or 102.11.

5. We evaluate speech deficits due to non-neurological disorders under 2.09.

L. What are neurodegenerative disorders of the central nervous system, such as Juvenile-onset Huntington's disease and Friedreich's ataxia, and how do we evaluate them under 111.17? Neurodegenerative disorders of the central nervous system are disorders characterized by progressive and irreversible degeneration of neurons or their supporting cells. Over time, these disorders impair many of the body's motor or cognitive and other mental functions. We consider neurodegenerative disorders of the central nervous system under 111.17 that we do not evaluate elsewhere in section 111.00, such as juvenile-onset Huntington's disease (HD) and Friedreich's ataxia. When these disorders result in solely cognitive and other mental functional limitations, we will evaluate the disorder under the mental disorder listings, 112.00.

M. What is traumatic brain injury, and how do we evaluate it under 111.18?

1. Traumatic brain injury (TBI) is damage to the brain resulting from skull fracture, collision with an external force leading to a closed head injury, or penetration by an object that enters the skull and makes contact with brain tissue. We evaluate a TBI that results in coma or persistent vegetative state (PVS) under 111.20.

2. We generally need evidence from at least 3 months after the TBI to evaluate whether you have disorganization of motor function under 111.18. In some cases, evidence of your TBI is sufficient to determine disability. If we are unable to allow your claim within 3 months post–TBI, we will defer adjudication of the claim until we obtain evidence of your neurological disorder at least 3 months post–TBI. If a finding of disability still is not possible at that time, we will again defer adjudication of the claim until we obtain evidence at least 6 months after your TBI.

N. What are coma and persistent vegetative state, and how do we evaluate them under 111.20? Coma is a state of unconsciousness in which a child does not exhibit a sleep/wake cycle, and is unable to perceive or respond to external stimuli. Children who do not fully emerge from coma may progress into persistent vegetative state (PVS). PVS is a condition of partial arousal in which a child may have a low level of consciousness but is still unable to react to external stimuli. In contrast to coma, a child in a PVS retains sleep/wake cycles and may exhibit some key lower brain functions, such as spontaneous movement, opening and moving eyes, and grimacing. Coma or PVS may result from a TBI, a nontraumatic insult to the brain (such as a vascular insult, infection, or brain tumor), or a neurodegenerative or metabolic disorder. Medically induced comas should be considered under the section pertaining to the underlying reason the coma was medically induced and not under this section.

O. What is multiple sclerosis, and how do we evaluate it under 111.21?

1. Multiple sclerosis (MS) is a chronic, inflammatory, degenerative disorder that damages the myelin sheath surrounding the nerve fibers in the brain and spinal cord. The damage disrupts the normal transmission of nerve impulses within the brain and between the brain and other parts of the body causing impairment in muscle coordination, strength, balance, sensation, and vision. There are several forms of MS, ranging from slightly to highly aggressive. Milder forms generally involve acute attacks (exacerbations) with partial or complete recovery from signs and symptoms (remissions). Aggressive forms generally exhibit a steady progression of signs and symptoms with few or no remissions. The effects of all forms vary from child to child.

2. We evaluate your signs and symptoms, such as flaccidity, spasticity, spasms, incoordination, imbalance, tremor, physical fatigue, muscle weakness, dizziness, tingling, and numbness when we determine your ability to stand up, balance, walk, or perform fine and gross motor movements, such as using your arms, hands, and fingers. If you have a vision impairment resulting from your MS, we may evaluate that impairment under the special senses body system, 102.00.

P. What are motor neuron disorders, and how do we evaluate them under 111.22? Motor neuron disorders are progressive neurological disorders that destroy the cells that control voluntary muscle activity, such as walking, breathing, swallowing, and speaking. The most common motor neuron disorders in children are progressive bulbar palsy and spinal muscular dystrophy syndromes. We evaluate the effects of these disorders on motor functioning or bulbar and neuromuscular functioning.

Q. How do we consider symptoms of fatigue in these listings? Fatigue is one of the most common and limiting symptoms of some neurological disorders, such as multiple sclerosis and myasthenia gravis. These disorders may result in physical fatigue (lack of muscle strength) or mental fatigue (decreased awareness or attention). When we evaluate your fatigue, we will consider the intensity, persistence, and effects of fatigue on your functioning. This may include information such as the clinical and laboratory data and other objective evidence concerning your neurological deficit, a description of fatigue considered characteristic of your disorder, and information about your functioning. We consider the effects of physical fatigue on your ability to stand up, balance, walk, or perform fine and gross motor movements using the criteria described in 111.00D.

R. How do we evaluate your neurological disorder when it does not meet one of these listings?

1. If your neurological disorder does not meet the criteria of any of these listings, we must also consider whether your impairment(s) meets the criteria of a listing in another body system. If you have a severe medically determinable impairment(s) that does not meet a listing, we will determine whether your impairment(s) medically equals a listing. See § 416.926 of this chapter.

2. If your impairment(s) does not meet or medically equal a listing, we will consider whether your impairment(s) functionally equals the listings. See § 416.926a of this chapter.

3. We use the rules in § 416.994a of this chapter when we decide whether you continue to be disabled.

111.01 Category of Impairments, Neurological Disorders

111.02 Epilepsy, documented by a detailed description of a typical seizure and characterized by A or B:

A. Generalized tonic-clonic seizures (see 111.00F1a), occurring at least once a month for at least 3 consecutive months (see 111.00F4) despite adherence to prescribed treatment (see 111.00C); or

B. Dyscognitive seizures (see 111.00F1b) or absence seizures (see 111.00F1c), occurring at least once a week for at least 3 consecutive months (see 111.00F4) despite adherence to prescribed treatment (see 111.00C).

111.03 [Reserved]

111.04 Vascular insult to the brain, characterized by disorganization of motor function in two extremities (see 111.00D1), resulting in an extreme limitation (see 111.00D2) in the ability to stand up from a seated position, balance while standing or walking, or use the upper extremities, persisting for at least 3 consecutive months after the insult.

111.05 Benign brain tumors, characterized by disorganization of motor function in two extremities (see 111.00D1), resulting in an extreme limitation (see 111.00D2) in the ability to stand up from a seated position, balance while standing or walking, or use the upper extremities.

111.06 [Reserved]

111.07 Cerebral palsy, characterized by disorganization of motor function in two extremities (see 111.00D1), resulting in an extreme limitation (see 111.00D2) in the ability to stand up from a seated position, balance while standing or walking, or use the upper extremities.

111.08 Spinal cord disorders, characterized by A or B:

A. Complete loss of function, as described in 111.00J2, persisting for 3 consecutive months after the disorder (see 111.00J4); or

B. Disorganization of motor function in two extremities (see 111.00D1), resulting in an extreme limitation (see 111.00D2) in the ability to stand up from a seated position, balance while standing or walking, or use the upper extremities persisting for 3 consecutive months after the disorder (see 111.00J4).

111.09 Communication impairment, associated with documented neurological disorder and one of the following:

A. Documented speech deficit that significantly affects (see 111.00K1) the clarity and content of the speech; or

B. Documented comprehension deficit resulting in ineffective verbal communication (see 111.00K2) for age; or

C. Impairment of hearing as described under the criteria in 102.10 or 102.11.

111.10 [Reserved]

111.11 [Reserved]

111.12 Myasthenia gravis, characterized by A or B despite adherence to prescribed treatment for at least 3 months (see 111.00C):

A. Disorganization of motor function in two extremities (see 111.00D1), resulting in an extreme limitation (see 111.00D2) in the ability to stand up from a seated position, balance while standing or walking, or use the upper extremities; or

B. Bulbar and neuromuscular dysfunction (see 111.00E), resulting in:

1. One myasthenic crisis requiring mechanical ventilation; or

2. Need for supplemental enteral nutrition via a gastrostomy or parenteral nutrition via a central venous catheter.

111.13 Muscular dystrophy, characterized by disorganization of motor function in two extremities (see 111.00D1), resulting in an extreme limitation (see 111.00D2) in the ability to stand up from a seated position, balance while standing or walking, or use the upper extremities.

111.14 Peripheral neuropathy, characterized by disorganization of motor function in two extremities (see 111.00D1), resulting in an extreme limitation (see

111.00D2) in the ability to stand up from a seated position, balance while standing or walking, or use the upper extremities.

111.15 [Reserved]

111.16 [Reserved]

111.17 Neurodegenerative disorders of the central nervous system, such as Juvenile-onset Huntington's disease and Friedreich's ataxia, characterized by disorganization of motor function in two extremities (see 111.00D1), resulting in an extreme limitation (see 111.00D2) in the ability to stand up from a seated position, balance while standing or walking, or use the upper extremities.

111.18 Traumatic brain injury, characterized by disorganization of motor function in two extremities (see 111.00D1), resulting in an extreme limitation (see 111.00D2) in the ability to stand up from a seated position, balance while standing or walking, or use the upper extremities, persisting for at least 3 consecutive months after the injury.

111.19 [Reserved]

111.20 Coma or persistent vegetative state, persisting for at least 1 month.

111.21 Multiple sclerosis, characterized by disorganization of motor function in two extremities (see 111.00D1), resulting in an extreme limitation (see 111.00D2) in the ability to stand up from a seated position, balance while standing or walking, or use the upper extremities.

111.22 Motor neuron disorders, characterized by A or B:

A. Disorganization of motor function in two extremities (see 111.00D1), resulting in an extreme limitation (see 111.00D2) in the ability to stand up from a seated position, balance while standing or walking, or use the upper extremities; or

B. Bulbar and neuromuscular dysfunction (see 111.00E), resulting in:

1. Acute respiratory failure requiring invasive mechanical ventilation; or

2. Need for supplemental enteral nutrition via a gastrostomy or parenteral nutrition via a central venous catheter.

112.00 Mental Disorders

A. How are the listings for mental disorders for children arranged, and what do they require?

1. The listings for mental disorders for children are arranged in 12 categories: neurocognitive disorders (112.02); schizophrenia spectrum and other psychotic disorders (112.03); depressive, bipolar and related disorders (112.04); intellectual disorder (112.05); anxiety and obsessive-compulsive disorders (112.06); somatic symptom and related disorders (112.07); personality and impulse-control disorders (112.08); autism spectrum disorder (112.10); neurodevelopmental disorders (112.11); eating disorders (112.13); developmental disorders in infants and toddlers (112.14); and trauma- and stressor-related disorders (112.15). All of these listings, with the exception of 112.14, apply to children from age three to attainment of age 18. Listing 112.14 is for children from birth to attainment of age 3.

2. Listings 112.07, 112.08, 112.10, 112.11, 112.13, and 112.14 have two paragraphs, designated A and B; your mental disorder must satisfy the requirements of both paragraphs A and B. Listings 112.02, 112.03, 112.04, 112.06, and 112.15 have three paragraphs, designated A, B, and C; your mental disorder must satisfy the requirements of both paragraphs A and B, or the requirements of both paragraphs A and C. Listing 112.05 has two paragraphs that are unique to that listing (see 112.00A3); your mental disorder must satisfy the requirements of either paragraph A or paragraph B.

a. Paragraph A of each listing (except 112.05) includes the medical criteria that must be present in your medical evidence.

b. Paragraph B of each listing (except 112.05) provides the functional criteria we assess to evaluate how your mental disorder limits your functioning. For children ages 3 to 18, these criteria represent the areas of mental functioning a child uses to perform age-appropriate activities. They are: understand, remember, or apply information; interact with others; concentrate, persist, or maintain pace; and adapt or manage oneself. (See 112.00I for a discussion of the criteria for children from birth to attainment of age 3 under 112.14.) We will determine the degree to which your medically determinable mental impairment affects the four areas of mental functioning and your ability to function age-appropriately in a manner comparable to that of other children your age who do not have impairments. (Hereinafter, the words "age-appropriately" incorporate the qualifying statement, "in a manner comparable to that of other children your age who do not have impairments.") To satisfy the paragraph B criteria, your mental disorder must result in "extreme" limitation of one, or "marked" limitation of two, of the four areas of mental functioning. (When we refer to "paragraph B criteria" or "area[s] of mental functioning" in the introductory text of this body system, we mean the criteria in paragraph B of every listing except 112.05 and 112.14.)

c. Paragraph C of listings 112.02, 112.03, 112.04, 112.06, and 112.15 provides the criteria we use to evaluate "serious and persistent mental disorders." To satisfy the paragraph C criteria, your mental disorder must be "serious and persistent"; that is, there must be a medically documented history of the existence of the disorder over a period of at least 2 years, and evidence that satisfies the criteria in both C1 and C2 (see 112.00G). (When we refer to "paragraph C" or "the paragraph C criteria" in the introductory text of this body system, we mean the criteria in paragraph C of listings 112.02, 112.03, 112.04, 112.06, and 112.15.)

3. Listing 112.05 has two paragraphs, designated A and B, that apply to only intellectual disorder. Each paragraph requires that you have significantly subaverage general intellectual functioning and significant deficits in current adaptive functioning.

B. Which mental disorders do we evaluate under each listing category for children?

1. Neurocognitive disorders (112.02).

a. These disorders are characterized in children by a clinically significant deviation in normal cognitive development or by a decline in cognitive functioning. Symptoms and signs may include, but are not limited to, disturbances in memory, executive functioning (that is, higher-level cognitive processes; for example, regulating attention, planning, inhibiting responses, decision-making), visual-spatial functioning, language and speech, perception, insight, and judgment.

b. Examples of disorders that we evaluate in this category include major neurocognitive disorder; mental impairments resulting from medical conditions such as a metabolic disease (for example, juvenile Tay–Sachs disease), human immunodeficiency virus infection, vascular malformation, progressive brain tumor, or traumatic brain injury; or substance-induced cognitive disorder associated with drugs of abuse, medications, or toxins. (We evaluate neurological disorders under that body system (see 111.00). We evaluate cognitive impairments that result from neurological disorders under 112.02 if they do not satisfy the requirements in 111.00. We evaluate catastrophic genetic disorders under listings in 110.00, 111.00, or 112.00, as appropriate. We evaluate genetic disorders that are not catastrophic under the affected body system(s).)

c. This category does not include the mental disorders that we evaluate under intellectual disorder (112.05), autism spectrum disorder (112.10), and neurodevelopmental disorders (112.11).

2. Schizophrenia spectrum and other psychotic disorders (112.03).

a. These disorders are characterized by delusions, hallucinations, disorganized speech, or grossly disorganized or catatonic behavior, causing a clinically significant decline in functioning. Symptoms and signs may include, but are not limited to, inability to initiate and persist in goal-directed activities, social withdrawal, flat or inappropriate affect, poverty of thought and speech, loss of interest or pleasure, disturbances of mood, odd beliefs and mannerisms, and paranoia.

b. Examples of disorders that we evaluate in this category include schizophrenia, schizoaffective disorder, delusional disorder, and psychotic disorder due to another medical condition.

3. Depressive, bipolar and related disorders (112.04).

a. These disorders are characterized by an irritable, depressed, elevated, or expansive mood, or by a loss of interest or pleasure in all or almost all activities, causing a clinically significant decline in functioning. Symptoms and signs may include, but are not limited to, feelings of hopelessness or guilt, suicidal ideation, a clinically significant change in body weight or appetite, sleep disturbances, an increase or decrease in energy, psychomotor abnormalities, disturbed concentration, pressured speech, grandiosity, reduced impulse control, sadness, euphoria, and social withdrawal. Depending on a child's age and developmental stage, certain features, such as somatic complaints, irritability, anger, aggression, and social withdrawal may be more commonly present than other features.

b. Examples of disorders that we evaluate in this category include bipolar disorders (I or II), cyclothymic disorder, disruptive mood dysregulation disorder, major depressive disorder, persistent depressive disorder (dysthymia), and bipolar or depressive disorder due to another medical condition.

4. Intellectual disorder (112.05).

a. This disorder is characterized by significantly subaverage general intellectual functioning and significant deficits in current adaptive functioning. Signs may include, but are not limited to, poor conceptual, social, or practical skills evident in your adaptive functioning.

b. The disorder that we evaluate in this category may be described in the evidence as intellectual disability, intellectual developmental disorder, or historically used terms such as "mental retardation."

c. This category does not include the mental disorders that we evaluate under neurocognitive disorders (112.02), autism spectrum disorder (112.10), or neurodevelopmental disorders (112.11).

5. Anxiety and obsessive-compulsive disorders (112.06).

a. These disorders are characterized by excessive anxiety, worry, apprehension, and fear, or by avoidance of feelings, thoughts, activities, objects, places, or people. Symptoms and signs may include, but are not limited to, restlessness, difficulty concentrating, hypervigilance, muscle tension, sleep disturbance, fatigue, panic attacks, obsessions and compulsions, constant thoughts and fears about safety, and frequent physical complaints. Depending on a child's age and developmental stage, other features may also include refusal to go to school, academic failure, frequent stomachaches and other physical complaints, extreme worries about sleeping away from home, being overly clinging, and exhibiting tantrums at times of separation from caregivers.

b. Examples of disorders that we evaluate in this category include separation anxiety disorder, social anxiety disorder, panic disorder, generalized anxiety disorder, agoraphobia, and obsessive-compulsive disorder.

c. This category does not include the mental disorders that we evaluate under trauma- and stressor-related disorders (112.15).

6. Somatic symptom and related disorders (112.07).

a. These disorders are characterized by physical symptoms or deficits that are not intentionally produced or feigned, and that, following clinical investigation, cannot be fully explained by a general medical condition, another mental disorder, the direct effects of a substance, or a culturally sanctioned behavior or experience. Symptoms and signs may include, but are not limited to, pain and other abnormalities of sensation, gastrointestinal symptoms, fatigue, abnormal motor movement, pseudoseizures, and pseudoneurological symptoms, such as blindness or deafness.

b. Examples of disorders that we evaluate in this category include somatic symptom disorder and conversion disorder.

7. Personality and impulse-control disorders (112.08).

a. These disorders are characterized by enduring, inflexible, maladaptive, and pervasive patterns of behavior. Onset may occur in childhood but more typically occurs in adolescence or young adulthood. Symptoms and signs may include, but are not limited to, patterns of distrust, suspiciousness, and odd beliefs; social detachment, discomfort, or avoidance; hypersensitivity to negative evaluation; an excessive need to be taken care of; difficulty making independent decisions; a preoccupation with orderliness, perfectionism, and control; and inappropriate, intense, impulsive anger and behavioral expression grossly out of proportion to any external provocation or psychosocial stressors.

b. Examples of disorders that we evaluate in this category include paranoid, schizoid, schizotypal, borderline, avoidant, dependent, obsessive-compulsive personality disorders, and intermittent explosive disorder.

8. Autism spectrum disorder (112.10).

a. These disorders are characterized by qualitative deficits in the development of reciprocal social interaction, verbal and nonverbal communication skills, and symbolic or imaginative play; restricted repetitive and stereotyped patterns of behavior, interests, and activities; and stagnation of development or loss of acquired skills. Symptoms and signs may include, but are not limited to, abnormalities and unevenness in the development of cognitive skills; unusual responses to sensory stimuli; and behavioral difficulties, including hyperactivity, short attention span, impulsivity, aggressiveness, or self-injurious actions.

b. Examples of disorders that we evaluate in this category include autism spectrum disorder with or without accompanying intellectual impairment, and autism spectrum disorder with or without accompanying language impairment.

c. This category does not include the mental disorders that we evaluate under neurocognitive disorders (112.02), intellectual disorder (112.05), and neurodevelopmental disorders (112.11).

9. Neurodevelopmental disorders (112.11).

a. These disorders are characterized by onset during the developmental period, that is, during childhood or adolescence, although sometimes they are not diagnosed until adulthood. Symptoms and signs may include, but are not limited to, underlying abnormalities in cognitive processing (for example, deficits in learning and applying verbal or nonverbal information, visual perception, memory, or a combination of these); deficits in attention or impulse control; low frustration tolerance; excessive or poorly planned motor activity; difficulty with organizing (time, space, materials, or tasks); repeated accidental injury; and deficits in social skills. Symptoms and signs specific to tic disorders include sudden, rapid, recurrent, non-rhythmic, motor movement or vocalization.

b. Examples of disorders that we evaluate in this category include specific learning disorder, borderline intellectual functioning, and tic disorders (such as Tourette syndrome).

c. This category does not include the mental disorders that we evaluate under neurocognitive disorders (112.02), autism spectrum disorder (112.10), or personality and impulse-control disorders (112.08).

10. Eating disorders (112.13).

a. These disorders are characterized in young children by persistent eating of nonnutritive substances or repeated episodes of regurgitation and re-chewing of food, or by persistent failure to consume adequate nutrition by mouth. In adolescence, these disorders are characterized by disturbances in eating behavior and preoccupation with, and excessive self-evaluation of, body weight and shape. Symptoms and signs may include, but are not limited to, failure to make expected weight gains; restriction of energy consumption when compared with individual requirements; recurrent episodes of binge eating or behavior intended to prevent weight gain, such as self-induced vomiting, excessive exercise, or misuse of laxatives; mood disturbances, social withdrawal, or irritability; amenorrhea; dental problems; abnormal laboratory findings; and cardiac abnormalities.

b. Examples of disorders that we evaluate in this category include anorexia nervosa, bulimia nervosa, binge-eating disorder, and avoidant/restrictive food disorder.

11. Developmental disorders in infants and toddlers (112.14).

a. Developmental disorders are characterized by a delay or deficit in the development of age-appropriate skills, or a loss of previously acquired skills, involving motor planning and control, learning, relating and communicating, and self-regulating.

b. Examples of disorders that we evaluate in this category include developmental coordination disorder, separation anxiety disorder, autism spectrum disorder, and regulation disorders of sensory processing (difficulties in regulating emotions, behaviors, and motor abilities in response to sensory stimulation). Some infants and toddlers may have only a general diagnosis of "developmental delay."

c. This category does not include eating disorders related to low birth weight and failure to thrive, which we evaluate under that body system (100.00).

12. Trauma- and stressor-related disorders (112.15).

a. These disorders are characterized by experiencing or witnessing a traumatic or stressful event, or learning of a traumatic event occurring to a close family member or close friend, and the psychological aftermath of clinically significant effects on functioning. Symptoms and signs may include, but are not limited to, distressing memories, dreams, and flashbacks related to the trauma or stressor; avoidant or withdrawn behavior; constriction of play and significant activities; increased frequency of negative emotional states (for example, fear, sadness) or reduced expression of positive emotions (for example, satisfaction, affection); anxiety; irritability; aggression; exaggerated startle response; difficulty concentrating; sleep disturbance; and a loss of previously acquired developmental skills.

b. Examples of disorders that we evaluate in this category include posttraumatic stress disorder, reactive attachment disorder, and other specified trauma- and stressor-related disorders (such as adjustment-like disorders with prolonged duration without prolonged duration of stressor).

c. This category does not include the mental disorders that we evaluate under anxiety and obsessive-compulsive disorders (112.06), and cognitive impairments that result from neurological disorders, such as a traumatic brain injury, which we evaluate under neurocognitive disorders (112.02).

C. What evidence do we need to evaluate your mental disorder?

1. General. We need objective medical evidence from an acceptable medical source to establish that you have a medically determinable mental disorder. We also need evidence to assess the severity of your mental disorder and its effects on your ability to function age-appropriately. We will determine the extent and kinds of evidence we need from medical and nonmedical sources based on the individual facts about your disorder. For additional evidence requirements for intellectual disorder (112.05), see 112.00H. For our basic rules on evidence, see §§ 416.912, 416.913, and 416.920b of this chapter. For our rules on evaluating medical opinions, see §§ 416.1520c and 416.927 of this chapter. For our rules on evidence about your symptoms, see § 416.929 of this chapter.

2. Evidence from medical sources. We will consider all relevant medical evidence about your disorder from your physician, psychologist, and other medical sources, which include health care providers such as physician assistants, psychiatric nurse practitioners, licensed clinical social workers, and clinical mental health counselors. Evidence from your medical sources may include:

a. Your reported symptoms.

b. Your developmental, medical, psychiatric, and psychological history.

c. The results of physical or mental status examinations, structured clinical interviews, psychiatric or psychological rating scales, measures of adaptive functioning, or other clinical findings.

d. Developmental assessments, psychological testing, imaging results, or other laboratory findings.

e. Your diagnosis.

f. The type, dosage, and beneficial effects of medications you take.

g. The type, frequency, duration, and beneficial effects of therapy you receive.

h. Side effects of medication or other treatment that limit your ability to function.

i. Your clinical course, including changes in your medication, therapy, or other treatment, and the time required for therapeutic effectiveness.

j. Observations and descriptions of how you function during examinations or therapy.

k. Information about sensory, motor, or speech abnormalities, or about your cultural background (for example, language or customs) that may affect an evaluation of your mental disorder.

l. The expected duration of your symptoms and signs and their effects on your ability to function age-appropriately, both currently and in the future.

3. Evidence from you and people who know you. We will consider all relevant evidence about your mental disorder and your daily functioning that we receive from you and from people who know you. If you are too young or unable to describe your symptoms and your functioning, we will ask for a description from the person who is most familiar with you. We will ask about your symptoms, your daily functioning, and your medical treatment. We will ask for information from third parties who can tell us about your mental disor-

der, but we must have permission to do so. This evidence may include information from your family, caregivers, teachers, other educators, neighbors, clergy, case managers, social workers, shelter staff, or other community support and outreach workers. We will consider whether your statements and the statements from third parties are consistent with the medical and other evidence we have.

4. Evidence from early intervention programs, school, vocational training, work, and work-related programs.

a. Early intervention programs. You may receive services in an Early Intervention Program (EIP) to help you with your developmental needs. If so, we will consider information from your Individualized Family Service Plan (IFSP) and the early intervention specialists who help you.

b. School. You may receive special education or related services at your preschool or school. If so, we will try to obtain information from your school sources when we need it to assess how your mental disorder affects your ability to function. Examples of this information include your Individualized Education Programs (IEPs), your Section 504 plans, comprehensive evaluation reports, school-related therapy progress notes, information from your teachers about how you function in a classroom setting, and information from special educators, nurses, school psychologists, and occupational, physical, and speech/language therapists about any special education services or accommodations you receive at school.

c. Vocational training, work, and work-related programs. You may have recently participated in or may still be participating in vocational training, work-related programs, or work activity. If so, we will try to obtain information from your training program or your employer when we need it to assess how your mental disorder affects your ability to function. Examples of this information include training or work evaluations, modifications to your work duties or work schedule, and any special supports or accommodations you have required or now require in order to work. If you have worked or are working through a community mental health program, sheltered or supported work program, rehabilitation program, or transitional employment program, we will consider the type and degree of support you have received or are receiving in order to work (see 112.00D).

5. Need for longitudinal evidence.

a. General. Longitudinal medical evidence can help us learn how you function over time, and help us evaluate any variations in the level of your functioning. We will request longitudinal evidence of your mental disorder when your medical providers have records concerning you and your mental disorder over a period of months or perhaps years (see § 416.912(d) of this chapter).

b. Non-medical sources of longitudinal evidence. Certain situations, such as chronic homelessness, may make it difficult for you to provide longitudinal medical evidence. If you have a severe mental disorder, you will probably have evidence of its effects on your functioning over time, even if you have not had an ongoing relationship with the medical community or are not currently receiving treatment. For example, family members, caregivers, teachers, neighbors, former employers, social workers, case managers, community support staff, outreach workers, or government agencies may be familiar with your mental health history. We will ask for information from third parties who can tell us about your mental disorder, but you must give us permission to do so.

c. Absence of longitudinal evidence. In the absence of longitudinal evidence, we will use current objective medical evidence and all other relevant evidence available to us in your case record to evaluate your mental disorder. If we purchase a consultative examination to document your disorder, the record will include the results of that examination (see § 416.914 of this chapter). We will take into consideration your medical history, symptoms, clinical and laboratory findings, and medical source opinions. If you do not have longitudinal evidence, the current evidence alone may not be sufficient or appropriate to show that you have a disorder that meets the criteria of one of the mental disorders listings. In that case, we will follow the rules in 112.00K.

6. Evidence of functioning in unfamiliar situations or supportive situations.

a. Unfamiliar situations. We recognize that evidence about your functioning in unfamiliar situations does not necessarily show how you would function on a sustained basis in a school or other age-appropriate setting. In one-time, time-limited, or other unfamiliar situations, you may function differently than you do in familiar situations. In unfamiliar situations, you may appear more, or less, limited than you do on a daily basis and over time.

b. Supportive situations. Your ability to function in settings that are highly structured, or that are less demanding or more supportive than settings in which children your age without impairments typically function, does not necessarily demonstrate your ability to function age-appropriately.

c. Our assessment. We must assess your ability to function age-appropriately by evaluating all the evidence, such as reports about your functioning from third parties who are familiar with you, with an emphasis on how well you can initiate, sustain, and complete age-appropriate activities despite your impairment(s), compared to other children your age who do not have impairments.

D. How do we consider psychosocial supports, structured settings, living arrangements, and treatment when we evaluate the functioning of children?

1. General. Psychosocial supports, structured settings, and living arrangements, including assistance from your family or others, may help you by reducing the demands made on you. In addition, treatment you receive may reduce your symptoms and signs and possibly improve your functioning, or may have side effects that limit your functioning. Therefore, when we evaluate the effects of your mental disorder and rate the limitation of your areas of mental functioning, we will consider the kind and extent of supports you receive, the characteristics of any structured setting in which you spend your time (compared to children your age without impairments), and the effects of any treatment. This evidence may come from reports about your functioning from third parties who are familiar with you, and other third-party statements or information. Following are some examples of the supports you may receive:

a. You receive help from family members or other people in ways that children your age without impairments typically do not need in order to function age-appropriately. For example, an aide may accompany you on the school bus to help you control your actions or to monitor you to ensure you do not injure yourself or others.

b. You receive one-on-one assistance in your classes every day; or you have a full-time personal aide who helps you to function in your classroom; or you are a student in a self-contained classroom; or you attend a separate or alternative school where you receive special education services.

c. You participate in a special education or vocational training program, or a psychosocial rehabilitation day treatment or community support program, where you receive training in daily living and entry-level work skills.

d. You participate in a sheltered, supported, or transitional work program, or in a competitive employment setting with the help of a job coach or supervisor.

e. You receive comprehensive "24/7 wrap-around" mental health services while living in a group home or transitional housing, while participating in a semi-independent living program, or while living at home.

f. You live in a residential school, hospital, or other institution with 24-hour care.

g. You receive assistance from a crisis response team, social workers, or community mental health workers who help you meet your physical needs, and who may also represent you in dealings with government or community social services.

2. How we consider different levels of support and structure in psychosocial rehabilitation programs.

a. Psychosocial rehabilitation programs are based on your specific needs. Therefore, we cannot make any assumptions about your mental disorder based solely on the fact that you are associated with such a program. We must know the details of the program(s) in which you are involved and the pattern(s) of your involvement over time.

b. The kinds and levels of supports and structures in psychosocial rehabilitation programs typically occur on a scale of "most restrictive" to "least restrictive." Participation in a psychosocial rehabilitation program at the most restrictive level would suggest greater limitation of your areas of mental functioning than would participation at a less restrictive level. The length of time you spend at different levels in a program also provides information about your functioning. For example, you could begin participation at the most restrictive crisis intervention level but gradually improve to the point of readiness for a lesser level of support and structure and, if you are an older adolescent, possibly some form of employment.

3. How we consider the help or support you receive.

a. We will consider the complete picture of your daily functioning, including the kinds, extent, and frequency of help and support you receive, when we evaluate your mental disorder and determine whether you are able to use the four areas of mental functioning age-appropriately. The fact that you have done, or currently do, some routine activities without help or support does not necessarily mean that you do not have a mental disorder or that you are not disabled. For example, you may be able to take age-appropriate care of your personal needs, or you may be old enough and able to cook, shop, and take public transportation. You may demonstrate both strengths and deficits in your daily functioning.

b. You may receive various kinds of help and support from others that enable you to do many things that, because of your mental disorder, you might not be able to do independently. Your daily functioning may depend on the special contexts in which you function. For example, you may spend your time among only familiar people or surroundings, in a simple and steady routine or an unchanging environment, or in a highly structured classroom or alternative school. However, this does not necessarily show whether you would function age-appropriately without those supports or contexts. (See 112.00H for further discussion of these issues regarding significant deficits in adaptive functioning for the purpose of 112.05.)

4. How we consider treatment. We will consider the effect of any treatment on your functioning when we evaluate your mental disorder. Treatment may include medication(s), psychotherapy, or other forms of intervention, which you receive in a doctor's office, during a hospitalization, or in a day program at a

hospital or outpatient treatment program. With treatment, you may not only have your symptoms and signs reduced, but may also be able to function age-appropriately. However, treatment may not resolve all of the limitations that result from your mental disorder, and the medications you take or other treatment you receive for your disorder may cause side effects that limit your mental or physical functioning. For example, you may experience drowsiness, blunted affect, memory loss, or abnormal involuntary movements.

E. What are the paragraph B criteria for children age 3 to the attainment of age 18?

1. Understand, remember, or apply information (paragraph B1). This area of mental functioning refers to the abilities to learn, recall, and use information to perform age-appropriate activities. Examples include: Understanding and learning terms, instructions, procedures; following one- or two-step oral instructions to carry out a task; describing an activity to someone else; asking and answering questions and providing explanations; recognizing a mistake and correcting it; identifying and solving problems; sequencing multi-step activities; and using reason and judgment to make decisions. These examples illustrate the nature of the area of mental functioning. We do not require documentation of all of the examples. How you manifest this area of mental functioning and your limitations in using it depends, in part, on your age.

2. Interact with others (paragraph B2). This area of mental functioning refers to the abilities to relate to others age-appropriately at home, at school, and in the community. Examples include: Engaging in interactive play; cooperating with others; asking for help when needed; initiating and maintaining friendships; handling conflicts with others; stating own point of view; initiating or sustaining conversation; understanding and responding to social cues (physical, verbal, emotional); responding to requests, suggestions, criticism, correction, and challenges; and keeping social interactions free of excessive irritability, sensitivity, argumentativeness, or suspiciousness. These examples illustrate the nature of this area of mental functioning. We do not require documentation of all of the examples. How you manifest this area of mental functioning and your limitations in using it depends, in part, on your age.

3. Concentrate, persist, or maintain pace (paragraph B3). This area of mental functioning refers to the abilities to focus attention on activities and stay on task age-appropriately. Examples include: Initiating and performing an activity that you understand and know how to do; engaging in an activity at home or in school at an appropriate and consistent pace; completing tasks in a timely manner; ignoring or avoiding distractions while engaged in an activity or task; changing activities without being disruptive; engaging in an activity or task close to or with others without interrupting or distracting them; sustaining an ordinary routine and regular attendance at school; and engaging in activities at home, school, or in the community without needing an unusual amount of rest. These examples illustrate the nature of this area of mental functioning. We do not require documentation of all of the examples. How you manifest this area of mental functioning and your limitations in using it depends, in part, on your age.

4. Adapt or manage oneself (paragraph B4). This area of mental functioning refers to the abilities to regulate emotions, control behavior, and maintain wellbeing in age-appropriate activities and settings. Examples include: Responding to demands; adapting to changes; managing your psychologically based symptoms; distinguishing between acceptable and unacceptable performance in community- or school-related activities; setting goals; making plans independently of others; maintaining personal hygiene; and protecting yourself from harm and exploitation by others. These examples illustrate the nature of this area of mental functioning. We do not require documentation of all of the examples. How you manifest this area of mental functioning and your limitations in using it depends, in part, on your age.

F. How do we use the paragraph B criteria to evaluate mental disorders in children?

1. General. We use the paragraph B criteria to rate the degree of your limitations. We consider only the limitations that result from your mental disorder(s). We will determine whether you are able to use each of the paragraph B areas of mental functioning in age-appropriate activities in a manner comparable to that of other children your age who do not have impairments. We will consider, for example, the range of your activities and whether they are age-appropriate; how well you can initiate, sustain, and complete your activities; the kinds and frequency of help or supervision you receive; and the kinds of structured or supportive settings you need in order to function age-appropriately (see 112.00D).

2. Degrees of limitation. We evaluate the effects of your mental disorder on each of the four areas of mental functioning. To satisfy the paragraph B criteria, your mental disorder must result in extreme limitation of one, or marked limitation of two, paragraph B areas of mental functioning. See §§ 416.925(b)(2)(ii) and 416.926a(e) of this chapter for the definitions of the terms marked and extreme as they apply to children.

3. Rating the limitations of your areas of mental functioning.

a. General. We use all of the relevant medical and non-medical evidence in your case record to evaluate your mental disorder: The symptoms and signs of your disorder, the reported limitations in your activities, and any help and support you receive that is necessary for you to function. The medical evidence may include descriptors regarding the diagnostic stage or level of your disorder, such as "mild" or "moderate." Clinicians may use these terms to characterize your medical condition. However, these terms will not always be the same as the degree of your limitation in a paragraph B area of mental functioning.

b. Areas of mental functioning in daily activities. You use the same four areas of mental functioning in daily activities at home, at school, and in the community. With respect to a particular task or activity, you may have trouble using one or more of the areas. For example, you may have difficulty understanding and remembering what to do; or concentrating and staying on task long enough to do it; or engaging in the task or activity with other people; or trying to do the task without becoming frustrated and losing self-control. Information about your daily functioning in your activities at home, at school, or in your community can help us understand whether your mental disorder limits one or more of these areas; and, if so, whether it also affects your ability to function age-appropriately.

c. Overall effect of limitations. Limitation of an area of mental functioning reflects the overall degree to which your mental disorder interferes with that area. The degree of limitation does not necessarily reflect a specific type or number of activities, including activities of daily living, that you have difficulty doing. In addition, no single piece of information (including test results) can establish whether you have extreme or marked limitation of an area of mental functioning.

d. Effects of support, supervision, structure on functioning. The degree of limitation of an area of mental functioning also reflects the kind and extent of supports or supervision you receive (beyond what other children your age without impairments typically receive) and the characteristics of any structured setting where you spend your time, which enable you to function. The more extensive the support you need from others (beyond what is age-appropriate) or the more structured the setting you need in order to function, the more limited we will find you to be (see 112.00D).

e. Specific instructions for paragraphs B1, B3, and B4. For paragraphs B1, B3, and B4, the greatest degree of limitation of any part of the area of mental functioning directs the rating of limitation of that whole area of mental functioning.

(i) To do an age-appropriate activity, you must be able to understand and remember and apply information required by the activity. Similarly, you must be able to concentrate and persist and maintain pace in order to complete the activity, and adapt and manage yourself age-appropriately. Limitation in any one of these parts (understand or remember or apply; concentrate or persist or maintain pace; adapt or manage oneself) may prevent you from completing age-appropriate activities.

(ii) We will document the rating of limitation of the whole area of mental functioning, not each individual part. We will not add ratings of the parts together. For example, with respect to paragraph B3, if you have marked limitation in concentrating, but your limitations in persisting and maintaining pace do not rise to a marked level, we will find that you have marked limitation in the whole paragraph B3 area of mental functioning.

(iii) Marked limitation in more than one part of the same paragraph B area of mental functioning does not satisfy the requirement to have marked limitation in two paragraph B areas of mental functioning.

4. How we evaluate mental disorders involving exacerbations and remissions.

a. When we evaluate the effects of your mental disorder, we will consider how often you have exacerbations and remissions, how long they last, what causes your mental disorder to worsen or improve, and any other relevant information. We will assess whether your mental impairment(s) causes marked or extreme limitation of the affected paragraph B area(s) of mental functioning (see 112.00F2). We will consider whether you can use the area of mental functioning age-appropriately on a sustained basis. We will not find that you function age-appropriately solely because you have a period(s) of improvement (remission), or that you are disabled solely because you have a period of worsening (exacerbation), of your mental disorder.

b. If you have a mental disorder involving exacerbations and remissions, you may be able to use the four areas of mental functioning at home, at school, or in the community for a few weeks or months. Recurrence or worsening of symptoms and signs, however, can interfere enough to render you unable to function age-appropriately.

G. What are the paragraph C criteria, and how do we use them to evaluate mental disorders in children age 3 to the attainment of age 18?

1. General. The paragraph C criteria are an alternative to the paragraph B criteria under listings 112.02, 112.03, 112.04, 112.06, and 112.15. We use the paragraph C criteria to evaluate mental disorders that are "serious and persistent." In the paragraph C criteria, we recognize that mental health interventions may control the more obvious symptoms and signs of your mental disorder.

2. Paragraph C criteria.

a. We find a mental disorder to be "serious and persistent" when there is a medically documented history of the existence of the mental disorder in the listing category over a period of at least 2 years, and evidence shows that your disorder satisfies both C1 and C2.

b. The criterion in C1 is satisfied when the evidence shows that you rely, on an ongoing basis, upon medical treatment, mental health therapy, psychosocial support(s), or a highly structured setting(s), to diminish the symptoms and signs of your mental disorder (see 112.00D). We consider that you receive ongoing medical treatment when the medical evidence establishes that you obtain medical treatment with a frequency consistent with accepted medical practice for the type of treatment or evaluation required for your medical condition. We will consider periods of inconsistent treatment or lack of compliance with treatment that may result from your mental disorder. If the evidence indicates that the inconsistent treatment or lack of compliance is a feature of your mental disorder, and it has led to an exacerbation of your symptoms and signs, we will not use it as evidence to support a finding that you have not received ongoing medical treatment as required by this paragraph.

c. The criterion in C2 is satisfied when the evidence shows that, despite your diminished symptoms and signs, you have achieved only marginal adjustment. "Marginal adjustment" means that your adaptation to the requirements of daily life is fragile; that is, you have minimal capacity to adapt to changes in your environment or to demands that are not already part of your daily life. We will consider that you have achieved only marginal adjustment when the evidence shows that changes or increased demands have led to exacerbation of your symptoms and signs and to deterioration in your functioning; for example, you have become unable to function outside of your home or a more restrictive setting, without substantial psychosocial supports (see 112.00D). Such deterioration may have necessitated a significant change in medication or other treatment. Similarly, because of the nature of your mental disorder, evidence may document episodes of deterioration that have required you to be hospitalized or absent from school, making it difficult for you to sustain age-appropriate activity over time.

H. How do we document and evaluate intellectual disorder under 112.05?

1. General. Listing 112.05 is based on the two elements that characterize intellectual disorder for children up to age 18: Significantly subaverage general intellectual functioning and significant deficits in current adaptive functioning.

2. Establishing significantly subaverage general intellectual functioning.

a. Definition. Intellectual functioning refers to the general mental capacity to learn, reason, plan, solve problems, and perform other cognitive functions. Under 112.05A, we identify significantly subaverage general intellectual functioning by the cognitive inability to function at a level required to participate in standardized intelligence testing. Our findings under 112.05A are based on evidence from an acceptable medical source. Under 112.05B, we identify significantly subaverage general intellectual functioning by an IQ score(s) on an individually administered standardized test of general intelligence that meets program requirements and has a mean of 100 and a standard deviation of 15. A qualified specialist (see 112.00H2c) must administer the standardized intelligence testing.

b. Psychometric standards. We will find standardized intelligence test results usable for the purposes of 112.05B1 when the measure employed meets contemporary psychometric standards for validity, reliability, normative data, and scope of measurement; and a qualified specialist has individually administered the test according to all pre-requisite testing conditions.

c. Qualified specialist. A "qualified specialist" is currently licensed or certified at the independent level of practice in the State where the test was performed, and has the training and experience to administer, score, and interpret intelligence tests. If a psychological assistant or paraprofessional administered the test, a supervisory qualified specialist must interpret the test findings and co-sign the examination report.

d. Responsibility for conclusions based on testing. We generally presume that your obtained IQ score(s) is an accurate reflection of your general intellectual functioning, unless evidence in the record suggests otherwise. Examples of this evidence include: A statement from the test administrator indicating that your obtained score is not an accurate reflection of your general intellectual functioning, prior or internally inconsistent IQ scores, or information about your daily functioning. Only qualified specialists, Federal and State agency medical and psychological consultants, and other contracted medical and psychological experts may conclude that your obtained IQ score(s) is not an accurate reflection of your general intellectual functioning. This conclusion must be well supported by appropriate clinical and laboratory diagnostic techniques and must be based on relevant evidence in the case record, such as:

(i) The data obtained in testing;

(ii) Your developmental history, including when your signs and symptoms began;

(iii) Information about how you function on a daily basis in a variety of settings; and

(iv) Clinical observations made during the testing period, such as your ability to sustain attention, concentration, and effort; to relate appropriately to the examiner; and to perform tasks independently without prompts or reminders.

3. Establishing significant deficits in adaptive functioning.

a. Definition. Adaptive functioning refers to how you learn and use conceptual, social, and practical skills in dealing with common life demands. It is your typical functioning at home, at school, and in the community, alone or among others. Under 112.05A, we identify significant deficits in adaptive functioning based on your dependence on others to care for your personal needs, such as eating and bathing (grossly in excess of age-appropriate dependence). We will base our conclusions about your adaptive functioning on evidence from a variety of sources (see 112.00H3b) and not on your statements alone. Under 112.05B2, we identify significant deficits in adaptive functioning based on whether there is extreme limitation of one, or marked limitation of two, of the paragraph B criteria (see 112.00E; 112.00F).

b. Evidence. Evidence about your adaptive functioning may come from:

(i) Medical sources, including their clinical observations;

(ii) Standardized tests of adaptive functioning (see 112.00H3c);

(iii) Third party information, such as a report of your functioning from a family member or your caregiver;

(iv) School records;

(v) A teacher questionnaire;

(vi) Reports from employers or supervisors; and

(vii) Your own statements about how you handle all of your daily activities.

c. Standardized tests of adaptive functioning. We do not require the results of an individually administered standardized test of adaptive functioning. If your case record includes these test results, we will consider the results along with all other relevant evidence; however, we will use the guidelines in 112.00E and F to evaluate and determine the degree of your deficits in adaptive functioning, as required under 112.05B2.

d. Standardized developmental assessments. We do not require the results of standardized developmental assessments, which compare your level of development to the level typically expected for your chronological age. If your case record includes test results, we will consider the results along with all other relevant evidence. However, we will use the guidelines in 112.00E and F to evaluate and determine the degree of your deficits in adaptive functioning, as required under 112.05B2.

e. How we consider common everyday activities.

(i) The fact that you engage in common everyday activities, such as caring for your personal needs, preparing simple meals, or driving a car, will not always mean that you do not have deficits in adaptive functioning as required by 112.05B2. You may demonstrate both strengths and deficits in your adaptive functioning. However, a lack of deficits in one area does not negate the presence of deficits in another area. When we assess your adaptive functioning, we will consider all of your activities and your performance of them.

(ii) Our conclusions about your adaptive functioning rest on the quality of your daily activities and whether you do them age-appropriately. If you receive help in performing your activities, we need to know the kind, extent, and frequency of help you receive in order to perform them. We will not assume that your ability to do some common everyday activities, or to do some things without help or support, demonstrates that your mental disorder does not meet the requirements of 112.05B2. (See 112.00D regarding the factors we consider when we evaluate your functioning, including how we consider any help or support you receive.)

f. How we consider work activity. The fact that you have engaged in work activity, or that you work intermittently or steadily in a job commensurate with your abilities, will not always mean that you do not have deficits in adaptive functioning as required by 112.05B2. When you have engaged in work activity, we need complete information about the work, and about your functioning in the work activity and work setting, before we reach any conclusions about your adaptive functioning. We will consider all factors involved in your work history before concluding whether your impairment satisfies the criteria for intellectual disorder under 112.05B. We will consider your prior and current work history, if any, and various other factors influencing how you function. For example, we consider whether the work was in a supported setting, whether you required more supervision than other employees, how your job duties compared to others in the same job, how much time it took you to learn the job duties, and the reason the work ended, if applicable.

I. What additional considerations do we use to evaluate developmental disorders of infants and toddlers?

1. General. We evaluate developmental disorders from birth to attainment of age 3 under 112.14. We evaluate your ability to acquire and maintain the motor, cognitive, social/communicative, and emotional skills that you need to function age-appropriately. When we rate your impairment-related limitations for this listing (see §§ 416.925(b)(2)(ii) and 416.926a(e) of this chapter), we consider only limitations you have because of your developmental disorder. If you have a chronic illness or physical abnormality(ies), we will evaluate it under the affected body system, for example, the cardiovascular or musculoskeletal system.

2. Age and typical development in early childhood.

a. Prematurity and age. If you were born prematurely, we will use your corrected chronological age (CCA) for comparison. CCA is your chronological age adjusted by a period of gestational prematurity. CCA = (chronological age)-(number of weeks premature). If you have not attained age 1, we will correct your chronological age, using the same formula. If you are over age 1, we will decide whether to correct your chronological age, based on our judgment and all the facts of your case (see § 416.924b(b) of this chapter).

b. Developmental assessment. We will use the results from a standardized developmental assessment to compare your level of development with that typically expected for your chronological age. When there are no results from a comprehensive standardized developmental assessment in the case record, we need narrative developmental reports from your medical sources in sufficient detail to assess the limitations resulting from your developmental disorder.

c. Variation. When we evaluate your developmental disorder, we will consider the wide variation in the range of normal or typical development in early childhood. At the end of a recognized milestone period, new skills typically begin to emerge. If your new skills begin to emerge later than is typically expected, the timing of their emergence may or may not indicate that you have a developmental delay or deficit that can be expected to last for 1 year.

3. Evidence.

a. Standardized developmental assessments. We use standardized test reports from acceptable medical sources or from early intervention specialists, physical or occupational therapists, and other qualified professionals. Only the qualified professional who administers the test, Federal and State agency medical and psychological consultants, and other contracted medical and psychological experts may conclude that the assessment results are not an accurate reflection of your development. This conclusion must be well supported by appropriate clinical and laboratory diagnostic techniques and must be based on relevant evidence in the case record. If the assessment results are not an accurate reflection of your development, we may purchase a new developmental assessment. If the developmental assessment is inconsistent with other information in your case record, we will follow the guidelines in § 416.920b of this chapter.

b. Narrative developmental reports. A narrative developmental report is based on clinical observations, progress notes, and well-baby check-ups, and includes your developmental history, examination findings (with abnormal findings noted on repeated examinations), and an overall assessment of your development (that is, more than one or two isolated skills) by the medical source. Although medical sources may refer to screening test results as supporting evidence in the narrative developmental report, screening test results alone cannot establish a diagnosis or the severity of developmental disorder.

4. What are the paragraph B criteria for 112.14?

a. General. The paragraph B criteria for 112.14 are slightly different from the paragraph B criteria for the other listings. They are the developmental abilities that infants and toddlers use to acquire and maintain the skills needed to function age-appropriately. An infant or toddler is expected to use his or her developmental abilities to achieve a recognized pattern of milestones, over a typical range of time, in order to acquire and maintain the skills needed to function age-appropriately. We will find that your developmental disorder satisfies the requirements of 112.14 if it results in extreme limitation of one, or marked limitation of two, of the 112.14 paragraph B criteria. (See §§ 416.925(b)(2)(ii) and 416.926a(e) of this chapter for the definitions of the terms marked and extreme as they apply to children.)

b. Definitions of the 112.14 paragraph B developmental abilities.

(i) Ability to plan and control motor movement. This criterion refers to the developmental ability to plan, remember, and execute controlled motor movements by integrating and coordinating perceptual and sensory input with motor output. Using this ability develops gross and fine motor skills, and makes it possible for you to engage in age-appropriate symmetrical or alternating motor activities. You use this ability when, for example, you grasp and hold objects with one or both hands, pull yourself up to stand, walk without holding on, and go up and down stairs with alternating feet. These examples illustrate the nature of the developmental ability. We do not require documentation of all of the examples. How you manifest this developmental ability and your limitations in using it depends, in part, on your age.

(ii) Ability to learn and remember. This criterion refers to the developmental ability to learn by exploring the environment, engaging in trial-and-error experimentation, putting things in groups, understanding that words represent things, and participating in pretend play. Using this ability develops the skills that help you understand what things mean, how things work, and how you can make things happen. You use this ability when, for example, you show interest in objects that are new to you, imitate simple actions, name body parts, understand simple cause-and-effect relationships, remember simple directions, or figure out how to take something apart. These examples illustrate the nature of the developmental ability. We do not require documentation of all of the examples. How you manifest this developmental ability and your limitations in using it depends, in part, on your age.

(iii) Ability to interact with others. This criterion refers to the developmental ability to participate in reciprocal social interactions and relationships by communicating your feelings and intents through vocal and visual signals and exchanges; physical gestures and contact; shared attention and affection; verbal turn taking; and understanding and sending increasingly complex messages. Using this ability develops the social skills that make it possible for you to influence others (for example, by gesturing for a toy or saying "no" to stop an action); invite someone to interact with you (for example, by smiling or reaching); and draw someone's attention to what interests you (for example, by pointing or taking your caregiver's hand and leading that person). You use this ability when, for example, you use vocalizations to initiate and sustain a "conversation" with your caregiver; respond to limits set by an adult with words, gestures, or facial expressions; play alongside another child; or participate in simple group activities with adult help. These examples illustrate the nature of the developmental ability. We do not require documentation of all of the examples. How you manifest this developmental ability and your limitations in using it depends, in part, on your age.

(iv) Ability to regulate physiological functions, attention, emotion, and behavior. This criterion refers to the developmental ability to stabilize biological rhythms (for example, by developing an age-appropriate sleep/wake cycle); control physiological functions (for example, by achieving regular patterns of feeding); and attend, react, and adapt to environmental stimuli, persons, objects, and events (for example, by becoming alert to things happening around you and in relation to you, and responding without overreacting or underreacting). Using this ability develops the skills you need to regulate yourself and makes it possible for you to achieve and maintain a calm, alert, and organized physical and emotional state. You use this ability when, for example, you recognize your body's needs for food or sleep, focus quickly and pay attention to things that interest you, cry when you are hurt but become quiet when your caregiver holds you, comfort yourself with your favorite toy when you are upset, ask for help when something frustrates you, or refuse help from your caregiver when trying to do something for yourself. These examples illustrate the nature of the developmental ability. We do not require documentation of all of the examples. How you manifest this developmental ability and your limitations in using it depends, in part, on your age.

5. Deferral of determination.

a. Full-term infants. In the first few months of life, full-term infants typically display some irregularities in observable behaviors (for example, sleep cycles, feeding, responding to stimuli, attending to faces, self-calming), making it difficult to assess the presence, extent, and duration of a developmental disorder. When the evidence indicates that you may have a significant developmental delay, but there is insufficient evidence to make a determination, we will defer making a disability determination under 112.14 until you are at least 6 months old. This deferral will allow us to obtain a longitudinal medical history so that we can more accurately evaluate your developmental patterns and functioning over time. In most cases, when you are at least 6 months old, any developmental delay you may have can be better assessed, and you can undergo standardized developmental testing, if indicated.

b. Premature infants. When the evidence indicates that you may have a significant developmental delay, but there is insufficient evidence to make a determination, we will defer your case until you attain a CCA (see 112.00I2a) of at least 6 months in order to better evaluate your developmental delay.

c. When we will not defer a determination. We will not defer our determination if we have sufficient evidence to determine that you are disabled under 112.14 or any other listing, or that you have an impairment or combination of impairments that functionally equals the listings. In addition, we will not defer our determination if the evidence demonstrates that you are not disabled.

J. How do we evaluate substance use disorders? If we find that you are disabled and there is medical evidence in your case record establishing that you have a substance use disorder, we will determine whether your substance use disorder is a contributing factor material to the determination of disability (see § 416.935 of this chapter).

K. How do we evaluate mental disorders that do not meet one of the mental disorders listings?

1. These listings include only examples of mental disorders that we consider serious enough to result in marked and severe functional limitations. If your severe mental disorder does not meet the criteria of any of these listings, we will consider whether you have an impairment(s) that meets the criteria of a listing in another body system. You may have another impairment(s) that is secondary to your mental disorder. For example, if you have an eating disorder and develop a cardiovascular impairment because of it, we will evaluate your cardiovascular impairment under the listings for the cardiovascular body system.

2. If you have a severe medically determinable impairment(s) that does not meet a listing, we will determine whether your impairment(s) medically equals a listing (see § 416.926 of this chapter).

3. If your impairment(s) does not meet or medically equal a listing, we will consider whether you have an impairment(s) that functionally equals the listings (see § 416.926a of this chapter).

4. Although we present these alternatives in a specific sequence above, each represents listing-level severity, and we can evaluate your claim in any order. For example, if the factors of your case indicate that the combination of your impairments may functionally equal the listings, we may start with that analysis. We use the rules in § 416.994a of this chapter, as appropriate, when we decide whether you continue to be disabled.

112.01 Category of Impairments, Mental Disorders

112.02 Neurocognitive disorders (see 112.00B1), for children age 3 to attainment of age 18, satisfied by A and B, or A and C:

A. Medical documentation of a clinically significant deviation in normal cognitive development or by significant cognitive decline from a prior level of functioning in one or more of the cognitive areas:

1. Complex attention;

2. Executive function;

3. Learning and memory;

4. Language;

5. Perceptual-motor; or

6. Social cognition.

AND

B. Extreme limitation of one, or marked limitation of two, of the following areas of mental functioning (see 112.00F):

1. Understand, remember, or apply information (see 112.00E1).

2. Interact with others (see 112.00E2).

3. Concentrate, persist, or maintain pace (see 112.00E3).

4. Adapt or manage oneself (see 112.00E4).

OR

C. Your mental disorder in this listing category is "serious and persistent;" that is, you have a medically documented history of the existence of the disorder over a period of at least 2 years, and there is evidence of both:

1. Medical treatment, mental health therapy, psychosocial support(s), or a highly structured setting(s) that is ongoing and that diminishes the symptoms and signs of your mental disorder (see 112.00G2b); and

2. Marginal adjustment, that is, you have minimal capacity to adapt to changes in your environment or to demands that are not already part of your daily life (see 112.00G2c).

112.03 Schizophrenia spectrum and other psychotic disorders (see 112.00B2), for children age 3 to attainment of age 18, satisfied by A and B, or A and C:

A. Medical documentation of one or more of the following:

1. Delusions or hallucinations;

2. Disorganized thinking (speech); or

3. Grossly disorganized behavior or catatonia.

AND

B. Extreme limitation of one, or marked limitation of two, of the following areas of mental functioning (see 112.00F):

1. Understand, remember, or apply information (see 112.00E1).

2. Interact with others (see 112.00E2).

3. Concentrate, persist, or maintain pace (see 112.00E3).

4. Adapt or manage oneself (see 112.00E4).

OR

C. Your mental disorder in this listing category is "serious and persistent;" that is, you have a medically documented history of the existence of the disorder over a period of at least 2 years, and there is evidence of both:

1. Medical treatment, mental health therapy, psychosocial support(s), or a highly structured setting(s) that is ongoing and that diminishes the symptoms and signs of your mental disorder (see 112.00G2b); and

2. Marginal adjustment, that is, you have minimal capacity to adapt to changes in your environment or to demands that are not already part of your daily life (see 112.00G2c).

112.04 Depressive, bipolar and related disorders (see 112.00B3), for children age 3 to attainment of age 18, satisfied by A and B, or A and C:

A. Medical documentation of the requirements of paragraph 1, 2, or 3:

1. Depressive disorder, characterized by five or more of the following:

a. Depressed or irritable mood;

b. Diminished interest in almost all activities;

c. Appetite disturbance with change in weight (or a failure to achieve an expected weight gain);

d. Sleep disturbance;

e. Observable psychomotor agitation or retardation;

f. Decreased energy;

g. Feelings of guilt or worthlessness;

h. Difficulty concentrating or thinking; or

i. Thoughts of death or suicide.

2. Bipolar disorder, characterized by three or more of the following:

a. Pressured speech;

b. Flight of ideas;

c. Inflated self-esteem;

d. Decreased need for sleep;

e. Distractibility;

f. Involvement in activities that have a high probability of painful consequences that are not recognized; or

g. Increase in goal-directed activity or psychomotor agitation.

3. Disruptive mood dysregulation disorder, beginning prior to age 10, and all of the following:

a. Persistent, significant irritability or anger;

b. Frequent, developmentally inconsistent temper outbursts; and

c. Frequent aggressive or destructive behavior.

AND

B. Extreme limitation of one, or marked limitation of two, of the following areas of mental functioning (see 112.00F):

1. Understand, remember, or apply information (see 112.00E1).

2. Interact with others (see 112.00E2).

3. Concentrate, persist, or maintain pace (see 112.00E3).

4. Adapt or manage oneself (see 112.00E4).

OR

C. Your mental disorder in this listing category is "serious and persistent;" that is, you have a medically documented history of the existence of the disorder over a period of at least 2 years, and there is evidence of both:

1. Medical treatment, mental health therapy, psychosocial support(s), or a highly structured setting(s) that is ongoing and that diminishes the symptoms and signs of your mental disorder (see 112.00G2b); and

2. Marginal adjustment, that is, you have minimal capacity to adapt to changes in your environment or to demands that are not already part of your daily life (see 112.00G2c).

112.05 Intellectual disorder (see 112.00B4), for children age 3 to attainment of age 18, satisfied by A or B:

A. Satisfied by 1 and 2 (see 112.00H):

1. Significantly subaverage general intellectual functioning evident in your cognitive inability to function at a level required to participate in standardized testing of intellectual functioning; and

2. Significant deficits in adaptive functioning currently manifested by your dependence upon others for personal needs (for example, toileting, eating, dressing, or bathing) in excess of age-appropriate dependence.

OR

B. Satisfied by 1 and 2 (see 112.00H):

1. Significantly subaverage general intellectual functioning evidenced by a or b:

a. A full scale (or comparable) IQ score of 70 or below on an individually administered standardized test of general intelligence; or

b. A full scale (or comparable) IQ score of 71–75 accompanied by a verbal or performance IQ score (or comparable part score) of 70 or below on an individually administered standardized test of general intelligence; and

2. Significant deficits in adaptive functioning currently manifested by extreme limitation of one, or marked limitation of two, of the following areas of mental functioning:

a. Understand, remember, or apply information (see 112.00E1); or

b. Interact with others (see 112.00E2); or

c. Concentrate, persist, or maintain pace (see 112.00E3); or

d. Adapt or manage oneself (see 112.00E4).

112.06 Anxiety and obsessive-compulsive disorders (see 112.00B5), for children age 3 to attainment of age 18, satisfied by A and B, or A and C:

A. Medical documentation of the requirements of paragraph 1, 2, 3, or 4:

1. Anxiety disorder, characterized by one or more of the following:

a. Restlessness;

b. Easily fatigued;

c. Difficulty concentrating;

d. Irritability;

e. Muscle tension; or

f. Sleep disturbance.

2. Panic disorder or agoraphobia, characterized by one or both:

a. Panic attacks followed by a persistent concern or worry about additional panic attacks or their consequences; or

b. Disproportionate fear or anxiety about at least two different situations (for example, using public transportation, being in a crowd, being in a line, being outside of your home, being in open spaces).

3. Obsessive-compulsive disorder, characterized by one or both:

a. Involuntary, time-consuming preoccupation with intrusive, unwanted thoughts; or;

b. Repetitive behaviors that appear aimed at reducing anxiety.

4. Excessive fear or anxiety concerning separation from those to whom you are attached.

AND

B. Extreme limitation of one, or marked limitation of two, of the following areas of mental functioning (see 112.00F):

1. Understand, remember, or apply information (see 112.00E1).

2. Interact with others (see 112.00E2).

3. Concentrate, persist, or maintain pace (see 112.00E3).

4. Adapt or manage oneself (see 112.00E4).

OR

C. Your mental disorder in this listing category is "serious and persistent;" that is, you have a medically documented history of the existence of the disorder over a period of at least 2 years, and there is evidence of both:

1. Medical treatment, mental health therapy, psychosocial support(s), or a highly structured setting(s) that is ongoing and that diminishes the symptoms and signs of your mental disorder (see 112.00G2b); and

2. Marginal adjustment, that is, you have minimal capacity to adapt to changes in your environment or to demands that are not already part of your daily life (see 112.00G2c).

112.07 Somatic symptom and related disorders (see 112.00B6), for children age 3 to attainment of age 18, satisfied by A and B:

A. Medical documentation of one or both of the following:

1. Symptoms of altered voluntary motor or sensory function that are not better explained by another medical or mental disorder; or

2. One or more somatic symptoms that are distressing, with excessive thoughts, feelings, or behaviors related to the symptoms.

AND

B. Extreme limitation of one, or marked limitation of two, of the following areas of mental functioning (see 112.00F):

1. Understand, remember, or apply information (see 112.00E1).

2. Interact with others (see 112.00E2).

3. Concentrate, persist, or maintain pace (see 112.00E3).

4. Adapt or manage oneself (see 112.00E4).

112.08 Personality and impulse-control disorders (see 112.00B7), for children age 3 to attainment of age 18, satisfied by A and B:

A. Medical documentation of a pervasive pattern of one or more of the following:

1. Distrust and suspiciousness of others;

2. Detachment from social relationships;

3. Disregard for and violation of the rights of others;

4. Instability of interpersonal relationships;

5. Excessive emotionality and attention seeking;

6. Feelings of inadequacy;

7. Excessive need to be taken care of;

8. Preoccupation with perfectionism and orderliness; or

9. Recurrent, impulsive, aggressive behavioral outbursts.

AND

B. Extreme limitation of one, or marked limitation of two, of the following areas of mental functioning (see 112.00F):

1. Understand, remember, or apply information (see 112.00E1).

2. Interact with others (see 112.00E2).

3. Concentrate, persist, or maintain pace (see 112.00E3).

4. Adapt or manage oneself (see 112.00E4).

112.09 [Reserved]

112.10 Autism spectrum disorder (see 112.00B8), for children age 3 to attainment of age 18), satisfied by A and B:

A. Medical documentation of both of the following:

1. Qualitative deficits in verbal communication, nonverbal communication, and social interaction; and

2. Significantly restricted, repetitive patterns of behavior, interests, or activities.

AND

B. Extreme limitation of one, or marked limitation of two, of the following areas of mental functioning (see 112.00F):

1. Understand, remember, or apply information (see 112.00E1).

2. Interact with others (see 112.00E2).

3. Concentrate, persist, or maintain pace (see 112.00E3).

4. Adapt or manage oneself (see 112.00E4).

112.11 Neurodevelopmental disorders (see 112.00B9), for children age 3 to attainment of age 18, satisfied by A and B:

A. Medical documentation of the requirements of paragraph 1, 2, or 3:

1. One or both of the following:

a. Frequent distractibility, difficulty sustaining attention, and difficulty organizing tasks; or

b. Hyperactive and impulsive behavior (for example, difficulty remaining seated, talking excessively, difficulty waiting, appearing restless, or behaving as if being "driven by a motor").

2. Significant difficulties learning and using academic skills; or

3. Recurrent motor movement or vocalization.

AND

B. Extreme limitation of one, or marked limitation of two, of the following areas of mental functioning (see 112.00F):

1. Understand, remember, or apply information (see 112.00E1).

2. Interact with others (see 112.00E2).

3. Concentrate, persist, or maintain pace (see 112.00E3).

4. Adapt or manage oneself (see 112.00E4).

112.12 [Reserved]

112.13 Eating disorders (see 112.00B10), for children age 3 to attainment of age 18, satisfied by A and B:

A. Medical documentation of a persistent alteration in eating or eating-related behavior that results in a change in consumption or absorption of food and that significantly impairs physical or psychological health.

AND

B. Extreme limitation of one, or marked limitation of two, of the following areas of mental functioning (see 112.00F):

1. Understand, remember, or apply information (see 112.00E1).

2. Interact with others (see 112.00E2).

3. Concentrate, persist, or maintain pace (see 112.00E3).

4. Adapt or manage oneself (see 112.00E4).

112.14 Developmental disorders in infants and toddlers (see 112.00B11, 112.00I), satisfied by A and B:

A. Medical documentation of one or both of the following:

1. A delay or deficit in the development of age-appropriate skills; or

2. A loss of previously acquired skills.

AND

B. Extreme limitation of one, or marked limitation of two, of the following developmental abilities (see 112.00F):

1. Plan and control motor movement (see 112.00I4b(i)).

2. Learn and remember (see 112.00I4b(ii)).

3. Interact with others (see 112.00I4b(iii)).

4. Regulate physiological functions, attention, emotion, and behavior (see 112.00I4b(iv)).

112.15 Trauma- and stressor-related disorders (see 112.00B11), for children age 3 to attainment of age 18, satisfied by A and B, or A and C:

A. Medical documentation of the requirements of paragraph 1 or 2:

1. Posttraumatic stress disorder, characterized by all of the following:

a. Exposure to actual or threatened death, serious injury, or violence;

b. Subsequent involuntary re-experiencing of the traumatic event (for example, intrusive memories, dreams, or flashbacks);

c. Avoidance of external reminders of the event;

d. Disturbance in mood and behavior (for example, developmental regression, socially withdrawn behavior); and

e. Increases in arousal and reactivity (for example, exaggerated startle response, sleep disturbance).

2. Reactive attachment disorder, characterized by two or all of the following:

a. Rarely seeks comfort when distressed;

b. Rarely responds to comfort when distressed; or

c. Episodes of unexplained emotional distress.

AND

B. Extreme limitation of one, or marked limitation of two, of the following areas of mental functioning (see 112.00F):

1. Understand, remember, or apply information (see 112.00E1).

2. Interact with others (see 112.00E2).

3. Concentrate, persist, or maintain pace (see 112.00E3).

4. Adapt or manage oneself (see 112.00E4).

OR

C. Your mental disorder in this listing category is "serious and persistent;" that is, you have a medically documented history of the existence of the disorder over a period of at least 2 years, and there is evidence of both:

1. Medical treatment, mental health therapy, psychosocial support(s), or a highly structured setting(s) that is ongoing and that diminishes the symptoms and signs of your mental disorder (see 112.00G2b); and

2. Marginal adjustment, that is, you have minimal capacity to adapt to changes in your environment or to demands that are not already part of your daily life (see 112.00G2c).

113.00 CANCER (MALIGNANT NEOPLASTIC DISEASES)

A. What impairments do these listings cover? We use these listings to evaluate all cancers (malignant neoplastic diseases) except certain cancers associated with human immunodeficiency virus (HIV) infection. We use the criteria in 114.11B to evaluate primary central nervous system lymphoma, 114.11C to evaluate primary effusion lymphoma, and 114.11E to evaluate pulmonary Kaposi sarcoma if you also have HIV infection. We evaluate all other cancers associated with HIV infection, for example, Hodgkin lymphoma or nonpulmonary Kaposi sarcoma, under this body system or under 114.11F–I in the immune system disorders body system.

B. What do we consider when we evaluate cancer under these listings? We will consider factors including:

1. Origin of the cancer.

2. Extent of involvement.

3. Duration, frequency, and response to anticancer therapy.

4. Effects of any post-therapeutic residuals.

C. How do we apply these listings? We apply the criteria in a specific listing to a cancer originating from that specific site.

D. What evidence do we need?

1. We need medical evidence that specifies the type, extent, and site of the primary, recurrent, or metastatic lesion. When the primary site cannot be identified, we will use evidence documenting the site(s) of metastasis to evaluate the impairment under 13.27 in part A.

2. For operative procedures, including a biopsy or a needle aspiration, we generally need a copy of both the:

a. Operative note, and

b. Pathology report.

3. When we cannot get these documents, we will accept the summary of hospitalization(s) or other medical reports. This evidence should include details of the findings at surgery and, whenever appropriate, the pathological findings.

4. In some situations, we may also need evidence about recurrence, persistence, or progression of the cancer, the response to therapy, and any significant residuals. (See 113.00G.)

E. When do we need longitudinal evidence?

1. Cancer with distant metastases. Most cancer of childhood consists of a local lesion with metastases to regional lymph nodes and, less often, distant metastases. We generally do not need longitudinal evidence for cancer that has metastasized beyond the regional lymph nodes because this cancer usually meets the requirements of a listing. Exceptions are for cancer with distant metastases that we expect to respond to anticancer therapy. For these exceptions, we usually need a longitudinal record of 3 months after therapy starts to determine whether the therapy achieved its intended effect, and whether this effect is likely to persist.

2. Other cancers. When there are no distant metastases, many of the listings require that we consider your response to initial anticancer therapy; that is, the initial planned treatment regimen. This therapy may consist of a single modality or a combination of modalities; that is, multimodal therapy (see 113.00I3).

3. Types of treatment.

a. Whenever the initial planned therapy is a single modality, enough time must pass to allow a determination about whether the therapy will achieve its intended effect. If the treatment fails, the failure often happens within 6 months after treatment starts, and there will often be a change in the treatment regimen.

b. Whenever the initial planned therapy is multimodal, we usually cannot make a determination about the effectiveness of the therapy until we can determine the effects of all the planned modalities. In some cases, we may need to defer adjudication until we can assess the effectiveness of therapy. However, we do not need to defer adjudication to determine whether the therapy will achieve its intended effect if we can make a fully favorable determination or decision based on the length and effects of therapy, or the residuals of the cancer or therapy (see 113.00G).

F. How do we evaluate impairments that do not meet one of the cancer listings?

1. These listings are only examples of cancers that we consider severe enough to result in marked and severe functional limitations. If your severe impairment(s) does not meet the criteria of any of these listings, we must also consider whether you have an impairment(s) that meets the criteria of a listing in another body system.

2. If you have a severe medically determinable impairment(s) that does not meet a listing, we will determine whether your impairment(s) medically equals a listing. (See §§ 404.1526 and 416.926 of this chapter.) If your impairment(s) does not meet or medically equal a listing, we will also consider whether you have an impairment(s) that functionally equals the listings. (See § 416.926a of this chapter.) We use the rules in § 416.994a of this chapter when we decide whether you continue to be disabled.

G. How do we consider the effects of anticancer therapy?

1. How we consider the effects of anticancer therapy under the listings. In many cases, cancers meet listing criteria only if the therapy is not effective and the cancer persists, progresses, or recurs. However, as explained in the following paragraphs, we will not delay adjudication if we can make a fully favorable determination or decision based on the evidence in the case record.

2. Effects can vary widely.

a. We consider each case on an individual basis because the therapy and its toxicity may vary widely. We will request a specific description of the therapy, including these items:

i. Drugs given.

ii. Dosage.

iii. Frequency of drug administration.

iv. Plans for continued drug administration.

v. Extent of surgery.

vi. Schedule and fields of radiation therapy.

b. We will also request a description of the complications or adverse effects of therapy, such as the following:

i. Continuing gastrointestinal symptoms.

ii. Persistent weakness.

iii. Neurological complications.

iv. Cardiovascular complications.

v. Reactive mental disorders.

3. Effects of therapy may change. The severity of the adverse effects of anticancer therapy may change during treatment; therefore, enough time must pass to allow us to evaluate the therapy's effect. The residual effects of treatment are temporary in most instances; however, on occasion, the effects may be disabling for a consecutive period of at least 12 months. In some situations, very serious adverse effects may interrupt and prolong multimodal anticancer therapy for a continuous period of almost 12 months. In these situations, we may determine there is an expectation that your impairment will preclude you from engaging in any age-appropriate activities for at least 12 months.

4. When the initial anticancer therapy is effective. We evaluate any post-therapeutic residual impairment(s) not included in these listings under the criteria for the affected body system. We must consider any complications of therapy. When the residual impairment(s) does not meet a listing, we must consider whether it medically equals a listing, or, as appropriate, functionally equals the listings.

H. How long do we consider your impairment to be disabling?

1. In some listings, we specify that we will consider your impairment to be disabling until a particular point in time (for example, until at least 12 months from the date of transplantation). We may consider your impairment to be disabling beyond this point when the medical and other evidence justifies it.

2. When a listing does not contain such a specification, we will consider an impairment(s) that meets or medically equals a listing in this body system to be disabling until at least 3 years after onset of complete remission. When the impairment(s) has been in complete remission for at least 3 years, that is, the original tumor or a recurrence (or relapse) and any metastases have not been evident for at least 3 years, the impairment(s) will no longer meet or medically equal the criteria of a listing in this body system.

3. Following the appropriate period, we will consider any residuals, including residuals of the cancer or therapy (see 113.00G), in determining whether you are disabled. If you have a recurrence or relapse of your cancer, your impairment may meet or medically equal one of the listings in this body system again.

I. What do we mean by the following terms?

1. Anticancer therapy means surgery, radiation, chemotherapy, hormones, immunotherapy, or bone marrow or stem cell transplantation. When we refer to surgery as an anticancer treatment, we mean surgical excision for treatment, not for diagnostic purposes.

2. Metastases means the spread of cancer cells by blood, lymph, or other body fluid. This term does not include the spread of cancer cells by direct extension of the cancer to other tissues or organs.

3. Multimodal therapy means anticancer therapy that is a combination of at least two types of treatment given in close proximity as a unified whole and usually planned before any treatment has begun. There are three types of treatment modalities: Surgery, radiation, and systemic drug therapy (chemotherapy, hormone therapy, and immunotherapy or biological modifier therapy). Examples of multimodal therapy include:

a. Surgery followed by chemotherapy or radiation.

b. Chemotherapy followed by surgery.

c. Chemotherapy and concurrent radiation.

4. Persistent means the planned initial anticancer therapy failed to achieve a complete remission of your cancer; that is, your cancer is evident, even if smaller, after the therapy has ended.

5. Progressive means the cancer becomes more extensive after treatment; that is, there is evidence that your cancer is growing after you have completed at least half of your planned initial anticancer therapy.

6. Recurrent or relapse means the cancer that was in complete remission or entirely removed by surgery has returned.

J. Can we establish the existence of a disabling impairment prior to the date of the evidence that shows the cancer satisfies the criteria of a listing? Yes. We will consider factors such as:

1. The type of cancer and its location.

2. The extent of involvement when the cancer was first demonstrated.

3. Your symptoms.

K. How do we evaluate specific cancers?

1. Lymphoma.

a. We provide criteria for evaluating lymphomas that are disseminated or have not responded to anticancer therapy in 113.05.

b. Lymphoblastic lymphoma is treated with leukemia-based protocols, so we evaluate this type of cancer under 113.06.

2. Leukemia.

a. Acute leukemia. The initial diagnosis of acute leukemia, including the accelerated or blast phase of chronic myelogenous (granulocytic) leukemia, is based on definitive bone marrow examination. Additional diagnostic information is based on chromosomal analysis, cytochemical and surface marker studies on the abnormal cells, or other methods consistent with the prevailing state of medical knowledge and clinical practice. Recurrent disease must be documented by peripheral blood, bone marrow, or cerebrospinal fluid examination, or by testicular biopsy. The initial and follow-up pathology reports should be included.

b. Chronic myelogenous leukemia (CML). We need a diagnosis of CML based on documented granulocytosis, including immature forms such as differentiated or undifferentiated myelocytes and myeloblasts, and a chromosomal analysis that demonstrates the Philadelphia chromosome. In the absence of a chromosomal analysis, or if the Philadelphia chromosome is not present, the diagnosis may be made by other methods consistent with the prevailing state of medical knowledge and clinical practice. The requirement for CML in the accelerated or blast phase is met in 113.06B if laboratory findings show the proportion of blast (immature) cells in the peripheral blood or bone marrow is 10 percent or greater.

c. Juvenile chronic myelogenous leukemia (JCML). JCML is a rare, Philadelphia-chromosome-negative childhood leukemia that is aggressive and clinically similar to acute myelogenous leukemia. We evaluate JCML under 113.06A.

d. Elevated white cell count. In cases of chronic leukemia (either myelogenous or lymphocytic), an elevated white cell count, in itself, is not a factor in determining the severity of the impairment.

3. Malignant solid tumors. The tumors we consider under 113.03 include the histiocytosis syndromes except for solitary eosinophilic granuloma. We do not evaluate thyroid cancer (see 113.09), retinoblastomas (see 113.12), primary central nervous system (CNS) cancers (see 113.13), neuroblastomas (see 113.21), or malignant melanoma (see 113.29) under this listing.

4. Primary central nervous system (CNS) cancers. We use the criteria in 113.13 to evaluate cancers that originate within the CNS (that is, brain and spinal cord cancers).

a. The CNS cancers listed in 113.13A are highly malignant and respond poorly to treatment, and therefore we do not require additional criteria to evaluate them. We do not list pituitary gland cancer (for example, pituitary gland carcinoma) in 113.13A, although this CNS cancer is highly malignant and responds poorly to treatment. We evaluate pituitary gland cancer under 113.13A and do not require additional criteria to evaluate it.

b. We consider a CNS tumor to be malignant if it is classified as Grade II, Grade III, or Grade IV under the World Health Organization (WHO) classification of tumors of the CNS (WHO Classification of Tumours of the Central Nervous System, 2007).

c. We evaluate benign (for example, WHO Grade I) CNS tumors under 111.05. We evaluate metastasized CNS cancers from non–CNS sites under the primary cancers (see 113.00C). We evaluate any complications of CNS cancers, such as resultant neurological or psychological impairments, under the criteria for the affected body system.

5. Retinoblastoma. The treatment for bilateral retinoblastoma usually results in a visual impairment. We will evaluate any resulting visual impairment under 102.02.

6. Melanoma. We evaluate malignant melanoma that affects the skin (cutaneous melanoma), eye (ocular melanoma), or mucosal membranes (mucosal melanoma) under 113.29. We evaluate melanoma that is not malignant that affects the skin (benign melanocytic tumor) under the listings in 108.00 or other affected body systems.

L. How do we evaluate cancer treated by bone marrow or stem cell transplantation, including transplantation using stem cells from umbilical cord blood? Bone marrow or stem cell transplantation is performed for a variety of cancers. We require the transplantation to occur before we evaluate it under these listings. We do not need to restrict our determination of the onset of disability to the date of transplantation (113.05 or 113.06). We may be able to establish an earlier onset date of disability due to your transplantation if the evidence in your case record supports such a finding.

1. Acute leukemia (including all types of lymphoblastic lymphomas and JCML) or accelerated or blast phase of CML. If you undergo bone marrow or stem cell transplantation for any of these disorders, we will consider you to be disabled until at least 24 months from the date of diagnosis or relapse, or at least 12 months from the date of transplantation, whichever is later.

2. Lymphoma or chronic phase of CML. If you undergo bone marrow or stem cell transplantation for any of these disorders, we will consider you to be disabled until at least 12 months from the date of transplantation.

3. Evaluating disability after the appropriate time period has elapsed. We consider any residual impairment(s), such as complications arising from:

a. Graft-versus-host (GVH) disease.

b. Immunosuppressant therapy, such as frequent infections.

c. Significant deterioration of other organ systems.

113.01 Category of Impairments, Cancer (Malignant Neoplastic Diseases)

113.01 Category of Impairments, Malignant Neoplastic Diseases

113.03 Malignant solid tumors. Consider under a disability:

A. For 24 months from the date of initial diagnosis. Thereafter, evaluate any residual impairment(s) under the criteria for the affected body system.

OR

B. For 24 months from the date of recurrence of active disease. Thereafter, evaluate any residual impairment(s) under the criteria for the affected body system.

113.05 Lymphoma (excluding all types of lymphoblastic lymphomas—113.06). (See 113.00K1.)

A. Non–Hodgkin lymphoma (including Burkitt's and anaplastic large cell), with either 1 or 2:

1. Bone marrow, brain, spinal cord, liver, or lung involvement at initial diagnosis. Consider under a disability for 24 months from the date of diagnosis. Thereafter, evaluate under 113.05A2, or any residual impairments(s) under the criteria for the affected body system.

2. Persistent or recurrent following initial anticancer therapy.

OR

B. Hodgkin lymphoma, with either 1 or 2:

1. Bone marrow, brain, spinal cord, liver, or lung involvement at initial diagnosis. Consider under a disability for 24 months from the date of diagnosis. Thereafter, evaluate under 113.05B2, or any residual impairment(s) under the criteria for the affected body system.

2. Persistent or recurrent following initial anticancer therapy.

OR

C. With bone marrow or stem cell transplantation. Consider under a disability until at least 12 months from the date of transplantation. Thereafter, evaluate any residual impairment(s) under the criteria of the affected body system.

OR

D. Mantle cell lymphoma.

113.06 Leukemia. (See 113.00K2.)

A. Acute leukemia (including all types of lymphoblastic lymphomas and juvenile chronic myelogenous leukemia (JCML)). Consider under a disability until at least 24 months from the date of diagnosis or relapse, or at least 12 months from the date of bone marrow or stem cell transplantation, whichever is later. Thereafter, evaluate any residual impairment(s) under the criteria for the affected body system.

OR

B. Chronic myelogenous leukemia (except JCML), as described in 1 or 2:

1. Accelerated or blast phase (see 113.00K2b). Consider under a disability until at least 24 months from the date of diagnosis or relapse, or at least 12 months from the date of bone marrow or stem cell transplantation, whichever is later. Thereafter, evaluate any residual impairment(s) under the criteria for the affected body system.

2. Chronic phase, as described in a or b:

a. Consider under a disability until at least 12 months from the date of bone marrow or stem cell transplantation. Thereafter, evaluate any residual impairment(s) under the criteria for the affected body system.

b. Progressive disease following initial antineoplastic therapy.

113.09 Thyroid gland.

A. Anaplastic (undifferentiated) carcinoma.

OR

B. Carcinoma with metastases beyond the regional lymph nodes progressive despite radioactive iodine therapy.

OR

C. Medullary carcinoma with metastases beyond the regional lymph nodes.

113.12 Retinoblastoma.

A. With extension beyond the orbit.

OR

B. Persistent or recurrent following initial anticancer therapy.

OR

C. With regional or distant metastases.

113.13 Nervous system. (See 113.00K4.) Primary central nervous system (CNS; that is, brain and spinal cord) cancers, as described in A, B, or C:

A. Glioblastoma multiforme, ependymoblastoma, and diffuse intrinsic brain stem gliomas (see 113.00K4a).

B. Any Grade III or Grade IV CNS cancer (see 113.00K4b), including astrocytomas, sarcomas, and medulloblastoma and other primitive neuroectodermal tumors (PNETs).

C. Any primary CNS cancer, as described in 1 or 2:

1. Metastatic.

2. Progressive or recurrent following initial anticancer therapy.

113.21 Neuroblastoma.

A. With extension across the midline.

OR

B. With distant metastases.

OR

C. Recurrent.

OR

D. With onset at age 1 year or older.

113.29 Malignant melanoma (including skin, ocular, or mucosal melanomas), as described in either A, B, or C:

A. Recurrent (except an additional primary melanoma at a different site, which is not considered to be recurrent disease) following either 1 or 2:

1. Wide excision (skin melanoma).

2. Enucleation of the eye (ocular melanoma).

OR

B. With metastases as described in 1, 2, or 3:

1. Metastases to one or more clinically apparent nodes; that is, nodes that are detected by imaging studies (excluding lymphoscintigraphy) or by clinical evaluation (palpable).

2. If the nodes are not clinically apparent, with metastases to four or more nodes.

3. Metastases to adjacent skin (satellite lesions) or distant sites (for example, liver, lung, or brain).

OR

C. Mucosal melanoma.

114.00 Immune System Disorders

A. What disorders do we evaluate under the immune system disorders listings?

1. We evaluate immune system disorders that cause dysfunction in one or more components of your immune system.

a. The dysfunction may be due to problems in antibody production, impaired cell-mediated immunity, a combined type of antibody/cellular deficiency, impaired phagocytosis, or complement deficiency.

b. Immune system disorders may result in recurrent and unusual infections, or inflammation and dysfunction of the body's own tissues. Immune system disorders can cause a deficit in a single organ or body system that results in extreme (that is, very serious) loss of function. They can also cause lesser degrees of limitations in two or more organs or body systems, and when associated with symptoms or signs, such as severe fatigue, fever, malaise, diffuse musculoskeletal pain, or involuntary weight loss, can also result in extreme limitation. In children, immune system disorders or their treatment may also affect growth, development, and the performance of age-appropriate activities.

c. We organize the discussions of immune system disorders in three categories: Autoimmune disorders; Immune deficiency disorders, excluding human immunodeficiency virus (HIV) infection; and HIV infection.

2. Autoimmune disorders (114.00D). Autoimmune disorders are caused by dysfunctional immune responses directed against the body's own tissues, resulting in chronic, multisystem impairments that differ in clinical manifestations, course, and outcome. They are sometimes referred to as rheumatic diseases, connective tissue disorders, or collagen vascular disorders. Some of the features of autoimmune disorders in children differ from the features of the same disorders in adults. The impact of the disorders or their treatment on physical, psychological, and developmental growth of pre-pubertal children may be considerable, and often differs from that of post-pubertal adolescents or adults.

3. Immune deficiency disorders, excluding HIV infection (114.00E). Immune deficiency disorders are characterized by recurrent or unusual infections that respond poorly to treatment, and are often associated with complications affecting other parts of the body. Immune deficiency disorders are classified as either primary (congenital) or acquired. Children with immune deficiency disorders also have an increased risk of malignancies and of having autoimmune disorders.

4. Human immunodeficiency virus (HIV) infection (114.00F). HIV infection may be characterized by increased susceptibility to common infections as well as opportunistic infections, cancers, or other conditions listed in 114.11.

B. What information do we need to show that you have an immune system disorder?

Generally, we need your medical history, a report(s) of a physical examination, a report(s) of laboratory findings, and in some instances, appropriate medically acceptable imaging or tissue biopsy reports to show that you have an immune system disorder. Therefore, we will make every reasonable effort to obtain your medical history, medical findings, and results of laboratory tests. We explain the information we need in more detail in the sections below.

C. Definitions

1. Appropriate medically acceptable imaging includes, but is not limited to, angiography, x-ray imaging, computerized axial tomography (CAT scan) or magnetic resonance imaging (MRI), with or without contrast material, myelography, and radionuclear bone scans. "Appropriate" means that the technique used is the proper one to support the evaluation and diagnosis of the impairment.

2. Constitutional symptoms or signs, as used in these listings, means severe fatigue, fever, malaise, or involuntary weight loss. Severe fatigue means a fre-

quent sense of exhaustion that results in significantly reduced physical activity or mental function. Malaise means frequent feelings of illness, bodily discomfort, or lack of well-being that result in significantly reduced physical activity or mental function.

3. Disseminated means that a condition is spread over a considerable area. The type and extent of the spread will depend on your specific disease.

4. Dysfunction means that one or more of the body regulatory mechanisms are impaired, causing either an excess or deficiency of immunocompetent cells or their products.

5. Extra-articular means "other than the joints"; for example, an organ(s) such as the heart, lungs, kidneys, or skin.

6. Inability to ambulate effectively has the same meaning as in 101.00B2b.

7. Inability to perform fine and gross movements effectively has the same meaning as in 101.00B2c.

8. Major peripheral joints has the same meaning as in 101.00F.

9. Persistent means that a sign(s) or symptom(s) has continued over time. The precise meaning will depend on the specific immune system disorder, the usual course of the disorder, and the other circumstances of your clinical course.

10. Recurrent means that a condition that previously responded adequately to an appropriate course of treatment returns after a period of remission or regression. The precise meaning, such as the extent of response or remission and the time periods involved, will depend on the specific disease or condition you have, the body system affected, the usual course of the disorder and its treatment, and the other facts of your particular case.

11. Resistant to treatment means that a condition did not respond adequately to an appropriate course of treatment. Whether a response is adequate or a course of treatment is appropriate will depend on the specific disease or condition you have, the body system affected, the usual course of the disorder and its treatment, and the other facts of your particular case.

12. Severe means medical severity as used by the medical community. The term does not have the same meaning as it does when we use it in connection with a finding at the second step of the sequential evaluation process in § 416.924.

D. How do we document and evaluate the listed autoimmune disorders?

1. Systemic lupus erythematosus (114.02).

a. General. Systemic lupus erythematosus (SLE) is a chronic inflammatory disease that can affect any organ or body system. It is frequently, but not always, accompanied by constitutional symptoms or signs (severe fatigue, fever, malaise, involuntary weight loss). Major organ or body system involvement can include: Respiratory (pleuritis, pneumonitis), cardiovascular (endocarditis, myocarditis, pericarditis, vasculitis), renal (glomerulonephritis), hematologic (anemia, leukopenia, thrombocytopenia), skin (photosensitivity), neurologic (seizures), mental (anxiety, fluctuating cognition ("lupus fog"), mood disorders, organic brain syndrome, psychosis), or immune system disorders (inflammatory arthritis). Immunologically, there is an array of circulating serum auto-antibodies and pro- and anti-coagulant proteins that may occur in a highly variable pattern.

b. Documentation of SLE. Generally, but not always, the medical evidence will show that your SLE satisfies the criteria in the current "Criteria for the Classification of Systemic Lupus Erythematosus" by the American College of Rheumatology found in the most recent edition of the Primer on the Rheumatic Diseases published by the Arthritis Foundation.

2. Systemic vasculitis (114.03).

a. General.

(i) Vasculitis is an inflammation of blood vessels. It may occur acutely in association with adverse drug reactions, certain chronic infections, and occasionally, malignancies. More often, it is chronic and the cause is unknown. Symptoms vary depending on which blood vessels are involved. Systemic vasculitis may also be associated with other autoimmune disorders; for example, SLE or dermatomyositis.

(ii) Children can develop the vasculitis of Kawasaki disease, of which the most serious manifestation is formation of coronary artery aneurysms and related complications. We evaluate heart problems related to Kawasaki disease under the criteria in the cardiovascular listings (104.00). Children can also develop the vasculitis of anaphylactoid purpura (Henoch–Schoenlein purpura), which may cause intestinal and renal disorders. We evaluate intestinal and renal disorders related to vasculitis of anaphylactoid purpura under the criteria in the digestive (105.00) or genitourinary (106.00) listings. Other clinical patterns include, but are not limited to, polyarteritis nodosa, Takayasu's arteritis (aortic arch arteritis), and Wegener's granulomatosis.

b. Documentation of systemic vasculitis. Angiography or tissue biopsy confirms a diagnosis of systemic vasculitis when the disease is suspected clinically. When you have had angiography or tissue biopsy for systemic vasculitis, we will make every reasonable effort to obtain reports of the results of that procedure. However, we will not purchase angiography or tissue biopsy.

3. Systemic sclerosis (scleroderma) (114.04).

a. General. Systemic sclerosis (scleroderma) constitutes a spectrum of disease in which thickening of the skin is the clinical hallmark. Raynaud's phenomenon, often medically severe and progressive, is present frequently and may be the peripheral manifestation of a vasospastic abnormality in the heart, lungs, and kidneys. The CREST syndrome (calcinosis, Raynaud's phenomenon, esophageal dysmotility, sclerodactyly, and telangiectasia) is a variant that may slowly progress over years to the generalized process, systemic sclerosis.

b. Diffuse cutaneous systemic sclerosis. In diffuse cutaneous systemic sclerosis (also known as diffuse scleroderma), major organ or systemic involvement can include the gastrointestinal tract, lungs, heart, kidneys, and muscle in addition to skin or blood vessels. Although arthritis can occur, joint dysfunction results primarily from soft tissue/cutaneous thickening, fibrosis, and contractures.

c. Localized scleroderma (linear scleroderma and morphea).

(i) Localized scleroderma (linear scleroderma and morphea) is more common in children than systemic scleroderma. To assess the severity of the impairment, we need a description of the extent of involvement of linear scleroderma and the location of the lesions. For example, linear scleroderma involving the arm but not crossing any joints is not as functionally limiting as sclerodactyly (scleroderma localized to the fingers). Linear scleroderma of a lower extremity involving skin thickening and atrophy of underlying muscle or bone can result in contractures and leg length discrepancy. In such cases, we may evaluate your impairment under the musculoskeletal listings (101.00).

(ii) When there is isolated morphea of the face causing facial disfigurement from unilateral hypoplasia of the mandible, maxilla, zygoma, or orbit, adjudication may be more appropriate under the criteria in the affected body system, such as special senses and speech (102.00) or mental disorders (112.00).

(iii) Chronic variants of these syndromes include disseminated morphea, Shulman's disease (diffuse fasciitis with eosinophilia), and eosinophilia-myalgia syndrome (often associated with toxins such as toxic oil or contaminated tryptophan), all of which can impose medically severe musculoskeletal dysfunction and may also lead to restrictive pulmonary disease. We evaluate these variants of the disease under the criteria in the musculoskeletal listings (101.00) or respiratory system listings (103.00).

d. Documentation of systemic sclerosis (scleroderma). Documentation involves differentiating the clinical features of systemic sclerosis (scleroderma) from other autoimmune disorders. However, there may be an overlap.

4. Polymyositis and dermatomyositis (114.05).

a. General.

(i) Polymyositis and dermatomyositis are related disorders that are characterized by an inflammatory process in striated muscle, occurring alone or in association with other autoimmune disorders. The most common manifestations are symmetric weakness, and less frequently, pain and tenderness of the proximal limb-girdle (shoulder or pelvic) musculature. There may also be involvement of the cervical, cricopharyngeal, esophageal, intercostal, and diaphragmatic muscles.

(ii) Polymyositis occurs rarely in children; the more common presentation in children is dermatomyositis with symmetric proximal muscle weakness and characteristic skin findings. The clinical course of dermatomyositis can be more severe when it is accompanied by systemic vasculitis rather than just localized to striated muscle. Late in the disease, some children with dermatomyositis develop calcinosis of the skin and subcutaneous tissues, muscles, and joints. We evaluate the involvement of other organs/body systems under the criteria for the listings in the affected body system.

b. Documentation of polymyositis and dermatomyositis. Generally, but not always, polymyositis is associated with elevated serum muscle enzymes (creatine phosphokinase (CPK), aminotransferases, and aldolase), and characteristic abnormalities on electromyography and muscle biopsy. In children, the diagnosis of dermatomyositis is supported largely by medical history, findings on physical examination that include the characteristic skin findings, and elevated serum muscle enzymes. Muscle inflammation or vasculitis depicted on MRI is additional evidence supporting the diagnosis of childhood dermatomyositis. When you have had electromyography, muscle biopsy, or MRI for polymyositis or dermatomyositis, we will make every reasonable effort to obtain reports of the results of that procedure. However, we will not purchase electromyography, muscle biopsy, or MRI.

c. Additional information about how we evaluate polymyositis and dermatomyositis under the listings.

(i) In newborn and younger infants (birth to attainment of age 1), we consider muscle weakness that affects motor skills, such as head control, reaching, grasping, taking solids, or self-feeding, under 114.05A. In older infants and toddlers (age 1 to attainment of age 3), we also consider muscle weakness affecting your ability to roll over, sit, crawl, or walk under 114.05A.

(ii) If you are of preschool age through adolescence (age 3 to attainment of age 18), weakness of your pelvic girdle muscles that results in your inability to rise independently from a squatting or sitting position or to climb stairs may be an indication that you are unable to ambulate effectively. Weakness of your shoulder girdle muscles may result in your inability to perform lifting, carrying, and reaching overhead, and also may seriously affect your ability to perform activities requiring fine movements. We evaluate these limitations under 114.05A.

5. Undifferentiated and mixed connective tissue disease (114.06).

a. General. This listing includes syndromes with clinical and immunologic features of several autoimmune disorders, but which do not satisfy the criteria for any of the specific disorders described. For example, you may have clinical features of SLE and systemic vasculitis, and the serologic (blood test) findings of rheumatoid arthritis. The most common pattern of undifferentiated autoimmune disorders in children is mixed connective tissue disease (MCTD).

b. Documentation of undifferentiated and mixed connective tissue disease. Undifferentiated connective tissue disease is diagnosed when clinical features and serologic (blood test) findings, such as rheumatoid factor or antinuclear antibody (consistent with an autoimmune disorder) are present but do not satisfy the criteria for a specific disease. Children with MCTD have laboratory findings of extremely high antibody titers to extractable nuclear antigen (ENA) or ribonucleoprotein (RNP) without high titers of anti-dsDNA or anti-SM antibodies. There are often clinical findings suggestive of SLE or childhood dermatomyositis. Many children later develop features of scleroderma.

6. Inflammatory arthritis (114.09).

a. General. The spectrum of inflammatory arthritis includes a vast array of disorders that differ in cause, course, and outcome. Clinically, inflammation of major peripheral joints may be the dominant manifestation causing difficulties with ambulation or fine and gross movements; there may be joint pain, swelling, and tenderness. The arthritis may affect other joints, or cause less limitation in ambulation or the performance of fine and gross movements. However, in combination with extra-articular features, including constitutional symptoms or signs (severe fatigue, fever, malaise, involuntary weight loss), inflammatory arthritis may result in an extreme limitation. You may also have impaired growth as a result of the inflammatory arthritis because of its effects on the immature skeleton, open epiphyses, and young cartilage and bone. We evaluate any associated growth impairment under the criteria in 100.00.

b. Inflammatory arthritis involving the axial spine (spondyloarthropathy). In children, inflammatory arthritis involving the axial spine may be associated with disorders such as:

(i) Reactive arthropathies;

(ii) Juvenile ankylosing spondylitis;

(iii) Psoriatic arthritis;

(iv) SEA syndrome (seronegative enthesopathy arthropathy syndrome);

(v) Behçet's disease; and

(vi) Inflammatory bowel disease.

c. Inflammatory arthritis involving the peripheral joints. In children, inflammatory arthritis involving peripheral joints may be associated with disorders such as:

(i) Juvenile rheumatoid arthritis;

(ii) Sjögren's syndrome;

(iii) Psoriatic arthritis;

(iv) Crystal deposition disorders (gout and pseudogout);

(v) Lyme disease; and

(vi) Inflammatory bowel disease.

d. Documentation of inflammatory arthritis. Generally, but not always, the diagnosis of inflammatory arthritis is based on the clinical features and serologic findings described in the most recent edition of the Primer on the Rheumatic Diseases published by the Arthritis Foundation.

e. How we evaluate inflammatory arthritis under the listings.

(i) Listing-level severity in 114.09A and 114.09C1 is shown by an impairment that results in an "extreme" (very serious) limitation. In 114.09A, the criterion is satisfied with persistent inflammation or deformity in one major peripheral weight-bearing joint resulting in the inability to ambulate effectively (as defined in 114.00C6) or one major peripheral joint in each upper extremity resulting in the inability to perform fine and gross movements effectively (as defined in 114.00C7). In 114.09C1, if you have the required ankylosis (fixation) of your cervical or dorsolumbar spine, we will find that you have an extreme limitation in your ability to see in front of you, above you, and to the side. Therefore, inability to ambulate effectively is implicit in 114.09C1, even though you might not require bilateral upper limb assistance.

(ii) Listing-level severity is shown in 114.09B and 114.09C2 by inflammatory arthritis that involves various combinations of complications of one or more major peripheral joints or involves other joints, such as inflammation or deformity, extra-articular features, repeated manifestations, and constitutional symptoms and signs. Extra-articular impairments may also meet listings in other body systems.

(iii) Extra-articular features of inflammatory arthritis may involve any body system; for example: Musculoskeletal (heel enthesopathy), ophthalmologic (iridocyclitis, keratoconjunctivitis sicca, uveitis), pulmonary (pleuritis, pulmonary fibrosis or nodules, restrictive lung disease), cardiovascular (aortic valve insufficiency, arrhythmias, coronary arteritis, myocarditis, pericarditis, Raynaud's phenomenon, systemic vasculitis), renal (amyloidosis of the kidney), hematologic (chronic anemia, thrombocytopenia), neurologic (peripheral neuropathy, radiculopathy, spinal cord or cauda equina compression with sensory and motor loss), mental (cognitive dysfunction, poor memory), and immune system (Felty's syndrome (hypersplenism with compromised immune competence)).

(iv) If both inflammation and chronic deformities are present, we evaluate your impairment under the criteria of any appropriate listing.

7. Sjögren's syndrome (114.10).

a. General.

(i) Sjögren's syndrome is an immune-mediated disorder of the exocrine glands. Involvement of the lacrimal and salivary glands is the hallmark feature, resulting in symptoms of dry eyes and dry mouth, and possible complications, such as corneal damage, blepharitis (eyelid inflammation), dysphagia (difficulty in swallowing), dental caries, and the inability to speak for extended periods of time. Involvement of the exocrine glands of the upper airways may result in persistent dry cough.

(ii) Many other organ systems may be involved, including musculoskeletal (arthritis, myositis), respiratory (interstitial fibrosis), gastrointestinal (dysmotility, dysphagia, involuntary weight loss), genitourinary (interstitial cystitis, renal tubular acidosis), skin (purpura, vasculitis,), neurologic (central nervous system disorders, cranial and peripheral neuropathies), mental (cognitive dysfunction, poor memory), and neoplastic (lymphoma). Severe fatigue and malaise are frequently reported. Sjögren's syndrome may be associated with other autoimmune disorders (for example, rheumatoid arthritis or SLE); usually the clinical features of the associated disorder predominate.

b. Documentation of Sjögren's syndrome. If you have Sjögren's syndrome, the medical evidence will generally, but not always, show that your disease satisfies the criteria in the current "Criteria for the Classification of Sjögren's Syndrome" by the American College of Rheumatology found in the most recent edition of the Primer on the Rheumatic Diseases published by the Arthritis Foundation.

E. How do we document and evaluate immune deficiency disorders, excluding HIV infection?

1. General.

a. Immune deficiency disorders can be classified as:

(i) Primary (congenital); for example, X-linked agammaglobulinemia, thymic hypoplasia (DiGeorge syndrome), severe combined immunodeficiency (SCID), chronic granulomatous disease (CGD), C1 esterase inhibitor deficiency.

(ii) Acquired; for example, medication-related.

b. Primary immune deficiency disorders are seen mainly in children. However, recent advances in the treatment of these disorders have allowed many affected children to survive well into adulthood. Occasionally, these disorders are first diagnosed in adolescence or adulthood.

2. Documentation of immune deficiency disorders. The medical evidence must include documentation of the specific type of immune deficiency. Documentation may be by laboratory evidence or by other generally acceptable methods consistent with the prevailing state of medical knowledge and clinical practice.

3. Immune deficiency disorders treated by stem cell transplantation.

a. Evaluation in the first 12 months. If you undergo stem cell transplantation for your immune deficiency disorder, we will consider you disabled until at least 12 months from the date of the transplant.

b. Evaluation after the 12–month period has elapsed. After the 12–month period has elapsed, we will consider any residuals of your immune deficiency disorder as well as any residual impairment(s) resulting from the treatment, such as complications arising from:

(i) Graft-versus-host (GVH) disease.

(ii) Immunosuppressant therapy, such as frequent infections.

(iii) Significant deterioration of other organ systems.

4. Medication-induced immune suppression. Medication effects can result in varying degrees of immune suppression, but most resolve when the medication is ceased. However, if you are prescribed medication for long-term immune suppression, such as after an organ transplant, we will evaluate:

a. The frequency and severity of infections.

b. Residuals from the organ transplant itself, after the 12–month period has elapsed.

c. Significant deterioration of other organ systems.

F. How do we document and evaluate HIV infection? Any child with HIV infection, including one with a diagnosis of acquired immune deficiency syndrome (AIDS), may be found disabled under 114.11 if his or her impairment meets the criteria in that listing or is medically equivalent to the criteria in that listing.

1. Documentation of HIV infection.

a. Definitive documentation of HIV infection. We may document a diagnosis of HIV infection by positive findings on one or more of the following definitive laboratory tests:

(i) HIV antibody screening test (for example, enzyme immunoassay, or EIA), confirmed by a supplemental HIV antibody test such as the Western blot (immunoblot) or immunofluorescence assay, for any child age 18 months or older.

(ii) HIV nucleic acid (DNA or RNA) detection test (for example, polymerase chain reaction, or PCR).

(iii) HIV p24 antigen (p24Ag) test, for any child age 1 month or older.

(iv) Isolation of HIV in viral culture.

(v) Other tests that are highly specific for detection of HIV and that are consistent with the prevailing state of medical knowledge.

b. We will make every reasonable effort to obtain the results of your laboratory testing. Pursuant to § 416.919f of this chapter, we will purchase examinations or tests necessary to make a determination in your claim if no other acceptable documentation exists.

c. Other acceptable documentation of HIV infection. We may also document HIV infection without definitive laboratory evidence.

(i) We will accept a persuasive report from a physician that a positive diagnosis of your HIV infection was confirmed by an appropriate laboratory test(s), such as those described in 114.00F1a. To be persuasive, this report must state that you had the appropriate definitive laboratory test(s) for diagnosing your HIV infection and provide the results. The report must also be consistent with the remaining evidence of record.

(ii) We may also document HIV infection by the medical history, clinical and laboratory findings, and diagnosis(es) indicated in the medical evidence, provided that such documentation is consistent with the prevailing state of medical knowledge and clinical practice and is consistent with the other evidence in your case record. For example, we will accept a diagnosis of HIV infection without definitive laboratory evidence of the HIV infection if you have an opportunistic disease that is predictive of a defect in cell-mediated immunity (for example, toxoplasmosis of the brain or Pneumocystis pneumonia (PCP)), and there is no other known cause of diminished resistance to that disease (for example, long-term steroid treatment or lymphoma). In such cases, we will make every reasonable effort to obtain full details of the history, medical findings, and results of testing.

2. Documentation of the manifestations of HIV infection.

a. Definitive documentation of manifestations of HIV infection. We may document manifestations of HIV infection by positive findings on definitive laboratory tests, such as culture, microscopic examination of biopsied tissue or other material (for example, bronchial washings), serologic tests, or on other generally acceptable definitive tests consistent with the prevailing state of medical knowledge and clinical practice.

b. We will make every reasonable effort to obtain the results of your laboratory testing. Pursuant to § 416.919f of this chapter, we will purchase examinations or tests necessary to make a determination of your claim if no other acceptable documentation exists.

c. Other acceptable documentation of manifestations of HIV infection. We may also document manifestations of HIV infection without definitive laboratory evidence.

(i) We will accept a persuasive report from a physician that a positive diagnosis of your manifestation of HIV infection was confirmed by an appropriate laboratory test(s). To be persuasive, this report must state that you had the appropriate definitive laboratory test(s) for diagnosing your manifestation of HIV infection and provide the results. The report must also be consistent with the remaining evidence of record.

(ii) We may also document manifestations of HIV infection without the definitive laboratory evidence described in 114.00F2a, provided that such documentation is consistent with the prevailing state of medical knowledge and clinical practice and is consistent with the other evidence in your case record. For example, many conditions are now commonly diagnosed based on some or all of the following: Medical history, clinical manifestations, laboratory findings (including appropriate medically acceptable imaging), and treatment responses. In such cases, we will make every reasonable effort to obtain full details of the history, medical findings, and results of testing.

3. Disorders associated with HIV infection (114.11A–E).

a. Multicentric Castleman disease (MCD, 114.11A) affects multiple groups of lymph nodes and organs containing lymphoid tissue. This widespread involvement distinguishes MCD from localized (or unicentric) Castleman disease, which affects only a single set of lymph nodes. While not a cancer, MCD is known as a lymphoproliferative disorder. Its clinical presentation and progression is similar to that of lymphoma, and its treatment may include radiation or chemotherapy. We require characteristic findings on microscopic examination of the biopsied lymph nodes or other generally acceptable methods consistent with the prevailing state of medical knowledge and clinical practice to establish the diagnosis. Localized (or unicentric) Castleman disease does not meet or medically equal the criterion in 114.11A, but we may evaluate it under the criteria in 114.11G or 14.11I in part A.

b. Primary central nervous system lymphoma (PCNSL, 114.11B) originates in the brain, spinal cord, meninges, or eye. Imaging tests (for example, MRI) of the brain, while not diagnostic, may show a single lesion or multiple lesions in the white matter of the brain. We require characteristic findings on microscopic examination of the cerebral spinal fluid or of the biopsied brain tissue, or other generally acceptable methods consistent with the prevailing state of medical knowledge and clinical practice to establish the diagnosis.

c. Primary effusion lymphoma (PEL, 114.11C) is also known as body cavity lymphoma. We require characteristic findings on microscopic examination of the effusion fluid or of the biopsied tissue from the affected internal organ, or other generally acceptable methods consistent with the prevailing state of medical knowledge and clinical practice to establish the diagnosis.

d. Progressive multifocal leukoencephalopathy (PML, 114.11D) is a progressive neurological degenerative syndrome caused by the John Cunningham (JC) virus in immunosuppressed children. Clinical findings of PML include clumsiness, progressive weakness, and visual and speech changes. Personality and cognitive changes may also occur. We require appropriate clinical findings, characteristic white matter lesions on MRI, and a positive PCR test for the JC virus in the cerebrospinal fluid to establish the diagnosis. We also accept a positive brain biopsy for JC virus or other generally acceptable methods consistent with the prevailing state of medical knowledge and clinical practice to establish the diagnosis.

e. Pulmonary Kaposi sarcoma (Kaposi sarcoma in the lung, 114.11E) is the most serious form of Kaposi sarcoma (KS). Other internal KS tumors (for example, tumors of the gastrointestinal tract) have a more variable prognosis. We require characteristic findings on microscopic examination of the induced sputum, bronchoalveolar lavage washings, or of the biopsied transbronchial tissue, or other generally acceptable methods consistent with the prevailing state of medical knowledge and clinical practice to establish the diagnosis.

4. CD4 measurement (114.11F). To evaluate your HIV infection under 114.11F, we require one measurement of your absolute CD4 count (also known as CD4 count or CD4+ T–helper lymphocyte count) or CD4 percentage for children from birth to attainment of age 5, or one measurement of your absolute CD4 count for children from age 5 to attainment of age 18. These measurements (absolute CD4 count or CD4 percentage) must occur within the period we are considering in connection with your application or continuing disability review. If you have more than one CD4 measurement within this period, we will use your lowest absolute CD4 count or your lowest CD4 percentage.

5. Complications of HIV infection requiring hospitalization (114.11G).

a. Complications of HIV infection may include infections (common or opportunistic), cancers, and other conditions. Examples of complications that may result in hospitalization include: Depression; diarrhea; immune reconstitution inflammatory syndrome; malnutrition; and PCP and other severe infections.

b. Under 114.11G, we require three hospitalizations within a 12–month period that are at least 30 days apart and that result from a complication(s) of HIV infection. The hospitalizations may be for the same complication or different complications of HIV infection and are not limited to the examples of complications that may result in hospitalization listed in 114.00F5a. All three hospitalizations must occur within the period we are considering in connection with your application or continuing disability review. Each hospitalization must last at least 48 hours, including hours in a hospital emergency department immediately before the hospitalization.

c. We will use the rules on medical equivalence in § 416.926 of this chapter to evaluate your HIV infection if you have fewer, but longer, hospitalizations, or more frequent, but shorter, hospitalizations, or if you receive nursing, rehabilitation, or other care in alternative settings.

6. Neurological manifestations specific to children (114.11H). The methods of identifying and evaluating neurological manifestations may vary depending on a child's age. For example, in an infant, impaired brain growth can be documented by a decrease in the growth rate of the head. In an older child, impaired brain growth may be documented by brain atrophy on a CT scan or MRI. Neurological manifestations may present in the loss of acquired developmental milestones (developmental regression) in infants and young children or, in the loss of acquired intellectual abilities in school-age children and adolescents. A child may demonstrate loss of intellectual abilities by a decrease in IQ scores, by forgetting information previously learned, by inability to learn new information, or by a sudden onset of a new learning disability. When infants and young children present with serious developmental delays (without regression), we evaluate the child's impairment(s) under 112.00.

7. Growth failure due to HIV immune suppression (114.11I).

a. To evaluate growth failure due to HIV immune suppression, we require documentation of the laboratory values described in 114.11I1 and the growth measurements in 114.11I2 or 114.11I3 within the same consecutive 12–month period. The dates of laboratory findings may be different from the dates of growth measurements.

b. Under 114.11I2 and 114.11I3, we use the appropriate table under 105.08B in the digestive system to determine whether a child's growth is less than the third percentile.

(i) For children from birth to attainment of age 2, we use the weight-for-length table corresponding to the child's gender (Table I or Table II).

(ii) For children from age 2 to attainment of age 18, we use the body mass index (BMI)-for-age corresponding to the child's gender (Table III or Table IV).

(iii) BMI is the ratio of a child's weight to the square of his or her height. We calculate BMI using the formulas in 105.00G2c.

G. How do we consider the effects of treatment in evaluating your autoimmune disorder, immune deficiency disorder, or HIV infection?

1. General. If your impairment does not otherwise meet the requirements of a listing, we will consider your medical treatment in terms of its effectiveness in improving the signs, symptoms, and laboratory abnormalities of your specific immune system disorder or its manifestations, and in terms of any side effects that limit your functioning. We will make every reasonable effort to obtain a specific description of the treatment you receive (including surgery) for your immune system disorder. We consider:

a. The effects of medications you take.

b. Adverse side effects (acute and chronic).

c. The intrusiveness and complexity of your treatment (for example, the dosing schedule, need for injections).

d. The effect of treatment on your mental functioning (for example, cognitive changes, mood disturbance).

e. Variability of your response to treatment (see 114.00G2).

f. The interactive and cumulative effects of your treatments. For example, many children with immune system disorders receive treatment both for their immune system disorders and for the manifestations of the disorders or co-occurring impairments, such as treatment for HIV infection and hepatitis C. The interactive and cumulative effects of these treatments may be greater than the effects of each treatment considered separately.

g. The duration of your treatment.

h. Any other aspects of treatment that may interfere with your ability to function.

2. Variability of your response to treatment. Your response to treatment and the adverse or beneficial consequences of your treatment may vary widely. The effects of your treatment may be temporary or long term. For example, some children may show an initial positive response to a drug or combination of drugs followed by a decrease in effectiveness. When we evaluate your response to treatment and how your treatment may affect you, we consider such factors as disease activity before treatment, requirements for changes in therapeutic regimens, the time required for therapeutic effectiveness of a particular drug or drugs, the limited number of drug combinations that may be available for your impairment(s), and the time-limited efficacy of some drugs. For example, a child with HIV infection or another immune deficiency disorder who develops otitis media may not respond to the same antibiotic regimen used in treating children without HIV infection or another immune deficiency disorder, or may not respond to an antibiotic that he or she responded to before. Therefore, we must consider the effects of your treatment on an individual basis, including the effects of your treatment on your ability to function.

3. How we evaluate the effects of treatment for autoimmune disorders on your ability to function. Some medications may have acute or long-term side effects. When we consider the effects of corticosteroids or other treatments for autoimmune disorders on your ability to function, we consider the factors in 114.00G1 and 114.00G2. Long-term corticosteroid treatment can cause ischemic necrosis of bone, posterior subcapsular cataract, impaired growth, weight gain, glucose intolerance, increased susceptibility to infection, and osteopenia that may result in a loss of function. In addition, medications used in the treatment of autoimmune disorders may also have effects on mental functioning, including cognition (for example, memory), concentration, and mood.

4. How we evaluate the effects of treatment for immune deficiency disorders, excluding HIV infection, on your ability to function. When we consider the effects of your treatment for your immune deficiency disorder on your ability to function, we consider the factors in 114.00G1 and 114.00G2. A frequent need for treatment such as intravenous immunoglobulin and gamma interferon therapy can be intrusive and interfere with your ability to function. We will also consider whether you have chronic side effects from these or other medications, including severe fatigue, fever, headaches, high blood pressure, joint swelling, muscle aches, nausea, shortness of breath, or limitations in mental function including cognition (for example, memory) concentration, and mood.

5. How we evaluate the effects of treatment for HIV infection on your ability to function.

a. General. When we consider the effects of antiretroviral drugs (including the effects of highly active antiretroviral therapy (HAART)) and the effects of treatments for the manifestations of HIV infection on your ability to function, we consider the factors in 114.00G1 and 114.00G2. Side effects of antiretroviral drugs include, but are not limited to: Bone marrow suppression, pancreatitis, gastrointestinal intolerance (nausea, vomiting, diarrhea), neuropathy, rash, hepatotoxicity, lipodystrophy (fat redistribution, such as "buffalo hump"), glucose intolerance, and lactic acidosis. In addition, medications used in the treatment of HIV infection may also have effects on mental functioning, including cognition (for example, memory), concentration, and mood, and may result in malaise, severe fatigue, joint and muscle pain, and insomnia. The symptoms of HIV infection and the side effects of medication may be indistinguishable from each other. We will consider all of your functional limitations, whether they result from your symptoms or signs of HIV infection or the side effects of your treatment.

b. Structured treatment interruptions. A structured treatment interruption (STI, also called a "drug holiday") is a treatment practice during which your treating source advises you to stop taking your medications temporarily. An STI in itself does not imply that your medical condition has improved; nor does it imply that you are noncompliant with your treatment because you are following your treating source's advice. Therefore, if you have stopped taking medication because your treating source prescribed or recommended an STI, we will not find that you are failing to follow treatment or draw inferences about the severity of your impairment on this fact alone. We will consider why your treating source has prescribed or recommended an STI and all the other information in your case record when we determine the severity of your impairment.

6. When there is no record of ongoing treatment. If you have not received ongoing treatment or have not had an ongoing relationship with the medical community despite the existence of a severe impairment(s), we will evaluate the medical severity and duration of your immune system disorder on the basis of the current objective medical evidence and other evidence in your case record, taking into consideration your medical history, symptoms, clinical and laboratory findings, and medical source opinions. If you have just begun treatment and we cannot determine whether you are disabled based on the evidence we have, we may need to wait to determine the effect of the treatment on your ability to develop and function in an age-appropriate manner. The amount of time we need to wait will depend on the facts of your case. If you have not received treatment, you may not be able to show an impairment that meets the criteria of one of the immune system disorders listings, but your immune system disorder may medically equal a listing or functionally equal the listings.

H. How do we consider your symptoms, including your pain, severe fatigue, and malaise?

Your symptoms, including pain, severe fatigue, and malaise, may be important factors in our determination whether your immune system disorder(s) meets or medically equals a listing or in our determination whether you otherwise have marked and severe functional limitations. In order for us to consider your symptoms, you must have medical signs or laboratory findings showing the existence of a medically determinable impairment(s) that could reasonably be expected to produce the symptoms. If you have such an impairment(s), we will evaluate the intensity, persistence, and functional effects of your symptoms using the rules throughout 114.00 and in our other regulations. See §§ 416.921 and 416.929. Additionally, when we assess the credibility of your complaints about your symptoms and their functional effects, we will not draw any inferences from the fact that you do not receive treatment or that you are not following treatment without considering all of the relevant evidence in your case record, including any explanations you provide that may explain why you are not receiving or following treatment.

I. How do we consider the impact of your immune system disorder on your functioning?

1. We will consider all relevant information in your case record to determine the full impact of your immune system disorder, including HIV infection, on your ability to function. Functional limitation may result from the impact of the disease process itself on your mental functioning, physical functioning, or both your mental and physical functioning. This could result from persistent or intermittent symptoms, such as depression, diarrhea, severe fatigue, or pain, resulting in a limitation of your ability to acquire information, to concentrate, to persevere at a task, to interact with others, to move about, or to cope with stress. You may also have limitations because of your treatment and its side effects (see 114.00G).

2. Important factors we will consider when we evaluate your functioning include, but are not limited to: Your symptoms (see 114.00H), the frequency and duration of manifestations of your immune system disorder, periods of exacerbation and remission, and the functional impact of your treatment, including the side effects of your medication (see 114.00G). See §§ 416.924a and 416.926a of this chapter for additional guidance on the factors we consider when we evaluate your functioning.

3. We will use the rules in §§ 416.924a and 416.926a of this chapter to evaluate your functional limitations and determine whether your impairment functionally equals the listings.

J. How do we evaluate your immune system disorder when it does not meet one of these listings?

1. These listings are only examples of immune system disorders that we consider severe enough to result in marked and severe functional limitations. If your impairment(s) does not meet the criteria of any of these listings, we must also consider whether you have an impairment(s) that satisfies the criteria of a listing in another body system.

2. Children with immune system disorders, including HIV infection, may manifest signs or symptoms of a mental impairment or of another physical impairment. For example, HIV infection may accelerate the onset of conditions such as diabetes or affect the course of or treatment options for diseases such as cardiovascular disease or hepatitis. We may evaluate these impairments under the affected body system. For example, we will evaluate:

a. Growth impairment under 100.00.

b. Musculoskeletal involvement, such as surgical reconstruction of a joint, under 101.00.

c. Ocular involvement, such as dry eye, under 102.00.

d. Respiratory impairments, such as pleuritis, under 103.00.

e. Cardiovascular impairments, such as cardiomyopathy, under 104.00.

f. Digestive impairments, such as hepatitis (including hepatitis C) or weight loss as a result of HIV infection that affects the digestive system, under 105.00.

g. Genitourinary impairments, such as nephropathy, under 106.00.

h. Hematologic abnormalities, such as anemia, granulocytopenia, and thrombocytopenia, under 107.00.

i. Skin impairments, such as persistent fungal and other infectious skin eruptions, and photosensitivity, under 108.00.

j. Neurologic impairments, such as neuropathy or seizures, under 111.00.

k. Mental disorders, such as depression, anxiety, or cognitive deficits, under 112.00.

l. Allergic disorders, such as asthma or atopic dermatitis, under 103.00 or 108.00 or under the criteria in another affected body system.

m. Syphilis or neurosyphilis under the criteria for the affected body system, for example, 102.00 Special senses and speech, 104.00 Cardiovascular system, or 111.00 Neurological.

3. If you have a severe medically determinable impairment(s) that does not meet a listing, we will determine whether your impairment(s) medically equals a listing. (See § 416.926.) If it does not, we will also consider whether you have an impairment(s) that functionally equals the listings. (See § 416.926a.) We use the rules in § 416.994a when we decide whether you continue to be disabled.

114.01 Category of Impairments, Immune System Disorders.

114.02 Systemic lupus erythematosus, as described in 114.00D1. With involvement of two or more organs/body systems, and with:

A. One of the organs/body systems involved to at least a moderate level of severity;

AND

B. At least two of the constitutional symptoms and signs (severe fatigue, fever, malaise, or involuntary weight loss).

114.03 Systemic vasculitis, as described in 114.00D2. With involvement of two or more organs/body systems, and with:

A. One of the organs/body systems involved to at least a moderate level of severity;

AND

B. At least two of the constitutional symptoms and signs (severe fatigue, fever, malaise, or involuntary weight loss).

114.04 Systemic sclerosis (scleroderma). As described in 114.00D3. With:

A. Involvement of two or more organs/body systems, with:

1. One of the organs/body systems involved to at least a moderate level of severity; and

2. At least two of the constitutional symptoms or signs (severe fatigue, fever, malaise, or involuntary weight loss).

or

B. With one of the following:

1. Toe contractures or fixed deformity of one or both feet, resulting in the inability to ambulate effectively as defined in 114.00C6; or

2. Finger contractures or fixed deformity in both hands, resulting in the inability to perform fine and gross movements effectively as defined in 114.00C7; or

3. Atrophy with irreversible damage in one or both lower extremities, resulting in the inability to ambulate effectively as defined in 114.00C6; or

4. Atrophy with irreversible damage in both upper extremities, resulting in the inability to perform fine and gross movements effectively as defined in 114.00C7.

or

C. Raynaud's phenomenon, characterized by:

1. Gangrene involving at least two extremities; or

2. Ischemia with ulcerations of toes or fingers, resulting in the inability to ambulate effectively or to perform fine and gross movements effectively as defined in 114.00C6 and 114.00C7.

114.05 Polymyositis and dermatomyositis. As described in 114.00D4. With:

A. Proximal limb-girdle (pelvic or shoulder) muscle weakness, resulting in inability to ambulate effectively or inability to perform fine and gross movements effectively as defined in 114.00C6 and 114.00C7.

or

B. Impaired swallowing (dysphagia) with aspiration due to muscle weakness.

or

C. Impaired respiration due to intercostal and diaphragmatic muscle weakness.

or

D. Diffuse calcinosis with limitation of joint mobility or intestinal motility.

114.06 Undifferentiated and mixed connective tissue disease, as described in 114.00D5. With involvement of two or more organs/body systems, and with:

A. One of the organs/body systems involved to at least a moderate level of severity;

AND

B. At least two of the constitutional symptoms and signs (severe fatigue, fever, malaise, or involuntary weight loss).

114.07 Immune deficiency disorders, excluding HIV infection. As described in 114.00E. With:

A. One or more of the following infections. The infection(s) must either be resistant to treatment or require hospitalization or intravenous treatment three or more times in a 12–month period.

1. Sepsis; or

2. Meningitis; or

3. Pneumonia; or

4. Septic arthritis; or

5. Endocarditis; or

6. Sinusitis documented by appropriate medically acceptable imaging.

or

B. Stem cell transplantation as described under 114.00E3. Consider under a disability until at least 12 months from the date of transplantation. Thereafter, evaluate any residual impairment(s) under the criteria for the affected body system.

114.08 [Reserved by 81 FR 86923]

114.09 Inflammatory arthritis. As described in 114.00D6. With:

A. Persistent inflammation or persistent deformity of:

1. One or more major peripheral weight-bearing joints resulting in the inability to ambulate effectively (as defined in 114.00C6); or

2. One or more major peripheral joints in each upper extremity resulting in the inability to perform fine and gross movements effectively (as defined in 114.00C7).

or

B. Inflammation or deformity in one or more major peripheral joints with:

1. Involvement of two or more organs/body systems with one of the organs/body systems involved to at least a moderate level of severity; and

2. At least two of the constitutional symptoms or signs (severe fatigue, fever, malaise, or involuntary weight loss).

or

C. Ankylosing spondylitis or other spondyloarthropathies, with:

1. Ankylosis (fixation) of the dorsolumbar or cervical spine as shown by appropriate medically acceptable imaging and measured on physical examination at 45° or more of flexion from the vertical position (zero degrees); or

2. Ankylosis (fixation) of the dorsolumbar or cervical spine as shown by appropriate medically acceptable imaging and measured on physical examination at 30° or more of flexion (but less than 45°) measured from the vertical position (zero degrees), and involvement of two or more organs/body systems with one of the organs/body systems involved to at least a moderate level of severity.

114.10 Sjögren's syndrome, as described in 114.00D7. With involvement of two or more organs/body systems, and with:

A. One of the organs/body systems involved to at least a moderate level of severity;

AND

B. At least two of the constitutional symptoms and signs (severe fatigue, fever, malaise, or involuntary weight loss).

114.11 Human immunodeficiency virus (HIV) infection. With documentation as described in 114.00F1 and one of the following:

A. Multicentric (not localized or unicentric) Castleman disease affecting multiple groups of lymph nodes or organs containing lymphoid tissue (see 114.00F3a).

OR

B. Primary central nervous system lymphoma (see 114.00F3b).

OR

C. Primary effusion lymphoma (see 114.00F3c).

OR

D. Progressive multifocal leukoencephalopathy (see 114.00F3d).

OR

E. Pulmonary Kaposi sarcoma (see 114.00F3e).

OR

F. Absolute CD4 count or CD4 percentage (see 114.00F4):

1. For children from birth to attainment of age 1, absolute CD4 count of 500 cells/mm^3 or less, or CD4 percentage of less than 15 percent; or

2. For children from age 1 to attainment of age 5, absolute CD4 count of 200 cells/mm^3 or less, or CD4 percentage of less than 15 percent; or

3. For children from age 5 to attainment of age 18, absolute CD4 count of 50 cells/mm^3 or less.

OR

G. Complication(s) of HIV infection requiring at least three hospitalizations within a 12–month period and at least 30 days apart (see 114.00F5). Each hospitalization must last at least 48 hours, including hours in a hospital emergency department immediately before the hospitalization.

OR

H. A neurological manifestation of HIV infection (for example, HIV encephalopathy or peripheral neuropathy) (see 114.00F6) resulting in one of the following:

1. Loss of previously acquired developmental milestones or intellectual ability (including the sudden onset of a new learning disability), documented on two examinations at least 60 days apart; or

2. Progressive motor dysfunction affecting gait and station or fine and gross motor skills, documented on two examinations at least 60 days apart; or

3. Microcephaly with head circumference that is less than the third percentile for age, documented on two examinations at least 60 days apart; or

4. Brain atrophy, documented by appropriate medically acceptable imaging.

OR

I. Immune suppression and growth failure (see 114.00F7) documented by 1 and 2, or by 1 and 3:

1. CD4 measurement:

a. For children from birth to attainment of age 5, CD4 percentage of less than 20 percent; or

b. For children from age 5 to attainment of age 18, absolute CD4 count of less than 200 cells/mm^3 or CD4 percentage of less than 14 percent; and

2. For children from birth to attainment of age 2, three weight-for-length measurements that are:

a. Within a consecutive 12–month period; and

b. At least 60 days apart; and

c. Less than the third percentile on the appropriate weight-for-length table under 105.08B1; or

3. For children from age 2 to attainment of age 18, three BMI–for-age measurements that are:

a. Within a consecutive 12–month period; and

b. At least 60 days apart; and

c. Less than the third percentile on the appropriate BMI–for-age table under 105.08B2.

[81 FR 66161, Sept. 26, 2016; 81 FR 86923, Dec. 2, 2016; 81 FR 86928, Dec. 2, 2016; 82 FR 5872, Jan. 18, 2017]

APPENDIX 2 TO SUBPART P OF PART 404—MEDICAL–VOCATIONAL GUIDELINES

Sec.

200.00 Introduction. (a) The following rules reflect the major functional and vocational patterns which are encountered in cases which cannot be evaluated on medical considerations alone, where an individual with a severe medically determinable physical or mental impairment(s) is not engaging in substantial gainful activity and the individual's impairment(s) prevents the performance of his or her vocationally relevant past work. They also reflect the analysis of the various vocational factors (i.e., age, education, and work experience) in combination with the individual's residual functional capacity (used to determine his or her maximum sustained work capability for sedentary, light, medium, heavy, or very heavy work) in evaluating the individual's ability to engage in substantial gainful activity in other than his or her vocationally relevant past work. Where the findings of fact made with respect to a particular individual's vocational factors and residual functional capacity coincide with all of the criteria of a particular rule, the rule directs a conclusion as to whether the individual is or is not disabled. However, each of these findings of fact is subject to rebuttal and the individual may present evidence to refute such findings. Where any one of the findings of fact does not coincide with the corresponding criterion of a rule, the rule does not apply in that particular case and, accordingly, does not direct a conclusion of disabled or not disabled. In any instance where a rule does not apply, full consideration must be given to all of the relevant facts of the case in accordance with the definitions and discussions of each factor in the appropriate sections of the regulations.

(b) The existence of jobs in the national economy is reflected in the "Decisions" shown in the rules; i.e., in promulgating the rules, administrative notice has been taken of the numbers of unskilled jobs that exist throughout the national economy at the various functional levels (sedentary, light, medium, heavy, and very heavy) as supported by the "Dictionary of Occupational Titles" and the "Occupational Outlook Handbook," published by the Department of Labor; the "County Business Patterns" and "Census Surveys" published by the Bureau of the Census; and occupational surveys of light and sedentary jobs prepared for the Social Security Administration by various State employment agencies. Thus, when all factors coincide with the criteria of a rule, the existence of such jobs is established. However, the existence of such jobs for individuals whose remaining functional capacity or other factors do not coincide with the criteria of a rule must be further considered in terms of what kinds of jobs or types of work may be either additionally indicated or precluded.

(c) In the application of the rules, the individual's residual functional capacity (i.e., the maximum degree to which the individual retains the capacity for sustained performance of the physical-mental requirements of jobs), age, education, and work experience must first be determined. When assessing the person's residual functional capacity, we consider his or her symptoms (such as pain), signs, and laboratory findings together with other evidence we obtain.

(d) The correct disability decision (i.e., on the issue of ability to engage in substantial gainful activity) is found by then locating the individual's specific vocational profile. If an individual's specific profile is not listed within this appendix 2, a conclusion of disabled or not disabled is not directed. Thus, for example, an individual's ability to engage in substantial gainful work where his or her residual functional capacity falls between the ranges of work indicated in the rules (e.g., the individual who can perform more than light but less than medium work), is decided on the basis of the principles and definitions in the regulations, giving consideration to the rules for specific case situations in this appendix 2. These rules represent various combinations of exertional capabilities, age, education and work experience and also provide an overall structure for evaluation of those cases in which the judgments as to each factor do not coincide with those of any specific rule. Thus, when the necessary judgments have been made as to each factor and it is found that no specific rule applies, the rules still provide guidance for decisionmaking, such as in cases involving combinations of impairments. For example, if strength limitations resulting from an individual's impairment(s) considered with the judgments made as to the individual's age, education and work experience correspond to (or closely approximate) the factors of a particular rule, the adjudicator then has a frame of reference for considering the jobs or types of work precluded by other, nonexertional impairments in terms of numbers of jobs remaining for a particular individual.

(e) Since the rules are predicated on an individual's having an impairment which manifests itself by limitations in meeting the strength requirements of jobs, they may not be fully applicable where the nature of an individual's impairment does not result in such limitations, e.g., certain mental, sensory, or skin impairments. In addition, some impairments may result solely in postural and manipulative limitations or environmental restrictions. Environmental restrictions are those restrictions which result in inability to tolerate some physical feature(s) of work settings that occur in certain industries or types of work, e.g., an inability to tolerate dust or fumes.

(1) In the evaluation of disability where the individual has solely a nonexertional type of impairment, determination as to whether disability exists shall be based on the principles in the appropriate sections of the regulations, giving consideration to the rules for specific case situations in this appendix 2. The rules do not direct factual conclusions of disabled or not disabled for individuals with solely nonexertional types of impairments.

(2) However, where an individual has an impairment or combination of impairments resulting in both strength limitations and nonexertional limitations, the rules in this subpart are considered in determining first whether a finding of disabled may be possible based on the strength limitations alone and, if not, the rule(s) reflecting the individual's maximum residual strength capabilities, age, education, and work experience provide a framework for consideration of how much the individual's work capability is further diminished in terms of any types of jobs that would be contraindicated by the nonexertional limitations. Also, in these combinations of nonexertional and exertional limitations which cannot be wholly determined under the rules in this appendix 2, full consideration must be given to all of the relevant facts in the case in accordance with the definitions and discussions of each factor in the appropriate sections of the regulations, which will provide insight into the adjudicative weight to be accorded each factor.

201.00 Maximum sustained work capability limited to sedentary work as a result of severe medically determinable impairment(s). (a) Most sedentary occupations fall within the skilled, semi-skilled, professional, administrative, technical, clerical, and benchwork classifications. Approximately 200 separate unskilled sedentary occupations can be identified, each representing numerous jobs in the national economy. Approximately 85 percent of these jobs are in the machine trades and benchwork occupational categories. These jobs (unskilled sedentary occupations) may be performed after a short demonstration or within 30 days.

(b) These unskilled sedentary occupations are standard within the industries in which they exist. While sedentary work represents a significantly restricted range of work, this range in itself is not so prohibitively restricted as to negate work capability for substantial gainful activity.

(c) Vocational adjustment to sedentary work may be expected where the individual has special skills or experience relevant to sedentary work or where age and basic educational competencies provide sufficient occupational mobility to adapt to the major segment of unskilled sedentary work. Inability to engage in substantial gainful activity would be indicated where an individual who is restricted to sedentary work because of a severe medically determinable impairment lacks special skills or experience relevant to sedentary work, lacks educational qualifications relevant to most sedentary work (e.g., has a limited education or less) and the individual's age, though not necessarily advanced, is a factor which significantly limits vocational adaptability.

(d) The adversity of functional restrictions to sedentary work at advanced age (55 and over) for individuals with no relevant past work or who can no longer perform vocationally relevant past work and have no transferable skills, warrants a finding of disabled in the absence of the rare situation where the individual has recently completed education which provides a basis for direct entry into skilled sedentary work. Advanced age and a history of unskilled work or no work experience would ordinarily offset any vocational advantages that might accrue by reason of any remote past education, whether it is more or less than limited education.

(e) The presence of acquired skills that are readily transferable to a significant range of skilled work within an individual's residual functional capacity would ordinarily warrant a finding of ability to engage in substantial gainful activity regardless of the adversity of age, or whether the individual's formal education is commensurate with his or her demonstrated skill level. The acquisition of work skills demonstrates the ability to perform work at the level of complexity demonstrated by the skill level attained regardless of the individual's formal educational attainments.

(f) In order to find transferability of skills to skilled sedentary work for individuals who are of advanced age (55 and over), there must be very little, if any, vocational adjustment required in terms of tools, work processes, work settings, or the industry.

(g) Individuals approaching advanced age (age 50–54) may be significantly limited in vocational adaptability if they are restricted to sedentary work. When such individuals have no past work experience or can no longer perform vocationally relevant past work and have no transferable skills, a finding of disabled ordinarily obtains. However, recently completed education which provides for direct entry into sedentary work will preclude such a finding. For this age group, even a high school education or more (ordinarily completed in the remote past) would have little impact for effecting a vocational adjustment unless relevant work experience reflects use of such education.

(h)(1) The term younger individual is used to denote an individual age 18 through 49. For individuals who are age 45–49, age is a less advantageous factor for making an adjustment to other work than for those who are age 18–44. Accordingly, a finding of "disabled" is warranted for individuals age 45–49 who:

(i) Are restricted to sedentary work,

(ii) Are unskilled or have no transferable skills,

(iii) Have no past relevant work or can no longer perform past relevant work, and

(iv) Are unable to communicate in English, or are able to speak and understand English but are unable to read or write in English.

(2) For individuals who are under age 45, age is a more advantageous factor for making an adjustment to other work. It is usually not a significant factor in limiting such individuals' ability to make an adjustment to other work, including an adjustment to unskilled sedentary work, even when the individuals are unable to communicate in English or are illiterate in English.

(3) Nevertheless, a decision of "disabled" may be appropriate for some individuals under age 45 (or individuals age 45–49 for whom rule 201.17 does not direct a decision of disabled) who do not have the ability to perform a full range of sedentary work. However, the inability to perform a full range of sedentary work does not necessarily equate with a finding of "disabled." Whether an individual will be able to make an adjustment to other work requires an adjudicative assessment of factors such as the type and extent of the individual's limitations or restrictions and the extent of the erosion of the occupational base. It requires an individualized determination that considers the impact of the limitations or restrictions on the number of sedentary, unskilled occupations or the total number of jobs to which the individual may be able to adjust, considering his or her age, education and work experience, including any transferable skills or education providing for direct entry into skilled work.

(4) "Sedentary work" represents a significantly restricted range of work, and individuals with a maximum sustained work capability limited to sedentary work have very serious functional limitations. Therefore, as with any case, a finding that an individual is limited to less than the full range of sedentary work will be based on careful consideration of the evidence of the individual's medical impairment(s) and the limitations and restrictions attributable to it. Such evidence must support the finding that the individual's residual functional capacity is limited to less than the full range of sedentary work.

(i) While illiteracy or the inability to communicate in English may significantly limit an individual's vocational scope, the primary work functions in the bulk of unskilled work relate to working with things (rather than with data or people) and in these work functions at the unskilled level, literacy or ability to communicate in English has the least significance. Similarly the lack of relevant work experience would have little significance since the bulk of unskilled jobs require no qualifying work experience. Thus, the functional capability for a full range of sedentary work represents sufficient numbers of jobs to indicate substantial vocational scope for those individuals age 18–44 even if they are illiterate or unable to communicate in English.

Table No. 1—Residual Functional Capacity: Maximum Sustained Work Capability Limited to Sedentary Work as a Result of Severe Medically Determinable Impairment(s)

Rule	Age	Education	Previous work experience	Decision
201.01	Advanced age	Limited or less	Unskilled or none	Disabled.
201.02	...do	...do	Skilled or semiskilled–skills not transferable [1].	Do.
201.03	...do	...do	Skilled or semiskilled–skills transferable [1].	Not disabled.
201.04	...do	High school graduate or more–does not provide for direct entry into skilled work [2].	Unskilled or none	Disabled.
201.05	...do	High school graduate or more–provides for direct entry into skilled work [2].	...do	Not disabled.
201.06	...do	High school graduate or more–does not provide for direct entry into skilled work [2].	Skilled or semiskilled–skills not transferable [1].	Disabled.
201.07	...do	...do	Skilled or semiskilled–skills transferable [1].	Not disabled.
201.08	...do	High school graduate or more–provides for direct entry into skilled work [2].	Skilled or semiskilled–skills not transferable [1].	Do.
201.09	Closely approaching advanced age.	Limited or less	Unskilled or none	Disabled.
201.10	...do	...do	Skilled or semiskilled–skills not transferable.	Do.
201.11	...do	...do	Skilled or semiskilled–skills transferable.	Not disabled.
201.12	...do	High school graduate or more–does not provide for direct entry into skilled work [3].	Unskilled or none	Disabled.
201.13	...do	High school graduate or more–provides for direct entry into skilled work [3].	...do	Not disabled.
201.14	...do	High school graduate or more–does not provide for direct entry into skilled work [3].	Skilled or semiskilled–skills not transferable.	Disabled.
201.15	...do	...do	Skilled or semiskilled–skills transferable.	Not disabled.
201.16	...do	High school graduate or more–provides for direct entry into skilled work [3].	Skilled or semiskilled–skills not transferable.	Do.
201.17	Younger individual age 45-49.	Illiterate or unable to communicate in English.	Unskilled or none	Disabled.
201.18	...do	Limited or less–at least literate and able to communicate in English.	...do	Not disabled.
201.19	...do	Limited or less	Skilled or semiskilled–skills not transferable.	Do.
201.20	...do	...do	Skilled or semiskilled–skills transferable.	Do.
201.21	...do	High school graduate or more	Skilled or semiskilled–skills not transferable.	Do.
201.22	...do	...do	Skilled or semiskilled–skills transferable.	Do.
201.23	Younger individual age 18-44.	Illiterate or unable to communicate in English.	Unskilled or none	Do.[4]
201.24	...do	Limited or less–at least literate and able to communicate in English.	...do	Do.[4]
201.25	...do	Limited or less	Skilled or semiskilled–skills not transferable.	Do.[4]
201.26	...do	...do	Skilled or semiskilled–skills transferable.	Do.[4]
201.27	...do	High school graduate or more	Unskilled or none	Do.[4]
201.28	...do	...do	Skilled or semiskilled–skills not transferable.	Do.[4]
201.29	...do	...do	Skilled or semiskilled–skills transferable.	Do.[4]

[1] See 201.00(f).
[2] See 201.00(d).
[3] See 201.00(g).
[4] See 201.00(h).

202.00 Maximum sustained work capability limited to light work as a result of severe medically determinable impairment(s). (a) The functional capacity to perform a full range of light work includes the functional capacity to perform sedentary as well as light work. Approximately 1,600 separate sedentary and light unskilled occupations can be identified in eight broad occupational categories, each occupation representing numerous jobs in the national economy. These jobs can be performed after a short demonstration or within 30 days, and do not require special skills or experience.

(b) The functional capacity to perform a wide or full range of light work represents substantial work capability compatible with making a work adjustment to substantial numbers of unskilled jobs and, thus, generally provides sufficient occupational mobility even for severely impaired individuals who are not of advanced age and have sufficient educational competencies for unskilled work.

(c) However, for individuals of advanced age who can no longer perform vocationally relevant past work and who have a history of unskilled work experience, or who have only skills that are not readily transferable to a significant range of semi-skilled or skilled work that is within the individual's functional capacity, or who have no work experience, the limitations in vocational adaptability represented by functional restriction to light work warrant a finding of disabled. Ordinarily, even a high school education or more which was completed in the remote past will have little positive impact on effecting a vocational adjustment unless relevant work experience reflects use of such education.

(d) Where the same factors in paragraph (c) of this section regarding education and work experience are present, but where age, though not advanced, is a factor which significantly limits vocational adaptability (i.e., closely approaching advanced age, 50–54) and an individual's vocational scope is further significantly limited by illiteracy or inability to communicate in English, a finding of disabled is warranted.

(e) The presence of acquired skills that are readily transferable to a significant range of semi-skilled or skilled work within an individual's residual functional capacity would ordinarily warrant a finding of not disabled regardless of the adversity of age, or whether the individual's formal education is commensurate with his or her demonstrated skill level. The acquisition of work skills demonstrates the ability to perform work at the level of complexity demonstrated by the skill level attained regardless of the individual's formal educational attainments.

(f) For a finding of transferability of skills to light work for persons of advanced age who are closely approaching retirement age (age 60 or older), there must be very little, if any, vocational adjustment required in terms of tools, work processes, work settings, or the industry.

(g) While illiteracy or the inability to communicate in English may significantly limit an individual's vocational scope, the primary work functions in the bulk of unskilled work relate to working with things (rather than with data or people) and in these work functions at the unskilled level, literacy or ability to communicate in English has the least significance. Similarly, the lack of relevant work experience would have little significance since the bulk of unskilled jobs require no qualifying work experience. The capability for light work, which includes the ability to do sedentary work, represents the capability for substantial numbers of such jobs. This, in turn, represents substantial vocational scope for younger individuals (age 18–49) even if illiterate or unable to communicate in English.

Table No. 2—Residual Functional Capacity: Maximum Sustained Work Capability Limited to Light Work as a Result of Severe Medically Determinable Impairment(s)

Rule	Age	Education	Previous work experience	Decision
202.01	Advanced age	Limited or less	Unskilled or none	Disabled.
202.02	...do	...do	Skilled or semiskilled–skills not transferable.	Do.
202.03	...do	...do	Skilled or semiskilled–skills transferable [1]	Not disabled.
202.04	...do	High school graduate or more–does not provide for direct entry into skilled work [2].	Unskilled or none	Disabled.
202.05	...do	High school graduate or more–provides for direct entry into skilled work [2].	...do	Not disabled.
202.06	...do	High school graduate or more–does not provide for direct entry into skilled work [2].	Skilled or semiskilled–skills not transferable.	Disabled.
202.07	...do	...do	Skilled or semiskilled–skills transferable [2]	Not disabled.
202.08	...do	High school graduate or more–provides for direct entry into skilled work [2].	Skilled or semiskilled–skills not transferable.	Do.

Rule	Age	Education	Previous work experience	Decision
202.09	Closely approaching advanced age. ...	Illiterate or unable to communicate in English.	Unskilled or none	Disabled.
202.10	...do	Limited or less–at least literate and able to communicate in English.	...do	Not disabled.
202.11	...do	Limited or less	Skilled or semiskilled–skills not transferable.	Do.
202.12	...do	...do	Skilled or semiskilled–skills transferable.	Do.
202.13	...do	High school graduate or more	Unskilled or none	Do.
202.14	...do	...do	Skilled or semiskilled–skills not transferable.	Do.
202.15	...do	...do	Skilled or semiskilled–skills transferable.	Do.
202.16	Younger individual	Illiterate or unable to communicate in English.	Unskilled or none	Do.
202.17	...do	Limited or less–at least literate and able to communicate in English.	...do	Do.
202.18	...do	Limited or less	Skilled or semiskilled–skills not transferable.	Do.
202.19	...do	...do	Skilled or semiskilled–skills transferable.	Do.
202.20	...do	High school graduate or more	Unskilled or none	Do.
202.21	...do	...do	Skilled or semiskilled–skills not transferable.	Do.
202.22	...do	...do	Skilled or semiskilled–skills transferable.	Do.

[1] See 202.00(f).
[2] See 202.00(c).

203.00 Maximum sustained work capability limited to medium work as a result of severe medically determinable impairment(s). (a) The functional capacity to perform medium work includes the functional capacity to perform sedentary, light, and medium work. Approximately 2,500 separate sedentary, light, and medium occupations can be identified, each occupation representing numerous jobs in the national economy which do not require skills or previous experience and which can be performed after a short demonstration or within 30 days.

(b) The functional capacity to perform medium work represents such substantial work capability at even the unskilled level that a finding of disabled is ordinarily not warranted in cases where a severely impaired person retains the functional capacity to perform medium work. Even the adversity of advanced age (55 or over) and a work history of unskilled work may be offset by the substantial work capability represented by the functional capacity to perform medium work. However, we will find that a person who (1) has a marginal education, (2) has work experience of 35 years or more doing only arduous unskilled physical labor, (3) is not working, and (4) is no longer able to do this kind of work because of a severe impairment(s) is disabled, even though the person is able to do medium work. (See § 404.1562(a) in this subpart and § 416.962(a) in subpart I of part 416.)

(c) However, the absence of any relevant work experience becomes a more significant adversity for persons of advanced age (55 and over). Accordingly, this factor, in combination with a limited education or less, militates against making a vocational adjustment to even this substantial range of work and a finding of disabled is appropriate. Further, for persons closely approaching retirement age (60 or older) with a work history of unskilled work and with marginal education or less, a finding of disabled is appropriate.

Table No. 3—Residual Functional Capacity: Maximum Sustained Work Capability Limited to Medium Work as a Result of Severe Medically Determinable Impairment(s)

Rule	Age	Education	Previous work experience	Decision
203.01	Closely approaching retirement age.	Marginal or none	Unskilled or none	Disabled.
203.02	...do	Limited or less	None	Do.
203.03	...do	Limited	Unskilled	Not disabled.
203.04	...do	Limited or less	Skilled or semiskilled–skills not transferable.	Do.
203.05	...do	...do	Skilled or semiskilled–skills transferable.	Do.
203.06	...do	High school graduate or more	Unskilled or none	Do.
203.07	...do	High school graduate or more–does not provide for direct entry into skilled work.	Skilled or semiskilled–skills not transferable.	Do.

Rule	Age	Education	Previous work experience	Decision
203.08	...do	...do	Skilled or semiskilled–skills transferable.	Do.
203.09	...do	High school graduate or more–provides for direct entry into skilled work.	Skilled or semiskilled–skills not transferable.	Do.
203.10	Advanced age	Limited or less	None	Disabled.
203.11	...do	...do	Unskilled	Not disabled.
203.12	...do	...do	Skilled or semiskilled–skills not transferable.	Do.
203.13	...do	...do	Skilled or semiskilled–skills transferable.	Do.
203.14	...do	High school graduate or more	Unskilled or none...........	Do.
203.15	...do	High school graduate or more–does not provide for direct entry into skilled work.	Skilled or semiskilled–skills not transferable.	Do.
203.16	...do	...do	Skilled or semiskilled–skills transferable.	Do.
203.17	...do	High school graduate or more–provides for direct entry into skilled work.	Skilled or semiskilled–skills not transferable.	Do.
203.18	Closely approaching advanced age.	Limited or less	Unskilled or none..........	Do.
203.19	...do	...do	Skilled or semiskilled–skills not transferable.	Do.
203.20	...do	...do	Skilled or semiskilled–skills transferable.	Do.
203.21	...do	High school graduate or more	Unskilled or none..........	Do.
203.22	...do	High school graduate or more–does not provide for direct entry into skilled work.	Skilled or semiskilled–skills not transferable.	Do.
203.23	...do	...do	Skilled or semiskilled–skills transferable.	Do.
203.24	...do	High school graduate or more–provides for direct entry into skilled work.	Skilled or semiskilled–skills not transferable.	Do.
203.25	Younger individual	Limited or less	Unskilled or none..........	Do.
203.26	...do	...do	Skilled or semiskilled–skills not transferable.	Do.
203.27	...do	...do	Skilled or semiskilled–skills transferable.	Do.
203.28	...do	High school graduate or more	Unskilled or none..........	Do.
203.29	...do	High school graduate or more–does not provide for direct entry into skilled work.	Skilled or semiskilled–skills not transferable.	Do.
203.30	...do	...do	Skilled or semiskilled–skills transferable.	Do.
203.31	...do	High school graduate or more–provides for direct entry into skilled work.	Skilled or semiskilled–skills not transferable.	Do.

204.00 Maximum sustained work capability limited to heavy work (or very heavy work) as a result of severe medically determinable impairment(s). The residual functional capacity to perform heavy work or very heavy work includes the functional capability for work at the lesser functional levels as well, and represents substantial work capability for jobs in the national economy at all skill and physical demand levels. Individuals who retain the functional capacity to perform heavy work (or very heavy work) ordinarily will not have a severe impairment or will be able to do their past work—either of which would have already provided a basis for a decision of "not disabled". Environmental restrictions ordinarily would not significantly affect the range of work existing in the national economy for individuals with the physical capability for heavy work (or very heavy work). Thus an impairment which does not preclude heavy work (or very heavy work) would not ordinarily be the primary reason for unemployment, and generally is sufficient for a finding of not disabled, even though age, education, and skill level of prior work experience may be considered adverse.

[56 FR 57944, Nov. 14, 1991; 66 FR 45166, Aug. 28, 2001; 68 FR 51164, Aug. 26, 2003; 73 FR 64197, Oct. 29, 2008]

SUBPART Q—DETERMINATIONS OF DISABILITY

Authority: Secs. 205(a), 221, and 702(a)(5) of the Social Security Act (42 U.S.C. 405(a), 421, and 902(a)(5)).

Source: 46 FR 29204, May 29, 1981; 52 FR 27541, July 22, 1987; 61 FR 5941, Feb. 15, 1996, unless otherwise noted.

GENERAL PROVISIONS

§ 404.1601 Purpose and scope.

This subpart describes the standards of performance and administrative requirements and procedures for

States making determinations of disability for the Commissioner under title II of the Act. It also establishes the Commissioner's responsibilities in carrying out the disability determination function.

(a) Sections 404.1601 through 404.1603 describe the purpose of the regulations and the meaning of terms frequently used in the regulations. They also briefly set forth the responsibilities of the Commissioner and the States covered in detail in other sections.

(b) Sections 404.1610 through 404.1618 describe the Commissioner's and the State's responsibilities in performing the disability determination function.

(c) Sections 404.1620 through 404.1633 describe the administrative responsibilities and requirements of the States. The corresponding role of the Commissioner is also set out.

(d) Sections 404.1640 through 404.1650 describe the performance accuracy and processing time standards for measuring State agency performance.

(e) Sections 404.1660 through 404.1661 describe when and what kind of assistance the Commissioner will provide State agencies to help them improve performance.

(f) Sections 404.1670 through 404.1675 describe the level of performance below which the Commissioner will consider a State agency to be substantially failing to make disability determinations consistent with the regulations and other written guidelines and the resulting action the Commissioner will take.

(g) Sections 404.1680 through 404.1683 describe the rules for resolving disputes concerning fiscal issues and providing hearings when we propose to find that a State is in substantial failure.

(h) Sections 404.1690 through 404.1694 describe when and what action the Commissioner will take and what action the State will be expected to take if the Commissioner assumes the disability determination function from a State agency.

[62 FR 38451, July 18, 1997; 71 FR 16445, March 31, 2006; 76 FR 24808, May 3, 2011]

§ 404.1602 Definitions.

For purposes of this subpart:

Act means the Social Security Act, as amended.

Class or classes of cases means the categories into which disability claims are divided according to their characteristics.

Commissioner means the Commissioner of Social Security or his or her authorized designee.

Compassionate allowance means a determination or decision we make under a process that identifies for expedited handling claims that involve impairments that invariably qualify under the Listing of Impairments in appendix 1 to subpart P based on minimal, but sufficient, objective medical evidence.

Determination of disability or disability determination means one or more of the following decisions:

(a) Whether or not a person is under a disability;

(b) The date a person's disability began; or

(c) The date a person's disability ended.

Disability means disability or blindness as defined in sections 216(i) and 223 of the Act or as defined in title IV of the Federal Mine Safety and Health Act of 1977, as amended.

Disability determination function means making determinations as to disability and carrying out related administrative and other responsibilities.

Disability program means, as appropriate, the Federal programs for providing disability insurance benefits under title II of the Act and disability benefits under title IV of the Federal Mine Safety and Health Act of 1977, as amended.

Initial means the first level of disability adjudication.

Other written guidelines means written issuances such as Social Security Rulings and memoranda by the Commissioner of Social Security, the Deputy Commissioner for Programs and Policy, or the Associate Commissioner for Disability and the procedures, guides, and operating instructions in the Disability Insurance sections of the Program Operations Manual System, that are instructive, interpretive, clarifying, and/or administrative and not designated as advisory or discretionary. The purpose of including the foregoing material in the definition is to assure uniform national application of program standards and service delivery to the public.

Quick disability determination means an initial determination on a claim that we have identified as one that reflects a high degree of probability that you will be found disabled and where we expect that your allegations will be easily and quickly verified.

Regulations means regulations in this subpart issued under sections 205(a), 221 and 1102 of the Act, unless otherwise indicated.

State means any of the 50 States of the United States, the Commonwealth of Puerto Rico, the District of Columbia, or Guam. It includes the State agency.

State agency means that agency of a State which has been designated by the State to carry out the disability determination function.

We, us, and our refers to the Social Security Administration (SSA).

[56 FR 11018, March 14, 1991; 62 FR 38452, July 18, 1997; 72 FR 51177, Sept. 6, 2007; 75 FR 62682, Oct. 13, 2010]

§ 404.1603 Basic responsibilities for us and the State.

(a) General. We will work with the State to provide and maintain an effective system for processing claims of those who apply for and who are receiving benefits under the disability program. We will provide program standards, leadership, and oversight. We do not intend to become involved in the State's ongoing management of the program except as is necessary and in accordance with these regulations. The State will comply with our regulations and other written guidelines.

(b) Our responsibilities. We will:

(1) Periodically review the regulations and other written guidelines to determine whether they insure effective and uniform administration of the disability program. To the extent feasible, we will consult with and take into consideration the experience of the States in issuing regulations and guidelines necessary to insure effective and uniform administration of the disability program;

(2) Provide training materials or in some instances conduct or specify training, see § 404.1622;

(3) Provide funds to the State agency for the necessary cost of performing the disability determination function, see § 404.1626;

(4) Monitor and evaluate the performance of the State agency under the established standards, see §§ 404.1644 and 404.1645; and

(5) Maintain liaison with the medical profession nationally and with national organizations and agencies whose interests or activities may affect the disability program.

(c) Responsibilities of the State. The State will:

(1) Provide management needed to insure that the State agency carries out the disability determination function so that disability determinations are made accurately and promptly;

(2) Provide an organizational structure, adequate facilities, qualified personnel, medical consultant services, designated quick disability determination examiners (§§ 404.1619 and 404.1620(c)), and a quality assurance function (§§ 404.1620 through 404.1624);

(3) Furnish reports and records relating to the administration of the disability program (§ 404.1625);

(4) Submit budgets (§ 404.1626);

(5) Cooperate with audits (§ 404.1627);

(6) Insure that all applicants for and recipients of disability benefits are treated equally and courteously;

(7) Be responsible for property used for disability program purposes (§ 404.1628);

(8) Take part in the research and demonstration projects (§ 404.1629);

(9) Coordinate with other agencies (§ 404.1630);

(10) Safeguard the records created by the State in performing the disability determination function (§ 404.1631);

(11) Comply with other provisions of the Federal law and regulations that apply to the State in performing the disability determination function;

(12) Comply with other written guidelines (§ 404.1633);

(13) Maintain liaison with the medical profession and organizations that may facilitate performing the disability determination function; and

(14) Assist us in other ways that we determine may promote the objectives of effective and uniform administration.

[72 FR 51177, Sept. 6, 2007]

RESPONSIBILITIES FOR PERFORMING THE DISABILITY DETERMINATION FUNCTION

§ 404.1610 How a State notifies us that it wishes to perform the disability determination function.

(a) Deemed notice. Any State that has in effect as of June 1, 1981, an agreement with us to make disability determinations will be deemed to have given us notice that it wishes to perform the disability determination function, in lieu of continuing the agreement in effect after June 1, 1981.

(b) Written notice. After June 1, 1981, a State not making disability determinations that wishes to perform the disability determination function under these regulations must notify us in writing. The notice must be from an official authorized to act for the State for this purpose. The State will provide an opinion from the State's Attorney General verifying the authority of the official who sent the notice to act for the State.

§ 404.1611 How we notify a State whether it may perform the disability determination function.

(a) If a State notifies us in writing that it wishes to perform the disability determination function, we will notify the State in writing whether or not it may perform the function. The State will begin performing the disability determination function beginning with the month we and the State agree upon.

(b) If we have previously found that a State agency has substantially failed to make disability determinations in accordance with the law or these regulations and other written guidelines or if the State has previously notified us in writing that it does not wish to make disability determinations, the notice will advise the State whether the State agency may again make the disability determinations and, if so, the date and the conditions under which the State may again make them.

§ 404.1613 Disability determinations the State makes.

(a) General rule. A State agency will make determinations of disability with respect to all persons in the State except those individuals whose cases are in a class specifically excluded by our written guidelines. A determination of disability made by the State is the determination of the Commissioner, except as described in § 404.1503(d)(1).

(b) New classes of cases. Where any new class or classes of cases arise requiring determinations of disability, we will determine the conditions under which a State may choose not to make the disability determinations. We will provide the State with the necessary funding to do the additional work.

(c) Temporary transfer of classes of cases. We will make disability determinations for classes of cases temporarily transferred to us by the State agency if the State agency asks us to do so and we agree. The State agency will make written arrangements with us which will specify the period of time and the class or classes of cases we will do.

[62 FR 38452, July 18, 1997]

§ 404.1614 Responsibilities for obtaining evidence to make disability determinations.

(a) We or the State agency will secure from the claimant or other sources any evidence the State agency needs to make a disability determination. When we secure the evidence, we will furnish it to the State agency for use in making the disability determination.

(b) At our request, the State agency will obtain and furnish medical or other evidence and provide assistance as may be necessary for us to carry out our responsibilities—

(1) For making disability determinations in those classes of cases described in the written guidelines for which the State agency does not make the determination; or

(2) Under international agreements with respect to social security benefits payable under section 233 of the Act.

[79 FR 33682, June 12, 2014]

§ 404.1615 Making disability determinations.

(a) When making a disability determination, the State agency will apply subpart P, part 404, of our regulations.

(b) The State agency will make disability determinations based only on the medical and nonmedical evidence in its files.

(c) Disability determinations will be made by:

(1) A State agency medical or psychological consultant and a State agency disability examiner;

(2) A State agency disability examiner alone when there is no medical evidence to be evaluated (i.e., no medical evidence exists or we are unable, despite making every reasonable effort, to obtain any medical evidence that may exist) and the individual fails or refuses, without a good reason, to attend a consultative examination (see § 404.1518);

(3) A State agency disability examiner alone if the claim is adjudicated under the quick disability determination process (see § 404.1619) or the compassionate allowance process (see § 404.1602), and the initial or reconsidered determination is fully favorable to you. This paragraph (c)(3) will no longer be effective on December 28, 2018 unless we terminate it earlier by publication of a final rule in the Federal Register; or

(4) A State agency disability hearing officer.

See § 404.1616 for the definition of medical or psychological consultant and § 404.915 for the definition of disability hearing officer. The State agency disability examiner and disability hearing officer must be qualified to interpret and evaluate medical reports and other evidence relating to the claimant's physical or mental impairments and as necessary to determine the capacities of the claimant to perform substantial gainful activity.

See § 404.1572 for what we mean by substantial gainful activity.

(d) The State agency will certify each determination of disability to us on forms we provide.

(e) The State agency will furnish us with all the evidence it considered in making its determination.

(f) The State agency will not be responsible for defending in court any determination made, or any procedure for making determinations, under these regulations.

(g) [Redesignated as subsection (f) by 82 FR 5872]

[52 FR 33926, Sept. 9, 1987; 56 FR 11018, March 14, 1991; 61 FR 11135, March 19, 1996; 62 FR 38452, July 18, 1997; 65 FR 34958, June 1, 2000; 75 FR 62682, Oct. 13, 2010; 78 FR 66639, Nov. 6, 2013; 79 FR 51243, Aug. 28, 2014; 80 FR 63093, Oct. 19, 2015; 81 FR 73028, Oct. 24, 2016; 82 FR 5872, Jan. 18, 2017]

§ 404.1616 Medical consultants and psychological consultants.

(a) What is a medical consultant? A medical consultant is a member of a team that makes disability determinations in a State agency (see § 404.1615), or who is a member of a team that makes disability determinations for us when we make disability determinations ourselves. The medical consultant completes the medical portion of the case review and any applicable residual functional capacity assessment about all physical impairment(s) in a claim.

(b) What qualifications must a medical consultant have? A medical consultant is a licensed physician, as defined in § 404.1502(a)(1).

(c) What is a psychological consultant? A psychological consultant is a member of a team that makes disability determinations in a State agency (see § 404.1615), or who is a member of a team that makes disability determinations for us when we make disability determinations ourselves. The psychological consultant completes the medical portion of the case review and any applicable residual functional capacity assessment about all mental impairment(s) in a claim. When we are unable to obtain the services of a qualified psychiatrist or psychologist despite making every reasonable effort (see § 404.1617) in a claim involving a mental impairment(s), a medical consultant will evaluate the mental impairment(s).

(d) What qualifications must a psychological consultant have? A psychological consultant can be either a licensed psychiatrist or psychologist. We will only consider a psychologist qualified to be a psychological consultant if he or she:

(1) Is licensed or certified as a psychologist at the independent practice level of psychology by the State in which he or she practices; and

(2)(i) Possesses a doctorate degree in psychology from a program in clinical psychology of an educational institution accredited by an organization recognized by the Council on Post–Secondary Accreditation; or

(ii) Is listed in a national register of health service providers in psychology which the Commissioner of Social Security deems appropriate; and

(3) Possesses 2 years of supervised clinical experience as a psychologist in health service, at least 1 year of which is post-masters degree.

(e) Cases involving both physical and mental impairments. In a case where there is evidence of both physical and mental impairments, the medical consultant will evaluate the physical impairments in accordance with paragraph (a) of this section, and the psychological consultant will evaluate the mental impairment(s) in accordance with paragraph (c) of this section.

[52 FR 33927, Sept. 9, 1987; 62 FR 38452, July 18, 1997; 65 FR 34958, June 1, 2000; 71 FR 16445, March 31, 2006; 76 FR 24808, May 3, 2011; 82 FR 5873, Jan. 18, 2017]

§ 404.1617 Reasonable efforts to obtain review by a physician, psychiatrist, and psychologist.

(a) When the evidence of record indicates the existence of a physical impairment, the State agency must make every reasonable effort to ensure that a medical consultant completes the medical portion of the case review and any applicable residual functional capacity assessment. When the evidence of record indicates the existence of a mental impairment, the State agency must make every reasonable effort to ensure that a psychological consultant completes the medical portion of the case review and any applicable residual functional capacity assessment. The State agency must determine if additional physicians, psychiatrists, and psychologists are needed to make the necessary reviews. When it does not have sufficient resources to make the necessary reviews, the State agency must attempt to obtain the resources needed. If the State agency is unable to obtain additional physicians, psychiatrists, and psychologists because of low salary rates or fee schedules, it should attempt to raise the State agency's levels of compensation to meet the prevailing rates for these services. If these efforts are unsuccessful, the State agency will seek assistance from us. We will assist the State agency as necessary. We will also monitor the State agency's efforts and where the State agency is unable to obtain the necessary services, we will make every reasonable effort to provide the services using Federal resources.

(b) Federal resources may include the use of Federal contracts for the services of qualified psychiatrists and psychologists to review mental impairment cases. Where Federal resources are required to perform these reviews, which are a basic State agency responsibility, and where appropriate, the State agency's budget will be reduced accordingly.

(c) Where every reasonable effort is made to obtain the services of a qualified psychiatrist or psychologist to review a mental impairment case, but the professional services are not obtained, a physician who is not a psychiatrist will review the mental impairment case. For these purposes, every reasonable effort to ensure that a qualified psychiatrist or psychologist review mental impairment cases will be considered to have been made only after efforts by both State and Federal agencies as set forth in paragraphs (a) and (b) of this section are made.

[52 FR 33927, Sept. 9, 1987; 82 FR 5873, Jan. 18, 2017]

§ 404.1618 Notifying claimants of the disability determination.

The State agency will prepare denial notices in accordance with subpart J of this part whenever it makes a disability determination which is fully or partially unfavorable to the claimant.

[75 FR 33168, June 11, 2010]

QUICK DISABILITY DETERMINATIONS

Source: 72 FR 51177, Sept. 6, 2007, unless otherwise noted.

§ 404.1619 Quick disability determination process.

(a) If we identify a claim as one involving a high degree of probability that the individual is disabled, and we expect that the individual's allegations will be easily and quickly verified, we will refer the claim to the State agency for consideration under the quick disability determination process pursuant to this section and § 404.1620(c).

(b) If we refer a claim to the State agency for a quick disability determination, a designated quick disability determination examiner must do all of the following:

(1) Subject to the provisions in paragraph (c) of this section, make the disability determination after consulting with a State agency medical or psychological consultant if the State agency disability examiner determines consultation is appropriate or if consultation is required under § 404.1526(c). The State agency may certify the disability determination forms to us without the signature of the medical or psychological consultant.

(2) Make the quick disability determination based only on the medical and nonmedical evidence in the file.

(3) Subject to the provisions in paragraph (c) of this section, make the quick disability determination by applying the rules in subpart P of this part.

(c) If the quick disability determination examiner cannot make a determination that is fully favorable, or if there is an unresolved disagreement between the disability examiner and the medical or psychological consultant (except when a disability examiner makes the determination alone under § 404.1615(c)(3)), the State agency will adjudicate the claim using the regularly applicable procedures in this subpart.

[75 FR 62682, Oct. 13, 2010]

ADMINISTRATIVE RESPONSIBILITIES AND REQUIREMENTS

§ 404.1620 General administrative requirements.

(a) The State will provide the organizational structure, qualified personnel, medical consultant services, and a quality assurance function sufficient to ensure that disability determinations are made accurately and promptly. We may impose specific administrative requirements in these areas and in those under "Administrative Responsibilities and Requirements" in order to establish uniform, national administrative practices or to correct the areas of deficiencies which may later cause the State to be substantially failing to comply with our regulations or other written guidelines. We will notify the State, in writing, of the administrative requirements being imposed and of any administrative deficiencies it is required to correct. We will allow the State 90 days from the date of this notice to make appropriate corrections. Once corrected, we will monitor the State's administrative practices for 180 days. If the State does not meet the requirements or correct all of the deficiencies, or, if some of the deficiencies recur, we may initiate procedures to determine if the State is substantially failing to follow our regulations or other written guidelines.

(b) The State is responsible for making accurate and prompt disability determinations.

(c) Each State agency will designate experienced disability examiners to handle claims we refer to it under § 404.1619(a).

[56 FR 11018, March 14, 1991; 72 FR 51177, Sept. 6, 2007]

§ 404.1621 Personnel.

(a) Equal employment opportunity. The State will comply with all applicable Federal statutes, executive orders and regulations concerned with equal employment opportunities.

(b) Selection, tenure, and compensation. The State agency will, except as may be inconsistent with paragraph (a) of this section, adhere to applicable State approved personnel standards in the selection, tenure, and compensation of any individual employed in the disability program.

(c) Travel. The State will make personnel available to attend meetings or workshops as may be sponsored or approved by us for furthering the purposes of the disability program.

(d) Restrictions. Subject to appropriate Federal funding, the State will, to the best of its ability, facilitate the processing of disability claims by avoiding personnel freezes, restrictions against overtime work, or curtailment of facilities or activities.

§ 404.1622 Training.

The State will insure that all employees have an acceptable level of competence. We will provide training and other instructional materials to facilitate basic and advanced technical proficiency of disability staff in order to insure uniformity and effectiveness in the administration of the disability program. We will conduct or specify training, as appropriate, but only if:

(a) A State agency's performance approaches unacceptable levels; or

(b) The material required for the training is complex or the capacity of the State to deliver the training is in doubt and uniformity of the training is essential.

§ 404.1623 Facilities.

(a) Space, equipment, supplies, and other services. Subject to appropriate Federal funding, the State will provide adequate space, equipment, supplies, and other services to facilitate making accurate and prompt disability determinations.

(b) Location of facilities. Subject to appropriate Federal funding, the State will determine the location where the disability determination function is to be performed so that disability determinations are made accurately and promptly.

(c) Access. The State will permit us access to the premises where the disability determination function is performed and also where it is managed for the purposes of inspecting and obtaining information about the work and activities required by our regulations and assuring compliance with pertinent Federal statutes and regulations. Access includes personal onsite visits and other means, such as telecommunications, of contacting the State agency to obtain information about its functions. We will contact the State agency and give reasonable prior notice of the times and purposes of any visits.

[56 FR 11019, March 14, 1991]

§ 404.1624 Medical and other purchased services.

The State will determine the rates of payment for purchasing medical or other services necessary to make determinations of disability. The rates may not exceed the highest rate paid by Federal or other agencies in the State for the same or similar type of service. The State will maintain documentation to support the rates of payment it uses.

[71 FR 16445, March 31, 2006; 76 FR 24808, May 3, 2011]

§ 404.1625 Records and reports.

(a) The State will establish and maintain the records and furnish the schedules, financial, cost, and other reports relating to the administration of the disability programs as we may require.

(b) The State will permit us and the Comptroller General of the United States (including duly authorized representatives) access to and the right to examine records relating to the work which the State performs under these regulations. These records will be retained by the State for the periods of time specified for retention of records in the Federal Procurement Regulations (41 CFR parts 1–20).

§ 404.1626 Fiscal.

(a) We will give the State funds, in advance or by way of reimbursement, for necessary costs in making disability determinations under these regulations. Necessary costs are direct as well as indirect costs as defined in 41 CFR part 1–15, subpart 1–15.7 of the Federal Procurement Regulations System for costs incurred before April 1, 1984; and 48 CFR part 31, subpart 31.6 of the Federal Acquisition Regulations System and Federal Management Circular A–74–4 [1] as amended or superseded for costs incurred after March 31, 1984.

(b) The State will submit estimates of anticipated costs in the form of a budget at the time and in the manner we require.

(c) We will notify the State of the amount which will be made available to it as well as what anticipated costs are being approved.

(d) The State may not incur or make expenditures for items of cost not approved by us or in excess of the amount we make available to the State.

(e) After the close of a period for which funds have been made available to the State, the State will submit a report of its expenditures. Based on an audit arranged by the State under Pub.L. 98–502, the Single Audit Act of 1984, or by the Inspector General of the Social Security Administration or based on an audit or review by the Social Security Administration (see § 404.1627), we will determine whether the expenditures were consistent with cost principles described in 41 CFR part 1–15, subpart 1–15.7 for costs incurred before April 1, 1984; and 48 CFR part 31, subpart 31.6 and Federal Management Circular A–741–4 for costs incurred after March 31, 1984: and in other applicable written guidelines in effect at the time the expenditures were made or incurred.

(f) Any monies paid to the State which are used for purposes not within the scope of these regulations will be paid back to the Treasury of the United States.

[56 FR 11019, March 14, 1991; 62 FR 38452, July 18, 1997]

§ 404.1627 Audits.

(a) Audits performed by the State—

(1) Generally. Audits of accounts and records pertaining to the administration of the disability program under the Act, will be performed by the States in accordance with the Single Audit Act of 1984 (Pub. L. 98–502) which establishes audit requirements for States receiving Federal assistance. If the audit performed by the State meets our program requirements, we will accept the findings and recommendations of the audit. The State will make every effort to act upon and resolve any items questioned in the audit.

(2) Questioned items. Items questioned as a result of an audit under the Single Audit Act of 1984 of a cross-cutting nature will be resolved by the Department of Health and Human Services, Office of Grant and Contract Financial Management. A cross-cutting issue is one that involves more than one Federal awarding agency. Questioned items affecting only the disability program will be resolved by SSA in accord with paragraph (b)(2) of this section,

(3) State appeal of audit determinations. The Office of Grant and Contract Financial Management will notify the State of its determination on questioned cross-cutting items. If the State disagrees with that determination, it may appeal in writing within 60 days of receiving the determination. State appeals of a cross-cutting issue as a result of an audit under the Single

[1] The circular is available from the Office of Administration, Publications Unit, Rm. G–236, New Executive Office Bldg., Washington, DC 20503.

Audit Act of 1984 will be made to the Department of Health and Human Services' Departmental Appeals Board. The rules for hearings and appeals are provided in 45 CFR part 16.

(b) Audits performed by the Commissioner—

(1) Generally. If the State does not perform an audit under the Single Audit Act of 1984 or the audit performed is not satisfactory for disability program purposes, the books of account and records in the State pertaining to the administrations of the disability programs under the Act will be audited by the SSA's Inspector General or audited or reviewed by SSA as appropriate. These audits or reviews will be conducted to determine whether the expenditures were made for the intended purposes and in amounts necessary for the proper and efficient administration of the disability programs. Audits or reviews will also be made to inspect the work and activities required by the regulations to ensure compliance with pertinent Federal statutes and regulations. The State will make every effort to act upon and resolve any items questioned in an audit or review.

(2) Questioned items. Expenditures of State agencies will be audited or reviewed, as appropriate, on the basis of cost principles and written guidelines in effect at the time the expenditures were made or incurred. Both the State and the State agency will be informed and given a full explanation of any items questioned. They will be given reasonable time to explain items questioned. Any explanation furnished by the State or State agency will be given full consideration before a final determination is made on the audit or review report.

(3) State appeal of audit determinations. The appropriate Social Security Administration Regional Commissioner will notify the State of his or her determination on the audit or review report. If the State disagrees with that determination, the State may request reconsideration in writing within 60 days of the date of the Regional Commissioner's notice of the determination. The written request may be made, through the Associate Commissioner, Office of Disability, to the Commissioner of Social Security, room 900, Altmeyer Building, 6401 Security Boulevard, Baltimore, Maryland 21235. The Commissioner will make a determination and notify the State of the decision in writing no later than 90 days from the date the Social Security Administration receives the State's appeal and all supporting documents. The decision by the Commissioner on other than monetary disallowances will be final and binding upon the State. The decision by the Commissioner on monetary disallowances will be final and binding upon the State unless the State appeals the decision in writing to the Department of Health and Human Services, Departmental Appeals Board within 30 days after receiving the Commissioner's decision. See § 404.1683.

[56 FR 11019, March 14, 1991; 62 FR 38452, July 18, 1997]

§ 404.1628 Property.

The State will have title to equipment purchased for disability program purposes. The State will be responsible for maintaining all property it acquires or which we furnish to it for performing the disability determination function. The State will identify the equipment by labeling and by inventory and will credit the SSA account with the fair market value of disposed property.

In the event we assume the disability determination function from a State, ownership of all property and equipment acquired with SSA funds will be transferred to us effective on the date the State is notified that we are assuming the disability determination function or we are notified that the State is terminating the relationship.

§ 404.1629 Participation in research and demonstration projects.

We will invite State participation in federally funded research and demonstration projects to assess the effectiveness of the disability program and to ascertain the effect of program policy changes. Where we determine that State participation is necessary for the project to be complete, for example, to provide national uniformity in a claims process, State participation is mandatory.

§ 404.1630 Coordination with other agencies.

(a) The State will establish cooperative working relationships with other agencies concerned with serving the disabled and, insofar as practicable, use their services, facilities, and records to:

(1) Assist the State in developing evidence and making determinations of disability; and

(2) Insure that referral of disabled or blind persons for rehabilitation services will be carried out effectively.

(b) The State may pay these agencies for the services, facilities, or records they provide. The State will include these costs in its estimates of anticipated costs and reports of actual expenditures.

§ 404.1631 Confidentiality of information and records.

The State will comply with the confidentiality of information, including the security of systems, and records requirements described in 20 CFR part 401 and pertinent written guidelines (see § 404.1633).

§ 404.1632 Other Federal laws and regulations.

The State will comply with the provisions of other Federal laws and regulations that directly affect its responsibilities in carrying out the disability determination function; for example, Treasury Department regulations on letters of credit (31 CFR part 205).

§ 404.1633 Policies and operating instructions.

(a) We will provide the State agency with written guidelines necessary for it to carry out its responsibilities in performing the disability determination function.

(b) The State agency making determinations of disability will comply with our written guidelines that are not designated as advisory or discretionary. (See § 404.1602 for what we mean by written guidelines.)

(c) A representative group of State agencies will be given an opportunity to participate in formulating disability program policies that have an affect on their role in carrying out the disability determination function. State agencies will also be given an opportunity to comment before changes are made in written guidelines unless delay in issuing a change may impair service to the public.

[56 FR 11020, March 14, 1991]

PERFORMANCE STANDARDS

§ 404.1640 General.

The following sections provide the procedures and guidelines we use to determine whether the State agency is substantially complying with our regulations and other written guidelines, including meeting established national performance standards. We use performance standards to help assure effective and uniform administration of our disability programs and to measure whether the performance of the disability determination function by each State agency is acceptable. Also, the standards are designed to improve overall State agency performance in the disability determination process and to ensure that benefits are made available to all eligible persons in an accurate and efficient manner. We measure the performance of a State agency in two areas—processing time and quality of documentation and decisions on claims. State agency compliance is also judged by State agency adherence to other program requirements.

[56 FR 11020, March 14, 1991]

§ 404.1641 Standards of performance.

(a) General. The performance standards include both a target level of performance and a threshold level of performance for the State agency. The target level represents a level of performance that we and the States will work to attain in the future. The threshold level is the minimum acceptable level of performance. Performance below the threshold level will be the basis for the Commissioner's taking from the State agency partial or complete responsibility for performing the disability determination function. Intermediate State agency goals are designed to help each State agency move from its current performance levels to the target levels.

(b) The target level. The target level is the optimum level of performance. There are three targets—one for combined title II and title XVI initial performance accuracy, one for title II initial processing time, and one for title XVI initial processing time.

(c) The threshold level. The threshold level is the minimum acceptable level of performance. There are three thresholds—one for combined title II and title XVI initial performance accuracy, one for title II initial processing time, and one for title XVI initial processing time.

(d) Intermediate goals. Intermediate goals are levels of performance between the threshold levels and the target levels established by our appropriate Regional Commissioner after negotiation with each State agency. The intermediate goals are designed to help the State agencies reach the target levels. Failure to meet these goals is not a cause for considering the State agency to be substantially failing to comply with the performance standards. However, failure to meet the intermediate goals may result in consultation and an offer of optional performance support depending on the availability of our resources.

[56 FR 11020, March 14, 1991; 62 FR 38452, July 18, 1997]

§ 404.1642 Processing time standards.

(a) General. Title II processing time refers to the average number of days, including Saturdays, Sundays, and holidays, it takes a State agency to process an initial disability claim from the day the case folder is received in the State agency until the day it is released to us by the State agency. Title XVI processing time refers to the average number of days, including Saturdays, Sundays, and holidays, from the day of receipt of the initial disability claim in the State agency until systems input of a presumptive disability decision or the day the case folder is released to us by the State agency, whichever is earlier.

(b) Target levels. The processing time target levels are:

(1) 37 days for title II initial claims.

(2) 43 days for title XVI initial claims.

(c) Threshold levels. The processing time threshold levels are:

(1) 49.5 days for title II initial claims.

(2) 57.9 days for title XVI initial claims.

[56 FR 11020, March 14, 1991]

§ 404.1643 Performance accuracy standard.

(a) General. Performance accuracy refers to the percentage of cases that do not have to be returned to State agencies for further development or correction of decisions based on evidence in the files and as such represents the reliability of State agency adjudication.

The definition of performance accuracy includes the measurement of factors that have a potential for affecting a decision, as well as the correctness of the decision. For example, if a particular item of medical evidence should have been in the file but was not included, even though its inclusion does not change the result in the case, that is a performance error. Performance accuracy, therefore, is a higher standard than decisional accuracy. As a result, the percentage of correct decisions is significantly higher than what is reflected in the error rate established by SSA's quality assurance system.

(b) Target level. The State agency initial performance accuracy target level for combined title II and title XVI cases is 97 percent with a corresponding decision accuracy rate of 99 percent.

(c) Intermediate goals. These goals will be established annually by SSA's regional commissioner after negotiation with the State and should be used as stepping stones to progress towards our targeted level of performance.

(d) Threshold levels. The State agency initial performance accuracy threshold level for combined title II and title XVI cases is 90.6 percent.

§ 404.1644 How and when we determine whether the processing time standards are met.

(a) How we determine processing times. For all initial title II cases, we calculate the mean number of days, including Saturdays, Sundays and holidays, from the day the case folder is received in the State agency until the day it is released to us by the State agency. For initial title XVI cases, we calculate the mean number of days, including Saturdays, Sundays, and holidays, from the day the case folder is received in the State agency until the day there is a systems input of a presumptive disability decision or the day the case folder is released to us by the State agency, whichever is earlier.

(b) Frequency of review. Title II processing times and title XVI processing times are monitored separately on a quarterly basis. The determination as to whether or not the processing time thresholds have been met is made at the end of each quarter each year. Quarterly State-by-State mean processing times are compared with the threshold levels for both title II and title XVI.

[56 FR 11020, March 14, 1991]

§ 404.1645 How and when we determine whether the performance accuracy standard is met.

(a) How we determine performance accuracy. We determine a State agency's performance accuracy rate on the basis of decision and documentation errors identified in our review of the sample cases.

(b) Frequency of review. Title II and title XVI initial performance accuracy are monitored together on a quarterly basis. The determinations as to whether the performance accuracy threshold has been met is made at the end of each quarter each year. Quarterly State-by-State combined initial performance accuracy rates are compared to the established threshold level.

§ 404.1650 Action we will take if a State agency does not meet the standards.

If a State agency does not meet two of the three established threshold levels (one of which must be performance accuracy) for two or more consecutive calendar quarters, we will notify the State agency in writing that it is not meeting the standards. Following our notification, we will provide the State agency appropriate performance support described in §§ 404.1660, 404.1661 and 404.1662 for a period of up to 12 months.

[56 FR 11020, March 14, 1991]

PERFORMANCE MONITORING AND SUPPORT

§ 404.1660 How we will monitor.

We will regularly analyze State agency combined title II and title XVI initial performance accuracy rate, title II initial processing time, and title XVI initial processing time. Within budgeted resources, we will also routinely conduct fiscal and administrative management reviews and special onsite reviews. A fiscal and administrative management review is a fact-finding mission to review particular aspects of State agency operations. During these reviews we will also review the quality assurance function. This regular monitoring and review program will allow us to determine the progress each State is making and the type and extent of performance support we will provide to help the State progress toward threshold, intermediate, and/or target levels.

[56 FR 11020, March 14, 1991]

§ 404.1661 When we will provide performance support.

(a) Optional support. We may offer, or a State may request, performance support at any time that the regular monitoring and review process reveals that support could enhance performance. The State does not have to be below the initial performance accuracy rate of 90.6 percent to receive performance support. Support will be offered, or granted upon request, based on available resources.

(b) Mandatory support.

(1) We will provide a State agency with mandatory performance support if regular monitoring and review reveal that two of three threshold levels (one of which must be performance accuracy) are not met for two consecutive calendar quarters.

(2) We may also decide to provide a State agency with mandatory performance support if regular monitoring and review reveal that any one of the three threshold levels is not met for two consecutive calendar quarters. Support will be provided based on available resources.

(3) The threshold levels are:

(i) Combined title II and title XVI initial performance accuracy rate—90.6 percent,

(ii) Title II initial processing time—49.5 days, and

(iii) Title XVI initial processing time—57.9 days.

[56 FR 11020, March 14, 1991]

§ 404.1662 What support we will provide.

Performance support may include, but is not limited to, any or all of the following:

(a) An onsite review of cases processed by the State agency emphasizing adherence to written guidelines.

(b) A request that necessary administrative measures be implemented (e.g., filling staffing vacancies, using overtime, assisting with training activities, etc.).

(c) Provisions for Federal personnel to perform onsite reviews, conduct training, or perform other functions needed to improve performance.

(d) Provisions for fiscal aid to allow for overtime, temporary hiring of additional staff, etc., above the authorized budget.

[56 FR 11020, March 14, 1991]

SUBSTANTIAL FAILURE

§ 404.1670 General.

After a State agency falls below two of three established threshold levels, one being performance accuracy, for two consecutive quarters, and after the mandatory performance support period, we will give the State agency a 3–month adjustment period. During this 3–month period we will not require the State agency to meet the threshold levels. Following the adjustment period, if the State agency again falls below two of three threshold levels, one being performance accuracy, in two consecutive quarters during the next 12 months, we will notify the State that we propose to find that the State agency has substantially failed to comply with our standards and advise it that it may request a hearing on that issue. After giving the State notice and an opportunity for a hearing, if it is found that a State agency has substantially failed to make disability determinations consistent with the Act, our regulations or other written guidelines, we will assume partial or complete responsibility for performing the disability determination function after we have complied with §§ 404.1690 and 404.1692.

[56 FR 11021, March 14, 1991]

§ 404.1671 Good cause for not following the Act, our regulations, or other written guidelines.

If a State has good cause for not following the Act, our regulations, or other written guidelines, we will not find that the State agency has substantially failed to meet our standards. We will determine if good cause exists. Some of the factors relevant to good cause are:

(a) Disasters such as fire, flood, or civil disorder, that—

(1) Require the diversion of significant personnel normally assigned to the disability determination function, or

(2) Destroyed or delayed access to significant records needed to make accurate disability determinations;

(b) Strikes of State agency staff or other government or private personnel necessary to the performance of the disability determination function;

(c) Sudden and unanticipated workload changes which result from changes in Federal law, regulations, or written guidelines, systems modification or systems malfunctions, or rapid, unpredictable caseload growth for a 6–month period or longer.

[56 FR 11021, March 14, 1991]

§ 404.1675 Finding of substantial failure.

A finding of substantial failure with respect to a State may not be made unless and until the State is afforded an opportunity for a hearing.

HEARINGS AND APPEALS

§ 404.1680 Notice of right to hearing on proposed finding of substantial failure.

If, following the mandatory performance support period and the 3–month adjustment period, a State agency again falls below two of three threshold levels (one being performance accuracy) in two consecutive quarters in the succeeding 12 months, we will notify the State in writing that we will find that the State agency has substantially failed to meet our standards unless the State submits a written request for a hearing with the Department of Health and Human Services' Departmental Appeals Board within 30 days after receiving the notice. The notice will identify the threshold levels that were not met by the State agency, the period during which the thresholds were not met and the accuracy and processing time levels attained by the State agency during this period. If a hearing is not requested, the State agency will be found to have substantially failed to meet our standards, and we will implement our plans to assume the disability determination function.

[56 FR 11021, March 14, 1991]

§ 404.1681 Disputes on matters other than substantial failure.

Disputes concerning monetary disallowances will be resolved in proceedings before the Department of Health and Human Services' Departmental Appeals Board if the issue cannot be resolved between us and the State. Disputes other than monetary disallowances will be resolved through an appeal to the Commissioner of Social Security, who will make the final decision. (See § 404.1627.)

[56 FR 11021, March 14, 1991]

§ 404.1682 Who conducts the hearings.

If a hearing is required, it will be conducted by the Department of Health and Human Services' Grant [1] Appeals Board (the Board).

[62 FR 38452, July 18, 1997]

§ 404.1683 Hearings and appeals process.

The rules for hearings and appeals before the Board are provided in 45 CFR part 16. A notice under § 404.1680 of this subpart will be considered a "final written decision" for purposes of Board review.

ASSUMPTION OF DISABILITY DETERMINATION FUNCTION

§ 404.1690 Assumption when we make a finding of substantial failure.

(a) Notice to State. When we find that substantial failure exists, we will notify the State in writing that we will assume responsibility for performing the disability determination function from the State agency, whether the assumption will be partial or complete, and the date on which the assumption will be effective.

(b) Effective date of assumption. The date of any partial or complete assumption of the disability determination function from a State agency may not be earlier than 180 days after our finding of substantial failure, and not before compliance with the requirements of § 404.1692.

§ 404.1691 Assumption when State no longer wishes to perform the disability determination function.

(a) Notice to the Commissioner. If a State no longer wishes to perform the disability determination function, it will notify us in writing. The notice must be from an official authorized to act for the State for this purpose. The State will provide an opinion from the State's Attorney General verifying the authority of the official who gave the notice.

(b) Effective date of assumption. The State agency will continue to perform whatever activities of the disability determination function it is performing at the time the notice referred to in paragraph (a) of this section is given for not less than 180 days or, if later, until we have complied with the requirements of § 404.1692. For example, if the State is not making disability determinations (because we previously assumed responsibility for making them) but is performing other activities related to the disability determination function at the time it gives notice, the State will continue to do these activities until the requirements of this paragraph are met. Thereafter, we will assume complete responsibility for performing the disability determination function.

[62 FR 38452, July 18, 1997]

§ 404.1692 Protection of State employees.

(a) Hiring preference. We will develop and initiate procedures to implement a plan to partially or completely assume the disability determination function from the State agency under § 404.1690 or § 404.1691, as appropriate. Except for the State agency's administrator, deputy administrator, or assistant administrator (or his equivalent), we will give employees of the State agency who are capable of performing duties in the disability determination function preference over any other persons in filling positions with us for which they are qualified. We may also give a preference in hiring to the State agency's administrator, deputy administrator, or assistant administrator (or his equivalent). We will establish a system for determining the hiring priority among the affected State agency employees in those instances where we are not hiring all of them.

(b) Determination by Secretary of Labor. We will not assume responsibility for performing the disability determination function from a State until the Secretary of Labor determines that the State has made fair and equitable arrangements under applicable Federal, State and local law to protect the interests of employees who will be displaced from their employment because of the assumption and who we will not hire.

§ 404.1693 Limitation on State expenditures after notice.

The State agency may not, after it receives the notice referred to in § 404.1690, or gives the notice referred to in § 404.1691, make any new commitments to spend funds allocated to it for performing the disability determination function without the approval of the appropriate SSA regional commissioner. The State will make every effort to close out as soon as possible all existing commitments that relate to performing the disability determination function.

§ 404.1694 Final accounting by the State.

The State will submit its final claims to us as soon as possible, but in no event later than 1 year from the

[1] So in original; probably should read "Departmental Appeals Board". See 62 FR 38452.

effective date of our assumption of the disability determination function unless we grant an extension of time. When the final claim(s) is submitted, a final accounting will be made by the State of any funds paid to the State under § 404.1626 which have not been spent or committed prior to the effective date of our assumption of the disability determination function. Disputes concerning final accounting issues which cannot be resolved between the State and us will be resolved in proceedings before the Departmental Appeals Board as described in 45 CFR part 16.

[62 FR 38452, July 18, 1997]

SUBPART R—REPRESENTATION OF PARTIES

Authority: Secs. 205(a), 206, 702(a)(5), and 1127 of the Social Security Act (42 U.S.C. 405(a), 406, 902(a)(5), and 1320a–6).

Source: 45 FR 52090, Aug. 5, 1980; 52 FR 27541, July 22, 1987; 61 FR 5941, Feb. 15, 1996; 72 FR 16724, April 5, 2007; 72 FR 44767, Aug. 9, 2007; 76 FR 45192, July 28, 2011; 76 FR 56109, Sept. 12, 2011; 80 FR 399, Jan. 6, 2015, unless otherwise noted.

§ 404.1700 Introduction.

You may appoint someone to represent you in any of your dealings with us. This subpart explains, among other things—

(a) Who may be your representative and what his or her qualifications must be;

(b) How you appoint a representative;

(c) The payment of fees to a representative;

(d) Our rules that representatives must follow; and

(e) What happens to a representative who breaks the rules.

§ 404.1703 Definitions.

As used in this subpart—

Date we notify him or her means 5 days after the date on the notice, unless the recipient shows us that he or she did not receive it within the 5-day period.

Eligible non-attorney means a non-attorney representative who we determine is qualified to receive direct payment of his or her fee under § 404.1717(a).

Entity means any business, firm, or other association, including but not limited to partnerships, corporations, for-profit organizations, and not-for-profit organizations.

Federal agency refers to any authority of the Executive branch of the Government of the United States.

Federal program refers to any program established by an Act of Congress or administered in whole or in part by a Federal agency.

Legal guardian or court-appointed representative means a court-appointed person, committee, or conservator who is responsible for taking care of and managing the property and rights of an individual who is considered incapable of managing his or her own affairs.

Past-due benefits means the total amount of benefits under title II of the Act that has accumulated to all beneficiaries because of a favorable administrative or judicial determination or decision, up to but not including the month the determination or decision is made. For purposes of calculating fees for representation, we determine past-due benefits before any applicable reduction under section 1127 of the Act (for receipt of benefits for the same period under title XVI). Past-due benefits do not include:

(1) Continued benefits paid pursuant to § 404.1597a of this part; or

(2) Interim benefits paid pursuant to section 223(h) of the Act.

Representational services means services performed for a claimant in connection with any claim the claimant has before us, any asserted right the claimant may have for an initial or reconsidered determination, and any decision or action by an administrative law judge or the Appeals Council.

Representative means an attorney who meets all of the requirements of § 404.1705(a), or a person other than an attorney who meets all of the requirements of § 404.1705(b), and whom you appoint to represent you in dealings with us.

We, our, or us refers to the Social Security Administration.

You or your refers to any person claiming a right under the old-age, disability, dependents', or survivors' benefits program.

[72 FR 16724, April 5, 2007; 72 FR 44767, Aug. 9, 2007; 74 FR 48384, Sept. 23, 2009; 76 FR 45192, July 28, 2011; 76 FR 80245, Dec. 23, 2011; 80 FR 399, Jan. 6, 2015]

§ 404.1705 Who may be your representative.

(a) You may appoint as your representative in dealings with us, any attorney in good standing who—

(1) Has the right to practice law before a court of a State, Territory, District, or island possession of the United States, or before the Supreme Court or a lower Federal court of the United States;

(2) Is not disqualified or suspended from acting as a representative in dealings with us; and

(3) Is not prohibited by any law from acting as a representative.

(b) You may appoint any person who is not an attorney to be your representative in dealings with us if the person—

(1) Is capable of giving valuable help to you in connection with your claim;

(2) Is not disqualified or suspended from acting as a representative in dealings with us;

(3) Is not prohibited by any law from acting as a representative; and

(4) Is generally known to have a good character and reputation. Persons lacking good character and reputation, include, but are not limited to, persons who have a final conviction of a felony (as defined by § 404.1506(c)) or any crime involving moral turpitude, dishonesty, false statements, misrepresentation, deceit, or theft.

(c) We may refuse to recognize the person you choose to represent you if the person does not meet the requirements in this section. We will notify you and the person you attempted to appoint as your representative if we do not recognize the person as a representative.

[76 FR 80245, Dec. 23, 2011; 83 FR 30854, July 2, 2018]

§ 404.1706 Notification of options for obtaining attorney representation.

If you are not represented by an attorney and we make a determination or decision that is subject to the administrative review process provided under subpart J of this part and it does not grant all of the benefits or other relief you requested or it adversely affects any entitlement to benefits that we have established or may establish for you, we will include with the notice of that determination or decision information about your options for obtaining an attorney to represent you in dealing with us. We will also tell you that a legal services organization may provide you with legal representation free of charge if you satisfy the qualifying requirements applicable to that organization.

[58 FR 64886, Dec. 10, 1993]

§ 404.1707 Appointing a representative.

We will recognize a person as your representative if the following things are done:

(a) You sign a written notice stating that you want the person to be your representative in dealings with us.

(b) That person signs the notice, agreeing to be your representative, if the person is not an attorney. An attorney does not have to sign a notice of appointment.

(c) The notice is filed at one of our offices if you have initially filed a claim or have requested reconsideration; with an administrative law judge if you requested a hearing; or with the Appeals Council if you have requested a review of the administrative law judge's decision.

§ 404.1710 Authority of a representative.

(a) What a representative may do. Your representative may, on your behalf—

(1) Obtain information about your claim to the same extent that you are able to do;

(2) Submit evidence;

(3) Make statements about facts and law; and

(4) Make any request or give any notice about the proceedings before us.

(b) What a representative may not do. A representative may not sign an application on behalf of a claimant for rights or benefits under title II of the Act unless authorized to do so under § 404.612.

§ 404.1713 Mandatory use of electronic services.

A representative must conduct business with us electronically at the times and in the manner we prescribe on matters for which the representative requests direct fee payment. (See § 404.1740(b)(4)).

[76 FR 56109, Sept. 12, 2011]

§ 404.1715 Notice or request to a representative.

(a) We shall send your representative—

(1) Notice and a copy of any administrative action, determination, or decision; and

(2) Requests for information or evidence.

(b) A notice or request sent to your representative, will have the same force and effect as if it had been sent to you.

§ 404.1717 Direct payment of fees to eligible non-attorney representatives.

(a) Criteria for eligibility. An individual who is a licensed attorney or who is suspended or disbarred from the practice of law in any jurisdiction may not be an eligible non-attorney. A non-attorney representative is eligible to receive direct payment of his or her fee out of your past-due benefits if he or she:

(1) Completes and submits to us an application as described in paragraph (b) of this section;

(2) Pays the application fee as described in paragraph (c) of this section;

(3) Demonstrates that he or she possesses:

(i) A bachelor's degree from an accredited institution of higher learning; or

(ii) At least four years of relevant professional experience and either a high school diploma or a General Educational Development certificate;

(4) Passes our criminal background investigation (including checks of our administrative records), and attests under penalty of perjury that he or she:

(i) Has not been suspended or disqualified from practice before us and is not suspended or disbarred from the practice of law in any jurisdiction;

(ii) Has not had a judgment or lien assessed against him or her by a civil court for malpractice or fraud;

(iii) Has not had a felony conviction; and

(iv) Has not misrepresented information provided on his or her application or supporting materials for the application;

(5) Takes and passes a written examination we administer;

(6) Provides proof of and maintains continuous liability insurance coverage that is underwritten by an entity that is legally permitted to provide professional liability insurance in the States in which the representative conducts business. The policy must include coverage for malpractice claims against the representative and be in an amount we prescribe; and

(7) Completes and provides proof that he or she has completed all continuing education courses that we prescribe by the deadline we prescribe.

(b) Application. An applicant must timely submit his or her completed application form during an application period that we prescribe. The application must be postmarked by the last day of the application period. If an applicant timely submits the application fee and a defective application, we will give the applicant 10 calendar days after the date we notify him or her of the defect to correct the application.

(c) Application fee. An applicant must timely submit his or her application fee during the application period. We will set the fee annually.

(1) We will refund the fee if:

(i) We do not administer an examination, and an applicant was unable to take the rescheduled examination; or

(ii) Circumstances beyond the applicant's control that could not have been reasonably anticipated and planned for prevent an applicant from taking a scheduled examination.

(2) We will not refund the fee if:

(i) An applicant took and failed the examination; or

(ii) An applicant failed to arrive on time for the examination because of circumstances within the applicant's control that could have been anticipated and planned for.

(d) Protest procedures.

(1) We may find that a non-attorney representative is ineligible to receive direct fee payment at any time because he or she fails to meet any of the criteria in paragraph (a) of this section. A non-attorney representative whom we find to be ineligible for direct fee payment may protest our finding only if we based it on the representative's failure to:

(i) Attest on the application or provide sufficient documentation that he or she possesses the required education or equivalent qualifications, as described in paragraph (a)(3) of this section;

(ii) Meet at all times the criminal background investigation criteria, as described in paragraph (a)(4) of this section;

(iii) Provide proof that he or she has maintained continuous liability insurance coverage, as described in paragraph (a)(6) of this section, after we previously determined the representative was eligible to receive direct fee payment; or

(iv) Complete continuing education courses or provide documentation of the required continuing education courses, as described in paragraph (a)(7) of this section.

(2) A non-attorney representative who wants to protest our finding under paragraph (d)(1) of this section must file a protest in writing and provide all relevant supporting documentation to us within 10 calendar days after the date we notify him or her of our finding.

(3) A representative may not file a protest for reasons other than those listed in paragraph (d)(1) of this section. If a representative files a protest for reasons other than those listed in paragraph (d)(1) of this section, we will not process the protest and will implement our finding as if no protest had been filed. Our finding in response to the protest is final and not subject to further review.

(e) Ineligibility and suspension.

(1) If an applicant does not protest, in accordance with paragraph (d)(2) of this section, our finding about the criteria in paragraphs (a)(3) or (a)(4) of this section, the applicant will be either ineligible to take the written examination for which he or she applied or ineligible to receive direct fee payment if the applicant already took and passed the examination prior to our finding. If an applicant protests in accordance with paragraph (d)(2) of this section and we uphold our finding, the applicant will be either ineligible to take the written examination for which he or she applied or ineligible to receive direct fee payment if the applicant already took and passed the examination prior to our finding.

(2) If an eligible non-attorney representative does not protest, in accordance with paragraph (d)(2) of this section, our finding about the criteria in paragraphs (a)(3) or (a)(4) of this section, the non-attorney representative will be ineligible to receive direct fee payment beginning with the month after the month the protest period ends. If the eligible non-attorney representative protests in accordance with paragraph (d)(2) of this section and we uphold our finding, the non-attorney representative will be ineligible to receive direct fee payment beginning with the month after the month we uphold our finding.

(3) If an eligible non-attorney representative does not protest, in accordance with paragraph (d)(2) of this section, our finding about the criteria in paragraph (a)(6) of this section, the non-attorney representative

will be ineligible to receive direct fee payment for 6 full calendar months beginning with the month after the month the protest period ends. If the eligible non-attorney representative protests in accordance with paragraph (d)(2) of this section and we uphold our finding, the non-attorney representative will be ineligible to receive direct fee payment for 6 full calendar months beginning with the month after the month we uphold our finding. In either case, the non-attorney representative may provide us with documentation that he or she has acquired and maintains the required liability insurance coverage described in paragraph (a)(6) of this section, no earlier than the sixth month of the ineligibility. The non-attorney representative will again be eligible to receive direct fee payment beginning in the first month after the month we find that we have received sufficient documentation that the non-attorney representative meets the requirements of paragraph (a)(6) of this section.

(4) If an eligible non-attorney representative does not protest, in accordance with paragraph (d)(2) of this section, our finding about the criteria in paragraph (a)(7) of this section, the non-attorney representative will be ineligible to receive direct fee payment for 6 full calendar months beginning with the month after the month the protest period ends. If the eligible non-attorney representative protests in accordance with paragraph (d)(2) of this section and we uphold our finding, the non-attorney will be ineligible to receive direct fee payment for 6 full calendar months beginning with the month after the month we uphold our finding. In either case, the non-attorney representative may provide us with documentation that he or she has satisfied the criteria in paragraph (a)(7) of this section at any time. The non-attorney representative will again be eligible to receive direct fee payment beginning in the first month after the month we find that we have received sufficient documentation, but not earlier than the month following the end of the 6 month ineligibility period.

(f) Reapplying. A representative may reapply to become eligible to receive direct fee payment under paragraph (a) of this section during any subsequent application period if he or she:

(1) Did not meet the initial criteria for eligibility in paragraphs (a)(1), (a)(2), (a)(3), or (a)(5) of this section in a prior application period; or

(2) Failed to timely correct a defective application in a prior application period, as described in paragraph (b) of this section.

[72 FR 16724, April 5, 2007; 72 FR 44767, Aug. 9, 2007; 76 FR 45192, July 28, 2011; 80 FR 399, 400, Jan. 6, 2015]

§ 404.1720 Fee for a representative's services.

(a) General. A representative may charge and receive a fee for his or her services as a representative only as provided in paragraph (b) of this section.

(b) Charging and receiving a fee.

(1) The representative must file a written request with us before he or she may charge or receive a fee for his or her services.

(2) We decide the amount of the fee, if any, a representative may charge or receive.

(3) Subject to paragraph (e) of this section, a representative must not charge or receive any fee unless we have authorized it, and a representative must not charge or receive any fee that is more than the amount we authorize.

(4) If your representative is an attorney or an eligible non-attorney, and you are entitled to past-due benefits, we will pay the authorized fee, or a part of the authorized fee, directly to the attorney or eligible non-attorney out of the past-due benefits, subject to the limitations described in § 404.1730(b)(1). If the representative is a non-attorney who is ineligible to receive direct fee payment, we assume no responsibility for the payment of any fee that we have authorized.

(c) Notice of fee determination. We shall mail to both you and your representative at your last known address a written notice of what we decide about the fee. We shall state in the notice—

(1) The amount of the fee that is authorized;

(2) How we made that decision;

(3) Whether we are responsible for paying the fee from past-due benefits; and

(4) That within 30 days of the date of the notice, either you or your representative may request us to review the fee determination.

(d) Review of fee determination—

(1) Request filed on time. We will review the decision we made about a fee if either you or your representative files a written request for the review at one of our offices within 30 days after the date of the notice of the fee determination. Either you or your representative, whoever requests the review, shall mail a copy of the request to the other person. An authorized official of the Social Security Administration who did not take part in the fee determination being questioned will review the determination. This determination is not subject to further review. The official shall mail a written notice of the decision made on review both to you and to your representative at your last known address.

(2) Request not filed on time.

(i) If you or your representative requests a review of the decision we made about a fee, but does so more than 30 days after the date of the notice of the fee determination, whoever makes the request shall state in writing why it was not filed within the 30–day period. We will review the determination if we decide that there was good cause for not filing the request on time.

(ii) Some examples of good cause follow:

(A) Either you or your representative was seriously ill and the illness prevented you or your representative from contacting us in person or in writing.

(B) There was a death or serious illness in your family or in the family of your representative.

(C) Material records were destroyed by fire or other accidental cause.

(D) We gave you or your representative incorrect or incomplete information about the right to request review.

(E) You or your representative did not timely receive notice of the fee determination.

(F) You or your representative sent the request to another government agency in good faith within the 30–day period, and the request did not reach us until after the period had ended.

(3) Payment of fees. We assume no responsibility for the payment of a fee based on a revised determination if the request for administrative review was not filed on time.

(e) When we do not need to authorize a fee. We do not need to authorize a fee when:

(1) An entity or a Federal, State, county, or city government agency pays from its funds the representative fees and expenses and both of the following conditions apply:

(i) You and your auxiliary beneficiaries, if any, are not liable to pay a fee or any expenses, or any part thereof, directly or indirectly, to the representative or someone else; and

(ii) The representative submits to us a writing in the form and manner that we prescribe waiving the right to charge and collect a fee and any expenses from you and your auxiliary beneficiaries, if any, directly or indirectly, in whole or in part; or

(2) A court authorizes a fee for your representative based on the representative's actions as your legal guardian or a court-appointed representative.

[72 FR 16724, April 5, 2007; 72 FR 44767, Aug. 9, 2007; 74 FR 48384, Sept. 23, 2009; 76 FR 45193, July 28, 2011; 80 FR 399, Jan. 6, 2015]

§ 404.1725 Request for approval of a fee.

(a) Filing a request. In order for your representative to obtain approval of a fee for services he or she performed in dealings with us, he or she shall file a written request with one of our offices. This should be done after the proceedings in which he or she was a representative are completed. The request must contain—

(1) The dates the representative's services began and ended;

(2) A list of the services he or she gave and the amount of time he or she spent on each type of service;

(3) The amount of the fee he or she wants to charge for the services;

(4) The amount of fee the representative wants to request or charge for his or her services in the same matter before any State or Federal court;

(5) The amount of and a list of any expenses the representative incurred for which he or she has been paid or expects to be paid;

(6) A description of the special qualifications which enabled the representative, if he or she is not an attorney, to give valuable help in connection with your claim; and

(7) A statement showing that the representative sent a copy of the request for approval of a fee to you.

(b) Evaluating a request for approval of a fee.

(1) When we evaluate a representative's request for approval of a fee, we consider the purpose of the social security program, which is to provide a measure of economic security for the beneficiaries of the program, together with—

(i) The extent and type of services the representative performed;

(ii) The complexity of the case;

(iii) The level of skill and competence required of the representative in giving the services;

(iv) The amount of time the representative spent on the case;

(v) The results the representative achieved;

(vi) The level of review to which the claim was taken and the level of the review at which the representative became your representative; and

(vii) The amount of fee the representative requests for his or her services, including any amount authorized or requested before, but not including the amount of any expenses he or she incurred.

(2) Although we consider the amount of benefits, if any, that are payable, we do not base the amount of fee we authorize on the amount of the benefit alone, but on a consideration of all the factors listed in this section. The benefits payable in any claim are determined by specific provisions of law and are unrelated to the efforts of the representative. We may authorize a fee even if no benefits are payable.

§ 404.1728 Proceedings before a State or Federal court.

(a) Representation of a party in court proceedings. We shall not consider any service the representative gave you in any proceeding before a State or Federal court to be services as a representative in dealings with us. However, if the representative also has given service to you in the same connection in any dealings with us, he or she must specify what, if any, portion of the fee he or she wants to charge is for services performed in dealings with us. If the representative charges any fee for those services, he or she must file the request and furnish all of the information required by § 404.1725.

(b) Attorney fee allowed by a Federal court. If a Federal court in any proceeding under title II of the Act makes a judgment in favor of a claimant who was represented before the court by an attorney, and the court, under section 206(b) of the Act, allows to the attorney as part of its judgment a fee not in excess of 25 percent of the total of past-due benefits to which the claimant is entitled by reason of the judgment, we may pay the attorney the amount of the fee out of, but not in addition to, the amount of the past-due benefits payable. We will not certify for direct payment any other fee your representative may request.

§ 404.1730 Payment of fees.

(a) Fees allowed by a Federal court. We will pay an attorney representative out of your past-due benefits the amount of the fee allowed by a Federal court in a proceeding under title II of the Act. The payment we make to the attorney is subject to the limitations described in paragraph (b)(1) of this section.

(b) Fees we may authorize—

(1) Attorneys and eligible non-attorneys. Except as provided in paragraph (c) of this section, if we make a determination or decision in your favor and you were represented by an attorney or an eligible non-attorney, and as a result of the determination or decision you have past-due benefits, we will pay the representative out of the past-due benefits, the smaller of the amounts in paragraph (b)(1)(i) or (ii) of this section, less the amount of the assessment described in paragraph (d) of this section.

(i) Twenty-five percent of the total of the past-due benefits; or

(ii) The amount of the fee that we set.

(2) Non-attorneys ineligible for direct payment. If the representative is a non-attorney who is ineligible to receive direct payment of his or her fee, we assume no responsibility for the payment of any fee that we authorized. We will not deduct the fee from your past-due benefits.

(c) Time limit for filing request for approval of fee to obtain direct payment.

(1) To receive direct fee payment from your past-due benefits, a representative who is an attorney or an eligible non-attorney should file a request for approval of a fee, or written notice of the intent to file a request, at one of our offices, or electronically at the times and in the manner that we prescribe if we give notice that such a method is available, within 60 days of the date we mail the notice of the favorable determination or decision.

(2)(i) If no request is filed within 60 days of the date the notice of the favorable determination is mailed, we will mail a written notice to you and your representative at your last known addresses. The notice will inform you and the representative that unless the representative files, within 20 days from the date of the notice, a written request for approval of a fee under § 404.1725, or a written request for an extension of time, we will pay all the past-due benefits to you.

(ii) The representative must send you a copy of any request made to us for an extension of time. If the request is not filed within 20 days of the date of the notice, or by the last day of any extension we approved, we will pay all past-due benefits to you. We must approve any fee the representative charges after that time, but the collection of any approved fee is a matter between you and the representative.

(d) Assessment when we pay a fee directly to a representative.

(1) Whenever we pay a fee directly to a representative from past-due benefits, we impose an assessment on the representative.

(2) The amount of the assessment is equal to the lesser of:

(i) The product we obtain by multiplying the amount of the fee we are paying to the representative by the percentage rate the Commissioner of Social Security determines is necessary to achieve full recovery of the costs of determining and paying fees directly to representatives, but not in excess of 6.3 percent; and

(ii) The maximum assessment amount. The maximum assessment amount was initially set at $75, but by law is adjusted annually to reflect the increase in the cost of living. (See §§ 404.270 through 404.277 for an explanation of how the cost-of-living adjustment is computed.) If the adjusted amount is not a multiple of $1, we round down the amount to the next lower $1, but the amount will not be less than $75. We will announce any increase in the maximum assessment amount and explain how the increase was determined in the Federal Register.

(3) We collect the assessment by subtracting it from the amount of the fee to be paid to the representative. The representative who is subject to an assessment may not, directly or indirectly, request or otherwise obtain reimbursement of the assessment from you.

[72 FR 16724, April 5, 2007; 72 FR 44767, Aug. 9, 2007; 76 FR 45193, July 28, 2011; 80 FR 399, Jan. 6, 2015]

§ 404.1735 [Reserved by 76 FR 80245]

[76 FR 80245, Dec. 23, 2011]

§ 404.1740 Rules of conduct and standards of responsibility for representatives.

(a) Purpose and scope.

(1) All attorneys or other persons acting on behalf of a party seeking a statutory right or benefit must, in their dealings with us, faithfully execute their duties as agents and fiduciaries of a party. A representative must provide competent assistance to the claimant and recognize our authority to lawfully administer the process. The following provisions set forth certain affirmative duties and prohibited actions that will govern the relationship between the representative and us, including matters involving our administrative procedures and fee collections.

(2) All representatives must be forthright in their dealings with us and with the claimant and must comport themselves with due regard for the nonadversarial nature of the proceedings by complying with our rules and standards, which are intended to ensure orderly and fair presentation of evidence and argument.

(b) Affirmative duties. A representative must, in conformity with the regulations setting forth our existing duties and responsibilities and those of claimants (see § 404.1512 in disability and blindness claims):

(1) Act with reasonable promptness to help obtain the information or evidence that the claimant must submit under our regulations, and forward the information or evidence to us for consideration as soon as practicable.

(2) Assist the claimant in complying, as soon as practicable, with our requests for information or evidence at any stage of the administrative decisionmaking process in his or her claim. In disability and blindness claims, this includes the obligation pursuant to § 404.1512(c) to assist the claimant in providing, upon our request, evidence about:

(i) The claimant's medical source(s);

(ii) The claimant's age;

(iii) The claimant's education and training;

(iv) The claimant's work experience;

(v) The claimant's daily activities both before and after the date the claimant alleges that he or she became disabled;

(vi) The claimant's efforts to work; and

(vii) Any other factors showing how the claimant's impairment(s) affects his or her ability to work. In §§ 404.1560 through 404.1569a, we discuss in more detail the evidence we need when we consider vocational factors.

(3) Conduct his or her dealings in a manner that furthers the efficient, fair, and orderly conduct of the administrative decision-making process, including duties to:

(i) Provide competent representation to a claimant. Competent representation requires the knowledge, skill, thoroughness, and preparation reasonably necessary for the representation. A representative must know the significant issue(s) in a claim, have reasonable and adequate familiarity with the evidence in the case, and have a working knowledge of the applicable provisions of the Social Security Act, as amended, the regulations, the Social Security Rulings, and any other applicable provisions of law.

(ii) Act with reasonable diligence and promptness in representing a claimant. This includes providing prompt and responsive answers to our requests for information pertinent to processing of the claim.

(iii) When requested, provide us, in a manner we specify, potential dates and times that the representative will be available for a hearing. We will inform the representative how many potential dates and times we require to coordinate the hearing schedule.

(iv) Only withdraw representation at a time and in a manner that does not disrupt the processing or adjudication of a claim and that provides the claimant adequate time to find new representation, if desired. A representative should not withdraw after we set the time and place for the hearing (see § 404.936) unless the representative can show that a withdrawal is necessary due to extraordinary circumstances, as we determine on a case-by-case basis.

(v) Maintain prompt and timely communication with the claimant, which includes, but is not limited to, reasonably informing the claimant of all matters concerning the representation, consulting with the claimant on an ongoing basis during the entire representational period, and promptly responding to a claimant's reasonable requests for information. When we evaluate whether a representative has maintained prompt and timely communication with the claimant, we will consider the difficulty the representative has in locating a particular claimant (e.g., because the claimant is homeless) and the representative's efforts to keep that claimant informed.

(4) Conduct business with us electronically at the times and in the manner we prescribe on matters for which the representative requests direct fee payment. (See § 404.1713).

(5) Disclose in writing, at the time a medical or vocational opinion is submitted to us or as soon as the representative is aware of the submission to us, if:

(i) The representative's employee or any individual contracting with the representative drafted, prepared, or issued the medical or vocational opinion; or

(ii) The representative referred or suggested that the claimant seek an examination from, treatment by, or the assistance of, the individual providing opinion evidence.

(6) Disclose to us immediately if the representative discovers that his or her services are or were used by the claimant to commit fraud against us.

(7) Disclose to us whether the representative is or has been disbarred or suspended from any bar or court to which he or she was previously admitted to practice, including instances in which a bar or court took administrative action to disbar or suspend the representative in lieu of disciplinary proceedings (e.g. acceptance of voluntary resignation pending disciplinary action). If the disbarment or suspension occurs after the appointment of the representative, the representative will immediately disclose the disbarment or suspension to us.

(8) Disclose to us whether the representative is or has been disqualified from participating in or appearing before any Federal program or agency, including instances in which a Federal program or agency took administrative action to disqualify the representative in lieu of disciplinary proceedings (e.g. acceptance of voluntary resignation pending disciplinary action). If the disqualification occurs after the appointment of the representative, the representative will immediately disclose the disqualification to us.

(9) Disclose to us whether the representative has been removed from practice or suspended by a professional licensing authority for reasons that reflect on the person's character, integrity, judgment, reliability, or fitness to serve as a fiduciary. If the removal or suspension occurs after the appointment of the representative, the representative will immediately disclose the removal or suspension to us.

(10) Ensure that all of the representative's employees, assistants, partners, contractors, or any person assisting the representative on claims for which the representative has been appointed, comply with these rules of conduct and standards of responsibility for representatives, when the representative has managerial or supervisory authority over these individuals or otherwise has responsibility to oversee their work. This includes a duty to take remedial action when:

(i) The representative's employees, assistants, partners, contractors or other individuals' conduct violates these rules of conduct and standards of responsibility; and

(ii) The representative has reason to believe a violation of these rules of conduct and standards of responsibility occurred or will occur.

(c) Prohibited actions. A representative must not:

(1) In any manner or by any means threaten, coerce, intimidate, deceive or knowingly mislead a claimant, or prospective claimant or beneficiary, regarding benefits or other rights under the Act. This prohibition includes misleading a claimant, or prospective claimant or beneficiary, about the representative's services and qualifications.

(2) Knowingly charge, collect or retain, or make any arrangement to charge, collect or retain, from any source, directly or indirectly, any fee for representational services in violation of applicable law or regulation. This prohibition includes soliciting any gift or any other item of value, other than what is authorized by law.

(3) Make or present, or participate in the making or presentation of, false or misleading oral or written statements, evidence, assertions, or representations about a material fact or law concerning a matter within our jurisdiction, in matters where the representative knows or should have known that those statements, evidence, assertions, or representations are false or misleading.

(4) Through his or her own actions or omissions, unreasonably delay or cause to be delayed, without good cause (see § 404.911(b)), the processing of a claim at any stage of the administrative decision-making process.

(5) Divulge, without the claimant's consent, except as may be authorized by regulations prescribed by us or as otherwise provided by Federal law, any information we furnish or disclose about a claim or prospective claim.

(6) Attempt to influence, directly or indirectly, the outcome of a decision, determination, or other administrative action by any means prohibited by law, or by offering or granting a loan, gift, entertainment, or anything of value to a presiding official, agency employee, or witness who is or may reasonably be expected to be involved in the administrative decision-making process, except as reimbursement for legitimately incurred expenses or lawful compensation for the services of an expert witness retained on a non-contingency basis to provide evidence.

(7) Engage in actions or behavior prejudicial to the fair and orderly conduct of administrative proceedings, including but not limited to:

(i) Repeated absences from or persistent tardiness at scheduled proceedings without good cause (see § 404.911(b));

(ii) Behavior that has the effect of improperly disrupting proceedings or obstructing the adjudicative process, including but not limited to:

(A) Directing threatening or intimidating language, gestures, or actions at a presiding official, witness, contractor, or agency employee;

(B) Providing misleading information or misrepresenting facts that affect how we process a claim, including, but not limited to, information relating to the claimant's work activity or the claimant's place of residence or mailing address in matters where the representative knows or should have known that the information was misleading and the facts would constitute a misrepresentation; and

(C) Communicating with agency staff or adjudicators outside the normal course of business or other prescribed procedures in an attempt to inappropriately influence the processing or outcome of a claim(s).

(8) Violate any section of the Act for which a criminal or civil monetary penalty is prescribed.

(9) Refuse to comply with any of our rules or regulations.

(10) Suggest, assist, or direct another person to violate our rules or regulations.

(11) Advise any claimant or beneficiary not to comply with any of our rules or regulations.

(12) Knowingly assist a person whom we suspended or disqualified to provide representational services in a proceeding under title II of the Act, or to exercise the authority of a representative described in § 404.1710.

(13) Fail to comply with our sanction(s) decision.

(14) Fail to oversee the representative's employees, assistants, partners, contractors, or any other person assisting the representative on claims for which the representative has been appointed when the representative has managerial or supervisory authority over these individuals or otherwise has responsibility to oversee their work.

[63 FR 41416, Aug. 4, 1998; 76 FR 56109, Sept. 12, 2011; 76 FR 80245, Dec. 23, 2011; 80 FR 14837, March 20, 2015; 83 FR 30854, July 2, 2018]

§ 404.1745 Violations of our requirements, rules, or standards.

When we have evidence that a representative fails to meet our qualification requirements or has violated the rules governing dealings with us, we may begin proceedings to suspend or disqualify that individual from acting in a representational capacity before us. We may file charges seeking such sanctions when we have evidence that a representative:

(a) Does not meet the qualifying requirements described in § 404.1705;

(b) Has violated the affirmative duties or engaged in the prohibited actions set forth in § 404.1740;

(c) Has been convicted of a violation under section 206 of the Act;

(d) Has been, by reason of misconduct, disbarred or suspended from any bar or court to which he or she was previously admitted to practice (see § 404.1770(a));

(e) Has been, by reason of misconduct, disqualified from participating in or appearing before any Federal program or agency (see § 404.1770(a)); or

(f) Who, as a non-attorney, has been removed from practice or suspended by a professional licensing authority for reasons that reflect on the person's character, integrity, judgment, reliability, or fitness to serve as a fiduciary.

[56 FR 24131, May 29, 1991; 62 FR 38452, July 18, 1997; 63 FR 41416, Aug. 4, 1998; 71 FR 2876, Jan. 18, 2006; 83 FR 30855, July 2, 2018]

§ 404.1750 Notice of charges against a representative.

(a) The General Counsel or other delegated official will prepare a notice containing a statement of charges that constitutes the basis for the proceeding against the representative.

(b) We will send this notice to the representative either by certified or registered mail, to his or her last known address, or by personal delivery.

(c) We will advise the representative to file an answer, within 14 business days from the date of the notice, or from the date the notice was delivered personally, stating why he or she should not be suspended or disqualified from acting as a representative in dealings with us.

(d) The General Counsel or other delegated official may extend the 14–day period specified in paragraph (c) of this section for good cause, in accordance with § 404.911.

(e) The representative must—

(1) Answer the notice in writing under oath (or affirmation); and

(2) File the answer with the Social Security Administration, at the address specified on the notice, within the 14–day time period specified in paragraph (c) of this section.

(f) If the representative does not file an answer within the 14–day time period specified in paragraph (c) of this section (or the period extended in accordance with paragraph (d) of this section), he or she does not have the right to present evidence, except as may be provided in § 404.1765(g).

[56 FR 24131, May 29, 1991; 62 FR 38452, July 18, 1997; 63 FR 41417, Aug. 4, 1998; 71 FR 2876, Jan. 18, 2006; 76 FR 80246, Dec. 23, 2011; 83 FR 30855, July 2, 2018]

§ 404.1755 Withdrawing charges against a representative.

The General Counsel or other delegated official may withdraw charges against a representative. We will withdraw charges if the representative files an answer, or we obtain evidence, that satisfies us that we should not suspend or disqualify the representative from acting as a representative. When we consider withdrawing charges brought under § 404.1745(d) through (f) based on the representative's assertion that, before or after our filing of charges, the representative has been reinstated to practice by the court, bar, or Federal program or Federal agency that suspended, disbarred, or disqualified the representative, the General Counsel or other delegated official will determine whether such reinstatement occurred, whether it remains in effect, and whether he or she is reasonably satisfied that the representative will in the future act in accordance with the provisions of section 206(a) of the Act and our rules and regulations. If the representative proves that reinstatement occurred and remains in effect and the General Counsel or other delegated official is so satisfied, the General Counsel or other delegated official will withdraw those charges. The action of the General Counsel or other delegated official regarding withdrawal of charges is solely that of the General Counsel or other delegated official and is not reviewable, or subject to consideration in decisions made under §§ 404.1770 and 404.1790. If we withdraw the charges, we will notify the representative by mail at the representative's last known address.

[71 FR 2876, Jan. 18, 2006; 76 FR 80246, Dec. 23, 2011; 83 FR 30855, July 2, 2018]

§ 404.1760 [Reserved]

[56 FR 24131, May 29, 1991]

§ 404.1765 Hearing on charges.

(a) Holding the hearing. If the General Counsel or other delegated official does not take action to withdraw the charges within 15 days after the date on which the representative filed an answer, we will hold a hearing and make a decision on the charges.

(b) Hearing officer.

(1) The Deputy Commissioner for the Office of Hearings Operations or other delegated official will assign an administrative law judge, designated to act as a hearing officer, to hold a hearing on the charges.

(2) No hearing officer shall hold a hearing in a case in which he or she is prejudiced or partial about any party, or has any interest in the matter.

(3) If the representative or any party to the hearing objects to the hearing officer who has been named to hold the hearing, we must be notified at the earliest opportunity. The hearing officer shall consider the objection(s) and either proceed with the hearing or withdraw from it.

(4) If the hearing officer withdraws from the hearing, another one will be named.

(5) If the hearing officer does not withdraw, the representative or any other person objecting may, after the hearing, present his or her objections to the Appeals Council explaining why he or she believes the hearing officer's decision should be revised or a new hearing held by another administrative law judge designated to act as a hearing officer.

(c) Time and place of hearing. The hearing officer will mail the parties a written notice of the hearing at their last known addresses, at least 14 calendar days before the date set for the hearing. The notice will inform the parties whether the appearance of the parties or any witnesses will be in person, by video teleconferencing, or by telephone. The notice will also include requirements and instructions for filing motions, requesting witnesses, and entering exhibits.

(d) Change of time and place for hearing.

(1) The hearing officer may change the time and place for the hearing, either on his or her own initiative, or at the request of the representative or the other party to the hearing. The hearing officer will not consider objections to the manner of appearance of parties or witnesses, unless the party shows good cause not to appear in the prescribed manner. To determine whether good cause exists for extending the deadline, we use the standards explained in § 404.911.

(2) The hearing officer may adjourn or postpone the hearing.

(3) Subject to the limitations in paragraph (g)(2) of this section, the hearing officer may reopen the hearing for the receipt of additional evidence at any time before mailing notice of the decision.

(4) The hearing officer shall give the representative and the other party to the hearing reasonable notice of any change in the time or place for the hearing, or of an adjournment or reopening of the hearing.

(e) Parties. The representative against whom charges have been made is a party to the hearing. The General Counsel or other delegated official will also be a party to the hearing.

(f) Subpoenas.

(1) The representative or the other party to the hearing may request the hearing officer to issue a subpoena for the attendance and testimony of witnesses and for the production of books, records, correspondence, papers, or other documents that are material to any matter being considered at the hearing. The hearing officer may, on his or her own initiative, issue subpoenas for the same purposes when the action is reasonably necessary for the full presentation of the facts.

(2) The representative or the other party who wants a subpoena issued shall file a written request with the hearing officer. This must be done at least 5 days before the date set for the hearing. The request must name the documents to be produced, and describe the address or location in enough detail to permit the witnesses or documents to be found.

(3) The representative or the other party who wants a subpoena issued shall state in the request for a subpoena the material facts that he or she expects to establish by the witness or document, and why the facts could not be established by the use of other evidence which could be obtained without use of a subpoena.

(4) We will pay the cost of the issuance and the fees and mileage of any witness subpoenaed, as provided in section 205(d) of the Act.

(g) Conduct of the hearing.

(1) The representative or the other party may file a motion for decision on the basis of the record prior to

the hearing. The hearing officer will give the representative and the other party a reasonable amount of time to submit any evidence and to file briefs or other written statements as to fact and law prior to deciding the motion. If the hearing officer concludes that there is no genuine dispute as to any material fact and the movant is entitled to a decision as a matter of law, the hearing officer may grant the motion and issue a decision in accordance with the provisions of § 404.1770.

(2) If the representative did not file an answer to the charges, he or she has no right to present evidence at the hearing. The hearing officer may make or recommend a decision on the basis of the record, or permit the representative to present a statement about the sufficiency of the evidence or the validity of the proceedings upon which the suspension or disqualification, if it occurred, would be based.

(3) The hearing officer will make the hearing open to the representative, to the other party, and to any persons the hearing officer or the parties consider necessary or proper. The hearing officer will inquire fully into the matters being considered, hear the testimony of witnesses, and accept any documents that are material.

(4) The hearing officer has the right to decide the order in which the evidence and the allegations will be presented and the conduct of the hearing.

(h) Evidence. The hearing officer may accept evidence at the hearing, even though it is not admissible under the rules of evidence that apply to Federal court procedure.

(i) Witnesses. Witnesses who testify at the hearing shall do so under oath or affirmation. Either the representative or a person representing him or her may question the witnesses. The other party and that party's representative must also be allowed to question the witnesses. The hearing officer may also ask questions as considered necessary, and shall rule upon any objection made by either party about whether any question is proper.

(j) Oral and written summation.

(1) The hearing officer shall give the representative and the other party a reasonable time to present oral summation and to file briefs or other written statements about proposed findings of fact and conclusions of law if the parties request it.

(2) The party that files briefs or other written statements shall provide enough copies so that they may be made available to any other party to the hearing who requests a copy.

(k) Record of hearing. In all cases, the hearing officer shall have a complete record of the proceedings at the hearing made.

(*l*) Representation. The representative, as the person charged, may appear in person and may be represented by an attorney or other representative. The General Counsel or other delegated official will be represented by one or more attorneys from the Office of the General Counsel.

(m) Failure to appear. If the representative or the other party to the hearing fails to appear after being notified of the time and place, the hearing officer may hold the hearing anyway so that the party present may offer evidence to sustain or rebut the charges. The hearing officer shall give the party who failed to appear an opportunity to show good cause for failure to appear. If the party fails to show good cause, he or she is considered to have waived the right to be present at the hearing. If the party shows good cause, the hearing officer may hold a supplemental hearing.

(n) Dismissal of charges. The hearing officer may dismiss the charges in the event of the death of the representative.

(*o*) Cost of transcript. If the representative or the other party to a hearing requests a copy of the transcript of the hearing, the hearing officer will have it prepared and sent to the party upon payment of the cost, unless the payment is waived for good cause.

[56 FR 24131, 24132, May 29, 1991; 62 FR 38452, July 18, 1997; 63 FR 41417, Aug. 4, 1998; 71 FR 2877, Jan. 18, 2006; 76 FR 80246, Dec. 23, 2011; 83 FR 30856, July 2, 2018]

§ 404.1770 Decision by hearing officer.

(a) General.

(1) After the close of the hearing, the hearing officer will issue a decision or certify the case to the Appeals Council. The decision must be in writing, will contain findings of fact and conclusions of law, and be based upon the evidence of record.

(2) In deciding whether a person has been, by reason of misconduct, disbarred or suspended by a court or bar, or disqualified from participating in or appearing before any Federal program or Federal agency, the hearing officer will consider the reasons for the disbarment, suspension, or disqualification action. If the action was taken for solely administrative reasons (e.g., failure to pay dues or to complete continuing legal education requirements), that will not disqualify the person from acting as a representative before us. However, this exception to disqualification does not apply if the administrative action was taken in lieu of disciplinary proceedings (e.g., acceptance of a voluntary resignation pending disciplinary action). Although the hearing officer will consider whether the disbarment, suspension, or disqualification action is based on misconduct when deciding whether a person should be disqualified from acting as a representative before us, the hearing officer will not re-examine or revise the factual or legal conclusions that led to the disbarment, suspension, or disqualification. For purposes of determining whether a person has been, by reason of misconduct, disqualified from participating in

or appearing before any Federal program or Federal agency, disqualified refers to any action that prohibits a person from participating in or appearing before any Federal program or Federal agency, regardless of how long the prohibition lasts or the specific terminology used.

(3) If the hearing officer finds that the charges against the representative have been sustained, he or she will either—

(i) Suspend the representative for a specified period of not less than 1 year, nor more than 5 years, from the date of the decision; or

(ii) Disqualify the representative from acting as a representative in dealings with us until he or she may be reinstated under § 404.1799. Disqualification is the sole sanction available if the charges have been sustained because the representative has been disbarred or suspended from any court or bar to which the representative was previously admitted to practice or disqualified from participating in or appearing before any Federal program or Federal agency, or because the representative has collected or received, and retains, a fee for representational services in excess of the amount authorized.

(4) The hearing officer shall mail a copy of the decision to the parties at their last known addresses. The notice will inform the parties of the right to request the Appeals Council to review the decision.

(b) Effect of hearing officer's decision.

(1) The hearing officer's decision is final and binding unless reversed or modified by the Appeals Council upon review.

(2) If the final decision is that a person is disqualified from being a representative in dealings with us, he or she will not be permitted to represent anyone in dealings with us until authorized to do so under the provisions of § 404.1799.

(3) If the final decision is that a person is suspended for a specified period of time from being a representative in dealings with us, he or she will not be permitted to represent anyone in dealings with us during the period of suspension unless authorized to do so under the provisions of § 404.1799.

[56 FR 24132, May 29, 1991; 63 FR 41417, Aug. 4, 1998; 71 FR 2877, Jan. 18, 2006; 76 FR 80246, Dec. 23, 2011]

§ 404.1775 Requesting review of the hearing officer's decision.

(a) General. After the hearing officer issues a decision, either the representative or the other party to the hearing may ask the Appeals Council to review the decision.

(b) Time and place of filing request for review. The party requesting review will file the request for review in writing with the Appeals Council within 14 business days from the date the hearing officer mailed the notice. The party requesting review will certify that a copy of the request for review and of any documents that are submitted have been mailed to the opposing party.

[83 FR 30856, July 2, 2018]

§ 404.1776 Assignment of request for review of the hearing officer's decision.

Upon receipt of a request for review of the hearing officer's decision, the matter will be assigned to a panel consisting of three members of the Appeals Council none of whom shall be the Chair of the Appeals Council. The panel shall jointly consider and rule by majority opinion on the request for review of the hearing officer's decision, including a determination to dismiss the request for review. Matters other than a final disposition of the request for review may be disposed of by the member designated chair of the panel.

[56 FR 24132, May 29, 1991]

§ 404.1780 Appeals Council's review of hearing officer's decision.

(a) Upon request, the Appeals Council will give the parties a reasonable time to file briefs or other written statements as to fact and law, and to request to appear before the Appeals Council to present oral argument. When oral argument is requested within the time designated by the Appeals Council, the Appeals Council will grant the request for oral argument and determine whether the parties will appear at the oral argument in person, by video teleconferencing, or by telephone. If oral argument is not requested within the time designated by the Appeals Council, the Appeals Council may deny the request.

(b) If a party files a brief or other written statement with the Appeals Council, he or she shall send a copy to the opposing party and certify that the copy has been sent.

[83 FR 30856, July 2, 2018]

§ 404.1785 Evidence permitted on review.

(a) General. Generally, the Appeals Council will not consider evidence in addition to that introduced at the hearing. However, if the Appeals Council finds the evidence offered is material to an issue it is considering, it may consider that evidence, as described in paragraph (b) of this section.

(b) Individual charged filed an answer.

(1) When the Appeals Council finds that additional evidence material to the charges is available, and the individual charged filed an answer to the charges, the Appeals Council will allow the party with the information to submit the additional evidence.

(2) Before the Appeals Council admits additional evidence into the record, it will mail a notice to the parties, informing them that evidence about certain

issues was submitted. The Appeals Council will give each party a reasonable opportunity to comment on the evidence and to present other evidence that is material to an issue it is considering.

(3) The Appeals Council will determine whether the additional evidence warrants a new review by a hearing officer or whether the Appeals Council will consider the additional evidence as part of its review of the case.

(c) Individual charged did not file an answer. If the representative did not file an answer to the charges, the representative may not introduce evidence that was not considered at the hearing.

[83 FR 30856, July 2, 2018]

§ 404.1790 Appeals Council's decision.

(a) The Appeals Council will base its decision upon the evidence in the hearing record and any other evidence it may permit on review. The Appeals Council will affirm the hearing officer's decision if the action, findings, and conclusions are supported by substantial evidence. If the hearing officer's decision is not supported by substantial evidence, the Appeals Council will either:

(1) Reverse or modify the hearing officer's decision; or

(2) Return the case to the hearing officer for further proceedings.

(b) The Appeals Council, in changing a hearing officer's decision to suspend a representative for a specified period, shall in no event reduce the period of suspension to less than 1 year. In modifying a hearing officer's decision to disqualify a representative, the Appeals Council shall in no event impose a period of suspension of less than 1 year. Further, the Appeals Council shall in no event impose a suspension when disqualification is the sole sanction available in accordance with § 404.1770(a)(3)(ii).

(c) If the Appeals Council affirms or changes a hearing officer's decision, the period of suspension or the disqualification is effective from the date of the Appeals Council's decision.

(d) If the hearing officer did not impose a period of suspension or a disqualification, and the Appeals Council decides to impose one or the other, the suspension or disqualification is effective from the date of the Appeals Council's decision.

(e) The Appeals Council shall make its decision in writing and shall mail a copy of the decision to the parties at their last known addresses.

(f) The Appeals Council may designate and publish certain final decisions as precedent for other actions brought under its representative conduct provisions. Prior to making a decision public, we will remove or redact personally identifiable information from the decision.

[56 FR 24132, May 29, 1991; 71 FR 2877, Jan. 18, 2006; 83 FR 30856, July 2, 2018]

§ 404.1795 When the Appeals Council will dismiss a request for review.

The Appeals Council may dismiss a request for the review of any proceeding to suspend or disqualify a representative in any of the following circumstances:

(a) Upon request of party. The Appeals Council may dismiss a request for review upon written request of the party or parties who filed the request if there is no other party who objects to the dismissal.

(b) Death of party. The Appeals Council may dismiss a request for review in the event of the death of the representative.

(c) Request for review not timely filed. The Appeals Council will dismiss a request for review if a party failed to file a request for review within the 30–day time period and the Appeals Council does not extend the time for good cause.

§ 404.1797 Reinstatement after suspension—period of suspension expired.

We shall automatically allow a person to serve again as a representative in dealings with us at the end of any suspension.

§ 404.1799 Reinstatement after suspension or disqualification—period of suspension not expired.

(a) After more than one year has passed, a person who has been suspended or disqualified may ask the Appeals Council for permission to serve as a representative again. The Appeals Council will assign and process a request for reinstatement using the same general procedures described in § 404.1776.

(b) The suspended or disqualified person must submit any evidence the person wishes to have considered along with the request to be allowed to serve as a representative again.

(c) The General Counsel or other delegated official, upon notification of receipt of the request, will have 30 days in which to present a written report of any experiences with the suspended or disqualified person subsequent to that person's suspension or disqualification. The Appeals Council will make available to the suspended or disqualified person a copy of the report.

(d)(1) The Appeals Council shall not grant the request unless it is reasonably satisfied that the person will in the future act according to the provisions of section 206(a) of the Act, and to our rules and regulations.

(2) If a person was disqualified because he or she had been disbarred, suspended, or removed from practice for the reasons described in § 404.1745(d) through (f), the Appeals Council will grant a request for reinstatement as a representative only if the criterion in

paragraph (d)(1) of this section is met and the disqualified person shows that he or she has been admitted (or readmitted) to and is in good standing with the court, bar, Federal program or agency, or other governmental or professional licensing authority from which he or she had been disbarred, suspended, or removed from practice.

(3) If a person was disqualified because the person had been disqualified from participating in or appearing before a Federal program or Federal agency, the Appeals Council will grant the request for reinstatement only if the criterion in paragraph (d)(1) of this section is met and the disqualified person shows that the person is now qualified to participate in or appear before that Federal program or Federal agency.

(4) If the person was disqualified as a result of collecting or receiving, and retaining, a fee for representational services in excess of the amount authorized, the Appeals Council will grant the request only if the criterion in paragraph (d)(1) of this section is met and the disqualified person shows that full restitution has been made.

(e) The Appeals Council will mail a notice of its decision on the request for reinstatement to the suspended or disqualified person. It will also mail a copy to the General Counsel or other delegated official.

(f) If the Appeals Council decides not to grant the request, it will not consider another request before the end of 3 years from the date of the notice of the previous denial.

[56 FR 24132, May 29, 1991; 62 FR 38452, July 18, 1997; 63 FR 41417, Aug. 4, 1998; 71 FR 2877, Jan. 18, 2006; 76 FR 80246, Dec. 23, 2011; 83 FR 30857, July 2, 2018]

SUBPART S—PAYMENT PROCEDURES

Authority: Secs. 205(a) and (n), 207, 702(a)(5), and 708(a) of the Social Security Act (42 U.S.C. 405(a) and (n), 407, 902(a)(5) and 909(a)).

Source: 45 FR 52095, Aug. 5, 1980; 52 FR 27541, July 22, 1987; 61 FR 5941, Feb. 15, 1996; 62 FR 6120, Feb. 11, 1997, unless otherwise noted.

§ 404.1800 Introduction.

After we have made a determination or decision that you are entitled to benefits under title II of the Act, we begin paying those benefits to you as soon as possible. This subpart explains—

(a) What we must do so that your benefits begin promptly;

(b) When and how you may request that payment of benefits be expedited;

(c) When we may cause your benefits to be withheld;

(d) Our obligation not to assign or transfer your benefits to someone; and

(e) When we will use one check to pay benefits to two or more persons in a family.

§ 404.1805 Paying benefits.

(a) As soon as possible after we have made a determination or decision that you are entitled to benefits, we certify to the Secretary of the Treasury, who is the Managing Trustee of the Trust Funds—

(1) Your name and address, or the name and address of the person to be paid if someone receives your benefits on your behalf as a representative payee;

(2) The amount of the payment or payments to be made from the appropriate Trust Fund; and

(3) The time at which the payment or payments should be made in accordance with § 404.1807.

(b) Under certain circumstances when you have had railroad employment, we will certify the information to the Railroad Retirement Board.

[62 FR 6120, Feb. 11, 1997]

§ 404.1807 Monthly payment day.

(a) General. Once we have made a determination or decision that you are entitled to recurring monthly benefits, you will be assigned a monthly payment day. Thereafter, any recurring monthly benefits which are payable to you will be certified to the Managing Trustee for delivery on or before that day of the month as part of our certification under § 404.1805(a)(3). Except as provided in paragraphs (c)(2) through (c)(6) of this section, once you have been assigned a monthly payment day, that day will not be changed.

(b) Assignment of payment day.

(1) We will assign the same payment day for all individuals who receive benefits on the earnings record of a particular insured individual.

(2) The payment day will be selected based on the day of the month on which the insured individual was born. Insured individuals born on the 1st through the 10th of the month will be paid on the second Wednesday of each month. Insured individuals born on the 11th through the 20th of the month will be paid on the third Wednesday of each month. Insured individuals born after the 20th of the month will be paid on the fourth Wednesday of each month. See paragraph (c) of this section for exceptions.

(3) We will notify you in writing of the particular monthly payment day that is assigned to you.

(c) Exceptions.

(1) If you or any other person became entitled to benefits on the earnings record of the insured individual based on an application filed before May 1, 1997, you will continue to receive your benefits on the 3rd day of the month (but see paragraph (c)(6) of this section). All persons who subsequently become entitled to benefits on that earnings record will be assigned to the 3rd day of the month as the monthly payment day.

(2) If you or any other person become entitled to benefits on the earnings record of the insured individual based on an application filed after April 30, 1997, and also become entitled to Supplemental Security Income (SSI) benefits or have income which is deemed to an SSI beneficiary (per § 416.1160), all persons who are or become entitled to benefits on that earnings record will be assigned to the 3rd day of the month as the monthly payment day. We will notify you in writing if your monthly payment day is being changed to the 3rd of the month due to this provision.

(3) If you or any other person become entitled to benefits on the earnings record of the insured individual based on an application filed after April 30, 1997, and also reside in a foreign country, all persons who are or become entitled to benefits on that earnings record will be assigned to the 3rd day of the month as the monthly payment day. We will notify you in writing if your monthly payment day is being changed to the 3rd of the month due to this provision.

(4) If you or any other person become entitled on the earnings record of the insured individual based on an application filed after April 30, 1997, and are not entitled to SSI but are or become eligible for the State where you live to pay your Medicare premium under the provisions of section 1843 of the Act, all persons who are or become entitled to benefits on that earnings record will be assigned to the 3rd day of the month as the monthly payment day. We will notify you in writing if your monthly payment day is being changed to the 3rd of the month due to this provision.

(5) After April 30, 1997, all individuals who become entitled on one record and later entitled on another record, without a break in entitlement, will be paid all benefits to which they are entitled no later than their current payment day. Individuals who are being paid benefits on one record on the 3rd of the month, and who become entitled on another record without a break in entitlement, will continue to receive all benefits on the 3rd of the month.

(6) If the day regularly scheduled for the delivery of your benefit payment falls on a Saturday, Sunday, or Federal legal holiday, you will be paid on the first preceding day that is not a Saturday, Sunday, or Federal legal holiday.

[62 FR 6120, Feb. 11, 1997]

§ 404.1810 Expediting benefit payments.

(a) General. We have established special procedures to expedite the payment of benefits in certain initial and subsequent claims. This section tells how you may request an expedited payment and when we will be able to hasten your payments by means of this process.

(b) Applicability of section.

(1) This section applies to monthly benefits payable under title II of the Act, except as indicated in paragraph (b)(2) of this section; and to those cases where we certify information to the Railroad Retirement Board.

(2) This section does not apply—

(i) If an initial determination has been made and a request for a reconsideration, a hearing, a review by the Appeals Council, or review by a Federal court is pending on any issue of entitlement to or payment of a benefit;

(ii) To any benefit for which a check has been cashed; or

(iii) To any benefit based on an alleged disability.

(c) Request for payment.

(1) You shall submit to us a written request for payment of benefits in accordance with paragraph (c)(2) or (c)(3) of this section. Paragraph (c)(2) of this section applies if you were receiving payments regularly and you then fail to receive payment for one or more months. Paragraph (c)(3) of this section applies if we have not made a determination about your entitlement to benefits, or if we have suspended or withheld payment due, for example, to excess earnings or recovery of an overpayment.

(2) If you received a regular monthly benefit in the month before the month in which a payment was allegedly due, you may make a written request for payment any time 30 days after the 15th day of the month in which the payment was allegedly due. If you request is made before the end of the 30–day period, we will consider it to have been made at the end of the period.

(3)(i) If you did not receive a regular monthly benefit in the month before the month in which a payment was allegedly due, you may make a written request for payment any time 90 days after the later of—

(A) The date on which the benefit is alleged to have been due; or

(B) The date on which you furnished us the last information we requested from you.

(ii) If your request is made before the end of the 90–day period we will consider it to have been made at the end of the period.

(d) Certification for payment. If we find that benefits are due, we shall certify the benefits for payment in sufficient time to permit the payment to be made within 15 days after the request for expedited payment is made, or considered to have been made, as provided in paragraph (c) of this section.

(e) Preliminary certification for payment. If we determine that there is evidence, although additional evidence may be required for a final decision, that a monthly benefit due to you in a particular month was not paid, we may make preliminary certification of payment even though the 30–day or 90–day periods described in paragraph (c) of this section have not elapsed.

§ 404.1815 Withholding certification or payments.

(a) When certification may be withheld. After a determination or decision, we may withhold certification to the Managing Trustee, or, if we have already made certification, we may notify the Managing Trustee to withhold payments. We may do this if a question about the validity of the payment or payments to be made under the determination or decision arises as the result of one of the following events:

(1) A reconsideration (whether at the request of a claimant or on our own motion), hearing, or review is being conducted, or a civil action has been filed in a Federal district court concerning the determination or decision.

(2) An application or request is pending concerning the payment of benefits or a lump sum to another person, and the application or request is inconsistent, in whole or in part, with the payment or payments under the determination or decision.

(b) When certification will not be withheld. We will not withhold certification or payment as explained in paragraph (a) of this section unless evidence is submitted with the request or application that is sufficient to raise a reasonable question about the validity of the payment or payments under the determination or decision. We will not withhold certification of any amount of the payment or payments not in question. Your acceptance of any payment or payments will not affect your right to reconsideration, hearing, or review about any additional payment or payments you may claim.

§ 404.1820 Transfer or assignment of payments.

(a) General. We shall not certify payment to—

(1) Any person designated as your assignee or transferee; or

(2) Any person claiming payment because of an execution, levy, attachment, garnishment, or other legal process, or because of any bankruptcy or insolvency proceeding against or affecting you.

(b) Enforcement of a child support or alimony obligation. If you have a legal obligation to provide child support or make alimony payments and legal process is issued to enforce this obligation, the provisions of paragraph (a) of this section do not apply.

§ 404.1821 Garnishment of payments after disbursement.

(a) Payments that are covered by section 207 of the Social Security Act and made by direct deposit are subject to 31 CFR part 212, Garnishment of Accounts Containing Federal Benefit Payments.

(b) This section may be amended only by a rulemaking issued jointly by the Department of Treasury and the agencies defined as a "benefit agency" in 31 CFR 212.3.

[76 FR 9960, Feb. 23, 2011; 78 FR 32109, May 29, 2013]

§ 404.1825 Joint payments to a family.

(a) Two or more beneficiaries in same family. If an amount is payable under title II of the Act for any month to two or more persons who are members of the same family, we may certify any two or more of the individuals for joint payment of the total benefits payable to them for the month.

(b) Joint payee dies before cashing a check.

(1) If a check has been issued for joint payment to an individual and spouse residing in the same household, and one of the joint payees dies before the check has been cashed, we may authorize the surviving payee to cash the check. We make the authorization by placing on the face of the check a stamped legend signed by an official of the Social Security Administration or the Treasury Disbursing Office redesignating the survivor as the payee of the check.

(2) If the uncashed check represents benefits for a month after the month of death, we will not authorize the surviving payee to cash the check unless the proceeds of the check are necessary to meet the ordinary and necessary living expenses of the surviving payee.

(c) Adjustment or recovery of overpayment. If a check representing payment of benefits to an individual and spouse residing in the same household is cashed by the surviving payee under the authorization in paragraph (b) of this section, and the amount of the check exceeds the amount to which the surviving payee is entitled, we shall make appropriate adjustment or recovery of the excess amount.

SUBPART T—TOTALIZATION AGREEMENTS

Authority: Secs. 205(a), 233, and 702(a)(5) of the Social Security Act (42 U.S.C. 405(a), 433, and 902(a)(5)).

Source: 61 FR 5941, Feb. 15, 1996, unless otherwise noted.

GENERAL PROVISIONS

Authority: Secs. 205(a), 233, and 1102 of the Social Security Act; 42 U.S.C. 405(a), 433, and 1302.

Source: 44 FR 42964, July 23, 1979; 52 FR 27541, July 22, 1987, unless otherwise noted.

§ 404.1901 Introduction.

(a) Under section 233 of the Social Security Act, the President may enter into an agreement establishing a totalization arrangement between the social security system of the United States and the social security system of a foreign country. An agreement permits entitlement to and the amount of old-age, survivors, disability, or derivative benefits to be based on a combination of a person's periods of coverage under the social security system of the United States and the social security system of the foreign country. An agreement also provides for the precluding of dual coverage and dual social security taxation for work covered under both systems. An agreement may provide that the provisions of the social security system of each country will apply equally to the nationals of both countries (regardless of where they reside). For this purpose, refugees, stateless persons, and other nonnationals who derive benefit rights from nationals, refugees, or stateless persons may be treated as nationals if they reside within one of the countries.

(b) The regulations in this subpart provide definitions and principles for the negotiation and administration of totalization agreements. Where necessary to accomplish the purposes of totalization, we will apply these definitions and principles, as appropriate and within the limits of the law, to accommodate the widely diverse characteristics of foreign social security systems.

§ 404.1902 Definitions.

For purposes of this subpart—

Act means the Social Security Act (42 U.S.C. 301 et seq.).

Agency means the agency responsible for the specific administration of a social security system including responsibility for implementing an agreement; the Social Security Administration (SSA) is the agency in the U.S.

Agreement means the agreement negotiated to provide coordination between the social security systems of the countries party to the agreement. The term agreement includes any administrative agreements concluded for purposes of administering the agreement.

Competent authority means the official with overall responsibility for administration of a country's social security system including applicable laws and international social security agreements; the Commissioner of Social Security is the competent authority in the U.S.

Period of coverage means a period of payment of contributions or a period of earnings based on wages for employment or on self-employment income, or any similar period recognized as equivalent under the social security system of the U.S. or under the social security system of the foreign country which is a party to an agreement.

Residence or ordinarily resides, when used in agreements, has the following meaning for the U.S. Residence or ordinarily resides in a country means that a person has established a home in that country intending to remain there permanently or for an indefinite period of time. Generally, a person will be considered to have established a home in a country if that person assumes certain economic burdens, such as the purchase of a dwelling or establishment of a business, and participates in the social and cultural activities of the community. If residence in a country is established, it may continue even though the person is temporarily absent from that country. Generally, an absence of six months or less will be considered temporary. If an absence is for more than six months, residence in the country will generally be considered to continue only if there is sufficient evidence to establish that the person intends to maintain the residence. Sufficient evidence would include the maintenance of a home or apartment in that country, the departure from the country with a reentry permit, or similar acts. The existence of business or family associations sufficient to warrant the person's return would also be considered.

Social security system means a social insurance or pension system which is of general application and which provides for paying periodic benefits, or the actuarial equivalent, because of old-age, death, or disability.

[62 FR 38452, July 18, 1997]

§ 404.1903 Negotiating totalization agreements.

An agreement shall be negotiated with the national government of the foreign country for the entire country. However, agreements may only be negotiated with foreign countries that have a social security system of general application in effect. The system shall be considered to be in effect if it is collecting social security taxes or paying social security benefits.

§ 404.1904 Effective date of a totalization agreement.

Section 233 of the Social Security Act provides that a totalization agreement shall become effective on any date provided in the agreement if—

(a) The date occurs after the expiration of a period during which at least one House of Congress has been in session on each of 60 days following the date on which the agreement is transmitted to Congress by the President; and

(b) Neither House of Congress adopts a resolution of disapproval of the agreement within the 60–day period described in paragraph (a) of this section.

[49 FR 29775, July 24, 1984]

§ 404.1905 Termination of agreements.

Each agreement shall contain provisions for its possible termination. If an agreement is terminated, entitlement to benefits and coverage acquired by an individual before termination shall be retained. The agreement shall provide for notification of termination to the other party and the effective date of termination.

BENEFIT PROVISIONS

§ 404.1908 Crediting foreign periods of coverage.

(a) General. To have foreign periods of coverage combined with U.S. periods of coverage for purposes of determining entitlement to and the amount of benefits payable under title II, an individual must have at least 6 quarters of coverage, as defined in section 213 of the Social Security Act, under the U.S. system. As a rule, SSA will accept foreign coverage information, as certified by the foreign country's agency, unless otherwise specified by the agreement. No credit will be given, however, for periods of coverage acquired before January 1, 1937.

(b) For quarters of coverage purposes.

(1) Generally, a quarter of coverage (QC) will be credited for every 3 months (or equivalent period), or remaining fraction of 3 months, of coverage in a reporting period certified to SSA by the other country's agency. A reporting period used by a foreign country may be one calendar year or some other period of time. QCs based on foreign periods of coverage may be credited as QCs only to calendar quarters not already QCs under title II. The QCs will be assigned chronologically beginning with the first calendar quarter (not already a QC under title II) within the reporting period and continuing until all the QCs are assigned, or the reporting period ends. Example: Country XYZ, which has an annual reporting period, certifies to SSA that a worker has 8 months of coverage in 1975, from January 1 to August 25. The worker has no QCs under title II in that year. Since 8 months divided by 3 months equals 2 QCs with a remainder of 2 months, the U.S. will credit the worker with 3 QCs. The QCs will be credited to the first 3 calendar quarters in 1975.

(2) If an individual fails to meet the requirements for currently insured status or the insured status needed for establishing a period of disability solely because of the assignment of QCs based on foreign coverage to calendar quarters chronologically, the QCs based on foreign coverage may be assigned to different calendar quarters within the beginning and ending dates of the reporting period certified by the foreign country, but only as permitted under paragraph (b)(1) of this section.

§ 404.1910 Person qualifies under more than one totalization agreement.

(a) An agreement may not provide for combining periods of coverage under more than two social security systems.

(b) If a person qualifies under more than one agreement, the person will receive benefits from the U.S. only under the agreement affording the most favorable treatment.

(c) In the absence of evidence to the contrary, the agreement that affords the most favorable treatment for purposes of paragraph (b) of this section will be determined as follows:

(1) If benefit amounts are the same under all such agreements, benefits will be paid only under the agreement which affords the earliest month of entitlement.

(2) If benefit amounts and the month of entitlement are the same under all such agreements, benefits will be paid only under the agreement under which all information necessary to pay such benefits is first available.

(3) If benefit amounts under all such agreements are not the same, benefits will be paid only under the agreement under which the highest benefit is payable. However, benefits may be paid under an agreement under which a lower benefit is payable for months prior to the month of first entitlement to such higher benefit.

[49 FR 29775, July 24, 1984]

§ 404.1911 Effects of a totalization agreement on entitlement to hospital insurance benefits.

A person may not become entitled to hospital insurance benefits under section 226 or section 226A of the Act by combining the person's periods of coverage under the social security system of the United States with the person's periods of coverage under the social security system of the foreign country. Entitlement to hospital insurance benefits is not precluded if the person otherwise meets the requirements.

COVERAGE PROVISIONS

§ 404.1913 Precluding dual coverage.

(a) General. Employment or self-employment or services recognized as equivalent under the Act or the social security system of the foreign country shall, on or after the effective date of the agreement, result in a period of coverage under the U.S. system or under the foreign system, but not under both. Methods shall be set forth in the agreement for determining under which system the employment, self-employment, or other service shall result in a period of coverage.

(b) Principles for precluding dual coverage.

(1) An agreement precludes dual coverage by assigning responsibility for coverage to the U.S. or a foreign country. An agreement may modify the coverage provisions of title II of the Act to accomplish this purpose. Where an agreement assigns coverage to the foreign country, it may exempt from coverage services otherwise covered by the Act. Where an agreement assigns coverage to the U.S., it may extend coverage to services not otherwise covered by the Act but only for taxable years beginning on or after April 20, 1983.

(2) If the work would otherwise be covered by both countries, an agreement will exempt it from coverage by one of the countries.

(3) Generally, an agreement will provide that a worker will be covered by the country in which he or she is employed and will be exempt from coverage by the other country.

Example: A U.S. national employed in XYZ country by an employer located in the United States will be covered by XYZ country and exempt from U.S. coverage.

(4) An agreement may provide exceptions to the principle stated in paragraph (b)(3) of this section so that a worker will be covered by the country to which he or she has the greater attachment.

Example: A U.S. national sent by his employer located in the United States to work temporarily for that employer in XYZ country will be covered by the United States and will be exempt from coverage by XYZ country.

(5) Generally, if a national of either country resides in one country and has self employment income that is covered by both countries, an agreement will provide that the person will be covered by the country in which he or she resides and will be exempt from coverage by the other country.

(6) Agreements may provide for variations from the general principles for precluding dual coverage to avoid inequitable or anomalous coverage situations for certain workers. However, in all cases coverage must be provided by one of the countries.

[50 FR 36575, Sept. 9, 1985; 50 FR 38113, Sept. 20, 1985]

§ 404.1914 Certificate of coverage.

Under some agreements, proof of coverage under one social security system may be required before the individual may be exempt from coverage under the other system. Requests for certificates of coverage under the U.S. system may be submitted by the employer, employee, or self-employed individual to SSA.

§ 404.1915 Payment of contributions.

On or after the effective date of the agreement, to the extent that employment or self-employment (or service recognized as equivalent) under the U.S. social security system or foreign system is covered under the agreement, the agreement shall provide that the work or equivalent service be subject to payment of contributions or taxes under only one system (see sections 1401(c), 3101(c), and 3111(c) of the Internal Revenue Code of 1954). The system under which contributions or taxes are to be paid is the system under which there is coverage pursuant to the agreement.

COMPUTATION PROVISIONS

§ 404.1918 How benefits are computed.

(a) General. Unless otherwise provided in an agreement, benefits will be computed in accordance with this section. Benefits payable under an agreement are based on a pro rata primary insurance amount (PIA), which we determine as follows:

(1) We establish a theoretical earnings record for a worker which attributes to all computation base years (see §§ 404.211(b) and 404.241(c)) the same relative earnings position (REP) as he or she has in the years of his or her actual U.S. covered work. As explained in paragraph (b)(3) of this section, the REP is derived by determining the ratio of the worker's actual U.S. covered earnings in each year to the average of the total U.S. covered wages of all workers for that year, and then averaging the ratios for all such years. This average is the REP and is expressed as a percentage.

(2) We compute a theoretical PIA as prescribed in § 404.1918(c) based on the theoretical earnings record and the provisions of subpart C of this part.

(3) We multiply the theoretical PIA by a fraction equal to the number of quarters of coverage (QC's) which the worker completed under the U.S. Social Security system over the number of calendar quarters in the worker's coverage lifetime (see paragraph (d)(2) of this section). See § 404.140 for the definition of QC.

(4) If the pro rata PIA is higher than the PIA which would be computed if the worker were insured under the U.S. system without totalization, the pro rata PIA will be reduced to the later PIA.

(b) Establishing a theoretical earnings record.

(1) To establish a worker's theoretical earnings record, we divide his or her U.S. earnings in each year credited with at least one U.S. QC by the average of the total wages of all workers for that year and express the quotient as a percentage. For the years 1937 through 1950, the average of the total wages is as follows:

Year	Average of the total wages of all workers
1937	$1,137.96
1938	1,053.24
1939	1,142.36
1940	1,195.00
1941	1,276.04
1942	1,454.28
1943	1,713.52
1944	1,936.32
1945	2,021.40
1946	1,891.76
1947	2,175.32
1948	2,361.64
1949	2,483.20
1950	2,543.96

(2) For years after 1950, the average of the total wages is as prescribed in § 404.211(c). If a worker has earnings in the year preceding the year of eligibility or death, or in a later year, we may not have been able to establish the average of the total wages of all workers for that year. Therefore, we will divide a worker's actual earnings in these years by the average of the total wages for the latest year for which that information is available. Average wage information is considered available on January 1 of the year following

the year in which it is published in the Federal Register.

(3) The percentages for all years of actual covered earnings are then averaged to give the worker's REP for the entire period of work in the U.S. In determining the percentages for all years of covered earnings and the REP, we make adjustments as necessary to take account of the fact that the covered earnings for some years may have involved less than four U.S. QC's. The actual earnings that are taken into account in determining the percentage for any year with 1, 2, or 3 QC's cannot exceed ¼, ½, or ¾, respectively, of the maximum creditable earnings for that year. When we determine the REP from the percentages for all years, we add the percentages for all years, divide this sum by the total number of QC's credited to the worker, and multiply this quotient by 4 (see Example 1 of paragraph (d) of this section). This has the effect of calculating the REP on a quarterly basis.

(4) For each of the worker's computation base years (see §§ 404.211(b), 404.221(b) and 404.241(c)), we multiply the average of the total wages of all workers for that year by the worker's REP. The product is the amount of earnings attributed to the worker for that year, subject to the annual wage limitation (see § 404.1047). The worker's theoretical earnings record consists of his or her attributed earnings based on his or her REP for all computation base years. However, we do not attribute earnings to computation base years before the year of attainment of age 22 or to computation base years beginning with the year of attainment of retirement age (or the year in which a period of disability begins), unless the worker is actually credited with U.S. earnings in those years. In death cases, earnings for the year of death will be attributed only through the quarter of death, on a proportional basis.

(c) *Determining the theoretical PIA.* We determine the worker's theoretical PIA based on his or her theoretical earnings record by applying the same computation method that would have applied under subpart C if the worker had these theoretical earnings and had qualified for benefits without application of an agreement. However, when the criteria in § 404.210(a) for the Average Indexed Monthly Earnings (AIME) computation method are met, only that method is used. If these criteria are not met but the criteria in § 404.220(a) for the Average Monthly Wage method are met, then only that method is used. If neither of these criteria are met, then the old-start method described in § 404.241 is used. If a theoretical PIA is to be determined based on a worker's AIME, theoretical earnings amounts for each year, determined under paragraph (b) of this section, are indexed in determining the AIME under § 404.211.

(d) *Determining the pro rata PIA.* We then determine a pro rata PIA from the theoretical PIA. The pro rata PIA is the product of—

(1) The theoretical PIA; and

(2) The ratio of the worker's actual number of U.S. QC's to the number of calendar quarters in the worker's coverage lifetime. A coverage lifetime means the worker's benefit computation years as determined under § 404.211(e), § 404.221(c), or § 404.241(d).

Example 1: C attains age 62 in 1982 and needs 31 QC's to be insured. C worked under the U.S. system from July 1, 1974 to December 31, 1980 and therefore has only 6½ years during which he worked under the U.S. system (26 QC's). C, however, has worked under the Social Security system of a foreign country that is party to a totalization agreement, and his total U.S. and foreign work, combined as described in § 404.1908, equals more than 31 QC's. Thus, the combined coverage gives C insured status. The benefit is computed as follows:

Step 1: Establish C's theoretical earnings record:

The following table shows: (1) C's actual U.S. covered earnings for each year, (2) the average of the total wages of all workers for that year and (3) the ratio of (1) to (2):

Year	QC's	C's actual U.S. covered earnings	National average wage	Percentage ratio of (1) to (2)
		(1)	(2)	(3)
1974	2	$2,045.08	$8,030.76	25.46558
1975	4	7,542.00	8,630.92	87.38350
1976	4	9,016.00	9,226.48	97.71874
1977	4	9,952.00	9,779.44	101.76452
1978	4	10,924.00	10,556.03	103.48587
1979	4	12,851.00	11,479.46	111.94777
1980	4	11,924.00	12,513.46	95.28939

C's REP is the average of the ratios in column 3, adjusted to take account of the fact that C had only 2 QC's in 1974. Thus, the REP equals the sum of the figures in column 3 (623.05537), divided by the total number of C's QC's (26) and multiplied by 4, or 95.85467 percent.

Since C attained age 62 in 1982, his computation base years are 1951 through 1981. To establish his theoretical earnings record we use 95.85467 percent of the national average wage for each of the years 1951 through 1981. Since national average wage data is not available for 1981, for that year we attribute 95.85467 percent of the national average wage for 1980 or $11,994.74. His theoretical earnings record would look like this:

1951	$ 2,683.13
1952	2,850.07
1953	3,009.30
1954	3,024.83
1955	3,164.58
1956	3,385.93
1957	3,490.76
1958	3,521.51
1959	3,695.96
1960	3,841.01
1961	3,917.35
1962	4,113.51
1963	4,214.38
1964	4,386.62
1965	4,465.60
1966	4,733.65
1967	4,997.33

1968	5,340.79
1969	5,649.44
1970	5,929.80
1971	6,227.75
1972	6,838.08
1973	7,265.94
1974	7,697.86
1975	8,273.14
1976	8,844.01
1977	9,374.05
1978	10,118.45
1979	11,003.60
1980	11,994.74
1981	11,994.74

Step 2: Compute the theoretical PIA: Since C attains age 62 in 1982, we determine his theoretical PIA using an AIME computation. In applying the AIME computation, we index each year's earnings on the theoretical earnings record in accordance with § 404.211(d). In this example, the theoretical PIA is $453.

Step 3: Compute the pro rata PIA:

$$\frac{\text{Theoretical PIA - Actual U.S.QC's}}{\text{calendar quarters in benefit computation years}}$$

$$\frac{\$453 \text{ - } 26 \text{ QC's } (6\tfrac{1}{2} \text{ years})}{104 \text{ quarters } (26 \text{ years})}$$

$$=\$113.20 \text{ pro rata PIA}$$

Example 2: M needs 27 QC's to be insured, but she has only 3 years of work (12 QC's) under the U.S. system. M has enough foreign work, however, to be insured. She attained age 62 in 1978, and her U.S. covered earnings were in 1947, 1948 and 1949. Based on M's date of birth, her theoretical PIA can be computed, in accordance with § 404.220, under a new start method. If M's earnings in 1947, 1948, and 1949 were 50 percent, 60 percent and 70 percent, respectively, of the average wage for each year, her REP would be 60 percent. For each year in the computation period, 60 percent of the average wage for that year will be attributed as M's assumed earnings. The theoretical PIA will then be computed as described in §§ 404.220 through 404.222.

To determine M's pro rata PIA, the theoretical PIA will be multiplied by the ratio of the actual number of U.S. QC's to the number of calendar quarters in the benefit computation years. There are 22 benefit computation years, or 88 quarters. The pro rata PIA would, therefore, be 12/88 x theoretical PIA.

(e) Rounding of benefits.

(1) If the effective date of the pro rata PIA is before June 1982, we will round to the next higher multiple of 10 cents if it is not already a multiple of 10 cents.

(2) If the effective date of the pro rata PIA is June 1982 or later, we will round to the next lower multiple of 10 cents if it is not already a multiple of 10 cents.

(f) Auxiliary and survivors benefits; reductions; family maximum. We will determine auxiliary and survivors benefit amounts (see subpart D) on the basis of the pro rata PIA. We will apply the regular reductions for age under section 202(q) of the Act to the benefits of the worker or to any auxiliaries or survivors which are based on the pro rata PIA (see § 404.410). Benefits will be payable subject to the family maximum (see § 404.403) derived from the pro rata PIA. If the pro rata PIA is less than the minimum PIA, the family maximum will be 1½ times the pro rata PIA.

[49 FR 29775, July 24, 1984]

§ 404.1919 How benefits are recomputed.

Unless otherwise provided in an agreement, we will recompute benefits in accordance with this section. We will recompute the pro rata PIA only if the inclusion of the additional earnings results in an increase in the benefits payable by the U.S. to all persons receiving benefits on the basis of the worker's earnings. Subject to this limitation, the pro rata PIA will be automatically recomputed (see § 404.285) to include additional earnings under the U.S. system. In so doing, a new REP will be established for the worker, taking the additional earnings into account, and assumed earnings in the computation base years used in the original computation will be refigured using the new REP. Assumed earnings will also be determined for the year of additional earnings using the new REP. The additional U.S. earnings will also be used in refiguring the ratio described in § 404.1918(d)(2).

[49 FR 29777, July 24, 1984]

§ 404.1920 Supplementing the U.S. benefit if the total amount of the combined benefits is less than the U.S. minimum benefit.

If a resident of the U.S. receives benefits under an agreement from both the U.S. and from the foreign country, the total amount of the two benefits may be less than the amount for which the resident would qualify under the U.S. system based on the minimum PIA as in effect for persons first becoming eligible for benefits before January 1982. An agreement may provide that in the case of an individual who first becomes eligible for benefits before January 1982, the U.S. will supplement the total amount to raise it to the amount for which the resident would have qualified under the U.S. system based on the minimum PIA. (The minimum benefit will be based on the first figure in column IV in the table in section 215(a) of the Act for a person becoming eligible for the benefit before January 1, 1979, or the PIA determined under section 215(a)(1)(C)(i)(I) of the Act (as in effect in December 1981) for a person becoming eligible for the benefit after December 31, 1978.)

[49 FR 29777, July 24, 1984]

§ 404.1921 Benefits of less than $1 due.

If the monthly benefit amount due an individual (or several individuals, e.g., children, where several benefits are combined in one check) as a result of a claim filed under an agreement is less than $1, the benefits may be accumulated until they equal or exceed $5.

OTHER PROVISIONS

§ 404.1925 Applications.

(a)(1) An application, or written statement requesting benefits, filed with the competent authority or agency of a country with which the U.S. has concluded an agreement shall be considered an application for benefits under title II of the Act as of the date it is filed with the competent authority or agency if—

(i) An applicant expresses or implies an intent to claim benefits from the U.S. under an agreement; and

(ii) The applicant files an application that meets the requirements in subpart G of this part.

(2) The application described in paragraph (a)(1)(ii) of this section must be filed, even if it is not specifically provided for in the agreement.

(b) Benefits under an agreement may not be paid on the basis of an application filed before the effective date of the agreement.

§ 404.1926 Evidence.

(a) An applicant for benefits under an agreement shall submit the evidence needed to establish entitlement, as provided in subpart H of this part. Special evidence requirements for disability benefits are in subpart P of this part.

(b) Evidence submitted to the competent authority or agency of a country with which the U.S. has concluded an agreement shall be considered as evidence submitted to SSA. SSA shall use the rules in §§ 404.708 and 404.709 to determine if the evidence submitted is sufficient, or if additional evidence is needed to prove initial or continuing entitlement to benefits.

(c) If an application is filed for disability benefits, SSA shall consider medical evidence submitted to a competent authority or agency, as described in paragraph (b) of this section, and use the rules of subpart P of this part for making a disability determination.

§ 404.1927 Appeals.

(a) A request for reconsideration, hearing, or Appeals Council review of a determination that is filed with the competent authority or agency of a country with which the U.S. has concluded an agreement, shall be considered to have been timely filed with SSA if it is filed within the 60–day time period provided in §§ 404.911, 404.918, and 404.946.

(b) A request for reconsideration, hearing, or Appeals Council review of a determination made by SSA resulting from a claim filed under an agreement shall be subject to the provisions in subpart J of this part. The rules governing administrative finality in subpart J of this part shall also apply.

§ 404.1928 Effect of the alien non-payment provision.

An agreement may provide that a person entitled to benefits under title II of the Social Security Act may receive those benefits while residing in the foreign country party to the agreement, regardless of the alien non-payment provision (see § 404.460).

§ 404.1929 Overpayments.

An agreement may not authorize the adjustment of title II benefits to recover an overpayment made under the social security system of a foreign country (see § 404.501). Where an overpayment is made under the U.S. system, the provisions in subpart F of this part will apply.

§ 404.1930 Disclosure of information.

The use of information furnished under an agreement generally shall be governed by the national statutes on confidentiality and disclosure of information of the country that has been furnished the information. (The U.S. will be governed by pertinent provisions of the Social Security Act, the Freedom of Information Act, the Privacy Act, the Tax Reform Act, and other related statutes.) In negotiating an agreement, consideration, should be given to the compatibility of the other country's laws on confidentiality and disclosure to those of the U.S. To the extent possible, information exchanged between the U.S. and the foreign country should be used exclusively for purposes of implementing the agreement and the laws to which the agreement pertains.

SUBPART U—REPRESENTATIVE PAYMENT

Authority: Secs. 205(a), (j), and (k), and 702(a)(5) of the Social Security Act (42 U.S.C. 405(a), (j), and (k), and 902(a)(5)).

Source: 26 FR 11827, Dec. 9, 1961; 26 FR 11938, Dec. 14, 1961; 46 FR 29204, May 29, 1981, as amended at 47 FR 30472, July 14, 1982; 52 FR 27541, July 22, 1987; 61 FR 5941, Feb. 15, 1996; 75 FR 7552, Feb. 22, 2010, unless otherwise noted.

§ 404.2001 Introduction.

(a) Explanation of representative payment. This subpart explains the principles and procedures that we follow in determining whether to make representative payment and in selecting a representative payee. It also explains the responsibilities that a representative payee has concerning the use of the funds he or she receives on behalf of a beneficiary. A representative payee may be either a person or an organization selected by us to receive benefits on behalf of a beneficiary. A representative payee will be selected if we believe that the interest of a beneficiary will be served by representative payment rather than direct payment of benefits. Generally, we appoint a representative payee if we have determined that the beneficiary is not able to manage or direct the management of benefit payments in his or her interest.

(b) Policy used to determine whether to make representative payment.

(1) Our policy is that every beneficiary has the right to manage his or her own benefits. However, some beneficiaries due to a mental or physical condition or due to their youth may be unable to do so. Under these circumstances, we may determine that the interests of the beneficiary would be better served if we certified benefit payments to another person as a representative payee.

(2) If we determine that representative payment is in the interest of a beneficiary, we will appoint a representative payee. We may appoint a representative payee even if the beneficiary is a legally competent individual. If the beneficiary is a legally incompetent individual, we may appoint the legal guardian or some other person as a representative payee.

(3) If payment is being made directly to a beneficiary and a question arises concerning his or her ability to manage or direct the management of benefit payments, we will, if the beneficiary is 18 years old or older and has not been adjudged legally incompetent, continue to pay the beneficiary until we make a determination about his or her ability to manage or direct the management of benefit payments and the selection of a representative payee.

§ 404.2010 When payment will be made to a representative payee.

(a) We pay benefits to a representative payee on behalf of a beneficiary 18 years old or older when it appears to us that this method of payment will be in the interest of the beneficiary. We do this if we have information that the beneficiary is—

(1) Legally incompetent or mentally incapable of managing benefit payments; or

(2) Physically incapable of managing or directing the management of his or her benefit payments.

(b) Generally, if a beneficiary is under age 18, we will pay benefits to a representative payee. However, in certain situations, we will make direct payments to a beneficiary under age 18 who shows the ability to manage the benefits. For example, we make direct payments to a beneficiary under age 18 if the beneficiary is—

(1) Receiving disability insurance benefits on his or her own Social Security earnings record; or

(2) Serving in the military services; or

(3) Living alone and supporting himself or herself; or

(4) A parent and files for himself or herself and/or his or her child and he or she has experience in handling his or her own finances; or

(5) Capable of using the benefits to provide for his or her current needs and no qualified payee is available; or

(6) Within 7 months of attaining age 18 and is initially filing an application for benefits.

[54 FR 35483, Aug. 28, 1989]

§ 404.2011 What happens to your monthly benefits while we are finding a suitable representative payee for you?

(a) We may pay you directly. We will pay current monthly benefits directly to you while finding a suitable representative payee unless we determine that paying you directly would cause substantial harm to you. We determine substantial harm as follows:

(1) If you are receiving disability payments and we have determined that you have a drug addiction or alcoholism condition, or you are legally incompetent, or you are under age 15, we will presume that substantial harm exists. However, we will allow you to rebut this presumption by presenting evidence that direct payment would not cause you substantial harm.

(2) If you do not fit any of these categories, we make findings of substantial harm on a case-by-case basis. We consider all matters that may affect your ability to manage your benefits in your own best interest. We decide that substantial harm exists if both of the following conditions exist:

(i) Directly receiving benefits can be expected to cause you serious physical or mental injury.

(ii) The possible effect of the injury would outweigh the effect of having no income to meet your basic needs.

(b) We may delay or suspend your payments. If we find that direct payment will cause substantial harm to you, we may delay (in the case of initial entitlement to benefits) or suspend (in the case of existing entitlement to benefits) payments for as long as one month while we try to find a suitable representative payee for you. If we do not find a payee within one month, we will pay you directly. If you are receiving disability payments and we have determined that you have a drug addiction and alcoholism condition, or you are legally incompetent, or you are under age 15, we will withhold payment until a representative payee is appointed even if it takes longer than one month. We will, however, as noted in paragraph (a)(1) of this section, allow you to present evidence to rebut the presumption that direct payment would cause you substantial harm. See § 404.2001(b)(3) for our policy on suspending benefits if you are currently receiving benefits directly.

Example 1: Substantial Harm Exists. We are unable to find a representative payee for Mr. X, a 67 year old retirement beneficiary who is an alcoholic. Based on contacts with the doctor and beneficiary, we determine that Mr. X was hospitalized recently for his drinking. Paying him directly will cause serious injury, so we may delay payment for as long as one month based on substantial harm while we locate a suitable representative payee.

Example 2: Substantial Harm Does Not Exist. We approve a claim for Mr. Y, a title II claimant who suffers from a combination of mental impairments but who is not legally incompetent. We determine that Mr. Y needs assistance in managing his benefits, but we have not found a representative payee. Although we believe that Mr. Y may not use the money wisely, there is no indication that receiving funds directly would cause him substantial harm (i.e., serious physical or mental injury). We must pay current benefits directly to Mr. Y while we locate a suitable representative payee.

(c) How we pay delayed or suspended benefits. Payment of benefits, which were delayed or suspended pending appointment of a representative payee, can be made to you or your representative payee as a single sum or in installments when we determine that installments are in your best interest.

[69 FR 60232, Oct. 7, 2004]

§ 404.2015 Information considered in determining whether to make representative payments.

In determining whether to make representative payment we consider the following information:

(a) Court determinations. If we learn that a beneficiary has been found to be legally incompetent, a certified copy of the court's determination will be the basis of our determination to make representative payment.

(b) Medical evidence. When available, we will use medical evidence to determine if a beneficiary is capable of managing or directing the management of benefit payments. For example, a statement by a physician or other medical professional based upon his or her recent examination of the beneficiary and his or her knowledge of the beneficiary's present condition will be used in our determination, if it includes information concerning the nature of the beneficiary's illness, the beneficiary's chances for recovery and the opinion of the physician or other medical professional as to whether the beneficiary is able to manage or direct the management of benefit payments.

(c) Other evidence. We will also consider any statements of relatives, friends and other people in a position to know and observe the beneficiary, which contain information helpful to us in deciding whether the beneficiary is able to manage or direct the management of benefit payments.

§ 404.2020 Information considered in selecting a representative payee.

In selecting a payee we try to select the person, agency, organization or institution that will best serve the interest of the beneficiary. In making our selection we consider—

(a) The relationship of the person to the beneficiary;

(b) The amount of interest that the person shows in the beneficiary;

(c) Any legal authority the person, agency, organization or institution has to act on behalf of the beneficiary;

(d) Whether the potential payee has custody of the beneficiary;

(e) Whether the potential payee is in a position to know of and look after the needs of the beneficiary; and

(f) The potential payee's criminal history.

[84 FR 4325, Feb. 15, 2019]

§ 404.2021 What is our order of preference in selecting a representative payee for you?

As a guide in selecting a representative payee, categories of preferred payees have been established. These preferences are flexible. Our primary concern is to select the payee who will best serve the beneficiary's interest. The preferences are:

(a) For beneficiaries 18 years old or older (except those described in paragraph (b) of this section), our preference is—

(1) A legal guardian, spouse (or other relative) who has custody of the beneficiary or who demonstrates strong concern for the personal welfare of the beneficiary;

(2) A friend who has custody of the beneficiary or demonstrates strong concern for the personal welfare of the beneficiary;

(3) A public or nonprofit agency or institution having custody of the beneficiary;

(4) A private institution operated for profit and licensed under State law, which has custody of the beneficiary; and

(5) Persons other than above who are qualified to carry out the responsibilities of a payee and who are able and willing to serve as a payee for a beneficiary; e.g., members of community groups or organizations who volunteer to serve as payee for a beneficiary.

(b) For individuals who are disabled and who have a drug addiction or alcoholism condition our preference is—

(1) A community-based nonprofit social service agency which is licensed by the State, or bonded;

(2) A Federal, State, or local government agency whose mission is to carry out income maintenance, social service, or health care-related activities;

(3) A State or local government agency with fiduciary responsibilities;

(4) A designee of an agency (other than a Federal agency) referred to in paragraphs (b)(1), (2), and (3) of this section, if appropriate; or

(5) A family member.

(c) For beneficiaries under age 18, our preference is—

(1) A natural or adoptive parent who has custody of the beneficiary, or a guardian;

(2) A natural or adoptive parent who does not have custody of the beneficiary, but is contributing toward the beneficiary's support and is demonstrating strong concern for the beneficiary's well being;

(3) A natural or adoptive parent who does not have custody of the beneficiary and is not contributing toward his or her support but is demonstrating strong concern for the beneficiary's well being;

(4) A relative or stepparent who has custody of the beneficiary;

(5) A relative who does not have custody of the beneficiary but is contributing toward the beneficiary's support and is demonstrating concern for the beneficiary's well being;

(6) A relative or close friend who does not have custody of the beneficiary but is demonstrating concern for the beneficiary's well being; and

(7) An authorized social agency or custodial institution.

[47 FR 30472, July 14, 1982; 47 FR 32936, July 30, 1982; 69 FR 60232, Oct. 7, 2004]

§ 404.2022 Who may not serve as a representative payee?

A representative payee applicant may not serve if he/she:

(a) Has been convicted of a violation under section 208, 811 or 1632 of the Social Security Act.

(b) Has been convicted of an offense resulting in imprisonment for more than 1 year. However, we may make an exception to this prohibition, if the nature of the conviction is such that selection of the applicant poses no risk to the beneficiary and the exception is in the beneficiary's best interest.

(c) Receives title II, VIII, or XVI benefits through a representative payee.

(d) Previously served as a representative payee and was found by us, or a court of competent jurisdiction, to have misused title II, VIII or XVI benefits. However, if we decide to make an exception to this prohibition, we must evaluate the payee's performance at least every 3 months until we are satisfied that the payee poses no risk to the beneficiary's best interest. Exceptions are made on a case-by-case basis if all of the following are true:

(1) Direct payment of benefits to the beneficiary is not in the beneficiary's best interest.

(2) No suitable alternative payee is available.

(3) Selecting the payee applicant as representative payee would be in the best interest of the beneficiary.

(4) The information we have indicates the applicant is now suitable to serve as a representative payee.

(5) The payee applicant has repaid the misused benefits or has a plan to repay them.

(e) Is a creditor. A creditor is someone who provides you with goods or services for consideration. This restriction does not apply to the creditor who poses no risk to you and whose financial relationship with you presents no substantial conflict of interest, and who is any of the following:

(1) A relative living in the same household as you do.

(2) Your legal guardian or legal representative.

(3) A facility that is licensed or certified as a care facility under the law of a State or a political subdivision of a State.

(4) A qualified organization authorized to collect a monthly fee from you for expenses incurred in providing representative payee services for you, under § 404.2040a.

(5) An administrator, owner, or employee of the facility in which you live, and we are unable to locate an alternative representative payee.

(6) Any other individual we deem appropriate based on a written determination.

Example 1: Sharon applies to be representative payee for Ron who we have determined cannot manage his benefits. Sharon has been renting a room to Ron for several years and assists Ron in handling his other financial obligations, as needed. She charges Ron a reasonable amount of rent. Ron has no other family or friends willing to help manage his benefits or to act as representative payee. Sharon has demonstrated that her interest in and concern for Ron goes beyond her desire to collect the rent each month. In this instance, we may select Sharon as Ron's representative payee because a more suitable payee is not available, she appears to pose no risk to Ron and there is minimal conflict of interest. We will document this decision.

Example 2: In a situation similar to the one above, Ron's landlord indicates that she is applying to be payee only to ensure receipt of her rent. If there is money left after payment of the rent, she will give it directly to Ron to manage on his own. In this situation, we would not select the landlord as Ron's representative payee because of the substantial conflict of interest and lack of interest in his well being.

(f) Was convicted under Federal or State law of a felony for: Human trafficking, false imprisonment, kidnapping, rape or sexual assault, first-degree homicide, robbery, fraud to obtain access to government assistance, fraud by scheme, theft of government funds or property, abuse or neglect, forgery, or identity theft or identity fraud. We will also apply this provision to a representative payee applicant with a felony conviction of an attempt to commit any of these crimes or conspiracy to commit any of these crimes.

(1) If the representative payee applicant is the custodial parent of a minor child beneficiary, custodial parent of a beneficiary who is under a disability which began before the beneficiary attained the age of 22, custodial spouse of a beneficiary, custodial court-appointed guardian of a beneficiary, or custodial grandparent of the minor child beneficiary for whom the applicant is applying to serve as representative payee, we will not consider the conviction for one of the crimes, or of attempt or conspiracy to commit one of the crimes, listed in this paragraph (f), by itself, to prohibit the applicant from serving as a representative payee. We will consider the criminal history of an applicant in this category, along with the factors in paragraphs (a) through (e) of this section, when we decide whether it is in the best interest of the individual entitled to benefits to appoint the applicant as a representative payee.

(2) If the representative payee applicant is the parent who was previously the representative payee for his or her minor child who has since turned age 18 and continues to be eligible for benefits, we will not consider the conviction for one of the crimes, or of attempt or conspiracy to commit one of the crimes, listed in this paragraph (f), by itself, to prohibit the applicant from serving as a representative payee for that beneficiary. We will consider the criminal history of an applicant in this category, along with the factors in paragraphs (a) through (e) of this section, when we decide whether it is in the best interest of the individual entitled to benefits to appoint the applicant as a representative payee.

(3) If the representative payee applicant received a Presidential or gubernatorial pardon for the relevant conviction, we will not consider the conviction for one of the crimes, or of attempt or conspiracy to commit one of the crimes, listed in this paragraph (f), by itself, to prohibit the applicant from serving as a representative payee. We will consider the criminal history of an applicant in this category, along with the factors in paragraphs (a) through (e) of this section, when we decide whether it is in the best interest of the individual entitled to benefits to appoint the applicant as a representative payee.

[69 FR 60232, Oct. 7, 2004; 71 FR 61407, Oct. 18, 2006; 84 FR 4325, Feb. 15, 2019]

§ 404.2024 How do we investigate a representative payee applicant?

Before selecting an individual or organization to act as your representative payee, we will perform an investigation.

(a) Nature of the investigation. As part of the investigation, we do the following:

(1) Conduct a face-to-face interview with the payee applicant unless it is impracticable as explained in paragraph (c) of this section.

(2) Require the payee applicant to submit documented proof of identity, unless information establishing identity has recently been submitted with an application for title II, VIII or XVI benefits.

(3) Verify the payee applicant's Social Security account number or employer identification number.

(4) Determine whether the payee applicant has been convicted of a violation of section 208, 811 or 1632 of the Social Security Act.

(5) Determine whether the payee applicant has previously served as a representative payee and if any previous appointment as payee was revoked or terminated for misusing title II, VIII or XVI benefits.

(6) Use our records to verify the payee applicant's employment and/or direct receipt of title II, VIII, or XVI benefits.

(7) Verify the payee applicant's concern for the beneficiary with the beneficiary's custodian or other interested person.

(8) Require the payee applicant to provide adequate information showing his or her relationship to the beneficiary and to describe his or her responsibility for the care of the beneficiary.

(9) Determine whether the payee applicant is a creditor of the beneficiary (see § 404.2022(e)).

(10) Conduct a criminal background check on the payee applicant.

(b) Subsequent face-to-face interviews. After holding a face-to-face interview with a payee applicant, subsequent face-to-face interviews are not required if that applicant continues to be qualified and currently is acting as a payee, unless we determine, within our discretion, that a new face-to-face interview is necessary. We base this decision on the payee's past performance and knowledge of and compliance with our reporting requirements.

(c) Impracticable. We may consider a face-to-face interview impracticable if it would cause the payee applicant undue hardship. For example, the payee applicant would have to travel a great distance to the field office. In this situation, we may conduct the investigation to determine the payee applicant's suitability to serve as a representative payee without a face-to-face interview.

[69 FR 60233, Oct. 7, 2004; 73 FR 66521, Nov. 10, 2008; 84 FR 4325, Feb. 15, 2019]

§ 404.2025 What information must a representative payee report to us?

Anytime after we select a representative payee for you, we may ask your payee to give us information showing a continuing relationship with you, a continuing responsibility for your care, and how he/she used the payments on your behalf. If your representative payee does not give us the requested information within a reasonable period of time, we may stop sending your benefit payment to him/her—unless we determine that he/she had a satisfactory reason for not meeting our request and we subsequently receive the requested information. If we decide to stop sending your payment to your representative payee, we will consider paying you directly (in accordance with § 404.2011) while we look for a new payee.

[69 FR 60233, Oct. 7, 2004]

§ 404.2026 How do we investigate an appointed representative payee?

After we select an individual or organization to act as your representative payee, we will conduct a criminal background check on the appointed representative payee at least once every 5 years.

[84 FR 4325, Feb. 15, 2019]

§ 404.2030 How will we notify you when we decide you need a representative payee?

(a) We notify you in writing of our determination to make representative payment. This advance notice explains that we have determined that representative payment is in your interest, and it provides the name of the representative payee we have selected. We provide this notice before we actually appoint the payee. If you are under age 15, an unemancipated minor under the age of 18, or legally incompetent, our written notice goes to your legal guardian or legal representative. The advance notice:

(1) Contains language that is easily understandable to the reader.

(2) Identifies the person designated as your representative payee.

(3) Explains that you, your legal guardian, or your legal representative can appeal our determination that you need a representative payee.

(4) Explains that you, your legal guardian, or your legal representative can appeal our designation of a particular person or organization to serve as your representative payee.

(5) Explains that you, your legal guardian, or your legal representative can review the evidence upon which our designation of a particular representative payee is based and submit additional evidence.

(b) If you, your legal guardian, or your legal representative objects to representative payment or to the designated payee, we will handle the objection as follows:

(1) If you disagree with the decision and wish to file an appeal, we will process it under subpart J of this part.

(2) If you received your advance notice by mail and you protest or file your appeal within 10 days after you receive this notice, we will delay the action until we make a decision on your protest or appeal. (If you received and signed your notice while you were in the local field office, our decision will be effective immediately.)

[47 FR 30472, July 14, 1982; 47 FR 32936, July 30, 1982; 69 FR 60233, Oct. 7, 2004]

§ 404.2035 What are the responsibilities of your representative payee?

A representative payee has a responsibility to—

(a) Use the benefits received on your behalf only for your use and benefit in a manner and for the purposes he or she determines, under the guidelines in this subpart, to be in your best interests;

(b) Keep any benefits received on your behalf separate from his or her own funds and show your ownership of these benefits unless he or she is your spouse or natural or adoptive parent or stepparent and lives in the same household with you or is a State or local government agency for whom we have granted an exception to this requirement;

(c) Treat any interest earned on the benefits as your property;

(d) Notify us of any event or change in your circumstances that will affect the amount of benefits you receive, your right to receive benefits, or how you receive them;

(e) Submit to us, upon our request, a written report accounting for the benefits received on your behalf, and make all supporting records available for review if requested by us; and

(f) Notify us of any change in his or her circumstances that would affect performance of his/her payee responsibilities.

[71 FR 61407, Oct. 18, 2006]

§ 404.2040 Use of benefit payments.

(a) Current maintenance.

(1) We will consider that payments we certify to a representative payee have been used for the use and benefit of the beneficiary if they are used for the beneficiary's current maintenance. Current maintenance includes cost incurred in obtaining food, shelter, clothing, medical care, and personal comfort items.

Example: An aged beneficiary is entitled to a monthly Social Security benefit of $400. Her son, who is her payee, disburses her benefits in the following manner:

Rent and utilities	$200
Medical	25
Food	60
Clothing (coat)	55
Savings	30
Miscellaneous	30

The above expenditures would represent proper disbursements on behalf of the beneficiary.

(2) Notwithstanding the provisions of paragraph (a)(1) of this section, if a beneficiary is a member of an Aid to Families With Dependent Children (AFDC) assistance unit, we do not consider it inappropriate for a representative payee to make the benefit payments available to the AFDC assistance unit.

(b) Institutional care. If a beneficiary is receiving care in a Federal, State, or private institution because of mental or physical incapacity, current maintenance includes the customary charges made by the institution, as well as expenditures for those items which will aid in the beneficiary's recovery or release from the institution or expenses for personal needs which will improve the beneficiary's conditions while in the institution.

Example: An institutionalized beneficiary is entitled to a monthly Social Security benefit of $320. The institution charges $700 a month for room and board. The beneficiary's brother, who is the payee, learns the beneficiary needs new shoes and does not have any funds to purchase miscellaneous items at the institution's canteen.

The payee takes his brother to town and buys him a pair of shoes for $29. He also takes the beneficiary to see a movie which costs $3. When they return to the institution, the payee gives his brother $3 to be used at the canteen.

Although the payee normally withholds only $25 a month from Social Security benefit for the beneficiary's personal needs, this month the payee deducted the above expenditures and paid the institution $10 less than he usually pays.

The above expenditures represent what we would consider to be proper expenditures for current maintenance.

(c) Support of legal dependents. If the current maintenance needs of the beneficiary are met, the payee may use part of the payments for the support of the beneficiary's legally dependent spouse, child, and/or parent.

Example: A disabled beneficiary receives a Veterans Administration (VA) benefit of $325 and a Social Security benefit of $525. The beneficiary resides in a VA hospital and his VA benefits are sufficient to provide for all of his needs; i.e., cost of care and personal needs. The beneficiary's legal dependents—his wife and two children—have a total income of $250 per month in Social Security benefits. However, they have expenses of approximately $450 per month.

Because the VA benefits are sufficient to meet the beneficiary's needs, it would be appropriate to use part of his Social Security benefits to support his dependents.

(d) Claims of creditors. A payee may not be required to use benefit payments to satisfy a debt of the beneficiary, if the debt arose prior to the first month for which payments are certified to a payee. If the debt arose prior to this time, a payee may satisfy it only if the current and reasonably foreseeable needs of the beneficiary are met.

Example: A retroactive Social Security check in the amount of $1,640, representing benefits due for July 1980 through January 1981, was issued on behalf of the beneficiary to the beneficiary's aunt who is the representative payee. The check was certified in February 1981.

The nursing home, where the beneficiary resides, submitted a bill for $1,139 to the payee for maintenance expenses the beneficiary incurred during the period from June 1980 through November 1980. (Maintenance charges for December 1980 through February 1981 had previously been paid.)

Because the benefits were not required for the beneficiary's current maintenance, the payee had previously saved over $500 for the beneficiary and the beneficiary had no foreseeable needs which would require large disbursements, the expenditure for the maintenance charges would be consistent with our guidelines.

[54 FR 35483, Aug. 28, 1989]

§ 404.2040a Compensation for qualified organizations serving as representative payees.

(a) Organizations that can request compensation. A qualified organization can request us to authorize it to collect a monthly fee from your benefit payment. A qualified organization is:

(1) Any State or local government agency with fiduciary responsibilities or whose mission is to carry out income maintenance, social service, or health care-related activities; or

(2) Any community-based nonprofit social service organization founded for religious, charitable or social welfare purposes, which is tax exempt under section 501(c) of the Internal Revenue Code and which is bonded/insured to cover misuse and embezzlement by officers and employees and which is licensed in each State in which it serves as representative payee (if licensing is available in the State). The minimum amount of bonding or insurance coverage must equal the average monthly amount of social security payments received by the organization plus the amount of the beneficiaries' conserved funds (i.e., beneficiaries' saved social security benefits) plus interest on hand. For example, an organization that has conserved funds of $5,000 and receives an average of $12,000 a month in social security payments must be bonded/insured for a minimum of $17,000. The license must be appropriate under the laws of the State for the type of services the organization provides. An example of an appropriately licensed organization is a community mental health center holding a State license to provide community mental health services.

(b) Requirements qualified organizations must meet. Organizations that are qualified under paragraphs (a)(1) or (a)(2) of this section must also meet the following requirements before we can authorize them to collect a monthly fee.

(1) A qualified organization must regularly provide representative payee services concurrently to at least five beneficiaries. An organization which has received our authorization to collect a fee for representative payee services, but is temporarily (not more than 6

months) not a payee for at least five beneficiaries, may request our approval to continue to collect fees.

(2) A qualified organization must demonstrate that it is not a creditor of the beneficiary. See paragraph (c) of this section for exceptions to the requirement regarding creditors.

(c) Creditor relationship. On a case-by-case basis, we may authorize an organization to collect a fee for payee services despite the creditor relationship. (For example, the creditor is the beneficiary's landlord.) To provide this authorization, we will review all of the evidence submitted by the organization and authorize collection of a fee when:

(1) The creditor services (e.g., providing housing) provided by the organization help to meet the current needs of the beneficiary; and

(2) The amount the organization charges the beneficiary for these services is commensurate with the beneficiary's ability to pay.

(d) Authorization process.

(1) An organization must request in writing and receive an authorization from us before it may collect a fee.

(2) An organization seeking authorization to collect a fee must also give us evidence to show that it is qualified, pursuant to paragraphs (a), (b), and (c) of this section, to collect a fee.

(3) If the evidence provided to us by the organization shows that it meets the requirements of this section, and additional investigation by us proves it suitable to serve, we will notify the organization in writing that it is authorized to collect a fee. If we need more evidence, or if we are not able to authorize the collection of a fee, we will also notify the organization in writing that we have not authorized the collection of a fee.

(e) Revocation and cancellation of the authorization.

(1) We will revoke an authorization to collect a fee if we have evidence which establishes that an organization no longer meets the requirements of this section. We will issue a written notice to the organization explaining the reason(s) for the revocation.

(2) An organization may cancel its authorization at any time upon written notice to us.

(f) Notices. The written notice we will send to an organization authorizing the collection of a fee will contain an effective date for the collection of a fee pursuant to paragraphs (a), (b) and (c) of this section. The effective date will be no earlier than the month in which the organization asked for authorization to collect a fee. The notice will be applicable to all beneficiaries for whom the organization was payee at the time of our authorization and all beneficiaries for whom the organization becomes payee while the authorization is in effect.

(g) Limitation on fees.

(1) An organization authorized to collect a fee under this section may collect from a beneficiary a monthly fee for expenses (including overhead) it has incurred in providing payee services to a beneficiary. The limit on the fee a qualified organization may collect for providing payee services increases by the same percentage as the annual cost of living adjustment (COLA). The increased fee amount (rounded to the nearest dollar) is taken beginning with the benefit for December (received in January).

(2) Any agreement providing for a fee in excess of the amount permitted shall be void and treated as misuse of your benefits by the organization under § 404.2041.

(3) A fee may be collected for any month during which the organization—

(i) Provides representative payee services;

(ii) Receives a benefit payment for the beneficiary; and

(iii) Is authorized to receive a fee for representative payee services.

(4) Fees for services may not be taken from any funds conserved for the beneficiary by a payee in accordance with § 404.2045.

(5) Generally, an organization may not collect a fee for months in which it does not receive a benefit payment. However, an organization will be allowed to collect a fee for months in which it did not receive a payment if we later issue payment for these months and the organization:

(i) Received our approval to collect a fee for the months for which payment is made;

(ii) Provided payee services in the months for which payment is made; and

(iii) Was the payee when the retroactive payment was paid by us.

(6) Fees for services may not be taken from beneficiary benefits for the months for which we or a court of competent jurisdiction determine(s) that the representative payee misused benefits. Any fees collected for such months will be treated as a part of the beneficiary's misused benefits.

(7) An authorized organization can collect a fee for providing representative payee services from another source if the total amount of the fee collected from both the beneficiary and the other source does not exceed the amount authorized by us.

[57 FR 23057, June 1, 1992; 69 FR 60234, Oct. 7, 2004; 71 FR 61407, Oct. 18, 2006]

§ 404.2041 Who is liable if your representative payee misuses your benefits?

(a) A representative payee who misuses your benefits is responsible for paying back misused benefits.

We will make every reasonable effort to obtain restitution of misused benefits so that we can repay these benefits to you.

(b) Whether or not we have obtained restitution from the misuser, we will repay benefits in cases when we determine that a representative payee misused benefits and the representative payee is an organization or an individual payee serving 15 or more beneficiaries. When we make restitution, we will pay you or your alternative representative payee an amount equal to the misused benefits less any amount we collected from the misuser and repaid to you.

(c) Whether or not we have obtained restitution from the misuser, we will repay benefits in cases when we determine that an individual representative payee serving 14 or fewer beneficiaries misused benefits and our negligent failure in the investigation or monitoring of that representative payee results in the misuse. When we make restitution, we will pay you or your alternative representative payee an amount equal to the misused benefits less any amount we collected from the misuser and repaid to you.

(d) The term "negligent failure" used in this subpart means that we failed to investigate or monitor a representative payee or that we did investigate or monitor a representative payee but did not follow established procedures in our investigation or monitoring. Examples of our negligent failure include, but are not limited to, the following:

(1) We did not follow our established procedures in this subpart when investigating, appointing, or monitoring a representative payee;

(2) We did not timely investigate a reported allegation of misuse; or

(3) We did not take the necessary steps to prevent the issuance of payments to the representative payee after it was determined that the payee misused benefits.

(e) Our repayment of misused benefits under these provisions does not alter the representative payee's liability and responsibility as described in paragraph (a) of this section.

(f) Any amounts that the representative payee misuses and does not refund will be treated as an overpayment to that representative payee. See subpart F of this part.

[69 FR 60234, Oct. 7, 2004; 71 FR 61408, Oct. 18, 2006]

§ 404.2045 Conservation and investment of benefit payments.

(a) General. After the representative payee has used benefit payments consistent with the guidelines in this subpart (see § 404.2040 regarding use of benefits), any remaining amount shall be conserved or invested on behalf of the beneficiary. Conserved funds should be invested in accordance with the rules followed by trustees. Any investment must show clearly that the payee holds the property in trust for the beneficiary.

Example: A State institution for children with intellectual disability, which is receiving Medicaid funds, is representative payee for several Social Security beneficiaries. The checks the payee receives are deposited into one account which shows that the benefits are held in trust for the beneficiaries. The institution has supporting records which show the share each individual has in the account. Funds from this account are disbursed fairly quickly after receipt for the current support and maintenance of the beneficiaries as well as for miscellaneous needs the beneficiaries may have. Several of the beneficiaries have significant accumulated resources in this account. For those beneficiaries whose benefits have accumulated over $150, the funds should be deposited in an interest-bearing account or invested relatively free of risk on behalf of the beneficiaries.

(b) Preferred investments. Preferred investments for excess funds are U.S. Savings Bonds and deposits in an interest or dividend paying account in a bank, trust company, credit union, or savings and loan association which is insured under either Federal or State law. The account must be in a form which shows clearly that the representative payee has only a fiduciary and not a personal interest in the funds. If the payee is the legally appointed guardian or fiduciary of the beneficiary, the account may be established to indicate this relationship. If the payee is not the legally appointed guardian or fiduciary, the accounts may be established as follows:

(1) For U.S. Savings Bonds—

__________ (Name of beneficiary) __________ (Social Security Number), for whom __________ (Name of payee) is representative payee for Social Security benefits;

(2) For interest or dividend paying accounts—

__________ (Name of beneficiary) by __________ (Name of payee), representative payee.

(c) Interest and dividend payments. The interest and dividends which result from an investment are the property of the beneficiary and may not be considered to be the property of the payee.

[54 FR 35483, Aug. 28, 1989; 78 FR 46501, Aug. 1, 2013]

§ 404.2050 When will we select a new representative payee for you?

When we learn that your interest is not served by sending your benefit payment to your present representative payee or that your present payee is no longer able or willing to carry out payee responsibilities, we will promptly stop sending your payment to the payee. We will then send your benefit payment to an alternative payee or directly to you, until we find a suitable payee. We may suspend payment as explained in § 404.2011(c) if we find that paying you directly would cause substantial harm and we cannot find a suitable alternative representative payee before your next payment is due. We will terminate payment of benefits to your representative payee and find a new payee or pay you directly if the present payee:

(a) Has been found by us or a court of competent jurisdiction to have misused your benefits;

(b) Has not used the benefit payments on your behalf in accordance with the guidelines in this subpart;

(c) Has not carried out the other responsibilities described in this subpart;

(d) Dies;

(e) No longer wishes to be your payee;

(f) Is unable to manage your benefit payments; or

(g) Fails to cooperate, within a reasonable time, in providing evidence, accounting, or other information we request.

[69 FR 60235, Oct. 7, 2004]

§ 404.2055 When representative payment will be stopped.

If a beneficiary receiving representative payment shows us that he or she is mentally and physically able to manage or direct the management of benefit payments, we will make direct payment. Information which the beneficiary may give us to support his or her request for direct payment include the following—

(a) A physician's statement regarding the beneficiary's condition, or a statement by a medical officer of the institution where the beneficiary is or was confined, showing that the beneficiary is able to manage or direct the management of his or her funds; or

(b) A certified copy of a court order restoring the beneficiary's rights in a case where a beneficiary was adjudged legally incompetent; or

(c) Other evidence which establishes the beneficiary's ability to manage or direct the management of benefits.

§ 404.2060 Transfer of accumulated benefit payments.

A representative payee who has conserved or invested benefit payments shall transfer these funds and the interest earned from the invested funds to either a successor payee, to the beneficiary, or to us, as we will specify. If the funds and the earned interest are returned to us, we will recertify them to a successor representative payee or to the beneficiary.

[47 FR 30472, July 14, 1982; 47 FR 34781, Aug. 11, 1982; 75 FR 7552, Feb. 22, 2010]

§ 404.2065 How does your representative payee account for the use of benefits?

Your representative payee must account for the use of your benefits. We require written reports from your representative payee at least once a year (except for certain State institutions that participate in a separate onsite review program). We may verify how your representative payee used your benefits. Your representative payee should keep records of how benefits were used in order to make accounting reports and must make those records available upon our request. If your representative payee fails to provide an annual accounting of benefits or other required reports, we may require your payee to receive your benefits in person at the local Social Security field office or a United States Government facility that we designate serving the area in which you reside. The decision to have your representative payee receive your benefits in person may be based on a variety of reasons. Some of these reasons may include the payee's history of past performance or our past difficulty in contacting the payee. We may ask your representative payee to give us the following information:

(a) Where you lived during the accounting period;

(b) Who made the decisions on how your benefits were spent or saved;

(c) How your benefit payments were used; and

(d) How much of your benefit payments were saved and how the savings were invested.

[69 FR 60235, Oct. 7, 2004; 71 FR 61408, Oct. 18, 2006]

SUBPART V—PAYMENTS FOR VOCATIONAL REHABILITATION SERVICES

Authority: Secs. 205(a), 222, and 702(a)(5) of the Social Security Act (42 U.S.C. 405(a), 422, and 902(a)(5)).

Source: 48 FR 6293, Feb. 10, 1983; 52 FR 27541, July 22, 1987; 55 FR 8453, March 8, 1990; 61 FR 5941, Feb. 15, 1996, unless otherwise noted.

GENERAL PROVISIONS

§ 404.2101 General.

Section 222(d) of the Social Security Act authorizes the transfer from the Federal Old–Age and Survivors Insurance Trust Fund and the Federal Disability Insurance Trust Fund of such sums as may be necessary to pay for the reasonable and necessary costs of vocational rehabilitation (VR) services provided certain disabled individuals entitled under section 223, 225(b), 202(d), 202(e) or 202(f) of the Social Security Act. The purpose of this provision is to make VR services more readily available to disabled individuals and ensure that savings accrue to the Federal Old–Age and Survivors Insurance Trust Fund and the Federal Disability Insurance Trust Fund. Payment will be made for VR services provided on behalf of such an individual in cases where—

(a) The furnishing of the VR services results in the individual's completion of a continuous 9–month period of substantial gainful activity (SGA) as specified in §§ 404.2110 through 404.2111; or

(b) The individual continues to receive disability payments from us, even though his or her disability has ceased, because of his or her continued participation in an approved VR program which we have determined will increase the likelihood that he or she will not return to the disability rolls (see § 404.2112).

[55 FR 8453, March 8, 1990; 68 FR 40123, July 7, 2003]

§ 404.2102 Purpose and scope.

This subpart describes the rules under which the Commissioner will pay the State VR agencies for VR services. Payment will be provided for VR services provided on behalf of disabled individuals under one or more of the provisions discussed in § 404.2101.

(a) Sections 404.2101 through 404.2103 describe the purpose of these regulations and the meaning of terms we frequently use in them.

(b) Section 404.2104 explains how State VR agencies may participate in the payment program under this subpart.

(c) [Reserved by 83 FR 62456.]

(d) Sections 404.2108 through 404.2109 describe the requirements and conditions under which we will pay a State VR agency under this subpart.

(e) Sections 404.2110 through 404.2111 describe when an individual has completed a continuous period of SGA and when VR services will be considered to have contributed to that period.

(f) Section 404.2112 describes when payment will be made to a VR agency because an individual's disability benefits are continued based on his or her participation in a VR program which we have determined will increase the likelihood that he or she will not return to the disability rolls.

(g) Sections 404.2114 through 404.2115 describe services for which payment will be made.

(h) Section 404.2116 describes the filing deadlines for claims for payment for VR services.

(i) Section 404.2117 describes the payment conditions.

(j) [Reserved by 83 FR 62456.]]

(k) Section 404.2119 describes how we will make payment to State VR agencies for rehabilitation services.

(*l*) Sections 404.2120 and 404.2121 describe the audits and the prepayment and postpayment validation reviews we will conduct.

(m) Section 404.2122 discusses confidentiality of information and records.

(n) Section 404.2123 provides for the applicability of other Federal laws and regulations.

(*o*) Section 404.2127 provides for the resolution of disputes.

[55 FR 8454, March 8, 1990; 59 FR 11912, March 15, 1994; 62 FR 38452, July 18, 1997; 68 FR 40123, July 7, 2003; 83 FR 62456, Dec. 4, 2018]

§ 404.2103 Definitions.

For purposes of this subpart:

Accept the beneficiary as a client for VR services means that the State VR agency determines that the individual is eligible for VR services and places the individual into an active caseload status for development of an individualized written rehabilitation program.

Act means the Social Security Act, as amended.

Commissioner means the Commissioner of Social Security or the Commissioner's designee.

Disability means "disability" or "blindness" as defined in sections 216(i) and 223 of the Act.

Disability beneficiary means a disabled individual who is entitled to benefits under section 223, 202(d), 202(e) or 202(f) of the act or is continuing to receive payment under section 225(b) of the Act after his or her disabling physical or mental impairments have ceased.

Medical recovery for purposes of this subpart is established when a beneficiary's disability entitlement ceases for any medical reason (other than death). The determination of medical recovery is made by the Commissioner in deciding a beneficiary's continuing entitlement to benefits.

Place the beneficiary into an extended evaluation process means that the State VR agency determines that an extended evaluation of the individual's VR potential is necessary to determine whether the individual is eligible for VR services and places the individual into an extended evaluation status.

SGA means substantial gainful activity performed by an individual as defined in §§ 404.1571 through 404.1575 or § 404.1584 of this subpart.

State means any of the 50 States of the United States, the Commonwealth of Puerto Rico, the District of Columbia, the Virgin Islands, or Guam. It includes the State VR agency.

Trust Funds means the Federal Old–Age and Survivors Insurance Trust Fund and the Federal Disability Insurance Trust Fund.

Vocational rehabilitation services has the meaning assigned to it under title I of the Rehabilitation Act of 1973.

VR agency means an agency of the State which has been designated by the State to provide vocational rehabilitation services under title I of the Rehabilitation Act of 1973.

Waiting period means a five consecutive calendar month period throughout which an individual must be under a disability and which must be served before disability benefits can be paid (see § 404.315(d)).

We, us and our refer to the Social Security Administration (SSA).

[55 FR 8454, March 8, 1990; 59 FR 11912, March 15, 1994; 62 FR 38452, July 18, 1997; 68 FR 40123, July 7, 2003; 83 FR 62456, Dec. 4, 2018]

§ 404.2104 Participation by State VR agencies.

(a) General. In order to participate in the payment program under this subpart through its VR agency(ies), a State must have a plan which meets the requirements of title I of the Rehabilitation Act of 1973, as amended.

(b) Participation by States.

(1) The opportunity to participate through its VR agency(ies) with respect to disability beneficiaries in the State will be offered first to the State in accordance with paragraph (c) of this section, unless the State has notified us in advance under paragraph (e)(1) of this section of its decision not to participate or to limit such participation.

(2) A State with one or more approved VR agencies may choose to limit participation of those agencies to a certain class(es) of disability beneficiaries. For example, a State with separate VR agencies for the blind and disabled may choose to limit participation to the VR agency for the blind. In such a case, we would give the State, through its VR agency for the blind, the opportunity to participate with respect to blind disability beneficiaries in the State in accordance with paragraph (d) of this section. A State that chooses to limit participation of its VR agency(ies) must notify us in advance under paragraph (e)(1) of this section of its decision to limit such participation.

(c) Opportunity for participation through State VR agencies.

(1) Unless a State has decided not to participate or to limit participation, we will give the State the opportunity to participate through its VR agency(ies) with respect to disability beneficiaries in the State by referring such beneficiaries first to the State VR agency(ies) for necessary VR services. A State, through its VR agency(ies), may participate with respect to any beneficiary so referred by accepting the beneficiary as a client for VR services or placing the beneficiary into an extended evaluation process and notifying us under paragraph (c)(2) of this section of such acceptance or placement.

(2)(i) In order for the State to participate with respect to a disability beneficiary whom we referred to a State VR agency, the State VR agency must notify the appropriate Regional Commissioner (SSA) in writing or through electronic notification of its decision either to accept the beneficiary as a client for VR services or to place the beneficiary into an extended evaluation process. The notice must be received by the appropriate Regional Commissioner (SSA) no later than the close of the fourth month following the month in which we referred the beneficiary to the State VR agency.

(ii) In any case in which a State VR agency notifies the appropriate Regional Commissioner (SSA) in writing within the stated time period under paragraph (c)(2)(i) of this section of its decision to place the beneficiary into an extended evaluation process, the State VR agency also must notify that Regional Commissioner in writing upon completion of the evaluation of its decision whether or not to accept the beneficiary as a client for VR services. If we receive a notice of a decision by the State VR agency to accept the beneficiary as a client for VR services following the completion of the extended evaluation, the State may continue to participate with respect to such beneficiary.

(d) Opportunity for limited participation through State VR agencies. If a State has decided under paragraph (e)(1) of this section to limit participation of its VR agency(ies) to a certain class(es) of disability beneficiaries in the State, we will give the State the opportunity to participate with respect to such class(es) of disability beneficiaries by referring such beneficiaries first to the State VR agency(ies) for necessary VR services. The State, through its VR agency(ies), may participate with respect to any beneficiary so referred by accepting the beneficiary as a client for VR services or placing the beneficiary into an extended evaluation process and notifying us under paragraph (c)(2) of this section of such acceptance or placement.

(e) Decision of a State not to participate or to limit participation.

(1) A State may choose not to participate through its VR agency(ies) with respect to any disability beneficiaries in the State, or it may choose to limit participation of its VR agency(ies) to a certain class(es) of disability beneficiaries in the State. A State which decides not to participate or to limit participation must provide advance written notice of that decision to the appropriate Regional Commissioner (SSA). Unless a State specifies a later month, a decision not to participate or to limit participation will be effective beginning with the third month following the month in which the notice of the decision is received by the appropriate Regional Commissioner (SSA). The notice of the State decision must be submitted by an official authorized to act for the State for this purpose. A State must provide to the appropriate Regional Commissioner (SSA) an opinion from the State's Attorney General verifying the authority of the official who sent the notice to act for the State. This opinion will not be necessary if the notice is signed by the Governor of the State.

(2) [Reserved]

(3) A State which has decided not to participate or to limit participation may participate later through its VR agency(ies) in accordance with paragraph (c) of this section. A State which decides to resume participation under paragraph (c) of this section must provide advance written notice of that decision to the appropriate

Regional Commissioner (SSA). A decision of a State to resume participation under paragraph (c) of this section will be effective beginning with the third month following the month in which the notice of the decision is received by the appropriate Regional Commissioner (SSA) or, if later, with a month specified by the State. The notice of the State decision must be submitted by an official authorized to act for the State as explained in paragraph (e)(1) of this section.

(f) [Reserved by 83 FR 62456]

[59 FR 11912, March 15, 1994; 83 FR 62456, Dec. 4, 2018]

§ 404.2106 [Reserved by 83 FR 62457]

[83 FR 62457, Dec. 4, 2018]

PAYMENT PROVISIONS

§ 404.2108 Requirements for payment.

(a) The State VR agency must file a claim for payment in each individual case within the time periods specified in § 404.2116;

(b) The claim for payment must be in a form prescribed by us and contain the following information:

(1) A description of each service provided;

(2) When the service was provided; and

(3) The cost of the service;

(c) The VR services for which payment is being requested must have been provided during the period specified in § 404.2115;

(d) The VR services for which payment is being requested must have been provided under a State plan for VR services approved under title I of the Rehabilitation Act of 1973, as amended, and must be services that are described in § 404.2114;

(e) The individual must meet one of the VR payment provisions specified in § 404.2101;

(f) The State VR agency must maintain, and provide as we may require, adequate documentation of all services and costs for all disability beneficiaries with respect to whom a State VR agency could potentially request payment for services and costs under this subpart; and

(g) The amount to be paid must be reasonable and necessary and be in compliance with the cost guidelines specified in § 404.2117.

[55 FR 8454, March 8, 1990; 59 FR 11914, March 15, 1994; 83 FR 62457, Dec. 4, 2018]

§ 404.2109 Responsibility for making payment decisions.

The Commissioner will decide—

(a) Whether a continuous period of 9 months of SGA has been completed;

(b) Whether a disability beneficiary whose disability has ceased should continue to receive benefits under § 404.316(c), 404.337(c), or 404.352(c) for a month after October 1984, based on his or her continued participation in a VR program;

(c) If and when medical recovery has occurred;

(d) Whether documentation of VR services and expenditures is adequate;

(e) If payment is to be based on completion of a continuous 9–month period of SGA, whether the VR services contributed to the continuous period of SGA;

(f) Whether a VR service is a service described in § 404.2114; and

(g) What VR costs were reasonable and necessary and will be paid.

[55 FR 8454, March 8, 1990; 59 FR 11914, March 15, 1994; 68 FR 40123, July 7, 2003]

§ 404.2110 What we mean by "SGA" and by "a continuous period of 9 months".

(a) What we mean by "SGA". In determining whether an individual's work is SGA, we will follow the rules in §§ 404.1572 through 404.1575. We will follow these same rules for individuals who are statutorily blind, but we will evaluate the earnings in accordance with the rules in § 404.1584(d).

(b) What we mean by "a continuous period of 9 months". A continuous period of 9 months ordinarily means a period of 9 consecutive calendar months. Exception: When an individual does not perform SGA in 9 consecutive calendar months, he or she will be considered to have done so if—

(1) The individual performs 9 months of SGA within 10 consecutive months and has monthly earnings that meet or exceed the guidelines in § 404.1574(b)(2), or § 404.1584(d) if the individual is statutorily blind; or

(2) The individual performs at least 9 months of SGA within 12 consecutive months, and the reason for not performing SGA in 2 or 3 of those months was due to circumstances beyond his or her control and unrelated to the impairment (e.g., the employer closed down for 3 months).

(c) What work we consider. In determining if a continuous period of SGA has been completed, all of an individual's work activity may be evaluated for purposes of this section, including work performed before October 1981, during the waiting period, during the trial work period and after entitlement to disability benefits terminated. We will ordinarily consider only the first 9 months of SGA that occur. The exception will be if an individual who completed 9 months of SGA later stops performing SGA, receives VR services and then performs SGA for a 9–month period. See § 404.2115 for the use of the continuous period in determining payment for VR services.

[55 FR 8454, March 8, 1990]

§ 404.2111 Criteria for determining when VR services will be considered to have contributed to a continuous period of 9 months.

The State VR agency may be paid for VR services if such services contribute to the individual's performance of a continuous 9–month period of SGA. The following criteria apply to individuals who received more than just evaluation services. If a State VR agency claims payment for services to an individual who received only evaluation services, it must establish that the individual's continuous period or medical recovery (if medical recovery occurred before completion of a continuous period) would not have occurred without the services provided. In applying the criteria below, we will consider services described in § 404.2114 that were initiated, coordinated or provided, including services before October 1, 1981.

(a) Continuous period without medical recovery. If an individual who has completed a "continuous period" of SGA has not medically recovered as of the date of completion of the period, the determination as to whether VR services contributed will depend on whether the continuous period began one year or less after VR services ended or more than one year after VR services ended.

(1) One year or less. Any VR services which significantly motivated or assisted the individual in returning to, or continuing in, SGA will be considered to have contributed to the continuous period.

(2) More than one year.

(i) If the continuous period was preceded by transitional work activity (employment or self-employment which gradually evolved, with or without periodic interruption, into SGA), and that work activity began less than a year after VR services ended, any VR services which significantly motivated or assisted the individual in returning to, or continuing in, SGA will be considered to have contributed to the continuous period.

(ii) If the continuous period was not preceded by transitional work activity that began less than a year after VR services ended, VR services will be considered to have contributed to the continuous period only if it is reasonable to conclude that the work activity which constitutes a continuous period could not have occurred without the VR services (e.g., training).

(b) Continuous period with medical recovery occurring before completion.

(1) If an individual medically recovers before a continuous period has been completed, VR services under paragraph (a) of this section will not be payable unless some VR services contributed to the medical recovery. VR services will be considered to have contributed to the medical recovery if—

(i) The individualized written rehabilitation program (IWRP) included medical services; and

(ii) The medical recovery occurred, at least in part, because of these medical services. (For example, the individual's medical recovery was based on improvement in a back condition which, at least in part, stemmed from surgery initiated, coordinated or provided under an IWRP).

(2) In some instances, the State VR agency will not have provided, initiated, or coordinated medical services. If this happens, payment for VR services may still be possible under paragraph (a) of this section if:

(i) The medical recovery was not expected by us; and

(ii) The individual's impairment is determined by us to be of such a nature that any medical services provided would not ordinarily have resulted in, or contributed to, the medical cessation.

[55 FR 8454, March 8, 1990; 83 FR 62457, Dec. 4, 2018]

§ 404.2112 Payment for VR services in a case where an individual continues to receive disability payments based on participation in an approved VR program.

Sections 404.1586(g), 404.316(c), 404.337(c), and 404.352(c) explain the criteria we will use in determining if an individual whose disability has ceased should continue to receive disability benefits from us because of his or her continued participation in a VR program. A VR agency can be paid for the cost of VR services provided to an individual if the individual was receiving benefits in a month or months, after October 1984, based on § 404.316(c), § 404.337(c), or § 404.352(c). If this requirement is met, a VR agency can be paid for the costs of VR services provided within the period specified in § 404.2115, subject to the other payment and administrative provisions of this subpart.

[55 FR 8454, 8455, March 8, 1990; 83 FR 62457, Dec. 4, 2018]

§ 404.2113 [Reserved]

[68 FR 40123, July 7, 2003]

§ 404.2114 Services for which payment may be made.

(a) General. Payment may be made for VR services provided by a State VR agency in accordance with title I of the Rehabilitation Act of 1973, as amended, subject to the limitations and conditions in this subpart. VR services for which payment may be made under this subpart include only those services described in paragraph (b) of this section which are—

(1) Necessary to determine an individual's eligibility for VR services or the nature and scope of the services to be provided; or

(2) Provided by a State VR agency under an IWRP, but only if the services could reasonably be expected to

motivate or assist the individual in returning to, or continuing in, SGA.

(b) Specific services. Payment may be made under this subpart only for the following VR services:

(1) An assessment for determining an individual's eligibility for VR services and vocational rehabilitation needs by qualified personnel, including, if appropriate, an assessment by personnel skilled in rehabilitation technology, and which includes determining—

(i) The nature and extent of the physical or mental impairment(s) and the resultant impact on the individual's employability;

(ii) The likelihood that an individual will benefit from vocational rehabilitation services in terms of employability; and

(iii) An employment goal consistent with the capacities of the individual and employment opportunities;

(2) Counseling and guidance, including personal adjustment counseling, and those referrals and other services necessary to help an individual secure needed services from other agencies;

(3) Physical and mental restoration services necessary to correct or substantially modify a physical or mental condition which is stable or slowly progressive and which constitutes an impediment to suitable employment at or above the SGA level;

(4) Vocational and other training services, including personal and vocational adjustment, books, tools, and other training materials, except that training or training services in institutions of higher education will be covered under this section only if maximum efforts have been made by the State VR agency to secure grant assistance in whole or in part from other sources;

(5) Maintenance expenses that are extra living expenses over and above the individual's normal living expenses and that are incurred solely because of and while the individual is participating in the VR program and that are necessary in order for the individual to benefit from other necessary VR services;

(6) Travel and related expenses necessary to transport an individual for purpose of enabling the individual's participation in other necessary VR services;

(7) Services to family members of a disabled individual only if necessary to the successful vocational rehabilitation of that individual;

(8) Interpreter services and note-taking services for an individual who is deaf and tactile interpreting for an individual who is deaf and blind;

(9) Reader services, rehabilitation teaching services, note-taking services, and orientation and mobility services for an individual who is blind;

(10) Telecommunications, sensory, and other technological aids and devices;

(11) Work-related placement services to secure suitable employment;

(12) Post-employment services necessary to maintain, regain or advance into suitable employment at or above the SGA level;

(13) Occupational licenses, tools, equipment, initial stocks, and supplies;

(14) Rehabilitation technology services; and

(15) Other goods and services that can reasonably be expected to motivate or assist the individual in returning to, or continuing in, SGA.

[55 FR 8454, March 8, 1990; 59 FR 11915, March 15, 1994; 83 FR 62457, Dec. 4, 2018]

§ 404.2115 When services must have been provided.

(a) In order for the VR agency to be paid, the services must have been provided—

(1) After September 30, 1981;

(2) No earlier than the beginning of the waiting period or the first month of entitlement, if no waiting period is required; and

(3) Before completion of a continuous 9–month period of SGA or termination of entitlement to disability benefits, whichever occurs first.

(b) If an individual who is entitled to disability benefits under this part also is or has been receiving disability or blindness benefits under part 416 of this chapter, the determination as to when services must have been provided may be made under this section or § 416.2215 of this chapter, whichever is advantageous to the State VR agency that is participating in both VR programs.

[55 FR 8454, 8455, March 8, 1990; 61 FR 31025, June 19, 1996; 83 FR 62457, Dec. 4, 2018]

§ 404.2116 When claims for payment for VR services must be made (filing deadlines).

The State VR agency must file a claim for payment in each individual case within the following time periods:

(a) A claim for payment for VR services based on the individual's completion of a continuous 9–month period of SGA must be filed within 12 months after the month in which the continuous 9–month period of SGA is completed.

(b) A claim for payment for VR services provided to an individual whose disability benefits were continued after disability has ceased because of that individual's continued participation in a VR program must be filed as follows:

(1) If a written notice requesting that a claim be filed was sent to the State VR agency, a claim must be filed within 90 days following the month in which VR

services end, or if later, within 90 days after receipt of the notice.

(2) If no written notice was sent to the State VR agency, a claim must be filed within 12 months after the month in which VR services end.

[55 FR 8455, March 8, 1990; 61 FR 31025, June 19, 1996; 68 FR 40124, July 7, 2003; 83 FR 62457, Dec. 4, 2018]

§ 404.2117 What costs will be paid.

In accordance with section 222(d) of the Social Security Act, the Commissioner will pay the State VR agency for the VR services described in § 404.2114 which were provided during the period described in § 404.2115 and which meet the criteria in § 404.2111 or § 404.2112, but subject to the following limitations:

(a) The cost must have been incurred by the State VR agency;

(b) The cost must not have been paid or be payable from some other source. For this purpose, State VR agencies will be required to seek payment or services from other sources in accordance with the "similar benefit" provisions under 34 CFR part 361, including making maximum efforts to secure grant assistance in whole or part from other sources for training or training services in institutions of higher education.

(c)(1) The cost must be reasonable and necessary, in that it complies with the written cost-containment policies of the State VR agency. A cost which complies with these policies will be considered necessary only if the cost is for a VR service described in § 404.2114. The State VR agency must maintain and use these cost-containment policies, including any reasonable and appropriate fee schedules, to govern the costs incurred for all VR services, including the rates of payment for all purchased services, for which payment will be requested under this subpart. For the purpose of this subpart, the written cost-containment policies must provide guidelines designed to ensure—

(i) The lowest reasonable cost for such services; and

(ii) Sufficient flexibility so as to allow for an individual's needs.

(2) The State VR agency shall submit to us before the end of the first calendar quarter of each year a written statement certifying that cost-containment policies are in effect and are adhered to in procuring and providing goods and services for which the State VR agency requests payment under this subpart. Such certification must be signed by the State's chief financial official or the head of the VR agency. Each certification must specify the basis upon which it is made, e.g., a recent audit by an authorized State, Federal or private auditor (or other independent compliance review) and the date of such audit (or compliance review). We may request the State VR agency to submit to us a copy(ies) of its specific written cost-containment policies and procedures (e.g., any guidelines and fee schedules for a given year) if we determine that such additional information is necessary to ensure compliance with the requirements of this subpart. The State VR agency must provide such information when requested by us.

(d) The total payment in each case, including any prior payments related to earlier continuous 9–month periods of SGA made under this subpart, must not be so high as to preclude a "net saving" to the trust funds (a "net saving" is the difference between the estimated saving to the trust funds, if disability benefits eventually terminate, and the total amount we pay to the State VR agency);

(e) Any payment to the State VR agency for either direct or indirect VR expenses must be consistent with the cost principles described in OMB Circular No. A–87, as revised;

(f) Payment for VR services or costs may be made under more than one of the VR payment provisions described in §§ 404.2111 and 404.2112 of this subpart and similar provisions in §§ 416.2211 and 416.2212 of subpart V of part 416. However, payment will not be made more than once for the same VR service or cost; and

(g) Payment will be made for administrative costs and for counseling and placement costs. This payment may be on a formula basis, or on an actual cost basis, whichever the State VR agency prefers. The formula will be negotiated. The payment will also be subject to the preceding limitations.

[55 FR 8454, 8455, March 8, 1990; 59 FR 11915, March 15, 1994; 62 FR 38452, July 18, 1997; 68 FR 40124, July 7, 2003; 83 FR 62457, Dec. 4, 2018]

ADMINISTRATIVE PROVISIONS

§ 404.2118 [Reserved by 83 FR 62458]

[83 FR 62458, Dec. 4, 2018]

§ 404.2119 Method of payment.

Payment to the State VR agencies pursuant to this subpart will be made either by advancement of funds or by payment for services provided (with necessary adjustments for any overpayments and underpayments), as decided by the Commissioner.

[55 FR 8454, 8455, March 8, 1990; 83 FR 62458, Dec. 4, 2018]

§ 404.2120 Audits.

(a) *General.* The State shall permit us and the Comptroller General of the United States (including duly authorized representatives) access to and the right to examine records relating to the services and costs for which payment was requested or made under these regulations. These records shall be retained by the State for the periods of time specified for retention of records in the Federal Acquisition Regulations (48 CFR part 4, subpart 4.7).

(b) Audit basis. Auditing will be based on cost principles and written guidelines in effect at the time services were provided and costs were incurred. The State VR agency will be informed and given a full explanation of any questioned items. It will be given a reasonable time to explain questioned items. Any explanation furnished by the State VR agency will be given full consideration before a final determination is made on questioned items in the audit report.

(c) Appeal of audit determinations. The appropriate SSA Regional Commissioner will notify the State VR agency in writing of his or her final determination on the audit report. If the State VR agency disagrees with that determination, it may request reconsideration in writing within 60 days after receiving the Regional Commissioner's notice of the determination. The Commissioner will make a determination and notify the State VR agency of that decision in writing, usually, no later than 45 days from the date of appeal. The decision by the Commissioner will be final and conclusive unless the State VR agency appeals that decision in writing in accordance with 45 CFR part 16 to the Department of Health and Human Services' Departmental Appeals Board within 30 days after receiving it.

[55 FR 8456, March 8, 1990; 62 FR 38452, July 18, 1997; 83 FR 62458, Dec. 4, 2018]

§ 404.2121 Validation reviews.

(a) General. We will conduct a validation review of a sample of the claims for payment filed by each State VR agency. We will conduct some of these reviews on a prepayment basis and some on a postpayment basis. We may review a specific claim, a sample of the claims, or all the claims filed by any State VR agency, if we determine that such review is necessary to ensure compliance with the requirements of this subpart. For each claim selected for review, the State VR agency must submit such records of the VR services and costs for which payment has been requested or made under this subpart, or copies of such records, as we may require to ensure that the services and costs meet the requirements for payment. For claims for cases described in § 404.2101(a), a clear explanation or existing documentation which demonstrates how the service contributed to the individual's performance of a continuous 9–month period of SGA must be provided. For claims for cases described in § 404.2101(b) or (c), a clear explanation or existing documentation which demonstrates how the service was reasonably expected to motivate or assist the individual to return to or continue in SGA must be provided. If we find in any prepayment validation review, that the scope or content of the information is inadequate, we will request additional information and will withhold payment until adequate information has been provided. The State VR agency shall permit us (including duly authorized representatives) access to, and the right to examine, any records relating to such services and costs. Any review performed under this section will not be considered an audit for purposes of this subpart.

(b) Purpose. The primary purpose of these reviews is—

(1) To ensure that the VR services and costs meet the requirements for payment under this subpart;

(2) To assess the validity of our documentation requirements; and

(3) To assess the need for additional validation reviews or additional documentation requirements for any State VR agency to ensure compliance with the requirements under this subpart.

(c) Determinations. In any validation review, we will determine whether the VR services and costs meet the requirements for payment and determine the amount of payment. We will notify in writing the State VR agency of our determination. If we find in any postpayment validation review that more or less than the correct amount of payment was made for a claim, we will determine that an overpayment or underpayment has occurred and will notify the State VR agency that we will make the appropriate adjustment.

(d) Appeals. If the State VR agency disagrees with our determination under this section, it may appeal that determination in accordance with § 404.2127. For purposes of this section, an appeal must be filed within 60 days after receiving the notice of our determination.

[59 FR 11916, March 15, 1994; 83 FR 62458, Dec. 4, 2018]

§ 404.2122 Confidentiality of information and records.

The State shall comply with the provisions for confidentiality of information, including the security of systems, and records requirements described in 20 CFR part 401 and pertinent written guidelines (see § 404.2123).

[83 FR 62459, Dec. 4, 2018]

§ 404.2123 Other Federal laws and regulations.

Each State VR agency shall comply with the provisions of other Federal laws and regulations that directly affect its responsibilities in carrying out the vocational rehabilitation function.

[83 FR 62459, Dec. 4, 2018]

§ 404.2127 Resolution of disputes.

(a) Disputes on the amount to be paid. The appropriate SSA official will notify the State VR agency in writing of his or her determination concerning the amount to be paid. If the State VR agency disagrees with that determination, the State VR agency may request reconsideration in writing within 60 days after receiving the notice of determination. The Commissioner will make a determination and notify the State VR agency of that decision in writing, usually no later than 45 days from the date of the State VR agency's appeal. The decision by the Commissioner will be final and conclusive upon the State VR agency unless the State VR agency appeals that decision in writing in accordance with 45 CFR part 16 to the Department of Health and Human Services' Departmental Appeals Board within 30 days after receiving the Commissioner's decision.

(b) Disputes on whether there was a continuous period of SGA and whether VR services contributed to a continuous period of SGA. The rules in paragraph (a) of this section will apply, except that the Commissioner's decision will be final and conclusive. There is no right of appeal to the Departmental Appeals Board.

(c) Disputes on determinations made by the Commissioner which affect a disability beneficiary's rights to benefits. Determinations made by the Commissioner which affect an individual's right to benefits (e.g., determinations that disability benefits should be terminated, denied, suspended, continued or begun at a different date than alleged) cannot be appealed by a State VR agency. Because these determinations are an integral part of the disability benefits claims process, they can only be appealed by the beneficiary or applicant whose rights are affected or by his or her authorized representative. However, if an appeal of an unfavorable determination is made by the individual and is successful, the new determination would also apply for purposes of this subpart. While a VR agency cannot appeal a determination made by the Commissioner which affects a beneficiary's or applicant's rights, the VR agency can furnish any evidence it may have which would support a revision of a determination.

[55 FR 8456, March 8, 1990; 62 FR 38452, July 18, 1997; 83 FR 62459, Dec. 4, 2018]

PART 405—[RESERVED]

Source: 81 FR 90994, Dec. 16, 2016, unless otherwise noted.

§§ 405.1 to 405.30 [Reserved by 81 FR 90994]

[81 FR 90994, Dec. 16, 2016]

APPENDIX [RESERVED BY 81 FR 90994]

[81 FR 90994, Dec. 16, 2016]

§§ 405.101 to 405.120 [Reserved by 81 FR 90994]

[81 FR 90994, Dec. 16, 2016]

§§ 405.201 to 405.240 [Reserved by 81 FR 90994]

[81 FR 90994, Dec. 16, 2016]

§§ 405.301 to 405.383 [Reserved by 81 FR 90994]

[81 FR 90994, Dec. 16, 2016]

§§ 405.401 to 405.430 [Reserved by 81 FR 90994]

[81 FR 90994, Dec. 16, 2016]

§§ 405.501 to 405.515 [Reserved by 81 FR 90994]

[81 FR 90994, Dec. 16, 2016]

§ 405.601 [Reserved by 81 FR 90994]

[81 FR 90994, Dec. 16, 2016]

§§ 405.701 to 405.725 [Reserved by 81 FR 90994]

[81 FR 90994, Dec. 16, 2016]

§§ 405.801 to 405.850 [Reserved by 81 FR 90994]

[81 FR 90994, Dec. 16, 2016]

§ 405.901 [Reserved by 81 FR 90994]

[81 FR 90994, Dec. 16, 2016]

PART 408—SPECIAL BENEFITS FOR CERTAIN WORLD WAR II VETERANS

SUBPART A—INTRODUCTION, GENERAL PROVISION AND DEFINITIONS

Sec.
408.101. What is this part about?
408.105. Purpose and administration of the program.
408.110. General definitions and use of terms.
408.120. Periods of limitations ending on Federal nonworkdays.

SUBPART B—SVB QUALIFICATION AND ENTITLEMENT

408.201. What is this subpart about?
408.202. How do you qualify for SVB?
408.204. What conditions will prevent you from qualifying for SVB or being entitled to receive SVB payments?
408.206. What happens when you apply for SVB?
408.208. What happens if you establish residence outside the United States within 4 calendar months?
408.210. What happens if you do not establish residence outside the United States within 4 calendar months?
408.212. What happens if you are a qualified individual already residing outside the United States?

AGE

408.214. Are you age 65?

MILITARY SERVICE

408.216. Are you a World War II veteran?

SSI ELIGIBILITY

408.218. Do you meet the SSI eligibility requirements?

OTHER BENEFIT INCOME

408.220. Do you have other benefit income?
408.222. How does your other benefit income affect your SVB?
408.224. How do we determine the monthly amount of your other benefit income?
408.226. What happens if you begin receiving other benefit income after you become entitled to SVB?

RESIDENCE OUTSIDE THE UNITED STATES

408.228. When do we consider you to be residing outside the United States?
408.230. When must you begin residing outside the United States?
408.232. When do you lose your foreign resident status?
408.234. Can you continue to receive SVB payments if you stay in the United States for more than 1 full calendar month?

SUBPART C—FILING APPLICATIONS

FILING YOUR APPLICATION

408.301. What is this subpart about?
408.305. Why do you need to file an application to receive benefits?

Sec.
408.310. What makes an application a claim for SVB?
408.315. Who may sign your application?
408.320. What evidence shows that a person has authority to sign an application for you?
408.325. When is your application considered filed?
408.330. How long will your application remain in effect?

FILING DATE BASED ON WRITTEN STATEMENT OR ORAL INQUIRY

408.340. When will we use a written statement as your filing date?
408.345. When will we use the date of an oral inquiry as your application filing date?

DEEMED FILING DATE BASED ON MISINFORMATION

408.351. What happens if we give you misinformation about filing an application?

WITHDRAWAL OF APPLICATION

408.355. Can you withdraw your application?
408.360. Can you cancel your request to withdraw your application?

SUBPART D—EVIDENCE REQUIREMENTS

GENERAL INFORMATION

408.401. What is this subpart about?
408.402. When do you need to give us evidence?
408.403. Where should you give us your evidence?
408.404. What happens if you fail to give us the evidence we ask for?
408.405. When do we require original records or copies as evidence?
408.406. How do we evaluate the evidence you give us?

AGE

408.410. When do you need to give us evidence of your age?
408.412. What kinds of evidence of age do you need to give us?
408.413. How do we evaluate the evidence of age you give us?

MILITARY SERVICE

408.420. What evidence of World War II military service do you need to give us?

SSI ELIGIBILITY

408.425. How do we establish your eligibility for SSI?

OTHER BENEFIT INCOME

408.430. When do you need to give us evidence of your other benefit income?
408.432. What kind of evidence of your other benefit income do you need to give us?

RESIDENCE

408.435. How do you prove that you are residing outside the United States?
408.437. How do you prove that you had good cause for staying in the United States for more than 1 full calendar month?

Authority: Secs. 702(a)(5), 808, and 1147 of the Social Security Act (42 U.S.C. 902(a)(5), 1008, and 1320b–17); 31 U.S.C. 3716; 31 U.S.C. 3720A.

Source: 68 FR 16418, April 4, 2003; 76 FR 65108, Oct. 20, 2011, unless otherwise noted.

SUBPART A—INTRODUCTION, GENERAL PROVISION AND DEFINITIONS

Authority: Secs. 702(a)(5) and 801–813 of the Social Security Act (42 U.S.C. 902(a)(5) and 1001–1013).

§ 408.101 What is this part about?

The regulations in this part 408 (Regulation No. 8 of the Social Security Administration) relate to the provisions of title VIII of the Social Security Act as added by Pub.L. 106–169 enacted December 14, 1999. Title VIII (Special Benefits for Certain World War II Veterans) established a program for the payment of benefits to certain World War II veterans. The regulations in this part are divided into the following subparts according to subject content.

(a) Subpart A contains this introductory section, a statement of the general purpose underlying the payment of special benefits to World War II veterans, general provisions applicable to the program and its administration, and defines certain terms that we use throughout part 408.

(b) Subpart B contains the requirements for qualification and entitlement to monthly title VIII benefits.

(c) Subpart C contains the provisions relating to the filing and withdrawal of applications.

(d) Subpart D contains the provisions relating to the evidence required for establishing qualification for and entitlement to monthly title VIII benefits.

(e) Subpart E contains the provisions about the amount and payment of monthly benefits.

(f) Subpart F is reserved for future use.

(g) Subpart G contains the provisions on your requirement to report certain events to us.

(h) Subpart H contains the provisions on suspension and termination of title VIII entitlement.

(i) Subpart I contains the provisions on underpayments and overpayments.

(j) Subpart J contains the provisions on determinations and the administrative review process.

(k) Subpart K contains the provisions on claimant representation.

(*l*) Subpart L contains the provisions on Federal administration of State recognition payments.

[69 FR 25955, May 10, 2004]

§ 408.105 Purpose and administration of the program.

The purpose of the title VIII program is to assure a basic income level for certain veterans who are entitled to supplemental security income (SSI) and who want to leave the United States to live abroad. The title VIII program is administered by the Social Security Administration.

§ 408.110 General definitions and use of terms.

(a) Terms relating to the Act and regulations.

(1) The Act means the Social Security Act as amended (42 U.S.C. Chap.7).

(2) Title means the title of the Act.

(3) Section or § means a section of the regulations in part 408 of this chapter unless the context indicates otherwise.

(b) Commissioner; Appeals Council; Administrative Law Judge defined.

(1) Commissioner means the Commissioner of Social Security.

(2) Appeals Council means the Appeals Council of the Office of Hearings and Appeals of the Social Security Administration or a member or members of the Council designated by the Chairman.

(3) Administrative Law Judge means an Administrative Law Judge in the Office of Hearings and Appeals in the Social Security Administration.

(c) Miscellaneous—

(1) A calendar month. The period including all of 24 hours of each day of January, February, March, April, May, June, July, August, September, October, November, or December.

(2) Federal benefit rate (FBR). The amount of the cash benefit payable under title XVI for the month to an eligible individual who has no income. The FBR does not include any State supplementary payment that is paid by the Commissioner pursuant to an agreement with a State under section 1616(a) of the Act or section 212(b) of Public Law 93–66.

(3) Qualified individual. An individual who meets all the requirements for qualification for SVB in § 408.202 and does not meet any of the conditions that prevent qualification in § 408.204.

(4) Special veterans benefits (SVB). The benefits payable to certain veterans of World War II under title VIII of the Act.

(5) State. Unless otherwise indicated, this means:

(i) A State of the United States

(ii) The District of Columbia; or

(iii) The Northern Mariana Islands.

(6) Supplemental Security Income (SSI). SSI is the national program for providing a minimum level of income to aged, blind, and disabled individuals under title XVI of the Act.

(7) United States. When used in the geographical sense, this is:

(i) The 50 States;

(ii) The District of Columbia; and

(iii) The Northern Mariana Islands.

(8) We, us or our means the Social Security Administration (SSA).

(9) World War II. The period beginning September 16, 1940 and ending on July 24, 1947.

(10) You or your means, as appropriate, the person who applies for benefits, the person for whom an application is filed, or the person who is considering applying for benefits.

§ 408.120 Periods of limitations ending on Federal nonworkdays.

Title VIII of the Act and the regulations in this part require you to take certain actions within specified time periods or you may lose your right to a portion or all of your benefits. If any such period ends on a Saturday, Sunday, Federal legal holiday, or any other day all or part of which is declared to be a nonworkday for Federal employees by statute or Executive Order, you will have until the next Federal workday to take the prescribed action.

SUBPART B—SVB QUALIFICATION AND ENTITLEMENT

Authority: Secs. 702(a)(5), 801, 802, 803, 804, 806, 810 and 1129A of the Social Security Act (42 U.S.C. 902(a)(5), 1001, 1002, 1003, 1004, 1006, 1010 and 1320a–8a); Sec. 251, Pub.L. 106–169, 113 Stat. 1844.

§ 408.201 What is this subpart about?

You are qualified for SVB if you meet the requirements listed in § 408.202 and if none of the conditions listed in § 408.204 exist. However, you cannot be entitled to receive benefits for any month before the first month in which you reside outside the United States on the first day of the month and meet all the qualification requirements. You must give us any information we request and evidence to prove that you meet these requirements. You continue to be qualified for SVB unless we determine that you no longer meet the requirements for qualification in § 408.202 or we determine that you are not qualified because one of the conditions listed in § 404.204 of this chapter exists. You continue to be entitled to receive benefits unless we determine you are no longer residing outside the United States.

§ 408.202 How do you qualify for SVB?

You qualify for SVB if you meet all of the following requirements.

(a) Age. You were age 65 or older on December 14, 1999 (the date on which Pub.L. 106–169 was enacted into law).

(b) World War II veteran. You are a World War II veteran as explained in § 408.216.

(c) SSI eligible. You were eligible for SSI, as explained in § 408.218, for both December 1999 (the month in which Pub.L. 106–169 was enacted into law) and for the month in which you file your application for SVB.

(d) Application. You file an application for SVB as explained in subpart C of this part.

(e) Other benefit income. You do not have other benefit income, as explained in § 408.220, which is equal to, or more than, 75 percent of the current FBR.

§ 408.204 What conditions will prevent you from qualifying for SVB or being entitled to receive SVB payments?

(a) General rule. Even if you meet all the qualification requirements in § 408.202, you will not be qualified for SVB for or entitled to receive SVB payments for any of the following months.

(1) Removal from the United States. Any month that begins after the month in which we are advised by the Attorney General that you have been removed (including deported) from the United States pursuant to section 237(a) or 212(a)(6)(A) of the Immigration and Nationality Act and before the month in which you are subsequently lawfully admitted to the United States for permanent residence.

(2) Fleeing felon. Any month during any part of which you are fleeing to avoid prosecution, or custody or confinement after conviction, under the laws of the United States or the jurisdiction in the United States from which you fled, for a crime or an attempt to commit a crime that is a felony under the laws of the place from which you fled, or in the case of the State of New Jersey, is a high misdemeanor.

(3) Parole violation. Any month during any part of which you violate a condition of probation or parole imposed under Federal or State law.

(4) Residence in certain countries. Any month during which you are not a citizen or national of the United States and reside in a country to which payments to residents of that country are withheld by the Treasury Department under section 3329 of title 31, United States Code.

(b) Condition occurs before we determine that you are qualified. If one of the conditions in paragraph (a) of this section occurs before we determine that you are qualified, we will deny your claim for SVB.

(c) Condition occurs after we determine that you are qualified. If one of the conditions in paragraph (a) of this section occurs after we determine that you are qualified for SVB, you cannot receive SVB payments for any month in which the condition exists.

§ 408.206 What happens when you apply for SVB?

(a) General rule. When you apply for SVB, we will ask you for documents and other information that we need to determine if you meet all the requirements for qualification. You must give us complete information (see subpart D of this part for our rules on evidence). If you do not meet all of the requirements for qualification listed in § 408.202, or if one of the conditions listed in § 408.204 exists, we will deny your claim.

(b) If you are a qualified individual residing in the United States. If you meet all the requirements for qualification listed in § 408.202 and if none of the conditions listed in § 408.204 exist, we will send you a letter telling you the following:

(1) You are qualified for SVB;

(2) In order to become entitled to SVB, you will have to begin residing outside the United States by the end of the fourth calendar month after the month in which your notice of qualification is dated. For example, if our letter is dated May 15, you must establish residence outside the United States before October 1 of that year; and

(3) What documents and information you must give us to establish that you are residing outside the United States.

§ 408.208 What happens if you establish residence outside the United States within 4 calendar months?

If you begin residing outside the United States within 4 calendar months after the month in which your SVB qualification notice is dated, we will send you a letter telling you that you are entitled to SVB and the first month for which SVB payments can be made to you. The letter will also tell you the amount of your monthly benefit payments, whether your payments are reduced because of your other benefit income, and what rights you have to a reconsideration of our determination.

§ 408.210 What happens if you do not establish residence outside the United States within 4 calendar months?

If you do not establish residence outside the United States within 4 calendar months after the month in which your SVB qualification notice is dated, we will deny your SVB claim. We will send you a notice explaining what rights you have to a reconsideration of our determination. You will have to file a new application and meet all the requirements for qualification and entitlement based on the new application to become entitled to SVB.

§ 408.212 What happens if you are a qualified individual already residing outside the United States?

If you meet all the requirements for qualification listed in § 408.202 and if none of the conditions listed in § 408.204 exist, we will ask you for documents and information to establish your residence outside the United States. If you establish that you are residing outside the United States, we will send you a letter telling you that you are entitled to SVB and the first month for which SVB payments can be made to you. The letter will also tell you the amount of your monthly benefit payments, whether your payments are reduced because of your other benefit income, and what rights you have to a reconsideration of our determination.

AGE

§ 408.214 Are you age 65?

You become age 65 on the first moment of the day before the anniversary of your birth corresponding to age 65. Thus, you must have been born on or before December 15, 1934 to be at least age 65 on December 14, 1999 and to qualify for SVB.

MILITARY SERVICE

§ 408.216 Are you a World War II veteran?

(a) Service requirements. For SVB purposes, you are a World War II veteran if you:

(1) Served in the active military, naval or air service of the United States during World War II at any time during the period beginning on September 16, 1940 and ending on July 24, 1947; or

(2) Served in the organized military forces of the Government of the Commonwealth of the Philippines, while the forces were in the service of the U.S. Armed Forces pursuant to the military order of the President dated July 26, 1941, including among the military forces organized guerrilla forces under commanders appointed, designated, or subsequently recognized by the Commander in Chief, Southwest Pacific Area, or other competent authority in the U.S. Army. This service must have been rendered at any time during the period beginning July 26, 1941 and ending on December 30, 1946.

(b) Discharge requirements. You must have been discharged or released from this service under conditions other than dishonorable after service of 90 days or more or, if your service was less than 90 days, because of a disability or injury incurred or aggravated in the line of active duty.

SSI ELIGIBILITY

§ 408.218 Do you meet the SSI eligibility requirements?

For SVB purposes, you are eligible for SSI for a given month if all of the following are met:

(a) You have been determined to be eligible for SSI (except as noted in paragraph (c) of this section); you do not have to actually receive a payment for that month;

(b) Your SSI eligibility has not been terminated for that month; and

(c) Your SSI benefits are not subject to a penalty under § 416.1340 of this chapter. This includes months in which a penalty has been imposed, as well as months in which a penalty cannot be imposed because you are in SSI nonpay status for some other reason.

OTHER BENEFIT INCOME

§ 408.220 Do you have other benefit income?

(a) Description of other benefit income. Other benefit income is any regular periodic payment (such as an annuity, pension, retirement or disability benefit) that you receive. For other benefit income to affect your SVB eligibility, you must have been receiving the other benefit income in any part of the 12–month period before the month in which you filed your application for SVB. Payments received after you become entitled to SVB can be included as other benefit income only if you received a similar payment from the same or a related source during any part of the 12–month period before the month in which you filed your application for SVB.

(b) When other benefit payments are considered to be similar payments from the same or a related source. Payments are similar payments from the same or a related source if they are received from sources substantially related to the sources of income received before you became entitled to SVB. For example, if you received U.S. Social Security spouse's benefits in the 12–month period before you filed your application for SVB and these were changed to widower's benefits after you became entitled to SVB, we would consider this to be from the same or a related source.

(c) Examples of other benefit income. Other benefit income can come from a source inside or outside the United States. It includes, but is not limited to, any of the following:

(1) Veterans' compensation or pension,

(2) Workers' compensation,

(3) U.S. or foreign Social Security benefits (not including SSI payments from the U.S.),

(4) Railroad retirement annuity or pension,

(5) Retirement or disability pension,

(6) Individual Retirement Account (IRA) payments, and

(7) Unemployment insurance benefit.

(d) If you receive a lump-sum payment. Regular periodic payments can also include lump-sum payments made at your request or as an administrative convenience or practice in place of more frequent payments. See § 408.224(e) for an explanation of how we determine the monthly amount of your benefit income if you receive a lump-sum payment.

§ 408.222 How does your other benefit income affect your SVB?

(a) Income began before you qualify for SVB. If, at the time you file your application for SVB, your other benefit income is equal to, or more than, the maximum SVB payment possible (see § 408.505), we will deny your SVB claim. If it is less, we will reduce any monthly SVB payments you become entitled to by the amount of your other benefit income (see § 408.510 for a description of how we make the reduction).

(b) Income begins after you qualify for SVB. If you have been determined to be qualified for SVB, we will reduce any monthly SVB payments you become entitled to by the amount of your other benefit income (see § 408.510 for a description of how we make the reduction).

§ 408.224 How do we determine the monthly amount of your other benefit income?

If your other benefit income is paid in other than monthly amounts, we will compute the equivalent monthly amount as follows:

(a) Weekly payments. We multiply the amount of the weekly payment by 52 and divide by 12 to determine the equivalent monthly payment amount.

(b) Bi-weekly payments. We multiply the amount of the bi-weekly payment by 26 and divide by 12 to determine the equivalent monthly payment amount.

(c) Quarterly payments. We multiply the amount of the quarterly payment by 4 and divide by 12 to determine the equivalent monthly payment amount.

(d) Semi-annual payments. We multiply the amount of the semi-annual payment by 2 and divide by 12 to determine the equivalent monthly payment amount.

(e) Lump sum payment. If the paying agency will not prorate the lump sum to determine the monthly amount, we will compute the amount as follows:

(1) If the payment is for a specific period. We divide the lump sum by the number of months in the period for which the payment was made to determine the equivalent monthly payment amount.

(2) If the payment is for a lifetime or for an unspecified period. We divide the lump sum amount by your life expectancy in months at the time the lump sum is paid.

§ 408.226 What happens if you begin receiving other benefit income after you become entitled to SVB?

If you begin receiving other benefit income after you become entitled to SVB, we will reduce your SVB by the amount of those payments only if you were receiving similar benefits from the same or a related source during the 12–month period before you filed for SVB. (See § 408.220(b) for a description of when we consider other benefit income to be from the same or a related source.)

RESIDENCE OUTSIDE THE UNITED STATES

§ 408.228 When do we consider you to be residing outside the United States?

(a) Effect of residency on SVB eligibility. You can be paid SVB only for those months in which you are residing outside the United States but you can not be paid for a month that is earlier than the month in which you filed your application for SVB. You are residing outside the United States in a month only if you reside outside the United States on the first day of that month. For SVB purposes, you can be a resident of only one country at a time. You cannot, for example, maintain a residence in the United States and a residence outside the United States at the same time.

(b) Definition of residing outside the United States. We consider you to be residing outside the United States if you:

(1) Have established an actual dwelling place outside the United States; and

(2) Intend to continue to live outside the United States.

(c) When we will assume you intend to continue living outside the United States. If you tell us, or the evidence shows, that you intend to reside outside the United States for at least 6 months, we will assume you meet the intent requirement in paragraph (b)(2) of this section. Otherwise we will assume, absent convincing evidence to the contrary, that your stay is temporary and that you are not residing outside the United States.

§ 408.230 When must you begin residing outside the United States?

(a) 4–month rule. Except as provided in paragraph (b) of this section, you must begin residing outside the United States by the end of the fourth calendar month after the month in which the notice explaining that you are qualified for SVB is dated, as explained in § 408.206. If you do not establish residence outside the United States within this 4–month period, we will deny your claim for SVB. You will have to file a new application and meet all the requirements for qualification and entitlement based on the new application to become entitled to SVB.

(b) When we will extend the 4–month period. We will extend the 4–month period for establishing residence outside the United States if you are in the United States and are appealing either:

(1) A determination that we made on your SVB claim, or

(2) A determination that we made on a title II and/or a title XVI claim but only if the determination affects your SVB qualification.

(c) How we extend the 4–month period. If the requirements in paragraph (b) of this section are met, the 4–month period begins with the month after the month in which your notice of our decision on your appeal is dated or the month in which your appeal rights have expired.

§ 408.232 When do you lose your foreign resident status?

(a) General rule. We consider you to have lost or abandoned your residence outside the United States if you:

(1) Enter the United States and stay for more than 1 full calendar month (see § 408.234 for exceptions to this rule);

(2) Tell us that you no longer consider yourself to be residing outside the United States; or

(3) Become eligible (as defined by title XVI) for SSI benefits.

(b) Resumption of SVB following a period of U.S. residence. Once you lose or abandon your residence outside the United States, you cannot receive SVB again until you meet all the requirements for SVB qualification and reestablish your residence outside the United States.

Example: You leave your home outside the United States on June 15 to visit your son in the United States and return to your home abroad on August 15. Your SVB payments will continue for the months of June and July. However, because you were in the United States for the entire calendar month of July (i.e., all of the first day through all of the last day of July), you are not entitled to an SVB payment for the month of August. Your SVB payments resume with September, the month you reestablished your residence outside the United States.

§ 408.234 Can you continue to receive SVB payments if you stay in the United States for more than 1 full calendar month?

(a) When we will consider your foreign residence to continue. We will continue to consider you to be a foreign resident and will continue to pay you SVB payments even if you have been in the United States for more than 1 full calendar month if you—

(1) Made a good faith effort to return to your home abroad within that 1–month period but were prevented from doing so by circumstances beyond your control (e.g., sickness, a death in the family, a transportation strike, etc.); or

(2) Are exercising your option to be personally present in the United States to present testimony and

other evidence in the appeal of an SSA decision on a claim filed under any SSA-administered program. This extension applies only as long as you are participating in activities where you are providing testimony and other evidence in connection with a determination or decision at a specific level of the appeals process (e.g., a hearing before an administrative law judge).

(b) When you must return to your home abroad. When the circumstance/event that was the basis for the continuation of your SVB payments ceases to exist, you must return to your home abroad within 1 full calendar month. If you do not return to your home abroad within this 1–calendar-month period, we will consider you to have lost or abandoned your foreign resident status for SVB purposes and we will stop your SVB payments with the first day of the month following the first full calendar month you remain in the United States.

SUBPART C—FILING APPLICATIONS

Authority: Secs. 702(a)(5), 802, 806, and 810 of the Social Security Act (42 U.S.C. 902(a)(5), 1102, 1106 and 1110); Sec. 251, Pub.L. 106–169, 113 Stat. 1844.

FILING YOUR APPLICATION

§ 408.301 What is this subpart about?

This subpart contains our rules about filing applications for SVB. It explains what an application is, who may sign it, where and when it must be signed and filed, the period of time it is in effect, and how it may be withdrawn. This subpart also explains when a written statement or an oral inquiry may be considered to establish your application filing date.

§ 408.305 Why do you need to file an application to receive benefits?

In addition to meeting other requirements, you must file an application to become entitled to SVB. If you believe you may be entitled to SVB, you should file an application. Filing an application will—

(a) Permit us to make a formal decision on whether you qualify for SVB;

(b) Assure that you receive SVB for any months you are entitled to receive payments; and

(c) Give you the right to appeal if you are dissatisfied with our determination.

§ 408.310 What makes an application a claim for SVB?

To be considered a claim for SVB, an application must generally meet all of the following conditions:

(a) It must be on the prescribed SVB application form (SSA–2000–F6, Application for Special Benefits for World War II Veterans).

(b) It must be completed and filed with SSA as described in § 408.325.

(c) It must be signed by you or by someone who may sign an application for you as described in § 408.315.

(d) You must be alive at the time it is filed.

§ 408.315 Who may sign your application?

(a) When you must sign. If you are mentally competent, and physically able to do so, you must sign your own application.

(b) When someone else may sign for you.

(1) If you are mentally incompetent, or physically unable to sign, your application may be signed by a court-appointed representative or a person who is responsible for your care, including a relative. If you are in the care of an institution, the manager or principal officer of the institution may sign your application.

(2) If it is necessary to protect you from losing benefits and there is good cause why you could not sign the application, we may accept an application signed by someone other than you or a person described in paragraph (b)(1) of this section.

Example: Mr. Smith comes to a Social Security office a few days before the end of a month to file an application for SVB for his neighbor, Mr. Jones. Mr. Jones, a 68–year–old widower, just suffered a heart attack and is in the hospital. He asked Mr. Smith to file the application for him. We will accept an application signed by Mr. Smith because it would not be possible to have Mr. Jones sign and file the application until the next calendar month and a loss of one month's benefits would result.

§ 408.320 What evidence shows that a person has authority to sign an application for you?

(a) A person who signs an application for you will be required to give us evidence of his or her authority to sign the application for you under the following rules:

(1) If the person who signs is a court-appointed representative, he or she must give us a certificate issued by the court showing authority to act for you.

(2) If the person who signs is not a court-appointed representative, he or she must give us a statement describing his or her relationship to you. The statement must also describe the extent to which the person is responsible for your care.

(3) If the person who signs is the manager or principal officer of an institution which is responsible for your care, he or she must give us a statement indicating the person's position of responsibility at the institution.

(b) We may, at any time, require additional evidence to establish the authority of a person to sign an application for you.

§ 408.325 When is your application considered filed?

(a) General rule. We consider an application for SVB filed on the day it is received by an SSA employee at one of our offices, by an SSA employee who is authorized to receive it at a place other than one of our offices, or by any office of the U.S. Foreign Service or by the Veterans Affairs Regional Office in the Philippines.

(b) Exceptions.

(1) When we receive an application that is mailed, we will use the date shown by the United States postmark as the filing date if using the date we receive it would result in your entitlement to additional benefits. If the postmark is unreadable, or there is no United States postmark, we will use the date the application is signed (if dated) or 5 days before the day we receive the signed application, whichever date is later.

(2) We consider an application to be filed on the date of the filing of a written statement or the making of an oral inquiry under the conditions in §§ 408.340 and 408.345.

(3) We will establish a deemed filing date of an application in a case of misinformation under the conditions described in § 408.351. The filing date of the application will be a date determined under § 408.351(b).

§ 408.330 How long will your application remain in effect?

Your application for SVB will remain in effect from the date it is filed until we make a final determination on it, unless there is a hearing decision on your application. If there is a hearing decision, your application will remain in effect until the hearing decision is issued.

FILING DATE BASED ON WRITTEN STATEMENT OR ORAL INQUIRY

§ 408.340 When will we use a written statement as your filing date?

If you file with us under the rules stated in § 408.325 a written statement, such as a letter, indicating your intent to claim SVB, we will use the filing date of the written statement as the filing date of your application. If the written statement is mailed, we will use the date the statement was mailed to us as shown by the United States postmark. If the postmark is unreadable or there is no United States postmark, we will use the date the statement is signed (if dated) or 5 days before the day we receive the written statement, whichever date is later, as the filing date. In order for us to use your written statement to protect your filing date, the following requirements must be met:

(a) The statement indicates your intent to file for benefits.

(b) The statement is signed by you, your spouse, or a person described in § 408.315.

(c) You file an application with us on an application form as described in § 408.310(a), or one is filed for you by a person described in § 408.315, within 60 days after the date of a notice we will send advising of the need to file an application. The notice will say that we will make an initial determination of your qualification if an application form is filed within 60 days after the date of the notice. We will send the notice to you. However, if it is clear from the information we receive that you are mentally incompetent, we will send the notice to the person who submitted the written statement.

(d) You are alive when the application is filed.

§ 408.345 When will we use the date of an oral inquiry as your application filing date?

We will use the date of an oral inquiry about SVB as the filing date of your application for SVB if the following requirements are met:

(a) The inquiry asks about your entitlement to SVB.

(b) The inquiry is made by you, your spouse, or a person who may sign an application on your behalf as described in § 408.315.

(c) The inquiry, whether in person or by telephone, is directed to an office or an official described in § 408.325(a).

(d) You, or a person on your behalf as described in § 408.315, file an application on a prescribed form within 60 days after the date of the notice we will send telling of the need to file an application. The notice will say that we will make an initial determination on whether you qualify for SVB if an application form is filed within 60 days after the date of the notice. However, if it is clear from the information we receive that you are mentally incompetent, we will send the notice to the person who made the inquiry.

(e) You are alive when the prescribed application is filed.

DEEMED FILING DATE BASED ON MISINFORMATION

§ 408.351 What happens if we give you misinformation about filing an application?

(a) General rule. You may have considered applying for SVB, for yourself or another person and you may have contacted us in writing, by telephone or in person to inquire about filing an application for SVB. It is possible that in responding to your inquiry, we may have given you misinformation about qualification for such benefits that caused you not to file an application at that time. If this happened and use of that date will result in entitlement to additional benefits, and you later file an application for SVB with us, we may establish an earlier filing date as explained in paragraphs (b) through (f) of this section.

(b) Deemed filing date of an application based on misinformation. Subject to the requirements and conditions in paragraphs (c) through (f) of this section, we may establish a deemed filing date of an application for SVB under the following provisions.

(1) If we determine that you failed to apply for SVB because we gave you misinformation about qualification for or entitlement to such benefits, we will deem an application for such benefits to have been filed with us on the later of—

(i) The date on which we gave you the misinformation; or

(ii) The date on which all of the requirements for qualification to SVB were met, other than the requirement of filing an application.

(2) Before we may establish a deemed filing date of an application for SVB under paragraph (b)(1) of this section, you or a person described in § 408.315 must file an application for such benefits.

(c) Requirements concerning the misinformation. We apply the following requirements for purposes of paragraph (b) of this section.

(1) The misinformation must have been provided to you by one of our employees while he or she was acting in his or her official capacity as our employee. For purposes of this section, an employee includes an officer of SSA, an employee of a U.S. Foreign Service office, and an employee of the SSA Division of the Veterans Affairs Regional Office in the Philippines who is authorized to take and develop Social Security claims.

(2) Misinformation is information which we consider to be incorrect, misleading, or incomplete in view of the facts which you gave to the employee, or of which the employee was aware or should have been aware, regarding your particular circumstances. In addition, for us to find that the information you were given was incomplete, the employee must have failed to provide you with the appropriate, additional information which he or she would be required to provide in carrying out his or her official duties.

(3) The misinformation may have been provided to you orally or in writing.

(4) The misinformation must have been provided to you in response to a specific request by you to us for information about your qualification for SVB.

(d) Evidence that misinformation was provided. We will consider the following evidence in making a determination under paragraph (b) of this section.

(1) Preferred evidence. Preferred evidence is written evidence which relates directly to your inquiry about your qualification for SVB and which shows that we gave you misinformation which caused you not to file an application. Preferred evidence includes, but is not limited to, the following—

(i) A notice, letter or other document which was issued by us and addressed to you; or

(ii) Our record of your telephone call, letter or in-person contact.

(2) Other evidence. In the absence of preferred evidence, we will consider other evidence, including your statements about the alleged misinformation, to determine whether we gave you misinformation, which caused you not to file an application. We will not find that we gave you misinformation, however, based solely on your statements. Other evidence which you provide or which we obtain must support your statements. Evidence which we will consider includes, but is not limited to, the following—

(i) Your statements about the alleged misinformation, including statements about—

(A) The date and time of the alleged contact(s);

(B) How the contact was made, e.g., by telephone or in person;

(C) The reason(s) the contact was made;

(D) Who gave the misinformation; and

(E) The questions you asked and the facts you gave us, and the questions we asked and the information we gave you, at the time of the contact;

(ii) Statements from others who were present when you were given the alleged misinformation, e.g., a neighbor who accompanied you to our office;

(iii) If you can identify the employee or the employee can recall your inquiry about benefits—

(A) Statements from the employee concerning the alleged contact, including statements about the questions you asked, the facts you gave, the questions the employee asked, and the information provided to you at the time of the alleged contact; and

(B) Our assessment of the likelihood that the employee provided the alleged misinformation;

(iv) An evaluation of the credibility and the validity of your allegations in conjunction with other relevant information; and

(v) Any other information regarding your alleged contact.

(e) Information which does not constitute satisfactory proof that misinformation was given. Certain kinds of information will not be considered satisfactory proof that we gave you misinformation which caused you not to file an application. Examples of such information include—

(1) General informational pamphlets that we issue to provide basic program information;

(2) General information which we review or prepare but which is disseminated by the media, e.g., radio, television, magazines, and newspapers; and

(3) Information provided by other governmental agencies, e.g., the Department of Veterans Affairs (except for certain employees of the SSA Division of the Veterans Affairs Regional Office in the Philippines as provided in paragraph (c)(1) of this section), the Department of Defense, State unemployment agencies, and State and local governments.

(f) Claim for benefits based on misinformation. You may make a claim for SVB based on misinformation at any time. Your claim must contain information that will enable us to determine if we did provide misinformation to you about qualification for SVB which caused you not to file an application. Specifically, your claim must be in writing and it must explain what information was provided, how, when and where it was provided and by whom, and why the information caused you not to file an application. If you give us this information, we will make a determination on such a claim for benefits if all of the following conditions are also met.

(1) An application for SVB is filed with us by you or someone described in § 408.315 who may file. The application must be filed after the alleged misinformation was provided. This application may be—

(i) An application on which we have made a previous final determination or decision awarding SVB, but only if the claimant continues to be entitled to benefits based on that application;

(ii) An application on which we have made a previous final determination or decision denying the benefits, but only if such determination or decision is reopened; or

(iii) A new application on which we have not made a final determination or decision.

(2) The establishment of a deemed filing date of an application for benefits based on misinformation could result in entitlement to benefits or payment of additional benefits.

(3) We have not made a previous final determination or decision to which you were a party on a claim for benefits based on alleged misinformation involving the same facts and issues. This provision does not apply, however, if the final determination or decision may be reopened.

WITHDRAWAL OF APPLICATION

§ 408.355 Can you withdraw your application?

(a) Request for withdrawal filed before a determination is made. You may withdraw your application for SVB before we make a determination on it if—

(1) You, or a person who may sign an application for you under § 408.315, file a written request for withdrawal at a place described in § 408.325; and

(2) You are alive at the time the request is filed.

(b) Request for withdrawal filed after a determination is made. An application may be withdrawn after we make a determination on it if you repay all benefits already paid based on the application being withdrawn or we are satisfied that the benefits will be repaid.

(c) Effect of withdrawal. If we approve your request to withdraw your application, we consider that the application was never filed. If we disapprove your request for withdrawal, we treat your application as though you did not file a request for withdrawal.

§ 408.360 Can you cancel your request to withdraw your application?

You may request to cancel your request to withdraw your application and have your application reinstated if all of the following requirements are met:

(a) You, or someone who may sign an application for you under § 408.315, file a written request for cancellation at a place described in § 408.325;

(b) You are alive at the time you file your request for cancellation; and

(c) A cancellation request received after we have approved your withdrawal must be filed no later than 60 days after the date of the notice of approval.

SUBPART D—EVIDENCE REQUIREMENTS

Authority: Secs. 702(a)(5), 806, and 810 of the Social Security Act (42 U.S.C. 902(a)(5), 1006, and 1010); sec. 251, Pub.L. 106–169, 113 Stat. 1844.

GENERAL INFORMATION

§ 408.401 What is this subpart about?

We cannot determine your entitlement to SVB based solely on your statements about your qualification for benefits or other facts concerning payments to you. We will ask you for specific evidence or additional information. We may verify the evidence you give us with other sources to ensure that it is correct. This subpart contains our rules about the evidence you need to give us when you claim SVB.

§ 408.402 When do you need to give us evidence?

When you apply for SVB, we will ask you for any evidence we need to make sure that you meet the SVB qualification and entitlement requirements. After you begin receiving SVB, we may ask you for evidence showing whether your SVB payments should be reduced or stopped. We will help you get any documents you need but do not have. If your evidence is a foreign-language record or document, we can have it translated for you. The evidence you give us will be kept confidential and not disclosed to anyone but you except under the rules set out in part 401 of this chapter. You should also be aware that section 811 of the Act provides criminal penalties for misrepresenting the facts or for making false statements to obtain SVB payments for yourself or someone else, or to continue entitlement to benefits.

§ 408.403 Where should you give us your evidence?

You should give your evidence to the people at a Social Security Administration office. In the Philippines, you should give your evidence to the people at the Veterans Affairs Regional Office. Elsewhere outside the United States, you should give your evidence to the people at the nearest U.S. Social Security office or a United States Foreign Service Office.

§ 408.404 What happens if you fail to give us the evidence we ask for?

(a) You have not yet qualified for SVB. Generally, we will ask you to give us specific evidence or information by a certain date to prove that you qualify for SVB or to prove your foreign residence. If we do not receive the evidence or information by that date, we may decide that you do not qualify for SVB or may not receive SVB and deny your claim.

(b) You have qualified for or become entitled to SVB. If you have already qualified for or become entitled to SVB, we may ask you to give us information by a specific date to decide whether you should receive benefits or, if you are already receiving benefits, whether your benefits should be stopped or reduced. If you do not give us the requested evidence or information by the date given, we may decide that you are no longer entitled to benefits or that your benefits should be stopped or reduced.

(c) If you need more time. You should let us know if you are unable to give us the evidence or information within the specified time and explain why there will be a delay. If this delay is due to illness, failure to receive timely evidence you have asked for from another source, or a similar circumstance, we will give you additional time to give us the evidence.

§ 408.405 When do we require original records or copies as evidence?

(a) General rule. To prove your qualification for or continuing entitlement to SVB, you may be asked to show us an original document or record. These original documents or records will be returned to you after we have photocopied them. We will also accept copies of original records that are properly certified and some uncertified birth certifications. These types of records are described in paragraphs (b) and (c) of this section.

(b) Certified copies of original records. You may give us copies of original records or extracts from records if they are certified as true and exact copies by:

(1) The official custodian of the record;

(2) A Social Security Administration employee authorized to certify copies;

(3) A Veterans Affairs employee if the evidence was given to that agency to obtain veteran's benefits;

(4) An employee of the Veterans Affairs Regional Office, Manila, Philippines who is authorized to certify copies; or

(5) A U.S. Consular Officer or employee of the Department of State authorized to certify evidence received outside the United States.

(c) Uncertified copies of original birth records. You may give us an uncertified photocopy of a birth registration notification as evidence of age where it is the practice of the local birth registrar to issue them in this way.

§ 408.406 How do we evaluate the evidence you give us?

When you give us evidence, we examine it to see if it is convincing evidence. This means that unless we have information in our records that raises a doubt about the evidence, other evidence of the same fact will not be needed. If the evidence you give us is not convincing by itself, we may ask you for additional evidence. In evaluating whether the evidence you give us is convincing, we consider such things as whether:

(a) The information contained in the evidence was given by a person in a position to know the facts;

(b) There was any reason to give false information when the evidence was created;

(c) The information in the evidence was given under oath, or with witnesses present, or with the knowledge that there was a penalty for giving false information;

(d) The evidence was created at the time the event took place or shortly thereafter;

(e) The evidence has been altered or has any erasures on it; and

(f) The information contained in the evidence agrees with other available evidence including our records.

AGE

§ 408.410 When do you need to give us evidence of your age?

To qualify for SVB you must establish that you were age 65 or older on December 14, 1999, the date on which Public Law 106–169 was enacted into law. If we have already established your age or date of birth in connection with your claim for other benefit programs that we administer, you will not have to give us evidence of your age for your SVB claim. If we have not established your age or date of birth, you must give us evidence of your age or date of birth. In the absence of information to the contrary, we generally will not ask for additional evidence of your age or date of birth if you state that you are at least age 68, and you submit documentary evidence that is at least 3 years old when the application is filed and supports your statement.

§ 408.412 What kinds of evidence of age do you need to give us?

For a description of the kinds of evidence of age you may need to give us, see § 416.802 of this chapter.

§ 408.413 How do we evaluate the evidence of age you give us?

In evaluating the evidence of age you give us, we use the rules in § 416.803 of this chapter.

MILITARY SERVICE

§ 408.420 What evidence of World War II military service do you need to give us?

(a) Kinds of evidence you can give us. To show that you are a World War II veteran as defined in § 408.216, you can give us any of the documents listed in § 404.1370(b)(1) through (5) of this chapter that were issued by a U.S. Government agency. However, depending on the type of document you give us and what the document shows, we may verify your military service, or the dates of your service, with the National Personnel Records Center (NPRC) in St. Louis, Missouri. If we do, we will use the information in NPRC's records to determine whether you meet the military service requirements for SVB.

(b) What the evidence must show. When you file an application for SVB, you must give us evidence of your World War II military service. The evidence you give us must show:

(1) Your name;

(2) The branch of service in which you served;

(3) The dates of your military service;

(4) Your military service serial number;

(5) The character of your discharge; and

(6) If your service was in the organized military forces of the Government of the Commonwealth of the Philippines (including the organized guerrilla forces), the period of your service that was under the control of U.S. Armed Forces.

SSI ELIGIBILITY

§ 408.425 How do we establish your eligibility for SSI?

To qualify for SVB, you must have been eligible for SSI for the month of December 1999, the month in which Public Law 106–169 was enacted, and for the month in which you filed your application for SVB. You do not have to submit evidence of this. We will use our SSI record of your eligibility to determine if you meet these requirements.

OTHER BENEFIT INCOME

§ 408.430 When do you need to give us evidence of your other benefit income?

If you tell us or if we have information indicating that you are receiving other benefit income that could affect your qualification for or the amount of your SVB payments, we will ask you to give us evidence of that income as explained in § 408.432.

§ 408.432 What kind of evidence of your other benefit income do you need to give us?

As evidence of your other benefit income, we may require a document such as an award notice or other letter from the paying agency or written notification from the former employer, insurance company, etc. The evidence should show the benefit payable, the current amount of the payment, and the date the payment began.

RESIDENCE

§ 408.435 How do you prove that you are residing outside the United States?

(a) General rule. To establish that you are residing outside the United States for SVB purposes, you must give us all of the following:

(1) Evidence of the date on which you arrived in the country in which you are residing;

(2) A statement signed by you showing the address at which you are living and that you intend to continue living there; and

(3) Evidence that you are actually living at the address given in your signed statement.

(b) Evidence of the date you entered the foreign country. To establish the date you arrived in the country in which you are residing, you can give us evidence such as:

(1) A visa or passport showing the date you entered that country;

(2) Your plane ticket showing the date you arrived in that country; or

(3) An entry permit showing the date you entered that country.

(c) Evidence of your actual place of residence. To establish your actual place of residence, you can give us evidence such as:

(1) A lease agreement showing where you live;

(2) Rental or mortgage receipts;

(3) Utility or other bills addressed to you at the address where you live;

(4) A signed statement from a local official showing that he or she knows where you live, when you began living there and how he or she knows this information; or

(5) A Standard Form 1199A, Direct Deposit Sign–Up Form, showing your address abroad and signed by an official of the financial institution after the date you arrived in the country in which you will be residing.

§ 408.437 How do you prove that you had good cause for staying in the United States for more than 1 full calendar month?

(a) General rule. If you believe that you meet the requirements in § 408.234 and that you should continue to receive SVB payments even though you have been in the United States for more than 1 full calendar month, you must give us evidence that you had good cause for staying in the United States.

(b) Circumstances prevent you from returning to your home abroad. To prove that you had good cause for staying in the United States for more than 1 full calendar month, you must give us evidence of your good faith effort to return to your home abroad before the 1–month period had elapsed and of the circumstances/event which prevented your return to your home abroad.

(1) Evidence of your good faith effort to return to your home abroad. Evidence of your plans to return to your home abroad can include, but is not limited to:

(i) A plane ticket showing that you intended to return to your home abroad before the expiration of 1 full calendar month; or

(ii) Notice from a travel agency or airline confirming the cancellation of your reservation to return to your home abroad on a date within 1 full calendar month.

(2) Evidence of the circumstances preventing your return to your home abroad. The evidence we will accept from you to support the circumstance or event that prevented you from returning to your home abroad will depend on the reason you are staying in the United States. It can include, but is not limited to, a:

(i) Newspaper article or other publication describing the event or natural disaster which prevented your return; or

(ii) Doctor's statement, etc. showing that you are unable to travel; or

(iii) Death certificate or notice if you are staying in the United States to attend the funeral of a member of your family.

(c) You are appealing a decision we made. To establish that you had good cause to stay in the United States for more than 1 full calendar month because you want to appear in person at the appeal of a decision on a claim filed under a program administered by the Social Security Administration, you must submit evidence of this. The evidence must identify the appeal proceeding and the dates you are scheduled to attend.

(d) When we may ask for more evidence. If you stay in the United States for several months, we may ask you to give us more evidence to prove that you are still unable to return to your home abroad.

SUBPART E—AMOUNT AND PAYMENT OF BENEFITS

Authority: Secs. 702(a)(5), 801, 805, and 810 of the Social Security Act (42 U.S.C. 902(a)(5), 1001, 1005, and 1010); Sec. 251, Pub.L. 106–169, 113 Stat. 1844.

§ 408.501 What is this subpart about?

This subpart explains how we compute the amount of your monthly SVB payment, including how we reduce your payments if you receive other benefit income. It also explains how we pay benefits under the SVB program.

§ 408.505 How do we determine the amount of your SVB payment?

(a) Maximum SVB payment. The maximum monthly SVB payment is equal to 75% of the FBR for an individual under title XVI of the Act. See § 416.410 of this chapter.

(b) Cost-of-living adjustments in the FBR. The maximum SVB amount will increase whenever there is a cost-of-living increase in the SSI FBR under the provisions of § 416.405 of this chapter. The basic SVB amount following such an increase is equal to 75 percent of the increased FBR.

(c) When we will reduce the amount of your basic benefit. We will reduce your basic benefit by the amount of the other benefit income you receive in that month, as explained in § 408.510.

§ 408.510 How do we reduce your SVB when you receive other benefit income?

(a) Amount of the reduction. If you receive other benefit income as defined in § 408.220, we will reduce your SVB payment by the amount of the other benefit income you receive in that month. The reduction is on a dollar-for-dollar and cents-for-cents basis. We do not round SVB payment amounts except as described in paragraph (b) of this section.

(b) Minimum benefit amount. If the reduction described in paragraph (a) of this section results in a benefit amount that is greater than zero but less than $1.00, we will pay you a benefit of $1.00 for that month.

§ 408.515 When do we make SVB payments?

SVB payments are made on the first day of each month and represent payment for that month. If the first day of the month falls on a Saturday, Sunday, or Federal legal holiday, payment will be made on the first day preceding such day that is not a Saturday, Sunday, or Federal legal holiday.

SUBPART F—REPRESENTATIVE PAYMENT

Authority: Secs. 702(a)(5), 807, and 810 of the Social Security Act (42 U.S.C. 902(a)(5), 1007, and 1010).

Source: 69 FR 60235, Oct. 7, 2004, unless otherwise noted.

§ 408.601 What is this subpart about?

(a) Explanation of representative payment. This subpart explains the policies and procedures we follow to determine whether to pay your benefits to a representative payee and to select a representative payee for you. It also explains the responsibilities your representative payee has for using the funds he or she receives on your behalf. A representative payee may be either an individual or an organization. We will select a representative payee to receive your benefits if we believe your interests will be better served by paying a representative payee than by paying you directly. Generally, we appoint a representative payee if we determine you are unable to manage or direct the management of your own benefit payments. Because the representative payment policies and procedures we use for the title VIII program closely parallel our title II policies and procedures, we provide cross-references to the appropriate material in our title II representative payment rules in subpart U of part 404 of this chapter.

(b) Policy we use to determine whether to make representative payment. For an explanation of the policy we use to determine whether to pay your SVB to a representative payee, see § 404.2001(b) of this chapter.

§ 408.610 When will we send your SVB payments to a representative payee?

In determining when we will pay your benefits to a representative payee, we follow the rules in § 404.2010(a) of this chapter.

§ 408.611 What happens to your monthly benefits while we are finding a suitable representative payee for you?

For an explanation of the policy we use to determine what happens to your monthly benefits while we are finding a suitable representative payee for you, see § 404.2011 of this chapter.

§ 408.615 What information do we consider in determining whether we will pay your benefits to a representative payee?

We determine whether to pay your benefits to a representative payee after considering the information listed in § 404.2015 of this chapter.

§ 408.620 What information do we consider in selecting the proper representative payee for you?

To select a proper representative payee for you, we consider the information listed in § 404.2020 of this chapter.

§ 408.621 What is our order of preference in selecting a representative payee for you?

We use the preference list in § 404.2021(a) of this chapter as a guide in selecting the proper representative payee for you.

§ 408.622 Who may not serve as a representative payee?

For a list of individuals who may not serve as a representative payee, see § 404.2022 of this chapter.

§ 408.624 How do we investigate a representative payee applicant?

Before selecting an individual or organization as your representative payee, we investigate him or her following the rules in § 404.2024 of this chapter.

§ 408.625 What information must a representative payee report to us?

Your representative payee must report to us information as described in § 404.2025 of this chapter.

§ 408.626 How do we investigate an appointed representative payee?

After we select an individual or organization as your representative payee, we investigate him or her following the rules in § 404.2026 of this chapter.

[84 FR 4325, Feb. 15, 2019]

§ 408.630 How will we notify you when we decide you need a representative payee?

(a) We notify you in writing of our determination to make representative payment. If you are legally incompetent, our written notice is sent to your legal guardian or legal representative. The notice explains that we have determined that representative payment is in your interest, and it provides the name of the representative payee we have selected. The notice:

(1) Contains language that is easily understandable to the reader.

(2) Identifies the person designated as your representative payee.

(3) Explains that you, your legal guardian, or your legal representative can appeal our determination that you need a representative payee.

(4) Explains that you, your legal guardian, or your legal representative can appeal our designation of a particular person to serve as representative payee.

(b) If you, your legal guardian, or your legal representative objects to representative payment or to the designated payee, you can file a formal appeal.

§ 408.635 What are the responsibilities of your representative payee?

For a list of your representative payee's responsibilities, see § 404.2035 of this chapter.

§ 408.640 How must your representative payee use your benefits?

Your representative payee must use your benefits in accordance with the rules in § 404.2040 of this chapter.

§ 408.641 Who is liable if your representative payee misuses your benefits?

For the rules we follow to determine who is liable for repayment of misused benefits, see § 404.2041 of this chapter.

§ 408.645 What must your representative payee do with unused benefits?

If your representative payee has accumulated benefits for you, he or she must conserve or invest them as provided in § 404.2045 of this chapter.

§ 408.650 When will we select a new representative payee for you?

We follow the rules in § 404.2050 of this chapter to determine when we will select a new representative payee for you.

§ 408.655 When will we stop making your payments to a representative payee?

To determine when we will stop representative payment for you, we follow the rules in § 404.2055 of this chapter.

§ 408.660 What happens to your accumulated funds when your representative payee changes?

For a description of what happens to your accumulated funds (including the interest earned on the funds) when we change your representative payee or when you begin receiving benefits directly, see § 404.2060 of this chapter.

§ 408.665 How does your representative payee account for the use of your SVB payments?[1]

Your representative payee must account for the use of your benefits. We require written reports from your representative payee at least once a year. We may verify how your representative payee used your benefits. Your representative payee should keep records of how benefits were used in order to provide accounting reports and must make those records available upon our request. If your representative payee fails to provide an annual accounting of benefits or other required report, we may require your payee to appear in person at the local Social Security field office or a United States Government facility that we designate serving the area in which you reside. The decision to have your representative payee receive your benefits in person may be based on a variety of reasons. Some of these reasons may include the payee's history of past performance or our past difficulty in contacting the payee. We may ask your representative payee to give us the following information:

(a) Where you lived during the accounting period;

(b) Who made the decisions on how your benefits were spent or saved;

(c) How your benefit payments were used; and

(d) How much of your benefit payments were saved and how the savings were invested.

[71 FR 61408, Oct. 18, 2006]

SUBPART G—REPORTING REQUIREMENTS

Authority: Secs. 702(a)(5), 802, 803, 804, 806, 807, and 810 of the Social Security Act (42 U.S.C. 902(a)(5), 1002, 1003, 1004, 1006, 1007, and 1010).

Source: 69 FR 25955, May 10, 2004, unless otherwise noted.

§ 408.701 What is this subpart about?

To achieve efficient administration of the Special Veterans Benefit (SVB) program, we require you (or your representative) to report certain events to us. It is important for us to know about these events because they may affect your right to receive SVB or the amount of your benefits. This subpart tells you what events you must report; what your reports must include; how you should make your report; and when reports are due.

§ 408.704 Who must make reports?

(a) If you receive your own benefits, you are responsible for making required reports to us.

(b) If you have a representative payee, and you have not been legally adjudged incompetent, either you or your representative payee must make the required reports.

(c) If you have a representative payee and you have been legally adjudged incompetent, you are not responsible for making reports to us; however, your representative payee is responsible for making required reports to us.

[1] So in official CFR; probably should read "benefits". See 71 FR 61408.

§ 408.708 What events must you report to us?

This section describes the events that you must report to us. They are—

(a) A change of address or residence. You must report to us any change in your mailing address and any change in your residence, i.e., the address where you live.

(b) A change in your other benefit income. You must report to us any increase or decrease in your other benefit income as described in § 408.220.

(c) Certain deaths.

(1) If you are a representative payee, you must report the death of the entitled individual.

(2) If you have a representative payee, you must report the death of your representative payee.

(d) Entry into the United States. You must report to us if you enter the United States to visit or live even if you have no intention of abandoning your residence outside the United States.

(e) Removal (including deportation) from the United States. You must report to us if you are removed (including deported) from the United States under section 237(a) or 212(a)(6)(A) of the Immigration and Nationality Act.

(f) Fleeing to avoid criminal prosecution or custody or confinement after conviction, or violating probation or parole. You must report to us that you are—

(1) Fleeing to avoid prosecution, under the laws of the United States or the jurisdiction within the United States from which you flee, for a crime, or an attempt to commit a crime, which is a felony under the laws of the place from which you flee (or which, in the case of the State of New Jersey, is a high misdemeanor under the laws of that State);

(2) Fleeing to avoid custody or confinement after conviction under the laws of the United States or the jurisdiction within the United States from which you flee, for a crime, or an attempt to commit a crime, which is a felony under the laws of the place from which you flee (or which, in the case of the State of New Jersey, is a high misdemeanor under the laws of that State); or

(3) Violating a condition of probation or parole imposed under Federal or State law.

§ 408.710 What must your report include?

When you make a report, you must tell us—

(a) The name and social security number of the person to whom the report applies;

(b) The event you are reporting and the date it happened; and

(c) Your name if you are not the person to whom the report applies.

§ 408.712 How should you make your report?

You should make your report in any of the ways described in this section.

(a) Written reports. You may write a report on your own paper or on a printed form supplied by us. You may mail a written report or bring it to one of our offices.

(b) Oral reports. You may report to us by telephone, or you may come to one of our offices and tell one of our employees what you are reporting.

(c) Other methods of reporting. You may use any other suitable method of reporting—for example, a telegram or a cable.

§ 408.714 When are reports due?

(a) A reportable event happens. You should report to us as soon as an event listed in § 408.708 happens.

(b) We request a report. We may request a report from you if we need information to determine continuing entitlement or the correct amount of your SVB payments. If you do not make the report within 30 days of our written request, we may determine that you may not continue to receive SVB. We will suspend your benefits effective with the month following the month in which we determine that you are not entitled to receive SVB because of your failure to give us necessary information (see § 408.803).

SUBPART H—SUSPENSIONS AND TERMINATIONS

Authority: Secs. 702(a)(5) and 810(d) of the Social Security Act (42 U.S.C. 902(a)(5) and 1010(d)).

Source: 69 FR 25955, 25957, May 10, 2004, unless otherwise noted.

§ 408.801 What is this subpart about?

This subpart explains the circumstances that will result in suspension of your SVB payments or termination of your SVB entitlement.

SUSPENSION

§ 408.802 When will we suspend your SVB payments?

(a) When suspension is proper. Suspension of SVB payments is required when you no longer meet the SVB qualification requirements (see subpart B of this part) and termination in accordance with §§ 408.814 through 408.818 does not apply. (This subpart does not cover suspension of payments for administrative reasons, as, for example, when mail is returned as undeliverable by the Postal Service and we do not have a valid mailing address for you or when your representative payee dies and a search is underway for a substitute representative payee.)

(b) Effect of suspension. When we correctly suspend your SVB payments, we will not resume them until you again meet all qualification requirements except the filing of a new application. If you request reinstatement, you are required to submit the evidence necessary to establish that you again meet all requirements for eligibility under this part. Your SVB payments will be reinstated effective with the first month in which you meet all requirements for eligibility except the filing of a new application.

§ 408.803 What happens to your SVB payments if you fail to comply with our request for information?

(a) Effective date of suspension. We will suspend your SVB payments effective with the month following the month in which we determine in accordance with § 408.714(b) that you may no longer receive SVB payments because you failed to comply with our request for necessary information.

(b) Resumption of payments. When we have information to establish that SVB is again payable, your benefit payments will be reinstated for any previous month for which you continue to meet the requirements of § 408.202.

(c) When we will not suspend your payments. We will not suspend your payments for failing to comply with our request for information for any month we can determine your eligibility for or the amount of your payment based on information on record. If we cannot determine your eligibility or the amount of your payment based on the information on record, we will send you a notice of suspension of payment because you failed to comply with our request for information in accordance with §§ 408.820 and 408.1005.

§ 408.806 What happens to your SVB payments if you are no longer residing outside the United States?

(a) Suspension effective date. We will suspend your SVB payments effective the first full calendar month you are no longer residing outside the United States.

(b) Resumption of payments. If otherwise payable, we will resume your SVB payments effective with the first full calendar month you are again residing outside the United States.

§ 408.808 What happens to your SVB payments if you begin receiving additional benefit income?

(a) Suspension effective date. We will suspend your SVB payments for any month your other benefit income (as described in § 408.220(a)) exceeds the maximum SVB amount payable for a month (see § 408.505(a)).

(b) Resumption of payments. If otherwise payable, we will resume your SVB payments effective with the first month your other benefit income is less than the maximum SVB amount payable for a month.

§ 408.809 What happens to your SVB payments if you are removed (including deported) from the United States?

(a) Suspension effective date. We will suspend your SVB payments effective with the month after the month in which we receive notice from the United States Citizenship and Immigration Service that you have been removed (including deported) from the United States under section 237(a) or 212(a)(6)(A) of the Immigration and Nationality Act.

(b) Resumption of payments. If otherwise payable, we will resume your SVB effective with the first month after the month of your removal that you were granted the status of a lawful permanent resident of the United States.

§ 408.810 What happens to your SVB payments if you are fleeing to avoid criminal prosecution or custody or confinement after conviction, or because you violate a condition of probation or parole?

(a) Basis for suspension. You may not receive SVB for any month during which you are—

(1) Fleeing to avoid prosecution under the laws of the United States or the jurisdiction within the United States from which you flee for a crime, or attempt to commit a crime, that is a felony under the laws of the place from which you flee (or that, in the case of the State of New Jersey, is a high misdemeanor under the laws of that State); or

(2) Fleeing to avoid custody or confinement after conviction under the laws of the United States or the jurisdiction within the United States from which you flee, for a crime, or an attempt to commit a crime, that is a felony under the laws of the place from which you flee (or that, in the case of the State of New Jersey, is a high misdemeanor under the laws of that State); or

(3) Violating a condition of probation or parole imposed under Federal or State law.

(b) Suspension effective date. Suspension of SVB payments because you are a fugitive as described in paragraph (a)(1) or (a)(2) of this section or a probation or parole violator as described in paragraph (a)(3) of this section is effective with the first day of whichever of the following months is earlier—

(1) The month in which a warrant or order for your arrest or apprehension, an order requiring your appearance before a court or other appropriate tribunal (e.g., a parole board), or similar order is issued by a court or other duly authorized tribunal in the United States on the basis of an appropriate finding that you—

(i) Are fleeing, or have fled, to avoid prosecution as described in paragraph (a)(1) of this section;

(ii) Are fleeing, or have fled, to avoid custody or confinement after conviction as described in paragraph (a)(2) of this section;

(iii) Are violating, or have violated, a condition of your probation or parole as described in paragraph (a)(3) of this section; or

(2) The first month during which you fled to avoid such prosecution, fled to avoid such custody or confinement after conviction, or violated a condition of your probation or parole, if indicated in such warrant or order, or in a decision by a court or other appropriate tribunal in the United States.

(c) Resumption of payments. If otherwise payable, we will resume your SVB payments beginning with the first month throughout which you are determined to be no longer fleeing to avoid prosecution, fleeing to avoid custody or confinement after conviction, or violating a condition of your probation or parole.

§ 408.812 What happens to your SVB payments if you are not a citizen or national of the United States and you begin residing in a Treasury-restricted country?

(a) Suspension effective date. If you are not a citizen or national of the United States, we will suspend your SVB payments effective with the first full calendar month you are residing in a country to which the Treasury Department restricts payments under 31 U.S.C. 3329.

(b) Resumption of payments. If benefits are otherwise payable, they will be resumed effective with the first day of the first month in which you are not residing in a Treasury-restricted country.

TERMINATION

§ 408.814 Can you request termination of your SVB entitlement?

You, your legal guardian, or your representative payee, may voluntarily terminate your SVB entitlement by filing a written request for termination. If your representative payee requests termination, it must be shown that no hardship would result to you if the request is processed. When a termination request is filed, your SVB entitlement ends effective with the month following the month you file your request with us unless you specify some other month. However, we will not terminate your entitlement for any month for which payment has been or will be made unless you repay (or there is an assurance you will repay) any amounts paid for those months. When we process a voluntary request for termination of your SVB entitlement, we will send you a notice of our determination in accordance with § 408.1005. Once terminated, your entitlement can be reestablished only if you file a new application, except as provided by § 408.1009.

§ 408.816 When does SVB entitlement end due to death?

Your SVB entitlement ends with the month in which you die. Payments are terminated effective with the month after the month of death.

§ 408.818 When does SVB entitlement terminate if your benefit payments have been in suspense for 12 consecutive months?

We will terminate your SVB entitlement following 12 consecutive months of benefit suspension for any reason beginning with the first month you were no longer entitled to SVB. We will count the 12–month suspension period from the start of the first month that you are no longer entitled to SVB (see § 408.802(a)). This termination is effective with the first day of the 13th month after the suspension began.

§ 408.820 Will we send you a notice of intended action affecting your SVB payment status?

(a) Advance written notice requirement. Before we suspend, reduce (see subpart E of this part), or terminate your SVB payments, we will send you a written notice explaining our intention to do so, except where we have factual information confirming your death, e.g., as specified in § 404.704(b) of this chapter, or a report by a surviving spouse, a legal guardian, a parent or other close relative, or a landlord.

(b) Continuation of payment pending an appeal. The written notice of our intent to suspend, reduce, or terminate payments will give you 60 days after the date you receive the notice to request the appropriate appellate review. If your benefit payments are reduced or suspended and you file an appeal within 10 days after you receive the notice, payments will be continued or reinstated at the previously established payment level (subject to the effects of intervening events on the payment which are not appealed within 10 days of receipt of a required advance notice or which do not require advance notice, e.g., an increase in the benefit amount) until a decision on your initial appeal is issued, unless you specifically waive in writing your right to continuation of payment at the previously established level in accordance with paragraph (c) of this section. Where the request for the appropriate appellate review is filed more than 10 days after the notice is received but within the 60–day period specified in § 408.1009 of this part, you have no right to continuation or reinstatement of payment at the previously established level unless you establish good cause under the criteria specified in § 408.1011 of this part for failure to appeal within 10 days after receipt of the notice. For purposes of this paragraph, we will presume you received our notice of intent to suspend, reduce, or terminate payments 5 days after the date on the face of the notice, unless there is a reasonable showing to the contrary.

(c) Waiver of right to continued payment. In order to avoid the possibility of an overpayment of benefits, you may waive continuation of payment at the previously established level (subject to intervening events which would have increased the benefit for the month in which the incorrect payment was made, in which case the higher amount shall be paid), after you receive a full explanation of your rights. Your request for waiver of continuation of payment must be in writing, state that waiver action is being initiated solely at your request, and state that you understand your right to receive continued payment at the previously established level.

SUBPART I—UNDERPAYMENTS AND OVERPAYMENTS

Authority: Secs. 702(a)(5), 808, and 1147 of the Social Security Act (42 U.S.C. 902(a)(5), 1008, and 1320b–17); 31 U.S.C. 3716; 31 U.S.C. 3720A.

Source: 69 FR 25955, 25959, May 10, 2004; 70 FR 15, Jan. 3, 2005; 70 FR 16113, March 30, 2005; 76 FR 65108, Oct. 20, 2011, unless otherwise noted.

GENERAL RULES

§ 408.900 What is this subpart about?

This subpart explains what happens when you receive less or more than the correct amount of SVB than you are entitled to receive. Sections 408.901 through 408.903 define overpayment and underpayment and describe how we determine the amount of the overpayment or underpayment. When you receive less than the correct amount of SVB (which we refer to as an underpayment), we will take the actions described in §§ 408.904 and 408.905. Waiver of recovery of overpayments (payments of more than the correct amount) is discussed in §§ 408.910 through 408.914, and the methods we use to recover overpayments are discussed in §§ 408.920 through 408.946. In § 408.950, we explain when we will accept a compromise settlement of an overpayment or suspend or terminate collection of an overpayment.

§ 408.901 What is an underpayment?

(a) An underpayment can occur only with respect to a period for which you filed an application for benefits and met all conditions of eligibility for benefits.

(b) An underpayment is:

(1) Nonpayment, where payment was due but was not made; or

(2) Payment of less than the amount due for a period.

(c) For purposes of this section, payment has been made when certified by the Social Security Administration to the Department of the Treasury. Payment is not considered to have been made where payment has not been received by the designated payee, or where payment was returned.

§ 408.902 What is an overpayment?

As used in this subpart, the term overpayment means payment of more than the amount due for any period. For purposes of this section, payment has been made when certified by the Social Security Administration to the Department of the Treasury. Payment is not considered to have been made where payment has not been received by the designated payee, or where payment was returned.

§ 408.903 How do we determine the amount of an underpayment or overpayment?

(a) General. The amount of an underpayment or overpayment is the difference between the amount you are paid and the amount you are due for a given period. An underpayment or overpayment period begins with the first month for which there is a difference between the amount paid and the amount actually due for that month. The period ends with the month in which we make the initial determination of the overpayment or underpayment. With respect to the period established, there can be no underpayment to you if we paid you more than the correct amount of SVB, even though we waived recovery of any overpayment to you for that period under the provisions of §§ 408.910 through 408.914. A later initial determination of an overpayment will require no change with respect to a prior determination of overpayment or to the period relating to such prior determination to the extent that the basis of the prior overpayment remains the same.

(b) Limited delay in payment of an underpayment. Where we have detected a potential overpayment but we have not made a determination of the overpayment (see § 408.918(a)), we will not delay making a determination of underpayment and paying you unless we can make an overpayment determination before the close of the month following the month in which we discovered the potential underpayment.

(c) Delay in payment of underpayment to ineligible individual. If you are no longer entitled to SVB, we will delay a determination and payment of an underpayment that is otherwise due you so that we can resolve all overpayments, incorrect payments, and adjustments.

§ 408.904 How will you receive an underpayment?

We will pay you the amount of any underpayment due you in a separate payment or by increasing the amount of your monthly payment. If you die before we pay you all or any part of an underpayment, the balance of the underpayment reverts to the general fund of the U.S. Treasury.

§ 408.905 Will we withhold or adjust an underpayment to reduce an overpayment if that overpayment occurred in a different period?

We will withhold or adjust any underpayment due you to reduce any overpayment to you that we determine for a different period, unless we have waived recovery of the overpayment under the provisions of §§ 408.910 through 408.914.

WAIVER OF RECOVERY OF SVB OVERPAYMENTS

§ 408.910 When will we waive recovery of an SVB overpayment?

We will waive recovery of an overpayment when:

(a) You are without fault in connection with the overpayment, and

(b) Recovery of such overpayment would either:

(1) Defeat the purpose of the title VIII program, or

(2) Be against equity and good conscience.

§ 408.911 What happens when we waive recovery of an SVB overpayment?

Waiver of recovery of an overpayment from you (or, after your death, from your estate) frees you and your estate from the obligation to repay the amount of the overpayment covered by the waiver. Example: You filed for waiver of recovery of a $600 overpayment. We found that you are eligible for waiver of recovery of $260 of that amount. Only $340 of the overpayment would be recoverable from you or your estate.

§ 408.912 When are you without fault regarding an overpayment?

(a) General—when fault is relevant. If you request waiver of recovery of an overpayment, we must determine whether you were without fault. You are not relieved of liability and are not without fault solely because we may have been at fault in making the overpayment.

(b) The factors we consider to determine whether you were without fault. When we determine whether you were without fault, we consider all the pertinent circumstances relating to the overpayment. We consider your understanding of your obligation to give us information affecting your payments, your agreement to report events, your knowledge of the occurrence of events that should have been reported, the efforts you made to comply with the reporting requirements, the opportunities you had to comply with the reporting requirements, your ability to comply with the reporting requirements (e.g., your age, comprehension, memory, physical and mental condition), and your understanding of the obligation to return payments that were not due. In determining whether you are without fault based on these factors, we will take into account any physical, mental, educational, or language limitations (including any lack of facility with the English language) you may have. We will determine that you were at fault if, after considering all of the circumstances, we find that the overpayment resulted from one of the following:

(1) Your failure to furnish information which you knew or should have known was material;

(2) An incorrect statement you made which you knew or should have known was incorrect (this includes furnishing your opinion or conclusion when you were asked for facts), or

(3) You did not return a payment, which you knew, or could have been expected to know, was incorrect.

§ 408.913 When would overpayment recovery defeat the purpose of the title VIII program?

We will waive recovery of an overpayment when you are without fault (as defined in § 408.912) and recovery of the overpayment would defeat the purpose of the title VIII program. Recovery of an overpayment would defeat the purpose of the title VIII program to the extent that our recovery action would deprive you of income and resources you need to meet your ordinary and necessary living expenses as described in § 404.508(a) of this chapter.

§ 408.914 When would overpayment recovery be against equity and good conscience?

We will waive recovery of an overpayment when you are without fault (as defined in § 408.912) and recovery would be against equity and good conscience. Recovery would be against equity and good conscience if you changed your position for the worse or gave up a valuable right in reliance on our notice that payment would be made or because of the incorrect payment itself. Example: Upon our notice that you are eligible for SVB payments, you signed a lease on an apartment renting for $15 a month more than the one you previously occupied. You were subsequently found ineligible for SVB and no benefits are payable. In this case, recovery of the overpayment would be considered "against equity and good conscience."

NOTICES

§ 408.918 What notices will you receive if you are overpaid or underpaid?

(a) Notice of overpayment or underpayment determination. Whenever we determine that you were overpaid or underpaid for a given period, as defined in

§ 408.903, we will send you a written notice of the correct and incorrect amounts you received for each month in the period, even if part or all of the underpayment must be withheld in accordance with § 408.905. The notice of overpayment will advise you about recovery of the overpayment, as explained in §§ 408.920–408.923, and your rights to appeal the determination and to request waiver of recovery of the overpayment under the provisions of § 408.910.

(b) Notice of waiver determination. Written notice of an initial determination regarding waiver of recovery will be mailed to you in accordance with § 408.1005 unless you were not given notice of the overpayment in accordance with paragraph (a) of this section.

REFUND OF OVERPAYMENTS

§ 408.920 When will we seek refund of an SVB overpayment?

We will seek refund of an SVB overpayment in every case in which we have not waived recovery. An overpayment may be refunded by you or by anyone on your behalf. If you are receiving SVB currently and you have not refunded the overpayment, adjustment as set forth in § 408.922 will be proposed. If you die before we recover the full overpayment, we will seek refund of the balance from your estate.

ADJUSTMENT OF SVB

§ 408.922 When will we adjust your SVB payments to recover an overpayment?

If you do not refund your overpayment to us, and waiver of recovery is not applicable, we will adjust any SVB payments due you to recover the overpayment. Adjustment will generally be accomplished by withholding each month the amount set forth in § 408.923 from the benefit payable to you.

§ 408.923 Is there a limit on the amount we will withhold from your SVB payments to recover an overpayment?

(a) Amount of the withholding limit. Except as provided in paragraphs (b) and (c) of this section, the amount we will withhold from your monthly SVB payment to recover an overpayment is limited to the lesser of (1) the amount of your Federal SVB payment or (2) an amount equal to 10 percent of the maximum SVB monthly payment amount as defined in § 408.505(a).

(b) Your right to request a different rate of withholding. When we notify you of the rate we propose to withhold from your monthly SVB payment, we will give you the opportunity to request a higher or lower rate of withholding than that proposed. If you request a rate of withholding that is lower than the one established under paragraph (a) of this section, we will set a rate that is appropriate to your financial condition after we evaluate all the pertinent facts. An appropriate rate is one that will not deprive you of income required for ordinary and necessary living expenses. We will evaluate your income, resources, and expenses as described in § 404.508 of this chapter.

(c) Fraud, misrepresentation or concealment of material information. If we determine that there was fraud, willful misrepresentation, or concealment of material information by you in connection with the overpayment, the limits in paragraph (a)(2) of this section do not apply and we will not lower the rate of withholding under paragraph (b) of this section. Concealment of material information means an intentional, knowing, and purposeful delay in making or in failing to make a report that will affect your SVB payment amount and/or eligibility. It does not include a mere omission on your part; it is an affirmative act to conceal.

ADJUSTMENT OF TITLE II BENEFITS

§ 408.930 Are title II and title XVI benefits subject to adjustment to recover title VIII overpayments?

(a) Definitions—

(1) Cross-program recovery. Cross-program recovery is the process that we will use to collect title VIII overpayments from benefits payable to you under title II or title XVI of the Social Security Act.

(2) Benefits payable. For purposes of this section, benefits payable means the amount of title II or title XVI benefits you actually would receive. For title II benefits, it includes your monthly benefit and your past-due benefits after any reductions or deductions listed in § 404.401(a) and (b) of this chapter. For title XVI benefits, it includes your monthly benefit and your past-due benefits as described in § 416.420 of this chapter.

(b) When may we collect title VIII overpayments using cross-program recovery? We may use cross-program recovery to collect a title VIII overpayment you owe when benefits are payable to you under title II, title XVI, or both.

[70 FR 15, Jan. 3, 2005; 70 FR 16113, March 30, 2005]

§ 408.931 How much will we withhold from your title II and title XVI benefits to recover a title VIII overpayment?

(a) If past-due benefits are payable to you, we will withhold the lesser of the entire overpayment balance or the entire amount of past-due benefits.

(b)(1) We will collect the overpayment from current monthly benefits due in a month under title II and title XVI by withholding the lesser of the amount of the entire overpayment balance or:

(i) 10 percent of the monthly title II benefits payable for that month and

(ii) in the case of title XVI benefits, an amount no greater than the lesser of the benefit payable for that month or an amount equal to 10 percent of your income for that month (including such monthly benefit but excluding payments under title II when recovery is also made from title II benefits and excluding income excluded pursuant to §§ 416.1112 and 416.1124 of this chapter).

(2) Paragraph (b)(1) of this section does not apply if:

(i) You request and we approve a different rate of withholding, or

(ii) You or your spouse willfully misrepresented or concealed material information in connection with the overpayment.

(c) In determining whether to grant your request that we withhold less than the amount described in paragraph (b)(1) of this section, we will use the criteria applied under § 408.923 to similar requests about withholding from title VIII benefits.

(d) If you or your spouse willfully misrepresented or concealed material information in connection with the overpayment, we will collect the overpayment by withholding the lesser of the overpayment balance or the entire amount of title II benefits and title XVI benefits payable to you. We will not collect at a lesser rate. (See § 408.923 for what we mean by concealment of material information.)

[70 FR 16, Jan. 3, 2005; 70 FR 16113, March 30, 2005]

§ 408.932 Will you receive notice of our intention to apply cross-program recovery?

Before we collect an overpayment from you using cross-program recovery, we will send you a written notice that tells you the following information:

(a) We have determined that you owe a specific overpayment balance that can be collected by cross-program recovery;

(b) We will withhold a specific amount from the title II or title XVI benefits (see § 408.931(b));

(c) You may ask us to review this determination that you still owe this overpayment balance;

(d) You may request that we withhold a different amount from your current monthly benefits (the notice will not include this information if § 408.931(d) applies); and

(e) You may ask us to waive collection of this overpayment balance.

[70 FR 16, Jan. 3, 2005; 70 FR 16113, March 30, 2005]

§ 408.933 When will we begin cross-program recovery from your current monthly benefits?

(a) We will begin collecting the overpayment balance by cross-program recovery from your title II and title XVI current monthly benefits no sooner than 30 calendar days after the date of the notice described in § 408.932. If within that 30–day period you pay us the full overpayment balance stated in the notice, we will not begin cross-program recovery from your current monthly benefits.

(b) If within that 30–day period you ask us to review our determination that you still owe us this overpayment balance, we will not begin cross-program recovery from your current monthly benefits before we review the matter and notify you of our decision in writing.

(c) If within that 30–day period you ask us to withhold a different amount than the amount stated in the notice, we will not begin cross-program recovery from your current monthly benefits until we determine the amount we will withhold. This paragraph does not apply when § 408.931(d) applies.

(d) If within that 30–day period you ask us to waive recovery of the overpayment balance, we will not begin cross-program recovery from your current monthly benefits before we review the matter and notify you of our decision in writing. See §§ 408.910 through 408.914.

[70 FR 16, Jan. 3, 2005; 70 FR 16113, March 30, 2005]

TAX REFUND OFFSET

§ 408.940 When will we refer an SVB overpayment to the Department of the Treasury for tax refund offset?

(a) General. The standards we will apply and the procedures we will follow before requesting the Department of the Treasury to offset income tax refunds due you to recover outstanding overpayments are set forth in §§ 408.940 through 408.946 of this subpart. These standards and procedures are authorized by 31 U.S.C. 3720A, as implemented through Department of the Treasury regulations at 31 CFR 285.2.

(b) We will use the Department of the Treasury tax refund offset procedure to collect overpayments that are certain in amount, past due and legally enforceable and eligible for tax refund offset under regulations issued by the Secretary of the Treasury. We will use these procedures to collect overpayments from you only when you are not currently entitled to monthly SVB under title VIII of the Act, and we are not recovering your SVB overpayment from your monthly benefits payable under title II of the Act. We refer overpayments to the Department of the Treasury for offset against Federal tax refunds regardless of the amount of time the debts have been outstanding.

[76 FR 65108, Oct. 20, 2011]

§ 408.941 Will we notify you before we refer an SVB overpayment for tax refund offset?

Before we request that an overpayment be collected by reduction of Federal and State income tax refunds, we will send a written notice of our action to the overpaid person. In our notice of intent to collect an overpayment through tax refund offset, we will state:

(a) The amount of the overpayment; and

(b) That we will collect the overpayment by requesting that the Department of the Treasury reduce any amounts payable to the overpaid person as refunds of Federal and State income taxes by an amount equal to the amount of the overpayment unless, within 60 calendar days from the date of our notice, the overpaid person:

(1) Repays the overpayment in full; or

(2) Provides evidence to us at the address given in our notice that the overpayment is not past due or legally enforceable; or

(3) Asks us to waive collection of the overpayment under section 204(b) of the Act.

(c) The conditions under which we will waive recovery of an overpayment under section 808(c) of the Act;

(d) That we will review any evidence presented that the overpayment is not past due or not legally enforceable;

(e) That you have the right to inspect and copy our records related to the overpayment as determined by us and you will be informed as to where and when the inspection and copying can be done after we receive notice from you requesting inspection and copying.

[76 FR 65108, Oct. 20, 2011]

§ 408.942 Will you have a chance to present evidence showing that the overpayment is not past due or is not legally enforceable?

(a) Notification. If you receive a notice as described in § 408.941 of this subpart, you have the right to present evidence that all or part of the overpayment is not past due or not legally enforceable. To exercise this right, you must notify us and present evidence regarding the overpayment within 60 calendar days from the date of our notice.

(b) Submission of evidence. You may submit evidence showing that all or part of the debt is not past due or not legally enforceable as provided in paragraph (a) of this section. Failure to submit the notification and evidence within 60 calendar days will result in referral of the overpayment to the Department of the Treasury, unless, within this 60–day time period, you ask us to waive collection of the overpayment under § 408.910 and we have not yet determined whether we can grant the waiver request. If you ask us to waive collection of the overpayment, we may ask you to submit evidence to support your request.

(c) Review of the evidence. If you submit evidence on a timely basis, we will consider all available evidence related to the overpayment. We will make findings based on a review of the written record, unless we determine that the question of indebtedness cannot be resolved by a review of the documentary evidence.

(d) Written findings. We will issue our written findings including supporting rationale to you, your attorney or other representative. The findings will be our final action with respect to the past-due status and enforceability of the overpayment.

§ 408.943 What happens after we make our determination on your request for review or your request for waiver?

(a) If we make a determination that all or part of the overpayment is past due and legally enforceable and/or your waiver request cannot be granted, we will refer the overpayment to the Department of the Treasury for recovery from any Federal income tax refund due you. We will not suspend our referral of the overpayment to the Department of the Treasury under § 408.945 of this subpart pending any further administrative review of the waiver determination that you may seek.

(b) We will not refer the overpayment to the Department of the Treasury if we reverse our prior finding that the overpayment is past due and legally enforceable or, upon consideration of a waiver request, we determine that waiver of recovery of the overpayment is appropriate.

§ 408.944 How can you review our records related to an SVB overpayment?

(a) What you must do. If you intend to inspect or copy our records related to the overpayment, you must notify us stating your intention to inspect or copy.

(b) What we will do. If you notify us that you intend to inspect or copy our records related to the overpayment as described in paragraph (a) of this section, we will notify you of the location and time when you may do so. We may also, at our discretion, mail copies of the overpayment-related records to you.

§ 408.945 When will we suspend tax refund offset?

If, within 60 days of the date of the notice described in § 408.941 of this subpart, you notify us that you are exercising a right described in § 408.942(a) of this subpart and submit evidence pursuant to § 408.942(b) of this subpart or request a waiver under § 408.910 of this subpart, we will suspend any notice to the Department of the Treasury until we have issued written findings that affirm that an overpayment is past due and legally enforceable and, if applicable, make a determination that a waiver request cannot be granted.

§ 408.946 What happens if your tax refund is insufficient to cover the amount of your SVB overpayment?

If your tax refund is insufficient to recover an overpayment in a given year, the case will remain with the

Department of the Treasury for succeeding years, assuming that all criteria for certification are met at that time.

COMPROMISE SETTLEMENTS, OR SUSPENSION OR TERMINATION OF COLLECTION

§ 408.950 Will we accept a compromise settlement of an overpayment debt or suspend or terminate collection of an overpayment?

(a) *General.* If we find that you do not, or your estate does not, have the present or future ability to pay the full amount of the overpayment within a reasonable time or the cost of collection is likely to exceed the amount of recovery, we may take any of the following actions, as appropriate.

(1) We may accept a compromise settlement (payment of less than the full amount of the overpayment) to discharge the entire overpayment debt.

(2) We may suspend our efforts to collect the overpayment.

(3) We may terminate our efforts to collect the overpayment.

(b) *Rules we apply.* In deciding whether to take any of the actions described in paragraph (a) of this section, we will apply the rules in § 404.515(b), (c), (d), (e), and (f) of this chapter and other applicable rules, including the Federal Claims Collection Standards (31 CFR 900.3 and parts 902 and 903).

(c) *Effect of compromise, suspension or termination.* When we suspend or terminate collection of the overpayment debt, we may take collection action in the future in accordance with provisions of the Social Security Act, other laws, and the standards set forth in 31 CFR chapter IX. A compromise settlement satisfies the obligation to repay the overpayment if you or your estate comply with the terms of the settlement. Failure to make payment in the manner and within the time that we require in the settlement will result in reinstatement of our claim for the full amount of the overpayment less any amounts paid.

SUBPART J—DETERMINATIONS AND THE ADMINISTRATIVE REVIEW PROCESS

Authority: Secs. 702(a)(5) and 809 of the Social Security Act (42 U.S.C. 902(a)(5) and 1009).

Source: 69 FR 25955, 25962, May 10, 2004, unless otherwise noted.

INTRODUCTION, DEFINITIONS, AND INITIAL DETERMINATIONS

§ 408.1000 What is this subpart about?

(a) *Explanation of the administrative review process.* This subpart explains the procedures we follow in determining your appeal rights under title VIII of the Social Security Act. The regulations describe the process of administrative review and explain your right to judicial review after you have taken all the necessary administrative steps. The administrative review process consists of several steps, which usually must be requested within certain time periods and in the following order:

(1) *Initial determination.* This is a determination we make about whether you qualify for and can become entitled to SVB or whether your SVB entitlement can continue. It can also be about any other matter, as discussed in § 408.1003, that gives you a right to further review.

(2) *Reconsideration.* If you are dissatisfied with an initial determination, you may ask us to reconsider it.

(3) *Hearing before an administrative law judge.* If you are dissatisfied with the reconsideration determination, you may request a hearing before an administrative law judge.

(4) *Appeals Council review.* If you are dissatisfied with the decision of the administrative law judge, you may request that the Appeals Council review the decision.

(5) *Federal court review.* When you have completed the steps of the administrative review process listed in paragraphs (a)(1) through (a)(4) of this section, we will have made our final decision. If you are dissatisfied with our final decision, you may request judicial review by filing an action in a Federal district court.

(6) *Expedited appeals process.* At some time after your initial determination has been reviewed, if you have no dispute with our findings of fact and our application and interpretation of the controlling laws, but you believe that a part of the law is unconstitutional, you may use the expedited appeals process. This process permits you to go directly to a Federal district court so that the constitutional issue may be resolved.

(b) *Nature of the administrative review process.* In making a determination or decision in your case, we conduct the administrative review process in an informal, nonadversary manner. In each step of the review process, you may present any information you feel is helpful to your case. Subject to the limitations on Appeals Council consideration of additional evidence, we will consider at each step of the review process any information you present as well as all the information in our records. You may present the information yourself or have someone represent you, including an attorney. If you are dissatisfied with our decision in the review process, but do not take the next step within the stated time period, you will lose your right to further administrative review and your right to judicial review, unless you can show us that there was good cause for your failure to make a timely request for review.

§ 408.1001 Definitions.

As used in this subpart:

Date you receive notice means 5 days after the date on the notice, unless you show us that you did not receive it within the 5–day period.

Decision means the decision made by an administrative law judge or the Appeals Council.

Determination means the initial determination or the reconsidered determination.

Mass change means a State-initiated change in the level(s) of federally administered State recognition payments applicable to all recipients of such payments due, for example, to State legislative or executive action.

Preponderance of the evidence means such relevant evidence that as a whole shows that the existence of the fact to be proven is more likely than not.

Remand means to return a case for further review.

SVB, for purposes of this subpart, includes qualification for SVB, entitlement to SVB and payments of SVB.

Vacate means to set aside a previous action.

Waive means to give up a right knowingly and voluntarily.

We, us, or our refers to the Social Security Administration.

You or your refers to any person claiming or receiving SVB.

[73 FR 76944, Dec. 18, 2008]

§ 408.1002 What is an initial determination?

Initial determinations are the determinations we make that are subject to administrative and judicial review. The initial determination will state the important facts and give the reasons for our conclusions. We will base our initial determination on the preponderance of the evidence.

[73 FR 76944, Dec. 18, 2008]

§ 408.1003 Which administrative actions are initial determinations?

Initial determinations regarding SVB include, but are not limited to, determinations about—

(a) Whether you qualify for SVB;

(b) Whether you are entitled to receive SVB payments on the basis of your residence outside the United States;

(c) The amount of your SVB payments;

(d) Suspension or reduction of your SVB payments;

(e) Termination of your SVB entitlement;

(f) Whether an overpayment of benefits must be repaid to us;

(g) Whether payments will be made, on your behalf, to a representative payee, unless you are legally incompetent;

(h) Who will act as your payee if we determine that representative payment will be made;

(i) A claim for benefits under § 408.351 based on alleged misinformation; and

(j) Our calculation of the amount of change in your federally administered State recognition payment amount (i.e., a reduction, suspension, or termination) which results from a mass change as defined in § 408.1001.

[69 FR 45586, July 30, 2004]

§ 408.1004 Which administrative actions are not initial determinations?

Administrative actions that are not initial determinations may be reviewed by us, but they are not subject to the administrative review process provided by this subpart and they are not subject to judicial review. These actions include, but are not limited to, an action about—

(a) Denial of a request to be made your representative payee;

(b) Denial of your request to use the expedited appeals process;

(c) Denial of your request to reopen a determination or a decision;

(d) Disqualifying or suspending a person from acting as your representative in a proceeding before us;

(e) Denial of your request to extend the time period for requesting review of a determination or a decision;

(f) Denial of your request to readjudicate your claim and apply an Acquiescence Ruling;

(g) Declining under § 408.351(f) to make a determination on a claim for benefits based on alleged misinformation because one or more of the conditions specified in § 408.351(f) are not met;

(h) Findings on whether we can collect an overpayment by using the Federal income tax refund offset procedure. (See § 408.943).

(i) The determination to reduce, suspend, or terminate your federally administered State recognition payments due to a State-initiated mass change, as defined in § 408.1001, in the levels of such payments, except as provided in § 408.1003(h).

§ 408.1005 Will we mail you a notice of the initial determination?

(a) We will mail a written notice of the initial determination to you at your last known address. Generally, we will not send a notice if your benefits are stopped because of your death, or if the initial determination is a redetermination that your eligibility for benefits and the amount of your benefits have not changed.

(b) The notice that we send will tell you—

(1) What our initial determination is;

(2) The reasons for our determination; and

(3) What rights you have to a reconsideration of the determination.

(c) If our initial determination is that we must suspend, reduce your SVB payments or terminate your SVB entitlement, the notice will also tell you that you have a right to a reconsideration before the determination takes effect (see § 408.820).

§ 408.1006 What is the effect of an initial determination?

An initial determination is binding unless you request a reconsideration within the stated time period, or we revise the initial determination.

RECONSIDERATION

§ 408.1007 What is reconsideration?

Reconsideration is the first step in the administrative review process that we provide if you are dissatisfied with the initial determination. If you are dissatisfied with our reconsideration determination, you may request a hearing before an administrative law judge.

§ 408.1009 How do you request reconsideration?

(a) When you must file your request. We will reconsider an initial determination if you file a written request within 60 days after the date you receive notice of the initial determination (or within the extended time period if we extend the time as provided in paragraph (c) of this section).

(b) Where to file your request. You can file your request for reconsideration at:

(1) Any of our offices;

(2) The Veterans Affairs Regional Office in the Philippines;

(3) An office of the Railroad Retirement Board if you have 10 or more years of service in the railroad industry; or

(4) A competent authority or agency of a country with which the United States has a totalization agreement (see § 404.1927 of this chapter).

(c) When we will extend the time period to request a reconsideration. If you want a reconsideration of the initial determination but do not request one within 60 days after the date you receive notice of the initial determination, you may ask us for more time to request a reconsideration. You must make your request in writing and explain why it was not filed within the stated time period. If you show us that you had good cause for missing the deadline, we will extend the time period. To determine whether good cause exists, we use the standards explained in § 408.1011.

§ 408.1011 How do we determine whether you had good cause for missing the deadline to request review?

(a) In determining whether you have shown that you have good cause for missing a deadline to request review we consider—

(1) What circumstances kept you from making the request on time;

(2) Whether our action misled you;

(3) Whether you did not understand the requirements of the Act resulting from amendments to the Act, other legislation, or court decisions; and

(4) Whether you had any physical, mental, educational, or linguistic limitations (including any lack of facility with the English language) which prevented you from filing a timely request or from understanding or knowing about the need to file a timely request for review.

(b) Examples of circumstances where good cause may exist include, but are not limited to, the following situations:

(1) You were seriously ill and were prevented from contacting us in person, in writing, or through a friend, relative, or other person.

(2) There was a death or serious illness in your immediate family.

(3) Important records were destroyed or damaged by fire or other accidental cause.

(4) You were trying very hard to find necessary information to support your claim but did not find the information within the stated time periods.

(5) You asked us for additional information explaining our action within the time limit, and within 60 days of receiving the explanation you requested reconsideration or a hearing, or within 30 days of receiving the explanation you requested Appeals Council review or filed a civil suit.

(6) We gave you incorrect or incomplete information about when and how to request administrative review or to file a civil suit.

(7) You did not receive notice of the initial determination or decision.

(8) You sent the request to another Government agency in good faith within the time limit and the request did not reach us until after the time period had expired.

(9) Unusual or unavoidable circumstances exist, including the circumstances described in paragraph (a)(4) of this section, which show that you could not

have known of the need to file timely, or which prevented you from filing timely.

§ 408.1013 What are the methods for reconsideration?

If you request reconsideration, we will give you a chance to present your case. How you can present your case depends upon the issue involved and whether you are asking us to reconsider an initial determination on an application or an initial determination on an SVB suspension, reduction or termination action. The methods of reconsideration include the following:

(a) Case review. We will give you an opportunity to review the evidence in our files and then to present oral and written evidence to us. We will then make a decision based on all of this evidence. The official who reviews the case will make the reconsidered determination.

(b) Informal conference. In addition to following the procedures of a case review, an informal conference allows you an opportunity to present witnesses. A summary record of this proceeding will become part of the case record. The official who conducts the informal conference will make the reconsidered determination.

(c) Formal conference. In addition to following the procedures of an informal conference, a formal conference allows you an opportunity to request us to subpoena adverse witnesses and relevant documents and to cross-examine adverse witnesses. A summary record of this proceeding will become a part of the case record. The official who conducts the formal conference will make the reconsidered determination.

§ 408.1014 What procedures apply if you request reconsideration of an initial determination on your application for SVB?

When you appeal an initial determination on your application for benefits, we will offer you a case review, and will make our determination on the basis of that review.

§ 408.1015 What procedures apply if you request reconsideration of an initial determination that results in suspension, reduction, or termination of your SVB?

If you have been entitled to SVB and we notify you that we are going to suspend, reduce or terminate your benefit payments, you can appeal our determination within 60 days of the date you receive our notice. The 60–day period may be extended if you have good cause for an extension of time under the conditions stated in § 408.1011(b). If you appeal, you have the choice of a case review, informal conference or formal conference.

§ 408.1016 What happens if you request a conference?

(a) As soon as we receive a request for a formal or informal conference, we will set the time, date and place for the conference. Formal and informal conferences are held only in the United States.

(b) We will send you a written notice about the conference (either by mailing it to your last known address or by personally serving you with it) at least 10 days before the conference. However, we may hold the conference sooner if we all agree. We will not send written notice of the time, date, and place of the conference if you waive your right to receive it.

(c) We will schedule the conference within 15 days after you request it, but, at our discretion or at your request, we will delay the conference if we think the delay will ensure that the conference is conducted efficiently and properly.

(d) We will hold the conference at one of our offices in the United States, by telephone or in person, whichever you prefer. However, if you are outside the United States, we will hold the conference by telephone only if you request that we do so and time and language differences permit. We will hold the conference in person elsewhere in the United States if you show circumstances that make this arrangement reasonably necessary.

§ 408.1020 How do we make our reconsidered determination?

After you request a reconsideration, we will review the evidence considered in making the initial determination and any other evidence we receive. We will make our determination based on the preponderance of the evidence in the record. The person who makes the reconsidered determination will have had no prior involvement with the initial determination.

[73 FR 76944, Dec. 18, 2008]

§ 408.1021 How does the reconsidered determination affect you?

The reconsidered determination is binding unless—

(a) You request a hearing before an administrative law judge within the stated time period and a decision is made;

(b) The expedited appeals process is used; or

(c) The reconsidered determination is revised.

§ 408.1022 How will we notify you of our reconsidered determination?

We will mail a written notice of the reconsidered determination to you at your last known address. We will state the specific reasons for the determination and tell you about your right to a hearing. If it is appropriate, we will also tell you how to use the expedited appeals process.

EXPEDITED APPEALS PROCESS

§ 408.1030 When can you use the expedited appeals process?

(a) General rules. Under the expedited appeals process (EAP), you may go directly to a Federal District Court without first completing the administrative review process. For purposes of this part, we use the same EAP rules we use in the title XVI program (see §§ 416.1423–416.1428 of this chapter) except as noted in paragraph (b) of this section.

(b) Exceptions. In § 416.1425, the words "one of our offices" in paragraph (b) are deemed to read "any of the offices listed in § 408.1009(b)" and the reference in the last sentence of paragraph (c) to "§ 416.1411" is deemed to read "§ 408.1011."

HEARING BEFORE AN ADMINISTRATIVE LAW JUDGE

§ 408.1040 When can you request a hearing before an administrative law judge (ALJ)?

(a) General rules. For purposes of this part, we use the same rules on hearings before an administrative law judge (ALJ) that we use in the title XVI program (see §§ 416.1429–1416.1440 of this chapter), except as noted in paragraph (b) of this section.

(b) Exceptions. In § 416.1433, the words "one of our offices" in paragraph (b) are deemed to read "any of the offices listed in § 408.1009(b)" and the reference in the last sentence of § 416.1433(c) to "§ 416.1411" is deemed to read "§ 408.1011."

ADMINISTRATIVE LAW JUDGE HEARING PROCEDURES

§ 408.1045 What procedures apply if you request an ALJ hearing?

(a) General rules. For purposes of this part, we use the same rules on ALJ hearing procedures that we use in the title XVI program (see §§ 416.1444–416.1461 of this chapter), except as noted in paragraph (b) of this section.

(b) Exceptions.

(1) In § 416.1446(b)(1), the last sentence does not apply under this part.

(2) In § 416.1452(a)(1)(i), the words "supplemental security income" are deemed to read "SVB."

(3) In § 416.1457, the provisions of paragraph (c)(4) do not apply under this part.

APPEALS COUNCIL REVIEW

§ 408.1050 When can you request Appeals Council review of an ALJ hearing decision or dismissal of a hearing request?

(a) General rules. For purposes of this part, we use the same rules on Appeals Council review that we use in the title XVI program (see §§ 416.1467–416.1482 of this chapter), except as noted in paragraph (b) of this section.

(b) Exceptions.

(1) In § 416.1468(b), the words "one of our offices" in the third sentence are deemed to read "any of the offices listed in § 408.1009(b)."

(2) In § 416.1469(d), the last sentence does not apply under this part.

(3) In § 416.1471, paragraph (b) does not apply under this part.

(4) In § 416.1482, the reference to "§ 416.1411" in the last sentence is deemed to read "§ 408.1011."

COURT REMAND CASES

§ 408.1060 What happens if a Federal Court remands your case to the Commissioner?

For purposes of this part, we use the same rules on court remand cases that we use in the title XVI program (see §§ 416.1483–416.1485 of this chapter).

REOPENING AND REVISING DETERMINATIONS AND DECISIONS

§ 408.1070 When will we reopen a final determination?

(a) General rules. For purposes of this part, we use the same rules on reopening and revising determinations and decisions that we use in the title XVI program (see §§ 416.1487–416.1494 of this chapter), except as noted in paragraph (b) of this section.

(b) Exceptions.

(1) In addition to the rule stated in § 416.1488, a determination, revised determination, or revised decision may be reopened at any time if it was fully or partially unfavorable to you, but only to correct—

(i) A clerical error; or

(ii) An error that appears on the face of the evidence that we considered when we made the determination or decision.

(2) In § 416.1492(b), the parenthetical clause is deemed to read "(see § 408.820)," and paragraph (d) does not apply to this part.

(3) In § 416.1494, the words "one of our offices" in the first sentence are deemed to read "any of the offices listed in § 408.1009(b)."

[75 FR 33168, June 11, 2010; 75 FR 44138, July 28, 2010]

SUBPART K—REPRESENTATION OF PARTIES

Authority: Secs. 702(a)(5) and 810(a) of the Social Security Act (42 U.S.C. 902(a)(5) and 1010(a)).

Source: 69 FR 25955, 25965, May 10, 2004, unless otherwise noted.

§ 408.1101 Can you appoint someone to represent you?

(a) General rules. You may appoint someone to represent you in any of your dealings with us. For purposes of this part, the rules on representation of parties in §§ 416.1500–416.1505, 416.1507–416.1515 and 416.1540–416.1599 of this chapter apply except as noted in paragraph (b) of this section.

(b) Exceptions. For purposes of this part:

(1) In § 416.1500, paragraph (c) does not apply.

(2) The last sentence of § 416.1503 is deemed to read: "You refers to any person claiming or receiving SVB."

(3) In § 416.1507(c), the words "one of our offices" are deemed to read "any of the offices listed in § 408.1009(b)."

(4) In § 416.1510(b), the reference to "title XVI of the Act" is deemed to read "title VIII of the Act," and the reference to "§ 416.315" is deemed to read "§ 408.315."

(5) In § 416.1540, the parenthetical clause in paragraph (b), the second sentences in paragraphs (b)(1) and (b)(2), and paragraph (c)(2) do not apply, and the references to "§ 416.1411(b)" in paragraphs (c)(4) and (c)(7)(i) are deemed to read "§ 408.1011(b)."

(6) In § 416.1545, paragraph (c) does not apply.

(7) In § 416.1599, paragraph (d) is deemed to read: "The Appeals Council will not grant the request unless it is reasonably satisfied that the person will in the future act according to the provisions of our regulations."

SUBPART L—FEDERAL ADMINISTRATION OF STATE RECOGNITION PAYMENTS

Authority: Secs. 702(a)(5) and 810A of the Social Security Act (42 U.S.C. 902(a)(5) and 1010a).

Source: 69 FR 25955, 25965, May 10, 2004, unless otherwise noted.

§ 408.1201 What are State recognition payments?

(a) State recognition payments; defined. State recognition payments are any payments made by a State or one of its political subdivisions to an individual who is entitled to SVB, if the payments are made:

(1) As a supplement to monthly SVB payments; and

(2) Regularly, on a periodic recurring, or routine basis of at least once a quarter; and

(3) In cash, which may be actual currency, or any negotiable instrument convertible into cash upon demand.

(b) State; defined. For purposes of this subpart, State means a State of the United States or the District of Columbia.

§ 408.1205 How can a State have SSA administer its State recognition payment program?

A State (or political subdivision) may enter into a written agreement with SSA, under which SSA will make recognition payments on behalf of the State (or political subdivision). The regulations in effect for the SVB program also apply in the Federal administration of State recognition payments except as necessary for the effective and efficient administration of both the SVB program and the State's recognition payment program.

§ 408.1210 What are the essential elements of an administration agreement?

(a) Payments. The agreement must provide that recognition payments can only be made to individuals who are receiving SVB payments.

(b) Administrative costs—

(1) General rule. SSA will assess each State that elects Federal administration of its recognition payments an administration fee for administering those payments.

(2) Determining the administration fee. The administration fee is assessed and paid monthly and is derived by multiplying the number of State recognition payments we make on behalf of a State for any month in a fiscal year by the applicable dollar rate for the fiscal year. The number of recognition payments we make in a month is the total number of checks we issue, and direct deposits we make, to recipients in that month, that are composed in whole or in part of State recognition funds. The dollar amounts are as follows:

(i) For fiscal year 2001, $8.10;

(ii) For fiscal year 2002, $8.50; and

(iii) For fiscal year 2003 and each succeeding fiscal year—

(A) The applicable rate in the preceding fiscal year, increased by the percentage, if any, by which the Consumer Price Index for the month of June of the calendar year of the increase exceeds the Consumer Price Index for the month of June of the calendar year preceding the calendar year of the increase, and rounded to the nearest whole cent; or

(B) A different rate if the Commissioner determines the different rate is appropriate for the State considering the complexity of administering the State's recognition payment program.

(c) Agreement period. The agreement period for a State that has elected Federal administration of its recognition payments extends for one year from the date the agreement was signed unless otherwise designated in the agreement. The agreement will be automatically renewed for a period of one year unless either the State or SSA gives written notice not to renew, at least 90 days before the beginning of the new period. For a State to elect Federal administration of its recognition payment program, it must notify SSA of its intent to enter into an agreement, furnishing the necessary payment specifications, at least 120 days before the first day of the month for which it wishes Federal administration to begin, and have executed such agreement at least 30 days before such day.

(d) Modification or termination. The agreement may be modified at any time by mutual consent. The State or SSA may terminate the agreement upon 90 days' written notice to the other party, provided the effective date of the termination is the last day of a quarter. However, the State may terminate the agreement upon 45 days written notice to SSA if: (1) The State does not wish to comply with a regulation promulgated by SSA after the execution of the agreement; and (2) the State provides its written notice within 30 days of the effective date of the regulation. The Commissioner is not precluded from terminating the agreement in less than 90 days if the State has failed to materially comply with the provisions of § 408.1235 on State transfer of funds to SSA.

§ 408.1215 How do you establish eligibility for Federally administered State recognition payments?

(a) Applications. When you file an application for SVB under subpart C of this part, you are deemed to have filed an application for any Federally administered State recognition payments for which you may be eligible unless you waive your right to such payments as provided for in § 408.1230. However, you will be required to give us a supplemental statement if additional information is necessary to establish your eligibility or to determine the correct amount of your State recognition payment.

(b) Evidence requirements. The evidence requirements and developmental procedures of this part also apply with respect to Federally administered State recognition payments.

(c) Determination. Where not inconsistent with the provisions of this subpart, we determine your eligibility for and the amount of your State recognition payment using the rules in subparts A through K of this part.

§ 408.1220 How do we pay Federally administered State recognition payments?

(a) Payment procedures. We make Federally administered State recognition payments on a monthly basis and we include them in the same check as your SVB payment. The State recognition payment is for the same month as your SVB payment.

(b) Maximum amount. Except as specified in paragraph (c) of this section, there is no restriction on the amount of a State recognition payment that SSA will administer on behalf of a State.

(c) Minimum amount. SSA will not administer State recognition payments in amounts less than $1 per month. Hence, recognition payment amounts of less than $1 will be raised to a dollar.

§ 408.1225 What happens if you receive an overpayment?

If we determine that you received an overpayment, we will adjust future Federally administered State recognition payments you are entitled to. Our rules and requirements (see §§ 408.910 through 408.941) that apply to recovery (or waiver) of SVB overpayments also apply to the recovery (or waiver) of Federally administered State recognition overpayments. If your entitlement to State recognition payments ends before you have repaid the overpayment, we will annotate your record (specifying the amount of the overpayment) to permit us to recoup the overpaid amount if you become reentitled to recognition payments from the same State.

§ 408.1226 What happens if you are underpaid?

If we determine that you are due an underpayment of State recognition payments, we will pay the amount you were underpaid directly to you, or to your representative.

§ 408.1230 Can you waive State recognition payments?

(a) Waiver request in writing. You may waive your right to receive State recognition payments if you make a written request. If you make your request before you become entitled to SVB, you will not be entitled to State recognition payments. If you make your request after you become entitled to SVB, your request will be effective with the month we receive your request, or with an earlier month if you refund to us the amount of any recognition payment(s) we made to you for the earlier period.

(b) Cancelling your waiver. You may cancel your waiver of State recognition payments at any time by making a written request with us. The cancellation will be effective the month in which it is filed. The date your request is received in a Social Security office or the postmarked date, if the written request was mailed, will be the filing date, whichever is earlier.

§ 408.1235 How does the State transfer funds to SSA to administer its recognition payment program?

(a) Payment transfer and adjustment.

(1) Any State that has entered into an agreement with SSA which provides for Federal administration of such State's recognition payments will transfer to SSA:

(i) An amount of funds equal to SSA's estimate of State recognition payments for any month which will be made by SSA on behalf of such State; and

(ii) An amount of funds equal to SSA's estimate of administration fees for any such month determined in the manner described in § 408.1210(b).

(3) In order for SSA to make State recognition payments on behalf of a State for any month as provided by the agreement, the estimated amount of State funds referred to in paragraph (a)(1)(i) of this section together with the estimated amount of administration fees referred to in paragraph (a)(1)(ii) of this section, for that month, must be on deposit with SSA on the State recognition payment transfer date, which is:

(i) the business day preceding the date that the Commissioner pays such monthly recognition payments; or

(ii) with respect to such monthly payments paid for the month that is the last month of the State's fiscal year, the fifth business day following such date.

(b) Accounting of State funds.

(1) As soon as feasible after the end of each calendar month, SSA will provide the State with a statement showing, cumulatively, the total amounts paid by SSA on behalf of the State during the current Federal fiscal year; the fees charged by SSA to administer such recognition payments; the State's total liability; and the end-of-month balance of the State's cash on deposit with SSA.

(2) SSA will provide the State with an accounting of State funds received as State recognition payments and administration fees within three calendar months following the termination of an agreement under § 408.1210(d).

(3) Adjustments will be made because of State funds due and payable or amounts of State funds recovered for calendar months for which the agreement was in effect. Interest will be incurred by SSA and the States with respect to the adjustment and accounting of State recognition payments funds in accordance with applicable laws and regulations of the United States Department of the Treasury.

(c) State audit. Any State entering into an agreement with SSA which provides for Federal administration of the State's recognition payments has the right to an audit (at State expense) of the payments made by SSA on behalf of such State. The Commissioner and the State shall mutually agree upon a satisfactory audit arrangement to verify that recognition payments paid by SSA on behalf of the State were made in accordance with the terms of the administration agreement under § 408.1205. Audit findings will be resolved in accordance with the provisions of the State's agreement with SSA.

PART 411—THE TICKET TO WORK AND SELF-SUFFICIENCY PROGRAM

SUBPART A—INTRODUCTION

Authority: Secs. 702(a)(5) and 1148 of the Social Security Act (42 U.S.C. 902(a)(5) and 1320b–19); sec. 101(b)-(e), Public Law 106–170, 113 Stat. 1860, 1873 (42 U.S.C. 1320b–19 note).

Source: 66 FR 67420, Dec. 28, 2001; 73 FR 29338, May 20, 2008, unless otherwise noted.

SUBPART A—INTRODUCTION

§ 411.100 Scope.

The regulations in this part 411 relate to the provisions of section 1148 of the Social Security Act which establishes the Ticket to Work and Self–Sufficiency Program (hereafter referred to as the "Ticket to Work program"). The regulations in this part are divided into ten subparts:

(a) Subpart A explains the scope of this part, explains the purpose and manner of implementation of the Ticket to Work program, and provides definitions of terms used in this part.

(b) Subpart B contains provisions relating to the ticket under the Ticket to Work program.

(c) Subpart C contains provisions relating to the suspension of continuing disability reviews for disabled beneficiaries who are considered to be using a ticket.

(d) Subpart D contains provisions relating to the use of one or more program managers to assist us in the administration of the Ticket to Work program.

(e) Subpart E contains provisions relating to employment networks in the Ticket to Work program.

(f) Subpart F contains provisions relating to State vocational rehabilitation agencies' participation in the Ticket to Work program.

(g) Subpart G contains provisions relating to individual work plans in the Ticket to Work program.

(h) Subpart H contains provisions establishing employment network payment systems.

(i) Subpart I contains provisions that establish a procedure for resolving disputes under the Ticket to Work program.

(j) [Reserved by 83 FR 62459]

[83 FR 62459, Dec. 4, 2018]

§ 411.105 What is the purpose of the Ticket to Work program?

The purpose of the Ticket to Work program is to expand the universe of service providers available to individuals who are entitled to Social Security benefits based on disability or eligible for Supplemental Security Income (SSI) benefits based on disability or blindness in obtaining the services necessary to find, enter and retain employment. Expanded employment opportunities for these individuals also will increase the likelihood that these individuals will reduce their dependency on Social Security and SSI cash benefits.

§ 411.110 [Reserved by 73 FR 29338]

[73 FR 29338, May 20, 2008]

§ 411.115 Definitions of terms used in this part.

As used in this part:

(a) *The Act* means the Social Security Act, as amended.

(b) *Commissioner* means the Commissioner of Social Security.

(c) *Cost reimbursement payment system* means the provisions for payment for vocational rehabilitation services under subpart V of part 404 and subpart V of part 416 of this chapter.

(d) *Disabled beneficiary* means a title II disability beneficiary or a title XVI disability beneficiary.

(e) *Employment network* or *EN* means a qualified public or private entity that has entered into an agreement with us to serve under the Ticket to Work program and that assumes responsibility for the coordination and delivery of employment services, vocational rehabilitation services, or other support services to beneficiaries assigning tickets to it. The rules on employment networks are described in subpart E of this part (§§ 411.300–411.330). A State vocational rehabilitation agency may choose, on a case-by-case basis, to function as an employment network with respect to a beneficiary under the Ticket to Work program. The rules on State vocational rehabilitation agencies' participation in the Ticket to Work program are described in subpart F of this part (§§ 411.350–411.435).

(f) Employment plan means an individual work plan described in paragraph (i) of this section, or an individualized plan for employment described in paragraph (j) of this section.

(g) Federal SSI cash benefits means a "Supplemental Security Income benefit under title XVI" based on blindness or disability as described in paragraphs (n) and (r) of this section.

(h) I, my, you, or your means the disabled beneficiary.

(i) Individual work plan or IWP means an employment plan under which an employment network (other than a State vocational rehabilitation agency) provides services to a disabled beneficiary under the Ticket to Work program. An individual work plan must be developed under, and meet the requirements of, the rules in subpart G of this part (§§ 411.450–411.470).

(j) Individualized plan for employment or IPE means an employment plan under which a State vocational rehabilitation agency provides services to individuals with disabilities (including beneficiaries assigning tickets to it under the Ticket to Work program) under a State plan approved under title I of the Rehabilitation Act of 1973, as amended (29 U.S.C. 720 et seq.). An individualized plan for employment must be developed under, and meet the requirements of, 34 CFR 361.45 and 361.46.

(k) Program manager or PM means an organization in the private or public sector that has entered into a contract with us to assist us in administering the Ticket to Work program. The rules on the use of one or more program managers to assist us in administering the program are described in subpart D of this part (§§ 411.230–411.250).

(*l*) Social Security disability benefits means the benefits described in paragraph (q) of this section.

(m) State vocational rehabilitation agency or State VR agency means a State agency administering or supervising the administration of the State plan approved under title I of the Rehabilitation Act of 1973, as amended (29 U.S.C. 720 et seq.). In those States that have one agency that provides VR services to non-blind individuals and another agency that provides services to blind individuals, this term refers to either State agency.

(n) Supplemental Security Income benefit under title XVI means a cash benefit under section 1611 or 1619(a) of the Act, and does not include a State supplementary payment, administered Federally or otherwise.

(*o*) Ticket means a document described in § 411.120 which the Commissioner may issue to disabled beneficiaries for participation in the Ticket to Work program.

(p) Ticket to Work program or program means the Ticket to Work and Self–Sufficiency Program under section 1148 of the Act.

(q) Title II disability beneficiary means an individual entitled to disability insurance benefits under section 223 or to monthly insurance benefits under section 202 of the Act based on such individual's disability as defined in section 223(d) of the Act. (See § 404.1505 of this chapter.) An individual is a title II disability beneficiary for each month for which such individual is entitled to such benefits.

(r) Title XVI disability beneficiary means an individual eligible for Supplemental Security Income benefits under title XVI on the basis of blindness (within the meaning of section 1614(a)(2) of the Act) (see §§ 416.981 and 416.982 of this chapter) or disability (within the meaning of section 1614(a)(3) of the Act) (see § 416.905 of this chapter). An individual is a title XVI disability beneficiary for each month for which such individual is eligible for such benefits.

(s) VR cost reimbursement option means an arrangement under which your ticket is not assigned to the State VR agency but you do receive services pursuant to an individualized plan for employment where the State VR agency has chosen to receive payment under the cost reimbursement payment system.

(t) We or us means the Social Security Administration.

[73 FR 29338, May 20, 2008; 83 FR 62459, Dec. 4, 2018]

SUBPART B—TICKETS UNDER THE TICKET TO WORK PROGRAM

§ 411.120 What is a ticket under the Ticket to Work program?

(a) A ticket under the Ticket to Work program is a document which provides evidence of the Commissioner's agreement to pay, under the rules in subpart H of this part, an employment network (EN) or a State VR agency to which a disabled beneficiary's ticket is assigned, for providing employment services, vocational rehabilitation services, and other support services to the beneficiary.

(b) The left side of the ticket includes the beneficiary's name, ticket number, claim account number, and the date we issued the ticket. The ticket number is 12 characters and comprises the beneficiary's own social security number, the letters "TW," and a number (1, 2, etc.) in the last position signifying that this is the first ticket, second ticket, etc., that the beneficiary has received.

(c) The right side of the ticket includes the signature of the Commissioner of Social Security and provides a description of the Ticket to Work program. The description of the program will tell you how you may offer the ticket to an EN or State VR agency. The description will also tell you how the EN provides services to you.

[73 FR 29339, May 20, 2008]

§ 411.125 Who is eligible to receive a ticket under the Ticket to Work program?

(a) You will be eligible to receive a Ticket to Work in a month in which—

(1) You are age 18 or older and have not attained age 65; and

(2)(i)(A) You are a title II disability beneficiary (other than a beneficiary receiving benefit payments under § 404.316(c), § 404.337(c), § 404.352(d), or § 404.1597a of this chapter); and

(B) You are in current pay status for monthly title II cash benefits based on disability (see subpart E of part 404 of this chapter for our rules on nonpayment of title II benefits); or

(ii)(A) You are a title XVI disability beneficiary (other than a beneficiary receiving disability or blindness benefit payments under § 416.996 or § 416.1338 of this chapter);

(B) If you are an individual described in § 416.987(a)(1) of this chapter, you are eligible for benefits under title XVI based on disability under the standard for evaluating disability for adults following a redetermination of your eligibility under § 416.987 of this chapter; and

(C) Your monthly Federal cash benefits based on disability or blindness under title XVI are not suspended (see subpart M of part 416 of this chapter for our rules on suspension of title XVI benefit payments).

(3) [Reserved by 73 FR 29339]

(b) You will not be eligible to receive more than one ticket during any period during which you are either—

(1) Entitled to title II benefits based on disability (see §§ 404.316(b), 404.337(b) and 404.352(b) of this chapter for when entitlement to title II disability benefits ends); or

(2) Eligible for title XVI benefits based on disability or blindness and your eligibility has not terminated (see subpart M of part 416 of this chapter for our rules on when eligibility for title XVI benefits terminates).

(c) If your entitlement to title II benefits based on disability ends and/or your eligibility for title XVI benefits based on disability or blindness terminates as described in § 411.155(b)(1) or (2), you will be eligible to receive a new ticket in a month in which—

(1) Your entitlement to title II benefits based on disability is reinstated under section 223(i) of the Act, or your eligibility for title XVI benefits based on disability or blindness is reinstated under section 1631(p) of the Act; and

(2) You meet the requirements of paragraphs (a)(1) and (2) of this section.

[73 FR 29339, May 20, 2008]

§ 411.130 How will we distribute tickets under the Ticket to Work program?

We may send you a ticket if you are eligible to receive one under § 411.125. All Ticket-eligible beneficiaries may receive a Ticket upon request.

[73 FR 29339, May 20, 2008; 77 FR 1864, Jan. 12, 2012; 78 FR 45453, July 29, 2013]

§ 411.135 What do I do when I receive a ticket?

Your participation in the Ticket to Work program is voluntary. When you receive your ticket, you are free to choose when and whether to assign it (see § 411.140 for information on assigning your ticket). If you want to participate in the program, you can take your ticket to any EN you choose or to your State VR agency. You may choose either to assign your ticket to an EN by signing an individual work plan (see §§ 411.450 through 411.470) or receive services from your State VR agency by entering into and signing an individualized plan for employment. If the State VR agency provides services to you, it will decide whether to accept your ticket. If it accepts your ticket, you will have assigned your ticket to the State VR agency and it will receive payment as an EN. If the State VR agency decides to be paid under the cost reimbursement payment system, you have not assigned your ticket and you may assign your ticket after the State VR agency has closed your case.

[73 FR 29339, May 20, 2008]

§ 411.140 When may I assign my ticket and how?

(a) You may assign your ticket during a month in which you meet the requirements of § 411.125(a)(1) and (a)(2). You may assign your ticket during the 90–day period after your case is closed by a State VR agency that elected the VR cost reimbursement option (see § 411.171(d)), without meeting the requirements of § 411.125(a)(2). You may assign your ticket to any EN which is serving under the program and is willing to provide you with services, or you may assign your ticket to a State VR agency acting as an EN if you are eligible to receive VR services under 34 CFR 361.42. You may not assign your ticket to more than one provider of services (i.e., an EN or a State VR agency) at a time. You may not assign your ticket until after the State VR agency has closed your case if you are receiving VR services pursuant to an individualized plan for employment from a State VR agency which has elected the VR cost reimbursement option. You also may not assign your ticket to a State VR agency if that VR agency previously served you and elected the VR cost reimbursement option and closed your case.

(b)(1) In determining which EN you want to work with, you may discuss your rehabilitation and employment plans with as many ENs in your area as you wish. You also may discuss your rehabilitation and employment plans with the State VR agency.

(2) You can obtain a list of the approved ENs in your area from the program manager (PM) we have enlisted to assist in the administration of the Ticket to Work program. (See § 411.115(k) for a definition of the PM.)

(c) If you choose to work with an EN serving under the program, both you and the EN of your choice need to agree upon an individual work plan (IWP) (see § 411.115(i) for a definition of an IWP). If you choose to work with a State VR agency, you must develop an individualized plan for employment (IPE) and your State VR counselor must agree to the terms of the IPE, according to the requirements established in 34 CFR 361.45 and 361.46. (See § 411.115(j) for a definition of an IPE.) The IWP or IPE outlines the services necessary to assist you in achieving your chosen employment goal.

(d) In order for you to assign your ticket to an EN or State VR agency acting as an EN, all of the following requirements must be met:

(1)(i) If you decide to work with an EN, you and a representative of the EN must agree to and sign an IWP; or

(ii) If you decide to work with a State VR agency, you and a representative of the State VR agency must agree to and sign both an IPE and a form that provides the information described in § 411.385(a)(1), (2) and (3).

(2) You must be eligible to assign your ticket under the rules in paragraph (a) of this section.

(3) A representative of the EN must submit a copy of the signed IWP to the PM, or a representative of the State VR agency, acting as an EN, must submit the completed and signed form (as described in § 411.385(a) and (b)) to the PM.

(4) The PM must receive the copy of the IWP or receive the required form, as appropriate.

(e) If all of the requirements in paragraph (d) of this section are met, we will consider your ticket assigned to the EN or State VR agency acting as an EN. The effective date of the assignment of your ticket will be the first day on which the requirements of paragraphs (d)(1) and (2) of this section are met. See §§ 411.160 through 411.225 for an explanation of how assigning your ticket may affect medical reviews that we conduct to determine if you are still disabled under our rules.

[73 FR 29339, May 20, 2008]

§ 411.145 When can my ticket be taken out of assignment?

(a) If you assigned your ticket to an EN or a State VR agency acting as an EN, you may take your ticket out of assignment for any reason. You must notify the PM in writing that you wish to take your ticket out of assignment. The ticket will be no longer assigned to that EN or State VR agency acting as an EN, effective with the first day of the month following the month in which you notify the PM in writing that you wish to take your ticket out of assignment. You will be sent a notice informing you that your ticket is no longer assigned to that EN or State VR agency. You may reassign your ticket under the rules in § 411.150.

(b) If your EN goes out of business or is no longer approved to participate as an EN in the Ticket to Work program, the PM will take your ticket out of assignment with that EN. The ticket will no longer be assigned to that EN effective on the first day of the month following the month in which the EN goes out of business or is no longer approved to participate in the Ticket to Work program. You will be sent a notice informing you that your ticket is no longer assigned to that EN. In addition, if your EN is no longer willing or able to provide you with services, or if your State VR agency acting as an EN stops providing services to you because you have been determined to be ineligible for VR services under 34 CFR 361.42, the EN or State VR agency acting as an EN may ask the PM to take your ticket out of assignment with that EN or State VR agency. The ticket will no longer be assigned to that EN or State VR agency acting as an EN effective on the first day of the month following the month in which the EN or State VR agency acting as an EN makes a request to the PM that the ticket be taken out of assignment. You will be sent a notice informing you that your ticket is no longer assigned to that EN or State VR agency acting as an EN. You may reassign your ticket under the rules in § 411.150.

(c) For information about how taking a ticket out of assignment may affect medical reviews that we conduct to determine if you are still disabled under our rules, see §§ 411.171(c) and 411.220.

[73 FR 29339, May 20, 2008]

§ 411.150 Can I reassign my ticket?

(a) If you previously assigned your ticket and your ticket is no longer assigned (see § 411.145), you may reassign your ticket, unless you are receiving benefit payments under § 404.316(c), § 404.337(c), § 404.352(d) or § 404.1597a of this chapter, or you are receiving disability or blindness benefit payments under § 416.996 or § 416.1338 of this chapter (the provisions of paragraph (b)(3) of this section notwithstanding). If you previously assigned your ticket to an EN, you may reassign your ticket to a different EN which is serving under the program and is willing to provide you with services, or you may reassign your ticket to a

State VR agency acting as an EN if you are eligible to receive VR services under 34 CFR 361.42. If you previously assigned your ticket to a State VR agency acting as an EN, you may reassign your ticket to an EN which is serving under the program and is willing to provide you with services, or to another State VR agency acting as an EN if you are eligible to receive VR services under 34 CFR 361.42.

(b) In order for you to reassign your ticket to an EN or State VR agency, all of the following requirements must be met:

(1) Your ticket must be unassigned. If your ticket is assigned to an EN or a State VR agency, you must first tell the PM in writing that you want to take your ticket out of assignment (see § 411.145).

(2)(i) You and a representative of the new EN must agree to and sign a new IWP; or

(ii) If you wish to reassign your ticket to a State VR agency, you and a representative of the State VR agency must agree to and sign both an IPE and a form that provides the information described in § 411.385(a)(1), (2) and (3).

(3) You must meet the requirements of § 411.125(a)(1) and (2) on or after the day you and a representative of the new EN sign your IWP or you and a representative of the State VR agency sign your IPE and the required form. You may reassign your ticket within 90 days of the effective date your ticket was no longer assigned, without meeting the requirements of § 411.125(a)(2).

(4) A representative of the EN must submit a copy of the signed IWP to the PM or a representative of the State VR agency must submit the completed and signed form (as described in § 411.385(a) and (b)) to the PM.

(5) The PM must receive the copy of the IWP or received the required form, as appropriate.

(c) If all of the requirements in paragraphs (a) and (b) of this section are met, we will consider your ticket reassigned to the new EN or State VR agency. The effective date of the reassignment of your ticket will be the first day on which the requirements of paragraphs (a) and (b)(1), (2) and (3) of this section are met. See §§ 411.160 through 411.225 for an explanation of how reassigning your ticket may affect medical reviews that we conduct to determine if you are still disabled under our rules.

[73 FR 29340, May 20, 2008]

§ 411.155 When does my ticket terminate?

(a) Your ticket will terminate if and when you are no longer eligible to participate in the Ticket to Work program. If your ticket terminates, you may not assign or reassign it to an EN or State VR agency. We will not pay an EN (including a State VR agency) for milestones or outcomes achieved in or after the month in which your ticket terminates (see § 411.525(c)). Your eligibility to participate in the Ticket to Work program will end, and your ticket will terminate, in the earliest of the following months:

(1) The month in which your entitlement to title II benefits based on disability ends for reasons other than your work activity or earnings, or the month in which your eligibility for benefits under title XVI based on disability or blindness terminates for reasons other than your work activity or earnings, whichever is later;

(2) If you are entitled to widow's or widower's insurance benefits based on disability (see §§ 404.335 and 404.336 of this chapter), the month in which you attain full retirement age;

(3) If you are eligible for benefits under title XVI based on disability or blindness, the month following the month in which you attain age 65; or

(4) The month after the month in which your outcome payment period ends (see § 411.500(b)).

(b) The rules in paragraph (c) of this section apply in determining when your eligibility to participate in the Ticket to Work program will end and your ticket will terminate if—

(1) You were not a concurrent title II/title XVI disability beneficiary, and your entitlement to title II benefits based on disability ends or your eligibility for title XVI benefits based on disability or blindness terminates because of your work activity or earnings; or

(2) You were a concurrent title II/title XVI disability beneficiary and—

(i) Your entitlement to title II benefits based on disability ends because of work activity or earnings and your eligibility for title XVI benefits based on disability or blindness terminates for any reason; or

(ii) Your eligibility for title XVI benefits based on disability or blindness terminates because of your work activity or earnings and your entitlement to title II benefits based on disability ends for any reason.

(c) For purposes of paragraph (b) of this section, the ticket which you received in connection with the previous period during which you were either entitled to title II benefits based on disability or eligible for title XVI benefits based on disability or blindness (as described in § 411.125(b)) will terminate, and your eligibility to participate in the Ticket to Work program based on that ticket will end, in the earliest of the following months:

(1) If we make a final determination or decision that you are not entitled to have title II benefits based on disability reinstated under section 223(i) of the Act or eligible to have title XVI benefits based on disability or blindness reinstated under section 1631(p) of the Act, the month in which we make that determination or decision;

(2) If we make a final determination or decision that you are not entitled to title II benefits based on disability or eligible for title XVI benefits based on disability or blindness after you file an application for benefits, the month in which we make that determination or decision;

(3) The month you attain retirement age (as defined in section 216(*l*) of the Act);

(4) The month in which you die;

(5) The month in which you become entitled to a title II benefit that is not based on disability or eligible for a title XVI benefit that is not based on disability or blindness;

(6) The month in which you again become entitled to title II benefits based on disability, or eligible for title XVI benefits based on disability or blindness, based on the filing of an application for such benefits;

(7) If your entitlement to title II benefits based on disability is reinstated under section 223(i) of the Act, or your eligibility for title XVI benefits based on disability or blindness is reinstated under section 1631(p) of the Act, the month in which you are eligible to receive a new ticket under § 411.125(c); or

(8) The month after the month in which your outcome payment period ends (see § 411.500(b)).

[73 FR 29340, May 20, 2008]

SUBPART C—SUSPENSION OF CONTINUING DISABILITY REVIEWS FOR BENEFICIARIES WHO ARE USING A TICKET

INTRODUCTION

§ 411.160 What does this subpart do?

(a) This subpart explains our rules about continuing disability reviews for disability beneficiaries who are participating in the Ticket to Work program.

(b) Continuing disability reviews are reviews that we conduct to determine if you are still disabled under our rules (see §§ 404.1589, 416.989 and 416.989a of this chapter for the rules on when we may conduct continuing disability reviews). For the purposes of this subpart, continuing disability reviews include the medical reviews we conduct to determine if your medical condition has improved (see §§ 404.1594 and 416.994 of this chapter), but not any review to determine if your disability has ended under § 404.1594(d)(5) of this chapter because you have demonstrated your ability to engage in substantial gainful activity (SGA), as defined in §§ 404.1571–404.1576 of this chapter.

§ 411.165 How does using a ticket under the Ticket to Work program affect my continuing disability reviews?

We periodically review your case to determine if you are still disabled under our rules. However, we will not begin a continuing disability review during the period in which you are using a ticket. Sections 411.170 and 411.171 describe when the period of using a ticket begins and ends. You must meet certain requirements for us to consider you to be using a ticket.

[73 FR 29340, May 20, 2008]

§ 411.166 Glossary of terms used in this subpart.

(a) Using a ticket means you have assigned a ticket to an Employment Network (EN) or a State VR agency that has elected to serve you as an EN, and you are making timely progress toward self-supporting employment as defined in § 411.180; or you have a ticket that would otherwise be available for assignment and are receiving VR services pursuant to an individualized plan for employment (IPE) and the State VR agency has chosen to be paid for these services under the cost reimbursement payment system, and you are making timely progress toward self-supporting employment as defined in § 411.180. (See § 411.171 for when the period of using a ticket ends.)

(b) Timely progress toward self-supporting employment means you have completed the specified goals of work and earnings, or completed the specified post-secondary education credits at an educational institution (see § 411.167) in pursuit of a degree or certificate, or completed specified course requirements for a vocational or technical training program at an educational institution consisting of a technical, trade or vocational school (see § 411.167), or completed a certain percentage of the work requirement and a certain percentage of the post-secondary education requirement or vocational or technical training requirement and the sum of the two percentages equals 100 or more (see § 411.180(c)), or obtained a high school diploma or General Education Development (GED) certificate in the applicable progress certification period as described in § 411.180.

(c) Timely progress guidelines mean the guidelines we use to determine if you are making timely progress toward self-supporting employment (see § 411.180).

(d) Progress certification period means any 12–month progress certification period described in § 411.180(b).

(e) Progress review means the reviews the PM conducts to determine if you are meeting the timely progress guidelines described in § 411.180. We explain the method for conducting progress reviews in § 411.200.

(f) Extension period is a period of up to 90 days during which you may reassign a ticket without being subject to continuing disability reviews. You may be eligible for an extension period if the ticket is in use and no longer assigned to an EN or State VR agency acting as an EN (see § 411.220).

(g) Inactive status is a status in which you may place your ticket if you are temporarily or otherwise unable to make timely progress toward self-supporting employment during a progress certification period. See § 411.192 for the rules on placing your ticket in inactive status and on reactivating your ticket.

(h) Variance tolerance means the margin of flexibility whereby we will consider you to have met the requirement for completing a specified amount of post-secondary credit hours in an educational degree or certification program or the course requirements in a vocational or technical training program under § 411.180 in the applicable progress certification period if your completion of credit hours or course requirements in this period is within 10% of the goal. Figures representing the number of credit hours required for the first and second progress certification periods as described in § 411.180 will be rounded by dropping any fractions. Under the variance tolerance, we also will consider you to have met the requirements in an applicable progress certification period if you complete a certain percentage of the work requirement and a certain percentage of the post-secondary education requirement or vocational or technical training requirement in the period and the sum of the two percentages is within 10% of the goal. See § 411.180(a) and (c).

(i) VR cost reimbursement option means an arrangement under which your ticket is not assigned to the State VR agency but you do receive services pursuant to an individualized plan for employment where the State VR agency has chosen to receive payment under the cost reimbursement payment system.

(j) VR cost reimbursement status means the status of your ticket under the arrangement described in paragraph (i) of this section. The period during which your ticket is in VR cost reimbursement status begins on the date described in § 411.170(b) and ends on the date your case is closed by the State VR agency.

[73 FR 29340, May 20, 2008]

§ 411.167 What is an educational institution or a technical, trade or vocational school?

(a) Educational institution means a school (including a technical, trade, or vocational school), junior college, college or university that is: operated or directly supported by the United States; operated or directly supported by any State or local government or by a political subdivision of any State or local government; or approved by a State agency or subdivision of the State, or accredited by a State-recognized or nationally recognized accrediting body.

(b) Technical, trade or vocational school is an educational institution that is approved by a State agency or subdivision of the State or accredited by a State-recognized or nationally recognized accrediting body to provide technical, trade or vocational training.

(c) State-recognized accrediting body means an entity designated or recognized by a State as the proper authority for accrediting schools, colleges or universities.

(d) Nationally recognized accrediting body means an entity determined to be such by the U.S. Department of Education.

(e) Approval by a State agency or subdivision of the State includes approval of a school, college or university as an educational institution, or approval of one or more of the courses offered by a school, college or university.

[73 FR 29341, May 20, 2008]

§ 411.170 When does the period of using a ticket begin?

(a) The period of using a ticket begins on the effective date of the assignment of your ticket to an EN or State VR agency under § 411.140.

(b) If you have a ticket that would otherwise be available for assignment and are receiving VR services pursuant to an individualized plan for employment (IPE) and the State VR agency has elected the VR cost reimbursement option, the period of using a ticket begins on the later of—

(1) The effective date of your IPE; or

(2) The first day your ticket would otherwise have been assignable if you had not been receiving services from a State VR agency that elected the VR cost reimbursement option.

[73 FR 29341, May 20, 2008]

§ 411.171 When does the period of using a ticket end?

The period of using a ticket ends with the earliest of the following—

(a) The last day of the month before the month in which the ticket terminates as a result of one of the events listed in § 411.155 (see § 411.155(a)(4) and (c)(8) for when your ticket terminates if your outcome payment period ends);

(b) The day before the effective date of a decision under § 411.200 or § 411.205 that you are no longer making timely progress toward self-supporting employment;

(c) The last day of the 90–day extension period which begins with the first day of the first month in which your ticket is no longer assigned to an EN or State VR agency acting as an EN (see § 411.145), unless you reassign your ticket within the 90–day extension period (see § 411.220 for an explanation of the 90–day extension period); or

(d) If your ticket was in VR cost reimbursement status as described in § 411.166(j), the 90th day following the date the State VR agency closes your case, unless you assign your ticket during this 90–day period.

[73 FR 29341, May 20, 2008]

§ 411.175 What if a continuing disability review is begun before my ticket is in use?

(a) If we begin a continuing disability review before the date on which your ticket is in use, you may still assign the ticket and receive services from an EN or a State VR agency acting as an EN under the Ticket to Work program, or you may still receive services from a State VR agency that elects the VR cost reimbursement option. However, we will complete the continuing disability review. If in this review we determine that you are no longer disabled, in most cases you will no longer be eligible to receive benefit payments. However, if your ticket was in use before we determined that you are no longer disabled, in certain circumstances you may continue to receive benefit payments (see §§ 404.316(c), 404.337(c), 404.352(d), and 416.1338 of this chapter). If you appeal the decision that you are no longer disabled, you may also choose to have your benefits continued pending reconsideration and/or a hearing before an administrative law judge on the cessation determination (see §§ 404.1597a and 416.996 of this chapter).

(b) The date on which we begin the continuing disability review is the date on the notice we send you that tells you that we are beginning to review your disability case.

[73 FR 29341, May 20, 2008]

§ 411.180 What is timely progress toward self-supporting employment?

(a) General. We consider you to be making timely progress toward self-supporting employment when you show progress as described below toward the ability to work at levels which will reduce your dependence on Social Security disability benefits or SSI benefits. We will also consider you to be making timely progress when you obtain a high school diploma or GED certificate in the first 12–month progress certification period, or if you show progress as described below toward obtaining an educational degree or certificate or vocational or technical training that will enhance your ability to return to work. In addition, if you complete a certain percentage of the work requirement and a certain percentage of the post-secondary education requirement or vocational or technical training requirement in the applicable progress certification period under the guidelines below, and the sum of the two percentages equals 100 or more, we will consider you to have met the timely progress requirements for purposes of the progress review conducted at the end of the 12–month progress certification period. For example, if you complete 33.3 percent of the work requirement during the first 12–month progress certification period as described in paragraph (c)(1)(i) of this section (i.e., one month of work with earnings equal to or greater than the amount representing a trial work service month), and complete 66.7 percent of the requisite credit hours in an educational program during this period as described in paragraph (c)(1)(iii) of this section (i.e., 40 percent of the post-secondary credit hours that are considered to represent an academic year of full-time study), we will consider you to have met the timely progress requirements for purposes of the progress review conducted at the end of the first 12–month progress certification period. In addition, we will apply the variance tolerance described in § 411.166(h) in determining whether you have met the requirements in paragraph (c)(1)(iii), (iv) or (v), paragraph (c)(2)(ii), (iii) or (iv), paragraph (c)(3)(iii) or (v), paragraph (c)(4)(ii) or (iii), or paragraph (c)(5)(ii) or (iii) of this section.

(b) 12–month progress certification periods. The first 12–month progress certification period begins with the month following the month in which you first assigned your ticket, or with the month beginning after the date described in § 411.170(b) if you have a ticket that would otherwise be available for assignment and are receiving VR services under an IPE from a State VR agency which has chosen the VR cost reimbursement option. Any subsequent 12–month progress certification period will begin with the month following the end of the previous 12–month progress certification period. In computing any 12–month progress certification period, we do not count any month during which—

(1) Your ticket is not assigned to an EN or State VR agency acting as an EN and is not in VR cost reimbursement status (as described in § 411.166(j)); or

(2) Your ticket is in inactive status (see § 411.192).

(c) Guidelines. We will determine if you are making timely progress toward self-supporting employment by using the following guidelines:

(1) During the first 12–month progress certification period, you must be making timely progress as follows:

(i) You must have worked in at least three months within this 12–month period and have earnings in each of those three months that are equal to or greater than the amount representing a trial work service month (see § 404.1592(b) of this chapter); or

(ii) You must have obtained a high school diploma or GED certificate within this 12–month period; or

(iii) You must have been enrolled in a two- or four-year degree or certification program at an educational institution and have completed 60 percent of the post-secondary credit hours that are considered to represent an academic year of full-time study in the program by the end of this 12–month period; or

(iv) You must have been enrolled in a vocational or technical training program at an educational institution consisting of a technical, trade or vocational school and have completed 60 percent of the course requirements that are considered to represent a year of full-time study in the program by the end of this 12–month period; or

(v) You must have completed a percentage of the required number of months of work and earnings described in paragraph (c)(1)(i) of this section and a percentage of the specified amount of post-secondary credit hours or course requirements required under paragraph (c)(1)(iii) or (iv) of this section within this 12–month period so that the sum of the two percentages equals 100 or more.

(2) During the second 12–month progress certification period, at the conclusion of 24 months of ticket use, you must be making timely progress as follows:

(i) You must have worked in at least six months within this 12–month period and have earnings in each of those six months that are equal to or greater than the amount representing a trial work service month (see § 404.1592(b) of this chapter); or

(ii) You must have been enrolled in a two- or four-year degree or certification program at an educational institution and have completed an additional 75 percent of the post-secondary credit hours that are considered to represent an academic year of full-time study in the program by the end of this 12–month period; or

(iii) You must have been enrolled in a vocational or technical training program at an educational institution consisting of a technical, trade or vocational school and have completed an additional 75 percent of the course requirements that are considered to represent a year of full-time study in the program by the end of this 12–month period; or

(iv) You must have completed a percentage of the required number of months of work and earnings described in paragraph (c)(2)(i) of this section and a percentage of the specified amount of post-secondary credit hours or course requirements required under paragraph (c)(2)(ii) or (iii) of this section within this 12–month period so that the sum of the two percentages equals 100 or more.

(3) During the third 12–month progress certification period, at the conclusion of 36 months of ticket use, you must be making timely progress as follows:

(i) You must have worked in at least nine months within this 12–month period and have gross earnings from employment (or net earnings from self-employment as defined in § 404.1080 of this chapter) in each of those nine months that are more than the SGA threshold amount specified in § 404.1574(b)(2) of this chapter; or

(ii) You must have completed the course work and earned a degree or certificate from a two-year degree or certification program at an educational institution by the end of this 12–month period; or

(iii) You must have been enrolled in a four-year degree or certification program at an educational institution and completed additional post-secondary credit hours that are considered to represent an academic year of full-time study in the program by the end of this 12–month period; or

(iv) You must have been enrolled in a vocational or technical training program at an educational institution consisting of a technical, trade or vocational school and have completed the course requirements of the program by the end of this 12–month period; or

(v) You must have completed a percentage of the required number of months of work and earnings described in paragraph (c)(3)(i) of this section and a percentage of the specified amount of post-secondary credit hours required under paragraph (c)(3)(iii) of this section within this 12–month period so that the sum of the two percentages equals 100 or more.

(4) During the fourth 12–month progress certification period, at the conclusion of 48 months of ticket use, you must be making timely progress as follows:

(i) You must have worked in at least nine months within this 12–month period and have gross earnings from employment (or net earnings from self-employment as defined in § 404.1080 of this chapter) in each of those nine months that are more than the SGA threshold amount specified in § 404.1574(b)(2) of this chapter; or

(ii) You must have been enrolled in a four-year degree or certification program at an educational institution and completed additional post-secondary credit hours that are considered to represent an academic year of full-time study in the program by the end of this 12–month period; or

(iii) You must have completed a percentage of the required number of months of work and earnings described in paragraph (c)(4)(i) of this section and a percentage of the specified amount of post-secondary credit hours required under paragraph (c)(4)(ii) of this section within this 12–month period so that the sum of the two percentages equals 100 or more.

(5) During the fifth 12–month progress certification period, at the conclusion of 60 months of ticket use, you must be making timely progress as follows:

(i) You must have worked in at least six months within this 12–month period and have earnings in each of those six months that preclude payment of Social Security disability benefits and Federal SSI cash benefits; or

(ii) You must have been enrolled in a four-year degree or certification program at an educational institution and either completed additional post-secondary credit hours that are considered to represent an academic year of full-time study in the program or completed the course work and earned a degree or certificate from the program by the end of this 12–month period; or

(iii) You must have completed a percentage of the required number of months of work and earnings described in paragraph (c)(5)(i) of this section and a percentage of the specified amount of post-secondary credit hours required under paragraph (c)(5)(ii) of this section within this 12–month period so that the sum of the two percentages equals 100 or more.

(6) During the sixth 12–month progress certification period, at the conclusion of 72 months of ticket use, you must be making timely progress as follows:

(i) You must have worked in at least six months within this 12–month period and have earnings in each of those six months that preclude payment of Social Security disability benefits and Federal SSI cash benefits; or

(ii) You must have completed the course work and earned a degree or certificate from a four-year degree or certification program at an educational institution by the end of this 12–month period.

(7) During all subsequent 12–month progress certification periods, you must have worked in at least six months within the 12–month period and have earnings in each of those six months that preclude payment of Social Security disability benefits and Federal SSI cash benefits.

[73 FR 29341, May 20, 2008]

§ 411.185 [Reserved by 73 FR 29343]

[73 FR 29343, May 20, 2008]

§ 411.190 [Reserved by 73 FR 29343]

[73 FR 29343, May 20, 2008]

§ 411.191 [Reserved by 73 FR 29343]

[73 FR 29343, May 20, 2008]

§ 411.192 What choices do I have if I am unable to make timely progress toward self-supporting employment?

(a) If you report to the PM that you are temporarily or otherwise unable to make timely progress toward self-supporting employment during a progress certification period, the PM will give you the choice of placing your ticket in inactive status or, if applicable, taking your ticket out of assignment with the EN or State VR agency acting as an EN. The choice of placing your ticket in inactive status applies whether your ticket is assigned or in VR cost reimbursement status (as described in § 411.166(j)).

(b) You may place your ticket in inactive status at any time by submitting a written request to the PM asking that your ticket be placed in inactive status. Your ticket will be placed in inactive status beginning with the first day of the month following the month in which you make your request. You are not considered to be using a ticket during months in which your ticket is in inactive status. Therefore, you will be subject to continuing disability reviews during those months. The months in which your ticket is in inactive status do not count toward the time limitations for making timely progress toward self-supporting employment.

(c) You may reactivate your ticket and return to in-use status if your ticket is still assigned to an EN or State VR agency acting as an EN. You may also reactivate your ticket and return to in-use status if you have a ticket which would otherwise be available for assignment, you were receiving services under an IPE from a State VR agency which chose the VR cost reimbursement option, and your VR case has not been closed by the State VR agency. You may reactivate your ticket by submitting a written request to the PM. Your ticket will be reactivated beginning with the first day of the month following the month in which the PM receives your request. The progress certification period will resume counting from the last month of in-use status, and the next progress review will be due when the progress certification period has been completed. Earnings from work, obtaining a high school diploma or GED certificate, or completion of post-secondary education credits in a two- or four-year degree or certification program or course requirements in a vocational or technical training program, as described in § 411.180, during the period your ticket is in inactive status may be counted toward meeting the requirements for the next progress review.

(d) You may take your ticket out of assignment under § 411.145(a) at any time.

[73 FR 29343, May 20, 2008]

§ 411.195 [Reserved by 73 FR 29343]

[73 FR 29343, May 20, 2008]

§ 411.200 How will the PM conduct my progress reviews?

The PM will conduct a progress review at the end of each 12–month progress certification period.

(a) The PM will first review the available administrative records to determine if you completed the work requirements as specified in § 411.180 in the applicable progress certification period.

(b) If the administrative records do not indicate that you met the work requirements, the PM will contact either you or your EN or State VR agency to request additional information to determine if you completed the work requirements or have met the educational or training requirements as specified in § 411.180 in the applicable progress certification period.

(c) If the PM finds that you completed the work requirements or met the educational or training requirements as specified in § 411.180 in the applicable progress certification period, the PM will find that you are making timely progress toward self-supporting employment. On the basis of that finding, we will consider you to be making timely progress toward self-supporting employment until your next scheduled progress review.

(d) If the PM finds that you did not complete the work requirements or meet the educational or training requirements as specified in § 411.180 in the applicable progress certification period, the PM will find that you are not making timely progress toward self-supporting employment. If the PM makes such a finding, the PM will send a written notice of the decision to you at your last known address. This notice will explain the reasons for the decision and inform you of the right to ask us to review the decision. This decision will be effective 30 days after the date on which the PM sends the notice of the decision to you, unless you request that we review the decision under § 411.205.

[73 FR 29343, May 20, 2008]

§ 411.205 What if I disagree with the PM's decision about whether I am making timely progress toward self-supporting employment?

If you disagree with the PM's decision, you may request that we review the decision. You must make the request before the 30th day after the date on which the PM sends the notice of its decision to you. We will consider you to be making timely progress toward self-supporting employment until we make a decision. We will send a written notice of our decision to you at your last known address. If we decide that you are no longer making timely progress toward self-supporting employment, our decision will be effective on the date on which we send the notice of the decision to you.

FAILURE TO MAKE TIMELY PROGRESS

§ 411.210 What happens if I do not make timely progress toward self-supporting employment?

(a) General. If it is determined that you are not making timely progress toward self-supporting employment, we will find that you are no longer using a ticket. If this happens, you will once again be subject to continuing disability reviews. However, you may continue participating in the Ticket to Work program. Your EN (including a State VR agency which is serving you as an EN) also may receive any milestone or outcome payments for which it is eligible under § 411.500 et seq. If you are working with a State VR agency which elected payment under the cost reimbursement payment system, your State VR agency may receive payment for which it is eligible under the cost reimbursement payment system (see subparts F and H of this part).

(b) Re-entering in-use status. If you failed to meet the timely progress guidelines for a 12–month progress certification period and you believe that you have now met the applicable requirements for that progress certification period as described in § 411.180, you may request that you be reinstated to in-use status. In order to do so, you must submit a written request to the PM asking that you be reinstated to in-use status and you must provide evidence showing that you have met the applicable requirements for the progress certification period. The PM will decide whether you have satisfied the applicable requirements for the progress certification period and may be reinstated to in-use status. If the PM determines you have met the applicable requirements for the progress certification period, you will be reinstated to in-use status, provided that your ticket is assigned to an EN or State VR agency acting as an EN or in VR cost reimbursement status (as described in § 411.166(j)). See paragraph (c) of this section for when your reinstatement to in-use status will be effective. The month after you are reinstated to in-use status, your next 12–month progress certification period will begin.

(c) Decisions on re-entering in-use status.

(1) After you have submitted a written request to the PM asking that you be reinstated to in-use status, the PM will decide whether you have satisfied the applicable requirements in this section for re-entering in-use status. The PM will send a written notice of the decision to you at your last known address. The notice will explain the reasons for the decision and inform you of the right to ask us to review the decision. If the PM decides that you have satisfied the requirements for re-entering in-use status (including the requirement that your ticket be assigned to an EN or State VR agency acting as an EN or in VR cost reimbursement status), you will be reinstated to in-use status effective with the date on which the PM sends the notice of the decision to you. If the PM decides that you have not satisfied the requirements for re-entering in-use status, you may request that we review the decision under paragraph (c)(2) of this section.

(2) If you disagree with the PM's decision, you may request that we review the decision. You must make the request before the 30th day after the date on which the PM sends the notice of its decision to you. We will send you a written notice of our decision at your last known address. If we decide that you have satisfied the requirements for re-entering in-use status (including the requirement that your ticket be assigned to an EN or State VR agency acting as an EN or in VR cost reimbursement status), you will be reinstated to in-use status effective with the date on which we send the notice of the decision to you.

[73 FR 29343, May 20, 2008]

THE EXTENSION PERIOD

§ 411.220 What if my ticket is no longer assigned to an EN or State VR agency?

(a) If your ticket was once assigned to an EN or State VR agency acting as an EN and is no longer assigned, you are eligible for an extension period of up to 90 days to reassign your ticket. You are eligible for an extension period if your ticket is in use and no longer assigned because—

(1) You retrieved your ticket because you were dissatisfied with the services being provided (see § 411.145(a)) or because you relocated to an area not served by your previous EN or State VR agency; or

(2) Your EN went out of business, is no longer approved to participate as an EN in the Ticket to Work program, or is no longer willing or able to provide you with services as described in § 411.145(b), or your State VR agency stopped providing services to you as described in § 411.145(b).

(b) During the extension period, the ticket will still be considered to be in use. This means that you will not be subject to continuing disability reviews during this period.

(c) Time spent in the extension period will not count toward the time limitations for the timely progress guidelines.

(d) The extension period—

(1) Begins on the first day on which the ticket is no longer assigned (see § 411.145); and

(2) Ends 90 days after it begins or when you assign your ticket to a new EN or State VR agency, whichever is sooner.

(e) If you do not assign your ticket by the end of the extension period, the ticket will no longer be in use and you will once again be subject to continuing disability reviews.

[73 FR 29344, May 20, 2008]

§ 411.225 What if I reassign my ticket after the end of the extension period?

(a) General. You may reassign your ticket after the end of the extension period under the conditions described in § 411.150. If you reassign your ticket after the end of the extension period, you will be reinstated to in-use status beginning on the day on which the reassignment of your ticket is effective under § 411.150(c).

(b) Time limitations for the timely progress guidelines. Any month during which your ticket is not assigned and not in VR cost reimbursement status (as described in § 411.166(j)), either during or after the extension period, will not count toward the time limitations for the timely progress guidelines.

(c) If you reassign your ticket after the end of the extension period. If you reassign your ticket after the end of the extension period, the period comprising the remaining months in the applicable 12–month progress certification period will begin with the first month beginning after the day on which the reassignment of your ticket is effective under § 411.150(c).

(d) [Reserved by 73 FR 29344]

[73 FR 29344, May 20, 2008]

§ 411.226 How will SSA determine if I am meeting the timely progress guidelines if I assign my ticket prior to July 21, 2008?

(a) If you assigned your ticket to an EN or State VR agency prior to July 21, 2008, we will determine which 12–month progress certification period in § 411.180 you are in as of July 21, 2008 using the rules in paragraph (a)(1) of this section. We will not conduct a progress review at the end of that progress certification period. We will conduct a progress review at the end of your next progress certification period as explained in paragraph (a)(2) of this section.

(1) We will consider you to be in the first or a subsequent 12–month progress certification period under § 411.180 as of July 21, 2008. We will determine your applicable 12–month progress certification period and the number of months remaining in that period as of July 21, 2008 by counting all months during which your ticket was assigned and in use during the period—

(i) Beginning with the month following the month in which you first assigned your ticket under the rules in effect prior to July 21, 2008; and

(ii) Ending with the close of June 2008.

(2) We will use the timely progress guidelines in § 411.180(c) beginning with your next 12–month progress certification period. At the conclusion of that progress certification period, we will conduct a progress review to determine whether you are making timely progress toward self-supporting employment using the guidelines in § 411.180(c) that apply in that period.

(b) Prior to the conclusion of your applicable 12–month progress certification period determined under paragraph (a)(1) of this section, we will send you a notice telling you that we will not conduct a progress review at the end of that progress certification period, and that we will conduct a progress review at the conclusion of your next 12–month progress certification period using the guidelines in § 411.180(c). We will tell you in the notice when this next 12–month progress certification period will begin and will describe the specific timely progress guidelines you must meet in this 12–month period.

(c) Subsequent 12–month progress certification periods will follow the rules in § 411.180.

(d) If, on June 30, 2008, your ticket is in use and assigned to a State VR agency which chose to be paid for services it provides to you under the cost reimbursement payment system, your period of using a ticket may continue under the rules in this subpart, including the rules in paragraphs (a), (b) and (c) of this section. While your ticket may still be considered in-use for the purpose of the suspension of continuing disability reviews, it will no longer be considered assigned to that State VR agency effective July 21, 2008. You may assign your ticket after the State VR agency has closed your case.

[73 FR 29344, May 20, 2008]

SUBPART D—USE OF ONE OR MORE PROGRAM MANAGERS TO ASSIST IN ADMINISTRATION OF THE TICKET TO WORK PROGRAM

§ 411.230 What is a PM?

A program manager (PM) is an organization in the private or public sector that has entered into a contract to assist us in administering the Ticket to Work program. We will use a competitive bidding process to select one or more PMs.

§ 411.235 What qualifications are required of a PM?

A PM must have expertise and experience in the field of vocational rehabilitation or employment services.

§ 411.240 What limitations are placed on a PM?

A PM is prohibited from directly participating in the delivery of employment services, vocational rehabilitation services, or other support services to beneficiaries with tickets in the PM's designated service delivery area. A PM is also prohibited from holding a financial interest in an employment network (EN) or service provider that provides services under the Ticket to Work program in the PM's designated service delivery area.

§ 411.245 What are a PM's responsibilities under the Ticket to Work program?

A PM will assist us in administering the Ticket to Work program by conducting the following activities:

(a) Recruiting, recommending, and monitoring ENs. A PM must recruit and recommend for selection by us public and private entities to function as ENs under the program. A PM is also responsible for monitoring the ENs operating in its service delivery area. Such monitoring must be done to the extent necessary and appropriate to ensure that adequate choices of services are made available to beneficiaries with tickets. A PM may not limit the number of public or private entities being recommended to function as ENs.

(b) Facilitating access by beneficiaries to ENs. A PM must assist beneficiaries with tickets in accessing ENs.

(1) A PM must establish and maintain lists of the ENs available to beneficiaries with tickets in its service delivery area and make these lists generally available to the public.

(2) A PM must ensure that all information provided to beneficiaries with tickets about ENs is in accessible formats. For purposes of this section, accessible format means by media that is appropriate to a particular beneficiary's impairment(s).

(3) A PM must take necessary measures to ensure that sufficient ENs are available and that each beneficiary under the Ticket to Work program has reasonable access to employment services, vocational rehabilitation services, and other support services. The PM shall ensure that services such as the following are available in each service area, including rural areas: case management, work incentives planning, supported employment, career planning, career plan development, vocational assessment, job training, placement, follow-up services, and other services that we may require in an agreement with a PM.

(4) A PM must ensure that each beneficiary with a ticket is allowed to change ENs. When a change in the EN occurs, the PM must reassign the ticket based on the choice of the beneficiary.

(c) Facilitating payments to ENs. A PM must facilitate payments to the ENs in its service delivery area. Subpart H explains the EN payment systems and the PM's role in administering these systems.

(1) A PM must maintain documentation and provide regular assurances to us that payments to an EN are warranted. The PM shall ensure that an EN is complying with the terms of its agreement and applicable regulations.

(2) Upon the request of an EN, the PM shall make a determination of the allocation of the outcome or milestone payments due to an EN based on the services provided by the EN when a beneficiary has been served by more than one EN.

(d) Administrative requirements. A PM will perform such administrative tasks as are required to assist us in administering and implementing the Ticket to Work program. Administrative tasks required for the implementation of the Program may include, but are not limited to:

(1) Reviewing individual work plans (IWPs) submitted by ENs for ticket assignment. These reviews will be conducted to ensure that the IWPs meet the requirements of § 411.465. (The PM will not review individualized plans for employment developed by State VR agencies and beneficiaries.)

(2) Reviewing amendments to IWPs to ensure that the amendments meet the requirements in § 411.465.

(3) Ensuring that ENs only refer an individual to a State VR agency for services pursuant to an agreement regarding the conditions under which such services will be provided.

(4) Resolving a dispute between an EN and a State VR agency with respect to agreements regarding the conditions under which services will be provided when an individual is referred by an EN to a State VR agency for services.

EVALUATION OF PROGRAM MANAGER PERFORMANCE

§ 411.250 How will SSA evaluate a PM?

(a) We will periodically conduct a formal evaluation of the PM. The evaluation will include, but not be limited to, an assessment examining the following areas:

(1) Quality of services;

(2) Cost control;

(3) Timeliness of performance;

(4) Business relations; and

(5) Customer satisfaction.

(b) Our Project Officer will perform the evaluation. The PM will have an opportunity to comment on the evaluation, and then the Contracting Officer will determine the PM's final rating.

(c) These performance evaluations will be made part of our database on contractor past performance to which any Federal agency may have access.

(d) Failure to comply with the standards used in the evaluation may result in early termination of our agreement with the PM.

SUBPART E—EMPLOYMENT NETWORKS

§ 411.300 What is an EN?

An employment network (EN) is any qualified entity that has entered into an agreement with us to function as an EN under the Ticket to Work program and assume responsibility for the coordination and delivery of employment services, vocational rehabilitation services, or other support services to beneficiaries who have assigned their tickets to that EN.

§ 411.305 Who is eligible to be an EN?

Any qualified agency or instrumentality of a State (or political subdivision thereof) or a private entity that assumes responsibility for the coordination and delivery of services under the Ticket to Work program to disabled beneficiaries is eligible to be an EN. A single entity or an association of or consortium of entities combining their resources is eligible to be an EN. The entity may provide these services directly or by entering into an agreement with other organizations or individuals to provide the appropriate services or other assistance that a beneficiary with a ticket may need to find and maintain employment that reduces dependency on disability benefits. ENs may include, but are not limited to:

(a) Any public or private entity, including charitable and religious organizations, that can provide directly, or arrange for other organizations or entities to provide, employment services, vocational rehabilitation services, or other support services.

(b) State agencies administering or supervising the administration of the State plan approved under title I of the Rehabilitation Act of 1973, as amended (29 U.S.C. 720 et seq.) may choose, on a case-by-case basis, to be paid as an EN under the payment systems described in subpart H of this part. For the rules on State VR agencies' participation in the Ticket to Work program, see subpart F of this part. The rules in this subpart E apply to entities other than State VR agencies.

(c) One-stop delivery systems established under subtitle B of title I of the Workforce Investment Act of 1998 (29 U.S.C. 2841 et seq.).

(d) [Reserved by 83 FR 62459]

(e) Organizations administering Vocational Rehabilitation Services Projects for American Indians with Disabilities authorized under section 121 of part C of title I of the Rehabilitation Act of 1973, as amended (29 U.S.C. 750 et seq.).

(f) Public or private schools that provide VR or employment services, conduct job training programs, or make services or programs available that can assist students with disabilities in acquiring specific job skills that lead to employment. This includes transition programs that can help students acquire work skills.

(g) Employers that offer job training or other support services or assistance to help individuals with disabilities obtain and retain employment or arrange for individuals with disabilities to receive relevant services or assistance.

[83 FR 62459, Dec. 4, 2018]

§ 411.310 How does an entity other than a State VR agency apply to be an EN and who will determine whether an entity qualifies as an EN?

(a) An entity other than a State VR agency applies by responding to our Request for Proposal (RFP), which we published in the Commerce Business Daily and which is available online through the Federal government's electronic posting system (http://www.eps.gov). This RFP also is available through SSA's website, http://www.ssa.gov/work. Since recruitment of ENs will be an ongoing process, the RFP is open and continuous. The entity must respond in a format prescribed in the RFP announcement. In its response, the entity must assure SSA that it is qualified to provide employment services, vocational rehabilitation services, or other support services to disabled beneficiaries, either directly or through arrangements with other entities.

(b) The PM will solicit service providers and other qualified entities to respond to the RFP on an ongoing basis. (See § 411.115(k) for a definition of the PM.) The PM will conduct a preliminary review of responses to the RFP from applicants located in the PM's service delivery area and make recommendations to the Commissioner regarding selection. The Commissioner will decide which applicants will be approved to serve as ENs under the program.

(c) State VR agencies must comply with the requirements in subpart F of this part to participate as an EN in the Ticket to Work program. (See § 411.360ff).

(d) One-stop delivery systems established under subtitle B of title I of the Workforce Investment Act of 1998 (29 U.S.C. 2811 et seq.) may participate in the Ticket to Work program as ENs and do not need to respond to the RFP. However, in order to participate in the Ticket to Work program, the one-stop delivery system must enter into an agreement with the Commissioner to be an EN and must maintain compliance with general and specific selection criteria as described in § 411.315 in order to remain an EN.

(e) Organizations administering Vocational Rehabilitation Services Projects for American Indians with Disabilities authorized under section 121 of part C of title I of the Rehabilitation Act of 1973, as amended (29 U.S.C. 741), may participate in the Ticket to Work program as ENs and do not need to respond to the RFP. However, in order to participate in the Ticket to Work program, the organization administering the project must enter into an agreement with the Commissioner to be an EN and must maintain compliance with general and specific selection criteria as described in § 411.315 in order to remain an EN.

[73 FR 29344, May 20, 2008]

§ 411.315 What are the minimum qualifications necessary to be an EN?

To serve as an EN under the Ticket to Work program, an entity must meet and maintain compliance with both general selection criteria and specific selection criteria.

(a) The general criteria include:

(1) having systems in place to protect the confidentiality of personal information about beneficiaries seeking or receiving services;

(2) being accessible, both physically and programmatically, to beneficiaries seeking or receiving services (examples of being programmatically accessible include the capability of making documents and literature available in alternate media including Braille, recorded formats, enlarged print, and electronic media; and insuring that data systems available to clients are fully accessible for independent use by persons with disabilities);

(3) not discriminating in the provision of services based on a beneficiary's age, gender, race, color, creed, or national origin;

(4) having adequate resources to perform the activities required under the agreement with us or the ability to obtain them;

(5) complying with the terms and conditions in the agreement with us, including delivering or coordinating the delivery of employment services, vocational rehabilitation services, and other support services; and

(6) implementing accounting procedures and control operations necessary to carry out the Ticket to Work program.

(b) The specific criteria that an entity must meet to qualify as an EN include:

(1)(i) Using staff who are qualified under applicable certification, licensing, or registration standards that apply to their profession including certification or accreditation by national accrediting or certifying organizations; or

(ii) Using staff that are otherwise qualified based on education or experience, such as by using staff with experience or a college degree in a field related to the services the EN wants to provide, such as vocational counseling, human relations, teaching, or psychology; and

(2) Taking reasonable steps to assure that if any medical and related health services are provided, such medical and health related services are provided under the formal supervision of persons licensed to prescribe or supervise the provision of these services in the State in which the services are performed.

(c) Any entity must have applicable certificates, licenses or other credentials if such documentation is required by State law to provide vocational rehabilitation services, employment services or other support services.

(d) We will not use the following as an EN:

(1) any entity that has had its license, accreditation, certification, or registration suspended or revoked for reasons concerning professional competence or conduct or financial integrity;

(2) any entity that has surrendered a license, accreditation, certification, or registration with a disciplinary proceeding pending; or

(3) any entity that is precluded from Federal procurement or non-procurement programs.

(e) One-stop delivery systems established under subtitle B of title I of the Workforce Investment Act of 1998 (29 U.S.C. 2811 et seq.) are qualified to be ENs. A one-stop delivery system must enter into an agreement with the Commissioner to be an EN and must maintain compliance with general and specific selection criteria of this section and § 411.305 in order to remain an EN.

(f) Organizations administering Vocational Rehabilitation Services Projects for American Indians with Disabilities authorized under section 121 of part C of title I of the Rehabilitation Act of 1973, as amended (29 U.S.C. 741), are qualified to be ENs. An organization administering such a project must enter into an agreement with the Commissioner to be an EN and must maintain compliance with general and specific selection criteria of this section and § 411.305 in order to remain an EN.

[73 FR 29344, May 20, 2008]

§ 411.320 What are an EN's responsibilities as a participant in the Ticket to Work program?

An EN must—

(a) Enter into an agreement with us.

(b) Serve a prescribed service area. The EN must designate the geographic area in which it will provide services. This will be designated in the EN's agreement with us.

(c) Provide services directly, or enter into agreements with other entities to provide employment services, vocational rehabilitation services, or other support services to beneficiaries with tickets.

(d) Ensure that employment services, vocational rehabilitation services, and other support services provided under the Ticket to Work program are provided under appropriate individual work plans (IWPs).

(e) Elect a payment system at the time of signing an agreement with us (see § 411.505).

(f) Develop and implement each IWP in partnership with each beneficiary receiving services in a manner that affords the beneficiary the opportunity to exercise informed choice in selecting an employment goal and specific services needed to achieve that employment goal. Each IWP must meet the requirements described in § 411.465.

§ 411.321 Under what conditions will SSA terminate an agreement with an EN due to inadequate performance?

We will terminate our agreement with an EN if it does not comply with the requirements under § 411.320, § 411.325, or the conditions in the agreement between SSA and the EN, including minimum performance standards relating to beneficiaries achieving self-supporting employment and leaving the benefit rolls.

§ 411.325 What reporting requirements are placed on an EN as a participant in the Ticket to Work program?

An EN must:

(a) Report to the PM in writing each time the EN accepts a ticket for assignment or the EN no longer wants a ticket assigned to it;

(b) Submit a copy of each signed IWP to the PM;

(c) Submit to the PM copies of amendments to a beneficiary's IWP;

(d) Submit to the PM a copy of any agreement the EN has established with a State VR agency regarding the conditions under which the State VR agency will provide services to beneficiaries who are referred by the EN under the Ticket to Work program;

(e) Submit information to assist the PM conducting the reviews necessary to assess a beneficiary's timely progress towards self-supporting employment to determine if a beneficiary is using a ticket for purposes of suspending continuing disability reviews (see subpart C of this part);

(f) Report to the PM the specific outcomes achieved with respect to specific services the EN provided or secured on behalf of beneficiaries whose tickets it accepted for assignment. Such reports shall conform to a national model prescribed by us and shall be submitted to the PM at least annually;

(g) Provide a copy of its most recent annual report on outcomes to each beneficiary considering assigning a ticket to it and assure that a copy of its most recent report is available to the public while ensuring that personal information on beneficiaries is kept confidential;

(h) Meet our financial reporting requirements. These requirements will be described in the agreements between ENs and the Commissioner, and will include submitting a financial report to the program manager on an annual basis;

(i) Collect and record such data as we shall require, in a form prescribed by us; and

(j) Adhere to all requirements specified in the agreement with the Commissioner and all regulatory requirements in this part 411.

[73 FR 29345, May 20, 2008]

§ 411.330 How will SSA evaluate an EN's performance?

(a) We will periodically review the results of the work of each EN to ensure effective quality assurance in the provision of services by ENs.

(b) In conducting such a review, we will solicit and consider the views of the individuals the EN serves and the PM which monitors the EN.

(c) ENs must make the results of these periodic reviews available to disabled beneficiaries to assist them in choosing among available ENs.

SUBPART F—STATE VOCATIONAL REHABILITATION AGENCIES' PARTICIPATION

PARTICIPATION IN THE TICKET TO WORK PROGRAM

§ 411.350 Must a State VR agency participate in the Ticket to Work program?

A State VR agency may elect, but is not required, to participate in the Ticket to Work program as an EN. The State VR agency may elect on a case-by-case basis to participate in the Ticket to Work program as an EN, or it may elect to provide services to beneficiaries under the VR cost reimbursement option. (See § 411.115(s) for a definition of the VR cost reimbursement option.)

[73 FR 29345, May 20, 2008]

§ 411.355 What payment options does a State VR agency have?

(a) The Ticket to Work program provides different payment options that are available to a State VR agency for providing services to disabled beneficiaries who have a ticket. A State VR agency participates in the program in one of two ways when providing services to a particular disabled beneficiary under the program. On a case-by-case basis, the State VR agency may participate either—

(1) As an employment network (EN); or

(2) Under the cost reimbursement payment system (see subpart V of part 404 and subpart V of part 416 of this chapter).

(b) When the State VR agency serves a beneficiary with a ticket as an EN, the State VR agency will use the EN payment system it has elected for this purpose, either the outcome payment system or the outcome-milestone payment system (described in subpart H of this part). The State VR agency will have periodic opportunities to change the payment system it uses when serving as an EN.

(c) The State VR agency may seek payment only under its elected EN payment system whenever it serves as an EN. When serving a beneficiary who does not have a ticket that can be assigned pursuant to § 411.140, the State VR agency may seek payment only under the cost reimbursement payment system.

(d) [Reserved by 73 FR 29345]

[73 FR 29345, May 20, 2008]

§ 411.360 [Reserved by 73 FR 29345]

[73 FR 29345, May 20, 2008]

§ 411.365 How does a State VR agency notify us about its choice of a payment system for use when functioning as an EN?

(a) The State VR agency must send us a letter telling us which EN payment system it will use when it functions as an EN with respect to a beneficiary who has a ticket.

(b) The director of the State agency administering or supervising the administration of the State plan approved under title I of the Rehabilitation Act of 1973, as amended (29 U.S.C. 720 et seq.), or the director's designee must sign the State VR agency's letter described in paragraph (a) of this section.

[73 FR 29345, May 20, 2008]

§ 411.370 [Reserved by 73 FR 29345]

[73 FR 29345, May 20, 2008]

§ 411.375 Does a State VR agency continue to provide services under the requirements of the State plan approved under title I of the Rehabilitation Act of 1973, as amended (29 U.S.C. 720 et seq.), when functioning as an EN?

Yes. The State VR agency must continue to provide services under the requirements of the State plan approved under title I of the Rehabilitation Act of 1973, as amended (29 U.S.C. 720 et seq.), even when functioning as an EN.

TICKET STATUS

§ 411.380 What does a State VR agency do if the State VR agency wants to determine whether a person seeking services has a ticket?

A State VR agency can contact the Program Manager (PM) to determine if a person seeking VR services has a ticket and, if so, whether the ticket may be assigned to the State VR agency (see § 411.140) or reassigned to the State VR agency (see § 411.150). (See § 411.115(k) for a definition of the PM.)

§ 411.385 What does a State VR agency do if a beneficiary who is eligible for VR services has a ticket that is available for assignment or reassignment?

(a) Once the State VR agency determines that a beneficiary is eligible for VR services, the beneficiary and a representative of the State VR agency must agree to and sign the individualized plan for employment (IPE) required under section 102(b) of the Rehabilitation Act of 1973, as amended (29 U.S.C. 722(b)). The State VR agency must submit the following information to the PM in order for the beneficiary's ticket to be considered in use:

(1) A statement that an IPE has been agreed to and signed by both the beneficiary and a representative of the State VR agency;

(2) A statement of the vocational goal outlined in the beneficiary's IPE; and

(3) A statement of the State VR agency's selection of the payment system (either the cost reimbursement payment system or the previously elected EN payment system) under which the State VR agency will seek payment for providing services to the beneficiary.

(b) This information must be submitted to the PM in a format prescribed by us and must include the signatures of both the beneficiary, or a representative of the beneficiary, and a representative of the State VR agency.

[73 FR 29345, May 20, 2008]

§ 411.390 What does a State VR agency do if a beneficiary to whom it is already providing services has a ticket that is available for assignment?

If a beneficiary who is receiving services from the State VR agency under an existing IPE becomes eligible for a ticket that is available for assignment, the State VR agency must submit the information required in § 411.385(a) to the PM. We require this information in order for the beneficiary's ticket to be considered in use. If a beneficiary who is receiving services from the State VR agency under an existing IPE becomes eligible for a ticket that is available for assignment, the State VR agency is limited to the cost reimbursement payment system, unless both the beneficiary and the State VR agency agree to have the ticket assigned to the State VR agency.

[73 FR 29345, May 20, 2008]

§ 411.395 Is a State VR agency required to provide periodic reports?

(a) For cases where a State VR agency provided services functioning as an EN, the State VR agency will be required to prepare periodic reports on the specific outcomes achieved with respect to the specific services the State VR agency provided to or secured for disabled beneficiaries whose tickets it accepted for assignment. These reports must be submitted to the PM at least annually.

(b) Regardless of the payment method selected, a State VR agency must submit information to assist the PM conducting the reviews necessary to assess a beneficiary's timely progress toward self-supporting employment to determine if a beneficiary is using a ticket for purposes of suspending continuing disability reviews (see §§ 411.190, 411.195 and 411.200).

REFERRALS BY EMPLOYMENT NETWORKS TO STATE VR AGENCIES

§ 411.400 Can an EN to which a beneficiary's ticket is assigned refer the beneficiary to a State VR agency for services?

Yes. An EN may refer a beneficiary it is serving under the Ticket to Work program to a State VR agency for services. However, a referral can be made only if the State VR agency and the EN have an agreement that specifies the conditions under which services will be provided by the State VR agency. This agreement must be in writing and signed by the State VR agency and the EN prior to the EN referring any beneficiary to the State VR agency for services.

AGREEMENTS BETWEEN EMPLOYMENT NETWORKS AND STATE VR AGENCIES

§ 411.405 When does an agreement between an EN and the State VR agency have to be in place?

Each EN must have an agreement with the State VR agency prior to referring a beneficiary it is serving under the Ticket to Work program to the State VR agency for specific services.

§ 411.410 Does each referral from an EN to a State VR agency require its own agreement?

No. The agreements between ENs and State VR agencies should be broad-based and apply to all beneficiaries who may be referred by the EN to the State VR agency for services, although an EN and a State VR agency may want to enter into an individualized agreement to meet the needs of a single beneficiary.

§ 411.415 Who will verify the establishment of agreements between ENs and State VR agencies?

The PM will verify the establishment of these agreements. Each EN is required to submit a copy of the agreement it has established with the State VR agency to the PM.

§ 411.420 What information should be included in an agreement between an EN and a State VR agency?

The agreement between an EN and a State VR agency should state the conditions under which the State VR agency will provide services to a beneficiary when the beneficiary is referred by the EN to the State VR agency for services. Examples of this information include—

(a) Procedures for making referrals and sharing information that will assist in providing services;

(b) A description of the financial responsibilities of each party to the agreement;

(c) The terms and procedures under which the EN will pay the State VR agency for providing services; and

(d) Procedures for resolving disputes under the agreement.

§ 411.425 What should a State VR agency do if it gets an attempted referral from an EN and no agreement has been established between the EN and the State VR agency?

The State VR agency should contact the EN to discuss the need to establish an agreement. If the State VR agency and the EN are not able to negotiate acceptable terms for an agreement, the State VR agency should notify the PM that an attempted referral has been made without an agreement.

§ 411.430 What should the PM do when it is informed that an EN has attempted to make a referral to a State VR agency without an agreement being in place?

The PM will contact the EN to explain that a referral cannot be made to the State VR agency unless an agreement has been established that sets out the conditions under which services will be provided when a beneficiary's ticket is assigned to the EN and the EN is referring the beneficiary to the State VR agency for specific services.

RESOLVING DISPUTES ARISING UNDER AGREEMENTS BETWEEN EMPLOYMENT NETWORKS AND STATE VR AGENCIES

§ 411.435 How will disputes arising under the agreements between ENs and State VR agencies be resolved?

Disputes arising under agreements between ENs and State VR agencies must be resolved using the following steps:

(a) When procedures for resolving disputes are spelled out in the agreement between the EN and the State VR agency, those procedures must be used.

(b) If procedures for resolving disputes are not included in the agreement between the EN and the State VR agency and procedures for resolving disputes under contracts and interagency agreements are provided for in State law or administrative procedures, the State procedures must be used to resolve disputes under agreements between ENs and State VR agencies.

(c) If procedures for resolving disputes are not spelled out in the agreement or in State law or administrative procedures, the EN or the State VR agency may request that the PM recommend a resolution to the dispute.

(1) The request must be in writing and include:

(i) a copy of the agreement;

(ii) information on the issue(s) in dispute; and

(iii) information on the position of both the EN and the State VR agency regarding the dispute.

(2) The PM has 20 calendar days after receiving a written request to recommend a resolution to the dispute. If either the EN or the State VR agency does not agree with the PM's recommended resolution to the dispute, the EN or the State VR agency has 30 calendar days after receiving the PM's recommendation to request a decision by us on the matter in dispute.

SUBPART G—REQUIREMENTS FOR INDIVIDUAL WORK PLANS

§ 411.450 What is an Individual Work Plan?

An individual work plan (IWP) is a required written document signed by an employment network (EN) (other than a State VR agency) and a beneficiary, or a representative of a beneficiary, with a ticket. It is developed and implemented in partnership when a beneficiary and an EN have come to a mutual understanding to work together to pursue the beneficiary's employment goal under the Ticket to Work program.

§ 411.455 What is the purpose of an IWP?

The purpose of an IWP is to outline the specific employment services, vocational rehabilitation services and other support services that the EN and beneficiary have determined are necessary to achieve the beneficiary's stated employment goal. An IWP provides written documentation for both the EN and beneficiary. Both parties should develop and implement the IWP in partnership. The EN shall develop and implement the plan in a manner that gives the beneficiary the opportunity to exercise informed choice in selecting an employment goal. Specific services needed to achieve the designated employment goal are discussed and agreed to by both parties.

§ 411.460 Who is responsible for determining what information is contained in the IWP?

The beneficiary and the EN share the responsibility for determining the employment goal and the specific services needed to achieve that employment goal. The EN will present information and options in a way that affords the beneficiary the opportunity to exercise informed choice in selecting an employment goal and specific services needed to achieve that employment goal.

§ 411.465 What are the minimum requirements for an IWP?

(a) An IWP must include at least—

(1) A statement of the vocational goal developed with the beneficiary, including, as appropriate, goals for earnings and job advancement;

(2) A statement of the services and supports necessary for the beneficiary to accomplish that goal;

(3) A statement of any terms and conditions related to the provision of these services and supports;

(4) A statement that the EN may not request or receive any compensation for the costs of services and supports from the beneficiary;

(5) A statement of the conditions under which an EN may amend the IWP or terminate the relationship;

(6) A statement of the beneficiary's rights under the Ticket to Work program, including the right to retrieve the ticket at any time if the beneficiary is dissatisfied with the services being provided by the EN;

(7) A statement of the remedies available to the beneficiary, including information on the availability of advocacy services and assistance in resolving disputes through the State Protection and Advocacy (P&A) System;

(8) A statement of the beneficiary's rights to privacy and confidentiality regarding personal information, including information about the beneficiary's disability;

(9) A statement of the beneficiary's right to seek to amend the IWP (the IWP can be amended if both the beneficiary and the EN agree to the change); and

(10) A statement of the beneficiary's right to have a copy of the IWP made available to the beneficiary, including in an accessible format chosen by the beneficiary.

(b) The EN will be responsible for ensuring that each IWP contains this information.

§ 411.470 When does an IWP become effective?

(a) An IWP becomes effective if the following requirements are met—

(1) It has been signed by the beneficiary or the beneficiary's representative, and by a representative of the EN;

(2)(i) The beneficiary is eligible to assign his or her ticket under § 411.140(a); or

(ii) The beneficiary is eligible to reassign his or her ticket under § 411.150(a) and (b); and

(3) A representative of the EN submits a copy of the signed IWP to the PM and the PM receives the copy of the IWP.

(b) If all of the requirements in paragraph (a) of this section are met, the IWP will be effective on the first day on which the requirements of paragraphs (a)(1) and (a)(2) of this section are met.

SUBPART H—EMPLOYMENT NETWORK PAYMENT SYSTEMS

§ 411.500 Definitions of terms used in this subpart.

(a) Payment calculation base means for any calendar year—

(1) In connection with a title II disability beneficiary (including a concurrent title II/title XVI disability beneficiary), the average monthly disability insurance benefit payable under section 223 of the Act for months during the preceding calendar year to all beneficiaries who are in current pay status for the month for which the benefit is payable; and

(2) In connection with a title XVI disability beneficiary (who is not concurrently a title II disability beneficiary), the average monthly payment of Supplemental Security Income (SSI) benefits based on disability payable under title XVI (excluding State supplementation) for months during the preceding calendar year to all beneficiaries who—

(i) Have attained age 18 but have not attained age 65;

(ii) Are not concurrent title II/title XVI beneficiaries; and

(iii) Are in current pay status for the month for which the payment is made.

(b) Outcome payment period means a period of 36 months for a title II disability beneficiary or a period of 60 months for a title XVI disability beneficiary who is not concurrently a title II disability beneficiary, not necessarily consecutive, for which Social Security disability benefits and Federal SSI cash benefits are not payable to the beneficiary because of the performance of substantial gainful activity (SGA) or by reason of earnings from work activity. The outcome payment period begins with the first month, ending after the date on which the ticket was first assigned to an EN (or to a State VR agency acting as an EN), for which such benefits are not payable to the beneficiary because of SGA or by reason of earnings from work activity. The outcome payment period ends as follows:

(1) For a title II disability beneficiary (including a concurrent title II/title XVI disability beneficiary), the outcome payment period ends with the 36th month, consecutive or otherwise, ending after the date on which the ticket was first assigned to an EN (or to a State VR agency acting as an EN), for which Social Security disability benefits and Federal SSI cash benefits are not payable to the beneficiary because of earnings from work activity (except as provided for in § 411.551).

(2) For a title XVI disability beneficiary who is not concurrently a title II disability beneficiary, the outcome payment period ends with the 60th month, consecutive or otherwise, ending after the date on which the ticket was first assigned to an EN (or to a State VR agency acting as an EN), for which Federal SSI cash benefits are not payable to the beneficiary by reason of earnings from work activity (except as provided for in § 411.551).

(c) Outcome payment system is a system providing a schedule of payments to an EN (or a State VR agency acting as an EN) for each month, during an individual's outcome payment period, for which Social Security disability benefits and Federal SSI cash benefits are not payable to the individual because of work or earnings.

(d) Outcome payment means the payment for an outcome payment month.

(e) Outcome payment month means a month, during the beneficiary's outcome payment period, for which Social Security disability benefits and Federal SSI cash benefits are not payable to the beneficiary because of work or earnings.

(f) Outcome–milestone payment system is a system providing a schedule of payments to an EN (or State VR agency acting as an EN) that includes, in addition to any outcome payments which may be made during the individual's outcome payment period, payments for completion by a title II or title XVI disability beneficiary of up to four Phase 1 milestones; and up to eleven Phase 2 milestones for a title II disability beneficiary or a concurrent beneficiary or up to eighteen Phase 2 milestones for a title XVI disability beneficiary who is not a concurrent title II disability beneficiary.

(1) Phase 1 milestones are based on the beneficiary achieving a level of earnings that reflects initial efforts at self-supporting employment. They are based on the earnings threshold that we use to establish a trial work period service month as defined in § 404.1592(b) of this chapter. We use this threshold amount as defined in § 404.1592(b) of this chapter in order to measure whether the beneficiary's earnings level meets the milestone objective.

(2) Phase 2 milestones are based on the beneficiary achieving a level of earnings that reflects substantial efforts at self-supporting employment. They are based on the earnings threshold that we use to determine if work activity is SGA. We use the SGA earnings threshold amount in § 404.1574(b)(2) of this chapter. We use the SGA threshold amounts in order to measure whether the beneficiary's gross earnings level meets the milestone objective.

(g) Transition case is a case where milestones or outcomes had been attained before July 21, 2008 (that is, the work required to meet such a milestone or outcome had been completed by that date). Section 411.551 explains how subsequent payments will be made to the EN (or State VR agency acting as an EN) on a transition case.

(h) Reconciliation payment is a final payment equal to the milestone payments that are unpaid when the beneficiary enters the outcome payment period before all the milestone payments are paid (see §§ 411.525(c) and 411.536).

[73 FR 29345, May 20, 2008]

§ 411.505 How is an EN paid?

An EN (including a State VR agency acting as an EN) can elect to be paid under either the outcome payment system or the outcome-milestone payment system. The EN will elect a payment system at the time the EN enters into an agreement with us. (For State VR agencies, see § 411.365.) The EN (or State VR agency) may periodically change its elected EN payment system as described in § 411.515.

[73 FR 29346, May 20, 2008]

§ 411.510 How is the State VR agency paid under the Ticket to Work program?

(a) The State VR agency's payment choices are described in § 411.355.

(b) The State VR agency's decision to serve the beneficiary must be communicated to the program manager (PM). (See § 411.115(k) for a definition of the PM.) At the same time, the State VR agency must notify the PM of its selected payment system for that beneficiary.

(c) If a beneficiary who is receiving services from the State VR agency under an existing IPE becomes eligible for a ticket that is available for assignment, the State VR agency is limited to the cost reimbursement payment system, unless both the beneficiary and the State VR agency agree to have the ticket assigned to the State VR agency (see § 411.390).

[73 FR 29346, May 20, 2008]

§ 411.515 Can the EN change its elected payment system?

(a) Yes. Any change by an EN in its elected EN payment system will apply to beneficiaries who assign their ticket to the EN after the EN's change in election becomes effective. A change in the EN's election will become effective with the first day of the month following the month in which the EN notifies us of the change. For beneficiaries who already assigned their ticket to the EN under the EN's earlier elected payment system, the EN's earlier elected payment system will continue to apply. These rules also apply to a change by a State VR agency in its elected EN payment system for cases in which the State VR agency serves a beneficiary as an EN.

(b) After an EN (or a State VR agency) first elects an EN payment system, the EN (or State VR agency) can choose to make one change in its elected payment system in each calendar year (January–December) thereafter. The first EN payment system election constitutes the only election an EN may make for that calendar year.

(c) [Reserved by 73 FR 29346]

[73 FR 29346, May 20, 2008]

§ 411.520 How are beneficiaries whose tickets are assigned to an EN affected by a change in that EN's elected payment system?

A change in an EN's (or State VR agency's) elected payment system has no effect upon the beneficiaries who have assigned their ticket to the EN (or State VR agency).

§ 411.525 What payments are available under each of the EN payment systems?

(a) For payments for outcome payment months, both EN payment systems use the payment calculation base as defined in § 411.500(a)(1) or (a)(2), as appropriate.

(1)(i) Under the outcome payment system, we can pay up to 36 outcome payments to the EN (or State VR agency acting as an EN) for a title II disability beneficiary (including a concurrent title II/title XVI disability beneficiary). We can pay up to 60 outcome payments to the EN (or State VR agency acting as an EN) for a title XVI disability beneficiary who is not concurrently a title II disability beneficiary. For each month during the beneficiary's outcome payment period for which Social Security disability benefits and Federal SSI cash benefits are not payable to the beneficiary because of the performance of SGA or by reason of earnings from work activity, the EN (or the State VR agency acting as an EN) is eligible for a monthly outcome payment. Payment for an outcome payment month under the outcome payment system is equal to 67% of the payment calculation base for the calendar year in which such month occurs, rounded to the nearest whole dollar (see § 411.550).

(ii) If a disabled beneficiary's entitlement to Social Security disability benefits ends (see §§ 404.316(b), 404.337(b) and 404.352(b) of this chapter) or eligibility for SSI benefits based on disability or blindness terminates (see § 416.1335 of this chapter) because of the performance of SGA or by reason of earnings from work activity, we will consider any month after the month with which such entitlement ends or eligibility terminates to be a month for which Social Security disability benefits and Federal SSI cash benefits are not payable to the individual because of work or earnings if—

(A) The individual has gross earnings from employment (or net earnings from self-employment as defined in § 416.1110(b) of this chapter) in that month that are more than the SGA threshold amount in § 404.1574(b)(2) of this chapter (or in § 404.1584(d) of this chapter for an individual who is statutorily blind); and

(B) The individual is not entitled to any monthly benefits under title II or eligible for any benefits under title XVI for that month.

(2) Under the outcome-milestone payment system:

(i) We can pay the EN (or State VR agency acting as an EN) for up to four Phase 1 milestones attained within the required earnings period for a title II or title XVI disability beneficiary who has assigned his or her ticket to the EN (or State VR agency acting as an EN). The first Phase 1 milestone is met when a beneficiary has worked in a month and earned at least 50% of the amount of earnings considered to represent a trial work period service month as defined in § 404.1592(b) of this chapter. The second Phase 1 milestone is met after a beneficiary has worked for three months within a six-month period and has gross earnings in each of those three months equal to or greater than a trial work period service amount as defined in § 404.1592(b) of this chapter. The third Phase 1 milestone is met after a beneficiary has worked for a total of six months within a twelve-month period and had gross earnings in each of those six months equal to a trial work period service amount as defined in § 404.1592(b) of this chapter. The fourth Phase 1 milestone is met after a beneficiary has worked a total of nine months within an 18–month period and had gross earnings in each of those nine months equal to a trial work period service amount as defined in § 404.1592(b) of this chapter and the EN has substantially completed the services agreed to in the IWP/IPE, including any amendments. Earnings used to meet the first, second or third Phase 1 milestone may be counted again when determining if a later Phase 1 milestone is met, provided the earlier earnings fall within the relevant time period for meeting the later milestone.

(ii) We can also pay the EN (or State VR agency acting as an EN) up to eleven Phase 2 milestones achieved by a title II disability beneficiary (including a concurrent title II/title XVI disability beneficiary) or up to eighteen Phase 2 milestones achieved by a title XVI disability beneficiary (who is not concurrently a title II disability beneficiary) who has assigned his or her ticket to the EN (or State VR agency acting as an EN). A Phase 2 milestone is met for each calendar month in which the beneficiary has worked and has gross earnings from employment (or net earnings from self-employment as defined in § 404.1080 of this chapter) in that month that are more than the SGA threshold amount as defined in § 404.1574 of this chapter.

(iii) We pay available milestone payments in sequence except when the beneficiary's outcome period begins before the beneficiary has achieved all Phase 1 and Phase 2 milestones. Example: The individual, in the first month of employment after assigning the ticket, earns above the SGA level. Despite having exceeded trial work period level earnings and earned above the SGA level as required for Phase 2 payments in paragraph (a)(2)(ii) of this section, based on the individual's earning we would pay the EN the sequentially available milestone, which in this case would be Phase 1, milestone 1.

(iv) In addition to the milestone payments, monthly outcome payments can be paid to the EN (or State VR agency acting as an EN) during the outcome payment period.

(b) The outcome-milestone payment system is designed so that the total payments to the EN (or the State VR agency acting as an EN) for a beneficiary are less than the total amount that would have been paid if the EN were paid under the outcome payment system. Under the outcome-milestone payment system, the total payment to the EN (or the State VR agency acting as an EN) is about 90% of the total that would have been potentially payable under the outcome payment system for the same beneficiary.

(c) Except as provided in § 411.536 (reconciliation payments) the milestones for which payments may be made must occur prior to the beginning of the beneficiary's outcome payment period.

(d) We will pay an EN (or State VR agency acting as an EN) to which the beneficiary has assigned a ticket for milestones or outcomes achieved only in months prior to the month in which the ticket terminates (see § 411.155). We will not pay a milestone or outcome payment to an EN (or State VR agency acting as an EN) based on a beneficiary's work or earnings activity in or after the month in which the ticket terminates.

(e) If a title XVI disability beneficiary becomes entitled to title II benefits after we authorize the first milestone or outcome payment, we will continue to calculate the EN payments using title XVI payment calculation base under the outcome payment system on the basis of paragraph (a)(1)(i) and under the outcome-milestone payment system on the basis of paragraph (a)(2). This applies even if the title XVI eligibility is subsequently terminated and the person becomes only a title II beneficiary.

[73 FR 29346, May 20, 2008]

§ 411.530 [Reserved by 73 FR 29347]

[73 FR 29347, May 20, 2008]

§ 411.535 Under what circumstances will milestones be paid?

(a)(1)(i) Under the outcome-milestone payment system, an EN (or a State VR agency acting as an EN) can earn up to four Phase 1 milestone payments for serving beneficiaries whose gross earnings were less than the trial work level in each of the 18 months before the ticket was first assigned to an EN. All work and earnings counted toward reaching the four Phase 1 milestones must occur after the ticket is assigned and before the beginning of the beneficiary's outcome payment period (see § 411.500(f)) except as provided in § 411.536 (reconciliation payments).

(ii) Significant work activity prior to ticket assignment will limit the availability of Phase 1 milestone payments. The PM will make this assessment of work activity prior to the first ticket assignment on each ticket, irrespective of the EN's chosen payment system, in order to determine how many milestone payments may be available for serving an individual in the Ticket to Work program. The first Phase 1 milestone payment is not available to be made to an EN if the beneficiary has worked above the trial work level in the calendar month prior to the first ticket assignment on each ticket in the Ticket to Work program. The second Phase 1 milestone payment is not available if the beneficiary has worked above the trial work level in three of the six months prior to the first ticket assignment on each ticket in the Ticket to Work program. The third Phase 1 milestone is not available if the beneficiary has worked above the trial work level in six of the twelve months prior to the first ticket assignment on each ticket in the Ticket to Work program. The fourth Phase 1 milestone is not available if the beneficiary has worked above the trial work level in nine of the 18 months prior to the first ticket assignment on each ticket in the Ticket to Work program.

(iii) If a beneficiary had a ticket that otherwise was available for assignment and chose to receive services under an IPE from a State VR agency that elected the VR cost reimbursement option, payment of Phase 1 milestones to an EN or a different VR agency acting as an EN with respect to the same ticket is precluded if the State VR Agency that elected the VR cost reimbursement option achieved an employment outcome (as described in 34 CFR 361.56) before case closure. An EN or a different VR agency acting as an EN can be paid Phase 2 milestones as described in paragraph (2) of this section with respect to this ticket.

(2) Under the outcome-milestone payment system, an EN can receive up to eleven Phase 2 milestone payments for work by a title II disability beneficiary (including a concurrent title II/title XVI disability beneficiary), or up to eighteen Phase 2 milestone payments for work by a title XVI disability beneficiary. Earnings prior to the first assignment of the ticket in the Ticket to Work program are not taken into account when determining whether sufficient earnings exist for payment of Phase 2 milestones.

(3) If the beneficiary's outcome payment period begins before the beneficiary has achieved all Phase 1 and Phase 2 milestones, then we will pay the EN a final payment in accordance with § 411.536 (reconciliation payments) to account for unpaid milestone payments that had been available when the ticket was first assigned.

(b) An EN can be paid for a milestone only if the milestone is attained after a beneficiary has assigned his or her ticket to the EN. See § 411.575 for other milestone payment criteria.

[73 FR 29347, May 20, 2008]

§ 411.536 Under what circumstances can we make a reconciliation payment under the outcome-milestone payment system?

When the beneficiary's outcome payment period begins before the beneficiary has attained all Phase 1 and Phase 2 milestones, we will pay the EN (or a State VR agency acting as an EN) a reconciliation payment. The reconciliation payment will equal the total amount of the milestone payments that were available with respect to that ticket, when the ticket was first assigned, but that have not yet been paid. The reconciliation payment will be based on the payment calculation base for the calendar year in which the first month of the beneficiary's outcome period occurs, rounded to the nearest whole dollar. The payment will be made after an EN has qualified for 12 outcome payments. Where multiple ENs had the ticket assigned at some time, the PM will apply the rule under § 411.560 to determine the allocation of the reconciliation payment.

[73 FR 29347, May 20, 2008]

§ 411.540 How are the payment amounts calculated for each of the milestones?

(a) For both title II disability beneficiaries and title XVI disability beneficiaries, the payment amount for each of the Phase 1 milestone payments is equal to 120% of the payment calculation base for title II (as defined in § 411.500(a)(1)) for the calendar year in which the month of attainment of the milestone occurs, rounded to the nearest whole dollar.

(b) The payment amount for each of the Phase 2 milestones:

(1) For title II disability beneficiaries (including concurrent title II/title XVI disability beneficiaries) is equal to 36% of the payment calculation base as defined in § 411.500(a)(1) for the calendar year in which the month of attainment of the milestone occurs, rounded to the nearest whole dollar;

(2) For title XVI beneficiaries (who are not concurrently title II disability beneficiaries) is equal to 36% of the payment calculation base as defined in § 411.500(a)(2) for the calendar year in which the month of attainment of the milestone occurs, rounded to the nearest whole dollar.

[73 FR 29347, May 20, 2008]

§ 411.545 How are the outcome payments calculated under the outcome-milestone payment system?

The amount of each monthly outcome payment under the outcome-milestone payment system is calculated as follows:

(a) For title II disability beneficiaries (including concurrent title II/title XVI disability beneficiaries), an outcome payment is equal to 36 percent of the payment calculation base as defined in § 411.500(a)(1) for the calendar year in which the month occurs, rounded to the nearest whole dollar;

(b) For title XVI disability beneficiaries (who are not concurrently title II/title XVI disability beneficiaries), an outcome payment is equal to 36% of the payment calculation base as defined in § 411.500(a)(2) for the calendar year in which the month occurs, rounded to the nearest whole dollar.

(c) The following chart provides an example of how an EN could receive milestone and outcome payments:

Outcome-Milestone Payment Table

Chart I—New Outcome-Milestone Payment Table

[2008 figures for illustration only]

Payment type	Beneficiary earnings	Title II amount of payment	Title XVI amount of payment
Phase 1 (120% of Title II PCB)			
Milestone 1	$335/mo. $670/mo. x 3 mo. work in a 6-month period	$1,177	$1,177
Milestone 2		$1,177	$1,177
Milestone 3	$670/mo. x 6 mo. work in a 12-month period	$1,177	$1,177
Milestone 4	$670/mo. x 9 mo. work in an 18-month period	$1,177	$1,177
Total Phase 1 milestones		$4,708	$4,708
Phase 2 (36% of PCB)	Gross Earnings>SGA		
Title II milestones 1-11		$353 x 11=$3,883	
Title XVI milestones 1-18			$203 x 18 = $3,654
Total Phase 1 + 2		$8,591	$8,362
	Outcome payments (36% of PCB)		
Title II = 1-36	Monthly cash benefit not payable due to SGA	$353 x 36 = $12,708	

Title XVI = 1-60 . . .	Sufficient earnings for federal cash . . benefits = "0"	203 x 60 = $12,180
Total milestone and outcome payments		$21,299 . . . $20,542

Definitions and amounts: Payment Calculation Base (PCB)—The average title II disability insurance benefit payable under section 223 of the Social Security Act for all beneficiaries for months during the preceding calendar year; and the average payment of supplemental security income benefits based on disability payable under title XVI (excluding State supplementation) for months during the preceding calendar year to all beneficiaries who have attained 18 years of age but have not attained 65 years of age. (2008 title II = $981.17, title XVI = $563.35).

Gross earnings requirements for Phase 1 are based on Trial Work level amounts.

For Phase 1 milestones only, the payments are calculated for both title XVI and title II beneficiaries using the higher title II payment calculation base. All other payments are based on a percentage of the Payment Calculation Base (PCB) for the respective program (title XVI or title II). See § 411.535 for a discussion of the circumstances under which we will pay milestones.

Phase 1 milestones = 120% of PCB.

Phase 2 milestones = 36% of PCB.

Outcome payments (under the outcome-milestone payment system) = 36% of PCB Earnings used to meet the first, second, or third Phase 1 milestone may be counted again when determining if a later milestone is met, provided the earlier earnings fall within the relevant time period for meeting the later Phase 1 milestone (see 411.525(a)(2) for the relevant time period for each milestone).

[73 FR 29348, May 20, 2008]

§ 411.550 How are the outcome payments calculated under the outcome payment system?

The amount of each monthly outcome payment under the outcome payment system is calculated as follows:

(1) For title II disability beneficiaries (including concurrent title II/title XVI disability beneficiaries), an outcome payment is equal to 67% of the payment calculation base as defined in § 411.500(a)(1) for the calendar year in which the month occurs, rounded to the nearest whole dollar;

(2) For title XVI disability beneficiaries (who are not concurrently title II/title XVI disability beneficiaries), an outcome payment is equal to 67% of the payment calculation base as defined in § 411.500(a)(2) for the calendar year in which the month occurs, rounded to the nearest whole dollar.

Chart II—New Outcome Payment System Table—Title II and Concurrent
[2008 figures for illustration only]

Payment type	Beneficiary earnings	Title II amount of monthly outcome payment	Title II total outcome payments
Outcome payments 1-36 (67% of PCB)	Monthly cash benefit not payable due to SGA	$657.00	$23,652

Chart III—New Outcome Payment System Table—Title XVI Only
[2008 figures for illustration only]

Payment type	Beneficiary earnings	Title XVI amount of monthly outcome payment	Title XVI total outcome payments
Outcome payments 1-60 (67% of PCB)	Earnings sufficient to "0" out Federal SSI cash benefits	$377.00	$22,620

Note: Outcome payment (outcome payment system) = 67% of PCB Individual payments are rounded to the nearest dollar amount.

2008 non-blind SGA level = $940.

2008 Blind SGA = $1570.

2008 TWP service amount = $670.

[73 FR 29348, May 20, 2008]

§ 411.551 How are EN payments calculated for transition cases pending on July 21, 2008?

A Transition case is a case where a ticket had been assigned and milestones or outcomes had been attained as of June 30, 2008 (that is, the individual has completed the necessary work to trigger a milestone or outcome payment before July 21, 2008 regardless of whether the payment has actually been made). We will pay outcome and milestone payments at the rate in effect when the work leading to such outcome or milestone is attained. Since milestone and outcome payments are numbered and attained in sequence, the EN must request the final payment for which it expects payment under the prior rules before we can determine the number of the milestone or outcome payment that represents the first payment after July 21, 2008. In addition, for cases on which an EN has attained an outcome payment before July 21, 2008 we must know the sum of the amount paid on the ticket before we can determine the remaining amount that can be paid in outcome payments on the ticket. Therefore, with respect to a ticket, we will only accept payment requests for milestones or outcomes attained under the prior rules until March 31, 2009 or until we make the first payment on the ticket under § 411.525. Payments to an EN (or State VR agency acting as an EN) after July 21, 2008 on a transition case will be made as follows:

(a) The four milestones under the prior rules will be equated with the four Phase 1 milestones available under the rules after July 21, 2008. For example, if a beneficiary had attained milestone 1 under our prior rules (1 month above the gross SGA level, e.g., $940 in 2008), then the next milestone to be achieved would be Phase 1 milestone 2 under these rules (work in three months with gross earnings in each of these months equal to a trial work period service month, e.g., $670 in 2008).

(b) If the beneficiary had attained all four of the milestones under the prior rules, the next milestone to be achieved would be the first Phase 2 milestone (a calendar month in which the beneficiary has worked and has gross earnings from employment or net earnings from self-employment that are more than the substantial gainful activity threshold level, e.g., $900 in 2007).

(c) The maximum number of outcome payments available to an EN with respect to a ticket for a transition case will be computed as follows:

(1) First, we will compute the total dollar amount already paid or payable with respect to a ticket, including all outcome and milestone payments.

(2) Then, we will subtract the total dollar amount already paid from the total value of the ticket under the new rules for the year when these rules take effect. The total value of the ticket will be calculated based on the elected payment system for the beneficiary, i.e., the outcome or the outcome-milestone payment system, and on the appropriate payment calculation base for either a title II disability beneficiary (including a concurrent title II and title XVI disability) or a title XVI disability beneficiary (see §§ 411.500 and 411.505). For accounting purposes, we will use the payment calculation base for 2008 and assume that all payments could be earned in that year in calculating the total value of the ticket.

(3) We then will divide this amount by the applicable outcome payment amount (whether title II or title XVI) payable for 2008 and round the result in accordance with customary rounding principles. The resulting number represents the number of outcome payments available to be paid with respect to the ticket. In no case can this number exceed 60.

[73 FR 29349, May 20, 2008]

§ 411.552 What effect will the subsequent entitlement to title II benefits have on EN payments for title XVI beneficiaries after they assign their ticket?

If a beneficiary is only eligible for title XVI benefits when we authorize the first milestone or outcome for which an EN can be paid, but the beneficiary later becomes entitled to title II benefits, we will continue to make payments as though the beneficiary were only a title XVI beneficiary, up to the maximum number of milestone and outcome payments payable for that ticket for title XVI beneficiaries. If a beneficiary who is eligible for title XVI disability benefits becomes entitled to title II disability benefits before we authorize the first milestone or outcome payment, we will make payments to the EN pursuant to the rate, payment calculation base and number of payments available for title II beneficiaries, as described in this subpart.

[73 FR 29349, May 20, 2008]

§ 411.555 Can the EN keep the milestone and outcome payments even if the beneficiary does not achieve all outcome months?

(a) Yes. The EN (or State VR agency acting as an EN) can keep each milestone and outcome payment for which the EN (or State VR agency acting as an EN) is eligible, even though the title II beneficiary does not achieve all 36 outcome months or the title XVI beneficiary does not achieve all 60 outcome months.

(b) Except as provided in paragraph (c) of this section, payments which we make or deny to an EN (or a State VR agency acting as an EN) may be subject to adjustment (including recovery, as appropriate) if we determine that more or less than the correct amount was paid. This may happen, for example, because we determine that the payment determination was in error or because of an allocation of payment under § 411.560.

(c) If we determine that an overpayment or underpayment to an EN has occurred, we will notify the EN (or State VR agency acting as an EN) of the adjustment. We will not seek an adjustment if a determination or decision about a beneficiary's right to benefits causes an overpayment to the EN. Any dispute which the EN (or State VR agency) has regarding the adjustment may be resolved under the rules in § 411.590(a) and (b).

[73 FR 29349, May 20, 2008]

§ 411.560 Is it possible to pay a milestone or outcome payment to more than one EN?

It is possible for more than one EN (including a State VR agency acting as an EN) to receive payment based on the same milestone or outcome. If the beneficiary has assigned the ticket to more than one

EN (or State VR agency acting as an EN) at different times, and more than one EN (or State VR agency) requests payment for the same milestone, outcome or reconciliation payment under its elected payment system, the PM will make a determination of the allocation of payment to each EN (or State VR agency acting as an EN). The PM will make this determination based upon the contribution of the services provided by each EN (or State VR agency acting as an EN) toward the achievement of the outcomes or milestones. Outcome and milestone payments will not be increased because the payments are shared between two or more ENs (including a State VR agency acting as an EN).

[73 FR 29350, May 20, 2008]

§ 411.565 What happens if two or more ENs qualify for payment on the same ticket but have elected different EN payment systems?

We will pay each EN (or State VR agency acting as an EN) according to its elected EN payment system in effect at the time the beneficiary assigned the ticket to the EN (or the State VR agency acting as an EN).

[73 FR 29350, May 20, 2008]

§ 411.566 May an EN use outcome or milestone payments to make payments to the beneficiary?

Yes, an EN may use milestone or outcome payments to make payments to a beneficiary.

[73 FR 29350, May 20, 2008]

§ 411.570 Can an EN request payment from the beneficiary who assigned a ticket to the EN?

No. Section 1148(b)(4) of the Act prohibits an EN from requesting or receiving compensation from the beneficiary for the services of the EN.

§ 411.575 How does the EN request payment for milestones or outcome payment months achieved by a beneficiary who assigned a ticket to the EN?

The EN (or State VR agency acting as an EN) will send its request for payment, evidence of the beneficiary's work or earnings, and other information to the PM. In addition, we or the PM may require a summary of the services provided as described in the IWP/IPE.

(a) Milestone payments.

(1) We will pay the EN (or State VR agency acting as an EN) for milestones only if—

(i) The outcome-milestone payment system was the EN's (or State VR agency's) elected payment system in effect at the time the beneficiary assigned a ticket to the EN (or the State VR agency acting as an EN);

(ii) The milestones occur prior to the outcome payment period (see § 411.500(b));

(iii) The requirements in § 411.535 are met; and

(iv) The ticket has not terminated for any of the reasons listed in § 411.155.

(2) The EN (or State VR agency acting as an EN) must request payment for each milestone attained by a beneficiary who has assigned a ticket to the EN (or State VR agency acting as an EN). The request must include evidence that the milestone was attained after ticket assignment and other information as we may require to evaluate the EN's (or State VR agency's) request. If the EN is requesting payment for months after the ticket is no longer assigned to it, the payment request shall include evidence that the services agreed to in the IWP/IPE were provided and those services contributed to the employment milestones or outcomes that the beneficiary attained in months after the ticket had been assigned to the EN. We do not have to stop monthly benefit payments to the beneficiary before we can pay the EN (or State VR agency acting as an EN) for milestones attained by the beneficiary.

(b) Outcome payments.

(1) We will pay an EN (or State VR agency acting as an EN) an outcome payment for a month if—

(i)(A) Social Security disability benefits and Federal SSI cash benefits are not payable to the individual for that month due to work or earnings; or

(B) The requirements of § 411.525(a)(1)(ii) are met in a case where the beneficiary's entitlement to Social Security disability benefits has ended or eligibility for SSI benefits based on disability or blindness has terminated because of work activity or earnings; and

(ii) We have not already paid for 36 outcome payment months for a title II disability beneficiary (or a concurrent title II/title XVI disability beneficiary), or paid for 60 outcome payment months for a title XVI disability beneficiary who is not concurrently a title II disability beneficiary, on the same ticket; and

(iii) The ticket has not terminated for any of the other reasons listed in § 411.155.

(2) The EN (or State VR agency acting as an EN) must request payment for outcome payment months. In its initial request, the EN (or State VR agency acting as an EN) must submit evidence of the beneficiary's work or earnings (e.g., a statement of monthly earnings from the employer or the employer's designated payroll preparer, or an unaltered copy of the beneficiary's pay stub). After we have started paying outcome payments to an EN (or State VR agency acting as an EN) based on evidence of the beneficiary's earnings, the EN (or State VR agency) must provide documentation of the beneficiary's continued work or earnings in such a manner or form and at such time or times as we may require. Exception: If the EN (or State VR agency) does not currently hold the ticket because it is assigned to another EN (or State VR

agency), the EN (or State VR agency) must request payment, but is not required to submit evidence of the beneficiary's work or earnings. However, if the payment request is for work the beneficiary attained in a month in which the EN no longer held the ticket, the payment request should include evidence that the services agreed to in the IWP/IPE were provided and those services contributed to the beneficiary's work.

(c) Evidence requirements for payment. As primary evidence, we require original pay slips, or oral or written statements from an employer or the employer's designated payroll preparer. In lieu of primary evidence, we accept two sources of secondary evidence, such as photocopies of pay slips, a signed beneficiary statement, State unemployment records or federal/state tax returns. The evidence must be clear and legible and include the beneficiary's name, gross earnings or net earnings from self employment, pay date and pay period of wages or monthly net earnings of self-employment earnings.

[73 FR 29350, May 20, 2008]

§ 411.580 Can an EN receive payments for milestones or outcome payment months that occur before the beneficiary assigns a ticket to the EN?

No. An EN (or State VR agency acting as an EN) may be paid only for milestones or outcome payment months that are achieved after the month in which the ticket is assigned to the EN or State VR agency acting as an EN (except as provided for in § 411.536).

[73 FR 29351, May 20, 2008]

§ 411.581 Can an EN receive milestone and outcome payments for months after a beneficiary takes his or her ticket out of assignment?

Yes. If an individual whose ticket is assigned to an EN (or State VR agency acting as an EN) takes his or her ticket out of assignment (see § 411.145), the EN (or State VR agency) can receive payments under its elected payment system for milestones or outcome payment months that occur after the ticket is taken out of assignment, provided the ticket has not terminated for any of the reasons listed in § 411.155. The PM will make a determination about eligibility for a payment based upon the contribution of services provided by an EN toward the achievement of the outcome or milestones. See § 411.560 for situations in which payment may be made to more than one EN or State VR agency based on the same milestone or outcome.

[73 FR 29351, May 20, 2008]

§ 411.582 Can a State VR agency receive payment under the cost reimbursement payment system if a continuous 9–month period of substantial gainful activity is completed after the ticket is assigned to an EN?

Yes. If a State VR agency provides services to a beneficiary under 34 CFR part 361, and elects payment under the cost reimbursement payment system under subpart V of part 404 (or subpart V of part 416) of this chapter, the State VR agency can receive payment under the cost reimbursement payment system for services provided to the beneficiary if all the requirements under subpart V of part 404 (or subpart V of part 416) of this chapter and § 411.585 are met even when these requirements are met after the ticket has been assigned to the EN. The EN can be paid during this period in accordance with §§ 411.525 and 411.535.

[73 FR 29351, May 20, 2008]

§ 411.585 Can a State VR agency and an EN both receive payment for serving the same beneficiary?

Yes. A State VR agency and an EN can both receive payment for serving the same beneficiary, but the ticket can only be assigned to one EN, including a State VR agency acting as an EN, at a time. It also cannot be assigned to an EN and placed in the VR cost reimbursement status at the same time.

(a) A State VR agency may act as an EN and serve a beneficiary. In this case, both the State VR agency acting as an EN and another EN may be eligible for payment based on the same ticket (see § 411.560).

(b) If a State VR agency is paid by us under the VR cost reimbursement option, such payment does not preclude payment by us to an EN or to another State VR agency acting as an EN under its elected EN payment system. A subsequent VR agency also may choose to be paid under the VR cost reimbursement option.

(c) If an EN or a State VR agency acting as an EN is paid by us under one of the EN payment systems, that does not preclude payment by us to a different State VR agency under the VR cost reimbursement option. The subsequent State VR agency also may choose to be paid under its elected EN payment system.

[73 FR 29351, May 20, 2008]

§ 411.587 [Reserved by 73 FR 29351]

[73 FR 29351, May 20, 2008]

§ 411.590 What can an EN do if the EN disagrees with our decision on a payment request?

(a) If an EN other than a State VR agency has a payment dispute with us, the dispute shall be resolved under the dispute resolution procedures contained in the EN's agreement with us.

(b) If a State VR agency serving a beneficiary as an EN has a dispute with us regarding payment under an

EN payment system, the State VR agency may, within 60 days of receiving notice of our decision, request reconsideration in writing. The State VR agency must send the request for reconsideration to the PM. The PM will forward to us the request for reconsideration and a recommendation. We will notify the State VR agency of our reconsidered decision in writing.

(c) An EN (including a State VR agency) cannot appeal determinations we make about an individual's right to benefits (e.g. determinations that disability benefits should be suspended, terminated, continued, denied, or stopped or started on a different date than alleged). Only the beneficiary or applicant or his or her representative can appeal these determinations. See §§ 404.900 et seq. and 416.1400 et seq. of this chapter.

(d) Determinations or decisions we make about a beneficiary's right to benefits may cause payments we have already made to an EN (or denial of payment to an EN) to be incorrect, resulting in an underpayment or overpayment to the EN. If this happens, we will make any necessary adjustments to future payments (see § 411.555). See § 411.555(c) for when we will not make an adjustment in a case in which an overpayment results from a determination or decision we make about a beneficiary's right to benefits.) While an EN cannot appeal our determination about an individual's right to benefits, the EN may furnish any evidence the EN has which relates to the issue(s) to be decided on appeal if the individual appeals our determination.
[73 FR 29351, May 20, 2008]

§ 411.595 What oversight procedures are planned for the EN payment systems?

We use audits, reviews, studies and observation of daily activities to identify areas for improvement. Internal reviews of our systems security controls are regularly performed. These reviews provide an overall assurance that our business processes are functioning as intended. The reviews also ensure that our management controls and financial management systems comply with the standards established by the Federal Managers' Financial Integrity Act and the Federal Financial Management Improvement Act. These reviews operate in accordance with the Office of Management and Budget Circulars A–123, A–127 and Appendix III to A–130. Additionally, our Executive Internal Control Committee meets periodically and provides further oversight of program and management control issues.

§ 411.597 Will SSA periodically review the outcome payment system and the outcome-milestone payment system for possible modifications?

(a) Yes. We will periodically review the system of payments and their programmatic results to determine if they provide an adequate incentive for ENs to assist beneficiaries to enter the work force, while providing for appropriate economies.

(b) We will specifically review the limitation on monthly outcome payments as a percentage of the payment calculation base, the difference in total payments between the outcome-milestone payment system and the outcome payment system, the length of the outcome payment period, and the number and amount of milestone payments, as well as the benefit savings and numbers of beneficiaries going to work. We will consider altering the payment system conditions based upon the information gathered and our determination that an alteration would better provide for the incentives and economies noted above.

SUBPART I—TICKET TO WORK PROGRAM DISPUTE RESOLUTION

DISPUTES BETWEEN BENEFICIARIES AND EMPLOYMENT NETWORKS

§ 411.600 Is there a process for resolving disputes between beneficiaries and ENs that are not State VR agencies?

Yes. After an IWP is signed, a process is available which will assure each party a full, fair and timely review of a disputed matter. This process has three steps.

(a) The beneficiary can seek a solution through the EN's internal grievance procedures.

(b) If the EN's internal grievance procedures do not result in an agreeable solution, either the beneficiary or the EN may seek a resolution from the PM. (See § 411.115(k) for a definition of the PM.)

(c) If either the beneficiary or the EN is dissatisfied with the resolution proposed by the PM, either party may request a decision from us.

§ 411.605 What are the responsibilities of the EN that is not a State VR agency regarding the dispute resolution process?

The EN must:

(a) Have grievance procedures that a beneficiary can use to seek a resolution to a dispute under the Ticket to Work program;

(b) Give each beneficiary seeking services a copy of its internal grievance procedures;

(c) Inform each beneficiary seeking services of the right to refer a dispute first to the PM for review, and then to us for a decision; and

(d) Inform each beneficiary of the availability of assistance from the State P&A system.

§ 411.610 When should a beneficiary receive information on the procedures for resolving disputes?

Each EN that is not a State VR agency must inform each beneficiary seeking services under the Ticket to Work program of the procedures for resolving disputes when—

(a) The EN and the beneficiary complete and sign the IWP;

(b) Services in the beneficiary's IWP are reduced, suspended or terminated; and

(c) A dispute arises related to the services spelled out in the beneficiary's IWP or to the beneficiary's participation in the program.

§ 411.615 How will a disputed issue be referred to the PM?

The beneficiary or the EN that is not a State VR agency may ask the PM to review a disputed issue. The PM will contact the EN to submit all relevant information within 10 working days. The information should include:

(a) A description of the disputed issue(s);

(b) A summary of the beneficiary's position, prepared by the beneficiary or a representative of the beneficiary, related to each disputed issue;

(c) A summary of the EN's position related to each disputed issue; and

(d) A description of any solutions proposed by the EN when the beneficiary sought resolution through the EN's grievance procedures, including the reasons the beneficiary rejected each proposed solution.

§ 411.620 How long does the PM have to recommend a resolution to the dispute?

The PM has 20 working days to provide a written recommendation. The recommendation should explain the reasoning for the proposed resolution.

§ 411.625 Can the beneficiary or the EN that is not a State VR agency request a review of the PM's recommendation?

(a) Yes. After receiving the PM's recommendation, either the beneficiary or the EN may request a review by us. The request must be in writing and received by the PM within 15 working days of the receipt of the PM's recommendation for resolving the dispute.

(b) The PM has 10 working days to refer the request for a review to us. The request for a review must include:

(1) A copy of the beneficiary's IWP;

(2) Information and evidence related to the disputed issue(s); and

(3) The PM's conclusion(s) and recommendation(s).

§ 411.630 Is SSA's decision final?

Yes. Our decision is final. If either the beneficiary or the EN that is not a State VR agency is unwilling to accept our decision, either has the right to terminate its relationship with the other.

§ 411.635 Can a beneficiary be represented in the dispute resolution process under the Ticket to Work program?

Yes. Both the beneficiary and the EN that is not a State VR agency may use an attorney or other individual of their choice to represent them at any step in the dispute resolution process. The P&A system in each State and U.S. Territory is available to provide assistance and advocacy services to beneficiaries seeking or receiving services under the Ticket to Work program, including assistance in resolving issues at any stage in the dispute resolution process.

DISPUTES BETWEEN BENEFICIARIES AND STATE VR AGENCIES

§ 411.640 Do the dispute resolution procedures of the Rehabilitation Act of 1973, as amended (29 U.S.C. 720 et seq.), apply to beneficiaries seeking services from the State VR agency?

Yes. The procedures in the Rehabilitation Act of 1973, as amended (29 U.S.C. 720 et seq.) apply to any beneficiary who has assigned a ticket to a State VR agency. ENs that are State VR agencies are subject to the provisions of the Rehabilitation Act. The Rehabilitation Act requires the State VR agency to provide each person seeking or receiving services with a description of the services available through the Client Assistance Program authorized under section 112 of the Rehabilitation Act of 1973, as amended (29 U.S.C. 732). It also provides the opportunity to resolve disputes using formal mediation services or the impartial hearing process in section 102(c) of the Rehabilitation Act of 1973, as amended (29 U.S.C. 722(c)). ENs that are not State VR agencies are not subject to the provisions of Title I of the Rehabilitation Act of 1973, as amended (29 U.S.C. 720 et seq.).

DISPUTES BETWEEN EMPLOYMENT NETWORKS AND PROGRAM MANAGERS

§ 411.650 Is there a process for resolving disputes between ENs that are not State VR agencies and PMs, other than disputes on a payment request?

Yes. Under the agreement to assist us in administering the Ticket to Work program, a PM is required to have procedures to resolve disputes with ENs that do not involve an EN's payment request. (See § 411.590 for the process for resolving disputes on EN payment requests.) This process must ensure that:

(a) The EN can seek a solution through the PM's internal grievance procedures; and

(b) If the PM's internal grievance procedures do not result in a mutually agreeable solution, the PM shall refer the dispute to us for a decision.

§ 411.655 How will the PM refer the dispute to us?

The PM has 20 working days from the failure to come to a mutually agreeable solution with an EN to refer the dispute to us with all relevant information. The information should include:

(a) A description of the disputed issue(s);

(b) A summary of the EN's and PM's position related to each disputed issue; and

(c) A description of any solutions proposed by the EN and PM when the EN sought resolution through the PM's grievance procedures, including the reasons each party rejected each proposed solution.

§ 411.660 Is SSA's decision final?

Yes. Our decision is final.

SUBPART J—THE TICKET TO WORK PROGRAM AND ALTERNATE PARTICIPANTS UNDER THE PROGRAMS FOR PAYMENTS FOR VOCATIONAL REHABILITATION SERVICES [RESERVED]

Source: 83 FR 62459, Dec. 4, 2018, unless otherwise noted.

§§ 411.700 to 411.730 [Reserved by 83 FR 62459]

[83 FR 62459, Dec. 4, 2018]

PART 416—SUPPLEMENTAL SECURITY INCOME FOR THE AGED, BLIND, AND DISABLED

SUBPART A—INTRODUCTION, GENERAL PROVISIONS AND DEFINITIONS

SUBPART B—ELIGIBILITY

GENERAL

REASONS WHY YOU MAY NOT GET SSI BENEFITS FOR WHICH YOU ARE OTHERWISE ELIGIBLE

ELIGIBILITY FOR INCREASED BENEFITS BECAUSE OF ESSENTIAL PERSONS

SPECIAL PROVISIONS FOR PEOPLE WHO WORK DESPITE A DISABLING IMPAIRMENT

SUBPART C—FILING OF APPLICATIONS

GENERAL PROVISIONS

APPLICATIONS

EFFECTIVE FILING PERIOD OF APPLICATION

FILING DATE BASED UPON A WRITTEN STATEMENT OR ORAL INQUIRY

DEEMED FILING DATE BASED ON MISINFORMATION

WITHDRAWAL OF APPLICATION

SUBPART D—AMOUNT OF BENEFITS

SUBPART N—DETERMINATIONS, ADMINISTRATIVE REVIEW PROCESS, AND REOPENING OF DETERMINATIONS AND DECISIONS

INTRODUCTION, DEFINITIONS, AND INITIAL DETERMINATIONS

RECONSIDERATION

EXPEDITED APPEALS PROCESS

HEARING BEFORE AN ADMINISTRATIVE LAW JUDGE

ADMINISTRATIVE LAW JUDGE HEARINGS PROCEDURES

APPEALS COUNCIL REVIEW

SUBPART A—INTRODUCTION, GENERAL PROVISIONS AND DEFINITIONS

Authority: Secs. 702(a)(5) and 1601–1635 of the Social Security Act (42 U.S.C. 902(a)(5) and 1381–1383d); sec. 212, Pub.L. 93–66, 87 Stat. 155 (42 U.S.C. 1382 note); sec. 502(a), Pub.L. 94–241, 90 Stat. 268 (48 U.S.C. 1681 note).

Source: 39 FR 28625, Aug. 9, 1974; 52 FR 27541, July 22, 1987; 53 FR 12941, April 20, 1988; 61 FR 5941, Feb. 15, 1996; 83 FR 62459, Dec. 4, 2018, unless otherwise noted.

§ 416.101 Introduction.

The regulations in this part 416 (Regulations No. 16 of the Social Security Administration) relate to the provisions of title XVI of the Social Security Act as amended by section 301 of Pub.L. 92–603 enacted October 30, 1972, and as may thereafter be amended. Title XVI (Supplemental Security Income For The Aged, Blind, and Disabled) of the Social Security Act, as amended, established a national program, effective January 1, 1974, for the purpose of providing supplemental security income to individuals who have attained age 65 or are blind or disabled. The regulations in this part are divided into the following subparts according to subject content:

(a) This subpart A contains this introduction, a statement of the general purpose underlying the supplemental security income program, general provisions applicable to the program and its administration, and definitions and use of terms occurring throughout this part.

(b) Subpart B of this part covers in general the eligibility requirements which must be met for benefits under the supplemental security income program. It sets forth the requirements regarding residence, citizenship, age, disability, or blindness, and describes the conditions which bar eligibility and generally points up other conditions of eligibility taken up in greater detail elsewhere in the regulations (e.g., limitations on income and resources, receipt of support and maintenance, etc.).

(c) Subpart C of this part sets forth the rules with respect to the filing of applications, requests for withdrawal of applications, cancellation of withdrawal requests and other similar requests.

(d) Subpart D of this part sets forth the rules for computing the amount of benefits payable to an eligible individual and eligible spouse.

(e) Subpart E of this part covers provisions with respect to periodic payment of benefits, joint payments, payment of emergency cash advances, payment of benefits prior to a determination of disability, prohibition against transfer or assignment of benefits, adjustment and waiver of overpayments, and payment of underpayments.

(f) Subpart F of this part contains provisions with respect to the selection of representative payees to receive benefits on behalf of and for the use of recipients and to the duties and responsibilities of representative payees.

(g) Subpart G of this part sets forth rules with respect to the reporting of events and circumstances affecting eligibility or the amount of benefits payable.

(h) Subpart H of this part sets forth rules and guidelines for the submittal and evaluation of evidence of age where age is pertinent to establishing eligibility or the amount of benefits payable.

(i) Subpart I of this part sets forth the rules for establishing disability or blindness where the establishment of disability or blindness is pertinent to eligibility.

(j) Subpart J of this part sets forth the standards, requirements and procedures for States making determinations of disability for the Commissioner. It also sets out the Commissioner's responsibilities in carrying out the disability determination function.

(k) Subpart K of this part defines income, earned income, and unearned income and sets forth the statutory exclusions applicable to earned and unearned income for the purpose of establishing eligibility for and the amount of benefits payable.

(*l*) Subpart L of this part defines the term resources and sets forth the statutory exclusions applicable to resources for the purpose of determining eligibility.

(m) Subpart M of this part deals with events or circumstances requiring suspension or termination of benefits.

(n) Subpart N of this part contains provisions with respect to procedures for making determinations with respect to eligibility, amount of benefits, representative payment, etc., notices of determinations, rights of appeal and procedures applicable thereto, and other procedural due process provisions.

(*o*) Subpart O of this part contains provisions applicable to attorneys and other individuals who represent applicants in connection with claims for benefits.

(p) Subpart P of this part sets forth the residence and citizenship requirements that are pertinent to eligibility.

(q) Subpart Q of this part contains provisions with respect to the referral of individuals for vocational rehabilitation, treatment for alcoholism and drug addiction, and application for other benefits to which an applicant may be potentially entitled.

(r) Subpart R of this part sets forth the rules for determining marital and other family relationships where pertinent to the establishment of eligibility for or the amount of benefits payable.

(s) Subpart S of this part explains interim assistance and how benefits may be withheld to repay such assistance given by the State.

(t) Subpart T of this part contains provisions with respect to the supplementation of Federal supplemental security income payments by States, agreements for Federal administration of State supplementation programs, and payment of State supplementary payments.

(u) Subpart U of this part contains provisions with respect to agreements with States for Federal determination of Medicaid eligibility of applicants for supplemental security income.

(v) Subpart V of this part explains when payments are made to State vocational rehabilitation agencies for vocational rehabilitation services.

[51 FR 11718, April 7, 1986; 62 FR 38454, July 18, 1997; 83 FR 62459, Dec. 4, 2018]

§ 416.105 Administration.

The Supplemental Security Income for the Aged, Blind, and Disabled program is administered by the Social Security Administration.

[51 FR 11718, April 7, 1986; 62 FR 38454, July 18, 1997]

§ 416.110 Purpose of program.

The basic purpose underlying the supplemental security income program is to assure a minimum level of income for people who are age 65 or over, or who are blind or disabled and who do not have sufficient income and resources to maintain a standard of living at the established Federal minimum income level. The supplemental security income program replaces the financial assistance programs for the aged, blind, and disabled in the 50 States and the District of Columbia for which grants were made under the Social Security Act. Payments are financed from the general funds of the United States Treasury. Several basic principles underlie the program:

(a) Objective tests. The law provides that payments are to be made to aged, blind, and disabled people who have income and resources below specified amounts. This provides objective measurable standards for determining each person's benefits.

(b) Legal right to payments. A person's rights to supplemental security income payments—how much he gets and under what conditions—are clearly defined in the law. The area of administrative discretion is thus limited. If an applicant disagrees with the decision on his claim, he can obtain an administrative review of the decision and if still not satisfied, he may initiate court action.

(c) Protection of personal dignity. Under the Federal program, payments are made under conditions that are as protective of people's dignity as possible. No restrictions, implied or otherwise, are placed on how recipients spend the Federal payments.

(d) Nationwide uniformity of standards. The eligibility requirements and the Federal minimum income level are identical throughout the 50 States and the District of Columbia. This provides assurance of a minimum income base on which States may build supplementary payments.

(e) Incentives to work and opportunities for rehabilitation. Payment amounts are not reduced dollar-for-dollar for work income but some of an applicant's income is counted toward the eligibility limit. Thus, recipients are encouraged to work if they can. Blind and disabled recipients with vocational rehabilitation potential are referred to the appropriate State vocational rehabilitation agencies that offer rehabilitation services to enable them to enter the labor market.

(f) State supplementation and Medicaid determinations.

(1) Federal supplemental security income payments lessen the variations in levels of assistance and provide a basic level of assistance throughout the nation. States are required to provide mandatory minimum State supplementary payments beginning January 1, 1974, to aged, blind, or disabled recipients of assistance for the month of December 1973 under such State's plan approved under title I, X, XIV, or XVI of the Act in order for the State to be eligible to receive title XIX funds (see subpart T of this part). These payments must be in an amount sufficient to ensure that individuals who are converted to the new program will not have their income reduced below what it was under the State program for December 1973. In addition, each State may choose to provide more than the Federal supplemental security income and/or mandatory minimum State supplementary payment to whatever extent it finds appropriate in view of the needs and resources of its citizens or it may choose to provide no more than the mandatory minimum payment where applicable. States which provide State supplementary payments can enter into agreements for Federal administration of the mandatory and optional State supplementary payments with the Federal Government paying the administrative costs. A State which elects Federal administration of its supplementation program must apply the same eligibility criteria (other than those pertaining to income) applied to determine eligibility for the Federal portion of the supplemental security income payment, except as provided in sec. 1616(c) of the Act (see subpart T of this part). There is a limitation on the amount payable to the Commissioner by a State for the amount of the supplementary pay-

ments made on its behalf for any fiscal year pursuant to the State's agreement with the Secretary. Such limitation on the amount of reimbursement is related to the State's payment levels for January 1972 and its total expenditures for calendar year 1972 for aid and assistance under the appropriate State plan(s) (see subpart T of this part).

(2) States with Medicaid eligibility requirements for the aged, blind, and disabled that are identical (except as permitted by § 416.2111) to the supplemental security income eligibility requirements may elect to have the Social Security Administration determine Medicaid eligibility under the State's program for recipients of supplemental security income and recipients of a federally administered State supplementary payment. The State would pay half of Social Security Administration's incremental administrative costs arising from carrying out the agreement.

[53 FR 12941, April 20, 1988; 62 FR 38454, July 18, 1997]

§ 416.120 General definitions and use of terms.

(a) Terms relating to acts and regulations. As used in this part:

(1) The Act means the Social Security Act as amended (42 U.S.C. Chap. 7).

(2) Wherever a title is referred to, it means such title of the Act.

(3) Vocational Rehabilitation Act means the act approved June 2, 1920 (41 Stat. 735), 29 U.S.C. 31–42, as amended, and as may be amended from time to time hereafter.

(b) Commissioner; Appeals Council; defined. As used in this part:

(1) Commissioner means the Commissioner of Social Security.

(2) Appeals Council means the Appeals Council of the Office of Hearings and Appeals in the Social Security Administration or such member or members thereof as may be designated by the Chairman.

(c) Miscellaneous. As used in this part unless otherwise indicated:

(1) Supplemental security income benefit means the amount to be paid to an eligible individual (or eligible individual and his eligible spouse) under title XVI of the Act.

(2) Income means the receipt by an individual of any property or service which he can apply, either directly or by sale or conversion, to meeting his basic needs (see subpart K of this part).

(3) Resources means cash or other liquid assets or any real or personal property that an individual owns and could convert to cash to be used for support and maintenance (see § 416.1201(a)).

(4) Attainment of age. An individual attains a given age on the first moment of the day preceding the anniversary of his birth corresponding to such age.

(5) Couple means an eligible individual and his eligible spouse.

(6) Institution (see § 416.201).

(7) Public institution (see § 416.201).

(8) Resident of a public institution (see § 416.201).

(9) State, unless otherwise indicated, means a State of the United States, the District of Columbia, or effective January 9, 1978, the Northern Mariana Islands.

(10) The term United States when used in a geographical sense means the 50 States, the District of Columbia, and effective January 9, 1978, the Northern Mariana Islands.

(11) Masculine gender includes the feminine, unless otherwise indicated.

(12) Section means a section of the regulations in part 416 of this chapter unless the context indicates otherwise.

(13) Eligible individual means an aged, blind, or disabled individual who meets all the requirements for eligibility for benefits under the supplemental security income program.

(14) Eligible spouse means an aged, blind, or disabled individual who is the husband or wife of another aged, blind, or disabled individual and who is living with that individual (see § 416.1801(c)).

(d) Periods of limitation ending on nonwork days. Pursuant to the Act, where any provision of title XVI, or any provision of another law of the United States (other than the Internal Revenue Code of 1954) relating to or changing the effect of title XVI, or any regulation of the Commissioner issued under title XVI, provides for a period within which an act is required to be done which affects eligibility for or the amount of any benefit or payment under title XVI or is necessary to establish or protect any rights under title XVI and such period ends on a Saturday, Sunday, or Federal legal holiday or on any other day all or part of which is declared to be a nonworkday for Federal employees by statute or Executive Order, then such act shall be considered as done within such period if it is done on the first day thereafter which is not a Saturday, Sunday, or legal holiday or any other day all or part of which is declared to be a nonworkday for Federal employees either by statute or Executive Order. For purposes of this paragraph, the day on which a period ends shall include the final day of any extended period where such extension is authorized by law or by the Commissioner pursuant to law. Such extension of any period of limitation does not apply to periods during which an application for benefits or payments may be accepted as such an application pursuant to subpart C of this part.

[39 FR 28625, Aug. 9, 1974, as amended at 43 FR 25091, June 9, 1978; 51 FR 11719, April 7, 1986; 60 FR 16374, March 30, 1995; 62 FR 38454, July 18, 1997]

§ 416.121 Receipt of aid or assistance for December 1973 under an approved State plan under title I, X, XIV, or XVI of the Social Security Act.

(a) Recipient of aid or assistance defined. As used in this part 416, the term individual who was a recipient of aid or assistance for December 1973 under a State plan approved under title I, X, XIV, or XVI of the Social Security Act means an individual who correctly received aid or assistance under such plan for December 1973 even though such aid or assistance may have been received subsequent to December 1973. It also includes an individual who filed an application prior to January 1974 and was otherwise eligible for aid or assistance for December 1973 under the provisions of such State plan but did not in fact receive such aid or assistance. It does not include an individual who received aid or assistance because of the provisions of 45 CFR 205.10(a) (pertaining to continuation of assistance until a fair hearing decision is rendered), as in effect in December 1973, and with respect to whom it is subsequently determined that such aid or assistance would not have been received without application of the provisions of such 45 CFR 205.10(a).

(b) Aid or assistance defined. As used in this part 416, the term aid or assistance means aid or assistance as defined in titles I, X, XIV, and XVI of the Social Security Act, as in effect in December 1973, and such aid or assistance is eligible for Federal financial participation in accordance with those titles and the provisions of 45 CFR chapter II as in effect in December 1973.

(c) Determinations of receipt of aid or assistance for December 1973. For the purpose of application of the provisions of this part 416, the determination as to whether an individual was a recipient of aid or assistance for December 1973 under a State plan approved under title I, X, XIV, or XVI of the Social Security Act will be made by the Social Security Administration. In making such determination, the Social Security Administration may take into consideration a prior determination by the appropriate State agency as to whether the individual was eligible for aid or assistance for December 1973 under such State plan. Such prior determination, however, shall not be considered as conclusive in determining whether an individual was a recipient of aid or assistance for December 1973 under a State plan approved under title I, X, XIV, or XVI of the Social Security Act for purposes of application of the provisions of this part 416.

(d) Special provision for disabled recipients. For purposes of § 416.907, the criteria and definitions enumerated in paragraphs (a) through (c) of this section are applicable in determining whether an individual was a recipient of aid or assistance (on the basis of disability) under a State plan approved under title XIV or XVI of the Act for a month prior to July 1973. It is not necessary that the aid or assistance for December 1973 and for a month prior to July 1973 have been paid under the State plan of the same State.

[39 FR 32024, Sept. 4, 1974; 39 FR 33207, Sept. 16, 1974; 51 FR 11719, April 7, 1986]

SUBPART B—ELIGIBILITY

Authority: Secs. 702(a)(5), 1110(b), 1602, 1611, 1614, 1619(a), 1631, and 1634 of the Social Security Act (42 U.S.C. 902(a)(5), 1310(b), 1381a, 1382, 1382c, 1382h(a), 1383, and 1383c); secs. 211 and 212, Pub.L. 93–66, 87 Stat. 154 and 155 (42 U.S.C. 1382 note); sec. 502(a), Pub.L. 94–241, 90 Stat. 268 (48 U.S.C. 1681 note); sec. 2, Pub.L. 99–643, 100 Stat. 3574 (42 U.S.C. 1382h note).

Source: 47 FR 3103, Jan. 22, 1982; 50 FR 48570, Nov. 26, 1985; 50 FR 51517, Dec. 18, 1985; 51 FR 13492, April 21, 1986; 51 FR 34464, Sept. 29, 1986; 52 FR 27541, July 22, 1987; 59 FR 41403, Aug. 12, 1994; 61 FR 1712, Jan. 23, 1996; 61 FR 5941, Feb. 15, 1996; 68 FR 40124, July 7, 2003, unless otherwise noted.

GENERAL

§ 416.200 Introduction.

You are eligible for SSI benefits if you meet all the basic requirements listed in § 416.202. However, the first month for which you may receive SSI benefits is the month after the month in which you meet these eligibility requirements. (See § 416.501.) You must give us any information we request and show us necessary documents or other evidence to prove that you meet these requirements. We determine your eligibility for each month on the basis of your countable income in that month. You continue to be eligible unless you lose your eligibility because you no longer meet the basic requirements or because of one of the reasons given in §§ 416.207 through 416.216.

[50 FR 48570, Nov. 26, 1985; 64 FR 31972, June 15, 1999; 68 FR 53508, Sept. 11, 2003]

§ 416.201 General definitions and terms used in this subpart.

Any 9–month period means any period of 9 full calendar months ending with any full calendar month throughout which (as defined in § 416.211) an individual is residing in a public emergency shelter for the homeless (as defined in this section) and including the immediately preceding 8 consecutive full calendar months. January 1988 is the earliest possible month in any 9–month period.

Educational or vocational training means a recognized program for the acquisition of knowledge or skills to prepare an individual for gainful employment. For purposes of these regulations, educational or vocational training does not include programs limited to the acquisition of basic life skills including but not limited to eating and dressing.

Emergency shelter means a shelter for individuals whose homelessness poses a threat to their lives or health.

Homeless individual is one who is not in the custody of any public institution and has no currently usable place to live. By custody we mean the care and control of an individual in a mandatory residency where the individual's freedom to come and go as he or she chooses is restricted. An individual in a public institution awaiting discharge and placement in the community is in the custody of that institution until discharged and is not homeless for purposes of this provision.

Institution means an establishment that makes available some treatment or services in addition to food and shelter to four or more persons who are not related to the proprietor.

Medical treatment facility means an institution or that part of an institution that is licensed or otherwise approved by a Federal, State, or local government to provide inpatient medical care and services.

Public emergency shelter for the homeless means a public institution or that part of a public institution used as an emergency shelter by the Federal government, a State, or a political subdivision of a State, primarily for making available on a temporary basis a place to sleep, food, and some services or treatment to homeless individuals. A medical treatment facility (as defined in § 416.201) or any holding facility, detoxification center, foster care facility, or the like that has custody of the individual is not a public emergency shelter for the homeless. Similarly, transitional living arrangements such as a halfway house that are part of an institution's plan to facilitate the individual's adjustment to community living are not public emergency shelters for the homeless.

Public institution means an institution that is operated by or controlled by the Federal government, a State, or a political subdivision of a State such as a city or county. The term public institution does not include a publicly operated community residence which serves 16 or fewer residents.

Resident of a public institution means a person who can receive substantially all of his or her food and shelter while living in a public institution. The person need not be receiving treatment and services available in the institution and is a resident regardless of whether the resident or anyone else pays for all food, shelter, and other services in the institution. A person is not a resident of a public institution if he or she is living in a public educational institution for the primary purpose of receiving educational or vocational training as defined in this section. A resident of a public institution means the same thing as an inmate of a public institution as used in section 1611(e)(1)(A) of the Social Security Act. (See § 416.211(b), (c), and (d) of this subpart for exceptions to the general limitation on the eligibility for Supplemental Security Income benefits of individuals who are residents of a public institution.)

SSI means supplemental security income.

State assistance means payments made by a State to an aged, blind, or disabled person under a State plan approved under title I, X, XIV, or XVI (AABD) of the Social Security Act which was in effect before the SSI Program.

We or Us means the Social Security Administration.

You or Your means the person who applies for or receives SSI benefits or the person for whom an application is filed.

[49 FR 19639, May 19, 1984; 50 FR 48570, Nov. 26, 1985; 50 FR 51517, Dec. 18, 1985; 54 FR 19164, May 4, 1989; 72 FR 50874, Sept. 5, 2007]

§ 416.202 Who may get SSI benefits.

You are eligible for SSI benefits if you meet all of the following requirements:

(a) You are—

(1) Aged 65 or older (subpart H);

(2) Blind (subpart I); or

(3) Disabled (subpart I).

(b) You are a resident of the United States (§ 416.1603), and—

(1) A citizen or a national of the United States (§ 416.1610);

(2) An alien lawfully admitted for permanent residence in the United States (§ 416.1615);

(3) An alien permanently residing in the United States under color of law (§ 416.1618); or

(4) A child of armed forces personnel living overseas as described in § 416.216.

(c) You do not have more income than is permitted (subparts K and D).

(d) You do not have more resources than are permitted (subpart L).

(e) You are disabled, drug addiction or alcoholism is a contributing factor material to the determination of disability (see § 416.935), and you have not previously received a total of 36 months of Social Security benefit payments when appropriate treatment was available or 36 months of SSI benefits on the basis of disability where drug addiction or alcoholism was a contributing factor material to the determination of disability.

(f) You are not—

(1) Fleeing to avoid prosecution for a crime, or an attempt to commit a crime, which is a felony under the laws of the place from which you flee (or which, in the case of the State of New Jersey, is a high misdemeanor under the laws of that State);

(2) Fleeing to avoid custody or confinement after conviction for a crime, or an attempt to commit a crime, which is a felony under the laws of the place from which you flee (or which, in the case of the State of New Jersey, is a high misdemeanor under the laws of that State); or

(3) Violating a condition of probation or parole imposed under Federal or State law.

(g) You file an application for SSI benefits (subpart C).

[58 FR 4897, Jan. 19, 1993; 60 FR 8149, Feb. 10, 1995; 61 FR 10277, March 13, 1996; 65 FR 40495, June 30, 2000]

§ 416.203 Initial determinations of SSI eligibility.

(a) What happens when you apply for SSI benefits. When you apply for SSI benefits we will ask you for documents and any other information we need to make sure you meet all the requirements. We will ask for information about your income and resources and about other eligibility requirements and you must answer completely. We will help you get any documents you need but do not have.

(b) How we determine your eligibility for SSI benefits. We determine that you are eligible for SSI benefits for a given month if you meet the requirements in § 416.202 in that month. However, you cannot become eligible for payment of SSI benefits until the month after the month in which you first become eligible for SSI benefits (see § 416.501). In addition, we usually determine the amount of your SSI benefits for a month based on your income in an earlier month (see § 416.420). Thus, it is possible for you to meet the eligibility requirements in a given month but receive no benefit payment for that month.

[50 FR 48570, Nov. 26, 1985; 64 FR 31972, June 15, 1999]

§ 416.204 Redeterminations of SSI eligibility.

(a) Redeterminations defined. A redetermination is a review of your eligibility to make sure that you are still eligible and that you are receiving the right amount of SSI benefits. This review deals with the requirements for eligibility other than whether you are still disabled or blind. Continuation of disability or blindness reviews are discussed in §§ 416.989 and 416.990.

(b) When we make redeterminations.

(1) We redetermine your eligibility on a scheduled basis at periodic intervals. The length of time between scheduled redeterminations varies depending on the likelihood that your situation may change in a way that affects your benefits.

(2) We may also redetermine your eligibility when you tell us (or we otherwise learn) of a change in your situation which affects your eligibility or the amount of your benefit.

(c) The period for which a redetermination applies:

(1) The first redetermination applies to—

(i) The month in which we make the redetermination;

(ii) All months beginning with the first day of the latest of the following:

(A) The month of first eligibility or re-eligibility; or

(B) The month of application; or

(C) The month of deferred or updated development; and

(iii) Future months until the second redetermination.

(2) All other redeterminations apply to—

(i) The month in which we make the redetermination;

(ii) All months beginning with the first day of the month the last redetermination was initiated; and

(iii) Future months until the next redetermination.

(3) If we made two redeterminations which cover the same month, the later redetermination is the one we apply to that month.

[50 FR 48570, Nov. 26, 1985; 58 FR 64893, Dec. 10, 1993]

REASONS WHY YOU MAY NOT GET SSI BENEFITS FOR WHICH YOU ARE OTHERWISE ELIGIBLE

§ 416.207 You do not give us permission to contact financial institutions.

(a) To be eligible for SSI payments you must give us permission to contact any financial institution and request any financial records that financial institution may have about you. You must give us this permission when you apply for SSI payments or when we ask for it at a later time. You must also provide us with permission from anyone whose income and resources we consider as being available to you, i.e., deemors (see §§ 416.1160, 416.1202, 416.1203, and 416.1204).

(b) Financial institution means any:

(1) Bank,

(2) Savings bank,

(3) Credit card issuer,

(4) Industrial loan company,

(5) Trust company,

(6) Savings association,

(7) Building and loan,

(8) Homestead association,

(9) Credit union,

(10) Consumer finance institution, or

(11) Any other financial institution as defined in section 1101(1) of the Right to Financial Privacy Act.

(c) Financial record means an original of, a copy of, or information known to have been derived from any record held by the financial institution pertaining to your relationship with the financial institution.

(d) We may ask any financial institution for information on any financial account concerning you. We may also ask for information on any financial accounts for anyone whose income and resources we consider as being available to you (see §§ 416.1160, 416.1202, 416.1203, and 416.1204).

(e) We ask financial institutions for this information when we think that it is necessary to determine your SSI eligibility or payment amount.

(f) Your permission to contact financial institutions, and the permission of anyone whose income and resources we consider as being available to you, i.e., a deemor (see §§ 416.1160, 416.1202, 416.1203, and 416.1204), remains in effect until a terminating event occurs. The following terminating events only apply prospectively and do not invalidate the permission for past periods.

(1) You cancel your permission in writing and provide the writing to us.

(2) The deemor cancels their permission in writing and provides the writing to us.

(3) The basis on which we consider a deemor's income and resources available to you ends, e.g. when spouses separate or divorce or a child attains age 18.

(4) Your application for SSI is denied, and the denial is final. A denial is final when made, unless you appeal the denial timely as described in §§ 416.1400 through 416.1499.

(5) You are no longer eligible for SSI as described in §§ 416.1331 through 416.1335.

(g) If you don't give us permission to contact any financial institution and request any financial records about you when we think it is necessary to determine your SSI eligibility or payment amount, or if you cancel the permission, you cannot be eligible for SSI payments. Also, except as noted in paragraph (h), if anyone whose income and resources we consider as being available to you (see §§ 416.1160, 416.1202, 416.1203, and 416.1204) doesn't give us permission to contact any financial institution and request any financial records about that person when we think it is necessary to determine your eligibility or payment amount, or if that person cancels the permission, you cannot be eligible for SSI payments. This means that if you are applying for SSI payments, you cannot receive them. If you are receiving SSI payments, we will stop your payments.

(h) You may be eligible for SSI payments if there is good cause for your being unable to obtain permission for us to contact any financial institution and request any financial records about someone whose income and resources we consider as being available to you (see §§ 416.1160, 416.1202, 416.1203, and 416.1204).

(1) Good cause exists if permission cannot be obtained from the individual and there is evidence that the individual is harassing you, abusing you, or endangering your life.

(2) Good cause may exist if an individual other than one listed in paragraph (h)(3) of this section refuses to provide permission and: you acted in good faith to obtain permission from the individual but were unable to do so through no fault of your own, or you cooperated with us in our efforts to obtain permission.

(3) Good cause does not apply if the individual is your representative payee and your legal guardian, if you are a minor child and the individual is your representative payee and your custodial parent, or if you are an alien and the individual is your sponsor or the sponsor's living-with spouse.

[68 FR 53508, Sept. 11, 2003]

§ 416.210 You do not apply for other benefits.

(a) General rule. You are not eligible for SSI benefits if you do not apply for all other benefits for which you may be eligible.

(b) What "other benefits" includes. "Other benefits" includes any payments for which you can apply that are available to you on an ongoing or one-time basis of a type that includes annuities, pensions, retirement benefits, or disability benefits. For example, "other benefits" includes veterans' compensation and pensions, workers' compensation payments, Social Security insurance benefits and unemployment insurance benefits. "Other benefits" for which you are required to apply do not include payments that you may be eligible to receive from a fund established by a State to aid victims of crime. (See § 416.1124(c)(17).)

(c) Our notice to you. We will give you a dated, written notice that will tell you about any other benefits that we think you are likely to be eligible for. In addition, the notice will explain that your eligibility for SSI benefits will be affected if you do not apply for those other benefits.

(d) What you must do to apply for other benefits. In order to apply for other benefits, you must file any required applications and do whatever else is needed so that your eligibility for the other benefits can be determined. For example, if any documents (such as a copy of a birth certificate) are required in addition to the application, you must submit them.

(e) What happens if you do not apply for the other benefits.

(1) If you do not apply for the other benefits within 30 days from the day that you receive our written notice, you are not eligible for SSI benefits. This means that if you are applying for SSI benefits, you cannot receive them. If you are receiving SSI bene-

fits, your SSI benefits will stop. In addition, you will have to repay us for any SSI benefits that you received beginning with the month that you received our written notice. We assume (unless you prove otherwise) that you received our written notice 5 days after the date shown on the notice. We will also find that you are not eligible for SSI benefits if you file the required application for other benefits but do not take other necessary steps to obtain them.

(2) We will not find you ineligible for SSI benefits if you have a good reason for not applying for the other benefits within the 30–day period or taking other necessary steps to obtain them. In determining whether a good reason exists, we will take into account any physical, mental, educational, or linguistic limitations (including any lack of facility with the English language) which may have caused you to fail to apply for other benefits. You may have a good reason if, for example—

(i) You are incapacitated (because of illness you were not able to apply); or

(ii) It would be useless for you to apply (you once applied for the benefits and the reasons why you were turned down have not changed).

[50 FR 5573, Feb. 11, 1985; 50 FR 14211, April 11, 1985; 58 FR 63889, Dec. 3, 1993; 59 FR 1635, Jan. 12, 1994; 61 FR 1712, Jan. 23, 1996]

§ 416.211 You are a resident of a public institution.

(a) General rule.

(1) Subject to the exceptions described in paragraphs (b), (c), and (d) of this section and § 416.212, you are not eligible for SSI benefits for any month throughout which you are a resident of a public institution as defined in § 416.201. In addition, if you are a resident of a public institution when you apply for SSI benefits and meet all other eligibility requirements, you cannot be eligible for payment of benefits until the first day of the month following the day of your release from the institution.

(2) By throughout a month we mean that you reside in an institution as of the beginning of a month and stay the entire month. If you have been a resident of a public institution, you remain a resident if you are transferred from one public institution to another or if you are temporarily absent for a period of not more than 14 consecutive days. A person also is a resident of an institution throughout a month if he or she is born in the institution during the month and resides in the institution the rest of the month or resides in the institution as of the beginning of a month and dies in the institution during the month.

(b) Exception—SSI benefits payable at a reduced rate. You may be eligible for SSI benefits at a reduced rate described in § 416.414, if—

(1)(i) You reside throughout a month in a public institution that is a medical treatment facility where Medicaid (title XIX of the Social Security Act) pays a substantial part (more than 50 percent) of the cost of your care; you are a child under the age of 18 residing throughout a month in a public institution that is a medical treatment facility where a substantial part (more than 50 percent) of the cost of your care is paid under a health insurance policy issued by a private provider of such insurance; or, you are a child under the age of 18 residing throughout a month in a public institution that is a medical treatment facility where a substantial part (more than 50 percent) of the cost of your care is paid by a combination of Medicaid payments and payments made under a health insurance policy issued by a private provider of such insurance; or

(ii) You reside for part of a month in a public institution and the rest of the month in a public institution or private medical treatment facility where Medicaid pays a substantial part (more than 50 percent) of the cost of your care; you are a child under the age of 18 residing for part of a month in a public institution and the rest of the month in a public institution or private medical treatment facility where a substantial part (more than 50 percent) of the cost of your care is paid under a health insurance policy issued by a private provider of such insurance; or you are a child under the age of 18 residing for part of a month in a public institution and the rest of the month in a public institution or private medical treatment facility where a substantial part (more than 50 percent) of the cost of your care is paid by a combination of Medicaid payments and payments made under a health insurance policy issued by a private provider; and

(2) You are ineligible in that month for a benefit described in § 416.212 that is payable to a person temporarily confined in a medical treatment facility.

(c) Exception for publicly operated community residences which serve no more than 16 residents—

(1) General rule. If you are a resident of a publicly operated community residence which serves no more than 16 residents, you may be eligible for SSI benefits.

(2) Services that a facility must provide in order to be a community residence. To be a community residence, a facility must provide food and shelter. In addition, it must make available some other services. For example, the other services could be—

(i) Social services;

(ii) Help with personal living activities;

(iii) Training in socialization and life skills; or

(iv) Providing occasional or incidental medical or remedial care.

(3) Serving no more than 16 residents. A community residence serves no more than 16 residents if—

(i) It is designed and planned to serve no more than 16 residents, or the design and plan were changed to serve no more than 16 residents; and

(ii) It is in fact serving 16 or fewer residents.

(4) Publicly operated. A community residence is publicly operated if it is operated or controlled by the Federal government, a State, or a political subdivision of a State such as a city or county.

(5) Facilities which are not a publicly operated community residence. If you live in any of the following facilities, you are not a resident of a publicly operated community residence:

(i) A residential facility which is on the grounds of or next to a large institution or multipurpose complex;

(ii) An educational or vocational training institution whose main function is to provide an approved, accredited, or recognized program to some or all of those who live there;

(iii) A jail or other facility where the personal freedom of anyone who lives there is restricted because that person is a prisoner, is being held under court order, or is being held until charges against that person are disposed of; or

(iv) A medical treatment facility (defined in § 416.201).

(d) Exception for residents of public emergency shelters for the homeless. For months after December 1987, if you are a resident of a public emergency shelter for the homeless (defined in § 416.201) you may be eligible for SSI benefits for any 6 months throughout which you reside in a shelter in any 9–month period (defined in § 416.201). The 6 months do not need to be consecutive and we will not count as part of the 6 months any prior months throughout which you lived in the shelter but did not receive SSI benefits. We will also not count any months throughout which you lived in the shelter and received SSI benefits prior to January 1988.

Example: You are receiving SSI benefits when you lose your home and enter a public emergency shelter for the homeless on March 10, 1988. You remain a resident of a shelter until October 10, 1988. Since you were not in the shelter throughout the month of March, you are eligible to receive your benefit for March without having this month count towards the 6–month period. The last full month throughout which you reside in the shelter is September 1988. Therefore, if you meet all eligibility requirements, you will also be paid benefits for April through September (6 months during the 9–month period September 1988 back through January 1988). If you are otherwise eligible, you will receive your SSI benefit for October when you left the shelter, since you were not a resident of the shelter throughout that month.

[50 FR 51518, Dec. 18, 1985; 51 FR 13492, April 21, 1986; 51 FR 17332, May 12, 1986; 51 FR 34464, Sept. 29, 1986; 54 FR 19164, May 4, 1989; 61 FR 10277, March 13, 1996; 62 FR 1055, Jan. 8, 1997; 62 FR 42412, Aug. 7, 1997; 64 FR 31972, June 15, 1999; 72 FR 50874, Sept. 5, 2007]

§ 416.212 Continuation of full benefits in certain cases of medical confinement.

(a) Benefits payable under section 1611(e)(1)(E) of the Social Security Act. Subject to eligibility and regular computation rules (see subparts B and D of this part), you are eligible for the benefits payable under section 1611(e)(1)(E) of the Social Security Act for up to 2 full months of medical confinement during which your benefits would otherwise be suspended because of residence in a public institution or reduced because of residence in a public or private institution where Medicaid pays a substantial part (more than 50 percent) of the cost of your care or, if you are a child under age 18, reduced because of residence in a public or private institution which receives payments under a health insurance policy issued by a private provider, or a combination of Medicaid and a health insurance policy issued by a private provider, pay a substantial part (more than 50 percent) of the cost of your care if—

(1) You were eligible under either section 1619(a) or section 1619(b) of the Social Security Act in the month before the first full month of residence in an institution;

(2) The institution agrees that no portion of these benefits will be paid to or retained by the institution excepting nominal sums for reimbursement of the institution for any outlay for a recipient's personal needs (e.g., personal hygiene items, snacks, candy); and

(3) The month of your institutionalization is one of the first 2 full months of a continuous period of confinement.

(b) Benefits payable under section 1611(e)(1)(G) of the Social Security Act.

(1) Subject to eligibility and regular computation rules (see subparts B and D of this part), you are eligible for the benefits payable under section 1611(e)(1)(G) of the Social Security Act for up to 3 full months of medical confinement during which your benefits would otherwise be suspended because of residence in a public institution or reduced because of residence in a public or private institution where Medicaid pays a substantial part (more than 50 percent) of the cost of your care or, if you are a child under age 18, reduced because of residence in a public or private institution which receives payments under a health insurance policy issued by a private provider, or a combination of Medicaid and a health insurance policy issued by a private provider, pay a substantial part (more than 50 percent) of the cost of your care if—

(i) You were eligible for SSI cash benefits and/or federally administered State supplementary payments for the month immediately prior to the first full month you were a resident in such institution;

(ii) The month of your institutionalization is one of the first 3 full months of a continuous period of confinement;

(iii) A physician certifies, in writing, that you are not likely to be confined for longer than 90 full consecutive days following the day you entered the institution, and the certification is submitted to SSA no later than the day of discharge or the 90th full day of confinement, whichever is earlier; and

(iv) You need to pay expenses to maintain the home or living arrangement to which you intend to return after institutionalization and evidence regarding your need to pay these expenses is submitted to SSA no later than the day of discharge or the 90th full day of confinement, whichever is earlier.

(2) We will determine the date of submission of the evidence required in paragraphs (b)(1)(iii) and (iv) of this section to be the date we receive it or, if mailed, the date of the postmark.

(c) Prohibition against using benefits for current maintenance. If the recipient is a resident in an institution, the recipient or his or her representative payee will not be permitted to pay the institution any portion of benefits payable under section 1611(e)(1)(G) excepting nominal sums for reimbursement of the institution for any outlay for the recipient's personal needs (e.g., personal hygiene items, snacks, candy). If the institution is the representative payee, it will not be permitted to retain any portion of these benefits for the cost of the recipient's current maintenance excepting nominal sums for reimbursement for outlays for the recipient's personal needs.

[61 FR 10277, March 13, 1996; 62 FR 1055, Jan. 8, 1997; 62 FR 42412, Aug. 7, 1997; 72 FR 50874, Sept. 5, 2007]

§ 416.213 [Reserved]

[68 FR 40124, July 7, 2003]

§ 416.214 You are disabled and drug addiction or alcoholism is a contributing factor material to the determination of disability.

(a) If you do not comply with treatment requirements. If you receive benefits because you are disabled and drug addiction or alcoholism is a contributing factor material to the determination of disability (see § 416.935), you must avail yourself of any appropriate treatment for your drug addiction or alcoholism at an approved institution or facility when this treatment is available and make progress in your treatment. You are not eligible for SSI benefits beginning with the month after the month you are notified in writing that we determined that you have failed to comply with the treatment requirements. If your benefits are suspended because you failed to comply with treatment requirements, you will not be eligible to receive benefits until you have demonstrated compliance with treatment for a period of time, as specified in § 416.1326. The rules regarding treatment for drug addiction and alcoholism are in subpart I of this part.

(b) If you previously received 36 months of SSI or Social Security benefits. You are not eligible for SSI benefits by reason of disability on the basis of drug addiction or alcoholism as described in § 416.935 if—

(1) You previously received a total of 36 months of SSI benefits on the basis of disability and drug addiction or alcoholism was a contributing factor material to the determination of disability for months beginning March 1995, as described in § 416.935. Not included in these 36 months are months before March 1995 and months for which your benefits were suspended for any reason. The 36–month limit is no longer effective for months beginning after September 2004; or

(2) You previously received a total of 36 months of Social Security benefits counted in accordance with the provisions of §§ 404.316, 404.337, and 404.352 by reason of disability on the basis of drug addiction or alcoholism as described in § 404.1535.

[60 FR 8149, Feb. 10, 1995; 61 FR 10277, March 13, 1996]

§ 416.215 You leave the United States.

You lose your eligibility for SSI benefits for any month during all of which you are outside of the United States. If you are outside of the United States for 30 days or more in a row, you are not considered to be back in the United States until you are back for 30 days in a row. You may again be eligible for SSI benefits in the month in which the 30 days end if you continue to meet all other eligibility requirements.

By United States, we mean the 50 States, the District of Columbia, and the Northern Mariana Islands.

[61 FR 10277, March 13, 1996]

§ 416.216 You are a child of armed forces personnel living overseas.

(a) General rule. For purposes of this part, overseas means any location outside the United States as defined in § 416.215; i.e., the 50 States, the District of Columbia and the Northern Mariana Islands. You may be eligible for SSI benefits if you live overseas and if—

(1) You are a child as described in § 416.1856;

(2) You are a citizen of the United States; and

(3) You are living with a parent as described in § 416.1881 who is a member of the armed forces of the United States assigned to permanent duty ashore overseas.

(b) Living with. You are considered to be living with your parent who is a member of the armed forces if—

(1) You physically live with the parent who is a member of the armed forces overseas; or

(2) You are not living in the same household as the military parent but your presence overseas is due to his or her permanent duty assignment.

[58 FR 4897, Jan. 19, 1993; 58 FR 9597, Feb. 22, 1993; 59 FR 41400, Aug. 12, 1994; 61 FR 10277, March 13, 1996; 70 FR 61366, Oct. 24, 2005]

ELIGIBILITY FOR INCREASED BENEFITS BECAUSE OF ESSENTIAL PERSONS

§ 416.220 General.

If you are a qualified individual and have an essential person you may be eligible for increased benefits. You may be a qualified individual and have an essential person only if you received benefits under a State assistance plan approved under title I, X, XIV, or XVI (AABD) of the Act for December 1973. Definitions and rules that apply to qualified individuals and essential persons are discussed in §§ 416.221 through 416.223.

§ 416.221 Who is a qualified individual.

You are a qualified individual if—

(a) You received aid or assistance for the month of December 1973 under a State plan approved under title I, X, XIV, or XVI (AABD) of the Act;

(b) The State took into account the needs of another person in deciding your need for the State assistance for December 1973;

(c) That other person was living in your home in December 1973; and

(d) That other person was not eligible for State assistance for December 1973.

§ 416.222 Who is an essential person.

(a) General rule. A person is an essential person if—

(1) That person has continuously lived in the home of the same qualified individual since December 1973;

(2) That person was not eligible for State assistance for December 1973;

(3) That person was never eligible for SSI benefits in his or her own right or as an eligible spouse; and

(4) There are State records which show that under a State plan in effect for June 1973, the State took that person's needs into account in determining the qualified individual's need for State assistance for December 1973.

Any person who meets these requirements is an essential person. This means that the qualified individual can have more than one essential person.

(b) Absence of an essential person from the home of a qualified individual. An essential person may be temporarily absent from the house of a qualified individual and still be an essential person. For example, the essential person could be hospitalized. We consider an absence to[1] temporary if—

(1) The essential person intends to return;

(2) The facts support this intention;

(3) It is likely that he or she will return; and

(4) The absence is not longer than 90 days.

(c) Absence of a qualified individual from his or her home. You may be temporarily absent from your home and still have an essential person. For example, you could be hospitalized. We consider an absence to be temporary if—

(1) You intend to return;

(2) The facts support your intention;

(3) It is likely that you will return; and

(4) Your absence does not exceed six months.

(d) Essential person becomes eligible for SSI benefits. If an essential person becomes eligible for SSI benefits, he or she will no longer be an essential person beginning with the month that he or she becomes eligible for the SSI benefits.

§ 416.223 What happens if you are a qualified individual.

(a) Increased SSI benefits. We may increase the amount of your SSI benefits if—

(1) You are a qualified individual; and

(2) You have one or more essential persons in your home.

In subpart D, we explain how these increased benefits are calculated.

(b) Income and resource limits. If you are a qualified individual, we consider the income and resources of an essential person in your home to be yours. You are eligible for increased SSI benefits if—

(1) Your resources which are counted do not exceed the limit for SSI eligibility purposes (see subpart L); and

(2) Your income which is counted for SSI eligibility purposes (see subpart K) does not exceed the sum of—

(i) The SSI Federal benefit rate (see subpart D); and

(ii) The proper number of essential person increments (for the value of an essential person increment see subpart D). One essential person increment is added to the SSI Federal benefit rate for each essential person in your home.

(c) Excluding the income and resources of an essential person.

[1] So in original; probably should read "to be". See 47 FR 3105.

(1) While an essential person increment increases your SSI Federal benefit rate, that person's income which we consider to be yours may actually result in a lower monthly payment to you. We will discuss this with you and explain how an essential person affects your benefit. If you choose to do so, you may ask us in writing to determine your eligibility without your essential person or, if you have more than one essential person, without one or more of your essential persons. We will then figure the amount of your SSI benefits without counting as your own income and resources of the essential persons that you specify and we will end the essential person increment for those essential persons. You should consider this carefully because once you make the request, you cannot withdraw it. We will make the change beginning with the month following the month that you make the request.

(2) We will not include the income and resources of the essential person if the person's income or resources would cause you to lose your eligibility. The loss of the essential person increment will be permanent.

§ 416.250 Experimental, pilot, and demonstration projects in the SSI program.

(a) Authority and purpose. Section 1110(b) of the Act authorizes the Commissioner to develop and conduct experimental, pilot, and demonstration projects to promote the objectives or improve the administration of the SSI program. These projects will test the advantages of altering certain requirements, conditions, or limitations for recipients and test different administrative methods that apply to title XVI applicants and recipients.

(b) Altering benefit requirements, limitations or conditions. Notwithstanding any other provision of this part, the Commissioner is authorized to waive any of the requirements, limitations or conditions established under title XVI of the Act and impose additional requirements, limitations or conditions for the purpose of conducting experimental, pilot, or demonstration projects. The projects will alter the provisions that currently apply to applicants and recipients to test their effect on the program. If, as a result of participation in a project under this section, a project participant becomes ineligible for Medicaid benefits, the Commissioner shall make arrangements to extend Medicaid coverage to such participant and shall reimburse the States for any additional expenses incurred due to such continued participation.

(c) Applicability and scope—

(1) Participants and nonparticipants. If you are selected to participate in an experimental, pilot, or demonstration project, we may temporarily set aside one or more current requirements, limitations or conditions of eligibility and apply alternative provisions to you. We may also modify current methods of administering title XVI as part of a project and apply alternative procedures or policies to you. The alternative provisions or methods of administration used in the projects will not substantially reduce your total income or resources as a result of your participation or disadvantage you in comparison to current provisions, policies, or procedures. If you are not selected to participate in the experimental, or pilot, or demonstration projects (or if you are placed in a control group which is not subject to the alternative requirements, limitations, or conditions) we will continue to apply the current requirements, limitations or conditions of eligibility to you.

(2) Alternative provisions or methods of administration. The alternative requirements, limitations or conditions that apply to you in an experimental, pilot, or demonstration project may include any of the factors needed for aged, blind, or disabled persons to be eligible for SSI benefits. Experiments that we conduct will include, to the extent feasible, applicants and recipients who are under age 18 as well as adults and will include projects to ascertain the feasibility of treating drug addicts and alcoholics.

(d) Selection of participants. Participation in the SSI project will be on a voluntary basis. The voluntary written consent necessary in order to participate in any experimental, pilot, or demonstration project may be revoked by the participant at any time.

(e) Duration of experimental, pilot, and demonstration projects. A notice describing each experimental, pilot, or demonstration project will be published in the Federal Register before each project is placed in operation. Each experimental, pilot and demonstration project will have a termination date (up to 10 years from the start of the project).

[48 FR 7576, Feb. 23, 1983; 52 FR 37605, Oct. 8, 1987; 62 FR 38454, July 18, 1997]

SPECIAL PROVISIONS FOR PEOPLE WHO WORK DESPITE A DISABLING IMPAIRMENT

§ 416.260 General.

The regulations in §§ 416.260 through 416.269 describe the rules for determining eligibility for special SSI cash benefits and for special SSI eligibility status for an individual who works despite a disabling impairment. Under these rules an individual who works despite a disabling impairment may qualify for special SSI cash benefits and in most cases for Medicaid benefits when his or her gross earned income exceeds the applicable dollar amount which ordinarily represents SGA described in § 416.974(b)(2). The calculation of this gross earned income amount, however, is not to be considered an actual SGA determination. Also, for purposes of determining eligibility or continuing eligibility for Medicaid benefits, a blind or disabled individual (no longer eligible for regular SSI benefits or for special SSI cash benefits) who, except for earnings, would otherwise be eligible for SSI cash benefits may be eligible for a special SSI eligibility status under which he or she is considered to be a blind or disabled individual receiving SSI benefits. We explain the rules for eligibility for special SSI cash benefits in §§ 416.261 and 416.262. We explain the rules for the special SSI eligibility status in §§ 416.264 through 416.269.

[47 FR 15324, Apr. 9, 1982; 50 FR 46763, Nov. 13, 1985; 59 FR 41403, Aug. 12, 1994]

§ 416.261 What are special SSI cash benefits and when are they payable.

Special SSI cash benefits are benefits that we may pay you in lieu of regular SSI benefits because your gross earned income in a month of initial eligibility for regular SSI benefits exceeds the amount ordinarily considered to represent SGA under § 416.974(b)(2). You must meet the eligibility requirements in § 416.262 in order to receive special SSI cash benefits. Special SSI cash benefits are not payable for any month in which your countable income exceeds the limits established for the SSI program (see subpart K of this part). If you are eligible for special SSI cash benefits, we consider you to be a disabled individual receiving SSI benefits for purposes of eligibility for Medicaid. We compute the amount of special SSI cash benefits according to the rules in subpart D of this part. If your State makes supplementary payments which we administer under a Federal–State agreement, and if your State elects to supplement the special SSI cash benefits, the rules in subpart T of this part will apply to these payments.

[50 FR 46763, Nov. 13, 1985; 59 FR 41403, Aug. 12, 1994]

§ 416.262 Eligibility requirements for special SSI cash benefits.

You are eligible for special SSI cash benefits if you meet the following requirements—

(a) You were eligible to receive a regular SSI benefit or a federally administered State supplementary payment (see § 416.2001) in a month before the month for which we are determining your eligibility for special SSI cash benefits as long as that month was not in a prior period of eligibility which has terminated according to §§ 416.1331 through 416.1335;

(b) In the month for which we are making the determination, your gross earned income exceeds the amount ordinarily considered to represent SGA under § 416.974(b)(2);

(c) You continue to have a disabling impairment;

(d) If your disability is based on a determination that drug addiction or alcoholism is a contributing factor material to the determination of disability as described in § 416.935, you have not yet received SSI cash benefits, special SSI cash benefits, or special SSI eligibility status for a total of 36 months, or Social Security benefit payments when treatment was available for a total of 36 months; and

(e) You meet all the nondisability requirements for eligibility for SSI benefits (see § 416.202).

We will follow the rules in this subpart in determining your eligibility for special SSI cash benefits.

[59 FR 41404, Aug. 12, 1994; 60 FR 8149, Feb. 10, 1995; 64 FR 31972, June 15, 1999]

§ 416.263 No additional application needed.

We do not require you to apply for special cash benefits nor is it necessary for you to apply to have the special SSI eligibility status determined. We will make these determinations automatically.

§ 416.264 When does the special SSI eligibility status apply.

The special SSI eligibility status applies for the purposes of establishing or maintaining your eligibility for Medicaid. For these purposes we continue to consider you to be a blind or disabled individual receiving benefits even though you are in fact no longer receiving regular SSI benefits or special SSI cash benefits. You must meet the eligibility requirements in § 416.265 in order to qualify for the special SSI eligibility status. Special SSI eligibility status also applies for purposes of reacquiring status as eligible for regular SSI benefits or special SSI cash benefits.

[59 FR 41404, Aug. 12, 1994]

§ 416.265 Requirements for the special SSI eligibility status.

In order to be eligible for the special SSI eligibility status, you must have been eligible to receive a regular SSI benefit or a federally administered State supplementary payment (see § 416.2001) in a month before the month for which we are making the special SSI eligibility status determination. The month you were eligible for a regular SSI benefit or a federally administered State supplementary payment may not be in a prior period of eligibility which has been terminated according to §§ 416.1331 through 416.1335. For periods prior to May 1, 1991, you must be under age 65. Also, we must establish that:

(a) You are blind or you continue to have a disabling impairment which, if drug addiction or alcoholism is a contributing factor material to the determination of disability as described in § 416.935, has not resulted in your receiving SSI cash benefits, special SSI cash benefits, or special SSI eligibility status for a total of 36 months, or Social Security benefit payments when treatment was available for a total of 36 months;

(b) Except for your earnings, you meet all the nondisability requirements for eligibility for SSI benefits (see § 416.202);

(c) The termination of your eligibility for Medicaid would seriously inhibit your ability to continue working (see § 416.268); and

(d) Your earnings after the exclusions in § 416.1112(c)(6), (8), and (9) are not sufficient to allow you to provide yourself with a reasonable equivalent of the benefits (SSI benefits, federally administered State supplementary payments, Medicaid, and publicly-funded attendant care services, including personal care assistance under § 416.269(d)) which would be available to you if you did not have those earnings (see § 416.269).

[59 FR 41404, Aug. 12, 1994; 59 FR 49291, Sept. 27, 1994; 60 FR 8149, Feb. 10, 1995]

§ 416.266 Continuation of SSI status for Medicaid.

If we stop your benefits because of your earnings and you are potentially eligible for the special SSI eligibility status you will continue to be considered an SSI recipient for purposes of eligibility for Medicaid during the time it takes us to determine whether the special eligibility status applies to you.

§ 416.267 General.

We determine whether the special SSI eligibility status applies to you by verifying that you continue to be blind or have a disabling impairment by applying the rules in subpart I of this part, and by following the rules in this subpart to determine whether you meet the requirements in § 416.265(b). If you do not meet these requirements we determine that the special eligibility status does not apply. If you meet these requirements, then we apply special rules to determine if you meet the requirements of § 416.265(c) and (d). If for the period being evaluated, you meet all of the requirements in § 416.265 we determine that the special status applies to you.

§ 416.268 What is done to determine if you must have Medicaid in order to work.

For us to determine that you need Medicaid benefits in order to continue to work, you must establish:

(a) That you are currently using or have received services which were paid for by Medicaid during the period which began 12 months before our first contact with you to discuss this use; or

(b) That you expect to use these services within the next 12 months; or

(c) That you would need Medicaid to pay for unexpected medical expenses in the next 12 months.

[59 FR 41404, Aug. 12, 1994]

§ 416.269 What is done to determine whether your earnings are too low to provide comparable benefits and services you would receive in the absence of those earnings.

(a) What we determine. We must determine whether your earnings are too low to provide you with benefits and services comparable to the benefits and services you would receive if you did not have those earnings (see § 416.265(d)).

(b) How the determination is made. In determining whether your earnings are too low to provide you with benefits and services comparable to the benefits and services you would receive if you did not have those earnings, we compare your anticipated gross earnings (or a combination of anticipated and actual gross earnings, as appropriate) for the 12–month period beginning with the month for which your special SSI eligibility status is being determined to a threshold amount for your State of residence. This threshold amount consists of the sum for a 12–month period of two items, as follows:

(1) The amount of gross earnings including amounts excluded under § 416.1112(c)(4), (5) and (7) that would reduce to zero the Federal SSI benefit and the optional State supplementary payment for an individual with no other income living in his or her own household in the State where you reside. This amount will vary from State to State depending on the amount of the State supplementary payment; and

(2) The average expenditures for Medicaid benefits for disabled and blind SSI cash recipients, including recipients of federally administered State supplementary payments only, in your State of residence.

(c) How the eligibility requirements are met.

(1) You meet the requirements in § 416.265(d) if the comparison shows that your gross earnings are equal to or less than the applicable threshold amount for your State, as determined under paragraphs (b)(1) and (2) of this section. However, if the comparison shows that these earnings exceed the applicable threshold amount for your State, we will establish (and use in a second comparison) an individualized threshold taking into account the total amount of:

(i) The amount determined under paragraph (b)(1) of this section that would reduce to zero the Federal SSI benefit and State supplementary payment for your actual living arrangement;

(ii) The average Medicaid expenditures for your State of residence under paragraph (b)(2) of this section or, if higher, your actual medical expenditures in the appropriate 12–month period;

(iii) Any amounts excluded from your income as impairment-related work expenses (see § 416.1112(c)(6)), work expenses of the blind (see § 416.1112(c)(8)), and income used or set aside for use under an approved plan for achieving self support (see § 416.1112(c)(9)); and

(iv) The value of any publicly-funded attendant care services as described in paragraph (d) of this section (including personal care assistance).

(2) If you have already completed the 12-month period for which we are determining your eligibility, we will consider only the expenditures made in that period.

(d) Attendant care services. Expenditures for attendant care services (including personal care assistance) which would be available to you in the absence of earnings that make you ineligible for SSI cash benefits will be considered in the individualized threshold (as described in paragraph (c)(1) of this section) if we establish that they are:

(1) Provided by a paid attendant;

(2) Needed to assist with work-related and/or personal functions; and

(3) Paid from Federal, State, or local funds.

(e) Annual update of information. The threshold amounts used in determinations of sufficiency of earnings will be based on information and data updated no less frequently than annually.

[59 FR 41404, Aug. 12, 1994; 59 FR 49291, Sept. 27, 1994]

SUBPART C—FILING OF APPLICATIONS

Authority: Secs. 702(a)(5), 1611, and 1631 (a), (d), and (e) of the Social Security Act (42 U.S.C. 902(a)(5), 1382, and 1383 (a), (d), and (e)).

Source: 45 FR 48120, July 18, 1980; 51 FR 13492, April 21, 1986; 52 FR 27541, July 22, 1987; 61 FR 5941, Feb. 15, 1996, unless otherwise noted.

GENERAL PROVISIONS

§ 416.301 Introduction.

This subpart contains the rules for filing a claim for supplemental security income (SSI) benefits. It tells you what an application is, who may sign it, who must file one to be eligible for benefits, the period of time it is in effect, and how it may be withdrawn. It also tells you when a written statement or an oral inquiry may be considered to establish an application filing date.

§ 416.302 Definitions.

For the purpose of this subpart—

Benefits means any payments made under the SSI program. SSI benefits also include any federally administered State supplementary payments.

Claimant means the person who files an application for himself or herself or the person on whose behalf an application is filed.

We or us means the Social Security Administration (SSA).

You or your means the person who applies for benefits, the person for whom an application is filed or anyone who may consider applying for benefits.

§ 416.305 You must file an application to receive supplemental security income benefits.

(a) General rule. In addition to meeting other requirements, you must file an application to become eligible to receive benefits. If you believe you may be eligible, you should file an application as soon as possible. Filing an application will—

(1) Permit us to make a formal determination whether or not you are eligible to receive benefits;

(2) Assure that you receive benefits for any months you are eligible to receive payment; and

(3) Give you the right to appeal if you disagree with the determination.

(b) Exceptions. You need not file a new application if—

(1) You have been receiving benefits as an eligible spouse and are no longer living with your husband or wife;

(2) You have been receiving benefits as an eligible spouse of an eligible individual who has died;

(3) You have been receiving benefits because you are disabled or blind and you are 65 years old before the date we determine that you are no longer blind or disabled.

(4) A redetermination of your eligibility is being made and it is found that you were not eligible for benefits during any part of a period for which we are making a redetermination but you currently meet the requirements for eligibility;

(5) You are notified that your payments of SSI benefits will be stopped because you are no longer eligible and you again meet the requirements for eligibility before your appeal rights are exhausted.

[60 FR 16374, March 30, 1995; 64 FR 31972, June 15, 1999]

APPLICATIONS

§ 416.310 What makes an application a claim for benefits.

An application will be considered a claim for benefits, if the following requirements are met:

(a) An application form prescribed by us must be filled out.

(b) It must be filed at a social security office, at another Federal or State office we have designated to receive applications for us, or with a person we have authorized to receive applications for us. See § 416.325.

(c) The claimant or someone who may sign an application for the claimant must sign the application. See §§ 416.315 and 416.320.

(d) The claimant must be alive at the time the application is filed. See §§ 416.340, 416.345, and 416.351 for exceptions.

[59 FR 44926, Aug. 31, 1994]

§ 416.315 Who may sign an application.

We will determine who may sign an application according to the following rules:

(a) If you are 18 years old or over, mentally competent, and physically able, you must sign your own application. If you are 16 years old or older and under age 18, you may sign the application if you are mentally competent, have no court appointed representative, and are not in the care of any other person or institution.

(b) If the claimant is under age 18, or is mentally incompetent, or is physically unable to sign the application, a court appointed representative or a person who is responsible for the care of the claimant, including a relative, may sign the application. If the claimant is in the care of an institution, the manager or principal officer of the institution may sign the application.

(c) To prevent a claimant from losing benefits because of a delay in filing an application when there is a good reason why the claimant cannot sign an application, we may accept an application signed by someone other than a person described in this section.

Example: Mr. Smith comes to a Social Security office to file an application for SSI disability benefits for Mr. Jones. Mr. Jones, who lives alone, just suffered a heart attack and is in the hospital. He asked Mr. Smith, whose only relationship is that of a neighbor and friend, to file the application for him. We will accept an application signed by Mr. Smith since it would not be possible to have Mr. Jones sign and file the application at this time. SSI benefits can be paid starting with the first day of the month following the month the individual first meets all eligibility requirements for such benefits, including having filed an application. If Mr. Smith could not sign an application for Mr. Jones, a loss of benefits would result if it is later determined that Mr. Jones is in fact disabled.

[51 FR 13492, April 21, 1986; 64 FR 31972, June 15, 1999]

§ 416.320 Evidence of authority to sign an application for another.

(a) A person who signs an application for someone else will be required to provide evidence of his or her authority to sign the application for the person claiming benefits under the following rules:

(1) If the person who signs is a court appointed representative, he or she must submit a certificate issued by the court showing authority to act for the claimant.

(2) If the person who signs is not a court appointed representative, he or she must submit a statement describing his or her relationship to the claimant. The statement must also describe the extent to which the person is responsible for the care of the claimant. This latter information will not be requested if the application is signed by a parent for a child with whom he or she is living. If the person signing is the manager or principal officer of an institution he or she should show his or her title.

(b) We may, at any time, require additional evidence to establish the authority of a person to sign an application for someone else.

[51 FR 13493, April 21, 1986]

§ 416.325 When an application is considered filed.

(a) General rule. We consider an application for SSI benefits filed on the day it is received by an employee at any social security office, by someone at another Federal or State office designated to receive applications for us, or by a person we have authorized to receive applications for us.

(b) Exceptions.

(1) When we receive an application that is mailed, we will use the date shown by the United States postmark as the filing date if using the date the application is received will result in a loss of benefits. If the postmark is unreadable or there is no postmark, we will use the date the application is signed (if dated) or 5 days before the day we receive the signed application, whichever date is later.

(2) We consider an application to be filed on the date of the filing of a written statement or the making of an oral inquiry under the conditions in §§ 416.340, 416.345 and 416.350.

(3) We will establish a "deemed" filing date of an application in a case of misinformation under the conditions described in § 416.351. The filing date of the application will be a date determined under § 416.351(b).

[51 FR 13493, April 21, 1986; 59 FR 44926, Aug. 31, 1994]

§ 416.327 Pilot program for photographic identification of disability benefit applicants in designated geographic areas.

(a) To be eligible for SSI disability or blindness benefits in the designated pilot geographic areas during the time period of the pilot, you or a person acting on your behalf must give SSA permission to take your photograph and make this photograph a part of the claims folder. You must give us this permission when you apply for benefits and/or when we ask for it at a later time. Failure to cooperate will result in denial of benefits. We will permit an exception to the photograph requirement when an individual has a sincere religious objection. This pilot will be in effect for a six-month period after these final rules become effective.

(b) Designated pilot geographic areas means:

(1) All SSA field offices in the State of South Carolina.

(2) The Augusta, Georgia SSA field office.

(3) All SSA field offices in the State of Kansas.

(4) Selected SSA field offices located in New York City.

[68 FR 23195, May 1, 2003]

EFFECTIVE FILING PERIOD OF APPLICATION

§ 416.330 Filing before the first month you meet the requirements for eligibility.

If you file an application for SSI benefits before the first month you meet all the other requirements for eligibility, the application will remain in effect from the date it is filed until we make a final determination on your application, unless there is a hearing decision on your application. If there is a hearing decision, your application will remain in effect until the hearing decision is issued.

(a) If you meet all the requirements for eligibility while your application is in effect, the earliest month for which we can pay you benefits is the month following the month that you first meet all the requirements.

(b) If you first meet all the requirements for eligibility after the period for which your application was in effect, you must file a new application for benefits. In this case, we can pay you benefits only from the first day of the month following the month that you meet all the requirements based on the new application.

[51 FR 13493, April 21, 1986; 64 FR 31973, June 15, 1999]

§ 416.335 Filing in or after the month you meet the requirements for eligibility.

When you file an application in the month that you meet all the other requirements for eligibility, the earliest month for which we can pay you benefits is the month following the month you filed the application. If you file an application after the month you first meet all the other requirements for eligibility, we cannot pay you for the month in which your application is filed or any months before that month. See §§ 416.340, 416.345 and 416.350 on how a written statement or an oral inquiry made before the filing of the application form may affect the filing date of the application.

[51 FR 13493, April 21, 1986; 64 FR 31973, June 15, 1999]

FILING DATE BASED UPON A WRITTEN STATEMENT OR ORAL INQUIRY

§ 416.340 Use of date of written statement as application filing date.

We will use the date a written statement, such as a letter, an SSA questionnaire or some other writing, is received at a social security office, at another Federal or State office designated by us, or by a person we have authorized to receive applications for us as the filing date of an application for benefits, only if the use of that date will result in your eligibility for additional benefits. If the written statement is mailed, we will use the date the statement was mailed to us as shown by a United States postmark. If the postmark is unreadable or there is no postmark, we will use the date the statement is signed (if dated) or 5 days before the day we receive the written statement, whichever date is later, as the filing date of an application for benefits. In order for us to use your written statement to protect your filing date, the following requirements must be met:

(a) The written statement shows an intent to claim benefits for yourself or for another person.

(b) You, your spouse or a person who may sign an application for you signs the statement.

(c) An application form signed by you or by a person who may sign an application for you is filed with us within 60 days after the date of a notice we will send telling of the need to file an application. The notice will say that we will make an initial determination of eligibility for SSI benefits if an application form is filed within 60 days after the date of the notice. (We will send the notice to the claimant, or where he or she is a minor or incompetent, to the person who gave us the written statement.)

(d)(1) The claimant is alive when the application is filed on a prescribed form, or

(2) If the claimant dies after the written statement is filed, the deceased claimant's surviving spouse or parent(s) who could be paid the claimant's benefits under § 416.542(b), or someone on behalf of the surviving spouse or parent(s) files an application form. If we learn that the claimant has died before the notice is sent or within 60 days after the notice but before an application form is filed, we will send a notice to such a survivor. The notice will say that we will make an initial determination of eligibility for SSI benefits only if an application form is filed on behalf of the deceased within 60 days after the date of the notice to the survivor.

[51 FR 13493, April 21, 1986; 58 FR 52912, Oct. 13, 1993]

§ 416.345 Use of date of oral inquiry as application filing date.

We will use the date of an oral inquiry about SSI benefits as the filing date of an application for benefits only if the use of that date will result in your eligibility for additional benefits and the following requirements are met:

(a) The inquiry asks about the claimant's eligibility for SSI benefits.

(b) The inquiry is made by the claimant, the claimant's spouse, or a person who may sign an application on the claimant's behalf as described in § 416.315.

(c) The inquiry, whether in person or by telephone, is directed to an office or an official described in § 416.310(b).

(d) The claimant or a person on his or her behalf as described in § 416.315 files an application on a prescribed form within 60 days after the date of the notice we will send telling of the need to file an application. The notice will say that we will make an initial determination of eligibility for SSI benefits if an application form is filed within 60 days after the date of the notice. (We will send the notice to the claimant or, where he or she is a minor or incompetent, to the person who made the inquiry.)

(e)(1) The claimant is alive when the application is filed on a prescribed form, or

(2) If the claimant dies after the oral inquiry is made, the deceased claimant's surviving spouse or parent(s) who could be paid the claimant's benefits under § 416.542(b), or someone on behalf of the surviving spouse or parent(s) files an application form. If we learn that the claimant has died before the notice is sent or within 60 days after the notice but before an application form is filed, we will send a notice to such a survivor. The notice will say that we will make an initial determination of eligibility for SSI benefits only if an application form is filed on behalf of the deceased within 60 days after the date of the notice to the survivor.

[51 FR 13493, April 21, 1986; 58 FR 52912, Oct. 13, 1993]

§ 416.350 Treating a title II application as an oral inquiry about SSI benefits.

(a) When a person applies for benefits under title II (retirement, survivors, or disability benefits) we will explain the requirements for receiving SSI benefits and give the person a chance to file an application for them if—

(1) The person is within 2 months of age 65 or older or it looks as if the person might qualify as a blind or disabled person, and

(2) It is not clear that the person's title II benefits would prevent him or her from receiving SSI or any State supplementary benefits handled by the Social Security Administration.

(b) If the person applying for title II benefits does not file an application for SSI on a prescribed form when SSI is explained to him or her, we will treat his or her filing of an application for title II benefits as an oral inquiry about SSI, and the date of the title II application form may be used to establish the SSI application date if the requirements of § 416.345 (d) and (e) are met.

DEEMED FILING DATE BASED ON MISINFORMATION

§ 416.351 Deemed filing date in a case of misinformation.

(a) General. You may have considered applying for SSI benefits for yourself or for another person, and you may have contacted us in writing, by telephone or in person to inquire about filing an application for these benefits. It is possible that in responding to your inquiry, we may have given you misinformation about your eligibility for such benefits, or the eligibility of the person on whose behalf you were considering applying for benefits, which caused you not to file an application at that time. If this happened, and later an application for such benefits is filed with us, we may establish an earlier filing date under this section.

Example 1: Ms. Jones calls a Social Security office to inquire about filing an application for SSI benefits. During her conversation with an SSA employee, she tells the employee about her resources. The SSA employee tells Ms. Jones that because her countable resources are above the allowable limit, she would be ineligible for SSI benefits. The employee fails to consider certain resource exclusions under the SSI program which would have reduced Ms. Jones' countable resources below the allowable limit, making her eligible for benefits. Because Ms. Jones thought that she would be ineligible, she decides not to file an application for SSI benefits. Ms. Jones later reads about resource exclusions under the SSI program. She recontacts the Social Security office to file an SSI application, and alleges that she had been previously misinformed about her eligibility for SSI benefits. She files an application for SSI benefits, provides the information required under paragraph (f) of this section to show that an SSA employee provided misinformation, and requests a deemed filing date based upon her receipt of misinformation.

Example 2: Mr. Adams resides in a State which provides State supplementary payments that are administered by SSA under the SSI program. He telephones a Social Security office and tells an SSA employee that he does not have enough income to live on and wants to file for SSI benefits. Mr. Adams states that his only income is his monthly Social Security benefit check. The SSA employee checks Mr. Adams' Social Security record and advises him that he is ineligible for SSI benefits based on the amount of his monthly Social Security benefit. The employee does not consider whether Mr. Adams would be eligible for State supplementary payments. Because Mr. Adams was told that he would not be eligible for benefits under the SSI program, he does not file an application. The employee does not make a record of Mr. Adams' oral inquiry or take any other action. A year later, Mr. Adams speaks to a neighbor who receives the same Social Security benefit amount that Mr. Adams does, but also receives payments under the SSI program. Thinking the law may have changed, Mr. Adams recontacts a Social Security office and learns from an SSA employee that he would be eligible for State supplementary payments under the SSI program and that he could have received these payments earlier had he filed an application. Mr. Adams explains that he did not file an application earlier because he was told by an SSA employee that he was not eligible for SSI benefits. Mr. Adams files an application for the benefits, provides the information required under paragraph (f) of this section to show that an SSA employee provided misinformation, and requests a deemed filing date based on the misinformation provided to him earlier.

(b) Deemed filing date of an application based on misinformation. Subject to the requirements and conditions in paragraphs (c) through (g) of this section, we may establish a deemed filing date of an application for SSI benefits under the following provisions.

(1)(i) If we determine that you failed to apply for SSI benefits for yourself because we gave you misinformation about your eligibility for such benefits, we will deem an application for such benefits to have been filed with us on the later of—

(A) The date on which the misinformation was provided to you; or

(B) The date on which you met all of the requirements for eligibility for such benefits, other than the requirement of filing an application.

(ii) Before we may establish a deemed filing date of an application for benefits for you under paragraph (b)(1)(i) of this section, you or a person described in § 416.315 must file an application for such benefits. If you die before an application for the benefits is filed with us, we will consider establishing a deemed filing date of an application for such benefits only if a person who would be qualified under § 416.542(b) to receive any benefits due you, or someone on his or her behalf, files an application for the benefits.

(2)(i) If you had authority under § 416.315 to sign an application for benefits for another person, and we determine that you failed to apply for SSI benefits for that person because we gave you misinformation about that person's eligibility for such benefits, we will deem an application for such benefits to have been filed with us on the later of—

(A) The date on which the misinformation was provided to you; or

(B) The date on which the person met all of the requirements for eligibility for such benefits, other than the requirement of filing an application.

(ii) Before we may establish a deemed filing date of an application for benefits for the person under paragraph (b)(2)(i) of this section, you, such person, or another person described in § 416.315 must file an application for such benefits. If the person referred to in paragraph (b)(2)(i) of this section dies before an application for the benefits is filed with us, we will consider establishing a deemed filing date of an application for such benefits only if a person who would be qualified under § 416.542(b) to receive any benefits due the deceased person, or someone on his behalf, files an application for the benefits.

(c) Requirements concerning the misinformation. We apply the following requirements for purposes of paragraph (b) of this section.

(1) The misinformation must have been provided to you by one of our employees while he or she was acting in his or her official capacity as our employee. For purposes of this section, an employee includes an officer of SSA.

(2) Misinformation is information which we consider to be incorrect, misleading, or incomplete in view of the facts which you gave to the employee, or of which the employee was aware or should have been aware, regarding your particular circumstances, or the particular circumstances of the person referred to in paragraph (b)(2)(i) of this section. In addition, for us to find that the information you received was incomplete, the employee must have failed to provide you with the appropriate, additional information which he or she would be required to provide in carrying out his or her official duties.

(3) The misinformation may have been provided to you orally or in writing.

(4) The misinformation must have been provided to you in response to a specific request by you to us for information about your eligibility for benefits or the eligibility for benefits of the person referred to in paragraph (b)(2)(i) of this section for which you were considering filing an application.

(d) Evidence that misinformation was provided. We will consider the following evidence in making a determination under paragraph (b) of this section.

(1) Preferred evidence. Preferred evidence is written evidence which relates directly to your inquiry about your eligibility for benefits or the eligibility of another person and which shows that we gave you misinformation which caused you not to file an application. Preferred evidence includes, but is not limited to, the following—

(i) A notice, letter, or other document which was issued by us and addressed to you; or

(ii) Our record of your telephone call, letter, or in-person contact.

(2) Other evidence. In the absence of preferred evidence, we will consider other evidence, including your statements about the alleged misinformation, to determine whether we gave you misinformation which caused you not to file an application. We will not find that we gave you misinformation, however, based solely on your statements. Other evidence which you provide or which we obtain must support your statements. Evidence which we will consider includes, but is not limited to, the following—

(i) Your statements about the alleged misinformation, including statements about—

(A) The date and time of the alleged contact(s);

(B) How the contact was made, e.g., by telephone or in person;

(C) The reason(s) the contact was made;

(D) Who gave the misinformation; and

(E) The questions you asked and the facts you gave us, and the questions we asked and the information we gave you at the time of the contact;

(ii) Statements from others who were present when you were given the alleged misinformation, e.g., a neighbor who accompanied you to our office;

(iii) If you can identify the employee or the employee can recall your inquiry about benefits—

(A) Statements from the employee concerning the alleged contact, including statements about the questions you asked, the facts you gave, the questions the employee asked, and the information provided to you at the time of the alleged contact; and

(B) Our assessment of the likelihood that the employee provided the alleged misinformation;

(iv) An evaluation of the credibility and the validity of your allegations in conjunction with other relevant information; and

(v) Any other information regarding your alleged contact.

(e) Information which does not constitute satisfactory proof that misinformation was given. Certain kinds of information will not be considered satisfactory proof that we gave you misinformation which caused you not to file an application. Examples of such information include—

(1) General informational pamphlets that we issue to provide basic program information;

(2) The SSI Benefit Estimate Letter that is based on an individual's reported and projected income and is an estimate which can be requested at any time;

(3) General information which we review or prepare but which is disseminated by the media, e.g., radio, television, magazines, and newspapers; and

(4) Information provided by other governmental agencies, e.g., the Department of Veterans Affairs, the Department of Defense, State unemployment agencies, and State and local governments.

(f) Claim for benefits based on misinformation. You may make a claim for benefits based on misinformation at any time. Your claim must contain information that will enable us to determine if we did provide misinformation to you about your eligibility for SSI benefits, or the eligibility of a person on whose behalf you were considering applying for benefits, which caused you not to file an application for the benefits. Specifically, your claim must be in writing and it must explain what information was provided; how, when, and where it was provided and by whom; and why the information caused you not to file an application. If you give us this information, we will make a determination on such a claim for benefits if all of the following conditions are also met.

(1) An application for the benefits described in paragraph (b)(1)(i) or (b)(2)(i) of this section is filed with us by someone described in paragraph (b)(1)(ii) or (b)(2)(ii) of this section, as appropriate. The application must be filed after the alleged misinformation was provided. This application may be—

(i) An application on which we have made a previous final determination or decision awarding the benefits, but only if the claimant continues to be eligible for benefits (or again could be eligible for benefits) based on that application;

(ii) An application on which we have made a previous final determination or decision denying the benefits, but only if such determination or decision is reopened under § 416.1488; or

(iii) A new application on which we have not made a final determination or decision.

(2) The establishment of a deemed filing date of an application for benefits based on misinformation could result in the claimant becoming eligible for benefits or for additional benefits.

(3) We have not made a previous final determination or decision to which you were a party on a claim for benefits based on alleged misinformation involving the same facts and issues. This provision does not apply, however, if the final determination or decision may be reopened under § 416.1488.

(g) Effective date. This section applies only to misinformation which we provided on or after December 19, 1989. In addition, this section is effective only for benefits payable for months after December 1989.

[59 FR 44926, Aug. 31, 1994]

WITHDRAWAL OF APPLICATION

§ 416.355 Withdrawal of an application.

(a) Request for withdrawal filed before we make a determination. If you make a request to withdraw your application before we make a determination on your claim, we will approve the request if the following requirements are met:

(1) You or a person who may sign an application for you signs a written request to withdraw the application and files it at a place described in § 416.325.

(2) You are alive when the request is filed.

(b) Request for withdrawal filed after a determination is made. If you make a request to withdraw your application after we make a determination on your claim, we will approve the request if the following requirements are met:

(1) The conditions in paragraph (a) of this section are met.

(2) Every other person who may lose benefits because of the withdrawal consents in writing (anyone who could sign an application for that person may give the consent).

(3) All benefits already paid based on the application are repaid or we are satisfied that they will be repaid.

(c) Effect of withdrawal. If we approve your request to withdraw an application, we will treat the application as though you never filed it. If we disapprove your request for withdrawal, we will treat the application as though you never requested the withdrawal.

§ 416.360 Cancellation of a request to withdraw.

You may cancel your request to withdraw your application and your application will still be good if the following requirements are met:

(a) You or a person who may sign an application for you signs a written request for cancellation and files it at a place described in § 416.325.

(b) You are alive at the time the request for cancellation is filed.

(c) For a cancellation request received after we have approved the withdrawal, the cancellation request is filed no later than 60 days after the date of the notice of approval of the withdrawal request.

SUBPART D—AMOUNT OF BENEFITS

Authority: Secs. 702(a)(5), 1611 (a), (b), (c), and (e), 1612, 1617, and 1631 of the Social Security Act (42 U.S.C. 902(a)(5), 1382 (a), (b), (c), and (e), 1382a, 1382f, and 1383).

Source: 39 FR 23053, June 26, 1974; 50 FR 48570, Nov. 26, 1985; 51 FR 10616, March 28, 1986; 51 FR 12606, April 14, 1986; 51 FR 13493, April 21, 1986; 52 FR 27541, July 22, 1987; 61 FR 5942, Feb. 15, 1996, unless otherwise noted.

§ 416.401 Scope of subpart.

This subpart D sets forth basic guidelines for establishing the amount of monthly benefits payable to an eligible individual or couple (as defined in § 416.120(c)(5)). This subpart does not contain provisions with respect to establishing the amount of State supplementary payments payable in accordance with an agreement entered into between a State and the Administration under the provisions of subpart T of this part. Provisions with respect to determination and payment of State supplementary payments under such agreements will be administered by the Administration in accordance with the terms set forth in such agreements.

§ 416.405 Cost-of-living adjustments in benefits.

Whenever benefit amounts under title II of the Act (part 404 of this chapter) are increased by any percentage effective with any month as a result of a determination made under Section 215(i) of the Act, each of the dollar amounts in effect for such month under §§ 416.410, 416.412, and 416.413, as specified in such sections or as previously increased under this section or under any provision of the Act, will be increased. We will increase the unrounded yearly SSI benefit amount by the same percentage by which the title II benefits are being increased based on the Consumer Price Index, or, if greater, the percentage they would be increased if the rise in the Consumer Price Index were currently the basis for the title II increase. (See §§ 404.270–404.277 for an explanation of how the title II cost-of-living adjustment is computed.) If the increased annual SSI benefit amount is not a multiple of $12, it will be rounded to the next lower multiple of $12.

[41 FR 20872, May 21, 1976; 48 FR 21945, May 16, 1983; 51 FR 12606, April 14, 1986; 51 FR 16016, April 30, 1986]

§ 416.410 Amount of benefits; eligible individual.

The benefit under this part for an eligible individual (including the eligible individual receiving benefits payable under the § 416.212 provisions) who does not have an eligible spouse, who is not subject to either benefit suspension under § 416.1325 or benefit reduction under § 416.414, and who is not a qualified individual (as defined in § 416.221) shall be payable at the rate of $5,640 per year ($470 per month) effective for the period beginning January 1, 1996. This rate is the result of a 2.6 percent cost-of-living adjustment (see § 416.405) to the December 1995 rate. For the period January 1, through December 31, 1995, the rate payable, as increased by the 2.8 percent cost-of-living adjustment, was $5,496 per year ($458 per month). For the period January 1, through December 31, 1994, the rate payable, as increased by the 2.6 percent cost-of-living adjustment, was $5,352 per year ($446 per month). The monthly rate is reduced by the amount of the individual's income which is not excluded pursuant to subpart K of this part.

[61 FR 10278, March 13, 1996]

§ 416.412 Amount of benefits; eligible couple.

The benefit under this part for an eligible couple (including couples where one or both members of the couple are receiving benefits payable under the § 416.212 provisions), neither of whom is subject to suspension of benefits based on § 416.1325 or reduction of benefits based on § 416.414 nor is a qualified individual (as defined in § 416.221) shall be payable at the rate of $8,460 per year ($705 per month), effective for the period beginning January 1, 1996. This rate is the result of a 2.6 percent cost-of-living adjustment (see § 416.405) to the December 1995 rate. For the period January 1, through December 31, 1995, the rate payable, as increased by the 2.8 percent cost-of-living adjustment, was $8,224 per year ($687 per month). For the period January 1, through December 31, 1994, the rate payable, as increased by the 2.6 percent cost-of-living adjustment, was $8,028 per year ($669 per month). The monthly rate is reduced by the amount of the couple's income which is not excluded pursuant to subpart K of this part.

[61 FR 10278, March 13, 1996]

§ 416.413 Amount of benefits; qualified individual.

The benefit under this part for a qualified individual (defined in § 416.221) is payable at the rate for an eligible individual or eligible couple plus an increment for each essential person (defined in § 416.222) in the household, reduced by the amount of countable income of the eligible individual or eligible couple as explained in § 416.420. A qualified individual will receive an increment of $2,820 per year ($235 per month), effective for the period beginning January 1, 1996. This rate is the result of the 2.6 percent cost-of-living adjustment (see § 416.405) to the December 1995 rate, and is for each essential person (as defined in § 416.222) living in the household of a qualified individual. (See § 416.532.) For the period January 1, through December 31, 1995, the rate payable, as increased by the 2.8 percent cost-of-living adjustment, was $2,748 per year ($229 per month). For the period January 1, through December 31, 1994, the rate payable, as increased by the 2.6 percent cost-of-living adjustment, was $2,676 per year ($223 per month). The total benefit rate, including the increment, is reduced by the amount of the individual's or couple's income that is not excluded pursuant to subpart K of this part.

[61 FR 10278, March 13, 1996]

§ 416.414 Amount of benefits; eligible individual or eligible couple in a medical treatment facility.

(a) General rule. Except where the § 416.212 provisions provide for payment of benefits at the rates specified under §§ 416.410 and 416.412, reduced SSI benefits are payable to persons and couples who are in medical treatment facilities where a substantial part (more than 50 percent) of the cost of their care is paid by a State plan under title XIX of the Social Security Act (Medicaid). This reduced SSI benefit rate applies to persons who are in medical treatment facilities where a substantial part (more than 50 percent) of the cost would have been paid by an approved Medicaid State plan but for the application of section 1917(c) of the Social Security Act due to a transfer of assets for less than fair market value. This reduced SSI benefit rate also applies to children under age 18 who are in medical treatment facilities where a substantial part (more than 50 percent) of the cost of their care is paid by a health insurance policy issued by a private provider of such insurance, or where a substantial part (more than 50 percent) of the cost of their care is paid for by a combination of Medicaid payments and payments made under a health insurance policy issued by a private provider of such insurance. Persons and couples to whom these reduced benefits apply are—

(1) Those who are otherwise eligible and who are in the medical treatment facility throughout a month. (By throughout a month we mean that you are in the medical treatment facility as of the beginning of the month and stay the entire month. If you are in a medical treatment facility you will be considered to have continuously been staying there if you are transferred from one medical treatment facility to another or if you are temporarily absent for a period of not more than 14 consecutive days.); and

(2) Those who reside for part of a month in a public institution and for the rest of the month are in a public or private medical treatment facility where Medicaid pays or would have paid (but for the application of section 1917(c) of the Act) a substantial part (more than 50 percent) of the cost of their care; and

(3) Children under age 18 who reside for part of a month in a public institution and for the rest of the month are in a public or private medical treatment facility where a substantial part (more than 50 percent) of the cost of their care is being paid under a health insurance policy issued by a private provider or by a combination of Medicaid and payments under a health insurance policy issued by a private provider.

(b) The benefit rates are—

(1) Eligible individual. For months after June 1988, the benefit rate for an eligible individual with no eligible spouse is $30 per month. The benefit payment is figured by subtracting the eligible individual's countable income (see subpart K) from the benefit rate as explained in § 416.420.

(2) Eligible couple both of whom are temporarily absent from home in medical treatment facilities as described in § 416.1149(c)(1). For months after June 1988, the benefit rate for a couple is $60 a month. The benefit payment is figured by subtracting the couple's countable income (see subpart K) from the benefit rate as explained in § 416.420.

(3) Eligible couple with one spouse who is temporarily absent from home as described in § 416.1149(c)(1). The couple's benefit rate equals:

(i) For months after June 1988, $30 per month for the spouse in the medical treatment facility; plus

(ii) The benefit rate for an eligible individual (see § 416.410) for the spouse who is not in the medical treatment facility. The benefit payment for each spouse is figured by subtracting each individual's own countable income in the appropriate month (see § 416.420) from his or her portion of the benefit rate shown in paragraphs (b)(3)(i) and (ii).

(c) Definition. For purposes of this section, a medical treatment facility means an institution or that part of an institution that is licensed or otherwise approved by a Federal, State, or local government to provide inpatient medical care and services.

[47 FR 3106, Jan. 22, 1982; 50 FR 48571, Nov. 26, 1985; 50 FR 51514, Dec. 18, 1985; 54 FR 19164, May 4, 1989; 58 FR 64894, Dec. 10, 1993; 60 FR 16374, March 30, 1995; 61 FR 10278, March 13, 1996; 62 FR 1056, Jan. 8, 1997; 62 FR

42412, Aug. 7, 1997; 72 FR 50874, Sept. 5, 2007; 72 FR 54350, Sept. 25, 2007]

§ 416.415 Amount of benefits; eligible individual is disabled child under age 18.

(a) If you are a disabled child under age 18 and meet the conditions in § 416.1165(i) for waiver of deeming, your parents' income will not be deemed to you and your benefit rate will be $30 a month.

(b) If you are a disabled child under age 18 and do not meet the conditions in § 416.1165(i) only because your parents' income is not high enough to make you ineligible for SSI but deeming of your parents' income would result in an SSI benefit less than the amount payable if you received benefits as a child under § 416.1165(i), your benefit will be the amount payable if you received benefits as a child under § 416.1165(i).

[60 FR 361, Jan. 4, 1995]

§ 416.420 Determination of benefits; general.

Benefits shall be determined for each month. The amount of the monthly payment will be computed by reducing the benefit rate (see §§ 416.410, 416.412, 416.413, and 416.414) by the amount of countable income as figured under the rules in subpart K of this part. The appropriate month's countable income to be used to determine how much your benefit payment will be for the current month (the month for which a benefit is payable) will be determined as follows:

(a) General rule. We generally use the amount of your countable income in the second month prior to the current month to determine how much your benefit amount will be for the current month. We will use the benefit rate (see §§ 416.410 through 416.414), as increased by a cost-of-living adjustment, in determining the value of the one-third reduction or the presumed maximum value, to compute your SSI benefit amount for the first 2 months in which the cost-of-living adjustment is in effect. If you have been receiving an SSI benefit and a Social Security insurance benefit and the latter is increased on the basis of the cost-of-living adjustment or because your benefit is recomputed, we will compute the amount of your SSI benefit for January, the month of an SSI benefit increase, by including in your income the amount by which your Social Security benefit in January exceeds the amount of your Social Security benefit in November. Similarly, we will compute the amount of your SSI benefit for February by including in your income the amount by which your Social Security benefit in February exceeds the amount of your Social Security benefit in December.

Example 1. Mrs. X's benefit amount is being determined for September (the current month). Mrs. X's countable income in July is used to determine the benefit amount for September.

Example 2. Mr. Z's SSI benefit amount is being determined for January (the current month). There has been a cost-of-living increase in SSI benefits effective January. Mr. Z's countable income in November is used to determine the benefit amount for January. In November, Mr. Z had in-kind support and maintenance valued at the presumed maximum value as described in § 416.1140(a). We will use the January benefit rate, as increased by the COLA, to determine the value of the in-kind support and maintenance Mr. Z received in November when we determine Mr. Z's SSI benefit amount for January.

Example 3. Mr. Y's SSI benefit amount is being determined for January (the current month). Mr. Y has Social Security income of $100 in November, $100 in December, and $105 in January. We find the amount by which his Social Security income in January exceeds his Social Security income in November ($5) and add that to his income in November to determine the SSI benefit amount for January.

(b) Exceptions to the general rule—

(1) First month of initial eligibility for payment or the first month of eligibility after a month of ineligibility. We use your countable income in the current month to determine your benefit amount for the first month you are initially eligible for payment of SSI benefits (see § 416.501) or for the first month you again become eligible for SSI benefits after at least a month of ineligibility. Your payment for a first month of reeligibility after at least one-month of ineligibility will be prorated according to the number of days in the month that you are eligible beginning with the date on which you reattain eligibility.

Example: Mrs. Y applies for SSI benefits in September and meets the requirements for eligibility in that month. (We use Mrs. Y's countable income in September to determine if she is eligible for SSI in September.) The first month for which she can receive payment is October (see § 416.501). We use Mrs. Y's countable income in October to determine the amount of her benefit for October. If Mrs. Y had been receiving SSI benefits through July, became ineligible for SSI benefits in August, and again became eligible for such benefits in September, we would use Mrs. Y's countable income in September to determine the amount of her benefit for September. In addition, the proration rules discussed above would also apply to determine the amount of benefits in September in this second situation.

(2) Second month of initial eligibility for payment or second month of eligibility after a month of ineligibility. We use your countable income in the first month prior to the current month to determine how much your benefit amount will be for the current month when the current month is the second month of initial eligibility for payment or the second month of reeligibility following at least a month of ineligibility. However, if you have been receiving both an SSI benefit and a Social Security insurance benefit and the latter is increased on the basis of the cost-of-living adjustment or because your benefit is recomputed, we will compute the amount of your SSI benefit for January, the month of an SSI benefit increase, by including in your income the amount by which your Social Security benefit in January exceeds the amount of your Social Security benefit in December.

Example: Mrs. Y was initially eligible for payment of SSI benefits in October. Her benefit amount for November will be based on her countable income in October (first prior month).

(3) Third month of initial eligibility for payment or third month of eligibility after a month of ineligibility. We use your countable income according to the rule set out in paragraph (a) of this section to determine how much your benefit amount will be for the third month of initial eligibility for payment or the third month of reeligibility after at least a month of ineligibility.

Example: Mrs. Y was initially eligible for payment of SSI benefits in October. Her benefit amount for December will be based on her countable income in October (second prior month).

(4) Income derived from certain assistance payments. We use your income in the current month from the programs listed below to determine your benefit amount for that same month. The assistance programs are as follows:

(i) Aid to Families with Dependent Children under title IV–A of the Social Security Act (the Act);

(ii) Foster Care under title IV–E of the Act;

(iii) Refugee Cash Assistance pursuant to section 412(e) of the Immigration and Nationality Act;

(iv) Cuban and Haitian Entrant Assistance pursuant to section 501(a) of Pub.L. 96–422; and

(v) Bureau of Indian Affairs general assistance and child welfare assistance pursuant to 42 Stat. 208 as amended.

(c) Reliable information which is currently available for determining benefits. The Commissioner has determined that no reliable information exists which is currently available to use in determining benefit amounts.

(1) Reliable information. For purposes of this section reliable information means payment information that is maintained on a computer system of records by the government agency determining the payments (e.g., Department of Veterans Affairs, Office of Personnel Management for Federal civil service information and the Railroad Retirement Board).

(2) Currently available information. For purposes of this section currently available information means information that is available at such time that it permits us to compute and issue a correct benefit for the month the information is pertinent.

(d) Payment of benefits. See subpart E of this part for the rules on payments and the minimum monthly benefit (as explained in § 416.503).

[50 FR 48571, Nov. 26, 1985; 50 FR 51514, Dec. 18, 1985; 54 FR 31657, Aug. 1, 1989; 62 FR 30751, June 5, 1997; 63 FR 33546, June 19, 1998; 64 FR 31973, June 15, 1999]

§ 416.421 Determination of benefits; computation of prorated benefits.

(a) In the month that you reacquire eligibility after a month or more of ineligibility (see § 416.1320(b)), your benefit will be prorated according to the number of days in the month that you are eligible beginning with the date on which you meet all eligibility requirements.

(b) In determining the amount of your benefit for a month in which benefits are to be prorated, we first compute the amount of the benefit that you would receive for the month as if proration did not apply. We then determine the date on which you meet all factors of eligibility. (The income limits must be met based on the entire month and the resource limit must be as of the first day of the month.) We then count the number of days in the month beginning with the day on which you first meet all factors of eligibility through the end of the month. We then multiply the amount of your unprorated benefit for the month by the number of days for which you are eligible for benefits and divide that figure by the number of days in the month for which your benefit is being determined. The result is the amount of the benefit that you are due for the month in which benefits are to be prorated.

[51 FR 13493, April 21, 1986; 64 FR 31973, June 15, 1999; 68 FR 53509, Sept. 11, 2003]

§ 416.426 Change in status involving an individual; ineligibility occurs.

Whenever benefits are suspended or terminated for an individual because of ineligibility, no benefit is payable for that month.

[50 FR 48571, Nov. 26, 1985]

§ 416.428 Eligible individual without an eligible spouse has an essential person in his home.

When an eligible individual without an eligible spouse has an essential person (as defined in § 416.222 of this part) in his home, the amount by which his rate of payment is increased is determined in accordance with §§ 416.220 through 416.223 and with 416.413 of this part. The essential person's income is deemed to be that of the eligible individual, and the provisions of §§ 416.401 through 416.426 will apply in determining the benefit of such eligible individual.

[51 FR 10616, March 28, 1986; 65 FR 16814, March 30, 2000]

§ 416.430 Eligible individual with eligible spouse; essential person(s) present.

(a) When an eligible individual with an eligible spouse has an essential person (§ 416.222) living in his or her home, or when both such persons each has an essential person, the increase in the rate of payment is determined in accordance with §§ 416.413 and 416.532. The income of the essential person(s) is included in the income of the couple and the payment due will be equally divided between each member of the eligible couple.

(b) When one member of an eligible couple is temporarily absent in accordance with § 416.1149(c)(1) and § 416.222(c) and either one or both individuals has an essential person, add the essential person increment to the benefit rate for the member of the couple who is actually residing with the essential person and include the income of the essential person in that member's income. See § 416.414(b)(3).

[51 FR 10616, March 28, 1986; 60 FR 16375, March 30, 1995]

§ 416.432 Change in status involving a couple; eligibility continues.

When there is a change in status which involves the formation or dissolution of an eligible couple (for example, marriage, divorce), a redetermination of the benefit amount shall be made for the months subsequent to the month of such formation or dissolution of the couple in accordance with the following rules:

(a) When there is a dissolution of an eligible couple and each member of the couple becomes an eligible individual, the benefit amount for each person shall be determined individually for each month beginning with the first month after the month in which the dissolution occurs. This shall be done by determining the applicable benefit rate for an eligible individual with no eligible spouse according to §§ 416.410 or 416.413 and 416.414 and applying § 416.420(a). See § 416.1147a for the applicable income rules when in-kind support and maintenance is involved.

(b) When two eligible individuals become an eligible couple, the benefit amount will be determined for the couple beginning with the first month following the month of the change. This shall be done by determining which benefit rate to use for an eligible couple according to §§ 416.412 or 416.413 and 416.414 and applying the requirements in § 416.420(a).

[39 FR 23053, June 26, 1974, as amended at 41 FR 20872, May 21, 1976; 50 FR 48571, Nov. 26, 1985; 54 FR 19164, May 4, 1989; 60 FR 16375, March 30, 1995]

§ 416.435 Change in status involving a couple; ineligibility occurs.

Whenever benefits are suspended or terminated for both members of a couple because of ineligibility, no benefits are payable for that month. However, when benefits are suspended or terminated for one member of a couple because of ineligibility for a month, the member who remains eligible assumes the eligibility status of an eligible individual without an eligible spouse for such month and the benefit rate and payment amount will be determined as an eligible individual for the month.

[50 FR 48572, Nov. 26, 1985]

SUBPART E—PAYMENT OF BENEFITS, OVERPAYMENTS, AND UNDERPAYMENTS

Authority: Secs. 702(a)(5), 1147, 1601, 1602, 1611(c) and (e), and 1631(a)-(d) and (g) of the Social Security Act (42 U.S.C. 902(a)(5), 1320b–17, 1381, 1381a, 1382(c) and (e), and 1383(a)-(d) and (g)); 31 U.S.C. 3716; 31 U.S.C. 3720A.

Source: 39 FR 8156, March 4, 1974; 50 FR 48572, Nov. 26, 1985; 51 FR 10616, March 28, 1986; 52 FR 8881, March 20, 1987; 52 FR 27541, July 22, 1987; 53 FR 16543, May 10, 1988; 55 FR 7313, March 1, 1990; 59 FR 1636, Jan. 12, 1994; 60 FR 8149, Feb. 10, 1995; 61 FR 5942, Feb. 15, 1996; 62 FR 49438, Sept. 22, 1997; 66 FR 38906, July 26, 2001; 76 FR 65108, Oct. 20, 2011, unless otherwise noted.

§ 416.501 Payment of benefits: General.

Payment of SSI benefits will be made for the month after the month of initial eligibility and for each subsequent month provided all requirements for eligibility (see § 416.202) and payment (see § 416.420) are met. In the month the individual re-establishes eligibility after at least a month of ineligibility, benefits are paid for such a month beginning with the date in the month on which the individual meets all eligibility requirements. In some months, while the factors of eligibility based on the current month may be established, it is possible to receive no payment for that month if the factors of eligibility for payment are not met. Payment of benefits may not be made for any period that precedes the first month following the date on which an application is filed or, if later, the first month following the date all conditions for eligibility are met.

[50 FR 48572, Nov. 26, 1985; 64 FR 31973, June 15, 1999]

§ 416.502 Manner of payment.

For the month an individual reestablishes eligibility after a month of ineligibility, an SSI payment will be made on or after the day of the month on which the individual becomes reeligible to receive benefits. In all other months, a payment will be made on the first day of each month and represents payment for that month. If the first day of the month falls on a Saturday, Sunday, or legal holiday, payments will be made on the first day preceding such day which is not a Saturday, Sunday, or legal holiday. Unless otherwise indicated, the monthly amount for an eligible couple will be divided equally and paid separately to each individual. Section 416.520 explains emergency advance payments.

[50 FR 48572, Nov. 26, 1985; 55 FR 4422, Feb. 8, 1990; 64 FR 31974, June 15, 1999]

§ 416.503 Minimum monthly benefit amount.

If you receive an SSI benefit that does not include a State supplement the minimum monthly SSI benefit amount payable is $1. When an SSI benefit amount of less than $1 is payable, the benefit amount will be increased to $1. If you receive an SSI benefit that does include a State supplement and the SSI benefit amount is less than $1 but when added to the State supplement exceeds $1, the SSI benefit amount will not be increased to $1. Rather, we pay the actual amount of the SSI benefit plus the State supplement.

[50 FR 48572, Nov. 26, 1985]

§ 416.520 Emergency advance payments.

(a) General. We may pay a one-time emergency advance payment to an individual initially applying for benefits who is presumptively eligible for SSI benefits and who has a financial emergency. The amount of this payment cannot exceed the Federal benefit rate (see §§ 416.410 through 416.414) plus the federally administered State supplementary payment, if any (see § 416.2020), which apply for the month for which the payment is made. Emergency advance payment is defined in paragraph (b)(1) of this section. The actual payment amount is computed as explained in paragraph (c) of this section. An emergency advance payment is an advance of benefits expected to be due that is recoverable as explained in paragraphs (d) and (e) of this section.

(b) Definition of terms. For purposes of this subpart—

(1) Emergency advance payment means a direct, expedited payment by a Social Security Administration field office to an individual or spouse who is initially applying (see paragraph (b)(3) of this section), who is at least presumptively eligible (see paragraph (b)(4) of this section), and who has a financial emergency (see paragraph (b)(2) of this section).

(2) Financial emergency is the financial status of an individual who has insufficient income or resources to meet an immediate threat to health or safety, such as the lack of food, clothing, shelter, or medical care.

(3) Initially applying means the filing of an application (see § 416.310) which requires an initial determination of eligibility, such as the first application for SSI benefits or an application filed subsequent to a prior denial or termination of a prior period of eligibility for payment. An individual or spouse who previously received an emergency advance payment in a prior period of eligibility which terminated may again receive such a payment if he or she reapplies for SSI and meets the other conditions for an emergency advance payment under this section.

(4) Presumptively eligible is the status of an individual or spouse who presents strong evidence of the likelihood of meeting all of the requirements for eligibility including the income and resources tests of eligibility (see subparts K and L of this part), categorical eligibility (age, disability, or blindness), and technical eligibility (United States residency and citizenship or alien status—see subpart P of this part).

(c) Computation of payment amount. To compute the emergency advance payment amount, the maximum amount described in paragraph (a) of this section is compared to both the expected amount payable for the month for which the payment is made (see paragraph (c)(1) of this section) and the amount the applicant requested to meet the emergency. The actual payment amount is no more than the least of these three amounts.

(1) In computing the emergency advance payment amount, we apply the monthly income counting rules appropriate for the month for which the advance is paid, as explained in § 416.420. Generally, the month for which the advance is paid is the month in which it is paid. However, if the advance is paid in the month the application is filed, the month for which the advance is paid is considered to be the first month of expected eligibility for payment of benefits.

(2) For a couple, we separately compute each member's emergency advance payment amount.

(d) Recovery of emergency advance payment where eligibility is established. When an individual or spouse is determined to be eligible and retroactive payments are due, any emergency advance payment amounts are recovered in full from the first payment(s) certified to the United States Treasury. However, if no retroactive payments are due and benefits are only due in future months, any emergency advance payment amounts are recovered through proportionate reductions in those benefits over a period of not more than 6 months. (See paragraph (e) of this section if the individual or spouse is determined to be ineligible.)

(e) Disposition of emergency advance payments where eligibility is not established. If a presumptively eligible individual (or spouse) or couple is determined to be ineligible, the emergency advance payment constitutes a recoverable overpayment. (See the exception in § 416.537(b)(1) when payment is made on the basis of presumptive disability or presumptive blindness.)

[50 FR 48572, Nov. 26, 1985; 55 FR 4422, Feb. 8, 1990; 55 FR 7411, March 1, 1990; 64 FR 31974, June 15, 1999]

§ 416.525 Reimbursement to States for interim assistance payments.

Notwithstanding § 416.542, the Social Security Administration may, in accordance with the provisions of subpart S of this part, withhold supplemental security income benefits due with respect to an individual and may pay to a State (or political subdivision thereof, if agreed to by the Social Security Administration and the State) from the benefits withheld, an amount sufficient to reimburse the State (or political subdivision) for interim assistance furnished on behalf of the individual.

[41 FR 20872, May 21, 1976]

§ 416.532 Method of payment when the essential person resides with more than one eligible person.

(a) When an essential person lives with an eligible individual and an eligible spouse, the State may report that the person is essential to one or both members of the couple. In either event, the income and resources of the essential person will be considered to be available to the family unit. The payment increment attributable to the essential person will be added to the rate of payment for the couple, the countable income subtracted, and the resulting total benefit divided equally between the eligible individual and the eligible spouse.

(b) Where the essential person lives with two eligible individuals (as opposed to an eligible individual and eligible spouse), one of whom has been designated the qualified individual, the income and resources of the essential person will be considered to be available only to the qualified individual (as defined in § 416.221) and any increase in payment will be made to such qualified individual.

(c) In those instances where the State has designated the essential person as essential to two or more eligible individuals so that both are qualified individuals, the payment increment attributable to the essential person must be shared equally, and the income and resources of the essential person divided and counted equally against each qualified individual.

(d) When an essential person lives with an eligible individual and an eligible spouse (or two or more eligible individuals) only one of whom is the qualified individual, essential person status is not automatically retained upon the death of the qualified individual or upon the separation from the qualified individual. A review of the State records established on or before December 31, 1973, will provide the basis for a determination as to whether the remaining eligible individual or eligible spouse meets the definition of qualified individual. Payment in consideration of the essential person will be dependent on whether the essential person continues to live with a qualified individual. If the essential person does reside with a qualified individual, status as an essential person is retained.

[39 FR 33796, Sept. 20, 1974; 50 FR 48572, Nov. 26, 1985; 51 FR 10616, March 28, 1986; 60 FR 16375, March 30, 1995]

§ 416.533 Transfer or assignment of benefits.

Except as provided in § 416.525 and subpart S of this part, the Social Security Administration will not certify payment of supplemental security income benefits to a transferee or assignee of a person eligible for such benefits under the Act or of a person qualified for payment under § 416.542. The Social Security Administration shall not certify payment of supplemental security income benefits to any person claiming such payment by virtue of an execution, levy, attachment, garnishment, or other legal process or by virtue of any bankruptcy or insolvency proceeding against or affecting the person eligible for benefits under the Act.

[41 FR 20873, May 21, 1976; 58 FR 52912, Oct. 13, 1993]

§ 416.534 Garnishment of payments after disbursement.

(a) Payments that are covered by section 1631(d)(1) of the Social Security Act and made by direct deposit are subject to 31 CFR part 212, Garnishment of Accounts Containing Federal Benefit Payments.

(b) This section may be amended only by a rulemaking issued jointly by the Department of Treasury and the agencies defined as a "benefit agency" in 31 CFR 212.3.

[76 FR 9961, Feb. 23, 2011; 78 FR 32109, May 29, 2013]

§ 416.535 Underpayments and overpayments.

(a) General. When an individual receives SSI benefits of less than the correct amount, adjustment is effected as described in §§ 416.542 and 416.543, and the additional rules in § 416.545 may apply. When an individual receives more than the correct amount of SSI benefits, adjustment is effected as described in § 416.570. Refund of overpayments is discussed in § 416.560 and waiver of recovery of overpayments is discussed in §§ 416.550 through 416.555.

(b) Additional rules for individuals whose drug addiction or alcoholism is a contributing factor material to the determination of disability. When an individual whose drug addiction or alcoholism is a contributing factor material to the determination of disability, as described in § 416.935, receives less than the correct amount of SSI benefits, adjustment is effected as described in §§ 416.542 and 416.543 and the additional rule described in § 416.544 applies.

(c) Additional rules for eligible individuals under age 18 who have a representative payee. When an eligible individual under age 18 has a representative payee and receives less than the correct amount of SSI benefits, the additional rules in § 416.546 may apply.

(d) Additional rules for eligible aliens and for their sponsors. When an individual who is an alien is overpaid SSI benefits during the 3–year period in which deeming from a sponsor applies (see § 416.1160(a)(3)), the sponsor and the alien may be jointly and individually liable for repayment of the overpayment. The sponsor is liable for the overpayment if he or she failed to report correct information that affected the alien's eligibility or payment amount. This means information about the income and resources of the sponsor and, if they live together, of the sponsor's spouse. However, the sponsor is not liable for repayment if the sponsor was without fault or had good cause for failing to report correctly. A special rule that applies to adjustment of other benefits due the alien and the sponsor to recover an overpayment is described in § 416.570(b).

(e) Sponsor without fault or good cause exists for failure to report. Without fault or good cause will be found to exist if the failure to report was not willful. To establish willful failure, the evidence must show that the sponsor knowingly failed to supply pertinent information regarding his or her income and resources.

[40 FR 47763, Oct. 10, 1975; 52 FR 8881, March 20, 1987; 60 FR 8149, Feb. 10, 1995; 61 FR 67205, Dec. 20, 1996]

§ 416.536 Underpayments—defined.

An underpayment can occur only with respect to a period for which a recipient filed an application, if required, for benefits and met all conditions of eligibility for benefits. An underpayment, including any amounts of State supplementary payments which are due and administered by the Social Security Administration, is:

(a) Nonpayment, where payment was due but was not made; or

(b) Payment of less than the amount due. For purposes of this section, payment has been made when certified by the Social Security Administration to the Department of the Treasury, except that payment has not been made where payment has not been received by the designated payee, or where payment was returned.

[40 FR 47763, Oct. 10, 1975; 50 FR 48572, Nov. 26, 1985; 58 FR 52912, Oct. 13, 1993]

§ 416.537 Overpayments—defined.

(a) Overpayments. As used in this subpart, the term overpayment means payment of more than the amount due for any period, including any amounts of State supplementary payments which are due and administered by the Social Security Administration. For purposes of this section, payment has been made when certified by the Social Security Administration to the Department of the Treasury, except that payment has not been made where payment has not been received by the designated payee, or where payment was returned. When a payment of more than the amount due is made by direct deposit to a financial institution to or on behalf of an individual who has died, and the financial institution credits the payment to a joint account of the deceased individual and another person who is the surviving spouse of the deceased individual and was eligible for a payment under title XVI of the Act (including any State supplementation payment paid by the Commissioner) as an eligible spouse (or as either member of an eligible couple) for the month in which the deceased individual died, the amount of the payment in excess of the correct amount will be an overpayment to the surviving spouse.

(b) Actions which are not overpayments—

(1) Presumptive disability and presumptive blindness. Any payment made for any month, including an advance payment of benefits under § 416.520, is not an overpayment to the extent it meets the criteria for payment under § 416.931. Payments made on the basis of presumptive disability or presumptive blindness will not be considered overpayments where ineligibility is determined because the individual or eligible spouse is not disabled or blind. However, where it is determined that all or a portion of the presumptive payments made are incorrect for reasons other than disability or blindness, these incorrect payments are considered overpayments (as defined in paragraph (a) of this section). Overpayments may occur, for example, when the person who received payments on the basis of presumptive disability or presumptive blindness is determined to be ineligible for all or any part of the payments because of excess resources or is determined to have received excess payment for those months based on an incorrect estimate of income.

(2) Penalty. The imposition of a penalty pursuant to § 416.724 is not an adjustment of an overpayment and is imposed only against any amount due the penalized recipient, or, after death, any amount due the deceased which otherwise would be paid to a survivor as defined in § 416.542.

[40 FR 47763, Oct. 10, 1975, as amended at 43 FR 17354, Apr. 24, 1978; 50 FR 48573, Nov. 26, 1985; 55 FR 7313, March 1, 1990; 58 FR 52912, Oct. 13, 1993; 62 FR 38454, July 18, 1997]

§ 416.538 Amount of underpayment or overpayment.

(a) General. The amount of an underpayment or overpayment is the difference between the amount paid to a recipient and the amount of payment actually due such recipient for a given period. An underpayment or overpayment period begins with the first month for which there is a difference between the amount paid and the amount actually due for that month. The period ends with the month the initial determination of overpayment or underpayment is made. With respect to the period established, there can be no underpayment to a recipient or his or her eligible spouse if more than the correct amount payable under title XVI of the Act has been paid, whether or not adjustment or recovery of any overpayment for that period to the recipient or his or her eligible spouse has been waived under the provisions of §§ 416.550 through 416.556. A subsequent initial determination of overpayment will require no change with respect to a prior determination of overpayment or to the period relating to such determination to the extent that the basis of the prior overpayment remains the same.

(b) Limited delay in payment of underpaid amount to recipient or eligible surviving spouse. Where an apparent overpayment has been detected but determination of the overpayment has not been made (see § 416.558(a)), a determination of an underpayment and payment of an underpaid amount which is otherwise due cannot be delayed to a recipient or eligible surviving spouse unless a determination with respect to the apparent overpayment can be made before the close of the month following the month in which the underpaid amount was discovered.

(c) Delay in payment of underpaid amount to ineligible individual or survivor. A determination of an underpayment and payment of an underpaid amount which is otherwise due an individual who is no longer eligible for SSI or is payable to a survivor pursuant to § 416.542(b) will be delayed for the resolution of all overpayments, incorrect payments, adjustments, and penalties.

(d) Limited delay in payment of underpaid amount to eligible individual under age 18 who has a representative payee. When the representative payee of an eligible individual under age 18 is required to establish a dedicated account pursuant to §§ 416.546 and 416.640(e), payment of past-due benefits which are otherwise due will be delayed until the representative payee has established the dedicated account as described in § 416.640(e). Once the account is established, SSA will deposit the past-due benefits payable directly to the account.

(e) Reduction of underpaid amount. Any underpayment amount otherwise payable to a survivor on account of a deceased recipient is reduced by the amount of any outstanding penalty imposed against the benefits payable to such deceased recipient or survivor under section 1631(e) of the Act (see § 416.537(b)(2)).

[40 FR 47763, Oct. 10, 1975; 50 FR 48573, Nov. 26, 1985; 58 FR 52912, Oct. 13, 1993; 61 FR 67205, Dec. 20, 1996]

§ 416.542 Underpayments—to whom underpaid amount is payable.

(a) Underpaid recipient alive—underpayment payable.

(1) If an underpaid recipient is alive, the amount of any underpayment due him or her will be paid to him or her in a separate payment or by increasing the amount of his or her monthly payment. If the underpaid amount meets the formula in § 416.545 and one of the exceptions does not apply, the amount of any past-due benefits will be paid in installments.

(2) If an underpaid recipient whose drug addiction or alcoholism is a contributing factor material to the determination of disability (as described in § 416.935) is alive, the amount of any underpayment due the recipient will be paid through his or her representative payee in installment payments. No underpayment may be paid directly to the recipient. If the recipient dies before we have paid all benefits due through his or her representative payee, we will follow the rules which apply to underpayments for the payment of any remaining amounts due to any eligible survivor of a deceased recipient as described in paragraph (b) of this section.

(3) If an underpaid individual under age 18 is alive and has a representative payee and is due past-due benefits which meet the formula in § 416.546, SSA will pay the past-due benefits into the dedicated account described in § 416.640(e). If the underpaid individual dies before the benefits have been deposited into the account, we will follow the rules which apply to underpayments for the payment of any unpaid amount due to any eligible survivor of a deceased individual as described in paragraph (b) of this section.

(b) Underpaid recipient deceased—underpaid amount payable to survivor.

(1) If a recipient dies before we have paid all benefits due or before the recipient endorses the check for the correct payment, we may pay the amount due to the deceased recipient's surviving eligible spouse or to his or her surviving spouse who was living with the underpaid recipient within the meaning of section 202(i) of the Act (see § 404.347) in the month he or she died or within 6 months immediately preceding the month of death.

(2) If the deceased underpaid recipient was a disabled or blind child when the underpayment occurred, the underpaid amount may be paid to the natural or adoptive parent(s) of the underpaid recipient who lived with the underpaid recipient in the month he or she died or within the 6 months preceding death. We consider the underpaid recipient to have been living with the natural or adoptive parent(s) in the period if the underpaid recipient satisfies the "living with" criteria we use when applying § 416.1165 or would have satisfied the criteria had his or her death not precluded the application of such criteria throughout a month.

(3) If the deceased individual was living with his or her spouse within the meaning of section 202(i) of the Act in the month of death or within 6 months immediately preceding the month of death, and was also living with his or her natural or adoptive parent(s) in the month of death or within 6 months preceding the month of death, we will pay the parent(s) any SSI underpayment due the deceased individual for months he or she was a blind or disabled child and we will pay the spouse any SSI underpayment due the deceased individual for months he or she no longer met the definition of "child" as set forth at § 416.1856. If no parent(s) can be paid in such cases due to death or other reason, then we will pay the SSI underpayment due the deceased individual for months he or she was a blind or disabled child to the spouse.

(4) No benefits may be paid to the estate of any underpaid recipient, the estate of the surviving spouse, the estate of a parent, or to any survivor other than those listed in paragraph (b)(1) through (3) of this section. Payment of an underpaid amount to an ineligible spouse or surviving parent(s) may only be made for benefits payable for months after May 1986. Payment to surviving parent(s) may be made only for months of eligibility during which the deceased underpaid recipient was a child. We will not pay benefits to a survivor other than the eligible spouse who requests payment of an underpaid amount more than 24 months after the month of the individual's death.

(c) Underpaid recipient's death caused by an intentional act. No benefits due the deceased individual may be paid to a survivor found guilty by a court of competent jurisdiction of intentionally causing the underpaid recipient's death.

[40 FR 47763, Oct. 10, 1975; 58 FR 52913, Oct. 13, 1993; 60 FR 8149, Feb. 10, 1995; 61 FR 67206, Dec. 20, 1996]

§ 416.543 Underpayments—applied to reduce overpayments.

We apply any underpayment due an individual to reduce any overpayment to that individual that we determine to exist (see § 416.558) for a different period, unless we have waived recovery of the overpayment under the provisions of §§ 416.550 through 416.556. Similarly, when an underpaid recipient dies, we first apply any amounts due the deceased recipient that would be payable to a survivor under § 416.542(b) against any overpayment to the survivor unless we have waived recovery of such overpayment under the provisions of §§ 416.550 through 416.556.

Example: A disabled child, eligible for payments under title XVI, and his parent, also an eligible individual receiving payments under title XVI, were living together. The disabled child dies at a time when he was underpaid $100. The deceased child's underpaid benefit is payable to the surviving parent. However, since the parent must repay an SSI overpayment of $225 on his own record, the $100 underpayment will be applied to reduce the parent's own overpayment to $125.

[40 FR 47763, Oct. 10, 1975; 58 FR 52913, Oct. 13, 1993]

§ 416.544 Paying benefits in installments: Drug addiction or alcoholism.

(a) General. For disabled recipients who receive benefit payments through a representative payee because drug addiction or alcoholism is a contributing factor material to the determination of disability, certain amounts due the recipient for a past period will be paid in installments. The amounts subject to payment in installments include:

(1) Benefits due but unpaid which accrued prior to the month payment was effectuated;

(2) Benefits due but unpaid which accrued during a period of suspension for which the recipient was subsequently determined to have been eligible; and

(3) Any adjustment to benefits which results in an accrual of unpaid benefits.

(b) Installment formula. Except as provided in paragraph (c) of this section, the amount of the installment payment in any month is limited so that the sum of (1) the amount due for a past period (and payable under paragraph (a) of this section) paid in such month and (2) the amount of any current benefit due cannot exceed twice the Federal Benefit Rate plus any federally-administered State supplementation payable to an eligible individual for the preceding month.

(c) Exception to installment limitation. An exception to the installment payment limitation in paragraph (b) of this section can be granted for the first month in which a recipient accrues benefit amounts subject to payment in installments if the recipient has unpaid housing expenses which result in a high risk of homelessness for the recipient. In that case, the benefit payment may be increased by the amount of the unpaid housing expenses so long as that increase does not exceed the amount of benefits which accrued during the most recent period of nonpayment. We consider a person to be at risk of homelessness if continued nonpayment of the outstanding housing expenses is likely to result in the person losing his or her place to live or if past nonpayment of housing expenses has resulted in the person having no appropriate personal place to live. In determining whether this exception applies, we will ask for evidence of outstanding housing expenses that shows that the person is likely to lose or has already lost his or her place to live. For purposes of this section, homelessness is the state of not being under the control of any public institution and having no appropriate personal place to live. Housing expenses include charges for all items required to maintain shelter (for example, mortgage payments, rent, heating fuel, and electricity).

(d) Payment through a representative payee. If the recipient does not have a representative payee, payment of amounts subject to installments cannot be made until a representative payee is selected.

(e) Underpaid recipient no longer eligible. In the case of a recipient who is no longer currently eligible for monthly payments, but to whom amounts defined in paragraph (a) of this section are still owing, we will continue to make installment payments of such benefits through a representative payee.

(f) Recipient currently not receiving SSI benefits because of suspension for noncompliance with treatment. If a recipient is currently not receiving SSI benefits because his or her benefits have been suspended for noncompliance with treatment (as defined in § 416.936), the payment of amounts under paragraph (a) of this section will stop until the recipient has demonstrated compliance with treatment as described in § 416.1326 and will again commence with the first month the recipient begins to receive benefits.

(g) Underpaid recipient deceased. Upon the death of a recipient, any remaining unpaid amounts as defined in paragraph (a) of this section will be treated as underpayments in accordance with § 416.542(b).

[60 FR 8150, Feb. 10, 1995]

§ 416.545 Paying large past-due benefits in installments.

(a) General. Except as described in paragraph (c) of this section, when an individual is eligible for past-due benefits in an amount which meets the formula in paragraph (b) of this section, payment of these benefits must be made in installments. If an individual becomes eligible for past-due benefits for a different period while installments are being made, we will notify the individual of the amount due and issue these benefits in the last installment payment. The amounts subject to payment in installments include:

(1) Benefits due but unpaid which accrued prior to the month payment was effectuated;

(2) Benefits due but unpaid which accrued during a period of suspension for which the recipient was subsequently determined to have been eligible; and

(3) Any adjustment to benefits which results in an accrual of unpaid benefits.

(b) Installment formula. Installment payments must be made if the amount of the past-due benefits, including any federally administered State supplementation, after applying § 416.525 (reimbursement to States for interim assistance) and applying § 416.1520 (payment of attorney fees), equals or exceeds 3 times the Federal Benefit Rate plus any federally administered State supplementation payable in a month to an eligible individual (or eligible individual and eligible spouse). These installment payments will be paid in not more than 3 installments and made at 6–month intervals. Except as described in paragraph (d) of this section, the amount of each of the first and second installment payments may not exceed the threshold amount of 3 times the maximum monthly benefit payable as described in this paragraph.

(c) Exception—When installments payments are not required. Installment payments are not required and the rules in this section do not apply if, when the determination of an underpayment is made, the individual is (1) afflicted with a medically determinable impairment which is expected to result in death within 12 months, or (2) ineligible for benefits and we determine that he or she is likely to remain ineligible for the next 12 months.

(d) Exception—Increased first and second installment payments.

(1) The amount of the first and second installment payments may be increased by the total amount of the following debts and expenses:

(i) Outstanding debt for food, clothing, shelter, or medically necessary services, supplies or equipment, or medicine; or

(ii) Current or anticipated expenses in the near future for medically necessary services, supplies or equipment, or medicine, or for the purchase of a home.

(2) The increase described in paragraph (d)(1) of this section only applies to debts or expenses that are not subject to reimbursement by a public assistance program, the Secretary of Health and Human Services under title XVIII of the Act, a State plan approved under title XIX of the Act, or any private entity that is legally liable for payment in accordance with an insurance policy, pre-paid plan, or other arrangement.

[61 FR 67206, Dec. 20, 1996; 76 FR 453, Jan. 5, 2011; 79 FR 33685, June 12, 2014]

§ 416.546 Payment into dedicated accounts of past-due benefits for eligible individuals under age 18 who have a representative payee.

For purposes of this section, amounts subject to payment into dedicated accounts (see § 416.640(e)) include the amounts described in § 416.545(a)(1), (2), and (3).

(a) For an eligible individual under age 18 who has a representative payee and who is determined to be eligible for past-due benefits (including any federally administered State supplementation) in an amount which, after applying § 416.525 (reimbursement to States for interim assistance) and § 416.1520 (payment of attorney fee), exceeds six times the Federal Benefit Rate plus any federally administered State supplementation payable in a month, this unpaid amount must be paid into the dedicated account established and maintained as described in § 416.640(e).

(b) After the account is established, the representative payee may (but is not required to) deposit into the account any subsequent funds representing past-due benefits under this title to the individual which are equal to or exceed the maximum Federal Benefit Rate (including any federally administered State supplementation).

(c) If the underpaid individual dies before all the benefits due have been deposited into the dedicated account, we will follow the rules which apply to underpayments for the payment of any unpaid amount due to any eligible survivor as described in § 416.542(b).

[61 FR 67206, Dec. 20, 1996; 76 FR 453, Jan. 5, 2011]

§ 416.550 Waiver of adjustment or recovery—when applicable.

Waiver of adjustment or recovery of an overpayment of SSI benefits may be granted when (EXCEPTION: This section does not apply to a sponsor of an alien):

(a) The overpaid individual was without fault in connection with an overpayment, and

(b) Adjustment or recovery of such overpayment would either:

(1) Defeat the purpose of title XVI, or

(2) Be against equity and good conscience, or

(3) Impede efficient or effective administration of title XVI due to the small amount involved.

[40 FR 47763, Oct. 10, 1975; 52 FR 8882, March 20, 1987; 53 FR 16543, May 10, 1988]

§ 416.551 Waiver of adjustment or recovery—effect of.

Waiver of adjustment or recovery of an overpayment from the overpaid person himself (or, after his death, from his estate) frees him and his eligible spouse from the obligation to repay the amount of the overpayment covered by the waiver. Waiver of adjustment or recovery of an overpayment from anyone other than the overpaid person himself or his estate (e.g., a surviving eligible spouse) does not preclude adjustment or recovery against the overpaid person or his estate.

Example: The recipient was overpaid $390. It was found that the overpaid recipient was eligible for waiver of adjustment or recovery of $260 of that amount, and such action was taken. Only $130 of the overpayment remained to be recovered by adjustment, refund, or the like.

[40 FR 47763, Oct. 10, 1975]

§ 416.552 Waiver of adjustment or recovery—without fault.

Without fault relates only to the situation of the individual seeking relief from adjustment or recovery of an overpayment. The overpaid individual (and any other individual from whom the Social Security Administration seeks to recover the overpayment) is not relieved of liability and is not without fault solely because the Social Security Administration may have been at fault in making the overpayment. In determining whether an individual is without fault, the fault of the overpaid person and the fault of the individual seeking relief under the waiver provision are considered. Whether an individual is without fault depends on all the pertinent circumstances surrounding the overpayment in the particular case. The Social Security Administration considers the individual's understanding of the reporting requirements, the agreement to report events affecting payments, knowledge of the occurrence of events that should have been reported, efforts to comply with the reporting requirements, opportunities to comply with the reporting requirements, understanding of the obligation to return checks which were not due, and ability to comply with the reporting requirements (e.g., age, comprehension, memory, physical and mental condition). In determining whether an individual is without fault based on a consideration of these factors, the Social Security Administration will take into account any physical, mental, educational, or linguistic limitations (including any lack of facility with the English language) the individual may have. Although the finding depends on all of the circumstances in the particular case, an individual will be found to have been at fault in connection with an overpayment when an incorrect payment resulted from one of the following:

(a) Failure to furnish information which the individual knew or should have known was material;

(b) An incorrect statement made by the individual which he knew or should have known was incorrect (this includes the individual's furnishing his opinion or conclusion when he was asked for facts), or

(c) The individual did not return a payment which he knew or could have been expected to know was incorrect.

[40 FR 47763, Oct. 10, 1975; 59 FR 1636, Jan. 12, 1994]

§ 416.553 Waiver of adjustment or recovery—defeat the purpose of the supplemental security income program.

We will waive adjustment or recovery of an overpayment when an individual on whose behalf waiver is being considered is without fault (as defined in § 416.552) and adjustment or recovery of the overpayment would defeat the purpose of the supplemental security income program.

(a) General rule. We consider adjustment or recovery of an overpayment to defeat the purpose of the supplemental security income (SSI) program if the individual's income and resources are needed for ordinary and necessary living expenses under the criteria set out in § 404.508(a) of this chapter.

(b) Alternative criteria for individuals currently eligible for SSI benefits. We consider an individual or couple currently eligible for SSI benefits to have met the test in paragraph (a) of this section if the individual's or couple's current monthly income (that is, the income upon which the individual's or couple's eligibility for the current month is determined) does not exceed—

(1) The applicable Federal monthly benefit rate for the month in which the determination of waiver is made (see subpart D of this part); plus

(2) The $20 monthly general income exclusion described in §§ 416.1112(c)(3) and 416.1124(c)(10); plus

(3) The monthly earned income exclusion described in § 416.1112(c)(4); plus

(4) The applicable State supplementary payment, if any (see subpart T of this part) for the month in which determination of waiver is made.

For those SSI recipients whose income exceeds these criteria, we follow the general rule in paragraph (a) of this section.

[45 FR 72649, Nov. 3, 1980; 50 FR 48573, Nov. 26, 1985]

§ 416.554 Waiver of adjustment or recovery—against equity and good conscience.

We will waive adjustment or recovery of an overpayment when an individual on whose behalf waiver is being considered is without fault (as defined in § 416.552) and adjustment or recovery would be against equity and good conscience. Adjustment or recovery is considered to be against equity and good conscience if an individual changed his or her position for the worse or relinquished a valuable right because of reliance upon a notice that payment would be made or because of the incorrect payment itself. In addition, adjustment or recovery is considered to be against equity and good conscience for an individual who is a member of an eligible couple that is legally separated and/or living apart for that part of an overpayment not received, but subject to recovery under § 416.570.

Example 1: Upon being notified that he was eligible for supplemental security income payments, an individual signed a lease on an apartment renting for $15 a month more than the room he had previously occupied. It was subsequently found that eligibility for the payment should not have been established. In such a case, recovery would be considered "against equity and good conscience."

Example 2: An individual fails to take advantage of a private or organization charity, relying instead on the award of supplemental security income payments to support himself. It was subsequently found that the money was improperly paid. Recovery would be considered "against equity and good conscience."

Example 3: Mr. and Mrs. Smith—members of an eligible couple—separate in July. Later in July, Mr. Smith receives earned income resulting in an overpayment to both. Mrs. Smith is found to be without fault in causing the overpayment. Recovery from Mrs. Smith of Mr. Smith's part of the couple's overpayment is waived as being against equity and good conscience. Whether recovery of Mr. Smith's portion of the couple's overpayment can be waived will be evaluated separately.

[40 FR 47764, Oct. 10, 1975; 53 FR 16543, May 10, 1988; 53 FR 19856, May 31, 1988; 53 FR 25484, July 7, 1988; 60 FR 16375, March 30, 1995]

§ 416.555 Waiver of adjustment or recovery—impede administration.

Waiver of adjustment or recovery is proper when the overpaid person on whose behalf waiver is being considered is without fault, as defined in § 416.552, and adjustment or recovery would impede efficient or effective administration of title XVI due to the small amount involved. The amount of overpayment determined to meet such criteria is measured by the current average administrative cost of handling such overpayment case through such adjustment or recovery processes. In determining whether the criterion is met, the overpaid person's financial circumstances are not considered.

[40 FR 47764, Oct. 10, 1975]

§ 416.556 Waiver of adjustment or recovery—countable resources in excess of the limits prescribed in § 416.1205 by $50 or less.

(a) If any overpayment with respect to an individual (or an individual and his or her spouse if any) is attributable solely to the ownership or possession by the individual (and spouse if any) of countable resources having a value which exceeds the applicable dollar figure specified in § 416.1205 by an amount of $50.00 or less, including those resources deemed to an individual in accordance with § 416.1202, such individual (and spouse if any) shall be deemed to have been without fault in connection with the overpayment, and waiver of adjustment or recovery will be made, unless the failure to report the value of the excess resources correctly and in a timely manner was willful and knowing.

(b) Failure to report the excess resources correctly and in a timely manner will be considered to be willful and knowing and the individual will be found to be at fault when the evidence clearly shows the individual (and spouse if any) was fully aware of the requirements of the law and of the excess resources and chose to conceal these resources. When an individual incurred a similar overpayment in the past and received an explanation and instructions at the time of the previous overpayment, we will generally find the individual to be at fault. However, in determining whether the individual is at fault, we will consider all aspects of the current and prior overpayment situations, and where we determine the individual is not at fault, we will waive adjustment or recovery of the subsequent overpayment. In making any determination or decision under this section concerning whether an individual is at fault, including a determination or decision of whether the failure to report the excess resources correctly and in a timely manner was willful and knowing, we will take into account any physical, mental, educational, or linguistic limitations (including any lack of facility with the English language) of the individual (and spouse if any).

[53 FR 16544, May 10, 1988; 59 FR 1636, Jan. 12, 1994]

§ 416.557 Personal conference.

(a) If waiver cannot be approved (i.e., the requirements in § 416.550 (a) and (b) are not met), the individual is notified in writing and given the dates, times and place of the file review and personal conference; the procedure for reviewing the claims file prior to the personal conference; the procedure for seeking a change in the scheduled date, time and/or place; and all other information necessary to fully inform the individual about the personal conference. The file review is always scheduled at least 5 days before the personal conference. We will offer to the individual the option of conducting the personal conference face-to-face at a place we designate, by telephone, or by video teleconference. The notice will advise the individual of the date and time of the personal conference.

(b) At the file review, the individual and the individual's representative have the right to review the claims file and applicable law and regulations with the decisionmaker or another of our representatives who is prepared to answer questions. We will provide copies of material related to the overpayment and/or waiver from the claims file or pertinent sections of the law or regulations that are requested by the individual or the individual's representative.

(c) At the personal conference, the individual is given the opportunity to:

(1) Appear personally, testify, cross-examine any witnesses, and make arguments;

(2) Be represented by an attorney or other representative (see § 416.1500), although the individual must be present at the conference; and

(3) Submit documents for consideration by the decisionmaker.

(d) At the personal conference, the decisionmaker:

(1) Tells the individual that the decisionmaker was not previously involved in the issue under review, that the waiver decision is solely the decisionmaker's, and that the waiver decision is based only on the evidence or information presented or reviewed at the conference;

(2) Ascertains the role and identity of everyone present;

(3) Indicates whether or not the individual reviewed the claims file;

(4) Explains the provisions of law and regulations applicable to the issue;

(5) Briefly summarizes the evidence already in file which will be considered;

(6) Ascertains from the individual whether the information presented is correct and whether he/she fully understands it;

(7) Allows the individual and the individual's representative, if any, to present the individual's case;

(8) Secures updated financial information and verification, if necessary;

(9) Allows each witness to present information and allows the individual and the individual's representative to question each witness;

(10) Ascertains whether there is any further evidence to be presented;

(11) Reminds the individual of any evidence promised by the individual which has not been presented;

(12) Lets the individual and the individual's representative, if any, present any proposed summary or closing statement;

(13) Explains that a decision will be made and the individual will be notified in writing; and

(14) Explains repayment options and further appeal rights in the event the decision is adverse to the individual.

(e) SSA issues a written decision to the individual (and his or her representative, if any) specifying the findings of fact and conclusions in support of the decision to approve or deny waiver and advising of the individual's right to appeal the decision. If waiver is denied, adjustment or recovery of the overpayment begins even if the individual appeals.

(f) If it appears that the waiver cannot be approved, and the individual declines a personal conference or fails to appear for a second scheduled personal conference, a decision regarding the waiver will be made based on the written evidence of record. Reconsideration is the next step in the appeals process.

[73 FR 1973, Jan. 11, 2008]

§ 416.558 Notice relating to overpayments and underpayments.

(a) Notice of overpayment and underpayment determination. Whenever a determination concerning the amount paid and payable for any period is made and it is found that, with respect to any month in the period, more or less than the correct amount was paid, written notice of the correct and incorrect amounts for each such month in the period will be sent to the individual against whom adjustment or recovery of the overpayment as defined in § 416.537(a) may be effected or to whom the underpayment as defined in §§ 416.536 and any amounts subject to installment payments as defined in § 416.544 would be payable, notwithstanding the fact that part or all of the underpayment must be withheld in accordance with § 416.543. When notifying an individual of a determination of overpayment, the Social Security Administration will, in the notice, also advise the individual that adjustment or recovery is required, as set forth in § 416.571, except under certain specified conditions, and of his or her right to request waiver of adjustment or recovery of the overpayment under the provisions of § 416.550.

(b) Notice of waiver determination. Written notice of an initial determination of waiver shall be given the individual in accordance with § 416.1404 unless the individual was not given notice of the overpayment in accordance with paragraph (a) of this section.

(c) Notice relating to installment payments to individuals whose drug addiction or alcoholism is a contributing factor material to the determination of disability. Whenever a determination is made concerning the amount of any benefits due for a period that must be paid in installments, the written notice will also explain the amount of the installment payment and when an increased initial installment payment may be made (as described in § 416.544). This written notice will be sent to the individual and his or her representative payee.

[40 FR 47764, Oct. 10, 1975; 55 FR 33668, Aug. 17, 1990; 60 FR 8150, Feb. 10, 1995]

§ 416.560 Recovery—refund.

An overpayment may be refunded by the overpaid recipient or by anyone on his or her behalf. Refund should be made in every case where the overpaid individual is not currently eligible for SSI benefits. If the individual is currently eligible for SSI benefits and has not refunded the overpayment, adjustment as set forth in § 416.570 will be proposed.

[40 FR 47764, Oct. 10, 1975; 55 FR 33669, Aug. 17, 1990]

§ 416.570 Adjustment.

(a) General. When a recipient has been overpaid, the overpayment has not been refunded, and waiver of adjustment or recovery is not applicable, any payment due the overpaid recipient or his or her eligible spouse (or recovery from the estate of either or both when either or both die before adjustment is completed) is adjusted for recovery of the overpayment. Adjustment will generally be accomplished by withholding each month the amount set forth in § 416.571 from the benefit payable to the individual except that, when the overpayment results from the disposition of resources as provided by §§ 416.1240(b) and 416.1244, the overpayment will be recovered by withholding any payments due the overpaid recipient or his or her eligible spouse before any further payment is made. Absent a specific request from the person from whom recovery is sought, no overpayment made under title XVIII of the Act will be recovered by adjusting SSI benefits. In no case shall an overpayment of SSI benefits be adjusted against title XVIII benefits. No funds properly deposited into a dedicated account (see §§ 416.546 and 416.640(e)) can be used to repay an overpayment while the overpaid individual remains subject to the provisions of those sections.

(b) Overpayment made to representative payee after the recipient's death. A representative payee or his estate is solely liable for repaying an overpayment made to the representative payee on behalf of a recipient after the recipient's death. In such case, we will recover the overpayment according to paragraph (a) of this section, except that:

(1) We will not adjust any other payment due to the eligible spouse of the overpaid representative payee to recover the overpayment, and

(2) If the overpaid representative payee dies before we complete adjustment, we will not seek to recover the overpayment from the eligible spouse or the estate of the eligible spouse.

[40 FR 47764, Oct. 10, 1975; 52 FR 8882, March 20, 1987; 55 FR 33669, Aug. 17, 1990; 55 FR 42148, Oct. 17, 1990; 61 FR 67206, Dec. 20, 1996; 66 FR 38906, July 26, 2001; 67 FR 38383, June 4, 2002; 70 FR 16, Jan. 3, 2005; 70 FR 16113, March 30, 2005; 73 FR 65543, Nov. 4, 2008]

§ 416.571 10-percent limitation of recoupment rate—overpayment.

Any adjustment or recovery of an overpayment for an individual in current payment status is limited in amount in any month to the lesser of (1) the amount of the individual's benefit payment for that month or (2) an amount equal to 10 percent of the individual's total income (countable income plus SSI and State supplementary payments) for that month. The countable income used is the countable income used in determining the SSI and State supplementary payments for that month under § 416.420. When the overpaid individual is notified of the proposed SSI and/or federally administered State supplementary overpayment adjustment or recovery, the individual will be given the opportunity to request that such adjustment or recovery be made at a higher or lower rate than that proposed. If a lower rate is requested, a rate of withholding that is appropriate to the financial condition of the overpaid individual will be set after an evaluation of all the pertinent facts. An appropriate rate is one that will not deprive the individual of income required for ordinary and necessary living expenses. This will include an evaluation of the individual's income, resources, and other financial obligations. The 10–percent limitation does not apply where it is determined that the overpayment occurred because of fraud, willful misrepresentation, or concealment of material information committed by the individual or his or her spouse. Concealment of material information means an intentional, knowing, and purposeful delay in making or failure to make a report that will affect payment amount and/or eligibility. It does not include a mere omission on the part of the recipient; it is an affirmative act to conceal. The 10–percent limitation does not apply to the recovery of overpayments incurred under agreements to dispose of resources pursuant to § 416.1240. In addition, the 10–percent limitation does not apply to the reduction of any future SSI benefits as a consequence of the misuse of funds set aside in accordance with § 416.1231(b) to meet burial expenses. Adjustment or recovery will be suspended if the recipient is subject to a reduced benefit rate under § 416.414 because of residing in a medical treatment facility in which Medicaid is paying a substantial portion of the recipient's cost of care.

[55 FR 33669, Aug. 17, 1990; 72 FR 50874, Sept. 5, 2007]

§ 416.572 Are title II and title VIII benefits subject to adjustment to recover title XVI overpayments?

(a) Definitions—

(1) Cross-program recovery. Cross-program recovery is the process that we will use to collect title XVI overpayments from benefits payable to you under title II or title VIII of the Social Security Act.

(2) Benefits payable. For purposes of this section, benefits payable means the amount of title II or title VIII benefits you actually would receive. For title II benefits, it includes your monthly benefit and your past-due benefits after any reductions or deductions listed in § 404.401(a) and (b) of this chapter. For title VIII benefits, it includes your monthly benefit and any past-due benefits after any reduction by the amount of income for the month as described in §§ 408.505 through 408.510 of this chapter.

(b) When may we collect title XVI overpayments using cross-program recovery? We may use cross-program recovery to collect a title XVI overpayment you owe when benefits are payable to you under title II, title VIII, or both.

[66 FR 38906, July 26, 2001; 67 FR 38383, June 4, 2002; 70 FR 16, Jan. 3, 2005; 70 FR 16113, March 30, 2005]

§ 416.573 How much will we withhold from your title II and title VIII benefits to recover a title XVI overpayment?

(a) If past-due benefits are payable to you, we will withhold the lesser of the entire overpayment balance or the entire amount of past-due benefits.

(b)(1) We will collect the overpayment from current monthly benefits due in a month by withholding the lesser of the amount of the entire overpayment balance or 10 percent of the monthly title II benefits and monthly title VIII benefits payable to you in the month.

(2) If we are already recovering a title II, title VIII or title XVI overpayment from your monthly title II benefit, we will figure your monthly withholding from title XVI payments (as described in § 416.571) without including your title II benefits in your total countable income.

(3) Paragraph (b)(1) of this section does not apply if:

(i) You request and we approve a different rate of withholding, or

(ii) You or your spouse willfully misrepresented or concealed material information in connection with the overpayment.

(c) In determining whether to grant your request that we withhold less than the amount described in paragraph (b)(1) of this section, we will use the criteria applied under § 416.571 to similar requests about withholding from title XVI benefits.

(d) If you or your spouse willfully misrepresented or concealed material information in connection with the overpayment, we will collect the overpayment by withholding the lesser of the overpayment balance or the entire amount of title II benefits and title VIII benefits payable to you. We will not collect at a lesser rate. (See § 416.571 for what we mean by concealment of material information.)

[70 FR 16, Jan. 3, 2005; 70 FR 16113, March 30, 2005]

§ 416.574 Will you receive notice of our intention to apply cross-program recovery?

Before we collect an overpayment from you using cross-program recovery, we will send you a written notice that tells you the following information:

(a) We have determined that you owe a specific overpayment balance that can be collected by cross-program recovery;

(b) We will withhold a specific amount from the title II or title VIII benefits (see § 416.573);

(c) You may ask us to review this determination that you still owe this overpayment balance;

(d) You may request that we withhold a different amount from your current monthly benefits (the notice will not include this information if § 416.573(d) applies); and

(e) You may ask us to waive collection of this overpayment balance.

[70 FR 16, Jan. 3, 2005; 70 FR 16113, March 30, 2005]

§ 416.575 When will we begin cross-program recovery from your current monthly benefits?

(a) We will begin collecting the overpayment balance by cross-program recovery from your current monthly title II and title VIII benefits no sooner than 30 calendar days after the date of the notice described in § 416.574. If within that 30–day period you pay us the full overpayment balance stated in the notice, we will not begin cross-program recovery.

(b) If within that 30–day period you ask us to review our determination that you still owe us this overpayment balance, we will not begin cross-program recovery from your current monthly benefits before we review the matter and notify you of our decision in writing.

(c) If within that 30–day period you ask us to withhold a different amount from your current monthly benefits than the amount stated in the notice, we will not begin cross-program recovery until we determine the amount we will withhold. This paragraph does not apply when § 416.573(d) applies.

(d) If within that 30–day period you ask us to waive recovery of the overpayment balance, we will not begin cross-program recovery from your current monthly benefits before we review the matter and notify you of our decision in writing. See §§ 416.550 through 416.556.

[70 FR 16, Jan. 3, 2005; 70 FR 16113, March 30, 2005]

§ 416.580 Referral of overpayments to the Department of the Treasury for tax refund offset—General.

(a) The standards we will apply and the procedures we will follow before requesting the Department of the Treasury to offset income tax refunds due taxpayers who have an outstanding overpayment are set forth in §§ 416.580 through 416.586 of this subpart. These standards and procedures are authorized by the Deficit Reduction Act of 1984 [31 U.S.C. § 3720A], as implemented through Department of the Treasury regulations at 31 CFR 285.2.

(b) We will use the Department of the Treasury tax refund offset procedure to collect overpayments that are certain in amount, past due and legally enforceable, and eligible for tax refund offset under regulations issued by the Secretary of the Treasury. We will use these procedures to collect overpayments only from persons who are not currently entitled to monthly supplemental security income benefits under title XVI of the Act. We refer overpayments to the Department of the Treasury for offset against Federal tax refunds regardless of the amount of time the debts have been outstanding.

[62 FR 49439, Sept. 22, 1997; 76 FR 65109, Oct. 20, 2011]

§ 416.581 Notice to overpaid person.

We will make a request for collection by reduction of Federal and State income tax refunds only after we determine that a person owes an overpayment that is past due and provide the overpaid person with written notice. Our notice of intent to collect an overpayment through tax refund offset will state:

(a) The amount of the overpayment; and

(b) That we will collect the overpayment by requesting that the Department of the Treasury reduce any amounts payable to the overpaid person as refunds of Federal and State income taxes by an amount equal to the amount of the overpayment unless, within 60 calendar days from the date of our notice, the overpaid person:

(1) Repays the overpayment in full; or

(2) Provides evidence to us at the address given in our notice that the overpayment is not past due or legally enforceable; or

(3) Asks us to waive collection of the overpayment under section 204(b) of the Act.

(c) The conditions under which we will waive recovery of an overpayment under section 1631(b)(1)(B) of the Act;

(d) That we will review any evidence presented that the overpayment is not past due or not legally enforceable;

(e) That the overpaid person has the right to inspect and copy our records related to the overpayment as determined by us and will be informed as to where and when the inspection and copying can be done after we receive notice from the overpaid person that inspection and copying are requested.

[62 FR 49439, Sept. 22, 1997; 76 FR 65109, Oct. 20, 2011]

§ 416.582 Review within SSA that an overpayment is past due and legally enforceable.

(a) Notification by overpaid individual. An overpaid individual who receives a notice as described in § 416.581 of this subpart has the right to present evidence that all or part of the overpayment is not past due or not legally enforceable. To exercise this right, the individual must notify us and present evidence regarding the overpayment within 60 calendar days from the date of our notice.

(b) Submission of evidence. The overpaid individual may submit evidence showing that all or part of the debt is not past due or not legally enforceable as provided in paragraph (a) of this section. Failure to submit the notification and evidence within 60 calendar days will result in referral of the overpayment to the Department of the Treasury, unless the overpaid individual, within this 60–day time period, has asked us to waive collection of the overpayment under section 1631(b)(1)(B) of the Act and we have not yet determined whether we can grant the waiver request. If the overpaid individual asks us to waive collection of the overpayment, we may ask that evidence to support the request be submitted to us.

(c) Review of the evidence. After a timely submission of evidence by the overpaid individual, we will consider all available evidence related to the overpayment. We will make findings based on a review of the written record, unless we determine that the question of indebtedness cannot be resolved by a review of the documentary evidence.

[62 FR 49439, Sept. 22, 1997]

§ 416.583 Findings by SSA.

(a) Following the review of the record, we will issue written findings which include supporting rationale for the findings. Issuance of these findings concerning whether the overpayment or part of the overpayment is past due and legally enforceable is the final Agency action with respect to the past-due status and enforceability of the overpayment. If we make a determination that a waiver request cannot be granted, we will issue a written notice of this determination in accordance with the regulations in subpart E of this part. Our referral of the overpayment to the Department of the Treasury will not be suspended under § 416.585 of this subpart pending any further administrative review of the waiver request that the individual may seek.

(b) Copies of the findings described in paragraph (a) of this section will be distributed to the overpaid individual and the overpaid individual's attorney or other representative, if any.

(c) If the findings referred to in paragraph (a) of this section affirm that all or part of the overpayment is past due and legally enforceable and, if waiver is requested and we determine that the request cannot be granted, we will refer the overpayment to the Department of the Treasury. However, no referral will be made if, based on our review of the overpayment, we reverse our prior finding that the overpayment is past due and legally enforceable or, upon consideration of a waiver request, we determine that waiver of our collection of the overpayment is appropriate.

[62 FR 49439, Sept. 22, 1997]

§ 416.584 Review of our records related to the overpayment.

(a) Notification by the overpaid individual. An overpaid individual who intends to inspect or copy our records related to the overpayment as determined by us must notify us stating his or her intention to inspect or copy.

(b) Our response. In response to a notification by the overpaid individual as described in paragraph (a) of this section, we will notify the overpaid individual of the location and time when the overpaid individual may inspect or copy our records related to the overpayment. We may also, at our discretion, mail copies of the overpayment-related records to the overpaid individual.

[62 FR 49439, Sept. 22, 1997]

§ 416.585 Suspension of offset.

If, within 60 days of the date of the notice described in § 416.581 of this subpart, the overpaid individual notifies us that he or she is exercising a right described in § 416.582(a) of this subpart and submits evidence pursuant to § 416.582(b) of this subpart or requests a waiver under § 416.550 of this subpart, we will suspend any notice to the Department of the Treasury until we have issued written findings that affirm that an overpayment is past due and legally enforceable and, if applicable, make a determination that a waiver request cannot be granted.

[62 FR 49439, Sept. 22, 1997]

§ 416.586 Tax refund insufficient to cover amount of overpayment.

If a tax refund is insufficient to recover an overpayment in a given year, the case will remain with the Department of the Treasury for succeeding years, assuming that all criteria for certification are met at that time.

[62 FR 49439, Sept. 22, 1997]

§ 416.590 Are there additional methods for recovery of title XVI benefit overpayments?

(a) General. In addition to the methods specified in §§ 416.560, 416.570, 416.572 and 416.580, we may recover an overpayment under title XVI of the Act from you under the rules in subparts D and E of part 422 of this chapter. Subpart D of part 422 of this chapter applies only under the following conditions:

(1) The overpayment occurred after you attained age 18;

(2) You are no longer entitled to benefits under title XVI of the Act; and

(3) Pursuant to paragraph (b) of this section, we have determined that the overpayment is otherwise unrecoverable under section 1631(b) of the Act.

(b) When we consider an overpayment to be otherwise unrecoverable. We consider an overpayment under title XVI of the Act to be otherwise unrecoverable under section 1631(b) of the Act if all of the following conditions are met:

(1) We have completed our billing system sequence (i.e., we have sent you an initial notice of the overpayment, a reminder notice, and a past-due notice) or we have suspended or terminated collection activity under applicable rules, such as, the Federal Claims Collection Standards in 31 CFR 903.2 or 903.3.

(2) We have not entered into an installment payment arrangement with you or, if we have entered into such an arrangement, you have failed to make any payment for two consecutive months.

(3) You have not requested waiver pursuant to § 416.550 or § 416.582 or, after a review conducted pursuant to those sections, we have determined that we will not waive collection of the overpayment.

(4) You have not requested reconsideration of the initial overpayment determination pursuant to §§ 416.1407 and 416.1409 or, after a review conducted pursuant to § 416.1413, we have affirmed all or part of the initial overpayment determination.

(5) We cannot recover your overpayment pursuant to § 416.570 by adjustment of benefits payable to any individual other than you. For purposes of this paragraph, if you are a member of an eligible couple that is legally separated and/or living apart, we will deem unrecoverable from the other person that part of your overpayment which he or she did not receive.

[66 FR 67081, Dec. 28, 2001; 68 FR 74184, Dec. 23, 2003]

SUBPART F—REPRESENTATIVE PAYMENT

Authority: Secs. 702(a)(5), 1631(a)(2) and (d)(1) of the Social Security Act (42 U.S.C. 902(a)(5) and 1383(a)(2) and (d)(1)).

Source: 39 FR 37634, Oct. 23, 1974, as amended at 47 FR 30475, July 14, 1982; 52 FR 27541, July 22, 1987; 61 FR 5942, Feb. 15, 1996; 75 FR 7552, Feb. 22, 2010, unless otherwise noted.

§ 416.601 Introduction.

(a) Explanation of representative payment. This subpart explains the principles and procedures that we follow in determining whether to make representative payment and in selecting a representative payee. It also explains the responsibilities that a representative payee has concerning the use of the funds he or she receives on behalf of a beneficiary. A representative payee may be either a person or an organization selected by us to receive benefits on behalf of a beneficiary. A representative payee will be selected if we believe that the interest of a beneficiary will be served by representative payment rather than direct payment of benefits. Generally, we appoint a representative payee if we have determined that the beneficiary is not able to manage or direct the management of benefit payments in his or her own interest.

(b) Policy used to determine whether to make representative payment.

(1) Our policy is that every beneficiary has the right to manage his or her own benefits. However, some beneficiaries due to a mental or physical condition or due to their youth may be unable to do so. Under these circumstances, we may determine that the interests of the beneficiary would be better served if we certified benefit payments to another person as a representative payee. However, we must select a representative payee for an individual who is eligible for benefits solely on the basis of disability if drug addic-

tion or alcoholism is a contributing factor material to the determination of disability.

(2) If we determine that representative payment is in the interest of a beneficiary, we will appoint a representative payee. We may appoint a representative payee even if the beneficiary is a legally competent individual. If the beneficiary is a legally incompetent individual, we may appoint the legal guardian or some other person as a representative payee.

(3) If payment is being made directly to a beneficiary and a question arises concerning his or her ability to manage or direct the management of benefit payments, we will, if the beneficiary is 18 years old or older and has not been adjudged legally incompetent, continue to pay the beneficiary until we make a determination about his or her ability to manage or direct the management of benefit payments and the selection of a representative payee.

[60 FR 8150, Feb. 10, 1995]

§ 416.610 When payment will be made to a representative payee.

(a) We pay benefits to a representative payee on behalf of a beneficiary 18 years old or older when it appears to us that this method of payment will be in the interest of the beneficiary. We do this if we have information that the beneficiary is—

(1) Legally incompetent or mentally incapable of managing benefit payments; or

(2) Physically incapable of managing or directing the management of his or her benefit payments; or

(3) Eligible for benefits solely on the basis of disability and drug addiction or alcoholism is a contributing factor material to the determination of disability.

(b) Generally, if a beneficiary is under age 18, we will pay benefits to a representative payee. However, in certain situations, we will make direct payments to a beneficiary under age 18 who shows the ability to manage the benefits. For example, we make direct payment to a beneficiary under age 18 if the beneficiary is—

(1) A parent and files for himself or herself and/or his or her child and he or she has experience in handling his or her own finances; or

(2) Capable of using the benefits to provide for his or her current needs and no qualified payee is available; or

(3) Within 7 months of attaining age 18 and is initially filing an application for benefits.

[54 FR 35483, Aug. 28, 1989; 60 FR 8150, Feb. 10, 1995]

§ 416.611 What happens to your monthly benefits while we are finding a suitable representative payee for you?

(a) We may pay you directly. We will pay current monthly benefits directly to you while finding a suitable representative payee unless we determine that paying you directly would cause substantial harm to you. We determine substantial harm as follows:

(1) If you are receiving disability payments and we have determined that you have a drug addiction or alcoholism condition, or you are legally incompetent, or you are under age 15, we will presume that substantial harm exists. However, we will allow you to rebut this presumption by presenting evidence that direct payment would not cause you substantial harm.

(2) If you do not fit any of these categories, we make findings of substantial harm on a case-by-case basis. We consider all matters that may affect your ability to manage your benefits in your own best interest. We decide that substantial harm exists if both of the following conditions exist:

(i) Directly receiving benefits can be expected to cause you serious physical or mental injury.

(ii) The possible effect of the injury would outweigh the effect of having no income to meet your basic needs.

(b) We may delay or suspend your payments. If we find that direct payment will cause substantial harm to you, we may delay (in the case of initial eligibility for benefits) or suspend (in the case of existing eligibility for benefits) payments for as long as one month while we try to find a suitable representative payee. If we do not find a payee within one month, we will pay you directly. If you are receiving disability payments and we have determined that you have a drug addiction or alcoholism condition, or you are legally incompetent, or you are under age 15, we will withhold payment until a representative payee is appointed even if it takes longer than one month. We will, however, as noted in paragraph (a)(1) of this section, allow you to present evidence to rebut the presumption that direct payment would cause you substantial harm. See § 416.601(b)(3) for our policy on suspending the benefits if you are currently receiving benefits directly.

Example 1: Substantial Harm Exists. We are unable to find a representative payee for Mr. X, a 67 year old claimant receiving title XVI benefits based on age who is an alcoholic. Based on contacts with the doctor and beneficiary, we determine that Mr. X was hospitalized recently for his drinking. Paying him directly will cause serious injury, so we may delay payment for as long as one month based on substantial harm while we locate a suitable representative payee.

Example 2: Substantial Harm Does Not Exist. We approve a claim for Mr. Y, a title XVI claimant who suffers from a combination of mental impairments but who is not legally incompetent. We determine that Mr. Y needs assistance in managing benefits, but we have not found a representative payee. Although we believe that Mr. Y may not use the money wisely, there is no indication that receiving funds directly would cause him substantial harm (i.e., serious physical or mental injury). We must pay current benefits directly to Mr. Y while we locate a suitable representative payee.

(c) How we pay delayed or suspended benefits. Payment of benefits, which were delayed or suspended pending appointment of a representative payee, can be made to you or your representative payee as a single sum or in installments when we determine that installments are in your best interest.

[69 FR 60236, Oct. 7, 2004]

§ 416.615 Information considered in determining whether to make representative payment.

In determining whether to make representative payment we consider the following information:

(a) Court determinations. If we learn that a beneficiary has been found to be legally incompetent, a certified copy of the court's determination will be the basis of our determination to make representative payment.

(b) Medical evidence. When available, we will use medical evidence to determine if a beneficiary is capable of managing or directing the management of benefit payments. For example, a statement by a physician or other medical professional based upon his or her recent examination of the beneficiary and his or her knowledge of the beneficiary's present condition will be used in our determination, if it includes information concerning the nature of the beneficiary's illness, the beneficiary's chances for recovery and the opinion of the physician or other medical professional as to whether the beneficiary is able to manage or direct the management of benefit payments.

(c) Other evidence. We will also consider any statements of relatives, friends and other people in a position to know and observe the beneficiary, which contain information helpful to us in deciding whether the beneficiary is able to manage or direct the management of benefit payments.

§ 416.620 Information considered in selecting a representative payee.

In selecting a payee we try to select the person, agency, organization or institution that will best serve the interest of the beneficiary. In making our selection we consider—

(a) The relationship of the person to the beneficiary;

(b) The amount of interest that the person shows in the beneficiary;

(c) Any legal authority the person, agency, organization or institution has to act on behalf of the beneficiary;

(d) Whether the potential payee has custody of the beneficiary;

(e) Whether the potential payee is in a position to know of and look after the needs of the beneficiary; and

(f) The potential payee's criminal history.

[84 FR 4325, Feb. 15, 2019]

§ 416.621 What is our order of preference in selecting a representative payee for you?

As a guide in selecting a representative payee, categories of preferred payees have been established. These preferences are flexible. Our primary concern is to select the payee who will best serve the beneficiary's interests. The preferences are:

(a) For beneficiaries 18 years old or older (except those described in paragraph (b) of this section), our preference is—

(1) A legal guardian, spouse (or other relative) who has custody of the beneficiary or who demonstrates strong concern for the personal welfare of the beneficiary;

(2) A friend who has custody of the beneficiary or demonstrates strong concern for the personal welfare of the beneficiary;

(3) A public or nonprofit agency or institution having custody of the beneficiary;

(4) A private institution operated for profit and licensed under State law, which has custody of the beneficiary; and

(5) Persons other than above who are qualified to carry out the responsibilities of a payee and who are able and willing to serve as a payee for the beneficiary; e.g., members of community groups or organizations who volunteer to serve as payee for a beneficiary.

(b) For individuals who are disabled and who have a drug addiction or alcoholism condition our preference is—

(1) A community-based nonprofit social service agency licensed by the State, or bonded;

(2) A Federal, State or local government agency whose mission is to carry out income maintenance, social service, or health care-related activities;

(3) A State or local government agency with fiduciary responsibilities;

(4) A designee of an agency (other than a Federal agency) referred to in paragraphs (b)(1), (2), and (3) of this section, if appropriate; or

(5) A family member.

(c) For beneficiaries under age 18, our preference is—

(1) A natural or adoptive parent who has custody of the beneficiary, or a guardian;

(2) A natural or adoptive parent who does not have custody of the beneficiary, but is contributing toward the beneficiary's support and is demonstrating strong concern for the beneficiary's well being;

(3) A natural or adoptive parent who does not have custody of the beneficiary and is not contributing

toward his or her support but is demonstrating strong concern for the beneficiary's well being;

(4) A relative or stepparent who has custody of the beneficiary;

(5) A relative who does not have custody of the beneficiary but is contributing toward the beneficiary's support and is demonstrating concern for the beneficiary's well being;

(6) A relative or close friend who does not have custody of the beneficiary but is demonstrating concern for the beneficiary's well being; and

(7) An authorized social agency or custodial institution.

[69 FR 60237, Oct. 7, 2004]

§ 416.622 Who may not serve as a representative payee?

A representative payee applicant may not serve if he/she:

(a) Has been convicted of a violation under section 208, 811 or 1632 of the Social Security Act.

(b) Has been convicted of an offense resulting in imprisonment for more than 1 year. However, we may make an exception to this prohibition, if the nature of the conviction is such that selection of the applicant poses no risk to the beneficiary and the exception is in the beneficiary's best interest.

(c) Receives title II, VIII, or XVI benefits through a representative payee.

(d) Previously served as a representative payee and was found by us, or a court of competent jurisdiction, to have misused title II, VIII or XVI benefits. However, if we decide to make an exception to the prohibition, we must evaluate the payee's performance at least every 3 months until we are satisfied that the payee poses no risk to the beneficiary's best interest. Exceptions are made on a case-by-case basis if all of the following are true:

(1) Direct payment of benefits to the beneficiary is not in the beneficiary's best interest.

(2) No suitable alternative payee is available.

(3) Selecting the payee applicant as representative payee would be in the best interest of the beneficiary.

(4) The information we have indicates the applicant is now suitable to serve as a representative payee.

(5) The payee applicant has repaid the misused benefits or has a plan to repay them.

(e) Is a creditor. A creditor is someone who provides you with goods or services for consideration. This restriction does not apply to the creditor who poses no risk to you and whose financial relationship with you presents no substantial conflict of interest, and is any of the following:

(1) A relative living in the same household as you do.

(2) Your legal guardian or legal representative.

(3) A facility that is licensed or certified as a care facility under the law of a State or a political subdivision of a State.

(4) A qualified organization authorized to collect a monthly fee from you for expenses incurred in providing representative payee services for you, under § 416.640a.

(5) An administrator, owner, or employee of the facility in which you live and we are unable to locate an alternative representative payee.

(6) Any other individual we deem appropriate based on a written determination.

Example 1: Sharon applies to be representative payee for Ron who we have determined needs assistance in managing his benefits. Sharon has been renting a room to Ron for several years and assists Ron in handling his other financial obligations, as needed. She charges Ron a reasonable amount of rent. Ron has no other family or friends willing to help manage his benefits or to act as representative payee. Sharon has demonstrated that her interest in and concern for Ron goes beyond her desire to collect the rent each month. In this instance, we may select Sharon as Ron's representative payee because a more suitable payee is not available, she appears to pose no risk to Ron and there is minimal conflict of interest. We will document this decision.

Example 2: In a situation similar to the one above, Ron's landlord indicates that she is applying to be payee only to ensure receipt of her rent. If there is money left after payment of the rent, she will give it directly to Ron to manage on his own. In this situation, we would not select the landlord as Ron's representative payee because of the substantial conflict of interest and lack of interest in his well being.

(f) Was convicted under Federal or State law of a felony for: Human trafficking, false imprisonment, kidnapping, rape or sexual assault, first-degree homicide, robbery, fraud to obtain access to government assistance, fraud by scheme, theft of government funds or property, abuse or neglect, forgery, or identity theft or identity fraud. We will also apply this provision to a representative payee applicant with a felony conviction of an attempt to commit any of these crimes or conspiracy to commit any of these crimes.

(1) If the representative payee applicant is the custodial parent of a minor child beneficiary, custodial parent of a beneficiary who is under a disability which began before the beneficiary attained the age of 22, custodial spouse of a beneficiary, custodial court-appointed guardian of a beneficiary, or custodial grandparent of the minor child beneficiary for whom the applicant is applying to serve as representative payee, we will not consider the conviction for one of the crimes, or of attempt or conspiracy to commit one of the crimes, listed in this paragraph (f), by itself, to prohibit the applicant from serving as a representative payee. We will consider the criminal history of an applicant in this category, along with the factors in paragraphs (a) through (e) of this section, when we

decide whether it is in the best interest of the individual entitled to benefits to appoint the applicant as a representative payee.

(2) If the representative payee applicant is the parent who was previously the representative payee for his or her minor child who has since turned age 18 and continues to be eligible for benefits, we will not consider the conviction for one of the crimes, or of attempt or conspiracy to commit one of the crimes, listed in this paragraph (f), by itself, to prohibit the applicant from serving as a representative payee for that beneficiary. We will consider the criminal history of an applicant in this category, along with the factors in paragraphs (a) through (e) of this section, when we decide whether it is in the best interest of the individual entitled to benefits to appoint the applicant as a representative payee.

(3) If the representative payee applicant received a Presidential or gubernatorial pardon for the relevant conviction, we will not consider the conviction for one of the crimes, or of attempt or conspiracy to commit one of the crimes, listed in this paragraph (f), by itself, to prohibit the applicant from serving as a representative payee. We will consider the criminal history of an applicant in this category, along with the factors in paragraphs (a) through (e) of this section, when we decide whether it is in the best interest of the individual entitled to benefits to appoint the applicant as a representative payee.

[69 FR 60237, Oct. 7, 2004; 71 FR 61408, Oct. 18, 2006; 84 FR 4325, Feb. 15, 2019]

§ 416.624 How do we investigate a representative payee applicant?

Before selecting an individual or organization to act as your representative payee, we will perform an investigation.

(a) Nature of the investigation. As part of the investigation, we do the following:

(1) Conduct a face-to-face interview with the payee applicant unless it is impracticable as explained in paragraph (c) of this section.

(2) Require the payee applicant to submit documented proof of identity, unless information establishing identity has recently been submitted with an application for title II, VIII or XVI benefits.

(3) Verify the payee applicant's Social Security account number or employer identification number.

(4) Determine whether the payee applicant has been convicted of a violation of section 208, 811 or 1632 of the Social Security Act.

(5) Determine whether the payee applicant has previously served as a representative payee and if any previous appointment as payee was revoked or terminated for misusing title II, VIII or XVI benefits.

(6) Use our records to verify the payee applicant's employment and/or direct receipt of title II, VIII, or XVI benefits.

(7) Verify the payee applicant's concern for the beneficiary with the beneficiary's custodian or other interested person.

(8) Require the payee applicant to provide adequate information showing his or her relationship to the beneficiary and to describe his or her responsibility for the care of the beneficiary.

(9) Determine whether the payee applicant is a creditor of the beneficiary (see § 416.622(e)).

(10) Conduct a criminal background check on the payee applicant.

(b) Subsequent face-to-face interviews. After holding a face-to-face interview with a payee applicant, subsequent face-to-face interviews are not required if that applicant continues to be qualified and currently is acting as a payee, unless we determine, within our discretion, that a new face-to-face interview is necessary. We base this decision on the payee's past performance and knowledge of and compliance with our reporting requirements.

(c) Impracticable. We may consider a face-to-face interview impracticable if it would cause the payee applicant undue hardship. For example, the payee applicant would have to travel a great distance to the field office. In this situation, we may conduct the investigation to determine the payee applicant's suitability to serve as a representative payee without a face-to-face interview.

[69 FR 60237, Oct. 7, 2004; 73 FR 66521, Nov. 10, 2008; 84 FR 4326, Feb. 15, 2019]

§ 416.625 What information must a representative payee report to us?

Anytime after we select a representative payee for you, we may ask your payee to give us information showing a continuing relationship with you, a continuing responsibility for your care, and how he/she used the payments on your behalf. If your representative payee does not give us the requested information within a reasonable period of time, we may stop sending your benefit payment to him/her—unless we determine that he/she had a satisfactory reason for not meeting our request and we subsequently receive the requested information. If we decide to stop sending your benefit payment to your representative payee, we will consider paying you directly (in accordance with § 416.611) while we look for a new payee.

[69 FR 60238, Oct. 7, 2004]

§ 416.626 How do we investigate an appointed representative payee?

After we select an individual or organization to act as your representative payee, we will conduct a criminal background check on the appointed representative payee at least once every 5 years.

[84 FR 4326, Feb. 15, 2019]

§ 416.630 How will we notify you when we decide you need a representative payee?

(a) We notify you in writing of our determination to make representative payment. This advance notice explains that we have determined that representative payment is in your interest, and it provides the name of the representative payee we have selected. We provide this notice before we actually appoint the payee. If you are under age 15, an unemancipated minor under the age of 18, or legally incompetent, our written notice goes to your legal guardian or legal representative. The advance notice:

(1) Contains language that is easily understandable to the reader.

(2) Identifies the person designated as your representative payee.

(3) Explains that you, your legal guardian, or your legal representative can appeal our determination that you need a representative payee.

(4) Explains that you, your legal guardian, or your legal representative can appeal our designation of a particular person to serve as your representative payee.

(5) Explains that you, your legal guardian, or your legal representative can review the evidence upon which our designation of a particular representative payee is based and submit additional evidence.

(b) If you, your legal guardian, or your legal representative objects to representative payment or to the designated payee, we will handle the objection as follows:

(1) If you disagree with the decision and wish to file an appeal, we will process it under subpart N of this part.

(2) If you received your advance notice by mail and you protest or file your appeal within 10 days after you receive the notice, we will delay the action until we make a decision on your protest or appeal. (If you received and signed your notice while you were in the local field office, our decision will be effective immediately.)

[69 FR 60238, Oct. 7, 2004]

§ 416.635 What are the responsibilities of your representative payee?

A representative payee has a responsibility to—

(a) Use the benefits received on your behalf only for your use and benefit in a manner and for the purposes he or she determines under the guidelines in this subpart, to be in your best interests;

(b) Keep any benefits received on your behalf separate from his or her own funds and show your ownership of these benefits unless he or she is your spouse or natural or adoptive parent or stepparent and lives in the same household with you or is a State or local government agency for whom we have granted an exception to this requirement;

(c) Treat any interest earned on the benefits as your property;

(d) Notify us of any event or change in your circumstances that will affect the amount of benefits you receive, your right to receive benefits, or how you receive them;

(e) Submit to us, upon our request, a written report accounting for the benefits received on your behalf, and make all supporting records available for review if requested by us;

(f) Notify us of any change in his or her circumstances that would affect performance of his/her payee responsibilities; and

(g) Ensure that you are receiving treatment to the extent considered medically necessary and available for the condition that was the basis for providing benefits (see § 416.994a(i)) if you are under age 18 (including cases in which your low birth weight is a contributing factor material to our determination that you are disabled).

[62 FR 6420, Feb. 11, 1997; 71 FR 61408, Oct. 18, 2006]

§ 416.640 Use of benefit payments.

(a) Current maintenance. We will consider that payments we certify to a representative payee have been used for the use and benefit of the beneficiary if they are used for the beneficiary's current maintenance. Current maintenance includes costs incurred in obtaining food, shelter, clothing, medical care and personal comfort items.

Example: A Supplemental Security Income beneficiary is entitled to a monthly benefit of $264. The beneficiary's son, who is the representative payee, disburses the benefits in the following manner:

Rent and Utilities	$166
Medical	20
Food	60
Clothing	10
Miscellaneous	8

The above expenditures would represent proper disbursements on behalf of the beneficiary.

(b) Institution not receiving Medicaid funds on beneficiary's behalf. If a beneficiary is receiving care in a Federal, State, or private institution because of mental or physical incapacity, current maintenance will include the customary charges for the care and services provided by an institution, expenditures for those items which will aid in the beneficiary's recovery or release from the institution, and nominal expenses for personal needs (e.g., personal hygiene items, snacks, candy) which will improve the beneficiary's condition. Except as provided under § 416.212, there is no restriction in using SSI benefits for a beneficiary's current maintenance in an institution. Any payments remaining from SSI benefits may be used for a temporary period to maintain the beneficiary's residence outside of the institution unless a physician has certified that the beneficiary is not likely to return home.

Example: A hospitalized disabled beneficiary is entitled to a monthly benefit of $264. The beneficiary, who resides in a boarding home, has resided there for over 6 years. It is doubtful that the beneficiary will leave the boarding home in the near future. The boarding home charges $215 per month for the beneficiary's room and board.

The beneficiary's representative payee pays the boarding home $215 (assuming an unsuccessful effort was made to negotiate a lower rate during the beneficiary's absence) and uses the balance to purchase miscellaneous personal items for the beneficiary. There are no benefits remaining which can be conserved on behalf of the beneficiary. The payee's use of the benefits is consistent with our guidelines.

(c) Institution receiving Medicaid funds on beneficiary's behalf. Except in the case of a beneficiary receiving benefits payable under § 416.212, if a beneficiary resides throughout a month in an institution that receives more than 50 percent of the cost of care on behalf of the beneficiary from Medicaid, any payments due shall be used only for the personal needs of the beneficiary and not for other items of current maintenance.

Example: A disabled beneficiary resides in a hospital. The superintendent of the hospital receives $30 per month as the beneficiary's payee. The benefit payment is disbursed in the following manner, which would be consistent with our guidelines:

Miscellaneous canteen items	$10
Clothing	15
Conserved for future needs of the beneficiary	5

(d) Claims of creditors. A payee may not be required to use benefit payments to satisfy a debt of the beneficiary, if the debt arose prior to the first month for which payments are certified to a payee. If the debt arose prior to this time, a payee may satisfy it only if the current and reasonably foreseeable needs of the beneficiary are met.

Example: A disabled beneficiary was determined to be eligible for a monthly benefit payment of $208 effective April 1981. The benefits were certified to the beneficiary's brother who was appointed as the representative payee. The payee conserved $27 of the benefits received. In June 1981 the payee received a bill from a doctor who had treated the beneficiary in February and March 1981. The bill was for $175.

After reviewing the beneficiary's current needs and resources, the payee decided not to use any of the benefits to pay the doctor's bill. (Approximately $180 a month is required for the beneficiary's current monthly living expenses—rent, utilities, food, and insurance—and the beneficiary will need new shoes and a coat within the next few months.)

Based upon the above, the payee's decision not to pay the doctor's bill is consistent with our guidelines.

(e) Dedicated accounts for eligible individuals under age 18.

(1) When past-due benefit payments are required to be paid into a separate dedicated account (see § 416.546), the representative payee is required to establish in a financial institution an account dedicated to the purposes described in paragraph (e)(2) of this section. This dedicated account may be a checking, savings or money market account subject to the titling requirements set forth in § 416.645. Dedicated accounts may not be in the form of certificates of deposit, mutual funds, stocks, bonds or trusts.

(2) A representative payee shall use dedicated account funds, whether deposited on a mandatory or permissive basis (as described in § 416.546), for the benefit of the child and only for the following allowable expenses—

(i) Medical treatment and education or job skills training;

(ii) If related to the child's impairment(s), personal needs assistance; special equipment; housing modification; and therapy or rehabilitation; or

(iii) Other items and services related to the child's impairment(s) that we determine to be appropriate. The representative payee must explain why or how the other item or service relates to the impairment(s) of the child. Attorney fees related to the pursuit of the child's disability claim and use of funds to prevent malnourishment or homelessness could be considered appropriate expenditures.

(3) Representative payees must keep records and receipts of all deposits to and expenditures from dedicated accounts, and must submit these records to us upon our request, as explained in §§ 416.635 and 416.665.

(4) The use of funds from a dedicated account in any manner not authorized by this section constitutes a misapplication of benefits. These misapplied benefits are not an overpayment as defined in § 416.537; however, if we determine that a representative payee knowingly misapplied funds in a dedicated account, that representative payee shall be liable to us in an amount equal to the total amount of the misapplied funds. In addition, if a recipient who is his or her own payee knowingly misapplies benefits in a dedicated account, we will reduce future benefits payable to that recipient (or to that recipient and his or her spouse) by an amount equal to the total amount of the misapplied funds.

(5) The restrictions described in this section and the income and resource exclusions described in §§ 416.1124(c)(20) and 416.1247 shall continue to apply

until all funds in the dedicated account are depleted or eligibility for benefits terminates, whichever comes first. This continuation of the restrictions and exclusions applies in situations where funds remain in the account in any of the following situations—

(i) A child attains age 18, continues to be eligible and receives payments directly;

(ii) A new representative payee is appointed. When funds remaining in a dedicated account are returned to us by the former representative payee, the new representative payee must establish an account in a financial institution into which we will deposit these funds, even if the amount is less than that prescribed in § 416.546; or

(iii) During a period of suspension due to ineligibility as described in § 416.1320, administrative suspension, or a period of eligibility for which no payment is due.

[61 FR 10278, March 13, 1996; 61 FR 67206, Dec. 20, 1996; 68 FR 53509, Sept. 11, 2003; 76 FR 453, Jan. 5, 2011]

§ 416.640a Compensation for qualified organizations serving as representative payees.

(a) Organizations that can request compensation. A qualified organization can request us to authorize it to collect a monthly fee from your benefit payment. A qualified organization is:

(1) Any State or local government agency with fiduciary responsibilities or whose mission is to carry out income maintenance, social service, or health care-related activities; or

(2) Any community-based nonprofit social service organization founded for religious, charitable or social welfare purposes, which is tax exempt under section 501(c) of the Internal Revenue Code and which is bonded/insured to cover misuse and embezzlement by officers and employees and which is licensed in each State in which it serves as representative payee (if licensing is available in the State). The minimum amount of bonding or insurance coverage must equal the average monthly amount of supplemental security income payments received by the organization plus the amount of the beneficiaries' conserved funds (i.e., beneficiaries' saved supplemental security income payments) plus interest on hand. For example, an organization that has conserved funds of $5,000 and receives an average of $12,000 a month in supplemental security income payments must be bonded/insured for a minimum of $17,000. The license must be appropriate under the laws of the State for the type of services the organization provides. An example of an appropriately licensed organization is a community mental health center holding a State license to provide community mental health services.

(b) Requirements qualified organizations must meet. Organizations that are qualified under paragraphs (a)(1) or (a)(2) of this section must also meet the following requirements before we can authorize them to collect a monthly fee.

(1) A qualified organization must regularly provide representative payee services concurrently to at least five beneficiaries. An organization which has received our authorization to collect a fee for representative payee services, but is temporarily (not more than 6 months) not a payee for at least five beneficiaries, may request our approval to continue to collect fees.

(2) A qualified organization must demonstrate that it is not a creditor of the beneficiary. See paragraph (c) of this section for exceptions to the requirement regarding creditors.

(c) Creditor relationship. On a case-by-case basis, we may authorize an organization to collect a fee for payee services despite the creditor relationship. (For example, the creditor is the beneficiary's landlord.) To provide this authorization, we will review all of the evidence submitted by the organization and authorize collection of a fee when:

(1) The creditor services (e.g., providing housing) provided by the organization help to meet the current needs of the beneficiary; and

(2) The amount the organization charges the beneficiary for these services is commensurate with the beneficiary's ability to pay.

(d) Authorization process.

(1) An organization must request in writing and receive an authorization from us before it may collect a fee.

(2) An organization seeking authorization to collect a fee must also give us evidence to show that it is qualified, pursuant to paragraphs (a), (b), and (c) of this section, to collect a fee.

(3) If the evidence provided to us by the organization shows that it meets the requirements of this section, and additional investigation by us proves it suitable to serve, we will notify the organization in writing that it is authorized to collect a fee. If we need more evidence, or if we are not able to authorize the collection of a fee, we will also notify the organization in writing that we have not authorized the collection of a fee.

(e) Revocation and cancellation of the authorization.

(1) We will revoke an authorization to collect a fee if we have evidence which establishes that an organization no longer meets the requirements of this section. We will issue a written notice to the organization explaining the reason(s) for the revocation.

(2) An organization may cancel its authorization at any time upon written notice to us.

(f) Notices. The written notice we will send to an organization authorizing the collection of a fee will contain an effective date for the collection of a fee pursuant to paragraphs (a), (b) and (c) of this section.

The effective date will be no earlier than the month in which the organization asked for authorization to collect a fee. The notice will be applicable to all beneficiaries for whom the organization was payee at the time of our authorization and all beneficiaries for whom the organization becomes payee while the authorization is in effect.

(g) Limitation on fees.

(1) An organization authorized to collect a fee under this section may collect from a beneficiary a monthly fee for expenses (including overhead) it has incurred in providing payee services to a beneficiary. The limit on the fee a qualified organization may collect for providing payee services increases by the same percentage as the annual cost of living adjustment (COLA). The increased fee amount (rounded to the nearest dollar) is taken beginning with the payment for January.

(2) Any agreement providing for a fee in excess of the amount permitted shall be void and treated as misuse of your benefits by the organization under § 416.641.

(3) A fee may be collected for any month during which the organization—

(i) Provides representative payee services;

(ii) Receives a benefit payment for the beneficiary; and

(iii) Is authorized to receive a fee for representative payee services.

(4) Fees for services may not be taken from any funds conserved for the beneficiary by a payee in accordance with § 416.645.

(5) Generally, an organization may not collect a fee for months in which it does not receive a benefit payment. However, an organization will be allowed to collect a fee for months in which it did not receive a payment if we later issue payment for these months and the organization:

(i) Received our approval to collect a fee for the months for which payment is made;

(ii) Provided payee services in the months for which payment is made; and

(iii) Was the payee when the retroactive payment was paid by us.

(6) Fees for services may not be taken from beneficiary benefits for the months for which we or a court of competent jurisdiction determine(s) that the representative payee misused benefits. Any fees collected for such months will be treated as a part of the beneficiary's misused benefits.

(7) An authorized organization can collect a fee for providing representative payee services from another source if the total amount of the fee collected from both the beneficiary and the other source does not exceed the amount authorized by us.

[57 FR 23057, June 1, 1992; 57 FR 27091, June 17, 1992; 69 FR 60238, Oct. 7, 2004; 71 FR 61408, Oct. 18, 2006]

§ 416.641 Who is liable if your representative payee misuses your benefits?

(a) A representative payee who misuses your benefits is responsible for paying back misused benefits. We will make every reasonable effort to obtain restitution of misused benefits so that we can repay these benefits to you.

(b) Whether or not we have obtained restitution from the misuser, we will repay benefits in cases when we determine that a representative payee misused benefits and the representative payee is an organization or an individual payee serving 15 or more beneficiaries. When we make restitution, we will pay you or your alternative representative payee an amount equal to the misused benefits less any amount we collected from the misuser and repaid to you.

(c) Whether or not we have obtained restitution form the misuser, we will repay benefits in cases when we determine that an individual representative payee serving 14 or fewer beneficiaries misused benefits and our negligent failure in the investigation or monitoring of that representative payee results in the misuse. When we make restitution, we will pay you or your alternative representative payee an amount equal to the misused benefits less any amount we collected from the misuser and repaid to you.

(d) The term "negligent failure" used in this subpart means that we failed to investigate or monitor a representative payee or that we did investigate or monitor a representative payee but did not follow established procedures in our investigation or monitoring. Examples of our negligent failure include, but are not limited to, the following:

(1) We did not follow our established procedures in this subpart when investigating, appointing, or monitoring a representative payee;

(2) We did not investigate timely a reported allegation of misuse; or

(3) We did not take the steps necessary to prevent the issuance of payments to the representative payee after it was determined that the payee misused benefits.

(e) Our repayment of misused benefits under these provisions does not alter the representative payee's liability and responsibility as described in paragraph (a) of this section.

(f) Any amounts that the representative payee misuses and does not refund will be treated as an overpayment to that representative payee. See subpart E of this part.

[69 FR 60239, Oct. 7, 2004; 71 FR 61409, Oct. 18, 2006]

§ 416.645 Conservation and investment of benefit payments.

(a) General. If payments are not needed for the beneficiary's current maintenance or reasonably foreseeable needs, they shall be conserved or invested on behalf of the beneficiary. Conserved funds should be invested in accordance with the rules followed by trustees. Any investment must show clearly that the payee holds the property in trust for the beneficiary.

Example: A State institution for children with intellectual disability, which is receiving Medicaid funds, is representative payee for several beneficiaries. The checks the payee receives are deposited into one account which shows that the benefits are held in trust for the beneficiaries. The institution has supporting records which show the share each individual has in the account. Funds from this account are disbursed fairly quickly after receipt for the personal needs of the beneficiaries. However, not all those funds were disbursed for this purpose. As a result, several of the beneficiaries have significant accumulated resources in this account. For those beneficiaries whose benefits have accumulated over $150, the funds should be deposited in an interest-bearing account or invested relatively free of risk on behalf of the beneficiaries.

(b) Preferred investments. Preferred investments for excess funds are U.S. Savings Bonds and deposits in an interest or dividend paying account in a bank, trust company, credit union, or savings and loan association which is insured under either Federal or State law. The account must be in a form which shows clearly that the representative payee has only a fiduciary and not a personal interest in the funds. If the payee is the legally appointed guardian or fiduciary of the beneficiary, the account may be established to indicate this relationship. If the payee is not the legally appointed guardian or fiduciary, the accounts may be established as follows:

(1) For U.S. Savings Bonds—

__________ (Name of beneficiary) ______ (Social Security Number), for whom __________ (Name of payee) is representative payee for Supplemental Security Income benefits;

(2) For interest or dividend paying accounts—

__________ (Name of beneficiary) by __________ (Name of payee), representative payee.

(c) Interest and dividend payments. The interest and dividends which result from an investment are the property of the beneficiary and may not be considered to be the property of the payee.

[78 FR 46501, Aug. 1, 2013]

§ 416.650 When will we select a new representative payee for you?

When we learn that your interest is not served by sending your benefit payment to your present representative payee or that your present payee is no longer able or willing to carry out payee responsibilities, we will promptly stop sending your payment to the payee. We will then send your benefit payment to an alternative payee or directly to you, until we find a suitable payee. We may suspend payment as explained in § 416.611(c) if we find that paying you directly would cause substantial harm and we cannot find a suitable alternative representative payee before your next payment is due. We will terminate payment of benefits to your representative payee and find a new payee or pay you directly if the present payee:

(a) Has been found by us or a court of competent jurisdiction to have misused your benefits;

(b) Has not used the benefit payments on your behalf in accordance with the guidelines in this subpart;

(c) Has not carried out the other responsibilities described in this subpart;

(d) Dies;

(e) No longer wishes to be your payee;

(f) Is unable to manage your benefit payments; or

(g) Fails to cooperate, within a reasonable time, in providing evidence, accounting, or other information we request.

[69 FR 60239, Oct. 7, 2004]

§ 416.655 When representative payment will be stopped.

If a beneficiary receiving representative payment shows us that he or she is mentally and physically able to manage or direct the management of benefit payments, we will make direct payment. Information which the beneficiary may give us to support his or her request for direct payment include the following—

(a) A physician's statement regarding the beneficiary's condition, or a statement by a medical officer of the institution where the beneficiary is or was confined, showing that the beneficiary is able to manage or direct the management of his or her funds; or

(b) A certified copy of a court order restoring the beneficiary's rights in a case where a beneficiary was adjudged legally incompetent; or

(c) Other evidence which establishes the beneficiary's ability to manage or direct the management of benefits.

§ 416.660 Transfer of accumulated benefit payments.

A representative payee who has conserved or invested benefit payments shall transfer these funds and the interest earned from the invested funds to either a successor payee, to the beneficiary, or to us, as we will specify. If the funds and the earned interest are returned to us, we will recertify them to a successor representative payee or to the beneficiary.

[75 FR 7552, Feb. 22, 2010]

§ 416.665 How does your representative payee account for the use of benefits?

Your representative payee must account for the use of your benefits. We require written reports from your representative payee at least once a year (except for certain State institutions that participate in a separate onsite review program). We may verify how your representative payee used your benefits. Your representative payee should keep records of how benefits were used in order to make accounting reports and must make those records available upon our request. If your representative payee fails to provide an annual accounting of benefits or other required reports, we may require your payee to receive your benefits in person at the local Social Security field office or a United States Government facility that we designate serving the area in which you reside. The decision to have your representative payee receive your benefits in person may be based on a variety of reasons. Some of these reasons may include the payee's history of past performance or our past difficulty in contacting the payee. We may ask your representative payee to give us the following information:

(a) Where you lived during the accounting period;

(b) Who made the decisions on how your benefits were spent or saved;

(c) How your benefit payments were used; and

(d) How much of your benefit payments were saved and how the savings were invested.

[69 FR 60239, Oct. 7, 2004; 71 FR 61409, Oct. 18, 2006]

SUBPART G—REPORTS REQUIRED

Authority: Secs. 702(a)(5), 1611, 1612, 1613, 1614, and 1631 of the Social Security Act (42 U.S.C. 902(a)(5), 1382, 1382a, 1382b, 1382c, and 1383); sec. 211, Pub.L. 93–66, 87 Stat. 154 (42 U.S.C. 1382 note); sec. 202, Pub.L. 108–203, 118 Stat. 509 (42 U.S.C. 902 note).

Source: 46 FR 5873, Jan. 21, 1981; 51 FR 10616, March 28, 1986; 52 FR 27541, July 22, 1987; 52 FR 31477, Aug. 20, 1987; 61 FR 5942, Feb. 15, 1996; 71 FR 66866, Nov. 17, 2006, unless otherwise noted.

INTRODUCTION

§ 416.701 Scope of subpart.

(a) Report provisions. The Social Security Administration, to achieve efficient administration of the Supplemental Security Income (SSI) program for the Aged, Blind, and Disabled, requires that you (or your representative) must report certain events to us. It is important for us to know about these events because they may affect your continued eligibility for SSI benefits or the amount of your benefits. This subpart tells you what events you must report; what your reports must include; and when reports are due. The rules regarding reports are in §§ 416.704 through 416.714.

(b) Penalty deductions. If you fail to make a required report when it is due, you may suffer a penalty. This subpart describes the penalties; discusses when we may impose them; and explains that we will not impose a penalty if you have good cause for failing to report timely. The rules regarding penalties are in §§ 416.722 through 416.732.

§ 416.702 Definitions.

For purposes of this subpart—

Essential person means someone whose presence was believed to be necessary for your welfare under the State program that preceded the SSI program. (See §§ 416.220 through 416.223 of this part.)

Parent means a natural parent, an adoptive parent, or the spouse of a natural or adoptive parent.

Representative payee means an individual, an agency, or an institution selected by us to receive and manage SSI benefits on your behalf. (See subpart F of this part for details describing when a representative payee is selected and a representative payee's responsibilities.)

Residence in the United States means that your permanent home is in the United States.

United States or U.S. means the 50 States, the District of Columbia, and the Northern Mariana Islands.

We, Us, or Our means the Social Security Administration.

You or Your means an applicant, an eligible individual, an eligible spouse, or an eligible child.

[65 FR 16814, March 30, 2000]

REPORT PROVISIONS

§ 416.704 Who must make reports.

(a) You are responsible for making required reports to us if you are—

(1) An eligible individual (see § 416.120(c)(13));

(2) An eligible spouse (see § 416.120(c)(14));

(3) An eligible child (see §§ 416.120(c)(13) and 416.1856); or

(4) An applicant awaiting a final determination upon an application.

(b) If you have a representative payee, and you have not been legally adjudged incompetent, either you or your representative payee must make the required reports.

(c) If you have a representative payee and you have been legally adjudged incompetent, you are not responsible for making reports to us; however, your representative payee is responsible for making required reports to us.

[51 FR 10616, March 28, 1986]

§ 416.708 What you must report.

This section describes the events that you must report to us. They are—

(a) A change of address. You must report to us any change in your mailing address and any change in the address where you live.

(b) A change in living arrangements. You must report to us any change in the make-up of your household: That is, any person who comes to live in your household and any person who moves out of your household.

(c) A change in income. You must report to us any increase or decrease in your income, and any increase or decrease in the income of—

(1) Your ineligible spouse who lives with you;

(2) Your essential person;

(3) Your parent, if you are an eligible child and your parent lives with you; or

(4) An ineligible child who lives with you.

However, you need not report an increase in your Social Security benefits if the increase is only a cost-of-living adjustment. (For a complete discussion of what we consider income, see subpart K. See subpart M, § 416.1323 regarding suspension because of excess income.) If you receive benefits based on disability, when you or your representative report changes in your earned income, we will issue a receipt to you or your representative until we establish a centralized computer file to record the information that you give us and the date that you make your report. Once the centralized computer file is in place, we will continue to issue receipts to you or your representative if you request us to do so.

(d) A change in resources. You must report to us any resources you receive or part with, and any resources received or parted with by—

(1) Your ineligible spouse who lives with you;

(2) Your essential person; or

(3) Your parent, if you are an eligible child and your parent lives with you. (For a complete discussion of what we consider a resource, see subpart L. See subpart M, § 416.1324 regarding suspension because of excess resources.)

(e) Eligibility for other benefits. You must report to us your eligibility for benefits other than SSI benefits. See §§ 416.210 and 416.1330 regarding your responsibility to apply for any other benefits for which you may be eligible.

(f) Certain deaths.

(1) If you are an eligible individual, you must report the death of your eligible spouse, the death of your ineligible spouse who was living with you, and the death of any other person who was living with you.

(2) If you are an eligible spouse, you must report the death of your spouse, and the death of any other person who was living with you.

(3) If you are an eligible child, you must report the death of a parent who was living with you, and the death of any other person who was living with you.

(4) If you are a representative payee, you must report the death of an eligible individual, eligible spouse, or eligible child whom you represent; and the death of any other person who was living in the household of the individual you represent.

(5) If you have a representative payee, you must report the death of your representative payee.

(g) A change in marital status. You must report to us—

(1) Your marriage, your divorce, or the annulment of your marriage;

(2) The marriage, divorce, or annulment of marriage of your parent who lives with you, if you are an eligible child;

(3) The marriage of an ineligible child who lives with you, if you are an eligible child; and

(4) The marriage of an ineligible child who lives with you if you are an eligible individual living with an ineligible spouse.

(h) Medical improvements. If you are eligible for SSI benefits because of disability or blindness, you must report any improvement in your medical condition to us.

(i) [Reserved]

(j) Refusal to accept treatment for drug addiction or alcoholism; discontinuance of treatment. If you have been medically determined to be a drug addict or an alcoholic, and you refuse to accept treatment for drug addiction or alcoholism at an approved facility or institution, or if you discontinue treatment, you must report your refusal or discontinuance to us.

(k) Admission to or discharge from a medical treatment facility, public institution, or private institution. You must report to us your admission to or discharge from—

(1) A medical treatment facility; or

(2) A public institution (defined in § 416.201); or

(3) A private institution. Private institution means an institution as defined in § 416.201 which is not administered by or the responsibility of a governmental unit.

(*l*) A change in school attendance. You must report to us—

(1) A change in your school attendance if you are an eligible child;

(2) A change in school attendance of an ineligible child who is at least age 18 but less than 21 and who lives with you if you are an eligible child; and

(3) A change in school attendance of an ineligible child who is at least age 18 but less than 21 and who lives with you if you are an eligible individual living with an ineligible spouse.

(m) A termination of residence in the U.S. You must report to us if you leave the United States voluntarily with the intention of abandoning your residence in the United States or you leave the United States involuntarily (for example, you are deported).

(n) Leaving the U.S. temporarily. You must report to us if you leave the United States for 30 or more consecutive days or for a full calendar month (without the intention of abandoning your residence in the U.S.).

(*o*) Fleeing to avoid criminal prosecution or custody or confinement after conviction, or violating probation or parole. You must report to us that you are—

(1) Fleeing to avoid prosecution for a crime, or an attempt to commit a crime, which is a felony under the laws of the place from which you flee (or which, in the case of the State of New Jersey, is a high misdemeanor under the laws of that State);

(2) Fleeing to avoid custody or confinement after conviction for a crime, or an attempt to commit a crime, which is a felony under the laws of the place from which you flee (or which, in the case of the State of New Jersey, is a high misdemeanor under the laws of that State); or

(3) Violating a condition of probation or parole imposed under Federal or State law.

[51 FR 10616, March 28, 1986; 65 FR 40495, June 30, 2000; 68 FR 40124, July 7, 2003; 71 FR 66866, Nov. 17, 2006; 72 FR 50874, Sept. 5, 2007]

§ 416.710 What reports must include.

When you make a report you must tell us—

(a) The name and social security number under which benefits are paid;

(b) The name of the person about whom you are reporting;

(c) The event you are reporting and the date it happened; and

(d) Your name.

§ 416.712 Form of the report.

You may make a report in any of the ways described in this section.

(a) Written reports. You may write a report on your own paper or on a printed form supplied by us. You may mail a written report or bring it to one of our offices.

(b) Oral reports. You may report to us by telephone, or you may come to one of our offices and tell one of our employees what you are reporting.

(c) Other forms. You may use any other suitable method of reporting—for example, a telegram or a cable.

§ 416.714 When reports are due.

(a) A reportable event happens. You should report to us as soon as an event listed in § 416.708 happens. If you do not report within 10 days after the close of the month in which the event happens, your report will be late. We may impose a penalty deduction from your benefits for a late report (see §§ 416.722 through 416.732).

(b) We request a report. We may request a report from you if we need information to determine continuing eligibility or the correct amount of your SSI benefit payments. If you do not report within 30 days of our written request, we may determine that you are ineligible to receive SSI benefits. We will suspend your benefits effective with the month following the month in which we determine that you are ineligible to receive SSI benefits because of your failure to give us necessary information.

[50 FR 48573, Nov. 26, 1985]

PENALTY DEDUCTIONS

§ 416.722 Circumstances under which we make a penalty deduction.

A penalty deduction is made from your benefits if—

(a) You fail to make a required report on time (see §§ 416.708 and 416.714);

(b) We must reduce, suspend, or terminate your benefits because of the event you have not reported;

(c) You received and accepted an SSI benefit for the penalty period (see §§ 416.724 through 416.728 for penalty period definitions); and

(d) You do not have good cause for not reporting on time (see § 416.732).

§ 416.724 Amounts of penalty deductions.

(a) Amounts deducted. If we find that we must impose a penalty deduction, you will lose from your SSI benefits a total amount of—

(1) $25 for a report overdue in the first penalty period;

(2) $50 for a report overdue in the second penalty period; and

(3) $100 for a report overdue in the third (or any following) penalty period.

(b) Limit on number of penalties. Even though more than one required report is overdue from you at the end of a penalty period, we will limit the number of penalty deductions imposed to one penalty deduction for any one penalty period.

§ 416.726 Penalty period: First failure to report.

(a) First penalty period. The first penalty period begins on the first day of the month you apply for SSI benefits and ends on the day we first learn that you should have made a required report, but did not do so within 10 days after the close of the month in which the event happened. There may be more than one required report overdue at the end of the first penalty period, but we will impose no more than one penalty deduction for the period.

(b) Extension of first penalty period. If you have good cause for not making a report on time (see § 416.732), we will extend the first penalty period to the day when we learn that you should have made another required report, but did not do so within 10 days after the close of the month in which the event happened. There may be more than one required report overdue at the end of the extended first penalty period, but we will impose no more than one penalty deduction for the extended period.

[50 FR 48573, Nov. 26, 1985]

§ 416.728 Penalty period: Second failure to report.

(a) Second penalty period. The second penalty period begins on the day after the first penalty period ends. The second penalty period ends on the day we first learn that you should have made a required report, but did not do so within 10 days after the close of the month in which the event happened. (The event may have happened during the first penalty period, with the reporting due date in the second penalty period. The due date and the failure to report on time are the important factors in establishing a penalty period.) There may be more than one required report overdue at the end of the second penalty period, but we will impose no more than one penalty deduction for the period.

(b) Extension of second penalty period. If you have good cause for not making a report on time (see § 416.732), we will extend the second penalty period to the day when we learn that you should have made another required report, but did not do so within 10 days after the close of the month in which the event happened. There may be more than one required report overdue at the end of the extended second penalty period, but we will impose no more than one penalty deduction for the extended period.

[50 FR 48573, Nov. 26, 1985]

§ 416.730 Penalty period: Three or more failures to report.

(a) Third (or a following) penalty period. A third (or a following) penalty period begins the day after the last penalty period ends. This penalty period ends on the day we first learn that you should have made a required report during the penalty period, but did not do so within 10 days after the close of the month in which the event happened. (The event may have happened during an earlier penalty period, with the reporting due date in the third (or a following) penalty period. The due date and the failure to report on time are the important factors in establishing a penalty period.) There may be more than one required report overdue at the end of a penalty period, but we will impose no more than one penalty deduction for any one penalty period.

(b) Extension of third (or a following) penalty period. Just as with the first and second penalty periods, if you have good cause for not making a report on time during the third (or a following) penalty period (see § 416.732), we will extend the penalty period to the day when we learn that you should have made another required report, but did not do so within 10 days after the close of the month in which the event happened. There may be more than one required report overdue at the end of an extended penalty period, but we will impose no more than one penalty deduction for any one extended penalty period.

[50 FR 48573, Nov. 26, 1985]

§ 416.732 No penalty deduction if you have good cause for failure to report timely.

(a) We will find that you have good cause for failure to report timely and we will not impose a penalty deduction, if—

(1) You are "without fault" as defined in § 416.552; or

(2) Your failure or delay in reporting is not willful. "Not willful" means that—

(i) You did not have full knowledge of the existence of your obligation to make a required report; or

(ii) You did not intentionally, knowingly, and purposely fail to make a required report.

However, in either case we may require that you refund an overpayment caused by your failure to report. See subpart E of this part for waiver of recovery of overpayments.

(b) In determining whether you have good cause for failure to report timely, we will take into account any physical, mental, educational, or linguistic limitations (including any lack of facility with the English language) you may have.

[59 FR 1636, Jan. 12, 1994]

SUBPART H—DETERMINATION OF AGE

Authority: Secs. 702(a)(5), 1601, 1614(a)(1) and 1631 of the Social Security Act (42 U.S.C. 902(a)(5), 1381, 1382c(a)(1), and 1383).

Source: 39 FR 12731, Apr. 8, 1974; 52 FR 27541, July 22, 1987; 61 FR 5942, Feb. 15, 1996, unless otherwise noted.

§ 416.801 Evidence as to age—when required.

An applicant for benefits under title XVI of the Act shall file supporting evidence showing the date of his birth if his age is a condition of eligibility for benefits or is otherwise relevant to the payment of benefits pursuant to such title XVI. Such evidence may also be required by the Administration as to the age of any other individual when such other individual's age is relevant to the determination of the applicant's eligibility or benefit amount. In the absence of evidence to the contrary, if the applicant alleges that he is at least 68 years of age and submits any documentary evidence at least 3 years old which supports his allegation, no further evidence of his age is required. In the absence of evidence to the contrary, if a State required reasonably acceptable evidence of age and provides a statement as to an applicant's age, no further evidence of his age is required unless a statistically valid quality control sample has shown that a State's determination of age procedures do not yield an acceptable low rate of error.

§ 416.802 Type of evidence to be submitted.

Where an individual is required to submit evidence of date of birth as indicated in § 416.801, he shall submit a public record of birth or a religious record of birth or baptism established or recorded before his fifth birthday, if available. Where no such document recorded or established before age 5 is available the individual shall submit as evidence of age another document or documents which may serve as the basis for a determination of the individual's date of birth provided such evidence is corroborated by other evidence or by information in the records of the Administration.

§ 416.803 Evaluation of evidence.

Generally, the highest probative value will be accorded to a public record of birth or a religious record of birth or baptism established or recorded before age 5. Where such record is not available, and other documents are submitted as evidence of age, in determining their probative value, consideration will be given to when such other documents were established or recorded, and the circumstances attending their establishment or recordation. Among the documents which may be submitted for such purpose are: school record, census record, Bible or other family record, church record of baptism or confirmation in youth or early adult life, insurance policy, marriage record, employment record, labor union record, fraternal organization record, military record, voting record, vaccination record, delayed birth certificate, birth certificate of child of applicant, physician's or midwife's record of birth, immigration record, naturalization record, or passport.

§ 416.804 Certified copy in lieu of original.

In lieu of the original of any record, except a Bible or other family record, there may be submitted as evidence of age a copy of such record or a statement as to the date of birth shown by such record, which has been duly certified (see § 404.701(g) of this chapter).

§ 416.805 When additional evidence may be required.

If the evidence submitted is not convincing, additional evidence may be required.

§ 416.806 Expedited adjudication based on documentary evidence of age.

Where documentary evidence of age recorded at least 3 years before the application is filed, which reasonably supports an aged applicant's allegation as to his age, is submitted, payment of benefits may be initiated even though additional evidence of age may be required by §§ 416.801 through 416.805. The applicant will be advised that additional evidence is required and that, if it is subsequently established that the prior finding of age is incorrect, the applicant will be liable for refund of any overpayment he has received. If any of the evidence initially submitted tends to show that the age of the applicant or such other person does not correspond with the alleged age, no benefits will be paid until the evidence required by §§ 416.801 through 416.805 is submitted.

SUBPART I—DETERMINING DISABILITY AND BLINDNESS

Authority: Secs. 221(m), 702(a)(5), 1611, 1614, 1619, 1631(a), (c), (d)(1), and (p), and 1633 of the Social Security Act (42 U.S.C. 421(m), 902(a)(5), 1382, 1382c, 1382h, 1383(a), (c), (d)(1), and (p), and 1383b); secs. 4(c) and 5, 6(c)-(e), 14(a), and 15, Pub.L. 98-460, 98 Stat. 1794, 1801, 1802, and 1808 (42 U.S.C. 421 note, 423 note, and 1382h note).

Source: 45 FR 55621, Aug. 20, 1980; 50 FR 50136, Dec. 6, 1985; 51 FR 16826, May 7, 1986; 52 FR 27541, July 22, 1987; 53 FR 29023, Aug. 2, 1988; 55 FR 11011, March 26, 1990; 56 FR 57944, Nov. 14, 1991; 56 FR 65683, Dec. 18, 1991; 57 FR 53853, Nov. 13, 1992; 59 FR 1636, Jan. 12, 1994; 60 FR 8150, Feb. 10, 1995; 61 FR 5942, Feb. 15, 1996; 65 FR 16814, March 30, 2000; 70 FR 57144, Sept. 30, 2005; 71 FR 10430, March 1, 2006; 71 FR 16458, March 31, 2006; 71 FR 66857, Nov. 17, 2006; 72 FR 51178, Sept. 6, 2007; 72 FR 59431, Oct. 19, 2007; 75 FR 62682, Oct. 13, 2010, unless otherwise noted.

GENERAL

§ 416.901 Scope of subpart.

In order for you to become entitled to any benefits based upon disability or blindness you must be disabled or blind as defined in title XVI of the Social Security Act. This subpart explains how we determine whether you are disabled or blind. We have organized the rules in the following way.

(a) We define general terms, then discuss who makes our disability or blindness determinations and state that disability and blindness determinations made under other programs are not binding on our determinations.

(b) We explain the term disability and note some of the major factors that are considered in determining whether you are disabled in §§ 416.905 through 416.910.

(c) Sections 416.912 through 416.918 contain our rules on evidence. We explain your responsibilities for submitting evidence of your impairment, state what we consider to be acceptable sources of medical evidence, and describe what information should be included in medical reports.

(d) Our general rules on evaluating disability for adults filing new applications are stated in §§ 416.920 through 416.923. We describe the steps that we go through and the order in which they are considered.

(e) Our general rules on evaluating disability for children filing new applications are stated in § 416.924.

(f) Our rules on medical considerations are found in §§ 416.925 through 416.930. We explain in these rules—

(1) The purpose and use of the Listing of Impairments found in appendix 1 of subpart P of part 404 of this chapter;

(2) What we mean by the terms medical equivalence and functional equivalence and how we make those findings;

(3) The effect of a conclusion by your physician that you are disabled;

(4) What we mean by symptoms, signs, and laboratory findings;

(5) How we evaluate pain and other symptoms; and

(6) The effect on your benefits if you fail to follow treatment that is expected to restore your ability to work or, if you are a child, to reduce your functional limitations to the point that they are no longer marked and severe, and how we apply the rule in § 416.930.

(g) In §§ 416.931 through 416.934 we explain that we may make payments on the basis of presumptive disability or presumptive blindness.

(h) In §§ 416.935 through 416.939 we explain the rules which apply in cases of drug addiction and alcoholism.

(i) In §§ 416.945 through 416.946 we explain what we mean by the term residual functional capacity, state when an assessment of residual functional capacity is required, and who may make it.

(j) Our rules on vocational considerations are in §§ 416.960 through 416.969a. We explain in these rules—

(1) When we must consider vocational factors along with the medical evidence;

(2) How we use our residual functional capacity assessment to determine if you can still do your past relevant work or other work;

(3) How we consider the vocational factors of age, education, and work experience;

(4) What we mean by "work which exists in the national economy";

(5) How we consider the exertional, nonexertional, and skill requirements of work, and when we will consider the limitations or restrictions that result from your impairment(s) and related symptoms to be exertional, nonexertional, or a combination of both; and

(6) How we use the Medical–Vocational Guidelines in appendix 2 of subpart P of part 404 of this chapter.

(k) Our rules on substantial gainful activity are found in §§ 416.971 through 416.974. These explain what we mean by substantial gainful activity and how we evaluate your work activity.

(*l*) In §§ 416.981 through 416.985 we discuss blindness.

(m) Our rules on when disability or blindness continues and stops are contained in §§ 416.986 and 416.988 through 416.998. We explain what your responsibilities are in telling us of any events that may cause a change in your disability or blindness status and when we will review to see if you are still disabled. We also explain how we consider the issue of medical improvement (and the exceptions to medical improvement) in determining whether you are still disabled.

[50 FR 50136, Dec. 6, 1985; 56 FR 5553, Feb. 11, 1991; 56 FR 57944, Nov. 14, 1991; 62 FR 6420, Feb. 11, 1997; 65 FR 42788, July 11, 2000; 65 FR 54777, Sept. 11, 2000; 68 FR 51164, Aug. 26, 2003]

§ 416.902 Definitions for this subpart.

As used in the subpart—

(a) Acceptable medical source means a medical source who is a:

(1) Licensed physician (medical or osteopathic doctor);

(2) Licensed psychologist, which includes:

(i) A licensed or certified psychologist at the independent practice level; or

(ii) A licensed or certified school psychologist, or other licensed or certified individual with another title who performs the same function as a school psychologist in a school setting, for impairments of intellectual disability, learning disabilities, and borderline intellectual functioning only;

(3) Licensed optometrist for impairments of visual disorders, or measurement of visual acuity and visual fields only, depending on the scope of practice in the State in which the optometrist practices;

(4) Licensed podiatrist for impairments of the foot, or foot and ankle only, depending on whether the State in which the podiatrist practices permits the practice of podiatry on the foot only, or the foot and ankle;

(5) Qualified speech-language pathologist for speech or language impairments only. For this source, qualified means that the speech-language pathologist must be licensed by the State professional licensing agency, or be fully certified by the State education agency in the State in which he or she practices, or hold a Certificate of Clinical Competence in Speech–Language Pathology from the American Speech–Language–Hearing Association;

(6) Licensed audiologist for impairments of hearing loss, auditory processing disorders, and balance disorders within the licensed scope of practice only (with respect to claims filed (see § 416.325) on or after March 27, 2017);

(7) Licensed Advanced Practice Registered Nurse, or other licensed advanced practice nurse with another title, for impairments within his or her licensed scope of practice (only with respect to claims filed (see § 416.325) on or after March 27, 2017); or

(8) Licensed Physician Assistant for impairments within his or her licensed scope of practice (only with respect to claims filed (see § 416.325) on or after March 27, 2017).

(b) Adult means a person who is age 18 or older.

(c) Child means a person who has not attained age 18.

(d) Commissioner means the Commissioner of Social Security or his or her authorized designee.

(e) Disability redetermination means a redetermination of your eligibility based on disability using the rules for new applicants appropriate to your age, except the rules pertaining to performance of substantial gainful activity. For individuals who are working and for whom a disability redetermination is required, we will apply the rules in §§ 416.260 through 416.269. In conducting a disability redetermination, we will not use the rules for determining whether disability continues set forth in § 416.994 or § 416.994a. (See § 416.987.)

(f) Impairment(s) means a medically determinable physical or mental impairment or a combination of medically determinable physical or mental impairments.

(g) Laboratory findings means one or more anatomical, physiological, or psychological phenomena that can be shown by the use of medically acceptable laboratory diagnostic techniques. Diagnostic techniques include chemical tests (such as blood tests), electrophysiological studies (such as electrocardiograms and electroencephalograms), medical imaging (such as X–rays), and psychological tests.

(h) Marked and severe functional limitations, when used as a phrase, means the standard of disability in the Social Security Act for children claiming SSI benefits based on disability. It is a level of severity that meets, medically equals, or functionally equals the listings. (See §§ 416.906, 416.924, and 416.926a.) The words "marked" and "severe" are also separate terms used throughout this subpart to describe measures of functional limitations; the term "marked" is also used in the listings. (See §§ 416.924 and 416.926a.) The meaning of the words "marked" and "severe" when used as part of the phrase marked and severe functional limitations is not the same as the meaning of the separate terms "marked" and "severe" used elsewhere in 404 and 416. (See §§ 416.924(c) and 416.926a(e).)

(i) Medical source means an individual who is licensed as a healthcare worker by a State and working within the scope of practice permitted under State or Federal law, or an individual who is certified by a State as a speech-language pathologist or a school psychologist and acting within the scope of practice permitted under State or Federal law.

(j) Nonmedical source means a source of evidence who is not a medical source. This includes, but is not limited to:

(1) You;

(2) Educational personnel (for example, school teachers, counselors, early intervention team members, developmental center workers, and daycare center workers);

(3) Public and private social welfare agency personnel; and

(4) Family members, caregivers, friends, neighbors, employers, and clergy.

(k) Objective medical evidence means signs, laboratory findings, or both.

(*l*) Signs means one or more anatomical, physiological, or psychological abnormalities that can be observed, apart from your statements (symptoms). Signs must be shown by medically acceptable clinical diagnostic techniques. Psychiatric signs are medically demonstrable phenomena that indicate specific psychological abnormalities, e.g., abnormalities of behavior, mood, thought, memory, orientation, development, or perception and must also be shown by observable facts that can be medically described and evaluated.

(m) State agency means an agency of a State designated by that State to carry out the disability or blindness determination function.

(n) Symptoms means your own description of your physical or mental impairment.

(*o*) The listings means the Listing of Impairments in appendix 1 of subpart P of part 404 of this chapter. When we refer to an impairment(s) that "meets, medically equals, or functionally equals the listings," we mean that the impairment(s) meets or medically equals the severity of any listing in appendix 1 of subpart P of part 404 of this chapter, as explained in §§ 416.925 and 416.926, or that it functionally equals the severity of the listings, as explained in § 416.926a.

(p) We or us means, as appropriate, either the Social Security Administration or the State agency making the disability or blindness determination.

(q) You, your, me, my and I mean, as appropriate, the person who applies for benefits, the person for whom an application is filed, or the person who is receiving benefits based on disability or blindness.

[46 FR 29211, May 29, 1981; 56 FR 5553, Feb. 11, 1991; 56 FR 36962, Aug. 1, 1991; 58 FR 47577, Sept. 9, 1993; 62 FR 6420, Feb. 11, 1997; 62 FR 13733, March 21, 1997; 65 FR 11878, March 7, 2000; 65 FR 54777, Sept. 11, 2000; 65 FR 80308, Dec. 21, 2000; 71 FR 16458, March 31, 2006; 76 FR 24810, May 3, 2011; 82 FR 5873, Jan. 18, 2017; 83 FR 51836, Oct. 15, 2018]

DETERMINATIONS

§ 416.903 Who makes disability and blindness determinations.

(a) State agencies. State agencies make disability and blindness determinations for the Commissioner for most persons living in the State. State agencies make these disability and blindness determinations under regulations containing performance standards and other administrative requirements relating to the disability and blindness determination function. States have the option of turning the function over to the Federal Government if they no longer want to make disability determinations. Also, the Commissioner may take the function away from any State which has substantially failed to make disability and blindness determinations in accordance with these regulations. Subpart J of this part contains the rules the States must follow in making disability and blindness determinations.

(b) Social Security Administration. The Social Security Administration will make disability and blindness determinations for—

(1) Any person living in a State which is not making for the Commissioner any disability and blindness determinations or which is not making those determinations for the class of claimants to which that person belongs; and

(2) Any person living outside the United States.

(c) What determinations are authorized. The Commissioner has authorized the State agencies and the Social Security Administration to make determinations about—

(1) Whether you are disabled or blind;

(2) The date your disability or blindness began; and

(3) The date your disability or blindness stopped.

(d) Review of State agency determinations. On review of a State agency determination or redetermination of disability or blindness we may find that—

(1) You are, or are not, disabled or blind, regardless of what the State agency found;

(2) Your disability or blindness began earlier or later than the date found by the State agency; and

(3) Your disability or blindness stopped earlier or later than the date found by the State agency.

(e) Determinations for childhood impairments. In making a determination under title XVI with respect to the disability of a child, we will make reasonable efforts to ensure that a qualified pediatrician or other individual who specializes in a field of medicine appropriate to the child's impairment(s) evaluates the case of the child.

(f) [Redesignated as subsection (e) by 82 FR 5874]

[46 FR 29211, May 29, 1981; 52 FR 33927, Sept. 9, 1987; 58 FR 47577, Sept. 9, 1993; 62 FR 38454, July 18, 1997; 65 FR 34958, June 1, 2000; 71 FR 16458, March 31, 2006; 72 FR 51178, Sept. 6, 2007; 82 FR 5874, Jan. 18, 2017]

§ 416.903a Program integrity.

We will not use in our program any individual or entity, except to provide existing medical evidence, who is currently excluded, suspended, or otherwise barred from participation in the Medicare or Medicaid programs, or any other Federal or Federally-assisted program; whose license to provide health care services is currently revoked or suspended by any State licensing authority pursuant to adequate due process procedures for reasons bearing on professional competence, professional conduct, or financial integrity; or who until a final determination is made has surrendered such a license while formal disciplinary proceedings involving professional conduct are pending. By individual or entity we mean a medical or psychological consultant, consultative examination provider, or diagnostic test facility. Also see §§ 416.919 and 416.919g(b).

[56 FR 36963, Aug. 1, 1991]

§ 416.903b Evidence from excluded medical sources of evidence.

(a) General. We will not consider evidence from the following medical sources excluded under section 223(d)(5)(C)(i) of the Social Security Act (Act), as amended, unless we find good cause under paragraph (b) of this section:

(1) Any medical source that has been convicted of a felony under section 208 or under section 1632 of the Act;

(2) Any medical source that has been excluded from participation in any Federal health care program under section 1128 of the Act; or

(3) Any medical source that has received a final decision imposing a civil monetary penalty or assessment, or both, for submitting false evidence under section 1129 of the Act.

(b) Good cause. We may find good cause to consider evidence from an excluded medical source of evidence under section 223(d)(5)(C)(i) of the Act, as amended, if:

(1) The evidence from the medical source consists of evidence of treatment that occurred before the date the source was convicted of a felony under section 208 or under section 1632 of the Act;

(2) The evidence from the medical source consists of evidence of treatment that occurred during a period in which the source was not excluded from participation in any Federal health care program under section 1128 of the Act;

(3) The evidence from the medical source consists of evidence of treatment that occurred before the date the source received a final decision imposing a civil monetary penalty or assessment, or both, for submitting false evidence under section 1129 of the Act;

(4) The sole basis for the medical source's exclusion under section 223(d)(5)(C)(i) of the Act, as amended, is that the source cannot participate in any Federal health care program under section 1128 of the Act, but the Office of Inspector General of the Department of Health and Human Services granted a waiver of the section 1128 exclusion; or

(5) The evidence is a laboratory finding about a physical impairment and there is no indication that the finding is unreliable.

(c) Reporting requirements for excluded medical sources of evidence. Excluded medical sources of evidence (as described in paragraph (a) of this section) must inform us in writing that they are excluded under section 223(d)(5)(C)(i) of the Act, as amended, each time they submit evidence related to a claim for initial or continuing benefits under titles II or XVI of the Act. This reporting requirement applies to evidence that excluded medical sources of evidence submit to us either directly or through a representative, claimant, or other individual or entity.

(1) Excluded medical sources of evidence must provide a written statement, which contains the following information:

(i) A heading stating: "WRITTEN STATEMENT REGARDING SECTION 223(d)(5)(C) OF THE SOCIAL SECURITY ACT—DO NOT REMOVE"

(ii) The name and title of the medical source;

(iii) The applicable excluding event(s) stated in paragraph (a)(1)-(a)(3) of this section;

(iv) The date of the medical source's felony conviction under sections 208 or 1632 of the Act, if applicable;

(v) The date of the imposition of a civil monetary penalty or assessment, or both, for the submission of false evidence, under section 1129 of the Act, if applicable; and

(vi) The basis, effective date, anticipated length of the exclusion, and whether the Office of the Inspector General of the Department of Health and Human Services waived the exclusion, if the excluding event was the medical source's exclusion from participation in any Federal health care program under section 1128 of the Act.

(2) The written statement provided by an excluded medical source of evidence may not be removed by any individual or entity prior to submitting evidence to us.

(3) We may request that the excluded medical source of evidence provide us with additional information or clarify any information submitted that bears on the medical source's exclusion(s) under section 223(d)(5)(C)(i) of the Act, as amended.

[81 FR 65540, Sept. 23, 2016]

§ 416.904 Decisions by other governmental agencies and nongovernmental entities.

Other governmental agencies and nongovernmental entities—such as the Department of Veterans Affairs, the Department of Defense, the Department of Labor, the Office of Personnel Management, State agencies, and private insurers—make disability, blindness, employability, Medicaid, workers' compensation, and other benefits decisions for their own programs using their own rules. Because a decision by any other governmental agency or a nongovernmental entity about whether you are disabled, blind, employable, or entitled to any benefits is based on its rules, it is not binding on us and is not our decision about whether you are disabled or blind under our rules. Therefore, in claims filed (see § 416.325) on or after March 27, 2017, we will not provide any analysis in our determination or decision about a decision made by any other governmental agency or a nongovernmental entity about whether you are disabled, blind, employable, or entitled to any benefits. However, we will consider all of the supporting evidence underlying the other governmental agency or nongovernmental entity's decision that we receive as evidence in your claim in accordance with § 416.913(a)(1) through (4).

[82 FR 5874, Jan. 18, 2017; 82 FR 15132, March 27, 2017]

DEFINITION OF DISABILITY

§ 416.905 Basic definition of disability for adults.

(a) The law defines disability as the inability to do any substantial gainful activity by reason of any medically determinable physical or mental impairment which can be expected to result in death or which has lasted or can be expected to last for a continuous period of not less than 12 months. To meet this definition, you must have a severe impairment(s) that makes you unable to do your past relevant work (see § 416.960(b)) or any other substantial gainful work that exists in the national economy. If your severe impairment(s) does not meet or medically equal a listing in appendix 1 to subpart P of part 404 of this chapter, we will assess your residual functional capacity as provided in §§ 416.920(e) and 416.945. (See § 416.920(g)(2) and 416.962 for an exception to this rule.) We will use this residual functional capacity assessment to determine if you can do your past relevant work. If we find that you cannot do your past relevant work, we will use the same residual functional capacity assessment and your vocational factors of age, education, and work experience to determine if you can do other work. (See § 416.920(h) for an exception to this rule.)

(b) There are different rules for determining disability for individuals who are statutorily blind. We discuss these in §§ 416.981 through 416.985.

[56 FR 5553, Feb. 11, 1991; 68 FR 51164, Aug. 26, 2003; 77 FR 43495, July 25, 2012]

§ 416.906 Basic definition of disability for children.

If you are under age 18, we will consider you disabled if you have a medically determinable physical or mental impairment or combination of impairments that causes marked and severe functional limitations, and that can be expected to cause death or that has lasted or can be expected to last for a continuous period of not less than 12 months. Notwithstanding the preceding sentence, if you file a new application for benefits and you are engaging in substantial gainful activity, we will not consider you disabled. We discuss our rules for determining disability in children who file new applications in §§ 416.924 through 416.924b and §§ 416.925 through 416.926a.

[56 FR 5553, Feb. 11, 1991; 62 FR 6420, Feb. 11, 1997; 65 FR 54777, Sept. 11, 2000]

§ 416.907 Disability under a State plan.

You will also be considered disabled for payment of supplemental security income benefits if—

(a) You were found to be permanently and totally disabled as defined under a State plan approved under title XIV or XVI of the Social Security Act, as in effect for October 1972;

(b) You received aid under the State plan because of your disability for the month of December 1973 and for at least one month before July 1973; and

(c) You continue to be disabled as defined under the State plan.

§ 416.908 [Reserved by 82 FR 5874]

[82 FR 5874, Jan. 18, 2017]

§ 416.909 How long the impairment must last.

Unless your impairment is expected to result in death, it must have lasted or must be expected to last for a continuous period of at least 12 months. We call this the duration requirement.

§ 416.910 Meaning of substantial gainful activity.

Substantial gainful activity means work that—

(a) Involves doing significant and productive physical or mental duties; and

(b) Is done (or intended) for pay or profit.

(See § 416.972 for further details about what we mean by substantial gainful activity.)

§ 416.911 Definition of disabling impairment.

(a) If you are an adult:

(1) A disabling impairment is an impairment (or combination of impairments) which, of itself, is so severe that it meets or equals a set of criteria in the Listing of Impairments in appendix 1 of subpart P of part 404 of this chapter or which, when considered with your age, education and work experience, would result in a finding that you are disabled under § 416.994, unless the disability redetermination rules in § 416.987(b) apply to you.

(2) If the disability redetermination rules in § 416.987 apply to you, a disabling impairment is an impairment or combination of impairments that meets the requirements in §§ 416.920(c) through (f).

(b) If you are a child, a disabling impairment is an impairment (or combination of impairments) that causes marked and severe functional limitations. This means that the impairment or combination of impairments:

(1) Must meet, medically equal, or functionally equal the listings, or

(2) Would result in a finding that you are disabled under § 416.994a.

(c) In determining whether you have a disabling impairment, earnings are not considered.

[49 FR 22273, May 29, 1984; 50 FR 50137, Dec. 6, 1985; 62 FR 6421, Feb. 11, 1997; 65 FR 54777, Sept. 11, 2000]

EVIDENCE

§ 416.912 Responsibility for evidence.

(a) Your responsibility.

(1) General. In general, you have to prove to us that you are blind or disabled. You must inform us about or submit all evidence known to you that relates to whether or not you are blind or disabled (see § 416.913). This duty is ongoing and requires you to disclose any additional related evidence about which you become aware. This duty applies at each level of the administrative review process, including the Appeals Council level if the evidence relates to the period on or before the date of the administrative law judge hearing decision. We will consider only impairment(s)

you say you have or about which we receive evidence. When you submit evidence received from another source, you must submit that evidence in its entirety, unless you previously submitted the same evidence to us or we instruct you otherwise. If we ask you, you must inform us about:

(i) Your medical source(s);

(ii) Your age;

(iii) Your education and training;

(iv) Your work experience;

(v) Your daily activities both before and after the date you say that you became disabled;

(vi) Your efforts to work; and

(vii) Any other factors showing how your impairment(s) affects your ability to work, or, if you are a child, your functioning. In §§ 416.960 through 416.969, we discuss in more detail the evidence we need when we consider vocational factors.

(2) Completeness. The evidence in your case record must be complete and detailed enough to allow us to make a determination or decision about whether you are disabled or blind. It must allow us to determine—

(i) The nature and severity of your impairment(s) for any period in question;

(ii) Whether the duration requirement described in § 416.909 is met; and

(iii) Your residual functional capacity to do work-related physical and mental activities, when the evaluation steps described in §§ 416.920(e) or (f)(1) apply, or, if you are a child, how you typically function compared to children your age who do not have impairments.

(3) Statutory blindness. If you are applying for benefits on the basis of statutory blindness, we will require an examination by a physician skilled in diseases of the eye or by an optometrist, whichever you may select.

(b) Our responsibility.

(1) Development. Before we make a determination that you are not disabled, we will develop your complete medical history for at least the 12 months preceding the month in which you file your application unless there is a reason to believe that development of an earlier period is necessary or unless you say that your disability began less than 12 months before you filed your application. We will make every reasonable effort to help you get medical evidence from your own medical sources and entities that maintain your medical sources' evidence when you give us permission to request the reports.

(i) Every reasonable effort means that we will make an initial request for evidence from your medical source or entity that maintains your medical source's evidence, and, at any time between 10 and 20 calendar days after the initial request, if the evidence has not been received, we will make one follow-up request to obtain the medical evidence necessary to make a determination. The medical source or entity that maintains your medical source's evidence will have a minimum of 10 calendar days from the date of our follow-up request to reply, unless our experience with that source indicates that a longer period is advisable in a particular case.

(ii) Complete medical history means the records of your medical source(s) covering at least the 12 months preceding the month in which you file your application. If you say that your disability began less than 12 months before you filed your application, we will develop your complete medical history beginning with the month you say your disability began unless we have reason to believe your disability began earlier.

(2) Obtaining a consultative examination. We may ask you to attend one or more consultative examinations at our expense. See §§ 416.917 through 416.919t for the rules governing the consultative examination process. Generally, we will not request a consultative examination until we have made every reasonable effort to obtain evidence from your own medical sources. We may order a consultative examination while awaiting receipt of medical source evidence in some instances, such as when we know a source is not productive, is uncooperative, or is unable to provide certain tests or procedures. We will not evaluate this evidence until we have made every reasonable effort to obtain evidence from your medical sources.

(3) Other work. In order to determine under § 416.920(g) that you are able to adjust to other work, we must provide evidence about the existence of work in the national economy that you can do (see §§ 416.960 through 416.969a), given your residual functional capacity (which we have already assessed, as described in § 416.920(e)), age, education, and work experience.

[56 FR 36963, Aug. 1, 1991; 62 FR 6421, Feb. 11, 1997; 65 FR 11878, March 7, 2000; 65 FR 34958, June 1, 2000; 68 FR 51164, Aug. 26, 2003; 71 FR 16458, March 31, 2006; 75 FR 62682, Oct. 13, 2010; 76 FR 24810, May 3, 2011; 77 FR 10656, Feb. 23, 2012; 79 FR 33685, June 12, 2014; 80 FR 14837, March 20, 2015; 82 FR 5874, Jan. 18, 2017]

§ 416.913 Categories of evidence.

(a) What we mean by evidence. Subject to the provisions of paragraph (b), evidence is anything you or anyone else submits to us or that we obtain that relates to your claim. We consider evidence under §§ 416.920b, 416.920c (or under § 416.927 for claims filed (see § 416.325) before March 27, 2017). We evaluate evidence we receive according to the rules pertaining to the relevant category of evidence. The categories of evidence are:

(1) Objective medical evidence. Objective medical evidence is medical signs, laboratory findings, or both, as defined in § 416.902(k).

(2) Medical opinion. A medical opinion is a statement from a medical source about what you can still do despite your impairment(s) and whether you have one or more impairment-related limitations or restrictions in the abilities listed in paragraphs (a)(2)(i)(A) through (D) and (a)(2)(ii)(A) through (F) of this section. (For claims filed (see § 416.325) before March 27, 2017, see § 416.927(a) for the definition of medical opinion.)

(i) Medical opinions in adult claims are about impairment-related limitations and restrictions in:

(A) Your ability to perform physical demands of work activities, such as sitting, standing, walking, lifting, carrying, pushing, pulling, or other physical functions (including manipulative or postural functions, such as reaching, handling, stooping, or crouching);

(B) Your ability to perform mental demands of work activities, such as understanding; remembering; maintaining concentration, persistence, or pace; carrying out instructions; or responding appropriately to supervision, co-workers, or work pressures in a work setting;

(C) Your ability to perform other demands of work, such as seeing, hearing, or using other senses; and

(D) Your ability to adapt to environmental conditions, such as temperature extremes or fumes.

(ii) Medical opinions in child claims are about impairment-related limitations and restrictions in your abilities in the six domains of functioning:

(A) Acquiring and using information (see § 416.926a(g));

(B) Attending and completing tasks (see § 416.926a(h));

(C) Interacting and relating with others (see § 416.926a(i));

(D) Moving about and manipulating objects (see § 416.926a(j));

(E) Caring for yourself (see § 416.926a(k)); and

(F) Health and physical well-being (see § 416.926a(*l*)).

(3) Other medical evidence. Other medical evidence is evidence from a medical source that is not objective medical evidence or a medical opinion, including judgments about the nature and severity of your impairments, your medical history, clinical findings, diagnosis, treatment prescribed with response, or prognosis. (For claims filed (see § 416.325) before March 27, 2017, other medical evidence does not include a diagnosis, prognosis, or a statement that reflects a judgment(s) about the nature and severity of your impairment(s)).

(4) Evidence from nonmedical sources. Evidence from nonmedical sources is any information or statement(s) from a nonmedical source (including you) about any issue in your claim. We may receive evidence from nonmedical sources either directly from the nonmedical source or indirectly, such as from forms we receive and our administrative records.

(5) Prior administrative medical finding. A prior administrative medical finding is a finding, other than the ultimate determination about whether you are disabled, about a medical issue made by our Federal and State agency medical and psychological consultants at a prior level of review (see § 416.1400) in your current claim based on their review of the evidence in your case record, such as:

(i) The existence and severity of your impairment(s);

(ii) The existence and severity of your symptoms;

(iii) Statements about whether your impairment(s) meets or medically equals any listing in the Listing of Impairments in Part 404, Subpart P, Appendix 1;

(iv) If you are a child, statements about whether your impairment(s) functionally equals the listings in Part 404, Subpart P, Appendix 1;

(v) If you are an adult, your residual functional capacity;

(vi) Whether your impairment(s) meets the duration requirement; and

(vii) How failure to follow prescribed treatment (see § 416.930) and drug addiction and alcoholism (see § 416.935) relate to your claim.

(b) Exceptions for privileged communications.

(1) The privileged communications listed in paragraphs (b)(1)(i) and (b)(1)(ii) of this section are not evidence, and we will neither consider nor provide any analysis about them in your determination or decision. This exception for privileged communications applies equally whether your representative is an attorney or a non-attorney.

(i) Oral or written communications between you and your representative that are subject to the attorney-client privilege, unless you voluntarily disclose the communication to us.

(ii) Your representative's analysis of your claim, unless he or she voluntarily discloses it to us. This analysis means information that is subject to the attorney work product doctrine, but it does not include medical evidence, medical opinions, or any other factual matter that we may consider in determining whether or not you are entitled to benefits (see paragraph (b)(2) of this section).

(2) The attorney-client privilege generally protects confidential communications between an attorney and his or her client that are related to providing or obtaining legal advice. The attorney work product doctrine generally protects an attorney's analyses, theories, mental impressions, and notes. In the context of your disability claim, neither the attorney-client privilege nor the attorney work product doctrine allow you to withhold factual information, medical opinions, or other medical evidence that we may consider in determining whether or not you are entitled to benefits.

For example, if you tell your representative about the medical sources you have seen, your representative cannot refuse to disclose the identity of those medical sources to us based on the attorney-client privilege. As another example, if your representative asks a medical source to complete an opinion form related to your impairment(s), symptoms, or limitations, your representative cannot withhold the completed opinion form from us based on the attorney work product doctrine. The attorney work product doctrine would not protect the source's opinions on the completed form, regardless of whether or not your representative used the form in his or her analysis of your claim or made handwritten notes on the face of the report.

[56 FR 5553, Feb. 11, 1991; 56 FR 36964, Aug. 1, 1991; 58 FR 47577, Sept. 9, 1993; 62 FR 6421, Feb. 11, 1997; 65 FR 11878, March 7, 2000; 65 FR 34958, June 1, 2000; 65 FR 54777, Sept. 11, 2000; 71 FR 16459, March 31, 2006; 72 FR 9242, March 1, 2007; 76 FR 24810, May 3, 2011; 78 FR 46502, Aug. 1, 2013; 82 FR 5875, Jan. 18, 2017]

§ 416.913a Evidence from our Federal or State agency medical or psychological consultants.

The following rules apply to our Federal or State agency medical or psychological consultants that we consult in connection with administrative law judge hearings and Appeals Council reviews:

(a) In claims adjudicated by the State agency, a State agency medical or psychological consultant may make the determination of disability together with a State agency disability examiner or provide medical evidence to a State agency disability examiner when the disability examiner makes the initial or reconsideration determination alone (see § 416.1015(c) of this part). The following rules apply:

(1) When a State agency medical or psychological consultant makes the determination together with a State agency disability examiner at the initial or reconsideration level of the administrative review process as provided in § 416.1015(c)(1), he or she will consider the evidence in your case record and make administrative findings about the medical issues, including, but not limited to, the existence and severity of your impairment(s), the existence and severity of your symptoms, whether your impairment(s) meets or medically equals the requirements for any impairment listed in appendix 1 to this subpart, and your residual functional capacity. These administrative medical findings are based on the evidence in your case but are not in themselves evidence at the level of the administrative review process at which they are made. See § 416.913(a)(5).

(2) When a State agency disability examiner makes the initial determination alone as provided in § 416.1015(c)(3), he or she may obtain medical evidence from a State agency medical or psychological consultant about one or more of the medical issues listed in paragraph (a)(1) of this section. In these cases, the State agency disability examiner will consider the medical evidence of the State agency medical or psychological consultant under §§ 416.920b, 416.920c, and 416.927.

(3) When a State agency disability examiner makes a reconsideration determination alone as provided in § 416.1015(c)(3), he or she will consider prior administrative medical findings made by a State agency medical or psychological consultant at the initial level of the administrative review process, and any medical evidence provided by such consultants at the initial and reconsideration levels, about one or more of the medical issues listed in paragraph (a)(1)(i) of this section under §§ 416.920b, 416.920c, and 416.927.

(b) Administrative law judges are responsible for reviewing the evidence and making administrative findings of fact and conclusions of law. They will consider prior administrative medical findings and medical evidence from our Federal or State agency medical or psychological consultants as follows:

(1) Administrative law judges are not required to adopt any prior administrative medical findings, but they must consider this evidence according to §§ 416.920b, 416.920c, and 416.927, as appropriate, because our Federal or State agency medical or psychological consultants are highly qualified and experts in Social Security disability evaluation.

(2) Administrative law judges may also ask for medical evidence from expert medical sources. Administrative law judges will consider this evidence under §§ 416.920b, 416.920c, and 416.927, as appropriate.

(c) When the Appeals Council makes a decision, it will consider prior administrative medical findings according to the same rules for considering prior administrative medical findings as administrative law judges follow under paragraph (b) of this section.

[82 FR 5876, Jan. 18, 2017]

§ 416.914 When we will purchase existing evidence.

We need specific medical evidence to determine whether you are disabled or blind. We will pay for the medical evidence we request, if there is a charge. We will also be responsible for the cost of medical evidence we ask you to get.

§ 416.915 Where and how to submit evidence.

You may give us evidence about your impairment at any of our offices or at the office of any State agency authorized to make disability or blindness determinations. You may also give evidence to one of our employees authorized to accept evidence at another place. For more information about this, see subpart C of this part.

§ 416.916 If you fail to submit medical and other evidence.

You (and if you are a child, your parent, guardian, relative, or other person acting on your behalf) must co-operate in furnishing us with, or in helping us to obtain or identify, available medical or other evidence about your impairment(s). When you fail to cooperate with us in obtaining evidence, we will have to make a decision based on information available in your case. We will not excuse you from giving us evidence because you have religious or personal reasons against medical examinations, tests, or treatment.

[56 FR 5554, Feb. 11, 1991; 58 FR 47577, Sept. 9, 1993]

§ 416.917 Consultative examination at our expense.

If your medical sources cannot or will not give us sufficient medical evidence about your impairment for us to determine whether you are disabled or blind, we may ask you to have one or more physical or mental examinations or tests. We will pay for these examinations. However, we will not pay for any medical examination arranged by you or your representative without our advance approval. If we arrange for the examination or test, we will give you reasonable notice of the date, time, and place the examination or test will be given, and the name of the person or facility who will do it. We will also give the examiner any necessary background information about your condition.

[56 FR 36964, Aug. 1, 1991]

§ 416.918 If you do not appear at a consultative examination.

(a) General. If you are applying for benefits and do not have a good reason for failing or refusing to take part in a consultative examination or test which we arrange for you to get information we need to determine your disability or blindness, we may find that you are not disabled or blind. If you are already receiving benefits and do not have a good reason for failing or refusing to take part in a consultative examination or test which we arranged for you, we may determine that your disability or blindness has stopped because of your failure or refusal. Therefore, if you have any reason why you cannot go for the scheduled appointment, you should tell us about this as soon as possible before the examination date. If you have a good reason, we will schedule another examination. We will consider your physical, mental, educational, and linguistic limitations (including any lack of facility with the English language) when determining if you have a good reason for failing to attend a consultative examination.

(b) Examples of good reasons for failure to appear. Some examples of what we consider good reasons for not going to a scheduled examination include—

(1) Illness on the date of the scheduled examination or test;

(2) Not receiving timely notice of the scheduled examination or test, or receiving no notice at all;

(3) Being furnished incorrect or incomplete information, or being given incorrect information about the physician involved or the time or place of the examination or test, or;

(4) Having had death or serious illness occur in your immediate family.

(c) Objections by your medical source(s). If any of your medical sources tell you that you should not take the examination or test, you should tell us at once. In many cases, we may be able to get the information we need in another way. Your medical source(s) may agree to another type of examination for the same purpose.

[59 FR 1636, Jan. 12, 1994; 82 FR 5877, Jan. 18, 2017]

STANDARDS TO BE USED IN DETERMINING WHEN A CONSULTATIVE EXAMINATION WILL BE OBTAINED IN CONNECTION WITH DISABILITY DETERMINATIONS

§ 416.919 The consultative examination.

A consultative examination is a physical or mental examination or test purchased for you at our request and expense from a treating source or another medical source, including a pediatrician when appropriate. The decision to purchase a consultative examination will be made on an individual case basis in accordance with the provisions of § 416.919a through § 416.919f. Selection of the source for the examination will be consistent with the provisions of § 416.903a and §§ 416.919g through 416.919j. The rules and procedures for requesting consultative examinations set forth in §§ 416.919a and 416.919b are applicable at the reconsideration and hearing levels of review, as well as the initial level of determination.

[56 FR 36964, Aug. 1, 1991; 65 FR 11879, March 7, 2000]

§ 416.919a When we will purchase a consultative examination and how we will use it.

(a) General. If we cannot get the information we need from your medical sources, we may decide to purchase a consultative examination. See § 416.912 for the procedures we will follow to obtain evidence from your medical sources and § 416.920b for how we consider evidence. Before purchasing a consultative examination, we will consider not only existing medical reports, but also the disability interview form containing your allegations as well as other pertinent evidence in your file.

(b) Situations that may require a consultative examination. We may purchase a consultative examination to try to resolve an inconsistency in the evidence or when the evidence as a whole is insufficient to support a determination or decision on your claim. Some examples of when we might purchase a consultative examination to secure needed medical evidence, such as clinical findings, laboratory tests, a diagnosis, or prognosis, include but are not limited to:

(1) The additional evidence needed is not contained in the records of your medical sources;

(2) The evidence that may have been available from your treating or other medical sources cannot be obtained for reasons beyond your control, such as death or noncooperation of a medical source;

(3) Highly technical or specialized medical evidence that we need is not available from your treating or other medical sources; or

(4) There is an indication of a change in your condition that is likely to affect your ability to work, or, if you are a child, your functioning, but the current severity of your impairment is not established.

[56 FR 36964, Aug. 1, 1991; 62 FR 6421, Feb. 11, 1997; 77 FR 10656, Feb. 23, 2012]

§ 416.919b When we will not purchase a consultative examination.

We will not purchase a consultative examination in situations including, but not limited to, the following situations:

(a) When any issues about your actual performance of substantial gainful activity have not been resolved;

(b) When you do not meet all of the nondisability requirements.

[56 FR 36965, Aug. 1, 1991]

STANDARDS FOR THE TYPE OF REFERRAL AND FOR REPORT CONTENT

§ 416.919f Type of purchased examinations.

We will purchase only the specific examinations and tests we need to make a determination in your claim. For example, we will not authorize a comprehensive medical examination when the only evidence we need is a special test, such as an X-ray, blood studies, or an electrocardiogram.

[56 FR 36965, Aug. 1, 1991]

§ 416.919g Who we will select to perform a consultative examination.

(a) We will purchase a consultative examination only from a qualified medical source. The medical source may be your own medical source or another medical source. If you are a child, the medical source we choose may be a pediatrician.

(b) By "qualified," we mean that the medical source must be currently licensed in the State and have the training and experience to perform the type of examination or test we will request; the medical source must not be barred from participation in our programs under the provisions of § 416.903a. The medical source must also have the equipment required to provide an adequate assessment and record of the existence and level of severity of your alleged impairments.

(c) The medical source we choose may use support staff to help perform the consultative examination. Any such support staff (e.g., X–ray technician, nurse) must meet appropriate licensing or certification requirements of the State. See § 416.903a.

[56 FR 36965, Aug. 1, 1991; 65 FR 11879, March 7, 2000; 82 FR 5877, Jan. 18, 2017]

§ 416.919h Your medical source.

When, in our judgment, your medical source is qualified, equipped, and willing to perform the additional examination or test(s) for the fee schedule payment, and generally furnishes complete and timely reports, your medical source will be the preferred source for the purchased examination or test(s).

[56 FR 36965, Aug. 1, 1991; 65 FR 11879, March 7, 2000; 82 FR 5877, Jan. 18, 2017]

§ 416.919i Other sources for consultative examinations.

We will use a different medical source than your medical source for a purchased examination or test in situations including, but not limited to, the following:

(a) Your medical source prefers not to perform such an examination or does not have the equipment to provide the specific data needed;

(b) There are conflicts or inconsistencies in your file that cannot be resolved by going back to your medical source;

(c) You prefer a source other than your medical source and have a good reason for your preference;

(d) We know from prior experience that your medical source may not be a productive source, such as when he or she has consistently failed to provide complete or timely reports; or

(e) Your medical source is not a qualified medical source as defined in § 416.919g.

[56 FR 36965, Aug. 1, 1991; 65 FR 11879, March 7, 2000; 82 FR 5877, Jan. 18, 2017]

§ 416.919j Objections to the medical source designated to perform the consultative examination.

You or your representative may object to your being examined by a medical source we have designated to perform a consultative examination. If there is a good reason for the objection, we will schedule the examination with another medical source. A good reason may be that the medical source we designated had previously represented an interest adverse to you. For example, the medical source may have represented your employer in a workers' compensation case or may have been involved in an insurance claim or legal action adverse to you. Other things we will consider include: The presence of a language barrier, the medical source's office location (e.g., 2nd floor, no elevator), travel restrictions, and whether the medical source had examined you in connection with a previous disability determination or decision that was unfavorable to you. If your objection is that a medical source allegedly "lacks objectivity" in general, but not in relation to you personally, we will review the allegations. See § 416.919s. To avoid a delay in processing your claim, the consultative examination in your case will be changed to another medical source while a review is being conducted. We will handle any objection to use of the substitute medical source in the same manner. However, if we had previously conducted such a review and found that the reports of the medical source in question conformed to our guidelines, we will not change your examination.

[56 FR 36965, Aug. 1, 1991; 65 FR 11879, March 7, 2000]

§ 416.919k Purchase of medical examinations, laboratory tests, and other services.

We may purchase medical examinations, including psychiatric and psychological examinations, X–rays and laboratory tests (including specialized tests, such as pulmonary function studies, electrocardiograms, and stress tests) from a medical source.

(a) The rate of payment for purchasing medical or other services necessary to make determinations of disability may not exceed the highest rate paid by Federal or public agencies in the State for the same or similar types of service. See §§ 416.1024 and 416.1026 of this part.

(b) If a physician's bill, or a request for payment for a physician's services, includes a charge for a laboratory test for which payment may be made under this part, the amount payable with respect to the test shall be determined as follows:

(1) If the bill or request for payment indicates that the test was personally performed or supervised by the physician who submitted the bill (or for whose services the request for payment was made) or by another physician with whom that physician shares his or her practice, the payment will be based on the physician's usual and customary charge for the test or the rates of payment which the State uses for purchasing such services, whichever is the lesser amount.

(2) If the bill or request for payment indicates that the test was performed by an independent laboratory, the amount of reimbursement will not exceed the billed cost of the independent laboratory or the rate of payment which the State uses for purchasing such services, whichever is the lesser amount. A nominal payment may be made to the physician for collecting, handling and shipping a specimen to the laboratory if the physician bills for such a service. The total reimbursement may not exceed the rate of payment which the State uses for purchasing such services.

(c) The State will assure that it can support the rate of payment it uses. The State shall also be responsible for monitoring and overseeing the rate of payment it uses to ensure compliance with paragraphs (a) and (b) of this section.

[56 FR 36965, Aug. 1, 1991; 65 FR 11879, March 7, 2000; 71 FR 16459, March 31, 2006; 76 FR 24810, May 3, 2011]

§ 416.919m Diagnostic tests or procedures.

We will request the results of any diagnostic tests or procedures that have been performed as part of a workup by your treating source or other medical source and will use the results to help us evaluate impairment severity or prognosis. However, we will not order diagnostic tests or procedures that involve significant risk to you, such as myelograms, arteriograms, or cardiac catheterizations for the evaluation of disability under the Supplemental Security Income program. A State agency medical consultant must approve the ordering of any diagnostic test or procedure when there is a chance it may involve significant risk. The responsibility for deciding whether to perform the examination rests with the medical source designated to perform the consultative examination.

[56 FR 36966, Aug. 1, 1991; 65 FR 11879, March 7, 2000; 71 FR 16459, March 31, 2006; 76 FR 24810, May 3, 2011]

§ 416.919n Informing the medical source of examination scheduling, report content, and signature requirements.

The medical sources who perform consultative examinations will have a good understanding of our disability programs and their evidentiary requirements. They will be made fully aware of their responsibilities and obligations regarding confidentiality as described in § 401.105(e). We will fully inform medical sources who perform consultative examinations at the time we first contact them, and at subsequent appropriate intervals, of the following obligations:

(a) Scheduling. In scheduling full consultative examinations, sufficient time should be allowed to permit the medical source to take a case history and perform the examination, including any needed tests. The following minimum scheduling intervals (i.e., time set aside for the individual, not the actual duration of the consultative examination) should be used.

(1) Comprehensive general medical examination—at least 30 minutes;

(2) Comprehensive musculoskeletal or neurological examination—at least 20 minutes;

(3) Comprehensive psychiatric examination—at least 40 minutes;

(4) Psychological examination—at least 60 minutes (Additional time may be required depending on types of psychological tests administered); and

(5) All others—at least 30 minutes, or in accordance with accepted medical practices.

We recognize that actual practice will dictate that some examinations may require longer scheduling intervals depending on the circumstances in a particular situation. We also recognize that these minimum intervals may have to be adjusted to allow for those claimants that do not attend their scheduled examination. The purpose of these minimum scheduling timeframes is to ensure that such examinations are complete and that sufficient time is made available to obtain the information needed to make an accurate determination in your case. State agencies will monitor the scheduling of examinations (through their normal consultative examination oversight activities) to ensure that any overscheduling is avoided, as overscheduling may lead to examinations that are not thorough.

(b) Report content. The reported results of your medical history, examination, requested laboratory findings, discussions and conclusions must conform to accepted professional standards and practices in the medical field for a complete and competent examination. The facts in a particular case and the information and findings already reported in the medical and other evidence of record will dictate the extent of detail needed in the consultative examination report for that case. Thus, the detail and format for reporting the results of a purchased examination will vary depending upon the type of examination or testing requested. The reporting of information will differ from one type of examination to another when the requested examination relates to the performance of tests such as ventilatory function tests, treadmill exercise tests, or audiological tests. The medical report must be complete enough to help us determine the nature, severity, and duration of the impairment, and your residual functional capacity (if you are an adult) or your functioning (if you are a child). The report should reflect your statement of your symptoms, not simply the medical source's statements or conclusions. The medical source's report of the consultative examination should include the objective medical facts as well as observations and opinions.

(c) Elements of a complete consultative examination. A complete consultative examination is one which involves all the elements of a standard examination in the applicable medical specialty. When the report of a complete consultative examination is involved, the report should include the following elements:

(1) Your major or chief complaint(s);

(2) A detailed description, within the area of specialty of the examination, of the history of your major complaint(s);

(3) A description, and disposition, of pertinent "positive" and "negative" detailed findings based on the history, examination and laboratory tests related to the major complaint(s), and any other abnormalities or lack thereof reported or found during examination or laboratory testing;

(4) The results of laboratory and other tests (e.g., X-rays) performed according to the requirements stated in the Listing of Impairments (see appendix 1 of subpart P of part 404 of this chapter);

(5) The diagnosis and prognosis for your impairment(s);

(6) A medical opinion. Although we will ordinarily request a medical opinion as part of the consultative examination process, the absence of a medical opinion in a consultative examination report will not make the report incomplete. See § 416.913(a)(3); and

(7) In addition, the medical source will consider, and provide some explanation or comment on, your major complaint(s) and any other abnormalities found during the history and examination or reported from the laboratory tests. The history, examination, evaluation of laboratory test results, and the conclusions will represent the information provided by the medical source who signs the report.

(d) When a complete consultative examination is not required. When the evidence we need does not require a complete consultative examination (for example, we need only a specific laboratory test result to complete the record), we may not require a report containing all of the elements in paragraph (c).

(e) Signature requirements. All consultative examination reports will be personally reviewed and signed by the medical source who actually performed the examination. This attests to the fact that the medical source doing the examination or testing is solely responsible for the report contents and for the conclusions, explanations or comments provided with respect to the history, examination and evaluation of laboratory test results. The signature of the medical source on a report annotated "not proofed" or "dictated but not read" is not acceptable. A rubber stamp signature of a medical source or the medical source's signature entered by any other person is not acceptable.

[56 FR 36966, Aug. 1, 1991; 62 FR 6421, Feb. 11, 1997; 62 FR 13733, March 21, 1997; 65 FR 11879, March 7, 2000; 65 FR 54778, Sept. 11, 2000; 82 FR 5877, Jan. 18, 2017]

§ 416.919o When a properly signed consultative examination report has not been received.

If a consultative examination report is received unsigned or improperly signed we will take the following action.

(a) When we will make determinations and decisions without a properly signed report. We will make a determination or decision in the circumstances specified in paragraphs (a)(1) and (a)(2) of this section without waiting for a properly signed consultative examination report. After we have made the determination or decision, we will obtain a properly signed report and include it in the file unless the medical source who performed the original consultative examination has died:

(1) Continuous period of disability allowance with an onset date as alleged or earlier than alleged; or

(2) Continuance of disability.

(b) When we will not make determinations and decisions without a properly signed report. We will not use an unsigned or improperly signed consultative examination report to make the determinations or decisions specified in paragraphs (b)(1), (b)(2), (b)(3), and (b)(4) of this section. When we need a properly signed consultative examination report to make these determinations or decisions, we must obtain such a report. If the signature of the medical source who performed the original examination cannot be obtained because the medical source is out of the country for an extended period of time, or on an extended vacation, seriously ill, deceased, or for any other reason, the consultative examination will be rescheduled with another medical source:

(1) Denial; or

(2) Cessation; or

(3) Allowance of disability which has ended; or

(4) Allowance with an onset date later than the filing date.

[56 FR 36967, Aug. 1, 1991; 65 FR 11880, March 7, 2000]

§ 416.919p Reviewing reports of consultative examinations.

(a) We will review the report of the consultative examination to determine whether the specific information requested has been furnished. We will consider the following factors in reviewing the report:

(1) Whether the report provides evidence which serves as an adequate basis for decisionmaking in terms of the impairment it assesses;

(2) Whether the report is internally consistent; Whether all the diseases, impairments and complaints described in the history are adequately assessed and reported in the clinical findings; Whether the conclusions correlate the findings from your medical history, clinical examination and laboratory tests and explain all abnormalities;

(3) Whether the report is consistent with the other information available to us within the specialty of the examination requested; Whether the report fails to mention an important or relevant complaint within that specialty that is noted in other evidence in the file (e.g., your blindness in one eye, amputations, pain, alcoholism, depression);

(4) Whether this is an adequate report of examination as compared to standards set out in the course of a medical education; and

(5) Whether the report is properly signed.

(b) If the report is inadequate or incomplete, we will contact the medical source who performed the consultative examination, give an explanation of our evidentiary needs, and ask that the medical source furnish the missing information or prepare a revised report.

(c) With your permission, or when the examination discloses new diagnostic information or test results that reveal a potentially life-threatening situation, we will refer the consultative examination report to your treating source. When we refer the consultative examination report to your treating source without your permission, we will notify you that we have done so.

(d) We will perform ongoing special management studies on the quality of consultative examinations purchased from major medical sources and the appropriateness of the examinations authorized.

(e) We will take steps to ensure that consultative examinations are scheduled only with medical sources who have access to the equipment required to provide an adequate assessment and record of the existence and level of severity of your alleged impairments.

[56 FR 36967, Aug. 1, 1991; 65 FR 11880, March 7, 2000]

§ 416.919q Conflict of interest.

All implications of possible conflict of interest between medical or psychological consultants and their medical or psychological practices will be avoided. Such consultants are not only those physicians and psychologists who work for us directly but are also those who do review and adjudication work in the State agencies. Physicians and psychologists who work for us directly as employees or under contract will not work concurrently for a State agency. Physicians and psychologists who do review work for us will not perform consultative examinations for us without our prior approval. In such situations, the physician or psychologist will disassociate himself or herself from further involvement in the case and will not participate in the evaluation, decision, or appeal actions. In addition, neither they, nor any member of their families, will acquire or maintain, either directly or indirectly, any financial interest in a medical partnership, corporation, or similar relationship in which consultative examinations are provided. Sometimes physicians and psychologists who do review work for us will have prior knowledge of a case; for example, when the claimant was a patient. Where this is so, the physician or psychologist will not participate in the review or determination of the case. This does not preclude the physician or psychologist from submitting medical evidence based on treatment or examination of the claimant.

[56 FR 36967, Aug. 1, 1991]

AUTHORIZING AND MONITORING THE REFERRAL PROCESS

§ 416.919s Authorizing and monitoring the consultative examination.

(a) Day-to-day responsibility for the consultative examination process rests with the State agencies that make disability determinations for us.

(b) The State agency will maintain a good working relationship with the medical community in order to recruit sufficient numbers of physicians and other providers of medical services to ensure ready availability of consultative examination providers.

(c) Consistent with Federal and State laws, the State agency administrator will work to achieve appropriate rates of payment for purchased medical services.

(d) Each State agency will be responsible for comprehensive oversight management of its consultative examination program, with special emphasis on key providers.

(e) A key consultative examination provider is a provider that meets at least one of the following conditions:

(1) Any consultative examination provider with an estimated annual billing to the disability programs we administer of at least $150,000; or

(2) Any consultative examination provider with a practice directed primarily towards evaluation examinations rather than the treatment of patients; or

(3) Any consultative examination provider that does not meet the above criteria, but is one of the top five consultative examination providers in the State by dollar volume, as evidenced by prior year data.

(f) State agencies have flexibility in managing their consultative examination programs, but at a minimum will provide:

(1) An ongoing active recruitment program for consultative examination providers;

(2) A process for orientation, training, and review of new consultative examination providers, with respect to SSA's program requirements involving consultative examination report content and not with respect to medical techniques;

(3) Procedures for control of scheduling consultative examinations;

(4) Procedures to ensure that close attention is given to specific evaluation issues involved in each case;

(5) Procedures to ensure that only required examinations and tests are authorized in accordance with the standards set forth in this subpart;

(6) Procedures for providing medical or supervisory approval for the authorization or purchase of consultative examinations and for additional tests or studies requested by consulting medical sources. This includes physician approval for the ordering of any diagnostic test or procedure where the question of significant risk to the claimant/beneficiary might be raised. See § 416.919m.

(7) Procedures for the ongoing review of consultative examination results to ensure compliance with written guidelines;

(8) Procedures to encourage active participation by physicians and psychologists in the consultative examination oversight program;

(9) Procedures for handling complaints;

(10) Procedures for evaluating claimant reactions to key providers; and

(11) A program of systematic, onsite reviews of key providers that will include annual onsite reviews of such providers when claimants are present for examinations. This provision does not contemplate that such reviews will involve participation in the actual examinations but, rather, offer an opportunity to talk with claimants at the provider's site before and after the examination and to review the provider's overall operation.

(g) The State agencies will cooperate with us when we conduct monitoring activities in connection with their oversight management of their consultative examination programs.

[56 FR 36967, Aug. 1, 1991; 65 FR 11880, March 7, 2000; 71 FR 16459, March 31, 2006; 75 FR 32846, June 10, 2010; 76 FR 24810, May 3, 2011]

PROCEDURES TO MONITOR THE CONSULTATIVE EXAMINATION

§ 416.919t Consultative examination oversight.

(a) We will ensure that referrals for consultative examinations and purchases of consultative examinations are made in accordance with our policies. We will also monitor both the referral processes and the product of the consultative examinations obtained. This monitoring may include reviews by independent medical specialists under direct contract with SSA.

(b) Through our regional offices, we will undertake periodic comprehensive reviews of each State agency to evaluate each State's management of the consultative examination process. The review will involve visits to key providers, with State staff participating, including a program physician when the visit will deal with medical techniques or judgment, or factors that go to the core of medical professionalism.

(c) We will also perform ongoing special management studies of the quality of consultative examinations purchased from key providers and other sources and the appropriateness of the examinations authorized.

[56 FR 36968, Aug. 1, 1991]

EVALUATION OF DISABILITY

§ 416.920 Evaluation of disability of adults, in general.

(a) General—

(1) Purpose of this section. This section explains the five-step sequential evaluation process we use to decide whether you are disabled, as defined in § 416.905.

(2) Applicability of these rules. These rules apply to you if you are age 18 or older and you file an application for Supplemental Security Income disability benefits.

(3) Evidence considered. We will consider all evidence in your case record when we make a determination or decision whether you are disabled. See § 416.920b.

(4) The five-step sequential evaluation process. The sequential evaluation process is a series of five "steps" that we follow in a set order. See paragraph (h) of this section for an exception to this rule. If we can find that you are disabled or not disabled at a step, we make our determination or decision and we do not go on to the next step. If we cannot find that you are disabled or not disabled at a step, we go on to the next step. Before we go from step three to step four, we assess your residual functional capacity. (See paragraph (e) of this section.) We use this residual functional capacity assessment at both step four and at step five when we evaluate your claim at these steps. These are the five steps we follow:

(i) At the first step, we consider your work activity, if any. If you are doing substantial gainful activity, we will find that you are not disabled. (See paragraph (b) of this section.)

(ii) At the second step, we consider the medical severity of your impairment(s). If you do not have a severe medically determinable physical or mental impairment that meets the duration requirement in § 416.909, or a combination of impairments that is severe and meets the duration requirement, we will find that you are not disabled. (See paragraph (c) of this section.)

(iii) At the third step, we also consider the medical severity of your impairment(s). If you have an impairment(s) that meets or equals one of our listings in appendix 1 to subpart P of part 404 of this chapter and meets the duration requirement, we will find that you are disabled. (See paragraph (d) of this section.)

(iv) At the fourth step, we consider our assessment of your residual functional capacity and your past relevant work. If you can still do your past relevant work, we will find that you are not disabled. See paragraphs (f) and (h) of this section and § 416.960(b).

(v) At the fifth and last step, we consider our assessment of your residual functional capacity and your age, education, and work experience to see if you can make an adjustment to other work. If you can make an adjustment to other work, we will find that you are not disabled. If you cannot make an adjustment to other work, we will find that you are disabled. See paragraphs (g) and (h) of this section and § 416.960(c).

(5) When you are already receiving disability benefits. If you are already receiving disability benefits, we will use a different sequential evaluation process to decide whether you continue to be disabled. We explain this process in § 416.994(b)(5).

(b) If you are working. If you are working and the work you are doing is substantial gainful activity, we will find that you are not disabled regardless of your medical condition or your age, education, and work experience.

(c) You must have a severe impairment. If you do not have any impairment or combination of impairments which significantly limits your physical or mental ability to do basic work activities, we will find that you do not have a severe impairment and are, therefore, not disabled. We will not consider your age, education, and work experience.

(d) When your impairment(s) meets or equals a listed impairment in appendix 1. If you have an impairment(s) which meets the duration requirement and is listed in appendix 1 or is equal to a listed impairment(s), we will find you disabled without considering your age, education, and work experience.

(e) When your impairment(s) does not meet or equal a listed impairment. If your impairment(s) does not meet or equal a listed impairment, we will assess and make a finding about your residual functional capacity based on all the relevant medical and other evidence in your case record, as explained in § 416.945. (See paragraph (g)(2) of this section and § 416.962 for an exception to this rule.) We use our residual functional capacity assessment at the fourth step of the sequential evaluation process to determine if you can do your past relevant work (paragraph (f) of this section) and at the fifth step of the sequential evaluation process (if the evaluation proceeds to this step) to determine if you can adjust to other work (paragraph (g) of this section).

(f) Your impairment(s) must prevent you from doing your past relevant work. If we cannot make a determination or decision at the first three steps of the sequential evaluation process, we will compare our residual functional capacity assessment, which we made under paragraph (e) of this section, with the physical and mental demands of your past relevant work. See paragraph (h) of this section and § 416.960(b). If you can still do this kind of work, we will find that you are not disabled.

(g) Your impairment(s) must prevent you from making an adjustment to any other work.

(1) If we find that you cannot do your past relevant work because you have a severe impairment(s) (or you do not have any past relevant work), we will consider the same residual functional capacity assessment we made under paragraph (e) of this section, together with your vocational factors (your age, education, and work experience) to determine if you can make an adjustment to other work. (See § 416.960(c).) If you can make an adjustment to other work, we will find you not disabled. If you cannot, we will find you disabled.

(2) We use different rules if you meet one of the two special medical-vocational profiles described in § 416.962. If you meet one of those profiles, we will find that you cannot make an adjustment to other work, and that you are disabled.

(h) Expedited process. If we do not find you disabled at the third step, and we do not have sufficient evidence about your past relevant work to make a finding at the fourth step, we may proceed to the fifth step of the sequential evaluation process. If we find that you can adjust to other work based solely on your age, education, and the same residual functional capacity assessment we made under paragraph (e) of this section, we will find that you are not disabled and will not make a finding about whether you can do your past relevant work at the fourth step. If we find that you may be unable to adjust to other work or if § 416.962 may apply, we will assess your claim at the fourth step and make a finding about whether you can perform your past relevant work. See paragraph (g) of this section and § 416.960(c).

[50 FR 8728, March 5, 1985; 50 FR 19164, May 7, 1985; 56 FR 5554, Feb. 11, 1991; 56 FR 36968, Aug. 1, 1991; 65 FR 80308, Dec. 21, 2000; 68 FR 51164, Aug. 26, 2003; 77 FR 10656, Feb. 23, 2012; 77 FR 43495, July 25, 2012]

§ 416.920a Evaluation of mental impairments.

(a) General. The steps outlined in §§ 416.920 and 416.924 apply to the evaluation of physical and mental impairments. In addition, when we evaluate the severity of mental impairments for adults (persons age 18 and over) and in persons under age 18 when Part A of the Listing of Impairments is used, we must follow a special technique at each level in the administrative review process. We describe this special technique in paragraphs (b) through (e) of this section. Using this technique helps us:

(1) Identify the need for additional evidence to determine impairment severity;

(2) Consider and evaluate functional consequences of the mental disorder(s) relevant to your ability to work; and

(3) Organize and present our findings in a clear, concise, and consistent manner.

(b) Use of the technique.

(1) Under the special technique, we must first evaluate your pertinent symptoms, signs, and laboratory findings to determine whether you have a medically determinable mental impairment(s). See § 416.921 for more information about what is needed to show a medically determinable impairment. If we determine that you have a medically determinable mental impairment(s), we must specify the symptoms, signs, and laboratory findings that substantiate the presence of the impairment(s) and document our findings in accordance with paragraph (e) of this section.

(2) We must then rate the degree of functional limitation resulting from the impairment(s) in accordance with paragraph (c) of this section and record our findings as set out in paragraph (e) of this section.

(c) Rating the degree of functional limitation.

(1) Assessment of functional limitations is a complex and highly individualized process that requires us to consider multiple issues and all relevant evidence to obtain a longitudinal picture of your overall degree of functional limitation. We will consider all relevant and available clinical signs and laboratory findings, the effects of your symptoms, and how your functioning may be affected by factors including, but not limited to, chronic mental disorders, structured settings, medication, and other treatment.

(2) We will rate the degree of your functional limitation based on the extent to which your impairment(s) interferes with your ability to function independently, appropriately, effectively, and on a sustained basis. Thus, we will consider such factors as the quality and level of your overall functional performance, any episodic limitations, the amount of supervision or assistance you require, and the settings in which you are able to function. See 12.00C through 12.00H of the Listing of Impairments in appendix 1 to subpart P of part 404 of this chapter for more information about the factors we consider when we rate the degree of your functional limitation.

(3) We have identified four broad functional areas in which we will rate the degree of your functional limitation: Understand, remember, or apply information; interact with others; concentrate, persist, or maintain pace; and adapt or manage oneself. See 12.00E of the Listing of Impairments in appendix 1 to subpart P of part 404 of this chapter.

(4) When we rate your degree of limitation in these areas (understand, remember, or apply information; interact with others; concentrate, persist, or maintain pace; and adapt or manage oneself), we will use the following five-point scale: None, mild, moderate, marked, and extreme. The last point on the scale represents a degree of limitation that is incompatible with the ability to do any gainful activity.

(d) Use of the technique to evaluate mental impairments. After we rate the degree of functional limitation resulting from your impairment(s), we will determine the severity of your mental impairment(s).

(1) If we rate the degrees of your limitation as "none" or "mild," we will generally conclude that your impairment(s) is not severe, unless the evidence otherwise indicates that there is more than a minimal limitation in your ability to do basic work activities (see § 416.922).

(2) If your mental impairment(s) is severe, we must then determine if it meets or is equivalent in severity to a listed mental disorder. We do this by comparing the medical findings about your impairment(s) and the rating of the degree of functional limitation to the criteria of the appropriate listed mental disorder. We will record the presence or absence of the criteria and the rating of the degree of functional limitation on a standard document at the initial and reconsideration levels of the administrative review process, or in the decision at the administrative law judge hearing and Appeals Council levels (in cases in which the Appeals Council issues a decision). See paragraph (e) of this section.

(3) If we find that you have a severe mental impairment(s) that neither meets nor is equivalent in severity to any listing, we will then assess your residual functional capacity.

(e) Documenting application of the technique. At the initial and reconsideration levels of the administrative review process, we will complete a standard document to record how we applied the technique. At the administrative law judge hearing and Appeals Council levels (in cases in which the Appeals Council issues a decision), we will document application of the technique in the decision. The following rules apply:

(1) When a State agency medical or psychological consultant makes the determination together with a State agency disability examiner at the initial or reconsideration level of the administrative review process as provided in § 416.1015(c)(1) of this part, the State agency medical or psychological consultant has overall responsibility for assessing medical severity. A State agency disability examiner may assist in preparing the standard document. However, our medical or psychological consultant must review and sign the document to attest that it is complete and that he or she is responsible for its content, including the findings of fact and any discussion of supporting evidence.

(2) When a State agency disability examiner makes the determination alone as provided in § 416.1015(c)(3), the State agency disability examiner has overall responsibility for assessing medical severity and for completing and signing the standard document.

(3) When a disability hearing officer makes a reconsideration determination as provided in § 416.1015(c)(4), the determination must document application of the technique, incorporating the disability hearing officer's pertinent findings and conclusions based on this technique.

(4) At the administrative law judge hearing and Appeals Council levels, the written decision must incorporate the pertinent findings and conclusions based on the technique. The decision must show the significant history, including examination and laboratory findings, and the functional limitations that were considered in reaching a conclusion about the severity of the mental impairment(s). The decision must include a specific finding as to the degree of limitation in each of the functional areas described in paragraph (c) of this section.

(5) If the administrative law judge requires the services of a medical expert to assist in applying the technique but such services are unavailable, the administrative law judge may return the case to the State agency or the appropriate Federal component, using the rules in § 416.1441 of this part, for completion of the standard document. If, after reviewing the case file and completing the standard document, the State agency or Federal component concludes that a determination favorable to you is warranted, it will process the case using the rules found in § 416.1441(d) or (e) of this part. If, after reviewing the case file and completing the standard document, the State agency or Federal component concludes that a determination favorable to you is not warranted, it will send the completed standard document and the case to the administrative law judge for further proceedings and a decision.

[50 FR 35070, Aug. 28, 1985; 55 FR 51236, Dec. 12, 1990; 65 FR 50782, Aug. 21, 2000; 65 FR 60584, Oct. 12, 2000; 71 FR 16459, March 31, 2006; 75 FR 62682, Oct. 13, 2010; 76 FR 24810, May 3, 2011; 81 FR 66178, Sept. 26, 2016; 82 FR 5877, Jan. 18, 2017]

§ 416.920b How we consider evidence.

After we review all of the evidence relevant to your claim, we make findings about what the evidence shows.

(a) Complete and consistent evidence. If all of the evidence we receive, including all medical opinion(s), is consistent and there is sufficient evidence for us to determine whether you are disabled, we will make our determination or decision based on that evidence.

(b) Incomplete or inconsistent evidence. In some situations, we may not be able to make our determination or decision because the evidence in your case record is insufficient or inconsistent. We consider evidence to be insufficient when it does not contain all the information we need to make our determination or decision. We consider evidence to be inconsistent when it conflicts with other evidence, contains an internal conflict, is ambiguous, or when the medical evidence does not appear to be based on medically acceptable clinical or laboratory diagnostic techniques. If the evidence in your case record is insufficient or inconsistent, we may need to take the additional actions in paragraphs (b)(1) through (4) of this section.

(1) If any of the evidence in your case record, including any medical opinion(s) and prior administrative medical findings, is inconsistent, we will consider the relevant evidence and see if we can determine whether you are disabled based on the evidence we have.

(2) If the evidence is consistent but we have insufficient evidence to determine whether you are disabled, or if after considering the evidence we determine we cannot reach a conclusion about whether you are disabled, we will determine the best way to resolve the inconsistency or insufficiency. The action(s) we take will depend on the nature of the inconsistency or insufficiency. We will try to resolve the inconsistency or insufficiency by taking any one or more of the actions listed in paragraphs (b)(2)(i) through (b)(2)(iv) of this section. We might not take all of the actions listed below. We will consider any additional evidence we receive together with the evidence we already have.

(i) We may recontact your medical source. We may choose not to seek additional evidence or clarification from a medical source if we know from experience that the source either cannot or will not provide the necessary evidence. If we obtain medical evidence over the telephone, we will send the telephone report to the source for review, signature, and return;

(ii) We may request additional existing evidence;

(iii) We may ask you to undergo a consultative examination at our expense (see §§ 416.917 through 416.919t); or

(iv) We may ask you or others for more information.

(3) When there are inconsistencies in the evidence that we cannot resolve or when, despite efforts to obtain additional evidence, the evidence is insufficient to determine whether you are disabled, we will make a determination or decision based on the evidence we have.

(c) Evidence that is inherently neither valuable nor persuasive. Paragraphs (c)(1) through (c)(3) apply in claims filed (see § 416.325) on or after March 27, 2017. Because the evidence listed in paragraphs ((c)(1)-(c)(3) of this section is inherently neither valuable nor persuasive to the issue of whether you are disabled or blind under the Act, we will not provide any analysis about how we considered such evidence in our determination or decision, even under § 416.920c:

(1) Decisions by other governmental agencies and nongovernmental entities. See § 416.904.

(2) Disability examiner findings. Findings made by a State agency disability examiner made at a previous level of adjudication about a medical issue, vocational issue, or the ultimate determination about whether you are disabled.

(3) Statements on issues reserved to the Commissioner. The statements listed in paragraphs (c)(3)(i) through (c)(3)(ix) of this section would direct our determination or decision that you are or are not disabled or blind within the meaning of the Act, but we are responsible for making the determination or decision about whether you are disabled or blind:

(i) Statements that you are or are not disabled, blind, able to work, or able to perform regular or continuing work;

(ii) Statements about whether or not you have a severe impairment(s);

(iii) Statements about whether or not your impairment(s) meets the duration requirement (see § 416.909);

(iv) Statements about whether or not your impairment(s) meets or medically equals any listing in the Listing of Impairments in Part 404, Subpart P, Appendix 1;

(v) If you are a child, statements about whether or not your impairment(s) functionally equals the listings in Part 404 Subpart P Appendix 1 (see § 416.926a);

(vi) If you are an adult, statements about what your residual functional capacity is using our programmatic terms about the functional exertional levels in Part 404, Subpart P, Appendix 2, Rule 200.00 instead of descriptions about your functional abilities and limitations (see § 416.945);

(vii) If you are an adult, statements about whether or not your residual functional capacity prevents you from doing past relevant work (see § 416.960);

(viii) If you are an adult, statements that you do or do not meet the requirements of a medical-vocational rule in Part 404, Subpart P, Appendix 2; and

(ix) Statements about whether or not your disability continues or ends when we conduct a continuing disability review (see § 416.994).

[77 FR 10656, Feb. 23, 2012; 82 FR 5877, Jan. 18, 2017]

§ 416.920c How we consider and articulate medical opinions and prior administrative medical findings for claims filed on or after March 27, 2017.

For claims filed (see § 416.325) on or after March 27, 2017, the rules in this section apply. For claims filed before March 27, 2017, the rules in § 416.927 apply.

(a) How we consider medical opinions and prior administrative medical findings. We will not defer or give any specific evidentiary weight, including controlling weight, to any medical opinion(s) or prior administrative medical finding(s), including those from your medical sources. When a medical source provides one or more medical opinions or prior administrative medical findings, we will consider those medical opinions or prior administrative medical findings from that medical source together using the factors listed in paragraphs (c)(1) through (c)(5) of this section, as appropriate.

The most important factors we consider when we evaluate the persuasiveness of medical opinions and prior administrative medical findings are supportability (paragraph (c)(1) of this section) and consistency (paragraph (c)(2) of this section). We will articulate how we considered the medical opinions and prior administrative medical findings in your claim according to paragraph (b) of this section.

(b) How we articulate our consideration of medical opinions and prior administrative medical findings. We will articulate in our determination or decision how persuasive we find all of the medical opinions and all of the prior administrative medical findings in your case record. Our articulation requirements are as follows:

(1) Source-level articulation. Because many claims have voluminous case records containing many types of evidence from different sources, it is not administratively feasible for us to articulate in each determination or decision how we considered all of the factors for all of the medical opinions and prior administrative medical findings in your case record. Instead, when a medical source provides multiple medical opinion(s) or prior administrative medical finding(s), we will articulate how we considered the medical opinions or prior administrative medical findings from that medical source together in a single analysis using the factors listed in paragraphs (c)(1) through (c)(5) of this section, as appropriate. We are not required to articulate how we considered each medical opinion or prior administrative medical finding from one medical source individually.

(2) Most important factors. The factors of supportability (paragraph (c)(1) of this section) and consistency (paragraph (c)(2) of this section) are the most important factors we consider when we determine how persuasive we find a medical source's medical opinions or prior administrative medical findings to be. Therefore, we will explain how we considered the supportability and consistency factors for a medical source's medical opinions or prior administrative medical findings in your determination or decision. We may, but are not required to, explain how we considered the factors in paragraphs (c)(3) through (c)(5) of this section, as appropriate, when we articulate how we consider medical opinions and prior administrative medical findings in your case record.

(3) Equally persuasive medical opinions or prior administrative medical findings about the same issue. When we find that two or more medical opinions or prior administrative medical findings about the same issue are both equally well-supported (paragraph (c)(1) of this section) and consistent with the record (paragraph (c)(2) of this section) but are not exactly the same, we will articulate how we considered the other most persuasive factors in paragraphs (c)(3) through (c)(5) of this section for those medical opinions or prior administrative medical findings in your determination or decision.

(c) Factors. We will consider the following factors when we consider the medical opinion(s) and prior administrative medical finding(s) in your case:

(1) Supportability. The more relevant the objective medical evidence and supporting explanations presented by a medical source are to support his or her medical opinion(s) or prior administrative medical finding(s), the more persuasive the medical opinions or prior administrative medical finding(s) will be.

(2) Consistency. The more consistent a medical opinion(s) or prior administrative medical finding(s) is with the evidence from other medical sources and nonmedical sources in the claim, the more persuasive the medical opinion(s) or prior administrative medical finding(s) will be.

(3) Relationship with the claimant. This factor combines consideration of the issues in paragraphs (c)(3)(i)-(v) of this section.

(i) Length of the treatment relationship. The length of time a medical source has treated you may help demonstrate whether the medical source has a longitudinal understanding of your impairment(s).

(ii) Frequency of examinations. The frequency of your visits with the medical source may help demonstrate whether the medical source has a longitudinal understanding of your impairment(s).

(iii) Purpose of the treatment relationship. The purpose for treatment you received from the medical source may help demonstrate the level of knowledge the medical source has of your impairment(s).

(iv) Extent of the treatment relationship. The kinds and extent of examinations and testing the medical source has performed or ordered from specialists or independent laboratories may help demonstrate the level of knowledge the medical source has of your impairment(s).

(v) Examining relationship. A medical source may have a better understanding of your impairment(s) if he or she examines you than if the medical source only reviews evidence in your folder.

(4) Specialization. The medical opinion or prior administrative medical finding of a medical source who has received advanced education and training to become a specialist may be more persuasive about medical issues related to his or her area of specialty than the medical opinion or prior administrative medical finding of a medical source who is not a specialist in the relevant area of specialty.

(5) Other factors. We will consider other factors that tend to support or contradict a medical opinion or prior administrative medical finding. This includes, but is not limited to, evidence showing a medical source has familiarity with the other evidence in the claim or an understanding of our disability program's policies and evidentiary requirements. When we consider a

medical source's familiarity with the other evidence in a claim, we will also consider whether new evidence we receive after the medical source made his or her medical opinion or prior administrative medical finding makes the medical opinion or prior administrative medical finding more or less persuasive.

(d) Evidence from nonmedical sources. We are not required to articulate how we considered evidence from nonmedical sources using the requirements in paragraphs (a) through (c) in this section.

[82 FR 5878, Jan. 18, 2017]

§ 416.921 Establishing that you have a medically determinable impairment(s).

If you are not doing substantial gainful activity, we will then determine whether you have a medically determinable physical or mental impairment(s) (see § 416.920(a)(4)(ii)). Your impairment(s) must result from anatomical, physiological, or psychological abnormalities that can be shown by medically acceptable clinical and laboratory diagnostic techniques. Therefore, a physical or mental impairment must be established by objective medical evidence from an acceptable medical source. We will not use your statement of symptoms, a diagnosis, or a medical opinion to establish the existence of an impairment(s). After we establish that you have a medically determinable impairment(s), then we determine whether your impairment(s) is severe.

[50 FR 8729, March 5, 1985; 56 FR 5554, Feb. 11, 1991; 82 FR 5879, Jan. 18, 2017]

§ 416.922 What we mean by an impairment(s) that is not severe in an adult.

(a) Non-severe impairment(s). An impairment or combination of impairments is not severe if it does not significantly limit your physical or mental ability to do basic work activities.

(b) Basic work activities. When we talk about basic work activities, we mean the abilities and aptitudes necessary to do most jobs. Examples of these include—

(1) Physical functions such as walking, standing, sitting, lifting, pushing, pulling, reaching, carrying, or handling;

(2) Capacities for seeing, hearing, and speaking;

(3) Understanding, carrying out, and remembering simple instructions;

(4) Use of judgment;

(5) Responding appropriately to supervision, co-workers and usual work situations; and

(6) Dealing with changes in a routine work setting.

[50 FR 8729, March 5, 1985; 82 FR 5879, Jan. 18, 2017]

§ 416.923 Multiple impairments.

(a) Unrelated severe impairments. We cannot combine two or more unrelated severe impairments to meet the 12–month duration test. If you have a severe impairment(s) and then develop another unrelated severe impairment(s) but neither one is expected to last for 12 months, we cannot find you disabled, even though the two impairments in combination last for 12 months.

(b) Concurrent impairments. If you have two or more concurrent impairments that, when considered in combination, are severe, we must determine whether the combined effect of your impairments can be expected to continue to be severe for 12 months. If one or more of your impairments improves or is expected to improve within 12 months, so that the combined effect of your remaining impairments is no longer severe, we will find that you do not meet the 12–month duration test.

(c) Combined effect. In determining whether your physical or mental impairment or impairments are of a sufficient medical severity that such impairment or impairments could be the basis of eligibility under the law, we will consider the combined effect of all of your impairments without regard to whether any such impairment, if considered separately, would be of sufficient severity. If we do find a medically severe combination of impairments, we will consider the combined impact of the impairments throughout the disability determination process. If we do not find that you have a medically severe combination of impairments, we will determine that you are not disabled (see §§ 416.920 and 416.924).

[50 FR 8729, March 5, 1985; 56 FR 5554, Feb. 11, 1991; 82 FR 5879, Jan. 18, 2017]

§ 416.924 How we determine disability for children.

(a) Steps in evaluating disability. We consider all relevant evidence in your case record when we make a determination or decision whether you are disabled. If you allege more than one impairment, we will evaluate all the impairments for which we have evidence. Thus, we will consider the combined effects of all your impairments upon your overall health and functioning. We will also evaluate any limitations in your functioning that result from your symptoms, including pain (see § 416.929). We will also consider all of the relevant factors in §§ 416.924a and 416.924b whenever we assess your functioning at any step of this process. We follow a set order to determine whether you are disabled. If you are doing substantial gainful activity, we will determine that you are not disabled and not review your claim further. If you are not doing substantial gainful activity, we will consider your physical or mental impairment(s) first to see if you have an impairment or combination of impairments that is severe. If your impairment(s) is not severe, we will determine that you are not disabled and not review your claim further. If your impairment(s) is severe, we will review your claim further to see if you have an impairment(s) that meets, medically equals, or functionally equals the listings. If you have such an impairment(s), and it meets the duration requirement, we will find that you are disabled. If you do not have such an impairment(s), or if it does not meet the duration requirement, we will find that you are not disabled.

(b) If you are working. If you are working and the work you are doing is substantial gainful activity, we will find that you are not disabled regardless of your medical condition or age, education, or work experience. (For our rules on how we decide whether you are engaging in substantial gainful activity, see §§ 416.971 through 416.976.)

(c) You must have a medically determinable impairment(s) that is severe. If you do not have a medically determinable impairment, or your impairment(s) is a slight abnormality or a combination of slight abnormalities that causes no more than minimal functional limitations, we will find that you do not have a severe impairment(s) and are, therefore, not disabled.

(d) Your impairment(s) must meet, medically equal, or functionally equal the listings. An impairment(s) causes marked and severe functional limitations if it meets or medically equals the severity of a set of criteria for an impairment in the listings, or if it functionally equals the listings.

(1) Therefore, if you have an impairment(s) that meets or medically equals the requirements of a listing or that functionally equals the listings, and that meets the duration requirement, we will find you disabled.

(2) If your impairment(s) does not meet the duration requirement, or does not meet, medically equal, or functionally equal the listings, we will find that you are not disabled.

(e) Other rules. We explain other rules for evaluating impairments at all steps of this process in §§ 416.924a, 416.924b, and 416.929. We explain our rules for deciding whether an impairment(s) meets a listing in § 416.925. Our rules for how we decide whether an impairment(s) medically equals a listing are in § 416.926. Our rules for deciding whether an impairment(s) functionally equals the listings are in § 416.926a.

(f) If you attain age 18 after you file your disability application but before we make a determination or decision. For the period during which you are under age 18, we will use the rules in this section. For the period starting with the day you attain age 18, we will use the disability rules we use for adults who file new claims, in § 416.920.

(g) How we will explain our findings. When we make a determination or decision whether you are disabled under this section or whether your disability continues under § 416.994a, we will indicate our findings at each step of the sequential evaluation process as we explain in this paragraph. At the initial and reconsideration levels of the administrative review process, State agency medical and psychological consultants will indicate their findings in writing in a manner that we prescribe. The State agency medical or psychological consultant (see § 416.1016) or other designee of the Commissioner has overall responsibility for completing the prescribed writing and must sign the prescribed writing to attest that it is complete, including the findings of fact and any discussion of supporting evidence. Disability hearing officers, administrative law judges and the administrative appeals judges on the Appeals Council (when the Appeals Council makes a decision) will indicate their findings at each step of the sequential evaluation process in their determinations or decisions. In claims adjudicated under the procedures in part 405 of this chapter, administrative law judges will also indicate their findings at each step of the sequential evaluation process in their decisions.

[50 FR 8729, March 5, 1985; 56 FR 5554, Feb. 11, 1991; 56 FR 13266, 13365, April 1, 1991; 58 FR 47577, Sept. 9, 1993; 62 FR 6421, Feb. 11, 1997; 65 FR 54778, Sept. 11, 2000; 71 FR 16460, March 31, 2006; 76 FR 24811, May 3, 2011; 76 FR 41687, July 15, 2011; 79 FR 36204, June 26, 2014]

§ 416.924a Considerations in determining disability for children.

(a) Basic considerations. We consider all evidence in your case record (see § 416.913). The evidence in your case record may include information from medical sources (such as your pediatrician or other physician; psychologist; qualified speech-language pathologist; and physical, occupational, and rehabilitation therapists) and nonmedical sources (such as your parents, teachers, and other people who know you).

(1) Medical evidence—

(i) General. Medical evidence of your impairment(s) must describe symptoms, signs, and laboratory findings. The medical evidence may include, but is not limited to, formal testing that provides information about your development or functioning in terms of standard deviations, percentiles, percentages of delay, or age or grade equivalents. It may also include opinions from medical sources about the nature and severity of your impairments. (See § 416.920c.)

(ii) Test scores. We consider all of the relevant information in your case record and will not consider any single piece of evidence in isolation. Therefore, we will not rely on test scores alone when we decide whether you are disabled. (See § 416.926a(e) for more information about how we consider test scores.)

(iii) Medical sources. Medical sources will report their findings and observations on clinical examination and the results of any formal testing. A medical source's report should note and resolve any material inconsistencies between formal test results, other medical findings, and your usual functioning. Whenever possible and appropriate, the interpretation of findings by the medical source should reflect consideration of information from your parents or other people who know you, including your teachers and therapists. When a medical source has accepted and relied on such information to reach a diagnosis, we may consider this information to be a sign, as defined in § 416.902(*l*).

(2) Statements from nonmedical sources. Every child is unique, so the effects of your impairment(s) on your functioning may be very different from the effects the same impairment(s) might have on another child. Therefore, whenever possible and appropriate, we will try to get information from people who can tell us about the effects of your impairment(s) on your activities and how you function on a day-to-day basis. These other people may include, but are not limited to:

(i) Your parents and other caregivers. Your parents and other caregivers can be important sources of information because they usually see you every day. In addition to your parents, other caregivers may include a childcare provider who takes care of you while your parent(s) works or an adult who looks after you in a before-or after-school program.

(ii) Early intervention and preschool programs. If you have been identified for early intervention services (in your home or elsewhere) because of your impairment(s), or if you attend a preschool program (e.g., Headstart or a public school kindergarten for children with special needs), these programs are also important sources of information about your functioning. We will ask for reports from the agency and individuals who provide you with services or from your teachers about how you typically function compared to other children your age who do not have impairments.

(iii) School. If you go to school, we will ask for information from your teachers and other school personnel about how you are functioning there on a day-to-day basis compared to other children your age who do not have impairments. We will ask for any reports that the school may have that show the results of formal testing or that describe any special education instruction or services, including home-based instruction, or any accommodations provided in a regular classroom.

(b) Factors we consider when we evaluate the effects of your impairment(s) on your functioning—

(1) General. We must consider your functioning when we decide whether your impairment(s) is "severe" and when we decide whether your impairment(s) functionally equals the listings. We will also consider your functioning when we decide whether your impairment(s) meets or medically equals a listing if the listing we are considering includes functioning among its criteria.

(2) Factors we consider when we evaluate your functioning. Your limitations in functioning must result from your medically determinable impairment(s). The information we get from your medical and nonmedical sources can help us understand how your impairment(s) affects your functioning. We will also consider any factors that are relevant to how you function when we evaluate your impairment or combination of impairments. For example, your symptoms (such as pain, fatigue, decreased energy, or anxiety) may limit your functioning. (See § 416.929.) We explain some other factors we may consider when we evaluate your functioning in paragraphs (b)(3)–(b)(9) of this section.

(3) How your functioning compares to the functioning of children your age who do not have impairments—

(i) General. When we evaluate your functioning, we will look at whether you do the things that other children your age typically do or whether you have limitations and restrictions because of your medically determinable impairment(s). We will also look at how well you do the activities and how much help you need from your family, teachers, or others. Information about what you can and cannot do, and how you function on a day-to-day basis at home, school, and in the community, allows us to compare your activities to the activities of children your age who do not have impairments.

(ii) How we will consider reports of your functioning. When we consider the evidence in your case record about the quality of your activities, we will consider the standards used by the person who gave us the information. We will also consider the characteristics of the group to whom you are being compared. For example, if the way you do your classwork is compared to other children in a special education class, we will consider that you are being compared to children who do have impairments.

(4) Combined effects of multiple impairments. If you have more than one impairment, we will sometimes be able to decide that you have a "severe" impairment or an impairment that meets, medically equals, or functionally equals the listings by looking at each of your impairments separately. When we cannot, we will look comprehensively at the combined effects of your impairments on your day-to-day functioning instead of considering the limitations resulting from each impairment separately. (See §§ 416.923 and 416.926a(c) for more information about how we will consider the interactive and cumulative effects of your impairments on your functioning.)

(5) How well you can initiate, sustain, and complete your activities, including the amount of help or adaptations you need, and the effects of structured or supportive settings—

(i) Initiating, sustaining, and completing activities. We will consider how effectively you function by examining how independently you are able to initiate, sustain, and complete your activities despite your impairment(s), compared to other children your age who do not have impairments. We will consider:

(A) The range of activities you do;

(B) Your ability to do them independently, including any prompting you may need to begin, carry through, and complete your activities;

(C) The pace at which you do your activities;

(D) How much effort you need to make to do your activities; and

(E) How long you are able to sustain your activities.

(ii) Extra help. We will consider how independently you are able to function compared to other children your age who do not have impairments. We will consider whether you need help from other people, or whether you need special equipment, devices, or medications to perform your day-to-day activities. For example, we may consider how much supervision you need to keep from hurting yourself, how much help you need every day to get dressed or, if you are an infant, how long it takes for your parents or other caregivers to feed you. We recognize that children are often able to do things and complete tasks when given help, but may not be able to do these same things by themselves. Therefore, we will consider how much extra help you need, what special equipment or devices you use, and the medications you take that enable you to participate in activities like other children your age who do not have impairments.

(iii) Adaptations. We will consider the nature and extent of any adaptations that you use to enable you to function. Such adaptations may include assistive devices or appliances. Some adaptations may enable you to function normally or almost normally (e.g., eyeglasses). Others may increase your functioning, even though you may still have functional limitations (e.g., ankle-foot orthoses, hand or foot splints, and specially adapted or custom-made tools, utensils, or devices for self-care activities such as bathing, feeding, toileting, and dressing). When we evaluate your functioning with an adaptation, we will consider the degree to which the adaptation enables you to function compared to other children your age who do not have impairments, your ability to use the adaptation effectively on a sustained basis, and any functional limitations that nevertheless persist.

(iv) Structured or supportive settings.

(A) If you have a serious impairment(s), you may spend some or all of your time in a structured or supportive setting, beyond what a child who does not have an impairment typically needs.

(B) A structured or supportive setting may be your own home in which family members or other people (e.g., visiting nurses or home health workers) make adjustments to accommodate your impairment(s). A structured or supportive setting may also be your classroom at school, whether it is a regular classroom in which you are accommodated or a special classroom. It may also be a residential facility or school where you live for a period of time.

(C) A structured or supportive setting may minimize signs and symptoms of your impairment(s) and help to improve your functioning while you are in it, but your signs, symptoms, and functional limitations may worsen outside this type of setting. Therefore, we will consider your need for a structured setting and the degree of limitation in functioning you have or would have outside the structured setting. Even if you are able to function adequately in the structured or supportive setting, we must consider how you function in other settings and whether you would continue to function at an adequate level without the structured or supportive setting.

(D) If you have a chronic impairment(s), you may have your activities structured in such a way as to minimize stress and reduce the symptoms or signs of your impairment(s). You may continue to have persistent pain, fatigue, decreased energy, or other symptoms or signs, although at a lesser level of severity. We will consider whether you are more limited in your functioning than your symptoms and signs would indicate.

(E) Therefore, if your symptoms or signs are controlled or reduced in a structured setting, we will consider how well you are functioning in the setting and the nature of the setting in which you are functioning (e.g., home or a special class); the amount of help you need from your parents, teachers, or others to function as well as you do; adjustments you make to structure your environment; and how you would function without the structured or supportive setting.

(6) Unusual settings. Children may function differently in unfamiliar or one-to-one settings than they do in their usual settings at home, at school, in childcare or in the community. You may appear more or less impaired on a single examination (such as a consultative examination) than indicated by the information covering a longer period. Therefore, we will apply the guidance in paragraph (b)(5) of this section when we consider how you function in an unusual or one-to-one situation. We will look at your performance in a special situation and at your typical day-to-day functioning in routine situations. We will not draw inferences about your functioning in other situations based only on how you function in a one-to-one, new, or unusual situation.

(7) Early intervention and school programs—

(i) General. If you are a very young child who has been identified for early intervention services, or if you attend school (including preschool), the records of people who know you or who have examined you are important sources of information about your impairment(s) and its effects on your functioning. Records from physicians, teachers and school psychologists, or physical, occupational, or speech-language therapists are examples of what we will consider. If you receive early intervention services or go to school or preschool, we will consider this information when it is relevant and available to us.

(ii) School evidence. If you go to school or preschool, we will ask your teacher(s) about your performance in your activities throughout your school day. We will consider all the evidence we receive from your school, including teacher questionnaires, teacher checklists, group achievement testing, and report cards.

(iii) Early intervention and special education programs. If you have received a comprehensive assessment for early intervention services or special education services, we will consider information used by the assessment team to make its recommendations. We will consider the information in your Individualized Family Service Plan, your Individualized Education Program, or your plan for transition services to help us understand your functioning. We will examine the goals and objectives of your plan or program as further indicators of your functioning, as well as statements regarding related services, supplementary aids, program modifications, and other accommodations recommended to help you function, together with the other relevant information in your case record.

(iv) Special education or accommodations. We will consider the fact that you attend school, that you may be placed in a special education setting, or that you receive accommodations because of your impairments along with the other information in your case record. The fact that you attend school does not mean that you are not disabled. The fact that you do or do not receive special education services does not, in itself, establish your actual limitations or abilities. Children are placed in special education settings, or are included in regular classrooms (with or without accommodation), for many reasons that may or may not be related to the level of their impairments. For example, you may receive one-to-one assistance from an aide throughout the day in a regular classroom, or be placed in a special classroom. We will consider the circumstances of your school attendance, such as your ability to function in a regular classroom or preschool setting with children your age who do not have impairments. Similarly, we will consider that good performance in a special education setting does not mean that you are functioning at the same level as other children your age who do not have impairments.

(v) Attendance and participation. We will also consider factors affecting your ability to participate in your education program. You may be unable to participate on a regular basis because of the chronic or episodic nature of your impairment(s) or your need for therapy or treatment. If you have more than one impairment, we will look at whether the effects of your impairments taken together make you unable to participate on a regular basis. We will consider how your temporary removal or absence from the program affects your ability to function compared to other children your age who do not have impairments.

(8) The impact of chronic illness and limitations that interfere with your activities over time. If you have a chronic impairment(s) that is characterized by episodes of exacerbation (worsening) and remission (improvement), we will consider the frequency and severity of your episodes of exacerbation as factors that may be limiting your functioning. Your level of functioning may vary considerably over time. Proper evaluation of your ability to function in any domain requires us to take into account any variations in your level of functioning to determine the impact of your chronic illness on your ability to function over time. If you require frequent treatment, we will consider it as explained in paragraph (b)(9)(ii) of this section.

(9) The effects of treatment (including medications and other treatment). We will evaluate the effects of your treatment to determine its effect on your functioning in your particular case.

(i) Effects of medications. We will consider the effects of medication on your symptoms, signs, laboratory findings, and functioning. Although medications may control the most obvious manifestations of your impairment(s), they may or may not affect the functional limitations imposed by your impairment(s). If your symptoms or signs are reduced by medications, we will consider:

(A) Any of your functional limitations that may nevertheless persist, even if there is improvement from the medications;

(B) Whether your medications create any side effects that cause or contribute to your functional limitations;

(C) The frequency of your need for medication;

(D) Changes in your medication or the way your medication is prescribed; and

(E) Any evidence over time of how medication helps or does not help you to function compared to other children your age who do not have impairments.

(ii) Other treatment. We will also consider the level and frequency of treatment other than medications that you get for your impairment(s). You may need frequent and ongoing therapy from one or more medical sources to maintain or improve your functional status. (Examples of therapy include occupational, physical, or speech and language therapy, nursing or home health services, psychotherapy, or psychosocial counseling.) Frequent therapy, although intended to improve your functioning in some ways, may also interfere with your functioning in other ways. Therefore, we will consider the frequency of any therapy you must have, and how long you have received or will need it. We will also consider whether the therapy interferes with your participation in activities typical of other children your age who do not have impairments, such as attending school or classes and socializing with your peers. If you must frequently interrupt your activities at school or at home for therapy, we will consider whether these interruptions interfere with your functioning. We will also consider the length and frequency of your hospitalizations.

(iii) Treatment and intervention, in general. With treatment or intervention, you may not only have your symptoms or signs reduced, but may also maintain, return to, or achieve a level of functioning that is not disabling. Treatment or intervention may prevent, eliminate, or reduce functional limitations.

[65 FR 54779, Sept. 11, 2000; 82 FR 5879, Jan. 18, 2017]

§ 416.924b Age as a factor of evaluation in the sequential evaluation process for children.

(a) General. In this section, we explain how we consider age when we decide whether you are disabled. Your age may or may not be a factor in our determination whether your impairment(s) meets or medically equals a listing, depending on the listing we use for comparison. However, your age is an important factor when we decide whether your impairment(s) is severe (see § 416.924(c)) and whether it functionally equals the listings (see § 416.926a). Except in the case of certain premature infants, as described in paragraph (b) of this section, age means chronological age.

(1) When we determine whether you have an impairment or combination of impairments that is severe, we will compare your functioning to that of children your age who do not have impairments.

(2) When we determine whether your impairment(s) meets a listing, we may or may not need to consider your age. The listings describe impairments that we consider of such significance that they are presumed to cause marked and severe functional limitations.

(i) If the listing appropriate for evaluating your impairment is divided into specific age categories, we will evaluate your impairment according to your age when we decide whether your impairment meets that listing.

(ii) If the listing appropriate for evaluating your impairment does not include specific age categories, we will decide whether your impairment meets the listing without giving consideration to your age.

(3) When we compare an unlisted impairment or a combination of impairments with the listings to determine whether it medically equals the severity of a listing, the way we consider your age will depend on the listing we use for comparison. We will use the same principles for considering your age as in paragraphs (a)(2)(i) and (a)(2)(ii) of this section; that is, we will consider your age only if we are comparing your impairment(s) to a listing that includes specific age categories.

(4) We will also consider your age and whether it affects your ability to be tested. If your impairment(s) is not amenable to formal testing because of your age, we will consider all information in your case record that helps us decide whether you are disabled. We will consider other generally acceptable methods consistent with the prevailing state of medical knowledge and clinical practice that will help us evaluate the existence and severity of your impairment(s).

(b) Correcting chronological age of premature infants. We generally use chronological age (a child's age based on birth date) when we decide whether, or the extent to which, a physical or mental impairment or combination of impairments causes functional limitations. However, if you were born prematurely, we may consider you younger than your chronological age when we evaluate your development. We may use a "corrected" chronological age (CCA); that is, your chronological age adjusted by a period of gestational prematurity. We consider an infant born at less than 37 weeks' gestation to be born prematurely.

(1) We compute your CCA by subtracting the number of weeks of prematurity (the difference between 40 weeks of full-term gestation and the number of actual weeks of gestation) from your chronological age. For example, if your chronological age is 20 weeks but you were born at 32 weeks gestation (8 weeks premature), then your CCA is 12 weeks.

(2) We evaluate developmental delay in a premature child until the child's prematurity is no longer a relevant factor, generally no later than about chronological age 2.

(i) If you have not attained age 1 and were born prematurely, we will assess your development using your CCA.

(ii) If you are over age 1 and have a developmental delay, and prematurity is still a relevant factor, we will decide whether to correct your chronological age. We will base our decision on our judgment and all the facts in your case. If we decide to correct your chronological age, we may correct it by subtracting the full number of weeks of prematurity or a lesser number of weeks. If your developmental delay is the result of your medically determinable impairment(s) and is not attributable to your prematurity, we will decide not to correct your chronological age.

(3) Notwithstanding the provisions in paragraph (b)(1) of this section, we will not compute a corrected chronological age if the medical evidence shows that your medical source has already considered your prematurity in his or her assessment of your development. We will not compute a CCA when we find you disabled under listing 100.04 of the Listing of Impairments.

[56 FR 5555, Feb. 11, 1991; 56 FR 13365, April 1, 1991; 58 FR 47578, Sept. 9, 1993; 62 FR 6422, Feb. 11, 1997; 65 FR 54778, Sept. 11, 2000; 72 FR 59431, Oct. 19, 2007; 80 FR 19529, April 13, 2015; 82 FR 5880, Jan. 18, 2017]

§ 416.924c [Reserved]

[65 FR 54778, Sept. 11, 2000]

§§ 416.924d, 416.924e [Reserved]

[62 FR 6424, Feb. 11, 1997]

MEDICAL CONSIDERATIONS

§ 416.925 Listing of Impairments in appendix 1 of subpart P of part 404 of this chapter.

(a) What is the purpose of the Listing of Impairments? The Listing of Impairments (the listings) is in appendix 1[1] of subpart P of part 404 of this chapter. For adults, it describes for each of the major body systems impairments that we consider to be severe enough to prevent an individual from doing any gainful activity, regardless of his or her age, education, or work experience. For children, it describes impairments that cause marked and severe functional limitations.

(b) How is appendix 1 organized? There are two parts in appendix 1:

(1) Part A contains criteria that apply to individuals age 18 and over. We may also use part A for individuals who are under age 18 if the disease processes have a similar effect on adults and children.

(2)(i) Part B contains criteria that apply only to individuals who are under age 18; we never use the listings in part B to evaluate individuals who are age 18 or older. In evaluating disability for a person under age 18, we use part B first. If the criteria in part B do not apply, we may use the criteria in part A when those criteria give appropriate consideration to the effects of the impairment(s) in children. To the extent possible, we number the provisions in part B to maintain a relationship with their counterparts in part A.

(ii) Although the severity criteria in part B of the listings are expressed in different ways for different impairments, "listing-level severity" generally means the level of severity described in § 416.926a(a); that is, "marked" limitations in two domains of functioning or an "extreme" limitation in one domain. (See § 416.926a(e) for the definitions of the terms marked and extreme as they apply to children.) Therefore, in general, a child's impairment(s) is of "listing-level severity" if it causes marked limitations in two domains of functioning or an extreme limitation in one. However, when we decide whether your impairment(s) meets the requirements of a listing, we will decide that your impairment is of "listing-level severity" even if it does not result in marked limitations in two domains of functioning, or an extreme limitation in one, if the listing that we apply does not require such limitations to establish that an impairment(s) is disabling.

(c) How do we use the listings?

(1) Most body system sections in parts A and B of appendix 1 are in two parts: an introduction, followed by the specific listings.

(2) The introduction to each body system contains information relevant to the use of the listings in that body system; for example, examples of common impairments in the body system and definitions used in the listings for that body system. We may also include specific criteria for establishing a diagnosis, confirming the existence of an impairment, or establishing that your impairment(s) satisfies the criteria of a particular listing in the body system. Even if we do not include specific criteria for establishing a diagnosis or confirming the existence of your impairment, you must still show that you have a severe medically determinable impairment(s), as defined in §§ 416.921 and 416.924(c).

(3) In most cases, the specific listings follow the introduction in each body system, after the heading, Category of Impairments. Within each listing, we specify the objective medical and other findings needed to satisfy the criteria of that listing. We will find that your impairment(s) meets the requirements of a listing when it satisfies all of the criteria of that listing, including any relevant criteria in the introduction, and meets the duration requirement (see § 416.909).

(4) Most of the listed impairments are permanent or expected to result in death. For some listings, we state a specific period of time for which your impairment(s) will meet the listing. For all others, the evidence must show that your impairment(s) has lasted or can be expected to last for a continuous period of at least 12 months.

(5) If your impairment(s) does not meet the criteria of a listing, it can medically equal the criteria of a listing. We explain our rules for medical equivalence in § 416.926. We use the listings only to find that you are disabled or still disabled. If your impairment(s) does not meet or medically equal the criteria of a listing, we may find that you are disabled or still disabled at a later step in the sequential evaluation process.

(d) Can your impairment(s) meet a listing based only on a diagnosis? No. Your impairment(s) cannot meet the criteria of a listing based only on a diagnosis. To meet the requirements of a listing, you must have a medically determinable impairment(s) that satisfies all of the criteria of the listing.

[1] See: 20 C.F.R. Pt. 404, Subpt. P, App. 1, et seq.

(e) How do we consider your symptoms when we determine whether your impairment(s) meets a listing? Some listed impairments include symptoms, such as pain, as criteria. Section 416.929(d)(2) explains how we consider your symptoms when your symptoms are included as criteria in a listing.

[56 FR 57944, Nov. 14, 1991; 62 FR 6424, Feb. 11, 1997; 62 FR 13538, March 21, 1997; 65 FR 54782, Sept. 11, 2000; 71 FR 10430, March 1, 2006; June 7, 2011; 76 FR 19698, April 8, 2011; 82 FR 5880, Jan. 18, 2017]

§ 416.926 Medical equivalence for adults and children.

(a) What is medical equivalence? Your impairment(s) is medically equivalent to a listed impairment in appendix 1 of subpart P of part 404 of this chapter if it is at least equal in severity and duration to the criteria of any listed impairment.

(b) How do we determine medical equivalence? We can find medical equivalence in three ways.

(1)(i) If you have an impairment that is described in the Listing of Impairments in appendix 1 of subpart P of part 404 of this chapter, but—

(A) You do not exhibit one or more of the findings specified in the particular listing, or

(B) You exhibit all of the findings, but one or more of the findings is not as severe as specified in the particular listing,

(ii) We will find that your impairment is medically equivalent to that listing if you have other findings related to your impairment that are at least of equal medical significance to the required criteria.

(2) If you have an impairment(s) that is not described in the Listing of Impairments in appendix 1 of subpart P of part 404 of this chapter, we will compare your findings with those for closely analogous listed impairments. If the findings related to your impairment(s) are at least of equal medical significance to those of a listed impairment, we will find that your impairment(s) is medically equivalent to the analogous listing.

(3) If you have a combination of impairments, no one of which meets a listing described in the Listing of Impairments in appendix 1 of subpart P of part 404 of this chapter (see § 416.925(c)(3)), we will compare your findings with those for closely analogous listed impairments. If the findings related to your impairments are at least of equal medical significance to those of a listed impairment, we will find that your combination of impairments is medically equivalent to that listing.

(4) Section 416.929(d)(3) explains how we consider your symptoms, such as pain, when we make findings about medical equivalence.

(c) What evidence do we consider when we determine if your impairment(s) medically equals a listing? When we determine if your impairment medically equals a listing, we consider all evidence in your case record about your impairment(s) and its effects on you that is relevant to this finding. We do not consider your vocational factors of age, education, and work experience (see, for example, § 416.960(c)(1)). We also consider the opinion given by one or more medical or psychological consultants designated by the Commissioner. (See § 416.1016.)

(d) Who is a designated medical or psychological consultant? A medical or psychological consultant designated by the Commissioner includes any medical or psychological consultant employed or engaged to make medical judgments by the Social Security Administration, the Railroad Retirement Board, or a State agency authorized to make disability determinations. See § 416.1016 for the necessary qualifications for medical consultants and psychological consultants.

(e) Who is responsible for determining medical equivalence?

(1) In cases where the State agency or other designee of the Commissioner makes the initial or reconsideration disability determination, a State agency medical or psychological consultant or other designee of the Commissioner (see § 416.1016 of this part) has the overall responsibility for determining medical equivalence.

(2) For cases in the disability hearing process or otherwise decided by a disability hearing officer, the responsibility for determining medical equivalence rests with either the disability hearing officer or, if the disability hearing officer's reconsideration determination is changed under § 416.1418 of this part, with the Associate Commissioner for Disability Policy or his or her delegate.

(3) For cases at the administrative law judge or Appeals Council level, the responsibility for deciding medical equivalence rests with the administrative law judge or Appeals Council.

[52 FR 33928, Sept. 9, 1987; 56 FR 5561, Feb. 11, 1991; 62 FR 6424, Feb. 11, 1997; 62 FR 13538, March 21, 1997; 65 FR 34959, June 1, 2000; 71 FR 10431, March 1, 2006; 71 FR 16460, March 31, 2006; 76 FR 24811, May 3, 2011; 82 FR 5880, Jan. 18, 2017; 82 FR 15132, March 27, 2017]

§ 416.926a Functional equivalence for children.

(a) General. If you have a severe impairment or combination of impairments that does not meet or medically equal any listing, we will decide whether it results in limitations that functionally equal the listings. By "functionally equal the listings," we mean that your impairment(s) must be of listing-level severity; i.e., it must result in "marked" limitations in two domains of functioning or an "extreme" limitation in one domain, as explained in this section. We will assess the functional limitations caused by your impairment(s); i.e., what you cannot do, have difficulty doing, need help doing, or are restricted from doing because of your impairment(s). When we make a finding regarding functional equivalence, we will assess the interactive and cumulative effects of all of the impairments for which we have evidence, including any impairments you have that are not "severe." (See § 416.924(c).) When we assess your functional limitations, we will consider all the relevant factors in §§ 416.924a, 416.924b, and 416.929 including, but not limited to:

(1) How well you can initiate and sustain activities, how much extra help you need, and the effects of structured or supportive settings (see § 416.924a(b)(5));

(2) How you function in school (see § 416.924a(b)(7)); and

(3) The effects of your medications or other treatment (see § 416.924a(b)(9)).

(b) How we will consider your functioning. We will look at the information we have in your case record about how your functioning is affected during all of your activities when we decide whether your impairment or combination of impairments functionally equals the listings. Your activities are everything you do at home, at school, and in your community. We will look at how appropriately, effectively, and independently you perform your activities compared to the performance of other children your age who do not have impairments.

(1) We will consider how you function in your activities in terms of six domains. These domains are broad areas of functioning intended to capture all of what a child can or cannot do. In paragraphs (g) through (*l*), we describe each domain in general terms. For most of the domains, we also provide examples of activities that illustrate the typical functioning of children in different age groups. For all of the domains, we also provide examples of limitations within the domains. However, we recognize that there is a range of development and functioning, and that not all children within an age category are expected to be able to do all of the activities in the examples of typical functioning. We also recognize that limitations of any of the activities in the examples do not necessarily mean that a child has a "marked" or "extreme" limitation, as defined in paragraph (e) of this section. The domains we use are:

(i) Acquiring and using information;

(ii) Attending and completing tasks;

(iii) Interacting and relating with others;

(iv) Moving about and manipulating objects;

(v) Caring for yourself; and,

(vi) Health and physical well-being.

(2) When we evaluate your ability to function in each domain, we will ask for and consider information that will help us answer the following questions about whether your impairment(s) affects your functioning and whether your activities are typical of other children your age who do not have impairments.

(i) What activities are you able to perform?

(ii) What activities are you not able to perform?

(iii) Which of your activities are limited or restricted compared to other children your age who do not have impairments?

(iv) Where do you have difficulty with your activities-at home, in childcare, at school, or in the community?

(v) Do you have difficulty independently initiating, sustaining, or completing activities?

(vi) What kind of help do you need to do your activities, how much help do you need, and how often do you need it?

(3) We will try to get information from sources who can tell us about the effects of your impairment(s) and how you function. We will ask for information from your medical sources who can give us medical evidence, including medical opinions, about your limitations and restrictions. We will also ask for information from your parents and teachers, and may ask for information from others who see you often and can describe your functioning at home, in childcare, at school, and in your community. We may also ask you to go to a consultative examination(s) at our expense. (See §§ 416.912–416.919a regarding medical evidence and when we will purchase a consultative examination.)

(c) The interactive and cumulative effects of an impairment or multiple impairments. When we evaluate your functioning and decide which domains may be affected by your impairment(s), we will look first at your activities and your limitations and restrictions. Any given activity may involve the integrated use of many abilities and skills; therefore, any single limitation may be the result of the interactive and cumulative effects of one or more impairments. And any given impairment may have effects in more than one domain; therefore, we will evaluate the limitations from your impairment(s) in any affected domain(s).

(d) How we will decide that your impairment(s) functionally equals the listings. We will decide that your impairment(s) functionally equals the listings if it is of listing-level severity. Your impairment(s) is of listing-level severity if you have "marked" limitations in two of the domains in paragraph (b)(1) of this section, or an "extreme" limitation in one domain. We will not compare your functioning to the requirements of any specific listing. We explain what the terms "marked" and "extreme" mean in paragraph (e) of this section. We explain how we use the domains in paragraph (f) of this section, and describe each domain in paragraphs (g)–(*l*). You must also meet the duration requirement. (See § 416.909.)

(e) How we define "marked" and "extreme" limitations—

(1) General.

(i) When we decide whether you have a "marked" or an "extreme" limitation, we will consider your functional limitations resulting from all of your impairments, including their interactive and cumulative effects. We will consider all the relevant information in your case record that helps us determine your functioning, including your signs, symptoms, and laboratory findings, the descriptions we have about your functioning from your parents, teachers, and other people who know you, and the relevant factors explained in §§ 416.924a, 416.924b, and 416.929.

(ii) The medical evidence may include formal testing that provides information about your development or functioning in terms of percentiles, percentages of delay, or age or grade equivalents. Standard scores (e.g., percentiles) can be converted to standard deviations. When you have such scores, we will consider them together with the information we have about your functioning to determine whether you have a "marked" or "extreme" limitation in a domain.

(2) Marked limitation.

(i) We will find that you have a "marked" limitation in a domain when your impairment(s) interferes seriously with your ability to independently initiate, sustain, or complete activities. Your day-to-day functioning may be seriously limited when your impairment(s) limits only one activity or when the interactive and cumulative effects of your impairment(s) limit several activities. "Marked" limitation also means a limitation that is "more than moderate" but "less than extreme." It is the equivalent of the functioning we would expect to find on standardized testing with scores that are at least two, but less than three, standard deviations below the mean.

(ii) If you have not attained age 3, we will generally find that you have a "marked" limitation if you are functioning at a level that is more than one-half but not more than two-thirds of your chronological age when there are no standard scores from standardized tests in your case record.

(iii) If you are a child of any age (birth to the attainment of age 18), we will find that you have a "marked" limitation when you have a valid score that is two standard deviations or more below the mean, but less than three standard deviations, on a comprehensive standardized test designed to measure ability or functioning in that domain, and your day-to-day functioning in domain-related activities is consistent with that score. (See paragraph (e)(4) of this section.)

(iv) For the sixth domain of functioning, "Health and physical well-being," we may also consider you to have a "marked" limitation if you are frequently ill because of your impairment(s) or have frequent exacerbations of your impairment(s) that result in significant, documented symptoms or signs. For purposes of this domain, "frequent means that you have episodes of illness or exacerbations that occur on an average of 3 times a year, or once every 4 months, each lasting 2 weeks or more. We may also find that you have a "marked" limitation if you have episodes that occur more often than 3 times in a year or once every 4 months but do not last for 2 weeks, or occur less often than an average of 3 times a year or once every 4 months but last longer than 2 weeks, if the overall effect (based on the length of the episode(s) or its frequency) is equivalent in severity.

(3) Extreme limitation.

(i) We will find that you have an "extreme" limitation in a domain when your impairment(s) interferes very seriously with your ability to independently initiate, sustain, or complete activities. Your day-to-day functioning may be very seriously limited when your impairment(s) limits only one activity or when the interactive and cumulative effects of your impairment(s) limit several activities. "Extreme" limitation also means a limitation that is "more than marked." "Extreme" limitation is the rating we give to the worst limitations. However, "extreme limitation" does not necessarily mean a total lack or loss of ability to function. It is the equivalent of the functioning we would expect to find on standardized testing with scores that are at least three standard deviations below the mean.

(ii) If you have not attained age 3, we will generally find that you have an "extreme" limitation if you are functioning at a level that is one-half of your chronological age or less when there are no standard scores from standardized tests in your case record.

(iii) If you are a child of any age (birth to the attainment of age 18), we will find that you have an "extreme" limitation when you have a valid score that is three standard deviations or more below the mean on a comprehensive standardized test designed to measure ability or functioning in that domain, and your day-to-day functioning in domain-related activities is consistent with that score. (See paragraph (e)(4) of this section.)

(iv) For the sixth domain of functioning, "Health and physical well-being," we may also consider you to have an "extreme" limitation if you are frequently ill because of your impairment(s) or have frequent exacerbations of your impairment(s) that result in significant, documented symptoms or signs substantially in excess of the requirements for showing a "marked" limitation in paragraph (e)(2)(iv) of this section. However, if you have episodes of illness or exacerbations of your impairment(s) that we would rate as "extreme" under this definition, your impairment(s) should meet or medically equal the requirements of a listing in most cases. See §§ 416.925 and 416.926.

(4) How we will consider your test scores.

(i) As indicated in § 416.924a(a)(1)(ii), we will not rely on any test score alone. No single piece of information taken in isolation can establish whether you have a "marked" or an "extreme" limitation in a domain.

(ii) We will consider your test scores together with the other information we have about your functioning, including reports of classroom performance and the observations of school personnel and others.

(A) We may find that you have a "marked" or "extreme" limitation when you have a test score that is slightly higher than the level provided in paragraph (e)(2) or (e)(3) of this section, if other information in your case record shows that your functioning in day-to-day activities is seriously or very seriously limited because of your impairment(s). For example, you may have IQ scores above the level in paragraph (e)(2), but other evidence shows that your impairment(s) causes you to function in school, home, and the community far below your expected level of functioning based on this score.

(B) On the other hand, we may find that you do not have a "marked" or "extreme" limitation, even if your test scores are at the level provided in paragraph (e)(2) or (e)(3) of this section, if other information in your case record shows that your functioning in day-to-day activities is not seriously or very seriously limited by your impairment(s). For example, you may have a valid IQ score below the level in paragraph (e)(2), but other evidence shows that you have learned to drive a car, shop independently, and read books near your expected grade level.

(iii) If there is a material inconsistency between your test scores and other information in your case record, we will try to resolve it. The interpretation of the test is primarily the responsibility of the psychologist or other professional who administered the test. But it is also our responsibility to ensure that the evidence in your case is complete and consistent or that any material inconsistencies have been resolved. Therefore, we will use the following guidelines when we resolve concerns about your test scores:

(A) We may be able to resolve the inconsistency with the information we have. We may need to obtain additional information; e.g., by recontact with your medical source(s), by purchase of a consultative examination to provide further medical information, by recontact with a medical source who provided a consultative examination, or by questioning individuals familiar with your day-to-day functioning.

(B) Generally, we will not rely on a test score as a measurement of your functioning within a domain when the information we have about your functioning is the kind of information typically used by medical professionals to determine that the test results are not the best measure of your day-to-day functioning. When we do not rely on test scores, we will explain our reasons for doing so in your case record or in our decision.

(f) How we will use the domains to help us evaluate your functioning.

(1) When we consider whether you have "marked" or "extreme" limitations in any domain, we examine all the information we have in your case record about how your functioning is limited because of your impairment(s), and we compare your functioning to the typical functioning of children your age who do not have impairments.

(2) The general descriptions of each domain in paragraphs (g)–(*l*) help us decide whether you have limitations in any given domain and whether these limitations are "marked" or "extreme."

(3) The domain descriptions also include examples of some activities typical of children in each age group and some functional limitations that we may consider. These examples also help us decide whether you have limitations in a domain because of your impairment(s). The examples are not all-inclusive, and we will not require our adjudicators to develop evidence about each specific example. When you have limitations in a given activity or activities in the examples, we may or may not decide that you have a "marked" or "extreme" limitation in the domain. We will consider the activities in which you are limited because of your impairment(s) and the extent of your limitations under the rules in paragraph (e) of this section. We will also consider all of the relevant provisions of §§ 416.924a, 416.924b, and 416.929.

(g) Acquiring and using information. In this domain, we consider how well you acquire or learn information, and how well you use the information you have learned.

(1) General.

(i) Learning and thinking begin at birth. You learn as you explore the world through sight, sound, taste, touch, and smell. As you play, you acquire concepts and learn that people, things, and activities have names. This lets you understand symbols, which prepares you to use language for learning. Using the concepts and symbols you have acquired through play and learning experiences, you should be able to learn to read, write, do arithmetic, and understand and use new information.

(ii) Thinking is the application or use of information you have learned. It involves being able to perceive relationships, reason, and make logical choices. People think in different ways. When you think in pictures, you may solve a problem by watching and imitating what another person does. When you think in words, you may solve a problem by using language to talk your way through it. You must also be able to use language to think about the world and to understand others and express yourself; e.g., to follow directions, ask for information, or explain something.

(2) Age group descriptors—

(i) Newborns and young infants (birth to attainment of age 1). At this age, you should show interest in, and explore, your environment. At first, your actions are random; for example, when you accidentally touch the mobile over your crib. Eventually, your actions should become deliberate and purposeful, as when you shake noisemaking toys like a bell or rattle. You should begin to recognize, and then anticipate, routine situations and events, as when you grin with expectation at the sight of your stroller. You should also recognize and gradually attach meaning to everyday sounds, as when you hear the telephone or your name. Eventually, you should recognize and respond to familiar words, including family names and what your favorite toys and activities are called.

(ii) Older infants and toddlers (age 1 to attainment of age 3). At this age, you are learning about the world around you. When you play, you should learn how objects go together in different ways. You should learn that by pretending, your actions can represent real things. This helps you understand that words represent things, and that words are simply symbols or names for toys, people, places, and activities. You should refer to yourself and things around you by pointing and eventually by naming. You should form concepts and solve simple problems through purposeful experimentation (e.g., taking toys apart), imitation, constructive play (e.g., building with blocks), and pretend play activities. You should begin to respond to increasingly complex instructions and questions, and to produce an increasing number of words and grammatically correct simple sentences and questions.

(iii) Preschool children (age 3 to attainment of age 6). When you are old enough to go to preschool or kindergarten, you should begin to learn and use the skills that will help you to read and write and do arithmetic when you are older. For example, listening to stories, rhyming words, and matching letters are skills needed for learning to read. Counting, sorting shapes, and building with blocks are skills needed to learn math. Painting, coloring, copying shapes, and using scissors are some of the skills needed in learning to write. Using words to ask questions, give answers, follow directions, describe things, explain what you mean, and tell stories allows you to acquire and share knowledge and experience of the world around you. All of these are called "readiness skills," and you should have them by the time you begin first grade.

(iv) School-age children (age 6 to attainment of age 12). When you are old enough to go to elementary and middle school, you should be able to learn to read, write, and do math, and discuss history and science. You will need to use these skills in academic situations to demonstrate what you have learned; e.g., by reading about various subjects and producing oral and written projects, solving mathematical problems, taking achievement tests, doing group work, and entering into class discussions. You will also need to use these skills in daily living situations at home and in the community (e.g., reading street signs, telling time, and making change). You should be able to use increasingly complex language (vocabulary and grammar) to share information and ideas with individuals or groups, by asking questions and expressing your own ideas, and by understanding and responding to the opinions of others.

(v) Adolescents (age 12 to attainment of age 18). In middle and high school, you should continue to demonstrate what you have learned in academic assignments (e.g., composition, classroom discussion, and laboratory experiments). You should also be able to use what you have learned in daily living situations without assistance (e.g., going to the store, using the library, and using public transportation). You should be able to comprehend and express both simple and complex ideas, using increasingly complex language (vocabulary and grammar) in learning and daily living situations (e.g., to obtain and convey information and ideas). You should also learn to apply these skills in practical ways that will help you enter the workplace after you finish school (e.g., carrying out instructions, preparing a job application, or being interviewed by a potential employer).

(3) Examples of limited functioning in acquiring and using information. The following examples describe some limitations we may consider in this domain. Your limitations may be different from the ones listed here. Also, the examples do not necessarily describe a "marked" or "extreme" limitation. Whether an example applies in your case may depend on your age and developmental stage; e.g., an example below may describe a limitation in an older child, but not a limitation in a younger one. As in any case, your limitations must result from your medically determinable impairment(s). However, we will consider all of the relevant information in your case record when we decide whether your medically determinable impairment(s) results in a "marked" or "extreme" limitation in this domain.

(i) You do not demonstrate understanding of words about space, size, or time; e.g., in/under, big/little, morning/night.

(ii) You cannot rhyme words or the sounds in words.

(iii) You have difficulty recalling important things you learned in school yesterday.

(iv) You have difficulty solving mathematics questions or computing arithmetic answers.

(v) You talk only in short, simple sentences and have difficulty explaining what you mean.

(h) Attending and completing tasks. In this domain, we consider how well you are able to focus and maintain your attention, and how well you begin, carry through, and finish your activities, including the pace at which you perform activities and the ease with which you change them.

(1) General.

(i) Attention involves regulating your levels of alertness and initiating and maintaining concentration. It involves the ability to filter out distractions and to remain focused on an activity or task at a consistent level of performance. This means focusing long enough to initiate and complete an activity or task, and changing focus once it is completed. It also means that if you lose or change your focus in the middle of a task, you are able to return to the task without other people having to remind you frequently to finish it.

(ii) Adequate attention is needed to maintain physical and mental effort and concentration on an activity or task. Adequate attention permits you to think and reflect before starting or deciding to stop an activity. In other words, you are able to look ahead and predict the possible outcomes of your actions before you act. Focusing your attention allows you to attempt tasks at an appropriate pace. It also helps you determine the time needed to finish a task within an appropriate timeframe.

(2) Age group descriptors—

(i) Newborns and young infants (birth to attainment of age 1). You should begin at birth to show sensitivity to your environment by responding to various stimuli (e.g., light, touch, temperature, movement). Very soon, you should be able to fix your gaze on a human face. You should stop your activity when you hear voices or sounds around you. Next, you should begin to attend to and follow various moving objects with your gaze, including people or toys. You should be listening to your family's conversations for longer and longer periods of time. Eventually, as you are able to move around and explore your environment, you should begin to play with people and toys for longer periods of time. You will still want to change activities frequently, but your interest in continuing interaction or a game should gradually expand.

(ii) Older infants and toddlers (age 1 to attainment of age 3). At this age, you should be able to attend to things that interest you and have adequate attention to complete some tasks by yourself. As a toddler, you should demonstrate sustained attention, such as when looking at picture books, listening to stories, or building with blocks, and when helping to put on your clothes.

(iii) Preschool children (age 3 to attainment of age 6). As a preschooler, you should be able to pay attention when you are spoken to directly, sustain attention to your play and learning activities, and concentrate on activities like putting puzzles together or completing art projects. You should also be able to focus long enough to do many more things by yourself, such as getting your clothes together and dressing yourself, feeding yourself, or putting away your toys. You should usually be able to wait your turn and to change your activity when a caregiver or teacher says it is time to do something else.

(iv) School-age children (age 6 to attainment of age 12). When you are of school age, you should be able to focus your attention in a variety of situations in order to follow directions, remember and organize your school materials, and complete classroom and homework assignments. You should be able to concentrate on details and not make careless mistakes in your work (beyond what would be expected in other children your age who do not have impairments). You should be able to change your activities or routines without distracting yourself or others, and stay on task and in place when appropriate. You should be able to sustain your attention well enough to participate in group sports, read by yourself, and complete family chores. You should also be able to complete a transition task (e.g., be ready for the school bus, change clothes after gym, change classrooms) without extra reminders and accommodation.

(v) Adolescents (age 12 to attainment of age 18). In your later years of school, you should be able to pay attention to increasingly longer presentations and discussions, maintain your concentration while reading textbooks, and independently plan and complete long-range academic projects. You should also be able to organize your materials and to plan your time in order to complete school tasks and assignments. In anticipation of entering the workplace, you should be able to maintain your attention on a task for extended periods of time, and not be unduly distracted by your peers or unduly distracting to them in a school or work setting.

(3) Examples of limited functioning in attending and completing tasks. The following examples describe some limitations we may consider in this domain. Your limitations may be different from the ones listed here. Also, the examples do not necessarily describe a "marked" or "extreme" limitation. Whether an example applies in your case may depend on your age and developmental stage; e.g., an example below may describe a limitation in an older child, but not a limitation in a younger one. As in any case, your limitations must result from your medically determinable impairment(s). However, we will consider all of the relevant information in your case record when we decide whether your medically determinable impairment(s) results in a "marked" or "extreme" limitation in this domain.

(i) You are easily startled, distracted, or overreactive to sounds, sights, movements, or touch.

(ii) You are slow to focus on, or fail to complete activities of interest to you, e.g., games or art projects.

(iii) You repeatedly become sidetracked from your activities or you frequently interrupt others.

(iv) You are easily frustrated and give up on tasks, including ones you are capable of completing.

(v) You require extra supervision to keep you engaged in an activity.

(i) Interacting and relating with others. In this domain, we consider how well you initiate and sustain emotional connections with others, develop and use the language of your community, cooperate with others, comply with rules, respond to criticism, and respect and take care of the possessions of others.

(1) General.

(i) Interacting means initiating and responding to exchanges with other people, for practical or social purposes. You interact with others by using facial expressions, gestures, actions, or words. You may interact with another person only once, as when asking a stranger for directions, or many times, as when describing your day at school to your parents. You may interact with people one-at-a-time, as when you are listening to another student in the hallway at school, or in groups, as when you are playing with others.

(ii) Relating to other people means forming intimate relationships with family members and with friends who are your age, and sustaining them over time. You may relate to individuals, such as your siblings, parents or best friend, or to groups, such as other children in childcare, your friends in school, teammates in sports activities, or people in your neighborhood.

(iii) Interacting and relating require you to respond appropriately to a variety of emotional and behavioral cues. You must be able to speak intelligibly and fluently so that others can understand you; participate in verbal turntaking and nonverbal exchanges; consider others' feelings and points of view; follow social rules for interaction and conversation; and respond to others appropriately and meaningfully.

(iv) Your activities at home or school or in your community may involve playing, learning, and working cooperatively with other children, one-at-a-time or in groups; joining voluntarily in activities with the other children in your school or community; and responding to persons in authority (e.g., your parent, teacher, bus driver, coach, or employer).

(2) Age group descriptors—

(i) Newborns and young infants (birth to attainment of age 1). You should begin to form intimate relationships at birth by gradually responding visually and vocally to your caregiver(s), through mutual gaze and vocal exchanges, and by physically molding your body to the caregiver's while being held. You should eventually initiate give-and-take games (such as pat-a-cake, peek-a-boo) with your caregivers, and begin to affect others through your own purposeful behavior (e.g., gestures and vocalizations). You should be able to respond to a variety of emotions (e.g., facial expressions and vocal tone changes). You should begin to develop speech by using vowel sounds and later consonants, first alone, and then in babbling.

(ii) Older infants and toddlers (age 1 to attainment of age 3). At this age, you are dependent upon your caregivers, but should begin to separate from them. You should be able to express emotions and respond to the feelings of others. You should begin initiating and maintaining interactions with adults, but also show interest in, then play alongside, and eventually interact with other children your age. You should be able to spontaneously communicate your wishes or needs, first by using gestures, and eventually by speaking words clearly enough that people who know you can understand what you say most of the time.

(iii) Preschool children (age 3 to attainment of age 6). At this age, you should be able to socialize with children as well as adults. You should begin to prefer playmates your own age and start to develop friendships with children who are your age. You should be able to use words instead of actions to express yourself, and also be better able to share, show affection, and offer to help. You should be able to relate to caregivers with increasing independence, choose your own friends, and play cooperatively with other children, one-at-a-time or in a group, without continual adult supervision. You should be able to initiate and participate in conversations, using increasingly complex vocabulary and grammar, and speaking clearly enough that both familiar and unfamiliar listeners can understand what you say most of the time.

(iv) School-age children (age 6 to attainment of age 12). When you enter school, you should be able to develop more lasting friendships with children who are your age. You should begin to understand how to work in groups to create projects and solve problems. You should have an increasing ability to understand another's point of view and to tolerate differences. You should be well able to talk to people of all ages, to share ideas, tell stories, and to speak in a manner that both familiar and unfamiliar listeners readily understand.

(v) Adolescents (age 12 to attainment of age 18). By the time you reach adolescence, you should be able to initiate and develop friendships with children who are your age and to relate appropriately to other children and adults, both individually and in groups. You should begin to be able to solve conflicts between yourself and peers or family members or adults outside your family. You should recognize that there are different social rules for you and your friends and for acquaintances or adults. You should be able to intelligibly express your feelings, ask for assistance in getting your needs met, seek information, describe events, and tell stories, in all kinds of environments (e.g., home, classroom, sports, extra-curricular activities, or part-time job), and with all types of people (e.g., parents, siblings, friends, classmates, teachers, employers, and strangers).

(3) Examples of limited functioning in interacting and relating with others. The following examples describe some limitations we may consider in this domain. Your limitations may be different from the ones listed here. Also, the examples do not necessarily describe a "marked" or "extreme" limitation. Whether an example applies in your case may depend on your age and developmental stage; e.g., an example below may describe a limitation in an older child, but not a limitation in a younger one. As in any case, your limitations must result from your medically determinable impairment(s). However, we will consider all of the relevant information in your case record when we decide whether your medically determinable impairment(s) results in a "marked" or "extreme" limitation in this domain.

(i) You do not reach out to be picked up and held by your caregiver.

(ii) You have no close friends, or your friends are all older or younger than you.

(iii) You avoid or withdraw from people you know, or you are overly anxious or fearful of meeting new people or trying new experiences.

(iv) You have difficulty playing games or sports with rules.

(v) You have difficulty communicating with others; e.g., in using verbal and nonverbal skills to express yourself, carrying on a conversation, or in asking others for assistance.

(vi) You have difficulty speaking intelligibly or with adequate fluency.

(j) Moving about and manipulating objects. In this domain, we consider how you move your body from one place to another and how you move and manipulate things. These are called gross and fine motor skills.

(1) General.

(i) Moving your body involves several different kinds of actions: Rolling your body; rising or pulling yourself from a sitting to a standing position; pushing yourself up; raising your head, arms, and legs, and twisting your hands and feet; balancing your weight on your legs and feet; shifting your weight while sitting or standing; transferring yourself from one surface to another; lowering yourself to or toward the floor as when bending, kneeling, stooping, or crouching; moving yourself forward and backward in space as when crawling, walking, or running, and negotiating different terrains (e.g., curbs, steps, and hills).

(ii) Moving and manipulating things involves several different kinds of actions: Engaging your upper and lower body to push, pull, lift, or carry objects from one place to another; controlling your shoulders, arms, and hands to hold or transfer objects; coordinating your eyes and hands to manipulate small objects or parts of objects.

(iii) These actions require varying degrees of strength, coordination, dexterity, pace, and physical ability to persist at the task. They also require a sense of where your body is and how it moves in space; the integration of sensory input with motor output; and the capacity to plan, remember, and execute controlled motor movements.

(2) Age group descriptors—

(i) Newborns and infants (birth to attainment of age 1). At birth, you should begin to explore your world by moving your body and by using your limbs. You should learn to hold your head up, sit, crawl, and stand, and sometimes hold onto a stable object and stand actively for brief periods. You should begin to practice your developing eye-hand control by reaching for objects or picking up small objects and dropping them into containers.

(ii) Older infants and toddlers (age 1 to attainment of age 3). At this age, you should begin to explore actively a wide area of your physical environment, using your body with steadily increasing control and independence from others. You should begin to walk and run without assistance, and climb with increasing skill. You should frequently try to manipulate small objects and to use your hands to do or get something that you want or need. Your improved motor skills should enable you to play with small blocks, scribble with crayons, and feed yourself.

(iii) Preschool children (age 3 to attainment of age 6). As a preschooler, you should be able to walk and run with ease. Your gross motor skills should let you climb stairs and playground equipment with little supervision, and let you play more independently; e.g., you should be able to swing by yourself and may start learning to ride a tricycle. Your fine motor skills should also be developing. You should be able to complete puzzles easily, string beads, and build with an assortment of blocks. You should be showing increasing control of crayons, markers, and small pieces in board games, and should be able to cut with scissors independently and manipulate buttons and other fasteners.

(iv) School-age children (age 6 to attainment of age 12). As a school-age child, your developing gross motor skills should let you move at an efficient pace about your school, home, and neighborhood. Your increasing strength and coordination should expand your ability to enjoy a variety of physical activities, such as running and jumping, and throwing, kicking, catching and hitting balls in informal play or organized sports. Your developing fine motor skills should enable you to do things like use many kitchen and household tools independently, use scissors, and write.

(v) Adolescents (age 12 to attainment of age 18). As an adolescent, you should be able to use your motor skills freely and easily to get about your school, the neighborhood, and the community. You should be able to participate in a full range of individual and group physical fitness activities. You should show mature skills in activities requiring eye-hand coordination, and should have the fine motor skills needed to write efficiently or type on a keyboard.

(3) Examples of limited functioning in moving about and manipulating objects. The following examples describe some limitations we may consider in this domain. Your limitations may be different from the ones listed here. Also, the examples do not necessarily describe a "marked" or "extreme" limitation. Whether an example applies in your case may depend on your age and developmental stage; e.g., an example below may describe a limitation in an older child, but not a limitation in a younger one. As in any case, your limitations must result from your medically determinable impairment(s). However, we will consider all of the relevant information in your case record when we decide whether your medically determinable impairment(s) results in a "marked" or "extreme" limitation in this domain.

(i) You experience muscle weakness, joint stiffness, or sensory loss (e.g., spasticity, hypotonia, neuropathy, or paresthesia) that interferes with your motor activities (e.g., you unintentionally drop things).

(ii) You have trouble climbing up and down stairs, or have jerky or disorganized locomotion or difficulty with your balance.

(iii) You have difficulty coordinating gross motor movements (e.g., bending, kneeling, crawling, running, jumping rope, or riding a bike).

(iv) You have difficulty with sequencing hand or finger movements.

(v) You have difficulty with fine motor movement (e.g., gripping or grasping objects).

(vi) You have poor eye-hand coordination when using a pencil or scissors.

(k) Caring for yourself. In this domain, we consider how well you maintain a healthy emotional and physical state, including how well you get your physical and emotional wants and needs met in appropriate ways; how you cope with stress and changes in your environment; and whether you take care of your own health, possessions, and living area.

(1) General.

(i) Caring for yourself effectively, which includes regulating yourself, depends upon your ability to respond to changes in your emotions and the daily demands of your environment to help yourself and cooperate with others in taking care of your personal needs, health and safety. It is characterized by a sense of independence and competence. The effort to become independent and competent should be observable throughout your childhood.

(ii) Caring for yourself effectively means becoming increasingly independent in making and following your own decisions. This entails relying on your own abilities and skills, and displaying consistent judgment about the consequences of caring for yourself. As you mature, using and testing your own judgment helps you develop confidence in your independence and competence. Caring for yourself includes using your independence and competence to meet your physical needs, such as feeding, dressing, toileting, and bathing, appropriately for your age.

(iii) Caring for yourself effectively requires you to have a basic understanding of your body, including its normal functioning, and of your physical and emotional needs. To meet these needs successfully, you must employ effective coping strategies, appropriate to your age, to identify and regulate your feelings, thoughts, urges, and intentions. Such strategies are based on taking responsibility for getting your needs met in an appropriate and satisfactory manner.

(iv) Caring for yourself means recognizing when you are ill, following recommended treatment, taking medication as prescribed, following safety rules, responding to your circumstances in safe and appropriate ways, making decisions that do not endanger yourself, and knowing when to ask for help from others.

(2) Age group descriptors—

(i) Newborns and infants (birth to attainment of age 1). Your sense of independence and competence begins in being able to recognize your body's signals (e.g., hunger, pain, discomfort), to alert your caregiver to your needs (e.g., by crying), and to console yourself (e.g., by sucking on your hand) until help comes. As you mature, your capacity for self-consolation should expand to include rhythmic behaviors (e.g., rocking). Your need for a sense of competence also emerges in things you try to do for yourself, perhaps before you are ready to do them, as when insisting on putting food in your mouth and refusing your caregiver's help.

(ii) Older infants and toddlers (age 1 to attainment of age 3). As you grow, you should be trying to do more things for yourself that increase your sense of independence and competence in your environment. You might console yourself by carrying a favorite blanket with you everywhere. You should be learning to cooperate with your caregivers when they take care of your physical needs, but you should also want to show what you can do; e.g., pointing to the bathroom, pulling off your coat. You should be experimenting with your independence by showing some degree of contrariness (e.g., "No! No!") and identity (e.g., hoarding your toys).

(iii) Preschool children (age 3 to attainment of age 6). You should want to take care of many of your physical needs by yourself (e.g., putting on your shoes, getting a snack), and also want to try doing some things that you cannot do fully (e.g., tying your shoes, climbing on a chair to reach something up high, taking a bath). Early in this age range, it may be easy for you to agree to do what your caregiver asks. Later, that may be difficult for you because you want to do things your way or not at all. These changes usually mean that you are more confident about your ideas and what you are able to do. You should also begin to understand how to control behaviors that are not good for you (e.g., crossing the street without an adult).

(iv) School-age children (age 6 to attainment of age 12). You should be independent in most day-to-day activities (e.g., dressing yourself, bathing yourself), although you may still need to be reminded sometimes to do these routinely. You should begin to recognize that you are competent in doing some activities and that you have difficulty with others. You should be able to identify those circumstances when you feel good about yourself and when you feel bad. You should begin to develop understanding of what is right and wrong, and what is acceptable and unacceptable behavior. You should begin to demonstrate consistent control over your behavior, and you should be able to avoid behaviors that are unsafe or otherwise not good for you. You should begin to imitate more of the behavior of adults you know.

(v) Adolescents (age 12 to attainment of age 18). You should feel more independent from others and should be increasingly independent in all of your day-to-day activities. You may sometimes experience confusion in the way you feel about yourself. You should begin to notice significant changes in your body's development, and this can result in anxiety or worrying about yourself and your body. Sometimes these worries can make you feel angry or frustrated. You should begin to discover appropriate ways to express your feelings, both good and bad (e.g., keeping a diary to sort out angry feelings or listening to music to calm yourself down). You should begin to think seriously about your future plans, and what you will do when you finish school.

(3) Examples of limited functioning in caring for yourself. The following examples describe some limitations we may consider in this domain. Your limitations may be different from the ones listed here. Also, the examples do not necessarily describe a "marked" or "extreme" limitation. Whether an example applies in your case may depend on your age and developmental stage; e.g., an example below may describe a limitation in an older child, but not a limitation in a younger one. As in any case, your limitations must result from your medically determinable impairment(s). However, we will consider all of the relevant information in your case record when we decide whether your medically determinable impairment(s) results in a "marked" or "extreme" limitation in this domain.

(i) You continue to place non-nutritive or inedible objects in your mouth.

(ii) You often use self-soothing activities showing developmental regression (e.g., thumbsucking, re-chewing food), or you have restrictive or stereotyped mannerisms (e.g., body rocking, headbanging).

(iii) You do not dress or bathe yourself appropriately for your age because you have an impairment(s) that affects this domain.

(iv) You engage in self-injurious behavior (e.g., suicidal thoughts or actions, self-inflicted injury, or refusal to take your medication), or you ignore safety rules.

(v) You do not spontaneously pursue enjoyable activities or interests.

(vi) You have disturbance in eating or sleeping patterns.

(*l*) Health and physical well-being. In this domain, we consider the cumulative physical effects of physical or mental impairments and their associated treatments or therapies on your functioning that we did not consider in paragraph (j) of this section. When your physical impairment(s), your mental impairment(s), or your combination of physical and mental impairments has physical effects that cause "extreme" limitation in your functioning, you will generally have an impairment(s) that "meets" or "medically equals" a listing.

(1) A physical or mental disorder may have physical effects that vary in kind and intensity, and may make it difficult for you to perform your activities independently or effectively. You may experience problems such as generalized weakness, dizziness, shortness of breath, reduced stamina, fatigue, psychomotor retardation, allergic reactions, recurrent infection, poor growth, bladder or bowel incontinence, or local or generalized pain.

(2) In addition, the medications you take (e.g., for asthma or depression) or the treatments you receive (e.g., chemotherapy or multiple surgeries) may have physical effects that also limit your performance of activities.

(3) Your illness may be chronic with stable symptoms, or episodic with periods of worsening and improvement. We will consider how you function during periods of worsening and how often and for how long these periods occur. You may be medically fragile and need intensive medical care to maintain your level of health and physical well-being. In any case, as a result of the illness itself, the medications or treatment you receive, or both, you may experience physical effects that interfere with your functioning in any or all of your activities.

(4) Examples of limitations in health and physical well-being. The following examples describe some limitations we may consider in this domain. Your limitations may be different from the ones listed here. Also, the examples do not necessarily describe a "marked" or "extreme" limitation. Whether an example applies

in your case may depend on your age and developmental stage; e.g., an example below may describe a limitation in an older child, but not a limitation in a younger one. As in any case, your limitations must result from your medically determinable impairment(s). However, we will consider all of the relevant information in your case record when we decide whether your medically determinable impairment(s) results in a "marked" or "extreme" limitation in this domain.

(i) You have generalized symptoms, such as weakness, dizziness, agitation (e.g., excitability), lethargy (e.g., fatigue or loss of energy or stamina), or psychomotor retardation because of your impairment(s).

(ii) You have somatic complaints related to your impairments (e.g., seizure or convulsive activity, headaches, incontinence, recurrent infections, allergies, changes in weight or eating habits, stomach discomfort, nausea, headaches, or insomnia).

(iii) You have limitations in your physical functioning because of your treatment (e.g., chemotherapy, multiple surgeries, chelation, pulmonary cleansing, or nebulizer treatments).

(iv) You have exacerbations from one impairment or a combination of impairments that interfere with your physical functioning.

(v) You are medically fragile and need intensive medical care to maintain your level of health and physical well-being.

(m) Examples of impairments that functionally equal the listings. The following are some examples of impairments and limitations that functionally equal the listings. Findings of equivalence based on the disabling functional limitations of a child's impairment(s) are not limited to the examples in this paragraph, because these examples do not describe all possible effects of impairments that might be found to functionally equal the listings. As with any disabling impairment, the duration requirement must also be met (see §§ 416.909 and 416.924(a)).

(1) Any condition that is disabling at the time of onset, requiring continuing surgical management within 12 months after onset as a life-saving measure or for salvage or restoration of function, and such major function is not restored or is not expected to be restored within 12 months after onset of this condition.

(2) Effective ambulation possible only with obligatory bilateral upper limb assistance.

(3) Any physical impairment(s) or combination of physical and mental impairments causing complete inability to function independently outside the area of one's home within age-appropriate norms.

(4) Requirement for 24–hour–a–day supervision for medical (including psychological) reasons.

(5) Major congenital organ dysfunction which could be expected to result in death within the first year of life without surgical correction, and the impairment is expected to be disabling (because of residual impairment following surgery, or the recovery time required, or both) until attainment of 1 year of age.

(n) Responsibility for determining functional equivalence. In cases where the State agency or other designee of the Commissioner makes the initial or reconsideration disability determination, a State agency medical or psychological consultant or other designee of the Commissioner (see § 416.1016 of this part) has the overall responsibility for determining functional equivalence. For cases in the disability hearing process or otherwise decided by a disability hearing officer, the responsibility for determining functional equivalence rests with either the disability hearing officer or, if the disability hearing officer's reconsideration determination is changed under § 416.1418 of this part, with the Associate Commissioner for Disability Programs or his or her delegate. For cases at the administrative law judge or Appeals Council level, the responsibility for deciding functional equivalence rests with the administrative law judge or Appeals Council.

[56 FR 5561, Feb. 11, 1991; 58 FR 47585, Sept. 9, 1993; 58 FR 52367, Oct. 7, 1993; 62 FR 6424, Feb. 11, 1997; 62 FR 13538, 13733, March 21, 1997; 65 FR 54782, Sept. 11, 2000; 65 FR 80308, Dec. 21, 2000; 66 FR 58045, Nov. 19, 2001; 71 FR 16460, March 31, 2006; 72 FR 59431, Oct. 19, 2007; 76 FR 24811, May 3, 2011; 80 FR 19530, April 13, 2015; 81 FR 37153, June 9, 2016; 82 FR 5880, Jan. 18, 2017]

§ 416.927 Evaluating opinion evidence for claims filed before March 27, 2017.

For claims filed (see § 416.325) before March 27, 2017, the rules in this section apply. For claims filed on or after March 27, 2017, the rules in § 416.920c apply.

(a) Definitions.

(1) Medical opinions. Medical opinions are statements from acceptable medical sources that reflect judgments about the nature and severity of your impairment(s), including your symptoms, diagnosis and prognosis, what you can still do despite impairment(s), and your physical or mental restrictions.

(2) Treating source. Treating source means your own acceptable medical source who provides you, or has provided you, with medical treatment or evaluation and who has, or has had, an ongoing treatment relationship with you. Generally, we will consider that you have an ongoing treatment relationship with an acceptable medical source when the medical evidence establishes that you see, or have seen, the source with a frequency consistent with accepted medical practice for the type of treatment and/or evaluation required for your medical condition(s). We may consider an acceptable medical source who has treated or evaluated you only a few times or only after long intervals (e.g., twice a year) to be your treating source if the nature and frequency of the treatment or evaluation is typical for

your condition(s). We will not consider an acceptable medical source to be your treating source if your relationship with the source is not based on your medical need for treatment or evaluation, but solely on your need to obtain a report in support of your claim for disability. In such a case, we will consider the acceptable medical source to be a nontreating source.

(b) How we consider medical opinions. In determining whether you are disabled, we will always consider the medical opinions in your case record together with the rest of the relevant evidence we receive. See § 416.920b.

(c) How we weigh medical opinions. Regardless of its source, we will evaluate every medical opinion we receive. Unless we give a treating source's medical opinion controlling weight under paragraph (c)(2) of this section, we consider all of the following factors in deciding the weight we give to any medical opinion.

(1) Examining relationship. Generally, we give more weight to the medical opinion of a source who has examined you than to the medical opinion of a medical source who has not examined you.

(2) Treatment relationship. Generally, we give more weight to medical opinions from your treating sources, since these sources are likely to be the medical professionals most able to provide a detailed, longitudinal picture of your medical impairment(s) and may bring a unique perspective to the medical evidence that cannot be obtained from the objective medical findings alone or from reports of individual examinations, such as consultative examinations or brief hospitalizations. If we find that a treating source's medical opinion on the issue(s) of the nature and severity of your impairment(s) is well-supported by medically acceptable clinical and laboratory diagnostic techniques and is not inconsistent with the other substantial evidence in your case record, we will give it controlling weight. When we do not give the treating source's medical opinion controlling weight, we apply the factors listed in paragraphs (c)(2)(i) and (c)(2)(ii) of this section, as well as the factors in paragraphs (c)(3) through (c)(6) of this section in determining the weight to give the medical opinion. We will always give good reasons in our notice of determination or decision for the weight we give your treating source's medical opinion.

(i) Length of the treatment relationship and the frequency of examination. Generally, the longer a treating source has treated you and the more times you have been seen by a treating source, the more weight we will give to the source's medical opinion. When the treating source has seen you a number of times and long enough to have obtained a longitudinal picture of your impairment, we will give the medical source's medical opinion more weight than we would give it if it were from a nontreating source.

(ii) Nature and extent of the treatment relationship. Generally, the more knowledge a treating source has about your impairment(s) the more weight we will give to the source's medical opinion. We will look at the treatment the source has provided and at the kinds and extent of examinations and testing the source has performed or ordered from specialists and independent laboratories. For example, if your ophthalmologist notices that you have complained of neck pain during your eye examinations, we will consider his or her medical opinion with respect to your neck pain, but we will give it less weight than that of another physician who has treated you for the neck pain. When the treating source has reasonable knowledge of your impairment(s), we will give the source's medical opinion more weight than we would give it if it were from a nontreating source.

(3) Supportability. The more a medical source presents relevant evidence to support a medical opinion, particularly medical signs and laboratory findings, the more weight we will give that medical opinion. The better an explanation a source provides for a medical opinion, the more weight we will give that medical opinion. Furthermore, because nonexamining sources have no examining or treating relationship with you, the weight we will give their medical opinions will depend on the degree to which they provide supporting explanations for their medical opinions. We will evaluate the degree to which these medical opinions consider all of the pertinent evidence in your claim, including medical opinions of treating and other examining sources.

(4) Consistency. Generally, the more consistent a medical opinion is with the record as a whole, the more weight we will give to that medical opinion.

(5) Specialization. We generally give more weight to the medical opinion of a specialist about medical issues related to his or her area of specialty than to the medical opinion of a source who is not a specialist.

(6) Other factors. When we consider how much weight to give to a medical opinion, we will also consider any factors you or others bring to our attention, or of which we are aware, which tend to support or contradict the medical opinion. For example, the amount of understanding of our disability programs and their evidentiary requirements that a medical source has, regardless of the source of that understanding, and the extent to which a medical source is familiar with the other information in your case record are relevant factors that we will consider in deciding the weight to give to a medical opinion.

(d) Medical source opinions on issues reserved to the Commissioner. Opinions on some issues, such as the examples that follow, are not medical opinions, as described in paragraph (a)(1) of this section, but are, instead, opinions on issues reserved to the Commissioner because they are administrative findings that are dispositive of a case; i.e., that would direct the determination or decision of disability.

(1) Opinions that you are disabled. We are responsible for making the determination or decision about whether you meet the statutory definition of disability. In so doing, we review all of the medical findings and other evidence that support a medical source's statement that you are disabled. A statement by a medical source that you are "disabled" or "unable to work" does not mean that we will determine that you are disabled.

(2) Other opinions on issues reserved to the Commissioner. We use medical sources, including your treating source, to provide evidence, including opinions, on the nature and severity of your impairment(s). Although we consider opinions from medical sources on issues such as whether your impairment(s) meets or equals the requirements of any impairment(s) in the Listing of Impairments in appendix 1 to subpart P of part 404 of this chapter, your residual functional capacity (see §§ 416.945 and 416.946), or the application of vocational factors, the final responsibility for deciding these issues is reserved to the Commissioner.

(3) We will not give any special significance to the source of an opinion on issues reserved to the Commissioner described in paragraphs (d)(1) and (d)(2) of this section.

(e) Evidence from our Federal or State agency medical or psychological consultants. The rules in § 416.913a apply except that when an administrative law judge gives controlling weight to a treating source's medical opinion, the administrative law judge is not required to explain in the decision the weight he or she gave to the prior administrative medical findings in the claim.

(f) Opinions from medical sources who are not acceptable medical sources and from nonmedical sources.

(1) Consideration. Opinions from medical sources who are not acceptable medical sources and from nonmedical sources may reflect the source's judgment about some of the same issues addressed in medical opinions from acceptable medical sources. Although we will consider these opinions using the same factors as listed in paragraph (c)(1) through (c)(6) in this section, not every factor for weighing opinion evidence will apply in every case because the evaluation of an opinion from a medical source who is not an acceptable medical source or from a nonmedical source depends on the particular facts in each case. Depending on the particular facts in a case, and after applying the factors for weighing opinion evidence, an opinion from a medical source who is not an acceptable medical source or from a nonmedical source may outweigh the medical opinion of an acceptable medical source, including the medical opinion of a treating source. For example, it may be appropriate to give more weight to the opinion of a medical source who is not an acceptable medical source if he or she has seen the individual more often than the treating source, has provided better supporting evidence and a better explanation for the opinion, and the opinion is more consistent with the evidence as a whole.

(2) Articulation. The adjudicator generally should explain the weight given to opinions from these sources or otherwise ensure that the discussion of the evidence in the determination or decision allows a claimant or subsequent reviewer to follow the adjudicator's reasoning, when such opinions may have an effect on the outcome of the case. In addition, when an adjudicator determines that an opinion from such a source is entitled to greater weight than a medical opinion from a treating source, the adjudicator must explain the reasons in the notice of decision in hearing cases and in the notice of determination (that is, in the personalized disability notice) at the initial and reconsideration levels, if the determination is less than fully favorable.

[56 FR 36968, Aug. 1, 1991; 62 FR 6428, Feb. 11, 1997; 62 FR 13538, March 21, 1997; 62 FR 38454, July 18, 1997; 65 FR 11880, March 7, 2000; 71 FR 16460, March 31, 2006; 75 FR 62683, Oct. 13, 2010; 76 FR 24811, May 3, 2011; 77 FR 10657, Feb. 23, 2012; 77 FR 43495, July 25, 2012; 82 FR 5880, Jan. 18, 2017; 82 FR 15133, March 27, 2017]

§ 416.928 [Reserved by 82 FR 5882]

[82 FR 5882, Jan. 18, 2017]

§ 416.929 How we evaluate symptoms, including pain.

(a) General. In determining whether you are disabled, we consider all your symptoms, including pain, and the extent to which your symptoms can reasonably be accepted as consistent with the objective medical evidence and other evidence. We will consider all of your statements about your symptoms, such as pain, and any description your medical sources or nonmedical sources may provide about how the symptoms affect your activities of daily living and your ability to work (or, if you are a child, your functioning). However, statements about your pain or other symptoms will not alone establish that you are disabled. There must be objective medical evidence from an acceptable medical source that shows you have a medical impairment(s) which could reasonably be expected to produce the pain or other symptoms alleged and that, when considered with all of the other evidence (including statements about the intensity and persistence of your pain or other symptoms which may reasonably be accepted as consistent with the medical signs and laboratory findings), would lead to a conclusion that you are disabled. In evaluating the intensity and persistence of your symptoms, including pain, we will consider all of the available evidence, including your medical history, the medical signs and laboratory findings, and statements about how your symptoms affect you. We will then determine the extent to which your alleged functional limitations and restrictions due to pain or other symptoms can reasonably be accepted as consistent with the medical signs and laboratory findings and other evidence to decide how your symptoms affect your ability to work (or if you are a child, your functioning).

(b) Need for medically determinable impairment that could reasonably be expected to produce your symptoms, such as pain. Your symptoms, such as pain, fatigue, shortness of breath, weakness, or nervousness, will not be found to affect your ability to do basic work activities unless medical signs or laboratory findings show that a medically determinable impairment(s) is present. Medical signs and laboratory findings, established by medically acceptable clinical or laboratory diagnostic techniques, must show the existence of a medical impairment(s) which results from anatomical, physiological, or psychological abnormalities and which could reasonably be expected to produce the pain or other symptoms alleged. In cases decided by a State agency (except in disability hearings under §§ 416.1414 through 416.1418 of this part and in fully favorable determinations made by State agency disability examiners alone under § 416.1015(c)(3) of this part), a State agency medical or psychological consultant or other medical or psychological consultant designated by the Commissioner directly participates in determining whether your medically determinable impairment(s) could reasonably be expected to produce your alleged symptoms. In the disability hearing process, a medical or psychological consultant may provide an advisory assessment to assist a disability hearing officer in determining whether your impairment(s) could reasonably be expected to produce your alleged symptoms. At the administrative law judge hearing or Appeals Council level of the administrative review process, the adjudicator(s) may ask for and consider the opinion of a medical or psychological expert concerning whether your impairment(s) could reasonably be expected to produce your alleged symptoms. The finding that your impairment(s) could reasonably be expected to produce your pain or other symptoms does not involve a determination as to the intensity, persistence, or functionally limiting effects of your symptoms. We will develop evidence regarding the possibility of a medically determinable mental impairment when we have information to suggest that such an impairment exists, and you allege pain or other symptoms but the medical signs and laboratory findings do not substantiate any physical impairment(s) capable of producing the pain or other symptoms.

(c) Evaluating the intensity and persistence of your symptoms, such as pain, and determining the extent to which your symptoms limit your capacity for work or, if you are a child, your functioning—

(1) General. When the medical signs or laboratory findings show that you have a medically determinable impairment(s) that could reasonably be expected to produce your symptoms, such as pain, we must then evaluate the intensity and persistence of your symptoms so that we can determine how your symptoms limit your capacity for work or, if you are a child, your functioning. In evaluating the intensity and persistence of your symptoms, we consider all of the available evidence from your medical sources and nonmedical sources about how your symptoms affect you. We also consider the medical opinions as explained in § 416.920c. Paragraphs (c)(2) through (c)(4) of this section explain further how we evaluate the intensity and persistence of your symptoms and how we determine the extent to which your symptoms limit your capacity for work (or, if you are a child, your functioning) when the medical signs or laboratory findings show that you have a medically determinable impairment(s) that could reasonably be expected to produce your symptoms, such as pain.

(2) Consideration of objective medical evidence. Objective medical evidence is evidence obtained from the application of medically acceptable clinical and laboratory diagnostic techniques, such as evidence of reduced joint motion, muscle spasm, sensory deficit or motor disruption. Objective medical evidence of this type is a useful indicator to assist us in making reasonable conclusions about the intensity and persistence of your symptoms and the effect those symptoms, such as pain, may have on your ability to work or, if you are a child, your functioning. We must always attempt to obtain objective medical evidence and, when it is obtained, we will consider it in reaching a conclusion as to whether you are disabled. However, we will not reject your statements about the intensity and persistence of your pain or other symptoms or about the effect your symptoms have on your ability to work (or if you are a child, to function independently, appropriately, and effectively in an age-appropriate manner) solely because the available objective medical evidence does not substantiate your statements.

(3) Consideration of other evidence. Because symptoms sometimes suggest a greater severity of impairment than can be shown by objective medical evidence alone, we will carefully consider any other information you may submit about your symptoms. The information that your medical sources or nonmedical sources provide about your pain or other symptoms (e.g., what may precipitate or aggravate your symptoms, what medications, treatments or other methods you use to alleviate them, and how the symptoms may affect your pattern of daily living) is also an important indicator of the intensity and persistence of your symptoms. Because symptoms, such as pain, are subjective and difficult to quantify, any symptom-related functional limitations and restrictions that your medical sources or nonmedical sources report, which can reasonably be accepted as consistent with the objective medical evidence and other evidence, will be taken into account as explained in paragraph (c)(4) of this section in reaching a conclusion as to whether you are disabled. We will consider all of the evidence presented, including infor-

mation about your prior work record, your statements about your symptoms, evidence submitted by your medical sources, and observations by our employees and other persons. If you are a child, we will also consider all of the evidence presented, including evidence submitted by your medical sources (such as physicians, psychologists, and therapists) and nonmedical sources (such as educational agencies and personnel, parents and other relatives, and social welfare agencies). Section 416.920c explains in detail how we consider medical opinions and prior administrative medical findings about the nature and severity of your impairment(s) and any related symptoms, such as pain. Factors relevant to your symptoms, such as pain, which we will consider include:

(i) Your daily activities;

(ii) The location, duration, frequency, and intensity of your pain or other symptoms;

(iii) Precipitating and aggravating factors;

(iv) The type, dosage, effectiveness, and side effects of any medication you take or have taken to alleviate your pain or other symptoms;

(v) Treatment, other than medication, you receive or have received for relief of your pain or other symptoms;

(vi) Any measures you use or have used to relieve your pain or other symptoms (e.g., lying flat on your back, standing for 15 to 20 minutes every hour, sleeping on a board, etc.); and

(vii) Other factors concerning your functional limitations and restrictions due to pain or other symptoms.

(4) How we determine the extent to which symptoms, such as pain, affect your capacity to perform basic work activities, or, if you are a child, your functioning). In determining the extent to which your symptoms, such as pain, affect your capacity to perform basic work activities (or if you are a child, your functioning), we consider all of the available evidence described in paragraphs (c)(1) through (c)(3) of this section. We will consider your statements about the intensity, persistence, and limiting effects of your symptoms, and we will evaluate your statements in relation to the objective medical evidence and other evidence, in reaching a conclusion as to whether you are disabled. We will consider whether there are any inconsistencies in the evidence and the extent to which there are any conflicts between your statements and the rest of the evidence, including your history, the signs and laboratory findings, and statements by your medical sources or other persons about how your symptoms affect you. Your symptoms, including pain, will be determined to diminish your capacity for basic work activities (or, if you are a child, your functioning) to the extent that your alleged functional limitations and restrictions due to symptoms, such as pain, can reasonably be accepted as consistent with the objective medical evidence and other evidence.

(d) Consideration of symptoms in the disability determination process. We follow a set order of steps to determine whether you are disabled. If you are not doing substantial gainful activity, we consider your symptoms, such as pain, to evaluate whether you have a severe physical or mental impairment(s), and at each of the remaining steps in the process. Sections 416.920 and 416.920a (for adults) and 416.924 (for children) explain this process in detail. We also consider your symptoms, such as pain, at the appropriate steps in our review when we consider whether your disability continues. The procedure we follow in reviewing whether your disability continues is explained in § 416.994 (for adults) and § 416.994a (for children).

(1) Need to establish a severe medically determinable impairment(s). Your symptoms, such as pain, fatigue, shortness of breath, weakness, or nervousness, are considered in making a determination as to whether your impairment or combination of impairment(s) is severe. (See § 416.920(c) for adults and § 416.924(c) for children.)

(2) Decision whether the Listing of Impairments is met. Some listed impairments include symptoms usually associated with those impairments as criteria. Generally, when a symptom is one of the criteria in a listing, it is only necessary that the symptom be present in combination with the other criteria. It is not necessary, unless the listing specifically states otherwise, to provide information about the intensity, persistence, or limiting effects of the symptom as long as all other findings required by the specific listing are present.

(3) Decision whether the Listing of Impairments is equaled. If your impairment is not the same as a listed impairment, we must determine whether your impairment(s) is medically equivalent to a listed impairment. Section 416.926 explains how we make this determination. Under § 416.926(b), we will consider medical equivalence based on all evidence in your case record about your impairment(s) and its effects on you that is relevant to this finding. In considering whether your symptoms, signs, and laboratory findings are medically equal to the symptoms, signs, and laboratory findings of a listed impairment, we will look to see whether your symptoms, signs, and laboratory findings are at least equal in severity to the listed criteria. However, we will not substitute your allegations of pain or other symptoms for a missing or deficient sign or laboratory finding to raise the severity of your impairment(s) to that of a listed impairment. (If you are a child and we cannot find equivalence based on medical evidence only, we will consider pain and other symptoms under §§ 416.924a and 416.926a in determining whether you have an impairment(s) that functionally equals the listings.) Regardless of whether you are an adult or a child, if the symptoms, signs, and

laboratory findings of your impairment(s) are equivalent in severity to those of a listed impairment, we will find you disabled. (If you are a child and your impairment(s) functionally equals the listings under the rules in § 416.926a, we will also find you disabled.) If they are not, we will consider the impact of your symptoms on your residual functional capacity if you are an adult. (See paragraph (d)(4) of this section.)

(4) Impact of symptoms (including pain) on residual functional capacity or, if you are a child, on your functioning. If you have a medically determinable severe physical or mental impairment(s), but your impairment(s) does not meet or equal an impairment listed in appendix 1 of subpart P of part 404 of this chapter, we will consider the impact of your impairment(s) and any related symptoms, including pain, or your residual functional capacity, if you are an adult, or, on your functioning if you are a child. (See §§ 416.945 and 416.924a–416.924b.)

[56 FR 57944, Nov. 14, 1991; 62 FR 6428, Feb. 11, 1997; 62 FR 13538, March 21, 1997; 62 FR 38454, July 18, 1997; 65 FR 16814, March 30, 2000; 65 FR 54789, Sept. 11, 2000; 71 FR 10431, March 1, 2006; 71 FR 16461, March 31, 2006; 75 FR 62683, Oct. 13, 2010; 76 FR 24811, May 3, 2011; 82 FR 5882, Jan. 18, 2017]

§ 416.930 Need to follow prescribed treatment.

(a) What treatment you must follow. In order to get benefits, you must follow treatment prescribed by your medical source(s) if this treatment is expected to restore your ability to work.

(b) When you do not follow prescribed treatment. If you do not follow the prescribed treatment without a good reason, we will not find you disabled or blind or, if you are already receiving benefits, we will stop paying you benefits.

(c) Acceptable reasons for failure to follow prescribed treatment. We will consider your physical, mental, educational, and linguistic limitations (including any lack of facility with the English language) when determining if you have an acceptable reason for failure to follow prescribed treatment. The following are examples of a good reason for not following treatment:

(1) The specific medical treatment is contrary to the established teaching and tenets of your religion.

(2) The prescribed treatment would be cataract surgery for one eye when there is an impairment of the other eye resulting in a severe loss of vision and is not subject to improvement through treatment.

(3) Surgery was previously performed with unsuccessful results and the same surgery is again being recommended for the same impairment.

(4) The treatment because of its enormity (e.g. open heart surgery), unusual nature (e.g., organ transplant), or other reason is very risky for you; or

(5) The treatment involves amputation of an extremity, or a major part of an extremity.

[59 FR 1636, Jan. 12, 1994; 62 FR 6429, Feb. 11, 1997; 82 FR 5882, Jan. 18, 2017]

PRESUMPTIVE DISABILITY AND BLINDNESS

§ 416.931 The meaning of presumptive disability or presumptive blindness.

If you are applying for supplemental security income benefits on the basis of disability or blindness, we may pay you benefits before we make a formal finding of whether or not you are disabled or blind. In order to receive these payments, we must find that you are presumptively disabled or presumptively blind. You must also meet all other eligibility requirements for supplemental security income benefits. We may make these payments to you for a period not longer than 6 months. These payments will not be considered overpayments if we later find that you are not disabled or blind.

[57 FR 53853, Nov. 13, 1992]

§ 416.932 When presumptive payments begin and end.

We may make payments to you on the basis of presumptive disability or presumptive blindness before we make a formal determination about your disability or blindness. The payments can not be made for more than 6 months. They start for a period of not more than 6 months beginning in the month we make the presumptive disability or presumptive blindness finding. The payments end the earliest of—

(a) The month in which we make a formal finding on whether or not you are disabled or blind;

(b) The month for which we make the sixth monthly payment based on presumptive disability or presumptive blindness to you; or

(c) The month in which you no longer meet one of the other eligibility requirements (e.g., your income exceeds the limits).

[57 FR 53853, Nov. 13, 1992]

§ 416.933 How we make a finding of presumptive disability or presumptive blindness.

We may make a finding of presumptive disability or presumptive blindness if the evidence available at the time we make the presumptive disability or presumptive blindness finding reflects a high degree of probability that you are disabled or blind. In the case of readily observable impairments (e.g., total blindness), we will find that you are disabled or blind for purposes of this section without medical or other evidence. For other impairments, a finding of disability or blindness must be based on medical evidence or other information that, though not sufficient for a formal determination of disability or blindness, is sufficient for us to find that there is a high degree of probability that you are disabled or blind. For example, for claims involving the human immunodeficiency virus (HIV), the Social Security Field Office may make a finding of presumptive disability if your medical source provides us with information that confirms that your disease manifestations meet the severity of listing-level criteria for HIV. Of course, regardless of the specific HIV manifestations, the State agency may make a finding of presumptive disability if the medical evidence or other information reflects a high degree of probability that you are disabled.

[58 FR 36063, July 2, 1993; 66 FR 58046, Nov. 19, 2001]

§ 416.934 Impairments that may warrant a finding of presumptive disability or presumptive blindness.

We may make findings of presumptive disability and presumptive blindness in specific impairment categories without obtaining any medical evidence. These specific impairment categories are—

(a) Amputation of a leg at the hip;

(b) Allegation of total deafness;

(c) Allegation of total blindness;

(d) Allegation of bed confinement or immobility without a wheelchair, walker, or crutches, due to a longstanding condition, excluding recent accident and recent surgery;

(e) Allegation of a stroke (cerebral vascular accident) more than 3 months in the past and continued marked difficulty in walking or using a hand or arm;

(f) Allegation of cerebral palsy, muscular dystrophy or muscle atrophy and marked difficulty in walking (e.g., use of braces), speaking, or coordination of the hands or arms.

(g) Allegation of Down syndrome.

(h) Allegation of intellectual disability or another neurodevelopmental impairment (for example, autism spectrum disorder) with complete inability to independently perform basic self-care activities (such as toileting, eating, dressing, or bathing) made by another person who files on behalf of a claimant who is at least 4 years old.

(i) Allegation of amyotrophic lateral sclerosis (ALS, Lou Gehrig's disease).

(j) Infants weighing less than 1200 grams at birth, until attainment of 1 year of age.

(k) Infants weighing at least 1200 but less than 2000 grams at birth, and who are small for gestational age, until attainment of 1 year of age. (Small for gestational age means a birth weight that is at or more than 2 standard deviations below the mean or that is less than the third growth percentile for the gestational age of the infant.)

[50 FR 5574, Feb. 11, 1985; 53 FR 3741, Feb. 9, 1988; 54 FR 53607, Dec. 29, 1989; 56 FR 65684, Dec. 18, 1991; 66 FR 58046, Nov. 19, 2001; 68 FR 51693, Aug. 28, 2003; 80 FR 19530, April 13, 2015; 81 FR 66178, Sept. 26, 2016]

DRUG ADDICTION AND ALCOHOLISM

§ 416.935 How we will determine whether your drug addiction or alcoholism is a contributing factor material to the determination of disability.

(a) General. If we find that you are disabled and have medical evidence of your drug addiction or alcoholism, we must determine whether your drug addiction or alcoholism is a contributing factor material to the determination of disability, unless we find that you are eligible for benefits because of your age or blindness.

(b) Process we will follow when we have medical evidence of your drug addiction or alcoholism.

(1) The key factor we will examine in determining whether drug addiction or alcoholism is a contributing factor material to the determination of disability is whether we would still find you disabled if you stopped using drugs or alcohol.

(2) In making this determination, we will evaluate which of your current physical and mental limitations, upon which we based our current disability determination, would remain if you stopped using drugs or alcohol and then determine whether any or all of your remaining limitations would be disabling.

(i) If we determine that your remaining limitations would not be disabling, we will find that your drug addiction or alcoholism is a contributing factor material to the determination of disability.

(ii) If we determine that your remaining limitations are disabling, you are disabled independent of your drug addiction or alcoholism and we will find that your drug addiction or alcoholism is not a contributing factor material to the determination of disability.

[60 FR 8151, Feb. 10, 1995]

§ 416.936 Treatment required for individuals whose drug addiction or alcoholism is a contributing factor material to the determination of disability.

(a) If we determine that you are disabled and drug addiction or alcoholism is a contributing factor material to the determination of disability, you must avail yourself of appropriate treatment for your drug addiction or alcoholism at an institution or facility approved by us when this treatment is available and make progress in your treatment. Generally, you are not expected to pay for this treatment. You will not be paid benefits for any month after the month we have notified you in writing that—

(1) You did not comply with the terms, conditions and requirements of the treatment which has been made available to you; or

(2) You did not avail yourself of the treatment after you had been notified that it is available to you.

(b) If your benefits are suspended for failure to comply with treatment requirements, your benefits can be reinstated in accordance with the rules in § 416.1326.

[60 FR 8151, Feb. 10, 1995]

§ 416.937 What we mean by appropriate treatment.

By appropriate treatment, we mean treatment for drug addiction or alcoholism that serves the needs of the individual in the least restrictive setting possible consistent with your treatment plan. These settings range from outpatient counseling services through a variety of residential treatment settings including acute detoxification, short-term intensive residential treatment, long-term therapeutic residential treatment, and long-term recovery houses. Appropriate treatment is determined with the involvement of a State licensed or certified addiction professional on the basis of a detailed assessment of the individual's presenting symptomatology, psychosocial profile, and other relevant factors. This assessment may lead to a determination that more than one treatment modality is appropriate for the individual. The treatment will be provided or overseen by an approved institution or facility. This treatment may include (but is not limited to)—

(a) Medical examination and medical management;

(b) Detoxification;

(c) Medication management to include substitution therapy (e.g., methadone);

(d) Psychiatric, psychological, psychosocial, vocational, or other substance abuse counseling in a residential or outpatient treatment setting; or

(e) Relapse prevention.

[60 FR 8151, Feb. 10, 1995]

§ 416.938 What we mean by approved institutions or facilities.

Institutions or facilities that we may approve include—

(a) An institution or facility that furnishes medically recognized treatment for drug addiction or alcoholism in conformity with applicable Federal or State laws and regulations;

(b) An institution or facility used by or licensed by an appropriate State agency which is authorized to refer persons for treatment of drug addiction or alcoholism;

(c) State licensed or certified care providers;

(d) Programs accredited by the Commission on Accreditation for Rehabilitation Facilities (CARF) and/or the Joint Commission for the Accreditation of Healthcare Organizations (JCAHO) for the treatment of drug addiction or alcoholism;

(e) Medicare or Medicaid certified care providers; or

(f) Nationally recognized self-help drug addiction or alcoholism recovery programs (e.g., Alcoholics Anonymous or Narcotics Anonymous) when participation in these programs is specifically prescribed by a treatment professional at an institution or facility described in paragraphs (a) through (e) of this section as part of an individual's treatment plan.

[60 FR 8151, Feb. 10, 1995]

§ 416.939 How we consider whether treatment is available.

Our determination about whether treatment is available to you for your drug addiction or your alcoholism will depend upon—

(a) The capacity of an approved institution or facility to admit you for appropriate treatment;

(b) The location of the approved institution or facility, or the place where treatment, services or resources could be provided to you;

(c) The availability and cost of transportation for you to the place of treatment;

(d) Your general health, including your ability to travel and capacity to understand and follow the prescribed treatment;

(e) Your particular condition and circumstances; and

(f) The treatment that is prescribed for your drug addiction or alcoholism.

[60 FR 8151, Feb. 10, 1995]

§ 416.940 Evaluating compliance with the treatment requirements.

(a) General. Generally, we will consider information from the treatment institution or facility to evaluate your compliance with your treatment plan. The treatment institution or facility will—

(1) Monitor your attendance at and participation in treatment sessions;

(2) Provide reports of the results of any clinical testing (such as, hematological or urinalysis studies for individuals with drug addiction and hematological studies and breath analysis for individuals with alcoholism) when such tests are likely to yield important information;

(3) Provide observational reports from the treatment professionals familiar with your individual case (subject to verification and Federal confidentiality requirements); or

(4) Provide their assessment or views on your noncompliance with treatment requirements.

(b) Measuring progress. Generally, we will consider information from the treatment institution or facility to evaluate your progress in completing your treatment plan. Examples of milestones for measuring your progress with the treatment which has been prescribed for your drug addiction or alcoholism may include (but are not limited to)—

(1) Abstinence from drug or alcohol use (initial progress may include significant reduction in use);

(2) Consistent attendance at and participation in treatment sessions;

(3) Improved social functioning and levels of gainful activity;

(4) Participation in vocational rehabilitation activities; or

(5) Avoidance of criminal activity.

[60 FR 8151, Feb. 10, 1995]

§ 416.941 Establishment and use of referral and monitoring agencies.

We will contract with one or more agencies in each of the States and the District of Columbia to provide services to individuals whose disabilities are based on a determination that drug addiction or alcoholism is a contributing factor material to the determination of disability (as described in § 416.935) and to submit information to us which we will use to make decisions about these individuals' benefits. These agencies will be known as referral and monitoring agencies. Their duties and responsibilities include (but are not limited to)—

(a) Identifying appropriate treatment placements for individuals we refer to them;

(b) Referring these individuals for treatment;

(c) Monitoring the compliance and progress with the appropriate treatment of these individuals; and

(d) Promptly reporting to us any individual's failure to comply with treatment requirements as well as failure to achieve progress through the treatment.

[60 FR 8152, Feb. 10, 1995]

RESIDUAL FUNCTIONAL CAPACITY

§ 416.945 Your residual functional capacity.

(a) General—

(1) Residual functional capacity assessment. Your impairment(s), and any related symptoms, such as pain, may cause physical and mental limitations that affect what you can do in a work setting. Your residual functional capacity is the most you can still do despite your limitations. We will assess your residual functional capacity based on all the relevant evidence in your case record. (See § 416.946.)

(2) If you have more than one impairment. We will consider all of your medically determinable impairments of which we are aware, including your medically determinable impairments that are not "severe," as explained in §§ 416.920(c), 416.921, and 416.923, when we assess your residual functional capacity. (See paragraph (e) of this section.)

(3) Evidence we use to assess your residual functional capacity. We will assess your residual functional capacity based on all of the relevant medical and other evidence. In general, you are responsible for providing the evidence we will use to make a finding about your residual functional capacity. (See § 416.912(c).) However, before we make a determination that you are not disabled, we are responsible for developing your complete medical history, including arranging for a consultative examination(s) if necessary, and making every reasonable effort to help you get medical reports from your own medical sources. (See §§ 416.912(d) through (e).) We will consider any statements about what you can still do that have been provided by medical sources, whether or not they are based on formal medical examinations. (See § 416.913.) We will also consider descriptions and observations of your limitations from your impairment(s), including limitations that result from your symptoms, such as pain, provided by you, your family, neighbors, friends, or other persons. (See paragraph (e) of this section and § 416.929.)

(4) What we will consider in assessing residual functional capacity. When we assess your residual functional capacity, we will consider your ability to meet the physical, mental, sensory, and other requirements of work, as described in paragraphs (b), (c), and (d) of this section.

(5) How we will use our residual functional capacity assessment.

(i) We will first use our residual functional capacity assessment at step four of the sequential evaluation process to decide if you can do your past relevant work. (See §§ 416.920(f) and 416.960(b).)

(ii) If we find that you cannot do your past relevant work, you do not have any past relevant work, or if we use the procedures in § 416.920(h) and § 416.962 does not apply, we will use the same assessment of your residual functional capacity at step five of the sequential evaluation process to decide if you can adjust to any other work that exists in the national economy. (See §§ 416.920(g) and 416.966.) At this step, we will not use our assessment of your residual functional capacity alone to decide if you are disabled. We will use the guidelines in §§ 416.960 through 416.969a, and consider our residual functional capacity assessment together with the information about your vocational background to make our disability determination or decision. For our rules on residual functional capacity assessment in deciding whether your disability continues or ends, see § 416.994.

(b) Physical abilities. When we assess your physical abilities, we first assess the nature and extent of your physical limitations and then determine your residual functional capacity for work activity on a regular and continuing basis. A limited ability to perform certain physical demands of work activity, such as sitting, standing, walking, lifting, carrying, pushing, pulling, or other physical functions (including manipulative or postural functions, such as reaching, handling, stooping or crouching), may reduce your ability to do past work and other work.

(c) Mental abilities. When we assess your mental abilities, we first assess the nature and extent of your mental limitations and restrictions and then determine your residual functional capacity for work activity on a regular and continuing basis. A limited ability to carry out certain mental activities, such as limitations in understanding, remembering, and carrying out instructions, and in responding appropriately to supervision, coworkers, and work pressures in a work setting, may reduce your ability to do past work and other work.

(d) Other abilities affected by impairment(s). Some medically determinable impairment(s), such as skin impairment(s), epilepsy, impairment(s) of vision, hearing or other senses, and impairment(s) which impose environmental restrictions, may cause limitations and restrictions which affect other work-related abilities. If you have this type of impairment(s), we consider any resulting limitations and restrictions which may reduce your ability to do past work and other work in deciding your residual functional capacity.

(e) Total limiting effects. When you have a severe impairment(s), but your symptoms, signs, and laboratory findings do not meet or equal those of a listed impairment in appendix 1 of subpart P of part 404 of this chapter, we will consider the limiting effects of all your impairment(s), even those that are not severe, in determining your residual functional capacity. Pain or other symptoms may cause a limitation of function beyond that which can be determined on the basis of the anatomical, physiological or psychological abnormalities considered alone; e.g., someone with a low back disorder may be fully capable of the physical demands consistent with those of sustained medium work activity, but another person with the same disorder, because of pain, may not be capable of more than the physical demands consistent with those of light work activity on a sustained basis. In assessing the total limiting effects of your impairment(s) and any related symptoms, we will consider all of the medical and nonmedical evidence, including the information described in § 416.929(c).

[56 FR 36970, Aug. 1, 1991; 56 FR 57947, Nov. 14, 1991; 68 FR 51165, Aug. 26, 2003; 77 FR 10657, Feb. 23, 2012; 77 FR 43495, July 25, 2012]

§ 416.946 Responsibility for assessing your residual functional capacity.

(a) Responsibility for assessing residual functional capacity at the State agency. When a State agency medical or psychological consultant and a State agency disability examiner make the disability determination as provided in § 416.1015(c)(1) of this part, a State agency medical or psychological consultant(s) is responsible for assessing your residual functional capacity. When a State agency disability examiner makes a disability determination alone as provided in § 416.1015(c)(3), the disability examiner is responsible for assessing your residual functional capacity.

(b) Responsibility for assessing residual functional capacity in the disability hearings process. If your case involves a disability hearing under § 416.1414, a disability hearing officer is responsible for assessing your residual functional capacity. However, if the disability hearing officer's reconsidered determination is changed under § 416.1418, the Associate Commissioner for the Office of Disability Determinations or his or her delegate is responsible for assessing your residual functional capacity.

(c) Responsibility for assessing residual functional capacity at the administrative law judge hearing or Appeals Council level. If your case is at the administrative law judge hearing level or at the Appeals Council review level, the administrative law judge or the administrative appeals judge at the Appeals Council (when the Appeals Council makes a decision) is responsible for assessing your residual functional capacity.

(d) [Reserved by 76 FR 24812]

[51 FR 304, Jan. 3, 1986; 52 FR 33928, Sept. 9, 1987; 56 FR 36970, Aug. 1, 1991; 62 FR 38454, July 18, 1997; 68 FR 51165, Aug. 26, 2003; 71 FR 16461, March 31, 2006; 75 FR 62683, Oct. 13, 2010; 76 FR 24812, May 3, 2011]

VOCATIONAL CONSIDERATIONS

§ 416.960 When we will consider your vocational background.

(a) General. If you are age 18 or older and applying for supplemental security income benefits based on disability, and we cannot decide whether you are disabled at one of the first three steps of the sequential evaluation process (see § 416.920), we will consider your residual functional capacity together with your vocational background, as discussed in paragraphs (b) and (c) of this section.

(b) Past relevant work. We will first compare our assessment of your residual functional capacity with the physical and mental demands of your past relevant work. See § 416.920(h) for an exception to this rule.

(1) Definition of past relevant work. Past relevant work is work that you have done within the past 15 years, that was substantial gainful activity, and that

lasted long enough for you to learn to do it. (See § 416.965(a).)

(2) Determining whether you can do your past relevant work. We will ask you for information about work you have done in the past. We may also ask other people who know about your work. (See § 416.965(b).) We may use the services of vocational experts or vocational specialists, or other resources, such as the "Dictionary of Occupational Titles" and its companion volumes and supplements, published by the Department of Labor, to obtain evidence we need to help us determine whether you can do your past relevant work, given your residual functional capacity. A vocational expert or specialist may offer relevant evidence within his or her expertise or knowledge concerning the physical and mental demands of a claimant's past relevant work, either as the claimant actually performed it or as generally performed in the national economy. Such evidence may be helpful in supplementing or evaluating the accuracy of the claimant's description of his past work. In addition, a vocational expert or specialist may offer expert opinion testimony in response to a hypothetical question about whether a person with the physical and mental limitations imposed by the claimant's medical impairment(s) can meet the demands of the claimant's previous work, either as the claimant actually performed it or as generally performed in the national economy.

(3) If you can do your past relevant work. If we find that you have the residual functional capacity to do your past relevant work, we will determine that you can still do your past work and are not disabled. We will not consider your vocational factors of age, education, and work experience or whether your past relevant work exists in significant numbers in the national economy.

(c) Other work.

(1) If we find that your residual functional capacity does not enable you to do any of your past relevant work or if we use the procedures in § 416.920(h), we will use the same residual functional capacity assessment when we decide if you can adjust to any other work. We will look at your ability to adjust to other work by considering your residual functional capacity and the vocational factors of age, education, and work experience, as appropriate in your case. (See § 416.920(h) for an exception to this rule.) Any other work (jobs) that you can adjust to must exist in significant numbers in the national economy (either in the region where you live or in several regions in the country).

(2) In order to support a finding that you are not disabled at this fifth step of the sequential evaluation process, we are responsible for providing evidence that demonstrates that other work exists in significant numbers in the national economy that you can do, given your residual functional capacity and vocational factors. We are not responsible for providing additional evidence about your residual functional capacity because we will use the same residual functional capacity assessment that we used to determine if you can do your past relevant work.

[55 FR 11011, March 26, 1990; 68 FR 51166, Aug. 26, 2003; 77 FR 43495, July 25, 2012]

§ 416.961 [Reserved]

[68 FR 51166, Aug. 26, 2003]

§ 416.962 Medical-vocational profiles showing an inability to make an adjustment to other work.

(a) If you have done only arduous unskilled physical labor. If you have no more than a marginal education (see § 416.964) and work experience of 35 years or more during which you did only arduous unskilled physical labor, and you are not working and are no longer able to do this kind of work because of a severe impairment(s) (see §§ 416.920(c), 416.921, and 416.923), we will consider you unable to do lighter work, and therefore, disabled.

Example to paragraph (a): B is a 58–year–old miner's helper with a fourth grade education who has a lifelong history of unskilled arduous physical labor. B says that he is disabled because of arthritis of the spine, hips, and knees, and other impairments. Medical evidence shows a "severe" combination of impairments that prevents B from performing his past relevant work. Under these circumstances, we will find that B is disabled.

(b) If you are at least 55 years old, have no more than a limited education, and have no past relevant work experience. If you have a severe, medically determinable impairment(s) (see §§ 416.920(c), 416.921, and 416.923), are of advanced age (age 55 or older, see § 416.963), have a limited education or less (see § 416.964), and have no past relevant work experience (see § 416.965), we will find you disabled. If the evidence shows that you meet this profile, we will not need to assess your residual functional capacity or consider the rules in appendix 2 to subpart P of part 404 of this chapter.

[68 FR 51166, Aug. 26, 2003]

§ 416.963 Your age as a vocational factor.

(a) General. "Age" means your chronological age. When we decide whether you are disabled under § 416.920(g)(1), we will consider your chronological age in combination with your residual functional capacity, education, and work experience. We will not consider your ability to adjust to other work on the basis of your age alone. In determining the extent to which age affects a person's ability to adjust to other work, we consider advancing age to be an increasingly limiting factor in the person's ability to make such an adjustment, as we explain in paragraphs (c) through (e) of this section. If you are unemployed but you still have the ability to adjust to other work, we will find that you are not disabled. In paragraphs (b) through (e) of this section and in appendix 2 of subpart P of part 404 of this chapter, we explain in more detail how we consider your age as a vocational factor.

(b) How we apply the age categories. When we make a finding about your ability to do other work under § 416.920(f)(1), we will use the age categories in paragraphs (c) through (e) of this section. We will use each of the age categories that applies to you during the period for which we must determine if you are disabled. We will not apply the age categories mechanically in a borderline situation. If you are within a few days to a few months of reaching an older age category, and using the older age category would result in a determination or decision that you are disabled, we will consider whether to use the older age category after evaluating the overall impact of all the factors of your case.

(c) Younger person. If you are a younger person (under age 50), we generally do not consider that your age will seriously affect your ability to adjust to other work. However, in some circumstances, we consider that persons age 45–49 are more limited in their ability to adjust to other work than persons who have not attained age 45. See Rule 201.17 in appendix 2 of subpart P of part 404 of this chapter.

(d) Person closely approaching advanced age. If you are closely approaching advanced age (age 50–54), we will consider that your age along with a severe impairment(s) and limited work experience may seriously affect your ability to adjust to other work.

(e) Person of advanced age. We consider that at advanced age (age 55 or older), age significantly affects a person's ability to adjust to other work. We have special rules for persons of advanced age and for persons in this category who are closely approaching retirement age (age 60 or older). See § 416.968(d)(4).

(f) Information about your age. We will usually not ask you to prove your age. However, if we need to know your exact age to determine whether you get disability benefits, we will ask you for evidence of your age.

[65 FR 18001, April 6, 2000; 68 FR 51166, Aug. 26, 2003; 73 FR 64197, Oct. 29, 2008]

§ 416.964 Your education as a vocational factor.

(a) General. Education is primarily used to mean formal schooling or other training which contributes to your ability to meet vocational requirements, for example, reasoning ability, communication skills, and arithmetical ability. However, if you do not have formal schooling, this does not necessarily mean that you are uneducated or lack these abilities. Past work experience and the kinds of responsibilities you had when you were working may show that you have intellectual abilities, although you may have little formal education. Your daily activities, hobbies, or the results of testing may also show that you have significant intellectual ability that can be used to work.

(b) How we evaluate your education. The importance of your educational background may depend upon how much time has passed between the completion of your formal education and the beginning of your physical or mental impairment(s) and by what you have done with your education in a work or other setting. Formal education that you completed many years before your impairment began, or unused skills and knowledge that were a part of your formal education, may no longer be useful or meaningful in terms of your ability to work. Therefore, the numerical grade level that you completed in school may not represent your actual educational abilities. These may be higher or lower. However, if there is no other evidence to contradict it, we will use your numerical grade level to determine your educational abilities. The term education also includes how well you are able to communicate in English since this ability is often acquired or improved by education. In evaluating your educational level, we use the following categories:

(1) Illiteracy. Illiteracy means the inability to read or write. We consider someone illiterate if the person cannot read or write a simple message such as instructions or inventory lists even though the person can sign his or her name. Generally, an illiterate person has had little or no formal schooling.

(2) Marginal education. Marginal education means ability in reasoning, arithmetic, and language skills which are needed to do simple, unskilled types of jobs. We generally consider that formal schooling at a 6th grade level or less is a marginal education.

(3) Limited education. Limited education means ability in reasoning, arithmetic, and language skills, but not enough to allow a person with these educational qualifications to do most of the more complex job duties needed in semi-skilled or skilled jobs. We generally consider that a 7th grade through the 11th grade level of formal education is a limited education.

(4) High school education and above. High school education and above means abilities in reasoning, arithmetic, and language skills acquired through formal schooling at a 12th grade level or above. We generally consider that someone with these educational abilities can do semi-skilled through skilled work.

(5) Inability to communicate in English. Since the ability to speak, read and understand English is generally learned or increased at school, we may consider this an educational factor. Because English is the dominant language of the country, it may be difficult for someone who doesn't speak and understand English to do a job, regardless of the amount of education the person may have in another language. Therefore, we consider a person's ability to communicate in En-

glish when we evaluate what work, if any, he or she can do. It generally doesn't matter what other language a person may be fluent in.

(6) Information about your education. We will ask you how long you attended school and whether you are able to speak, understand, read and write in English and do at least simple calculations in arithmetic. We will also consider other information about how much formal or informal education you may have had through your previous work, community projects, hobbies, and any other activities which might help you to work.

§ 416.965 Your work experience as a vocational factor.

(a) General. Work experience means skills and abilities you have acquired through work you have done which show the type of work you may be expected to do. Work you have already been able to do shows the kind of work that you may be expected to do. We consider that your work experience applies when it was done within the last 15 years, lasted long enough for you to learn to do it, and was substantial gainful activity. We do not usually consider that work you did 15 years or more before the time we are deciding whether you are disabled applies. A gradual change occurs in most jobs so that after 15 years it is no longer realistic to expect that skills and abilities acquired in a job done then continue to apply. The 15–year guide is intended to insure that remote work experience is not currently applied. If you have no work experience or worked only off-and-on or for brief periods of time during the 15–year period, we generally consider that these do not apply. If you have acquired skills through your past work, we consider you to have these work skills unless you cannot use them in other skilled or semi-skilled work that you can now do. If you cannot use your skills in other skilled or semi-skilled work, we will consider your work background the same as unskilled. However, even if you have no work experience, we may consider that you are able to do unskilled work because it requires little or no judgment and can be learned in a short period of time.

(b) Information about your work. Under certain circumstances, we will ask you about the work you have done in the past. If you cannot give us all of the information we need, we may try, with your permission, to get it from your employer or other person who knows about your work, such as a member of your family or a co-worker. When we need to consider your work experience to decide whether you are able to do work that is different from what you have done in the past, we will ask you to tell us about all of the jobs you have had in the last 15 years. You must tell us the dates you worked, all of the duties you did, and any tools, machinery, and equipment you used. We will need to know about the amount of walking, standing, sitting, lifting and carrying you did during the work day, as well as any other physical or mental duties of your job. If all of your work in the past 15 years has been arduous and unskilled, and you have very little education, we will ask you to tell us about all of your work from the time you first began working. This information could help you to get disability benefits.

[77 FR 43495, July 25, 2012]

§ 416.966 Work which exists in the national economy.

(a) General. We consider that work exists in the national economy when it exists in significant numbers either in the region where you live or in several other regions of the country. It does not matter whether—

(1) Work exists in the immediate area in which you live;

(2) A specific job vacancy exists for you; or

(3) You would be hired if you applied for work.

(b) How we determine the existence of work. Work exists in the national economy when there is a significant number of jobs (in one or more occupations) having requirements which you are able to meet with your physical or mental abilities and vocational qualifications. Isolated jobs that exist only in very limited numbers in relatively few locations outside of the region where you live are not considered work which exists in the national economy. We will not deny you disability benefits on the basis of the existence of these kinds of jobs. If work that you can do does not exist in the national economy, we will determine that you are disabled. However, if work that you can do does exist in the national economy, we will determine that you are not disabled.

(c) Inability to obtain work. We will determine that you are not disabled if your residual functional capacity and vocational abilities make it possible for you to do work which exists in the national economy, but you remain unemployed because of—

(1) Your inability to get work;

(2) Lack of work in your local area;

(3) The hiring practices of employers;

(4) Technological changes in the industry in which you have worked;

(5) Cyclical economic conditions;

(6) No job openings for you;

(7) You would not actually be hired to do work you could otherwise do, or;

(8) You do not wish to do a particular type of work.

(d) Administrative notice of job data. When we determine that unskilled, sedentary, light, and medium jobs exist in the national economy (in significant numbers either in the region where you live or in several regions of the country), we will take administrative notice of reliable job information available from various governmental and other publications. For example, we will take notice of—

(1) Dictionary of Occupational Titles, published by the Department of Labor;

(2) County Business Patterns, published by the Bureau of the Census;

(3) Census Reports, also published by the Bureau of the Census;

(4) Occupational Analyses prepared for the Social Security Administration by various State employment agencies; and

(5) Occupational Outlook Handbook, published by the Bureau of Labor Statistics.

(e) Use of vocational experts and other specialists. If the issue in determining whether you are disabled is whether your work skills can be used in other work and the specific occupations in which they can be used, or there is a similarly complex issue, we may use the services of a vocational expert or other specialist. We will decide whether to use a vocational expert or other specialist.

§ 416.967 Physical exertion requirements.

To determine the physical exertion requirements of work in the national economy, we classify jobs as sedentary, light, medium, heavy, and very heavy. These terms have the same meaning as they have in the Dictionary of Occupational Titles, published by the Department of Labor. In making disability determinations under this subpart, we use the following definitions:

(a) Sedentary work. Sedentary work involves lifting no more than 10 pounds at a time and occasionally lifting or carrying articles like docket files, ledgers, and small tools. Although a sedentary job is defined as one which involves sitting, a certain amount of walking and standing is often necessary in carrying out job duties. Jobs are sedentary if walking and standing are required occasionally and other sedentary criteria are met.

(b) Light work. Light work involves lifting no more than 20 pounds at a time with frequent lifting or carrying of objects weighing up to 10 pounds. Even though the weight lifted may be very little, a job is in this category when it requires a good deal of walking or standing, or when it involves sitting most of the time with some pushing and pulling of arm or leg controls. To be considered capable of performing a full or wide range of light work, you must have the ability to do substantially all of these activities. If someone can do light work, we determine that he or she can also do sedentary work, unless there are additional limiting factors such as loss of fine dexterity or inability to sit for long periods of time.

(c) Medium work. Medium work involves lifting no more than 50 pounds at a time with frequent lifting or carrying of objects weighing up to 25 pounds. If someone can do medium work, we determine that he or she can also do sedentary and light work.

(d) Heavy work. Heavy work involves lifting no more than 100 pounds at a time with frequent lifting or carrying of objects weighing up to 50 pounds. If someone can do heavy work, we determine that he or she can also do medium, light, and sedentary work.

(e) Very heavy work. Very heavy work involves lifting objects weighing more than 100 pounds at a time with frequent lifting or carrying of objects weighing 50 pounds or more. If someone can do very heavy work, we determine that he or she can also do heavy, medium, light, and sedentary work.

§ 416.968 Skill requirements.

In order to evaluate your skills and to help determine the existence in the national economy of work you are able to do, occupations are classified as unskilled, semi-skilled, and skilled. In classifying these occupations, we use materials published by the Department of Labor. When we make disability determinations under this subpart, we use the following definitions:

(a) Unskilled work. Unskilled work is work which needs little or no judgment to do simple duties that can be learned on the job in a short period of time. The job may or may not require considerable strength. For example, we consider jobs unskilled if the primary work duties are handling, feeding and offbearing (that is, placing or removing materials from machines which are automatic or operated by others), or machine tending, and a person can usually learn to do the job in 30 days, and little specific vocational preparation and judgment are needed. A person does not gain work skills by doing unskilled jobs.

(b) Semi-skilled work. Semi-skilled work is work which needs some skills but does not require doing the more complex work duties. Semi-skilled jobs may require alertness and close attention to watching machine processes; or inspecting, testing or otherwise looking for irregularities; or tending or guarding equipment, property, materials, or persons against loss, damage or injury; or other types of activities which are similarly less complex than skilled work, but more complex than unskilled work. A job may be classified as semi-skilled where coordination and dexterity are necessary, as when hands or feet must be moved quickly to do repetitive tasks.

(c) Skilled work. Skilled work requires qualifications in which a person uses judgment to determine the machine and manual operations to be performed in order to obtain the proper form, quality, or quantity of material to be produced. Skilled work may require laying out work, estimating quality, determining the suitability and needed quantities of materials, making precise measurements, reading blueprints or other specifications, or making necessary computations or mechanical adjustments to control or regulate the work. Other skilled jobs may require dealing with people, facts, or figures or abstract ideas at a high level of complexity.

(d) Skills that can be used in other work (transferability)—

(1) What we mean by transferable skills. We consider you to have skills that can be used in other jobs, when the skilled or semi-skilled work activities you did in past work can be used to meet the requirements of skilled or semi-skilled work activities of other jobs or kinds of work. This depends largely on the similarity of occupationally significant work activities among different jobs.

(2) How we determine skills that can be transferred to other jobs. Transferability is most probable and meaningful among jobs in which—

(i) The same or a lesser degree of skill is required;

(ii) The same or similar tools and machines are used; and

(iii) The same or similar raw materials, products, processes, or services are involved.

(3) Degrees of transferability. There are degrees of transferability of skills ranging from very close similarities to remote and incidental similarities among jobs. A complete similarity of all three factors is not necessary for transferability. However, when skills are so specialized or have been acquired in such an isolated vocational setting (like many jobs in mining, agriculture, or fishing) that they are not readily usable in other industries, jobs, and work settings, we consider that they are not transferable.

(4) Transferability of skills for persons of advanced age. If you are of advanced age (age 55 or older), and you have a severe impairment(s) that limits you to sedentary or light work, we will find that you cannot make an adjustment to other work unless you have skills that you can transfer to other skilled or semiskilled work (or you have recently completed education which provides for direct entry into skilled work) that you can do despite your impairment(s). We will decide if you have transferable skills as follows. If you are of advanced age and you have a severe impairment(s) that limits you to no more than sedentary work, we will find that you have skills that are transferable to skilled or semiskilled sedentary work only if the sedentary work is so similar to your previous work that you would need to make very little, if any, vocational adjustment in terms of tools, work processes, work settings, or the industry. (See § 416.967(a) and Rule 201.00(f) of appendix 2 of subpart P of part 404 of this chapter.) If you are of advanced age but have not attained age 60, and you have a severe impairment(s) that limits you to no more than light work, we will apply the rules in paragraphs (d)(1) through (d)(3) of this section to decide if you have skills that are transferable to skilled or semiskilled light work (see § 416.967(b)). If you are closely approaching retirement age (age 60 or older) and you have a severe impairment(s) that limits you to no more than light work, we will find that you have skills that are transferable to skilled or semiskilled light work only if the light work is so similar to your previous work that you would need to make very little, if any, vocational adjustment in terms of tools, work processes, work settings, or the industry. (See § 416.967(b) and Rule 202.00(f) of appendix 2 of subpart P of part 404 of this chapter.)

[65 FR 18001, April 6, 2000; 73 FR 64197, Oct. 29, 2008]

§ 416.969 Listing of Medical–Vocational Guidelines in appendix 2 of subpart P of part 404 of this chapter.

The Dictionary of Occupational Titles includes information about jobs (classified by their exertional and skill requirements) that exist in the national economy. Appendix 2 provides rules using this data reflecting major functional and vocational patterns. We apply these rules in cases where a person is not doing substantial gainful activity and is prevented by a severe medically determinable impairment from doing vocationally relevant past work. (See § 416.920(h) for an exception to this rule.) The rules in appendix 2 do not cover all possible variations of factors. Also, as we explain in § 200.00 of appendix 2, we do not apply these rules if one of the findings of fact about the person's vocational factors and residual functional capacity is not the same as the corresponding criterion of a rule. In these instances, we give full consideration to all relevant facts in accordance with the definitions and discussions under vocational considerations. However, if the findings of fact made about all factors are the same as the rule, we use that rule to decide whether a person is disabled.

[77 FR 43495, July 25, 2012]

§ 416.969a Exertional and nonexertional limitations.

(a) General. Your impairment(s) and related symptoms, such as pain, may cause limitations of function or restrictions which limit your ability to meet certain demands of jobs. These limitations may be exertional, nonexertional, or a combination of both. Limitations are classified as exertional if they affect your ability to meet the strength demands of jobs. The classification of a limitation as exertional is related to the United States Department of Labor's classification of jobs by various exertional levels (sedentary, light, medium, heavy, and very heavy) in terms of the strength demands for sitting, standing, walking, lifting, carrying, pushing, and pulling. Sections 416.967 and 416.969 explain how we use the classification of jobs by exertional levels (strength demands) which is contained in the Dictionary of Occupational Titles published by the Department of Labor, to determine the exertional requirements of work which exists in the national economy. Limitations or restrictions which affect your ability to meet the demands of jobs other than the strength demands, that is, demands other than sitting, standing, walking, lifting, carrying, pushing or pulling, are considered nonexertional. When we decide whether you can do your past relevant work (see §§ 416.920(f) and 416.994(b)(5)(vi)), we will compare our assessment of your residual functional capacity with the demands of your past relevant work. If you cannot do your past relevant work, we will use the same residual functional capacity assessment along with your age, education, and work experience to decide if you can adjust to any other work which exists in the national economy. (See §§ 416.920(g) and 416.994(b)(5)(vii).) Paragraphs (b), (c), and (d) of this section explain how we apply the medical-vocational guidelines in appendix 2 of subpart P of part 404 of this chapter in making this determination, depending on whether the limitations or restrictions imposed by your impairment(s) and related symptoms, such as pain, are exertional, nonexertional, or a combination of both.

(b) Exertional limitations. When the limitations and restrictions imposed by your impairment(s) and related symptoms, such as pain, affect only your ability to meet the strength demands of jobs (sitting, standing, walking, lifting, carrying, pushing, and pulling), we consider that you have only exertional limitations. When your impairment(s) and related symptoms only impose exertional limitations and your specific vocational profile is listed in a rule contained in appendix 2, we will directly apply that rule to decide whether you are disabled.

(c) Nonexertional limitations.

(1) When the limitations and restrictions imposed by your impairment(s) and related symptoms, such as pain, affect only your ability to meet the demands of jobs other than the strength demands, we consider that you have only nonexertional limitations or restrictions. Some examples of nonexertional limitations or restrictions include the following:

(i) You have difficulty functioning because you are nervous, anxious, or depressed;

(ii) You have difficulty maintaining attention or concentrating;

(iii) You have difficulty understanding or remembering detailed instructions;

(iv) You have difficulty in seeing or hearing;

(v) You have difficulty tolerating some physical feature(s) of certain work settings, e.g., you cannot tolerate dust or fumes; or

(vi) You have difficulty performing the manipulative or postural functions of some work such as reaching, handling, stooping, climbing, crawling, or crouching.

(2) If your impairment(s) and related symptoms, such as pain, only affect your ability to perform the nonexertional aspects of work-related activities, the rules in appendix 2 do not direct factual conclusions of disabled or not disabled. The determination as to whether disability exists will be based on the principles in the appropriate sections of the regulations, giving consideration to the rules for specific case situations in appendix 2.

(d) Combined exertional and nonexertional limitations. When the limitations and restrictions imposed by your impairment(s) and related symptoms, such as pain, affect your ability to meet both the strength and demands of jobs other than the strength demands, we consider that you have a combination of exertional and nonexertional limitations or restrictions. If your impairment(s) and related symptoms, such as pain, affect your ability to meet both the strength and demands of jobs other than the strength demands, we will not directly apply the rules in appendix 2 unless there is a rule that directs a conclusion that you are disabled based upon your strength limitations; otherwise the rules provide a framework to guide our decision.

[56 FR 57947, Nov. 14, 1991; 68 FR 51166, Aug. 26, 2003]

SUBSTANTIAL GAINFUL ACTIVITY

§ 416.971 General.

The work, without regard to legality, that you have done during any period in which you believe you are disabled may show that you are able to work at the substantial gainful activity level. If you are able to engage in substantial gainful activity, we will find that you are not disabled. (We explain the rules for persons who are statutorily blind in § 416.984.) Even if the work you have done was not substantial gainful activity, it may show that you are able to do more work than you actually did. We will consider all of the medical and vocational evidence in your file to decide whether or not you have the ability to engage in substantial gainful activity.

[65 FR 42788, July 11, 2000]

§ 416.972 What we mean by substantial gainful activity.

Substantial gainful activity is work activity that is both substantial and gainful:

(a) Substantial work activity. Substantial work activity is work activity that involves doing significant physical or mental activities. Your work may be substantial even if it is done on a part-time basis or if you do less, get paid less, or have less responsibility than when you worked before.

(b) Gainful work activity. Gainful work activity is work activity that you do for pay or profit. Work activity is gainful if it is the kind of work usually done for pay or profit, whether or not a profit is realized.

(c) Some other activities. Generally, we do not consider activities like taking care of yourself, household tasks, hobbies, therapy, school attendance, club activities, or social programs to be substantial gainful activity.

§ 416.973 General information about work activity.

(a) The nature of your work. If your duties require use of your experience, skills, supervision and responsibilities, or contribute substantially to the operation of a business, this tends to show that you have the ability to work at the substantial gainful activity level.

(b) How well you perform. We consider how well you do your work when we determine whether or not you are doing substantial gainful activity. If you do your work satisfactorily, this may show that you are working at the substantial gainful activity level. If you are unable, because of your impairments, to do ordinary or simple tasks satisfactorily without more supervision or assistance than is usually given other people doing similar work, this may show that you are not working at the substantial gainful activity level. If you are doing work that involves minimal duties that make little or no demands on you and that are of little or no use to your employer, or to the operation of a business if you are self-employed, this does not show that you are working at the substantial gainful activity level.

(c) If your work is done under special conditions. The work you are doing may be done under special conditions that take into account your impairment, such as work done in a sheltered workshop or as a patient in a hospital. If your work is done under special conditions, we may find that it does not show that you have the ability to do substantial gainful activity. Also, if you are forced to stop or reduce your work because of the removal of special conditions that were related to your impairment and essential to your work, we may find that your work does not show that you are able to do substantial gainful activity. However, work done under special conditions may show that you have the necessary skills and ability to work at the substantial gainful activity level. Examples of the special conditions that may relate to your impairment include, but are not limited to, situations in which—

(1) You required and received special assistance from other employees in performing your work;

(2) You were allowed to work irregular hours or take frequent rest periods;

(3) You were provided with special equipment or were assigned work especially suited to your impairment;

(4) You were able to work only because of specially arranged circumstances, for example, other persons helped you prepare for or get to and from your work;

(5) You were permitted to work at a lower standard of productivity or efficiency than other employees; or

(6) You were given the opportunity to work, despite your impairment, because of family relationship, past association with your employer, or your employer's concern for your welfare.

(d) If you are self-employed. Supervisory, managerial, advisory or other significant personal services that you perform as a self-employed individual may show that you are able to do substantial gainful activity.

(e) Time spent in work. While the time you spend in work is important, we will not decide whether or not you are doing substantial gainful activity only on that basis. We will still evaluate the work to decide whether it is substantial and gainful regardless of whether you spend more time or less time at the job than workers who are not impaired and who are doing similar work as a regular means of their livelihood.

[65 FR 42788, July 11, 2000]

§ 416.974 Evaluation guides if you are an employee.

(a) We use several guides to decide whether the work you have done shows that you are able to do substantial gainful activity. If you are working or have worked as an employee, we will use the provisions in paragraphs (a) through (d) of this section that are relevant to your work activity. We will use these provisions whenever they are appropriate in connection with your application for supplemental security income benefits (when we make an initial determination on your application and throughout any appeals you may request) to determine if you are eligible.

(1) Your earnings may show you have done substantial gainful activity. Generally, in evaluating your work activity for substantial gainful activity purposes, our primary consideration will be the earnings you derive from the work activity. We will use your earnings to determine whether you have done substantial gainful activity unless we have information from you, your employer, or others that shows that we should not count all of your earnings. The amount of your earnings from work you have done (regardless of whether it is unsheltered or sheltered work) may show that you have engaged in substantial gainful activity. Generally, if you worked for substantial earnings, we will find that you are able to do substantial gainful activity. However, the fact that your earnings were not substantial will not necessarily show that you are not able to do substantial gainful activity. We generally consider work that you are forced to stop or to reduce below the substantial gainful activity level after a short time because of your impairment to be an unsuccessful work attempt. Your earnings from an unsuccessful work attempt will not show that you are able to do substantial gainful activity. We will use the criteria in paragraph (c) of this section to determine if the work you did was an unsuccessful work attempt.

(2) We consider only the amounts you earn. When we decide whether your earnings show that you have done substantial gainful activity, we do not consider any income that is not directly related to your productivity. When your earnings exceed the reasonable value of the work you perform, we consider only that part of your pay which you actually earn. If your earnings are being subsidized, we do not consider the amount of the subsidy when we determine if your earnings show that you have done substantial gainful activity. We consider your work to be subsidized if the true value of your work, when compared with the same or similar work done by unimpaired persons, is less than the actual amount of earnings paid to you for your work. For example, when a person with a serious impairment does simple tasks under close and continuous supervision, our determination of whether that person has done substantial gainful activity will not be based only on the amount of the wages paid. We will first determine whether the person received a subsidy; that is, we will determine whether the person was being paid more than the reasonable value of the actual services performed. We will then subtract the value of the subsidy from the person's gross earnings to determine the earnings we will use to determine if he or she has done substantial gainful activity.

(3) If you are working in a sheltered or special environment. If you are working in a sheltered workshop, you may or may not be earning the amounts you are being paid. The fact that the sheltered workshop or similar facility is operating at a loss or is receiving some charitable contributions or governmental aid does not establish that you are not earning all you are being paid. Since persons in military service being treated for severe impairments usually continue to receive full pay, we evaluate work activity in a therapy program or while on limited duty by comparing it with similar work in the civilian work force or on the basis of reasonable worth of the work, rather than on the actual amount of the earnings.

(b) Earnings guidelines—

(1) General. If you are an employee, we first consider the criteria in paragraph (a) of this section and § 416.976, and then the guides in paragraphs (b)(2) and (3) of this section. When we review your earnings to determine if you have been performing substantial gainful activity, we will subtract the value of any subsidized earnings (see paragraph (a)(2) of this section) and the reasonable cost of any impairment-related work expenses from your gross earnings (see § 416.976). The resulting amount is the amount we use to determine if you have done substantial gainful activity. We will generally average your earnings for comparison with the earnings guidelines in paragraphs (b)(2) and (3) of this section. See § 416.974a for our rules on averaging earnings.

(2) Earnings that will ordinarily show that you have engaged in substantial gainful activity. We will consider that your earnings from your work activity as an employee (including earnings from work in a sheltered workshop or a comparable facility especially set up for severely impaired persons) show that you have engaged in substantial gainful activity if:

(i) Before January 1, 2001, they averaged more than the amount(s) in Table 1 of this section for the time(s) in which you worked.

(ii) Beginning January 1, 2001, and each year thereafter, they average more than the larger of:

(A) The amount for the previous year, or

(B) An amount adjusted for national wage growth, calculated by multiplying $700 by the ratio of the national average wage index for the year 2 calendar years before the year for which the amount is being calculated to the national average wage index for the year 1998. We will then round the resulting amount to the next higher multiple of $10 where such amount is a multiple of $5 but not of $10 and to the nearest multiple of $10 in any other case.

Table 1

For months:	Your monthly earnings averaged more than:
In calendar years before 1976	$200
In calendar year 1976	230
In calendar year 1977	240
In calendar year 1978	260
In calendar year 1979	280
In calendar years 1980-1989	300
January 1990-June 1999	500
July 1999-December 2000	700

(3) Earnings that will ordinarily show that you have not engaged in substantial gainful activity.

(i) General. If your average monthly earnings are equal to or less than the amount(s) determined under paragraph (b)(2) of this section for the year(s) in which you work, we will generally consider that the earnings from your work as an employee (including earnings from work in a sheltered workshop or comparable facility) will show that you have not engaged in substantial gainful activity. We will generally not consider other information in addition to your earnings except in the circumstances described in paragraph (b)(3)(ii) of this section.

(ii) When we will consider other information in addition to your earnings. Unless you meet the criteria set forth in section 416.990 (h) and (i), we will generally consider other information in addition to your earnings if there is evidence indicating that you may be engaging in substantial gainful activity or that you are in a position to control when earnings are paid to you or the amount of wages paid to you (for example, if you are working for a small corporation owned by a relative). Examples of other information we may consider include, whether—

(A) Your work is comparable to that of unimpaired people in your community who are doing the same or similar occupations as their means of livelihood, taking into account the time, energy, skill, and responsibility involved in the work; and

(B) Your work, although significantly less than that done by unimpaired people, is clearly worth the amounts shown in paragraph (b)(2) of this section, according to pay scales in your community.

(c) The unsuccessful work attempt—

(1) General. Ordinarily, work you have done will not show that you are able to do substantial gainful activity if, after working for a period of 6 months or less, you were forced by your impairment to stop working or to reduce the amount of work you do so that your earnings from such work fall below the substantial gainful activity earnings level in paragraph (b)(2) of this section and you meet the conditions described in paragraphs (c)(2), (3), (4), and (5) of this section.

(2) Event that must precede an unsuccessful work attempt. There must be a significant break in the continuity of your work before we will consider you to have begun a work attempt that later proved unsuccessful. You must have stopped working or reduced your work and earnings below the substantial gainful activity earnings level because of your impairment or because of the removal of special conditions that were essential to the further performance of your work. We explain what we mean by special conditions in § 416.973(c). We will consider your prior work to be "discontinued" for a significant period if you were out of work at least 30 consecutive days. We will also consider your prior work to be "discontinued" if, because of your impairment, you were forced to change to another type of work or another employer.

(3) If you worked 6 months or less. We will consider work of 6 months or less to be an unsuccessful work attempt if you stopped working or you reduced your work and earnings below the substantial gainful activity earnings level because of your impairment or because of the removal of special conditions that took into account your impairment and permitted you to work.

(4) If you worked more than 6 months. We will not consider work you performed at the substantial gainful activity earnings level for more than 6 months to be an unsuccessful work attempt regardless of why it ended or was reduced below the substantial gainful activity earnings level.

(d) Work activity in certain volunteer programs. If you work as a volunteer in certain programs administered by the Federal government under the Domestic Volunteer Service Act of 1973 or the Small Business Act, we will not count any payments you receive from these programs as earnings when we determine whether you are engaging in substantial gainful activity. These payments may include a minimal stipend, payments for supportive services such as housing, supplies and equipment, an expense allowance, or reimbursement of out-of-pocket expenses. We will also disregard the services you perform as a volunteer in applying any of the substantial gainful activity tests discussed in paragraph (b)(6) of this section. This exclusion from the substantial gainful activity provisions will apply only if you are a volunteer in a program explicitly mentioned in the Domestic Volunteer Service Act of 1973 or the Small Business Act. Programs explicitly mentioned in those Acts include Volunteers in Service to America, University Year for ACTION, Special Volunteer Programs, Retired Senior Volunteer Program, Foster Grandparent Program, Service Corps of Retired Executives, and Active Corps of Executives. We will not exclude under this paragraph volunteer work you perform in other programs or any nonvolunteer work you may perform, including nonvolunteer work under one of the specified programs. For civilians in certain government-sponsored job training and employment programs, we evaluate the work activity on a case-by-case basis under the substantial gainful activity earnings test. In programs such as these, subsidies often occur. We will subtract the value of any subsidy and use the remainder to determine if you have done substantial gainful activity. See paragraphs (a)(2)–(3) of this section.

(e) Work activity as a member or consultant of an advisory committee established under the Federal Advisory Committee Act (FACA), 5 U.S.C. App. 2. If you are serving as a member or consultant of an advisory committee, board, commission, council, or similar group established under FACA, we will not count any payments you receive from serving on such committees as earnings when we determine whether you are engaging in substantial gainful activity. These payments may include compensation, travel expenses, and special assistance. We also will exclude the services you perform as a member or consultant of an advisory committee established under FACA in applying any of the substantial gainful activity tests discussed in paragraph (b)(6) of this section. This exclusion from the substantial gainful activity provision will apply only if you are a member or consultant of an advisory committee specifically authorized by statute, or by the President, or determined as a matter of formal record by the head of a federal government agency. This exclusion from the substantial gainful activity provisions will not apply if your service as a member or consultant of an advisory committee is part of your duties or is required as an employee of any governmental or non-governmental organization, agency, or business.

[46 FR 4871, Jan. 19, 1981; 48 FR 21939, May 16, 1974; 49 FR 22274, May 29, 1984; 54 FR 53605, Dec. 29, 1989; 64 FR 18570, April 15, 1999; 64 FR 22903, April 28, 1999; 65 FR

42788, July 11, 2000; 65 FR 82911, Dec. 29, 2000; 71 FR 3219, Jan. 20, 2006; 71 FR 66857, Nov. 17, 2006; 81 FR 71369, Oct. 17, 2016]

§ 416.974a When and how we will average your earnings.

(a) To determine your initial eligibility for benefits, we will average any earnings you make during the month you file for benefits and any succeeding months to determine if you are doing substantial gainful activity. If your work as an employee or as a self-employed person was continuous without significant change in work patterns or earnings, and there has been no change in the substantial gainful activity earnings levels, your earnings will be averaged over the entire period of work requiring evaluation to determine if you have done substantial gainful activity.

(b) If you work over a period of time during which the substantial gainful activity earnings levels change, we will average your earnings separately for each period in which a different substantial gainful activity earnings level applies.

(c) If there is a significant change in your work pattern or earnings during the period of work requiring evaluation, we will average your earnings over each separate period of work to determine if any of your work efforts were substantial gainful activity.

[65 FR 42790, July 11, 2000]

§ 416.975 Evaluation guides if you are self-employed.

(a) If you are a self-employed person. If you are working or have worked as a self-employed person, we will use the provisions in paragraphs (a) through (d) of this section that are relevant to your work activity. We will use these provisions whenever they are appropriate in connection with your application for supplemental security income benefits (when we make an initial determination on your application and throughout any appeals you may request). We will consider your activities and their value to your business to decide whether you have engaged in substantial gainful activity if you are self-employed. We will not consider your income alone because the amount of income you actually receive may depend on a number of different factors, such as capital investment and profit-sharing agreements. We will generally consider work that you were forced to stop or reduce to below substantial gainful activity after 6 months or less because of your impairment as an unsuccessful work attempt. See paragraph (d) of this section. We will evaluate your work activity based on the value of your services to the business regardless of whether you receive an immediate income for your services. We determine whether you have engaged in substantial gainful activity by applying three tests. If you have not engaged in substantial gainful activity under test one, then we will consider tests two and three. The tests are as follows:

(1) Test One: You have engaged in substantial gainful activity if you render services that are significant to the operation of the business and receive a substantial income from the business. Paragraphs (b) and (c) of this section explain what we mean by significant services and substantial income for purposes of this test.

(2) Test Two: You have engaged in substantial gainful activity if your work activity, in terms of factors such as hours, skills, energy output, efficiency, duties, and responsibilities, is comparable to that of unimpaired individuals in your community who are in the same or similar businesses as their means of livelihood.

(3) Test Three: You have engaged in substantial gainful activity if your work activity, although not comparable to that of unimpaired individuals, is clearly worth the amount shown in § 416.974(b)(2) when considered in terms of its value to the business, or when compared to the salary that an owner would pay to an employee to do the work you are doing.

(b) What we mean by significant services.

(1) If you are not a farm landlord and you operate a business entirely by yourself, any services that you render are significant to the business. If your business involves the services of more than one person, we will consider you to be rendering significant services if you contribute more than half the total time required for the management of the business, or you render management services for more than 45 hours a month regardless of the total management time required by the business.

(2) If you are a farm landlord, that is, you rent farm land to another, we will consider you to be rendering significant services if you materially participate in the production or the management of the production of the things raised on the rented farm. (See § 404.1082 of this chapter for an explanation of "material participation".) If you were given social security earnings credits because you materially participated in the activities of the farm and you continue these same activities, we will consider you to be rendering significant services.

(c) What we mean by substantial income. We deduct your normal business expenses from your gross income to determine net income. Once net income is determined, we deduct the reasonable value of any significant amount of unpaid help furnished by your spouse, children, or others. Miscellaneous duties that ordinarily would not have commercial value would not be considered significant. We deduct impairment-related work expenses that have not already been deducted in determining your net income. Impairment-related work expenses are explained in § 416.976. We deduct unincurred business expenses paid for you by another individual or agency. An unincurred business expense occurs when a sponsoring agency or another person incurs responsibility for the payment of certain business expenses, e.g., rent, utilities, or purchases and repair of equipment, or provides you with equipment, stock, or other material for the operation of your business. We deduct soil bank payments if they were included as farm income. That part of your income remaining after we have made all applicable deductions represents the actual value of work performed. The resulting amount is the amount we use to determine if you have done substantial gainful activity. We will generally average your income for comparison with the earnings guidelines in §§ 416.974(b)(2) and 416.974(b)(3). See § 416.974a for our rules on averaging of earnings. We will consider this amount to be substantial if—

(1) It averages more than the amounts described in § 416.974(b)(2); or

(2) It averages less than the amounts described in § 416.974(b)(2) but it is either comparable to what it was before you became seriously impaired if we had not considered your earnings or is comparable to that of unimpaired self-employed persons in your community who are in the same or a similar business as their means of livelihood.

(d) The unsuccessful work attempt—

(1) General. Ordinarily, work you have done will not show that you are able to do substantial gainful activity if, after working for a period of 6 months or less, you were forced by your impairment to stop working or to reduce the amount of work you do so that you are no longer performing substantial gainful activity and you meet the conditions described in paragraphs (d)(2), (3), and (4) of this section.

(2) Event that must precede an unsuccessful work attempt. There must be a significant break in the continuity of your work before we will consider you to have begun a work attempt that later proved unsuccessful. You must have stopped working or reduced your work and earnings below substantial gainful activity because of your impairment or because of the removal of special conditions which took into account your impairment and permitted you to work. Examples of such special conditions may include any significant amount of unpaid help furnished by your spouse, children, or others, or unincurred business expenses, as described in paragraph (c) of this section, paid for you by another individual or agency. We will consider your prior work to be "discontinued" for a significant period if you were out of work at least 30 consecutive days. We will also consider your prior work to be "discontinued" if, because of your impairment, you were forced to change to another type of work.

(3) If you worked 6 months or less. We will consider work of 6 months or less to be an unsuccessful work attempt if you stopped working or you reduced your work and earnings below the substantial gainful activity earnings level because of your impairment or because of the removal of special conditions that took into account your impairment and permitted you to work.

(4) If you worked more than 6 months. We will not consider work you performed at the substantial gainful activity level for more than 6 months to be an unsuccessful work attempt regardless of why it ended or was reduced below the substantial gainful activity level.

[46 FR 4872, Jan. 19, 1981; 48 FR 21940, May 16, 1983; 49 FR 22274, May 29, 1984; 65 FR 42790, July 11, 2000; 81 FR 71369, Oct. 17, 2016]

§ 416.976 Impairment-related work expenses.

(a) General. When we figure your earnings in deciding if you have done substantial gainful activity, and in determining your countable earned income (see § 416.1112(c)(5)), we will subtract the reasonable costs to you of certain items and services which, because of your impairment(s), you need and use to enable you to work. The costs are deductible even though you also need or use the items and services to carry out daily living functions unrelated to your work. Paragraph (b) of this section explains the conditions for deducting work expenses. Paragraph (c) of this section describes the expenses we will deduct. Paragraph (d) of this section explains when expenses may be deducted. Paragraph (e) of this section describes how expenses may be allocated. Paragraph (f) of this section explains the limitations on deducting expenses. Paragraph (g) of this section explains our verification procedures.

(b) Conditions for deducting impairment-related work expenses. We will deduct impairment-related work expenses if—

(1) You are otherwise disabled as defined in §§ 416.905 through 416.907;

(2) The severity of your impairment(s) requires you to purchase (or rent) certain items and services in order to work;

(3) You pay the cost of the item or service. No deduction will be allowed to the extent that payment has been or will be made by another source. No deduction will be allowed to the extent that you have been, could be, or will be reimbursed for such cost by any other source (such as through a private insurance plan, Medicare or Medicaid, or other plan or agency). For example, if you purchase crutches for $80 but you were, could be, or will be reimbursed $64 by some agency, plan, or program, we will deduct only $16;

(4) You pay for the item or service in accordance with paragraph (d) of this section; and

(5) Your payment is in cash (including checks or other forms of money). Payment in kind is not deductible.

(c) What expenses may be deducted—

(1) Payments for attendant care services.

(i) If because of your impairment(s) you need assistance in traveling to and from work, or while at work you need assistance with personal functions (e.g., eating, toileting) or with work-related functions (e.g., reading, communicating), the payments you make for those services may be deducted.

(ii) If because of your impairment(s) you need assistance with personal functions (e.g., dressing, administering medications) at home in preparation for going to and assistance in returning from work, the payments you make for those services may be deducted.

(iii)(A) We will deduct payments you make to a family member for attendant care services only if such person, in order to perform the services, suffers an economic loss by terminating his or her employment or by reducing the number of hours he or she worked.

(B) We consider a family member to be anyone who is related to you by blood, marriage or adoption, whether or not that person lives with you.

(iv) If only part of your payment to a person is for services that come under the provisions of paragraph (c)(1) of this section, we will only deduct that part of the payment which is attributable to those services. For example, an attendant gets you ready for work and helps you in returning from work, which takes about 2 hours a day. The rest of his or her 8 hour day is spent cleaning your house and doing your laundry, etc. We would only deduct one-fourth of the attendant's daily wages as an impairment-related work expense.

(2) Payments for medical devices. If your impairment(s) requires that you utilize medical devices in order to work, the payments you make for those devices may be deducted. As used in this subparagraph, medical devices include durable medical equipment which can withstand repeated use, is customarily used for medical purposes, and is generally not useful to a person in the absence of an illness or injury. Examples of durable medical equipment are wheelchairs, hemodialysis equipment, canes, crutches, inhalators and pacemakers.

(3) Payments for prosthetic devices. If your impairment(s) requires that you utilize a prosthetic device in order to work, the payments you make for that device may be deducted. A prosthetic device is that which replaces an internal body organ or external body part. Examples of prosthetic devices are artificial replacements of arms, legs and other parts of the body.

(4) Payments for equipment—

(i) Work-related equipment. If your impairment(s) requires that you utilize special equipment in order to do your job, the payments you make for that equipment may be deducted. Examples of work-related equipment are one-hand typewriters, telecommunication devices for the deaf and tools specifically designed to accommodate a person's impairment(s).

(ii) Residential modifications. If your impairment(s) requires that you make modifications to your residence, the location of your place of work will determine if the cost of these modifications will be deducted. If you are employed away from home, only the cost of changes made outside of your home to permit you to get to your means of transportation (e.g., the installation of an exterior ramp for a wheel-chair confined person or special exterior railings or pathways for someone who requires crutches) will be deducted. Costs relating to modifications of the inside of your home will not be deducted. If you work at home, the costs of modifying the inside of your home in order to create a working space to accommodate your impairment(s) will be deducted to the extent that the changes pertain specifically to the space in which you work. Examples of such changes are the enlargement of a doorway leading into the work space or modification of the work space to accommodate problems in dexterity. However, if you are self-employed at home, any cost deducted as a business expense cannot be deducted as an impairment-related work expense.

(iii) Nonmedical appliances and equipment. Expenses for appliances and equipment which you do not ordinarily use for medical purposes are generally not deductible. Examples of these items are portable room heaters, air conditioners, humidifiers, dehumidifiers, and electric air cleaners. However, expenses for such items may be deductible when unusual circumstances clearly establish an impairment-related and medically verified need for such an item because it is essential for the control of your disabling condition, thus enabling you to work. To be considered essential, the item must be of such a nature that if it were not available to you there would be an immediate adverse impact on your ability to function in your work activity. In this situation, the expense is deductible whether the item is used at home or in the working place. An example would be the need for an electric air cleaner by an individual with severe respiratory disease who cannot function in a non-purified air environment. An item such as an exercycle is not deductible if used for general physical fitness. If it is prescribed and used as necessary treatment of your impairment and necessary to enable you to work, we will deduct payments you make toward its cost.

(5) Payments for drugs and medical services.

(i) If you must use drugs or medical services (including diagnostic procedures) to control your impairment(s), the payments you make for them may be deducted. The drugs or services must be prescribed (or utilized) to reduce or eliminate symptoms of your impairment(s) or to slow down its progression. The diagnostic procedures must be performed to ascertain how the impairment(s) is progressing or to determine what type of treatment should be provided for the impairment(s).

(ii) Examples of deductible drugs and medical services are anticonvulsant drugs to control epilepsy or anticonvulsant blood level monitoring; antidepressant medication for mental disorders; medication used to allay the side effects of certain treatments; radiation treatment or chemotherapy for cancer patients; corrective surgery for spinal disorders; electroencephalograms and brain scans related to a disabling epileptic condition; tests to determine the efficacy of medication on a diabetic condition; and immunosuppressive medications that kidney transplant patients regularly take to protect against graft rejection.

(iii) We will only deduct the costs of drugs or services that are directly related to your impairment(s). Examples of non-deductible items are routine annual physical examinations, optician services (unrelated to a disabling visual impairment) and dental examinations.

(6) Payments for similar items and services—

(i) General. If you are required to utilize items and services not specified in paragraph (c)(1) through (5) of this section but which are directly related to your impairment(s) and which you need to work, their costs are deductible. Examples of such items and services are medical supplies and services not discussed above, and transportation.

(ii) Medical supplies and services not described above. We will deduct payments you make for expendable medical supplies, such as incontinence pads, catheters, bandages, elastic stockings, face masks, irrigating kits, and disposable sheets and bags. We will also deduct payments you make for physical therapy which you require because of your impairment(s) and which you need in order to work.

(iii) Payments for transportation costs. We will deduct transportation costs in these situations:

(A) Your impairment(s) requires that in order to get to work you need a vehicle that has structural or operational modifications. The modifications must be critical to your operation or use of the vehicle and directly related to your impairment(s). We will deduct the costs of the modifications, but not the cost of the vehicle. We will also deduct a mileage allowance for the trip to and from work. The allowance will be based on data compiled by the Federal Highway Administration relating to vehicle operating costs.

(B) Your impairment(s) requires you to use driver assistance, taxicabs or other hired vehicles in order to work. We will deduct amounts paid to the driver and, if your own vehicle is used, we will also deduct a mileage allowance, as provided in paragraph (c)(6)(iii)(A) of this section, for the trip to and from work.

(C) Your impairment(s) prevents your taking available public transportation to and from work and you must drive your (unmodified) vehicle to work. If we can verify through your physician or other sources that the need to drive is caused by your impairment(s) (and not due to the unavailability of public transportation), we will deduct a mileage allowance as provided in paragraph (c)(6)(iii)(A) of this section, for the trip to and from work.

(7) Payments for installing, maintaining, and repairing deductible items. If the device, equipment, appliance, etc., that you utilize qualifies as a deductible item as described in paragraphs (c)(2), (3), (4), and (6) of this section, the costs directly related to installing, maintaining and repairing these items are also deductible. (The costs which are associated with modifications to a vehicle are deductible. Except for a mileage allowance, as provided for in paragraph (c)(6)(iii) of this section, the costs which are associated with the vehicle itself are not deductible.)

(d) When expenses may be deducted—

(1) Effective date. To be deductible an expense must be incurred after November 30, 1980. An expense may be considered incurred after that date if it is paid thereafter even though pursuant to a contract or other arrangement entered into before December 1, 1980.

(2) Payments for services. For the purpose of determining SGA, a payment you make for services may be deducted if the services are received while you are working and the payment is made in a month you are working. We consider you to be working even though you must leave work temporarily to receive the services. For the purpose of determining your SSI monthly payment amount, a payment you make for services may be deducted if the payment is made in the month your earned income is received and the earned income is for work done in the month you received the services. If you begin working and make a payment before the month earned income is received, the payment is also deductible. If you make a payment after you stop working, and the payment is made in the month you received earned income for work done in the month you received the services, the payment is also deductible.

(3) Payment for items. For the purpose of determining SGA, a payment you make toward the cost of a deductible item (regardless of when it is acquired) may be deducted if payment is made in a month you are working. For the purpose of determining your SSI monthly payment amount, a payment you make toward the cost of a deductible item (regardless of when it is acquired) may be deducted if the payment is made in the month your earned income is received and the earned income is for work done in the month you used the item. If you begin working and make a payment before the month earned income is received, the payment is also deductible. If you make a payment after you stop working, and the payment is made in the month you received earned income for work done in the month you used the item, the payment is also deductible. See paragraph (e)(4) of this section when purchases are made in anticipation of work.

(e) How expenses are allocated—

(1) Recurring expenses. You may pay for services on a regular periodic basis, or you may purchase an item on credit and pay for it in regular periodic installments or you may rent an item. If so, each payment you make for the services and each payment you make toward the purchase or rental (including interest) is deductible as described in paragraph (d) of this section.

Example: B starts work in October 1981 at which time she purchases a medical device at a cost of $4,800 plus interest charges of $720. Her monthly payments begin in October. She earns and receives $400 a month. The term of the installment contract is 48 months. No downpayment is made. The monthly allowable deduction for the item would be $115 ($5520 divided by 48) for each month of work (for SGA purposes) and for each month earned income is received (for SSI payment purposes) during the 48 months.

(2) Nonrecurring expenses. Part or all of your expenses may not be recurring. For example, you may make a one-time payment in full for an item or service or make a downpayment. For the purpose of determining SGA, if you are working when you make the payment we will either deduct the entire amount in the month you pay it or allocate the amount over a 12 consecutive month period beginning with the month of payment, whichever you select. For the purpose of determining your SSI monthly payment amount, if you are working in the month you make the payment and the payment is made in a month earned income is received, we will either deduct the entire amount in that month, or we will allocate the amount over a 12 consecutive month period, beginning with that month, whichever you select. If you begin working and do not receive earned income in the month you make the payment, we will either deduct or begin allocating the payment amount in the first month you do receive earned income. If you make a payment for services or items after you stopped working, we will deduct the payment if it was made in the month you received earned income for work done in the month you received the services or used the item.

Example: A begins working in October 1981 and earns and receives $525 a month. In the same month he purchases and pays for a deductible item at a cost of $250. In this situation we could allow a $250 deduction for both SGA and SSI payment purposes for October 1981, reducing A's earnings below the SGA level for that month.

If A's earnings had been $15 above the SGA earnings amount, A probably would select the option of projecting the $250 payment over the 12–month period, October 1981–September 1982, giving A an allowable deduction of $20.83 a month for each month of work (for SGA purposes) and for each month earned income is received (for SSI payment purposes) during that period. This deduction would reduce A's earnings below the SGA level for 12 months.

(3) Allocating downpayments. If you make a downpayment we will, if you choose, make a separate calculation for the downpayment in order to provide for uniform monthly deductions. In these situations we will determine the total payment that you will make over a 12 consecutive month period beginning with the month of the downpayment and allocate that amount over the 12 months. Beginning with the 13th month, the regular monthly payment will be deductible. This allocation process will be for a shorter period if your regular monthly payments will extend over a period of less than 12 months.

Example 1. C starts working in October 1981, at which time he purchases special equipment at a cost of $4,800, paying $1,200 down. The balance of $3,600, plus interest of $540, is to be repaid in 36 installments of $115 a month beginning November 1981. C earns and receives $500 a month. He chooses to have the downpayment allocated. In this situation we would allow a deduction of $205.42 a month for each month of work (for SGA purposes) and for each month earned income is received (for SSI payment purposes) during the period October 1981 through September 1982. After September 1982, the deduction amount would be the regular monthly payment of $115 for each month of work (for SGA purposes) and for each month earned income is received (for SSI payment purposes) during the remaining installment period.

Explanation:

Downpayment in 10/81	$1,200	
Monthly payments 11/81 through 09/82	1,265	
	12) 2,465	=$205.42.

Example 2. D, while working, buys a deductible item in July 1981, paying $1,450 down. (D earns and receives $500 a month.) However, his first monthly payment of $125 is not due until September 1981. D chooses to have the downpayment allocated. In this situation we would allow a deduction of $225 a month for each month of work (for SGA purposes) and for each month earned income is received (for SSI payment purposes) during the period July 1981 through June 1982. After June 1982, the deduction amount would be the regular monthly payment of $125 for each month of work (for SGA purposes) and for each month earned income is received (for SSI payment purposes).

Explanation:

Downpayment in 07/81	$1,450	
Monthly payments 09/81 through 06/82	1,250	
	12) 2,700	=225.

(4) Payments made in anticipation of work. A payment toward the cost of a deductible item that you made in any of the 11 months preceding the month you started working will be taken into account in determining your impairment-related work expenses. When an item is paid for in full during the 11 months preceding the month you started working the payment will be allocated over the 12–consecutive month period beginning with the month of the payment. However, the only portion of the payment which may be deductible is the portion allocated to the month work begins and the following months. For example, if an item is pur-

chased 3 months before the month work began and is paid for with a one-time payment of $600, the deductible amount would be $450 ($600 divided by 12, multiplied by 9). Installment payments (including a downpayment) that you made for a particular item during the 11 months preceding the month you started working will be totaled and considered to have been made in the month of your first payment for that item within this 11 month period. The sum of these payments will be allocated over the 12–consecutive month period beginning with the month of your first payment (but never earlier than 11 months before the month work began). However, the only portion of the total which may be deductible is the portion allocated to the month work begins and the following months. For example, if an item is purchased 3 months before the month work began and is paid for in 3 monthly installments of $200 each, the total payment of $600 will be considered to have been made in the month of the first payment, that is, 3 months before the month work began. The deductible amount would be $450 ($600 divided by 12, multiplied by 9). The amount, as determined by these formulas, will then be considered to have been paid in the first month of work for the purpose of determining SGA and in the first month earned income is received for the purpose of determining the SSI monthly payment amount. For the purpose of determining SGA, we will deduct either the entire amount in the first month of work or allocate it over a 12 consecutive month period beginning with the first month of work, whichever you select. In the above examples, the individual would have the choice of having the entire $450 deducted in the first month of work or of having $37.50 a month ($450 divided by 12) deducted for each month that he works over a 12–consecutive month period, beginning with the first month of work. For the purpose of determining the SSI payment amount, we will either deduct the entire amount in the first month earned income is received or allocate it over a 12–consecutive month period beginning with the first month earned income is received, whichever you select. In the above examples, the individual would have the choice of having the entire $450 deducted in the first month earned income is received or of having $37.50 a month ($450 divided by 12) deducted for each month he receives earned income (for work) over a 12–consecutive month period, beginning with the first month earned income is received. To be deductible the payments must be for durable items such as medical devices, prostheses, work-related equipment, residential modifications, nonmedical appliances and vehicle modifications. Payments for services and expendable items such as drugs, oxygen, diagnostic procedures, medical supplies and vehicle operating costs are not deductible for purposes of this paragraph.

(f) Limits on deductions.

(1) We will deduct the actual amounts you pay toward your impairment-related work expenses unless the amounts are unreasonable. With respect to durable medical equipment, prosthetic devices, medical services, and similar medically related items and services, we will apply the prevailing charges under Medicare (part B of title XVIII, Health Insurance for the Aged and Disabled) to the extent that this information is readily available. Where the Medicare guides are used, we will consider the amount that you pay to be reasonable if it is no more than the prevailing charge for the same item or service under the Medicare guidelines. If the amount you actually pay is more than the prevailing charge for the same item under the Medicare guidelines, we will deduct from your earnings the amount you paid to the extent you establish that the amount is consistent with the standard or normal charge for the same or similar item or service in your community. For items and services that are not listed in the Medicare guidelines, and for items and services that are listed in the Medicare guidelines but for which such guides cannot be used because the information is not readily available, we will consider the amount you pay to be reasonable if it does not exceed the standard or normal charge for the same or similar item(s) or service(s) in your community.

(2) The decision as to whether you performed substantial gainful activity in a case involving impairment-related work expenses for items or services necessary for you to work generally will be based upon your "earnings" and not on the value of "services" you rendered. (See §§ 416.974(b)(6)(i) and (ii), and 416.975(a)). This is not necessarily so, however, if you are in a position to control or manipulate your earnings.

(3) The amount of the expenses to be deducted must be determined in a uniform manner in both the disability insurance and SSI programs. The amount of deductions must, therefore, be the same for determinations as to substantial gainful activity under both programs. The deductions that apply in determining the SSI payment amounts, though determined in the same manner as for SGA determinations, are applied so that they correspond to the timing of the receipt of the earned income to be excluded.

(4) No deduction will be allowed to the extent that any other source has paid or will pay for an item or service. No deduction will be allowed to the extent that you have been, could be, or will be, reimbursed for payments you made. (See paragraph (b)(3) of this section.)

(5) The provisions described in the foregoing paragraphs of this section are effective with respect to expenses incurred on and after December 1, 1980, although expenses incurred after November 1980 as a result of contractual or other arrangements entered into before December 1980, are deductible. For months before December 1980 we will deduct impairment-related work expenses from your earnings only

to the extent they exceeded the normal work-related expenses you would have had if you did not have your impairment(s). We will not deduct expenses, however, for those things which you needed even when you were not working.

(g) Verification. We will verify your need for items or services for which deductions are claimed, and the amount of the charges for those items or services. You will also be asked to provide proof that you paid for the items or services.

[48 FR 21940, May 16, 1983; 65 FR 42791, July 11, 2000]

BLINDNESS

§ 416.981 Meaning of blindness as defined in the law.

We will consider you blind under the law for payment of supplemental security income benefits if we determine that you are statutorily blind. Statutory blindness is central visual acuity of 20/200 or less in the better eye with the use of a correcting lens. An eye which has a limitation in the field of vision so that the widest diameter of the visual field subtends an angle no greater than 20 degrees is considered to have a central visual acuity of 20/200 or less.

§ 416.982 Blindness under a State plan.

We shall also consider you blind for the purposes of payment of supplemental security income benefits if—

(a) You were found to be blind as defined under a State plan approved under title X or title XVI of the Social Security Act, as in effect for October 1972;

(b) You received aid under the State plan because of your blindness for the month of December 1973; and

(c) You continue to be blind as defined under the State plan.

§ 416.983 How we evaluate statutory blindness.

We will find that you are blind if you are statutorily blind within the meaning of § 416.981. For us to find that you are statutorily blind, it is not necessary—

(a) That your blindness meet the duration requirement; or

(b) That you be unable to do any substantial gainful activity.

§ 416.984 If you are statutorily blind and still working.

There is no requirement that you be unable to work in order for us to find that you are blind. However, if you are working, your earnings will be considered under the income and resources rules in subparts K and L of this part. This means that if your income or resources exceed the limitations, you will not be eligible for benefits, even though you are blind.

§ 416.985 How we evaluate other visual impairments.

If you are not blind as defined in the law, we will evaluate a visual impairment the same as we evaluate other impairments in determining disability. Although you will not qualify for benefits on the basis of blindness, you may still be eligible for benefits if we find that you are disabled as defined in §§ 416.905 through 416.907.

§ 416.986 Why and when we will find that you are no longer entitled to benefits based on statutory blindness.

(a) If your vision does not meet the definition of blindness. If you become entitled to payments as a statutorily blind person and your statutory blindness ends, your eligibility for payments generally will end 2 months after your blindness ends. We will find that your statutory blindness has ended beginning with the earliest of the following months—

(1) The month your vision, based on current medical evidence, does not meet the definition of blindness and you were disabled only for a specified period of time in the past;

(2) The month your vision based on current medical evidence, does not meet the definition of blindness, but not earlier than the month in which we mail you a notice saying that the information we have shows that you are not now blind; or

(3) The first month in which you fail to follow prescribed treatment that can restore your ability to work (see § 416.930).

(b) If you were found blind as defined in a State plan. If you become eligible for payments because you were blind as defined in a State plan, we will find that your blindness has ended beginning with the first month in which your vision, as shown by medical or other evidence, does not meet the criteria of the appropriate State plan or the first month in which your vision does not meet the definition of statutory blindness (§ 416.981), whichever is later, and in neither event earlier than the month in which we mail you a notice saying that we have determined that you are not now blind under a State plan or not now statutorily blind, as appropriate.

(c) If you do not cooperate with us. If you are asked to give us medical or other evidence or to go for a physical or mental examination by a certain date, we will find that your blindness ended if you fail, without good cause, to do what we ask. Section 416.1411 explains the factors we consider and how we will determine generally whether you have good cause for failure to cooperate. In addition, § 416.918 discusses how we determine whether you have good cause for failing to attend a consultative examination. The month in which your blindness ends will be the month in which you fail to do what we asked.

(d) Before we stop your payments. Before we stop payment of your benefits we will give you a chance to give us your reasons why we should not stop payment. Subpart M of this part describes your rights and the procedures we will follow.

[50 FR 50137, Dec. 6, 1985; 51 FR 7063, Feb. 28, 1986; 59 FR 1636, Jan. 12, 1994]

DISABILITY REDETERMINATIONS FOR INDIVIDUALS WHO ATTAIN AGE 18

§ 416.987 Disability redeterminations for individuals who attain age 18.

(a) Who is affected by this section?

(1) We must redetermine your eligibility if you are eligible for SSI disability benefits and:

(i) You are at least 18 years old; and

(ii) You became eligible for SSI disability benefits as a child (i.e., before you attained age 18); and

(iii) You were eligible for such benefits for the month before the month in which you attained age 18.

(2) We may find that you are not now disabled even though we previously found that you were disabled.

(b) What are the rules for age–18 redeterminations? When we redetermine your eligibility, we will use the rules for adults (individuals age 18 or older) who file new applications explained in § 416.920(c) through (h). We will not use the rule in § 416.920(b) for people who are doing substantial gainful activity, and we will not use the rules in § 416.994 for determining whether disability continues. If you are working and we find that you are disabled under § 416.920(d) or (g), we will apply the rules in §§ 416.260ff.

(c) When will my eligibility be redetermined? We will redetermine your eligibility either during the 1–year period beginning on your 18th birthday or, in lieu of a continuing disability review, whenever we determine that your case is subject to redetermination under the Act.

(d) Will I be notified?—

(1) We will notify you in writing before we begin your disability redetermination. We will tell you:

(i) That we are redetermining your eligibility for payments;

(ii) Why we are redetermining your eligibility;

(iii) Which disability rules we will apply;

(iv) That our review could result in a finding that your SSI payments based on disability could be terminated;

(v) That you have the right to submit medical and other evidence for our consideration during the redetermination; and

(vi) That we will notify you of our determination, your right to appeal the determination, and your right to request continuation of benefits during appeal.

(2) We will notify you in writing of the results of the disability redetermination. The notice will tell you what our determination is, the reasons for our determination, and your right to request reconsideration of the determination. If our determination shows that we should stop your SSI payments based on disability, the notice will also tell you of your right to request that your benefits continue during any appeal. Our initial disability redetermination will be binding unless you request a reconsideration within the stated time period or we revise the initial determination.

(e) When will we find that your disability ended? If we find that you are not disabled, we will find that your disability ended in the earliest of:

(1) The month the evidence shows that you are not disabled under the rules in this section, but not earlier than the month in which we mail you a notice saying that you are not disabled.

(2) The first month in which you failed without good cause to follow prescribed treatment under the rules in § 416.930.

(3) The first month in which you failed without good cause to do what we asked. Section 416.1411 explains the factors we will consider and how we will determine generally whether you have good cause for failure to cooperate. In addition, § 416.918 discusses how we determine whether you have good cause for failing to attend a consultative examination.

[62 FR 6429, Feb. 11, 1997; 65 FR 54789, Sept. 11, 2000; 70 FR 36508, June 24, 2005; 77 FR 43495, July 25, 2012]

CONTINUING OR STOPPING DISABILITY OR BLINDNESS

§ 416.988 Your responsibility to tell us of events that may change your disability or blindness status.

If you are entitled to payments because you are disabled or blind, you should promptly tell us if—

(a) Your condition improves;

(b) Your return to work;

(c) You increase the amount of your work; or

(d) Your earnings increase.

§ 416.989 We may conduct a review to find out whether you continue to be disabled.

After we find that you are disabled, we must evaluate your impairment(s) from time to time to determine if you are still eligible for payments based on disability. We call this evaluation a continuing disability review. We may begin a continuing disability review for any number of reasons including your failure to follow the provisions of the Social Security Act or these regulations. When we begin such a review, we will notify you that we are reviewing your eligibility for payments, why we are reviewing your eligibility, that in medical reviews the medical improvement review standard will apply, that our review could result in the termination of your payments, and that you have the right to submit medical and other evidence for our consideration during the continuing disability review. In doing a medical review, we will develop a complete medical history of at least the preceding 12 months in any case in which a determination is made that you are no longer under a disability. If this review shows that we should stop your payments, we will notify you in writing and give you an opportunity to appeal. In § 416.990 we describe those events that may prompt us to review whether you continue to be disabled.

[51 FR 16826, May 7, 1986]

§ 416.989a We may conduct a review to find out whether you continue to be blind.

After we find that you are blind, we must evaluate your impairment(s) from time to time to determine if you are still eligible for payments based on blindness. We call this evaluation a continuing disability review. We may begin a continuing disability review for any number of reasons including your failure to follow the provisions of the Social Security Act or these regulations. When we begin such a review, we will notify you that we are reviewing your eligibility for payments, why we are reviewing your eligibility, that our review could result in the termination of your payments, and that you have the right to submit medical and other evidence for our consideration during the continuing disability review. In doing a medical review, we will develop a complete medical history of at least the preceding 12 months in any case in which a determination is made that you are no longer blind. If this review shows that we should stop your payments, we will notify you in writing and give you an opportunity to appeal. In § 416.990 we describe those events that may prompt us to review whether you continue to be blind.

[51 FR 16826, May 7, 1986]

§ 416.990 When and how often we will conduct a continuing disability review.

(a) General. We conduct continuing disability reviews to determine whether or not you continue to meet the disability or blindness requirements of the law. Payment ends if the medical or other evidence shows that you are not disabled or blind as determined under the standards set out in section 1614(a) of the Social Security Act if you receive benefits based on disability or § 416.986 of this subpart if you receive benefits based on blindness. In paragraphs (b) through (g) of this section, we explain when and how often we conduct continuing disability reviews for most individuals. In paragraph (h) of this section, we explain special rules for some individuals who are participating in the Ticket to Work program. In paragraph (i) of this section, we explain special rules for some individuals who work and have received social security benefits as well as supplemental security income payments.

(b) When we will conduct a continuing disability review. Except as provided in paragraphs (h) and (i) of this section, we will start a continuing disability review if—

(1) You have been scheduled for a medical improvement expected diary review;

(2) You have been scheduled for a periodic review (medical improvement possible or medical improvement not expected) in accordance with the provisions of paragraph (d) of this section;

(3) We need a current medical or other report to see if your disability continues. (This could happen when, for example, an advance in medical technology, such as improved treatment for Alzheimer's disease, or a change in vocational therapy or technology raises a disability issue);

(4) You return to work;

(5) Substantial earnings are reported to your wage record;

(6) You tell us that—

(i) You have recovered from your disability; or

(ii) You have returned to work;

(7) Your State Vocational Rehabilitation Agency tells us that—

(i) The services have been completed; or

(ii) You are now working; or

(iii) You are able to work;

(8) Someone in a position to know of your physical or mental condition tells us any of the following, and it appears that the report could be substantially correct:

(i) You are not disabled or blind; or

(ii) You are not following prescribed treatment; or

(iii) You have returned to work; or

(iv) You are failing to follow the provisions of the Social Security Act or these regulations;

(9) Evidence we receive raises a question whether your disability or blindness continues;

(10) You have been scheduled for a vocational reexamination diary review; or

(11) By your first birthday, if you are a child whose low birth weight was a contributing factor material to our determination that you were disabled; i.e., whether we would have found you disabled if we had not considered your low birth weight. However, we will conduct your continuing disability review later if at the

time of our initial determination that you were disabled:

(i) We determine that you have an impairment that is not expected to improve by your first birthday; and

(ii) We schedule you for a continuing disability review after your first birthday.

(c) Definitions. As used in this section—

Medical improvement expected diary—refers to a case which is scheduled for review at a later date because the individual's impairment(s) is expected to improve. Generally, the diary period is set for not less than 6 months or for not more than 18 months. Examples of cases likely to be scheduled for medical improvement expected diary are fractures and cases in which corrective surgery is planned and recovery can be anticipated.

Permanent impairment—medical improvement not expected—refers to a case in which any medical improvement in a person's impairment(s) is not expected. This means an extremely severe condition determined on the basis of our experience in administering the disability programs to be at least static, but more likely to be progressively disabling either by itself or by reason of impairment complications, and unlikely to improve so as to permit the individual to engage in substantial gainful activity or, if you are a child, unlikely to improve to the point that you will no longer have marked and severe functional limitations. The interaction of the individual's age, impairment consequences and the lack of recent attachment to the labor market may also be considered in determining whether an impairment is permanent. Improvement which is considered temporary under § 416.994(b)(2)(iv)(D) or § 416.994(c)(2)(iv), as appropriate, will not be considered in deciding if an impairment is permanent. Examples of permanent impairments taken from the list contained in our other written guidelines which are available for public review are as follows and are not intended to be all inclusive:

(1) Parkinsonian Syndrome which has reached the level of severity necessary to meet the Listing in appendix 1 of subpart P or part 404 of this chapter.

(2) Amyotrophic Lateral Sclerosis which has reached the level of severity necessary to meet the Listing in appendix 1 of subpart P of part 404 of this chapter.

(3) Diffuse pulmonary fibrosis in an individual age 55 or over which has reached the level of severity necessary to meet the Listing in appendix 1 of subpart P of part 404 of this chapter.

(4) Amputation of leg at hip.

Nonpermanent impairment—refers to a case in which any medical improvement in the person's impairment(s) is possible. This means an impairment for which improvement cannot be predicted based on current experience and the facts of the particular case but which is not at the level of severity of an impairment that is considered permanent. Examples of nonpermanent impairments are: Regional enteritis, hyperthyroidism, and chronic ulcerative colitis.

Vocational reexamination diary—refers to a case which is scheduled for review at a later date because the individual is undergoing vocational therapy, training or an educational program which may improve his or her ability to work so that the disability or blindness requirement of the law is no longer met. Generally, the diary period will be set for the length of the training, therapy, or program of education.

(d) Frequency of review. If your impairment is expected to improve, generally we will review your continuing eligibility for payments based on disability or blindness at intervals from 6 months to 18 months following our most recent decision. Our notice to you about the review of your case will tell you more precisely when the review will be conducted. If your disability is not considered permanent but is such that any medical improvement in your impairment(s) cannot be accurately predicted, we will review your continuing eligibility for payments at least once every 3 years. If your disability is considered permanent, we will review your continuing eligibility for payments no less frequently than once every 7 years but no more frequently than once every 5 years. Regardless of your classification we will conduct an immediate continuing disability review if a question of continuing disability is raised pursuant to paragraph (b) of this section.

(e) Change in classification of impairment. If the evidence developed during a continuing disability review demonstrates that your impairment has improved, is expected to improve, or has worsened since the last review, we may reclassify your impairment to reflect this change in severity. A change in the classification of your impairment will change the frequency with which we will review your case. We may also reclassify certain impairments because of improved tests, treatment, and other technical advances concerning those impairments.

(f) Review after administrative appeal. If you were found eligible to receive or to continue to receive, payments on the basis of a decision by an administrative law judge, the Appeals Council or a Federal court, we will not conduct a continuing disability review earlier than 3 years after that decision unless your case should be scheduled for a medical improvement expected or vocational reexamination diary review or a question of continuing disability is raised pursuant to paragraph (b) of this section.

(g) Waiver of timeframes. All cases involving a nonpermanent impairment will be reviewed by us at least once every 3 years unless we, after consultation with the State agency, determine that the requirement should be waived to ensure that only the appropriate number of cases are reviewed. The appropriate number of cases to be reviewed is to be based on such considerations as the backlog of pending reviews, the projected number of new applications, and projected staffing levels. Such waiver shall be given only after good faith effort on the part of the State to meet staffing requirements and to process the reviews on a timely basis. Availability of independent medical resources may also be a factor. A waiver in this context refers to our administrative discretion to determine the appropriate number of cases to be reviewed on a State by State basis. Therefore, your continuing disability review may be delayed longer than 3 years following our original decision or other review under certain circumstances. Such a delay would be based on our need to ensure that backlogs, reviews required to be performed by the Social Security Disability Benefits Reform Act (Pub.L. 98–460), and new disability claims workloads are accomplished within available medical and other resources in the State agency and that such reviews are done carefully and accurately.

(h) If you are participating in the Ticket to Work program. If you are participating in the Ticket to Work program, we will not start a continuing disability review during the period in which you are using a ticket. See subpart C of part 411 of this chapter.

(i) If you are working and have received social security disability benefits for at least 24 months—

(1) General. Notwithstanding the provisions in paragraphs (b)(4), (b)(5), (b)(6)(ii), (b)(7)(ii), and (b)(8)(iii) of this section, we will not start a continuing disability review based solely on your work activity if—

(i) You are currently entitled to disability insurance benefits as a disabled worker, child's insurance benefits based on disability, or widow's or widower's insurance benefits based on disability under title II of the Social Security Act (see subpart D of part 404 of this chapter); and

(ii) You have received such benefits for at least 24 months (see paragraph (i)(2) of this section).

(2) The 24–month requirement.

(i) The months for which you have actually received disability insurance benefits as a disabled worker, child's insurance benefits based on disability, or widow's or widower's insurance benefits based on disability that you were due under title II of the Social Security Act, or for which you have constructively received such benefits, will count for the 24–month requirement under paragraph (i)(1)(ii) of this section, regardless of whether the months were consecutive. We will consider you to have constructively received a benefit for a month for purposes of the 24–month requirement if you were otherwise due a social security disability benefit for that month and your monthly benefit was withheld to recover an overpayment. Any month for which you were entitled to social security disability benefits but for which you did not actually or constructively receive a benefit payment will not be counted for the 24–month requirement. Months for which your social security disability benefits are continued under § 404.1597a pending reconsideration and/or a hearing before an administrative law judge on a medical cessation determination will not be counted for the 24–month requirement. Months for which you received only supplemental security income payments will not be counted for the 24–month requirement.

(ii) In determining whether paragraph (i)(1) of this section applies, we consider whether you have received disability insurance benefits as a disabled worker, child's insurance benefits based on disability, or widow's or widower's insurance benefits based on disability under title II of the Social Security Act for at least 24 months as of the date on which we start a continuing disability review. For purposes of this provision, the date on which we start a continuing disability review is the date on the notice we send you that tells you that we are beginning to review your disability case.

(3) When we may start a continuing disability review even if you have received social security disability benefits for at least 24 months. Even if you meet the requirements of paragraph (i)(1) of this section, we may still start a continuing disability review for a reason(s) other than your work activity. We may start a continuing disability review if we have scheduled you for a periodic review of your continuing disability, we need a current medical or other report to see if your disability continues, we receive evidence which raises a question as to whether your disability or blindness continues, or you fail to follow the provisions of the Social Security Act or these regulations. For example, we will start a continuing disability review when you have been scheduled for a medical improvement expected diary review, and we may start a continuing disability review if you failed to report your work to us.

(4) Erroneous start of the continuing disability review. If we start a continuing disability review based solely on your work activity that results in a medical cessation determination, we will vacate the medical cessation determination if—

(i) You provide us evidence that establishes that you met the requirements of paragraph (i)(1) of this section as of the date of the start of your continuing disability review and that the start of the review was erroneous; and

(ii) We receive the evidence within 12 months of the date of the notice of the initial determination of medical cessation.

[51 FR 16826, May 7, 1986; 62 FR 6430, Feb. 11, 1997; 65 FR 54790, Sept. 11, 2000; 71 FR 66858, Nov. 17, 2006]

§ 416.991 If your medical recovery was expected and you returned to work.

If your impairment was expected to improve and you returned to full-time work with no significant medical limitations and acknowledge that medical improvement has occurred, we may find that your disability ended in the month you returned to work. Unless there is evidence showing that your disability has not ended, we will use the medical and other evidence already in your file and the fact that you returned to full-time work without significant limitations to determine that you are no longer disabled.

Example: Evidence obtained during the processing of your claim showed that you had an impairment that was expected to improve about 18 months after your disability began. We, therefore, told you that your claim would be reviewed again at that time. However, before the time arrived for your scheduled medical re-examination, you told us that you had returned to work and your impairment had improved. We reviewed your claim immediately and found that, in the 16th month after your disability began, you returned to full-time work without any significant medical restrictions. Therefore, we would find that your disability ended in the first month you returned to full-time work.

[50 FR 50137, Dec. 6, 1985; 65 FR 42791, July 11, 2000]

§ 416.992 What happens if you fail to comply with our request for information.

We will suspend your payments before we make a determination regarding your continued eligibility for disability payments if you fail to comply, without good cause (see § 416.1411), with our request for information for your continuing disability review or age–18 redetermination. The suspension is effective with the month in which it is determined in accordance with § 416.1322 that your eligibility for disability payments has ended due to your failure to comply with our request for necessary information. When we have received the information, we will reinstate your payments for any previous month for which they are otherwise payable, and continue with the CDR or age–18 redetermination process. We will terminate your eligibility for payments following 12 consecutive months of payment suspension as discussed in § 416.1335.

[71 FR 60823, Oct. 17, 2006]

§ 416.992a [Reserved]

[65 FR 42791, July 11, 2000]

§ 416.993 Medical evidence in continuing disability review cases.

(a) General. If you are entitled to benefits because you are disabled, we will have your case file with the supporting medical evidence previously used to establish or continue your entitlement. Generally, therefore, the medical evidence we will need for a continuing disability review will be that required to make a current determination or decision as to whether you are still disabled, as defined under the medical improvement review standard. See §§ 416.987 and 416.994.

(b) Obtaining evidence from your medical sources. You must provide us with reports from your physician, psychologist, or others who have treated or evaluated you, as well as any other evidence that will help us determine if you are still disabled. See § 416.912. You must have a good reason for not giving us this information or we may find that your disability has ended. See § 416.994(e)(2). If we ask you, you must contact your medical sources to help us get the medical reports. We will make every reasonable effort to help you in getting medical reports when you give us permission to request them from your physician, psychologist, or other medical sources. See § 416.912(b)(1)(i) concerning what we mean by every reasonable effort. In some instances, such as when a source is known to be unable to provide certain tests or procedures or is known to be nonproductive or uncooperative, we may order a consultative examination while awaiting receipt of medical source evidence. See § 416.912(b)(1)(ii). See § 416.912(c)

(c) When we will purchase a consultative examination. A consultative examination may be purchased when we need additional evidence to determine whether or not your disability continues. As a result, we may ask you, upon our request and reasonable notice, to undergo consultative examinations and tests to help us determine if you are still disabled. See § 416.917. We will decide whether or not to purchase a consultative examination in accordance with the standards in §§ 416.919a through 416.919b.

[50 FR 50137, Dec. 6, 1985; 56 FR 36970, Aug. 1, 1991; 65 FR 16815, March 30, 2000; 82 FR 5882, Jan. 18, 2017]

§ 416.994 How we will determine whether your disability continues or ends, disabled adults.

(a) General. There is a statutory requirement that, if you are entitled to disability benefits, your continued entitlement to such benefits must be reviewed periodically. Our rules for deciding whether your disability continues are set forth in paragraph (b) of this section. Additional rules apply if you were found disabled under a State plan, as set forth in paragraph (c) of this section.

(b) Disabled persons age 18 or over (adults). If you are entitled to disability benefits as a disabled person age 18 or over (adult) there are a number of factors we consider in deciding whether your disability continues. We must determine if there has been any medical improvement in your impairment(s) and, if so, whether this medical improvement is related to your ability to work. If your impairment(s) has not so medically improved, we must consider whether one or more of the exceptions to medical improvement applies. If medical improvement related to your ability to work has not occurred and no exception applies, your benefits will continue. Even where medical improvement related to your ability to work has occurred or an exception applies, in most cases, (see paragraph (b)(4) of this section for exceptions) we must also show that you are currently able to engage in substantial gainful activity before we can find that you are no longer disabled.

(1) Terms and definitions. There are several terms and definitions which are important to know in order to understand how we review whether your disability continues. In addition, see paragraph (b)(8) of this section if you work during your current period of eligibility based on disability or during certain other periods.

(i) Medical improvement. Medical improvement is any decrease in the medical severity of your impairment(s) which was present at the time of the most recent favorable medical decision that you were disabled or continued to be disabled. A determination that there has been a decrease in medical severity must be based on changes (improvement) in the symptoms, signs, or laboratory findings associated with your impairment(s).

Example 1: You were awarded disability benefits due to a herniated nucleus pulposus. At the time of our prior decision granting you benefits you had had a laminectomy. Postoperatively, a myelogram still shows evidence of a persistent deficit in your lumbar spine. You had pain in your back, and pain and a burning sensation in your right foot and leg. There were no muscle weakness or neurological changes and a modest decrease in motion in your back and leg. When we reviewed your claim your medical source who has treated you reported that he or she had seen you regularly every 2 to 3 months for the past 2 years. No further myelograms had been done, complaints of pain in the back and right leg continued especially on sitting or standing for more than a short period of time. Your doctor further reported a moderately decreased range of motion in your back and right leg, but again no muscle atrophy or neurological changes were reported. Medical improvement has not occurred because there has been no decrease in the severity of your back impairment as shown by changes in symptoms, signs or laboratory findings.

Example 2: You were awarded disability benefits due to rheumatoid arthritis. At the time, laboratory findings were positive for this condition. Your doctor reported persistent swelling and tenderness of your fingers and wrists and that you complained of joint pain. Current medical evidence shows that while laboratory tests are still positive for rheumatoid arthritis, your impairment has responded favorably to therapy so that for the last year your fingers and wrists have not been significantly swollen or painful. Medical improvement has occurred because there has been a decrease in the severity of your impairment as documented by the current symptoms and signs reported by your physician. Although your impairment is subject to temporary remissions and exacerbations, the improvement that has occurred has been sustained long enough to permit a finding of medical improvement. We would then determine if this medical improvement is related to your ability to work.

(ii) Medical improvement not related to ability to do work. Medical improvement is not related to your ability to work if there has been a decrease in the severity of the impairment(s) as defined in paragraph (b)(1)(i) of this section, present at the time of the most recent favorable medical decision, but no increase in your functional capacity to do basic work activities as defined in paragraph (b)(1)(iv) of this section. If there has been any medical improvement in your impairment(s), but it is not related to your ability to do work and none of the exceptions applies, your benefits will be continued.

Example: You are 65 inches tall and weighed 246 pounds at the time your disability was established. You had venous insufficiency and persistent edema in your legs. At the time, your ability to do basic work activities was affected because you were able to sit for 6 hours, but were able to stand or walk only occasionally. At the time of our continuing disability review, you had undergone a vein stripping operation. You now weigh 220 pounds and have intermittent edema. You are still able to sit for 6 hours at a time and to stand or work only occasionally although you report less discomfort on walking. Medical improvement has occurred because there has been a decrease in the severity of the existing impairment as shown by your weight loss and the improvement in your edema. This medical improvement is not related to your ability to work, however, because your functional capacity to do basic work activities (i.e., the ability to sit, stand and walk) has not increased.

(iii) Medical improvement that is related to ability to do work. Medical improvement is related to your ability to work if there has been a decrease in the severity, as defined in paragraph (b)(1)(i) of this section, of the impairment(s) present at the time of the most recent favorable medical decision and an increase in your functional capacity to do basic work activities as discussed in paragraph (b)(1)(iv) of this section. A determination that medical improvement related to your ability to do work has occurred does not, necessarily, mean that your disability will be found to have ended unless it is also shown that you are currently able to engage in substantial gainful activity as discussed in paragraph (b)(1)(v) of this section.

Example 1: You have a back impairment and had a laminectomy to relieve the nerve root impingement and weakness in your left leg. At the time of our prior decision, basic work activities were affected because you were able to stand less than 6 hours, and sit no more than ½ hour at a time. You had a successful fusion operation on your back about 1 year before our review of your entitlement. At the time of our review, the weakness in your leg has decreased. Your functional capacity to perform basic work activities now is unimpaired because you now have no limitation on your ability to sit, walk, or stand. Medical improvement has occurred because there has been a decrease in the severity of your impairment as demonstrated by the decreased weakness in your leg. This medical improvement is related to your ability to work because there has also been an increase in your functional capacity to perform basic work activities (or residual functional capacity) as shown by the absence of limitation on your ability to sit, walk, or stand. Whether or not your disability is found to have ended, however, will depend on our determination as to whether you can currently engage in substantial gainful activity.

Example 2: You were injured in an automobile accident receiving a compound fracture to your right femur and a fractured pelvis. When you applied for disability benefits 10 months after the accident your doctor reported that neither fracture had yet achieved solid union based on his clinical examination. X-rays supported this finding. Your doctor estimated that solid union and a subsequent return to full weight bearing would not occur for at least 3 more months. At the time of our review 6 months later, solid union had occurred and you had been returned to weight-bearing for over a month. Your doctor reported this and the fact that your prior fractures no longer placed any limitation on your ability to walk, stand, lift, etc., and, that in fact, you could return to fulltime work if you so desired.

Medical improvement has occurred because there has been a decrease in the severity of your impairments as shown by X-ray and clinical evidence of solid union and your return to full weight-bearing. This medical improvement is related to your ability to work because you no longer meet the same listed impairment in appendix 1 of subpart P of part 404 of this chapter (see paragraph (b)(2)(iii)(A) of this section). In fact, you no longer have an impairment which is severe (see § 416.921) and your disability will be found to have ended.

(iv) Functional capacity to do basic work activities. Under the law, disability is defined, in part, as the inability to do any substantial gainful activity by reason of any medically determinable physical or mental impairment(s). In determining whether you are disabled under the law, we must measure, therefore, how and to what extent your impairment(s) has affected your ability to do work. We do this by looking at how your functional capacity for doing basic work activities has been affected. Basic work activities means the abilities and aptitudes necessary to do most jobs. Included are exertional abilities such as walking, standing, pushing, pulling, reaching and carrying, and nonexertional abilities and aptitudes such as seeing, hearing, speaking, remembering, using judgment, dealing with changes and dealing with both supervisors and fellow workers. A person who has no impairment(s) would be able to do all basic work activities at normal levels; he or she would have an unlimited functional capacity to do basic work activities. Depending on its nature and severity, an impairment will result in some limitation to the functional capacity to do one or more of these basic work activities. Diabetes, for example, can result in circulatory problems which could limit the length of time a person could stand or walk and damage to his or her eyes as well, so that the person also had limited vision. What a person can still do despite an impairment, is called his or her residual functional capacity. How the residual functional capacity is assessed is discussed in more detail in § 416.945. Unless an impairment is so severe that it is deemed to prevent you from doing substantial gainful activity (see §§ 416.925 and 416.926) it is this residual functional capacity that is used to determine whether you can still do your past work or, in conjunction with your age, education and work experience, any other work.

(A) A decrease in the severity of an impairment as measured by changes (improvement) in symptoms, signs or laboratory findings can, if great enough, result in an increase in the functional capacity to do work activities. Vascular surgery (e.g., femoropopliteal bypass) may sometimes reduce the severity of the circulatory complications of diabetes so that better circulation results and the person can stand or walk for longer periods. When new evidence showing a change in symptoms, signs and laboratory findings establishes that both medical improvement has occurred and your functional capacity to perform basic work activities, or residual functional capacity, has increased, we say that medical improvement which is related to your ability to do work has occurred. A residual functional capacity assessment is also used to determine whether you can engage in substantial gainful activity and, thus, whether you continue to be disabled (see paragraph (b)(1)(vi) of this section).

(B) Many impairment-related factors must be considered in assessing your functional capacity for basic work activities. Age is one key factor. Medical literature shows that there is a gradual decrease in organ function with age; that major losses and deficits become irreversible over time and that maximum exercise performance diminishes with age. Other changes related to sustained periods of inactivity and the aging process include muscle atrophy, degenerative joint changes, decrease in range of motion, and changes in the cardiac and respiratory systems which limit the exertional range.

(C) Studies have also shown that the longer an individual is away from the workplace and is inactive, the more difficult it becomes to return to ongoing gainful employment. In addition, a gradual change occurs in most jobs so that after about 15 years, it is no longer realistic to expect that skills and abilities acquired in these jobs will continue to apply to the current workplace. Thus, if you are age 50 or over and have been receiving disability benefits for a considerable period of time, we will consider this factor along with your age in assessing your residual functional capacity. This will ensure that the disadvantages resulting from inactivity and the aging process during a long period of disability will be considered. In some instances where available evidence does not resolve what you can or cannot do on a sustained basis, we will provide special work evaluations or other appropriate testing.

(v) Ability to engage in substantial gainful activity. In most instances, we must show that you are able to engage in substantial gainful activity before your benefits are stopped. When doing this, we will consider all your current impairments not just that impairment(s) present at the time of the most recent favorable determination. If we cannot determine that you are still disabled based on medical consideration alone (as discussed in §§ 416.925 and 416.926), we will use the new symptoms, signs and laboratory findings to make an objective assessment of your functional capacity to do basic work activities or residual functional capacity and we will consider your vocational factors. See §§ 416.945 through 416.969.

(vi) Evidence and basis for our decision. Our decisions under this section will be made on a neutral basis without any initial inference as to the presence or absence of disability being drawn from the fact that you have previously been determined to be disabled. We will consider all evidence you submit and that we obtain from your medical sources and nonmedical sources. What constitutes "evidence" and our procedures for obtaining it are set out in §§ 416.912 through 416.918. Our determination regarding whether your disability continues will be made on the basis of the weight of the evidence.

(vii) Point of comparison. For purpose of determining whether medical improvement has occurred, we will compare the current medical severity of that impairment(s) which was present at the time of the most recent favorable medical decision that you were disabled or continued to be disabled to the medical severity of that impairment(s) at that time. If medical improvement has occurred, we will compare your current functional capacity to do basic work activities (i.e., your residual functional capacity) based on the previously existing impairments with your prior residual functional capacity in order to determine whether the medical improvement is related to your ability to do work. The most recent favorable medical decision is the latest decision involving a consideration of the medical evidence and the issue of whether you were disabled or continued to be disabled which became final.

(2) Determining medical improvement and its relationship to your abilities to do work. Paragraphs (b)(1)(i) through (b)(1)(iii) of this section discuss what we mean by medical improvement, medical improvement not related to your ability to work, and medical improvement that is related to your ability to work. (In addition, see paragraph (b)(8) of this section if you work during your current period of eligibility based on disability or during certain other periods.) How we will arrive at the decision that medical improvement has occurred and its relationship to the ability to do work, is discussed below.

(i) Medical improvement. Medical improvement is any decrease in the medical severity of impairment(s) present at the time of the most recent favorable medical decision that you were disabled or continued to be disabled and is determined by a comparison of prior and current medical evidence which must show that there have been changes (improvement) in the symptoms, signs or laboratory findings associated with that impairment(s).

(ii) Determining if medical improvement is related to ability to work. If there is a decrease in medical severity as shown by the symptoms, signs and laboratory findings, we then must determine if it is related to your ability to do work. In paragraph (b)(1)(iv) of this section, we explain the relationship between medical severity and limitation on functional capacity to do basic work activities (or residual functional capacity) and how changes in medical severity can affect your residual functional capacity. In determining whether medical improvement that has occurred is related to your ability to do work, we will assess your residual functional capacity (in accordance with paragraph (b)(1)(iv) of this section) based on the current severity of the impairment(s) which was present at your last favorable medical decision.

(iii) Your new residual functional capacity will then be compared to your residual functional capacity at the time of our most recent favorable medical decision. Unless an increase in the current residual functional capacity is based on actual changes in the signs, symptoms, or laboratory findings any medical improvement that has occurred will not be considered to be related to your ability to do work.

(iv) Following are some additional factors and considerations which we will apply in making these determinations.

(A) Previous impairment met or equaled listings. If our most recent favorable decision was based on the fact that your impairment(s) at the time met or equaled the severity contemplated by the Listing of Impairments in appendix 1 of subpart P of part 404 of this chapter, an assessment of your residual functional capacity would not have been made. If medical improvement has occurred and the severity of the prior impairment(s) no longer meets or equals the same listing section used to make our most recent favorable decision, we will find that the medical improvement was related to your ability to work. Appendix 1 of subpart P of part 404 of this chapter describes impairments which, if severe enough, affect a person's ability to work. If the appendix level severity is met or equaled the individual is deemed, in the absence of evidence to the contrary, to be unable to engage in gainful activity. If there has been medical improvement to the degree that the requirement of the listing section is no longer met or equaled, then the medical improvement is related to your ability to work. We must, of course, also establish that you can currently engage in substantial gainful activity before finding that your disability has ended.

(B) Prior residual functional capacity assessment made. The residual functional capacity assessment used in making the most recent favorable medical decision will be compared to the residual functional capacity assessment based on current evidence in order to determine if your functional capacity for basic work activities has increased. There will be no attempt made to reassess the prior residual functional capacity.

(C) Prior residual functional capacity assessment should have been made, but was not. If the most recent favorable medical decision should have contained an assessment of your residual functional capacity (i.e., your impairments did not meet or equal the level of severity contemplated by the Listing of Impairments in appendix 1 of subpart P of part 404 of this chapter) but does not, either because this assessment is missing from your file or because it was not done, we will reconstruct the residual functional capacity. This reconstructed residual functional capacity will accurately and objectively assess your functional capacity to do basic work activities. We will assign the maximum functional capacity consistent with a decision of allowance.

Example: You were previously found to be disabled on the basis that "while your impairment did not meet or equal a listing, it did prevent you from doing your past or any other work." The prior adjudicator did not, however, include a residual functional capacity assessment in the rationale of this decision and a review of the prior evidence does not show that such an assessment was ever made. If a decrease in medical severity, i.e., medical improvement, has occurred, the residual functional capacity based on the current level of severity of your impairment will have to be compared with your residual functional capacity based on its prior severity in order to determine if the medical improvement is related to your ability to do work. In order to make this comparison, we will review the prior evidence and make an objective assessment of your residual functional capacity at the time of our most recent favorable medical determination, based on the symptoms, signs and laboratory findings as they then existed.

(D) Impairment subject to temporary remission. In some cases the evidence shows that an individual's impairments are subject to temporary remission. In assessing whether medical improvement has occurred in persons with this type of impairment, we will be careful to consider the longitudinal history of the impairment, including the occurrence of prior remission, and prospects for future worsenings. Improvement in such impairments that is only temporary will not warrant a finding of medical improvement.

(E) Prior file cannot be located. If the prior file cannot be located, we will first determine whether you are able to now engage in substantial gainful activity based on all your current impairments. (In this way, we will be able to determine that your disability continues at the earliest point without addressing the often lengthy process of reconstructing prior evidence.) If you cannot engage in substantial gainful activity currently, your benefits will continue unless one of the second group of exceptions applies (see paragraph (b)(4) of this section). If you are able to engage in substantial gainful activity, we will determine whether an attempt should be made to reconstruct those portions of the missing file that were relevant to our most recent favorable medical decision (e.g., work history, medical evidence, and the results of consultative examinations). This determination will consider the potential availability of old records in light of their age, whether the source of the evidence is still in operation, and whether reconstruction efforts will yield a complete record of the basis for the most recent favorable medical decision. If relevant parts of the prior record are not reconstructed either because it is determined not to attempt reconstruction or because such efforts fail, medical improvement cannot be found. The documentation of your current impairments will provide a basis for any future reviews. If the missing file is later found, it may serve as a basis for reopening any decision under this section in accordance with § 416.988.

(3) First group of exceptions to medical improvement. The law provides for certain limited situations when your disability can be found to have ended even though medical improvement has not occurred, if you can engage in substantial gainful activity. These exceptions to medical improvement are intended to provide a way of finding that a person is no longer disabled in those limited situations where, even though there has been no decrease in severity of the impairment(s), evidence shows that the person should no longer be considered disabled or never should have been considered disabled. If one of these exceptions applies, we must also show that, taking all your current impairment(s) into account, not just those that existed at the time of our most recent favorable medical decision, you are now able to engage in substantial gainful activity before your disability can be found to have ended. As part of the review process, you will be asked about any medical or vocational therapy you received or are receiving. Your answers and the evidence gathered as a result as well as all other evidence, will serve as the basis for the finding that an exception applies.

(i) Substantial evidence shows that you are the beneficiary of advances in medical or vocational therapy or technology (related to your ability to work). Advances in medical or vocational therapy or technology are improvements in treatment or rehabilitative methods which have increased your ability to do basic work activities. We will apply this exception when substantial evidence shows that you have been the beneficiary of services which reflect these advances and they have favorably affected the severity of your impairment or your ability to do basic work activities. This decision will be based on new medical evidence and a new residual functional capacity assessment. (See § 416.945.) This exception does not apply if you are eligible to receive special Supplemental Security Income cash benefits as explained in § 416.261. In many instances, an advanced medical therapy or technology will result in a decrease in severity as shown by symptoms, signs and laboratory findings which will meet the definition of medical improvement. This exception will, therefore, see very limited application.

(ii) Substantial evidence shows that you have undergone vocational therapy (related to your ability to work). Vocational therapy (related to your ability to work) may include, but is not limited to, additional education, training, or work experience that improves your ability to meet the vocational requirements of more jobs. This decision will be based on substantial evidence which includes new medical evidence and a new residual functional capacity assessment. (See § 416.945.) This exception does not apply if you are eligible to receive special Supplemental Security Income cash benefits as explained in § 416.261. If, at the time of our review, you have not completed vocational therapy which could affect the continuance of your disability, we will review your claim upon completion of the therapy.

Example 1: You were found to be disabled because the limitations imposed on you by your impairment allowed you to only do work that was at a sedentary level of exertion. Your prior work experience was work that required a medium level of exertion. Your age and education at the time would not have qualified you for work that was below this medium level of exertion. You enrolled in and completed a specialized training course which qualifies you for a job in data processing as a computer programmer in the period since you were awarded benefits. On review of your claim, current evidence shows that there is no medical improvement and that you can still do only sedentary work. As the work of a computer programmer is sedentary in nature, you are now able to engage in substantial gainful activity when your new skills are considered.

Example 2: You were previously entitled to benefits because the medical evidence and assessment of your residual functional capacity showed you could only do light work. Your prior work was considered to be heavy in nature and your age, education and the nature of your prior work qualified you for work which was no less than medium in exertion. The current evidence and residual functional capacity show there has been no medical improvement and that you can still do only light work. Since you were originally entitled to benefits, your vocational rehabilitation agency enrolled you in and you successfully completed a trade school course so that you are now qualified to do small appliance repair. This work is light in nature, so when your new skills are considered, you are now able to engage in substantial gainful activity even though there has been no change in your residual functional capacity.

(iii) Substantial evidence shows that based on new or improved diagnostic or evaluative techniques your impairment(s) is not as disabling as it was considered to be at the time of the most recent favorable decision. Changing methodologies and advances in medical and other diagnostic or evaluative techniques have given, and will continue to give, rise to improved methods for measuring and documenting the effect of various impairments on the ability to do work. Where, by such new or improved methods, substantial evidence shows that your impairment(s) is not as severe as was determined at the time of our most recent favorable medical decision, such evidence may serve as a basis for finding that you are no longer disabled, if you can currently engage in substantial gainful activity. In order to be used under this exception, however, the new or improved techniques must have become generally available after the date of our most recent favorable medical decision.

(A) How we will determine which methods are new or improved techniques and when they become generally available. New or improved diagnostic techniques or evaluations will come to our attention by several methods. In reviewing cases, we often become aware of new techniques when their results are presented as evidence. Such techniques and evaluations are also discussed and acknowledged in medical literature by medical professional groups and other governmental entities. Through these sources, we develop listings of new techniques and when they become generally available. For example, we will consult the Health Care Financing Administration for its experience regarding when a technique is recognized for payment under Medicare and when they began paying for the technique.

(B) How you will know which methods are new or improved techniques and when they become generally available. We will let you know which methods we consider to be new or improved techniques and when they become available through two vehicles.

(1) Some of the future changes in the Listing of Impairments in appendix 1 of subpart P of part 404 of this chapter will be based on new or improved diagnostic or evaluation techniques. Such listings changes will clearly state this fact as they are published as Notices of Proposed Rulemaking and the new or improved techniques will be considered generally available as of the date of the final publication of that particular listing in the Federal Register.

(2) A cumulative list since 1970 of new or approved diagnostic techniques or evaluations, how they changed the evaluation of the applicable impairment and the month and year they became generally available, will be published in the Notices section of the Federal Register. Included will be any changes in the Listing of Impairments published in the Code of Federal Regulations since 1970 which are reflective of new or improved techniques. No cases will be processed under this exception until this cumulative listing is so published. Subsequent changes to the list will be published periodically. The period will be determined by the volume of changes needed.

Example: The electrocardiographic exercise test has replaced the Master's 2–step test as a measurement of heart function since the time of your last favorable medical decision. Current evidence could show that your condition, which was previously evaluated based on the Master's 2–step test, is not now as disabling as was previously thought. If, taking all your current impairments into account, you are now able to engage in substantial gainful activity, this exception would be used to find that you are no longer disabled even if medical improvement has not occurred.

(iv) Substantial evidence demonstrates that any prior disability decision was in error. We will apply the exception to medical improvement based on error if substantial evidence (which may be evidence on the record at the time any prior determination of the entitlement to benefits based on disability was made, or newly obtained evidence which relates to that determination) demonstrates that a prior determination was in error. A prior determination will be found in error only if:

(A) Substantial evidence shows on its face that the decision in question should not have been made (e.g., the evidence in your file such as pulmonary function study values was misread or an adjudicative standard such as a listing in appendix 1 of subpart P of part 404 of this chapter or a medical/vocational rule in appendix 2 of subpart P of part 404 of this chapter was misapplied).

Example 1: You were granted benefits when it was determined that your epilepsy met Listing 11.02. This listing calls for a finding of major motor seizures more frequently than once a month as documented by electroencephalogram evidence and by a detailed description of a typical seizure pattern. A history of either diurnal episodes or nocturnal episodes with residuals interfering with daily activities is also required. On review, it is found that a history of the frequency of your seizures showed that they occurred only once or twice a year. The prior decision would be found to be in error, and whether you were still considered to be disabled would be based on whether you could currently engage in substantial gainful activity.

Example 2: Your prior award of benefits was based on vocational rule 201.12 in appendix 2 of subpart P of part 404 of this chapter. This rule applies to a person age 50–54 who has at least a high school education, whose previous work was entirely at a semiskilled level, and who can do only sedentary work. On review, it is found that at the time of the prior determination you were actually only age 46 and vocational rule 201.21 should have been used. This rule would have called for a denial of your claim and the prior decision is found to have been in error. Continuation of your disability would depend on a finding of your current ability to engage in substantial gainful activity.

(B) At the time of the prior evaluation, required and material evidence of the severity of your impairment(s) was missing. That evidence becomes available upon review, and substantial evidence demonstrates that had such evidence been present at the time of the prior determination, disability would not have been found.

Example: You were found disabled on the basis of chronic obstructive pulmonary disease. The severity of your impairment was documented primarily by pulmonary function testing results. The evidence showed that you could do only light work. Spirometric tracings of this testing, although required, were not obtained, however. On review, the original report is resubmitted by the consultative examining physician along with the corresponding spirometric tracings. A review of the tracings shows that the test was invalid. Current pulmonary function testing supported by spirometric tracings reveals that your impairment does not limit your ability to perform basic work activities in any way. Error is found based on the fact that required, material evidence which was originally missing now becomes available and shows that if it had been available at the time of the prior determination, disability would not have been found.

(C) Substantial evidence which is new evidence which relates to the prior determination (of allowance or continuance) refutes the conclusions that were based upon the prior evidence (e.g., a tumor thought to be malignant was later shown to have actually been benign). Substantial evidence must show that had the new evidence, (which relates to the prior determination) been considered at the time of the prior decision, the claim would not have been allowed or continued. A substitution of current judgment for that used in the prior favorable decision will not be the basis for applying this exception.

Example: You were previously found entitled to benefits on the basis of diabetes mellitus which the prior adjudicator believed was equivalent to the level of severity contemplated in the Listing of Impairments. The prior record shows that you had "brittle" diabetes for which you were taking insulin. Your urine was 3+ for sugar, and you alleged occasional hypoglycemic attacks caused by exertion. On review, symptoms, signs and laboratory findings are unchanged. The current adjudicator feels, however, that your impairment clearly does not equal the severity contemplated by the listings. Error cannot be found because it would represent a substitution of current judgment for that of the prior adjudicator that your impairment equaled a listing.

(D) The exception for error will not be applied retroactively under the conditions set out above unless the conditions for reopening the prior decision (see §§ 416.1488 through 416.1489) are met.

(4) Second group of exceptions to medical improvement. In addition to the first group of exceptions to medical improvement, the following exceptions may result in a determination that you are no longer disabled. In these situations the decision will be made without a determination that you have medically improved or can engage in substantial gainful activity.

(i) A prior determination or decision was fraudulently obtained. If we find that any prior favorable determination or decision was obtained by fraud, we may find that you are not disabled. In addition, we may reopen your claim under the rules in § 416.1488. In determining whether a prior favorable determination or decision was fraudulently obtained, we will take into account any physical, mental, educational, or linguistic limitations (including any lack of facility with the English language) which you may have had at the time.

(ii) You do not cooperate with us. If there is a question about whether you continue to be disabled and we ask you to give us medical or other evidence or to go for a physical or mental examination by a certain date, we will find that your disability has ended if you fail, without good cause, to do what we ask. Section 416.1411 explains the factors we consider and how we will determine generally whether you have good cause for failure to cooperate. In addition, § 416.918 discusses how we determine whether you have good cause for failing to attend a consultative examination. The month in which your disability ends will be the first month in which you failed to do what we asked.

(iii) We are unable to find you. If there is a question about whether you continue to be disabled and we are unable to find you to resolve the question, we will suspend your payments. The month your payments are suspended will be the first month in which the question arose and we could not find you.

(iv) You fail to follow prescribed treatment which would be expected to restore your ability to engage in substantial gainful activity. If treatment has been prescribed for you which would be expected to restore your ability to work, you must follow that treatment in order to be paid benefits. If you are not following that treatment and you do not have good cause for failing to follow that treatment, we will find that your disability has ended (see § 416.930(c)). The month your disability ends will be the first month in which you failed to follow the prescribed treatment.

(5) Evaluation steps. To assure that disability reviews are carried out in a uniform manner, that a decision of continuing disability can be made in the most expeditious and administratively efficient way, and that any decisions to stop disability benefits are made objectively, neutrally, and are fully documented, we will follow specific steps in reviewing the question of whether your disability continues. Our review may cease and benefits may be continued at any point if we determine there is sufficient evidence to find that you are still unable to engage in substantial gainful activity. The steps are as follows. (See paragraph (b)(8) of this section if you work during your current period of eligibility based on disability or during certain other periods.)

(i) Step 1. Do you have an impairment or combination of impairments which meets or equals the severity of an impairment listed in appendix 1 of subpart P of part 404 of this chapter? If you do, your disability will be found to continue.

(ii) Step 2. If you do not, has there been medical improvement as defined in paragraph (b)(1)(i) of this section? If there has been medical improvement as shown by a decrease in medical severity, see step 3 in paragraph (b)(5)(iii) of this section. If there has been no decrease in medical severity, there has been no medical improvement. (See step 4 in paragraph (b)(5)(iv) of this section.)

(iii) Step 3. If there has been medical improvement, we must determine whether it is related to your ability to do work in accordance with paragraphs (b)(1)(i) through (b)(1)(iv) of this section; i.e., whether or not there has been an increase in the residual functional capacity based on the impairment(s) that was present at the time of the most recent favorable medical determination. If medical improvement is not related to your ability to do work, see step 4 in paragraph (b)(5)(iv) of this section. If medical improvement is related to your ability to do work, see step 5 in paragraph (b)(5)(v) of this section.

(iv) Step 4. If we found at step 2 in paragraph (b)(5)(ii) of this section that there has been no medical improvement or if we found at step 3 in paragraph (b)(5)(iii) of this section that the medical improvement is not related to your ability to work, we consider whether any of the exceptions in paragraphs (b)(3) and (b)(4) of this section apply. If none of them apply, your disability will be found to continue. If one of the first group of exceptions to medical improvement applies, see step 5 in paragraph (b)(5)(v) of this section. If an exception from the second group of exceptions to medical improvement applies, your disability will be found to have ended. The second group of exceptions to medical improvement may be considered at any point in this process.

(v) Step 5. If medical improvement is shown to be related to your ability to do work or if one of the first group of exceptions to medical improvement applies, we will determine whether all your current impairments in combination are severe (see § 416.921). This determination will consider all your current impairments and the impact of the combination of these impairments on your ability to function. If the residual functional capacity assessment in step 3 in paragraph (b)(5)(iii) of this section shows significant limitation of your ability to do basic work activities, see step 6 in paragraph (b)(5)(vi) of this section. When the evidence shows that all your current impairments in combination do not significantly limit your physical or mental abilities to do basic work activities, these impairments will not be considered severe in nature. If so, you will no longer be considered to be disabled.

(vi) Step 6. If your impairment(s) is severe, we will assess your current ability to do substantial gainful activity in accordance with § 416.960. That is, we will assess your residual functional capacity based on all your current impairments and consider whether you can still do work you have done in the past. If you can do such work, disability will be found to have ended.

(vii) Step 7. If you are not able to do work you have done in the past, we will consider whether you can do other work given the residual functional capacity assessment made under paragraph (b)(5)(vi) of this section and your age, education, and past work experience (see paragraph (b)(5)(viii) of this section for an exception to this rule). If you can, we will find that your disability has ended. If you cannot, we will find that your disability continues.

(viii) Step 8. We may proceed to the final step, described in paragraph (b)(5)(vii) of this section, if the evidence in your file about your past relevant work is not sufficient for us to make a finding under paragraph (b)(5)(vi) of this section about whether you can perform your past relevant work. If we find that you can adjust to other work based solely on your age, education, and residual functional capacity, we will find that you are no longer disabled, and we will not make a finding about whether you can do your past relevant work under paragraph (b)(5)(vi) of this section. If we find that you may be unable to adjust to other work or if § 416.962 may apply, we will assess your claim under paragraph (b)(5)(vi) of this section and make a finding about whether you can perform your past relevant work.

(6) The month in which we will find you are no longer disabled. If the evidence shows that you are no longer disabled, we will find that your disability ended in the earliest of the following months.

(i) The month the evidence shows that you are no longer disabled under the rules set out in this section, and you were disabled only for a specified period of time in the past;

(ii) The month the evidence shows that you are no longer disabled under the rules set out in this section, but not earlier than the month in which we mail you a notice saying that the information we have shows that you are not disabled;

(iii) The month in which you return to full-time work, with no significant medical restrictions and acknowledge that medical improvement has occurred, and we expected your impairment(s) to improve (see § 416.991);

(iv) The first month in which you fail without good cause to follow prescribed treatment, when the rule set out in paragraph (b)(4)(iv) of this section applies;

(v) The first month you were told by your physician that you could return to work, provided there is no substantial conflict between your physician's and your statements regarding your awareness of your capacity for work and the earlier date is supported by substantial evidence; or

(vi) The first month in which you failed without good cause to do what we asked, when the rule set out in paragraph (b)(4)(ii) of this section applies.

(7) Before we stop your benefits. If we find you are no longer disabled, before we stop your benefits, we will give you a chance to explain why we should not do so. Subparts M and N of this part describe your rights and the procedures we will follow.

(8) If you work during your current period of eligibility based on disability or during certain other periods.

(i) We will not consider the work you are doing or have done during your current period of eligibility based on disability (or, when determining whether you are eligible for expedited reinstatement of benefits under section 1631(p) of the Act, the work you are doing or have done during or after the previously terminated period of eligibility referred to in section 1631(p)(1)(B) of the Act) to be past relevant work under paragraph (b)(5)(vi) of this section or past work experience under paragraph (b)(5)(vii) of this section. In addition, if you are currently entitled to disability benefits under title II of the Social Security Act, we may or may not consider the physical and mental activities that you perform in the work you are doing or have done during your current period of entitlement based on disability, as explained in paragraphs (b)(8)(ii) and (iii) of this section.

(ii) If you are currently entitled to disability insurance benefits as a disabled worker, child's insurance benefits based on disability, or widow's or widower's insurance benefits based on disability under title II of the Social Security Act, and at the time we are making a determination on your case you have received such benefits for at least 24 months, we will not consider the activities you perform in the work you are doing or have done during your current period of entitlement based on disability if they support a finding that your disability has ended. (We will use the rules in § 416.990(i)(2) to determine whether the 24–month requirement is met.) However, we will consider the activities you do in that work if they support a finding that your disability continues or they do not conflict with a finding that your disability continues. We will not presume that you are still disabled if you stop working.

(iii) If you are not a person described in paragraph (b)(8)(ii) of this section, we will consider the activities you perform in your work at any of the evaluation steps in paragraph (b)(5) of this section at which we need to assess your ability to function. However, we will not consider the work you are doing or have done during your current period of eligibility based on disability (or, when determining whether you are eligible for expedited reinstatement of benefits under section 1631(p) of the Act, the work you are doing or have done during or after the previously terminated period of eligibility referred to in section 1631(p)(1)(B) of the Act) to be past relevant work under paragraph (b)(5)(vi) of this section or past work experience under paragraph (b)(5)(vii) of this section.

(c) Persons who were found disabled under a State plan. If you became entitled to benefits because you were found to be disabled under a State plan, we will first evaluate your impairment(s) under the rules explained in paragraph (b) of this section. We will apply the same steps as described in paragraph (b) of this section to the last decision granting or affirming entitlement to benefits under the State plan. If we are not able to find that your disability continues on the basis of these rules, we will then evaluate your impairment(s) under the appropriate State plan. If we are not able to find that your disability continues under these State plan criteria, we will find that your disability ends. Disability will be found to end the month the evidence shows that you are no longer disabled under the criteria in paragraph (b) of this section (or appropriate State plan criteria), subject to the rules set out in paragraph (b)(6) of this section.

[49 FR 22274, May 29, 1984; 50 FR 50137, Dec. 6, 1985; 51 FR 7063, Feb. 28, 1986; 51 FR 16015, April 30, 1986; 52 FR 44971, Nov. 24, 1987; 56 FR 5562, Feb. 11, 1991; 57 FR 10287, March 25, 1992; 59 FR 1636, Jan. 12, 1994; 65 FR 42791, July 11, 2000; 68 FR 51167, Aug. 26, 2003; 68 FR 53219, Sept. 9, 2003; 71 FR 66859, Nov. 17, 2006; 77 FR 43496, July 25, 2012; 82 FR 5882, Jan. 18, 2017]

§ 416.994a How we will determine whether your disability continues or ends, and whether you are and have been receiving treatment that is medically necessary and available, disabled children.

(a) Evaluation of continuing disability, in general. There is a statutory requirement that, if you are eligible for disability benefits as a disabled child, your continued eligibility for such benefits must be reviewed periodically. There are a number of factors we consider when we decide whether your disability continues.

(1) We will first consider whether there has been medical improvement in your impairment(s). We define "medical improvement" in paragraph (c) of this section. If there has been no medical improvement, we will find you are still disabled unless one of the exceptions in paragraphs (e) or (f) of this section applies. If there has been medical improvement, we will consider whether the impairments(s) you had at the time of our most recent favorable determination or decision now meets or medically or functionally equals the severity of the listing it met or equalled at that time. If so, we will find you are still disabled, unless one of the exceptions in paragraphs (e) or (f) of this section applies. If not, we will consider whether your current impairment(s) are disabling under the rules in § 416.924. These steps are described in more detail in paragraph (b) of this section. Even where medical improvement or an exception applies, in most cases, we will find that your disability has ended only if we also find that you are not currently disabled.

(2) Our determinations and decisions under this section will be made on a neutral basis, without any initial inference as to the presence or absence of disability being drawn from the fact that you have been previously found disabled. We will consider all evidence you submit and that we obtain from your medical and nonmedical sources. What constitutes "evidence" and our procedures for obtaining it are set out in §§ 416.912 through 416.918. Our determination regarding whether your disability continues will be made on the basis of the weight of the evidence.

(b) Sequence of evaluation. To ensure that disability reviews are carried out in a uniform manner, that decisions of continuing disability can be made in the most expeditious and administratively efficient way, and that any decisions to stop disability benefits are made objectively, neutrally, and are fully documented, we follow specific steps in determining whether your disability continues. However, we may skip steps in the sequence if it is clear this would lead to a more prompt finding that your disability continues. For example, we might not consider the issue of medical improvement if it is obvious on the face of the evidence that a current impairment meets the severity of a listed impairment. If we can make a favorable determination or decision at any point in the sequence, we do not review further. The steps are:

(1) Has there been medical improvement in your condition(s)? We will determine whether there has been medical improvement in the impairment(s) you had at the time of our most recent favorable determination or decision. (The term medical improvement is defined in paragraph (c) of this section.) If there has been no medical improvement, we will find that your disability continues, unless one of the exceptions to medical improvement described in paragraph (e) or (f) of this section applies.

(i) If one of the first group of exceptions to medical improvement applies, we will proceed to step 3.

(ii) If one of the second group of exceptions to medical improvement applies, we may find that your disability has ended.

(2) Does your impairment(s) still meet or equal the severity of the listed impairment that it met or equaled before? If there has been medical improvement, we will consider whether the impairment(s) that we considered at the time of our most recent favorable determination or decision still meets or equals the severity of the listed impairment it met or equaled at that time. In making this decision, we will consider the current severity of the impairment(s) present and documented at the time of our most recent favorable determination or decision, and the same listing section used to make that determination or decision as it was written at that time, even if it has since been revised or removed from the Listing of Impairments. If that impairment(s) does not still meet or equal the severity of that listed impairment, we will proceed to the next step. If that impairment(s) still meets or equals the severity of that listed impairment as it was written at that time, we will find that you are still disabled, unless one of the exceptions to medical improvement described in paragraphs (e) or (f) of this section applies.

(i) If one of the first group of exceptions to medical improvement applies, we will proceed to step 3.

(ii) If one of the second group of exceptions to medical improvement applies, we may find that your disability has ended.

(3) Are you currently disabled? If there has been medical improvement in the impairment(s) that we considered at the time of our most recent favorable determination or decision, and if that impairment(s) no

longer meets or equals the severity of the listed impairment that it met or equaled at that time, we will consider whether you are disabled under the rules in § § 416.924(c) and (d). In determining whether you are currently disabled, we will consider all impairments you now have, including any you did not have at the time of our most recent favorable determination or decision, or that we did not consider at that time. The steps in determining current disability are summarized as follows:

(i) Do you have a severe impairment or combination of impairment? If there has been medical improvement in your impairment(s), or if one of the first group of exceptions applies, we will determine whether your current impairment(s) is severe, as defined in § 416.924(c). If your impairment(s) is not severe, we will find that your disability has ended. If your impairment(s) is severe, we will then consider whether it meets or medically equals the severity of a listed impairment.

(ii) Does your impairment(s) meet or medically equal the severity of any impairment listed in appendix 1 of subpart P of part 404 of this chapter? If your current impairment(s) meets or medically equals the severity of any listed impairment, as described in §§ 416.925 and 416.926, we will find that your disability continues. If not, we will consider whether it functionally equals the listings.

(iii) Does your impairment(s) functionally equal the listings? If your current impairment(s) functionally equals the listings, as described in § 416.926a, we will find that your disability continues. If not, we will find that your disability has ended.

(c) What we mean by medical improvement. Medical improvement is any decrease in the medical severity of your impairment(s) which was present at the time of the most recent favorable decision that you were disabled or continued to be disabled. Although the decrease in severity may be of any quantity or degree, we will disregard minor changes in your signs, symptoms, and laboratory findings that obviously do not represent medical improvement and could not result in a finding that your disability has ended. A determination that there has been a decrease in medical severity must be based on changes (improvement) in the symptoms, signs, or laboratory findings associated with your impairment(s).

(1) The most recent favorable decision is the latest final determination or decision involving a consideration of the medical evidence and whether you were disabled or continued to be disabled.

(2) The terms symptoms, signs, and laboratory findings are defined in § 416.902. For children, our definitions of the terms symptoms, signs, and laboratory findings may include any abnormalities of physical and mental functioning that we used in making our most recent favorable decision.

(3) Some impairments are subject to temporary remissions, which can give the appearance of medical improvement when in fact there has been none. If you have the kind of impairment that is subject to temporary remissions, we will be careful to consider the longitudinal history of the impairment, including the occurrence of prior remissions and prospects for future worsenings, when we decide whether there has been medical improvement. Improvements that are only temporary will not warrant a finding of medical improvement.

(d) Prior file cannot be located. If we cannot locate your prior file, we will first determine whether you are currently disabled under the sequence set forth in § 416.924. (In this way, we will determine that your benefits continue at the earliest time without reconstructing prior evidence.) If so, your benefits will continue unless one of the second group of exceptions applies (see paragraph (f) of this section). If not, we will determine whether an attempt should be made to reconstruct those portions of the missing file that were relevant to our most recent favorable determination or decision (e.g., school records, medical evidence, and the results of consultative examinations). This determination will consider the potential availability of old records in light of their age, whether the source of the evidence is still in operation, and whether reconstruction efforts will yield a complete record of the basis for the most recent favorable decision. If relevant parts of the prior record are not reconstructed, either because we decide not to attempt reconstruction or because our efforts failed, we will not find that you have medically improved. The documentation of your current impairment(s) will provide a basis for any future reviews. If the missing file is later found, it may serve as a basis for reopening any determination or decision under this section, in accordance with § 416.1488.

(e) First group of exceptions to medical improvement. The law provides certain limited situations when your disability can be found to have ended even though medical improvement has not occurred, if your impairment(s) no longer results in marked and severe functional limitations. These exceptions to medical improvement are intended to provide a way of finding that a person is no longer disabled in those situations where, even though there has been no decrease in severity of the impairment(s), evidence shows that the person should no longer be considered disabled or never should have been considered disabled. If one of these exceptions applies, we must also show that your impairment(s) does not now result in marked and severe functional limitations, before we can find you are no longer disabled, taking all your current impairments into account, not just those that existed at the time of our most recent favorable determination or decision. The evidence we gather will serve as the basis for the finding that an exception applies.

(1) Substantial evidence shows that, based on new or improved diagnostic techniques or evaluations, your impairment(s) is not as disabling as it was considered to be at the time of the most recent favorable decision. Changing methodologies and advances in medical and other diagnostic techniques or evaluations have given rise to, and will continue to give rise to, improved methods for determining the causes of (i.e., diagnosing) and measuring and documenting the effects of various impairments on children and their functioning. Where, by such new or improved methods, substantial evidence shows that your impairment(s) is not as severe as was determined at the time of our most recent favorable decision, such evidence may serve as a basis for a finding that you are no longer disabled, provided that you do not currently have an impairment(s) that meets, medically equals, or functionally equals the listings, and therefore results in marked and severe functional limitations. In order to be used under this exception, however, the new or improved techniques must have become generally available after the date of our most recent favorable decision.

(i) How we will determine which methods are new or improved techniques and when they become generally available. New or improved diagnostic techniques or evaluations will come to our attention by several methods. In reviewing cases, we often become aware of new techniques when their results are presented as evidence. Such techniques and evaluations are also discussed and acknowledged in medical literature by medical professional groups and other governmental entities. Through these sources, we develop listings of new techniques and when they become generally available. For example, we will consult the Health Care Financing Administration for its experience regarding when a technique is recognized for payment under Medicare and when they began paying for the technique.

(ii) How you will know which methods are new or improved techniques and when they become generally available. We will let you know which methods we consider to be new or improved techniques and when they become available through two vehicles.

(A) Some of the future changes in the Listing of Impairments in appendix 1 of subpart P of part 404 of this chapter will be based on new or improved diagnostic or evaluative techniques. Such listings changes will clearly state this fact as they are published as Notices of Proposed Rulemaking and the new or improved technique will be considered generally available as of the date of the final publication of that particular listing in the Federal Register.

(B) From time to time, we will publish in the Federal Register cumulative lists of new or approved diagnostic techniques or evaluations that have been in use since 1970, how they changed the evaluation of the applicable impairment and the month and year they became generally available. We will include any changes in the Listing of Impairments published in the Code of Federal Regulations since 1970 that are reflective of new or improved techniques. We will not process any cases under this exception using a new or improved diagnostic technique that we have not included in a published notice until we have published an updated cumulative list. The period between publications will be determined by the volume of changes needed.

(2) Substantial evidence demonstrates that any prior disability decision was in error. We will apply the exception to medical improvement based on error if substantial evidence (which may be evidence on the record at the time any prior determination or decision of the entitlement to benefits based on disability was made, or newly obtained evidence which relates to that determination or decision) demonstrates that a prior determination or decision (of allowance or continuance) was in error. A prior determination or decision will be found in error only if:

(i) Substantial evidence shows on its face that the determination or decision in question should not have been made (e.g., the evidence in your file, such as pulmonary function study values, was misread, or an adjudicative standard, such as a listing in appendix 1 of subpart P of part 404 of this chapter, was misapplied).

(ii) At the time of the prior evaluation, required and material evidence of the severity of your impairment(s) was missing. That evidence becomes available upon review, and substantial evidence demonstrates that, had such evidence been present at the time of the prior determination or decision, disability would not have been found.

(iii) New substantial evidence that relates to the prior determination or decision refutes the conclusions that were based upon the prior evidence at the time of that determination or decision (e.g., a tumor thought to be malignant was later shown to have actually been benign). Substantial evidence must show that, had the new evidence (which relates to the prior determination or decision) been considered at the time of the prior determination or decision, the claim would not have been allowed or continued. A substitution of current judgment for that used in the prior favorable determination or decision will not be the basis for applying this exception.

(iv) The exception for error will not be applied retroactively under the conditions set out above unless the conditions for reopening the prior decision (see §§ 416.1488 and 416.1489) are met.

(f) Second group of exceptions to medical improvement. In addition to the first group of exceptions to medical improvement, the following exceptions may result in a determination or decision that you are no longer disabled. In these situations, the determination or decision will be made without a finding that you have demonstrated medical improvement or that you are currently not disabled under the rules in § 416.924. There is no set point in the continuing disability review sequence described in paragraph (b) of this section at which we must consider these exceptions; exceptions in the second group may be considered at any point in the process.

(1) A prior determination or decision was fraudulently obtained. If we find that any prior favorable determination or decision was obtained by fraud, we may find that you are not disabled. In addition, we may reopen your claim under the rules in § 416.1488. In determining whether a prior favorable determination or decision was fraudulently obtained, we will take into account any physical, mental, educational, or linguistic limitations (including any lack of facility with the English language) which you may have had at the time.

(2) You do not cooperate with us. If there is a question about whether you continue to be disabled and we ask you to give us medical or other evidence or to go for a physical or mental examination by a certain date, we will find that your disability has ended if you fail, without good cause, to do what we ask. Section 416.1411 explains the factors we consider and how we will determine generally whether you have good cause for failure to cooperate. In addition, § 416.918 discusses how we determine whether you have good cause for failing to attend a consultative examination. The month in which your disability ends will be the first month in which you failed to do what we asked.

(3) We are unable to find you. If there is a question about whether you continue to be disabled and we are unable to find you to resolve the question, we will suspend your payments. The month your payments are suspended will be the first month in which the question arose and we could not find you.

(4) You fail to follow prescribed treatment which would be expected to improve your impairment(s) so that it no longer results in marked and severe functional limitations. If treatment has been prescribed for you which would be expected to improve your impairment(s) so that it no longer results in marked and severe functional limitations, you must follow that treatment in order to be paid benefits. If you are not following that treatment and you do not have good cause for failing to follow that treatment, we will find that your disability has ended (see § 416.930(c)). The month your disability ends will be the first month in which you failed to follow the prescribed treatment.

(g) The month in which we will find you are no longer disabled. If the evidence shows that you are no longer disabled, we will find that your disability ended in the following month—

(1) The month the evidence shows that you are no longer disabled under the rules set out in this section, and you were disabled only for a specified period of time in the past;

(2) The month the evidence shows that you are no longer disabled under the rules set out in this section, but not earlier than the month in which we mail you a notice saying that the information we have shows that you are not disabled;

(3) The month in which you return to, or begin, full-time work with no significant medical restrictions, and acknowledge that medical improvement has occurred, and we expected your impairment(s) to improve (see § 416.991);

(4) The first month in which you fail without good cause to follow prescribed treatment, when the rule set out in paragraph (f)(4) of this section applies;

(5) The first month in which you were told by your physician that you could return to normal activities, provided there is no substantial conflict between your physician's and your statements regarding your awareness of your capacity, and the earlier date is supported by substantial evidence; or

(6) The first month in which you failed without good cause to do what we asked, when the rule set out in paragraph (f)(2) of this section applies.

(h) Before we stop your benefits. If we find you are no longer disabled, before we stop your benefits, we will give you a chance to explain why we should not do so. Subparts M and N of this part describe your rights and the procedures we will follow.

(i) Requirement for treatment that is medically necessary and available. If you have a representative payee, the representative payee must, at the time of the continuing disability review, present evidence demonstrating that you are and have been receiving treatment, to the extent considered medically necessary and available, for the condition(s) that was the basis for providing you with SSI benefits, unless we determine that requiring your representative payee to provide such evidence would be inappropriate or unnecessary considering the nature of your impairment(s). If your representative payee refuses without good cause to comply with this requirement, and if we decide that it is in your best interests, we may pay your benefits to another representative payee or to you directly.

(1) What we mean by treatment that is medically necessary. Treatment that is medically necessary means treatment that is expected to improve or restore your functioning and that was prescribed by your medical source. If you do not have a medical source, we will decide whether there is treatment that is medically necessary that could have been prescribed by a medical source. The treatment may include (but is not limited to)—

(i) Medical management;

(ii) Psychological or psychosocial counseling;

(iii) Physical therapy; and

(iv) Home therapy, such as administering oxygen or giving injections.

(2) How we will consider whether medically necessary treatment is available. When we decide whether medically necessary treatment is available, we will consider such things as (but not limited to)—

(i) The location of an institution or facility or place where treatment, services, or resources could be provided to you in relationship to where you reside;

(ii) The availability and cost of transportation for you and your payee to the place of treatment;

(iii) Your general health, including your ability to travel for the treatment;

(iv) The capacity of an institution or facility to accept you for appropriate treatment;

(v) The cost of any necessary medications or treatments that are not paid for by Medicaid or another insurer or source; and

(vi) The availability of local community resources (e.g., clinics, charitable organizations, public assistance agencies) that would provide free treatment or funds to cover treatment.

(3) When we will not require evidence of treatment that is medically necessary and available. We will not require your representative payee to present evidence that you are and have been receiving treatment if we find that the condition(s) that was the basis for providing you benefits is not amenable to treatment.

(4) Removal of a payee who does not provide evidence that a child is and has been receiving treatment that is medically necessary and available. If your representative payee refuses without good cause to provide evidence that you are and have been receiving treatment that is medically necessary and available, we may, if it is in your best interests, suspend payment of benefits to the representative payee, and pay benefits to another payee or to you. When we decide whether your representative payee had good cause, we will consider factors such as the acceptable reasons for failure to follow prescribed treatment in § 416.930(c) and other factors similar to those describing good cause for missing deadlines in § 416.1411.

(5) If you do not have a representative payee. If you do not have a representative payee and we make your payments directly to you, the provisions of this paragraph do not apply to you. However, we may still decide that you are failing to follow prescribed treatment under the provisions of § 416.930, if the requirements of that section are met.

[56 FR 5562, Feb. 11, 1991; 56 FR 13365, April 1, 1991; 58 FR 47586, Sept. 9, 1993; 59 FR 1637, Jan. 12, 1994; 62 FR 6430, Feb. 11, 1997; 62 FR 13538, 13733, March 21, 1997; 62 FR 36460, July 8, 1997; 65 FR 16815, March 30, 2000; 65 FR 54790, Sept. 11, 2000; 82 FR 5882, Jan. 18, 2017]

§ 416.995 If we make a determination that your physical or mental impairment(s) has ceased, did not exist or is no longer disabling (Medical Cessation Determination).

If we make a determination that the physical or mental impairment(s) on the basis of which disability or blindness benefits were payable has ceased, did not exist or is no longer disabling (a medical cessation determination), your benefits will stop. You will receive a written notice explaining this determination and the month your benefits will stop. The written notice will also explain your right to appeal if you disagree with our determination and your right to request that your disability or blindness benefits be continued under § 416.996. The continued benefit provisions of this section do not apply to an initial determination on an application for disability or blindness benefits or to a determination that you were disabled or blind only for a specified period of time.

[53 FR 29023, Aug. 2, 1988]

§ 416.996 Continued disability or blindness benefits pending appeal of a medical cessation determination.

(a) General. If we determine that you are not eligible for disability or blindness benefits because the physical or mental impairment(s) on the basis of which such benefits were payable is found to have ceased, not to have existed, or to no longer be disabling, and you appeal that determination, you may choose to have your disability or blindness benefits, including special cash benefits or special SSI eligibility status under §§ 416.261 and 416.264, continued pending reconsideration and/or a hearing before an administrative law judge on the disability/blindness cessation determination. If you appeal a medical cessation under both title II and title XVI (a concurrent case), the title II claim will be handled in accordance with title II regulations while the title XVI claim will be handled in accordance with the title XVI regulations.

(1) Benefits may be continued under this section only if the determination that your physical or mental impairment(s) has ceased, has never existed, or is no longer disabling is made after October 1984.

(2) Continued benefits under this section will stop effective with the earlier of: (i) The month before the month in which an administrative law judge's hearing decision finds that your physical or mental impairment(s) has ceased, has never existed, or is no longer disabling or the month before the month of a new administrative law judge decision (or final action is taken by the Appeals Council on the administrative law judge's recommended decision) if your case was sent back to an administrative law judge for further action; or (ii) the month before the month in which no timely request for reconsideration or administrative law judge hearing is pending after notification of our initial or

reconsideration cessation determination. These benefits may be stopped or adjusted because of certain events (such as, change in income or resources or your living arrangements) which may occur while you are receiving these continued benefits, in accordance with § 416.1336(b).

(b) Statement of choice. If you or another party (see § 416.1432(a)) request reconsideration under § 416.1409 or a hearing before an administrative law judge in accordance with § 416.1433 on our determination that your physical or mental impairment(s) has ceased, has never existed, or is no longer disabling, or if your case is sent back (remanded) to an administrative law judge for further action, we will explain your right to receive continued benefits and ask you to complete a statement indicating that you wish to have benefits continued pending the outcome of the reconsideration or administrative law judge hearing. If you request reconsideration and/or hearing but you do not want to receive continued benefits, we will ask you to complete a statement declining continued benefits indicating that you do not want to have your benefits continued during the appeal. A separate election must be made at each level of appeal.

(c) What you must do to receive continued benefits pending notice of our reconsideration determination.

(1) If you want to receive continued benefits pending the outcome of your request for reconsideration, you must request reconsideration and continuation of benefits no later than 10 days after the date you receive the notice of our initial determination that your physical or mental impairment(s) has ceased, has never existed, or is no longer disabling. Reconsideration must be requested as provided in § 416.1409, and you must request continued benefits using a statement in accordance with paragraph (b) of this section.

(2) If you fail to request reconsideration and continued benefits within the 10–day period required by paragraph (c)(1) of this section, but later ask that we continue your benefits pending a reconsidered determination, we will use the rules in § 416.1411 to determine whether good cause exists for your failing to request benefit continuation within 10 days after receipt of the notice of the initial cessation determination. If you request continued benefits after the 10–day period, we will consider the request to be timely and will pay continued benefits only if good cause for delay is established.

(d) What you must do to receive continued benefits pending an administrative law judge's decision.

(1) To receive continued benefits pending an administrative law judge's decision on our reconsideration determination, you must request a hearing and continuation of benefits no later than 10 days after the date you receive the notice of our reconsideration determination that your physical or mental impairment(s) has ceased, has never existed, or is no longer disabling. A hearing must be requested as provided in § 416.1433, and you must request continued benefits using a statement in accordance with paragraph (b) of this section.

(2) If you fail to request a hearing and continued benefits within the 10–day period required under paragraph (d)(1) of this section, but you later ask that we continue your benefits pending an administrative law judge's decision, we will use the rules as provided in § 416.1411 to determine whether good cause exists for your failing to request benefit continuation within 10 days after receipt of the reconsideration determination. If you request continued benefits after the 10–day period, we will consider the delayed request to be timely and will pay continued benefits only if good cause for delay is established.

(e) What you must do when your case is remanded to an administrative law judge. If we send back (remand) your case to an administrative law judge for further action under the rules provided in § 416.1477, and the administrative law judge's decision or dismissal order issued on your medical cessation appeal is vacated and is no longer in effect, you may be eligible for continued benefits pending a new decision by the administrative law judge or final action by the Appeals Council on the administrative law judge's recommended decision.

(1) When your case is remanded to an administrative law judge, and you have elected to receive continued benefits, we will contact you to update our file to verify that you continue to meet the nonmedical requirements to receive benefits based on disability or blindness. To determine your correct payment amount, we will ask you to provide information about events such as changes in living arrangements, income, or resources since our last contact with you. If you have returned to work, we will request additional information about this work activity. Unless your earnings cause your income to be too much to receive benefits, your continued benefits will be paid while your appeal of the medical cessation of your disability/blindness is still pending, unless you have completed a trial work period and are engaging in substantial gainful activity. If you have completed a trial work period and previously received continued benefits you may still be eligible for special cash benefits under § 416.261 or special SSI eligibility status under § 416.264. (Effective July 1, 1987, a title XVI individual is no longer subject to a trial work period or cessation based on engaging in substantial gainful activity in order to be eligible for special benefits under § 416.261 or special status under § 416.264.) If we determine that you no longer meet a requirement to receive benefits, we will send you a written notice. The written notice will explain why your continued benefits will not be reinstated or will be for an amount less than you received before the prior administrative law judge's decision. The notice will also explain your right to reconsideration under § 416.1407, if you dis-

agree. If you request a reconsideration, you will have the chance to explain why you believe your benefits should be reinstated or should be at a higher amount. If the final decision on your appeal of your medical cessation is a favorable one, we will send you a written notice in which we will advise you of any right to reentitlement to benefits including special benefits under § 416.261 or special status under § 416.264. If you disagree with our determination on your appeal, you will have the right to appeal this decision.

(2) After we verify that you meet all the nonmedical requirements to receive benefits as stated in paragraph (e)(1) of this section, and if you previously elected to receive continued benefits pending the administrative law judge's decision, we will start continued benefits again. We will send you a notice telling you this. You do not have to complete a request to have these same benefits continued through the month before the month the new decision or order of dismissal is issued by the administrative law judge or through the month before the month the Appeals Council takes final action on the administrative law judge's recommended decision. These continued benefits will begin again with the first month of nonpayment based on the prior administrative law judge hearing decision or dismissal order. Our notice explaining continued benefits will also tell you to report to us any changes or events that affect your receipt of benefits.

(3) When your case is remanded to an administrative law judge, and if you did not previously elect to have benefits continued pending an administrative law judge decision, we will send you a notice telling you that if you want to change that election, you must request to do so no later than 10 days after you receive our notice. If you do make this new election, and after we verify that you meet all the nonmedical requirements as explained in paragraph (e)(1) of this section, benefits will begin with the month of the Appeals Council remand order and will continue as stated in paragraph (e)(2) of this section.

(4) If a court orders that your case be sent back to us (remanded) and your case is sent to an administrative law judge for further action under the rules provided in § 416.1483, the administrative law judge's decision or dismissal order on your medical cessation appeal is vacated and is no longer in effect. You may be eligible for continued benefits pending a new decision by the administrative law judge or final action by the Appeals Council on the administrative law judge's recommended decision. In these court-remanded cases reaching the administrative law judge, we will follow the same rules provided in paragraph (e)(1), (2), and (3) of this section.

(f) What if your benefits are suspended, reduced or terminated for other reasons. If we determine that your payments should be reduced, suspended or terminated for reasons not connected with your medical condition (see subpart M of Regulations No. 16) benefits may be continued under the procedure described in § 416.1336.

(g) Responsibility to pay back continued benefits.

(1) If the final decision of the Secretary affirms the determination that you are not entitled to benefits, you will be asked to pay back any continued benefits you receive. However, you will have the right to ask that you not be required to pay back the benefits as described in the overpayment recovery and waiver provisions of subpart E of this part.

(2) Waiver of recovery of an overpayment resulting from continued benefits to you may be considered as long as the cessation determination was appealed in good faith. We will assume that your appeal was made in good faith and, therefore, you have the right to waiver consideration unless you fail to cooperate in connection with the appeal, e.g., if you fail (without good reason) to give us medical or other evidence we request, or to go for a physical or mental examination when requested, in connection with the appeal. In determining whether you have good cause for failure to cooperate and, thus, whether an appeal was made in good faith, we will take into account any physical, mental, educational, or linguistic limitations (including any lack of facility with the English language) you may have which may have caused your failure to cooperate.

[53 FR 29023, Aug. 2, 1988; 53 FR 39015, Oct. 4, 1988; 59 FR 1637, Jan. 12, 1994]

§ 416.998 If you become disabled by another impairment(s).

If a new severe impairment(s) begins in or before the month in which your last impairment(s) ends, we will find that your disability is continuing. The new impairment(s) need not be expected to last 12 months or to result in death, but it must be severe enough to keep you from doing substantial gainful activity, or severe enough so that you are still disabled under § 416.994, or, if you are a child, to result in marked and severe functional limitations.

[50 FR 50147, Dec. 6, 1985; 51 FR 16015, April 30, 1986; 62 FR 6432, Feb. 11, 1997]

§ 416.999 What is expedited reinstatement?

The expedited reinstatement provision provides you another option for regaining eligibility for benefits when we previously terminated your eligibility for disability benefits due to your work activity. The expedited reinstatement provision provides you the option of requesting that your prior eligibility for disability benefits be reinstated, rather than filing a new application for a new period of eligibility. Since January 1, 2001, you can request to be reinstated to benefits if you stop doing substantial gainful activity within 60 months of your prior termination. You must not be able to do substantial gainful activity because of your medical condition. Your current impairment must be the same as or related to your prior impairment and you must be disabled. To determine if you are disabled, we will use our medical improvement review standard that we use in our continuing disability review process. The advantage of using the medical improvement review standard is that we will generally find that you are disabled unless your impairment has improved so that you are able to work or unless an exception under the medical improvement review standard process applies. We explain the rules for expedited reinstatement in §§ 416.999a through 416.999d.

[70 FR 57144, Sept. 30, 2005]

§ 416.999a Who is eligible for expedited reinstatement?

(a) You can have your eligibility to benefits reinstated under expedited reinstatement if—

(1) You were previously eligible for a benefit based on disability or blindness as explained in § 416.202;

(2) Your disability or blindness eligibility referred to in paragraph (a)(1) of this section was terminated because of earned income or a combination of earned and unearned income;

(3) You file your request for reinstatement timely under § 416.999b; and

(4) In the month you file your request for reinstatement—

(i) You are not able or become unable to do substantial gainful activity because of your medical condition as determined under paragraph (c) of this section.

(ii) Your current impairment is the same as or related to the impairment that we used as the basis for your previous eligibility referred to in paragraph (a)(2) of this section,

(iii) You are disabled or blind, as determined under the medical improvement review standard in §§ 416.994 or 416.994a, and

(iv) You meet the non-medical requirements for eligibility as explained in § 416.202.

(b) You are eligible for reinstatement if you are the spouse of an individual who can be reinstated under § 416.999a if—

(1) You were previously an eligible spouse of the individual;

(2) You meet the requirements for eligibility as explained in § 416.202 except the requirement that you must file an application; and

(3) You request reinstatement.

(c) We will determine that you are not able to do substantial gainful activity because of your medical condition, under paragraph (a)(4)(i) of this section, when:

(1) You certify under § 416.999b(e) that you are unable to do substantial gainful activity because of your medical condition;

(2) You are not able or become unable to do substantial gainful activity in the month you file your request for reinstatement; and

(3) We determine that you are disabled under paragraph (a)(4)(iii) of this section.

[70 FR 57144, Sept. 30, 2005; 81 FR 71370, Oct. 17, 2016]

§ 416.999b How do I request reinstatement?

(a) You must make your request for reinstatement in writing.

(b) You must have filed your request on or after January 1, 2001.

(c) You must provide the information we request so that we can determine whether you meet the eligibility requirements listed in § 416.999a.

(d) We must receive your request within the consecutive 60–month period that begins with the month in which your eligibility terminated due to earned income, or a combination of earned and unearned income. If we receive your request after the 60–month period, we can grant you an extension if we determine you had good cause, under the standards explained in § 416.1411, for not filing the request timely.

(e) You must certify that you are disabled, that your current impairment(s) is the same as or related to the impairment(s) that we used as the basis for the eligibility you are requesting to be reinstated, that you are unable to do substantial gainful activity because of your medical condition, and that you meet the non-medical requirements for eligibility for benefits.

[70 FR 57144, Sept. 30, 2005]

§ 416.999c How do we determine provisional benefits?

(a) You may receive up to six consecutive months of provisional cash benefits and Medicaid during the provisional benefit period, while we determine whether we can reinstate your disability benefit eligibility under § 416.999a—

(1) We will pay you provisional benefits beginning with the month after you file your request for reinstatement under § 416.999a(a).

(2) If you are an eligible spouse, you can receive provisional benefits with the month your spouse's provisional benefits begin.

(3) If you do not have an eligible spouse, we will pay you a monthly provisional benefit amount equal to the monthly amount that would be payable to an eligible individual under §§ 416.401 through 416.435 with the same kind and amount of income as you have.

(4) If you have an eligible spouse, we will pay you and your spouse a monthly provisional benefit amount equal to the monthly amount that would be payable to an eligible individual and eligible spouse under

§ 416.401 through 416.435 with the same kind and amount of income as you and your spouse have.

(5) Your provisional benefits will not include state supplementary payments payable under §§ 416.2001 through 416.2176.

(b) You cannot receive provisional cash benefits or Medicaid a second time under this section when—

(1) You request reinstatement under § 416.999a;

(2) You previously received provisional cash benefits or Medicaid under this section based upon a prior request for reinstatement filed under § 416.999a(a); and

(3) Your requests under paragraphs (b)(1) and (b)(2) are for the same previous disability eligibility referred to in § 416.999a(a)(2) of this section.

(4) Examples:

Example 1: Mr. K files a request for reinstatement in April 2004. His disability benefit had previously terminated in January 2003. Since Mr. K meets the other factors for possible reinstatement (i.e., his prior eligibility was terminated within the last 60 months because of his work activity) we start paying him provisional benefits beginning May 2004 while we determine whether he is disabled and whether his current impairment(s) is the same as or related to the impairment(s) that we used as the basis for the benefit that was terminated in January 2003. In July 2004 we determine that Mr. K cannot be reinstated because he is not disabled under the medical improvement review standard; therefore we stop his provisional benefits. Mr. K does not request review of the determination. In January 2005 Mr. K again requests reinstatement on the eligibility that terminated in January 2003. Since this request again meets all the other factors for possible reinstatement mentioned above, and his request is still within 60 months from January 2003, we will make a new determination on whether he is disabled and whether his current impairment(s) is the same as or related to the impairment(s) that we used as the basis for the benefit that was terminated in January 2003. Since the January 2005 request and the April 2004 request both request reinstatement on the same benefit that terminated in January 2003, and since we already paid Mr. K provisional benefits based upon the April 2004 request, we will not pay additional provisional benefits on the January 2005 request for reinstatement.

Example 2: Assume the same facts as shown in Example 1 of this section, with the addition of these facts. We approve Mr. K's January 2005 request for reinstatement and start his reinstated benefits beginning February 2005. Mr. K subsequently returns to work and his benefits are again terminated due to his work activity in January 2008. Mr. K again stops work and requests reinstatement in January 2010. Since Mr. K meets the other factors for possible reinstatement (i.e., his prior eligibility was terminated within the last 60 months because of his work activity) we start paying him provisional benefits beginning February 2010 while we determine whether he is disabled and whether his current impairment(s) is the same as or related to the impairment(s) that we used as the basis for the benefit that was terminated in January 2008.

(c) We will not pay you a provisional benefit for a month where you are not eligible for a payment under §§ 416.1322, 416.1323, 416.1325, 416.1327, 416.1329, 416.1330, 416.1334, and 416.1339.

(d) We will not pay you a provisional benefit for any month that is after the earliest of either: the month we send you notice of our determination on your request for reinstatement; or, the sixth month following the month you requested expedited reinstatement.

(e) You are not eligible for provisional benefits if—

(1) Prior to starting your provisional benefits we determine that you do not meet the requirements for reinstatement under §§ 416.999a(a); or

(2) We determine that your statements on your request for reinstatement, made under § 416.999b(d)(2), are false.

(f) Determinations we make regarding your provisional benefits under paragraphs (a) through (e) of this section are final and are not subject to administrative and judicial review under subpart N of part 416.

(g) If you were previously overpaid benefits under title II or title XVI of the Act, we will not recover the overpayment from your provisional benefits unless you give us permission.

(h) If we determine you are not eligible to receive reinstated benefits, provisional benefits we have already paid you under this section that were made prior to the termination month under paragraph (d) of this section will not be subject to recovery as an overpayment unless we determine that you knew, or should have known, you did not meet the requirements for reinstatement in § 416.999a. If we inadvertently pay you provisional benefits when you are not entitled to them because we have already made a determination described in paragraph (e) of this section, they will be subject to recover as an overpayment under subpart E of part 416.

[70 FR 57144, Sept. 30, 2005]

§ 416.999d How do we determine reinstated benefits?

(a) If you meet the requirements for reinstatement under § 416.999a(a), we will reinstate your benefits with the month after the month you filed your request for reinstatement. We cannot reinstate your eligibility for any month prior to February 2001.

(b) We will compute your reinstated benefit amount and determine benefits payable under the applicable paragraphs in §§ 416.401 through 416.435. We will reduce your reinstated benefit due in a month by a provisional benefit we already paid you for that month. If your provisional benefit paid for a month equals or exceeds the reinstated benefit due, we will treat the difference as an overpayment under § 416.536.

(c) Once you have been reinstated under § 416.999a you cannot be reinstated again until you have completed a 24–month initial reinstatement period. Your initial reinstatement period begins with the month your reinstated benefits begin under paragraph (a) of this section and ends when you have had 24 payable months of reinstated benefits. We consider you to have a payable month for the purposes of this paragraph when you are due a cash benefit of any amount for the month based upon our normal computation and payment rules in § 416.401 through § 416.435 or if you are considered to be receiving SSI benefits in a month under section 1619(b) of the Social Security Act. If your entire benefit payment due you for a month is adjusted for recovery of an overpayment under § 416.570 and § 416.571 or if the amount of the provisional benefit already paid you for a month exceeds the amount of the reinstated benefit payable for that month so that no additional payment is due, we will consider the month a payable month.

(d) Your eligibility for reinstated benefits ends with the month preceding the earliest of the following months—

(1) The month an applicable terminating event in §§ 416.1331 through 416.1339 occurs;

(2) The third month following the month in which your disability ceases; or

(3) The month in which you die.

(e) Determinations we make under this section are initial determinations under § 416.1402 and are subject to review under subpart N of part 416.

(f) If we determine you are not eligible for reinstated benefits, we will consider your request filed under § 416.999a(a) your intent to claim benefits under § 416.340.

[70 FR 57144, Sept. 30, 2005]

SUBPART J—DETERMINATIONS OF DISABILITY

Authority: Secs. 702(a)(5), 1614, 1631, and 1633 of the Social Security Act (42 U.S.C. 902(a)(5), 1382c, 1383, and 1383b).

Source: 46 FR 29211, May 29, 1981; 52 FR 27541, July 22, 1987; 61 FR 5942, Feb. 15, 1996, unless otherwise noted.

GENERAL PROVISIONS

§ 416.1001 Purpose and scope.

This subpart describes the standards of performance and administrative requirements and procedures for States making determinations of disability for the Commissioner under title XVI of the Act. It also establishes the Commissioner's responsibilities in carrying out the disability determination function.

(a) Sections 416.1001 through 416.1003 describe the purpose of the regulations and the meaning of terms frequently used in the regulations. They also briefly set forth the responsibilities of the Commissioner and the States covered in detail in other sections.

(b) Sections 416.1010 through 416.1018 describe the Commissioner's and the State's responsibilities in performing the disability determination function.

(c) Sections 416.1020 through 416.1033 describe the administrative responsibilities and requirements of the States. The corresponding role of the Commissioner is also set out.

(d) Sections 416.1040 through 416.1050 describe the performance accuracy and processing time standards for measuring State agency performance.

(e) Sections 416.1060 through 416.1061 describe when and what kind of assistance the Commissioner will provide State agencies to help them improve performance.

(f) Sections 416.1070 through 416.1075 describe the level of performance below which the Commissioner will consider a State agency to be substantially failing to make disability determinations consistent with the regulations and other written guidelines and the resulting action the Commissioner will take.

(g) Sections 416.1080 through 416.1083 describe the rules for resolving disputes concerning fiscal issues and providing hearings when we propose to find that a State is in substantial failure.

(h) Sections 416.1090 through 416.1094 describe when and what action the Commissioner will take and what action the State will be expected to take if the Commissioner assumes the disability determination function from a State agency.

[62 FR 38454, July 18, 1997; 71 FR 16461, March 31, 2006; 76 FR 24812, May 3, 2011]

§ 416.1002 Definitions.

For purposes of this subpart:

Act means the Social Security Act, as amended.

Class or classes of cases means the categories into which disability claims are divided according to their characteristics.

Commissioner means the Commissioner of Social Security or his or her authorized designee.

Compassionate allowance means a determination or decision we make under a process that identifies for expedited handling claims that involve impairments that invariably qualify under the Listing of Impairments in appendix 1 to subpart P of part 404 of this chapter based on minimal, but sufficient, objective medical evidence.

Determination of disability or disability determination means one or more of the following decisions:

(a) Whether or not a person is under a disability;

(b) The date a person's disability began; or

(c) The date a person's disability ended.

Disability means disability or blindness as defined in sections 1614(a)(2) and (3) of the Act.

Disability determination function means making determinations as to disability or blindness and carrying out related administrative and other responsibilities.

Disability program means the Federal program for providing supplemental security income benefits for the blind and disabled under title XVI of the Act, as amended.

Initial means the first level of disability or blindness adjudication.

Other written guidelines means written issuances such as Social Security Rulings and memoranda by the Commissioner of Social Security, the Deputy Commissioner for Programs and Policy, or the Associate Commissioner for Disability and the procedures, guides, and operating instructions in the Disability Insurance sections of the Program Operations Manual System that are instructive, interpretive, clarifying, and/or administrative and not designated as advisory or discretionary. The purpose of including the foregoing material in the definition is to assure uniform national application of program standards and service delivery to the public.

Quick disability determination means an initial determination on a claim that we have identified as one that reflects a high degree of probability that you will be found disabled and where we expect that your allegations will be easily and quickly verified.

Regulations means regulations in this subpart issued under sections 1102, 1631(c) and 1633(a) of the Act, unless otherwise indicated.

State means any of the 50 States of the United States and the District of Columbia. It includes the State agency.

State agency means that agency of a State which has been designated by the State to carry out the disability determination function.

We, us, and our refers to the Social Security Administration (SSA).

[56 FR 11021, March 14, 1991; 62 FR 38454, July 18, 1997; 72 FR 51178, Sept. 6, 2007; 75 FR 62683, Oct. 13, 2010]

§ 416.1003 Basic responsibilities for us and the State.

(a) General. We will work with the State to provide and maintain an effective system for processing claims of those who apply for and who are receiving benefits under the disability program. We will provide program standards, leadership, and oversight. We do not intend to become involved in the State's ongoing management of the program except as is necessary and in accordance with these regulations. The State will comply with our regulations and other written guidelines.

(b) Our responsibilities. We will:

(1) Periodically review the regulations and other written guidelines to determine whether they insure effective and uniform administration of the disability program. To the extent feasible, we will consult with and take into consideration the experience of the States in issuing regulations and guidelines necessary to insure effective and uniform administration of the disability program;

(2) Provide training materials or in some instances conduct or specify training (see § 416.1022);

(3) Provide funds to the State agency for the necessary cost of performing the disability determination function (see § 416.1026);

(4) Monitor and evaluate the performance of the State agency under the established standards (see §§ 416.1044 and 416.1045); and

(5) Maintain liaison with the medical profession nationally and with national organizations and agencies whose interests or activities may affect the disability program.

(c) Responsibilities of the State. The State will:

(1) Provide management needed to insure that the State agency carries out the disability determination function so that disability determinations are made accurately and promptly;

(2) Provide an organizational structure, adequate facilities, qualified personnel, medical consultant services, designated quick disability determination examiners (§§ 416.1019 and 416.1020(c)), and a quality assurance function (§§ 416.1020 through 416.1024);

(3) Furnish reports and records relating to the administration of the disability program (§ 416.1025);

(4) Submit budgets (§ 416.1026);

(5) Cooperate with audits (§ 416.1027);

(6) Insure that all applicants for and recipients of disability benefits are treated equally and courteously;

(7) Be responsible for property used for disability program purposes (§ 416.1028);

(8) Take part in the research and demonstration projects (§ 416.1029);

(9) Coordinate with other agencies (§ 416.1030);

(10) Safeguard the records created by the State in performing the disability determination function (§ 416.1031);

(11) Comply with other provisions of the Federal law and regulations that apply to the State in performing the disability determination function;

(12) Comply with other written guidelines (§ 416.1033);

(13) Maintain liaison with the medical profession and organizations that may facilitate performing the disability determination function; and

(14) Assist us in other ways that we determine may promote the objectives of effective and uniform administration.

[72 FR 51178, Sept. 6, 2007]

RESPONSIBILITIES FOR PERFORMING THE DISABILITY DETERMINATION FUNCTION

§ 416.1010 How a State notifies us that it wishes to perform the disability determination function.

(a) Deemed notice. Any State that has in effect as of June 1, 1981, an agreement with us to make disability determinations will be deemed to have given us notice that it wishes to perform the disability determination function, in lieu of continuing the agreement in effect after June 1, 1981.

(b) Written notice. After June 1, 1981, a State not making disability determinations that wishes to perform the disability determination function under these regulations must notify us in writing. The notice must be from an official authorized to act for the State for this purpose. The State will provide an opinion from the State's Attorney General verifying the authority of the official who sent the notice to act for the State.

§ 416.1011 How we notify a State whether it may perform the disability determination function.

(a) If a State notifies us in writing that it wishes to perform the disability determination function, we will notify the State in writing whether or not it may perform the function. The State will begin performing the disability determination function beginning with the month we and the State agree upon.

(b) If we have previously found that a State agency has substantially failed to make disability determinations in accordance with the law or these regulations and other written guidelines or if the State has previously notified us in writing that it does not wish to make disability determinations, the notice will advise the State whether the State agency may again make the disability determinations and, if so, the date and the conditions under which the State may again make them.

§ 416.1013 Disability determinations the State makes.

(a) General rule. A State agency will make determinations of disability with respect to all persons in the State except those individuals whose cases are in a class specifically excluded by our written guidelines. A determination of disability made by the State is the determination of the Commissioner, except as described in § 416.903(d)(1).

(b) New classes of cases. Where any new class or classes of cases arise requiring determinations of disability, we will determine the conditions under which a State may choose not to make the disability determinations. We will provide the State with the necessary funding to do the additional work.

(c) Temporary transfer of classes of cases. We will make disability determinations for classes of cases temporarily transferred to us by the State agency if the State agency asks us to do so and we agree. The State agency will make written arrangements with us which will specify the period of time and the class or classes of cases we will do.

[62 FR 38455, July 18, 1997]

§ 416.1014 Responsibilities for obtaining evidence to make disability determinations.

(a) We or the State agency will secure from the claimant or other sources any evidence the State agency needs to make a disability determination. When we secure the evidence, we will furnish it to the State agency for use in making the disability determination.

(b) At our request, the State agency will obtain and furnish medical or other evidence and provide assistance as may be necessary for us to carry out our responsibility for making disability determinations in those classes of cases described in the written guidelines for which the State agency does not make the determination.

[79 FR 33682, June 12, 2014]

§ 416.1015 Making disability determinations.

(a) When making a disability determination, the State agency will apply subpart I, part 416, of our regulations.

(b) The State agency will make disability determinations based only on the medical and nonmedical evidence in its files.

(c) Disability determinations will be made by:

(1) A State agency medical or psychological consultant and a State agency disability examiner;

(2) A State agency disability examiner alone when there is no medical evidence to be evaluated (i.e., no medical evidence exists or we are unable, despite making every reasonable effort, to obtain any medical evidence that may exist) and the individual fails or refuses, without a good reason, to attend a consultative examination (see § 416.918);

(3) A State agency disability examiner alone if you are not a child (a person who has not attained age 18), and the claim is adjudicated under the quick disability determination process (see § 416.1019) or the compassionate allowance process (see § 416.1002), and the initial or reconsidered determination is fully favorable to you. This paragraph (c)(3) will no longer be effective on December 28, 2018 unless we terminate it earlier by publication of a final rule in the Federal Register; or

(4) A State agency disability hearing officer.

See § 416.1016 for the definition of medical or psychological consultant and § 416.1415 for the definition of disability hearing officer. The State agency disability examiner and disability hearing officer must be qualified to interpret and evaluate medical reports and other evidence relating to the claimant's physical or mental impairments and as necessary to determine the capacities of the claimant to perform substantial gainful activity. See § 416.972 for what we mean by substantial gainful activity.

(d) In making a determination under title XVI with respect to the disability of a child to whom paragraph (d) of this section does not apply, we will make reasonable efforts to ensure that a qualified pediatrician or other individual who specializes in a field of medicine appropriate to the child's impairment(s) evaluates the case of the child.

(e) The State agency will certify each determination of disability to us on forms we provide.

(f) The State agency will furnish us with all the evidence it considered in making its determination.

(g) The State agency will not be responsible for defending in court any determination made, or any procedure for making determinations, under these regulations.

(h) [Redesignated as subsection (g) by 82 FR 5883]

[46 FR 29211, May 29, 1981; 46 FR 42063, Aug. 19, 1981; 52 FR 33928, Sept. 9, 1987; 56 FR 11021, March 14, 1991; 58 FR 47587, Sept. 9, 1993; 61 FR 11136, March 19, 1996; 62 FR 38455, July 18, 1997; 65 FR 34959, June 1, 2000; 75 FR 62684, Oct. 13, 2010; 78 FR 66639, Nov. 6, 2013; 79 FR 51243, Aug. 28, 2014; 80 FR 63093, Oct. 19, 2015; 81 FR 73028, Oct. 24, 2016; 82 FR 5883, Jan. 18, 2017]

§ 416.1016 Medical consultants and psychological consultants.

(a) What is a medical consultant? A medical consultant is a member of a team that makes disability determinations in a State agency (see § 416.1015), or who is a member of a team that makes disability determinations for us when we make disability determinations ourselves. The medical consultant completes the medical portion of the case review and any applicable residual functional capacity assessment about all physical impairment(s) in a claim.

(b) What qualifications must a medical consultant have? A medical consultant is a licensed physician, as defined in § 416.902(a)(1).

(c) What is a psychological consultant? A psychological consultant is a member of a team that makes disability determinations in a State agency (see § 416.1015), or who is a member of a team that makes disability determinations for us when we make disability determinations ourselves. The psychological consultant completes the medical portion of the case review and any applicable residual functional capacity assessment about all mental impairment(s) in a claim. When we are unable to obtain the services of a qualified psychiatrist or psychologist despite making every reasonable effort (see § 416.1017) in a claim involving a mental impairment(s), a medical consultant will evaluate the mental impairment(s).

(d) What qualifications must a psychological consultant have? A psychological consultant can be either a licensed psychiatrist or psychologist. We will only consider a psychologist qualified to be a psychological consultant if he or she:

(1) Is licensed or certified as a psychologist at the independent practice level of psychology by the State in which he or she practices; and

(2)(i) Possesses a doctorate degree in psychology from a program in clinical psychology of an educational institution accredited by an organization recognized by the Council on Post–Secondary Accreditation; or

(ii) Is listed in a national register of health service providers in psychology which the Commissioner of Social Security deems appropriate; and

(3) Possesses 2 years of supervised clinical experience as a psychologist in health service, at least 1 year of which is post-masters degree.

(e) Cases involving both physical and mental impairments. In a case where there is evidence of both physical and mental impairments, the medical consultant will evaluate the physical impairments in accordance with paragraph (a) of this section, and the psychological consultant will evaluate the mental impairment(s) in accordance with paragraph (c) of this section.

[52 FR 33928, Sept. 9, 1987; 62 FR 38455, July 18, 1997; 65 FR 34959, June 1, 2000; 71 FR 16461, March 31, 2006; 76 FR 24812, May 3, 2011; 82 FR 5883, Jan. 18, 2017]

§ 416.1017 Reasonable efforts to obtain review by a physician, psychiatrist, and psychologist.

(a) When the evidence of record indicates the existence of a physical impairment, the State agency must make every reasonable effort to ensure that a medical consultant completes the medical portion of the case review and any applicable residual functional capacity assessment. When the evidence of record indicates the existence of a mental impairment, the State agency must make every reasonable effort to ensure that a psychological consultant completes the medical portion of the case review and any applicable residual functional capacity assessment. The State agency must determine if additional physicians, psychiatrists, and psychologists are needed to make the necessary reviews. When it does not have sufficient resources to make the necessary reviews, the State agency must attempt to obtain the resources needed. If the State agency is unable to obtain additional physicians, psychiatrists, and psychologists because of low salary rates or fee schedules, it should attempt to raise the State agency's levels of compensation to meet the prevailing rates for these services. If these efforts are unsuccessful, the State agency will seek assistance from us. We will assist the State agency as necessary. We will also monitor the State agency's efforts and where the State agency is unable to obtain the necessary services, we will make every reasonable effort to provide the services using Federal resources.

(b) Federal resources may include the use of Federal contracts for the services of qualified psychiatrists and psychologists to review mental impairment cases. Where Federal resources are required to perform these reviews, which are a basic State agency responsibility, and where appropriate, the State agency's budget will be reduced accordingly.

(c) Where every reasonable effort is made to obtain the services of a qualified psychiatrist or psychologist to review a mental impairment case, but the professional services are not obtained, a physician who is not a psychiatrist will review the mental impairment case. For these purposes, every reasonable effort to ensure that a qualified psychiatrist or psychologist review mental impairment cases will be considered to have been made only after efforts by both State and Federal agencies as set forth in paragraphs (a) and (b) of this section are made.

[52 FR 33928, Sept. 9, 1987; 82 FR 5883, Jan. 18, 2017; 82 FR 15133, March 27, 2017]

§ 416.1018 Notifying claimant of the disability determination.

The State agency will prepare denial notices in accordance with subpart N of this part whenever it makes a disability determination which is fully or partially unfavorable to the claimant.

[75 FR 33169, June 11, 2010]

QUICK DISABILITY DETERMINATIONS

Source: 72 FR 51178, Sept. 6, 2007, unless otherwise noted.

§ 416.1019 Quick disability determination process.

(a) If we identify a claim as one involving a high degree of probability that the individual is disabled, and we expect that the individual's allegations will be easily and quickly verified, we will refer the claim to the State agency for consideration under the quick disability determination process pursuant to this section and § 416.1020(c).

(b) If we refer a claim to the State agency for a quick disability determination, a designated quick disability determination examiner must do all of the following:

(1) Subject to the provisions in paragraph (c) of this section, make the disability determination after consulting with a State agency medical or psychological consultant if the State agency disability examiner determines consultation is appropriate or if consultation is required under § 416.926(c). The State agency may certify the disability determination forms to us without the signature of the medical or psychological consultant.

(2) Make the quick disability determination based only on the medical and nonmedical evidence in the file.

(3) Subject to the provisions in paragraph (c) of this section, make the quick disability determination by applying the rules in subpart I of this part.

(c) If the quick disability determination examiner cannot make a determination that is fully favorable, or if there is an unresolved disagreement between the disability examiner and the medical or psychological consultant (except when a disability examiner makes the determination alone under § 416.1015(c)(3)), the State agency will adjudicate the claim using the regularly applicable procedures in this subpart.

[75 FR 62684, Oct. 13, 2010]

ADMINISTRATIVE RESPONSIBILITIES AND REQUIREMENTS

§ 416.1020 General administrative requirements.

(a) The State will provide the organizational structure, qualified personnel, medical consultant services, and a quality assurance function sufficient to ensure that disability determinations are made accurately and promptly. We may impose specific administrative requirements in these areas and in those under "Administrative Responsibilities and Requirements" in order to establish uniform, national administrative practices or to correct the areas of deficiencies which may later cause the State to be substantially failing to comply with our regulations or other written guidelines. We will notify the State, in writing, of the administrative requirements being imposed and of any administrative deficiencies it is required to correct. We will allow the State 90 days from the date of this notice to make appropriate corrections. Once corrected, we will monitor the State's administrative practices for 180 days. If the State does not meet the requirements or correct all of the deficiencies, or, if some of the deficiencies recur, we may initiate procedures to determine if the State is substantially failing to follow our regulations or other written guidelines.

(b) The State is responsible for making accurate and prompt disability determinations.

(c) Each State agency will designate experienced disability examiners to handle claims we refer to it under § 416.1019(a).

[56 FR 11021, March 14, 1991; 56 FR 13365, April 1, 1991; 72 FR 51178, Sept. 6, 2007]

§ 416.1021 Personnel.

(a) Equal Employment Opportunity. The State will comply with all applicable Federal statutes, executive orders and regulations concerned with equal employment opportunities.

(b) Selection, tenure, and compensation. The State agency will, except as may be inconsistent with paragraph (a) of this section, adhere to applicable State approved personnel standards in the selection, tenure, and compensation of any individual employed in the disability program.

(c) Travel. The State will make personnel available to attend meetings or workshops as may be sponsored or approved by us for furthering the purposes of the disability program.

(d) Restrictions. Subject to appropriate Federal funding, the State will, to the best of its ability, facilitate the processing of disability claims by avoiding personnel freezes, restrictions against overtime work, or curtailment of facilities or activities.

§ 416.1022 Training.

The State will insure that all employees have an acceptable level of competence. We will provide training and other instructional materials to facilitate basic and advanced technical proficiency of disability staff in order to insure uniformity and effectiveness in the administration of the disability program. We will conduct or specify training, as appropriate but only if:

(a) A State agency's performance approaches unacceptable levels or

(b) The material required for the training is complex or the capacity of the State to deliver the training is in doubt and uniformity of the training is essential.

§ 416.1023 Facilities.

(a) Space, equipment, supplies, and other services. Subject to appropriate Federal funding, the State will provide adequate space, equipment, supplies, and other services to facilitate making accurate and prompt disability determinations.

(b) Location of facilities. Subject to appropriate Federal funding, the State will determine the location where the disability determination function is to be performed so that disability determinations are made accurately and promptly.

(c) Access. The State will permit us access to the premises where the disability determination function is performed and also where it is managed for the purposes of inspecting and obtaining information about the work and activities required by our regulations and assuring compliance with pertinent Federal statutes and regulations. Access includes personal onsite visits and other means, such as telecommunications, of contacting the State agency to obtain information about its functions. We will contact the State agency and give reasonable prior notice of the times and purposes of any visits.

[56 FR 11022, March 14, 1991]

§ 416.1024 Medical and other purchased services.

The State will determine the rates of payment for purchasing medical or other services necessary to make determinations of disability. The rates may not exceed the highest rate paid by Federal or other agencies in the State for the same or similar type of service. The State will maintain documentation to support the rates of payment it uses.

[71 FR 16461, March 31, 2006; 76 FR 24812, May 3, 2011]

§ 416.1025 Records and reports.

(a) The State will establish and maintain the records and furnish the schedules, financial, cost, and other reports relating to the administration of the disability programs as we may require.

(b) The State will permit us and the Comptroller General of the United States (including duly authorized representatives) access to and the right to examine records relating to the work which the State performs under these regulations. These records will be retained by the State for the periods of time specified for retention of records in the Federal Procurement Regulations (41 CFR parts 1–20).

§ 416.1026 Fiscal.

(a) We will give the State funds, in advance or by way of reimbursement, for necessary costs in making disability determinations under these regulations. Necessary costs are direct as well as indirect costs as defined in 41 CFR part 1–15, subpart 1–15.7 of the Federal Procurement Regulations System for costs incurred before April 1, 1984; and 48 CFR part 31, subpart 31.6 of the Federal Acquisition Regulations System and Federal Management Circular A–74–4 [1] as amended or superseded for costs incurred after March 31, 1984.

(b) The State will submit estimates of anticipated costs in the form of a budget at the time and in the manner we require.

(c) We will notify the State of the amount which will be made available to it as well as what anticipated costs are being approved.

(d) The State may not incur or make expenditures for items of cost not approved by us or in excess of the amount we make available to the State.

[1] The circular is available from the Office of Administration, Publications Unit, Rm. G–236, New Executive Office Bldg., Washington, DC 20503.

(e) After the close of a period for which funds have been made available to the State, the State will submit a report of its expenditures. Based on an audit arranged by the State under Pub.L. 98–502, the Single Audit Act of 1984, or by the Inspector General of the Social Security Administration or based on an audit or review by the Social Security Administration (see § 416.1027), we will determine whether the expenditures were consistent with cost principles described in 41 CFR part 1–15, subpart 1–15.7 for costs incurred before April 1, 1984; and 48 CFR part 31, subpart 31.6 and Federal Management Circular A–74–4 for costs incurred after March 31, 1984; and in other applicable written guidelines in effect at the time the expenditures were made or incurred.

(f) Any monies paid to the State which are used for purposes not within the scope of these regulations will be paid back to the Treasury of the United States.

[56 FR 11022, March 14, 1991; 62 FR 38455, July 18, 1997]

§ 416.1027 Audits.

(a) Audits performed by the State—

(1) Generally. Audits of account and records pertaining to the administration of the disability program under the Act, will be performed by the States in accordance with the Single Audit Act of 1984 (Pub.L. 98–502) which establishes audit requirements for States receiving Federal assistance. If the audit performed by the State meets our program requirements, we will accept the findings and recommendations of the audit. The State will make every effort to act upon and resolve any items questioned in the audit.

(2) Questioned items. Items questioned as a result of an audit under the Single Audit Act of 1984 of a cross-cutting nature will be resolved by the Department of Health and Human Services, Office of Grant and Contract Financial Management. A cross-cutting issue is one that involves more than one Federal awarding agency. Questioned items affecting only the disability program will be resolved by SSA in accord with paragraph (b)(2) of this section.

(3) State appeal of audit determinations. The Office of Grant and Contract Financial Management will notify the State of its determination on questioned cross-cutting items. If the State disagrees with that determination, it may appeal in writing within 60 days of receiving the determination. State appeals of a cross-cutting issue as a result of an audit under the Single Audit Act of 1984 will be made to the Department of Health and Human Services' Departmental Appeals Board. The rules for hearings and appeals are provided in 45 CFR part 16.

(b) Audits performed by the Commissioner—

(1) Generally. If the State does not perform an audit under the Single Audit Act of 1984 or the audit performed is not satisfactory for disability program purposes, the books of account and records in the State pertaining to the administration of the disability programs under the Act will be audited by the SSA's Inspector General or audited or reviewed by SSA as appropriate. These audits or reviews will be conducted to determine whether the expenditures were made for the intended purposes and in amounts necessary for the proper and efficient administration of the disability programs. Audits or reviews will also be made to inspect the work and activities required by the regulations to ensure compliance with pertinent Federal statutes and regulations. The State will make every effort to act upon and resolve any items questioned in an audit or review.

(2) Questioned items. Expenditures of State agencies will be audited or reviewed, as appropriate, on the basis of cost principles and written guidelines in effect at the time the expenditures were made or incurred. Both the State and the State agency will be informed and given a full explanation of any items questioned. They will be given reasonable time to explain items questioned. Any explanation furnished by the State or State agency will be given full consideration before a final determination is made on the audit or review report.

(3) State appeal of audit determinations. The appropriate Social Security Administration Regional Commissioner will notify the State of his or her determination on the audit or review report. If the State disagrees with that determination, the State may request reconsideration in writing within 60 days of the date of the Regional Commissioner's notice of the determination. The written request may be made, through the Associate Commissioner, Office of Disability, to the Commissioner of Social Security, Room 900, Altmeyer Building, 6401 Security Boulevard, Baltimore, MD 21235. The Commissioner will make a determination and notify the State of the decision in writing no later than 90 days from the date the Social Security Administration receives the State's appeal and all supporting documents. The decision by the Commissioner on other than monetary disallowances will be final and binding upon the State. The decision by the Commissioner on monetary disallowances will be final and binding upon the State unless the State appeals the decision in writing to the Department of Health and Human Services' Departmental Appeals Board within 30 days after receiving the Commissioner's decision. See § 416.1083.

[46 FR 29211, May 29, 1981; 46 FR 42063, Aug. 19, 1981; 56 FR 11022, March 14, 1991; 62 FR 38455, July 18, 1997]

§ 416.1028 Property.

The State will have title to equipment purchased for disability program purposes. The State will be responsible for maintaining all property it acquires or which we furnish to it for performing the disability determination function. The State will identify the equipment by labeling and by inventory and will credit the SSA account with the fair market value of disposed property. In the event we assume the disability determination function from a State, ownership of all property and equipment acquired with SSA funds will be transferred to us effective on the date the State is notified that we are assuming the disability determination function or we are notified that the State is terminating the relationship.

§ 416.1029 Participation in research and demonstration projects.

We will invite State participation in federally funded research and demonstration projects to assess the effectiveness of the disability program and to ascertain the effect of program policy changes. Where we determine that State participation is necessary for the project to be complete, for example, to provide national uniformity in a claims process, State participation is mandatory.

§ 416.1030 Coordination with other agencies.

(a) The State will establish cooperative working relationships with other agencies concerned with serving the disabled and, insofar as practicable, use their services, facilities, and records to:

(1) Assist the State in developing evidence and making determinations of disability; and

(2) Insure that referral of disabled or blind persons for rehabilitation services will be carried out effectively.

(b) The State may pay these agencies for the services, facilities, or records they provide. The State will include these costs in its estimates of anticipated costs and reports of actual expenditures.

§ 416.1031 Confidentiality of information and records.

The State will comply with the confidentiality of information, including the security of systems, and records requirements described in 20 CFR part 401 and pertinent written guidelines (see § 416.1033).

§ 416.1032 Other Federal laws and regulations.

The State will comply with the provisions of other Federal laws and regulations that directly affect its responsibilities in carrying out the disability determination function; for example, Treasury Department regulations on letters of credit (31 CFR part 205).

§ 416.1033 Policies and operating instructions.

(a) We will provide the State agency with written guidelines necessary for it to carry out its responsibilities in performing the disability determination function.

(b) The State agency making determinations of disability will comply with our written guidelines that are not designated as advisory or discretionary. (See § 416.1002 for what we mean by written guidelines.)

(c) A representative group of State agencies will be given an opportunity to participate in formulating disability program policies that have an effect on their role in carrying out the disability determination function. State agencies will also be given an opportunity to comment before changes are made in written guidelines unless delay in issuing a change may impair service to the public.

[56 FR 11023, March 14, 1991]

PERFORMANCE STANDARDS

§ 416.1040 General.

The following sections provide the procedures and guidelines we use to determine whether the State agency is substantially complying with our regulations and other written guidelines, including meeting established national performance standards. We use performance standards to help assure effective and uniform administration of our disability program and to measure whether the performance of the disability determination function by each State agency is acceptable. Also, the standards are designed to improve overall State agency performance in the disability determination process and to ensure that benefits are made available to all eligible persons in an accurate and efficient manner. We measure the performance of a State agency in two areas—processing time and quality of documentation and decisions on claims. State agency compliance is also judged by State agency adherence to other program requirements.

[56 FR 11023, March 14, 1991]

§ 416.1041 Standards of performance.

(a) General. The performance standards include both a target level of performance and a threshold level of performance for the State agency. The target level represents a level of performance that we and the States will work to attain in the future. The threshold level is the minimum acceptable level of performance. Performance below the threshold level will be the basis for the Commissioner's taking from the State agency partial or complete responsibility for performing the disability determination function. Intermediate State agency goals are designed to help each State agency move from its current performance levels to the target levels.

(b) The target level. The target level is the optimum level of performance. There are three targets—one for combined title II and title XVI initial performance accuracy, one for title II initial processing time, and one for title XVI initial processing time.

(c) The threshold level. The threshold level is the minimum acceptable level of performance. There are three thresholds—one for combined title II and title XVI initial performance accuracy, one for title II initial processing time, and one for title XVI initial processing time.

(d) Intermediate goals. Intermediate goals are levels of performance between the threshold levels and the target levels established by our appropriate Regional Commissioner after negotiation with each State agency. The intermediate goals are designed to help the State agencies reach the target levels. Failure to meet these goals is not a cause for considering the State agency to be substantially failing to comply with the performance standards. However, failure to meet the intermediate goals may result in consultation and an offer of optional performance support depending on the availability of our resources.

[56 FR 11023, March 14, 1991; 62 FR 38455, July 18, 1997]

§ 416.1042 Processing time standards.

(a) General. Title II processing time refers to the average number of days (including Saturdays, Sundays, and holidays) it takes a State agency to process an initial disability claim from the day the case folder is received in the State agency until the day it is released to us by the State agency. Title XVI processing time refers to the average number of days, including Saturdays, Sundays, and holidays, from the day of receipt of the initial disability claim in the State agency until systems input of a presumptive disability decision or the day the case folder is released to us by the State agency, whichever is earlier.

(b) Target levels. The processing time target levels are:

(1) 37 days for title II initial claims.

(2) 43 days for title XVI initial claims.

(c) Threshold levels. The processing time threshold levels are:

(1) 49.5 days for title II initial claims.

(2) 57.9 days for title XVI initial claims.

[56 FR 11023, March 14, 1991]

§ 416.1043 Performance accuracy standard.

(a) General. Performance accuracy refers to the percentage of cases that do not have to be returned to State agencies for further development or correction of decisions based on evidence in the files and as such represents the reliability of State agency adjudication. The definition of performance accuracy includes the measurement of factors that have a potential for affecting a decision, as well as the correctness of the decision. For example, if a particular item of medical evidence should have been in the file but was not included, even though its inclusion does not change the result in the case, that is a performance error. Performance accuracy, therefore, is a higher standard than decisional accuracy. As a result, the percentage of correct decisions is significantly higher than what is reflected in the error rate established by SSA's quality assurance system.

(b) Target level. The State agency initial performance accuracy target level for combined title II and title XVI cases is 97 percent with a corresponding decision accuracy rate of 99 percent.

(c) Intermediate goals. These goals will be established annually by SSA's regional commissioner after negotiation with the State and should be used as stepping stones to progress towards our targeted level of performance.

(d) Threshold levels. The State agency initial performance accuracy threshold level for combined title II and title XVI cases is 90.6 percent.

§ 416.1044 How and when we determine whether the processing time standards are met.

(a) How we determine processing times. For all initial title II cases, we calculate the mean number of days, including Saturdays, Sundays, and holidays, from the day the case folder is received in the State agency until the day it is released to us by the State agency. For initial title XVI cases, we calculate the mean number of days, including Saturdays, Sundays, and holidays, from the day the case folder is received in the State agency until the day there is systems input of a presumptive disability decision or the day the case folder is released to us by the State agency, whichever is earlier.

(b) Frequency of review. Title II processing times and title XVI processing times are monitored separately on a quarterly basis. The determination as to whether or not the processing time thresholds have been met is made at the end of each quarter each year. Quarterly State-by-State mean processing times are compared with the threshold levels for both title II and title XVI.

[56 FR 11023, March 14, 1991]

§ 416.1045 How and when we determine whether the performance accuracy standard is met.

(a) How we determine performance accuracy. We determine a State agency's performance accuracy rate on the basis of decision and documentation errors identified in our review of the sample cases.

(b) Frequency of review. Title II and title XVI initial performance accuracy are monitored together on a quarterly basis. The determinations as to whether the performance accuracy threshold has been met is made at the end of each quarter each year. Quarterly State-by-State combined initial performance accuracy rates are compared to the established threshold level.

§ 416.1050 Action we will take if a State agency does not meet the standards.

If a State agency does not meet two of the three established threshold levels (one of which must be performance accuracy) for two or more consecutive calendar quarters, we will notify the State agency in writing that it is not meeting the standards. Following our notification, we will provide the State agency appropriate performance support described in §§ 416.1060, 416.1061 and 416.1062 for a period of up to 12 months.

[56 FR 11023, March 14, 1991]

PERFORMANCE MONITORING AND SUPPORT

§ 416.1060 How we will monitor.

We will regularly analyze State agency combined title II and title XVI initial performance accuracy rate, title II initial processing time, and title XVI initial processing time. Within budgeted resources, we will also routinely conduct fiscal and administrative management reviews and special onsite reviews. A fiscal and administrative management review is a fact-finding mission to review particular aspects of State agency operations. During these reviews we will also review the quality assurance function. This regular monitoring and review program will allow us to determine the progress each State is making and the type and extent of performance support we will provide to help the State progress toward threshold, intermediate, and/or target levels.

[56 FR 11023, March 14, 1991]

§ 416.1061 When we will provide performance support.

(a) Optional support. We may offer, or a State may request, performance support at any time that the regular monitoring and review process reveals that support could enhance performance. The State does not have to be below the initial performance accuracy rate of 90.6 percent to receive performance support. Support will be offered, or granted upon request, based on available resources.

(b) Mandatory support.

(1) We will provide a State agency with performance support if regular monitoring and review reveal that two of three threshold levels (one of which must be performance accuracy) are not met for two consecutive calendar quarters.

(2) We may also decide to provide a State agency with mandatory performance support if regular monitoring and review reveal that any one of the three threshold levels is not met for two consecutive calendar quarters. Support will be provided based on available resources.

(3) The threshold levels are:

(i) Combined title II and title XVI initial performance accuracy rate—90.6 percent,

(ii) Title II initial processing time—49.5 days, and

(iii) Title XVI initial processing time—57.9 days.

[56 FR 11023, March 14, 1991]

§ 416.1062 What support we will provide.

Performance support may include, but is not limited to, any or all of the following:

(a) An onsite review of cases processed by the State agency emphasizing adherence to written guidelines.

(b) A request that necessary administrative measures be implemented (e.g., filling staffing vacancies, using overtime, assisting with training activities, etc.).

(c) Provisions for Federal personnel to perform onsite reviews, conduct training, or perform other functions needed to improve performance.

(d) Provisions for fiscal aid to allow for overtime, temporary hiring of additional staff, etc., above the authorized budget.

[56 FR 11024, March 14, 1991]

SUBSTANTIAL FAILURE

§ 416.1070 General.

After a State agency falls below two of three established threshold levels, one being performance accuracy, for two consecutive quarters, and after the mandatory performance support period, we will give the State agency a 3–month adjustment period. During this 3–month period we will not require the State agency to meet the threshold levels. Following the adjustment period, if the State agency again falls below two of three threshold levels, one being performance accuracy, in two consecutive quarters during the next 12 months, we will notify the State that we propose to find that the State agency has substantially failed to comply with our standards and advise it that it may request a hearing on that issue. After giving the State notice and an opportunity for a hearing, if it is found that a State agency has substantially failed to make disability determinations consistent with the Act, our regulations, or other written guidelines, we will assume partial or complete responsibility for performing the disability determination function after we have complied with §§ 416.1090 and 416.1092.

[56 FR 11024, March 14, 1991]

§ 416.1071 Good cause for not following the Act, our regulations, or other written guidelines.

If a State has good cause for not following the Act, our regulations, or other written guidelines, we will not find that the State agency has substantially failed to meet our standards. We will determine if good cause exists. Some of the factors relevant to good cause are:

(a) Disasters such as fire, flood, or civil disorder, that—

(1) Require the diversion of significant personnel normally assigned to the disability determination function, or

(2) Destroyed or delayed access to significant records needed to make accurate disability determinations;

(b) Strikes of State agency staff or other government or private personnel necessary to the performance of the disability determination function;

(c) Sudden and unanticipated workload changes which result from changes in Federal law, regulations, or written guidelines, systems modification or systems malfunctions, or rapid, unpredictable caseload growth for a 6–month period or longer.

[56 FR 11024, March 14, 1991]

§ 416.1075 Finding of substantial failure.

A finding of substantial failure with respect to a State may not be made unless and until the State is afforded an opportunity for a hearing.

HEARINGS AND APPEALS

§ 416.1080 Notice of right to hearing on proposed finding of substantial failure.

If, following the mandatory performance support period and the 3–month adjustment period, a State agency again falls below two of three threshold levels (one being performance accuracy) in two consecutive quarters in the succeeding 12 months, we will notify the State in writing that we will find that the State agency has substantially failed to meet our standards unless the State submits a written request for a hearing with the Department of Health and Human Services' Departmental Appeals Board within 30 days after receiving the notice. The notice will identify the threshold levels that were not met by the State agency, the period during which the thresholds were not met, and the accuracy and processing time levels attained by the State agency during this period. If a hearing is not requested, the State agency will be found to have substantially failed to meet our standards, and we will implement our plans to assume the disability determination function.

[56 FR 11024, March 14, 1991]

§ 416.1081 Disputes on matters other than substantial failure.

Disputes concerning monetary disallowances will be resolved in proceedings before the Department of Health and Human Services, Departmental Appeals Board if the issue cannot be resolved between us and the State. Disputes other than monetary disallowances will be resolved through an appeal to the Commissioner of Social Security, who will make the final decision. (See § 416.1027.)

[56 FR 11024, March 14, 1991]

§ 416.1082 Who conducts the hearings.

If a hearing is required, it will be conducted by the Department of Health and Human Services' Departmental Appeals Board (the Board).

[62 FR 38455, July 18, 1997]

§ 416.1083 Hearings and appeals process.

The rules for hearings and appeals before the Board are provided in 45 CFR part 16. A notice under § 416.1080 of this subpart will be considered a "final written decision" for purposes of Board review.

ASSUMPTION OF DISABILITY DETERMINATION FUNCTION

§ 416.1090 Assumption when we make a finding of substantial failure.

(a) Notice to State. When we find that substantial failure exists, we will notify the State in writing that we will assume responsibility for performing the disability determination function from the State agency, whether the assumption will be partial or complete, and the date on which the assumption will be effective.

(b) Effective date of assumption. The date of any partial or complete assumption of the disability determination function from a State agency may not be earlier than 180 days after our finding of substantial failure, and not before compliance with the requirements of § 416.1092.

§ 416.1091 Assumption when State no longer wishes to perform the disability determination function.

(a) Notice to the Commissioner. If a State no longer wishes to perform the disability determination function, it will notify us in writing. The notice must be from an official authorized to act for the State for this purpose. The State will provide an opinion from the State's Attorney General verifying the authority of the official who gave the notice.

(b) Effective date of assumption. The State agency will continue to perform whatever activities of the disability determination function it is performing at the time the notice referred to in paragraph (a) of this section is given for not less than 180 days or, if later, until we have complied with the requirements of § 416.1092. For example, if the State is not making disability determinations (because we previously assumed responsibility for making them) but is performing other activities related to the disability determination function at the time it gives notice, the State will continue to do these activities until the requirements of this paragraph are met. Thereafter, we will assume complete responsibility for performing the disability determination function.

[62 FR 38455, July 18, 1997]

§ 416.1092 Protection of State employees.

(a) Hiring preference. We will develop and initiate procedures to implement a plan to partially or completely assume the disability determination function from the State agency under § 416.1090 or § 416.1091, as appropriate. Except for the State agency's administrator, deputy administrator, or assistant administrator (or his equivalent), we will give employees of the State agency who are capable of performing duties in the disability determination function preference over any other persons in filling positions with us for which they are qualified. We may also give a preference in hiring to the State agency's administrator, deputy administrator, or assistant administrator (or his equivalent). We will establish a system for determining the hiring priority among the affected State agency employees in those instances where we are not hiring all of them.

(b) Determination by Secretary of Labor. We will not assume responsibility for performing the disability determination function from a State until the Secretary of Labor determines that the State has made fair and equitable arrangements under applicable Federal, State and local law to protect the interests of employees who will be displaced from their employment because of the assumption and who we will not hire.

§ 416.1093 Limitation on State expenditures after notice.

The State agency may not, after it receives the notice referred to in § 416.1090, or gives the notice referred to in § 416.1091, make any new commitments to spend funds allocated to it for performing the disability determination function without the approval of the appropriate SSA regional commissioner. The State will make every effort to close out as soon as possible all existing commitments that relate to performing the disability determination function.

§ 416.1094 Final accounting by the State.

The State will submit its final claims to us as soon as possible, but in no event later than 1 year from the effective date of our assumption of the disability determination function unless we grant an extension of time. When the final claim(s) is submitted, a final accounting will be made by the State of any funds paid to the State under § 416.1026 which have not been spent or committed prior to the effective date of our assumption of the disability determination function. Disputes concerning final accounting issues which cannot be resolved between the State and us will be resolved in proceedings before the Grant Appeals Board as described in 45 CFR part 416.

SUBPART K—INCOME

Authority: Secs. 702(a)(5), 1602, 1611, 1612, 1613, 1614(f), 1621, 1631, and 1633 of the Social Security Act (42 U.S.C. 902(a)(5), 1381a, 1382, 1382a, 1382b, 1382c(f), 1382j, 1383, and 1383b); sec. 211, Pub.L. 93–66, 87 Stat. 154 (42 U.S.C. 1382 note).

Source: 45 FR 65547, Oct. 3, 1980; 50 FR 48573, Nov. 26, 1985; 51 FR 10616, March 28, 1986; 51 FR 34464, Sept. 29, 1986; 51 FR 39523, Oct. 29, 1986; 52 FR 8882, March 20, 1987; 52 FR 27541, July 22, 1987; 56 FR 36000, July 30, 1991; 57 FR 1384, Jan. 14, 1992; 57 FR 48562, Oct. 27, 1992; 57 FR 53850, Nov. 13, 1992; 57 FR 55088, Nov. 24, 1992; 59 FR 41405, Aug. 12, 1994; 61 FR 1712, Jan. 23, 1996; 61 FR 5942, Feb. 15, 1996; 71 FR 28264, May 16, 2006, unless otherwise noted.

GENERAL

§ 416.1100 Income and SSI eligibility.

You are eligible for supplemental security income (SSI) benefits if you are an aged, blind, or disabled person who meets the requirements described in subpart B and who has limited income and resources. Thus, the amount of income you have is a major factor in deciding whether you are eligible for SSI benefits and the amount of your benefit. We count income on a monthly basis. Generally, the more income you have the less your benefit will be. If you have too much income, you are not eligible for a benefit. However, we do not count all of your income to determine your eligibility and benefit amount. We explain in the following sections how we treat your income for the SSI program. These rules apply to the Federal benefit and to any optional State supplement paid by us on behalf of a State (§ 416.2025) except as noted in subpart T and in the Federal–State agreements with individual States. While this subpart explains how we count income, subpart D of these regulations explains how we determine your benefits, including the provision that we generally use countable income in a prior month to determine how much your benefit amount will be for a month in which you are eligible (§ 416.420).

[50 FR 48573, Nov. 26, 1985]

§ 416.1101 Definition of terms.

As used in this subpart—

Calendar quarter means a period of three full calendar months beginning with January, April, July, or October.

Child means someone who is not married, is not the head of a household, and is either under age 18 or is under age 22 and a student. (See § 416.1856)

Couple means an eligible individual and his or her eligible spouse.

Current market value means the price of an item on the open market in your locality.

Federal benefit rate means the monthly payment rate for an eligible individual or couple. It is the figure from which we subtract countable income to find out how much your Federal SSI benefit should be.

The Federal benefit rate does not include the rate for any State supplement paid by us on behalf of a State.

Institution means an establishment which makes available some treatment or services beyond food and shelter to four or more persons who are not related to the proprietor. (See § 416.201)

Spouse means someone who lives with another person as that person's husband or wife. (See § 416.1806)

We, Us, or Our means the Social Security Administration.

You or Your means a person who is applying for, or already receiving, SSI benefits.

[50 FR 48570, 48573, Nov. 26, 1985; 51 FR 10616, March 28, 1986; 60 FR 16375, March 30, 1995]

§ 416.1102 What is income?

Income is anything you receive in cash or in kind that you can use to meet your needs for food and shelter. Sometimes income also includes more or less than you actually receive (see § 416.1110 and § 416.1123(b)). In-kind income is not cash, but is actually food or shelter, or something you can use to get one of these.

[56 FR 3212, Jan. 29, 1991; 70 FR 6344, Feb. 7, 2005]

§ 416.1103 What is not income?

Some things you receive are not income because you cannot use them as food or shelter, or use them to obtain food or shelter. In addition, what you receive from the sale or exchange of your own property is not income; it remains a resource. The following are some items that are not income:

(a) Medical care and services. Medical care and services are not income if they are any of the following:

(1) Given to you free of charge or paid for directly to the provider by someone else;

(2) Room and board you receive during a medical confinement;

(3) Assistance provided in cash or in kind (including food or shelter) under a Federal, State, or local government program whose purpose is to provide medical care or medical services (including vocational rehabilitation);

(4) In-kind assistance (except food or shelter) provided under a nongovernmental program whose purpose is to provide medical care or medical services;

(5) Cash provided by any nongovernmental medical care or medical services program or under a health insurance policy (except cash to cover food or shelter) if the cash is either:

(i) Repayment for program-approved services you have already paid for; or

(ii) A payment restricted to the future purchase of a program-approved service.

Example: If you have paid for prescription drugs and get the money back from your health insurance, the money is not income.

(6) Direct payment of your medical insurance premiums by anyone on your behalf.

(7) Payments from the Department of Veterans Affairs resulting from unusual medical expenses.

(b) Social services. Social services are not income if they are any of the following:

(1) Assistance provided in cash or in kind (but not received in return for a service you perform) under any Federal, State, or local government program whose purpose is to provide social services including vocational rehabilitation (Example: Cash given you by the Department of Veterans Affairs to purchase aid and attendance);

(2) In-kind assistance (except food or shelter) provided under a nongovernmental program whose purpose is to provide social services; or

(3) Cash provided by a nongovernmental social services program (except cash to cover food or shelter) if the cash is either:

(i) Repayment for program-approved services you already have paid for; or

(ii) A payment restricted to the future purchase of a program-approved service.

Example: If you are unable to do your own household chores and a private social services agency provides you with cash to pay a homemaker the cash is not income.

(c) Receipts from the sale, exchange, or replacement of a resource. Receipts from the sale, exchange, or replacement of a resource are not income but are resources that have changed their form. This includes any cash or in-kind item that is provided to replace or repair a resource (see subpart L) that has been lost, damaged, or stolen. Sections 416.1150 and 416.1151 discuss treatment of receipts to replace or repair a resource following a major disaster or following some other event causing damage or loss of a resource.

Example: If you sell your automobile, the money you receive is not income; it is another form of a resource.

(d) Income tax refunds. Any amount refunded on income taxes you have already paid is not income.

(e) Payments by credit life or credit disability insurance. Payments made under a credit life or credit disability insurance policy on your behalf are not income.

Example: If a credit disability policy pays off the mortgage on your home after you become disabled in an accident, we do not consider either the payment or your increased equity in the home to be income.

(f) Proceeds of a loan. Money you borrow or money you receive as repayment of a loan is not income. However, interest you receive on money you have lent is income. Buying on credit is treated as though you were borrowing money and what you purchase this way is not income.

(g) Bills paid for you. Payment of your bills by someone else directly to the supplier is not income. However, we count the value of anything you receive because of the payment if it is in-kind income as defined in § 416.1102.

Examples: If your daughter uses her own money to pay the grocer to provide you with food, the payment itself is not your income because you do not receive it. However, because of your daughter's payment, the grocer provides you with food; the food is in-kind income to you. Similarly, if you buy food on credit and your son later pays the bill, the payment to the store is not income to you, but the food is in-kind income to you. In this example, if your son pays for the food in a month after the month of purchase, we will count the in-kind income to you in the month in which he pays the bill. On the other hand, if your brother pays a lawn service to mow your grass, the payment is not income to you because the mowing cannot be used to meet your needs for food or shelter. Therefore, it is not in-kind income as defined in § 416.1102.

(h) Replacement of income you have already received. If income is lost, destroyed, or stolen and you receive a replacement, the replacement is not income.

Example: If your paycheck is stolen and you get a replacement check, we count the first check as income. The replacement check is not income.

(i) Weatherization assistance. Weatherization assistance (Examples: Insulation, storm doors and windows) is not income.

(j) Receipt of certain noncash items. Any item you receive (except shelter as defined in § 416.1130 or food) which would be an excluded nonliquid resource (as described in subpart L of this part) if you kept it, is not income.

Example 1: A community takes up a collection to buy you a specially equipped van, which is your only vehicle. The value of this gift is not income because the van does not provide you with food or shelter and will become an excluded nonliquid resource under § 416.1218 in the month following the month of receipt.

Example 2: You inherit a house which is your principal place of residence. The value of this inheritance is income because the house provides you with shelter and shelter is income. However, we value the house under the rule in § 416.1140.

[49 FR 48038, Nov. 26, 1984; 57 FR 53850, Nov. 13, 1992; 59 FR 33907, July 1, 1994; 70 FR 6344, Feb. 7, 2005]

§ 416.1104 Income we count.

We have described generally what income is and is not for SSI purposes (§ 416.1103). There are different types of income, earned and unearned, and we have rules for counting each. The earned income rules are described in §§ 416.1110 through 416.1112 and the unearned income rules are described in §§ 416.1120 through 416.1124. One type of unearned income is in-kind support and maintenance (food or shelter). The way we value it depends on your living arrangement. These rules are described in §§ 416.1130 through 416.1148 of this part. In some situations we must consider the income of certain people with whom you live as available to you and part of your income. These rules are described in §§ 416.1160 through 416.1169. We use all of these rules to determine the amount of your countable income—the amount that is left after we subtract what is not income or is not counted.

[65 FR 16815, March 30, 2000; 70 FR 6345, Feb. 7, 2005]

EARNED INCOME

§ 416.1110 What is earned income.

Earned income may be in cash or in kind. We may include more of your earned income than you actually receive. We include more than you actually receive if amounts are withheld from earned income because of a garnishment or to pay a debt or other legal obligation, or to make any other payments. Earned income consists of the following types of payments:

(a) Wages—

(1) Wages paid in cash—general. Wages are what you receive (before any deductions) for working as someone else's employee. Wages are the same for SSI purposes as for the social security retirement program's earnings test. (See § 404.429(c) of this chapter.) Wages include salaries, commissions, bonuses, severance pay, and any other special payments received because of your employment.

(2) Wages paid in cash to uniformed service members. Wages paid in cash to uniformed service members include basic pay, some types of special pay, and some types of allowances. Allowances for on-base housing or privatized military housing are unearned income in the form of in-kind support and maintenance. Cash allowances paid to uniformed service members for private housing are wages.

(3) Wages paid in kind. Wages may also include the value of food, clothing, shelter, or other items provided instead of cash. We refer to this type of income as in-kind earned income. However, if you are a domestic or agricultural worker, the law requires us to treat your in-kind pay as unearned income.

(b) Net earnings from self-employment. Net earnings from self-employment are your gross income from any trade or business that you operate, less allowable deductions for that trade or business. Net earnings also include your share of profit or loss in any partnership to which you belong. For taxable years beginning before January 1, 2001, net earnings from self-employment under the SSI program are the same net earnings that we would count under the social security retirement insurance program and that you would report on your Federal income tax return. (See § 404.1080 of this chapter.) For taxable years beginning on or after January 1, 2001, net earnings from self-employment under the SSI program will also include the earnings of statutory employees. In addition, for SSI purposes only, we consider statutory employees to be self-employed individuals. Statutory employees are agent or commission drivers, certain full-time life insurance salespersons, home workers, and traveling or city salespersons. (See § 404.1008 of this chapter for a more detailed description of these types of employees).

(c) Refunds of Federal income taxes and advance payments by employers made in accordance with the earned income credit provisions of the Internal Revenue Code. Refunds on account of earned income credits are payments made to you under the provisions of section 32 of the Internal Revenue Code of 1986, as amended. These refunds may be greater than taxes you have paid. You may receive earned income tax credit payments along with any other Federal income tax refund you receive because of overpayment of your income tax, (Federal income tax refunds made on the basis of taxes you have already paid are not income to you as stated in § 416.1103(d).) Advance payments of earned income tax credits are made by your employer under the provisions of section 3507 of the same code. You can receive earned income tax credit payments only if you meet certain requirements of family composition and income limits.

(d) Payments for services performed in a sheltered workshop or work activities center. Payments for services performed in a sheltered workshop or work activities center are what you receive for participating in a program designed to help you become self-supporting.

(e) Certain royalties and honoraria. Royalties that are earned income are payments to an individual in connection with any publication of the work of the individual. (See § 416.1110(b) if you receive a royalty as part of your trade or business. See § 416.1121(c) if you receive another type of royalty.) Honoraria that are earned income are those portions of payments, such as an honorary payment, reward, or donation, received in consideration of services rendered for which no payment can be enforced by law. (See § 416.1120 if you receive another type of honorarium.)

[48 FR 23179, May 24, 1983; 50 FR 48574, Nov. 26, 1985; 56 FR 3212, Jan. 29, 1991; 59 FR 43471, Aug. 24, 1994; 75 FR 1273, Jan. 11, 2010; 75 FR 54287, Sept. 7, 2010]

§ 416.1111 How we count earned income.

(a) Wages. We count wages at the earliest of the following points: when you receive them or when they are credited to your account or set aside for your use. We determine wages for each month. We count wages for services performed as a member of a uniformed service (as defined in § 404.1330 of this chapter) as received in the month in which they are earned.

(b) Net earnings from self-employment. We count net earnings from self-employment on a taxable year basis. However, we divide the total of these earnings equally among the months in the taxable year to get your earnings for each month. For example, if your net earnings for a taxable year are $2,400, we consider that you received $200 in each month. If you have net losses from self-employment, we divide them over the taxable year in the same way, and we deduct them only from your other earned income.

(c) Payments for services in a sheltered workshop or activities center. We count payments you receive for services performed in a sheltered workshop or work activities center when you receive them or when they are set aside for your use. We determine the amount of the payments for each calendar quarter.

(d) In-kind earned income. We use the current market value of in-kind earned income for SSI purposes. (See § 416.1101 for a definition of current market value.) If you receive an item that is not fully paid for and are responsible for the unpaid balance, only the paid-up value is income to you. (See the example in § 416.1123(c)).

(e) Royalties and honoraria. We count payments of royalties to you in connection with any publication of your work, and honoraria, to the extent received for services rendered, at the earliest of the following points: when you receive them, when they are credited to your account, or when they are set aside for your use. (See § 416.1111(b) if you receive royalties as part of your trade or business.)

[48 FR 23179, May 24, 1983; 48 FR 30357, July 1, 1983; 50 FR 48574, Nov. 26, 1985; 58 FR 63889, Dec. 3, 1993; 59 FR 43471, Aug. 24, 1994; 71 FR 45378, Aug. 9, 2006]

§ 416.1112 Earned income we do not count.

(a) General. While we must know the source and amount of all of your earned income for SSI, we do not count all of it to determine your eligibility and benefit amount. We first exclude income as authorized by other Federal laws (see paragraph (b) of this section). Then we apply the other exclusions in the order listed in paragraph (c) of this section to the rest of your income in the month. We never reduce your earned income below zero or apply any unused earned income exclusion to unearned income.

(b) Other Federal laws. Some Federal laws other than the Social Security Act provide that we cannot count some of your earned income for SSI purposes. We list the laws and exclusions in the appendix to this subpart which we update periodically.

(c) Other earned income we do not count. We do not count as earned income—

(1) Any refund of Federal income taxes you receive under section 32 of the Internal Revenue Code (relating to earned income tax credit) and any payment you receive from an employer under section 3507 of the Internal Revenue Code (relating to advance payment of earned income tax credit);

(2) The first $30 of earned income received in a calendar quarter if you receive it infrequently or irregularly. We consider income to be received infrequently if you receive it only once during a calendar quarter from a single source and you did not receive it in the month immediately preceding that month or in the month immediately subsequent to that month. We consider income to be received irregularly if you cannot reasonably expect to receive it.

(3) If you are under age 22 and a student who is regularly attending school as described in § 416.1861:

(i) For earned income beginning January 1, 2002, monthly and yearly maximum amounts that are the larger of:

(A) The monthly and yearly amounts for the previous year, or

(B) Monthly and yearly maximum amounts increased for changes in the cost-of-living, calculated in the same manner as the Federal benefit rates described in § 416.405, except that we will use the calendar year 2001 amounts as the base amounts and will round the resulting amount to the next higher multiple of $10 where such amount is a multiple of $5 but not of $10 and to the nearest multiple of $10 in any other case.

(ii) For earned income before January 1, 2002, the amounts indicated in Table 1 of this section.

Table 1

For months	Up to per month	But not more than in a calendar year
In calendar years before 2001	$400	$1,620
In calendar year 2001	1,290	5,200

(4) Any portion of the $20 monthly exclusion in § 416.1124(c)(10) which has not been excluded from your unearned income in that same month;

(5) $65 of earned income in a month;

(6) Earned income you use to pay impairment-related work expenses described in § 416.976, if you are disabled (but not blind) and under age 65 or you are disabled (but not blind) and received SSI as a disabled individual (or received disability payments under a former State plan) for the month before you reached age 65.

(i) For periods prior to December 1, 1990, you must be able, however, to establish your initial eligibility for Federal benefits without the use of the impairment-related work expense exclusion. Once you establish your initial eligibility without the use of the impairment-related work expense exclusion, the exclusion applies for determining your eligibility for all subsequent consecutive months for which you are eligible for regular SSI benefits, federally administered optional State supplementary payments, special SSI cash benefits or special SSI eligibility status. If, in a subsequent month, you are not eligible for any of these benefits, you cannot reestablish your eligibility for Federal SSI benefits or federally administered optional State supplementary payments before December 1, 1990, using the impairment-related work expense exclusion.

(ii) For periods after November 30, 1990, you may also use the impairment-related work expense exclusion to establish initial eligibility and reeligibility following a month in which you were not eligible for regular SSI benefits, a federally administered optional State supplementary payment, special SSI cash benefits or special SSI eligibility status.

(7) One-half of remaining earned income in a month;

(8) Earned income used to meet any expenses reasonably attributable to the earning of the income if you are blind and under age 65 or if you receive SSI as a blind person for the month before you reach age 65. (We consider that you "reach" a certain age on the day before that particular birthday.);

(9) Any earned income you receive and use to fulfill an approved plan to achieve self-support if you are blind or disabled and under age 65 or blind or disabled and received SSI as a blind or disabled person for the month before you reached age 65. See §§ 416.1180 through 416.1182 for an explanation of plans to achieve self-support and for the rules on when this exclusion applies; and

(10) Payments made to participants in AmeriCorps State and National and AmeriCorps National Civilian Community Corps (NCCC). Payments to participants in AmeriCorps State and National and AmeriCorps NCCC may be made in cash or in-kind and may be made directly to the AmeriCorps participant or on the AmeriCorps participant's behalf. These payments include, but are not limited to: Living allowance payments, stipends, educational awards, and payments in lieu of educational awards.

[48 FR 21943, May 16, 1983; 50 FR 48574, Nov. 26, 1985; 58 FR 63890, Dec. 3, 1993; 59 FR 41405, Aug. 12, 1994; 65 FR 82912, Dec. 29, 2000; 71 FR 45378, Aug. 9, 2006; 71 FR 66866, Nov. 17, 2006; 75 FR 54287, Sept. 7, 2010]

UNEARNED INCOME

§ 416.1120 What is unearned income.

Unearned income is all income that is not earned income. We describe some of the types of unearned income in § 416.1121. We consider all of these items as unearned income, whether you receive them in cash or in kind.

§ 416.1121 Types of unearned income.

Some types of unearned income are—

(a) Annuities, pensions, and other periodic payments. This unearned income is usually related to prior work or service. It includes, for example, private pensions, social security benefits, disability benefits, veterans benefits, worker's compensation, railroad retirement annuities and unemployment insurance benefits.

(b) Alimony and support payments. For SSI purposes, alimony and support payments are cash or in-kind contributions to meet some or all of a person's needs for food or shelter. Support payments may be made voluntarily or because of a court order. Alimony (sometimes called maintenance) is an allowance made by a court from the funds of one spouse to the other spouse in connection with a suit for separation or divorce.

(c) Dividends, interest, and certain royalties. Dividends and interest are returns on capital investments, such as stocks, bonds, or savings accounts. Royalties are compensation paid to the owner for the use of property, usually copyrighted material or natural resources such as mines, oil wells, or timber tracts. Royalty compensation may be expressed as a percentage of receipts from using the property or as an amount per unit produced. (See § 416.1110(b) if you receive royalties as part of your trade or business and § 416.1110(e) if you receive royalties in connection with the publication of your work.)

(d) Rents. Rents are payments you receive for the use of real or personal property such as land, housing, or machinery. We deduct from rental payments your ordinary and necessary expenses in the same taxable year. These include only those expenses necessary for the production or collection of the rental income and they must be deducted when paid, not when they are incurred. Some examples of deductible expenses are interest on debts, State and local taxes on real and personal property and on motor fuels, general sales taxes, and expenses of managing or maintaining the property. (Sections 163, 164, and 212 of the Internal Revenue Code of 1954 and related regulations explain this in more detail.) We do not consider depreciation or depletion of property a deductible expense. (See § 416.1110(b) for rules on rental income that is earned from self-employment. For example, you may be in the business of renting properties.)

(e) Death benefits. We count payments you get which were occasioned by the death of another person except for the amount of such payments that you spend on the deceased person's last illness and burial expenses. Last illness and burial expenses include related hospital and medical expenses, funeral, burial plot and interment expenses, and other related costs.

Example: If you receive $2,000 from your uncle's life insurance policy and you spend $900 on his last illness and burial expenses, the balance, $1,100, is unearned income. If you spend the entire $2,000 for the last illness and burial, there is no unearned income.

(f) Prizes and awards. A prize is generally something you win in a contest, lottery or game of chance. An award is usually something you receive as the result of a decision by a court, board of arbitration, or the like.

(g) Gifts and inheritances. A gift is something you receive which is not repayment to you for goods or services you provided and which is not given to you because of a legal obligation on the giver's part. An inheritance is something that comes to you as a result of someone's death. It can be in cash or in kind, including any right in real or personal property. Gifts and inheritances occasioned by the death of another person, to the extent that they are used to pay the expenses of the deceased's last illness and burial, as defined in paragraph (e) of this section, are not considered income.

(h) Support and maintenance in kind. This is food, or shelter furnished to you. Our rules for valuing this income depend on your living arrangement. We use one rule if you are living in the household of a person who provides you with both food and shelter. We use different rules for other situations where you receive food or shelter. We discuss all of the rules in §§ 416.1130 through 416.1147.

[56 FR 36000, July 30, 1991; 59 FR 43471, Aug. 24, 1994; 70 FR 6345, Feb. 7, 2005]

§ 416.1123 How we count unearned income.

(a) When we count unearned income. We count unearned income at the earliest of the following points: when you receive it or when it is credited to your account or set aside for your use. We determine your unearned income for each month. We describe exceptions to the rule on how we count unearned income in paragraphs (d), (e) and (f) of this section.

(b) Amount considered as income. We may include more or less of your unearned income than you actually receive.

(1) We include more than you actually receive where another benefit payment (such as a social security insurance benefit) (see § 416.1121) has been reduced to recover a previous overpayment. You are repaying a legal obligation through the withholding of portions of your benefit amount, and the amount of the debt reduction is also part of your unearned income. Exception: We do not include more than you actually receive if you received both SSI benefits and the other benefit at the time the overpayment of the other benefit occurred and the overpaid amount was included in figuring your SSI benefit at that time.

Example: Joe, an SSI beneficiary, is also entitled to social security insurance benefits in the amount of $200 per month. However, because of a prior overpayment of his social security insurance benefits, $20 per month is being withheld to recover the overpayment. In figuring the amount of his SSI benefits, the full monthly social security insurance benefit of $200 is included in Joe's unearned income. However, if Joe was receiving both benefits when the overpayment of the social security insurance benefit occurred and we then included the overpaid amount as income, we will compute his SSI benefit on the basis of receiving $180 as a social security insurance benefit. This is because we recognize that we computed his SSI benefit on the basis of the higher amount when he was overpaid.

(2) We also include more than you actually receive if amounts are withheld from unearned income because of a garnishment, or to pay a debt or other legal obligation, or to make any other payment such as payment of your Medicare premiums.

(3) We include less than you actually receive if part of the payment is for an expense you had in getting the payment. For example, if you are paid for damages you receive in an accident, we subtract from the amount of the payment your medical, legal, or other expenses connected with the accident. If you receive a retroactive check from a benefit program other than SSI, legal fees connected with the claim are subtracted. We do not subtract from any taxable unearned income the part you have to use to pay personal income taxes. The payment of taxes is not an expense you have in getting income.

(4) In certain situations, we may consider someone else's income to be available to you, whether or not it actually is. (For the rules on this process, called deeming, see §§ 416.1160 through 416.1169.)

(c) In-kind income. We use the current market value (defined in § 416.1101) of in-kind unearned income to determine its value for SSI purposes. We describe some exceptions to this rule in §§ 416.1131 through 416.1147. If you receive an item that is not fully paid for and are responsible for the balance, only the paid-up value is income to you.

Example: You are given a $1500 automobile but must pay the $1000 due on it. You are receiving income of $500.

(d) Retroactive monthly social security benefits. We count retroactive monthly social security benefits according to the rule in paragraph (d)(1) of this section, unless the exception in paragraph (d)(2) of this section applies:

(1) Periods for which SSI payments have been made. When you file an application for social security benefits and retroactive monthly social security benefits are payable on that application for a period for which you also received SSI payments (including federally-administered State supplementary payments), we count your retroactive monthly social security benefits as unearned income received in that period. Rather than reducing your SSI payments in months prior to your receipt of a retroactive monthly social security benefit, we will reduce the retroactive social security benefits by an amount equal to the amount of SSI payments (including federally-administered State supplementary payments) that we would not have paid to you if your social security benefits had been paid when regularly due rather than retroactively (see § 404.408b(b)). If a balance is due you from your retroactive social security benefits after this reduction, for SSI purposes we will not count the balance as unearned income in a subsequent month in which you receive it. This is because your social security benefits were used to determine the amount of the reduction. This exception to the unearned income counting rule does not apply to any monthly social security benefits for a period for which you did not receive SSI.

(2) Social security disability benefits where drug addiction or alcoholism is a contributing factor material to the determination of disability. If your retroactive social security benefits must be paid in installments because of the limitations on paying lump sum retroactive benefits to disabled recipients whose drug addiction or alcoholism is a contributing factor material to the determination of disability as described in § 404.480, we will count the total of such retroactive social security benefits as unearned income in the first month such installments are paid, except to the extent the rule in paragraph (d)(1) of this section would provide that such benefits not be counted.

(e) Certain veterans benefits.

(1) If you receive a veterans benefit that includes an amount paid to you because of a dependent, we do not count as your unearned income the amount paid to you because of the dependent.

(2) If you are a dependent of an individual who receives a veterans benefit and a portion of the benefit is attributable to you as a dependent, we count the amount attributable to you as your unearned cash income if—

(i) You reside with the individual who receives the veterans benefit, or

(ii) You receive your own separate payment from the Department of Veterans Affairs.

(f) Uniformed service compensation. We count compensation for services performed as a member of a uniformed service (as defined in § 404.1330 of this chapter) as received in the month in which it is earned.

(Reporting and recordkeeping requirements in paragraph (b) have been approved by the Office of Management and Budget under control number 0960–0128)

[45 FR 65547, Oct. 3, 1980, as amended at 47 FR 4988, Feb. 3, 1982; 47 FR 13794, Apr. 1, 1982; 50 FR 48574, Nov. 26, 1985; 55 FR 20599, May 18, 1990; 56 FR 3212, Jan. 29, 1991; 59 FR 59364, Nov. 17, 1994; 60 FR 8152, Feb. 10, 1995; 71 FR 45378, Aug. 9, 2006]

§ 416.1124 Unearned income we do not count.

(a) General. While we must know the source and amount of all of your unearned income for SSI, we do not count all of it to determine your eligibility and benefit amount. We first exclude income as authorized by other Federal laws (see paragraph (b) of this section). Then we apply the other exclusions in the order listed in paragraph (c) of this section to the rest of your unearned income in the month. We never reduce your unearned income below zero or apply any unused unearned income exclusion to earned income except for the $20 general exclusion described in paragraph (c)(12) of this section.

(b) Other Federal laws. Some Federal laws other than the Social Security Act provide that we cannot count some of your unearned income for SSI purposes. We list the laws and the exclusions in the appendix to this subpart which we update periodically.

(c) Other unearned income we do not count. We do not count as unearned income—

(1) Any public agency's refund of taxes on real property or food;

(2) Assistance based on need which is wholly funded by a State or one of its political subdivisions. (For purposes of this rule, an Indian tribe is considered a political subdivision of a State.) Assistance is based on need when it is provided under a program which uses the amount of your income as one factor to determine your eligibility. Assistance based on need includes State supplementation of Federal SSI benefits as defined in subpart T of this part but does not include payments under a Federal/State grant program such as Temporary Assistance for Needy Families under title IV–A of the Social Security Act;

(3) Any portion of a grant, scholarship, fellowship, or gift used or set aside for paying tuition, fees, or other necessary educational expenses. However, we do count any portion set aside or actually used for food or shelter;

(4) Food which you or your spouse raise if it is consumed by you or your household;

(5) Assistance received under the Disaster Relief and Emergency Assistance Act and assistance provided under any Federal statute because of a catastrophe which the President of the United States declares to be a major disaster. See § 416.1150 for a more detailed discussion of this assistance, particularly the treatment of in-kind support and maintenance received as the result of a major disaster;

(6) The first $60 of unearned income received in a calendar quarter if you receive it infrequently or irregularly. We consider income to be received infrequently if you receive it only once during a calendar quarter from a single source and you did not receive it in the month immediately preceding that month or in the month immediately subsequent to that month. We consider income to be received irregularly if you cannot reasonably expect to receive it.

(7) Alaska Longevity Bonus payments made to an individual who is a resident of Alaska and who, prior to October 1, 1985: met the 25–year residency requirement for receipt of such payments in effect prior to January 1, 1983; and was eligible for SSI;

(8) Payments for providing foster care to an ineligible child who was placed in your home by a public or private nonprofit child placement or child care agency;

(9) Any interest earned on excluded burial funds and any appreciation in the value of an excluded burial arrangement which are left to accumulate and become a part of the separate burial fund. (See § 416.1231 for an explanation of the exclusion of burial assets.) This exclusion from income applies to interest earned on burial funds or appreciation in the value of excluded burial arrangements which occur beginning November 1, 1982, or the date you first become eligible for SSI benefits, if later;

(10) Certain support and maintenance assistance as described in § 416.1157;

(11) One-third of support payments made to or for you by an absent parent if you are a child;

(12) The first $20 of any unearned income in a month other than income in the form of in-kind support and maintenance received in the household of another (see § 416.1131) and income based on need. Income based on need is a benefit that uses financial need as measured by your income as a factor to determine your eligibility. The $20 exclusion does not apply to a benefit based on need that is totally or partially funded by the Federal government or by a nongovernmental agency. However, assistance which is based on need and funded wholly by a State or one of its political subdivisions is excluded totally from income as described in § 416.1124(c)(2). If you have less than $20 of unearned income in a month and you have earned income in that month, we will use the rest of the $20 exclusion to reduce the amount of your countable earned income;

(13) Any unearned income you receive and use to fulfill an approved plan to achieve self-support if you are blind or disabled and under age 65 or blind or disabled and received SSI as a blind or disabled person for the month before you reached age 65. See §§ 416.1180 through 416.1182 for an explanation of plans to achieve self-support and for the rules on when this exclusion applies;

(14) The value of any assistance paid with respect to a dwelling unit under—

(i) The United States Housing Act of 1937;

(ii) The National Housing Act;

(iii) Section 101 of the Housing and Urban Development Act of 1965;

(iv) Title V of the Housing Act of 1949; or

(v) Section 202(h) of the Housing Act of 1959.

(15) Any interest accrued on and left to accumulate as part of the value of an excluded burial space purchase agreement. This exclusion from income applies to interest accrued on or after April 1, 1990;

(16) The value of any commercial transportation ticket, for travel by you or your spouse among the 50 States, the District of Columbia, the Commonwealth of Puerto Rico, the Virgin Islands, Guam, American Samoa, and the Northern Mariana Islands, which is received as a gift by you or your spouse and is not converted to cash. If such a ticket is converted to cash, the cash you receive is income in the month you receive the cash;

(17) Payments received by you from a fund established by a State to aid victims of crime;

(18) Relocation assistance provided you by a State or local government that is comparable to assistance provided under title II of the Uniform Relocation Assistance and Real Property Acquisition Policies Act of 1970 that is subject to the treatment required by section 216 of that Act;

(19) Special pay received from one of the uniformed services pursuant to 37 U.S.C. 310;

(20) Interest or other earnings on a dedicated account which is excluded from resources. (See § 416.1247);

(21) Gifts from an organization as described in section 501(c)(3) of the Internal Revenue Code of 1986 which is exempt from taxation under section 501(a) of such Code, to, or for the benefit of, an individual who has not attained 18 years of age and who has a life-threatening condition. We will exclude any in-kind gift that is not converted to cash and cash gifts to the extent that the total gifts excluded pursuant to this paragraph do not exceed $2000 in any calendar year. In-kind gifts converted to cash are considered under income counting rules in the month of conversion;

(22) Interest and dividend income from a countable resource or from a resource excluded under a Federal statute other than section 1613(a) of the Social Security Act; and

(23) AmeriCorps State and National and AmeriCorps National Civilian Community Corps cash or in-kind payments to AmeriCorps participants or on AmeriCorps participants' behalf. These include, but are not limited to: Food and shelter, and clothing allowances;

(24) Any annuity paid by a State to a person (or his or her spouse) based on the State's determination that the person is:

(i) A veteran (as defined in 38 U.S.C. 101); and

(ii) Blind, disabled, or aged.

[45 FR 65547, Oct. 3, 1980, and 47 FR 55213, Dec. 8, 1982; 48 FR 21943, May 16, 1983; 48 FR 33258, July 21, 1983; 48 FR 57127, Dec. 28, 1983; 50 FR 48574, Nov. 26, 1985; 51 FR 39523, Oct. 29, 1986; 54 FR 19164, May 4, 1989; 55 FR 28378, July 11, 1990; 57 FR 1384, Jan. 14, 1992; 57 FR 53850, Nov. 13, 1992; 58 FR 63888, Dec. 3, 1993; 61 FR 1712, Jan. 23, 1996; 61 FR 49964, Sept. 24, 1996; 61 FR 67207, Dec. 20, 1996; 70 FR 6345, Feb. 7, 2005; 70 FR 41137, July 18, 2005; 71 FR 45378, Aug. 9, 2006; 75 FR 7554, Feb. 22, 2010; 75 FR 54287, Sept. 7, 2010]]

IN–KIND SUPPORT AND MAINTENANCE

§ 416.1130 Introduction.

(a) General. Both earned income and unearned income include items received in kind (§ 416.1102). Generally, we value in-kind items at their current market value and we apply the various exclusions for both earned and unearned income. However, we have special rules for valuing food or shelter that is received as unearned income (in-kind support and maintenance). This section and the ones that follow discuss these rules. In these sections (§§ 416.1130 through 416.1148) we use the in-kind support and maintenance you receive in the month as described in § 416.420 to determine your SSI benefit. We value the in-kind support and maintenance using the Federal benefit rate for the month in which you receive it. Exception: For the first 2 months for which a cost-of-living adjustment applies, we value in-kind support and maintenance you receive using the VTR or PMV based on the Federal benefit rate as increased by the cost-of-living adjustment.

Example: Mr. Jones receives an SSI benefit which is computed by subtracting one-third from the Federal benefit rate. This one-third represents the value of the income he receives because he lives in the household of a son who provides both food and shelter (in-kind support and maintenance). In January, we increase his SSI benefit because of a cost-of-living adjustment. We base his SSI payment for that month on the food and shelter he received from his son two months earlier in November. In determining the value of that food and shelter he received in November, we use the Federal benefit rate for January.

(b) How we define in-kind support and maintenance. In-kind support and maintenance means any food or shelter that is given to you or that you receive because someone else pays for it. Shelter includes room, rent, mortgage payments, real property taxes, heating fuel, gas, electricity, water, sewerage, and garbage collection services. You are not receiving in-kind support and maintenance in the form of room or rent if you are paying the amount charged under a business arrangement. A business arrangement exists when the amount of monthly rent required to be paid equals the current market rental value (see § 416.1101). Exception: In the States in the Seventh Circuit (Illinois, Indiana, and Wisconsin), a business arrangement exists when the amount of monthly rent required to be paid equals or exceeds the presumed maximum value described in § 416.1140(a)(1). In those States, if the required amount of rent is less than the presumed maximum value, we will impute as in-kind support and maintenance, the difference between the required amount of rent and either the presumed maximum value or the current market value, whichever is less. In addition, cash payments to uniformed service members as allowances for on-base housing or privatized military housing are in-kind support and maintenance.

(c) How we value in-kind support and maintenance. Essentially, we have two rules for valuing the in-kind support and maintenance which we must count. The one-third reduction rule applies if you are living in the household of a person who provides you with both food and shelter (§§ 416.1131 through 416.1133). The presumed value rule applies in all other situations where you are receiving countable in-kind support and maintenance (§§ 416.1140 through 416.1145). If certain conditions exist, we do not count in-kind support and maintenance. These are discussed in §§ 416.1141 through 416.1145.

[50 FR 48574, Nov. 26, 1985; 51 FR 13488, April 21, 1986; 60 FR 16375, March 30, 1995; 63 FR 33546, June 19, 1998; 70 FR 6345, Feb. 7, 2005; 75 FR 54287, Sept. 7, 2010]

§ 416.1131 The one-third reduction rule.

(a) What the rule is. Instead of determining the actual dollar value of in-kind support and maintenance, we count one-third of the Federal benefit rate as additional income if you (or you and your eligible spouse)—

(1) Live in another person's household (see § 416.1132) for a full calendar month except for temporary absences (see § 416.1149), and

(2) Receive both food and shelter from the person in whose household you are living. (If you do not receive both food and shelter from this person, see § 416.1140.)

(b) How we apply the one-third reduction rule. The one-third reduction applies in full or not at all. When you are living in another person's household, and the one-third reduction rule applies, we do not apply any income exclusions to the reduction amount. However, we do apply appropriate exclusions to any other earned or unearned income you receive. If you have an eligible spouse we apply the rules described in § 416.1147.

(c) If you receive other support and maintenance. If the one-third reduction rule applies to you, we do not count any other in-kind support and maintenance you receive.

[50 FR 48574, Nov. 26, 1985]

§ 416.1132 What we mean by "living in another person's household".

(a) Household. For purposes of this subpart, we consider a household to be a personal place of residence. A commercial establishment such as a hotel or boarding house is not a household but a household can exist within a commercial establishment. If you live in a commercial establishment, we do not automatically consider you to be a member of the household of the proprietor. You may, however, live in the household of a roomer or boarder within the hotel or boarding house. An institution is not a household and a household cannot exist within an institution. (Institution is defined in § 416.1101.)

(b) Another person's household. You live in another person's household if paragraph (c) of this section does not apply and if the person who supplies the support and maintenance lives in the same household and is not—

(1) Your spouse (as defined in § 416.1806);

(2) A minor child; or

(3) An ineligible person (your spouse, parent, or essential person) whose income may be deemed to you as described in §§ 416.1160 through 416.1169.

(c) Your own household—not another person's household. You are not living in another person's household (you live in your own household) if—

(1) You (or your spouse who lives with you or any person whose income is deemed to you) have an ownership interest or a life estate interest in the home;

(2) You (or your spouse who lives with you or any person whose income is deemed to you) are liable to the landlord for payment of any part of the rental charges;

(3) You live in a noninstitutional care situation as described in § 416.1143;

(4) You pay at least a pro rata share of household and operating expenses (see § 416.1133); or

(5) All members of the household receive public income—maintenance payments (§ 416.1142).

[50 FR 48574, Nov. 26, 1985]

§ 416.1133 What is a pro rata share of household operating expenses.

(a) General. If you pay your pro rata share toward monthly household operating expenses, you are living in your own household and are not receiving in-kind support and maintenance from anyone else in the household. The one-third reduction, therefore, does not apply to you. (If you are receiving food or shelter from someone outside the household, we value it under the rule in § 416.1140.)

(b) How we determine a pro rata share. Your pro rata share of household operating expenses is the average monthly household operating expenses (based on a reasonable estimate if exact figures are not available) divided by the number of people in the household, regardless of age.

(c) Average household operating expenses. Household operating expenses are the household's total monthly expenditures for food, rent, mortgage, property taxes, heating fuel, gas, electricity, water, sewerage, and garbage collection service. (The term does not include the cost of these items if someone outside the household pays for them.) Generally, we average household operating expenses over the past 12 months to determine a pro rata share.

[70 FR 6345, Feb. 7, 2005]

§ 416.1140 The presumed value rule.

(a) How we apply the presumed value rule.

(1) When you receive in-kind support and maintenance and the one-third reduction rule does not apply, we use the presumed value rule. Instead of determining the actual dollar value of any food or shelter you receive, we presume that it is worth a maximum value. This maximum value is one-third of your Federal benefit rate plus the amount of the general income exclusion described in § 416.1124(c)(12).

(2) The presumed value rule allows you to show that your in-kind support and maintenance is not equal to the presumed value. We will not use the presumed value if you show us that—

(i) The current market value of any food or shelter you receive, minus any payment you make for them, is lower than the presumed value; or

(ii) The actual amount someone else pays for your food or shelter is lower than the presumed value.

(b) How we determine the amount of your unearned income under the presumed value rule.

(1) If you choose not to question the use of the presumed value, or if the presumed value is less than the actual value of the food or shelter you receive, we use the presumed value to figure your unearned income.

(2) If you show us, as provided in paragraph (a)(2) of this section, that the presumed value is higher than the actual value of the food or shelter you receive, we use the actual amount to figure your unearned income.

[50 FR 48574, Nov. 26, 1985; 58 FR 63888, Dec. 3, 1993; 70 FR 6345, Feb. 7, 2005]

§ 416.1141 When the presumed value rule applies.

The presumed value rule applies whenever we must count in-kind support and maintenance as unearned income and the one-third reduction rule does not apply. This means that the presumed value rule applies if you are living—

(a) In another person's household (as described in § 416.1132(b)) but not receiving both food and shelter from that person;

(b) In your own household (as described in § 416.1132(c)). For exceptions, see § 416.1142 if you are in a public assistance household and § 416.1143 if you are in a noninstitutional care situation;

(c) In a nonmedical institution including any—

(1) Public nonmedical institution if you are there for less than a full calendar month;

(2) Public or private nonprofit educational or vocational training institution;

(3) Private nonprofit retirement home or similar institution where there is an express obligation to provide your full support and maintenance or where someone else pays for your support and maintenance. For exceptions, see § 416.1144; and

(4) For-profit institution where someone else pays for your support and maintenance. If you or the institution pay for it, see § 416.1145.

§ 416.1142 If you live in a public assistance household.

(a) Definition. A public assistance household is one in which every member receives some kind of public income-maintenance payments. These are payments made under—

(1) Title IV–A of the Social Security Act (Temporary Assistance for Needy Families);

(2) Title XVI of the Social Security Act (SSI, including federally administered State supplements and State administered mandatory supplements);

(3) The Refugee Act of 1980 (Those payments based on need);

(4) The Disaster Relief and Emergency Assistance Act;

(5) General assistance programs of the Bureau of Indian Affairs;

(6) State or local government assistance programs based on need (tax credits or refunds are not assistance based on need); and

(7) U.S. Department of Veterans Affairs programs (those payments based on need).

(b) How the presumed value rule applies. If you live in a public assistance household, we consider that you are not receiving in-kind support and maintenance from members of the household. In this situation, we use the presumed value rule only if you receive food or shelter from someone outside the household.

[57 FR 53850, Nov. 13, 1992; 70 FR 6345, Feb. 7, 2005; 70 FR 41137, July 18, 2005]

§ 416.1143 If you live in a noninstitutional care situation.

(a) Definitions. For purposes of this subpart you live in a noninstitutional care situation if all the following conditions exist:

(1) You are placed by a public or private agency under a specific program such as foster or family care;

(2) The placing agency is responsible for your care;

(3) You are in a private household (not an institution) which is licensed or approved by the placing agency to provide care; and

(4) You, a public agency, or someone else pays for your care.

(b) How the presumed value rule applies. You are not receiving in-kind support and maintenance and the presumed value rule does not apply if you pay the rate the placing agency establishes. We consider this established rate to be the current market value for the in-kind support and maintenance you are receiving. The presumed value rule applies if you pay less than the established rate and the difference is paid by someone else other than a public or private agency providing social services described in § 416.1103(b) or assistance based on need described in § 416.1124(c)(2).

§ 416.1144 If you live in a nonprofit retirement home or similar institution.

(a) Definitions. For purposes of this section the following definitions apply:

(1) Nonprofit retirement home or similar institution means a nongovernmental institution as defined under § 416.1101, which is, or is controlled by, a private nonprofit organization and which does not provide you with—

(i) Services which are (or could be) covered under Medicaid, or

(ii) Education or vocational training.

(2) Nonprofit organization means a private organization which is tax exempt under section 501(a) of the Internal Revenue Code of 1954 and is of the kind described in section 501(c) or (d) of that code.

(3) An express obligation to provide your full support and maintenance means there is either a legally enforceable written contract or set of membership rules providing that the home, institution, or organization—

(i) Will provide at least all of your food and shelter needs; and

(ii) Does not require any current or future payment for that food and shelter. (For purposes of this paragraph, a lump sum prepayment for lifetime care is not a current payment.)

(b) How the presumed value rule applies. The presumed value rule applies if you are living in a nonprofit retirement home or similar institution where there is an express obligation to provide your full support and maintenance or where someone else pays for your support and maintenance. The rule does not apply to the extent that—

(1) The home, institution, or nonprofit organization does not have an express obligation to provide your full support and maintenance; and

(2) The home, institution, or nonprofit organization receives no payment for your food or shelter, or receives payment from another nonprofit organization.

[51 FR 34464, Sept. 29, 1986; 70 FR 6345, Feb. 7, 2005]

§ 416.1145 How the presumed value rule applies in a nonmedical for-profit institution.

If you live in a nonmedical for-profit institution, we consider the amount accepted by that institution as payment in full to be the current market value of whatever food or shelter the institution provides. If you are paying or are legally indebted for that amount, you are not receiving in-kind support and maintenance. We do not use the presumed value rule unless someone else pays for you.

[70 FR 6345, Feb. 7, 2005]

IN-KIND SUPPORT AND MAINTENANCE IN SPECIAL CIRCUMSTANCES

§ 416.1147 How we value in-kind support and maintenance for a couple.

(a) Both members of a couple live in another person's household and receive food and shelter from that person. When both of you live in another person's household throughout a month and receive food and shelter from that person, we apply the one-third reduction to the Federal benefit rate for a couple (§ 416.1131).

(b) One member of a couple lives in another person's household and receives food and shelter from that person and the other member of the couple is in a medical institution.

(1) If one of you is living in the household of another person who provides you with both food and shelter, and the other is temporarily absent from the household as provided in § 416.1149(c)(1) (in a medical institution that receives substantial Medicaid payments for his or her care (§ 416.211(b))), and is ineligible in the month for either benefit payable under § 416.212, we compute your benefits as if you were separately eligible individuals (see § 416.414(b)(3)). This begins with the first full calendar month that one of you is in the medical institution. The one living in another person's household is eligible at an eligible individual's Federal benefit rate and one-third of that rate is counted as income not subject to any income exclusions. The one in the medical institution cannot receive more than the reduced benefit described in § 416.414(b)(3)(i).

(2) If the one member of the couple in the institution is eligible for one of the benefits payable under the § 416.212 provisions, we compute benefits as a couple at the rate specified under § 416.412. However, if that one member remains in the institution for a full month after expiration of the period benefits based on § 416.212 can be paid, benefits will be computed as if each person were separately eligible as described under paragraph (c)(1) of this section. This begins with the first calendar month after expiration of the period benefits based on § 416.212 can be paid.

(c) Both members of a couple are subject to the presumed value rule. If the presumed value rule applies to both of you, we value any food or shelter you and your spouse receive at one-third of the Federal benefit rate for a couple plus the amount of the general income exclusion (§ 416.1124(c)(12)), unless you can show that their value is less as described in § 416.1140(a)(2).

(d) One member of a couple is subject to the presumed value rule and the other member is in a medical institution.

(1) If one of you is subject to the presumed value rule and the other is temporarily absent from the household as provided in § 416.1149(c)(1) (in a medical institution that receives substantial Medicaid payments for his or her care (§ 416.211(b))), and is ineligible in that month for either benefit payable under § 416.212, we compute your benefits as if both members of the couple are separately eligible individuals (see § 416.414(b)(3)). This begins with the first full calendar month that one of you is in the medical institution (see § 416.211(b)). We value any food or shelter received by the one outside of the medical institution at one-third of an eligible individual's Federal benefit rate, plus the amount of the general income exclusion (§ 416.1124(c)(12)), unless you can show that their value is less as described in § 416.1140(a)(2). The member of the couple in the medical institution cannot receive more than the reduced benefit described in § 416.414(b)(3)(i).

(2) If one of you is subject to the presumed value rule and the other in the institution is eligible for one of the benefits payable under § 416.212, we compute the benefits as a couple at the rate specified under § 416.412. However, if the one in the institution remains in the institution after the period benefits based on § 416.212 can be paid, we will compute benefits as if each member of the couple were separately eligible as described in paragraph (d)(1) of this section.

[50 FR 48574, Nov. 26, 1985; 60 FR 16375, March 30, 1995; 61 FR 10279, March 13, 1996; 70 FR 6345, Feb. 7, 2005]

§ 416.1147a Income rules in change-of-status situations involving in-kind support and maintenance.

(a) General. This section explains the rules for determining countable income, including in-kind support and maintenance, when eligible individuals become an eligible couple or when an eligible couple becomes eligible individuals. Generally, under retrospective monthly accounting, income in a prior month, including in-kind support and maintenance, affects benefit amounts for a current month. The prior month may be the first or second month prior to the current month (as explained in § 416.420(a)) and the rules in this section apply when a change-of-status becomes effective between the prior month and the current month.

(b) Eligible individuals become an eligible couple. If you and your spouse have been eligible individuals and become an eligible couple, we combine the earned and unearned income each of you had as an eligible individual in the prior month. If either or both of you received in-kind support and maintenance, we include its value as income. This may be one-third of the Federal benefit rate that applied in the prior month for one or both of you who lived in the household of another. It may be the presumed maximum value (one-third of the Federal benefit rate plus $20 as explained in § 416.1140) for one or both of you as appropriate. It may also be a combination of the two if each of you received income in one of these forms. We also include income deemed to either or both of you in the prior month.

(c) Eligible couple becomes one or two eligible individuals. If you are an eligible individual in the current month but were a member of an eligible couple in the prior month, we determine your countable income in the prior month separately from that of your spouse. We determine the value of any in-kind support and maintenance you and your spouse received in the prior month using the rules contained in § 416.1147. For example, if both of you lived in the household of another and the one-third reduction applied, each of you would have income equal to one-sixth of the Federal benefit rate for a couple. Also, for example, if you received in-kind support and maintenance and the presumed maximum value applied, you would have income equal to one-sixth of the Federal benefit rate for a couple, plus $10. We divide any other income you had as an eligible couple according to who owned the income. If ownership of jointly owned income cannot be determined, we allocate one-half of it to you.

[50 FR 48575, Nov. 26, 1985]

§ 416.1148 If you have both in-kind support and maintenance and income that is deemed to you.

(a) The one-third reduction and deeming of income. If you live in the household of your spouse, parent, essential person, or sponsor whose income can be deemed to you, or the household of a parent whose income is not deemed to you because of the provisions of § 416.1165(i), the one-third reduction does not apply to you. The rules on deeming income are in §§ 416.1160 through 416.1169. However, if you live in another person's household as described in § 416.1131, and someone whose income can be deemed to you lives in the same household, we must apply both the one-third reduction and the deeming rules to you.

(b) The presumed value rule and deeming of income.

(1) If you live in the same household with someone whose income can be deemed to you (§§ 416.1160 through 416.1169), or with a parent whose income is not deemed to you because of the provisions of

§ 416.1165(i), any food or shelter that person provides is not income to you. However, if you receive any food or shelter from another source, it is income and we value it under the presumed value rule (§ 416.1140). We also apply the deeming rules.

(2) If you are a child under age 18 who lives in the same household with an ineligible parent whose income may be deemed to you, and you are temporarily absent from the household to attend school (§ 416.1167(b)), any food or shelter you receive at school is income to you unless your parent purchases it. Unless otherwise excluded, we value this income under the presumed value rule (§ 416.1140). We also apply the deeming rules to you (§ 416.1165).

[50 FR 48575, Nov. 26, 1985; 52 FR 8882, March 20, 1987; 60 FR 361, Jan. 4, 1995; 70 FR 6345, Feb. 7, 2005]

TEMPORARY ABSENCE

§ 416.1149 What is a temporary absence from your living arrangement.

(a) General. A temporary absence may be due to employment, hospitalization, vacations, or visits. The length of time an absence can be temporary varies depending on the reason for your absence. For purposes of valuing in-kind support and maintenance under §§ 416.1130 through 416.1148, we apply the rules in this section. In general, we will find a temporary absence from your permanent living arrangement if you (or you and your eligible spouse)—

(1) Become a resident of a public institution, or a public or private medical treatment facility where you otherwise would be subject to the reduced benefit rate described in § 416.414, and you are eligible for the benefits payable under § 416.212; or

(2) Were in your permanent living arrangement for at least 1 full calendar month prior to the absence and intend to, and do, return to your permanent living arrangement in the same calendar month in which you (or you and your spouse) leave, or in the next month.

(b) Rules we apply during a temporary absence. During a temporary absence, we continue to value your support and maintenance the same way that we did in your permanent living arrangement. For example, if the one-third reduction applies in your permanent living arrangement, we continue to apply the same rule during a temporary absence. However, if you receive in-kind support and maintenance only during a temporary absence we do not count it since you are still responsible for maintaining your permanent quarters during the absence.

(c) Rules for temporary absence in certain circumstances.

(1)(i) If you enter a medical treatment facility where you are eligible for the reduced benefits payable under § 416.414 for full months in the facility, and you are not eligible for either benefit payable under § 416.212 (and you have not received such benefits during your current period of confinement) and you intend to return to your prior living arrangement, we consider this a temporary absence regardless of the length of your stay in the facility. We use the rules that apply to your permanent living arrangement to value any food or shelter you receive during the month (for which reduced benefits under § 416.414 are not payable) you enter or leave the facility. During any full calendar month you are in the medical treatment facility, you cannot receive more than the Federal benefit rate described in § 416.414(b)(1). We do not consider food or shelter provided during a medical confinement to be income.

(ii) If you enter a medical treatment facility and you are eligible for either benefit payable under § 416.212, we also consider this a temporary absence from your permanent living arrangement. We use the rules that apply to your permanent living arrangement to value any food or shelter you receive during the month you enter the facility and throughout the period you are eligible for these benefits. We consider your absence to be temporary through the last month benefits under § 416.212 are paid unless you are discharged from the facility in the following month. In that case, we consider your absence to be temporary through the date of discharge.

(2)(i) Generally, if you are a child under age 22, you are temporarily absent while you are away at school, regardless of how long you are away, if you come home on some weekends, lengthy holidays, and vacations (or for extended visits as provided in school regulations).

(ii) However, if you are a child under age 18, and your permanent living arrangement is with an ineligible parent or essential person (§ 416.222), we follow the rules in § 416.1148(b)(2). When you reach age 18, or if you are under age 18 and deeming does not apply, we consider the circumstances of your permanent living arrangement to value any in-kind support and maintenance you receive.

[50 FR 48575, Nov. 26, 1985; 52 FR 8882, March 20, 1987; 61 FR 10279, March 13, 1996; 62 FR 1056, Jan. 8, 1997; 62 FR 42412, Aug. 7, 1997; 70 FR 6345, Feb. 7, 2005; 72 FR 50874, Sept. 5, 2007]

DISASTERS

§ 416.1150 How we treat income received because of a major disaster.

(a) General. The Disaster Relief and Emergency Assistance Act and other Federal statutes provide assistance to victims of major disasters. In this section we describe when we do not count certain kinds of assistance you receive under these statutes.

(b) Support and maintenance.

(1) We do not count the value of support and maintenance (in cash or in kind) received from a Federal,

State, or local government source, or from a disaster assistance organization, and the one-third reduction rule does not apply if—

(i) You live in a household which you or you and another person maintain as your home when a catastrophe occurs in the area;

(ii) The President of the United States declares the catastrophe to be a major disaster for purposes of the Disaster Relief and Emergency Assistance Act;

(iii) You stop living in the home because of the catastrophe and within 30 days after the catastrophe you begin to receive support and maintenance; and

(iv) You receive the support and maintenance while living in a residential facility maintained by another person.

(2) We do not count the value of support and maintenance (in cash or in kind) received from any other source, such as from a private household, and the one-third reduction rule does not apply for up to 18 months after you begin to receive it if—

(i) You live in a household which you or you and another person maintain as your home when a catastrophe occurs in the area;

(ii) The President of the United States declares the catastrophe to be a major disaster for purposes of the Disaster Relief and Emergency Assistance Act;

(iii) You stop living in the home because of the catastrophe and within 30 days after the catastrophe you begin to receive support and maintenance; and

(iv) You receive the support and maintenance while living in a residential facility (including a private household) maintained by another person.

(c) Other assistance you receive. We do not consider other assistance to be income if you receive it under the Disaster Relief and Emergency Assistance Act or under another Federal statute because of a catastrophe which the President declares to be a major disaster or if you receive it from a State or local government or from a disaster assistance organization. For example, you may receive payments to repair or replace your home or other property.

(d) Interest payments. We do not count any interest earned on the assistance payments described in paragraph (c) of this section.

[57 FR 53850, Nov. 13, 1992]

§ 416.1151 How we treat the repair or replacement of lost, damaged, or stolen resources.

(a) General rule. If a resource is lost, damaged, or stolen, you may receive cash to repair or replace it or the resource may be repaired or replaced for you. We do not count the cash or the repair or replacement of the resource as your income.

(b) Interest on cash for repair or replacement of a noncash resource. We do not count any interest earned on the cash you receive for repair or replacement of a noncash resource if the interest is earned within 9 months of the date you receive the cash. We can extend the 9–month period for up to an additional 9 months if we find you have good cause for not repairing or replacing the resource within the initial period. Good cause exists, for example, if you show that circumstances beyond your control prevent the repair or replacement, or contracting for the repair or replacement, of the resource within the first 9–month period.

(c) Temporary replacement of a damaged or destroyed home. In determining the amount of in-kind support and maintenance you receive (§§ 416.1130 through 416.1140), we do not count temporary housing if—

(1) Your excluded home is damaged or destroyed, and

(2) You receive the temporary housing only until your home is repaired or replaced.

HOME ENERGY ASSISTANCE

§ 416.1157 Support and maintenance assistance.

(a) General. Section 2639 of Pub.L. 98–369, effective October 1, 1984, amended section 1612(b)(13) to provide that certain support and maintenance assistance, which includes home energy assistance, be excluded from countable income for SSI purposes. This section discusses how we apply section 1612(b)(13).

(b) Definitions. For support and maintenance assistance purposes—

Appropriate State agency means the agency designated by the chief executive officer of the State to handle the State's responsibilities as set out in paragraph (c) of this section.

Based on need means that the provider of the assistance:

(1) Does not have an express obligation to provide the assistance;

(2) States that the aid is given for the purpose of support or maintenance assistance or for home energy assistance (e.g., vouchers for heating or cooling bills, storm doors); and

(3) Provides the aid for an SSI claimant, a member of the household in which an SSI claimant lives or an SSI claimant's ineligible spouse, parent, sponsor (or the sponsor's spouse) of an alien, or essential person.

Private nonprofit agency means a religious, charitable, educational, or other organization such as described in section 501(c) of the Internal Revenue Code of 1954. (Actual tax exempt certification by IRS is not necessary.)

Rate-of-return entity means an entity whose revenues are primarily received from the entity's charges to the public for goods or services and such charges are based on rates regulated by a State or Federal governmental body.

Support and maintenance assistance means cash provided for the purpose of meeting food or shelter needs or in-kind support and maintenance as defined in § 416.1121(h). Support and maintenance assistance includes home energy assistance. Home energy assistance means any assistance related to meeting the costs of heating or cooling a home. Home energy assistance includes such items as payments for utility service or bulk fuels; assistance in kind such as portable heaters, fans, blankets, storm doors, or other items which help reduce the costs of heating and cooling such as conservation or weatherization materials and services; etc.

(c) What assistance we do not count as income. We do not count as income certain support and maintenance assistance received on or after October 1, 1984, by you or your ineligible spouse, parent, sponsor (or your sponsor's spouse) if you are an alien, or an essential person. We also do not consider certain support and maintenance assistance in determining a pro rata share of household operating expenses under § 416.1133. We do not count that assistance which is certified in writing by the appropriate State agency to be both based on need and—

(1) Provided in kind by a private nonprofit agency; or

(2) Provided in cash or in kind by—

(i) A supplier of home heating oil or gas;

(ii) A rate-of-return entity providing home energy; or

(iii) A municipal utility providing home energy.

[51 FR 39523, Oct. 29, 1986; 51 FR 43709, Dec. 3, 1986; 53 FR 35808, Sept. 15, 1988; 70 FR 6345, Feb. 7, 2005]

DEEMING OF INCOME

§ 416.1160 What is deeming of income?

(a) General. We use the term deeming to identify the process of considering another person's income to be your own. When the deeming rules apply, it does not matter whether the income of the other person is actually available to you. We must apply these rules anyway. There are four categories of individuals whose income may be deemed to you.

(1) Ineligible spouse. If you live in the same household with your ineligible spouse, we look at your spouse's income to decide whether we must deem some of it to you. We do this because we expect your spouse to use some of his or her income to take care of some of your needs.

(2) Ineligible parent. If you are a child to whom deeming rules apply (see § 416.1165), we look at your ineligible parent's income to decide whether we must deem some of it to be yours. If you live with both your parent and your parent's spouse (i.e., your stepparent), we also look at your stepparent's income to decide whether we must deem some of it to be yours. We do this because we expect your parent (and your stepparent, if living with you and your parent) to use some of his or her income to take care of your needs.

(3) Sponsor of an alien. If you are an alien who has a sponsor and you first apply for SSI benefits after September 30, 1980, we look at your sponsor's income to decide whether we must deem some of it to be yours. This rule applies for 3 years after you are admitted to the United States for permanent residence and regardless of whether you live in the same household as your sponsor. We deem your sponsor's income to you because your sponsor agreed to support you (signed an affidavit of support) as a condition of your admission to the United States. If two deeming rules could apply to you because your sponsor is also your ineligible spouse or parent who lives with you, we use the appropriate spouse-to-spouse or parent-to-child deeming rules instead of the sponsor-to-alien rules. If you have a sponsor and also have an ineligible spouse or parent who is not your sponsor and whose income can be deemed to you, both rules apply. If your sponsor is not your parent or spouse but is the ineligible spouse or parent of another SSI beneficiary, we use the sponsor-to-alien deeming rules for you and the appropriate spouse-to-spouse or parent-to-child deeming rules for the other SSI beneficiary.

(4) Essential person. If you live in the same household with your essential person (as defined in § 416.222), we must look at that person's income to decide whether we must deem some of it to you. We do this because we have increased your benefit to help meet the needs of your essential person.

(b) When we deem. We deem income to determine whether you are eligible for a benefit and to determine the amount of your benefit. However, we may consider this income in different months for each purpose.

(1) Eligibility. We consider the income of your ineligible spouse, ineligible parent, sponsor or essential person in the current month to determine whether you are eligible for SSI benefits for that month.

(2) Amount of benefit. We consider the income of your ineligible spouse, ineligible parent, sponsor, or essential person in the second month prior to the current month to determine your benefit amount for the current month. Exceptions:

(i) We use the income from the first month you are initially eligible for payment of SSI benefits (see § 416.501) to determine your benefit amount for that month. In the following month (the second month you are eligible for payment), we use the same countable income that we used in the preceding month to determine your benefit amount.

(ii) To determine your benefit amount for the first month you again become eligible after you have been ineligible for at least a month, we use the same countable income that we use to determine your eligibility for that month. In the following month (the second month of reeligibility), we use the same countable income that we used in the preceding month to determine your benefit amount.

(iii) To determine the amount of your benefit in the current month, if there are certain changes in your situation which we list below, we use only your own countable income in a prior month, excluding any income deemed to you in that month from an ineligible spouse or parent. These changes are the death of your spouse or parent, your attainment of age 18, or your becoming subject to the $30 Federal benefit rate (§ 416.211(b)).

(iv) To determine the amount of your benefit for the current month, we do not use income deemed from your essential person beginning with the month you can no longer qualify for the essential person increment (§ 416.413). We use only your own countable income in a prior month to determine the amount of your benefit for the current month.

(c) Steps in deeming. Although the way we deem income varies depending upon whether you are an eligible individual, an eligible child, an alien with a sponsor, or an individual with an essential person, we follow several general steps to determine how much income to deem.

(1) We determine how much earned and unearned income your ineligible spouse, ineligible parent, sponsor, or essential person has, and we apply the appropriate exclusions. (See § 416.1161(a) for exclusions that apply to an ineligible parent or spouse, and § 416.1161(b) for those that apply to an essential person or to a sponsor.)

(2) Before we deem income to you from either your ineligible spouse or ineligible parent, we allocate an amount for each ineligible child in the household. (Allocations for ineligible children are explained in § 416.1163(b) and § 416.1165(b).) We also allocate an amount for each eligible alien who is subject to deeming from your ineligible spouse or parent as a sponsor. (Allocations for eligible aliens are explained in § 416.1163(c).)

(3) We then follow the deeming rules which apply to you.

(i) For deeming income from your ineligible spouse, see § 416.1163.

(ii) For deeming income from your ineligible parent, see § 416.1165.

(iii) For deeming income from your ineligible spouse when you also have an eligible child, see § 416.1166.

(iv) For deeming income from your sponsor if you are an alien, see § 416.1166a.

(v) For deeming income from your essential person, see § 416.1168. The rules on when we stop deeming income from your essential person are in § 416.1169.

(vi) For provisions on change in status involving couples see § 416.1163(f) and for those involving parents see § 416.1165(g).

(d) Definitions for deeming purposes. For deeming purposes—

Combat zone means

(i) Any area the President of the United States designates by Executive Order under 26 U.S.C. 112 as an area in which Armed Forces of the United States are or have engaged in combat;

(ii) A qualified hazardous duty area (QHDA) Congress designates be treated in the same manner as an area designated by the President under 26 U.S.C. 112, provided the member of the uniformed services serving in this area is entitled to special pay under 37 U.S.C. 310; or

(iii) An area where the Secretary of Defense or his or her designated representative has certified that Armed Forces members provide direct support for military operations in an area designated by the President under 26 U.S.C. 112 or a QHDA, provided the member of the uniformed services serving in the area certified by the Secretary of Defense or his or her designated representative is entitled to special pay under 37 U.S.C. 310.

Date of admission to or date of entry into the United States means the date established by the U.S. Citizenship and Immigration Services as the date the alien is admitted for permanent residence.

Dependent means the same thing as it does for Federal income tax purposes—we mean someone for whom you are entitled to take a deduction on your personal income tax return. Exception: An alien and an alien's spouse are not considered to be dependents of the alien's sponsor for the purposes of these rules.

Essential person means someone who was identified as essential to your welfare under a State program that preceded the SSI program. (See §§ 416.220 through 416.223 for the rules on essential persons.)

Ineligible child means your natural child or adopted child, or the natural or adopted child of your spouse, or the natural or adopted child of your parent or of your parent's spouse (as the term child is defined in § 416.1101 and the term spouse is defined in § 416.1806), who lives in the same household with you, and is not eligible for SSI benefits.

Ineligible parent means a natural or adoptive parent, or the spouse (as defined in § 416.1101) of a natural or adoptive parent, who lives with you and is not eligible for SSI benefits. The income of ineligible parents affects your benefit only if you are a child under age 18.

Ineligible spouse means someone who lives with you as your husband or wife and is not eligible for SSI benefits.

Sponsor means an individual (but not an organization such as the congregation of a church or a service club, or an employer who only guarantees employment for an alien upon entry but does not sign an affidavit of support) who signs an affidavit of support agreeing to support you as a condition of your admission as an alien for permanent residence in the United States.

[50 FR 48575, Nov. 26, 1985; 51 FR 10616, March 28, 1986; 52 FR 8882, March 20, 1987; 54 FR 19164, May 4, 1989; 64 FR 31974, June 15, 1999; 73 FR 28035, May 15, 2008; 75 FR 7554, Feb. 22, 2010]

§ 416.1161 Income of an ineligible spouse, ineligible parent, and essential person for deeming purposes.

The first step in deeming is determining how much income your ineligible spouse, ineligible parent (if you are a child), your sponsor (if you are an alien), or your essential person, has. We do not always include all of their income when we determine how much income to deem. In this section we explain the rules for determining how much of their income is subject to deeming. As part of the process of deeming income from your ineligible spouse or parent, we must determine the amount of income of any ineligible children in the household.

(a) *For an ineligible spouse or parent.* We do not include any of the following types of income (see § 416.1102) of an ineligible spouse or parent:

(1) Income excluded by Federal laws other than the Social Security Act (See the appendix to this subpart.)

(2) Any public income-maintenance payments (§ 416.1142(a)) your ineligible spouse or parent receives, and any income which was counted or excluded in figuring the amount of that payment;

(3) Any of the income of your ineligible spouse or parent that is used by a public income-maintenance program (§ 416.1142(a)) to determine the amount of that program's benefit to someone else;

(4) Any portion of a grant, scholarship, fellowship, or gift used or set aside to pay tuition, fees or other necessary educational expenses;

(5) Money received for providing foster care to an ineligible child;

(6) The value of food stamps and the value of Department of Agriculture donated foods;

(7) Food raised by your parent or spouse and consumed by members of the household in which you live;

(8) Tax refunds on income, real property, or food purchased by the family;

(9) Income used to fulfill an approved plan for achieving self-support (see §§ 416.1180 through 416.1182);

(10) Income used to comply with the terms of court-ordered support, or support payments enforced under title IV–D of the Act;

(11) The value of in-kind support and maintenance;

(12) Alaska Longevity Bonus payments made to an individual who is a resident of Alaska and who, prior to October 1, 1985: met the 25–year residency requirement for receipt of such payments in effect prior to January 1, 1983; and was eligible for SSI;

(13) Disaster assistance as described in § § 416.1150 and 416.1151;

(14) Income received infrequently or irregularly (see § § 416.1112(c)(1) and 416.1124(c)(6));

(15) Work expenses if the ineligible spouse or parent is blind;

(16) Income of your ineligible spouse or ineligible parent which was paid under a Federal, State, or local government program (For example, payments under title XX of the Social Security Act) to provide you with chore, attendant or homemaker services;

(17) Certain support and maintenance assistance as described in § 416.1157(c);

(18) Housing assistance as provided in § 416.1124(c)(14);

(19) The value of a commercial transportation ticket as described in § 416.1124(c)(16). However, if such a ticket is converted to cash, the cash is income in the month your spouse or parent receives the cash;

(20) Refunds of Federal income taxes and advances made by an employer relating to an earned income tax credit, as provided in § 416.1112(c);

(21) Payments from a fund established by a State to aid victims of crime (see § 416.1124(c)(17));

(22) Relocation assistance, as described in § 416.1124(c)(18);

(23) Special pay received from one of the uniformed services pursuant to 37 U.S.C. 310;

(24) Impairment-related work expenses, as described in 20 CFR 404.1576, incurred and paid by an ineligible spouse or parent, if the ineligible spouse or parent receives disability benefits under title II of the Act;

(25) Interest earned on excluded burial funds and appreciation in the value of excluded burial arrangements which are left to accumulate and become part of separate burial funds, and interest accrued on and left to accumulate as part of the value of agreements representing the purchase of excluded burial spaces (see § 416.1124(c)(9) and (15));

(26) Interest and dividend income from a countable resource or from a resource excluded under a Federal statute other than section 1613(a) of the Social Security Act;

(27) Earned income of a student as described in § 416.1112(c)(3); and

(28) Any additional increment in pay, other than any increase in basic pay, received while serving as a member of the uniformed services, if—

(i) Your ineligible spouse or parent received the pay as a result of deployment to or service in a combat zone; and

(ii) Your ineligible spouse or parent was not receiving the additional pay immediately prior to deployment to or service in a combat zone.

(b) For an essential person or for a sponsor of an alien. We include all the income (as defined in § 416.1102) of an essential person or of a sponsor of an alien and of the spouse of the sponsor (if the sponsor and spouse live in the same household) except for support and maintenance assistance described in § 416.1157(c), and income excluded under Federal laws other than the Social Security Act. For information on these laws see the appendix to this subpart.

(c) For an ineligible child. Although we do not deem any income to you from an ineligible child, we reduce his or her allocation if the ineligible child has income (see § 416.1163(b)(2)). For this purpose, we do not include any of the child's income listed in paragraph (a) of this section. In addition, if the ineligible child is a student (see § 416.1861), we exclude his/her earned income subject to the amounts set in § 416.1112(c)(3).

(d) For an eligible alien. Although we do not deem any income to you from an eligible alien, if your ineligible spouse or ineligible parent is also a sponsor of an eligible alien, we reduce the alien's allocation if he or she has income (see § 416.1163(c)(2)). For this purpose exclude any of the alien's income listed in paragraph (a) of this section.

[45 FR 65547, Oct. 3, 1980, as amended at 46 FR 57276, Nov. 23, 1981; 48 FR 33259, July 21, 1983; 50 FR 48576, Nov. 26, 1985; 51 FR 39523, Oct. 29, 1986; 52 FR 8883, March 20, 1987; 52 FR 44971, Nov. 24, 1987; 55 FR 28378, July 11, 1990; 58 FR 63888, 63890, Dec. 3, 1993; 61 FR 1712, Jan. 23, 1996; 61 FR 49964, Sept. 24, 1996; 67 FR 11034, March 12, 2002; 71 FR 45378, Aug. 9, 2006; 71 FR 66866, Nov. 17, 2006; 75 FR 7554, Feb. 22, 2010]

§ 416.1161a Income for deeming purposes where Medicaid eligibility is affected.

(a) General. In many States, an individual who is eligible for SSI or a Federally administered State optional supplementary payment is in turn eligible for Medicaid. Also, several other States use SSI deeming rules in determining eligibility for Medicaid. In all of these States, in extraordinary cases, the Department will not apply the usual rules on deeming of income where those rules would result in an individual's being ineligible for SSI (or a Federally administered State optional supplementary payment) and Medicaid. Any determination made under this section may at any time be revised based on new information or changed circumstances.

(b) When special deeming rules apply:

(1) The Department will consider not applying the usual deeming rules only upon application by a State Medicaid agency (requirement approved under OMB No. 0960–0304) and on condition that the agency must show:

(i) Deeming would result in lack of Medicaid eligibility for the individual.

(ii) Medicaid eligibility would, prospectively, result in savings to the Medicaid program; and

(iii) The quality of medical care necessary for the individual would be maintained under the arrangements contemplated.

(2) The Department may also in particular cases require that additional facts be demonstrated, or that other criteria or standards be met, before it determines not to apply the usual deeming rules.

(c) Amount of income to be deemed. If the usual rules of deeming do not apply, the Department will determine an amount, if any, to be deemed.

(d) Temporary effect of special deeming rules. This provision is temporary and will be continued only through December 31, 1984. Determinations made under this section will nevertheless remain in effect unless they are revised based on changed circumstances (including establishment in the State of a Medicaid program of home and community-based services or eligibility under a State plan provision) or new information.

[47 FR 24277, June 4, 1982; 49 FR 5747, Feb. 15, 1984]

§ 416.1163 How we deem income to you from your ineligible spouse.

If you have an ineligible spouse who lives in the same household, we apply the deeming rules to your ineligible spouse's income in the following order.

(a) Determining your ineligible spouse's income. We first determine how much earned and unearned income your ineligible spouse has, using the appropriate exclusions in § 416.1161(a).

(b) Allocations for ineligible children. We then deduct an allocation for ineligible children in the household to help meet their needs. Exception: We do not allocate for ineligible children who are receiving public income-maintenance payments (see § 416.1142(a)).

(1) The allocation for each ineligible child is the difference between the Federal benefit rate for an eligible couple and the Federal benefit rate for an

eligible individual. The amount of the allocation automatically increases whenever the Federal benefit rate increases. The amount of the allocation that we use to determine the amount of a benefit for a current month is based on the Federal benefit rate that applied in the second prior month unless one of the exceptions in § 416.1160(b)(2) applies.

(2) Each ineligible child's allocation is reduced by the amount of his or her own income as described in § 416.1161(c).

(3) We first deduct the allocations from your ineligible spouse's unearned income. If your ineligible spouse does not have enough unearned income to cover the allocations we deduct the balance from your ineligible spouse's earned income.

(c) Allocations for aliens sponsored by your ineligible spouse. We also deduct an allocation for eligible aliens who have been sponsored by and who have income deemed from your ineligible spouse.

(1) The allocation for each alien who is sponsored by and who has income deemed from your ineligible spouse is the difference between the Federal benefit rate for an eligible couple and the Federal benefit rate for an eligible individual. The amount of the allocation automatically increases whenever the Federal benefit rate increases. The amount of the allocation that we use to compute your benefit for a current month is based on the Federal benefit rate that applied in the second prior month (unless the current month is the first or second month of eligibility or re-eligibility as explained in § 416.420(a) and (b)(2) and (3)).

(2) Each alien's allocation is reduced by the amount of his or her own income as described in § 416.1161(d).

(3) We first deduct the allocations from your ineligible spouse's unearned income. If your ineligible spouse does not have enough unearned income to cover the allocations, we deduct the balance from your ineligible spouse's earned income.

(d) Determining your eligibility for SSI.

(1) If the amount of your ineligible spouse's income that remains after appropriate allocations is not more than the difference between the Federal benefit rate for an eligible couple and the Federal benefit rate for an eligible individual, there is no income to deem to you from your spouse. In this situation, we subtract only your own countable income from the Federal benefit rate for an individual to determine whether you are eligible for SSI benefits.

(2) If the amount of your ineligible spouse's income that remains after appropriate allocations is more than the difference between the Federal benefit rate for an eligible couple and the Federal benefit rate for an eligible individual, we treat you and your ineligible spouse as an eligible couple. We do this by:

(i) Combining the remainder of your spouse's unearned income with your own unearned income and the remainder of your spouse's earned income with your earned income;

(ii) Applying all appropriate income exclusions in §§ 416.1112 and 416.1124; and

(iii) Subtracting the couple's countable income from the Federal benefit rate for an eligible couple. (See § 416.2025(b) for determination of the State supplementary payment amount.)

(e) Determining your SSI benefit.

(1) In determining your SSI benefit amount, we follow the procedure in paragraphs (a) through (d) of this section. However, we use your ineligible spouse's income in the second month prior to the current month. We vary this rule if any of the exceptions in § 416.1160(b)(2) applies (for example, if this is the first month you are eligible for payment of an SSI benefit or if you are again eligible after at least a month of being ineligible). In the first month of your eligibility for payment (or re-eligibility), we deem your ineligible spouse's income in the current month to determine both whether you are eligible for a benefit and the amount of your benefit. In the second month, we deem your ineligible spouse's income in that month to determine whether you are eligible for a benefit but we deem your ineligible spouse's income in the first month to determine the amount of your benefit.

(2) Your SSI benefit under the deeming rules cannot be higher than it would be if deeming did not apply. Therefore, your benefit is the lesser of the amount computed under the rules in paragraph (d)(2) of this section or the amount remaining after we subtract only your own countable income from an individual's Federal benefit rate.

(f) Special rules for couples when a change in status occurs. We have special rules to determine how to deem your spouse's income to you when there is a change in your situation.

(1) Ineligible spouse becomes eligible. If your ineligible spouse becomes eligible for SSI benefits, we treat both of you as newly eligible. Therefore, your eligibility and benefit amount for the first month you are an eligible couple will be based on your income in that month. In the second month, your benefit amount will also be based on your income in the first month.

(2) Spouses separate or divorce. If you separate from your ineligible spouse or your marriage to an ineligible spouse ends by divorce, we do not deem your ineligible spouse's income to you to determine your eligibility for benefits beginning with the first month following the event. If you remain eligible, we determine your benefit amount by following the rule in paragraph (e) of this section provided deeming from your spouse applied in the prior month.

(3) Eligible individual begins living with an ineligible spouse. If you begin to live with your ineligible spouse, we deem your ineligible spouse's income to you

in the first month thereafter to determine whether you continue to be eligible for SSI benefits. If you continue to be eligible, we follow the rule in § 416.420(a) to determine your benefit amount.

(4) Ineligible spouse dies. If your ineligible spouse dies, we do not deem your spouse's income to you to determine your eligibility for SSI benefits beginning with the month following the month of death. In determining your benefit amount beginning with the month following the month of death, we use only your own countable income in a prior month, excluding any income deemed to you in that month from your ineligible spouse.

(5) You become subject to the $30 Federal benefit rate. If you become a resident of a medical care facility and the $30 Federal benefit rate applies, we do not deem your ineligible spouse's income to you to determine your eligibility for SSI benefits beginning with the first month for which the $30 Federal benefit rate applies. In determining your benefit amount beginning with the first month for which the $30 Federal benefit rate applies, we use only your own countable income in a prior month, excluding any income deemed to you in that month from your ineligible spouse.

(g) Examples. These examples show how we deem income from an ineligible spouse to an eligible individual in cases which do not involve any of the exceptions in § 416.1160(b)(2). The income, the income exclusions, and the allocations are monthly amounts. The Federal benefit rates used are those effective January 1, 1986.

Example 1. In September 1986, Mr. Todd, an aged individual, lives with his ineligible spouse, Mrs. Todd, and their ineligible child, Mike. Mr. Todd has a Federal benefit rate of $336 per month. Mrs. Todd receives $252 unearned income per month. She has no earned income and Mike has no income at all. Before we deem any income, we allocate to Mike $168 (the difference between the September Federal benefit rate for an eligible couple and the September Federal benefit rate for an eligible individual). We subtract the $168 allocation from Mrs. Todd's $252 unearned income, leaving $84. Since Mrs. Todd's $84 remaining income is not more than $168, which is the difference between the September Federal benefit rate for an eligible couple and the September Federal benefit rate for an eligible individual, we do not deem any income to Mr. Todd. Instead, we compare only Mr. Todd's own countable income with the Federal benefit rate for an eligible individual to determine whether he is eligible. If Mr. Todd's own countable income is less than his Federal benefit rate, he is eligible. To determine the amount of his benefit, we determine his countable income, including any income deemed from Mrs. Todd, in July and subtract this income from the appropriate Federal benefit rate for September.

Example 2. In September 1986, Mr. Jones, a disabled individual, lives with his ineligible spouse, Mrs. Jones, and ineligible child, Christine. Mr. Jones and Christine have no income. Mrs. Jones has earned income of $401 a month and unearned income of $252 a month. Before we deem any income, we allocate $168 to Christine. We take the $168 allocation from Mrs. Jones' $252 unearned income, leaving $84 in unearned income. Since Mrs. Jones' total remaining income ($84 unearned plus $401 earned) is more than $168, which is the difference between the September Federal benefit rate for an eligible couple and the September Federal benefit rate for an eligible individual, we compute the combined countable income as we do for a couple. We apply the $20 general income exclusion to the unearned income, reducing it further to $64. We then apply the earned income exclusion ($65 plus one-half the remainder) to Mrs. Jones' earned income of $401, leaving $168. We combine the $64 countable unearned income and $168 countable earned income, and compare it ($232) with the $504 September Federal benefit rate for a couple, and determine that Mr. Jones is eligible. Since Mr. Jones is eligible, we determine the amount of his benefit by subtracting his countable income in July (including any deemed from Mrs. Jones) from September's Federal benefit rate for a couple.

Example 3. In September 1986, Mr. Smith, a disabled individual, lives with his ineligible spouse, Mrs. Smith, who earns $201 per month. Mr. Smith receives a pension (unearned income) of $100 a month. Since Mrs. Smith's income is greater than $168, which is the difference between the September Federal benefit rate for an eligible couple and the September Federal benefit rate for an eligible individual, we deem all of her income to be available to both Mr. and Mrs. Smith and compute the combined countable income for the couple. We apply the $20 general income exclusion to Mr. Smith's $100 unearned income, leaving $80. Then we apply the earned income exclusion ($65 plus one-half of the remainder) to Mrs. Smith's $201, leaving $68. This gives the couple total countable income of $148. This is less than the $504 September Federal benefit rate for a couple, so Mr. Smith is eligible based on deeming. Since he is eligible, we determine the amount of his benefit based on his income (including any deemed from Mrs. Smith) in July.

Example 4. In September 1986, Mr. Simon has a disabled spouse, Mrs. Simon, and has sponsored an eligible alien, Mr. Ollie. Mrs. Simon has monthly unearned income of $100 and Mr. Simon has earned income of $405. From Mr. Simon's earned income we allocate to Mr. Ollie $168, which is the difference between the Federal benefit rate for an eligible couple and the rate for an eligible individual. Mr. Ollie has no other income. This reduces Mr. Simon's earned income from $405 to $237. Since $237 is more than $168 (the difference between the Federal benefit rate for an eligible couple and the rate for an eligible individual), we deem all of Mr. Simon's remaining income to be available to Mr. and Mrs. Simon and compute the combined countable income for the couple. We apply the $20 general income exclusion to Mrs. Simon's unearned income, leaving $80. Then we apply the general earned income exclusion ($65 plus one-half the remainder) to Mr. Simon's $237 earned income, leaving $86. This gives the couple total income of $166 ($80 + $86.). The $166 is less than the $504 Federal benefit rate for a couple so Mrs. Simon would be eligible based on deeming. Since she is eligible, we determine the amount of her benefit based on her income (including any deemed from Mr. Simon) in July. For the way we deem Mr. Simon's income to Mr. Ollie, see the rules in § 416.1166a.

[50 FR 48576, Nov. 26, 1985; 52 FR 8883, March 20, 1987; 53 FR 25151, July 5, 1988; 54 FR 19164, May 4, 1989; 64 FR 31974, June 15, 1999]

§ 416.1165 How we deem income to you from your ineligible parent(s).

If you are a child living with your parents, we apply the deeming rules to you through the month in which you reach age 18. We follow the rules in paragraphs (a) through (e) of this section to determine your eligibility. To determine your benefit amount, we follow the rules in paragraph (f) of this section. The rules in paragraph (g) of this section apply to changes in your family situation. Paragraph (i) of this section discusses the conditions under which we will not deem your ineligible parents' income to you if you are a disabled child living with your parents.

(a) Determining your ineligible parent's income. We first determine how much current monthly earned and unearned income your ineligible parents have, using the appropriate exclusions in § 416.1161(a).

(b) Allocations for ineligible children. We next deduct an allocation for each ineligible child in the household as described in § 416.1163(b).

(c) Allocations for aliens who are sponsored by and have income deemed from your ineligible parent. We also deduct an allocation for eligible aliens who have been sponsored by and have income deemed from your ineligible parent as described in § 416.1163(c).

(d) Allocations for your ineligible parent(s). We next deduct allocations for your parent(s). We do not deduct an allocation for a parent who is receiving public income-maintenance payments (see § 416.1142(a)). The allocations are calculated as follows:

(1) We first deduct $20 from the parents' combined unearned income, if any. If they have less than $20 in unearned income, we subtract the balance of the $20 from their combined earned income.

(2) Next, we subtract $65 plus one-half the remainder of their earned income.

(3) We total the remaining earned and unearned income and subtract—

(i) The Federal benefit rate for the month for a couple if both parents live with you; or

(ii) The Federal benefit rate for the month for an individual if only one parent lives with you.

(e)(1) When you are the only eligible child. If you are the only eligible child in the household, we deem any of your parents' current monthly income that remains to be your unearned income. We combine it with your own unearned income and apply the exclusions in § 416.1124 to determine your countable unearned income in the month. We add this to any countable earned income you may have and subtract the total from the Federal benefit rate for an individual to determine whether you are eligible for benefits.

(2) When you are not the only eligible child. If your parents have more than one eligible child under age 18 in the household, we divide the parental income to be deemed equally among those eligible children.

(3) When one child's income makes that child ineligible. We do not deem more income to an eligible child than the amount which, when combined with the child's own income, reduces his or her SSI benefit to zero. (For purposes of this paragraph, an SSI benefit includes any federally administered State supplement). If the share of parental income that would be deemed to a child makes that child ineligible (reduces the amount to zero) because that child has other countable income, we deem any remaining parental income to other eligible children under age 18 in the household in the manner described in paragraph (e)(2) of this section.

(f) Determining your SSI benefit. In determining your SSI benefit amount, we follow the procedure in paragraphs (a) through (d) of this section. However, we use your ineligible parents' income in the second month prior to the current month. We vary this rule if any of the exceptions in § 416.1160(b)(2) applies (for example, if this is the first month you are eligible for payment of an SSI benefit or if you are again eligible after at least a month of being ineligible). In the first month of your eligibility for payment (or re-eligibility) we deem your ineligible parents' income in the current month to determine both whether you are eligible for a benefit and the amount of your benefit. In the second month we deem your ineligible parents' income in that month to determine whether you are eligible for a benefit but we again use your countable income (including any that was deemed to you) in the first month to determine the amount of your benefit.

(g) Special rules for a change in status. We have special rules to begin or stop deeming your ineligible parents' income to you when a change in your family situation occurs.

(1) Ineligible parent becomes eligible. If your ineligible parent becomes eligible for SSI benefits, there will be no income to deem from that parent to you to determine your eligibility for SSI benefits beginning with the month your parent becomes eligible. However, to determine your benefit amount, we follow the rule in § 416.420.

(2) Eligible parent becomes ineligible. If your eligible parent becomes ineligible, we deem your parents' income to you in the first month of the parents' ineligibility to determine whether you continue to be eligible for SSI benefits. However, if you continue to be eligible, in order to determine your benefit amount, we follow the regular rule of counting your income in the second month prior to the current month.

(3) Ineligible parent dies. If your ineligible parent dies, we do not deem that parent's income to you to determine your eligibility for SSI benefits beginning with the month following the month of death. In determining your benefit amount beginning with the

month following the month of death, we use only your own countable income in a prior month, excluding any income deemed to you in that month from your deceased ineligible parent (see § 416.1160(b)(2)(iii)). If you live with two ineligible parents and one dies, we continue to deem income from the surviving ineligible parent who is also your natural or adoptive parent. If you live with a stepparent following the death of your natural or adoptive parent, we do not deem income from the stepparent.

(4) Ineligible parent and you no longer live in the same household. If your ineligible parent and you no longer live in the same household, we do not deem that parent's income to you to determine your eligibility for SSI benefits beginning with the first month following the month in which one of you leaves the household. We also will not deem income to you from your parent's spouse (i.e., your stepparent) who remains in the household with you if your natural or adoptive parent has permanently left the household. To determine your benefit amount if you continue to be eligible, we follow the rule in § 416.420 of counting your income including deemed income from your parent and your parent's spouse (i.e., your stepparent) (if the stepparent and parent lived in the household with you) in the second month prior to the current month.

(5) Ineligible parent and you begin living in the same household. If your ineligible parent and you begin living in the same household, we consider that parent's income to determine whether you continue to be eligible for SSI benefits beginning with the month following the month of change. However (if you continue to be eligible), to determine your benefit amount, we follow the rule in § 416.420 of counting your income in the second month prior to the current month.

(6) You become subject to the $30 Federal benefit rate. If you become a resident of a medical treatment facility and the $30 Federal benefit rate applies, we do not deem your ineligible parent's income to you to determine your eligibility for SSI benefits beginning with the first month for which the $30 Federal benefit rate applies. In determining your benefit amount beginning with the first month for which the $30 Federal benefit rate applies, we only use your own countable income in a prior month, excluding any income deemed to you in that month from your ineligible parent.

(7) You attain age 18. In the month following the month in which you attain age 18 and thereafter, we do not deem your ineligible parent's income to you to determine your eligibility for SSI benefits. In determining your benefit amount beginning with the month following your attainment of age 18, we only use your own countable income in a prior month, excluding any income deemed to you in that month from your ineligible parent (see § 416.1160(b)(2)(B)). Your income for the current and subsequent months must include any income in the form of cash or in-kind support and maintenance provided by your parents. If you attain age 18 and stop living in the same household with your ineligible parent, these rules take precedence over paragraph (g)(4) of this section which requires continued use of deemed income in the benefit computation for 2 months following the month you no longer live in the same household.

(h) Examples. These examples show how we deem an ineligible parent's income to an eligible child when none of the exceptions in § 416.1160(b)(2) applies. The Federal benefit rates are those effective January 1, 1992.

Example 1. Henry, a disabled child, lives with his mother and father and a 12–year-old ineligible brother. His mother receives a pension (unearned income) of $365 per month and his father earns $1,165 per month. Henry and his brother have no income. First we deduct an allocation of $211 for Henry's brother from the unearned income. This leaves $154 in unearned income. We reduce the remaining unearned income further by the $20 general income exclusion, leaving $134. We then reduce the earned income of $1,165 by $65 leaving $1,100. Then we subtract one-half of the remainder, leaving $550. To this we add the remaining unearned income of $134 resulting in $684. From this, we subtract the parent allocation of $633 (the Federal benefit rate for a couple) leaving $51 to be deemed as Henry's unearned income. Henry has no other income. We apply Henry's $20 general income exclusion which reduces his countable income to $31. Since that amount is less than the $422 Federal benefit rate for an individual, Henry is eligible. We determine his benefit amount by subtracting his countable income (including deemed income) in a prior month from the Federal benefit rate for an individual for the current month. See § 416.420.

Example 2. James and Tony are disabled children who live with their mother. The children have no income but their mother receives $542 a month in unearned income. We reduce the unearned income by the $20 general income exclusion, leaving $522. We then subtract the amount we allocate for the mother's needs, $422 (the Federal benefit rate for an individual). The amount remaining to be deemed to James and Tony is $100, which we divide equally between them resulting in $50 deemed unearned income to each child. We then apply the $20 general income exclusion, leaving each child with $30 countable income. The $30 of unearned income is less than the $422 Federal benefit rate for an individual, so the children are eligible. We then determine each child's benefit by subtracting his countable income (including deemed income) in a prior month from the Federal benefit rate for an individual for the current month. See § 416.420.

Example 3. Mrs. Jones is the ineligible mother of two disabled children, Beth and Linda, and has sponsored an eligible alien, Mr. Sean. Beth, Linda, and Mr. Sean have no income; Mrs. Jones has unearned income of $924 per month. We reduce the mother's unearned income by the $211 allocation for Mr. Sean, leaving $713. We further reduce her income by the $20 general income exclusion, which leaves a balance of $693. Next, we subtract the amount we allocate for the mother's needs, $422 (the amount of the Federal benefit rate for an individual). The balance of $271 to be deemed is divided equally between Beth and Linda. Each now has unearned income of $135.50 from which we deduct the $20 general income exclusion, leaving each child with $115.50

countable income. Since this is less than the $422 Federal benefit rate for an individual, the girls are eligible. We then determine each child's benefit by subtracting her countable income (including deemed income) in a prior month from the Federal benefit rate for an individual for the current month. See § 416.420. (For the way we deem the mother's income to Mr. Sean, see examples No. 3 and No. 4 in § 416.1166a.)

Example 4. Jack, a disabled child, lives with his mother, father, and two brothers, none of whom are eligible for SSI. Jack's mother receives a private pension of $350 per month and his father works and earns $1,525 per month. We allocate a total of $422 for Jack's ineligible brothers and subtract this from the parents' total unearned income of $350; the parents' unearned income is completely offset by the allocations for the ineligible children with an excess allocation of $72 remaining. We subtract the excess of $72 from the parents' total earned income leaving $1,453. We next subtract the combined general income and earned income exclusions of $85 leaving a remainder of $1,368. We subtract one-half the remainder, leaving $684 from which we subtract the parents' allocation of $633. This results in $51 deemed to Jack. Jack has no other income, so we subtract the general income exclusion of $20 from the deemed income leaving $31 as Jack's countable income. Since this is below the $422 Federal benefit rate for an individual, Jack is eligible. We determine his payment amount by subtracting his countable income (including deemed income) in a prior month from the Federal benefit rate for an individual for the current month. See § 416.420.

(i) Disabled child under age 18. If you are a disabled child under the age of 18 living with your parents, we will not deem your parents' income to you if—

(1) You previously received a reduced SSI benefit while a resident of a medical treatment facility, as described in § 416.414;

(2) You are eligible for medical assistance under a Medicaid State home care plan approved by the Secretary under the provisions of section 1915(c) or authorized under section 1902(e)(3) of the Act; and

(3) You would otherwise be ineligible for a Federal SSI benefit because of the deeming of your parents' income or resources.

[50 FR 48578, Nov. 26, 1985; 50 FR 51514, Dec. 18, 1985; 52 FR 8885, March 20, 1987; 54 FR 19164, May 4, 1989; 57 FR 48562, Oct. 27, 1992; 60 FR 361, Jan. 4, 1995; 62 FR 1056, Jan. 8, 1997; 62 FR 42412, Aug. 7, 1997; 64 FR 31974, June 15, 1999; 72 FR 50874, Sept. 5, 2007; 73 FR 28036, May 15, 2008]

§ 416.1166 How we deem income to you and your eligible child from your ineligible spouse.

If you and your eligible child live in the same household with your ineligible spouse, we deem your ineligible spouse's income first to you, and then we deem any remainder to your eligible child. For the purpose of this section, SSI benefits include any federally administered State supplement. We then follow the rules in § 416.1165(e) to determine the child's eligibility for SSI benefits and in § 416.1165(f) to determine the benefit amount.

(a) Determining your ineligible spouse's income. We first determine how much earned and unearned income your ineligible spouse has, using the appropriate exclusions in § 416.1161(a).

(b) Allocations for ineligible children. We next deduct an allocation for each ineligible child in the household as described in § 416.1163(b).

(c) Allocations for aliens who are sponsored by and have income deemed from your ineligible spouse. We also deduct an allocation for eligible aliens who have been sponsored by and have income deemed from your ineligible spouse as described in § 416.1163(c).

(d) Determining your eligibility for SSI benefits and benefit amount. We then follow the rules in § 416.1163(c) to find out if any of your ineligible spouse's current monthly income is deemed to you and, if so, to determine countable income for a couple. Next, we follow paragraph (e) of this section to determine your child's eligibility. However, if none of your spouse's income is deemed to you, none is deemed to your child. Whether or not your spouse's income is deemed to you in determining your eligibility, we determine your benefit amount as explained in § 416.1163(e).

(e) Determining your child's eligibility and amount of benefits.

(1) If you are eligible for SSI benefits after your spouse's income has been deemed to you, we do not deem any income to your child. To determine the child's eligibility, we subtract the child's own countable income without deeming from the benefit rate for an individual.

(2) If you are not eligible for SSI benefits after your ineligible spouse's income has been deemed to you, we deem to your eligible child any of your spouse's income which was not used to reduce your SSI benefits to zero.

(f) Examples. These examples show how we deem income to an eligible individual and an eligible child in the same household. The Federal benefit rates used are those effective January 1, 1984.

Example 1. Mary, a blind individual, lives with her husband, John, and their disabled child, Peter. Mary and Peter have no income, but John is employed and earns $605 per month. We determine Mary's eligibility first. Since John's income is more than $157, which is one-half of the Federal benefit rate for an eligible individual, we treat the entire $605 as earned income available to John and Mary as a couple. Because they have no unearned income, we reduce the $605 by the $20 general income exclusion, and then by the earned income exclusion of $65 plus one-half the remainder. This leaves John and Mary with $260 in countable income. The $260 countable income is less than the $472 Federal benefit rate for a couple, so Mary is eligible; therefore, there is no income to be deemed to Peter.

Example 2. Al, a disabled individual, resides with his ineligible spouse, Dora, and their disabled son, Jeff. Al and

Jeff have no income, but Dora is employed and earns $1,065 a month. Since Dora's income is more than $157, which is one-half of the Federal benefit rate for an eligible individual, we treat the entire $1,065 as earned income available to Al and Dora as a couple. We reduce this income by the $20 general income exclusion and then by $65 plus one-half the remainder (earned income exclusion), leaving $490 in countable income. Al is ineligible because the couple's $490 countable income exceeds the $472 Federal benefit rate for a couple. Since Al is ineligible, we deem to Jeff $18, the amount of income over and above the amount which causes Al to be ineligible (the difference between the countable income and the Federal benefit rate for a couple). We treat the $18 deemed to Jeff as unearned income, and we apply the $20 general income exclusion, reducing Jeff's countable income to zero. Jeff is eligible.

[50 FR 48578, Nov. 26, 1985; 52 FR 8887, March 20, 1987; 64 FR 31975, June 15, 1999]

§ 416.1166a How we deem income to you from your sponsor if you are an alien.

Before we deem your sponsor's income to you if you are an alien, we determine how much earned and unearned income your sponsor has under § 416.1161(b). We then deduct allocations for the sponsor and the sponsor's dependents. This is an amount equal to the Federal benefit rate for an individual for the sponsor (or for each sponsor even if two sponsors are married to each other and living together) plus an amount equal to one-half the Federal benefit rate for an eligible individual for each dependent of the sponsor. An ineligible dependent's income is not subtracted from the sponsor's dependent's allocation. We deem the balance of the income to be your unearned income.

(a) If you are the only alien applying for or already eligible for SSI benefits who has income deemed to you from your sponsor. If you are the only alien who is applying for or already eligible for SSI benefits and who is sponsored by your sponsor, all the deemed income is your unearned income.

(b) If you are not the only alien who is applying for or already eligible for SSI benefits and who has income deemed from your sponsor. If you and other aliens applying for or already eligible for SSI benefits are sponsored by the same sponsor, we deem the income to each of you as though you were the only alien sponsored by that person. The income deemed to you becomes your unearned income.

(c) When you are an alien and income is no longer deemed from your sponsor. If you are an alien and have had your sponsor's income deemed to you, we stop deeming the income with the month in which the third anniversary of your admission into the United States occurs.

(d) When sponsor deeming rules do not apply to you if you are an alien. If you are an alien, we do not apply the sponsor deeming rules to you if—

(1) You are a refugee. You are a refugee admitted to the United States as the result of application of one of three sections of the Immigration and Nationality Act: (1) Section 203(a)(7), effective before April 1, 1980; (2) Section 207(c)(1), effective after March 31, 1980; or (3) Section 212(d)(5);

(2) You have been granted asylum. You have been granted political asylum by the Attorney General of the United States; or

(3) You become blind or disabled. If you become blind or disabled as defined in § 416.901 (at any age) after your admission to the United States, we do not deem your sponsor's income to you to determine your eligibility for SSI benefits beginning with the month in which your disability or blindness begins. However, to determine your benefit payment, we follow the rule in § 416.420 of counting your income in the second month prior to the current month.

(e) Examples. These examples show how we deem a sponsor's income to an eligible individual who is an alien when none of the exceptions in § 416.1160(b)(2) applies. The income, income exclusions, and the benefit rates are in monthly amounts. The Federal benefit rates are those effective January 1, 1986.

Example 1. Mr. John, an alien who has no income, has been sponsored by Mr. Herbert who has monthly earned income of $1,300 and unearned income of $70. Mr. Herbert's wife and three children have no income. We add Mr. Herbert's earned and unearned income for a total of $1,370 and apply the allocations for the sponsor and his dependents. Allocations total $1,008. These are made up of $336 (the Federal benefit rate for an eligible individual) for the sponsor, plus $672 (one-half the Federal benefit rate for an eligible individual, $168 each) for Mr. Herbert's wife and three children. The $1,008 is subtracted from Mr. Herbert's total income of $1,370 which leaves $362 to be deemed to Mr. John as his unearned income. Mr. John's only exclusion is the $20 general income exclusion. Since the $342 balance exceeds the $336 Federal benefit rate, Mr. John is ineligible.

Example 2. Mr. and Mrs. Smith are an alien couple who have no income and who have been sponsored by Mr. Hart. Mr. Hart has earned income of $1,350 and his wife, Mrs. Hart, who lives with him, has earned income of $150. Their two children have no income. We combine Mr. and Mrs. Hart's income ($1,350 + $150 = $1,500). We deduct the allocations of $336 for Mr. Hart (the Federal benefit rate for an individual) and $504 for Mrs. Hart and the two children ($168 or one-half the Federal benefit rate for an eligible individual for each), a total of $840. The allocations ($840) are deducted from the total $1,500 income which leaves $660. This amount must be deemed independently to Mr. and Mrs. Smith. Mr. and Mrs. Smith would qualify for SSI benefits as a couple in the amount of $504 if no income had been deemed to them. The $1,320 ($660 each to Mr. and Mrs. Smith) deemed income is unearned income to Mr. and Mrs. Smith and is subject to the $20 general income exclusion, leaving $1,300. This exceeds the couple's rate of $504 so Mr. and Mrs. Smith are ineligible for SSI benefits.

Example 3. Mr. Bert and Mr. Davis are aliens sponsored by their sister Mrs. Jean, who has earned income of $800. She also receives $250 as survivors' benefits for her two minor children. We do not consider the $250 survivors' benefits to be Mrs. Jean's income because it is the children's income. We exclude $336 for Mrs. Jean (the Federal benefit rate for an individual) plus $336 ($168, one-half the Federal benefit rate for an eligible individual for each child), a total of $672. We subtract the $672 from Mrs. Jean's income of $800, which leaves $128 to be deemed to Mr. Bert and Mr. Davis. Each of the brothers is liable for rent in the boarding house (a commercial establishment) where they live. Each lives in his own household, receives no in-kind support and maintenance, and is eligible for the Federal benefit rate of $336. The $128 deemed income is deemed both to Mr. Bert and to Mr. Davis. As a result, each has countable income of $108 ($128 minus the $20 general income exclusion). This is less than $336, the Federal benefit rate for an individual, so that both are eligible for SSI. We use their income in a prior month to determine their benefit payments.

Example 4. The same situation applies as in example 3 except that one of Mrs. Jean's children is disabled and eligible for SSI benefits. The eligibility of the disabled child does not affect the amount of income deemed to Mr. Bert and Mr. Davis since the sponsor-to-alien and parent-to-child rules are applied independently. The child's countable income is computed under the rules in § 416.1165.

[52 FR 8887, March 20, 1987]

§ 416.1167 Temporary absences and deeming rules.

(a) General. During a temporary absence, we continue to consider the absent person a member of the household. A temporary absence occurs when—

(1) You, your ineligible spouse, parent, or an ineligible child leaves the household but intends to and does return in the same month or the month immediately following; or

(2) You enter a medical treatment facility and are eligible for either benefit payable under § 416.212. We consider your absence to be temporary through the last month benefits under § 416.212 were paid unless you were discharged from the facility in the following month. In that case, we consider your absence to be temporary through the date of discharge.

(b) Child away at school. If you are an eligible child who is away at school but comes home on some weekends or lengthy holidays and if you are subject to the control of your parents, we consider you temporarily absent from your parents' household. However, if you are not subject to parental control, we do not consider your absence temporary and we do not deem parental income (or resources) to you. Being subject to parental control affects deeming to you only if you are away at school.

(c) Active duty military service. If your ineligible spouse or parent is absent from the household due solely to a duty assignment as a member of the Armed Forces on active duty, we continue to consider that person to be living in the same household as you, absent evidence to the contrary. If we determine that during such an absence, evidence indicates that your spouse or parent should no longer be considered to be living in the same household as you, then deeming will cease. When such evidence exists, we determine the month in which your spouse or parent should no longer be considered to be living in the same household as you and stop deeming his or her income and resources beginning with the month following that month.

Example: Tom is a child who receives SSI. In January 1996, Tom's father leaves the household due solely to an active duty assignment as a member of the Armed Forces. Five months later in June 1996, while Tom's father is still on an active duty assignment, Tom's parents file for divorce. As a result, Tom's father will not be returning to live in Tom's household. Therefore, Tom's father should no longer be considered to be living in the same household with Tom. Beginning July 1, 1996, deeming from Tom's father will cease.

[50 FR 48579, Nov. 26, 1985; 61 FR 10280, March 13, 1996; 62 FR 42411, Aug. 7, 1997; 72 FR 50874, Sept. 5, 2007]

§ 416.1168 How we deem income to you from your essential person.

(a) Essential person's income. If you have an essential person, we deem all of that person's income (except any not counted because of other Federal statutes as described in § 416.1161(b)) to be your own unearned income. If your essential person is also your ineligible spouse, or if you are a child whose essential person is your ineligible parent, we apply the essential person deeming rules in this section. See § 416.1169 for the rules that apply when an ineligible spouse or parent ceases to be your essential person.

(b) Determining your eligibility for an SSI benefit. We apply the exclusions to which you are entitled under §§ 416.1112 and 416.1124 to your earned income and to your unearned income which includes any income deemed from your essential person. After combining the remaining amounts of countable income, we compare the total with the Federal benefit rate for a qualified individual (see § 416.413) to determine whether you are eligible for an SSI benefit.

(c) Determining your SSI benefit amount. We determine your SSI benefit amount in the same way that we determine your eligibility. However, in following the procedure in paragraphs (a) and (b) of this section we use your essential person's income that we deemed to you in the second month prior to the current month. Exception: Beginning with the month in which you no longer have your essential person, we do not use any of the income deemed to you from that essential person in a prior month to determine the amount of your benefit (see § 416.1160(a)(3)(ii)(C)). We use only your own countable income in a prior month.

[50 FR 48579, Nov. 26, 1985]

§ 416.1169 When we stop deeming income from an essential person.

If including the income deemed to you from your essential person causes you to be ineligible for an SSI benefit, you are no longer considered to have that essential person whose income makes you ineligible. To determine your eligibility for that month we deduct only your own countable income from your Federal benefit rate. However, other deeming rules may then apply as follows:

(a) Essential person is your spouse. If the person who was your essential person is your ineligible spouse, we apply the deeming rules in § 416.1163 beginning with the month that the income of your essential person is no longer deemed to you.

(b) Essential person is your parent. If you are a child under age 18, and the person who was your essential person is your ineligible parent, we apply the deeming rules in § 416.1165 beginning with the month that the income of your essential person is no longer deemed to you.

[50 FR 48579, Nov. 26, 1985]

ALTERNATIVE INCOME COUNTING RULES FOR CERTAIN BLIND INDIVIDUALS

§ 416.1170 General.

(a) What the alternative is. If you are blind and meet the requirements in § 416.1171, we use one of two rules to see how much countable income you have. We use whichever of the following rules results in the lower amount of countable income:

(1) The SSI income exclusions in §§ 416.1112 and 416.1124; or

(2) The disregards that would have applied under the State plan for October 1972.

(b) State plan. As used in this subpart, State plan for October 1972 means a State plan for providing assistance to the blind under title X or XVI (AABD) of the Social Security Act. That plan must have been approved under the provisions of 45 CFR chapter II as in effect for October 1972.

§ 416.1171 When the alternative rules apply.

(a) Eligibility for the alternative. We use the alternative income counting rules for you if you meet all the following conditions:

(1) You were eligible for, and received, assistance for December 1973 under a State plan for October 1972;

(2) You have continued to live in that same State since December 1973;

(3) You were transferred to the SSI rolls and received a benefit for January 1974; and

(4) You have not been ineligible for an SSI benefit for any period of more than 6 consecutive months. (For purposes of this section, an SSI benefit means a Federal benefit; it does not include any State supplementation.)

(b) Living in the same State. For purposes of this section, you have continued to live in the same State since December 1973 unless you have left it at any time with the intention of moving to another State. If there is no evidence to the contrary, we assume that—

(1) If you leave the State for 90 calendar days or less, the absence is temporary and you still live in that State; and

(2) If you leave the State for more than 90 calendar days, you are no longer living there.

RULES FOR HELPING BLIND AND DISABLED INDIVIDUALS ACHIEVE SELF–SUPPORT

§ 416.1180 General.

One of the objectives of the SSI program is to help blind or disabled persons become self-supporting. If you are blind or disabled, we will pay you SSI benefits and will not count the part of your income (for example, your or a family member's wages, title II benefits, or pension income) that you use or set aside to use for expenses that we determine to be reasonable and necessary to fulfill an approved plan to achieve self-support. (See §§ 416.1112(c)(9) and 1124(c)(13).) You may develop a plan to achieve self-support on your own or with our help. As appropriate, we will refer you to a State rehabilitation agency or agency for the blind for additional assistance in developing a plan.

[51 FR 10616, March 28, 1986; 62 FR 59813, Nov. 5, 1997; 71 FR 28264, May 16, 2006]

§ 416.1181 What is a plan to achieve self-support (PASS)?

(a) A PASS must—

(1) Be designed especially for you;

(2) Be in writing;

(3) Be approved by us (a change of plan must also be approved by us);

(4) Have a specific employment goal that is feasible for you, that is, a goal that you have a reasonable likelihood of achieving;

(5) Have a plan to reach your employment goal that is viable and financially sustainable, that is, the plan—

(i) Sets forth steps that are attainable in order to reach your goal, and

(ii) Shows that you will have enough money to meet your living expenses while setting aside income or resources to reach your goal;

(6) Be limited to one employment goal; however, the employment goal may be modified and any changes related to the modification must be made to the plan;

(7) Show how the employment goal will generate sufficient earnings to substantially reduce or eliminate your dependence on SSI or eliminate your need for title II disability benefits;

Example 1: A Substantial Reduction Exists. Your SSI monthly payment amount is $101 and your PASS employment goal earnings will reduce your SSI payment by $90. We may consider that to be a substantial reduction.

Example 2: A Substantial Reduction Exists. You receive a title II benefit of $550 and an SSI payment of $73. Your PASS employment goal will result in work over the SGA level that eliminates your title II benefit but increases your SSI payment by $90. We may consider that a substantial reduction because your work will eliminate your title II payment while only slightly increasing your SSI payment.

Example 3: A Substantial Reduction Does Not Exist. Your SSI monthly payment amount is $603 and your PASS employment goal earnings will reduce your SSI payment by $90. We may not consider that to be a substantial reduction.

(8) Contain a beginning date and an ending date to meet your employment goal;

(9) Give target dates for meeting milestones towards your employment goal;

(10) Show what expenses you will have and how they are reasonable and necessary to meet your employment goal;

(11) Show what money you have and will receive, how you will use or spend it to attain your employment goal, and how you will meet your living expenses; and

(12) Show how the money you set aside under the plan will be kept separate from your other funds.

(b) You must propose a reasonable ending date for your PASS. If necessary, we can help you establish an ending date, which may be different than the ending date you propose. Once the ending date is set and you begin your PASS, we may adjust or extend the ending date of your PASS based on progress towards your goal and earnings level reached.

(c) If your employment goal is self-employment, you must include a business plan that defines the business, provides a marketing strategy, details financial data, outlines the operational procedures, and describes the management plan.

(d) Your progress will be reviewed at least annually to determine if you are following the provisions of your plan.

[71 FR 28264, May 16, 2006]

§ 416.1182 When we begin to count the income excluded under the plan.

We will begin to count the earned and unearned income that would have been excluded under your plan in the month in which any of the following circumstances first exist:

(a) You fail to follow the conditions of your plan;

(b) You abandon your plan;

(c) You complete the time schedule outlined in the plan; or

(d) You reach your goal as outlined in the plan.

[50 FR 48579, Nov. 26, 1985]

APPENDIX TO SUBPART K OF PART 416—LIST OF TYPES OF INCOME EXCLUDED UNDER THE SSI PROGRAM AS PROVIDED BY FEDERAL LAWS OTHER THAN THE SOCIAL SECURITY ACT

Many Federal statutes in addition to the Social Security Act provide assistance or benefits for individuals and specify that the assistance or benefit will not be considered in deciding eligibility for SSI. We have listed these statutes in this appendix and have placed them in categories according to the kind of income or assistance they provide. The list gives the name of the Federal statute (where possible), the public law number, and the citation. Each item briefly describes what the statute provides that will not reduce or eliminate an SSI payment. More detailed information is available from a social security office or by reference to the statutes.

We update this list periodically. However, when new Federal statutes of this kind are enacted, or existing statutes are changed, we apply the law currently in effect, even before this appendix is updated.

I. Food

(a) Value of food coupons under the Food Stamp Act of 1977, section 1301 of Pub.L. 95–113 (91 Stat. 968, 7 U.S.C. 2017(b)).

(b) Value of federally donated foods distributed under section 32 of Pub.L. 74–320 (49 Stat. 774) or section 416 of the Agriculture Act of 1949 (63 Stat. 1058, 7 CFR 250.6(e)(9)).

(c) Value of free or reduced price food for women and children under the—

(1) Child Nutrition Act of 1966, section 11(b) of Pub.L. 89–642 (80 Stat. 889, 42 U.S.C. 1780(b)) and section 17 of that Act as added by Pub.L. 92–433 (86 Stat. 729, 42 U.S.C. 1786); and

(2) National School Lunch Act, section 13(h)(3), as amended by section 3 of Pub.L. 90–302 (82 Stat. 119, 42 U.S.C. 1761(h)(3)).

(d) Services, except for wages paid to residents who assist in providing congregate services such as meals and personal care, provided a resident of an eligible housing project under a congregate services program under section 802 of the Cranston–Gonzales National Affordable Housing Act, Public Law 101–625 (104 Stat. 4313, 42 U.S.C. 8011).

II. Housing and Utilities

(a) Assistance to prevent fuel cut-offs and to promote energy efficiency under the Emergency Energy Conservation Services Program or the Energy Crisis Assistance Program as authorized by section 222(a)(5) of the Economic Opportunity Act of 1964, as amended by section 5(d)(1) of Pub.L. No. 93–644 and section

5(a)(2) of Pub.L. 95–568 (88 Stat. 2294 as amended, 42 U.S.C. 2809(a)(5)).

(b) Home energy assistance payments or allowances under title XXVI of the Omnibus Budget Reconciliation Act of 1981, Public Law 97–35, as amended (42 U.S.C. 8624(f)).

Note: This exclusion applies to a sponsor's income only if the alien is living in the housing unit for which the sponsor receives the home energy assistance payments or allowances.

(c) Value of any assistance paid with respect to a dwelling unit under—

(1) The United States Housing Act of 1937;

(2) The National Housing Act;

(3) Section 101 of the Housing and Urban Development Act of 1965; or

(4) Title V of the Housing Act of 1949.

Note: This exclusion applies to a sponsor's income only if the alien is living in the housing unit for which the sponsor receives the housing assistance.

(d) Payments for relocating, made to persons displaced by Federal or federally assisted programs which acquire real property, under section 216 of Pub.L. 91–646, the Uniform Relocation Assistance and Real Property Acquisition Policies Act of 1970 (84 Stat. 1902, 42 U.S.C. 4636).

III. Education and Employment

(a) Grants or loans to undergraduate students made or insured under programs administered by the Secretary of Education under section 507 of the Higher Education Amendments of 1968, Pub.L. 90–575 (82 Stat. 1063).

(b) Any wages, allowances, or reimbursement for transportation and attendant care costs, unless excepted on a case-by-case basis, when received by an eligible handicapped individual employed in a project under title VI of the Rehabilitation Act of 1973 as added by title II of Pub.L. 95–602 (92 Stat. 2992, 29 U.S.C. 795(b)(c)).

(c) Student financial assistance for attendance costs received from a program funded in whole or in part under title IV of the Higher Education Act of 1965, as amended, or under Bureau of Indian Affairs student assistance programs if it is made available for tuition and fees normally assessed a student carrying the same academic workload, as determined by the institution, including costs for rental or purchase of any equipment, materials, or supplies required of all students in the same course of study and an allowance for books, supplies, transportation, and miscellaneous personal expenses for a student attending the institution on at least a half-time basis, as determined by the institution, under section 14(27) of Public Law 100–50, the Higher Education Technical Amendments Act of 1987 (20 U.S.C. 1087uu).

IV. Native Americans

(a) Types of Payments Excluded Without Regard to Specific Tribes or Groups—

(1) Indian judgment funds that are held in trust by the Secretary of the Interior or distributed per capita pursuant to a plan prepared by the Secretary of the Interior and not disapproved by a joint resolution of the Congress under Public Law 93–134 as amended by section 4 of Public Law 97–458 (96 Stat. 2513, 25 U.S.C. 1408). Indian judgment funds include interest and investment income accrued while such funds are so held in trust. This exclusion extends to initial purchases made with Indian judgment funds. This exclusion does not apply to sales or conversions of initial purchases or to subsequent purchases.

Note: This exclusion applies to the income of sponsors of aliens only if the alien lives in the sponsor's household.

(2) All funds held in trust by the Secretary of the Interior for an Indian tribe and distributed per capita to a member of that tribe are excluded from income under Public Law 98–64 (97 Stat. 365, 25 U.S.C. 117b). Funds held by Alaska Native Regional and Village Corporations (ANRVC) are not held in trust by the Secretary of the Interior and therefore ANRVC dividend distributions are not excluded from countable income under this exclusion. For ANRVC dividend distributions, see paragraph IV.(a)(3) of this appendix.

Note: This exclusion applies to the income of sponsors of aliens only if the alien lives in the sponsor's household.

(3) Distributions received by an individual Alaska Native or descendant of an Alaska Native from an Alaska Native Regional and Village Corporation pursuant to the Alaska Native Claims Settlement Act, as follows: cash, including cash dividends on stock received from a Native Corporation, to the extent that it does not, in the aggregate, exceed $2,000 per individual each year; stock, including stock issued or distributed by a Native Corporation as a dividend or distribution on stock; a partnership interest; land or an interest in land, including land or an interest in land received from a Native Corporation as a dividend or distribution on stock; and an interest in a settlement trust. This exclusion is pursuant to section 15 of the Alaska Native Claims Settlement Act Amendments of 1987, Public Law 100–241 (101 Stat. 1812, 43 U.S.C. 1626(c)), effective February 3, 1988.

Note: This exclusion does not apply in deeming income from sponsors to aliens.

(4) Up to $2,000 per year received by Indians that is derived from individual interests in trust or restricted lands under section 13736 of Public Law 103–66 (107 Stat. 663, 25 U.S.C. 1408, as amended).

(b) Payments to Members of Specific Indian Tribes and Groups—

(1) Per capita payments to members of the Red Lake Band of Chippewa Indians from the proceeds of the sale of timber and lumber on the Red Lake Reser-

vation under section 3 of Public Law 85–794 (72 Stat. 958).

(2) Per capita distribution payments by the Blackfeet and Gros Ventre tribal governments to members which resulted from judgment funds to the tribes under section 4 of Public Law 92–254 (86 Stat. 65) and under section 6 of Public Law 97–408 (96 Stat. 2036).

(3) Settlement fund payments and the availability of such funds to members of the Hopi and Navajo Tribes under section 22 of Public Law 93–531 (88 Stat. 1722) as amended by Public Law 96–305 (94 Stat. 929).

Note: This exclusion applies to the income of sponsors of aliens only if the alien lives in the sponsor's household.

(4) Judgment funds distributed per capita to, or held in trust for, members of the Sac and Fox Indian Nation, and the availability of such funds under section 6 of Public Law 94–189 (89 Stat. 1094).

Note: This exclusion applies to the income of sponsors of aliens only if the alien lives in the sponsor's household.

(5) Judgment funds distributed per capita to, or held in trust for, members of the Grand River Band of Ottawa Indians, and the availability of such funds under section 6 of Public Law 94–540 (90 Stat. 2504).

Note: This exclusion applies to the income of sponsors of aliens only if the alien lives in the sponsor's household.

(6) Any judgment funds distributed per capita to members of the Confederated Tribes and Bands of the Yakima Indian Nation or the Apache Tribe of the Mescalero Reservation under section 2 of Public Law 95–433 (92 Stat. 1047, 25 U.S.C. 609c–1).

(7) Any judgment funds distributed per capita or made available for programs for members of the Delaware Tribe of Indians and the absentee Delaware Tribe of Western Oklahoma under section 8 of Public Law 96–318 (94 Stat. 971).

(8) All funds and distributions to members of the Passamaquoddy Tribe, the Penobscot Nation, and the Houlton Band of Maliseet Indians under the Maine Indian Claims Settlement Act, and the availability of such funds under section 9 of Public Law 96–420 (94 Stat. 1795, 25 U.S.C. 1728(c)).

Note: This exclusion applies to the income of sponsors of aliens only if the alien lives in the sponsor's household.

(9) Any distributions of judgment funds to members of the San Carlos Apache Indian Tribe of Arizona under section 7 of Public Law 93–134 (87 Stat. 468) and Public Law 97–95 (95 Stat. 1206).

Note: This exclusion applies to the income of sponsors of aliens only if the alien lives in the sponsor's household.

(10) Any distribution of judgment funds to members of the Wyandot Tribe of Indians of Oklahoma under section 6 of Public Law 97–371 (96 Stat. 1814).

(11) Distributions of judgment funds to members of the Shawnee Tribe of Indians (Absentee Shawnee Tribe of Oklahoma, the Eastern Shawnee Tribe of Oklahoma and the Cherokee Band of Shawnee descendants) under section 7 of Public Law 97–372 (96 Stat. 1816).

(12) Judgment funds distributed per capita or made available for programs for members of the Miami Tribe of Oklahoma and the Miami Indians of Indiana under section 7 of Public Law 97–376 (96 Stat. 1829).

(13) Distributions of judgment funds to members of the Clallam Tribe of Indians of the State of Washington (Port Gamble Indian Community, Lower Elwha Tribal Community and the Jamestown Band of Clallam Indians) under section 6 of Public Law 97–402 (96 Stat. 2021).

(14) Judgment funds distributed per capita or made available for programs for members of the Pembina Chippewa Indians (Turtle Mountain Band of Chippewa Indians, Chippewa Cree Tribe of Rocky Boy's Reservation, Minnesota Chippewa Tribe, Little Shell Band of the Chippewa Indians of Montana, and the nonmember Pembina descendants) under section 9 of Public Law 97–403 (96 Stat. 2025).

(15) Per capita distributions of judgment funds to members of the Assiniboine Tribe of Fort Belknap Indian Community and the Papago Tribe of Arizona under sections 6 and 8(d) of Public Law 97–408 (96 Stat. 2036, 2038).

(16) Up to $2,000 of per capita distributions of judgment funds to members of the Confederated Tribes of the Warm Springs Reservation under section 4 of Public Law 97–436 (96 Stat. 2284).

Note: This exclusion applies to the income of sponsors of aliens only if the alien lives in the sponsor's household.

(17) Judgment funds distributed to the Red Lake Band of Chippewa Indians under section 3 of Public Law 98–123 (97 Stat. 816).

(18) Funds distributed per capita or family interest payments for members of the Assiniboine Tribe of Fort Belknap Indian Community of Montana and the Assiniboine Tribe of the Fort Peck Indian Reservation of Montana under section 5 of Public Law 98–124 (97 Stat. 818).

(19) Distributions of judgment funds and income derived therefrom to members of the Shoalwater Bay Indian Tribe under section 5 of Public Law 98–432 (98 Stat. 1672).

(20) All distributions to heirs of certain deceased Indians under section 8 of the Old Age Assistance Claims Settlement Act, Public Law 98–500 (98 Stat. 2319).

Note: This exclusion applies to the income of sponsors of aliens only if the alien lives in the sponsor's household.

(21) Judgment funds distributed per capita or made available for any tribal program for members of the Wyandotte Tribe of Oklahoma and the Absentee Wyandottes under section 106 of Public Law 98–602 (98 Stat. 3151).

(22) Per capita and dividend payment distributions of judgment funds to members of the Santee Sioux Tribe of Nebraska, the Flandreau Santee Sioux Tribe, the Prairie Island Sioux, Lower Sioux, and Shakopee Mdewakanton Sioux Communities of Minnesota under section 8 of Public Law 99–130 (99 Stat. 552) and section 7 of Public Law 93–134 (87 Stat. 468), as amended by Public Law 97–458 (96 Stat. 2513; 25 U.S.C. 1407).

(23) Funds distributed per capita or held in trust for members of the Chippewas of Lake Superior and the Chippewas of the Mississippi under section 6 of Public Law 99–146 (99 Stat. 782).

(24) Distributions of claims settlement funds to members of the White Earth Band of Chippewa Indians as allottees, or their heirs, under section 16 of Public Law 99–264 (100 Stat. 70).

(25) Payments or distributions of judgment funds, and the availability of any amount for such payments or distributions, to members of the Saginaw Chippewa Indian Tribe of Michigan under section 6 of Public Law 99–346 (100 Stat. 677).

Note: This exclusion applies to the income of sponsors of aliens only if the alien lives in the sponsor's household.

(26) Judgment funds distributed per capita or held in trust for members of the Chippewas of Lake Superior and the Chippewas of the Mississippi under section 4 of Public Law 99–377 (100 Stat. 805).

(27) Judgment funds distributed to members of the Cow Creek Band of Umpqua Tribe of Indians under section 4 of Public Law 100–139 (101 Stat. 822).

(28) Per capita payments of claims settlement funds to members of the Coushatta Tribe of Louisiana under section 2 of Public Law 100–411 (102 Stat. 1097) and section 7 of Public Law 93–134 (87 Stat. 468), as amended by Public Law 97–458 (96 Stat. 2513; 25 U.S.C. 1407).

Note: This exclusion applies to the income of sponsors of aliens only if the alien lives in the sponsor's household.

(29) Funds distributed per capita for members of the Hoopa Valley Indian Tribe and the Yurok Indian Tribe under sections 4, 6 and 7 of Public Law 100–580 (102 Stat. 2929, 2930, 2931) and section 3 of Public Law 98–64 (97 Stat. 365; 25 U.S.C. 117b).

Note: This exclusion applies to the income of sponsors of aliens only if the alien lives in the sponsor's household.

(30) Judgment funds held in trust by the United States, including interest and investment income accruing on such funds, and judgment funds made available for programs or distributed to members of the Wisconsin Band of Potawatomi (Hannahville Indian Community and Forest County Potawatomi) under section 503 of Public Law 100–581 (102 Stat. 2945).

Note: This exclusion applies to the income of sponsors of aliens only if the alien lives in the sponsor's household.

(31) All funds, assets, and income from the trust fund transferred to the members of the Puyallup Tribe under section 10 of the Puyallup Tribe of Indians Settlement Act of 1989, Public Law 101–41 (103 Stat. 88, 25 U.S.C. 1773h(c)).

Note: This exclusion does not apply in deeming income from sponsors to aliens.

(32) Judgment funds distributed per capita, or held in trust, or made available for programs, for members of the Seminole Nation of Oklahoma, the Seminole Tribe of Florida, the Miccosukee Tribe of Indians of Florida and the independent Seminole Indians of Florida under section 8 of Public Law 101–277 (104 Stat. 145).

Note: This exclusion applies to the income of sponsors of aliens only if the alien lives in the sponsor's household.

(33) Payments, funds, distributions, or income derived from them to members of the Seneca Nation of New York under section 8(b) of the Seneca Nation Settlement Act of 1990, Public Law 101–503 (104 Stat. 1297, 25 U.S.C. 1774f).

Note: This exclusion does not apply in deeming income from sponsors to aliens.

(34) Per capita distributions of settlement funds under section 102 of the Fallon Paiute Shoshone Indian Tribes Water Rights Settlement Act of 1990, Public Law 101–618 (104 Stat. 3289) and section 7 of Public Law 93–134 (87 Stat. 468), as amended by Public Law 97–458 (96 Stat. 2513; 25 U.S.C. 1407).

(35) Settlement funds, assets, income, payments, or distributions from Trust Funds to members of the Catawba Indian Tribe of South Carolina under section 11(m) of Public Law 103–116 (107 Stat. 1133).

(36) Settlement funds held in trust (including interest and investment income accruing on such funds) for, and payments made to, members of the Confederated Tribes of the Colville Reservation under section 7(b) of Public Law 103–436 (108 Stat. 4579).

Note: This exclusion applies to the income of sponsors of aliens only if the alien lives in the sponsor's household.

(37) Judgment funds distributed under section 111 of the Michigan Indian Land Claims Settlement Act, (Pub.L. 105–143, 111 Stat. 2665).

(38) Judgment funds distributed under section 4 of the Cowlitz Indian Tribe Distribution of Judgment Funds Act, (Pub.L. 108–222, 118 Stat. 624).

(c) Receipts from Lands Held in Trust for Certain Tribes or Groups—

(1) Receipts from land held in trust by the Federal government and distributed to members of certain Indian tribes under section 6 of Public Law 94–114 (89 Stat. 579, 25 U.S.C. 459e).

Note: This exclusion applies to the income of sponsors of aliens only if the alien lives in the sponsor's household.

(2) Receipts derived from trust lands awarded to the Pueblo of Santa Ana and distributed to members of

that tribe under section 6 of Public Law 95–498 (92 Stat. 1677).

(3) Receipts derived from trust lands awarded to the Pueblo of Zia of New Mexico and distributed to members of that tribe under section 6 of Public Law 95–499 (92 Stat. 1680).

V. Other

(a) Compensation provided to volunteers by the Corporation for National and Community Service (CNCS), unless determined by the CNCS to constitute the minimum wage in effect under the Fair Labor Standards Act of 1938 (29 U.S.C. 201 et seq.), or applicable State law, pursuant to 42 U.S.C. 5044(f)(1).

Note: This exclusion does not apply to the income of sponsors of aliens.

(b) Any assistance to an individual (other than wages or salaries) under the Older Americans Act of 1965, as amended by section 102(h)(1) of Pub.L. 95–478 (92 Stat. 1515, 42 U.S.C. 3020a).

(c) Amounts paid as restitution to certain individuals of Japanese ancestry and Aleuts for losses suffered as a result of evacuation, relocation, and internment during World War II, under the Civil Liberties Act of 1988 and the Aleutian and Pribilof Islands Restitution Act, sections 105(f) and 206(d) of Public Law 100–383 (50 U.S.C. App. 1989 b and c).

(d) Payments made on or after January 1, 1989, from the Agent Orange Settlement Fund or any other fund established pursuant to the settlement in the In Re Agent Orange product liability litigation, M.D.L. No. 381 (E.D.N.Y.) under Public Law 101–201 (103 Stat. 1795) and section 10405 of Public Law 101–239 (103 Stat. 2489).

(e) Payments made under section 6 of the Radiation Exposure Compensation Act, Public Law 101–426 (104 Stat. 925, 42 U.S.C. 2210).

(f) The value of any child care provided or arranged (or any payment for such care or reimbursement for costs incurred for such care) under the Child Care and Development Block Grant Act, as amended by section 8(b) of Public Law 102–586 (106 Stat. 5035).

(g) Payments made to individuals because of their status as victims of Nazi persecution excluded pursuant to section 1(a) of the Victims of Nazi Persecution Act of 1994, Public Law 103–286 (108 Stat. 1450).

(h) Any matching funds from a demonstration project authorized by the Community Opportunities, Accountability, and Training and Educational Services Act of 1998 (Pub.L. 105–285) and any interest earned on these matching funds in an Individual Development Account, pursuant to section 415 of Pub.L. 105–285 (112 Stat. 2771).

(i) Any earnings, Temporary Assistance for Needy Families matching funds, and interest in an Individual Development Account, pursuant to section 103 of the Personal Responsibility and Work Opportunity Reconciliation Act of 1996 (Pub.L. 104–193, 42 U.S.C. 604(h)(4)).

(j) Payments made to individuals who were captured and interned by the Democratic Republic of Vietnam as a result of participation in certain military operations, pursuant to section 606 of the Departments of Labor, Health and Human Services and Education and Related Agencies Appropriations Act of 1996 (Pub.L. 105–78).

(k) Payments made to certain Vietnam veterans' children with spina bifida, pursuant to section 421 of the Departments of Veterans Affairs and Housing and Urban Development, and Independent Agencies Appropriations Act of 1997 (Pub.L. 104–204, 38 U.S.C. 1805(a)).

(*l*) Payments made to the children of women Vietnam veterans who suffer from certain birth defects, pursuant to section 401 of the Veterans Benefits and Health Care Improvement Act of 2000 (Pub.L. 106–419 (38 U.S.C. 1833(c)).

(m) Payments of the refundable child tax credit made under section 24 of the Internal Revenue Code of 1986, pursuant to section 203 of the Economic Growth and Tax Relief Reconciliation Act of 2001, Public Law 107–16 (115 Stat. 49, 26 U.S.C. 24 note).

(n) Assistance provided for flood mitigation activities as provided under section 1324 of the National Flood Insurance Act of 1968, pursuant to section 1 of Public Law 109–64 (119 Stat. 1997, 42 U.S.C. 4031).

(*o*) Payments made to individuals under the Energy Employees Occupational Illness Compensation Program Act of 2000, pursuant to section 1 [Div. C, Title XXXVI section 3646] of Public Law 106–398 (114 Stat. 1654A–510, 42 U.S.C. 7385e).

[52 FR 8888, March 20, 1987; 57 FR 53851, Nov. 13, 1992; 57 FR 55088, Nov. 24, 1992; 59 FR 8538, Feb. 23, 1994; 62 FR 30982, June 6, 1997; 70 FR 41137, July 18, 2005; 75 FR 1273, Jan. 11, 2010]

SUBPART L—RESOURCES AND EXCLUSIONS

Authority: Secs. 702(a)(5), 1602, 1611, 1612, 1613, 1614(f), 1621, 1631, and 1633 of the Social Security Act (42 U.S.C. 902(a)(5), 1381a, 1382, 1382a, 1382b, 1382c(f), 1382j, 1383, and 1383b); sec. 211, Pub.L. 93–66, 87 Stat. 154 (42 U.S.C. 1382 note).

Source: 40 FR 48915, Oct. 20, 1975; 51 FR 10616, March 28, 1986; 51 FR 39523, Oct. 29, 1986; 52 FR 8888, March 20, 1987; 52 FR 27541, July 22, 1987; 52 FR 29841, Aug. 12, 1987; 52 FR 31762, Aug. 24, 1987; 56 FR 36001, July 30, 1991; 57 FR 53851, Nov. 13, 1992; 57 FR 55089, Nov. 24, 1992; 61 FR 1712, Jan. 23, 1996; 61 FR 5942, Feb. 15, 1996; 61 FR 5944, Feb. 15, 1996; 71 FR 28265, May 16, 2006, unless otherwise noted.

§ 416.1201 Resources; general.

(a) Resources; defined. For purposes of this subpart L, resources means cash or other liquid assets or any real or personal property that an individual (or spouse, if any) owns and could convert to cash to be used for his or her support and maintenance.

(1) If the individual has the right, authority or power to liquidate the property or his or her share of the property, it is considered a resource. If a property right cannot be liquidated, the property will not be considered a resource of the individual (or spouse).

(2) Support and maintenance assistance not counted as income under § 416.1157(c) will not be considered a resource.

(3) Except for cash reimbursement of medical or social services expenses already paid for by the individual, cash received for medical or social services that is not income under § 416.1103(a) or (b), or a retroactive cash payment which is income that is excluded from deeming under § 416.1161(a)(16), is not a resource for the calendar month following the month of its receipt. However, cash retained until the first moment of the second calendar month following its receipt is a resource at that time.

(i) For purposes of this provision, a retroactive cash payment is one that is paid after the month in which it was due.

(ii) This provision applies only to the unspent portion of those cash payments identified in this paragraph (a)(3). Once the cash from such payments is spent, this provision does not apply to items purchased with the money, even if the period described above has not expired.

(iii) Unspent money from those cash payments identified in this paragraph (a)(3) must be identifiable from other resources for this provision to apply. The money may be commingled with other funds, but if this is done in such a fashion that an amount from such payments can no longer be separately identified, that amount will count toward the resource limit described in § 416.1205.

(4) Death benefits, including gifts and inheritances, received by an individual, to the extent that they are not income in accordance with paragraphs (e) and (g) of § 416.1121 because they are to be spent on costs resulting from the last illness and burial of the deceased, are not resources for the calendar month following the month of receipt. However, such death benefits retained until the first moment of the second calendar month following their receipt are resources at that time.

(b) Liquid resources. Liquid resources are cash or other property which can be converted to cash within 20 days, excluding certain nonwork days as explained in § 416.120(d). Examples of resources that are ordinarily liquid are stocks, bonds, mutual fund shares, promissory notes, mortgages, life insurance policies, financial institution accounts (including savings, checking, and time deposits, also known as certificates of deposit) and similar items. Liquid resources, other than cash, are evaluated according to the individual's equity in the resources. (See § 416.1208 for the treatment of funds held in individual and joint financial institution accounts.)

(c) Nonliquid resources.

(1) Nonliquid resources are property which is not cash and which cannot be converted to cash within 20 days excluding certain nonwork days as explained in § 416.120(d). Examples of resources that are ordinarily nonliquid are loan agreements, household goods, automobiles, trucks, tractors, boats, machinery, livestock, buildings and land. Nonliquid resources are evaluated according to their equity value except as otherwise provided. (See § 416.1218 for treatment of automobiles.)

(2) For purposes of this subpart L, the equity value of an item is defined as:

(i) The price that item can reasonably be expected to sell for on the open market in the particular geographic area involved; minus

(ii) Any encumbrances.

[40 FR 48915, Oct. 20, 1975, as amended at 44 FR 43266, July 24, 1979; 47 FR 55213, Dec. 8, 1982; 48 FR 33259, July 21, 1983; 51 FR 39523, Oct. 29, 1986; 52 FR 4283, Feb. 11, 1987; 52 FR 16845, May 6, 1987; 53 FR 23231, June 21, 1988; 56 FR 36001, July 30, 1991; 57 FR 35461, Aug. 10, 1992; 57 FR 55089, Nov. 24, 1992; 59 FR 27988, May 31, 1994]

§ 416.1202 Deeming of resources.

(a) Married individual. In the case of an individual who is living with a person not eligible under this part and who is considered to be the husband or wife of such individual under the criteria in §§ 416.1802 through 416.1835 of this part, such individual's resources shall be deemed to include any resources, not otherwise excluded under this subpart, of such spouse whether or not such resources are available to such individual. In addition to the exclusions listed in § 416.1210, we also exclude the following items:

(1) Pension funds that the ineligible spouse may have. Pension funds are defined as funds held in individual retirement accounts (IRA), as described by the Internal Revenue Code, or in work-related pension plans (including such plans for self-employed persons, sometimes referred to as Keogh plans);

(2) For 9 months beginning with the month following the month of receipt, the unspent portion of any retroactive payment of special pay an ineligible spouse received from one of the uniformed services pursuant to 37 U.S.C. 310; and

(3) For 9 months beginning with the month following the month of receipt, the unspent portion of any retroactive payment of family separation allowance an ineligible spouse received from one of the uniformed services pursuant to 37 U.S.C. 427 as a result of

deployment to or service in a combat zone (as defined in § 416.1160(d)).

(b) Child—

(1) General. In the case of a child (as defined in § 416.1856) who is under age 18, we will deem to that child any resources, not otherwise excluded under this subpart, of his or her ineligible parent who is living in the same household with him or her (as described in § 416.1851). We also will deem to the child the resources of his or her ineligible stepparent. As used in this section, the term "parent" means the natural or adoptive parent of a child, and the term "stepparent" means the spouse (as defined in § 416.1806) of such natural or adoptive parent who is living in the same household with the child and parent. We will deem to a child the resources of his or her parent and stepparent whether or not those resources are available to him or her. We will deem to a child the resources of his or her parent and stepparent only to the extent that those resources exceed the resource limits described in § 416.1205. (If the child is living with only one parent, we apply the resource limit for an individual. If the child is living with both parents, or the child is living with one parent and a stepparent, we apply the resource limit for an individual and spouse.) We will not deem to a child the resources of his or her parent or stepparent if the child is excepted from deeming under paragraph (b)(2) of this section. In addition to the exclusions listed in § 416.1210, we also exclude the following items:

(i) Pension funds of an ineligible parent (or stepparent). Pension funds are defined as funds held in IRAs, as described by the Internal Revenue Code, or in work-related pension plans (including such plans for self-employed persons, sometimes referred to as Keogh plans);

(ii) For 9 months beginning with the month following the month of receipt, the unspent portion of any retroactive payment of special pay an ineligible parent (or stepparent) received from one of the uniformed services pursuant to 37 U.S.C. 310; and

(iii) For 9 months beginning with the month following the month of receipt, the unspent portion of any retroactive payment of family separation allowance an ineligible parent (or stepparent) received from one of the uniformed services pursuant to 37 U.S.C. 427 as a result of deployment to or service in a combat zone (as defined in § 416.1160(d)).

(2) Disabled child under age 18. In the case of a disabled child under age 18 who is living in the same household with his or her parents, the deeming provisions of paragraph (b)(1) of this section shall not apply if such child—

(i) Previously received a reduced SSI benefit while a resident of a medical treatment facility, as described in § 416.414;

(ii) Is eligible for medical assistance under a Medicaid State home care plan approved by the Secretary under the provisions of section 1915(c) or authorized under section 1902(e)(3) of the Act; and

(iii) Would otherwise be ineligible because of the deeming of his or her parents' resources or income.

(c) Applicability. When used in this subpart L, the term individual refers to an eligible aged, blind, or disabled person, and also includes a person whose resources are deemed to be the resources of such individual (as provided in paragraphs (a) and (b) of this section).

[50 FR 38982, Sept. 26, 1985; 52 FR 8888, March 20, 1987; 52 FR 29841, Aug. 12, 1987; 52 FR 32240, Aug. 26, 1987; 60 FR 361, Jan. 4, 1995; 62 FR 1056, Jan. 8, 1997; 62 FR 42412, Aug. 7, 1997; 65 FR 16815, March 30, 2000; 72 FR 50875, Sept. 5, 2007; 73 FR 28036, May 15, 2008; 75 FR 7554, Feb. 22, 2010]

§ 416.1203 Deeming of resources of an essential person.

In the case of a qualified individual (as defined in § 416.221) whose payment standard has been increased because of the presence of an essential person (as defined in § 416.222), the resources of such qualified individual shall be deemed to include all the resources of such essential person with the exception of the resources explained in § 416.1210(t) and § 416.1249. If such qualified individual would not meet the resource criteria for eligibility (as defined in §§ 416.1205 and 416.1260) because of the deemed resources, then the payment standard increase because of the essential person will be nullified and the provision of this section will not apply; essential person status is lost permanently. However, if such essential person is an ineligible spouse of a qualified individual or a parent (or spouse of a parent) of a qualified individual who is a child under age 21, then the resources of such person will be deemed to such qualified individual in accordance with the provision in § 416.1202.

[39 FR 33797, Sept. 20, 1974; 51 FR 10616, March 28, 1986; 70 FR 41138, July 18, 2005]

§ 416.1204 Deeming of resources of the sponsor of an alien.

The resources of an alien who first applies for SSI benefits after September 30, 1980, are deemed to include the resources of the alien's sponsor for 3 years after the alien's date of admission into the United States. The date of admission is the date established by the U.S. Citizenship and Immigration Services as the date the alien is admitted for permanent residence. The resources of the sponsor's spouse are included if the sponsor and spouse live in the same household. Deeming of these resources applies regardless of whether the alien and sponsor live in the same household and regardless of whether the resources are actually available to the alien. For rules that apply in specific situations, see § 416.1166a(d).

(a) Exclusions from the sponsor's resources. Before we deem a sponsor's resources to an alien, we exclude the same kinds of resources that are excluded from the resources of an individual eligible for SSI benefits. The applicable exclusions from resources are explained in § 416.1210 (paragraphs (a) through (i), (k), and (m) through (t)) through § 416.1239 and § 416.1247 through § 416.1249. For resources excluded by Federal statutes other than the Social Security Act, as applicable to the resources of sponsors deemed to aliens, see the appendix to subpart K of part 416. We next allocate for the sponsor or for the sponsor and spouse (if living together). (The amount of the allocation is the applicable resource limit described in § 416.1205 for an eligible individual and an individual and spouse.)

(b) An alien sponsored by more than one sponsor. The resources of an alien who has been sponsored by more than one person are deemed to include the resources of each sponsor.

(c) More than one alien sponsored by one individual. If more than one alien is sponsored by one individual the deemed resources are deemed to each alien as if he or she were the only one sponsored by the individual.

(d) Alien has a sponsor and a parent or a spouse with deemable resources. Resources may be deemed to an alien from both a sponsor and a spouse or parent (if the alien is a child) provided that the sponsor and the spouse or parent are not the same person and the conditions for each rule are met.

(e) Alien's sponsor is also the alien's ineligible spouse or parent. If the sponsor is also the alien's ineligible spouse or parent who lives in the same household, the spouse-to-spouse or parent-to-child deeming rules apply instead of the sponsor-to-alien deeming rules. If the spouse or parent deeming rules cease to apply, the sponsor deeming rules will begin to apply. The spouse or parent rules may cease to apply if an alien child reaches age 18 or if either the sponsor who is the ineligible spouse or parent, or the alien moves to a separate household.

(f) Alien's sponsor also is the ineligible spouse or parent of another SSI beneficiary. If the sponsor is also the ineligible spouse or ineligible parent of an SSI beneficiary other than the alien, the sponsor's resources are deemed to the alien under the rules in paragraph (a), and to the eligible spouse or child under the rules in §§ 416.1202, 1205, 1234, 1236, and 1237.

[52 FR 8888, March 20, 1987; 61 FR 1712, Jan. 23, 1996; 70 FR 41138, July 18, 2005; 73 FR 28036, May 15, 2008]

§ 416.1204a Deeming of resources where Medicaid eligibility is affected.

Section 416.1161a of this part describes certain circumstances affecting Medicaid eligibility in which the Department will not deem family income to an individual. The Department will follow the same standards, procedures, and limitations set forth in that section with respect to deeming of resources.

[47 FR 24277, June 4, 1982; 49 FR 5747, Feb. 15, 1984]

§ 416.1205 Limitation on resources.

(a) Individual with no eligible spouse. An aged, blind, or disabled individual with no spouse is eligible for benefits under title XVI of the Act if his or her nonexcludable resources do not exceed $1,500 prior to January 1, 1985, and all other eligibility requirements are met. An individual who is living with an ineligible spouse is eligible for benefits under title XVI of the Act if his or her nonexcludable resources, including the resources of the spouse, do not exceed $2,250 prior to January 1, 1985, and all other eligibility requirements are met.

(b) Individual with an eligible spouse. An aged, blind, or disabled individual who has an eligible spouse is eligible for benefits under title XVI of the Act if their nonexcludable resources do not exceed $2,250 prior to January 1, 1985, and all other eligibility requirements are met.

(c) Effective January 1, 1985 and later. The resources limits and effective dates for January 1, 1985 and later are as follows:

Effective date	Individual	Individual and spouse
Jan. 1, 1985	$1,600	$2,400
Jan. 1, 1986	1,700	$2,550
Jan. 1, 1987	1,800	$2,700
Jan. 1, 1988	1,900	$2,850
Jan. 1, 1989	2,000	$3,000

[50 FR 38982, Sept. 26, 1985]

§ 416.1207 Resources determinations.

(a) General. Resources determinations are made as of the first moment of the month. A resource determination is based on what assets an individual has, what their values are, and whether or not they are excluded as of the first moment of the month.

(b) Increase in value of resources. If, during a month, a resource increases in value or an individual acquires an additional resource or replaces an excluded resource with one that is not excluded, the increase in the value of the resources is counted as of the first moment of the next month.

(c) Decrease in value of resources. If, during a month, a resource decreases in value or an individual spends a resource or replaces a resource that is not excluded with one that is excluded, the decrease in the value of the resources is counted as of the first moment of the next month.

(d) Treatment of items under income and resource counting rules. Items received in cash or in kind during a month are evaluated first under the income counting rules and, if retained until the first moment of the following month, are subject to the rules for counting resources at that time.

(e) Receipts from the sale, exchange, or replacement of a resource. If an individual sells, exchanges or replaces a resource, the receipts are not income. They are still considered to be a resource. This rule includes resources that have never been counted as such because they were sold, exchanged or replaced in the month in which they were received. See § 416.1246 for the rule on resources disposed of for less than fair market value (including those disposed of during the month of receipt).

Example: Miss L., a disabled individual, receives a $350 unemployment insurance benefit on January 10, 1986. The benefit is unearned income to Miss L. when she receives it. On January 14, Miss L. uses the $350 payment to purchase shares of stock. Miss L. has exchanged one item (cash) for another item (stock). The $350 payment is never counted as a resource to Miss L. because she exchanged it in the same month she received it. The stock is not income; it is a different form of a resource exchanged for the cash. Since a resource is not countable until the first moment of the month following its receipt, the stock is not a countable resource to Miss L. until February 1.

[52 FR 4283, Feb. 11, 1987]

§ 416.1208 How funds held in financial institution accounts are counted.

(a) General. Funds held in a financial institution account (including savings, checking, and time deposits, also known as certificates of deposit) are an individual's resource if the individual owns the account and can use the funds for his or her support and maintenance. We determine whether an individual owns the account and can use the funds for his or her support and maintenance by looking at how the individual holds the account. This is reflected in the way the account is titled.

(b) Individually-held account. If an individual is designated as sole owner by the account title and can withdraw funds and use them for his or her support and maintenance, all of the funds, regardless of their source, are that individual's resource. For as long as these conditions are met, we presume that the individual owns 100 percent of the funds in the account. This presumption is non-rebuttable.

(c) Jointly-held account—

(1) Account holders include one or more SSI claimants or recipients. If there is only one SSI claimant or recipient account holder on a jointly held account, we presume that all of the funds in the account belong to that individual. If there is more than one claimant or recipient account holder, we presume that all the funds in the account belong to those individuals in equal shares.

(2) Account holders include one or more deemors. If none of the account holders is a claimant or recipient, we presume that all of the funds in a jointly-held account belong to the deemor(s), in equal shares if there is more than one deemor. A deemor is a person whose income and resources are required to be considered when determining eligibility and computing the SSI benefit for an eligible individual (see §§ 416.1160 and 416.1202).

(3) Right to rebut presumption of ownership. If the claimant, recipient, or deemor objects or disagrees with an ownership presumption as described in paragraph (c)(1) or (c)(2) of this section, we give the individual the opportunity to rebut the presumption. Rebuttal is a procedure as described in paragraph (c)(4) of this section, which permits an individual to furnish evidence and establish that some or all of the funds in a jointly- held account do not belong to him or her. Successful rebuttal establishes that the individual does not own some or all of the funds. The effect of successful rebuttal may be retroactive as well as prospective.

Example: The recipient's first month of eligibility is January 1993. In May 1993 the recipient successfully establishes that none of the funds in a 5–year-old jointly-held account belong to her. We do not count any of the funds as resources for the months of January 1993 and continuing.

(4) Procedure for rebuttal. To rebut an ownership presumption as described in paragraph (c)(1) or (c)(2) of this section, the individual must:

(i) Submit his/her statement, along with corroborating statements from other account holders, regarding who owns the funds in the joint account, why there is a joint account, who has made deposits to and withdrawals from the account, and how withdrawals have been spent;

(ii) Submit account records showing deposits, withdrawals, and interest (if any) in the months for which ownership of funds is at issue; and

(iii) Correct the account title to show that the individual is no longer a co-owner if the individual owns none of the funds; or, if the individual owns only a portion of the funds, separate the funds owned by the other account holder(s) from his/her own funds and correct the account title on the individual's own funds to show they are solely-owned by the individual.

[59 FR 27989, May 31, 1994]

§ 416.1210 Exclusions from resources; general.

In determining the resources of an individual (and spouse, if any), the following items shall be excluded:

(a) The home (including the land appertaining thereto) to the extent its value does not exceed the amount set forth in § 416.1212;

(b) Household goods and personal effects as defined in § 416.1216;

(c) An automobile, if used for transportation, as provided in § 416.1218;

(d) Property of a trade or business which is essential to the means of self-support as provided in § 416.1222;

(e) Nonbusiness property which is essential to the means of self-support as provided in § 416.1224;

(f) Resources of a blind or disabled individual which are necessary to fulfill an approved plan for achieving self-support as provided in § 416.1226;

(g) Stock in regional or village corporations held by natives of Alaska during the twenty-year period in which the stock is inalienable pursuant to the Alaska Native Claims Settlement Act (see § 416.1228);

(h) Life insurance owned by an individual (and spouse, if any) to the extent provided in § 416.1230;

(i) Restricted allotted Indian lands as provided in § 416.1234;

(j) Payments or benefits provided under a Federal statute other than title XVI of the Social Security Act where exclusion is required by such statute;

(k) Disaster relief assistance as provided in § 416.1237;

(*l*) Burial spaces and certain funds up to $1,500 for burial expenses as provided in § 416.1231;

(m) Title XVI or title II retroactive payments as provided in § 416.1233;

(n) Housing assistance as provided in § 416.1238;

(*o*) Refunds of Federal income taxes and advances made by an employer relating to an earned income tax credit, as provided in § 416.1235;

(p) Payments received as compensation for expenses incurred or losses suffered as a result of a crime as provided in § 416.1229;

(q) Relocation assistance from a State or local government as provided in § 416.1239;

(r) Dedicated financial institution accounts as provided in § 416.1247;

(s) Gifts to children under age 18 with life-threatening conditions as provided in § 416.1248;

(t) Restitution of title II, title VIII or title XVI benefits because of misuse by certain representative payees as provided in § 416.1249;

(u) Any portion of a grant, scholarship, fellowship, or gift used or set aside for paying tuition, fees, or other necessary educational expenses as provided in § 416.1250;

(v) Payment of a refundable child tax credit, as provided in § 416.1235; and

(w) Any annuity paid by a State to a person (or his or her spouse) based on the State's determination that the person is:

(1) A veteran (as defined in 38 U.S.C. 101); and

(2) Blind, disabled, or aged.

[40 FR 48915, Oct. 20, 1975, as amended at 41 FR 13338, March 30, 1976; 44 FR 15664, March 15, 1979; 47 FR 55213, Dec. 8, 1982; 48 FR 57127, Dec. 28, 1983; 51 FR 34464, Sept. 29, 1986; 55 FR 28378, July 11, 1990; 58 FR 63890, Dec. 3, 1993; 59 FR 8538, Feb. 23, 1994; 61 FR 1712, Jan. 23, 1996; 61 FR 67207, Dec. 20, 1996; 70 FR 6345, Feb. 7, 2005; 70 FR 41138, July 18, 2005; 71 FR 45378, Aug. 9, 2006; 75 FR 1273, Jan. 11, 2010; 75 FR 54287, Sept. 7, 2010]

§ 416.1212 Exclusion of the home.

(a) Defined. A home is any property in which an individual (and spouse, if any) has an ownership interest and which serves as the individual's principal place of residence. This property includes the shelter in which an individual resides, the land on which the shelter is located and related outbuildings.

(b) Home not counted. We do not count a home regardless of its value. However, see §§ 416.1220 through 416.1224 when there is an income-producing property located on the home property that does not qualify under the home exclusion.

(c) If an individual changes principal place of residence. If an individual (and spouse, if any) moves out of his or her home without the intent to return, the home becomes a countable resource because it is no longer the individual's principal place of residence. If an individual leaves his or her home to live in an institution, we still consider the home to be the individual's principal place of residence, irrespective of the individual's intent to return, as long as a spouse or dependent relative of the eligible individual continues to live there. The individual's equity in the former home becomes a countable resource effective with the first day of the month following the month it is no longer his or her principal place of residence.

(d) If an individual leaves the principal place of residence due to domestic abuse. If an individual moves out of his or her home without the intent to return, but is fleeing the home as a victim of domestic abuse, we will not count the home as a resource in determining the individual's eligibility to receive, or continue to receive, SSI payments. In that situation, we will consider the home to be the individual's principal place of residence until such time as the individual establishes a new principal place of residence or otherwise takes action rendering the home no longer excludable.

(e) Proceeds from the sale of an excluded home.

(1) The proceeds from the sale of a home which is excluded from the individual's resources will also be excluded from resources to the extent they are intended to be used and are, in fact, used to purchase another home, which is similarly excluded, within 3 months of the date of receipt of the proceeds.

(2) The value of a promissory note or similar installment sales contract constitutes a "proceed" which can be excluded from resources if—

(i) The note results from the sale of an individual's home as described in § 416.1212(a);

(ii) Within 3 months of receipt (execution) of the note, the individual purchases a replacement home as described in § 416.1212(a) (see paragraph (f) of this section for an exception); and

(iii) All note-generated proceeds are reinvested in the replacement home within 3 months of receipt (see paragraph (g) of this section for an exception).

(3) In addition to excluding the value of the note itself, other proceeds from the sale of the former home are excluded resources if they are used within 3 months of receipt to make payment on the replacement home. Such proceeds, which consist of the downpayment and that portion of any installment amount constituting payment against the principal, represent a conversion of a resource.

(f) Failure to purchase another excluded home timely. If the individual does not purchase a replacement home within the 3–month period specified in paragraph (e)(2)(ii) of this section, the value of a promissory note or similar installment sales contract received from the sale of an excluded home is a countable resource effective with the first moment of the month following the month the note is executed. If the individual purchases a replacement home after the expiration of the 3–month period, the note becomes an excluded resource the month following the month of purchase of the replacement home provided that all other proceeds are fully and timely reinvested as explained in paragraph (g) of this section.

(g) Failure to reinvest proceeds timely.

(1) If the proceeds (e.g., installment amounts constituting payment against the principal) from the sale of an excluded home under a promissory note or similar installment sales contract are not reinvested fully and timely (within 3 months of receipt) in a replacement home, as of the first moment of the month following receipt of the payment, the individual's countable resources will include:

(i) The value of the note; and

(ii) That portion of the proceeds, retained by the individual, which was not timely reinvested.

(2) The note remains a countable resource until the first moment of the month following the receipt of proceeds that are fully and timely reinvested in the replacement home. Failure to reinvest proceeds for a period of time does not permanently preclude exclusion of the promissory note or installment sales contract. However, previously received proceeds that were not timely reinvested remain countable resources to the extent they are retained.

Example 1. On July 10, an SSI recipient received his quarterly payment of $200 from the buyer of his former home under an installment sales contract. As of October 31, the recipient has used only $150 of the July payment in connection with the purchase of a new home. The exclusion of the unused $50 (and of the installment contract itself) is revoked back to July 10. As a result, the $50 and the value of the contract as of August 1, are included in a revised determination of resources for August and subsequent months.

Example 2. On April 10, an SSI recipient received a payment of $250 from the buyer of his former home under an installment sales contract. On May 3, he reinvested $200 of the payment in the purchase of a new home. On May 10, the recipient received another $250 payment, and reinvested the full amount on June 3. As of July 31, since the recipient has used only $200 of the April payment in connection with the purchase of the new home, the exclusion of the unused $50 (and of the installment contract itself) is revoked back to April 10. As a result, the $50 and the value of the contract as of May 1 are includable resources. Since the recipient fully and timely reinvested the May payment, the installment contract and the payment are again excludable resources as of June 1. However, the $50 left over from the previous payment remains a countable resource.

(h) Interest payments. If interest is received as part of an installment payment resulting from the sale of an excluded home under a promissory note or similar installment sales contract, the interest payments do not represent conversion of a resource. The interest is income under the provisions of §§ 416.1102, 416.1120, and 416.1121(c).

[40 FR 48915, Oct. 20, 1975, as amended at 42 FR 40192, Aug. 9, 1977; 50 FR 42686, Oct. 22, 1985; 51 FR 7437, March 4, 1986; 59 FR 43285, Aug. 23, 1994; 75 FR 1273, Jan. 11, 2010]

§ 416.1216 Exclusion of household goods and personal effects.

(a) Household goods.

(1) We do not count household goods as a resource to an individual (and spouse, if any) if they are:

(i) Items of personal property, found in or near the home, that are used on a regular basis; or

(ii) Items needed by the householder for maintenance, use and occupancy of the premises as a home.

(2) Such items include but are not limited to: Furniture, appliances, electronic equipment such as personal computers and television sets, carpets, cooking and eating utensils, and dishes.

(b) Personal effects.

(1) We do not count personal effects as resources to an individual (and spouse, if any) if they are:

(i) Items of personal property ordinarily worn or carried by the individual; or

(ii) Articles otherwise having an intimate relation to the individual.

(2) Such items include but are not limited to: Personal jewelry including wedding and engagement rings, personal care items, prosthetic devices, and educational or recreational items such as books or musical instruments. We also do not count as resources items of cultural or religious significance to an individual and items required because of an individual's impairment.

However, we do count items that were acquired or are held for their value or as an investment because we do not consider these to be personal effects. Such items can include but are not limited to: Gems, jewelry that is not worn or held for family significance, or collectibles. Such items will be subject to the limits in § 416.1205.

[40 FR 48915, Oct. 20, 1975, as amended at 44 FR 43266, July 24, 1979; 70 FR 6345, Feb. 7, 2005]

§ 416.1218 Exclusion of the automobile.

(a) Automobile; defined. As used in this section, the term automobile includes, in addition to passenger cars, other vehicles used to provide necessary transportation.

(b) Limitation on automobiles. In determining the resources of an individual (and spouse, if any), automobiles are excluded or counted as follows:

(1) Total exclusion. One automobile is totally excluded regardless of value if it is used for transportation for the individual or a member of the individual's household.

(2) Other automobiles. Any other automobiles are considered to be nonliquid resources. Your equity in the other automobiles is counted as a resource. (See § 416.1201(c).)

[40 FR 48915, Oct. 20, 1975, as amended at 44 FR 43266, July 24, 1979; 50 FR 42687, Oct. 22, 1985; 70 FR 6345, Feb. 7, 2005]

§ 416.1220 Property essential to self-support; general.

When counting the value of resources an individual (and spouse, if any) has, the value of property essential to self-support is not counted, within certain limits. There are different rules for considering this property depending on whether it is income-producing or not. Property essential to self-support can include real and personal property (for example, land, buildings, equipment and supplies, motor vehicles, and tools, etc.) used in a trade or business (as defined in § 404.1066 of part 404), nonbusiness income-producing property (houses or apartments for rent, land other than home property, etc.) and property used to produce goods or services essential to an individual's daily activities. Liquid resources other than those used as part of a trade or business are not property essential to self-support. If the individual's principal place of residence qualifies under the home exclusion, it is not considered in evaluating property essential to self-support.

[50 FR 42687, Oct. 22, 1985]

§ 416.1222 How income-producing property essential to self-support is counted.

(a) General. When deciding the value of property used in a trade or business or nonbusiness income-producing activity, only the individual's equity in the property is counted. We will exclude as essential to self-support up to $6,000 of an individual's equity in income-producing property if it produces a net annual income to the individual of at least 6 percent of the excluded equity. If the individual's equity is greater than $6,000, we count only the amount that exceeds $6,000 toward the allowable resource limit specified in § 416.1205 if the net annual income requirement of 6 percent is met on the excluded equity. If the activity produces less than a 6–percent return due to circumstances beyond the individual's control (for example, crop failure, illness, etc.), and there is a reasonable expectation that the individual's activity will again produce a 6–percent return, the property is also excluded. If the individual owns more than one piece of property and each produces income, each is looked at to see if the 6–percent rule is met and then the amounts of the individual's equity in all of those properties producing 6 percent are totaled to see if the total equity is $6,000 or less. The equity in those properties that do not meet the 6–percent rule is counted toward the allowable resource limit specified in § 416.1205. If the individual's total equity in the properties producing 6–percent income is over the $6,000 equity limit, the amount of equity exceeding $6,000 is counted as a resource toward the allowable resource limit.

Example 1. Sharon has a small business in her home making hand-woven rugs. The looms and other equipment used in the business have a current market value of $7,000. The value of her equity is $5,500 since she owes $1,500 on the looms. Sharon's net earnings from self-employment is $400. Since Sharon's equity in the looms and other equipment ($5,500) is under the $6,000 limit for property essential to self-support and her net income after expenses ($400) is greater than 6 percent of her equity, her income-producing property is excluded from countable resources. The home is not considered in any way in valuing property essential to self-support.

Example 2. Charlotte operates a farm. She owns 3 acres of land on which her home is located. She also owns 10 acres of farm land not connected to her home. There are 2 tool sheds and 2 animal shelters located on the 10 acres. She has various pieces of farm equipment that are necessary for her farming activities. We exclude the house and the 3 acres under the home exclusion (see § 416.1212). However, we look at the other 10 acres of land, the buildings and equipment separately to see if her total equity in them is no more than $6,000 and if the annual rate of return is 6 percent of her equity. In this case, the 10 acres and buildings are valued at $4,000 and the few items of farm equipment and other inventory are valued at $1,500. Charlotte sells produce which nets her more than 6 percent for this year. The 10 acres and other items are excluded as essential to her self-support and they continue to be excluded as long as she meets the 6–percent annual return requirement and the equity value of the 10 acres and other items remains less than $6,000.

Example 3. Henry has an automobile repair business valued at $5,000. There are no debts on the property and bills are paid monthly. For the past 4 years the business has just broken even. Since Henry's income from the business is less then 6 percent of his equity, the entire $5,000 is counted as his resources. Since this exceeds the resources limit as described in § 416.1205, he is not eligible for SSI benefits.

(b) Exception. Property that represents the authority granted by a governmental agency to engage in an income-producing activity is excluded as property essential to self-support if it is:

(1) Used in a trade or business or nonbusiness income-producing activity; or

(2) Not used due to circumstances beyond the individual's control, e.g., illness, and there is a reasonable expectation that the use will resume.

Example: John owns a commercial fishing permit granted by the State Commerce Commission, a boat, and fishing tackle. The boat and tackle have an equity value of $6,500. Last year, John earned $2,000 from his fishing business. The value of the fishing permit is not determined because the permit is excluded under the exception. The boat and tackle are producing in excess of a 6 percent return on the excluded equity value, so they are excluded under the general rule (see paragraph (a) of this section) up to $6,000. The $500 excess value is counted toward the resource limit as described in § 416.1205.

[50 FR 42687, Oct. 22, 1985]

§ 416.1224 How nonbusiness property used to produce goods or services essential to self-support is counted.

Nonbusiness property is considered to be essential for an individual's (and spouse, if any) self-support if it is used to produce goods or services necessary for his or her daily activities. This type of property includes real property such as land which is used to produce vegetables or livestock only for personal consumption in the individual's household (for example, corn, tomatoes, chicken, cattle). This type of property also includes personal property necessary to perform daily functions exclusive of passenger cars, trucks, boats, or other special vehicles. (See § 416.1218 for a discussion on how automobiles are counted.) Property used to produce goods or services or property necessary to perform daily functions is excluded if the individual's equity in the property does not exceed $6,000. Personal property which is required by the individual's employer for work is not counted, regardless of value, while the individual is employed. Examples of this type of personal property include tools, safety equipment, uniforms and similar items.

Example: Bill owns a small unimproved lot several blocks from his home. He uses the lot, which is valued at $4,800, to grow vegetables and fruit only for his own consumption. Since his equity in the property is less than $6,000, the property is excluded as necessary to self-support.

[50 FR 42687, Oct. 22, 1985]

§ 416.1225 An approved plan to achieve self-support; general.

If you are blind or disabled, we will pay you SSI benefits and will not count resources that you use or set aside to use for expenses that we determine to be reasonable and necessary to fulfill an approved plan to achieve self-support.

[50 FR 42688, Oct. 22, 1985 71 FR 28265, May 16, 2006]

§ 416.1226 What is a plan to achieve self-support (PASS)?

(a) A PASS must—

(1) Be designed especially for you;

(2) Be in writing;

(3) Be approved by us (a change of plan must also be approved by us);

(4) Have a specific employment goal that is feasible for you, that is, a goal that you have a reasonable likelihood of achieving;

(5) Have a plan to reach your employment goal that is viable and financially sustainable, that is, the plan—

(i) Sets forth steps that are attainable in order to reach your goal, and

(ii) Shows that you will have enough money to meet your living expenses while setting aside income or resources to reach your goal;

(6) Be limited to one employment goal; however, the employment goal may be modified and any changes related to the modification must be made to the plan;

(7) Show how the employment goal will generate sufficient earnings to substantially reduce your dependence on SSI or eliminate your need for title II disability benefits;

Example 1: A Substantial Reduction Exists. Your SSI monthly payment amount is $101 and your PASS employment goal earnings will reduce your SSI payment by $90. We may consider that to be a substantial reduction.

Example 2: A Substantial Reduction Exists. You receive a title II benefit of $550 and an SSI payment of $73. Your PASS employment goal will result in work over the SGA level that eliminates your title II benefit but increases your SSI payment by $90. We may consider that a substantial reduction because your work will eliminate your title II payment while only slightly increasing your SSI payment.

Example 3: A Substantial Reduction Does Not Exist. Your SSI monthly payment amount is $603 and your PASS employment goal earnings will reduce your SSI payment by $90. We may not consider that to be a substantial reduction.

(8) Contain a beginning date and an ending date to meet your employment goal;

(9) Give target dates for meeting milestones towards your employment goal;

(10) Show what expenses you will have and how they are reasonable and necessary to meet your employment goal;

(11) Show what resources you have and will receive, how you will use them to attain your employment goal, and how you will meet your living expenses; and

(12) Show how the resources you set aside under the plan will be kept separate from your other resources.

(b) You must propose a reasonable ending date for your PASS. If necessary, we can help you establish an ending date, which may be different than the ending date you propose. Once the ending date is set and you begin your PASS, we may adjust or extend the ending date of your PASS based on progress towards your goal and earnings level reached.

(c) If your employment goal is self-employment, you must include a business plan that defines the business, provides a marketing strategy, details financial data, outlines the operational procedures, and describes the management plan.

(d) Your progress will be reviewed at least annually to determine if you are following the provisions of your plan.

[50 FR 42688, Oct. 22, 1985; 51 FR 10616, March 28, 1986; 71 FR 28265, May 16, 2006]

§ 416.1227 When the resources excluded under a plan to achieve self-support begin to count.

The resources that were excluded under the individual's plan will begin to be counted as of the first day of the month following the month in which any of these circumstances occur:

(a) Failing to follow the conditions of the plan:

(b) Abandoning the plan;

(c) Completing the time schedule outlined in the plan; or

(d) Reaching the goal as outlined in the plan.

[50 FR 42688, Oct. 22, 1985]

§ 416.1228 Exclusion of Alaskan natives' stock in regional or village corporations.

(a) In determining the resources of a native of Alaska (and spouse, if any) there will be excluded from resources, shares of stock held in a regional or village corporation during the period of 20 years in which such stock is inalienable, as provided by sections 7(h) and 8(c) of the Alaska Native Claims Settlement Act (43 U.S.C. 1606, 1607). The 20–year period of inalienability terminates on January 1, 1992.

(b) As used in this section, native of Alaska has the same meaning as that contained in section 3(b) of the Alaska Native Claims Settlement Act (43 U.S.C. 1602(b)).

§ 416.1229 Exclusion of payments received as compensation for expenses incurred or losses suffered as a result of a crime.

(a) In determining the resources of an individual (and spouse, if any), any amount received from a fund established by a State to aid victims of crime is excluded from resources for a period of 9 months beginning with the month following the month of receipt.

(b) To be excluded from resources under this section, the individual (or spouse) must demonstrate that any amount received was compensation for expenses incurred or losses suffered as the result of a crime.

[61 FR 1712, Jan. 23, 1996]

§ 416.1230 Exclusion of life insurance.

(a) General. In determining the resources of an individual (and spouse, if any), life insurance owned by the individual (and spouse, if any) will be considered to the extent of its cash surrender value. If, however, the total face value of all life insurance policies on any person does not exceed $1,500, no part of the cash surrender value of such life insurance will be taken into account in determining the resources of the individual (and spouse, if any). In determining the face value of life insurance on the individual (and spouse, if any), term insurance and burial insurance will not be taken into account.

(b) Definitions—

(1) Life insurance. Life insurance is a contract under which the insurer agrees to pay a specified amount upon the death of the insured.

(2) Insurer. The insurer is the company or association which contracts with the owner of the insurance.

(3) Insured. The insured is the person upon whose life insurance is effected.

(4) Owner. The owner is the person who has the right to change the policy. This is normally the person who pays the premiums.

(5) Term insurance. Term insurance is a form of life insurance having no cash surrender value and generally furnishing insurance protection for only a specified or limited period of time.

(6) Face value. Face value is the basic death benefit of the policy exclusive of dividend additions or additional amounts payable because of accidental death or under other special provisions.

(7) Cash surrender value. Cash surrender value is the amount which the insurer will pay (usually to the owner) upon cancellation of the policy before death of the insured or before maturity of the policy.

(8) Burial insurance. Burial insurance is insurance whose terms specifically provide that the proceeds can be used only to pay the burial expenses of the insured.

§ 416.1231 Burial spaces and certain funds set aside for burial expenses.

(a) Burial spaces—

(1) General. In determining the resources of an individual, the value of burial spaces for the individual, the individual's spouse or any member of the individual's immediate family will be excluded from resources.

(2) Burial spaces defined. For purposes of this section "burial spaces" include burial plots, gravesites, crypts, mausoleums, urns, niches and other customary and traditional repositories for the deceased's bodily

remains provided such spaces are owned by the individual or are held for his or her use. Additionally, the term includes necessary and reasonable improvements or additions to or upon such burial spaces including, but not limited to, vaults, headstones, markers, plaques, or burial containers and arrangements for opening and closing the gravesite for burial of the deceased.

(3) An agreement representing the purchase of a burial space. The value of an agreement representing the purchase of a burial space, including any accumulated interest, will be excluded from resources. We do not consider a burial space "held for" an individual under an agreement unless the individual currently owns and is currently entitled to the use of the space under that agreement. For example, we will not consider a burial space "held for" an individual under an installment sales agreement or other similar device under which the individual does not currently own nor currently have the right to use the space, nor is the seller currently obligated to provide the space, until the purchase amount is paid in full.

(4) Immediate family defined. For purposes of this section immediate family means an individual's minor and adult children, including adopted children and step-children; an individual's brothers, sisters, parents, adoptive parents, and the spouses of those individuals. Neither dependency nor living-in-the-same-household will be a factor in determining whether a person is an immediate family member.

(b) Funds set aside for burial expenses—

(1) Exclusion. In determining the resources of an individual (and spouse, if any) there shall be excluded an amount not in excess of $1,500 each of funds specifically set aside for the burial expenses of the individual or the individual's spouse. This exclusion applies only if the funds set aside for burial expenses are kept separate from all other resources not intended for burial of the individual (or spouse) and are clearly designated as set aside for the individual's (or spouse's) burial expenses. If excluded burial funds are mixed with resources not intended for burial, the exclusion will not apply to any portion of the funds. This exclusion is in addition to the burial space exclusion.

(2) Exception for parental deeming situations. If an individual is an eligible child, the burial funds (up to $1,500) that are set aside for the burial arrangements of the eligible child's ineligible parent or parent's spouse will not be counted in determining the resources of such eligible child.

(3) Burial funds defined. For purposes of this section "burial funds" are revocable burial contracts, burial trusts, other burial arrangements (including amounts paid on installment sales contracts for burial spaces), cash, accounts, or other financial instruments with a definite cash value clearly designated for the individual's (or spouse's, if any) burial expenses and kept separate from nonburial-related assets. Property other than listed in this definition will not be considered "burial funds."

(4) Recipients currently receiving SSI benefits. Recipients currently eligible as of July 11, 1990, who have had burial funds excluded which do not meet all of the requirements of paragraphs (b)(1) and (3) of this section must convert or separate such funds to meet these requirements unless there is an impediment to such conversion or separation; i.e., a circumstance beyond an individual's control which makes conversion/separation impossible or impracticable. For so long as such an impediment or circumstance exists, the burial funds will be excluded if the individual remains otherwise continuously eligible for the exclusion.

(5) Reductions. Each person's (as described in §§ 416.1231(b)(1) and 416.1231(b)(2)) $1,500 exclusion must be reduced by:

(i) The face value of insurance policies on the life of an individual owned by the individual or spouse (if any) if the cash surrender value of those policies has been excluded from resources as provided in § 416.1230; and

(ii) Amounts in an irrevocable trust (or other irrevocable arrangement) available to meet the burial expenses.

(6) Irrevocable trust or other irrevocable arrangement. Funds in an irrevocable trust or other irrevocable arrangement which are available for burial are funds which are held in an irrevocable burial contract, an irrevocable burial trust, or an amount in an irrevocable trust which is specifically identified as available for burial expenses.

(7) Increase in value of burial funds. Interest earned on excluded burial funds and appreciation in the value of excluded burial arrangements which occur beginning November 1, 1982, or the date of first SSI eligibility, whichever is later, are excluded from resources if left to accumulate and become part of the separate burial fund.

(8) Burial funds used for some other purpose.

(i) Excluded burial funds must be used solely for that purpose.

(ii) If any excluded funds are used for a purpose other than the burial arrangements of the individual or the individual's spouse for whom the funds were set aside, future SSI benefits of the individual (or the individual and eligible spouse) will be reduced by an amount equal to the amount of excluded burial funds used for another purpose. This penalty for use of excluded burial funds for a purpose other than the burial arrangements of the individual (or spouse) will apply only if, as of the first moment of the month of use, the individual would have had resources in excess of the limit specified in § 416.1205 without application of the exclusion.

(9) Extension of burial fund exclusion during suspension. The exclusion of burial funds and accumulated interest and appreciation will continue to apply throughout a period of suspension as described in § 416.1320, so long as the individual's eligibility has not been terminated as described in §§ 416.1331 through 416.1335.

[47 FR 55213, Dec. 8, 1982; 48 FR 57127, Dec. 28, 1983; 55 FR 28377, July 11, 1990; 57 FR 1384, Jan. 14, 1992; 68 FR 53509, Sept. 11, 2003]

§ 416.1232 Replacement of lost, damaged, or stolen excluded resources.

(a) Cash (including any interest earned on the cash) or in-kind replacement received from any source for purposes of repairing or replacing an excluded resource (as defined in § 416.1210) that is lost, damaged, or stolen is excluded as a resource. This exclusion applies if the cash (and the interest) is used to repair or replace the excluded resource within 9 months of the date the individual received the cash. Any of the cash (and interest) that is not used to repair or replace the excluded resource will be counted as a resource beginning with the month after the 9–month period expires.

(b) The initial 9–month time period will be extended for a reasonable period up to an additional 9 months where we find the individual had good cause for not replacing or repairing the resource. An individual will be found to have good cause when circumstances beyond his or her control prevented the repair or replacement or the contracting for the repair or replacement of the resource. The 9–month extension can only be granted if the individual intends to use the cash or in-kind replacement items to repair or replace the lost, stolen, or damaged excluded resource in addition to having good cause for not having done so. If good cause is found for an individual, any unused cash (and interest) is counted as a resource beginning with the month after the good cause extension period expires. Exception: For victims of Hurricane Andrew only, the extension period for good cause may be extended for up to an additional 12 months beyond the 9–month extension when we find that the individual had good cause for not replacing or repairing an excluded resource within the 9–month extension.

(c) The time period described in paragraph (b) of this section (except the time period for individuals granted an additional extension under the Hurricane Andrew provision) may be extended for a reasonable period up to an additional 12 months in the case of a catastrophe which is declared to be a major disaster by the President of the United States if the excluded resource is geographically located within the disaster area as defined by the Presidential order; the individual intends to repair or replace the excluded resource; and, the individual demonstrates good cause why he or she has not been able to repair or replace the excluded resource within the 18–month period.

(d) Where an extension of the time period is made for good cause and the individual changes his or her intent to repair or replace the excluded resource, funds previously held for replacement or repair will be counted as a resource effective with the month that the individual reports this change of intent.

[44 FR 15662, Mar. 15, 1979; 50 FR 48579, Nov. 26, 1985; 59 FR 12545, March 17, 1994; 61 FR 5944, Feb. 15, 1996]

§ 416.1233 Exclusion of certain underpayments from resources.

(a) General. In determining the resources of an eligible individual (and spouse, if any), we will exclude, for 9 months following the month of receipt, the unspent portion of any title II or title XVI retroactive payment received on or after March 2, 2004. Exception: We will exclude for 6 months following the month of receipt the unspent portion of any title II or title XVI retroactive payment received before March 2, 2004. This exclusion also applies to such payments received by any other person whose resources are subject to deeming under this subpart.

(b) Retroactive payments. For purposes of this exclusion, a retroactive payment is one that is paid after the month in which it was due. A title XVI retroactive payment includes any retroactive amount of federally administered State supplementation.

(c) Limitation on exclusion. This exclusion applies only to any unspent portion of retroactive payments made under title II or XVI. Once the money from the retroactive payment is spent, this exclusion does not apply to items purchased with the money, even if the 6–month or 9–month period, whichever is applicable (see paragraph (a) of this section), has not expired. However, other exclusions may be applicable. As long as the funds from the retroactive payment are not spent, they are excluded for the full 6–month or 9–month period, whichever is applicable.

(d) Funds must be identifiable. Unspent money from a retroactive payment must be identifiable from other resources for this exclusion to apply. The money may be commingled with other funds but, if this is done in such a fashion that the retroactive amount can no longer be separately identified, that amount will count toward the resource limit described in § 416.1205.

(e) Written notice. We will give each recipient a written notice of the exclusion limitation when we make the retroactive payment.

[51 FR 34464, Sept. 29, 1986; 54 FR 19164, May 4, 1989; 70 FR 41138, July 18, 2005]

§ 416.1234 Exclusion of Indian lands.

In determining the resources of an individual (and spouse, if any) who is of Indian descent from a federally recognized Indian tribe, we will exclude any interest of the individual (or spouse, if any) in land which is held in trust by the United States for an individual Indian or tribe, or which is held by an individual Indian or tribe and which can only be sold, transferred, or otherwise disposed of with the approval of other individuals, his or her tribe, or an agency of the Federal Government.

[59 FR 8538, Feb. 23, 1994]

§ 416.1235 Exclusion of certain payments related to tax credits.

(a) In determining the resources of an individual (and spouse, if any), we exclude for the 9 months following the month of receipt the following funds received on or after March 2, 2004, the unspent portion of:

(1) Any payment of a refundable credit pursuant to section 32 of the Internal Revenue Code (relating to the earned income tax credit);

(2) Any payment from an employer under section 3507 of the Internal Revenue Code (relating to advance payment of the earned income tax credit); or

(3) Any payment of a refundable credit pursuant to section 24 of the Internal Revenue Code (relating to the child tax credit).

(b) Any unspent funds described in paragraph (a) of this section that are retained until the first moment of the tenth month following their receipt are countable as resources at that time.

(c) Exception: For any payments described in paragraph (a) of this section received before March 2, 2004, we will exclude for the month following the month of receipt the unspent portion of any such payment.

[58 FR 63890, Dec. 3, 1993; 70 FR 41138, July 18, 2005; 75 FR 1273, Jan. 11, 2010]

§ 416.1236 Exclusions from resources; provided by other statutes.

(a) For the purpose of § 416.1210(j), payments or benefits provided under a Federal statute other than title XVI of the Social Security Act where exclusion from resources is required by such statute include:

(1) Payments made under title II of the Uniform Relocation Assistance and Real Property Acquisition Policies Act of 1970 (84 Stat. 1902, 42 U.S.C. 4636).

(2) Payments made to Native Americans as listed in paragraphs (b) and (c) of section IV of the appendix to subpart K of part 416, as provided by Federal statutes other than the Social Security Act.

(3) Indian judgment funds held in trust by the Secretary of the Interior or distributed per capita pursuant to a plan prepared by the Secretary of the Interior and not disapproved by a joint resolution of the Congress under Public Law 93–134, as amended by Public Law 97–458 (25 U.S.C. 1407). Indian judgment funds include interest and investment income accrued while the funds are so held in trust. This exclusion extends to initial purchases made with Indian judgment funds. This exclusion will not apply to proceeds from sales or conversions of initial purchases or to subsequent purchases.

(4) The value of the coupon allotment in excess of the amount paid for the coupons under the Food Stamp Act of 1964 (78 Stat. 705, as amended, 7 U.S.C. 2016(c)).

(5) The value of assistance to children under the National School Lunch Act (60 Stat. 230, 42 U.S.C. 1751 et seq.) as amended by Pub.L. 90–302 (82 Stat. 117, 42 U.S.C. 1761(h)(3)).

(6) The value of assistance to children under the Child Nutrition Act of 1966 (80 Stat. 889, 42 U.S.C. 1780(b)).

(7) Any grant or loan to any undergraduate student for educational purposes made or insured under any program administered by the Commissioner of Education as provided by section 507 of the Higher Education Amendments of 1968, Pub.L. 90–575 (82 Stat. 1063).

(8) Incentive allowances received under title I of the Comprehensive Employment and Training Act of 1973 (87 Stat. 849, 29 U.S.C. 821(a)).

(9) Compensation provided to volunteers by the Corporation for National and Community Service (CNCS), unless determined by the CNCS to constitute the minimum wage in effect under the Fair Labor Standards Act of 1938 (29 U.S.C. 201 et seq.), or applicable State law, pursuant to 42 U.S.C. 5044(f)(1).

(10) Distributions received by an individual Alaska Native or descendant of an Alaska Native from an Alaska Native Regional and Village Corporation pursuant to the Alaska Native Claims Settlement Act, as follows: cash, including cash dividends on stock received from a Native Corporation, is disregarded to the extent that it does not, in the aggregate, exceed $2,000 per individual each year (the $2,000 limit is applied separately each year, and cash distributions up to $2,000 which an individual received in a prior year and retained into subsequent years will not be counted as resources in those years); stock, including stock issued or distributed by a Native Corporation as a dividend or distribution on stock; a partnership interest; land or an interest in land, including land or an interest in land received from a Native Corporation as a dividend or distribution on stock; and an interest in a settlement trust. This exclusion is pursuant to the exclusion under section 15 of the Alaska Native Claims Settlement Act Amendments of 1987, Public Law 100–241 (43 U.S.C. 1626(c)), effective February 3, 1988.

(11) Value of Federally donated foods distributed pursuant to section 32 of Pub.L. 74–320 or section 416 of the Agriculture Act of 1949 (7 CFR 250.6(e)(9) as authorized by 5 U.S.C. 301).

(12) All funds held in trust by the Secretary of the Interior for an Indian tribe and distributed per capita to a member of that tribe under Public Law 98–64. Funds held by Alaska Native Regional and Village Corporations (ANRVC) are not held in trust by the Secretary of the Interior and therefore ANRVC dividend distributions are not excluded from resources under this exclusion. For the treatment of ANRVC dividend distributions, see paragraph (a)(10) of this section.

(13) Home energy assistance payments or allowances under the Low-Income Home Energy Assistance Act of 1981, as added by title XXVI of the Omnibus Budget Reconciliation Act of 1981, Public Law 97–35 (42 U.S.C. 8624(f)).

(14) Student financial assistance for attendance costs received from a program funded in whole or in part under title IV of the Higher Education Act of 1965, as amended, or under Bureau of Indian Affairs student assistance programs if it is made available for tuition and fees normally assessed a student carrying the same academic workload, as determined by the institution, including costs for rental or purchase of any equipment, materials, or supplies required of all students in the same course of study; and an allowance for books, supplies, transportation, and miscellaneous personal expenses for a student attending the institution on at least a half-time basis, as determined by the institution, under section 14(27) of Public Law 100–50, the Higher Education Technical Amendments Act of 1987 (20 U.S.C. 1087uu), or under Bureau of Indian Affairs student assistance programs.

(15) Amounts paid as restitution to certain individuals of Japanese ancestry and Aleuts under the Civil Liberties Act of 1988 and the Aleutian and Pribilof Islands Restitution Act, sections 105(f) and 206(d) of Public Law 100–383 (50 U.S.C. app. 1989 b and c).

(16) Payments made on or after January 1, 1989, from the Agent Orange Settlement Fund or any other fund established pursuant to the settlement in the In Re Agent Orange product liability litigation, M.D.L. No. 381 (E.D.N.Y.) under Public Law 101–201 (103 Stat. 1795) and section 10405 of Public Law 101–239 (103 Stat. 2489).

(17) Payments made under section 6 of the Radiation Exposure Compensation Act, Public Law 101–426 (104 Stat. 925, 42 U.S.C. 2210).

(18) Payments made to individuals because of their status as victims of Nazi persecution excluded pursuant to section 1(a) of the Victims of Nazi Persecution Act of 1994, Public Law 103–286 (108 Stat. 1450).

(19) Any matching funds and interest earned on matching funds from a demonstration project authorized by Public Law 105–285 that are retained in an Individual Development Account, pursuant to section 415 of Public Law 105–285 (112 Stat. 2771).

(20) Any earnings, Temporary Assistance for Needy Families matching funds, and accrued interest retained in an Individual Development Account, pursuant to section 103 of Public Law 104–193 (42 U.S.C. 604(h)(4)).

(21) Payments made to individuals who were captured and interned by the Democratic Republic of Vietnam as a result of participation in certain military operations, pursuant to section 606 of Public Law 105–78 and section 657 of Public Law 104–201 (110 Stat. 2584).

(22) Payments made to certain Vietnam veterans' children with spina bifida, pursuant to section 421 of Public Law 104–204 (38 U.S.C. 1805(d)).

(23) Payments made to the children of women Vietnam veterans who suffer from certain birth defects, pursuant to section 401 of Public Law 106–419, (38 U.S.C. 1833(c)).

(24) Assistance provided for flood mitigation activities under section 1324 of the National Flood Insurance Act of 1968, pursuant to section 1 of Public Law 109–64 (119 Stat. 1997, 42 U.S.C. 4031).

(25) Payments made to individuals under the Energy Employees Occupational Illness Compensation Program Act of 2000, pursuant to section 1, app. [Div. C. Title XXXVI section 3646] of Public Law 106–398 (114 Stat. 1654A–510, 42 U.S.C. 7385e).

(b) In order for payments and benefits listed in paragraph (a) to be excluded from resources, such funds must be segregated and not commingled with other countable resources so that the excludable funds are identifiable.

[41 FR 13338, March 30, 1976, as amended at 42 FR 44221, Sept. 2, 1977; 42 FR 54945, Oct. 12, 1977; 43 FR 45555, Oct. 3, 1978; 55 FR 28378, July 11, 1990; 57 FR 53851, Nov. 13, 1992; 57 FR 55089, Nov. 24, 1992; 59 FR 8538, Feb. 23, 1994; 62 FR 30983, June 6, 1997; 70 FR 41138, July 18, 2005; 75 FR 1274, Jan. 11, 2010]

§ 416.1237 Assistance received on account of major disaster.

(a) Assistance received under the Disaster Relief and Emergency Assistance Act or other assistance provided under a Federal statute because of a catastrophe which is declared to be a major disaster by the President of the United States or comparable assistance received from a State or local government, or from a disaster assistance organization, is excluded in determining countable resources under § 416.1210.

(b) Interest earned on the assistance is excluded from resources.

[44 FR 15664, Mar. 15, 1979; 57 FR 53852, Nov. 13, 1992]

§ 416.1238 Exclusion of certain housing assistance.

The value of any assistance paid with respect to a dwelling under the statutes listed in § 416.1124(c)(14) is excluded from resources.

[55 FR 28378, July 11, 1990]

§ 416.1239 Exclusion of State or local relocation assistance payments.

In determining the resources of an individual (or spouse, if any), relocation assistance provided by a State or local government (as described in § 416.1124(c)(18)) is excluded from resources for a period of 9 months beginning with the month following the month of receipt.

[61 FR 1712, Jan. 23, 1996]

§ 416.1240 Disposition of resources.

(a) Where the resources of an individual (and spouse, if any) are determined to exceed the limitations prescribed in § 416.1205, such individual (and spouse, if any) shall not be eligible for payment except under the conditions provided in this section. Payment will be made to an individual (and spouse, if any) if the individual agrees in writing to:

(1) Dispose of, at current market value, the nonliquid resources (as defined in § 416.1201(c)) in excess of the limitations prescribed in § 416.1205 within the time period specified in § 416.1242; and

(2) Repay any overpayments (as defined in § 416.1244) with the proceeds of such disposition.

(b) Payment made for the period during which the resources are being disposed of will be conditioned upon the disposition of those resources as prescribed in paragraphs (a)(1) and (a)(2) of this section. Any payments so made are (at the time of disposition) considered overpayments to the extent they would not have been paid had the disposition occurred at the beginning of the period for which such payments were made.

(c) If an individual fails to dispose of the resources as prescribed in paragraphs (a)(1) and (a)(2) of this section, regardless of the efforts he or she makes to dispose of them, the resources will be counted at their current market value and the individual will be ineligible due to excess resources. We will use the original estimate of current market value unless the individual submits evidence establishing a lower value (e.g., an estimate from a disinterested knowledgeable source).

[52 FR 31762, Aug. 24, 1987; 75 FR 1274, Jan. 11, 2010]

§ 416.1242 Time limits for disposing of resources.

(a) In order for payment conditioned on the disposition of nonliquid resources to be made, the individual must agree in writing to dispose of real property within 9 months and personal property within 3 months. The time period for disposal of property begins on the date we accept the individual's signed written agreement to dispose of the property. If we receive a signed agreement on or after the date we have determined that the individual meets the eligibility requirements described in § 416.202 of this part, with the exception of the resource requirements described in this subpart, our acceptance of the written agreement will occur on the date the individual receives our written notice that the agreement is in effect. If we receive a signed agreement prior to the date we determine that all nonresource requirements are met, our acceptance of the written agreement will not occur until the date the individual receives our written notice that all nonresource requirements are met and that the agreement is in effect. When the written notice is mailed to the individual, we assume that the notice was received 5 days after the date shown on the notice unless the individual shows us that he or she did not receive it within the 5–day period.

(b) The 3–month time period for disposition of personal property will be extended an additional 3 months where it is found that the individual had "good cause" for failing to dispose of the resources within the original time period. The rules on the valuation of real property not disposed of within 9 months are described in § 416.1245(b).

(c) An individual will be found to have "good cause" for failing to dispose of a resource if, despite reasonable and diligent effort on his part, he was prevented by circumstances beyond his control from disposing of the resource.

(d) In determining whether the appropriate time limits discussed in paragraphs (a) and (b) of this section have elapsed, no month will be counted for which an individual's benefits have been suspended as described in § 416.1320, provided that the reason for the suspension is unrelated to the requirements in § 416.1245(b) and that the individual's eligibility has not been terminated as defined in §§ 416.1331 through 416.1335.

[53 FR 13257, April 22, 1988; 55 FR 10419, March 21, 1990; 58 FR 60105, Nov. 15, 1993; 68 FR 53509, Sept. 11, 2003]

§ 416.1244 Treatment of proceeds from disposition of resources.

(a) Upon disposition of the resources, the net proceeds to the individual from the sale are considered available to repay that portion of the payments that would not have been made had the disposition occurred at the beginning of the period for which payment was made.

(b) The net proceeds from disposition will normally be the sales price less any encumbrance on the resource and the expenses of sale such as transfer taxes, fees, advertising costs, etc. where, however, a resource has been sold (or otherwise transferred) by an individual to a friend or relative for less than its current market value, the net proceeds will be the current market value less costs of sale and encumbrance.

(c) After deducting any amount necessary to raise the individual's (and spouse's, if any) resources to the applicable limits described in § 416.1205, as of the beginning of the disposition period, the balance of the net proceeds will be used to recover the payments made to the individual (and spouse, if any). Any remaining proceeds are considered liquid resources.

(d) The overpayment to be recovered is equal to the balance of the net proceeds (as described in paragraph (c) of this section) or the total payments made to the individual (and spouse, if any) for the period of disposition, whichever is less.

[50 FR 38982, Sept. 26, 1985]

§ 416.1245 Exceptions to required disposition of real property.

(a) Loss of housing for joint owner. Excess real property which would be a resource under § 416.1201 is not a countable resource for conditional benefit purposes when: it is jointly owned; and sale of the property by an individual would cause the other owner undue hardship due to loss of housing. Undue hardship would result when the property serves as the principal place of residence for one (or more) of the other owners, sale of the property would result in loss of that residence, and no other housing would be readily available for the displaced other owner (e.g., the other owner does not own another house that is legally available for occupancy). However, if undue hardship ceases to exist, its value will be included in countable resources as described in § 416.1207.

(b) Reasonable efforts to sell.

(1) Excess real property is not included in countable resources for so long as the individual's reasonable efforts to sell it have been unsuccessful. The basis for determining whether efforts to sell are reasonable, as well as unsuccessful, will be a 9–month disposal period described in § 416.1242. If it is determined that reasonable efforts to sell have been unsuccessful, further SSI payments will not be conditioned on the disposition of the property and only the benefits paid during the 9–month disposal period will be subject to recovery. In order to be eligible for payments after the conditional benefits period, the individual must continue to make reasonable efforts to sell.

(2) A conditional benefits period involving excess real property begins as described at § 416.1242(a). The conditional benefits period ends at the earliest of the following times:

(i) Sale of the property;

(ii) Lack of continued reasonable efforts to sell;

(iii) The individual's written request for cancellation of the agreement;

(iv) Countable resources, even without the conditional exclusion, fall below the applicable limit (e.g., liquid resources have been depleted); or

(v) The 9–month disposal period has expired.

(3) Reasonable efforts to sell property consist of taking all necessary steps to sell it in the geographic area covered by the media serving the area in which the property is located, unless the individual has good cause for not taking these steps. More specifically, making a reasonable effort to sell means that:

(i) Except for gaps of no more than 1 week, an individual must attempt to sell the property by listing it with a real estate agent or by undertaking to sell it himself;

(ii) Within 30 days of receiving notice that we have accepted the individual's signed written agreement to dispose of the property, and absent good cause for not doing so, the individual must:

(A) List the property with an agent; or

(B) Begin to advertise it in at least one of the appropriate local media, place a "For Sale" sign on the property (if permitted), begin to conduct "open houses" or otherwise show the property to interested parties on a continuous basis, and attempt any other appropriate methods of sale; and

(iii) The individual accepts any reasonable offer to buy and has the burden of demonstrating that an offer was rejected because it was not reasonable. If the individual receives an offer that is at least two-thirds of the latest estimate of current market value, the individual must present evidence to establish that the offer was unreasonable and was rejected.

(4) An individual will be found to have "good cause" for failing to make reasonable efforts to sell under paragraph (b)(3) of this section if he or she was prevented by circumstances beyond his or her control from taking the steps specified in paragraph (b)(3)(i) through (ii) of this section.

(5) An individual who has received conditional benefits through the expiration of the 9 month disposal period and whose benefits have been suspended as described at § 416.1320 for reasons unrelated to the property excluded under the conditional benefits agreement, but whose eligibility has not been terminated as defined at §§ 416.1331 through 416.1335, can continue to have the excess real property not included in countable resources upon reinstatement of SSI payments if reasonable efforts to sell the property resume within 1 week of reinstatement. Such an individual will not have to go through a subsequent conditional benefits period. However, the individual whose eligibility has been terminated as defined at §§ 416.1331 through 416.1335 and who subsequently reapplies would be subject to a new conditional benefits period if there is still excess real property.

[53 FR 13257, April 22, 1988; 55 FR 10419, March 21, 1990; 62 FR 30983, June 6, 1997; 64 FR 31975, June 15, 1999; 68 FR 53509, Sept. 11, 2003]

§ 416.1246 Disposal of resources at less than fair market value.

(a) General.

(1) An individual (or eligible spouse) who gives away or sells a nonexcluded resource for less than fair market value for the purpose of establishing SSI or Medicaid eligibility will be charged with the difference between the fair market value of the resource and the amount of compensation received. The difference is referred to as uncompensated value and is counted toward the resource limit (see § 416.1205) for a period of 24 months from the date of transfer.

(2) If the transferred resource (asset) is returned to the individual, the uncompensated value is no longer counted as of the date of return. If the transferred asset is cash, the uncompensated value is reduced as of the date of return by the amount of cash that is returned. No income will be charged as a result of such returns. The returned asset will be evaluated as a resource according to the rules described in §§ 416.1201 through 416.1230 as of the first day of the following month.

(3) If the individual receives additional compensation in the form of cash for the transferred asset the uncompensated value is reduced, as of the date the additional cash compensation is received, by the amount of that additional compensation.

(b) Fair market value. Fair market value is equal to the current market value of a resource at the time of transfer or contract of sale, if earlier. See § 416.1101 for definition of current market value.

(c) Compensation. The compensation for a resource includes all money, real or personal property, food, shelter, or services received by the individual (or eligible spouse) at or after the time of transfer in exchange for the resource if the compensation was provided pursuant to a binding (legally enforceable) agreement in effect at the time of transfer. Compensation also includes all money, real or personal property, food, shelter, or services received prior to the actual transfer if they were provided pursuant to a binding (legally enforceable) agreement whereby the eligible individual would transfer the resource or otherwise pay for such items. In addition, payment or assumption of a legal debt owed by the eligible individual in exchange for the asset is considered compensation.

(d)(1) Uncompensated value—General. The uncompensated value is the fair market value of a resource at the time of transfer minus the amount of compensation received by the individual (or eligible spouse) in exchange for the resource. However, if the transferred resource was partially excluded, we will not count uncompensated value in an amount greater than the countable value of the resources at the time of transfer.

(2) Suspension of counting as a resource the uncompensated value where necessary to avoid undue hardship. We will suspend counting as a resource the uncompensated value of the transferred asset for any month in the 24-month period if such counting will result in undue hardship. We will resume counting the uncompensated value as a resource for any month of the 24-month period in which counting will not result in undue hardship. We will treat as part of the 24-month period any months during which we suspend the counting of uncompensated value.

(3) When undue hardship exists. Undue hardship exists when:

(i) An individual alleges that failure to receive SSI benefits would deprive the individual of food or shelter; and

(ii) The applicable Federal benefit rate (plus the federally-administered State supplementary payment level) exceeds the sum of: The individual's monthly countable and excludable income and monthly countable and excludable liquid resources.

(e) Presumption that resource was transferred to establish SSI or Medicaid eligibility. Transfer of a resource for less than fair market value is presumed to have been made for the purpose of establishing SSI or Medicaid eligibility unless the individual (or eligible spouse) furnishes convincing evidence that the resource was transferred exclusively for some other reason. Convincing evidence may be pertinent documentary or non-documentary evidence which shows, for example, that the transfer was ordered by a court, or that at the time of transfer the individual could not have anticipated becoming eligible due to the existence of other circumstances which would have precluded eligibility. The burden of rebutting the presumption that a resource was transferred to establish SSI or Medicaid eligibility rests with the individual (or eligible spouse).

(f) Applicability. This section applies only to transfers of resources that occurred before July 1, 1988. Paragraphs (d)(2) and (d)(3) of this section, regarding undue hardship, are effective for such transfers on or after April 1, 1988.

[48 FR 40885, Sept. 12, 1983; 50 FR 38982, Sept. 26, 1985; 53 FR 13257, April 22, 1988; 55 FR 10419, March 21, 1990]

§ 416.1247 Exclusion of a dedicated account in a financial institution.

(a) General. In determining the resources of an individual (or spouse, if any), the funds in a dedicated account in a financial institution established and maintained in accordance with § 416.640(e) will be excluded from resources. This exclusion applies only to benefits which must or may be deposited in such an account, as specified in § 416.546, and accrued interest or other earnings on these benefits. If these funds are commingled with any other funds (other than accumulated earnings or interest) this exclusion will not apply to any portion of the funds in the dedicated account.

(b) Exclusion during a period of suspension or termination—

(1) Suspension. The exclusion of funds in a dedicated account and interest and other earnings thereon continues to apply during a period of suspension due to ineligibility as described in § 416.1320, administrative suspension, or a period of eligibility for which no payment is due, so long as the individual's eligibility has not been terminated as described in §§ 416.1331 through 416.1335.

(2) Termination. Once an individual's eligibility has been terminated, any funds previously excluded under paragraph (a) of this section may not be excluded if the individual establishes a subsequent period of eligibility by filing a new application.

[61 FR 67207, Dec. 20, 1996; 68 FR 53509, Sept. 11, 2003]

§ 416.1248 Exclusion of gifts to children with life-threatening conditions.

In determining the resources of an individual who has not attained 18 years of age and who has a life-threatening condition, we will exclude any gifts from an organization described in section 501(c)(3) of the Internal Revenue Code of 1986 which is exempt from taxation under section 501(a) of such Code. We will exclude any in-kind gift that is not converted to cash and cash gifts to the extent that the total gifts excluded pursuant to this paragraph do not exceed $2000 in any calendar year. In-kind gifts converted to cash are considered under income counting rules in the month of conversion.

[70 FR 41139, July 18, 2005]

§ 416.1249 Exclusion of payments received as restitution for misuse of benefits by a representative payee.

In determining the resources of an individual (and spouse, if any), the unspent portion of any payment received by the individual as restitution for title II, title VIII or title XVI benefits misused by a representative payee under § 404.2041, § 408.641 or § 416.641, respectively, is excluded for 9 months following the month of receipt.

[70 FR 41139, July 18, 2005]

§ 416.1250 How we count grants, scholarships, fellowships or gifts.

(a) When we determine your resources (or your spouse's, if any), we will exclude for 9 months any portion of any grant, scholarship, fellowship, or gift that you use or set aside to pay the cost of tuition, fees, or other necessary educational expenses at any educational institution, including vocational or technical institutions. The 9 months begin the month after the month you receive the educational assistance.

(b)(1) We will count as a resource any portion of a grant, scholarship, fellowship, or gift you (or your spouse, if any) did not use or set aside to pay tuition, fees, or other necessary educational expenses. We will count such portion of a grant, scholarship, fellowship or gift as a resource in the month following the month of receipt.

(2) If you use any of the funds that were set aside for tuition, fees, or other necessary educational expenses for another purpose within the 9–month exclusion period, we will count such portion of the funds used for another purpose as income in the month you use them.

(3) If any portion of the funds are no longer set aside for paying tuition, fees, or other necessary educational expenses within the 9–month exclusion period, we will count the portion of the funds no longer set aside as income in the month when they are no longer set aside for paying tuition, fees, or other necessary educational expenses. We will consider any remaining funds that are no longer set aside or used to pay tuition, fees, or other educational expenses as a resource in the month following the month we count them as income.

(4) We will count any portion of grants, scholarships, fellowships, or gifts remaining unspent after the 9–month exclusion period as a resource beginning with the 10th month after you received the educational assistance.

[71 FR 45378, Aug. 9, 2006]

§ 416.1260 Special resource provision for recipients under a State plan.

(a) General. In the case of any individual (or individual and spouse, as the case may be) who for the month of December 1973 was a recipient of aid or assistance under a State plan approved under title I, X, XIV, or XVI, of the Act (see § 416.121), the resources of such individual (or individual and spouse, as the case may be) shall be deemed not to exceed the amount specified in § 416.1205 during any period that the resources of such individual (or individual and spouse, as the case may be) do not exceed the maximum amount of resources specified in such State plan as in effect in October 1972, provided that such individual:

(1) Has, since December 1973, resided continuously in the State under whose plan he was eligible for the month of December 1973; and

(2) Has not, since December 1973, been ineligible for an SSI benefit for a period exceeding 6 consecutive months. An SSI benefit means a Federal benefit only; it does not include any State supplementation.

(b) For purposes of this section, an individual will cease to reside continuously in a State if he leaves the State with the present intention to abandon his home there. In the absence of evidence to the contrary,

(1) If an individual leaves the State for a period of 90 calendar days or less, his absence from the State will be considered temporary and he will be considered to continue to reside in such State; and

(2) If an individual leaves the State for a period in excess of 90 calendar days, he will no longer be considered to reside continuously in such State.

(c) State plan; defined. As used in this subpart, an approved State plan as in effect in October 1972 and State plan for October 1972 means a State plan as approved under the provisions of 45 CFR Ch. II as in effect in October 1972.

[41 FR 47424, Oct. 29, 1976; 52 FR 29841, Aug. 12, 1987]

§ 416.1261 Application of special resource provision.

In determining the resources of an individual (and spouse, if any) who meets the conditions specified in § 416.1260(a), either the State plan resource limit and exclusions (as specified in § 416.1260) or the resource limit (as specified in § 416.1205) and exclusions (as specified in § 416.1210), whichever is most advantageous to the individual (and spouse, if any) will be used.

§ 416.1262 Special resource provision applicable in cases involving essential persons.

(a) Essential persons continuously meet criteria of eligibility. In determining the resources of an individual (and spouse, if any) who meet the conditions specified in § 416.1260 and whose payment standard is increased because such individual has in his home an essential person (as defined in § 416.222), either the State plan resource limit and exclusions (as specified in § 416.1260) applicable to cases in which the needs of an essential person are taken into account in determining the individual's needs, or the resource limit as specified in § 416.1205 and exclusions as specified in § 416.1210, whichever is most advantageous to the individual (and spouse), will be used.

(b) Essential person fails to meet criteria of eligibility. If for any month after December 1973 a person fails to meet the criteria for an essential person as specified in § 416.222, in determining the resources of an individual (and spouse, if any) either the State plan resource limit and criteria as specified in § 416.1260 applicable to the individual or individual and spouse, as the case may be, or the resource limit as specified in § 416.1205 and exclusions as specified in § 416.1210, whichever is most advantageous to the individual (and spouse), will be used.

[39 FR 33797, Sept. 20, 1974; 51 FR 10616, March 28, 1986]

§ 416.1264 Spouse ineligible under a State plan in December 1973.

In the case of an individual who meets the conditions specified in § 416.1260 but whose spouse does not meet such conditions, whichever of the following is most advantageous for the individual (and spouse, if any) will be applied:

(a) The resource limitation and exclusions for an individual as in effect under the approved State plan for October 1972, or

(b) The resource limitation (as specified in § 416.1205) and exclusions (as specified in § 416.1210) for an individual and eligible spouse or an individual living with an ineligible spouse.

§ 416.1266 Individual under special resource provision dies after December 1973.

Where only one person, either the eligible individual or the eligible spouse, meets the conditions specified in § 416.1260 and that person dies after December 1973, the State plan resource limitation and exclusions will not be applied to determine the amount of resources of the surviving individual. The resource limitation (as specified in § 416.1205) and exclusions (as specified in § 416.1210) will be applied for the now eligible individual beginning with the month such person is considered the eligible individual as defined in subpart A of this part.

SUBPART M—SUSPENSIONS AND TERMINATIONS

Authority: Secs. 702(a)(5), 1129A, 1611–1614, 1619, and 1631 of the Social Security Act (42 U.S.C. 902(a)(5), 1320a–8a, 1382–1382c, 1382h, and 1383).

Source: 40 FR 1510, Jan. 8, 1975; 50 FR 46763, Nov. 13, 1985; 50 FR 51518, Dec. 18, 1985; 51 FR 13494, April 21, 1986; 51 FR 17618, May 14, 1986; 52 FR 27541, July 22, 1987; 56 FR 55453, Oct. 28, 1991; 61 FR 5942, Feb. 15, 1996; 65 FR 42286, July 10, 2000; 67 FR 20893, April 29, 2002; 68 FR 40124, July 7, 2003, 70 FR 36508, June 24, 2005, unless otherwise noted.

§ 416.1320 Suspensions; general.

(a) When suspension is proper. Suspension of benefit payments is required when a recipient is alive but no longer meets the requirements of eligibility under title XVI of the Act (see subpart B of this part) and termination in accordance with §§ 416.1331 through 416.1335 does not apply. (This subpart does not cover suspension of payments for administrative reasons, as, for example, when mail is returned as undeliverable by the Postal Service and the Administration does not have a valid mailing address for a recipient or when the representative payee dies and a search is underway for a substitute representative payee.)

(b) Effect of suspension.

(1) When payments are correctly suspended due to the ineligibility of a recipient, payments shall not be resumed until the individual again meets all requirements for eligibility except the filing of a new application. Such recipient, upon requesting reinstatement, shall be required to submit such evidence as may be necessary (except evidence of age, disability, or blindness) to establish that he or she again meets all

requirements for eligibility under this part. Payments to such recipient shall be reinstated effective with the first day such recipient meets all requirements for eligibility except the filing of a new application.

(2) A month of ineligibility for purposes of determining when to prorate the SSI benefit payment for a subsequent month, is a month for which the individual is ineligible for any Federal SSI benefit and any federally administered State supplementation.

(c) Actions which are not suspensions. Payments are not "suspended," but the claim is disallowed, when it is found that:

(1) The claimant was notified in accordance with § 416.210(c) at or about the time he filed application and before he received payment of a benefit that he should file a claim for a payment of the type discussed in § 416.1330 and such claimant has failed, without good cause (see § 416.210(e)(2)), to take all appropriate steps within 30 days after receipt of such notice to file and prosecute an application for such payment;

(2) Upon initial application, payment of benefits was conditioned upon disposal of specified resources which exceeded the permitted amount and the claimant did not comply with the agreed-upon conditions;

(3) Payment was made to an individual faced with a financial emergency who was later found to have been not eligible for payment; or

(4) Payment was made to an individual presumed to be disabled and such disability is not established.

(d) Exception. Even though conditions described in paragraph (a) of this section apply because your impairment is no longer disabling or you are no longer blind under § 416.986(a)(1), (a)(2) or (b), we will not suspend your benefits for this reason if—

(1) You are participating in an appropriate program of vocational rehabilitation services, employment services, or other support services, as described in § 416.1338(c) and (d);

(2) You began participating in the program before the date your disability or blindness ended; and

(3) We have determined under § 416.1338(e) that your completion of the program, or your continuation in the program for a specified period of time, will increase the likelihood that you will not have to return to the disability or blindness benefit rolls.

[40 FR 1510, Jan. 8, 1975 and 47 FR 31544, July 21, 1982; 47 FR 52693, Nov. 23, 1982; 51 FR 13494, April 21, 1986; 51 FR 17618, May 14, 1986; 56 FR 55453, Oct. 28, 1991; 68 FR 53509, Sept. 11, 2003; 70 FR 36508, June 24, 2005]

§ 416.1321 Suspension for not giving us permission to contact financial institutions.

(a) If you don't give us permission to contact any financial institution and request any financial records about you when we think it is necessary to determine your SSI eligibility or payment amount, or if you cancel the permission, you cannot be eligible for SSI payments (see § 416.207) and we will stop your payments. Also, if anyone whose income and resources we consider as being available to you (see §§ 416.1160, 416.1202, 416.1203 and 416.1204) doesn't give us permission to contact any financial institution and request any financial records about that person when we think it is necessary to determine your SSI eligibility or payment amount, or that person cancels the permission, you cannot be eligible for SSI payments and we will stop your payments. We will not find you ineligible and/or stop your payments if the person whose income and resources we consider as being available to you fails to give or continue permission and good cause, as discussed in § 416.207(h), exists.

(b) We will suspend your payments starting with the month after the month in which we notify you in writing that:

(1) You failed to give us permission to contact any financial institution and request any financial records about you, or

(2) The person(s) whose income and resources we consider as being available to you failed to give us such permission.

(c) If you are otherwise eligible, we will start your benefits in the month following the month in which:

(1) You give us permission to contact any financial institution and request any financial records about you, or

(2) The person(s) whose income and resources we consider as being available to you gives us such permission.

[68 FR 53509, Sept. 11, 2003]

§ 416.1322 Suspension due to failure to comply with request for information.

(a) Suspension of benefit payments is required effective with the month following the month in which it is determined in accordance with § 416.714(b) that the individual is ineligible for payment due to his or her failure to comply with our request for necessary information. When we have information to establish that benefit payments are again payable, the benefit payments will be reinstated for any previous month for which the individual continued to meet the eligibility requirements of § 416.202. If the reason that an individual's benefits were suspended was failure to comply with our request for information, the payments for the months that benefits are reinstated will not be prorated under § 416.421.

(b) A suspension of payment for failure to comply with our request for information will not apply with respect to any month for which a determination as to eligibility for or amount of payment can be made based on information on record, whether or not furnished by an individual specified in § 416.704(a). Where it is determined that the information of record does not permit a determination with respect to eligibility for or amount of payment, notice of a suspension of payment due to a recipient's failure to comply with a request for information will be sent in accordance with §§ 416.1336 and 416.1404.

[42 FR 39099, Aug. 2, 1977; 51 FR 13494, April 21, 1986]

§ 416.1323 Suspension due to excess income.

(a) Effective date. Suspension of payments due to ineligibility for benefits because of excess income is effective with the first month in which "countable income" (see §§ 416.1100 through 416.1124 of this part) equals or exceeds the amount of benefits otherwise payable for such month (see subpart D of this part). This rule applies regardless of the month in which the income is received.

(b) Resumption of payments. If benefits are otherwise payable, they will be resumed effective with the first month in which a recipient's monthly countable income becomes less than the applicable Federal benefit rate (or the sum of that rate and the level for any federally administered State supplementary payment) for that month. If the reason that a recipient's benefits were suspended was excess income, the payment for the first month that benefits are reinstated will not be prorated under § 416.421.

[51 FR 13494, April 21, 1986; 65 FR 16815, March 30, 2000]

§ 416.1324 Suspension due to excess resources.

(a) Effective date. Except as specified in §§ 416.1240 through 416.1242, suspension of benefit payments because of excess resources is required effective with the month in which:

(1) Ineligibility exists because countable resources are in excess of:

(i) The resource limits prescribed in § 416.1205 for an individual and an individual and spouse, or

(ii) In the case of an eligible individual (and eligible spouse, if any) who for the month of December 1973 was a recipient of aid or assistance under a State plan approved under title I, X, XIV, or XVI of the Act, the maximum amount of resources specified in such State plan as in effect for October 1972, if greater than the amounts specified in § 416.1205, as applicable; or

(2) After eligibility has been established, payment of benefits was conditioned upon disposal of specified resources, which exceeded the permitted amount and the claimant did not comply with the agreed upon conditions.

(3) The amount of an individual's or couple's countable resources is determined as of the first moment of each calendar quarter.

(b) Resumption of payments. If benefits are otherwise payable, they will be resumed effective with the start of the month after the month in which a recipient's countable resources no longer exceed the limit that applies. If the reason that a recipient's benefits were suspended was excess resources, the payment for the first month that benefits are reinstated will not be prorated under § 416.421.

[50 FR 38982, Sept. 26, 1985; 51 FR 13494, April 21, 1986]

§ 416.1325 Suspension due to status as a resident of a public institution.

(a) Except as provided in § 416.211 (b) and (c), a recipient is ineligible for benefits for the first full calendar month in which he or she is a resident of a public institution (as defined in § 416.201) throughout the calendar month (as defined in § 416.211(a)), and payments are suspended effective with such first full month. Such ineligibility continues for so long as such individual remains a resident of a public institution.

(b) Resumption of payments. If benefits are otherwise payable, they will be resumed effective with the earliest day of the month in which a recipient is no longer a resident of a public institution. See § 416.421. A transfer from one public institution to another or a temporary absence from the institution lasting 14 days or less, however, will not change his or her status as a resident, and the suspension will continue.

[50 FR 51518, Dec. 18, 1985; 51 FR 13494, April 21, 1986]

§ 416.1326 Suspension for failure to comply with treatment for drug addiction or alcoholism.

(a) Basis for suspension. If you are disabled and drug addiction or alcoholism is a contributing factor material to the determination of disability as described in § 416.935, we will refer you to appropriate treatment as defined in § 416.937. You will not be an eligible individual and we will suspend your benefits if you do not comply with the terms, conditions and requirements of treatment prescribed by the institution or facility. (See § 416.940 which explains how we evaluate compliance with treatment.)

(b) Date of suspension. We will suspend your benefits for a period starting with the first month after we notify you in writing that you failed to comply with prescribed treatment.

(c) Resumption of benefits. If you are complying with prescribed treatment and are otherwise eligible for benefits, we will resume benefits effective with the first day of the month after you demonstrate and maintain compliance with appropriate treatment for these periods—

(1) 2 consecutive months for the first determination of noncompliance;

(2) 3 consecutive months for the second determination of noncompliance; and

(3) 6 consecutive months for the third and all subsequent determinations of noncompliance.

[51 FR 13494, April 21, 1986; 60 FR 8152, Feb. 10, 1995]

§ 416.1327 Suspension due to absence from the United States.

(a) Suspension effective date. A recipient is not eligible for SSI benefits if he is outside the United States for a full calendar month. For purposes of this paragraph—

(1) United States means the 50 States, the District of Columbia, and the Northern Mariana Islands:

(2) Day means a full 24-hour day; and

(3) In determining whether a recipient has been outside the United States for a full calendar month, it must be established whether the recipient is outside the United States for 30 consecutive days or more. If yes, he or she will be treated as remaining outside the United States until he or she has returned to and remained in the United States for a period of 30 consecutive days. When a recipient has been outside the United States, the first period of 30 consecutive days of absence is counted beginning with the day after the day the recipient departs from the United States and ending with the day before the day on which he or she returns to the United States. When a recipient has returned to the United States, the second period of 30 consecutive days starts on the day the individual returned and ends on the 30th day of continuous presence in the United States. Benefits will be suspended effective with the first full calendar month in which a recipient is outside the United States.

(b) Resumption of payments after absence from the United States. If benefits are otherwise payable they will be resumed—

(1) Effective with the day following the 30th day of continuous presence in the United States after the recipient's return if the absence was for 30 consecutive days or more.

(2) Effective with the day the recipient returned to the United States, if the absence from the United States was for a full calendar month, but for less than 30 consecutive days (this can occur only for the calendar month of February).

Example 1: Mike left the United States on March 1 and returned on April 1. Counting March 2 through March 31, he was outside the United States for 30 consecutive days; thus he is also deemed to be outside the United States for 30 additional consecutive days. Therefore, for April 1 through April 30, he is deemed to be outside the United States and not eligible for the calendar month of April. Payments start effective May 1.

Example 2: Mary left the United States on April 15 and returned on July 1. Counting April 16 through June 30, she was actually outside the United States and not eligible for the calendar months of May and June. Since she was absent for more than 30 consecutive days, she is deemed to be outside the United States for 30 additional consecutive days. Therefore, for July 1 through July 30, she is deemed to be outside the United States and not eligible for payment until July 31.

[40 FR 1510, Jan. 8, 1975, as amended at 43 FR 25092, June 9, 1978; 51 FR 13494, April 21, 1986; 51 FR 17332, May 12, 1986]

§ 416.1328 [Reserved]

[68 FR 40124, July 7, 2003]

§ 416.1329 Suspension due to loss of United States residency, United States citizenship, or status as an alien lawfully admitted for permanent residence or otherwise permanently residing in the United States under color of law.

(a) A recipient ceases to be an eligible individual or eligible spouse, under section 1614(a)(1)(B) of the Act, when he or she ceases to meet the requirement of § 416.202(b) with respect to United States residency, United States citizenship, or status as an alien lawfully admitted for permanent residence or otherwise permanently residing in the United States under color of law. Payments are suspended effective with the first month after the last month in which a recipient meets the requirements of § 416.202(b).

(b) Resumption of payments. If benefits are otherwise payable, they will be resumed effective with the earliest day of the month on which the recipient again meets both the residence and citizenship or lawfully admitted alien or color of law requirements. See § 416.421.

[51 FR 13495, April 21, 1986]

§ 416.1330 Suspension due to failure to apply for and obtain other benefits.

(a) Suspension effective date. A recipient ceases to be an eligible individual or eligible spouse when, in the absence of a showing of incapacity to do so, or other good cause, he or she fails within 30 days after notice from the Social Security Administration of probable eligibility, to take all appropriate steps to apply for and, if eligible, to obtain payments such as an annuity, pension, retirement, or disability benefit, including veterans' compensation, old-age, survivors, and disability insurance benefit, railroad retirement annuity or pension, or unemployment insurance benefit. Benefit payments are suspended due to such ineligibility effective with the month in which the recipient was notified in writing of the requirement that he or she file and take all appropriate steps to receive the other benefits. See § 416.210(e).

(b) Resumption of payment. If benefits are otherwise payable, they will be resumed effective with the earliest day of the month on which the recipient takes the necessary steps to obtain the other benefits. See § 416.421.

[51 FR 13495, April 21, 1986]

§ 416.1331 Termination of your disability or blindness payments.

(a) General. The last month for which we can pay you benefits based on disability or blindness is the second month after the month in which your disability or blindness ends. (See §§ 416.987(e), 416.994(b)(6) and 416.994a(g) for when disability ends, and § 416.986 for when blindness ends.) See § 416.1338 for an exception to this rule if you are participating in an appropriate program of vocational rehabilitation services, employment services, or other support services. You must meet the income, resources, and other eligibility requirements to receive any of the benefits referred to in this paragraph. We will also stop payment of your benefits if you have not cooperated with us in getting information about your disability or blindness.

(b) After we make a determination that you are not now disabled or blind. If we determine that you do not meet the disability or blindness requirements of the law, we will send you an advance written notice telling you why we believe you are not disabled or blind and when your benefits should stop. The notice will explain your right to appeal if you disagree with our determination. You may still appeal our determination that you are not now disabled or blind even though your payments are continuing because of your participation in an appropriate program of vocational rehabilitation services, employment services, or other support services. You may also appeal a determination that your completion of, or continuation for a specified period of time in, an appropriate program of vocational rehabilitation services, employment services, or other support services will not increase the likelihood that you will not have to return to the disability or blindness benefit rolls and, therefore, you are not eligible to continue to receive benefits.

(c) When benefits terminate due to 12 consecutive suspension months for failure to comply with treatment for drug addiction or alcoholism. If you are disabled and drug addiction or alcoholism is a contributing factor material to the determination of disability as described in § 416.935, your benefits will terminate after 12 consecutive months of suspension for noncompliance with treatment requirements as described in § 416.1326.

(d) When benefits terminate due to payment of 36 months of benefits based on disability when drug addiction or alcoholism is a contributing factor material to the determination of disability. If you are disabled and drug addiction or alcoholism is a contributing factor material to the determination of disability as described in § 416.935, your benefits will terminate after you receive a total of 36 months of SSI benefits. The 36–month limit is no longer effective for benefits for months beginning after September 2004.

(e) Months we count in determining the 36 months of benefits when drug addiction or alcoholism is a contributing factor material to the determination of disability. Beginning March 1995, we will count all months for which you were paid an SSI benefit, a federally-administered State supplement, a special SSI cash benefit, or you were in special SSI eligibility status, toward the 36 months described in paragraph (d) of this section. Months for which you were not eligible for benefits will not count toward the 36 months.

[47 FR 31544, July 21, 1982; 49 FR 22274, May 29, 1984; 60 FR 8152, Feb. 10, 1995; 65 FR 42792, July 11, 2000; 70 FR 36508, June 24, 2005]

§ 416.1332 Termination of benefit for disabled individual: Exception.

Special SSI cash benefits (see § 416.261) will be payable for the period beginning January 1, 1981, and ending June 30, 1987 if you meet eligibility requirements in § 416.262. These requirements apply if you, as a disabled recipient, are no longer eligible for regular SSI benefits because you demonstrate that you are able to engage in SGA.

[46 FR 6908, Jan. 22, 1981, as amended at 47 FR 15325, Apr. 9, 1982; 50 FR 46763, Nov. 13, 1985]

§ 416.1333 Termination at the request of the recipient.

A recipient, his legal guardian, or his representative payee, may terminate his eligibility for benefits under this part by filing a written request for termination which shows an understanding that such termination may extend to other benefits resulting from eligibility under this part. In the case of a representative payee there must also be a showing which establishes that no hardship would result if an eligible recipient were not covered by the supplemental security income program. When such a request is filed, the recipient ceases to be an eligible individual, or eligible spouse, effective with the month following the month the request is filed with the Social Security Administration unless the recipient specifies some other month. However, the Social Security Administration will not effectuate the request for any month for which payment has been or will be made unless there is repayment, or assurance of repayment, of any amounts paid for those months (e.g., from special payments which would be payable for such months under section 228 of the Act). When the Social Security Administration effectuates a termination of eligibility at the request of the recipient, his legal guardian, or his representative payee, notice of the determination will be sent in accordance with § 416.1404, and eligibility, once terminated, can be reestablished, except as provided by § 416.1408, only upon the filing of a new application.

[42 FR 39100, Aug. 2, 1977]

§ 416.1334 Termination due to death of recipient.

Eligibility for benefits ends with the month in which the recipient dies. Payments are terminated effective with the month after the month of death.

§ 416.1335 Termination due to continuous suspension.

We will terminate your eligibility for benefits following 12 consecutive months of benefit suspension for any reason beginning with the first month you were no longer eligible for regular SSI cash benefits, federally-administered State supplementation, special SSI cash benefits described in § 416.262, or special SSI eligibility status described in § 416.265. We will count the 12–month suspension period from the start of the first month that you are no longer eligible for SSI benefits (see § 416.1320(a)) or the start of the month after the month your special SSI eligibility status described in § 416.265 ended. This termination is effective with the start of the 13th month after the suspension began.

[60 FR 8153, Feb. 10, 1995; 64 FR 31975, June 15, 1999; 68 FR 53509, Sept. 11, 2003]

§ 416.1336 Notice of intended action affecting recipient's payment status.

(a) Advance written notice requirement. Advance written notice of intent to discontinue payment because of an event requiring suspension, reduction (see subpart D of this part), or termination of payments shall be given in all cases, prior to effectuation of the action, except where the Social Security Administration has factual information confirming the death of the recipient, e.g., as enumerated in § 404.704(b) of this chapter, or a report by a surviving spouse, a legal guardian, a parent or other close relative, or a landlord.

(b) Continuation of payment pending an appeal. The written notice of intent to suspend, reduce, or terminate payments shall allow 60 days after the date of receipt of the notice for the recipient to request the appropriate appellate review (see subpart N of this part). If appeal is filed within 10 days after the individual's receipt of the notice, the payment shall be continued or reinstated at the previously established payment level (subject to the effects of intervening events on the payment which are not appealed within 10 days of receipt of a required advance notice or which do not require advance notice, e.g., an increase in the benefit amount) until a decision on such initial appeal is issued, unless the individual specifically waives in writing his right to continuation of payment at the previously established level in accordance with paragraph (c) of this section. (See § 416.1337 for exceptions to the continuation of payment level.) Where the request for the appropriate appellate review is filed more than 10 days after the notice is received but within the 60–day period specified in § 416.1413 or § 416.1425 of this part, there shall be no right to continuation or reinstatement of payment at the previously established level unless good cause is established under the criteria specified in § 416.1411 of this part for failure to appeal within 10 days after receipt of the notice. For purposes of this paragraph, the date of receipt of the notice of intent to suspend, reduce, or terminate payments shall be presumed to be 5 days after the date on the face of such notice, unless there is a reasonable showing to the contrary.

(c) Waiver of right to continued payment. Notwithstanding any other provisions of this section, the recipient, in order to avoid the possibility of an overpayment of benefits, may waive continuation of payment at the previously established level (subject to intervening events which would have increased the benefit for the month in which the incorrect payment was made, in which case the higher amount shall be paid), after having received a full explanation of his rights. The request for waiver of continuation of payment shall be in writing, state that waiver action is being initiated solely at the recipient's request, and state that the recipient understands his right to receive continued payment at the previously established level.

[43 FR 18170, April 28, 1978; 65 FR 16815, March 30, 2000]

§ 416.1337 Exceptions to the continuation of previously established payment level.

(a) Multiple payments exception.

(1) Where it is determined that a recipient is receiving two or more regular monthly payments in one month, the Social Security Administration shall determine the correct payment amount and, as soon as practicable thereafter, send the recipient an advance written notice of intent to make subsequent payment in that amount. Payment for the following month shall be made in the correct amount, except as provided in paragraph (a)(3) of this section.

(2) The advance notice shall explain:

(i) That multiple payments were made in the one or more months identified in the notice;

(ii) The correct amount of monthly benefits that the recipient is eligible to receive; and

(iii) The recipient's appeal rights.

(3) If an appeal is filed within 10 days after receipt of the written notice of intent, the highest of the two or more check amounts, or the correct amount if higher (subject to the dollar limitation provisions), shall be continued until a decision on such initial level of appeal is issued. See § 416.1474 for criteria as to good cause for failure to file a timely appeal. For purposes of this paragraph, the date of receipt of the notice of intent shall be presumed to be 5 days after the date on the face of such notice, unless there is a reasonable showing to the contrary.

(4) The fact that a recipient is receiving multiple payments is established if the records of the Social Security Administration show that:

(i) Two or more checks are being sent to an individual under the same name or a common logical spelling variation of the name;

(ii) The social security number is the same or a pseudo number appears;

(iii) The checks are being sent to the same address;

(iv) The sex code for such individual is the same; and

(v) The date of birth for such individual is the same.

(b) Dollar limitation exception.

(1) Where it is determined that a recipient is receiving an erroneous monthly payment which exceeds the dollar limitation applicable to the recipient's payment category, as set forth in paragraph (b)(4) of this section, the Social Security Administration shall determine the correct payment amount and, as soon as practicable thereafter, send the recipient an advance written notice of intent to make subsequent payment in that amount. Payment for the following month shall be made in the correct amount, except as provided in paragraph (b)(3) of this section.

(2) The advance notice shall explain:

(i) That an erroneous monthly payment which exceeds the dollar limitation applicable to the recipient's payment category was made in the one or more months identified in the notice;

(ii) The correct amount of monthly benefits that the recipient is eligible to receive; and

(iii) The recipient's appeal rights.

(3) If an appeal is filed within 10 days after receipt of the written notice of the intent (see § 416.1474 for criteria as to good cause for failure to file a timely appeal), the amount of payment to be continued, pending decision on appeal, shall be determined as follows:

(i) Recipient in payment status. Where the recipient is in payment status, the payment shall be in the amount the recipient received in the month immediately preceding the month the dollar limitation was first exceeded (subject to intervening events which would have increased the benefit for the month in which the incorrect payment was made, in which case the higher amount shall be paid).

(ii) Recipient in nonpayment status. If the recipient's benefits were suspended in the month immediately preceding the month the dollar limitation was first exceeded, the payment shall be based on that amount which should have been paid in the month in which the incorrect payment was made. However, if the individual's benefits had been correctly suspended as provided in §§ 416.1320 through 416.1330 or § 416.1339 and they should have remained suspended but a benefit that exceeded the dollar limitation was paid, no further payment shall be made to him or her at this time and notice of the planned action shall not contain any provision regarding continuation of payment pending appeal.

For purposes of this paragraph, the date of receipt of the notice of planned action shall be presumed to be 5 days after the date on the face of such notice, unless there is a reasonable showing to the contrary.

(4) The payment categories and dollar limitations are as follows:

Payment Category and Dollar Limitation

(i) Federal supplemental security income benefit only—$200.

Recipients whose records indicate eligibility for Federal supplemental security income benefits for the month before the month the dollar limitation was first exceeded.

(ii) Federal supplemental security income benefit and optional supplementation, or optional supplementation only—$700

Recipients whose records indicate they were eligible for Federal supplemental security income benefits plus federally-administered optional supplementation, or eligible for federally-administered optional supplementation only, for the month before the month the dollar limitation was first exceeded.

(iii) Federal supplemental security income benefit and mandatory or other supplementation, or mandatory supplementation only—$2,000

Recipients whose records show eligibility for Federal supplemental security income benefits and federally-administered mandatory supplementation or essential person increment for the month before the month the dollar limitation was first exceeded. This category also includes those eligible for federally-administered mandatory supplementation only and those eligible for Federal supplemental security income benefits plus an essential person increment and federally-administered optional supplementation.

[43 FR 18170, April 28, 1978; 65 FR 40495, June 30, 2000; 68 FR 53509, Sept. 11, 2003]

§ 416.1338 If you are participating in an appropriate program of vocational rehabilitation services, employment services, or other support services.

(a) When may your benefits based on disability or blindness be continued? Your benefits based on disability or blindness may be continued after your impairment is no longer disabling, you are no longer blind as determined under § 416.986(a)(1), (a)(2) or (b), or your disability has ended as determined under § 416.987(b) and (e)(1) in an age–18 redetermination, if—

(1) You are participating in an appropriate program of vocational rehabilitation services, employment services, or other support services, as described in paragraphs (c) and (d) of this section;

(2) You began participating in the program before the date your disability or blindness ended; and

(3) We have determined under paragraph (e) of this section that your completion of the program, or your continuation in the program for a specified period of time, will increase the likelihood that you will not have to return to the disability or blindness benefit rolls.

(b) When will we stop your benefits? We generally will stop your benefits with the earliest of these months—

(1) The month in which you complete the program; or

(2) The month in which you stop participating in the program for any reason (see paragraph (d) of this section for what we mean by "participating" in the program); or

(3) The month in which we determine under paragraph (e) of this section that your continuing participation in the program will no longer increase the likelihood that you will not have to return to the disability or blindness benefit rolls.

Exception to paragraph (b): In no case will we stop your benefits with a month earlier than the second month after the month your disability or blindness ends, provided that you are otherwise eligible for benefits through such month.

(c) What is an appropriate program of vocational rehabilitation services, employment services, or other support services? An appropriate program of vocational rehabilitation services, employment services, or other support services means—

(1) A program that is carried out under an individual work plan with an employment network under the Ticket to Work and Self-Sufficiency Program under part 411 of this chapter;

(2) A program that is carried out under an individualized plan for employment with—

(i) A State vocational rehabilitation agency (i.e., a State agency administering or supervising the administration of a State plan approved under title I of the Rehabilitation Act of 1973, as amended (29 U.S.C. 720–751)) under 34 CFR part 361; or

(ii) An organization administering a Vocational Rehabilitation Services Project for American Indians with Disabilities authorized under section 121 of part C of title I of the Rehabilitation Act of 1973, as amended (29 U.S.C. 741);

(3) A program of vocational rehabilitation services, employment services, or other support services that is carried out under a similar, individualized written employment plan with—

(i) An agency of the Federal government (for example, the Department of Veterans Affairs);

(ii) A one-stop delivery system or specialized one-stop center described in section 134(c) of the Workforce Investment Act of 1998 (29 U.S.C. 2864(c)); or

(iii) Another provider of services approved by us; providers we may approve include, but are not limited to—

(A) A public or private organizations with expertise in the delivery or coordination of vocational rehabilitation services, employment services, or other support services; or

(B) A public, private or parochial school that provides or coordinates a program of vocational rehabilitation services, employment services, or other support services carried out under an individualized program or plan;

(4) An individualized education program developed under policies and procedures approved by the Secretary of Education for assistance to States for the education of individuals with disabilities under the Individuals with Disabilities Education Act, as amended (20 U.S.C. 1400 et seq.); you must be age 18 through age 21 for this provision to apply.

(d) When are you participating in the program?

(1) You are participating in a program described in paragraph (c)(1), (c)(2) or (c)(3) of this section when you are taking part in the activities and services outlined in your individual work plan, your individualized plan for employment, or your similar individualized written employment plan, as appropriate.

(2) If you are a student age 18 through 21 receiving services under an individualized education program described in paragraph (c)(4) of this section, you are participating in your program when you are taking part in the activities and services outlined in your program or plan.

(3) You are participating in your program under paragraph (d)(1) or (2) of this section during temporary interruptions in your program. For an interruption to be considered temporary, you must resume taking part in the activities and services outlined in your plan or program, as appropriate, no more than three months after the month the interruption occurred.

(e) How will we determine whether or not your completion of the program, or your continuation in the program for a specified period of time, will increase the likelihood that you will not have to return to the disability or blindness benefit rolls?

(1) We will determine that your completion of the program, or your continuation in the program for a specified period of time, will increase the likelihood that you will not have to return to the disability or blindness benefit rolls if your completion of or your continuation in the program will provide you with—

(i) Work experience (see § 416.965) so that you would more likely be able to do past relevant work (see § 416.960(b)), despite a possible future reduction in your residual functional capacity (see § 416.945); or

(ii) Education (see § 416.964) and/or skilled or semi-skilled work experience (see § 416.968) so that you would more likely be able to adjust to other work that exists in the national economy (see § 416.960(c)), despite a possible future reduction in your residual functional capacity (see § 416.945).

(2) If you are a student age 18 through age 21 participating in an individualized education program described in paragraph (c)(4) of this section, we will find that your completion of or continuation in the program will increase the likelihood that you will not have to return to the disability or blindness benefit rolls.

(3) If you are receiving transition services after having completed an individualized education program as described in paragraph (e)(2) of this section, we will determine that the transition services will increase the likelihood that you will not have to return to the disability benefit rolls if they meet the requirements in paragraph (e)(1) of this section.

[47 FR 31544, July 21, 1982, as amended at 47 FR 52693, Nov. 23, 1982; 51 FR 17618, May 14, 1986; 70 FR 36508, June 24, 2005]

§ 416.1339 Suspension due to flight to avoid criminal prosecution or custody or confinement after conviction, or due to violation of probation or parole.

For statute(s) affecting validity, see: 42 USCA §§ 902(a)(5), 1320a-8a, 1382-1382c, 1382h, and 1383.

(a) Basis for suspension. An individual is ineligible for SSI benefits for any month during which he or she is—

(1) Fleeing to avoid prosecution for a crime, or an attempt to commit a crime, which is a felony under the laws of the place from which the individual flees (or which, in the case of the State of New Jersey, is a high misdemeanor under the laws of that State); or

(2) Fleeing to avoid custody or confinement after conviction for a crime, or an attempt to commit a crime, which is a felony under the laws of the place from which the individual flees (or which, in the case of the State of New Jersey, is a high misdemeanor under the laws of that State); or

(3) Violating a condition of probation or parole imposed under Federal or State law.

(b) Suspension effective date.

(1) Suspension of benefit payments because an individual is a fugitive as described in paragraph (a)(1) or (a)(2) of this section or a probation or parole violator as described in paragraph (a)(3) of this section is effective with the first day of whichever of the following months is earlier—

(i) The month in which a warrant or order for the individual's arrest or apprehension, an order requiring the individual's appearance before a court or other appropriate tribunal (e.g., a parole board), or similar order is issued by a court or other duly authorized tribunal on the basis of an appropriate finding that the individual—

(A) Is fleeing, or has fled, to avoid prosecution as described in paragraph (a)(1) of this section;

(B) Is fleeing, or has fled, to avoid custody or confinement after conviction as described in paragraph (a)(2) of this section;

(C) Is violating, or has violated, a condition of his or her probation or parole as described in paragraph (a)(3) of this section; or

(ii) The first month during which the individual fled to avoid such prosecution, fled to avoid such custody or confinement after conviction, or violated a condition of his or her probation or parole, if indicated in such warrant or order, or in a decision by a court or other appropriate tribunal.

(2) An individual will not be considered to be ineligible for SSI benefits and benefit payments will not be suspended under this section for any month prior to August 1996.

(c) Resumption of payments. If benefits are otherwise payable, they will be resumed effective with the first month throughout which the individual is determined to be no longer fleeing to avoid such prosecution, fleeing to avoid such custody or confinement after conviction, or violating a condition of his or her probation or parole.

[65 FR 40495, June 30, 2000]

§ 416.1340 Penalty for making false or misleading statements or withholding information.

(a) Why would SSA penalize me? You will be subject to a penalty if:

(1) You make, or cause to be made, a statement or representation of a material fact, for use in determining any initial or continuing right to, or the amount of, monthly insurance benefits under title II or benefits or payments under title XVI, that you know or should know is false or misleading; or

(2) You make a statement or representation of a material fact for use as described in paragraph (a)(1) of this section with knowing disregard for the truth; or

(3) You omit from a statement or representation made for use as described in paragraph (a)(1) of this section, or otherwise withhold disclosure (for example, fail to come forward to notify us) of, a fact which you

know or should know is material to the determination of any initial or continuing right to, or the amount of, monthly insurance benefits under title II or benefits or payments under title XVI, if you know, or should know, that the statement or representation with such omission is false or misleading or that the withholding of such disclosure is misleading.

(b) What is the penalty? The penalty is ineligibility for cash benefits under title XVI (including State supplementary payments made by SSA according to § 416.2005) and nonpayment of any benefits under title II that we would otherwise pay you.

(c) How long will the penalty last? The penalty will last—

(1) Six consecutive months the first time we penalize you;

(2) Twelve consecutive months the second time we penalize you; and

(3) Twenty-four consecutive months the third or subsequent time we penalize you.

(d) Will this penalty affect any of my other government benefits? If we penalize you, the penalty will apply only to your eligibility for benefits under titles II and XVI (including State supplementary payments made by us according to § 416.2005). The penalty will not affect—

(1) Your eligibility for benefits that you would otherwise be eligible for under titles XVIII and XIX but for the imposition of the penalty; and

(2) The eligibility or amount of benefits payable under titles II or XVI to another person. For example, if you and your spouse are receiving title XVI benefits, those benefit payments to your spouse based on the benefit rate for a couple will not be affected because of the penalty. Your spouse will receive one half of the couple rate.

(e) How will SSA make its decision to penalize me? In order to impose a penalty on you, we must find that you knowingly (knew or should have known or acted with knowing disregard for the truth) made a false or misleading statement or omitted or failed to report a material fact if you knew, or should have known, that the omission or failure to disclose was misleading. We will base our decision to penalize you on the evidence and the reasonable inferences that can be drawn from that evidence, not on speculation or suspicion. Our decision to penalize you will be documented with the basis and rationale for that decision. In determining whether you knowingly made a false or misleading statement or omitted or failed to report a material fact so as to justify imposition of the penalty, we will consider all evidence in the record, including any physical, mental, educational, or linguistic limitations (including any lack of facility with the English language) which you may have had at the time. In determining whether you acted knowingly, we will also consider the significance of the false or misleading statement or omission or failure to disclose in terms of its likely impact on your benefits.

(f) What should I do if I disagree with SSA's initial determination to penalize me? If you disagree with our initial determination to impose a penalty, you have the right to request reconsideration of the penalty decision as explained in § 416.1407. We will give you a chance to present your case, including the opportunity for a face-to-face conference. If you request reconsideration of our initial determination to penalize you, you have the choice of a case review, informal conference, or formal conference, as described in § 416.1413(a) through (c). If you disagree with our reconsidered determination you have the right to follow the normal administrative and judicial review process by requesting a hearing before an administrative law judge, Appeals Council review and Federal court, review as explained in § 416.1400.

(g) When will the penalty period begin and end? Subject to the additional limitations noted in paragraphs (g)(1) and (g)(2) of this section, the penalty period will begin the first day of the month for which you would otherwise receive payment of benefits under title II or title XVI were it not for imposition of the penalty. Once a sanction begins, it will run continuously even if payments are intermittent. If more than one penalty has been imposed, but they have not yet run, the penalties will not run concurrently.

(1) If you do not request reconsideration of our initial determination to penalize you, the penalty period will begin no earlier than the first day of the second month following the month in which the time limit for requesting reconsideration ends. The penalty period will end on the last day of the final month of the penalty period. For example, if the time period for requesting reconsideration ends on January 10, a 6–month period of nonpayment begins on March 1 if you would otherwise be eligible to receive benefits for that month, and ends on August 31.

(2) If you request reconsideration of our initial determination to penalize you and the reconsidered determination does not change our original decision to penalize you, the penalty period will begin no earlier than the first day of the second month following the month we notify you of our reconsidered determination. The penalty period will end on the last day of the final month of the penalty period. For example, if we notify you of our reconsidered determination on August 31, 2001, and you are not otherwise eligible for payment of benefits at that time, but would again be eligible to receive payment of benefits on October 1, 2003, a 6–month period of nonpayment would begin on October 1, 2003 and end on March 31, 2004.

[65 FR 42286, July 10, 2000; 67 FR 20893, April 29, 2002; 71 FR 61409, Oct. 18, 2006]

SUBPART N—DETERMINATIONS, ADMINISTRATIVE REVIEW PROCESS, AND REOPENING OF DETERMINATIONS AND DECISIONS

Authority: Secs. 702(a)(5), 1631, and 1633 of the Social Security Act (42 U.S.C. 902(a)(5), 1383, and 1383b); sec. 202, Pub.L. 108–203, 118 Stat. 509 (42 U.S.C. 902 note).

Source: 45 FR 52096, Aug. 5, 1980; 50 FR 21438, May 24, 1985; 51 FR 8809, March 14, 1986; 51 FR 15472, April 24, 1986; 51 FR 28545, Aug. 8, 1986; 51 FR 44983, Dec. 16, 1986; 52 FR 4004, Feb. 9, 1987; 52 FR 27541, July 22, 1987; 57 FR 23058, June 1, 1992; 59 FR 8532, Feb. 23, 1994; 59 FR 41405, Aug. 12, 1994; 60 FR 34132, June 30, 1995; 62 FR 49440, Sept. 22, 1997; 66 FR 67081, Dec. 28, 2001; 71 FR 66867, Nov. 17, 2006, unless otherwise noted.

INTRODUCTION, DEFINITIONS, AND INITIAL DETERMINATIONS

§ 416.1400 Introduction.

(a) Explanation of the administrative review process. This subpart explains the procedures we follow in determining your rights under title XVI of the Social Security Act. The regulations describe the process of administrative review and explain your right to judicial review after you have taken all the necessary administrative steps. The administrative review process consists of several steps, which usually must be requested within certain time periods and in the following order:

(1) Initial determination. This is a determination we make about your eligibility or your continuing eligibility for benefits or about any other matter, as discussed in § 416.1402, that gives you a right to further review.

(2) Reconsideration. If you are dissatisfied with an initial determination, you may ask us to reconsider it.

(3) Hearing before an administrative law judge. If you are dissatisfied with the reconsideration determination, you may request a hearing before an administrative law judge.

(4) Appeals Council review. If you are dissatisfied with the decision of the administrative law judge, you may request that the Appeals Council review the decision.

(5) Federal court review. When you have completed the steps of the administrative review process listed in paragraphs (a)(1) through (a)(4) of this section, we will have made our final decision. If you are dissatisfied with our final decision, you may request judicial review by filing an action in a Federal district court.

(6) Expedited appeals process. At some time after your initial determination has been reviewed, if you have no dispute with our findings of fact and our application and interpretation of the controlling laws, but you believe that a part of the law is unconstitutional, you may use the expedited appeals process. This process permits you to go directly to a Federal district court so that the constitutional issue may be resolved.

(b) Nature of the administrative review process. In making a determination or decision in your case, we conduct the administrative review process in an informal, non-adversarial manner. Subject to certain time-frames at the hearing level (see § 416.1435) and the limitations on Appeals Council consideration of additional evidence (see § 416.1470), we will consider at each step of the review process any information you present as well as all the information in our records. You may present the information yourself or have someone represent you, including an attorney. If you are dissatisfied with our decision in the review process, but do not take the next step within the stated time period, you will lose your right to further administrative review and your right to judicial review, unless you can show us that there was good cause for your failure to make a timely request for review.

[51 FR 305, Jan. 3, 1986; 52 FR 4004, Feb. 9, 1987; 80 FR 14838, March 20, 2015; 81 FR 90995, Dec. 16, 2016]

§ 416.1401 Definitions.

As used in this subpart:

Date you receive notice means 5 days after the date on the notice, unless you show us that you did not receive it within the 5–day period.

Decision means the decision made by an administrative law judge or the Appeals Council.

Determination means the initial determination or the reconsidered determination.

Mass change means a State-initiated change in the level(s) of federally administered State supplementary payments applicable to all recipients of such payments, or to categories of such recipients, due, for example, to State legislative or executive action.

Preponderance of the evidence means such relevant evidence that as a whole shows that the existence of the fact to be proven is more likely than not.

Remand means to return a case for further review.

Substantial evidence means such relevant evidence as a reasonable mind might accept as adequate to support a conclusion.

Vacate means to set aside a previous action.

Waive means to give up a right knowingly and voluntarily.

We, us, or our refers to the Social Security Administration.

You or your refers to any person or the eligible spouse of any person claiming or receiving supplemental security income benefits.

[59 FR 43038, Aug. 22, 1994; 73 FR 76944, Dec. 18, 2008]

§ 416.1402 Administrative actions that are initial determinations.

Initial determinations are the determinations we make that are subject to administrative and judicial review. We will base our initial determination on the preponderance of the evidence. We will state the important facts and give the reasons for our conclusions in the initial determination. Initial determinations regarding supplemental security income benefits include, but are not limited to, determinations about—

(a) Your eligibility for, or the amount of, your supplemental security income benefits or your special SSI cash benefits under § 416.262, except actions solely involving transitions to eligibility between these types of benefits (see §§ 416.1403 (a)(13) and (a)(14)).

(b) Suspension, reduction, or termination of your SSI benefits or special SSI cash benefits (see §§ 416.261 and 416.262) or suspension or termination of your special SSI eligibility status (see §§ 416.264 through 416.269);

(c) Whether an overpayment of benefits must be repaid to us;

(d) Whether the payment of your benefits will be made, on your behalf, to a representative payee;

(e) Who will act as your payee if we determine that representative payment will be made;

(f) Imposing penalties for failing to report important information;

(g) Your drug addiction or alcoholism;

(h) Whether you are eligible for special SSI eligibility status under § 416.265;

(i) Your disability;

(j) Whether your completion of, or continuation for a specified period of time in, an appropriate program of vocational rehabilitation services, employment services, or other support services will increase the likelihood that you will not have to return to the disability or blindness benefit rolls, and thus, whether your benefits may be continued even though you are not disabled or blind;

(k) Whether or not you have a disabling impairment as defined in § 416.911;

(*l*) How much and to whom benefits due a deceased individual will be paid;

(m) A claim for benefits under § 416.351 based on alleged misinformation;

(n) Our calculation of the amount of change in your federally administered State supplementary payment amount (i.e., a reduction, suspension, or termination) which results from a mass change, as defined in § 416.1401; and

(*o*) Whether we were negligent in investigating or monitoring or failing to investigate or monitor your representative payee, which resulted in the misuse of benefits by your representative payee.

[45 FR 52096, Aug. 5, 1980, as amended at 46 FR 6908, Jan. 22, 1981; 47 FR 15325, April 9, 1982; 47 FR 31545, July 21, 1982; 49 FR 22275, May 29, 1984; 58 FR 52913, Oct. 13, 1993; 59 FR 41405, Aug. 12, 1994; 59 FR 43039, Aug. 22, 1994; 59 FR 44928, Aug. 31, 1994; 60 FR 8153, Feb. 10, 1995; 60 FR 14215, March 16, 1995; 69 FR 60240, Oct. 7, 2004; 70 FR 36509, June 24, 2005; 73 FR 76944, Dec. 18, 2008]

§ 416.1403 Administrative actions that are not initial determinations.

(a) Administrative actions that are not initial determinations may be reviewed by us, but they are not subject to the administrative review process provided by this subpart and they are not subject to judicial review. These actions include, but are not limited to, an action about—

(1) Presumptive disability or presumptive blindness;

(2) An emergency advance payment (as defined in § 416.520(b));

(3) Denial of a request to be made a representative payee;

(4) Denial of a request to use the expedited appeals process;

(5) Denial of a request to reopen a determination or a decision;

(6) The fee that may be charged or received by a person who has represented you in connection with a proceeding before us;

(7) Refusing to recognize, disqualifying, or suspending a person from acting as your representative in a proceeding before us (see §§ 416.1505 and 416.1545);

(8) Denying your request to extend the time period for requesting review of a determination or a decision;

(9) Determining whether (and the amount of) travel expenses incurred are reimbursable in connection with proceedings before us;

(10) Denying your request to readjudicate your claim and apply an Acquiescence Ruling;

(11) Determining whether an organization may collect a fee from you for expenses it incurs in serving as your representative payee (see § 416.640a);

(12) Declining under § 416.351(f) to make a determination on a claim for benefits based on alleged misinformation because one or more of the conditions specified in § 416.351(f) are not met;

(13) Transition to eligibility for special SSI cash benefits (§ 416.262) in a month immediately following a month for which you were eligible for regular SSI benefits;

(14) Transition to eligibility for regular SSI benefits in a month immediately following a month for which you were eligible for special SSI cash benefits (§ 416.262);

(15) The determination to reduce, suspend, or terminate your federally administered State supplementary payments due to a State-initiated mass change, as defined in § 416.1401, in the levels of such payments, except as provided in § 416.1402(n);

(16) Termination of Federal administration of State supplementary payments;

(17) Findings on whether we can collect an overpayment by using the Federal income tax refund offset procedure (see § 416.583);

(18) Determining whether we will refer information about your overpayment to a consumer reporting agency (see §§ 416.590 and 422.305 of this chapter);

(19) Determining whether we will refer your overpayment to the Department of the Treasury for collection by offset against Federal payments due you (see §§ 416.590 and 422.310 of this chapter);

(20) Determining whether we will order your employer to withhold from your disposable pay to collect an overpayment you received under title XVI of the Social Security Act (see part 422, subpart E, of this chapter);

(21) Determining when provisional benefits are payable, the amount of the provisional benefit payable, and when provisional benefits terminate (see § 416.999c);

(22) Determining whether to select your claim for the quick disability determination process under § 416.1019;

(23) The removal of your claim from the quick disability determination process under § 416.1019;

(24) Starting or discontinuing a continuing disability review;

(25) Issuing a receipt in response to your report of a change in your earned income; and

(26) Determining whether a non-attorney representative is eligible to receive direct fee payment as described in § 416.1517 of this part.

(b) We send some notices of actions that are not initial determinations:

(1) If you receive an emergency advance payment; presumptive disability or presumptive blindness payment, or provisional payment, we will provide a notice explaining the nature and conditions of the payments.

(2) If you receive presumptive disability or presumptive blindness payments, or provisional payments, we shall send you a notice when those payments are exhausted.

(3) If there is a termination of Federal administration of State supplementary payments.

[51 FR 8809, March 14, 1986; 55 FR 1020, Jan. 11, 1990; 55 FR 4423, Feb. 8, 1990; 57 FR 23058, June 1, 1992; 59 FR 41405, Aug. 12, 1994; 59 FR 43039, Aug. 22, 1994; 59 FR 44928, Aug. 31, 1994; 62 FR 49440, Sept. 22, 1997; 66 FR 67081, Dec. 28, 2001; 68 FR 74184, Dec. 23, 2003; 70 FR 57146, Sept. 30, 2005; 71 FR 16461, March 31, 2006; 71 FR 66859, 66867, Nov. 17, 2006; 72 FR 51178, Sept. 6, 2007; 76 FR 45194, July 28, 2011; 76 FR 80247, Dec. 23, 2011; 80 FR 399, 400, Jan. 6, 2015]

§ 416.1404 Notice of the initial determination.

(a) We will mail a written notice of our initial determination to you at your last known address. The written notice will explain in simple and clear language what we have determined and the reasons for and the effect of our determination. If our determination involves a determination of disability that is in whole or in part unfavorable to you, our written notice also will contain in understandable language a statement of the case setting forth the evidence on which our determination is based. The notice also will inform you of your right to reconsideration. We will not mail a notice if the beneficiary's entitlement to benefits has ended because of his or her death.

(b) If our initial determination is that we must suspend, reduce or terminate your benefits, the notice will also tell you that you have a right to a reconsideration before the determination takes effect (see § 416.1336).

[51 FR 305, Jan. 3, 1986; 72 FR 51179, Sept. 6, 2007]

§ 416.1405 Effect of an initial determination.

An initial determination is binding unless you request a reconsideration within the stated time period, or we revise the initial determination.

[51 FR 305, Jan. 3, 1986]

§ 416.1406 Testing modifications to the disability determination procedures.

(a) Applicability and scope. Notwithstanding any other provision in this part or part 422 of this chapter, we are establishing the procedures set out in this section to test modifications to our disability determination process. These modifications will enable us to test, either individually or in one or more combinations, the effect of: having disability claim managers assume primary responsibility for processing an application for SSI payments based on disability; providing persons who have applied for benefits based on disability with the opportunity for an interview with a decisionmaker when the decisionmaker finds that the evidence in the file is insufficient to make a fully favorable determination or requires an initial determination denying the claim; having a single decisionmaker make the initial determination with assistance from medical consultants, where appropriate; and eliminating the reconsideration step in the administrative review process and having a claimant who is dissatisfied with the initial determination request a hearing before an administrative law judge. The model procedures we test will be designed to provide us with information regarding the effect of these procedural modifications and enable us to decide whether and to what degree the disability determination process would be improved if they were implemented on a national level.

(b) Procedures for cases included in the tests. Prior to commencing each test or group of tests in selected site(s), we will publish a notice in the Federal Register. The notice will describe which model or combinations of models we intend to test, where the specific test site(s) will be, and the duration of the test(s). The individuals who participate in the test(s) will be randomly assigned to a test group in each site where the tests are conducted. Paragraph (b)(1) through (4) of this section lists descriptions of each model.

(1) In the disability claim manager model, when you file an application for SSI payments based on disability, a disability claim manager will assume primary responsibility for the processing of your claim. The disability claim manager will be the focal point for your contacts with us during the claims intake process and until an initial determination on your claim is made. The disability claim manager will explain the SSI disability program to you, including the definition of disability and how we determine whether you meet all the requirements for SSI payments based on disability. The disability claim manager will explain what you will be asked to do throughout the claims process and how you can obtain information or assistance through him or her. The disability claim manager will also provide you with information regarding your right to representation, and he or she will provide you with appropriate referral sources for representation. The disability claim manager may be either a State agency employee or a Federal employee. In some instances, the disability claim manager may be assisted by other individuals.

(2) In the single decisionmaker model, the decisionmaker will make the disability determination and may also determine whether the other conditions of eligibility for SSI payments based on disability are met. The decisionmaker will make the disability determination after any appropriate consultation with a medical or psychological consultant. The medical or psychological consultant will not be required to sign the disability determination forms we use to have the State agency certify the determination of disability to us (see § 416.1015). However, before an initial determination is made in any case where there is evidence which indicates the existence of a mental impairment, the decisionmaker will make every reasonable effort to ensure that a qualified psychiatrist or psychologist has completed the medical portion of the case review and any applicable residual functional capacity assessment pursuant to our existing procedures (see § 416.1017). Similarly, in making an initial determination with respect to the disability of a child under age 18 claiming SSI payments based on disability, the decisionmaker will make reasonable efforts to ensure that a qualified pediatrician, or other individual who specializes in a field of medicine appropriate to the child's impairment(s), evaluates the claim of such child (see § 416.903(f)). In some instances the decisionmaker may be the disability claim manager described in paragraph (b)(1) of this section. When the decisionmaker is a State agency employee, a team of individuals that includes a Federal employee will determine whether the other conditions of eligibility for SSI payments are met.

(3) In the predecision interview model, if the decisionmaker(s) finds that the evidence in your file is insufficient to make a fully favorable determination or requires an initial determination denying your claim, a predecision notice will be mailed to you. The notice will tell you that, before the decisionmaker(s) makes an initial determination about whether you are disabled, you may request a predecision interview with the decisionmaker(s). The notice will also tell you that you may also submit additional evidence. You must request a predecision interview within 10 days after the date you receive the predecision notice. You must also submit any additional evidence within 10 days after the date you receive the predecision notice. If you request a predecision interview, the decisionmaker(s) will conduct the predecision interview in person, by videoconference, or by telephone as the decisionmaker(s) determines is appropriate under the circumstances. If you make a late request for a predecision interview, or submit additional evidence late, but show in writing that you had good cause under the standards in § 416.1411 for missing the deadline, the decisionmaker(s) will extend the deadline. If you do not request the predecision interview or if you do not appear for a scheduled predecision interview and do not submit additional evidence, or if you do not respond to our attempts to communicate with you, the decisionmaker(s) will make an initial determination based upon the evidence in your file. If you identify additional evidence during the predecision interview, which was previously not available, the decisionmaker(s) will advise you to submit the evidence. If you are unable to do so, the decisionmaker(s) may assist you in obtaining it. The decisionmaker(s) also will advise you of the specific timeframes you have for submitting any additional evidence identified during the predecision interview. If you have no treating source(s) (see § 416.902), or your treating source(s) is unable or unwilling to provide the necessary evidence, or there is a conflict in the evidence that cannot be resolved through evidence from your treating source(s), the decisionmaker(s) may arrange a consultative examination or resolve conflicts according to existing procedures (see § 416.919a). If you attend the predecision interview, or do not attend the predecision interview but you submit additional evidence, the decisionmaker(s) will make an initial determination based on the evidence in your file, including the additional evidence you submit or the evidence obtained as a result of the predecision notice or interview, or both.

(4) In the reconsideration elimination model, we will modify the disability determination process by eliminating the reconsideration step of the administrative

review process. If you receive an initial determination on your claim for SSI payments based on disability, and you are dissatisfied with the determination, we will notify you that you may request a hearing before an administrative law judge.

[51 FR 15473, April 24, 1986; 60 FR 20026, April 24, 1995; 73 FR 2416, Jan. 15, 2008; 73 FR 10381, Feb. 27, 2008; 76 FR 24812, May 3, 2011; 82 FR 5883, Jan. 18, 2017]

RECONSIDERATION

§ 416.1407 Reconsideration—general.

Reconsideration is the first step in the administrative review process that we provide if you are dissatisfied with the initial determination. If you are dissatisfied with our reconsideration determination, you may request a hearing before an administrative law judge.

[51 FR 305, Jan. 3, 1986]

§ 416.1408 Parties to a reconsideration.

(a) Who may request a reconsideration. If you are dissatisfied with the initial determination, you may request that we reconsider it. In addition, a person who shows in writing that his or her rights may be adversely affected by the initial determination may request a reconsideration.

(b) Who are parties to a reconsideration. After a request for the reconsideration, you and any person who shows in writing that his or her rights are adversely affected by the initial determination will be parties to the reconsideration.

§ 416.1409 How to request reconsideration.

(a) We shall reconsider an initial determination if you or any other party to the reconsideration files a written request at one of our offices within 60 days after the date you receive notice of the initial determination (or within the extended time period if we extend the time as provided in paragraph (b) of this section).

(b) Extension of time to request a reconsideration. If you want a reconsideration of the initial determination but do not request one in time, you may ask us for more time to request a reconsideration. Your request for an extension of time must be in writing and it must give the reasons why the request for reconsideration was not filed within the stated time period. If you show us that you had good cause for missing the deadline, we will extend the time period. To determine whether good cause exists, we use the standards explained in § 416.1411.

§ 416.1411 Good cause for missing the deadline to request review.

(a) In determining whether you have shown that you have good cause for missing a deadline to request review we consider—

(1) What circumstances kept you from making the request on time;

(2) Whether our action misled you;

(3) Whether you did not understand the requirements of the Act resulting from amendments to the Act, other legislation, or court decisions; and

(4) Whether you had any physical, mental, educational, or linguistic limitations (including any lack of facility with the English language) which prevented you from filing a timely request or from understanding or knowing about the need to file a timely request for review.

(b) Examples of circumstances where good cause may exist include, but are not limited to, the following situations:

(1) You were seriously ill and were prevented from contacting us in person, in writing, or through a friend, relative, or other person.

(2) There was a death or serious illness in your immediate family.

(3) Important records were destroyed or damaged by fire or other accidental cause.

(4) You were trying very hard to find necessary information to support your claim but did not find the information within the stated time periods.

(5) You asked us for additional information explaining our action within the time limit, and within 60 days of receiving the explanation you requested reconsideration or a hearing, or within 30 days of receiving the explanation you requested Appeals Council review or filed a civil suit.

(6) We gave you incorrect or incomplete information about when and how to request administrative review or to file a civil suit.

(7) You did not receive notice of the initial determination or decision.

(8) You sent the request to another Government agency in good faith within the time limit and the request did not reach us until after the time period had expired.

(9) Unusual or unavoidable circumstances exist, including the circumstances described in paragraph (a)(4) of this section, which show that you could not have known of the need to file timely, or which prevented you from filing timely.

[59 FR 1637, Jan. 12, 1994]

§ 416.1413 Reconsideration procedures.

If you request reconsideration, we will give you a chance to present your case. How you can present your case depends upon the issue involved and whether you are asking us to reconsider an initial determination on an application or an initial determination on a suspension, reduction or termination of benefits. The methods of reconsideration include the following:

(a) Case review. We will give you and the other parties to the reconsideration an opportunity to review the evidence in our files and then to present oral and written evidence to us. We will then make a decision based on all of this evidence. The official who reviews the case will make the reconsidered determination.

(b) Informal conference. In addition to following the procedures of a case review, an informal conference allows you and the other parties to the reconsideration an opportunity to present witnesses. A summary record of this proceeding will become part of the case record. The official who conducts the informal conference will make the reconsidered determination.

(c) Formal conference. In addition to following the procedures of an informal conference, a formal conference allows you and the other parties to a reconsideration an opportunity to request us to subpoena adverse witnesses and relevant documents and to cross-examine adverse witnesses. A summary record of this proceeding will become a part of the case record. The official who conducts the formal conference will make the reconsidered determination.

(d) Disability hearing. If you have been receiving supplemental security income benefits because you are blind or disabled and you request reconsideration of an initial or revised determination that, based on medical factors, you are not now blind or disabled, we will give you and the other parties to the reconsideration an opportunity for a disability hearing. (See §§ 416.1414 through 416.1418.)

[51 FR 305, Jan. 3, 1986]

§ 416.1413a Reconsiderations of initial determinations on applications.

The method of reconsideration we will use when you appeal an initial determination on your application for benefits depends on the issue involved in your case.

(a) Nonmedical issues. If you challenge our finding on a nonmedical issue, we shall offer you a case review or an informal conference, and will reach our reconsidered determination on the basis of the review you select.

(b) Medical issues. If you challenge our finding on a medical issue (even if you received payments because we presumed you were blind or disabled), we shall reach our reconsidered determination on the basis of a case review.

[51 FR 305, Jan. 3, 1986]

§ 416.1413b Reconsideration procedures for post-eligibility claims.

If you are eligible for supplemental security income benefits and we notify you that we are going to suspend, reduce or terminate your benefits, you can appeal our determination within 60 days of the date you receive our notice. The 60–day period may be extended if you have good cause for an extension of time under the conditions stated in § 416.1411(b). If you appeal a suspension, reduction, or termination of benefits, the method of reconsideration we will use depends on the issue in your case. If the issue in your case is that you are no longer blind or disabled for medical reasons, you will receive an opportunity for a disability hearing. If any other issue is involved, you have the choice of a case review, informal conference or formal conference.

[51 FR 305, Jan. 3, 1986]

§ 416.1413c Arrangement for conferences.

(a) As soon as we receive a request for a formal or informal conference, we shall set the time, date and place for the conference.

(b) We shall send you and any other parties to the reconsideration a written notice about the conference (either by mailing it to your last known address or by personally serving you with it) at least 10 days before the conference. However, we may hold the conference sooner if we all agree. We will not send written notice of the time, date, and place of the conference if you waive your right to receive it.

(c) We shall schedule the conference within 15 days after you request it, but, at our discretion or at your request, we will delay the conference if we think the delay will ensure that the conference is conducted efficiently and properly.

(d) We shall hold the conference at one of our offices, by telephone or in person, whichever you prefer. We will hold the conference elsewhere in person if you show circumstances that make this arrangement reasonably necessary.

[51 FR 305, Jan. 3, 1986]

§ 416.1414 Disability hearing—general.

(a) Availability. We will provide you with an opportunity for a disability hearing if:

(1) You have been receiving supplemental security income benefits based on a medical impairment that renders you blind or disabled;

(2) We have made an initial or revised determination based on medical factors that you are not blind or disabled because your impairment:

(i) Has ceased;

(ii) Did not exist; or

(iii) Is no longer disabling; and

(3) You make a timely request for reconsideration of the initial or revised determination.

(b) Scope. The disability hearing will address only the initial or revised determination, based on medical factors, that you are not now blind or disabled. Any other issues you raise in connection with your request for reconsideration will be reviewed in accordance with the reconsideration procedures described in § 416.1413 (a) through (c).

(c) Time and place—

(1) General. Either the State agency or the Associate Commissioner for Disability Determinations or his or her delegate, as appropriate, will set the time and place of your disability hearing. We will send you a notice of the time and place of your disability hearing at least 20 days before the date of the hearing. You may be expected to travel to your disability hearing. (See §§ 416.1495–416.1499 regarding reimbursement for travel expenses.)

(2) Change of time or place. If you are unable to travel or have some other reason why you cannot attend your disability hearing at the scheduled time or place, you should request at the earliest possible date that the time or place of your hearing be changed. We will change the time or place if there is good cause for doing so under the standards in § 416.1436 (c) and (d).

(d) Combined issues. If a disability hearing is available to you under paragraph (a) of this section, and you file a new application for benefits while your request for reconsideration is still pending, we may combine the issues on both claims for the purpose of the disability hearing and issue a combined initial/reconsidered determination which is binding with respect to the common issues on both claims.

(e) Definition. For purposes of the provisions regarding disability hearings (§§ 416.1414 through 416.1418) we, us, or our means the Social Security Administration or the State agency.

[51 FR 305, Jan. 3, 1986; 51 FR 8809, March 14, 1986; 71 FR 10432, March 1, 2006]

§ 416.1415 Disability hearing—disability hearing officers.

(a) General. Your disability hearing will be conducted by a disability hearing officer who was not involved in making the determination you are appealing. The disability hearing officer will be an experienced disability examiner, regardless of whether he or she is appointed by a State agency or by the Associate Commissioner for Disability Determinations or his or her delegate, as described in paragraphs (b) and (c) of this section.

(b) State agency hearing officers—

(1) Appointment of State agency hearing officers. If a State agency made the initial or revised determination that you are appealing, the disability hearing officer who conducts your disability hearing may be appointed by a State agency. If the disability hearing officer is appointed by a State agency, that individual will be employed by an adjudicatory unit of the State agency other than the adjudicatory unit which made the determination you are appealing.

(2) State agency defined. For purposes of this subpart, State agency means the adjudicatory component in the State which issues disability determinations.

(c) Federal hearing officers. The disability hearing officer who conducts your disability hearing will be appointed by the Associate Commissioner for Disability Determinations or his or her delegate if:

(1) A component of our office other than a State agency made the determination you are appealing; or

(2) The State agency does not appoint a disability hearing officer to conduct your disability hearing under paragraph (b) of this section.

[51 FR 305, Jan. 3, 1986; 71 FR 10432, March 1, 2006]

§ 416.1416 Disability hearing—procedures.

(a) General. The disability hearing will enable you to introduce evidence and present your views to a disability hearing officer if you are dissatisfied with an initial or revised determination, based on medical factors, that you are not now blind or disabled, as described in § 416.1414(a)(2).

(b) Your procedural rights. We will advise you that you have the following procedural rights in connection with the disability hearing process:

(1) You may request that we assist you in obtaining pertinent evidence for your disability hearing and, if necessary, that we issue a subpoena to compel the production of certain evidence or testimony. We will follow subpoena procedures similar to those described in § 416.1450(d) for the administrative law judge hearing process;

(2) You may have a representative at the hearing appointed under subpart O of this part, or you may represent yourself;

(3) You or your representative may review the evidence in your case file, either on the date of your hearing or at an earlier time at your request, and present additional evidence;

(4) You may present witnesses and question any witnesses at the hearing; and

(5) You may waive your right to appear at the hearing. If you do not appear at the hearing, the disability hearing officer will prepare and issue a written reconsidered determination based on the information in your case file.

(c) Case preparation. After you request reconsideration, your case file will be reviewed and prepared for the hearing. This review will be conducted in the component of our office (including a State agency) that made the initial or revised determination, by personnel who were not involved in making the initial or revised determination. Any new evidence you submit in connection with your request for reconsideration will be included in this review. If necessary, further development of evidence, including arrangements for medical examinations, will be undertaken by this component. After the case file is prepared for the hearing, it will be forwarded by this component to the disability hearing officer for a hearing. If necessary, the case file may be sent back to this component at any time prior to the issuance of the reconsidered determination for additional development. Under paragraph (d) of this section, this component has the authority to issue a favorable reconsidered determination at any time in its development process.

(d) Favorable reconsidered determination without a hearing. If the evidence in your case file supports a finding that you are now blind or disabled, either the component that prepares your case for hearing under paragraph (c) or the disability hearing officer will issue a written favorable reconsidered determination, even if a disability hearing has not yet been held.

(e) Opportunity to submit additional evidence after the hearing. At your request, the disability hearing officer may allow up to 15 days after your disability hearing for receipt of evidence which is not available at the hearing, if:

(1) The disability hearing officer determines that the evidence has a direct bearing on the outcome of the hearing; and

(2) The evidence could not have been obtained before the hearing.

(f) Opportunity to review and comment on evidence obtained or developed by us after the hearing. If, for any reason, additional evidence is obtained or developed by us after your disability hearing, and all evidence taken together can be used to support a reconsidered determination that is unfavorable to you with regard to the medical factors of eligibility, we will notify you, in writing, and give you an opportunity to review and comment on the additional evidence. You will be given 10 days from the date you receive our notice to submit your comments (in writing or, in appropriate cases, by telephone), unless there is good cause for granting you additional time, as illustrated by the examples in § 416.1411(b). Your comments will be considered before a reconsidered determination is issued. If you believe that it is necessary to have further opportunity for a hearing with respect to the additional evidence, a supplementary hearing may be scheduled at your request. Otherwise, we will ask for your written comments on the additional evidence, or, in appropriate cases, for your telephone comments.

[51 FR 306, Jan. 3, 1986]

§ 416.1417 Disability hearing—disability hearing officer's reconsidered determination.

(a) General. The disability hearing officer who conducts your disability hearing will prepare and will issue a written reconsidered determination, unless:

(1) The disability hearing officer sends the case back for additional development by the component that prepared the case for the hearing, and that component issues a favorable determination, as permitted by § 416.1416(c);

(2) It is determined that you are engaging in substantial gainful activity and that you are therefore not disabled; or

(3) The reconsidered determination prepared by the disability hearing officer is reviewed under § 416.1418.

(b) Content. The disability hearing officer's reconsidered determination will give the findings of fact and the reasons for the reconsidered determination. The disability hearing officer must base the reconsidered determination on the preponderance of the evidence offered at the disability hearing or otherwise included in your case file.

(c) Notice. We will mail you and the other parties a notice of reconsidered determination in accordance with § 416.1422.

(d) Effect. The disability hearing officer's reconsidered determination, or, if it is changed under § 416.1418, the reconsidered determination that is issued by the Associate Commissioner for Disability Determinations or his or her delegate, is binding in accordance with § 416.1421, subject to the exceptions specified in that section.

[51 FR 306, Jan. 3, 1986; 71 FR 10432, March 1, 2006; 73 FR 76944, Dec. 18, 2008]

§ 416.1418 Disability hearing—review of the disability hearing officer's reconsidered determination before it is issued.

(a) General. The Associate Commissioner for Disability Determinations or his or her delegate may select a sample of disability hearing officers' reconsidered determinations, before they are issued, and review any such case to determine its correctness on any grounds he or she deems appropriate. The Associate Commissioner or his or her delegate shall review any case within the sample if:

(1) There appears to be an abuse of discretion by the hearing officer;

(2) There is an error of law; or

(3) The action, findings or conclusions of the disability hearing officer are not supported by substantial evidence.

Note to paragraph (a): If the review indicates that the reconsidered determination prepared by the disability hearing officer is correct, it will be dated and issued immediately upon completion of the review. If the reconsidered determination prepared by the disability hearing officer is found by the Associate Commissioner or his or her delegate to be deficient, it will be changed as described in paragraph (b) of this section.

(b) Methods of correcting deficiencies in the disability hearing officer's reconsidered determination. If the reconsidered determination prepared by the disability hearing officer is found by the Associate Commissioner for Disability Determinations or his or her delegate to be deficient, the Associate Commissioner or his or her delegate will take appropriate action to assure that the deficiency is corrected before a reconsidered determination is issued. The action taken by the Associate Commissioner or his or her delegate will take one of two forms:

(1) The Associate Commissioner or his or her delegate may return the case file either to the component responsible for preparing the case for hearing or to the disability hearing officer, for appropriate further action; or

(2) The Associate Commissioner or his or her delegate may issue a written reconsidered determination which corrects the deficiency.

(c) Further action on your case if it is sent back by the Associate Commissioner for Disability Determinations or his or her delegate either to the component that prepared your case for hearing or to the disability hearing officer. If the Associate Commissioner for Disability Determinations or his or her delegate sends your case back either to the component responsible for preparing the case for hearing or to the disability hearing officer for appropriate further action, as provided in paragraph (b)(1) of this section, any additional proceedings in your case will be governed by the disability hearing procedures described in § 416.1416(f) or if your case is returned to the disability hearing officer and an unfavorable determination is indicated, a supplementary hearing may be scheduled for you before a reconsidered determination is reached in your case.

(d) Opportunity to comment before the Associate Commissioner for Disability Determinations or his or her delegate issues a reconsidered determination that is unfavorable to you. If the Associate Commissioner for Disability Determinations or his or her delegate proposes to issue a reconsidered determination as described in paragraph (b)(2) of this section, and that reconsidered determination is unfavorable to you, he or she will send you a copy of the proposed reconsidered determination with an explanation of the reasons for it, and will give you an opportunity to submit written comments before it is issued. At your request, you will also be given an opportunity to inspect the pertinent materials in your case file, including the reconsidered determination prepared by the disability hearing officer, before submitting your comments. You will be given 10 days from the date you receive the Associate Commissioner's notice of proposed action to submit your written comments, unless additional time is necessary to provide access to the pertinent file materials or there is good cause for providing more time, as illustrated by the examples in § 416.1411(b). The Associate Commissioner or his or her delegate will consider your comments before taking any further action on your case.

[51 FR 306, Jan. 3, 1986; 71 FR 10432, March 1, 2006]

§ 416.1419 Notice of another person's request for reconsideration.

If any other person files a request for reconsideration of the initial determination in your case, we shall notify you at your last known address before we reconsider the initial determination. We shall also give you an opportunity to present any evidence you think helpful to the reconsidered determination.

[51 FR 306, Jan. 3, 1986]

§ 416.1420 Reconsidered determination.

After you or another person requests a reconsideration, we will review the evidence we considered in making the initial determination and any other evidence we receive. We will make our determination based on the preponderance of the evidence. The person who makes the reconsidered determination will have had no prior involvement with the initial determination.

[51 FR 306, Jan. 3, 1986; 73 FR 76945, Dec. 18, 2008]

§ 416.1421 Effect of a reconsidered determination.

The reconsidered determination is binding unless—

(a) You or any other party to the reconsideration requests a hearing before an administrative law judge within the stated time period and a decision is made;

(b) The expedited appeals process is used; or

(c) The reconsidered determination is revised.

[51 FR 306, 307, Jan. 3, 1986]

§ 416.1422 Notice of a reconsidered determination.

We shall mail a written notice of the reconsidered determination to the parties at their last known address. We shall state the specific reasons for the determination and tell you and any other parties of the right to a hearing. If it is appropriate, we will also tell you and any other parties how to use the expedited appeals process.

[51 FR 306, Jan. 3, 1986]

EXPEDITED APPEALS PROCESS

§ 416.1423 Expedited appeals process—general.

By using the expedited appeals process you may go directly to a Federal district court without first completing the administrative review process that is generally required before the court will hear your case.

§ 416.1424 When the expedited appeals process may be used.

You may use the expedited appeals process if all of the following requirements are met:

(a) We have made an initial and a reconsidered determination; an administrative law judge has made a hearing decision; or Appeals Council review has been requested, but a final decision has not been issued.

(b) You are a party to the reconsidered determination or the hearing decision.

(c) You have submitted a written request for the expedited appeals process.

(d) You have claimed, and we agree, that the only factor preventing a favorable determination or decision is a provision in the law that you believe is unconstitutional.

(e) If you are not the only party, all parties to the determination or decision agree to request the expedited appeals process.

§ 416.1425 How to request expedited appeals process.

(a) Time of filing request. You may request the expedited appeals process—

(1) Within 60 days after the date you receive notice of the reconsidered determination (or within the extended time period if we extend the time as provided in paragraph (c) of this section);

(2) At any time after you have filed a timely request for a hearing but before you receive notice of the administrative law judge's decision;

(3) Within 60 days after the date you receive a notice of the administrative law judge's decision or dismissal (or within the extended time period if we extend the time as provided in paragraph (c) of this section); or

(4) At any time after you have filed a timely request for Appeals Council review, but before you receive notice of the Appeals Council's action.

(b) Place of filing request. You may file a written request for the expedited appeals process at one of our offices.

(c) Extension of time to request expedited appeals process. If you want to use the expedited appeals process but do not request it within the stated time period, you may ask for more time to submit your request. Your request for an extension of time must be in writing and it must give the reasons why the request for the expedited appeals process was not filed within the stated time period. If you show that you had good cause for missing the deadline, the time period will be extended. To determine whether good cause exists, we use the standards explained in § 416.1411.

§ 416.1426 Agreement in expedited appeals process.

If you meet all the requirements necessary for the use of the expedited appeals process, our authorized representative shall prepare an agreement. The agreement must be signed by you, by every other party to the determination or decision, and by our authorized representative. The agreement must provide that—

(a) The facts in your claim are not in dispute;

(b) The sole issue in dispute is whether a provision of the Act that applies to your case is unconstitutional;

(c) Except for your belief that a provision of the Act is unconstitutional, you agree with our interpretation of the law;

(d) If the provision of the Act that you believe is unconstitutional were not applied to your case, your claim would be allowed; and

(e) Our determination or the decision is final for the purpose of seeking judicial review.

§ 416.1427 Effect of expedited appeals process agreement.

After an expedited appeals process agreement is signed, you will not need to complete the remaining steps of the administrative review process. Instead, you may file an action in a Federal district court within 60 days after the date you receive notice (a signed copy of the agreement will be mailed to you and will constitute notice) that the agreement has been signed by our authorized representative.

[49 FR 46370, Nov. 26, 1984]

§ 416.1428 Expedited appeals process request that does not result in agreement.

If you do not meet all of the requirements necessary to use the expedited appeals process, we shall tell you that your request to use this process is denied and that your request will be considered as a request for a hearing, or Appeals Council review, whichever is appropriate.

HEARING BEFORE AN ADMINISTRATIVE LAW JUDGE

§ 416.1429 Hearing before an administrative law judge-general.

If you are dissatisfied with one of the determinations or decisions listed in § 416.1430, you may request a hearing. The Deputy Commissioner for Disability Adjudication and Review, or his or her delegate, will appoint an administrative law judge to conduct the hearing. If circumstances warrant, the Deputy Commissioner, or his or her delegate, may assign your case to another administrative law judge. At the hearing, you may appear in person, by video teleconferencing, or, under certain extraordinary circumstances, by telephone. You may submit new evidence (subject to the provisions of § 416.1435), examine the evidence used in making the determination or decision under review, and present and question witnesses. The administrative law judge who conducts the hearing may ask you questions. He or she will issue a decision based on the preponderance of the evidence in the hearing record. If you waive your right to appear at the hearing, in person, by video teleconferencing, or by telephone, the administrative law judge will make a decision based on the preponderance of the evidence that is in the file and, subject to the provisions of § 416.1435, any new evidence that may have been submitted for consideration.

[51 FR 307, Jan. 3, 1986; 68 FR 5219, Feb. 3, 2003; 68 FR 69009, Dec. 11, 2003; 79 FR 35933, June 25, 2014; 81 FR 90995, Dec. 16, 2016]

§ 416.1430 Availability of a hearing before an administrative law judge.

(a) You or another party may request a hearing before an administrative law judge if we have made—

(1) A reconsidered determination;

(2) A reconsideration of a revised determination of an initial or reconsidered determination that involves a suspension, reduction or termination of benefits;

(3) A revised initial determination or revised reconsidered determination that does not involve a suspension, reduction or termination of benefits; or

(4) A revised decision based on evidence not included in the record on which the prior decision was based.

(b) We will hold a hearing only if you or another party to the hearing file a written request for a hearing.

(c) [Reserved by 76 FR 24812]

[51 FR 307, Jan. 3, 1986; 73 FR 2416, Jan. 15, 2008; 73 FR 10381, Feb. 27, 2008; 76 FR 24812, May 3, 2011]

§ 416.1432 Parties to a hearing before an administrative law judge.

(a) Who may request a hearing. You may request a hearing if a hearing is available under § 416.1430. In addition, a person who shows in writing that his or her rights may be adversely affected by the decision may request a hearing.

(b) Who are parties to a hearing. After a request for a hearing is made, you, the other parties to the initial, reconsidered, or revised determination, and any other person who shows in writing that his or her rights may be adversely affected by the hearing, are parties to the hearing. In addition, any other person may be made a party to the hearing if his or her rights may be adversely affected by the decision, and we notify the person to appear at the hearing or to present evidence supporting his or her interest.

[51 FR 307, Jan. 3, 1986; 75 FR 39160, July 8, 2010]

§ 416.1433 How to request a hearing before an administrative law judge.

(a) Written request. You may request a hearing by filing a written request. You should include in your request—

(1) Your name and social security number;

(2) The name and social security number of your spouse, if any;

(3) The reasons you disagree with the previous determination or decision;

(4) A statement of additional evidence to be submitted and the date you will submit it; and

(5) The name and address of any designated representative.

(b) When and where to file. The request must be filed at one of our offices within 60 days after the date you receive notice of the previous determination or decision (or within the extended time period if we extend the time as provided in paragraph (c) of this section).

(c) Extension of time to request a hearing. If you have a right to a hearing but do not request one in time, you may ask for more time to make your request. The request for an extension of time must be in writing and it must give the reasons why the request for a hearing was not filed within the stated time period. You may file your request for an extension of time at one of our offices. If you show that you had good cause for missing the deadline, the time period will be extended. To determine whether good cause exists, we use the standards explained in § 416.1411.

[51 FR 307, Jan. 3, 1986]

§ 416.1435 Submitting written evidence to an administrative law judge.

(a) When you submit your request for hearing, you should also submit information or evidence as required by § 416.912 or any summary of the evidence to the administrative law judge. Each party must make every effort to ensure that the administrative law judge receives all of the evidence and must inform us about or submit any written evidence, as required in § 416.912, no later than 5 business days before the date of the scheduled hearing. If you do not comply with this requirement, the administrative law judge may decline to consider or obtain the evidence unless the circumstances described in paragraph (b) of this section apply.

(b) If you have evidence required under § 416.912 but you have missed the deadline described in paragraph (a) of this section, the administrative law judge will accept the evidence if he or she has not yet issued a decision and you did not inform us about or submit the evidence before the deadline because:

(1) Our action misled you;

(2) You had a physical, mental, educational, or linguistic limitation(s) that prevented you from informing us about or submitting the evidence earlier; or

(3) Some other unusual, unexpected, or unavoidable circumstance beyond your control prevented you from

informing us about or submitting the evidence earlier. Examples include, but are not limited to:

(i) You were seriously ill, and your illness prevented you from contacting us in person, in writing, or through a friend, relative, or other person;

(ii) There was a death or serious illness in your immediate family;

(iii) Important records were destroyed or damaged by fire or other accidental cause; or

(iv) You actively and diligently sought evidence from a source and the evidence was not received or was received less than 5 business days prior to the hearing.

(c) Claims Not Based on an Application For Benefits. Notwithstanding the requirements in paragraphs (a)-(b) of this section, for claims that are not based on an application for benefits, the evidentiary requirement to inform us about or submit evidence no later than 5 business days before the date of the scheduled hearing will not apply if our other regulations allow you to submit evidence after the date of an administrative law judge decision.

[51 FR 307, Jan. 3, 1986; 80 FR 14838, March 20, 2015; 81 FR 90995, Dec. 16, 2016]

§ 416.1436 Time and place for a hearing before an administrative law judge.

(a) General. We may set the time and place for any hearing. We may change the time and place, if it is necessary. After sending you reasonable notice of the proposed action, the administrative law judge may adjourn or postpone the hearing or reopen it to receive additional evidence any time before he or she notifies you of a hearing decision.

(b) Where we hold hearings. We hold hearings in the 50 States, the District of Columbia, American Samoa, Guam, the Northern Mariana Islands, the Commonwealth of Puerto Rico, and the United States Virgin Islands. The "place" of the hearing is the hearing office or other site(s) at which you and any other parties to the hearing are located when you make your appearance(s) before the administrative law judge, whether in person, by video teleconferencing, or by telephone.

(c) Determination how appearances will be made. In setting the time and place of the hearing, we will consider the following:

(1) We will consult with the administrative law judge to determine the status of case preparation and to determine whether your appearance, or the appearance of any other party to the hearing, will be made in person, by video teleconferencing or, under extraordinary circumstances, by telephone. The administrative law judge will determine that your appearance, or the appearance of any other party to the hearing, be conducted by video teleconferencing if video teleconferencing equipment is available to conduct the appearance, use of video teleconferencing to conduct the appearance would be more efficient than conducting the appearance in person, and the administrative law judge determines there is no circumstance in the particular case that prevents the use of video teleconferencing to conduct the appearance. The administrative law judge will direct you or another party to the hearing to appear by telephone when:

(i) An appearance in person is not possible, such as if you are incarcerated, the facility will not allow a hearing to be held at the facility, and video teleconferencing is not available; or

(ii) The administrative law judge determines, either on his or her own, or at your request or at the request of any other party to the hearing, that extraordinary circumstances prevent you or another party to the hearing from appearing at the hearing in person or by video teleconferencing.

(2) The administrative law judge will determine whether any person, other than you or any other party to the hearing, including a medical expert or a vocational expert, will appear at the hearing in person, by video teleconferencing, or by telephone. If you or any other party to the hearing objects to any other person appearing by video teleconferencing or by telephone, the administrative law judge will decide, either in writing or at the hearing, whether to have that person appear in person, by video teleconferencing, or by telephone. The administrative law judge will direct a person, other than you or any other party to the hearing if we are notified as provided in paragraph (e) of this section that you or any other party to the hearing objects to appearing by video teleconferencing, to appear by video teleconferencing or telephone when the administrative law judge determines:

(i) Video teleconferencing or telephone equipment is available,

(ii) Use of video teleconferencing or telephone equipment would be more efficient than conducting an examination of a witness in person, and

(iii) The administrative law judge determines there is no other reason why video teleconferencing or telephone should not be used.

(d) Objecting to appearing by video teleconferencing. Prior to scheduling your hearing, we will notify you that we may schedule you to appear by video teleconferencing. If you object to appearing by video teleconferencing, you must notify us in writing within 30 days after the date you receive the notice. If you notify us within that time period and your residence does not change while your request for hearing is pending, we will set your hearing for a time and place at which you may make your appearance before the administrative law judge in person.

(1) Notwithstanding any objections you may have to appearing by video teleconferencing, if you change your residence while your request for hearing is pend-

ing, we may determine how you will appear, including by video teleconferencing, as provided in paragraph (c)(1) of this section. For us to consider your change of residence when we schedule your hearing, you must submit evidence verifying your new residence.

(2) If you notify us that you object to appearing by video teleconferencing more than 30 days after the date you receive our notice, we will extend the time period if you show you had good cause for missing the deadline. To determine whether good cause exists for extending the deadline, we use the standards explained in § 416.1411.

(e) Objecting to the time or place of the hearing. If you object to the time or place of your hearing, you must:

(1) Notify us in writing at the earliest possible opportunity, but not later than 5 days before the date set for the hearing or 30 days after receiving notice of the hearing, whichever is earlier (or within the extended time period if we extend the time as provided in paragraph (e)(3) of this section); and

(2) State the reason(s) for your objection and state the time and place you want the hearing to be held. We will change the time or place of the hearing if the administrative law judge finds you have good cause, as determined under paragraph (f) of this section. Section 416.1438 provides procedures we will follow when you do not respond to a notice of hearing.

(3) If you notify us that you object to the time or place of hearing less than 5 days before the date set for the hearing or, if earlier, more than 30 days after receiving notice of the hearing, we will extend the time period if you show you had good cause for missing the deadline. To determine whether good cause exists for extending the deadline, we use the standards explained in § 416.1411.

(f) Good cause for changing the time or place. The administrative law judge will determine whether good cause exists for changing the time or place of your scheduled hearing. However, a finding that good cause exists to reschedule the time or place of your hearing will not change the assignment of the administrative law judge for your case, unless we determine reassignment will promote more efficient administration of the hearing process.

(1) We will reschedule your hearing, if your reason is one of the following circumstances and is supported by the evidence:

(i) A serious physical or mental condition or incapacitating injury makes it impossible for you or your representative to travel to the hearing, or a death in the family occurs; or

(ii) Severe weather conditions make it impossible for you or your representative to travel to the hearing.

(2) In determining whether good cause exists in circumstances other than those set out in paragraph (f)(1) of this section, the administrative law judge will consider your reason(s) for requesting the change, the facts supporting it, and the impact of the proposed change on the efficient administration of the hearing process. Factors affecting the impact of the change include, but are not limited to, the effect on the processing of other scheduled hearings, delays that might occur in rescheduling your hearing, and whether we previously granted you any changes in the time or place of your hearing. Examples of such other circumstances that you might give for requesting a change in the time or place of the hearing include, but are not limited to, the following:

(i) You unsuccessfully attempted to obtain a representative and need additional time to secure representation;

(ii) Your representative was appointed within 30 days of the scheduled hearing and needs additional time to prepare for the hearing;

(iii) Your representative has a prior commitment to be in court or at another administrative hearing on the date scheduled for the hearing;

(iv) A witness who will testify to facts material to your case would be unavailable to attend the scheduled hearing and the evidence cannot be otherwise obtained;

(v) Transportation is not readily available for you to travel to the hearing; or

(vi) You are unrepresented, and you are unable to respond to the notice of hearing because of any physical, mental, educational, or linguistic limitations (including any lack of facility with the English language) which you may have.

(g) Good cause in other circumstances. In determining whether good cause exists in circumstances other than those set out in paragraph (e) of this section, the administrative law judge will consider your reason for requesting the change, the facts supporting it, and the impact of the proposed change on the efficient administration of the hearing process. Factors affecting the impact of the change include, but are not limited to, the effect on the processing of other scheduled hearings, delays which might occur in rescheduling your hearing, and whether any prior changes were granted to you. Examples of such other circumstances, which you might give for requesting a change in the time or place of the hearing, include, but are not limited to, the following:

(1) You have attempted to obtain a representative but need additional time;

(2) Your representative was appointed within 30 days of the scheduled hearing and needs additional time to prepare for the hearing;

(3) Your representative has a prior commitment to be in court or at another administrative hearing on the date scheduled for the hearing;

(4) A witness who will testify to facts material to your case would be unavailable to attend the scheduled hearing and the evidence cannot be otherwise obtained;

(5) Transportation is not readily available for you to travel to the hearing;

(6) You live closer to another hearing site; or

(7) You are unrepresented, and you are unable to respond to the notice of hearing because of any physical, mental, educational, or linguistic limitations (including any lack of facility with the English language) which you may have.

(h) Consultation procedures. Before we exercise the authority to set the time and place for an administrative law judge's hearings, we will consult with the appropriate hearing office chief administrative law judge to determine if there are any reasons why we should not set the time and place of the administrative law judge's hearings. If the hearing office chief administrative law judge does not state a reason that we believe justifies the limited number of hearings scheduled by the administrative law judge, we will then consult with the administrative law judge before deciding whether to begin to exercise our authority to set the time and place for the administrative law judge's hearings. If the hearing office chief administrative law judge states a reason that we believe justifies the limited number of hearings scheduled by the administrative law judge, we will not exercise our authority to set the time and place for the administrative law judge's hearings. We will work with the hearing office chief administrative law judge to identify those circumstances where we can assist the administrative law judge and address any impediment that may affect the scheduling of hearings.

(i) Pilot program. The provisions of the first and second sentences of paragraph (a), the first sentence of paragraph (c)(1), and paragraph (g) of this section are a pilot program. These provisions will no longer be effective on August 11, 2017, unless we terminate them earlier or extend them beyond that date by notice of a final rule in the Federal Register.

[51 FR 307, Jan. 3, 1986; 59 FR 1637, Jan. 12, 1994; 68 FR 5220, Feb. 3, 2003; 68 FR 69009, Dec. 11, 2003; 75 FR 39161, July 8, 2010; 78 FR 29628, May 21, 2013; 78 FR 45452, July 29, 2013; 79 FR 35933, June 25, 2014; 79 FR 41883, July 18, 2014; 80 FR 37971, July 2, 2015; 81 FR 41214, June 24, 2016]

§ 416.1437 Protecting the safety of the public and our employees in our hearing process.

(a) Notwithstanding any other provision in this part or part 422 of this chapter, we are establishing the procedures set out in this section to ensure the safety of the public and our employees in our hearing process.

(b)(1) At the request of any hearing office employee, the Hearing Office Chief Administrative Law Judge will determine, after consultation with the presiding administrative law judge, whether a claimant or other individual poses a reasonable threat to the safety of our employees or other participants in the hearing. The Hearing Office Chief Administrative Law Judge will find that a claimant or other individual poses a threat to the safety of our employees or other participants in the hearing when he or she determines that the individual has made a threat and there is a reasonable likelihood that the claimant or other individual could act on the threat or when evidence suggests that a claimant or other individual poses a threat. In making a finding under this paragraph, the Hearing Office Chief Administrative Law Judge will consider all relevant evidence, including any information we have in the claimant's record and any information we have regarding the claimant's or other individual's past conduct.

(2) If the Hearing Office Chief Administrative Law Judge determines that the claimant or other individual poses a reasonable threat to the safety of our employees or other participants in the hearing, the Hearing Office Chief Administrative Law Judge will either:

(i) Require the presence of a security guard at the hearing; or

(ii) Require that the hearing be conducted by video teleconference or by telephone.

(c) If we have banned a claimant from any of our facilities, we will provide the claimant with the opportunity for a hearing that will be conducted by telephone.

(d) The actions of the Hearing Office Chief Administrative Law Judge taken under this section are final and not subject to further review.

[76 FR 13508, March 14, 2011; 77 FR 10658, Feb. 23, 2012]

§ 416.1438 Notice of a hearing before an administrative law judge.

(a) Issuing the notice. After we set the time and place of the hearing, we will mail notice of the hearing to you at your last known address, or give the notice to you by personal service, unless you have indicated in writing that you do not wish to receive this notice. We will mail or serve the notice at least 75 days before the date of the hearing.

(b) Notice information. The notice of hearing will tell you:

(1) The specific issues to be decided in your case;

(2) That you may designate a person to represent you during the proceedings;

(3) How to request that we change the time or place of your hearing;

(4) That your hearing may be dismissed if neither you nor the person you designate to act as your representative appears at your scheduled hearing without good reason under § 416.1457;

(5) Whether your appearance or that of any other party or witness is scheduled to be made in person, by video teleconferencing, or by telephone. If we have scheduled you to appear at the hearing by video teleconferencing, the notice of hearing will tell you that the scheduled place for the hearing is a video teleconferencing site and explain what it means to appear at your hearing by video teleconferencing;

(6) That you must make every effort to inform us about or submit all written evidence that is not already in the record no later than 5 business days before the date of the scheduled hearing, unless you show that your circumstances meet the conditions described in § 416.1435(b); and

(7) Any other information about the scheduling and conduct of your hearing.

(c) Acknowledging the notice of hearing. The notice of hearing will ask you to return a form to let us know that you received the notice. If you or your representative do not acknowledge receipt of the notice of hearing, we will attempt to contact you for an explanation. If you tell us that you did not receive the notice of hearing, an amended notice will be sent to you by certified mail. See § 416.1436 for the procedures we will follow in deciding whether the time or place of your scheduled hearing will be changed if you do not respond to the notice of hearing.

[51 FR 307, Jan. 3, 1986; 68 FR 5220, Feb. 3, 2003; 68 FR 69009, Dec. 11, 2003; 75 FR 39161, July 8, 2010; 78 FR 29628, May 21, 2013; 79 FR 35934, June 25, 2014; 81 FR 90995, Dec. 16, 2016]

§ 416.1439 Objections to the issues.

If you object to the issues to be decided at the hearing, you must notify the administrative law judge in writing at the earliest possible opportunity, but no later than 5 business days before the date set for the hearing, unless you show that your circumstances meet the conditions described in § 416.1435(b). You must state the reason(s) for your objection(s). The administrative law judge will make a decision on your objection(s) either at the hearing or in writing before the hearing.

[81 FR 90995, Dec. 16, 2016]

§ 416.1440 Disqualification of the administrative law judge.

An administrative law judge shall not conduct a hearing if he or she is prejudiced or partial with respect to any party or has any interest in the matter pending for decision. If you object to the administrative law judge who will conduct the hearing, you must notify the administrative law judge at your earliest opportunity. The administrative law judge shall consider your objections and shall decide whether to proceed with the hearing or withdraw. If he or she withdraws, the Associate Commissioner for Hearings and Appeals, or his or her delegate, will appoint another administrative law judge to conduct the hearing. If the administrative law judge does not withdraw, you may, after the hearing, present your objections to the Appeals Council as reasons why the hearing decision should be revised or a new hearing held before another administrative law judge.

§ 416.1441 Prehearing case review.

(a) General. After a hearing is requested but before it is held, we may, for the purposes of a prehearing case review, forward the case to the component of our office (including a State agency) that issued the determination being reviewed. That component will decide whether it should revise the determination based on the preponderance of the evidence. A revised determination may be fully or partially favorable to you. A prehearing case review will not delay the scheduling of a hearing unless you agree to continue the review and delay the hearing. If the prehearing case review is not completed before the date of the hearing, the case will be sent to the administrative law judge unless a favorable revised determination is in process or you and the other parties to the hearing agree in writing to delay the hearing until the review is completed.

(b) When a prehearing case review may be conducted. We may conduct a prehearing case review if—

(1) Additional evidence is submitted;

(2) There is an indication that additional evidence is available;

(3) There is a change in the law or regulation; or

(4) There is an error in the file or some other indication that the prior determination may be revised.

(c) Notice of a prehearing revised determination. If we revise the determination in a prehearing case review, we will mail a written notice of the revised determination to all parties at their last known addresses. We will state the basis for the revised determination and advise all parties of the effect of the revised determination on the request for a hearing.

(d) Effect of a fully favorable revised determination. If the revised determination is fully favorable to you, we will tell you in the notice that an administrative law judge will dismiss the request for a hearing. We will also tell you that you or another party to the hearing may request that the administrative law judge vacate the dismissal and reinstate the request for a hearing if you or another party to the hearing disagrees with the revised determination for any reason. If you wish to make this request, you must do so in writing and send it to us within 60 days of the date you receive notice of the dismissal. If the request is timely, an administrative law judge will vacate the dismissal, reinstate the request for a hearing, and offer you and all parties an opportunity for a hearing. The administrative law judge will extend the time limit if you show that you had good cause for missing the deadline. The administrative law judge will use the standards in § 416.1411 to determine whether you had good cause.

(e) Effect of a partially favorable revised determination. If the revised determination is partially favorable to you, we will tell you in the notice what was not favorable. We will also tell you that an administrative law judge will hold the hearing you requested unless you and all other parties to the hearing agree in writing to dismiss the request for a hearing. An administrative law judge will dismiss the request for a hearing if we receive the written statement(s) agreeing to dismiss the request for a hearing before an administrative law judge mails a notice of his or her hearing decision.

[73 FR 76945, Dec. 18, 2008; 75 FR 33169, June 11, 2010; 76 FR 65370, Oct. 21, 2011]

§ 416.1442 Prehearing proceedings and decisions by attorney advisors.

(a) General. After a hearing is requested but before it is held, an attorney advisor may conduct prehearing proceedings as set out in paragraph (c) of this section. If after the completion of these proceedings we can make a decision that is fully favorable to you and all other parties based on the preponderance of the evidence, an attorney advisor, instead of an administrative law judge, may issue the decision. The conduct of the prehearing proceedings by the attorney advisor will not delay the scheduling of a hearing. If the prehearing proceedings are not completed before the date of the hearing, the case will be sent to the administrative law judge unless a fully favorable decision is in process or you and all other parties to the hearing agree in writing to delay the hearing until the proceedings are completed.

(b) When prehearing proceedings may be conducted by an attorney advisor. An attorney advisor may conduct prehearing proceedings if you have filed a claim for SSI benefits based on disability and—

(1) New and material evidence is submitted;

(2) There is an indication that additional evidence is available;

(3) There is a change in the law or regulations; or

(4) There is an error in the file or some other indication that a fully favorable decision may be issued.

(c) Nature of the prehearing proceedings that may be conducted by an attorney advisor. As part of the prehearing proceedings, the attorney advisor, in addition to reviewing the existing record, may—

(1) Request additional evidence that may be relevant to the claim, including medical evidence; and

(2) If necessary to clarify the record for the purpose of determining if a fully favorable decision is warranted, schedule a conference with the parties.

(d) Notice of a decision by an attorney advisor. If an attorney advisor issues a fully favorable decision under this section, we will mail a written notice of the decision to all parties at their last known addresses. We will state the basis for the decision and advise all parties that they may request that an administrative law judge reinstate the request for a hearing if they disagree with the decision for any reason. Any party who wants to make this request must do so in writing and send it to us within 60 days of the date he or she receives notice of the decision. The administrative law judge will extend the time limit if the requestor shows good cause for missing the deadline. The administrative law judge will use the standards in § 416.1411 to determine whether there is good cause. If the request is timely, an administrative law judge will reinstate the request for a hearing and offer all parties an opportunity for a hearing.

(e) Effect of an attorney advisor's decision. An attorney advisor's decision under this section is binding unless—

(1) You or another party to the hearing submits a timely request that an administrative law judge reinstate the request for a hearing under paragraph (d) of this section;

(2) The Appeals Council reviews the decision on its own motion pursuant to § 416.1469 as explained in paragraph (f)(3) of this section; or

(3) The decision of the attorney advisor is revised under the procedures explained in § 416.1487.

(f) Ancillary provisions. For the purposes of the procedures authorized by this section, the regulations of part 416 shall apply to—

(1) Authorize an attorney advisor to exercise the functions performed by an administrative law judge under §§ 416.913a, 416.920a, 416.926, and 416.946.

(2) Define the term "decision" to include a decision made by an attorney advisor, as well as the decisions identified in § 416.1401; and

(3) Make the decision of an attorney advisor under paragraph (d) of this section subject to review by the Appeals Council if the Appeals Council decides to review the decision of the attorney advisor anytime within 60 days after the date of the decision under § 416.1469.

(g) [Reserved by 83 FR 40453]

[60 FR 34132, June 30, 1995; 62 FR 35074, June 30, 1997; 63 FR 35516, June 30, 1998; 64 FR 13678, March 22, 1999; 64 FR 51894, Sept. 27, 1999; 65 FR 16815, March 30, 2000; 72 FR 44765, Aug. 9, 2007; 73 FR 11353, March 3, 2008; 73 FR 76945, Dec. 18, 2008; 74 FR 33328, July 13, 2009; 76 FR 18384, April 4, 2011; 76 FR 65371, Oct. 21, 2011; 78 FR 45460, July 29, 2013; 80 FR 31991, June 5, 2015; 82 FR 5884, Jan. 18, 2017; 82 FR 34401, July 25, 2017; 83 FR 712, Jan. 8, 2018; 83 FR 28993, June 22, 2018; 83 FR 40453, Aug. 15, 2018]

§ 416.1443 Responsibilities of the adjudication officer.

(a)(1) General. Under the procedures set out in this section we will test modifications to the procedures we follow when you file a request for a hearing before an administrative law judge in connection with a claim for benefits based on disability where the question of whether you are under a disability as defined in §§ 416.905 and 416.906 is at issue. These modifications will enable us to test the effect of having an adjudication officer be your primary point of contact after you file a hearing request and before you have a hearing with an administrative law judge. The tests may be conducted alone, or in combination with the tests of the modifications to the disability determination procedures which we conduct under § 416.1406. The adjudication officer, working with you and your representative, if any, will identify issues in dispute, develop evidence, conduct informal conferences, and conduct any other prehearing proceeding as may be necessary. The adjudication officer has the authority to make a decision fully favorable to you if the evidence so warrants. If the adjudication officer does not make a decision on your claim, your hearing request will be assigned to an administrative law judge for further proceedings.

(2) Procedures for cases included in the tests. Prior to commencing tests of the adjudication officer position in selected site(s), we will publish a notice in the Federal Register. The notice will describe where the specific test site(s) will be and the duration of the test(s). We will also state whether the tests of the adjudication officer position in each site will be conducted alone, or in combination with the tests of the modifications to the disability determination procedures which we conduct under § 416.1406. The individuals who participate in the test(s) will be assigned randomly to a test group in each site where the tests are conducted.

(b)(1) Prehearing procedures conducted by an Adjudication Officer. When you file a request for a hearing before an administrative law judge in connection with a claim for benefits based on disability where the question of whether you are under a disability as defined in §§ 416.905 and 416.906 is at issue, the adjudication officer will conduct an interview with you. The interview may take place in person, by telephone, or by videoconference, as the adjudication officer determines is appropriate under the circumstances of your case. If you file a request for an extension of time to request a hearing in accordance with § 416.1433(c), the adjudication officer may develop information on, and may decide where the adjudication officer issues a fully favorable decision to you that you had good cause for missing the deadline for requesting a hearing. To determine whether you had good cause for missing the deadline, the adjudication officer will use the standards contained in § 416.1411.

(2) Representation. The adjudication officer will provide you with information regarding the hearing process, including your right to representation. As may be appropriate, the adjudication officer will provide you with referral sources for representation, and give you copies of necessary documents to facilitate the appointment of a representative. If you have a representative, the adjudication officer will conduct an informal conference with the representative, in person or by telephone, to identify the issues in dispute and prepare proposed written agreements for the approval of the administrative law judge regarding those issues which are not in dispute and those issues proposed for the hearing. If you decide to proceed without representation, the adjudication officer may hold an informal conference with you. If you obtain representation after the adjudication officer has concluded that your case is ready for a hearing, the administrative law judge will return your case to the adjudication officer who will conduct an informal conference with you and your representative.

(3) Evidence. You, or your representative, may submit, or may be asked to obtain and submit, additional evidence to the adjudication officer. As the adjudication officer determines is appropriate under the circumstances of your case, the adjudication officer may refer the claim for further medical or vocational evidence.

(4) Referral for a hearing. The adjudication officer will refer the claim to the administrative law judge for further proceedings when the development of evidence is complete, and you or your representative agree that a hearing is ready to be held. If you or your representative are unable to agree with the adjudication officer that the development of evidence is complete, the adjudication officer will note your disagreement and refer the claim to the administrative law judge for further proceedings. At this point, the administrative law judge conducts all further hearing proceedings, including scheduling and holding a hearing, (§ 416.1436), considering any additional evidence or arguments submitted (§§ 416.1435, 416.1444, 416.1449, 416.1450), and issuing a decision or dismissal of your request for a hearing, as may be appropriate (§§ 416.1448, 416.1453, 416.1457). In addition, if the administrative law judge determines on or before the date of your hearing that the development of evidence is not complete, the administrative law judge may return the claim to the adjudication officer to complete the development of the evidence and for such other action as necessary.

(c)(1) Fully favorable decisions issued by an adjudication officer. If, after a hearing is requested but before it is held, the adjudication officer decides that the evidence in your case warrants a decision which is fully favorable to you, the adjudication officer may issue such a decision. For purposes of the tests authorized under this section, the adjudication officer's decision shall be considered to be a decision as defined in § 416.1401. If the adjudication officer issues a decision under this section, it will be in writing and will give the findings of fact and the reasons for the decision. The adjudication officer will evaluate the issues relevant to determining whether or not you are disabled in accordance with the provisions of the Social Security Act, the rules in this part and part 422 of this chapter and applicable Social Security Rulings. For cases in which the adjudication officer issues a decision, he or she may determine your residual functional capacity in the same manner that an administrative law judge is authorized to do so in § 416.946. The adjudication officer may also evaluate the severity of your mental impairments in the same manner that an administrative law judge is authorized to do so under § 416.920a. The adjudication officer's decision will be based on the evidence which is included in the record and, subject to paragraph (c)(2) of this section, will complete the actions that will be taken on your request for hearing. A copy of the decision will be mailed to all parties at their last known address. We will tell you in the notice that the administrative law judge will not hold a hearing unless a party to the hearing requests that the hearing proceed. A request to proceed with the hearing must be made in writing within 30 days after the date the notice of the decision of the adjudication officer is mailed.

(2) Effect of a decision by an adjudication officer. A decision by an adjudication officer which is fully favorable to you under this section, and notification thereof, completes the administrative action on your request for hearing and is binding on all parties to the hearing and not subject to further review, unless—

(i) You or another party requests that the hearing continue, as provided in paragraph (c)(1) of this section;

(ii) The Appeals Council decides to review the decision on its own motion under the authority provided in § 416.1469;

(iii) The decision is revised under the procedures explained in §§ 416.1487 through 416.1489; or

(iv) In a case remanded by a Federal court, the Appeals Council assumes jurisdiction under the procedures in § 416.1484.

(3) Fee for a representative's services. The adjudication officer may authorize a fee for your representative's services if the adjudication officer makes a decision on your claim that is fully favorable to you, and you are represented. The actions of, and any fee authorization made by, the adjudication officer with respect to representation will be made in accordance with the provisions of subpart O of this part.

(d) Who may be an adjudication officer. The adjudication officer described in this section may be an employee of the Social Security Administration or a State agency that makes disability determinations for us.

[60 FR 47476, Sept. 13, 1995; 75 FR 33169, June 11, 2010]

ADMINISTRATIVE LAW JUDGE HEARINGS PROCEDURES

§ 416.1444 Administrative law judge hearing procedures—general.

A hearing is open to the parties and to other persons the administrative law judge considers necessary and proper. At the hearing, the administrative law judge looks fully into the issues, questions you and the other witnesses, and, subject to the provisions of § 416.1435: Accepts as evidence any documents that are material to the issues; may stop the hearing temporarily and continue it at a later date if he or she finds that there is material evidence missing at the hearing; and may reopen the hearing at any time before he or she mails a notice of the decision in order to receive new and material evidence. The administrative law judge may decide when the evidence will be presented and when the issues will be discussed.

[51 FR 307, Jan. 3, 1986; 81 FR 90995, Dec. 16, 2016]

§ 416.1446 Issues before an administrative law judge.

(a) General. The issues before the administrative law judge include all the issues brought out in the initial, reconsidered or revised determination that were not decided entirely in your favor. However, if evidence presented before or during the hearing causes the administrative law judge to question a fully favorable determination, he or she will notify you and will consider it an issue at the hearing.

(b) New issues—

(1) General. The administrative law judge may consider a new issue at the hearing if he or she notifies you and all the parties about the new issue any time after receiving the hearing request and before mailing notice of the hearing decision. The administrative law judge or any party may raise a new issue; an issue may be raised even though it arose after the request for a hearing and even though it has not been considered in an initial or reconsidered determination. However, it may not be raised if it involves a claim that is within the jurisdiction of a State agency under a Federal–State agreement concerning the determination of disability.

(2) Notice of a new issue. The administrative law judge shall notify you and any other party if he or she will consider any new issue. Notice of the time and place of the hearing on any new issues will be given in the manner described in § 416.1438, unless you have indicated in writing that you do not wish to receive the notice.

[51 FR 307, Jan. 3, 1986]

§ 416.1448 Deciding a case without an oral hearing before an administrative law judge.

(a) Decision fully favorable. If the evidence in the hearing record supports a finding in favor of you and all the parties on every issue, the administrative law judge may issue a hearing decision based on a preponderance of the evidence without holding an oral hearing. The notice of the decision will state that you have the right to an oral hearing and to examine the evidence on which the administrative law judge based the decision.

(b) Parties do not wish to appear.

(1) The administrative law judge may decide a case on the record and not conduct an oral hearing if—

(i) You and all the parties indicate in writing that you do not wish to appear before the administrative law judge at an oral hearing; or

(ii) You live outside the United States, you do not inform us that you wish to appear, and there are no other parties who wish to appear.

(2) When an oral hearing is not held, the administrative law judge shall make a record of the material evidence. The record will include the applications, written statements, certificates, reports, affidavits, and other documents which were used in making the determination under review and any additional evidence you or any other party to the hearing present in writing. The decision of the administrative law judge must be based on this record.

(c) Case remanded for a revised determination.

(1) The administrative law judge may remand a case to the appropriate component of our office for a revised determination if there is reason to believe that the revised determination would be fully favorable to you. This could happen if the administrative law judge receives new and material evidence or if there is a change in the law that permits the favorable determination.

(2) Unless you request the remand the administrative law judge shall notify you that your case has been remanded and tell you that if you object, you must notify him or her of your objections within 10 days of the date the case is remanded or we will assume that you agree to the remand. If you object to the remand, the administrative law judge will consider the objection and rule on it in writing.

[51 FR 307, Jan. 3, 1986; 73 FR 76945, Dec. 18, 2008; 75 FR 33169, June 11, 2010; 76 FR 65371, Oct. 21, 2011]

§ 416.1449 Presenting written statements and oral arguments.

You or a person you designate to act as your representative may appear before the administrative law judge to state your case, present a written summary of your case, or enter written statements about the facts and law material to your case in the record. If presenting written statements prior to hearing, you must provide a copy of your written statements for each party no later than 5 business days before the date set for the hearing, unless you show that your circumstances meet the conditions described in § 416.1435(b).

[81 FR 90996, Dec. 16, 2016]

§ 416.1450 Presenting evidence at a hearing before an administrative law judge.

(a) The right to appear and present evidence. Any party to a hearing has a right to appear before the administrative law judge, either in person, or, when the conditions in § 416.1436(c)(1) exist, by video teleconferencing or telephone, to present evidence and to state his or her position. A party may also make his or her appearance by means of a designated representative, who may make the appearance in person, or, when the conditions in § 416.1436(c)(1) exist, by video teleconferencing or telephone.

(b) Waiver of the right to appear. You may send the administrative law judge a waiver or a written statement indicating that you do not wish to appear at the hearing. You may withdraw this waiver any time before a notice of the hearing decision is mailed to you. Even if all of the parties waive their right to appear at a hearing, we may notify them of a time and a place for an oral hearing, if the administrative law judge believes that a personal appearance and testimony by you or any other party is necessary to decide the case.

(c) Admissible evidence. Subject to the provisions of § 416.1435, the administrative law judge may receive any evidence at the hearing that he or she believes is material to the issues, even though the evidence would not be admissible in court under the rules of evidence used by the court.

(d) Subpoenas.

(1) When it is reasonably necessary for the full presentation of a case, an administrative law judge or a member of the Appeals Council may, on his or her own initiative or at the request of a party, issue subpoenas for the appearance and testimony of witnesses and for the production of books, records, correspondence, papers, or other documents that are material to an issue at the hearing.

(2) Parties to a hearing who wish to subpoena documents or witnesses must file a written request for the issuance of a subpoena with the administrative law judge or at one of our offices at least 10 business days before the hearing date, unless you show that your circumstances meet the conditions described in § 416.1435(b). The written request must give the names of the witnesses or documents to be produced; describe the address or location of the witnesses or documents with sufficient detail to find them; state the important facts that the witness or document is expect-

ed to prove; and indicate why these facts could not be proven without issuing a subpoena.

(3) We will pay the cost of issuing the subpoena.

(4) We will pay subpoenaed witnesses the same fees and mileage they would receive if they had been subpoenaed by a Federal district court.

(e) Witnesses at a hearing. Witnesses may appear at a hearing in person or, when the conditions in § 416.1436(c)(2) exist, by video teleconferencing or telephone. They will testify under oath or affirmation unless the administrative law judge finds an important reason to excuse them from taking an oath or affirmation. The administrative law judge may ask the witness any questions material to the issues and will allow the parties or their designated representatives to do so.

(f) Collateral estoppel—issues previously decided. An issue at your hearing may be a fact that has already been decided in one of our previous determinations or decisions in a claim involving the same parties, but arising under a different title of the Act or under the Federal Coal Mine Health and Safety Act. If this happens, the administrative law judge will not consider the issue again, but will accept the factual finding made in the previous determination or decision unless there are reasons to believe that it was wrong.

[51 FR 307, Jan. 3, 1986; 68 FR 5221, Feb. 3, 2003; 68 FR 69009, Dec. 11, 2003; 75 FR 39161, July 8, 2010; 78 FR 29628, May 21, 2013; 81 FR 90996, Dec. 16, 2016]

§ 416.1451 Official record.

(a) Hearing recording. All hearings will be recorded. The hearing recording will be prepared as a typed copy of the proceedings if—

(1) The case is sent to the Appeals Council without a decision or with a recommended decision by the administrative law judge;

(2) You seek judicial review of your case by filing an action in a Federal district court within the stated time period, unless we request the court to remand the case; or

(3) An administrative law judge or the Appeals Council asks for a written record of the proceedings.

(b) Contents of the official record. All evidence upon which the administrative law judge relies for the decision must be contained in the record, either directly or by appropriate reference. The official record will include the applications, written statements, certificates, reports, affidavits, medical records, and other documents that were used in making the decision under review and any additional evidence or written statements that the administrative law judge admits into the record under §§ 416.1429 and 416.1435. All exhibits introduced as evidence must be marked for identification and incorporated into the record. The official record of your claim will contain all of the marked exhibits and a verbatim recording of all testimony offered at the hearing. It also will include any prior initial determinations or decisions on your claim.

[51 FR 308, Jan. 3, 1986; 81 FR 90996, Dec. 16, 2016]

§ 416.1452 Consolidated hearings before an administrative law judge.

(a) General.

(1) A consolidated hearing may be held if—

(i) You have requested a hearing to decide your eligibility for supplemental security income benefits and you have also requested a hearing to decide your rights under another law we administer; and

(ii) One or more of the issues to be considered at the hearing you requested are the same issues that are involved in another claim you have pending before us.

(2) If the administrative law judge decides to hold the hearing on both claims, he or she decides both claims, even if we have not yet made an initial or reconsidered determination on the other claim.

(b) Record, evidence, and decision. There will be a single record at a consolidated hearing. This means that the evidence introduced in one case becomes evidence in the other(s). The administrative law judge may make either a separate or consolidated decision.

[51 FR 308, Jan. 3, 1986]

§ 416.1453 The decision of an administrative law judge.

(a) General. The administrative law judge shall issue a written decision which gives the findings of fact and the reasons for the decision. The administrative law judge must base the decision on the preponderance of the evidence offered at the hearing or otherwise included in the record. The administrative law judge shall mail a copy of the decision to all the parties at their last known address. The Appeals Council may also receive a copy of the decision.

(b) Fully favorable oral decision entered into the record at the hearing. The administrative law judge may enter a fully favorable oral decision based on the preponderance of the evidence into the record of the hearing proceedings. If the administrative law judge enters a fully favorable oral decision into the record of the hearing proceedings, the administrative law judge may issue a written decision that incorporates the oral decision by reference. The administrative law judge may use this procedure only in those categories of cases that we identify in advance. The administrative law judge may only use this procedure in those cases where the administrative law judge determines that no changes are required in the findings of fact or the reasons for the decision as stated at the hearing. If a fully favorable decision is entered into the record at the hearing, the administrative law judge will also include in the record, as an exhibit entered into the record at the hearing, a document that sets forth the key data, findings of fact, and narrative rationale for the decision. If the decision incorporates by reference the findings and the reasons stated in an oral decision at the hearing, the parties shall also be provided, upon written request, a record of the oral decision.

(c) Time for the administrative law judge's decision.

(1) The administrative law judge must issue the hearing decision no later than 90 days after the request for hearing is filed, unless—

(i) The matter to be decided is whether you are disabled; or

(ii) There is good cause for extending the time period because of unavoidable circumstances.

(2) Good cause for extending the time period may be found under the following circumstances:

(i) Delay caused by you or by your representative's action. The time period for decision in this instance may be extended by the total number of days of the delays. The delays include delays in submitting evidence, briefs, or other statements, postponements or adjournments made at your request, and any other delays caused by you or your representative.

(ii) Other delays. The time period for decision may be extended where delays occur through no fault of the Commissioner. In this instance, the decision will be issued as soon as practicable.

(d) Recommended decision. Although an administrative law judge will usually make a decision, the administrative law judge may send the case to the Appeals Council with a recommended decision based on a preponderance of the evidence when appropriate. The administrative law judge will mail a copy of the recommended decision to the parties at their last known addresses and send the recommended decision to the Appeals Council.

[51 FR 308, Jan. 3, 1986; 54 FR 37793, Sept. 13, 1989; 62 FR 38455, July 18, 1997; 69 FR 61597, Oct. 20, 2004; 73 FR 76945, Dec. 18, 2008; 75 FR 33169, June 11, 2010]

§ 416.1455 The effect of an administrative law judge's decision.

The decision of the administrative law judge is binding on all parties to the hearing unless—

(a) You or another party request a review of the decision by the Appeals Council within the stated time period, and the Appeals Council reviews your case;

(b) You or another party requests a review of the decision by the Appeals Council within the stated time period, the Appeals Council denies your request for review, and you seek judicial review of your case by filing an action in a Federal district court;

(c) The decision is revised by an administrative law judge or the Appeals Council under the procedures explained in § 416.1487;

(d) The expedited appeals process is used;

(e) The decision is a recommended decision directed to the Appeals Council; or

(f) In a case remanded by a Federal court, the Appeals Council assumes jurisdiction under the procedures in § 416.1484.

[51 FR 308, Jan. 3, 1986; 54 FR 37793, Sept. 13, 1989]

§ 416.1456 Removal of a hearing request from an administrative law judge to the Appeals Council.

If you have requested a hearing and the request is pending before an administrative law judge, the Appeals Council may assume responsibility for holding a hearing by requesting that the administrative law judge send the hearing request to it. If the Appeals Council holds a hearing, it shall conduct the hearing according to the rules for hearings before an administrative law judge. Notice shall be mailed to all parties at their last known address telling them that the Appeals Council has assumed responsibility for the case.

[51 FR 308, Jan. 3, 1986]

§ 416.1457 Dismissal of a request for a hearing before an administrative law judge.

An administrative law judge may dismiss a request for a hearing under any of the following conditions:

(a) At any time before notice of the hearing decision is mailed, you or the party or parties that requested the hearing ask to withdraw the request. This request may be submitted in writing to the administrative law judge or made orally at the hearing.

(b)(1)(i) Neither you nor the person you designate to act as your representative appears at the time and place set for the hearing and you have been notified before the time set for the hearing that your request for a hearing may be dismissed without further notice if you did not appear at the time and place of hearing, and good cause has not been found by the administrative law judge for your failure to appear; or

(ii) Neither you nor the person you designate to act as your representative appears at the time and place set for the hearing and within 10 days after the administrative law judge mails you a notice asking why you did not appear, you do not give a good reason for the failure to appear.

(2) In determining good cause or good reason under this paragraph, we will consider any physical, mental, educational, or linguistic limitations (including any lack of facility with the English language) which you may have.

(c) The administrative law judge decides that there is cause to dismiss a hearing request entirely or to refuse to consider any one or more of the issues because—

(1) The doctrine of res judicata applies in that we have made a previous determination or decision under this subpart about your rights on the same facts and on the same issue or issues, and this previous determination or decision has become final by either administrative or judicial action;

(2) The person requesting a hearing has no right to it under § 416.1430;

(3) You did not request a hearing within the stated time period and we have not extended the time for requesting a hearing under § 416.1433(c); or

(4) You die, there are no other parties, and we have no information to show that you may have a survivor who may be paid benefits due to you under § 416.542(b) and who wishes to pursue the request for hearing, or that you authorized interim assistance reimbursement to a State pursuant to section 1631(g) of the Act. The administrative law judge, however, will vacate a dismissal of the hearing request if, within 60 days after the date of the dismissal:

(i) A person claiming to be your survivor, who may be paid benefits due to you under § 416.542(b), submits a written request for a hearing, and shows that a decision on the issues that were to be considered at the hearing may adversely affect him or her; or

(ii) We receive information showing that you authorized interim assistance reimbursement to a State pursuant to section 1631(g) of the Act.

[50 FR 21439, May 24, 1985; 51 FR 308, Jan. 3, 1986; 58 FR 52913, Oct. 13, 1993; 59 FR 1637, Jan. 12, 1994]

§ 416.1458 Notice of dismissal of a request for a hearing before an administrative law judge.

We shall mail a written notice of the dismissal of the hearing request to all parties at their last known address. The notice will state that there is a right to request that the Appeals Council vacate the dismissal action.

[51 FR 308, Jan. 3, 1986]

§ 416.1459 Effect of dismissal of a request for a hearing before an administrative law judge.

The dismissal of a request for a hearing is binding, unless it is vacated by an administrative law judge or the Appeals Council.

[51 FR 308, Jan. 3, 1986]

§ 416.1460 Vacating a dismissal of a request for a hearing before an administrative law judge.

(a) Except as provided in paragraph (b) of this section, an administrative law judge or the Appeals Council may vacate a dismissal of a request for a hearing if you request that we vacate the dismissal. If you or another party wish to make this request, you must do so within 60 days of the date you receive notice of the dismissal, and you must state why our dismissal of your request for a hearing was erroneous. The administrative law judge or Appeals Council will inform you in writing of the action taken on your request. The Appeals Council may also vacate a dismissal of a request for a hearing on its own motion. If the Appeals Council decides to vacate a dismissal on its own motion, it will do so within 60 days of the date we mail the notice of dismissal and will inform you in writing that it vacated the dismissal.

(b) If you wish to proceed with a hearing after you received a fully favorable revised determination under the prehearing case review process in § 416.1441, you must follow the procedures in § 416.1441(d) to request that an administrative law judge vacate his or her order dismissing your request for a hearing.

[51 FR 308, Jan. 3, 1986; 76 FR 65371, Oct. 21, 2011]

§ 416.1461 Prehearing and posthearing conferences.

The administrative law judge may decide on his or her own, or at the request of any party to the hearing, to hold a prehearing or posthearing conference to facilitate the hearing or the hearing decision. The administrative law judge shall tell the parties of the time, place and purpose of the conference at least seven days before the conference date, unless the parties have indicated in writing that they do not wish to receive a written notice of the conference. At the conference, the administrative law judge may consider matters in addition to those stated in the notice, if the parties consent in writing. A record of the conference will be made. The administrative law judge shall issue an order stating all agreements and actions resulting from the conference. If the parties do not object, the agreements and actions become part of the hearing record and are binding on all parties.

§ 416.1465 [Reserved]

APPEALS COUNCIL REVIEW

§ 416.1466 Testing elimination of the request for Appeals Council review.

(a) Applicability and scope. Notwithstanding any other provision in this part or part 422 of this chapter, we are establishing the procedures set out in this section to test elimination of the request for review by the Appeals Council. These procedures will apply in randomly selected cases in which we have tested a combination of model procedures for modifying the disability claim process as authorized under §§ 416.1406 and 416.1443, and in which an administrative law judge has issued a decision (not including a recommended decision) that is less than fully favorable to you.

(b) Effect of an administrative law judge's decision. In a case to which the procedures of this section apply, the decision of an administrative law judge will be binding on all the parties to the hearing unless—

(1) You or another party file an action concerning the decision in Federal district court;

(2) The Appeals Council decides to review the decision on its own motion under the authority provided in § 416.1469, and it issues a notice announcing its decision to review the case on its own motion no later than the day before the filing date of a civil action establishing the jurisdiction of a Federal district court; or

(3) The decision is revised by the administrative law judge or the Appeals Council under the procedures explained in § 416.1487.

(c) Notice of the decision of an administrative law judge. The notice of decision the administrative law judge issues in a case processed under this section will advise you and any other parties to the decision that you may file an action in a Federal district court within 60 days after the date you receive notice of the decision.

(d) Extension of time to file action in Federal district court. Any party having a right to file a civil action under this section may request that the time for filing an action in Federal district court be extended. The request must be in writing and it must give the reasons why the action was not filed within the stated time period. The request must be filed with the Appeals Council. If you show that you had good cause for missing the deadline, the time period will be extended. To determine whether good cause exists, we will use the standards in § 416.1411.

[62 FR 49603, Sept. 23, 1997; 75 FR 33169, June 11, 2010]

§ 416.1467 Appeals Council review—general.

If you or any other party is dissatisfied with the hearing decision or with the dismissal of a hearing request, you may request that the Appeals Council review that action. The Appeals Council may deny or dismiss the request for review, or it may grant the request and either issue a decision or remand the case to an administrative law judge. The Appeals Council shall notify the parties at their last known address of the action it takes.

§ 416.1468 How to request Appeals Council review.

(a) Time and place to request Appeals Council review. You may request Appeals Council review by filing a written request. You should submit any evidence you wish to have considered by the Appeals Council with your request for review, and the Appeals Council will consider the evidence in accordance with § 416.1470. You may file your request at one of our offices within 60 days after the date you receive notice of the hearing decision or dismissal (or within the extended time period if we extend the time as provided in paragraph (b) of this section).

(b) Extension of time to request review. You or any party to a hearing decision may ask that the time for filing a request for the review be extended. The request for an extension of time must be in writing. It must be filed with the Appeals Council, and it must give the reasons why the request for review was not filed within the stated time period. If you show that you had good cause for missing the deadline, the time period will be extended. To determine whether good cause exists, we use the standards explained in § 416.1411.

[81 FR 90996, Dec. 16, 2016]

§ 416.1469 Appeals Council initiates review.

(a) General. Anytime within 60 days after the date of a decision or dismissal that is subject to review under this section, the Appeals Council may decide on its own motion to review the action that was taken in your case. We may refer your case to the Appeals Council for it to consider reviewing under this authority.

(b) Identification of cases. We will identify a case for referral to the Appeals Council for possible review under its own-motion authority before we effectuate a decision in the case. We will identify cases for referral to the Appeals Council through random and selective sampling techniques, which we may use in association with examination of the cases identified by sampling. We will also identify cases for referral to the Appeals Council through the evaluation of cases we conduct in order to effectuate decisions.

(1) Random and selective sampling and case examinations. We may use random and selective sampling to identify cases involving any type of action (i.e., fully or partially favorable decisions, unfavorable decisions,or dismissals) and any type of benefits (i.e., benefits based on disability and benefits not based on disability). We will use selective sampling to identify cases that exhibit problematic issues or fact patterns that increase the likelihood of error. Neither our random sampling procedures nor our selective sampling procedures will identify cases based on the identity of the decisionmaker or the identity of the office issuing the decision. We may examine cases that have been identified through random or selective sampling to refine the identification of cases that may meet the criteria for review by the Appeals Council.

(2) Identification as a result of the effectuation process. We may refer a case requiring effectuation to the Appeals Council if, in the view of the effectuating component, the decision cannot be effectuated because it contains a clerical error affecting the outcome of the claim; the decision is clearly inconsistent with the Social Security Act, the regulations, or a published ruling; or the decision is unclear regarding a matter that affects the claim's outcome.

(c) *Referral of cases.* We will make referrals that occur as the result of a case examination or the effectuation process in writing. The written referral based on the results of such a case examination or the effectuation process will state the referring component's reasons for believing that the Appeals Council should review the case on its own motion. Referrals that result from selective sampling without a case examination may be accompanied by a written statement identifying the issue(s) or fact pattern that caused the referral. Referrals that result from random sampling without a case examination will only identify the case as a random sample case.

(d) *Appeals Council's action.* If the Appeals Council decides to review a decision or dismissal on its own motion, it will mail a notice of review to all the parties as provided in § 416.1473. The Appeals Council will include with that notice a copy of any written referral it has received under paragraph (c) of this section. The Appeals Council's decision to review a case is established by its issuance of the notice of review. If it is unable to decide within the applicable 60–day period whether to review a decision or dismissal, the Appeals Council may consider the case to determine if the decision or dismissal should be reopened pursuant to §§ 416.1487 and 416.1488. If the Appeals Council decides to review a decision on its own motion or to reopen a decision as provided in §§ 416.1487 and 416.1488, the notice of review or the notice of reopening issued by the Appeals Council will advise, where appropriate, that interim benefits will be payable if a final decision has not been issued within 110 days after the date of the decision that is reviewed or reopened, and that any interim benefits paid will not be considered overpayments unless the benefits are fraudulently obtained.

[63 FR 36571, July 7, 1998; 75 FR 33169, June 11, 2010]

§ 416.1470 Cases the Appeals Council will review.

(a) The Appeals Council will review a case if—

(1) There appears to be an abuse of discretion by the administrative law judge;

(2) There is an error of law;

(3) The action, findings or conclusions of the administrative law judge are not supported by substantial evidence;

(4) There is a broad policy or procedural issue that may affect the general public interest; or

(5) Subject to paragraph (b) of this section, the Appeals Council receives additional evidence that is new, material, and relates to the period on or before the date of the hearing decision, and there is a reasonable probability that the additional evidence would change the outcome of the decision.

(b) In reviewing decisions other than those based on an application for benefits, the Appeals Council will consider the evidence in the administrative law judge hearing record and any additional evidence it believes is material to an issue being considered. However, in reviewing decisions based on an application for benefits, the Appeals Council will only consider additional evidence under paragraph (a)(5) of this section if you show good cause for not informing us about or submitting the evidence as described in § 416.1435 because:

(1) Our action misled you;

(2) You had a physical, mental, educational, or linguistic limitation(s) that prevented you from informing us about or submitting the evidence earlier; or

(3) Some other unusual, unexpected, or unavoidable circumstance beyond your control prevented you from informing us about or submitting the evidence earlier. Examples include, but are not limited to:

(i) You were seriously ill, and your illness prevented you from contacting us in person, in writing, or through a friend, relative, or other person;

(ii) There was a death or serious illness in your immediate family;

(iii) Important records were destroyed or damaged by fire or other accidental cause;

(iv) You actively and diligently sought evidence from a source and the evidence was not received or was received less than 5 business days prior to the hearing; or

(v) You received a hearing level decision on the record and the Appeals Council reviewed your decision.

(c) If you submit additional evidence that does not relate to the period on or before the date of the administrative law judge hearing decision as required in paragraph (a)(5) of this section, or the Appeals Council does not find you had good cause for missing the deadline to submit the evidence in § 416.1435, the Appeals Council will send you a notice that explains why it did not accept the additional evidence and advises you of your right to file a new application. The notice will also advise you that if you file a new application within 60 days after the date of the Appeals Council's notice, your request for review will constitute a written statement indicating an intent to claim benefits under § 416.340. If you file a new application within 60 days of the Appeals Council's notice, we will use the date you requested Appeals Council review as the filing date for your new application.

[52 FR 4004, Feb. 9, 1987; 81 FR 90996, Dec. 16, 2016]

§ 416.1471 Dismissal by Appeals Council.

The Appeals Council will dismiss your request for review if you did not file your request within the stated period of time and the time for filing has not been extended. The Appeals Council may also dismiss any proceedings before it if—

(a) You and any other party to the proceedings files a written request for dismissal; or

(b) You die, there are no other parties, and we have no information to show that you may have a survivor who may be paid benefits due to you under § 416.542(b) and who wishes to pursue the request for review, or that you authorized interim assistance reimbursement to a State pursuant to section 1631(g) of the Act. The Appeals Council, however, will vacate a dismissal of the request for review if, within 60 days after the date of the dismissal:

(1) A person claiming to be your survivor, who may be paid benefits due to you under § 416.542(b), submits a written request for review, and shows that a decision on the issues that were to be considered on review may adversely affect him or her; or

(2) We receive information showing that you authorized interim assistance reimbursement to a State pursuant to section 1631(g) of the Act.

[58 FR 52914, Oct. 13, 1993]

§ 416.1472 Effect of dismissal of request for Appeals Council review.

The dismissal of a request for Appeals Council review is binding and not subject to further review.

§ 416.1473 Notice of Appeals Council review.

When the Appeals Council decides to review a case, it shall mail a notice to all parties at their last known address stating the reasons for the review and the issues to be considered.

§ 416.1474 Obtaining evidence from Appeals Council.

You may request and receive copies or a statement of the documents or other written evidence upon which the hearing decision or dismissal was based and a copy or summary of the transcript of oral evidence. However, you will be asked to pay the costs of providing these copies unless there is a good reason why you should not pay.

§ 416.1475 Filing briefs with the Appeals Council.

Upon request, the Appeals Council shall give you and all other parties a reasonable opportunity to file briefs or other written statements about the facts and law relevant to the case. A copy of each brief or statement should be filed for each party.

§ 416.1476 Procedures before the Appeals Council on review.

(a) Limitation of issues. The Appeals Council may limit the issues it considers if it notifies you and the other parties of the issues it will review.

(b) Oral argument. You may request to appear before the Appeals Council to present oral argument. The Appeals Council will grant your request if it decides that your case raises an important question of law or policy or that oral argument would help to reach a proper decision. If your request to appear is granted, the Appeals Council will tell you the time and place of the oral argument at least 10 business days before the scheduled date. The Appeals Council will determine whether your appearance, or the appearance of any other person relevant to the proceeding, will be in person, by video teleconferencing, or by telephone.

[52 FR 4004, Feb. 9, 1987; 81 FR 6171, Feb. 5, 2016; 81 FR 90997, Dec. 16, 2016]

§ 416.1477 Case remanded by Appeals Council.

(a) When the Appeals Council may remand a case. The Appeals Council may remand a case to an administrative law judge so that he or she may hold a hearing and issue a decision or a recommended decision. The Appeals Council may also remand a case in which additional evidence is needed or additional action by the administrative law judge is required.

(b) Action by administrative law judge on remand. The administrative law judge shall take any action that is ordered by the Appeals Council and may take any additional action that is not inconsistent with the Appeals Council's remand order.

(c) Notice when case is returned with a recommended decision. When the administrative law judge sends a case to the Appeals Council with a recommended decision, a notice is mailed to the parties at their last known address. The notice tells them that the case has been sent to the Appeals Council, explains the rules for filing briefs or other written statements with the Appeals Council, and includes a copy of the recommended decision.

(d) Filing briefs with and obtaining evidence from the Appeals Council.

(1) You may file briefs or other written statements about the facts and law relevant to your case with the Appeals Council within 20 days of the date that the recommended decision is mailed to you. Any party may ask the Appeals Council for additional time to file briefs or statements. The Appeals Council will extend this period, as appropriate, if you show that you had good cause for missing the deadline.

(2) All other rules for filing briefs with and obtaining evidence from the Appeals Council follow the procedures explained in this subpart.

(e) Procedures before the Appeals Council.

(1) The Appeals Council after receiving a recommended decision will conduct its proceedings and issue its decision according to the procedures explained in this subpart.

(2) If the Appeals Council believes that more evidence is required, it may again remand the case to an administrative law judge for further inquiry into the issues, rehearing, receipt of evidence, and another

decision or recommended decision. However, if the Appeals Council decides that it can get the additional evidence more quickly, it will take appropriate action.

§ 416.1479 Decision of Appeals Council.

After it has reviewed all the evidence in the administrative law judge hearing record and any additional evidence received, subject to the limitations on Appeals Council consideration of additional evidence in § 416.1470, the Appeals Council will make a decision or remand the case to an administrative law judge. The Appeals Council may affirm, modify or reverse the administrative law judge hearing decision or it may adopt, modify or reject a recommended decision. If the Appeals Council issues its own decision, it will base its decision on the preponderance of the evidence. A copy of the Appeals Council's decision will be mailed to the parties at their last known address.

[52 FR 4005, Feb. 9, 1987; 73 FR 76945, Dec. 18, 2008; 81 FR 90997, Dec. 16, 2016]

§ 416.1481 Effect of Appeals Council's decision or denial of review.

The Appeals Council may deny a party's request for review or it may decide to review a case and make a decision. The Appeals Council's decision, or the decision of the administrative law judge if the request for review is denied, is binding unless you or another party file an action in Federal district court, or the decision is revised. You may file an action in a Federal district court within 60 days after the date you receive notice of the Appeals Council's action.

§ 416.1482 Extension of time to file action in Federal district court.

Any party to the Appeals Council's decision or denial of review, or to an expedited appeals process agreement, may request that the time for filing an action in a Federal district court be extended. The request must be in writing and it must give the reasons why the action was not filed within the stated time period. The request must be filed with the Appeals Council, or if it concerns an expedited appeals process agreement, with one of our offices. If you show that you had good cause for missing the deadline, the time period will be extended. To determine whether good cause exists, we use the standards explained in § 416.1411.

COURT REMAND CASES

§ 416.1483 Case remanded by a Federal court.

When a Federal court remands a case to the Commissioner for further consideration, the Appeals Council, acting on behalf of the Commissioner, may make a decision, or it may remand the case to an administrative law judge with instructions to take action and issue a decision or return the case to the Appeals Council with a recommended decision. If the case is remanded by the Appeals Council, the procedures explained in § 416.1477 will be followed. Any issues relating to your claim may be considered by the administrative law judge whether or not they were raised in the administrative proceedings leading to the final decision in your case.

[54 FR 37793, Sept. 13, 1989; 62 FR 38455, July 18, 1997]

§ 416.1484 Appeals Council review of administrative law judge decision in a case remanded by a Federal court.

(a) General. In accordance with § 416.1483, when a case is remanded by a Federal court for further consideration, the decision of the administrative law judge will become the final decision of the Commissioner after remand on your case unless the Appeals Council assumes jurisdiction of the case. The Appeals Council may assume jurisdiction based on written exceptions to the decision of the administrative law judge which you file with the Appeals Council or based on its authority pursuant to paragraph (c) of this section. If the Appeals Council assumes jurisdiction of your case, any issues relating to your claim may be considered by the Appeals Council whether or not they were raised in the administrative proceedings leading to the final decision in your case or subsequently considered by the administrative law judge in the administrative proceedings following the court's remand order. The Appeals Council will either make a new, independent decision based on the preponderance of the evidence in the record that will be the final decision of the Commissioner after remand, or it will remand the case to an administrative law judge for further proceedings.

(b) You file exceptions disagreeing with the decision of the administrative law judge.

(1) If you disagree with the decision of the administrative law judge, in whole or in part, you may file exceptions to the decision with the Appeals Council. Exceptions may be filed by submitting a written statement to the Appeals Council setting forth your reasons for disagreeing with the decision of the administrative law judge. The exceptions must be filed within 30 days of the date you receive the decision of the administrative law judge or an extension of time in which to submit exceptions must be requested in writing within the 30–day period. A timely request for a 30–day extension will be granted by the Appeals Council. A request for an extension of more than 30 days should include a statement of reasons as to why you need the additional time.

(2) If written exceptions are timely filed, the Appeals Council will consider your reasons for disagreeing with the decision of the administrative law judge and all the issues presented by your case. If the Appeals Council concludes that there is no reason to change the decision of the administrative law judge, it will issue a notice to you addressing your exceptions

and explaining why no change in the decision of the administrative law judge is warranted. In this instance, the decision of the administrative law judge is the final decision of the Commissioner after remand.

(3) When you file written exceptions to the decision of the administrative law judge, the Appeals Council may assume jurisdiction at any time, even after the 60–day time period which applies when you do not file exceptions. If the Appeals Council assumes jurisdiction, it will make a new, independent decision based on the preponderance of the evidence in the entire record affirming, modifying, or reversing the decision of the administrative law judge, or it will remand the case to an administrative law judge for further proceedings, including a new decision. The new decision of the Appeals Council is the final decision of the Commissioner after remand.

(c) Appeals Council assumes jurisdiction without exceptions being filed. Any time within 60 days after the date of the decision of the administrative law judge, the Appeals Council may decide to assume jurisdiction of your case even though no written exceptions have been filed. Notice of this action will be mailed to all parties at their last known address. You will be provided with the opportunity to file briefs or other written statements with the Appeals Council about the facts and law relevant to your case. After the Appeals Council receives the briefs or other written statements, or the time allowed (usually 30 days) for submitting them has expired, the Appeals Council will either issue a final decision of the Commissioner based on the preponderance of the evidence affirming, modifying, or reversing the decision of the administrative law judge, or remand the case to an administrative law judge for further proceedings, including a new decision.

(d) Exceptions are not filed and the Appeals Council does not otherwise assume jurisdiction. If no exceptions are filed and the Appeals Council does not assume jurisdiction of your case, the decision of the administrative law judge becomes the final decision of the Commissioner after remand.

[54 FR 37793, Sept. 13, 1989; 62 FR 38455, July 18, 1997; 73 FR 76945, Dec. 18, 2008]

§ 416.1485 Application of circuit court law.

The procedures which follow apply to administrative determinations or decisions on claims involving the application of circuit court law.

(a) General. We will apply a holding in a United States Court of Appeals decision that we determine conflicts with our interpretation of a provision of the Social Security Act or regulations unless the Government seeks further judicial review of that decision or we relitigate the issue presented in the decision in accordance with paragraphs (c) and (d) of this section. We will apply the holding to claims at all levels of the administrative review process within the applicable circuit unless the holding, by its nature, applies only at certain levels of adjudication.

(b) Issuance of an Acquiescence Ruling. When we determine that a United States Court of Appeals holding conflicts with our interpretation of a provision of the Social Security Act or regulations and the Government does not seek further judicial review or is unsuccessful on further review, we will issue a Social Security Acquiescence Ruling. The Acquiescence Ruling will describe the administrative case and the court decision, identify the issue(s) involved, and explain how we will apply the holding, including, as necessary, how the holding relates to other decisions within the applicable circuit. These Acquiescence Rulings will generally be effective on the date of their publication in the Federal Register and will apply to all determinations, redeterminations, and decisions made on or after that date unless an Acquiescence Ruling is rescinded as stated in paragraph (e) of this section. The process we will use when issuing an Acquiescence Ruling follows:

(1) We will release an Acquiescence Ruling for publication in the Federal Register for any precedential circuit court decision that we determine contains a holding that conflicts with our interpretation of a provision of the Social Security Act or regulations no later than 120 days from the receipt of the court's decision. This timeframe will not apply when we decide to seek further judicial review of the circuit court decision or when coordination with the Department of Justice and/or other Federal agencies makes this timeframe no longer feasible.

(2) If we make a determination or decision on your claim between the date of a circuit court decision and the date we publish an Acquiescence Ruling, you may request application of the published Acquiescence Ruling to the prior determination or decision. You must demonstrate that application of the Acquiescence Ruling could change the prior determination or decision in your case. You may demonstrate this by submitting a statement that cites the Acquiescence Ruling or the holding or portion of a circuit court decision which could change the prior determination or decision in your case. If you can so demonstrate, we will readjudicate the claim in accordance with the Acquiescence Ruling at the level at which it was last adjudicated. Any readjudication will be limited to consideration of the issue(s) covered by the Acquiescence Ruling and any new determination or decision on readjudication will be subject to administrative and judicial review in accordance with this subpart. Our denial of a request for readjudication will not be subject to further administrative or judicial review. If you file a request for readjudication within the 60–day appeal period and we deny that request, we shall extend the time to file an appeal on the merits of the claim to 60 days after the date that we deny the request for readjudication.

(3) After we receive a precedential circuit court decision and determine that an Acquiescence Ruling

may be required, we will begin to identify those claims that are pending before us within the circuit and that might be subject to readjudication if an Acquiescence Ruling is subsequently issued. When an Acquiescence Ruling is published, we will send a notice to those individuals whose cases we have identified which may be affected by the Acquiescence Ruling. The notice will provide information about the Acquiescence Ruling and the right to request readjudication under that Acquiescence Ruling, as described in paragraph (b)(2) of this section. It is not necessary for an individual to receive a notice in order to request application of an Acquiescence Ruling to his or her claim, as described in paragraph (b)(2) of this section.

(c) Relitigation of court's holding after publication of an Acquiescence Ruling. After we have published an Acquiescence Ruling to reflect a holding of a United States Court of Appeals on an issue, we may decide under certain conditions to relitigate that issue within the same circuit. We may relitigate only when the conditions specified in paragraphs (c)(2) and (3) of this section are met, and, in general, one of the events specified in paragraph (c)(1) of this section occurs.

(1) Activating events:

(i) An action by both Houses of Congress indicates that a circuit court decision on which an Acquiescence Ruling was based was decided inconsistently with congressional intent, such as may be expressed in a joint resolution, an appropriations restriction, or enactment of legislation which affects a closely analogous body of law;

(ii) A statement in a majority opinion of the same circuit indicates that the court might no longer follow its previous decision if a particular issue were presented again;

(iii) Subsequent circuit court precedent in other circuits supports our interpretation of the Social Security Act or regulations on the issue(s) in question; or

(iv) A subsequent Supreme Court decision presents a reasonable legal basis for questioning a circuit court holding upon which we base an Acquiescence Ruling.

(2) The General Counsel of the Social Security Administration, after consulting with the Department of Justice, concurs that relitigation of an issue and application of our interpretation of the Social Security Act or regulations to selected claims in the administrative review process within the circuit would be appropriate.

(3) We publish a notice in the Federal Register that we intend to relitigate an Acquiescence Ruling issue and that we will apply our interpretation of the Social Security Act or regulations within the circuit to claims in the administrative review process selected for relitigation. The notice will explain why we made this decision.

(d) Notice of relitigation. When we decide to relitigate an issue, we will provide a notice explaining our action to all affected claimants. In adjudicating claims subject to relitigation, decisionmakers throughout the SSA administrative review process will apply our interpretation of the Social Security Act and regulations, but will also state in written determinations or decisions how the claims would have been decided under the circuit standard. Claims not subject to relitigation will continue to be decided under the Acquiescence Ruling in accordance with the circuit standard. So that affected claimants can be readily identified and any subsequent decision of the circuit court or the Supreme Court can be implemented quickly and efficiently, we will maintain a listing of all claimants who receive this notice and will provide them with the relief ordered by the court.

(e) Rescission of an Acquiescence Ruling. We will rescind as obsolete an Acquiescence Ruling and apply our interpretation of the Social Security Act or regulations by publishing a notice in the Federal Register when any of the following events occurs:

(1) The Supreme Court overrules or limits a circuit court holding that was the basis of an Acquiescence Ruling;

(2) A circuit court overrules or limits itself on an issue that was the basis of an Acquiescence Ruling;

(3) A Federal law is enacted that removes the basis for the holding in a decision of a circuit court that was the subject of an Acquiescence Ruling; or

(4) We subsequently clarify, modify or revoke the regulation or ruling that was the subject of a circuit court holding that we determined conflicts with our interpretation of the Social Security Act or regulations, or we subsequently publish a new regulation(s) addressing an issue(s) not previously included in our regulations when that issue(s) was the subject of a circuit court holding that conflicted with our interpretation of the Social Security Act or regulations and that holding was not compelled by the statute or Constitution.

[55 FR 1020, Jan. 11, 1990; 62 FR 38455, July 18, 1997; 63 FR 24933, May 6, 1998]

REOPENING AND REVISING DETERMINATIONS AND DECISIONS

§ 416.1487 Reopening and revising determinations and decisions.

(a) General. Generally, if you are dissatisfied with a determination or decision made in the administrative review process, but do not request further review within the stated time period, you lose your right to further review and that determination or decision becomes final. However, a determination or a decision made in your case which is otherwise final and binding may be reopened and revised by us.

(b) Procedure for reopening and revision. We may reopen a final determination or decision on our own initiative, or you may ask that a final determination or a decision to which you were a party be reopened. In either instance, if we reopen the determination or decision, we may revise that determination or decision. The conditions under which we may reopen a previous determination or decision, either on our own initiative or at your request, are explained in § 416.1488.

[59 FR 8535, Feb. 23, 1994]

§ 416.1488 Conditions for reopening.

A determination, revised determination, decision, or revised decision may be reopened—

(a) Within 12 months of the date of the notice of the initial determination, for any reason;

(b) Within two years of the date of the notice of the initial determination if we find good cause, as defined in § 416.1489, to reopen the case; or

(c) At any time if it was obtained by fraud or similar fault. In determining whether a determination or decision was obtained by fraud or similar fault, we will take into account any physical, mental, educational, or linguistic limitations (including any lack of facility with the English language) which you may have had at the time.

[59 FR 1637, Jan. 12, 1994]

§ 416.1489 Good cause for reopening.

(a) We will find that there is good cause to reopen a determination or decision if—

(1) New and material evidence is furnished;

(2) A clerical error was made; or

(3) The evidence that was considered in making the determination or decision clearly shows on its face that an error was made.

(b) We will not find good cause to reopen your case if the only reason for reopening is a change of legal interpretation or administrative ruling upon which the determination or decision was made.

§ 416.1491 Late completion of timely investigation.

We may revise a determination or decision after the applicable time period in § 416.1488(a) or § 416.1488(b) expires if we begin an investigation into whether to revise the determination or decision before the applicable time period expires. We may begin the investigation either based on a request by you or by an action on our part. The investigation is a process of gathering facts after a determination or decision has been reopened to determine if a revision of the determination or decision is applicable.

(a) If we have diligently pursued the investigation to its conclusion, we may revise the determination or decision. The revision may be favorable or unfavorable to you. "Diligently pursued" means that in light of the facts and circumstances of a particular case, the necessary action was undertaken and carried out as promptly as the circumstances permitted. Diligent pursuit will be presumed to have been met if we conclude the investigation and if necessary, revise the determination or decision within 6 months from the date we began the investigation.

(b) If we have not diligently pursued the investigation to its conclusion, we will revise the determination or decision if a revision is applicable and if it will be favorable to you. We will not revise the determination or decision if it will be unfavorable to you.

[49 FR 46370, Nov. 26, 1984; 49 FR 48036, Dec. 10, 1984]

§ 416.1492 Notice of revised determination or decision.

(a) When a determination or decision is revised, notice of the revision will be mailed to the parties at their last known address. The notice will state the basis for the revised determination or decision and the effect of the revision. The notice will also inform the parties of the right to further review.

(b) If a determination is revised and the revised determination requires that your benefits be suspended, reduced, or terminated, the notice will inform you of your right to continued payment (see § 416.1336 and the exceptions set out in § 416.1337) and of your right of reconsideration.

(c) If a determination is revised and the revised determination does not require that your benefits be suspended, reduced, or terminated, the notice will inform you of your right to a hearing before an administrative law judge.

(d) If a reconsidered determination that you are blind or disabled, based on medical factors, is reopened for the purpose of being revised, you will be notified, in writing, of the proposed revision and of your right to request that a disability hearing be held before a revised reconsidered determination is issued. If a revised reconsidered determination is issued, you may request a hearing before an administrative law judge.

(e) If an administrative law judge or the Appeals Council proposes to revise a decision, and the revision would be based on evidence not included in the record on which the prior decision was based, you and any other parties to the decision will be notified, in writing, of the proposed action and of your right to request that a hearing be held before any further action is taken. If a revised decision is issued by an administrative law judge, you and any other party may request that it be reviewed by the Appeals Council, or the Appeals Council may review the decision on its own initiative.

(f) If an administrative law judge or the Appeals Council proposes to revise a decision, and the revision would be based only on evidence included in the record on which the prior decision was based, you and any other parties to the decision will be notified, in writing, of the proposed action. If a revised decision is issued by an administrative law judge, you and any other party may request that it be reviewed by the Appeals Council, or the Appeals Council may review the decision on its own initiative.

(g) An administrative law judge may, in connection with a valid request for a hearing, propose to reopen an issue other than the issue on which the request for a hearing was based. The administrative law judge will follow the time limits for reopenings set out in § 416.1488. The administrative law judge shall mail to the parties at their last known address a notice of the reopening.

[51 FR 308, Jan. 3, 1986]

§ 416.1493 Effect of revised determination or decision.

A revised determination or decision is binding unless—

(a) You or a party to the revised determination file a written request for a reconsideration or a hearing;

(b) You or another party to the revised decision file, as appropriate, a request for review by the Appeals Council or a hearing;

(c) The Appeals Council reviews the revised decision; or

(d) The revised determination or decision is further revised.

§ 416.1494 Time and place to request further review or a hearing on revised determination or decision.

You or another party to the revised determination or decision may request, as appropriate, further review or a hearing on the revision by filing a request in writing at one of our offices within 60 days after the date you receive notice of the revision. Further review or a hearing will be held on the revision according to the rules of this subpart.

PAYMENT OF CERTAIN TRAVEL EXPENSES

§ 416.1495 Payment of certain travel expenses—general.

When you file a claim for supplemental security income (SSI) benefits, you may incur certain travel expenses in pursuing your claim. Sections 416.1496 through 416.1499 explain who may be reimbursed for travel expenses, the types of travel expenses that are reimbursable, and when and how to claim reimbursement. Generally, the agency that requests you to travel will be the agency that reimburses you. No later than when it notifies you of the examination or hearing described in § 416.1496(a), that agency will give you information about the right to travel reimbursement, the right to advance payment and how to request it, the rules on means of travel and unusual travel costs, and the need to submit receipts.

[51 FR 8810, March 14, 1986]

§ 416.1496 Who may be reimbursed.

(a) The following individuals may be reimbursed for certain travel expenses—

(1) You, when you attend medical examinations upon request in connection with disability determinations; these are medical examinations requested by the State agency or by us when additional medical evidence is necessary to make a disability determination (also referred to as consultative examinations, see § 416.917);

(2) You, your representative (see § 416.1505 (a) and (b)), and all unsubpoenaed witnesses we or the State agency determines to be reasonably necessary who attend disability hearings; and

(3) You, your representative, and all unsubpoenaed witnesses we determine to be reasonably necessary who attend hearings on any claim for SSI benefits before an administrative law judge.

(b) Sections 416.1495 through 416.1499 do not apply to subpoenaed witnesses. They are reimbursed under §§ 416.1450(d) and 416.1416(b)(1).

[51 FR 8810, March 14, 1986]

§ 416.1498 What travel expenses are reimbursable.

Reimbursable travel expenses include the ordinary expenses of public or private transportation as well as unusual costs due to special circumstances.

(a) Reimbursement for ordinary travel expenses is limited—

(1) To the cost of travel by the most economical and expeditious means of transportation available and appropriate to the individual's condition of health as determined by the State agency or by us, considering the available means in the following order—

(i) Common carrier (air, rail, or bus);

(ii) Privately owned vehicles;

(iii) Commercially rented vehicles and other special conveyances;

(2) If air travel is necessary, to the coach fare for air travel between the specified travel points involved unless first-class air travel is authorized in advance by the State agency or by the Secretary in instances when—

(i) Space is not available in less-than-first-class accommodations on any scheduled flights in time to accomplish the purpose of the travel;

(ii) First-class accommodations are necessary because you, your representative, or reasonably necessary witness is so handicapped or otherwise impaired that other accommodations are not practical and the impairment is substantiated by competent medical authority;

(iii) Less-than-first-class accommodations on foreign carriers do not provide adequate sanitation or health standards; or

(iv) The use of first-class accommodations would result in an overall savings to the government based on economic considerations, such as the avoidance of additional subsistence costs that would be incurred while awaiting availability of less-than-first-class accommodations.

(b) Unusual travel costs may be reimbursed but must be authorized in advance and in writing by us or the appropriate State official, as applicable, unless they are unexpected or unavoidable; we or the State agency must determine their reasonableness and necessity and must approve them before payment can be made. Unusual expenses that may be covered in connection with travel include, but are not limited to—

(1) Ambulance services;

(2) Attendant services;

(3) Meals;

(4) Lodging; and

(5) Taxicabs.

(c) If we reimburse you for travel, we apply the rules in §§ 416.1496 through 416.1499 and the same rates and conditions of payment that govern travel expenses for Federal employees as authorized under 41 CFR chapter 301. If a State agency reimburses you, the reimbursement rates shall be determined by the rules in §§ 416.1496 through 416.1499 and that agency's rules and regulations and may differ from one agency to another and also may differ from the Federal reimbursement rates.

(1) When public transportation is used, reimbursement will be made for the actual costs incurred, subject to the restrictions in paragraph (a)(2) of this section on reimbursement for first-class air travel.

(2) When travel is by a privately owned vehicle, reimbursement will be made at the current Federal or State mileage rate specified for that geographic location plus the actual costs of tolls and parking, if travel by a privately owned vehicle is determined appropriate under paragraph (a)(1) of this section. Otherwise, the amount of reimbursement for travel by privately owned vehicle cannot exceed the total cost of the most economical public transportation for travel between the same two points. "Total cost" includes the cost for all the authorized travelers who travel in the same privately owned vehicle. Advance approval of travel by privately owned vehicle is not required (but could give you assurance of its approval).

(3) Sometimes your health condition dictates a mode of transportation different from most economical and expeditious. In order for your health to require a mode of transportation other than common carrier or passenger car, you must be so handicapped or otherwise impaired as to require special transportation arrangements and the condition must be substantiated by competent medical authority.

(d) For travel to a hearing—

(1) Reimbursement is limited to travel within the U.S. For this purpose, the U.S. includes the U.S. as defined in § 416.120(c)(10).

(2) When the travel is performed after September 30, 1981, we or the State agency will reimburse you, your representative, or an unsubpoenaed witness only if the distance from the person's residence or office (whichever he or she travels from) to the hearing site exceeds 75 miles.

(3) For travel expenses incurred on or after April 1, 1991, the amount of reimbursement under this section for travel by your representative to attend a disability hearing or a hearing before an administrative law judge shall not exceed the maximum amount allowable under this section for travel to the hearing site from any point within the geographic area of the office having jurisdiction over the hearing.

(i) The geographic area of the office having jurisdiction over the hearing means, as appropriate—

(A) The designated geographic service area of the State agency adjudicatory unit having responsibility for providing the disability hearing;

(B) If a Federal disability hearing officer holds the disability hearing, the geographic area of the State (as defined in § 416.120(c)(9)) in which the claimant resides or, if the claimant is not a resident of a State, in which the hearing officer holds the disability hearing; or

(C) The designated geographic service area of the Office of Hearings and Appeals hearing office having responsibility for providing the hearing before an administrative law judge.

(ii) We or the State agency determine the maximum amount allowable for travel by a representative based on the distance to the hearing site from the farthest point within the appropriate geographic area. In determining the maximum amount allowable for travel between these two points, we or the State agency apply the rules in paragraphs (a) through (c) of this section and the limitations in paragraph (d)(1) and (4) of this section. If the distance between these two points does not exceed 75 miles, we or the State agency will not reimburse any of your representative's travel expenses.

(4) If a change in the location of the hearing is made at your request from the location we or the State agency selected to one farther from your residence or office, neither your additional travel expenses nor the additional travel expenses of your representative and witnesses will be reimbursed.

[51 FR 8810, March 14, 1986; 59 FR 8532, Feb. 23, 1994]

§ 416.1499 When and how to claim reimbursement.

(a)(1) Generally, you will be reimbursed for your expenses after your trip. However, travel advances may be authorized if you request prepayment and show that the requested advance is reasonable and necessary.

(2) You must submit to us or the State agency, as appropriate, an itemized list of what you spent and supporting receipts to be reimbursed.

(3) Arrangements for special means of transportation and related unusual costs may be made only if we or the State agency authorizes the costs in writing in advance of travel, unless the costs are unexpected or unavoidable. If they are unexpected or unavoidable we or the State agency must determine their reasonableness and necessity and must approve them before payment may be made.

(4) If you receive prepayment, you must, within 20 days after your trip, provide to us or the State agency, as appropriate, an itemized list of your actual travel costs and submit supporting receipts. We or the State agency will require you to pay back any balance of the advanced amount that exceeds any approved travel expenses within 20 days after you are notified of the amount of that balance. (State agencies may have their own time limits in place of the 20–day periods in the preceding two sentences.)

(b) You may claim reimbursable travel expenses incurred by your representative for which you have been billed by your representative, except that if your representative makes a claim for them to us or the State, he or she will be reimbursed directly.

(Approved by the Office of Management and Budget under control number 0960–0434)

[51 FR 8810, March 14, 1986; 51 FR 28545, Aug. 8, 1986; 51 FR 44983, Dec. 16, 1986]

SUBPART O—REPRESENTATION OF PARTIES

Authority: Secs. 702(a)(5), 1127, and 1631(d) of the Social Security Act (42 U.S.C. 902(a)(5), 1320a–6, and 1383(d)).

Source: 45 FR 52106, Aug. 5, 1980; 52 FR 27541, July 22, 1987; 61 FR 5942, Feb. 15, 1996; 72 FR 16725, April 5, 2007; 72 FR 44767, Aug. 9, 2007; 76 FR 45194, July 28, 2011; 76 FR 56109, Sept. 12, 2011; 80 FR 399, Jan. 6, 2015, unless otherwise noted.

§ 416.1500 Introduction.

You may appoint someone to represent you in any of your dealings with us. This subpart explains, among other things—

(a) Who may be your representative and what his or her qualifications must be;

(b) How you appoint a representative;

(c) The payment of fees to a representative;

(d) Our rules that representatives must follow; and

(e) What happens to a representative who breaks the rules.

§ 416.1503 Definitions.

As used in this subpart:

Date we notify him or her means 5 days after the date on the notice, unless the recipient shows us that he or she did not receive it within the 5–day period.

Eligible non-attorney means a non-attorney representative who we determine is qualified to receive direct payment of his or her fee under § 416.1517(a).

Entity means any business, firm, or other association, including but not limited to partnerships, corporations, for-profit organizations, and not-for-profit organizations.

Federal agency refers to any authority of the Executive branch of the Government of the United States.

Federal program refers to any program established by an Act of Congress or administered in whole or in part by a Federal agency.

Legal guardian or court-appointed representative means a court-appointed person, committee, or conservator who is responsible for taking care of and managing the property and rights of an individual who is considered incapable of managing his or her own affairs.

Past-due benefits means the total amount of payments under title XVI of the Act, the Supplemental Security Income (SSI) program, including any Federally administered State payments, that has accumulated to you and your spouse because of a favorable administrative or judicial determination or decision, up to but not including the month the determination or decision is made. For purposes of calculating fees for representation, we first determine the SSI past-due benefits before any applicable reduction for reimbursement to a State (or political subdivision) for interim assistance reimbursement, and before any applicable reduction under section 1127 of the Act (for receipt of benefits for the same period under title II). We then reduce that figure by the amount of any reduction of title II or title XVI benefits that was required by section 1127. We do this whether the actual offset, as provided under section 1127, reduced the title II or title XVI benefits. Past-due benefits do not include:

(1) Continued benefits paid pursuant to § 416.996 of this part;

(2) Continued benefits paid pursuant to § 416.1336(b) of this part; or

(3) Interim benefits paid pursuant to section 1631(a)(8) of the Act.

Representational services means services performed for a claimant in connection with any claim the claimant has before us, any asserted right the claimant may have for an initial or reconsidered determination, and any decision or action by an administrative law judge or the Appeals Council.

Representative means an attorney who meets all of the requirements of § 416.1505(a), or a person other than an attorney who meets all of the requirements of § 416.1505(b), and whom you appoint to represent you in dealings with us.

We, our, or us refers to the Social Security Administration (SSA).

You or your refers to any person or the eligible spouse of any person claiming or receiving supplemental security income benefits.

[62 FR 38455, July 18, 1997; 72 FR 16725, April 5, 2007; 72 FR 44767, Aug. 9, 2007; 74 FR 48384, Sept. 23, 2009; 76 FR 45194, July 28, 2011; 76 FR 80247, Dec. 23, 2011; 80 FR 399, Jan. 6, 2015]

§ 416.1505 Who may be your representative.

(a) You may appoint as your representative in dealings with us any attorney in good standing who—

(1) Has the right to practice law before a court of a State, Territory, District, or island possession of the United States, or before the Supreme Court or a lower Federal court of the United States;

(2) Is not disqualified or suspended from acting as a representative in dealings with us; and

(3) Is not prohibited by any law from acting as a representative.

(b) You may appoint any person who is not an attorney to be your representative in dealings with us if the person—

(1) Is capable of giving valuable help to you in connection with your claim;

(2) Is not disqualified or suspended from acting as a representative in dealings with us;

(3) Is not prohibited by any law from acting as a representative; and

(4) Is generally known to have a good character and reputation. Persons lacking good character and reputation, include, but are not limited to, persons who have a final conviction of a felony (as defined by § 404.1506(c) of this chapter), or any crime involving moral turpitude, dishonesty, false statement, misrepresentations, deceit, or theft.

(c) We may refuse to recognize the person you choose to represent you if the person does not meet the requirements in this section. We will notify you and the person you attempted to appoint as your representative if we do not recognize the person as a representative.

[76 FR 80247, Dec. 23, 2011; 83 FR 30857, July 2, 2018]

§ 416.1506 Notification of options for obtaining attorney representation.

If you are not represented by an attorney and we make a determination or decision that is subject to the administrative review process provided under subpart N of this part and it does not grant all of the benefits or other relief you requested or it adversely affects any eligibility to benefits that we have established or may establish for you, we will include with the notice of that determination or decision information about your options for obtaining an attorney to represent you in dealing with us. We will also tell you that a legal services organization may provide you with legal representation free of charge if you satisfy the qualifying requirements applicable to that organization.

[58 FR 64886, Dec. 10, 1993]

§ 416.1507 Appointing a representative.

We will recognize a person as your representative if the following things are done:

(a) You sign a written notice stating that you want the person to be your representative in dealings with us.

(b) That person signs the notice, agreeing to be your representative, if the person is not an attorney. An attorney does not have to sign a notice of appointment.

(c) The notice is filed at one of our offices if you have initially filed a claim or requested reconsideration; with an administrative law judge if you have requested a hearing; or with the Appeals Council if you have requested a review of the administrative law judge's decision.

§ 416.1510 Authority of a representative.

(a) What a representative may do. Your representative may, on your behalf—

(1) Obtain information about your claim to the same extent that you are able to do;

(2) Submit evidence;

(3) Make statements about facts and law; and

(4) Make any request or give any notice about the proceedings before us.

(b) What a representative may not do. A representative may not sign an application on behalf of a claimant for rights or benefits under title XVI of the Act unless authorized to do so under § 416.315.

§ 416.1513 Mandatory use of electronic services.

A representative must conduct business with us electronically at the times and in the manner we prescribe on matters for which the representative requests direct fee payment. (See § 416.1540(b)(4)).

[76 FR 56109, Sept. 12, 2011]

§ 416.1515 Notice or request to a representative.

(a) We shall send your representative—

(1) Notice and a copy of any administrative action, determination, or decision; and

(2) Requests for information or evidence.

(b) A notice or request sent to your representative will have the same force and effect as if it had been sent to you.

§ 416.1517 Direct payment of fees to eligible non-attorney representatives.

(a) Criteria for eligibility. An individual who is a licensed attorney or who is suspended or disbarred from the practice of law in any jurisdiction may not be an eligible non-attorney. A non-attorney representative is eligible to receive direct payment of his or her fee out of your past-due benefits if he or she:

(1) Completes and submits to us an application as described in paragraph (b) of this section;

(2) Pays the application fee as described in paragraph (c) of this section;

(3) Demonstrates that he or she possesses:

(i) A bachelor's degree from an accredited institution of higher learning; or

(ii) At least four years of relevant professional experience and either a high school diploma or a General Educational Development certificate;

(4) Passes our criminal background investigation (including checks of our administrative records), and attests under penalty of perjury that he or she:

(i) Has not been suspended or disqualified from practice before us and is not suspended or disbarred from the practice of law in any jurisdiction;

(ii) Has not had a judgment or lien assessed against him or her by a civil court for malpractice or fraud;

(iii) Has not had a felony conviction; and

(iv) Has not misrepresented information provided on his or her application or supporting materials for the application;

(5) Takes and passes a written examination we administer;

(6) Provides proof of and maintains continuous liability insurance coverage that is underwritten by an entity that is legally permitted to provide professional liability insurance in the States in which the representative conducts business. The policy must include coverage for malpractice claims against the representative and be in an amount we prescribe; and

(7) Completes and provides proof that he or she has completed all continuing education courses that we prescribe by the deadline we prescribe.

(b) Application. An applicant must timely submit his or her completed application form during an application period that we prescribe. The application must be postmarked by the last day of the application period. If an applicant timely submits the application fee and a defective application, we will give the applicant 10 calendar days after the date we notify him or her of the defect to correct the application.

(c) Application fee. An applicant must timely submit his or her application fee during the application period. We will set the fee annually.

(1) We will refund the fee if:

(i) We do not administer an examination, and an applicant was unable to take the rescheduled examination; or

(ii) Circumstances beyond the applicant's control that could not have been reasonably anticipated and planned for prevent an applicant from taking a scheduled examination.

(2) We will not refund the fee if:

(i) An applicant took and failed the examination; or

(ii) An applicant failed to arrive on time for the examination because of circumstances within the applicant's control that could have been anticipated and planned for.

(d) Protest procedures.

(1) We may find that a non-attorney representative is ineligible to receive direct fee payment at any time because he or she fails to meet any of the criteria in paragraph (a) of this section. A non-attorney representative whom we find to be ineligible for direct fee payment may protest our finding only if we based it on the representative's failure to:

(i) Attest on the application or provide sufficient documentation that he or she possesses the required education or equivalent qualifications, as described in paragraph (a)(3) of this section;

(ii) Meet at all times the criminal background investigation criteria, as described in paragraph (a)(4) of this section;

(iii) Provide proof that he or she has maintained continuous liability insurance coverage, as described in paragraph (a)(6) of this section, after we previously determined the representative was eligible to receive direct fee payment; or

(iv) Complete continuing education courses or provide documentation of the required continuing education courses, as described in paragraph (a)(7) of this section.

(2) A non-attorney representative who wants to protest our finding under paragraph (d)(1) of this section must file a protest in writing and provide all relevant supporting documentation to us within 10 calendar days after the date we notify him or her of our finding.

(3) A representative may not file a protest for reasons other than those listed in paragraph (d)(1) of this section. If a representative files a protest for reasons other than those listed in paragraph (d)(1) of this section, we will not process the protest and will implement our finding as if no protest had been filed. Our finding in response to the protest is final and not subject to further review.

(e) Ineligibility and suspension.

(1) If an applicant does not protest, in accordance with paragraph (d)(2) of this section, our finding about the criteria in paragraphs (a)(3) or (a)(4) of this section, the applicant will be either ineligible to take the written examination for which he or she applied or ineligible to receive direct fee payment if the applicant already took and passed the examination prior to our finding. If an applicant protests in accordance with paragraph (d)(2) of this section and we uphold our finding, the applicant will be either ineligible to take the written examination for which he or she applied or ineligible to receive direct fee payment if the applicant already took and passed the examination prior to our finding.

(2) If an eligible non-attorney representative does not protest, in accordance with paragraph (d)(2) of this section, our finding about the criteria in paragraphs (a)(3) or (a)(4) of this section, the non-attorney representative will be ineligible to receive direct fee payment beginning with the month after the month the protest period ends. If the eligible non-attorney representative protests in accordance with paragraph (d)(2) of this section and we uphold our finding, the non-attorney representative will be ineligible to receive direct fee payment beginning with the month after the month we uphold our finding.

(3) If an eligible non-attorney representative does not protest, in accordance with paragraph (d)(2) of this section, our finding about the criteria in paragraph (a)(6) of this section, the non-attorney representative will be ineligible to receive direct fee payment for 6 full calendar months beginning with the month after the month the protest period ends. If the eligible non-attorney representative protests in accordance with paragraph (d)(2) of this section and we uphold our finding, the non-attorney representative will be ineligible to receive direct fee payment for 6 full calendar months beginning with the month after the month we uphold our finding. In either case, the non-attorney representative may provide us with documentation that he or she has acquired and maintains the required liability insurance coverage described in paragraph (a)(6) of this section, no earlier than the sixth month of the ineligibility. The non-attorney representative will again be eligible to receive direct fee payment beginning in the first month after the month we find that we have received sufficient documentation that the non-attorney representative meets the requirements of paragraph (a)(6) of this section.

(4) If an eligible non-attorney representative does not protest, in accordance with paragraph (d)(2) of this section, our finding about the criteria in paragraph (a)(7) of this section, the non-attorney representative will be ineligible to receive direct fee payment for 6 full calendar months beginning with the month after the month the protest period ends. If the eligible non-attorney representative protests in accordance with paragraph (d)(2) of this section and we uphold our finding, the non-attorney will be ineligible to receive direct fee payment for 6 full calendar months beginning with the month after the month we uphold our finding. In either case, the non-attorney representative may provide us with documentation that he or she has satisfied the criteria in paragraph (a)(7) of this section at any time. The non-attorney representative will again be eligible to receive direct fee payment beginning in the first month after the month we find that we have received sufficient documentation, but not earlier than the month following the end of the 6 month ineligibility period.

(f) Reapplying. A representative may reapply to become eligible to receive direct fee payment under paragraph (a) of this section during any subsequent application period if he or she:

(1) Did not meet the initial criteria for eligibility in paragraph (a)(1), (2), (3), or (5) of this section in a prior application period; or

(2) Failed to timely correct a defective application in a prior application period as described in paragraph (b) of this section.

[72 FR 16725, April 5, 2007; 72 FR 44767, Aug. 9, 2007; 76 FR 45194, July 28, 2011; 80 FR 399, 400, Jan. 6, 2015]

§ 416.1520 Fee for a representative's services.

(a) General. A representative may charge and receive a fee for his or her services as a representative only as provided in paragraph (b) of this section.

(b) Charging and receiving a fee.

(1) The representative must file a written request with us before he or she may charge or receive a fee for his or her services.

(2) We decide the amount of the fee, if any, a representative may charge or receive.

(3) Subject to paragraph (e) of this section, a representative must not charge or receive any fee unless we have authorized it, and a representative must not charge or receive any fee that is more than the amount we authorize.

(4) If your representative is an attorney or an eligible non-attorney, and you are entitled to past-due benefits, we will pay the authorized fee, or a part of the authorized fee, directly to the attorney or eligible non-attorney out of the past-due benefits, subject to the limitations described in § 416.1530(b)(1). If the repre-

sentative is a non-attorney who is ineligible to receive direct fee payment, we assume no responsibility for the payment of any fee that we have authorized.

(c) Notice of fee determination. We shall mail to both you and your representative at your last known address a written notice of what we decide about the fee. We shall state in the notice—

(1) The amount of the fee that is authorized;

(2) How we made that decision;

(3) Whether we are responsible for paying the fee from past-due benefits; and

(4) That within 30 days of the date of the notice, either you or your representative may request us to review the fee determination.

(d) Review of fee determination—

(1) Request filed on time. We will review the decision we made about a fee if either you or your representative files a written request for the review at one of our offices within 30 days after the date of the notice of the fee determination. Either you or your representative, whoever requests the review, shall mail a copy of the request to the other person. An authorized official of the Social Security Administration who did not take part in the fee determination being questioned will review the determination. This determination is not subject to further review. The official shall mail a written notice of the decision made on review both to you and to your representative at your last known address.

(2) Request not filed on time.

(i) If you or your representative requests a review of the decision we made about a fee, but does so more than 30 days after the date of the notice of the fee determination, whoever makes the request shall state in writing why it was not filed within the 30–day period. We will review the determination if we decide that there was good cause for not filing the request on time.

(ii) Some examples of good cause follow:

(A) Either you or your representative was seriously ill and the illness prevented you or your representative from contacting us in person or in writing.

(B) There was a death or serious illness in your family or in the family of your representative.

(C) Material records were destroyed by fire or other accidental cause.

(D) We gave you or your representative incorrect or incomplete information about the right to request review.

(E) You or your representative did not timely receive notice of the fee determination.

(F) You or your representative sent the request to another government agency in good faith within the 30–day period, and the request did not reach us until after the period had ended.

(3) Payment of fees. We assume no responsibility for the payment of a fee based on a revised determination if the request for administrative review was not filed on time.

(e) When we do not need to authorize a fee. We do not need to authorize a fee when:

(1) An entity or a Federal, State, county, or city government agency pays from its funds the representative fees and expenses and both of the following conditions apply:

(i) You are not liable to pay a fee or any expenses, or any part thereof, directly or indirectly, to the representative or someone else; and

(ii) The representative submits to us a writing in the form and manner we prescribe waiving the right to charge and collect a fee and any expenses from you directly or indirectly, in whole or in part; or

(2) A court authorizes a fee for your representative based on the representative's actions as your legal guardian or a court-appointed representative.

[72 FR 16725, April 5, 2007; 72 FR 44767, Aug. 9, 2007; 74 FR 48384, Sept. 23, 2009; 76 FR 45195, July 28, 2011; 80 FR 399, Jan. 6, 2015]

§ 416.1525 Request for approval of a fee.

(a) Filing a request. In order for your representative to obtain approval of a fee for services he or she performed in dealings with us, he or she shall file a written request with one of our offices. This should be done after the proceedings in which he or she was a representative are completed. The request must contain—

(1) The dates the representative's services began and ended;

(2) A list of the services he or she gave and the amount of time he or she spent on each type of service;

(3) The amount of the fee he or she wants to charge for the services;

(4) The amount of fee the representative wants to request or charge for his or her services in the same matter before any State or Federal court;

(5) The amount of and a list of any expenses the representative incurred for which he or she has been paid or expects to be paid;

(6) A description of the special qualifications which enabled the representative, if he or she is not an attorney, to give valuable help to you in connection with your claim; and

(7) A statement showing that the representative sent a copy of the request for approval of a fee to you.

(b) Evaluating a request for approval of a fee.

(1) When we evaluate a representative's request for approval of a fee, we consider the purpose of the

supplemental security income program, which is to assure a minimum level of income for the beneficiaries of the program, together with—

(i) The extent and type of services the representative performed;

(ii) The complexity of the case;

(iii) The level of skill and competence required of the representative in giving the services;

(iv) The amount of time the representative spent on the case;

(v) The results the representative achieved;

(vi) The level of review to which the claim was taken and the level of the review at which the representative became your representative; and

(vii) The amount of fee the representative requests for his or her services, including any amount authorized or requested before, but not including the amount of any expenses he or she incurred.

(2) Although we consider the amount of benefits, if any, that are payable, we do not base the amount of fee we authorize on the amount of the benefit alone, but on a consideration of all the factors listed in this section. The benefits payable in any claim are determined by specific provisions of law and are unrelated to the efforts of the representative. We may authorize a fee even if no benefits are payable.

§ 416.1528 Proceedings before a State or Federal court.

(a) Representation of a party in court proceedings. We shall not consider any service the representative gave you in any proceeding before a State or Federal court to be services as a representative in dealings with us. However, if the representative also has given service to you in the same connection in any dealings with us, he or she must specify what, if any, portion of the fee he or she wants to charge is for services performed in dealings with us. If the representative charges any fee for those services, he or she must file the request and furnish all of the information required by § 416.1525.

(b) Attorney fee allowed by a Federal court. If a Federal court in any proceeding under title XVI of the Act makes a judgment in favor of the claimant who was represented before the court by an attorney, and the court, under section 1631(d)(2) of the Act, allows to the attorney as part of its judgment a fee not in excess of 25 percent of the total of past-due benefits to which the claimant is eligible by reason of the judgment, we may pay the attorney the amount of the fee out of, but not in addition to, the amount of the past-due benefits payable. We will not pay directly any other fee your representative may request.

[72 FR 16725, April 5, 2007; 72 FR 44767, Aug. 9, 2007]

§ 416.1530 Payment of fees.

(a) Fees allowed by a Federal court. We will pay an attorney representative out of your past-due benefits the amount of the fee allowed by a Federal court in a proceeding under title XVI of the Act. The payment we make to the attorney is subject to the limitations described in paragraph (b)(1) of this section.

(b) Fees we may authorize—

(1) Attorneys and eligible non-attorneys. Except as provided in paragraph (c) of this section, if we make a determination or decision in your favor and you were represented by an attorney or an eligible non-attorney, and as a result of the determination or decision you have past-due benefits, we will pay the representative out of the past-due benefits, the smallest of the amounts in paragraphs (b)(1)(i) through (iii) of this section, less the amount of the assessment described in paragraph (d) of this section.

(i) Twenty-five percent of the total of the past-due benefits, as determined before any payment to a State (or political subdivision) to reimburse the State (or political subdivision) for interim assistance furnished you, as described in § 416.525 of this part, and reduced by the amount of any reduction in benefits under this title or title II pursuant to section 1127 of the Act;

(ii) The amount of past-due benefits remaining after we pay to a State (or political subdivision) an amount sufficient to reimburse the State (or political subdivision) for interim assistance furnished you, as described in § 416.525 of this part, and after any applicable reductions under section 1127 of the Act; or

(iii) The amount of the fee that we set.

(2) Non-attorneys ineligible for direct payment. If the representative is a non-attorney who is ineligible to receive direct payment of his or her fee, we assume no responsibility for the payment of any fee that we authorized. We will not deduct the fee from your past-due benefits.

(c) Time limit for filing request for approval of fee to obtain direct payment.

(1) To receive direct fee payment from your past-due benefits, a representative who is an attorney or an eligible non-attorney should file a request for approval of a fee, or written notice of the intent to file a request, at one of our offices, or electronically at the times and in the manner that we prescribe if we give notice that such a method is available, within 60 days of the date we mail the notice of the favorable determination or decision.

(2)(i) If no request is filed within 60 days of the date the notice of the favorable determination is mailed, we will mail a written notice to you and your representative at your last known addresses. The notice will inform you and the representative that unless the representative files, within 20 days from the date of the notice, a written request for approval of a fee under

§ 416.1525, or a written request for an extension of time, we will pay all the past-due benefits to you.

(ii) The representative must send you a copy of any request made to us for an extension of time. If the request is not filed within 20 days of the date of the notice, or by the last day of any extension we approved, we will pay to you all past-due benefits remaining after we reimburse the State for any interim assistance you received. We must approve any fee the representative charges after that time, but the collection of any approved fee is a matter between you and the representative.

(d) Assessment when we pay a fee directly to a representative.

(1) Whenever we pay a fee directly to a representative from past-due benefits, we impose an assessment on the representative.

(2) The amount of the assessment is equal to the lesser of:

(i) The product we obtain by multiplying the amount of the fee we are paying to the representative by the percentage rate the Commissioner of Social Security determines is necessary to achieve full recovery of the costs of determining and paying fees directly to representatives, but not in excess of 6.3 percent; and

(ii) The maximum assessment amount. The maximum assessment amount was initially set at $75, but by law is adjusted annually to reflect the increase in the cost of living. (See §§ 404.270 through 404.277 for an explanation of how the cost-of-living adjustment is computed.) If the adjusted amount is not a multiple of $1, we round down the amount to the next lower $1, but the amount will not be less than $75. We will announce any increase in the maximum assessment amount, and explain how that increase was determined in the Federal Register.

(3) We collect the assessment by subtracting it from the amount of the fee to be paid to the representative. The representative who is subject to an assessment may not, directly or indirectly, request or otherwise obtain reimbursement of the assessment from you.

(e) Effective dates for extension of direct payment of fee to attorneys. The provisions of this subpart authorizing the direct payment of fees to attorneys and the withholding of title XVI benefits for that purpose, apply in claims for benefits with respect to which the agreement for representation is entered into before March 1, 2010.

[72 FR 16726, April 5, 2007; 72 FR 44767, Aug. 9, 2007; 76 FR 45195, July 28, 2011; 80 FR 399, Jan. 6, 2015]

§ 416.1535 [Reserved by 76 FR 80247]

[76 FR 80247, Dec. 23, 2011]

§ 416.1540 Rules of conduct and standards of responsibility for representatives.

(a) Purpose and scope.

(1) All attorneys or other persons acting on behalf of a party seeking a statutory right or benefit must, in their dealings with us, faithfully execute their duties as agents and fiduciaries of a party. A representative must provide competent assistance to the claimant and recognize our authority to lawfully administer the process. The following provisions set forth certain affirmative duties and prohibited actions that will govern the relationship between the representative and us, including matters involving our administrative procedures and fee collections.

(2) All representatives must be forthright in their dealings with us and with the claimant and must comport themselves with due regard for the nonadversarial nature of the proceedings by complying with our rules and standards, which are intended to ensure orderly and fair presentation of evidence and argument.

(b) Affirmative duties. A representative must, in conformity with the regulations setting forth our existing duties and responsibilities and those of claimants (see § 416.912 in disability and blindness claims):

(1) Act with reasonable promptness to help obtain the information or evidence that the claimant must submit under our regulations, and forward the information or evidence to us for consideration as soon as practicable.

(2) Assist the claimant in complying, as soon as practicable, with our requests for information or evidence at any stage of the administrative decisionmaking process in his or her claim. In disability and blindness claims, this includes the obligation pursuant to § 416.912(c) to assist the claimant in providing, upon our request, evidence about:

(i) The claimant's medical source(s);

(ii) The claimant's age;

(iii) The claimant's education and training;

(iv) The claimant's work experience;

(v) The claimant's daily activities both before and after the date the claimant alleges that he or she became disabled;

(vi) The claimant's efforts to work; and

(vii) Any other factors showing how the claimant's impairment(s) affects his or her ability to work. In §§ 416.960 through 416.969a, we discuss in more detail the evidence we need when we consider vocational factors.

(3) Conduct his or her dealings in a manner that furthers the efficient, fair, and orderly conduct of the administrative decision-making process, including duties to:

(i) Provide competent representation to a claimant. Competent representation requires the knowledge, skill, thoroughness, and preparation reasonably necessary for the representation. A representative must know the significant issue(s) in a claim, have reasonable and adequate familiarity with the evidence in the case, and have a working knowledge of the applicable provisions of the Social Security Act, as amended, the regulations, the Social Security Rulings, and any other applicable provisions of law.

(ii) Act with reasonable diligence and promptness in representing a claimant. This includes providing prompt and responsive answers to our requests for information pertinent to processing of the claim.

(iii) When requested, provide us, in a manner we specify, potential dates and times that the representative will be available for a hearing. We will inform the representative how many potential dates and times we require to coordinate the hearing schedule.

(iv) Only withdraw representation at a time and in a manner that does not disrupt the processing or adjudication of a claim and that provides the claimant adequate time to find new representation, if desired. A representative should not withdraw after we set the time and place for the hearing (see § 416.1436) unless the representative can show that a withdrawal is necessary due to extraordinary circumstances, as we determine on a case-by-case basis.

(v) Maintain prompt and timely communication with the claimant, which includes, but is not limited to, reasonably informing the claimant of all matters concerning the representation, consulting with the claimant on an ongoing basis during the entire representational period, and promptly responding to a claimant's reasonable requests for information. When we evaluate whether a representative has maintained prompt and timely communication with the claimant, we will consider the difficulty the representative has in locating a particular claimant (e.g., because the claimant is homeless) and the representative's efforts to keep that claimant informed.

(4) Conduct business with us electronically at the times and in the manner we prescribe on matters for which the representative requests direct fee payment. (See § 416.1513).

(5) Disclose in writing, at the time a medical or vocational opinion is submitted to us or as soon as the representative is aware of the submission to us, if:

(i) The representative's employee or any individual contracting with the representative drafted, prepared, or issued the medical or vocational opinion; or

(ii) The representative referred or suggested that the claimant seek an examination from, treatment by, or the assistance of, the individual providing opinion evidence.

(6) Disclose to us immediately if the representative discovers that his or her services are or were used by the claimant to commit fraud against us.

(7) Disclose to us whether the representative is or has been disbarred or suspended from any bar or court to which he or she was previously admitted to practice, including instances in which a bar or court took administrative action to disbar or suspend the representative in lieu of disciplinary proceedings (e.g. acceptance of voluntary resignation pending disciplinary action). If the disbarment or suspension occurs after the appointment of the representative, the representative will immediately disclose the disbarment or suspension to us.

(8) Disclose to us whether the representative is or has been disqualified from participating in or appearing before any Federal program or agency, including instances in which a Federal program or agency took administrative action to disqualify the representative in lieu of disciplinary proceedings (e.g. acceptance of voluntary resignation pending disciplinary action). If the disqualification occurs after the appointment of the representative, the representative will immediately disclose the disqualification to us.

(9) Disclose to us whether the representative has been removed from practice or suspended by a professional licensing authority for reasons that reflect on the person's character, integrity, judgment, reliability, or fitness to serve as a fiduciary. If the removal or suspension occurs after the appointment of the representative, the representative will immediately disclose the removal or suspension to us.

(10) Ensure that all of the representative's employees, assistants, partners, contractors, or any person assisting the representative on claims for which the representative has been appointed, comply with these rules of conduct and standards of responsibility for representatives, when the representative has managerial or supervisory authority over these individuals or otherwise has responsibility to oversee their work. This includes a duty to take remedial action when:

(i) The representative's employees, assistants, partners, contractors or other individuals' conduct violates these rules of conduct and standards of responsibility; and

(ii) The representative has reason to believe a violation of these rules of conduct and standards of responsibility occurred or will occur.

(c) Prohibited actions. A representative must not:

(1) In any manner or by any means threaten, coerce, intimidate, deceive or knowingly mislead a claimant, or prospective claimant or beneficiary, regarding benefits or other rights under the Act. This prohibition includes misleading a claimant, or prospective claimant or beneficiary, about the representative's services and qualifications.

(2) Knowingly charge, collect or retain, or make any arrangement to charge, collect or retain, from any source, directly or indirectly, any fee for representational services in violation of applicable law or regulation. This prohibition includes soliciting any gift or any other item of value, other than what is authorized by law.

(3) Make or present, or participate in the making or presentation of, false or misleading oral or written statements, evidence, assertions, or representations about a material fact or law concerning a matter within our jurisdiction, in matters where the representative knows or should have known that those statements, evidence, assertions or representations are false or misleading.

(4) Through his or her own actions or omissions, unreasonably delay or cause to be delayed, without good cause (see § 416.1411(b)), the processing of a claim at any stage of the administrative decision-making process.

(5) Divulge, without the claimant's consent, except as may be authorized by regulations prescribed by us or as otherwise provided by Federal law, any information we furnish or disclose about a claim or prospective claim.

(6) Attempt to influence, directly or indirectly, the outcome of a decision, determination, or other administrative action by any means prohibited by law, or offering or granting a loan, gift, entertainment, or anything of value to a presiding official, agency employee, or witness who is or may reasonably be expected to be involved in the administrative decision-making process, except as reimbursement for legitimately incurred expenses or lawful compensation for the services of an expert witness retained on a non-contingency basis to provide evidence.

(7) Engage in actions or behavior prejudicial to the fair and orderly conduct of administrative proceedings, including but not limited to:

(i) Repeated absences from or persistent tardiness at scheduled proceedings without good cause (see § 416.1411(b));

(ii) Behavior that has the effect of improperly disrupting proceedings or obstructing the adjudicative process, including but not limited to:

(A) Directing threatening or intimidating language, gestures, or actions at a presiding official, witness, contractor, or agency employee;

(B) Providing misleading information or misrepresenting facts that affect how we process a claim, including, but not limited to, information relating to the claimant's work activity or the claimant's place of residence or mailing address in matters where the representative knows or should have known that the information was misleading and the facts would constitute a misrepresentation; and

(C) Communicating with agency staff or adjudicators outside the normal course of business or other prescribed procedures in an attempt to inappropriately influence the processing or outcome of a claim(s).

(8) Violate any section of the Act for which a criminal or civil monetary penalty is prescribed.

(9) Refuse to comply with any of our rules or regulations.

(10) Suggest, assist, or direct another person to violate our rules or regulations.

(11) Advise any claimant or beneficiary not to comply with any of our rules or regulations.

(12) Knowingly assist a person whom we suspended or disqualified to provide representational services in a proceeding under title XVI of the Act, or to exercise the authority of a representative described in § 416.1510.

(13) Fail to comply with our sanction(s) decision.

(14) Fail to oversee the representative's employees, assistants, partners, contractors, or any other person assisting the representative on claims for which the representative has been appointed when the representative has managerial or supervisory authority over these individuals or otherwise has responsibility to oversee their work.

[63 FR 41417, Aug. 4, 1998; 76 FR 56109, Sept. 12, 2011; 76 FR 80247, Dec. 23, 2011; 80 FR 14838, March 20, 2015; 83 FR 30857, July 2, 2018]

§ 416.1545 Violations of our requirements, rules, or standards.

When we have evidence that a representative fails to meet our qualification requirements or has violated the rules governing dealings with us, we may begin proceedings to suspend or disqualify that individual from acting in a representational capacity before us. We may file charges seeking such sanctions when we have evidence that a representative:

(a) Does not meet the qualifying requirements described in § 416.1505;

(b) Has violated the affirmative duties or engaged in the prohibited actions set forth in § 416.1540;

(c) Has been convicted of a violation under section 1631(d) of the Act;

(d) Has been, by reason of misconduct, disbarred or suspended from any bar or court to which he or she was previously admitted to practice (see § 416.1570(a));

(e) Has been, by reason of misconduct, disqualified from participating in or appearing before any Federal program or agency (see § 416.1570(a)); or

(f) Who, as a non-attorney, has been removed from practice or suspended by a professional licensing authority for reasons that reflect on the person's character, integrity, judgment, reliability, or fitness to serve as a fiduciary.

[56 FR 24132, May 29, 1991; 63 FR 41418, Aug. 4, 1998; 71 FR 2877, Jan. 18, 2006; 83 FR 30858, July 2, 2018]

§ 416.1550 Notice of charges against a representative.

(a) The General Counsel or other delegated official will prepare a notice containing a statement of charges that constitutes the basis for the proceeding against the representative.

(b) We will send this notice to the representative either by certified or registered mail, to his or her last known address, or by personal delivery.

(c) We will advise the representative to file an answer, within 14 business days from the date of the notice, or from the date the notice was delivered personally, stating why he or she should not be suspended or disqualified from acting as a representative in dealings with us.

(d) The General Counsel or other delegated official may extend the 14–day period specified in paragraph (c) of this section for good cause in accordance with § 416.1411.

(e) The representative must—

(1) Answer the notice in writing under oath (or affirmation); and

(2) File the answer with the Social Security Administration, at the address specified on the notice, within the 14–day time period specified in paragraph (c) of this section.

(f) If the representative does not file an answer within the 14–day time period specified in paragraph (c) of this section (or the period extended in accordance with paragraph (d) of this section), he or she does not have the right to present evidence, except as may be provided in § 416.1565(g).

[56 FR 24132, May 29, 1991; 62 FR 38455, July 18, 1997; 63 FR 41418, Aug. 4, 1998; 71 FR 2878, Jan. 18, 2006; 76 FR 80247, Dec. 23, 2011; 83 FR 30858, July 2, 2018]

§ 416.1555 Withdrawing charges against a representative.

The General Counsel or other delegated official may withdraw charges against a representative. We will withdraw charges if the representative files an answer, or we obtain evidence, that satisfies us that we should not suspend or disqualify the representative from acting as a representative. When we consider withdrawing charges brought under § 416.1545(d) through (f) based on the representative's assertion that, before or after our filing of charges, the representative has been reinstated to practice by the court, bar, or Federal program or Federal agency that suspended, disbarred, or disqualified the representative, the General Counsel or other delegated official will determine whether such reinstatement occurred, whether it remains in effect, and whether he or she is reasonably satisfied that the representative will in the future act in accordance with the provisions of section 206(a) of the Act and our rules and regulations. If the representative proves that reinstatement occurred and remains in effect and the General Counsel or other delegated official is so satisfied, the General Counsel or other delegated official will withdraw those charges. The action of the General Counsel or other delegated official regarding withdrawal of charges is solely that of the General Counsel or other delegated official and is not reviewable, or subject to consideration in decisions made under §§ 416.1570 and 416.1590. If we withdraw the charges, we will notify the representative by mail at the representative's last known address.

[71 FR 2878, Jan. 18, 2006; 76 FR 80248, Dec. 23, 2011; 83 FR 30859, July 2, 2018]

§ 416.1560 [Reserved]

[56 FR 24132, May 29, 1991]

§ 416.1565 Hearing on charges.

(a) Holding the hearing. If the General Counsel or other delegated official does not take action to withdraw the charges within 15 days after the date on which the representative filed an answer, we will hold a hearing and make a decision on the charges.

(b) Hearing officer.

(1) The Deputy Commissioner for the Office of Hearings Operations or other delegated official will assign an administrative law judge, designated to act as a hearing officer, to hold a hearing on the charges.

(2) No hearing officer shall hold a hearing in a case in which he or she is prejudiced or partial about any party, or has any interest in the matter.

(3) If the representative or any party to the hearing objects to the hearing officer who has been named to hold the hearing, we must be notified at the earliest opportunity. The hearing officer shall consider the objection(s) and either proceed with the hearing or withdraw from it.

(4) If the hearing officer withdraws from the hearing, another one will be named.

(5) If the hearing officer does not withdraw, the representative or any other person objecting may, after the hearing, present his or her objections to the Appeals Council explaining why he or she believes the hearing officer's decision should be revised or a new hearing held by another administrative law judge designated to act as a hearing officer.

(c) Time and place of hearing. The hearing officer shall mail the parties a written notice of the hearing at their last known addresses, at least 14 calendar days before the date set for the hearing. The notice will inform the parties whether the appearance of the parties or any witnesses will be in person, by video teleconferencing, or by telephone. The notice will also include requirements and instructions for filing motions, requesting witnesses, and entering exhibits.

(d) Change of time and place for hearing.

(1) The hearing officer may change the time and place for the hearing, either on his or her own initiative, or at the request of the representative or the other party to the hearing. The hearing officer will not consider objections to the manner of appearance of parties or witnesses, unless the party shows good cause not to appear in the prescribed manner. To determine whether good cause exists for extending the deadline, we use the standards explained in § 416.1411.

(2) The hearing officer may adjourn or postpone the hearing.

(3) Subject to the limitations in paragraph (g)(2) of this section, the hearing officer may reopen the hearing for the receipt of additional evidence at any time before mailing notice of the decision.

(4) The hearing officer shall give the representative and the other party to the hearing reasonable notice of any change in the time or place for the hearing, or of an adjournment or reopening of the hearing.

(e) Parties. The representative against whom charges have been made is a party to the hearing. The General Counsel or other delegated official will also be a party to the hearing.

(f) Subpoenas.

(1) The representative or the other party to the hearing may request the hearing officer to issue a subpoena for the attendance and testimony of witnesses and for the production of books, records, correspondence, papers, or other documents that are material to any matter being considered at the hearing. The hearing officer may, on his or her own, initiative, issue subpoenas for the same purposes when the action is reasonably necessary for the full presentation of the facts.

(2) The representative or the other party who wants a subpoena issued shall file a written request with the hearing officer. This must be done at least 5 days before the date set for the hearing. The request must name the documents to be produced, and describe the address or location in enough detail to permit the witnesses or documents to be found.

(3) The representative or the other party who wants a subpoena issued shall state in the request for a subpoena the material facts that he or she expects to establish by the witness or document, and why the facts could not be established by the use of other evidence which could be obtained without use of a subpoena.

(4) We will pay the cost of the issuance and the fees and mileage of any witness subpoenaed, as provided in section 205(d) of the Act.

(g) Conduct of the hearing.

(1) The representative or the other party may file a motion for decision on the basis of the record prior to the hearing. The hearing officer will give the representative and the other party a reasonable amount of time to submit any evidence and to file briefs or other written statements as to fact and law prior to deciding the motion. If the hearing officer concludes that there is no genuine dispute as to any material fact and the movant is entitled to a decision as a matter of law, the hearing officer may grant the motion and issue a decision in accordance with the provisions of § 416.1570.

(2) If the representative did not file an answer to the charges, he or she has no right to present evidence at the hearing. The hearing officer may make or recommend a decision on the basis of the record, or permit the representative to present a statement about the sufficiency of the evidence or the validity of the proceedings upon which the suspension or disqualification, if it occurred, would be based.

(3) The hearing officer will make the hearing open to the representative, to the other party, and to any persons the hearing officer or the parties consider necessary or proper. The hearing officer will inquire fully into the matters being considered, hear the testimony of witnesses, and accept any documents that are material.

(4) The hearing officer has the right to decide the order in which the evidence and the allegations will be presented and the conduct of the hearing.

(h) Evidence. The hearing officer may accept evidence at the hearing, even though it is not admissible under the rules of evidence that apply to Federal court procedure.

(i) Witnesses. Witnesses who testify at the hearing shall do so under oath or affirmation. Either the representative or a person representing him or her may question the witnesses. The other party and that party's representative must also be allowed to question the witnesses. The hearing officer may also ask questions as considered necessary, and shall rule upon any objection made by either party about whether any question is proper.

(j) Oral and written summation.

(1) The hearing officer shall give the representative and the other party a reasonable time to present oral summation and to file briefs or other written statements about proposed findings of fact and conclusions of law if the parties request it.

(2) The party that files briefs or other written statements shall provide enough copies so that they may be made available to any other party to the hearing who requests a copy.

(k) Record of hearing. In all cases, the hearing officer shall have a complete record of the proceedings at the hearing made.

(*l*) Representation. The representative, as the person charged, may appear in person and may be represented by an attorney or other representative. The General Counsel or other delegated official will be represented by one or more attorneys from the Office of the General Counsel.

(m) Failure to appear. If the representative or the other party to the hearing fails to appear after being notified of the time and place, the hearing officer may hold the hearing anyway so that the party present may offer evidence to sustain or rebut the charges. The hearing officer shall give the party who failed to appear an opportunity to show good cause for failure to appear. If the party fails to show good cause, he or she is considered to have waived the right to be present at the hearing. If the party shows good cause, the hearing officer may hold a supplemental hearing.

(n) Dismissal of charges. The hearing officer may dismiss the charges in the event of the death of the representative.

(*o*) Cost of transcript. If the representative or the other party to a hearing requests a copy of the transcript of the hearing, the hearing officer will have it prepared and sent to the party upon payment of the cost, unless the payment is waived for good cause.

[56 FR 24132, May 29, 1991; 62 FR 38455, July 18, 1997; 63 FR 41418, Aug. 4, 1998; 71 FR 2878, Jan. 18, 2006; 76 FR 80248, Dec. 23, 2011; 83 FR 30859, July 2, 2018]

§ 416.1570 Decision by hearing officer.

(a) General.

(1) After the close of the hearing, the hearing officer will issue a decision or certify the case to the Appeals Council. The decision must be in writing, will contain findings of fact and conclusions of law, and be based upon the evidence of record.

(2) In deciding whether a person has been, by reason of misconduct, disbarred or suspended by a court or bar, or disqualified from participating in or appearing before any Federal program or Federal agency, the hearing officer will consider the reasons for the disbarment, suspension, or disqualification action. If the action was taken for solely administrative reasons (e.g., failure to pay dues or to complete continuing legal education requirements), that will not disqualify the person from acting as a representative before us. However, this exception to disqualification does not apply if the administrative action was taken in lieu of disciplinary proceedings (e.g., acceptance of a voluntary resignation pending disciplinary action). Although the hearing officer will consider whether the disbarment, suspension, or disqualification action is based on misconduct when deciding whether a person should be disqualified from acting as a representative before us, the hearing officer will not re-examine or revise the factual or legal conclusions that led to the disbarment, suspension, or disqualification. For purposes of determining whether a person has been, by reason of misconduct, disqualified from participating in or appearing before any Federal program or Federal agency, disqualified refers to any action that prohibits a person from participating in or appearing before any Federal program or Federal agency, regardless of how long the prohibition lasts or the specific terminology used.

(3) If the hearing officer finds that the charges against the representative have been sustained, he or she will either—

(i) Suspend the representative for a specified period of not less than 1 year, nor more than 5 years, from the date of the decision; or

(ii) Disqualify the representative from acting as a representative in dealings with us until he or she may be reinstated under § 416.1599. Disqualification is the sole sanction available if the charges have been sustained because the representative has been disbarred or suspended from any court or bar to which the representative was previously admitted to practice or disqualified from participating in or appearing before any Federal program or Federal agency, or because the representative has collected or received, and retains, a fee for representational services in excess of the amount authorized.

(4) The hearing officer shall mail a copy of the decision to the parties at their last known addresses. The notice will inform the parties of the right to request the Appeals Council to review the decision.

(b) Effect of hearing officer's decision.

(1) The hearing officer's decision is final and binding unless reversed or modified by the Appeals Council upon review.

(2) If the final decision is that a person is disqualified from being a representative in dealings with us, he or she will not be permitted to represent anyone in dealings with us until authorized to do so under the provisions of § 416.1599.

(3) If the final decision is that a person is suspended for a specified period of time from being a representative in dealings with us, he or she will not be permitted to represent anyone in dealings with us during the period of suspension unless authorized to do so under the provisions of § 416.1599.

[56 24132, May 29, 1991; 71 FR 2878, Jan. 18, 2006; 76 FR 80248, Dec. 23, 2011]

§ 416.1575 Requesting review of the hearing officer's decision.

(a) General. After the hearing officer issues a decision, either the representative or the other party to the hearing may ask the Appeals Council to review the decision.

(b) Time and place of filing request for review. The party requesting review will file the request for review in writing with the Appeals Council within 14 business days from the date the hearing officer mailed the notice. The party requesting review will certify that a copy of the request for review and of any documents that are submitted have been mailed to the opposing party.

[83 FR 30859, July 2, 2018]

§ 416.1576 Assignment of request for review of the hearing officer's decision.

Upon receipt of a request for review of the hearing officer's decision, the matter will be assigned to a panel consisting of three members of the Appeals Council none of whom shall be the Chair of the Appeals Council. The panel shall jointly consider and rule by majority opinion on the request for review of the hearing officer's decision, including a determination to dismiss the request for review. Matters other than a final disposition of the request for review may be disposed of by the member designated chair of the panel.

[56 FR 24132, May 29, 1991]

§ 416.1580 Appeals Council's review of hearing officer's decision.

(a) Upon request, the Appeals Council will give the parties a reasonable time to file briefs or other written statements as to fact and law, and to request to appear before the Appeals Council to present oral argument. When oral argument is requested within the time designated by the Appeals Council, the Appeals Council will grant the request for oral argument and determine whether the parties will appear at the oral argument in person, by video teleconferencing, or by telephone. If oral argument is not requested within the time designated by the Appeals Council, the Appeals Council may deny the request.

(b) If a party files a brief or other written statement with the Appeals Council, he or she shall send a copy to the opposing party and certify that the copy has been sent.

[83 FR 30859, July 2, 2018]

§ 416.1585 Evidence permitted on review.

(a) General. Generally, the Appeals Council will not consider evidence in addition to that introduced at the hearing. However, if the Appeals Council finds the evidence offered is material to an issue it is considering, it may consider that evidence, as described in paragraph (b) of this section.

(b) Individual charged filed an answer.

(1) When the Appeals Council finds that additional evidence material to the charges is available, and the individual charged filed an answer to the charges, the Appeals Council will allow the party with the information to submit the additional evidence.

(2) Before the Appeals Council admits additional evidence into the record, it will mail a notice to the parties, informing them that evidence about certain issues was submitted. The Appeals Council will give each party a reasonable opportunity to comment on the evidence and to present other evidence that is material to an issue it is considering.

(3) The Appeals Council will determine whether the additional evidence warrants a new review by a hearing officer or whether the Appeals Council will consider the additional evidence as part of its review of the case.

(c) Individual charged did not file an answer. If the representative did not file an answer to the charges, the representative may not introduce evidence that was not considered at the hearing.

[83 FR 30859, July 2, 2018]

§ 416.1590 Appeals Council's decision.

(a) The Appeals Council will base its decision upon the evidence in the hearing record and any other evidence it may permit on review. The Appeals Council will affirm the hearing officer's decision if the action, findings, and conclusions are supported by substantial evidence. If the hearing officer's decision is not supported by substantial evidence, the Appeals Council will either:

(1) Reverse or modify the hearing officer's decision; or

(2) Return a case to the hearing officer for further proceedings.

(b) The Appeals Council, in changing a hearing officer's decision to suspend a representative for a specified period, shall in no event reduce the period of suspension to less than 1 year. In modifying a hearing officer's decision to disqualify a representative, the Appeals Council shall in no event impose a period of suspension of less than 1 year. Further, the Appeals Council shall in no event impose a suspension when disqualification is the sole sanction available in accordance with § 416.1570(a)(3)(ii).

(c) If the Appeals Council affirms or changes a hearing officer's decision, the period of suspension or the disqualification is effective from the date of the Appeals Council's decision.

(d) If the hearing officer did not impose a period of suspension or a disqualification, and the Appeals Council decides to impose one or the other, the suspension or disqualification is effective from the date of the Appeals Council's decision.

(e) The Appeals Council shall make its decision in writing and shall mail a copy of the decision to the parties at their last known addresses.

(f) The Appeals Council may designate and publish certain final decisions as precedent for other actions brought under its representative conduct provisions. Prior to making a decision public, we will remove or redact personally identifiable information from the decision.

[56 FR 24133, May 29, 1991; 71 FR 2878, Jan. 18, 2006; 83 FR 30860, July 2, 2018]

§ 416.1595 When the Appeals Council will dismiss a request for review.

The Appeals Council may dismiss a request for the review of any proceeding to suspend or disqualify a representative in any of the following circumstances:

(a) Upon request of party. The Appeals Council may dismiss a request for review upon written request of the party or parties who filed the request, if there is no other party who objects to the dismissal.

(b) Death of party. The Appeals Council may dismiss a request for review in the event of the death of the representative.

(c) Request for review not timely filed. The Appeals Council will dismiss a request for review if a party failed to file a request for review within the 30–day time period and the Appeals Council does not extend the time for good cause.

§ 416.1597 Reinstatement after suspension—period of suspension expired.

We shall automatically allow a person to serve again as a representative in dealings with us at the end of any suspension.

§ 416.1599 Reinstatement after suspension or disqualification—period of suspension not expired.

(a) After more than one year has passed, a person who has been suspended or disqualified may ask the Appeals Council for permission to serve as a representative again. The Appeals Council will assign and process a request for reinstatement using the same general procedures described in § 416.1576.

(b) The suspended or disqualified person must submit any evidence the person wishes to have considered along with the request to be allowed to serve as a representative again.

(c) The General Counsel or other delegated official, upon notification of receipt of the request, will have 30 days in which to present a written report of any experiences with the suspended or disqualified person subsequent to that person's suspension or disqualification. The Appeals Council will make available to the suspended or disqualified person a copy of the report.

(d)(1) The Appeals Council shall not grant the request unless it is reasonably satisfied that the person will in the future act according to the provisions of section 206(a) of the Act, and to our rules and regulations.

(2) If a person was disqualified because he or she had been disbarred, suspended, or removed from practice for the reasons described in § 416.1545(d) through (f), the Appeals Council will grant a request for reinstatement as a representative only if the criterion in paragraph (d)(1) of this section is met and the disqualified person shows that he or she has been admitted (or readmitted) to and is in good standing with the court, bar, Federal program or agency, or other governmental or professional licensing authority from which he or she had been disbarred, suspended, or removed from practice.

(3) If a person was disqualified because the person had been disqualified from participating in or appearing before a Federal program or Federal agency, the Appeals Council will grant the request for reinstatement only if the criterion in paragraph (d)(1) of this section is met and the disqualified person shows that the person is now qualified to participate in or appear before that Federal program or Federal agency.

(4) If the person was disqualified as a result of collecting or receiving, and retaining, a fee for representational services in excess of the amount authorized, the Appeals Council will grant the request only if the criterion in paragraph (d)(1) of this section is met and the disqualified person shows that full restitution has been made.

(e) The Appeals Council will mail a notice of its decision on the request for reinstatement to the suspended or disqualified person. It will also mail a copy to the General Counsel or other delegated official.

(f) If the Appeals Council decides not to grant the request, it will not consider another request before the end of 3 years from the date of the notice of the previous denial.

[56 FR 24133, May 29, 1991; 62 FR 38455, July 18, 1997; 63 FR 41418, Aug. 4, 1998; 71 FR 2878, Jan. 18, 2006; 76 FR 80248, Dec. 23, 2011; 83 FR 30860, July 2, 2018]

SUBPART P—RESIDENCE AND CITIZENSHIP

Authority: Secs. 702(a)(5), 1614(a)(1)(B) and (e), and 1631 of the Social Security Act (42 U.S.C. 902(a)(5), 1382c(a)(1)(B) and (e), and 1383); 8 U.S.C. 1254a; sec. 502, Pub.L. 94–241, 90 Stat. 268 (48 U.S.C. 1681 note).

Source: 47 FR 3106, Jan. 22, 1982; 52 FR 21943, June 10, 1987; 52 FR 27541, July 22, 1987; 58 FR 41182, Aug. 3, 1993; 61 FR 5942, Feb. 15, 1996, unless otherwise noted.

§ 416.1600 Introduction.

You are eligible for supplemental security income (SSI) benefits if you meet the requirements in subpart B. Among these are requirements that you must be a resident of the United States and either a citizen, a national, or an alien with a lawful right to reside permanently in the United States. In this subpart, we tell you what kinds of evidence show that you are a resident of the United States (see § 416.1603) and—

(a) A citizen or a national of the United States (see § 416.1610);

(b) An alien lawfully admitted for permanent residence in the United States (see § 416.1615); or

(c) An alien permanently residing in the United States under color of law (see § 416.1618).

§ 416.1601 Definitions and terms used in this subpart.

We or Us means the Social Security Administration.

You or Your means the person who applies for or receives SSI benefits or the person for whom an application is filed.

§ 416.1603 How to prove you are a resident of the United States.

(a) What you should give us. Your home address in the United States may be sufficient to establish that you are a resident. However, if we have any reason to question that you are a resident of the United States we will ask for evidence. You can prove you are a resident of the United States by giving us papers or documents showing that you live in the United States such as—

(1) Property, income, or other tax forms or receipts;

(2) Utility bills, leases or rent payment records;

(3) Documents that show you participate in a social services program in the United States; or

(4) Other records or documents that show you live in the United States.

(b) What "resident of the United States" means. We use the term resident of the United States to mean a person who has established an actual dwelling place within the geographical limits of the United States with the intent to continue to live in the United States.

(c) What "United States" means. We use the term United States in this section to mean the 50 States, the District of Columbia, and the Northern Mariana Islands.

[62 FR 59813, Nov. 5, 1997]

§ 416.1605 [Reserved]

[56 FR 55075, Oct. 24, 1991]

§ 416.1610 How to prove you are a citizen or a national of the United States.

(a) What you should give us. You can prove that you are a citizen or a national of the United States by giving us—

(1) A certified copy of your birth certificate which shows that you were born in the United States;

(2) A certified copy of a religious record of your birth or baptism, recorded in the United States within 3 months of your birth, which shows you were born in the United States;

(3) Your naturalization certificate;

(4) Your United States passport;

(5) Your certificate of citizenship;

(6) An identification card for use of resident citizens in the United States (Immigration and Naturalization Service Form I–197); or

(7) An identification card for use of resident citizens of the United States by both or naturalization of parents (INS Form I–179).

(b) How to prove you are an interim citizen of the United States if you live in the Northern Mariana Islands. As a resident of the Northern Mariana Islands you must meet certain conditions to prove you are an interim citizen of the United States. You must prove that you were domiciled in the Northern Mariana Islands as required by section 8 of the Schedule of Transitional Matters of the Constitution of the Northern Mariana Islands, or that you were born there after March 6, 1977. By "domiciled" we mean that you maintained a residence with the intention of continuing that residence for an unlimited or indefinite period, and that you intended to return to that residence whenever absent, even for an extended period. You must also give us proof of your citizenship if you are a citizen of the Trust Territory of the Pacific Islands of which the Marianas are a part.

(1) You can prove you were domiciled in the Northern Mariana Islands by giving us—

(i) Statements of civil authorities; or

(ii) Receipts or other evidence that show you were domiciled there.

(2) You can prove that you are a citizen of the Trust Territory of the Pacific Islands by giving us—

(i) Your identification card issued by the Trust Territory of the Pacific Islands and a public or religious record of age which shows you were born in this territory;

(ii) Your voter's registration card;

(iii) A Chammoro Family Record showing your birth in the Trust Territory of the Pacific Islands; or

(iv) Your naturalization certificate.

(c) What to do if you cannot give us the information listed in paragraph (a) or (b). If you cannot give us any of the documents listed in paragraph (a) or (b), we may find you to be a citizen or a national of the United States if you—

(1) Explain why you cannot give us any of the documents; and

(2) Give us any information you have which shows or results in proof that you are a citizen or a national of the United States. The kind of information we are most concerned about shows—

(i) The date and place of your birth in the United States;

(ii) That you have voted or are otherwise known to be a citizen or national of the United States; or

(iii) The relationship to you and the citizenship of any person through whom you obtain citizenship.

(d) What "United States" means. We use the term United States in this section to mean the 50 States, the District of Columbia, Puerto Rico, Guam, the Virgin Islands of the United States, American Samoa, Swain's Island, and the Northern Mariana Islands.

[62 FR 59813, Nov. 5, 1997]

§ 416.1615 How to prove you are lawfully admitted for permanent residence in the United States.

(a) What you should give us. You can prove that you are lawfully admitted for permanent residence in the United States by giving us—

(1) An Alien Registration Receipt Card issued by the Immigration and Naturalization Service (INS) in accordance with that Agency's current regulations;

(2) A reentry permit;

(3) An alien identification card issued by the government of the Northern Mariana Islands showing that you are admitted to the Northern Mariana Islands for permanent residence; or

(4) INS Form I–688 which shows that you have been granted lawful temporary resident status under section 210 or section 210A of the Immigration and Nationality Act.

(b) What to do if you cannot give us the information listed in paragraph (a). If you cannot give us any of the documents listed in paragraph (a), we may find you to be lawfully admitted for permanent residence in the United States if you—

(1) Explain why you cannot give us any of the documents; and

(2) Give us any information you have which shows or results in proof that you are lawfully admitted for permanent residence in the United States.

(c) What "United States" means. We use the term United States in this section to mean the 50 States, the District of Columbia, and the Northern Mariana Islands.

(Approved by the Office of Management and Budget under control number 0960–0451)

[52 FR 21943, June 10, 1987; 56 FR 55075, Oct. 24, 1991; 61 FR 56134, Oct. 31, 1996]

§ 416.1618 When you are considered permanently residing in the United States under color of law.

(a) General. We will consider you to be permanently residing in the United States under color of law and you may be eligible for SSI benefits if you are an alien residing in the United States with the knowledge and permission of the Immigration and Naturalization Service and that agency does not contemplate enforcing your departure. The Immigration and Naturalization Service does not contemplate enforcing your departure if it is the policy or practice of that agency not to enforce the departure of aliens in the same category or if from all the facts and circumstances in your case it appears that the Immigration and Naturalization Service is otherwise permitting you to reside in the United States indefinitely. We make these decisions by verifying your status with the Immigration and Naturalization Service following the rules contained in paragraphs (b) through (e) of this section.

(b) Categories of aliens who are permanently residing in the United States under color of law. Aliens who are permanently residing in the United States under color of law are listed below. None of the categories includes applicants for an Immigration and Naturalization status other than those applicants listed in paragraph (b)(6) of this section or those covered under paragraph (b)(17) of this section. None of the categories allows SSI eligibility for nonimmigrants; for example, students or visitors. Also listed are the most common documents that the Immigration and Naturalization Service provides to aliens in these categories:

(1) Aliens admitted to the United States pursuant to 8 U.S.C. 1153(a)(7), (section 203(a)(7) of the Immigration and Nationality Act). We ask for INS Form I–94 endorsed "Refugee–Conditional Entry";

(2) Aliens paroled into the United States pursuant to 8 U.S.C. 1182(d)(5) (section 212(d)(5) of the Immigration and Nationality Act) including Cuban/Haitian Entrants. We ask for INS Form I–94 with the notation that the alien was paroled pursuant to section 212(d)(5) of the Immigration and Nationality Act. For Cuban/Haitian Entrants, we ask for INS Form I–94 stamped "Cuban/Haitian Entrant (Status Pending) reviewable January 15, 1981. Employment authorized until January 15, 1981." (Although the forms bear this notation, Cuban/Haitian Entrants are admitted under section 212(d)(5) of the Immigration and Nationality Act.);

(3) Aliens residing in the United States pursuant to an indefinite stay of deportation. We ask for an Immigration and Naturalization Service letter with this information or INS Form I–94 with such a notation;

(4) Aliens residing in the United States pursuant to an indefinite voluntary departure. We ask for an Immigration and Naturalization Service letter or INS Form I–94 showing that a voluntary departure has been granted for an indefinite time period;

(5) Aliens on whose behalf an immediate relative petition has been approved and their families covered by the petition, who are entitled to voluntary departure (under 8 CFR 242.5(a)(2)(vi)) and whose departure the Immigration and Naturalization Service does not con-

template enforcing. We ask for a copy of INS Form I–94 or I–210 letter showing that status;

(6) Aliens who have filed applications for adjustment of status pursuant to section 245 of the Immigration and Nationality Act (8 U.S.C. 1255) that the Immigration and Naturalization Service has accepted as "properly filed" (within the meaning of 8 CFR 245.2(a)(1) or (2)) and whose departure the Immigration and Naturalization Service does not contemplate enforcing. We ask for INS Form I–181 or a passport properly endorsed;

(7) Aliens granted stays of deportation by court order, statute or regulation, or by individual determination of the Immigration and Naturalization Service pursuant to section 106 of the Immigration and Nationality Act (8 U.S.C. 1105a) or relevant Immigration and Naturalization Service instructions, whose departure that agency does not contemplate enforcing. We ask for INS Form I–94 or a letter from the Immigration and Naturalization Service, or copy of a court order establishing the alien's status;

(8) Aliens granted asylum pursuant to section 208 of the Immigration and Nationality Act (8 U.S.C. 1158). We ask for INS Form I–94 and a letter establishing this status;

(9) Aliens admitted as refugees pursuant to section 207 of the Immigration and Nationality Act (8 U.S.C. 1157) or section 203(a)(7) of the Immigration and Nationality Act (8 U.S.C. 1153(a)(7)). We ask for INS Form I–94 properly endorsed;

(10) Aliens granted voluntary departure pursuant to section 242(b) of the Immigration and Nationality Act (8 U.S.C. 1252(b)) or 8 CFR 242.5 whose departure the Immigration and Naturalization Service does not contemplate enforcing. We ask for INS Form I–94 or I–210 bearing a departure date;

(11) Aliens granted deferred action status pursuant to Immigration and Naturalization Service Operations Instruction 103.1(a)(ii) prior to June 15, 1984 or 242.1(a)(22) issued June 15, 1984 and later. We ask for INS Form I–210 or a letter showing that departure has been deferred;

(12) Aliens residing in the United States under orders of supervision pursuant to section 242 of the Immigration and Nationality Act (8 U.S.C. 1252(d)). We ask for INS Form I–220B;

(13) Aliens who have entered and continuously resided in the United States since before January 1, 1972 (or any date established by section 249 of the Immigration and Nationality Act, 8 U.S.C. 1259). We ask for any proof establishing this entry and continuous residence;

(14) Aliens granted suspension of deportation pursuant to section 244 of the Immigration and Nationality Act (8 U.S.C. 1254) and whose departure the Immigration and Naturalization Service does not contemplate enforcing. We ask for an order from the immigration judge;

(15) Aliens whose deportation has been withheld pursuant to section 243(h) of the Immigration and Nationality Act (8 U.S.C. 1253(h)). We ask for an order from an immigration judge showing that deportation has been withheld;

(16) Aliens granted lawful temporary resident status pursuant to section 245A of the Immigration and Nationality Act (8 U.S.C. 1255a). We ask for INS form I–688 showing that status; or

(17) Any other aliens living in the United States with the knowledge and permission of the Immigration and Naturalization Service and whose departure that agency does not contemplate enforcing.

(c) How to prove you are in a category listed in paragraph (b) of this section. You must give us proof that you are in one of the categories in paragraph (b) of this section. You may give us—

(1) Any of the documents listed in paragraph (b) of this section; or

(2) Other information which shows that you are in one of the categories listed in paragraph (b) of this section.

(d) We must contact the Immigration and Naturalization Service.

(1) We must contact the Immigration and Naturalization Service to verify the information you give us to prove you are permanently residing in the United States under color of law.

(2) If you give us any of the documents listed in paragraphs (b)(1), (2), (3), (4), (8), (9), (11), (12), (13), (15), or (16) of this section, we will pay you benefits if you meet all other eligibility requirements. We will contact the Immigration and Naturalization Service to verify that the document you give us is currently valid.

(3) If you give us any of the documents listed in paragraphs (b)(5), (6), (7), (10), or (14) of this section, or documents that indicate that you meet paragraph (b)(17) of this section, or any other information to prove you are permanently residing in the United States under color of law, we will contact the Immigration and Naturalization Service to verify that the document or other information is currently valid. We must also get information from the Immigration and Naturalization Service as to whether that agency contemplates enforcing your departure. We will apply the following rules:

(i) If you have a document that shows that you have an Immigration and Naturalization Service status that is valid for an indefinite period we will assume that the Immigration and Naturalization Service does not contemplate enforcing your departure. Therefore, we will pay you benefits if you meet all other eligibility requirements. If, based on the information we get from the Immigration and Naturalization Service, we find that your document is currently valid, we will consider this sufficient proof that the Immigration and Naturalization Service does not contemplate enforcing your departure. We will continue your benefits. However, if we find that your document is not currently valid, we will suspend your benefits under § 416.1320.

(ii) If you have a document that appears currently valid and shows you have an Immigration and Naturalization Service status for at least 1 year, or that shows the Immigration and Naturalization Service is allowing you to remain in the United States for a specified period due to conditions in your home country, we will assume that the Immigration and Naturalization Service does not contemplate enforcing your departure. Therefore, we will pay you benefits if you meet all other eligibility requirements. If, based on the information we get from the Immigration and Naturalization Service, we learn that your document is currently valid and that agency does not contemplate enforcing your departure, we will continue your benefits. However, if we learn that your document is not currently valid or that the Immigration and Naturalization Service does contemplate enforcing your departure, we will suspend your benefits under § 416.1320.

(iii) If you have a document that shows you have an Immigration and Naturalization Service status valid for less than 1 year, or if your document has no expiration date, or if you have no document, we will not pay you benefits until the Immigration and Naturalization Service confirms that your document is currently valid and we get information from that agency that indicates whether it contemplates enforcing your departure. If that agency does not contemplate enforcing your departure, we will pay you benefits if you meet all other eligibility requirements.

(iv) If at any time after you begin receiving benefits we receive information from the Immigration and Naturalization Service which indicates that the Immigration and Naturalization Service contemplates enforcing your departure, we will suspend your benefits under § 416.1320 and any benefits you have received after the date that the Immigration and Naturalization Service began contemplating enforcing departure will be overpayments under subpart E of this part.

(e) What "United States" means. We use the term United States in this section to mean the 50 States, the District of Columbia, and the Northern Mariana Islands.

(Approved by the Office of Management and Budget under control number 0960–0451)

[52 FR 21943, June 10, 1987; 52 FR 34773, Sept. 15, 1987; 52 FR 35836, Sept. 23, 1987; 56 FR 55075, Oct. 24, 1991; 56 FR 61287, Dec. 2, 1991; 68 FR 53509, Sept. 11, 2003]

§ 416.1619 When you cannot be considered permanently residing in the United States under color of law.

We will not consider you to be permanently residing in the United States under color of law and you are not eligible for SSI benefits during a period in which you have been granted temporary protected status by the Immigration and Naturalization Service under section 244A of the Immigration and Nationality Act.

[58 FR 41182, Aug. 3, 1993]

SUBPART Q—REFERRAL OF PERSONS ELIGIBLE FOR SUPPLEMENTAL SECURITY INCOME TO OTHER AGENCIES

Authority: Secs. 702(a)(5), 1611(e)(3), 1615, and 1631 of the Social Security Act (42 U.S.C. 902(a)(5), 1382(e)(3), 1382d, and 1383).

Source: 45 FR 70859, Oct. 27, 1980; 52 FR 27541, July 22, 1987; 60 FR 8153, Feb. 10, 1995; 61 FR 5942, Feb. 15, 1996, unless otherwise noted.

GENERAL

§ 416.1701 Scope of subpart.

This subpart describes whom we refer to agencies for (a) vocational rehabilitation services or (b) treatment for alcoholism or drug addiction. The purpose of these services or treatments is to restore your ability to work. This subpart also describes the conditions under which you can refuse treatment after we have referred you. If these conditions are not met, this subpart describes how your benefits are affected when you refuse treatment.

[68 FR 40124, July 7, 2003]

§ 416.1705 Definitions.

As used in this subpart—

Vocational rehabilitation services refers to services provided blind or disabled persons under the State plan approved under the Rehabilitation Act of 1973 (see 45 CFR 401.120ff for requirements of these State plans).

We or us refers to either the Social Security Administration or the State agency making the disability or blindness determination.

You or your refers to the person who applies for or receives benefits or the person for whom an application is filed.

REFERRAL FOR VOCATIONAL REHABILITATION SERVICES

§ 416.1710 Whom we refer and when.

(a) Whom we refer. If you are 16 years of age or older and under 65 years old, and receiving supplemental security income (SSI) benefits, we will refer you to the State agency providing vocational rehabilitation services. If you are under age 16, we will refer you to an agency administering services under the Maternal and Child Health Services (Title V) Block Grant Act.

(b) When we refer. We will make this referral when we find you eligible for benefits or at any other time that we find you might be helped by vocational rehabilitation services.

[45 FR 70859, Oct. 27, 1980, as amended at 48 FR 6297, Feb. 23, 1983]

§ 416.1715 [Reserved]

[68 FR 40124, July 7, 2003]

REFERRAL FOR TREATMENT OF ALCOHOLISM OR DRUG ADDICTION

§ 416.1720 Whom we refer.

We will refer you to an approved facility for treatment of your alcoholism or drug addiction if—

(a) You are disabled;

(b) You are not blind;

(c) You are not 65 years old or older; and

(d) Alcoholism or drug addiction is a contributing factor to your disability.

§ 416.1725 Effect of your failure to comply with treatment requirements for your drug addiction or alcoholism.

(a) Suspension of benefits. Your eligibility for benefits will be suspended beginning with the first month after we notify you in writing that we have determined that you have failed to comply with the treatment requirements for your drug addiction or alcoholism as defined in § 416.940. Your benefits will be suspended and reinstated in accordance with the provisions in § 416.1326.

(b) Termination of benefits. If your benefits are suspended for 12 consecutive months for failure to comply with treatment in accordance with § 416.1326, your eligibility for disability benefits will be terminated in accordance with § 416.1331.

[60 FR 8153, Feb. 10, 1995]

SUBPART R—RELATIONSHIP

Authority: Secs. 702(a)(5), 1612(b), 1614(b), (c), and (d), and 1631(d)(1) and (e) of the Social Security Act (42 U.S.C. 902(a)(5), 1382a(b), 1382c(b), (c), and (d) and 1383(d)(1) and (e)).

Source: 45 FR 71795, Oct. 30, 1980; 46 FR 29211, May 29, 1981; 46 FR 42063, Aug. 19, 1981; 52 FR 8889, March 20, 1987; 52 FR 27542, July 22, 1987; 61 FR 5942, Feb. 15, 1996; 71 FR 66867, Nov. 17, 2006, unless otherwise noted.

§ 416.1801 Introduction.

(a) What is in this subpart. This subpart contains the basic rules for deciding for SSI purposes whether a person is considered married and, if so, to whom; whether a person is considered a child; and whether a person is considered another person's parent. It tells what information and evidence we need to decide these facts.

(b) Related subparts. Subpart D discusses how to determine the amount of a person's benefits; subpart G discusses what changes in a person's situation he or she must report to us; subpart K discusses how we count income; and subpart L discusses how we count resources (money and property). The questions of whether a person is married, to whom a person is married, whether a person is a child, and who is a person's parent must be answered in order to know which rules in subparts D, G, K, and L apply.

(c) Definitions. In this subpart—

Eligible spouse means a person—

(1) Who is eligible for SSI,

(2) Whom we consider the spouse of another person who is eligible for SSI, and

(3) Who was living in the same household with that person on—

(i) The first day of the month following the date the application is filed (for the initial month of eligibility for payment based on that application);

(ii) The date a request for reinstatement of eligibility is filed (for the month of such request); or

(iii) The first day of the month, for all other months. An individual is considered to be living with an eligible spouse during temporary absences as defined in § 416.1149 and while receiving continued benefits under section 1611(e)(1)(E) or (G) of the Act.

Spouse means a person's husband or wife under the rules of §§ 416.1806 through 416.1835 of this part.

We and us mean the Social Security Administration.

You means a person who has applied for or has been receiving SSI benefits, or a person for whom someone else has applied for or has been receiving SSI benefits.

[60 FR 16376, March 30, 1995; 64 FR 31975, June 15, 1999; 65 FR 16815, March 30, 2000]

WHO IS CONSIDERED YOUR SPOUSE

§ 416.1802 Effects of marriage on eligibility and amount of benefits.

(a) If you have an ineligible spouse—

(1) Counting income. If you apply for or receive SSI benefits, and you are married to someone who is not eligible for SSI benefits and are living in the same household as that person, we may count part of that person's income as yours. Counting part of that person's income as yours may reduce the amount of your

benefits or even make you ineligible. Section 416.410 discusses the amount of benefits and § 416.1163 explains how we count income for an individual with an ineligible spouse.

(2) Counting resources. If you are married to someone who is not eligible for SSI benefits and are living in the same household as that person, we will count the value of that person's resources (money and property), minus certain exclusions, as yours when we determine your eligibility. Section 416.1202(a) gives a more detailed statement of how we count resources and § 416.1205(a) gives the limit of resources allowed for eligibility of a person with an ineligible spouse.

(b) If you have an eligible spouse—

(1) Counting income. If you apply for or receive SSI benefits and have an eligible spouse as defined in § 416.1801(c), we will count your combined income and calculated the benefit amount for you as a couple. Section 416.412 gives a detailed statement of the amount of benefits and subpart K of this part explains how we count income for an eligible couple.

(2) Counting resources. If you have an eligible spouse as defined in § 416.1801(c), we will count the value of your combined resources (money and property), minus certain exclusions, and use the couple's resource limit when we determine your eligibility. Section 416.1205(b) gives a detailed statement of the resource limit for an eligible couple.

(c) If you are married, we do not consider you a child. The rules for counting income and resources are different for children than for adults. (Section 416.1851 discusses the effects of being considered a child on eligibility and amount of benefits.) Regardless of your age, if you are married we do not consider you to be a child.

(d)(1) General rule: Benefits depend on whether you are married or not married at the beginning of each month. If you get married, even on the first day of a month we will treat you as single until the next month. If your marriage ends, even on the first day of a month, we will treat you as married until the next month.

(2) Exception: If you both meet eligibility requirements after your date of marriage or after your marriage ends. If, in the month that you marry, each of you first meets all eligibility requirements after the date of your marriage, we will treat you as an eligible couple for that month. If, in the month that your marriage ends, each of you first meets all eligibility requirements after the date your marriage ends, we will treat you as eligible individuals. (See subparts D and E regarding how your benefits will be prorated.)

[51 FR 13495, April 21, 1985; 60 FR 16376, March 30, 1995]

§ 416.1806 Whether you are married and who is your spouse.

(a) We will consider someone to be your spouse (and therefore consider you to be married) for SSI purposes if—

(1) You are legally married under the laws of the State where your and his or her permanent home is (or was when you lived together);

(2) We have decided that either of you is entitled to husband's or wife's Social Security insurance benefits as the spouse of the other (this decision will not affect your SSI benefits for any month before it is made); or

(3) You and an unrelated person of the opposite sex are living together in the same household at or after the time you apply for SSI benefits, and you both lead people to believe that you are husband and wife.

(b) if more than one person would qualify as your husband or wife under paragraph (a) of this section, we will consider the person you are presently living with to be your spouse for SSI purposes.

[60 FR 16376, March 30, 1995]

§ 416.1811 [Reserved]

[60 FR 16376, March 30, 1995]

§ 416.1816 Information we need concerning marriage when you apply for SSI.

When you apply for SSI benefits, we will ask whether you are married. If you are married, we will ask whether you are living with your spouse. If you are unmarried or you are married but not living with your spouse, we will ask whether you are living in the same household with anyone of the opposite sex who is not related to you. If you are, we will ask whether you and that person lead other people to believe that you are husband and wife.

§ 416.1821 Showing that you are married when you apply for SSI.

(a) General rule: Proof is unnecessary. If you tell us you are married we will consider you married unless we have information to the contrary. We will also consider you married, on the basis of your statement, if you say you are living with an unrelated person of the opposite sex and you both lead people to believe you are married. However, if we have information contrary to what you tell us, we will ask for evidence as described in paragraph (c).

(b) Exception: If you are a child to whom parental deeming rules apply. If you are a child to whom the parental deeming rules apply and we receive information from you or others that you are married, we will ask for evidence of your marriage. The rules on deeming parental income are in §§ 416.1165 and 416.1166. The rules on deeming of parental resources are in § 416.1202.

(c) Evidence of marriage. If paragraph (a) or (b) of this section indicates that you must show us evidence that you are married, you must show us your marriage certificate (which can be the original certificate, a certified copy of the public record of marriage, or a certified copy of the church record) if you can. If you cannot, you must tell us why not and give us whatever evidence you can.

[52 FR 8889, March 20, 1987]

§ 416.1826 Showing that you are not married when you apply for SSI.

(a) General rule: Proof is unnecessary. If you do not live with an unrelated person of the opposite sex and you say that you are not married, we will generally accept your statement unless we have information to the contrary.

(b) Exception: If you are under age 22 and have been married. If you are under age 22 and have been married, to prove that your marriage has ended you must show us the decree of divorce or annulment or the death certificate if you can. If you cannot, you must tell us why not and give us whatever evidence you can.

(c) Exception: If you are living with an unrelated person of the opposite sex.

(1) If you are living with an unrelated person of the opposite sex, you and the person you are living with must explain to us what your relationship is and answer questions such as the following:

(i) What names are the two of you known by?

(ii) Do you introduce yourselves as husband and wife? If not, how are you introduced?

(iii) What names are used on mail for each of you?

(iv) Who owns or rents the place where you live?

(v) Do any deeds, leases, time payment papers, tax papers, or any other papers show you as husband and wife?

(2) We will consider you married to the person you live with unless the information we have, including the answers to the questions in paragraph (c)(1) of this section, all considered together, show that the two of you do not lead people to believe that you are each other's husband and wife.

§ 416.1830 When we stop considering you and your spouse an eligible couple.

We will stop considering you and your spouse an eligible couple, even if you both remain eligible, at the beginning of whichever of these months comes first—

(a) The calendar month after the month you stopped living with your eligible spouse, or

(b) The calendar month after the month in which your marriage ends.

[60 FR 16376, March 30, 1995]

§ 416.1832 When we consider your marriage ended.

We consider your marriage ended when—

(a) Your spouse dies;

(b) Your divorce or annulment becomes final;

(c) We decide that either of you is not a spouse of the other for purposes of husband's or wife's social security insurance benefits, if we considered you married only because of § 416.1806(a)(2); or

(d) You and your spouse stop living together, if we considered you married only because of § 416.1806(a)(3).

[60 FR 16376, March 30, 1995]

§ 416.1835 Information we need about separation or end of marriage after you become eligible for SSI.

(a) If you and your spouse stop living together. If you and your spouse stop living together, you must promptly report that fact to us, so that we can decide whether there has been a change that affects either person's benefits. You must also answer questions such as the following. If you cannot answer our questions you must tell us why not and give us whatever information you can.

(1) When did you stop living together?

(2) Do you expect to live together again?

(3) If so, when?

(4) Where is your husband or wife living?

(5) Is either of you living with someone else as husband and wife?

(b) Evidence of end of marriage—

(1) Death. We will accept your statement that your husband or wife died unless we have information to the contrary. If we have contrary information, you must show us the death certificate if you can. If you cannot, you must tell us why not and give us whatever evidence you can.

(2) Divorce or annulment. If your marriage ends by divorce or annulment, you must show us the decree of divorce or annulment if you can. If you cannot, you must tell us why not and give us whatever evidence you can.

(3) Other reason. If your marriage ends for reasons other than death, divorce, or annulment, you must give us any information we ask you to give us about the end of the marriage. If you cannot, you must explain why you cannot. We will consider all of the relevant information to decide if and when your marriage ends.

WHO IS CONSIDERED A CHILD

§ 416.1851 Effects of being considered a child.

If we consider you to be a child for SSI purposes, the rules in this section apply when we determine your eligibility for SSI and the amount of your SSI benefits.

(a) If we consider you to be a student, we will not count all of your earned income when we determine your SSI eligibility and benefit amount. Section 416.1110 tells what we mean by earned income. Section 416.1112(c)(2) tells how much of your earned income we will not count.

(b) If you have a parent who does not live with you but who pays money to help support you, we will not count one-third of that money when we count your income. Section 416.1124(c)(9) discusses this rule.

(c) If you are under age 18 and live with your parent(s) who is not eligible for SSI benefits, we consider (deem) part of his or her income and resources to be your own. If you are under age 18 and live with both your parent and your parent's spouse (stepparent) and neither is eligible for SSI benefits, we consider (deem) part of their income and resources to be your own. Sections 416.1165 and 416.1166 explain the rules and the exception to the rules on deeming your parent's income to be yours, and § 416.1202 explains the rules and the exception to the rules on deeming your parent's resources to be yours.

[52 FR 8889, March 20, 1987; 73 FR 28036, May 15, 2008]

§ 416.1856 Who is considered a child.

We consider you to be a child if—

(a)(1) You are under 18 years old; or

(2) You are under 22 years old and you are a student regularly attending school or college or training that is designed to prepare you for a paying job;

(b) You are not married; and

(c) You are not the head of a household.

§ 416.1861 Deciding whether you are a child: Are you a student?

(a) Are you a student? You are a student regularly attending school or college or training that is designed to prepare you for a paying job if you are enrolled for one or more courses of study and you attend class—

(1) In a college or university for at least 8 hours a week under a semester or quarter system;

(2) In grades 7–12 for at least 12 hours a week;

(3) In a course of training to prepare you for a paying job, and you are attending that training for at least 15 hours a week if the training involves shop practice or 12 hours a week if it does not involve shop practice (this kind of training includes anti-poverty programs, such as the Job Corps, and government-supported courses in self-improvement); or

(4) Less than the amount of time given in paragraph (a)(1), (2), or (3) of this section for reasons you cannot control, such as illness, if the circumstances justify your reduced credit load or attendance.

(b) If you are instructed at home. You may be a student regularly attending school if you are instructed at home in grades 7–12 in accordance with a home school law of the State or other jurisdiction in which you reside and for at least 12 hours a week.

(c) If you have to stay home. You may be a student regularly attending school, college, or training to prepare you for a paying job if—

(1) You have to stay home because of your disability;

(2) You are studying at home a course or courses given by a school (grades 7–12), college, university, or government agency; and

(3) A home visitor or tutor directs your study or training.

(d) When you are not in school—

(1) When school is out. We will consider you to be a student regularly attending school, college, or training to prepare you for a paying job even when classes are out if you actually attend regularly just before the time classes are out and you—

(i) Tell us that you intend to resume attending regularly when school opens again; or

(ii) Actually do resume attending regularly when school opens again.

(2) Other times. Your counselor or teacher may believe you need to stay out of class for a short time during the course or between courses to enable you to continue your study or training. That will not stop us from considering you to be a student regularly attending school, college, or training to prepare you for a paying job if you are in—

(i) A course designed to prepare disabled people for work; or

(ii) A course to prepare you for a job that is specially set up for people who cannot work at ordinary jobs.

(e) Last month of school. We will consider you to be a student regularly attending school, college, or training to prepare you for a paying job for the month in which you complete or stop your course of study or training.

(f) When we need evidence that you are a student. We need evidence that you are a student if you are 18 years old or older but under age 22, because we will not consider you to be a child unless we consider you to be a student.

(g) What evidence we need. If we need evidence that you are a student, you must—

(1) Show us any paper you have that shows you are a student in a school, college, or training program, such as a student identification card or tuition receipt; and

(2) Tell us—

(i) What courses you are taking;

(ii) How many hours a week you spend in classes;

(iii) The name and address of the school or college you attend or the agency training you; and

(iv) The name and telephone number of someone at the school, college, or agency who can tell us more about your courses, in case we need information you cannot give us.

[71 FR 66867, Nov. 17, 2006]

§ 416.1866 Deciding whether you are a child: Are you the head of a household?

(a) Meaning of head of household. You are the head of a household if you have left your parental home on a permanent basis and you are responsible for the day-to-day decisions on the operation of your own household. If you live with your parent(s) or stepparents, we will ordinarily assume you are not the head of a household. However, we will consider you to be the head of a household if for some reason (such as your parent's illness) you are the one who makes the day-to-day decisions. You need not have someone living with you to be the head of a household.

(b) If you share decision-making equally. If you live with one or more people and everyone has an equal voice in the decision-making (for example, a group of students who share off-campus housing), that group is not a household. Each person who has left the parental home on a permanent basis is the head of his or her own household.

WHO IS CONSIDERED A STUDENT FOR PURPOSES OF THE STUDENT EARNED INCOME EXCLUSION

Source: 71 FR 66867, Nov. 17, 2006, unless otherwise noted.

§ 416.1870 Effect of being considered a student.

If we consider you to be a student, we will not count all of your earned income when we determine your SSI eligibility and benefit amount. If you are an ineligible spouse or ineligible parent for deeming purposes and we consider you to be a student, we will not count all of your income when we determine how much of your income to deem. Section 416.1110 explains what we mean by earned income. Section 416.1112(c)(3) explains how much of your earned income we will not count. Section 416.1161(a)(27) explains how the student earned income exclusion applies to deemors.

§ 416.1872 Who is considered a student.

We consider you to be a student if you are under 22 years old and you regularly attend school or college or training that is designed to prepare you for a paying job as described in § 416.1861(a) through (e).

[71 FR 66867, Nov. 17, 2006]

§ 416.1874 When we need evidence that you are a student.

We need evidence that you are a student if you are under age 22 and you expect to earn over $65 in any month. Section 416.1861(g) explains what evidence we need.

[71 FR 66867, Nov. 17, 2006]

WHO IS CONSIDERED YOUR PARENT

§ 416.1876 Effects a parent (or parents) can have on the child's benefits.

Section 416.1851 (b) and (c) tells what effects a parent's income and resources can have on his or her child's benefits.

§ 416.1881 Deciding whether someone is your parent or stepparent.

(a) We consider your parent to be—

(1) Your natural mother or father; or

(2) A person who legally adopted you.

(b) We consider your stepparent to be the present husband or wife of your natural or adoptive parent. A person is not your stepparent if your natural or adoptive parent, to whom your stepparent was married, has died, or if your parent and stepparent have been divorced or their marriage has been annulled.

(c) Necessary evidence. We will accept your statement on whether or not someone is your parent or stepparent unless we have information to the contrary. If we have contrary information, you must show us, if you can, one or more of the following kinds of evidence that would help to prove whether or not the person is your parent or stepparent: Certificate of birth, baptism, marriage, or death, or decree of adoption, divorce, or annulment. If you cannot, you must tell us why not and show us any other evidence that would help to show whether or not the person is your parent or stepparent.

SUBPART S—INTERIM ASSISTANCE PROVISIONS

Authority: Secs. 702(a)(5) and 1631 of the Social Security Act (42 U.S.C. 902(a)(5) and 1383).

Source: 46 FR 47449, Sept. 27, 1981; 52 FR 27542, July 22, 1987; 61 FR 5942, Feb. 15, 1996, unless otherwise noted.

INTRODUCTION

§ 416.1901 Scope of subpart S.

(a) General. This subpart explains that we may withhold your SSI benefit and/or State supplementary payments and send them to the State (or a political subdivision of the State) as repayment for interim assistance it gave you while your application for SSI was pending, or while your SSI benefits were suspended or terminated if you are subsequently found to have been eligible for such benefits. Before we will do this, the State must have entered into an interim assistance agreement with us authorizing such reimbursement, and you must have given written authorization for us to repay the State (or a political subdivision of the State).

(b) Organization of this subpart. We have organized this subpart as follows:

(1) Definitions. Section 416.1902 contains definitions of terms used in this subpart.

(2) Authorizations. Sections 416.1904 through 416.1908 give the rules that apply to your written authorization.

(3) Interim assistance agreements. Section 416.1910 gives the requirements for interim assistance agreements between us and the State.

(4) Appeals. Sections 416.1920 through 416.1922 describe your appeal rights in the State and in SSA.

[56 FR 19262, April 26, 1991]

§ 416.1902 Definitions.

For purposes of this subpart—

Authorization means your written permission, in a form legally acceptable to us and to the State from which you received interim assistance, for us to withhold the appropriate SSI benefit payment and send it to the State.

Interim assistance means assistance the State gives you, including payments made on your behalf to providers of goods or services, to meet your basic needs, beginning with the first month for which you are eligible for payment of SSI benefits and ending with, and including, the month your SSI payments begin, or assistance the State gives you beginning with the day for which your eligibility for SSI benefits is reinstated after a period of suspension or termination and ending with, and including, the month the Commissioner makes the first payment of benefits following the suspension or termination if it is determined subsequently that you were eligible for benefits during that period. It does not include assistance the State gives to or for any other person. If the State has prepared and cannot stop delivery of its last assistance payment to you when it receives your SSI benefit payment from us, that assistance payment is included as interim assistance to be reimbursed. Interim assistance does not include assistance payments financed wholly or partly with Federal funds.

SSI benefit payment means your Federal benefit and any State supplementary payment made by us to you on behalf of a State (see subpart T of this part) which is due you at the time we make the first payment of benefits or when your benefits are reinstated after suspension or termination. Advance payment, as defined in § 416.520, payment based upon presumptive disability or presumptive blindness, as defined in § 416.931, or certain payments made under the administrative immediate payment procedure, are not considered SSI benefit payments for interim assistance purposes.

State for purposes of an interim assistance agreement, means a State of the United States, the District of Columbia, or the Northern Mariana Islands. For all other purposes (for example, payment, appeals, notices) State also means a political subdivision of any of these.

We, Us, or Our means the Social Security Administration.

You or Your means someone who has applied for or is already receiving SSI benefits.

[46 FR 47449, Sept. 28, 1981; 46 FR 50947, Oct. 16, 1981; 56 FR 19262, April 26, 1991; 56 FR 25446, June 4, 1991; 62 FR 38455, July 18, 1997; 64 FR 31975, June 15, 1999]

AUTHORIZATIONS

§ 416.1904 Authorization to withhold SSI benefits.

We may withhold your SSI benefit payment and send it to the State to repay the State for the interim assistance it gave to you, if—

(a) We have an interim assistance agreement with the State at the time your authorization goes into effect; and

(b) Your authorization is in effect at the time we make the SSI benefit payment.

§ 416.1906 When your authorization is in effect.

Your authorization for us to withhold your SSI benefit payment, to repay the State for interim assistance the State gives you, is effective when we receive it, or (if our agreement with the State allows) when we receive notice from the State that it has received your authorization. It remains in effect until—

(a) We make the first SSI benefit payment on your initial application for benefits or, in the case of an authorization effective for a period of suspense or termination, until the initial payment following the termination or suspension of your benefits.

(b) We make a final determination on your claim (if your SSI claim is denied, the denial is the final determination, unless you file a timely appeal as described in subpart N of this part);

(c) You and the State agree to terminate your authorization; or

(d) If earlier than the event in paragraph (a), (b), or (c) of this section, the date (if any) specified in your authorization.

[56 FR 19262, April 26, 1991]

§ 416.1908 When we need another authorization.

Once an event described in § 416.1906 occurs, your authorization is no longer effective. If you reapply for SSI benefits, or the authorization has expired, the State must obtain a new authorization from you in order for us to repay the State for interim assistance it gives you.

INTERIM ASSISTANCE AGREEMENTS

§ 416.1910 Requirements for interim assistance agreement.

An interim assistance agreement must be in effect between us and the State if we are to repay the State for interim assistance. The following requirements must be part of the agreement:

(a) SSA to repay the State. We must agree to repay the State for interim assistance it gives you. Repayment to the State takes priority over any underpayments due you (see §§ 416.525 and 416.542).

(b) State to pay any excess repayment to you. The State must agree that, if we repay it an amount greater than the amount of interim assistance it gave to you, the State will—

(1) Pay the excess amount to you no later than 10 working days from the date the State receives repayment from us; or

(2) Refund the excess amount to us for disposition under the rules in subpart E of the this part on payment of benefits if the State cannot pay it to you (for example, you die or you move and the State cannot locate you).

(c) State to notify you. The State must agree to give you written notice explaining—

(1) How much we have repaid the State for interim assistance it gave you;

(2) The excess amount, if any, due you; and

(3) That it will give you an opportunity for a hearing if you disagree with State's actions regarding repayment of interim assistance.

(d) Duration of the agreement. We and the State must agree to the length of time that the agreement will remain in effect.

(e) State to comply with other regulations. The State must agree to comply with any other regulations that we find necessary to administer the interim assistance provisions.

APPEALS

§ 416.1920 Your appeal rights in the State.

Under its interim assistance agreement with us, the State must agree to give you an opportunity for a hearing if you disagree with the State's actions regarding repayment of interim assistance. For example, you are entitled to a hearing by the State if you disagree with the State regarding the amount of the repayment the State keeps or the amount of any excess the State pays to you. You are not entitled to a Federal hearing on the State's actions regarding repayment of interim assistance.

§ 416.1922 Your appeal rights in SSA.

If you disagree with the total amount of money we have withheld and sent to the State for the interim assistance it gave to you, you have a right to appeal to us, as described in subpart N of this part.

SUBPART T—STATE SUPPLEMENTATION PROVISIONS; AGREEMENTS; PAYMENTS

Authority: Secs. 702(a)(5), 1616, 1618, and 1631 of the Social Security Act (42 U.S.C. 902(a)(5), 1382e, 1382g, and 1383); sec. 212, Pub.L. 93–66, 87 Stat. 155 (42 U.S.C. 1382 note); sec. 8(a), (b)(1)–(b)(3), Pub.L. 93–233, 87 Stat. 956 (7 U.S.C. 612c note, 1431 note and 42 U.S.C. 1382e note); secs. 1(a)–(c) and 2(a), 2(b)(1), 2(b)(2), Pub.L. 93–335, 88 Stat. 291 (42 U.S.C. 1382 note, 1382e note).

Source: 40 FR 7640, Feb. 21, 1975; 50 FR 48579, Nov. 26, 1985; 51 FR 10616, March 28, 1986; 52 FR 27542, July 22, 1987; 56 FR 55453, Oct. 28, 1991; 61 FR 5942, Feb. 15, 1996, unless otherwise noted.

§ 416.2001 State supplementary payments; general.

(a) State supplementary payments; defined. State supplementary payments are any payments made by a State or one of its political subdivisions (including any such payments for which reimbursement is available from the Social Security Administration pursuant to Pub.L. 94–23, as amended) to a recipient of supplemental security income benefits (or to an individual who would be eligible for such benefits except for income), if the payments are made:

(1) In supplementation of the Federal supplemental security income benefits; i.e., as a complement to the Federal benefit amount, thereby increasing the amount of income available to the recipient to meet his needs; and

(2) Regularly, on a periodic recurring, or routine basis of at least once a quarter; and

(3) In cash, which may be actual currency or any negotiable instrument, convertible into cash upon demand; and

(4) In an amount based on the need or income of an individual or couple.

(b) State; defined. For purposes of this subpart, State means a State of the United States or the District of Columbia.

(c) Mandatory minimum supplementary payments. In order for a State to be eligible for payments pursuant to title XIX of the Act with respect to expenditures for any quarter beginning after December 1973, such State must have in effect an agreement with the Commissioner under which such State will provide to aged, blind, and disabled individuals (as defined in § 416.202) residing in the State who were recipients of aid or assistance for December 1973 as defined in § 416.121, under such State's plan approved under title I, X, XIV, or XVI of the Act, mandatory minimum supplementary payments beginning in January 1974 in an amount determined in accordance with § 416.2050 in order to maintain their income levels of December 1973. (See §§ 416.2065 and 416.2070.)

(d) Supplementary payments for recipients of special SSI cash benefits. A State which makes supplementary payments (regardless of whether they are mandatory or optional and whether the payments are federally administered), has the option of making those payments to individuals who receive cash benefits under section 1619(a) of the Act (see § 416.261), or who would be eligible to receive cash benefits except for their income.

[40 FR 7640, Feb. 21, 1975, as amended at 41 FR 36017, Aug. 26, 1976; 43 FR 48995, Oct. 20, 1978; 45 FR 54748, July 18, 1980, Jan. 22, 1981; 47 FR 15326, April 9, 1982; 62 FR 38455, July 18, 1997]

§ 416.2005 Administration agreements with SSA.

(a) Agreement-mandatory only. Subject to the provisions of paragraph (d) of this section, any State having an agreement with the Social Security Administration (SSA) under § 416.2001(c) may enter into an administration agreement with SSA under which SSA will make the mandatory minimum supplementary payments on behalf of such State. An agreement under § 416.2001(c) and an administration agreement under this paragraph may be consolidated into one agreement.

(b) Agreement—mandatory and optional payments. Subject to the provisions of paragraph (d) of this section, any State may enter into an agreement with SSA under which the State will provide both mandatory and optional State supplementary payments and elect Federal administration of such State supplementary payment programs. If SSA agrees to administer such State's optional supplementary payments, the State must also have SSA administer its mandatory minimum supplementary payments unless the State is able to provide sufficient justification for exemption from this requirement.

(c) Administration—combination. Any State may enter into an agreement with SSA under which the State will provide mandatory minimum supplementary payments and elect Federal administration of such payments while providing optional State supplementary payments which it shall administer itself. If the State chooses to administer such payment itself, it may establish its own criteria for determining eligibility requirements as well as the amounts.

(d) Conditions of administration agreement. The State and SSA may, subject to the provisions of this subpart, enter into a written agreement, in such form and containing such provisions not inconsistent with this part as are found necessary by SSA, under which SSA will administer the State supplementary payments on behalf of a State (or political subdivision). Under such an agreement between SSA and a State, specific Federal and State responsibilities for administration and fiscal responsibilities will be stipulated. The regulations in effect for the supplemental security income program shall be applicable in the Federal administration of State supplementary payments except as may otherwise be provided in this subpart as found by SSA to be necessary for the effective and efficient administration of both the basic Federal benefit and the State supplementary payment. If the State elects options available under this subpart (specified in §§ 416.2015–416.2035), such options must be specified in the administration agreement.

[62 FR 312, Jan. 3, 1997]

§ 416.2010 Essentials of the administration agreements.

(a) Payments. Any agreement between SSA and a State made pursuant to § 416.2005 must provide that, if for optional supplementation, such State supplementary payments are made to all individuals and/or couples who are:

(1) Receiving (or at the option of the State would, but for the amount of their income, be eligible to receive) supplemental security income benefits under title XVI of the Social Security Act, and

(2) Within the variations and categories (as defined in § 416.2030) for which the State (or political subdivision) wishes to provide a supplementary payment, and

(3) Residing, subject to the provisions of § 416.2035(a), in such State (or political subdivision thereof).

(b) Administrative costs.

(1) SSA shall assess each State that had elected Federal administration of optional and/or mandatory State supplementary payments an administration fee for administering those payments. The administration fee is assessed and paid monthly and is derived by multiplying the number of State supplementary payments made by SSA on behalf of a State for any month in a fiscal year by the applicable dollar rate for the fiscal year. The number of supplementary payments made by SSA in a month is the total number of checks issued, and direct deposits made, to recipients in that month, that are composed in whole or in part of State supplementary funds. The dollar rates are as follows:

(i) For fiscal year 1994, $1.67;

(ii) For fiscal year 1995, $3.33;

(iii) For fiscal year 1996, $5.00;

(iv) For fiscal year 1997, $5.00;

(v) For fiscal year 1998, $6.20;

(vi) For fiscal year 1999, $7.60;

(vii) For fiscal year 2000, $7.80;

(viii) For fiscal year 2001, $8.10;

(ix) For fiscal year 2002, $8.50; and

(x) For fiscal year 2003 and each succeeding fiscal year—

(A) The applicable rate in the preceding fiscal year, increased by the percentage, if any, by which the Consumer Price Index for the month of June of the calendar year of the increase exceeds the Consumer Price Index for the month of June of the calendar year preceding the calendar year of the increase, and rounded to the nearest whole cent; or

(B) Such different rate as the Commissioner determines is appropriate for the State taking into account the complexity of administering the State's supplementary payment program.

(2) SSA shall charge a State an additional services fee if, at the request of the State, SSA agrees to provide the State with additional services beyond the level customarily provided in the administration of State supplementary payments. The additional services fee shall be in an amount that SSA determines is necessary to cover all costs, including indirect costs, incurred by the Federal Government in furnishing the additional services. SSA is not required to perform any additional services requested by a State and may, at its sole discretion, refuse to perform those additional services. An additional services fee charged a State may be a one-time charge or, if the furnished services result in ongoing costs to the Federal Government, a monthly or less frequent charge to the State for providing such services.

(c) Agreement period. The agreement period for a State which has elected Federal administration of its supplementary payments will extend for one year from the date the agreement was signed unless otherwise designated. The agreement will be automatically renewed for a period of one year unless either the State or SSA gives written notice not to renew, at least 90 days before the beginning of the new period. For a State to elect Federal administration, it must notify SSA of its intent to enter into an agreement, furnishing the necessary payment specifications, at least 120 days before the first day of the month for which it wishes Federal administration to begin, and have executed such agreement at least 30 days before such day.

(d) Modification or termination. The agreement may be modified at any time by mutual consent. The State or SSA may terminate the agreement upon 90 days written notice to the other party, provided the effective date of the termination is the last day of a quarter. However, the State may terminate the agreement upon 45 days written notice to SSA where:

(1) The State does not wish to comply with a regulation promulgated by SSA subsequent to the execution of the agreement; and

(2) the State provides such written notice within 30 days of the effective date of the regulation. The Secretary[1] is not precluded from terminating the agreement in less than 90 days where he finds that a State has failed to materially comply with the provisions of paragraph (f) of this section or § 416.2090.

(e) Mandatory minimum State supplementation. Any administration agreement between SSA and a State under which SSA will make such State's mandatory minimum State supplementary payments shall provide that the State will:

(1) Certify income and payment amount. Certify to SSA the names of each individual who, for December 1973 was eligible for and a recipient of aid or assistance in the form of money payments under a plan of such State approved under title I, X, XIV, or XVI of the Act (§ 416.121), together with the amount of such aid or assistance payable to each such individual and the amount of such individual's other income (as defined in § 416.2050(b)(2)), and

(2) Additional data. Provide SSA with such additional data at such times as SSA may reasonably require in order to properly, economically, and efficiently carry out such administration agreement. This shall include required information on changes in countable income as well as changes in special needs and circumstances that would result in a decrease in the mandatory income level being maintained by the State, unless the State has specified in the agreement that the minimum income level shall not be lowered by such changes.

[62 FR 313, Jan. 3, 1997; 63 FR 33849, June 22, 1998]

§ 416.2015 Establishing eligibility.

(a) Applications. Any person who meets the application requirements of subpart C of this part is deemed to have filed an application for any federally administered State supplementation for which he may be eligible unless supplementation has been waived pursuant to § 416.2047. However, a supplemental statement will be required where additional information is necessary to establish eligibility or to determine the correct payment amount.

(b) Evidentiary requirements. The evidentiary requirements and developmental procedures of this part

[1] So in official CFR; probably should read "SSA". See 62 FR 313.

are applicable with respect to federally administered State supplementary payments.

(c) Determination. Where not inconsistent with the provisions of this subpart, eligibility for and the amount of the State supplementary payment will be determined pursuant to the provisions of subparts A through Q of this part.

(d) Categories; aged, blind, disabled. An applicant will be deemed to have filed for the State supplementary payment amount provided for the category under which his application for a Federal supplemental security income benefit is filed. As in the Federal supplemental security income program, an individual who establishes eligibility as a blind or disabled individual, and continually remains on the rolls, will continue to be considered blind or disabled after he attains age 65.

(e) Concurrent categories.

(1) In States where the supplementary payment provided for the aged category is higher than for the blind or disabled category aged individuals will be paid the State supplement on the basis of age.

(2) If the administration agreement pursuant to § 416.2005(b) provides for higher supplementary payments to the blind or disabled than to the aged category, then, at the option of the State, the agreement may provide that individuals who are age 65 or over at time of application and who are blind or disabled may elect to receive such higher supplementary payments.

§ 416.2020 Federally administered supplementary payments.

(a) Payment procedures. A federally administered State supplementary payment will be made on a monthly basis and will be included in the same check as a Federal benefit that is payable. A State supplementary payment shall be for the same month as the Federal benefit.

(b) Maximum amount. There is no restriction on the amount of a State supplementary payment that the Federal Government will administer on behalf of a State.

(c) Minimum amount. The Federal Government will not administer optional State supplementary payments in amounts less than $1 per month. Hence, optional supplementary payment amounts of less than $1 will be raised to a dollar.

(d) Optional supplementation: nine categories possible. A State may elect Federal administration of its supplementary payments for up to nine categories, depending on the assistance titles in effect in that State in January 1972 (i.e., title I, X, XIV, or XVI). It can have no more than two categories (one for individuals and one for couples) for each title in effect for January 1972:

(1) Since a State with a title XVI program had just the one title in effect, it can supplement only to two categories, the individual (aged, blind, or disabled), the couple (both of whom are aged, blind, or disabled).

(2) Other States could supplement up to nine categories, depending on the plans they had in effect. Six of these categories would be for:

(i) Aged Individual,

(ii) Aged Couple,

(iii) Blind Individual,

(iv) Blind Couple,

(v) Disabled Individual,

(vi) Disabled Couple.

(3) In addition to those enumerated in paragraph (d)(2) of this section, there are three additional couple categories for which a State may elect to provide a federally administered supplement. These categories are created when one individual in the couple is:

(i) Aged and the other blind, or

(ii) Aged and the other disabled, or

(iii) Blind and the other disabled.

[50 FR 48579, Nov. 26, 1985]

§ 416.2025 Optional supplementation: Countable income.

(a) Earned and unearned income. No less than the amounts of earned or unearned income which were excluded in determining eligibility for or amount of a title XVI supplemental security income benefit must be excludable by a State in the Federal–State agreement for purposes of determining eligibility for or amount of the State supplementary payment.

(b) Effect of countable income on payment amounts. Countable income of an eligible individual or eligible couple is determined in the same manner as such income is determined under the title XVI supplemental security income program. Countable income will affect the amount of the State supplementary payments as follows:

(1) As provided in § 416.420, countable income will first be deducted from the Federal benefit rate applicable to an eligible individual or eligible couple. In the case of an eligible individual living with an ineligible spouse with income (the deeming provisions of § 416.1163 apply), the Federal benefit rate from which countable income will be deducted is the Federal benefit rate applicable to an eligible couple, except that an eligible individual's payment amount may not exceed the amount he or she would have received if he or she were not subject to the deeming provisions (§ 416.1163(e)(2)).

(2) If countable income is equal to or less than the amount of the Federal benefit rate, the full amount of the State supplementary payment as specified in the Federal agreement will be made.

(3) If countable income exceeds the amount of the Federal benefit rate, the State supplementary benefit will be reduced by the amount of such excess. In the case of an eligible individual living with an ineligible spouse with income (the deeming methodology of § 416.1163 applies), the State supplementary payment rate from which the excess income will be deducted is the higher of the State supplementary rates for an eligible couple or an eligible individual, except that an eligible individual's payment amount may not exceed the amount he or she would have received if he or she were not subject to the deeming provisions (see § 416.1163(e)(2)). For purposes of determining the State supplementary couple rate, the ineligible spouse is considered to be in the same category as the eligible individual.

(4) No State supplementary payment will be made where countable income is equal to or exceeds the sum of the Federal benefit rate and the State supplementary payment rate.

(c) Effect of additional income exclusions on payment amounts. A State has the option of excluding amounts of earned and unearned income in addition to the amounts it is required to exclude under paragraph (a) of this section in determining a person's eligibility for State supplementary payments. Such additional income exclusions affect the amount of the State supplementary payments as follows:

(1) Countable income (as determined under the Federal eligibility rules) will first be deducted from the Federal benefit rate applicable to an eligible individual or eligible couple.

(2) Such countable income is then reduced by the amount of the additional income exclusion specified by the State.

(3) If the remaining countable income is equal to or less than the amount of the Federal benefit rate, the full amount of the State supplementary payment will be made.

(4) If the remaining countable income exceeds the amount of the Federal benefit rate, the State supplementary payment will be reduced by the amount of such excess.

(Authority: Secs. 1102, 1614(f), 1616(a), 1631, Social Security Act, as amended, 49 Stat. 647, as amended, 86 Stat. 1473, 1474(a), and 1475 (42 U.S.C. 1302, 1382c(f), 1382e(a), 1383))

[40 FR 7640, Feb. 21, 1975, as amended at 43 FR 39570, Sept. 6, 1978; 53 FR 25151, July 5, 1988]

§ 416.2030 Optional supplementation: Variations in payments.

(a) Payment level. The level of State supplementary payments may vary for each category the State elects to include in its federally administered supplement. These categorical variations of payment levels must be specified in the agreement between the Commissioner and the State. If any State has in effect for July 1974 an agreement which provides for variations in addition to those specified in this section, the State may, at its option, continue such variations but only for periods ending before July 1, 1976.

(1) Geographical variations. A State may elect to include two different geographical variations. A third may be elected if adequate justification, e.g., substantial differences in living costs, can be demonstrated. All such variations must be readily identifiable by county or ZIP code or other readily identifiable factor.

(2) Living arrangements. In addition, a State may elect up to six variations in recognition of the different needs which result from various living arrangements. If a State elects six payment level variations based on differences in living arrangements, one of these six variations must apply only to individuals in Medicaid facilities, that is, facilities receiving title XIX payments with respect to such persons for the cost of their care (see § 416.211(b)(1)). In any event, States are limited to one payment level variation for residents of Medicaid facilities. Types of other living arrangements for which payment variations may be allowed include arrangements such as:

(i) Living alone;

(ii) Living with an ineligible spouse;

(iii) Personal care facility; or,

(iv) Domiciliary or congregate care facility.

(b) Relationship to actual cost differences. Under the agreement, variations in State supplementary payment levels will be permitted for each living arrangement the State elects. These differences must be based on rational distinctions between both the types of living arrangements and the costs of those arrangements.

(c) Effective month of State supplementary payment category. The State supplementary payment category which applies in the current month will be used to determine the State payment level in that month. This rule applies even if the countable income in a prior month is used to determine the amount of State supplementary payment.

[50 FR 48579, Nov. 26, 1985; 56 FR 41455, Aug. 21, 1991; 62 FR 38455, July 18, 1997]

§ 416.2035 Optional supplementation: Additional State options.

(a) Residency requirement. A State or political subdivision may impose, as a condition of eligibility, a residency requirement which excludes from eligibility for State supplementary payment any individual who has resided in such State (or political subdivision thereof) for less than a minimum period prescribed by the State. Any such residency requirement will be specified in the agreement.

(b) Lien and relative responsibility. A State which elects Federal administration of its supplementary payments may place a lien upon property of an individual as a consequence of the receipt of such payments or may require that a relative of the individual contribute to a reasonable extent to the support of the individual, providing it is stated in the agreement that:

(1) The Commissioner has determined that the specific State laws and their enforcement are consistent with the supplemental security income program purpose of providing unencumbered cash payments to recipients; and

(2) The Federal Government is not involved in the administration of such laws and will not vary the State supplementary payment amount it makes to comply with such laws; and

(3) Neither the basic Federal benefit nor any part of the State supplementary payment financed by Federal funds will be subject to the liens or encumbrances of such laws.

[62 FR 38455, July 18, 1997]

§ 416.2040 Limitations on eligibility.

Notwithstanding any other provision of this subpart, the eligibility of an individual (or couple) for optional State supplementary payments administered by the Federal Government in accordance with this subpart shall be limited as follows:

(a) Inmate of public institution. A person who is a resident in a public institution for a month, is ineligible for a Federal benefit for that month under the provision of § 416.211(a), and does not meet the requirements for any of the exceptions in § 416.211 (b), (c), or (d), or § 416.212, also shall be ineligible for a federally administered State supplementary payment for that month.

(b) Ineligible persons. No person who is ineligible for a Federal benefit for any month under sections 1611(e)(1)(A), (2), (3), or (f) of the Act (failure to file; refuses treatment for drug addiction or alcoholism; outside the United States) or other reasons (other than the amount of income) shall be eligible for such State supplementation for such month.

(c) Recipient eligible for benefits under § 416.212. A recipient who is institutionalized and is eligible for either benefit payable under § 416.212 for a month or months may also receive federally administered State supplementation for that month. Additionally, a recipient who would be eligible for benefits under § 416.212 but for countable income which reduces his or her Federal SSI benefit to zero, may still be eligible to receive federally administered State supplementation.

[56 FR 41455, Aug. 21, 1991; 61 FR 10280, March 13, 1996; 68 FR 40124, July 7, 2003]

§ 416.2045 Overpayments and underpayments; federally administered supplementation.

(a) Overpayments. Upon determination that an overpayment has been made, adjustments will be made against future federally administered State supplementary payments for which the person is entitled. Rules and requirements (see §§ 416.550 through 416.586) in effect for recovery (or waiver) of supplemental security income benefit overpayments shall also apply to the recovery (or waiver) of federally administered State supplementary overpaid amounts. If the overpaid person's entitlement to the State supplementary payments is terminated prior to recoupment of the overpaid State supplementary payment amount, and the overpayment cannot be recovered from a Federal benefit payable under this part, the person's record will be annotated (specifying the amount of the overpayment) to permit recoupment if the person becomes reentitled to supplementary payments of such State or to a Federal benefit under this part.

(b) Underpayments. Upon determination that an underpayment of State supplementary payments is due and payable, the underpaid amount shall be paid to the underpaid claimant directly, or his representative. If the underpaid person dies before receiving the underpaid amount of State supplementary payment the underpaid amount shall be paid to the claimant's eligible spouse. If the deceased claimant has no eligible spouse, no payment of the underpaid amount shall be made. (See §§ 416.538 through 416.543.)

[65 FR 16815, March 30, 2000]

§ 416.2047 Waiver of State supplementary payments.

(a) Waiver request in writing. Any person who is eligible to receive State supplementary payments or who would be eligible to receive such State supplementary payments may waive his right to receive such payments if such person makes a written request for waiver of State supplementary payments. Any such request made at time of application for the Federal benefit shall be effective immediately. Any such request filed after the application is filed shall be effective the month the request is received in a social security office, or earlier if the recipient refunds to the Social Security Administration the amount of any supplementary payment(s) made to him for the subject period.

(b) Revocation of waiver. Any individual who has waived State supplementary payments may revoke such waiver at any time by making a written request to any social security office. The revocation will be effective the month in which it is filed. The date such request is received in a social security office or the postmarked date, if the written request was mailed, will be the filing date, whichever is earlier.

§ 416.2050 Mandatory minimum State supplementation.

(a) Determining the amount. The amount of a mandatory State supplementary payment in the case of any eligible individual or couple for any month is equal to:

(1) The amount by which such individual or couple's December 1973 income (as defined in paragraph (b) of this section) exceeds the amount of such individual or couple's title XVI benefit plus other income which would have been used by such State in computing the assistance payable under the State's approved plan for such month; or

(2) Such greater amount as the State may specify.

(b) December 1973 income. "December 1973 income" means an amount equal to the aggregate of:

(1) Money payments. The amount of the aid or assistance in the form of money payments (as defined in 45 CFR § 234.11(a)) which an individual would have received (including any part of such amount which is attributable to meeting special needs or special circumstances) under a State plan approved under title I, X, XIV, or XVI of the Act in accordance with the terms and conditions of such plan relating to eligibility for and amount of such aid or assistance payable thereunder which were in effect for the month of June 1973 together with the bonus value of food stamps for January 1972 if for such month such individual resides in a State which SSA has determined provides supplementary payments the level of which has been found by SSA pursuant to section 8 of Pub.L. 93–233 (87 Stat. 956) to have been specifically increased so as to include the bonus value of food stamps, and

(2) Income. The amount of the income of such individual other than aid or assistance, received by such individual in December 1973, remaining after application of all appropriate income exclusions and used in computation of the amount of aid or assistance, minus any such income which did not result, but which if properly reported, would have resulted in a reduction in the amount of such aid or assistance. Income, which because a State paid less than 100% of its standard of need, did not cause a reduction in the amount of aid or assistance is included.

(c) Special needs or circumstances. Special needs or circumstances include needs of essential persons (as defined in § 416.222), special allowances for housing, and such other situations for which money payments to or for an eligible individual were made under a State plan approved under title I, X, XIV, or XVI of the Act as in effect for June 1973.

(d) Optional supplement payable. A recipient meeting the requirements of paragraph (a) of this section who would otherwise qualify for a payment under a State's program of optional State supplementation (provided for by § 416.2010) which is greater than the amount required by paragraph (a) of this section, shall be paid such greater amount.

[51 FR 10616, March 28, 1986; 62 FR 313, Jan. 3, 1997]

§ 416.2055 Mandatory minimum supplementation reduced.

If for any month after December 1973 there is a change with respect to any special need or special circumstance which, if such change had existed in December 1973, would have caused a reduction in the amount of such individual's aid or assistance payment, then, for such month and for each month thereafter, the amount of the mandatory minimum supplement payable to such individual may, at the option of the State, be reduced in accordance with the terms and conditions of the State's plan approved under title I, X, XIV, or XVI of the Act in effect for the month of June 1973.

§ 416.2060 Mandatory minimum supplementary payments not applicable.

An individual eligible for mandatory minimum supplementary payments from a State beginning in January 1974 shall not be eligible for such payments:

(a) Month after the month of death. Beginning with the month after the month in which the individual dies; or

(b) Not aged, blind, or disabled. Beginning with the first month after the month in which such individual ceases to be an aged, blind, or disabled individual (as defined in § 416.202); or

(c) Not entitled to a Federal payment. During any month in which such individual was ineligible to receive supplemental income benefits under title XVI of the Social Security Act by reason of the provisions of section 1611(e)(1)(A), (2) or (3), 1611(f), or 1615(c) of such Act; or

(d) Month of change in residence. During any full month such individual is not a resident of such State.

§ 416.2065 Mandatory minimum State supplementation: Agreement deemed.

A State shall be deemed to have entered into an agreement with the Commissioner under which such State shall provide mandatory minimum supplementary payments if such State has entered into an agreement with the Commissioner under section 1616 of the Act under which:

(a) Other eligible individuals. Supplementary payments are made to individuals other than those aged, blind, and disabled individuals who were eligible to receive aid or assistance in the form of money payments for the month of December 1973 under a State plan approved under title I, X, XIV, or XVI of the Act, under terms and conditions of such plan in effect for June 1973, and

(b) Minimum requirements. Supplementary payments which meet the mandatory minimum requirements of this subpart are payable to all aged, blind, or disabled individuals who were eligible to receive aid or assistance in the form of money payments for the month of December 1973 under a State plan approved under title I, X, XIV, or XVI of the Act, under terms and conditions of such plan in effect for June 1973.

[62 FR 38455, July 18, 1997]

§ 416.2070 Mandatory supplementation: State compliance not applicable.

The requirement that a State must have in effect an agreement with the Commissioner whereby such State shall provide individual aged, blind, and disabled recipients residing in the State mandatory minimum supplementary payments beginning in January 1974 shall not be applicable in the case of any State where:

(a) State constitution. The State constitution limits expenditures that may be paid as public assistance to, or on behalf of, any needy person to an amount that does not exceed the amount of State public assistance payments that are matched by Federal funds under title I, IV, X, XIV, XVI or XIX of the Social Security Act making it impossible for such State to enter into and commence carrying out (on January 1, 1974) such agreement with the Commissioner, and

(b) Attorney General decision. The Attorney General (or other appropriate State official) has, prior to July 1, 1973, made a finding that the State constitution of such State contains limitations which prevent such State from making supplementary payments of the type described in section 1616 of the Act.

[62 FR 38455, July 18, 1997]

§ 416.2075 Monitoring of mandatory minimum supplementary payments.

(a) Access to records. Any State entering into an agreement with the Commissioner whereby such State will provide mandatory minimum supplementary payments in accordance with § 416.2001(c) shall agree that the Commissioner shall have access to and the right to examine any directly pertinent books, documents, papers, and records of the State involving transactions related to this agreement.

(b) Additional data. Any State entering into an agreement in accordance with § 416.2005 shall provide the Commissioner with such additional data at such times as the Commissioner may reasonably require in order to properly, economically, and efficiently be assessed of such State's compliance with such State agreements.

[62 FR 38455, July 18, 1997]

§ 416.2090 State funds transferred for supplementary payments.

(a) Payment transfer and adjustment.

(1) Any State which has entered into an agreement with SSA which provides for Federal administration of such State's supplementary payments shall transfer to SSA:

(i) An amount of funds equal to SSA's estimate of State supplementary payments for any month which shall be made by SSA on behalf of such State; and

(ii) An amount of funds equal to SSA's estimate of administration fees for any such month determined in the manner described in § 416.2010(b)(1); and

(iii) If applicable, an amount of funds equal to SSA's determination of the costs incurred by the Federal government in furnishing additional services for the State as described in § 416.2010(b)(2).

(2) In order for SSA to make State supplementary payments on behalf of a State for any month as provided by the agreement, the estimated amount of State funds referred to in paragraph (a)(1)(i) of this section, necessary to make those payments for the month, together with the estimated amount of administration fees referred to in paragraph (a)(1)(ii) of this section, for that month, must be on deposit with SSA on the State supplementary payment transfer date, which is the fifth Federal business day following the day in the month that the regularly recurring monthly supplemental security income payments are issued. The additional services fee referred to in paragraph (a)(1)(iii) of this section shall be on deposit with SSA on the date specified by SSA. The amount of State funds paid to SSA for State supplementary payments and the amount paid for administration fees will be adjusted as necessary to maintain the balance with State supplementary payments paid out by SSA on behalf of the State, and administration fees owed to SSA, respectively.

(b) Accounting of State funds.

(1) As soon as feasible, after the end of each calendar month, SSA will provide the State with a statement showing, cumulatively, the total amounts paid by SSA on behalf of the State during the current Federal fiscal year; the fees charged by SSA to administer such supplementary payments; any additional services fees charged the State; the State's total liability therefore; and the end-of-month balance of the State's cash on deposit with SSA.

(2) SSA shall provide an accounting of State funds received as State supplementary payments, administration fees, and additional services fees, within three calendar months following the termination of an agreement under § 416.2005.

(3) Adjustments will be made because of State funds due and payable or amounts of State funds recovered for calendar months for which the agreement was in effect. Interest will be incurred by SSA and the States with respect to the adjustment and accounting of State supplementary payments funds in accordance with applicable laws and regulations of the United States Department of the Treasury.

(c) State audit. Any State entering into an agreement with SSA which provides for Federal administration of the State's supplementary payments has the right to an audit (at State expense) of the payments made by SSA on behalf of such State. The Secretary and the State shall mutually agree upon a satisfactory audit arrangement to verify that supplementary payments paid by SSA on behalf of the State were made in accordance with the terms of the administration agreement under § 416.2005. Resolution of audit findings shall be made in accordance with the provisions of the State's agreement with SSA.

(d) Advance payment and adjustment not applicable. The provisions of paragraphs (a) and (b) of this section shall not apply with respect to any State supplementary payment for which reimbursement is available from the Social and Rehabilitation Service pursuant to the Indochina Migration and Refugee Assistance Act of 1975 (Pub.L. 94–23; 89 Stat. 87), as amended, since such amounts are not considered to be State supplementary payments.

[40 FR 7640, Feb. 21, 1975, as amended at 41 FR 36018, Aug. 26, 1976; 62 FR 313, Jan. 3, 1997]

§ 416.2095 Pass-along of Federal benefit increases.

(a) General. This section and the four sections that follow describe the rules for passing along increases in the Federal SSI benefit to recipients of State supplementary payments.

(1) Section 416.2095(b) indicates when the pass-along rules apply to State supplementary payments.

(2) Section 416.2096 describes the basic pass-along rules. The States must have an agreement to "pass-along" increases in Federal SSI benefits. A State passes along an increase when it maintains (rather than decreases) the levels of all its supplementary payments after a Federal benefit increase has occurred. Generally, a pass-along of the increase permits recipients to receive an additional amount in combined benefits equal to the Federal benefit increase. Except for the supplementary payment level made to residents of Medicaid facilities (see § 416.2096(d)), a State can decrease one or more of its payment levels if it meets an annual total expenditures test.

(3) Section 416.2097 explains the required combined supplementary/SSI payment level.

(4) Section 416.2098 explains how to compute the March 1983, December 1981, and December 1976 supplementary payment levels.

(5) Section 416.2099 discusses what information a State must provide to the Commissioner concerning its supplementation programs so that the Commissioner can determine whether the State is in compliance. That section also discusses the basis for findings of noncompliance and what will occur if a State is found out of compliance.

(b) When the pass-along provisions apply:

(1) The pass-along requirements apply to all States (and the District of Columbia) that make supplementary payments on or after June 30, 1977, and wish to participate in the Medicaid program.

(2) The pass-along requirements apply to both optional State supplementary payments of the type described in § 416.2001(a) and mandatory minimum State supplementary payments as described in § 416.2001(c), whether or not these State supplementary payments are Federally administered.

(3) The requirements apply to State supplementary payments both for recipients who receive Federal SSI benefits and those who, because of countable income, receive only a State supplementary payment.

(4) The requirements apply to State supplementary payments for recipients eligible for a State supplementary payment on or after June 30, 1977.

(5) Supplementary payments made by a State include payments made by a political subdivision (including Indian tribes) where—

(i) The payment levels are set by the State; and

(ii) The payments are funded in whole or in part by the State.

[45 FR 54749, July 18, 1980; 52 FR 36241, Sept. 28, 1987; 54 FR 19165, May 4, 1989; 62 FR 38455, July 18, 1997]

§ 416.2096 Basic pass-along rules.

(a) State agreements to maintain supplementary payment levels.

(1) In order to be eligible to receive Medicaid reimbursement, any State that makes supplementary payments, other than payments to residents of Medicaid facilities where Medicaid pays more than 50 percent of the cost of their care (see paragraph (d) of this section for definition of Medicaid facility and § 416.414 for discussion of the reduced SSI benefit amount payable to residents of Medicaid facilities), on or after June 30, 1977, must have in effect an agreement with the Commissioner. In this agreement—

(i) The State must agree to continue to make the supplementary payments;

(ii) For months from July 1977 through March 1983, the State must agree to maintain the supplementary payments at levels at least equal to the December 1976 levels (or, if a State first makes supplementary payments after December 1976, the levels for the first month the State makes supplementary payments). For months in the period July 1, 1982 through March 31, 1983, a State may elect to maintain the levels described in paragraph (b)(2) of this section; and

(iii) For months after March 1983, the State must agree to maintain supplementary payments at least sufficient to maintain the combined supplementary/SSI payment levels in effect in March 1983, increased by any subsequent SSI benefit increases, except as provided in § 416.2097(b) and § 416.2097(c).

(2) We will find that the State has met the requirements of paragraph (a)(1) of this section if the State has the appropriate agreement in effect and complies

with the conditions in either paragraph (b) or (c) of this section. We will consider a State to have made supplementary payments on or after June 30, 1977, unless the State furnishes us satisfactory evidence to the contrary.

(b) Meeting the pass-along requirements—supplementary payment levels. The provisions of this paragraph do not apply to the supplementary payment level for residents of Medicaid facilities (see paragraph (d) of this section).

(1) We will consider a State to have met the requirements for maintaining its supplementary payment levels (described in § 416.2098) for a particular month or months after March 1983 if the combined supplementary/SSI payment levels have not been reduced below the levels in effect in March 1983 (or if a State first made supplementary payments after March 1983, the combined supplementary/SSI payment levels in effect the first month the State made supplementary payments), increased by any subsequent Federal SSI benefit increases, except as provided in § 416.2097(b) and § 416.2097(c). We will consider a State to have met the requirements for maintaining its supplementary payment levels for a particular month or months between June 1977 and April 1983 if the supplementary payment levels have not been reduced below the levels in effect in December 1976 (or if a State first made supplementary payments after December 1976, the levels in effect the first month the State made supplementary payments, or in certain cases described in paragraph (b)(2) of this section, the levels in effect in December 1981.)

(2) We will also consider a State to have met the requirements for maintaining its supplementary payment levels for a particular month or months in the period July 1, 1982, through March 31, 1983, if the State had met the requirements of paragraph (c) of this section for a particular month or months in the 12–month period July 1, 1981 through June 30, 1982, and, with respect to any month in the period July 1, 1982 through March 31, 1983, the State maintained the payment levels in effect in December 1981.

(3) If a State reduced any of its supplementary payment levels for a month or months within any 12–month period beginning with the effective date of a Federal benefit increase, we will consider the State to have met the requirement to maintain its supplementary payment levels if—

(i) Within 12 months after the relevant 12–month period, the State restores the levels retroactively; and

(ii) The State makes a single retroactive benefit payment to each of the beneficiaries eligible for the retroactive payment.

(c) Meeting the passalong requirement—total expenditures. Exception—The provisions of this paragraph do not apply to the supplementary payment level for residents of Medicaid facilities (see paragraph (d) of this section).

(1) If a State does not meet the conditions in paragraph (b) of this section, we will consider a State to have met the requirement for maintaining supplementary payment levels for a particular month or months if total State expenditures for supplementary payments in the 12–month period within which the month or months fall, beginning on the effective date of a Federal SSI benefit increase, are at least equal to the total State expenditures for supplementary payments in the 12–month period immediately before the Federal SSI benefit increase provided that the State was in compliance for such preceding 12–month period. The combined Federal/State payment level for those persons receiving a mandatory minimum State supplementary payment can be no lower than the recipient's total income for December 1973 as defined in section 212(a)(3)(B) of Pub.L. 93–66.

(2) If total State expenditures in the relevant 12–month period are less than the total expenditures in the preceding 12–month period (a "shortfall"), we also will consider a State to have met the requirement for maintaining supplementary payment levels for the relevant 12–month period if in the following 12–month period the State increases the total expenditures required for that period by an amount at least equal to the amount of the shortfall in the relevant 12–month period. The increased amount up to the amount needed to correct the shortfall shall be deemed to be an expenditure in the relevant 12–month period, for passalong purposes only. (See paragraph (c)(5) of this section.)

(3)(i) Exception for the 6–month period from July 1, 1983 through December 31, 1983: We will consider the State to have met the total-expenditures requirement for the 6–month period July 1, 1983 through December 31, 1983, if—

(A) Total expenditures for State supplementary payments for the period July 1, 1983 through December 31, 1983, equal or exceed the total of such expenditures for the period July l, 1982 through December 31, 1982;

(B) Total expenditures for State supplementary payments for the period January 1, 1983 through December 31, 1983, equal or exceed the total of such expenditures for the period January 1, 1982 through December 31, 1982; or

(C) Total expenditures for State supplementary payments for the period July 1, 1983 through December 31, 1983 equal or exceed one-half of the total of such expenditures for the period July 1, 1982 through June 30, 1983. The provisions of paragraphs (c)(4) and (c)(5) of this section and of § 416.2099 (b), (c), and (d) shall apply to this 6–month period in the same manner as they apply to the 12–month periods referred to therein.

(ii) Exception for the 12–month period ending June 30, 1981: If a State did not meet the conditions in paragraph (b) of this section, we will consider a State to have met the maintenance-of-supplementary-payment-levels requirement for this 12–month period if the State's expenditures for supplementary payments in that period were at least equal to its expenditures for such payments for the 12–month period ending June 30, 1977 (or, if the State made no supplementary payments in that period, the expenditures for the first 12–month period ending June 30 in which the State made such payments); if a State made additional State supplementary payments during the period July 1, 1981 through June 30, 1982, in order to make up a shortfall in the 12–month period ending June 30, 1981 (determined by a comparison with the preceding 12–month period) which later resulted in an excess payment (determined by comparison with the 12–month period July 1, 1976 through June 30, 1977) we will credit the State with the amount of the excess payments if the State so requests. This credit will be applied to any shortfall(s) in total expenditures (should one exist) in any period(s) ending on or before December 31, 1986.

(4) Total State expenditures for supplementary payments are the State's total payments for both mandatory minimum and optional State supplementary payments in the appropriate 12–month period less any amounts deemed to be expenditures for another 12–month period under paragraph (c)(2) of this section, less the amount of any payments recovered and other adjustments made in that period. Total State expenditures do not include State administrative expenses, interim assistance payments, vendor payments, or payments made under other Federal programs, such as titles IV, XIX, or XX of the Social Security Act.

(5) Adjustments in total State supplementary payments made after the expiration of the relevant 12–month period for purposes of meeting total State expenditures under paragraph (c) of this section shall be considered a State expenditure in the relevant 12–month period only for purposes of the pass-along requirement. For purposes of § 416.2090 of this part, which discusses the rules for limitation on fiscal liability of States (hold harmless), these retroactive adjustments are State expenditures when made and shall be counted as a State expenditure in the fiscal year in which the adjustments are made.

(6) To determine whether a State's expenditures for supplementary payments in the 12–month period beginning on the effective date of any increase in the level of SSI benefits are not less than the State's expenditures for the payments in the preceding 12–month period, in computing the State's expenditures, we disregard, pursuant to a one-time election of the State, all expenditures by the State for the retroactive supplementary payments that are required to be made under the Sullivan v. Zebley, 493 U.S. 521 (1990) class action.

(d) Payments to residents to Medicaid facilities. A Medicaid facility is a medical care facility where Medicaid pays more than 50 percent of the cost of a person's care. In order to be eligible to receive Medicaid reimbursement, any State that has a supplementary payment level for residents of Medicaid facilities on or after October 1, 1987, must have in effect an agreement with the Commissioner to maintain such supplementary payment level at least equal to the October 1987 level (or if a State first makes such supplementary payments after October 1, 1987, but before July 1, 1988, the level for the first month the State makes such supplementary payments).

[45 FR 54749, July 18, 1980; 45 FR 59143, Sept. 8, 1980; 45 FR 64173, Sept. 29, 1980; 52 FR 36241, Sept. 28, 1987; 54 FR 19165, May 4, 1989; 56 FR 55453, Oct. 28, 1991; 62 FR 30984, June 6, 1997; 62 FR 38455, July 18, 1997; 65 FR 16815, March 30, 2000]

§ 416.2097 Combined supplementary/SSI payment levels.

(a) Other than the level for residents of Medicaid facilities (see paragraph (d) of this section), the combined supplementary/SSI payment level for each payment category that must be provided in any month after March 1983 (or if a State first made supplementary payments after March 1983, the combined supplementary SSI payment levels in effect the first month the State made supplementary payments) in order for a State to meet the requirement of the first sentence of § 416.2096(b) is the sum of—

(1) The SSI Federal benefit rate (FBR) for March 1983 for a recipient with no countable income;

(2) That portion of the July 1983 benefit increase computed in accordance with paragraph (b) of this section;

(3) The full amount of all SSI benefit increases after July 1983; and

(4) The State supplementary payment level for March 1983 as determined under § 416.2098.

(b) The monthly FBR's were increased in July 1983 by $20 for an eligible individual and $30 for an eligible couple, and the monthly increment for essential persons was increased by $10 in lieu of the expected cost-of-living adjustment which was delayed until January 1984. However, in computing the required combined supplementary/SSI payment levels for the purpose of determining pass-along compliance, we use only the amounts by which the FBR's and the essential person increment would have increased had there been a cost-of-living adjustment in July 1983 (a 3.5 percent increase would have occurred). These amounts are $9.70 for an eligible individual, $14.60 for an eligible couple and $4.50 for an essential person.

(c) For the 24–month period January 1, 1984, through December 31, 1985, a State will not be found out of compliance with respect to its payment levels if in the period January 1, 1986, through December 31, 1986, its supplementary payment levels are not less than its supplementary payment levels in effect in December 1976 increased by the percentage by which the FBR has increased after December 1976 and before February 1986. The FBR for an individual in December 1976 was $167.80. The FBR for an individual in effect on January 31, 1986, was $336.00, an increase of 100.24 percent over the December 1976 FBR. In order for a State to take advantage of this provision for the 24–month period January 1, 1984, through December 31, 1985, the State supplementary payment levels in effect for calendar year 1986 must be at least 100.24 percent higher than the State supplementary payment levels in effect in December 1976. This provision does not apply to State supplementary payments to recipients in Federal living arrangement "D" (residents of a medical facility where title XIX pays more than 50 percent of the costs).

(d) The combined supplementary/SSI payment level which must be maintained for residents of Medicaid facilities is the State supplement payable on October 1, 1987, or if no such payments were made on October 1, 1987, the supplementary payment amount made in the first month that a supplementary payment was made after October 1987 but before July 1, 1988, plus the Federal benefit rate in effect in October 1987 increased by $5 for an individual/$10 for a couple effective July 1, 1988.

[52 FR 36242, Sept. 28, 1987; 54 FR 19165, May 4, 1989; 54 FR 23018, May 30, 1989]

§ 416.2098 Supplementary payment levels.

(a) General. For the purpose of determining the combined supplementary/SSI payment levels described in § 416.2097(a) (i.e., the levels that must be provided in any month after March 1983), the supplementary payment level, except for the level for residents of Medicaid facilities (see § 416.2097(d)), for each payment category must be no less than the total State payment for March 1983 for that payment category that a State provided an eligible individual (or couple) with no countable income in excess of the FBR for March 1983. For States that did not make supplementary payments in March 1983, the supplementary payment level for each payment category must be no less than the total State payment for the first month after March 1983 in which a State makes supplementary payments.

(b) Calculation of the required mandatory minimum State supplementary payment level.

(1) Except for States described in paragraph (b)(2) of this section, the mandatory minimum State supplementary payment level for March 1983 is a recipient's December 1973 income, as defined in section 212(a)(3)(B) of Pub.L. 93–66, plus any State increases prior to April 1983, less any reductions made at any time after December 1973 due to changes in special needs or circumstances, less the March 1983 FBR. The amount determined under the previous sentence shall continue for April, May, and June 1983. For July 1983 and later the amount calculated in the first sentence shall continue except that it may be reduced by the amount of the July 1983 Federal increase that was not related to the cost of living (i.e., $10.30), so long as that reduction does not cause the mandatory minimum State supplementary level to fall below that required by section 212(a)(3)(A) of Pub.L. 93–66.

(2) Section 1618(c) of the Act permitted any State that had satisfied the requirements of section 1618 of the Act by the total-expenditures method for the 12–month period July 1, 1981, through June 30, 1982, and that elected to change and meet the section 1618 requirements by the maintenance-of-payment-levels method for the period July 1, 1982, through June 30, 1983, to do so by paying benefits at levels no lower than the levels of such payments in effect for December 1981. However, a recipient's December 1981 total income (December 1981 mandatory minimum State supplement plus the FBR) could not be less than the recipient's total income for December 1973 as defined in section 212(a)(3)(B) of Pub.L. 93–66. For a State that elected the option in the preceding two sentences, the mandatory minimum State supplementary payment level for March 1983 is a recipient's December 1981 total income (but not less than the total income for December 1973 as defined by section 212(a)(3)(B) of Pub.L. 93–66) plus any State increases after December 1981 and prior to April 1983, less any reductions made at any time after December 1981 due to changes in special needs or circumstances, less the March 1983 FBR. The amount determined under the previous sentence shall continue for April, May, and June 1983. For July 1983 and later, the amount calculated under the preceding sentence defining the required March 1983 mandatory minimum State supplementary payment level would continue except that it may be reduced by the amount of the July 1983 Federal increase that was not related to the cost of living (i.e., $10.30), so long as that reduction does not cause the mandatory minimum State supplementary level to fall below that required by section 212(a)(3)(A) of Pub.L. 93–66.

(c) Calculation of the required optional State supplementary payment level for flat grant amounts. The optional State supplementary payment level for March 1983 for flat grant amounts is the total amount that an eligible individual (or couple) with no countable income received for March 1983 in excess of the FBR for March 1983. The amount determined under the previous sentence shall continue for April, May, and June 1983. For July 1983 and later the amount calculated in the first sentence shall continue except that it may be reduced by the amount of the July 1983 Federal increase that was not related to the cost of living (i.e., $10.30). If the State varied its payment levels for different groups of recipients (e.g., paid recipients different amounts based on eligibility categories, geographic areas, living arrangements, or marital status), each variation represents a separate supplementary payment level.

(d) Calculation of the required optional State supplementary payment level for individually budgeted grant amounts. The optional State supplementary payment level for individually budgeted grant amounts for March 1983 is the amount that the State budgeted for March 1983 in excess of the March 1983 FBR for an eligible individual (or couple) having the same needs and no countable income. The amount determined under the previous sentence shall continue for April, May, and June 1983. For July 1983 and later the amount calculated in the first sentence shall continue except that it may be reduced by the amount of the July 1983 Federal increase that was not related to the cost of living (i.e., $10.30).

(e) Optional State supplementary payment level for per diem based grant amounts.

(1) The optional State supplementary payment level for March 1983 for per diem grant amounts is the total dollar amount that the State paid to an eligible individual (or couple) with no countable income at rates in effect for March 1983 (number of days in the calendar month multiplied by the March 1983 per diem rate plus any March 1983 personal needs allowance) in excess of the March 1983 FBR.

Example:

March 1983:	
$15.40	Per diem rate.
×31	Days in month.
477.40	
477.40	
+42.00	Personal needs allowance.
519.40	
519.40	Combined State supplementary/SSI payment.
−284.30	March 1983 FBR.
235.10	State supplementary payment level.

(2) The optional State supplementary payment level for months subsequent to March 1983 for per diem grant amounts is the total dollar amount that the State paid to an individual (or couple) with no countable income at rates in effect in March 1983 (number of days in the calendar month multiplied by the March 1983 per diem rate plus any March 1983 personal needs allowance) in excess of the March 1983 FBR for an individual (or couple) with no countable income increased by all FBR increases subsequent to March 1983 with the exception of the July 1, 1983 increase. For the July 1, 1983 increase to the FBR, a State need pass-along only that portion of the increase which represented the increase in the cost of living adjustment (3.5 percent).

Example:

Note: Example assumes the State passed along only $9.70 of the $20.00 increase in the FBR effective July 1, 1983.

The March 1983 combined supplementary/SSI payment level for a 31–day month was $519.40.

July 1983 level:	
$519.40	March 1983 combined payment.
+9.70	July 1983 COLA-equivalent.
529.10	Required July 1983 combined payment level.
529.10	Required July 1983 combined payment level.
−304.30	July 1983 FBR.
224.80	Required State Supplementary payment level.
529.10	Required July 1983 combined payment level.
−42.00	Personal needs allowance.
487.10	
487.10	
÷31	Days in month.
15.71	Per diem rate.

The required July 1983 combined supplementary/SSI payment level for a 31–day month was $529.10. This amount is equal to the March 1983 combined payment amount for a 31–day month plus the July 1983 COLA-equivalent ($519.40+$9.70).

(f) Required optional State supplementary payment level for months prior to April 1983. In determining pass-along compliance under the maintenance-of-payment-levels test for months from July 1977 through March 1983, we used December 1976 (or December 1981 under the circumstances described in paragraph (g) of this section) as the standard month for determining the required State supplementary payment level. To determine the December 1976 State supplementary payment levels for categories described in paragraphs (a) through (e) of this section substitute "December 1976" for "March 1983" and "January 1977" for "April 1983" whenever they appear in these paragraphs only.

(g) Alternative required optional State supplementary payment level for July 1982 through March 1983. States which were in compliance solely under the total-expenditures test for the 12–month period ending June 30, 1982, had the option of substituting December 1981 for December 1976 and switching to the maintenance-of-payment-levels test for July 1982 through March 1983 (see § 416.2096(b)(2)). If this situation applies, determine the December 1981 State supplementary payment levels for categories described in paragraphs (a) through (e) of this section by substituting "December 1981" for "March 1983" and "January 1982" for "April 1983" whenever they appear in these paragraphs only.

[45 FR 54750, July 18, 1980; 52 FR 36242, 36243, Sept. 28, 1987; 53 FR 4135, Feb. 12, 1988; 54 FR 19165, May 4, 1989; 54 FR 23018, May 30, 1989]

§ 416.2099 Compliance with pass-along.

(a) Information regarding compliance. Any State required to enter into a pass-along agreement with the Commissioner shall provide appropriate and timely information to demonstrate to the Commissioner's satisfaction that the State is meeting the pass-along requirements. The information shall include, where relevant—

(1) The State's December 1976 supplementary payment levels, any subsequent supplementary payment levels, and any change in State eligibility requirements. If the State made no supplementary payments in December 1976, it shall provide such information about the first month in which it makes supplementary payments;

(2) The State's March 1983 supplementary payment levels, any subsequent supplementary payment levels, and any changes in State eligibility requirements;

(3) The total State expenditures for supplementary payments in the 12–month period beginning July 1976 through June 1977, in each subsequent 12–month period, and in any other 12–month period beginning on the effective date of a Federal SSI benefit increase. The State shall also submit advance estimates of its total supplementary payments in each 12–month period covered by the agreement;

(4) The total State expenditures for supplementary payments in the 6–month periods July 1, 1982 through December 31, 1982 and July 1, 1983 through December 31, 1983; and

(5) The State supplementary payment level payable to residents of Medicaid facilities (see § 416.2096(d)) on October 1, 1987 (or, if a State first makes such supplementary payments after October 1, 1987, but before July 1, 1988, the level for the month the State first makes such supplementary payments). The State shall also report all changes in such payment levels.

(b) Records. Except where the Commissioner administers the State supplementary payments, the State shall maintain records about its supplementary payment levels and total 12–month (or 6–month where applicable) expenditures for supplementary payments and permit inspection and audit by the Commissioner or someone designated by the Commissioner.

(c) Noncompliance by the States. Any State that makes supplementary payments on or after June 30, 1977, and does not have a pass-along agreement with the Commissioner in effect, shall be determined by the Commissioner to be ineligible for payments under title XIX of the Act. A State does not have an agreement in effect if it has not entered into an agreement or has not complied with the terms of the agreement. Ineligibility shall apply to total expenditures for any calendar quarter beginning after June 30, 1977, for which a State has not entered into an agreement. A State that enters into an agreement but does not maintain its payment levels or meet the total-expenditures test in a particular 12–month or transitional 6–month period, shall be determined by the Commissioner not to have an agreement in effect for any month that the State did not meet the pass-along requirements during that particular period. The State shall then be ineligible for title XIX payments for any calendar quarter containing a month for which an agreement was not in effect. If a State first makes supplementary payments beginning with a month after June 1977, ineligibility shall apply to any calendar quarter beginning after the calendar quarter in which the State first makes payments.

(d) Notices to States about potential noncompliance. Within 90 days after the end of the relevant 12–month period, the Commissioner shall send a notice to any State that has not maintained its supplementary payment levels and that appears not to have maintained its total expenditures during the period. The notice will advise the State of the available methods of compliance and the time within which corrective action must be taken (see §§ 416.2096(b)(3) and 416.2096(c)(2)) in order to avoid a determination of noncompliance. If the State fails to take the corrective action, the Commissioner shall make a timely determination of noncompliance.

(Approved by the Office of Management and Budget under control number 0960–0240)

[45 FR 54750, July 18, 1980; 52 FR 36242, 36244, Sept. 28, 1987; 54 FR 19165, May 4, 1989; 62 FR 38455, July 18, 1997]

SUBPART U—MEDICAID ELIGIBILITY DETERMINATIONS

Authority: Secs. 702(a)(5), 1106, 1631(d)(1), and 1634 of the Social Security Act (42 U.S.C. 902(a)(5), 1306, 1383(d)(1), and 1383c).

Source: 53 FR 12941, April 20, 1988; 61 FR 5942, Feb. 15, 1996, unless otherwise noted.

§ 416.2101 Introduction.

(a) What is in this subpart. This subpart describes the agreements we make with States under which we determine the Medicaid eligibility of individuals who receive Supplemental Security Income (SSI) benefits. It includes a general description of the services we will provide under these agreements and the costs to the States for the services.

(b) Related regulations. The comprehensive regulations on eligibility for the Medicaid program, administered by the Health Care Financing Administration, are in part 435 of title 42 of the Code of Federal Regulations.

(c) Definitions. In this subpart—

SSI benefits means Federal SSI benefits, including special SSI cash benefits under section 1619(a) of the Social Security Act. In addition, we consider a person who has special SSI eligibility status under section 1619(b) of the Social Security Act to be receiving SSI benefits.

State Medicaid Plan means a State's medical assistance plan which the Secretary has approved under title XIX of the Act for Federal payment of a share of the State's medical assistance expenses.

State supplementary payments means supplementary payments we administer for a State under subpart T of this part.

We, us, or *our* refers to the Social Security Administration.

§ 416.2111 Conditions for our agreeing to make Medicaid eligibility determinations.

We will agree to make Medicaid eligibility determinations for a State only if the State's Medicaid eligibility requirements for recipients of SSI benefits and for recipients of State supplementary payments are the same as the requirements for receiving SSI benefits and the requirements for receiving State supplementary payments, respectively. Exceptions: We may agree to make Medicaid eligibility determinations—

(a) For one, two, or all of the three categories of people (i.e., aged, blind, and disabled) who receive SSI benefits or State supplementary payments; or

(b) Even though the State's Medicaid eligibility requirements for recipients of SSI benefits or of State supplementary payments, or both, differ from the requirements for SSI or State supplementary payments, or both, in ways mandated by Federal law.

§ 416.2116 Medicaid eligibility determinations.

If a State requests, we may agree, under the conditions in this subpart, to make Medicaid eligibility determinations on behalf of the State. Under these agreements, we make the Medicaid determinations when determinations or redeterminations are necessary for SSI purposes. Our determinations may include non-SSI requirements that are mandated by Federal law. When we determine that a person is eligible for Medicaid in accordance with § 416.2111 or that we are not making the determination, we notify the State of that fact.

§ 416.2130 Effect of the agreement and responsibilities of States.

(a) An agreement under this subpart does not change—

(1) The provisions of a State's Medicaid plan;

(2) The conditions under which the Secretary will approve a State's Medicaid plan; or

(3) A State's responsibilities under the State Medicaid plan.

(b) Following are examples of functions we will not agree to carry out for the State:

(1) Stationing of our employees at hospitals or nursing homes to take Medicaid applications;

(2) Determining whether a person is eligible for Medicaid for any period before he or she applied for SSI benefits;

(3) Giving approval for emergency medical care under Medicaid before a determination has been made on whether a person is eligible for SSI benefits;

(4) Setting up or running a State's system for requiring a person to pay part of the cost of services he or she receives under Medicaid; or

(5) Giving identification cards to people to show that they are eligible for Medicaid.

§ 416.2140 Liability for erroneous Medicaid eligibility determinations.

If the State suffers any financial loss, directly or indirectly, through using any information we provide under an agreement described in this subpart, we will not be responsible for that loss. However, if we erroneously tell a State that a person is eligible for Medicaid and the State therefore makes erroneous Medicaid payments, the State will be paid the Federal share of those payments under the Medicaid program as if they were correct.

§ 416.2145 Services other than Medicaid determinations.

We will agree under authority of section 1106 of the Act and 31 U.S.C. 6505 to provide services other than Medicaid determinations to help the State administer its Medicaid program. We will do this only if we determine it is the most efficient and economical way to accomplish the State's purpose and does not interfere with administration of the SSI program. The services can be part of a Medicaid eligibility determination agreement or a separate agreement. Under either agreement we will—

(a) Give the State basic information relevant to Medicaid eligibility from individuals' applications for SSI benefits;

(b) Give the State answers to certain purely Medicaid-related questions (in addition to any that may be necessary under § 416.2111(b)), such as whether the SSI applicant has any unpaid medical expenses for the current month or the previous 3 calendar months;

(c) Conduct statistical or other studies for the State; and

(d) Provide other services the State and we agree on.

§ 416.2161 Charges to States.

(a) States with Medicaid eligibility determination agreement. A State with which we have an agreement to make Medicaid eligibility determinations is charged in the following manner:

(1) If making Medicaid determinations and providing basic SSI application information for a State causes us additional cost, the State must pay half of that additional cost. "Additional cost" in this section means cost in addition to costs we would have had anyway in administering the SSI program.

(2) The State must pay half our additional cost caused by providing any information that we collect for Medicaid purposes and by any other services directly related to making Medicaid eligibility determinations.

(3) The State must pay our full additional cost for statistical or other studies and any other services that are not directly related to making Medicaid eligibility determinations.

(b) States without Medicaid eligibility determination agreement. A State with which we do not have an agreement to make Medicaid eligibility determinations is charged in the following manner:

(1) If providing basic SSI application information causes us additional cost, the State must pay our full additional cost.

(2) The State must pay our full additional cost caused by providing any information that we collect for Medicaid purposes and for statistical or other studies and any other services.

§ 416.2166 Changing the agreement.

The State and we can agree in writing to change the agreement at any time.

§ 416.2171 Duration of agreement.

An agreement under this subpart is automatically renewed for 1 year at the end of the term stated in the agreement and again at the end of each 1–year renewal term, unless—

(a) The State and we agree in writing to end it at any time;

(b) Either the State or we end it at any time without the other's consent by giving written notice at least 90 days before the end of a term, or 120 days before any other ending date selected by whoever wants to end the agreement; or

(c)(1) The State fails to pay our costs as agreed;

(2) We notify the State in writing, at least 30 days before the ending date we select, why we intend to end the agreement; and

(3) The State does not give a good reason for keeping the agreement in force beyond the ending date we selected. If the State does provide a good reason, the termination will be postponed or the agreement will be kept in force until the end of the term.

§ 416.2176 Disagreements between a State and us.

(a) If a State with which we have an agreement under this subpart and we are unable to agree about any question of performance under the agreement, the State may appeal the question to the Commissioner of Social Security. The Commissioner or his or her designee will, within 90 days after receiving the State's appeal, give the State either a written decision or a written explanation of why a decision cannot be made within 90 days, what is needed before a decision can be made, and when a decision is expected to be made.

(b) The Commissioner's decision will be the final decision of the Social Security Administration.

[62 FR 38456, July 18, 1997]

SUBPART V—PAYMENTS FOR VOCATIONAL REHABILITATION SERVICES

Authority: Secs. 702(a)(5), 1615, 1631(d)(1) and (e), and 1633(a) of the Social Security Act (42 U.S.C. 902(a)(5), 1382d, 1383(d)(1) and (e), and 1383b(a)).

Source: 48 FR 6297, Feb. 10, 1983; 52 FR 27542, July 22, 1987; 55 FR 8456, March 8, 1990; 61 FR 5942, Feb. 15, 1996; 61 FR 31026, June 19, 1996; 68 FR 40124, July 7, 2003, unless otherwise noted.

GENERAL PROVISIONS

§ 416.2201 General.

In general, sections 1615(d) and (e) of the Social Security Act (the Act) authorize payment from the general fund for the reasonable and necessary costs of vocational rehabilitation (VR) services provided certain disabled or blind individuals who are eligible for supplemental security income (SSI) benefits, special SSI eligibility status, or federally administered State supplementary payments. In this subpart, such benefits, status, or payments are referred to as disability or blindness benefits (see § 416.2203). Subject to the provisions of this subpart, payment may be made for VR services provided an individual during a month(s) for which the individual is eligible for disability or blindness benefits, including the continuation of such benefits under section 1631(a)(6) of the Act, or for which the individual's disability or blindness benefits are suspended (see § 416.2215). Paragraphs (a) and (b) of this section describe the cases in which the State VR agencies can be paid for the VR services provided such an individual under this subpart. The purpose of sections 1615(d) and (e) of the Act is to make VR services more readily available to disabled or blind individuals and ensure that savings accrue to the general fund. Payment will be made for VR services provided on behalf of such an individual in cases where—

(a) The furnishing of the VR services results in the individual's completion of a continuous 9–month period of substantial gainful activity (SGA) as specified in §§ 416.2210 through 416.2211; or

(b) The individual continues to receive disability or blindness benefits, even though his or her disability or blindness has ceased, under section 1631(a)(6) of the Act because of his or her continued participation in an approved VR program which we have determined will increase the likelihood that he or she will not return to the disability or blindness rolls (see § 416.2212).

[55 FR 8456, March 8, 1990; 61 FR 31026, June 19, 1996; 68 FR 40124, July 7, 2003; 83 FR 62459, Dec. 4, 2018]

§ 416.2202 Purpose and scope.

This subpart describes the rules under which the Commissioner will pay the State VR agencies for VR services. Payment will be provided for VR services provided on behalf of disabled or blind individuals under one or more of the provisions discussed in § 416.2201.

(a) Sections 416.2201 through 416.2203 describe the purpose of these regulations and the meaning of terms we frequently use in them.

(b) Section 416.2204 explains how State VR agencies may participate in the payment program under this subpart.

(c) [Reserved by 83 FR 62460]

(d) Sections 416.2208 through 416.2209 describe the requirements and conditions under which we will pay a State VR agency under this subpart.

(e) Sections 416.2210 through 416.2211 describe when an individual has completed a continuous period of SGA and when VR services will be considered to have contributed to that period.

(f) Section 416.2212 describes when payment will be made to a VR agency because an individual's disability or blindness benefits are continued based on his or her participation in a VR program which we have determined will increase the likelihood that he or she will not return to the disability rolls.

(g) Sections 416.2214 through 416.2215 describe services for which payment will be made.

(h) Section 416.2216 describes the filing deadlines for claims for payment for VR services.

(i) Section 416.2217 describes the payment conditions.

(j) [Reserved by 83 FR 62460]

(k) Section 416.2219 describes how we will make payment to State VR agencies for rehabilitation services.

(*l*) Sections 416.2220 and 416.2221 describe the audits and the prepayment and postpayment validation reviews we will conduct.

(m) Section 416.2222 discusses confidentiality of information and records.

(n) Section 416.2223 provides for the applicability of other Federal laws and regulations.

(*o*) Section 416.2227 provides for the resolution of disputes.

[55 FR 8456, March 8, 1990; 59 FR 11916, March 15, 1994; 62 FR 38456, July 18, 1997; 68 FR 40124, July 7, 2003; 83 FR 62460, Dec. 4, 2018]

§ 416.2203 Definitions.

For purposes of this subpart:

Accept the recipient as a client for VR services means that the State VR agency determines that the individual is eligible for VR services and places the individual into an active caseload status for development of an individualized written rehabilitation program.

Act means the Social Security Act, as amended.

Blindness means "blindness" as defined in section 1614(a)(2) of the Act.

Commissioner means the Commissioner of Social Security or the Commissioner's designee.

Disability means "disability" as defined in section 1614(a)(3) of the Act.

Disability or blindness benefits, as defined for this subpart only, refers to regular SSI benefits under section 1611 of the Act (see § 416.202), special SSI cash benefits under section 1619(a) of the Act (see § 416.261), special SSI eligibility status under section 1619(b) of the Act (see § 416.264), and/or a federally administered State supplementary payment under section 1616 of the Act or section 212(b) of Public Law 93–66 (see § 416.2001), for which an individual is eligible based on disability or blindness, as appropriate.

Medical recovery for purposes of this subpart is established when a disabled or blind recipient's eligibility ceases for any medical reason (other than death). The determination of medical recovery is made by the Commissioner in deciding a recipient's continuing eligibility for benefits.

Place the recipient into an extended evaluation process means that the State VR agency determines that an extended evaluation of the individual's VR potential is necessary to determine whether the individual is eligible for VR services and places the individual into an extended evaluation status.

SGA means substantial gainful activity performed by an individual as defined in §§ 416.971 through 416.975 of this subpart or § 404.1584 of this chapter.

Special SSI eligibility status refers to the special status described in §§ 416.264 through 416.269 relating to eligibility for Medicaid.

State means any of the 50 States of the United States, the District of Columbia, or the Northern Mariana Islands. It includes the State VR agency.

Vocational rehabilitation services has the meaning assigned to it under title I of the Rehabilitation Act of 1973.

VR agency means an agency of the State which has been designated by the State to provide vocational rehabilitation services under title I of the Rehabilitation Act of 1973.

We, us, and *our* refer to the Social Security Administration (SSA).

[55 FR 8456, March 8, 1990; 55 FR 19423, May 9, 1990; 59 FR 1637, Jan. 12, 1994; 59 FR 11916, March 15, 1994; 61 FR 31026, June 19, 1996; 62 FR 38456, July 18, 1997; 68 FR 40125, July 7, 2003; 83 FR 62460, Dec. 4, 2018]

§ 416.2204 Participation by State VR agencies.

(a) *General.* In order to participate in the payment program under this subpart through its VR agency(ies), a State must have a plan which meets the requirements of title I of the Rehabilitation Act of 1973, as amended.

(b) *Participation by States.*

(1) The opportunity to participate through its VR agency(ies) with respect to disabled or blind recipients in the State will be offered first to the State in accordance with paragraph (c) of this section, unless the State has notified us in advance under paragraph (e)(1) of this section of its decision not to participate or to limit such participation.

(2) A State with one or more approved VR agencies may choose to limit participation of those agencies to a certain class(es) of disabled or blind recipients. For example, a State with separate VR agencies for the blind and disabled may choose to limit participation to the VR agency for the blind. In such a case, we would give the State, through its VR agency for the blind, the opportunity to participate with respect to blind recipients in the State in accordance with paragraph (d) of this section. A State that chooses to limit participation of its VR agency(ies) must notify us in advance under paragraph (e)(1) of this section of its decision to limit such participation.

(c) *Opportunity for participation through State VR agencies.*

(1) Unless a State has decided not to participate or to limit participation, we will give the State the opportunity to participate through its VR agency(ies) with respect to disabled or blind recipients in the State by referring such recipients first to the State VR agency(ies) for necessary VR services. A State, through its VR agency(ies), may participate with respect to any recipient so referred by accepting the recipient as a client for VR services or placing the recipient into an extended evaluation process and notifying us under paragraph (c)(2) of this section of such acceptance or placement.

(2)(i) In order for the State to participate with respect to a disabled or blind recipient whom we referred to a State VR agency, the State VR agency must notify the appropriate Regional Commissioner (SSA) in writing or through electronic notification of its decision either to accept the recipient as a client for VR services or to place the recipient into an extended evaluation process. The notice must be received by the appropriate Regional Commissioner (SSA) no later than the close of the fourth month following the month in which we referred the recipient to the State VR agency.

(ii) In any case in which a State VR agency notifies the appropriate Regional Commissioner (SSA) in writing within the stated time period under paragraph (c)(2)(i) of this section of its decision to place the recipient into an extended evaluation process, the State VR agency also must notify that Regional Commissioner in writing upon completion of the evaluation of its decision whether or not to accept the recipient as a client for VR services. If we receive a notice of a decision by the State VR agency to accept the recipient as a client for VR services following the completion of the extended evaluation, the State may continue to participate with respect to such recipient.

(d) *Opportunity for limited participation through State VR agencies.* If a State has decided under paragraph (e)(1) of this section to limit participation of its VR agency(ies) to a certain class(es) of disabled or blind recipients in the State, we will give the State the opportunity to participate with respect to such class(es) of disabled or blind recipients by referring such recipients first to the State VR agency(ies) for necessary VR services. The State, through its VR agency(ies), may participate with respect to any recipient so referred by accepting the recipient as a client for VR services or placing the recipient into an extended evaluation process and notifying us under paragraph (c)(2) of this section of such acceptance or placement.

(e) *Decision of a State not to participate or to limit participation.*

(1) A State may choose not to participate through its VR agency(ies) with respect to any disabled or blind recipients in the State, or it may choose to limit participation of its VR agency(ies) to a certain class(es) of disabled or blind recipients in the State. A State which decides not to participate or to limit participation must provide advance written notice of that decision to the appropriate Regional Commissioner (SSA). Unless a State specifies a later month, a decision not to participate or to limit participation will be effective beginning with the third month following the month in which the notice of the decision is received by the appropriate Regional Commissioner (SSA). The notice of the State decision must be

submitted by an official authorized to act for the State for this purpose. A State must provide to the appropriate Regional Commissioner (SSA) an opinion from the State's Attorney General, verifying the authority of the official who sent the notice to act for the State. This opinion will not be necessary if the notice is signed by the Governor of the State.

(2) [Reserved by 83 FR 62460]

(3) A State which has decided not to participate or to limit participation may participate later through its VR agency(ies) in accordance with paragraph (c) of this section. A State that decides to resume participation under paragraph (c) of this section must provide advance written notice of that decision to the appropriate Regional Commissioner (SSA). A decision of a State to resume participation under paragraph (c) of this section will be effective beginning with the third month following the month in which the notice of the decision is received by the appropriate Regional Commissioner (SSA) or, if later, with a month specified by the State. The notice of the State decision must be submitted by an official authorized to act for the State as explained in paragraph (e)(1) of this section.

(f) [Reserved by 83 FR 62460]

[59 FR 11917, March 15, 1994; 83 FR 62460, Dec. 4, 2018]

§ 416.2206 [Reserved by 83 FR 62460]

[83 FR 62460, Dec. 4, 2018]

PAYMENT PROVISIONS

§ 416.2208 Requirements for payment.

(a) The State VR agency must file a claim for payment in each individual case within the time periods specified in § 416.2216;

(b) The claim for payment must be in a form prescribed by us and contain the following information:

(1) A description of each service provided;

(2) When the service was provided; and

(3) The cost of the service;

(c) The VR services for which payment is being requested must have been provided during the period specified in § 416.2215;

(d) The VR services for which payment is being requested must have been provided under a State plan for VR services approved under title I of the Rehabilitation Act of 1973, as amended, and must be services that are described in § 416.2214;

(e) The individual must meet one of the VR payment provisions specified in § 416.2201;

(f) The State VR agency must maintain, and provide as we may require, adequate documentation of all services and costs for all disabled or blind recipients with respect to whom a State VR agency could potentially request payment for services and costs under this subpart; and

(g) The amount to be paid must be reasonable and necessary and be in compliance with the cost guidelines specified in § 416.2217.

[55 FR 8456, March 8, 1990; 59 FR 11918, March 15, 1994; 83 FR 62460, Dec. 4, 2018]

§ 416.2209 Responsibility for making payment decisions.

The Commissioner will decide:

(a) Whether a continuous period of 9 months of SGA has been completed;

(b) Whether a disability or blindness recipient whose disability or blindness has ceased should continue to receive benefits under section 1631(a)(6) of the Social Security Act for a month after October 1984 or, in the case of a blindness recipient, for a month after March 1988, based on his or her continued participation in a VR program;

(c) If and when medical recovery has occurred;

(d) Whether documentation of VR services and expenditures is adequate;

(e) If payment is to be based on completion of a continuous 9–month period of SGA, whether the VR services contributed to the continuous period of SGA;

(f) Whether a VR service is a service described in § 416.2214; and

(g) What VR costs were reasonable and necessary and will be paid.

[55 FR 8456, March 8, 1990; 59 FR 11918, March 15, 1994; 61 FR 31026, June 19, 1996; 68 FR 40125, July 7, 2003]

§ 416.2210 What we mean by "SGA" and by "a continuous period of 9 months".

(a) What we mean by "SGA". In determining whether an individual's work is SGA, we will follow the rules in §§ 416.972 through 416.975. We will follow these same rules for individuals who are statutorily blind, but we will evaluate the earnings in accordance with the rules in § 404.1584(d) of this chapter.

(b) What we mean by "a continuous period of 9 months". A continuous period of 9 months ordinarily means a period of 9 consecutive calendar months. Exception: When an individual does not perform SGA in 9 consecutive calendar months, he or she will be considered to have done so if—

(1) The individual performs 9 months of SGA within 10 consecutive months and has monthly earnings that meet or exceed the guidelines in § 416.974(b)(2), or § 404.1584(d) of this chapter if the individual is statutorily blind, or

(2) The individual performs at least 9 months of SGA within 12 consecutive months, and the reason for not performing SGA in 2 or 3 of those months was due to circumstances beyond his or her control and unrelat-

ed to the impairment (e.g., the employer closed down for 3 months).

(c) What work we consider. In determining if a continuous period of SGA has been completed, all of an individual's work activity may be evaluated for purposes of this section, including work performed before October 1, 1981, during a trial work period, and after eligibility for disability or blindness payments ended. We will ordinarily consider only the first 9 months of SGA that occurs. The exception will be if an individual who completed 9 months of SGA later stops performing SGA, received VR services and then performs SGA for a 9–month period. See § 416.2215 for the use of the continuous period in determining payment for VR services.

[55 FR 8457, March 8, 1990]

§ 416.2211 Criteria for determining when VR services will be considered to have contributed to a continuous period of 9 months.

The State VR agency may be paid for VR services if such services contribute to the individual's performance of a continuous 9–month period of SGA. The following criteria apply to individuals who received more than just evaluation services. If a State VR agency claims payment for services to an individual who received only evaluation services, it must establish that the individual's continuous period or medical recovery (if medical recovery occurred before completion of a continuous period) would not have occurred without the services provided. In applying the criteria below, we will consider services described in § 416.2214 that were initiated, coordinated or provided, including services before October 1, 1981.

(a) Continuous period without medical recovery. If an individual who has completed a "continuous period" of SGA has not medically recovered as of the date of completion of the period, the determination as to whether VR services contributed will depend on whether the continuous period began one year or less after VR services ended or more than one year after VR services ended.

(1) One year or less. Any VR services which significantly motivated or assisted the individual in returning to, or continuing in, SGA will be considered to have contributed to the continuous period.

(2) More than one year.

(i) If the continuous period was preceded by transitional work activity (employment or self-employment which gradually evolved, with or without periodic interruption, into SGA), and that work activity began less than a year after VR services ended, any VR services which significantly motivated or assisted the individual in returning to, or continuing in, SGA will be considered to have contributed to the continuous period.

(ii) If the continuous period was not preceded by transitional work activity that began less than a year after VR services ended, VR services will be considered to have contributed to the continuous period only if it is reasonable to conclude that the work activity which constitutes a continuous period could not have occurred without the VR services (e.g., training).

(b) Continuous period with medical recovery occurring before completion.

(1) If an individual medically recovers before a continuous period has been completed, VR services under paragraph (a) of this section will not be payable unless some VR services contributed to the medical recovery. VR services will be considered to have contributed to the medical recovery if—

(i) The individualized written rehabilitation program (IWRP), included medical services; and

(ii) The medical recovery occurred, at least in part, because of these medical services. (For example, the individual's medical recovery was based on improvement in a back condition which, at least in part, stemmed from surgery initiated, coordinated or provided under an IWRP).

(2) In some instances, the State VR agency will not have provided, initiated, or coordinated medical services. If this happens, payment for VR services may still be possible under paragraph (a) of this section if:

(i) The medical recovery was not expected by us; and

(ii) The individual's impairment is determined by us to be of such a nature that any medical services provided would not ordinarily have resulted in, or contributed to, the medical cessation.

[55 FR 8457, March 8, 1990; 59 FR 11918, March 15, 1994; 83 FR 62460, Dec. 4, 2018]

§ 416.2212 Payment for VR services in a case where an individual continues to receive disability or blindness benefits based on participation in an approved VR program.

Section 1631(a)(6) of the Act contains the criteria we will use in determining if an individual whose disability or blindness has ceased should continue to receive disability or blindness benefits because of his or her continued participation in an approved VR program. A VR agency can be paid for the cost of VR services provided to an individual if the individual was receiving benefits based on this provision in a month(s) after October 1984 or, in the case of a blindness recipient, in a month(s) after March 1988. If this requirement is met, a VR agency can be paid for the costs of VR services provided within the period specified in § 416.2215, subject to the other payment and administrative provisions of this subpart.

[55 FR 8457, March 8, 1990; 61 FR 31026, June 19, 1996; 83 FR 62461, Dec. 4, 2018]

§ 416.2213 [Reserved]

[68 FR 40125, July 7, 2003]

§ 416.2214 Services for which payment may be made.

(a) General. Payment may be made for VR services provided by a State VR agency in accordance with title I of the Rehabilitation Act of 1973, as amended, subject to the limitations and conditions in this subpart. VR services for which payment may be made under this subpart include only those services described in paragraph (b) of this section which are—

(1) Necessary to determine an individual's eligibility for VR services or the nature and scope of the services to be provided; or

(2) Provided by a State VR agency under an IWRP, but only if the services could reasonably be expected to motivate or assist the individual in returning to, or continuing in, SGA.

(b) Specific services. Payment may be made under this subpart only for the following VR services:

(1) An assessment for determining an individual's eligibility for VR services and vocational rehabilitation needs by qualified personnel, including, if appropriate, an assessment by personnel skilled in rehabilitation technology, and which includes determining—

(i) The nature and extent of the physical or mental impairment(s) and the resultant impact on the individual's employability;

(ii) The likelihood that an individual will benefit from vocational rehabilitation services in terms of employability; and

(iii) An employment goal consistent with the capacities of the individual and employment opportunities;

(2) Counseling and guidance, including personal adjustment counseling, and those referrals and other services necessary to help an individual secure needed services from other agencies;

(3) Physical and mental restoration services necessary to correct or substantially modify a physical or mental condition which is stable or slowly progressive and which constitutes an impediment to suitable employment at or above the SGA level;

(4) Vocational and other training services, including personal and vocational adjustment, books, tools, and other training materials, except that training or training services in institutions of higher education will be covered under this section only if maximum efforts have been made by the State VR agency to secure grant assistance in whole or in part from other sources;

(5) Maintenance expenses that are extra living expenses over and above the individual's normal living expenses and that are incurred solely because of and while the individual is participating in the VR program and that are necessary in order for the individual to benefit from other necessary VR services;

(6) Travel and related expenses necessary to transport an individual for purpose of enabling the individual's participation in other necessary VR services;

(7) Services to family members of a disabled or blind individual only if necessary to the successful vocational rehabilitation of that individual;

(8) Interpreter services and note-taking services for an individual who is deaf and tactile interpreting for an individual who is deaf and blind;

(9) Reader services, rehabilitation teaching services, note-taking services, and orientation and mobility services for an individual who is blind;

(10) Telecommunications, sensory, and other technological aids and devices;

(11) Work-related placement services to secure suitable employment;

(12) Post-employment services necessary to maintain, regain or advance into suitable employment at or above the SGA level;

(13) Occupational licenses, tools, equipment, initial stocks, and supplies;

(14) Rehabilitation technology services; and

(15) Other goods and services that can reasonably be expected to motivate or assist the individual in returning to, or continuing in, SGA.

[55 FR 8457, March 8, 1990; 59 FR 11919, March 15, 1994; 83 FR 62461, Dec. 4, 2018]

§ 416.2215 When services must have been provided.

(a) In order for the VR agency to be paid, the services must have been provided—

(1) After September 30, 1981;

(2) During a month(s) for which—

(i) The individual is eligible for disability or blindness benefits or continues to receive such benefits under section 1631(a)(6) of the Act (see § 416.2212); or

(ii) The disability or blindness benefits of the individual are suspended due to his or her ineligibility for the benefits (see subpart M of this part concerning suspension for ineligibility); and

(3) Before completion of a continuous 9–month period of SGA or termination of disability or blindness benefits, whichever occurs first (see subpart M of this part concerning termination of benefits).

(b) If an individual who is receiving disability or blindness benefits under this part, or whose benefits under this part are suspended, also is entitled to disability benefits under part 404 of this chapter, the determination as to when services must have been provided may be made under this section or § 404.2115 of this chapter, whichever is advantageous to the State VR agency that is participating in both VR programs.

[55 FR 8457, March 8, 1990; 61 FR 31026, June 19, 1996; 83 FR 62461, Dec. 4, 2018]

§ 416.2216 When claims for payment for VR services must be made (filing deadlines).

The State VR agency must file a claim for payment in each individual case within the following time periods:

(a) A claim for payment for VR services based on the completion of a continuous 9–month period of SGA must be filed within 12 months after the month in which the continuous 9–month period of SGA is completed.

(b) A claim for payment for VR services provided to an individual whose disability or blindness benefits were continued after disability or blindness has ceased because of that individual's continued participation in a VR program must be filed as follows:

(1) If a written notice requesting that a claim be filed was sent to the State VR agency, a claim must be filed within 90 days following the month in which VR services end, or if later, within 90 days after receipt of the notice.

(2) If no written notice was sent to the State VR agency, a claim must be filed within 12 months after the month in which VR services end.

[55 FR 8457, March 8, 1990; 61 FR 31026, June 19, 1996; 68 FR 40125, July 7, 2003; 83 FR 62461, Dec. 4, 2018]

§ 416.2217 What costs will be paid.

In accordance with section 1615(d) and (e) of the Social Security Act, the Commissioner will pay the State VR agency for the VR services described in § 416.2214 which were provided during the period described in § 416.2215 and which meet the criteria in § 416.2211 or § 416.2212, but subject to the following limitations:

(a) The cost must have been incurred by the State VR agency;

(b) The cost must not have been paid or be payable from some other source. For this purpose, State VR agencies will be required to seek payment or services from other sources in accordance with the "similar benefit" provisions under 34 CFR part 361, including making maximum efforts to secure grant assistance in whole or part from other sources for training or training services in institutions of higher education.

(c)(1) The cost must be reasonable and necessary, in that it complies with the written cost-containment policies of the State VR agency. A cost which complies with these policies will be considered necessary only if the cost is for a VR service described in § 416.2214. The State VR agency must maintain and use these cost-containment policies, including any reasonable and appropriate fee schedules, to govern the costs incurred for all VR services, including the rates of payment for all purchased services, for which payment will be requested under this subpart. For the purpose of this subpart, the written cost-containment policies must provide guidelines designed to ensure—

(i) The lowest reasonable cost for such services; and

(ii) Sufficient flexibility so as to allow for an individual's needs.

(2) The State VR agency shall submit to us before the end of the first calendar quarter of each year a written statement certifying that cost-containment policies are in effect and are adhered to in procuring and providing goods and services for which the State VR agency requests payment under this subpart. Such certification must be signed by the State's chief financial official or the head of the VR agency. Each certification must specify the basis upon which it is made, e.g., a recent audit by an authorized State, Federal or private auditor (or other independent compliance review) and the date of such audit (or compliance review). We may request the State VR agency to submit to us a copy(ies) of its specific written cost-containment policies and procedures (e.g., any guidelines and fee schedules for a given year), if we determine that such additional information is necessary to ensure compliance with the requirements of this subpart. The State VR agency shall provide such information when requested by us.

(d) The total payment in each case, including any prior payments related to earlier continuous 9–month periods of SGA made under this subpart, must not be so high as to preclude a "net saving" to the general funds (a "net saving" is the difference between the estimated savings to the general fund, if payments for disability or blindness remain reduced or eventually terminate, and the total amount we pay to the State VR agency);

(e) Any payment to the State VR agency for either direct or indirect VR expenses must be consistent with the cost principles described in OMB Circular No. A–87, as revised;

(f) Payment for VR services or costs may be made under more than one of the VR payment provisions described in §§ 416.2211 and 416.2212 of this subpart and similar provisions in §§ 404.2111 and 404.2112 of subpart V of part 404. However, payment will not be made more than once for the same VR service or cost; and

(g) Payment will be made for administrative costs and for counseling and placement costs. This payment may be on a formula basis, or on an actual cost basis, whichever the State VR agency prefers. The formula will be negotiated. The payment will also be subject to the preceding limitations.

[55 FR 8457, 8458, March 8, 1990; 55 FR 14916, April 19, 1990; 59 FR 11919, March 15, 1994; 61 FR 31027, June 19, 1996; 62 FR 38456, July 18, 1997; 68 FR 40125, July 7, 2003; 83 FR 62461, Dec. 4, 2018]

ADMINISTRATIVE PROVISIONS

§ 416.2218 [Reserved by 83 FR 62462]

[83 FR 62462, Dec. 4, 2018]

§ 416.2219 Method of payment.

Payment to the State VR agencies pursuant to this subpart will be made either by advancement of funds or by payment for services provided (with necessary adjustments for any overpayments and underpayments), as decided by the Commissioner.

[55 FR 8457, 8458, March 8, 1990; 83 FR 62462, Dec. 4, 2018]

§ 416.2220 Audits.

(a) General. The State shall permit us and the Comptroller General of the United States (including duly authorized representatives) access to and the right to examine records relating to the services and costs for which payment was requested or made under these regulations. These records shall be retained by the State for the periods of time specified for retention of records in the Federal Acquisition Regulations (48 CFR part 4, subpart 4.7).

(b) Audit basis. Auditing will be based on cost principles and written guidelines in effect at the time services were provided and costs were incurred. The State VR agency will be informed and given a full explanation of any questioned items. They will be given a reasonable time to explain questioned items. Any explanation furnished by the State VR agency will be given full consideration before a final determination is made on questioned items in the audit report.

(c) Appeal of audit determinations. The appropriate SSA Regional Commissioner will notify the State VR agency in writing of his or her final determination on the audit report. If the State VR agency disagrees with that determination, it may request reconsideration in writing within 60 days after receiving the Regional Commissioner's notice of the determination. The Commissioner will make a determination and notify the State VR agency of that decision in writing, usually, no later than 45 days from the date of the appeal. The decision by the Commissioner will be final and conclusive unless the State VR agency appeals that decision in writing in accordance with 45 CFR part 16 to the Department of Health and Human Services' Departmental Appeals Board within 30 days after receiving it.

[55 FR 8458, March 8, 1990; 62 FR 38456, July 18, 1997; 83 FR 62462, Dec. 4, 2018]

§ 416.2221 Validation reviews.

(a) General. We will conduct a validation review of a sample of the claims for payment filed by each State VR agency. We will conduct some of these reviews on a prepayment basis and some on a postpayment basis. We may review a specific claim, a sample of the claims, or all the claims filed by any State VR agency, if we determine that such review is necessary to ensure compliance with the requirements of this subpart. For each claim selected for review, the State VR agency must submit such records of the VR services and costs for which payment has been requested or made under this subpart, or copies of such records, as we may require to ensure that the services and costs meet the requirements for payment. For claims for cases described in § 416.2201(a), a clear explanation or existing documentation which demonstrates how the service contributed to the individual's performance of a continuous 9–month period of SGA must be provided. For claims for cases described in § 416.2201(b) or (c), a clear explanation or existing documentation which demonstrates how the service was reasonably expected to motivate or assist the individual to return to or continue in SGA must be provided. If we find in any prepayment validation review that the scope or content of the information is inadequate, we will request additional information and will withhold payment until adequate information has been provided. The State VR agency shall permit us (including duly authorized representatives) access to, and the right to examine, any records relating to such services and costs. Any review performed under this section will not be considered an audit for purposes of this subpart.

(b) Purpose. The primary purpose of these reviews is—

(1) To ensure that the VR services and costs meet the requirements for payment under this subpart;

(2) To assess the validity of our documentation requirements; and

(3) To assess the need for additional validation reviews or additional documentation requirements for any State VR agency to ensure compliance with the requirements under this subpart.

(c) Determinations. In any validation review, we will determine whether the VR services and costs meet the requirements for payment and determine the amount of payment. We will notify in writing the State VR agency of our determination. If we find in any postpayment validation review that more or less than the correct amount of payment was made for a claim, we will determine that an overpayment or underpayment has occurred and will notify the State VR agency that we will make the appropriate adjustment.

(d) Appeals. If the State VR agency disagrees with our determination under this section, it may appeal that determination in accordance with § 416.2227. For purposes of this section, an appeal must be filed within 60 days after receiving the notice of our determination.

[59 FR 11920, March 15, 1994; 83 FR 62462, Dec. 4, 2018]

§ 416.2222 Confidentiality of information and records.

The State shall comply with the provisions for confidentiality of information, including the security of systems, and records requirements described in 20 CFR part 401 and pertinent written guidelines (see § 416.2223).

[83 FR 62462, Dec. 4, 2018]

§ 416.2223 Other Federal laws and regulations.

Each State VR agency shall comply with the provisions of other Federal laws and regulations that directly affect its responsibilities in carrying out the vocational rehabilitation function.

[83 FR 62462, Dec. 4, 2018]

§ 416.2227 Resolution of disputes.

(a) Disputes on the amount to be paid. The appropriate SSA official will notify the State VR agency in writing of his or her determination concerning the amount to be paid. If the State VR agency disagrees with that determination, the State VR agency may request reconsideration in writing within 60 days after receiving the notice of determination. The Commissioner will make a determination and notify the State VR agency of that decision in writing, usually, no later than 45 days from the date of the State VR agency's appeal. The decision by the Commissioner will be final and conclusive upon the State VR agency unless the State VR agency appeals that decision in writing in accordance with 45 CFR part 16 to the Department of Health and Human Services' Departmental Appeals Board within 30 days after receiving the Commissioner's decision.

(b) Disputes on whether there was a continuous period of SGA and whether VR services contributed to a continuous period of SGA. The rules in paragraph (a) of this section will apply, except that the Commissioner's decision will be final and conclusive. There is no right of appeal to the Departmental Appeals Board.

(c) Disputes on determinations made by the Commissioner which affect a disabled or blind beneficiary's rights to benefits. Determinations made by the Commissioner which affect an individual's right to benefits (e.g., determinations that disability or blindness benefits should be terminated, denied, suspended, continued or begun at a different date than alleged) cannot be appealed by a State VR agency. Because these determinations are an integral part of the disability or blindness benefits claims process, they can only be appealed by the beneficiary or applicant whose rights are affected or by his or her authorized representative. However, if an appeal of an unfavorable determination is made by the individual and is successful, the new determination would also apply for purposes of this subpart. While a VR agency cannot appeal a determination made by the Commissioner which affects a beneficiary's or applicant's rights, the VR agency can furnish any evidence it may have which would support a revision of a determination.

[55 FR 8458, March 8, 1990; 62 FR 38456, July 18, 1997; 83 FR 62462, Dec. 4, 2018]

PART 418—MEDICARE SUBSIDIES

SUBPART B—MEDICARE PART B INCOME-RELATED MONTHLY ADJUSTMENT AMOUNT

INTRODUCTION, GENERAL PROVISIONS, AND DEFINITIONS

DETERMINATION OF THE INCOME-RELATED MONTHLY ADJUSTMENT AMOUNT

DETERMINATIONS USING A MORE RECENT TAX YEAR'S MODIFIED ADJUSTED GROSS INCOME

DETERMINATIONS AND THE ADMINISTRATIVE REVIEW PROCESS

SUBPART C—INCOME-RELATED MONTHLY ADJUSTMENTS TO MEDICARE PRESCRIPTION DRUG COVERAGE PREMIUMS

INTRODUCTION, GENERAL PROVISIONS, AND DEFINITIONS

Authority: Secs. 702(a)(5) and 1860D–1, 1860D–14 and -15 of the Social Security Act (42 U.S.C. 902(a)(5),1395w–101, 1395w–114, and -115).

Source: 70 FR 77675, Dec. 30, 2005, unless otherwise noted.

SUBPART A—[RESERVED]

SUBPART B—MEDICARE PART B INCOME-RELATED MONTHLY ADJUSTMENT AMOUNT

Authority: Secs. 702(a)(5) and 1839(i) of the Social Security Act (42 U.S.C. 902(a)(5) and 1395r(i)).

Source: 71 FR 62931, Oct. 27, 2006, unless otherwise noted.

INTRODUCTION, GENERAL PROVISIONS, AND DEFINITIONS

§ 418.1001 What is this subpart about?

This subpart relates to section 1839(i) of the Social Security Act (the Act), as amended. Section 1839(i) establishes an income-related monthly adjustment to the Medicare Part B premium. Beneficiaries enrolled in Medicare Part B who have modified adjusted gross income over a threshold amount established in the statute will pay an income-related monthly adjustment amount in addition to the Medicare Part B standard monthly premium and any applicable premium increases as described in 42 CFR 408.20. The regulations in this subpart explain how we decide whether you are required to pay an income-related monthly adjustment amount, and if you are, the amount of your adjustment. The rules are divided into the following groups of sections:

(a) Sections 418.1001 through 418.1010 contain the introduction, a statement of the general purpose of the income-related monthly adjustment amount, general provisions that apply to the income-related monthly adjustment amount, and definitions of terms that we use in this subpart.

(b) Sections 418.1101 through 418.1150 describe what information about your modified adjusted gross income we will use to determine if you are required to pay an income-related monthly adjustment amount. In these sections, we also describe how the income-related monthly adjustment amount will affect your total Medicare Part B premium.

(c) Sections 418.1201 through 418.1270 contain an explanation of the standards that you must meet for us to grant your request to use modified adjusted gross income information that you provide for a more recent tax year rather than the information described in paragraph (b) of this section. These sections explain when we may consider such a request, and the evidence that you will be required to provide. These sections also explain when income-related monthly adjustment amount determinations based on information you provide will be effective, and how long they will remain in effect. Additionally, these sections describe how retroactive adjustments of the income-related monthly adjustment amount will be made based on information you provide, updated information you provide, and information we later receive from the Internal Revenue Service (IRS).

(d) Sections 418.1301 through 418.1355 contain the rules that we will apply when you disagree with our determination regarding your income-related monthly adjustment amount. These sections explain your appeal rights and the circumstances under which you may request that we make a new initial determination of your income-related monthly adjustment amount.

[78 FR 57259, Sept. 18, 2013; 79 FR 11706, March 3, 2014; 83 FR 55628, Nov. 7, 2018]

§ 418.1005 Purpose and administration.

(a) The purpose of the income-related monthly adjustment amount is to reduce the Federal subsidy of the Medicare Part B program for beneficiaries with modified adjusted gross income above an established threshold. These beneficiaries will pay a greater share of actual program costs. Medicare Part B premiums paid by beneficiaries cover approximately 25 percent of total Medicare Part B program costs and the remaining 75 percent of program costs are subsidized by the Federal Government's contributions to the Federal Supplementary Medical Insurance Trust Fund. The reduction in the Medicare Part B premium subsidy results in an increase in the total amount that affected beneficiaries pay for Medicare Part B coverage. A beneficiary with modified adjusted gross income above the threshold amount will pay:

(1) The Medicare Part B standard monthly premium; plus

(2) Any applicable increase in the standard monthly premium for late enrollment or reenrollment; plus

(3) An income-related monthly adjustment amount.

(b) The Centers for Medicare & Medicaid Services (CMS) in the Department of Health and Human Services (HHS) publishes the Medicare Part B standard monthly premium each year. CMS also establishes rules for entitlement to a nonstandard premium, as well as premium penalties for late enrollment or reenrollment (42 CFR 408.20 through 408.27).

(c) We use information that we get from IRS to determine if beneficiaries who are enrolled in Medicare Part B are required to pay an income-related monthly adjustment amount. We also change income-related monthly adjustment amount determinations using information provided by a beneficiary under certain circumstances. In addition, we notify beneficiaries when the social security benefit amounts they receive will change based on our income-related monthly adjustment amount determination.

§ 418.1010 Definitions.

(a) Terms relating to the Act and regulations. For the purposes of this subpart:

(1) Administrator means the Administrator of the Centers for Medicare & Medicaid Services (CMS) in HHS.

(2) CMS means the Centers for Medicare & Medicaid Services in HHS.

(3) Commissioner means the Commissioner of Social Security.

(4) HHS means the Department of Health and Human Services which oversees the Centers for Medicare & Medicaid Services, the Office of Medicare Hearings and Appeals (OMHA) and the Medicare Appeals Council (MAC).

(5) IRS means the Internal Revenue Service in the Department of the Treasury.

(6) MAC means the Medicare Appeals Council in HHS.

(7) OMHA means the Office of Medicare Hearings and Appeals in HHS.

(8) Section means a section of the regulations in this part unless the context indicates otherwise.

(9) The Act means the Social Security Act, as amended.

(10) Title means a title of the Act.

(11) We, our, or us means the Social Security Administration (SSA).

(b) Miscellaneous. For the purposes of this subpart:

(1) Amended tax return means a Federal income tax return for which an amended tax return using the required IRS form(s) has been filed by an individual or couple and accepted by IRS.

(2) Effective year means the calendar year for which we make an income-related monthly adjustment amount determination.

(3) Federal premium subsidy is the portion of the full cost of providing Medicare Part B coverage that is paid by the Federal Government through transfers into the Federal Supplementary Medical Insurance Trust Fund.

(4) Income-related monthly adjustment amount is an additional amount of premium that you will pay for Medicare Part B coverage if you have income above the threshold. The amount of your income-related monthly adjustment amount is based on your modified adjusted gross income.

(5) Medicare Part B standard monthly premium means the monthly Medicare Part B premium amount which is set annually by CMS, according to regulations in 42 CFR 408.20 through 408.27.

(6) Modified adjusted gross income is your adjusted gross income as defined by the Internal Revenue Code, plus the following forms of tax-exempt income:

(i) Tax-exempt interest income;

(ii) Income from United States savings bonds used to pay higher education tuition and fees;

(iii) Foreign earned income;

(iv) Income derived from sources within Guam, American Samoa, or the Northern Mariana Islands; and

(v) Income from sources within Puerto Rico.

(7) Modified adjusted gross income ranges are the groupings of modified adjusted gross income above the threshold. There are four ranges for most individuals, based on their tax filing status. There are two ranges for those with a tax filing status of married, filing separately, who also lived with their spouse for part of the year. The dollar amounts of the modified adjusted gross income ranges are specified in § 418.1115.

(8) Non-standard premium means a Medicare Part B premium that some beneficiaries pay for Medicare Part B, rather than the standard premium. The rules for applying a non-standard premium are in 42 CFR 408.20(e). The non-standard premium does not apply to beneficiaries who must pay an income-related monthly adjustment amount.

(9) Premium is a payment that an enrolled beneficiary pays for Medicare Part B coverage. The rules that CMS uses to annually establish the premium amount are found in 42 CFR 408.20 through 408.27.

(10) Representative means, for the purposes of the initial determination and reconsidered determination, an individual as defined in § 404.1703 of this chapter, and for purposes of an ALJ hearing or review by the MAC, an individual as defined in 42 CFR 405.910.

(11) Tax filing status means the filing status shown on your individual income tax return. It may be single, married filing jointly, married filing separately, head of household, or qualifying widow(er) with dependent child.

(12) Tax year means the year for which your Federal income tax return has been filed or will be filed with the IRS.

(13) Threshold means a modified adjusted gross income amount above which the beneficiary will have to pay an income-related monthly adjustment amount described in paragraph (b)(4) of this section. The dollar amount of the threshold is specified in § 418.1105.

(14) You or your means the person or representative of the person who is subject to the income-related monthly adjustment amount.

DETERMINATION OF THE INCOME–RELATED MONTHLY ADJUSTMENT AMOUNT

§ 418.1101 What is the income-related monthly adjustment amount?

(a) The income-related monthly adjustment amount is an amount that you will pay in addition to the Medicare Part B standard monthly premium plus any applicable increase in that premium as described in 42 CFR 408.22 for your Medicare Part B coverage when your modified adjusted gross income is above the threshold described in § 418.1105.

(b) Your income-related monthly adjustment amount is based on your applicable modified adjusted gross income as described in § 418.1115 and your tax filing status.

(c) We will determine your income-related monthly adjustment amount using the method described in § 418.1120.

[78 FR 57259, Sept. 18, 2013; 79 FR 11706, March 3, 2014]

§ 418.1105 What is the threshold?

(a) The threshold is a level of modified adjusted gross income above which the beneficiary will have to pay the income-related monthly adjustment amount.

(b) From January 1, 2011 through December 31, 2019, the modified adjusted gross income threshold is $170,000 for individuals with a Federal income tax filing status of married filing jointly. The threshold is $85,000 for individuals with any other filing status.

(c) Starting on January 1, 2020, the threshold amounts will resume adjustment for inflation as required by section 1839(i)(5) of the Act. In each year thereafter, CMS will set all modified adjusted gross income threshold amounts for the following year by increasing the preceding year's threshold amounts by any percentage increase in the Consumer Price Index rounded to the nearest $1,000. CMS will publish the amounts in the Federal Register in September of each year. Published threshold amounts will be effective January 1 of the next calendar year, for the full calendar year.

[78 FR 57259, Sept. 18, 2013; 79 FR 11706, March 3, 2014]

§ 418.1110 What is the effective date of our initial determination about your income-related monthly adjustment amount?

(a) Generally, an income-related monthly adjustment amount will be effective for all months that you are enrolled in Medicare Part B during the year for which we determine you must pay an income-related monthly adjustment amount. We will follow the rules in 42 CFR part 408, subpart C, regarding premium collections to withhold your income-related monthly adjustment amount from a benefit payment or to determine if you will be billed directly.

(b) When we have used modified adjusted gross income information from IRS for the tax year 3 years prior to the effective year to determine your income-related monthly adjustment amount and modified adjusted gross income information for the tax year 2 years prior later becomes available from IRS, we will review the new information to determine if we should revise our initial determination. If we revise our initial determination, the effective date of the new initial determination will be January 1 of the effective year, or the first month you were enrolled or re-enrolled in Medicare Part B if later than January.

(c) When we use your amended tax return, as described in § 418.1150, the effective date will be January 1 of the year(s) that is affected, or the first month in that year that you were enrolled or reenrolled in Medicare Part B if later than January.

Example: You are enrolled in Medicare Part B throughout 2011. We use your 2009 modified adjusted gross income as reported to us by IRS to determine your 2011 income-related monthly adjustment amount. In 2012 you submit to us a copy of your 2009 amended tax return that you filed with IRS. The modified adjusted gross income reported on your 2009 amended tax return is significantly less than originally reported to IRS. We use the modified adjusted gross income that was reported on your 2009 amended tax return to determine your income-related monthly adjustment amount. That income-related monthly adjustment amount is effective January 1, 2011. We will retroactively adjust for any differences between the amount paid in 2011 and the amount that should have been paid based on the amended tax return.

(d) When we use evidence that you provide which proves that the IRS modified adjusted gross income information we used is incorrect, as described in § 418.1335, the effective date will be January of the year(s) that is affected or the first month in that year that you were enrolled or reenrolled in Medicare Part B if later than January.

(e) When we use information from a more recent tax year that you provide due to a major life-changing event, as described in § 418.1201, the effective date is described in § 418.1230.

§ 418.1115 What are the modified adjusted gross income ranges?

(a) We list the modified adjusted gross income ranges for the calendar years 2011 through and including 2017, 2018, and for years beginning in 2019 for each Federal tax filing category in paragraphs (b), (c) and (d) of this section. We will use your modified adjusted gross income amount together with your tax filing status to determine the amount of your income-related monthly adjustment for these calendar years.

(b) The modified adjusted gross income ranges for individuals with a Federal tax filing status of single, head of household, qualifying widow(er) with dependent child, and married filing separately when the individual has lived apart from his/her spouse for the entire tax year for the year we use to make our income-related monthly adjustment amount determination are as follows.

(1) For calendar years 2011 through and including 2017—

(i) Greater than $85,000 but less than or equal to $107,000;

(ii) Greater than $107,000 but less than or equal to $160,000;

(iii) Greater than $160,000 but less than or equal to $214,000; and

(iv) Greater than $214,000.

(2) For calendar year 2018—

(i) Greater than $85,000 but less than or equal to $107,000;

(ii) Greater than $107,000 but less than or equal to $133,500;

(iii) Greater than $133,500 but less than or equal to $160,000; and

(iv) Greater than $160,000

(3) For calendar years beginning with 2019—

(i) Greater than $85,000 but less than or equal to $107,000;

(ii) Greater than $107,000 but less than or equal to $133,500;

(iii) Greater than $133,500 but less than or equal to $160,000;

(iv) Greater than $160,000 but less than $500,000; and

(v) Greater than or equal to $500,000.

(c) The modified adjusted gross income ranges for individuals who are married and filed a joint tax return for the tax year we use to make the income-related monthly adjustment amount determination are as follows.

(1) For calendar years 2011 through and including 2017—

(i) Greater than $170,000 but less than or equal to $214,000;

(ii) Greater than $214,000 but less than or equal to $320,000;

(iii) Greater than $320,000 but less than or equal to $428,000; and

(iv) Greater than $428,000.

(2) For calendar year 2018—

(i) Greater than $170,000 but less than or equal to $214,000;

(ii) Greater than $214,000 but less than or equal to $267,000;

(iii) Greater than $267,000 but less than or equal to $320,000; and

(iv) Greater than $320,000.

(3) For calendar years beginning in 2019—

(i) Greater than $170,000 but less than or equal to $214,000;

(ii) Greater than $214,000 but less than or equal to $267,000;

(iii) Greater than $267,000 but less than or equal to $320,000;

(iv) Greater than $320,000 but less than $750,000; and

(v) Greater than or equal to $750,000.

(d) The modified adjusted gross income ranges for married individuals who file a separate return and have lived with their spouse at any time during the tax year we use to make the income-related monthly adjustment amount determination are as follows.

(1) For calendar years 2011 through and including 2017—

(i) Greater than $85,000 but less than or equal to $129,000; and

(ii) Greater than $129,000.

(2) For calendar year 2018—Greater than $85,000.

(3) For calendar years beginning in 2019—

(i) Greater than $85,000 but less than $415,000; and

(ii) Greater than or equal to $415,000.

(e)(1) Subject to paragraph (e)(2) of this section, in 2019, CMS will set the modified adjusted gross income ranges for 2020 and publish them in the Federal Register. In each year thereafter, CMS will set the modified adjusted gross income ranges by increasing the preceding year's ranges by any percentage increase in the Consumer Price Index rounded to the nearest $1,000 and will publish the amounts for the following year in September of each year.

(2) The amounts listed in paragraphs (b), (c), and (d) of $415,000, $500,000, and $750,000 will not be adjusted under paragraph (e)(1) of this section until 2028. Beginning in 2027, and in each year thereafter, CMS will adjust these range amounts for the following year under paragraph (e)(1) of this section and publish the updated ranges in the Federal Register.

[78 FR 57259, Sept. 18, 2013; 79 FR 11706, March 3, 2014; 83 FR 55628, Nov. 7, 2018]

§ 418.1120 How do we determine your income-related monthly adjustment amount?

(a) We will determine your income-related monthly adjustment amount by using your tax filing status and modified adjusted gross income.

(b) Tables of applicable percentage. The tables in paragraphs (b)(1) through (b)(3) of this section contain the modified adjusted gross income ranges for calendar years 2011 through and including 2017, 2018, and beginning in 2019 in the column on the left in each table. The middle column in each table shows the percentage of the unsubsidized Medicare Part B premium that will be paid by individuals with modified adjusted gross income that falls within each of the ranges. The column on the right in each table shows the percentage of the Medicare Part B premium that will be subsidized by contributions from the Federal Government. We use your tax filing status and your modified adjusted gross income for the tax year to determine which income-related monthly adjustment amount to apply to you. The dollar amount of income-related monthly adjustment for each range will be set annually for each year after 2019 as described in paragraph (c) of this section. The modified adjusted gross income ranges will be adjusted annually after 2019 as described in § 418.1115(e).

(1) General tables of applicable percentages. If, for the tax year, we use your filing status for your Federal income taxes for the tax year is single; head of household; qualifying widow(er) with dependent child; or married filing separately and you lived apart from your spouse for the entire tax year, we will use the general tables of applicable percentages. When your modified adjusted gross income for the year we use is in the range listed in the left column in the following tables, then the Federal Government's Part B premium subsidy of 75 percent is reduced to the percentage listed in the right column. You will pay an amount based on the percentage listed in the center column.

Table 1 to paragraph (b)(1): Modified adjusted gross income effective in 2011-2017	Beneficiary percentage (percent)	Federal premium subsidy (percent)
Greater than $85,000 but less than or equal to $107,000	35	65
Greater than $107,000 but less than or equal to $160,000	50	50
Greater than $160,000 but less than or equal to $214,000	65	35
Greater than $214,000	80	20

Table 2 to paragraph (b)(1): Modified adjusted gross income effective in 2018	Beneficiary percentage (percent)	Federal premium subsidy (percent)
Greater than $85,000 but less than or equal to $107,000	35	65
Greater than $107,000 but less than or equal to $133,500	50	50

Greater than $133,500 less than or equal to $160,000	65	35
Greater than $160,000	80	20

Table 3 to paragraph (b)(1): Modified adjusted gross income effective beginning in 2019	Beneficiary percentage (percent)	Federal premium subsidy (percent)
Greater than $85,000 but less than or equal to $107,000	35	65
Greater than $107,000 but less than or equal to $133,500	50	50
Greater than $133,500 but less than or equal to $160,000	65	35
Greater than $160,000 but less than $500,000	80	20
Greater than or equal to $500,000	85	15

(2) *Tables of applicable percentages for joint returns.* If, for the tax year, we use your Federal tax filing status is married filing jointly for the tax year and your modified adjusted gross income for that tax year is in the range listed in the left column in the following tables, then the Federal Government's Part B premium subsidy of 75 percent is reduced to the percentage listed in the right column. You will pay an amount based on the percentage listed in the center column.

Table 1 to paragraph (b)(2): Modified adjusted gross income effective in 2011-2017	Beneficiary percentage (percent)	Federal premium subsidy (percent)
Greater than $170,000 but less than or equal to $214,000	35	65
Greater than $214,000 but less than or equal to $320,000	50	50
Greater than $320,000 but less than or equal to $428,000	65	35
Greater than $428,000	80	20

Table 2 to paragraph (b)(2): Modified adjusted gross income effective in 2018	Beneficiary percentage (percent)	Federal premium subsidy (percent)
Greater than $170,000 but less than or equal to $214,000	35	65
Greater than $214,000 but less than or equal to $267,000	50	50
Greater than $267,000 but less than or equal to $320,000	65	35
Greater than $320,000	80	20

Table 3 to paragraph (b)(2): Modified adjusted gross income effective beginning in 2019	Beneficiary percentage (percent)	Federal premium subsidy (percent)
Greater than $170,000 but less than or equal to $214,000	35	65
Greater than $214,000 but less than or equal to $267,000	50	50
Greater than $267,000 but less than or equal to $320,000	65	35
Greater than $320,000 but less than $750,000	80	20
Greater than or equal to $750,000	85	15

(3) *Tables of applicable percentages for married individuals filing separate returns.* If, for the tax year, we use your Federal tax filing status is married filing separately, you lived with your spouse at some time during that tax year, and your modified adjusted gross income is in the range listed in the left column in the following tables, then the Federal Government's Part B premium subsidy of 75 percent is reduced to the percentage listed in the right column. You will pay an amount based on the percentage listed in the center column.

Table 1 to paragraph (b)(3): Modified adjusted gross income effective in 2011-2017	Beneficiary percentage (percent)	Federal premium subsidy (percent)
Greater than $85,000 but less than or equal to $129,000	65	35
Greater than $129,000	80	20

Table 2 to paragraph (b)(3): Modified adjusted gross income effective in 2018	Beneficiary percentage (percent)	Federal premium subsidy (percent)
Greater than $85,000	80	20

Table 3 to paragraph (b)(3): Modified adjusted gross income effective beginning in 2019	Beneficiary percentage (percent)	Federal premium subsidy (percent)
Greater than $85,000 but less than $415,000	80	20
Greater than or equal to $415,000	85	15

(c) For each year after 2019, CMS will annually publish in the Federal Register the dollar amounts for the income-related monthly adjustment amount described in paragraph (b) of this section.

[78 FR 57259, Sept. 18, 2013; 79 FR 11706, March 3, 2014; 83 FR 55628, Nov. 7, 2018]

§ 418.1125 How will the income-related monthly adjustment amount affect your total Medicare Part B premium?

(a) If you must pay an income-related monthly adjustment amount, your total Medicare Part B premium will be the sum of:

(1) The Medicare Part B standard monthly premium, determined using the rules in 42 CFR 408.20; plus

(2) Any applicable increase in the Medicare Part B standard monthly premium as described in 42 CFR 408.22; plus

(3) Your income-related monthly adjustment amount.

(b) The nonstandard Medicare Part B premium amount described in 42 CFR 408.20 does not apply to individuals who must pay an income-related monthly adjustment amount. Such individuals must pay the full Medicare Part B standard monthly premium plus any applicable penalties for late enrollment or reenrollment plus the income-related adjustment.

[78 FR 57260, Sept. 18, 2013; 79 FR 11706, March 3, 2014]

§ 418.1130 [Reserved by 78 FR 57260]

[78 FR 57260, Sept. 18, 2013; 79 FR 11706, March 3, 2014]

§ 418.1135 What modified adjusted gross income information will we use to determine your income-related monthly adjustment amount?

(a) In general, we will use your modified adjusted gross income provided by IRS for the tax year 2 years prior to the effective year of the income-related monthly adjustment amount determination. Modified adjusted gross income is based on information you provide to IRS when you file your Federal income tax return.

(b) We will use your modified adjusted gross income for the tax year 3 years prior to the effective year of the income-related monthly adjustment amount determination when IRS does not provide the information specified in paragraph (a) of this section. If IRS can provide modified adjusted gross income for the tax year 3 years prior to the income-related monthly adjustment amount effective year, we will temporarily use that information to determine your income-related monthly adjustment amount and make adjustments as described in § 418.1110(b) to all affected income-related monthly adjustment amounts when information for the year specified in paragraph (a) of this section is provided by IRS.

(c) When we have used the information in paragraph (b) of this section, you may provide us with evidence of your modified adjusted gross income for the year in paragraph (a) of this section. You must provide a retained copy of your signed Federal income tax return for that year, if available. If you filed a return for that year, but did not retain a copy, you must request a transcript or a copy of your return from IRS and provide it to us. When we use this evidence, we will later confirm this information with IRS records.

(d) When you meet the conditions specified in § 418.1150 because you have amended your Federal income tax return, or when you believe we have used information provided by IRS which is incorrect, as described in § 418.1335, we will use information that you provide directly to us regarding your modified adjusted gross income.

(e) We may use information that you give us about your modified adjusted gross income for a more recent tax year than those discussed in paragraphs (a) or (b) of this section as described in §§ 418.1201 through 418.1270.

(f) If you fail to file an income tax return for any year after 2004 and IRS informs us that you had modified adjusted gross income above the threshold applicable 2 years after the tax year when you failed to file an income tax return, we will impose the highest income-related adjustment percentage applicable to your income filing status for the effective year. If we later determine that the amount of the income-related monthly adjustment amount imposed was inconsistent with your modified adjusted gross income, we will correct it. The rules in 42 CFR 408.40 through 408.92 will apply to the collection of any retroactive premiums due.

§ 418.1140 What will happen if the modified adjusted gross income information from IRS is different from the modified adjusted gross income information we used to determine your income-related monthly adjustment amount?

In general, we will use modified adjusted gross income information from IRS to determine your income-related monthly adjustment. We will make retroactive adjustments to your income-related monthly adjustment amount as described in paragraphs (a), (b), and (d) of this section.

(a) When we have used modified adjusted gross income from the tax year 3 years prior to the effective year as described in § 418.1135(b), and IRS provides modified adjusted gross income information from the tax year 2 years prior to the effective year, we will use the new information to make an initial determination for the effective year. We will make retroactive adjustments back to January 1 of the effective year, or the first month you were enrolled or reenrolled in Medicare Part B if later than January.

(b) When we have used the modified adjusted gross income information that you provided for the tax year 2 years prior to the effective year and the modified adjusted gross income information we receive from IRS for that same year is different from the information you provided, we will use the modified adjusted gross income information provided to us by IRS to make a new initial determination. We will make retroactive adjustments back to January 1 of the effective year, or the first month you were enrolled or reenrolled in Medicare Part B if later than January.

(c) When we have used information from your amended Federal tax return that you provide, as explained in § 418.1150, or you provide proof that the information IRS provided to us is incorrect as described in § 418.1335, we will not make any adjustments to your income-related monthly adjustment amount for the effective year or years based on IRS information we receive later from IRS.

(d) When we use modified adjusted gross income information that you provided due to a qualifying life-changing event and we receive different information from IRS, we will use the IRS information to make retroactive corrections to all months in the effective year(s) during which you were enrolled in Medicare Part B, except when paragraph (c) of this section applies.

(e) When we used the table in § 418.1120(b)(3) to determine your income-related monthly adjustment amount, and you lived apart from your spouse throughout that year, we will ask you for a signed statement or attestation that you lived apart from your spouse throughout that year. We will also ask you to provide information about the addresses of you and your spouse during that year. If you provide a signed statement or attestation that you lived apart from your spouse throughout that year, and information about your respective addresses that year, we will use the table in § 418.1120(b)(1) to determine your income-related monthly adjustment amount.

§ 418.1145 How do we determine your income-related monthly adjustment amount if IRS does not provide information about your modified adjusted gross income?

In general, if we do not receive any information for you from IRS showing that you had modified adjusted gross income above the threshold in the tax year we request, we will not make an income-related monthly adjustment amount determination.

§ 418.1150 When will we use your amended tax return filed with IRS?

You may provide your amended tax return for a tax year we used within 3 calendar years following the close of the tax year for which you filed the amended tax return. You must provide us with your retained copy of your amended U.S. Individual Income Tax Return on the required IRS form and a copy of the IRS letter confirming the amended tax return was filed or a transcript from IRS if they did not send a letter. If you cannot provide your retained copy of the amended tax return, you must obtain a copy of the return from IRS. We will then make any necessary retroactive corrections as defined in § 418.1110(c) to your income-related monthly adjustment amount.

DETERMINATIONS USING A MORE RECENT TAX YEAR'S MODIFIED ADJUSTED GROSS INCOME

§ 418.1201 When will we determine your income-related monthly adjustment amount based on the modified adjusted gross income information that you provide for a more recent tax year?

We will use a more recent tax year than the years described in § 418.1135(a) or (b) to reduce or eliminate your income-related monthly adjustment amount when all of the following occur:

(a) You experience a major life-changing event as defined in § 418.1205; and

(b) That major life-changing event results in a significant reduction in your modified adjusted gross income for the year which you request we use and the next year, if applicable. For purposes of this section, a significant reduction in your modified adjusted gross income is one that results in the decrease or elimination of your income-related monthly adjustment amount; and

(c) You request that we use a more recent tax year's modified adjusted gross income; and

(d) You provide evidence as described in §§ 418.1255 and 418.1265.

§ 418.1205 What is a major life-changing event?

For the purposes of this subpart, we will consider the following to be major life-changing events:

(a) Your spouse dies;

(b) You marry;

(c) Your marriage ends through divorce or annulment;

(d) You or your spouse stop working or reduce the hours you work;

(e) You or your spouse experiences a loss of income-producing property, provided the loss is not at the direction of you or your spouse (e.g., due to the sale or transfer of the property) and is not a result of the ordinary risk of investment. Examples of the type of property loss include, but are not limited to: Loss of real property within a Presidentially or Gubernatorially-declared disaster area, destruction of livestock or crops by natural disaster or disease, loss from real property due to arson, or loss of investment property as a result of fraud or theft due to a criminal act by a third party;

(f) You or your spouse experiences a scheduled cessation, termination, or reorganization of an employer's pension plan;

(g) You or your spouse receives a settlement from an employer or former employer because of the employer's closure, bankruptcy, or reorganization.

[75 FR 41086, July 15, 2010; 76 FR 38554, July 1, 2011]

§ 418.1210 What is not a major life-changing event?

We will not consider events other than those described in § 418.1205 to be major life-changing events. Certain types of events are not considered major life-changing events for the purposes of this subpart, such as:

(a) Events that affect your expenses, but not your income; or

(b) Events that result in the loss of dividend income because of the ordinary risk of investment.

[75 FR 41086, July 15, 2010; 76 FR 38554, July 1, 2011]

§ 418.1215 What is a significant reduction in your income?

For purposes of this subpart, we will consider a reduction in your income to be significant if your modified adjusted gross income decreases; and

(a) The decrease reduces the percentage of the income-related monthly adjustment amount you must pay according to the Table of Applicable Percentages in § 418.1120; or

(b) The decrease reduces your modified adjusted gross income to an amount below the threshold described in § 418.1105 and eliminates any income-related monthly adjustment amount you must pay.

§ 418.1220 What is not a significant reduction in your income?

For purposes of this subpart, we will not consider a reduction in your income to be significant unless the reduction affects the amount of income-related monthly adjustment you must pay.

§ 418.1225 Which more recent tax year will we use?

We will consider evidence of your modified adjusted gross income that you provide for a tax year that is more recent than the year described in § 418.1135 (a) or (b) when you meet all of the requirements described in § 418.1201. We will always ask you for your retained copy of your filed Federal income tax return for the more recent year you request that we use and will use that information to make an initial determination. If you have not filed your Federal income tax return for the more recent year you request that we use, you must provide us with evidence that is equivalent to a copy of a filed Federal income tax return. Evidence that is equivalent to a copy of a filed Federal income tax return is defined in § 418.1265(c).

§ 418.1230 What is the effective date of an income-related monthly adjustment amount initial determination that is based on a more recent tax year?

(a) Subject to paragraph (b) of this section, when your modified adjusted gross income for the more recent tax year is significantly reduced as a result of a major life-changing event, our initial determination is generally effective on January 1 of the year in which you make your request. If your first month of enrollment or reenrollment in Medicare Part B is after January of the year for which you make your request, our initial determination is effective on the first day of your Medicare Part B enrollment or reenrollment.

(b) We will make a determination about your income-related monthly adjustment amount for the year preceding the year that you make your request in the limited circumstances explained in § 418.1310(a)(4). When we make a determination for the preceding year, our initial determination is generally effective on January 1 of that year. If your first month of enrollment or reenrollment in Medicare Part B is after January of that year, our initial determination is effective on the first day of your Medicare Part B enrollment or reenrollment.

(c) Our initial determination will be effective January 1 of the year following the year you make your request, when your modified adjusted gross income will not be significantly reduced as a result of one or more of the events described in § 418.1205(a) through (g) until the year following the year you make your request.

[75 FR 41086, July 15, 2010; 76 FR 38554, July 1, 2011; 78 FR 57260, Sept. 18, 2013; 79 FR 11706, March 3, 2014]

§ 418.1235 When will we stop using your more recent tax year's modified adjusted gross income to determine your income-related monthly adjustment amount?

We will use your more recent tax year's modified adjusted gross income to determine your income-related monthly adjustment amount effective with the month and year described in § 418.1230 and for each year thereafter until one of the following occurs:

(a) We receive your modified adjusted gross income from IRS for the more recent tax year we used or a later tax year;

(b) Your more recent tax year modified adjusted gross income that we used is for a tax year more than 3 years prior to the income-related monthly adjustment amount effective year;

(c) You request we use a more recent tax year based on another major life-changing event as described in § 418.1201; or

(d) You notify us of a change in your modified adjusted gross income for the more recent tax year we used as described in § 418.1240.

§ 418.1240 Should you notify us if the information you gave us about your modified adjusted gross income for the more recent tax year changes?

If you know that the information you provided to us about the more recent tax year that we used has changed, you should tell us so that we can determine if your income-related monthly adjustment amount should be eliminated or adjusted. We will accept new modified adjusted gross income information at any time after your request until the end of the calendar year following the more recent tax year(s) that we used. For us to make a new initial determination using your new modified adjusted gross income information, you must provide evidence as described in § 418.1265 to support the reduction or increase in your modified adjusted gross income. If you amend your Federal income tax return for the more recent tax year we used, we will use the rules in § 418.1150.

§ 418.1245 What will happen if you notify us that your modified adjusted gross income for the more recent tax year changes?

(a) If you notify us that your modified adjusted gross income for the more recent tax year has changed from what is in our records, we may make a new initial determination for each effective year involved. To make a new initial determination(s) we will take into account:

(1) The new modified adjusted gross income information for the more recent tax year you provide; and

(2) Any modified adjusted gross income information from IRS, as described in § 418.1135, that we have available for each effective year; and

(3) Any modified adjusted gross income information from you, as described in § 418.1135, that we have available for each effective year.

(b) For each new initial determination that results in a change in your income-related monthly adjustment amount, we will make retroactive adjustments that will apply to all enrolled months of the effective year.

(c) We will continue to use a new initial determination described in paragraph (a) of this section to determine additional yearly income-related monthly adjustment amount(s) until an event described in § 418.1235 occurs.

(d) We will make a new determination about your income-related monthly adjustment amount when we receive modified adjusted gross income for the effective year from IRS, as described in § 418.1140(d).

§ 418.1250 What evidence will you need to support your request that we use a more recent tax year?

When you request that we use a more recent tax year to determine your income-related monthly adjustment amount, we will ask for evidence of the major life-changing event and how the event significantly reduced your modified adjusted gross income as described in §§ 418.1255 and 418.1265. Unless we have information in our records that raises a doubt about the evidence, additional evidence documenting the major life-changing event(s) will not be needed.

§ 418.1255 What kind of major life-changing event evidence will you need to support your request for us to use a more recent tax year?

(a) If your spouse died and we do not have evidence of the death in our records, we will require proof of death as described in § 404.720(b) or (c) or § 404.721 of this chapter.

(b) If you marry and we do not have evidence of the marriage in our records, we will require proof of marriage as described in §§ 404.725 through 404.727 of this chapter.

(c) If your marriage ends and we do not have evidence that the marriage has ended in our records, we will require proof that the marriage has ended as described in § 404.728(b) or (c) of this chapter.

(d) If you or your spouse stop working or reduce your work hours, we will require evidence documenting the change in work activity. Examples of acceptable documentation include, but are not limited to, documents we can corroborate such as a signed statement from your employer, proof of the transfer of your business, or your signed statement under penalty of perjury, describing your work separation or a reduction in hours.

(e) If you or your spouse experiences a loss of income-producing property, we will require evidence documenting the loss. Examples of acceptable evidence include, but are not limited to, insurance claims or an insurance adjuster's statement. If the claim of loss is due to criminal fraud or theft by a third party, we will also require proof of conviction for the fraud or theft, such as a court document.

(f) If you or your spouse experiences a scheduled cessation, termination, or reorganization of an employer's pension plan, we will require evidence documenting the change in or loss of the pension. An example of acceptable evidence includes, but is not limited to, a statement from your pension fund administrator explaining the reduction or termination of your benefits.

(g) If you or your spouse receives a settlement from an employer or former employer because of the employer's closure, bankruptcy, or reorganization, we will require evidence documenting the settlement and the reason(s) for the settlement. An example of acceptable evidence includes, but is not limited to, a letter from the former employer stating the settlement terms and how they affect you or your spouse.

[75 FR 41086, July 15, 2010; 76 FR 38554, July 1, 2011]

§ 418.1260 What major life-changing event evidence will we not accept?

(a) We will not accept evidence of death that fails to meet the requirements in §§ 404.720 through 404.721 of this chapter.

(b) We will not accept evidence of marriage that fails to meet the requirements in §§ 404.725 through 404.727 of this chapter.

(c) We will not accept evidence that your marriage has ended if the evidence fails to meet the requirements in § 404.728 of this chapter.

(d) We will not accept documents supporting loss of income from income-producing property, or failure of or loss from a defined benefit pension plan unless the documents are original documents or copies from the original source.

(e) We will not accept evidence of work reduction or work stoppage that cannot be substantiated.

§ 418.1265 What kind of significant modified adjusted gross income reduction evidence will you need to support your request?

(a) You must provide evidence that one or more of the major life-changing events described in § 418.1205 resulted in a significant reduction in your modified adjusted gross income for the tax year you request we use.

(b) The preferred evidence is your retained copy of your filed Federal income tax return, your retained copy of your amended tax return with an IRS letter of receipt of the amended tax return, your copy of proof of a correction of the IRS information we used or a copy of your return or amended or proof of a correction of tax return information that you obtain from IRS for the more recent tax year you request we use.

(c) When a copy of your filed Federal income tax return is not available for the more recent tax year in which your modified adjusted gross income was significantly reduced, we will accept equivalent evidence. Equivalent evidence is the appropriate proof(s) in paragraphs (c)(1), (2) and (3) of this section, plus your signed statement under penalty of perjury that the information you provide is true and correct. When the major life-changing event changes your tax filing status, or the income-related monthly adjustment amount determination could be affected by your tax filing status, you will also be required to sign a statement regarding your intended income tax filing status for the tax year you request we use.

(1) If you experience one or more of the events described in § 418.1205(a), (b), or (c), you must provide evidence as to how the event(s) significantly reduced your modified adjusted gross income. Examples of the type of evidence include, but are not limited to, evidence of your spouse's modified adjusted gross income and/or your modified adjusted gross income for the tax year we use.

(2) If you experience one or more of the events described in § 418.1205(d), (e), (f), or (g), you must provide evidence of how the event(s) significantly reduced your modified adjusted gross income, such as a statement explaining any modified adjusted gross income changes for the tax year we used and a copy of your filed Federal income tax return (if you have filed one).

(3) If your spouse experiences one or more of the events described in § 418.1205(d), (e), (f), or (g), you must provide evidence of the resulting significant reduction in your modified adjusted gross income. The evidence requirements are described in paragraph (c)(2) of this section.

(d) When we use information described in paragraph (c) of this section, we will request that you provide your retained copy of your Federal income tax return for the year we used when you file your taxes. We will use that information to make timely adjustments to your Medicare premium, if necessary. We will later verify the information you provide when we receive information about that tax year from IRS, as described in § 418.1140(d).

[75 FR 41087, July 15, 2010; 76 FR 38554, July 1, 2011]

§ 418.1270 What modified adjusted gross income evidence will we not accept?

We will not accept a correction or amendment of your income tax return without a letter from IRS acknowledging the change. We will also not accept illegible or unsigned copies of income tax returns or attestations or other statements of income unless they are provided under penalty of perjury.

DETERMINATIONS AND THE ADMINISTRATIVE REVIEW PROCESS

§ 418.1301 What is an initial determination regarding your income-related monthly adjustment amount?

An initial determination is the determination we make about your income-related monthly adjustment amount that is subject to administrative review. For the purposes of administering the income-related monthly adjustment amount, initial determinations include but are not limited to determinations about:

(a) The amount of your income-related monthly adjustment amount based on information provided by IRS; and

(b) Any change in your income-related monthly adjustment amount based on one of the circumstances listed in § 418.1310(a)(1) through (a)(4).

§ 418.1305 What is not an initial determination regarding your income-related monthly adjustment amount?

Administrative actions that are not initial determinations may be reviewed by us, but they are not subject to the administrative review process as provided by §§ 418.1320 through 418.1325 and §§ 418.1340 through 418.1355, and they are not subject to judicial review. These actions include, but are not limited to, our dismissal of a request for reconsideration as described in § 418.1330 and our dismissal of a request for a new initial determination as described in § 418.1310(d).

§ 418.1310 When may you request that we make a new initial determination?

(a) You may request that we make a new initial determination in the following circumstances:

(1) You provide a copy of your filed Federal income tax return for the tax year 2 years prior to the effective year when IRS has provided information for the tax year 3 years prior to the effective year. You may request a new initial determination beginning with the date you receive a notice from us regarding your income-related monthly adjustment amount until the end of the effective year, with one exception. If you receive the notice during the last 3 months of a calendar year, you may request a new initial determination beginning with the date you receive the notice until March 31 of the following year. We will follow the rules and procedures in §§ 418.1110(b) and 418.1140(b) to make a new initial determination and any necessary retroactive adjustments back to January 1 of the effective year, or the first month you were enrolled in Medicare Part B in the effective year if later than January.

(2) You provide a copy of an amended tax return filed with IRS, as defined in § 418.1010(b)(1). We will use your amended tax return for the same tax year as the year used to determine your income-related monthly adjustment amount. You must request the new initial determination within the timeframe described in § 418.1150.

(3) You provide proof that the tax return information about your modified adjusted gross income or tax filing status IRS gave us is incorrect. We will use proof that you obtain from IRS of a correction of your tax return information for the same tax year instead of the information that was provided to us by IRS, as explained in § 418.1335(a). You may request a new initial determination at any time after you receive a notice from us regarding your income-related monthly adjustment amount if you have such proof. We will use the rules and procedures in § 418.1335.

(4) You have a major life-changing event. You may request a new initial determination based on a major life-changing event when you meet all the requirements described in § 418.1201. You may make such a request at any time during the calendar year in which you experience a significant reduction in your modified adjusted gross income caused by a major life-changing event. When you have a major life-changing event that occurs in the last 3 months of a calendar year and your modified adjusted gross income for that year is significantly reduced as a result of the event, you may request that we make a new initial determination based on your major life-changing event from the date of the event until March 31 of the next year. We will follow the rules in § 418.1230 when we make a new initial determination based on your major life-changing event.

(b) If a request for a new initial determination based on any of the circumstances in paragraph (a) of this section is made after the time frame provided for each type of listed circumstance, we will review the request under the rules in § 404.911 of this chapter to determine if there is good cause for a late request.

(c) We will notify you of the new initial determination as described in § 418.1315.

(d) We will dismiss your request to make a new initial determination if it does not meet one of the circumstances specified in paragraphs (a)(1) through (a)(4) of this section. Our dismissal of your request for a new initial determination is not an initial determination subject to further administrative or judicial review.

§ 418.1315 How will we notify you and what information will we provide about our initial determination?

(a) We will mail a written notice of all initial determinations to you. The notice of the initial determination will state the important facts and give the reasons for our conclusions. Generally, we will not send a notice if your income-related monthly adjustment amount stops because of your death.

(b) The written notice that we send will tell you:

(1) What our initial determination is;

(2) What modified adjusted gross income information we used to make our determination;

(3) The reason for our determination;

(4) The effect of the initial determination; and

(5) Your right to a reconsideration or a new initial determination.

§ 418.1320 What is the effect of an initial determination?

An initial determination is binding unless you request a reconsideration within the time period described in §§ 404.909 and 404.911 of this chapter or we revise the initial determination or issue a new initial determination.

§ 418.1322 How will a Medicare prescription drug coverage income-related monthly adjustment amount determination for the effective year affect your Medicare Part B?

If we make an income-related monthly adjustment amount determination for you for the effective year under subpart C of this part (Medicare Prescription Drug Coverage Income–Related Monthly Adjustment Amount), we will apply that income-related monthly adjustment amount determination under this subpart to determine your Part D income-related monthly adjustment amount for the same effective year. Therefore, if you become enrolled in Medicare Part B in the effective year after we make an income-related monthly adjustment amount determination about your Medicare prescription drug coverage, the income-related monthly adjustment amount determination for your Medicare prescription drug coverage will also be used to determine your Medicare Part B income-related monthly adjustment amount. Any change in your net benefit due will be accompanied by a letter explaining the change in your net benefit and your right to appeal the change.

[75 FR 75890, Dec. 7, 2010; 77 FR 43498, July 25, 2012]

§ 418.1325 When may you request a reconsideration?

If you are dissatisfied with our initial determination about your income-related monthly adjustment amount, you may request that we reconsider it. In addition, a person who shows that his or her rights may be adversely affected by the initial determination may request a reconsideration. We may accept requests for reconsideration that are filed by electronic or other means that we determine to be appropriate. Subject to the provisions of this section and § 418.1330, when you request a reconsideration, we will use the rules in §§ 404.907 through 404.922 of this chapter.

§ 418.1330 Can you request a reconsideration when you believe that the IRS information we used is incorrect?

If you request a reconsideration solely because you believe that the information that IRS gave us is incorrect, we will dismiss your request for a reconsideration and notify you to obtain proof of a correction from IRS and request a new initial determination (§ 418.1335).

Our dismissal of your request for reconsideration is not an initial determination subject to further administrative or judicial review.

§ 418.1335 What should you do if our initial determination is based on modified adjusted gross income information you believe to be incorrect?

If you believe that IRS or you provided incorrect modified adjusted gross income information to us that we used to determine your income-related monthly adjustment amount, you can request information from us on how to contact IRS regarding the information we used.

(a) If IRS determines that the information it provided is not correct, IRS will provide you with documentation of the error, such as a copy of your Federal income tax return. If you would like us to use the revised or corrected information to determine your income-related monthly adjustment amount, you will need to request that we use that information and provide us with the IRS documentation confirming the error. We will make any necessary retroactive corrections as described in § 418.1110(d) to your income-related monthly adjustment amount.

(b) If you provided information to us about your modified adjusted gross income that we used to determine your income-related monthly adjustment amount, and that information is not correct, you may provide revised or corrected information. We will use the revised or corrected information if it reduces or eliminates your income-related monthly adjustment amount. We will make any necessary retroactive corrections as described in § 418.1110 to your income-related monthly adjustment amount. If you are providing corrected information about a more recent tax year's modified adjusted gross income that we used due to your major life-changing event, as described in § 418.1240, we will use the rules in § 418.1245 to determine how it will affect your income-related monthly adjustment amount.

§ 418.1340 What are the rules for our administrative review process?

To the extent that they are not inconsistent with the rules in this subpart for making initial determinations and reconsidered determinations, we will use the same rules for the administrative review process that we use for determinations and decisions about your rights regarding non-medical issues under title II of the Act, as described in subpart J of part 404 of this chapter. We will accept oral requests as well as the written requests required in subpart J of part 404 of this chapter for requesting administrative review of our determination. If you are dissatisfied with our reconsidered determination, you may request review in accordance with § 418.1350 for this subpart. A request for a new initial determination, described in § 418.1310, is not the same as a request for reconsideration or further administrative review.

§ 418.1345 Is reopening of an initial or reconsidered determination made by us ever appropriate?

We may reopen an initial or reconsidered determination made by us when the conditions for reopening are met as described in § 404.988 of this chapter. We will use the rules in §§ 404.987 through 404.991a of this chapter when we reopen determinations made by us.

§ 418.1350 What are the rules for review of a reconsidered determination or an administrative law judge decision?

You may request a hearing before an OMHA administrative law judge consistent with HHS' regulations at 42 CFR part 405. You may seek further review of the administrative law judge's decision by requesting MAC review and judicial review in accordance with HHS' regulations.

[78 FR 57260, Sept. 18, 2013; 79 FR 11706, March 3, 2014]

§ 418.1355 What are the rules for reopening a decision by an administrative law judge of the Office of Medicare Hearings and Appeals (OMHA) or by the Medicare Appeals Council (MAC)?

The rules in 42 CFR 405.980 through 405.986 govern reopenings of decisions by an administrative law judge of the OMHA and decisions by the MAC. A decision by an administrative law judge of the OMHA may be reopened by the administrative law judge or by the MAC. A decision by the MAC may be reopened only by the MAC.

SUBPART C—INCOME-RELATED MONTHLY ADJUSTMENTS TO MEDICARE PRESCRIPTION DRUG COVERAGE PREMIUMS

Authority: Secs. 702(a)(5), 1860D–13(a) and (c) of the Social Security Act (42 U.S.C. 902(a)(5), 1395w–113(a) and (c)).

Source: 75 FR 75891, Dec. 7, 2010; 77 FR 43498, July 25, 2012, unless otherwise noted.

INTRODUCTION, GENERAL PROVISIONS, AND DEFINITIONS

§ 418.2001 What is this subpart about?

This subpart implements sections 1860D–13(a)(7) and 1860D–13(c)(4) of the Social Security Act (the Act), as added by section 3308 of the Affordable Care Act (Pub.L. 111–148). Section 3308(a) establishes an income-related monthly adjustment to Medicare prescription drug coverage premiums. Persons enrolled in Medicare prescription drug plans, Medicare Advantage plans with prescription drug coverage, Programs of All–Inclusive Care for the Elderly plans, and cost plans offering prescription drug coverage who have modified adjusted gross income over a threshold amount established in the statute will pay an income-related monthly adjustment amount in addition to their Medicare prescription drug coverage plan's monthly premium and any applicable premium increases as described in 42 CFR 423.286. The regulations in this subpart explain how we determine whether you are required to pay an income-related monthly adjustment amount, and if you are, the amount of your adjustment. We have divided the rules into the following groups of sections:

(a) Sections 418.2001 through 418.2010 contain the introduction, a statement of the general purpose of the income-related monthly adjustment amount, general provisions that apply to the income-related monthly adjustment amount, and definitions of terms that we use in this subpart.

(b) Sections 418.2101 through 418.2150 describe what information about your modified adjusted gross income we will use to determine if you are required to pay an income-related monthly adjustment amount. In these sections, we also describe how the income-related monthly adjustment amount will affect your total Medicare prescription drug coverage premium.

(c) Sections 418.2201 through 418.2270 contain an explanation of the standards that you must meet for us to grant your request to use modified adjusted gross income information that you provide for a more recent tax year rather than the information described in paragraph (b) of this section. These sections explain when we may consider such a request, and the evidence that you will be required to provide. These sections also explain when an income-related monthly adjustment amount determination based on information you provide will be effective, and how long it will remain in effect. Additionally, these sections describe how we make retroactive adjustments of the income-related monthly adjustment amount based on information you provide, updated information you provide, and information we later receive from the Internal Revenue Service.

(d) Sections 418.2301 through 418.2355 explain how we will notify you of our determination regarding your income-related monthly adjustment amount and contain the rules that we will apply when you disagree with our determination. These sections explain your appeal rights and the circumstances under which you may request that we make a new initial determination of your income-related monthly adjustment amount.

§ 418.2005 Purpose and administration.

(a) The purpose of the income-related monthly adjustment amount is for beneficiaries who have modified adjusted gross income above an established threshold to reimburse the Federal Government for a portion of the Federal subsidy of the Medicare prescription drug coverage. Persons who have modified adjusted gross income above the thresholds described in § 418.2105 will pay an income-related monthly adjustment amount in addition to the premium for their prescription drug coverage. The income-related monthly adjustment amount due will be determined based on the base beneficiary premium amount that represents 25.5 percent of the cost of the basic Medicare prescription drug coverage. The application of an income-related monthly adjustment amount results in an increase in the total amount that those who are affected pay for Medicare prescription drug coverage plans. A person who has modified adjusted gross income above the threshold amount will pay:

(1) The Medicare prescription drug coverage plan monthly premium; plus

(2) Any applicable increase for late enrollment or reenrollment;

(3) An income-related monthly adjustment amount; and

(b) The Centers for Medicare & Medicaid Services in the Department of Health and Human Services establishes rules for eligibility for Medicare prescription drug coverage and enrollment in Medicare prescription drug coverage plans, as well as premium penalties for late enrollment or reenrollment (42 CFR 423.30 through 423.56).

(c) We use information from CMS about enrollment in Medicare prescription drug coverage plans to determine the records that we must send to the IRS.

(d) We use information that we get from the IRS to determine if persons enrolled in Medicare prescription drug coverage plans are required to pay an income-related monthly adjustment amount. We also change income-related monthly adjustment amount determinations using information you provide under certain circumstances. In addition, we notify beneficiaries when the social security benefit amounts they receive will change based on our income-related monthly adjustment amount determination.

§ 418.2010 Definitions.

(a) Terms relating to the Act and regulations. For the purposes of this subpart:

(1) Administrator means the Administrator of CMS in HHS.

(2) ALJ means administrative law judge.

(3) CMS means the Centers for Medicare & Medicaid Services in HHS.

(4) Commissioner means the Commissioner of Social Security.

(5) HHS means the Department of Health and Human Services, which oversees the Centers for Medicare & Medicaid Services (CMS), the Office of Medicare Hearings and Appeals (OMHA) and the Medicare Appeals Council (MAC)

(6) IRS means the Internal Revenue Service in the Department of the Treasury.

(7) MAC means the Medicare Appeals Council in HHS.

(8) Medicare Prescription Drug Coverage Plan means a Medicare prescription drug plan, a Medicare Advantage plan with prescription drug coverage, a Program for All-inclusive Care for the Elderly plan offering qualified prescription drug coverage, or a cost plan offering qualified prescription drug coverage.

(9) OMHA means the Office of Medicare Hearings and Appeals in HHS.

(10) Section means a section of the regulations in this part unless the context indicates otherwise.

(11) The Act means the Social Security Act, as amended.

(12) Title means a title of the Act.

(13) We, our, or us means the Social Security Administration (SSA).

(b) Miscellaneous. For the purposes of this subpart:

(1) Amended tax return means a Federal income tax return for which an individual or couple has filed an amended tax return that has been accepted by the IRS.

(2) Effective year means the calendar year for which we make an income-related monthly adjustment amount determination.

(3) Federal premium subsidy is the portion of the cost of providing Medicare prescription drug coverage that is paid by the Federal Government. The Federal Government pays this amount to Medicare Prescription Drug coverage Plans from payments made into the Medicare Prescription Drug Account in the Federal Supplementary Medical Insurance Trust Fund.

(4) Income-related monthly adjustment amount is an additional amount of premium that you will pay for Medicare prescription drug coverage if you have modified adjusted gross income above the threshold described in 418.2105.

(5) Modified adjusted gross income is your adjusted gross income as defined by the Internal Revenue Code, plus the following forms of tax-exempt income:

(i) Tax-exempt interest income;

(ii) Income from United States savings bonds used to pay higher education tuition and fees;

(iii) Foreign earned income;

(iv) Income derived from sources within Guam, American Samoa, or the Northern Mariana Islands; and

(v) Income from sources within Puerto Rico.

(6) Modified adjusted gross income ranges are the groupings of modified adjusted gross income above the threshold. There are four ranges for most individuals, based on their tax filing status. There are two ranges for those with a tax filing status of married, filing separately, who also lived with their spouse for part of the year. The dollar amounts of the modified adjusted gross income ranges are specified in § 418.2115.

(7) Premium is a payment that an enrolled beneficiary pays for Medicare prescription drug coverage to a Medicare prescription drug plan, a Medicare Advantage plan with prescription drug coverage, a Program of All–Inclusive Care for the Elderly Plan offering qualified prescription drug coverage, or a cost plan offering qualified prescription drug coverage. The rules that CMS use annually to establish premium amounts for Medicare prescription drug coverage are contained in 42 CFR 423.286.

(8) Representative means, for the purposes of the initial determination and reconsidered determination, an individual as defined in § 404.1703 of this chapter, and for purposes of an ALJ hearing or review by the MAC, an individual as defined in 42 CFR 423.560.

(9) Tax filing status means the filing status shown on your individual income tax return. It may be single, married filing jointly, married filing separately, head of household, or qualifying widow(er) with dependent child.

(10) Tax year means the year for which you have filed or will file your Federal income tax return with the IRS.

(11) Threshold means a modified adjusted gross income amount above which you will have to pay an income-related monthly adjustment amount described in paragraph (b)(4) of this section. The dollar amount of the threshold is specified in § 418.2105.

(12) You or your means the person or representative of the person who is subject to the income-related monthly adjustment amount.

DETERMINATION OF THE INCOME–RELATED MONTHLY ADJUSTMENT AMOUNT

§ 418.2101 What is the income-related monthly adjustment amount?

(a) The income-related monthly adjustment amount is an amount that you will pay in addition to the Medicare prescription drug coverage plan monthly premium, plus any applicable increase in that premium as described in 42 CFR 423.286, for your Medicare prescription drug coverage plan when your modified adjusted gross income is above the threshold described in § 418.2105.

(b) Your income-related monthly adjustment amount is based on your applicable modified adjusted gross income as described in § 418.2115 and your tax filing status.

(c) We will determine your income-related monthly adjustment amount using the method described in § 418.2120.

§ 418.2105 What is the threshold?

(a) The threshold is a level of modified adjusted gross income above which you will have to pay the income-related monthly adjustment amount.

(b) For calendar years 2011 through and including 2019, the modified adjusted gross income threshold is $85,000 for individuals with a Federal income tax filing status of single, married filing separately, head of household, and qualifying widow(er) with dependent child. The threshold is $170,000 for individuals with a Federal income tax filing status of married filing jointly.

(c) Starting at the end of calendar year 2019 and for each calendar year thereafter, CMS will set the threshold amounts for the following year. CMS will publish the threshold amounts annually in the Federal Register. Published threshold amounts will be effective January 1 of the next calendar year, and remain unchanged for the full calendar year.

§ 418.2110 What is the effective date of our initial determination about your income-related monthly adjustment amount?

(a) Generally, an income-related monthly adjustment amount determination will be effective for all months that you are enrolled in a prescription drug coverage plan during the year for which we determine you must pay an income-related monthly adjustment amount.

(b) When we have used modified adjusted gross income information from the IRS for the tax year 3 years prior to the effective year to determine your income-related monthly adjustment amount, and modified adjusted gross income information for the tax year 2 years prior later becomes available from the IRS, we will review the new information to determine if we should revise our initial determination concerning the income-related monthly adjustment amount. If we revise our initial determination, the effective date of the new initial determination will be January 1 of the effective year, or the first month your enrollment or re-enrollment in a Medicare prescription drug coverage plan became effective if later than January.

(c) When we use your amended tax return, as described in § 418.2150, the effective date will be January 1 of the year(s) that is affected, or the first month in that year that your enrollment or re-enrollment in a Medicare prescription drug coverage plan became effective if later than January.

Example: You are enrolled in Medicare prescription drug coverage throughout 2011. We use your 2009 modified adjusted gross income as reported to us by the IRS to determine your 2011 income-related monthly adjustment amount. In 2012, you submit to us a copy of your 2009 amended tax return that you filed with the IRS. The modified adjusted gross income reported on your 2009 amended tax return is significantly less than originally reported to the IRS. We use the modified adjusted gross income reported on your 2009 amended tax return to determine your income-related monthly adjustment amount. That income-related monthly adjustment amount is effective January 1, 2011. We will retroactively correct any differences between the amount paid in 2011 and the amount you should have paid based on the amended tax return.

(d) When we use evidence that you provide to proves the IRS modified adjusted gross income information we used was incorrect, as described in § 418.2335, the effective date will be January of the year(s) that is affected or the first month in that year that your enrollment or re-enrollment in a Medicare prescription drug coverage plan became effective if later than January.

(e) When we use information from a more recent tax year that you provide due to a major life-changing event, as described in § 418.2201, the effective date is described in § 418.2230.

§ 418.2112 Paying your income-related monthly adjustment amount.

(a) We will deduct the income-related monthly adjustment amount from your Social Security benefits if they are sufficient to cover the amount owed. If the amount of your Social Security benefits is not sufficient to pay the full amount of your income-related monthly adjustment amount, CMS will bill you for the full amount owed.

(b) If you do not receive Social Security or Railroad Retirement Board benefits, but you receive benefits from the Office of Personnel Management, the Office of Personnel Management will deduct the income-related monthly adjustment amount from your benefits if they are sufficient to cover the amount owed. If the amount of your Office of Personnel Management benefits is not sufficient to pay the full amount of your income-related monthly adjustment amount, CMS will bill you for the full amount owed.

(c) If you do not receive Social Security, Railroad Retirement Board, or Office of Personnel Management benefits, CMS will bill you for your income-related monthly adjustment amount.

§ 418.2115 What are the modified adjusted gross income ranges?

(a) We list the modified adjusted gross income ranges for the calendar years 2011 through and including 2017, 2018, and beginning in 2019 for each Federal tax filing category in paragraphs (b), (c) and (d) of this section. We will use your modified adjusted gross income amount together with your tax filing status to determine the amount of your income-related monthly adjustment for these calendar years.

(b) The modified adjusted gross income ranges for individuals with a Federal tax filing status of single, head of household, qualifying widow(er) with dependent child, and married filing separately when the individual has lived apart from his/her spouse for the entire tax year for the year we use to make our income-related monthly adjustment amount determination are as follows:

(1) For calendar years 2011 through and including 2017—

(i) Greater than $85,000 but less than or equal to $107,000;

(ii) Greater than $107,000 but less than or equal to $160,000;

(iii) Greater than $160,000 but less than or equal to $214,000; and

(iv) Greater than $214,000.

(2) For calendar year 2018—

(i) Greater than $85,000 but less than $107,000;

(ii) Greater than $107,000 but less than $133,500;

(iii) Greater than $133,500 but less than $160,000; and

(iv) Greater than $160,000.

(3) For calendar years beginning in 2019—

(i) Greater than $85,000 but less than or equal to $107,000;

(ii) Greater than $107,000 but less than or equal to $133,500;

(iii) Greater than $133,500 but less than or equal to $160,000;

(iv) Greater than $160,000 but less than $500,000; and

(v) Greater than or equal to $500,000.

(c) The modified adjusted gross income ranges for individuals who are married and filed a joint tax return for the tax year we use to make the income-related monthly adjustment amount determination are as follows.

(1) For calendar years 2011 through 2017—

(i) Greater than $170,000 but less than or equal to $214,000;

(ii) Greater than $214,000 but less than or equal to $320,000;

(iii) Greater than $320,000 but less than or equal to $428,000; and

(iv) Greater than $428,000.

(2) For calendar year 2018—

(i) Greater than $170,000 but less than or equal to $214,000;

(ii) Greater than $214,000 but less than or equal to $267,000;

(iii) Greater than $267,000 but less than or equal to $320,000; and

(iv) Greater than $320,000.

(3) For calendar years beginning in 2019—

(i) Greater than $170,000 but less than or equal to $214,000;

(ii) Greater than $214,000 but less than or equal to $267,000;

(iii) Greater than $267,000 but less than or equal to $320,000;

(iv) Greater than $320,000 but less than $750,000; and

(v) Greater than or equal to $750,000.

(d) The modified adjusted gross income ranges for married individuals who file a separate return and have lived with their spouse at any time during the tax year we use to make the income-related monthly adjustment amount determination are as follows:

(1) For calendar years 2011 through and including 2017—

(i) Greater than $85,000 but less than or equal to $129,000; and

(ii) Greater than $129,000.

(2) For calendar year 2018—Greater than $85,000.

(3) For calendar years beginning in 2019—

(i) Greater than $85,000 but less than $415,000; and

(ii) Greater than or equal to $415,000.

(e)(1) Subject to paragraph (e)(2) of this section, in 2019, CMS will set the modified adjusted gross income ranges for 2020 and publish them in the Federal Register. In each year thereafter, CMS will set the modified adjusted gross income ranges by increasing the preceding year's ranges by any percentage increase in the Consumer Price Index rounded to the nearest $1,000 and will publish the amounts for the following year in September of each year.

(2) The amounts listed in paragraphs (b), (c), and (d) of $415,000, $500,000, and $750,000 will not be adjusted under paragraph (e)(1) of this section until 2028. Beginning in 2027, and in each year thereafter, CMS will adjust these range amounts for the following year under paragraph (e)(1) of this section and publish the updated ranges in the Federal Register.

[83 FR 55630, Nov. 7, 2018]

§ 418.2120 How do we determine your income-related monthly adjustment amount?

(a) We will determine your income-related monthly adjustment amount by using your tax filing status and modified adjusted gross income.

(b) Tables of applicable percentage. The tables in paragraphs (b)(1) through (b)(3) of this section contain the modified adjusted gross income ranges for calendar years 2011 through and including 2017, 2018, and 2019, and the corresponding percentage of the cost of basic Medicare prescription drug coverage that individuals with modified adjusted gross incomes that fall within each of the ranges will pay. The monthly dollar amounts will be determined by CMS using the formula in section 1860D–13(a)(7)(B) of the Act. Based on your tax filing status for the tax year we use to make a determination about your income-related monthly adjustment amount, we will determine which table is applicable to you. We will use your modified adjusted gross income to determine which income-related monthly adjustment amount to apply to you. The dollar amounts used for each of the ranges of income-related monthly adjustment will be set annually after 2019 as described in paragraph (c) of this section. The modified adjusted gross income ranges will be adjusted annually after 2019 as described in § 418.2115(e).

(1) General tables of applicable percentages. If your filing status for your Federal income taxes for the tax year we use is single; head of household; qualifying widow(er) with dependent child; or married filing separately and you lived apart from your spouse for the entire tax year, we will use the general tables of applicable percentages. When your modified adjusted gross income for the year we use is in the range listed in the left column in the following tables, you will pay an amount based on the percentage listed in the right column, which represents a percentage of the cost of basic Medicare prescription drug coverage.

Table 1 to paragraph (b)(1): Modified adjusted gross income effective in 2011-2017	Beneficiary percentage (percent)
Greater than $85,000 but less than or equal to $107,000	35
Greater than $107,000 but less than or equal to $160,000	50
Greater than $160,000 but less than or equal to $214,000	65
Greater than $214,000	80

Table 2 to paragraph (b)(1): Modified adjusted gross income effective in 2018	Beneficiary percentage (percent)
Greater than $85,000 but less than or equal to $107,000	35
Greater than $107,000 but less than or equal to $133,500	50
Greater than $133,500 but less than or equal to $160,000	65
Greater than $160,000	80

Table 3 to paragraph (b)(1): Modified adjusted gross income effective beginning in 2019	Beneficiary percentage (percent)

Greater than $85,000 but less than or equal to $107,000	35
Greater than $107,000 but less than or equal to $133,500	50
Greater than $133,500 but less than or equal to $160,000	65
Greater than $160,000 but less than $500,000	80
Greater than or equal to $500,000	85

(2) *Tables of applicable percentages for joint returns.* If your Federal tax filing status is married filing jointly for the tax year we use and your modified adjusted gross income for that tax year is in the range listed in the left column in the following tables, you will pay an amount based on the percentage listed in the right column, which represents a percentage of the cost of basic Medicare prescription drug coverage.

Table 1 to paragraph (b)(2): Modified adjusted gross income effective in 2011-2017	Beneficiary percentage (percent)
Greater than $170,000 but less than or equal to $214,000	35
Greater than $214,000 but less than or equal to $320,000	50
Greater than $320,000 but less than or equal to $428,000	65
Greater than $428,000	80

Table 2 to paragraph (b)(2): Modified adjusted gross income effective in 2018	Beneficiary percentage (percent)
Greater than $170,000 but less than or equal to $214,000	35
Greater than $214,000 but less than or equal to $267,000	50
Greater than $267,000 but less than or equal to $320,000	65
Greater than $320,000	80

Table 3 to paragraph (b)(2): Modified adjusted gross income effective beginning in 2019	Beneficiary percentage (percent)
Greater than $170,000 but less than or equal to $214,000	35
Greater than $214,000 but less than or equal to $267,000	50
Greater than $267,000 but less than or equal to $320,000	65
Greater than $320,000 but less than $750,000	80
Greater than or equal to $750,000	85

(3) *Tables of applicable percentages for married individuals filing separate returns.* If, for the tax year we use, your Federal tax filing status is married filing separately, you lived with your spouse at some time during that tax year, and your modified adjusted gross income is in the range listed in the left column in the

following tables, you will pay an amount based on the percentage listed in the right column, which represents a percentage of the cost of basic Medicare prescription drug coverage.

Table 1 to paragraph (b)(3): Modified adjusted gross income effective in 2011-2017	Beneficiary percentage (percent)
Greater than $85,000 but less than or equal to $129,000	65
Greater than $129,000	80

Table 2 to paragraph (b)(3): Modified adjusted gross income effective in 2018	Beneficiary percentage (percent)
Greater than $85,000	80

Table 3 to paragraph (b)(3): Modified adjusted gross income effective beginning in 2019	Beneficiary percentage (percent)
Greater than $85,000 but less than $415,000 ...	80
Greater than or equal to $415,000	85

(c) For each year after 2019, CMS will announce the modified adjusted gross income ranges for the income-related monthly adjustment amount described in paragraph (b) of this section.

[83 FR 55631, Nov. 7, 2018]

§ 418.2125 How will the income-related monthly adjustment amount affect your total Medicare prescription drug coverage premium?

(a) If you must pay an income-related monthly adjustment amount, your total Medicare prescription drug coverage premium will be the sum of:

(1) Your prescription drug coverage monthly premium, as determined by your plan; plus

(2) Any applicable increase in the prescription drug coverage monthly premium as described in 42 CFR 423.286; plus

(3) Your income-related monthly adjustment amount.

(b) Regardless of the method you use to pay your Medicare prescription drug coverage premiums to your Medicare prescription drug coverage plan, you will pay any income-related monthly adjustment amount you owe using the method described in 418.2112.

§ 418.2135 What modified adjusted gross income information will we use to determine your income-related monthly adjustment amount?

We will follow the rules in § 418.1135, except that any references in that section to regulations in subpart B of this part shall be treated as references to the corresponding regulation in this subpart.

§ 418.2140 What will happen if the modified adjusted gross income information from the IRS is different from the modified adjusted gross income information we used to determine your income-related monthly adjustment amount?

We will follow the rules in § 418.1140, except that any references in that section to regulations in subpart B of this part shall be treated as references to the corresponding regulation in this subpart.

§ 418.2145 How do we determine your income-related monthly adjustment amount if the IRS does not provide information about your modified adjusted gross income?

We will follow the rules in § 418.1145, except that any references in that section to regulations in subpart B of this part shall be treated as references to the corresponding regulation in this subpart.

§ 418.2150 When will we use your amended tax return filed with the IRS?

We will follow the rules in § 418.1150, except that any references in that section to regulations in subpart B of this part shall be treated as references to the corresponding regulation in this subpart.

DETERMINATIONS USING A MORE RECENT TAX YEAR'S MODIFIED ADJUSTED GROSS INCOME

§ 418.2201 When will we determine your income-related monthly adjustment amount based on the modified adjusted gross income information that you provide for a more recent tax year?

We will follow the rules in § 418.1201, except that any references in that section to regulations in subpart B of this part shall be treated as references to the corresponding regulation in this subpart.

§ 418.2205 What is a major life-changing event?

We will follow the rules in § 418.1205, except that any references in that section to regulations in subpart B of this part shall be treated as references to the corresponding regulation in this subpart.

§ 418.2210 What is not a major life-changing event?

We will follow the rules in § 418.1210, except that any references in that section to regulations in subpart B of this part shall be treated as references to the corresponding regulation in this subpart.

§ 418.2215 What is a significant reduction in your income?

We will follow the rules in § 418.1215, except that any references in that section to regulations in subpart B of this part shall be treated as references to the corresponding regulation in this subpart.

§ 418.2220 What is not a significant reduction in your income?

We will follow the rules in § 418.1220, except that any references in that section to regulations in subpart B of this part shall be treated as references to the corresponding regulation in this subpart.

§ 418.2225 Which more recent tax year will we use?

We will follow the rules in § 418.1225, except that any references in that section to regulations in subpart B of this part shall be treated as references to the corresponding regulation in this subpart.

§ 418.2230 What is the effective date of an income-related monthly adjustment amount initial determination based on a more recent tax year?

We will follow the rules in § 418.1230, except that any references in that section to regulations in subpart B of this part shall be treated as references to the corresponding regulation in this subpart.

§ 418.2235 When will we stop using your more recent tax year's modified adjusted gross income to determine your income-related monthly adjustment amount?

We will follow the rules in § 418.1235, except that any references in that section to regulations in subpart B of this part shall be treated as references to the corresponding regulation in this subpart.

§ 418.2240 Should you notify us if the information you gave us about your modified adjusted gross income for the more recent tax year changes?

We will follow the rules in § 418.1240, except that any references in that section to regulations in subpart B of this part shall be treated as references to the corresponding regulation in this subpart.

§ 418.2245 What will happen if you notify us that your modified adjusted gross income for the more recent tax year changes?

(a) If you notify us that your modified adjusted gross income for the more recent tax year has changed from what is in our records, we may make a new initial determination for each effective year involved. To make a new initial determination(s) we will take into account:

(1) The new modified adjusted gross income information for the more recent tax year you provide; and

(2) Any modified adjusted gross income information from the IRS, as described in § 418.2135, that we have available for each effective year; and

(3) Any modified adjusted gross income information from you, as described in § 418.2135, that we have available for each effective year.

(b) For each new initial determination that results in a change in your income-related monthly adjustment amount, we will make retroactive corrections that will apply to all enrolled months of the effective year.

(c) We will continue to use a new initial determination described in paragraph (a) of this section to determine additional yearly income-related monthly adjustment amount(s) until an event described in § 418.2235 occurs.

(d) We will make a new determination about your income-related monthly adjustment amount when we receive modified adjusted gross income for the effective year from the IRS, as described in § 418.1140(d).

§ 418.2250 What evidence will you need to support your request that we use a more recent tax year?

We will follow the rules in § 418.1250, except that any references in that section to regulations in subpart B of this part shall be treated as references to the corresponding regulation in this subpart.

§ 418.2255 What kind of evidence of a major life-changing event will you need to support your request for us to use a more recent tax year?

We will follow the rules in § 418.1255, except that any references in that section to regulations in subpart B of this part shall be treated as references to the corresponding regulation in this subpart.

§ 418.2260 What major life-changing event evidence will we not accept?

We will follow the rules in § 418.1260, except that any references in that section to regulations in subpart

B of this part shall be treated as references to the corresponding regulation in this subpart.

§ 418.2265 What kind of evidence of a significant modified adjusted gross income reduction will you need to support your request?

We will follow the rules in § 418.1265, except that any references in that section to regulations in subpart B of this part shall be treated as references to the corresponding regulation in this subpart.

§ 418.2270 What modified adjusted gross income evidence will we not accept?

We will follow the rules in § 418.1270, except that any references in that section to regulations in subpart B of this part shall be treated as references to the corresponding regulation in this subpart.

DETERMINATIONS AND THE ADMINISTRATIVE REVIEW PROCESS

§ 418.2301 What is an initial determination regarding your income-related monthly adjustment amount?

We will follow the rules in § 418.1301, except that any references in that section to regulations in subpart B of this part shall be treated as references to the corresponding regulation in this subpart.

§ 418.2305 What is not an initial determination regarding your income-related monthly adjustment amount?

We will follow the rules in § 418.1305, except that any references in that section to regulations in subpart B of this part shall be treated as references to the corresponding regulation in this subpart.

§ 418.2310 When may you request that we make a new initial determination?

We will follow the rules in § 418.1310, except that any references in that section to regulations in subpart B of this part shall be treated as references to the corresponding regulation in this subpart.

§ 418.2315 How will we notify you and what information will we provide about our initial determination?

We will follow the rules in § 418.1315, except that any references in that section to regulations in subpart B of this part shall be treated as references to the corresponding regulation in this subpart.

§ 418.2320 What is the effect of an initial determination?

We will follow the rules in § 418.1320, except that any references in that section to regulations in subpart B of this part shall be treated as references to the corresponding regulation in this subpart.

§ 418.2322 How will a Medicare Part B income-related monthly adjustment amount determination for the effective year affect your Medicare prescription drug coverage?

If we make an income-related monthly adjustment amount determination for you for the effective year under subpart B of this part (Medicare Part B Income–Related Monthly Adjustment Amount), we will apply that income-related monthly adjustment amount determination under this subpart to determine your Part D income-related monthly adjustment amount for the same effective year. Therefore, if you obtain Medicare prescription drug coverage in the effective year after we make an income-related monthly adjustment amount determination about your Medicare Part B, the income-related monthly adjustment amount determination we made for your Medicare Part B will also apply to your Medicare prescription drug coverage. Any change in your net benefit due will be accompanied by a letter explaining the change in your net benefit and your right to appeal the change.

§ 418.2325 When may you request a reconsideration?

We will follow the rules in § 418.1325, except that any references in that section to regulations in subpart B of this part shall be treated as references to the corresponding regulation in this subpart.

§ 418.2330 Can you request a reconsideration when you believe that the IRS information we used is incorrect?

If you request a reconsideration solely because you believe that the information that the IRS gave us is incorrect, we will dismiss your request for a reconsideration and notify you to obtain proof of a correction from the IRS and request a new initial determination (§ 418.2335). Our dismissal of your request for reconsideration is not an initial determination subject to further administrative or judicial review.

§ 418.2332 Can you request a reconsideration when you believe that the CMS information we used is incorrect?

If you request a reconsideration solely because you believe that the information that CMS gave us about your participation in a Medicare prescription drug coverage plan is incorrect, we will dismiss your request for a reconsideration and notify you that you must contact CMS to get your records corrected. Our dismissal of your request for reconsideration is not an initial determination subject to further administrative or judicial review.

§ 418.2335 What should you do if we base our initial determination on modified adjusted gross income information you believe to be incorrect?

We will follow the rules in § 418.1335, except that any references in that section to regulations in subpart B of this part shall be treated as references to the corresponding regulation in this subpart.

§ 418.2340 What are the rules for our administrative review process?

We will follow the rules in § 418.1340, except that any references in that section to regulations in subpart B of this part shall be treated as references to the corresponding regulation in this subpart.

§ 418.2345 Is reopening of an initial or reconsidered determination made by us ever appropriate?

We will follow the rules in § 418.1345, except that any references in that section to regulations in subpart B of this part shall be treated as references to the corresponding regulation in this subpart.

§ 418.2350 What are the rules for review of a reconsidered determination or an ALJ decision?

You may request a hearing before an OMHA administrative law judge consistent with HHS' regulations at 42 CFR part 423. You may seek further review of the administrative law judge's decision by requesting MAC review and judicial review in accordance with HHS' regulations.

§ 418.2355 What are the rules for reopening a decision by an ALJ of the Office of Medicare Hearings and Appeals (OMHA) or by the Medicare Appeals Council (MAC)?

The rules in 42 CFR 423.1980 through 423.1986 govern reopenings of decisions by an administrative law judge of the OMHA and decisions by the MAC. A decision by an administrative law judge of the OMHA may be reopened by the administrative law judge or the MAC. A decision by the MAC may be reopened only by the MAC.

SUBPART D—MEDICARE PART D SUBSIDIES

INTRODUCTION, GENERAL PROVISIONS, AND DEFINITIONS

§ 418.3001 What is this subpart about?

This subpart D relates to sections 1860D–1 through 1860D–24 of title XVIII of the Social Security Act (the Act) as added by section 101 of the Medicare Prescription Drug, Improvement, and Modernization Act of 2003 (Pub.L. 108–173). Sections 1860D–1 through 1860D–24 established Part D of title XVIII of the Act to create a Medicare program known as the Voluntary Prescription Drug Benefit Program. Section 1860D–14, codified into the Act by section 101, includes a provision for subsidies of prescription drug premiums and of Part D cost-sharing requirements for Medicare beneficiaries whose income and resources do not exceed certain levels. The regulations in this subpart explain how we decide whether you are eligible for a Part D premium subsidy as defined in 42 CFR 423.780 and cost-sharing subsidy as defined in 42 CFR 423.782. The rules are divided into the following groups of sections according to subject content:

(a) Sections 418.3001 through 418.3010 contain the introduction, a statement of the general purpose underlying the subsidy program for the Voluntary Prescription Drug Benefit Program under Medicare Part D, general provisions that apply to the subsidy program, a description of how we administer the program, and definitions of terms that we use in this subpart.

(b) Sections 418.3101 through 418.3125 contain the general requirements that you must meet in order to be eligible for a subsidy. These sections set forth the subsidy eligibility requirements of being a Medicare beneficiary, of having income and resources below certain levels, and of filing an application. These sections also explain when we will redetermine your eligibility for a subsidy and the period covered by a redetermination.

(c) Sections 418.3201 through 418.3230 contain the rules that relate to the filing of subsidy applications.

(d) Sections 418.3301 through 418.3350 contain the rules that explain how we consider your income (and your spouse's income, if applicable) and define what income we count when we decide whether you are eligible for a subsidy.

(e) Sections 418.3401 through 418.3425 contain the rules that explain how we consider your resources (and your spouse's resources, if applicable) and define what resources we count when we decide whether you are eligible for a subsidy.

(f) Sections 418.3501 through 418.3515 contain the rules that explain when we will adjust or when we will terminate your eligibility for a subsidy.

(g) Sections 418.3601 through 418.3680 contain the rules that we apply when you appeal our determination regarding your subsidy eligibility or our determination of whether you should receive a full or partial subsidy. They also contain the rules that explain that our decision is binding unless you file an action in Federal district court seeking review of our final decision and what happens if your case is remanded by a Federal court.

§ 418.3005 Purpose and administration of the program.

The purpose of the subsidy program is to offer help with the costs of prescription drug coverage for individuals who meet certain income and resources requirements under the law as explained in this subpart. The Centers for Medicare & Medicaid Services (CMS) in the Department of Health and Human Services has responsibility for administration of the Medicare program, including the new Medicare Part D Voluntary Prescription Drug Benefit Program. We notify Medicare beneficiaries who appear to have limited income, based on our records, about the availability of the subsidy if they are not already eligible for this help, and take applications for and determine the eligibility of individuals for a subsidy.

§ 418.3010 Definitions.

(a) Terms relating to the Act and regulations.

(1) CMS means the Centers for Medicare & Medicaid Services in the Department of Health and Human Services.

(2) Commissioner means the Commissioner of Social Security.

(3) Section means a section of the regulations in part 418 of this chapter unless the context indicates otherwise.

(4) The Act means the Social Security Act, as amended.

(5) Title means a title of the Act.

(6) We, our or us means the Social Security Administration (SSA).

(b) Miscellaneous.

(1) Claimant means the person who files an application for himself or herself or the person on whose behalf an application is filed.

(2) Date you receive a notice means 5 calendar days after the date on the notice, unless you show us you did not receive it within the 5–day period.

(3) Decision means the decision we make after a hearing.

(4) Determination means the initial determination that we make as defined in § 418.3605.

(5) Family size, for purposes of this subpart, means family size as defined in 42 CFR 423.772.

(6) Federal poverty line, for purposes of this subpart, has the same meaning as Federal poverty line in 42 CFR 423.772.

(7) Full-benefit dual eligible individual for purposes of this subpart, has the same meaning as full-benefit dual eligible individual in 42 CFR 423.772.

(8) Medicare beneficiary means an individual who is entitled to or enrolled in Medicare Part A (Hospital Insurance) or enrolled in Part B (Supplementary Medical Insurance) or both under title XVIII of the Act.

(9) Periods of limitations ending on Federal nonworkdays Title XVIII of the Act and regulations in this subpart require you to take certain actions within specified time periods or you may lose your right to a portion of or your entire subsidy. If any such period ends on a Saturday, Sunday, Federal legal holiday, or any other day all or part of which is declared to be a nonworkday for Federal employees by statute or Executive Order, you will have until the next Federal workday to take the prescribed action.

(10) Representative or personal representative means a personal representative as defined in 42 CFR 423.772.

(11) State, unless otherwise indicated, means:

(i) A State of the United States; or

(ii) The District of Columbia.

(12) Subsidy eligible individual, for purposes of this subpart, has the same meaning as subsidy eligible individual as defined in 42 CFR 423.773.

(13) Subsidy means an amount CMS will pay on behalf of Medicare beneficiaries who are eligible for a subsidy of their Medicare Part D costs. The amount of a subsidy for a Medicare beneficiary depends on the beneficiary's income as related to household size, resources, and late enrollment penalties (if any) as explained in 42 CFR 423.780 and 42 CFR 423.782. We do not determine the amount of the subsidy, only whether or not the individual is eligible for a full or partial subsidy.

(14) United States when used in a geographical sense means:

(i) The 50 States; and

(ii) The District of Columbia

(1) [1] You or your means the person who applies for the subsidy, the person for whom an application is filed or anyone who may consider applying for a subsidy.

ELIGIBILITY FOR A MEDICARE PRESCRIPTION DRUG SUBSIDY

§ 418.3101 How do you become eligible for a subsidy?

Unless you are deemed eligible as explained in § 418.3105 and 42 CFR 423.773(c), you are eligible for a Medicare Part D prescription drug subsidy if you meet all of the following requirements:

(a) You are entitled to or enrolled in Medicare Part A (Hospital Insurance) or enrolled in Medicare Part B

[1] So in original. See 70 FR 77677.

(Supplementary Medical Insurance) or both under title XVIII of the Act.

(b) You are enrolled in a Medicare prescription drug plan or Medicare Advantage plan with prescription drug coverage. We can also determine your eligibility for a subsidy before you enroll in one of the above programs. However, as explained in § 418.3225(b), if we determine that you would be eligible for a subsidy before you have enrolled in a Medicare prescription drug plan or Medicare Advantage plan with prescription drug coverage, you must enroll in one of these plans to actually receive a subsidy.

(c) You reside in the United States as defined in § 418.3010.

(d) You (and your spouse, if applicable) meet the income requirements as explained in §§ 418.3301 through 418.3350 and 42 CFR 423.773.

(e) You (and your spouse, if applicable) meet the resources requirements as explained in §§ 418.3401 through 418.3425 and 42 CFR 423.773.

(f) You or your personal representative file an application for a subsidy as explained in §§ 418.3201 through 418.3230.

§ 418.3105 Who does not need to file an application for a subsidy?

Regulations in 42 CFR 423.773(c) explain who is deemed eligible and does not need to file an application for a subsidy to be eligible for this assistance. Full-benefit dual eligible beneficiaries are in this category. If beneficiaries have deemed eligibility status because they receive Medicaid coverage, are enrolled in a Medicare Savings Program within their State, or receive SSI and have Medicare, then their subsidy is effective with the first month they have deemed eligibility status.

§ 418.3110 What happens when you apply for a subsidy?

(a) When you or your personal representative apply for a subsidy, we will ask for information that we need to determine if you meet all the requirements for a subsidy. You must give us complete information. If, based on the information you present to us, you do not meet all the requirements for eligibility listed in § 418.3101, or if one of the events listed in § 418.3115 exists, or you fail to submit information we request, we will deny your claim.

(b) If you meet all the requirements for eligibility listed in § 418.3101, or you meet all the requirements except for enrollment in a Medicare Part D plan or Medicare Advantage plan with prescription drug coverage, we will send you a notice telling you the following:

(1) You are eligible for a full or partial subsidy for a period not to exceed 1 year;

(2) What information we used to make this determination including how we calculated your income and resources;

(3) What you may do if your circumstances change as described in § 418.3120; and

(4) Your appeal rights.

(c) If you are not already enrolled with a Medicare prescription drug plan or a Medicare Advantage plan with prescription drug coverage, you must enroll in order to receive your subsidy.

(d) If you do not meet all the requirements for eligibility listed in § 418.3101 or if § 418.3115 applies to you except for enrollment in a Medicare Part D plan or Medicare Advantage plan with prescription drug coverage as described in § 418.3225, we will send you a notice telling you the following:

(1) You are not eligible for a subsidy;

(2) The information we used to make this determination including how we calculated your income or resources;

(3) You may reapply if your situation changes; and

(4) Your appeal rights.

§ 418.3115 What events will make you ineligible for a subsidy?

Generally, even if you meet the other requirements in §§ 418.3101 through 418.3125, we will deny your claim or you will lose your subsidy if any of the following apply to you:

(a) You lose entitlement to or are not enrolled in Medicare Part A and are not enrolled in Medicare Part B.

(b) You do not enroll or lose your enrollment in a Medicare Part D plan or Medicare Advantage plan with prescription drug coverage.

(c) You do not give us information we need to determine your eligibility and if eligible, whether you should receive a full or partial subsidy; or you do not give us information we need to determine whether you continue to be eligible for a subsidy and if eligible, whether you should receive a full or partial subsidy.

(d) You knowingly give us false or misleading information.

§ 418.3120 What happens if your circumstances change after we determine you are eligible for a subsidy?

(a) After we determine that you are eligible for a subsidy, your subsidy eligibility could change if:

(1) You marry.

(2) You and your spouse, who lives with you, divorce.

(3) Subject to the provisions of paragraph (b)(4) of this section, your spouse, who lives with you, dies.

(4) You and your spouse separate (i.e., you or your spouse move out of the household and you are no longer living with your spouse) unless the separation is a temporary absence as described in § 404.347 of this chapter.

(5) You and your spouse resume living together after having been separated.

(6) You and your spouse, who lives with you, have your marriage annulled.

(7) You (or your spouse, who lives with you, if applicable) expect your estimated annual income to increase or decrease in the next calendar year.

(8) You (or your spouse, who lives with you, if applicable) expect your resources to increase or decrease in the next calendar year.

(9) Your family size as defined in 42 CFR 423.772 has changed or will change (other than a change resulting from one of the events in paragraphs (a)(1) through (6) of this section).

(10) You become eligible for one of the programs listed in 42 CFR 423.773(c).

(b)(1) When you report one of the events listed in paragraphs (a)(1) through (a)(6) of this section, or we receive such a report from another source (e.g., a data exchange of reports of death), we will send you a redetermination form upon receipt of the report. You must return the completed form within 90 days of the date of the form.

(2) When you report one of the events listed in paragraphs (a)(7) through (a)(9) of this section or we receive such a report from another source (e.g., a data exchange involving income records), we will send you a redetermination form between August and December to evaluate the change. You must return the completed form to us within 30 days of the date of the form.

(3) If we increase, decrease, or terminate your subsidy as a result of the redetermination, we will send you a notice telling you:

(i) Whether you can receive a full or partial subsidy as described in 42 CFR 423.780 and 423.782.

(ii) How we calculated your income and resources;

(iii) When the change in your subsidy is effective;

(iv) Your appeal rights;

(v) What to do if your situation changes.

(4) If your spouse who lives with you dies, your spouse's death may result in changes in your income or resources that could decrease or eliminate your subsidy. If we are informed of the death of your spouse and the death would cause a decrease in or elimination of your subsidy, we will notify you that we will not immediately change your subsidy because of your spouse's death. We will defer your redetermination for 1 year from the month following the month we are notified of the death of your spouse, unless we receive a report of another event specified in 418.3120(a) that would affect your eligibility for a subsidy.

(c) If you become eligible for one of the programs listed in 42 CFR 423.773(c), CMS will notify you of any change in your subsidy.

[75 FR 81845, Dec. 29, 2010; 77 FR 2448, Jan. 18, 2012]

§ 418.3123 When is a change in your subsidy effective?

(a) If we redetermine your subsidy as described in § 418.3120(b)(1), any change in your subsidy will be effective the month following the month of your report.

(b) If we redetermine your subsidy as described in § 418.3120(b)(2), any change in your subsidy will be effective in January of the next year.

(c) If you do not return the redetermination form described in § 418.3120(b)(1), we will terminate your subsidy effective with the month following the expiration of the 90–day period described in § 418.3120(b)(1).

(d) If you do not return the redetermination forms described in § 418.3120(b)(2), we will terminate your subsidy effective in January of the next year.

(e) Special rule for widows and widowers. If your spouse who lives with you dies and the changes in your income or resources resulting from your spouse's death would decrease or eliminate your subsidy, we will defer your next redetermination for 1 year from the month following the month we are notified of the death of your spouse, unless we receive a report of another event specified in 418.3120(a) that would affect your eligibility for a subsidy.

[75 FR 81845, Dec. 29, 2010; 77 FR 2448, Jan. 18, 2012]

§ 418.3125 What are redeterminations?

(a) Redeterminations defined. A redetermination is a periodic review of your eligibility to make sure that you are still eligible for a subsidy and if so, to determine whether you should continue to receive a full or partial subsidy. This review deals with evaluating your income and resources (and those of your spouse, who lives with you) and will not affect past months of eligibility. It will be used to determine your future subsidy eligibility and whether you should receive a full or partial subsidy for future months. We will redetermine your eligibility if we made the initial determination of your eligibility or if you are deemed eligible because you receive SSI benefits. Rules regarding redeterminations of initial eligibility determinations made by a State are described in 42 CFR 423.774.

(b) When we make redeterminations.

(1) We will redetermine your subsidy eligibility within one year after we determine that you are eligible for the subsidy.

(2) After the first redetermination, we will redetermine your subsidy eligibility at intervals determined by the Commissioner. The length of time between redeterminations varies depending on the likelihood that your situation may change in a way that affects your eligibility and whether you should receive a full or partial subsidy.

(3) We may also redetermine your eligibility and whether you should receive a full or partial subsidy when you tell us of a change in your circumstances described in § 418.3120.

(4) We may redetermine your eligibility when we receive information from you or from data exchanges with Federal and State agencies that may affect whether you should receive a full or partial subsidy or your eligibility for the subsidy.

(5) We will also redetermine eligibility on a random sample of cases for quality assurance purposes. For each collection of sample cases, all factors affecting eligibility and/or whether you should receive a full or partial subsidy may be verified by contact with primary repositories of information relevant to each individual factor (e.g., we may contact employers to verify wage information). Consequently, we may contact a variety of other sources, in addition to recontacting you, to verify the completeness and accuracy of our information.

FILING OF APPLICATION

§ 418.3201 Must you file an application to become eligible for a subsidy?

Unless you are a person covered by § 418.3105, in addition to meeting other requirements, you or your personal representative must file an application to become eligible for a subsidy. If you believe you may be eligible for a subsidy, you should file an application. Filing a subsidy application does not commit you to participate in the Part D program. Filing an application will:

(a) Permit us to make a formal determination on your eligibility for the subsidy and whether you should receive a full or partial subsidy;

(b) Assure that you can receive the subsidy for any months that you are eligible and are enrolled in a Medicare Part D plan or Medicare Advantage plan with prescription drug coverage; and

(c) Give you the right to appeal if you disagree with our determination.

§ 418.3205 What makes an application a claim for a subsidy?

We will consider your application a claim for the subsidy if:

(a) You, or someone acting on your behalf as described in § 418.3215, complete an application on a form prescribed by us;

(b) You, or someone acting on your behalf as described in § 418.3215, file the application with us pursuant to § 418.3220; and

(c) You are alive on the first day of the month in which the application is filed.

§ 418.3210 What is a prescribed application for a subsidy?

If you choose to apply with SSA, you must file for the subsidy on an application prescribed by us. A prescribed application may include a printed form, an application our employees complete on computer screens, or an application available online on our Internet Web site (www.socialsecurity.gov). See § 418.3220 for places where an application for the subsidy may be filed and when it is considered filed.

§ 418.3215 Who may file your application for a subsidy?

You or your personal representative (as defined in 42 CFR 423.772) may complete and file your subsidy application.

§ 418.3220 When is your application considered filed?

(a) General rule. We consider an application for a subsidy as described in § 418.3210 to be filed with us on the day it is received by either one of our employees at one of our offices or by one of our employees who is authorized to receive it at a place other than one of our offices or it is considered filed on the day it is submitted electronically through our Internet Web site. If a State Medicaid agency forwards to us a subsidy application that you gave to it, we will consider the date you submitted that application to the State Medicaid agency as the filing date. (See 42 CFR 423.774 for applications filed with a State Medicaid agency.)

(b) Exceptions.

(1) When we receive an application that is mailed, we will assume that we received it 5 days earlier (unless you can show us that you did not receive it within the 5 days) and use the earlier date as the application filing date if it would result in another month of subsidy eligibility.

(2) We may consider an application to be filed on the date a written or oral inquiry about your subsidy eligibility is made, or the date we receive a partially completed Internet subsidy application from our Internet Web site where the requirements set forth in § 418.3230 are met.

§ 418.3225 How long will your application remain in effect?

(a) Your application will remain in effect until our determination or decision has become final and binding under § 418.3620. If you appeal our initial determination, the determination does not become final until we issue a decision on any appeal you have filed under § 418.3655 (see § 418.3675) or dismiss the request for a hearing under § 418.3670.

(b) If, at the time your application is filed or before our determination or decision becomes final and binding, you meet all the requirements for a subsidy as described in 42 CFR 423.773 except for enrollment in a Medicare Part D plan or Medicare Advantage plan with prescription drug coverage, we will send you a notice advising you of your eligibility for the subsidy and the requirement to enroll in such a plan.

(c) If you are not entitled to Medicare Part A and/or enrolled in Medicare Part B at the time your subsidy application is filed but you appear to be in an enrollment period, we will send you a notice advising you that we will not make a determination on your application until you become entitled to Medicare Part A and/or enrolled in Medicare Part B. If you are not entitled to Medicare Part A and/or enrolled in Medicare Part B at the time your application is filed and you do not appear to be in an enrollment period, we will send you a notice advising you that you are not eligible for the subsidy because you are not entitled to Medicare Part A and/or enrolled in Medicare Part B and explain your appeal rights.

§ 418.3230 When will we use your subsidy inquiry as your filing date?

If you or your personal representative (as defined in 42 CFR 423.772) make an oral or written inquiry about the subsidy, or partially complete an Internet subsidy application on our Web site, we will use the date of the inquiry or the date the partial Internet application was started as your filing date if the following requirements are met:

(a) The written or oral inquiry indicates your intent to file for the subsidy, or you submit a partially completed Internet application to us;

(b) The inquiry, whether in person, by telephone, or in writing, is directed to an office or an official described in § 418.3220, or a partially completed Internet subsidy application is received by us;

(c) You or your personal representative (as defined in 42 CFR 423.772) file an application (as defined in § 418.3210) within 60 days after the date of the notice we will send in response to the inquiry. The notice will say that we will make an initial determination of your eligibility for a subsidy, if an application is filed within 60 days after the date of the notice. We will send the notice to you. Where you are a minor or adjudged legally incompetent and your personal representative made the inquiry, we will send the notice to your personal representative; and

(d) You are alive on the first day of the month in which the application is filed.

INCOME

§ 418.3301 What is income?

Income is anything you and your spouse, who lives with you, receive in cash or in-kind that you can use to meet your needs for food and shelter. Income can be earned income or unearned income.

§ 418.3305 What is not income?

Some things you receive are not considered income because you cannot use them to meet your needs for food or shelter. The things that are not income for purposes of determining eligibility and whether you should receive a full or partial subsidy are described in § 416.1103 of this chapter.

§ 418.3310 Whose income do we count?

(a) We count your income. If you are married and live with your spouse in the month you file for a subsidy, or when we redetermine your eligibility for a subsidy as described in § 418.3125, we count your income and your spouse's income regardless of whether one or both of you apply or are eligible for the subsidy.

(b) We will determine your eligibility based on your income alone if you are not married or if you are married but you are separated from your spouse (i.e., you or your spouse move out of the household and you are no longer living with your spouse) at the time you apply for a subsidy or when we redetermine your eligibility for a subsidy as described in § 418.3125.

(c) If your subsidy is based on your income and your spouse's income and we redetermine your subsidy as described in § 418.3120(b)(1), we will stop counting the income of your spouse in the month following the month that we receive a report that your marriage ended due to death, divorce, or annulment; or a report that you and your spouse stopped living together.

(d) If your subsidy is based on your income and your spouse's income, we will continue counting the income of both you and your spouse if one of you is temporarily away from home as described in § 404.347 of this chapter.

§ 418.3315 What is earned income?

Earned income is defined in § 416.1110 of this chapter and may be in cash or in kind. We may count more of your earned income than you actually receive. We count gross income, which is more than you actually receive, if amounts are withheld from earned income because of a garnishment, or to pay a debt or other legal obligation such as taxes, or to make any other similar payments.

§ 418.3320 How do we count your earned income?

(a) Wages. We count your wages at the earliest of the following points: when you receive them, when they are credited to you, or when they are set aside for your use.

(b) Net earnings from self-employment. We count net earnings from self-employment on a taxable year basis. If you have net losses from self-employment, we deduct them from your other earned income. We do not deduct the net losses from your unearned income.

(c) Payments for services performed in a sheltered workshop or work activities center. We count payments you receive for services performed in a sheltered workshop or work activities center when you receive them or when they are set aside for your use.

(d) In-kind earned income. We count the current market value of in-kind earned income. For purposes of this part, we use the definition of current market value in § 416.1101 of this chapter. If you receive an item that is not fully paid for and you are responsible for the unpaid balance, only the paid-up value is income to you (see example in § 416.1123(c) of this chapter).

(e) Certain honoraria and royalties. We count honoraria for services rendered and royalty payments that you receive in connection with any publication of your work. We will consider these payments as available to you when you receive them, when they are credited to your account, or when they are set aside for your use, whichever is earliest.

(f) Period for which earned income is counted. For purposes of determining subsidy eligibility and, if eligible, whether you should receive a full or partial subsidy, we consider all of the countable earned income you receive (or expect to receive) during the year for which we are determining your eligibility for this subsidy. However, in the first year that you or your spouse apply for the subsidy, we consider all of the countable earned income you and your living-with spouse receive (or expect to receive) starting in the month for which we determine your eligibility based on your application for a subsidy through the end of the year for which we are determining your eligibility. If we count your income for only a portion of the year, the income limit for subsidy eligibility will be adjusted accordingly. For example, if we count your income for 6 consecutive months of the year (July through December), the income limit for subsidy eligibility will be half of the income limit applicable for the full year.

§ 418.3325 What earned income do we not count?

(a) While we must know the source and amount of all of your earned income, we do not count all of it to determine your subsidy eligibility and whether you should receive a full or partial subsidy. We apply these income exclusions in the order listed in paragraph (b) of this section to your income. We never reduce your earned income below zero or apply any unused earned income exclusion to unearned income.

(b) For the year or partial year that we are determining your eligibility for the subsidy, we do not count as earned income:

(1) Any refund of Federal income taxes you or your living-with spouse receive under section 32 of the Internal Revenue Code (relating to the earned income tax credit) and payment you receive from an employer under section 3507 of the Internal Revenue Code (relating to advance payments of earned income tax credit);

(2) Earned income which is received infrequently or irregularly as explained in § 416.1112(c)(2) of this chapter;

(3) Any portion of the $20 per month exclusion described in § 416.1124(c)(12) of this chapter which has not been excluded from your combined unearned income (or the combined unearned income of you and your living-with spouse);

(4) $65 per month of your earned income (or the combined earned income you and your living-with spouse receive in that same year);

(5) Earned income you use to pay impairment-related work expenses described in § 416.976 of this chapter, if you are receiving a social security disability insurance benefit, your disabling condition(s) does not include blindness and you are under age 65. We consider that you attain age 65 on the day before your 65th birthday. In lieu of determining the actual amount of these expenses, we will assume that the value of these work expenses is equal to a standard percentage of your total earned income per month if you tell us that you have impairment-related work expenses. The amount we exclude will be equal to the average percentage of gross earnings excluded for SSI recipients who have such expenses. Initially, the exclusion for impairment-related work expenses will be 16.3 percent of the gross earnings. We may adjust the percentages if the average percentage of gross earnings excluded for supplemental security income (SSI) recipients changes. If we make such a change we will publish a notice in the Federal Register. If excluding impairment-related work expenses greater than the standard percentage of your earned income would affect your eligibility or subsidy amount, you may establish that your actual expenses are greater than the standard percentage of your total earned income. You may do so by contacting us and providing evidence of your actual expenses. The exclusion of impairment-related work expenses also applies to the earnings of your living-with spouse if he or she is receiving a social security disability insurance benefit, the disabling condition(s) does not include blindness and he or she is under age 65;

(6) One-half of your remaining earned income (or combined earned income of you and your living-with spouse); and

(7) Earned income as described in § 416.1112(c)(8) of this chapter that you use to meet any expenses reasonably attributable to the earning of the income if you receive a social security disability insurance benefit based on blindness and you are under age 65. We consider that you attain age 65 on the day before your 65th birthday. In lieu of determining the actual amount of these expenses, we will assume that the value of these expenses is equal to a standard percentage of your total earned income per month. The amount we exclude will be equal to the average percentage of gross earnings excluded for SSI recipients who have such expenses. Initially, the exclusion for blind work expenses will be 25 percent of the gross earnings. We may adjust the percentages if the average percentage of gross earnings excluded for SSI recipients changes. If we make such a change we will publish a notice in the Federal Register. If excluding work expenses greater than the standard percentage of your earned income would affect your eligibility or subsidy amount, you may establish that your actual expenses are greater than the standard percentage of your earned income. You may do so by contacting us and providing evidence of your actual expenses. The exclusion of work expenses also applies to the earnings of your living-with spouse if he or she receives a social security disability insurance benefit based on blindness and is under age 65.

§ 418.3330 What is unearned income?

Unearned income is all income that is not earned income. We describe some of the types of unearned income we count in § 418.3335.

§ 418.3335 What types of unearned income do we count?

(a) Some of the types of unearned income we count are described in § 416.1121(a) through (g) of this chapter.

(b) For claims filed before January 1, 2010, and redeterminations that are effective before January 1, 2010, we also count in-kind support and maintenance as unearned income. In-kind support and maintenance is any food and shelter given to you or that you receive because someone else pays for it.

[75 FR 81845, Dec. 29, 2010; 77 FR 2448, Jan. 18, 2012]

§ 418.3340 How do we count your unearned income?

(a) When income is received. We count unearned income as available to you at the earliest of the following points: when you receive it, when it is credited to your account, or when it is set aside for your use.

(b) When income is counted. For purposes of determining eligibility and whether you should receive a full or partial subsidy, we consider all of the countable unearned income you and your living-with spouse receive (or expect to receive) during the year for which we are determining your eligibility for this benefit. However, in the first year you or your spouse apply for the subsidy, we consider all of the countable unearned income both you and your living-with spouse receive (or expect to receive) starting in the month for which we determine eligibility for you or your living-with spouse based on an application for the subsidy. If we count your income for only a portion of the year, the income limits for subsidy eligibility will be adjusted accordingly. For example, if we count your income for 6 consecutive months of the year (July through December), the income limit for subsidy eligibility will be half of the income limit applicable for the full year.

(c) Amount considered as income. We may include more or less of your income than you actually receive.

(1) We include more than you actually receive where another benefit payment (such as a social security benefit) has been reduced to recover an overpayment. In such a situation, you are repaying a legal obligation through the withholding of portions of your benefit amount, and the amount of this withholding is part of your unearned income.

(2) We also include more than you actually receive if amounts are withheld from unearned income because of a garnishment, or to pay a debt or other legal obligation, or to make any other payment such as payment of your Medicare premiums.

(3) We include less than you actually receive if part of the payment is for an expense you had in getting the payment. For example, if you are paid for damages you receive in an accident, we subtract from the amount of the payment your medical, legal, or other expenses connected with the accident. If you receive a retroactive check from a benefit program, we subtract legal fees connected with the claim. We do not subtract from any taxable unearned income the part you have to use to pay personal income taxes. The payment of taxes is not an expense you have in getting income.

(d) Retroactive benefits. We count retroactive monthly benefits such as social security benefits as unearned income in the year you receive the retroactive benefits.

(e) Certain veterans benefits. If you receive a veterans benefit that includes an amount paid to you because of a dependent, we do not count as your unearned income the amount paid to you because of the dependent. If you are a dependent of an individual who receives a veterans benefit and a portion of the benefit is attributable to you as a dependent, we count the amount attributable to you as your unearned income if you reside with the veteran or you receive your own separate payment from the Department of Veterans Affairs.

(f) Social Security cost-of-living adjustment. We will not count as income the amount of the cost-of-living adjustment for social security benefits for any month through the month following the month in which the annual revision of the Federal poverty guidelines is published.

§ 418.3345 [Reserved by 75 FR 81846]

[75 FR 81846, Dec. 29, 2010; 77 FR 2448, Jan. 18, 2012]

§ 418.3350 What types of unearned income do we not count?

(a) For claims filed on or after January 1, 2010 and redeterminations that are effective on or after January 1, 2010, we do not count as income in-kind support and maintenance.

(b) While we must know the source and amount of all of your unearned income, we do not count all of it to determine your eligibility for the subsidy. We apply to your unearned income the exclusions in § 418.3350(c) in the order listed. However, we do not reduce your unearned income below zero, and we do not apply any unused unearned income exclusion to earned income except for the $20 per month exclusion described in § 416.1124(c)(12) of this chapter. For purposes of determining eligibility for a subsidy and whether you should receive a full or partial subsidy, we treat the $20 per month exclusion as a $240 per year exclusion.

(c) We do not count as income the unearned income described in § 416.1124(b) and (c) of this chapter, except for paragraph (c)(13).

(d) We do not count as income any dividends or interest earned on resources you or your spouse owns.

[75 FR 81846, Dec. 29, 2010; 77 FR 2448, Jan. 18, 2012]

RESOURCES

§ 418.3401 What are resources?

For purposes of this subpart, resources are cash or other assets that an individual owns and could convert to cash to be used for his or her support and maintenance.

§ 418.3405 What types of resources do we count?

(a) We count liquid resources. Liquid resources are cash, financial accounts, and other financial instruments that can be converted to cash within 20 workdays, excluding certain non-workdays as explained in § 416.120(d) of this chapter. Examples of resources that are ordinarily liquid include: stocks, bonds, mutual fund shares, promissory notes, mortgages, life insurance policies (for claims filed before January 1, 2010, and redeterminations that are effective before January 1, 2010), financial institution accounts (including savings, checking, and time deposits, also known as certificates of deposit), retirement accounts (such as individual retirement accounts or 401(k) accounts), revocable trusts, funds in an irrevocable trust if the trust beneficiary can direct the use of the funds, and similar items. We will presume that these types of resources can be converted to cash within 20 workdays and are countable as resources for subsidy determinations. However, if you establish that a particular resource cannot be converted to cash within 20 workdays, we will not count it as a resource.

(b) We count the equity value of real property as a resource regardless of whether it can be sold within 20 workdays. However, we do not count the home that is your principal place of residence and the land on which it is situated as a resource as defined in § 418.3425(a).

[75 FR 81846, Dec. 29, 2010; 77 FR 2448, Jan. 18, 2012]

§ 418.3410 Whose resources do we count?

(a) We count your resources. We count the resources of both you and your spouse regardless of whether one or both of you apply or are eligible for the subsidy if you are married and live with your spouse as of the month for which we determine your eligibility based on an application for a subsidy, as of the month for which we redetermine your eligibility for a subsidy as described in § 418.3125, or as of the month for which we determine your eligibility due to a change you reported as described in § 418.3120.

(b) We will determine your eligibility based on your resources alone if you are not married or if you are married but you are separated from your spouse at the time you apply for a subsidy or at the time we redetermine your eligibility for a subsidy as described in § 418.3125.

(c) If your subsidy is based on the resources of you and your spouse and we redetermine your subsidy as described in § 418.3120(b)(1), we will stop counting the resources of your spouse in the month following the month that we receive a report that your marriage ended due to death, divorce, or annulment; or a report that you and your spouse stopped living together.

(d) If your subsidy is based on the resources of you and your spouse, we will continue counting the resources of both you and your spouse if one of you is temporarily away from home as described in § 404.347 of this chapter.

§ 418.3415 How do we determine countable resources?

(a) General rule. Your countable resources are determined as of the first moment of the month for which we determine your eligibility based on your application for a subsidy or for which we redetermine your eligibility for a subsidy. A resource determination is based on what assets you (and your living-with spouse, if any) have, what their values are, and whether they are excluded as of the first moment of the month. We will use this amount as your countable resources at the point when we determine your eligibility for the subsidy unless you report to us that the value of your resources has changed as described in § 418.3120.

(b) Equity value. Resources, other than cash, are evaluated according to your (and your spouse's, if any) equity in the resources. For purposes of this subpart, the equity value of an item is defined as the price for which that item, minus any encumbrances, can reasonably be expected to sell on the open market in the particular geographic area involved.

(c) Relationship of income to resources. Cash you receive during a month is evaluated under the rules for counting income during the month of receipt. If you retain the cash until the first moment of the following month, the cash is countable as a resource unless it is otherwise excludable.

§ 418.3420 How are funds held in financial institution accounts counted?

(a) Owner of the account. Funds held in a financial institution account (including savings, checking, and time deposits also known as certificates of deposit) are considered your resources if you own the account and can use the funds for your support and maintenance. We determine whether you own the account and can use the funds by looking at how the account is held.

(b) Individually-held account. If you are designated as the sole owner by the account title and you can withdraw and use funds from that account for your support and maintenance, all of that account's funds are your resource regardless of the source. For as long as these conditions are met, we presume that you own 100 percent of the funds in the account. This presumption is not rebuttable.

(c) Jointly-held account.

(1) If you are the only subsidy claimant or subsidy recipient who is an account holder on a jointly held account, we presume that all of the funds in the account belong to you. If more than one subsidy claimant or subsidy recipient are account holders, we presume that the funds in the account belong to those individuals in equal shares.

(2) If you disagree with the ownership presumption as described in paragraph (c)(1) of this section, you may rebut the presumption. Rebuttal is a procedure which permits you to furnish evidence and establish that some or all of the funds in a jointly-held account do not belong to you.

§ 418.3425 What resources do we exclude from counting?

In determining your resources (and the resources of your spouse, if any) the following items shall be excluded:

(a) Your home. For purposes of this exclusion, a home is any property in which you (and your spouse, if any) have an ownership interest and which serves as your principal place of residence. This property includes the shelter in which an individual resides, the land on which the shelter is located, and outbuildings;

(b) Non-liquid resources, other than nonhome real property. Non-liquid resources are resources that are not liquid resources as defined in § 418.3405. Irrevocable burial trusts and the irrevocable portion of prepaid burial contracts are considered non-liquid resources;

(c) Property of a trade or business which is essential to the means of self-support as provided in § 416.1222 of this chapter;

(d) Nonbusiness property which is essential to the means of self-support as provided in § 416.1224 of this chapter;

(e) Stock in regional or village corporations held by natives of Alaska during the twenty-year period in which the stock is inalienable pursuant to the Alaska Native Claims Settlement Act (see § 416.1228 of this chapter);

(f) For claims filed on or after January 1, 2010, and redeterminations that are effective on or after January 1, 2010, life insurance owned by an individual (and spouse, if any);

(g) Restricted allotted Indian lands as provided in § 416.1234 of this chapter;

(h) Payments or benefits provided under a Federal statute where exclusion is required by such statute;

(i) Disaster relief assistance as provided in § 416.1237 of this chapter;

(j) Funds up to $1,500 for the individual and $1,500 for the spouse who lives with the individual if these funds are expected to be used for burial expenses of the individual and spouse;

(k) Burial spaces, as provided in § 416.1231(a) of this chapter;

(*l*) Title XVI or title II retroactive payments as provided in § 416.1233 of this chapter;

(m) Housing assistance as provided in § 416.1238 of this chapter;

(n) Refunds of Federal income taxes and advances made by an employer relating to an earned income tax credit, as provided in § 416.1235 of this chapter;

(*o*) Payments received as compensation incurred or losses suffered as a result of a crime, as provided in § 416.1229 of this chapter;

(p) Relocation assistance from a State or local government, as provided in § 416.1239 of this chapter;

(q) Dedicated financial institution accounts as provided in § 416.1247 of this chapter;

(r) A gift to, or for the benefit of, an individual who has not attained 18 years of age and who has a life-threatening condition, from an organization described in section 501(c)(3) of the Internal Revenue Code of

1986 which is exempt from taxation under section 501(a) of such Code. The resource exclusion applies to any in-kind gift that is not converted to cash, or to a cash gift that does not exceed $2,000; and

(s) Funds received and conserved to pay for medical and/or social services as provided in § 416.1103 of this chapter.

[75 FR 81846, Dec. 29, 2010; 77 FR 2448, Jan. 18, 2012]

ADJUSTMENTS AND TERMINATIONS

§ 418.3501 What could cause us to increase or reduce your subsidy or terminate your subsidy eligibility?

(a) Certain changes in your circumstances could cause us to increase or reduce your subsidy or terminate your subsidy eligibility. These changes include (but are not limited to) changes to:

(1) Your income;

(2) Your spouse's income if you are married and living with your spouse;

(3) Your resources;

(4) Your spouse's resources if you are married and living with your spouse; and

(5) Your family size.

(b) We will periodically review your circumstances (as described in § 418.3125) to make sure you are still eligible for a subsidy and, if eligible, whether you should receive a full or partial subsidy.

(c) If you report that your circumstances have changed or we receive other notice of such a change after we determine that you are eligible, we will review your circumstances as described in § 418.3120 to determine if you are still eligible.

§ 418.3505 How would an increase, reduction or termination affect you?

(a) An increase in your subsidy means that you would be able to pay a lower premium to participate in the Medicare Part D prescription drug program. An increased subsidy may also result in a reduction in any deductible or copayments for which you are responsible.

(b) A reduction in your subsidy means that you would have to begin to pay a premium or a higher premium to participate in the Medicare Part D prescription drug program. You may also have to begin to pay a deductible and higher copayments or increase the amounts of these payments.

(c) A termination means that you would no longer be eligible for a subsidy under the Medicare Part D prescription drug program.

§ 418.3510 When would an increase, reduction or termination start?

We are required to give you a written notice of our proposed action before increasing, reducing, or terminating your subsidy. We will not give this advance notice where we have factual information confirming your death, such as through a report by your surviving spouse, a legal guardian, a close relative, or a landlord. The notice will tell you the first month that we plan to make the change. The notice will also give you appeal rights which are explained in detail in §§ 418.3601 through 418.3670. Your appeal rights for a reduction or termination will include the right to continue to receive your subsidy at the previously established level until there is a decision on your appeal request if your appeal is filed within 10 days after you receive our notice. You will not be required to pay back any subsidy you received while your appeal was pending.

§ 418.3515 How could you qualify for a subsidy again?

Unless you subsequently qualify as a deemed eligible person (per 42 CFR 423.773(c)), you must file a new application for a subsidy and meet all the requirements in § 418.3101.

DETERMINATIONS AND THE ADMINISTRATIVE REVIEW PROCESS

§ 418.3601 When do you have the right to administrative review?

You have the right to an administrative review of the initial determination we make about your eligibility and about your continuing eligibility for a subsidy and any other matter that gives you the right to further review as discussed in § 418.3605. If you are married and living with your spouse and your spouse's eligibility for a subsidy may be adversely affected by our decision upon review, we will notify your spouse before our review and give him or her the opportunity to present additional information for us to consider.

§ 418.3605 What is an initial determination?

Initial determinations are the determinations we make that are subject to administrative and judicial review. The initial determination will state the relevant facts and will give the reasons for our conclusions. Examples of initial determinations that are subject to administrative and judicial review include but are not limited to:

(a) The initial calculation of your income and/or resources;

(b) The determination about whether or not you are eligible for a subsidy and if so, whether you receive a full or partial subsidy;

(c) The determination to reduce your subsidy; and

(d) The determination to terminate your subsidy.

§ 418.3610 Is there administrative or judicial review for administrative actions that are not initial determinations?

Administrative actions that are not initial determinations may be reviewed by us, but they are not subject to the administrative or judicial review process as provided by these sections. For example, changes in your prescription drug program or voluntary disenrollment in the Part D program are not initial determinations that are subject to the administrative review process.

§ 418.3615 Will we mail you a notice of the initial determination?

(a) We will mail a written notice of the initial determination to you at your last known address. Generally, we will not send a notice if your premium subsidy stops because of your death or if the initial determination is a redetermination that your eligibility for a subsidy and the amount of your subsidy has not changed.

(b) The written notice that we send will tell you:

(1) What our initial determination is;

(2) The reasons for our determination; and

(3) The effect of our determination on your right to further review.

(c) We will mail you a written notice before increasing, reducing, or terminating your subsidy. The notice will tell you the first month that we plan to make the change and give you appeal rights. Your appeal rights for a reduction or termination will include the right to continue to receive your subsidy at the previously established level until there is a decision on your appeal request if your appeal is filed within 10 days after you receive our notice.

§ 418.3620 What is the effect of an initial determination?

An initial determination is binding unless you request an appeal within the time period stated in § 418.3630(a) or we revise it as provided in § 418.3678.

§ 418.3625 What is the process for administrative review?

The process for administrative review of initial determinations is either a hearing conducted by telephone or a case review. We will provide you with a hearing by telephone when you appeal the initial determination made on your claim, unless you choose not to participate in a telephone hearing. If you choose not to participate in a telephone hearing, the review will consist of a case review. The hearing will be conducted by an individual who was not involved in making the initial determination. The individual who conducts the hearing will make the final decision after the hearing. If you are dissatisfied after we have made a final decision, you may file an action in Federal district court.

(a) Notice scheduling the telephone hearing. Once you request a telephone hearing, we will schedule the hearing and send you a notice of the date and time of the hearing at least 20 days before the hearing. The notice will contain a statement of the specific issues to be decided and tell you that you may designate a personal representative (as defined in 42 CFR 423.772) to represent you during the proceedings. The notice will explain the opportunity and procedure for reviewing your file and for submitting additional evidence prior to the hearing. It also will provide a brief explanation of the proceedings, of the right and process to subpoena witnesses and documents, of the procedures for requesting a change in the time or date of your hearing, and of the procedure for requesting interpreter services.

(b) Opportunity to review your file. Prior to the telephone hearing, you will be able to review the information that was used to make an initial determination in your case. You can provide us with additional information you wish to have considered at the hearing.

(c) Hearing waived, rescheduled, or missed. If you decide you do not want a hearing by telephone or if you are not available at the time of the scheduled hearing, the decision in your case will be made by a case review. This means that the decision will be based on the information in your file and any additional information you provide. You may ask for a change in the time and date of the telephone hearing; this should be done at the earliest possible opportunity prior to the hearing. Your request must state your reason(s) for needing the change in time or date and state the new time and date you want the hearing to be held. We will change the time and date, but not necessarily to your preferred time or date, of the telephone hearing if you have good cause. If you miss the scheduled hearing and the decision in your case is decided by a case review, we will provide a hearing, at your written request, if we decide you had good cause for missing the scheduled hearing. Examples of good cause include, but are not limited to, the following:

(1) You have attempted to obtain a representative but need additional time;

(2) Your representative was appointed within 30 days of the scheduled hearing and needs additional time to prepare for the hearing;

(3) Your representative has a prior commitment to be in court or at another administrative hearing on the date scheduled for your hearing;

(4) A witness who will testify to facts material to your case would be unavailable to participate in the

scheduled hearing and the evidence cannot be obtained any other way;

(5) You are unrepresented, and you are unable to respond to the notice of hearing because of any physical, mental, educational, or linguistic limitations (including any lack of facility with the English language) that you may have; or

(6) You did not receive notice of the hearing appointment.

(d) Witnesses at hearing. When we determine that it is reasonably necessary for the full presentation of a case, we may issue a subpoena to compel the production of certain evidence or testimony.

§ 418.3630 How do you request administrative review?

(a) Time period for requesting review. You must request administrative review within 60 days after the date you receive notice of the initial determination (or within the extended time period if we extend the time as provided in paragraph (c) of this section). You can request administrative review in person, by phone, fax, or mail. If you miss the time frame for requesting administrative review, you may ask us for more time to request a review. The process for requesting an extension is explained further in paragraph (c) of this section.

(b) Where to file your request. You can request administrative review by mailing or faxing a request or calling or visiting any Social Security office.

(c) When we will extend the time period to request administrative review. If you want a review of the initial determination but do not request one within 60 days after the date you receive notice of the initial determination, you may ask us for more time to request a review. Your request for an extension must explain why it was not filed within the stated time period. If you show us that you had good cause for missing the deadline, we will extend the time period. To determine whether good cause exists, we use the standards explained in § 418.3640.

§ 418.3635 Can anyone request administrative review on your behalf?

Your personal representative (as defined in 42 CFR 423.772) may request administrative review on your behalf. That person can send additional information to us on your behalf and participate in the hearing.

§ 418.3640 How do we determine if you had good cause for missing the deadline to request administrative review?

(a) In determining whether you have shown that you have good cause for missing a deadline to request review we consider:

(1) What circumstances kept you from making the request on time;

(2) Whether our action misled you;

(3) Whether you did not understand the requirements of the Act resulting from amendments to the Act, other legislation, or court decisions; and

(4) Whether you had any physical, mental, educational, or linguistic limitations (including any lack of facility with the English language) which prevented you from filing a timely request or from understanding or knowing about the need to file a timely request for review.

(b) Examples of circumstances where good cause may exist include, but are not limited to, the following situations:

(1) You were seriously ill and were prevented from contacting us in person, in writing, or through a friend, relative, or other person.

(2) There was a death or serious illness in your immediate family.

(3) Important records were destroyed or damaged by fire or other accidental cause.

(4) You were trying very hard to find necessary information to support your claim but did not find the information within the stated time periods.

(5) You asked us for additional information explaining our action within the time limit, and within 60 days of receiving the explanation you requested a review.

(6) We gave you incorrect or incomplete information about when and how to request administrative review.

(7) You did not receive notice of the initial determination.

(8) You sent the request to another Government agency in good faith within the time limit and the request did not reach us until after the time period had expired.

(9) Unusual or unavoidable circumstances exist, including the circumstances described in paragraph (a)(4) of this section, which show that you could not have known the need to file timely, or which prevented you from filing timely.

§ 418.3645 Can you request that the decision-maker be disqualified?

The person designated to conduct your hearing will not conduct the hearing if he or she is prejudiced or partial with respect to any party or has any interest in the matter pending for decision. If you object to the person who will be conducting your hearing, you must notify us at your earliest opportunity. The Commissioner or the Commissioner's designee will decide whether to appoint another person to conduct your hearing.

§ 418.3650 How do we make our decision upon review?

After you request review of our initial determination, we will review the information that we considered in making the initial determination and any other information we receive. We will make our decision based on this information. The issues that we will review are the issues with which you disagree. We may consider other issues, but we will provide you with advance notice of these other issues as explained in § 418.3625. If you are dissatisfied with our final decision, you may file an action in Federal district court.

§ 418.3655 How will we notify you of our decision after our review?

We will mail a written notice of our decision on the issue(s) you appealed to you at your last known address. Generally, we will not send a notice if your subsidy stops because of your death. The written notice that we send will tell you:

(a) What our decision is;

(b) The reasons for our decision;

(c) The effect of our decision; and

(d) Your right to judicial review of the decision.

§ 418.3665 Can your request for a hearing or case review be dismissed?

We will dismiss your request for a hearing or case review under any of the following conditions:

(a) At any time before notice of the decision is mailed, you ask that your request for administrative review be withdrawn; or

(b) You failed to request administrative review timely and did not have good cause for missing the deadline for requesting review.

§ 418.3670 How will you be notified of the dismissal?

We will mail a written notice of the dismissal of your request for administrative review to you at your last known address. The dismissal is not subject to judicial review and is binding on you unless we vacate it. The decision-maker may vacate any dismissal of your request for administrative review if, within 60 days after the date you receive the dismissal notice, you request that the dismissal be vacated and show good cause why the request should not be dismissed. The decision-maker shall advise you in writing of any action he or she takes.

§ 418.3675 How does our decision affect you?

Our decision is binding unless you file an action in Federal district court seeking review of our final decision or we revise it as provided in § 418.3678. You may file an action in Federal district court within 60 days after the date you receive notice of the decision. You may request that the time for filing an action in Federal district court be extended. The request must be in writing and it must give the reasons why the action was not filed within the stated time period. The request must be filed with the decision-maker who issued the final decision in your case. If you show that you had good cause for missing the deadline, we will extend the deadline. We will use the standards in § 418.3640 to decide if you had good cause to miss the deadline.

§ 418.3678 What is the process for correcting Agency clerical errors?

If we become aware within 60 days of the date of our initial determination or our decision following a case review or telephone hearing, that a clerical error was made in determining whether or not you are eligible for a subsidy (either in whole or in part), we may issue a revised initial determination which would be effective back to the date you originally filed your application or the effective date of a subsidy changing event, provided you meet the requirements in § 418.3101. We may revise an initial determination or decision regardless of whether such revised determination or decision is favorable or unfavorable to you. If the revised determination or decision (which is a new initial determination) is not favorable to you, you will not be responsible for paying back any subsidy received prior to the revised determination or decision. We will mail you a notice of the revised determination which will explain to you that we have made a revised determination and that this determination replaces an earlier determination, how this determination affects your subsidy eligibility, and your right to request a hearing.

§ 418.3680 What happens if your case is remanded by a Federal court?

When a Federal court remands a case to the Commissioner for further consideration, the decision-maker (as described in § 418.3625) acting on behalf of the Commissioner, may make a decision. That component will follow the procedures in § 418.3625, unless we decide that we can make a decision that is fully favorable to you without another hearing. Any issues relating to your subsidy may be considered by the decision-maker whether or not they were raised in the administrative proceedings leading to the final decision in your case.

[75 FR 33169, June 11, 2010]

PART 422—ORGANIZATION AND PROCEDURES

SUBPART A—ORGANIZATION AND FUNCTIONS OF THE SOCIAL SECURITY ADMINISTRATION

SUBPART B—GENERAL PROCEDURES

SUBPART C—PROCEDURES OF THE OFFICE OF DISABILITY ADJUDICATION AND REVIEW

SUBPART D—CLAIMS COLLECTION

SUBPART E—COLLECTION OF DEBTS BY ADMINISTRATIVE WAGE GARNISHMENT

SUBPART F—APPLICATIONS AND RELATED FORMS

SUBPART G—ADMINISTRATIVE REVIEW PROCESS UNDER THE COAL INDUSTRY RETIREE HEALTH BENEFIT ACT OF 1992

SUBPART H—USE OF SSA TELEPHONE LINES

SUBPART I—ADMINISTRATIVE CLAIMS COLLECTION

SUBPART J—PROTECTING THE PUBLIC AND OUR PERSONNEL TO ENSURE OPERATIONAL EFFECTIVENESS

Source: 32 FR 13653, Sept. 29, 1967; 61 FR 5942, Feb. 15, 1996, unless otherwise noted.

SUBPART A—ORGANIZATION AND FUNCTIONS OF THE SOCIAL SECURITY ADMINISTRATION

Authority: Secs. 205, 218, 221, and 701–704 of the Social Security Act (42 U.S.C. 405, 418, 421, and 901–904).

Source: 61 FR 5942, Feb. 15, 1996, unless otherwise noted.

§ 422.1 Organization and functions.

(a) General. A complete description of the organization and functions of the Social Security Administration (pursuant to 5 U.S.C. 552(a), as amended by Pub.L. 90–23, the Public Information Act) was published in the Federal Register of July 15, 1967 (32 FR 10458), and was subsequently revised on April 16, 1968 (33 FR 5828), and amended on July 18, 1968 (33 FR 10292). Further amendments to or revisions of the description will be published in the Federal Register when and if required by changes in the organization or functions of the Social Security Administration. Such description (referred to as the SSA Statement of Organization, Functions, and Delegations of Authority) is printed and kept up to date in the Social Security Administration Organizational Manual, a copy of which is maintained in each district office and branch office of the Social Security Administration and is available for inspection and copying.

(b) Information included in description. This description includes information about the organization and functions of each component of the Social Security Administration. It also includes a listing of all district offices and branch offices within the organization of the Bureau of District Office Operations, and a listing of field offices within the organization of the Bureau of Hearings and Appeals where the public may secure information, make submittals or requests, or obtain decisions.

[34 FR 435, Jan. 11, 1969; 62 FR 38456, July 18, 1997]

§ 422.5 District offices and branch offices.

There are over 700 social security district offices and branch offices located in the principal cities and other urban areas or towns of the United States. In addition, there are over 3,300 contact stations, located in population and trading centers, which are visited on a regularly, recurring, preannounced basis. A schedule of these visits can be obtained from the nearest district office or branch office. The address of the nearest district office or branch office can be obtained from the local telephone directory or from the post office. Each district office and branch office has a list of all district offices and branch offices throughout the country and their addresses. The principal officer in each district office is the manager. The principal officer in each branch office is the officer-in-charge. Each district office and branch office also has a list of field offices of the Bureau of Hearings and Appeals and their addresses. The administrative hearing examiner is the principal officer in each field office. For procedures relating to claims see § 422.130, subpart J of part 404 of this chapter, and § 404.1520 of this chapter (the latter relating to disability determinations). For procedures on request for hearing by an Administrative Law Judge and review by the Appeals Council see subpart C of this part 422.

SUBPART B—GENERAL PROCEDURES

Authority: Secs. 205, 232, 702(a)(5), 1131, 1143 of the Social Security Act (42 U.S.C. 405, 432, 902(a)(5), 1320b–1, and 1320b–13), and sec. 7213(a)(1)(A) of Pub.L. 108–458.

Source: 55 FR 46664, Nov. 6, 1990; 57 FR 54919, Nov. 23, 1992; 60 FR 32446, June 22, 1995; 60 FR 42433, Aug. 16, 1995; 61 FR 5942, Feb. 15, 1996; 70 FR 74651, Dec. 16, 2005; 71 FR 16461, March 31, 2006; 71 FR 43056, July 31, 2006, unless otherwise noted.

§ 422.101 Material included in this subpart.

This subpart describes the procedures relating to applications for and assignment of social security numbers, maintenance of earnings records of individuals by the Social Security Administration, requests for statements of earnings or for revision of earnings records, and general claims procedures, including filing of applications, submission of evidence, determinations, and reconsideration of initial determinations.

§ 422.103 Social security numbers.

Text of section amended by 71 FR 43056, retroactively effective Dec. 16, 2005.

(a) General. The Social Security Administration (SSA) maintains a record of the earnings reported for each individual assigned a social security number. The individual's name and social security number identify the record so that the wages or self-employment income reported for or by the individual can be properly posted to the individual's record. Additional procedures concerning social security numbers may be found in Internal Revenue Service, Department of the Treasury regulation 26 CFR 31.6011(b)–2.

(b) Applying for a number—

(1) Application. An individual needing a Social Security number may apply for one by completing a prescribed application and submitting the required evidence. An individual outside the United States (U.S.) may apply for a Social Security number card at the Department of Veterans Affairs Regional Office, Manila, Philippines, at any U.S. Foreign Service post, or at a U.S. military post outside the United States. (See § 422.106 for special procedures for filing applications with other government agencies.) Additionally, a U.S. resident may apply for a Social Security number for a nonresident dependent when the number is necessary for U.S. tax purposes or some other valid reason, the evidence requirements of § 422.107 are met, and we determine that a personal interview with the dependent is not required.

(2) Birth registration document. We may enter into an agreement with officials of a State, including, for this purpose, the District of Columbia, Puerto Rico, Guam, the U.S. Virgin Islands, and New York City, to establish, as part of the official birth registration process, a procedure to assist us in assigning Social Security numbers to newborn children. Where an agreement is in effect, a parent, as part of the official birth registration process, need not complete a prescribed application and may request that we assign a Social Security number to the newborn child.

(3) Immigration form. We may enter into an agreement with the Department of State (DOS) and the Department of Homeland Security (DHS) to assist us by collecting enumeration data as part of the immigration process. Where an agreement is in effect, an alien need not complete a prescribed application and may request, through DOS or DHS, as part of the immigration process, that we assign a Social Security number and issue a Social Security number card to him or her. An alien will request the assignment of a Social Security number through this process in the manner provided by DOS and DHS.

(c) How numbers are assigned—

(1) Application. If you complete a prescribed application, we will require you to furnish evidence, as necessary, to assist us in establishing your age, U.S. citizenship or alien status, true identity, and previously assigned Social Security number(s), if any. (See § 422.107 for evidence requirements.) We may require you to undergo a personal interview before we assign a Social Security number. If you request evidence to show that you have filed a prescribed application for a Social Security number card, we may furnish you with a receipt or equivalent document. We will electronically screen the data from the prescribed application against our files. If we find that you have not been assigned a Social Security number previously, we will assign one to you and issue a Social Security number card. However, if we find that you have been assigned a Social Security number previously, we will issue a replacement Social Security number card.

(2) Request on birth registration document. Where a parent has requested a social security number for a newborn child as part of an official birth registration process described in paragraph (b)(2) of this section, the State vital statistics office will electronically transmit the request to SSA's central office in Baltimore, MD, along with the child's name, date and place of birth, sex, mother's maiden name, father's name (if shown on the birth registration), address of the mother, and birth certificate number. This birth registration information received by SSA from the State vital statistics office will be used to establish the age, identity, and U.S. citizenship of the newborn child. Using this information, SSA will assign a number to the child and send the social security number card to the child at the mother's address.

(3) Request on immigration document. Where an alien has requested a social security number as part of the immigration process described in paragraph (b)(3) of this section, Department of Homeland Security will electronically transmit to SSA's central office in Baltimore, MD, the data elements collected for immigration purposes, by both Department of Homeland Security and DOS, that SSA needs to assign the alien a social security number along with other data elements as agreed upon by SSA and DOS or Department of Homeland Security. The data elements received by

SSA will be used to establish the age, identity, and lawful alien status or authority to work of the alien. Using this data, SSA will assign a social security number to the alien and send the social security number card to him/her at the address the alien provides to DOS or Department of Homeland Security (or to the sponsoring agency of a refugee, if no personal mailing address is available).

(d) Social security number cards. A person who is assigned a social security number will receive a social security number card from SSA within a reasonable time after the number has been assigned. (See § 422.104 regarding the assignment of social security number cards to aliens.) Social security number cards are the property of SSA and must be returned upon request.

(e) Replacement of social security number card—

(1) When we may issue you a replacement card. We may issue you a replacement Social Security number card, subject to the limitations in paragraph (e)(2) of this section. You must complete a prescribed application to receive a replacement Social Security number card. We follow the evidence requirements in § 422.107 when we issue you a replacement Social Security number card.

(2) Limits on the number of replacement cards. There are limits on the number of replacement social security number cards we will issue to you. You may receive no more than three replacement social security number cards in a year and ten replacement social security number cards per lifetime. We may allow for reasonable exceptions to these limits on a case-by-case basis in compelling circumstances. We also will consider name changes (i.e., verified legal changes to the first name and/or surname) and changes in alien status which result in a necessary change to a restrictive legend on the SSN card (see paragraph (e)(3) of this section) to be compelling circumstances, and will not include either of these changes when determining the yearly or lifetime limits. We may grant an exception if you provide evidence establishing that you would experience significant hardship if the card were not issued. An example of significant hardship includes, but is not limited to, providing SSA with a referral letter from a governmental social services agency indicating that the social security number card must be shown in order to obtain benefits or services.

(3) Restrictive legend change defined. Based on a person's immigration status, a restrictive legend may appear on the face of an SSN card to indicate that work is either not authorized or that work may be performed only with Department of Homeland Security (DHS) authorization. This restrictive legend appears on the card above the individual's name and SSN. Individuals without work authorization in the U.S. receive SSN cards showing the restrictive legend, "Not Valid for Employment;" and SSN cards for those individuals who have temporary work authorization in the U.S. show the restrictive legend, "Valid For Work Only With DHS Authorization." U.S. citizens and individuals who are permanent residents receive SSN cards without a restrictive legend. For the purpose of determining a change in restrictive legend, the individual must have a change in immigration status or citizenship which results in a change to or the removal of a restrictive legend when compared to the prior SSN card data. An SSN card request based upon a change in immigration status or citizenship which does not affect the restrictive legend will count toward the yearly and lifetime limits, as in the case of Permanent Resident Aliens who attain U.S. citizenship.

[44 FR 10370, Feb. 22, 1979; 55 FR 7315, March 1, 1990; 55 FR 10030, March 16, 1990; 55 FR 46664, Nov. 6, 1990; 63 FR 56554, Oct. 22, 1998; 69 FR 55076, Sept. 13, 2004; 70 FR 74651, Dec. 16, 2005; 71 FR 43056, July 31, 2006; 80 FR 47833, Aug. 10, 2015]

§ 422.104 Who can be assigned a social security number.

(a) Persons eligible for SSN assignment. We can assign you a social security number if you meet the evidence requirements in § 422.107 and you are:

(1) A United States citizen; or

(2) An alien lawfully admitted to the United States for permanent residence or under other authority of law permitting you to work in the United States (§ 422.105 describes how we determine if a nonimmigrant alien is permitted to work in the United States); or

(3) An alien who cannot provide evidence of alien status showing lawful admission to the U.S., or an alien with evidence of lawful admission but without authority to work in the U.S., if the evidence described in § 422.107(e) does not exist, but only for a valid nonwork reason. We consider you to have a valid nonwork reason if:

(i) You need a social security number to satisfy a Federal statute or regulation that requires you to have a social security number in order to receive a Federally-funded benefit to which you have otherwise established entitlement and you reside either in or outside the U.S.; or

(ii) You need a social security number to satisfy a State or local law that requires you to have a social security number in order to receive public assistance benefits to which you have otherwise established entitlement, and you are legally in the United States.

(b) Annotation for a nonwork purpose. If we assign you a social security number as an alien for a nonwork purpose, we will indicate in our records that you are not authorized to work. We will also mark your social security card with a legend such as "NOT VALID FOR EMPLOYMENT." If earnings are reported to us on your number, we will inform the Department of Homeland Security of the reported earnings.

[44 FR 10371, Feb. 20, 1979; 56 FR 41790, Aug. 23, 1991; 63 FR 56554, Oct. 22, 1998; 68 FR 55308, Sept. 25, 2003]

§ 422.105 Presumption of authority of nonimmigrant alien to engage in employment.

(a) General rule. Except as provided in paragraph (b) of this section, if you are a nonimmigrant alien, we will presume that you have permission to engage in employment if you present a Form I–94 issued by the Department of Homeland Security that reflects a classification permitting work. (See 8 CFR 274a.12 for Form I–94 classifications.) If you have not been issued a Form I–94, or if your Form I–94 does not reflect a classification permitting work, you must submit a current document authorized by the Department of Homeland Security that verifies authorization to work has been granted e.g., an employment authorization document, to enable SSA to issue an SSN card that is valid for work. (See 8 CFR 274a.12(c)(3).)

(b) Exception to presumption for foreign academic students in immigration classification F–1. If you are an F–1 student and do not have a separate DHS employment authorization document as described in paragraph (a) of this section and you are not authorized for curricular practical training (CPT) as shown on your Student and Exchange Visitor Information System (SEVIS) Form I–20, Certificate of Eligibility for Nonimmigrant (F–1) Student Status, we will not presume you have authority to engage in employment without additional evidence. Before we will assign an SSN to you that is valid for work, you must give us proof (as explained in § 422.107(e)(2)) that:

(1) You have authorization from your school to engage in employment, and

(2) You are engaging in, or have secured, employment.

[44 FR 10371, Feb. 20, 1979; 44 FR 20078, April 4, 1979; 55 FR 46665, Nov. 6, 1990; 63 FR 56554, Oct. 22, 1998; 69 FR 55075, Sept. 13, 2004]

§ 422.106 Filing applications with other government agencies.

(a) Agreements. In carrying out its responsibilities to assign social security numbers, SSA enters into agreements with the United States Attorney General, other Federal officials, and State and local welfare agencies. An example of these agreements is discussed in paragraph (b) of this section.

(b) States. SSA and a State may enter into an agreement that authorizes employees of a State or one of its subdivisions to accept social security number card applications from some individuals who apply for or are receiving welfare benefits under a State-administered Federal program. Under such an agreement, a State employee is also authorized to certify the application to show that he or she has reviewed the required evidence of the applicant's age, identity, and U.S. citizenship. The employee is also authorized to obtain evidence to assist SSA in determining whether the applicant has previously been assigned a number. The employee will then send the application to SSA which will issue a social security number card.

[44 FR 10371, Feb. 20, 1979; 55 FR 46665, Nov. 6, 1990; 63 FR 56555, Oct. 22, 1998]

§ 422.107 Evidence requirements.

(a) General. To obtain an original Social Security number card, you must submit convincing evidence of your age, U.S. citizenship or alien status, and true identity, as described in paragraphs (b) through (e) of this section. If you apply for a replacement Social Security number card, you must submit convincing evidence of your true identity, as described in paragraph (c) of this section, and you may also be required to submit convincing evidence of your age and U.S. citizenship or alien status, as described in paragraphs (b), (d), and (e) of this section. If you apply for an original or replacement Social Security number card, you are also required to submit evidence to assist us in determining the existence and identity of any previously assigned Social Security number(s). We will not assign a Social Security number or issue an original or replacement card unless we determine that you meet all of the evidence requirements. We require an in-person interview if you are age 12 or older and are applying for an original Social Security number, unless you are an alien who requests a Social Security number as part of the immigration process described in § 422.103(b)(3). We may require an in-person interview of other applicants. All paper or other tangible documents submitted as evidence must be originals or copies of the original documents certified by the custodians of the original records and are subject to verification. We may also verify your eligibility factors, as described in paragraphs (b) through (e) of this section, through other means, including but not limited to data matches or other agreements with government agencies or other entities that we determine can provide us with appropriate and secure verification of your eligibility factors.

(b) Evidence of age. An applicant for an original social security number is required to submit convincing evidence of age. An applicant for a replacement social security number card may also be required to submit evidence of age. Examples of the types of evidence which may be submitted are a birth certificate, a religious record showing age or date of birth, a hospital record of birth, or a passport. (See § 404.716.)

(c) Evidence of identity.

(1) If you apply for an original Social Security number or a replacement Social Security number card, you are required to submit convincing evidence of your identity. Evidence of identity may consist of a driver's

license, identification card, school record, medical record, marriage record, passport, Department of Homeland Security document, or other similar evidence serving to identify you. The evidence must contain sufficient information to identify you, including your name and:

(i) Your age, date of birth, or parents' names; or

(ii) Your photograph or physical description.

(2) A birth record is not sufficient evidence to establish identity for these purposes.

(d) Evidence of U.S. citizenship. Generally, an applicant for an original or replacement social security number card may prove that he or she is a U.S. citizen by birth by submitting a birth certificate or other evidence, as described in paragraphs (b) and (c) of this section, that shows a U.S. place of birth. Where a foreign-born applicant claims U.S. citizenship, the applicant for a social security number or a replacement social security number card is required to present documentary evidence of U.S. citizenship. If required evidence is not available, a social security number card will not be issued until satisfactory evidence of U.S. citizenship is furnished. Any of the following is generally acceptable evidence of U.S. citizenship for a foreign-born applicant:

(1) Certificate of naturalization;

(2) Certificate of citizenship;

(3) U.S. passport;

(4) U.S. citizen identification card issued by the Department of Homeland Security;

(5) Consular report of birth (State Department form FS-240 or FS-545); or

(6) Other verification from the Department of Homeland Security, U.S. Department of State, or Federal or State court records confirming citizenship.

(e) Evidence of alien status—

(1) General evidence rules. When a person who is not a U.S. citizen applies for an original social security number or a replacement social security number card, he or she is required to submit, as evidence of alien status, a current document issued by the Department of Homeland Security in accordance with that agency's regulations. The document must show that the applicant has been lawfully admitted to the United States, either for permanent residence or under authority of law permitting him or her to work in the United States, or that the applicant's alien status has changed so that it is lawful for him or her to work. If the applicant fails to submit such a document, a social security number card will not be issued. If the applicant submits an unexpired Department of Homeland Security document(s) which shows current authorization to work, a social security number will be assigned or verified and a card which can be used for work will be issued. If the authorization of the applicant to work is temporary or subject to termination by the Department of Homeland Security, the SSA records may be so annotated. If the document(s) does not provide authorization to work and the applicant wants a social security number for a work purpose, no social security number will be assigned. If the applicant requests the number for a nonwork purpose and provides evidence documenting that the number is needed for a valid nonwork purpose, the number may be assigned and the card issued will be annotated with a nonwork legend. The SSA record will be annotated to show that a number has been assigned and a card issued for a nonwork purpose. In that case, if earnings are later reported to SSA, the Department of Homeland Security will be notified of the report. SSA may also notify that agency if earnings are reported for a social security number that was valid for work when assigned but for which work authorization expired or was later terminated by the Department of Homeland Security. SSA may also annotate the record with other remarks, if appropriate.

(2) Additional evidence rules for F–1 students—

(i) Evidence from your designated school official. If you are an F–1 student and do not have a separate DHS employment authorization document as described in § 422.105(a) and you are not authorized for curricular practical training (CPT) as shown on your SEVIS Form I–20, Certificate of Eligibility for Nonimmigrant (F–1) Student Status, you must give us documentation from your designated school official that you are authorized to engage in employment. You must submit your SEVIS Form I–20, Certificate of Eligibility for Nonimmigrant (F–1) Student Status. You must also submit documentation from your designated school official that includes:

(A) The nature of the employment you are or will be engaged in, and

(B) The identification of the employer for whom you are or will be working.

(ii) Evidence of your employment. You must also provide us with documentation that you are engaging in, or have secured, employment; e.g., a statement from your employer.

(f) Failure to submit evidence. If the applicant does not comply with a request for the required evidence or other information within a reasonable time, SSA may attempt another contact with the applicant. If there is still no response, a social security number card will not be issued.

(g) Inability to verify eligibility factors. We will not issue an original or replacement Social Security number card when you present invalid or expired documents or when we are unable to verify the required evidence through other means, as described in paragraph (a) of this section. Invalid documents are either forged documents that supposedly were issued by the custodian of the record, or properly issued documents that were improperly changed after they were issued. An expired document is one that was valid for only a limited time and that time has passed.

[44 FR 10371, Feb. 20, 1979; 55 FR 46665, Nov. 6, 1990; 60 FR 32446, June 22, 1995; 62 FR 38456, July 18, 1997; 63 FR 56555, Oct. 22, 1998; 68 FR 55308, Sept. 25, 2003; 69 FR 55076, Sept. 13, 2004; 70 FR 74651, Dec. 16, 2005; 71 FR 43056, July 31, 2006; 80 FR 47834, Aug. 10, 2015]

§ 422.108 Criminal penalties.

A person may be subject to criminal penalties for furnishing false information in connection with earnings records or for wrongful use or misrepresentation in connection with social security numbers, pursuant to section 208 of the Social Security Act and sections of title 18 U.S.C. (42 U.S.C. 408; 18 U.S.C. 1001 and 1546).

[39 FR 10242, March 19, 1974]

§ 422.110 Individual's request for change in record.

(a) Application. If you wish to change the name or other personal identifying information you previously submitted in connection with an application for a Social Security number card, you must complete a prescribed application, except as provided in paragraph (b) of this section. You must prove your identity, and you may be required to provide other evidence. (See § 422.107 for evidence requirements.) You may complete a request for change in records in the manner we designate, including at any Social Security office, or, if you are outside the U.S., to the Department of Veterans Affairs Regional Office, Manila, Philippines, or to any U.S. Foreign Service post or U.S. military post. If your request is for a change of name on the card (that is, verified legal changes to the first name or surname, or both), we may issue you a replacement Social Security number card bearing the same number and the new name. We will grant an exception to the limitations specified in § 422.103(e)(2) for replacement Social Security number cards representing a change in name or, if you are an alien, a change to a restrictive legend shown on the card. (See § 422.103(e)(3) for the definition of a change to a restrictive legend.)

(b) Assisting in enumeration. We may enter into an agreement with officials of the Department of State and the Department of Homeland Security to assist us by collecting, as part of the immigration process, information to change the name or other personal identifying information you previously submitted in connection with an application or request for a social security number card. If your request is to change a name on the card (i.e., verified legal changes to the first name and/or surname) or to correct the restrictive legend on the card to reflect a change in alien status, we may issue you a replacement card bearing the same number and the new name or legend. We will grant an exception from the limitations specified in § 422.103(e)(2) for replacement social security number cards representing a change of name or, if you are an alien, a change to a restrictive legend shown on the card. (See § 422.103(e)(3) for the definition of a change to a restrictive legend.)

[44 FR 10372, Feb. 20, 1979; 55 FR 46666, Nov. 6, 1990; 63 FR 56555, Oct. 22, 1998; 69 FR 55076, Sept. 13, 2004; 70 FR 74652, Dec. 16, 2005; 71 FR 43056, July 31, 2006; 80 FR 47834, Aug. 10, 2015]

§ 422.112 Employer identification numbers.

(a) General. Most employers are required by section 6109 of the Internal Revenue Code and by Internal Revenue Service (IRS) regulations at 26 CFR 31.6011(b)–1 to obtain an employer identification number (EIN) and to include it on wage reports filed with SSA. A sole proprietor who does not pay wages to one or more employees or who is not required to file any pension or excise tax return is not subject to this requirement. To apply for an EIN, employers file Form SS–4, "Application for Employer Identification Number," with the IRS. For the convenience of employers, Form SS–4 is available at all SSA and IRS offices. Household employers, agricultural employers, and domestic corporations which elect social security coverage for employees of foreign subsidiaries who are citizens or residents of the U.S. may be assigned an EIN by IRS without filing an SS–4.

(b) State and local governments. When a State submits a modification to its agreement under section 218 of the Act, which extends coverage to periods prior to 1987, SSA will assign a special identification number to each political subdivision included in that modification. SSA will send the State a Form SSA–214–CD, "Notice of Identifying Number," to inform the State of the special identification number(s). The special number will be used for reporting the pre–1987 wages to SSA. The special number will also be assigned to an interstate instrumentality if pre–1987 coverage is obtained and SSA will send a Form SSA–214–CD to the interstate instrumentality to notify it of the number assigned.

[32 FR 13653, Sept. 29, 1967. Redesignated at 39 FR 10242, Mar. 19, 1974; 55 FR 46666, Nov. 6, 1990; 60 FR 42433, Aug. 16, 1995; 64 FR 33016, June 21, 1999]

§ 422.114 Annual wage reporting process.

(a) General. Under the authority of section 232 of the Act, SSA and IRS have entered into an agreement that sets forth the manner by which SSA and IRS will ensure that the processing of employee wage reports is effective and efficient. Under this agreement, employers are instructed by IRS to file annual wage reports with SSA on paper Forms W–2, "Wage and Tax Statement," and Forms W–3, "Transmittal of Income and Tax Statements," or equivalent W–2 and W–3 magnetic media reports. Special versions of these forms for Puerto Rico, Guam, American Samoa, the Virgin Islands, and the Commonwealth of the Northern Mariana Islands are also filed with SSA. SSA processes all wage reporting forms for updating to SSA's earnings records and IRS tax records, identifies employer reporting errors and untimely filed forms for IRS penalty assessment action, and takes action to correct any reporting errors identified, except as provided in paragraph (c) of this section. SSA also processes Forms W–3c, "Transmittal of Corrected Income Tax Statements," and W–2c, "Statement of Corrected Income and Tax Amounts" (and their magnetic media equivalents) that employers are required to file with SSA when certain previous reporting errors are discovered.

(b) Magnetic media reporting requirements. Under IRS regulations at 26 CFR 301.6011–2, employers who file 250 or more W–2 wage reports per year must file them on magnetic media in accordance with requirements provided in SSA publications, unless IRS grants the employer a waiver. Basic SSA requirements are set out in SSA's Technical Instruction Bulletin No. 4, "Magnetic Media Reporting." Special filing requirements for U.S. territorial employers are set out in SSA Technical Instruction Bulletins No. 5 (Puerto Rico), No. 6 (Virgin Islands), and No. 7 (Guam and American Samoa). At the end of each year, SSA mails these technical instructions to employers (or third parties who file wage reports on their behalf) for their use in filing wage reports for that year.

(c) Processing late and incorrect magnetic media wage transmittals. If an employer's transmittal of magnetic media wage reports is received by SSA after the filing due date, SSA will notify IRS of the late filing so that IRS can decide whether to assess penalties for late filing, pursuant to section 6721 of the Internal Revenue Code. If reports do not meet SSA processing requirements (unprocessable reports) or are out of balance on critical money amounts, SSA will return them to the employer to correct and resubmit. In addition, beginning with wage reports filed for tax year 1993, if 90 percent or more of an employer's magnetic media wage reports have no social security numbers or incorrect employee names or social security numbers so that SSA is unable to credit their wages to its records, SSA will not attempt to correct the errors, but will instead return the reports to the employer to correct and resubmit (see also § 422.120(b)). An employer must correct and resubmit incorrect and unprocessable magnetic media wage reports to SSA within 45 days from the date of the letter sent with the returned report. Upon request, SSA may grant the employer a 15–day extension of the 45–day period. If an employer does not submit corrected reports to SSA within the 45–day (or, if extended by SSA, 60–day) period, SSA will notify IRS of the late filing so that IRS can decide whether to assess a penalty. If an employer timely resubmits the reports as corrected magnetic media reports, but they are unprocessable or out of balance on W–2 money totals, SSA will return the resubmitted reports for the second and last time for the employer to correct and return to SSA. SSA will enclose with the resubmitted and returned forms a letter informing the employer that he or she must correct and return the reports to SSA within 45 days or be subject to IRS penalties for late filing.

(d) Paper form reporting requirements. The format and wage reporting instructions for paper forms are determined jointly by IRS and SSA. Basic instructions on how to complete the forms and file them with SSA are provided in IRS forms materials available to the public. In addition, SSA provides standards for employers (or third parties who file wage reports for them) to follow in producing completed reporting forms from computer software; these standards appear in SSA publication, "Software Specifications and Edits for Annual Wage Reporting." Requests for this publication should be sent to: Social Security Administration, Office of Financial Policy and Operations, Attention: AWR Software Standards Project, P.O. Box 17195, Baltimore, MD 21235.

(e) Processing late and incorrect paper form reports. If SSA receives paper form wage reports after the due date, SSA will notify IRS of the late filing so that IRS can decide whether to assess penalties for late filing, pursuant to section 6721 of the Internal Revenue Code. SSA will ask an employer to provide replacement forms for illegible, incomplete, or clearly erroneous paper reporting forms, or will ask the employer to provide information necessary to process the reports without having to resubmit corrected forms. (For wage reports where earnings are reported without a social security number or with an incorrect name or social security number, see § 422.120.) If an employer fails to provide legible, complete, and correct W–2 reports within 45 days, SSA may identify the employers to IRS for assessment of employer reporting penalties.

(f) Reconciliation of wage reporting errors. After SSA processes wage reports, it matches them with the information provided by employers to the IRS on Forms 941, "Employer's Quarterly Federal Tax Return," for that tax year. Based upon this match, if the total social security or medicare wages reported to SSA for employees is less than the totals reported to IRS, SSA will write to the employer and request corrected reports or an explanation for the discrepancy. If the total social security or medicare wages reported to SSA for employees is more than the totals reported to IRS, IRS will resolve the difference with the employer. If the employer fails to provide SSA with corrected reports or information that shows the wage reports filed with SSA are correct, SSA will ask IRS to investigate the employer's wage and tax reports to resolve the discrepancy and to assess any appropriate reporting penalties.

[60 FR 42433, Aug. 16, 1995]

§ 422.115 [Reserved]

[60 FR 42434, Aug. 16, 1995]

§ 422.120 Earnings reported without a social security number or with an incorrect employee name or social security number.

(a) Correcting an earnings report. If an employer reports an employee's wages to SSA without the employee's social security number or with a different employee name or social security number than shown in SSA's records for him or her, SSA will write to the employee at the address shown on the wage report and request the missing or corrected information. If the wage report does not show the employee's address or shows an incomplete address, SSA will write to the employer and request the missing or corrected employee information. SSA notifies IRS of all wage reports filed without employee social security numbers so that IRS can decide whether to assess penalties for erroneous filing, pursuant to section 6721 of the Internal Revenue Code. If an individual reports self-employment income to IRS without a social security number or with a different name or social security number than shown in SSA's records, SSA will write to the individual and request the missing or corrected information. If the employer, employee, or self-employed individual does not provide the missing or corrected report information in response to SSA's request, the wages or self-employment income cannot be identified and credited to the proper individual's earnings records. In such cases, the information is maintained in a "Suspense File" of uncredited earnings. Subsequently, if identifying information is provided to SSA for an individual whose report is recorded in the Suspense File, the wages or self-employment income then may be credited to his or her earnings record.

(b) Returning incorrect reports. SSA may return to the filer, unprocessed, an employer's annual wage report submittal if 90 percent or more of the wage reports in that submittal are unidentified or incorrectly identified. In such instances, SSA will advise the filer to return corrected wage reports within 45 days to avoid any possible IRS penalty assessment for failing to file correct reports timely with SSA. (See also § 422.114(c).) Upon request, SSA may grant the employer a 15–day extension of the 45–day period.

[55 FR 46666, Nov. 6, 1990; 60 FR 42434, Aug. 16, 1995]

§ 422.122 Information on deferred vested pension benefits.

(a) Claimants for benefits. Each month, SSA checks the name and social security number of each new claimant for social security benefits or for hospital insurance coverage to see whether the claimant is listed in SSA's electronic pension benefit record. This record contains information received from IRS on individuals for whom private pension plan administrators have reported to IRS, as required by section 6057 of the Internal Revenue Code, as possibly having a right to future retirement benefits under the plan. SSA sends a notice to each new claimant for whom it has pension benefit information, as required by section 1131 of the Act. If the claimant filed for the lump-sum death payment on the social security account of a relative, SSA sends the claimant the pension information on the deceased individual. In either case, SSA sends the notice after it has made a decision on the claim for benefits. The notice shows the type, payment frequency, and amount of pension benefit, as well as the name and address of the plan administrator as reported to the IRS. This information can then be used by the claimant to claim any pension benefits still due from the pension plan.

(b) Requesting deferred vested pension benefit information from SSA files. Section 1131 of the Act also requires SSA to provide available pension benefit information on request. SSA will provide this pension benefit information only to the individual who has the pension coverage (or a legal guardian or parent, in the case of a minor, on the individual's behalf). However, if the individual is deceased, the information may be provided to someone who would be eligible for any underpayment of benefits that might be due the individual under section 204(d) of the Act. All requests for such information must be in writing and should contain the following information: the individual's name, social security number, date of birth, and any information the requestor may have concerning the name of the pension plan involved and the month and year coverage under the plan ended; the name and address of the person to whom the information is to be sent; and the requester's signature under the following statement: "I am the individual to whom the information applies (or "I am related to the individual as his or her __________"). I know that if I make any representation which I know is false to obtain information from Social Security records, I could be punished by a fine or imprisonment or both." Such requests should be sent to: Social Security Administration, Office of Central Records Operations, P.O. Box 17055, Baltimore, Maryland 21235.

[60 FR 42434, Aug. 16, 1995]

§ 422.125 Statements of earnings; resolving earnings discrepancies.

(a) Obtaining a statement of earnings and estimated benefits. An individual may obtain a statement of the earnings on his earnings record and an estimate of social security benefits potentially payable on his record either by writing, calling, or visiting any social security office, or by waiting until we send him one under the procedure described in § 404.812 of this chapter. An individual may request this statement by completing the proper form or by otherwise providing the information the Social Security Administration requires, as explained in § 404.810(b) of this chapter.

(b) Statement of earnings and estimated benefits. Upon receipt of such a request or as required by section 1143(c) of the Social Security Act, the Social Security Administration will provide the individual, without charge, a statement of earnings and benefit estimates or an earnings statement. See §§ 404.811 through 404.812 of this chapter concerning the information contained in these statements.

(c) Detailed earnings statements. A more detailed earnings statement will be furnished upon request, generally without charge, where the request is program related under § 402.170 of this part. If the request for a more detailed statement is not program related under § 402.170 of this part, a charge will be imposed according to the guidelines set out in § 402.175 of this part.

(d) Request for revision of earnings records. If an individual disagrees with a statement of earnings credited to his social security account, he may request a revision by writing to the Bureau of Data Processing and Accounts, Social Security Administration, Baltimore, MD 21235, or by calling at or writing to any social security district office or branch office or, if the individual is in the Philippines, by calling at or writing to the Veterans' Administration Regional Office, Manila, Philippines. Upon receipt of a request for revision, the Social Security Administration will initiate an investigation of the individual's record of earnings. Form OAR–7008, "Statement of Employment for Wages and Self–Employment," is used by the Social Security Administration for obtaining information from the individual requesting a revision to aid the Administration in the investigation. These forms are available at any of the sources listed in this paragraph. If an individual receives a Form OAR–7008 from the Bureau of Data Processing and Accounts, the completed form should be returned to that office. In the course of the investigation the district office or branch office, where appropriate, contacts the employer and the employee or the self-employed individual, whichever is applicable, for the purpose of obtaining the information and evidence necessary to reconcile any discrepancy between the allegations of the individual and the records of the Administration. See subpart I of part 404 of this chapter for requirements for filing requests for revision, and for limitation on the revision of records of earnings.

(e) Notice to individual of determination. After the investigation has been completed and a determination affecting the individual's earnings record has been made, the Social Security Administration will notify the individual in writing of the status of his earnings record and inform him at the same time of the determination made in his case and of his right to a reconsideration if he is dissatisfied with such determination (see § 422.140).

(f) Notice to individual of adverse adjustment of his account. Written notice is given to an individual or his survivor in any case where the Social Security Administration adversely adjusts the individual's self-employment income. Where, subsequent to the issuance of a statement of earnings to an individual, an adverse adjustment is made of an amount of wages included in the statement, written notice of the adverse adjustment is given to the individual or his survivor. Written notice of the adverse adjustment is also given to the survivor if the statement of earnings had been given to such survivor. The individual or his survivor is requested to notify the Social Security Administration promptly if he disagrees, and he is informed that the adjustment will become final unless he notifies the Administration of his disagreement (if any) within 6 months from the date of the letter, or within 3 years, 3 months, and 15 days after the year to which the adjustment relates, whichever is later.

[32 FR 13653, Sept. 29, 1967, as amended at 35 FR 7891, May 22, 1970; 35 FR 8426, May 29, 1970; 39 FR 26721, July 23, 1974; 41 FR 50998, Nov. 19, 1976; 50 FR 28568, July 15, 1985; 57 FR 54919, Nov. 23, 1992; 61 FR 18078, April 24, 1996; 65 FR 16816, March 30, 2000]

§ 422.130 Claim procedure.

(a) General. The Social Security Administration provides facilities for the public to file claims and to obtain assistance in completing them. An appropriate application form and related forms for use in filing a claim for monthly benefits, the establishment of a period of disability, a lump-sum death payment, or entitlement to hospital insurance benefits or supplementary medical insurance benefits can be obtained from any district office, branch office, contact station, or resident station of the Social Security Administration, from the Division of Foreign Claims, Post Office Box 1756, Baltimore, MD 21203, or from the Veteran's Administration Regional Office, Manila, Philippines. See § 404.614 of this chapter for offices at which applications may be filed. See 42 CFR part 405, subpart A, for conditions of entitlement to hospital insurance benefits and 42 CFR part 405, subpart B, for information relating to enrollment under the supplementary medical insurance benefits program.

(b) Submission of evidence. An individual who files an application for monthly benefits, the establishment of a period of disability, a lump-sum death payment, or entitlement to hospital insurance benefits or supplementary medical insurance benefits, either on his own behalf or on behalf of another, must establish by satisfactory evidence the material allegations in his application, except as to earnings shown in the Social Security Administration's records (see subpart H of part 404 of this chapter for evidence requirements in nondisability cases and subpart P of part 404 of this chapter for evidence requirements in disability cases). Instructions, report forms, and forms for the various proofs necessary are available to the public in district offices, branch offices, contact stations, and resident stations of the Social Security Administration, and the Veteran's Administration Regional Office, Manila, Philippines. These offices assist individuals in preparing their applications and in obtaining the proofs required in support of their applications.

(c) Determinations and notice to individuals. In the case of an application for benefits, the establishment of a period of disability, a lump-sum death payment, a recomputation of a primary insurance amount, or entitlement to hospital insurance benefits or supplementary medical insurance benefits, after obtaining the necessary evidence, we will determine, based on the preponderance of the evidence (see §§ 404.901 and 416.1401 of this chapter) as to the entitlement of the individual claiming or for whom is claimed such benefits, and will notify the applicant of the determination and of his right to appeal. Section 404.1503 of this chapter has a discussion of the respective roles of State agencies and the Administration in the making of disability determinations and information regarding initial determinations as to entitlement or termination of entitlement in disability claims. See section 1869(a) of the Social Security Act for determinations under the health insurance for the aged program and sections 1816 and 1842 of the Act for the role of intermediaries, carriers, and State agencies in performing certain functions under such program, e.g., payment of claims pursuant to an agreement with the Social Security Administration.

[32 FR 13653, Sept. 29, 1967, as amended at 44 FR 34942, June 18, 1979; 65 FR 16816, March 30, 2000; 71 FR 16461, March 31, 2006; 73 FR 76945, Dec. 18, 2008; 76 FR 24812, May 3, 2011]

§ 422.135 Reports by beneficiaries.

(a) A recipient of monthly benefits and a person for whom a period of disability has been established are obligated to report to the Social Security Administration the occurrence of certain events which may suspend or terminate benefits or which may cause a cessation of a period of disability. (See §§ 404.415 et seq. and 404.1571 of this chapter.)

(b) A person who files an application for benefits receives oral and written instructions about events which may cause a suspension or termination, and also appropriate forms and instruction cards for reporting such events. Pursuant to section 203(h)(1)(A) of the Act, under certain conditions a beneficiary must, within 3 months and 15 days after the close of a taxable year, submit to the Social Security Administration and annual report of his earnings and of any substantial services in self-employment performed during such taxable year. The purpose of the annual report is to furnish the Social Security Administration with information for making final adjustments in the payment of benefits for that year. An individual may also be requested to submit other reports to the Social Security Administration from time to time.

[65 FR 16816, March 30, 2000]

§ 422.140 Reconsideration of initial determination.

If you are dissatisfied with an initial determination with respect to entitlement to monthly benefits, a lump-sum death payment, a period of disability, a revision of an earnings record, with respect to any other right under title II of the Social Security Act, or with respect to entitlement to hospital insurance benefits or supplementary medical insurance benefits, you may request that we reconsider the initial determination. The information in § 404.1503 of this chapter as to the respective roles of State agencies and the Social Security Administration in making disability determinations is also generally applicable to the reconsideration of initial determinations involving disability. However, in cases in which a disability hearing as described in §§ 404.914 through 404.918 and §§ 416.1414 through 416.1418 of this chapter is available, the reconsidered determination may be issued by a disability hearing officer or the Associate Commissioner for Disability Programs or his or her delegate. After the initial determination has been reconsidered, we will mail you written notice and inform you of your right to a hearing before an administrative law judge (see § 422.201).

[51 FR 308, Jan. 3, 1986; 71 FR 16462, March 31, 2006; 76 FR 24812, May 3, 2011]

SUBPART C—PROCEDURES OF THE OFFICE OF DISABILITY ADJUDICATION AND REVIEW

Authority: Secs. 205, 221, and 702(a)(5) of the Social Security Act (42 U.S.C. 405, 421, and 902(a)(5)); 30 U.S.C. 923(b).

Source: 54 FR 4268, Jan. 30, 1989; 61 FR 5942, Feb. 15, 1996; 76 FR 24812, May 3, 2011, unless otherwise noted.

§ 422.201 Material included in this subpart.

This subpart describes in general the procedures relating to hearings before an administrative law judge of the Office of Disability Adjudication and Review, review by the Appeals Council of the hearing decision or dismissal, and court review in cases decided under the procedures in parts 404, 405, 408, 410, and 416 of this chapter. It also describes the procedures for requesting such hearing or Appeals Council review, and for instituting a civil action for court review for cases decided under these parts. Procedures related to hearings before an administrative law judge, review by the Appeals Council, or court review in claims adjudicated under the procedures in part 405 of this chapter are explained in subparts D, E, and F of part 405 of this chapter. For detailed provisions relating to hearings before an administrative law judge, review by the Appeals Council, and court review, see the following references as appropriate to the matter involved:

(a) Title II of the Act, §§ 404.929 through 404.983 of this chapter;

(b) Title VIII of the Act, §§ 408.1040 through 408.1060 of this chapter;

(c) Title XVI of the Act, §§ 416.1429 through 416.1483 of this chapter;

(d) Part B of title IV of the Federal Mine Safety and Health Act of 1977 as amended, §§ 410.630 through 410.670.

[41 FR 53791, Dec. 9, 1976, as amended at 44 FR 34942, June 18, 1979; 54 FR 4268, Jan. 30, 1989; 71 FR 16462, March 31, 2006; 76 FR 24812, May 3, 2011]

§ 422.203 Hearings.

(a) Right to request a hearing.

(1) After a reconsidered or a revised determination (i) of a claim for benefits or any other right under title II of the Social Security Act; or (ii) of eligibility or amount of benefits or any other matter under title XVI of the Act, except where an initial or reconsidered determination involving an adverse action is revised, after such revised determination has been reconsidered; or (iii) as to entitlement under part A or part B of title XVIII of the Act, or as to the amount of benefits under part A of such title XVIII (where the amount in controversy is $100 or more); or of health services to be provided by a health maintenance organization without additional costs (where the amount in controversy is $100 or more); or as to the amount of benefits under part B of title XVIII (where the amount in controversy is $500 or more); or as to a determination by a peer review organization (PRO) under title XI (where the amount in controversy is $200 or more); or as to certain determinations made under section 1154, 1842(1), 1866(f)(2), or 1879 of the Act; any party to such a determination may, pursuant to the applicable section of the Act, file a written request for a hearing on the determination. After a reconsidered determination of a claim for benefits under part B of title IV (Black Lung benefits) of the Federal Mine Safety and Health Act of 1977 (30 U.S.C. 921 through 925), a party to the determination may file a written request for hearing on the determination.

(2) After (i) a reconsidered or revised determination that an institution, facility, agency, or clinic does not qualify as a provider of services, or (ii) a determination terminating an agreement with a provider of services, such institution, facility, agency, or clinic may, pursuant to section 1866 of the Act, file a written request for a hearing on the determination.

(3) After (i) a reconsidered or revised determination that an independent laboratory, supplier of portable X-ray services, or end-stage renal disease treatment facility or other person does not meet the conditions for coverage of its services or (ii) a determination that it no longer meets such conditions has been made, such laboratory, supplier, treatment facility may, under 42 CFR 498.40 of this chapter, file a written request for a hearing on the determination. (For hearing rights of independent laboratories, suppliers of portable X-ray services, and end-stage renal disease treatment facilities and other person see 42 CFR 498.5.)

(b) Request for hearing.

(1) A request for a hearing under paragraph (a) of this section may be made on Form HA–501, "Request for Hearing," or Form HA–501.1, "Request for Hearing, part A Hospital Insurance Benefits," or by any other writing requesting a hearing. The request shall be filed at an office of the Social Security Administration, usually a district office or a branch office, or at the Veterans' Administration Regional Office in the Philippines (except in title XVI cases), or at a hearing office of the Office of Hearings and Appeals, or with the Appeals Council. A qualified railroad retirement beneficiary may, if he prefers, file a request for a hearing under part A of title XVIII with the Railroad Retirement Board. Form HA–501 may be obtained from any social security district office or branch office, from the Office of Hearings and Appeals, Social Security Administration, P.O. Box 3200, Arlington, VA 22203, or from any other office where a request for a hearing may be filed.

(2) Unless for good cause shown an extension of time has been granted, a request for hearing must be filed within 60 days after the receipt of the notice of the reconsidered or revised determination, or after an initial determination described in 42 CFR 498.3(b) and (c) (see §§ 404.933, 410.631, and 416.1433 of this chapter and 42 CFR 405.722, 498.40, and 417.260.)

(c) Hearing decision or other action. Generally, the administrative law judge will either decide the case after hearing (unless hearing is waived) or, if appropriate, dismiss the request for hearing. With respect to a hearing on a determination under paragraph (a)(1) of this section, the administrative law judge may certify the case with a recommended decision to the Appeals Council for decision. If the determination on which the hearing request is based relates to the amount of benefits under part A or B of title XVIII of the Act, to health services to be provided by a health maintenance organization without additional costs, or to PRO determinations, the administrative law judge shall dismiss the request for hearing if he or she finds that the amount in controversy is less than $100 for appeals arising under part A or concerning health maintenance organization benefits; less than $200 for appeals arising from PRO determinations; and less than $500 for appeals arising under part B. The administrative law judge, or an attorney advisor under §§ 404.942 or 416.1442 of this chapter, must base the hearing decision on the preponderance of the evidence offered at the hearing or otherwise included in the record.

[41 FR 53791, Dec. 9, 1976, as amended at 44 FR 34942, June 18, 1979; 51 FR 308, Jan. 3, 1986; 54 FR 4268, Jan. 30, 1989; 73 FR 76945, Dec. 18, 2008]

§ 422.205 Review by Appeals Council.

(a) Any party to a hearing decision or dismissal may request a review of such action by the Appeals Council. The Health Care Financing Administration or, as appropriate, the Office of the Inspector General is a party to a hearing on a determination under § 422.203 (a)(2) and (a)(3) and to administrative appeals involving matters under section 1128(b)(6) of the Act (see 42 CFR 498.42). This request may be made on Form HA–520, "Request for Review of Hearing Decision/Order," or by any other writing specifically requesting review. Form HA–520 may be obtained from any social security district office or branch office, from the Office of Hearings and Appeals Social Security Administration, P.O. Box 3200, Arlington, VA 22203, or at any other office where a request for a hearing may be filed. (For time and place of filing, see §§ 404.968, 410.661, and 416.1468 of this chapter, and 42 CFR 405.724, 498.82 and 417.261.)

(b) Whenever the Appeals Council reviews a hearing decision under §§ 404.967 or 404.969, 410.662, 416.1467, or 416.1469 of this chapter, or 42 CFR 405.724 or 417.261 or 473.46 and the claimant does not appear personally or through representation before the Council to present oral argument, such review will be conducted by a panel of not less than two members of the Council designated in the manner prescribed by the Chairman or Deputy Chairman of the Council. In the event of disagreement between a panel composed of only two members, the Chairman or Deputy Chairman, or his delegate, who must be a member of the Council, shall participate as a third member of the panel. When the claimant appears in person or through representation before the Council in the location designated by the Council, the review will be conducted by a panel of not less than three members of the Council designated in the manner prescribed by the Chairman or Deputy Chairman. Concurrence of a majority of a panel shall constitute the decision of the Appeals Council unless the case is considered as provided under paragraph (e) of this section.

(c) The denial of a request for review of a hearing decision concerning a determination under § 422.203(a)(1) shall be by such appeals officer or appeals officers or by such member or members of the Appeals Council as may be designated in the manner prescribed by the Chair or Deputy Chair. The denial of a request for review of a hearing dismissal, the dismissal of a request for review, the denial of a request for review of a hearing decision whenever such hearing decision after such denial would not be subject to judicial review as explained in § 422.210(a), or the refusal of a request to reopen a hearing or Appeals Council decision concerning a determination under § 422.203(a)(1) shall be by such member or members of the Appeals Council as may be designated in the manner prescribed by the Chair or Deputy Chair.

(d) A review or a denial of review of a hearing decision or a dismissal of a request for review with respect to requests by parties under 42 CFR 498.82 or 1001.128 in accordance with § 498.83 will be conducted by a panel of at least two members of the Appeals Council designated by the Chairman or Deputy Chairman and one person from the U.S. Public Health Service designated by the Surgeon General, Public Health Service, Department of Health and Human Services, or his delegate. This person shall serve on an ad hoc basis and shall be considered for this purpose as a member of the Appeals Council. Concurrence of a majority of the panel shall constitute the decision of the Appeals Council unless the case is considered as provided under paragraph (e) of this section.

(e) On call of the Chairman, the Appeals Council may meet en banc or a representative body of Appeals Council members may be convened to consider any case arising under paragraph (b), (c), or (d) of this section. Such representative body shall be comprised of a panel of not less than five members designated by the Chairman as deemed appropriate for the matter to be considered, including a person from the U.S. Public Health Service in a matter under paragraph (d) of this section. The Chairman or Deputy Chairman shall preside, or in his absence, the Chairman shall designate a member of the Appeals Council to preside. A majority vote of the designated panel, or of the members present and voting shall constitute the decision of the Appeals Council.

(f) The Chairman may designate an administrative law judge to serve as a member of the Appeals Council for temporary assignments. An administrative law judge shall not be designated to serve as a member on any panel where such panel is conducting review on a case in which such individual has been previously involved.

[41 FR 53792, Dec. 9, 1976, as amended at 44 FR 34942, June 18, 1979; 54 FR 4268, Jan. 30, 1989; 60 FR 7120, Feb. 7, 1995]

§ 422.210 Judicial review.

(a) General. A claimant may obtain judicial review of a decision by an administrative law judge if the Appeals Council has denied the claimant's request for review, or of a decision by the Appeals Council when that is the final decision of the Commissioner. A claimant may also obtain judicial review of a reconsidered determination, or of a decision of an administrative law judge, where, under the expedited appeals procedure, further administrative review is waived by agreement under §§ 404.926, 410.629d, or 416.1426 of this chapter or 42 CFR 405.718a-e as appropriate. For judicial review as to the amount of benefits under part A or part B of title XVIII of the Social Security Act, or of health services to be provided by a health maintenance organization without additional cost, the amount in controversy must be $1,000 or more as provided under section 1869(b) and section 1876(c)(5)(B) of the Act. For judicial review of a determination by a PRO, the amount in controversy must be $2,000 or more. An institution or agency may obtain judicial review of a decision by the Appeals Council that it is not a provider of services, or of a decision by the Appeals Council terminating an agreement entered into by the institution or agency with the Commissioner (see section 1866(b)(2) of the Act). The Social Security Act does not provide for a right to judicial review of a final decision of the Commissioner regarding the status of an entity which is not a "provider of services", such as an independent laboratory. Providers of services or other persons may seek judicial review of a final administrative determination made pursuant to section 1128(b)(6) of the Act. There are no amount-in-controversy limitations on these rights of appeal.

(b) Court in which to institute civil action. Any civil action described in paragraph (a) of this section must be instituted in the district court of the United States for the judicial district in which the claimant resides or where such individual or institution or agency has his principal place of business. If the individual does not reside within any such judicial district, or if such individual or institution or agency does not have his principal place of business within any such judicial district, the civil action must be instituted in the District Court of the United States for the District of Columbia.

(c) Time for instituting civil action. Any civil action described in paragraph (a) of this section must be instituted within 60 days after the Appeals Council's notice of denial of request for review of the administrative law judge's decision or notice of the decision by the Appeals Council is received by the individual, institution, or agency, except that this time may be extended by the Appeals Council upon a showing of good cause. For purposes of this section, the date of receipt of notice of denial of request for review of the presiding officer's decision or notice of the decision by the Appeals Council shall be presumed to be 5 days after the date of such notice, unless there is a reasonable showing to the contrary. Where pursuant to the expedited appeals procedures an agreement has been entered into under 42 CFR 405.718c, a civil action under section 205(g) of the Act must be commenced within 60 days from the date of the signing of such agreement by, or on behalf of, the Commissioner, except where the time described in the first sentence of this paragraph (c) has been extended by the Commissioner upon a showing of good cause. Where pursuant to the expedited appeals procedures an agreement has been entered into under §§ 404.926, 410.629d, or 416.1426 of this chapter, a civil action under section 205(g) of the Act must be commenced within 60 days after the date the individual receives notice (a signed copy of the agreement will be mailed to the individual and will constitute notice) of the signing of such agreement by, or on behalf of, the Commissioner, except where the time described in this paragraph (c) has been extended by the Commissioner upon a showing of good cause.

(d) Proper defendant. Where any civil action described in paragraph (a) of this section is instituted, the person holding the Office of the Commissioner shall, in his official capacity, be the proper defendant. Any such civil action properly instituted shall survive notwithstanding any change of the person holding the Office of the Commissioner or any vacancy in such office. If the complaint is erroneously filed against the United States or against any agency, officer, or employee of the United States other than the Commissioner, the plaintiff will be notified that he has named an incorrect defendant and will be granted 60 days from the date of receipt of such notice in which to commence the action against the correct defendant, the Commissioner.

[41 FR 53792, Dec. 9, 1976, as amended at 44 FR 34942, June 18, 1979; 49 FR 46370, Nov. 26, 1984; 49 FR 48036, Dec. 10, 1984; 54 FR 4268, Jan. 30, 1989; 62 FR 38456, July 18, 1997]

SUBPART D—CLAIMS COLLECTION

Authority: Secs. 204(f), 205(a), 702(a)(5), and 1631(b) of the Social Security Act (42 U.S.C. 404(f), 405(a), 902(a)(5), and 1383(b)); 5 U.S.C. 5514; 31 U.S.C. 3711(e); 31 U.S.C. 3716.

Source: 62 FR 64278, Dec. 5, 1997; 66 FR 67081, Dec. 28, 2001; 71 FR 38070, July 5, 2006, unless otherwise noted.

§ 422.301 Scope of this subpart.

(a) Except as provided in paragraphs (b) and (c) of this section, this subpart describes the procedures relating to collection of:

(1) Overdue administrative debts, and

(2) Overdue program overpayments described in §§ 404.527 and 416.590 of this chapter.

(b) This subpart does not apply to administrative debts owed by employees of the Social Security Administration, including, but not limited to, overpayment of pay and allowances.

(c) The following exceptions apply only to Federal salary offset as described in § 422.310(a)(1).

(1) We will not use this subpart to collect a debt while the debtor's disability benefits are stopped during the reentitlement period, under § 404.1592a(a)(2) of this chapter, because the debtor is engaging in substantial gainful activity.

(2) We will not use this subpart to collect a debt while the debtor's Medicare entitlement is continued because the debtor is deemed to be entitled to disabili-

ty benefits under section 226(b) of the Social Security Act (42 U.S.C. 426(b)).

(3) We will not use this subpart to collect a debt if the debtor has decided to participate in the Ticket to Work and Self–Sufficiency Program and the debtor's ticket is in use as described in §§ 411.170 through 411.225 of this chapter.

[66 FR 67081, Dec. 28, 2001; 71 FR 38070, July 5, 2006]

§ 422.303 Interest, late payment penalties, and administrative costs of collection.

We may charge the debtor with interest, late payment penalties, and our costs of collection on delinquent debts covered by this subpart when authorized by our regulations issued in accordance with the Federal Claims Collection Standards (31 CFR 901.9).

[71 FR 38070, July 5, 2006]

§ 422.305 Report of overdue program overpayment debts to consumer reporting agencies.

(a) Debts we will report. We will report to consumer reporting agencies all overdue program overpayment debts over $25.

(b) Notice to debtor. Before we report any such debt to a consumer reporting agency, we will send the debtor written notice of the following:

(1) We have determined that payment of the debt is overdue;

(2) We will refer the debt to a consumer reporting agency at the expiration of not less than 60 calendar days after the date of the notice unless, within that 60–day period, the debtor pays the full amount of the debt or takes either of the actions described in paragraphs (b)(6) or (b)(7) of this section;

(3) The specific information we will provide to the consumer reporting agency, including information that identifies the debtor (e.g., name, address, and social security number) and the amount, status, and history of the debt;

(4) The debtor has the right to a complete explanation of the debt;

(5) The debtor may dispute the accuracy of the information to be provided to the consumer reporting agency;

(6) The debtor may request a review of the debt by giving us evidence showing that he or she does not owe all or part of the amount of the debt or that we do not have the right to collect it; and

(7) The debtor may request an installment payment plan.

(c) Disputing the information that we would send to consumer reporting agencies. If a debtor believes that the information we propose to send to consumer reporting agencies is incorrect, the debtor may ask us to correct such information. If, within 60 calendar days from the date of our notice described in paragraph (b) of this section, the debtor notifies us that any information to be sent to consumer reporting agencies is incorrect, we will not send the information to consumer reporting agencies until we determine the correct information.

[66 FR 67081, Dec. 28, 2001]

§ 422.306 Report of overdue administrative debts to credit reporting agencies.

(a) Debts we will report. We will report to credit reporting agencies all overdue administrative debts over $25. Some examples of administrative debts are as follows: debts for civil monetary penalties imposed under section 1140(b) of the Act, debts for unpaid fees for reimbursable services performed by SSA (e.g., disclosures of information), and contractor debts.

(b) Notice to debtor. Before we report any administrative debt to a credit reporting agency, we will send the debtor written notice of the following:

(1) We have determined that payment of the debt is overdue;

(2) We will refer the debt to a credit reporting agency at the expiration of not less than 60 calendar days after the date of the notice unless, within that 60–day period, the debtor pays the full amount of the debt or takes either of the actions described in paragraphs (b)(6) or (b)(7) of this section;

(3) The specific information we will provide to the credit reporting agency, including information that identifies the debtor (e.g., name, address, social security number, and employer identification number) and the amount, status, and history of the debt;

(4) The debtor has the right to a complete explanation of the debt;

(5) The debtor may dispute the accuracy of the information to be provided to the credit reporting agency;

(6) The debtor may request a review of the debt by giving us evidence showing that he or she does not owe all or part of the amount of the debt or that we do not have the right to collect it; and

(7) The debtor may request an installment payment plan.

[71 FR 38070, July 5, 2006]

§ 422.310 Collection of overdue debts by administrative offset.

(a) Referral to the Department of the Treasury for offset.

(1) We recover overdue debts by offsetting Federal and State payments due the debtor through the Treasury Offset Program (TOP). TOP is a Government-wide delinquent debt matching and payment offset process operated by the Department of the Treasury, whereby debts owed to the Federal Government are

collected by offsetting them against Federal and State payments owed the debtor. Federal payments owed the debtor include current "disposable pay," defined in 5 CFR 550.1103, owed by the Federal Government to a debtor who is an employee of the Federal Government. Deducting from such disposable pay to collect an overdue debt owed by the employee is called "Federal salary offset" in this subpart.

(2) Except as provided in paragraphs (b) and (c) of § 422.301, we will use Federal salary offset to collect overdue debts from Federal employees, including employees of the Social Security Administration. A Federal employee's involuntary payment of all or part of a debt collected by Federal salary offset does not amount to a waiver of any rights which the employee may have under any statute or contract, unless a statute or contract provides for waiver of such rights.

(b) Debts we refer. We refer for administrative offset all qualifying debts that meet or exceed the threshold amounts used by the Department of the Treasury for collection from State and Federal payments, including Federal salaries.

(c) Notice to debtor. Before we refer any debt for collection by administrative offset, we will send the debtor written notice that explains all of the following:

(1) The nature and amount of the debt.

(2) We have determined that payment of the debt is overdue.

(3) We will refer the debt for administrative offset (except as provided in paragraph (c)(9) of this section) at the expiration of not less than 60 calendar days after the date of the notice unless, within that 60–day period:

(i) The debtor pays the full amount of the debt, or

(ii) The debtor takes any of the actions described in paragraphs (c)(6) or (c)(7) of this section.

(4) The frequency and amount of any Federal salary offset deduction (the payment schedule) expressed as a fixed dollar amount or percentage of disposable pay.

(5) The debtor may inspect or copy our records relating to the debt. If the debtor or his or her representative cannot personally inspect the records, the debtor may request and receive a copy of such records.

(6) The debtor may request a review of the debt by giving us evidence showing that the debtor does not owe all or part of the amount of the debt or that we do not have the right to collect it. The debtor may also request review of any payment schedule for Federal salary offset stated in the notice. If the debtor is an employee of the Federal Government and Federal salary offset is proposed, an official designated in accordance with 5 U.S.C. 5514(a)(2) will conduct the review.

(7) The debtor may request to repay the debt voluntarily through an installment payment plan.

(8) If the debtor knowingly furnishes any false or frivolous statements, representations, or evidence, the debtor may be subject to:

(i) Civil or criminal penalties under applicable statutes;

(ii) Appropriate disciplinary procedures under applicable statutes or regulations, when the debtor is a Federal employee.

(9) We will refer the debt for Federal salary offset at the expiration of not less than 30 calendar days after the date of the notice unless, within that 30 day period the debtor takes any actions described in paragraphs (c)(3)(i), (c)(6) or (c)(7) of this section.

(d) Federal salary offset: amount, frequency and duration of deductions.

(1) We may collect the overdue debt from an employee of the Federal Government through the deduction of an amount not to exceed 15% of the debtor's current disposable pay each payday.

(2) Federal salary offset will begin no sooner than the first payday following 30 calendar days after the date of the notice to the debtor described in paragraph (c) of this section.

(3) Once begun, Federal salary offset will continue until we recover the full amount of the debt, the debt is otherwise resolved, or the debtor's Federal employment ceases, whichever occurs first.

(4) After Federal salary offset begins, the debtor may request a reduction in the amount deducted from disposable pay each payday. When we determine that the amount deducted causes financial harm under the rules in § 422.415(b), (c), and (d) of this chapter, we will reduce that amount.

(e) Refunds. We will promptly refund to the debtor any amounts collected that the debtor does not owe. Refunds do not bear interest unless required or permitted by law or contract.

[71 FR 38070, July 5, 2006; 76 FR 65109, Oct. 20, 2011]

§ 422.315 Review of our records related to the debt.

(a) Notification by the debtor. The debtor may request to inspect or copy our records related to the debt.

(b) Our response. In response to a request from the debtor described in paragraph (a) of this section, we will notify the debtor of the location and time at which the debtor may inspect or copy our records related to the debt. We may also, at our discretion, mail to the debtor copies of the records relating to the debt.

§ 422.317 Review of the debt.

(a) Notification and presentation of evidence by the debtor. A debtor who receives a notice described in

§ 422.305(b), § 422.306(b), or § 422.310(c) has a right to have a review of the debt and the payment schedule for Federal salary offset stated in the notice. To exercise this right, the debtor must notify us and give us evidence that he or she does not owe all or part of the debt, or that we do not have the right to collect it, or that the payment schedule for Federal salary offset stated in the notice would cause financial hardship.

(1) If the debtor notifies us and presents evidence within 60 calendar days from the date of our notice (except as provided for Federal salary offset in paragraph (a)(3) of this section), we will not take the action described in our notice unless and until review of all of the evidence is complete and we send the debtor the findings that all or part of the debt is overdue and legally enforceable.

(2) If the debtor notifies us and presents evidence after that 60 calendar-day period expires (except as provided for Federal salary offset in paragraph (a)(4) of this section) and paragraph (b) of this section does not apply, the review will occur, but we may take the actions described in our notice without further delay.

(3) If the debtor notifies us and presents evidence within 30 calendar days from the date of our notice, we will not refer the debt for Federal salary offset unless and until review of all of the evidence is complete and we send the debtor the findings that all or part of the debt is overdue and legally enforceable and (if appropriate) the findings on the payment schedule for Federal salary offset.

(4) If the debtor notifies us and presents evidence after that 30 calendar-day period expires and paragraph (b) of this section does not apply, the review will occur, but we may refer the debt for Federal salary offset without further delay.

(b) Good cause for failure to timely request review.

(1) If we decide that the debtor has good cause for failing to request review within the applicable period mentioned in paragraphs (a)(1) and (a)(3) of this section, we will treat the request for review as if we received it within the applicable period.

(2) We will determine good cause under the rules in § 422.410(b)(1) and (2) of this chapter.

(c) Review of the evidence. The review will cover our records and any evidence and statements presented by the debtor.

(d) Special rules regarding Federal salary offset.

(1) When we use Federal salary offset to collect a debt owed by an employee of the Federal Government, an official designated in accordance with 5 U.S.C. 5514(a)(2) will conduct the review described in this section and will issue the findings.

(2) In addition to the requirements in paragraphs (a) and (b) of this section, the Federal employee must submit the request for review in writing. The request must

(i) Be signed by the employee,

(ii) Explain with reasonable specificity the facts and evidence that support the employee's position, and

(iii) Include the names of any witnesses.

(3) In reviewing the payment schedule described in the notice to the Federal employee, the reviewing official must apply the rules in § 422.415(b), (c), and (d) of this chapter regarding financial hardship.

(4) The reviewing official will review our records and any documents, written statements, or other evidence submitted by the debtor and issue written findings.

(5) The reviewing official will complete the review within 60 calendar days from the date on which the request for review and the debtor's evidence are received. If the reviewing official does not complete the review within that 60–day period and the debt was referred to the Department of the Treasury for Federal salary offset, we will notify the Department of the Treasury to suspend Federal salary offset. Offset will not begin or resume before we send the debtor findings that all or part of the debt is overdue and legally enforceable or (if appropriate) findings on the payment schedule.

(e) The findings.

(1) Following the review described in paragraphs (c) or (d) of this section, we will send the written findings to the debtor. The findings will state the nature and origin of the debt, the analysis, findings and conclusions regarding the amount and validity of the debt, and, when appropriate, the repayment schedule for Federal salary offset. Issuance of these findings will be the final action on the debtor's request for review.

(2) If the findings state that an individual does not owe the debt, or the debt is not overdue, or we do not have the right to collect it, we will not send information about the debt to consumer or other credit reporting agencies or refer the debt to the Department of the Treasury for administrative offset. If we had referred the debt to the Department of the Treasury for administrative offset, we will cancel that action. If we had informed consumer or credit reporting agencies about the debt, we will inform them of the findings.

(3) If the findings state that the payment schedule for Federal salary offset would cause financial hardship, we will notify the debtor and the Department of the Treasury of the new payment schedule.

[71 FR 38071, July 5, 2006]

SUBPART E—COLLECTION OF DEBTS BY ADMINISTRATIVE WAGE GARNISHMENT

Authority: Secs. 205(a), 702(a)(5) and 1631(d)(1) of the Social Security Act (42 U.S.C. 405(a), 902(a)(5) and 1383(d)(1)) and 31 U.S.C. 3720D.

Source: 68 FR 74184, Dec. 23, 2003, unless otherwise noted.

§ 422.401 What is the scope of this subpart?

This subpart describes the procedures relating to our use of administrative wage garnishment under 31 U.S.C. 3720D to recover past due debts that you owe.

§ 422.402 What special definitions apply to this subpart?

(a) Administrative wage garnishment is a process whereby we order your employer to withhold a certain amount from your disposable pay and send the withheld amount to us. The law requires your employer to comply with our garnishment order.

(b) Debt means any amount of money or property that we determine is owed to the United States and that arises from a program that we administer or an activity that we perform. These debts include program overpayments made under title II or title XVI of the Social Security Act and any other debt that meets the definition of "claim" or "debt" at 31 U.S.C. 3701(b).

(c) Disposable pay means that part of your total compensation (including, but not limited to, salary or wages, bonuses, commissions, and vacation pay) from your employer after deduction of health insurance premiums and amounts withheld as required by law. Amounts withheld as required by law include such things as Federal, State and local taxes but do not include amounts withheld under court order.

(d) We, our, or us means the Social Security Administration.

(e) You means an individual who owes a debt to the United States within the scope of this subpart.

§ 422.403 When may we use administrative wage garnishment?

(a) General. Subject to the exceptions described in paragraph (b) of this section and the conditions described in paragraphs (c) and (d) of this section, we may use administrative wage garnishment to collect any debt that is past due. We may use administrative wage garnishment while we are taking other action regarding the debt, such as, using tax refund offset under §§ 404.520–404.526 and 416.580–416.586 of this chapter and taking action under subpart D of this part.

(b) Exceptions.

(1) We will not use this subpart to collect a debt from salary or wages paid by the United States Government.

(2) If you have been separated involuntarily from employment, we will not order your employer to withhold amounts from your disposable pay until you have been reemployed continuously for at least 12 months. You have the burden of informing us about an involuntary separation from employment.

(3) We will not use this subpart to collect a debt while your disability benefits are stopped during the reentitlement period, under § 404.1592a(a)(2) of this chapter, because you are engaging in substantial gainful activity.

(4) We will not use this subpart to collect a debt while your Medicare entitlement is continued because you are deemed to be entitled to disability benefits under section 226(b) of the Social Security Act (42 U.S.C. 426(b)).

(5) We will not use this subpart to collect a debt if you have decided to participate in the Ticket to Work and Self–Sufficiency Program and your ticket is in use as described in §§ 411.170 through 411.225 of this chapter.

(c) Overpayments under title II of the Social Security Act. This subpart applies to overpayments under title II of the Social Security Act if all of the following conditions are met:

(1) You are not receiving title II benefits.

(2) We have completed our billing system sequence (i.e., we have sent you an initial notice of the overpayment, a reminder notice, and a past-due notice) or we have suspended or terminated collection activity in accordance with applicable rules, such as, the Federal Claims Collection Standards in 31 CFR 903.2 or 31 CFR 903.3.

(3) We have not made an installment payment arrangement with you or, if we have made such an arrangement, you have failed to make any payment for two consecutive months.

(4) You have not requested waiver pursuant to § 404.506 or § 404.522 of this chapter or, after a review conducted pursuant to those sections, we have determined that we will not waive collection of the overpayment.

(5) You have not requested reconsideration of the initial overpayment determination pursuant to §§ 404.907 and 404.909 of this chapter or, after a review conducted pursuant to § 404.913 of this chapter, we have affirmed all or part of the initial overpayment determination.

(6) We cannot recover your overpayment pursuant to § 404.502 of this chapter by adjustment of benefits payable to any individual other than you. For purposes of this paragraph, an overpayment will be deemed to be unrecoverable from any individual who was living in a separate household from yours at the time of the overpayment and who did not receive the overpayment.

(d) Overpayments under title XVI of the Social Security Act. This subpart applies to overpayments under title XVI of the Social Security Act if all of the following conditions are met:

(1) You are not receiving benefits under title XVI of the Social Security Act.

(2) We are not collecting your title XVI overpayment by reducing title II benefits payable to you.

(3) We have completed our billing system sequence (i.e., we have sent you an initial notice of the overpayment, a reminder notice, and a past-due notice) or we have suspended or terminated collection activity under applicable rules, such as, the Federal Claims Collection Standards in 31 CFR 903.2 or 31 CFR 903.3.

(4) We have not made an installment payment arrangement with you or, if we have made such an arrangement, you have failed to make any payment for two consecutive months.

(5) You have not requested waiver pursuant to § 416.550 or § 416.582 of this chapter or, after a review conducted pursuant to those sections, we have determined that we will not waive collection of the overpayment.

(6) You have not requested reconsideration of the initial overpayment determination pursuant to §§ 416.1407 and 416.1409 of this chapter or, after a review conducted pursuant to § 416.1413 of this chapter, we have affirmed all or part of the initial overpayment determination.

(7) We cannot recover your overpayment pursuant to § 416.570 of this chapter by adjustment of benefits payable to any individual other than you. For purposes of this paragraph, if you are a member of an eligible couple that is legally separated and/or living apart, we will deem unrecoverable from the other person that part of your overpayment which he or she did not receive.

§ 422.405 What notice will we send you about administrative wage garnishment?

(a) General. Before we order your employer to collect a debt by deduction from your disposable pay, we will send you written notice of our intention to do so.

(b) Contents of the notice. The notice will contain the following information:

(1) We have determined that payment of the debt is past due;

(2) The nature and amount of the debt;

(3) Information about the amount that your employer could withhold from your disposable pay each payday (the payment schedule);

(4) No sooner than 60 calendar days after the date of the notice, we will order your employer to withhold the debt from your disposable pay unless, within that 60–day period, you pay the full amount of the debt or take either of the actions described in paragraphs (b)(6) or (7) of this section;

(5) You may inspect and copy our records about the debt (see § 422.420);

(6) You may request a review of the debt (see § 422.425) or the payment schedule stated in the notice (see § 422.415); and

(7) You may request to pay the debt by monthly installment payments to us.

(c) Mailing address. We will send the notice to the most current mailing address that we have for you in our records.

(d) Electronic record of the notice. We will keep an electronic record of the notice that shows the date we mailed the notice to you and the amount of your debt.

§ 422.410 What actions will we take after we send you the notice?

(a) General.

(1) We will not send an administrative wage garnishment order to your employer before 60 calendar days elapse from the date of the notice described in § 422.405.

(2) If paragraph (b) of this section does not apply and you do not pay the debt in full or do not take either of the actions described in § 422.405(b)(6) or (7) within 60 calendar days from the date of the notice described in § 422.405, we may order your employer to withhold and send us part of your disposable pay each payday until your debt is paid.

(3) If you request review of the debt or the payment schedule after the end of the 60 calendar day period described in paragraph (a)(2) of this section and paragraph (b) of this section does not apply, we will conduct the review. However, we may send the administrative wage garnishment order to your employer without further delay. If we sent the administrative wage garnishment order to your employer and we do not make our decision on your request within 60 calendar days from the date that we received your request, we will tell your employer to stop withholding from your disposable pay. Withholding will not resume before we conduct the review and notify you of our decision.

(4) We may send an administrative wage garnishment order to your employer without further delay if:

(i) You request an installment payment plan after receiving the notice described in § 422.405, and

(ii) We arrange such a plan with you, and

(iii) You fail to make payments in accordance with that arrangement for two consecutive months.

(b) Good cause for failing to request review on time. If we decide that you had good cause for failing to request review within the 60–day period mentioned in paragraph (a)(2) of this section, we will treat your request for review as if we received it within that 60–day period.

(1) Determining good cause. In determining whether you had good cause, we will consider—

(i) Any circumstances that kept you from making the request on time;

(ii) Whether our action misled you;

(iii) Whether you had any physical, mental, educational, or linguistic limitations (including any lack of facility with the English language) which prevented you from making a request on time or from understanding the need to make a request on time.

(2) Examples of good cause. Examples of facts supporting good cause include, but are not limited to, the following.

(i) Your serious illness prevented you from contacting us yourself or through another person.

(ii) There was a death or serious illness in your family.

(iii) Fire or other accidental cause destroyed important records.

(iv) You did not receive the notice described in § 422.405.

(v) In good faith, you sent the request to another government agency within the 60–day period, and we received the request after the end of that period.

(3) If we issued the administrative wage garnishment order. If we determine that you had good cause under paragraph (b) of this section and we already had sent an administrative wage garnishment order to your employer, we will tell your employer to stop withholding from your disposable pay. Withholding will not resume until we conduct the review and notify you of our decision.

§ 422.415 Will we reduce the amount that your employer must withhold from your pay when withholding that amount causes financial hardship?

(a) General. Unless paragraph (d) of this section applies, we will reduce the amount that your employer must withhold from your pay when you request the reduction and we find financial hardship. In any event, we will not reduce the amount your employer must withhold each payday below $10. When we decide to reduce the amount that your employer withholds, we will give you and your employer written notice.

(1) You may ask us at any time to reduce the amount due to financial hardship.

(2) If you request review of the payment schedule stated in the notice described in § 422.405 within the 60–day period stated in the notice, we will not issue a garnishment order to your employer until we notify you of our decision.

(b) Financial hardship. We will find financial hardship when you show that withholding a particular amount from your pay would deprive you of income necessary to meet your ordinary and necessary living expenses. You must give us evidence of your financial resources and expenses.

(c) Ordinary and necessary living expenses. Ordinary and necessary living expenses include:

(1) Fixed expenses such as food, clothing, housing, utilities, maintenance, insurance, tax payments;

(2) Medical, hospitalization and similar expenses;

(3) Expenses for the support of others for whom you are legally responsible; and

(4) Other reasonable and necessary miscellaneous expenses which are part of your standard of living.

(d) Fraud and willful concealment or failure to furnish information.

(1) We will not reduce the amount that your employer withholds from your disposable pay if your debt was caused by:

(i) Your intentional false statement, or

(ii) Your willful concealment of, or failure to furnish, material information.

(2) "Willful concealment" means an intentional, knowing and purposeful delay in providing, or failure to reveal, material information.

§ 422.420 May you inspect and copy our records related to the debt?

You may inspect and copy our records related to the debt. You must notify us of your intention to review our records. After you notify us, we will arrange with you the place and time the records will be available to you. At our discretion, we may send copies of the records to you.

§ 422.425 How will we conduct our review of the debt?

(a) You must request review and present evidence. If you receive a notice described in § 422.405, you have the right to have us review the debt. To exercise this right, you must request review and give us evidence that you do not owe all or part of the debt or that we do not have the right to collect it. If you do not request review and give us this evidence within 60 calendar days from the date of our notice, we may issue the garnishment order to your employer without further delay. If you request review of the debt and present evidence within that 60 calendar-day period, we will not send a garnishment order to your employer unless and until we consider all of the evidence and send you our findings that all or part of the debt is overdue and we have the right to collect it.

(b) Review of the evidence. If you request review of the debt, we will review our records related to the debt and any evidence that you present.

(c) Our findings. Following our review of all of the evidence, we will send you written findings, including the supporting rationale for the findings. Issuance of these findings will be our final action on your request for review. If we find that you do not owe the debt, or the debt is not overdue, or we do not have the right to collect it, we will not send a garnishment order to your employer.

§ 422.430 When will we refund amounts of your pay withheld by administrative wage garnishment?

If we find that you do not owe the debt or that we have no right to collect it, we will promptly refund to you any amount withheld from your disposable pay under this subpart that we received and cancel any administrative wage garnishment order that we issued. Refunds under this section will not bear interest unless Federal law or contract requires interest.

§ 422.435 What happens when we decide to send an administrative wage garnishment order to your employer?

(a) The wage garnishment order. The wage garnishment order that we send to your employer will contain only the information necessary for the employer to comply with the order. This information includes:

(1) Your name, address, and social security number,

(2) The amount of the debt,

(3) Information about the amount to be withheld, and

(4) Information about where to send the withheld amount.

(b) Electronic record of the garnishment order. We will keep an electronic record of the garnishment order that shows the date we mailed the order to your employer.

(c) Employer certification. Along with the garnishment order, we will send your employer a certification form to complete about your employment status and the amount of your disposable pay available for withholding. Your employer must complete the certification and return it to us within 20 days of receipt.

(d) Amounts to be withheld from your disposable pay. After receipt of the garnishment order issued under this section, your employer must begin withholding from your disposable pay each payday the lesser of:

(1) The amount indicated on the order (up to 15% of your disposable pay); or

(2) The amount by which your disposable pay exceeds thirty times the minimum wage as provided in 15 U.S.C. 1673(a)(2).

(e) Multiple withholding orders. If your disposable pay is subject to more than one withholding order, we apply the following rules to determine the amount that your employer will withhold from your disposable pay:

(1) Unless otherwise provided by Federal law or paragraph (e)(2) of this section, a garnishment order issued under this section has priority over other withholding orders served later in time.

(2) Withholding orders for family support have priority over garnishment orders issued under this section.

(3) If at the time we issue a garnishment order to your employer amounts are already being withheld from your pay under another withholding order, or if a withholding order for family support is served on your employer at any time, the amounts to be withheld under this section will be the lesser of:

(i) The amount calculated under paragraph (d) of this section; or

(ii) The amount calculated by subtracting the amount(s) withheld under the withholding order(s) with priority from 25% of your disposable pay.

(4) If you owe more than one debt to us, we may issue multiple garnishment orders. If we issue more than one garnishment order, the total amount to be withheld from your disposable pay under such orders will not exceed the amount set forth in paragraph (d) or (e)(3) of this section, as appropriate.

(f) You may request that your employer withhold more. If you request in writing that your employer withhold more than the amount determined under paragraphs (d) or (e) of this section, we will order your employer to withhold the amount that you request.

§ 422.440 What are your employer's responsibilities under an administrative wage garnishment order?

(a) When withholding must begin. Your employer must withhold the appropriate amount from your disposable pay on each payday beginning on the first payday after receiving the garnishment order issued under this section. If the first payday is within 10 days after your employer receives the order, then your employer must begin withholding on the first or second payday after your employer receives the order. Withholding must continue until we notify your employer to stop withholding.

(b) Payment of amounts withheld. Your employer must promptly pay to us all amounts withheld under this section.

(c) Other assignments or allotments of pay. Your employer cannot honor an assignment or allotment of your pay to the extent that it would interfere with or prevent withholding under this section, unless the assignment or allotment is made under a family support judgement or order.

(d) Effect of withholding on employer pay and disbursement cycles. Your employer will not be required to vary its normal pay and disbursement cycles in order to comply with the garnishment order.

(e) When withholding ends. When we have fully recovered the amounts you owe, including interest, penalties, and administrative costs that we charge you as allowed by law, we will tell your employer to stop withholding from your disposable pay. As an added precaution, we will review our debtors' accounts at least annually to ensure that withholding has been terminated for accounts paid in full.

(f) Certain actions by an employer against you are prohibited. Federal law prohibits an employer from using a garnishment order issued under this section as the basis for discharging you from employment, refusing to employ you, or taking disciplinary action against you. If your employer violates this prohibition, you may file a civil action against your employer in a Federal or State court of competent jurisdiction.

§ 422.445 May we bring a civil action against your employer for failure to comply with our administrative wage garnishment order?

(a) We may bring a civil action against your employer for any amount that the employer fails to withhold from your disposable pay in accordance with § 422.435(d), (e) and (f). Your employer may also be liable for attorney fees, costs of the lawsuit and (in the court's discretion) punitive damages.

(b) We will not file a civil action against your employer before we terminate collection action against you, unless earlier filing is necessary to avoid expiration of any applicable statute of limitations period. For purposes of this section, "terminate collection action" means that we have terminated collection action in accordance with the Federal Claims Collection Standards (31 CFR 903.3) or other applicable standards. In any event, we will consider that collection action has been terminated if we have not received any payments to satisfy the debt for a period of one year.

SUBPART F—APPLICATIONS AND RELATED FORMS

Authority: Sec. 1140(a)(2)(A) of the Social Security Act. 42 U.S.C. 1320b–10(a)(2)(A) (Pub.L. 103–296, Sec. 312(a)).

Source: 32 FR 18030, Dec. 16, 1967; 51 FR 41952, Nov. 20, 1986; 61 FR 5943, Feb. 15, 1996; 72 FR 73261, Dec. 27, 2007, unless otherwise noted.

§ 422.501 Applications and other forms used in Social Security Administration programs.

This subpart lists the applications and some of the related forms prescribed by the Social Security Administration for use by the public in applying for benefits under titles II and XVIII of the Social Security Act and the black lung benefits program (Part B, title IV of the Federal Coal Mine Health and Safety Act of 1969, as amended).

[38 FR 11450, May 8, 1973]

§ 422.505 What types of applications and related forms are used to apply for retirement, survivors, and disability insurance benefits?

(a) Applications. Prescribed applications include our traditional pre-printed forms, and applications our employees complete on computer screens based on information you give us. We then print a copy on paper, have you sign it and process the signed application electronically. You may also use SSA's Internet website to submit an SSA–approved application to us. You can complete an Internet application on a computer (or other suitable device, such as an electronic kiosk) and electronically transmit the form to us using an SSA–approved electronic signature. If, however, we do not have an approved electronic signature established when you file your Internet application, you must print and sign the completed application and deliver the form to us.

(b) Related forms. The following are some related forms:

SSA–3—Marriage Certification. (For use in connection with Application for Wife's or Husband's Insurance Benefits, (Form SSA–2))

SSA–11—Request to be Selected as Payee. (For use when an individual proposing to be substituted for the current payee files an application to receive payment of benefits on behalf of disabled child, or a child under 18, or an incapable or incompetent beneficiary or for himself/herself if he/she has a payee.)

SSA–21—Supplement to Claim of Person Outside of the United States. (To be completed by or on behalf of a person who is, was, or will be outside the United States.)

SSA–25—Certificate of Election for Reduced Spouse's Benefits. (For use by a wife or husband age 62 to full retirement age who has an entitled child in his or her care and elects to receive reduced benefits for months during which he or she will not have a child in his or her care.)

SSA–721—Statement of Death by Funeral Director. (This form may be used as evidence of death (see § 404.704 of this chapter).)

SSA–760—Certificate of Support (Parent's, Husband's or Widower's). (For use in collecting evidence of support.)

SSA–766—Statement of Self–Employment Income. (For use by a claimant to establish insured status based on self-employment income in the current year.)

SSA–783—Statement Regarding Contributions. (This form may be used as evidence of total contributions for a child.)

SSA–787—Physician's/Medical Officer's Statement of Patient's Capability to Manage Benefits. (This form may be used to request evidence of capability from various medical sources.)

SSA–824—Report on Individual with Mental Impairment. (For use in obtaining medical evidence from medical sources when the claimant has been treated for a mental impairment.)

SSA–827—Authorization for Source to Release Information to the Social Security Administration. (To be completed by a disability claimant to authorize release of medical or other information.)

SSA–1002—Statement of Agricultural Employer (Years Prior to 1988). (For use by employer to provide evidence of annual wage payments for agricultural work.)

SSA–1372—Student's Statement Regarding School Attendance. (For use in connection with request for payment of child's insurance benefits for a child who is age 18 through 19 and a full-time student.

SSA–1724—Claim for Amount Due in the Case of a Deceased Beneficiary. (For use in requesting amounts payable under title II to a deceased beneficiary.)

SSA–3368—Disability Report—Adult. (For use in recording information about the claimant's condition, source of medical evidence and other information needed to process the claim to a determination or decision.)

SSA–3369—Disability Report—Work History. (For use in recording work history information.)

SSA–3826–F4—Medical Report—General. (For use in helping disability claimants in obtaining medical records from their doctors or other medical sources.)

SSA–3827—Medical Report—(Individual with Childhood Impairment). (For use in requesting information to determine if an individual's impairment meets the requirements for payment of childhood disability benefits.)

SSA–4111—Certificate of Election for Reduced Widow(er)s Benefits. (For use by applicants for certain reduced widow's or widower's benefits.)

SSA–7156—Farm Self–Employment Questionnaire. (For use in connection with claims for benefits based on farm income to determine whether the income is covered under the Social Security Act.)

SSA–7160—Employment Relationship Questionnaire. (For use by an individual and the alleged employer to determine the individual's employment status.)

SSA–7163—Questionnaire about Employment or Self–Employment Outside the United States.

(To be completed by or on behalf of a beneficiary who is, was, or will be employed or self-employed outside the United States.)

[38 FR 11450, May 8, 1973; 51 FR 41952, Nov. 20, 1986; 55 FR 25826, June 25, 1990; 69 FR 499, Jan. 6, 2004; 70 FR 14978, March 24, 2005]

§ 422.510 Applications and related forms used in the health insurance for the aged program.

(a) Application forms. The following forms are prescribed for use in applying for entitlement to benefits under the health insurance for the aged program:

SSA–18—Application for Hospital Insurance Entitlement. (For use by individuals who are not entitled to retirement benefits under title II of the Social Security Act or under the Railroad Retirement Act. This form may also be used for enrollment in the supplementary medical insurance benefits plan.)

SSA–40—Application for Enrollment in the Supplementary Medical Insurance Program. (This form is mailed directly to beneficiaries at the beginning of their initial enrollment period.)

SSA–40A—Application for Enrollment in Supplementary Medical Insurance. (For use by civil service employees who are not eligible for enrollment in the hospital insurance plan.)

SSA–40B—Application for Medical Insurance. (For general use in requesting medical insurance protection.)

SSA–40C—Application for Enrollment. (This form is mailed to beneficiaries as a followup on Form SSA–40 (Application for Enrollment in the Supplementary Medical Insurance Program).)

SSA–40F—Application for Medical Insurance. (For use by beneficiaries residing outside the United States.)

An individual who upon attainment of age 65 is entitled to a monthly benefit based on application OA–C1, SSA–2, OA–C7, OA–C10, SSA–10A, OA–C13, or SSA–14 is automatically entitled to hospital insurance protection. (For conditions of entitlement to hospital insurance benefits, see 42 CFR part 405, subpart A. For medical insurance protection, an applicant must request supplementary medical insurance coverage (see Forms SSA–40, SSA–40A, SSA–40B, SSA–40C, and SSA–40F under § 422.510(a)). (For conditions of entitlement to supplementary medical insurance benefits, see 42 CFR part 405, subpart B.)

(b) Related forms. The following are the prescribed forms for use in requesting payment for services under the hospital insurance benefits program and the supplementary medical insurance benefits program and other related forms:

SSA–1453—Inpatient Hospital and Extended Care Admission and Billing. (To be completed by hospital for payment of hospital expenses for treatment of patient confined in hospital.)

SSA–1483—Provider Billing for Medical and Other Health Services. (To be completed by hospital for payment of hospital expenses for treatment of patient who is not confined in the hospital.)

SSA–1484—Explanation of Accommodation Furnished. (To be completed by the hospital to explain accommodation of a patient in other than a semiprivate (two- to four-bed) room.)

SSA–1486—Inpatient Admission and Billing—Christian Science Sanatorium. (To be completed by a Christian Science sanatorium for payment for treatment of patients confined in the sanatorium.)

SSA–1487—Home Health Agency Report and Billing. (For use by an organization providing home health services.)

SSA–1490—Request for Medicare Payment. (For use by patient or physician to request payment for medical expenses.)

SSA–1554—Provider Billing for Patient Services by Physicians. (For use by hospital for payment for services provided by hospital-based physicians.)

SSA–1556—Prepayment Plan for Group Medical Practices Dealing Through a Carrier. (For use by organizations (which have been determined to be group practice prepayment plans for medicare purposes) for reimbursement for medical services provided to beneficiaries.)

SSA–1660—Request for Information—Medicare Payment For Services to a Patient Now Deceased. (For use in requesting amounts payable under title XVIII to a deceased beneficiary.)

SSA–1739—Request for Enrollment Card Information by Foreign Beneficiary. (Used to notify beneficiaries approaching age 65 who reside in foreign countries that they are eligible to enroll for SMI. They return this form if they wish additional information and an application, SSA–40F.)

SSA–1966—Health Insurance Card. (This card is issued to a person entitled to benefits under the health insurance for the aged program and designates whether he is entitled to hospital insurance benefits or supplementary medical insurance benefits or both.)

SSA–1980—Carrier or Intermediary Request for SSA Assistance.

SSA–2384—Third Party Premium Billing Request. (For use by a nonbeneficiary enrollee who must pay premiums by direct remittance and is having his premium notices sent to a third party to assure continuance of supplementary medical insurance.)

[32 FR 18030, Dec. 16, 1967, as amended at 38 FR 11451, May 8, 1973; 44 FR 34943, June 18, 1979]

§ 422.512 Applications and related forms used in the black lung benefits program.

(a) Application forms. The following forms are prescribed for use in applying for entitlement to benefits under part B of title IV of the Federal Coal Mine Health and Safety Act of 1969, as amended by the Black Lung Benefits Act of 1972:

SSA–46—Application for Benefits Under the Federal Coal Mine Health and Safety Act of 1969, as Amended (Coal Miner's Claim of Total Disability).

SSA–47—Application for Benefits Under the Federal Coal Mine Health and Safety Act of 1969, as Amended (Widow's Claim).

SSA–48—Application for Benefits Under the Federal Coal Mine Health and Safety Act of 1969, as Amended (Child's Claim).

SSA–49—Application for Benefits Under the Federal Coal Mine Health and Safety Act of 1969, as Amended (Parent's, Brother's and Sister's Claim).

(b) Related forms. The following are some related forms:

SSA–50—Request To Be Selected as Payee. (For use when the individual proposing to be substituted for current payee files application to receive payment of black lung benefits on behalf of himself, a disabled child or child under age 18, a student beneficiary, or an incompetent beneficiary.)

SSA–2179—Report by Person Entitled to Black Lung Benefits. (For use by person entitled to black lung benefits to report events which affect benefits.)

SSA–2210—Statement of Coal Mine Employment by United Mine Workers of America.

SSA–2325—Medical Report (Pneumoconiosis).

[38 FR 11451, May 8, 1973]

§ 422.515 Forms used for withdrawal, reconsideration and other appeals, and appointment of representative.

The following is a list of forms prescribed by the Social Security Administration for use by the public to request a withdrawal of an application, a reconsideration of an initial determination, a hearing, a review of an administrative law judge's decision, or for use where a person is authorized to represent a claimant.

SSA–521—Request for Withdrawal of Application. (For use by an individual to cancel his application.)

SSA–561—Request for Reconsideration. (For use by an individual who disagrees with an initial determination concerning (a) entitlement to benefits or any other right under title II of the Social Security Act, or (b) entitlement to hospital insurance benefits or supplementary medical insurance benefits under title XVIII of the act, or (c) entitlement to black lung benefits under title IV of the Federal Coal Mine Health and Safety Act. See § 422.140 for a discussion of the reconsideration procedure.)

SSA–1696—Appointment of Representative. (For use by person other than an attorney authorized by a claimant to act for him in a claim or related matter.)

SSA–1763—Request for Termination of Supplementary Medical Insurance. (For use by an enrollee in requesting that his supplementary medical insurance coverage be terminated.)

SSA–1965—Request for Hearing—Part B Medicare Claim. (For use by an individual enrollee or his assignee to obtain a hearing before a hearing officer designated by the carrier concerning benefits payable under part B of title XVIII.)

HA–501—Request for Hearing. (For use by an individual or institution to obtain a hearing on a claim for title II benefits before an administrative law judge of the Social Security Administration.)

Note: This form is also used to request a hearing regarding entitlement to hospital insurance benefits or supplementary medical insurance benefits under title XVIII of the act. (See § 422.203 for a discussion of the hearing procedure.)

HA–501.1—Request for Hearing—Part A Health Insurance. (For use by an individual or institution to obtain a hearing before an administrative law judge of the Social Security Administration concerning the amount of hospital insurance benefits under title XVIII.)

HA–512.1—Notice by Attorney of Appointment as Representative. (For use by an attorney authorized by a claimant to act for him in a claim or related matter.)

HA–520—Request for Review of Hearing Examiner's Action. (For use by an individual or institution to obtain a review of a decision by an administrative law judge of the Social Security Administration.)

[38 FR 11452, May 8, 1973]

§ 422.520 Forms related to maintenance of earnings records.

The following forms are used by the Social Security Administration and by the public in connection with the maintenance of earnings records of wage-earners and self-employed persons:

SS–4—Application for Employer Identification Number.

SS–4A—Agricultural Employer's Application. (For use by employers of agricultural workers to request an employer identification number under the FICA.)

SS–5—Application for a Social Security Number (or Replacement of Lost Card).

SS–15—Certificate Waiving Exemption From Taxes Under the FICA. (For use by certain nonprofit organizations requesting coverage of its employees.)

SS–15a—List of Concurring Employees. (To be signed by each employee who concurs in the filing of the Certificate Waiving Exemption From Taxes Under the FICA, Form SS–15.)

SSI–21—Social Security and Your Household Employee. (For use by employers of household workers to request information from the Internal Revenue Service Center regarding filing employee tax returns.)

OA–702—Social Security Number Card.

Form 2031—Waiver Certificate To Elect Social Security Coverage for Use by Ministers, Certain Members of Religious Orders, and Christian Science Practitioners.

Form 4029—Application for Exemption from Tax on Self–Employment Income and Waiver of Benefits. (To be completed by self-employed individuals who are members of certain recognized religious sects (or division thereof) and do not wish to pay FICA taxes or participate in the programs provided under titles II and XVIII.)

Form 4361—Application for Exemption From Self–Employment Tax for Use by Ministers, Members of Religious Orders, and Christian Science Practitioners.

Form 4415—Election To Exempt From Self–Employment Coverage Fees Received by Certain Public Officers and Employees of a State or Political Subdivision Thereof.

OAAN–5028—Evidence of Application for Social Security Number Card.

OAAN–7003—Request for Change in Social Security Records. (For use by an individual to change information given on original application for a social security number.)

OAR–7004—Request for Statement of Earnings. (For use by worker to obtain a statement of earnings recorded in his earnings record.)

OAR–7008—Request for Correction of Earnings Record. (For use by an individual who wishes to have his earnings record revised.)

SSA–7011—Statement of Employer. (For use by an employer to provide evidence of wage payments in cases of a wage discrepancy in an individual's earnings record.)

[38 FR 11452, May 8, 1973]

§ 422.525 Where applications and other forms are available.

All applications and related forms prescribed for use in the programs administered by the Social Security Administration pursuant to the provisions of titles II and XVIII of the act, and part B of title IV of the Federal Coal Mine Health and Safety Act of 1969 are printed under the specifications of the Administration and distributed free of charge to the public, institutions, or organizations for the purposes described therein. All prescribed forms can be obtained upon request from any social security district office or branch office (see § 422.5). Forms appropriate for use in requesting payment for services provided under the health insurance for the aged and disabled programs can also be obtained from the intermediaries or carriers (organizations under contract with the Social Security Administration to make payment for such services) without charge. Form 2031 (Waiver Certificate to Elect Social Security Coverage for Use by Ministers, Certain Members of Religious Orders, and Christian Science Practitioners), Form 4029 (Application for Exemption From Tax on Self–Employment Income and Waiver of Benefits), Form 4361 (Application for Exemption From Self–Employment Tax for Use by Ministers, Members of Religious Orders, and Christian Science Practitioners), Form 4415 (Election to Exempt From Self–Employment Coverage Fees Received by Certain Public Officers and Employees of a State or a Political Subdivision Thereof), Form SS–4 (Application for Employer Identification Number), Form SS–4A (Agricultural Employer's Application for Identification Number), Form SS–5 (Application for a Social Security Number (or Replacement of Lost Card)), Form SS–15 (Certificate Waiving Exemption From Taxes Under the FICA), and Form SS–15a (List of Concurring Employees) can also be obtained without charge from offices of the Internal Revenue Service. For other offices where applications and certain other forms can be obtained, see subparts B and C of this part 422.

[38 FR 11452, May 8, 1973]

§ 422.527 Private printing and modification of prescribed applications, forms, and other publications.

Any person, institution, or organization wishing to reproduce, reprint, or distribute any application, form, or publication prescribed by the Administration must obtain prior approval if he or she intends to charge a fee. Requests for approval must be in writing and include the reason or need for the reproduction, reprinting, or distribution; the intended users of the application, form, or publication; the fee to be charged; any proposed modification; the proposed format; the type of machinery (e.g., printer, burster, mail handling), if any, for which the application, form, or publication is being designed; estimated printing quantity; estimated printing cost per thousand; estimated annual usage; and any other pertinent information required by the Administration. Forward all requests for prior approval to: Office of Publications Management, 6401 Security Boulevard, Baltimore, MD 21235–6401.

[33 FR 11281, Aug. 8, 1968; 72 FR 73261, Dec. 27, 2007]

SUBPART G—ADMINISTRATIVE REVIEW PROCESS UNDER THE COAL INDUSTRY RETIREE HEALTH BENEFIT ACT OF 1992

Authority: 26 U.S.C. 9701–9708.

Source: 58 FR 52916, Oct. 13, 1993; 61 FR 5943, Feb. 15, 1996, unless otherwise noted.

§ 422.601 Scope and purpose.

The regulations in this subpart describe how the Social Security Administration (SSA) will conduct reviews of assignments it makes under provisions of the Coal Industry Retiree Health Benefit Act of 1992 (the Coal Act). Under the Coal Act, certain retired coal miners and their eligible family members (beneficiaries) are assigned to particular coal operators (or related persons). These operators are then responsible for paying the annual health and death benefit premiums for these beneficiaries as well as the annual premiums for certain unassigned coal miners and eligible members of their families. We will notify the assigned operators of these assignments and give each operator an opportunity to request detailed information about an assignment and to request review of an assignment. We also inform the United Mine Workers of America (UMWA) Combined Benefit Fund Trustees of each assignment made and the unassigned beneficiaries so they can assess appropriate annual premiums against the assigned operators. This subpart explains how assigned operators may request such additional information, how they may request review of an assignment, and how reviews will be conducted.

§ 422.602 Terms used in this subpart.

Assignment means our selection of the coal operator or related person to be charged with the responsibility of paying the annual health and death benefit premiums of certain coal miners and their eligible family members.

Beneficiary means either a coal industry retiree who, on July 20, 1992, was eligible to receive, and receiving, benefits as an eligible individual under the 1950 or the 1974 UMWA Benefit Plan, or an individual who was eligible to receive, and receiving, benefits on July 20, 1992 as an eligible relative of a coal industry retiree.

Evidence of a prima facie case of error means documentary evidence, records, and written statements submitted to us by the assigned operator (or related person) that, standing alone, shows our assignment was in error. The evidence submitted must, when considered by itself without reference to other contradictory evidence that may be in our possession, be sufficient to persuade a reasonable person that the assignment was erroneous. Examples of evidence that may establish a prima facie case of error include copies of Federal, State, or local government tax records; legal documents such as business incorporation, merger, and bankruptcy papers; health and safety reports filed with Federal or State agencies that regulate mining activities; payroll and other employment business records; and information provided in trade journals and newspapers.

A related person to a signatory operator means a person or entity which as of July 20, 1992, or, if earlier, the time immediately before the coal operator ceased to be in business, was a member of a controlled group of corporations which included the signatory operator, or was a trade or business which was under common control with a signatory operator, or had a partnership interest (other than as a limited partner) or joint venture with a signatory operator in a business within the coal industry which employed eligible beneficiaries, or is a successor in interest to a person who was a related person.

We or us refers to the Social Security Administration.

You as used in this subpart refers to the coal operator (or related person) assigned premium responsibility for a specific beneficiary under the Coal Act.

[62 FR 38456, July 18, 1997]

§ 422.603 Overview of the review process.

Our notice of assignment will inform you as the assigned operator (or related person) which beneficiaries have been assigned to you, the reason for the assignment, and the dates of employment on which the assignment was based. The notice will explain that, if you disagree with the assignment for any beneficiary listed in the notice of assignment, you may request from us detailed information as to the work history of the miner and the basis for the assignment. Such request must be filed with us within 30 days after you receive the notice of assignment, as explained in § 422.604. The notice will also explain that if you still disagree with the assignment after you have received the detailed information, you may submit evidence that shows there is a prima facie case of error in that assignment and request review. Such request must be filed with us within 30 days after you receive the detailed information, as explained in § 422.605. Alternatively, you may request review within 30 days after you receive the notice of assignment, even if you have not first requested the detailed information. In that case, you still may request the detailed information within that 30–day period. (See § 422.606(c) for further details.)

§ 422.604 Request for detailed information.

(a) General. After you receive our notice of assignment listing the beneficiaries for whom you have premium responsibility, you may request detailed information as to the work histories of any of the listed miners and the basis for the assignment. Your request for detailed information must:

(1) Be in writing;

(2) Be filed with us within 30 days of receipt of that notice of assignment. Unless you submit evidence showing a later receipt of the notice, we will assume the notice was received by you within 5 days of the date appearing on the notice. We will consider the request to be filed as of the date we receive it. However, if we receive the request after the 30–day period, the postmark date on the envelope may be used as the filing date. If there is no postmark or the postmark is illegible, the filing date will be deemed to be the fifth day prior to the day we received the request; and

(3) Identify the individual miners about whom you are requesting the detailed information.

(b) The detailed information we will provide. We will send you detailed information as to the work history and the basis for the assignment for each miner about whom you requested such information. This information will include the name and address of each employer for whom the miner has worked since 1978 or since 1946 (whichever period is appropriate), the amount of wages paid by each employer and the period for which the wages were reported. We will send you the detailed information with a notice informing you that you have 30 days from the date you receive the information to submit to SSA evidence of a prima facie case of error (as defined in § 422.602) and request review of the assignment if you have not already requested review. The notice will also inform you that, if you are seeking evidence to make a case of prima facie error, you may include with a timely filed request for review a written request for additional time to obtain and submit such evidence to us. Under these circumstances, you will have 90 days from the date of your request to submit the evidence before we determine whether we will review the assignment.

§ 422.605 Request for review.

We will review an assignment if you request review and show that there is a prima facie case of error regarding the assignment. This review is a review on the record and will not entail a face-to-face hearing. We will review an assignment if:

(a) You are an assigned operator (or related person);

(b) Your request is in writing and states your reasons for believing the assignment is erroneous;

(c) Your request is filed with us no later than 30 days from the date you received the detailed information described in § 422.604, or no later than 30 days from the date you received the notice of assignment if you choose not to request detailed information. Unless you submit evidence showing a later receipt of the notice, we will assume you received the detailed information or the notice of assignment within 5 days of the date shown thereon. We will consider the request to be filed as of the date we receive it. However, if we receive the request after the 30–day period, the postmark date on the envelope may be used as the filing date. If there is no postmark or the postmark is illegible, the filing date will be deemed to be the fifth day prior to the day we received the request; and

(d) Your request is accompanied by evidence establishing a prima facie case of error regarding the assignment. If your request for review includes a request for additional time to submit such evidence, we will give you an additional 90 days from the date of your request for review to submit such evidence to us.

§ 422.606 Processing the request for review.

Upon receipt of your written request for review of an assignment and where relevant, the expiration of any additional times allowed under §§ 422.605(d) and 422.606(c), we will take the following action:

(a) Request not timely filed. If your request is not filed within the time limits set out in § 422.605(c), we will deny your request for review on that basis and send you a notice explaining that we have taken this action;

(b) Lack of evidence. If your request is timely filed under § 422.605(c) but you have not provided evidence constituting a prima facie case of error, we will deny your request for review on that basis and send you a notice explaining that we have taken this action;

(c) Request for review without requesting detailed information. If your request is filed within 30 days after you received the notice of assignment and you have not requested detailed information, we will not process your request until at least 30 days after the date you received the notice of assignment. You may still request detailed information within that 30–day period, in which case we will not process your request for review until at least 30 days after you received the detailed information, so that you may submit additional evidence if you wish;

(d) Reviewing the evidence. If your request meets the filing requirements of § 422.605 and is accompanied by evidence constituting a prima facie case of error, we will review the assignment. We will review all evidence submitted with your request for review, together with the evidence used in making the assignment. An SSA employee who was not involved in the original assignment will perform the review. The review will be a review on the record and will not involve a face-to-face hearing.

(e) Original decision correct. If, following this review of the evidence you have submitted and the evidence in our file, we make a determination that the assignment is correct, we will send you a notice explaining the basis for our decision. We will not review the decision again, except as provided in § 422.607.

(f) Original decision erroneous. If, following this review of the evidence you have submitted and the evidence in our file, we make a determination that the assignment is erroneous, we will send you a notice to this effect. We will then determine who the correct operator is and assign the affected beneficiary(s) to that coal operator (or related person). If no assigned operator can be identified, the affected beneficiary(s) will be treated as "unassigned." We will notify the UMWA Combined Benefit Fund Trustees of the review decision so that any premium liability of the initial assigned operator can be adjusted.

§ 422.607 Limited reopening of assignments.

On our own initiative, we may reopen and revise an assignment, whether or not it has been reviewed as described in this subpart, under the following conditions:

(a) The assignment reflects an error on the face of our records or the assignment was based upon fraud; and

(b) We sent to the assigned operator (or related person) notice of the assignment within 12 months of the time we decided to reopen that assignment.

SUBPART H—USE OF SSA TELEPHONE LINES

Authority: Secs. 205(a) and 702(a)(5) of the Social Security Act (42 U.S.C. 405 and 902(a)(5)).

Source: 63 FR 57058, Oct. 26, 1998, unless otherwise noted.

§ 422.701 Scope and purpose.

The regulations in this subpart describe the limited circumstances under which SSA is authorized to listen-in to or record telephone conversations. The purpose of this subpart is to inform the public and SSA employees of those circumstances and the procedures that SSA will follow when conducting telephone service observation activities.

§ 422.705 When SSA employees may listen-in to or record telephone conversations.

SSA employees may listen-in to or record telephone conversations on SSA telephone lines under the following conditions:

(a) Law enforcement/national security. When performed for law enforcement, foreign intelligence, counterintelligence or communications security purposes when determined necessary by the Commissioner of Social Security or designee. Such determinations shall be in writing and shall be made in accordance with applicable laws, regulations and Executive Orders governing such activities. Communications security monitoring shall be conducted in accordance with procedures approved by the Attorney General. Line identification equipment may be installed on SSA telephone lines to assist Federal law enforcement officials in investigating threatening telephone calls, bomb threats and other criminal activities.

(b) Public safety. When performed by an SSA employee for public safety purposes and when documented by a written determination by the Commissioner of Social Security or designee citing the public safety needs. The determination shall identify the segment of the public needing protection and cite examples of the possible harm from which the public requires protection. Use of SSA telephone lines identified for reporting emergency and other public safety-related situations will be deemed as consent to public safety monitoring and recording. (See § 422.710(a)(1))

(c) Public service monitoring. When performed by an SSA employee after the Commissioner of Social Security or designee determines in writing that monitoring of such lines is necessary for the purposes of measuring or monitoring SSA's performance in the delivery of service to the public; or monitoring and improving the integrity, quality and utility of service provided to the public. Such monitoring will occur only on telephone lines used by employees to provide SSA–related information and services to the public. Use of such telephone lines will be deemed as consent to public service monitoring. (See § 422.710(a)(2) and (c)).

(d) All-party consent. When performed by an SSA employee with the prior consent of all parties for a specific instance. This includes telephone conferences, secretarial recordings and other administrative practices. The failure to identify all individuals listening to a conversation by speaker phone is not prohibited by this or any other section.

§ 422.710 Procedures SSA will follow.

SSA component(s) that plan to listen-in to or record telephone conversations under § 422.705(b) or (c) shall comply with the following procedures.

(a) Prepare a written certification of need to the Commissioner of Social Security or designee at least 30 days before the planned operational date. A certification as used in this section means a written justification signed by the Deputy Commissioner of the requesting SSA component or designee, that specifies general information on the following: the operational need for listening-in to or recording telephone conversations; the telephone lines and locations where monitoring is to be performed; the position titles (or a statement about the types) of SSA employees involved in the listening-in to or recording of telephone conversations; the general operating times and an expiration date for the monitoring. This certification of need must identify the telephone lines which will be subject to monitoring, e.g., SSA 800 number voice and text telephone lines, and include current copies of any documentation, analyses, determinations, policies and procedures supporting the application, and the name and telephone number of a contact person in the SSA component which is requesting authority to listen-in to or record telephone conversations.

(1) When the request involves listening-in to or recording telephone conversations for public safety purposes, the requesting component head or designee must identify the segment of the public needing protection and cite examples of the possible harm from which the public requires protection.

(2) When the request involves listening-in to or recording telephone conversations for public service monitoring purposes, the requesting component head or designee must provide a statement in writing why such monitoring is necessary for measuring or monitoring the performance in the delivery of SSA service to the public; or monitoring and improving the integrity, quality and utility of service provided to the public.

(b) At least every 5 years, SSA will review the need for each determination authorizing listening-in or recording activities in the agency. SSA components or authorized agents involved in conducting listening-in or recording activities must submit documentation as described in § 422.710(a) to the Commissioner of Social Security or a designee to continue or terminate telephone service observation activities.

(c) SSA will comply with the following controls, policies and procedures when listening-in or recording is associated with public service monitoring.

(1) SSA will provide a message on SSA telephone lines subject to public service monitoring that will inform callers that calls on those lines may be monitored for quality assurance purposes. SSA will also continue to include information about telephone monitoring activities in SSA brochures and/or pamphlets as notification that some incoming and outgoing SSA telephone calls are monitored to ensure SSA's clients are receiving accurate and courteous service.

(2) SSA employees authorized to listen-in to or record telephone calls are permitted to annotate personal identifying information about the calls, such as a person's name, Social Security number, address and/or telephone number. When this information is obtained from public service monitoring as defined in § 422.705(c), it will be used for programmatic or policy purposes; e.g., recontacting individuals to correct or supplement information relating to benefits, for assessment of current/proposed policies and procedures, or to

correct SSA records. Privacy Act requirements must be followed if data are retrievable by personal identifying information.

(3) SSA will take appropriate corrective action, when possible, if information obtained from monitoring indicates SSA may have taken an incorrect action which could affect the payment of or eligibility to SSA benefits.

(4) Telephone instruments subject to public service monitoring will be conspicuously labeled.

(5) Consent from both parties is needed to tape record SSA calls for public service monitoring purposes.

(d) The recordings and records pertaining to the listening-in to or recording of any conversations covered by this subpart shall be used, safeguarded and destroyed in accordance with SSA records management program.

SUBPART I—ADMINISTRATIVE CLAIMS COLLECTION

Authority: Sec. 97, Pub.L. 97–365, 96 Stat. 1749; Sec. 104, Pub.L. 104–134, 110 Stat. 1321; 5 U.S.C. 552; 5 U.S.C. 553; 31 U.S.C. 3711; 31 U.S.C. 3716; 31 U.S.C. 3717; 31 U.S.C. 3720A; 31 U.S.C. 3720B; 31 U.S.C. 3720C; 31 U.S.C. 3720D; 31 U.S.C. 3720E; 31 CFR parts 901–904; 31 CFR part 285; 5 U.S.C. 5514; 5 CFR part 550; 42 U.S.C. 902(a)(5).

Source: 80 FR 61734, Oct. 14, 2015, unless otherwise noted.

§ 422.801 Scope of this subpart.

(a) The regulations in this part are issued under the Debt Collection Act of 1982, as amended by the Debt Collection Improvement Act of (DCIA) 1996 (31 U.S.C. 3701, et seq.) and the Federal Claims Collection Standards (31 CFR parts 901–904) issued pursuant to the DCIA by the Department of the Treasury (Treasury) and the Department of Justice (DOJ). These authorities prescribe government-wide standards for administrative collection, compromise, suspension, or termination of agency collection action, disclosure of debt information to credit reporting agencies, referral of claims to private collection contractors for resolution, and referral to the DOJ for litigation to collect debts owed the Government. The regulations under this part also are issued under the Commissioner's general rule-making authority in the Social Security Act at section 702(a)(5), 42 U.S.C. 902(a)(5), the Treasury's regulations implementing the DCIA (31 CFR part 285), and related statutes and regulations governing the offset of Federal salaries (5 U.S.C. 5512, 5514; 5 CFR part 550, subpart K) and the administrative offset of tax refunds (31 U.S.C. 3720A).

(b) This subpart describes the procedures relating to the collection, compromise, and suspension of administrative debts owed to us, the Social Security Administration (SSA).

(c) Administrative debts include claims against current employees, separated employees, and non-employee debtors.

(1) Employee debts include salary overpayments; advanced sick and annual leave, advanced religious compensatory time, overpayments of health benefit premiums, leave buy back, emergency employee payments, travel, and transit subsidies.

(2) Non-employee debts include vendor overpayments, reimbursable agreements, Supplemental Security Income Medicaid determinations, and economic recovery payments.

(d) This subpart does not apply to programmatic overpayments described in subparts D and E of this part, and §§ 404.527 and § 416.590 of this title.

(e) This subpart does not apply to civil monetary penalties arising from sections 1129 and 1140 of the Social Security Act and collected pursuant to part 498 of this title.

§ 422.803 Collection activities.

(a) We will collect all administrative debts arising out of our activities or that are referred or transferred to us, the Social Security Administration, for collection actions. We will send an initial written demand for payment no later than 30 days after an appropriate official determines that a debt exists.

(b) In accordance with 31 CFR 285.12(c) and (g), we transfer legally enforceable administrative debts that are 120 calendar days or more delinquent to Treasury for debt collection services (i.e., cross-servicing). This requirement does not apply to any debt that:

(1) Is in litigation or foreclosure;

(2) Will be disposed of under an approved asset sale program within one year of becoming eligible for sale;

(3) Has been referred to a private collection contractor for a period acceptable to the Secretary of the Treasury;

(4) Is at a debt collection center for a period of time acceptable to Treasury (see paragraph (c) of this section);

(5) Will be collected under internal offset procedures within three years after the debt first became delinquent; or

(6) Is exempt from this requirement based on a determination by Treasury that exemption for a certain class of debt is in the best interest of the United States.

(c) Pursuant to 31 CFR 285.12(h), we may refer debts less than 120 calendar days delinquent to Treasury or, with the consent of Treasury, to a Treasury-designated debt collection center to accomplish efficient, cost effective debt collection. Referrals to debt collection centers will be at the discretion of, and for a period acceptable to, the Secretary of the Treasury.

Referrals may be for servicing, collection, compromise, suspension, or termination of collection action.

(d) We may refer delinquent administrative debts to Treasury for offset through the Treasury Offset Program (TOP). Administered by Treasury, TOP's centralized offset process permits Treasury to withhold funds payable by the United States to a person to collect and satisfy delinquent debts the person owes Federal agencies and States.

(e) We may collect an administrative debt by using Administrative Wage Garnishment.

(f) We may collect an administrative debt by using Federal Salary Offset.

§ 422.805 Demand for payment.

(a) Written demand for payment.

(1) We will make a written demand, as described in paragraph (b) of this section, promptly to a debtor in terms that inform the debtor of the consequences of failing to cooperate with us to resolve the debt.

(2) We will send a demand letter no later than 30 days after the appropriate official determines that the debt exists. We will send the demand letter to the debtor's last known address.

(3) When necessary to protect the Government's interest, we may take appropriate action under this part, including immediate referral to DOJ for litigation, before sending the written demand for payment.

(b) Demand letters. The specific content, timing, and number of demand letters will depend upon the type and amount of the debt and the debtor's response, if any, to our letters or telephone calls.

(1) The written demand for payment will include the following information:

(i) The nature and amount of the debt, including the basis for the indebtedness;

(ii) The date by which payment should be made to avoid late charges and enforced collection, which must be no later than 30 days from the date the demand letter is mailed;

(iii) Where applicable, the standards for imposing any interest, penalties, or administrative costs as specified under § 422.807;

(iv) The rights, if any, the debtor may have to:

(A) Seek review of our determination of the debt, and for purposes of salary offset or Administrative Wage Garnishment, request a hearing. To request a hearing see §§ 422.810(h) and 422.833(f)); and

(B) Enter into a reasonable repayment agreement when necessary and authorized.

(v) An explanation of how the debtor may exercise any of the rights described in paragraph (b)(1)(iv) of this section;

(vi) The name, address, and phone number of a contact person or office to address any debt-related matters; and

(vii) Our remedies to enforce payment of the debt, which may include:

(A) Garnishing the debtor's wages through Administrative Wage Garnishment;

(B) Offsetting any Federal or State payments due the debtor, including income tax refunds, salary, certain benefit payments;

(C) Referring the debt to a private collection contractor;

(D) Reporting the debt to a credit bureau or other automated database;

(E) Referring the debt to the DOJ for litigation; and

(F) Referring the debt to the Department of the Treasury for any of the collection actions described in paragraphs (b)(1)(vii)(A) through (E) of this section.

(2) The written demand for payment should also include the following information:

(i) The debtor's right to review our records pertaining to the debt, or, if the debtor or the debtor's representative cannot personally review the records, to request and receive copies of such records;

(ii) Our willingness to discuss alternative methods of payment with the debtor;

(iii) If a Federal employee, the debtor may be subject to disciplinary action under 5 CFR part 752 or other applicable authority;

(iv) Any amounts collected and ultimately found to not be owed by the debtor will be refunded;

(v) For salary offset, up to 15 percent of the debtor's current disposable pay may be deducted every pay period until the debt is paid in full; and

(vi) Dependent upon applicable statutory authority, the debtor may be entitled to consideration for a waiver.

(c) Evidence retention. We will retain evidence of service indicating the date of mailing of the demand letter. The evidence of service may be retained electronically so long as the manner of retention is sufficient for evidentiary purposes.

(d) Pursue offset. Prior to, during, or after the completion of the demand process, if we determine to pursue, or are required to pursue offset, the procedures applicable to offset should be followed (see § 422.821). The availability of funds for debt satisfaction by offset and our determination to pursue collection by offset will release us from the necessity of further compliance with paragraphs (a), (b), and (c) of this section.

(e) Communications from debtors. Where feasible, we will respond promptly to communications from debtors within 30 days, and will advise debtors who dispute debts to furnish available evidence to support their contentions.

(f) Exception. This section does not require duplication of any notice already contained in a written agreement, letter, or other document signed by, or provided to, the debtor.

§ 422.807 Interest, penalties, and administrative costs.

(a) Except as provided in paragraphs (g), (h), and (i) of this section, we will charge interest, penalties, and administrative costs on delinquent debts owed to the United States. These charges will continue to accrue until the debtor pays the debt in full or otherwise resolves the debt through compromise, termination, or an approved waiver.

(b) Interest. We will charge interest on delinquent administrative debts owed the agency as follows:

(1) Interest will accrue from the date of delinquency or as otherwise provided by law. For debts not paid by the date specified in the written demand for payment made under § 422.805, the date of delinquency is the date of mailing of the notice. The date of delinquency for an installment payment is the due date specified in the payment agreement.

(2) Unless a different rate is prescribed by statute, contract, or a repayment agreement, the rate of interest charged will be the rate established annually by the Treasury pursuant to 31 U.S.C. 3717. We may charge a higher rate if necessary to protect the rights of the United States, and the Commissioner has determined and documented a higher rate for delinquent debt is required to protect the Government's interests.

(3) Unless prescribed by statute or contract, the initial rate of interest charged will remain fixed for the duration of the indebtedness. A debtor who defaults on a repayment agreement may seek to enter into a new agreement. If we agree to a new agreement, we may require additional financial information and payment of interest at a new rate that reflects the Treasury rate in effect at the time the new agreement is executed or at a higher rate consistent with paragraph (b)(2) of this section. Interest will not be compounded. That is, we will not charge interest on the interest, penalties, or administrative costs required by this section, except as permitted by statute or contract. If, however, the debtor defaults on a previous repayment agreement, we will add charges that accrued but were not collected under the defaulted agreement to the principal of any new repayment agreement.

(c) Penalty. Unless otherwise established by contract, repayment agreement, or statute, we will charge a penalty pursuant to 31 U.S.C. 3717(e)(2) and 31 CFR 901.9 on the amount due on a debt that is delinquent for more than 90 days. This charge will accrue from the date of delinquency.

(d) Administrative costs. We will assess administrative costs incurred for processing and handling delinquent debts. We will base the calculation of administrative costs on actual costs incurred or a valid estimate of the actual costs. Calculation of administrative costs will include all direct (personnel, supplies, etc.) and indirect collection costs, including the cost of providing a hearing or any other form of administrative review requested by a debtor and any costs charged by a collection agency under § 422.837. We will assess these charges monthly or per payment period throughout the period that the debt is overdue. Such costs may also be in addition to other administrative costs if collection is being made for another Federal agency or unit.

(e) Cost of living adjustment. When there is a legitimate reason to do so, such as when calculating interest and penalties on a debt would be extremely difficult because of the age of the debt, we may increase an administrative debt by the cost of living adjustment in lieu of charging interest and penalties under this section. The cost of living adjustment is the percentage by which the Consumer Price Index for the month of June of the calendar year preceding the adjustment exceeds the Consumer Price Index for the month of June of the calendar year in which the debt was determined or last adjusted. We will manually compute such increases to administrative debts.

(f) Priority. When a debt is paid in partial or installment payments, amounts received will be applied first to outstanding penalties, second to administrative charges, third to interest, and last to principal.

(g) Waiver.

(1) We will waive the collection of interest and administrative costs imposed pursuant to this section on the portion of the debt that is paid within 30 days after the date on which interest began to accrue. Excepting debt affected by fraud or other misconduct, we may extend this 30–day period on a case-by-case basis if we determine that such action is in the best interest of the Government or is otherwise warranted by equity and good conscience.

(2) We may waive interest, penalties, and administrative charges charged under this section, in whole or in part, without regard to the amount of the debt, based on:

(i) The criteria set forth at § 422.846 (b)(1) for the compromise of debts; or

(ii) A determination by the agency that collection of these charges is:

(A) Against equity and good conscience; or

(B) Not in the best interest of the United States.

(h) Review.

(1) Except as provided in paragraph (h)(2) of this section, administrative review of a debt will not sus-

pend the assessment of interest, penalties, and administrative costs. While agency review of a debt is pending, the debtor may either pay the debt or be liable for interest and related charges on the uncollected debt. When agency review results in a final determination that any amount was properly a debt and the debtor failed to pay the full amount of the disputed debt, we will collect from the debtor the amount determined to be due, and interest, penalties and administrative costs on the debt amount. We will calculate and assess interest, penalties, and administrative costs under this section starting from the date the debtor was first made aware of the debt and ending when the debt is repaid.

(2) Exception. Interest, penalties, and administrative cost charges will not be imposed on a debt for periods during which collection activity has been suspended under § 422.848(c)(1) pending agency review or consideration of waiver, if a statute prohibits collection of the debt during this period. This exception does not apply to interest, penalties, and administrative cost charges on debts affected by fraud or other misconduct unless a statute so requires.

(i) Common law or other statutory authority. We may impose and waive interest and related charges on debts not subject to 31 U.S.C. 3717 in accordance with the common law or other statutory authority.

§ 422.809 Collection in installments.

Whenever feasible, we will collect the total amount of a debt in one lump sum payment. If a debtor claims a financial inability to pay a debt in one lump sum, by funds or Administrative Offset, we may accept payment in regular installments provided the debtor establishes the financial need and no evidence indicates that fraud or similar fault affected the debt. We will request financial statements from debtors who represent that they are unable to pay in one lump sum and independently verify such representations as described in § 422.846.

(a) When we agree to accept payments in regular installments, we will obtain a legally enforceable written agreement from the debtor that specifies all the terms and conditions of the agreement and includes a provision accelerating the debt in the event of a default.

(b) The size and frequency of the payments will reasonably relate to the size of the debt and the debtor's ability to pay. Whenever feasible, the installment agreement will provide for full payment of the debt, including interest and charges, in three years or less.

(c) When appropriate, the agreement will include a provision identifying security obtained from the debtor for the deferred payments, such as a surety bond or confession of judgment supporting a lien on any property of the debtor.

(d) An approved installment agreement does not prevent the use of Administrative Wage Garnishment or other collection tools in this subpart.

§ 422.810 Salary offset for current employees.

(a) Purpose. This part prescribes the Social Security Administration's (SSA) standards and procedures for the collection of debts owed by current SSA employees to SSA through involuntary salary offset.

(b) Authority. 5 U.S.C. 5514; 5 CFR part 550.

(c) Scope.

(1) This part applies to internal collections of debt by Administrative Offset from the current pay accounts of SSA employees without his or her consent. The part does not apply to current SSA employees indebted to another Federal agency or employees who separate from SSA.

(2) The procedures contained in this part do not apply to any case where an employee consents to collection through deduction(s) from the employee's pay account, or to debts arising under the Internal Revenue Code or the tariff laws of the United States, or where another statute explicitly provides for or prohibits collection of a debt by salary offset (e.g., travel advances in 5 U.S.C. 5705 and employee training expenses in 5 U.S.C. 4108).

(3) This part does not preclude an employee from requesting a waiver of an erroneous payment under 5 U.S.C. 5584, 10 U.S.C. 2774, or 32 U.S.C. 716, or in any way questioning the amount or validity of a debt. Similarly, this part does not preclude an employee from requesting waiver of the collection of a debt under any other applicable statutory authority.

(4) Provided a debt is not affected by fraud and does not exceed $100,000, nothing in this part precludes the compromise of the debt or the suspension or termination of collection actions in accordance with §§ 422.846 and 422.848 of this title.

(d) Definitions.

Administrative Offset means withholding funds payable by the United States to, or held by the United States for, a person to satisfy a debt owed by the payee.

Agency means an executive department or agency, a military department, the United States Postal Service, the Postal Rate Commission, the United States Senate, the United States House of Representatives, a court, court administrative office, or instrumentality in the judicial or legislative branches of the Government, or a Government Corporation.

Creditor agency means the agency to which the debt is owed or SSA, including a debt collection center when acting on behalf of a creditor agency in matters pertaining to the collection of a debt.

Day means calendar day. For purposes of computation, the last day of the period will be included unless it is a Saturday, Sunday, or a Federal holiday, in which case the next business day will be considered the last day of the period.

Debt means an amount of funds or other property determined by an appropriate official of the Federal Government to be owed to the United States from any person, organization, or entity or any other debt that meets the definition of "claim" or "debt" under 31 U.S.C. 3701(b), excluding program overpayments made under title II or title XVI of the Social Security Act.

Debt collection center means the Department of the Treasury (Treasury) or other Government agency or division designated by the Secretary of the Treasury with authority to collect debts on behalf of creditor agencies in accordance with 31 U.S.C. 3711(g).

Debtor means an employee currently employed by SSA who owes a delinquent non-tax debt to the United States.

Delinquent debt means a debt that the debtor does not pay or otherwise resolve by the date specified in the initial demand for payment, or in an applicable written repayment agreement or other instrument, including a post-delinquency repayment agreement.

Disposable pay means that part of the debtor's current basic, special, incentive, retired, and retainer pay, or other authorized pay remaining after deduction of amounts we are required by law to withhold. For purposes of calculating disposable pay, legally required deductions that must be applied first include: Tax levies pursuant to the Internal Revenue Code (title 26, United States Code); properly withheld taxes; Federal Insurance Contributions Act (FICA); Medicare; health, dental, vision, and life insurance premiums; and Thrift Savings Plan and retirement contributions. Amounts deducted under garnishment orders, including child support garnishment orders, are not legally permissible deductions when calculating disposable pay as specified in 5 CFR 550.1103.

Employee means any individual currently employed by SSA, as defined in this section, including seasonal and temporary employees and current members of the Armed Forces or a Reserve of the Armed Forces (Reserves).

Evidence of service means information retained by the agency indicating the nature of the document to which it pertains, the date of mailing the document, and the address and name of the debtor to whom it is being sent. A copy of the dated and signed notice provided to the debtor pursuant to this part may be considered evidence of service for purposes of this part. We may retain evidence of service electronically so long as the manner of retention is sufficient for evidentiary purposes.

Hearing means a review of the documentary evidence to confirm the existence or amount of a debt or the terms of a repayment schedule. If we determine that the issues in dispute cannot be resolved by such a review, such as when the validity of the claim turns on the issue of credibility or veracity, we may provide an oral hearing.

Hearing official means an administrative law judge or appropriate alternate.

Paying agency means the agency employing the employee and authorizing the payment of his or her current pay.

Salary offset means an Administrative Offset to collect a debt under 5 U.S.C. 5514 owed by a current SSA employee through deductions at one or more officially established pay intervals from the current pay account of the current SSA employee without his or her consent.

Waiver means the cancellation, remission, forgiveness, or non-recovery of a debt owed by an employee to the agency or another agency as required or permitted by 5 U.S.C. 5584, 8346(b), 10 U.S.C. 2774, 32 U.S.C. 716, or any other law.

(e) General rule.

(1) Whenever an employee owes us a delinquent debt, we may, subject to paragraph (e)(3) of this section, involuntarily offset the amount of the debt from the employee's disposable pay.

(2) Except as provided in paragraph (e)(3) of this section, prior to initiating collection through salary offset under this part, we will first provide the employee with the following:

(i) A notice as described in paragraph (f) of this section; and

(ii) An opportunity to petition for a hearing, and, if a hearing is provided, to receive a written decision from the hearing official within 60 days on the following issues:

(A) The determination concerning the existence or amount of the debt; and

(B) The repayment schedule, unless it was established by written agreement between the employee and us.

(3) The provisions of paragraph (e)(2) of this section do not apply to:

(i) Any adjustment to pay arising out of an employee's election of coverage or a change in coverage under a federal benefits program requiring periodic deduction from pay, if the amount to be recovered was accumulated over four pay periods or less;

(ii) A routine intra-agency adjustment of pay that is made to correct an overpayment of pay attributable to clerical or administrative errors or delays in processing pay documents, if the overpayment occurred within four pay periods preceding the adjustment and, at the time of such adjustment, or as soon thereafter as practical, the individual is provided a notice of the nature and the amount of the adjustment and point of contact for contesting such adjustment; or

(iii) Any adjustment to collect a debt amount in accordance with the amount stated in 5 U.S.C. 5514 as amended by the DCIA, if, at the time of such adjustment, or as soon thereafter as practical, the individual is provided a notice of the nature and the amount of the adjustment and a point of contact for contesting such adjustment.

(f) Notice requirements before offset.

(1) At least 30 days before the initiation of salary offset under this part, we will send a notice to the employee's last known address, informing the debtor of the following:

(i) We have reviewed the records relating to the debt and have determined that a debt is owed, the amount of the debt, and the facts giving rise to the debt;

(ii) Our intention to collect the debt by means of deduction from the employee's current disposable pay until the debt and all accumulated interest, penalties, and administrative costs are paid in full;

(iii) The amount, stated either as a fixed dollar amount or as a percentage of pay not to exceed 15 percent of disposable pay, the frequency, the commencement date, and the duration of the intended deductions;

(iv) An explanation of our policies concerning the assessment of interest, penalties, and administrative costs, stating that such assessments must be made unless waived in accordance with 31 CFR 901.9 and § 422.807 of this part;

(v) The employee's right to review and copy all of our records pertaining to the debt or, if the employee or the employee's representative cannot personally review the records, to request and receive copies of such records;

(vi) If not previously provided, the opportunity to establish a schedule for the voluntary repayment of the debt through offset or to enter into an agreement to establish a schedule for repayment of the debt in lieu of offset provided the agreement is in writing, signed by both the employee and us, and documented in our files;

(vii) The right to a hearing conducted by an impartial hearing official with respect to the existence and amount of the debt, or the repayment schedule, so long as a petition is filed by the employee as prescribed in paragraph (h) of this section;

(viii) Time limits and other procedures or conditions for reviewing our records pertaining to the debt, establishing an alternative repayment agreement, and requesting a hearing;

(ix) The name, address, and telephone number of the person or office who may be contacted concerning the procedures for reviewing our records, establishing an alternative repayment agreement, and requesting a hearing;

(x) The name and address of the office to send the petition for a hearing;

(xi) A timely and properly filed petition for a hearing will suspend the commencement of the collection proceeding;

(xii) We will initiate action to effect salary offset not less than 30 days from the date of mailing the notice, unless the employee properly files a timely petition for a hearing,

(xiii) A final decision on a hearing, if one is requested, will be issued at the earliest practical date, but not later than 60 days after the filing of the petition requesting the hearing unless the employee requests and the hearing official grants a delay in the proceeding;

(xiv) Notice that an employee who knowingly makes false or frivolous statements or submits false or frivolous representations or evidence may be subject to disciplinary procedures under chapter 75 of title 5, United States Code, Part 752 of title 5, CFR, or any other applicable statutes or regulations;

(xv) Any other rights and remedies available to the employee under statutes or regulations governing the program for which the collection is being made;

(xvi) Unless there are applicable contractual or statutory provisions to the contrary, amounts paid on or deducted for the debt that are later waived or found not owed to the United States will be promptly refunded to the employee; and

(xvii) Proceedings with respect to such debt are governed by 5 U.S.C. 5514.

(2) We will retain evidence of service indicating the date of mailing of the notice.

(g) Review of records relating to the debt.

(1) To review or copy our records relating to the debt, the employee must send a written request stating his or her intention. We must receive the written request within 15 days from the employee's receipt of the notice.

(2) In response to a timely request as described in paragraph (1) of this section, we will notify the employee of the location and time when the employee may review and copy such records. If the employee or employee's representative is unable to review personally such records as the result of geographical or other constraints, we will arrange to send copies of such records to the employee.

(h) Hearings—

(1) Petitions for hearing.

(i) To request a hearing concerning the existence or amount of the debt or the offset schedule established by us, the employee must send a written petition to the office we identified in the notice (see paragraph (f)(1)(x) of this section) within 15 days of receipt of the notice.

(ii) The petition must:

(A) Be signed by the employee;

(B) Fully identify and explain with reasonable specificity all the facts, evidence, and witnesses, if any, that the employee believes support his or her position; and

(C) Specify whether an oral or paper hearing is requested. If an oral hearing is requested, the request should explain why the matter cannot be resolved by a paper hearing, which is a determination of the request for reconsideration based upon a review of the written record.

(iii) The timely filing of a petition for hearing will suspend any further collection proceedings.

(2) Failure to timely request a hearing.

(i) If the petition for hearing is filed after the 15–day period provided in paragraph (h)(1)(i) of this section, we may grant the request if the employee can establish either that the delay was the result of circumstances beyond the employee's control or that the employee failed to receive actual notice of the filing deadline.

(ii) An employee waives the right to a hearing and will have his or her disposable pay offset in accordance with the offset schedule established by us, if the employee:

(A) Fails to file a timely request for a hearing unless such failure is excused; or

(B) Fails to appear at an oral hearing of which the employee was notified unless the hearing official determines that the failure to appear was due to circumstances beyond the employee's control.

(3) Form of hearings—

(i) General. After the employee requests a hearing, the hearing official must notify the employee of the type of hearing that will occur. If an oral hearing will occur, the notice will state the date, time, and location of the hearing. If a paper hearing will occur, the employee will be notified and required to submit evidence and arguments in writing to the hearing official by the date specified in the notice, after which the record will be closed.

(ii) Oral hearing. An employee who requests an oral hearing will be provided an oral hearing if the hearing official determines that the matter cannot be resolved by review of documentary evidence alone because an issue of credibility or veracity is involved. Where an oral hearing is appropriate, the hearing is not an adversarial adjudication and need not take the form of an evidentiary hearing (e.g., the formal rules of evidence need not apply). Oral hearings may take the form of, but are not limited to:

(A) Informal conferences with the hearing official in which the employee and agency representative will be given full opportunities to present evidence, witnesses, and arguments;

(B) Informal meetings in which the hearing official interviews the employee by phone or videoconferencing; or

(C) Formal written submissions with an opportunity for oral presentations.

(iii) Paper hearing. If the hearing official determines that an oral hearing is not necessary, the hearing official will make the determination based upon a review of the available written record.

(iv) Record. The hearing official will maintain a summary record of any hearing conducted under this part. Witnesses who testify in oral hearings will do so under oath or affirmation.

(4) Written decision—

(i) Date of decision. The hearing officer will issue a written opinion stating his or her decision. This opinion is based upon documentary evidence and information developed at the hearing, as soon as practicable after the hearing, but not later than 60 days after the date on which the hearing petition was received by the creditor agency. This is dependent upon whether the employee requested a delay in the proceedings and the hearing official grants it, in which case the 60–day decision period will be extended by the number of days by which the hearing was postponed. The recipient of an employee's request for a hearing must forward the request expeditiously to the hearing official to avoid jeopardizing the hearing official's ability to issue a decision within this 60–day period.

(ii) Content of decision. The written decision will include:

(A) A statement of the facts presented to support the origin, nature, and amount of the debt;

(B) The hearing official's findings, analysis, and conclusions, including a determination whether the employee's petition for hearing was baseless and resulted from an intent to delay the creditor agency's collection activity; and

(C) The terms of any repayment schedule, if applicable.

(5) Failure to appear. In the absence of good cause shown, an employee who fails to appear at a hearing will be deemed, for the purpose of this part, to admit the existence and amount of the debt as described in the notice. If the representative of the creditor agency fails to appear, the hearing official will proceed with the hearing as scheduled and make a determination based upon oral testimony presented and the documentary evidence submitted by both parties. With the

agreement of both parties, the hearing official will schedule a new hearing date, and both parties will be given notice of the time and place of the new hearing.

(i) Obtaining the services of a hearing official. The office designated in paragraph (f)(1)(x) of this section will schedule a hearing, if one is requested by an employee, before a hearing official.

(1) When we cannot provide a prompt and appropriate hearing before an administrative law judge or a hearing official furnished pursuant to another lawful arrangement, the office designated in paragraph (f)(1)(x) of this section may contact an agent of any agency designated in 5 CFR part 581, appendix A to arrange for a hearing official.

(2)(i) When another agency is the creditor agency, not SSA, it is the responsibility of that agency to arrange for a hearing if one is requested. We will provide a hearing official upon the request of a creditor agency when the debtor is employed by us and the creditor agency cannot provide a prompt and appropriate hearing before a hearing official furnished pursuant to another lawful arrangement.

(ii) Services rendered to a creditor agency under paragraph (i)(2)(i) of this section will be provided on a fully reimbursable basis pursuant to the Economy Act of 1932, as amended by 31 U.S.C. 1535.

(3) The determination of a hearing official designated under this section is considered an official certification regarding the existence and amount of the debt for purposes of executing salary offset under 5 U.S.C. 5514 and this part. A creditor agency may make a certification to the Secretary of the Treasury under 5 CFR 550.1108 or a paying agency under 5 CFR 550.1109 regarding the existence and amount of the debt based on the certification of a hearing official. If a hearing official determines that a debt may not be collected via salary offset, but we find that the debt is still valid, we may still seek collection of the debt through other means, such as offset of other Federal payments or litigation.

(j) Voluntary repayment agreement in lieu of salary offset.

(1)(i) In response to the notice, the employee may propose to establish an alternative schedule for the voluntary repayment of the debt by submitting a written request. An employee who wishes to repay the debt without salary offset will also submit a proposed written repayment agreement. The proposal will admit the existence of the debt, and the agreement must be in such form that it is legally enforceable. The agreement must:

(A) Be in writing;

(B) Be signed by both the employee and the agency;

(C) Specify all the terms of the arrangement for payment; and

(D) Contain a provision accelerating the debt in the event of default by the employee, but such an increase may not result in a deduction that exceeds 15 percent of the employee's disposable pay unless the employee has agreed in writing to a deduction of a greater amount.

(ii) Any proposal under paragraph (j)(1)(i) of this section must be received within 30 days of the date of the notice.

(2) In response to a timely request as described in paragraph (j)(1) of this section, we will notify the employee whether the proposed repayment schedule is acceptable. It is within our discretion to accept a proposed alternative repayment schedule and to set the necessary terms of a voluntary repayment agreement.

(3) No voluntary repayment agreement will be binding on us unless it is in writing and signed by the employee and us.

(k) Special review.

(1) At any time, an employee subject to salary offset or a voluntary repayment agreement may request a special review by the agency of the amount of the salary offset or voluntary repayment installments based on materially changed circumstances, such as, but not limited to, catastrophic illness, divorce, death, or disability.

(2)(i) In determining whether an offset would prevent the employee from meeting essential subsistence expenses (e.g., food, housing, clothing, transportation, and medical care), the employee must submit a detailed statement and supporting documents for the employee, his or her spouse, and dependents indicating:

(A) Income from all sources;

(B) Assets and liabilities;

(C) Number of dependents;

(D) Food, housing, clothing, transportation, and medical expenses; and

(E) Exceptional and unusual expenses, if any.

(ii) When requesting a special review under this section, the employee must file an alternative proposed offset or payment schedule and a statement, with supporting documents as described in paragraph (k)(2)(i) of this section, stating why the current salary offset or payments result in an extreme financial hardship to the employee.

(3)(i) We will evaluate the statement and supporting documents and determine whether the original offset or repayment schedule impose extreme financial hardship on the employee.

(ii) Within 30 calendar days of the receipt of the request and supporting documents, we will notify the employee in writing of such determination, including, if appropriate, a revised offset or repayment schedule.

(4) If the special review results in a revised offset or repayment schedule, we will do a new certification based on the result of the review.

(*l*) Procedures for salary offset—

(1) Method and source of deductions. Unless the employee and the agency have agreed to an alternative repayment arrangement under paragraph (j) of this section, the agency will collect a debt in a lump sum or by installment deductions at officially established pay intervals from an employee's current pay account.

(2) Limitation on amount of deduction. Ordinarily, the size of installment deductions must bear a reasonable relationship to the size of the debt and the employee's ability to pay. However, the amount deducted for any pay period must not exceed 15 percent of the disposable pay from which the deduction is made unless the employee has agreed in writing to the deduction of a greater amount, as outlined in paragraph (j) of this seciton [1].

(3) Duration of deductions—

(i) Lump sum. If the amount of the debt is equal to or less than 15 percent of the employee's disposable pay for an officially established pay interval, the agency will collect the debt in one lump-sum deduction including lump-sum annual leave amounts.

(ii) If the employee is deemed financially unable to pay in one lump sum or the amount of the debt exceeds 15 percent of the employee's disposable pay for an officially established pay interval, the agency will collect the debt in installments. Except as provided in paragraphs (k)(5) and (6) of this section, installment deductions must be made over a period no longer than the anticipated period of active duty or employment.

(4) When deductions may begin.

(i) Deductions will begin on the date stated in the notice, unless the agency and individual have agreed to an alternative repayment agreement under paragraph (j) of this section or the employee has filed a timely request for a hearing.

(ii) If the employee files a timely petition for hearing as provided in paragraph (h) of this section, the agency will begin deductions after the hearing official has provided the employee with a hearing and a final written decision has been rendered in favor of the agency.

(5) Liquidation from final check. If an employee retires, resigns, or the period of employment ends before collection of the debt is completed, the agency will offset the remainder under 31 U.S.C. 3716 from subsequent agency payments of any nature (e.g., final salary payment or lump-sum leave) due the employee as of the date of separation.

(6) Recovery from other payments due a separated employee. If the debt cannot be satisfied by offset from any final payment due the employee on the date of separation, we will liquidate the debt, where appropriate, by Administrative Offset under 31 U.S.C. 3716 from later payments of any kind due the former employee (e.g., lump-sum leave payment).

(m) Exception to internal salary offset. SSA may follow Administrative Offset notification requirements when attempting the collection of delinquent travel advances and training expenses, not those associated with Federal employee salary offset. Once the notification procedures have been followed, SSA has the authority to withhold all or part of an employee's salary, retirement benefits, or other amount due the employee including lump-sum payments to recover the amounts owed. No statutory or regulatory limits exist on the amount that can be withheld or offset.

(n) Salary offset when we are the paying agency but not the creditor agency. When we are the paying agency and another agency is the creditor agency, the creditor agency must provide written certification to Treasury that the employee owes the debt, the amount and basis of the debt, the date on which payment(s) is due, the date the Government's right to collect the debt first accrued, and that the Office of Personnel Management has approved the creditor agency's regulations implementing 5 U.S.C. 5514. We are not required or authorized to review the merits of the determination with respect to the amount or validity of the debt certified by the creditor agency.

(*o*) Interest, penalties, and administrative costs. Debts owed will be assessed interest, penalties, and administrative costs in accordance with § 422.807.

(p) Non-waiver of rights. An employee's involuntary payment of all or any portion of a debt collected under this part will not be construed as a waiver of any rights the employee may have under 5 U.S.C. 5514 or any other provision of law or contract unless there are statutory or contractual provisions to the contrary.

(q) Refunds.

(1) We will promptly refund any amounts paid or deducted under this part when:

(i) A debt is waived or otherwise found not owed to us; or

(ii) We are directed by administrative or judicial order to refund amount deducted from the employee's current pay.

(2) Unless required or permitted by law or contract, refunds will not bear interest.

(r) Additional administrative collection action. Nothing contained in this part is intended to preclude the use of any other appropriate administrative remedy.

[1] So in original; see 80 FR 61734.

§ 422.811 Discretionary referral for cross-servicing.

We may refer legally enforceable non-tax administrative debts that are less than 120 calendar days delinquent to the Department of the Treasury (Treasury) or to Treasury-designated "debt collection centers" in accordance with 31 CFR 285.12 to accomplish efficient, cost effective debt collection.

§ 422.813 Mandatory referral for cross-servicing.

(a) Pursuant to the cross-servicing process, creditor agencies must transfer any eligible debt more than 120 calendar days delinquent to the Department of the Treasury (Treasury) for debt collection services. As one such agency, pursuant to 31 CFR 285.12, we are required to transfer to Treasury any legally enforceable nontax debt in excess of $25. We may transfer to Treasury any combination of legally enforceable nontax debts less than $25 that exceeds $25 (in the case of a debtor whose taxpayer identification number (TIN) is unknown, the applicable threshold is $100) that has or have been delinquent for a period of 120 calendar days. Treasury will take appropriate action on behalf of the creditor agency to collect, compromise, suspend, or terminate collection of the debt, including use of debt collection centers and private collection contractors to collect the debt or terminate collection action.

(b) Debts not eligible for mandatory referral of paragraph (a) of this section include:

(1) Debts owed by a Federal agency;

(2) Debts owed by a deceased debtor;

(3) Debts not legally enforceable: A debt is considered legally enforceable for purposes of referral to the Treasury's Bureau of the Fiscal Service if there has been a final agency determination that the debt is due and there are no legal bars to collection;

(4) Debts that are the subject of an administrative appeal until the appeal is concluded and the amount of the debt is fixed;

(5) Debts owed by a debtor who has filed for bankruptcy protection or the debt has been discharged in bankruptcy proceeding; or

(6) Debts that are less than $25 (including interest, penalties, and administrative costs).

(c) A debt is considered delinquent for purposes of this section if it is 120 calendar days past due and is legally enforceable. A debt is past due if it has not been paid by the date specified in the agency's initial written demand for payment or applicable agreement or instrument (including a post-delinquency payment agreement) unless other satisfactory payment arrangements have been made. A debt is legally enforceable if there has been a final agency determination that the debt, in the amount stated, is due and there are no legal bars to collection action. Where, for example, a debt is the subject of a pending administrative review process required by statute or regulation and collection action during the review process is prohibited, the debt is not considered legally enforceable for purposes of mandatory transfer to the Treasury and is not to be transferred even if the debt is more than 120 calendar days past due. When a final agency determination is made after an administrative appeal or review process, the creditor agency must transfer such debt to Treasury, if more than 120 calendar days delinquent, within 30 days after the date of the final decision.

(d) We may also refer debts owed by a foreign country upon consultation with our Office of the General Counsel.

§ 422.815 Referral of administrative debts to the Department of the Treasury.

(a) Agencies are required by law to transfer delinquent, nontax, and legally enforceable debts to Department of the Treasury (Treasury) for collection through cross-servicing and through centralized Administrative Offset. Additionally, we may transfer debts to the Treasury for collection through Administrative Wage Garnishment. Agencies need not make duplicate referrals to Treasury for all these purposes; we may refer a debt to Treasury for purposes of simultaneous collection by cross-servicing, centralized Administrative Offset, and Administrative Wage Garnishment where applicable. However, in some instances a debt exempt from cross-servicing collection may be subject to collection by centralized Administrative Offset, so simultaneous referrals are not always appropriate.

(b) When we refer or transfer administrative debts to Treasury, or Treasury-designated debt collection centers under the authority of 31 U.S.C. 3711(g), Treasury will service, collect, or compromise the debts, or Treasury will suspend or terminate the collection action, in accordance with the statutory requirements and authorities applicable to the collection of such debts.

(c) Debts that are not required for referral include:

(1) Debts delinquent for 120 calendar days or less;

(2) Debts less than $100 and we are unable to obtain the debtor's taxpayer identification number;

(3) Debts in litigation or foreclosure as defined in 31 CFR 285.12(d)(2);

(4) Debts that have been referred to a private collection contractor for a period acceptable to Treasury;

(5) Debts that will be disposed of under an approved asset sale program as defined in 31 CFR 285.12(d)(3)(i);

(6) Debts that will be collected under internal offset procedures within three years after the debt first became delinquent;

(7) Debts at a debt collection center for a period of time acceptable to Treasury; or

(8) Debts exempt from this requirement based on a determination by the Secretary of the Treasury that exemption for a certain class of debt is in the best interest of the United States. Federal agencies may request that the Secretary of the Treasury exempt specific classes of debts. Any such request by an agency must be sent to the Fiscal Assistant Secretary of the Treasury by the agency's Chief Financial Officer.

§ 422.817 Required certification.

Before referring delinquent administrative debts to the Department of the Treasury (Treasury) for collection, we will certify, in writing, that:

(a) The debts we are transferring are valid and legally enforceable;

(b) There are no legal bars to collection; and

(c) We have complied with all prerequisites to a particular collection action under the laws, regulations, or policies applicable to us, unless we agree that Treasury will do so on our behalf.

§ 422.819 Fees.

Federal agencies operating Department of the Treasury-designated debt collection centers are authorized to charge a fee for services rendered regarding referred or transferred debts. The fee may be paid out of amounts collected and may be added to the debt as an administrative cost.

§ 422.821 Administrative offset.

(a) Scope.

(1) Administrative Offset is the withholding of funds payable by the United States to, or held by the United States for, a person to satisfy a debt. We will use Administrative Offset to recover administrative debts.

(2) This section does not apply to:

(i) Debts arising under the Social Security Act;

(ii) Payments made under the Social Security Act, except as provided for in 31 U.S.C. 3716(c), and 31 CFR 285.4;

(iii) Debts arising under, or payments made under the Internal Revenue Code or the tariff laws of the United States;

(iv) Offsets against Federal salaries to the extent these standards are inconsistent with regulations published to implement such offsets under 5 U.S.C. 5514 and 31 U.S.C. 3716 (see 5 CFR part 550, subpart K; 31 CFR 285.7; §§ 422.810 and 422.829 of this part);

(v) Offsets under 31 U.S.C. 3728 against a judgment obtained by a debtor against the United States;

(vi) Offsets or recoupments under common law, State law, or Federal statutes specifically prohibiting offsets or recoupments for particular types of debts; or

(vii) Offsets in the course of judicial proceedings, including bankruptcy.

(3) Unless otherwise provided for by contract or law, debts or payments that are not subject to Administrative Offset under 31 U.S.C. 3716 may be collected by Administrative Offset under the common law or other applicable statutory authority.

(4) In bankruptcy cases, the agency may seek legal advice from the Office of the General Counsel concerning the impact of the Bankruptcy Code, particularly 11 U.S.C. 106, 362, and 553, on pending or contemplated collections by offset.

(b) [Reserved]

§ 422.822 Notification of intent to collect by administrative offset.

(a) Prior to initiation of collection by Administrative Offset, we will:

(1) Send the debtor a notice by mail or hand-delivery. The notice will include the type and amount of the debt, the intention of the agency using internal offset or non-centralized Administrative Offset to collect the debt 30 days after the date of the notice, and the name of the Federal agency from which the creditor agency wishes to collect in the case of a non-centralized Administrative Offset. Additionally, if the debt is not satisfied by offset within the Social Security Administration or by agreement with another Federal agency, the notice will include the intent to refer the debt to the Department of the Treasury (Treasury) for collection through centralized Administrative Offset, including offset of tax refunds 60 days after the date of the notice as well as an explanation of the debtor's rights under 31 U.S.C. 3716.

(2) Give the debtor the opportunity:

(i) To make a voluntary payment;

(ii) To review and copy agency records related to the debt;

(iii) For a review within the agency of the determination of indebtedness;

(iv) To make a written agreement to repay the debt.

(b) The procedures set forth in paragraph (a) of this section are not required when:

(1) The offset is in the nature of a recoupment;

(2) The debt arises under a contract subject to the Contracts Disputes Act or Federal Acquisition Regulations;

(3) In the case of a non-centralized Administrative Offset (see § 422.824), the agency first learns of the existence of the amount owed by the debtor when there is insufficient time before payment would be made to the debtor/payee to allow for prior notice and an opportunity for review. When prior notice and an opportunity for review are omitted, we will give the debtor such notice and an opportunity for review as

soon as practicable and will promptly refund any money ultimately found not to have been owed to the agency; or

(4) The agency previously has given a debtor any of the notice and review opportunities required under this part, with respect to a particular debt. Subsequently, any interest accrued or any installments coming due after we initiate an offset would not require a new notice and opportunity to review.

(c) The notice will be included as part of a demand letter issued under § 422.805 to advise the debtor of all debt collection possibilities that the agency will seek to employ.

§ 422.823 Debtor rights to review or copy records, submit repayment proposals, or request administrative review.

(a) A debtor who intends to review or copy our records with respect to the debt must notify us in writing within 30 days of the date of the notice as described in section § 422.822. In response, we will notify the debtor of the location, time, and any other conditions for reviewing and copying. The debtor may be liable for reasonable copying expenses.

(b) In response to the notice as described in section § 422.822, the debtor may propose a written agreement to repay the debt as an alternative to Administrative Offset. Any debtor who wishes to do this must submit a written proposal for repayment of the debt, which we must receive within 30 days of the date of the notice as described in section § 422.822 or 15 days after the date of a decision adverse to the debtor. In response, we will notify the debtor whether we need additional information, for example, financial status information. We will obtain any necessary authorization required to approve the agreement, and we will issue a written determination whether the proposed agreement is acceptable. In exercising our discretion, we will balance the Government's interest in collecting the debt against fairness to the debtor.

(c) A debtor must request an administrative review of the debt within 30 days of the date of the notice as described in section § 422.822 for purposes of a proposed collection by non-centralized Administrative Offset pursuant to § 422.824. A debtor must request an administrative review of the debt within 60 days of the date of the notice as described in section § 422.822 for purposes of a proposed collection by centralized Administrative Offset for offset against other Federal payments that would include tax refunds pursuant to § 422.825.

(1) For purposes of this section, whenever we are required to provide a debtor a review within the agency, we will give the debtor a reasonable opportunity for an oral hearing, either by telephone or in person, when the debtor requests reconsideration of the debt and we determine that the question of the indebtedness cannot be resolved by review of the documentary evidence.

(2) Unless otherwise required by law, an oral hearing under this section is not required to be a formal evidentiary hearing, although we will carefully document all significant matters discussed at the hearing.

(3) An oral hearing is not required with respect to debts where determinations of indebtedness rarely involve issues of credibility or veracity, and we have determined that a review of the written record is adequate to correct prior mistakes.

(4) In those cases when an oral hearing is not required by this section, we will provide the debtor a paper hearing, that is, a determination of the request for reconsideration based upon a review of the written record.

§ 422.824 Non-centralized administrative offset.

(a) Unless otherwise prohibited by law, when centralized Administrative Offset under § 422.825 is not available or appropriate, we may collect a past due, legally enforceable, nontax delinquent debt by conducting non-centralized Administrative Offset internally or in cooperation with the agency certifying or authorizing payments to the debtor. Generally, non-centralized Administrative Offsets are ad hoc case-by-case offsets that an agency conducts at its own discretion, internally or in cooperation with a second agency certifying or authorizing payments to the debtor. In these cases, we may make a request directly to a payment-authorizing agency to offset a payment due a debtor to collect a delinquent debt. We adopt the procedures in 31 CFR 901.3(c) so that we may request the Department of the Treasury or any other payment-authorizing agency to conduct a non-centralized Administrative Offset.

(b) Administrative Offset may be initiated only after:

(1) The debtor has been sent a notice of the type and amount of the debt, the intention to initiate Administrative Offset to collect the debt, and an explanation of the debtor's rights under 31 U.S.C. 3716; and

(2) The debtor has been given:

(i) The opportunity to review and copy records related to the debt;

(ii) The opportunity for a review within the department of the determination of indebtedness; and

(iii) The opportunity to make a written agreement to repay the debt.

(c) The agency may omit the requirements under paragraph (b) of this section when:

(1) Offset is in the nature of a recoupment (i.e., the debt and the payment to be offset arise out of the same transaction or occurrence);

(2) The debt arises under a contract as set forth in Cecile Industries, Inc. v. Cheney, 995 F.2d 1052 (Fed. Cir. 1993) (notice and other procedural protections set forth in 31 U.S.C. 3716(a) do not supplant or restrict established procedures for contractual offsets covered by the Contracts Disputes Act); or

(3) In the case of non-centralized Administrative Offset conducted under paragraph (a) of this section, the agency first learns of the existence of the amount owed by the debtor when there is insufficient time before payment would be made to the debtor to allow for prior notice and an opportunity for review. When prior notice and an opportunity for review are omitted, we will give the debtor such notice and an opportunity for review as soon as practical and will promptly refund any money ultimately found not to have been owed to the Government.

(d) When the debtor previously has been given any of the required notice and review opportunities with respect to a particular debt, such as under § 422.805, we need not duplicate such notice and review opportunities before Administrative Offset may be initiated.

(e) Before requesting that a payment-authorizing agency conduct non-centralized Administrative Offset, we will:

(1) Provide the debtor with due process as set forth in paragraph (b) of this section; and

(2) Provide the payment-authorizing agency written certification that the debtor owes the past due, legally enforceable delinquent debt in the amount stated and that we have fully complied with this section.

(f) When a creditor agency requests that we, as the payment authorizing agency, conduct non-centralized Administrative Offset, we will comply with the request, unless the offset would not be in the best interest of the United States with respect to the program of the agency, or would otherwise be contrary to law. Appropriate use should be made of the cooperative efforts of other agencies in effecting collection by Administrative Offset, including salary offset.

(g) When collecting multiple debts by non-centralized Administrative Offset, we will apply the recovered amounts to those debts in accordance with the best interests of the United States, as determined by the facts and circumstances of the particular case, particularly the applicable statute of limitations.

§ 422.825 Centralized administrative offset.

(a) Mandatory referral. After we provide and meet the notice and review opportunity requirements of § 422.822, we will refer debts that are over 120 calendar days delinquent to the Department of the Treasury (Treasury) for collection through centralized Administrative Offset 61 days after the date of the notice provided in accordance with § 422.822. If the debtor seeks review, referral of the debt must occur within 30 days of the final decision upholding our decision to offset the debt if the debt is more than 120 calendar days delinquent.

(b) Discretionary referral. After we provide and meet the notice and review opportunity requirements of § 422.822, and the debtor does not request administrative review or the result of the review is unsuccessful for the debtor, we may refer a debt that is less than 120 calendar days delinquent.

(c) Procedures for referral. We will refer debts to Treasury for collection in accordance with Treasury procedures set forth in 31 CFR 285.5 and 31 CFR 901.3(b).

§ 422.827 Offset against tax refunds.

We will take action to effect Administrative Offset against tax refunds due to debtors in accordance with the provisions of 31 U.S.C. 3720A through referral for centralized Administrative Offset under § 422.825.

§ 422.829 Federal salary offset.

(a) Referral to the Department of the Treasury for offset.

(1) The Department of the Treasury (Treasury) will recover overdue administrative debts by offsetting Federal payments due the debtor through the Treasury Offset Program (TOP). TOP is a government-wide delinquent debt matching and payment offset process operated by Treasury, whereby debts owed to the Federal Government are collected by offsetting them against Federal payments owed the debtor. Federal payments owed the debtor include current "disposable pay," defined in 5 CFR 550.1103, owed by the Federal Government to a debtor who is an employee of the Federal Government. Deducting from such disposable pay to collect an overdue debt owed by the employee is called "Federal Salary Offset" in this subpart.

(2) Treasury will use Federal Salary Offset to collect overdue administrative debts from Federal employees, including employees of the Social Security Administration. A Federal employee's involuntary payment of all or part of a debt collected by Federal Salary Offset does not amount to a waiver of any rights that the employee may have under any statute or contract, unless a statute or contract provides for waiver of such rights.

(b) Debts we will refer. We will refer all qualifying administrative debts that meet or exceed the threshold amounts used by Treasury for collection from Federal payments, including Federal salaries.

(c) Notice to debtor. Before we refer any administrative debt for collection by Administrative Offset, we will send the debtor a notice that explains all of the following:

(1) The nature and amount of the debt;

(2) That we have determined that payment of the debt is overdue; and

(3) That we will refer the debt for Administrative Offset (except as provided in paragraph (c)(9) of this section) at the expiration of not less than 60 calendar days after the date of the notice unless, within that 60–day period:

(i) The debtor pays the full amount of the debt, or

(ii) The debtor takes any of the actions described in paragraphs (c)(6) or (c)(7) of this section.

(4) The frequency and amount of any Federal Salary Offset deduction (the payment schedule) expressed as a fixed dollar amount or percentage of disposable pay.

(5) The debtor may review or copy our records relating to the debt. If the debtor or his or her representative cannot personally review the records, the debtor may request and receive a copy of such records.

(6) The debtor may request a review of the debt by giving us evidence showing that the debtor does not owe all or part of the amount of the debt or that we do not have the right to collect it. The debtor may also request review of any payment schedule for Federal Salary Offset stated in the notice. If the debtor is an employee of the Federal Government and Federal Salary Offset is proposed, an official designated in accordance with 5 U.S.C. 5514(a)(2) will conduct the review.

(7) The debtor may request to repay the debt voluntarily through an installment payment plan.

(8) If the debtor knowingly furnishes any false or frivolous statements, representations, or evidence, the debtor may be subject to appropriate disciplinary procedures under applicable statutes or regulations when the debtor is a Federal employee.

(9) We will refer the debt for Federal Salary Offset at the expiration of not less than 60 calendar days after the date of the notice unless, within that 60 day period, the debtor takes any actions described in paragraphs (c)(3)(i), (c)(6), or (c)(7) of this section.

(d) Federal Salary Offset: amount, frequency and duration of deductions.

(1) Treasury may collect the overdue debt from an employee of the Federal Government through the deduction of an amount not to exceed 15 percent of the debtor's current disposable pay each payday.

(2) [1] Federal Salary Offset will begin not less than 60 calendar days after the date of the notice to the debtor described in paragraph (c) of this section.

(3) Once begun, Federal Salary Offset will continue until Treasury recovers the full amount of the debt, the debt is otherwise resolved, or the debtor's Federal employment ceases, whichever occurs first.

[1] So in original; there are two subsections (d)(2). See 80 FR 61743.

(4) After Federal Salary Offset begins, the debtor may request a reduction in the amount deducted from disposable pay each payday. When Treasury determines that the amount deducted causes financial harm under the rules in § 422.833(j), they will reduce that amount. Treasury will not reduce the amount from the debtor's disposable pay if the debt was caused by:

(A) An intentional false statement by the debtor, or

(B) The debtor's willful concealment of, or failure to furnish, material information.

(2) [1] "Willful concealment" means an intentional, knowing and purposeful delay in providing, or failure to reveal, material information.

(e) Refunds. Treasury will promptly refund to the debtor any amounts collected that the debtor does not owe. Refunds do not bear interest unless required or permitted by law or contract.

§ 422.833 Administrative wage garnishment for administrative debts.

(a) Purpose. This part prescribes the standards and procedures for collecting money from a debtor's disposable pay by means of Administrative Wage Garnishment to satisfy delinquent non-tax debts owed to us, the Social Security Administration.

(b) Authority. These standards and procedures are authorized under the wage garnishment provisions of the Debt Collection Improvement Act of 1996, codified at 31 U.S.C. 3720D, and the Department of the Treasury's (Treasury) Administrative Wage Garnishment regulation at 31 CFR 285.11.

(1) This part will apply notwithstanding any provision of State law.

(2) Nothing in this part precludes the compromise of a debt or the suspension or termination of collection action in accordance with § 422.803 of this title or other applicable law or regulation, and the Commissioner has retained the authority. The Department of Justice has exclusive authority to suspend or terminate collection action on a debt affected by fraud.

(3) The receipt of payments pursuant to this part does not preclude us from pursuing other debt collection remedies, including the offset of Federal or State payments to satisfy delinquent non-tax debt owed to the United States. We will pursue such debt collection remedies separately or in conjunction with Administrative Wage Garnishment.

(4) This section does not apply to the collection of delinquent non-tax debts owed to the United States from the wages of Federal employees from their Federal employment. Federal pay is subject to the Federal Salary Offset procedures set forth in 5 U.S.C. 5514 and other applicable laws.

[1] So in original; there are two subsections (d)(2). See 80 FR 61743.

(5) Nothing in this section requires us to duplicate notices or administrative proceedings required by contract or other laws or regulations.

(c) Definitions. In this section, the following definitions will apply:

(1) Business day means Monday through Friday. For purposes of computation, the last day of the period will be included unless it is a Federal legal holiday, in which case the next business day following the holiday will be considered the last day of the period.

(2) Day means calendar day. For purposes of computation, the last day of the period will be included unless it is a Saturday, Sunday, or a Federal legal holiday, in which case the next business day will be considered the last day of the period.

(3) Debt means an amount of funds or other property determined by an appropriate official of the Federal Government to be owed to the United States from any person, organization, or entity or any other debt that meets the definition of "claim" or "debt" under 31 U.S.C. 3701(b), excluding program overpayments made under title II or title XVI of the Social Security Act.

(4) Debtor means an individual who owes a delinquent non-tax debt to the United States.

(5) Delinquent debt means any non-tax debt that has not been paid by the date specified in the agency's initial written demand for payment, or applicable payment agreement or instrument, unless other satisfactory payment arrangements have been made. For purposes of this part, "delinquent" and "overdue" have the same meaning.

(6) Disposable pay means that part of the debtor's compensation (including, but not limited to, salary, bonuses, commissions, and vacation pay) from an employer remaining after the deduction of health insurance premiums and any amounts required by law to be withheld. For purposes of this part, "amounts required by law to be withheld" include amounts for deductions such as social security taxes and withholding taxes, but do not include any amount withheld pursuant to a court order.

(7) Employer means a person or entity that employs the services of others and that pays their wages or salaries. The term employer includes, but is not limited to, State and local Governments, but does not include an agency of the Federal Government as defined by 31 CFR 285.11(c).

(8) Garnishment means the process of withholding amounts from an employee's disposable pay and paying those amounts to a creditor in satisfaction of a withholding order.

(9) Hearing means a review of the documentary evidence concerning the existence or amount of a debt or the terms of a repayment schedule, provided such repayment schedule is established other than by a written agreement entered into pursuant to this part. If the hearing official determines that the issues in dispute cannot be resolved solely by review of the written record, such as when the validity of the debt turns on the issue of credibility or veracity, an oral hearing may be provided.

(10) Hearing official means an administrative law judge or appropriate alternate.

(11) Treasury means the Department of the Treasury.

(12) Withholding order for purposes of this part means "Wage Garnishment Order (SF329B)." Also for purposes of this part, the terms "wage garnishment order" and "garnishment order" have the same meaning as "withholding order."

(d) General rule.

(1) Except as provided in paragraph (d)(2) of this section, whenever an individual owes a delinquent debt, the agency or another Federal agency collecting a debt on our behalf (see § 422.803) may initiate administrative proceedings to garnish the wages of the delinquent debtor.

(2) Treasury will not garnish the wages of a debtor who we know has been involuntarily separated from employment until the debtor has been re-employed continuously for at least 12 months. The debtor has the burden to inform the agency of the circumstances surrounding an involuntary separation from employment.

(e) Notice—

(1) Notice requirements. At least 30 days before the initiation of garnishment proceedings, Treasury will mail, by first class mail, to the debtor's last known address, a notice informing the debtor of:

(i) The nature and amount of the debt;

(ii) The intention to initiate proceedings to collect the debt through deductions from pay until the debt and all accumulated interest, penalties, and administrative costs are paid in full;

(iii) The debtor's right:

(A) To review and copy our records related to the debt;

(B) To enter into a written repayment which is agreeable to the agency;

(C) To a hearing, in accordance with paragraph (f) of this section, concerning the existence or the amount of the debt or the terms of the proposed repayment schedule under the garnishment order, except that the debtor is not entitled to a hearing concerning the proposed repayment schedule if the terms were established by written agreement pursuant to paragraph (1)(iii)(B) of this section; and

(iv) The periods within which the debtor may exercise his or her rights.

(2) Treasury will keep a copy of the dated notice. The notice may be retained electronically so long as the manner of retention is sufficient for evidentiary purposes.

(f) Hearing—

(1) In general. Upon timely written request of the debtor, Treasury will provide a paper or oral hearing concerning the existence or amount of the debt, or the terms of a repayment schedule established other than by written agreement under paragraph (e)(1)(iii)(B) of this section.

(2) Request for hearing.

(i) The request for a hearing must be signed by the debtor, state each issue being disputed, and identify and explain with reasonable specificity all facts and evidence that the debtor believes support the debtor's position. Supporting documentation identified by the debtor should be attached to the request.

(ii) Effect of timely request: Subject to paragraph (e)(10) of this section, if the debtor's written request is received on or before the 15 business days following the mailing of the notice required under this part, a withholding order will not be issued under paragraph (g) of this section until the debtor has been provided the requested hearing, and a decision in accordance with paragraphs (e)(7) and (8) of this section has been rendered.

(iii) Failure to timely request a hearing: If the debtor's written request is received after the 15th business day following the mailing of the notice required under this part, Treasury will provide a hearing to the debtor. However, Treasury may not delay the issuance of a withholding order unless they determine that the delay in submitting such request was caused by factors beyond the control of the debtor, or receive information that they determine justifies a delay or cancellation of the withholding order.

(3) Oral hearing.

(i) For purposes of this section, a debtor will be provided a reasonable opportunity for an oral hearing when the hearing official determines that the issues in dispute cannot be resolved by review of the documentary evidence, such as when the validity of the claim turns on the issue of credibility or veracity.

(ii) If the hearing official decides to have a hearing, a debtor can specify to Treasury whether he or she wants to appear in person or by telephone. At the debtor's option, the oral hearing may be conducted in person or by telephone conference. The hearing official will notify the debtor of the date, time, and in the case of an in-person hearing, the location of the hearing. All travel expenses incurred by the debtor in connection with an in-person hearing will be borne by the debtor.

(4) Paper hearing.

(i) If the hearing official determines an oral hearing is not required by this section, the hearing official will afford the debtor a paper hearing, that is, the issues in dispute will be decided based upon a review of the written record.

(ii) The hearing official will notify the debtor of the deadline for the submission of additional evidence if necessary for a review of the record.

(5) Burden of proof.

(i) Treasury has the initial burden of proving the existence or amount of the debt.

(ii) Thereafter, if the debtor disputes the existence or amount of the debt, the debtor must present Treasury preponderant evidence that no debt exists or that the amount is incorrect. Debtors challenging the terms of a repayment schedule must provide preponderant evidence to Treasury that the terms of the repayment schedule are unlawful, would cause the debtor financial hardship, or that operation of law prohibits collection of the debt.

(6) Record. The hearing official will maintain a summary record of any hearing provided under this part. A hearing is not required to be a formal evidentiary-type hearing, but witnesses who testify in an oral hearing must do so under oath or affirmation.

(7) Date of decision.

(i) The hearing official will issue a written decision, as soon as practicable, but no later than 60 days after the date on which the request for the hearing was received by the agency.

(ii) If the hearing official is unable to provide the debtor with a hearing and render a decision within 60 days after the receipt of the request for such hearing:

(A) A withholding order may not be issued until the hearing is held and a decision is rendered; or

(B) A withholding order previously issued to the debtor's employer must be suspended beginning on the 61st day after the receipt of the hearing request and continuing until a hearing is held and a decision is rendered.

(8) Content of decision. The written decision will include:

(i) A summary of the facts presented;

(ii) The hearing official's findings, analysis, and conclusions; and

(iii) The terms of any repayment schedule, if applicable.

(9) Final agency action. The hearing official's decision will be the final agency action for the purposes of judicial review under the Administrative Procedure Act. 5 U.S.C. 701 et seq.

(10) Failure to appear. In the absence of good cause shown, a debtor who fails to appear at a hearing

will be deemed as not having timely filed a request for a hearing.

(g) Withholding order. Unless Treasury receives information that determines a justified delay or cancellation of a withholding order, Treasury will send, by first class mail, an SF–329A "Letter to Employer & Important Notice to Employer," an SF–329B "Wage Garnishment Order," an SF–329C "Wage Garnishment Worksheet," and an SF–329D "Employer Certification" to the debtor's employer within 30 days after the debtor fails to make a timely request for a hearing or, if the timely request for a hearing is made by the debtor, within 30 days after a final decision is made by the agency to proceed with garnishment.

(h) Certification by employer. The employer must complete and return the SF–329D "Employer Certification" within 20 days of receipt.

(i) Amounts withheld.

(1) After receipt of a withholding order issued under this part, the employer will deduct from all disposable pay paid to the debtor during each pay period the amount of garnishment described in paragraph (h)(2) of this section. The employer may use the SF–329C "Wage Garnishment Worksheet" to calculate the amount to be deducted from the debtor's disposable pay.

(2) Subject to paragraphs (h)(3)(i) and (h)(4) of this section, the amount of garnishment will be the lesser of:

(i) The amount indicated on the garnishment order up to 15 percent of the debtor's disposable pay; or

(ii) The amount set forth in 15 U.S.C. 1673(a)(2) (Maximum allowable garnishment). The amount set forth at 15 U.S.C. 1673(a)(2) is the amount by which a debtor's disposable pay exceeds an amount equivalent to thirty times the minimum wage. See 29 CFR 870.10.

(3)(i) Except as provided in paragraph (h)(3)(ii) of this section, when a debtor's pay is subject to multiple withholding orders, unless otherwise provided by Federal law, withholding orders issued pursuant to this part will have priority over other withholding orders that are served later.

(ii) Notwithstanding the foregoing, withholding orders for family support will have priority over withholding orders issued under this part.

(iii) If amounts are being withheld from a debtor's pay pursuant to a withholding order served on an employer before a withholding order issued pursuant to this part, or if a withholding order for family support is served on an employer at any time, the amounts withheld pursuant to a withholding order issued under this part will be the lesser of:

(A) The amount calculated under paragraph (h)(3)(iii)(B) of this section; or

(B) An amount equal to 25 percent of the debtor's disposable pay less the amount(s) withheld under the withholding order(s) with priority.

(4) If the debtor owes more than one debt to the agency, Treasury will issue multiple withholding orders provided that the total amount garnished from the debtor's pay for such orders does not exceed the amount set forth in paragraph (h)(2) of this section.

(5) An amount greater than that set forth in paragraphs (h)(2) or (3) of this section may be withheld with the debtor's written consent.

(6) The employer will promptly pay all amounts withheld in accordance with the withholding order issued pursuant to this part.

(7) The employer is not required to vary its normal pay and disbursement cycles in order to comply with the withholding order.

(8) Any assignment or allotment by an employee will be void to the extent it interferes with or prohibits execution of the withholding order issued under this part, except for any assignment or allotment made pursuant to a family support judgment or order.

(9) The employer will withhold the appropriate amount from the debtor's wages for each pay period until the employer receives notification from the agency to discontinue wage withholding.

(10) The withholding order, SF–329B "Wage Garnishment Order," sent to the employer under paragraph (g) of this section, requires the employer to commence wage withholding on the first payday after the employer receives the order. However, if the first payday is within 10 days after receipt of the order, the employer may elect to begin deductions on the second payday.

(11) An employer may not discharge, refuse to employ, or take disciplinary action against any debtor because of the issuance of a withholding order under this part.

(j) Financial hardship.

(1) A debtor whose wages are subject to a withholding order may, at any time, request a review by Treasury of the amount garnished, based on materially changed circumstances, such as disability, divorce, or catastrophic illness, which result in financial hardship.

(2) A debtor requesting review under paragraph (i)(1) of this section will submit the basis for the claim that the current amount of garnishment results in a financial hardship to the debtor, along with supporting documentation. Treasury will consider any information submitted in accordance with this part.

(3) If Treasury finds financial hardship, to reflect the debtor's financial condition, Treasury will downwardly adjust the amount garnished by an amount and for a period established by the agency. Treasury will

notify the employer of any adjustments in the amount to be withheld.

(k) Fraud and willful concealment or failure to furnish information. Treasury will not reduce the amount that the employer withholds from disposable pay if the debt was caused by an intentional false statement.

(*l*) Refunds.

(1) If the hearing official, pursuant to a hearing under this part, determines that a debt is not legally due and owing to the United States, Treasury will promptly refund any amount collected by means of Administrative Wage Garnishment.

(2) Unless required by Federal law or contract, refunds under this part will not bear interest.

(m) Ending garnishment.

(1) Once Treasury has fully recovered the amounts owed by the debtor, including interest, penalties, and administrative costs assessed pursuant to and in accordance with § 422.803 of this title, Treasury will send the debtor's employer notification to discontinue wage withholding.

(2) At least annually, Treasury will review debtors' accounts to ensure that garnishment has ended for accounts that have been paid in full.

(n) Employers' responsibilities and right of action.

(1) The employer of a debtor subject to wage withholding pursuant to this part will pay the agency as directed in a withholding order issued under this part.

(2) Treasury may bring suit against an employer for any amount that the employer fails to withhold from wages owed and payable to a debtor in accordance with paragraphs (g) and (i) of this section, plus attorney's fees, costs, and, if applicable, punitive damages.

(3) A suit under this section may not be filed before the end of the collection action involving a particular debtor, unless earlier filing is necessary to avoid expiration of any applicable statute of limitations period. For purposes of this section, "end of collection action" occurs when we have completed taking collection action in accordance with part 422, subpart I of this title or other applicable law or regulation.

(4) Notwithstanding any other provision or action referred to in this section, the end of the collection action will be deemed to occur one (1) year after the agency does not receive any payment of wages that were subject to a garnishment order issued under this part.

§ 422.835 Debt reporting and use of credit reporting agencies.

(a) Reporting delinquent debts

(1) We may report delinquent debts over $25 to credit bureaus or other automated databases.

(2) We will report administrative debts owed by individuals to consumer reporting agencies pursuant to 5 U.S.C. 552a(b)(12). We may disclose only the individual's name, address, and Social Security number and the nature, amount, status, and history of the debt.

(3) Once we refer a debt to the Department of the Treasury (Treasury) for collection, Treasury may handle any subsequent reporting to or updating of a credit bureau or other automated database.

(4) Where there is reason to believe that a debtor has filed a bankruptcy petition, prior to proceeding under this paragraph (a), we will contact the Office of the General Counsel for legal advice concerning the impact of the Bankruptcy Code, particularly with respect to the applicability of the automatic stay, 11 U.S.C. 362, and the procedures for obtaining relief from such stay.

(5) If the debtor has not received prior notice under § 422.805, before reporting a delinquent debt under this section, we will provide the debtor at least 60 days notice including:

(i) The amount and nature of the debt;

(ii) That the debt is delinquent and that we intend to report the debt to a credit bureau;

(iii) The specific information that we will disclose;

(iv) The right to dispute the accuracy and validity of the information being disclosed; and

(v) If a previous opportunity was not provided, the right to request review of the debt or rescheduling of payment.

(b) Use of credit reporting agencies. We may use credit-reporting agencies to determine a debtor's ability to repay a debt and to locate debtors. In the case of an individual, we may disclose, as a routine use under 5 U.S.C. 552a(b)(3), only the individual's name, address, and Social Security number, and the purpose for which the information will be used.

§ 422.837 Contracting with private collection contractors and with entities that locate and recover unclaimed assets.

(a) Subject to the provisions of paragraph (b) of this section, we may contract with private collection contractors to recover delinquent debts, if:

(1) We retain the authority to resolve disputes, compromise debts, suspend or terminate collection action, and, as appropriate, to refer debts to the Department of Justice for review and litigation;

(2) The private collection contractor is not allowed to offer the debtor, as an incentive for payment, the opportunity to pay the debt less the private collection contractor's fee, unless we have granted such authority prior to the offer;

(3) The contract provides that the private collection contractor is subject to the Privacy Act of 1974 to the

extent specified in 5 U.S.C. 552a(m) and to applicable Federal and State laws and regulations pertaining to debt collection practices, including, but not limited, to the Fair Debt Collection Practices Act, 15 U.S.C. 1692; and

(4) The private collection contractor is required to account for all amounts collected.

(b) We will use government-wide debt collection contracts to obtain debt collection services provided by private collection contractors. However, we may refer debts to private collection contractors pursuant to a contract between the agency and the private collection contractor only if such debts are not subject to the requirement to transfer debts to the Treasury for debt collection under 31 U.S.C. 3711(g) and 31 CFR 285.12(e).

(c) Debts arising under the Social Security Act (which can be collected by private collection contractors only by Department of the Treasury (Treasury) after the debt has been referred to Treasury for collection) are excluded from this section.

(d) We may fund private collection contractor contracts in accordance with 31 U.S.C. 3718(d) or as otherwise permitted by law. A contract under paragraph (a) of this section may provide that the fee a private collection contractor charges the agency for collecting the debt is payable from the amounts collected.

(e) We may enter into contracts for locating and recovering assets of the United States, including unclaimed assets. However, before entering into a contract to recover assets of the United States that may be held by a State Government or financial institution, we must establish procedures that are acceptable to the Secretary of the Treasury.

(f) We enter into contracts for debtor asset and income search reports. In accordance with 31 U.S.C. 3718(d), such contracts may provide that the fee a contractor charges the agency for such services may be payable from the amounts recovered unless otherwise prohibited by statute.

§ 422.839 Offset against amounts payable from civil service retirement and disability fund and the Federal employees' retirement system.

Upon providing the Office of Personnel Management (OPM) written certification that a debtor has been afforded the procedures provided in § 422.823 of this part, we may request OPM to offset a debtor's anticipated or future benefit payments under the Civil Service Retirement and Disability Fund (Fund) and the Federal Employees' Retirement System (FERS) in accordance with regulations codified at 5 CFR 831.1801 through 831.1808, and 5 CFR part 845 Subpart D. Upon receipt of such a request, OPM will identify and "flag" a debtor's account in anticipation of the time when the debtor requests, or becomes eligible to receive, payments from the Fund or FERS.

§ 422.842 Liquidation of collateral.

(a)(1) If the debtor fails to pay the debt(s) within a reasonable time after demand and if such action is in the best interests of the United States, we will liquidate security or collateral through the exercise of a power of sale in the security instrument or a non-judicial foreclosure and apply the proceeds to the applicable debt(s).

(2) Collection from other sources, including liquidation of security or collateral, is not a prerequisite to requiring payment by a surety, insurer, or guarantor unless such action is expressly required by statute or contract.

(3) We will give the debtor reasonable notice of the sale and an accounting of any surplus proceeds and will comply with other requirements under law or contract.

(b) Where there is reason to believe that a bankruptcy petition has been filed with respect to a debtor, we will contact the Office of the General Counsel for legal advice concerning the impact of the Bankruptcy Code, particularly with respect to the applicability of the automatic stay, 11 U.S.C. 362, and the procedures for obtaining relief from such stay prior to proceeding under paragraph (a) of this section.

§ 422.846 Bases for compromise.

(a) Scope and application—

(1) Scope. The standards set forth in this subpart apply to the compromise of administrative debts pursuant to 31 U.S.C. 3711. We may exercise such compromise authority for debts arising out of activities of, or referred or transferred for collection services to, the agency when the amount of the debt then due, exclusive of interest, penalties, and administrative costs, does not exceed $100,000 or any higher amount authorized by the Attorney General.

(2) Application. Unless otherwise provided by law, when the principal balance of a debt, exclusive of interest, penalties, and administrative costs, exceeds $100,000 or any higher amount authorized by the Attorney General, the authority to accept a compromise rests with the Department of Justice (DOJ). We will evaluate the compromise offer using the factors set forth in this subpart. If an offer to compromise any debt in excess of $100,000 is acceptable to the agency, we will refer the debt to the Civil Division or other appropriate litigating division in the DOJ using a Claims Collection Litigation Report (CCLR). A CCLR may be obtained from the DOJ's National Central Intake Facility. The referral will include appropriate financial information and a recommendation for the acceptance of the compromise offer. DOJ approval is not required if we reject a compromise offer.

(b) Bases for compromise—

(1) Compromise. We may compromise a debt if the agency cannot collect the full amount based upon the debtor's inability to pay, inability to collect the full debt, the cost of collection, or if we are doubtful that the debt can be proven in court.

(i) Inability to pay. We may compromise a debt if the debtor is unable to pay the full amount in a reasonable time, as verified through credit reports or other financial information. In determining a debtor's inability to pay the full amount of the debt within a reasonable time, we will obtain and verify the debtor's claim of inability to pay by using credit reports and/or a current financial statement from the debtor, executed under penalty of perjury, showing the debtor's assets, liabilities, income, and expenses. We may use a financial information form used in connection with the agency's programs or may request suitable forms from the DOJ or the local United States Attorney's Office. We also may consider other relevant factors such as:

(A) Age and health of the debtor;

(B) Present and potential income;

(C) Inheritance prospects;

(D) The possibility that assets have been concealed or improperly transferred by the debtor; and

(E) The availability of assets or income that may be realized by enforced collection proceedings.

(ii) Inability to collect full debt. We may compromise a debt if the Government is unable to collect the debt in full within a reasonable time by enforced collection proceedings.

(A) In determining the Government's ability to enforce collection, we will consider the applicable exemptions available to the debtor under State and Federal law, and we may also consider uncertainty as to the price any collateral or other property will bring at a forced sale.

(B) A compromise affected under this section should be for an amount that bears a reasonable relation to the amount that can be recovered by enforced collection procedures, with regard to any exemptions available to the debtor and the time that collection will take.

(iii) Cost of collection. We may compromise a debt if the cost of collecting the debt does not justify the enforced collection of the full amount.

(A) The amount accepted in compromise of such debts may reflect an appropriate discount for the administrative and litigation costs of collection, with consideration given to the time it will take to effect collection. Collection costs may be a substantial factor in the settlement of small debts.

(B) In determining whether the costs of collection justify enforced collection of the full amount, we will consider whether continued collection of the debt, regardless of cost, is necessary to further an enforcement principal, such as the Government's willingness to pursue aggressively defaulting and uncooperative debtors.

(iv) Doubtful debt can be proven in court. We may compromise a debt if there is significant doubt concerning the Government's ability to prove its case in court.

(A) If significant doubt exists concerning the Government's ability to prove its case in court for the full amount claimed, either because of the legal issues involved or because of a legitimate dispute as to the facts, then the amount accepted in compromise should fairly reflect the probabilities of successful prosecution to judgment, with due regard to the availability of witnesses and other evidentiary support for the Government's claim.

(B) In determining the litigation risks involved, we will consider the probable amount of court costs and attorney fees a court may impose pursuant to the Equal Access to Justice Act, 28 U.S.C. 2412, if the Government is unsuccessful in litigation.

(2) Installments. We may not accept compromises payable in installments. This is not an advantageous form of compromise in terms of time and administrative expense. If, however, payment in installments is necessary in cases of compromise based on paragraphs (b)(1)(i) through (iii) of this section, we will obtain a legally enforceable written agreement providing that, in the event of default, the full original principal balance of the debt prior to compromise, less sums paid thereon, is reinstated. In cases of compromise based on paragraph (b)(1)(iv) of this section, we will consult with the Office of the General Counsel concerning the appropriateness of including such a requirement in the legally enforceable written agreement. Whenever possible, we will obtain security for repayment in the manner set forth in § 422.809.

(c) Enforcement policy. Subject to the Commissioner's approval, we may compromise statutory penalties, forfeitures, or claims established as an aid to enforcement and to compel compliance if our enforcement policy, in terms of deterrence and securing compliance, present, and future, will be adequately served by the agency's acceptance of the sum to be agreed upon.

(d) Joint and several liability.

(1) When two or more debtors are jointly and severally liable, we will pursue collection against all debtors, as appropriate. We will not attempt to allocate the burden of payment between the debtors but will proceed to liquidate the indebtedness as quickly as possible.

(2) We will ensure that a compromise agreement with one debtor does not automatically release the agency's claim against the remaining debtor(s). The amount of a compromise with one debtor will not be considered a precedent or binding in determining the

amount that will be required from other debtors jointly and severally liable on the claim.

(e) Further review of compromise offers. If we are uncertain whether to accept a firm, written, substantive compromise offer on a debt that is within the agency's statutory compromise authority, we may use a CCLR with supporting data and particulars concerning the debt to refer the offer to the DOJ's Civil Division or other appropriate litigating division. The DOJ may act upon such an offer or return it to the agency with instructions or advice.

(f) Consideration of tax consequences to the Government. In negotiating a compromise, we will consider the tax consequences to the Government. In particular, we will consider requiring a waiver of tax-loss-carry-forward and tax-loss-carry-back rights of the debtor. For information on discharge of indebtedness reporting requirements, see § 422.848(e).

(g) Mutual release of the debtor and the Government. In all appropriate instances, a compromise that is accepted will be implemented by means of a mutual release. The terms of such mutual release will provide that the debtor is released from further non-tax liability on the compromised debt in consideration of payment in full of the compromise amount, and the Government and its officials, past and present, are released and discharged from any and all claims and causes of action arising from the same transaction that the debtor may have. In the event a mutual release is not executed when a debt is compromised, unless prohibited by law, the debtor is still deemed to have waived any and all claims and causes of action against the Government and its officials related to the transaction giving rise to the compromised debt.

§ 422.848 Suspension and termination of collection activities.

(a) Scope and application—

(1) Scope. The standards set forth in this subpart apply to the suspension or termination of collection activity pursuant to 31 U.S.C. 3711 on debts that do not appear to be fraudulent or that do not exceed $100,000, or such other amount as the Attorney General may direct, exclusive of interest, penalties, and administrative costs, after deducting the amount of partial payments or collections, if any. Prior to referring a debt to the Department of Justice (DOJ) for litigation, we may suspend or terminate collection under this subpart with respect to such debts that arise out of the activities of, or are referred or transferred for collection services to, the agency.

(2) Application.

(i) If the debt stems from a claim that appears to be fraudulent, false, or misrepresented by a party with an interest in the claim or after deducting the amount of partial payments or collections, the principal amount of the debt exceeds $100,000, or such other amount as the Attorney General may direct, exclusive of interest, penalties, and administrative costs, the authority to suspend or terminate rests solely with the DOJ.

(ii) If we believe that suspension or termination of any debt that relates to a claim that appears to be fraudulent, false, or misrepresented by a party with an interest in the claim or that exceeds $100,000 may be appropriate, we will use the Claims Collection Litigation Report to refer the debt to the Civil Division or other appropriate litigating division in the DOJ. The referral will specify the reasons for our recommendation. If, prior to referral to the DOJ, we determine that a debt is plainly erroneous or clearly without merit, we may terminate collection activity regardless of the suspected fraud or amount involved without obtaining the DOJ's concurrence.

(b) Suspension of collection activity.

(1) We may suspend collection activity on a debt when:

(i) The debtor cannot be located;

(ii) The debtor's financial condition is not expected to improve; or

(iii) The debtor has requested a legally permissible waiver or review of the debt.

(2) Financial condition. Based on the current financial condition of a debtor, we may suspend collection activity on a debt when the debtor's future prospects justify retention of the debt for periodic review and collection activity, and:

(i) No applicable statute of limitations has expired; or

(ii) Future collection can be effected by Administrative Offset, notwithstanding the expiration of the applicable statute of limitations for litigation of claims, with due regard to any statute of limitation for Administrative Offset prescribed by 31 U.S.C. 3716(e)(1); or

(iii) The debtor agrees to pay interest on the amount of the debt on which collection will be suspended and suspension is likely to enhance the debtor's ability to pay the full amount of the principal of the debt with interest at a later date.

(3) Waiver or review.

(i) We will suspend collection activity during the time required for consideration of the debtor's request for waiver or administrative review of the debt if the statute under which the request is sought prohibits us from collecting the debt during that time.

(ii) If the statute under which the waiver or administrative review request is sought does not prohibit collection activity pending consideration of the request, we may use discretion, on a case-by-case basis, to suspend collection. We will ordinarily suspend collection action upon a request for waiver or review if we are prohibited by statute or regulation from issuing a refund of amounts collected prior to agency consideration of the debtor's request. However, we will not suspend collection when we determine that the request for waiver or review is frivolous or was made primarily to delay collection.

(4) Bankruptcy. Upon learning that a bankruptcy petition has been filed with respect to a debtor, we must suspend collection activity on the debt, pursuant to the provisions of 11 U.S.C. 362, 1201, and 1301, unless we can clearly establish that the automatic stay has been lifted or is no longer in effect. In such cases, we will consult our Office of the General Counsel for advice. When appropriate, the Offices of the Regional Chief Counsel will take the necessary legal steps to ensure that no funds or money are paid by the agency to the debtor until relief from the automatic stay is obtained.

(c) Termination of collection activity.

(1) We may terminate collection activity when:

(i) We are unable to collect any substantial amount through our own efforts or through the efforts of others;

(ii) We are unable to locate the debtor;

(iii) Costs of collection are anticipated to exceed the amount recoverable;

(iv) The debt is legally without merit or enforcement of the debt is barred by any applicable statute of limitations;

(v) The debt cannot be substantiated; or

(vi) The debt against the debtor has been discharged in bankruptcy.

(2)(i) Collection activity will not be terminated before we have pursued all appropriate means of collection and determined, based upon the results of the collection activity, that the debt is uncollectible.

(ii) Termination of collection activity ceases active collection of the debt. The termination of collection activity does not preclude us from retaining a record of the account for purposes of:

(A) Selling the debt, if the Secretary of the Department of the Treasury (Treasury) determines that such sale is in the best interest of the United States;

(B) Pursuing collection at a subsequent date in the event there is a change in the debtor's status or a new collection tool becomes available;

(C) Offsetting against future income or assets not available at the time of termination of collection activity; or

(D) Screening future applicants for prior indebtedness.

(3) We will terminate collection activity on a debt that has been discharged in bankruptcy, regardless of the amount. We may continue collection activity, however, subject to the provisions of the Bankruptcy Code, for any payments provided under a plan of reorganization. Offset and recoupment rights may survive the discharge of the debtor in bankruptcy and, under some circumstances, claims also may survive the discharge. For example, when we are a known creditor of a debtor, the claims of the agency may survive a discharge if we did not receive notice of the bankruptcy proceeding or the debt was affected by fraud. When we believe that the agency has claims or offsets that may have survived the discharge of the debtor, we will contact the Office of the General Counsel for legal advice.

(d) Exception to termination. When a significant enforcement policy is involved or recovery of a judgment is a prerequisite to the imposition of administrative sanctions, we may refer debts to the DOJ for litigation even though termination of collection activity may otherwise be appropriate.

(e) Discharge of indebtedness; reporting requirements.

(1)(i) Before discharging a delinquent debt, also referred to as close out of the debt, we will take all appropriate steps to collect the debt in accordance with 31 U.S.C. 3711(g)(9), and §§ 422.803 and 422.810 of this part, including, as applicable, Administrative Offset; tax refund offset; Federal Salary Offset; credit bureau reporting; Administrative Wage Garnishment; litigation; foreclosure; and referral to the Treasury, Treasury-designated debt collection centers, or private collection contractors.

(ii) Discharge of indebtedness is distinct from termination or suspension of collection activity under this subpart, and is governed by the Internal Revenue Code. When collection action on a debt is suspended or terminated, the debt remains delinquent and further collection action may be pursued at a later date in accordance with the standards set forth in this part and 31 CFR parts 900 through 904.

(iii) When we discharge a debt in full or in part, further collection action is prohibited. Therefore, before discharging a debt, we must:

(A) Make the determination that collection action is no longer warranted; and

(B) Terminate debt collection action.

(2) In accordance with 31 U.S.C. 3711(i), we will use competitive procedures to sell a delinquent debt upon termination of collection action if the Secretary of the Treasury determines such a sale is in the best interests of the United States. Since the discharge of a debt precludes any further collection action, including the sale of a delinquent debt, we may not discharge a debt until the requirements of 31 U.S.C. 3711(i) have been met.

(3) Upon discharge of indebtedness, we must report the discharge to the Internal Revenue Service (IRS) in accordance with the requirements of 26 U.S.C. 6050P and 26 CFR 1.6050P–1. We may request that Trea-

sury or Treasury-designated debt collection centers file such a discharge report to the IRS on our behalf.

(4) When discharging a debt, we must request that litigation counsel release any liens of record securing the debt.

§ 422.850 Referrals to the Department of Justice.

(a) Prompt referral.

(1)(i) We will promptly refer to the Department of Justice (DOJ) for litigation debts on which aggressive collection activity has been taken in accordance with § 422.803, and that cannot be compromised, or on which collection activity cannot be suspended or terminated, in accordance with § 422.848.

(ii) We may refer debts arising out of activities of, or referred or transferred for collection services to, the agency to DOJ for litigation.

(2)(i) Debts for which the principal amount is over $100,000 or such other amount as the Attorney General may direct, exclusive of interest, penalties, and administrative costs will be referred to the Civil Division or other division responsible for litigating such debts at the DOJ.

(ii) Debts for which the principal amount is $1,000,000 or less, or such other amount as the Attorney General may direct, exclusive of interest, penalties, and administrative costs will be referred to the Nationwide Central Intake Facility at the DOJ as required by the Claims Collections Litigation Report (CCLR) instructions.

(3)(i) Consistent with aggressive agency collection activity and the standards contained in this part and 31 CFR parts 900 through 904, debts will be referred to the DOJ as early as possible and, in any event, well within the period for initiating timely lawsuits against the debtors.

(ii) We will make every effort to refer delinquent debts to the DOJ for litigation within one year of the date such debts last became delinquent. In the case of guaranteed or insured loans, we will make every effort to refer these delinquent debts to the DOJ for litigation within one year from the date the debt was known to the agency.

(4) The DOJ has exclusive jurisdiction over debts referred to it pursuant to this subpart. Upon referral of a debt to the DOJ, we will:

(i) Immediately terminate the use of any administrative collection activities to collect the debt;

(ii) Advise the DOJ of the collection tools utilized and the results of activities to date; and

(iii) Refrain from having any contact with the debtor and direct all debtor inquiries concerning the debt to the DOJ.

(5) After referral of a debt under this subpart, we will immediately notify the DOJ of any payments credited by the agency to the debtor's account. Pursuant to 31 CFR 904.1(b), after referral of the debt under this subpart, the DOJ will notify the agency of any payment received from the debtor.

(b) Claims Collection Litigation Report.

(1)(i) Unless excepted by the DOJ, we will complete a CCLR and associated signed Certificate of Indebtedness to refer all administratively uncollectible claims to the DOJ for litigation.

(ii) We will complete all sections of the CCLR appropriate to each debt as required by the CCLR instructions and furnish such other information as may be required in specific cases.

(2) We will indicate clearly on the CCLR the actions that we wish the DOJ to take with respect to the referred debt. We may indicate specifically any of a number of litigation activities the DOJ may choose to pursue, including enforced collection, judgment lien only, renew judgment lien only, renew judgment lien and enforced collection, program enforcement, foreclosure only, and foreclosure and deficiency judgment.

(3) We will also use the CCLR to refer a debt to the DOJ for the purpose of obtaining any necessary approval of a proposal to compromise a debt or to suspend or terminate administrative collection activity on a debt.

(c) Preservation of evidence. We will maintain and preserve all files and records that may be needed by the DOJ to prove our claim in court. When referring debts to the DOJ for litigation, certified copies of the documents that form the basis for the claim should be provided along with the CCLR. Upon its request, the original documents will be provided to the DOJ.

(d) Minimum amount of referrals.

(1) Except as provided in paragraph (d)(2) of this section, we will not refer for litigation claims of less than $2,500 exclusive of interest, penalties, and administrative costs, or such other amount as the Attorney General may prescribe.

(2) We will not refer claims of less than the minimum amount unless:

(i) Litigation to collect such smaller amount is important to ensure compliance with the agency's policies and programs;

(ii) The agency is referring the claim solely for the purpose of securing a judgment against the debtor, which will be filed as a lien against the debtor's property pursuant to 28 U.S.C. 3201 and returned to the agency for enforcement; or

(iii) The debtor has the clear ability to pay the claim and the Government can enforce payment effectively, with due regard for the exemptions available to the debtor under State and Federal law and the judicial remedies available to the Government.

(3) We will consult with the Financial Litigation Staff of the Executive Office for United States Attorneys at DOJ prior to referring claims valued at less than the minimum amount.

SUBPART J—PROTECTING THE PUBLIC AND OUR PERSONNEL TO ENSURE OPERATIONAL EFFECTIVENESS

Authority: Sec. 702(a)(4)–(5) of the Social Security Act (42 U.S.C. 902(a)(4)–(5)).

Source: 76 FR 54702, Sept. 2, 2011, unless otherwise noted.

§ 422.901 Scope and purpose.

The regulations in this subpart describe the process we will follow when we decide whether to ban you from entering our offices. Due to increasing reports of threats to our personnel and the public, we are taking steps to increase the level of protection we provide to our personnel and to the public. The purpose of this subpart is to inform the public and our personnel of the conduct that will subject an individual to a ban and the procedures we will follow when banning an individual from entering our offices. We expect that the regulations will result in a safer environment for our personnel and the public who visit our facilities, while ensuring that our personnel can continue to serve the American people with as little disruption to our operations as possible.

§ 422.902 Definition of personnel for purposes of this subpart.

We will construe the term "personnel" broadly to mean persons responsible for or engaged in carrying out the responsibilities, programs, or services of or on behalf of the agency. Personnel includes, but is not limited to, our employees, contractors, consultants, and examiners and State disability determination services (DDS) employees, contractors, consultants, and examiners.

§ 422.903 Prohibited conduct.

We will ban you from entering our offices if you:

(a) Physically or verbally assault our personnel or a member of the public in our occupied space;

(b) Use force or threats of force against our personnel or offices, including but not limited to communicating threats in person or by phone, facsimile, mail, or electronic mail;

(c) Engage in disruptive conduct that impedes our personnel from performing their duties; or

(d) Engage in disruptive conduct that impedes members of the public from obtaining services from our personnel.

§ 422.904 Notice of the ban.

If an agency manager makes a decision in writing that you pose a threat to the safety of our personnel, visitors, office, or the operational effectiveness of the agency, we will send you a notice banning you from our offices. The notice will contain the following information:

(a) Type of restriction. If we ban you from entering our offices, the ban will apply to all of our offices, and you must obtain all future service through alternate means. We will provide you in-person service only if you establish that there are no alternate means available. You must direct your request for in-person service to the manager of the office you are requesting to visit. If we determine that an office visit is warranted, we will schedule an appointment for you and send you a certified letter notifying you of the date, time, and location of the appointment.

(b) Prohibited conduct. We will provide you with specific details of the prohibited conduct that served as the basis for our decision to ban you.

(c) Alternate means of service. If you are banned from entering our offices, you still have several means to receive services:

(1) You may use the online services available through our Web site at http://www.socialsecurity.gov;

(2) You may call your local office. Your notice will include the contact information for your local office. You should ask to speak with the office manager or a supervisor;

(3) You may call our national toll-free number at 1–800–772–1213 between the hours of 7 a.m. and 7 p.m., Monday through Friday. You should not attempt to schedule an in-person appointment through this number. If you are deaf or hard of hearing, you may call our toll-free TTY number at 1–800–325–0778;

(4) You may write to your local office. You should address all correspondence to the attention of the office manager;

(5) With your written consent, another person may call, write, or visit us to conduct business on your behalf.

(d) Appeal rights. The notice will provide you with information on how to appeal the ban.

(e) Periodic request for review of ban decision. The notice will provide you with information on how to request review of the ban determination every three years from the date of the ban notice, or if you appeal the ban, the date of the appeal decision.

§ 422.905 Appeal rights.

You may appeal our decision to ban you. You must submit your appeal in writing to the address identified in the notice within 60 days of the date of the notice. You should identify your name, address, Social Security number, and the office that issued the notice of the ban. The appeal should clearly state why we should reconsider our decision and provide any supporting documentation. We may allow an additional 10 days for the late filing of an appeal if you show good cause for the late filing. The ban will remain in effect while the appeal is pending. We will notify you of our decision in writing.

§ 422.906 Periodic request for review of ban decision.

You may request review of our ban decision every three years. The three-year cycle to request review will begin on the date we issued notice of the ban, or if you appealed, the date of our appeal decision. You must submit your request for review of a ban decision in writing to the address identified in the original notice of the ban. Your request for review should identify your name, address, Social Security number, and office that issued the notice of the ban. Your request should clearly state why we should lift the ban and provide relevant documentation that supports removal of the restriction, including medical documentation, applicable psychiatric evaluations, work history, and any criminal record. You must prove by a preponderance of the evidence (meaning that it is more likely than not) that you no longer pose a threat to the safety of our personnel or visitors or the operational effectiveness of the agency. We will notify you of our decision in writing.

§ 422.907 Posting requirement.

We will post the regulation in this subpart in a conspicuous place in our offices that serve the public.

PART 498—CIVIL MONETARY PENALTIES, ASSESSMENTS AND RECOMMENDED EXCLUSIONS

Authority: Secs. 702(a)(5), 1129, and 1140 of the Social Security Act (42 U.S.C. 902(a)(5), 1320a–8, and 1320b–10).

Source: 60 FR 58226, Nov. 27, 1995; 61 FR 18079, April 24, 1996, unless otherwise noted.

§ 498.100 Basis and purpose.

(a) Basis. This part implements sections 1129 and 1140 of the Social Security Act (42 U.S.C. 1320a–8 and 1320b–10).

(b) Purpose. This part provides for the imposition of civil monetary penalties and assessments, as applicable, against persons who—

(1) Make or cause to be made false statements or representations or omissions or otherwise withhold disclosure of a material fact for use in determining any right to or amount of benefits under title II or benefits or payments under title VIII or title XVI of the Social Security Act;

(2) Convert any payment, or any part of a payment, received under title II, title VIII, or title XVI of the Social Security Act for the use and benefit of another individual, while acting in the capacity of a representative payee for that individual, to a use that such person knew or should have known was other than for the use and benefit of such other individual; or

(3) Misuse certain Social Security program words, letters, symbols, and emblems; or

(4) With limited exceptions, charge a fee for a product or service that is available from SSA free of charge without including a written notice stating the product or service is available from SSA free of charge.

[61 FR 18079, April 24, 1996; 71 FR 28579, May 17, 2006]

§ 498.101 Definitions.

As used in this part:

Agency means the Social Security Administration.

Assessment means the amount described in § 498.104, and includes the plural of that term.

Commissioner means the Commissioner of Social Security or his or her designees.

Department means the U.S. Department of Health and Human Services.

General Counsel means the General Counsel of the Social Security Administration or his or her designees.

Inspector General means the Inspector General of the Social Security Administration or his or her designees.

Material fact means a fact which the Commissioner of Social Security may consider in evaluating whether an applicant is entitled to benefits under title II or eligible for benefits or payments under title VIII or title XVI of the Social Security Act.

Otherwise withhold disclosure means the failure to come forward to notify the SSA of a material fact when such person knew or should have known that the withheld fact was material and that such withholding was misleading for purposes of determining eligibility or Social Security benefit amount for that person or another person.

Penalty means the amount described in § 498.103 and includes the plural of that term.

Person means an individual, organization, agency, or other entity.

Respondent means the person upon whom the Commissioner or the Inspector General has imposed, or intends to impose, a penalty and assessment, as applicable.

Secretary means the Secretary of the U.S. Department of Health and Human Services or his or her designees.

SSA means the Social Security Administration.

SSI means Supplemental Security Income.

[61 FR 18079, April 24, 1996; 71 FR 28580, May 17, 2006]

§ 498.102 Basis for civil monetary penalties and assessments.

(a) The Office of the Inspector General may impose a penalty and assessment, as applicable, against any person who it determines in accordance with this part—

(1) Has made, or caused to be made, a statement or representation of a material fact for use in determining any initial or continuing right to or amount of:

(i) Monthly insurance benefits under title II of the Social Security Act; or

(ii) Benefits or payments under title VIII or title XVI of the Social Security Act; and

(2)(i) Knew, or should have known, that the statement or representation was false or misleading, or

(ii) Made such statement with knowing disregard for the truth; or

(3) Omitted from a statement or representation, or otherwise withheld disclosure of, a material fact for use in determining any initial or continuing right to or amount of benefits or payments, which the person knew or should have known was material for such use and that such omission or withholding was false or misleading.

(b) The Office of the Inspector General may impose a penalty and assessment, as applicable, against any representative payee who receives a payment under title II, title VIII, or title XVI for the use and benefit of another individual and who converts such payment, or any part thereof, to a use that such representative payee knew or should have known was other than for the use and benefit of such other individual.

(c) The Office of the Inspector General may impose a penalty against any person who it determines in accordance with this part has made use of certain Social Security program words, letters, symbols, or emblems in such a manner that the person knew or should have known would convey, or in a manner which reasonably could be interpreted or construed as conveying, the false impression that a solicitation, advertisement or other communication was authorized, approved, or endorsed by the Social Security Administration, or that such person had some connection with, or authorization from, the Social Security Administration.

(1) Civil monetary penalties may be imposed for misuse, as set forth in paragraph (c) of this section, of—

(i) The words "Social Security," "Social Security Account," "Social Security Administration," "Social Security System," "Supplemental Security Income Program," "Death Benefits Update," "Federal Benefit Information," "Funeral Expenses," "Final Supplemental Program," or any combination or variation of such words; or

(ii) The letters "SSA," or "SSI," or any other combination or variation of such letters; or

(iii) A symbol or emblem of the Social Security Administration (including the design of, or a reasonable facsimile of the design of, the Social Security card, the check used for payment of benefits under title II, or envelopes or other stationery used by the Social Security Administration) or any other combination or variation of such symbols or emblems.

(2) Civil monetary penalties will not be imposed against any agency or instrumentality of a State, or political subdivision of a State, that makes use of any words, letters, symbols or emblems of the Social Security Administration or instrumentality of the State or political subdivision.

(d) The Office of the Inspector General may impose a penalty against any person who offers, for a fee, to assist an individual in obtaining a product or service that the person knew or should have known the Social Security Administration provides free of charge, unless:

(1) The person provides sufficient notice before the product or service is provided to the individual that the product or service is available free of charge and:

(i) In a printed solicitation, advertisement or other communication, such notice is clearly and prominently placed and written in a font that is distinguishable from the rest of the text;

(ii) In a broadcast or telecast such notice is clearly communicated so as not to be construed as misleading or deceptive.

(2) Civil monetary penalties will not be imposed under paragraph (d) of this section with respect to offers—

(i) To serve as a claimant representative in connection with a claim arising under title II, title VIII, or title XVI; or

(ii) To prepare, or assist in the preparation of, an individual's plan for achieving self-support under title XVI.

(e) The use of a disclaimer of affiliation with the United States Government, the Social Security Administration or its programs, or any other agency or instrumentality of the United States Government will not be considered as a defense in determining a violation of section 1140 of the Social Security Act.

[61 FR 18079, April 24, 1996; 71 FR 28580, May 17, 2006]

§ 498.103 Amount of penalty.

(a) Under § 498.102(a), the Office of the Inspector General may impose a penalty of not more than $5,000 for each false statement or representation, omission, or receipt of payment or benefit while withholding disclosure of a material fact.

(b) Under § 498.102(b), the Office of the Inspector General may impose a penalty of not more than $5,000 against a representative payee for each time the representative payee receives a payment under title II, title VIII, or title XVI of the Social Security Act for the use and benefit of another individual, and who converts such payment, or any part thereof, to a use that such representative payee knew or should have known was other than for the use and benefit of such other individual.

(c) Under § 498.102(c), the Office of the Inspector General may impose a penalty of not more than $5,000 for each violation resulting from the misuse of Social Security Administration program words, letters, symbols, or emblems relating to printed media and a penalty of not more than $25,000 for each violation in the case that such misuse related to a broadcast or telecast.

(d) Under § 498.102(d), the Office of the Inspector General may impose a penalty of not more than $5,000 for each violation resulting from insufficient notice relating to printed media regarding products or services provided free of charge by the Social Security Administration and a penalty of not more than $25,000 for each violation in the case that such insufficient notice relates to a broadcast or telecast.

(e) For purposes of paragraphs (c) and (d) of this section, a violation is defined as—

(1) In the case of a mailed solicitation, advertisement, or other communication, each separate piece of mail which contains one or more program words, letters, symbols, or emblems or insufficient notice related to a determination under § 498.102(c) or (d); and

(2) In the case of a broadcast or telecast, each airing of a single commercial or solicitation related to a determination under § 498.102(c) or (d).

(f) [Reserved]

(g) (1) The amount of the penalties described in paragraphs (a) through (d) of this section are the maximum penalties which may be assessed under these paragraphs for violations made after June 16, 2006, but before August 1, 2016.

(2) (i) After August 1, 2016 penalties are adjusted in accordance with the Federal Civil Penalties Inflation Adjustment Act of 1990 (Pub.L. 101–410), as amended by the Debt Collection Improvement Act of 1996 (Pub.L. 104–134), as further amended by the Bipartisan Budget Act of 2015, Section 701: Federal Civil Penalties Inflation Adjustment Act Improvements Act of 2015 (Section 701 of Pub.L. 114–74).

(ii) The maximum penalties which may be assessed under this section is the larger of:

(A) The amount for the previous calendar year; or

(B) An amount adjusted for inflation, calculated by multiplying the amount for the previous calendar year by the percentage by which the Consumer Price Index for all urban consumers for the month of October preceding the current calendar year exceeds the Consumer Price Index for all urban consumers for the month of October of the calendar year two years prior to the current calendar year, adding that amount to the amount for the previous calendar year, and rounding the total to the nearest dollar.

(iii) Notice of the maximum penalty which may be assessed under this section for calendar years after 2016 will be published in the Federal Register on an annual basis on or before January 15 of each calendar year.

[61 FR 18080, April 24, 1996; 71 FR 28580, May 17, 2006; 81 FR 41440, June 27, 2016]

§ 498.104 Amount of assessment.

A person subject to a penalty determined under § 498.102(a) may be subject, in addition, to an assessment of not more than twice the amount of benefits or payments paid under title II, title VIII or title XVI of the Social Security Act as a result of the statement, representation, omission, or withheld disclosure of a material fact which was the basis for the penalty. A representative payee subject to a penalty determined under § 498.102(b) may be subject, in addition, to an assessment of not more than twice the amount of benefits or payments received by the representative payee for the use and benefit of another individual and converted to a use other than for the use and benefit of such other individual. An assessment is in lieu of damages sustained by the United States because of such statement, representation, omission, withheld disclosure of a material fact, or conversion, as referred to in § 498.102(a) and (b).

[61 FR 18080, April 24, 1996; 71 FR 28581, May 17, 2006]

§ 498.105 [Reserved]

§ 498.106 Determinations regarding the amount or scope of penalties and assessments.

(a) In determining the amount or scope of any penalty and assessment, as applicable, in accordance with § 498.103(a) and (b) and 498.104, the Office of the Inspector General will take into account:

(1) The nature of the statements, representations, or actions referred to in § 498.102(a) and (b) and the circumstances under which they occurred;

(2) The degree of culpability of the person committing the offense;

(3) The history of prior offenses of the person committing the offense;

(4) The financial condition of the person committing the offense; and

(5) Such other matters as justice may require.

(b) In determining the amount of any penalty in accordance with § 498.103(c) and (d), the Office of the Inspector General will take into account—

(1) The nature and objective of the advertisement, solicitation, or other communication, and the circumstances under which they were presented;

(2) The frequency and scope of the violation, and whether a specific segment of the population was targeted;

(3) The prior history of the individual, organization, or entity in their willingness or refusal to comply with informal requests to correct violations;

(4) The history of prior offenses of the individual, organization, or entity in their misuse of program words, letters, symbols, and emblems;

(5) The financial condition of the individual or entity; and

(6) Such other matters as justice may require.

(c) In cases brought under section 1140 of the Social Security Act, the use of a disclaimer of affiliation with the United States Government, the Social Security Administration or its programs will not be considered as a mitigating factor in determining the amount of a penalty in accordance with § 498.106.

[61 FR 18080, April 24, 1996; 71 FR 28581, May 17, 2006]

§ 498.107 [Reserved]

§ 498.108 Penalty and assessment not exclusive.

Penalties and assessments, as applicable, imposed under this part are in addition to any other penalties prescribed by law.

[61 FR 18080, April 24, 1996]

§ 498.109 Notice of proposed determination.

(a) If the Office of the Inspector General seeks to impose a penalty and assessment, as applicable, it will serve written notice of the intent to take such action. The notice will include:

(1) Reference to the statutory basis for the proposed penalty and assessment, as applicable;

(2) A description of the false statements, representations, other actions (as described in § 498.102(a) and (b)), and incidents, as applicable, with respect to which the penalty and assessment, as applicable, are proposed;

(3) The amount of the proposed penalty and assessment, as applicable;

(4) Any circumstances described in § 498.106 that were considered when determining the amount of the proposed penalty and assessment, as applicable; and

(5) Instructions for responding to the notice, including

(i) A specific statement of respondent's right to a hearing; and

(ii) A statement that failure to request a hearing within 60 days permits the imposition of the proposed penalty and assessment, as applicable, without right of appeal.

(b) Any person upon whom the Office of the Inspector General has proposed the imposition of a penalty and assessment, as applicable, may request a hearing on such proposed penalty and assessment.

(c) If the respondent fails to exercise the respondent's right to a hearing within the time permitted under this section, and does not demonstrate good cause for such failure before an administrative law judge, any penalty and assessment, as applicable, becomes final.

[61 FR 18080, April 24, 1996; 71 FR 28581, May 17, 2006]

§ 498.110 Failure to request a hearing.

If the respondent does not request a hearing within the time prescribed by § 498.109(a), the Office of the Inspector General may seek the proposed penalty and assessment, as applicable, or any less severe penalty and assessment. The Office of the Inspector General shall notify the respondent by certified mail, return receipt requested, of any penalty and assessment, as applicable, that has been imposed and of the means by which the respondent may satisfy the amount owed.

[61 FR 18080, April 24, 1996]

§ 498.114 Collateral estoppel.

In a proceeding under section 1129 of the Social Security Act that—

(a) Is against a person who has been convicted (whether upon a verdict after trial or upon a plea of guilty or nolo contendere) of a Federal or State crime; and

(b) Involves the same transactions as in the criminal action, the person is estopped from denying the essential elements of the criminal offense.

[61 FR 18080, April 24, 1996; 71 FR 28581, May 17, 2006]

§§ 498.115 to 498.125 [Reserved]

§ 498.126 Settlement.

The Inspector General has exclusive authority to settle any issues or case, without the consent of the administrative law judge or the Commissioner, at any time prior to a final determination. Thereafter, the Commissioner or his or her designee has such exclusive authority.

§ 498.127 Judicial review.

Sections 1129 and 1140 of the Social Security Act authorize judicial review of any penalty and assessment, as applicable, that has become final. Judicial review may be sought by a respondent only in regard to a penalty and assessment, as applicable, with respect to which the respondent requested a hearing, unless the failure or neglect to urge such objection is excused by the court because of extraordinary circumstances.

[61 FR 18080, April 24, 1996]

§ 498.128 Collection of penalty and assessment.

(a) Once a determination has become final, collection of any penalty and assessment, as applicable, will be the responsibility of the Commissioner or his or her designee.

(b) In cases brought under section 1129 of the Social Security Act, a penalty and assessment, as applicable, imposed under this part may be compromised by the Commissioner or his or her designee and may be recovered in a civil action brought in the United States District Court for the district where the violation occurred or where the respondent resides.

(c) In cases brought under section 1140 of the Social Security Act, a penalty imposed under this part may be compromised by the Commissioner or his or her designee and may be recovered in a civil action brought in the United States district court for the district where, as determined by the Commissioner, the:

(1) Violations referred to in § 498.102(c) or (d) occurred; or

(2) Respondent resides; or

(3) Respondent has its principal office; or

(4) Respondent may be found.

(d) As specifically provided under the Social Security Act, in cases brought under section 1129 of the Social Security Act, the amount of a penalty and assessment, as applicable, when finally determined, or the amount agreed upon in compromise, may also be deducted from:

(1) Monthly title II, title VIII, or title XVI payments, notwithstanding section 207 of the Social Security Act as made applicable to title XVI by section 1631(d)(1) of the Social Security Act;

(2) A tax refund to which a person is entitled to after notice to the Secretary of the Treasury under 31 U.S.C. § 3720A;

(3) By authorities provided under the Debt Collection Act of 1982, as amended, 31 U.S.C. 3711, to the extent applicable to debts arising under the Social Security Act; or

(4) Any combination of the foregoing.

(e) Matters that were raised or that could have been raised in a hearing before an administrative law judge or in an appeal to the United States Court of Appeals under sections 1129 or 1140 of the Social Security Act may not be raised as a defense in a civil action by the United States to collect a penalty and assessment, as applicable, under this part.

[61 FR 18080, April 24, 1996; 71 FR 28581, May 17, 2006]

§ 498.129 Notice to other agencies.

As provided in section 1129 of the Social Security Act, when a determination to impose a penalty and assessment, as applicable, with respect to a physician or medical provider becomes final, the Office of the Inspector General will notify the Secretary of the final determination and the reasons therefore.

[61 FR 18081, April 24, 1996]

§ 498.132 Limitations.

The Office of the Inspector General may initiate a proceeding in accordance with § 498.109(a) to determine whether to impose a penalty and assessment, as applicable—

(a) In cases brought under section 1129 of the Social Security Act, after receiving authorization from the Attorney General pursuant to procedures agreed upon by the Inspector General and the Attorney General; and

(b) Within 6 years from the date on which the violation was committed.

[61 FR 18081, April 24, 1996]

§ 498.200 [Reserved]

§ 498.201 Definitions.

As used in this part—

ALJ refers to an Administrative Law Judge of the Departmental Appeals Board.

Civil monetary penalty cases refer to all proceedings arising under any of the statutory bases for which the Inspector General, Social Security Administration has been delegated authority to impose civil monetary penalties.

DAB refers to the Departmental Appeals Board of the U.S. Department of Health and Human Services.

[61 FR 65468, Dec. 13, 1996]

§ 498.202 Hearing before an administrative law judge.

(a) A party sanctioned under any criteria specified in §§ 498.100 through 498.132 may request a hearing before an ALJ.

(b) In civil monetary penalty cases, the parties to a hearing will consist of the respondent and the Inspector General.

(c) The request for a hearing must be:

(1) In writing and signed by the respondent or by the respondent's attorney; and

(2) Filed within 60 days after the notice, provided in accordance with § 498.109, is received by the respondent or upon a showing of good cause, the time permitted by an ALJ.

(d) The request for a hearing shall contain a statement as to the:

(1) Specific issues or findings of fact and conclusions of law in the notice letter with which the respondent disagrees; and

(2) Basis for the respondent's contention that the specific issues or findings and conclusions were incorrect.

(e) For purposes of this section, the date of receipt of the notice letter will be presumed to be five days after the date of such notice, unless there is a reasonable showing to the contrary.

(f) The ALJ shall dismiss a hearing request where:

(1) The respondent's hearing request is not filed in a timely manner and the respondent fails to demonstrate good cause for such failure;

(2) The respondent withdraws or abandons respondent's request for a hearing; or

(3) The respondent's hearing request fails to raise any issue which may properly be addressed in a hearing under this part.

[61 FR 65468, Dec. 13, 1996]

§ 498.203 Rights of parties.

(a) Except as otherwise limited by this part, all parties may:

(1) Be accompanied, represented, and advised by an attorney;

(2) Participate in any conference held by the ALJ;

(3) Conduct discovery of documents as permitted by this part;

(4) Agree to stipulations of fact or law which will be made part of the record;

(5) Present evidence relevant to the issues at the hearing;

(6) Present and cross-examine witnesses;

(7) Present oral arguments at the hearing as permitted by the ALJ; and

(8) Submit written briefs and proposed findings of fact and conclusions of law after the hearing.

(b) Fees for any services performed on behalf of a party by an attorney are not subject to the provisions of section 206 of title II of the Social Security Act, which authorizes the Commissioner to specify or limit these fees.

[61 FR 65468, Dec. 13, 1996]

§ 498.204 Authority of the administrative law judge.

(a) The ALJ will conduct a fair and impartial hearing, avoid delay, maintain order and assure that a record of the proceeding is made.

(b) The ALJ has the authority to:

(1) Set and change the date, time, and place of the hearing upon reasonable notice to the parties;

(2) Continue or recess the hearing in whole or in part for a reasonable period of time;

(3) Hold conferences to identify or simplify the issues, or to consider other matters that may aid in the expeditious disposition of the proceeding;

(4) Administer oaths and affirmations;

(5) Issue subpoenas requiring the attendance of witnesses at hearings and the production of documents at or in relation to hearings;

(6) Rule on motions and other procedural matters;

(7) Regulate the scope and timing of documentary discovery as permitted by this part;

(8) Regulate the course of the hearing and the conduct of representatives, parties, and witnesses;

(9) Examine witnesses;

(10) Receive, exclude, or limit evidence;

(11) Take official notice of facts;

(12) Upon motion of a party, decide cases, in whole or in part, by summary judgment where there is no disputed issue of material fact; and

(13) Conduct any conference or argument in person, or by telephone upon agreement of the parties.

(c) The ALJ does not have the authority to:

(1) Find invalid or refuse to follow Federal statutes or regulations, or delegations of authority from the Commissioner;

(2) Enter an order in the nature of a directed verdict;

(3) Compel settlement negotiations;

(4) Enjoin any act of the Commissioner or the Inspector General; or

(5) Review the exercise of discretion by the Office of the Inspector General to seek to impose a civil monetary penalty or assessment under §§ 498.100 through 498.132.

[61 FR 65468, Dec. 13, 1996]

§ 498.205 Ex parte contacts.

No party or person (except employees of the ALJ's office) will communicate in any way with the ALJ on any matter at issue in a case, unless on notice and opportunity for all parties to participate. This provision does not prohibit a person or party from inquiring about the status of a case or asking routine questions concerning administrative functions or procedures.

[61 FR 65468, Dec. 13, 1996]

§ 498.206 Prehearing conferences.

(a) The ALJ will schedule at least one prehearing conference, and may schedule additional prehearing conferences as appropriate, upon reasonable notice to the parties.

(b) The ALJ may use prehearing conferences to address the following:

(1) Simplification of the issues;

(2) The necessity or desirability of amendments to the pleadings, including the need for a more definite statement;

(3) Stipulations and admissions of fact as to the contents and authenticity of documents and deadlines for challenges, if any, to the authenticity of documents;

(4) Whether the parties can agree to submission of the case on a stipulated record;

(5) Whether a party chooses to waive appearance at a hearing and to submit only documentary evidence (subject to the objection of other parties) and written argument;

(6) Limitation of the number of witnesses;

(7) The time and place for the hearing and dates for the exchange of witness lists and of proposed exhibits;

(8) Discovery of documents as permitted by this part;

(9) Such other matters as may tend to encourage the fair, just, and expeditious disposition of the proceedings; and

(10) Potential settlement of the case.

(c) The ALJ shall issue an order containing the matters agreed upon by the parties or ordered by the ALJ at a prehearing conference.

[61 FR 65468, Dec. 13, 1996]

§ 498.207 Discovery.

(a) For the purpose of inspection and copying, a party may make a request to another party for production of documents which are relevant and material to the issues before the ALJ.

(b) Any form of discovery other than that permitted under paragraph (a) of this section, such as requests for admissions, written interrogatories and depositions, is not authorized.

(c) For the purpose of this section, the term documents includes information, reports, answers, records, accounts, papers, memos, notes and other data and documentary evidence. Nothing contained in this section will be interpreted to require the creation of a document, except that requested data stored in an electronic data storage system will be produced in a form accessible to the requesting party.

(d)(1) A party who has been served with a request for production of documents may file a motion for a protective order. The motion for protective order shall describe the document or class of documents to be protected, specify which of the grounds in § 498.207(d)(2) are being asserted, and explain how those grounds apply.

(2) The ALJ may grant a motion for a protective order if he or she finds that the discovery sought:

(i) Is unduly costly or burdensome;

(ii) Will unduly delay the proceeding; or

(iii) Seeks privileged information.

(3) The burden of showing that discovery should be allowed is on the party seeking discovery.

[61 FR 65468, Dec. 13, 1996]

§ 498.208 Exchange of witness lists, witness statements and exhibits.

(a) At least 15 days before the hearing, the parties shall exchange:

(1) Witness lists;

(2) Copies of prior written statements of proposed witnesses; and

(3) Copies of proposed hearing exhibits, including copies of any written statements that the party intends to offer in lieu of live testimony in accordance with § 498.216.

(b)(1) Failure to comply with the requirements of paragraph (a) of this section may result in the exclusion of evidence or testimony upon the objection of the opposing party.

(2) When an objection is entered, the ALJ shall determine whether good cause justified the failure to timely exchange the information listed under paragraph (a) of this section. If good cause is not found, the ALJ shall exclude from the party's case-in-chief:

(i) The testimony of any witness whose name does not appear on the witness list; and

(ii) Any exhibit not provided to the opposing party as specified in paragraph (a) of this section.

(3) If the ALJ finds that good cause exists, the ALJ shall determine whether the admission of such evidence would cause substantial prejudice to the objecting party due to the failure to comply with paragraph (a) of this section. If the ALJ finds no substantial prejudice, the evidence may be admitted. If the ALJ finds substantial prejudice, the ALJ may exclude the evidence, or at his or her discretion, may postpone the hearing for such time as is necessary for the objecting party to prepare and respond to the evidence.

(c) Unless a party objects by the deadline set by the ALJ's prehearing order pursuant to § 498.206 (b)(3) and (c), documents exchanged in accordance with paragraph (a) of this section will be deemed authentic for the purpose of admissibility at the hearing.

[61 FR 65468, Dec. 13, 1996]

§ 498.209 Subpoenas for attendance at hearing.

(a) A party wishing to procure the appearance and testimony of any individual, whose appearance and testimony are relevant and material to the presentation of a party's case at a hearing, may make a motion requesting the ALJ to issue a subpoena.

(b) A subpoena requiring the attendance of an individual may also require the individual (whether or not the individual is a party) to produce evidence at the hearing in accordance with § 498.207.

(c) A party seeking a subpoena will file a written motion not less than 30 days before the date fixed for the hearing, unless otherwise allowed by the ALJ for good cause shown. Such request will:

(1) Specify any evidence to be produced;

(2) Designate the witness(es); and

(3) Describe the address and location with sufficient particularity to permit such witness(es) to be found.

(d) Within 20 days after the written motion requesting issuance of a subpoena is served, any party may file an opposition or other response.

(e) If the motion requesting issuance of a subpoena is granted, the party seeking the subpoena will serve the subpoena by delivery to the individual named, or by certified mail addressed to such individual at his or her last dwelling place or principal place of business.

(f) The subpoena will specify the time and place at which the witness is to appear and any evidence the witness is to produce.

(g) The individual to whom the subpoena is directed may file with the ALJ a motion to quash the subpoena within 10 days after service.

(h) When a subpoena is served by a respondent on a particular individual or particular office of the Office of the Inspector General, the OIG may comply by designating any of its representatives to appear and testify.

(i) In the case of contumacy by, or refusal to obey a subpoena duly served upon any person, the exclusive remedy is specified in section 205(e) of the Social Security Act (42 U.S.C. 405(e)).

[61 FR 65468, Dec. 13, 1996]

§ 498.210 Fees.

The party requesting a subpoena will pay the cost of the fees and mileage of any witness subpoenaed in the amounts that would be payable to a witness in a proceeding in United States District Court. A check for witness fees and mileage will accompany the subpoena when served, except that when a subpoena is issued on behalf of the Inspector General, a check for witness fees and mileage need not accompany the subpoena.

[61 FR 65468, Dec. 13, 1996]

§ 498.211 Form, filing and service of papers.

(a) Form.

(1) Unless the ALJ directs the parties to do otherwise, documents filed with the ALJ will include an original and two copies.

(2) Every document filed in the proceeding will contain a caption setting forth the title of the action, the case number, and a designation of the pleading or paper.

(3) Every document will be signed by, and will contain the address and telephone number of the party or the person on whose behalf the document was filed, or his or her representative.

(4) Documents are considered filed when they are mailed.

(b) Service. A party filing a document with the ALJ will, at the time of filing, serve a copy of such document on every other party. Service upon any party of any document will be made by delivering a copy, or placing a copy of the document in the United States mail, postage prepaid and addressed, or with a private delivery service, to the party's last known address. When a party is represented by an attorney, service will be made upon such attorney. Proof of service should accompany any document filed with the ALJ.

(c) Proof of service. A certificate of the individual serving the document by personal delivery or by mail, setting forth the manner of service, will be proof of service.

[61 FR 65468, Dec. 13, 1996]

§ 498.212 Computation of time.

(a) In computing any period of time under this part or in an order issued thereunder, the time begins with the day following the act, event or default, and includes the last day of the period unless it is a Saturday, Sunday or legal holiday observed by the Federal Government, in which event it includes the next business day.

(b) When the period of time allowed is less than 7 days, intermediate Saturdays, Sundays and legal holidays observed by the Federal Government will be excluded from the computation.

(c) Where a document has been served or issued by placing it in the mail, an additional 5 days will be added to the time permitted for any response. This paragraph does not apply to requests for hearing under § 498.202.

[61 FR 65468, Dec. 13, 1996]

§ 498.213 Motions.

(a) An application to the ALJ for an order or ruling will be by motion. Motions will:

(1) State the relief sought, the authority relied upon and the facts alleged; and

(2) Be filed with the ALJ and served on all other parties.

(b) Except for motions made during a prehearing conference or at a hearing, all motions will be in writing.

(c) Within 10 days after a written motion is served, or such other time as may be fixed by the ALJ, any party may file a response to such motion.

(d) The ALJ may not grant or deny a written motion before the time for filing responses has expired, except upon consent of the parties or following a hearing on the motion.

(e) The ALJ will make a reasonable effort to dispose of all outstanding motions prior to the beginning of the hearing.

(f) There is no right to appeal to the DAB any interlocutory ruling by the ALJ.

[61 FR 65468, Dec. 13, 1996]

§ 498.214 Sanctions.

(a) The ALJ may sanction a person, including any party or attorney, for:

(1) Failing to comply with an order or procedure;

(2) Failing to defend an action; or

(3) Misconduct that interferes with the speedy, orderly or fair conduct of the hearing.

(b) Such sanctions will reasonably relate to the severity and nature of the failure or misconduct. Such sanction may include—

(1) In the case of refusal to provide or permit discovery under the terms of this part, drawing negative factual inferences or treating such refusal as an admission by deeming the matter, or certain facts, to be established;

(2) Prohibiting a party from introducing certain evidence or otherwise supporting a particular claim or defense;

(3) Striking pleadings, in whole or in part;

(4) Staying the proceedings;

(5) Dismissal of the action; or

(6) Entering a decision by default.

(c) In addition to the sanctions listed in paragraph (b) of this section, the ALJ may:

(1) Order the party or attorney to pay attorney's fees and other costs caused by the failure or misconduct; or

(2) Refuse to consider any motion or other action that is not filed in a timely manner.

[61 FR 65468, 65471, Dec. 13, 1996]

§ 498.215 The hearing and burden of proof.

(a) The ALJ will conduct a hearing on the record in order to determine whether the respondent should be found liable under this part.

(b) In civil monetary penalty cases under §§ 498.100 through 498.132:

(1) The respondent has the burden of going forward and the burden of persuasion with respect to affirmative defenses and any mitigating circumstances; and

(2) The Inspector General has the burden of going forward and the burden of persuasion with respect to all other issues.

(c) The burden of persuasion will be judged by a preponderance of the evidence.

(d) The hearing will be open to the public unless otherwise ordered by the ALJ for good cause.

(e)(1) A hearing under this part is not limited to specific items and information set forth in the notice letter to the respondent. Subject to the 15–day requirement under § 498.208, additional items or information may be introduced by either party during its case-in-chief, unless such information or items are inadmissible under § 498.217.

(2) After both parties have presented their cases, evidence may be admitted on rebuttal as to those issues presented in the case-in-chief, even if not previously exchanged in accordance with § 498.208.

[61 FR 65468, 65471, Dec. 13, 1996]

§ 498.216 Witnesses.

(a) Except as provided in paragraph (b) of this section, testimony at the hearing will be given orally by witnesses under oath or affirmation.

(b) At the discretion of the ALJ, testimony (other than expert testimony) may be admitted in the form of a written statement. Any such written statement must be provided to all other parties along with the last known address of such witness, in a manner that allows sufficient time for other parties to subpoena such witness for cross-examination at the hearing. Prior written statements of witnesses proposed to testify at the hearing will be exchanged as provided in § 498.208.

(c) The ALJ will exercise reasonable control over the mode and order of witness direct and cross examination and evidence presentation so as to:

(1) Make the examination and presentation effective for the ascertainment of the truth;

(2) Avoid repetition or needless waste of time; and

(3) Protect witnesses from harassment or undue embarrassment.

(d) The ALJ may order witnesses excluded so that they cannot hear the testimony of other witnesses. This does not authorize exclusion of:

(1) A party who is an individual;

(2) In the case of a party that is not an individual, an officer or employee of the party appearing for the entity pro se or designated as the party's representative; or

(3) An individual whose presence is shown by a party to be essential to the presentation of its case, including an individual engaged in assisting the attorney for the Inspector General.

[61 FR 65468, 65471, Dec. 13, 1996]

§ 498.217 Evidence.

(a) The ALJ will determine the admissibility of evidence.

(b) Except as provided in this part, the ALJ will not be bound by the Federal Rules of Evidence, but may be guided by them in ruling on the admissibility of evidence.

(c) Although relevant, evidence may be excluded if its probative value is substantially outweighed by the danger of unfair prejudice, confusion of the issues, or by considerations of undue delay or needless presentation of cumulative evidence.

(d) Although relevant, evidence must be excluded if it is privileged under Federal law, unless the privilege is waived by a party.

(e) Evidence concerning offers of compromise or settlement made in this action will be inadmissible to the extent provided in Rule 408 of the Federal Rules of Evidence.

(f)(1) Evidence of crimes, wrongs or acts other than those at issue in the instant case is admissible in order to show motive, opportunity, intent, knowledge, preparation, identity, lack of mistake, or existence of a scheme.

(2) Such evidence is admissible regardless of whether the crimes, wrongs or acts occurred during the statute of limitations period applicable to the acts which constitute the basis for liability in the case, and regardless of whether they were referenced in the IG's notice sent in accordance with § 498.109.

(g) The ALJ will permit the parties to introduce rebuttal witnesses and evidence as to those issues raised in the parties' case-in-chief.

(h) All documents and other evidence offered or taken for the record will be open to examination by all parties, unless otherwise ordered by the ALJ for good cause.

[61 FR 65468, 65471, Dec. 13, 1996]

§ 498.218 The record.

(a) The hearing shall be recorded and transcribed. Transcripts may be obtained following the hearing from the ALJ.

(b) The transcript of testimony, exhibits and other evidence admitted at the hearing, and all papers and requests filed in the proceeding constitute the record for the decision by the ALJ.

(c) The record may be inspected and copied (upon payment of a reasonable fee) by any person, unless otherwise ordered by the ALJ for good cause.

[61 FR 65468, 65471, Dec. 13, 1996]

§ 498.219 Post-hearing briefs.

(a) Any party may file a post-hearing brief.

(b) The ALJ may require the parties to file post-hearing briefs and may permit the parties to file reply briefs.

(c) The ALJ will fix the time for filing briefs, which is not to exceed 60 days from the date the parties receive the transcript of the hearing or, if applicable, the stipulated record.

(d) The parties' briefs may be accompanied by proposed findings of fact and conclusions of law.

[61 FR 65468, 65471, Dec. 13, 1996]

§ 498.220 Initial decision.

(a) The ALJ will issue an initial decision, based only on the record, which will contain findings of fact and conclusions of law.

(b) The ALJ may affirm, deny, increase, or reduce the penalties or assessments proposed by the Inspector General.

(c) The ALJ will issue the initial decision to all parties within 60 days after the time for submission of post-hearing briefs or reply briefs, if permitted, has expired. The decision will be accompanied by a statement describing the right of any party to file a notice of appeal with the DAB and instructions for how to file such appeal. If the ALJ cannot issue an initial decision within the 60 days, the ALJ will notify the parties of the reason for the delay and will set a new deadline.

(d) Unless an appeal or request for extension pursuant to § 498.221(a) is filed with the DAB, the initial decision of the ALJ becomes final and binding on the parties 30 days after the ALJ serves the parties with a copy of the decision. If service is by mail, the date of service will be deemed to be five days from the date of mailing.

[61 FR 65468, 65472, Dec. 13, 1996]

§ 498.221 Appeal to DAB.

(a) Any party may appeal the decision of the ALJ to the DAB by filing a notice of appeal with the DAB within 30 days of the date of service of the initial decision. The DAB may extend the initial 30-day period for a period of time not to exceed 30 days if a party files with the DAB a request for an extension within the initial 30–day period and shows good cause.

(b) If a party files a timely notice of appeal with the DAB, the ALJ will forward the record of the proceeding to the DAB.

(c) A notice of appeal will be accompanied by a written brief specifying exceptions to the initial decision and reasons supporting the exceptions, and identifying which finding of fact and conclusions of law the party is taking exception to. Any party may file a brief in opposition to exceptions, which may raise any relevant issue not addressed in the exceptions, within 30 days of receiving the notice of appeal and accompanying brief. The DAB may permit the parties to file reply briefs.

(d) There is no right to appear personally before the DAB, or to appeal to the DAB any interlocutory ruling by the ALJ.

(e) No party or person (except employees of the DAB) will communicate in any way with members of the DAB on any matter at issue in a case, unless on notice and opportunity for all parties to participate. This provision does not prohibit a person or party from inquiring about the status of a case or asking routine questions concerning administrative functions or procedures.

(f) The DAB will not consider any issue not raised in the parties' briefs, nor any issue in the briefs that could have been, but was not, raised before the ALJ.

(g) If any party demonstrates to the satisfaction of the DAB that additional evidence not presented at such hearing is relevant and material and that there were reasonable grounds for the failure to adduce such evidence at such hearing, the DAB may remand the matter to the ALJ for consideration of such additional evidence.

(h) The DAB may remand a case to an ALJ for further proceedings, or may issue a recommended decision to decline review or affirm, increase, reduce, or reverse any penalty or assessment determined by the ALJ.

(i) When the DAB reviews a case, it will limit its review to whether the ALJ's initial decision is supported by substantial evidence on the whole record or contained error of law.

(j) Within 60 days after the time for submission of briefs or, if permitted, reply briefs has expired, the DAB will issue to each party to the appeal and to the Commissioner a copy of the DAB's recommended decision and a statement describing the right of any respondent who is found liable to seek judicial review upon a final decision.

[61 FR 65468, 65472, Dec. 13, 1996]

§ 498.222 Final decision of the Commissioner.

(a) Except with respect to any penalty or assessment remanded to the ALJ, the DAB's recommended decision, including a recommended decision to decline review of the initial decision, shall become the final decision of the Commissioner 60 days after the date on which the DAB serves the parties to the appeal and the Commissioner with a copy of the recommended decision, unless the Commissioner reverses or modifies the DAB's recommended decision within that 60–day period. If the Commissioner reverses or modifies the DAB's recommended decision, the Commissioner's decision is final and binding on the parties. In either event, a copy of the final decision will be served on the parties. If service is by mail, the date of service will be deemed to be five days from the date of mailing.

(b) There shall be no right to personally appear before or submit additional evidence, pleadings or briefs to the Commissioner.

(c)(1) Any petition for judicial review must be filed within 60 days after the parties are served with a copy of the final decision. If service is by mail, the date of service will be deemed to be five days from the date of mailing.

(2) In compliance with 28 U.S.C. 2112(a), a copy of any petition for judicial review filed in any U.S. Court of Appeals challenging a final action of the Commissioner will be sent by certified mail, return receipt requested, to the SSA General Counsel. The petition copy will be time-stamped by the clerk of the court when the original is filed with the court.

(3) If the SSA General Counsel receives two or more petitions within 10 days after the final decision is issued, the General Counsel will notify the U.S. Judicial Panel on Multidistrict Litigation of any petitions that were received within the 10–day period.

[61 FR 65468, 65472, Dec. 13, 1996]

§ 498.223 Stay of initial decision.

(a) The filing of a respondent's request for review by the DAB will automatically stay the effective date of the ALJ's decision.

(b)(1) After issuance of the final decision, pending judicial review, the respondent may file a request for stay of the effective date of any penalty or assessment with the ALJ. The request must be accompanied by a copy of the notice of appeal filed with the Federal court. The filing of such a request will automatically act to stay the effective date of the penalty or assessment until such time as the ALJ rules upon the request.

(2) The ALJ may not grant a respondent's request for stay of any penalty or assessment unless the respondent posts a bond or provides other adequate security.

(3) The ALJ will rule upon a respondent's request for stay within 10 days of receipt.

[61 FR 65468, 65472, Dec. 13, 1996]

§ 498.224 Harmless error.

No error in either the admission or the exclusion of evidence, and no error or defect in any ruling or order or in any act done or omitted by the ALJ or by any of the parties is ground for vacating, modifying or otherwise disturbing an otherwise appropriate ruling or order or act, unless refusal to take such action appears to the ALJ or the DAB to be inconsistent with substantial justice. The ALJ and the DAB at every stage of the proceeding will disregard any error or defect in the proceeding that does not affect the substantial rights of the parties.

[61 FR 65468, 65472, Dec. 13, 1996]

FEDERAL SOCIAL SECURITY LAWS AND REGULATIONS INDEX

INDEX

INDEX

INDEX

INDEX

INDEX

INDEX

INDEX

INDEX

INDEX

INDEX

INDEX

INDEX